BIOGRAPHICAL REGISTER OF THE ENGLISH CATHEDRAL PRIORIES OF THE PROVINCE OF CANTERBURY

*c.*1066 to 1540

BIOGRAPHICAL REGISTER OF THE ENGLISH CATHEDRAL PRIORIES OF THE PROVINCE OF CANTERBURY

*c.*1066 to 1540

Joan Greatrex

OXFORD · CLARENDON PRESS
1997

Oxford University Press, Great Clarendon Street, Oxford OX2 6DP
Oxford New York
Athens Auckland Bangkok Bogota Bombay
Buenos Aires Calcutta Cape Town Dar es Salaam
Delhi Florence Hong Kong Istanbul Karachi
Kuala Lumpur Madras Madrid Melbourne
Mexico City Nairobi Paris Singapore
Taipei Tokyo Toronto
and associated companies in
Berlin Ibadan

Oxford is a trade mark of Oxford University Press

Published in the United States
by Oxford University Press Inc., New York

British Library Cataloguing in Publication Data
Data available

Library of Congress Cataloging in Publication Data
Data applied for
ISBN 0-19-820424-8

1 3 5 7 9 10 8 6 4 2

Typeset by Hope Services (Abingdon) Ltd.
Printed in Great Britain
on acid-free paper by
Biddles Ltd, Guildford & King's Lynn

Ad totam familiam patris nostri Benedicti per saecula hoc registrum oblatio est oblate abbatie sancte Marie consolationis, quia omnes unum sumus per amorem Christi et in gaudio studii et in servitio Domini

ACKNOWLEDGEMENTS

During the course of some twenty years of wide-ranging research in the preparation of this Register I have been constantly encouraged by colleagues and friends and, indeed, also by strangers, many of whom have become friends. To all of them I remain profoundly grateful, whether it be for questions answered, information supplied, sections of text scrutinized, financial assistance provided, or hospitality extended. Here I can do no more than mention as many of them as possible by name in order to express my thanks for their contributions to this project now completed and to acknowledge gratefully their share in bringing it to fruition.

Among those whom I consulted at various stages of the work and who were unfailingly generous with their time and their constructive comments are Professor Christopher Brooke, Professor Barrie Dobson, Miss Barbara Harvey, and Professor David Smith. I am especially indebted to David Smith for reading through the entire text and suggesting many improvements. Others who have given valuable assistance whenever it was sought and have provided additional information from their own research or have pointed my investigations in new directions are Dr Roger Bowers, Dr Peter Cunich, Dr Virginia Davis, Dr Antonia Gransden, Dr Diana Greenway, Professor Christopher Harper-Bill, Professor Rosalind Hill, Professor Donald Logan, Mr Alan Piper, Professor Jane Sayers, Dr Richard Sharpe, Dr Nicholas Vincent, and Professor Andrew Watson.

The librarians and archivists of several Cambridge colleges, namely Corpus Christi, Emmanuel, St John's, and Trinity, have kindly permitted me to consult manuscripts in their care, and I have been the recipient of similar courtesies from their Oxford counterparts at Corpus Christi, Pembroke, and New College. The Manuscripts Room of Cambridge University Library proved to be the ideal setting in which to complete the final drafts of this work, and I should like to record my gratitude to its superintendent Godfrey Waller for his many acts of kindness. Miss Jayne Ringrose also came to my rescue on a number of occasions when I was baffled by the handwriting in a manuscript. At the Bodleian Library, Oxford, I have received help from all members of the staff on my many visits to Duke Humfrey's library; they have always responded to my requests and have come to my aid without delay. The assistant keepers in the Department of Manuscripts in the British Library and their counterparts in the Public Record Office in Chancery Lane have also been helpful in answering queries and resolving difficulties.

For assistance and advice in preparing the Bath section of this Register I am above all indebted to Dr R. W. Dunning, who read both the text and the introduction and offered sound advice on a number of points where I had stumbled. Mr Holborn, librarian at Lincoln's Inn, kindly made available for my use the Bath priory register, Mr Mayberry of the Somerset Record Office resolved one of my last-minute queries, and a former student of mine, Mrs Miriam Van Husen, used up part of her holiday in returning to a state of subservience as my research assistant.

I am sure that I may speak for the Canterbury monks as well as for myself when I express my gratitude to all those who have shown interest in this section of the Register and have been most generous in sharing their knowledge and expertise. At Canterbury the cathedral archivist Mrs Hodgson and her assistants, Miss Anne Oakley and Dr Michael Stansfield, and at Lambeth Palace library Miss Melanie Barber have all endured my endless questions with patience and courtesy and have been unsparing in their efforts to enlighten me. Dr Nigel Ramsay took it upon himself to check all the entries and has provided me with many additional references from his own research.

For assistance with the Coventry section I should like to acknowledge the helpful advice and comments from Professor Peter Coss, the late Mrs Joan Lancaster Lewis, and Dr Robert Swanson. The staff of the Lichfield Joint Record Office were obliging on my several visits there as was Mrs Bancroft of the cathedral library in Lichfield in allowing me to consult the Magnum Registrum Album.

I owe a lasting debt of gratitude to the late Dean Seiriol Evans who, without hesitation, lent me his collection of records of the Ely monks and welcomed my endeavours in the field in which he had already laboured for many years. Dr Dorothy Owen and, more recently, Mr Peter Meadows have also been most willing to share with me their knowledge of the Ely archive and to put all the documents at my disposal.

The Norwich entries have greatly benefited from the comments and suggestions of Miss Barbara Dodwell, who went over all the entries with me after reading them first herself. It behoves me also to acknowledge the help of Mr Ian Dunn, formerly of the Norfolk Record Office, of Mr Frank Meeres his successor there, and of Mr Paul Rutledge, deputy archivist. Dr Eleanor Scarfe at Windsor Castle kindly allowed me to examine the Norwich accounts that have come to rest among the Windsor muniments, and Miss Ruth Frost, Dr Margaret Harvey, and Mrs Joyce Horn have passed on to me information that has turned up during the course of their research.

When I began work on Rochester I discovered that Anne Oakley had already compiled a list of the monks which she most generously shared with me and on which I was able to build. The final draft of the entries and the introduction have been read by Dr Martin Brett, with beneficial results in the form of a number of improvements and refinements where the text was inaccurate or ambiguous. I am also grateful to Dr Irene Zadnik for passing on to me information which she came across while working on her doctoral thesis.

Winchester cathedral was the scene of my doctoral research and, as such, my introduction to monastic chapters. Some of those whose forbearance and courtesy on my first appearance I recall with gratitude are no longer with us: Canon Frank Bussby and Miss Beatrice Forder at the Cathedral and Mrs Eleanor Cottrill at the Hampshire Record Office. They spurred me on my way as, indeed, have their successors, Mr John Hardacre and Miss Caroline Humphreys; and Dr John Crook has also clarified a number of problems about the layout of the buildings within the monastic precincts. Dr Barker Benfield of the Bodleian Library and Mr Simon Bailey of the Oxford University Archives were most obliging in helping me to identify a manuscript belonging to a Winchester monk student at Oxford.

There are many at Worcester to whom I am indebted for continuing kindness and assistance on my frequent visits to the Cathedral and to St Helen's Record Office. Canon Iain Mackenzie, the cathedral librarian has generously allowed me to consult the manuscripts and muniments at my convenience, and has taken an active interest in the progress of the work; Mr Ronald Stratton and Mrs Ruth Piggott have unearthed many a relevant document to put at my disposal. Miss Margaret Henderson, now retired, and Mr Robin Whitaker, her successor at St Helen's, have never failed to provide for all my needs when examining manuscripts in their charge. I am also grateful to Professor Rodney Thompson, Mrs Mary Cheney and Dr Emma Mason for information on points where our studies overlap.

At the beginning of this project the Canada Council, as it was then called, provided me with a leave fellowship to enable me to spend a sabbatical year in searching cathedral archives and consulting manuscripts in the British Library and other major repositories. More recently the British Academy, the Leverhulme Trust, and the Marc Fitch Fund have awarded generous grants for the completion of this project. A Bye fellowship at Robinson College, Cambridge, enabled me to spend four terms among colleagues and friends, who provided stimulation and encouragement by their constant interest and challenging comments and questions; it was an ideal atmosphere in which the monks and I flourished, and my gratitude for all these blessings goes far beyond these few words.

For hospitality offered and gratefully received on my research travels around the country I should like to thank Nancy Christoff in London, Finola Hurley in Cambridge, Patrick Llewellyn-Davies and Michael Stansfield on Canterbury visits, Mr and Mrs Solloway in Norwich, and Mrs Tennant in Winchester.

Finally I wish to thank Carol Porter for typing the first drafts and Denise Bilton for her competence in preparing the final drafts for the press. Without their persevering work this volume would never have seen the light of day.

It remains for me to express my lasting indebtedness to a forbearing husband for his patience and support through many years when he has had to endure my lengthy periods of absence from home and, at home, my long hours closeted with the monks behind closed study doors. He has also entered into the project by serving as my willing assistant in preparing the first typescripts of the introductions. My youngest son, a historian of the late Roman world, has on occasion given advice on the translation of Latin words and phrases, for which I am grateful; the monks, however, would probably be reluctant to express their thanks if they knew of his disparaging comments on the debased vocabulary and syntax which they employed.

CONTENTS

ABBREVIATIONS OF WORDS AND PHRASES

abp	archbishop
acc.	according
acct(s)	account(s)
acol.	acolyte
adcn	archdeacon
adm.	admission, admit, admitted
appndx	appendix
apptd	appointed
apptment	appointment
B.A.	Bachelor of Arts
B.C.L.	Bachelor of Civil Law
B.Cn.L.	Bachelor of Canon Law
bp	bishop
B.Th.	Bachelor of Theology
c.	*circa* or century
cart.	cartulary
comm.	commission, commissioned
d.	death, died
D.C.L.	Doctor of Civil Law
dcn	deacon
D.Cn.L.	Doctor of Canon Law
D.Th.	Doctor of Theology
ed.	edited
el.	elect, elected, election
fl.	*floruit*
fo(s)	folio(s)
lit. dim.	letters dimissory
M.	Magister, i.e. a person who has a degree
m.	mark(s)
Ms(s)	manuscript(s)
n.	note
n.d.	no date
no(s)	number(s)
nom.	nominated
occ.	occurs
ord	ordained, ordination

p.a.	per annum
pd	paid
pr.	priest
prob.	probably
prof.	professed, profession
pt	part
rec.	receive
recd	received
ref.	reference, refers
reg.	register
res.	resignation, resigned
s. d.	shillings, pence
sed. vac.	*sede vacante*
subdcn	subdeacon
succ.	succeed(ed)
temp.	*tempore*
vs	*versus*
wk(s)	week(s)
yr(s)	year(s)

GENERAL BIBLIOGRAPHY OF WORKS CITED WITH ABBREVIATIONS

Amundesham, *Annales*	*Annales Monasterii S. Albani, a Johanne Amundesham, monacho ut videtur, conscripti, A.D. 1421–1440, quibus praefigitur chronicon rerum gestarum in monasterio S. Albani, A.D. 1422–1431, a quodam auctore ignoto compilatum*, Rolls Series, 2 vols, 1870–1871.
Anglia Sacra	H. Wharton, *Anglia Sacra*, 2 vols, London, 1691.
Ann. Burton *Ann. Dunstable* *Ann. Tewkes.*	H. R. Luard, ed., *Annales Monastici*, Rolls Series, 5 vols, 1864–1869; vols i (Tewkesbury and Burton) and iii (Dunstable).
Anstey, *Epist. Oxon*	H. Anstey, ed., *Epistolae Academicae Oxon (Registrum F.)*, Oxford Historical Society, 2 vols, 1898.
Anstey, *Munimenta Acad.*	H. Anstey, ed., *Munimenta Academica or Documents Illustrative of Academica Studies at Oxford*, Rolls Series, 2 vols, 1868.
Bale, *Catalogus*	John Bale, *Scriptorum Illustrium Maioris Brytanniae Catalogus*, 2 vols, Basle, 1557, 1559, facsimile reprint, Farnborough, Hants, 1971.
Bale, *Index Brit. Script.*	R. L. Poole and M. Bateson, eds, *Index Britanniae Scriptorum*, rev. edn., Cambridge, 1990.
BRUC	A. B. Emden, *A Biographical Register of the University of Cambridge to A.D. 1500*, Cambridge, 1963.
BRUO	A. B. Emden, *A Biographical Register of the University of Oxford to A.D. 1500*, 3 vols, Oxford, 1957–1959.
BRUO, 1501–1540	A.B. Emden, *A Biographical Register of the University of Oxford, A.D. 1501 to 1540*, Oxford, 1974.
Cal. Inq. Misc.	*Calendar of Inquisitions Miscellaneous*, Public Record Office Texts and Calendars, 1916– .
Cal. Inq. P.M.	*Calendar of Inquisitions Post Mortem, and other Analogous Documents*, Public Record Office, 1904– .
Cart. Ramsey	W. Hart and P. Lyons, eds, *Cartularium Monasterii de Rameseia*, Rolls Series, 3 vols, 1884–1893.
Catto, *Hist. Univ. Oxford*	J. Catto and R. Evans, eds, *The History of the University of Oxford*, i. *The Early Schools*, Oxford, 1984; ii. *Late Medieval Oxford*, Oxford, 1992.
CChR	*Calendar of Charter Rolls preserved in the Public Record Office*, Public Record Office Texts and Calendars, 1903– .
CClR	*Calendar of Close Rolls preserved in the Public Record Office*, Public Record Office Texts and Calendars, 1892– .
Chambers, *Faculty Office Regs*	D. S. Chambers, *Faculty Office Registers, 1534–1549, a Calendar of the first two Registers of the Archbishop of Canterbury's Faculty Office*, Oxford, 1966.
Cheney, *Letters Innocent III*	C. and M. Cheney, eds, *The Letters of Innocent III (1198–1216) concerning England and Wales*, Oxford, 1967.
Cheney, *Selected Letters, Innocent III*	C. Cheney and W. Semple, eds, *Selected Letters of Innocent III concerning England, 1198–1216*, London, 1953.
Chron. Evesham	W. Macray, ed., *Chronicon Abbatiae de Evesham, ad annum 1418*, Rolls Series, 1863.
Chron. Hovedene	W. Stubbs, ed., *Chronica Rogeri de Hovedene*, Rolls Series, 4 vols, 1868–1871.
Chron. Oxenedes	H. Ellis, ed., *Chronica Johannis de Oxenedes*, Rolls Series, 1859.
Chron. Ramsey	W. D. Macray, ed., *Chronicon Abbatiae Rameseiensis, a saec. X usque ad an. circiter 1200, in quatuor partibus*, Rolls Series, 1886.

Churchill, *Cant. Admin.*	I. J. Churchill, *Canterbury Administration: the Administrative Machinery of the Archbishop of Canterbury illustrated from Original Records*, 2 vols, London, 1933.
Coggeshall, *Chron.*	J. Stevenson, ed., *Radulphi de Coggeshall Chronicon Anglicanum*, Rolls Series, 1875.
Councils and Synods	F. Powicke and C. Cheney, eds, *Councils and Synods with other Documents relating to the English Church*, ii. 1205–1313, 2 parts, Oxford, 1964; continuous pagination.
CPL	W. Bliss, C. Johnston, J. Twemlow *et al*, eds, *Entries in the Papal Registers relating to Great Britain and Ireland, Papal Letters, 1894–* .
CPP	W. Bliss, ed., *Entries in the Papal Registers relating to Great Britain and Ireland, Petitions to the Pope*, i (1342–1419), 1897.
CPR	*Calendar of Patent Rolls*, Public Record Office Texts and Calendars, 1891– .
CSL Henry IV and V	J. L. Kirby, ed., *Calendar of Signet Letters of Henry IV and Henry V (1399–1422)*, HMSO, 1978.
CU Grace Book A	S. M. Leathes, ed., *Grace Book A, containing the Proctors' Accounts and other Records of the University of Cambridge for the years 1454–1488*, Cambridge Antiquarian Society, Luard Memorial Series, 1897.
CU Grace Book B	M. Bateson, ed., *Grace Book B, Part i, containing the Proctor's Accounts and other Records of the University of Cambridge for the years 1488–1511; Part ii, containing the Accounts of the Proctors of the University of Cambridge, 1511–1544*, Cambridge Antiquarian Society, Luard Memorial Series, 1903, 1905.
CU Grace Book Γ	W. G. Searle, ed., *Grace Book Γ, containing the Records of the University of Cambridge for the years 1501–1542*, Cambridge, 1908.
Curia Regis Rolls	*Curia Regis Rolls, Richard I to 26 Henry III*, Public Record Office, 1923– .
Delisle, *Rouleaux des Morts*	L. Delisle, *Rouleaux des Morts du IX*^{e} *au XV*^{e} *siècle*, Paris, 1866.
Delisle, *Rouleau Mortuaire*	L. Delisle, *Rouleau Mortuaire du B. Vital Abbé de Savigni*, Paris, 1909.
Diceto, Opera	W. Stubbs, ed., *Radulfi de Diceto Decani Lundoniensis, Opera Historica*, Rolls Series, 2 vols, 1876.
DK 7th Report *DK 8th Report*	*Annual Reports of the Deputy Keepers of the Public Records*, House of Lords Record Publications, 1965, 1966.
DNB	*The Dictionary of National Biography*, 63 vols, Oxford, 1882– .
Dugdale, *Monasticon*	W. Dugdale, *Monasticon Anglicanum*, rev. edn. by J. Caley, H. Ellis, and B. Bandinel, 6 vols in 8, London, 1817–1830.
Eng. Epis. Acta	See under the appropriate section.
Fasti, ii	D. E. Greenway, comp., *John Le Neve, Fasti Ecclesiae Anglicanae, 1066–1300*, ii. *Monastic Cathedrals*, London, 1971.
Fasti, iv	B. Jones, comp., *John Le Neve, Fasti Ecclesiae Anglicanae, 1300–1541*, iv. *Monastic Cathedrals*, London, 1963.
Fasti, 1541–1857, iii	J. Horn, comp., *John Le Neve, Fasti Ecclesiae Anglicanae, 1541–1857*, iii. *Canterbury, Rochester and Winchester Dioceses*, London, 1974.
Fasti, 1541–1857, vii.	J. Horn, comp., *John Le Neve, Fasti Ecclesiae Anglicanae*, vii, *Ely, Norwich, Westminster and Worcester Dioceses*, London, 1992.
Flores Hist.	H. R. Luard, ed., *Flores Historiarum*, Rolls Series, 3 vols, 1890.
Foliot Letters	Z. N. Brooke, A. Morey, C. N. L. Brooke, eds, *The Letters and Charters of Gilbert Foliot*, Cambridge, 1967.
Foster, *Alumni Oxon.*	J. Foster, *Alumni Oxoniensis*, 4 vols, Oxford, 1891–1892.
Giraldi Camb. Opera	J. Brewer, J. Dimock, G. Warner, eds, *Giraldi Cambrensis Opera*, Rolls Series, 8 vols, 1861–1891.

Graham, *Eng. Eccles. Studies*	R. Graham, *English Ecclesiastical Studies*, London, 1929.
Gransden, *Hist. Writing*	A. Gransden, *Historical Writing in England*, i. c.550 to c.1307, London, 1974; ii. *c.1307 to the early 16th century*, London, 1982.
Greatrex, 'Statistics'	J. Greatrex, 'Some Statistics of Religious Motivation', *Studies in Church History*, 15 (1978), 179–186.
Hardy, *Catalogue*	T. Hardy, *Descriptive Catalogue of Materials Relating to the History of Great Britain and Ireland, to the End of the Reign of Henry VII*, Rolls Series, 3 vols in 4, 1892–1871.
HBC	E. Fryde, D. Greenway, S. Porter, and I. Roy, eds, *Handbook of British Chronology*, 3rd edn, Royal Historical Society, 1986.
Hearne, *Antiq. Glastonbury*	T. Hearne, *The History and Antiquities of Glastonbury*, Oxford, 1722.
Hist. Mon. Gloucester	W. Hart, ed., *Historia et Cartularium Monasterii Sancti Petri Gloucestriae*, Rolls Series, 3 vols, 1863–1867.
Hist. Mss. Comm. Reports	*Reports and Calendars issued by the Royal Commission on Historical Manuscripts*, 1874– .
Holtzmann, *Papsturkunden*	W. Holtzmann, ed., *Papsturkunden in England*, 3 vols, Abhandlungen der Gesellschaft der Wissenschaften zu Göttingen, 1930–1952.
HRH	D. Knowles, C. N. L. Brooke, V. London, eds, *The Heads of Religious Houses, England and Wales, 940–1216*, Cambridge, 1972.
Index, Placita de Banco	*Index of Placita de Banco, 1327–28*, two parts, Public Record Office, 1910.
Ker, *Books, Collectors, Libraries*	A.G. Watson, ed., *Books, Collectors and Libraries, Studies in the Medieval Heritage*, London, 1985.
Knowles, *MO*	D. Knowles, *The Monastic Order in England*, Cambridge, 1966.
Knowles, *RO*	D. Knowles, *The Religious Orders in England*, 3 vols, Cambridge, 1948–1959.
Knowles and Hadcock, *MRH*	D. Knowles and R. N. Hadcock, *Medieval Religious Houses, England and Wales*, London, 1971.
L and P Henry VIII	*Letters and Papers, Foreign and Domestic, Henry VIII*, vols 1–16, 1867–1920.
Little and Pelster, *Oxford Theology*	A.G. Little and F. Pelster, *Oxford Theology and Theologians, c.A.D. 1282–1302*, Oxford Historical Society, 96, 1934.
Malmesbury, *Gest. Pont.*	N. E. S. A. Hamilton, ed., *Willelmi Malmesburiensis, Monachi, De Gestis Pontificum Anglorum*, Rolls Series, 1870.
Memorials Bury	Thomas Arnold, ed., *Memorials of St Edmund's Abbey*, Rolls Series, 3 vols, 1890–1896.
MLGB	N. Ker, ed., *Medieval Libraries of Great Britain*, 2nd edn, Royal Historical Society, London, 1964.
MLGB Suppl.	N. Ker and A. Watson, eds, *Medieval Libraries of Great Britain, a List of Surviving Books: Supplement to the Second Edition*, Royal Historical Society, London, 1987.
MMBL	N. Ker, *Medieval Manuscripts in British Libraries*, 4 vols, Oxford, 1969–1992; vol 4 was completed by A. J. Piper.
Orderic, *Eccl. Hist.*	M. Chibnall, ed., *The Ecclesiastical History of Orderic Vitalis*, Oxford Medieval Texts, 6 vols, 1969–1980.
Pantin, *BMC*	W. Pantin, ed., *Documents illustrating the Activities of the General and Provincial Chapters of the English Black Monks, 1215–1540*, Camden Society, 3rd series, 45[i], 47[ii], 54[iii], 1931–1937.
Paris, *Chron. Majora*	H. R. Luard, ed., *Matthaei Parisiensis, monachi sancti Albani, Chronica Majora*, Rolls Series, 7 vols, 1872–1883.
Parl. Writs	F. Palgrave, ed., *Parliamentary Writs and Writs of Military Summons, with Records and Muniments relating to Suit and Service to Parliament, etc.*, 2 vols, 1827–1834.

RB	H. Rochais and E. Manning, eds, *Règle de Saint Benoît*, Paris, 1980.
Reg. Cancell. Oxon. 1434–1469	H. Salter, ed., *Registrum Cancellarii Oxoniensis, 1434–1469*, Oxford Historical Society, 2 vols, 1932.
Reg. Cancell. Oxon. 1498–1506	W. Mitchell, ed., *Registrum Cancellarii Oxoniensis, 1498–1506*, Oxford Historical Society, new series, 28, 1980.
Reg. Univ. Oxon.	C. W. Boase, ed., *Register of the University of Oxford*, i. *1449–1463, 1505–1571*, Oxford Historical Society, 1885.
Reg. Whethamstede	*Registra quorundam Abbatum Monasterii S. Albani, qui Saeculo XVmo Floruere*, Rolls Series, 2 vols, 1872–1873.
Rouse and Mynors, *Reg. Anglie de Libris*	M. and R. Rouse and R. Mynors, *Registrum Anglie de Libris Doctorum et Auctorum Veterum*, Corpus of Mediaeval Library Catalogues, London, 1991.
Rymer, *Foedera*	T. Rymer, *Foedera, Conventiones, Litterae, et cujuscumque Generis Acta Publica inter Reges Angliae et alios quosvis Imperatores, Reges, Pontifices, Principes, vel Communitates, 1101–1654*, new edn, 1069–1381, ed. by A. Clark, F. Holbrooke, and J. Caley, 4 vols in 7 parts, Record Commission, 1816–1869.
Salisbury Letters	W. J. Miller and H. E. Butler, eds, revised by C. N. L. Brooke, *The Letters of John of Salisbury*, 2 vols; i. *The Early Letters (1153–1161)*, London, 1955; ii. *The Later Letters (1163–1180)*, Oxford, 1979.
Selden Society, *Select Cases Eccles.*	N. Adams and C. Donahue junior, eds, *Select Cases from the Ecclesiastical Courts of the Province of Canterbury, c.1200–1301*, Selden Society, xcv, 1981.
Selden Society, *Select Cases King's Bench*	G. Sayles, ed., *Select Cases in the Court of King's Bench under Edward I*, 3 vols, 1936–1939; also *ib.*, under Edward II, 1955.
Sharpe, *Eng. Benedictine Libraries*, iv	R. Sharpe, J. Carley, R. Thomson, A. Watson, *English Benedictine Libraries: Lesser Catalogues*, British Academy Corpus of British Medieval Library Catalogues, iv, London, 1996.
Sharpe, *Latin Writers*	R. Sharpe, *A Checklist of the Latin Writers of Great Britain and Ireland before 1540*, London 1996.
Snappe's Formulary	H. Salter, ed., *Snappe's Formulary and other Records*, Oxford Historical Society, 1924.
Sullivan, *Benedictine Monks at Paris*	T. Sullivan, *Benedictine Monks at the University of Paris, A.D. 1229–1500, a Biographical Register*, Leiden, 1995.
Talbot and Hammond, *Medical Practitioners*	C. H. Talbot and E. A. Hammond, *The Medical Practitioners in Medieval England*, London, 1965.
Tanner, *Bibliotheca Brit.*	Thomas Tanner, *Bibliotheca Britannico-Hibernica*, London, 1748.
Tanner, *Notitia*	T. Tanner, *Notitia Monastica*, London, 1744.
Trokelow, *Chron. St. Alban's*	H. Riley, ed., *Johannis de Trokelowe et Henrici de Blaneforde, Monachorum. S. Albani necnon quorundam Anonymorum, Chronica et Annales*, Rolls Series, 1866.
Turner and Coxe, *Charters and Rolls*	W. H. Turner and H. O. Coxe, eds, *Calendar of the Charters and Rolls in the Bodleian Library*, Oxford, 1878.
Twysden, *Hist. Angl. Script.*	R. Twysden, *Historiae Anglicanae Scriptores X*, 2 vols, London, 1652.
Valor Eccles.	J. Caley and J. Hunter, eds, *Valor Ecclesiasticus, temp. Henrici VIII, Auctoritate Regia Institutus*, Record Commissioners Publications, 6 vols, 1810–1834.
VCH	*The Victoria History of the Counties of England*, London, 1900– .
Venn, *Alumni*	J. and J. A. Venn, comps, *Alumni Cantabrigiensis, a Biographical list of all known students, graduates and holders of office at the University of Cambridge, from the earliest times to 1900*, pt 1, 4 vols, Cambridge, 1922.

Venn, *Gonville & Caius*	J. Venn, comp., *Biographical History of Gonville & Caius College, 1349–1891*, i. *1349–1713*, Cambridge, 1897.
Walsingham, *Gesta Abbatum*	H. Riley, ed., *Gesta Abbatum Monasterii sancti Albani, a Thoma Walsingham*, Rolls Series, 3 vols, 1867–1869.
Walsingham, *Hist. Anglicana*	H. Riley, ed., *Thomae Walsingham quondam Monachi S. Albani, Historia Anglicana*, Rolls Series, 2 vols, 1863–1864.
Watson, *Dated and Datable Mss*	A. G. Watson, *Catalogue of Dated and Datable Manuscripts c. 435–1600 in Oxford Libraries*, 2 vols, Oxford, 1984.
Wilkins, *Concilia*	D. Wilkins, *Concilia Magnae Britanniae et Hiberniae*, 4 vols, London, 1737.
Willis, *Mitred Abbies*	Browne Willis, *An History of the Mitred Parliamentary Abbies and Conventual Churches*, 2 vols, Coventry, 1718–1719.
Wood, *Athenae Oxon.*	A. Wood and P. Bliss, *Athenae Oxoniensis*, 5 vols, London, 1813–1820.
Wright, *Satirical Poets*	T. Wright, ed., *The Anglo-Latin Satirical Poets and Epigrammatists of the Twelfth Century*, Rolls Series, 2 vols, 1872.

SCHEMA FOR THE REFERENCES IN EACH SECTION

A. Manuscript Sources
   i Episcopal Registers
   ii Priory Registers and Cartularies

B. Other Manuscript Sources

C. Printed Sources
   i Episcopal Registers
   ii Priory Registers and Cartularies

D. Other Printed Sources and References

Note: in the case of some frequently cited manuscripts abbreviated titles have been used; for others, especially loose deeds and rolls, the class marks, where these have been assigned by archivist or librarian, have proved more satisfactory. In all cases the present location of the manuscripts and the means of identification have been included.

GENERAL INTRODUCTION

This volume had its origin many years ago on record cards filed in shoe boxes. These were intended to serve as primary source material for a comparative study of the monastic cathedral chapters, a project that remains unfinished but will now move to first place on my agenda.[1] The decision to give this register priority over the comparative study was prompted by a request from the British Academy which, in generously providing funds, pointed out that as a valuable reference work it should be completed as soon as possible.

It need hardly be stated that these pages will make available to medieval scholars a wide range of data that are not exclusively confined to monastic or ecclesiastical history, despite the fact that the subjects are all black monks. Information on matters as diverse as illness and life expectancy, intellectual pursuits and university study, financial administration, business and social connections, political influence and, conversely, the impact of governmental pressures on religious houses, all have a place. Moreover, given the nature of the evidence, it will be understood that in almost every entry the details provided may be regarded as prosopographical rather than biographical; however, case studies of some five thousand monks, all members of communities subject to the same Benedictine Rule, permit us to fill in many of the gaps in the life of the individual monk. In so doing, we are able to fill in many details of the typical monk's daily routine and activities both within the cloister and in the world outside; for he was to be found not only in choir and chapter house but also in the market place purchasing provisions and on the manors supervising the labour force and inspecting crops and stock. We should also hope to be made more aware of the obligations and responsibilities that formed the basis of community life within the cloister.

The entries have been arranged alphabetically within each of the eight sections (Bath, Canterbury, Coventry, Ely, Norwich, Rochester, Winchester, and Worcester). Moreover, each section is preceded by a list of References with abbreviations followed by a short introductory essay; the purpose of this last is to explain the general historical background to the entries, with more particular details of some events in order to elucidate the surrounding circumstances, and with references to the primary and printed sources consulted accompanied by a brief commentary on their interpretation and use. There is also a general bibliography of references that occur frequently throughout the Register; it is to be found on p. xv–xix.

For each entry the biographical details are arranged according to the following *schema*, with a space to indicate the transition from one section to the next:

for a prior:

- dates of appointment or election and of death or resignation;

for all the monks:

- dates of admission, profession, and ordination;

[1] It is envisaged that the comparative study will appear in two separate volumes; the first focusing mainly on the 14th c., and the second on the 15th and early 16th cs. The earlier of these will be mine while the later volume will be undertaken by Professor R. B. Dobson.

- dates of appointment to and dismissal from obedientiary office, and of periods of office holding;[2]
- dates of university study;
- dates of all other activities.

Note that the entries within each of the above sections are chronologically arranged and the dates are conspicuously placed against the left margin for ease of perusal. The slash has been preferred to the dash except in the case of priors; thus 1326/9 should be read as 1326 to 1329, and, when references are to obedientiary or manorial accounts, it may be assumed that the accounting year, from Michaelmas (29 Sept.) to Michaelmas, is understood unless otherwise stated. Like square brackets surrounding a date, a slash between two days of the month denotes uncertainty and should be read as either of the days concerned, or possibly both days.

The remaining sections of each entry include the names of books donated or used by the monk,[3] his family connections, and other miscellaneous information that cannot be readily accommodated within the chronological framework.

My aim throughout has been to provide the facts in a format that is easy to read and to use, and, in furthering this end, Anne Gelling and the Oxford University Press have been most understanding and co-operative. Abbreviations have thus been kept to a minimum and proper sentence structure favoured in most of the entries. When a place-name alone is given as the site of an ordination, the parish church is understood. In many cases Latin words, phrases, and quotations have been retained, to enable the readers to make their own judgement rather than to have to depend on mine; there is no substitute for direct exposure to the original forms of expression used by contemporaries or near contemporaries to describe, record, and interpret acts and events close to themselves but remote from us. Consistency has been kept in mind, but it must also be remembered that our medieval forebears did not always observe this precept, and difficulty may arise in the attempt to achieve certainty when faced with two accounts of a similar, very likely the same, action occurring on different dates; in such cases the only safe course is to adhere closely to the wording of the texts under scrutiny. With regard to omissions that may appear surprising and irritating to the reader, most, if not all, of these have already had the same effect on me and have led me to return to the source, only to verify again that the desired point of information is missing. References are given first to works in print followed, in many cases, by the original manuscript source in order to give the reader the possibility of immediate access to the latter. On occasion two manuscript references are included for one entry, or one date in an entry, where it has been judged helpful to the reader to be furnished with both.[4]

[2] In some cases, notably that of the office of penitentiary, or *primarius*, the sources are often unclear if the reference is to what I have treated here as an obedientiary office, that is to an appointment either by the bishop (or archbishop) or by the prior to office within the monastery as confessor to the monks. Most bishops also licensed monks as confessors in the cathedral, city, and diocese; these appointments have been assigned to the last of the chronological sections.

[3] To indicate ownership inscriptions I have adapted the usage of N. R. Ker in substituting—for the name of the monk.

[4] Experience has taught me that, with regard to obedientiary office holding, it is necessary to provide all the dates on which a given monk is known to have held a given office; this is because there are too many frequent changes or rotations of office to allow us to take the earliest and latest dates in one office and assume that there was continuity throughout the time-span. On the contrary, the pattern is often that of appointment, dismissal, and reappointment, sometimes in fairly quick succession.

There are many decisions required of those who attempt to produce a volume of this kind and not all of them can hope to meet with universal approval. One of the most obvious examples is that of the method employed in citing the monks' toponymics, which were generally the villages or towns from which they came. Some scholars prefer to modernize the spellings, thereby eliminating all possible variations, but I remain unconvinced by their arguments when applied to this Register. The difficulty is that some of the variations are so unlike the modern forms as to be unrecognizable, and some unusual spellings or spellings in which the same letters have been combined in a variety of ways are prone to misinterpretation.[5] Apart from a few exceptions, to avoid these pitfalls I have retained the spellings found in the original sources with plenty of cross-references to help the reader.

Like A. B. Emden's invaluable biographical registers of the medieval universities of Cambridge and Oxford, to which I make frequent reference, this volume is presented in what may be described as index form.[6] However, a single index has been provided incorporating the names from all eight cathedrals, with a letter code beside each to indicate the section in which the name is to be found. In addition, there is an appendix consisting of lists of the relevant archbishops, bishops, and priors accompanied by dates for ready reference.

The first register of monks of an English Benedictine house and, until now, the only one in print is that compiled by Canon Pearce for Westminster abbey some eighty years ago.[7] It is to be sincerely hoped that Alan Piper of Durham university will soon gladden us by the publication of his register of Durham monks, thus completing the biographical record for all the English Benedictine cathedral chapters. Among the other major black monk houses blessed with an abundant supply of original records are Bury St Edmunds, Reading, and St Alban's, all of which are currently receiving the attentions of medieval scholars.[8] If one of the fruits of their labours will be to shed light on the lives and careers of members of these monastic communities, medieval prosopography will be substantially enriched.

My own contribution in these pages is no more than a beginning, a foundation now

[5] The variations Bruton and Burton, Hengham, Hingham, and Ingham, Bilney and Tilney, Saham and Soham, Stratton and Stretton, Tottington and Tuttington, Watton, Wootton, and Wotton, and so on arouse grave doubts when one tries to distinguish between them. Uncertainties cannot be resolved by assuming that monks always came from the town or village closest to the monastery when there are several possibilities from which to choose. Moreover, in this period before spellings became stabilized, sound was the determining factor and the result is at times unrecognizable in terms of modern place-names. In my view, it is safer to adhere to the spellings found in the sources and to provide many cross-references. Those who are familiar with the place-names and history of a particular locality may be able to apply their expertise and clear up some of these problems; but let them not fail to take into account that medieval scribes neither confined themselves to the variations in spelling found in volumes like Ekwall's useful *Dictionary of English Place-Names* (Oxford, 1947), nor formed their letters with a greater degree of legibility than we do today.

[6] In many of my entries regarding the university studies of monks I have not referred to Emden's registers. Some of my information supplements his, some comes from different sources, and on a few points we differ. I have drawn attention, however, to those monks not included in Emden and, since his register like mine is arranged alphabetically, I have deemed it unnecessary to include reference to volume number and page. Similarly, I have not felt bound to refer to the volumes of *Fasti* for the details of prioral elections unless my entry is identical in every point.

[7] E. H. Pearce, *The monks of Westminster, being a Register of the Brethren of the Convent from the time of the Confessor to the Dissolution* (Cambridge, 1916).

[8] I have in mind Dr Antonia Gransden, whose scholarly writings on Bury St Edmunds are widely known; Dr Alan Coates, who is currently working on the monks of Reading abbey and their book collections; and James Clark, who is completing a doctoral thesis on St Alban's abbey in the later Middle Ages.

offered to other scholars on which I hope they will build. I am painfully aware that even in the final draft of this work some errors and omissions have failed to be rectified. The painstaking scrutiny of the text by several colleagues, who are acknowledged on another page, has eliminated many of these and resulted in a number of additions and improvements; any remaining mistakes I regret and acknowledge as my own. I shall be most grateful if those who make use of this volume will notify me (via the Oxford University Press) of any additional information or any corrections that may come to their attention during the course of their research.

Feast of St Scholastica 1996

JOAN GREATREX
Cambridge

BATH CATHEDRAL PRIORY

INTRODUCTION

The cathedral church of St Peter, Bath, was one of two monastic cathedral chapters in England that shared their bishop with a chapter of secular canons.[1] From 1245 by papal decree the diocese and its ruler were to have the double-barrelled appellation 'Bath and Wells', but the harmonious relationship between the two chapters which this implied was achieved only after a prolonged period of friction and bitter controversy.[2] Prior to this date the bishopric underwent several changes in its location and jurisdiction, while monks and canons became involved not only in the practical problems concerning their mutual relations but also in those concerning their respective positions under a diocesan who, in the case of Bath, was also titular abbot.

For the purposes of this Register our history begins c. 1090 with the episcopate of John de Villula or Tours (1088–1122), who was a skilled medical practitioner. Soon after his appointment as bishop of Wells by William Rufus he transferred his see to the more important centre of Bath and proceeded to convert the three-centuries-old abbey into a cathedral priory.[3] This elevation in rank, however, was accompanied by the confiscation of most of the monastic estates held before the Conquest. The new, foreign abbot/bishop, according to William of Malmesbury, introduced monks of his own choosing into the priory while at the same time encouraging learning in the cloister, where, on his arrival, he had found ignorance and barbarity.[4] Prosperity and prestige ensued after bishop John restored the chapter estates, added endowments of his own, and undertook to rebuild and enlarge the monastic church on such a grand scale that the length of its nave was exceeded only by Winchester, Ely, and Norwich.

The early priors, of whom the first recorded is John [I], q.v., c. 1106, were appointed by the bishop who also had (and retained until the end) the right of collation to the offices of sacrist and precentor. Free election of priors was granted in 1261 by bishop William Bitton I after the death of prior Thomas [I], q.v., as the *Priory Register* records in some detail.[5] It was during Thomas's lengthy rule (1223–1261) that the dispute over the procedures to be followed in episcopal elections was finally settled between the Bath and Wells chapters after several earlier unsuccessful attempts to resolve their rival claims. In 1173, for example, conflict arose when both chapters acted independently but, fortunately, both concurred in their choice of Reginald Fitzjocelin; not surprisingly the papal confirmation was accompanied by a recommendation that in future

[1] According to Dugdale, as early as the time of prior Robert de Bath [I], q.v., c. 1198–1223, its dedication also included St Paul, *Monasticon*, ii, 258.

[2] See below; and see also the Introduction to the Coventry section, p. 000 for an account of a similar situation and outcome there.

[3] For a brief study of this bishop see R. A. L. Smith, 'John of Tours, Bishop of Bath, 1088–1122', in his *Collected Papers* (London, 1947), 74–82.

[4] Malmesbury, *Gest. Pont.*, 195. See also L. Cochrane, *Adelard of Bath, the first English Scientist* (London, 1994), 1–10.

[5] Item numbers 251–259 (Ms pp. 75–76) are some of the official instruments relating to the election of Walter de Anno, q.v.

the two chapters should proceed jointly.[6] On the next occasion, however, the monks successfully ignored this injunction despite objections from Wells, but in 1206 both monks and canons participated by way of compromise [*via compromissi*] in the election of Jocelin of Wells; the prior and all forty monks appended their signatures to their letter to Innocent III requesting his confirmation.[7]

Tension between the two chapters recurred until the dispute came to a climax on the death of bishop Jocelin in November 1242 in Wells; since he had preferred to reside in Wells he was now buried there notwithstanding the protests of the monks. The subsequent course of events can be pieced together from the entries in the Bath Priory Register and the Wells Liber Albus; a brief summary will be sufficient to explain the historical setting in which the relevant entries in this present Register belong.

Protests having been publicly exchanged between both chapters in the month following the bishop's death, on 29 December two monks, Thomas de Kardif and Thomas de Theukesbiry, q.v., were appointed to confer with representatives from Wells at Farrington Gurney midway between Bath and Wells. With no agreement resulting from this encounter, prior Thomas [I], q.v., and the chapter sent Gilbert de Dunstorr and Richard de Kanynges, q.v., to Bordeaux to procure from the king, Henry III, licence to elect a bishop; they returned to Bath some three weeks later bearing the desired document allowing them to proceed, saving the rights of Wells. On learning of this move the canons followed suit, requesting both a *congé d'élire* and leave to appeal to Rome. Elated with their success, the monks informed the Wells chapter of their intention to conduct an election on 6 February in Bath and invited the canons to attend but without right of participation. This bold and unjustified step produced further letters of protest delivered in person on the eve of the election by a delegation from Wells whom the prior refused to meet. Roger, precentor of Salisbury, was forthwith elected by the monks; Gilbert de Dunstorr and Thomas de Theukesbiry, q.v., were sent to inform the king and obtain his assent; two other brethren, Robert de Ely and Thomas de Kardif, q.v., were appointed proctors for the convent in the counter appeal against an appeal initiated by Wells; and the former two monks must have proceeded to Rome.[8] In the meantime letters had reached Bath from the king and queen pressing the nomination of Peter Chaceporc, royal clerk and archdeacon of Wells. While the monks respectfully stood firm against royal pressure the king provided the canons with a licence to elect, saving the rights of Bath.[9] At this juncture, however, further action on the part of the canons was impeded by the appeals to Rome which remained pending, during the vacancy of the holy see, until June 1243 when Innocent IV was raised to the papal throne. Eight months later, on 3 February 1244, the new pope confirmed Roger as bishop and decreed that in future episcopal elections both chapters were to exercise equal rights.[10] This decision failed to satisfy the Wells canons, who raised further protests, with the result that both chapters renewed their appeals at the curia. In October 1244 Gilbert de Dunstorr, q.v., was still, or once

[6] See C. M. Church, 'Roger of Salisbury, first bishop of Bath and Wells, 1244–1247', *Archaeologia*, 52 (1890), 103–104.

[7] The original of this survives at Wells, as Wells Charter 40(iv). See Church, 'Roger of Salisbury', 104–105, and also, by the same author, 'Jocelin, bishop of Bath, 1206–1242', *Archaeologia*, 51 pt 2 (1888), 281–344; the latter provides a detailed account of his life and career, with documents. Further relevant details are to be found in J. A. Robinson, *Somerset Historical Essays* (London, 1921), 141–159.

[8] *Priory Register*, nos 196–200 (Ms pp. 55–56).

[9] *Priory Register*, nos 190–191 (Ms p. 53).

[10] Church, 'Roger of Salisbury', 111–112.

again, in Rome acting on behalf of the Bath chapter. In January 1245 the pope amended his earlier judgement to include the requirement that future elections were to be held alternately in Bath and in Wells and that the official title was to include both names. The following year bishop Roger himself drew up a final concord, based on the papal decrees, to which both chapters subscribed.[11] The fact that he and his episcopal successors had their main residence at Wells removed them from the possibility of interference in the everyday affairs of the priory, and co-operation with the canons over episcopal elections in accordance with the procedures laid down lasted until the dissolution.[12]

Like Coventry the community at Bath was small in number. The forty monks named in 1206 were probably down to just over thirty a few years before the Black Death and in 1377 barely half that number are recorded.[13] The prioral election of 1447 lists twenty-six monks, that of 1499 twenty-two, and twenty-two participated in the last election in 1525. Since twenty-one signatures are attached to the surrender list in January 1539 we may conclude that in the fifty years before the dissolution the monastic population at Bath suffered no decline.[14] From their names, which were usually toponymic, it is clear that most of the monks were recruited locally and a few came from priory manors, e.g. Dunster, Lyncombe, Corston, Olveston (Gloucestershire), and parishes, e.g. Chew and Compton [Dando].[15]

Long before the time of the episcopal election of 1206 the major obedientiary offices must have been in place. This event, however, provides the earliest record of some fifteen offices, namely, those of subprior, third prior, treasurer, sacrist, cellarer, granator, infirmarer, almoner, precentor, chamberlain, *custos operum*, refectorer, subcellarer, subsacrist, and succentor. The presence of a fourth prior (William Pensford, q.v.), a pittancer (John Lacok, q.v.), a hostiller (William Salford I, q.v.), a kitchener (John Norton II, q.v.), a *custos* of the Lady chapel (William Salford I, q.v.), and a subalmoner (Richard Lyncombe, q.v.) are also attested in the fifteenth century.[16] With almost as many offices as monks it is hardly surprising to find that one monk sometimes held several offices concurrently despite episcopal objections. John Laycok, q.v., for example, was in charge of three in 1447 and William Salford I, q.v., of four the same year.

Two other offices occur with frequency, those of prior or *custos* of the two dependent cells at Dunster, Somerset, and at Waterford, Ireland. The priory of St George at Dunster, where three or four monks were usually in residence, had its origin in the gift of the church there, together with lands and tithes, in the late eleventh century; however, the first known prior is Martin [I], q.v., whose dates are uncertainly placed

[11] See Hunt's introduction to the *Priory Register*, liv–lix, and Church, 'Roger of Salisbury', 107–111.

[12] Bishop Reginald Fitzjocelin was given the churches of Carhampton in the form of a prebend of Wells cathedral and they were later appropriated to Bath. The priors, who then became the patrons of Carhampton, appointed secular clerks to the living (*Priory Register*, no 18, Ms p. 17) but never occupied a stall at Wells. See n. 15 below.

[13] *Priory Register*, no 344 (Ms p. 119), *ib.*, lxv, from PRO E179/4/2; in 1377, however, the monks in the cell at Dunster were not included.

[14] *Ib.*, lxvi–lxviii where original records from episcopal registers have been transcribed.

[15] It should be noted that, although the Carhampton church had the prior and chapter as patron and the incumbent or his deputy sat in the prebendal stall in Wells cathedral, this does not signify that the prior himself held the prebend, as seems to be accepted by *Eng. Epis. Acta*, x, no 72 n. See the lists of dignitaries in the appendix of *Fasti*, viii, 85 which refute the statement in *ib.*, 21 that the prior held a prebend by this name. For lack of evidence uncertainty remains over this anomalous relationship; see the Introduction to the Coventry section, p. 339 as it is probable that a similar connection evolved there.

[16] In 1242 Walter [VII], q.v., was *quisinarius*, probably kitchener.

between the late twelfth and mid-thirteenth centuries. The priory or hospital of St John the Evangelist at Waterford, Ireland, with its scattered properties became attached to Bath in 1204 by the voluntary surrender of the Irish brethren.[17] While the cell at Dunster provided some financial benefits and served as an alternative location for a few of the monks, the Irish custody was a drain on the resources and the manpower of the community at Bath, who had to maintain at least two of the brethren there for administrative and supervisory purposes. The fact that some of the monks who were sent to Ireland could not speak the language only compounded the problems they faced.[18]

Unfortunately for Bath and for us, there is a dearth of the kind of evidence that is provided by the extant obedientiary and manorial accounts of most of the other cathedral priories. This precludes a fuller insight into the day-to-day running of the monastery and into its manorial administration. The economic and financial history of the cathedral priory and its estates has yet to be written, although the outlines were sketched by T. Scott Holmes and William Hunt almost a century ago, and the latter has provided a transcription of the cartulary now in Corpus Christi College, Cambridge.[19]

The internal state of the community is also hidden from view for the same reason; moreover, what has been revealed at Bath and elsewhere tends to focus on the reprehensible behaviour of monks who were singled out by the episcopal visitor for correction, since a few details were recorded in the extant bishops' registers. Although these registers for Bath and Wells survive between 1309 and 1540, except for a forty-year gap from 1363 to 1401, the visitation entries are few and incomplete. Bishop Drokensford's visitation in 1321, for example, brings to light the incompetence and maladministration of prior Robert de Clopcote, q.v., but the mismanagement of Hugh de Dovor, q.v., while in charge at Waterford is known only because of the visitation of archbishop Meopham in 1332 recorded in the *Priory Register*.[20] A visitation certificate issued by the prior on the eve of the *sede vacante* visitation of archbishop Morton in 1495 has furnished us with a list of the monks, but nothing more. Four years later, however, bishop Oliver King's visitation revealed the material and spiritual state of the community to be in great need of reform: the Rule was not being strictly observed, discipline was lax, the monks were idle, the cathedral church was in a state of disrepair, the provision of food was inadequate, and the monks had private property. The bishop's reform programme, issued the following year, aimed to correct all these and other defects and shortcomings. He himself undertook some of the financial responsibility for the rebuilding of the cathedral church, with the aid of the newly appointed prior William Birde, q.v., who had succeeded John Cantlow, q.v.[21]

By the time of prior Birde's death in 1525 royal interference was beginning to be felt by some religious houses, as evidenced by the 'election' proceedings at Bath.

[17] H. S. Sweetman, ed., *Calendar of Documents relating to Ireland*, 5 vols, 1875–1886, i, nos 219, 220.

[18] See John Lamport.

[19] T. Scott Holmes, 'Benedictine Houses, the Cathedral Priory of Bath', *VCH Somerset*, ii, 1911, 69–81, and W. Hunt, ed., *Bath Chartulary* and *Priory Register* under Bath References; the cartulary is Ms 111 in the Corpus catalogue. In the light of recent archaeological investigations the architectural history has been reviewed by J. Manco, 'The Buildings of Bath Priory', for which the details are also given in the Bath References.

[20] Archbishop Meopham's register does not survive.

[21] The injunctions are summarized in *Priory Register*, lxviii, from Reg. King, fo 62; see also William Birde.

Instead of an electoral body of *compromissorii* chosen by and consisting only of monks, in accordance with the provisions of bishop Bitton I almost three centuries earlier, there were only five monks and two seculars, the latter being the bishop's deputy in the form of his vicar-general and another secular cleric. Moreover, the seven were required to choose one of two candidates already named; they dutifully 'elected' William Holleway [II], q.v.[22] Ten years later the pressure increased on account of the restrictions laid upon the prior and chapter by Cromwell in the wake of the visitation of the royal commissioner, Richard Layton, who reported the house in good repair, the prior virtuous, but the monks licentious and a £400 debt.[23] Like other abbots and priors Holleway sent gifts to Cromwell to win his favour.[24]

Little can be said about the state of learning in the priory after the death of bishop John de Villula in 1122. There can be no doubt that monastic studies were pursued in the cloister and that the library was equipped with an adequate supply of texts; but the records are silent. Only a handful of volumes has been preserved, most of them works of the early church fathers, Jerome, Augustine, and Gregory, manuscripts dating from the twelfth century; in addition, six volumes that no longer survive are named in a list noted by Leland of which four were medical treatises.[25] Two other books were mentioned at the time of the 1535 visitation: a copy of Anselm's works which was sent to the king by prior Holleway in response to the royal request and 'a book of our Lady's miracles' which Layton disparagingly likened to the *Canterbury Tales*.[26] There are also frustratingly brief references to gifts of unnamed volumes to the library by two twelfth-century bishops, Geoffrey, John de Villula's successor and Reginald Fitzjocelin, who 'bibliotecam . . . ecclesiae nostrae pluribus libris ditavit'.[27] There was presumably an almonry school for young boys, to which there may be a single ambiguous reference in a grant of prior Robert de Bath (1198–1235), q.v.; when providing a corrody for a secular chaplain's boy servant it specified that the chaplain's boy was to receive the same allowance of food as one of 'the boys of the monastery'.[28]

Monk scholars from Bath known to have been at university number only seven. All but one of these studied at Oxford between the mid-1440s and the early sixteenth century, three obtaining a first degree in theology, and one in canon law.[29] Although in 1343 the Black Monk Chapter named Bath among the religious houses that had no monk students at university, there is no further evidence to indicate whether this was a frequent, or rare, failure to abide by the Chapter regulations that one monk in twenty should be sent.[30] The reason for this very poor showing may be wholly due to the already mentioned loss of the obedientiary accounts which record frequent payments to the monk students of Worcester, Ely, and Norwich at Oxford and Cambridge.

[22] The bishop at this time was John Clerk, who had been chaplain to cardinal Wolsey and acted as his agent on a number of occasions. For similar 'elections' at Winchester and Worcester see the respective Introductions, pp. 000 and 000.

[23] *L and P Henry VIII*, ix, no 42.

[24] In his letter to Cromwell Layton also mentions a gift of a 'leash of laners', falcons from the Irish estates, *ib.*

[25] See *MLGB* and Sharpe under Bath in *Eng. Benedictine Libraries*, iv, B8.

[26] *L and P Henry VIII*, ix, nos 426, 42.

[27] *Priory Register*, no 808 (Ms pp. 314–315).

[28] *Priory Register*, no 70 (Ms p. 20).

[29] The seven are M. Walter de Bathonia, William Birde, William Bristowe II, Thomas Browne, John Cantlow, John Lacok, John Temple, q.v. There was a Bath chamber at Canterbury college, Oxford, Pantin, *Cant. Coll. Ox.*, iv, 143 (Canterbury reference).

[30] Pantin, *BMC*, ii, 22.

Only a few glimpses of the monks' involvement in charitable works may be obtained from the surviving records. One of these relates to their responsibilities for the hospital of St John the Baptist in Bath founded by bishop Reginald Fitzjocelin c. 1180. The bishop gave the prior and convent charge of its administration as may be inferred from the entries referring to the appointments of masters.[31] Evidence of the almoner's activities on behalf of the poor may be reflected in the feeding of one hundred poor people on the anniversaries of all the bishops from Geoffrey to John Drokensford.[32] One recluse, Matilda of Stapleton, is named in a grant of 1244, which provided her with a daily allowance of bread and ale by way of alms.[33]

Corrodies were sometimes charitable gifts to relatives and retired priory or manorial lay servants; they commonly took the form of a daily supply of food and often lodging. The elderly mother of prior Hugh I, q.v., was one of these and Edith Cryst, probably a relative of prior Thomas Crist, q.v., may have been another; G. Vaillanto, who was employed as the priory messenger, and John Marshal, domestic servant, were given corrodies during their working lives that were to be extended to include their retirement.[34] Not infrequently, however, corrodies were purchased for life, usually by the down payment of a fixed sum which could provide welcome cash for the monks in time of need but could and did sometimes become a financial drain when the corrodian outlasted his estimated life-span. In addition, the king burdened many religious houses including Bath with the expense of providing accommodation for retired royal servants, and the proximity of a spa to Bath priory may have been an attractive prospect to pensioners with aching limbs.[35]

The prior was an important figure in Bath and beyond. In 1295 he was summoned with other spiritual lords to attend parliament although no records of his attendance appear in the *Priory Register*.[36] Prior Robert Clopcote, q.v., made an unsuccessful bid to obtain the right to assume pontifical regalia in 1321, but it was over a century later that one of his successors in office, Thomas Lacok, q.v., was granted the papal privilege and took his place among the mitred abbots and priors. As to the relations between the citizens of Bath and the monks, there is evidence of only one incident in the early fifteenth century which briefly marred what seems otherwise to have been an amicable association, preserved and strengthened by the presence of at least twelve sons of city families in the monastic community.[37] The lone dispute broke out over a matter of precedence in the ringing of the priory bells and of those of the parish churches, the former by custom long established having been both the first to sound at the beginning of each day and the last to sound each evening. When this custom was flouted by a reversal of the order of procedure in February 1412, the monks complained that the resulting noise disturbed them during the office. The disagreement

[31] Kemp, *Deeds of St John's Hospital*, 7–11; the patronage of the hospital was, however, a source of dispute between later bishops and priors, *ib.*

[32] Details for twelve bishops are given in *Priory Register*, no 808 (Ms pp. 314–317).

[33] *Priory Register*, no 144 (Ms p. 37).

[34] *Ib.*, nos 89, 149 (Ms pp. 24, 38). John de Bathon' physician, was granted a corrody in 1328 in return for his services, *ib.*, nos 630, 631 (Ms p. 235).

[35] *Ib.*, nos 584, 623, 681, 722, 911 (Ms pp. 213, 228, 256, 274, 386).

[36] *Parl. Writs*, i, 24. The prior's name was included in the mandate addressed to the bishop in *Reg. Shrewsbury*, no 1468; see William de Hampton I.

[37] See the entries under Bath, Bathe, Bathon', etc. I am making the reasonable assumption that the toponymic signifies domicile.

was brought to an end in 1421 with final judgement in the monks' favour delivered by the royal justices.[38]

The fact that three monks, two of them future priors, obtained degrees between about 1480 and 1500, and that the monastic community showed no sign of a decline in numbers in the final years before the dissolution should provide sufficient evidence on which to base a concluding comment. Taken together these facts strongly suggest that, although always a small monastic chapter, and despite earlier crises in the community's temporal and spiritual affairs, in the sixteenth century the house was in a reasonably healthy state and was continuing to attract recruits.[39]

BATH REFERENCES WITH ABBREVIATIONS

Note: if the particular reference sought does not appear below, turn to the General Bibliography on pp. xv–xix, or the Canterbury section, pp. 58–65.

A. Manuscript Sources

i Episcopal Registers, in the Somerset Record Office (SRO)

Note: Reg. [Walter] Giffard (1265–1266), fragment only, in York, Borthwick Institute, BI, Reg. 2.

Reg. [John] Drokensford/Droxford (1309–1329)	D/D/B.Reg.1
Reg. [Ralph] Shrewsbury (1329–1363)	D/D/B.Reg.2
Reg. [Henry] Bowett (1401–1407)	D/D/B.Reg.3
Reg. [Nicholas] Bubwith (1408–1424)	D/D/B.Reg.4
Reg. [John] Stafford (1425–1443)	D/D/B.Reg.5
Reg. [Thomas] Bekynton/Beckington (1443–1465)	D/D/B.Reg.6
Reg. [Robert] Stillington (1466–1491)	D/D/B.Reg.7
Reg. [Richard] Fox (1492–1494)	D/D/B.Reg.8
Reg. [Oliver] King (1496–1503)	D/D/B.Reg.9
Reg. [Adrian de] Castello (1504–1518)	D/D/B.Reg.10
Reg. [Thomas] Wolsey (1518–1523)	D/D/B.Reg.11
Reg. [John] Clerk (1523–1541)	D/D/B.Reg.12

Note: all the above are printed in calendar form; see Section C.i below.

Also Reg. Sed. Vac. (1465/6, 1495/6, 1503/4), D/D/B.Reg.29 a register covering three vacancies of the see.

ii Priory Registers and Cartularies

Bath Chartulary	Cambridge, Corpus Christi College Ms 111; Cartulary, 9th/12th cs.
BL Ms Egerton 3316	Cartulary, 11th/14th cs.
BL Ms Harley 317	Priory Register, 16th c.
BS Ms Harley 3970	Priory Register, 16th c.; briefly calendared in Hunt, *Two Chartularies*, lxxii–lxxiv; see Section C.ii below.
Priory Reg.	London, Lincoln's Inn, Ms 185 (Ms Hale); c. 1200 to mid-14th c., calendared by Hunt; see Section C.ii below. Note: This has been paginated, although some of the numbering has been crossed through. I have followed the page references in the ms which are also in Hunt.

[38] *Cal. Inq. Misc.*, vii, 582; *Reg. Bubwith*, no 1266.

[39] Cf. R. Dunning, 'Revival at Glastonbury 1530–9', *Studies in Church History*, 14 (1977), 213–222.

B. Other Manuscript Sources

Court Rolls in the Somerset Record Office (SRO); there are a few records of Dunster borough which occasionally name the prior of Dunster; the references are prefixed DD/L P.

C. Printed Sources

i Episcopal Registers (in chronological order)

Reg. Giffard T. S. Holmes, ed., *The Registers of Walter Giffard, Bishop of Bath and Wells, 1265/6. and of Henry Bowett, Bishop of Bath and Wells, 1401–7*, Somerset Record Society 13, 1899.

Reg. Drokensford E. Hobhouse, ed., *Calendar of the Register of John de Drokensford, Bishop of Bath and Wells (AD 1309–1329)*, Somerset Record Society 1, 1887.

Reg. Shrewsbury T. S. Holmes, ed., *The Register of Ralph of Shrewsbury, Bishop of Bath and Wells, 1329–1363*, Somerset Record Society, 2 vols, 9, 10, 1896.

Reg. Bowett See under *Reg. Giffard* above.

Reg. Bubwith T. S. Holmes, ed., *The Register of Nicholas Bubwith, Bishop of Bath and Wells, 1407–1424*, Somerset Record Society, 2 vols, 29, 30, 1914.

Reg. Stafford T. S. Holmes, ed., *The Register of John Stafford, Bishop of Bath and Wells, 1425–1443*, Somerset Record Society, 2 vols, 31, 32, 1915–1916.

Reg. Bekynton H. C. Maxwell Lyte and M. C. B. Dawes, eds, *The Register of Thomas Bekynton, Bishop of Bath and Wells, 1443–1465*, Somerset Record Society, 2 vols, 49, 50, 1934–1935.

Reg. Stillington H. C. Maxwell Lyte, ed., *The Registers of Robert Stillington, Bishop of Bath and Wells, 1466–1491, and Richard Fox, Bishop of Bath and Wells, 1492–1494*, Somerset Record Society 52, 1937.

Reg. Fox See under *Reg. Stillington* above.

Reg. King H. C. Maxwell Lyte, ed., *The Registers of Oliver King, Bishop of Bath and Wells, 1496–1503 and Hadrian de Castello, Bishop of Bath and Wells, 1503–1518*, Somerset Record Society 54, 1939.

Reg. Castello See under *Reg. King* above.

Reg. Wolsey H. C. Maxwell Lyte, ed., *The Registers of Thomas Wolsey, Bishop of Bath and Wells, 1518–1523, John Clerke, Bishop of Bath and Wells, 1524–1547, and Gilbert Bourne, Bishop of Bath and Wells, 1554–1559*, Somerset Record Society 55, 1940.

Reg. Clerk See under *Reg. Wolsey* above.

Note: These are mainly calendars, and some omit ordination lists.

ii Priory Registers and Cartularies

Bath Chartulary W. Hunt, ed., *Two Chartularies of the Priory of St Peter at Bath*, i. *The Chartulary in*
Priory Reg. *Ms cxi in the Library of Corpus Christi College, Cambridge*; ii, *Calendar of the Ms Register in the Library of the Hon. Society of Lincoln's Inn*, Somerset Record Society 7, 1893. In the latter the entries have been numbered.

D. Other Printed Sources and References

Chron. Devizes J. Giles, ed., *The Chronicle of Richard of Devizes concerning the Deeds of Richard I, King of England*, London, 1841.

Domerham, *Hist. Glaston.* T. Hearne, ed., *Adam de Domerham Historia de Rebus Gestis Glastoniensibus*, Rolls Series, 2 vols, London, 1727.

Eng. Epis. Acta, x F. M. R. Ramsey, ed., *English Episcopal Acta*, x, *Bath and Wells, 1061–1205*, British Academy, London, 1995.

Fasti, viii	B. Jones, comp., *John Le Neve, Fasti Ecclesiae Anglicanae*, viii. *Bath and Wells Diocese, 1300–1541*, London, 1964.
	J. Fowler, 'The Benedictines in Bath', *Downside Review*, 14 (1895), 54–74, 182–211, 316–337.
Hancock, *Dunster*	F. Hancock, *Dunster Church and Priory*, Taunton, 1905.
Hist. Monast. Gloucester	W. Hart, ed., *Historia et Cartularium Monasterii sancti Petri Gloucestrie*, Rolls Series, 3 vols, 1863–1867.
Kemp, *Deeds of St John's Hospital*	B. Kemp, ed., *Medieval Deeds of Bath and District*, i. *Deeds of St John's Hospital, Bath*, Somerset Record Society 73, 1974.
Manco, 'Buildings of Bath Priory'	J. Manco, 'The Buildings of Bath Priory', *Somerset Archaeology and Natural History*, 137 (1993), 75–109.
Maxwell Lyte, *Dunster*	H. C. Maxwell Lyte, *A History of Dunster and the Families of Mohun and Luttrell*, 2 vols, London, 1909.
Maxwell Lyte, 'Dunster and its Lords'	H. C. Maxwell Lyte, 'Dunster and its Lords', *The Archaeological Journal*, 38 (1881), 207–228.
Weaver, *Somerset Incumbents*	F. W. Weaver, *Somerset Incumbents*, Bristol, 1889 (privately printed).
Weaver, *Somerset Medieval Wills*	F. W. Weaver, *Somerset Medieval Wills*, Somerset Record Society, 2 vols (1st series, 16, 1383–1500; 2nd series, 19, 1501–1530), 1901, 1903.
Wells Liber Albus, i *Wells Liber Albus*, ii *Wells Liber Ruber* *Wells Charters*	W. H. Bird and W. P. Baildon, eds, *Historical Manuscripts Commission, 10th Report, Appendix 3, Calender of the Manuscripts of Albus, the Dean and Chapter of Wells*, 2 vols, 1907, 1914. *Liber Albus* i and ii and *Liber Ruber* are in the first volume, pp. 1–304, 305–528 and 529–551 respectively; *Wells Charters* is in vol. ii, 546–724.

BATH CATHEDRAL PRIORY
1090–1539

John ABYNDON
occ. 1463 occ. 1495

1463, 24 Sept., ord subdcn, chapel of the hospital of St John the Baptist, Wells, *Reg. Bekynton*, no 1782.

1466, 20 Sept., ord dcn, Muchelney abbey, Reg. Stillington, fo 172.

1467, 23 May, ord pr., chapel of the hospital of St John the Baptist, Wells, *ib.*, fo 175.

1473, 7 Dec., collated to the office of precentor, *Reg. Stillington*, no 588.

1489, 6 Nov., prior of Dunster, *Reg. Fox* no 1125.

1494, 1 July, as prior of Dunster instituted, jointly, with a lay patron, the vicar of Carhampton, *Reg. Fox* no 1126.

1495, 30 Jan., 4th in order on the *sed. vac.* visitation certificate, *Reg. abp Morton*, ii, no 347.

I ADAM
occ. 1206

1206, 3 Feb., present at the el. of bp Jocelin and 9th to put his signature on the letter to the pope requesting his confirmation, Wells Cathedral Muniments, Charter no 40 (iv).

II ADAM
occ. [1292]

[1292, before 25 Oct.], [subdcn], granted *lit. dim.* for dcn's orders by the vicar general of bp Robert [Burnell], *Priory Reg.*, no 419 (p. 149).

III ADAM
occ. 1326

1326, 14 Jan., one of twelve monks who made their prof. before the bp, Reg. Drokensford, fo 270.

Note: this may be Adam de Cheddre, q.v.

ADELSTAN
see Arleston

ALNETO
see Anno

ALURED [Aluredus
occ. 1206

1206, 3 Feb., present at the el. of bp Jocelin, and 2nd to put his signature on the letter to the pope requesting his confirmation, Wells Cathedral Muniments, Charter no 40 (iv).

Walter de ALYNTON [Alyngton
occ. 1341 occ. 1364

1364, 9 Jan., almoner, Reg. abp Islip, fo 242^{v}; *Wells Liber Albus*, i, 266 (fo 251).

1341, 19 Apr. (St Alphege), described as rector of English Combe [Inglescomb], and made a grant of land to tenants there, *Priory Reg.*, no 828 (p. 324).

1344, 5 Oct., 13th in order among those in chapter for the purpose of appointing general proctors, *Priory Reg.*, no 344 (p. 119).

1364, 9 Jan., with John [de Berwyk, q.v.], prior, and other monks was cleared by the abp of the censures illegally published against them because of an el. dispute, *sed. vac.*, *Wells Liber Albus*, i, 266 (fo 251) and Reg. abp Islip, fo 242^{v}.

Roger de ANNA
[1267 × 1283]

[1267 × 1283], in a memorandum concerning arrangements for the funerals and obits of deceased brethren there is ref. to the concern of Roger and of Robert de Rading, q.v., about this matter in their day; now, *temp.* prior Clopcote, q.v., further provisions were made which included prayers for the souls of these two monks who had been *honestatis zelae divinitus insperati* [*sic*], *Priory Reg.*, no 811 (p. 318).

Martin de ANNO [de Alneto, Anna, Danno
occ. 1264

1264, 22 May, named by the prior and chapter as one of the four monk electors to meet with the electors of the Wells chapter in order to el. a bp on this day, *Priory Reg.*, no 304 (p. 93), *Wells Liber Albus*, i, 102.

Thomas de ANNO [Anna, Aune
occ. 1261 occ. 1276

1261, c. 27 June, chosen by the chapter as one of seven *compromissorii* in the el. of a prior, *Priory Reg.*, nos 255, 257 (pp.75–76).

1264, 22 May, named by the prior and chapter as one of the four monk electors to meet with the electors of the Wells chapter in order to el. a bp on this day, *ib.*, no 304 (p. 93), *Wells Liber Albus*, i, 102.

1267, 9 Jan., named as one of six monks to join with the six representatives of the Wells chapter in the el. of a bp, *Priory Reg.*, no 319 (p. 99).

1276, 15 Sept., with Henry de Aune, recd royal letters of protection after being apptd attorneys for the prior in Ireland, *CPR (1272–1281)*, 160.

Walter de ANNO [Aune, d'Aune, Dune
occ. 1261 d. 1290

1261–1290, prior: el. announced 27 June 1261, *Priory Reg.*, nos 256, 257 (p. 76); d. before 14 Jan. 1290, *ib.*, no 394 (p. 142).

1261, before 27 June, cellarer, *Priory Reg.*, no 256 (p. 76).

1261, c. 27 June, chosen as prior by *via compromissi*, *ib.*, no 257 (p. 76).

1264/6, sought absolution for the community from excommunication incurred because of their support for the barons vs the king, *Priory Reg.*, no 266 (p. 80).

1267, 9 Jan., a W., prior was named as one of six monk proctors who were to meet with their six counterparts from the Wells chapter in order to [arrange to] el. a bp, *Priory Reg.*, no 319 (p. 99).

1267, 10 Feb., one of the six representatives of the Bath chapter who, with the dean and five other representatives of the Wells chapter, elected a bp, *Priory Reg.*, nos 320, 321 (p. 99).

1277, 25 May, summoned to the Black Monk Chapter at Reading, *Priory Reg.*, no 371 (p. 131).

Many of his *acta* are recorded in the *Priory Reg.*; see the index there under his name [Anno]. There are also a number of grants made by him in BL Ms Egerton 3316, e.g. on fos 59^v, 60, 62, 63, 67, 79; see also the entry under Gilbert Herebert.

He and the other monks of the same name presumably came from a family which had long had close connections with the priory, e.g. *Priory Reg.*, nos 3A, 68, 121, 122, 480, 808.

Note: Dune is a misreading or perhaps an alternative rendering of the name Anno or d'Aune.

ANSELM [Anselmus
occ. 1206

1206, 3 Feb., succentor, Wells Cathedral Muniments, Charter no 40 (iv).

1206, 3 Feb., present at the el. of bp Jocelin and 15th to put his signature on the letter to the pope requesting his confirmation, *ib.*

John APPLEBY [Appelby, Appulby
occ. 1413 occ. before 1447

1413, 10 Jan., the prior was comm. to rec. his prof., *Reg. Bubwith*, no 386.

1413, 23 Sept., ord subdcn, Banwell, *ib.*, no 1292.

1414, 3 Mar., ord dcn, Banwell, *ib.*, no 1294.

1418, 24 Sept., ord pr., Banwell, *ib.*, no 1302.

1447, 5 July, declared apostate at the el. of a prior as he had left some yrs previously, *Reg. Bekynton*, no 1639; see also Robert Veyse.

ARCHER
see Virtue

John ARLESTON [Adelstan, *alias* Browne
occ. 1539

1539, 27 Jan., 13th on the surrender list and assigned a pension of £6 p.a., *L and P Henry VIII*, xiv, pt i, no 148; on 20 Feb., he was dispensed to change his habit and hold a benefice, Chambers, *Faculty Office Regs*, 175.

ARNALD [Arnaldus
occ. 1206

1206, 3 Feb., present at the el. of bp Jocelin and 23rd to put his signature on the letter to the pope requesting his confirmation, Wells Cathedral Muniments, Charter no 40 (iv).

ASKETILLUS
see Chiuton

John ASSHLEY [?Asshwell
occ. 1505 occ. 1509

1505, 20 Dec., ord subdcn, St Mary's chapel by the cloister, Wells cathedral, Reg. Castello, fo 141.

1506, 28 Mar., ord dcn., St Mary's chapel by the cloister, Wells cathedral, ib, fo 141.

1506, 11 Apr., ord pr., St Mary's chapel by the cloister, Wells cathedral, ib, fo 142.

1509, 15 Nov., recd š2d. in a bequest from a parishioner of Dunster, Weaver, *Somerset Medieval Wills*, ii, 139.

AUNE
see Anno

AURELIANUS
occ. 1206

1206, 3 Feb., present at the el. of bp Jocelin and 7th to put his signature on the letter to the pope requesting his confirmation, Wells Cathedral Muniments, Charter no 40 (iv).

Thomas AVERY [Averay, Averee, Averey
occ. 1502 occ. 1534

1502, 12 Mar., ord acol., St Mary's chapel behind the new altar, Bath cathedral, Reg. King, fo 126.

1507, 20 Mar., ord pr., St Mary Redcliffe, Bristol, Reg. Castello, fo 144.

1525, 25 June/5 July, subprior, *Reg. Clerk*, no 477.

1525, 5 July, presided at the 'el.' of a prior, and was named as one of the five monk *compromissorii*, *Reg. Clerk*, no 477, (fo 81); see William Holleway II.

1534, 22 Sept., 4th to subscribe to the Act of Supremacy, *DK 7th Report*, Appndx 2, 280.

Thomas AXBRUGGE
occ. 1430/1

1430, 23 Sept., ord dcn, Bath cathedral, *Reg. Stafford*, no 950.

1431, 31 Mar., ord pr., Bath cathedral, *ib.*, no 954.

Note: on 24 Sept. 1429, a Thomas Axbrigge of the diocese of Worcester was ord subdcn to the title of the prior and convent of Bath, *Reg. Stafford*, no 946.

John de AXEBRIGGE [Axebrygg, *alias* Countevyle

occ. 1323 occ. 1369

1323, 11 Dec., dcn, granted *lit. dim.* for pr.'s orders on the prior's request, Reg. Drokensford, fo 207v.

1344, 5 Feb., provided by the pope to the hospital/cell of St John the Evangelist at Waterford to succ. Thomas de Foxcote, q.v.; the provision was on the grounds of failure to appt within the specified time, *CPL*, iii (1342–1362), 97.

1369, 6 Sept., with Geoffrey Flori, q.v., accused of various misdeeds including forgery, with the aid of the priory seals; the entry is very faded, but it appears that the two may have gone to the curia as the prior seems to have sent a proctor there, Priory Reg., p.332 (no. 840).

BA

see Bath

William de BADMYNGTON

occ. 1323 occ. 1344

1323, 8 Jan., apptd precentor 'at pleasure', Reg. Drokensford, fo 195v.

1342, 23 Nov.; 1344, 5 Oct., subprior, *Priory Reg.*, nos 835 and 344 (pp. 327, 119); in 1342 he was named as 'W. de B'.

1329, 2 June, named by the prior and chapter to be one of the five monk electors to meet with their counterparts from the Wells chapter in order to el. a bp on this day, *Priory Reg.*, nos 338, 340 (pp. 111, 114).

1332, 6 Mar., apptd *scrutator* with Robert de Sutton, q.v., in the el. of a prior, *ib.*, no 734 (p. 281).

1344, 5 Oct., 2nd in order among those in chapter for the purpose of appointing general proctors, *ib.*, no 344 (p. 119).

William BAKELER

occ. 1384

1384, 24 Sept., ord pr., Yeovil, Reg. abp Courtenay, i, fo 306v (while on visitation).

William BALDYNGTON

occ. 1369

1369, recd a bequest of 5s from Gilbert Scut of Dunster to celebrate two trentals, Hancock, *Dunster*, 20, 66, 68.

Note: this prob. means that he was or had been a resident of the cell at Dunster.

Adam BARET [Balet, Barret

occ. 1505 occ. 1510

1505, 20 Dec., ord subdcn, St Mary's chapel by the cloister, Wells cathedral, Reg. Castello, fo 141.

1507, 20 Mar., ord dcn, St Mary Redcliffe, Bristol, *ib.*, fo 144.

1510, 22 Sept., ord pr., St Mary's chapel by the cloister, Wells cathedral, fo 151.

Robert de BASYNGG'

occ. 1283

1283, 10 Feb., cellarer, BL Ms Egerton 3316, fo 62.

1283, 10 Feb., with Richard de Chernbury, q.v., witnessed a grant of the prior, *ib.*

Henry BATECOMBE

occ. 1365

1365, 28 Feb., with a clerk, nom. by the prior as his attorney in Ireland for two yrs, *CPR (1364–1367)*, 97.

I Nicholas de BATH [Bathon

occ. 1364

1364, 9 Jan., fourth prior, *Wells Liber Albus*, i, 266 (fo 251).

1364, 9 Jan., the abp revoked the censures against him and other monks, because of a disputed el., *sed. vac.*, as they had been published illegally, *Wells Liber Albus*, i, 266 (fo 251); also Reg. abp Islip, fo 242v.

II Nicholas BATH B.Th. [Bathe, *alias* Jobben, Jobbyn

occ. 1508 occ. 1539

1508, 18 Mar., ord dcn, St Mary's chapel by the cloister, Wells cathedral, Reg. Castello, fo 146.

1510, 21 Dec., ord pr., St Mary's chapel by the cloister, Wells cathedral, *ib.*, fo 152.

1525, 28 June/5 July, third prior, *Reg. Clerk*, no 477 (fo 82).

1539, 27 Jan., named as B.Th., *BRUO, 1501–1540*, Appndx A.

1525, 5 July, 7th in order at the 'el.' of a prior, and was named as one of the five monk *compromissorii*, *Reg. Clerk*, no 477; see William Holleway II.

1539, 27 Jan., 5th on the surrender list and assigned a pension of £8 p.a., *L and P Henry VIII*, xiv pt i, no 148; on 20 Feb., he was dispensed to change his habit and hold a benefice, Chambers, *Faculty Office Regs*, 175.

I Robert de BATH

occ. c. 1198 occ. 1235

c. 1198–1223, prior: first occ. as prior c. 1198; el. abbot of Glastonbury 1223, after 10 May, *HRH*, 29.

[1198–1205], witnessed an episcopal grant in favour of St John's hospital, Bath, Kemp, *Deeds of St John's Hospital*, nos. 9 and 12.

[1206 x 1223], witnessed another grant in favour of St John's hospital, Bath, *ib.*, no 117.

1206, 3 Feb., presided at the el. of bp Jocelin and was the first to put his signature on the letter to the pope requesting his confirmation, Wells Cathedral Muniments, Charter no 40 (iv). Prior to the el., he had been one of the Bath proctors in the negotiations with the dean and canons of Wells, *Wells Liber Albus*, i, 63 (fo 54^{v}).

1235, res. from the abbacy and returned to Bath with a pension of £60 p.a., *Priory Reg.*, no 16 (p. 7) and note.

He may have been in the *familia* of bp Savaric (1191–1205), *Priory Reg.*, no 16 and note (Domerham, *Hist. Glaston.*, ii, 478–502). See also *Eng. Epis. Acta*, x, pp. lvi-lvii.

Some of his *acta* may be found in the Priory Reg., q.v., under Robert, prior.

II Robert BATH [Bathe

occ. 1410 occ. 1447

1410, 20 Dec., ord acol. and subdcn, chapel of St Mary by the cloister, Wells cathedral, *Reg. Bubwith*, no 1287.

1412, 2 Apr., ord dcn, Wells cathedral, *ib.*, no 1290.

1412, 17 Dec., ord pr., bp's chapel, Wookey, *ib.*, no 1291; this entry is repeated on 23 Sept. 1413, *ib.*, no 1292 (at Banwell).

1447, 5 July, precentor, *Reg. Bekynton*, no 1639.

1412, 10 Mar., subdcn, prof., and 18th in order at the el. of a prior, *Reg. Bubwith*, no 1271 (pp.447–448); he had been a subdcn for two yrs, *ib.*

1447, 5 July, 3rd in order at the el. of a prior, *Reg. Bekynton*, no 1639.

I Thomas BATH [Bathe

occ. 1443 ?occ. 1499

1443, 21 Dec., ord dcn, St Cuthbert's church, Wells, *Reg. Bekynton*, no 1652; this entry is repeated on 26 Mar. 1444 (no. 1653). His ordination as dcn is also recorded on 22 Sept. 1442 in *Reg. Stafford*, no 1004.

1447, 5 July, 15th in order at the el. of a prior, *Reg. Bekynton*, no 1639.

1499, 30 Aug., 4th at the el. of a prior, Reg. King, fo 139^{v}.

Note: He would have been in his seventies in 1499, but Thomas Bath II below was far too junior to have been fourth in order. Some of the lists of monks are patently not in order of seniority.

II Thomas BATH [Bathe, *alias* Sexten (?Copten)

occ. 1487 occ. 1539

1487, 31 Mar., ord subdcn, St Mary Redcliffe, Bristol, Reg. Stillington, fo 220.

1488, 22 Mar., ord dcn, Bruton priory, *ib.*, fo 226.

1489, 4 Apr., ord pr., chapel of the hospital of St John the Baptist, Wells, *ib.*, fo 231.

1525, 23 June, 5 July, prior of Dunster, *Reg. Clerk*, no 477.

1495, 30 Jan., 15th in order on the *sed. vac.* visitation certificate, *Reg. abp Morton*, ii, no 347.

1499, 30 Aug., 10th in order at the el. of a prior, Reg. King, fo 139^{v}.

1525, 23 June, with Richard Widecombe, q.v., obtained licence to el. a prior from the abp of York at Westminster, *Reg. Clerk*, no 477. He and William Holleway II, q.v, were the two candidates selected by prearrangement before the 'el.'.

1525, 5 July, 4th at the el. of a prior, and acted as proctor for Richard Keynesham, q.v., *Reg. Clerk*, no 477.

1534, 22 Sept., 3rd to subscribe to the Act of Supremacy, *DK 7th Report*, Appndx 2, 280.

1539, 27 Jan., 4th on the surrender list where he was described as 'impotent' and assigned a pension of £8 p.a., *L and P Henry VIII*, xiv, pt i, no 148; on 20 Feb., he was dispensed to change his habit and hold a benefice, Chambers, *Faculty Office Regs*, 175.

Note: see also Thomas III.

John BATHE

occ. 1453 occ. 1456

1453, 26 May, ord dcn, St Cuthbert's church, Wells, *Reg. Bekynton*, no 1707.

1456, 18 Sept., ord pr., bp's chapel, Banwell, *ib.*, no 1731.

John de BATHON'

occ. 1344

1344, 5 Oct., 23rd in order among those in chapter for the purpose of appointing general proctors, *Priory Reg.*, no 344 (p. 119).

Matthew de BATHON'

occ. 1311

1311, 5 Nov., collated to the office of precentor, *Reg. Drokensford*, 67 (fo 57^{v}).

Philip de BATHON'

occ. 1290 occ. 1308

1292, 29/30 Dec.; 1295, 15 Aug.; 1297, 20 Mar., subprior, *Wells Liber Ruber*, 530, (fo 2^{v}), *Priory Reg.*, no 436 (p. 154), as Philip, and no 444 (p. 158), as Philip.

1290, 14 Jan., with Richard de Chernbury, q.v., recd from the bp in London licence to el. a prior, *Priory Reg.*, no 394 (p. 142).

1292, 30 Dec., with Richard de Warewik, proctor who met the Wells chapter proctors at Fernton [?Farrington Gurney] to fix a day for the joint el. of a bp, *Wells Liber Ruber*, 530 (fo 2v).

1302, 19 June, with William de Hampton I, q.v., sent by the prior and chapter as proctor to treat with the Wells chapter concerning obtaining the king's licence to el. a bp, *Priory Reg.*, no 592 (p. 216).

1308, 17 Dec., with John de Essex, q.v., apptd proctor by the prior and chapter to take part in the preliminary discussions with proctors of the Wells chapter concerning the el. of a bp, *Priory Reg.*, no 614 (p. 226); on the next day the two were named as the monk proctors to go to the king to obtain the necessary licence, *ib.*, no 615 (p. 226).

Thomas de BATHONIA

occ. 1317

1317, 18 Feb., with William de Hampton I and John de Essex, q.v. named as proctor to meet the Wells chapter proctors in order to come to an agreement over the advowson and appropriation of Bathampton church, *Wells Liber Albus*, i, 172 (fo 134).

M. Walter de BATHONIA

occ. 1275 occ. 1292

1275, 24 Jan., apptd proctor for the convent with Thomas de Winton, q.v., and two Wells proctors to inform the abp of the el. of Robert Burnell as bp, *Wells Liber Albus*, i, 113 (fo 91v). He is styled Magister and not identified as a monk.

1292, 29/30 Dec., with Richard de Warewik, q.v., acted as monk proctor in meeting with the proctors of the Wells chapter for the el. of a bp, *Wells Liber Ruber*, 530 (fo 2v).

Note: these two entries may apply to two different monks.

William BEACHYNE [Bewachyn, Bewchyn, Bewschyrn, Bewshyn

occ. 1523 occ. 1539

1523, 21 Mar., ord subdcn, St Mary's chapel by the cloister, Wells cathedral, Reg. Wolsey, fo 30.

1524, 12 Mar., ord dcn, Bath cathedral, Reg. Clerk, fo 110v.

1525, 5 July, 17th in order at the el. of a prior, *Reg. Clerk*, no 477.

1534, 22 Sept., 9th to subscribe to the Act of Supremacy, *DK 7th Report*, Appndx 2, 280.

1539, 27 Jan., 19th on the surrender list and assigned a pension of £5 6s. 8d. p.a., *L and P Henry VIII*, xiv pt i, no 148; on 20 Feb., he was dispensed to change his habit and hold a benefice, Chambers, *Faculty Office Regs*, 175.

John BEKYNTON [Bekenton *alias* Romeseton' Romesey

occ. 1517 occ. 1539

1517, 7 Mar., ord dcn, St Mary's chapel by the cloister, Wells cathedral, Reg. Castello, fo 159.

1520, 22 Sept., ord pr., St Mary's chapel by the cloister, Wells cathedral, Reg. Wolsey, fo 26.

1534, 22 Sept., 6th to subscribe to the Act of Supremacy, *DK 7th Report*, Appndx 2, 280.

1539, 27 Jan., 8th on the surrender list and assigned a pension of £6 13s. 4d., *L and P Henry VIII*, xiv pt i, no 148.

1539, 20 Feb., dispensed to change his habit and hold a benefice, Chambers, *Faculty Office Regs*, 175.

Thomas BEKYNTON

occ. 1495 occ. 1499

1497, 22 Sept., ord dcn, St Mary's chapel by the cloister, Wells cathedral, Reg. King, fo 117.

1495, 30 Jan., 22nd and last in order, and not prof., on the *sed. vac.* visitation certificate, *Reg. abp Morton*, ii, no 347.

1499, 30 Aug., 14th in order at the el. of a prior, Reg. King, fo 139.

BENEDICT

occ. 1136 occ. 1157

1136 x 1157: prior, *HRH*, 28; see Peter I.

1151, 24 June, witnessed an episcopal instrument, *Eng. Epis. Acta*, x, no 43.

c. 1157, may have d. in Italy, *Hist. Monast. Gloucester*, ii, 106.

See *Bath Chartulary* for a letter to him as prior from the bp of Exeter (no 71) and for one of his *acta*, (no 75).

John BENET [*alias* Parnell, Pennell

occ. 1534 occ. 1539

1534, 22 Sept., 16th to subscribe to the Act of Supremacy, *DK 7th Report*, Appndx 2, 280.

1539, 27 Jan., 20th on the surrender list and assigned a pension of £5 6s. 8d. p.a., *L and P Henry VIII*, xiv pt i, no 148; on 20 Feb., he was dispensed to change his habit and hold a benefice, Chambers, *Faculty Office Regs*, 175.

John de BEREWYK

occ. 1344 occ. 1379

c. 1362–1379, prior: occ. as prior 20 June 1362, *CPR (1361–1364)*, 225; occ. 11 Oct. 1379, BL Ms Egerton 3316, fo 99v.

1344, 5 Oct., 12th in order among those in chapter for the purpose of appointing general proctors, *Priory Reg.*, no 344 (p. 119).

1364, 9 Jan., with other monks cleared by the abp from the censures against them; they had been published illegally because of an el. dis-

pute, *sed. vac.*, *Wells Liber Albus*, i, 266 (fo 251), Reg. abp Islip, fo 242v.
1362, 20 June, apptd two attorneys in Ireland, *CPR (1361–1364)*, 225.
1377, 1st in order on the clerical subsidy list and he pd 12d, PRO E179/4/2.

For a memorandum of one of his *acta* see *Priory Reg.*, no 85 (p. 23).

John BERYNGTON [Buryngton, Byrynton
occ. 1412 occ. 1447

1412, 10 Mar., 12th in order at the el. of a prior, *Reg. Bubwith*, no 1271 (p. 477).
1419/21, recd 69s. 4d. p.a. from the receiver of Dunster [castle], Maxwell Lyte, 'Dunster and its Lords', 207, 209.
1447, 5 July, residing in the cell at Dunster and present at the el. of a prior as proctor for the Dunster monks *Reg. Bekynton*, no 1639.

Note: There may be two Beryngtons here; on the other hand this could be John Buryton, q.v.

William BEWACHYN, Bewchyn
see Beachyne

BIGG
see Lyncombe

William BIRDE B.Th. [Birt, Bridde, Byrde
occ. 1481 d. 1525

1499–1525, prior: apptd by the bp 30 Aug. 1499, after having been postulated by the subprior and chapter and released from excommunication by the bp 'ex criminibus inobediencie et contemptus nostri inhabilitatis', Reg. King, fo 139v, and see below; d. 22 May 1525, *Reg. Clerk*, no 477 (fo 81v).
Note: the bp stated that he collated Birde to the office, which pertained to him by right on this occasion [because the monks had neglected to obtain his licence previously]. The marginal heading on fo 139v is *electio prioris per postulacionem*.
1481, 7 Apr., ord dcn, chapel of the hospital of St John the Baptist, Wells, Reg. Stillington, fo 208.
1484, 18 Sept., ord pr., chapel of the hospital of St John the Baptist, Wells, *ib.*, fo 214.
1499, 17 Apr., collated to the office of sacrist, *Reg. King*, no 178.
1495, 30 Jan., student at Oxford, *Reg. abp Morton*, ii, no 347; acc. to *BRUO* (where the date is given as 1492), he was prob. at Canterbury College.
n.d., granted a grace to be adm. B.Th., *BRUO* with no ref.
1493, 29 Apr., with the prior apptd proctor in all causes, *Wells Liber Albus*, ii, 456, (fo 305v).
1495, 30 Jan., 10th in order on the *sed. vac.* visitation certificate, *Reg. abp Morton*, ii, no 347.

Name in BL Ms Royal 5 B.xiv, Augustine Confessions (12th c.); on an end flyleaf—'Ecclesie cathedralis Bathonie servus, Anno nostre salutis 1502'.

He was responsible for carrying on the rebuilding of the cathedral church begun by bp King and for the construction of his own chantry chapel on the south side of the choir; see Manco, 'Buildings of Bath Priory', 98.

BIRDE
see also Byrde

John BLOXHAM [Blockesham, Blokesham, Bloxam
occ. 1344 occ. 1360

1346, 1 Mar., apptd by the prior and chapter as prior of the hospital/cell of St John the Evangelist at Waterford, with the custody of their lands and possessions in Ireland, *Priory Reg.*, no 885 (p. 359); on 3 Mar. he was apptd proctor for the purposes required by this office, *ib.*, no 886 (p. 359); he had some initial difficulties with his predecessor, Thomas de Foxcote, q.v.
1357, 16 Sept., with a citizen of Waterford, apptd to the above custody as guardians and administrators in Ireland, *Priory Reg.*, no 941 (p. 411).
1344, 5 Oct., 30th in order (and last but one) among those in chapter for the purpose of appointing general proctors, *Priory Reg.*, no 344, (p. 119).
1355, 8 Feb., with another, nominated by the prior as his attorney in Ireland for two yrs, *CPR (1354–1358)*, 169.
1357, 16 Aug., a similar apptment for two yrs, *ib.*, 597.
1360, 22 Feb., the above apptment renewed for two yrs, *CPR (1358–1361)*, 337 and 343; on 18 May, a similar apptment, *ib.*, 356.

Robert de BOCLAND
occ. 1261

1261, 27 June, named by the subprior and chapter as one of seven *compromissorii* in the el. of a prior, *Priory Reg.*, nos 255, 257 (pp.75, 76).

John de BOCSTON [Boeston
occ. 1344

1344, 5 Oct., 9th in order among those in chapter for the purpose of appointing general proctors, *Priory Reg.*, no 344 (p. 119).

William BONAR [Boner, Bonere, Bonour
occ. 1423 occ. 1447

1423, 30 Aug., one of four novices whose prof. the bp comm. the prior to rec., *Reg. Bubwith*, no 1189.
1425, 22 Sept., ord acol. and subdcn, Bath cathedral, *Reg. Stafford*, no 935.

1426, 16 Mar., ord dcn, St Cuthbert's church, Wells, *ib.*, no 21.
1428, 18 Sept., ord pr., bp's chapel, Wookey, *ib.*, no 942.

1447, 5 July, one of five monks residing at Dunster; he did not go to the el. of a prior at Bath but named John Beryngton, q.v., as his proctor, *Reg. Bekynton*, no 1639.

Stephen le BOTYLER
occ. 1344

1344, 5 Oct., 3rd in order among those in chapter for the purpose of appointing general proctors, *Priory Reg.*, no 344, (p. 119).

BOTYLER
see also Butteler

Henry BRADELEGH [Bradeley
occ. 1413 occ. 1417

1413, 12 Sept., the prior was comm. to rec. his prof., *Reg. Bubwith*, no 434.
1413, 23 Sept., ord subdcn, Banwell, *ib.*, no 1292.
1414, 3 Mar., ord dcn., Banwell, *ib.*, no 1294.
1417, 6 Mar., ord pr., Yeovil, *ib.*, no 1299.

John de BRADELEGH
occ. 1344 occ. 1377

1344, 5 Oct., 26th in order among those in chapter for the purpose of appointing general proctors, *Priory Reg.*, no 344 (p. 119).
1377, 2nd in order on the clerical subsidy list and pd 12d., PRO E179/4/2.

Thomas BRADFORD [Bradeford
occ. 1444 occ. 1447

1444, 26 Mar., ord acol., Bath cathedral, *Reg. Bekynton*, no 1653.

1447, 5 July, 17th in order at the el. of a prior, *Reg. Bekynton*, no 1639.

William BRADFORD [Bradeforde
occ. 1440

1440, 26 Mar., ord acol. and subdcn, Bath cathedral, *Reg. Stafford*, no 991.

William BRIDDE
see Birde

BRISTOLL
see Brystoll

Alexander BRISTOW [Brystow *alias* Bull
occ. 1517 occ. 1539

1517, 7 Mar., ord dcn, St Mary's chapel by the cloister, Wells cathedral, Reg. Castello, fo 159.
1520, 22 Sept., ord pr., St Mary's chapel by the cloister, Wells cathedral, Reg. Wolsey, fo 26.

1525, 28 June/5 July, fourth prior, *Reg. Clerk*, no 477.
1525, 5 July, 12th in order at the el. of a prior, *Reg. Clerk*, no 477.

1539, 27 Jan., 6th on the surrender list and assigned a pension of £6 13s. 4d. p.a., *L and P Henry VIII*, xiv pt i, no 148; on 20 Feb., he was dispensed to change his habit and hold a benefice, Chambers, *Faculty Office Regs*, 175.

Thomas BRISTOWE [Brystow
occ. 1481 occ. 1499

1481, 7 Apr., ord dcn, chapel of the hospital of St John the Baptist, Wells, Reg. Stillington, fo 208.

1495, 30 Jan., 9th in order on the *sed. vac.* visitation certificate, *Reg. abp Morton*, ii, no 347.
1499, 30 Aug., 6th at the el. of a prior, Reg. King, fo 139^v^.

I William BRISTOW [Brystowe
occ. 1411 occ. 1417

1412, 10 Mar., prior of Dunster, *Reg. Bubwith*, no 1271.
Note: Maxwell Lyte, *Dunster*, ii, 552, provides the dates 1411 to 1417 from SRO DD/L P11/1 and DCB no 71.

1412, 10 Mar., 9th in order at the el. of a prior, *Reg. Bubwith*, no 1271.

II William BRISTOWE [Brystowe
occ. 1446 occ. 1470

1446, 24 Sept., ord dcn, St Mary Magdalen's church, Taunton, *Reg. Bekynton*, no 1669.
1451, 20 Mar., ord pr., Lady chapel, Wells cathedral, *ib.*, no 1687.
[1470], prior of Dunster, Maxwell Lyte, *Dunster*, ii, 552, (SRO DD/L P12/3).

1447, June, 5 July, student at Oxford, Pantin, *Cant. Coll. Ox.*, ii, 173, *Reg. Bekynton*, ii, no 436; he was possibly living at Canterbury College.
1448/9, student, to whom the warden of Canterbury College pd a debt of 30s. owed to him (named as William, monk of Bath), on behalf of Robert Lynton I, q.v. (under Canterbury), who had d., Pantin, *Cant. Coll. Ox.*, ii, 173.

BRISTOWE
see also Brystoll

John de BROK [Broke
occ. 1364 occ. 1377

1364, 9 Jan., precentor, Reg. abp Islip, fo 242^v^, *Wells Liber Albus*, i, 266 (fo 251).

1364, 9 Jan., involved in an el. dispute that had arisen *sed. vac.*, and the abp revoked the censure against him and other monks as it had been published illegally, *Wells Liber Albus*, i, 266 (fo 251).
21377, 4th in order on the clerical subsidy list and pd 12d., PRO E179/4/2.

John BROWNE
see Arleston

Thomas BROWNE ?B.Th.
occ. 1481 occ. 1500

1481, 7 Apr., ord dcn, chapel of the hospital of St John the Baptist, Wells, Reg. Stillington, fo 208.

1499, before 31 May, prior of Dunster, *Reg. King*, no 211; see William Gilys.

1500, must have previously been a student at Oxford for about seven yrs as he opposed in theology this yr, for his B.Th., *BRUO*.

1495, 30 Jan., 11th in order on the *sed. vac.* visitation certificate, *Reg. abp Morton*, ii, no 347.

1499, before 31 May, as prior of Dunster, with his brethren came to an agreement with the vicar and parishioners of Dunster, *Reg. King*, no 211. See Maxwell Lyte, *Dunster*, ii, 402–404.

1499, 30 Aug., 7th in order at the el. of a prior, Reg. King, fo 139^{v}.

William de BRUGES
occ. 1292/3

1292/3, exorcist, to whom the prior of Christ Church, Canterbury [*sed. vac.* both Bath and Canterbury] wrote concerning his ordination [as acol.], *Priory Reg.*, no 415 (p. 148).

Thomas de BRUTON [Brueton
occ. 1344 occ. 1352/3

1344, 5 Oct., 18th in order among those in chapter for the purpose of appointing general proctors, *Priory Reg.*, no 344 (p. 119).

1352/3, 12 Feb., with the prior, John de Iford, q.v., and two others accused of binding themselves on oath to maintain a quarrel and thus cause disturbance vs the law; the jury at Bristol found him guilty, *ib.*, no 939 (p. 410).

Hugh de BRYSTOLL
occ. 1344

1344, 5 Oct., 27th in order among those in chapter for the purpose of appointing general proctors, *Priory Reg.*, no 344 (p. 119).

BRYSTOW
see also Bristow

Alexander BULL
see Bristow

Robert BURNET
occ. 1425/6

1425, 22 Sept., ord acol. and subdcn, Bath cathedral, *Reg. Stafford*, no 935.

1426, 16 Mar., ord dcn, St Cuthbert's church, Wells, *ib.*, no 21.

1426, 25 May, ord pr., Bruton priory, *ib.*, no 28.

John BURTON
occ. 1425

1425, 22 Sept., ord acol. and subdcn, Bath cathedral, *Reg. Stafford*, no 935.

John BURYTON
occ. 1406 occ. [1423]

[1423], prior of Dunster, Maxwell Lyte, *Dunster*, ii, 552, using as ref. SRO DD/L P12/1.

1406, monk residing at Dunster to whom Hugh Luttrell made an allowance, Maxwell Lyte, *Dunster*, i, 100, where it is stated that this payment was recorded annually for a number of yrs and was possibly connected with the celebration of masses.

Note: see John Beryngton who could be the same monk.

Robert BUTTELER [Boteler
occ. 1444 occ. 1447

1444, 26 Mar., ord acol., Bath cathedral, *Reg. Bekynton*, no 1653.

1447, 5 July, 16th in order at the el. of a prior, *Reg. Bekynton*, no 1639.

BUTTELER
see also Botyler

Richard BYGGE
see Lyncombe

Cuthbert BYRDE
occ. 1524

1524, 12 Mar., ord dcn, Bath cathedral, Reg. Clerk, fo 110^{v}.

1524, 21 May, ord pr., St Mary's chapel by the cloister, Wells cathedral, *ib.*, fo 111^{v}.

BYRDE
see also Birde

BYRYNTON
see Beryngton

W. de CALN
n.d.

n.d., [?late 13th c.], *temp.* W[?alter de Anno], prior, sacrist, *Priory Reg.*, no 408 (p. 146).

n.d., [?late 13th c.], drew up a bond for 4m. in favour of the abbot of Stanley, *ib.*

John CANTLOW B.Th. [Cauntlowe
occ. 1472 d. 1499

?1489–1499, prior: occ. 6 Nov. 1489, *Reg. Stillington*, no 1125; d. before 30 Aug. 1499, *Reg. King*, no 518; see Peter II and William Birde.

1472, 19 Dec., ord pr., Taunton, Reg. Stillington, fo 187.

1483, 24 July, sacrist, *Priory Reg.*, no 942 (p. 412).

1495, 30 Jan., named as *magister*, *Reg. abp Morton*, ii, no 347.

1483, 24 July, witnessed the apptment of a master of the hospital of St John the Baptist, Bath, *Priory Reg.*, no 942 (p. 412).

1490, 3 Mar., granted papal dispensation to hold a benefice *in commendam* as well as the priorate, *CPL*, xv (1484–1492), 262 (transcribed as Greatlow).

1495 30 Jan., present at the *sed. vac.* visitation, *Reg. abp Morton*, ii, no 347.

Bp King's visitation of the priory in 1499 shortly before the prior's d., found him guilty of allowing the cathedral fabric to decay and the monks' observance of the Rule to slacken, *Priory Reg.* lxviii (introd.) and Reg. King, fo 62.

He was the donor of the east window of St Catherine's church Batheaston and a window of St Thomas', Widcombe, Manco, 'Buildings of Bath Priory', 91.

CANYNG, CANYNGES
see Kaninges, Kanyng, Kanynggs

CARDIFF
see Kardif

John CARY
occ. 1451

1451, 18 Sept., ord pr., bp's chapel, Wookey, *Reg. Bekynton*, no 1690.

William CARY
occ. 1397 occ. 1437

1397, 22 Dec., ord subdcn, bp's chapel, Highclere, by lit. dim., *Reg. Wykeham*, (Winchester), i, 343.

1398, 23 Mar., ord dcn, bp's chapel, Farnham castle, by lit. dim., *ib.*, i, 344.

1398, 1 July, ord pr., bp's chapel, Esher, *ib.*, i, 346.

[1437], prior of Dunster, Maxwell Lyte, *Dunster*, ii, 552 (SRO DD/L P18/6).

1400, 22 Apr., with William Southbroke, q.v., named as monk proctor to meet with their counterparts from the Wells chapter and go to the king to request a licence to el. a bp, *Wells Charters* no 498.

1411, 2 July, apptd proctor by the prior to attend the Black Monk Chapter at Northampton, Pantin, *BMC*, iii, 199, 212.

1412, 10 Mar., 10th at the el. of a prior, *Reg. Bubwith*, no 1271.

Geoffrey de CHAUMPENEYS
occ. 1293

1292/3, acol., to whom the prior of Christ Church, Canterbury [*sed. vac.*] wrote concerning his ordination [as subdcn] *Priory Reg.*, no 415 (p. 148).

Adam de CHEDDRE
occ. 1337 occ. ?1346

1337, 5 July, apptd prior of Dunster to succ. Robert de Sutton q.v., *Priory Reg.*, no 780 (p. 303); he was prior on 25 June 1340, *ib.*, no 812 (p. 319). He was also prior in 1344, *ib.*, no 878 and presumably retired in 1345, see Roger de Lolham and below.

1345, 6 Oct., described as having served as prior of Dunster and also as chamberlain of Bath, [presumably on separate occasions], *Priory Reg.*, p. 353 (no. 876).

1340, 25 June, apptd by the prior and chapter as their proctor in a tithe dispute, *Priory Reg.*, no 812 (p. 319).

1345, 6 Oct., assigned by the prior and convent an annual rent of 5s from the revenues of the cell of Dunster to be used for an anniversary [?mass] for him at Dunster, because of the 'sumptuous buildings he has constructed and the many and notable good works he has done'; during his lifetime it was to be observed on the feast of St Katherine the virgin and after his d. on his obit, *Priory Reg.*, p. 353 (no. 876).

1346, 9 Jan., the grant for his anniversary was raised by the prior and convent to 6s 8d., *Priory Reg.*, no 885 (p. 359).

Note: see also Adam III who may be this monk.

Richard de CHERNBURY [Chernibury, Chervibury,
occ. 1275 occ. 1290

1283, 11 Feb., sacrist, BL Ms Egerton 3316, fo 62.

1275, 23 Jan., named as one of the seven monk electors to meet with their counterparts from the Wells chapter in order to el. a bp, *Priory Reg.*, no 325 (p. 103) and *Wells Liber Albus* i, 113 (fo 91).

1283, 10 Feb., witnessed a grant by the prior, BL Ms Egerton 3316, fo 62.

1290, 14 Jan., with Philip de Bathon', q.v., recd from the bp in London licence to el. a prior, *Priory Reg.*, no 394 (p. 142); see Walter de Anno.

John CHESTRE [Chester
occ. 1508 occ. 1525

1508, 18 Mar., ord subdcn, St Mary's chapel by the cloister, Wells cathedral, Reg. Castello, fo 146^{v}.

1513, 21 May, ord dcn, bp's palace chapel, Wells, *ib.*, fo 155.

1517, 7 Mar., ord pr., St Mary's chapel by the cloister, Wells cathedral, *ib.*, fo 159.

1525, 5 July, 8th in order at the el. of a prior, *Reg. Clerk*, no 477.

John CHIEWE [Chiwe, Chw
occ. 1458 occ. 1499

1458, 25 Feb., ord subdcn, bp's palace chapel, Wells, *Reg. Bekynton*, no 1744.

1459, 19 May, ord dcn, bp's chapel, Banwell, *ib.*, no 1755.
1460, 20 Sept., ord pr., St Cuthbert's church, Wells, *ib.*, no 1763.
1499, 30 Aug., 3rd in order at the el. of a prior, Reg. King, fo 139^v^.

Robert CHIEWE [Chiew
occ. 1414 occ. 1447

1414, 3 Mar., one of two novices whose prof. the prior was comm. to rec., *Reg. Bubwith*, no 483.
1417, 6 Mar., ord acol. and subdcn, Yeovil, *ib.*, no 1299.
1418, 24 Sept., ord dcn., Bruton priory, *ib.*, no 1301.
1419, 23 Sept., ord pr., St Cuthbert's church, Wells, *ib.*, no 1304.
1447, 5 July, third prior, *Reg. Bekynton*, no 1639.
1447, 5 July, 4th in order at the el. of a prior, *Reg. Bekynton*, no 1639.

Richard de CHILDESTON
occ. [?1357]

[?1357], Jan., prior of Dunster, Maxwell Lyte, *Dunster*, ii, 393.

Note: his name occ. in an agreement made between the prior and monks and the parishioners of St George's, Dunster, on which the yr is given only as 13 Edward [*recte* 31 Edward]. On the strength of the date Friday after the feast of St Wulstan, Maxwell Lyte has deduced that the yr is prob. 1357, *Dunster*, ii, 393; but it could be 1303. See R. II.

Asketillus de CHIUTON [?Churton
n.d.

n.d., monk *ad succurrendum* who gave land in Redcliffe, Bristol for the observance of his anniversary, *Priory Reg.*, no 808 (p. 317).

Note: in a deed dated 1155 one of the witnesses is Asketillus de Churton; this is prob. the same person, *Bath Chartulary*, no 75.

CHIWE
see Chiewe

Thomas CHRISTI
see Crist

John de CIRCESTRE
occ. 1377

1377, 6th in order on the clerical subsidy list and pd 12d., PRO E179/4/2.

CIRCESTRE
see also Cyrcestre

John CLEMENT
occ. 1497 occ. 1502

1497, 23 Sept., ord subdcn, St Mary's chapel by the cloister, Wells cathedral, Reg. King, fo 117.
1498, 22 Sept., ord dcn, St Mary's chapel by the cloister, Wells cathedral, *ib.*, fo 119.
1502, 12 Mar., ord pr., St Mary's chapel behind the new altar, Bath cathedral, *ib.*, fo 126^v^.
1499, 30 Aug., 16th in order at the el. of a prior, Reg. King, fo 139^v^.

William CLEMENT [Clemente, Clementt
occ. 1523 occ. 1539

1523, 21 Mar., ord subdcn, St Mary's chapel by the cloister, Wells cathedral, Reg. Wolsey, fo 30.
1524, 12 Mar., ord dcn, Bath cathedral, Reg. Clerk, fo 110^v^.
1525, 5 July, 19th in order at the el. of a prior, *Reg. Clerk*, no 477.
1534, 22 Sept., 11th to subscribe to the Act of Supremacy, *DK 7th Report*, Appndx 2, 280.
1539, 27 Jan., 12th on the surrender list and assigned a pension of £5 6s. 8d. p.a., *L and P Henry VIII*, xiv pt i, no 148; on 20 Feb., he was dispensed to change his habit and hold a benefice, Chambers, *Faculty Office Regs*, 175.

Robert de CLOPCOTE [Clopecote, Clopkote, Cloppcot, Cloppecote
occ. 1292/3 d. 1332

1301–1332, prior: el. 14 Apr. 1301, *Priory Reg.*, no 580; d. before 27 Feb., 1332, *Reg. Shrewsbury*, no 356, *Priory Reg.*, nos 704 and 720 (pp.266, 273). However, he had previously sent in his res. to the pope; see Thomas Crist.

1292/3, acol., to whom the prior of Christ Church, Canterbury [*sed. vac.*] wrote concerning his ord [as subdcn], *Priory Reg.*, no 415 (p. 148).
1299, 29 Oct., sent as proctor, by the subprior and chapter to the abp, *Priory Reg.*, no 547 (p. 199).
1306, 4 May; 1307, 15 Apr., was visiting the Irish estates, *ib.*, nos 554, 521 (pp.201, 185); see John Symonis.
[1308], recd a bequest of £100 from bp Haselshaw who d. on 11 Dec., *Priory Reg.*, no 808 (p. 316).
1312, 28 Sept., one of the cathedral priors summoned to meet the papal nuncios in London, *Councils and Synods*, ii, 1377.
1316, 15 Aug., with the assent of the subprior and chapter made detailed arrangements concerning the better observation of the obits of deceased monks, *Priory Reg.*, no 810 (p. 318).
1321, 26 Aug., accused by the bp of incompetence and waste of the priory revenues and inadequate provision of food for the monks and urged to be more careful and also more gentle in word and deed, *Reg. Drokensford*, 193 (fo 177).
1321, 25 Oct., was refused the privilege of wearing pontifical insignia for which he had petitioned, with the support of Edmund, earl of

Kent, *Priory Reg.*, lxi-lxii, where the papal document from the Vatican archives is printed.

[1332], 6 Apr., (that is, Mon. before Palm Sunday), a memorandum ref. to the report that bulls containing his res. were expected from Rome, together with the pope's acceptance of the res. and the provision of Thomas Crist, q.v., as his successor, *Priory Reg.*, no 710 (p. 268).

Some of his *acta* are in the *Priory Reg.*; see the index there under his name. A chantry for him and for a number of others [benefactors] was set up and endowed on 10 June [1332] at the altar of St Martin in the cathedral, Priory Reg., p. 305 (no. 785) which says 1302, Wed. in the vigil of St Barnabas, surely a mistake, because of the omission of 'tricesimo'.

John COK
n.d.

n.d., [1223 × 1261], *temp.* prior Thomas [Stokton], q.v., involved in a dispute over the sale of a horse, *Priory Reg.*, no 425 (p. 150).

John COLYN
see Humylyte

Michael de COMB
occ. 1377

1377, 7th in order on the clerical subsidy list and pd 12d., PRO E179/4/2.

Richard COMBE
occ. 1509 occ. 1511

1509, 22 Dec., ord subdcn, chapel of All Saints [*sic*] by the cloister, Wells cathedral, Reg. Castello, fo 150.

1510, 22 Sept., ord dcn, chapel of St Mary by the cloister, Wells cathedral, *ib.*, fo 151.

1511, 5 Apr., ord pr., chapel of St Mary by the cloister, Wells cathedral, *ib.*, fo 152.

I John de COMPTON [Cumpton, Cumptona
occ. [1298] occ. 1319

1319, 28 Sept., apptd sacrist, Reg. Drokensford, fo 123v (p. 136).

1298, 23 Apr., apptd by the prior, Thomas de Winton, q.v., to take charge of the hospital/cell of St John the Evangelist at Waterford, *Priory Reg.*, nos 392, 535 (pp.196, 141). There is another apptment dated 18 Apr. in *ib.*, p. 197 (no 537).

[1298], W[?illiam of March] bp., wrote a letter of recommendation of behalf of Compton, prior of the hospital/cell of St John the Evangelist at Waterford, to the king's chancellor in Ireland, *Priory Reg.*, no 502 (p. 176), also no 538 (p. 197).

1302, 6 Nov., provided with royal letters of protection, having been named by the prior as one of his two attorneys in Ireland for two yrs, *CPR (1301–1307)*, 70.

1309, 2 Jan., sent by the prior and convent, with Robert de Sutton, q.v., to Fernton [?Farrington Gurney] to arrange with the Wells proctors a date for their joint el. of a bp., *Priory Reg.*, nos 619, 621 (pp. 227, 228).

1309, before 15 May, as proctor for the chapter, with a canon of Wells, informed the abp of the el. of John de Drokensford as bp, *Reg. abp Winchelsey*, 1112–1113.

II John COMPTON
occ. 1487 occ. 1495

1487, 31 Mar., ord subdcn, St Mary Redcliffe, Bristol, Reg. Stillington, fo 220.

1488, 22 Mar., ord dcn, Bruton priory, *ib.*, fo 226.

1492, 18 Mar., ord pr., chapel of the hospital of St John the Baptist, Wells, *Reg. abp Morton*, ii, no 65d.

1495, 30 Jan., 18th in order on the *sed. vac.* visitation certificate, *Reg. abp Morton*, ii, no 347.

?COPTEN
see Thomas Bath II

William de CORBUIL [?Corbeil
occ. [1198 × 1223]

n.d., [1198 × 1223], occ. as witness to a grant by prior Robert [de Bath], q.v., *Priory Reg.*, no 16 (p. 7).

Note: Hunt suggests that he and Urban, q.v., may have come to England with Reginald Fitzjocelin, q.v., who had been abbot of Corbeil, *ib.*, no 16, note.

M Simon de CORNUBIA [Cornub'
occ. [1198 × 1223]

[1198 × 1223], recd a licence from prior Robert [de Bath I, q.v.] and the convent to become a monk of their house, 'et reditum ad nos qu[ando]cumque voluerit habitum nostrum suscipere', Priory Reg., p.20 (no. 69).

Richard CORSTON
occ. 1453/5

1453, 26 May, ord dcn, St Cuthbert's church, Wells, *Reg. Bekynton*, no 1707.

1455, 20 Sept., ord pr., bp's palace chapel, Wells, *ib.*, no 1720.

William de CORSTON [*alias* Uppehulle
occ. 1325

1325, 11 Mar., *conversus*, recd licence to set off for the Holy Land, and permission from the prior to wear secular clothing if he found himself in dangerous circumstances, Priory Reg., p.252 (no. 670); see also William de Nubbeley.

John COTELE
occ. 1292/3

1292/3, exorcist, on behalf of whom the prior of Christ Church, Canterbury [*sed. vac.* both Bath and Canterbury] wrote to the official of Bath and Wells concerning his ordination [as acol.], *Priory Reg.*, no 415 (p. 148).

John COUNTEVYLE
see Axebrigge

John COWPER [Coupar
occ. 1492 occ. 1499

1492, 18 Mar., ord subdcn, chapel of the hospital of St John the Baptist, Wells, *Reg. abp Morton*, ii, no 65b.
1497, 23 Sept., ord pr., St Mary's chapel by the cloister, Wells cathedral, Reg. King, fo 117.
1495, 30 Jan., 21st (and last) in order on the *sed. vac.* visitation certificate and, with Robert Pavy, q.v., (mistakenly) described as acol., *Reg. abp Morton*, ii, no 347.
1499, 30 Aug., residing at Dunster, absent from the el. of a prior but represented by Thomas Gregory, q.v., Reg. King, fo 139v.

Thomas CRIST [Christi, Cristi, Cryst
occ. 1329 occ. 1340

1332–1340, prior: apptd by papal provision 12 July 1332, *CPL*, ii (1305–1342), 357, and confirmed by the bp, 24 Sept., *Reg. Shrewsbury*, no 449; res. before 12 Aug. 1340, *ib.*, no 1397; see John de Iforde.
1329, 12 May, with William de Hampton II apptd proctor to meet the proctors from the Wells chapter in order to make arrangements for obtaining the king's licence to el. a bp, *Wells Liber Albus* i, 218 (fo 177); see also Priory Reg. nos 330, 333A (pp 106, 107). They recd licence to el. on 23 May, *CPR (1327–1330)*, 391.
1329, 2 June, named as one of five monk proctors to meet with their counterparts from the Wells chapter in order to el. a bp on this day, *Priory Reg.*, nos 338, 340 (pp.111, 114).
[1332], 6 Apr., (that is, Mon. before Palm Sunday), a memorandum ref. to the report that bulls containing the res. of Robert Clopcote, q.v., as prior were expected from Rome, together with the pope's acceptance of the res. and the provision of Crist as his successor, *Priory Reg.*, no 710 (p. 268).
1337, before 15 May, was put in charge of the collection of clerical tenths, *Reg. Shrewsbury*, nos 1266, 1267.
1340, 27 Aug., his needs in retirement were provided for by the bp's ordinance: he was to be given a house for himself, his monk chaplain and his esquire and groom; adequate food was to be allocated and wood for fuel; the manor and advowson of Northstoke were also granted to him [by way of pension], *Reg. Shrewsbury*, no 1400.

Many of his *acta* are preserved in the *Priory Reg.*, see the index under his name; the section beginning with item no 737 reads 'Registrum de primo anno Domini Thome prioris'.

On 9 Sept., 1337, a corrody was granted to Edith Cryst of Malmesbury who may have been a relative, *Priory Reg.*, no 782 (p. 303). A Richard Cryst, also of Malmesbury, had recd a corrody from prior Clopcote, q.v., *ib.*, no 534 (p. 195).

Adam de CRISTMARLEFORD [Cristenalford, Crystamalford
occ. 1344 occ. 1364

1364, 9 Jan., subprior, Reg. abp Islip, fo 243, *Wells Liber Albus* i, 266 (fo 251).
1344, 5 Oct., 31st and last in order of those assembled in chapter for the purpose of appointing general proctors, *Priory Reg.*, no 344 (p. 119).
[1363/4], one of the monks involved in a disputed el., *sed. vac.*, Reg. abp Islip, fo 243; on 9 Jan. 1364, the abp removed the censures against him and other monks because they had been published illegally, during the dispute, *Wells Liber Albus* i, 266 (fo 251).

CRUTELYNGTONE
see Roger de Grutelyngthon

CUMPTON
see Compton

Thomas de CYRCESTRE
occ. 1332 occ. 1344

1332, 30 Mar., acc. to the prior's letter to Hugh de Dovor, q.v., he had been in charge of livestock in Ireland and had been badly treated by Hugh, Priory Reg., pp. 268, 270 (nos 708, 715).
1344, 5 Oct., 4th in order among those in chapter for the purpose of appointing general proctors, *Priory Reg.*, no 344 (p. 119).

CYRCESTRE
see also Circestre

DANNO, Daune
see Anno

John DENOROUS [?Devorons
occ. 1481

1481, 7 Apr., ord dcn, chapel of the hospital of St John the Baptist, Wells, Reg. Stillington, fo 208.

John de DERHAM
occ. 1301

1301, 11 Apr., subprior, *Priory Reg.*, no 580 (p. 212).

[?1290s], acted as proctor for the prior in an appeal on behalf of Geoffrey, q.v., accused of an offence before he became a monk, Priory Reg., p. 158 (no. 443).

DONESTERRE
see Dunster, Dunstorr

Hugh de DOVOR [Dovere, le Dovere
occ. 1320 occ. 1344

1320, 5 Feb., apptd precentor, Reg. Drokensford, fo 126v (p. 140).
1325, 20 Feb., apptd sacrist, with the general monition that the office was in need of better management and no one else was to lay claim to the office, *ib.*, fo 236 (p. 241).
1332, 30 Mar., the prior wrote to recall him from Waterford, where he had been prior, on order of the abp of Canterbury, after the latter's visitation of Bath, *Priory Reg.*, no 708 (p. 268); a second letter was sent commanding a reply, *ib.*, no 715 (p. 270); see Thomas de Cyrcestre and Thomas de Foxcote.
1344, 5 Oct., 5th in order among those in chapter for the purpose of appointing general proctors, *Priory Reg.*, no 344, (transcribed as Dowe), (p. 119).

Note: see also Hugh V.

John DRAPER
occ. 1468 occ. 1471

1468, 11 June, ord subdcn, Bridgwater, Reg. Stillington, fo 177.
1470, 16 June, ord dcn, chapel of the hospital of St John the Baptist, Wells, *ib.*, fo 183.
1471, 21 Sept., ord pr., chapel of the hospital of St John the Baptist, Wells, *ib.*, fo 185.

Walter de DUNE
see Walter de Anno

Note: this is a misreading or, perhaps, an alternative rendering of d'Aune.

I John de DUNSTER [Dunsterre (Prior I)
occ. 1397 d. 1412

c. 1397–1412, prior: occ. 3 May 1397, *CPL*, v (1396–1404), 50; d. 6 Feb., 1412, *Reg. Bubwith*, no 1271.

1397, 3 May, granted papal dispensation to choose his own confessor, *CPL*, v (1396–1404), 50.
1411, 2 July, apptd William Cary, q.v., his proctor to attend the Black Monk Chapter, his excuse being *diversis corporis mei membrorum collisionibus* and business affairs, Pantin, *BMC*, iii, 212–213.

One of his *acta* (undated) has been added as a memorandum in a blank space in the *Priory Reg.*, no 279 (p. 83).

II John DUNSTER (Prior II)
occ. 1450 occ. 1480

c. 1468–1480, prior: occ. 18 Feb. 1468, *CPR (1467–1477)*, 65; provided to the abbacy of St Augustine's, Canterbury, 13 Aug. 1480, *CPL*, xiii (1471–1484), 5, but still called prior on 16 June 1481, *CPR (1476–1485)*, 278; royal assent to his el. and renewal of the papal provision followed in 1482, *CPR (1476–1485)*, 310, *CPL*, xiii (1471–1484) pt ii, 812–813.

1450, 21 Mar., ord pr., chapel of the bp's hospice in the Strand, London, *Reg. Bekynton*, no 1683.
1458, 2 Oct., collated to the office of precentor, *Reg. Bekynton*, no 1166.

He was responsible for rebuilding the refectory but in so doing left the priory in debt, Manco, 'Buildings of Bath Priory', 89.

Martin de DUNSTER [Donesterre
occ. 1275

1275, 23 Jan., apptd as one of seven monk electors to meet with their counterparts from the Wells chapter in order to el. a bp, *Priory Reg.*, no 325 (p. 103) and *Wells Liber Albus* i, 113 (fo 91).

Note: this may be Martin I, q.v.

Matthew de DUNSTER [Donesterre
occ. 1275

1275, 23 Jan., apptd as one of seven monk electors to meet with their counterparts from the Wells chapter in order to el. a bp, *Priory Reg.*, no 325 (p. 103) and *Wells Liber Albus* i, 113 (fo 91).

Richard DUNSTER
occ. 1423 occ. 1426

1423, 30 Aug., one of four novices whose prof. the bp comm. the prior to rec., *Reg. Bubwith*, no 1189.
1423, 18 Sept., ord acol. and subdcn, St Mary's chapel by the cloister, Wells cathedral, *ib.*, no 1315.
1425, 22 Sept., ord dcn, Bath cathedral, *Reg. Stafford*, no 935.
1426, 21 Sept., ord pr., Yeovil, *ib.*, no 936.

David de DUNSTORR'
occ. 1292/3

1292/3, subdcn, to whom the prior of Christ Church, Canterbury [*sed. vac.* both Bath and Canterbury] wrote concerning his ordination [as dcn], *Priory Reg.*, no 415 (p. 148).

Gilbert de DUNSTORR [Dunestorra, Dunset', ?Kaerdine
occ. [1242] occ. 1267

1264, 22 May, subprior, *Priory Reg.*, no 304 (p. 93).
1267, 8 Jan., almoner, *ib.*, no 316 (p. 98).

[1242, c.19 Nov.], with Richard III q.v., sent as proctor to the king to inform him of the d. of bp Jocelin and to obtain licence to el. a bp, *Priory Reg.*, no 183 (p. 51); named as Gilbert.

1243, 6 Jan., with Richard de Kaninges, q.v., recd licence from the king at Bordeaux to el. a bp, *CPR (1232–1247)*, 354.

1243, 5 Feb., one of the monks who with the prior, Thomas I, q.v., was present in the guest hall when the subdean of Wells appeared to appeal vs the monks' proposed el. on the following day (where he is Gilbert de Kaerdine), *Wells Liber Albus*, i, 91–92 (fo 74). With Walter VIII, q.v., he was present on 7 Feb., in a chapel of Salisbury cathedral when the proctors of the Wells chapter appealed vs the el. of Roger, precentor of Salisbury by the Bath monks, *ib.*, i, 93–94 (fo 75^v^). On 15 Feb. he was named as proctor, with Thomas [de Theukesbiry], q.v., to inform the king of the el. of Roger de Salisbury as bp, *Priory Reg.*, no 187 (p. 52); and on 28 Feb., with other monks he was named in the course of an appeal vs the dean and chapter of Wells concerning the el., *ib.*, no 189 (p. 52). On 17 Sept., the two were apptd proctors to go to Rome concerning the el. with letters from the prior bearing this date, *ib.*, nos 197, 196 (pp. 56, 55).

1244, 3 Feb., with Thomas [de Theukesbiry], q.v., announced the el. of Roger de Salisbury to the pope, *CPL*, i (1198–1304), 205.

1244, 27 Oct., apptd proctor in the curia, *Priory Reg.*, no 202 (p. 57); see Thomas de Theukesbiry. On this same day he was authorized to procure a loan of 10m., for expenses there, *ib.*, no 204 (p. 57).

Note: this second apptment as proctor is prob. a confirmation of the earlier apptment issued in conjunction with the request for a loan; he may have remained at the curia between Sept. 1243 and Oct. 1244.

[1246], 30 Sept., was sent to Wells with official documents, *Wells Liber Albus* i, 3 (fo 8).

[1250], sent to the bp to explain the monks' inability to pay the clerical subsidy he had levied in aid of the bpric, *Priory Reg.*, no 208 (p. 57), (as Gilbert).

1264, 25 Apr., with Nicholas II, q.v., arranged with the Wells proctors a date for the el. of a bp, *Priory Reg.*, no 303 (p. 93), and *Wells Liber Albus* i, 102 (fo 82^v^); on 22 May he was one of the four monk electors who with the Wells representatives met at Fernton [?Farrington Gurney] to carry out the el., *Priory Reg.*, no 304 (p. 93), *Wells Liber Albus* i, 102.

1267, 8 Jan., named, with Nicholas II, q.v., as the monk proctors who were to meet with the Wells chapter proctors in order to arrange the date for the el. of a bp, *Priory Reg.*, no 316 (p. 98).

John EDGAR [Edger *alias* Godbury/?Sodbury

occ. 1539

1539, 27 Jan., 14th on the surrender list and assigned a pension of £5 6s. 8d., *L and P Henry VIII*, xiv pt i, no 148.

Note: see John Sudbury who is prob. the same monk.

EDMUND

occ. 1326

1326, 14 Jan., one of twelve monks who made their prof. before the bp, Reg. Drokensford, fo 270.

Edward EDWY [Edwey *alias* Style

occ. 1534 occ. 1539

1534, 22 Sept., 12th to subscribe to the Act of Supremacy, *DK 7th Report*, Appndx 2, 280.

1539, 27 Jan., 15th on the surrender list and assigned a pension of £5 6s. 8d. p.a., *L and P Henry VIII*, xiv pt 1, no 148; on 20 Feb., he was dispensed to change his habit and hold a benefice, Chambers, *Faculty Office Regs*, 175.

Robert de ELY [Hely

occ. 1243

1243, 26 Feb., almoner, *Priory Reg.*, no 189 (p. 52).

1243, 26 Feb., named with Thomas de Kardif, q.v., as proctor on behalf of the chapter's rights in the el. of Roger de Salisbury, *Priory Reg.*, no 188 (p. 52); on 28 Feb., with other monks named in the course of an appeal vs the dean and chapter of Wells concerning the el., *ib.*, no 189 (p. 52). See also Gilbert de Dunstorr.

John de ESSEX [Estsex

occ. 1308 occ. 1317

1308, 17 Dec., with Philip de Bathon', q.v., apptd proctor by the prior and chapter to take part in the preliminary discussions with proctors of the Wells chapter concerning the el. of a bp; *Priory Reg.*, no 614 (p. 226); on 18 Dec. they were named as the monk proctors to go to the king to obtain the necessary licence, *ib.*, no 615 (p. 226).

[1315], 3 June, as proctor for the prior recd absolution from excommunication for failure to pay the required subsidy to the king, Reg. Drokensford, fo 77^v^ (printed reg. p. 89).

1317, 18 Feb., with William de Hampton I and Thomas de Bathonia, q.v., named as proctors to meet the Wells proctors to come to an agreement over the advowson and appropriation of Bathampton church, *Wells Liber Albus* i, 172 (fo 134).

John de ESTON

occ. 1326

1326, 2 Sept., presented a petition to the bp from the prior requesting his collation to the office of precentor, Reg. Drokensford, fo 254^{v} (printed reg. p. 265); insisting on his right of apptment, the bp granted this as a concession, *ib.*

1327, 28 Aug., replaced as precentor by Simon de Schawe, q.v., *ib.*, fo 266^{v} (p. 273).

EUGENIUS

occ. 1299

1299, 10 Dec., made his prof. of obedience after having been adm. to the community at the request of Queen Margaret; he had previously been an abbot in a German monastery, *Priory Reg.*, no 447 (p. 159).

John EXETRE

occ. 1412

1412, 10 Mar., pr., and 17th in order at the el. of a prior, *Reg. Bubwith*, no 1271.

William EYLES

see Gilys

John EYTON

occ. 1497 occ. 1525

1497, 23 Sept., ord dcn, St Mary's chapel by the cloister, Wells cathedral, Reg. King, fo 117.

1499, 30 Aug., 17th in order at the el. of a prior, Reg. King, fo 139^{v}.

1525, 28 June, absent from the el. of a prior as he was reported *in partibus transmarinis*, *Reg. Clerk*, no 477.

Robert de la FFELDE

occ. 1319

1319, granted licence by the prior to leave the monastery, in order to try his vocation elsewhere, 'ad arciorem religionem posse transvolare', Priory Reg., p. 239 (no. 638).

Reginald FITZJOCELIN

occ. 1191

1191, 27 Nov., bp of Bath, elected abp of Canterbury, *HBC*, 232.

1191, 26 Dec., d. at Dogmersfield shortly after receiving the Benedictine habit from Walter I, prior, q.v., *Chron. Devizes*, 44. See *Eng. Epis. Acta*, ii (Canterbury), appndx 1, 276.

See William de Corbuil and Urban I.

Geoffrey FLORI

occ. 1369

1369, 6 Sept., with John de Axebrigge, q.v., accused of various misdeeds including forgery, with the aid of the priory seals; the entry is very faded, but it appears that the two may have gone to the curia, as the prior seems to have sent a proctor there, Priory Reg., p. 332 (no. 840).

John de FORD

see Iforde

Richard FORDE

occ. 1463 occ. 1495

1463, 24 Sept., ord subdcn, chapel of the hospital of St John the Baptist, Wells, *Reg. Bekynton*, no 1782.

1465, 21 Sept., ord dcn, chapel of the hospital of St John the Baptist, Wells, Reg. *sed. vac.*, fo 13 (third series of foliation).

1467, 23 May, ord pr., chapel of the hospital of St John the Baptist, Wells, Reg. Stillington, fo 175.

1495, 30 Jan., chamberlain, *Reg. abp Morton*, ii, no 347.

1495, 30 Jan., 5th in order on the *sed. vac.* visitation certificate, *Reg. abp Morton*, ii, no 347.

Thomas de FOXCOTE

occ. 1320 occ. 1346

1320, 26 Feb., collated to the office of precentor, Reg. Drokensford, fo 119 (p. 130).

1332, 30 Aug., apptd as proctor of the prior and chapter and as custodian of the Irish estates, *Priory Reg.*, no 719 (p. 273); see John de Axebrigge.

1334, 27 Nov., [renewal of his] apptment as proctor and custodian in Ireland with authority to revoke any of the alienations for which Hugh de Dovor, q.v. had been responsible, *Priory Reg.*, no 754 (p. 292).

1337, 22 Apr., removed from the above office and replaced by John de Kingeswode, q.v., *ib.*, no 774 (p. 299).

1346, 1 Mar., removed [?again] and followed by John de Bloxham, q.v., *ib.*, no 885 (p. 359).

n.d., remained in Ireland, and the prior ordered that he be given a room in the infirmary of the hospital of St John, Waterford and be provided with a groom and [a pension of] 100s. for the two of them; Bloxham had been made responsible for Foxcote, his predecessor, who was reported to have misused the hospital's funds and who made life difficult for him, *Priory Reg.*, nos 889, 896, 897 (pp. 364, 372).

FREDYNGTHORN

see Tredyngthon

FROMLOK

see William Lacock

FULCO

occ. 1206

1206, 3 Feb., present at the el. of bp Jocelin and 35th to put his signature on the letter to the pope requesting his confirmation, Wells Cathedral Muniments, Charter no 40 (iv).

G.[?ILBERT
n.d.

n.d., occ. as prior, prob. *temp.* Alexander, dean of Wells, *Wells Liber Albus* i, 25 (fo 24[v]); see *HRH*, 29.

Note: Alexander was dean of Wells late 1189 x June 1209, *Eng. Epis. Acta*, x, 214.

Some of his *acta* occ. in the *Priory Reg.*, nos 1–3, 4–13 (pp. 2–6).

John GABRIEL [Gabriell *alias* Style
occ. 1539

1539, 27 Jan., 18th on the surrender list and assigned a pension of £5 6s. 8d. p.a., *L and P Henry VIII*, xiv pt i, no 148.

See also Edward Edwy who had the same patronymic.

Ralph de GANARD [Gannard
occ. 1308 occ. 1332

1308, 18 Dec., chamberlain, *Priory Reg.*, no 615 (p. 226).

1308, 18 Dec., with William de Hampton I, q.v., apptd proctor to join the Wells chapter proctors in seeking from the king licence to el. a bp, *Priory Reg.*, no 615 (p. 226); they recd the licence on 25 Dec., *CPR (1307–1313)*, 97.

1332, 24 Sept., acting as proctor for Thomas Crist, q.v., recd a letter from the bp at Dogmersfield confirming Crist's provision to the priorate, *Reg. Shrewsbury*, no 449, and also *Priory Reg.*, no 527A (p. 187).

See also Ralph III.

I GEOFFREY [Galfridus
occ. [?1290s]

[?1290s], accused in the bp of Worcester's consistory court at Bristol of an unspecified offence before he became a monk while he was vicar of ?Hutton, and John de Derham, q.v., as proctor for the prior initiated an appeal to the pope to forestall his possible suspension or excommunication, Priory Reg., p. 158 (no. 443); see John de Derham.

II GEOFFREY
occ. 1326

1326, 14 Jan., one of twelve monks who made their prof. before the bp, Reg. Drokensford, fo 270.

Richard GIBBS
see Gules

William GIBBS
see William Holleway II

I GILBERT
see G.

II GILBERT
occ. [1242]

[1242, c. 19 Nov.], sent by the prior as proctor with Richard III, q.v., to inform the king of the d. of bp Jocelin, *Priory Reg.*, no 183 (p. 51).

Note: this is almost certainly Gilbert de Dunstorr, q.v.

GILBERT
see also under William de Hampton I, Herebert

William GILYS [Eyles, Giles, Gyles, Gylys
occ. 1468 occ. 1499

1468, 11 June, ord subdcn, Bridgwater, Reg. Stillington, fo 177.

1470, 16 June, ord dcn, chapel of the hospital of St John the Baptist, Wells, *ib.*, fo 183.

1471, 21 Sept., ord pr., chapel of the hospital of St John the Baptist, Wells, *ib.*, fo 185.

1495, 30 Jan., prior of Dunster, *Reg. abp Morton*, ii, no 347.

1495, 30 Jan., 7th in order on the *sed. vac.* visitation certificate, *Reg. abp Morton*, ii, no 347 (transcribed as Eyles).

1499, 30 Aug., 4th at the el. of a prior, Reg. King, fo 139[v].

Stephen GLASTONBURY
occ. 1447

1447, 5 July, 2nd in order at the el. of a prior, *Reg. Bekynton*, no 1639.

GODBURY
see Edgar

John GODDE
occ. 1282 or 1305

1282 or 1305, 2 May, subprior, Priory Reg., p. 6 (no. 15).

1282 or 1305, 2 May, witness to the apptment of a master of St John's hospital, Bath, *ib.*

Note: this entry is clearly dated 1281/2 [10 Edward I] and Robert Clopcote, q.v., fourth yr (i.e. 1304/5), and so we are left with an unresolved problem.

Henry de GODLEYE
occ. 1377

1377, 11th in order on the clerical subsidy list and pd 12d., PRO E179/4/2.

Hugh de GODMER
occ. 1292 occ. 1302

1292, 16 Dec.; 1300, 9 Nov.; 1301, 10 Apr., precentor, *CPR (1292–1302)*, 2; *Priory Reg.*, no 575 (p. 210); Priory Reg., p. 212 (not in printed text).

1302, 13/30 Apr., subprior, Pantin, *BMC*, i, 156–157, *Reg. Sed. Vac.* (Worcester), 78.

1292, 16 Dec., with William de Hampton I, q.v., and two canons of the Wells chapter obtained royal licence to el. a bp, *CPR (1292–1301)*, 2.

1299, 29 Oct., apptd proctor by the prior and chapter to go to London to a council called by the abp, *Councils and Synods*, ii, 1202, *Priory Reg.*, no 548 (p. 199).

1300, 9 Nov., apptd proctor by the prior and chapter with regard to their obtaining absolution from excommunication incurred because they pd a subsidy to the king vs papal ruling, *ib.*, no 575 (p. 210).

1301, 10 Apr., with Robert de Sutton, sent as proctor to obtain licence from the bp to el. a prior, Priory Reg., p.212 (not in printed text).

1302, 30 Apr., with the prior of Shrewsbury on behalf of the Black Monk Chapter conducted a visitation of the cathedral priory of Worcester, after having announced their intention in a letter dated 13 Apr., Pantin, *BMC*, i, 156–157, *Reg. Sed. Vac.* (Worcester), 78.

GODWINUS
occ. [1088 × 1106]

[1088, July × 1106], witness to an episcopal charter, *Eng. Epis. Acta*, x, no 2 (*Bath Chartulary*, no 51).

John GOLDCLYF
occ. 1412

1412, 10 Mar., pr., 11th in order at the el. of a prior, *Reg. Bubwith*, no 1271.

John GOOSE
see Joce

Thomas GREGORY [Gregorye
occ. 1481 occ. 1499

1481, 7 Apr., ord dcn, chapel of the hospital of St John the Baptist, Wells, Reg. Stillington, fo 208.

1495, 30 Jan., residing at Dunster and 12th in order on the *sed. vac.* visitation certificate, *Reg. abp Morton*, ii, no 347.

1499, 30 Aug., 9th in order at the el. of a prior, Reg. King, fo 139v; he acted as proxy for three Dunster monks, *ib.*

GRETELINTON
see Grutelyngthon

Richard GRIFFITHS [Griffyn, Griffyth, Gryffett, Gryffyth
occ. 1502 occ. 1539

1502, 12 Mar., ord acol., St Mary's chapel behind the new altar, Bath cathedral, Reg. King, fo 126.

1505, 20 Dec., ord dcn, St Mary's chapel by the cloister, Wells cathedral, Reg. Castello, fo 141.

1508, 18 Mar., ord pr., St Mary's chapel by the cloister, Wells cathedral, *ib.*, fo 146.

1535, 1539, 27 Jan., prior of Dunster, *Valor Eccles.* i, 220, (where he is John), *L and P Henry VIII*, xiv, pt 1, no 148.

1525, 5 July, 5th in order at the el. of a prior, *Reg. Clerk*, no 477.

1539, 27 Jan., 3rd on the surrender list and assigned a pension of £8 p.a., *L and P Henry VIII*, xiv, pt 1, no 148; on 20 Feb., he was dispensed to change his habit and hold a benefice, Chambers, *Faculty Office Regs*, 175.

Robert de GRUTELYNGTHON [Grittelyngton
occ. 1292/3 occ. 1344

1292/3, acol., to whom the prior of Christ Church, Canterbury, [*sed. vac.*, both Bath and Canterbury] wrote concerning his ordination [as subdcn] *Priory Reg.*, no 415 (p. 148).

1344, 5 Oct., 7th in order among those in chapter for the purpose of appointing general proctors, *Priory Reg.*, no 344 (p. 119).

Note: it is possible that there are two monks here.

Roger de GRUTELYNGTHON [Crutelyngtone, Gretelinton, Gretlington
occ. 1292/3 occ. 1332

1292/3, subdcn, on behalf of whom the prior of Christ Church, Canterbury [*sed. vac.* both Bath and Canterbury] wrote concerning his ordination [as dcn], *Priory Reg.*, no 415 (p. 148).

[1323], before 11 June, apptd prior of Dunster, Reg. Drokensford, fo 203v.

1310, 23 Jan., licensed to hear confessions, *Reg. Drokensford*, 28 (fo 28v).

[1323], absolved from the office of penitentiary before being apptd to Dunster above, Reg. Drokensford, fo 203v.

1332, 7 Aug., licensed to hear confessions, *Reg. Shrewsbury*, no 430 (transcribed as Crutelyngtone).

Richard GULES [Gule, Guley, Gwles *alias* Gybbs
occ. 1524 occ. 1539

1523, 21 Mar., ord subdcn, chapel of St Mary by the cloister, Wells cathedral, Reg. Wolsey, fo 30.

1524, 12 Mar., ord dcn, Bath cathedral, Reg. Clerk, fo 110v.

1525, 5 July, 16th in order at the el. of a prior, *Reg. Clerk*, no 477 (transcribed as Gate).

1534, 22 Sept., 8th to subscribe to the Act of Supremacy, *DK 7th Report*, Appndx 2, 280.

1539, 27 Jan., 10th on the surrender list and assigned a pension of £5 6s. 8d. p.a., *L and P Henry VIII*, xiv pt 1, no 148; on 20 Feb., he was dispensed to change his habit and hold a benefice, Chambers, *Faculty Office Regs*, 175.

HAIMON
see Hamo

John HALLE
occ. 1412/13

1412, 10 Mar., precentor, *Reg. Bubwith*, no 1271.
1413, 12 Sept., collated to the office of sacrist, *ib.*, no 436.

1412, 13 Feb., with William Southbroke, q.v., as proctor of the subprior and chapter recd licence from the bp to el. a prior, *Reg. Bubwith*, no 1271.
1412, 10 Mar., 3rd in order at the above el., *ib.*

HAMO [Haimon
occ. 1206

1206, 3 Feb., present at the el. of bp Jocelin and 4th to put his signature on the letter to the pope requesting his confirmation, Wells Cathedral Muniments, Charter no 40 (iv); his name was also on the el. certificate, *Wells Liber Albus* i, 63 (fo 55ᵛ).

Note: as M. Kam' [?recte Ham'] he may also have been one of the monk proctors for the Bath chapter in the el. negotiations, *Wells Liber Albus* i, 63 (fo 54ᵛ); see Robert de Bath I.

William de HAMPTESHYRE [Hampteshyr
occ. 1297 occ. 1302

1302, 23 June, cellarer, Priory Reg., p.217 (no. 595).

1297, 20 Mar., apptd by Philip subprior, q.v., and the chapter as proctor to attend convocation *Councils and Synods*, ii, 1163, *Priory Reg.*, no 444 (p. 158).
[1298], appted by the subprior to atend convocaton in London on 25 June, *Councils and Synods*, ii, 1189, *Priory Reg.*, no 539 (p. 197).
1302, 20 June, named as one of two monk proctors to go to the king at Devizes, with two canons of Wells, to obtain a licence to el. a bp, *Priory Reg.*, no 594 (p. 216); see also *CPR (1301–1307)*, 41. The other monk was William de Hampton I, q.v.

Thomas HAMPTON
occ. 1377

1377, 14th in order on the clerical subsidy list and pd 12d., PRO E179/4/2.

I William de HAMPTON [Hamton
occ. 1291 occ. 1332

1302, 30 June, sacrist, Priory Reg., p.217 (no. 595).
1308, 18 Dec., *magister operis*, Priory Reg., p.226 (no. 615).
1315, 25 Dec., apptd sacrist, *Reg. Drokensford*, 103 (fo 94).
1321, 19 Aug., sacrist, Reg. Drokensford, fo 176ᵛ.

[1291], 13 Feb., apptd by Richard subprior q.v., proctor to attend convocation beginning on this day at the New Temple, London, *Councils and Synods*, ii, 1100, *Priory Reg.*, no 467 (p. 166).
1292, 16 Dec., with Hugh Godmer, q.v., and two canons of the Wells chapter obtained royal licence to el. a bp, *CPR (1292–1302)*, 2.
1295, 9 Nov., named by the prior as proctor to attend convocation, *Priory Reg.*, no 556 (p. 202); on 22 Nov., the subprior [and convent] also named him as their proctor, *ib.*, no 557 (p. 202).
1298, 26 Jan., apptd proctor for the episcopal visitation of Keynsham church, *Priory Reg.*, no 445 (p. 158).
1300, 8 Mar., apptd proctor to represent the prior who was too weak to attend parliament, *ib.*, no 448 (p. 159).
1302, 19 June, named, with Philip de Bathon', q.v., to treat with the proctors of the Wells chapter concerning obtaining the king's licence to el. a bp, *ib.*, no 592 (p. 216); on 20 June he was apptd, with William de Hampteshyre, q.v., to go to the king at Devizes in order to obtain the licence, *ib.*, no 594 (p. 216); see also *CPR (1301–1307)*, 41.
1308, 18 Dec., named, with Ralph Ganard, q.v., as proctor to go to the king for a licence to el. a bp, *Priory Reg.*, no 615 (p. 226); they recd the licence on 25 Dec., *CPR (1307–1313)*, 97.
1309, before 15 May, with Robert de Sutton, q.v., acted as *instructores* at the examination of the el. of bp Drokensford by the abp, *Reg. abp Winchelsey*, 1112.
[1311], Thurs. 2 Dec., as proctor for the subprior John Symonis, q.v., and chapter, attended parliament which opened at Westminster, *Priory Reg.*, no 611 (p. 225).
1317, 18 Feb., with John de Essex and Thomas de Bathonia, q.v., named as proctor to meet the Wells proctors in order to come to an agreement over the advowson and appropriation of Bathampton church, *Wells Liber Albus* i, 172 (fo 134).
1329, 12 May, with Thomas Crist, q.v., named as proctor in the preliminary discussions with the Wells chapter concerning the el. of a bp, *Priory Reg.*, nos 330, 333A (pp. 106, 107) and *Wells Liber Albus* i, 218 (fo 177), and recd licence from the king to el. on 23 May, *CPR (1327–1330)*, 391; he was also one of the five monk electors in the el. on 2 June, *Priory Reg.*, nos 338–340 (pp.111–114).
1332, 6 Mar., named as one of the three *scrutatores* in the el. of a prior, *ib.*, no 734 (p. 281).
[1334 × 1348], 13 Feb., *temp.* abp Stratford, apptd by Richard subprior, proctor to attend convocation beginning on this day at the New Temple, *ib.*, no 467 (p. 166).

II William HAMPTON
occ. 1420 occ. [1463]

1420, 21 Sept., ord acol. and subdcn, St Cuthbert's church, Wells, *Reg. Bubwith*, no 1306.

1421, 22 Mar., ord dcn, bp's chapel, Wookey, *ib.*, no 1308.

1447, 5 July, subprior, *Reg. Bekynton*, no 1639.

[1463], prior of Dunster, Maxwell Lyte, *Dunster*, ii, 552.

1447, 5 July, presided at the el. of a prior when the chapter made the bp the sole *compromissorius*, *Reg. Bekynton*, no 1639; see Thomas Lacok.

William de HAUKESBURY
occ. 1329 occ. 1344

1330, 6 Feb., removed from the office of sacrist, *Reg. Shrewsbury*, no 118.

1329, 2 June, chosen as one of the five monk electors to meet with their Wells chapter counterparts in order to el. a bp on this day, *Priory Reg.*, nos 338–340 (pp. 111–114).

[1332], 21 Oct., was in the priory prison undergoing 'correction', and the harsh treatment he was enduring led the bp to write to the prior and chapter to urge them to show him mercy, *Reg. Shrewsbury*, no 470.

1344, 5 Oct., 16th in order among those in chapter for the purpose of appointing general proctors, *Priory Reg.*, no 344 (p. 119).

John HAWKYNG [Haukyn
occ. 1468 occ. 1471

1468, 11 June, ord subdcn, Bridgwater, Reg. Stillington, fo 177.

1470, 16 June, ord dcn, chapel of the hospital of St John the Baptist, Wells, *ib.*, fo 183.

1471, 21 Sept., ord pr., chapel of the hospital of St John the Baptist, Wells, *ib.*, fo 185.

HELY
see Ely

Robert HENDEMAN [Hyndeman
occ. 1401 occ. 1412

1401, 28 Oct., pr., granted papal licence, because of the danger of infection and the unhealthy atmosphere in Bath, to go to Dunster or Waterford when ill, *CPL*, v (1396–1404), 414.

1412, 10 Mar., pr., and 5th in order at the el. of a prior, *Reg. Bubwith*, no 1271.

John HENTON
occ. 1412 occ. 1425

1425, 28 July, appted prior of Dunster by the bp, *sed. vac.* priory, *Reg. Stafford*, no 46.

1412, 10 Mar., pr., and 7th in order at the el. of a prior, *Reg. Bubwith*, no 1271.

Gilbert HEREBERT
occ. 1277

1277, 26 Mar., with Richard de Kaninges, q.v., cited by name to be present, with all the monks, at the visitation of the adcn of Bath acting as the bp's commissary; the prior objected on the grounds that the priory was subject to visitation only by the bp in person; and these two monks may have been his spokesmen, Priory Reg., p. 89 (no. 291).

John HERVEY
occ. [1376]

[1376], prior of Dunster, Maxwell Lyte, *Dunster*, ii, 552, (SRO DD/L P1/4).

I William de HOLEWEYE
occ. 1292/3

1292/3, subdcn, on behalf of whom the prior of Christ Church, Canterbury, [*sed. vac.* both Bath and Canterbury], wrote concerning his ordination [as dcn], *Priory Reg.*, no 415 (p. 148); the undated licence given by the prior of Christ Church is *ib.*, no 420 (p. 149).

II William HOLLEWAY [Holewey, Holowey, Holwey, *alias* Gibbs, Gybbs, Gybes
occ. 1509 occ. 1539

1525–1539, prior: 'el.' 5 July 1525, *Reg. Clerk*, no 477; still prior at the surrender, see below.

1509, 22 Dec., ord subdcn, chapel of All Saints [*sic*] by the cloister, Wells cathedral, Reg. Castello, fo 150.

1510, 22 Sept., ord dcn, chapel of St Mary by the cloister, Wells cathedral, *ib.*, fo 151.

1510, 21 Dec., ord pr., chapel of St Mary by the cloister, Wells cathedral, *ib.*, fo 152.

1525, 25 June/5 July, pittancer [*pretensarius*], *Reg. Clerk*, no 477.

1525, 5 July, 9th in order at the 'el.' of a prior, which was conducted *per viam compromissi*, the electoral body consisting of five monks, the vicar general and another secular cleric; the choice was predetermined between Holleway and Thomas Bathe, q.v., *Reg. Clerk*, no 477. Cf. Henry Holbech's 'el.' at Worcester in 1536 (under the Worcester section).

1534, 22 Sept., subscribed to the Act of Supremacy, *DK 7th Report*, Appndx 2, 280.

1535, [Aug.], described by the commissioner, Richard Layton, in a letter to Cromwell as 'a ryghte virtuose man', 'simple and not of the greteste wite', *L and P Henry VIII*, ix, no 42; but see below.

1535, 24 Sept., wrote to Cromwell requesting a licence for him and the cellarer to leave the priory precincts in order to conduct their business affairs (the monks had recd an injunction confining them to the monastery). He also said that he was sending a copy of the works of Anselm from his library at the king's request, *L and P Henry VIII*, ix, no 426. There is another letter from him to Cromwell dated 7 Feb., 1537 in *ib.*, xii, pt 1, no 360; in this he asked for 'liberties for recreation' and made a grant of £5.

1538, before 3 Oct., wrote to Lord Hungerford requesting him to come to examine Richard Lyncmbe, q.v., concerning his accusations vs Thomas Powell, q.v., *L and P Henry VIII*, xiii, pt 2, no 532.

1539, 27 Jan., headed the surrender list and was assigned a pension of £80 p.a., and a house in Stall Street, Southgate, Bath, *L and P Henry VIII*, xiv pt i, no 148; on 20 Feb., he was dispensed to change his habit and hold a benefice, Chambers, *Faculty Office Regs*, 175.

His register, now BL Ms Harley 3970 (briefly calendared in *Priory Reg.*, lxxii-lxxiv), consists mainly of grants and leases of the 1530s.

Thomas Charnock, the alchemist, described Holleway as a learned man in the science of alchemy in his *The Breviary of Natural Philosophy*. This is in the form of a poem and is one of the treatises included in E. Ashmole, *Theatricum Chemicum Britannicum*, (London, 1552) 291–303, where the ref. to Holleway appears on p. 297. Charnock described his interviews with the former prior who told him that he had been taught by 'Ripley the Canon his Boy', which I take to mean the assistant of George Ripley, an Augustinian, who was also an alchemist, *ib*.

Thomas HOLT
occ. 1462

1462, 18 Sept., ord dcn, Lady chapel, Wells cathedral, *Reg. Bekynton*, no 1776.

John HOLTE
occ. 1402 occ. 1412

1412, 10 Mar., subprior, *Reg. Bubwith*, no 1271.

1402, 16 Jan., granted papal licence to go to, remain at, and leave the curia when and as he desired, no other permission being necessary, *CPL*, v (1396–1404), 409.

1412, 10 Mar., presided at the el. of a prior, *Reg. Bubwith*, no 1271.

HOLWEY
see Holleway

Richard HOPAR [Hoper
occ. 1447

1447, 5 July, one of five monks resident at Dunster at the time of the el. of a prior, and absent from the el., *Reg. Bekynton*, no 1639; see John Beryngton.

Note: see the entry below.

Robert HOPER [Hopere
occ. 1430 occ. 1433

1430, 23 Sept., ord acol., Bath cathedral, *Reg. Stafford*, no 950.

1432, 20 Dec., ord subdcn, Montacute, *ib.*, no 964.

1433, 19 Sept., ord dcn, Bath cathedral, *ib.*, no 966.

Note: this entry and the one above may refer to the same monk.

I HUGH [Hugo
occ. 1174 × c. 1184

1174 × c. 1184, prior, *temp.* bp Reginald Fitzjocelin, *Priory Reg.*, no 42 (p. 14), *HRH*, 29; see Peter and M. Walter.

His mother Wimarche recd from R[?obert de Bath, q.v.], prior, a corrody [*plenum corredium monachalem*] for life, Priory Reg., p. 12 (no. 32).

II HUGH
occ. 1186

1186, 8 Nov., prior of Dunster, *HRH*, 88.

III HUGH [Hugo
occ. 1206

1206, 3 Feb., present at the el. of bp Jocelin and 5th to put his signature on the letter to the pope requesting his confirmation, Wells Cathedral Muniments, Charter no 40 (iv).

IV HUGH [Hugo
occ. 1206

1206, 3 Feb., present at the el. of a bp Jocelin and 37th to put his signature on the letter to the pope requesting his confirmation, Wells Cathedral Muniments, Charter no 40 (iv).

V HUGH
occ. 1304

1304, 26 July, subprior, *Priory Reg.*, no 551 (p. 200).

Note: it is possible that this is Hugh de Dovor, q.v.

John HUMYLYTE [Humiliter, *alias* Colyn
occ. 1534 occ. 1539

1534, 22 Sept., acknowledged the Act of Supremacy, *DK 7th Report*, Appndx 2, 280.

1539, 27 Jan., 17th on the surrender list and assigned a pension of £5 6s. 8d., p.a., *L and P Henry VIII*, xiv pt i, no 148.

Nicholas HUSE
occ. 1377

1377, 15th in order on the clerical subsidy list and pd 12d., PRO E/179/4/2.

M. Walter de HYDA
see Walter I

HYNDEMAN
see Hendeman

John de IFORDE [Ford, Ilford, Yford
occ. 1323 occ. 1359

1340–1359, prior: el. c. 12 Aug. 1340, *Reg. Shrewsbury*, no 1397; possibly last occ. before 31

July 1359, when the subprior presented a vicar to a church in Bath, *Priory Reg.*, no 917 (p. 396).

1323, 11 Dec., granted *lit. dim.*, for the order of pr., Reg. Drokensford, fo 207v.

1330, 6 Feb., apptd sacrist, *Reg. Shrewsbury*, nos 117, 118.

1329, 13 Sept., involved in negotiations for obtaining a loan, *Reg. Shrewsbury*, no 6.

1330, 2 Jan., with the bp's steward comm. to audit the accts of the episcopal manors, *ib.*, no 88.

1344, 5 Oct., present in chapter for the purpose of appointing general proctors, *Priory Reg.*, no 344 (p. 119).

1346, 7 Aug., reported by the bp of Worcester, in a letter to the bp of Bath and Wells, as having committed adultery in the manor of Hammeswelle in Worcester diocese, *Reg. Shrewsbury*, no 1962.

[1348/9], in his ninth yr as prior, made two aptments to the mastership of the hospital of St John the Baptist, Bath, *Priory Register*, no 40 (p 13).

1350, 7 June, granted papal dispensation to choose his own confessor who was authorized to give plenary remission at the hour of d., *CPL*, iii (1342–1362), 368.

1352/3, 12 Feb., with Thomas de Bruton, q.v., and two others were taken into custody, accused of binding themselves on oath to maintain a quarrel and thus cause disturbance vs the law; the jury at Bristol acquitted him, *Priory Reg.*, no 939 (p. 410).

Nicholas de IWLEGH
occ. 1267

1267, 9 Jan., named as one of six monk electors to join with the six representatives of the Wells chapter in the el. of a bp, Priory Reg., p. 99 (no. 319 where it is transcribed as Irelegh; the name may derive from Uley, Gloucestershire).

Nicholas JOBBYN
see Nicholas Bath II

John JOCE [Goose
occ. 1453/5

1453, 26 May, ord dcn, St Cuthbert's church, Wells, *Reg. Bekynton*, no 1707.

1455, 20 Sept., ord pr., bp's palace chapel, Wells, *ib.*, no 1720.

I JOHN [Johannes
occ. 1106 × 1109 occ. 1122

1106 × 1109 and 1122, prior: see *HRH*, 28; he may have been apptd by bp John de Villula, *Priory Reg.*, lxxviii (introd.).

1106 × 1109, recd a letter from abp Anselm, addressed to him and the whole community, urging them to love one another and be obedient to the will of God even in those things which seemed of minor importance, *Anselm Letters*, v, no 450.

II JOHN [Johannes
occ. 1206

1206, 3 Feb., subprior; see below.

1206, 3 Feb., present at the el. of bp Jocelin and 6th to put his signature on the letter to the pope requesting his confirmation, Wells Cathedral Muniments, Charter no 40 (iv); he had also been one of the four Bath monk electors, *Wells Liber Albus* i, 63 (fos 55v, 54v); see Robert de Bath I.

III JOHN [Johannes
occ. 1206

1206, 3 Feb., *custos operum*, Wells Cathedral Muniments, Charter no 40 (iv).

1206, 3 Feb., present at the el. as in the previous entry and 30th to put his signature on the letter, *ib.*

IV JOHN [Johannes
occ. 1206

1206, 3 Feb., almoner, Wells Cathedral Muniments, Charter no 40 (iv).

1206, 3 Feb., present at the el. as in the previous entries and 31st to put his signature on the letter, *ib.*

V JOHN [Johannes
occ. 1206

1206, 3 Feb., third prior, Wells Cathedral Muniments, Charter no 40 (iv).

1206, 3 Feb., present at the el., as in the previous entries and 34th to put his signature on the letter, *ib.*

VI JOHN [Johannes
occ. 1206

1206, 3 Feb., present at the el. as in the previous entries and 38th to put his signature on the letter, *ib.*

VII JOHN [Johannes
occ. 1206

1206, 3 Feb., present at the el. as in the previous entries and 41st and last to put his signature on the letter, Wells Cathedral Muniments, Charter no 40 (iv); the handwriting of the document appears to be very close to this monk's signature acc. to Dr Hunt in *Priory Reg.*, lii (introd.), n. 1.

VIII JOHN
occ. 1267

1267, 9 Jan., succentor, *Priory Reg.*, no 319 (p. 99).

1267, 9 Jan., named as one of six monk electors to join with the six representatives from the

Wells chapter in the el. of a bp, *Priory Reg.*, no 319 (p. 99).

IX JOHN
occ. 1274/5

1274, 13 Dec.; 1275, 23 Jan., precentor, *Priory Reg.*, no 325 (p. 103), *Wells Liber Albus* i, 111 (fo 90v).

1274, 13 Dec., with Thomas de Winton, q.v., and the Wells chapter proctors named to go to the king for a licence to el. a bp, *Wells Liber Albus* i, 111 (fo 90v).

1275, 23 Jan., named as one of the seven monk electors to meet with their counterparts from the Wells chapter in order to el. a bp, *Priory Reg.*, no 325 (p. 103) and *Wells Liber Albus* i, 113 (fo 91).

Note: John VIII and John IX may be identical.

X JOHN
occ. 1326

1326, 14 Jan., one of twelve monks who made their prof. before the bp, Reg. Drokensford, fo 270.

XI JOHN
occ. 1326

1326, 14 Jan., one of twelve monks who made their prof. before the bp, Reg. Drokensford, fo 270.

XII JOHN
occ. 1326

1326, 14 Jan., one of twelve monks who made their prof. before the bp, Reg. Drokensford, fo 270.

XIII JOHN
occ. 1326

1326, 14 Jan., one of twelve monks who made their prof. before the bp, Reg. Drokensford, fo 270.

XIV JOHN
occ. 1326

1326, 14 Jan., one of twelve monks who made their prof. before the bp, Reg. Drokensford, fo 270.

Note: at least some of these five monks named John, who were prof. on the same day, prob. occ. elsewhere in this list under their toponymic.

XV JOHN
occ. 1359

1359, 31 July, subprior, *Priory Reg.*, no 917 (p. 396).

1359, 31 July, presented a vicar to a church in Bath, *ib.*

John KADDOK
occ. 1242

1242, 30 Dec., with the prior, Thomas I, q.v., and other monks, met the subdean of Wells and other representatives of the Wells chapter to discuss arrangements for the el. of a bp, *Wells Liber Albus* i, 92 (fo 74).

KAERDINE
see Gilbert de Dunstorr

KAM'
see Hamo

Richard de KANINGES [Kaning, Kanning junior, Kanyng
occ. 1242 occ. 1277

1242, 30 Dec., with the prior, Thomas I, q.v., and other monks, met the subdean of Wells and representatives of the Wells chapter to protest vs the delay in making arrangements for the el. of a bp, *Wells Liber Albus* i, 91–92 (fo 74).

1243, 6 Jan., with Gilbert de Dunstorr', q.v., recd licence from the king at Bordeaux to el. a bp, *CPR (1232–1247)*, 354.

1243, 28 Feb., one of several monks involved in appeals vs the Wells chapter after the el. of bp Roger de Salisbury by the Bath chapter, and the protest of the Wells chapter that followed in consequence, *Priory Reg.*, no 189 (p. 52).

1261, 23 June, with N[icholas II], precentor, q.v., sent by the subprior and chapter to obtain licence from the bp to el. a prior, *ib.*, no 253 (p. 75).

1277, 26 Mar., with Gilbert Herebert, q.v., cited by name to be present, with all the monks, at the visitation of the adcn of Bath acting as the bp's commissary; the prior objected on the grounds that the priory was subject to visitation only by the bp in person; and these two monks may have been his spokesmen, Priory Reg., p.89, (no. 291).

I William de KANYNG [Cannyng, Canyng, Kanynges, Kanynggs
occ. 1292/3 occ. 1320

1292/3, subdcn, on behalf of whom the prior of Christ Church, Canterbury [*sed. vac.* both Bath and Canterbury] concerning his ord [as dcn], *Priory Reg.*, no 415 (p. 148).

1316, 22 Apr., apptd sacrist, *Reg. Drokensford*, 110, (fo 96).

1320, 25 Sept., [re]apptd sacrist, *Reg. Drokensford*, 180, (fo 162).

II William de KANYNGGS [Canyng, Kanyngges junior
occ. 1336 occ. 1344

1336, precentor; the heading above no 767 (p. 297) in the *Priory Reg.*, reads 'Registrum de tempore Willelmi de Kanyngges junioris precentoris'; the first entry is dated 5 Oct.

1344, 5 Oct., 20th in order among those in chapter for the purpose of appointing general proctors, *Priory Reg.*, no 344 (p. 119).

Note: because there are two contemporary monks by this name it is not possible to ascribe the biographical details with certainty.

Thomas de KARDIF [Cardiff
occ. 1243/4

1242, 29 Dec., with Thomas de Theukesbiry, q.v., and a clerk, apptd proctors to confer with representatives of the Wells chapter concerning arrangements for the el. of a bp, *Priory Reg.*, no 184 (p. 51); on 26 Feb. 1243, with Robert de Ely, q.v., he was named proctor on behalf of the chapter's rights in the el. of Roger de Salisbury, *ib.*, nos 188, 189 (p. 52), the latter entry is dated 28 Feb.

John de KAYNESFORD
occ. 1344

1344, 5 Oct., 19th in order among those in chapter for the purpose of appointing general proctors, *Priory Reg.*, no 344 (p. 119).

Elias de KAYNESHAM
occ. 1261

1261, 27 June, named as one of seven *compromissorii* in the el. of a prior, *Priory Reg.*, nos 255, 257 (pp.75, 76); see Walter de Anno.

I John KEYNESHAM
occ. 1440 occ. 1447

1440, 26 Mar., ord acol. and subdcn, Bath cathedral, *Reg. Stafford*, no 991, where it states monk of Farley as it does in the ms reg.

1443, 21 Dec., ord dcn, St Cuthbert's church, Wells, *Reg. Bekynton*, no 1652; this entry is repeated on 26 Mar. 1444 (no. 1653). His ord as dcn is also in *Reg. Stafford*, no 1004, dated 22 Sept., 1442.

1447, 5 July, 14th in order at the el. of a prior, *Reg. Bekynton*, no 1639.

II John KEYNESHAM [Keynysham
occ. 1487 occ. 1499

1487, 31 Mar., ord subdcn, St Mary Redcliffe, Bristol, Reg. Stillington, fo 220.

1488, 22 Mar., ord dcn, Bruton priory church, *ib.*, fo 226.

1489, 4 Apr., ord pr., chapel of the hospital of St John the Baptist, Wells, *ib.*, fo 231.

1495, 30 Jan., 19th in order on the *sed. vac.* visitation certificate, *Reg. abp Morton*, ii, no 347.

1499, 30 Aug., residing at Dunster and apptd Thomas Gregory, q.v. his proxy in the el. of a prior, Reg. King, fo 139v.

I Thomas de KEYNSHAM
occ. 1344

1344, 5 Oct., 6th in order among those in chapter for the purpose of appointing general proctors, *Priory Reg.*, no 344 (p. 119).

II Thomas KEYNSHAM [Keynesham
occ. 1497 occ. 1525

1497, 23 Sept., ord subdcn, St Mary's chapel by the cloister, Wells cathedral, Reg. King, fo 117.

1498, 22 Sept., ord subdcn, St Mary's chapel by the cloister, Wells cathedral, *ib.*, fo 119.

1501, 6 Mar., ord pr., St Mary's chapel by the cloister, Wells cathedral, *ib.*, fo 123.

1499, 30 Aug., 15th in order at the el. of a prior, Reg. King, fo 139v.

1509, 15 Nov., recd 12d. in a bequest from a parishioner of Dunster, Weaver, *Somerset Medieval Wills*, ii, 139.

1525, 5 July, absent from the el. of a prior but Thomas Bath II, q.v., was his proctor, *Reg. Clerk*, no 477 (fo 81v).

Note: since Thomas Bath II, q.v., was prior of Dunster in 1525 it is prob. that Keynsham was residing in that cell.

John de KINGESWODE [Kingeswod, Kyngeswode
occ. 1337 occ. 1344

1337, 22 Apr., apptd by the prior, with a secular clerk, to have custody of the hospital/cell of St John the Evangelist at Waterford in succession to Thomas de Foxcote, q.v., *Priory Reg.*, no 774 (p. 299); four days later this apptment was revoked in favour of the secular clerk alone, *ib.*, no 775 (p. 299).

1344, 5 Oct., 15th in order among those in chapter for the purpose of appointing general proctors, *Priory Reg.*, no 344 (p. 119).

John de KYMEILTON
occ. 1377

1377, 9th in order on the clerical subsidy list and pd 12d., PRO E179/4/2.

Roger de KYNARDESLEGH
occ. [1332] occ. 1344

[1332], 24 Aug., apptd precentor, *Reg. Shrewsbury*, no.425.

1344, 5 Oct., 11th in order among those in chapter for the purpose of appointing general proctors, *Priory Reg.*, no 344 (p. 119).

William LACOCK [?Fromlok
occ. 1453/5

1453, 26 May, ord dcn, St Cuthbert's church, Wells, *Reg. Bekynton*, no 1707.

1455, 20 Sept., ord pr., bp's palace chapel, Wells, *ib.*, no 1720 (as Fromlok).

John LACOK B.Cn.L. [Lacocke
occ. 1433 occ. 1461

1433, 19 Sept., ord acol., Bath cathedral, *Reg. Stafford*, no 966.

1435, 2 Apr., ord subdcn, Bath cathedral, *ib.*, no 973.

1436, 22 Sept., ord dcn, St Mary Redcliffe, Bristol, *ib.*, no 976.
1439, 19 Sept., ord pr., St Mary Magdalen, Taunton, *ib.*, no 989.
1447, 5 July, infirmarer, pittancer and refectorer, *Reg. Bekynton*, no 1639.
1458, 22 Jan., precentor, *ib.*, no 1108.
1458, 2 Oct., apptd sacrist, *ib.*, no 1165; 1461, 9 Jan., sacrist, ib,. no 1349.

c. 1444 × 1452, student at Oxford [prob. intermittently], as on 31 Mar. 1452, he supplicated for B.Cn.L.; see *BRUO.*

1447, 5 July, 11th in order at the el. of a prior, *Reg. Bekynton*, no 1639; on 10 July he was sent, with Richard Whalley, q.v., to inform the bp of the chapter's decision to make him [the bp] sole *compromissorius*, *ib.*
1447, 16 Sept., sent as proctor to present the elect to the bp, *ib.*
1457, 8 Apr., licensed to preach in Latin or English throughout the diocese, *ib.*, no 1041.
1458, 22 Jan., comm., with the prior, Thomas Lacok, q.v., and another to look into the problems of the hospital of St John the Baptist, Bath, *ib.*, no 1108.
1461, 9 Jan., comm. to induct a new master into the above hospital, *ib.*, no 1349.

Thomas LACOK [Lacock
occ. 1421 occ. 1467

1447–?1467, prior: chosen by the bp 16 Sept. 1447, the subprior and chapter having agreed at the el. on 10 July to name the bp as their sole *compromissorius*, *Reg. Bekynton*, no 1639; occ. 9 Oct. 1467, *CPR (1467–1477)*, 10. See John Dunster II.

1421, 20 Sept., ord pr., bp's chapel, Banwell, *Reg. Bubwith*, no 1309.

1443, Apr.; 1444, Dec.; 1447, 24 June/12 July, prior of Dunster, Maxwell Lyte, *Dunster*, ii, 552 (SRO DD/L P12/3), *Reg. Bekynton*, no 1639.
1452, 14 May, had been charged with unspecified crimes which came to light during the bp's visitation and the bp now comm. three canons of Wells to arrange his purgation, *Reg. Bekynton*, no 660.
1453, 16 Nov., accused of simony and usurpation of the bp's ordinary jurisdiction, and the bp ordered an inquiry, *ib.*, no 801.
1457, 16 Feb., granted papal privilege of using pontifical regalia including mitre, ring and staff, *CPL*, xi (1455–1464), 293.
1457, 29 Nov., dispensed to eat meat during Advent on acct of his weak physical condition, *Reg. Bekynton*, no 1093.
1467, 9 Oct., petitioned to have a clerk cited for not returning a book worth 5m., *CPR (1467–1477)*, 10.

Robert de LAKE [Lak'
occ. 1344 occ. 1364

1364, 9 Jan., sacrist, Reg. abp Islip, fo 242v, *Wells Liber Albus* i, 266 (fo 251).

1344, 5 Oct., 17th in order in chapter among those assembled for the purpose of appointing general proctors, *Priory Reg.*, no 344 (p. 119).
1364, 9 Jan., the abp revoked the censures pronounced against him and other monks, on acct of a disputed el., as they had been published illegally, *Wells Liber Albus* i, 266 (fo 251).

John LAMPORT [Lampart, Lamporte
occ. 1425 occ. 1463

1425, 22 Sept., ord acol. and subdcn, Bath cathedral, *Reg. Stafford*, no 935.
1426, 16 Mar., ord dcn, St Cuthbert's church, Wells, *ib.*, no 21.
1426, 25 May, ord pr., Bruton priory, *ib.*, no 28.

1463, 22 Nov., prior of Waterford, *CPL*, xi (1455–1464), 500.
1463, 22 Nov., accused of neglecting the cure of souls in Waterford because he did not know the language; the pope ordered an inquiry and his removal if required, *CPL*, xi (1455–1464), 500.

William LANGPORT
occ. 1462/3

1462, 18 Sept., ord subdcn, Lady chapel, Wells cathedral, *Reg. Bekynton*, no 1776.
1463, 24 Sept., ord dcn, chapel of the hospital of St John the Baptist, Wells, *ib.*, no 1782.

LAURENCE
occ. 1432

1432, 20 Sept., ord pr., Bridgwater, *Reg. Stafford*, no 963.

Roger de LOLHAM [Lulham
occ. 1344

1344, 5 Oct., 21st in order in chapter among those assembled for the purpose of appointing general proctors, *Priory Reg.*, no 344 (p. 119).
1344, dwelling at Dunster and was one of the participants, as proctor for Adam de Cheddre, q.v., prior of Dunster, in an agreement concerning tithes signed in the Lady chapel at Wells cathedral, *ib.*, no 878 (p. 354).

John LONG
see Pacyence

Richard de LUCY
occ. 1283

1283, 11 Feb., almoner, BL Ms Egerton 3316, fo 62.

1283, 11 Feb., witnessed a grant of the prior, *ib.*

LULHAM
see Lolham

Richard LYNCOMBE [Lyncolne, Lynkcomb *alias* Bygge
occ. 1517 occ. 1539

1517, 7 Mar., ord dcn, St Mary's chapel by the cloister, Wells cathedral, Reg. Castello, fo 159.
1521, 21 Dec., ord pr., St Mary's chapel by the cloister, Wells cathedral, Reg. Wolsey, fo 29.

1525, 25 June/5 July, subalmoner, *Reg. Clerk*, no 477.

1525, 5 July, 13th in order at the el. of a prior, *Reg. Clerk*, no 477.
1534, 22 Sept., 5th to subscribe to the Act of Supremacy, *DK 7th Report*, Appndx 2, 280.
1538, 3 Oct., deposed before Lord Hungerford and the prior [William Holleway II, q.v.], that Thomas Powell, q.v., had rebuked him and violently laid hands upon him because he had changed the wording in a service book from *regibus et principibus nostris* to *regi et principi nostro*; as a result both monks were confined to ward, *L and P Henry VIII*, xiii, pt 2, no 532.
1539, 27 Jan., 7th on the surrender list and assigned a pension of £6 p.a., *L and P Henry VIII*, xiv pt i, no 148; on 20 Feb., he was dispensed to change his habit and hold a benefice, Chambers, *Faculty Office Regs*, 175.

John LYNDE
occ. 1421 occ. 1447

1421, 20 Sept., ord pr., bp's chapel, Banwell, *Reg. Bubwith*, no 1309.

1447, 5 July, 5th in order at the el. of a prior, *Reg. Bekynton*, no 1639.

MARK [Marchus
occ. 1206

1206, 3 Feb., present at the el. of bp Jocelin and 27th to put his signature on the letter to the pope requesting his confirmation, Wells Cathedral Muniments, Charter no 40 (iv).

I MARTIN
occ. [?late 12th c.]

[?late 12th c.], prior of Dunster, *HRH*, 88.

Note: using as refs. SRO DD/L P8/2, P17/1 and the cartulary of Buckland, Maxwell Lyte gave his dates as prior as 1257 to 1274, *Dunster*, ii, 552; perhaps there is a confusion of identity here with Martin de Dunster, q.v.

II MARTIN [Martinus
occ. 1206

1206, 3 Feb., chamberlain, Wells Cathedral Muniments, Charter no 40 (iv).

1206, 3 Feb., present at the el. of bp Jocelin and 8th to put his signature on the letter to the pope requesting his confirmation; he had been sent as one of the four monk electors for the Bath chapter in the el. and was one of the signatories of the el. certificate, *Priory Reg.*, lii (introd.), *Wells Liber Albus* i, 63, (fos 55^{v}, 54^{v}); see Robert de Bath I.

MARTIN
see also Dunster

MATTHEW
occ. 1311

1311, 5 Nov., apptd precentor, Reg. Drokensford, fo 57^{v} (p. 67); the date is wrong in the printed text.

Note: this may possibly be Matthew de Dunster, q.v.

John MEARE
occ. 1423

1423, 27 Feb., ord pr., St Mary's chapel by the cloister, Wells cathedral, *Reg. Bubwith*, no 1314.

Robert de MELKESHAM
occ. 1412

1412, 10 Mar., pr., and 14th in order at the el. of a prior, *Reg. Bubwith*, no 1271.

Roger de MERKESBURY
occ. 1321

1321, 13 Aug., apptd precentor, Reg. Drokensford, fo 176^{v}; this is crossed out and the entry repeated lower down and dated 25 Aug., *ib.*

John MILL'
occ. 1425

1425, 22 Sept., ord acol., Bath cathedral, *Reg. Stafford*, no 935.

John de MILVERTON
occ. 1377

1377, 17th and last on the clerical subsidy list and pd 12d, PRO E179/4/2.

Thomas MORTYMER
occ. 1502 occ. 1508

1502, 12 Mar., ord acol., St Mary's chapel behind the new altar, Bath cathedral, Reg. King, fo 126.
1505, 20 Dec., ord dcn, St Mary's chapel by the cloister, Wells cathedral, Reg. Castello, fo 141.
1508, 18 Mar., ord pr., St Mary's chapel by the cloister, Wells cathedral, *ib.*, fo 146.

N.
occ. [c. 1290 × 1301]

[c. 1290 × 1301], licensed by Thomas [de Winton] prior, q.v., to visit the curia, *Priory Reg.*, no 489 (p. 173).

Note: it is possible, though unlikely, that this entry was intended for use as a *pro forma* licence.

N.
see also Nicholas II

I NICHOLAS [Nicholaus
occ. 1206

1206, 3 Feb., present at the el. of bp Jocelin and 22nd to put his signature on the letter to the pope requesting his confirmation, Wells Cathedral Muniments, Charter no 40 (iv).

II NICHOLAS
occ. 1261 occ. 1267

1261, 23 June; 1264, 9 Apr.; 1267, [Jan.], precentor, *Priory Reg.*, nos 253, 295, 311 (pp. 75, 91, 97).

1261, 23 June, sent with Richard de Kaninges, q.v., by the subprior and chapter to obtain licence from the bp to el. a prior, *Priory Reg.*, no 253 (p. 75).

1264, 9 Apr., with Richard le Norreys, q.v., apptd proctor by the prior and chapter [for preliminary discussions concerning the el. of a bp] with the dean and chapter of Wells, *ib.*, no 295 (p. 91). On 25 Apr., with Gilbert [de Dunstorr], q.v., met at Fernton [?Farrington Gurney] with the Wells proctors to arrange the date of the el. and settled on 22 May, *ib.*, no 303 (p. 93), *Wells Liber Albus* i, 102 (fo 82v).

1266, [Dec.], with Robert [de Rading], q.v., sent as proctor to the dean and chapter of Wells to make preliminary arrangements for the el. of a bp, *Priory Reg.*, no 311 (p. 97); they met the proctors of the Wells dean and chapter on 28 Dec., *ib.*, no 313 (p. 97); on 8 Jan. 1267, with Gilbert de Dunstorr, q.v., named as the monk proctors who were to meet with the Wells chapter proctors in order to arrange the date for the el. of a bp, *Priory Reg.*, no 316 (p. 98).

Note: see Nicholas de Iwlegh who may be this monk.

Thomas NORMANNUS
occ. 1261

1261, 27 June, named as one of seven *compromissorii* in the el. of a prior, *Priory Reg.*, nos 255, 257 (pp. 75, 76); see Walter de Anno.

Richard le NORREYS [Noreys, Norrey
occ. 1264 occ. 1267

1264, 9 Apr., cellarer, *Priory Reg.*, no 295 (p. 91).
1267, 2 Jan., subprior, *ib.*, no 315 (p. 98).

1264, 9 Apr., with Nicholas II, q.v., apptd proctors by the prior and chapter to the dean and chapter of Wells [for preliminary discussions concerning the el. of a bp], *Priory Reg.*, no 295 (p. 91). On 15 Apr., with John de Rading, q.v., and the Wells proctors recd from the king at Nottingham licence to el. a bp, *ib.*, no 299 (p. 92); these items are also entered in *Wells Liber Albus* i, 101–102, (fo 82, 82v), *CPR (1258–1266)*, 312.

1267, 2 Jan., with Robert de Rading, q.v., and the Wells proctors obtained licence to el. a bp from the king at Windsor, *Priory Reg.*, no 315 (p. 98).

Note: see also Richard V, who is prob. this monk.

I John de NORTON
occ. 1344

1344, 5 Oct., 24th among those present in chapter for the purpose of appointing general proctors, *Priory Reg.*, no 344 (p. 119).

II John NORTON
occ. 1412

1412, 10 Mar., kitchener, *Reg. Bubwith*, no 1271.
1412, 10 Mar., 4th in order at the el. of a prior, *ib.*

III John NORTON [senior
occ. 1447

1447, 5 July, absent from the el. of a prior because he was residing at Dunster; John Beryngton, q.v., was his proctor, *Reg. Bekynton*, no 1639.

IV John NORTON
occ. 1444 occ. 1499

1444, 26 Mar., ord acol., Bath cathedral, *Reg. Bekynton*, no 1653.
1451, 20 Mar., ord pr., Lady chapel, Wells cathedral, *ib.*, no 1687.

1495, 30 Jan., precentor, *Reg. abp Morton*, ii, no 347.

1447, 5 July, 19th and last at the el. of a prior, *Reg. Bekynton*, no 1639.
1495, 30 Jan., 2nd in order on the *sed. vac.* visitation certificate, *Reg. abp Morton*, ii, no 347.
1499, 30 Aug., 2nd at the el. of a prior, Reg. King, fo 139v.

Note: it seems odd that a monk in his late sixties would be chosen to lead the singing; however, his seniority indicates his longevity.

William de NUBBELEY
occ. 1325

1325, 4 Mar., *conversus*, recd licence to set off for the Holy Land, and permission from the prior to wear secular clothing if he found himself in dangerous circumstances, Priory Reg., p. 252 (no. 669); see also William de Corston.

Robert de OLVESTON
occ. 1292/3

1292/3, dcn, on behalf of whom the prior of Christ Church, Canterbury [*sed. vac.*, both Bath and Canterbury] wrote concerning his ordination [as pr.], *Priory Reg.*, no 415 (p. 148).

The prior of Bath wrote to the prior of Christ Church requesting permission to present him for ordination by the bp of Cork in Bath cathedral on 21 Feb. 1293, *ib.*, no 416 (p. 148); he also wrote to the bp el. of Bath making the same request, *ib.*, no 417 (p. 148).

1293, 21 Feb., the ordination took place and the prior wrote to inform the prior of Christ Church, *ib.*, no 418.

John de OVERTON
occ. 1344

1344, 5 Oct., 10th in order among those present in chapter for the purpose of appointing general proctors, *Priory Reg.*, no 344 (p. 119).

John PACYENCE [Pacienc' *alias* Long
occ. 1534 occ. 1539

1534, 22 Sept., 15th to subscribe to the Act of Supremacy, *DK 7th Report*, Appndx 2, 280.

1539, 27 Jan., 21st and last on the surrender list and recd a pension of £4 13s. 4d. p.a., *L and P Henry VIII*, xiv pt 1, no 148; on 20 Feb., he was dispensed to change his habit and hold a benefice, Chambers, *Faculty Office Regs*, 175.

John PANTER
occ. 1435

1435, 2 Apr., ord subdcn, Bath cathedral, *Reg. Stafford*, no 973.

John PARNELL
see Benet

Robert PAVY
occ. 1492 occ. 1525

1492, 18 Mar., ord subdcn, chapel of the hospital of St John the Baptist, Wells, *Reg. abp Morton*, ii, no 65b.

1495, 30 Jan., 20th (out of 22) in order on the *sed. vac.* visitation certificate, *Reg. abp Morton*, ii, no 347 where he is (surely mistakenly) described as an acol.

1499, 30 Aug., 13th at the el. of a prior, Reg. King, fo 139v.

1525, 5 July, absent from the el. of a prior, *causa infirmitatis*, *Reg. Clerk*, no 477.

Philip PEKELYNCH
occ. 1377

1377, 15th in order on the clerical subsidy list and pd 12d., PRO E179/4/2.

PENNELL
see Benet

David PENSFORD [Pensforde
occ. 1465 occ. 1520

1465, 21 Sept., ord subdcn, chapel of the hospital of St John the Baptist, Wells, Reg. *sed. vac.*, fo 13 (third series of foliation).

1466, 20 Sept., ord dcn, Muchelney abbey, Reg. Stillington, fo 172v.

1467, 23 May, ord pr., chapel of the hospital of St John the Baptist, Wells, *ib.*, fo 175v.

1495, 30 Jan.; c. 30 Aug. 1499, subprior, *Reg. abp Morton*, ii, no 347; *Reg. King*, no 517.

1520, 8 Nov., subprior, *Priory Reg.*, no 943 (p. 412).

1495, 30 Jan., 2nd in order on the *sed. vac.* visitation certificate, *Reg. abp Morton*, ii, no 347.

1499, 30 Aug., presided at the el. of a prior and announced the chapter's unanimous choice of William Birde, q.v., Reg. King, fo 139v.

1520, 8 Nov., witnessed the apptment of a master of St John's hospital, Bath, *Priory Reg.*, no 943 (p. 412).

William PENSFORD [Pennesford
occ. 1423 occ. 1448

1423, 30 Aug., one of four novices whose prof. the bp comm. the prior to rec., *Reg. Bubwith*, no 1189.

1423, 18 Sept., ord acol. and subdcn, St Mary's chapel by the cloister, Wells cathedral, *ib.*, no 1315.

1425, 22 Sept., ord dcn, Bath cathedral, *Reg. Stafford*, no 935.

1426, 21 Sept., ord pr., Yeovil, *ib.*, no 936.

1447, 5 July, subsacrist and fourth prior, *Reg. Bekynton*, no 1639.

1448, 12 Nov., with Richard Whalley, q.v., accused of celebrating mass at Pensford while the parish was under interdict, *Reg. Bekynton*, no 382.

Richard PESTELL [Pestall
occ. 1484 occ. 1504

1484, 18 Sept., ord dcn, chapel of the hospital of St John the Baptist, Wells, Reg. Stillington, fo 213.

1486, 23 Dec., ord pr., chapel of the hospital of St John the Baptist, Wells, *ib.*, fo 218.

1504, 25 Mar./8 May, prior of Dunster, Weaver, *Somerset Medieval Wills*, ii, 61 (transcribed as Pester).

1495, 30 Jan., 13th in order on the *sed. vac.* visitation certificate, and residing at Dunster, *Reg. abp Morton*, ii, no 347.

1499, 30 Aug., residing at Dunster and apptd Thomas Gregory his proxy in the el. of a prior, Reg. King, fo 139v.

1504, 8 May, recd 20s in a bequest from a parishioner of Dunster, Weaver, *Somerset Medieval Wills*, ii, 61.

I PETER (Prior I)
occ. 1157 occ. [1175]

1157 × [1175], prior: occ. 13 Dec. 1157, 4 Nov., 1159, [1162 × 1166], [1168 × 1175], *HRH*, 29; see Benedict and Hugh I.

1151, 24 June, with prior Benedict, q.v., witnessed an episcopal instrument, *Eng. Epis. Acta*, x, no 43.

II PETER (Prior II)
occ. 1482

1482, 13 Oct., 7 Nov., prior: occ. on both these dates, *CPR (1476–1485)*, 571, when he sat on a commission of the peace for the county of Somerset.

Note: this may be Peter Twiverton, q.v.; as Peter only, he was el. prior at the age of c. 51 and prob. only in office for a yr or so between John Dunster and John Cantlow, q.v.

I PHILIP
occ. [1292]

[1292, before 25 Oct.], [acol.], granted *lit. dim.* for subdcn's orders by the vicar general of bp Robert [Burnell], *Priory Reg.*, no 419 (p. 149).

Note: this is prob. Philip de Wodewyke, q.v.

II PHILIP
occ. 1295/7

1295, 22 Nov., subprior, *Priory Reg.*, no 557 (p. 202).

1295, 22 Nov., informed the king that he and the chapter had apptd William de Hampton I, q.v., proctor for parliament, *ib.*, no 557 (p. 202).

1297, 20 Mar., appted William de Hampteshyre to attend the church council, *Councils and Synods*, ii, 1163, *Priory Reg.*, no 444 (p. 158).

PITT
see Pytte

John PLONTE
occ. 1377

1377, 13th in order on the clerical subsidy list and pd 12d., PRO E179/4/2.

Note: the name was transcribed by Hunt, *Priory Reg.*, lxv (introd.) as Pleicce.

Stephen POPE
occ. 1412

1412, 10 Mar., pr., and 13th in order at the el. of a prior, *Reg. Bubwith*, no 1271.

Thomas POWELL
occ. 1525 occ. 1539

1538, 3 Oct., precentor, *L and P Henry VIII*, xiii, pt 2, no 532.

1525, 5 July, 15th in order at the el. of a prior, *Reg. Clerk*, no 477.

1534, 22 Sept., 7th to subscribe to the Act of Supremacy, *DK 7th Report*, Appndx 2, 280.

1538, 3 Oct., confined [in the priory prison] as a result of the accusation of treason made vs him for attacking Robert Lyncombe, q.v., who had altered words in a service book in favour of the royal supremacy, *L and P Henry VIII*, xiii, pt 2, no 532.

1539, 27 Jan., 9th on the surrender list and assigned a pension of £5 p.a., *L and P Henry VIII*, xiv pt i, no 148; on 20 Feb., he was dispensed to change his habit and hold a benefice, Chambers, *Faculty Office Regs*, 175.

John PRESTON
occ. 1377

1377, 12th in order on the clerical subsidy list and pd 12d, PRO E179/4/2.

John PYTTE [Pitt, Pyt, Pytt
occ. 1509 occ. 1539

1509, 22 Dec., ord subdcn, chapel of All Saints [*sic*] by the cloister, Wells cathedral, Reg. Castello, fo 150.

1510, 22 Sept., ord dcn, chapel of St Mary by the cloister, Wells cathedral, *ib.*, fo 151.

1513, 21 May, ord pr., chapel of the bp's palace, Wells, *ib.*, fo 155.

1534, 22 Sept.; 1539, 27 Jan., subprior, *DK 7th Report*, Appndx 2, 280, *L and P Henry VIII*, xiv, pt i, no 148.

1525, 5 July, 10th in order at the el. of a prior, *Reg. Clerk*, no 477.

1534, 22 Sept., subscribed to the Act of Supremacy, *DK 7th Report*, Appndx 2, 280.

1539, 27 Jan., 2nd on the surrender list and assigned a pension of £9 p.a., *L and P Henry VIII*, xiv pt i, no 148; on 20 Feb., he was dispensed to change his habit and hold a benefice, Chambers, *Faculty Office Regs*, 175.

R., prior
see Richard IX, Richard X, Robert de Bath I, Robert Clopcote

R., subprior
see Richard IV, Richard V, Richard VI, Richard le Norreys

I R.
see Robert de Rading

II R.
occ. 1301

1301, 11 Apr., prior of Dunster, *Priory Reg.*, no 580 (p. 212).

1301, 11 Apr., commanded by the subprior to return to Bath to take part in the el. of a prior, *ib.*

Note: Maxwell Lyte suggested that this may have been a Richard de Childeston, *Dunster*, ii, 552, but he has also tentatively inserted Childeston, q.v., as prior in 1357, *ib.*

Seward de RADENE
n.d.

n.d., monk *ad succurrendum* who gave to the monastery a large silver gilt thurible, *Priory Reg.*, no 808 (p. 317).

John de RADING' [Redingge
occ. 1264 occ. 1275

1264, 15 Apr., with Richard le Norreys, q.v., and the Wells proctors recd from the king at Nottingham licence to el. a bp, *Priory Reg.*, no 299 (p. 92); see also *Wells Liber Albus* i, 101–102, (fo 82, 82v), *CPR (1258–1266)*, 312.
1264, 22 May, named by the prior and chapter as one of the four monk electors to meet on this day with the electors chosen by the Wells chapter in order to el. a bp, *Priory Reg.*, no 304 (p. 93).
1267, 9 Jan., named as one of six monk electors to meet with their six counterparts from the Wells chapter in order to el. a bp, *ib.*, no 319 (p. 99); they met to el. at Bath on 10 Feb., *ib.*, no 320 (p. 99).
1275, 23 Jan., named as one of the seven monk electors to meet with their counterparts from the Wells chapter in order to el. a bp, *ib.*, no 325 (p. 103), and *Wells Liber Albus* i, 113 (fo 91).

Robert de RADING [Radyngg
occ. 1266 occ. 1283

1267, 9 Jan., almoner, Priory Reg., p.97 (no. 311), as Robert only.
1283, 11 Feb., cellarer, BL Ms Egerton 3316, fo 62.
1266, [Dec.], with Nicholas II, q.v., apptd proctor by the prior and chapter for the purpose of making preliminary arrangements with the dean and chapter of Wells concerning the el. of a bp, *Priory Reg.*, no 311 (p. 97); they met the Wells proctors on 28 Dec., *ib.*, no 313 (p. 97), (as Robert only).
1267, 2 Jan., with Richard le Norreys, q.v. and the Wells proctors obtained licence to el. a bp from the king at Windsor, *ib.*, no 315 (p. 98).
1267, 9 Jan., named as one of six monk electors to join with their six counterparts from the Wells chapter in order to el. a bp, *ib.*, no 319 (p. 99).
1283, 11 Feb., witnessed a grant by the prior, BL Ms Egerton 3316, fo 62.
[1301 × 1332], a memorandum concerning arrangements for the funerals and obits of deceased brethren refers to the concern of Robert and of Roger de Anna, q.v., about this matter in their day; further provisions were now made [*temp.* prior Clopcote, q.v.] which included prayers for the souls of these two monks who had been 'honestatis zelae divinitus insperati [*sic*]', *Priory Reg.*, no 811 (p. 319).

Note: *Wells Liber Albus* i, 113, has, not surprisingly, become confused by the two contemporary Radings and tried to make them into one.

Walter de RADING
occ. 1260

1260, 26 Dec., monk and proctor in Ireland to whom the prior sent a writ concerning seisin of certain properties, *Priory Reg.*, nos 215, 218 (pp.61, 62); see Thomas de Theukesbiry [prior of Waterford].

I RALPH [Radulphus
occ. 1206

1206, 3 Feb., infirmarer, Wells Cathedral Muniments, Charter no 40 (iv).
1206, 3 Feb., present at the el. of bp Jocelin and 25th to put his signature on the letter to the pope requesting his confirmation, *ib.*

II RALPH
occ. [1298]

[1298], subprior, *Councils and Synods*, ii, 1189.
[1298], wrote to the abp to say that he was sending William de Hampteshyre to the convocation in London on 25 June, *ib.*, and *Priory Reg.*, no 539 (p. 197).

Note: this may be Ralph de Ganard, q.v.

III RALPH [Radulfus
occ. before 1329

1329, before, a citizen of Bath and afterwards 'monachus ejusdem ecclesiae per biennium et professus'; his benefactions included the gift of a silver gilt reliquary and three properties, and he also pd for the construction of two bells and for the completion of the main [?central] tower of the cathedral church. His obit was observed by a *splendida refectione*, *Priory Reg.*, no 808 (p. 317).

Note: this is Ralph de Salopia or Shrewsbury, el. bp in 1329.

John RAPHAEL
occ. 1534

1534, 22 Sept., 17th and last to subscribe to the Act of Supremacy, *DK 7th Report*, Appndx 2, 280.

REDING(GE)
see Rading

REGINALD [Reginaldus
occ. 1206

1206, 3 Feb., present at the el. of bp Jocelin and 10th to put his signature on the letter to the pope requesting his confirmation, Wells Cathedral Muniments, Charter no 40 (iv).

William REINOLDE
occ. 1282 or 1305

1282 or 1305, 2 May, cellarer, *Priory Reg.*, no 15 (p. 6).

1282 or 1305, 2 May, witnessed the apptment of a master of the hospital of St John, Bath, *ib.*, no 15 (p. 6).

Note: this entry is clearly dated 10 Edward I (1281/2) and Robert Clopcote, q.v., fourth yr, (which would be 1304/5) and so we are left with an unresolved problem.

RIALL
see Ryall

I RICHARD [Ricardus
occ. 1206

1206, 3 Feb., present at the el. of bp Jocelin and 11th to put his signature on the letter to the pope requesting his confirmation, Wells Cathedral Muniments, Charter no 40 (iv).

II RICHARD
occ. 1206

1206, 3 Feb., subsacrist, Wells Cathedral Muniments, Charter no 40 (iv).

1206, 3 Feb., present at the el. of bp Jocelin and 13th to put his signature on the letter to the pope requesting his confirmation, *ib.*

III RICHARD
occ. 1242

1242, 30 Dec., former almoner, *Wells Liber Albus* i, 91–92 (fo 74).

[1242, c. 19 Nov.], sent by the prior as proctor with Gilbert de Dunstorr, q.v., to the king to inform him of the d. of bp Jocelin, *Priory Reg.*, no 183 (p. 51).

1242, 30 Dec., one of the monks who, with the prior Thomas I, q.v., met the subdean and other representatives of the Wells chapter in the guest hall of the priory to protest vs the delay in making arrangements for the el. of a bp, *Wells Liber Albus* i, 91–92 (fo 74); see Thomas I.

IV RICHARD
occ. 1248

1248, 25 Feb., subprior, *Wells Charters* no 53.

1248, 25 Feb., with Henry de Sokerwyk, q.v., as proctors and with their Wells counterparts announced the el. of William de Bitton I as bp, *ib.*

Note: Richard III and Richard IV may be identical.

V RICHARD
occ. 1267 occ. 1275

1267, 10 Feb.; 1275, 23 Jan., subprior, *Priory Reg.*, nos 322, 325 (pp. 100, 103).

1267, 10 Feb., took to the papal legate the letter from the prior and the dean of Wells requesting confirmation of their el. of a bp, *Priory Reg.*, no 322 (p. 100).

1275, 23 Jan., named as one of the seven monk electors to meet their counterparts from the Wells chapter in order to el. a bp, *ib.*, no 325 (p. 103) and *Wells Liber Albus* i, 113 (fo 91).

Note: see Richard le Norreys who is prob. this monk.

VI RICHARD
occ. [1292]

[1292], 13 Feb., subprior, *Priory Reg.*, no 467 (p. 166).

[1292], 13 Feb., apptd William de Hampton I, q.v. as proctor to attend convocation, *ib.*

VII RICHARD
occ. [1292]

[1292, before 25 Oct.], [acol.], granted *lit. dim.*, for subdcn's orders by the vicar general of bp Robert [Burnell], *Priory Reg.*, no 419 (p. 149); see also Philip.

VIII RICHARD
occ. [1334 × 1348]

[1334 × 1348], 13 Feb., *temp.* abp Stratford, subprior, *Priory Reg.*, no 467 (p. 166).

[1334 × 1348], 13 Feb., apptd proctor to attend convocation, *ib.*; see Willam Hampton I.

IX RICHARD
occ. 1449

1449, prior of Dunster acc. to Maxwell Lyte, *Dunster*, ii, 552 (SRO DD/L P12/3).

[X RICHARD
occ. 1476

1476, prior, acc. to *Anglia Sacra*, i, 587.]

Note: There is uncertainty as to the number of monks named Richard; several of the above may overlap.

I ROBERT, prior
see Robert de Bath I

II ROBERT
occ. 1206

1206, 3 Feb., granator, Wells Cathedral Muniments, Charter no 40 (iv).

1206, 3 Feb., present at the el. of bp Jocelin and 18th to put his signature on the letter to the pope requesting his confirmation, *ib.*

III ROBERT
occ. 1206

1206, 3 Feb., present at the el. of bp Jocelin and 26th to put his signature on the letter as above.

IV ROBERT
occ. 1206

1206, 3 Feb., present at the el. of bp Jocelin and 32nd to put his signature on the letter as above.

V ROBERT
occ. 1206

1206, 3 Feb., present at the el. of bp Jocelin and 40th and last but one to put his signature on the letter as above.

VI ROBERT
see Robert de Rading

VII ROBERT
occ. 1243

1243, 5 Feb., was present in the guest hall when the subdean of Wells appeared to appeal vs the monks' proposed el. on the following day, *Wells Liber Albus* i, 93 (fo 75^{v}) see also Thomas I.

VIII ROBERT
occ. 1326

1326, 14 Jan., one of twelve monks who made their prof. before the bp, Reg. Drokensford, fo 270.

John ROKEBOURNE
occ. 1377

1377, 10th in order on the clerical subsidy list and pd 12d., PRO E179/4/2.

ROMSEY
see John Bekynton

William RYALL [Riall, Royall
occ. 1481 occ. 1525

1481, 7 Apr., ord subdcn, chapel of the hospital of St John the Baptist, Wells, Reg. Stillington, fo 207.
1484, 18 Sept., ord pr., chapel of the hospital of St John the Baptist, Wells, *ib.*, fo 214.
1495, 30 Jan., 14th in order at the *sed. vac.* visitation, *Reg. abp Morton*, ii, no 347.
1499, 30 Aug., 8th at the el. of a prior, Reg. King, fo 139^{v}.
1525, 5 July, 3rd at the 'el.' of a prior and was named as one of the five monk *compromissorii*, *Reg. Clerk*, no 477; see William Holleway II.

Simon de ST LAUD [Sancto Laudo
n.d.

n.d., monk *ad succurrendum* who gave a meadow and an annual rent of ½m., *Priory Reg.*, no 808 (p. 317).

John de SAKEFORD
occ. 1307

1307, 14 Sept., apptd by the prior as *custos* of the hospital/cell of St John the Evangelist, Waterford, Priory Reg., p. 185 (no 522, where it is transcribed as Sukeford).

John SALESBURY [Saresbury
occ. 1440 occ. 1447

1440, 26 Mar., ord acol. and subdcn, Axbridge, *Reg. Stafford*, no 991 (where it states monk of Farley as in the ms reg.).
1440, 24 Sept., ord dcn, Axbridge, *Reg. Stafford*, no 993.
1442, 22 Sept., ord pr., St Cuthbert's church, Wells, *ib.*, no 1004.
1447, 5 July, subalmoner, *Reg. Bekynton*, no 1639.
1447, 5 July, 13th in order at the el. of a prior, *Reg. Bekynton*, no 1639.

I William SALFORD [Saltford
occ. 1420 occ. 1449

1420, 21 Sept., ord acol. and subdcn, St Cuthbert's church, Wells, *Reg. Bubwith*, no 1306.
1421, 22 Mar., ord dcn, bp's chapel, Wookey, *ib.*, no 1308.
1423, 18 Sept., ord pr., St Mary's chapel by the cloister, Wells cathedral, *ib.*, no 1315.
1447, 5 July, sacrist, cellarer, custos of the Lady chapel, and hostiller, *Reg. Bekynton*, no 1639.
1449, 23 Oct., collated to the office of sacrist, *ib.*, no 459.
1447, 16 June, sent by the subprior and chapter to the bp for licence to el. a prior, *Reg. Bekynton*, no 1639.
1447, 5 July, 6th in order at the above el., *ib.*

Name possibly in BL Ms Arundel 86; see William Salford II.

II William SALFORD [Salforde
occ. 1502 occ. 1525

1502, 12 Mar., ord acol., St Mary's chapel behind the new altar, Bath cathedral, Reg. King, fo 126.
1505, 20 Dec., ord dcn, St Mary's chapel by the cloister, Wells cathedral, Reg. Castello, fo 141.
1507, 20 Mar., ord pr., St Mary Redcliffe, Bristol, *ib.*, fo 144.
1524, 4 Feb., collated to the office of precentor, *Reg. Clerk*, no 179, replacing John Worceter, q.v.; 1525, 5 July, precentor, *ib.*, no 477.
1525, 5 July, 6th in order at the 'el.' of a prior; he was named as one of the five monk *compromissorii*, *Reg. Clerk*, no 477; see William Holleway II.

Name possibly in BL Ms Arundel 86, Polychronicon (14th/15th c.), which he acquired from John Lutton who 'wrote' it.

Note: it is uncertain which William Salford acquired this volume.

RALPH DE SALOPIA
see Ralph III

Walter SAMUEL
occ. 1344

1344, 5 Oct., 29th in order among those in chapter for the purpose of appointing general proctors, *Priory Reg.*, no 344 (p. 119).

SARESBURY
see Salesbury

Simon de SCHAWE [Shawe
occ. 1327 occ. 1344

1327, 28 Aug., apptd to the office of precentor, succ. John de Eston, q.v., Reg. Drokensford, fo 266ᵛ (p. 273).

1344, 5 Oct., 8th in order among those in chapter for the purpose of appointing general proctors, *Priory Reg.*, no 344 (p. 119).

SERLO
occ. 1206

1206, 3 Feb., subcellarer, Wells Cathedral Muniments, Charter no 40 (iv).

1206, 3 Feb., present at the el. of bp Jocelin and 17th to put his signature on the letter to the pope requesting his confirmation, *ib.*

Thomas SEXTEN
see Thomas Bath II

SHAWE
see Schawe

John de SHEPTON
occ. 1344

1344, 5 Oct., 25th in order among those in chapter for the purpose of appointing general proctors, Priory Reg., p. 119 (no 344, where it has been transcribed as Shopton).

William SHIRBORN [Shyrborn
occ. 1414 occ. 1419

1414, 3 Mar., one of two novices whose prof. the prior was comm. to rec., *Reg. Bubwith*, no 483.
1417, 6 Mar., ord acol. and subdcn, Yeovil, *ib.*, no 1299.
1418, 24 Sept., ord dcn, Bruton priory, *ib.*, no 1301.
1419, 23 Sept., ord pr., St Cuthbert's church, Wells, *ib.*, no 1304.

SIMON
see Symon

John SLAPTON
occ. 1412

1412, 10 Mar., pr., and 15th in order at the el. of a prior, *Reg. Bubwith*, no 1271.

William SMALCOMBE
occ. 1412

1412, 10 Mar., pr. and 8th in order at the el. of a prior, *Reg. Bubwith*, no 1271.

SODBURY
see Edgar

Henry de SOKERWYK
occ. 1248

1248, 25 Feb., with Richard IV, q.v., as monk proctors and with their counterparts of the Wells chapter, announced the el. of William de Bitton I as bp, *Wells Charters* no 53.

William SOUTHBROKE [Southbrokes, Southbrook, Sowthbroke, Suthbroke
occ. 1400 d. 1447

?1425–1447, prior: occ. 20 Apr. 1426, *Reg. Stafford*, no 73; his predecessor John Telesford, q.v., having d. before 28 July 1425, *ib.*, no 46; d. 7 June 1447, *Reg. Bekynton*, no 1639.
1412, 10 Mar., sacrist, *Reg. Bubwith*, no 1271.
1413, 12 Sept., collated to the office of precentor, *ib.*, no 435.
1400, 22 Apr., with William Cary, q.v., named as monk proctor to meet with their counterparts from the Wells chapter and go to the king to request a licence to el. a bp, *Wells Charters* no 498.
1412, 13 Feb., with John Halle, q.v., proctor of the subprior and chapter and recd licence from the bp to el. a prior, *Reg. Bubwith*, no 1271.
1412, 10 Mar., 2nd in order at the above el., *ib.*, no 1271.
1417, 26 Nov., appeared in the cloister of the Dominican convent, London, as proctor for the prior and chapter in a dispute with the mayor and citizens of Bath over the ringing of bells in the city, BL Ms Egerton 3316, fo 96.
1430, 18 Apr., with others, comm. as vicar general, *Reg. Stafford*, no 267.
1435, 23 May, as prior petitioned against the continuation of grants of corrodies in spite of letters patent of Edward III, granting exemption, PRO SC8/346/65.

One of his *acta* has been inserted as a memorandum in a blank space in the *Priory Reg.*, no 279 (p. 83).

Reginald de STANFORD
occ. 1261

1261, 27 June, named as one of seven *compromissorii*, in the el. of a prior, *Priory Reg.*, nos 255, 257 (pp. 75, 76); see Walter de Anno.

Thomas STILLARD [Stilband
occ. 1539

1539, 20 Feb., dispensed to change his habit and hold a benefice, Chambers, *Faculty Office Regs*, 175.

Note: see Thomas Worceter *alias* Styllard who is the same monk; the 'Stilband' is the result of trying to read a difficult hand.

Thomas de STOKTON
see Thomas I

John de STONE [atte Stone
occ. 1361 occ. 1377

1361, 12 Nov., wrote to inform the prior that, in accordance with directions recd on 1 Nov., he had inducted the rector of St Mary's church, Bath, *Priory Reg.*, no 343 (p. 118).
1362, 20 June, with a clerk, named by the prior as attorney in Ireland for one yr, *CPR (1361–1364)*, 225.
1365, 28 Feb., reported to have letters similar to those above, *CPR (1364–1367)*, 97.
1367, 24 May, a similar apptment for three yrs, *ib.*, 400.
1371, 11 June, a similar apptment for two yrs, *CPR (1370–1374)*, 93.
1373, 28 Nov., a similar apptment for one yr, *ib.*, 372.
1377, 28 Apr., a similar apptment for three yrs, *CPR (1374–1377)*, 460; and again on 18 Oct. for three years, *CPR (1377–1381)*, 33.

John de STONYESTON
occ. 1344

1344, 5 Oct., 14th in order among those in chapter for the purpose of appointing general proctors, *Priory Reg.*, no 344 (p. 119).

Edward STYLE
see Edwy

John STYLE
see Gabriel

Thomas STYLLARD
see Worceter

John SUDBURY
occ. 1539

1539, 20 Feb., dispensed to change his habit and hold a benefice, Chambers, *Faculty Office Regs*, 175.
Note: this is prob. John Edgar, q.v.

SUKEFORD
see Sakeford

John de SUTTON
see Robert de Sutton

Robert de SUTTON [Sotton
occ. 1292/3 d. [1347]

1332, prior: el. 6 Mar. 1332, Priory Reg., p.266 (no. 704) and installed on 14 Mar., *ib.*; but it seems that Thomas Crist, q.v., had been designated as prior by Robert Clopcote who had written to the pope expressing his desire to res. and requesting the apptment of Crist. Clopcote d. before receiving an answer, and by 6 Apr., Sutton had begun to make inquiries about Clopcote's letters and the pope's response, *ib.*, pp. 268, 269, (nos 710–712). He res. c. 14 July, *CPL*, ii (1305–1342), 357.
Some of his *acta* during his few months as prior are in *Priory Reg.*, nos 705–719, 721.
1292/3, acol., on behalf of whom the prior of Christ Church, Canterbury, [*sed. vac.* both Bath and Canterbury] wrote concerning his ordination [as subdcn], *Priory Reg.*, no 415 (p. 148).
1310, 3 Feb., apptd cellarer and also sacrist for the time being until the bp's arrival, Reg. Drokensford, fo 29 (p. 29).
1332, 30 Sept., apptd prior of Dunster, *Reg. Shrewsbury*, no.697; in 1337, 5 July, Adam de Cheddre, q.v., succ. as prior of Dunster.
1301, 10 Apr., with Hugh de Godmer, sent as proctors to obtain licence from the bp to el. a prior, Priory Reg., p.212 (not in printed text).
[1308], had been the *familiaris* of bp Haselshaw who d. in 1308 and left him a legacy of 20m., *Priory Reg.*, no 808 (p. 316).
1309, 2 Jan., with John de Compton I, q.v., met with proctors of the Wells chapter at Fernton [?Farrington Gurney] to arrange for the episcopal el., *Priory Reg.*, nos 619, 621 (pp.227, 228).
1309, before May 15, with William de Hampton I, q.v., acted as *instructores* at the examination of the el. of bp Drokensford by the abp, *Reg. abp Winchelsey*, 1112.
1309, 18 Nov., apptd by the subprior and convent to attend convocation, *Councils and Synods*, ii, 1255, *Priory Reg.*, no 564 (p. 205).
1329, 2 June, named as one of the five monk proctors to meet with the proctors of the Wells chapter on this day in order to el. a bp, *Priory Reg.*, nos 338, 340 (pp. 111, 114).
1332, 6 Mar., apptd as one of three *scrutatores* in the el. of a prior; this was his own el., *ib.*, no 734 (p. 281).
1332, 30 Sept., this is the date of the earliest form of his post resignation settlement, granting him a £20 annual pension and the office of prior of Dunster, *Reg. Shrewsbury*, no 697.
1332, 18 Oct., the awarding of a pension of £20 p.a. by the new prior, Thomas Crist, q.v., differs slightly from the later one below as the revenues were to be pd from four different sources, *Priory Reg.*, no 736 (p. 282); presumably the later arrangements were the final settlement. This award was also entered in the bp's register where there are further provisions laid down to safeguard his position as prior of Dunster, with the choice of returning to Bath should he become ill or infirm, *Reg. Shrewsbury*, no 486 (dated 24 Oct.).
1332, 16 Nov., was granted by the new prior, an annual pension of 205s., *Priory Reg.*, nos 525, 526, 529 (pp.186, 187); this income was to come from three separate sources and it must reflect another revision of the arrangements.

n.d., ref. to a chamber in the priory constructed by him which was granted to a knight on 26 July 1339, *ib.*, no 799 (p. 309).
1347, 3 Mar., d. before this date when the prior granted to a clerk the dwellings, adjoining the garden gate of the priory, which had been constructed by him, Priory Reg., p. 368 (no. 892).

John SWAYNYSWYKE
occ. 1495

1495, 30 Jan., 6th in order on the *sed. vac.* visitation certificate, *Reg. abp Morton*, ii, no 347.

SYMON
occ. 1206

1206, 3 Feb., precentor, Wells Cathedral Muniments, Charter no 40 (iv).
1206, 3 Feb., present at the el. of bp Jocelin and 33rd to put his signature on the letter to the pope requesting his confirmation, *ib.*

John SYMONIS [*dictus* Symonis
occ. 1306 occ. [1311]

1306, 4 May; 1307, 15 Apr.; 1309, 18 Nov.; [1311], 2 Dec., subprior, *Priory Reg.*, nos 554, 521, 564, 611 (pp. 201, 185, 205, 225).
1306, 4 May, acted on behalf of the absent prior Robert de Clopcote, q.v., in drawing up a bond, *Priory Reg.*, no 554 (p. 201).
1307, 15 Apr., acted for the prior in presenting to a benefice, *ib.*, no 521 (p. 185).
1309, 18 Nov., as subprior he and the chapter apptd Robert de Sutton, q.v., proctor for convocation, *Councils and Synods*, ii, 1255, *Priory Reg.*, no 564 (p. 205).
[1311], Thursday, 2 Dec., as subprior, he and the chapter apptd William de Hampton I, q.v., their proctor to attend parliament, *ib.*, no 611 (p. 225).

John TELESFORD
occ. [1382] d. 1424/5

1412–1424, prior: el. 10 Mar. 1412, *Reg. Bubwith*, no 1271; occ. 26 Dec. 1424, *CPR (1422–1429)*, 265; see William Southbroke. He had died by 28 July, 1425; see John Henton.
[1382], ord pr., acc. to the statement at his el. that he had been in pr.'s orders for more than 30 yrs; he therefore prob. entered the priory some yrs before this date, *Reg. Bubwith*, no 1271.
1412, 10 Mar., 6th in order at the el. of a prior, and he was himself el., *via inspirationis*, *Reg. Bubwith*, no 1271.
1417, Nov./Dec., one a number of cathedral priors who were apptd by the abp to serve on a committee to look into the poverty of undergraduates, *Reg. abp Chichele*, iii, 37.
1420, 8 July, attended the Black Monk Chapter at Northampton, Pantin, *BMC*, ii, 96.

John TEMPLE
occ. 1430 occ. 1443

1430, 23 Sept., ord acol., Bath cathedral, *Reg. Stafford*, no 950.
1432, 20 Dec., ord subdcn, Montacute, *ib.*, no 964.
1433, 19 Sept., ord dcn, Bath cathedral, *ib.*, no 966.
1436, 22 Sept., ord pr., St Mary Redcliffe, Bristol, *ib.*, no 976.
1443, before this date, student at Oxford, prob. living at Canterbury College, Pantin, *Cant. Coll. Ox*, i, 2, 10.

Gave a painted cloth portraying Christ and Saints Peter and John to Canterbury College, Pantin, *Cant. Coll. Ox*, i, 2, 10. In the college inventories of 1443 and 1459 one item is 'j pannus intinctus cum 3[bus] ymaginibus viridis coloris, videlicet Christi, Johannis ewangeliste et sancti Petri, Iohannis Temple monachi Bath'.

Thomas de THEUKESBIRY [Theokesburia, Theukesburi
occ. 1242 occ. 1260

1242, 29 Dec.; 1243, 15 Feb., 6 June; 1245, 26 Jan.; 1246, 26 Aug., precentor, *Priory Reg.*, no 184 (p. 51); no 187 (p. 52, as Thomas), no 195 (p. 55); no 206 (p. 57, as Thomas); *Wells Liber Albus*, i, 3, (fo 8).
1260, July, 26 Dec., *custos* of Waterford, *Priory Reg.*, nos 212, 215, 218 (pp. 59, 61, 62; the first and last as Thomas).
1242, 29 Dec., with Thomas de Kardif, q.v., and a clerk apptd proctor to confer with representatives of the Wells chapter concerning arrangements for the el. of a bp, *Priory Reg.*, no 184 (p. 51); on 30 Dec. with other monks met the subdean and other Wells representatives in the guest hall of the priory to discuss the el. of a bp, *Wells Liber Albus*, i, 91–92 (fo 74). See Thomas I.
1243, 15 Feb., with Gilbert de Dunstorr, q.v., apptd proctor to inform the king of the el. of Roger de Salisbury as bp, *Priory Reg.*, no 187 (p. 52); on 28 Feb., with other monks, named in the course of an appeal vs the dean and chapter of Wells concerning the el., *ib.*, no 189 (p. 52).
1243, 6 June, with a clerk, apptd proctor by the prior and chapter to plead the case of the bp el., *ib.*, no 195 (p. 55); there is an undated apptment naming him as their proctor at the curia which prob. relates to this episode, *ib.*, no 119 (p. 31).
1244, 3 Feb., with Gilbert [de Dunstorr], q.v., announced the el. of bp Roger to the pope, *CPL*, i (1198–1304), 205; the letter from the prior, which they took to the pope, is dated 17 Sept., 1243, *Priory Reg.*, no 196 (p. 55), and on the same day letters of apptment as proctors were issued for him and Gilbert [Dunstorr],

q.v., Priory Reg., p.56 (no. 197), on the same day authorisation to take out loans, *ib.*, p.56 (nos 199, 200).

1244, 27 Oct., authorized by the prior and chapter to procure a loan of 10m., for expenses at the curia, ib,. no 205 (p. 57); see Gilbert de Dunstorr. On 26 Jan. 1245, similar authorization was given to Thomas, *cantor*, *ib.*, no 206 (p. 57).

1260, as prior of Waterford, issued a grant of land to a citizen there which Thomas I, prior of Bath, q.v., confirmed in July 1260, *Priory Reg.*, nos 211, 212 (p. 259); in a grant of the latter dated in the same yr there is a ref. to possible dangers which might delay the former's arrival in Cork, *ib.*, no 218 (p. 62).

1260, 26 Dec., the prior of Bath addressed a writ to him and to Walter de Rading, q.v., concerning seisin of certain properties, *ib.*, no 215 (p. 61).

I THOMAS [de Stokton

occ. c. 1223 d. 1261

c. 1223–1261, prior: occ. c.1223, after the departure of Robert de Bath I, q.v.; d. 23 June 1261, *Priory Reg.*, no 253 (p. 75); see Walter de Anno.

1242, 30 Dec., met the subdean and other representatives of the Wells chapter in the priory guest hall concerning the delay in making arrangements for the el. of a bp, *Wells Liber Albus* i, 91–92 (fo 74).

1243, 5 Feb., present in the guest hall when the subdean of Wells appeared to appeal vs the monks' proposed el. on the following day, *Wells Liber Albus* i, 93 (fo 75^v^).

Note: after the d. of bp Jocelin the dispute over the two chapters' rights in the el. of his successor came to a head, and the monks went ahead on their own and elected Roger of Salisbury on 6 Feb. 1243, *Wells Liber Albus* i, 93 (fo 75^v^).

[1223 × 1261] witnessed two grants in favour of St John's hospital, Bath, Kemp, *Deeds of St John's hospital*, nos 50, 51.

1251, Jan., witnessed another grant in favour of the same, *ib.*, no 96.

[1251 × 1257], again witnessed a grant to the same, *ib.*, no 97.

Many of his *acta* are recorded in the *Priory Reg.*; see the index under Thomas, prior. A number of these are concerned with the dispute arising out of the el. of Roger de Salisbury as bp in 1243/4 and the correspondence involved in seeking support from king, queen and pope; see also Gilbert de Dunstorr and Thomas de Theukesbiry.

Note: he is named 'Stokton' in BL Ms Egerton 3316, fo 106^v^; 'Scolton' in *CClR (1333–1337)*, 201 is a scribal slip or a misreading. (*CClR* ref. to an act of his c. 1249.)

II THOMAS

occ. 1326

1326, 14 Jan., one of twelve monks who made their prof. before the bp, Reg. Drokensford, fo 270.

III THOMAS

occ. [1509]

[1509], prior of Dunster, acc to Maxwell Lyte, *Dunster*, ii, 553 (SRO DD/L P13/1). See Thomas Bath II who may be this monk.

THOMAS

see also Theukesbiry, Winton

John THORNBURY

occ. 1412

1412, 10 Mar., pr., and 16th in order at the el. of a prior, *Reg. Bubwith*, no 1271.

THOUER

see Tondre

TIVERTON

see Twiverton

William TONDRE [Thouer, Toner, Tover

occ. [1354/5] occ. 1377

[1354/5], prior of Dunster, Maxwell Lyte, *Dunster*, ii, 552 (PRO Just 1/772/1/membrane 27).

1377, 3rd in order on the clerical subsidy list and pd 12d, PRO E179/4/2.

Robert de TREDYNGTHON

occ. 1293

1292/3, acol., on behalf of whom the prior of Christ Church, Canterbury [*sed. vac.* both Bath and Canterbury] wrote concerning his ord [as subdcn], *Priory Reg.*, no 415 (p. 148), transcribed as Fredyngthorn.

Peter TWIVERTON [Tiverton

occ. 1444 occ. 1451

1444, 26 Mar., ord acol., Bath cathedral, *Reg. Bekynton*, no 1653.

1451, 20 Mar., ord pr., Lady chapel, Wells cathedral, *ib.*, no 1687.

1447, 5 July, 18th in order at the el. of a prior, *Reg. Bekynton*, no 1639.

Note: see Peter II who was briefly prior and may be this monk.

Stephen TYSBERY [Tyssebury

occ. 1509 occ. 1525

1509, 22 Dec., ord subdcn, chapel of All Saints [*sic*] by the cloister, Wells cathedral, Reg. Castello, fo 150.

1510, 22 Sept., ord dcn, chapel of St Mary by the cloister, Wells cathedral, *ib.*, fo 151.

1525, 25 June/5 July, refectorer, *Reg. Clerk*, no 477.

1525, 5 July, 11th in order at the el. of a prior, *ib.*

William UPPEHULLE
see Corston

I URBAN [Urbanus
n.d.

n.d., [1198 × 1223], *temp.* Robert de Bath I, prior, q.v., with William de Corbuil, q.v., witness to two grants, *Priory Reg.*, nos 16, 17 (p. 7).

Note: Hunt suggests that Urban and William may have come with Reginald Fitzjocelin, q.v., from Corbeil, where Reginald had been abbot, *Priory Reg.*, no 16, note.

II URBAN
occ. 1206

1206, 3 Feb., cellarer, Wells Cathedral Muniments, Charter no 40 (iv).

1206, 3 Feb., present at the el. of bp Jocelin and 24th to put his signature on the letter to the pope requesting his confirmation *ib.*

Note: it is possible that these two Urbans may be one and the same.

VERTU
see Virtue

Robert VEYSE [Vise, Vyse, de la Vyse
occ. 1410 occ. 1445

1410, 20 Dec., ord acol. and subdcn, chapel of St Mary by the cloister, Wells cathedral, *Reg. Bubwith*, no 1287.

1412, 10 Mar., named as a prof. monk who had been a subdcn for two yrs, *Reg. Bubwith*, no 1271.

1412, 2 Apr., ord dcn, Wells cathedral, *ib.*, no 1290.

1412, 10 May, 19th and last in order at the el. of a prior, *Reg. Bubwith*, no 1271.

1444, 29 Aug., cited to appear before the bp to explain his disobedience and his activities at Stogursey, *Reg. Bekynton*, no 54.

1445, 14 May, the bp requested the king for a writ vs him as an apostate, *ib.*, no 115.

1445, 20 June, having been arrested and imprisoned he was to be returned to Bath to undergo punishment acc. to the Rule, *ib.*, no 123. On 24 June the bp ordered the prior and chapter to put him in the priory prison because he had left the cloister without permission and had been living for some time as a secular in the rectory at Stogursey which he had taken at farm; he was also suspected of living in adultery, *ib.*, no 126.

1445, 27 Dec., had escaped from the priory and returned to Stogursey and the bp now accused the prior of negligence, *ib.*, no 184.

1447, 5 July, was summoned to the el. of a prior, but declared apostate, *ib.*, no 1639; see also John Appleby.

VINCENT [Vincentius
occ. 1206

1206, 3 Feb., present at the el. of bp Jocelin, and 3rd to put his signature on the letter to the pope requesting his confirmation, Wells Cathedral Muniments, Charter no 40 (iv).

Nicholas VINOZ
occ. 1377

1377, 8th in order on the clerical subsidy list and pd 12d., PRO E179/4/2.

Patrick VIRTUE [Vertu *alias* Archer
occ. 1534 occ. 1539

1534, 22 Sept., subscribed to the Act of Supremacy, *DK 7th Report*, Appndx 2, 280.

1539, 27 Jan., 16th on the surrender list and assigned a pension of £5 6s. 8d. p.a., *L and P Henry VIII*, xiv, pt i, no 148.

VISE, Vyse
see Veyse

W., prior
see Walter de Anno

W., sacrist
see Walter VIII

W.
occ. 1243

1243, 5 Feb., present with the prior [Thomas I, q.v], in the guest hall when the subdean of Wells appeared to appeal vs the monks' proposed el. of a bp on the following day, *Wells Liber Albus* i, 93 (fo 75^{v}).

Richard WALLEIGH
see Whalley

I M. WALTER [de Hyda
occ. [by 1184] d. 1198

1184, by this date, prior; see below: previously subprior of Hyde; buried at Bath, 31 May 1198, *Ann. Wint.*, 68; see also *HRH*, 29, and under G.

[1174, 23 June × c. 1184], episcopal confirmation was given to him, as prior, of a grant made by him and the chapter, *Eng. Epis. Acta*, x, no 73; see also *Priory Reg.*, nos 757, 756.

[c. 1189 × 1191], as prior mentioned in grants by the bp in favour of St John's hospital, Bath, Kemp, *Deeds of St John's Hospital*, nos 3, 5.

1191, Nov./Dec., accompanied the bp, Reginald Fitzjocelin, q.v., elect of Canterbury on his way to Canterbury and recd him as a monk on his death bed at Dogmersfield, *Chron. Devizes*, 44.

Described as 'vir multae scientiae et religionis'; he left Bath c. 1190 for a time to try his vocation as a Carthusian at Witham, but was persuaded, if not pressed, to return and resume office, having discerned that his path to holiness was to save many souls, not just his own. He d. at Wherwell, *Ann. Wint.*, 68.

Four of his *acta* are in *Priory Reg.*, nos 452, 453, 756, 757 (pp. 160, 293).

II WALTER
occ. 1206

1206, 3 Feb., present at the el. of bp Jocelin and 16th to put his signature on the letter to the pope requesting his confirmation, Wells Cathedral Muniments, Charter no 40 (iv).

III WALTER
occ. 1206

1206, 3 Feb., present at the el. of bp Jocelin and 19th to put his signature on the letter as above.

IV WALTER
occ. 1206

1206, 3 Feb., present at the el. of bp Jocelin and 20th to put his signature on the letter as above.

V WALTER
occ. 1206

1206, 3 Feb., refectorer, Wells Cathedral Muniments, Charter no 40 (iv).

1206, 3 Feb., present at the el. of bp Jocelin and 29th to put his signature on the letter, *ib.*

VI WALTER
occ. 1206

1206, 3 Feb., present at the el. of bp Jocelin and 39th to put his signature on the letter as above.

VII WALTER
occ. 1242

1242, 30 Dec., *quisinarius*, *Wells Liber Albus* i, 92 (fo 74).

1242, 30 Dec., with the prior Thomas I, q.v, and other monks met the subdean and other representatives of the Wells chapter to discuss the el. of a bp, *ib.* See Thomas I.

VIII WALTER
occ. 1243

1243, 7 Feb., sacrist, *Wells Liber Albus* i, 93–94 (fo 75^{v}).

1243, 5 Feb., was present in the guest hall when the subdean and representatives of the Wells chapter came to protest against the monks' proposed el. of a bp on the following day, *Wells Liber Albus* i, 93 (fo 75^{v}). On 7 Feb., he was present with Gilbert de Dunstorr, q.v., in a chapel of Salisbury cathedral when the proctors of the Wells chapter appealed vs the el. of Roger, precentor of Salisbury by the Bath monks, *ib.*, i, 93–94 (fo 75^{v}).

Note: Walter VII and Walter VIII may be one and the same.

WALTER
see also Anno

Richard de WAREWIK
occ. 1292

1292, 30 Dec., almoner, *Wells Liber Ruber*, 530 (fo 2^{v}).

1292, 30 Dec., with Philip de Bathon', q.v., acted as monk proctor in meeting with the proctors of the Wells chapter at Fernton [?Farrington Gurney] to fix a day for the el. of a bp, *ib.*

John WEKE
see Wyke

John de WELL'
occ. 1289 occ. 1294

1289, 19 June, 1294, 10 Apr., apptd [?and 5 yrs later reapptd] by the prior as *custos* of the hospital/cell of St John the Evangelist, Waterford, *Priory Reg.*, no 388 (p. 139), no 427 (p. 151).

I William de WELL'
occ. 1377

1377, 5th in order on the clerical subsidy list and pd 12d., PRO E179/4/2.

II William WELLES [Wellys
occ. 1440 occ. 1447

1440, 26 Mar., ord acol. and subdcn, Axbridge, *Reg. Stafford*, no 991 (monk of Farley in the ms reg.)

1440, 24 Sept., ord dcn, Axbridge, *Reg. Stafford*, no 993.

1442, 22 Sept., ord pr., St Cuthbert's church, Wells, *ib.*, no 1004.

1447, 5 July, 12th in order at the el. of a prior, *Reg. Bekynton*, no 1639.

John de WESTBURI [Westbyr'
occ. 1261

1261, 27 June, named as one of seven *compromissorii* in the el. of a prior, *Priory Reg.*, nos 255, 257 (pp.75, 76); see Walter de Anno.

Richard WHALLEY [Wallay, Walleigh, Walley
occ. 1433 occ. 1448

1433, 19 Sept., ord acol., Bath cathedral, *Reg. Stafford*, no 966.

1435, 2 Apr., ord subdcn, Bath cathedral, *ib.*, no 973.

1436, 22 Sept., ord dcn, St Mary Redcliffe, Bristol, *ib.*, no 976.

1439, 19 Sept., ord pr., Taunton, *ib.*, no 989.

1447, 5 July, kitchener, *Reg. Bekynton*, no 1639.

1447, 5 July, 10th in order at the el. of a prior, *Reg. Bekynton*, no 1639; on 10 July he was sent with John Lacok, q.v., as proctors to inform the bp that the chapter had made him [the bp] their sole *compromissorius*, *ib.*; see Thomas Lacok.

1448, 12 Nov., with William Pensford, q.v., accused of celebrating mass at Pensford while the parish was under interdict, *ib.*, no 382.

John WHITE
occ. 1433 occ. 1436

1433, 19 Sept., ord acol., Bath cathedral, *Reg. Stafford*, no 966.

1436, 22 Sept., ord dcn, St Mary Redcliffe, Bristol, *ib.*, no 976.

WHITE
see also Whyte

Richard WHITYNG [Whiting, Whitynge
occ. 1430 occ. 1447

1430, 23 Sept., ord subdcn, Bath cathedral, *Reg. Stafford*, no 950.

1431, 31 Mar., ord dcn, Bath cathedral, *ib.*, no 954.

1432, 20 Sept., ord pr., Bridgwater, *ib.*, no 963.

1447, 5 July, chamberlain, *Reg. Bekynton*, no 1639.

1447, 5 July, 9th in order at the el. of a prior, *Reg. Bekynton*, no 1639.

John le WHYTE
occ. 1344

1344, 5 Oct., 28th in order among those in chapter for the purpose of appointing general proctors, *Priory Reg.*, no 344 (p. 119).

Richard WIDECOMBE [Witcombe, Wydycombe, Wytcombe
occ. 1481 occ. 1525

1481, 7 Apr., ord dcn, chapel of the hospital of St John the Baptist, Wells, Reg. Stillington, fo 208.

1484, 18 Sept., ord pr., chapel of the hospital of St John the Baptist, Wells, *ib.*, fo 214.

1520, 8 Nov., cellarer, *Priory Reg.*, no 943 (p. 412).

1525, 5 July, chamberlain, *Reg. Clerk*, no 477.

1495, 30 Jan., 8th in order on the *sed. vac.* visitation certificate, *Reg. abp Morton*, ii, no 347.

1499, 30 Aug., 5th in order at the el. of a prior, Reg. King, fo 139^v.

1520, 8 Nov., witnessed the apptment of a master of St John's hospital, Bath, *Priory Reg.*, no 943 (p. 412).

1525, 23 June, with Thomas Bath II, q.v., obtained licence to el. a prior from the abp of York at Westminster, *Reg. Clerk*, no 477.

1525, 5 July, 3rd in order at the 'el.' of a prior and named as one of five monk *compromissorii*, *Reg. Clerk*, no 477; see William Holleway II.

WIDECOMBE
see also Wydecombe

I WILLIAM
occ. 1151

1151, 24 June, a monk of this name witnessed an episcopal instrument, *Eng. Epis. Acta*, x, no 43.

II WILLIAM
occ. 1151

1151, 24 June, a monk of this name witnessed an episcopal instrument, *Eng. Epis. Acta*, x, no 43.

III WILLIAM [Willelmus
occ. 1155

1155, formerly a tenant of the priory and now a monk, who, with the consent of the prior and chapter, made over his property to his son Wlwinus, *Bath Chartulary*, no 75.

Note: one of the two Williams above may be this monk.

IV WILLIAM
occ. 1206

1206, 3 Feb., treasurer, Wells Cathedral Muniments, Charter no 40 (iv).

1206, 3 Feb., present at the el. of bp Jocelin and 12th to put his signature on the letter to the pope requesting his confirmation, *ib.*

V WILLIAM
occ. 1206

1206, 3 Feb., present at the el. of bp Jocelin and 14th to put his signature on the letter as above.

VI WILLIAM
occ. 1206

1206, 3 Feb., present at the el. of bp Jocelin and 21st to put his signature on the letter as above.

VII WILLIAM
occ. 1206

1206, 3 Feb., sacrist, Wells Cathedral Muniments, Charter no 40 (iv).

1206, 3 Feb., present at the el. of bp Jocelin and 28th to put his signature on the letter to the pope requesting his confirmation, *ib.*

VIII WILLIAM
occ. 1206

1206, 3 Feb., absent [*deest*] from the el. of bp Jocelin but 36th in order among the signatories of the letter to the pope requesting his confirmation, Wells Cathedral Muniments, Charter no 40 (iv).

IX WILLIAM
occ. 1326

1326, 14 Jan., one of twelve monks who made their prof. before the bp, Reg. Drokensford, fo 270.

X WILLIAM
occ. 1326

1326, 14 Jan., one of twelve monks who made their prof. before the bp, Reg. Drokensford, fo 270.

WILLIAM
see also William Bristowe II

Thomas de WINTON [Wynthon', Wynton
occ. 1274 occ. 1301

1290–1301, prior: el. soon after 14 Jan. 1290, *Priory Reg.*, no 394 (p. 142); 27 Jan. 1290, the bp confirmed his el., Priory Reg., p.142 (not in printed text); occ. 9 July 1290, *ib.*, no 391 (p. 140); res. because of illness and age, 10 Apr. 1301, and was granted a pension 'de camera communi . . . pro vestibus sicut ceteri monachi'; he was also assigned a *competentem cameram* for himself and two monks in the monastery, *ib.*, pp.211–212 (no. 578). See below.

1289/90, before his el., sacrist, *Priory Reg.*, no 702 (p. 265).

1274, 13 Dec., with other monks and Wells proctors went to the king for a licence to el. a bp, *Wells Liber Albus* i, 111 (fo 90v).

1275, 23 Jan., named as one of the seven monk proctors to meet with their counterparts from the Wells chapter in order to el. a bp, *Priory Reg.*, no 325 (p. 103), and *Wells Liber Albus* i, 113 (fo 91); on 24 Jan. he and M. Walter de Bathonia, q.v., with the Wells proctors were apptd to inform the abp of the el. of Robert Burnell, *ib.* (fo 91v).

1277, 26 Mar., on the grounds that the chapter was not subject to visitation except by the bp *in propria persona*, made a formal objection to the apptment of the adcn of Bath to visit as the bp's commissary, Priory Reg., p. 89 (no 291).

1291, 11 Sept., present at the Black Monk Chapter meeting in Salisbury, Pantin, *BMC*, i, 130.

1295, June, summoned by writ with other prelates and magnates to attend parliament at Westminster on 1 Aug., *Priory Reg.*, lx and *Parl. Writs*, i, 453.

1301, 31 Jan., a letter from the abp to the bp of Bath and Wells (addressed as Walter, *recte* William), reprimanded the bp for failing to punish the prior after learning of his manifest offences during a visitation, *Reg. abp Winchelsey*, 726–727.

WINTON
see also Wynthon

WITCOMBE
see Widecomb

WOCESTRE
see Worceter

John de WODEHOUS
occ. 1344

1344, 5 Oct., 22nd in order among those in chapter for the purpose of appointing general proctors, *Priory Reg.*, no 344 (p. 119).

Philip de WODEWYKE
occ. 1292/3

1292 [before 25 Oct.], [acol.], granted *lit. dim.* for subdcn's orders by the vicar general of bp Robert [Burnell], *Priory Reg.*, no 419 (p. 149, as Philip).

1292/3, subdcn, on behalf of whom the prior of Christ Church, Canterbury [*sed. vac.* both Bath and Canterbury] wrote concerning his ordination [as dcn], *Priory Reg.*, no 415 (p. 148).

Note: see Philip I.

John WORCETER [Worcetour, Worcetur, Wurcetur
occ. 1487 d. 1524

1487, 31 Mar., ord subdcn, St Mary Redcliffe, Bristol, Reg. Stillington, fo 220.

1488, 22 Mar., ord dcn, Bruton priory, *ib.*, fo 226.

1492, 18 Mar., ord pr., chapel of the hospital of St John the Baptist, Wells, *Reg. abp Morton*, ii, no 65d.

1524, 4 Feb., before this date precentor, *Reg. Clerk*, no 179.

1495, 30 Jan., 17th in order on the *sed. vac.* visitation certificate, *Reg. abp Morton*, ii, no 347.

1499, 30 Aug., 12th at the el. of a prior, Reg. King, fo 139v.

1524, 4 Feb., d. before this date, *Reg. Clerk*, no 179.

Thomas WORCETER [Wocestre, Worcetur, *alias* Styllard
occ. 1523 occ. 1539

1523, 21 Mar., ord subdcn, St Mary's chapel by the cloister, Wells cathedral, Reg. Wolsey, fo 30.

1524, 12 Mar., ord dcn, Bath cathedral, Reg. Clerk, fo 110.

1525, 5 July, 18th in order (out of 19) at the el. of a prior, *Reg. Clerk*, no 477.

1534, 22 Sept., subscribed to the Act of Supremacy, *DK 7th Report*, Appndx 2, 280.

1539, 27 Jan., 11th on the surrender list and assigned a pension of £5 6s. 8d., *L and P Henry VIII*, xiv pt i, no 148.

Note: see also Thomas Stillard who is the same monk.

John WYDECOMBE
occ. 1423 occ. 1447

1423, 30 Aug., one of four novices whose prof. the bp comm. the prior to rec., *Reg. Bubwith*, no 1189.
1423, 18 Sept., ord acol. and subdcn, St Mary's chapel by the cloister, Wells cathedral, *ib.*, no 1315.

1447, 5 July, 7th in order at the el. of a prior, *Reg. Bekynton*, no 1639.

WYDECOMBE
see also Widecombe

John WYKE [Weke, Wyk, Wykys
occ. 1487 occ. 1509

1487, 31 Mar., ord subdcn, St Mary Redcliffe, Bristol, Reg. Stillington, fo 220.
1488, 22 Mar., ord dcn, Bruton priory, *ib.*, fo 226.
1489, 4 Apr., ord pr., chapel of the hospital of St John the Baptist, Wells, *ib.*, fo 231.
1495, 30 Jan., 16th in order at the *sed. vac.* visitation and residing at Dunster, *Reg. abp Morton*, ii, no 347.
1499, 30 Aug., 11th at the el. of a prior, Reg. King, fo 139v.
1509, 15 Nov., recd 12d. in a bequest from a parishioner of Dunster, Weaver, *Somerset Medieval Wills*, ii, 139.

Richard WYKE
occ. 1433 occ. 1439

1433, 19 Sept., ord acol., Bath cathedral, *Reg. Stafford*, no 966.
1435, 2 Apr., ord subdcn, Bath cathedral, *ib.*, no 973.
1436, 22 Sept., ord dcn, St Mary Redcliffe, Bristol, *ib.*, no 976.
1439, 19 Sept., ord pr., Taunton, *ib.*, no 989.

John de WYNTHON
occ. 1261

1261, 27 June, named as one of seven *compromissorii* in the el. of a prior, *Priory Reg.*, nos 255, 257 (pp.75, 76); see Walter de Anno.

WYNTHON
see also Winton

John WYTTON
occ. 1425

1425, 22 Sept., ord dcn, Bath cathedral, *Reg. Stafford*, no 935 (fo 208).

YFORD
see Iforde

Thomas YORKE
occ. 1499 occ. 1503

1501, 6 Mar., ord subdcn, St Mary's chapel by the cloister, Wells cathedral, Reg. King, fo 123.
1502, 12 Mar., ord dcn, St Mary's chapel behind the new altar, Bath cathedral, *ib.*, fo 126.
1503, 10 Apr., ord pr., St Mary's chapel behind the new altar, Bath cathedral, *ib.*, fo 131.
1499, 30 Aug., 18th in order at the el. of a prior, Reg. King, fo 139v.

CANTERBURY CATHEDRAL PRIORY

INTRODUCTION

The history of a monastic community at Christ Church began with the arrival of Augustine in AD 597 leading a band of some forty monks; nine and a half centuries later at the dissolution fifty-six monks signed the deed of surrender.[1] The long history of the intervening years is a record of contrasting chapters of vitality and quiescence, controversy and reconciliation, crisis and composure which reveal the universal human condition constantly leaving its imprint on monastic life and affairs.

The tenth-century monastic reformers of whom Dunstan, as abbot of Glastonbury and later as archbishop of Canterbury, was the leader, set out not only to reform monasteries but also to revive monastic chapters in cathedrals like Canterbury, Winchester, and Worcester;[2] and Lanfranc's appointment to the archiepiscopal see by William the Conqueror was to ensure the permanent implementation of the norms of monastic observance based on the Benedictine Rule.[3]

A rough estimate suggests that during the five centuries covered by this register about seventeen hundred and fifty monks would have been professed members of the Christ Church community.[4] More than three-quarters of this number are included in the entries below, which add up to a total of some fifteen hundred and fifteen names, the highest proportion of identified monks from any of the cathedral priories of the southern province. This is not surprising in view of the fact that Christ Church is blessed by the survival of a far greater abundance of original records than other cathedral monasteries excluding Durham. There are, for example, well over twenty priory registers, and most of the archiepiscopal registers remain *in situ* at Lambeth. In addition, there are obedientiary accounts for most of the major obediences, except for the precentor. The quantity and variety of original source material, including charters, correspondence, notarial instruments, inventories, lists, and miscellaneous deeds and papers, is as impressive as it is daunting; not surprisingly, calendars and descriptive lists of the cathedral archive are still in progress. The sheer abundance in itself presents a problem in that many records, regarded at the time or later as important, were duplicated for future reference; but the originals (where these can be identified) and

[1] The surrender deed has not survived but twenty-eight monks received pensions and twenty-eight were appointed to offices in the new foundation, *L and P, Henry VIII*, xv, no 452.

[2] During the three centuries between Augustine and Dunstan it is probable that Christ Church was a mixed community of clerks and monks, with some form of monastic observance and discipline such as that imposed by reforming archbishops like Wulfred (805–832) and Oda (941–958); see N. Brooks, 'The Anglo-Saxon Cathedral Community, 597–1070', in Collinson, *Canterbury Cathedral*, 1–37.

[3] See T. Symons, ed., *Regularis Concordia* (Nelson's Medieval Classics, London, 1953) for the document drawn up by Dunstan and his episcopal colleagues, and D. Knowles, ed., *Decreta Lanfranci* (Nelson's Medieval Classics, London, 1951) for the constitutions of Lanfranc.

[4] The method employed for these calculations postulates a twenty-year average monastic lifespan for each individual monk, and takes into account the average number of monks based on the figures recorded only at irregular intervals and probably never completely reliable. Estimates where needed have been set low rather than high.

the copies are not necessarily identical depending upon the particular purpose which they were intended to serve.

Christ Church has never lacked historians from early times to the present day. Many members of the medieval cathedral community, notably Eadmer, Gervase, William Glastynbury, and John Stone I, q.v., compiled chronicles and histories of past and contemporary events mainly centred on the cathedral, the priory, and their titular abbot, who, as archbishop of the southern province and primate of all England, frequently played a significant role on the national and international stage. The sixteenth-century dissolution altered the perspective but did not curb the interest of new generations of antiquarian writers and historians who worked through the monastic records, transcribed and translated some of them, and wrote their own accounts of the cathedral and its illustrious past. Among these were William Somner in the mid-seventeenth century, John Dart in the early eighteenth, J. Brigstocke Sheppard in the late nineteenth, and C. E. Woodruff in the early part of the present century.[5] There are also a large number of books and articles of a more specialized nature devoted to a particular aspect of the medieval cathedral and its chapter: the monastic library, the administration of the monastic estates, and the reconstruction of the architectural history to name but three.[6]

These preliminary observations will have shown the necessity for certain changes in this section to the criteria that have been applied in compiling the entries in the other sections of the Register. Where biographical details provided elsewhere have been more or less comprehensive, for the Canterbury monks it has been necessary to be selective; where the other Introductions have aimed to provide a historical background to the entries, for Canterbury it will be preferable to confine the background to a few important incidents to which allusion is made in many of the entries and, for the rest, to make frequent reference to the pertinent writings of some of the host of modern scholars. The following paragraphs will thus blend historical narrative with explanatory comment in the hope that readers will obtain sufficient enlightenment for a fruitful perusal of the entries that they intend to consult, and additional references that they may wish to follow up.

Canterbury is unique among the eight southern cathedral priories in the survival of a partial record of monastic professions.[7] The earliest names in it, twenty-nine in all, state merely 'isti fuerunt in exilio'; since this is less than half the number who were reported to have been expelled from their monastery by king John in 1207, the compiler of the list presumably lacked precise information for that dismal hiatus when most of the community fled abroad.[8] The next section of this list begins with the heading *Post exilium* (i.e. after 1214) but is no more than a series of names until the 1280s, when

[5] The works of these and other writers are listed in the References.

[6] See James, *Ancient Libraries*, Smith, *Canterbury Cathedral Priory*, and Willis, 'Arch. Hist. Christ Church' in the References, Sections D.i and v. Collinson, *Canterbury Cathedral* (D.i) is the most recent volume containing chapters on the medieval archives and library by Nigel Ramsay, an appendix listing the monastic estates by Margaret Sparks, and references to architectural developments in the chapters by Nicholas Brooks, Margaret Gibson, and Barrie Dobson.

[7] This is now Lit. Ms D.12 in the Canterbury cathedral archives, with another copy, Ms 298, in Corpus Christi College, Cambridge. For the somewhat confusing printed version with its interpolations see under Searle in Section D.i of the References.

[8] *Chron. Oxenedes*, 121, states that while sixty-four monks went into exile thirteen others were [too] ill [to go].

dates first appear; later on, from the mid-fourteenth century, other snippets of information are added, and in the fifteenth century more details appear in the case of certain individual monks, some of which amount to a thumbnail biography. Between 1214 and 1533 the information provided by this record forms the initial entry of almost all the monks in the Register and after c. 1285 enables us to fix the precise date of admission to Christ Church because profession usually occurred within a year after entry.[9] For the majority of monks the date of death has also been preserved in this same manuscript, that is, covering the period from 1286 to 1507 with a lengthy gap between 1361 and 1395. In addition, the several obituary lists used for commemoration must here be taken into account. It was customary for every monastic house to keep a record, usually in kalendar form, of the day of death of all the brethren so that the individual monk's name could be read out, probably in chapter, each year on the anniversary of his death thus ensuring the continuity of prayer on his behalf. The day on which the name was entered was in most cases either the exact date of death or one very close to it but, of course, the year was irrelevant and was therefore rarely supplied. There are other problems in dealing with these obit lists in that only the Christian names of the monks were entered, with few exceptions, until at least the early thirteenth century; thus, with frequent repetition of popular names like John, William, Robert, etc., no certain identification is possible. Selectivity has therefore operated here by the inclusion of, for the most part, only the more uncommon names, although these too have sometimes turned up more often than anticipated. The three lists in BL Mss Cotton Nero C.ix and Arundel 68 and in Lambeth Ms 20 have much in common, and the Lambeth manuscript closely resembles the Arundel. I have used the Arundel most extensively but have added some references to the other two on a selective basis, with the purpose of drawing attention to some of the omissions and inclusions that should suggest the need for a thorough comparative examination of all three; this seemed preferable, though admittedly with inconsistent results, to confining myself to the entries in a single manuscript.[10]

There are many other lists of monks, usually in order of seniority, scattered *passim* in the priory and episcopal registers. These occur, as in other monasteries, on the occasion of elections, both prioral and archiepiscopal, and of archiepiscopal visitations.[11] Elections of priors *sede vacante* were free from outside interference after 1174, and the following century Pope Gregory IX granted the monks the right of free election *sede plena*, with the archbishop present to scrutinize the votes and to announce the *prefectio*.[12] Archiepiscopal elections were often fraught with tension, the monks being seldom left to make their own choice for the supreme ecclesiastical dignitary of the

[9] There are still some uncertainties about dating in a number of instances due to questionable or contradictory evidence, but these are noted where they occur.

[10] The Lambeth and Arundel manuscripts, dating from the 15th and 16th cs, were written later than the 13th-c. Cotton manuscript. Dr Robin Fleming has recently examined the Cotton and Arundel manuscripts, her interest being to study the early patrons and benefactors of Christ Church who were also commemorated, 'Christchurch's Sisters and Brothers: An Edition and Discussion of Canterbury Obituary Lists' in M. A. Meyer, ed., *The Culture of Christendom: Essays in Medieval History in Commemoration of Denis L. T. Bethell* (London, 1993), 115–153. See also A. Boutemy 'Two Obituaries of Christ Church, Canterbury', *English Historical Review*, 50 (1935), 292–299, for a discussion of the dating problems of the Cotton Ms.

[11] The compiler of the 1466 list of the monks' *jocalia* also recorded their names in order of seniority, a commendable procedure from the historian's point of view in that it helps to fill the noticeable gap in the mid-15th-c. records.

[12] Smith, *Canterbury Cathedral Priory*, 29–30.

realm since it was an appointment over which the crown if not the papacy usually asserted, in the final resort, a controlling influence.[13] The prior and chapter always went through the formalities of the election procedures but were only once successful in promoting one of their own community, Richard de Dover, q.v., in 1173.[14]

It was inevitable that the cathedral chapter of the primatial see experienced the adverse effects of confrontations between crown and metropolitan as, for example, when the monks found themselves exposed in a vulnerable position during the years of exile of archbishops Anselm and Thomas Becket by both of whom they felt deserted. However, their own rather unedifying disputes with archbishops Baldwin, Hubert Walter, and Edmund of Abingdon, in the late twelfth and early thirteenth centuries, show that even the most peace-loving primate had a formidable opponent to contend with on his home ground if he should challenge what the monks considered to be their rights or prerogative. Baldwin proposed to establish a secular college of canons at Hackington, on the outskirts of Canterbury, intended to serve as headquarters for his professional entourage in the conduct of archiepiscopal affairs; but the prior and convent saw this relocation of his administration away from the cathedral as a threat to their status and influence. A dramatic account of the monks' unrelenting and successful pursuit of their cause in the court of Rome has been preserved in the correspondence of the monastic participants (including priors Honorius [III] and Geoffrey [II], and also John de Bremble, q.v.) at home and abroad and in the chronicle by Gervase [I], q.v. Both of these also include the record of their equally victorious encounter with his successor, Hubert Walter, who had thought to establish a similar collegiate foundation this time at Lambeth.[15] The disagreement with archbishop Edmund in the 1230s had a similar project as one of its components, and the monks may not have been deceived when they thought that they were involved in a struggle for the survival of the primacy of Christ Church.[16] However, the focus of dissension shifted with the exposure of the forgery scandal, when Ralph de Orpynton II, q.v., broke ranks by confessing his role in the forging of the so-called charter of St Thomas to the archbishop. The prior, John de Chatham, q.v., was thus denounced and had to resign. The subprior and chapter responded by proceeding to elect a new prior, Roger de la Lee, q.v., without the archbishop's presence or authorization, an act which kept both parties at odds until the latter's death in 1240.

Appointments to obedientiary office within the priory also proved a source of contention from time to time with a number of archbishops. The positions in question were those of subprior, chamberlain, sacrist, cellarer, precentor, and penitentiary (of whom there were usually two). On several occasions the monks resorted to papal judgement in the matter, in an attempt to obtain freedom to appoint to all offices.[17] However, it is clear from archbishop Winchelsey's register that they were unable to rid themselves of this aspect of archiepiscopal intervention in their affairs, and that his successors continued to insist on the custom by which the prior and seniors provided

[13] To hold out against the king after their election of Stephen Langton in 1206, resulted in the monks' expulsion and exile.

[14] It is to be noted that this election was not long after Becket's murder. Simon Langham, monk of Westminster and bishop of Ely, was translated to Canterbury in 1366, the only other Benedictine to hold the primatial see.

[15] The letters were transcribed and printed by bishop Stubbs from Lambeth Ms 415; see the References Section D.iv under *Epist. Cant.* For Gervase's account see *Gervase Cant.*, i, 19–68.

[16] Lawrence, *St Edmund*, 165–167.

[17] For example in 1191 and 1219, Reg. I, fos 35, 40, 83.

the names of three suitable candidates for each office from whom the archbishop selected one.[18] However, in 1295 Winchelsey alleged that the monks had left him no choice by presenting him with three candidates of whom two were *inhabiles*.[19] In 1344 another method of influencing the appointment was employed by prior Robert Hathbrand, q.v., who followed up some of the nominations sent to the archbishop by a second letter in which he urged the selection of the one he deemed most competent.[20] It must also have been a frequent source of aggravation for the prior and seniors, when allocating the offices that were in their charge, to find that one or more of those whom they considered competent for the position were not available because they were serving in offices in the archbishop's collation, and permission was required from him for their release.[21]

There was, finally, recurring contention between the archbishop and the prior and convent over the status of St Martin's priory, Dover. Archbishop Theobald declared it to be a cell of Canterbury over which he had the right of appointment and removal of the prior, who was always to be a Christ Church monk. When Christ Church asserted its superiority over St Martin's on a number of occasions there was prolonged and costly litigation between Canterbury and Dover, and also with the archbishop over the prior of Canterbury's right *sede vacante* to appoint a prior for Dover. St Martin's was gradually able to reduce its subjugation to Christ Church, but almost all its priors continued to be Canterbury monks until the mid-fifteenth century.[22]

The Christ Church obedientiaries in name and office resembled those elsewhere except for a few appointments peculiar to Canterbury's unique circumstances. The presence of additional shrine keepers, for example, resulted from the martyrdom of Thomas Becket, by whose death the cathedral profited more than it ever had by his life. There was, thus, a *custos* or warden of the *corona* which was the eastern extension of the Trinity chapel where fragments of his skull were preserved, the *custos* of the martyrdom (*martyrii*) in the north-west transept where he died, and the *custos* of his tomb in the eastern crypt.[23] There was also a monk bartoner in charge of the home farm or barton as well as a monk granator who was responsible for the granary and its stores on the north side of the monastic *curia*.[24] The manorial properties were divided into four custodies with a monk *custos* for each, although on occasion, as in the 1380s, there

[18] *Reg. abp Winchelsey*, 1305–1306. This custom also applied to the office of warden of Canterbury college, Oxford.

[19] *Ib.*, 18–19.

[20] e.g. Reg. L, fo 79. Pantin notes archbishop Courtenay's wholesale removal of all seven obedientiaries over whom he had the right of *prefectio* soon after his consecration, *Cant. Coll. Ox.*, iv, 41 (Reg. abp Courtenay, fo 22); and, in 1392, the archbishop reprimanded the monks for an instance of failure to adhere to the prescribed customs of his predecessors, Reg. abp Courtenay, ii, fo 224.

[21] Archbishop Islip was co-operative in Feb. 1351, Reg. abp Islip, fo 39^{v}, when such a request was made, but stated that it must be regarded as a concession and not as a precedent.

[22] See *Theobald Charters*, 76–77, Haines, *Dover Priory*, 88–94 and *Lit. Cant.*, nos 641, 653, 717 (Scrap Book A.147, Reg. L, fos 71^{v}, 77^{v}).

[23] Note that the *custos* of the Lady chapel at Canterbury was known as the *custos beate Marie in criptis*. The keepers of the martyrdom and of the tomb of Becket benefited from the wine of St Thomas, as it was called and to which reference is made in a few entries. It originated as the gift of Louis VII of France to the Christ Church community, the custodians of the mortal remains of the martyred archbishop; the complex arrangements for its collection and transport to Canterbury are well documented in the cathedral muniments; see R. B. Dobson, 'Canterbury in the Later Middle Ages', in Collinson, *Canterbury Cathedral*, 142.

[24] Ely was the only other cathedral priory to have a monk granator and Winchester alone had a monk bartoner; in the northern province, however, Durham cathedral priory also had a granator.

was a sole warden of all the manors, in this case William Woghope I, q.v.[25] The convent chancery was in the hands of two chancellors whose responsibilities included keeping the registers up to date by entering all official *acta* and correspondence. Obedientiary accounts unfortunately do not survive in great numbers; but what remains includes a complex accumulation of rough drafts, day-to-day expenses, and miscellaneous and supplementary accounts many of which are difficult to interpret.[26]

The cathedral's primatial status is reflected in the significance attached to the prior's administrative authority *sede vacante*, an authority which was on occasion challenged by the suffragans of the province and by cathedral chapters of other dioceses where the episcopal throne became vacant during the Canterbury voidance. The procedures that came into play at such times have been examined and illustrated in Irene Churchill's *Canterbury Administration* where she has provided lists of commissaries-general and also of officials of the court of Canterbury appointed by the prior; among the former are a number of monks like Richard de Clyve, James de Oxney I, and the prior Thomas Chillenden, q.v., and among the latter Robert de Selesia and Peter Lumbardus, q.v.[27] At these times the principal concern was the safeguarding of the archbishop's spiritual overlordship in the diocese and province, as the *sede vacante* registers, F, G, Q, and R amply attest. The priors who, like Henry Eastry, q.v., acted as vicars-general for an absent prelate were also guided by similar concerns when acting in this official capacity.[28]

Archiepiscopal visitations of the Canterbury chapter reveal and reflect the usual problems that afflict a cloistered community. The first of the surviving registers, that of archbishop Pecham, brings to light the critical situation that had arisen in 1279 and 1281 because of the financial mismanagement of prior Thomas de Ryngmer, q.v., and the consequently disturbed state of the community. Archbishop Winchelsey issued injunctions in 1298 and 1303 with the aim of restoring discipline and religious zeal, with lasting effect it would seem, since archbishop Stratford found the chapter in a healthy state in 1335 on his first visit.[29] While archbishop Sudbury in 1377 had warned the monks to reduce their debts and live more simply, archbishop Bourgchier a century later found nothing of importance that required attention. However, Warham's *detecta* of 1511 suggest that, although there were apparently no signs of financial difficulty nor of internal dissension, there were indications of slackening discipline, with the decline in religious zeal that tends to develop when a routine characterized by

[25] The four custodies were those of east Kent, the Weald (west Kent), Surrey (including Oxford and Buckinghamshire), and Essex (with Suffolk and Norfolk). Some expense accounts of the *custodes* on supervisory visits survive as CCA DCc RE40 (1447), RE131 (1490), and RE6 (1493); CCA DCc DE70 is a similar account for 1518.

[26] The treasurer's accounts, for example, the earliest of which is dated 1198, although there are only a few for the 13th and 14th cs; see Smith, *Canterbury Cathedral Priory*, 14–28, 190–197 where there is a discussion of the central financial system and its later developments under prior Thomas Chillenden. Rough drafts of the accounts of the prior and other obedientiaries in the 13th and 14th cs are preserved in Lambeth Mss 242 and 243; and see William Ingram I and William Glastynbury for their account books. There is only one late 14th-c. feretrar's account and two 16th-c. infirmarers' accounts, but not one of the precentor has survived.

[27] See Churchill, *Cant. Admin.*, i, 551–564 for explanation and commentary and ii, 229–230, 237 for the lists. Robert Poucyn, Hugh de St Margaret and Richard Vaughan, q.v., also carried out special *sede vacante* commissions for the prior.

[28] Dobson, 'Canterbury in the Later Middle Ages', in Collinson, *Canterbury Cathedral*, 79.

[29] *Reg. abp Winchelsey*, 813–827, 1303–1306; also C. R. Cheney, *Episcopal Visitation of Monasteries in the Thirteenth Century* (Manchester, 1931), 59–61. Stratford's visitation is in Reg. Q, fo 197^{v}.

monotony replaces one of challenge and growth; at such times accidie finds its way into the cloister.[30] In this respect the monks of Christ Church were in no way different from their brethren elsewhere, exhibiting the same weaknesses to which all human nature is prone.

However, there was another area in which the prior and convent continuously asserted the difference between them and all other Benedictine houses. In their position as resident chapter of the 'mother church' of the primatial see, the monks considered it inappropriate for them to have to participate as equals with other Benedictines in the triennial chapter meetings that were set up in England after the Lateran council of 1215. Appeals to the papal curia by Christ Church to be dispensed from this obligation and by the other black monks to compel universal attendance were lengthy and at times acrimonious but eventually successful for Canterbury. Their case won the support of a number of archbishops including Simon Langham, whose influence was especially effective at Avignon after 1368 when he took up residence there as a cardinal. In 1379 Urban VI granted the long-awaited bull of exemption.[31]

While this dispute had been running its course the Black Monk Chapter had been engaged in setting up a house of study for Benedictine monk students at Oxford, a project in which Canterbury chose to have no part. Prior Eastry sent several monks to study in Paris during the early and middle years of his priorate, but by 1331, the year of his death, a small contingent of Christ Church monks had been established in Oxford.[32] Nevertheless, the permanent foundation of what came to be a cell of Christ Church, known as Canterbury college, was not assured until after the bull of 1379 for the early years were precarious, there being a succession of opposing forces to thwart the monks; these difficulties have been described by W. A. Pantin in detail.[33] In 1384, with the publication of archbishop Courtenay's statutes for the college, its future became secure. Pantin's four volumes relating its history over almost two centuries include transcriptions of a wide range of documents culled from the Canterbury and Lambeth archives and other sources. He lists about one hundred and thirty monk students, whose names and university careers are also in this Register; and most of these were at Canterbury college.[34] Nearly half obtained at least a first degree, usually in theology, but ten read canon law.[35] This indicates that about one out of every six monks benefited from the Oxford experience, the process of selection normally involving the archbishop who chose one monk from every three nominations sent to him. The average number at the college at any one time was probably three, not including the warden, although this was increased to five or six in the late fifteenth century, a commendable quota for a community that usually consisted of between seventy-five and eighty-five members.[36]

[30] Reg. abp Sudbury, fo 32, *Reg. abp Bourgchier*, 457–460, Wood-Legh, *Visit.*, 294–296.

[31] Earlier, the prior and convent had obtained a *prohibicio* from Edward III ordering the presidents of the Black Monk Chapter to cease their attempts to enforce attendance upon a house which was a royal foundation, Reg. I, fo 446. The 1379 bull is in Wilkins, *Concilia*, iii, 126 (Reg. abp Sudbury, fo 58^{v}). See also the letter prob. addressed to cardinal Langham at the curia c. 1373, seeking his aid in the matter of exemption and of the foundation at Oxford, *Lit. Cant.*, no 943 (Reg. H, fo 79^{v}).

[32] See Richard de Clyve, Stephen de Faversham, Andrew de Hardys, students at Paris, and Hugh de St Ives who was involved in setting up a hall to accommodate Canterbury monks at Oxford.

[33] Pantin, *Cant. Coll. Ox.*, iv, 9–50.

[34] *Ib.*, iv, 216–228; the majority of these are in *BRUO*.

[35] The degrees total fifty-five; there were twenty-three doctorates in theology and three in canon law; some fifteen monks had a degree before entering the monastery, and the university connections of another small group with the title *magister* remain unknown.

[36] Pantin, *Cant. Coll. Ox.*, iv, 55–57.

The monastic library was well furnished to provide for the needs of both the young novices and the university graduates. The former received instruction not only from the novice master but also from a lector, and from a *magister ordinum* who prepared them for an examination [*redditus*], the requirements for which included committing to memory parts of the divine office and mastering the customs of the house and the observance of the Rule.[37] Several library catalogues survive to provide us with much valuable information about the size and contents of the Christ Church collection at different periods.[38] In prior Eastry's early fourteenth-century catalogue 1,850 books are listed;[39] and there are also a number of inventories of books in the possession of individual monks, some of them Oxford students.[40] Summaries of the scholarly and literary activities and output of individual monks are provided in this Register.

The final decades of monastic life at Christ Church must have been fraught with uncertainty; its prestige did not save it from the impending disaster. Under the observant eye of a new and hostile archbishop, Thomas Cranmer, who was the king's protagonist in the royal divorce, prior Thomas Goldwell, q.v., displayed neither the strength of character nor the leadership qualities of some of his predecessors, and the community became increasingly demoralized and divided by apprehension and fear. The executions of Edward Bockyng and John Deryng, q.v., at Tyburn in April 1534 because of their association with Elizabeth Barton, an outspoken denouncer of the king's divorce, followed by the passage of the Act of Supremacy in December only served to make the monks more vulnerable to outside pressures. The royal commissioner's visitation in 1535 played on the internal divisions and encouraged individual monks to report 'treasonable' behaviour to the authorities, as Thomas Beckett II, q.v., found to his cost. Others like Richard Thornden, q.v., began to concern themselves with their own preferment, while Robert Anthony, q.v., probably in a state of confusion and anxiety, made a trip to Rome without permission and on his return to the priory was interrogated by Cranmer. A few like William Arundell II, q.v., left, after being dispensed by the new faculty office to take a secular benefice; but of the seventy who acknowledged the Act of 1534 fifty-six stayed on to the end. Professor Dobson's perceptive observation that the growing individualism within the Christ Church community paved the way for its downfall exposes the heart of the problem.[41] The list of monks probably prepared for Cromwell in 1538 described many of them as 'symple', that is, humble, and 'good' men, but in faith and practice they had ceased to function as St Benedict's disciples, brethren who dwelt together in unity.

[37] *Ib.*, iv, 53–55. In the late 13th c. the novices were expected to learn the whole of the psalter and the Rule by heart, Pantin, *BMC*, i, 73–74.

[38] See *MLGB*, 29.

[39] M. R. James has transcribed this catalogue as well as earlier and later ones in *Ancient Libraries*, and N. Ramsay has analysed the Eastry list in 'The Cathedral Archives and Library', in Collinson, *Canterbury Cathedral*, 355–359. It is to be hoped that a volume devoted to the medieval catalogues of Christ Church will be included in the Corpus of British Medieval Library Catalogues as planned, despite the untimely death of Dr Margaret Gibson.

[40] See e.g. Richard Stone, Robert Holyngborne (under the year c. 1495), prior Thomas Goldwell [II], and William Ingram I.

[41] See his conclusions in 'Canterbury in the Later Middle Ages', in Collinson, *Canterbury Cathedral*, 152–153.

CANTERBURY REFERENCES WITH ABBREVIATIONS

Note: if the particular reference sought does not appear below, turn to the General Bibliography on pp. xv–xix.

A. Manuscript Sources

i Episcopal Registers, in Lambeth Palace Library

Reg. abp [John] Pecham (1279–1292)
Reg. abp [Robert] Winchelsey (1294–1313)
Reg. abp [Walter] Reynolds (1313–1327)
Reg. abp [Simon] Islip (1349–1366)
Reg. abp [Simon] Langham (1366–1368)
Reg. abp [William] Wittlesey (1368–1374)
Reg. abp [Simon] Sudbury (1375–1381)
Reg. abp [William] Courtenay (1381–1396), 2 vols, of which vol ii is bound in Reg. abp Morton, fos 181–228.
Reg. abp [Thomas] Arundel (1396–1397, 1399–1414), 2 vols.
Reg. abp [Henry] Chichele (1414–1443), 2 vols.
Reg. abp [John] Stafford (1443–1452)
Reg. abp [John] Kemp (1452–1454), bound with Reg. abp Stafford, fos 210–347.
Reg. abp [Thomas] Bourgchier (1454–1486), 2 vols.
Reg. abp [John] Morton (1486–1500), 2 vols.
Reg. abp [Henry] Deane (1501–1503), bound in Reg. abp Morton, ii, fos 169–171.
Reg. abp [William] Warham (1503–1532), 2 vols.
Reg. abp [Thomas] Cranmer (1533–1553)

ii Priory Registers and Cartularies

(*a*) Canterbury Cathedral Archives (CCA DCc)

Reg. A General cartulary.
Reg. B Cartulary, estates.
Reg. C Cartulary, estates.
Reg. D Cartulary, estates.
Reg. E General cartulary, cf. BL Ms Cotton Galba E.iv in Section ii (*b*) below.
Reg. F *Sede Vacante* (commissary court, 1501–1503).
Reg. G *Sede Vacante*, 1348–1413, and some general register business.
Reg. H General register, 1355–1373 with other material of earlier and later date.
Reg. I Cartulary of prior Eastry, royal writs and letters patent 1290–1340, 14th-c. catalogue of muniments.
Reg. J Rental and custumal, register of John Gore, q.v. as manorial warden.
Reg. K Register of prior Eastry, q.v.
Reg. L Letter book, 1318–1367.
Reg. N General register, 1438–1474, from fo 172 onward.
Reg. O Register *temp.* prior Eastry, rural and domestic economy.
Reg. P Similar in content to the preceding of which it originally formed the first part.
Reg. Q *Sede Vacante*, 1292–1349; also *sede plene.*
Reg. R *Sede Vacante*, 1486–1503.
Reg. S General register, 1390–1500.
Reg. T General register, 1501–1532; foliation begins 411–454, then 53–end.

Note: Extracts from most of the above registers have been summarized by J. B. Sheppard and published by the Historical Manuscripts Commission:

Hist. Mss Comm. 8th Report, Appndx pt i (1881), 316–355 (Regs A to I).

Hist. Mss. Comm. 9th Report, Appndx	pt i (1893), 72–129 (Regs I to T).
Lit. Ms C.11	Registrum Penitenciariorum, 1511–1532 (see the entry under William Ingram).
Lit. Ms E.27	14th–16th-c. miscellanea including Eastry inventories and possible fragments from a 16th-c. register.

(*b*) London, British Library (BL)

Add. Ms 6159	Composite register, 13th/14th cs; see *Hist. Mss Comm. Letters* in section D.iv below.
Ms Cotton Galba E.iv	Memoriale multorum Henrici prioris, register of prior Eastry, of which an edition has been provided in the form of a Ph.D. thesis for London University, 1966, by T.L. Hogan who has called it a memorandum book. The library catalogue drawn up by Eastry is on fos 128–147v.
Ms Cotton Nero C.ix	Register with obituary list, 13th c.

(*c*) Cambridge University Library (CUL)

Ms Ee.5.31 General register, *temp.* prior Eastry.

(*d*) Oxford, Bodleian Library (Oxford, Bod.)

Ms Ashmole 794	Fragments, 1341–1348, 1381–1388.
Ms Tanner 165	Register of prior William Molassh, q.v., 1427–1438.

B. Other Manuscript Sources

i *Obedientiary Accounts*

(*a*) Canterbury (CCA DCc)

Alm.	Almoner	1269–1392
Anniv.	Anniversarian	1348–1534
Bart.	Bartoner	1299–1460
Cel.	Cellarer	1391–1494
Caruc. Serg.	Carucate Sergeant	1250–1472
Chamb.	Chamberlain	1308–1521
Feret.	Feretrar	1397/8
Gran.	Granator/Granger	1307–1505
Infirm.	Infirmarer	1518–1521
Prior	Prior	1372–c.1470
Prior's Chaplain	Prior's Chaplain	1347–1443
Rec.	Receiver	1425–1537
Sac.	Sacrist	1341–1533
Sheep Warden	Warden of abp Islip's sheep	1372–1382
Treas.	Treasurer	1198–1536
Warden of Manors	Warden of manors	[1257 × 1262]–1523

In addition there are some accounts of the bartoner, cellarer, chamberlain, and granator for 1299, 1334, and supplementary accounts of these and other obedientiaries in Regs O and P and under miscellaneous accts (MA) below in ii (*b*) of this section.

Note: the dates provided above are those of the earliest and latest accounts in each case; there are many accts missing in between. The accounts are identified by the date and the number assigned in the manuscript catalogue.

(*b*) Lambeth Palace Library

ED	Estate documents
Mss 242, 243	Accounts of obedientiaries, 13th and 14th cs.

(*c*) Oxford, Corpus Christi College Ms 256

Chron. Wm Glastynbury The notebook of William Glastynbury, q.v.; see also Section D.iii below.

ii Other Accounts at Canterbury (CCA DCc)

(*a*) Manorial Accounts

Note: these are identified by manor, date, and the number assigned in the manuscript catalogue.

(*b*) Miscellaneous Accounts

Arrears Arrears
AS *Assisa Scaccarii*
DE Domestic economy
Lit. Ms D.4 Early treasurers' accounts
MA Miscellaneous or supplementary accounts
RE Rural economy

iii Chronicles and Miscellaneous Manuscripts

Note: because of their large number these are grouped according to location.

(*a*) Canterbury (CCA DCc, CCL)

Cart. Antiq. Loose documents classified as *C[h]artae Antiquae*, some of which have been calendared by J. B. Sheppard in *Historical Manuscripts Commission, 5th Report*, Appndx, 1876, 427–462.

EC Eastry correspondence.

Lit. Ms C.14 'Anonymous chronicle' which includes a summary of the achievements of priors between 1338 and 1415; the printed version is listed in Section D.iii below.

Lit. Ms D.12 contains lists of monks admitted or professed, c.1207–1533 and obits of monks, c.1286–1507; sometimes referred to as the Causton Ms (see Thomas Causton). For a printed version see under *SL* (Searle) in Section D.i below.

Ms Scrap Books three vols (A, B, C) of miscellaneous, formerly loose, documents.

(*b*) Cambridge, Corpus Christi College

Ms 298 List of monks similar to CCA Lit. Ms D.12 above and other miscellaneous material. (This is only partially foliated.)

Ms 417 Fifteenth-century chronicle written by John Stone, q.v.; see also Section D.iii below.

(*c*) London, British Library (BL)

Add. Ms 59616 Customary of Thomas Becket's shrine; see also under Turner in Section D.v below.

Ms Arundel 68 An obit book, fos 12ᵛ–51ᵛ.

Ms Cotton Nero C.ix also contains Canterbury obits, fos 3–18ᵛ, 19–21.

Ms Cotton Julius D.v Annals of Dover.

Ms Royal 10 B.ix Notebook of Henry Cranbroke II, q.v.

(*d*) London, Lambeth Palace Library

Ms 20 An obit book, fos 157–249.
Ms 241 Cartulary of St Martin's, Dover.
Mss 242, 243 See Section B.i (*b*) above.
Ms 414 Epistolae Cantuarienses; see also under *Epist. Cant.* in Section D.iv below.
Ms 1212 Charters, 13th/14th cs.

iv Unpublished Thesis

See Section A.ii (*b*) above under BL Ms Cotton Galba E.iv.

C. Printed Sources

i Archiepiscopal Registers (in chronological order)

Reg. abp Pecham F. N. Davis et al, eds, *The Register of John Pecham, Archbishop of Canterbury, 1279–1292*, Canterbury and York Society, 2 vols, 64, 65, i (1969); Decima Douie, ed., *ib.*, ii (1968).

Reg. abp Winchelsey Rose Graham, ed., *Registrum Roberti Winchelsey Cantuariensis Archiepiscopi, A.D. 1294–1313*, Canterbury and York Society, 2 vols, 51, 52 (1952, 1956); vol. i (pp. 1–511), vol. ii (pp. 513–1473).

Reg. abp Langham A. C. Wood, ed., *Registrum Simonis Langham, Cantuariensis Archiepiscopi [1366–8]*, Canterbury and York Society, 53, 1956.

Reg. abp Chichele E. F. Jacob, ed., *The Register of Henry Chichele Archbishop of Canterbury, 1414–1443*, Canterbury and York Society, 4 vols, 45, 42, 46, 47, 1943, 1937, 1945, 1947.

Reg. abp Bourgchier F. R. H. Du Boulay, ed., *Registrum Thome Bourgchier Cantuariensis Archiepiscopi, A.D. 1454–1486*, Canterbury and York Society, 54, 1957.

Reg. abp Morton C. Harper-Bill, ed., *The Register of John Morton, Archbishop of Canterbury, 1486–1500*, Canterbury and York Society, 3 vols, 75, 78, 1987, 1991; the third volume is in the press.

ii Priory Registers and Cartularies

Note: none have been published in full or in calendar form but there are many extracts; see Section A. ii (*a*) above, e.g. under *Hist. Mss Comm.* and under *Lit. Cant.*. in D iv below.

D. Other Printed Sources and References

i General

Churchill, *Cant. Admin.* See under General Bibliography.

Collinson, *Canterbury Cathedral* P. Collinson, N. Ramsay, and M. Sparks, eds, *History of Canterbury Cathedral*, Oxford, 1995.

Dart, *Antiq. Cant.* J. Dart, *History and Antiquities of the Cathedral Church of Canterbury*, London, 1726; the appendices include extracts from BL Ms Cotton Galba E.iv; see Section A. ii (*b*) above.

Dodwell, *Cant. School* C. R. Dodwell, *The Canterbury School of Illumination, 1066–1200*, Cambridge, 1954.

Douglas, *Domesday Monachorum* D. C. Douglas, *Domesday Monachorum of Christ Church Canterbury*, London, 1944.

Foreville, *Église et Royauté* R. Foreville, *L'Église et la Royauté en Angleterre sous Henri II Plantagenet (1154–1189)*, Paris, 1943.

Haines, *Dover Priory* C. Haines, *Dover Priory, a History of the Priory of St Mary the Virgin and St Martin of the New Work*, Cambridge, 1930.

Hasted, *Kent* E. Hasted, *The History of Canterbury and Topographical Survey of the County of Kent*, 12 vols, Canterbury, 1797–1801.

James, *Ancient Libraries* M. R. James, *The Ancient Libraries of Canterbury and Dover*, Cambridge, 1903.

Legg and Hope, *Inventories* J. Wickham Legg and W. St John Hope, eds, *Inventories of Christ Church Canterbury with historical and topographical introductions*, Westminster, 1902.

Materials Becket	J. C. Robertson, ed., *Materials for the History of Thomas Becket, Archbishop of Canterbury, canonized by Pope Alexander III, A.D. 1173*, Rolls Series, 7 vols, 1875–1885; vol. vii, ed. by Robertson and J. B. Sheppard.
Pantin, *Cant. Coll. Ox.*	W. Pantin, *Canterbury College, Oxford*, Oxford Historical Society, new series, 4 vols, i and ii (1947), iii (1950), iv (1985).
Selden Society, *Select Cases Eccles.*	N. Adams and C. Donahue junior, eds, *Select Cases from the Ecclesiastical Courts of the Province of Canterbury, c.1200–1301*, Selden Society, xcv, 1981.
SL	W. G. Searle, comp., *List of the Deans, Priors and Monks of Christ Church Monastery*, Cambridge Antiquarian Society, Octavo Publications, no 34 (1902); compiled from Canterbury, Lit. Ms D.12 (B.iii (*a*)) above) and Cambridge, Corpus Christi College Ms 298 (B.iii (b)) above).
Smith, *Canterbury Cathedral Priory*	R. A. L. Smith, *Canterbury Cathedral Priory, a study in monastic administration*, Cambridge, 1969.
Somner, *Antiq. Cant.*	W. Somner and N. Battely, *The Antiquities of Canterbury*, 2nd edn, London, 1703.
Urry, *Canterbury*	W. Urry, *Canterbury under the Angevin Kings*, London, 1967.
Weiss, *Humanism*	R. Weiss, *Humanism in England during the Fifteenth Century*, 3rd edn, Oxford, 1967.
Wood-Legh, *Visit.*	K. Wood-Legh, ed., *Visitations of Archbishop William Warham and his Deputies, 1511–1512*, Kent Records, 1984.
Woodruff, *Christ Church Mss Catalogue*	C. Woodruff, comp., *A Catalogue of the Manuscript Books in the Library of Christ Church, Canterbury*, Canterbury, 1911.
Woodruff, *Memorials Cant.*	C. Woodruff and W. Danks, *Memorials of the Cathedral and Priory of Christ Church in Canterbury*, London, 1912.

ii Archbishops' Acta, Charters, and Lives

Acta Guala	N. Vincent, ed., *The Acta of the Legate Guala, 1216–1218*, Canterbury and York Society, forthcoming.
'Acta Lanfranci'	C. Plummer and J. Earle, eds, *Two of the Saxon Chronicles Parallel with Supplementary Extracts from the Others*, 2 vols, Oxford, 1892, 1899; the *acta* are in i, 287–292.
Anselm Memorials	R. Southern and F. Schmitt, eds, *Memorials of St Anselm*, Auctores Medii Aevi, i, Oxford, 1969.
Barlow, *Becket*	F. Barlow, *Thomas Becket*, London, 1986.
Dunstan Memorials	W. Stubbs, ed., *Memorials of St Dunstan, Archbishop of Canterbury, edited from various Manuscripts*, Rolls Series, 1874.
Eadmer, *Vita Anselmi*	R. Southern, *The Life of St Anselm by Eadmer*, Oxford, 1963.
Eng. Epis. Acta, ii	C. Cheney and B. Jones, eds, *English Episcopal Acta*, ii. *Canterbury 1162–1190*, British Academy, London, 1986.
Eng. Epis. Acta, iii	C. Cheney and E. John, eds, *English Episcopal Acta*, iii. *Canterbury 1193–1205*, British Academy, London, 1986.
Eng. Epis. Acta, Canterbury 1070–1161	M. Brett, ed., *English Episcopal Acta*, Canterbury 1070–1161, forthcoming.
Gibson, *Lanfranc*	M. Gibson, *Lanfranc of Bec*, Oxford, 1978.
Langton Acta	K. Major, ed., *Acta Stephani Langton (1207–1228)*, Canterbury and York Society, 1950.
Lawrence, *St Edmund*	C. Lawrence, *Edmund of Abingdon*, Oxford, 1960.
Southern, *St Anselm* (1963)	R. Southern, *St Anselm and his Biographer*, Cambridge, 1963.
Southern, *St Anselm* (1990)	R. Southern, *St Anselm, a Portrait in a Landscape*, Cambridge, 1990.

Theobald Charters — A. Saltman, *Theobald, Archbishop of Canterbury*, London, 1956.

Wallace, *St Edmund* — W. Wallace, *Life of St Edmund of Canterbury*, London, 1893.

iii Chronicles and Histories

'Anon. Chron.' — C. E. Woodruff, 'A Monastic Chronicle of Christ Church (1331–1414) lately Discovered', *Archaeologia Cantiana*, 29 (1911), 47–84; transcription and translation of Canterbury Cathedral, Lit. Ms C.14 (Section B.iii above).

Chron. Stone — W. Searle, ed. and comp., *The Chronicle of John Stone, Monk of Christ Church, 1415–1471*, Cambridge Antiquarian Society, Octavo Publications, no 34 (1902); transcript of Cambridge, Corpus Christi College Ms 417.

'Chron. Wm Glastynbury' — C. E. Woodruff, ed., 'Chronicle of William Glastynbury, Monk of the Priory of Christ Church, Canterbury', *Archaeologia Cantiana*, 37 (1925), 121–151; an incomplete transcript, partly in translation, of Oxford, Corpus Christi College Ms 256 (Section B.i (*c*)) above).

Eadmer, *Hist. Nov.* — M. Rule, ed., *Eadmeri Historia Novorum in Anglia et Opuscula duo de Vita Sancti Anselmi et quibusdam miraculis ejus*, Rolls Series, 1884.

Gervase Cant. — W. Stubbs, ed., *Gervasii Cantuariensis Opera Historica*, Rolls Series, 2 vols, 1879–1880.

iv Archiepiscopal Letters and Priory Correspondence

Anselm Letters — F. Schmitt, ed., *S. Anselmi Opera*, 6 vols, Edinburgh, 1946–1961; the letters are in iii (nos 1–147), iv (nos 148–309), v (nos 310–475).

Anstruther, *Epist. Losinga* — R. Anstruther, ed., *Epistolae Herberti de Losinga, Primi Episcopi Norwicensis, Osberti de Clara et Elmeri Prioris Cantuariensis*, Brussels, 1846.

Christ Church Letters — J. B. Sheppard, ed., *Christ Church Letters*, Camden Society, new series, no 19 (1877).

Epist. Cant. — W. Stubbs, ed., *Chronicles and Memorials of the Reign of Richard I*, Rolls Series, 2 vols, 1864–1865; vol ii. *Epistolae Cantuarienses, 1187–1199*.

Epist. Pecham — C. T. Martin, ed., *Registrum epistolarum fratris Johannis Peckham, archiepiscopi Cantuariensis*, Rolls Series, 3 vols, 1882–1885; the volumes are paginated continuously throughout and the letters numbered likewise. Vol. i, pp. 1–392, vol. ii, pp. 393–743, vol. iii, pp. 773– .

Hist. Mss Comm. Letters — R. Poole, ed., *Historical Manuscripts Commission, Reports, Various Collections*, i (1901), Appendix, 250–281; extracts from letters of Prior Eastry (from BL Add Ms 6159).

Lanfranc Letters — M. Gibson and H. Clover, eds, *The Letters of Lanfranc, Archbishop of Canterbury*, Oxford Medieval Texts, Oxford, 1979.

Lit. Cant. — J. B. Sheppard, ed., *Litterae Cantuarienses*, Rolls Series, 3 vols, 1887–1889; extracts mainly from priory registers; the items are numbered continuously throughout. Vol. i, nos 1–494, ii, nos 495–943, iii, nos 944 up to Appendix.

Salisbury Letters — W. J. Millor, H. E. Butler and C. N. L. Brooke, eds, *The Letters of John of Salisbury*, i. *Early Letters*, Nelson's Medieval Texts, 1955 (reprinted, Oxford Medieval Texts, 1986); W. J. Millor and C. N. L. Brooke, eds, ii. *Later Letters*, Oxford Medieval Texts, 1979.

v Miscellaneous Articles

	C. N. L. Brooke, 'The Canterbury Forgeries and their Author', *Downside Review*, 68 (1950), 462–476, 69 (1951), 210–231.
Cheney 'Cant. Forgery'	C. R. Cheney, 'Magna Carta Beati Thome: another Canterbury Forgery', *Bulletin of the Institute of Historical Research*, 36 (1963), 1–26; reprinted in his *Medieval Texts and Studies*, Oxford, 1973, 78–110.
Cheney, 'Mortuary Rolls'	C. R. Cheney, 'Two Mortuary Rolls from Canterbury', in D. Greenway, C. Holdsworth, and J. Sayers, eds, *Tradition and Change, Essays in honour of Marjorie Chibnall presented by her friends on the occasion of her seventieth birthday*, Cambridge, 1985.
Cowdrey, 'An Early Record at Dijon'	H. E. J. Cowdrey, 'An Early Record at Dijon of the Export of Becket's Relics', in H. E. J. Cowdrey, *Popes, Monks and Crusaders*, London, 1984, no xviii, 251–253.
Gasquet, 'Cant. Claustral School'	F. A. Gasquet, 'The Canterbury Claustral School in the Fifteenth Century', in *The Old English Bible and other Essays* 2nd edn, London, 1908, 225–246.
	J. Greatrex, 'Prosopography of English Benedictine Cathedral Chapters: some Monastic *Curricula Vitae*', *Medieval Prosopography*, 16 (1995), 1–26.
Holmes, 'Crusade vs the Hussites'	G. Holmes, 'Cardinal Beaufort and the Crusade against the Hussites', *English Historical Review*, 88 (1973), 721–750.
Hope, 'Inventories of Priors'	W. St John Hope, 'Inventories of the Goods of Henry of Eastry (1331), Richard of Oxenden (1334), and Robert Hathbrand (1339), successively Priors of the Monastery of Christchurch, Canterbury', *Archaeological Journal*, 53 (1896), 258–283.
Hussey, 'Kentish Wills'	A. Hussey, 'Further Notes from Kentish Wills', *Archaeologia Cantiana*, 31, (1915), 37–43.
Kissan, 'London Deanery'	B. Kissan, 'The London Deanery of Arches', in *Transactions of the London and Middlesex Archaeological Soeicty*, new series, 8 (1940), 195–233.
Knowles, 'Cant. Election of 1205–6'	D. Knowles, 'The Canterbury Election of 1205–6', *English Historical Review*, 53 (1938), 211–220.
Lawrence, 'Exile of Abp Edmund'	C. H. Lawrence, 'The Alleged Exile of archbishop Edmund', *Journal of Ecclesiastical History*, 7 (1956), 160–173.
Rooke, 'William Ingram'	G. Rooke, 'Dom William Ingram and his Account-Book, 1504–1533', *Journal of Ecclesiastical History*, 7 (1956), 30–44.
Sayers, 'Cant. Proctors'	J. Sayers, 'Canterbury Proctors at the Court of "Audientia Litterarum Contradictarum" ', *Traditio*, 22 (1966), 311–345.
	R. Southern, 'The Canterbury Forgeries', *English Historical Review*, 73 (1958), 193–226.
Turner, 'Customary'	D. Turner, 'The Customary of the Shrine of Thomas Becket', *Canterbury Cathedral Chronicle*, no. 70 (1976), 16–22.
Willis, 'Arch. Hist. Christ Church'	R. Willis, 'The Architectural History of the Conventual Buildings of the Monastery of Christ Church in Canterbury', *Archaeologia Cantiana*, 7 (1868), 1–206; see also his collected papers (1848–1863) reissued as *Architectural History of some English Cathedrals*, 2 parts, Chicheley, 1972, pt 1, 1–140.
Woodruff, 'Election of Winchelsey'	C. E. Woodruff, 'The Election of Robert Winchelsey', *Church Quarterly Review*, 121 (1936), 210–232
Woodruff, 'Letters to Eastry'	C. E. Woodruff, 'Letters to the Prior of Christ Church, Canterbury, from University Students', *Archaeologia Cantiana*, 39 (1927), 1–33.

Woodruff, 'Sacrist's Rolls' C. E. Woodruff, 'The Sacrist's Rolls, of Christ Church, Canterbury', *Archaeologia Cantiana*, 48 (1936), 38–80.

Woodruff, '*Sede Vacante Wills*' C. E. Woodruff, *Sede Vacante Wills: a Calendar of Wills proved before the Commissary of the Prior and Chapter of Christ Church, Canterbury, during Vacancies in the Primacy*, Kent Archaeological Society, Records Branch, 3 (1914).

CANTERBURY CATHEDRAL PRIORY
c.1066–1540

M. AARON
occ. 1187 occ. 1190

1187, 10 June, with Simon de Dover, q.v., sent to abp Baldwin by the prior and chapter with letters from the pope prohibiting him from carrying out his plan to build a collegiate church at Lambeth, *Epist. Cant.*, 67.
1189, May, one of several monks with whom the abp refused to negotiate, *ib.*, 292.
1189, 5/8 Nov., one of the party of monks sent by the convent to London to the king over the dispute with the abp, *ib.*, 315; during these negotiations, he, with other brethren, refused to go along with the terms put forward and left the court, *ib.*, 317; see M. William.
1190, Nov., confessor of the monks, and one of those to whom abp Baldwin made his confession not long before his d., Coggeshall, *Chron.*, 156.

Name in Distinctiones super psalmos and two books of sermons in the Eastry catalogue, nos 111, 261, 262, James, *Ancient Libraries*, 30, 47.

ABEL [Abell
occ. 1206

1206, 30 Mar., one of the monks summoned by the pope to Rome to give evidence in the dispute over their el. of Reginald, subprior, q.v., as abp, *CPL*, i (1198–1304), 26; while there they el. Stephen Langton, *Fasti*, ii, 6.

Note: n.d., the obit of an Abel occ. on 20 Apr. in BL Ms Arundel 68, fo 24ᵛ and Lambeth Ms 20, fo 181; there is another obit of an acol. by this name on 24 Sept. in BL Ms Cotton Nero C.ix, fo 12.

ACELINI
see Ascelin, Azelinus

John ACHARDE [*dictus* Achard, Hachard
occ. [c. 1283] d. 1298

[c. 1283], one of five prof., *SL*, 177, CCA Lit. Ms D.12, fo 3.
1285, 21 Sept., ord dcn, collegiate church of South Malling, *Reg. abp Pecham*, i, 222.
1296/7, treasurer, CCA MA1, fo 205.
1293, 24 Feb., present at Leighton Buzzard [Lecton] at Robert Winchelsey's consent to his el. as abp, *Reg. abp Winchelsey*, 1273–1274.
1298, 28 July, sent by the prior and chapter with Robert de Clyve, q.v. to Rome, and they were provided with authority to contract loans, CUL Ms Ee.5.31, fo 77, 77ᵛ.
1298, 21 Sept., d., CCA Lit. Ms D.12, fo 15.
1299, 14 Feb., accused of having allowed Benedicta de Burne to have goods belonging to Christ Church; she said that she had recd only *unam nucem nudam* which she had made into a cup, *Reg. abp Winchesley*, 1320–1321, Reg. I, fo 157.

I ADAM
n.d.

n.d., 14 May, obit occ. in BL Ms Arundel 68, fo 27ᵛ.

II ADAM
n.d.

n.d., 20 July, pr., whose obit occ. in BL Ms Arundel 68, fo 35ᵛ.

III ADAM
n.d.

n.d., the obit of another Adam occ. on 11 Sept. in BL Ms Cotton Nero C.ix, fo 11ᵛ.

Note: there are several more Adams included in the obituary lists which should be checked by those who are looking for other dates.

IV ADAM
occ. 1252 × 1262

1252 × 1262, sacrist, CCA DCc AS accts, Reg. H, fos 172–.

ADAM prior
see Chillenden

ADDRICUS
n.d.

n.d., pr., whose obit occ. on 21 June, BL MS Arundel 68, fo 31ᵛ.

Edmund de ADESHAM [Adisham
occ. 1298 d. 1342

1298, 18 Oct., one of seven prof., *SL*, 178, CCA Lit. Ms D.12, fo 3.
1313/14, 10 May, subchamberlain, CCA DCc Chamb. acct 8, MA2, fos 44ᵛ–52.
1320/3, warden of manors, CCA DCc Chartham acct 13, Ickham acct 22, Chartham acct 14.
1325/9, bartoner, CCA MA2, fos 146–184ᵛ, Bart. accts 14, 15, 16, 18.

1329/32, warden of manors, CCA DCc MA2, fos 182–209.
1332, Oct., apptd penitentiary by the abp after receiving the three names sent in by the prior and chapter *Lit. Cant.* no 479 (Reg. L, fo 25).
1333, Apr./1334, cellarer, CCA DCc DE3, fos 4, 25.
1333, 27 Aug., named as subprior by authority of the abp, CCA DCc DE3, fo 21ᵛ.
1333, warden of St Mary in crypt, CCA DCc MA2, fo 221.
1335/6, penitentiary, CCA DCc AS 14, MA2 fo 250ᵛ.
1337/40, warden of manors, CCA DCc West Farleigh acct 3, Adisham accts 15, 16.
1341/2, sacrist, CCA DCc Sac. acct 2.

1318, Jan., sent with William de Ledebury, q.v. to the abp with letters of credence, CUL Ms Ee.5.31, fo 186ᵛ. By 20 Feb. they were at the curia where they had been sent in connection with the troubles caused by Robert de Thaneto, q.v., *ib.*, fos 188ᵛ–189.
1327, 11 Dec., named as one of seven *compromissorii* in the el. of an abp, Reg. Q, fo 123 and *CPL*, ii (1305–1342), 272.
1331, one of four monks sent to the abp for licence to el. a prior, Lambeth Ms 243, fo 26ᵛ.
1332/3, with Richard de Ikham, q.v., pd supervisory visits to Godmersham, CCA DCc Godmersham acct 15.
1333, 3 Nov., named as one of seven *compromissorii* in the el. of an abp, Reg. Q, fo 193ᵛ, Reg. G, fos xxxii, xxxvii.
1335, 26 Oct., one of the monks who approved the apptment of a steward of the liberty, *Lit. Cant.*, no 587 (Reg.L, fo 107ᵛ).
1342, 29 Aug., d., CCA Lit. Ms D.12, fo 16ᵛ.

Note: see Edmund Albone.

Ralph de ADESHAM [Adisham
occ. 1280 d. 1300

n.d., the name Ralph occ. in the list in *SL*, 175, CCA Lit. Ms D.12, fo 2ᵛ.

1280/1, bartoner, CCA DCc MA1, fos 132ᵛ–135.
1281, granator, CCA DCc MA1, fo 135.
1282/3, 1284/5, 1286/95, subprior, CCA DCc Ickham acct 5, Meopham accts 5, 7, Agney acct 11, Cliffe acct 8, Adisham acct 1, Great Chart acct 13, Meopham acct 12, Great Chart acct 14, Hadleigh acct 4, Barksore acct 11.
1295, 12 Apr., apptd second penitentiary by the abp, and two days later penitentiary, *Reg. abp Winchelsey*, 18, 20; see also Reg. I, fo 175.
1296, May/Sept., penitentiary CCA DCc Cliffe acct 16.
1299, 7 Dec., penitentiary, who, by the abp's order, was not for the present to be nom. to another office, *Reg. abp Winchelsey*, 367–368, 1315; see also Reg. Q, fos 37ᵛ–38ᵛ where there are details of the abp's dispute with the monks over their manner of presenting to him nominations for obedientiary office.

[1285], 5 Jan., one of several monks imprisoned by royal officers for whose release into his charge the abp now gave orders, *Epist. Pecham*, 876–877.
1289, 7 Mar. and 20 Dec., sent with Robert de Selesya, q.v., with letters of credence to the abp, CUL Ms Ee.5.31, fos 29ᵛ, 30ᵛ.
1293, 13 Feb., one of seven *compromissorii* named by the prior and chapter in the el. of an abp, *Reg. abp Winchelsey*. 1265 (also Reg. Q, fo 19ᵛ, CUL Ms Ee.5.31, fo 38). See also Woodruff, 'Election of Winchelsey', 214.
1298, 25 Nov., with Robert Poucyn, q.v., chosen from among the *antiquioribus fratribus* as proctors, CUL Ms Ee.5.31, fo 76ᵛ.
1300, 22 Mar., d., CCA Lit. Ms D.12, fo 15.

Name in seven volumes in the Eastry catalogue, nos 1563–1569, James, *Ancient Libraries*, 130; these include sermons, treatises on contemplation and on the prof. of monks, and the Summa Raymundi.

An inventory of vestments, *temp.* prior Eastry, includes a green samite chasuble, a cope and an alb of his [?gift], Legg and Hope, *Inventories*, 52, 54, 59. Two silver *ciphi* and one *de murra* are listed as his in the 1328 inventory of the refectory, Dart *Antiq. Cant.* xx, xxiii (BL Ms Cotton Galba E.iv, fos 112ᵛ, 113, 115 for the vestments; 178ᵛ, 180 for the *ciphi*).

Note:
(1) Many of his *acta* as subprior are recorded in CUL Ms Ee.5.31, fos 29–65.
(2) A Ralph, subprior, d. at Rome, 9 May, acc. to the obit in BL Ms Arundel 68, fo 27.
(3) There are two letters among the Eastry correspondence written by R. de Adesham to the prior about the abp's apptment of a Dover monk as prior of Dover, CCA DCc EC III/15, 16.

ADESHAM
see also Adysham

ADEWINUS [Adewynus
occ. [1109 × 1125]

[1109 × 1125] sacrist, *temp.* prior Ernulf, *Anglia Sacra*, i, 137.

He and Edmund I, q.v., his successor, are described as *strenuissimi secretarii*, *ib.*

ADRICUS [?Alricus
n.d.

n.d., 15 Aug., dcn, whose obit occ. in BL Ms Arundel 68, fo 38.

See also Addricus.

ADRIANUS
occ. [?c. 1100]

[?c. 1100] described as apostate because he had left the monastery; abp Anselm wrote to urge him to repent and return, *Anselm Letters*, no 431; see Airardus.

Note: an Adrian, *bonae indolis adolescens*, gave Osbern I, q.v., the acct of the encounter of Edward, q.v., with St Dunstan, *Dunstan Memorials*, 156.

Henry ADYSHAM [Addesham, Addysham, Adisham, Adsham, Attysham
occ. 1480 d. 1518/19

1480, 25 Jan., one of six prof., *SL*, 191, CCA Lit. Ms D.12, fo 8v.
1480, 1 Apr., ord acol., Canterbury cathedral, *Reg. abp Bourgchier*, 430.
1480, 23 Sept., ord subdcn, Canterbury cathedral, *ib.*, 431.
1483, 29 Mar., ord dcn, Canterbury cathedral, *ib.*, 439.
1486, 25 Mar., ord pr., Canterbury cathedral, *ib.*, 455.
1504/5, anniversarian, Lambeth, ED47.
1493, 1 May, 39th in order at the ratification of an agreement, Reg. S, fo 383v.
1501, 26 Apr., 25th at the el. of an abp, Reg. R, fo 56v.
1508, 11 June, delegated to celebrate the Sun. mass, CCA Lit. Ms C.11, fo 17v.
1511, 2 Sept., 11th in order on the visitation certificate, Wood-Legh, *Visit.*, 3 (Reg. abp Warham, i, fo 35).
1518, with the prior witnessed the will of a parishioner of St Alphege, Canterbury, Hussey, 'Kentish Wills', 36.
1518/19, spent time in the infirmary, CCA DCc Infirm. acct 1.
1518/19, his d. is recorded on the treasurer's acct, Pantin, *Cant. Coll. Ox.*, iv, 206; his obit is on 25 Sept. in BL Ms Arundel 68, fo 43.

Richard ADYSHAM [Addysham, Adesham, Hadesham
occ. 1426 d. 1458

1426, 7 May, one of three prof., *SL*, 187, CCA Lit. Ms D.12, fo 7.
1427, 5 Dec., ord subdcn, bp's chapel, Trottiscliffe, Reg. Langdon (Rochester), fo 59v.
1428, 3 Apr., ord dcn, Rochester cathedral, *ib.*, fo 65.
1444/5, feretrar, CCA DCc, MA4, fo 29v.
1450/3, second anniversarian with Robert Chelmynton, q.v., CCA DCc Anniv. accts 10, 11, Prior acct 9.
1451, 21 Oct., *magister ordinis*, *SL*, 189, CCA Lit. Ms D.12, fo 7v.
1456/7, third prior with John Cross, q.v., CCA DCc Sac. acct 40.
1439, 3 Feb., one of several monks given licence to leave the priory *pro recreacione*, Chron. Wm Glastynbury, fo 182v/177v.
1451, 28 Dec., ill for 15 days and his expenses were 5s., CCA Lit. Ms E.6, fo 64v.
1457, 13 Aug., ill and unable to participate in the examination [*redditus*] of a novice, *Chron. Stone*, 68.
1458, *conventualis*, d., CCA Lit. Ms D.12, fo 26; his obit on 12 Aug. occ. in BL Ms Arundel 68, fo 38.

AEGELMER
occ ?late 11th c.

A monk of Canterbury by this name is listed among the friends and benefactors of Hyde Abbey, Birch, *Hyde Liber Vitae*, 57.

Note: is this Aelmer, q.v.?

AEGELREDUS [Aethelred
occ. [1071 × 1089]

n.d., subprior and precentor acc. to Eadmer in his life of St Dunstan, *Dunstan Memorials*, 163.
n.d., he later went to Worcester 'ob religiosam prudentiam et prudentem religiositatem' where he held office, *ib.*, 163–164; see under Worcester.
n.d., 12 Jan, the obit of an Aegelredus occ in BL Ms Arundel 68, fo 13, and Lambeth Ms 20, fo 158v.

AEGELWARD [Aethelweard
occ. [1073]

[1073], there is a possible ref to this monk by abp Lanfranc to the effect that he had gone mad while serving at the altar, *Lanfranc Letters*, no 15.
n.d., the life of St Dunstan by Osbern I, q.v., gives a detailed acct of his possession by an evil spirit while serving abp Lanfranc at mass and of his eventual cure by Dunstan, *Dunstan Memorials*, 144–150.

AEGELWINUS [Aethelwine, Egelwin
n.d.

n.d., went on a successful pilgrimage to Jerusalem, Constantinople and Rome with the intention of bringing back a finer pall [*pallium*] for Dunstan's tomb than the one he then had; Eadmer q.v, relates his perilous journeyings, *Dunstan Memorials*, 245–246.

AELFWORDUS
see Alfwordus

AELFWYNUS
see Alfwynus

AELGAR [Aelgarus, Elgarus
[?c. 1160]

[?c. 1160], pr., who gave his church to the monastery at the time of his entry, with the proviso that his relatives be vicars, beginning with his son, *Lit. Cant.* iii, Appndx no 7 (CCA DCc Cart. Antiq. L.2).

n.d. 26 Jan., the obit of an Elgar, pr., occ. in BL Ms Arundel 68, fo 14^{v}.

AELMER
n.d.

n.d., witnessed a grant in Saxmundham, *Text Roff.*, ii, fo 185^{v}, and cap 120 (see Rochester refs).

AELMER
see also Elmer

[AELNOTH
occ. [c. 1122]

[c. 1122], wrote Gesta Swenomagni regis et filiorum eius; see Sharpe, *Latin Writers*.]

Note: it is not certain that he was a Christ Church monk.

AELRICUS
see Ailricus

AERNALDUS
see Ernaldus

AESSEHFORD
see Assheforde

AETHELRED
see Aegelredus

AETHELWEARD
see Aegelward

AGELNODUS
n.d.

n.d., 29 Jan., obit occ. in BL Ms Arundel 68, fo 14^{v}.

I AGELREDUS [Egelredus
n.d.

n.d., 26 Feb., dcn, whose obit occ. in BL Ms Arundel 68, fo 18.

II AGELREDUS
n.d.

n.d., 2 Apr., pr., whose obit occ. in BL Ms Arundel 68, fo 22^{v}.

See also Aegelredus.

AILBRIGHTON
see Elbrighton

AILFWINUS
n.d.

n.d., sacrist, *temp.* the writing of Eadmer's, *Vita Wulfridi*; see Eadmer.

AILFWINUS
see also Alfwinus

AILMER
see Elmer

AILRICUS [Aelricus
occ. 1152 occ. [1153 × 1161]

[1153 × 1161], chamberlain, *temp.* abp Theobald and prior Wibert, q.v., *Theobald Charters*, no 40.

n.d., mentioned as chamberlain in a letter of Theobald to the pope, *Salisbury Letters*, i, no 59.

1152, witness to a purchase of land in Canterbury by prior Wibert, q.v., Urry, *Canterbury*, 392.

[1153 × 1161], attested a grant of the prior and convent in response to a request from the abp, *Theobald Charters*, no 40 (Reg. B, fo 146^{v}).

AIMERY
see under Azelinus

AIRARDUS
occ. [?c. 1100]

[?c. 1100] described as apostate because he had left the monastery with Adrianus, q.v.; in a letter to the latter abp Anselm urged him to share its contents with Airardus in the hope that they might both repent and return, *Anselm Letters*, no 431.

AISSHE
see Asshe

AISSHEY
see Asshelee

I M. ALAN [Alanus
occ. before 1170 occ. 1186

1179–1186, prior: apptd by the abp with the convent's approval, 6 Aug. 1179; el. abbot of Tewkesbury, May 1186, *Fasti*, ii, 10, *HRH*, 34. See *Gervase Cant.*, i, 293.

[1160s], *temp.* abp Becket, sacrist, Hasted, *Kent*, xi, 434.

[1183, 25 Sept. x 1184, 16 Feb.], witnessed a confirmation of abp Richard, *Eng. Epis. Acta*, ii, no 54.

1184, c. June/Dec., played a prominent role in the negotiations over the method of el. of an abp, in which the bps as well as the king were involved; he asserted the right of free el. of the abp by the chapter but reluctantly agreed to accept Baldwin of Worcester, the bps' choice, *Gervase Cant.*, i, 310–325.

Name in a number of vols in the Eastry catalogue, nos 110, 358, 1240–1245, James, *Ancient Libraries*, 29, 52, 109.

Though an Englishman, he had previously been a canon of Benevento, *HRH*, 34. He was a friend of Becket and compiled a volume of the latter's letters, *Gervase Cant.*, ii, 391. For a detailed description of and commentary on this collection see *Salisbury Letters*, ii, l-liv, lviii-lxiii, and Sharpe, *Latin Writers*. A list of his writings including sermons, a life of Becket and some of his correspondence in ms and in print is also in Sharpe. Among his correspondents as prior were Philip, king of France, and Henry II; Ms 288 in Corpus Christi College, Cambridge contains some of these letters on fos 1–9. See John Elham II.

II ALAN
occ. 1189

1189, Sept., third prior, *Epist. Cant.*, 307.

1189, c. 3 Aug., summoned to appear with S. treasurer and R. de Cripta, q.v., before the abp, *Epist. Cant.*, 298; in Sept. he was instructed by Geoffrey II, subprior, q.v., [*sed. vac.* priory] to stand firm vs the abp's scheme for the new collegiate church at Lambeth, *ib.*, 307–308.

III ALAN
occ. 1215 occ. 1227

[1207 × 1214], the name Alan de Wy, q.v., prob. this monk, occ. in the list of monks who were in exile, *SL*, 172, CCA Lit. Ms D.12, fo 1.

1215, before 29 Sept., almoner, CCA DCc MA1, fo 57ᵛ.

1227, subprior, *ib.*, fo 71.

IV ALAN
occ. 1239/41

1241, 1 Feb., penitentiary, *Gervase Cant.*, ii, 186, 187, 190.

1239, 12 Apr., named by the abp to a committee to arrange discussions for settlement with the abp in the controversy over the el. of Roger de la Lee as prior, *Gervase Cant.*, ii, 163.

1241, 1 Feb., one of seven *compromissorii* named by the prior and chapter in the el. of an abp, *Gervase Cant.*, ii, 186, 187, 190.

Note: some of the above entries placed under Alan III and IV overlap and may ref. to one and the same monk.

ALAN
see also Orpynton, Rufus, Wy.

ALAYN
see Aleyn

ALBAN
occ. [1096 × 1107]

[1096 × 1107], *temp.* prior Ernulf, bp of Rochester, q.v., (as monk of Canterbury), with Warner, q.v., witnessed an agreement, *Text Roff*, ii, fo 199, 199ᵛ and cap 183; he also witnessed a grant to the monks of Rochester, *ib.*, ii, fo 191ᵛ and cap 163 (Rochester refs).

Richard ALBANE
occ. 1527/8

1527, 25 May, one of twelve tonsured, *SL*, 195, CCA Lit. Ms D.12, fo 12.

1528, 2 Mar., prof., *ib.*

Edmund ALBONE, D.Th.
occ. [?1331 × 1338]

[?1331 × 1338], acc. to Dart, *Antiq. Cant.*, 184, he was a monk scholar *temp.* prior Oxenden, q.v., whose writings include a commentary on Boethius and a treatise on the Trinity.

Note: is this Edmund de Adesham, q.v.?

ALDING
see Audinges

Robert de ALDON [Aledon, Alendon, Allyndon, Alyndone
occ. 1309 occ. 1349

1309, 18 Oct., one of nine prof., *SL*, 179, CCA Lit. Ms D.12, fo 3ᵛ.

1317, 28 May, ord pr., Lambeth palace chapel, Reg. abp Reynolds, fo 178.

1317, 7 Mar., the subprior and chapter recorded their objection to his appeal vs the prior as unseemly for religious, CUL Ms Ee.5.31, fo 176.

[1318], 18 Sept., the abp wrote to the prior requesting that his penance be mitigated, *Lit. Cant.*, no 43 (CCA DCc Cart. Antiq. C.1294g); see also CCA DCc EC I/18.

[c. 1320], with Robert de Thaneto, q.v., and other monks involved in a dispute with prior Eastry, q.v., CCA DCc Cart. Antiq. C.1294, C.1296; he and they were imprisoned for a time by the prior because of their rebellious behaviour, but the abp was pressed by the king, himself under pressure from influential persons of Sandwich, to request their release. Sheppard has summarized the case in *Hist. Mss Comm. 5th Report*, Appndx, 438 and *Hist. Mss Comm. 9th Report*, Appndx, 94. See also CCA DCc EC I/29, 32, 44, this last being an undated letter of support for him from his friends and relatives.

1325, 1 Oct., an inquisition was held by the prior and chapter to consider the case vs him which centred on the forgery of a *littera famosa* which he had placed on the bed of John de Maldon, q.v., and 64 brethren were examined and were convinced of his guilt; this report was sent to the abp; it is transcribed in *Lit. Cant.*, no 156 (Reg. L, fo 142, 142ᵛ); see also CCA DCc EC I/52 and Cart. Antiq. C.1294 where the names of the monks are given.

1325, 10 Nov., in a letter to the abp, the prior listed the crimes of which he was accused and because of which he had been separated from the rest of the community; these included forgery, theft of plate and books and feigned illnesses; and the prior was concerned that he might abscond, *Lit. Cant.*, no 157 (Reg. L, fo 128, 128v and Cart. Antiq. C.1294).

1325, 1 Dec., the prior wrote to the abp about his future; he was restless and had expressed a desire to join the Dominicans in Oxford, *Lit. Cant.*, no 163a (Reg. L, fo 143).

[1327], 27 May, the abp ordered his punishment to be remitted by royal command, *Lit. Cant.*, no 215 (CCA DCc Cart. Antiq. C.1294b); see also Thomas de Sandwyco and John de Valoyns.

1338, 1 Mar., two missing books, one being Miracula beatae Mariae in lingua Gallicana belonging to John de Thaneto, were listed as being charged out to him, *Lit. Cant.*, no 618 (Reg. L, fo 104).

1349, 22 Jan., had been to London to consult the abp el., John de Offord, who now urged the prior to treat him less harshly in correction; the prior replied on 16 Feb., to the effect that the punishment meted out was in accordance with the Rule and had been decided on by common consent of the brethren, *Lit. Cant.*, nos 767, 768 (Reg. L, fos 81v, 82).

1349, 4 June, 9th in order at the el. of an abp, Reg. G, fo 60v.

1349, 8/9 Sept., 9th in order at the el. of an abp, *ib.*, fo 76.

ALDRETHONE
see Elbrighton

William de ALDYNG
see Audinges

John ALDYNTON [Aldyngton
occ. 1401 d. 1413

1401, 25 Mar., one of seven prof., *SL*, 185, CCA Lit. Ms D.12, fo 5v.

1401, 17 Dec., ord subdcn, Canterbury cathedral, Reg. abp Arundel, i, fo 329.

1403, 14 Apr., ord dcn, Canterbury cathedral, *ib.*, i, 331.

1404, 29 Mar., ord pr., Canterbury cathedral, *ib.*, i, 332v.

1413, 13 Oct., d. of the plague in the twelfth yr of his prof., CCA Lit. Ms D.12, fo 19v; his obit occ. in BL Ms Arundel 68, fo 45.

Note: this may be John Bastard, q.v.

Thomas ALDYNGTON
see Alyngton

I ALEXANDER
occ. [1101] occ. c. 1109

[1101/2], sent to Rome to pope Pascal with Baldwin, monk of Bec, on behalf of abp Anselm, Eadmer, *Hist. Nov.*, 132, *Anselm Letters*, nos 223, 284.

From c. 1100/1109, he was with abp Anselm and kept records of his sermons and conversations, as Eadmer, q.v., had done previously; see Southern, *St Anselm* (1990), 389–394 and *Anselm Memorials*, 105–270 which provides a transcription of his Liber ex dictis beati Anselmi and his Miracula. See also Cambridge, Corpus Christi College Ms 457, Dicta Anselmi (early 12th c.).

He is mentioned in two letters written by abp Anselm in exile, *Anselm Letters*, nos 311, 325; see Eadmer.

See also Sharpe, *Latin Writers*.

II ALEXANDER
occ. [1152 × 1167]

[1152 × 1167], *temp.* prior Wibert, q.v., *ortulanus*, Urry, *Canterbury*, 393.

[1152 × 1167], witnessed the purchase of land in Canterbury by prior Wibert, *ib.*, 392.

III ALEXANDER
occ. 1199 occ. 1216

1199/1200, prior's chaplain, CCA Lit. Ms D.4, fo 9.

1215/16, granator, CCA DCc, MA1, fos 56v, 58v.

Note:
(1) the obit of an Alexander occ. on 14 Apr. in BL Ms Arundel 68, fo 24.
(2) the obit of an Allexand', *conversus*, occ. on 22 Apr. in BL Ms Arundel 68, fo 25.

See Alexander de Oxon'.

ALEXANDER
see also Cambrig', Dover, Ha. . .dn, London.

Hugh ALEYN
occ. [1395] d. 1401

[1395], 12 Mar., one of eight prof., *SL*, 184, CCA Lit. Ms D.12, fo 5.

1396, 1 Apr., ord subdcn, Canterbury cathedral, Reg. abp Courtenay, ii, fo 186v.

1396, 7 Aug., 76th in order at the el. of an abp, Reg. G, fo 234v.

1401, 28 Sept., d., and abp Arundel celebrated the requiem mass, CCA Lit. Ms D.12, fo 18.

I John ALEYN D.Th. [Alayn
occ. 1365 occ. 1385

1365, one of eight prof., *SL*, 182, CCA Lit. Ms D.12, fo 4v; however, on 16 Dec. 1370, a John Aleyn, M.A., and James Hegham, q.v., as novices, made their prof. before the prior, Reg. abp Wittlesey, fo 36v.

1371, 22 Mar., ord subdcn, St Paul's cathedral, *Reg. Sudbury* (London), ii, 101, by *lit. dim.*

1371, 31 May, ord pr., abp's chapel, Charing, Reg. abp Wittlesey, fo 167.

1382, 18 Oct., removed from the office of warden of Canterbury college, Pantin, *Cant. Coll. Ox.*, iii, 39 (Reg. abp Courtenay, i, fo 23v).

1383, 23 Aug., apptd subprior, Reg. abp Courtenay, i, fo 43v; subprior 1383/4, Lambeth Ms 243, fo 192v.
1385, 22 June, apptd penitentiary, Reg. abp Courtenay, i, fo 61.

1375/6, student, recd 21s. 4d. for his expenses *versus Oxoniam*, Pantin, *Cant. Coll. Ox.*, iv, 186.
1376/9, student, recd similar amounts for his expenses, but in 1378/9 it was raised to 73s. 4d. 'cum foret bacularius in theologia', *ib.*, 187.
1380/1, student, recd 5s. *pro benedictione* [before leaving] for Oxford, *ib.*, iv, 188.
1381/2, D.Th., incepted, *ib.*, iv, 188; he was described as *sacre pagine professor* on 9 Aug. 1383, when the prior included his name among the three names sent to the abp for apptment to the office of warden of Canterbury college, Reg. abp Courtenay, i, fo 43.
1382/3, at Oxford and recd 13s. 4d. and 53s. 4d. for expenses, and 20s. 'pro capa sua scholastica', Pantin, *Cant. Coll. Ox.*, iv, 189.
1383/4, the treasurer's accts recorded payment of a debt of £30 13s. 4d. incurred to cover his inception expenses and those of Thomas Chillenden I, q.v., *ib.*, iv, 189.
1384/5, at Oxford, and recd 13s. 4d. *per feretrarios*, *ib.*, iv, 190.

1371, 3 June, with Stephen Mongeham, q.v., apptd proctors to present the papal bull which required the exclusion of seculars from Canterbury college, *Lit. Cant.*, no 939; see Pantin, *Cant. Coll. Ox.*, iv, 34–35.
[1372], the chamberlain purchased cloth [for his habit], CCA DCc, Chamb. acct, no 50.
1374, 30 June, 42nd in order at the 2nd el. of Simon Langham as abp, Reg. G, fos 173v–175v.
1374/5, ill and the anniversarian pd him a 'pension' of 10d., CCA DCc, Anniv. acct 6.
1381, 30 July, 29th in order at the el. of an abp, Reg. G, fo 225v.

1384/5, lector in the cloister, Reg. G, fo 229v; and see below.
n.d., 23 Mar., obit occ. in BL Ms Arundel 68, fo 21v where it states that he had been claustral lector for four yrs.

II John ALEYN [Alayn
occ. 1417 d. 1425

1417, 13 Dec., one of five [?clothed/professed], *SL*, 186, CCA Lit. Ms D.12, fo 6v.
Note: this entry has taken into account two conflicting accts:
(1) *SL* and Lit. Ms D.12 give the date 1417, 13 Dec. without specifying whether this ref. to tonsure, clothing or prof. and
(2) *Chron. Stone*, 5, states that John Stone [I, q.v.], one of the five, was clothed on 13 Dec. 1418.
1418, 26 Mar., ord acol., Canterbury cathedral, *Reg. abp Chichele*, iv, 332.
1419, 1 Apr., ord subdcn, chapel within the cathedral priory, *ib.*, i, 191.
1420, 6 Apr., ord dcn, Canterbury cathedral, *ib.*, iv, 342.

1425, 4 Aug., d., *Chron. Stone*, 12, BL Ms Arundel, 68, fo 37.

ALFWORDUS [Aelfwordus
n.d.

n.d., 21 May, obit occ. in Lambeth Ms 20, fo 188 and BL Ms Arundel 68, fo 28.

ALFWYNUS [Aelfwynus
n.d.

n.d., 11 Mar, obit occ. in BL Ms Arundel 68, fo 20.

ALLYNDON
see Aldon

ALMER, Almerus
see Aelmer, Elmer

ALNODUS
n.d.

n.d., 27 Feb., the obit occ. of a pr. who gave [?the manor of] Orpington [at the time of his entry], BL Ms Arundel 68, fo 14v.

ALRICUS
see Adricus

ALSELL
see Honorius III

I ALSTANUS
n.d.

n.d., 2 Jan., pr., whose obit occ. in BL Ms Arundel 68, fo 12.

II ALSTANUS
n.d.

n.d., 21 May, pr., whose obit occ. in BL Ms Arundel 68, fo 28 and Lambeth Ms 20, fo 188.

ALSTANUS
see also Over

ALYNDONE
see Aldone

John ALYNGTON
occ. 1524 d. 1524

1524, 21/22 July, one of eleven granted adm. [*ingressum*] to Christ Church, CCA Lit. Ms D.12, fos 11v–12.
1524, 4 Aug., one of eleven tonsured, *SL*, 195, CCA Lit. Ms D.12, fo 11v.

1524, 23/24 Sept.``, *conversus*, d., the 52nd day after his entry. Details of his funeral and burial are given in *SL*, 195 (from Cambridge,

Corpus Christi College, Ms 298). Roger Eastry, q.v., officiated at the exequies and the prior celebrated the requiem mass. At the same hour William Chichele celebrated mass in the infirmary in the presence of the corpse, after which Alexander Staple II, q.v., performed the burial rites, *ib.*

Thomas ALYNGTON [Aldyngton
occ. 1457 d. 1501

1457, 13 Dec., one of six adm. as monks, *Chron. Stone*, 71. *sl*, 189.
1458, 12 Feb., *venerunt ad parvum servitium*, and on 26 Feb., *ad commune servicium*, *ib.*
1458, 21 Apr., one of the same six who made their prof., *ib.*
1459, 24 Mar., ord dcn, Canterbury cathedral, *Reg. abp Bourgchier*, 371.
1462, 17 Apr., ord pr., Canterbury cathedral, *ib.*, 382.
1477, Apr./Nov. *magister ordinis*, *SL*, 191 (Cambridge, Corpus Christi College, Ms 298).
1490/1, 1492/1500, bartoner, CCA DCc MA7, fo 154v; MA9, fos 2, 45, 66; MA10, fo 23; MA9, fos 109, 123v; MA10, fos 51, 84.
1460, 31 Aug., was examined [*de redditu suo*] by the precentor in the presence of the seniors, *Chron. Stone*, 82.
1466, 17 Feb., 57th in order in an inventory listing *jocalia fratrum* [given by him and/or assigned for his use], Reg. N, fo 234.
1493, 1 May, 15th in order at the ratification of an agreement, but see John Crosse I, Reg. S, fo 383v.
1501, 26 Apr., 5th in order at the el. of an abp, Reg. R, fo 56v.
1501, 27 Aug., d. of the plague in the 45th yr of his prof., and at the age of 62, CCA Lit. Ms D.12, fo 28v; the obit records that he was 'in extronomia bene et valde instructus', *ib.* The obit is also in BL Ms Arundel 68, fo 39v.

ALYNGTON
see also Aldynton

AMANDUS
n.d.

n.d., 17 Apr., pr., whose obit occ. in BL Ms Arundel 68, fo 24v.

AMBROSE
n.d.

n.d., 29 Mar., pr., whose obit occ. in BL Ms Arundel 68, fo 22v.

John AMBROSE [Ambros
occ. 1517 occ. 1538

1517, 12 Mar (deposition of St Gregory), one of six tonsured, *SL*, 194, CCA Lit. Ms D.12, fo 11–11v.
1517, 29 Sept., one of six who made their prof. before the abp on the day on which Thomas Goldwell, q.v., celebrated his first pontifical high mass, *ib.*, fo 11v.
1523/4, celebrated his first mass, Woodruff, 'Sacrist's Rolls', 71 (CCA DCc Sac Acct?).
[1538, 8 Feb., after], one of the two chancellors, Pantin, *Cant. Coll. Ox.*, iii, 152.
1518/19, possibly a student at Canterbury college, as he and Richard Mokell rode to Oxford *cum scolaribus*, Pantin, *Cant. Coll. Ox.*, iv, 206.
1520/1, student at Oxford, CCA DCc, Treas. acct 25.
1528/9, student, Pantin, *Cant. Coll. Ox.*, ii, 259.
1520/1, spent time in the infirmary, CCA DCc Infirm. acct 2.
[1538, 8 Feb., after], on a list of monks prob. prepared for Thomas Cromwell, he was described as a 'witty' man, of 38 yrs, Pantin, *Cant. Coll. Ox.*, iii, 152.

His father and mother, John and Margaret Croge, were recd into confraternity with Christ Church in 1519, BL Ms Arundel 68, fo 11.

AMBROSE
see also Laurence Newynham

William de ANDEVILLE
occ. before 1142 occ. 1149

1142, before this date, sacrist, *HRH*, 87.
1142, apptd prior of Dover, *ib.*
1149, res. to become abbot of Evesham, *ib.*
1159, d., *HRH*, 87; on 3 Jan., his obit occ. in BL Ms Arundel 68, fo 12. He was buried at Christ Church in the crypt, *Chron. Evesham*, 99–100.

I ANDREW
n.d.

n.d., 17 Apr., dcn, [*levita*] whose obit occ. in BL Ms Arundel 68, fo 24v.

II ANDREW
occ. before 1098 × 1100

1098 × 1100, before, on being prof. as a monk he gave to Christ Church the churches of St Dunstan in the East and St Alphege, London, Kissan, 'London Deanery', 204.

III ANDREW
occ. [1198 × 1200]

[1198, 25 Sept. × ?1200, Nov.], with Geoffrey III, q.v., chaplain to abp Hubert Walter and witness to one of his *acta*, *Eng. Epis. Acta*, iii, no 384.

Note: it is not certain that these chaplains were Christ Church monks.

IV ANDREW
occ. 1201 occ. 1216

1201/3, 1207, 1213, sacrist, CCA Lit. Ms D4, fos 12v, 14, 15v, CCA DCc MA1, fos 59v, 53v.

1206, 30 Mar., infirmarer, *CPL*, i (1198–1304), 23, 26.
1215, 1216, granator, CCA DCc MA1, fos 56ᵛ, 58ᵛ.
1206, 30 Mar., one of the monks summoned by the pope to Rome to give evidence in the dispute over their el. of Reginald, q.v., as abp, *CPL*, i (1198–1304), 26; while there, they el. Stephen Langton, *Fasti*, ii, 6.

Note:
(1) this may be Andrew de Tumba, q.v.
(2) it is possible that Andrew III and IV may be the same monk.

V ANDREW
occ. 1244 occ. 1248

1244/8, chamberlain, CCA DCc AS16, MA1, fos 86ᵛ–89ᵛ.

John ANDREW [Andreu
occ. [1316] d. 1358

[1316], 6 Nov., one of five prof., *SL*, 179, CCA Lit. Ms D.12, fo 3ᵛ.
1318, 17 June, ord acol., Maidstone, Reg. abp Reynolds, fo 180.
1318, 23 Dec., ord subdcn, Maidstone, *ib.*, fo 181ᵛ.
Note: a John Andrew monk of Canterbury was ord pr. at Halling on 25 May 1331, Reg. Hethe, fo 144ᵛ; this is prob. a scribal error.
1333, Jan./1335, bartoner, CCA DCc Bart. acct 21, MA2, fos 222ᵛ–241ᵛ; he succ. Denys de St Margaret, q.v.
1334/7, *magister corone*, CCA DCc MA2, fos 231–255.
1337, Feb./Apr., granator, CCA DCc Gran. acct 7.
1340/3, warden of manors, CCA DCc Meopham accts 80, 81, Borley acct 4.
1342/3, 1344, 13 Mar., sacrist, CCA DCc Bart. acct 26, Oxford, Bod. Ms Ashmole 794, fo 209.
1331/2, recd 14s. from the prior for lights for [the altar of] St Mary in the nave, CCA DCc DE3, fo 33ᵛ.
1332/3, visited Godmersham with his *socius* and the sergeant charged 6s. 9d. to his acct, CCA DCc Godmersham acct 15.
1344, 13 Mar., one of the monks named as present in chapter for the apptment of proctors, Oxford, Bod. Ms Ashmole 794, fo 209.
1349, 4 June, 13th in order at the el. of an abp, Reg. G, fo 60ᵛ.
1349, 8/9 Sept., 13th at the el. of an abp, *ib.*, fo 76.
1358, 5 Mar., d., CCA Lit. Ms D.12, fo 17.

Thomas ANDREWE
occ. 1338

1338, 1 Mar., a list of missing books belonging to living monks included his psalter, *Lit. Cant.*, no 618 (Reg. L, fo 104).

Note: he prob. occ. elsewhere in this list under his toponymic.

ANDREW, Andrewe
see also Andrew John

ANKENUS
n.d.

n.d., pr. whose obit occ. on 8 Oct in BL Ms Cotton Nero C.ix, fo 13.

Walter ANSELL
occ. [?1230 × 1260]

n.d., name occ. in the list in *SL*, 174, CCA Lit. Ms D.12, fo 1ᵛ.

I ANSELM
n.d.

n.d., 13 Aug., *conversus*, whose obit occ. in BL Ms Arundel 68, fo 38.

II ANSELM
occ. 1270 occ. 1284

1270, 1271, 1272, treasurer, CCA DCc MA1, fos 113, 114ᵛ, 116; see Randulph.
1284, bartoner, CCA DCc MA1, fo 142.
Note: this may be Anselm de Eastry, q.v.

ANSELM
see also Ascelin

I Thomas ANSELME [Ansell, Annselme, Awncelme
occ. 1493 d. 1518/19

1493, 26 July, one of ten tonsured, *SL*, 192, CCA Lit. Ms D.12, fo 9ᵛ.
[1493, 19 Apr.], feast of the passion of St Elphege, made his prof. before the abp, CCA Lit. Ms D.12, fo 9–9ᵛ.
1494, 29 Mar., ord acol., Canterbury cathedral, *Reg. abp Morton*, i, no 443a.
1495, 18 Apr., ord subdcn, Canterbury cathedral, *ib.*, i, no 444b.
1496, 2 Apr., ord dcn, Canterbury cathedral, *ib.*, i, no 445c.
1498, 14 Apr., ord pr., Canterbury cathedral, *ib.*, i, no 447d.
1497/8, celebrated his first mass and recd 8d. from the sacrist, Woodruff, 'Sacrist's Rolls', 66 (transcribed as Austen).
1507, 26 Nov., subsacrist, CCA DCc DE61.
1510, Apr./1511, July, warden of St Mary in the crypt, CCA DCc MA36.
1501, 26 Apr., 45th in order at the el. of an abp, Reg. R, fo 56ᵛ.
1502, recd a bequest of 20d from a parishioner of St Margaret's Canterbury, Hussey, 'Kentish Wills', 43.
1511, 2 Sept., 27th on the visitation certificate, Wood-Legh, *Visit.*, 3 (Reg. abp Warham, i, fo 35ᵛ).

1517, Mar./June, borrowed 3s. 4d from William Ingram I, q.v., Lit. Ms C.11, fo 128ᵛ.
1518/19, d. acc. to the treasurer's acct., Pantin, *Cant. Coll. Ox.*, iv, 206; his obit is on 20 Sept. in BL Ms Arundel 68, fo 42ᵛ.

There is a list of books which he pledged [?1510 x 1518] to three fellow monks, William Austen, Roger Benet, William Wynchepe IV, q.v., in repayment of debts; it has been printed in Pantin, *Cant. Coll. Ox.*, i, 91–92 (CCA DCc DE56 and DE57A).

His sister, Alicia Hall, was recd into confraternity with Christ Church on 17 Feb., 1518, BL Ms Arundel 68, fo 11.

II Thomas ANSELME [Auncell
occ. 1527 occ. 1540

1527, 25 May, one of twelve tonsured, *SL*, 195, CCA Lit. Ms D.12, fo 12.
1528, 2 Mar., prof., *ib.*
[1538, 8 Feb., after] chaplain to the subprior, Pantin, *Cant. Coll. Ox.*, iii, 153.
1540, 4 Apr., third precentor; *L and P Henry VIII*, xv, no 452.
[1538, 8 Feb., after] student at Canterbury college, Pantin, *Cant. Coll. Ox.*, iii, 153.
1534, 12 Dec., acknowledged the Act of Supremacy, *DK 7th Report*, Appndx 2, 282.
[1538, 8 Feb., after] in a list of monks prob. prepared for Thomas Cromwell he was described as 'a good man', 31 yrs old, Pantin, *Cant. Coll. Ox.*, iii, 153.
1540, 4 Apr., awarded £3 and became a petty canon in the new foundation, *L and P Henry VIII*, xv, no 452.

I ANTHONY [Antonius
occ. c. 1089 occ. [1094 × 1096]

c. 1089, subprior, Dodwell, *Cant. School*, 25.
[1094 × 1096], subprior, *Anselm Letters*, no 182 which is a letter of Anselm to prior Henry and to Anthony subprior and the monks. In another letter written to him during this period, the abp commended him *pro bono zelo*, *ib.* no 313.
c. 1089, with 23 other Christ Church monks was sent to St Augustine's to fill the places of the rebellious monks there who had been dispersed to other monasteries, *ib.*; see Norman and Wido. He was named prior at St Augustine's, 'Acta Lanfranci', 292.
n.d., 14 Apr., subprior, whose obit occ. in BL Ms Arundel 68, fo 24.

Note: it is possible that the obit ref. to another subprior named Anthony; see below.

II ANTHONY
occ. 1108

1108, subprior; see below.
1108, sent by abp Anselm to Rochester on negotiations concerning the installation of Ralph as bp there, Eadmer, *Hist. Nov.*, 197.

Note: The two monks above may be identical.

John ANTONY [Antone, Antoni, Antonye
occ. 1485 d. 1517

1485, 12 Mar., one of six tonsured, *SL*, 191, CCA Lit. Ms D.12, fo 8ᵛ.
1485, 2 Apr., ord acol., Canterbury cathedral, *Reg. abp Morton*, i, no 438d; also in *Reg. abp Bourgchier*, 450.
1485, 6 Dec., prof., *SL*, 191.
1490, 10 Apr., ord pr., Canterbury cathedral, *Reg. abp Morton*, i, no 438d.
1504/5; 1506, Mar./Sept.; 1507/8, Oct. to Apr.; 1508, 25 Apr., third prior, CCA DCc Gran. acct 63; *SL*, 193, CCA Lit. Ms D.12, fo 10ᵛ; CCA Lit. Ms D.12, fo 36; CCA Lit. Ms D.12, fo 10ᵛ.
1506, Mar. to Sept., 1507/8, Oct. to Apr., *magister ordinis*, *SL*, 193, CCA Lit. Ms D.12, fo 10ᵛ.
1505/6, 1507/8, novice master, CCA DCc, Sac. accts 66, 64; MA11, fos 3ᵛ, 65ᵛ.
1513, 29 Sept., 1517, 25 Mar., bartoner, CCA DCc DE170, CCA, Lit. Ms C.11, fo 58.
1516/17, Dec. to Mar. only, infirmarer, CCA DCc MA14, fo 2ᵛ.
1493, 1 May, 50th in order at the ratification of an agreement, Reg. S, fo 383ᵛ; but see John Crosse I.
1501, 26 Apr., 34th in order at the el. of an abp, Reg. R, fo 56ᵛ.
1511, 2 Sept., 18th in order on the visitation certificate, Wood-Legh, *Visit.*, 3 (Reg. abp Warham, i, fo 35).
1516/17, d., Woodruff, 'Sacrist's Rolls', 69; since his obit in BL Ms Arundel 68, fo 38ᵛ, is on 18 Aug., he prob. d. c. 18 Aug. 1517.

Robert ANTONY [Anthonye
occ. 1522 occ. 1540

1522, 11 Feb., one of ten tonsured, *SL*, 195, CCA Lit. Ms D.12, fo 11ᵛ.
1522, 24 Nov., prof., *ib.*
1524/5, celebrated his first mass, Woodruff, 'Sacrist's Rolls', 71.
1538, 3 Aug., before, subcellarer, *L and P Henry VIII*, xiii, pt 2, no 24.
1534, 12 Dec., acknowledged the Act of Supremacy, *DK 7th Report*, Appndx 2, 282.
[1538, 8 Feb., after] in a list of monks prob. prepared for Thomas Cromwell he was described as 'wytty' and 'in the keeping of my Lorde of Caunterbury', and 34 yrs old, Pantin, *Cant. Coll. Ox.*, iii, 153.
1538, 3 Aug., a letter from abp Cranmer to Thomas Cromwell reports that he had left the priory without permission, gone to Rome and on his return had been readmitted by the prior

and chapter, *L and P Henry VIII*, xiii, pt 2, no 24. On 15 Aug., Cranmer announced that he had sent for Antony to explain his departure for Rome, *ib.*, xiii, pt 2, no 97.
1540, 4 Apr., awarded £6 p.a., *L and P Henry VIII*, xv, no 452.

John APULDOR [Appuldor, Apuldir, Apuldore
occ. 1493 occ. 1511
1493, 26 July, one of ten tonsured, *SL*, 192, CCA Lit. Ms D.12, fo 9ᵛ.
[1493, 19 Apr.], feast of the passion of St Elphege, made his prof. before the abp, CCA Lit. Ms D.12, fo 9–9ᵛ.
1494, 29 Mar., ord acol., Canterbury cathedral, *Reg. abp Morton*, i, no 443a.
1495, 18 Apr., ord subdcn, Canterbury cathedral, *ib.*, i, no 444b.
1496, 2 Apr., ord dcn, Canterbury cathedral, *ib.*, i, no 445c.
1501, 26 Apr., 46th in order at the el., Reg. R, fo 56–56ᵛ.
1505/6, repaired a *tapetus* for the sacrist, CCA DCc Sac. acct, 66.
1511, 2 Sept., 28th in order on the visitation certificate, Wood-Legh, *Visit.*, 3 (Reg. abp Warham, i, fo 35).
n.d., *recessit*, CCA Lit. Ms D.12, fo 9ᵛ; *SL* has *recessit capacitate habita*, 192 (from Cambridge, Corpus Christi College Ms 298).

Ralph de APULDOR [Apeldre, Apuldore, Apuldre
occ. 1289 occ. [1296]
1289, 19 Dec., one of nine prof., *SL*, 177, CCA Lit. Ms D.12, fo 3.
[1296], included among the juniors accused by the abp of being lax in attendance at divine office and in the performance of other monastic duties, *Reg. abp Winchelsey*, 92.
n.d., 14 Feb., obit occ. in BL Ms Arundel 68, fo 16.

An inventory of the refectory dated 1328 includes a *ciphus* of wood described as his, Dart, *Antiq. Cant.*, xxiii (BL Ms Cotton Galba E.iv, fo 180).

ARKILLUS
n.d.
n.d., 4 July, pr., whose obit occ. in BL Ms Arundel 68, fo 32ᵛ.

ARNALDUS
see Ernaldus

ARNOLD [Arnoldus
n.d.
n.d., 18 Apr., obit occ. in BL Ms Arundel 68, fo 24ᵛ.

[ARNOST [Arnostus, Ernostus
occ. [1070 × 1075]
[1070 × 1075], came from Bec with or soon after Lanfranc and was briefly bp of Rochester in 1075/6, *Fasti*, ii, 75, and Gibson, *Lanfranc*, 176.

Note: possibly never a monk of Christ Church.]

Henry ARUNDEL [Arundell
occ. 1485 d. 1511
1485, 12 Mar., one of six tonsured, *SL*, 191, CCA Lit. Ms D.12, fo 8ᵛ.
1485, 2 Apr., ord acol., Canterbury cathedral, *Reg. abp Bourgchier*, 450.
1485, 6 Dec., prof., *SL*, 191 (from Cambridge, Corpus Christi College, Ms 298).
1490, 10 Apr., ord pr., Canterbury cathedral, Reg. abp Morton, i, no 438d.
1511, 7 June, *magister mense*, and was apptd penitentiary by the chapter, CCA Lit. Ms C.11, fo 1.

1493, 1 May, 47th in order at the ratification of an agreement, Reg. S, fo 383ᵛ; but see John Crosse I.
1501, 26 Apr., 31st at the el. of an abp, Reg. R, fo 56ᵛ.
1510/11, d., Woodruff, 'Sacrist's Rolls', 69 (CCA DCc Sac. acct 73); his obit occ. on 8 June in BL Ms Arundel 68, fo 30.

There is an inventory of his belongings drawn up by William Ingram I, q.v., which includes books and several musical instruments, CCA Lit. Ms C.11, fo 1, where his d. is recorded on 7 June 1511.

Ralph de ARUNDEL
occ. [1167/8]
[late 1167/early 1168], recd a letter from John of Salisbury, *Salisbury Letters*, ii, no 246.
n.d., in writing to William Brito, q.v., John of Salisbury praised him for maintaining his devotion to the abp and his faithfulness to the pope, *ib.*, ii, no 247.

Note: this is possibly the monk who later became prior of Hurley and abbot of Westminster, *HRH*, 92, 77.

See also under Ralph.

I William ARUNDELL [Arundelle
occ. 1431 d. 1470
1431, 18 Apr., one of four prof., *SL*, 187, CCA Lit. Ms D.12, fo 7.
1433, 28 Mar., ord dcn, Charing, *Reg. abp Chichele*, iv, 327.
1434, 13 Mar., ord pr., infirmary chapel in the priory, *ib.*, iv, 379.
[1470], before his d., *magister mense*, CCA Lit. Ms D.12, fo 26.
1470, 13 May, d., *Chron. Stone*, 114; his obit occ. on 15 May in BL Ms Arundel 68, fo 27ᵛ.

II William ARUNDELL [Orundell, *alias* Pemble

occ. 1514 occ. 1536

1514, 1 Sept., one of seven tonsured, *SL*, 194, CCA Lit. Ms D.12, fo 11.
1515, 19 Apr., prof., *ib.*
1518/19, celebrated his first mass, and recd 8d. from the sacrist, Woodruff, 'Sacrist's Rolls', 70.

[c. 1514 × 1524], at Canterbury college but not applying himself to his work, Pantin, *Cant. Coll. Ox.*, iii, 143 (CCA DCc Ms Scrap Book B.193).

[c. 1514], had Thomas Goldston V, q.v. as his *magister regule*, Pantin, *Cant. Coll. Ox.*, iv, 54 (CCA DCc Ms Scrap Book B.186).
1518/19, spent time in the infirmary, CCA DCc Infirm. acct 1.
1534, 12 Dec., acknowledged the Act of Supremacy, *DK 7th Report*, Appndx 2, 282.
1536, 1 May, dispensed to hold a benefice and wear the habit of his order beneath the attire of a secular pr., Chambers, *Faculty Office Regs*, 53.

ASCELIN [Ascelinus

occ. before 1139

1139, before, sacrist, *HRH*, 87.
1139, apptd prior of Dover, *ib.*
1142, res. to become bp of Rochester, *ib.*

The name Acelin occ. in a Penitenciale in the Eastry catalogue, no 228, James, *Ancient Libraries*, 42.

Note: he is called Anselm in the Annals of Dover, *Theobald Charters*, 542 (BL Ms Cotton Julius D.v, fo 23v).

ASCELIN, Ascelinus

see also Anselm, Azelinus

ASCHEFORD

see Assheforde, Asshforde

ASCHEX

see Essex

ASKETILLUS [Askatillus

n.d.

n.d., 5 Apr., *conversus*, whose obit occ. in BL Ms Arundel 68, fo 23 and Lambeth Ms 20, fo 177v.

John ASSHE [Asch, Esche, Esshe

occ. [1390] d. 1435

[1390], 28 Sept., one of seven prof., *SL*, 184, CCA Lit. Ms D.12, fo 5.
1394, 18 Apr., ord dcn, Canterbury cathedral, Reg. abp Courtenay, ii, fo 185.
1413, 6 Oct., *magister ordinis*, *SL*, 185, CCA Lit. Ms D.12, fo 6.
1422/3, chaplain to the prior, with William Molasshe, q.v., CCA DCc, Prior acct, 5.
1424, 13/14 Nov., *magister ordinis*; he was succ. by John Elham II, q.v., during the yr, *SL*, 187, CCA Lit. Ms D.12, fo 7.
1429, part yr, *magister ordinis*, *SL*, 187, CCA Lit. Ms D.12, fo 7.

1396, 7 Aug., 65th in order at the el. of an abp, Reg. G, fo 234v.
1435, 27 Oct., d. of an *epidemia*, CCA Lit. Ms D.12, fo 24; Chron. Wm Glastynbury, fo 117v has 24 Oct.

In a letter prob. written by John Wodnesburgh III, q.v., (when warden of Canterbury college), he is named as *amicus meus specialissimus*, Pantin, *Cant. Coll. Ox.*, iii, 92 (Chron. Wm Glastynbury, fo 185v).

I Thomas ASSHE B.Th. [Asch, Assh, Aysshe

occ. 1408/9 d. 1472

1408/9, 21 Mar., one of six prof., CCA Lit. Ms D.12, fo 6 (*SL*, 185), Reg. abp Arundel, i, fo 451.
1409, 23 Mar., ord subdcn, Canterbury cathedral, Reg. abp Arundel, ii, fo 95.
1410, 13 Sept. ord pr., abp's chapel, Ford, *ib.*, ii, fo 99.

1421, 25 Dec., nom. for the office of penitentiary by the prior and chapter, *Reg. abp Chichele*, iv, 241–242, and apptd the next day, *ib.*
1435, penitentiary, with Robert Colbroke, q.v., *Lit. Cant.*, iii, 176, 'Chron. Wm Glastynbury', 129.
1437, Sept., apptd warden of Canterbury college, Pantin, *Cant. Coll. Ox.*, ii, 151 (CCA DCc Cart. Antiq. O.151.9);
1438, Feb., warden, *ib.*, iii, 95 (Reg. S, fo 126), but he had been removed by 23 Aug. of this yr, *ib.*, iii, 95.
1443/4, third prior, CCA DCc, Gran. acct 51, Sac. acct 31.
1449/50, 1451, Sept./Dec., granator, CCA DCc Gran. accts, 56, 57.

1414, Feb., student at Oxford, Pantin, *Cant. Coll. Ox.*, iii, 72 (Reg. S, fo 68v).
Note: Emden's entry in *BRUO* that he was BA by 1408 and B.Th., n.d., lacks any ref. and seems unlikely unless he had a degree at the time of his adm.
1437, 4 Aug., departed for Oxford and recd 15s. *pro capa scolari* and 21s. 8d. for expenses, Pantin, *Cant. Coll. Ox.*, iv, 192.
1441, 29 Oct., recd 6s. 8d. for his expenses in returning from Oxford, *ib.*, iv, 193; he also recd the same sum for another journey from Oxford to Canterbury on 19 Nov., *ib.*
1444, 13 Sept., was given 23s. 4d. for returning from Oxford to Canterbury, *ib.*, iv, 194.
Note: it does seem unusual to have a monk return to Oxford, though only for a year, as warden after an absence of over 20 yrs and also strange that he should rec. money for his

capa scolaris like the young monk students going up to Oxford for the first time. There are no other monks by this name to whom the later refs to study in Oxford in the 1440s could apply, but see Thomas Asshford.

1414, 12 Mar., 69th in order at the el. of an abp, *Reg. abp Chichele*, i, 4.

1428, [30/31 Mar.], preached at the el. of the prior [William Molassh], q.v., from the text 'Inspiravit in faciem eius spiraculum vite' (Gen. 2, 7), Oxford, Bod. Ms Tanner 165, fo 4^v.

[1429, Jan.], was appted preacher and confessor in the diocese for the crusade vs the Hussites, Holmes, 'Crusade vs the Hussites', 740.

1431, 9/10 Dec., preached to the clergy and people in the cathedral nave on the occasion of the reconciliation of two Lollard heretics, *Lit. Cant.*, no 1008 (Reg. S, fo 109).

[1443], 9 Oct., ordered by the prior to produce all the money and goods including books which were in his charge by 19 Oct. for examination by himself and other monks, *Lit. Cant.*, no 1021 (Reg. N, fo 213); he did not comply and was excommunicated and ordered to be separated from the community, *ib.*, no 1022 (Reg. N, fo 213–213^v).

1452, 22 Sept., preached to his brethren in choir on the text, 'Ecce servus meus, electus, suscipiam eum' (Is. 42, 1), after which he read the papal bull confirming abp Kemp's translation from York to Canterbury, *Chron. Stone*, 55.

1466, 17 Feb., 3rd in order in an inventory listing *jocalia fratrum* [given by him and/or assigned for his use], Reg. N, fo 230.

1472, 11 Feb., *stationarius*, d. in the 63rd yr of his monastic life and was buried the following day, *ib.*, 118. His obit occ. on 13 Feb., BL Ms Arundel 68, fo 16.

He gave a vestment to Canterbury college, which is listed in the 1443 inventory, Pantin, *Cant. Coll. Ox.*, i, 2 (CCA DCc Cart. Antiq. O.134).

See Pantin, *Cant. Coll. Ox.*, iii, 88, for a possible ref. to him [T.A.] in a letter written by John Wodnesburgh III, q.v.

II Thomas ASSHE [Aisshe, Asche

occ. 1488 occ. 1511

1488, 12 Mar., one of six tonsured, *SL*, 191, CCA Lit. Ms D.12, fo 8^v.

1488, 30 Sept., made his prof. before the cardinal abp, *ib.*

1490, 10 Apr., ord subdcn, Canterbury cathedral, *Reg. abp Morton*, i, no 438b.

1491, 2 Apr., ord dcn., Canterbury cathedral, *ib.*, i, no 439c.

1495, 18 Apr., ord pr., Canterbury cathedral, *ib.*, i no 444d.

1493, 1 May, 54th in order at the ratification of an agreement, Reg. S, fo 383^v; but see John Crosse I.

1501, 26 Apr., 38th at the el. of an abp, Reg. R, fo 56^v.

1511, 2 Sept., 22nd on the visitation certificate, Wood-Legh, *Visit.*, 3 (Reg. abp Warham, i, fo 35).

ASSHE

see also Essche

I John ASSHEFORDE [Ascheford, Aschyfford, Asschford, Asshford, Esshford, Osford

occ. [1399] d. 1452

[1399], one of four prof. *SL*, 184, CCA Lit. Ms D.12, fo 5^v.

1399, 20 Dec., ord subdcn, Canterbury cathedral, Reg. abp Arundel, i, fo 325 (as Osford).

1400, 3 Apr., ord dcn, Hoath chapel in Reculver parish, *ib.*, i, fo 325.

1404, 29 Mar., ord pr., Canterbury cathedral, *ib.*, i, fo 332^v.

1435, 1436/7, *custos corone*, 'Chron. Wm Glastynbury', 129, CCA DCc Prior acct 7.

1439/40, 1442/3, 1444/7, chamberlain, Lambeth ED34, CCA DCc Prior acct 6, MA4, fos 32^v, 35, Lambeth ED74.

1414, 12 Mar., 46th in order at the el. of an abp, *Reg. abp Chichele*, i, 4.

1449, 6 Dec., a vestment embroidered with gryphons, [?a gift] of his was blessed, *Chron. Stone*, 47.

1452, 31 July, d. after 52 yrs of monastic life, *Chron. Stone*, 54.

II John ASSHEFORDE [Aessehford, Aesthefford, Ascheford

occ. 1454 d. [1472 × 1480]

1454, 28 Apr., one of eight prof., *SL*, 189, CCA Lit. Ms D.12, fo 8.

1455, 5 Apr., ord acol., Canterbury cathedral, *Reg. abp Bourgchier*, 359.

1455, 20 Sept., ord subdcn, Canterbury cathedral, *ib.*, 361.

1457, 2 Apr., ord dcn, Canterbury cathedral, *ib.*, 366.

1460, 12 Apr., ord pr., Canterbury cathedral, *ib.*, 376.

1460, celebrated his first mass and recd 8d from the chamberlain, CCA DCc Chamb. acct 65.

1471, chancellor, with William Sellyng I, q.v, Reg. S, fo 248^v.

1471, 25 Jan., *magister ordinis*, *SL*, 190, CCA Lit. Ms D.12, fo 8–8^v.

n.d., [1472 × 1481], *magister* of St Mary in crypt, CCA Lit. Ms D.12, fo 26.

1466, 17 Feb., 51st in order in an inventory listing *jocalia fratrum* [given by him and/or assigned for his use], and he had none, Reg. N, fo 234.

[1472 × 1480], d., CCA Lit. Ms D.12, fo 26; on 16

Oct. his obit occ. in BL Ms Arundel 68, fo 45v. These dates are based on the known date of the d. of Thomas Asshe I, q.v., who occ. fairly near him in the list of those who died on fo 26 of CCA Lit. Ms D.12.

ASSHEFORDE
see also Asshforde

Richard ASSHELEE [Aisshey, Aschle, Asshele, Astle
occ. 1485 d. 1508

1485, 12 Mar., one of six [tonsured], *SL*, 191, CCA Lit. Ms D.12, fo 8v.
1485, 2 Apr., ord acol., Canterbury cathedral, *Reg. abp Bourgchier*, 450.
1485, 6 Dec., prof., *SL*, 191 (from Cambridge, Corpus Christi College Ms 298).
1492, 21 Apr., ord pr., Canterbury cathedral, *Reg. abp Morton*, i, no 441d.
1493, 1 May, 51st in order at the ratification of an agreement, Reg. S, fo 383v; but see John Crosse I.
1501, 26 Apr., 35th at the el. of an abp, Reg. R, fo 56v.
1508/9, d., Woodruff, 'Sacrist's Rolls', 68 (CCA DCc Sac. acct 71); since the obit date is 27 Oct., in BL Ms Arundel 68, fo 46v, he prob. d. on 27 Oct. 1508.

ASSHEX
see Essex

I John ASSHFORDE [Ascheford
occ. 1491 d. 1507/8

1491, 11 Sept., one of four tonsured, *SL*, 192, CCA Lit. Ms D.12, fo 9; he made his prof., n.d., before the abp, CCA Lit. Ms D.12, *ib.*
1492, 21 Apr., ord acol., Canterbury cathedral, *Reg. abp Morton*, i, no 441a.
1494, 29 Mar., ord subdcn, Canterbury cathedral, *ib.*, i, no 443b.
1495, 18 Apr., ord dcn, Canterbury cathedral, *ib.*, i, no 443c.
1498, 14 Apr., ord pr., Canterbury cathedral, *ib.*, i, no 447d.
1497/8, celebrated his first mass and recd 8d. from the sacrist, Woodruff, 'Sacrist's Rolls', 66.
1493, 1 May, 65th and last in order at the ratification of an agreement, Reg. S, fo 383v; but see John Crosse I.
1501, 26 Apr., 44th at the el. of an abp, Reg. R, fo 56v.
1507/8, d., Woodruff, 'Sacrist's Rolls', 68 (CCA DCc Sac. acct 64).

II John ASSHFORDE [Aschford
occ. 1509 occ. 1530

1509, 22 Dec., ord acol., Canterbury cathedral, Reg. abp Warham, ii, fo 264v.
1510, 16 June, one of eight tonsured, *SL*, 194, CCA Lit. Ms D.12, fo 11.
1511, 1 Jan., prof., *ib.*
1511, 19 Apr., ord subdcn, Canterbury cathedral, Reg. abp Warham, ii, fo 265v.
1516, [Apr.], celebrated his first mass and recd 4d. from William Ingram I, penitentiary, q.v., CCA Lit. Ms C.22 fo, 126v.
1530, 25 Mar., *magister corone*, CCA Lit. Ms C.11, fo 66.
1511, 2 Sept., 80th and last of the prof. monks on the visitation certificate, Wood-Legh, *Visit.*, 3 (Reg. abp Warham, i, fo 35v.
n.d., his *magister regule* was John Shepay II, q.v., Pantin, *Cant. Coll. Ox.*, iv, 54 (CCA DCc Ms Scrap Book B.186).

Thomas ASSHFORD [Aescheford, Asshetisford, Esshforde
occ. 1417 d. 1452

1417, 13 Dec., one of five [?clothed/professed], *SL*, 186, CCA Lit. Ms D.12, fo 6v.
Note: this entry takes into account two conflicting accts: 1) *SL* and Lit. Ms D.12 give the date 1417, 13 Dec. without specifying whether this ref. to tonsure, clothing or prof., and 2) *Chron. Stone*, 5, states that John Stone [I, q.v.], one of the five, was clothed on 13 Dec. 1418.
1418, 26 Mar., ord acol., Canterbury cathedral, *Reg. abp Chichele*, iv, 332.
1419, 1 Apr., ord subdcn, chapel within the cathedral priory, *ib.*, i, 191.
1420, 6 Apr., ord dcn, Canterbury cathedral, *ib.*, iv, 342.
1421, 20 Dec., ord pr., St Paul's cathedral, London, *ib.*, iv, 349.
1452, 23 Dec., one of several monks promoted *ad primam mensam*, i.e. one of twenty senior monks, *Chron. Stone*, 56.
[1430s], 2 Dec., [*in die regressionis* of Thomas Becket], he 'ascendit in superiori choro', Chron. Wm Glastynbury, fo 117v.
1451/2, recd 6s. 8d. from the prior towards his travelling expenses to Rome, Pantin, *Cant. Coll. Ox.*, iv, 195.
1452, 20 Mar., set out for Rome on pilgrimage where he d. on 25 July and was buried in the monastery of Santa Balbina, *Chron. Stone*, 53; the usual rites and services for one of the deceased brethren took place on 12 Feb. 1453, *ib.* His obit is in BL Ms Arundel 68, fo 36, on 25 July.

Dr Pantin suggested that he may have composed a metrical life of our Lady, *Cant. Coll. Ox.*, iv, 79, but has found no ref. to any connection with Canterbury college. However, see Thomas Asshe I's [?]second period of study at Oxford.

ASSHFORD
see also Esshetyford

ASTANUS
n.d.

n.d., 19 May, obit occ. in Lambeth Ms 20, fo 187ᵛ.

ASTEN
see Austen

ASTHILLUS
n.d.

n.d., 22 July, pr., whose obit occ. in BL Ms Arundel 68, fo 36.

ASTLE
see Asshelee

AT GATE
see Gate

ATHEBRANDE
see Hathbrande

ATHELRICUS
n.d.

n.d., 12 Jan., pr., whose obit occ. in Lambeth Ms 20, fo 158ᵛ.

Eustace de ATLEE
n.d. 2nd half 13th c.

n.d., name occ. in the list in *SL*, CCA Lit. Ms D.12, fo 2ᵛ.

ATSO(N)
see Azo

ATTYSHAM
see Adysham

Gregory de AUDINGES [Alding, Ealdinges, Eldyng
occ. 1239 occ. [1244 × 1258]

n.d., name occ. in the list in *SL*, 173, CCA Lit. Ms D.12, fo 1ᵛ.

1239, 7 Feb., with Simon de Leycestria, q.v., sent by the subprior and chapter to the abp in the difficulties which arose over their el. of Roger de La Lee, q.v., as prior, *Gervase Cant.*, ii, 154.

[1244 × 1258], one of the monks who were carrying out manorial visits and recd a warning letter from prior Nicholas de Sandwyco, q.v., about their absence from Canterbury for long periods, their excessive hospitality on the manors and their failure to alleviate the financial distress of the priory, CCA DCc Cart. Antiq. B.393(23).

William de AUDINGES [Alding
occ. 1239

n.d., name occ. near the beginning of the *post exilium* list in *SL*, 172, CCA Lit. Ms D.12, fo 1.

1239, 4 Jan., one of the monks who were accused of contumacy by the abp in the wake of the forgery scandal and summoned to appear before him, *Gervase Cant.*, ii, 144; see Simon de Hertlepe. On 1 Feb., he was one of those summoned to appear before the abp after the monks' el. of Roger de La Lee q.v., as prior, *ib.*, ii, 153.

AUDOEN
n.d.

n.d., subdcn whose obit occ. on 12 Sept. in BL Ms Cotton Nero C.ix, fo 11ᵛ.

Henry AUDOEN [Audoene, Awdewyn, Awdroyn
occ. 1517 occ. 1540

1517, 12 Mar. [deposition of St Gregory], one of six who were tonsured, *SL*, 194, CCA Lit. Ms D.12, fo 11–11ᵛ.

1517, 29 Sept., one of six who made their prof. before the abp on the day on which prior Thomas Goldwell, q.v. celebrated his first pontifical high mass, *ib.*

1523/4, celebrated his first mass, Woodruff, 'Sacrist's Rolls', 71.

[1538, 8 Feb., after], 1540, 4 Apr., fourth prior, Pantin, *Cant. Coll. Ox.*, iii, 153, *L and P Henry VIII*, xv, no 452.

1534, 12 Dec., acknowledged the Act of Supremacy, *DK 7th Report*, Appndx 2, 282.

[1538, 8 Feb., after], in a list of monks prob. prepared for Thomas Cromwell he was described as 'a good man' 36 yrs old, Pantin, *Cant. Coll. Ox.*, iii, 153.

1540, 4 Apr., awarded £3 and became a petty canon in the new foundation, *L and P Henry VIII*, xv, no 452.

AUGUSTINUS
occ. [1175 × 1177]

[1175 × 1177], cellarer, Urry, *Canterbury*, 403.

[1175 × 1177], witnessed a grant of prior Benedict, q.v., *ib.*

n.d., 10 Apr., the obit of a dcn named Augustinus occ. in BL Ms Arundel 68, fo 23ᵛ.

AUGUSTUS
n.d.

n.d., 25 Oct., obit occ. in BL Ms Arundel 68, fo 46ᵛ.

AUNCELL
see Anselme

John AURIFABER
n.d. [after 1214]

n.d., name occ. in the *post exilium* list in *SL*, 173, CCA Lit. Ms D.12, fo 1.

n.d., apptd subprior of Dover, *Lit. Cant.*, iii, Appndx no 35 (CCA DCc Z.D.4, 23).

A silver gilt *ciphus* belonging to him is included in an inventory of the refectory, dated 1328, Dart, *Antiq. Cant.*, Appndx, xix (BL MS Cotton Galba E.iv., fo 178).

Simon AUSTEN [Austin, Austyn
occ. 1480 d. 1511

1480, 25 Jan., one of six prof., *SL*, 191, CCA Lit. Ms D.12, fo 8^{v}.
1480, 1 Apr., ord acol., Canterbury cathedral, *Reg. abp Bourgchier*, 430.
1480, 23 Sept., ord subdcn, Canterbury cathedral, *ib.*, 431.
1483, 29 Mar., ord dcn, Canterbury cathedral, *ib.*, 439.
1486, 25 Mar., ord pr., Canterbury cathedral, *ib.*, 455.

1497/8, 1500/1, anniversarian, CCA DCc Anniv. acct 17, Lambeth, ED46.

1493, 1 May, 41st in order at the ratification of an agreement, Reg. S, fo 383^{v}; but see John Crosse I.
1501, 26 Apr., 27th at the el. of an abp., Reg. R, fo 56^{v}.
1508, 18 June, delegated to celebrate the Sun. mass, CCA Lit. Ms C.11, fo 17^{v}.
1510/11, d., Woodruff, 'Sacrist's Rolls', 69 (CCA DCc Sac. acct 73); since his obit in BL Ms Arundel, 68, fo 14 is 24 Jan., we may assume he d. on 24 Jan. 1511.

Thomas AUSTEN
occ. 1497/8

1497/8, celebrated his first mass and received 8d. from the sacrist, Woodruff, 'Sacrist's Rolls', 66.

Note: this must be Thomas Anselme I, q.v.

William AUSTEN [Asten, Austyn
occ. 1519 occ. 1540

1519, 6 May, one of nine tonsured, *SL*, 194, CCA Lit. Ms D.12, fo 11^{v}.
1520, 3 Feb., prof., *ib.*

1534, 12 Dec., acknowledged the Act of Supremacy, *DK 7th Report*, Appndx 2, 282.
[1538, 8 Feb., after], in a list of monks prob. prepared for Thomas Cromwell he was described as 'a good man', 40 yrs of age, Pantin, *Cant. Coll. Ox.*, iii, 153.
1540, 4 Apr., awarded £3 and became a petty canon in the new foundation, *L and P Henry VIII*, xv, no 452.

This is prob. one of the monks to whom Thomas Anselme I, q.v., pledged several books in payment of a debt, [?1510 × 1518] before he was adm. to Christ Church, Pantin, *Cant. Coll. Ox.*, i, 91–92 (CCA DCc DE57A).

AWDEWYN, Awdroyn
see Audoen

AWNCELME
see Anselme

John de AYLESFORD [Elisford, Elysford, Eylesford
occ. 1289 d. 1337

1289, 19 Dec., one of nine prof., *SL*, 177, CCA Lit. Ms D.12, fo 3.

1312/16, granator, CCA DCc Gran. accts, 5, 26, 66, 6, Ebony acct 28.

1337, 13 Feb., d., CCA Lit. Ms D.12, fo 16^{v}; his obit is in BL Ms Arundel 68, fo 16.

AYSSHE
see Asshe

William AZELINUS [Acellini
occ. 1189

1189, Oct./Nov., along with Robert de Sancto Martino *medicus*, described as *proditores* by a monk writing to Geoffrey subprior, q.v., *Epist. Cant.*, 311; reported to have left Christ Church (perhaps only figuratively as they are also described as in league with Roger Norreys I, q.v.), *ib.*, 312 and both were therefore considered apostate, *ib.*, 313, 322.

The name Acelin occ. in a Penitenciale in the Eastry catalogue, no 228, James, *Ancient Libraries*, 42. See also Ascelin.
With an otherwise unknown monk [?of Christ Church] named Aimery he travelled in the retinue of abp Baldwin in Mar. 1190 and carried relics of Becket to the monks of Dijon, Cowdrey, 'An Early Record at Dijon', 252–253. As Cowdrey observes, it seems odd that an apostate should be carrying out such a comm.

AZO [Athso, Atso, Atson'
occ. [1153 × 1161] occ. [c. 1168]

[1153 × 1161], infirmarer, *Theobald Charters*, no 40.

[1153 × 1161], *temp.* abp Theobald and prior Wibert, q.v., witnessed a grant of the prior and convent in response to a request from the abp, *Theobald Charters*, no 40 (Reg. B, fo 146^{v}).
[c. 1168], recd a letter from John of Salisbury in which the latter asked him to send the copy of Quintilian previously requested, *Salisbury Letters*, ii, no 263.

The name Azo is attached to two vols in the Eastry catalogue, both glossed psalters, nos 1015, 1016, James, *Ancient Libraries*, 98.

Note: there are two obits for priests named Azo in BL Ms Arundel 68, one on 28 Mar. (fo 22^{v}) and the other on 20 Oct. (fo 45^{v}); in the BL Ms Cotton Nero C.ix it is rendered Adzo on fo 8^{v} (28 Mar.).

Walter de BA [Bath
occ. 1189

1189, 11 Oct., chaplain of prior Roger Norreys I, q.v., *Epist. Cant.*, 312.

BAC
see Godwin

BAKER
see Thomas Becket I

BALDWIN [Badewinus
occ. 1152 occ. [late 1189]

1152, sacrist, Urry *Canterbury*, 392.
1152, witnessed the purchase of land in Canterbury by prior Wibert, *ib.*
[1189, late], with O[?do] de Tumba, q.v., forcibly detained by the abp after they had been sent by the chapter as messengers to him, *Epist. Cant.*, 311.

Note: there may be two Baldwins here.

John de BANBERY [Bannbery, Bannebery, Bannebury
occ. 1361 d. 1396

1361, 28 Oct., one of nine prof., *SL*, 181, CCA Lit. Ms D.12, fo 4^v.
1371, warden of St Mary in crypt, CCA DCc MA2, fo 266.
1374/5, second anniversarian with James de Dover, q.v., CCA DCc Anniv. acct, 6.
1379, 25 June, apptd cellarer, Reg. abp Sudbury, fo 56^v; removed 1380, 7 Apr., *ib.*, fo 61^v.
1383/4, third prior for two terms, Lambeth Ms 243, fo 192^v.
1385, *custos martyrii*, CCA DCc, MA2, fo 334^v.
1374, 30 June, 27th in order at the el. of an abp, Reg. G, fos 173^v–175^v.
1374/5, ill during the yr and recd a 'pension' of 2s. from the anniversarian's acct, CCA DCc Anniv. acct 6.
1381, 31 July, 19th at the el. of an abp, Reg. G, fo 225^v.
1383/4, as third prior recd *dona* of 15s. from the prior, Lambeth Ms 243, fo 192^v.
1396, 20 May, d., CCA Lit. Ms D.12, fo 17^v, and his obit is in BL Ms Arundel 68, fo 28.

[BANERS]
see Robert de Thaneto

BANNYNTON
see Bonyngton

Thomas BARBOR
see Saint Andrew

BARHAM
see Berham

BARKING
see also Berkyng

Edward BARKING
see Bockyng

BARKSORE
see Berkesore

BARNARD
see Bernarde

William BARNET [Bernett
occ. 1429 d. 1448

1429, 19 Apr., *adjunctus*, *SL*, 187, CCA Lit. Ms D.12, fo 7.
[1429, summer], ord acol. and subdcn, place not named, Reg. Langdon (Rochester), fo 74.
1433, 28 Mar., ord pr., Charing, *Reg. abp Chichele*, iv, 378.
1435, 12 Nov., Dec., apptd *parvus sacrista*, Chron. Wm Glastynbury, fo 117^v.
1439/48, for the last nine yrs of his life he was 'quasi stationarius in infirmitate mirabili detentus', CCA Lit. Ms D.12, fo 25^v.
1448, 4 Dec., d., *ib.*, and *Chron. Stone*, 45; his obit is in BL Ms Arundel 68, fo 50.

Name on front flyleaf of CCA Lit. Ms E.6, Quaternus W. Barnett; the contents are mainly manorial accts of 1451/2, rough drafts on paper.

[In his yrs in the infirmary] he was responsible for having a new [infirmary] kitchen built, and he redecorated the chamber next to the infirmary chapel, the chamber in which he d., *Chron. Stone*, 45.

BARTELOT
see Bertolot

I BARTHOLOMEW
occ. 1227 occ. 1233/4

1227, sacrist, CCA DCc MA1, fo 71.
1233/4, subsacrist, *ib.*, fos 76–77^v.

Note: this is prob. Bartholomew de Sandwyco, q.v.

II BARTHOLOMEW
occ. 1285

1285, 22 Sept., ord dcn., collegiate church of South Malling, *Reg. abp Pecham*, i, 222.

III BARTHOLOMEW
occ. 1373 occ. 1387/8

1373, *custos tumbe*, CCA DCc MA2, fo 276.
1387/8, recd 12d. from the prior, Lambeth Ms 243, fo 208^v.

Note: there may be two Bartholomews here; equally, both entries may ref. to Bartholomew de Lovelond, q.v.

BARTYN
see Bertyn

John BASTARD
occ. 1401

1401, 19 Mar., ord acol., Canterbury cathedral, Reg. abp Arundel, i, fo 327^v.

Note: this monk prob. occ. elsewhere in this list under his toponymic; see John Aldynton.

John BATAYLE [Bathelay, Botayle
occ. 1406 occ. 1414

1406, 21 Oct., one of three *adjuncti* among seven prof., *SL*, 185, CCA Lit. Ms D.12, fos 5^v–6.
1407, 26 Mar., ord acol., Canterbury cathedral, Reg. abp Arundel, i, fo 340^v.
1407, 24 Sept., ord subdcn, collegiate church, Maidstone, *ib.*, i, 341.
1414, 12 Mar., 65th in order at the el. of an abp, *Reg. abp Chichele*, i, 4.
n.d., became a Cistercian at Robertsbridge, *SL*, 185, CCA Lit. Ms D.12, fo 6. However, acc. to Chron. Wm Glastynbury, fo 168^v/162^v he departed *in apostesia* [*sic*].

BATH
see Ba

BATTLE
see Bello

BEATRISDEN
see Bedyrsden

William de BEAUMOND' [Beamund, Beumond, Bewmund
occ. 1328 d. 1349

1328, 25 Nov., one of seven prof., *SL*, 179, CCA Lit. Ms D.12, fo 3^v.
1334/6, *custos martyrii*, CCA DCc MA2, fos 231–241, DE3, fo 37.
1346/7, 1348, 3 Aug., 1349, 4 June, subprior, CCA DCc, Godmersham acct 19, Reg. G, fos 30^v, 31, 61^v.
1348, 30 Aug., named by the initial three *compromissorii* as one of seven *compromissorii* in the el. of an abp, Reg. G, fos 30^v, 82.
1349, 4 June, 2nd in order and one of thirteen *compromissorii* in the el. of an abp, Reg. G, fo 61^v.
1349, 27 June, one of four who d. of the plague within little more than a month, CCA Lit. Ms D.12, fo 16^v.

BEAUMOND
see also Bemond

BECFORD
see Bekforde

I Thomas BECKET [Beket, Bekett, ?*alias* Baker
occ. 1505 occ. 1518/19

1505, 13 Jan., one of six who were tonsured, *SL*, 193, CCA Lit. Ms D.12, fo 10.
1505, 22 Mar., ord acol., Canterbury cathedral, Reg. abp Warham, ii, fo 262.
1505, 11 July, prof., *SL*, 193, CCA Lit. Ms D.12, fo 10.
1506, 11 Apr., ord subdcn, Canterbury cathedral, Reg. abp Warham, ii, fo 262^v.
1507, 3 Apr., ord dcn, Canterbury cathedral, *ib.*, ii, fo 263.
1511, 19 Apr., ord pr, Canterbury cathedral, *ib.*, ii, fo 265^v.
1510/11, celebrated his first mass and recd a gift from the sacrist, Woodruff 'Sacrist's Rolls', 69 (CCA DCc Sac. acct 73). A Thomas Baker celebrated his first mass on the first Sunday in May 1511 and recd 4d. from the *custos martyrii*, CCA Lit. Ms C.11, fo 52.
1516, 25 Dec., almoner, CCA Lit. Ms C.11, fo 58.
1517/18, succentor, BL Ms Arundel 68, fo 11.
1511, 2 Sept., 58th in order on the visitation certificate, Wood-Legh, *Visit.*, 3 (Reg. abp Warham, i, fo 35^v).
1517/18 as succentor he was in charge of the confraternity list, BL Ms Arundel 68, fo 11.
1518/19, spent time in the infirmary on several occasions during the yr, CCA DCc Infirm. acct 1.
n.d., 1 July, obit occ. in BL Ms Arundel 68, fo 32^v.

Note: see John Clement III whose family name was also Baker.

II Thomas BECKETT [Bekett
occ. 1527 occ. 1540

1527, 25 May, one of twelve tonsured, *SL*, 195, CCA Lit. Ms D.12, fo 12.
1528, 2 Mar., prof., *ib.*
[1538, 8 Feb., after], subalmoner, Pantin, *Cant. Coll. Ox.*, iii, 153.
1534, 12 Dec., acknowledged the Act of Supremacy, *DK 7th Report*, Appndx 2, 282.
1537, c. 28 Jan, one of several monks examined on accusations of speaking vs the king by naming the popes in chapter house suffrages, *L and P Henry VIII*, xii, pt 1, no 256.
[1538, 8 Feb., after], in a list of monks prob. prepared for Thomas Cromwell he was described as 'wytty' and 32 yrs old, Pantin, *Cant. Coll. Ox.*, iii, 153.
1540, 4 Apr., awarded £3 and became a scholar in the new foundation, *L and P Henry VIII*, xv, no 452.

Name in Oxford, New College Ms 300, Miscellanea theologica, with the date AD 1531; did he write it? See also Robert Holyngbourne.

Note: it is not possible to assign with certainty all the refs to these two contemporaries with the same name. Since there are no entries which state 'junior' or 'senior' it is prob. that Thomas Becket I had d. by 1527.

BEDELYNGWELL
see Redelyngwell

Germanus BEDYRSDEN [Beatrisden, Bedrysden, Bethersden, Betrisden
occ. [1461] d. [1465]

1461, 4 Apr., ord acol. and subdcn, Canterbury cathedral, *Reg. abp Bourgchier*, 377, 378.
[1461], 19 Apr., one of six prof., *SL*, 190, CCA Lit. Ms D.12, fo 8.
1463, 9 Apr., ord dcn, Canterbury cathedral, *Reg. abp Bourgchier*, 386.
1465, 8 June, ord pr., Canterbury cathedral, *ib.*, 395.
[1465], 24 June, *convent[ualis*, d., CCA Lit. Ms D.12, fo 26; his obit occ. in BL Ms Arundel 68, fo 31v.

John de BEGBROKE [Bagebroke, Beggebroke, Bekebroke, Berkruke
occ. 1272/3 d. 1289

n.d., name occ. in the list in *SL*, 175, CCA Lit. Ms D.12, fo 2v; in Cambridge, Corpus Christi College, Ms 298, it appears as Dekebroke.
1272/3, treasurer, CCA DCc, Great Chart acct 1 (as William).
1276/8, chamberlain, CCA DCc MA1, fos 123v–128, Reg. H, fo 210.
1282, first treasurer with Henry de Eastry and John de Well I, q.v., CCA DCc Treas. acct 1, MA1, fo 136.
1283, 1285, chamberlain, CCA DCc MA1, fo 139v, Treas. acct 2; and see R de Esshe.
1287/8, *custos tumbe*, CCA DCc MA1, fo 153v.
1279/80, procured oil for 'our master' [?lector], Pantin, *Cant. Coll. Ox.*, iv, 168 (Lambeth Ms 243, fo 51).
1289, 29 Oct., d., CCA Lit. Ms D.12, fo 15.

BEKET(T)
see Becket

John de BEKFORDE [Becford, Bekford
occ. 1349 d. [1396/7]

1349, 9 Oct., one of six prof., *SL*, 181, CCA Lit. Ms D.12, fo 4.
1350, 18 Sept., ord subdcn, Goudhurst, Reg. abp Islip, fo 310.
1351, 24 Sept., ord dcn, chapel of Herne church, *ib.*, fo 312.
1353, 21 Dec., ord pr., abp's chapel, Maidstone, *ib.*, fo 314v.
1361/2, subsacrist, CCA DCc Sac. acct 3.
1362, June/Sept., sacrist, CCA DCc, Sac. acct 4.
1362/3, treasurer, Lambeth Ms 243, fo 120v.
1368/9, chaplain to the prior, CCA DCc Adisham acct 33.
1369, 22 June, apptd precentor, but removed at the prior's request, Reg. abp Wittlesey, fo 13; see below.
1366, 12 Feb., granted by the king an annuity of £20 to be pd by the exchequer, *CPR (1364–1371)*, 221.
1371, 19 Feb., presented to the church of Bishopsbourne in the abp's gift, as rector, and the prior and convent gave their ratification on 23 Feb., Reg. H, fo 73v.
1388, 5 Sept., his estate was reported ratified as rector of Chartham, *CPR (1385–1389)*, 504.
n.d., described as 'quondam de Chartham beneficiatus et rector', *SL*, 181, CCA Lit. Ms D.12, fo 4.
1392/3, gave 3s. 4d. to the sacrist *pro dealbatione chori*, CCA DCc Sac. acct 11.
[1396/7] 24 Mar., d., CCA Lit. Ms D.12, fo 17v, where he is described as precentor.

Henry de BELLO
occ. 1285

1285, 22 Sept., ord pr., collegiate church, South Malling, *Reg. abp Pecham*, i, 222.

Note: this may be Henry Moth, q.v.

John de BELLO
occ. 1277 d. 1293

n.d., name occ. in the list in *SL*, 175, CCA Lit. Ms D.12, fo 2v.
1277, was replaced as proctor at the curia by Robert Poucyn, q.v., *Hist. Mss Comm. 5th Report*, Appndx, 451 (CCA DCc Ms Scrap Book C.9).
1293, 30 Nov., d., CCA Lit. Ms D.12, fo 15.

Thomas de BELLO
occ. 1285

1285, 22 Sept., ord pr., collegiate church, South Malling, *Reg. abp Pecham*, i, 222.

Thomas BELOYZELL [Beloysell, Beloysoll
occ. 1292 d. 1296

[?c. 1260], name occ. several yrs after Henry de Eastry, q.v., in the list in *SL*, 176, CCA Lit. Ms D.12, fo 2v.
1294/5, chamberlain, CCA DCc MA1, fos 190–194.
1296, granator, *ib.*, MA1, fo 200.
1292, 5 Oct., with Geoffrey de Chilham, q.v., sent by the prior to Thomas Ryngmer, q.v., to inquire into his welfare, CUL Ms Ee.5.31, fo 34v.
1292/3, visited Meopham, CCA Dcc Meopham acct 17.

1296, 2 July, d., CCA Lit. Ms D.12, fo 15; obit in BL Ms Arundel 68, fo 32v.

John BEMOND [Bemonde, Bemound, Bemunde, Bewmond, Bewmund, Bomund
occ. 1395 d. 1432

[1395], 12 Mar., one of eight prof., *SL*, 184, CCA Lit. Ms D.12, fo 5.
1396, 1 Apr., ord subdcn, Canterbury cathedral, Reg. abp Courtenay, ii, fo 186v.
1419, 3 Oct., apptd chamberlain, *Reg. abp Chichele*, iv, 197.
1420/1, first anniversarian, with John Elham, II, q.v., CCA DCc, Anniv. acct 8.
1421/2, bartoner, CCA DCc, Bart. acct 84.
1422/3, anniversarian with John Elham, CCA DCc, Prior acct 5.
1429, 19 Apr., *magister ordinis*, *SL*, 187, CCA Lit. Ms D.12, fo 7.
1396, 7 Aug., 78th (out of 81) in order at the el. of an abp, Reg. G, fo 234v.
1414, 21 Mar., 30th at the el. of an abp, Reg. G, fo 288.
1432, 9 Aug., d. of plague and was buried at once, the subprior (in the absence of the prior) and monks having read the *commendatio* in the infirmary chapel, and all the brethren having done all on his behalf acc. to custom, *Chron. Stone*, 17 and CCA Lit. Ms D.12, fo 23v.

BEMOND
see also Beaumond

Richard de BENDINGEHAM [Bentingeham
occ 1206

1206, 30 Mar., one of the monks summoned to Rome by the pope to give evidence in the dispute over their el. of Reginald, q.v., as abp, *CPL* (1198–1304), 26. While there they el. Stephen Langton, *Fasti*, ii, 6.

Henry de BENE
occ. [?c. 1260]

[?c. 1260], name occ. several yrs after that of Henry de Eastry, q.v., in the list in *SL*, 176, CCA Lit. Ms D.12, fo 2v.

I BENEDICT [Benedictus
n.d.

n.d., 17 Mar., subdcn, whose obit occ. in BL Ms Arundel 68, fo 20v.

II BENEDICT
occ. [1174] occ. 1177

1175, July × Sept. to 1177, prior: el. July x Sept. 1175, *Eng. Epis. Acta*, ii, no 111 note; 1177, 29 May, res. because el. abbot of Peterborough, *Fasti*, ii, 10, *HRH*, 34.
n.d., chaplain to the abp, Cambridge, Corpus Christi College Ms 298, fo 115.
[?1174, Aug. × 1175, Sept.], abp's chancellor and witness to his *acta*, *Eng. Epis. Acta*, ii, nos 111, 168.
[1175, July × 1176, 24 Mar.], witnessed a confirmation of the abp, *ib.*, ii, no 215.
1193, d., *HRH*, 61; his obit is on 29 Sept., in BL Ms Arundel 68, fo 43v.

Author of a treatise on the miracles of Thomas Becket which he himself had witnessed, *Gervase Cant.*, ii, 391.

Acc. to Hasted, *Kent*, xi, 433, he was a favourite of Richard I and a doctor of divinity of Oxford.

III BENEDICT
occ. 1244 occ. 1252

1244, Nov., cellarer, CCA DCc AS16.
1251/2, anniversarian, Reg. H, fo 172v.

John BENETT
occ. 1461 d. 1481

1461, 4 Apr., ord acol. and subdcn, Canterbury cathedral, *Reg. abp Bourgchier*, 377.
[1461], 19 Apr., one of six prof., *SL*, 189, CCA Lit. Ms D.12, fo 8.
1462, 17 Apr., ord dcn, Canterbury cathedral, *Reg. abp Bourgchier*, 381.
1463, 9 Apr., ord pr., Canterbury cathedral, *ib.*, 386.
1462/3, celebrated his first mass and recd 8d. from the sacrist, Woodruff, 'Sacrist's Rolls', 62 (CCA DCc Sac. acct 43).
1481, before 5 June, feretrar, CCA Lit. Ms D.12, fo 26v.
1466, 17 Feb., 66th in order in an inventory listing *jocalia fratrum* [given by him and/or assigned for his use], and he had none, Reg. N, fo 234v.
1481, 5 June, d. and had *omnia servicia* on 9 June [the eve of Pentecost], CCA Lit. Ms D.12, fo 26v; obit in BL Ms Arundel 68, fo 29v.

Nicholas BENETT [Bennet
occ. 1524 occ. [c. 1534]

1524, 21/22 July, one of eleven granted adm. to Christ Church, [*ingressum*], CCA Lit. Ms D.12, fos 11v–12.
1524, 4 Aug., one of eleven tonsured, *SL*, 195, CCA Lit. Ms D.12, *ib.*
1525, 19 Apr., prof., *ib.*

n.d., subcellarer, see below.
1528/9, student at Canterbury college, Pantin, *Cant. Coll. Ox.*, ii, 259.
[c. 1535 × 1538], left Oxford and returned to Canterbury, *ib.*, iii, 149–150. Pantin suggests these dates and this assignation for a letter written to Thomas Tystede, q.v. (under

Winchester) by a monk in Canterbury signing himself 'Benedictus nomine'. However, it is prob. that this Benett had d. by 12 December 1534 as his name does not appear among the signatories to the Act of Supremacy. In the letter he said that he was not returning to Oxford and was occupied with the office of subcellarer; and he gave instructions for his belongings to be sent back to Canterbury, Pantin, *Cant. Coll. Ox.*, iii, 150.

Roger BENETT B.Th [Benet
occ. 1485 d. 1523/4

1485, 25 Mar., clothed in the habit, having been *adjunctus* in the place of William Gloucestre, q.v., *SL*, 191, CCA Lit. Ms D.12, fo 8ᵛ.
1485, 2 Apr., ord acol., Canterbury cathedral, *Reg. abp Bourgchier*, 450 (transcribed as Robert).
1485, 6 Dec., prof. *SL*, 191 (Cambridge, Corpus Christi College, Ms 298).
1491, 2 Apr., ord pr., Canterbury cathedral, Reg. abp Morton, i, no 439d.

1501, 2 Sept., 1504, 1505, 1506, one of the chancellors, *Hist. Mss Comm. 8th Report*, Appndx, 331 (Reg. E, fo 1), Reg. T, fos 411, 415, 425ᵛ, 442, 442ᵛ, 443, 448.
1492/3, prob. student at Oxford who was given 1s. by the prior for half a yr, Pantin, *Cant. Coll. Ox.*, iv, 202.
1495, 8 Feb., one of six scholars at Canterbury college from whom letters of proxy were obtained at the time of the el. of a prior, *ib.*, iv, 203.
1496, Mar./Sept., scholar, with a pension of £4, Pantin, *Cant. Coll. Ox.*, ii, 224 (CCA DCc Cart. Antiq. O.151.29).
1497, 2 Apr., returned from Oxford with the warden, Pantin, *ib.*, iv, 204.
1498/1501, scholar, Pantin, *ib.*, ii, 226, 229, 232 (Cart. Antiq. O.151, 30, 31, 32).
1500/1, recd money from the treasurer for his travelling expenses between Oxford and Canterbury, and for returning to Canterbury with his belongings [*pannis*], Pantin, *ib.*, iv, 205.
By 1501, B.Th., *BRUO*.

1501, 26 Apr., absent from the el. of an abp [because he was at Oxford], Reg. R, fo 56ᵛ.
1511, 2 Sept., 19th in order on the visitation certificate, Wood-Legh, *Visit.*, 3 (Reg. abp Warham, i, fo 35).
1523/4, d., Woodruff, 'Sacrist's Rolls', 71.

Name in BL Ms Egerton 2867, Biblia (13th c.).

One of the monks to whom Thomas Anselme I, q.v., pledged several books as payment of a debt, [?1510 × 1518], Pantin, *Cant. Coll. Ox.*, i, 91–92 (CCA DCc DE57A).

Gave silver spoons to Canterbury college, Pantin, *ib.*, i, 37, *ib.*, iv, 148, (CCA DCc Inventory Box no 21; date 1501).

John BENIND' [?Beninden
n.d.

n.d., 9 Aug., obit occ. in BL Ms Arundel 68, fo 37ᵛ.

I BENJAMIN [Beniaminus
n.d. [1104 × 1105]

[1104 × 1105], with Farman and Ordwy, q.v., recd a letter from abp Anselm, *Anselm Letters*, no 355.

II BENJAMIN
occ. 1189

1189, Oct., one of the monks who was ordered by abp Bonface to appear before him and cooperate in the el. of a prior; he did not do so, *Epist. Cant.*, 312 In this letter, written to Geoffrey II, subprior, q.v., by an unnamed monk, the writer says 'Benjamin quem non cognosco', and so presumably the writer was not a monk of Canterbury, *ib.*

III BENJAMIN
occ. 2nd half 13th c.

n.d., name occ. in the list in *SL*, 174, CCA Lit. Ms D.12, fo 2.

Note: the obits of two Benjamins, priests, occ. on 4 Feb., BL Ms Arundel, 68, fo 15.

BENNET
see Benett

BENTINGEHAM
see Bendingeham

Richard de BERE
occ. 1253 occ. 1257

1253/7, granator, Reg. H, fos 179, 182ᵛ, 184ᵛ, 188.

William de BERE
occ. 1281 occ. 1286/7

1281, bartoner, CCA DCc, Arrears acct 46.
1286/7, sacrist, CCA DCc Treas. acct 3.

William BEREGINGE
see William Berkynge junior

Thomas BEREHAM
see Kyngston

William de BERGATE [Beregate, Berygate
occ. 1333 d. 1361

1338, 9 Oct., one of eleven prof., *SL*, 180, CCA Lit. Ms D.12, fo 4.

1350/1, *custos tumbe*, CCA DCc, Treas. acct 27, fo 2ᵛ.

1349, 4 June, 39th in order at the el. of an abp, Reg. G, fo 60ᵛ.

1349, 8/9 Sept., 38th at the el. of an abp, *ib.*, fo 76^v.
1361, 13 Aug., d. in an epidemic which carried off c.25 monks, CCA Lit. Ms D.12, fo 17.

BERGATE
see also Berigate, Burgate

Henry BERHAM [Borham
occ. [1420] d. 1462

[1420], 31 May, *adjunctus*, *SL*, 186, CCA Lit. Ms D.12, fo 6^v.
1421, 4 Apr., one of six prof., *SL*, 186, CCA Lit. Ms D.12, fo 6^v.
1422, 11 Apr., recd first tonsure. *Reg. abp Chichele*, iv, 352.
1423, 18 Dec., ord subdcn, Rochester cathedral, *ib.*, iv, 358 (transcribed as Dereham).
1427, 5 Dec., ord pr., bp's chapel, Trottiscliffe, Reg. Langdon (Rochester), fo 59^v.
1435, second precentor, 'Chron. Wm Glastynbury', 129.
1448/9, 1449, 7 Dec., third prior, CCA DCc Sac. acct 35, *Chron. Stone*, 47.
1456/7, 1458, 2 Feb., 1460/1, subprior, CCA DcC Sac. acct 40, *Chron. Stone*, 72, CCA DCc Sac. acct 42; acc. to *Chron. Stone*, 69, he was apptd subprior on 15 Aug. 1457, and was succ. by John Oxney, II, q.v., *ib.*, 86.
1449, 7 Dec., was one of the 'examining board' for the novice, John Charyng, q.v., *Chron. Stone*, 47.
1462, 3 May, d., in the 42nd yr of monastic life, and was buried in the infirmary chapel, *ib.*, 86.

See John Dunstan I.

John BERHAM [Bereham
occ. 1381 d. 1415

1381, 6 May, one of eight prof., *SL*, 183, CCA Lit. Ms D.12, fo 5.
1385, 23 Dec., ord pr., abp's chapel, Otford, Reg. abp Courtenay, i, fo 308.
[1404/5], *custos martyrii*, CCA DCc, Prior acct 20.
1410/11, feretrar, *ib.*, Prior acct 2.
1383/4, possibly went up to Oxford to study as he recd a small sum *pro benedictione* from the prior, Lambeth Ms 243, fo 192^v.
1387/8, 1388/9, prob. student with small sums from the prior, *ib.*, fos 208^v, 212^v; in the latter yr he recd 5s. for travelling expenses, Pantin, *Cant. Coll. Ox.*, iv, 190 (Lambeth Ms 243, fo 212^v).
1396, 7 Aug., 35th in order at the el. of an abp, Reg. G, fo 234^v.
1411/12, recd pittance money from the chamberlain, CCA DCc Chamb. acct 71.
1415, 10 Feb., d. in the 33rd yr of his monastic life; his body and that of John Colchestre, q.v., who d. 9 Feb., lay together in the choir for the funeral rites, CCA Lit. Ms D.12, fo 20. His obit is 9 Feb., in BL Ms Arundel 68, fo 16.

Michael BERHAM [Barham
occ. [c. 1389] d. 1403/4

[c. 1389], one of eight who were prof., *SL*, 183, CCA Lit. Ms D.12, fo 5.
1391, 25 Mar., ord dcn, Canterbury cathedral, Reg. abp Courtenay, i, fo 312.
1396, 7 Aug., 54th in order at the el. of an abp, Reg. G, fo 234^v.
1403/4, 12 Oct,. d., CCA Lit. Ms D.12, fo 18.

Walter de BERHAM [Bereham, Boreham
occ. 1328 d. 1350

1328, 25 Nov., one of seven prof., *SL*, 179, CCA Lit. Ms D.12, fo 3^v.
1332, *magister corone*, CCA DCc MA2, fo 211^v.
1336, Aug./1337, Jan., 1337/8, 1339/40, 1342/3, subalmoner, CCA DCc Alm. accts 22 and 45, Eastry accts 64, 66, Monkton acct 70.
1348, June/Sept., chamberlain, CCA DCc Chamb. acct 40.
1348/9, first anniversarian with William de Eyorne, q.v., CCA DCc Anniv. acct 3.
1349, 4 June, 23rd in order at the el. of an abp, Reg. G, fo 60^v.
1349, 8/9 Sept., 22nd at the el. of an abp, *ib.*, fo 76.
1350, 10 July, d., CCA Lit. Ms D.12, fo 16^v.

William BERHAM
occ. 1520/1

1520/1, ill in the infirmary during the yr, CCA DCc Infirm. acct 2.

Note: this monk must be concealed elsewhere under his patronymic.

BERHAM
see also Borham

John de BERIGATE [Borgat'
occ. 1316 d. 1342

1316/18, 1319/21, July, granator [*interior*], CCA DCc, Gran. accts, 9, 10, 11, 12.
1329/31, *magister corone*, CCA DCc MA21, fos 183^v–201^v.
1332, *custos martyrii*, *ib.*, MA2, fo 211^v.
1342, 10 July, d., CCA Lit. Ms D.12, fo 16^v.

BERIGATE
see also Bergate, Burgate

Richard de BERKESORE [Barksore, Berkysore
occ. [1207 × 1214] occ. [1222 × 1228]

[1207 × 1214], name occ. on the list of those who were in exile, *SL*, 172, CCA Lit. Ms D.12, fo 1.
[1222 × 1228], warden of manors, Reg. B, fo 143 [possibly to 1238].
n.d., 24 Mar., obit occ. in BL Ms Arundel 68, fo 21^v.

The 1328 inventory of the refectory includes a *ciphus de murra* described as his, Dart, *Antiq. Cant.*, xxi (BL Ms Cotton Galba E.iv, fo 179v).

William de BERKRUKE
see John Begbroke

Adam de BERKYNG
occ. 1353 occ. 1359/60

1353, 27 Sept., one of five prof., *SL*, 181, CCA Lit. Ms D.12, fo 4.

1359/60, ill and recd a 'pension' of 5s. from the anniversarian, CCA DCc Anniv. acct 5.

Robert de BERKYNG
occ. 1st half 13th c.

n.d., name occ. in the *post exilium* list in *SL*, 174, CCA Lit. Ms D.12, fo 1v.

I William de BERKYNGE [Berkinge (senior)
occ. 1270

n.d., name occ. in the list in *SL*, 174, CCA Lit. Ms D.12, fo 2.

1270, 7 Sept., named as one of seven *compromissorii* in the el. of an abp, *Gervase Cant.*, ii, 252–253.

The 1328 inventory of the refectory includes two silver *ciphi* and a third of wood described as his, Dart, *Antiq. Cant.*, xix, xxii (BL Ms Cotton Galba E.iv, fos 178v, 180).

Note: the date of d. of William de Berkynge II may ref. to this monk.

II William de BERKYNGE [Bereginge junior, Berkyngg
occ. 1270 d. 1291

n.d., name occ. in the list in *SL*, 175, CCA Lit. Ms D.12, fo 2v.

1289, warden of manors, CCA DCc EC II/9.

1270, 7 Sept., named as one of seven *compromissorii* in the el. of an abp, *Gervase Cant.*, ii, 252–253 (transcribed as Bereginge junior); see Adam de Chillenden.

1291, 14 Mar., d., CCA Lit. Ms D.12, fo 15, his obit is in BL Ms Arundel 68, fo 20.

Name attached to several vols in the Eastry catalogue, nos 525–528, James, *Ancient Libraries*, 63. Also, a list of missing service books dated 1 Mar. 1338 includes an ordinale formerly his, *Lit. Cant.*, no 618 (Reg. L, fo 104).

An inventory of vestments, *temp.* prior Eastry, includes a red chasuble embroidered with castles, roses, birds and fleurs de lys described as his [?gift], Legg and Hope, *Inventories*, 52 (BL Ms Cotton Galba E.iv, fo 112); two *ciphi de murra*, formerly his, are in the 1328 inventory of the refectory, *ib.*, fo 179v.

BERKYSORE
see Berkesore

BERNARD [Bernardus
n.d.

n.d., 28 Apr., obit occ. in BL Ms Arundel 68, fo 26.

John BERNARDE [Barnard, Bernard
occ. 1384 d. 1397

1384, 29 Aug., clothed in the habit, *SL*, 183, CCA Lit. Ms D.12, fo 5.

1386, 21 Apr., ord subdcn, Canterbury cathedral, Reg. abp Courtenay, i, fo 308v.

1387, 6 Apr., ord pr., Canterbury cathedral, *ib.* i, fo 309v.

1385/8, 1389/1, each yr recd small sums, usually 12d., from the prior, Lambeth Ms 243, fos 200v, 204v, 208v, 216v, 220v.

1396, 7 Aug., 47th in order at the el. of an abp, Reg. G, fo 234v.

1397, 28 Apr., d., CCA Lit. Ms D.12, fo 17v.

BERNETT
see Barnet

BERTEN
see Bertyn

Andrew BERTOLOT [Barteloo, Bartelot, Bertolott
occ. 1339 d. 1360

1339, 13 Dec., one of five prof., *SL*, 180, CCA Lit. Ms D.12, fo 4.

1349, 4 June, 50th in order at the el. of an abp, Reg. G, fo 60v.

1349, 8/9 Sept., 49th at the el. of an abp, *ib.*, fo 76v.

1360, 15 Mar., d., CCA Lit. Ms D.12, fo 17.

John BERTRAM
occ. 1372 occ. 1382

1372, 18 Sept., the prior was comm. to clothe him in the monastic habit, Reg. abp Wittlesey, fo 56v.

1373, 12 Mar., prof., *ib.*, fo 59 (*SL*, 182, and CCA Lit. Ms D.12, fo 4v are confused).

1373, 16 Apr., ord subdcn, Canterbury cathedral, Reg. abp Wittlesey, fo 170v.

1375/6, ord pr., in London and recd 13s. 6d. from the treasurer for his travelling expenses, Pantin, *Cant. Coll. Ox.*, iv, 186.

1382, 15 Sept., absolved from the office of penitentiary in the priory, Reg. abp Courtenay, i, fo 21v.

1375/6, student at Oxford and recd 18s. for his expenses as he set out on a return journey from Oxford to Canterbury, 20s. as he set out on the way back to Oxford, and 20s. *pro capa scholastica*, Pantin, *Cant. Coll. Ox.*, iv, 186.

1377, at Oxford, CCA DCc MA2, fo 298; he was there on 2 Jan. 1377 at the time of abp Subdury's visitation of Christ Church, Reg. abp Sudbury, fo 32.

1374, 30 June, 61st and last in order and subdcn at the second el. of Langham, Reg. G, fos 173v–175v.

1381, 31 July, 45th in order at the el. of an abp, *ib.*, fo 225v.

BERTRAM
see also Eastry

Nicholas BERTYN [Bartyn, Berten
occ. 1435 occ. 1462

1435, 11 Nov., one of five who were clothed in the monastic habit, Chron. Wm Glastynbury, fo 117v (*SL*, 188, CCA Lit. Ms D.12, fo 7v).

1436, 3 Mar., ord acol., infirmary chapel in the priory, *Reg. abp Chichele*, iv, 383.

1439, 19 Dec., ord dcn, prior's chapel, 'Chron. Wm Glastynbury', 133 (transcribed as R. Bertyn; but see fo 119 in the ms).

1453/4, 1455/6, feretrar, CCA DCc Prior accts 9, 10.

1358, chancellor with Alexander Staple I, q.v., Reg. S, fo 200.

1439, 3 Feb., one of eight monks granted exit leave *pro recreacione*, Chron. Wm Glastynbury, fo 182v/177v.

1462, 25 Jan, *recessit*, Reg. S, fo 209; he transferred to Dover priory with the required licence, *ib.* (CCA Lit. Ms D.12, fo 26).

BERY
see also Bury

BERYGATE
see Bergate

BETHERSDEN
see Bedyrsden

BEUMOND, Bewmond
see Beaumond, Bemond

Richard de BEX
occ. [1149 × 1154]

[1149 × 1154], with Simon de Dover and Hervey, q.v., witnessed a charter concerning Dover priory, *Theobald Charters*, 542.

John de BEYNAM
occ. late 13th c.

n.d., name occ. in the list in *SL*, 175, CCA Lit. Ms D.12, fo 2v, next to that of William de Berkynge II, q.v.

BIDENDEN
see Bydynden

Andrew de BIHAM [Byham
occ. 1239/41 occ. [1244 × 1258]

1239, 4 Jan., one of the monks who were accused of contumacy by the abp after the forgery scandal, *Gervase Cant.*, ii, 144; see Simon de Hertlepe. On 1 Feb. he was among those summmoned to appear before the abp after the monks' el. of Roger de La Lee, q.v., as prior, *ib.*, ii, 153.

1241, 1 Feb., one of seven *compromissorii* named by the chapter in the el. of an abp, *ib.*, ii, 186, 187, 190.

[1244 × 1258], sent by the prior and chapter, with Walter de Hatfeld, q.v., to the king to confer with him, CCA DCc Cart. Antiq. B.393(20).

Note: this is prob. Andrew de Brau, q.v.

BIRCHINTON
see Byrchyngton

Gilbert de BISSHOPPISTON [Bisshopeston, Bissopeston, Byschoppystone, Bysshoppyston
occ. 1289 d. 1329

1289, 19 Dec., one of nine prof., *SL*, 177, CCA Lit. Ms D.12, fo 3.

1309, treasurer, CCA DCc MA2, fo 15.

1314/15, warden of manors, CCA DCc Cheam acct 31.

1316, Nov./1317, Oct., almoner, *ib.*, Alm. acct 20.

1317, Nov./1320, Mar., bartoner, *ib.*, Bart. acct 9, Ebony acct 31, Bart. acct 103.

n.d., prob. feretrar; see below.

[1293 × 1313], chaplain to abp Winchelsey for four yrs, and one of those who testified at the inquiry [in 1319] into the abp's sanctity, Wilkins, *Concilia*, ii, 488, CUL Ms Ee.5.31, fo 204.

1307, 3 Oct., with Guy de Smerden, q.v., named as proctor to attend parliament at Northampton, *Parl. Writs*, ii, pt 3, 546 (CUL Ms Ee.5.31, fo 107v).

1308, 19 Sept., 1313, 13 May, with Robert de Clive, q.v., apptd general proctors for the prior and chapter, *ib.*, fo 109–109v, 121.

1313, 28 May, named as one of seven *compromissorii* in the el. of an abp, Reg. Q, fo 61v/75v.

1313, 4 July/8 Nov., one of the monks who had been named to go to Avignon to seek confirmation of the el. of Thomas Cobham as abp, but they were recalled when news was recd of the papal provision of Walter Reynolds; he was also involved in preparing for the arrival and reception of Reynolds, CUL Ms Ee.5.31, fos 131–138v, Reg. Q, fo 86v.

[1313 × 1327], 19 Aug., had been accused of insubordination and the prior urged the abp to treat him leniently as he had been given outside support from 'certain influential men', CCA DCc EC I/34.

[1313 × 1327], 3 July, with John Ryngmer and

Hugh de St Ives, q.v., was released from the penalties imposed by the abp at his visitation, CCA DCc EC V/31.

1314, 27 June, again apptd as proctor for convocation, with William de Coventre, q.v., CUL Ms Ee.5.31, fo 147v.

1315, 17 Jan., with Hugh de St Margaret, q.v., named as proctors for parliament, *ib.*, fo 155v.

1316, 21 Apr., named as parliamentary proctor for both the prior and the chapter, *ib.*, fo 166v; (for these two proctorial apptments see also *Parl. Writs*, ii, pt 3, 546).

1329, 2 Apr., d., CCA Lit. Ms D.12, fo 16 [as Galfridus]; obit in BL Ms Arundel 68, fo 22v.

He had a nephew named Robert de Mersch, CCA DCc EC II/70.

An inventory of vestments, acquired *temp.* prior Eastry, includes a long list of vestments under the heading 'Vestimenta Gilberti de Bisshopestone', Legg and Hope, *Inventories*, 77 (BL Ms Cotton Galba E.iv, fo 122). The preceding entry in this inventory suggests that these were lists of vestments in the care of the feretrars.

BLACHMANNUS [Blakemannus

occ. [?1089]

[?1089], mentioned with Farman and Edwius, q.v., by Eadmer who in his early days at Christ Church knew them, Eadmer, *Hist. Nov.*, 107.

n.d., 21 Feb., obit occ. in BL Ms Arundel 68, fo 17v.

Roger de BLASTINGLEGH [Blechyngelegh, Blecingelee

occ. 1259/60

n.d., name occ. in the list in *SL*, 175, CCA Lit. Ms D.12, fo 2.

1259/60, pd a visit to Meopham, CCA DCc Meopham acct 1.

Note: the 1328 inventory of the refectory includes a *ciphus* described as that of R. de Blechyngelegh, Dart, *Antiq. Cant.*, xix (BL Ms Cotton Galba E.iv, fo 178v).

Adam BLASYNG'

occ. 1st half 13th c.

n.d., name occ. in the list in *SL*, 174, CCA Lit. Ms D.12, fo 1v.

Richard BLUNDEL [Blondell, Blundell

occ. 1294 d. 1313

1294, 18 Oct., one of eight prof., *SL*, 178, CCA Lit. Ms D.12, fo 3.

1299, 19 Sept., ord pr., Littlebourne, *Reg. abp Winchelsey*, 931.

c. 1300, with Hugh de Cretyng, q.v., denounced for their prolonged stay on the manors and their consequent secular behaviour, *Hist. Mss Comm. 5th Report*, Appndx, 438 (CCA DCc Cart. Antiq. M.368).

1313, 23 Apr., d., CCA Lit. Ms D.12, fo 15; obit in BL Ms Arundel 68, fo 24v.

Robert BLUNDEL

occ. 1239

n.d., name occ. in the list in *SL*, 174, CCA Lit. Ms D.12, fo 1v.

1239, 4 Jan., one of the monks who were accused of contumacy by the abp after the forgery scandal, *Gervase Cant.*, ii, 144; see Simon de Hertlepe. On 1 Feb. he was among those summmoned to appear before the abp after the monks' el. of Roger de La Lee, q.v., as prior, *ib.*, ii, 153.

n.d., 26/7 Feb., obit in BL Ms Arundel 68, fo 18.

In the 1328 inventory of the refectory there is a silver gilt *ciphus*, *cum angelo in fundo*, formerly his, Dart, *Antiq. Cant.*, xix (BL Ms Cotton Galba E.iv, fo 178–178v).

BLYNKHAM

see Bokyngham

BOCHAR

see Boughier

BOCHINGE

see Bockyng

BOCKINGHAM

see Buckingham

Edward BOCKYNG D.Th. [Boking, Bokkin, Bokyng

occ. 1500 d. 1534

1500, 28 July, one of eight tonsured, *SL*, 193, CCA Lit. Ms D.12, fos 9v–10; each of these novices recd a gold noble worth 6s. 8d. for their labours with regard to the funeral of abp Morton who d. c. 15 Sept. 1500, *SL*, 193 (CCA Lit. Ms D.12, fo 10).

1501, 19 Apr., made his prof. before the prior, *sed. vac.*, CCA Lit. Ms D.12, fo 10.

1503/4, celebrated his first mass and recd 8d. from the sacrist, CCA DCc Sac. acct 61.

1510/11, 1516/17, warden of Canterbury college, Pantin, *Cant. Coll. Ox.*, ii, 252–257 (CCA DCc Cart. Antiq. O.151.43, 44 his accts), *ib.*, i, 45 (CCA DCc Cart. Antiq. O.136, an inventory).

1518, 1519, 1521, 1522, 1523, 1525, 1526, 1527, 1528, on 25 Mar., of each of these yrs, cellarer, CCA Lit. Ms C.11, fos 59v, 61, 61v, 62, 63v, 64, 64v, 65. He was also cellarer on 15 July 1533, *L and P Henry VIII*, vi, no 835. His recall, on 13 Aug. 1518, from Oxford to take up this post is in Pantin, *Cant. Coll. Ox.*, iii, 142 (Reg. T, fo 155v).

[1533], possibly novice master, *L and P Henry VIII*, vi, no 1519.

1504/5, adm. as scholar at Canterbury college; in

his supplication for his D.Th. he stated that he had studied logic, philosophy and theology for 13 yrs, Pantin, *Cant. Coll. Ox.*, iii, 247.

1504/7, 1508/9, student, Pantin, *Cant. Coll. Ox.*, ii, 241, 245, 248, 250 (CCA DCc Cart. Antiq. O.151.38, 39, 41, 42).

1512, recd travelling expenses returning from Oxford to Canterbury, Pantin, *Cant. Coll. Ox.*, iv, 205.

1513, 16 June, B.Th., Pantin, *ib.*, iii, 246–247.

1514, 1 Mar., university preacher on Ash Wed., Pantin, *ib.*, iv, 219.

1518, June, D.Th., Pantin, *ib.*, iii, 247–248.

1501, 24 Apr., 51st in order on the list of those eligible to el. an abp, but on 26 Apr., his name is absent, Reg. R, fo 56.

1511, 2 Sept., absent from the abp's visitation because at Oxford, but 45th in order on the visitation certificate, Wood-Legh, *Visit.*, 3 (Reg. abp Warham, i, fo 35v).

1523, 30 May, apptd proctor for convocation, Reg. T, fo 215.

1525, apptd confessor to Elizabeth Barton, Knowles, *RO*, iii, 183.

1533, c. 25 Sept., arrested, with William Hadlegh II, q.v. and accused of being in league with Elizabeth Barton the 'holy maid' of Kent, who was holding forth vs the king's remarriage, *L and P Henry VIII*, vi, no 1149.

1534, 20 Apr., with John Deryng, q.v, executed at Tyburn, *L and P Henry VIII*, vii, pt 1, no 522; the charges against him are in *ib.* no 72.

Name in

(1) Ampleforth Abbey Joannes Franciscus (printed book), Venice, 1500, which he gave to Thomas Goldstone, q.v.

(2) Cambridge, Trinity College Ms 61, Mirror of life of Christ (in English) etc. (?14th/15th c.).

He gave an *ordinale ex papiro*, red vestments and hangings, a silver bowl [*cratera*], three *mirre*, a feather bed to Canterbury college, Pantin, *Cant. Coll. Ox.*, i, 57, 58, 63, 64, 68 (CCA DCc Cart. Antiq. O.135 A).

His obituary records that he was a *predicator egregius*, *SL*, 193 (Cambridge, Corpus Christi College, Ms 298).

Note: there is a biased acct of his connection with Elizabeth Barton in *DNB* to which Knowles' acct is to be preferred in Knowles, *RO*, iii, 182–191.

I John de BOCKYNG [Bochinge

occ. [1187] occ. 1189

[1187, c.Apr.], with Ralph de Orpynton, I, q.v., prob. wardens of manors to whom the abp issued orders that both should be deprived of office and forbidden to go out of the cloister, *Eng. Epis. Acta*, ii, no 251, *Epist. Cant.*, 28.

[1187, 23 June × 25 July], both were excommunicated for disobeying the above, *Eng. Epis. Acta*, ii, no 252, *Epist. Cant.*, 60, 64; but they were absolved on reaching the curia where they had gone with the prior, Honorius, q.v., and other monks to appeal vs the abp, *Epist. Cant.*, 70–71, 90.

1189, 5/8 Nov., one of the party of monks sent to confer with the king in London over their dispute with the abp, *Epist. Cant.*, 315.

See note below John Bockyng III.

II John de BOCKYNG [Bockynge

occ. 2nd half 13th c.

n.d., name occ. in the list in *SL*, 176, CCA Lit. Ms D.12, fo 2v.

Note: several vols in the Eastry catalogue bear the name J. Bokkinge, nos 99, 1362–1364, James, *Ancient Libraries*, 27,116.

III John BOCKYNG [Bokkyng

occ. 1473 d. c. 1490

1473, 13 Mar., ord acol., Canterbury cathedral, *Reg. abp Bourgchier*, 410.

1473, 28 Apr., one of six prof., *SL*, 190, CCA Lit. Ms D.12, fo 8v.

1480, 1 Apr., ord pr., Canterbury cathedral, *Reg. abp Bourgchier*, 430.

n.d. [c. 1490], subsacrist, CCA Lit. Ms D.12, fo 31v.

n.d., [c. 1490], d., *SL*, 190, CCA Lit. Ms D.12, fo 31v.

Note: there are two obits for monks by this name in BL Ms Arundel 68: 14 May (fo 27v) and 21 Oct. (fo 46).

Thomas de BOCKYNG [Bockynge, Bockyngg, Bokkynge

occ. 1337 d. 1357

1337, 20 Sept., described as chaplain at the time of his presentation to the abp, after his adm. (he was one of four), *Lit. Cant.*, no 633 (Reg. L, fo 68v).

1337, 30 Sept., one of three prof., *SL*, 180, CCA Lit. Ms D.12, fo 4.

1350/1, *custos* of St Mary in crypt, CCA DCc Treas. acct 27, fo 2v.

1340, June, possibly at Canterbury college, Oxford, with James de Oxney and John de Frome, q.v., (as T. de B), Pantin, *Cant. Coll. Ox.*, iv, 6, quoting *Lit. Cant.*, no 691 (Reg. L, fo 75).

1349, 4 June, 47th in order at the el. of an abp, Reg. G, fo 60v.

1349, 8/9 Sept., 46th at the el. of an abp and one of thirteen *compromissorii*, *ib.*, fos 76v, 77.

1357, 2 Aug., d., CCA Lit. Ms D.12, fo 17; his obit is in BL Ms Arundel 68, fo 36v.

Name in Cambridge, Trinity College Ms 85, Matheus et Marcus (13th c.)

William BOCKYNG [Bockynge, Bokking, Bokkyng
occ. 1432 d. 1457

1432, 19 Sept., one of six prof., *SL*, 18, CCA Lit. Ms D.12, fo 7.
1434, 13 Mar., ord acol. and subdcn, infirmary chapel in the priory, *Reg. abp Chichele*, iv, 378.
1435, 2 Apr., ord dcn, infirmary chapel, *ib.*, iv, 389.
1436, 3 Mar., ord pr., infirmary chapel, *ib.*, iv, 384.
1448/9, feretrar, CCA DCc MA4, fo 216.
1457, before d., penitentiary, *Chron. Stone*, 70.
1457, 18 Sept., d., *ib.*, 70 and CCA Lit. Ms D.12, fo 25ᵛ; his obit is in BL Ms Arundel 68, fo 42.

BOCKYNG
see also Bokkyng, Bokkynge

BOCLONDE
see Buklond

Eudo de BOCTON [Ewdo, Ivo or Odo, Boughton
occ. [c.1281] d. 1309

[c.1281], one of four prof. *SL*, 176, CCA Lit. Ms D.12, fo 3.
1295, 12/14 Apr., apptd chamberlain (as Odo), *Reg. abp Winchelsey*, 18, 20; also Reg. Q, fo 38, Reg. I, fo 175.
1299, 2 Feb., moved from the above office to that of warden of the East Kent manors, *Reg. abp Winchelsey*, 321, and Reg. Q, fo 40ᵛ. On 7 Dec., the abp wrote to the prior permitting, for this time only, his transfer from the office of his nomination to one of theirs, CCA DCc EC V/5.
1303, 23 Nov., removed from the office of sacrist, *Reg. abp Winchelsey*, 1305 (Reg. Q, fo 30ᵛ/42).
1309, 27 Oct., d., CCA Lit. Ms D.12, fo 15ᵛ.

An inventory of vestments, *temp.* prior Eastry, includes an alb 'consuta cum scutis' described as his [?gift], Legg and Hope, *Inventories*, 60 (BL Ms Cotton Galba E.iv, fo 115).

John de BOCTON [Boctune, Boughton
occ. 1259/60 d. 1307

n.d., name occ. in the list in *SL*, 175, CCA Lit. Ms D.12, fo 2.
1260, Dec./1261, Dec., treasurer, one of three this yr, CCA DCc MA1, fos 102ᵛ, 103ᵛ.
1268, cellarer, *ib.*, fo 112.
1259/60 pd a visit to Meopham, CCA DCc Meopham acct 1.
1270, 7 Sept., one of seven *compromissorii* named for the el. of an abp, *Gervase Cant.*, ii, 252.
1270, 14/15 Oct., penitentiary, who presided over the court of Canterbury as commissary for Geoffrey de Romenal, q.v., official, *sed. vac.*, Selden Soc., *Select Cases Eccles.*, 19.
1307, d., *SL*, 175 (Cambridge, Corpus Christi College, Ms 298).

Name heads a list of vols in the Eastry catalogue, nos 635–?641, James, *Ancient Libraries*, 72.

Name also in several of the missing books in a list dated 1 Mar. 1338: the Senatoris of Cassiodorus, Grecismus (of Everard de Béthune), Brito super prologos bibliae, and an ordinale, *Lit. Cant.*, no 618 (Reg. L, fo 104).

A list of vestments, *temp.* prior Eastry, includes an embroidered chasuble of samite, a cope and other vestments, described as his [gift], Legg and Hope, *Inventories*, 52, 54, 58 (BL MS Cotton Galba E.iv, fos 114ᵛ, 114, 113). One silver *ciphus* and one *de murra* of his are listed in the 1328 inventory of the refectory, Dart, *Antiq. Cant.*, xxii (BL Ms Cotton Galba E.iv, fos 178, 180).

Stephen de BOCTON [Boctone, Boughton
occ. 1330 d. 1361

1330, 9 Oct., one of six prof., *SL*, 180, CCA Lit. Ms D.12, fo 3ᵛ.
1340/1, subchamberlain, CCA DCc Chamb. acct, 35.
1356, 14 Oct., apptd chamberlain after the prior and chapter had sent in the usual three nominations on 11 Oct., Reg. abp Islip, fo 127.
1356/60, chamberlain, Lambeth Ms 1025/8, CCA DCc Ebony acct 57, Chamb. accts 43, 44. He also seems to have served in the office of cellarer in 1356/8, CCA DCc Bart accts 35, 36.
1362/3, cellarer, CCA DCc, Arrears acct 70.
1349, 4 June, 29th in order at the el. of an abp, Reg. G, fo 60ᵛ.
1349, 8/9 Sept., 28th at the el. of an abp, *ib.*, fo 76–76ᵛ.
1355, 10 Feb., was granted a papal licence to choose his own confessor, *CPL*, iii (1342–1362), 578.
1361, 7 Aug., d. in an epidemic which carried off c.25 monks, CCA Lit. Ms D.12, fo 17.

Walter de BOCTON [Boctone
occ. 1299 occ. 1338/9

1299, 24 Aug., one of seven prof., *SL*, 178, CCA Lit. Ms D.12, fo 3ᵛ.
1300, 4 June, ord subdcn, chapel of Smeeth by Aldington, *Reg. abp Winchelsey*, 934.
1338/9, master of the infirmary, CCA DCc Bart. acct 22.

BODRICUS
see Godric

M. John BODY [Bodi
occ. 1337 occ. 1357

1337, 20 Sept., one of four presented to the abp after having been adm. by the prior and chapter, *Lit. Cant.*, no 633 (Reg. L, fo 68ᵛ).

1357, 20 Dec., the university authorities condemned a bachelor in theology for ridiculing him and was required to make a public retractation and apology, Anstey, *Munimenta Acad.* i, 203.

See John de Frome who is prob. this monk.

John de BOKKYNG [Bockynge
occ. [?1241]

n.d., name occ. in the list in *SL*, 174, CCA Lit. Ms D.12, fo 2; he was prob. one of the twelve prof. with Richard de Wynchepe, q.v., c. 1241.

Peter de BOKKYNGE
n.d.

Name occ. only in connection with a lost psalter; see Laurence de Cheyham.

BOKKYNGE
see also Bockyng

John BOKYNGHAM [Blynkham, Bukkyngham
occ. 1480 d. [1493 × 1495]

1480, 25 Jan., one of six prof., *SL*, 191, CCA Lit. Ms D.12, fo 8^{v}.
1480, 1 Apr., ord acol., Canterbury cathedral, *Reg. abp Bourgchier*, 430 (transcribed as Blynkham).
1480, 23 Sept., ord subdcn, Canterbury cathedral, *ib.*, 431.
1481, 22 Sept., ord dcn, Sevenoaks, *ib.*, 432.
1484, 17 Apr., ord pr., Canterbury cathedral, *ib.*, 445.

n.d., fourth prior, *SL*, 191, CCA Lit. Ms D.12, fo 31^{v}.
1493, 1 May, 38th in order at the ratification of an agreement, Reg. S, fo 383^{v}; but see John Crosse I.
[1493 × 1495], d., CCA Lit. Ms D.12, fos 27^{v}, 31^{v}.

I Richard BOKYNGHAM
occ. 1428 d. c. 1474

1428, 2 Jan., prof., *SL*, 187, CCA Lit. Ms D.12, fo 7.
1429, 21 May, ord acol., bp's chapel, Trottisclife, Reg. Langdon (Rochester), fo 74.
[1432], 11 June, ord dcn, place not named, *ib.*, fo 74^{v}.
1433, 28 Mar., ord pr., Charing, *Reg. abp Chichele*, iv, 378.
1437, 30 Oct., apptd *parvus sacrista*, Chron. Wm Glastynbury, fo 117^{v}.
1437, 30 Oct., was *proclamatus de redditu suo*, Chron. Wm Glastynbury, fo 117^{v}. On 11 Nov. he was *absolutus*, *ib.*
1452, 24 Feb., ill and his expenses were 6s. 8d., CCA, Lit. Ms E.6, fo 64^{v}.
1466, 17 Feb., 15th in order in an inventory of *jocalia fratrum* [given by him and/or assigned for his use], and he had none, Reg. N, fo 231.
[c. 1474], described as *stacionarius* at the time of his d., CCA Lit. Ms D.12, fo 26; his obit occ. on 31 Aug., BL Ms Arundel 68, fo 40.

II Richard BOKYNGHAM [Bokenham
occ. 1494 occ. 1511

1494, 1 Aug., one of four tonsured, *SL*, 192, CCA Lit. Ms D.12, fo 9^{v}.
1496, 2 Apr., ord acol., Canterbury cathedral, *Reg. abp Morton*, i, no 445a.
1496, 4 Apr., prof., *SL*, 192, CCA Lit. Ms D.12, fo 9^{v}.
1497, 25 Mar., ord subdcn, Canterbury cathedral, *Reg. abp Morton*, i, no 446b.
1500/1, celebrated his first mass and recd a gift from the sacrist, CCA DCc Sac. acct 70.
1511, 10 Sept., fourth prior, Wood-Legh, *Visit.*, 5.
1501, 26 Apr., 53rd in order at the el. of an abp, Reg. R, fo 56^{v}.
1511, 2 Sept., 36th on the visitation certificate, Wood-Legh, *Visit.* 3 (Reg. abp Warham, i, fo 35^{v}); on 10 Sept he was one of six obedientiaries who, with the prior, were apptd to oversee corrections in the priory after the abp's visitation, Wood-Legh, *Visit.*, 5 (transcribed as John).
n.d., licensed by the abp to transfer to Folkestone, *SL*, 192, CCA Lit. Ms D.12, fo 9^{v}.

William BOLDE [Boolde
occ. 1443 d. [1489 × 1492]

1443, 25 Mar., one of six prof., *SL*, 188, CCA Lit. Ms D.12, fo 7^{v}.
1444, 11 Apr., ord subdcn, Canterbury cathedral, Reg. abp Stafford, fo 196^{v}.
1445, 27 Mar., ord dcn, Canterbury cathedral, *ib.*, fo 198^{v}.
1449, 12 Apr., ord pr., Canterbury cathedral, *ib.*, fo 203^{v}.

[c. 1490], *magister tumbe*, *SL*, 188, CCA Lit. Ms D.12, fos 27, 31^{v}.
1466, 17 Feb, 31st in order in an inventory of *jocalia fratrum* [given by him and/or assigned for his use], Reg. N, fo 232^{v}.
[1489 × 1492], d., *SL*, 188, CCA Lit. Ms D.12, fos 27, 31^{v}; his obit is on 4 Feb. in BL Ms Arundel 68, fo 15.

Name in Oxford, Bod. Ms 648, Miscellanea (15th c.) which includes treatises on medicine, astrology and doctrine as well as lists of religious houses, popes, abps etc; on fo 6, *iste liber constat*—, 1468. There is no evidence that he was the author of any part of this volume. See William Molassh I.

Possibly a relative of the M. William Boolde, notary, who was el. mayor of Canterbury in 1457, *Chron. Stone*, 71.

William BOLWELL
occ. 2nd half 13th c.

n.d., name occ. in the list in SL 174, CCA Lit. Ms D.12, fo 2.

BOMUND
see Bemond

Geoffrey BONDE [Boonde, Bounde, Bownd, Bownde
occ. 1408/9 d. 1446

1408/9, 13 Oct. (feast of translation of Edward, king), formerly monk of St Albans, made his prof. at Christ Church, *SL*, 185, CCA Lit. Ms D.12, fo 6.

1421, 20 Dec., apptd precentor, *Reg. abp Chichele*, iv, 242.

1428, Mar., 1435, precentor, Oxford Bod. Ms Tanner 165, fo 3, 'Chron. Wm Glastynbury', 129.

1414, 12 Mar., 48th in order at the el. of an abp, *Reg. abp Chichele*, i, 4 and Reg. G, fo 290.

1428, c. 1 Mar., with Thomas Goldwell I, q.v., sent to the abp at Lambeth to inform him of the d. of prior John Wodnesburgh, q.v., Oxford, Bod. Ms Tanner 165, fo 3–3^{v}.

1439, 7 Jan., one of six who were granted exit leave *pro recreacione* and returned 20 Jan., Chron. Wm Glastynbury, fo 182^{v}.

1446, 5 Oct., d., in his 37th yr as a monk at Christ Church; the writer of CCA Lit. Ms D.12 adds this eulogy on fo 25: 'Flos precentorum laicorum vel monachorum.' Obit in BL Ms Arundel 68, fo 44.

His departure from St Albans caused a stir, more especially since it was said to have been due to the attraction of higher standards of musical performance at Christ Church, Amundesham, *Annales*, i, 89, where he is not mentioned by name but is described as the despicable monk who lured William Powns, q.v., to follow his example. See F. D. Logan, *Runaway Religious*, Cambridge, 1996.

BONDO
n.d.

n.d., pr., whose obit occ. on 22 July in BL Ms Arundel 68, fo 35^{v}.

BONG(H)AY
see Bungay

I Richard de BONYNGTON
occ. 1333 d. 1346

1333, 9 Oct., one of eleven prof., *SL*, 180, CCA Lit. Ms D.12, fo 4.

1346, 25 Oct., d., CCA Lit. Ms D.12, fo 16^{v}.

II Richard BONYNGTON [Bonnyngton
occ. 1510 occ. 1540

1509, 22 Dec., ord acol., Canterbury cathedral, Reg. abp Warham, ii, fo 264^{v}.

1510, 16 June, one of eight tonsured, *SL*, 194, CCA Lit. Ms D.12, fo 11.

1511, 1 Jan., prof., *ib.*,

1511, 19 Apr., ord dcn, Canterbury cathedral, Reg. abp Warham, ii, fo 265^{v}.

1516 [Apr.], celebrated his first mass and recd 4d. from the penitentiary, William Ingram I, q.v., Lit. Ms C.11, fo 126^{v}.

[1538, 8 Feb., after] *custos tumbe*, Pantin, *Cant. Coll. Ox.*, iii, 152.

n.d., as a junior he was instructed by William Molassh II, q.v., *et non perfecit*, Pantin, *Cant. Coll. Ox.*, iv, 54 (CCA DCc Ms Scrap Book B.186).

1511, 2 Sept., 75th in order on the visitation certificate, Wood-Legh, *Visit.*, 3 (Reg. abp Warham, i, fo 35^{v}).

1534, 12 Dec., acknowledged the Act of Supremacy, *DK 7th Report*, Appndx 2, 282.

[1538, 8 Feb., after], in a list of monks prob. prepared for Thomas Cromwell he was described as a 'symple' man, 53 yrs old, Pantin, *Cant. Coll. Ox.*, iii, 152.

1540, 4 Apr., awarded £8, *L and P Henry VIII*, xv, no 452.

Thomas de BONYNGTON [?Bovynton
occ. 1294 d. 1329

1294, 18 Oct., one of eight prof., *SL*, 178, CCA Lit. Ms D.12, fo 3.

1299, 19 Sept., ord pr., Littlebourne, *Reg. abp Winchelsey*, 931.

1324/9, *custos tumbe*, CCA DCc MA2, fos 137^{v}–183^{v}.

1329, 4 Oct., d., CCA Lit. Ms D.12, fo 16.

I William BONYNGTON [Bannynton, Bonnyton, Bonynton, Bonyntone
occ. 1381 d. 1412.

1381, 6 May, one of eight prof., *SL*, 183, CCA Lit. Ms D.12, fo 5.

1385, 23 Sept., ord pr., Mayfield, Reg. abp Courtenay, i, fo 307^{v}.

1408/9, 21 Mar., *magister ordinis*, *SL*, 185, CCA Lit. Ms D.12, fo 6.

1383/4, 1387/8, recd small sums from the prior [?for his organ playing; see below], Lambeth Ms 243, fos 192^{v}, 208^{v}.

1388/9, recd similar small gifts, one was 2s. *pro benedictione*, *ib.*, fo 212^{v}.

1390/1, recd two gifts of 12d. as above, *ib.*, fo 212^{v}.

1396, 7 Aug., 34th in order at the el. of an abp Reg. G, fo 234^{v}.

[1412], 1 Sept., d., described as 'in cantu et ludo organico egregie eruditus', CCA Lit. Ms D.12, fo 19^{v}. His obit, on 2 Sept., is in BL Ms Arundel 68, fo 40.

II William BONYNGTON
occ. 1468 d. 1485

1468, 12 Oct., one of four to rec. the tonsure, *SL*, 190, CCA Lit. Ms D.12, fo 8 (where 1469 has been added later in the margin); *Chron. Stone*, 106, gives the date as 1468, 12 Oct., and adds that he was one of four almonry [school] boys to be clothed on this day.
1469, 1 Apr., ord acol., Canterbury cathedral, *Reg. abp Bourgchier*, 402.
1469, 21 Apr., made his prof., *SL*, 190 (Cambridge, Corpus Christi College, Ms 298).
1470, 21 Apr., ord subdcn, Canterbury cathedral, *Reg. abp Bourgchier*, 406.
1471, 9 Mar., ord dcn, Canterbury cathedral, *Reg. abp Bourgchier*, 405.
1473, 13 Mar., ord pr., Canterbury cathedral, *ib.*, 410.
1485, Oct., one of four monks who d. on the same day of *le Swete*, CCA Lit. Ms D.12, fo 26v; their obit on 15 Oct. is in BL Ms Arundel 68, fo 45.

Name in
(1) Oxford, Bod. Ms Rawlinson B.188, Giraldus Cambrensis (13th c.); *liber— reparatus* A.D.1483; see Cheney, 'Mortuary Rolls', 104.
(2) Manchester, John Rylands University Library, Ms Lat. 474, Biblia (13th c.); *in custodia*— A.D.1483. See John Langdon II.

BOOLDE
see Bolde

BOONDE
see Bonde

BOORNE
see Borne

BORAM
see Borham

BORDEN
see Burden

BOREHAM
see Berham

BORGAT'
see Berigate

William BORHAM [Boram
occ. 1424 d. 1431

1424, 20 Mar., a boy chorister who had been sponsored by abp Chichele at Canterbury college Oxford, now *adjunctus* and tonsured, *SL*, 187, CCA Lit. Ms D.12, fo 7.
1425, 22 Dec., ord subdcn, Charing, *Reg. abp Chichele*, iv, 374.
1426, 30 Mar., ord dcn, Canterbury cathedral, *ib.*, iv, 375.
1428, 3 Apr., ord pr., Rochester cathedral, Reg. Langdon (Rochester), fo 65v.
1431, 9 Aug., d. of the plague and was buried at once; in the absence of the prior, John Salisbury, I, q.v., subprior, performed the funeral rites, *Chron. Stone*, 16–17, where it mistakenly says, in his 36th yr of monastic life. According to CCA Lit. Ms D.12, fo 23, he d. in his 6th yr.

BORHAM
see also Berham

I John BORNE [Boorne, Bourne, Broune, Burne
occ. 1381 d. 1420

1381, 6 May, one of eight prof., *SL*, 183, CCA Lit. Ms D.12, fo 5.
1386, 17 Mar., ord pr., St Stephen's chapel, Westminster, Reg. abp Courtenay, i, fo 308v.
1414, 12 Mar., precentor, *Reg. abp Chichele*, i, 4 (and Reg. G, fo 288).
1416, 24 June, absolved from the above office, *Reg. abp Chichele*, iv, 152.
1423, 3 May, apptd subprior, *ib.*, iv, 247.
n.d., for about 30 yrs, he served as third cantor, succentor and precentor because he had 'inter omnes religiosos regni excellentissimam vocem', CCA Lit. Ms D.12, fo 21v.
1382, 1383/4, 1387/8, 1390/1, recd small sums from the prior, usually 12d. and *pro benedictionibus*, Lambeth Ms 243, fos 183, 192v, 208v, 220v.
1396, 7 Aug., 36th in order at the el. of an abp, Reg. G, fo 234v.
1414, 12 Mar., 8th at the el. of an abp, *Reg. abp Chichele*, i, 4.
1420, 22 Sept., d. of the plague, CCA Lit. Ms D.12, fo 21v; his obit occ. in BL Ms Arundel 68, fo 42v. His obit is also in *Chron. Stone*, 11, which notes that 'stetit in capite quasi per quatuor annos'.

II John BORNE [Bourne, Burne
occ. 1493 occ. 1511

1493, 26 July, one of ten tonsured, *SL*, 192, CCA Lit. Ms D.12, fo 9v.
1494, 29 Mar., ord acol., Canterbury cathedral, *Reg. abp Morton*, i, no 443a.
1494, 19 Apr., prof., *SL*, 192, CCA Lit. Ms D.12, fo 9v.
1495, 18 Apr., ord subdcn, Canterbury cathedral, *Reg. abp Morton*, i, no 444b.
1496, 2 Apr., ord dcn, Canterbury cathedral, *ib.*, i, no 445c.
1501, 26 Apr., 47th in order at the el. of an abp, Reg. R, fo 56v.
1511, 2 Sept., 30th on the visitation certificate, Wood-Legh, *Visit.*, 3 (Reg. abp Warham, i, fo 35v).
n.d., recd licence from the abp to transfer to the Carmelite priory in Coventry, CCA Lit. Ms D.12, fo 9v.

I Nicholas de BORNE [Boorne, Bourn, Bourne, Burn, Burne

occ. [c. 1283] d. 1328

[c. 1283], one of five prof., *SL*, 177, CCA Lit. Ms D.12, fo 3.

1285, 22 Sept., ord dcn, collegiate church, South Malling, *Reg. abp Pecham*, i, 222.

1309, chaplain to the prior, CCA DCc MA2, fo 17ᵛ.

1310, 6 Dec., one of three nom. for the office of cellarer by the prior and chapter and apptd by the abp on 13 Dec., Reg. Q, fo 41/53. See Richard de Sharstede.

1311/12, cellarer, CCA DCc MA2, fos 30–37; on 28 Aug. 1312 he was removed, Reg. Q, fo 38/50; see Simon de St Paul.

1316/17, 1320/1, warden of manors, CCA DCc Bocking acct 11, Illeigh acct 5.

1323/6, *magister corone*, CCA DCc MA2, fos 128ᵛ–154ᵛ.

1292, 11 Nov., sent with Geoffrey de Chilham, q.v., as proctors to the abp, CUL Ms Ee.5.31, fo 34ᵛ.

1309, 25 Apr., apptd proctor in parliament, with Thomas de Wynchelse I, q.v., CUL Ms Ee.5.31, fo 111; on 19 Nov. of this yr, these two were named to attend the provincial council at St Paul's London, *ib.*, fo 112.

1323, 8 Jan., with the prior, subprior and other monks acted as witness at the adm. of a rector, *ib.*, fo 228.

1323/4, pd the lector, Stephen de Faversham, q.v., 20s. de *corona*, Pantin, *Cant. Coll. Ox.*, iv, 177.

1328, 10 Oct., d., CCA Lit. Ms D.12, fo 16.

His name heads a list of vestments recorded in an inventory of those acquired *temp.* prior Eastry, Legg and Hope, *Inventories*, 67 (BL Ms Cotton Galba E.iv, fo 118). A *cuppa de murra*, with a silver cover, two silver *ciphi*, thirteen spoons and three *ciphi de murra* are listed as his in an inventory of the refectory dated 29 Sept., 1328, Dart, *Antiq. Cant.*, xviii, xx, xxiii (BL Ms Cot. Galba E.iv, fos 178, 179, 180ᵛ).

II Nicholas BORNE [Boorne, Bourne

occ. 1473 d. 1487

1473, 13 Mar., ord acol., Canterbury cathedral, *Reg. abp Bourgchier*, 410 (as Richard).

1473, 28 Apr., one of six prof., *SL*, 190, CCA Lit. Ms D.12, fo 8ᵛ).

1475, 23 Sept., ord dcn, Canterbury cathedral, *Reg. abp Bourgchier*, 418.

1487, 18 July, d., *de frenesi*, CCA Lit. Ms D.12, fo 27; the obit of Nicholas Borne, dcn, occ. on 10 July in BL Ms Arundel 68, fo 33ᵛ.

I Thomas de BORNE [Bourne, Burne

occ. 1295 d. 1345

1295, 23 Nov., one of five prof., *SL*, 178, CCA Lit. Ms D.12, fo 3.

1299, 19 Sept., ord dcn, Littlebourne, *Reg. abp Winchelsey*, 930.

1300, 4 June, ord pr., Smeeth Chapel by Aldington, *ib.*, 936.

1307/8, Dec., subchamberlain, CCA DCc MA2, fos 11ᵛ–17ᵛ, Chamb. acct 1.

1315/21, 1323/4, warden of manors, CCA DCc Agney acct 30, Loose acct 32, West Farleigh acct 30, Agney acct 31, Ebony accts 32 and 33, MA2, fos 126–135.

1324/7, treasurer, CCA DCc MA2, fos 135–162.

1327/9, warden of manors, CCA DCc MA2, fos 162–182.

1329/30, cellarer, CCA DCc MA2, fos 184ᵛ–193.

1330/1, warden of manors, CCA DCc Ebony acct 39.

1330/1, May, bartoner, CCA DCc Bart acct 19.

1331/6, warden of manors, CCA DCc MA2, fos 199–248.

1336, chaplain to the prior, CCA DCc MA2, fo 250ᵛ.

1336/7, granator, CCA DCc, Gran. acct 30.

1337, Jan./Sept., 1337/44, almoner, CCA DCc Alm. accts 43, 46, Eastry accts 65, 66, 68, Monkton acct 70, Eastry acct 71, Monkton acct 70.

1335, 26 Oct., one of the senior monks who approved the apptment of the steward of the liberty, *Lit. Cant.*, no 587 (Reg. L, fo 107ᵛ).

1337, 20 Sept., presented four candidates to the abp who had been adm. to the monastery, *Lit. Cant.*, no 633 (Reg. L, fo 68ᵛ); see John Frome (Body), Thomas de Bockyng, Edmund de Chymbeham, William de Hethe.

1345, 31 Aug., d., CCA Lit. Ms D.12, fo 16ᵛ.

II Thomas BORNE

occ. 1384 d. 1435

1384, 29 Aug., one of seven prof., *SL*, 183, CCA Lit. Ms D.12, fo 5.

1386, 21 Apr., ord subdcn, Canterbury cathedral, Reg. abp Courtenay, i, fo 308ᵛ.

1389, 12 June, ord dcn, St Dunstan's church, London, *ib.*, i, fo 311ᵛ.

1391, 25 Mar., ord pr., Canterbury cathedral, *ib.*, i, fo 312.

1414, 2nd day after the abp's enthronement, apptd subprior, *Reg. abp Chichele*, iv, 115.

1423, 3 May, [re]apptd subprior, *ib.*, iv, 247.

1435, before his d., *coronarius*, CCA Lit. Ms D.12, fo 23ᵛ.

1392/3, gave the sacrist 3s. 4d. *pro dealbacione chori*, CCA DCc Sac. acct 11.

1396, 7 Aug., 46th in order at the el. of an abp, Reg. G, fo 234ᵛ.

1414, 12 Mar., 15th at the el. of an abp, *Reg. abp Chichele*, i, 4.

[1435], 18 Mar. (St Ethelbert), d., in the 50th yr of his monastic life; he was buried at once because of '?fetrie apostema[tioni]s in capite emergentis', CCA Lit. Ms D.12, fo 23ᵛ.

III Thomas BORNE [Boorne, Bourne
occ. 1465 d. c. 1471

1465, 4 Apr., one of seven prof., SS, 190, CCA Lit. Ms D.12. fo 8.
1465, 13 Apr., ord subdcn, no place named, *Reg. abp Bourgchier*, 391.
1467, 28 Mar., ord dcn, Canterbury cathedral, *ib*., 399.
1470, 21 Apr., ord pr., Canterbury cathedral, *ib*., 406.
1469/70, celebrated his first mass and recd a gift from the sacrist, Woodruff, 'Sacrist's Rolls', 63 (CCA DCc Sac. acct 48).
c. 1471, d., and described as *conventualis*, CCA Lit. Ms D.12, fo 26.

Walter de BORNE [Bourne
occ. 2nd half 13th c.

n.d., name occ. in the list in *SL*, 174, CCA Lit. Ms D.12, fo 2.
n.d., subprior of Dover, *Lit. Cant.* iii, Appndx no 34 (CCA DCc Z.D.4, 23).
An inventory of the refectory of 1328 includes a *ciphus de murra* of his, BL Ms Cotton Galba E.iv, fo 179^{v}.
See note in the entry below.

William de BORNE [Bourne, Burn
occ. 1280 d. 1300

n.d., name occ. in the list in *SL*, 176,. CCA Lit. Ms D.12, fo 2^{v}.
1280, 1284/95, 1298/9, 1300, sacrist, CCA DCc MA1 fos 132^{v}–139^{v}, 215^{v}–222, 225.
1300, 28 May, d., CCA Lit. Ms D.12, fo 15^{v}; obit in BL Ms Arundel 68, fo 28^{v}.

Note
(1) a W. de Bourne is named in:
 (a) one of the missing books (in an inventory of 1 Mar. 1338): Vitae Beati Thomae et Anselmi which Edward II had borrowed and failed to return, *Lit. Cant.*, no 618 (Reg. L, fo 104);
 (b) Benedictionale cum exequiis mortuorum of——, *temp.* prior Eastry, Legg and Hope, *Inventories*, 75 (BL Ms Cotton Galba E.iv, fo 121).
(2) There is also a chasuble of W. de Bourne *de panno de Inde brudat'* in an inventory of vestments, acquired *temp.* prior Eastry, Legg and Hope, *Inventories*, 52 (BL Ms Cotton Galba E.iv, fo 112); also two silver *ciphi* in the 1328 inventory of the refectory are denoted as having belonged to W. de Bourne, Dart, *Antiq. Cant.*, xx (BL Ms Cotton Galba E.iv, fo 178^{v}).

BOTAYLE
see Batayle

Thomas BOUGHIER [Bochar, Bowcer, Bowser
occ. 1527 occ. 1540

1527, 15 May, one of twelve tonsured, *SL*, 195, CCA Lit. Ms D.12, fo 12.
1528, 2 Mar., prof., *ib.*
[1538, 8 Feb., after], third cantor, Pantin, *Cant. Coll. Ox.*, iii, 153.
1534, 12 Dec., acknowledged the Act of Supremacy, *DK 7th Report*, Appndx 2, 282.
[1538, 8 Feb., after], in a list of monks prob. prepared for Thomas Cromwell he was described as 'a good man' and 29 yrs old, Pantin, *Cant. Coll. Ox.*, iii, 153.
1540, 4 Apr., awarded £3 p.a. and became epistoler in the new foundation, *L and P Henry VIII*, xv, no 452.

BOUGHTON
see Bocton

BOUNDE, BOWNDE
see Bonde

BOURNE
see Borne

BOVYNTON
see Bonyngton

BOWCER, Bowser
see Boughier

Robert BOXLEE [Boxle, Boxley
occ. 1506 occ. 1540

1506, 21 Mar., one of six tonsured, *SL*, 193, CCA Lit. Ms D.12, fo 10^{v}.
1506, 11 Apr., ord acol., Canterbury cathedral, Reg. abp Warham, ii, fo 262^{v}.
1506, 30 Sept., prof., *SL*, 193, CCA Lit. Ms D.12, fo 10^{v}.
1507, 3 Apr., ord subdcn, Canterbury cathedral, Reg. abp Warham, ii, fo 263.
1508, 22 Apr., ord dcn, Canterbury cathedral, *ib.*, ii, fo 263^{v}.
1511, 19 Apr., ord pr., Canterbury cathedral, *ib.*, ii, fo 265^{v}.
1510/11, celebrated his first mass and recd a gift from the sacrist, Woodruff, 'Sacrist's Rolls', 69 (CCA DCc 5ac.acct 73); the date was the third Sunday in April 1511, when the *custos martyrii* gave him 4d., CCA Lit. Ms C.11, fo 52.
[1538, 8 Feb., after], 1540, 4 Apr., 'master of the table halle' [*magister mense*], Pantin, *Cant. Coll. Ox.*, iii, 152, *L and P Henry VIII*, xv, no 542.
n.d., as a junior he was instructed by Alexander Staple II, q.v., Pantin, *Cant. Coll. Ox.*, iv, 54 (CCA DCc Ms Scrap Book B.186).
1511, 2 Sept., 65th in order on the visitation certificate, Wood-Legh, *Visit.*, 3 (Reg. abp Warham, i, fo 35^{v}).

1520/1, spent some time ill in the infirmary, CCA DCc Infirm. acct 2.
1534, 12 Dec., acknowledged the Act of Supremacy, *DK 7th Report*, Appndx 2, 282.
[1538, 8 Feb., after], in a list of monks prob. prepared for Thomas Cromwell he was described as 'a good man' aged 54 yrs, Pantin, *Cant. Coll. Ox.*, iii, 152.
1540, 4 Apr., awarded £8 p.a., *L and P Henry VIII*, xv, no 452.

John BOXWELL B.Th.
occ. 1488 d. 1504

1488, 30 Sept., one of six tonsured, *SL*, 192, CCA Lit. Ms D.12, fo 9.
1490, 4 Apr., made his prof. before the abp, CCA Lit. Ms D.12, *ib.*; the delay in prof. did not preclude the six from having 'pecunias sicut ceteri fratres cum ebd' servicio et assignacione ad refect' et mensam conventus' by permission of the prior and *magister ordinis*, *ib.*
1491, 2 Apr., ord acol., Canterbury cathedral, *Reg. abp Morton*, i, no 439a.
1493, 6 Apr., ord subdcn, Canterbury cathedral, *ib.*, i, no 442b.
1495, 14 Mar., ord dcn, Abingdon, Reg. Blythe (Salisbury), fo 104ᵛ, by *lit. dim.*
1498/9, celebrated his first mass, CCA DCc MA9, fo 153.
1495, 8 Feb., one of six scholars at Canterbury college from whom letters of proxy were obtained at the time of the el. of a prior, Pantin, *Cant. Coll. Ox.*, iv, 203.
1500/1, student and recd money for travelling expenses between Oxford and Canterbury, *ib.*, iv, 205. He was absent from the archiepiscopal el. on 26 Apr. 1501, Reg. R, fo 56ᵛ.
n.d., B.Th., CCA Lit. Ms D.12, fo 34ᵛ. A letter, undated as to the yr, from him to the treasurer asking for his grace which 'must coste me a marke or a xs' is in Pantin, *Cant. Coll. Ox.*, iii, 131–132.
1493, 1 May, 61st in order at the ratification of an agreement, Reg. S, fo 383ᵛ; but see John Crosse I.
1504, 9 Mar., d. *ex febribus et consumpcione*; he was 'ultimus senior in superiori choro', was 28 yrs old and had been a monk for fourteen, CCA Lit. Ms D.12, fo 34ᵛ.

Nicholas de BOYWYKE [Boywik, Boywyk
occ. 1329 d. 1359

1329, 9 Oct., one of eight prof., *SL*, 180, CCA Lit. Ms D.12, fo 3ᵛ.
1349, 4 June, 25th in order at the el. of an abp, Reg. G, fo 60ᵛ.
1349, 8/9 Sept., 24th at the el. of an abp, *ib.*, fo 76.
[1357], recd 15s. from the treasurer, Lambeth Ms 243, fo 104ᵛ.
1359, 25 Feb., d., CCA Lit. Ms D.12, fo 17.

John BRACY
occ. 1450 d. 1454

1450, 25 Jan., one of seven prof., *SL*, 189, CCA Lit. Ms D.12, fo 7ᵛ.
1450, 3 Apr., ord acol., Canterbury cathedral, Reg. abp Stafford, fo 204.
1451, 20 Mar., ord subdcn, Canterbury cathedral, *ib.*, fo 205ᵛ.
1452, 8 Apr., ord dcn, Canterbury cathedral, *ib.*, fo 206ᵛ.
1452, 5 Apr., ill and his expenses were 3s. 4d., CCA Lit. Ms E.6, fo 64ᵛ.
1454, 19 Apr., dcn, d., CCA Lit. Ms D.12, fo 25ᵛ and *Chron. Stone*, 59. His d. is also recorded on the prior's acct (CCA DCc Prior acct 9) which reports that he left 52s. *de peculis.*

Peter BRADGARE [Bredyar
occ. 1527 occ. 1534

1527, 25 May, one of twelve tonsured, *SL*, 195, CCA Lit. Ms D.12, fo 12.
1528, 2 Mar., prof., *ib.*
1534, 12 Dec., acknowledged the Act of Supremacy, *DK 7th Report*, Appndx 2, 282.

Thomas BRADGARE [Bradgour, Bredgar
occ. 1462 d. 1510/11

1462, 17 Apr., ord acol., Canterbury cathedral, *Reg. abp Bourgchier*, 380.
[1462], 6 Dec., one of six prof., *SL*, 190, CCA Lit. Ms D.12, fo 8.
Note: this has been incorrectly dated 1464 in the margin of the ms; 1462 (or 1463) seems more likely.
1464, 31 Mar., ord subdcn, Canterbury cathedral, *Reg. abp Bourgchier*, 390.
1469, 1 Apr., ord pr., Canterbury cathedral, *ib.*, 402.
1468/9, celebrated his first mass and recd a gift from the sacrist, CCA DCc Sac. acct 47.
1475, 29 Sept., second warden of manors, CCA DCc Monk Warden acct 7.
1479, chancellor with William Garard, q.v., Reg. S, fo 300–300ᵛ.
1482/4, second treasurer, Lambeth ED85, CCA DCc Treas. acct 20.
1487, Apr., warden of manors, CCA DCc Ms Scrap Book B.47.
1490/1509, sacrist, CCA DCc MA5 fo 48; the accts for each yr from 1493/1509 in order are as follows: CCA DCc Sac. accts 63, 59, MA10 fo 1, Sac. acct 67, MA9 fo 119, MA9 fo 153, MA10 fo 81, MA10 fo 97, MA10 fo 145, Sac. acct 61, MA10 fo 206, Sac. acct 66, MA11 fo 32, Sac. accts 64, 71.
1466, 17 Feb., 75th in order in an inventory of *jocalia fratrum* [given by him and/or assigned for his use], Reg. N, fo 235.
1487, 12 Feb., appted proctor for convocation, Reg. S, fo 346ᵛ.

1501, 26 Apr., 9th in order at the el. of an abp, Reg. R, fo 56[v]; he was 7th on 24 Apr. among those present and eligible to el., *ib.*, fo 56.
1510/11, d., Woodruff 'Sacrist's Rolls', 69 (CCA DCc Sac. acct 73).

Gave two embroidered albs and amices of white damask, Legg and Hope, *Inventories*, 218, 228.

William BRADGARE [Bredgar, Bredgare
occ. 1502 occ. 1519

1502, 25 Aug., one of eight tonsured, *SL*, 193, CCA Lit. Ms D.12, fo 10.
1503, 4 Apr., made his prof. before the prior, *sed. vac.*, *ib.*
1505, 22 Mar., ord dcn, Canterbury cathedral, Reg. abp Warham, ii, fo 262.
1507, 3 Apr., ord pr., Canterbury cathedral, *ib.*, ii, fo 263; he celebrated on the first Sunday in May and recd 4d. from the *custos martyrii*, CCA Lit. Ms C.11, fo 49[v].
1517, 29 Sept., 1519, 25 Mar., feretrar, CCA DCc CCA Lit. Ms C.11, fos 58[v], 59[v].

1511, 2 Sept., 55th in order on the visitation certificate, Wood-Legh, *Visit.*, 3 (Reg. abp Warham, i, fo 35[v]).

William BRADLE [?Bradel', Bradlee
occ. 1st half 13th c.

n.d., name occ. in the list in *SL*, 174, CCA Lit. Ms D.12, fo 1[v].

?1244, a W. de Bradel' was cellarer, CCA DCc MA1 fo 85[v].

Peter BRAMBLYNG'
occ. 2nd half 13th c.

n.d., name occ. in the list in *SL*, 175, CCA Lit. Ms D.12, fo 2[v].

BRAMBLYNG'
see also Bremble, Bremblyng

BRAN
see Brau

M. Helyas de BRANDEFELD [Brantefeld
occ. 1206/7

1206/7, foremost [*praecipuus*] among the monks whom the king sent to Rome concerning the confirmation of John de Grey bp of Norwich as abp, *Flores Hist.*, ii, 131, Paris, *Chronica Majora*, ii, 494. (He was postulated by the monks in Dec. 1205, *Fasti*, ii, 5.) Knowles has thrown doubt on the identification of Brandefeld as a monk in 'Cant. Election of 1205–6', 219.
1207, refused to consent to the el. of Stephen Langton as abp, Paris, *Chronica Majora*, ii, 515.

See Elias III who may be the same monk.

Robert BRANDREDE [Brandred
occ. 1363 occ. 1381

1363, 6 Aug., ord acol., apb's chapel, Canterbury, Reg. abp Islip, fo 323.
1364, n.d., one of eleven prof., *SL*, 182, CCA Lit. Ms D.12, fo 4[v].
1364, 9 Mar., ord subdcn, apb's chapel, Charing, Reg. abp Islip, fo 325.
1365, 29 Mar., ord dcn, apb's chapel, Charing, *ib.*, fo 326.
1367, 18 Sept., ord pr., Lambeth palace chapel, *Reg. abp Langham*, 383.
1374, 30 June, 40th in order at the el. of an abp, Reg. R, fos 173[v]–175[v].
1381, 31 July, 28th at the el. of an abp, *ib.*, fo 225[v].

Andrew de BRAU [?Bran, Braun
occ. 1st half 13th c.

n.d., name occ. in the list in *SL*, 173, CCA Lit. Ms D.12, fo 1[v].

Note: see Andrew de Biham who may be the same monk.

Thomas BRAY
occ. 1416 d. 1427

1416, 22 June, one of eight prof., *SL*, 186, CCA Lit. Ms D.12, fo 6.
1417, 10 Apr., ord acol., Canterbury cathedral, *Reg. abp Chichele*, iv, 327.
1419, 1 Apr., ord subdcn, chapel in the priory, *ib.*, i, 191.
1420, 6 Apr., ord dcn, Canterbury cathedral, *ib.*, iv, 342.
1427, before d., sacrist, CCA Lit. Ms D.12, fo 22.
1427, 9 Mar., d., described as 'languens in infirmaria tilitus et ethicus'; the exequies and burial rites on the same day were performed by Henry [Sutton], q.v., subprior, CCA Lit. Ms D.12, fo 22; his obit, on 6 Mar. is in BL Ms Arundel 68, fo 19.

BREDGAR(E), Bredyar
see Bradgare

BREGG, Breggar
see Brygge

BREIDLINTONE
see Brydlyntone

John de BREMBLE
occ. 1188/9

1188, [Jan.], one of the monks who followed prior Honorius, q.v., to Rome during the appeal vs the abp, *Epist. Cant.* 181.
1188, Feb./1189, Aug., wrote a series of letters to the subprior, Geoffrey, II, q.v., and brethren in Canterbury in the course of his travels; these provide a narrative of events and furnish

insight into the operations of papal policy and administration. He and his companions crossed the St Bernard pass in Feb. (*Epist. Cant.*, 181), reached Rome on 27 Feb. (*ib.*, 193–194), were at Arras in or before July (*ib.*, 226), and at the monastery of S. Bertin in Aug. (*ib.*, 229–230), back in Rome in Jan. 1189 where Honorius d. (*ib.*, 275), in Paris in Apr. (*ib.*, 287–288), and on their way to deliver the papal mandate they had obtained to the kings of England and France and to the abp at Le Mans (*ib.*, 289–290), where John had a direct encounter with the abp (*ib.*, 292).

1189, 3 Aug., the abp, not surprisingly, demanded the removal of John as well as of the subprior (*ib.*, 298).

John de BREMBLYNG
occ. 2nd half 13th c.

n.d., name occ. in the list in *SL*, 174, CCA Lit. Ms D.12, fo 2.

Edmund BRENKLE [Brenkele, Rrenkle, Rreulee
occ. 1423 d. 1440

1423, 23 Feb., pr., and formerly a monk of Chester, made his prof. before the prior at Christ Church, *SL*, 187, CCA Lit. Ms D.12, fo 6v.

1440, 10 Oct., d., CCA Lit. Ms D.12, fo 24, *Chron. Stone*, 27; his obit occ. in BL Ms Arundel 68, fo 44v.

BRIAN
see Bryan

BRICE
n.d.

n.d., his nephew, Eadwyne clerk, gave land to the Dover monks, Lambeth MS 241, fo 90.

BRIDLINTONE
see Brydlynton

BRIGIA
see Brygge

BRIHTELINUS
n.d.

n.d., 7 Feb., pr., whose obit occ. in BL Ms Arundel 68, fo 15v.

Thomas BRINGHAY
n.d.

n.d., 31 Oct., obit occ. in BL Ms Arundel 68, fo 47.

Osbern/Osbert de BRISTOL [Bristo, Bristou
occ. 1189/91

1191, prior: apptd by the abp Jan./Feb. 1191, but expelled by the monks 10 May, *Fasti*, ii, 10, *HRH*, 34.

1189, 26 Mar., described by Gervase, q.v., as *cucullatus non monachus* in company with Roger Norreys I, q.v., 'the other Judas', *Gervase Cant.*, i, 443, *Epist. Cant.*, 285, 286. Like Roger he took the abp's side vs the monks in the controversy over the abp's proposed collegiate foundation at Hackington and prob. left the cloister with him, only to return when Roger was apptd prior by the abp. on 6 Oct. 1189, *Gervase Cant.*, i, 460.

1189, 6 Oct., after, given charge of all the priory manors under the regime of the new prior, and the abp, *Epist. Cant.*, 312.

1191, 10 May, expelled by the monks, taking authority into their own hands, *Gervase Cant.*, i, 495; he was succ. by Geoffrey II, q.v., and 'honorifice in camera honestiori infirmorum exhibitus est', *ib.*, i, 496, and see *Epist. Cant.*, 334.

Note: see the note under Osbern about the vol. in the 12th c. catalogue entitled Musica Osberni.

BRITHRICUS
n.d.

n.d., 27 Nov., obit occ. in BL Ms Arundel 68, fo 49v.

BRITHWALDUS
n.d.

n.d., 23 Aug., obit occ. in BL Ms Arundel 68, fo 39.

William BRITO [Briton
occ. [1159] occ. [1174/5]

[1159, 1167 × 1170, 1174 × 1175], subprior, in succ. to Wibert, q.v., *Salisbury Letters*, i, no 111, ii, nos 294, 323.

[1159], there is a derogatory remark in a letter of John of Salisbury complaining of his failure to return John's Policraticus, *Salisbury Letters*, i, no 111.

[1167/70], recd several letters from John, *ib.*, nos 242, 243 (in which he is rebuked for his failure to support the abp), 245, 247, 293, 294, 303 (and see Robert III, sacrist).

[1174 × 1175], recd a letter addressed jointly to prior Odo, q.v., and to him, *ib.*, no 323.

n.d., 6 Dec., obit— *quondam* subprior, BL Mss Cotton Nero C.ix, fo 17 and Arundel 68, fo 50.

Name attached to three vols in the late 12th-c. library catalogue, nos 6, 49, 203, James, *Ancient Libraries*, 7, 8, 12; and to a number of items in the Eastry catalogue, nos 108, 350, 397, 985–989, James, *Ancient Libraries*, 29, 52, 53, 96; see below.

Name in

(1) Oxford, Bod. Ms Digby 5, Seneca (12th c.).

(2) CUL Ms Gg.4.17, P.Cantor Liber de tropis loquendi, possibly no 988 in the Eastry catalogue (see above); the hand is late 12th/early 13th c., but there is some doubt that the list

of vols beneath his name extends to include this item.

BROCHULL
see Brokhell

John BROKE [Brook
occ. 1459 occ. 1511

1459, 30 Nov., one of six prof., *SL*, 189, CCA Lit. Ms D.12, fo 8.
1461, 4 Apr., ord dcn, Canterbury cathedral, *Reg. abp Bourgchier*, 378.
1464, 22 Dec., ord pr., abp's chapel, Otford, *ib.*, 388.
1472/3, first anniversarian, CCA DCc Anniv. acct 14.
1477/82, treasurer, CCA DCc MA27, fos 113–215.
1489/1503, chamberlain, CCA DCc MA7, fos 131, 147^{v}, 168^{v}; MA9, fos 3^{v}, 44, 68; MA10, fo 4; MA9, fos 94, 122; MA10, fos 50, 87, 34^{v}, 100, 147^{v}.
1466, 17 Feb., 63rd in order in an inventory of *jocalia fratrum* [given by him and/or assigned for his use], and he had none, Reg. N, fo 234^{v}.
1493, 1 May, 17th in order at the ratification of an agreement, Reg. S, fo 383^{v}; but see John Crosse I.
1501, 26 Apr., 6th in order at the el. of an abp, Reg. R, fo 56^{v}.
1511, 2 Sept., 2nd on the visitation certificate, Wood-Legh, *Visit.*, 3 (Reg. abp Warham, i, fo 35).
n.d., 14 Apr., obit occ. in BL Ms Arundel 68, fo 24.

Name in CUL Ms Ii.3.1, Polychronicon (14th c.); on an end flyleaf: *Iste liber constat*—.

Walter BROKE [Brook
occ. 1431 d. 1457

1431, 18 Apr., one of four prof., *SL*, 187, CCA Lit. Ms D.12, fo 7.
1433, 28 Mar., ord acol., Charing, *Reg. abp Chichele*, iv, 377.
1434, 13 Mar., ord dcn, infirmary chapel in the priory, *ib.*, iv, 379.
1435, 2 Apr., ord pr., infirmary chapel, *ib.*, iv, 389.
1457, 27 Mar., d. and his body lay in the choir through the night, *Chron. Stone*, 66; he is described as *conventualis* in the notice in CCA Lit. Ms D.12, fo 25^{v}, and his obit is in BL MS Arundel 68, fo 18, on 24 Feb.

John de BROKHELL [Brochull, Brokheld, Brokehell
occ. 1353 occ. 1381

1353, 27 Sept., one of five prof., *SL*, 181, CCA Lit. Ms D.12, fo 4.
1374, 30 June, 14th in order at the el. of an abp, Reg. G, fos 173^{v}, 199.
1380, recd a small sum from the prior, Lambeth Ms 243, fo 180^{v}.
1381, 31 July, 8th at the el. of an abp, Reg. G, fo 225^{v}.
n.d., 8 Apr., obit in BL Ms Arundel 68, fo 23.

Possibly a relative of the contemporary Thomas de Brokhull who was bailiff of the liberty 1340/2, CCA DCc Eastry acct 69, Agney acct 44.

BROOK
see Broke

BROUNE
see John Borne I

I John BROWNE [Brome, Broun, Broune, Brun
occ. c. 1380 d. 1412

c. 1380, one of four prof., *SL*, 183, CCA Lit. Ms D.12, fo 5.
1380, 24 Mar., ord subdcn, Canterbury cathedral, Reg. abp Sudbury, fo 147^{v}.
1381, 31 July, 59th in order at the el. of an abp, Reg. G, fo 225^{v}.
1387/8, journeyed to London and recd a gift of 3s. from the prior, Lambeth Ms 243, fo 208^{v}.
1389/90, recd 12d. *pro benedictione* from the prior, *ib.*, fo 216^{v}.
1396, 7 Aug., 31st at the el. of an abp, Reg. G, fo 234^{v}.
1412, 17 July, d., in the 31st yr of monastic life; he is described as *natione teutonicus*, CCA Lit. Ms D.12, fo 19^{v}. The obit in BL Ms Arundel 68, fo 35 is 18 July.

II John BROWNE [Brown
occ. [1461] d. 1503

[1461], 19 Apr., one of six prof., CCA Lit. Ms D.12, fo 8 (SL, 189).
1462, 17 Apr., ord dcn, Canterbury cathedral, *Reg. abp Bourgchier*, 381.
1463, 9 Apr., ord pr., Canterbury cathedral, *ib.*, 386.
1462/3, celebrated his first mass and recd a gift of 8d. from the sacrist, Woodruff, 'Sacrist's Rolls', 62 (CCA DCc Sac. acct 43).
1496/8, infirmarer, CCA DCc Sac. acct 67, Treas. acct 30, also MA9, fos 94^{v}, 124^{v}, 154^{v}.
1466, 17 Feb., 65th in order in an inventory listing *jocalia fratrum*, [given by him and/or assigned for his use] Reg. N, fo 234^{v}.
1486, c. 15 Apr., took part in the funeral of abp Bourgchier, Cambridge, Corpus Christi College Ms 298, fo 128^{v}.
1493, 1 May, 18th in order at the ratification of an agreement, Reg. S, fo 383^{v}; but see John Crosse I.
1501, 26 Apr., 7th in order at the el. of an abp, Reg. R, fo 56^{v}.
1503, 16 Dec., d., 'ex infirmitate vocata Empematis, id est Tussus et de la murre'; he

was 64 yrs of age and the 'primus senior de prima mensa', CCA Lit. Ms D.12, fo 34. The obit in BL Ms Arundel 68, fo 51 is 17 Dec. See Richard London II.

Note: there is a third obit for a John Browne in BL Ms Arundel 68 on 17 Apr. (fo 24^v^).

Thomas BROWNE [Broun, Brown
occ. 1410 d. 1421

1410, 13 Dec., one of eight prof., *SL*, 185, CCA Lit. Ms D.12, fo 6.
1413, 2 Apr., ord subdcn, Canterbury cathedral, Reg. abp Arundel, ii, fo 101.
1418, 21 May, ord pr., bp's chapel, Halling, Reg. Yonge (Rochester), fo 5^v^.
1414, Feb., scholar at Canterbury college, Pantin, *Cant. Coll. Ox.*, iii, 72 (Reg. S, fo 68^v^).
1414, 12 Mar., 74th in order at the el. of an abp, *Reg. abp Chichele*, i, 4.
1421, 29 Oct., d., *ex asmatica passione*, as did John Wykham, q.v., the same wk, CCA Lit. Ms D.12, fo 21^v^. In *Chron. Stone*, 11, the yrs of monastic life have been incorrectly transcribed as six, instead of eleven.

John BROWNYNG [Brounyng
occ. 1399 d. 1408

1399, n.d., one of six prof., *SL*, 185, CCA Lit. Ms D.12, fo 5^v^.
1399, 20 Dec., ord subdcn, Canterbury cathedral, Reg. abp Arundel, i, fo 325.
1400, 3 Apr., ord dcn, Hoath chapel in Reculver parish, *ib.*, i, fo 326.
1401, 19 Mar., ord pr., Canterbury cathedral, *ib.*, i, fo 328.
1408, 5 Jan., d., CCA Lit. Ms D.12, fo 18^v^; obit in BL Ms Arundel 68, fo 12.

Robert BROWNYNG [Brounyng
occ. 1406 d. 1466

1406, 21 Oct., one of seven prof., *SL*, 185, CCA Lit. Ms D.12, fo 5^v^.
1407, 26 Mar., ord acol., Canterbury cathedral, Reg. abp Arundel, i, fo 340^v^.
1407, 24 Sept., ord subdcn, collegiate church, Maidstone, *ib.*, i, fo 341.
1410, 22 Mar., ord pr., Canterbury cathedral, *ib.*, ii, fo 98^v^.
1419/20, treasurer and warden of manors, Lambeth ED81, CCA DCc RE 113; there were normally two treasurers and two monk wardens at this date.
1439, 14/15 Dec., *magister ordinis*, *SL*, 188, CCA Lit. Ms D.12, fo 7^v^.
1414, 12 Mar., 62nd in order at the el. of an abp, *Reg. abp Chichele*, i, 4.
1439, 3 Feb., one of eight monks granted exit leave *pro recreacione*, Chron. Wm Glastynbury, fo 182^v^/177^v^.
1441, 14 Apr., obtained a papal indult granting a plenary indulgence, *CPL*, ix (1431–1447), 231 (as William).
1466, 17 Feb., 1st in order (after the prior) in an inventory of *jocalia fratrum* [given by him and/or assigned for his use], Reg. N, fo 230.
1466, 25 June, d., in his 59th yr of monastic life and was buried the following day; the subprior, John Oxney, q.v., took the *commendatio* and said the requiem, *Chron. Stone*, 96, where the date is incorrectly printed. In CCA Lit. Ms D.12, fo 26, he is described as *stationarius*, but this section of the obit list lacks dates and the names are not in chronological order. BL Ms Arundel 68, fo 32 prob. has the correct date which is the one given here.

BRUGG
see Brygge

BRUN
see Browne

I Richard BRYAN [senior
occ. before 1207

[1207 × 1214], name in the list of those who were in exile, *SL*, 172, CCA Lit. Ms D.12, fo 1.

Three *ciphi* of wood [*murre*] in an inventory of the refectory dated 1328 are described as [formerly] his, Dart, *Antiq. Cant.*, xxi (BL MS Cotton Galba E.iv, fo 179).

See note below the next entry.

II Richard BRYAN [Brianus
occ. after 1207

n.d., name occ. in the *post exilium* list, *SL*, 173, CCA Lit. Ms D.12, fo 1.

1224/5, one of the acctants on CCA DCc AS acct 1.

A *ciphus de murra* in the 1328 inventory of the refectory is listed as that of R. Brian, Dart, *Antiq. Cant.*, xxii (BL Ms Cotton Galba E.iv, fo 180).

Note: one of these two monks was among those appointed [1222 x 1237] by M. Laurence de St Nicholas to arrange for his obit celebrations, *Acta Guala*, no 155.

Thomas BRYAN
occ. 1287 d. 1310

1287, 16 Mar., one of five prof., *SL*, 177, CCA Lit. Ms D.12, fo 3.

[1296], included among the juniors accused by the abp of being lax in attendance at divine office and in the performance of other monastic duties, *Reg. abp Winchelsey*, 92.
1310, 19 Nov., d., CCA Lit. Ms D.12, fo 15^v^.

In an inventory of vestments, *temp.* prior Eastry, a linen alb with the arms of 'Northwode et Ponying' is described as his [?gift], Legg and

Hope, *Inventories*, 59 (BL Ms Cotton Galba E.iv, fo 115).

Thomas de BRYDLYNTON [Breidlintone, Bridellinton, Bridlintone
occ. 1239 d. 1241

n.d., name occ. in the list in *SL*, 173, CCA Lit. Ms D.12, fo 4.

1239, 12 Apr., the abp included his name, with that of Roger de la Lee, Stephen, third prior, and Alan IV, q.v., when he proposed that a committee be set up to discuss the convent's complaints, *Gervase Cant.*, ii, 163.

1241, 1 Feb., named as one of seven *compromissorii* in the el. of an abp, *Gervase Cant.*, ii, 186, 187, 190.

1241, 10 June, accompanied the subprior, Stephen de Cranebroke, q.v., to Rome to request papal confirmation for the el. of Boniface of Savoy as abp. A note in the margin of Gervase's Ms (Gesta regum continuata) states that the party was captured by Emperor Frederick II and that Thomas d., *ib.*, ii, 191, 198n.

I William de BRYGGE [Bregge, ?Brigia
occ. 1323 d. 1361

1323, one of six clothed [in the monastic habit], CCA Lit. Ms D.12, fo 3^{v} (*SL*, 179).

[1325], 18 Oct., prof. Reg. L, fo 141^{v}.

1334/5, subchamberlain, CCA DCc, Chamb. acct 27, MA2 fo 241^{v}.

1337, *custos martyrii*, CCA DCc MA2 fo 255.

1349/50, sacrist, CCA DCc, Arrears acct 30.

1356/7, chaplain of the prior, CCA DCc, Ickham acct 43.

1357/9, [1360/1], 1362/3, sacrist, CCA DCc, Bart. accts 36, 37, 40, Arrears acct, 70.

1349, 4 June, 18th in order at the el. of an abp, Reg. G, fo 60^{v}.

1349, 8/9 Sept., 17th at the el. of an abp, *ib.*, fo 76.

1361, 3 Aug., d. in an epidemic which carried off c. 25 monks, CCA Lit. Ms D.12, fo 17. It is prob. his obit that is given under 2 Aug. in BL Ms Arundel 68, fo 36^{v}.

II William BRYGGE [Bregg, Breggar, Bregge, Breghe, Brugg
occ. [1369] d. [?1389]

[1369], one of four prof., *SL*, 182, CCA Lit. Ms D.12, fo 4^{v}.

1370, 15 Sept., ord acol., abp's chapel, Saltwood, Reg. abp Wittlesey, fo 166.

1370, 21 Sept., ord subdcn, Saltwood, *ib.*, fo 166^{v}.

1371, 20 Dec., ord dcn, abp's chapel, Otford, *ib.*, fo 168.

1372, 21 Feb., ord pr., abp's chapel, Croydon, *ib.*, fo 168^{v}.

1383/4, chamberlain, CCA DCc, Treas. acct 26, fo 7; he was apptd on 1 Sept. 1383, Reg. abp Courtenay, i, fo 44^{v}.

n.d., described as *quondam* precentor, CCA Lit. Ms D.12, fo 4^{v}.

1374, 30 June, 55th in order at the el. of an abp, Reg. G, fos 173^{v}–175^{v}.

1374/5, ill in the infirmary and the anniversarian pd him a 'pension' of 2s. 10d., CCA DCc Anniv. acct 6.

1381, 31 July, 41st at the el. of an abp, Reg. G, fo 225^{v}.

1383, 19 July, with Thomas Chillenden I, q.v., sent to the abp by the prior and chapter to discuss the future of Canterbury college, Pantin, *Cant. Coll. Ox.*, iv, 43 (Oxford Bod. Ms Ashmole 794, fo 258).

1388, Sept., obtained a letter of recommendation for his journey [to Rome], *ib.*, fo 220 (summary in *Hist. Mss Comm. 8th Report*, Appndx, 339).

[?1389], d., *iuxta Romam*, CCA Lit. Ms D.12, fo 4^{v}.

Simon BRYTEWELL
occ. 2nd half 13th c.

n.d., name occ. in the list in *SL*, 176, CCA Lit. Ms D.12, fo 2^{v}.

Roger BUCH [Roger Russel Bussh
occ. 1294 d. 1299

1294, 18 Oct., one of eight prof., *SL*, 178, CCA Lit. Ms D.12, fo 3.

[1296], one of the juniors accused by the abp of being lax in attendance at divine office and in the performance of other monastic duties, *Reg. abp Winchelsey*, 92.

1299, 22 Sept., d., CCA Lit. Ms D.12, fo 15.

Note: the three names together as above are given in CCA Lit. Ms D.12, fo 15.

BUCKINGHAM
see Bokyngham

Hamo de BUKLOND [Boclond
occ. 1257

n.d., name occ. in the list in *SL*, 175, CCA Lit. Ms D.12, fo 2.

1257, named on an acct of several manors, Reg. H, fo 188.

n.d., 27/28 Feb., obit occ. in BL Ms Arundel, 68, fo 18.

In an inventory of the refectory dated 1328 two silver *ciphi* and a wooden one described as *nux . . . cum gemmis* are listed as [formerly] his, Dart, *Antiq. Cant.*, xix, xxi (BL Ms Cotton Galba E.iv, fos 178^{v}, 179^{v}).

William de BUKLOND [Buclond
occ. 1241/3

n.d., name occ. in the *post exilium* list in *SL*, 173, CCA Lit. Ms D.12, fo 1.

1241/3, cellarer, CCA DCc MA1, fos 82^{v}–84^{v}.

William de BUCKWELLE [Bockwalle, Bocwelle
occ. c. 1252 occ. 1260

1252, sacrist, Reg. H, fo 172.
1257, Mar./Sept., 1257/60, Apr., sacrist, *ib.*, fo 187^{v}, CCA DCc MA1, fos 99–101^{v}, Reg. H, fo 200^{v}. See Richard de Wynchepe.
1260, Apr., apptd prior of Dover; his installation is in *Gervase Cant.*, ii, 211.

1259/60, pd a visit to Meopham, CCA DCc Meopham acct 1.
1268, 12 Oct., d., and was buried at Christ Church, BL Ms Cotton Julius D.v, fo 49^{v}, Lambeth Ms 20, fo 231^{v}; obit occ. also in BL Ms Arundel 68, fo 45.

Name at the head of a list of four vols in the Eastry catalogue, nos 521–524, James, *Ancient Libraries*, 62–63.

Thomas BUNGAY [Bongay, Bonghay, Bungeye
occ. c. 1389 d. 1421

c. 1389, 6 Nov., one of eight prof., *SL*, 183, CCA Lit. Ms D.12, fo 5; he had previously been a canon of Lesnes, *Chron. Stone*, 11.
1394, with William Elmore, q.v., chancellor, Reg. S, fo 1; he also shared the office with Thomas Dene, q.v., *ib.*, fo 35.
1400, Apr./1406, Nov., sacrist, CCA DCc CR 90, Prior acct 20.
1411, chancellor with Alexander London, q.v., Reg. S, fo 61^{v}.
1416, 2 July, apptd precentor, *Reg. abp Chichele*, iv, 152.
1396, 7 Aug., 53rd in order at the el. of an abp, Reg. G, fo 234^{v}.
1414, 12 Mar., 18th at the el. of an abp, *Reg. abp Chichele*, i, 4.
1421, 30 Oct., d., *ex asmatica passione*, as did Thomas Browne and John Wykham I, q.v., the same wk, CCA Lit. Ms D.12, fo 21^{v}. According to *ib.*, and *Chron. Stone*, 11, he had held *diversa officia honorabilia*.

Richard BURDEN [Bordon
occ. 1426 d. 1461

1426, 7 May, one of three prof., *SL*, 187, CCA Lit. Ms D.12, fo 7.
[1432], 11 June, ord dcn, place not named, Reg. Langdon (Rochester), fo 74^{v}.
1433, 28 Mar., ord pr., Charing, *Reg. abp Chichele*, iv, 378.
1435, *parvus sacrista*, 'Chron. Wm Glastynbury', 129 (Ms fo 117).
1439, 27 Dec., apptd subalmoner, Chron. Wm Glastynbury, fo 119.
1440/1, treasurer, CCA DCc MA 26; he was apptd on 31 Oct., Chron Wm Glastynbury, fo 119^{v}.
1446, Dec./1448, chaplain to the prior, Lambeth ED74, CCA DCc MA4, fos 133, 175; see below.
1452/4, 1455/9, bartoner, CCA DCc Caruc. Serg. acct 30, Prior accts 9, 10, 15, Bart. accts 98, 99.
1439, 3 Feb., one of eight monks granted exit leave *pro recreacione*, Chron. Wm Glastynbury, fo 182^{v}/177^{v}.
1455/6, one of the eight barons of the exchequer, CCA DCc, Prior acct 10.
1461, 10 Mar., d., described as chaplain to the prior, prob. at the time of d.; the prior read the *commendatio* and burial rites, *Chron. Stone*, 82.

Michael de BURDOUN [Borden, Bordenne, Bordeun, Bordonn, Bordoun
occ. 1353 d. 1361

1353, 27 Sept., one of five prof., *SL*, 181, CCA Lit. Ms D.12, fo 4.
1355, 30 May, ord acol., abp's chapel, Maidstone, Reg. abp Islip, fo 315^{v}.
1355, 19 Sept., ord subdcn, abp's chapel, Saltwood, *ib.*, fo 315^{v}.
1356, 18 June, ord dcn, Hoath chapel in Reculver parish, *ib.*, fo 316.
1356, 24 Sept., ord pr., abps' chapel, Tenham, *ib.*, fo 316.
1360/1, recd a small sum [from the prior] *pro magna missa*, Lambeth Ms 243, fo 115^{v}.
1361, 4 Oct., d. in an epidemic which carried off c.25 monks, CCA Lit. Ms D.12, fo 17.

Henry de BURGATE
occ. 2nd half 13th c.

n.d., name occ. in the list in *SL*, 174, CCA Lit. Ms D.12, fo 2.

In an inventory of the refectory of 1328 a *ciphus* of *murre* is described as [formerly] his, Dart, *Antiq. Cant.*, xxi (BL Ms Cotton Galba, E.iv, fo 179^{v}).

BURGATE
see also Bergate, Berigate

BURN(E)
see Borne

James BURTON
occ. 1465 d. 1516

1465, 4 Apr., one of seven prof., *SL*, 190, CCA Lit. Ms D.12, fo 8.
1465, 13 Apr., ord subdcn, no place named, *Reg. abp Bourgchier*, 391.

1467, 28 Mar., ord dcn, Canterbury cathedral, *ib.*, 399.
1470, 21 Apr., ord pr., Canterbury cathedral, *ib.*, 406.
1469/70, celebrated his first mass and recd 8d. from the sacrist, Woodruff, 'Sacrist's Rolls', 63, as John (CCA DCc Sac. acct 48).
1479/80, 2nd anniversarian, CCA DCc, Anniv. acct, 16.
1483, 1484, 1485, 1487, all on 29 Sept., warden of manors, CCA DCc, Monk warden accts 18, 19, 20,22.
1488/94, granator, CCA DCc, MA7, fos 110^{v}, 132^{v}, 153^{v}, 173, MA9, fos 5, 61.
1501, 26 Apr., *capellanus principalis* [to the prior], Reg. R, fo 56^{v}.
1504/9, bartoner, CCA DCc MA10, fo 227, MA11, fos 8^{v}, 36, 66, 101^{v}.
1486, Easter/Sept., described as *vicecustos maneriorum* making his progress around the manors and delivering money to Canterbury college, Pantin, *Cant. Coll. Ox.*, ii, 213 (CCA DCc Cart. Antiq. O.151.21).
1493, 1 May, 21st in order at the ratification of an agreement, Reg. S, fo 383^{v}; but see John Crosse I.
1501, 26 Apr., 10th in order at the el. of an abp, Reg. R, fo 56^{v}.
n.d., left to be prior of Folkestone; but after his res. from this office he retired to Christ Church with a pension from Folkestone, and was assigned St Mary's chamber in the infirmary. With the permission of the prior he did not join in the monastic routine, CCA Lit. Ms C.11, fos 2–4 where there is a lengthy inventory of his belongings (summarized in *Hist. Mss Comm. 9th Report*, Appndx, 125). See Rooke, 'William Ingram', 36.
1508, 2 Apr., delegated to celebrate the Sun. mass, CCA Lit. Ms C.11, fo 17^{v}.
1511, 2 Sept., 3rd in order on the visitation certificate, Wood-Legh, *Visit.*, 3 (Reg. abp Warham, i, fo 35).
1516, d., CCA Lit. Ms C.11 fo 2, his obit on 21 Jan. is in BL Ms Arundel 68, fo 13^{v}.

Richard de BURY [Bery
occ. 2nd half 13th c.

n.d., name occ. in the list in *SL*, 174, CCA Lit. Ms D.12, fo 2.

Thomas BURY [Bery, Byrry
occ. 1470 d. 1504

1470, 25 Jan., one of eight prof., *SL*, 190, CCA Lit. Ms D.12, fo 8.
1470, 21 Apr., ord acol., Canterbury cathedral, *Reg. abp Bourgchier*, 405.
1471, 9 Mar., ord subdcn, Canterbury cathedral, *ib.*, 404.
1473, 13 Mar., ord dcn, Canterbury cathedral, *ib.*, 410.
1475, 23 Sept., ord pr., prior's chapel, Canterbury cathedral, *ib.*, 419.
1496, succentor, BL Ms Arundel 68, fo 6.
1500, after 19 May, 1503, 7 June, *custos martyrii*, CCA Lit. Ms C.11, fos 26, 32. He d. in office, Legg and Hope, *Inventories*, 129.
1493, 1 May, 27th in order at the ratification of an agreement, Reg. S, fo 383^{v}; but see John Crosse I.
1496, as succentor responsible for recording the names of those recd into confraternity with Christ Church, BL Ms Arundel 68, fo 8.
1501, 26 Apr., 15th in order at the el. of an abp, Reg. R, fo 56^{v}.
1504, 17 June, d., *ex fluxu*; he was 54 and [at the time] *de prima mensa*, CCA Lit. Ms D.12, fo 34^{v}; his obit is on 20 June in BL Ms Arundel 68, fo 31^{v}.

The inventory dated 1500, 19 May, when he became *custos martyrii*, includes a set of red vestments *per t.b.*, Legg and Hope, *Inventories*, 127.

BUSSH
see Buch

I John BYDYNDEN [Bidindon, Bydyndenne, Bydyndon, Byndene
occ. [1358/9] occ. 1376

[1358/9], 28 Oct., one of nine prof., *SL*, 181, CCA Lit. Ms D.12, fo 4.
1362, 24 Sept., ord acol., Charing, Reg. abp Islip, fo 322.
1363, 23 Sept., ord dcn, Faversham monastery, *ib.*, fo 323^{v}.
1364, 21 Sept., ord pr., place not named, *ib.*, fo 325^{v} (by the bp of Worcester).
1371, 29 July, apptd warden of Canterbury college, Pantin, *Cant. Coll. Ox.*, iii, 20–21 (Reg. abp Wittlesey, fo 86^{v}, where the date is 10 Aug.). On 14 Sept. 1371 he was absolved from this office, Pantin, *ib.*, iv, 22 (Reg. abp Wittlesey, fo 86^{v}).
1371, 10 Oct., apptd penitentiary for the priory, Reg. abp Wittlesey, fo 48^{v}.
1364/5, recd 5s. for the hire of a horse to convey him to Oxford, 28s. for his *cappa scolastica* and 6s. 6d. for linen cloth, Pantin, *Cant. Coll. Ox.*, iv, 182.
1367/8, one of the scholars at Canterbury college to whom a letter was sent requiring their presence at Christ Church for an archiepiscopal visitation, Pantin, *Cant. Coll. Ox.*, iii, 18 (Reg. L, fo 98).
1369/70, with William Woghope, q.v., recd an allowance for clothing [because they were at Oxford], CCA DCc, Chamb. acct 48.
1374, 30 June, 24th in order at the el. of an abp, Reg. G, fos 173^{v}–175^{v}.

1376, Apr., one of ten nom. to the committee set up for regulating the infirmary, *Lit. Cant.*, no 945 (CCA DCc Cart. Antiq. C.206).

II John BYDYNDEN [Bedenden, Bodendon
occ. [1429] d. 1431

[1429, summer], ord acol., place not named, Reg. Langdon (Rochester), fo 74 (as Bodendon).

1430, 4 Apr., one of five prof., *SL*, 187, CCA Lit. Ms D.12, fo 7.

[1430, 23 Dec., ord acol. [*recte* subdcn], bp's chapel, Trottiscliffe, Reg. Langdon (Rochester), fo 72x.

Note: Langdon's register is in a state of confusion here.]

1431, 18 July, subdcn [*levita*], d. of the plague and was buried at once; the funeral and burial rites were performed by the subprior, CCA Lit. Ms D.12, fo 23. His obit is in BL Ms Arundel 68, fo 35.

Richard BYDYNDEN [Bidenden, Bydenden, Bydyndenne
occ. 1408/9 d. 1440

1408/9, 21 Mar., one of six prof., CCA Lit. Ms D.12, fo 6 (*SL*, 185).

1410, 22 Mar., ord dcn, Canterbury cathedral, Reg. abp Arundel, ii, fo 98ᵛ.

1413, 2 Apr., ord pr., Canterbury cathedral, *ib.*, ii, fo 101ᵛ.

1414, 12 Mar., 67th in order at the el. of an abp, *Reg. abp Chichele*, i, 4.

1439, 20 Jan., one of several monks who were granted exit leave *pro recreacione*; they returned on 31 Jan., Chron. Wm Glastynbury, fo 182ᵛ/177ᵛ.

1440, 12 June, d., *Chron. Stone*, 28; his obit is in BL Ms Arundel 68, fo 30ᵛ.

Simon de BYFORD
d. 1316

1316, 31 May, d., CCA Lit. Ms D.12, fo 15ᵛ.

Note: this may be Simon de Valoyns, q.v.

BYHAM
see Biham

BYNDENE
see Bydynden

Robert BYNNE [Bynnee, Bynny
occ. 1424 occ. [c. 1475]

1424, 13/14 Nov., one of two clothed, *SL*, 187, CCA Lit. Ms D.12, fo 7.

1426, 20 Mar., prof., *SL*, 126 (Cambridge, Corpus Christi College Ms 298).

1427, 5 Dec., ord subdcn, bp's chapel, Trottiscliffe, Reg. Langdon (Rochester), fo 59ᵛ.

[1428, 3 Apr., ord pr. [*recte* dcn], Rochester cathedral, *ib.*, fo 65.

Note: Langdon's register is in a state of confusion here.]

1431, 26 May, ord pr., Higham Ferrers, *Reg. abp Chichele*, iv, 383.

1435, chaplain to the subprior, 'Chron. Wm Glastynbury', 129 (Ms fo 117).

1436/7, feretrar, CCA DCc, Prior acct 7; he remained in office until he was apptd subsacrist; see below.

[1441], 5 Jan., apptd subsacrist, Chron. Wm Glastynbury, fo 119ᵛ.

[1448], 25 Jan., *magister ordinis*, *SL*, 189, CCA Lit. Ms D.12, fo 7ᵛ.

1457, 13 Aug., 1460, 31 Aug., 1468, 29 Apr., precentor, *Chron. Stone*, 68, 82, 103.

[1431], prob. at Canterbury college, *Reg. abp Chichele*, iv, 383.

1432/3, recd travelling expenses for journeys between Canterbury and Oxford, Pantin, *Cant. Coll. Ox.*, iv, 192.

1439, 20 Jan., one of several monks granted exit leave pro *recreacione*; they returned on 31 Jan., Chron. Wm Glastynbury, fo 182ᵛ/177ᵛ.

1457, 13 Aug., 1460, 31 Aug., 1468, 29 Apr., sat on the examining board to hear the *redditus* of novices, *Chron. Stone*, 68, 82, 103.

1465, 17 Feb., 14th in order in an inventory listing *jocalia fratrum* [given by him and/or assigned for his use], Reg. N, fo 231.

1473/4, ill in the infirmary, CCA DCc, Prior acct 14.

[c. 1475], 5 Oct., described as *stationarius*, CCA Lit. Ms D.12, fo 26; his obit is in BL Ms Arundel 68, fo 44.

I John BYRCHYNGTON [Birchinton, Byrchynton
occ. 1432 d. [1489 × 1492]

1432, 19 Sept., one of six prof., *SL*, 188, CCA Lit. Ms D.12, fo 7–7ᵛ.

1434, 13 Mar., ord acol. and subdcn, infirmary chapel in the priory, *Reg. abp Chichele*, iv, 378.

1435, 2 Apr., ord dcn, infirmary chapel, *ib.*, iv, 389 (transcribed as Bytchynton).

1460/1, 2nd anniversarian, with Thomas Well, q.v., CCA DCc, Anniv. acct 12.

1466, 17 Feb., 21st in order in an inventory listing *jocalia fratrum* [given by him and/or assigned for his use], and he had none, Reg. N, fo 231ᵛ.

[1489 × 1492], d., c. 23 Nov., *stationarius*, CCA Lit. Ms D.12, fos 27, 31ᵛ; his obit is in BL Ms Arundel 68, fo 49.

II John BYRCHYNGTON
occ. 1517 occ. 1534

1517, 12 Mar., [deposition of St Gregory], one of six tonsured, *SL*, 194, CCA Lit. Ms D.12 fo 11–11ᵛ.

1517, 29 Sept., made his prof. before the abp on the day on which Thomas Goldwell, prior, q.v., celebrated his first pontifical mass, *ib*.

1518/19, spent time in the infirmary, CCA DCc Infirm. acct. 1.

1534, 12 Dec., acknowledged the Act of Supremacy, *DK 7th Report*, Appndx 2, 282.

Stephen BYRCHYNGTON [Birchinton, Byrchynton

occ. 1382 d. [c. 1407]

1382, 5 Sept., one of six who were clothed in the monastic habit, *SL*, 183, CCA Lit. Ms D.12, fo 5.

1383, c. 11 Aug., the prior was comm. to rec. his and their prof., Reg. abp Courtenay, i, fo 42ᵛ.

1395/1400, treasurer, CCA DCc, Bailiff of the Liberty accts 6–10.

1401/2, June to June, 1402/5, monk warden, CCA DCc Adisham acct 42. Ebony acct 70, Chartham acct 45, Treas. acct 6.

1402/5, chaplain to the prior, Chaplain accts 5, 6, Prior acct 20.

[1407], before 12 Aug., cellarer, CCA Lit. Ms D.12, fo 18ᵛ.

1408/9, warden of manors, CCA DCc Ebony acct, 72.

Note: the dating of this acct may be inaccurate.

1396, 7 Aug., 41st in order at the el. of an abp, Reg. G, fo 234ᵛ.

[1407], 21 Aug., d., *beatissimo fine quievit in pace*, CCA Lit. Ms D.12, fo 18ᵛ; his obit is in BL Ms Arundel 68, fo 38ᵛ.

Name in Lambeth Ms 30, Gervase Cantuar' [15th c.].

The acct of the lives of the abps of Canterbury (Lambeth Ms 99) which was transcribed by Wharton in *Anglia Sacra* and attributed to him, has been shown to be an incorrect ascription, acc. to Gransden, *Hist. Writing*, ii, 70, n. 71 with refs. See also Sharpe, *Latin Writers* for other writings attributed to him.

BYRRY

see Bury

BYSSHOPPYSTON

see Bisshoppiston

Hugh de CAEN [Cadamo, Cadumo

occ. 1143 occ. 1149

1146, soon after 19 Aug., cellarer, *Theobald Charters*, 538 (as Hugh).

n.d., sacrist, [*secretarius*], before his departure for Dover, *Gervase Cant.*, i, 141.

n.d. [1143 x 1148], with the prior, Walter [Durdent, q.v.] and Richard [de Dover I, q.v.], witnessed a confirmation by the abp of the possessions of Dover priory, *Theobald Charters*, no 86; [were the latter the abp's chaplains?].

1145, 1 Sept., witnessed an *inspeximus* of Gundulf's (possibly spurious) charter to Rochester, *ib*., no 222 (as Hugh).

1149, apptd prior of Dover by the abp, *Theobald Charters*, 542, *HRH*, 87.

[1157, Feb., d., *HRH*, 87.]

See also Hugh I who may be the same monk.

Ralph de CAEN

occ. 1070 occ. before 1107

1070, chaplain to abp Lanfranc with whom he came from Bec, *Text. Roff.* (Rochester), fos 172ᵛ–173, and cap 87.

1107, before, prior of Rochester, q.v., under Ralph I in the Rochester section.

CALAIS

see Calys

John CALDERUN [Caudrun

occ. [1175 × 1177]

[1175 × 1177] *temp.* prior Benedict, q.v., granted property to the monks at the time of his adm., and they undertook to provide a corrody for his wife, Urry, *Canterbury*, 423.

CALEY

see Galy

[CALVELLUS [?Robert Calvellus

n.d.

n.d., 17 Oct., obit in BL Ms Arundel 68, fo 45ᵛ.

Item no 190 in the late 12th c. library catalogue is Libellus Roberti Calvelli, James, *Ancient Libraries*, 11.

Note: there is no certainty that this person was a monk.]

Thomas CALYS [Calais, Calees, Caleys, Calis, Calyes

occ. 1450 d. [1489 × 1492]

1450, 25 Jan., one of seven prof., *SL*, 189, CCA Lit. Ms D.12, fo 7ᵛ.

1450, 3 Apr., ord acol., Canterbury cathedral, Reg. abp Stafford, fo 204.

1451, 20 Mar., ord subdcn, Canterbury cathedral, *ib*., fo 205ᵛ.

1452, 8 Apr., ord dcn, Canterbury cathedral, *ib*., fo 206ᵛ.

1455, 5 Apr., ord pr., chapel within the cathedral priory, *Reg. abp Bourgchier*, 360.

[1489 x 1492], *magister mense*, CCA Lit. Ms D.12, fos 27, 31ᵛ.

1466, 17 Feb., 44th in order in an inventory listing *jocalia fratrum* [given by him and/or assigned for his use] and he had only a *ciphus de mora* [*sic*], Reg. N, fo 233ᵛ.

[1489 × 1492], d., CCA Lit. Ms D.12, fos 27, 31ᵛ.

Alexander CAMBRIG' [Cambregg, Cantebregge, Cantebrygg', Caumbrig', Cauntibrugge

occ. 1367 d. 1397

1367, 11 Nov., one of nine prof., *SL*, 182, CCA Lit. Ms D.12, fo 4^{v}.
1368, 4 Mar., ord acol., Canterbury cathedral, *Reg. abp Langham*, 387.
1369, 22 Dec., ord subdcn, abp's chapel, Charing, Reg. abp Wittlesey, fo 165^{v}.
1370, 21 Sept., ord dcn, abp's chapel, Saltwood, *ib.*, fo 166^{v}.
1371, 31 May, ord pr., abp's chapel, Charing, *ib.*, fo 167.

1377, *custos tumbe*, CCA DCc MA2, fo 312.
1382, Sept., apptd penitentiary in the priory, Reg. abp Courtenay, i, fo 22, but absolved the following June, *ib.*, fo 39.
1386, chaplain to the prior, CCA DCc, Arrears acct 117 (as Alexander).

1374, 30 June, 46th in order at the el. of an abp, Reg. G, fos 173^{v}–175^{v}.
1381, 31 July, 34th at the el. of an abp, *ib.*, fo 225^{v}.
1382, 1383/4, recd small sums from the prior in these and other yrs, sometimes *pro benedictione*, Lambeth Ms 243, fos 180^{v}, 183.
1396, 7 Aug., 16th in order at the el. of an abp, Reg. G, fo 234^{v}.
[c. 1383], went to Flanders with the bp of Norwich [Henry Despenser, see *DNB*] but returned, *SL*, 182, CCA Lit. Ms D.12, fo 4^{v}.
1397, 17 Sept., d. in his bed in the dormitory, CCA Lit. Ms D.12, fo 17^{v}.

Geoffrey de CANTEBRYGGE

see Grantebrygge

I John CANTORBURY [Canterbyry, Cantirbury, Cantuar', Caunterbury

occ. 1376 d. 1432

1376, 14/15 Nov., one of seven who were clothed in the monastic habit, CCA Lit. Ms D.12, fo 4^{v} (*SL*, 183).
1377, 28 Mar., ord acol., Canterbury cathedral, Reg. abp Sudbury, fo 141.
1377, 19 Sept., ord subdcn, Lambeth palace chapel, *ib.*, fo 142.
1378, 17 Apr., ord dcn, Canterbury cathedral, *ib.*, fo 145^{v}.

1401, 25 Mar., *magister ordinis*, *SL*, 185, CCA Lit. Ms D.12, fo 5^{v}.

1381, 31 July, 57th in order at the el. of an abp, Reg. G, fo 225^{v}.
1383/4, 1386/7, 1387/8, recd small sums from the prior, in the first instance, and prob. in the other yrs, *pro benedictione*, Lambeth Ms 243, fos 192^{v}, 204^{v}, 208^{v}.
1396, 7 Aug., 29th at the el. of an abp, Reg. G, fo 234^{v}.
1414, 12 Mar., 7th at the el. of an abp, *Reg. abp Chichele*, i, 4.
1432, 13 Dec., *stacionarius*, [residing] in the infirmary and d., after receiving the sacraments; the prior performed the burial office, *Chron. Stone*, 17, CCA Lit. Ms D.12, fo 23^{v}. The obit is 12 Dec. in BL Ms Arundel, 68, fo 51.

II John CANTORBURY [Caunterbyry

occ. 1439 d. 1462

1439, 4 or 15 Dec., [St Barbara] one of six clothed in the monastic habit, *SL*, 188, CCA Lit. Ms D.12, fo 7^{v}.
[1440], 8 or 20 July [St Margaret], made his prof. before the prior, Chron. Wm Glastynbury, fo 119^{v}.
1444, 11 Apr., ord pr., Canterbury cathedral, Reg. abp Stafford, fo 197.
1450, 7 Jan., was examined *de redditu suo* [examination at the end of the noviciate], *Chron. Stone*, 47–48.
1452, May, ill and his expenses were 2s. 4d., CCA Lit. Ms E.6, fo 64^{v}.
1462, 18 Feb., d., described as a *conventualis*, CCA Lit. Ms D.12, fo 26, *Chron. Stone*, 85.

Nicholas CANTORBURY [Canterbury, Cantyrbery

occ. [1395] d. 1403

[1395], 12 Mar., one of eight prof., *SL*, 184, CCA Lit. Ms D.12, fo 5^{v}.
1396, 1 Apr., ord subdcn, Canterbury cathedral,, Reg. abp Courtenay, ii, fo 186^{v}.

1396, 7 Aug., 79th in order (out of 81) at the el. of an abp, Reg. G, fo 234^{v}.
1403, 17 Nov., d.; his body was the first to be placed on the new stone before the image of the Cross in the chapel of the infirmary [*capell' infirmarie interiore?m*], CCA Lit. Ms D.12, fo 18.

I William de CANTORBURY [Canterbyry, Cantuar'

occ. 1333 d. 1361

1333, 9 Oct., one of eleven prof., *SL*, 180, CCA Lit. Ms D.12, fo 4.

1343/4, subalmoner, CCA DCc Monkton acct 70.
1353/4, 1355/7, warden of manors, CCA DCc Bocking acct 32, Cliffe acct 37, London acct 25.

1337, *custos* of the refectory spoons, CCA DCc DE3, fo 10.
1338, 1 Mar., an inventory of missing books records that he was *in nota* for Vita Sancti Thomae martiris, *Lit. Cant.*, no 618 (Reg. L, fo 104).
1349, 4 June, 38th in order at the el. of an abp, Reg. G, fo 60^{v}.
1349, 8/9 Sept., 37th at the el. of an abp, *ib.*, fo 76^{v}.
1357, 14 Sept., one of the monks *in remotis agentibus* and unable to be present at the abp's visitation, Reg. L, fos 89^{v}–90.

1360, 3 Oct., absent from the house but cited to return for the visitation, Reg. H, fo 98.
1361, 11 Aug., d., one of about 25 monks who were carried off by an epidemic, CCA Lit. Ms D.12, fo 17.

II William CANTORBURY [Canterbury, Cantirbury, Cantyrbery, Cauntirbury
occ. [1395] occ. 1425

[1395], 12 Mar., one of eight prof., *SL*, 184, CCA Lit. Ms D.12, fo 5v.
1396, 1 Apr., ord subdcn, Canterbury cathedral, Reg. abp Courtenay, ii, fo 186v.
1401, 19 Mar., ord pr., Canterbury cathedral, Reg. Arundel, i, fo 328.

1396, 7 Aug., 80th in order (out of 81) at the el. of an abp, Reg. G, fo 234v.
1414, 12 Mar., 38th at the el. of an abp, *Reg. abp Chichele*, i, 4.
1425, 10 Mar., granted licence to transfer to a stricter, more contemplative monastery, *Reg. abp Chichele*, iv, 263. This licence is followed by an undated letter from the prior to the prior of Farley [?Monkton Farleigh] requesting the latter to accept him there, *ib*. Acc. to Chron. Wm Glastynbury, fo 168v/162v, he was *expulsi*.

III William CANTORBURY [Cantorburie, Caunterbury
occ. 1524 occ. 1540

1524, 21/22 July, one of eleven granted adm. [*ingressum*] to Christ Church, CCA Lit. Ms D.12, fos 11v–12.
1524, 4 Aug., one of eleven tonsured, *SL*, 195, CCA Lit. Ms D.12, fo 12.
1525, 9 Apr., prof., *ib*.

[1538, 8 Feb., after], one of four subsacrists [*parvi sacristae*], Pantin, *Cant. Coll. Ox.*, iii, 153.

1534, 12 Dec., acknowledged the Act of Supremacy, *DK 7th Report*, Appndx 2, 282.
[1538, 8 Feb., after], in a list of monks prob. prepared for Thomas Cromwell he was described as 'a good man', 31 yrs old, Pantin, *Cant. Coll. Ox.*, iii, 153.
1540, 4 Apr., awarded £6 p.a., *L and P Henry VIII*, xv, no 452.

Denys de CANTUAR' [Dionisius
occ. 1st half 13th c.

n.d., name occ. in the *post exilium* list in *SL*, 173, CCA Lit. Ms D.12, fo 1.

The Eastry catalogue includes Libri Dionisii, no 1369, ?1369[a], James, *Ancient Libraries*, 117; these may have been his or possibly Denys de St Margaret's, q.v., or merely the title of a book or books. Nos 1370 and 1371 may also have belonged to one of them.

An inventory of the refectory dated 1328 includes one *ciphus de murra* [formerly] belonging to a Dionysius, prob. this one, Dart, *Antiq. Cant.*, xxi (BL Ms Cotton Galba E.iv, fo 179).

Geoffrey de CANTUAR'[Galfridus
occ. 1st half 13th c.

n.d., name occ. in the *post exilium* list in *SL*, 173, CCA Lit. Ms D.12, fo 1v.

John de CANTUAR' [Cantuaria
occ. 1300

1300, 4 June, ord dcn, Smeeth chapel by Aldington, *Reg. abp Winchelsey*, 935.

Note: see John le Spycer who may be the same monk.

Paulinus de CANTUAR'
occ. 1st half 13th c.

n.d., name occ. in the *post exilium* list in *SL*, 173, CCA Lit. Ms D.12, fo 1v.

Philip de CANTUAR'
occ. 1st half 13th c.

n.d., name occ. in the *post exilium* list in *SL*, 173, CCA Lit. Ms D.12, fo 1v.

Richard de CANTUARIA
occ. 1285

1285, 22 Sept., ord pr., collegiate church, South Malling, *Reg. abp Pecham*, i, 222.

Note: this monk prob. occ. in the list in *SL* under his toponymic; see Richard de Rawe.

Walter de CANTUARIA
see Walter V

William CANTUARIENSIS
occ. [late 12th c.]

[late 12th c.], wrote an acct of the life and miracles of Thomas Becket, Gervase, *Gervase Cant.*, ii, 391, 396; this has been printed in *Materials Becket*, i, 137–546.

See William IV to William VI who were contemporaries and one of whom may be this monk.

Ysaac CANTUARIENSIS
occ. 1189

1189, 4 Oct., sent to Tenham to tell the abp that the convent would not accept his imposition of a prior without the subprior's consent; and he was detained in the abp's prison at Otford, *Epist. Cant.*, 311.
1189, 6 Oct., one of the monks excommunicated by the abp, *ib.*, 311.
1189, c. 14 Nov., with Walter de Stura, q.v., sent away by the convent as they had heard reports that the abp was about to lay hands on the excommunicated monks, *Epist. Cant.*, 317.

See also Isaac.

Marcellus de CAPELLA
see Marcellus

CARLOMANNUS
see Karlemannus

CAROLUS
n.d.

n.d., pr. whose obit occ. on 7 Feb. in BL Ms Cotton Nero C.ix, fo 5.

CAUDRUN
see Calderun

Nicholas de CAUNTEBRUG'
see Gra[n]tebrygg

CAUNTERBYRY
see Cantorbury

CAUNTIBRUGGE
see Cambrig'

Robert CAUSTON [Cawston
occ. 1514/15

1514, 1 Sept., one of seven tonsured, *SL*, 194, CCA Lit. Ms D.12, fo 11.
1515, 19 Apr., prof., *ib.*
n.d., 16 Aug., *levita*, whose obit occ. in BL Ms Arundel 68, fo 38v.

Thomas CAUSTON [Cawston, Kawston
occ. 1454 d. 1504

1454, 28 Apr., one of eight prof., *SL*, 189, CCA Lit. Ms D.12, fo 7v.
1455, 5 Apr., ord acol. and subdcn, chapel in the priory, *Reg. abp Bourgchier*, 359.
1455, 20 Sept., ord dcn, Canterbury cathedral, *ib.*, 361.
1457, 2 Apr., ord pr., Canterbury cathedral, *ib.*, 366.
1470, 15 Aug., *magister in criptis*, *Chron. Stone*, 113.
1471, apptd feretrar by the subprior, *sed. vac.* priory, Reg. S, fo 248v.
1474/7, treasurer, CCA DCc MA27, fos 40–94.
1483/5, *magister ordinis*, *SL*, 191, CCA Lit. Ms D.12 fo 8v.
1486/93, 1495, 19 Apr., infirmarer, CCA DCc MA7, fos 35, 72, 95, 134, 154, 175, MA9, fo 4v, Monk Warden acct 28.
n.d., chancellor, third prior, feretrar, sacrist, *coronarius*, CCA Lit. Ms D.12, fo 35.

1466, 17 Feb., 49th in order in an inventory listing *jocalia fratrum* [given by him and/or assigned for his use], Reg. N, fo 234.
1470, 15 Aug. (feast of the Assumption), acc. to custom he provided a *magnum convivium* for the convent on this day, *Chron. Stone*, 113.
[1486], one of three monks apptd by the prior, *sed. vac.*, to be confessors in the diocese, Reg. N, fo 172.
1493, 1 May, 14th in order at the ratification of an agreement, Reg. S, fo 383v; but see John Crosse I.
1501, 26 Apr., 2nd in order of seniority at the el. of an abp, Reg. R, fo 56v; the subprior, Richard Copton, q.v., is 20th.
1504, 4 July, d., CCA Lit. Ms D.12, fo 35, which also specifies the night of the visitation of our Lady, i.e., 2/3 July, and BL Ms Arundel 68, fo 32v records the obit on 3 July. He was 76 yrs of age and 56 yrs a monk. The continuator of his own work records that he 'bene et laudabiliter gubernavit se in temporalibus et spiritualibus', CCA Lit. Ms D.12, fo 35.

Name in CCA Lit. Ms D.12, Nomina monachorum vivorum et mortuorum istius ecclesie . . . ab anno Johannis, regis octavo usque ad annum Henrici regis vii^mi^, xix^mo^.

Walter CAUSTON
occ. 1367 d. 1419

1367, 11 Nov., one of nine prof., *SL*, 182, CCA Lit. Ms D.12, fo 4v.
1368, 24 Feb., prof. acc. to *SL*, 128 with no ref., but see below.

1383, 25 Nov., apptd master of St Thomas' hospital [Eastbridge], *Chron. Stone*, 10 (Reg. abp Courtenay, i, fo 252v).
1396/7, precentor, CCA DCc Prior acct 4.

1381, 31 July, 46th in order at the el. of an abp, Reg. G, fo 225v.
1391/2, chaplain to the abp and recd 40s. *pro cameraria* from the chamberlain, CCA DCc Chamb. acct 56.
1396, 7 Aug., 19th at the el. of an abp, Reg. G, fo 234v.
1396, after Sept., apptd prior of Dover by abp Arundel; removed by abp Chichele and returned to Christ Church, CCA Lit. Ms D.12, fo 21v, *Chron. Stone*, 10, records that he returned to Canterbury in 1421 which must be a scribal error prob. for 1412. He was provided by Dover with a pension of £10 [p.a.] and at Christ Church was given a private chamber for himself and his servant; he dined with the prior or cellarer and pd 10m. p.a. for room and board, but took no part in chapter or other community activities.
1419, d., after c.52 yrs of monastic life, and all was performed for him as for William Dover III, q.v., *Chron. Stone*, 10 and CCA Lit. Ms D.12, fo 12v.

Abp Courtenay left him a legacy of 10m., in Sept., 1396, L. Duncan, 'The Will of William Courtenay, Archbishop of Canterbury', in *Archaeologia Cantiana*, xxiii, 62.

William CAUSTON [Kauston, Kauxton, Kawston
occ. 1519 occ. 1540

1519, 6 May, one of nine tonsured, *SL*, 194, CCA Lit. Ms D.12, fo 11^{v}.
1520, 3 Feb., prof., *ib.*
1525/6, celebrated his first mass and recd 9d. from the sacrist, Woodruff, 'Sacrist's Rolls', 72. He also recd a gift from William Ingram I penitentiary, q.v., CCA Lit. Ms C.11, fo 139^{v}.

[1538, 8 Feb., after] in a list of monks prob. prepared for Thomas Cromwell he was described as 'a good man', 39 yrs old, Pantin, *Cant. Coll. Ox.*, iii, 153.
1540, 4 Apr., awarded £6 p.a., *L and P Henry VIII*, xv, no 452.

CAWYN
see Colkin

CELESEYA
see Selesia

CELLING
see Sellyng

CERRINGE
see Charyng, Cherryng

Thomas CHALMYSFORD
occ. 2nd half 13th c.

n.d., name occ. in the list in *SL*, 177, CCA Lit. Ms D.12, fo 2.

Note: see John de Shamelysford who may be the same monk.

William CHALONER
see Kenerton

CHANDELER
see Chaundeler

CHARING(E)
see Charyng, Cherryng

CHARLES
occ. 1206

1206, 30 Mar., one of the monks summoned by the pope to Rome to give evidence in the dispute over their el. of Reginald, q.v., as abp. *CPL*, i (1198–1304), 26; while there, they el. Stephen Langton, *Fasti*, ii, 6.

Reginald CHARLYS [Charles
occ. 1314 d. 1329

1314, 13 Dec., one of five prof., *SL*, 179, CCA Lit. Ms D.12, fo 3^{v}.
1315, 20 Dec., ord subdcn, Maidstone, Reg. abp Reynolds, fo 173^{v}.

1329, 1 Aug., d., CCA Lit. Ms D.12, fo 16 (as Richard).

In an inventory of missing service books dated 1338, 1 Mar., his name was associated with Psalterium Sancti Silvestri and Exequiae, *Lit. Cant.* no 618 (Reg. L, fo 104).

I John CHART [Charte
occ. 1403 occ. 1427/8

1403, 22 Dec., one of six prof., *SL*, 185, CCA Lit. Ms D.12, fo 5^{v}.
1404, 29 Mar., ord acol., Canterbury cathedral, Reg. abp Arundel, i, fo 332^{v}.
1405, 18 Apr., ord subdcn, Canterbury cathedral, *ib.*, i, fo 333^{v}.
1407, 26 Mar., ord dcn, Canterbury cathedral, *ib.*, i, fo 340^{v}.
1410, 13 Sept., ord pr., abp's chapel, Ford, *ib.*, ii, fo 99.
1419, 25 Jan., *magister ordinis*, *SL*, 186, CCA Lit. Ms D.12, fo 6^{v}.
1422/3, warden of manors, CCA DCc, Prior acct 5.
1422/4, bartoner, CCA DCc, Bart. accts, 85, 86.
1426, 7 May, *magister ordinis*, *SL*, 187, CCA Lit. Ms D.12, fo 7.
1426/7, bartoner and warden of manors, CCA DCc, Bart. acct 89, Adisham acct 54.
1427/8, warden of manors, CCA DCc, Bocking acct 57.

1414, 12 Mar., 56th in order at the el. of an abp, *Reg. abp Chichele*, i, 4.
n.d., licensed to go to the Roman curia *sed non est reversus*, Chron. Wm Glastynbury, fo 168^{v}/162^{v}.

II John CHART [Charte
occ. 1511 occ. 1540

1511, 1 Sept., one of eight tonsured, *SL*, 194, CCA Lit. Ms D.12, fo 11.
1512, 19 Apr., prof., *ib.*
1513, 26 Mar., ord subdcn, Canterbury cathedral, Reg. abp Warham, ii, fo 266^{v}.
1516/17, celebrated his first mass and recd 8d. from the sacrist, Woodruff, 'Sacrist's Rolls', 69.
1532, 24 June, [1538, 8 Feb., after], warden of St Mary in crypt, CCA Lit. Ms C.11, fo 68, Pantin, *Cant. Coll. Ox.*, iii, 153.
1540, 4 Apr., *magister mense*, *L and P Henry VIII*, xv, no 452.

1518/19, student, provided with travelling expenses from Canterbury to Oxford, Pantin, *Cant. Coll. Ox*, iv, 206.
1521/2, student, whose stipend amounted to £6 10s., Pantin, *ib.*, ii, 258 (CCA DCc Cart. Antiq. O.151.46).

1511, 2 Sept., not prof., 87th and last but one in order on the visitation certificate, Wood-Legh, *Visit.*, 3 (Reg. abp Warham, i, fo 35^{v}).
n.d., as a novice had Thomas Goldston III q.v., as his *magister regule*, Pantin, *Cant. Coll. Ox.*, iv,

54 (CCA DCc Ms Scrap Book B.186). He was examined by John Sudbury, q.v.

[1538, 8 Feb., after], in a list of monks prob. prepared for Thomas Cromwell he was described as a 'symple' man, 28 (xxviii) yrs old, Pantin, *Cant. Coll. Ox.*, iii, 153.

Note: this cannot be correct, possibly it should be xxxviii.

1540, 4 Apr., awarded £3 p.a., and became a petty canon in the new foundation, *L and P Henry VIII*, xv, no 452.

I Thomas CHART [Chartham

occ. [1393] d. 1448

[1393], 21 Nov., one of six prof., *SL*, 184, CCA Lit. Ms D.12, fo 5.

1394, 18 Apr., ord subdcn, Canterbury cathedral, Reg. abp Courtenay, ii, fo 184ᵛ.

1396, 1 Apr., ord dcn, Canterbury cathedral, *ib.*, ii, fo 186ᵛ.

1419/22, bartoner, CCA DCc, Bart. accts 81–83.

1422, 20 Apr., apptd penitentiary in the priory, *Reg. abp Chichele*, iv, 246; see Richard Godmersham I.

1428, 2 Jan., *magister ordinis*, *SL*, 189, CCA Lit. Ms D.12, fo 7.

1429/31, anniversarian with John Elham II, q.v., Lambeth ED37A, 38.

1431, 25 June, treasurer, CCA DCc, MA25, fo 31a.

1435, 1436/7, *custos tumbe*, 'Chron. Wm Glastynbury', 129, CCA DCc Prior Acct 7.

1438/9, 1440/2, granator, CCA DCc, Gran. accts 47, 48, 50.

1396, 7 Aug., 73rd in order at the el. of an abp, Reg. G, fo 234ᵛ.

1414, 12 Mar., 33rd at the el. of an abp, *Reg. abp Chichele*, i, 4.

1448, 13 Mar., d., 'tempore collationis monachatus sui anno lj', CCA Lit. Ms D.12, fo 25ᵛ but *Chron. Stone*, 43, records 'per annos lv et amplius' which seems more accurate. In CCA Lit. Ms D.12, *ib.*, he is described as 'vir religiosus et elegantis stature, pius, hillaris largus singulisque affabilis' who served faithfully and prudently in many offices.

Note: he seems to have been known indifferently as Chart and Chartham.

II Thomas CHART [Charte

occ. 1446 d. 1501

1446, adm., at the age of 15; see below.

1451, 21 Oct., one of four prof., *SL*, 189, CCA Lit. Ms D.12, fo 7ᵛ.

1452, 8 Apr., ord acol., Canterbury cathedral, Reg. abp Stafford, fo 206ᵛ.

1453, 31 Mar., ord subdcn, Canterbury cathedral, Reg. abp Kemp, fo 254ᵛ.

1457, 2 Apr., ord pr., Canterbury cathedral, *Reg. abp Bourgchier*, 366.

1466, 17 Feb., 46th in order in an inventory listing *jocalia fratrum* [given by him and/or assigned for his use], Reg. N, fo 233ᵛ.

1486/9, 1490/2, recd small sums (rewards) as organist, CCA DCc MA7, fos 38, 68ᵛ, 93, 151, 171.

1492/3, recd 6s. 8d. from the sacrist for playing the organ, Woodruff, 'Sacrist's Rolls', 64.

1493, 1 May, 12th in order at the ratification of an agreement, Reg. S, fo 383ᵛ; but see John Crosse I.

1501, 14 Mar., d., CCA DCc Sac. acct 70 and the notice in CCA Lit. Ms D.12, fo 33. The latter records that he had been a monk for 55 yrs and was aged 70. He was 'in musicis et organis bene instructus et valde devotus', CCA Lit. Ms D.12, *ib.*

An inventory of the martyrdom dated 19 May, 1500 includes linen cloth and hangings of his [?gift] on which were painted images of the Crucified and of Sts Mary and John, Legg and Hope, *Inventories*, 128. A similar inventory dated 6 July 1503 includes a set of purple vestments described as *quondam* his, *ex dono* Thomas Goldston IV prior, q.v., *ib.*, 130.

III Thomas CHART

occ. 1502 d. 1508/9

1502, 25 Aug., one of eight tonsured, *SL*, 193, CCA Lit. Ms D.12, fo 10.

1503, 4 Apr., made his prof. before the prior, *sed. vac.*, *ib.*

1505, 22 Mar., ord subdcn, Canterbury cathedral, Reg. abp Warham, ii, fo 262.

1506, 11 Apr., ord dcn, Canterbury cathedral, *ib.*, ii, fo 262ᵛ.

1508, 22 Apr., ord pr., Canterbury cathedral, *ib.*, ii, fo 263ᵛ.

1507/8, celebrated his first mass and recd a gift of 10d. from the sacrist, Woodruff, 'Sacrist's Rolls', 68 (CCA DCc Sac. acct, 64). He celebrated on the second Sunday in May [1508] and recd 4d. from the *custos martyrii*, CCA Lit. Ms C.11, fo 50.

1508/9, d., Woodruff, 'Sacrist's Rolls', 68 (CCA DCc Sac. acct 71);

I William CHART B.Cn.L. [Charte, Chert

occ. 1370 d. 1418

1370, 2 or 6 June, one of four tonsured, *SL*, 182, CCA Lit. Ms D.12, fo 4ᵛ.

1372, 14 Mar., the prior was comm. to rec. his prof., Reg. abp Wittlesey, fo 52.

1372, 18 Sept., ord subdcn, abp's chapel, Saltwood, *ib.*, fo 169ᵛ.

1373, 12 Mar., ord dcn, abp's chapel, Charing, *ib.*, fo 170.

1373, 16 Apr., ord pr., Canterbury cathedral, *ib.*, fo 170ᵛ.

1381, 14 May, apptd penitentiary for the priory, Reg. abp Sudbury, fo 76.

1382, 15 Sept., apptd 2nd penitentiary, Reg. abp Courtenay, i, fo 22.
1386/7; 1387/91, cellarer, Lambeth Ms 243, fo 205, CCA DCc Arrears acct 117; Agney acct 60.
1390/1, treasurer, with William Stone, q.v., Lambeth Ms 243, fo 219.
1391/2, almoner, CCA DCc Alm. acct 1.
1393, 1397, warden of Canterbury college at the time of the *nova constructura*, CCA Lit. Ms D.12, fo 21; see below. His accts as warden 1393/7 provide details of the building operations, Pantin, *Cant. Coll. Ox.*, ii, 132–147 (CCA DCc Cart. Antiq. O.151.2, 3, O.141.C).
1410/11, subprior, CCA DCc Prior acct 2; subprior for ten yrs, CCA Lit. Ms D.12, fo 21 (thirteen yrs, in *Chron. Stone*, 9).
n.d., *coronarius*, CCA Lit. Ms D.12, fo 21.
n.d., granator, his last office, *ib.*

1376/7, recd 6s. 8d. from the treasurer for his [?first] journey to Oxford, Pantin, *Cant. Coll. Ox.*, iv, 187.
1383, B.Cn.L. by this date, *ib.*, iii, 45.
1396/7, recd £167 6s. 8d. from the prior for the construction of new buildings at Canterbury college of which he had oversight, *ib.*, iv, 191.
1397/8, still at Oxford and one of six who recd a small sum from the feretrars *pro benedictione*, CCA DCc, Feret. acct 1.

1374, 30 June, 57th in order at the el. of an abp, Reg. G, fos 173^v–175^v.
1377, 2 Jan., absent from the visitation because he was a student at Oxford, Reg. abp Sudbury, fo 32.
1381, 31 July, 43rd at the el. of an abp, and named as one of the six *compromissorii* chosen by the three previously named, Reg. G, fo 225^v, Oxford, Bod. Ms Ashmole 794, fo 254^v.
1382/3, with John Gloucestre I, q.v. and others involved in negotiations with the abp over the apptment of William de Dover III, q.v. to the wardenship of Canterbury college, Pantin, *Cant. Coll. Ox.*, iv, 188, 189.
1396, 7 Aug., 23rd at the el. of an abp, Reg. G, fo 234^v.
1414, 12 Mar., 4th at the el. of an abp, *Reg. abp Chichele*, i, 4.
1418, 17 Oct., d. in his 48th yr of monastic life, having spent his last yrs as a *stationarius* in St John's chamber in the infirmary; he was buried in the infirmary chapel before the altar of St Benedict and St Leonard, *Chron. Stone*, 9. His obit is in BL Ms Arundel 68, fo 45^v.

II William CHART [Charte

occ. 1438 d. 1458

1438, 9 Jan., one of four prof., *SL*, 188, CCA Lit. Ms D.12, fo 7^v.
1439, 19 Dec., ord subdcn, prior's chapel, 'Chron. Wm Glastynbury', 133 (Ms fo 119).
1455/6, 1st anniversarian, with William Covyntre II, q.v., CCA DCc Prior acct 10.
1442, 20 Oct., set out for Oxford with 20s. for expenses, Pantin, *Cant. Coll. Ox.*, iv, 193.
1444, Mar., at Canterbury college and excused from attendance at a visitation, *ib.*, iii, 101 (Reg. S, fo 159); he was reported as one of those unable to be present at the visitation because *ad studium generale transmissis*, Reg. abp Stafford, fo 41.

1440, Feb., novice and 'proclaimed' by Thomas Newton, q.v. [his *magister regule*] to appear for his final examination [*redditus*] on 21 Feb., at which time he 'respondit de vi historiis vii responsoriis', Pantin, *Cant. Coll. Ox.*, iv, 53 (Chron. Wm Glastynbury, fo 119^v).
1456/7, recd money from the treasurer on his departure for Ireland, CCA DCc Treas. acct 17.
1458, 14 July, d., in Ireland and was buried before the high altar at Tintern abbey, *Chron. Stone*, 75, CCA Lit. Ms D.12, fo 26. His obit is in BL Ms Arundel 68, fo 34.

For the collection of humanist texts compiled by him see K. Nishimoto, ed., *Codex Streeterianus*, University of Tokyo, 1987 and further refs in Weiss, *Humanism*, 129, n. 4, and B. Dobson, 'Canterbury in the Later Middle Ages' in Collinson, *Canterbury Cathedral*, 113, n. 218.

I John de CHARTHAM

occ. 1294 occ. 1299

1294, 18 Oct., one of eight prof., *SL*, 178, CCA Lit. Ms D.12, fo 3.
1299, 19 Sept., ord pr., Littlebourne, *Reg. abp Winchelsey*, 931.

II John de CHARTHAM [Chertham

occ. c. 1302 d. 1331

c. 1302, 24 Oct., one of four prof., *SL*, 178 (which has the wrong month), CCA Lit. Ms D.12, fo 3^v.
1325/27, warden of manors, CCA DCc MA2 fos 143–162.
1331, 22 July, d., CCA Lit. Ms D.12, fo 16.

An inventory of missing service books, dated 1 Mar. 1338, holds him responsible for the missale of Anselm de Eastry q.v., *Lit. Cant.* no 618 (Reg. L, fo 104).

I Thomas de CHARTHAM [Chertham

occ. 1370 occ. 1374

1370, 2 or 6 June, one of four tonsured, *SL*, 182, CCA Lit. Ms D.12, fo 4^v.
1372, 14 Mar., the prior was comm. to rec. his prof., Reg. abp Wittlesey, fo 52.
1373, 12 Mar., ord dcn, abp's chapel, Charing, *ib.*, fo 170.
1373, 16 Apr., ord pr., Canterbury cathedral, *ib.*, fo 170^v.

1374, 30 June, 59th in order at the el. of an abp, Reg. G, fos 173v–175v.
1374/5, ill and the anniversarian pd him a 'pension' of 11s. 10d., CCA DCc Anniv. acct 6.

II Thomas CHARTHAM
see I Thomas Chart

III Thomas CHARTHAM B.Cn.L.
occ. 1457 d. 1471

1457, 13 Dec., one of six who were adm. as monks, *Chron. Stone*, 71, *SL*, 189.
1458, 12 Feb., 'venerunt ad parvum servitium', *ib.*; and on 26 Feb. *ad commune servitium*, *ib.*
1458, 1 Apr., ord acol. Canterbury cathedral, *Reg. abp Bourgchier*, 368.
1458, 21 Apr., one of the same six who made their prof., *Chron. Stone*, 71.
1459, 24 Mar., ord dcn, Canterbury cathedral, *ib.*, 371.
1462, 12 June, ord pr., abp's chapel, Otford, *ib.*, 382.
1470, one of the chancellors, Reg. S, fo 245v; see William Sellyng.
1466/8, scholar at Canterbury college, Pantin, *Cant. Coll. Ox.*, ii, 185, 188 (CCA DCc Cart. Antiq. O.151.18, 19), *ib.*, iv, 206.
1470, by this date B.Cn.L., Reg. S, fo 245v.
1466, 17 Feb., 55th in order in an inventory listing *jocalia fratrum* [given by him and/or assigned for his use], Reg. N., fo 234.
1471, 17 Aug., d. in his bed, *Chron. Stone*, 116; his obit is in BL Ms Arundel 68, fo 38v.

I William de CHARTHAM [Chertham
occ. 1329 occ. 1356

1329, 9 Oct., one of eight prof., *SL*, 180, CCA Lit. Ms D.12, fo 3v.
1335/6, subcellarer, CCA DCc AS 14, MA2 fo 250v.
1336/7, treasurer, CCA DCc MA2 fo 253.
1342/6, warden of manors, CCA DCc, Bocking accts 24–26, Illeigh acct 20.
1345/6, chaplain to the prior, CCA DCc Adisham acct 21.
1346/8, warden of manors, CCA DCc Bocking acct 29, Cliffe acct 35.
1348/9, chaplain to the prior, CCA DCc Meopham acct 86.
1351/2, subprior, CCA DCc Lydden acct 63; he was apptd 11 Mar. [1351], Reg. abp Islip, fo 42.
1352, Apr./1355, almoner, CCA DCc Alm. acct 48, Eastry accts 85–87.
1349, 4 June, 26th in order at the el. of an abp and named as one of thirteen *compromissorii*, Reg. G, fos 60v–61v.
1349, 8/9 Sept., 25th at the el. of an abp and named as one of three *compromissorii* who were authorized to choose ten more to augment their number, *ib.*, fos 76, 77.
1356, 7 July, apptd prior of Dover, Reg. abp Islip, fo 272v; on 6 Oct. 1357 he was apptd for life, *ib.*, fo 136v.
1366, d., and was succ. as prior by James de Stone I, q.v.

II William CHARTHAM [Charteham, Chatham
occ. 1403 d. 1448

1403, 22 Dec., one of six prof., *SL*, 185, CCA Lit. Ms D.12, fo 5v.
1404, 29 Mar., ord acol. and subdcn, Canterbury cathedral, Reg. Arundel, i, fo 332v.
1421, 4 Apr., *magister ordinis*, *SL*, 186, CCA Lit. Ms D.12, fo 6v.
1421/2, fourth prior, CCA DCc, Sac. acct 21.
1435, 25 Dec., apptd third prior, Chron. Wm Glastynbury, fo 117v.
1442/3, *coronarius*, CCA DCc, Prior acct 6.
1443/5, 1446/7, granator, Gran. accts 51, 53, 55.
1414, 12 Mar., 59th in order at the el. of an abp, *Reg. abp Chichele*, i, 4.
1439, 20 Jan., one of several monks licensed to leave the priory *pro recreacione*, and he returned on 31 Jan., Chron. Wm Glastynbury, fo 182v/177v.
1448, 14 Feb., d., *Chron. Stone*, 42; his obit, as William Chatham, occ. on 15 Feb., in BL Ms Arundel 68, fo 16.

Name [Chartham] in Lambeth Ms 78, Speculum parvulorum 'liber compositus et perquisitus A.D. 1448'; see also John Salisbury III and *Anglia Sacra*, i, xx, 49. He was possibly the author of this ms.

III William CHARTHAM [Charteham
occ. 1473 d. 1487

1473, 13 Mar., ord acol., Canterbury cathedral, *Reg. abp Bourgchier*, 410.
1474, 26 Mar., ord subdcn, Canterbury cathedral, *ib.*, 416.
1477, 20 Dec., ord dcn, Winchester cathedral, by *lit. dim.*, from the abp, Reg. Waynflete (Winchester), ii, fo 179.
1481, 22 Sept., ord pr., Sevenoaks, *Reg. abp Bourgchier*, 433.
1476, 21 Apr., scholar at Canterbury college and recd 10s. for his *capa*, Pantin, *Cant. Coll. Ox.*, iv, 199.
1478/9, 1481/2, 1486/7, recd a scholar's stipend of £8, *ib.*, ii, 207, 211, 216 (CCA DCc Cart. Antiq. O.151.22.b, 24.a, 26).
[c. 1476 × 1487], his misbehaviour and subsequent repentance were reported to the prior by Thomas Goldstone IV, q.v., Pantin, *Cant. Coll. Ox.*, iii, 117–118.
[1486], student at Oxford, licensed to preach in Canterbury diocese, Reg. R, fo 8v.
1487, 12 Aug., d. at Oxford, aged 28, of the plague and was buried at St Frideswide's pri-

ory, CCA Lit. Ms D.12, fo 26v. The obit of a William Chartham occ. in BL Ms Arundel 68, fo 37v, on 10 Aug. A letter from the warden to the prior, dated 15 Nov. [1487] concerning his books, belongings and debts is in Pantin, *Cant. Coll. Ox.*, iii, 128–129.

IV William CHARTHAM [Charteham, *alias* Parett
occ. 1488 occ. 1515

1488, 12 Mar., one of six tonsured, SL 191, CCA Lit. Ms D.12, fo 9.
1488, 30 Sept., made his prof. before the cardinal abp, *ib.*
1490, 10 Apr., ord subdcn, Canterbury cathedral, *Reg. abp Morton*, i, no 438b.
1491, 2 Apr., ord dcn, Canterbury cathedral, *ib.*, i, no 439c.
1493, 6 Apr., ord pr., Canterbury cathedral, *ib.*, i, no 442d.
1500/1, fourth prior, CCA DCc MA10, fo 36.
1501/2, novice master and fourth prior, CCA DCc MA10, fo 99.
1502/3, Aug. to Apr., third prior and *magister ordinis*, CCA Lit. Ms D.12, fo 10.
1504, 5 June, chancellor with Roger Benett, q.v., Reg. T, fos 442–443; see Richard Sellyng.
1508/10, 1511/13, treasurer, Lambeth ED88 and Ms 951/1/31, CCA DCc, Treas. acct 24, Lambeth Ms 951/1/32.
1513, 1514, 1515, all on 25 Dec., treasurer, CCA Lit. Ms C.11 fos 55v, 56v, 57v.

1493, 1 May, 53rd in order at the ratification of an agreement, Reg. S, fo 383v; but see John Crosse I.
1501, 26 Apr., 37th in order at the el. of an abp, Reg. R, fo 56v.
1511, 2 Sept., 21st on the visitation certificate, Wood-Legh, *Visit.*, 3 (Reg. abp Warham, i, fo 35).
n.d., 26 Jan., the obit of a William Chartham *alias* Parett has been added to BL Ms Arundel 68, fo 14v.

Several brothers and sisters named Parett were recd into confraternity with Christ Church c. 1516, BL Ms Arundel 68, fo 11v.

V William CHARTHAM
occ. 1519 occ. 1525/6

1519, 6 May, one of nine tonsured, *SL*, 194, CCA Lit. Ms D.12, fo 11v.
1520, 3 Feb., prof., *ib.*
1525/6, celebrated his first mass and recd 9d. from the sacrist, Woodruff, 'Sacrist's Rolls', 72; he also recd a small sum from William Ingram I, q.v., CCA Lit. Ms C.11, fo 139v.

CHARTHAM
see also Chertham

John CHARYNG [Charinge, Charryng
occ. 1446 d. 1482

1446, 21 Dec., one of seven tonsured, *SL*, 188, CCA Lit. Ms D.12, fo 7v.
1447, 4 Mar., ord acol., Canterbury cathedral, Reg. abp Stafford, fo 199.
1447, 27 Aug., made his prof. before the abp, *Chron. Stone*, 41–42.
1447, 23 Dec., ord subdcn, Canterbury cathedral, Reg. abp Stafford, fo 201v.
1448, 17 Feb., ord dcn, Canterbury cathedral, *ib.*, fo 202.
1451, 20 Mar., ord pr., Canterbury cathedral, *ib.*, fo 205v.

1449, 7 Dec., was examined by a board of senior monks de *redditu*, *Chron. Stone*, 47.
1466, 17 Feb., 37th in order in an inventory listing *jocalia fratrum* [given by him and/or assigned for his use], Reg. N, fo 233v.
1482, 28 Oct., d., and all the funeral rites took place immediately before the office of none, CCA Lit. Ms D.12, fo 26v; the obit is in BL Ms Arundel 68, fo 46v.

CHARYNG
see also Cherryng

John de CHATHAM [Chetham, ?Chertham
occ. 1222/3 occ. 1238

[1236]–1238, prior: prob. occ. [but unnamed] before 11 Aug. 1236, when he was apparently apptd by the abp with the consent of the convent; forced to res. by the abp, Nov. 1238, *Fasti*, ii, ll; and see below.

1222/3, July, cellarer, CCA DCc MA1 fo 67v; see below.

[1222 × 1237], before he became prior he was one of the monks named by M. Laurence de St Nicholas to arrange for his obit celebrations, *Acta Guala*, no 155.
1236, visited Dover priory, *sed. vac*; the prior Robert de Holekumbe, q.v., and the monks objected but had to submit, Haines, *Dover Priory*, 328 with no ref.
1236/7, was privy to the forging of the torn charter of St Thomas and held responsible with the offenders, Simon de Hertlepe and Bartholomew de Sandwyco, q.v. His treatment of Ralph de Orpynton, q.v., whom he had called in to assist in the forgery, and his admission under examination by the papal legate, Otto, that he had altered and later had had destroyed a papal deocument that contained material not in the chapter's interests, led to his res. and departure and 'cum summa festinatione ad habitum Chertehusiensem convolavit', *Gervase Cant.*, ii, 133, Paris, *Chron Majora*, iii, 492.
n.d., described as *quondam prior*, his obit occ. on 8 July in BL Ms Arundel 68, fo 33v.

In the list of missing books dated 1 Mar. 1338, a Bible, formerly belonging to him or to Robert VIII, q.v., was charged out to John de Wynchelse I, q.v., *Lit. Cant.*, no 618 (Reg. L, fo 104).

Note: this is prob. not the John de Chertham q.v., who occ. in the *post exilium* list, *SL*, 172, CCA Lit. Ms D.12, fo 1; however, either of the two could have been cellarer.

CHATHAM
see also Chartham, Chetham

Thomas CHAUNDELER D.Th. [Chandeler, Chandellor, Chandler, Chaundler, Chawndeler
occ. 1481 occ. 1501

1481, 21 Dec., one of four prof., *SL*, 191, CCA Lit. Ms D.12, fo 8v.
1483, 29 Mar., ord subdcn, Canterbury cathedral, *Reg. abp Bourgchier*, 439.
1484, 17 Apr., ord dcn, Canterbury cathedral, *ib.*, 444.
1485, 24 Sept., ord pr., Canterbury cathedral, *ib.*, 452.

1496, 1498/1501, warden of Canterbury college, Pantin, *Cant. Coll. Ox.*, ii, 223–232 (CCA DCc Cart. Antiq. O.151.29–32); these are his accts as warden. The inventory at the time of his relinquishing office is in *ib.*, i, 18–34 (CCA DCc, Cart. Antiq. O.137).
1501, 27 July, apptd penitentiary of the priory by the abp, CCA DCc DE64.
1501/4, granator, CCA DCc MA10, fos 101v, 166, 181v.

[1487], student at Canterbury college for half the yr, Pantin, *Cant. Coll. Ox.*, ii, 268 (CCA DCc Ms Scrap Book B.49).
1489/90, scholar at Canterbury college, Pantin, *Cant. Coll. Ox.*, ii, 221 (CCA DCc Cart. Antiq. O.151.28).
1492/3, at Oxford and recd £4 for his stipend for half a yr, Pantin, *Cant. Coll. Ox.*, iv, 202.
1494, Mar., recd 18s. for travel expenses from Oxford to Canterbury, and 36s. for the return journey to Oxford in May, *ib.*
1495, 2/8 Feb., returned to Canterbury to participate in the el. of a new prior, *ib.*, iv, 203; he was prob. at Oxford for half the yr, *ib.*, ii, 270 (CCA DCc Ms Scrap Book B.49).
1496, 1 May, spent 12s. on a journey from Oxford to Canterbury, Pantin, *Cant. Coll. Ox.*, iv, 204.
1497, Feb./Mar., returned to Canterbury to preach during Lent, *ib.*
1500/1, described as *doctor*, *ib.*, iv, 205; *BRUO* states that he was D.Th. by 1498.
1501, 26 Apr., absent from the archiepiscopal el. because he was at Oxford, Reg. R, fo 56v.
1501, 27 July, apptd prior of Horsham St Faith (Norfolk); he went on to be abbot of Wymondham in 1511/14, and abbot of Eynsham in 1517, *BRUO*, with refs.
1516, described by cardinal Wolsey, who recommended that he be apptd abbot of Eynsham, as 'the flower of St Benet's order', *L and P Henry VIII*, ii, pt. 1, no 2724; see above.

John CHEKYR
see John Molond I

CHELESEYE
see Selesia

CHELHAM
see Chilham

Robert CHELMYNTON [Chelmeston, Chelmyston, Chilmyngton, Chilmynton, Chylmynton
occ. 1416 d. 1470

1416, 22 June, one of eight prof., *SL*, 186, CCA Lit. Ms D.12, fo 6.
1417, 10 Apr., ord acol., Canterbury cathedral, *Reg. abp Chichele*, iv, 327.
1418, 26 Mar., ord subdcn, Canterbury cathedral, *ib.*, iv, 332.
1419, 1 Apr., ord dcn, chapel within the priory, *ib.*, i, 191.

1435, 11 Nov., absolved from the office of *custos martyrii*, Chron. Wm Glastynbury, fo 117v.
1435, 11 Nov., apptd *magister ordinis*, *ib.*
1436/7, feretrar, CCA DCc Prior acct 7.
1438/44, anniversarian, Chron. Wm Glastynbury, fos 146v–151.
1442/3, warden of St Mary in crypt, CCA DCc Prior acct 6.
1444/5, chaplain to the prior, CCA DCc MA4, fo 32.
1445/7, third prior, CCA DCc Sac. acct 33, Gran. acct 55.
1450/2, 1453/4, anniversarian, CCA DCc Anniv. accts 10, 11, Prior acct 9.
1462, 26 Dec., penitentiary, *Lit. Cant.*, no 1051 (Reg. S, fo 199v).

1439, 7 Jan., one of several monks licensed to leave the priory *pro recreacione*, and he returned on 20 Jan., Chron. Wm Glastynbury, fo 182v/177v.
1462, 26 Dec., as penitentiary, signed with the cross a pilgrim who had made a private vow to go to the Holy Land, *Lit. Cant.* no 1051 (Reg. S, fo 199v); see William Thornden.
1466, 17 Feb., 8th in order in an inventory listing *jocalia fratrum* [given by him and/or assigned for his use], Reg. N, fo 230v.
1470, 4 Dec., d., described as penitentiary *per multos annos*; he had been a monk for 55 yrs, 'et non fit absolutus a tabula', *Chron. Stone*, 114.

Name in
(1) CCA Lit. Ms B.10, T. de Chabham etc. (14th c.); his name and the date 1452 on the front cover.

(2) Oxford, Bod. Ms Rawlinson C.269, R. Rolle etc. (15th c.); his name and the date 1454; see William Dover IV.

William de CHERRYNG [Cerringe
occ. 1270 d. 1296

n.d., occ. in the list in *SL*, 175, CCA Lit. Ms D.12, fo 2v.

[1274 × 1275], 1276/7, warden of manors, Reg. B, fo 138, Reg. H, fo 204v; see Stephen de Ikham.
1286/7, granator, CCA DCc Thes. acct 3.

1270, 9 Sept., named as one of the seven *compromissorii* in the el. of an abp, *Gervase Cant.*, ii, 253; see Adam de Chillenden.
1296, 3 Mar., d., CCA Lit. Ms D.12, fo 15.

In an inventory of missing books dated 1 Mar. 1338 the Biblus which had belonged to him or to Robert Sacriste, q.v. is included and also his psalterium beate Marie which had been lost by Richard de Rawe, q.v., *Lit. Cant.*, no 618 (Reg. L, fo 104).

A list of vestments, *temp.* prior Eastry, includes an alb of linen *consuta* with shields and black letters [?formerly his], Legg and Hope, *Inventories*, 59 (BL Ms Cotton Galba E.iv, fo 115).

CHERRYNG
see also Charyng

CHERT
see Chart

John de CHERTHAM
occ. first half 12th c.

n.d., name occ. in the *post exilium* list in *SL*, 172, CCA Lit. Ms D.12, fo 1.

n.d., 28 July, obit occ. in BL Ms Arundel 68, fo 36.

Note: see also John de Chartham I who may be this monk.

CHERTHAM
see also Chartham

Simon de CHESTERFORDE [Chestrefford
occ. 1363 occ. 1367

1363, 6 Aug., ord acol., abp's chapel, Canterbury, Reg. abp Islip, fo 323.
1364, n.d., one of eleven prof., *SL*, 182, CCA Lit. Ms D.12, fo 4v.
1364, 9 Mar., ord subdcn, abp's chapel, Charing, Reg. abp Islip, fo 325.
1365, 29 Mar., ord dcn, abp's chapel, Charing, *ib.*, fo 326.
1367, 18 Sept., ord pr., Lambeth palace chapel, *Reg. abp Langham*, 383 (as Chesterfeld).

n.d., 19 Mar., obit occ. in BL Ms Arundel 68, fo 21.

Richard de CHETHAM
occ. 2nd half 13th c.

n.d., name occ. in the list in *SL*, 175, CCA Lit. Ms D.12, fo 2v; *SL* has rendered it as Cheteham.

CHETHAM
see also Chatham

CHEVENE
see Chyvene

Laurence de CHEYHAM
occ. 1294 occ. 1302

[1286, 8 June, a Laurence de Cheyham was ord acol. at Wimbledon, *Epist. Pecham*, 1039 and *Reg. abp Pecham*, i, 231.]
1294, 18 Oct., one of eight prof., *SL*, 178, CCA Lit. Ms D.12, fo 3.

[1296], one of the monks accused of laxity in attendance at divine office, *Reg. abp Winchelsey*, 92.
1302, 10 May, with Alexander de Sandwyco, q.v., present as witnesses in the prior's chapel to the oath of obedience of a rector, CUL Ms Ee.5.31, fo 85.

In an inventory of missing service books dated 1 Mar. 1338, he was held responsible for the loss of a psalter which [?had] belonged to Peter de Bokkynge, q.v., *Lit. Cant.*, no 618 (Reg. L, fo 104).

I William CHICHELE B.Th. [Chichelee, Chicheley, Chichilee, Chichiley, Chychele
occ. 1459 d. 1474

1459, 30 Nov., one of six prof., *SL*, 189, CCA Lit. Ms D.12, fo 8.
1460, 12 Apr., ord dcn, Canterbury cathedral, *Reg. abp Bourgchier*, 376.
1465, 21 Sept., ord pr., Mersham, *ib.*, 392.

1471, 13 Oct., [1473], warden of Canterbury college, and he was still warden when he d. in 1474, Pantin, *Cant. Coll. Ox.*, iv, 197, *ib.*, ii, 263; see also Pantin, *ib.*, iii, 110–112, 113 and CCA Lit. Ms D.12, fo 26.

1462/3, 1466/8, 1469/71, scholar at Canterbury college, Pantin, *Cant. Coll. Ox.*, ii, 183, 185, 188, 190, 193 (CCA DCc Cart. Antiq., O.151.17, 18, 19, 20, 4).
1469/70, acting *custos* there in the absence of Reginald Goldston I, q.v., *ib.*, ii, 190 (Cart. Antiq. O.151.20).

1466, 17 Feb., 59th in order in an inventory listing *jocalia fratrum* [given by him and/or assigned for his use], Reg. N, fo 234v.
1468, 13 Mar., with Reginald Goldston I, q.v., recd money for travel expenses between Oxford and Canterbury *pro sermonibus dicendis*, Pantin, *Cant. Coll. Ox.*, iv, 196.
1468, 18 Sept., 1471, 6 Oct., recd sums for similar journeys, *ib.*, iv, 196, 197.

1472/3, recd 40s. on being adm. B.Th., *ib.*, iv, 198. In this yr the *CU Grace Bk A*, 97, records 'concessa est gracia monacho priori collegii Cantuarie Oxonie ut possit cum forma ibi habita apponere hic in sacra theologia' (quoted in Pantin, *Cant. Coll. Ox.*, iv, 199.

1473, 9 May, 1474, 24 Apr., continued to make regular journeys between Oxford and Canterbury, Pantin, *Cant. Coll. Ox.*, iv, 199.

1472/3, returned to Canterbury to give the Good Friday sermon and recd expenses of 6s. 8d., Pantin, *Cant. Coll. Ox.*, iv, 198.

[1474], 7 July, d. at Oxford, *BRUO*; his obit is in BL Ms Arundel 68, fo 33.

II William CHICHELE [Chichelee, Chychele, Chychley

occ. 1477 occ. 1524

1477, 22 Mar., ord subdcn, Canterbury cathedral, *Reg. abp Bourgchier*, 422.

1477, 19 Apr., one of four tonsured, *SL*, 191, CCA Lit. Ms D.12, fo 8v.

1477, 11 Nov., prof., *SL*, 191 and (Cambridge, Corpus Christi College, Ms 298).

1478, 7 Mar., ord dcn, Canterbury cathedral, *Reg. abp Bourgchier*, 425.

1483, 29 Mar., ord pr., Canterbury cathedral, *ib.*, 440.

1524, 23 Sept., *magister mense*, *SL*, 195.

1493, 1 May, 36th in order at the ratification of an agreement, Reg. S, fo 383v; but see John Crosse I.

1501, 26 Apr., 23rd in order at the el. of an abp, Reg. R, fo 56v.

1511, 2 Sept., 9th on the visitation certificate, Wood-Legh, *Visit.*, 3 (Reg. abp Warham, i, fo 35).

1518/19, spent time in the infirmary on several occasions, CCA DCc Infirm. acct 1.

CHILD

see Chyld

Anselm CHILD

see St Margaret

Geoffrey de CHILHAM [Chileham, Chyleham

occ. 1276 d. 1315

1276/7, 1278, 1279, 1280, 1281, treasurer, Reg. H, fo 216, CCA DCc, MA1 fos 127, 129v, 131, 134.

1282/3, cellarer, CCA DCc MA1 fos 137v–139v.

1285/7, 1287/99, 1300, warden of manors, CCA DCc Meopham acct 6, Treas. acct 3, MA1 fos 150v–222, 225.

1306/8, almoner, CCA DCc Meopham acct 47, Monkton acct 35.

1286, 7 Mar., brought in to replace Lambert de Clyve, q.v., in an agreement with St Augustine's abbey over the el. of monks, CUL Ms Ee.5.31, fo 27.

1292, 5 Oct., with Thomas Beloyzell, q.v., sent by the prior to Thomas Ryngmer, q.v., to inquire into his welfare, CUL Ms Ee.5.31, fo 34v.

1292, 11 Nov., sent with Nicholas de Borne I, q.v., as proctors to the abp, CUL Ms Ee.5.31, fo 34v.

1292/3, with John de Thaneto II, q.v., visited Meopham, *circa comp[otum audiend[um*, CCA DCc Meopham acct 17.

1295, 22 Nov., with Richard de Clyve, q.v., apptd parliamentary proctors by the prior and chapter, *Parl. Writs*, i, 531 (CUL Ms Ee.5.31, fo 66v).

1297, 7 Jan., with Robert de Elham, q.v., apptd proctors for convocation, *ib.*, fo 69–69v; in Nov., he and John de Hardys q.v., were named general proctors, *ib.*, fo 75v.

1301, 16 May, apptd proctor in negotiations with the abp, *ib.*, fo 85; and on the same day he recd a similar apptment to negotiate with the king over the payment of a papal subsidy, *ib.*

1315, 17 Feb., d., CCA Lit. Ms D.12, fo 15v; his obit is in BL Ms Arundel 68, fo 16v.

Name attached to a list of five vols in the Eastry catalogue which include Brito, Isidore and Peter Lombard, nos 1725–1729 in James, *Ancient Libraries*, 139.

An inventory of vestments, *temp.* prior Eastry, includes two chasubles of his [?gift] and an alb, Legg and Hope, *Inventories*, 52, 59 (BL Ms Cotton Galba E.iv, fos 112v, 115).

An inventory of the refectory dated 1328 includes a *ciphus de murra* of his, BL Ms Cotton Galba E.iv, fo 179v.

Henry CHILHAM [Chelham, Chylham

occ. 1381 occ. 1387/8

1381, 6 May, one of eight prof., *SL*, 183, CCA Lit. Ms D.12, fo 5.

1385, 23 Dec., ord pr., abp's chapel, Otford, Reg. abp Courtenay, i, fo 308.

1383, 1 Sept., proposed by the prior and convent as one of three nominations sent to the abp to be second scholar at Oxford in place of Thomas Dover, q.v., Pantin, *Cant. Coll. Ox.*, iii, 47 (Reg. abp Courtenay, i, fo 44v).

1385/6, recd 12d. from the prior *pro benedictione*, Lambeth Ms 243, fo 200v.

1386/7, recd 5s. *pro benedictione versus Oxoniam*, Pantin, *Cant. Coll. Ox*, iv, 190; the two refs above suggest that this was prob. not his first yr at Canterbury college, but they remain uncertain.

1387/8, recd 5s. from the prior as in the previous yr, and so he may have continued his Oxford studies, Lambeth Ms 243, fo 208v.

CHILHAM

see also Chylham

Adam de CHILLENDEN [Chilendenne, Chillendenne, Chillinden, Chylyndene
occ. 1260 d. 1274

1263 × 1264–1274, prior: el., and recd the abp's confirmation late 1263/early 1264; d. 13 Sept. 1274, *Fasti*, ii, 12.

n.d., name occ. in the list in *SL*, 175, CCA Lit. Ms D.12, fo 2.

1260, Dec./1261, Dec., treasurer, CCA DCc MA1 fos 101ᵛ, 102ᵛ.

1262/4, chamberlain, CCA DCc MA1 fos 104ᵛ–106ᵛ, AS9.

1263, with Richard de Wynchepe, q.v., *quasi* treasurers to the abp, *Gervase Cant.*, ii, 227.

1264, 24 Jan., confirmed as prior at Amiens, where he had gone to meet the abp and convey money to him acc. to Gervase, *ib.*, ii, 228: 'sors super Adam, non sors Mathiae apostoli sed voluntas archiepiscopi' and the love of money.

1270, 9 Sept., was el. abp, the seven *compromissorii* having chosen him *via inspirationis*, *ib.*, ii, 253.

1270/2, went to Rome to advance his case but res. there, possibly 16 Sept. 1272, *Fasti*, ii, 7.

1274, 13 Sept., d., as above and the obit is in BL Ms Arundel 68, fo 41ᵛ.

Name in CCA Lit. Ms D.11, J. Hispanus etc. (13th c.); on flyleaf 'Casus decretal' Adame prioris secundum Johis hyspan' '.

A list of his books is in the Eastry catalogue, nos 601–?615 in James, *Ancient Libraries*, 69–70; these vols include sermons, canon law and medical treatises, one of which was at Canterbury college in 1459, Pantin, *Cant. Coll. Ox.*, i, 100.

An inventory of vestments, *temp.* prior Eastry, includes a chasuble and three copes of his [?gift], and other vestments, Legg and Hope, *Inventories*, 52, 53, 57, 58 (BL Ms Cotton Galba E.iv, fos 112, 113, 114–114ᵛ).

Anthony CHILLENDEN
see Horden

Guy de CHILLENDEN [Chillynden, Chilynden, Chyllynden
occ. 1507 d. 1518/19

1507, 12 Oct., one of six tonsured, *SL*, 193, CCA Lit. Ms D.12, fo 10ᵛ.

1508, 22 Apr., ord acol., Canterbury cathedral, Reg. abp Warham, ii, fo 263ᵛ.

1508, 25/26 Apr., one of six who made their prof. before the abp, *SL*, 194, CCA Lit. Ms D.12, fo 10ᵛ.

1509, 7 Apr., ord subdcn, Canterbury cathedral, Reg. abp Warham, *ib.*, i, fo 264.

1509, 22 Dec., ord dcn, Canterbury cathedral, *ib.*, i, fo 264ᵛ.

1513, 26 Mar., ord pr., Canterbury cathedral, *ib.*, i, fo 266ᵛ.

n.d., as a novice was instructed by John Garard, q.v. *et perfecit* [i.e., completed his studies successfully], Pantin, *Cant. Coll. Ox.*, iv, 54 (CCA DCc Ms Scrap Book B.186).

1511, 2 Sept., 72nd in order on the visitation certificate, Wood-Legh, *Visit.*, 3 (Reg. abp Warham, i, fo 35ᵛ).

1518/19, spent time in the infirmary, CCA DCc Infirm. acct 1.

1518/19, d., recorded on the treasurer's acct, Pantin, *Cant. Coll. Ox.*, iv, 206.

John CHILLENDEN [Chillynden, Chyllynden, *alias* Daniel
occ. 1519 occ. 1540

1519, 6 May, one of nine tonsured, *SL*, 193, CCA Lit. Ms D.12, fo 11ᵛ.

1520, 3 Feb., prof., *ib.*

1536/7; 1540, 4 Apr., chaplain [to the prior], 'receptor in officio capellani', CCA DCc AS 24, this acct has 'God save the king, Amen' added to the heading; *L and P Henry VIII*, xv, no 452.

1534, 12 Dec., acknowledged the Act of Supremacy, *DK 7th Report*, Appndx 2, 282.

[1538, 8 Feb., after], in a list of monks prob. prepared for Thomas Cromwell he was described as a 'witty man', 38 yrs of age, Pantin, *Cant. Coll. Ox.*, iii, 153.

1540, 4 Apr., awarded £3 p.a., *L and P Henry VIII*, xv, no 452; the following yr he was apptd canon of the 11th prebend, *Fasti 1541–1857*, iii, 36.

Name in Cambridge, Trinity College Ms 829, Miscellanea (15th c.); libellus—, A.D. 1531. This volume may have previously been in the possession of [John] Holyngbourne, III, q.v.

I Thomas CHILLENDEN D.CnL [Chelenden, Chellenden, Chilinden, Chillendene, Chillynden, Chilyenden, Chyllenden, Chylynden
occ. 1365 d. 1411

1391–1411, prior: el. 15 Feb. 1391, the abp's *prefectio* was on 16 Feb., Reg. abp Courtenay, i, fos 336ᵛ–337; he was *stupefactus* at the abp's announcement and prostrated himself before him; the abp raised him and placed the ring on his right hand; d. 15 Aug. 1411, Reg. S, fo 61ᵛ, cf. *Fasti*, iv, 6.

1365, n.d., one of eight prof., *SL*, 182, CCA Lit. Ms D.12, fo 4ᵛ.

[1377], treasurer with William Woghope under prior John Fynch, q.v., *Anon. Chron.*, 61.

1384, 29 Sept./1385, Apr., warden of Canterbury college, CCA DCc Cart. Antiq. O.140a.

1389, almoner, CCA DCc BB 79/3.

1377/8, recd 20s. from the treasurer for his *capa scolastica*, [for Oxford], Pantin, *Cant. Coll. Ox.*, iv, 187. However, since he was B.Cn.L. by

1378, he must have begun his studies at Canterbury college some yrs earlier. See *BRUO*.

1378/9, 1379/80, at the curia where he studied canon law, and recd money for his expenses, *ib.*, iv, 187, 188.

1380/1, recd money to cover his travelling expenses to Oxford [from Canterbury], *ib.*, iv, 188.

1381/2, incepted in canon law, and D.CnL by 9 Aug. [1383], *ib.*, iv, 188, Reg. abp Courtenay, i, fo 43. For his *lib[eratione* and that of John Aleyn, q.v., *inceptorum*, the 1383/4 treasurer's acct records an expenditure of £30 13s. 4d., *ib.*, iv, 189.

1384/5, returned from Oxford to Canterbury for a visitation, *ib.*, iv, 190.

1378, 21 July, granted licence by the prior and chapter to go to Rome and to study canon law there for two yrs, Pantin, *Cant. Coll. Ox.*, iii, 34 (Reg. G, fo 217).

1379, 25 Mar., obtained a bull which gave Christ Church *ultimam exemptionem* from attendance at the Black Monk chapters, Anglia Sacra, i, 143, Pantin, *Cant. Coll. Ox.*, iv, 40, quoting Wilkins, *Concilia*, iii, 126; see also the summary of the later stages of the dispute with the Black Monk Chapter during Chillenden's priorate in Pantin, BMC, iii, 57. While at the curia he also obtained for the prior the papal privilege of the use of staff and sandals and of giving solemn benediction, *Anglia Sacra*, i, 143.

1381, 31 July, 30th in order at the el. of an abp, and one of three *compromissorii* who chose six more to add to their number, Reg. G, fo 225; he preached at the el., Oxford, Bod. Ms Ashmole 794, fo 254.

1382/3, one of the monks involved in negotiations with the abp over the apptment of William de Dover III, q.v. to the wardenship of Canterbury college, Pantin, *Cant. Coll. Ox.*, iv, 188, 189. On 19 July 1383 he and William Brygge II went to the abp to discuss the future of the college, *ib.*, iv, 43 (Oxford, Bod. Ms Ashmole 794, fo 258).

1385/7, in charge of the monk ordinands, that is in conducting them to their ordinations, Lambeth Ms 243, fos 201, 203.

1389, 30 Sept., accompanied the abp on his visitation of Spalding priory (Lincs.) and preached on the text *Videamus si floruerit vinea* (Cant. 7, 12), Pantin, *Cant. Coll. Ox.*, iv, 220 (Reg. abp Courtenay, i, fo 143^{v}). See also Churchill, *Cant. Admin.*, i, 325n.

1390, Sept. × 1391, June, recd a letter of confraternity from Rochester cathedral priory, BL Ms Cotton Faustina C.v, fo 53; the previous yr [1389], for some unknown reason the Rochester monks had spoken ill of him, *ib.*, fo 39, and the subprior and 72 monks wrote to the Rochester chapter on 11 May 1389 testifying to his unimpeachable character and reputation, *ib.*, fo 39–39^{v}. The Rochester monks replied in two placatory letters, one to the Christ Church monks on 14 May, and the other to Chillenden on 15 May, under their secret seal, *ib.*, fos 39^{v}–40.

1396, 7 Aug., presided at the el. of an abp, Reg. G, fo 234^{v}.

1396, 15 Sept., one of the executors of abp Courtenay, L. Duncan, 'The Will of William Courtenay, Archbishop of Canterbury', in *Archaeologia Cantiana*, xxiii, 57, 66.

1397, 13 Jan., apptd commissary general, Reg. abp Arundel i, fo 3^{v}, and see Churchill, *Cant. Admin.*, i, 60.

1397, 27 Oct., apptd vicar general by the abp at the time of the latter's suspension, Churchill, *Cant. Admin.*, i, 264, 569.

1399, 17 Jan., was one of the prelates summoned by Richard II to meet him at Oxford and advise him on the schism in the church, *CClR* (1396–1399), 367–368; see also Thomas Nevyle under Winchester.

1401, 20–23 Sept., accompanied abp Arundel on his visitation of the Ely chapter and witnessed the consent of John de St Ives (q.v., under Ely), who was ill in the infirmary, to the el. of William Powcher as prior there, Reg. abp Arundel, i, fo 494.

1404, Apr., el. bp of Rochester, but refused the honour, *Fasti*, iv, 38.

1404, 12 July, one of two comm. by the abp to act as his commissaries in carrying out corrections after his visitation of Battle Abbey, Reg. Arundel, i, fo 129.

1409, 1 Apr., gave charge of the priory to John Wodnesbrugh, q.v., and departed for the council of Pisa, as a member of the English delegation, 'Anon. Chron.', 76–77. For his contacts with Cluny see R. Graham *Eng. Eccles. Studies*, 59–61.

1411, 15 Aug., d., at 'Meister Omers' in the priory precincts, Reg. S, fo 61^{v}, CCA Lit. Ms D.12, fo 19; the latter records that in appearance he was reduced to skin and bone. Details of the funeral rites, requiem, burial in the cathedral nave and of the large numbers who came to pay their respects are also in CCA Lit. Ms D.12, *ib.*

Name in or attached to:

(1) Cambridge, Trinity College Ms 154, Augustinus (late 14th c.); — on a flyleaf now fo 367.

(2) Oxford, Bod. Ms Lat. misc. b.12, fo 8, J. Andreae (14th/15th c.); Ker suggests that this may be no 16 (Johannes in novellam primam super sextum) in the Chillenden list of books, *Lit. Cant.*, no 992 (CCA DCc Cart. Antiq. C.166). See *MLGB*, 38 and below.

He also wrote and compiled a number of works which survive:

(1) Oxford, All Souls College, Ms 53, art. 2, Reportorium quarti libri Decretalium.

(2) Hereford Cathedral Ms P.8.iii, Sexti Libri Decretalium Reportorium. Other copies of this are in Oxford, New College Ms 204, BL Ms Royal 11 C.ii, Cambridge, Trinity Hall Ms 7, Cambridge, Gonville and Caius Ms 308.
(3) Oxford, All Souls College Ms 53, art. i, Reportata on the Clementines; this is also included in Hereford Cathedral Ms, P.8.iii.
(4) Longleat, Wilts, marquis of Bath Ms 35, fos 187–206, contain his commentary on the Regulae juris.

Note: see Sharpe, *Latin Writers*, for further details.

A list of 34 volumes acquired by him or during his priorate is given in James, *Ancient Libraries*, 150–151, *Lit. Cant.*, no 992 (pp 121–122) (from CCA DCc Cart. Antiq. C.166); at least 25 of these are canon and civil law texts.

His *sed. vac.* register begins on fo 235 of Reg. G; his *acta* as prior are in Reg. S, fos 1–61.

He gave many gifts to Canterbury college including two silver basins [*pelves*], vestments, red silk altar hangings, which are listed in a number of inventories, e.g. Pantin, *Cant. Coll. Ox.*, i, 1, 9, 10, 30, 34, 51, 65 (CCA DCc Cart. Antiq. O.134, 135, 137, Inventory box no 21, O.136, 135C). There is a list of the ornaments and jewels, newly acquired, and of old ones repaired during his priorate, Legg and Hope, *Inventories*, 105–107 (CCA DCc Prior acct for 1410/11 has a list of all his 'good works' on the dorse; see also Legg and Hope, *Inventories*, 108–114.

Chillenden's other achievements were chiefly in the sphere of building and reconstruction both at Oxford and at Canterbury. The author of the *Anon. Chron.* has provided a chronological summary, for the yrs 1391–1397, 1405–1406, of the improvements at Christ Church and on the manors, 60–73, 74–76. Under the heading 'nova opera et adquisita' there is a long list of what was completed under his direction, *Lit. Cant.*, no 992 (pp 114–116, from CCA DCc Cart. Antiq. C.166), and this also includes repairs and construction on the manors, *ib.*, 116–120. In brief, his work survives in the nave which was rebuilt during his priorate, and also in the choir screen, chapter house and cloister vaulting. A *nova Schola monachorum* is included in the list in *Lit. Cant.* no 992 (p.116).

His grasp of financial adminstration and his reforms in this sphere involved his self apptment as prior-treasurer and included the introduction of leasing of the demesnes, see R.A.L. Smith, *Canterbury Cathedral Priory*, 190–197.

His mother Cecilia was remembered on 23 Aug., BL Ms Arundel 68, fo 35ᵛ.

Dr Smith also wrote a short biographical sketch in *Cant. Cath. Chron.*, no 35 (1941), 22–25.

II Thomas CHILLENDEN [Chyllynden
occ. 1470 d. [1487]

1470, 25 Jan., one of eight prof., *SL*, 190, CCA Lit. Ms D.12, fo 8.
1470, 21 Apr., ord acol., Canterbury cathedral, *Reg. abp Bourgchier*, 405.
1471, 9 Mar., ord subdcn, Canterbury cathedral, *ib.*, 404.
1473, 13 Mar., ord dcn, Canterbury cathedral, *ib.*, 410.
1473/4, celebrated his first mass and recd 10d. from the sacrist, Woodruff, 'Sacrist's Rolls', 64 (CCA DCc Sac. acct 56).

[1487], 24 Aug., d., *ex vehementi pestilencia*, aged 38, and was buried without delay, CCA Lit. Ms D.12, fo 27.

Walter de CHILLENDEN [Chelinden, Chelyndenn', Chilindenn, Chyllynden
occ. 1272 d. 1304

n.d., name occ. in the list in *SL*, 175, CCA Lit. Ms D.12, fo 2ᵛ.

1272, 1273, 1274, treasurer, CCA DCc MA1, fos 116, 117ᵛ, 119.
1275/7, 1285/8, cellarer, CCA DCc MA1, fos 121ᵛ–126, Reg. H, fo 208, CCA DCc, London acct 2, MA1, fos 144ᵛ–154ᵛ.
1287/8, chaplain to the prior, CCA DCc MA1, fos 150ᵛ–154ᵛ.
1288/94, warden of manors, CCA DCc MA1, fos 154ᵛ–190.
1295/9, subprior, CCA DCc, Brook acct 8, Little Chart acct 4, Appledore acct 6, Agney acct 18; his apptment on 12/14 Apr. 1295 is in *Reg. abp Winchelsey*, 18, 20, and Reg. I, fo 175; he was succ by Robert Poucyn, q.v.
1299/1300, almoner, CCA DCc Alm. acct 18.

1285/6, pd a visit to Meopham, CCA DCc Meopham acct 8.
1287, 23 May, with Robert de Fox[hele, q.v., sent by the prior and chapter to the bp of Bath and Wells and to the king on negotiations concerning Dover priory, CUL Ms Ee, 5.31, fo 27ᵛ.
1292, 22 Dec., sent to Newcastle-on-Tyne with John de Wy, q.v., as proctors to the king to obtain licence to el. an abp, *Reg. abp Winchelsey*, 1258–1259, CUL Ms Ee.5.31, fo 35ᵛ; they were also sent to the bp of Durham for his *consilium et auxilium*, and to the Earl of Lincoln, CUL Ms Ee.5.31, *ib.*
1293, 24 Feb., one of the monks who were present with the prior at Leighton Buzzard, [Lecton], to ask for and rec. Robert Winchelsey's acceptance of his el. as abp, *Reg. abp Winchelsey*, 1273–1274.
1294, 7 Aug., d., CCA Lit. Ms D.12, fo 15ᵛ.

The inventory of new vestments, acquired *temp.* prior Eastry, includes a set made of red samite designated as his, Legg and Hope, *Inventories*, 64 (BL Ms Cotton Galba E.iv, fo 116ᵛ).

An inventory of the refectory dated 1328 includes two *ciphi de murra* of is, with silver gilt covers Dart, *Antiq. Cant.* xxiii (BL Ms Cotton Galba E.iv, fo 180).

CHILMYN(G)TON
see Chelmynton

CHIVALER
see Chyveler

CHRISTIANUS [Cristianus
n.d.

n.d., 14 Apr., obit occ. in BL Mss Cotton Nero C.ix, fo 9ᵛ and Arundel 68, fo 24.

CHYCHELE
see Chichele

John CHYLDE
occ. 1341

1341, 13 Dec., one of nine prof., *SL*, 180, CCA Lit. Ms D.12, fo 4.

I John de CHYLHAM
occ. 1286 d. 1298

1286, 9 Oct. one of five prof., *SL*, 177, CCA Lit. Ms D.12, fo 3.

1298, 31 Oct., d., CCA Lit. Ms D.12, fo 15.

A list of books in the Eastry catalogue that were formerly his are nos 1524–1537 in James, *Ancient Libraries*, 128–129.

An inventory of the refectory dated 1328 includes a silver *ciphus* of J. de Chilham, Dart, *Antiq. Cant.*, xix [as Chilcham] (BL Ms Cotton Galba E.iv, fo 178ᵛ).

II John CHYLHAM
occ. 1421 d. 1458

1421, 4 Apr., one of six prof., *SL*, 186, CCA Lit. Ms D.12, fo 6ᵛ.
1423, 18 Dec., ord subdcn, Rochester cathedral, *Reg. abp Chichele*, iv, 358.
1425, 22 Dec., ord dcn, Charing, *ib.*, iv, 374.
1428, 3 Apr., ord pr., Rochester cathedral, Reg. Langdon (Rochester), fo 65ᵛ.

[1441], 5 Jan., removed from the office of fourth prior, Chron. Wm Glastynbury, fo 119ᵛ.
1446/7, anniversarian with William Sutton, q.v., Lambeth ED74.

1458, 6 Oct., pr. and *conventualis*, d., in the 37th yr of his monastic life; the subprior performed the *commendatio* and the prior celebrated the mass and conducted the burial, *Chron. Stone*, 75–76, CCA Lit. Ms D.12, fo 26; his obit, on 5 Oct., is in BL Ms Arundel 68, fo 44.

CHYLHAM
see also Chilham

CHYLLYNGHAM
see Gyllyngham

CHYLMYNTON
see Chelmynton

CHYLYNDENE
see Chillenden

M. Edmund de CHYMBHAM
occ. 1336 d. 1361

1336, 24 July, the prior was reproved by the abp for having adm. Edmund as a novice without his express approval, *Lit. Cant.*, no 630 (Reg. L, fo 68). He was already a *magister*, *ib.*, but is not in *BRUO* or *BRUC*.
1337, 30 Sept., one of three prof., *SL*, 180, CCA Lit. Ms D.12, fo 4.
Note: there are several other letters written by the prior to the abp resulting from this alleged breach in the customary procedures, Reg. L, fo 68–68ᵛ.

1358, 25 Oct., apptd penitentiary [in the priory] with James Oxney I, q.v., Reg. abp Islip, fo 144.
1358/9, 28 Oct., *magister ordinis*, *SL*, 181, CCA Lit. Ms D.12, fo 4.

1348/9, recd a *liberatioß* from the anniversarian, CCA DCc Anniv. acct 3.
1349, 4 June, 45th in order at the el. of an abp, Reg. G, fo 60ᵛ.
1349, 8/9 Sept., 44th at the el. of an abp, *ib.*, fo 76ᵛ.
1361, 27 July, d., one of c.25 monks who were carried off by an epidemic this yr, CCA Lit. Ms D.12, fo 17.

John CHYVELER [Chivaler, Chyvaleyr
occ. 1414/15 d. 1437

1414/15, n.d., one of five clothed in the monastic habit, *SL*, 186, CCA Lit. Ms D.12, fo 6.
1415, 10 Nov., the prior was comm. to rec. his prof., *Reg. abp Chichele*, iv, 142.
1416, 8 Apr., ord acol., Canterbury cathedral, *ib.*, iv, 319.
1417, 10 Apr., ord subdcn, Canterbury cathedral, *ib.*, iv, 327.
1419, 1 Apr., ord dcn, chapel in the priory, *ib.*, i, 191.
1421, 20 Dec., ord pr., St Paul's cathedral, London, *ib.*, iv, 349.

1433/4, [1435], before 29 Mar., warden of manors, CCA DCc Bocking acct 61, 'Chron. Wm Glastynbury', 129 (Ms fo 117).
[1435] before 29 Mar., chaplain to the prior, Chron. Wm Glastynbury, fo 117.
[1435], 29 Mar., apptd cellarer, in place of the newly apptd prior of Dover, John Coumbe II, q.v.; on 28 Apr. it was decided that he should take on the offices of both cellarer and bartoner as John Coumbe II, had done, *ib.*

1436/7, cellarer and warden of manors (or more prob. bartoner), CCA DCc Prior acct 7, Great Chart acct 108; he also seems to have been [still] chaplain to the prior, Prior acct 7.

1437, 27 Dec., d. *ex calido ydropici*, CCA Lit. Ms D.12, fo 24; his obit occ. 26 Dec. in BL Ms Arundel 68, fo 52.

Samuel de CHYVENE
occ. [1207 × 1214]

[1207 × 1214], name occ. in the list of those who went into exile, *SL*, 172, CCA Lit. Ms D.12, fo 1.

Gilbert de CLARE [Clara
occ. [c. 1139 × 1153]

[1139 × 1140], attested a charter of abp Theobald, *Theobald Charters*, no 161.
[1141 × 1148], chaplain to the abp, with Walter de Meri, q.v., *ib.*, nos 164, 165.
[1150 × 1153], chaplain to the abp with Walter de Gloucestre, q.v., *ib.*, no 255.

Note: there are four other charters which he witnessed in this same period: *ib.*, nos 42, 59, 63 and p.545.

Richard de CLARE [Clara
occ. [1148 × 1182]

[1150 × 1153], with Walter de Gloucestre, q.v., chaplains of abp Theobald and witnessed a confirmation made by him, *Theobald Charters*, no 255.
[1150 × 1161], with Walter above, witnessed a deed of the abp, *ib.*, no 225.
[1148 × 1182], *temp.* bp Walter of Rochester, witnessed an agreement between this bp and the adcn of Rochester, *Reg. Roff*, 58 (see Rochester refs).

I CLEMENT
occ. 1145

1145, 1 Sept., attested abp Theobald's (prob. spurious) *inspeximus* and confirmation of bp Gundulf's (wholly spurious) charter in favour of Rochester cathedral priory, *Theobald Charters*, no 222; see Hugh I, Reynaldus and Walter Durdent, prior.

II CLEMENT
occ. 1317

1317, 5 Nov., with an unnamed monk reported to have circulated letters containing false and harmful statements about which the abp ordered an inquiry, CUL Ms Ee.5.31, fo 181^{v}; see Walter de Eastry and Nicholas de Ivynghoe.

I John CLEMENT
occ. 1429 d. 1457

1429, one of two [tonsured], *SL*, 187, CCA Lit. Ms D.12, fo 7.
[1429, summer], ord acol. and subdcn, place not given, Reg. Langdon (Rochester), fo 74.
1434, 13 Mar., ord pr., infirmary chapel, *Reg. abp Chichele*, iv, 379.

1451, 20 Mar., 1455/6, subsacrist, *Chron. Stone*, 51, CCA DCc Prior acct 10; he was prob. subsacrist at the time of his d., CCA Lit. Ms D.12, fo 25^{v}, and see below.

1439, 19 Jan., given licence to leave the priory *pro recreacione*, Chron. Wm Glastynbury, fo 182^{v}/177^{v}.
1441, 2 Aug., obtained a dispensation to allow him to rec. and hold a benefice with cure of souls, *CPL*, ix (1431–1447), 206.
1451, 20 Mar., present at the blessing of the bells in St George's belfry, *Chron. Stone*, 51.
1457, 31 July, d.; his *exequies* in the choir were 'sine nota, nec habuit [the usual] psalmos l^{mos}', CCA Lit. Ms D.12, fo 25^{v}.

See note below.

II John CLEMENT
occ. 1480 d. 1487

1480, 25 Jan., one of six prof., *SL*, 191, CCA Lit. Ms D.12, fo 8^{v}.
1480, 1 Apr., ord acol., Canterbury cathedral, *Reg. abp Bourgchier*, 430.
1481, 22 Sept., ord subdcn, Sevenoaks, *ib.*, 432.
1483, 29 Mar., ord dcn, Canterbury cathedral, *ib.*, 439.
1487, 14 Apr., ord pr., Canterbury cathedral, *Reg. abp Morton*, i, no 433d.

1487, before 9 Aug., *parvus sacrista*, CCA Lit. Ms D.12, fo 26^{v}.

1487, 9 Aug., d., *ex vehementi pestilentia* at the age of 24, CCA Lit. Ms D.12, fo 26^{v}; the obit of a John Clement occ. on 17 Aug. in BL Ms Arundel 68, fo 38^{v}.

Note: a John Clement gave a silver gilt chalice inscribed with his name to Canterbury college, Pantin, *Cant. Coll. Ox.*, i, 28 (CCA DCc Cart. Antiq. O.137).

III John CLEMENT
occ. 1517 d. [1518]

1517, 12 Mar. [deposition of St Gregory], one of six tonsured, *SL*, 194, CCA Lit. Ms D.12, fo 11.
1517, 29 Sept., one of six who made their prof. before the abp, and the new prior, Thomas Goldwell q.v., who celebrated his first pontifical mass that day, *ib.*

1518/19, spent time in the infirmary, CCA DCc Infirm. acct 1.
1518/19, his d., recorded on the treasurer's acct, Pantin, *Cant. Coll. Ox.*, iv, 206; on 23 Oct., the obit of a John Clement, acol., occ. in BL Ms Arundel 68, fo 46.

See note above, under John Clement II.

His family name was Baker; his parents were recd into confraternity with Christ Church in 1518, BL Ms Arundel 68, fo 11. See Thomas Becket I.

Nicholas CLEMENT
occ. 1488 occ. 1540

1488, 30 Sept., one of six tonsured, *SL*, 192, CCA Lit. Ms D.12, fo 9.
1490, 4 Apr., made his prof. before the abp, CCA Lit. Ms D.12, ib; the delay in prof. did not preclude the six from having 'pecunias sicut ceteri fratres cum ebd' servicio et assignacione ad refect' et mensam conventus' by permission of the prior and the *magister ordinis*, *ib*.
1491, 2 Apr., ord acol., Canterbury cathedral, *Reg. abp Morton*, i, no 439a.
1492, 21 Apr., ord subdcn, Canterbury cathedral, *ib*., i, no 441b.
1493, 6 Apr., ord dcn, Canterbury cathedral, *ib*., i, no 442c.
1495, 18 Apr., ord pr., Canterbury cathedral, *ib*., i, no 444d.

1500, succentor, BL Ms Arundel 68, fo 10.
[?1530s], infirmarer, *L and P Henry VIII*, xii, pt. 1, no 485; see below.

1493, 1 May, 57th in order at the ratification of an agreement, Reg. S, fo 383ᵛ; but see John Crosse I.
1500, [as succentor], was responsible for the record of names of those recd into confraternity, BL Ms Arundel 68, fo 10.
1501, 26 Apr., 39th in order at the el. of an abp, Reg. R, fo 56ᵛ.
1511, 2 Sept., 25th on the visitation certificate, Wood-Legh, *Visit.*, 3 (Reg. abp Warham, i, fo 35ᵛ).
1518/19, spent time in the infirmary, CCA DCc Infirm. acct 1.
1534, 12 Dec., acknowledged the Act of Supremacy, *DK 7th Report*, Appndx 2, 282.
1537, 22 Feb., wrote two letters to Lord Lisle, the second undated; in both he begged for [financial] assistance as he had been robbed of c. £8 while in the office of infirmarer and the prior expected him to pay [it back]. He described himself as a 'stagyar, beyng ympotent and lame yn all parts of my body', *L and P Henry VIII*, xii, pt. 1, nos 484, 485.
[1538, 8 Feb., after], in a list of monks prob. prepared for Thomas Cromwell he was described as a good man, a 'stacionar', 71 yrs of age, Pantin, *Cant. Coll. Ox.*, iii, 152.
1540, 4 Apr., awarded £10 p.a., *L and P Henry VIII*, xv, no 452.

I Richard CLEMENT
occ. 1457 d. 1472

1457, 13 Dec., one of six who were adm. as monks, *Chron. Stone*, 71, *SL*, 189.
1458, 12 Feb., *venerunt ad parvum servicium*, and on 26 Feb. *ad commune servicium*, *ib*.
1458, 21 Apr., one of the same six who made their prof., *ib*.
1459, 24 Mar., ord subdcn, Canterbury cathedral, *Reg. abp Bourgchier*, 371.
1460, 12 Apr., ord dcn, Canterbury cathedral, *ib*., 376.
1463, 9 Apr., ord pr., Canterbury cathedral, *ib*., 386.

1466, 17 Feb., 56th in order in an inventory listing *jocalia fratrum* [given by him and/or assigned for his use], Reg. N, fo 234.
[1471/2], *stationarius* and *conventualis*, d., CCA Lit. Ms D.12, fo 26; in *Chron. Stone*, 118, the date is 13 Feb. 1472, and the obit in BL Ms Arundel 68, fo 16, is 15 Feb.

II Richard CLEMENT
occ. 1524 occ. 1534

1524, 21/22 July, one of eleven granted adm. [*ingressum*] to Christ Church, CCA Lit. Ms D.12, fos 11ᵛ–12.
1524, 4 Aug., one of eleven tonsured, *SL*, 195, CCA Lit. Ms D.12, fo 12.
1525, 19 Apr., prof., *ib*.
1527/8, celebrated his first mass and recd a small gift from the sacrist, Woodruff, 'Sacrist's Rolls', 72.

1534, 12 Dec., acknowledged the Act of Supremacy, *DK 7th Report*, Appndx 2, 282.

Peter de CLIMPING [Clympingg'
occ. [1296]

[1296], one of the juniors, accused by the abp of laxity in attendance at divine office and in the performance of other monastic duties, *Reg. abp Winchelsey*, 92.

Note: there are several other more or less contemporary monks named Peter of whom he is prob. one, but either this one or one of the others is using an alternative name or an *alias*; see for example Peter Lumbardus.

CLIVE
see Clyve

Nicholas de CLOPTON
occ. 2nd half 13th c.

n.d., name occ. in the list in *SL*, 174, CCA Lit. Ms D.12, fo 2.

CLYMPINGG
see Climping

CLYNSTEDE
see Klynstede

Edmund CLYVE
occ. [1393] d. 1398

[1393], 21 Nov., one of six prof., *SL*, 184, CCA Lit. Ms D.12, fo 5.
1394, 18 Apr., ord subdcn, Canterbury cathedral, *Reg. abp Courtenay*, ii, fo 184v.
1395, 10 Apr., ord dcn, Canterbury cathedral, *ib.*, fo 185v.

1398, 28 July, d., CCA Lit. Ms D.12, fo 18.

John de CLYVE
occ. [1241]

n.d., name occ. in the list in *SL*, 174, CCA Lit. Ms D.12, fo 2; he was prob. one of the twelve prof. with Richard de Wynchepe, q.v.

Lambert de CLYVE
occ. 1262 d. [1286]

n.d., name occ. in the list in *SL*, 184, CCA Lit. Ms D.12, fo 2.

1262; 1263; 1264, 29 Sept., treasurer, CCA DCc MA1, fos 104v, 105v, 106v.
1268/9, sacrist, CCA DCc AS10.

1276, 31 Aug., with J[ohn] de Eastry, q.v., involved in an agreement settling a dispute with St Augustine's abbey, CUL Ms Ee.5.31, fo 26v; in 1286, 7 Mar., Geoffrey de Chilham, q.v., was brought in to replace him in accordance with an agreement that had been reached in this matter.
[1286, before 7 Mar.], d., see above and below.
n.d., 15 Feb., obit occ. in BL Ms Arundel 68, fo 16 where it notes that 'de perquisito suo dedit ad fabricam ecclesie' 40 m.

An inventory of missing service books dated 1 Mar. 1338 includes his diurnale for which Richard de Ikham, q.v. was held responsible, *Lit. Cant.*, no 618 (Reg. L, fo 104).

Two silver *ciphi* and two *nux*, formerly his, are included in an inventory of the refectory dated 1328, Dart, *Antiq. Cant.*, xix, xxi (BL Ms Cotton Galba, E.iv, fos 178, 178v, 179v).

Note: see also Lambert II who is prob. this monk.

M. Martin de CLYVE
occ. [1256] d. 1301

n.d., name occ. in the list in *SL*, 175, CCA Lit. Ms D.12, fo 2.

1293, Feb/1294, July, penitentiary, *Reg. abp Winchelsey*, 1262 (CUL Ms Ee.5.31, fo 61).
1295, 20 Oct., lector, *Reg. abp Winchelsey*. 1309.

[1256, Feb., with another appted by the abp vicar and commissary general for the creation of officials in vacant dioceses, Churchill, *Cant. Admin.*, i, 185.]
Note: this may be another monk, perhaps of St Augustine's, as this monk must have been very young to have been given this apptment.

1293, 13 Feb., accompanied Geoffrey de Romenal, q.v., and a notary when they went to inform William de Codelawe, q.v., who was ill, of the impending el. of an abp, *Reg. abp Winchelsey*, 1262 (Reg. Q, fo 25v).
1293, 13 Feb., named as one of seven *compromissorii* in the el. of an abp, *ib.*, 1265 and Reg. Q, fo 19v, CUL Ms Ee.5.31, fo 38.
1294, 25 July, with Richard de Clyve, q.v., recd a comm. from the prior to install the pr. at St Gregory's church, CUL Ms Ee.5.31, fo 61.
1295, 20 Oct., lector who had been providing instruction in dialectic and theology [in the cloister] and who was now, by special concession authorized by the abp, on acct of his age, to be relieved of his other duties of service in choir and kitchen and of reading in the refectory, *Reg. abp Winchelsey*, 1309 (CCA DCc EC V/13).
1296, before 5 Mar., with Roger de Wroteham, q.v., and the prior [Henry de Eastry, q.v.] were examined by the abp on the state of the priory on his first visitation, *ib.*, 1303 (Reg. Q, fo 40).
1301, 3 May., d., CCA Lit. Ms D.12, fo 15v.
Name in CCA Lit. Ms A.12, Hugh de S. Caro (13th c.) in which the title 'magister' appears and 'liber — quem perquisivit et eidem ecclesie dedit'.

A list of books which he donated to the library is in James, *Ancient Libraries*, 131–133 (nos 1586–1613); a *penitentiale* of his was in Canterbury college in the warden's study in 1521, Pantin, *Cant. Coll. Ox.*, i, 61 (CCA DCc Cart. Antiq. O.135A).

An inventory of vestments, *temp.* prior Eastry, includes an embroidered alb matching that of Geoffrey de Chilham,q.v., Legg and Hope, Inventories, 59 (BL Ms Cotton Galba E.iv, fo 115).

An inventory of the refectory dated 1328 includes a *ciphus de murra* of his, Dart, *Antiq. Cant.*, xxi (BL Ms Cotton Galba E.iv, fo 179v).

Described as a famous preacher 'who left behind him a Volume of Sermons', Dart, *Antiq. Cant.*, 188.

Richard de CLYVE [Clyffe
occ. 1286 d. 1326

1286, 16 Mar., one of five prof., *SL*, 177, CCA Lit. Ms D.12, fo 3.

1315/18, subprior, CCA DCc Chartham accts 10, 11, Adisham acct 4; his apptment on 13 Jan. 1316 is in Reg. abp Reynolds, fo 124v.
1324, Mar./1326, July, almoner, CCA DCc Monkton acct 52, Alm. accts 26, 32.

1288, student at Paris, and wrote to the prior about the sale of the wine of St Thomas (from French vineyards that had been given to Christ Church by Louis IX), *Hist. Ms Comm.*

Letters, i, 277; see also CCA DCc EC III/18,19. He is included by Sullivan in *Benedictine Monks at Paris*, no 185.

Note: Pantin suggests that he had prob. obtained an M.A. and possibly studied law before being adm. as a monk, *Cant. Coll. Ox.*, iv, 217. Little and Pelster have found disputations possibly by him at Oxford, c. 1300, *Oxford Theology*, 259; see below.

1292, 14 Dec., apptd by the prior, *sed. vac.* as commissary with jurisdiction in spiritual causes, CUL Ms Ee.5.31, fo 35 (printed in Churchill, *Cant. Admin.*, ii, 13). Two of his subsequent *acta* over the next few months are in *ib.*, fos 43^{v}, 44, and he was still named by the prior as 'our commissary' on 8 Aug. 1293, *ib.*, fo 48, and again in Dec., *ib.*, fo 55^{v}. See Selden Soc., *Select Cases Eccles.*, 34.

1293, 13 Feb., apptd as one of seven *compromissorii* in the el. of an abp, *Reg. abp Winchelsey*, 1265 (Reg. Q, fo 31^{v}, CUL Ms Ee.5.31, fo 38).

1293, 4 Mar., during the vacancy of the see apptd by the prior to carry out visitations and corrections in the city and diocese, CUL Ms Ee.5.31, fo 38^{v}; see also C.E. Woodruff, 'Some Early Visitation Rolls Preserved at Canterbury', *Archaeologia Cantiana*, 32 (1917), 143–180, which are transcriptions of Clyve's activities as commissary during this vacancy of the see.

1293, 13 Aug., with Robert Poucyn, q.v. named general proctors, CUL Ms Ee.5.31, fo 47^{v}. On 10 Aug. the two were ordered by the prior and chaper, *sed. vac.* to take charge of the enthronement of the bp of Bath and Wells, in default of the adcn of Canterbury, *ib.*, fo 49^{v}, and see Churchill, *Cant. Admin.*, i, 560, ii, 224.

1294, 25 July, with Martin de Clyve, q.v., comm. by the prior to install the prior at St Gregory's, Canterbury, CUL Ms Ee.5.31, fo 61.

1295, 22 Nov., with Geoffrey de Chilham, q.v., apptd parliamentary proctors by the prior and chapter, *Parl. Writs*, i, 537 (CUL Ms Ee.5.31, fo 66^{v}).

1298, 28 July, sent by the prior and chapter, with John de Acharde, q.v., to Rome *ad impetrand' privilegia*; and they were provided with authority to contract loans, *ib.*, fo 77, 77^{v}.

1307, 11 Mar., with Henry Moth, q.v. apptd general proctors in the legal and judicial affairs of the priory, *ib.*, fo 106.

1308, 19 Sept., 1313, 13 May, with Gilbert de Bisshoppiston, q.v., apptd general proctors, *ib.*, fos 109–109^{v}, 121.

1313, 13 May, with a secular apptd by the prior to exercise *sed. vac.* jurisdiction as his commissaries, *ib.*, fo 121.

1313, 28 May, named as one of seven *compromissorii* at the el. of an abp, Reg. Q, fos 61^{v}–62/75^{v}–76.

1313, June, comm. by the prior, to exercise provincial jurisdiction until the official of the new abp arrived, and also to make corrections in the religious houses in the diocese after the visitation of the late abp, Reg. Q, fos 111^{v}, 116; see the letter in *Reg. Reynolds* (Worcester), 67.

1317, 13 Oct., with Geoffrey de Poterel, q.v. sent to the abp to discuss the rights of the prior and convent in *cella nostra* of Dover, CUL Ms Ee.5.31, fo 179^{v}; discussions were still continuing between the abp and the two monk proctors on 25 June 1319 *ib.*, fo 207^{v}.

c. 1318, before 22 May, with Stephen de Faversham, Thomas de Stoyl and William de Ledebury, q.v., had protested vs the abp's injunctions and the latter agreed to hear their case, CCA DCc EC I/51.

1325/6, was in the infirmary and contributed 40s. from his office for his expenses, CCA DCc Alm. acct 32.

1326, 6 July, d., CCA Lit. Ms D.12, fo 16; his obit occ. in BL Ms Arundel 68, fo 33.

Although his name does not occ. in any surviving mss, he left a collection of legal texts and sermons to the library, James, *Ancient Libraries*, 140 (Eastry catalogue, nos 1756–1772).

An inventory of vestments, acquired *temp.* prior Eastry, includes two embroidered albs, Legg and Hope, Inventories, 60 (BL Ms Cotton Galba E.iv, fo 115); another inventory includes a silver gilt chalice and paten, *ib.*, 70 (*ib.*, fo 119).

An inventory of the refectory dated 1328 includes six silver *ciphi* and three *de murra*, Dart *Antiq. Cant.*, xx, xxiii (BL Ms Cotton Galba E.iv, fos 179, 180).

William de COBEHAM

occ. 1st half 13th c.

n.d., name occ. in the list in *SL*, 173, CCA Lit. Ms D.12, fo 1^{v}.

William de CODELAWE [Codelaue, Codelowe, Cudelawe, Godelaue, Godelawe

occ. [1281/2] d. 1307

[1281/2], name occ. in the list in *SL*, 177, CCA Lit. Ms D.12, fo 3.

1294/5, subcellarer, CCA DCc MA1, fos 190–194; he may have held this office in 1292, see the following entry.

1293, 13 Feb., was unable to attend the impending el. of an abp as he was confined to his bed, *in cellario in lecto*, and so he apptd Geoffrey de Romenal, q.v. as his proxy, *Reg. abp Winchelsey*, 1262, Reg. Q, fo 25^{v}. He was asked which way of proceeding he favoured in the el. and replied *per viam compromissi*, *ib.*

1307, 3 Jan., d., CCA Lit. Ms D.12, fo 15; his obit is in BL Ms Arundel 68, fo 12.

An inventory of vestments, *temp.* prior Eastry, includes two linen albs of his [?gift], BL Ms Cotton Galba E.iv, fo 115.

An inventory of the refectory dated 1328 includes three silver *ciphi* and four *de murra*, Dart, *Antiq. Cant.*, xx, xxiii, BL Ms Cotton Galba E.iv, fos 179, 180.

Robert COLBROKE [Colbrok, Colebroke
occ. 1408/9 d. 1447

1408/9, 21 Mar., one of six prof., CCA Lit. Ms D.12, fo 6 (*SL*, 185).
1410, 22 Mar., ord dcn, Canterbury cathedral, Reg. Arundel, ii, fo 98v.
1413, 2 Apr., ord pr., Canterbury cathedral, *ib.*, ii, fo 101v.

1426/7, fourth prior, CCA DCc Bart. acct 89.
1430, 4 Apr., *magister ordinis*, SL 187, CCA Lit. Ms D.12, fo 7.
1435, penitentiary with Thomas Asshe I, q.v., 'Chron. Wm Glastynbury', 129; on 6 Nov. 1444 he was absolved from this position, Reg. abp Stafford, fo 17.
1444/6, 1447, 10 June, 29 Aug., sacrist, CCA DCc Sac. accts 32, 33, CR 95, CCA Lit. Ms D.12, fo 25; he was apptd sacrist on 6 Nov. 1444, Reg. abp Stafford, fo 17.

1414, Feb., scholar at Canterbury college, Pantin, *Cant. Coll. Ox.*, iii, 72 (Reg. S, fo 68v).

1414, 12 Mar., 72nd in order at the el. of an abp, *Reg. abp Chichele*, i, 4.
[1432], Aug., prob. referred to in letters of John Wodnesburgh to William Glastynbury, q.v., Pantin, *Cant. Coll. Ox.*, iii, 88–89 (Chron. Wm Glastynbury, fo 185/190), as R.C; referred to also as R. Colbroke, *ib.*, iii, 92, 93 (fo 185v/190v).
1447, 29 Aug., d., and was buried the next day by the prior, but the abp celebrated the first requiem mass, *Chron. Stone*, 42; his obit is on 30 Aug. in BL Ms Arundel 68, fo 39v. He was in his 39th yr as a monk, CCA Lit. Ms D.12, fo 25.

Thomas de COLCESTR'
occ. 2nd half 13th c.

n.d., name occ. in the list in *SL*, 175, CCA Lit. Ms D.12, fo 2.
n.d., 4 Jan., dcn, whose obit occ. in BL Ms Arundel 68, fo 12.

John de COLCHESTRE [Colcestr', Colcestria
occ. 1361 d. 1414

1361, 28 Oct., one of nine prof., *SL*, 182, CCA Lit. Ms D.12, fo 4v.
1362, 24 Sept., ord acol., Charing, Reg. abp Islip, fo 322.
1363, 23 Sept., ord dcn, Faversham monastery of St Saviour, *ib.*, fo 323v.
1363, 23 Dec., ord pr., Charing, *ib.*, fo 324v.

1373/4, 1375, 1379, *custos tumbe*, CCA DCc Treas acct 5, MA2 fos 291, 318.
1385, *custos martyrii* and of St Mary in crypt, CCA DCc MA2, fo 334v.
1396/7, infirmarer, CCA DCc Prior acct 4.

1366, 10 May, present at the el. of an abp, Reg. G, fo 147.
1374, 30 June, 31st in order at the el. of an abp, Reg. G, fos 173v–175v.
1381, 31 July, 22nd at the el. of an abp, *ib.*, fo 225v.
c. 1390, became blind, CCA Lit. Ms D.12, fo 20.
1396, 7 Aug., 10th at the el. of an abp, *ib.*, fo 234v.
1414, 9 Feb., d., after 24 yrs and more of blindness, CCA Lit. Ms D.12, fo 20; his obit is in BL Ms Arundel 68, fo 16.

COLEMAN [Colemannus
n.d.

n.d., 3 Apr., obit occ. in BL Ms Arundel 68, fo 23.

John COLESHULL [Colleshelle, Colselle, Colshill, Goleshull
occ. 1320 d. 1357

1320, 9 Oct., one of five prof., *SL*, 179, CCA Lit. Ms D.12, fo 3v.

1334, 25 July, before, subchaplain to the prior, Hope, 'Inventories of Priors', 280 (CCA Lit. Ms E.27, fo 7).
1334/6, *custos* of the high altar, CCA DCc MA2, fos 231–250.
1337, *magister corone*, CCA DCc MA2, fo 255.
1343, June/Sept.; 1344, 13 Mar.; 1345/6, chamberlain, CCA DCc, Chamb. acct 68; Oxford, Bod. Ms Ashmole 794, fo 209; CCA DCc Chamb. acct 39.
1348/9, subprior, CCA DCc Adisham acct 24.
1356/7, sacrist, CCA DCc Bart acct 35.

1344, 13 Mar., one of the monks named as present in chapter for the apptment of proctors, Oxford, Bod. Ms Ashmole 794, fo 209.
1349, June, 15th in order at the el. of an abp, Reg. G, fo 60v.
1349, 8/9 Sept., as subprior, 2nd in order at the el. of an abp, *ib.*, fo 76–76v.
1357, 27 Dec., d., CCA Lit. Ms D.12, fo 17.

Walter COLIWESTON
occ. c. 1503

1503, 6 July, before, gave a 'Missale pulchrum de percomino cum capitalibus cum auro sculptis' for the use of the secular priests, Legg and Hope, *Inventories*, 132.

John COLKYN
occ. 1349 d. 1361

1349, 9 Oct., one of six prof., *SL*, 181, CCA Lit. Ms D.12, fo 4.
1350, 18 Sept., ord subdcn, Goudhurst, Reg. abp Islip, fo 310.

1351, 24 Sept., ord dcn, chapel of Herne church, *ib.*, fo 312.
1353, 21 Dec., ord pr., abp's chapel, Maidstone, *ib.*, fo 314v.
1361, 16 Aug., d.; one of about 25 monks who were carried off in an epidemic, CCA Lit. Ms D.12, fo 17.

William COLKYN
occ. 1362 occ. 1377

1362, n.d., one of eight prof., *SL*, 182, CCA Lit. Ms D.12, fo 4v.
1367, 18 Sept., ord subdcn, Lambeth palace chapel, *Reg. abp Langham*, 383.
1368, 4 Mar., ord dcn., Canterbury cathedral, *ib.*, 388.
1368, 25 Mar., ord pr., abp's chapel, Charing, *ib.*, 389.
1374, 30 June, 44th in order at the el. of an abp, Reg. G, fos 173v–175v.
1377, recd a small sum from the prior [*dona*], Lambeth Ms 243, fo 176.

John COLMAN
occ. [1511/12]

[1511/12] receiver, Lit. Ms C.11, fos 17v–22.

COLSELLE
see Goleshull

Roger COLSTON
occ. 1st half 13th c.

n.d., name occ. in the list in *SL*, 173, CCA Lit. Ms D.12, fo 1v.

COMBE
see Coumbe

John de COMPYS
see Kompys

CONRAD
occ. 1108 × 1109 occ. 1125 × 1126

1108 × 1109–1125 × 1126, prior: apptd by the abp between 1108, June and 1109, Apr., following a vacancy after the d. of Ernulf I, q.v.; el. abbot of St Benet of Hulme, 1125 Jan. × 1126, Oct., *Fasti*, ii, 9.
1108, June × 1109, Apr., before this date sacrist, *Fasti*, ii, *ib.*
1108 × 1109, as prior occ. as witness in a prob. spurious charter of abp Anselm to St Gregory's priory, A.M Woodcock, *Cartulary of the Priory of St Gregory, Canterbury*, Camden Society, third series, 88 (1956), no 2.
1109, 21 Apr., with the assent of the bps he compelled the abp of York to make prof. to Canterbury, *sed. vac.*, *Gervase Cant.*, ii, 70.
1127, 16/18 Feb., d., *HRH*, 68, where it states that he was abbot for only eighteen wks. His obit occ. on 18 Feb. in Lambeth Ms 20, fos 164v–165. See also J. Harvey, ed., *William Worcestre Itineraries* (Oxford, 1969), 232–233 which reports that he was 'the wise confessor of King Henry I'.

He was responsible for the rebuilding and extension of the choir which was burned in 1174, *Gervase Cant.*, i, 3, 12. His gifts of vestments and ornaments to Christ Church are listed in Legg and Hope, *Inventories*, 44 (Lambeth Ms 20, fo 165). See also the chapter by M. Gibson in Collinson, *Canterbury Cathedral*, 53–55 for a recent summary of his achievements.

COORTNEY
see Courtney

COPIUS
n.d.

n.d., obit occ. on 4 Jan., in BL Ms Arundel 68, fo 12, and Lambeth Ms 20, fo 157.

Henry COPTON
occ. 1522 occ. 1534

1522, 11 Feb., one of ten tonsured, *SL*, 195, CCA Lit. Ms D.12, fo 11v.
1522, 24 Nov., prof., *ib.*
1525/6, celebrated his first mass and recd 9d. from the sacrist, Woodruff, 'Sacrist's Rolls', 72; he also recd a small sum from William Ingram I, q.v., CCA Lit. Ms C.11, fo 139v.
1534, 12 Dec., acknowledged the Act of Supremacy, *DK 7th Report*, Appndx 2, 282.

Jasper COPTON [Coptun
occ. 1506 occ. 1511

1506, 21 Mar., one of six tonsured, *SL*, 193, CCA Lit. Ms D.12, fo 10v.
1506, 11 Apr., ord acol., Canterbury cathedral, Reg. abp Warham, ii, fo 262v.
1506, 30 Sept., prof., *SL*, 193 CCA Lit. Ms D. 12, fo 10v.
1507, 3 Apr., ord subdcn, Canterbury cathedral, *ib.*, ii, fo 263.
1508, 22 Apr., ord dcn, Canterbury cathedral, *ib.*, ii, fo 263v.
1509/10, celebrated his first mass and recd a small gift from the sacrist, CCA DCc, Sac. acct 72. When he celebrated on the third Sunday in Apr. 1510 the *custos martyrii* gave him 4d., CCA Lit. Ms C.11, fo 51v.
1510/11, scholar at Canterbury college for half the yr, Pantin, *Cant. Coll. Ox.*, ii, 253 (CCA DCc Cart. Antiq. O.151.43).
1511, 9 Sept., absent from the visitation because he was at Oxford; he was 63rd in order on the visitation certificate, Wood-Legh, *Visit.*, 3 (Reg. abp Warham, i, fo 35v).
n.d., 29 Apr., obit occ. in BL Ms Arundel 68, fo 26.

Name in Oxford, New College Ω.13.2, Bernardus (printed book), Paris A.D.1494; 'attinens ad— ex dono doctoris Coptons', (i.e. Richard Copton, q.v.).

John de COPTON
occ. c. 1302 d.1333

c. 1302, 19 Oct., one of four prof., *SL*, 178, CCA Lit. Ms D.12, fo 3v; *SL* has the wrong month and Causton (Ms D.12) the wrong yr.
1305, 12 June, ord dcn, Smeeth chapel by Aldington, *Reg. abp Winchelsey*, 977.
1332/3, *custos* of the high altar, CCA DCc MA2, fos 211v–221.
1331, borrowed 60s. from the prior, gave 20s. towards the new organ and later borrowed 20s. [more], CCA DCc DE3, fo 32.
1333, 23 June, d., CCA Lit. Ms D.12, fo 16; his obit is in BL Ms Arundel 68, fo 31v and BL Ms Arundel 155, fo 4v.

There is a letter copied into Worcester cathedral Ms Q.20, fo 34v, possibly written by John de St Germans, q.v., (under Worcester) in which he is mentioned.

Richard COPTON, D.Th.
occ. 1473 d. 1519/20

1473, 13 Mar., ord acol., Canterbury cathedral, *Reg. abp Bourgchier*, 410 (transcribed as Capton).
1473, 28 Apr., one of six prof., *SL*, 190, CCA Lit. Ms D.12, fo 8v.
1474, 26 Mar., ord subdcn, Canterbury cathedral, *Reg. abp Bourgchier*, 416.
1478, 7 Mar., ord pr., Canterbury cathedral, *ib.*, 426.
1486, Easter/Sept., subwarden, Canterbury college, Pantin, *Cant. Coll. Ox.*, ii, 213–215 (CCA DCc Cart. Antiq. O.151.21); this is his acct.
1493, one of the chancellors, Reg. S, fo 381.
1494, 19 Apr.; 1495, Apr. and Nov., warden of manors, CCA DCc MA8, fo 158, Monk Warden acct 28, Treas acct 35.
1496, after 25 Dec., cellarer, CCA DCc DE32.
1498/1501; 1500, 19 May; 1501, 26 Apr.; 1503, 6 July; 1504, 13 May; 1507, 19 Aug.; 1512, June, subprior, CCA DCc DE27; CCA Lit. Ms C.11, fos 26, 32; Reg. R, fo 56v; CCA Lit. Ms D.12, fo 34v; *ib.*, fo 36; CCA Lit. Ms C.11, fo 54v.
[1482/5], student, at Canterbury college, recd 50s. each yr 'per assignacionem domini prioris', Pantin, *Cant. Coll. Ox.*, ii, 266–268 (CCA DCc Cart. Antiq. O.151.8).
1487, student, recd £2 10s. [for his half-yr stipend] and 15s. *pro cameraria*, Pantin, *Cant. Coll. Ox.*, ii, 268.
1489/90, student, who recd his stipend and pension, *ib.*, ii, 221, (CCA DCc Cart. Antiq. O.151.28), 270.
c. 1491, B.Th., *BRUO*.
1498/9, D.Th.; the inception feast cost over £17 and included a buck purchased from a servant at Magdalen college, Pantin, *Cant. Coll. Ox.*, iii, 132–134.
1486, Apr., student at Oxford, licensed to preach in Canterbury diocese, Reg. R, fo 8v.
1493, 1 May, 31st in order at the ratification of an agreement, Reg. S, fo 383v; but see John Crosse I.
1501, 26 Apr., 19th in order of seniority at the el. of an abp; he was also subprior, Reg. R, fo 56v.
1503, 28 Feb., apptd one of the abp's *auditores causarum in audiencia*, Reg. T, fo 427.
1511, 2 Sept., 7th in order on the visitation certificate, Wood-Legh, *Visit.*, 3 (Reg. abp Warham, i, fo 35).
1518/19, *stationarius* in the infirmary, CCA DCc Infirm. acct 1.
1519/20, d., Woodruff, 'Sacrist's Rolls' 70; his obit is 29 Nov. in BL Ms Arundel 68, fo 49v.

Name in Oxford, New College Ω.13.2, Bernardus (printed book), Paris A.D.1494; he gave it to Jasper Copton, q.v.

An inventory of the *custos martyrii* dated 1509, includes a silver gilt chalice *ex dono—subprioris*, Legg and Hope, *Inventories*, 133.

CORNELIUS
n.d.

n.d., 14 Mar., pr., whose obit occ. in BL Ms Arundel 68, fo 20.

Laurence CORNEWAYLE [de Cornubia
occ. 1361 occ. 1374

1361, 28 Oct., one of nine prof., *SL*, 182, CCA Lit. Ms D.12, fo 4v.
1362, 24 Sept., ord acol., Charing, Reg. abp Islip, fo 322.
1363, 23 Sept., ord dcn, Faversham monastery, *ib.*, fo 323v.
1363, 23 Dec., ord pr., Charing, *ib.*, fo 324v.
1374, 30 June, 32nd in order at the el. of an abp, Reg. G, fos 173v–175v.

Michael de CORNUBIA
occ. 1339 d. 1361

1339, 13 Dec., one of five prof., *SL*, 180, CCA Lit. Ms D.12, fo 4.
[1344 × 1348], one of three nominees sent to the abp by the prior and chapter for apptment as penitentiary. The letter urged the abp to choose him as the most worthy for the office, for the sake of unity in the convent, and the abp complied, *Lit. Cant.*, no 759 (Reg. L, fo 81).
[1358 × 1360], precentor, Reg. L, fo 92.
c. 1358/60, prob. a student at Oxford, see below.
1348, 30 Aug., one of three *compromissorii* chosen by the chapter to name seven *compromissorii* for the el. of an abp, Reg. G, fo 31, Reg. Q, fo 234v.

1349, 4 June, 48th in order at the el. of an abp, and chosen as one of thirteen *compromissorii*, Reg. G, fo 60v.

1349, 8/9 Sept., 47th at the el. of an abp, *ib.*, fo 76v.

1357, 14 Sept., one of the monks in *remotis agentibus* and unable to be present at the abp's visitation, Reg. L, fos 89v–90.

[1359], 9 Nov., commended to the subprior by the abp as eager and ready to resume his university studies more diligently than previously; the abp urged that he be sent without delay, *Lit. Cant.*, nos 861, 862 (Reg. L, fo 92, summary in *Hist. Mss Comm. 9th Report*, Appndx, 89).

1361, 22 July, d. in an epidemic which carried off about 25 of the community, CCA Lit. Ms D.12, fo 17.

Gave a volume of abp Fitzralph's lectures on the Sentences to Canterbury college, see Pantin, *Cant. Coll. Ox.*, i, 42, 103.

CORYDON
see Croydon

William de COTYNDON
n.d.

n.d., precentor, BL Ms Arundel 68, fo 32.

n.d., 27 June, obit occ. in *ib.*

I John COUMBE [Cumbe
n.d.

n.d., subprior of Dover, *Lit. Cant.*, iii, 377 (CCA DCc Z.D4.23).

Note: this cannot be John Coumbe II; was this monk ever a monk of Canterbury?

II John COUMBE [Combe, Cumbe
occ. 1413 occ. 1444

1413, 6 Oct., one of six tonsured, *SL*, 186, CCA Lit. Ms D.12, fo 6; it seems certain that this date ref. to tonsure rather than prof. because none of the six took part in the el. of abp Chichele on 12 Mar. 1414, *Reg. abp Chichele*, i, 4.

1414, 22 Dec., ord acol. and subdcn, Canterbury cathedral, *Reg. abp Chichele*, iv, 317.

1416, 18 Apr., ord dcn, Canterbury cathedral, *ib.*, iv, 320.

1418, 21 May, ord pr., bp's chapel, Halling, Reg. Yonge (Rochester), fo 5v.

1429/30, Mar., cellarer, CCA DCc Great Chart acct 104, Lambeth ED58.

1430/1, warden of manors, CCA DCc Great Chart acct 105.

1431, 25 June, treasurer, CCA DCc MA25, fo 301a.

1432/3, cellarer, CCA DCc Great Chart acct 107.

1433/5, Mar., bartoner, CCA DCc Bart. accts 92, 93, Chron. Wm Glastynbury, fo 117.

1435, 20 Mar., apptd prior of Dover, *Reg. abp Chichele*, i, 286.

1444, 14 Apr., apptd prior of Dover for life, Reg. abp Stafford, fo 23 (Reg. S, fo 159v).

Note: acc. to Chron. Wm Glastynbury, fo 168v/162v, he was *postea prior de Folstan* [Folkestone].

William COURTNEY [Coortney, Courteney, Curtney
occ. 1505 d. 1508

1505, 13 Jan., one of six tonsured, *SL*, 193, CCA Lit. Ms D.12, fo 10.

1505, 22 Mar., ord acol., Canterbury cathedral, Reg. abp Warham, ii, fo 262.

1505, 11 July, prof., *SL*, 193, CCA Lit. Ms D.12, fo 10.

1506, 11 Apr., ord subdcn, Canterbury cathedral, Reg. abp Warham, ii, fo 262v.

1508, 22 Apr., ord dcn, Canterbury cathedral, *ib.*, ii, fo 263v.

1508/9, d., Woodruff, 'Sacrist's Rolls', 68 (CCA DCc Sac. acct 71); his obit, on 4 Oct., describes him as *levita*, BL Ms Arundel 68, fo 44.

John de COVELE [Couele
occ. [1284] d. 1333

[1284], prof. by this date acc. to his place in the list in *SL*, 177, CCA Lit. Ms D.12, fo 3.

[1296], included among the juniors accused by the abp of laxity in attendance at divine office and in the performance of other monastic duties, *Reg. abp Winchelsey*, 92.

1300/1, one of many monks who visited Meopham during the yr, CCA DCc Meopham acct 38.

1333, 26 Jan., d., CCA Lit. Ms D.12, fo 16; his obit is on 29 Jan. in BL Ms Arundel 68, fo 14v.

John COVENTRE [Covintre
occ. 1462 d. 1511

1462, 17 Apr., ord acol., Canterbury cathedral, *Reg. abp Bourgchier*, 380.

[1462], 6 Dec., one of six prof., *SL*, 190; CCA Lit. Ms D.12, fo 8.

Note: this must have been incorrectly dated 1464 in the margin of the ms; 1462 (or 1463) is prob. more accurate.

1463, 9 Apr., ord subdcn, Canterbury cathedral, *ib.*, 385.

1464, 31 Mar., ord dcn, Canterbury cathedral, *ib.*, 390.

1464, 6 Dec., one of six prof., *SL*, 190; CCA Lit. Ms D.12, fo 8.

1486, 1493, chancellor, Reg. S, fos 362v, 383v.

1466, 17 Feb., 73rd in order in an inventory listing *jocalia fratrum* [given by him and/or assigned for his use], and he had none, Reg. N, fo 235.

1493, 1 May, 19th in order at the ratification of an agreement, Reg. S, fo 383v; but see John Crosse I.
1501, 26 Apr., 8th in order at the el. of an abp, Reg. R, fo 56v.
1510/11, d., Woodruff, 'Sacrist's Rolls', 69; the obit is on 13 Feb. in BL Ms Arundel 68, fo 16.

Name in Cambridge (USA), Harvard University, Houghton Library, Typ.3, Biblia, pars i (13th c.); see also Arnold Parmistede.

I William de COVENTRE [Covyntre
occ. 1295 d. 1338

1295, 23 Nov., one of five prof., *SL*, 178; CCA Lit. Ms D.12, fo 3.
1314/16, chaplain to the prior, CCA DCc MA2, fos 52–70.
1316/20, warden of manors, CCA DCc Chartham accts 11, 12, Eastry acct 47, Ickham acct 21.
1321/4, cellarer, CCA DCc MA2, fos 112–138.
1324/7, *custos* of the tomb of abp Winchelsey, CCA DCc MA2, fos 137v–164v.
1324/8, subprior, CCA DCc MA2, fos 138v–175v, and also warden of St Mary in crypt, MA2 fos 137v–175v.
1331/4, sacrist, CCA DCc MA2, fos 202v–232; he was sacrist by 25 Apr., 1331, Hope, 'Inventories of Priors', 270.
1335/6, chamberlain, CCA DCc AS 14.
1336/7, former subalmoner, CCA DCc Alm. acct 44.
1337, Mar./Nov., chamberlain, CCA DCc Chamb. accts 29, 13.
1300/1, one of many monks who visited Meopham during the yr, CCA DCc Meopham acct 38.
1314, 27 June, with Gilbert de Bisshoppiston, q.v. apptd proctors to attend convocation, CUL Ms Ee.v.31, fo 147.
1323, 15 May, with William de Ledebury, q.v., sent by the prior and convent to negotiate for the purchase of the manor of Wickham, *Lit. Cant.*, no 109 (Reg. L, fo 125v).
1332, July, apptd to carry out negotiations with the abbot of St Augustine's, *Lit. Cant.*, no 457 (Reg. L, fo 22v).
1333, 3 Nov., one of the seven *compromissorii* in the el. of an abp, Reg. G, fos xxxii, xxxvii, Reg. Q, fo 193v.
1338, 1 Mar., in an inventory of missing books he was held responsible for Transfiguratus in Crucifixum, *Lit. Cant.*, no 618 (Reg. L, fo 104).
1338, 20 Sept., d., CCA Lit. Ms D.12, fo 16.

Name in CCA Lit. Ms E.27, with the date 1331 (see References, section A ii a).

II William COVENTRE [Covyntre
occ. 1439 d. 1460

1439, 4 or 15 Dec., [St Barbara] one of six clothed in the monastic habit, *SL*, 188; CCA Lit. Ms D.12, fo 7v.
[1440], 8 or 20 July [St Margaret], made his prof., Chron. Wm Glastynbury, fo 119v.
1455/7, anniversarian, CCA DCc, Prior accts 10, 15.
n.d., *magister mense*, prob. just before his d., CCA Lit. Ms D.12, fo 26.
1460, 30 Aug., d.; the prior took the *commendatio* in the infirmary chapel and also conducted the burial, *Chron. Stone*, 82; the obit is in BL Ms Arundel 68, fo 39v.

Gervase CRANBROKE [Crambrok, Crambroke, Cranebrok
occ. 1507 d. 1511

1507, 12 Oct., one of six tonsured, *SL*, 193; CCA Lit. Ms D.12, fo 10v.
1508, 22 Apr., ord acol., Canterbury cathedral, Reg. abp Warham, ii, fo 263v.
1508, 25 Apr., made his prof. before the abp, *SL*, 193, CCA Lit. Ms D.12, fo 10v.
1509, 7 Apr., ord subdcn, Canterbury cathedral, Reg. abp Warham, ii, fo 264.
1509, 22 Dec., ord dcn, Canterbury cathedral, *ib.*, ii, fo 264v.
1509/10, celebrated his first mass and recd a small sum from the sacrist, CCA DCc Sac. acct 72.
1511, 2 Sept., 67th in order on the visitation certificate, Wood-Legh, *Visit.*, 3 (Reg. abp Warham, i, fo 35v).
1511, d., in St John's chamber, CCA Lit. Ms C.11, fo 2; his obit is in BL Ms Arundel 68, fo 44 on 4 Oct.

I Henry CRANBROKE [Crambroke, Cranbrok, Cranebroke, Cranebrook, Cravenebroke
occ. 1370 d. 1430

1370, 2 or 6 June, one of four [tonsured], *SL*, 182; CCA Lit. Ms D.12, fo 4v.
1372, 14 Mar., the prior was comm. to rec. his prof., Reg. abp Wittlesey, fo 52.
1372, [17 Sept.], ord acol., abp's chapel, Saltwood, Reg. abp Wittlesey, fo 169v.
Note: the entry is an insertion and the copyist has written 13 kal.Oct., i.e. the day after his ord as subdcn.
1372, 18 Sept. (or 1373, 12 Mar.), ord subdcn Canterbury cathedral, Reg. abp Wittlesey, fo 169v, fo 170 (there are two entries).
1373, 16 Apr., ord dcn, Canterbury cathedral, *ib.*, fo 170v.
1383/4, 1389/90, treasurer, CCA DCc MA2, fo 333, Lambeth Ms 243, fo 215; see also William Stone.
1390/1, chamberlain, replaced in 1391/2 by William Milton, q.v., CCA DCc Chamb. acct 56.
1391, Apr./Sept., 1393/8, cellarer, CCA DCc Cell. acct 1, Eastry acct 119, Copton acct 39,

Cell. accts 2, 3; he was apptd on 7 May 1392, Reg. abp Courtenay, ii, fo 224v.
1397/8, 1399/1400, 1413, Apr./Sept., sacrist, CCA DCc Sac. accts 14, 13, 18.
1412/13, sacrist with Stephen de St Laurence, q.v., CCA DCc Treas. acct 11 (prob. a prior's acct).
1415/16, 1417/18, 1419/21, sacrist, CCA DCc Sac. accts 19, 20, 69, 65; he was [re]apptd two days after the enthronement of the abp, and absolved from the office on 17 Sept. 1421, *Reg. abp Chichele*, iv, 115, 226.

1374, 30 June, in dcn's orders and 58th in order at the el. of an abp, Reg. G, fos 173v–175v.
1381, 31 July, 44th at the el. of an abp, *ib.*, fo 225v.
1396, 7 Aug., 24th at the el. of an abp, *ib.*, fo 234v.
1414, 12 Mar., 6th at the el. of an abp, *Reg. abp Chichele*, i, 4.
1430, 20 Sept., d.; he was a *stationarius* in the infirmary and rec. the sacrament on his deathbed. The subprior performed the exequies, and the following day the prior celebrated the mass and then buried him in the crypt before St Nicholas' altar, *Chron. Stone*, 15, which seems to have copied or been copied by CCA Lit. Ms D.12, fos 22v–23.

II Henry CRANBROKE [Crambroke, Cranbrook, Cranebroke, Cranebrook
occ. 1435 d. 1466

1435, 11 Nov., one of five clothed in the monastic habit, Chron. Wm Glastynbury, fo 117v (*SL*, 188; CCA Lit. Ms D.12, fo 7v).
1436, 5 Mar., ord acol., infirmary chapel, *Reg. abp Chichele*, iv, 383.
1444, 11 Apr., ord pr., Canterbury cathedral, Reg. abp Stafford, fo 197.
1462/3, 1464, 1465/6, warden of manors, CCA DCc Cliffe acct 73, Monk Warden acct 2, MA153.
1443, adm. scholar at Canterbury college, Pantin, *Cant. Coll. Ox.*, ii, 163 (CCA DCc, Cart. Antiq. O.151.12).
1464, 26 June, apptd by the prior and chapter as their proctor for convocation, Reg. S, fo 213v.
1466, 17 Feb., 25th in order in an inventory listing *jocalia fratrum* [given by him and/or assigned for his use], Reg. N., fo 232v.
1466, 8 Dec., d., *Chron. Stone*, 97; his obit is in BL Ms Arundel 68, fo 50v.

Name in
(1) BL Ms Royal 10 B.ix, Epistole etc. (15th c.); acquired in 1452; see Pantin, *Cant. Coll. Ox.*, iii, 68–72, 103–105; he himself added a number of letters and articles, e.g. on fos 46v–56v, fos 64v–67v.
(2) Oxford, Bod. Ms Selden supra 65, Artes dictandi (treatises, letters etc.) (early 15th c.); on fo 72v is his monogram 'hc'. This was in the library of Canterbury college, Pantin, *Cant. Coll. Ox.*, i, 112. See John Throwley II.
(3) Oxford, Bod. Ms Ashmole 393, Miscellanea (15th c.), which contains extracts from astrological treatises 'per—, alias Gruftorrentem'.

His interest in Italian humanist writings and his friendship, from student days at Oxford, and correspondence with John Tiptoft, earl of Worcester are discussed in R.J. Mitchell, *John Tiptoft, 1427–1470*, (London, 1938) 20, 21–23 and R. Weiss, *Humanism*, 21, 85, 113, 119, 130–131, 154. His notebook contains copies of some of his letters; see 1) above.

I John CRANBROKE [Cranbrok, Cranebroke
occ. 1406 d. 1447

1406, 21 Oct., one of three *adjuncti* among seven prof., *SL*, 185; CCA Lit. Ms D.12, fo 6.
1407, 26 Mar., ord acol., Canterbury cathedral, Reg. abp Arundel, i, fo 340v.
1440, 17 Feb., named to the office of refectorer, Chron. Wm Glastynbury, fo 119.
1414, 12 Mar., 66th in order at the el. of an abp, *Reg. abp Chichele*, i, 4.
n.d., described as an *organista eximius*, CCA Lit. Ms D.12, fo 25.
1447, 20 Oct., d. of the plague, *ib.*, and *Chron. Stone*, 42; his obit is on 21 Oct. in BL Ms Arundel 68, fo 46.

II John CRANBROKE [Crambroke, Cranebroke
occ. 1514 occ. 1540

1514, 1 Sept., one of seven tonsured, *SL*, 194; CCA Lit. Ms D.12, fo 11.
1515, 19 Apr., prof., *ib.*
1521, 15 Jan., celebrated his first mass, CCA DCc DE63; the bill of expenses for food served afterwards is in CCA DCc DE62A and B. Items served included beer, wine, dates and spices and a gift of seven capons from his father.
1529, 1530, 1531, 1532, all on 25 Mar., warden of St Mary in crypt, CCA Lit. Ms C.11, fos 65v, 66v, 67, 68.
[1538, 8 Feb., after], 1540, 4 Apr., succentor, Pantin, *Cant. Coll. Ox.*, iii, 153, *L and P Henry VIII*, xv, no 452.
1515/17, 1518/20, his tutor [*magister regule*] was Alexander Staple II, q.v., CCA DCc DE63. This is Staple's acct [1515/20] of his expenditures incurred on behalf of his charge and includes clothing needs, medical expenses and pocket money.
1518/19, spent time in the infirmary on two occasions, CCA DCc Infirm. acct 1.
1534, 12 Dec., acknowledged the Act of Supremacy, *DK 7th Report*, Appndx 2, 282.
[1538, after 8 Feb.], in a list of monks prob. prepared for Thomas Cromwell he was described

as 'a good man', 42 yrs old, Pantin, *Cant. Coll. Ox.*, iii, 153.

1540, 4 Apr., awarded no pension because apptd petty canon in the new foundation, *L and P Henry VIII*, xv, no 452.

Stephen de CRANEBROKE [Crambroke, Cranebroc

occ. 1239/41

n.d., name in the *post exilium* list in *SL*, 172; CCA Lit. Ms D.12, fo 1.

1239, 1 Feb., Mar., third prior, *Gervase Cant.*, ii, 153, 157.

1241, Feb., 10 May, subprior; *ib.*, ii, 186, 197.

n.d., included in a list of subpriors of Dover, *Lit. Cant.*, iii, Appndx no 34 (CCA DCc Z.D4, 23).

1239, 3 Jan., sent with Ralph the cellarer, q.v., and two seculars to the abp as proctors; on 4 Jan. he was numbered among the group of monks accused by the abp of contumacy after the forgery scandal, and ordered to appear before him. *Gervase Cant.*, ii, 142, 144; see Simon de Hertlepe.

1239, 7 Jan., named by the chapter as one of five *compromissorii* for the el. of a prior, *ib.*, ii, 146; they were excommunicated the following wk for their irregular el., *ib.*, ii, 147, 151, 153; see Roger de La Lee.

1241, 1 Feb., one of seven *compromissorii* named by the prior and chapter in the el. of an abp, *ib.*, ii, 186, 187, 189, 190–191.

1241, 10 June, sent to Rome with Thomas de Brydlynton, John de Thaneto I, q.v., and others, to obtain confirmation of the above el., *ib.*, ii, 191, 197–200; see also *CPL*, i (1198–1304), 200, 201.

His perseverance, apparently on his own when other spirits flagged, in the chapter's cause vs the abp was strongly commended by Gervase, *ib.*, ii, 198–199.

Note: see the obits under Stephen I and II.

CRANEBROKE

see also Kranbroke

Hugh de CRETYNG [Cretynge

occ. 2nd half 13th c.

n.d., name occ. in the list in *SL*, 174; CCA Lit. Ms D.12, fo 1v.

c. 1300, with Richard Blundel, q.v., denounced for their prolonged stay on the manors and their consequent secular behaviour, CCA DCc Cart. Antiq. M.368 (*Hist. Mss Comm. 5th Report*, Appndx, 438).

In an inventory of missing books, dated 1 Mar. 1338, he was named as having had in his possession a Codex valued at 4m., Lit. Cant., no 618 (Reg. L, fo 104v). A list of his books in the Eastry catalogue is given in James, *Ancient Libraries*, 67–68 (nos 546–563), of which the Codex is no 556. In this same list occ. a Digesta vetus worth 40s. Both of these volumes had been lent to seculars, and not returned, *ib*. There was also one digestum novum of his in the library at Canterbury college, Pantin, *Cant. Coll. Ox.*, i, 6 (CCA DCc Cart. Antiq. O.34).

R. de CRIPTA

occ. 1189

1189, c. 3 Aug., sent with S., treasurer and Alan II, q.v., to appear before the abp at Wingham, *Epist. Cant.*, 298.

Miles ?CRISPIN [Milo

occ. [1142 × 1152]

[1142 × 1148], with Gilbert de Clare, q.v., witnessed an archiepiscopal confirmation, *Theobald Charters*, no 59.

[1150 × 1152], Miles, Felix and Walter I, q.v., chaplains of the abp witnessed a grant with Walter [Meri], prior, q.v., *ib.*, no 310.

Note: Saltman suggests that Miles Crispin was precentor of Bec and author of the Compendium Vitae Theobaldi, *Theobald Charters*, 79; and he may never have been a monk of Christ Church; and this Miles, witness, may not be Crispin!

CRISTIANUS

see Christianus

CROIDONE

see Croydon

Richard CROPHELL [Crophill, Crophull, Cropphell, Cropphyl

occ. 1389 d. c. 1436

1389, 6 Nov., one of eight prof., *SL*, 184; CCA Lit. Ms D.12, fo 5.

1391, 25 Mar., ord dcn, Canterbury cathedral, Reg. abp Courtenay, i, fo 312.

1435, *magister mense* with Alexander London, q.v., 'Chron. Wm Glastynbury', 129; he was absolved from this office *causa debilitatis* on 24 Dec., Chron. Wm Glastynbury, fo 117v.

1435, 24 Dec., apptd refectorer, Chron. Wm Glastynbury, *ib*.

1390/1, recd 12d. *pro benedictione* from the prior, Lambeth Ms 243, fo 220v.

1396, 7 Aug., 58th in order at the el. of an abp, Reg. G, fo 234v.

1411/12, recd pittance money from the chamberlain, CCA DCc Chamb. acct 71.

1414, 12 Mar., 22nd at the el. of an abp, *Reg. abp Chichele*, i, 4.

c. 1436, d., CCA Lit. Ms D.12, fo 24; his obit on 24/25 Feb. is in BL Ms Arundel 68, fo 18; acc. to Chron. Wm Glastynbury, fo 117v, he d. on the feast of St Ethelbert, king, 24 Feb.

I John CROSSE [Cros, Crows

occ. 1432 d. c. 1494

1432, 19 Sept., one of six prof., *SL*, 188; CCA Lit. Ms D.12, fo 7.

1434, 13 Mar., ord acol. and subdcn, infirmary chapel, *Reg. abp Chichele*, iv, 378.
1435, 2 Apr., ord dcn, infirmary chapel, *ib.*, i, 389 (transcribed as Cirs).
1456/7, third prior, CCA DCc Sac. acct 40.
1464/7, granator, CCA DCc Gran. acts 59–61.
1472/4, *custos corone*, CCA DCc Prior accts 12, 13.
1435, 24 Dec., proclaimed [as ready for examination] by his *magister regule* William Wynchepe II, q.v., Chron. Wm Glastynbury, fo 117ᵛ; 30 Dec. was the day of his examination [*redditus*], *et bene reddit*, Pantin, *Cant. Coll. Ox.*, iv, 53 (Chron. Wm Glastynbury, fo 117ᵛ). On 24 Feb. 1436 he was *absolutus a redditu*, Chron. Wm Glastynbury, fo 117ᵛ.
1493, 1 May, the most senior monk present at the ratification of an agreement, but listed as 9th in order, coming after the prior, subprior and six obedientiaries, Reg. S, fo 383ᵛ.
c. 1494, d., described as *stationarius*, CCA Lit. Ms D.12, fos 27ᵛ and 31ᵛ; his obit on 15 May is in BL Ms Arundel 68, fo 27ᵛ.

II John CROSSE [Crose, Crost

occ. 1497 occ. 1540

1497, 28 July, one of nine tonsured, CCA Lit. Ms D.12, fo 9ᵛ (SL 192, has 1498).
1498, 14 Apr., ord acol., Canterbury cathedral, *Reg. abp Morton*, i, no 447a.
1498, 19 Apr., prof., *SL*, 192; CCA Lit. Ms D.12, fo 9ᵛ.
1505, 22 Mar., ord pr., Canterbury cathedral, Reg. abp Warham, ii, fo 262.
1517, Dec., 1519, Dec., treasurer, CCA Lit. Ms C.11, fos 58ᵛ, 59ᵛ.
1520/1, first treasurer, CCA DCc Treas. acct 25; on the top of this acct are the words 'conserva me Domine'.
1525/7, warden of manors, CCA Lit. Ms C.11, fos 63ᵛ, 64ᵛ.
1534, 2 Jan., [1538, 8 Feb., after], 1540, 4 Apr., cellarer, Reg. T, fo 18ᵛ, Pantin, *Cant. Coll. Ox.*, iii, 152, *L and P Henry VIII*, xv, no 452.
[c. 1500], scholar at Canterbury college, *Lit. Cant.*, no 1109 (CCA DCc L.B.182).
1501, 26 Apr., dcn and 62nd in order at the el. of an abp, Reg. R, fo 56ᵛ.
1511, 2 Sept., 42nd on the visitation certificate, Wood-Legh, *Visit.*, 3 (Reg. abp Warham, i, fo 35ᵛ).
[1538, 8 Feb., after], in a list of monks prob. prepared for Thomas Cromwell, he was reported as 59 yrs of age, Pantin, *Cant. Coll. Ox.*, iii, 152.
1540, 4 Apr., awarded £30 p.a., *L and P Henry VIII*, xv, no 452.

See the note below John Crosse III.

III John CROSSE

occ. 1524 occ. 1540

1524, 21/22 July, one of eleven granted adm. [*ingressum*] to Christ Church, CCA Lit. Ms D.12, fos 11ᵛ–12.
1524, 4 Aug., one of eleven tonsured, *SL*, 195, CCA Lit. Ms D.12, *ib.*
1525, 19 Apr., prof., *ib.*, (both refs).
1532/3, celebrated his first mass, Woodruff, 'Sacrist's Rolls', 73 (CCA DCc Sac. acct 75).
[1538, 8 Feb., after], fellow of Canterbury college, Pantin, *Cant. Coll. Ox.*, iii, 153.
[1538, 8 Feb., after], in a list of monks prob. prepared for Thomas Cromwell he was described as a 'witty' man, 29 yrs of age, Pantin, *Cant. Coll. Ox.*, iii, 153.
1540, 4 Apr., awarded £3 and became a scholar in the new foundation, *L and P Henry VIII*, xv, no 452.

Note: John Crosse II and III both signed the surrender deed but only one of them (?which one) subscribed to the Act of Supremacy, *DK 7th Report*, Appndx 2, 282.

William CROSTON

occ. 1502 occ. 1511

1502, 25 Aug., one of eight tonsured, *SL*, 193, CCA Lit. Ms D.12, fo 10.
1503, 4 Apr., made his prof. before the prior, *sed. vac.*, *ib.*
1511, 2 Sept., 51st in order on the visitation certificate, Wood-Legh, *Visit.*, 3 (Reg. abp Warham, i, fo 35ᵛ).
n.d., 3 Feb., pr., whose obit occ. in BL Ms Arundel 68, fo 15.

CROWS

see Crosse

Henry de CROYDON [Corydon, Croidone, Croyden, Croyndon

occ. [?1364] occ. 1384

[?1364], one of eleven [?clothed], *SL*, 182; CCA Lit. Ms D.12, fo 4ᵛ.
Note: the date, which has been added later in the margin, does not seem to fit for this monk as well as it does for the others; see, for example, Robert Brandrede.
1368, 18 Aug., the prior was comm. to rec. his prof., *Reg. abp Langham*, 199.
1374, 30 June, listed as 38th in order at the el. of an abp, Reg. G, fos 173ᵛ–175ᵛ, but he was absent at the curia, *ib.*, fos 174, 200. He did not agree to the decision to el. by way of scrutiny, *ib.*
1384, 20 May, given permission by the prior and convent to become the rector of Bradwell, London diocese, and licensed by the abp on 28 May, Oxford, Bod. Ms Ashmole 794, fos 263ᵛ, 264.

In the will of cardinal Langham dated 1375, he was to receive 150 florins of the chamber, R. Widmore, *An Enquiry into the Time of the First Foundation of Westminster Abbey*, London, 1743, Appndx vi, 186.

Alan de CRUCE [Cruche
occ. 1299 d. 1343

1299, 24 Aug., one of seven prof., *SL*, 178; CCA Lit. Ms D.12, fo 3v.
Note: an Alan de Cruce was ord subdcn and dcn in 1292 *ad titulum patrimonii*, *Reg. ab Winchelsey*, 903, 907.
1315, accused by the abp of having done violence to Robert de Aldon, q.v., and was therefore to remain under the greater excommunication, Reg. abp Reynolds, fo 69.
1324, 29 May, had been subjected to penance after a visitation and the abp now ordered the relaxation of his penance, CUL Ms Ee.5.31, fo 236–236v; see John de Maldon.
[c. 1320], in the dossier which is now CCA DCc Cart. Antiq. C.1294, 1296, he was, with Robert de Aldon above, Robert de Thaneto, q.v. and others, one of a group of rebellious and unruly monks who made life difficult for prior Henry Eastry, q.v.; there is a brief résumé in *Hist. Mss Comm. 5th Report*, Appndx, 438.
1326/7, recd two pittances from the almoner, CCA DCc Alm. acct 38.
1338, 1 Mar., in an inventory of missing books he was held responsible for three service books, all belonging to other monks, *Lit. Cant.*, no 618 (Reg. L, fo 104).
1343, 24 Mar., d., CCA Lit. Ms D.12, fo 16v.

Richard de CRUCE
occ. 1st half 13th c.

n.d., name occ. in the *post exilium* list in *SL*, 173; CCA Lit. Ms D.12, fo 1v.

Name attached to two vols in the Eastry catalogue, one containing a collection of miscellaneous treatises, biblical books, sermons etc., and the other lives of Thomas Becket and Anselm, James, *Ancient Libraries*, nos 1394, 1395 (p. 119).

See note below the next entry.

Richard de CRUCE SIGNATA [Signatus
occ. 1st half 13th c.

n.d., name occ. in the *post exilium* list in *SL*, 173; CCA Lit. Ms D.12, fo 1.

Name attached to a list of four vols in the Eastry catalogue, nos 1311–1314, James, *Ancient Libraries*, 113.

Note: James gives the dates of d. as 1240 and 1239 (*ib.*, 535) respectively without refs. Which is which?

John de CRUNDALE
occ. 1220/1 occ. 1224/5

[1207 × 1214], name occ. in the list of those who were in exile, *SL*, 172; CCA Lit. Ms D.12, fo 1.
1220, Nov./1221, Nov.; 1223, July/1225, Jan., cellarer, CCA DCc MA1 fos 65, 67v–69v, AS1 (as John only).
n.d., sacrist, and also chaplain to the abp, Amundesham, *Annales*, ii, 330.

He was the uncle of the monk, Hamo, who served as sacrist and chamberlain at St Alban's abbey. He gave a ring to St Alban's and the monks in return adm. him into their confraternity, Amundesham, *Annales*, ii, 330.

In the Eastry catalogue, a volume on church councils is listed as his, James, *Ancient Libraries*, 117 (no 1372).

CUDELAWE
see Codelawe

CUMBE
see Coumbe

CURTNEY
see Courtney

John ?CYRCHY
occ. 1518/19

1518/19, ill in the infirmary, CCA DCc Infirm. acct 1.

DANIEL
occ. [1144 × 1152]

[1144 × 1152], with Walter [Durdent or Meri q.v.] prior, and other monks witnessed a grant, *Theobald Charters*, no 63.

DANIEL
see also Sifflington, Sutton

John DANIEL
see Chillenden

I DAVID
n.d.

n.d., 1 Jan., pr., whose obit occ. in BL Ms Arundel 68, fo 12.

II DAVID
n.d.

n.d., 25 Oct., obit occ. in BL Ms Arundel 68, fo 46v.

Note: in 1152 Odo, the father of a David, monk, witnessed a purchase of land by prior Wibert, *ib.*, Urry *Canterbury*, 392.

Robert DENE [Deane, Deene
occ. [1461] d. c. 1478/9

1461, 4 Apr., ord subdcn, Canterbury cathedral, *Reg. abp Bourgchier*, 378.
[1461], 19 Apr., one of six prof., CCA Lit. Ms D.12, fo 8 (*SL*, 189).

1462, 17 Apr., ord dcn, Canterbury cathedral, *Reg. abp Bourgchier*, 381.

1465, 8 June, ord pr., Canterbury cathedral, *ib.*, 395.

1464/5, celebrated his first mass and recd an 8d gift from the sacrist, CCA DCc Sac. acct 45.

1472/6, 1477/8, anniversarian, CCA DCc Anniv. acct 14, Prior acct 14, Lambeth ED43, 44, CCA DCc Anniv. acct 15; in 1472/3 he was second anniversarian and in 1477/8 first.

1466, 17 Feb., 68th in order in an inventory listing *jocalia fratrum* [given by him and/or assigned for his use], Reg. N, fo 234^v.

1468, 29 Apr., was examined [*de redditu*] by the precentor and seniors, *Chron. Stone*, 103.

c. 1478/9, d., CCA Lit. Ms D.12, fo 26; his obit on 31 Aug. is in BL Ms Arundel 68, fo 40.

William DENE

occ. [1448] d. 1457

1448, n.d., one of four prof., *SL*, 189; CCA Lit. Ms D.12, fo 7^v.

1448, 17 Feb., ord acol., Canterbury cathedral, Reg. abp Stafford, fo 202.

1449, 12 Apr., ord subdcn, Canterbury cathedral, *ib.*, fo 203^v.

1450, 3 Apr., ord dcn, Canterbury cathedral, *ib.*, fo 204^v.

1452, 8 Apr., ord pr., Canterbury cathedral, *ib.*, fo 207.

n.d., prob. 1457, chaplain to the subprior [Henry Berham, q.v.], CCA Lit. Ms D.12, fo 25^v.

1457, 21 Oct., d. of the plague in his ninth yr of monastic life; the subprior celebrated the first requiem mass and buried him, *Chron. Stone*, 70; obit on 22 Oct., in BL Ms Arundel 68, fo 46.

DENYS or DIONISIUS

see Cantuar', St Margaret

Quintin DENYSE [Denysse, Denny, Quentin Dennys

occ. 1522 occ. 1540

1522, 11 Feb., one of ten to be tonsured, *SL*, 195; CCA Lit. Ms D.12, fo 11^v.

1525/6, celebrated his first mass and recd 9d from the sacrist, Woodruff, 'Sacrist's Rolls', 72.

[1538, 8 Feb., after], 1540, 4 Apr., one of four subsacrists [*parvus sacrista*], Pantin, *Cant. Coll. Ox.*, iii, 153, *L and P Henry VIII*, xv, no 452.

1534, 12 Dec., acknowledged the Act of Supremacy, *DK 7th Report*, Appndx 2, 282 (transcribed as Devuy).

1538 [8 Feb., after], in a list of monks prob. prepared for Thomas Cromwell, he was described as 'a good man', 36 yrs old, Pantin, *Cant. Coll. Ox.*, iii, 153.

1540, 4 Apr., awarded £6 13s. 4d., *L and P Henry VIII*, xv, no 452.

M. Henry de DEPHAM [Diepham, Depeham

occ. 1271 d. 1292

n.d., name occ. in the list in *SL*, 175; CCA Lit. Ms D.12, fo 2^v.

1272, Oct./Nov., penitentiary, CCA DCc ES Roll 222, 310.

1275/6, 1290/1, Feb., almoner, CCA DCc Monkton acct 5, Meopham acct 10.

1271, June, acted as commissary *sed. vac.* of the official, Geoffrey de Romenal, q.v., Selden Soc., *Select Cases Eccles.*, 19 (CCA DCc ES Roll 310 and Roll 222 for Dec. 1272).

1277/8, attended the general chapter of the Friars Minor *pro lectore nostro*, and was given his expenses of 10s., Pantin, *Cant. Coll. Ox.*, iv, 168.

1292, 11 Oct., d., CCA Lit. Ms D.12, fo 15.

Name in CCA Lit. Ms B3, Summa decretalium (late 13th c.); name on front flyleaf.

The inventory of missing books dated 1 Mar. 1338 includes two of his service books for which William de Mallyng q.v. was held responsible, *Lit. Cant.*, no 618 (Reg. L, fo 104). In the Eastry catalogue, his books include canon law texts and commentaries, sermons, works of Augustine and a copy of the Rule, James, *Ancient Libraries*, 53, 125–128 (nos 387, 1487–1522). A book of decretals of his was also in the library at Canterbury college, Pantin, *Cant. Coll. Ox.*, i, 5 (CCA DCc Cart. Antiq. O.34).

His silver gilt *ciphus* is included in an inventory of the refectory of 1328, Dart, *Antiq. Cant.*, xix (BL Ms Cotton Galba E.iv, fo 178^v).

John DERYNG B.Th [Derryng

occ. 1519 d. 1534

1519, 6 May, one of nine tonsured, *SL*, 194; CCA Lit. Ms D.12, fo 11^v.

1520, 3 Feb., prof., *ib.*

1525/6, celebrated his first mass and recd 9d from the sacrist, Woodruff, 'Sacrist's Rolls', 72.

1528/9, scholar at Canterbury college, Pantin, *Cant. Coll. Ox.*, ii, 259.

1532, July, supplicated for B.Th., *BRUO, 1501–1540*.

[1534], 28 Jan., his books and papers were sent by Richard Thornden, q.v., warden of Canterbury college, to Thomas Cromwell, Pantin, *Cant. Coll. Ox.*, iii, 147.

1533, 24 Nov., with Edward Bockyng, q.v., supported Elizabeth Barton, the nun of Kent who denounced Henry VIII's divorce, *L and P Henry VIII*, vi, no 1460. At some time during this yr he was sent for from Oxford to be interrogated, *ib.*, nos 1381, 1468.

1534, 5 Jan., as the author of a controversial tract De Duplici Spiritu, abp Cranmer reported questioning him, *ib.*, vii, pt. 1, nos 17, 72; the

latter item notes that in the tract he 'erred more by oversight than of malice'.
1534, 20 Apr., was executed at Tyburn, *L and P Henry VIII*, vii, pt. 1, no 522; see Edward Bockyng.

Richard DERYNG [Dering, Derynge
occ. 1475 d. 1518/19

1475, 27 Mar., one of four prof., *SL*, 191; CCA Lit. Ms D.12, fo 8v.
1475, 23 Sept., ord subdcn, prior's chapel, *Reg. abp Bourgchier*, 418.
1476, 21 Sept., ord dcn, Canterbury cathedral, *ib.*, 421 (as William).
1481, 1 Apr., ord pr., Canterbury cathedral, *ib.*, 430.
1486, c. 15 Apr., subchaplain [to the prior], Cambridge, Corpus Christi College, Ms 298, fo 128v.
1492, Mar., 1493, Mar., anniversarian, CCA DCc U15/24/17.
1495, chancellor with Richard Sellyng II, q.v., Reg. S, fo 396.
1495, 11 May; 1496, 6 May; 1497, 29 Apr., 23 Oct.; 1498, 23 Oct.; 1499, 28 Oct., warden of manors, CCA DCc Treas acct 35, pts 1, 2; MA109; MA110; MA111.
1501, 26 Apr.; 1503, 21 Feb.; 1516, 25 Mar.; 1517, 25 Mar., cellarer, Reg. R, fo 56v; Reg. T, fo 15v; CCA Lit. Ms C.11, fos 57v; *ib.*, fo 58.
1486, c. 15 Apr., took part in the funeral of abp Bourgchier, Cambridge, Corpus Christi College, Ms 298, fo 128v.
1493, 1 May, 33rd in order at the ratification of an agreement, Reg. S, fo 383v; but see John Crosse I.
1501, 26 Apr., 20th in order at the el. of an abp, Reg. R, fo 56v.
1511, 2 Sept., 8th on the visitation certificate, Wood-Legh, *Visit.*, 3 (Reg. abp Warham, i, fo 35).
1511, gave hangings on the north side of the choir, Hasted, *Kent*, xi, 365–366. These are now at Aix-en-Provence, Collinson, *Canterbury Cathedral*, 161, n. 39.
1518/19, d. acc. to the treasurer's acct, Pantin, *Cant. Coll. Ox.*, iv, 206. His obit occ. on 4 Aug. in BL Ms Arundel 68, fo 37.

His name, arms and rebus were in the windows of the cellarer's office acc. to Hasted, *Kent*, xi, 513 n.

DIEPHAM
see Depham

DIERMANNUS
n.d.

n.d., pr., whose obit occ. on 5 Mar. in BL Ms Cotton Nero C.ix, fo 7.

DIGARUS
n.d.

n.d., 22 Nov., *conversus*, whose obit occ. in Lambeth Ms 20, fo 240v.

DIGOUN, Digun
see Dygon

DIONISIUS
see Cantuar', St Margaret

DODINTON, Dodintune
see Dudynton

DONATUS [Donngus
occ. [before 1085]

[1085 before], sent by bp Patrick of Dublin [q.v. under Worcester] to be trained as a monk of Christ Church before succeeding Patrick in the see in 1085, Mason, *Wulfstan*, 251 (Worcester). Acc. to the 'Acta Lanfranci', 290, the yr of his consecration was 1086/7; see also J.A. Watt, *The Church in Medieval Ireland*, Dublin, 1972, 3.

Note: Dublin then came under the jurisdiction of the abp of Canterbury.

John DORKING
occ. 1474

1474, 26 Mar., ord subdcn, Canterbury cathedral, *Reg. abp Bourgchier*, 416.

Gervase DOROB[ERNENSIS
see Gervase, Sampson

DOROBERNENSIS
see Richard Pluto

DOUFFOLDE
see Duffelde

Alexander de DOVER [Dovoria
occ. 1187/9

1187, Sept., one of several monks sent to the king in Normandy to explain the convent's case vs the abp, *Epist. Cant.*, 94–95. However he became ill and returned, *ib.*
1189, May, one of the monks named by the abp with whom he refused to negotiate, *Epist. Cant.*, 292.
1189, Sept., with John de Bremble, q.v., given permission by Geoffrey II, subprior, q.v., to remain abroad; see *Epist. Cant.*, 308.
1189, 6 Oct., chosen by the abp to be one of the electors in the el. of a prior, and was the only one who complied, *ib.*, 311–312.

Name attached to two volumes which are listed in the Eastry catalogue, James, *Ancient Libraries*, 101 (nos 1077, 1088).

Eustace de DOVER [Dovor, Dovorr'
occ. 1st half 12th c.

n.d., name occ. in the list in *SL*, 173; CCA Lit. Ms D.12, fo 1^{v}.

Note: is this Eustace de Faversham, q.v.?

James de DOVER [Dovor, Dovorr'
occ. 1349 d. 1397

1349, 9 Oct., one of six prof., *SL*, 181; CCA Lit. Ms D.12, fo 4.
1350, 18 Sept., ord subdcn, Goudhurst, Reg. abp Islip, fo 310.
1351, 24 Sept., ord dcn, chapel of Herne parish church, *ib.*, fo 312.
1353, 21 Dec., ord pr., apb's chapel, Maidstone, *ib.*, fo 314^{v}.
1365, *magister ordinis*, *SL*, 182 (transcribed as John); CCA Lit. Ms D.12, fo 4^{v}.
1368/70, 1372/4, almoner, CCA DCc Alm. acct 36, Eastry acct 102, Alm. acct 24, Eastry acct 107.
1374/5, first anniversarian with John de Banbery, q.v., CCA DCc Anniv. acct 6.
1378/81, feretrar, CCA DCc MA2, fos 314^{v}–325.
1381, 31 July, subprior, Reg. G, fo 223^{v}.
1383, Jan./1384, Sept., 1385/1386, July, sacrist, CCA DCc Sac. accts 7,8.

1366, 10 May, present at the el. of an abp, Reg. G, fo 147.
1374, 30 June, 11th in order at the el. of an abp, *ib.*, fos 173^{v}–175^{v}.
1381, 31 July, (subprior and) 5th in order at the el. of an abp, and was named by the first three *compromissorii* when adding to their number six others, *ib.*, fo 223^{v}, Oxford, Bod. Ms Ashmole 794, fo 254^{v}.
1396, 7 Aug., 3rd at the el. of an abp, Reg. G, fo 234^{v}.
1397, 27 Apr., d., and was buried in the crypt before St Nicholas' altar; he was 'vir religiosus et senex venerabilis', CCA Lit. Ms D.12, fo 17^{v}. His obit is in BL Ms Arundel 68, fo 26.

A silver pyx of his is listed in Canterbury college inventories, e.g. that of 1443, Pantin, *Cant. Coll. Ox.*, i, 1 (CCA DCc Cart. Antiq. O.134).

I John de DOVER [Dovor, Duvra
occ. [1198] occ. 1200

[1198, July], chaplain of abp Hubert Walter, *Eng. Epis. Acta*, iii, no 377.
1197/8, 21 Jan., acted as cross bearer for the abp when the latter came to the chapter house to discuss his Lambeth project with the monks, *Diceto Opera*, ii, 151; see also C.R. Cheney, *Hubert Walter* (London, 1967), 137–157.
1198, 4 May, with Ralph de Orpynton I, q.v., apptd proctor in a suit over land, CCA DCc, Cart. Antiq. S.231.
1200, 1 May, el. abbot of Battle, *HRH*, 29.

II John DOVER [Dovor, Dovore, Dovorr
occ. 1403 d. 1463

1403, 22 Dec., one of six prof., *SL*, 185; CCA Lit. Ms D.12, fo 5^{v}.
1404, 29 Mar., ord acol., Canterbury cathedral, Reg. abp Arundel, i, fo 332^{v}.
1405, 18 Apr., ord subdcn, Canterbury cathedral, *ib.*, i, fo 333^{v}.
1410, 22 Mar., ord pr., Canterbury cathedral, *ib.*, ii, fo 98^{v}.

1435, 1440, before 17 Feb., refectorer, 'Chron. Wm Glastynbury', 129 (Ms fos 118, 119).
1440, 17 Feb., apptd feretrar, Chron. Wm Glastynbury, fos 118, 119; on 1 Feb. [1441] he was replaced by Thomas Wakeryng, q.v., *ib.*, fo 119^{v}.
1452/3, granator, CCA DCc Gran. acct 58.

1408/9, scholar at Canterbury college, with John Wotton I, for whom the treasurer pd the expenses of transporting his clothing from Oxford to Christ Church, Pantin, *Cant. Coll. Ox.*, iv, 191.

1414, 21 Mar., 45th in order at the el. of an abp, Reg. G, fo 290.
1463, 21 Apr., *stationarius*, d., after almost 60 yrs as a prof. monk, *Chron. Stone*, 88, CCA Lit. Ms D.12, fo 26; his obit on 22 Apr. is in BL Ms Arundel 68, fo 24^{v}.

III John DOVER [Dovor
occ. 1485

1485, 2 Apr., ord acol., Canterbury cathedral, *Reg. abp Bourgchier*, 450.

IV John DOVER [Dovor
occ. 1493 occ. 1522/3

1493, 26 July, one of ten who were tonsured, *SL*, 192; CCA Lit. Ms D.12, fo 9^{v}.
1494, 29 Mar., ord acol., Canterbury cathedral, *Reg. abp Morton*, i, no 443a.
1496, 2 Apr., ord subdcn, Canterbury cathedral, *ib.*, i, no 445b.
1497, 25 Mar., ord dcn, Canterbury cathedral, *ib.*, i, no 446c.

1505/6, third cantor, CCA Lit. Ms C.11, fo 48^{v}.
1521/3, anniversarian, Lambeth ED49, 50.
1524, Jan., apptd precentor, Reg. T, fo 228^{v}.

1501, 26 Apr., 48th in order at the el. of an abp, Reg. R, fo 56^{v}.
1511, 2 Sept., 31st on the visitation certificate, Wood-Legh, *Visit.*, 3 (Reg. abp Warham, i, fo 35^{v}).

Note: the obit of a John Dovyr, precentor, occ. on 28 July in BL Ms Arundel 68, fo 36.

Nicholas de DOVER [Dovor, Dovoria, Dovorr
occ. 1294 d. 1300

1294, 18 Oct., one of eight prof., *SL*, 178; CCA Lit. Ms D.12, fo 3.

1299, 19 Sept., ord pr., Littlebourne, *Reg. abp Winchelsey*, 931.

1300, 31 Aug., d., CCA Lit. Ms D.12, fo 15v.

Richard de DOVER
occ. [1143 × 1148] occ. 1173

[1143 × 1148], with Walter [Durdent, q.v.], prior, and Hugh de Caen q.v. witnessed a charter of abp Theobald, *Theobald Charters*, no 86; Gervase described him as a former chaplain to the abp, *Gervase Cant.*, ii, 397.

1157, apptd prior of Dover by the abp, *HRH*, 88.

1173, 3 June, el. abp at Westminster, and went to Rome where he was consecrated by the pope, *Gervase Cant.*, i, 244, *Fasti*, ii, 4. Gervase observed that he was Norman by birth and 'ab ineunte aetate in ecclesia Cantuariensi monachicum gesserat habitum', *ib.*, ii, 397. For details of royal influence and intervention in the el. to the primatial see, see *Foliot Letters*, no 220 and the note. See also R. Foreville, *Église et la Royauté*, 376, n. 7, and H. Mayr-Harting, 'Henry II and the Papacy, 1170–1189', in *Journal of Ecclesiastical History*., 16 (1965), 50–53.

According to *Gervase Cant.*, ii, 397, he was *artium liberalium scholas egressus*.

Robert de DOVER [Dovor, Dovoria, Dovorr
occ. [c. 1280] occ. 1336/7

[c. 1280], one of four prof., *SL*, 176; CCA Lit. Ms D.12, fo 3.

1285, 22 Sept., ord pr., collegiate church, South Malling, *Reg. abp Pecham*, i, 222.

1303, 6 Dec., apptd sacrist by the abp, *Reg. abp Winchelsey*, 1306, and Reg. Q, fo 30/42.

1304/7, 1308/13, sacrist, CCA DCc MA1, fos 251v–271, MA2, fos 11v–44v.

1313, 28 May, chamberlain, Reg. Q, fo 74.

1313, June/1314, May, subprior, CCA DCc Copton acct 8, Chamb. acct 8.

1319/24, sacrist, CCA DCc MA2, fos 97–138, DE24 (for 21 Oct. 1323).

1324, 10 Apr., 1329/30, precentor, CCA DCc EC V/46, Chartham acct 17.

1332/4, subprior, CCA DCc Godmersham acct 15, Agney acct 39.

1335/7, sacrist, CCA DCc AS 14, MA2, fos 241v–256.

1313, 28 May, named as one of the initial three *compromissorii* who were called upon to select seven *compromissorii* for the el. of an abp, Reg. Q, fo 61/75.

1321, 3 Nov., with William de London I, q.v., accepted delivery of the inventory of *ornamenta*, *textus*, and *reliquie*, Legg and Hope, *Inventories*, 51, 78 (BL Ms Cotton Galba E.iv, fos 112, 127).

1327, 11 Dec., again, one of three *compromissorii* apptd to choose seven for the el. of an abp, Reg. Q, fo 108/123 (and see *CPL*, ii (1305–1342), 272).

1333, 3 Nov., named as one of the three *compromissorii* apptd to name seven for the el. of an abp, Reg. G, fo xxxii, xxxvii, also Reg. Q, fo 193.

Simon de DOVER [Dovor, Dovorr', Dovra
occ. [1149 × 1154] occ. 1187

[1149 × 1154], with Richard de Bex and Hervey, q.v., witnessed a charter concerning Dover priory, *Theobald Charters*, 542.

1187, 10 June, with M. Aaron, q.v., sent to abp Baldwin by the prior and chapter with letters from the pope prohibiting him from carrying out his plan to build a collegiate church at Lambeth, *Epist. Cant.* 67.

Thomas DOVER [Dovor, Dovorre
occ. 1376 d. 1413

1376, 14/15 Nov., one of seven who were clothed in the monastic habit, CCA Lit. Ms D.12, fo 4v.

1376, 20 Dec., ord acol., Canterbury cathedral, Reg. abp Sudbury, fo 140v.

1377, 19 Sept., ord subdcn, Lambeth palace chapel, *ib.*, fo 142.

1378, 17 Apr., ord dcn, Canterbury cathedral, *ib.*, fo 145v.

1381, 8 June, ord pr., Lambeth palace chapel, *ib.*, fo 150v.

c. 1390, *magister ordinis*, *SL*, 184, CCA Lit. Ms D.12, fo 5.

1391, 25 Apr., one of three monk penitentiaries apptd for the priory, Reg. abp Courtenay, i, fo 338.

n.d., subprior twice, CCA Lit. Ms D.12, fo 20.

1381/2, scholar at Canterbury college, recd 20s. from the treasurer 'pro capa sua scholastica', Pantin, *Cant. Coll. Ox.*, iv, 188.

1383, 20 Aug., named as first scholar, Pantin, *ib.*, iii, 46 (Reg. abp Courtenay i, fo 43).

1393/5, payments for his battels and commons were recd by the warden, Pantin, *ib.*, ii, 132, 133, 135, 136, 138, 140 (CCA DCc Cart. Antiq. O.151.2, 3).

1391, 28 Apr., apptd penitentiary in the city of Canterbury, Reg. abp Courtenay, i, fo 338v.

1381, 31 July, 55th in order at the el. of an abp, Reg. G, fo 225v.

1396, 7 Aug., 28th at the el. of an abp, *ib.*, fo 234v.

1413, 31 Oct., d., after reciting [first] vespers of All Saints with his chaplains; having begun to say his own *commendatio*, after he had just uttered the words 'Sancta Maria magdalena ora pro anima . . .' he breathed his last. Because of his devotion to this saint, the obit notes, this was most appropriate. Details of his funeral, which was deferred because of the feast, are given; on 2 Nov. the requiem was attended by monks of St Augustine's and other religious because 'vir erat magne fame et quasi unus de senioribus', CCA Lit. Ms D.12, fo 20.

W. de DOVER [Dovoria
occ. 1187/8

Note:
(1) The name *W. prior Dovorie* is attached to two vols in the Eastry catalogue, nos 1315–1319, which are mainly concerned with canon law, James, *Ancient Libraries*, 113.
(2) The name W. de Dovoria, subprior of Dover is attached to two vols in the Eastry catalogue, nos 1377, 1378, James, *Ancient Libraries*, 117.

Which of the William Dovers are these?

I William de DOVER [Dovor, Dovoria, Dovorr
occ. 1238

n.d., name occ. in the *post exilium* list in *SL*, 173; CCA Lit. Ms D.12, fo 1.

1238, was sent with the subprior and Richard Dygon, q.v. to Rome in the case over the forged charter, *Gervase Cant.*, ii, 133; see Simon de Hertlepe.

II William de DOVER [Dovere, Dovor, Dovorr
occ. 1st half of 13th c.

n.d., name occ. in the list in *SL*, 173; CCA Lit. Ms D.12, fo 1ᵛ
n.d., name occ. in a list of subpriors of Dover, *Lit. Cant.*, iii, Appndx no 34 (CCA DCc Z.D4, 23).

His three *ciphi de murra* are listed in an inventory of the refectory dated 1328, Dart, *Antiq. Cant.*, xxi (BL Ms Cotton Galba E.iv, fo 179).

Note: William de Dover I and II must have been near contemporaries and therefore it is not certain that the entries have been correctly assigned. One of them was prob. prior of Dover and former confessor to the abp. See William de Sandford, who is possibly this monk, also known as M. William.

The M. William, prior of Dover, in 1233 made an unsuccessful claim to take part in the el. of an abp, Wallace, *Abp Edmund*, 153. On 7 Feb. 1235 a papal mandate addressed to the monks at Christ Church ordered them not to molest the prior of Dover on acct of his objection to the el. of abp Edmund, *CPL*, i (1198–1304), 131. He is briefly mentioned in BL Ms Cotton Julius D.v, fo 29ᵛ.

See William de Sandford.

III William de DOVER B.Cn.L. [Dovere, Dovor, Dovore, Dovorr'
occ. 1361 d. [1414]

1361, 28 Oct., one of nine prof., *SL*, 182; CCA Lit. Ms D.12, fo 4ᵛ.
1362, 24 Sept., ord acol., Charing, Reg. abp Islip, fo 322.
1363, 23 Sept., ord dcn, Faversham monastery, *ib.*, fo 323ᵛ.
1367, 18 Sept., ord pr., Lambeth palace chapel, *Reg. abp Langham*, 383.

1369/72, 1373/4, treasurer, CCA DCc MA2 fos 265–275, 290.
1375/6, 1377/9, warden of manors, CCA DCc Ebony acct 66, MA2, fos 311–316.
1380, 1382, 1383, 1385, Apr./Sept., warden of Canterbury college, Pantin, *Cant. Coll. Ox.*, iv, 229; his apptment on 27 Mar. 1380 is in Pantin, *ib.*, iii, 36–37 (Reg. abp Sudbury, fo 131ᵛ); he replaced John Aleyn, q.v., on 18 Oct. 1382 as *yconomus*, Reg. abp Courtenay, i, fo 23ᵛ (printed in Pantin, *ib.*, iii, 39); the apptment was renewed on 9 Aug. [1383], *ib.*, fo 43. On 29 Jan. 1384 he recd an apptment as 'perpetual master or warden', Pantin, *ib.*, iii, 48 (Oxford, Bod. Ms Ashmole 794, fos 258ᵛ–259). He was still custos on 27 Jan. 1391, Reg. S, fo 1ᵛ.
1382, 15 Sept., dismissed from the office of cellarer, Reg. abp Courtenay, i, fo 21ᵛ.

1379/80, scholar at Canterbury college, who with two others recd money for their expenses *versus Oxoniam* and for *capis suis scolasticis*, Pantin, *Cant. Coll. Ox.*, iv, 188.
1382/3, recd 5s. *pro benedicione*, *ib.* In this yr there were a number of expenditures on monk delegations to the abp *causa W. Dovorre* [?re his apptment as administrator], *ib.*, iv, 188–189.
1384/5, recd 110s. 4d. from the treasurer *pro statutis colegii Oxonie emendandis* and other purposes, Pantin, *ib.*, iv, 190.
1385/6, recd 5s. *pro benediccione versus Oxoniam*, *ib.*
n.d., B.Cn.L., CCA Lit. Ms D.12, fo 20ᵛ.

1374, 30 June, 29th in order at the el. of an abp, and apptd as proxy for James Hegham, q.v. on 27 June, Reg. G, fos 173ᵛ–175ᵛ, 172ᵛ.
1374/5, spent time in the infirmary and recd a 4s. pension from the anniversarian, CCA DCc Anniv. acct 6.
1376, Apr., one of ten nom. to the committee set up for regulating the infirmary, *Lit. Cant.*, no 945 (CCA DCc Cart. Antiq. C.206).
1376, 31 Aug., with William Woghope, q.v., brought news to the abp of the d. of prior Richard Gyllyngham, q.v., Reg. abp Sudbury, fo 27ᵛ.
1381, 31 July, 21st in order at the el. of an abp, Reg. G, fo 225ᵛ.
1393, 16 Aug., apptd prior of Dover, Reg. abp Courtenay, ii, fo 212.
n.d., 'removed' from the above position and returned to Canterbury, living not as an ordinary member of the community but at his own expense on his pension from Dover of 20m [p.a.] and paying 10m. 'pro mensa sua et famuli sui', CCA Lit. Ms D.12, fo 20ᵛ. He res.

c. 1396/7 (information from Miss M. Barber, Lambeth Palace Library).

[1414], 6 Jan., d., CCA Lit. Ms D.12, *ib.* The obituary praises his policy, when serving as manorial warden, of leasing out the manors to the 'inestimable' benefit of Christ Church; he was buried among his brethren, with the usual offices but without some of the usual accompanying ceremonies, *ib.*

IV William DOVER [Dovere, Dovor, Dovorr, Dovyr

occ. 1450 d. 1470

1450, 25 Jan., one of seven prof., *SL*, 189; CCA Lit. Ms D.12, fo 7v.

1450, 3 Apr., ord acol. Canterbury cathedral, Reg. abp Stafford, fo 204.

1452, 8 Apr., ord subdcn, Canterbury cathedral, *ib.*, fo 206v.

1452, 23 Sept., ord dcn, Canterbury cathedral, Reg. abp Kemp, fo 254.

1455, 20 Sept., ord pr., Canterbury cathedral, *Reg. abp Bourgchier*, 362.

1465/9, anniversarian, CCA DCc U15/24/7, Anniv. acct 20, Lambeth ED42, CCA DCc Prior acct 11.

1469/70, fourth prior with William Vowle, q.v., CCA DCc Sac. acct 48.

1466, 17 Feb., 45th in order in an inventory listing *jocalia fratrum* [given by him and/or assigned for his use], Reg. N, fo 233v.

1470, 25 Sept., d. of the plague, *Chron. Stone*, 114; his d. (1469/70) is also noted in CCA Lit. Ms D.12, fo 26, CCA DCc Sac. acct 48, and his obit is in BL Ms Arundel 68, fo 43 and Lambeth Ms 20, fo 224v.

Name in Oxford, Bod. Ms Rawlinson C.269, Richard Rolle (15th c.); also the date 1464; see Robert Chelmynton.

DROWLE

see John Throwley I

Peter de DUDYNTON [Dodintune

occ. 1238/9

n.d., name occ. in the *post exilium* list in *SL*, 173; CCA Lit. Ms D.12, fo 1v.

1238, 27 Dec., suspended by the abp's official because of his failure to appear when cited to the abp's court to answer a charge laid against him and four tenants at Meopham, *Gervase Cant.*, ii, 141–2; this was when the priory was vacant. Peter and two brethren then went to see the abp, *ib.*

1239, 4 Jan., one of the group of monks accused by the abp of contumacy after the forgery scandal, *Gervase Cant.*, ii, 144; see Simon de Hertlepe. On 1 Feb. he was among those summoned by the abp after the monks' el. of Roger de La Lee, q.v., as prior, *ib.*, ii, 153.

Robert de DUFFELDE [Douffolde

occ. [1336] d. 1353

[1336], n.d., one of seven adm., *SL*, 180; CCA Lit. Ms D.12, fo 4.

1337, 19 June, one of five of the above seven who, although they had not yet completed their yr of probation were urging the prior to rec. their prof.; the prior therefore consulted the abp as he was afraid that they would, if denied, return to the world, Reg. L, fo 67v. The abp's reply was no, *ib.*

1348/9, spent time in the infirmary and recd 3s. 6d. as *liberatio* from the anniversarian, CCA DCc Anniv. acct 3.

1349, 4 June, 43rd in order at the el. of an abp, Reg. G, fo 60v.

1349, 8/9 Sept., 42nd at the el. of an abp, *ib.*, fo 76v.

1353, 9 Oct., d., CCA Lit. Ms D.12, fo 16v.

Robert de DUNHAM

occ. 2nd half 13th c.

n.d., name occ. in the list in *SL*, 176; CCA Lit. Ms D.12, fo 2v.

I DUNSTAN [Dunstanus

occ. 1146

1146, [soon after 19 Aug.], with Walter [Durdent], prior, q.v. and others attested an archiepiscopal grant to Christ Church, *Theobald Charters*, 538.

II DUNSTAN

occ. 1239 occ. [1244 × 1258]

n.d., name occ. in the *post exilium* list in *SL*, 173; CCA Lit. Ms D.12, fo 1v.

1244/5, bartoner, CCA DCc AS16.

[1248 × 1249], warden of manors, Reg. B, fo 138.

1239, 4 Jan., one of the group of monks accused of contumacy by the abp after the forgery scandal, *Gervase Cant.*, ii, 144; see Simon de Hertlepe. On 1 Feb. he was among those summoned to appear before the abp after the monks' el. of Roger de La Lee, q.v., as prior, *ib.*, ii, 153.

[1244 × 1258], sent by the prior with letters to Colchester, CCA DCc Cart. Antiq. B.393.

I John DUNSTAN [Dunston, Dunstone

occ. 1451 d. 1458

1451, 21 Oct., one of four prof., *SL*, 189; CCA Lit. Ms D.12, fo 7v.

1452, 8 Apr., ord acol., Canterbury cathedral, Reg. abp Stafford, fo 206v.

1452, 23 Sept., ord subdcn, Canterbury cathedral, Reg. abp Kemp, fo 254.

1453, 31 Mar., ord dcn, Canterbury cathedral, *ib.*, fo 254v.

1458, before 25 Jan., scholar at Canterbury college, *Chron. Stone*, 72, CCA Lit. Ms D.12, fo 25v.

1458, 25 Jan., d. at Canterbury; the subprior, Henry Berham, q.v. took the *commendatio* and burial, *Chron. Stone*, 72. His obit in BL Ms Arundel 68, fo 14 notes that he was in priest's orders.

II John DUNSTAN [Dunston, Dunstone
occ. 1488 occ. 1535

1488, 12 Mar., one of six tonsured, *SL*, 191; CCA Lit. Ms D.12, fo 9.
1488, 30 Sept., made his prof. before the cardinal abp, *ib.*
1490, 9 Apr., ord subdcn, Canterbury cathedral, *Reg. abp Morton*, i, no 438b.
1492, 21 Apr., ord dcn, Canterbury cathedral, *ib.*, i, no 441c.
1493, 6 Apr., ord pr., Canterbury cathedral, *ib.*, i, no 442d.
1493/4, celebrated his first mass and recd a small sum from the sacrist, CCA DCc Sac. acct 63.
1504, Easter, apptd warden of Canterbury college, Pantin, *Cant. Coll. Ox.*, ii, 240.
1506, 9 June, replaced by Robert Holyngbourne, q.v., *ib.*, ii, 138 (Reg. T, fo 52).
1506, 29 June, 6 July; 1511, 25 Dec., warden of manors, CCA DCc MA116, CCA Lit. Ms C.11, fo 54; for 1510/11 Pantin *Cant. Coll. Ox.*, ii, 252 (CCA DCc Cart. Antiq. O.151.43). On 10 Sept. 1511, he was described as granator, Wood-Legh, *Visit.*, 5.
1512, Dec.; 1513, 25 Dec.; 1515, 25 Mar., 25 Dec.; 1517/23, all on 25 Mar.; 1525, 25 Mar., 29 Sept.; 1527/8, both on 25 Mar.; 1529, 25 Dec., 1532/3, both on 25 Mar., subprior, CCA Lit. Ms C.11, fos 55–68.
1535, 25 Nov., subprior, *L and P Henry VIII*, ix, no 880 and see below under 1534.
1495, 8 Feb., one of six scholars at Canterbury college from whom letters of proxy were obtained at the time of the el. of a prior, Pantin, *Cant. Coll. Ox.*, iv, 203.
1498/9, scholar, and 6s. 1d. spent on medicines during his illness, Pantin, *ib.*, ii, 228 (CCA DCc Cart. Antiq. O.151.30).
1500/1, recd travel money for journeys between Oxford and Canterbury, *ib.*, iv, 205.
1501/4, Easter, scholar, who recd an £8 pension, *ib.*, ii, 233, 236, 239 (CCA DCc Cart. Antiq. O.151.33, 35, 37).
1493, 1 May, 55th in order at the ratification of an agreement, Reg. S, fo 383v; but see John Crosse I.
1501, 26 Apr., absent [at Oxford] from the el. of an abp, Reg. R, fo 56v.
1511, 2 Sept., 23rd in order on the visitation certificate, Wood-Legh, *Visit.*, 3 (Reg. abp Warham, i, fo 35). On 10 Sept., he was one of six obedientiaries who, with the prior, were apptd to oversee corrections after the abp's visitations, Wood-Legh, *Visit.*, 5.
1534, 2 Dec., acknowledged the Act of Supremacy, *DK 7th Report*, Appndx 2, 282; his signature follows that of the prior.
1535, 25 Nov., supported the prior, Thomas Goldwell II, q.v., when accusations were made vs him by some of the monks, *L and P Henry VIII*, ix, no 879; on this same day he himself wrote to thank Cromwell for a dispensation concerning his oversight of St James' hospital and another to permit him to take meals in his chamber, *ib.*, ix, no 880.

A list of four books which he had had at Canterbury college in 1500/1 is in Pantin, *Cant. Coll. Ox.*, i, 83 (CCA DCc Cart. Antiq. Z.142).

Walter DURDENT [Duredent
occ. c. 1143 × 1149

c. 1143 × 1149, prior: apptd by the abp after deposing Jeremias, q.v., c. 1143, but first occ. 1 Sept. 1145 (see below); el. bp of Coventry/Lichfield, Oct. 1149, *Fasti*, ii, 9 (*Gervase Cant.*, i, 141).
1142/3, his apptment as prior is in *Gervase Cant.*, i, 30, 44, who said that when Jeremias q.v. was [briefly] restored to office by the papal legate in 1143, he had gone to stay at Dover priory, *ib.*, i, 127.
1145, 1 Sept., witnessed the abp's confirmation of bp Gundulf's (spurious) charter to Rochester cathedral priory, *Theobald Charters*, no 222. The confirmation is also prob. spurious.
1149, el. bp of Coventry/Lichfield; consecrated 2 Oct., *HBC*, 253.

Several volumes in the Eastry catalogue, mainly biblical texts, are listed under his name, James, *Ancient Libraries*, 45, 97 (nos 250, 251, 997–999), and a volume of Priscian in the 12th c. catalogue, *ib.*, 7 (no 9).

DUVRA
see John de Dover I

Richard DYGON [Digon, Digoun, Digun
occ. [1207 × 1214] occ. 1238

[1207 × 1214], name occ. in the list of those who were in exile, *SL*, 172, CCA Lit. Ms D.12, fo 1.
[1222 × 1237], one of the monks named by M. Laurence de St Nicholas to arrange for his obit celebrations, *Acta Guala*, no 155.
1238, accompanied the subprior and William de Dover I, q.v., to Rome in the aftermath of the forgery of the charter of St Thomas, *Gervase Cant.*, ii, 133; see Simon de Hertlepe.
[?1239/40], 4 Jan., d. at Rome, BL Ms Arundel 68, fo 12, where it lists him as a pr., and notes that he was the first monk to die on this day.

EADMER [Edmerus
occ. [1096] [?d. 1128]

[1073, after], taught by Ernulf I, q.v., when the latter was schoolmaster in the cloister, Gibson, *Lanfranc*, 177.

[?1121], precentor, prob. on his return from St Andrews, see below.

[1096 × 1120], *familiaris* in the households of abps Anselm and Ralph and as such witnessed several archiepiscopal acta:

(1) 1096 × 1107, *Text Roff.*, ii, fo 179 and cap 93 (Rochester refs).

(2) 1115 × 1122, *ib.*, fo 179ᵛ, ii, and cap 94.

Note: these two deeds are 'slightly suspicious' (the judgement and phrase are Dr Brett's).

He also witnessed:

(3) 1126 × 1135, *Text Roff.*, ii, fos 179ᵛ–180 and cap 95; this is supposedly a charter of abp William but is spurious.

(4) 1131, *Reg. Roff.*, 346, 349; this, too, is spurious.

Note: these four will appear in *Eng. Epis. Acta*, Canterbury, 1070–1161, as nos. 24, 51, 86, 88.

1097, went into exile with abp Anselm; see his *Vita Anselmi*, 386–389; see also *Anselm Letters*, no 208, and *ib.*, no 311, in which Anselm commended him and Alexander I, q.v, to prior Ernulf, q.v.

1114/20, was the main adviser to abp Ralph d'Escures, q.v.; from 1116 to 1119 they were abroad in Normandy, Southern, *St Anselm* (1990), 417.

1118, returned to England and Canterbury; see his *Hist. Nov.*, 249.

1120, was offered the bpric of St Andrews, *ib.*, 279–281; he soon relinquished this office before being consecrated, and returned to Canterbury, *ib.*, 283–286; see Southern, *St Anselm* (1990), 417–418.

[?1128], d., or possibly a few yrs later, see Southern, *St Anselm* (1990), 421; his obit on 13 Jan. names him as precentor, BL Ms Arundel 68, fo 13.

In the Eastry catalogue one volume is entitled Sermo Edmeri cantoris and contains a number of his own writings including the lives of Anselm and Dunstan, James, *Ancient Libraries*, 46 (no 257). See Cambridge, Corpus Christi College Ms 371.

His two main works, the *Vita Anselmi* and the *Historia Novorum* (of which some details of the printed editions are given in the Canterbury references) were written between 1093 and 1125. However, he also wrote the lives of other saints including Dunstan, Wilfrid and Oswald (of Worcester). See Sharpe, *Latin Writers* for a list of all his known writings and the printed editions. As constant companion of Anselm and keeper of his chapel he had access to numerous documents from which he freely copied extracts. His love for his own community and devotion to abp Anselm as well as his writing technique and influence on the Christ Church scriptorium and his merits as an historian of contemporary events and people are evaluated at length in Gransden, *Hist. Writing*, i, 129–141. See also R. Southern's two volumes, *St Anselm* (1963), passim, and *St Anselm* (1990), 404–436.

A letter survives which he wrote to advise the Worcester monks to el. one of their brethren as bp (printed in *Anglia Sacra*, ii, 238). See also Nicholas II (in the Worcester section) who wrote to him c. 1120. Aegelredus, q.v., was one of his informants for his life of Dunstan.

He was described by Anselm as 'carissimus filius meus et baculus senectutis meae', *Anselm Letters*, no 209.

EADMUND

see Edmund

EADWINE [Eadwinus, Eadwyne, Edwin

occ. mid 12th c.

n.d., monastic scribe responsible for the production of the tripartite psalter of St Jerome, now Cambridge, Trinity College Ms R. 17.1. This has recently been the subject of a detailed examination by a team of experts under the editorship of Margaret Gibson, T.A. Heslop and Richard Pfaff; *The Eadwine Psalter : text, image and monastic culture in twelfth-century Canterbury* (Modern Humanities Research Association, 1993).

Three of his books are listed in the Eastry catalogue, nos 319, 322, 323 (the tripartite psalter, as above), James, *Ancient Libraries*, 51.

EALDING

see Audinges

Anselm de EASTRY [Eastria, Ascelinus de Estria

occ. 1270 occ. 1283

n.d., name occ. in the list in *SL*, 176; CCA Lit. Ms D.12, fo 2ᵛ.

1275, 21 Dec., before this date, subprior, CCA Lit. Ms D.12, fo 2ᵛ.

1270, arrived at Dover priory with a mandate threatening excommunication unless the Dover monks submitted to the official, *sed. vac.*, *Gervase Cant.*, ii, 256, see Richard de Wynchepe.

1275, 21 Dec., apptd prior of Dover by abp Kilwardby, CCA Lit. Ms D.12, fo 2ᵛ; he was removed by abp Pecham 24 Sept. 1283, and presumably returned to Canterbury.

Note: see *Gervase Cant.*, ii, 282.

In the inventory of missing service books dated 1 Mar. 1338, his missale is reported to have last been seen when it was passed on to John de Chartham II q.v., *Lit. Cant.*, no 618 (Reg. L, fo 104).

Two silver *ciphi* and one *de murra*, formerly his, occ. in an inventory of the refectory dated 1328, Dart, *Antiq. Cant.*, xix, xxi (BL Ms Cotton Galba E.iv, fos 178ᵛ, 180ᵛ).

Note:

(1) Haines says that he was brother of Henry de Eastry, *Dover Priory*, 235, n.

(2) a clerk of abp Pecham by the same name should not be confused with this monk.

Bartholomew EASTRY [Estrey, Estry
occ. 1403 occ. 1414

1403, 22 Dec., one of six prof., *SL*, 185; CCA Lit. Ms D.12, fo 5v.
1404, 29 Mar., ord acol., Canterbury cathedral, Reg. abp Arundel, i, fo 332v.
1405, 18 Apr., ord subdcn, Canterbury cathedral, *ib.*, i, fo 333v.
1414, 12 Mar., 60th in order at the el. of an abp, *Reg. abp Chichele*, i, 4.
n.d., migrated to Totnes priory, Devon, 'sperans se in priorem ejusdem ecclesie fore promovendum, sed deceptus erat', CCA Lit. Ms D.12, fo 5v.

Bertram de EASTRY [Eastria, Bertrannus de Estria
occ. 1289 d. 1323

1289, 19 Dec., one of nine prof., *SL*, 177; CCA Lit. Ms D.12, fo 3.
1314/16, 1315/23, 1317/19, 1320/2, chamberlain, CCA DCc MA2, fo 52, Chamb. accts 7, 9, MA2, fos 61v–129, Chamb. accts 14–17.
[1293 × 1313], chaplain to abp Winchelsey for six yrs, and one of those who testified at the inquiry into the abp's sanctity, Wilkins' *Concilia*, ii, 489, CUL Ms Ee.5.31, fo 204.
1323, 22 Aug., d., CCA Lit. Ms D.12, fo 16; his obit is in BL Ms Arundel 68, fo 38v.

An inventory of vestments, acquired *temp.* prior Eastry, contains a set described as his [?gift], Legg and Hope, *Inventories*, 66 (BL Ms Cotton Galba E.iv, fo 117).

Christopher EASTRY [Estrey, Estry
occ. 1497 d. 1507

1497, 28 July, one of nine tonsured, *SL*, 192; CCA Lit. Ms D.12, fo 9v.
1498, 14 Apr., ord acol., Canterbury cathedral, *Reg. abp Morton*, i, no 447a.
1498, 19 Apr., prof., *SL*, 192; CCA Lit. Ms D.12, fo 9v.
1502/7, student at Canterbury college, Pantin, *Cant. Coll. Ox.*, ii, 236 (for half the yr), 239, 241, 245, 248 (CCA DCc Cart. Antiq. O.151.37, 38, 39, 41).
1501, 26 Apr., dcn and 58th in order at the el. of an abp, Reg. R, fo 56v.
1507, 17 Aug., d. at Oxford *ex vehementi pestilencia* and was buried at St Frideswide's in the Lady chapel. On the following Sun. the monks at Christ Church celebrated his exequies; the prior said the requiem mass and all was done for him as for monks who d. at Oxford or in other places outside the monastery, CCA Lit. Ms D.12, fo 36.

Henry de EASTRY [Estria
occ. [?before 1255] d. 1331

1285–1331, prior: el. 8 Apr. 1285; d. 8 Apr. 1331, *Fasti*, ii, 12.
n.d., name occ. in the list in *SL*, 176, CCA Lit. Ms D.12, fo 2v.
1275, 1276, 1282, 1284, treasurer, CCA DCc MA1, fos 120v, 122v, 136, 141v, also Treas. acct 1 (1282/3) where he was one of three; see John de Begbroke, John de Well I.
[1280/82], played an official role in the unsuccessful el. of adcn Richard de la More as bp of Winchester, BL Ms Arundel 68, fos 54v–55, and *Fasti*, ii, 87.
1285/6, as prior, visited Meopham, CCA DCc Meopham acct 8.
1292, 14 Dec., apptd Richard de Clyve, q.v. as his commissary in spiritual causes *sed. vac.*, CUL Ms Ee.5.31, fo 35.
1293, 24 Feb., present at Leighton Buzzard [Lecton], at Robert Winchelsey's consent to his el. as abp, *Reg. abp Winchelsey*, 1273–1274.
1297, 1 Mar., 26 Mar., 1 Apr., letters were sent from the subprior and convent to the prior [in London], advising him to support the abp in his trials with the king and seeking his advice on certain matters, CUL Ms Ee.5.31, fos 71–72.
1300, 22 Jan., rebuked by the abp for his alleged attempt to influence some monks to oppose any reconciliation between the former prior, Thomas Ryngmer, q.v., and the chapter, *Reg. abp Winchelsey*, 372–373, 378.
1300, 17 Mar., present at Lambeth when the abp confirmed the el. of John Dalderby as bp of Lincoln, *Reg. abp Winchelsey*, 702.
1300, c. 12 July/19 Oct., was abroad [*transmarinis*], and the subprior acted in his stead, CUL Ms Ee.5.31, fos 82v, 83.
1304, 6 Sept., sent a messenger with letters and money to the monk students in Paris, *ib.*, fo 101v; see Andrew de Hardres and Stephen de Feversham; another letter and more money were sent with Geoffrey de Poterel, q.v. in Apr. 1305, *ib.*, fo 102v.
1307, 5 Mar., obtained a letter from the Count Palatine authorizing him to appt three public notaries, Reg. I, fo 265.
1308, 28 Jan., comm. by the abp as his vicar general, *Reg. abp Winchelsey*, 1331, and also Reg. I, fo 282 where some of his acta follow on fos 293, 298v.
1312, one of the cathedral priors summoned to London to meet the papal nuncios, *Councils and Synods*, 1377.
1313, 29 May, had been named as one of abp Winchelsey's executors but refused to act, *Reg. abp Winchelsey*, 1342, xxxii.
1318/19, the fact that the subprior appears to have been acting in the place of the prior suggests that the latter was absent during part of

this yr, as Pantin remarks in *Cant. Coll. Ox.*, iv, 176, n. 1 (Lambeth Ms 242, fo 331).

1318, 8 Oct., apptd a proctor to go to the York parliament in his place, because he was not well, CUL Ms Ee.5.31, fo 196^{v}.

1319, 13 Nov., was apptd vicar general by the abp, Reg. I, fo 366; however, on 28 Nov. the subprior and chapter wrote to the abp on his behalf asking that he be relieved of the apptment, CUL Ms Ee.5.31, fo 211.

1325, 8 Feb., 31 July, 15 Aug., wrote letters to the abp offering advice about ecclesiastical affairs and the political crisis, *Lit. Cant.*, nos 146, 153, 154 (Reg. L, fos 140^{v}, 141, 141^{v}). More letters follow, e.g.

[1325], in reply to a visitation mandate he referred to and protested vs the complaints sent to the abp vs him and asked for the names of the culprits, *Lit. Cant.*, no 158 (Reg. L, fo 102^{v}).

[?1326], 14 Mar., the king had threatened action on learning of dissension in the priory and the abp mollified him by promising to make a visitation, all of which the latter revealed to the prior in a letter, *Lit. Cant.*, no 174 (CCA DCc Cart. Antiq. C.1294l); and see Robert de Aldon and Robert de Thaneto.

[1327], 3 Jan., excused himself to the abp from his personal attendance at the parliament at which the king was deposed, *Lit. Cant.*, no 199 (Reg. L, fo 147^{v}).

[1327], 2 Aug., absent from the monastery while carrying out a visitation of some of the priory manors in Kent and ?Surrey, *Lit. Cant.*, no 224 (Reg. L, fo 153).

1328, 16 Dec., wrote the first of what was to be a series of letters to the new abp, Simon Meopham, giving advice as he entered upon his high office, *Lit. Cant.*, no 260 (Reg. L, fo 164^{v}). Some of these were reprimanding in tone (e.g. *Lit. Cant.* no 275, Reg. L, fo 167^{v}) and others verged on the dictatorial (e.g. *ib.*, nos 290, 292, Reg. L, fo 171–171^{v}).

1331, 8 Apr., d. in the 92nd yr of his age, BL Ms Arundel 68, fo 23^{v}. According to the writer, incorrectly named as Stephen Byrchyngton, q.v., he had entered the monastery at an early age and from his studies in the claustral school had become 'fluent in Scriptures' (*Anglia Sacra*, i, 141; see also BL Ms Arundel 68, fo 23^{v}). He was buried between the images of saints Sytha and Appolonia, Cambridge, Corpus Christi College Ms 298, fo 118^{v}; and see Hope, 'Inventories of Priors', 259, where it is suggested that this was in the north choir aisle where his recumbent effigy had previously been identified as that of abp Reynolds. His tomb cost over £20, *ib.*, (from the treasurers' accts 1330/1).

An inventory of 80 of his books, mainly theology and civil and canon law, is printed in James, *Ancient Libraries* (nos 1–80) 143–145 (from CCA DCc Ms E.27).

The inventory of his 'goods' including his books has been printed by Hope in 'Inventories of Priors', 262–275 (from CCA Lit. Ms E.27).

A collection of letters addressed to him concerning the el. of abp Winchelsey 1293/4 has been printed in *Reg. abp Winchelsey*, 1278–1287; several are endorsed in his own hand, e.g. CCA DCc Cart. Antiq., S.380.

Many of the *acta* and achievements of prior Eastry remain to this day visible and tangible. While the biographical details do not readily emerge from the vast bulk of records and correspondence, his concerns, his programme of reforms within the priory and his influence outside are clearly indicated. His career has been summarized by T.F. Tout in *DNB* to which M. Mate has added in *DNB: Missing Persons*, supplement (Oxford, 1993). R.L. Smith, in *Canterbury Cathedral Priory* has dealt at length with his financial policy and administration and N.L. Ramsay with the archives and library during his priorate; see below.

His orderly mind and organizational skills led him to institute careful record keeping of all documents issued and recd, and to overhaul the muniments in order to compile cartularies containing copies of the deeds concerning all the convent properties and possessions (Regs E, I, J). Some registers compiled under his direction contained his outgoing correspondence (Reg. L), *acta* (Reg. K, CUL Ms Ee.5.31), and *acta* during vacancies of the see when the prior had spiritual jurisdiction (Reg. Q). Matters pertaining to rural and domestic economy were copied into another (Reg. O). Finally, there is the register known as 'Memoriale multorum Henrici prioris (BL Ms Cotton Galba E.iv., which has been ed. by T.L. Hogan as 'The Memorandum Book of Henry of Eastry, Prior of Christ Church, Canterbury', 2 vols, unpublished Ph.D thesis, London university, 1966). In addition to the catalogue of the monastic library for which Eastry was responsible, the Cotton ms contains inventories of vestments and ornaments acquired during his priorate and a record of the building works he completed. The chapter by N.L. Ramsay on Eastry's priorate in Collinson, *Canterbury Cathedral*, 353–362 provides a detailed discussion of his reorganisation of the archives and library, and in the same vol., R. B. Dobson a general appraisal of his priorate, 84–99 *passim*.

During his lengthy and autocratic rule it is not surprising to find evidence of occasional unrest among a minority of unruly monks like Robert de Aldon and Robert de Thaneto, q.v.

The Eastry Correspondence in the cathedral archives is a large and miscellaneous collection of letters mainly to, but also a few from, him; they have recently been listed and calendared.

Hugh de EASTRY [Estria
occ. [1207 × 1214]

[1207 × 1214], name occ. in the list of monks who were in exile, *SL*, 172; CCA Lit. Ms D.12, fo 1.

I John de EASTRY [Eastria
occ. 1268/9 d. 1292

n.d., name occ. in the list in *SL*, 175; CCA Lit. Ms D.12, fo 2.

1268/9, 1269/75, bartoner, CCA DCc AS10, MA1, fos 112–121^v.
1275/6, chamberlain, CCA DCc MA1, fos 121^v–123^v.
1277/80, warden of manors, CCA DCc Great Chart accts 3, 4, Ickham acct 3.
1283/5, chamberlain, CCA DCc MA1, fos 139^v–144^v.
1285/7, bartoner, CCA DCc MA1, fos 144^v–150^v, Treas accts 1, 2.
1288, granator, CCA DCc, Gran. acct 13.

1276, 31 Aug., with Lambert de Clyve, q.v., involved in an agreement settling a dispute with St Augustine's abbey, CUL Ms Ee.5.31, fo 26^v.
1292, 9 July, d., CCA Lit. Ms D.12, fo 15.

Four of his books are found in the Eastry catalogue, James, *Ancient Libraries*, 77 (nos 707–710).

A wooden *ciphus* of his is listed in an inventory of the refectory dated 1328, Dart, *Antiq. Cant.*, xxii (BL Ms Cotton Galba E.iv, fo 179^v).

II John EASTRY [Eastri, Estri, Estry
occ. 1367 occ. 1381

1367, 11 Nov., one of nine prof., *SL*, 182; CCA Lit. Ms D.12, fo 4^v.
1368, 4 Mar., ord acol., Canterbury cathedral, *Reg. abp Langham*, 387.
1369, 22 Dec., ord subdcn, abp's chapel, Charing, Reg. abp Wittlesey, fo 165^v.
1370, 21 Sept., ord dcn, Saltwood, *ib.*, fo 166^v.
1371, 20 Dec., ord pr., abp's chapel, Otford, *ib.*, fo 168.

1370, prob. one of the chancellors/keepers of the archives, *Hist. Mss Comm. 5th Report*, Appndx, 435 (CCA DCc Cart. Antiq. C.232); see John de Gloucestre I.
1374, *custos martyrii*, CCA DCc MA2, fo 281^v.
1382, Sept., apptd precentor, Reg. abp Courtenay, i, fo 22; he was removed the following yr on 20 Aug., *ib.*, i, fo 43^v.

1375/6, scholar at Canterbury college, CCA DCc MA2, fo 298; the treasurer also pd out 5s. 'pro libris domini I. Estry querendis Oxonie', Pantin, *Cant. Coll. Ox.*, iv, 186.

1374, 30 June, 49th in order at the el. of an abp, Reg. G, fos 173^v–175^v.
1380, recd a small sum from the prior, Lambeth Ms 243, fo 180.
1381, 31 July, 37th at the el. of an abp, Reg. G, fo 225^v.
n.d., 7 July, obit in BL Ms Arundel 68, fo 33.

Nicholas de EASTRY [Eastria
occ. [late 1260s] d. [c. 1286/7]

[late 1260s], one of a group of five prof., *SL*, 176; CCA Lit. Ms D.12, fo 3.
[c. 1286/7], 21 Sept., d., CCA Lit. Ms D.12, fo 15.

Osward de EASTRY [Eastria, Oswald, *alias* Heye
occ. 1267 d. 1292

n.d., name occ. in the list in *SL*, 175; CCA Lit. Ms D.12, fo 2^v.

1267/70, each yr on 29 Sept., 1271, treasurer, CCA DCc MA1, fos 110, 111, 112, 113, 114^v (as Heye).

1275, apptd abbot of Faversham by abp Kilwardby, CCA Lit. Ms D.12, fo 2^v, and *Gervase Cant.*, ii, 282.
1292, d., *Gervase Cant.*, ii, 300, his obit occ. on 10 May in BL Ms Arundel 68, fo 27 (as Heye).

R. de EASTRY [Eastreia, Eastria
occ. 1189

1189, 12 Oct., after, with Ralph de Orpynton I, q.v., sent to the king to offer gifts and gain his support in the monks' dispute with the abp; and again on 5/8 Nov. he was sent to the king in London with other brethren, *Epist. Cant.*, 313, 315; see Aaron.

Richard de EASTRY [Eastria
occ. 1st half 13th c.

n.d., name occ. in the list in *SL*, 173; CCA Lit. Ms D.12, fo 1.

Robert EASTRY B.Th. [Eastre, Estre
occ. 1473 d. 1496

1473, 13 Mar., ord acol., Canterbury cathedral, *Reg. abp Bourgchier*, 410.
1473, 28 Apr., one of five prof., *SL*, 190; CCA Lit. Ms D.12, fo 8^v.
1474, 26 Mar., ord subdcn, Canterbury cathedral, *Reg. abp Bourgchier*, 416.
1477, 20 Dec., ord dcn, Winchester cathedral, per *lit. dim.*, Reg. Waynflete (Winchester), ii, fo 179.
1481, 22 Sept., ord pr., Sevenoaks, *Reg. abp Bourgchier*, 433.

1490, apptd one of the chancellors, Reg. S, fo 363^v.
1492, May; 1493, Apr., 1492/3, warden of manors, CCA DCc MA8, fos 41^v, 574, Pantin, *Cant. Coll. Ox.*, iv, 201.
1493, 1 May; 1494, 6 July, 30 Nov., treasurer, Reg. S, fo 383^v, Pantin, *Cant. Coll. Ox.*, iv, 202, 203.

1495, before 5 Apr., apptd warden of Canterbury college, Pantin, *Cant. Coll. Ox.*, iv, 203; he d. in office.

1475/6, adm. to Canterbury college and recd an £8 stipend, Pantin, *Cant. Coll. Ox.*, ii, 195 (CCA DCc Cart. Antiq. O.151.21).

1478, 20 Sept., recd travel expenses from Oxford to Canterbury, Pantin, *Cant. Coll. Ox.*, iv, 200.

1478/9, 1480/2, 1486/8, 1489/90, at Canterbury college and receiving £8 stipend, Pantin, *Cant. Coll. Ox.*, ii, 204, 207, 211, 216, 218, 221 (CCA DCc Cart. Antiq. O.151.22b, 23, 24, 24a, 26, 27). His travelling expenses and those of Thomas Goldston IV, q.v., in Mar. 1483 from Oxford to Canterbury via London are in Pantin, *Cant. Coll. Ox.*, iii, 127–128 (CCA DCc DE96).

n.d., B.Th., CCA Lit. Ms D.12, fo 27v.

[1486, Apr.], student, licensed to preach in Canterbury diocese, Reg. R, fo 8v, Reg. N, fo 172. Between Apr. and Oct., the prior apptd him as one of several confessors, *sed. vac.*, Reg. N, fo 172.

1490, 30 Aug., together with Thomas Goldston IV, q.v., apptd general proctors, Reg. S, fos 361v–362.

1493, 1 May, 8th in order at the ratification of an agreement, Reg. S, fo 383v; but see John Crosse I.

1496, 16 Mar., d. at Oxford, and was buried in the Lady chapel at St Frideswide's priory, CCA Lit. Ms D.12, fo 27v; and see *BRUO* for additional refs.

Name occ. in CCA Lit. Ms B.1 Duns Scotus (later 13th c.) in a memorandum, see *MLGB*, supplement, 81.

There is an inventory of his books and belongings at Oxford made after his d., in Pantin, *Cant. Coll. Ox.*, i, 82–83, 107 (CCA DCc Inventory box no 27).

I Roger de EASTRY [Eastria

occ. [1241]

[1241], name occ. in the list in *SL*, 174; CCA Lit. Ms D.12, fo 2; he was prob. one of the twelve prof. with Richard de Wynchepe, q.v.

II Roger EASTRY [Estry, Estray

occ. 1507 occ. 1524

1507, 12 Oct., one of six tonsured, *SL*, 193; CCA Lit. Ms D.12, fo 10v.

1508, 19 Apr., made his prof. before abp Warham, *SL*, 194, CCA Lit. Ms D.12, *ib.*

1508, 22 Apr., ord acol., Canterbury cathedral, Reg. abp Warham, ii, fo 263v.

1509, 7 Apr., ord subdcn, Canterbury cathedral, *ib.*, ii, fo 264.

1509, 22 Dec., ord dcn, Canterbury cathedral, *ib.*, ii, fo 264v.

1513, 26 Mar., ord pr., Canterbury cathedral, *ib.*, ii, fo 266v.

n.d., as a novice was instructed by John Garard, q.v., *et perfecit*, Pantin, *Cant. Coll. Ox.*, iv, 54 (CCA DCc Ms Scrap Book B.186).

1511, 2 Sept., 68th in order on the visitation certificate, Wood-Legh, *Visit.*, 3 (Reg. abp Warham, i, fo 35v).

1524, 23 Sept., officiated at the exequies of John Alyngton q.v., *SL*, 195 (Cambridge, Corpus Christi College, Ms 298).

Thomas EASTRY [Eastri, Estri, Estry

occ. 1384 d. 1440

1384, 29 Aug., one of seven prof., *SL*, 183, CCA Lit. Ms D.12, fo 5.

1386, 21 Apr., ord subdcn, Canterbury cathedral, Reg. abp Courtenay, i, fo 308v.

1387, 6 Apr., ord dcn, Canterbury cathedral, *ib.*, i, fo 309v.

1389, 12 June, ord pr., St Dunstan's church, London, *ib.*, i, fo 311v.

1415/18, 1421/6, 1429/30, granator, CCA DCc Eastry accts 136, 139, 140, 146, Gran. accts 38–41, 43.

1385/6, recd 12d. *pro benedictione* from the prior, Lambeth Ms 243, fo 200v.

1390/1, recd 12d. from the prior, *ib.*, fo 220v.

1396, 7 Aug., 50th in order at the el. of an abp, Reg. G, fos 234v–235.

1414, 12 Mar., 17th at the el. of an abp, *Reg. abp Chichele*, i, 4.

1440, 10 Nov., d., after 51 yrs of monastic life, *Chron. Stone*, 28; his obit is in BL Ms Arundel 68, fo 47v.

Walter de EASTRY [Eastria, Estria

occ. 1314 d. 1351

1314, 13 Dec., one of five prof., *SL*, 179, CCA Lit. Ms D.12, fo 3v.

1315, 20 Dec., ord subdcn, Maidstone, Reg. abp Reynolds, fo 173v.

1328, chaplain to the prior, Lambeth Ms 243, fo 9v.

1330/1, *custos* of the high altar, CCA DCc MA2, fos 192–201v.

1332, *custos martyrii*, CCA DCc MA2, fo 211v.

1317, 5 Nov., one of three monks who, with the prior, examined all their brethren as required by the abp in connection with an inquiry over the circulation of letters containing false and harmful statements, CUL Ms Ee.5.31, fo 181v. See Clement II and Nicholas de Ivynghoe.

[1327], 27 May, witnessed the rec. of a letter from the abp, *Lit. Cant.*, no 215 (CCA DCc Cart. Antiq. C.1294b) (as William).

1349, 4 June, 12th in order at the el. of an abp, Reg. G, fo 60v.

1349, 8/9 Sept., 12th at the el. of an abp, *ib.*, fo 76.

1348/9, ill in the infirmary, CCA DCc Anniv. acct 3.

1351, 5 June, d., CCA Lit. Ms D.12, fo 16v.

William ECH
see Ethe

John ECHYNGHAM
occ. 1438 d. 1439

1438, 9 Jan., one of four prof., *SL*, 188, CCA Lit. Ms D.12, fo 7^{v}.

1439, 18 Jan., d., CCA Lit. Ms D.12, fo 24; his obit is in BL Ms Arundel, 68, fo 13^{v}. *Chron. Stone*, 22, has 17 Jan.

EDECRONE
see Hedecron

EDGAR [Edgarus
n.d.

n.d., 14 Apr., obit occ. in BL Ms Arundel 68, fo 24.

EDMERUS
see Eadmer, Elmer

I EDMUND
occ. [1108 × 1125]

[1108 × 1125], *temp.* prior Conrad, sacrist, *Anglia Sacra*, i, 137; he succ. Adewinus, q.v., and both were described as *strenuissimi secretarii*, *ib.*

Acc. to Dart he wrote about the quarrel between the king and abp Anselm, *Antiq. Cant.*, 179.

II M. EDMUND [Eadmundus
occ. 1187/8

1187, was with the prior Honorius, Hamo II and Humphrey I, q.v., in Rome where they persuaded the pope to write to the abp to urge him not to bear malice vs them, *Epist. Cant.* 43.
1188, Jan./Mar., one of the monks at the curia conducting the chapter's appeal vs abp Baldwin and wrote letters to the brethren in Canterbury with news of their progress in the case, *ib.*, 178–180, 191–192; and see Humphrey I.
1188, after 18 July, prior Honorius, q.v., also in Rome, wrote to report to the monks at home that Edmund and four other monks had d., *ib.*, 254. It is prob. his obit that occ. on 11 July in BL Ms Arundel 68, fo 34.

III EDMUND [Eadhmunde
occ. 1206

1206, 30 Mar., one of the monks summoned by the pope to Rome to give evidence in the dispute over their el. of Reginald, q.v., as abp. *CPL*, i (1198–1304), 26; while there, they el. Stephen Langton, *Fasti*, ii, 6.

EDWARD
occ. [1070 × 1089] d. before 1096

[1070 × 1089] former adcn of London, became a monk *temp.* abp Lanfranc, had regrets and wished to return to the world; but he was prevented by Dunstan, confessed to prior Henry, q.v., and d., *Dunstan Memorials*, 155–156, 241–244 (as Osbern, q.v., and Eadmer, q.v. relate).

EDWIN
see Eadwine

EDWIUS [Edwy
occ. [?c. 1089]

[?c. 1089], one of three monks who had talked in the presence of the boy Eadmer, q.v., about their recollections of past events in the priory, Eadmer, *Hist. Nov.*, 107. See Blachmannus, Farman.

EFFYNGTON
see Offynton

EGELRIDUS
see Agelredus

EGELSINUS
n.d.

n.d., *conversus*, whose obit occ. on 9 Jan. in BL Ms Cotton Nero C.ix, fo 3^{v}.

EGELWIN
see Aegelwinus

EGIDIUS [Giles
occ. 2nd half 13th c.

n.d., name occ. in the list in *SL*, 174, CCA Lit. Ms D.12, fo 2.

EGTHORN
see Eythorne

William EGYRTON [Egerton
occ. 1457 d. 1472

1457, 13 Dec., one of six prof. adm. as monks, *SL*, 189, *Chron. Stone*, 71, CCA Lit. Ms D.12, fo 8.
1459, 24 Mar., ord dcn, Canterbury cathedral, *Reg. abp Bourgchier*, 371.
1463, 9 Apr., ord pr., Canterbury cathedral, *ib.*, 386.
1462/3, celebrated his first mass and recd a gift of 8d. from the sacrist, Woodruff, 'Sacrist's Rolls', 61–62 (CCA DCc Sac. acct 43).

n.d., prob. at the time of his d., anniversarian, CCA Lit. Ms D.12, fo 26.

1466, 17 Feb., 58th in order in an inventory listing *jocalia fratrum* [given by him and/or assigned for his use], Reg. N., fo 234.
1471/2, d., CCA DCc Treas. acct, 22; his obit is on 23 July in BL Ms Arundel 68, fo 31^{v}.

ELAM
see Elham

Robert ELBRIGHTON [Ailbrighton, Ailbrigthton, Aldrethone, Elbryzton
occ. 1376 occ. 1381

1376, 14 or 15 Nov., one of seven who were clothed in the monastic habit, CCA Lit. Ms D.12, fo 4v, *SL*, 183.
1376, 20 Dec., ord acol., Canterbury cathedral, Reg. abp Sudbury, fo 140v.
1377, 19 Sept., ord subdcn, Lambeth palace chapel, *ib.*, fo 142.
1378, 17 Apr., ord dcn, Canterbury cathedral, *ib.*, fo 145v.
1380, recd a small sum from the prior, Lambeth Ms 243, fo 180v.
1381, 31 July, 53rd in order at the el. of an abp, Reg. G, fo 225v.

Gregory de ELDYNG
occ. 1st half 13th c.

n.d., name occ. in the list in *SL*, 173, CCA Lit. Ms D.12, fo 1v.

Note: this is Gregory de Audinges, q.v.

ELFE, Elfy
see Elphe

ELFNODUS
n.d.

n.d., *conversus*, whose obit occ. on 27 Jan., and who gave Orpington on his adm. as a monk, acc. to BL Ms Cotton Nero C.ix, fo 4v.

Note: there is also an Elfnothus, *levita* whose obit occ. on 10 Nov., *ib.*, fo 15v.

ELGARUS
see Aelgar

I John ELHAM [Elam
occ. [1369] d. 1397

[1369], one of four prof., *SL*, 182, CCA Lit. Ms D.12, fo 4v.
1370, 15 Sept., ord acol., abp's chapel, Saltwood, Reg. abp Wittlesey, fo 166.
1370, 21 Sept., ord subdcn, Saltwood, *ib.*, fo 166v.
1371, 20 Dec., ord dcn, abp's chapel, Otford, *ib.*, fo 168.
1372, 21 Feb., ord pr., abp's chapel, Croydon, *ib.*, fo 168v.

n.d., *magister mense*, CCA Lit. Ms D.12, fo 4v.
n.d., at time of d., *diu quondam magister infirmarie*, *ib.*, fo 17v.

1374, 30 June, 53rd in order at the el. of an abp, Reg. G, fos 173v–175v.
1381, 31 July, 39th at the el. of an abp, *ib.*, fo 225v.
1383/4, 1385/6, 1388/91, recd small sums from the prior in each of these yrs, usually *pro benedictione*, Lambeth Ms 243, fos 192v, 200v ,212v, 216v, 220v.
1396, 7 Aug., 20th at the el. of an abp, Reg. G, fo 234v.
1397, 25 Oct., d., CCA Lit. Ms D.12, fo 17v.

II John ELHAM [Elam
occ. [1399] d. 1449

1446–1449, prior: el. 13 Apr., 1446, *Chron. Stone*, 39, Reg. abp Stafford, fo 22; d. 19 Feb. 1449, Lambeth Ms 20, fo 165v, but see below.

[1399], one of four prof., *SL*, CCA Lit. Ms D.12, fo 5v.
1399, 20 Dec., ord subdcn, Canterbury cathedral, Reg. abp Arundel, i, fo 325.
1404, 29 Mar., ord pr., Canterbury cathedral, *ib.*, i, fo 332v.

1420/1, 1422/3, 1429/31, anniversarian, CCA DCc Anniv. acct 8, Prior acct 5, Lambeth ED37A, 38.
1424, 13/14 Nov., *magister ordinis*; succ. by John Asshe, q.v., during the yr., *SL*, 187, CCA Lit. Ms D.12, fo 7.
1429/31, *custos anniversariorum* with Thomas Chart I, q.v., Lambeth ED37A, 38.
1430, Dec./1431, Sept., cellarer, Lambeth ED58.
1435, 1436/7, chamberlain, 'Chron. Wm Glastynbury', 129, CCA DCc Prior acct 7.
1441/2, 1443, 12 Apr., 22 Apr., 1443/5, subprior, CCA DCc Sac. acct 29, CCA Lit. Ms D.12, fo 24v, *Chron. Stone*, 31, CCA DCc Sac. accts 31, 32.

1414, 12 Mar., 44th in order at the el. of an abp, *Reg. abp Chichele*, i, 4.
1430, 28 Nov., apptd by the prior and convent as one of several proctors in an appeal in the Court of Arches, Reg. S, fo 106v.
1443, 22 Apr., with Robert Lynton, I, q.v., sent by the prior and chapter to the king for licence to el. an abp, *Chron. Stone*, 31.
1449, 20 Feb., d. at Meister Omers after 50 yrs of monastic life, and was buried with other priors in the nave, *Chron. Stone*, 45–46, (Reg. S, fo 150).

There is a letter written in English by him to the prior from London on 13 or 14 Nov. [?c. 1430], printed in *Christ Church Letters*, 7–9 (CCA DCc Cart. Antiq. 79). This is in the form of a report of his activities in carrying out various business affairs for the convent, which included a meeting with Cardinal Beaufort.

Name in Cambridge, Corpus Christi College Ms 288, Alanus prior etc. (12th/13th c.) on a flyleaf; see M. Alan I.

III John ELHAM
occ. 1467 d. 1485

1467, 28 Mar., ord acol., Canterbury cathedral, *Reg. abp Bourgchier*, 399.
1467, 19 Sept., one of six prof., *SL*, 190, CCA Lit. Ms D.12, fo 8.
1468, 12 Mar., ord subdcn, Canterbury cathedral, *Reg. abp Bourgchier*, 398.

1468, 16 Apr., ord dcn, Canterbury cathedral, *ib.*, 400 (as William).
1470, 21 Apr., ord pr., Canterbury cathedral, *ib.*, 406.
1485, Oct./Nov., one of nine who d. of 'le Swete' within sixteen days, CCA Lit. Ms D.12, fo 26v; see Nicholas Herst I.

IV John ELHAM [Eleham
occ. 1488 d. [1494/5]

1488, 12 Mar., one of six tonsured, *SL*, 192, CCA Lit. Ms D.12, fo 9.
1488, 30 Sept., made his prof. before the cardinal abp, *ib.*
1490, 10 Apr., ord subdcn, Canterbury cathedral, *Reg. abp Morton*, i, no 438b.
1492, 21 Apr., ord dcn, Canterbury cathedral, *ib.*, i, no 441c.
1495, 18 Apr., ord pr., Canterbury cathedral, *ib.*, i, no 444d.
1493, 1 May, 56th in order at the ratification of an agreement, Reg. S, fo 383v; but see John Crosse I.
[1494/5], d., pr. and *conventualis*, CCA Lit. Ms D.12, fos 27v, 31v.

V John ELHAM [Elam, Elane
occ. 1507 d. 1518

1507, 12 Oct., one of six tonsured, *SL*, 193, CCA Lit. Ms D.12, fo 10v.
1508, 22 Apr., ord acol., Canterbury cathedral, Reg. abp Warham, ii, fo 263v.
1508, 25 Apr., made his prof. before the abp, *SL*, 194, CCA Lit. Ms D.12, fo 10v.
1509, 7 Apr., ord subdcn, Canterbury cathedral, Reg. abp Warham, ii, fo 264.
1511, 2 Sept., 69th in order on the visitation certificate, Wood-Legh, *Visit.*, 3 (Reg. abp Warham, i, fo 35v).
1518/19, d. recorded on the treasurer's acct, Pantin, *Cant. Coll. Ox.*, iv, 206; Woodruff, 'Sacrist's Rolls', 70 has 1517/18, and so the yr is prob. 1518.

Note: there are two obits for John Elhams in BL Ms Arundel 68 which cannot yet be assigned: 5 Sept. (fo 40v), 19 Oct. (fo 45v).

Robert de ELHAM [*dictus* de Elham, Helham
occ. [?mid 1260s] d. 1301

[?mid 1260s], one of seven prof., *SL*, 176, CCA Lit. Ms D.12, fo 2v.
1285/6, prob. *custos martyrii*, CCA DCc Treas. acct 2.
1295, Apr./1298, 1301, 29 Sept., sacrist, CCA DCc MA1, fos 194–215v, Arrears acct 46; the apptment on 14 Apr. 1295 is in *Reg. abp Winchelsey*, 20.
1284, 1 Oct., apptd proctor in the appeal of the prior and chapter concerning the el. and consecration of the bp of Salisbury, *Reg. abp Pecham*, i, 215–216; *Epist. Pecham*, 1036.
1292, 19 Dec., attended abp Pecham's funeral in the cathedral, *Reg. abp Winchelsey*, 1258.
1293, 23 Mar., apptd proctor, with John de Well I, q.v., *sed. vac.*, with regard to the el. of an abp, CUL Ms Ee.5.31, fo 42v; a second *procuratorium* was issued to them by the prior, Henry de Eastry, q.v., sending them to the curia, *ib.*, fo 43 and Reg. Q, fo 20.
1293, 2 Nov., in Rome with Geoffrey de Romenal, q.v. and others where they were authorized by the prior and chapter to obtain a loan, *ib.*, fo 52.
1294, 14 Oct., one of the monks present in Siena when abp Winchelsey made an apptment to the see of Llandaff, *Reg. abp Winchelsey*, 5–6.
1297, 7 Jan., named by the prior and chapter, with Geoffrey de Chilham, q.v. as proctors for convocation, CUL Ms Ee.5.31, fo 69–69v.
[1298], 4 Nov., named as proctor to take letters to the pope with regard to the chapter's dispute with the adcn of Canterbury, *ib.*, fo 78v; another proctorial comm. was issued to him and to Stephen de Worth, q.v. on 1 Nov. 1300, the purpose of which was 'ad contradicendum in audiencia et ad impetrandum privilegia', *ib.*, fos 83v–84.
1301, 20 Mar., still in Rome, *ib.*, fo 84v, but must have set out on the return journey shortly after as he d. at Bologna on 7 Apr., CCA Lit. Ms D.12, fo 15v. His obit in BL Ms Arundel 68, fo 22 is on 7 kal. Apr. (26 Mar.) and not 7 ides as in CCA Lit. Ms D.12.

Several volumes of his are in the Eastry catalogue: nos 381, 719 and prob. 720, James, *Ancient Libraries*, 53, 78.

An inventory of the refectory, dated 1328, includes a silver *ciphus* formerly his, and three *de murra*, Dart, *Antiq. Cant.*, xix, xx, xxi (BL Ms Cotton Galba E.iv, fos 178, 179, 179v).

Thomas de ELHAM
occ. 1st half 13th c.

n.d., name occ. in the list in *SL*, 173, CCA Lit. Ms D.12, fo 1v.

His Diadema monachorum is no 1343 in the Eastry catalogue, James, *Ancient Libraries*, 114.

I ELIAS [Helias
occ. [1109]

He reported that he had seen a vision of Anselm and of Dunstan three months before Anselm's death and gave the details to Eadmer, q.v., who included them in his *Vita Anselmi*, 154–156.

Eadmer described him as a monk 'bonis memoribus et simplicitate decoratus, vitae innocentis', *ib.*

Note: James suggests that this is Helyas Thes[aurarius whose name is attached to four vols in the Eastry catalogue nos 1096–1099,

James, *Ancient Libraries*, 102, 536. See note 1) under Elias III.

II ELIAS [Helyas
occ. [1144 × 1152]

[1144 × 1152], with prior Walter [?Durdent or de Meri, q.v.] attested a grant of abp Theobald, *Theobald Charters*, no 63.

III ELIAS
occ. 1188/9

1188, after 9 Dec., one of the monks who accompanied Geoffrey II, subprior, q.v., to Rome and was resident at the curia where he had been assigned to keep watch on the progress of the monk's appeal vs abp Baldwin's project for a collegiate church at Lambeth, *Epist. Cant.*, 271, 272; he was still there in Jan. 1189, *ib.*, 276; and with John [?Bremble] q.v., had an interview with the pope in Feb., *ib.*, 279. In Apr. he and John were in Paris on their way to meet the king, *ib.*, 287–289, and they wrote to the prior and convent after 20 May reporting on their meeting with the abp at Le Mans, *ib.*, 290, after which he was sent back to Canterbury, *ib.*, 293.

1189, c. 12 Oct., sent with James II, q.v., to the king concerning the removal of the college, *Epist. Cant.* 312.

Note:

(1) There may not be three monks named Elias, but the known dates seem sufficiently spread out to warrant this supposition. One of them—or yet another!—was commemorated on 25 Oct. in BL Ms Arundel 68, fo 46v. There is also an Elye Thes[aurarius] whose wooden *ciphus* [i.e. prob. formerly his] is included in an inventory of the refectory dated 1328, Dart, *Antiq. Cant.*, xxii (BL Ms Cotton Galba E.iv, fo 180). See note under Elias I.

(2) There is an Helias, whose name is in a former Canterbury ms, now Dublin, Trinity College Ms 124, Gilbert Altissiodorensis (12th/13th cs).

ELISFORD
see Aylesford

ELIZAEUS
n.d.

n.d., 12 June, obit occ. in Lambeth Ms 20, fo 193v.

ELLFFY
see Elphe

I ELMER
occ. [before 1109]

[1109, before], monk of Canterbury, ?formerly of Bec, greeted by abp Anselm, *Anselm Letters*, no 69.

II ELMER [Ailmer, Almer, Eilmer, Elmerus
occ. 1130 d. 1137

1130–1137, prior: in office at the dedication of the cathedral church, 4 May 1130; d. 1137, *Fasti*, ii, 9.

[1128 × 1136], attested a charter of abp William, Reg. abp Warham, i, fo 136 (this will appear in *Eng. Epis. Acta*, Canterbury, 1070–1161, as no 83).

[1130 × 1136], with the monks confirmed that they had witnessed a charter of abp William, F.R.H. Du Boulay, 'Bexley Church: some Early Documents', *Archaeologia Cantiana*, lxxii (1958), 51–52.

1137, 11 May, d., acc. to the obit in BL Ms Arundel 68, fo 27.

There is a list of the treatises written by him in Dart, *Antiq. Cant.*, 180. A collection of fifteen letters written by him has been printed by Robert Anstruther in *Epist. Losinga* (see Norwich refs); but for a more recent and more accurate edition of the letters and a sermon, see J. Leclercq, 'Écrits spirituels d'Elmer de Cantorbéry', *Studia Anselmiana, Analecta Monastica* 2me série xxxi (1953), 45–117. See also Sharpe, *Latin Writers*.

James lists three of his books in the Eastry catalogue, nos 104, 253, 349 *Ancient Libraries*, 28, 45, 52. No 253 is Sermo Edmeri prioris super regulam beati Benedicti.

Gervase described him as 'vir magnae simplicitatis et eximiae religionis', *Gervase Cant.*, i, 98.

William ELMORE [Elmer
occ. 1384 d. 1399

1384, 29 Aug., one of seven prof., *SL*, 183, CCA Lit. Ms D.12, fo 5.

1394, one of the chancellors, with Thomas Bungay, q.v., Reg. S, fo 1.

1397/8, feretrar, CCA DCc Feret. acct 1.

[1399], prob. at time of d., bartoner, see below.

1387/8, recd a small sum from the prior, Lambeth Ms 243, fo 208v.

1392/3, gave 6s. 8d. to the sacrist *pro dealbatione chori*, CCA DCc Sac. acct 11.

1396, 7 Aug., absent from the el. of abp Arundel, Reg. G, fo 234v.

1399, 4 Jan., d., CCA Lit. Ms D.12, fo 18; his obit is in BL Ms Arundel 68, fo 12, where he is listed as pr.

John ELMYSTON [Elmeston, Elmiston
occ. 1384 d. 1430

1384, 29 Aug., one of seven prof., *SL*, 183, CCA Lit. Ms D.12, fo 5.

1386, 21 Apr., ord subdcn, Canterbury cathedral, Reg. abp Courtenay, i, fo 308v.

1387, 6 Apr., ord dcn, Canterbury cathedral, *ib.*, i, fo 309v.

1389, 12 June, ord pr., St Dunstan's church, London, *ib.*, fo 311v.

1426/7, *magister mense*, CCA DCc Adisham acct 54; and see below.

1390/1, recd 12d. *pro benedictione* from the prior, Lambeth Ms 243, fo 220v.

1396, 7 Aug., 45th in order at the el. of an abp, Reg. G, fo 234v.

1414, 12 Mar., 14th at the el. of an abp, *Reg. abp Chichele*, i, 4.

1430, 8 Aug., d., *stationarius*, CCA Lit. Ms D.12, fo 22v; the obituaries in Ms D.12, *ib.*, and *Chron. Stone*, 15, note that he held *diversa officia* until he was released *de communa tabula* and given a chamber in the infirmary. His obit is in BL Ms Arundel 68, fo 37v.

John ELPHE [Ellffy, Elphee, Elphye
occ. 1506 occ. 1540

1506, 21 Mar., one of six tonsured, *SL*, 193, CCA Lit. Ms D.12, fo 10v.

1506, 11 Apr., ord acol., Canterbury cathedral, Reg. abp Warham, ii, fo 262v.

1506, 30 Sept., prof., *SL*, 193, CCA Lit. Ms D.12, fo 10v.

1507, 3 Apr., ord subdcn, Canterbury cathedral, Reg. abp Warham, ii, fo 263.

1508, 22 Apr., ord dcn, Canterbury cathedral, *ib.*, ii, fo 263v.

1513, 26 Mar., ord pr., Canterbury cathedral, *ib.*, ii, fo 266v.

1526, Aug., appted precentor, Reg. T, fo 272.

[1538, 8 Feb., after], 1540, 4 Apr., precentor, Pantin, *Cant. Coll. Ox.*, iii, 152, *L and P Henry VIII*, xv, no 452.

1511, 2 Sept., 64th in order on the visitation certificate, Wood-Legh, *Visit.*, 3 (Reg. abp Warham, i, fo 35v).

1518/19, spent time in the infirmary, CCA DCc, Infirm. acct 1.

1534, 12 Dec., acknowledged the Act of Supremacy, *DK 7th Report*, Appndx 2, 282.

[1538, 8 Feb., after], in a list of monks prob. prepared for Thomas Cromwell he was described as a 'symple' man, 50 yrs old, Pantin, *Cant. Coll. Ox.*, iii, 152.

1540, 4 Apr., awarded £3 6s. 8d. p.a., *L and P Henry VIII*, x, no 452 and became a petty canon in the new foundation.

I William de ELPHE [Elfy, Elphee, Elphego, St Elphege
occ. 1367 occ. 1371

1367, 11 Nov., one of nine prof., *SL*, 182, CCA Lit. Ms D.12, fo 4v.

1368, 4 Mar., ord acol., Canterbury cathedral, *Reg. abp Langham*, 387.

1369, 22 Dec., ord subdcn, abp's chapel, Charing, Reg. abp Wittlesey, fo 165v.

1370, 21 Sept., ord dcn, Saltwood, *ib.*, fo 166v.

1371, 31 May, ord pr., abp's chapel, Charing, *ib.*, fo 167.

II William ELPHE [Elfe, Elfy, St Elphege
occ. 1431 d. 1455

1431, 18 Apr., one of four prof., *SL*, 187, CCA Lit. Ms D.12, fo 7.

1433, 28 Mar., ord subdcn, Charing, *Reg. abp Chichele*, iv, 377.

1434, 13 Mar., ord dcn, infirmary chapel, *ib.*, iv, 379.

1455, before 30 Mar., *custos martyrii*; see below.

1455, 30 Mar., d., in the 24th yr of his monastic life, *Chron. Stone*, 63 (CCA Lit. Ms D.12, fo 25v); the obit of a William Elphe, prob. this one, is on 29 Mar. in BL Ms Arundel 68, fo 22v.

III William ELPHE [Elphe, Elphi
occ. 1470 d. 1504

1470, 25 Jan., one of eight prof., *SL*, 190, CCA Lit. Ms D.12, fo 8.

1470, 21 Apr., ord acol., Canterbury cathedral, *Reg. abp Bourgchier*, 405.

1471, 9 Mar., ord subdcn, Canterbury cathedral, *Reg. abp Bourgchier*, 404.

1473, 13 Mar., ord dcn, Canterbury cathedral, *ib.*, 410.

1475, 23 Sept., ord pr., prior's chapel, *ib.*, 419.

1488/9, Sept. to Apr., *magister ordinis*, *SL*, 192, CCA Lit. Ms D.12, fo 9.

1489/90, novice master, CCA DCc MA7, fo 134.

1496/1501, granator, CCA DCc MA9 fos 111, 126, MA10, fos 53v, 88v, 36.

1501/3, [1504], infirmarer, CCA DCc MA10, fos 101, 149, and still prob. at the time of his d.; see below.

1493, 1 May, 29th in order at the ratification of an agreement, Reg. S, fo 383v; but see John Crosse I.

1501, 26 Apr., 17th at the el. of an abp, Reg. R, fo 56v.

1504, 17 Oct., d. *ex magno fluxu* at the age of 51, CCA Lit. Ms D.12, fo 35. The obituary in *ib.*, describes him as 'magister infirmarie ad primam mensam'. His obit is in BL Ms Arundel 68, fo 45v.

ELPHE [de Sancto Elphego
see also St Elphege

John ELPHEGUS
n.d.

n.d., 29 Mar., *levita*, whose obit is in BL Ms Arundel 68, fo 22v.

William de ELY
occ. [1207 × 1214]

[1207 × 1214], name occ. in the list of those who were in exile, *SL*, 172, CCA Lit. Ms D.12, fo 1.

Volume nos 1226–1230 in the Eastry catalogue were his, James, *Ancient Libraries*, 107–108.

ELYAS
see Elias

Peter de ELYNGE
occ. 1287

1287, 16 Mar., one of five prof., *SL*, 177, CCA Lit. Ms D.12, fo 3.

Thomas ELYS
occ. 1367 occ. 1405

1367, 11 Nov., one of nine prof., *SL*, 182, CCA Lit. Ms D.12, fo 4v.
1368, 4 Mar., ord acol., Canterbury cathedral, *Reg. abp Langham*, 387.
1369, 22 Dec., ord subdcn, abp's chapel, Charing, Reg. abp Wittlesey, fo 165v.
1370, 21 Sept., ord dcn, Saltwood, *ib.*, fo 166v.
1371, 31 May, ord pr., abp's chapel, Charing, *ib.*, fo 167.
1378, *custos tumbe*, CCA DCc MA2, fo 314v.
1380/1, feretrar, CCA DCc MA2, fos 321v–325.
1382, Sept./1383, Aug., *magister ordinis*, *SL*, 183, CCA Lit. Ms D.12, fo 5.
1382, 1384/5, fourth prior, Lambeth Ms 243, fos 183, 196v.
1390/1, third prior, *ib.*, fo 220v.
1396/1402, 1403/5, anniversarian, with William Stone, q.v., CCA DCc Prior acct 4, Anniv. accts 7, 23.
1374, 30 June, 47th in order at the el. of an abp, Reg. G, fos 173v–175v.
1381, 31 July, 35th at the el. of an abp, *ib.*, fo 225v.
1391/2, gave 6s. 8d. to the sacrist towards the repair of the choir vault, CCA DCc Sac. acct 10.
1396, 7 Aug., 17th at the el. of an abp, *ib.*, fo 234v.

ENEFELD
see Henfeld

John EPYSWYCHE [Ypeswyche
occ. [1393] d. 1395

[1393], 21 Nov., one of six prof., *SL*, 184, CCA Lit. Ms D.12, fo 5.
1394, 18 Apr., ord subdcn, Canterbury cathedral, Reg. abp Courtenay, ii, fo 184v.
1395, 6 Jan., d., suddenly in the dormitory in his second yr of monastic life, CCA Lit. Ms D.12, fo 17.

ERNALDUS [Aernaldus
occ. 1155 occ. [1163 × 1167]

1155, 28 Mar., with William V, subprior, and Felix I, q.v. and others witnessed an agreement made between Christ Church and Godfrey de Malling, *Theobald Charters*, 536.
[1163 × 1167], name occ. in a rental along with his brother, William the Goldsmith, who held land in the parish of St. Elphege, Canterbury, Urry, *Canterbury*, 154, 226. Ernaldus was also called *aurifaber*, *ib.*, 155.

ERNOSTUS
see Arnost

I ERNULF [Arnulf, Ernulph, Hernostus
occ. [c. 1073] occ. 1107

c. 1096–1107, prior: apptd c. 1096 by the abp to succ. Henry, q.v.; el. abbot of Peterborough 1107, *HRH*, 33, *Fasti*, ii, 8; in 1114 became bp of Rochester, *ib.*, 75.
[c. 1073], schoolmaster in the cloister, Gibson, *Lanfranc*, 177.
[1086], alleged to have attested a spurious charter of abp Lanfranc, *Reg. Roff.*, 441 (Rochester ref.).
As prior he attested the following charters:
(1) [1096 × 1107], a grant of abp Anselm to Rochester, *Text Roff.*, ii, fo 179 and cap 93 (Rochester ref.).
(2) [1096 × 1107], two spurious charters of abp Anselm, *Reg. Roff.*, 359–360, 441–442, 446 (Rochester ref.).
(3) [1101], another spurious charter of abp Anselm, *ib.*, 442.
Note: nos 1), 2) and 3) will appear in *Eng. Epis. Acta*, Canterbury, 1070–1161, as nos 24, 27, 28.
[1096 × 1107], named in a grant of land by the prior and convent to Calvellus, Urry, *Canterbury*, 387.

Name in BL Ms Royal 5 D.i and 5 D.ii, Augustine (on the psalms), (early 12th c.) which he gave to Rochester cathedral library; 5 D.i, has, on fo 1, *liber de claustro Roffensis . . . Arnulphi prioris* and 5 D.ii has, in the same hand . . . *Ernulphi episcopi*.

Previously a monk of Beauvais who came to Christ Church with or soon after abp Lanfranc; he was a scholar and as schoolmaster taught Eadmer, Gibson *Lanfranc*, 177. He must have been a great influence at Rochester, perhaps the compiler of the Textus Roffensis, Dr Martin Brett has suggested. Southern notes his keen interest in the revival of Anglo-Saxon liturgical practices and the collection of Old English laws, *St Anselm* (1990), 322, with further refs. Among Anselm's correspondence the following letters were addressed to him or written by him as prior, *Anselm Letters*, nos 286, 289, 291, 292, 307, 310, 311, 331, 349, 357, 364, 374, 376, 380. See Sharpe, *Latin Writers*, for a full list of his known writings. See also P. Cramer, 'Ernulf of Rochester and Early Anglo-Norman Canon Law', in *Journal of Ecclesiastical History*, 40 (1989), 483–490, which provides many details of his early monastic career and his priorate at Christ Church; it also refers to the poem Malchus sent to him that had been composed by the author, Reginald of Canterbury and the poems by the same author addressed to him as a *vir clarus*.

His obit (under 18 Feb.) in BL Ms Arundel 68, fos 16v–17 gives a résumé of his achievements. His principal monument is the Norman library and scriptorium which, with abp Lanfranc, he founded, Gibson, 'Normans and Angevins, 1070–1220' in Collinson, *Canterbury Cathedral*, 51–52.

II ERNULF
occ. [1153 × 1167]

[1153 × 1161], *temp.* abp Theobald and prior Wibert, q.v., cellarer; see below.

[1153 × 1161], with William V subprior q.v., and others witnessed a grant made by the prior and convent at the request of the abp, *Theobald Charters*, no 40 (Reg. B, fo 146v).

[1153 × 1167], name occ. in a rental of prior Wibert, q.v., where his brother Robert de Suanetuna is also named, Urry *Canterbury*, 225.

John ESCHARE
occ. 1436

1436, 3 Mar., ord dcn, infirmary chapel, *Reg. abp Chichele*, iv, 384.

John ESCHE
see Asshe

John le ESPICER
see Spycer

Alexander ESSCHE [*alias* Goodschep
occ. 1394/5

1394, 18 Apr., ord subdcn, Canterbury cathedral, Reg. abp Courtenay, ii, fo 184v.

1395, 10 Apr., ord dcn, Canterbury cathedral, *ib.*, ii, fo 185v (as Goodschep).

Note: this is prob. Alexander London, q.v.

John ESSEX [Aschex, Asshex, Esex
occ. 1416 d. 1420

1416, 22 June, one of eight prof., *SL*, 186, CCA Lit. Ms D.12, fo 6.

1417, 10 Apr., ord acol., Canterbury cathedral, *Reg. abp Chichele*, iv, 327.

1418, 26 Mar., ord subdcn, Canterbury cathedral, *ib.*, iv, 332.

n.d., [prob. at the time of his d.], scholar at Canterbury college, *Chron. Stone*, 11.

1420, 5 Aug., subdcn, d., *ex pestilentia*, CCA Lit. Ms D.12, fo 21v; his obit is in BL Ms Arundel, 68, fo 37.

Walter de ESSEXIA [Essexe
occ. 1239

1239, 4 Jan., one of the group of monks accused of contumacy by the abp after the forgery scandal, *Gervase Cant.*, ii, 144; see Simon de Hertlepe. On 1 Feb. he was among those summoned to appear before the abp after the monks' el. of Roger de La Lee, q.v., as prior, *ib.*, ii, 153.

R. de ESSHE
occ. 1286

1286, chamberlain, CCA DCc, Treas. acct 2; see John de Begbroke.

Roger de ESSHETYFORD
occ. 1st half 13th c.

n.d., name occ. in the list in *SL*, 173, CCA Lit. Ms D.12, fo 1v.

ESSHFORD(E)
see Assheforde, Asshford

ESTRY
see Eastry

William ETHE [Ech, Eth, Hethe
occ. 1451 d. 1456

1451, 21 Oct., one of four prof., *SL*, 189, CCA Lit. Ms D.12, fo 7v.

1452, 8 Apr., ord acol., Canterbury cathedral, Reg. abp Stafford, fo 206v.

1455, 5 Apr., ord dcn, chapel in Canterbury cathedral, *Reg. abp Bourgchier*, 360.

1456, 8 Jan., d., *Chron. Stone*, 65, CCA Lit. Ms D.12, fo 25v; his obit is in BL Ms Arundel 68, fo 12v.

ETHE
see also Hethe

ETHELRED [?*alias* Nicholas

According to Eadmer, he held the offices of subprior and cantor and later, because of his knowledge of [the new] monastic discipline, he became an obedientiary at Worcester under bp Wulstan, *Dunstan Memorials*, 163–164.

Note: was he a monk of Worcester sent for training to Christ Church in the late 11th c.? See under Nicholas II in the Worcester section.

ETON
see Eyton, Heton

I EUDO [Eudes
occ. 1228 occ. 1238

1236/8, almoner, CCA DCc MA1, fos 78v–80.

1228, 3 Aug., named as one of five *compromissorii* in the unsuccessful el. of Walter de Eynesham, q.v., as abp, *Gervase Cant.*, ii, 120, 121, 123.

II EUDO [Eudes
occ. 1295 occ. 1306

1295/9, chamberlain, CCA DCc MA1, fos 194–222.

1299, warden of manors, CCA DCc MA1, fo 222.
1300/3, sacrist, CCA DCc MA1, fos 225–244v.
1306, granator, CCA DCc MA1, fo 264v.

n.d., the obit of a Eudo in BL Ms Arundel 68, fo 21 is recorded on 19 Mar.

EUDO
see also Guido

EUSTACE
occ. 1234 occ. 1237

1234, 1235/6, 1235/7, chamberlain, CCA DCc MA1, fo 77v, AS4, MA1, fos 78, 79.

Note: this is prob. Eustace de Faversham, q.v.

EUSTACE
see also Dover, Faversham

EUSTON
see Guston

EVENFELD
see Henfeld

EVERARD [Everardus
occ. 1104

1104, conveyed letters from the king to abp Anselm, Eadmer, *Hist. Nov.*, 159.
[1096 × 1107], *temp.* prior Ernulf, q.v., mentioned in three letters written by Anselm, *Anselm Letters*, nos 307, 330, 331; this last implies that he was an envoy to the abp in exile.

I John EVERARD [Euorarde
occ. [1316] d. 1328

[1316], 6 Nov., one of five prof., *SL*, 179, CCA Lit. Ms D.12, fo 3v.
1318, 17 June, ord subdcn, Maidstone, Reg. abp Reynolds, fo 180v.
1316, 23 Dec., ord dcn, Maidstone, *ib.*, fo 182.
1322/8, treasurer, CCA DCc MA2, fos 126–173v.
1324, 20 Feb., present in chapter with the chancellors at the apptment of a parliamentary proctor, CUL Ms Ee.5.31, fo 235.
1327, 11 Dec., named as one of seven *compromissorii* in the el. of an abp, Reg. Q, fo 123; see also *CPL*, ii (1305–1342), 272.
1328, 27 Aug., d. in Brabant and was buried at Antwerp, CCA Lit. Ms D.12, fo 16.

In an inventory of missing books dated 1 Mar. 1338, his name was in Logica vetus et nova which William de Thaneto, q.v., had failed to return, *Lit. Cant.*, no 618 (Reg. L, fo 104).

A list of his books is in the Eastry catalogue, nos 1796–1803, James, *Ancient Libraries*, 141.

An inventory of the refectory, dated 1328, includes two *ciphi de murra* formerly his, Dart, *Antiq. Cant.*, xxiii (BL Ms Cotton Galba E.iv, fo 180v).

II John EVERARD
see Garard

Thomas EVERARD D.Th. [Everarde
occ. 1376 d. 1398

1376, 14 or 15 Nov., one of seven who were clothed in the monastic habit, *SL*, 183, CCA Lit. Ms D.12, fo 4v.
1376, 20 Dec., ord acol., Canterbury cathedral, Reg. abp Sudbury, fo 140v.
1377, 19 Sept., ord subdcn, Lambeth palace chapel, *ib.*, fo 142.
1378, 17 Apr., ord dcn, Canterbury cathedral, *ib.*, fo 145v.

1388/9, treasurer, Lambeth Ms 243, fo 211.

1379/80, scholar at Canterbury college and recd money from the treasurers for expenses and for his *capa scolatsica*, Pantin, *Cant. Coll. Ox.*, iv, 188.
1383, 20 Aug., apptd scholar, Pantin, *Cant. Coll. Ox.*, iii, 46 (Reg. Courtenay, i, fo 43).
1383/4, 1388/9, scholar at Oxford, *ib.*, iv, 189, 190.
1393/4, 1394/5, payments of his battels and commons recd by the warden, Pantin, *Cant. Coll. Ox.*, ii, 132, 135, 136, 137, 138, 140 (CCA DCc Cart. Antiq. O.151.2, 3); he also recd a pittance for preaching, Pantin, *ib.* ii, 135, and £13 was pd by the prior in 1394/5, prob. for his inception, *ib.*, ii, 137.
[1395], D.Th., the expenses for his inception and that of William Gyllyngham I, q.v. are in Pantin, *Cant. Coll. Ox*, iii, 54–56 (CCA DCc Cart. Antiq. O.151.3b). He is given the title *sacre pagine* professor in a document dated 3 Aug. 1396, Reg. G, fo 242.

1381, 31 July, 52nd in order at the el. of an abp, Reg. G, fo 225v.
1385/6, recd 5s. from the prior *pro benedictione*, Lambeth Ms 243, fo 200v.
1396, 7 Aug., 26th at the el. of an abp, and with John Wodnesburgh, q.v., was sent as proctor to inform bp Thomas Arundel of his postulation, Reg. G, fos 234v, 239v.
1398, 8 Apr., d. (2nd feria in Easter wk) and was buried in the infirmary chapel, CCA Lit. Ms D.12, fo 17v.

Walter de EVESHAM
occ. 1st half 13th c.

n.d., name occ. in the list in *SL*, 173, CCA Lit. Ms D.12, fo 1v.

Two books of M. Gaterius de Evesham are in the Eastry catalogue, nos 1341, 1342, James, *Ancient Libraries*, 114.

Note: is this Walter de Eynesham, q.v.?

John de EXETRE [Excestre
occ. 1336 occ. 1381

[1336], n.d., one of seven adm., *SL*, 180; CCA Lit. Ms D.12, fo 4.

1337, 19 June, one of five of the above seven who, although they had not yet completed their yr of probation, were urging the prior to rec. their prof.; the prior therefore consulted the abp as he was afraid that they would, if denied, return to the world, Reg. L, fo 67^{v}. The abp's reply was a firm negative, *ib*.

1349, 4 June, 44th in order at the el. of an abp, Reg. G, fo 60^{v}.

1349, 8/9 Sept., 43rd at the el. of an abp, *ib*., fo 76^{v}.

1355/6, was responsible for some of the payments to the *custod' vini*, Lambeth Ms 243, fo 99^{v}.

1374, 30 June, 7th in order at the el. of an abp, Reg. G, fos 173^{v}–175^{v}.

1380, recd a small sum [*dona*] from the prior, Lambeth Ms 243, fo 180^{v}.

1381, 31 July, 4th in order at the el. of an abp, Reg. G, fo 225^{v}.

Alexander de EXON'
see Oxon

EYHAM
see Hegham

EYHORN(E)
see Eythorn

EYLESFORD
see Aylesford

William EYLESTON
occ. 1373

1373, 16 Apr., ord dcn, abp's chapel, Charing, Reg. abp Wittlesey, fo 170^{v}.

John de EYNESFORD [Eynysford
occ. 1354 d. 1355

1354, 28 Nov., one of seven who were clothed in the monastic habit, *SL*, 181, CCA Lit. Ms D.12, fos 4, 16^{v}.

1355, 5 May, d., as a *conversus*, and not yet prof.; because there ensued a discussion about whether or not he should have a cross and other *necessaria sicut professus*, a new ordinance had to be issued to clarify the uncertainty, CCA Lit. Ms D.12, fo 17.

William de EYNESFORD
n.d.

n.d., 31 Mar., obit in BL Ms Arundel 68, fo 22^{v}.

EYNESFORD
see also Eynysford

M. Walter de EYNESHAM
occ. 1228

1228, 3 Aug., el. abp by the monks, *Gervase Cant*., ii, 117–124; the king objected and the el. was quashed by the pope, 5 Jan. 1229, *ib*., ii, 127, and see *Fasti*, ii, 6.

Note: since this name does not occ. in the lists *in exilio* and *post exilium*, *SL*, 173 suggests that Walter de Evesham, q.v. is the same monk.

Simon de EYNYSFORD
occ. [1207 × 1214]

[1207 × 1214], name occ. in the list of monks who were in exile, *SL*, 172, CCA Lit. Ms D.12, fo 1.

A wooden *ciphus cum leone in fundo*, formerly his, was included in an inventory of the refectory dated 1328; Dart, *Antiq. Cant*., xxii (BL Ms Cotton Galba E.iv, fo 180).

William de EYNYSFORD [Eynsford, son of Ralf
occ. c. 1135

c. 1135, a knight who became a monk of Canterbury after 1130, Douglas, *Domesday Monachorum*, 46.

Details of his family connections and their manor of Eynsford, which they held as one of abp Lanfranc's knights, are in *ib*., 46–47.

Stephen EYTHORNE [Eyerorn, Eyorn, Eyorne
occ. 1459 occ. c. 1472/3

1459, 30 Nov., one of six prof., *SL*, 189, CCA Lit. Ms D.12, fo 8.

1462, 17 Apr., ord dcn, Canterbury cathedral, *Reg. abp Bourgchier*, 381.

1464, 31 Mar., ord pr., Canterbury cathedral, *ib*., 390 (transcribed as Everorn).

1463/4, celebrated his first mass and recd a gift from the sacrist, CCA DCc Sac. acct 44.

1466, 17 Feb., 64th in order in an inventory listing *jocalia fratrum* [given by him and/or assigned for his use], and he had none, Reg. N, fo 234^{v}.

[1472/3], *migravit*, and *recessit* (the latter added in the margin), *SL*, 189, CCA Lit. Ms D.12, fo 26; this entry is in the obit section.

William de EYTHORNE [Egthorn, Eydorne, Eyhorne, Eyorne, Hayhorne, Heyhorne
occ. 1330 occ. 1381

1330, 9 Oct., one of six prof., *SL*, 180, CCA Lit. Ms D.12, fo 3^{v}.

1333, 12 Oct., chancellor, his name occ. at the top of the *sed. vac.* section of the reg. after the d. of abp Meopham, Reg. G, fo xxvi.

1340/1, 1342/3, subalmoner, CCA DCc Eastry accts, 68, 71.

1348/9, second anniversarian, with Walter de Berham, q.v., CCA DCc Anniv. acct 3.

1350, 10 Aug./25 Dec., chamberlain, CCA DCc Chamb. acct 73; there is an undated letter from the prior to the abp, requesting his release from

this office, which he himself conveyed in order to explain in person, Reg. L, fo 84^{v}.
1358/60, warden of manors, CCA DCc Ebony accts 58, 59.
1362, 7 Jan., 1366, 10 May, subprior, Woodruff, *Sede Vacante Wills*, 79, Reg. G, fo 149.
1367, 11 Oct., apptd precentor, *Reg. abp Langham*, 293.
1369/70, July, bartoner, CCA DCc Bart. acct 45.
1371/3, feretrar, CCA DCc MA2, fos 266–276.
1374, *custos martyrii*, CCA DCc MA2, fo 281^{v}.
1374, 30 June, subprior, Reg. G, fo 175^{v}.
1349, 4 June, 28th in order at the el. of an abp, Reg. G, fo 60^{v}.
1349, 8/9 Sept., 27th at the el. of an abp, *ib.*, fo 76^{v}.
1366, 10 May, one of three *compromissorii* named by the prior and chapter to el. seven *compromissorii* for the el. of an abp, *ib.*, fo 149.
1374, 30 June, 5th in order and named as one of three *scrutatores* in the el. of an abp, *ib.*, fos 173^{v}–175^{v}.
1376, Apr., one of ten nominated to the committee set up for regulating the infirmary, *Lit. Cant.*, no 945 (CCA DCc Cart. Antiq. C.206).
1381, 31 July, 2nd in order (but not subprior) at the el. of an abp, *ib.*, fo 225^{v}.

Gave a red vestment to Canterbury college for use on Sundays, Pantin, *Cant. Coll. Ox.*, i, 2 (CCA DCc Cant. Antiq. O.34).

Robert EYTON [Eton
occ. [1392] occ. 1396

[1392], 21 Nov., one of four prof., *SL*, 184, CCA Lit. Ms D.12, fo 5.
1394, 18 Apr., ord pr., Canterbury cathedral, Reg. abp Courtenay, ii, fo 185.
1396, 7 Aug., 68th in order at the el. of an abp, Reg. G, fo 236.

Robert de FAGHE [ffaghe
occ. 2nd half 13th c.

n.d., name occ. in the list in *SL*, 175, CCA Lit. Ms D.12, fo 2.

FAIREFORD
see Fayrford

Robert de FALEWEYE [Faleway
occ. 1st half 13th c.

n.d., name occ. in the *post exilium* list in *SL*, 173, CCA Lit. Ms D.12, fo 1^{v}.

Note: a Robert de Forlee d. 23 Mar. 1292, CCA Lit. Ms D.12, fo 15; is this another spelling?

I Thomas FARLEY [Farle, Farlegh, Farleigh
occ. 1462 d. 1473

1462, 17 Apr., ord acol., Canterbury cathedral, *Reg. abp Bourgchier*, 380.
[1462], 6 Dec., one of six prof., *SL*, 190, CCA Lit. Ms D.12, fo 8.
Note: this must have been incorrectly dated 1464 in the margin of the ms; 1462 (or 1463) is more likely.
1463, 9 Apr., ord subdcn, Canterbury cathedral, *Reg. abp Bourgchier*, 385.
1464, 31 Mar., ord dcn, Canterbury cathedral, *ib.*, 390.
1467, 28 Mar., ord pr., Canterbury cathedral, *ib.*, 399.

n.d., treasurer, prob. at the time of his d., CCA Lit. Ms D.12, fo 26; see below.

1466, 17 Feb., 70th in order in an inventory listing *jocalia fratrum* [given by him and/or assigned for his use], Reg. N, fo 234^{v}.
1472/3, d., Woodruff, 'Sacrist's Rolls', 64 (CCA DCc Sac. acct 53), CCA Lit. Ms D.12, fo 26; his obit on 25 July is in BL Ms Arundel, fo 36.

II Thomas FARLEY [Farle, Farlegh
occ. 1483 d. [1489 × 1492]

1483, 30 Sept., one of six tonsured, *SL*, 191, CCA Lit. Ms D.12, fo 8^{v}.
1484, 10 June, prof., *ib.*
1485, 2 Apr., ord subdcn, Canterbury cathedral, *Reg. abp Bourgchier*, 450.
1485, 24 Sept., ord dcn, Canterbury cathedral, *ib.*, 452.
1487, 14 Apr., ord pr., Canterbury cathedral, *Reg. abp Morton*, i, no 433d.

[?1491/2], *parvus sacrista*, CCA Lit. Ms D.12, fos 27^{v}, 31^{v}.

[1489 × 1492], d., CCA Lit. Ms D.12, fos 27, 31^{v}; his obit is on 29 July in BL Ms Arundel 68, fo 36.

III Thomas FARLEY
occ. 1527 occ. 1534

1527, 25 May, one of twelve tonsured, *SL*, 195, CCA Lit. Ms D.12, fo 12.
1528, 2 Mar., prof., *ib.*

1534, 12 Dec., last on the list of those who acknowledged the Act of Supremacy, *DK 7th Report*, Appndx 2, 282.

William FARLEY [Fareley, Farlegh, Farleygh, Farnlegh
occ. 1502 d. 1518/19

1502, 25 Aug., one of eight tonsured, *SL*, 193, CCA Lit. Ms D.12, fo 10.
1503, 4 Apr., made his prof. before the prior, *sed. vac.*, *ib.*
1505, 22 Mar., ord dcn, Canterbury cathedral, Reg. abp Warham, ii, fo 262.
1508, 22 Apr., ord pr., Canterbury cathedral, *ib.*, ii, fo 263^{v}.
1507/8, celebrated his first mass and recd a 10d. gift from the sacrist, Woodruff, 'Sacrist's Rolls', 68 (CCA DCc Sac. acct 64). He

celebrated on the first Sun. in May [1508] and recd 4d. from the *custos martyrii*, CCA Lit. Ms C.11, fo 50.

1514, 25 Dec., almoner, CCA Lit. Ms C.11, fo 56v.

1511, 2 Sept., 54th in order on the visitation certificate, Wood-Legh, *Visit.*, 3 (Reg. abp Warham, i, fo 35v).

1518/19, d., acc. to the treasurer's acct, Pantin, *Cant. Coll. Ox.*, iv, 206; his obit is on 25 Sept. in BL Ms Arundel 68, fo 43.

FARMAN [Farmannus

occ. [?c. 1089] occ. [1094 × 1105]

[1089], one of several monks who had talked in the presence of the boy Eadmer, q.v., about past events in the priory, Eadmer, *Hist. Nov.*, 107. See Blachmannus, Edwius.

[1104 × 1105], with Benjamin I and Ordwius, q.v., recd a letter from abp Anselm, *Anselm Letters*, no 355; he is mentioned in *ib.*, no 173 (possibly dated 1094).

n.d., 28 Sept., obit in BL Ms Arundel 68, fo 43v.

Item no 370 in the Eastry catalogue, listed as 'Earmmannus' has been identified by James, *Ancient Libraries*, 52, as his.

Roger de FARNINGHAM [Frenyngham

occ. 1261 occ. 1263/4

1261, 19 Dec., treasurer, CCA DCc MA1, fo 103v.

1262/6 and 1263/4, cellarer, CCA DCc MA1, fos 104v–109, AS9.

An inventory of the refectory, dated 1328, includes two *ciphi de murra* formerly his, Dart, *Antiq. Cant.*, xxi, xxii (BL Ms Cotton Galba E.iv, fos 179v, 180).

FARNLEGH

see Farley

Thomas FAUELEY [Faveley

occ. 1472/3

1472/3, treasurer, CCA DCc MA27, fo 1.

Eustace de FAVERSHAM

occ. 1237 occ. 1240

1237, Dec., before, apptd chaplain to the abp, Lawrence, 'Exile of Abp Edmund', 170.

1237, 1239, 5 Jan., chamberlain, *Gervase Cant.*, ii, 131, 146.

1237, went to Rome with the abp without licence of the prior and convent, *Gervase Cant.*, ii, 131.

1239, 7 Jan., and later in the yr, chaplain to the abp; though summoned to the irregular el. of a prior (without the involvement of the abp) he declined to be present as the abp had no other chaplain and the abp sent a letter to excuse his absence, *Gervase Cant.*, ii, 145–146, 155.

7 Mar., 1240, apptd prior of Dover by abp Edmund [Abingdon], CCA DCc Cart. Antiq. D.76; but see Robert de Holekumbe.

Note: he never held the office of prior despite the abp's nomination; see Lawrence, *St Edmund*, 318–319, 41. It is this apptment that identiifes him as Eustace de Faversham; Gervase refs to him only as Eustace.

Author of a life of abp Edmund de Abingdon; see both Wallace, *St Edmund*, and Lawrence, *St Edmund*; the former has transcribed it, pp. 543–588 from a copy preserved in BL Ms Cotton Julius D.vi. Lawrence's 'Exile of Abp Edmund', 170–172 discusses his awkward position attached to the abp with whom the chapter were at odds, and also his authorship of the Life.

John FAVERSHAM

occ. 1499/1500

1499/1500, celebrated his first mass and recd 8d. as a gift from the sacrist, Woodruff, 'Sacrist's Rolls', 66 (CCA DCc Sac. acct 60).

Note: this is prob. Richard Faversham below, q.v.

Richard FAVERSHAM [Feversham, Fevyrsham

occ. 1493 d. 1519

1493, 26 July, one of ten tonsured, *SL*, 192, CCA Lit. Ms D.12, fo 9v.

1494, 29 Mar., ord acol., Canterbury cathedral, *Reg. abp Morton*, i, no 443a.

1494, 19 Apr., prof., SL., 192; CCA Lit. Ms D.12, fo 9v.

1496, 2 Apr., ord subdcn, Canterbury cathedral, *Reg. abp Morton*, i, no 446c.

[1499/1500, celebrated his first mass]; see John Faversham above.

1509/10, 1511/13; and in 1513, 1514, 1515, all on 25 Dec., 1517, 25 Mar.; 1517/18, treasurer, Lambeth Ms 951/1/31, CCA DCc Treas. acct 24, Lambeth Ms 951/1/32; CCA Lit. Ms C.11, fos 55v, 56v, 57v, 58; Lambeth ED89.

1501, 26 Apr., 50th in order at the el. of an abp, Reg. R, fo 56v.

1511, Feb., gave the penitentiary, William Ingram I, q.v. 10d. *pro obitu matris sue*, CCA Lit. Ms C.11, fo 55.

1511, 2 Sept., 33rd on the visitation certificate, Wood-Legh, *Visit.*, 3 (Reg. abp Warham, i, fo 35v).

1519, 13 July, d. *in capella nostra aput London*, and the penitentiary recd 48s. 6d. from his *bursa*, CCA Lit. Ms C.11, fo 4v; his obit occ. in BL Ms Arundel 68, fo 34.

I Thomas de FAVERSHAM [Faveresham

occ. 1317

1317, 28 May, ord pr., Lambeth palace chapel, Reg. abp Reynolds, fo 178.

II Thomas FAVERSHAM [Favershame
occ. 1522 occ. 1540

1522, 11 Feb., one of ten tonsured, *SL*, 195, CCA Lit. Ms D.12, fo 11v.
1522, 24 Nov., prof., *ib.*
1526/7, celebrated his first mass and recd a small gift from the sacrist, Woodruff, 'Sacrist's Rolls', 72.
[1538, 8 Feb., after], subrefectorer, Pantin, *Cant. Coll. Ox.*, iii, 153.
1540, 4 Apr., refectorer, *L and P Henry VIII*, xv, no 452.

1534, 12 Dec., acknowledged the Act of Supremacy, *DK 7th Report*, Appndx 2, 282.
[1538, 8 Feb., after], in a list of monks prob. prepared for Thomas Cromwell he was described as 'a good man', 32 yrs old, Pantin, *Cant. Coll. Ox.*, iii, 153.
1540, 4 Apr., awarded £3 p.a. and became a scholar in the new foundation, *L and P Henry VIII*, xv, no 452.

FAVERSHAM
see also Feversham

Thomas FAY [ffay
occ. 1st half 13th c.

n.d., name occ. in the list in *SL*, 174, CCA Lit. Ms D.12, fo 1v.

Note: is this Thomas le Jay, q.v.?

John FAYRFORD [Faireford, Fayrforde, Ferford
occ. 1373/4

[1373], name occ. in the list in *SL*, 183, CCA Lit. Ms D.12, fo 4v.
1373, 8 Aug., one of two *clerici*, adm. and clothed by the prior comm. by the abp, Reg. abp Wittlesey, fo 62v.
1374, 27 Apr., one of six novices whose prof. the prior was comm. to rec., *ib.*, fo 130v.

FEER
see Ferr'

Thomas de FELBREG
occ. 1278

1278, subchamberlain, CCA DCc MA1, fo 128.

I FELIX
occ. [1115 × 1122] occ. 1155

[1115 × 1122], with Theodore I, q.v., attested a charter of abp Ralph d'Escures, *Eng. Epis. Acta*, Canterbury, 1070–1136, no 47, forthcoming.
1146, [soon after 19 Aug.], with Walter [Durdent], prior, q.v. and others attested an archiepiscopal grant to Christ Church, *Theobald Charters*, 538.
[1150 × 1152], with Milo [Crispin] and Walter I, q.v., all three chaplains of abp Theobald, witnessed a grant made by the abp, *ib.*, no 310.
[1153 × 1161], with William V subprior, q.v, and others witnessed a grant made by prior Wibert, q.v., and the convent at the request of abp Theobald, *ib.*, no 40.
1155, 28 Mar., with William V subprior, and others witnessed an agreement between Christ Church and Geoffrey de Malling, *ib.*, 536.

Note: there may be two monks by the same name conflated here.

II FELIX
occ. 1189/91

1189, c.6 Aug., named cellarer by abp Boniface vs the monks' request, *Epist. Cant.*, 299.
1189, 6 Oct., one of those cited by the abp to el. a prior, but was the only one who was willing to obey, *Epist. Cant.*, 312; see Benjamin II, Herveus II, Ludovicus and Zacharias.
1191, May, removed from office and expelled as a traitor by the prior and convent, *ib.*, 333–334.

III FELIX
occ. [?1201 × 1203]
n.d. [?1201, Feb., × 1203, 24 Aug.], a Felix, prior of Dover witnessed an archiepiscopal instrument, *Eng. Epis. Acta*, iii, no 445.

Note:
(1) This must be Felix de Rosa, q.v., who in *Lit. Cant.* iii, Appndx no 34 was apptd prior by abp Richard de Dover (1174–1184); this information, from CCA DCc Z.D4, 23, written much later may well be inaccurately dated, for *HRH*, 88, dates his apptment from 1197.
(2) In the Eastry catalogue, item nos 1023–1031 are listed as 'Libri Felicis', James, *Ancient Libraries*, 98.

William FERE[?N]BRAS
occ. 1st half 12th c.

n.d., name occ. in the list in *SL*, 173, CCA Lit. Ms D.12, fo 1v.

A wooden *ciphus*, formerly his, appears in an inventory of the refectory dated 1328, Dart, *Antiq. Cant.*, xxi (BL Ms Cotton Galba E.iv, fo 179).

FERFORD
see Fayrford

Adam FERR' [?Feer, Ferre
occ. 1st half 12th c.

n.d., name occ. in the list in *SL*, 173, CCA Lit. Ms D.12, fo 1v.

An inventory of the refectory, dated 1328, includes a silver *ciphus* formerly his, Dart, *Antiq. Cant.*, xix (BL Ms Cotton Galba E.iv, fo 178v).

John de FEVERSHAM [Fevirsham
d. 1326

1326, 2 July, d., CCA Lit. Ms D.12, fo 16.

Note: this is surely Stephen de Feversham II, q.v.

I Stephen de FEVERSHAM
d. 1295

n.d., name occ. in the list in *SL*, 175, CCA Lit. Ms D.12, fo 2.
1295, 26 Oct., d., CCA Lit. Ms D.12, fo 15.

II Stephen de FEVERSHAM
[Faveresham, Fevirsham, Fevresham
occ. 1295 d. [1326]

1295, 23 Nov., one of five prof., *SL*, 178, CCA Lit. Ms D.12, fo 3.
1299, 19 Sept., ord dcn, Littlebourne, *Reg. abp Winchelsey*, 930.
1300, 4 June, ord pr., Smeeth chapel by Aldington, *ib.*, 936.
[1314/26], lector, see below.
1303/4, sent with Andrew de Hardys q.v., to study at the university of Paris and provided by the treasurers with £46 19s. 3d., for travel and other necessities, Pantin, *Cant. Coll. Ox.*, iv, 173. See Sullivan, *Benedictine Monks at Paris*, no 246.
1304/5, recd more funds through the agent who had been sent to arrange for the collection of the wine from the priory's French vineyards, Pantin, *ib.*, iv, 173–174; the agent carried with him a letter from the prior dated 6 Sept., CUL Ms Ee.5.31, fo 101^v. Geoffrey Poterel, q.v., was also a student this yr and £33 19s. were provided for the two of them, *ib.*, iv, 174.
1305/6, with Poterel returned from Paris, having recd £13 8s. to cover their expenses from Christmas until their return, Pantin, *ib.*
1314/15, first mention of his apptment as lector in the cloister; he recd 10s. 'pro tunica et corsetto', Pantin, *Cant. Coll. Ox.*, iv, 176 (Lambeth Ms 242, fo 301).
1316, 1 Apr., sent with Walter de Norwyco, q.v., to inform the abp of the state of affairs concerning Robert de Thaneto, q.v., CUL Ms Ee.5.31, fo 165.
1318/19, as claustral lector recd money for parchment, and also 10s. for his clerk; his own 'salary' was 20s., Pantin, *ib.*, iv, 176 (Lambeth Ms 242, fo 331–331^v).
1322/4, lector, Pantin, *ib.*, iv, 177 (Lambeth Ms, 242, fos 135^v, 141). On 10 Sept. 1324 bp Hamo de Hethe (q.v., under Rochester) wrote to the prior and chapter to require them to be more generous in rewarding their lector and ordering them to provide him with better quarters for study, *Reg. Hethe* (Rochester), 341.
[1326], 2/3 July, d., CCA Lit. Ms D.12, fo 16, states 'John' de Feversham, q.v. which is a mistake. BL Ms Arundel 68, fo 32^v gives his obit as 3 July and notes that he had been first lector in the cloister for a period of twelve yrs.

His own collection of books is listed in the Eastry catalogue, nos 1738–1748 in James, *Ancient Libraries*, 139; and one volume is noted in Canterbury college inventories, e.g. that of 1443, Pantin, *Cant. Coll. Ox.*, i, 5 (CCA DCc Cart. Antiq. O.134). Note, however, that James attributes this collection to Stephen de Feversham I which would be correct if the latest entries in the catalogue are those of abp Winchelsey as he stated (*ib.*, xxxix); however, this Stephen seems a more likely candidate.

An inventory of missing service books dated 1 Mar. 1338 held him responsible for a missing ordinale, *Lit. Cant.*, no 618 (Reg. L, fo 104).

His name heads a list of vestments acquired *temp.* prior Eastry and printed in Legg and Hope, *Inventories*, 67 (BL Ms Cotton Galba E.iv, fo 117^v).

An inventory of the refectory, dated 1328, includes a silver *ciphus* formerly his, and three *de murra*, Dart, *Antiq. Cant.*, xviii, xxii, xxiii (BL Ms Cotton Galba E.iv, fos 179, 180, 180^v).

I William de FEVERSHAM [Fevirsham
occ. 1st half 13th c.

n.d., name occ. in the list in *SL*, 174, CCA Lit. Ms D.12, fo 1^v.

II William FEVERSHAM
occ. 1421/3

1421, 4 Apr., one of six prof., *SL*, 186, CCA Lit. Ms D.12, fo 6^v.
1423, 18 Dec., ord subdcn, Rochester cathedral, *Reg. abp Chichele*, iv, 358.
n.d., acc. to Chron Wm Glastynbury, fo 168^v/162^v he departed *in apostesia* [*sic*].

FEVERSHAM
see also Faversham

Thomas FLETE
occ. 1450 d. 1457

1450, 25 Jan., one of seven prof., *SL*, 189, CCA Lit. Ms D.12, fo 7^v.
1450, 3 Apr., ord acol., Canterbury cathedral, Reg. abp Stafford, fo 204.
1451, 20 Mar., ord subdcn, Canterbury cathedral, *ib.*, fo 205^v.
1452, 8 Apr., ord dcn, Canterbury cathedral, *ib.*, fo 206^v.
1457, 15 Aug., pr., d., and the funeral rites took place in the infirmary chapel, *Chron. Stone*, 69; described as *conventualis* in CCA Lit. Ms D.12, fo 25^v. His obit is in BL Ms Arundel 68, fo 38.

FLORENTIUS [Florencius
occ. [1153 × 1161]

[1153 × 1161], *temp.* abp Theobald and prior Wibert, q.v., with William V subprior, q.v.

and others witnessed a grant made by the prior and convent at the request of the abp, *Theobald Charters*, no 40.

n.d., 17 Mar., pr., whose obit occ. in BL Ms Arundel 68, fo 20^v.

FOLCARDUS [Folcher

occ. [before 1068]

n.d., the obit of a monk, *levita*, by this name occ. on 10 Aug., in BL Ms Arundel 68, fo 37^v.

According to Dart, *Antiq. Cant.*, 179, a Folcard fl. *temp.* Ernulf, prior, q.v., wrote the life of John of Beverley (which is now BL Ms Cotton Faustina B.iv.8) at the request of abp Aldred of York (d. c. 1069), and also the life of Odo. See Sharpe, *Latin Writers.*

Note: this is prob. the same monk who was acting abbot of Thorney c. 1068–1084 and a former monk of St Bertin; see *HRH*, 74.

John FOLKESTON [Folkston

occ. 1467 d. [1489 × 1492]

1467, 28 Mar., ord acol., Canterbury cathedral, *Reg. abp Bourgchier*, 399.

1467, 19 Sept., one of six prof., *SL*, 190, CCA Lit. Ms D.12, fo 8.

1468, 12 Mar., ord subdcn, Canterbury cathedral, *Reg. abp Bourgchier*, 398.

1468, 16 Apr., ord dcn, Canterbury cathedral, *ib.*, 400.

1471, 13 Apr., ord pr., Canterbury cathedral, *ib.*, 407.

[1489 × 1492], *conventualis*, d., CCA Lit. Ms D.12, fos 27, 31^v; his obit on 22 Jan. is in BL Ms Arundel 68, fo 14.

William de FOLKESTON

occ. 2nd half 13th c.

n.d., name occ. in the list in *SL*, 174, CCA Lit. Ms D.12, fo 2.

Robert FONTEYN [Fonten, Fonteyne

occ. 1506 occ. 1516

1506, 21 Mar., one of six tonsured, *SL*, 193, CCA Lit. Ms D.12, fo 10^v.

1506, 11 Apr., ord acol., Canterbury cathedral, Reg. abp Warham, ii, fo 262^v.

1506, 30 Sept., prof., SL., 193, CCA Lit. Ms D.12, fo 10^v.

1507, 3 Apr., ord subdcn, Canterbury cathedral, Reg. abp Warham, ii, fo 263.

n.d., as a junior he was instructed by William Molassh, II, q.v., his *magister regule, et perfecit*, Pantin, *Cant. Coll. Ox.*, iv, 54 (CCA DCc Ms Scrap Book B.186).

1511, 2 Sept., 66th in order on the visitation certificate, Wood-Legh, *Visit.*, 3 (Reg. abp Warham, i, fo 35^v).

1516, Sept./Oct., recd 4d. from William Ingram I, q.v., CCA Lit. Ms C.11, fo 128.

n.d., a slip containing two short inventories of his goods [*boni*] and those of *senioris mei defuncti* is now CCA DCc DE191.

William FONTEYN [Fontayn, Fontayne, Fonten, Founteyn, Funteyn

occ. 1431 d. [1489 × 1492]

1431, 18 Apr., one of four prof., *SL*, 187, CCA Lit. Ms D.12, fo 7.

1433, 28 Mar., ord subdcn, Charing, *Reg. abp Chichele*, iv, 377.

1434, 13 Mar., ord dcn, infirmary chapel, *ib.*, iv, 379.

1436, 3 Mar., ord pr., infirmary chapel, *ib.*, iv, 384.

1449/50, treasurer, Lambeth ED82.

1450, Apr., warden of manors, CCA DCc Bocking acct 72.

1451, 20 July, 8 Dec.; 1454, 21 Oct., treasurer, CCA DCc DE15C/28, 20, 24.

1455/6, first treasurer and one of the eight *barones*, CCA DCc Prior acct 10, Treas. acct 16.

1456, 28 Oct.; 1457, 4 Jan., treasurer, CCA DCc DE15C/3, 7.

1458, 18 Oct., 1460/1, sacrist, CCA DCc BB 62/6, Sac. acct 42.

1466/7, chamberlain, CCA DCc Chamb. acct 64.

1468/9, 1471/2, 25 Dec., bartoner, Lambeth ED56, ED57, CCA DCc Carucate Sergeant acct 36.

1473/4, treasurer, CCA DCc MA27, fo 12.

1466, 17 Feb., 20th in order in an inventory listing *jocalia fratrum* [given by him and/or assigned for his use], Reg. N, fo 231^v.

[1489 × 1492], *stationarius*, d., CCA Lit. Ms D.12, fos 27, 31^v; his obit on 22 Apr. is in BL Ms Arundel 68, fo 24^v.

A vol. acquired by [*perquisito*] him is listed among the books in the 1506 inventory of Richard Stone, q.v., Pantin, *Cant. Coll. Ox.*, i, 88 (CCA DCc Inventory Box A, no 3).

John FORDE [Foorde, Ford

occ. 1399 d. 1403

1399, n.d., one of six prof. *SL*, 185, CCA Lit. Ms D.12, fo 5^v.

1399, 20 Dec., ord subdcn, Canterbury cathedral, Reg abp Arundel, i, fo 325.

1400, 3 Apr., ord dcn, Hoath chapel in Reculver parish, *ib.*, i, fo 326.

1401, 19 Mar., ord pr., Canterbury cathedral, *ib.*, i, fo 328.

1403, 10 Oct., d., CCA Lit. Ms D.12, fo 18.

Robert de FORLEE

see Faghe, Faleweye, Foxhele

William FOWGHELL, FOWLE

see Vowle

Robert de FOXHELE [Foxele, Foxle
occ. [1281/2] occ. 1287

[1281/2], one of five prof., *SL*, 177, CCA Lit. Ms D.12, fo 3.

1287, 23 May, with Walter de Chillenden, q.v., sent by the prior and chapter to the bp of Bath and Wells and to the king on negotiations concerning Dover priory, CUL Ms Ee.5.31, fo 27v.

An inventory of missing service books dated 1 Mar. 1338 includes his *diurnale*, *Lit. Cant.*, no 618 (Reg. L, fo 104).

Two of his books are in the Eastry catalogue, nos 1485–1486, James, *Ancient Libraries*, 125.

Richard de FRAKYNHAM
occ. 1st half 13th c.

n.d., name occ. in the *post exilium* list in *SL*, 172, CCA Lit. Ms D.12, fo 1.

Note: *Gervase Cant.*, ii, 131 and Wallace, *St Edmund*, 163 have a M. Thomas Frakenham, possibly this monk, who accompanied the abp to Rome and d. en route.

FREBEL
see Frevell

FREMBULDUS
n.d.

n.d., 9 Feb, obit occ. in BL Ms Arundel 68, fo 16.

Andrew FRENGHAM [Frengeham, Frengsham
occ. 1416 d. 1427

1416, 22 June, one of eight prof., *SL*, 186, CCA Lit. Ms D.12, fo 6.

1417, 10 Apr., ord acol., Canterbury cathedral, *Reg. abp Chichele*, iv, 327.

1418, 26 Mar., ord subdcn, Canterbury cathedral, *ib.*, iv, 332.

1419, 1 Apr., ord dcn, chapel within the priory, *ib.*, i, 191.

1419, 15 Apr., ord pr., chapel within the priory, *ib.*, i, 193.

1427, 2/3 Dec., d., after being ill in the infirmary for six months *diu ante mortem inunctus est*; the mass and *commendatio* were taken by the subprior, Henry Sutton, q.v., *Chron. Stone*, 14. His obit on 4 Dec. is in BL Ms Arundel 68, fo 50.

R de FRENINGEHAM
occ. 1261

1261, one of three treasurers, CCA DCc MA1, fo 103v; see John de Bocton and Roger de Wroteham.

Thomas FRENSHE
occ. 1353

1353, 27 Sept., one of five prof., *SL*, 181, CCA Lit. Ms D.12, fo 4.

John FRENYNGHAM [Fernyngham, Framyngham, Fremyngham, Frennyngham
occ. 1465 d. 1470

1465, 4 Apr., one of seven prof., *SL*, 190, CCA Lit. Ms D.12, fo 8.

1465, 13 Apr., ord acol., no place named, *Reg. abp Bourgchier*, 391.

1465, 8 June, ord subdcn, Canterbury cathedral, *ib.*, 395.

1467, 28 Mar., ord dcn, Canterbury cathedral, *ib.*, 399.

1470, 21 Apr., ord pr., Canterbury cathedral, *ib.*, 406.

1470, 8 July, was vested with all the brethren at the high mass attended by the abp, 'tunc existente in cursu diaconorum', *Chron. Stone*, 112.

1470, 9 Oct., d. of plague, *Chron. Stone*, 114; in CCA Lit. Ms D.12, fo 26 described as *conventualis*. His obit is in BL Ms Arundel 68, fo 44v.

Note: there is also a second John Frenyngham whose obit occ. on 15 May, BL Ms Arundel 68, fo 27v.

FRENYNGHAM
see also Farningham

George FREVELL [Frebel, Frevel, Frydell
occ. 1527 occ. 1540

1527, 25 May, one of twelve tonsured, *SL*, 195, CCA Lit. Ms D.12, fo 12.

1528, 2 Mar., prof., *ib.*

[1538, 8 Feb., after], 1540, 4 Apr., subchaplain to the prior, Pantin, *Cant. Coll. Ox.*, iii, 153, *L and P Henry VIII*, xv, no 452.

1540 and possibly before, prob. scholar at Canterbury college; scholar in the new foundation, *L and P Henry VIII*, xv, no 452.

1534, 12 Dec., acknowledged the Act of Supremacy, *DK 7th Report*, Appndx 2, 282.

[1538, 8 Feb., after], in a list of monks prob. prepared for Thomas Cromwell he was described as 'wytty' and 30 yrs old, Pantin, *Cant. Coll. Ox.*, iii, 153.

1540, 4 Apr., awarded £3 p.a., *L and P Henry VIII*, xv, no 452.

BRUO, 1501–1540, suggests that he is the Mr. Frewell who is found as a monk of the newly refounded Westminster Abbey in c. 1556; see E.H. Pearce, *The Monks of Westminster* (Cambridge, 1916), 214. See also John Langdon III.

FREVELL
see also John Menys

FREWINUS
n.d.

n.d., 24 Dec., obit occ. in BL Ms Cotton Nero C.ix, fo 18.

John de FROME D.Th. [?*alias* Bodi, Body
occ. 1337 occ. 1365/6

1337, 30 Sept., one of three prof., *SL*, 180, CCA Lit. Ms D.12, fo 4.

1351/7, lector, who recd regular payments for his office, Pantin, *Cant. Coll. Ox.*, iv, 181 (Lambeth Ms 243, fos 78ᵛ, 83ᵛ, 88ᵛ, 89, 92, 92ᵛ, 97, 97ᵛ, 98, 102ᵛ; also Reg. L, fos 85, 88).
1365/6, recd similar payments as above but not named as lector, Pantin, *ib.*, iv, 183 (Lambeth Ms 243, fo 136); see below.

1340, [June], scholar at Canterbury college, who was given licence to remain in Oxford during the vacation but for whom a horse was provided in case he wished to return to Canterbury for a visit, *Lit. Cant.*, nos 690, 691 (Reg. L, fo 75).
1342, Aug.; 1343, July; 1350/1, at Oxford, Pantin, *Cant. Coll. Ox.*, iv, 180–181.
n.d., D.Th., so described in BL Ms Arundel 68, fo 12ᵛ.

1349, 4 June, 46th in order at the el. of a bp, and one of the three *compromissorii* who were named to choose ten more *compromissorii* to join them in the el., Reg. G, fos 60ᵛ, 61.
1349, 8/9 Sept., 45th in order at the el. and again chosen as one of three to choose ten more to form the electoral body; he also preached at the el., *ib.*, fos 76ᵛ–78.
1357, 14 Sept., one of the monks *in remotis agentibus* and unable to be present for the abp's visitation, Reg. L, fos 89ᵛ–90.
n.d., 10 Jan., obit in BL Ms Arundel, fo 12ᵛ, which says that he was claustral lector for 'ten yrs and more'.

Name in
(1) CCA Lit. Ms A.1, Richard de Middleton (14th c.) which he obtained *de perquisicione*; the name, on fo 192ᵛ, has been partially obliterated but J. Fro' remains. This volume is no 22 in Ingram's list, James, *Ancient Libraries*, 153. See William Ingram I.
(2) CUL Ms Ff.5.31, James de Voragine (late 13th c.) which is no 1793 in the Eastry catalogue, James, *Ancient Libraries*, 141, 511; his name is on fo 1.

Note: Pantin suggests that his patronymic may have been Bodi, a monk, who turns up at Oxford in 1357, *Cant. Coll. Ox.*, iv, 6. See the entry under Body.

FRYDELL
see Frevell

FULLER
see John Holyngborne II

FUNTEYN
see Fonteyn

FURSEUS
n.d.

n.d., 18 Nov., pr. whose obit occ. in BL Mss Cotton Nero C.ix, fo 16 and Arundel 68, fo 48ᵛ.

John FYNCH [Fynche, Vynch, Wynch, de Wynchelsee, Wynchilse
occ. 1358/9 d. 1391

1377–1391, prior: el. c.27 June 1377, apptd [*prefecit*] by the abp on 25 July, Reg. abp Sudbury, fo 39, but see below; d. 25 Jan. 1391, Reg. abp Courtenay, i, fo 333ᵛ.

1358/9, 28 Oct., one of nine prof., *SL*, 181, CCA Lit. Ms D.12, fo 4.
1360, 29 Feb., ord acol., abp's chapel, Otford, Reg. abp Islip, fo 318 (as Wynchelse).
1360, 4 Apr., ord subdcn, abp's chapel, Saltwood, *ib.*, fo 318ᵛ (as Wynchelse).
1361, 18 Dec., ord dcn, Charing, *ib.*, fo 320.
1362, 11 June, ord pr., Mayfield, *ib.*, fo 321ᵛ (where he is named John Vynch de Wynchilse).

1368/Apr. 1370, chamberlain, CCA DCc Chamb accts 47, 48; his apptment on 6 Oct. 1368 is in *Reg. abp Langham*, 315, and the renewal of the apptment in Reg. abp Wittlesey, fo 13, dated 22 June 1369.
1370, July/Sept., 1370/1, bartoner, CCA DCc, Bart. accts, 46, 47.
1371, chamberlain and chaplain to the prior, CCA DCc MA2, fo 266ᵛ.
1371/6, also 1372/7, bartoner, CCA DCc Bart. accts 49–53, MA2 fos 270ᵛ–312.
1376, 14/15 Nov., *magister ordinis*, CCA Lit. Ms D.12, fo 4ᵛ.
While prior he held the following office:
1378/9, warden of manors, CCA DCc MA2, fos 313ᵛ–316ᵛ.

1377, 27 June was the date fixed by the abp to preside at the el. [by scrutiny], which seems reasonable since prior Mongeham, q.v. had d. on 14 June; however, when the reg. goes on to speak of the next day as 8k Aug. and the day after the el., the latter would appear to have been on 24 July, Reg. abp Sudbury, fo 39–39ᵛ. It seems unusual to delay the el., or to delay his announcement of the result of the scrutiny, for a month. There is confusion in the register because the scribe who made the entries was trying to save time and space by referring back to earlier entries which were similar apart from the names and dates.
1378/9, was successful in obtaining from pope Urban VI the grant of pontificals through the negotiations of Thomas Chillenden I, q.v., at the curia. See Walter III.
1391, 25 Jan., d., and was buried in the martyrdom, Dart, *Antiq. Cant.*, 185, on 14 Feb., acc. to Reg. abp Courtenay, i, fo 336ᵛ. His obit is

in BL Ms Arundel 68, fo 14, where it states that he was prior for 13 yrs, 6 months, 2 wks, which would take us back to an early July date for the el.!

A few leaves of the *sed. vac.* register of letters of prior Fynch, for the yr 1381 together with several other items dated c. 1381–1384, occ. in Oxford, Bod. Ms Ashmole 794, fos 248–265.

The 'Anon. Chron.', 58–61 described him as a man 'innocens manibus et mundo corde, venerabilis ac Deo devotus' who relieved the debt which he had inherited from his predecessor [Stephen Mongeham, q.v.] mainly by the power of prayer and with the practical aid of Thomas Chillenden and William Woghope, q.v. Cambridge, Corpus Christi College Ms 298, fo 119, describes him as a 'vir nobilis de genere de Vynchis de Wynchilsee' and observes that he began the new nave, *ib.* The obit in Lambeth Ms 20, fo 161, adds the following: 'in cuius tempore in spiritualibus et temporalibus multipliciter vig[ora]vit ecclesia X[i] Cant.'

William le FYNCH [Fync', Vynch

d. 1295

n.d., name occ. in the list in *SL*, 176, CCA Lit. Ms D.12, fo 2ᵛ.

1295, 19 Oct., d., CCA Lit. Ms D.12, fo 15.

Thomas FYNDEN [Fyndenn

occ. 1431 occ. 1438

1431, 25 Nov., previously a prof. monk of Westminster who signed and read [aloud] his prof. in front of the high altar before the prior at the solemn mass; he was then assigned his place as first *in cursu diaconatus* after John Tenham, q.v., *SL*, 187 and CCA Lit. Ms D.12, fo 7 (Reg. S, fos 108ᵛ–109 where the date is 25 Oct.).

1438, 12 May, left the monastery *in apostasia*, *ib.* According to CCA Lit. Ms D.12, fo 24, 'per unum terminum apostatavit et consumptis expensis in habutu seculari revenit', and was granted licence to transfer to Folkestone; but with the help of friends he returned to Westminster.

Note: he had been prof. at Westminster in 1428/9 and had been given licence to transfer to Canterbury; see E.H. Pearce, *The Monks of Westminster* (Cambridge, 1916), 143.

G.

occ. 1266 occ. 1314

1266, chamberlain, CCA DCc MA1, fo 109.

1282, cellarer, CCA DCc Treas. acct 1.

1313/14, subprior, CCA DCc Great Chart acct 28.

Note: there are prob. several monks included here!

GABRIEL

n.d.

n.d., 1 Sept., dcn, whose obit. occ. in BL Ms Arundel 68, fo 40.

Walter GABRIEL [de Maydystan

occ. 1364 occ. 1386

1364, one of eleven prof., *SL*, 182, CCA Lit. Ms D.12, fo 4ᵛ.

1374, 1377, *custos* of St Mary in crypt, CCA DCc MA2, fos 281ᵛ, 312.

1386, *magister ordinis* with Thomas Wykyng, q.v., *SL*, 183, CCA Lit. Ms D.12, fo 5.

n.d., precentor, CCA Lit. Ms D.12, fo 4ᵛ.

1374, 30 June, 37th in order at the el. of an abp, Reg. G, fos 173ᵛ–175ᵛ as Walter Gabriel de Maidest[on.

1381, 31 July, 26th at the el. of an abp, *ib.*, fo 225ᵛ.

1383/4, recd 12d. from the prior *pro benedictione*, Lambeth Ms 243, fo 192ᵛ.

Note: of these entries all but one specify Walter Gabriel, but see Walter Maydeston I and II.

Nicholas GALEYE [Galy, Galye, Gayly

occ. 1365 d. 1405

1365, one of eight prof., *SL*, 182, CCA Lit. Ms D.12, fo 4ᵛ.

1367, 18 Sept., ord subdcn, Lambeth palace chapel, *Reg. abp Langham*, 383.

1368, 4 Mar., ord dcn, Canterbury cathedral, *ib.*, 388 (transcribed as Caly).

1370, 21 Sept., ord pr., Saltwood, Reg. abp Wittlesey, fo 166ᵛ.

1380/1, 1386/90, fourth prior, Lambeth Ms 243, fos 180ᵛ, 204ᵛ, 208ᵛ, 212ᵛ, 216ᵛ; in 1389/90 William Kenerton, q.v. was also fourth prior, and so he prob. succ. Galeye in office.

[1394], 21 Nov., *magister ordinis*, *SL*, 184, CCA Lit. Ms D.12, fo 5.

1374, 30 June, 42nd in order at the el. of an abp, Reg. G, fos 173ᵛ–175ᵛ.

1381, 31 July, 31st at the el. of an abp, *ib.*, fo 225ᵛ.

1381/2, 1383/4, recd small sums *pro benedictione*, Lambeth Ms 243, fos 188ᵛ, 192ᵛ.

1386/90, as fourth prior he recd from the prior annual gifts of 20s., *ib.*, fos 204ᵛ, 208ᵛ, 212ᵛ, 216ᵛ.

1396, 7 Aug., 13th at the el. of an abp, Reg. G, fo 234ᵛ.

1405, 12 June, d., in the 41st yr of monastic life, CCA Lit. Ms D.12, fo 18.

GALEYE

see also Calys

GALFRIDUS

see Geoffrey

John GARARD [Garrard, Garrarde, Garrod, Gerard, Girrard

occ. 1493 occ. 1540

1493, 26 July, one of ten tonsured, *SL*, 192, CCA Lit. Ms D.12, fo 9v.

1494, 29 Mar., ord acol., Canterbury cathedral, *Reg. abp Morton*, i, no 443a.

1494, 19 Apr., prof., *SL*, 192, CCA Lit. Ms D.12, fo 9v.

1496, 2 Apr., ord subdcn, Canterbury cathedral, *Reg. abp Morton*, i, no 445b.

1497, 25 Mar., ord dcn, Canterbury cathedral, *ib.*, i, no 446c.

1500/1, celebrated his first mass and recd a small sum from the sacrist, CCA DCc Sac. acct 70.

1512, Apr., subsacrist, CCA Lit. Ms C.11, fo 54v.

1514/15, Sept. to Apr., *magister ordinis* and fourth prior, CCA Lit. Ms D.12, fo 11, CCA Lit. Ms C.11, fo 57.

1518, 25 Mar.; 1518, 25 Dec; 1519/20, May to Feb.; 1520, 3 Feb., *magister ordinis* and third prior, CCA Lit. Ms C.11, fos 59v, 60. Acc. to CCA DCc MA14, fo 69, he was *magister ordinis* in 1518/19.

1520/33, 1533/8 May; 1539, May; 1540, 4 Apr., bartoner, CCA DCc MA14, fos 142, 203v, 215, 252v, 285, MA30, fo 156, MA15, fos 37, 87, 155, 195v, MA16, fos 53v, 96, 142v, U15/17/4, 7, *L and P Henry VIII*, x, no 452.

1533/4, May to Mar., bartoner, as above, and *magister ordinis*, *SL*, 196, CCA Lit. Ms D.12, fo 12v.

n.d., *magister regule*, who instructed a number of monk novices: [Roger] Eastry, [Guy] Chillenden, [William] Wyngham, N[icholas] Herst, T[homas] Wylfryde, R[ichard] Godmersham [II] and [Thomas] Milton, q.v., Pantin, *Cant. Coll. Ox.*, iv, 54 (CCA DCc Ms Scrap Book B.186).

1501, 26 Apr., 49th in order at the el. of an abp, Reg. R, fo 56v.

1511, 2 Sept., 32nd on the visitation certificate, Wood-Legh, *Visit.*, 3 (Reg. abp Warham, i, fo 35v).

1518/19, 1520/1, spent time in the infirmary, CCA DCc Infirm. accts 1, 2.

1534, 12 Dec., acknowledged the Act of Supremacy, *DK 7th Report*, Appndx 2, 282.

[1538, 8 Feb., after], in a list of monks prob. prepared for Thomas Cromwell he was described as a 'symple' man, aged 60 yrs, Pantin, *Cant. Coll. Ox.*, iii, 152.

1540, 4 Apr., awarded £8 p.a., *L and P Henry VIII*, xv, no 452.

William GARARD [Gerard

occ. 1465 d. 1487

1465, 4 Apr., one of seven prof., *SL*, 190, CCA Lit. Ms D.12, fo 8.

1465, 13 Apr., ord subdcn, no place named, *Reg. abp Bourgchier*, 391.

1467, 28 Mar., ord dcn, Canterbury cathedral, *ib.*, 399.

1469, 1 Apr., ord pr., Canterbury cathedral, *ib.*, 402.

1468/9, celebrated his first mass and recd a gift from the sacrist, CCA DCc Sac. acct 47.

1479, chancellor with Thomas Bradgare, q.v., Reg. S, fo 300–300v.

1487, 20 Nov., d. 'ex calido idrepio infecto' at the age of 42, CCA Lit. Ms D.12, fos 27, 31; his obit is in BL Ms Arundel, fos 27, 31.

On 20 Apr. 1454, a Thomas Garard, son of T. Garard of Canterbury, was baptized in the cathedral and had for one of his godparents the prior, *Chron. Stone*, 60; these were prob. relatives.

William GARDINER

see Sandwych

[Thomas dictus GARDYN

?occ. 1307

1307, a monk of Worcester, q.v., who possibly transferred to Canterbury.]

Lambert GARGATE [Garegate

occ. [1163 × 1167]

[1163 × 1167], in an agreement issued by prior Wibert, q.v., there is ref. to property to be given by him to the monks when he recd the habit on his death bed, Urry, *Canterbury*, 400–401. Some of his relatives are named in another deed dated before 23 Mar. 1167, before he became a monk, *ib.*, 399.

See also Lambert I.

GARROD

see Garard

John GARWYNTON [Garrynton, Garyngton, Garynton,

occ. 1480 d. 1486

1480, 25 Jan., one of six prof., *SL*, 191, CCA Lit. Ms D.12, fo 8v.

1480, 1 Apr., ord acol., Canterbury cathedral, *Reg. abp Bourgchier*, 430.

1480, 23 Sept., ord subdcn, Canterbury cathedral, *ib.*, 431.

1483, 29 Mar., ord dcn, Canterbury cathedral, *ib.*, 439.

1486, 25 Mar., ord pr., Canterbury cathedral, *ib.*, 455 (transcribed as Earwynton).

1486, 22 Sept., d., at the age of 26 of an illness called *strangwyr*'; at his funeral 'presente in choro cuius seneys dat' est per dominum Willelmum Sellyng prior [*sic*] matri sue', CCA Lit. Ms D.12, fo 26v/31. His obit, on 24 Sept., is in BL Ms Arundel 68, fo 42v.

Thomas de GARWYNTON [Garwenton, Gawynton
occ. 1328 occ. 1374

1328, 25 Nov., one of seven prof., *SL*, 179, CCA Lit. Ms D.12, fo 3^v.

1333, subcellarer, CCA DCc DE3, fo 3c.
1336/7, subchaplain to the prior, CCA DCc Chartham acct 23.
1337, *custos* of the high altar, CCA DCc MA2, fo 255.
1339/44, chaplain to the prior, CCA DCc Agney acct 43, Meopham acct 80, MA68, Bocking accts 24, 25.
1346/7, Apr., cellarer, CCA DCc Agney acct 47.
1348/9, June, warden of manors, CCA DCc Bocking acct 30.
1349/50, cellarer, CCA DCc Arrears acct 30.
1350/1, chaplain to the prior, CCA DCc Treas. acct 27, fo 3^v; see Peter de Sales.
1352/3, Mar., granator, CCA DCc Gran. acct 36.
1352/3, 1354, Dec./6 Aug., chaplain to the prior, CCA DCc Bocking acct 31, Chartham accts 33, 34.
1355/6, cellarer, CCA DCc Ebony acct 55.
1356/7, granator, Lambeth Ms 1025/8.
1359/60, 1361/2, cellarer, CCA DCc Barksore acct 46, Ebony acct 60; his apptment, on 24 Sept. 1359 is in Reg. abp Islip, fo 151–151^v and the abp chose him (from the three nominees) to succ. John Richemonde, q.v., because he was *aptiorem et utiliorem*.
1362/3, granator, CCA DCc Arrears acct 70.
1366, 10 May, 1366/7, sacrist, Reg. G, fo 147^v, CCA DCc Bart. acct 43.
1371/3, Jan., cellarer, CCA MA2, fos 266^v–282, which lists him as still cellarer in 1374; however, he was absolved from the office on 19 Jan. 1373, acc. to Reg. abp Wittlesey, fo 58.

1338, 1 Mar., in an inventory of missing service books, he was reported to have mislaid a psalter belonging to Peter [de Sales] q.v., *Lit. Cant.*, no 618 (Reg. L, fo 104).

1349, 4 June, 21st in order at the el. of an abp and named as one of the ten *compromissorii* chosen by the initially named three *compromissorii* to form an electoral body of thirteen, Reg. G, fo 60^v.

1349, 8/9 Sept., 20th at the el. of an abp and named as one of the thirteen *compromissorii*, *ib.*, fos 76, 77.

1366, 10 May, chosen again, this time as one of seven *compromissorii* in the el. of an abp, *ib.*, fo 148.

1374, 30 June, 3rd in order at the el. of an abp, *ib.*, fos 173^v–175^v.

John at GATE
n.d.

n.d., 7 May, obit occ. in BL Ms Arundel 68, fo 26^v.

Robert de GATHERST [Catehurst, Gattherst
occ. 1329 d. 1334

1329, 9 Oct., one of eight prof., *SL*, 180, CCA Lit. Ms D.12, fo 3^v.

1334, 22 Nov., d., CCA Lit. Ms D.12, fo 16.

In an inventory of missing books dated 1 Mar. 1883, his Processionale was reported missing, *Lit., Cant.*, no 618 (Reg. L, fo 104).

GAWYNTON
see Garwynton

GAUFRIDUS
see Geoffrey

GAYLY
see Galeye

GELDWIN [Geldewinus
occ. [?c. 1180]

[?c. 1180], there is a fragmentary ref. to a gift of land in Canterbury by Joseph the pr., *pro Geldewino patre suo*, which suggests a later conversion [to monastic life], Urry, *Canterbury*, 156 (CCA DCc Shadwell Mss no 13). (Urry suggested the date c. 1180.)

GELYNGHAM
see Gyllyngham

I GEOFFREY [Goffridus, Gosfrid (Prior I)
occ. 1125/8

1125–1128, prior: first occ. after May 1125; apptd abbot of Dunfermline, 1128, *Fasti*, ii, 9.

n.d., 9 June, obit in BL Ms Arundel 68, fo 30^v and Lambeth Ms 20, fo 193.

II GEOFFREY (Prior II)
occ. 1187 d. 1213

1191–1213, prior: el. *sed. vac.* 10 May 1191 by the monks after expelling Osbern de Bristol q.v.; went into exile with the community in July 1207 and d. 15 June 1213, *Fasti*, ii, 10–11, *HRH*, 34.

1187, Mar./[91], subprior, *Epist. Cant.*, 21, 47 (as G.); and see below.

1187/8, during the absence of prior Honorius II q.v., at the curia he wrote a series of letters to Honorius to keep him informed of the state of affairs in Canterbury; some of these are in *Epist. Cant.* 31, 49, 154, 286, 314–15, 320. While the prior was pleading the convent's case vs abp Baldwin at Rome he, as subprior, came under great pressure from the king and other bps as well as the abp to submit, as Gervase recounts in detail, *Gervase Cant.*, i, 394–408. He and other monks were excommunicated 17 Jan. 1188, before his flight, *Gervase Cant.*, i, 400–402, 452, 454, *Epist. Cant.*, 302–303, 307–308.

1189, May, one of the monks with whom the abp refused to negotiate, *Epist. Cant.*, 292.

1189, Aug., fled to Arras from Canterbury after the abp demanded his removal from office and threatened to seize him, *Epist. Cant.*, 298, 299, 302; in Sept. he wrote to Alan II, q.v., third prior, *ib.*, 314. See also John de Bocking and Ralph de Orpynton.

[1191, late Sept.], recd. a letter from Godfrey de Lucy, bp of Winchester, *Eng. Epis. Acta*, viii, no 196.

n.d., travelled to Rouen accompanied by some of his brethren taking relics of Becket and was arrested at Amiens and held for a time, *Materials Becket*, ii, 268–269.

1198, Oct./1199, the dispute with the abp was resumed after the el. of Hubert Walter and the prior and chapter renewed their appeal; he set out for Rome after the convent property had been seized by the king, *Gervase Cant.*, i, 574–575. Letters written to the Christ Church community give details of his travels: he was in Pisa in late Nov., after meeting Salomon q.v. in Lucca, and in Dec. reached Rome where he had a 'hopeful interview' with the pope, *Epist. Cant.*, 451–452, 458, 477–478.

1205, c. 13 July, was present with abp Hubert Walter during his last moments, *Gervase Cant.*, ii, 413.

1213, 15 June, d. *in transmarinis*, *Gervase Cant.*, ii, 108.

Items 1012–1014, biblical works, described as 'Libri Gaufredi rubricani' were his according to James, *Ancient Libraries*, 98.

Some of his *acta* as prior *sed. vac.* and some of his letters to the pope, the monks at the curia, and others are in *Epist. Cant.*, 332–366. The convent for its part wrote many letters to him during his two periods of absence, see *Epist. Cant.*, index.

The chronicle found in Cambridge, Corpus Christi College Ms 298, fo 117, sums up his character as follows: 'diu gubernavit laudabiliter et multa adversa sustinuit pro libertate ecclesie . . .'.

III GEOFFREY

occ. [1198 × 1200]

[1198, 25 Sept. × ?1200, Nov.], with Andrew, q.v., chaplains to abp Hubert and witnesses to one of his *acta*, *Eng. Epis. Acta*, iii, no 384.

Note: it is not certain that these chaplains were Christ Church monks.

IV GEOFFREY

n.d.

n.d., 2 May, dcn, whose obit is in BL Ms Arundel 68, fo 26v.

V GEOFFREY, priest [Galfridus sacerdos

occ. 1st half 12th c.

n.d., name occ. in the list in *SL*, 174, CCA Lit. Ms D.12, fo 1v.

VI GEOFFREY

occ. 1279

1279, 30 Aug., 24 Oct., precentor, *Epist. Pecham*, 58, 60, *Reg. Giffard* (Worcester), 117.

1279, 30 Aug., was, with the prior, in difficulties over the collection of a papal tenth and recd letters from the abp with advice and encouragement and a testimony to their good behaviour in performing their duty, *Epist. Pecham*, 58, 60.

1279, 24 Oct., present at Lambeth when the abp pronounced a sentence of excommunication vs certain clerks of Canterbury, *Reg. Giffard* (Worcester), 117.

I GEORGE [Georgius

occ. [c. 1206]

[c. 1206], chamberlain, Urry, *Canterbury*, 321.

[c. 1206], named in a schedule of cathedral tenants in Canterbury along with his nephew, Salomon, *ib.*

n.d., 7 Apr., obit occ. in BL Ms Arundel 68, fo 23.

II GEORGE

n.d.

n.d., 7 Mar., dcn, whose obit occ. in BL Ms Arundel 68, fo 19.

Note: there is another obit for a pr. named George on 24 Mar. in Lambeth Ms 20, fo 175.

GERAM

see Jerom

GERARD

n.d.

n.d., 3 Apr., obit occ. in BL Ms Arundel 68, fo 23.

GERARD

see also Garard

GERMANUS

occ. [1153 × 1167]

[1153 × 1167], had a relative named Martin who was the brother of Edwin from whom prior Wibert, q.v., bought land, Urry, *Canterbury*, 225. In 1153 or earlier, Martin, a witness to a grant, was described as the nephew of Germanus, *ib*, 394.

n.d., 20 May, the obit of a Germanus occ. in BL Ms Arundel 68, fo 28.

Hugh de GEROUND [Gerunde, Girunde

occ. 1221 occ. 1239

n.d., name occ. in the list in *SL*, 173, CCA Lit. Ms D.12, fo 1.

1224/5, refectorer, CCA DCc AS1.

1221, was pd 2s. for moving the bell of St Thomas and placing it in another location,

Hist. Mss Comm. 5th Report, Appndx, 441 (CCA DCc DE C.165).

1239, 4 Jan., one of the group of monks accused of contumacy by the abp after the forgery scandal, *Gervase Cant.*, ii, 144; see Simon de Hertlepe. On 1 Feb. he was among those summoned to appear before the abp after the monks' el. of Roger de La Lee, q.v., as prior, *ib.*, ii, 153.

Name in Cambridge, Corpus Christi College Ms 222, Ric. de S. Victore (13th c.); name on fos 1 and 2. On fo 1 *liber*—de penitencia magdal[ene; this is no 1310 in the Eastry catalogue, James, *Ancient Libraries*, 113.

I [?M.] GERVASE [Cantuariensis or Dorobernensis, Dorobornensis

occ. 1163 d. c. 1210

1163, 16 Feb., became a monk [*monachatum*], *Gervase Cant.*, i, 173; he made his prof. before abp Thomas Becket and was ord by him, *ib.*, i, 231. Acc. to a survey of cathedral holdings in Canterbury, dated 1163–1167 two *mansurae* were given to Christ Church at the time of his entry, Urry, *Canterbury*, 230.

1193, sacrist, *Gervase Cant.*, i, 521.

1183, 19 Aug., present at the prof. of [Waleran] bp of Rochester to Canterbury, *Gervase Cant.*, i, 307.

1189, 5/8 Nov., was one of the party of monks who were sent to London to confer with the king over their dispute with the abp, *Epist. Cant.*, 315.

1193, 3 Nov., delivered the cross to the new abp, Hubert Walter, at Lewisham and made a speech which is recorded in *Gervase Cant.*, i, 521–522.

c. 1210, d., *Gervase Cant.*, i, xxx–xxxii.

Note: There are obits for monks named Gervase in BL Ms Arundel 68: 1) 1 Jan. (fo 12); 2) 2 Apr. (fo 26); 3) 21 May (fo 28).

His writings include chronicles of Christ Church, Gesta regum, Acta pontificum Cantuariensis ecclesiae, printed by Stubbs in the Rolls Series (see refs, section D.iii under Gervase). See also Sharpe, *Latin Writers*. A 13th-15th c. copy of some of his writings is in Cambridge, Corpus Christi College Ms 438.

Four volumes of M. Gervasius occ. in the Eastry catalogue, nos 1196–1199, James, *Ancient Libraries*, 106.

Dr Gransden regards Gervase as 'the best example of a chronicler writing in the monastic traditions', with a 'devotion to Christ Church [which] moulded his historiography', *Hist. Writing*, i, 253. The dramatic murder of abp Becket in 1170, followed by the disastrous fire of 1174 and the bitter dispute with abp Baldwin, all formed part of the background in which he wrote his Chronica, Gesta Regum and lives of the abps. However, he showed himself to be a copyer rather than a critical historian, with the result that he produced little more than 'a patchwork of secondary authorities even for the period which he could remember', Gransden *ib.*, i, 260. See her critical appreciation of his writings in *ib.*, i, 253–260.

His brother Thomas II, q.v. was also a monk of Christ Church.

II GERVASE

occ. 1225

1225, chaplain to the prior, CCA DCc MA1, fo 69v.

Note: is this possibly Gervase de Hogle, q.v.?

I GILBERT

occ. [?1143 × 1148]

[?1143 × 1148], with Walter de Gloucestre, q.v., chaplains of abp Theobald and witnessed a grant made by him, *Theobald Charters*, 545.

Note: this is prob. Gilbert de Clare, q.v.

II GIL1BERT

occ. 1206

1206, 30 Mar., chamberlain, *CPL*, i (1198–1304), 26.

1206, 30 Mar., one of the monks summoned by the pope to Rome to give evidence in the dispute over their el. of Reginald, q.v., as abp. *CPL*, i (1198–1304), 26; while there, they el. Stephen Langton, *Fasti*, ii, 6.

n.d., 17 Oct., the obit of a Gilbert who d. *in itinere versus Romam*, BL Ms Arundel 68, fo 45v.

Note: c. 1180 a rental names a Gilebert, whose sister Reeingard, had land in Canterbury, Urry, *Canterbury*, 155 (CCA DCc X2, fo 7v).

GILES

see Egidius, Gyles

GILLYNGHAM

see Gyllyngham

GIRRARD

see Garard

GIRUNDE

see Geround

Edward GLASTYNBURY [Glastonburie, Glossenbery

occ. 1514 occ. 1540

1514, 1 Sept., one of seven tonsured, *SL*, 194, CCA Lit. Ms D.12, fo 11.

1515, 19 Apr., prof., *ib.*

1529, 25 Dec., subalmoner, CCA Lit. Ms C.11, fo 66.

[1538, 8 Feb., after], 1540, 4 Apr., anniversarian, Pantin, *Cant. Coll. Ox.*, iii, 153, *L and P Henry VIII*, xv, no 452.

1523, scholar at Canterbury college with an exhibition from the bequest of cardinal Morton, Pantin, *Cant. Coll. Ox.*, ii, 274.

1534, 12 Dec., acknowledged the Act of Supremacy, *DK 7th Report*, Appndx 2, 282.

[1538, 8 Feb., after], in a list of monks prob. prepared for Thomas Cromwell he was described as 'a good man', 42 yrs old, Pantin, *Cant. Coll. Ox.*, iii, 153.

1540, 4 Apr., awarded £6 p.a., *L and P Henry VIII*, xv, no 452.

Note: *SL*, 194 gives his date of birth as c. 1496 with no ref.

Geoffrey GLASTYNBURY [Glastinbury, Glastyngbery

occ. [1461] d. 1496

1461, 4 Apr., ord subdcn, Canterbury cathedral, *Reg. abp Bourgchier*, 378.

[1461], 19 Apr., one of six prof., *SL*, 189, CCA Lit. Ms D.12, fo 8.

1463, 9 Apr., ord dcn, Canterbury cathedral, *Reg. abp Bourgchier*, 386.

1475, 27 Mar., *magister ordinis*, *SL*, 191, CCA Lit. Ms D.12, fo 8ᵛ.

1493, 1 May; [1496], penitentiary in the priory, Reg. S, fo 383ᵛ, CCA Lit. Ms D.12, fo 27ᵛ.

1466, 17 Feb., 69th in order in an inventory listing *jocalia fratrum* [given by him and/or assigned for his use], and he had none, Reg. N, fo 234ᵛ.

[1486], Apr. × Oct., licensed by the prior as confessor, *sed. vac.*, Reg. N, fo 172.

1493, 1 May, 6th in order at the ratification of an agreement, Reg. S, fo 383ᵛ; but see John Crosse I.

1496, 14 Sept., d., *ex consumptione*, *ib.* His obit on 16 Sept. is in BL Ms Arundel 68, fo 41ᵛ.

n.d., gave four pairs of linen altar cloths with frontals, for the altar of St Thomas, Legg and Hope, *Inventories*, 127; see also John Sandwych II.

William GLASTYNBURY [Glastonbyry, Glastynbery, Glastyngbury, Glastyngbyry

occ. 1415 d. 1449

1415, c. 14 Feb., *adjunctus est* to the group of five monks who had entered in 1414, *SL*, 186, CCA Lit. Ms D.12, fo 6.

1415, 10 Nov., the prior was comm. to rec his prof., *Reg. abp Chichele*, iv, 142.

1416, 18 Apr., ord acol. and subdcn, Canterbury cathedral, *Reg. abp Chichele*, iv, 319.

1417, 18 Apr., ord dcn, Canterbury cathedral, *ib.*, iv, 327.

1419, 1 Apr., ord pr., chapel in the priory, *ib.*, i, 192.

1435, Apr., 1438, Feb./Mar., fourth prior, Chron. Wm Glastynbury, fos 117, 118; his apptment was on 19 Apr., *ib.*, fo 117.

1437/8, anniversarian, with William Sutton, q.v., *ib.*, fo 145.

1438/40, *magister ordinis/magister regule*, *SL*, 188, CCA Lit. Ms D.12, fo 7ᵛ.

[1440], 29 June, apptd *magister mense*, Chron Wm Glastynbury, fo 119ᵛ; his acct from this date until Sept. is *ib.*, fo 183.

1441, Nov., 1442/3, Dec. to Mar., chaplain to the prior, Chron. Wm Glastynbury, fo 26, CCA DCc Chaplain acct 18; he was apptd on 4 Nov. 1441 and his acct for 1441/2 is in Chron. Wm Glastynbury, fos 26, 130.

1443, Dec./1446, Nov., bartoner, CCA DCc, Bart. acct 95, Chron. Wm Glastynbury, fo 35, CCA DCc Carucate Serjeant accts 26, 38, RE100B; he was apptd on 8 Dec., Chron Wm Glastynbury, fo 35.

1415, drew up a list of items which the monk postulant was required to bring with him at the time of his adm., Pantin, *Cant. Coll. Ox*, iv, 118 (Chron. Wm Glastynbury, fo 180).

[1432], 25 Aug., in a letter recd from John Wodnesburgh, q.v., the latter described R[?obert] C[?olbroke], q.v. as 'vinculo amoris specialiter penes vos habetis ligatum', Pantin, *Cant. Coll. Ox.*, iii, 89 (Chron. Wm Glastynbury, fo 185/190).

1439, 19 Jan., with Alexander [Staple I], q.v., licensed to leave the priory *pro recreacione* and returned on 21 or 28 Jan. [St Agnes], Chron. Wm Glastynbury, fo 182ᵛ/177.

[1440] 8 or 20 July [St Margaret], proclaimed [*proclamatus*] in chapter that Alexander Staple I, q.v., his novice, was ready for his final examination [*redditus*], Pantin, *Cant. Coll. Ox.*, iv, 53 (Chron. Wm Glastynbury, fo 119ᵛ).

1449, 25 Dec., d., and was buried on the same day, *Chron. Stone*, 48; his obit., on 24 Dec., is in BL Ms Arundel 68, fo 52.

His so called chronicle, now Oxford, Corpus Christi College Ms 256 is a miscellany of c. 200 folios and has been described and in part summarized by C.E. Woodruff in *Archaeologia Cantiana*, 37 (1925), 121–151. There is much autobiographical material of an uneventful monastic career with added comments, reflections, extracts from poems etc., which are of great interest; these are discussed in J. Greatrex 'Monastic Memoranda from Christ Church, Canterbury as Biographical Source Material', as yet unpublished.

Eight of the letters in Glastynbury's ms above have been transcribed in Pantin, *Cant. Coll. Ox.*, iii, 88–93; see also John Waltham, John Wodnesburgh III.

I John GLOUCESTRE [Glawcestre, Glowcestr'

occ. 1361 d. 1395

1361, 28 Oct., one of nine prof., *SL*, 181, CCA Lit. Ms D.12, fo 4ᵛ.

1362, 24 Sept., ord acol., Charing, Reg. abp Islip, fo 322.
1363, 23 Sept., ord dcn, Faversham monastery, *ib.*, fo 323^v.
1365, 29 Mar., ord pr., Charing, *ib.*, fo 326^v.
1370, with John Eastry II, q.v., keepers of the archives/chancellors, *Hist. Mss Comm. 5th Report*, Appndx, 435 (CCA DCc Cart. Antiq. C.232).
1370, 11 Oct., apptd penitentiary in the priory, Reg. abp Wittlesey, fo 34^v.
1372/3, cellarer, with Thomas Garwynton, q.v., CCA DCc Bart. acct 50.
1373/4, 1374/8, 1379/80, cellarer, CCA DCc Treas. acct 5, MA2 fos 282–315, 318–321^v; he was apptd on 4 Feb. 1373, Reg. abp Wittlesey, fo 58^v.
1381/2, *custos* of abp Islip's sheep, CCA DCc, Sheep Warden acct 5.
1381/3, treasurer, CCA DCc Treas. acct 26.
1385, third prior for two terms, Lambeth Ms 243, fo 196^v; he was also warden of manors, CCA DCc MA2, fo 333.
1388/9, 1390/1, bartoner, CCA DCc Bart. accts 64, 65.
1389, 6 Nov., *magister ordinis*, *SL*, 183, CCA Lit. Ms D.12, fo 5.
1391/4, sacrist, CCA DCc, Sac. accts 10, 11, 9; he was apptd on 9 May, 1391, Reg. abp Courtenay, i, fo 338^v.

1362/3, student at Canterbury college, for whom cloth *de burneto* was purchased for his *cappa scolastica*, Pantin, *Cant. Coll. Ox*, iv, 182; see below.
1370, 11 Oct., as chancellor this yr he was engaged in compiling a catalogue of the archives, see above.
1374, 30 June, 28th in order at the el. of an abp, Reg. G, fos 173^v–175^v.
1376, Apr., one of ten nominated to the committee set up for regulating the infirmary, *Lit. Cant.*, no 945 (CCA DCc Cart. Antiq. C.206).
1381, 31 July, 20th at the el. of an abp and selected as one of six *compromissorii* by the previously appointed three, Reg. G, fo 225^v, Oxford, Bod. Ms Ashmole 794, fo 254^v.
1382/3, with William Chart I, q.v., involved in negotiations with the abp over the apptment of William de Dover III, q.v., to the wardenship of Canterbury college, Pantin, *Cant. Coll. Ox.*, iv, 188, 189.
1395, 29 Apr., d. in his 34th yr of monastic life, CCA Lit. Ms D.12, fo 17; his obit is in BL Ms Arundel 68, fo 26.

II John GLOUCESTRE [Gloucetyr, Glowcestre

occ. 1416 d. 1426

1416, 22 June, one of eight prof., *SL*, 186, CCA Lit. Ms D.12, fo 6.
1417, 10 Apr., ord acol., Canterbury cathedral, *Reg. abp Chichele*, iv, 327.
1418, 26 Mar., ord subdcn, Canterbury cathedral, *ib.*, iv, 332.
1419, 1 Apr., ord dcn, chapel in the priory, *ib.*, i, 191.
1420, 6 Apr., ord pr., Canterbury cathedral, *ib.*, iv, 342.
1426, 18 Apr., d.; the *magister mense* and his chaplains and other brethren said the *commendatio* over his body in the infirmary chapel, *Chron. Stone*, 13, CCA Lit. Ms D.12, fo 22; the obit is in BL Ms Arundel 68, fo 24^v.

Walter de GLOUCESTRE

occ. [1143 × 1161] occ. [1148 × 1182]

[?1143 × 1148], with Gilbert [?de Clare] q.v., chaplains of abp Theobald and witnessed a grant made by him, *Theobald Charters*, 545 (as Walter).
[1150 × 1153], with Richard de Clare, q.v., chaplains of the abp and witnessed a confirmation, *Theobald Charters*, no 255.
[1150 × 1161], with Richard de Clare, witnessed a deed, *ib.*, no 225.
[1148 × 1182], *temp* bp Walter of Rochester, witnessed an agreement between this bp and the adcn of Rochester, *Reg. Roff.*, 58 (see Rochester refs).

GOBOSTON

see Reginald Goldston I

GODELAWE

see Codelawe

I GODFREY [Godefridus

n.d.

n.d., 22 Jan., *conversus*, whose obit occ. in BL Ms Arundel 68, fo 14.

II GODFREY

n.d.

n.d., 30 Mar., obit in BL Ms Arundel 68, fo 22.

III GODFREY [Godfridus, Gosfridus

n.d.

n.d., dcn, whose obit occ. on 1 Mar., BL Ms Arundel 68, fo 18.

I Richard GODMERSHAM, D.CnL

occ. [1390] d. 1442

[1390], 28 Sept., one of seven prof. *SL*, 184, CCA Lit. Ms D.12, fo 5; and see below.
1391, 25 Mar., ord subdcn, Canterbury cathedral, Reg. abp Courtenay, i, fo 312.
1394, 18 Apr., ord pr., Canterbury cathedral, Reg. abp Courtenay, ii, fo 185.
1403, 1 Jan./1403, June, penitentiary in the priory, Reg. abp Arundel, i, fo 437, ii, fo 125.
1403/10, warden of Canterbury college, apptd 19 June 1403 and removed Sept. 1410, Pantin,

Cant. Coll. Ox., iii, 60 (Reg. abp Arundel, i, fo 397), Pantin, *ib.*, iii, 68 (Reg. abp Arundel., ii, fo 125).

1410, Sept., apptd penitentiary, Reg. abp Arundel, ii, fo 125.

1416, 25 May, apptd penitentiary in the priory, *Reg. abp Chichele*, iv, 152.

1422, 19 Apr., apptd penitentiary for the priory but the following day a new apptment was made, *Reg. abp Chichele*, iv, 246; see Thomas Chart.

[?c. 1412/41], lector in the claustral school, Pantin, *Cant. Coll. Ox.*, iv, 71–73, where he gives the evidence for suggesting these dates, based on livery lists on which his name and his servants occ. See also below.

[1431/42], almoner, CCA Lit. Ms D.12, fo 24ᵛ; he held this office for 12 yrs and d. in office, *ib.*

1393/4, scholar at Canterbury college for whom the warden recd payments for battels and commons, Pantin, *Cant. Coll. Ox.*, ii, 132, 133, 136 (CCA DCc Cart. Antiq. O.151.2).

1397/8, one of six scholars who recd money from the feretrars, *pro benedictione*, CCA DCc Feret. acct 1.

1410/11, incepted in canon law and the inception expenses for him and for John Langdon I, q.v. were £118 3s. 5d., Pantin, *ib.*, iii, 63–67 (CCA DCc Prior acct 2 and Oxford, Bod. Ms Tanner 165, fos 146–147ᵛ).

1396, 7 Aug., 62nd in order at the el. of an abp Reg. G, fo 234ᵛ.

1414, 12 Mar., 24th in order at the el. of an abp, *Reg. abp Chichele*, i, 4 and acted as proxy for Thomas Tokenam, q.v.

1427, 16 Oct., 15 Dec., acted as commissary for the abp, *ib.*, i, 107, 108.

1428, 28 Feb., preached at the funeral of prior John Wodnesburgh, q.v., on the text 'transit de morte ad vitam', Oxford, Bod. Ms Tanner 165, fo 4ᵛ.

1442, 7 Feb., d. He is described as 'vir laudabilis vite et honeste et religiose conversationis' and among the *diversa officia* which he held was that of lector 'in scola claustrali [quem] laudabiliter annis plurimis regebat'. He had been a monk for 50 yrs (and so the prof. date may have been 1391 or 1392), CCA Lit. Ms D.12, fo 24ᵛ. His obit on 6 Feb. is in BL Ms Arundel, 68, fo 15ᵛ.

II Richard GODMERSHAM

occ. 1450 d. 1468

1450, 25 Jan., one of seven prof., *SL*, 189, CCA Lit. Ms D.12, fo 7ᵛ.

1450, 3 Apr., ord acol., Canterbury cathedral, Reg. abp Stafford, fo 204.

1451, 20 Mar., ord subdcn, Canterbury cathedral, *ib.*, fo 205ᵛ.

1452, 8 Apr., ord dcn, Canterbury cathedral, *ib.*, fo 206ᵛ (transcribed as Bodmersham).

1464/5, anniversarian, CCA DCc U15/24/7.

1466/8, warden of manors, CCA DCc MA154 and MA155; warden in 1468, prob. at the time of his d., *Chron. Stone*, 105.

1457, 13 Aug., [novice], was examined *de redditu* by the precentor Robert Bynne, q.v., *Chron. Stone*, 68.

1466, 17 Feb., 42nd in order in an inventory listing *jocalia fratrum* [given by him and/or assigned for his use], Reg. N, fo 233ᵛ.

1468, 27 Aug., d., *Chron. Stone*, 105; he was described as 'bonus et prudens atque ab omnibus multum dilectus', *ib.*

III Richard GODMERSHAM [Godmarsham

occ. 1509 occ. 1540

1509, 22 Dec., ord acol., Canterbury cathedral, Reg. abp Warham, ii, fo 264ᵛ.

1510, 16 June, one of eight tonsured, *SL*, 194, CCA Lit. Ms D.12, fo 11.

1511, 1 Jan., prof., *ib.*,

1511, 19 Apr., ord dcn, Canterbury cathedral, Reg. abp Warham, ii, fo 265ᵛ.

1517, 26 Apr., celebrated his first mass and recd 4d. from William Ingram I, q.v., CCA Lit. Ms C.11, fo 128ᵛ.

1525, 1526, 1529, all on 29 Sept.; 1531, 25 Mar., 1532, 24 June, feretrar, CCA Lit. Ms C.11, fos 63ᵛ, 64, 65ᵛ; *ib.*, fos 67, 68.

[1538, 8 Feb., after], 1540, 4 Apr., infirmarer, Pantin, *Cant. Coll. Ox.*, iii, 152, *L and P Henry VIII*, xv, no 452.

n.d., had John Garard as his *magister regule*, Pantin, *Cant. Coll. Ox.*, iv, 54 (CCA DCc Ms Scrap Book B.186).

n.d., in a statement on the behaviour of some monks he was reported as not having learned the Rule [by heart], Pantin, *ib.*, iii, 143 (CCA DCc Ms Scrap Book B.193).

1511, 2 Sept., 74th in order on the visitation certificate, Wood-Legh, *Visit.*, 3 (Reg. abp Warham, i, fo 35ᵛ).

1534, 12 Dec., acknowledged the Act of Supremacy, *DK 7th Report*, Appndx 2, 282.

[1538, 8 Feb., after], in a list of monks prob. prepared for Thomas Cromwell he was described as a 'good man' of 51 yrs, Pantin, *Cant. Coll. Ox.*, iii, 152.

1540, 4 Apr., awarded £10 p.a., *L and P Henry VIII*, xv, no 452.

Roger de GODMERSHAM

occ. 1320 d. 1331

1320, 9 Oct., one of five prof., *SL*, 179, CCA Lit. Ms D.12, fo 3ᵛ.

1321, 19 Dec., ord acol., Rochester cathedral, *Reg. Hethe* (Rochester), 1105, 101.

1331 [before 28 Oct.], *magister corone*, CCA DCc MA2, fo 201ᵛ.

1331, 28 Oct., one of three monk students sent to Oxford, the other two being James de Oxney and Hugh de St Ives, q.v., Pantin, *Cant. Coll. Ox.*, iv, 5, 178; see also *Hist. Mss Comm. 9th Report*, Appndx, 79.
1327, recd money for expenses, Lambeth Ms 243, fo 2v.
1331, 16 Dec., d. at Oxford, CCA Lit. Ms D.12, fo 16, which settles the date, and Pantin, *Cant. Coll. Ox.*, iv, 211 which settles the place in the transcription of a letter [from the prior] to Hugh de St Ives (from Reg. L, fo 13v).

William GODMERSHAM
occ. 1468/9 d. 1511

1468, 12 Oct., one of four to rec. the tonsure, *SL*, 190, CCA Lit. Ms D.12, fo 8 (which has inserted 1469); *Chron. Stone*, 106, gives the date as 1468, 12 Oct., and adds that he was one of four almonry [school] boys to be clothed on this day.
1469, 1 Apr., ord acol., Canterbury cathedral, *Reg. abp Bourgchier*, 402.
1469, 21 Apr., prof., *SL*, 190 (Cambridge, Corpus Christi College Ms 298).
1470, 21 Apr., ord subdcn, Canterbury cathedral, *Reg. abp Bourgchier*, 406.
1471, 9 Mar., ord dcn, Canterbury cathedral, *ib.*, 405.
1471/2, celebrated his first mass and recd a small sum from the sacrist, Woodruff, 'Sacrist's Rolls', 63 (CCA DCc Sac. acct 51).
1492/6, infirmarer, CCA DCc MA9, fos 2v, 46, 66v, MA10, fo 3, *SL*, 192 (CCA Lit. Ms D.12, fo 9v).
1494, apptd one of the chancellors, Reg. S, fo 389; see Richard Sellyng III.
1494/6, Apr., *magister ordinis* CCA DCc MA9, fo 66v, *SL*, 192 (CCA Lit. Ms D.12, fo 9v).
1501, 26 Apr., *alter penitentiarius* and 13th in order at the el. of an abp, Reg. R, fo 56v.
1503, 21 Feb., penitentiary, Reg. T, fo 15v.
1493, 1 May, 24th in order at the ratification of an agreement, Reg. S, fo 383v; but see John Crosse I.
1502, recd 20d. in a bequest from a parishioner of St Margaret's, Canterbury, Hussey, 'Kentish Wills', 43.
1510/11, d., Woodruff, 'Sacrist's Rolls', 69 (CCA DCc Sac. acct 73); the obit on 25 May, states that he was penitentiary [prob. at time of d.], BL Ms Arundel 68, fo 28v.

Richard GODNYSTON [Godwynstone, Goodusstun
occ. 1533/4

1533, 12 May, one of eight tonsured, *SL*, 196, CCA Lit. Ms D.12, fo 12.
1534, 21 Mar., made his prof. before the prior who had recd a comm. from the abp, *ib.*
1534, 12 Dec., acknowledged the Act of Supremacy, *DK 7th Report*, Appndx 2, 282.
n.d., 13 Apr., obit in BL Ms Arundel 68, fo 24.

Note: there are no other known monks by this name.

GODNYSTON
see Goodnyston

GODRIC
occ. before 1070

1023, 1045 × 1047, 1044 × 1048, 1052 × 1070, occ. as prior: possibly the predecessor of Henry, q.v., *HRH*, 33.
Note: it seems doubtful that these dates apply to a single monk.
n.d., 8 July, obit occ. in BL Ms Arundel 68, fo 33v.

GODWIN [Godwinus Bac
occ. before 1100

1100, before, *clericus*, who, on becoming a monk gave the church of St Denis Baccherche (Bachchirche), London, to Christ Church, Kissan, 'London Deanery', 206.

Note: there are a number of obits of monks named Godwin in the obituary lists, e.g., 10 Feb., in BL Ms Cotton Nero C.ix, fo 5, 14 Apr. and 7 May in BL Ms Arundel 68, fos 24 and 26v, and 16 May and 31 May in Lambeth Ms 20, fos 187 and 190v.

GODWYNSTON(E)
see Goodnyston

GOFFRIDUS
see Geoffrey

GOLDSMITH
see William Molassh II

I Reginald GOLDSTON, B.Th. [Goboston, Goldstone, Goldestone, Golston
occ. 1457 d. 1504

1457, 13 Dec., one of six adm. as monks, *Chron. Stone*, 71 (*SL*, 189, CCA Lit. Ms D.12, fo 8).
1458, 12 Feb. 'venerunt ad parvum servitium', and on 26 Feb. 'ad commune servicium', *Chron. Stone*, 71.
1458, 1 Apr., ord acol. and subdcn, Canterbury cathedral, *Reg. abp Bourgchier*, 368.
1458, 21 Apr., one of the same six who made their prof., *Chron. Stone*, 71.
1459, 24 Mar., ord dcn, Canterbury cathedral, *Reg. abp Bourgchier*, 371.
1466/71, warden of Canterbury college; his accts for 1466/8, 1469/71 are in Pantin, *Cant. Coll. Ox.*, ii, 184–194 (CCA DCc Cart. Antiq. O.151.18, 19, 20, 4).
1471, 29 Sept., warden of manors, CCA DCc Bocking acct 78.

c. 1472, c. 1480, chaplain to the prior, Reg. S, fo 362^{v}, *Lit. Cant.*, no 1094.
1472/82, treasurer, CCA DCc MA27, fos 1–215.
1486, 6 Apr., penitentiary, Cambridge, Corpus Christi College Ms 298, fo 130^{v}, Reg. N, fo 172, but prob. in the diocese, *sed. vac.*
1487, 23 Sept., 1489/91, 1493/4, cellarer, CCA DCc DE46, Cell. accts 10, 11, 9. He was removed on 2 Apr. 1494, CCA DCc DE33.
1493/4, subprior, CCA DCc Sac. acct 63, and infirmarer, MA9, fo 45.
Note: some of the above offices may have been held for only a few months; for example, he was infirmarer on 6 July 1494, Pantin, *Cant. Coll. Ox.*, iv, 202, but prob. for only part of the yr. See William Godmersham.
1494/6, granator, CCA DCc MA9, fo 90^{v}, MA10, fo 28.
1501, 26 Apr., penitentiary, Reg. R, fo 56^{v}.
1458/9, scholar at Canterbury college for two terms, CCA DCc Chamb. acct 62.
1459/60, scholar and recd stipend of £5 15s., Pantin, *Cant. Coll. Ox.*, ii, 180 (CCA DCc Cart. Antiq., O.151.16).
1460, scholar for the whole yr, CCA DCc Chamb. acct 65.
1462/3, scholar for the whole yr and recd £8 6s. 8d., Pantin, *Cant. Coll. Ox.*, ii, 183 (CCA DCc Cart. Antiq. O.151.17).
1463/4, 1467, Apr., at Oxford and recd travelling expenses for journeys back and forth between Canterbury and Oxford, Pantin, *Cant. Coll. Ox.*, iv, 196.
1468, 10 Mar., 10 Apr., 18 Sept.; 1469, 19 and 26 Feb., at Oxford as above, Pantin, *ib.*, iv, 196–197.
1468, 13 Mar., with William Chichele I, q.v., returned from Oxford to preach, *ib.*, iv, 196.
[1469], B.Th. by 8 Feb. 1370, *CPL*, xii (1458–1471), 772 (transcribed as Goboston).

1466, 17 Feb., 53rd in order in an inventory listing *jocalia fratrum* [given by him and/or assigned for his use], Reg. N, fo 234.
1469/70, accompanied William Sellyng, q.v. to Rome, on business connected with the jubilee of St Thomas Becket; the supporting letters from the king, queen and others are in Reg. S, fos 237^{v}–240 (and summarized in *Hist. Mss Comm. 9th Report*, Appndx, 116). Their expenses are in Pantin, *Cant. Coll. Ox.*, iii, 108–109 (CCA DCc Ms Scrap Book C loose). While there, on 8 Feb. 1370 he was granted a papal indult of plenary remission of sins at the hour of d., *CPL*, xii (1458–1471), 772.
1478, 8 Apr., 1481, 14 Mar., apptd proctor in convocation by the prior and convent, Reg. S, fos 286, 316.
[1486], Apr., one of several monks licensed to preach by the prior, *sed. vac.*, Reg. N, fo 172.
1486, 6 April, with Thomas Humfrey, q.v., was sent to the king for a licence to el. an abp, Cambridge, Corpus Christi College Ms 298, fo 130^{v}.
1486, 31 July, apptd commissary general by the prior and convent, *sed. vac*, Reg R, fo 14–14^{v}.
1487, recd a bequest of 20d., from a parishioner of St Margaret's, Canterbury, Hussey, 'Kentish Wills', 41.
1493, 1 May, 3rd in order at the ratification of an agreement, Reg. S, fo 383^{v}; but see John Crosse I.
1501, 26 Apr., 4th in order at the el. of an abp, Reg. R, fo 56^{v}.
n.d., acted as *senior* for William Ingram I, q.v., BL Ms Harley 1587, fo 188^{v}.
1504, 26 Sept., d. at the age of 68, 'tandem senio et debilitate confractus', he had retired [*stationarius*] to a room in the infirmary, CCA Lit. Ms D.12, fo 35.

Name in BL Ms Harley 1587, Grammatica etc. (1396 to 15th/16th c.), on fo 188^{v}, where it states that he passed it on to William Ingram I, q.v.

Gave an alb 'et inter albas ceteras optima' to Canterbury college, Pantin, *Cant. Coll. Ox.*, i, 30 (CCA DCc Cart. Antiq. O.137); also a legenda to the small chapel [*sacellum*], *ib.*, i, 36.

Three of his letters addressed to the prior, dated c. 1476 and referring to the convent's legal and business affairs, have been printed in *Christ Church Letters*, 31, 32; in all of these, written in English, he signed himself 'your chapelayn'. There is also in this volume a letter to him from the abbot of Abingdon, dated, Apr. 1488, *ib.*, 53. Other letters are found in *Lit. Cant*, no 1087 (to him from an agent in London, c. 1478), no 1094 (from him to the prior, c. 1480).

II Reginald GOLDSTON
occ. 1522/3

1522, 11 Feb., one of ten tonsured, *SL*, 195, CCA Lit. Ms D.12 fo 11^{v}.
1522, 24 Nov., prof., *ib.*
1523, Sept./Dec., recd a *tunica nocturnalis* from William Ingram I, q.v, who also paid his medical expenses of 4s., CCA Lit. Ms C.11, fo 137^{v}.
n.d., 9 June, dcn whose obit occ. in BL Ms Arundel 68, fo 30^{v}.

Note: I have assumed that the obit is his since he does not appear in any later records.

I Thomas GOLDSTON [Golston
occ. 1309 d. 1334

1309, 18 Oct., one of nine prof., *SL*, 179, CCA Lit. Ms D.12, fo 3^{v}.

1324, 20 Feb., one of the chancellors, CUL Ms Ee.5.31, fo 235; see Richard de Ikham.
1326/9, subalmoner, CCA DCc Blean acct 2, Eastry acct 53, Monkton acct 61.
1329/30, Mar., almoner, CCA DCc, Alm. acct 40.
1329, 13 July, apptd third cantor by the abp, Reg. L, fo 170 and printed in *Lit. Cant.*, no 298,

where the date is given as 20 Feb. 1330 (feast of St Mildred).

1331/2, *custos martyrii*, CCA DCc DE3, fo 23.

1333, 3 Nov., precentor, Reg. G, fos xxxii, xxxviii.

1333, 3 Nov., named as one of seven *compromissorii* in the el. of an abp, Reg. G, fos xxxii, xxxviii, and Reg. Q, fo 193v.

1334, 23 Dec., d., CCA Lit. Ms D.12, fo 16.

II Thomas GOLDSTON [Golstan, Golston

occ. [1392] d. 1415

[1392], 21 Nov., one of four prof., *SL*, 184, CCA Lit. Ms D.12, fo 5.

1394, 18 Apr., ord subdcn, Canterbury cathedral, Reg. abp Courtenay ii, fo 184v.

1395, 10 Apr., ord dcn, Canterbury cathedral, *ib.*, ii, fo 185v.

1404/5, *custos* of St Mary in crypt, CCA DCc, Prior acct 20.

1410/11, first treasurer, CCA DCc Treas. acct 10.

1396, 7 Aug., 69th in order at the el. of an abp, Reg. G, fo 234v.

1414, 12 Mar., 30th at the el. of an abp, *Reg. abp Chichele*, i, 4.

1415, 1 Mar., d., in the tenth yr of his monastic life, CCA Lit. Ms D.12, fo 20v. This is clearly a slip of the pen, 'x', in place of 'xxiii' or 'xxii'.

III Thomas GOLDSTON (Prior I)

occ. 1419 d. 1468

1449–1468, prior: el. 26 Mar., 1449,, Reg. S, fo 178v, *nominatio* and *prefectio*, 9 Apr., *ib.*, fo 180, *sublimatus* 16 Apr., *ib.*, fo 181; see also *Chron. Stone*, 46 (Reg. abp Stafford, fo 32); d. 6 Aug. 1468, Reg. S, fo 230v.

1419, 25 Jan., one of four prof., *SL*, 186, CCA Lit. Ms D.12, fo 6v.

1419, 15 Apr., ord acol., chapel in priory, *Reg. abp Chichele*, i, 192.

1420, 6 Apr., ord subdcn, Canterbury cathedral, *ib.*, iv, 341.

1431, 25 June, 1432/3, 1433, 1435, 1437, 9 Apr., treasurer, CCA DCc MA25, fo 301, Treas. acct 12, MA25, fo 289, 'Chron. Wm Glastynbury', 129, CCA DCc Lalling acct 22.

1437/8, warden of manors, Lambeth ED73.

1443, Sept./Dec., bartoner, Chron. Wm Glastynbury, fo 35.

1444, 14 Apr., apptd cellarer, Reg. abp Stafford, fo 14v; he was cellarer until at least 16 Jan. 1446, CCA DCc MA4, fos 38, 83v.

1445/6, subprior, CCA DCc Sac. acct 33; he was apptd 20 Apr. 1446, acc. to *Chron. Stone*, 39 (Reg. abp Stafford, fo 22).

1435, 24 Oct., one of three promoted to the upper choir, Chron. Wm Glastynbury, fo 117v.

1454, Aug., made a prolonged visitation of Canterbury college for which the expenses amounted to £9 3s., Pantin, *Cant. Coll. Ox.*, iv, 195 (CCA DCc Prior acct 9); at this time the library was under construction and he supervised the 'new work', *ib.* The acct of this supervision 1454/5 is in *ib.*, ii, 173–176 (CCA DCc Cart. Antiq. O.151.15).

1458, Jan./Feb., absent in London *in negociis regni* and was licensed by the abp to celebrate in the chapel of Lambeth palace on 2 Feb., *cum baculo pastorali*, *Chron. Stone*, 72.

1461, 28 June, did not attend the coronation of Edward IV, *ib.*, 83.

1465, 26 May, did not attend the coronation of Edward's wife, *ib.*, 92.

1465, two of his ordinances concerning the observance of certain feasts are recorded, *ib.*, 94–95; this same yr he repaired the *lavacrum aqueductus* which was adjoining his chapel, *ib.*

1467, 17 Apr., unwell, and by 7 July gravely ill, *ib.*, 102–103.

1468, 6 Aug., d., monk for 50 yrs and prior for 19; the funeral took place the following day and the burial followed in the new chapel of St Mary, which he had built next to the *martyrium* and close to the door leading to the cloister, *ib.*, 104–105. His obit is in BL Ms Arundel 68, fo 37.

Among his gifts to Canterbury college were a set of green vestments, new hangings for the hall, two *ciphi de murra* inscribed with his name, and a silver gilt chalice similarly inscribed, Pantin, *Cant. Coll. Ox.*, i, 10, 16, 17, 28 (CCA DCc Cart. Antiq. O.135, 137).

An inventory of plate in the prior's office, dated 1466, 17 Feb., is provided in Reg N, fos 223–226.

Some of his *acta* are in Reg. S, fos 153–230, and his rough accts for 1451/2 are in CCA Lit. Ms E.6.

He is described as 'affabilis atque benevolus' and a man who was on friendly terms with high and low, *Anglia Sacra*, i, 144–145. His obituary in BL Ms Arundel 68, fo 5, praises him for completing the library at Canterbury college and for building the Lady chapel on the north side of the cathedral, where he was buried.

IV Thomas GOLDSTON, D.Th. (Prior II) [Goldstone, Goldestone, Goleston, Golston, *alias* Quylter, Quilter

occ. 1470 d. 1517

1495–1517, prior: el. 19 Jan. 1495, Reg. S, fo 394–394v; d. 16 Sept., 1517, Reg. T, fo 141.

1470, 25 Jan., one of eight prof., *SL*, 190. CCA Lit. Ms D.12, fo 10.

1470, 21 Apr., ord acol., Canterbury cathedral, *Reg. abp Bourgchier*, 405.

1471, 9 Mar., ord subdcn, Canterbury cathedral, *Reg. abp Bourgchier*, 404.

1473/4, celebrated his first mass and recd 10d. from the sacrist, Woodruff, 'Sacrist's Rolls', 64 (CCA DCc Sac. acct 56).

1483/4, subwarden, Canterbury college, CCA DCc Monk Warden accts 18, 19; his travelling expenses, and those of Robert Eastry q.v., from Oxford to Canterbury via London, Mar. 1483 are in Pantin, *Cant. Coll. Ox.*, iii, 127–128 (CCA DCc DE96).

1485, warden of the college, *ib.*, Monk Warden acct 20.

1488/90, Apr. and Sept. in each case; 1491, Apr.; 1492, May; 1493, Apr. and Oct., warden of manors, CCA DCc Monk Warden accts 21, 24, 23, 25–7, MA8, fos 5, 21^{v}, 74, 139^{v}.

1494, 29 Sept., cellarer, CCA DCc, Cel. acct 13.

1473, 21 Feb., scholar at Canterbury college and recd his *capa scolaris*, Pantin, *Cant. Coll. Ox.*, iv, 199.

1475/6, 1476/8, at Canterbury college and shared a room with a monk of Battle, Pantin, *Cant. Coll. Ox.*, ii, 195, 200.

1478, 17 May, 20 Sept.; recd money for travel expenses between Oxford and Canterbury, *ib.*, iv, 200; see also *ib.*, ii, 204 for 1478/9 (CCA DCc Cart. Antiq. O.151.22.b).

1479, 10 Jan., again given money for travel expenses, *ib.*

1480/2, scholar and recd the annual stipend of £8, *ib.*, ii, 207, 211 (CCA DCc Cart. Antiq. O.151.23, 24).

1486, 23 Apr., by this date, B.Th., Reg. R, fo 14.

1493, 30 Jan., adm. to the fraternity of the English hospice in Rome, B. Newns, 'The Hospice of St Thomas and the English Crown 1474–1538', *The English Hospice in Rome* (The Venerabile), vol. xxi (1962), 190.

1493, 6 Apr., D.Th., Bologna, Pantin, *Cant. Coll. Ox.*, iii, 130–131 (Reg. S, fo 382); it was possibly an honorary degree, Pantin, *ib.*, iv, 81.

1498, offered an S.T.P. in 1498 at Oxford, Pantin, *ib.*, iv, 122.

1486, 23 Apr., appt`d commissary general with others by the prior and convent, *sed. vac.*, Reg. R, fo 14.

1490, 30 Aug., with Robert Eastry, q.v., apptd proctors for convocation, Reg. S, fos 361^{v}–362.

1491, apptd proctor for convocation, Reg. S, fo 365^{v}.

1492, 4 Dec., sent as proctor for the prior and convent to Rome, Reg. S, fos 376–377; while there he may have continued his studies for a short period, as above.

1493, 1 May, 26th in order at the ratification of an agreement, Reg. S, fo 383^{v}; but see John Crosse I.

1500/1, apptd commissary general of Canterbury, *sed. vac.*; some of his *acta* are in Reg. T, fos 427–432; there is a brief summary in *Hist. Mss Comm. 9th Report*, Appndx, 109.

1501, 26 Apr., presided at the el. of an abp, Reg. R, fos 56–57^{v}.

1506, 9 Mar., installed abp Warham, Reg. T, fo 448.

1508, 22 Apr., present at the opening of the tomb of St Dunstan in the cathedral, *Dunstan Memorials*, 426–427; and his correspondence with the abbot of Glastonbury is in CCA Lit. Ms E.27, fos 1–6 (brief summary in *Hist. Mss Comm. 9th Report*, Appndx, 110.

1511, 10 Sept., with six obedientiaries apptd to oversee corrections in the priory after the abp's visitation, Wood-Legh, *Visit.*, 5.

1517, 16 Sept., d., Reg. T, fo 146; his obit on 17 Sept. is in BL Ms Arundel 68, fo 41^{v}, and fos 64–66^{v} give a summary of his achievements.

Name in

(1) Oxford, Bod. Ms Tanner 15, J. Capgrave; the date AD 1499 is in it and the name of the ?scribe who copied it for him, see *MLGB*.

(2) Ampleforth Abbey, Joannes Franciscus, Brixianus (printed book), Venice, 1500.

Among the books he, or his namesake, prior, gave to Canterbury college are a commentary on Genesis, Pantin, *Cant. Coll. Ox*, i, 50 (CCA DCc Cart. Antiq. O.136).

The family name was Quylter; his brother Simon's obit occ. on 13 Apr., in BL Ms Arundel 68, fo 24 and that of his mother, Elizabeth on 16 Dec., *ib.*, fo 51.

His initials and rebus are on the piers of the central tower [angyll stepyll'] which was completed under his direction, and the 'new lodging' for distinguished guests visiting the priory was also his work. He initiated the building of Christ Church gate and left money for its completion. He also provided beautiful new service books for the choir and high altar; see Woodruff, *Memorials Cant.*, 210–212, 280 and *BRUO*. A summary of his character attributes to him the qualities of both Martha and Mary, *Anglia Sacra*, i, 146; and the Causton obituary (Lit. Ms D.12), states that he was 'valde dilectus a conventu suo propter sua egregia et bona opera', *SL*, 190, Cambridge, Corpus Christi College Ms 298. A list of his good works and gifts is recorded with his obit in Lambeth Ms 20, fos 219^{v}–222 and see Legg and Hope, *Inventories*, 122–124 for the several sets of vestments given by him and described in an inventory of the *custos martyrii* (dated 1503), *ib.*, 130, 131; he was himself buried in the martyrdom (north transept), *ib.*, 126, n. 3.

Among his gifts to Canterbury college are a silver gilt *nux*, several *panni* for the hall and an alb, Pantin, *Cant. Coll. Ox.*, i, 37, 38 (CCA DCc Inventory Box No 21). There is also a separate list of plate given by him to the college in Pantin, *ib.*, i, 83 (CCa DCc Cart. Antiq. O.134A).

Some of his correspondence has been transcribed in *Christ Church Letters*, 64–66, 68–69.

For his *acta* see Reg. S, fos 405–444 and Reg. T, fos 411–453, 53–145 (formerly the *libellus* bound in at the end of Reg. E).

V Thomas GOLDSTON [Goldestone, Goldstone

occ. 1504 occ. 1526

1504, 13 Jan., one of six tonsured, Sl., 193, CCA Lit. Ms D.12, fo 10.

1505, 22 Mar., ord acol., Canterbury cathedral, Reg. abp Warham, ii, fo 262.

1505, 11 July, prof., SL 193, CCA Lit. Ms D.12, fo 10.

1506, 11 Apr., ord subdcn, Canterbury cathedral, Reg. abp Warham, ii, fo 262v.

1507, 3 Apr., ord dcn, Canterbury cathedral, *ib.*, ii, fo 263.

1509, 7 Apr., ord pr., Canterbury cathedral, *ib.*, ii, fo 264.

[c. 1511 × 1514], *magister regule* for William Arundell II, Robert Holden, Laurence Newynham, John Salisbury III, q.v., Pantin, *Cant. Coll. Ox.*, iv, 54 (CCA DCc Ms Scrap Book B.186).

1519, Aug., chancellor with Thomas Lee II, q.v., Reg. T, fo 162v.

1525, 25 Mar., 29 Sept.; 1526, 29 Sept., feretrar, CCA Lit. Ms C.11, fos 63v, 64.

[c. 1514 × 1524], at Canterbury college and reported as being rarely if ever at compline and not eager to work, Pantin, *Cant. Coll. Ox.*, iii, 142 (CCA DCc Ms Scrap Book B.193).

1511, 2 Sept., 57th in order on the visitation certificate, Wood-Legh, *Visit.*, 3 (Reg. abp Warham, i, fo 35v).

VI Thomas GOLDSTON [Goldeston, Goldstone

occ. 1533 occ. 1540

1533, 12 May, one of eight tonsured, *SL*, 196, CCA Lit. Ms D.12, fo 12.

1534, 21 Mar., made his prof. before the prior who had been comm. by the abp, *ib.*

1534, 12 Dec., acknowledged the Act of Supremacy, *DK 7th Report*, Appndx 2, 282.

[1538, 8 Feb., after], in a list of monks prob. prepared for Thomas Cromwell he was described as 'wytty' and 25 yrs old, Pantin, *Cant. Coll. Ox.*, iii, 153.

1540, 4 Apr., awarded £6 p.a., *L and P Henry VIII*, xv, no 452.

Note: only one Thomas Goldston signed the act of 1534 and only one is on the dissolution list; thus it is prob. that the entries above have been correctly assigned.

I John GOLDWELL [Goldewele, Goldewell, Goldwel

occ. 1406 d. 1465

1406, 21 Oct., one of three *adjuncti* among seven prof., *SL*, 185, CCA Lit. Ms D.12, fo 6.

1407, 26 Mar., ord acol., Canterbury cathedral, Reg. abp Arundel, i, fo 340v.

1407, 24 Sept., ord subdcn, collegiate church, Maidstone, *ib.*, fo 341.

1431, 18 Apr., until *magister ordinis*, *SL*, 187, CCA Lit. Ms D.12, fo 7.

1432/3, 1435, until 24 Dec., third prior, CCA DCc Sac. acct 27, 'Chron. Wm Glastynbury', 129, (Ms fo 117v).

1436/7, first anniversarian with John Westgate, q.v., CCA DCc, Anniv. acct 7.

1439/41, May to May, 1441/4, sacrist, CCA DCc CR92, Sac. accts 29–31.

[1446], 14 Oct., apptd precentor, Reg. abp Stafford, fo 24v.

1447, 2 Sept., 1448, 10 June, 1448/51, 1452/4, 1456/7, sacrist, CCA DCc DE49, CR96, Sac. accts 35, 36, 38, 39, Prior acct 9, Sac. acct 40; his apptment in Aug. [1447] is in Reg. abp Stafford, fo 27v.

1414, 12 Mar., 68th in order at the el. of an abp, *Reg. abp Chichele*, i, 4.

1432/3, as third prior recd a pittance of 18d. from the sacrist, CCA DCc Sac. acct 27.

1454, 4 Apr., sent with Walter Hertford, q.v., by the prior and chapter to the king to obtain licence to el. an abp, *Chron. Stone*, 59.

1455/6, one of the monk *barones*, CCA DCc Prior acct 10.

1461, recd a bequest of 6s, 8d., from a parishioner of St Paul's, Canterbury, Hussey, 'Kentish Wills', 41.

1465, 2 Nov., *stationarius*, d. and was buried the same day, *Chron. Stone*, 95; his obit on 4 Nov. is in BL Ms Arundel 68, fo 47.

II John GOLDWELL

occ. 1519/20

1519, 6 May, one of nine tonsured, *SL*, 194, CCA Lit. Ms D.12, fo 11v.

1520, 3 Feb., prof., *ib.*

n.d., 18 Dec., his obit or that of another John Goldwell, dcn, occ. in BL Ms Arundel 68, fo 51v.

I Thomas GOLDWELL [Goldewell, Goldwelle

occ. 1410 d. 1439

1410, 13 Dec., one of eight prof., *SL*, 185, CCA Lit. Ms D.12, fo 6.

1413, 2 Apr., ord dcn, Canterbury cathedral, Reg. abp Arundel, ii, fo 101.

1417, 10 Apr., ord pr., Canterbury cathedral, *Reg. abp Chichele*, iv, 328.

1428, c. 1 Mar., *custos* of St Mary in crypt, Oxford Bod. Ms Tanner 165, fo 3–3v.

1432/3, 1435, 1437, 1438/9, treasurer, CCA DCc Treas. acct 12, 'Chron. Wm Glastynbury', 129, CCA DCc DE1 15C/21, London acct 38.

1428, c. 1 Mar., with Geoffrey Bonde, q.v., sent to inform the abp at Lambeth of the d. of prior John Wodnesburgh, q.v., Oxford Bod. Ms Tanner 165, fo 3–3v.

1439, 3 Feb., one of several monks licensed to leave the priory *pro recreacione*, Chron. Wm Glastynbury, fo 182^{v}/177^{v}.

1439, 10 Mar., d. *Chron. Stone*, 23–24; 'iste frater multa bona fecit in ista ecclesia', *ib.*

II Thomas GOLDWELL D.Th.
[Goldewell, Goldwel, ?*alias* Gyfford
occ. 1493 occ. 1540

1517–1540, prior: el. very shortly before 29 Sept. 1517, the day on which he celebrated his first pontifical mass, *SL*, 194, CCA Lit. Ms D.12, fo 11^{v}; 1540, 4 Apr., res., see below.

1493, 26 July, one of ten tonsured, *SL*, 192, CCA Lit. Ms D.12, fo 9^{v}.

1494, 29 Mar., ord acol., Canterbury cathedral, *Reg. abp Morton*, i, no 443a.

1494, 19 Apr., prof., *SL*, 192, CCA Lit. Ms D.12, fo 9^{v}.

1495, 18 Apr., ord subdcn, Canterbury cathedral, *Reg. abp Morton*, i, no 444b.

1496, 2 Apr., ord dcn, Canterbury cathedral, *ib.*, i, no 445c.

1499/1500, celebrated his first mass and recd 8d. from the sacrist, Woodruff, 'Sacrist's Rolls', 66 (CCA DCc Sac. acct 60).

1512, Dec.; 1513, 25 Dec.; 1514, 25 Dec.; 1516, 25 Mar.; 1517, 25 Mar., warden of manors, CCA Lit. Ms C.11, fos 55, 55^{v}, 56^{v}, 57^{v}, 58.

1496, May, given travelling expenses of 23s. 4d. to go to Oxford; in Oct. he recd 10s. to pay for his *cappa scolaris*, Pantin, *Cant. Coll. Ox.*, iv, 204; see also *ib.*, ii, 224.

1498/1507, at Oxford, *ib.*, ii, 224, 226, 232, 233, 236, 239, 241, 245, 248 (CCA DCc Cart. Antiq. O.151.30, 31, 32, 33, 35, 37, 38, 39, 41).

1506, 20 Mar., and again on 14 May, supplicated for reduction of grace for B.Th., Pantin, *Cant. Coll. Ox.*, iii, 248–249 (Oxford Univ. Archives, Reg. G, fos 13^{v}, 16^{v}).

1506, 14 Dec., adm. B.Th., Pantin, *Cant. Coll. Ox.*, iii, 249 (Reg. G, fo 28^{v}).

1511, 1 May, with William Gyllyngham III, q.v., given licence by the prior and convent to study abroad, Pantin, *Cant. Coll. Ox.*, iii, 140–141 (Reg. T, fo 92^{v}). See below.

1501, 26 Apr., [at Oxford] and absent from the el. of an abp, Reg. R, fo 56.

1511, 2 Sept., absent from the visitation, but 29th in order on the certificate; he was *in studio Parisiensi* with William Gyllyngham III, q.v., Wood-Legh, *Visit.*, 3 (Reg. abp Warham, i, fo 35^{v}).

1512, 9 Apr., with William Gyllyngham III, recalled to Canterbury from Louvain by the prior who considered the 'world so jeobardous', Pantin, *Cant. Coll. Ox*, iii, 141. Here, both are described as doctors.

1518, witnessed the will of a parishioner of St Alphege, Canterbury, Hussey, 'Kentish Wills', 36.

1533, wrote [to Cromwell] in connection with Elizabeth Barton, nun and visionary, *L and P Henry VIII*, vi, no 1470.

1534, 12 Dec., headed the list of monks who signed the Act of Supremacy, *DK 7th Report*, Appndx 2, 282.

1535, 7 Nov., begged Cromwell to modify some of his [harsh] injunctions, *L and P Henry VIII*, ix, no 784. Some of the monks complained to Cromwell in a letter dated 25 Nov., that the prior was not adhering to the diet prescribed by the royal injunctions, *ib.*, no 879.

1536, 4 June, sought to be relieved from attendance at convocation on grounds of age and infirmity, *L and P Henry VIII*, x, no 1053; Cromwell's favourable reply is *ib.*, no 1199.

[1538, 8 Feb., after], in a list of monks prob. prepared for Thomas Cromwell, he was reported as 61 yrs of age, Pantin, *Cant. Coll. Ox.*, iii, 152.

1538, 20 Aug., in a letter to Cromwell he observed that 'religious men have been in this church 900 year and more . . . [he had] made his profession to serve God in a religious habit' and was relieved to know that Cromwell had said he would not constrain the monks to forsake their religious vows, *L and P Henry VIII*, xiii, pt 2, no 139. In Dec. he sent a gift of £20 in gold to the king and 'a poor token' to Cromwell, *ib.*, no 1158.

1540, 24 Feb., wrote to Cromwell expressing the wish to be apptd dean but had heard that Richard Thornden q.v. was being apptd; he was loathe to leave his present quarters as he was old and soon to die, *L and P Henry VIII*, xv, no 254.

1540, 4 Apr., retired with a pension of £80 p.a., Pantin, *Cant. Coll. Ox.*, iii, 152.

An inventory of seventeen books, dated c. 1496, given for his use at Canterbury college is printed in Pantin, *Cant. Coll. Ox.*, i, 81.

His family name was prob. Gyfford as the obit of his brother John, of that name, is in BL Ms Arundel 68, fo 24^{v} and Lambeth Ms 20, fo 240^{v}.

William GOLDWELL
occ. 1524 occ. 1540

1524, 21/22 July, one of eleven granted adm. [*ingressum*] to Christ Church, CCA Lit. Ms D.12, fos 11^{v}–12.

1524, 4 Aug., one of eleven tonsured, *SL*, 195, CCA Lit. Ms D.12, fo 12.

1525, 19 Apr., prof., *ib.*

1534, 12 Dec., acknowledged the Act of Supremacy, *DK 7th Report*, Appndx 2, 282 (transcribed as Holdwell).

[1538, 8 Feb., after], in a list of monks prob. prepared for Thomas Cromwell, he was described as 'a good man', 30 yrs old, Pantin, *Cant. Coll. Ox.*, iii, 153.

1540, 4 Apr., awarded £6 p.a., *L and P Henry VIII*, xv, no 452.

GOLDWIN [Goldwinus
occ. [1070 × 1089]

[1070 × 1089], sent by abp Lanfranc to Queen Margaret of Scotland with regard to the founding of a monastery at Dunfermline, *Lanfranc Letters*, no 50.

Note: can there be any connection with Godfrey III?

[1114, before], monk keeper of the manor of Mucheberdesham [*sic*] which had been given to Christ Church, *Theobald Charters*, 537–538; the only clue to the date is 'before the time of Ralph, abp', *ib.*

Note: there may, of course, be two monks involved here, but if so they were prob. contemporaries.

GOLDWIN
see also Geldwin

GOLDYNSTONE
see John de Goodnyston II

GOLESHULL
see Coleshull

GOLSTANUS
n.d.

n.d., 3 Nov., obit in BL Ms Arundel 68, fo 47.

GOLSTON
see Goldston

I John de GOODNYSTON [Godeneston, Godneston, Godnistone, Godwynston, Guodnyston
occ. 1349 d. 1397

1349, 9 Oct., one of six prof., *SL*, 181, CCA Lit. Ms D.12, fo 4.
1350, 18 Sept., ord subdcn, Goudhurst, Reg. abp Islip, fo 310.
1351, 24 Sept., ord dcn, chapel of Herne parish church, *ib.*, fo 312.
1353, 21 Dec., ord pr., abp's chapel, Maidstone, *ib.*, fo 314^{v}.

1365/7, chamberlain, CCA DCc, Chamb. accts 67, 45.
1367, 28 Mar., [re]apptd chamberlain, *Reg. abp Langham*, 283.
1368, 6 Oct., apptd precentor, *ib.*, 315; he was [re]apptd precentor by abp Wittlesey on 22 June 1369, Reg. abp Wittlesey, fo 13, but replaced in Oct. 1370 by John de Otford I, q.v.; apptd precentor again on 25 Jan. 1371, *ib.*, fo 37, and was precentor still or again in June 1374, Reg. G, fo 175^{v}.
1376, Apr., 1377, 27 June, subprior, *Lit. Cant.*, no 945 (CCA DCc Cart. Antiq. C206), Reg. abp Sudbury, fo 39. On 18 June 1381 he was also subprior, Oxford Bod. Ms Ashmole 794, fo 248^{v}; see below and William Recolver.
1382/4, granator, CCA DCc Treas. acct 26, fos 2–7.
1383/4, 1385, cellarer, CCA DCc Treas. acct 26, fo 7, MA2, fo 335. He was apptd on 1 Sept. 1383, Reg. abp Courtenay, i, fo 44^{v}.
1391/2, subprior, CCA DCc Sac. acct 10; prob. subprior at the time of d., see below.

1360, 3 Oct., absent from the house and cited to return for the visitation, Reg. H, fo 98.
1374, 30 June, 13th in order at the el. of an abp, Reg. G, fos 173^{v}–175^{v}.
1376, Apr., one of ten monks apptd to the committee set up for regulating the infirmary, *Lit. Cant.*, no 945 (CCA DCc Cart. Antiq. C206).
1381, 18 June, papal letters were recd and read in chapter allowing him, in response to his petition, to remain in the office of subprior for life because of the exemplary way in which he had been carrying out his duties in that office for three yrs or more. However, the prior and chapter ordered him to renounce this privilege since it contravened the rights and customs of the church; he complied and swore obedience to the prior, Oxford, Bod. Ms Ashmole 794, fo 248^{v}.
1381, 31 July, 7th in order at the el. of an abp and one of six chosen by the previously named three *compromissorii* to add to their number, Reg. G, fo 225^{v}, Oxford, Bod. Ms Ashmole 794, fo 254^{v}.
1391/2, gave the sacrist 3s. 4d. for candles to burn before the image of our Lady during the hours of night, CCA DCc Sac. acct 10.
1396, 7 Aug., 2nd in order at the el. of an abp, Reg. G, fo 234^{v}.
1397, 8 May, d., prob. while subprior since the obituary states that he twice held this office, the first time for seven yrs and the second for thirteen; see above. He was described as 'venerabilis senex cunctis preteribus et magnatibus regni multum acceptus', CCA Lit. Ms D.12, fo 17^{v}; he was buried on the south side of the nave before the great cross and close to the grave of Catherine Lovel, *ib.*

A silver pax and a *ciphus* of wood, formerly his are included in Canterbury college inventories, e.g. that of 1443, Pantin, *Cant. Coll. Ox.*, i, 1, 7 (CCA DCc Cart. Antiq. O.34).

II John de GOODNYSTON [Godenyston, Godneston, Goldynstone
occ. 1483 occ. [1538]

1483, 30 Sept., one of six tonsured, *SL*, 191, CCA Lit. Ms D.12, fo 8^{v}.
1484, 10 June, prof., *ib.*
1485, 2 Apr., ord subdcn, Canterbury cathedral, *Reg. abp Bourgchier*, 450.
1485, 24 Sept., ord dcn, Canterbury cathedral, *ib.*, 452.

1496, chancellor, with Richard Sellyng III, q.v., Reg. S, fo 405v; also in 1499 with John Menys, q.v., *ib.*, fo 430v.
1496/7, he was described as *magister operum*, CCA DCc MA9, fo 109v.
1500/1; 1503, 21 Feb.; 1504, 25 Aug., treasurer, Lambeth ED86; Reg. T, fo 15v; CCA DCc Ms Scrap Book A.90A.
1504/9, granator, CCA DCc Gran. acct 63, MA11, fos 6v, 55, 63, 120v.
1509/11; 1516, 25 Mar.; 1516/30, sacrist, CCA DCc Sac. accts 72, 73, CCA Lit. Ms C.11, fo 57v, CCA DCc MA14, fos 1, 37, 67, 102, Sac. acct 74, MA14, fo 175, MA30, fo 129, MA14, fos 222, 279, MA30, fo 151, MA15, fos 2, 51, CCA Lit. Ms C.11, fo 65, CCA DCc MA15, fos 101, 159. MA5, fo 108–168v, shows that he was also in office continuously from 1510 to 1529. He res. in 1530 and his *dimissio* dated 23 Apr. is in Reg. T, fo 346.

1493, 1 May, 44th in order at the ratification of an agreement, Reg. S, fo 383v; but see John Crosse I.
1501, 26 Apr., 28th in order at the el. of an abp, Reg. R, fo 56v.
1508, wk of 25 Apr., served as *ebdomodarius* for the high mass, CCA Lit. Ms D.12, fo 11.
1511, 2 Sept., 13th on the visitation certificate, Wood-Legh, *Visit.*, 3 (Reg. abp Warham, i, fo 35).
[1538, 8 Feb., after], in a list of monks prob. prepared for Thomas Cromwell he was described as a good man, a 'stecionar', 76 yrs of age, Pantin, *Cant. Coll. Ox.*, iii, 152.

Joseph de GOODNYSTON [Godeneston, Godneston, Godnistone, Godwyneston, Godwynstone, Jodwynstone
occ. 1349 occ. 1381

1349, 9 Oct., one of six prof., *SL*, 181, CCA Lit. Ms D.12, fo 4.
1350, 18 Sept., ord acol. Goudhurst, Reg Islip, fo 310; see also John de Goodnyston I, who was his contemporary.
1350, 18 Dec., ord subdcn, Maidstone, *ib.*, fo 310v.
1351, 24 Sept., ord dcn, chapel of Herne parish church, *ib.*, fo 312.
1353, 21 Dec., ord pr., abp's chapel, Maidstone, *ib.*, fo 314v.
1371, 1373/4, *custos corone*, CCA DCc MA2, fo 266, Treas. acct 5 (as Joseph).
1383/4, 1385, *custos corone*, CCA DCc Treas. acct 26, fos 2–6v, MA2, fo 334v; also 1373 through to 1382 in MA2, fos 276–329v.
1366, 10 May, present at the el. of an abp, Reg. G, fo 147.
1374, 30 June, 12th in order at the el. of an abp, *ib.*, fos 173v–175v.
1381, 31 July, 6th at the el. of an abp, *ib.*, fo 225v.

I Thomas de GOODNYSTON [Godneston, Godnyston, Godwenstone, Guodwyneston
occ. 1323 occ. 1374

1323, one of six [clothed in the monastic habit], *SL*, 179, CCA Lit. Ms D.12, fo 3v.
[1325], 18 Oct., prof. Reg. L, fo 141v.
1336, feretrar, CCA DCc MA2, fo 250.
1341/2, anniversarian, Lambeth, ED37.
1349/50, sacrist, CCA DCc Arrears acct 22.
1367, 27 Mar., apptd penitentiary [in the priory], *Reg. abp Langham*, 282–283.
1331/3, chaplain to abp Meopham, CCA DCc DE3, fos 1, 2, Lambeth Ms 243, fo 41, Reg. L, fos 10, 174v, CCA DCc Godmersham acct 15.
[1331], recd a letter from the prior asking him to intercede with the abp on behalf of a clerk in prison, *Lit. Cant.*, no 396 (Reg. L, fo 12).
1348, 30 Aug., named as one of the three initial *compromissorii* who were to choose seven *compromissorii* for the el. of an abp, Reg. G, fo 31.
1349, 4 June, 19th in order at the el. of an abp and was named as one of the thirteen *compromissorii*, *ib.*, fo 61v.
1349, 8/9 Sept., 18th at the el. of an abp, and once again named as one of the thirteen *compromissorii*, *ib.*, fos 76, 77.
1374, 30 June, 2nd in order at the el. of an abp, Reg. G, fos 173v–175v.

II Thomas de GOODNYSTON [Goodnyshton
occ. 1421 d. 1457

1421, 4 Apr., one of six prof., *SL*, 186, CCA Lit. Ms D.12, fo 6v.
1446, 21 Dec., *magister ordinis*, *SL*, 188, CCA Lit. Ms D.12, fo 7v.
1449/50, third prior, CCA DCc, Sac. acct 36.
1448, 24 Mar., one of four monks who conveyed the reliquary containing the bones of St Fleogild, abp, from the high altar to the *corona*, *Chron. Stone*, 44.
1449/50, recd a 6d. pittance from the granator, CCA DCc Gran. acct 56.
1457, 1 July, d., *Chron. Stone*, 57.

Alexander GOODSCHEP
see Essche, London

GOODUSSTUN
see Godnyston

John de GORE [Goore, ?Gorle
occ. 1298 d. 1326

1298, 18 Oct., one of seven prof., *SL*, 178, CCA Lit. Ms D.12, fo 3.
1299, 19 Sept., ord subdcn, Littlebourne, *Reg. abp Winchelsey*, 930 (which states dcn, prob. mistakenly; see below).
1300, 4 June, ord dcn, Smeeth chapel by Aldington, *ib.*, 935.

1305, 1308/9, subalmoner, Reg. B, fo 426, CCA DCc Alm. acct 21.
1310/13, treasurer, CCA DCc MA2, fos 27v–42v.
1311, subcellarer, CCA DCc MA2, fo 30.
1314/16, warden of manors, CCA DCc East Farleigh acct 10, Agney acct 30.
1318/21, chaplain to the prior, CCA DCc MA2, fos 88v–112.
1320/3, treasurer, CCA DCc MA2, fos 109v–126.

1319, 5 Mar., with Richard de Clyve, q.v., recd an apptment as general proctors, CUL Ms Ee.5.31, fo 199.
1324, 29 May, one of the monks who had been subjected to penance after the abp's visitation, and on behalf of whom the prior and chapter now wrote to ask that the penance be lessened, CUL Ms Ee.5.31, fo 236–236v.
1325, 19 Oct., at the inquisition concerning the *littera famosa* which Robert de Aldon, q.v. said he had found on John de Gore's bed he declared his innocence of the forgery, and 57 brethren agreed and accused Aldon of guilt, *Lit. Cant.*, no 156 (Reg. L, fo 142, CCA DCc Cart. Antiq. C.1294).
1326, 17 June, d., CCA Lit. Ms D.12, fo 16; his obit is in BL Ms Arundel 68, fo 31.
n.d., sent by the prior and convent to the king in Scotland, CCA DCc, DE3, fo 3.

Name in Reg. J, which is known as his register. It contains treatises on husbandry, manorial extents and other material relating to the priory estates, prob. compiled when he was warden of manors or treasurer.

Item nos 1749–1755 in the Eastry catalogue belonged to him; two of these are partly in French and one, listed as registrum de consuetudinibus Thes' (no 1754) may be Reg. J above, James, *Ancient Libraries*, 139–140.

The inventory of missing books, dated 1 Mar. 1338 lists two service books of his, *Lit. Cant.*, no 618 (Reg. L, fo 104).

A list of vestments acquired *temp.* prior Eastry, q.v., has his name at its head, Legg and Hope, *Inventories*, 66 (BL Ms Cotton Galba E.iv, fo 117v).

An inventory of the refectory, dated 1328, includes five silver *ciphi*, eighteen spoons and four wooden *ciphi* of his, Dart, *Antiq. Cant.*, xx (BL Ms Cotton Galba E.iv, fos 179, 180).

Nicholas de GORE [Goore

occ. 1286 d. 1330

1286, 9 Oct., one of five prof., *SL*, 177, CCA Lit. Ms D.12, fo 3 (the name has been, confusingly, repeated, the second time as Richard).

1301, 1302/6, bartoner, CCA DCc MA1, fos 231v, 237v–264v.
1319, Jan./Sept., almoner, CCA DCc Alm. acct no 6.
1325/6, warden of manors, CCA DCc MA2, fos 143–152.
1326/9, *magister corone*, CCA DCc MA2, fos 154v–183v.
1330, *custos tumbe*, CCA DCc MA2, fo 192.

[1296], one of the monks accused of laxity in attendance at divine office during a visitation, *Reg. abp Winchelsey*, 92.
1297, 7 July, visited Meopham, CCA DCc Meopham acct 26.
1324, 29 May, subjected to penance after a visitation, and the prior and chapter now wrote to ask that the penance be mitigated as he was reduced to skin and bone by fasting, CUL Ms Ee.5.31, fo 236v.
1330, 9 May, d., CCA Lit. Ms D.12, fo 16; obit in BL Ms Arundel 68, fo 27.

An inventory of missing service books dated 1 Mar. 1338 includes his Exequiae for which Alan de Cruce, q.v. was held responsible, *Lit. Cant.*, no 618 (Reg. L, fo 104).

Thomas GORE [Goore

occ. 1382 d. 1417

1382, 5 Sept., one of six who recd the habit, *SL*, 183, CCA Lit. Ms D.12, fo 5.
1383, 11 Aug., made his prof. before the prior who had been comm. by the abp, Reg. abp Courtenay, i, fo 42v.

1396/7, *custos* of St Mary in crypt, CCA DCc Prior acct 4.
1397/8, feretrar, CCA DCc Feret. acct 1.
1398/1403, bartoner, CCA DCc Bart. accts 66, 68, Eastry accts 123, 124, Bart. acct 69.
1403/4, treasurer, CCA DCc Bailiff of Liberty acct 14.
1404/5, *magister corone*, CCA DCc Prior acct 20.
1407/10, chamberlain, CCA DCc Chamb. accts 57, 70, 58.
1412/14, bartoner, CCA DCc Bart. accts 74, 75.
1415, 1 Mar., apptd chamberlain, *Reg. abp Chichele*, iv, 115; absolved *ex certis causis*, 10 May, 1416, *ib.*, iv, 150.

1396, 7 Aug., 39th in order at the el. of an abp, Reg. G, fo 234v.
1414, 12 Mar., 10th at the el. of an abp, *Reg. abp Chichele*, i, 4.
1417, 16 Sept., d., after holding a number of offices *laudabiliter*, CCA Lit. Ms D.12, fo 21. His claim to fame in *Chron. Stone*, 8, is that it was he who brought about the inclusion of the name of St Blaise *in collecta Propiciare.* His obit is in BL Ms Arundel 68, fo 41v.

An inventory of the martyrdom dated 1500 includes a set of red vestments of his [?gift] Legg and Hope, *Inventories*, 127.

M. GOSCELIN [Goscelinus

occ. [c. 1080 × c. 1114]

[c. 1080 × c. 1114], wrote the life of St Edith, Gibson, *Lanfranc*, 138 n., 170 n.; he dedicated it to Lanfranc, *ib.*, 172. See Sharpe, *Latin Writers*.

Note: a M. Goscelin, presumably this monk, wrote the life of St Augustine of Canterbury, of which a copy is in Lambeth Ms 159, fos 186–200v.

GOSFRID(US)
see Geoffrey I, Godfrey III

GRACIANUS
n.d.

n.d., 28 July, pr., whose obit occ. in BL Ms Arundel 68, fo 36.

Geoffrey de GRANTEBRYGG
occ. 2nd half 13th c.

n.d., name occ. in the list in *SL*, 175 (transcribed as Cantebrygge), CCA Lit. Ms D.12, fo 2v.

Nicholas de GRA[N]TEBRYGG [Cauntebrug', Grantebrigge
occ. [1244 × 1258] occ. 1286

n.d., name occ. in the list in *SL*, 174, CCA Lit. Ms D.12, fo 2.

[1244 × 1248], with Walter de Hatfeld, q.v., sent as proctors by prior Nicholas de Sandwyco, q.v., to the abbot of Anglesey to procure the return of a volume containing John Chrysostom's De laude apostoli and other writings, *Acta Guala*, no 156.

[1281], 9 Nov., mentioned with John de Shamelysford, q.v., in a letter from the abp to the prior and convent, *Epist. Pecham*, 245.

1285/6, visited Meopham, CCA DCc Meopham acct 8.

1286, 13 Sept., granted licence by the prior and convent to transfer to the abbey of Geraldun [?Garendon] in order to lead a stricter life, CUL Ms Ee.5.31, fo 24v.

There are up to twelve volumes of an N. de Grantebregge in the Eastry catalogue, items 692–703, James, *Ancient Libraries*, 76–77.

Richard de GRAVENAL
occ. 1st half 13th c.

n.d., name occ. in the *post exilium* list in *SL*, 173, CCA Lit. Ms D.12, fo 1.

Richard GRAVENE B.CnL [Gravenay, Graveney, Graveneye
occ. 1423 d. 1472/3

1423, 30 Sept., one of five prof., *SL*, 187, CCA Lit. Ms D.12, fo 6v.

1425, 22 Dec., ord subdcn, Charing, *Reg. abp Chichele*, i, 374.

1426, 30 Mar., ord dcn, Canterbury cathedral, *ib.*, iv, 375.

1427, 5 Dec., ord pr., bp's chapel, Trottiscliffe, Reg. Langdon (Rochester), fo 59v.

1443, 25 Mar., *magister ordinis*, *SL*, 188, CCA Lit. Ms D.12, fo 7v.

1449, 21 Apr., apptd warden of Canterbury college; absolved by 27 Oct. 1454, Pantin, *Cant. Coll. Ox.*, iii, 103, 106 (Reg. abp Stafford, fo 32v, *Reg. abp Bourgchier*, 16), *Chron. Stone*, 54. His acct as warden 1448/9 is in Pantin, *Cant. Coll. Ox.*, ii, 170–176 (CCA DCc Cart. Antiq. O.151.14).

1432/3, scholar at Canterbury college, provided with horses and travelling expenses by the treasurers, Pantin, *Cant. Coll. Ox.*, iv, 192.

[1435], one of three students at Oxford, 'Chron. Wm Glastynbury', 129 (Ms fo 116v).

1446/7, at Oxford, and recd 13s. 4d. *pro exhibitione sua*, CCA Lit. Ms E.6, fo 75.

1451, 6 Apr., supplicated for B.CnL stating that he had studied for three yrs in the faculty of arts, two yrs in canon law and six yrs 'quos habuit in claustro in decretis'. This was granted on payment of 40s. 'ad fabricam novarum scolarum', Pantin, *Cant. Coll. Ox.*, iii, 249–250 (Oxford Univ. Archives, Reg. Aa, fo 53).

1439, 24 Dec., promoted to the upper [stalls in the] choir, 'Chron. Wm Glastynbury', 135.

1452, 29 June, with Walter Hertford, q.v., sent as proctors to the king and the abp elect [John Kemp], *Chron. Stone*, 54.

1466, 17 Feb., 12th in order in an inventory of *jocalia fratrum* [given by him and/or assigned for his use], Reg. N, fo 231.

1472/3, d., Woodruff, 'Sacrist's Rolls', 64 (CCA DCc Sac. acct 53); in CCA Lit. Ms D.12, fo 26, described as *conventualis*.

Note: the obit of a Richard Gravene, pr. on 28 Jan. is in BL Ms Arundel 68, fo 14v.

He left a blood red alb [embroidered] with pelicans and gryphons to Canterbury college, Pantin, *Cant. Coll. Ox.*, i, 11 (Cart. Antiq. O.135).

I GREGORY
n.d.

n.d., 30 July, acol., prof., whose obit occ. in BL Ms Arundel 68, fo 36v.

II GREGORY
occ. 1233 occ. 1237

1233, 29 Oct., 1234, 27 Oct., treasurer, CCA DCc MA1, fos 76, 77v.

1235, Dec./1237, Apr., cellarer, CCA DCc AS4, AS5.

III GREGORY
occ. 1254/6

1254, 13 Nov., 1255, 3 Dec., 1256, 15 Nov., treasurer, CCA DCc MA1, fos 95, 96, 97v.

Note: see Gregory de Audinges and Gregory de Hasting, both of whom were contemporaries of Gregory II and Gregory III, who may of course be one and the same; but if so, which?

William GREGORY [Gregorie
occ. 1522 occ. 1540

1522, 11 Feb., one of ten tonsured, *SL*, 195, CCA Lit. Ms D.12, fo 11^{v}.
1522, 24 Nov., prof., *ib.*
1526/7, celebrated his first mass and recd a small gift from the sacrist, Woodruff, 'Sacrist's Rolls', 72.
[1538, 8 Feb., after], *magister martyrii*, Pantin, *Cant. Coll. Ox.*, iii, 153.
1534, 12 Dec., acknowledged the Act of Supremacy, *DK 7th Report*, Appndx 2, 282.
[1538, 8 Feb., after], in a list of monks prob. prepared for Thomas Cromwell, he was described as a 'witty' man, 32 yrs old, Pantin, *Cant. Coll. Ox.*, ii, 153.
1540, 4 Apr., awarded £6 p.a, *L and P Henry VIII*, xv, no 452.

William GRENE
occ. 1401 d. 1408

1401, 19 Mar., ord acol., Canterbury cathedral, Reg. abp Arundel, i, fo 327^{v}.
1401, 25 Mar., one of seven prof., *SL*, 185, CCA Lit. Ms D.12, fo 5^{v}.
1401, 17 Dec., ord subdcn, Canterbury cathedral, Reg. abp Arundel, i, fo 329.
1403, 14 Apr., ord dcn, Canterbury cathedral, *ib.*, i, fo 331.
1408, 22 Sept., d., and the requiem mass was celebrated at the high altar, CCA Lit. Ms D.12, fo 19.

William de GRENEHELD [Grenchilde, Grenehelle, Grenehilde, Grenhulle
occ. 1275 d. 1293

n.d., name occ. in the list in *SL*, 175, CCA Lit. Ms D.12, fo 2.
1275/9, bartoner, CCA DCc MA1, fos 123^{v}–130.
1277/8, granator, CCA DCc AS11, Reg. H, fo 208 (granator *exterior*)
1287, warden of manors, CCA DCc MA1, fo 150^{v}.
1293, 11 May, d., CCA Lit. Ms D.12, fo 15.

He left two *ciphi*, one of silver and three of wood (*murra*), acc. to the inventory of the refectory dated 1328, Dart, *Antiq. Cant.*, xix, xxii (BL Ms Cotton Galba E.iv, fos 178^{v}, 180).

John de GRENEHULL [Grenehall, Grenhull
occ. 1346 occ. 1366

1346, 11 Nov., one of eight prof., *SL*, 181, CCA Lit. Ms D.12, fo 4.
1350, 18 Sept., ord pr., Goudhurst, Reg. abp Islip, fo 310^{v}.
1366, 10 May, penitentiary, Reg. G, fo 147^{v}.
1348, 30 Aug., not yet in sacred orders and therefore had no voice in the el. of an abp, Reg. G, fo 30.
1366, 10 May, named as one of seven *compromissorii* in the el. of an abp and acted as spokesman for the seven in announcing the choice, Reg. G, fos 147^{v}, 148, 150, 152.
1366, 6 July, one of four monks apptd by the prior *sed. vac.*, to carry out a visitation of St Gregory's priory, Canterbury, *ib.*, fo 127^{v}.

Thomas de GRENEWAY [Grenewey, Greneweye
occ. 1299 d. 1333

1299, n.d., one of seven prof., *SL*, 178, CCA Lit. Ms D.12, fo 3^{v}.
1300, 4 June, ord acol., Smeeth chapel by Aldington, *Reg. abp Winchelsey*, 933.
1319/20, treasurer, CCA DCc MA2, fo 102.
1323/33, feretrar, CCA DCc MA2, fos 128^{v}–221, DE3, fo 1 (1331).
1327, 11 Dec., one of three initial *compromissorii* chosen by the prior and chapter to name seven *compromissorii* in the el. of an abp, Reg. Q, fo 123; see also *CPL*, ii (1305–1342), 272.
1333, 15 July, d., CCA Lit. Ms D.12, fo 16; his obit is in BL Ms Arundel 68, fo 34.

His name is attached to a set of vestments acquired *temp.* prior Eastry, q.v., Legg and Hope, *Inventories* 65 (BL Ms Cotton Galba E.iv, fo 116^{v}); he is also associated with Richard de Rawe, q.v., with regard to another set, Legg and Hope, *Inventories*, 77 (BL Ms Cotton Galba E.iv, fo 122). On the 1328 inventory of the refectory, he and Rawe, *custodes feretrii*, acct for a dozen silver *scutelli*, Dart, *Antiq. Cant.*, xviii (BL Ms Cotton Galba E.iv, fo 178).

John GRENEWYCH
occ. [1390] d. 1413

[1390], 28 Sept., one of seven prof., *SL*, 184, CCA Lit. Ms D.12, fo 5.
1396, 7 Aug., 60th in order at the el. of an abp, Reg. G, fo 234^{v}.
1413, 23 June, d., after suffering from blindness for a yr, CCA Lit. Ms D.12, fo 19^{v}; he had previously been a canon regular of Lesnes, *ib.* His obit is in BL Ms Arundel 68, fo 31^{v}.

Hubert GROSSUS
see Hubert

James GROVE
occ. [1393] d. 1430

[1393], 21 Nov., one of six prof., *SL*, 184, CCA Lit. Ms D.12, fo 5.
1394, 18 Apr., ord subdcn, Canterbury cathedral, Reg. abp Courtenay, ii, fo 184^{v}.
1396, 1 Apr., ord dcn, Canterbury cathedral, Reg. abp Courtenay, ii, fo 186^{v}.
1401, 2 Apr., ord pr., Canterbury cathedral, Reg. abp Arundel, i, fo 328^{v}.

1414, 2nd day after the abp's enthronement, apptd second penitentiary, *Reg abp Chichele*, iv, 115–116.
1414 × 1428, warden of Canterbury college, Pantin, *Cant. Coll. Ox.*, i, 7, 8.
1421/3, May, sacrist, CCA DCc Sac. accts 21, 22; he was apptd on 22 Dec. 1421, *Reg. abp Chichele*, iv, 242.
1423, 16 Apr., apptd penitentiary, *ib.*, iv, 246. He was still (or again) penitentiary on 31 Mar., 1428, Oxford Bod. Ms Tanner 165, fo 6^{v}.
1428/9, subprior, CCA DCc Sac. acct 25; see Henry Sutton.

1397/8, with William Chart, Richard Holden q.v., and four others recd money 'pro benedictione fratrum . . . versus Oxon' ', CCA DCc Feret. acct 1.
1396, 7 Aug., 70th in order at the el. of an abp, Reg. G, fo 234^{v}.
1414, 12 Mar., 31st at the el. of an abp, *Reg. abp Chichele*, i, 4.
1428, 31 Mar., one of the monks invited to the abp's palace after the *prefectio* of William Molassh as prior, q.v., Oxford, Bod. Ms Tanner 165, fo 6^{v}.
[1429, Jan.], appted preacher and confessor in the diocese for the crusade vs the Hussites, Holmes, 'Crusades vs the Hussites', 740.
1430, 27 Dec., d., *propter quedam infirmitatis incommodem* after receiving the sacraments of communion and extreme unction; he was buried in the infirmary chapel in front of the altar of Saints Leonard and Benedict, near the door leading to the garden, *Chron. Stone*, 16 and CCA Lit. Ms D.12, fo 23; his obit is in BL Ms Arundel 68, fo 52.

He left table linen, bed linen, a *ciphus de radice*, eight spoons and a new chest to Canterbury college, Pantin, *Cant. Coll. Ox.*, i, 7, 8 (CCA DCc Cart. Antiq. O.34).

John GROVE
occ. 1417 d. 1425

1417, 13 Dec., one of five [?clothed/prof.], *SL*, 186, CCA Lit. Ms D.12, fo 6^{v}.
Note: this entry takes into account two conflicting statements:
(1) *SL* and Lit. Ms D.12 give the date 1417, 13 Dec. without specifying whether this ref. to tonsure, clothing or prof. and
(2) *Chron. Stone*, 5, states that John Stone I, q.v., one of the five, was clothed on 13 Dec. 1418.
1418, 26 Mar., ord acol., Canterbury cathedral, *Reg. abp Chichele*, iv, 332.
1419, 1 Apr., ord subdcn, chapel in the priory, *ib.*, i, 191.
1420, 6 Apr., ord dcn, Canterbury cathedral, *ib.*, iv, 342.
1424, 22 Apr., ord pr., Canterbury cathedral, *ib.*, iv, 360.
1425, 29 Dec., d. as the result of a fall from the south west tower of the cathedral then under construction, *Chron. Stone*, 12, CCA Lit. Ms D.12, fo 22; his obit is in BL Ms Arundel 68, fo 52^{v}.

John GRYFFUN [Gryffyn
occ. 1333 d. [1340/1]

1333, 9 Oct., one of twelve prof., *SL*, 180, CCA Lit. Ms D.12, fo 4.

[1340/1], 23 June, d., CCA Lit. Ms D.12, fo 16^{v}.

GUARNERIUS
see Warner

GUIBERTUS
see Wibert

I GUIDO [Guy, Wido
occ. 1233 occ. 1254

1233, 29 Oct., 1234, 27 Oct., treasurer, CCA DCc MA1, fos 76, 77^{v}.
1244/5, 1245/54, sacrist, CCA DCc AS16, MA1, fos 86^{v}–95 and Reg. H, fos 172, 174^{v}, 177^{v} (for the yrs 1252, 1253, 1254).
1239, 4 Jan., one of the group of monks accused of contumacy by the abp after the forgery scandal, *Gervase Cant.*, ii, 144; see Simon de Hertlepe.
1239, 1 Feb., one of those accused by the abp of being a ringleader in the el. of Roger de La Lee, q.v. as prior without his permission or presence, *ib.*, ii, 153.
Note: see also Guido de Walda.

II GUIDO
occ. 1251

1251, prior of Dover after John [de Northflete], q.v., acc. to Gervase, *Gervase Cant.*, ii, 203, but see Walter de Cantuaria.
Note: this must be Guy de Walda, q.v.

III GUIDO
occ. 1285/6 occ. 1308

1285/6, chaplain to the prior, CCA DCc Cliffe acct 7.
1288, cellarer, CCA DCc MA1, fo 154^{v}.
1288/9, chaplain to the prior, CCA DCc MA1, fos 154^{v}–158^{v}.
1291/5, bartoner, CCA DCc MA1, fos 173–194.
1300/7, 1308, chaplain to the prior, CCA DCc MA2, fo 11^{v}.

Note: is this Guy de Smerden, q.v.?
See also Wido

[GUNDULF
occ. [1070] occ. 1077

[1070], prior of St Étienne, Caen, who came to Canterbury with Lanfranc 'to help . . . in organizing the community and running the estates', Gibson, *Lanfranc*, 175, which provides a bibliography.

1077, before 19 Mar., apptd bp of Rochester by the abp and consecrated on 19 Mar., *Fasti*, ii, 75.

A monk of Rochester, prob. one of his chaplains, wrote a Vita Gundulfi, c. 1114 × 1124; Rodney Thomson has ed. and transcribed it from BL Ms Cotton Nero A.viii, fos 42–86, *The Life of Gundulf, Bishop of Rochester* (Centre for Medieval Studies, Toronto, 1977).

Note: He may never have been considered as a prof. member of the community at Christ Church.]

GUODNYSTON, Guodwyneston

see John de Goodnyston, I, Thomas de Goodnyston I

John de GUSTON [Gustone

occ. 1333 occ. 1381

1333, 9 Oct., one of eleven prof., *SL*, 180, CCA Lit. Ms D.12, fo 4.

1349/50, warden of manors, CCA DCc Chartham acct 28.

1356/7, chamberlain, CCA DCc Chamb. acct 42; he was apptd on 14 Oct., Reg. abp Islip, fo 127 (where the scribe has somewhat confused the names and apptments).

1362/3, chamberlain, CCA DCc Arrears acct 70 (where the initial appears to be 'S' rather than 'J').

1366, 9 Sept., feretrar, Reg. G, fo 148.

1367, 27 Mar., apptd subprior, *Reg. abp Langham*, 282–283.

1369, 20 June, [re]apptd subprior, Reg. abp Wittlesey, fo 13.

1371, 10 Oct., apptd sacrist, *ib.*, fo 48ᵛ.

1372, *magister corone*, CCA DCc MA2, fo 270.

1373/85, sacrist, CCA DCc MA2, fos 276ᵛ–329ᵛ, Sac. acct 6, Treas. acct, fos 2ᵛ–7, MA2, fo 335; but see John de Otford I.

Note: it appears that abp Courtenay may have allowed him to remain in office if the prior and chapter chose to have him continue, if not Otford was to be apptd.

1348, 30 Aug., named by the three initial *compromissorii* to be one of seven *compromissorii* in the el. of an abp, Reg. G, fo 30ᵛ, 82.

1349, 4 June, 33rd in order at the el. of an abp, Reg. G, fo 60ᵛ.

1349, 8/9 Sept., 32nd in order and named as one of thirteen *compromissorii* in the el. of an abp Reg. G, fos 76ᵛ, 77.

1366, 10 May, named as one of seven *compromissorii* in the el. of an abp, *ib.*, fo 148.

1374, 30 June, 6th in order and named as one of three *scrutatores* in the el. of an abp, *ib.*, fos 173ᵛ–175ᵛ.

1376, Apr., one of ten monks apptd to the committee set up for regulating the infirmary, *Lit. Cant.*, no 945 (CCA DCc Cart. Antiq. C.206).

1381, 31 July, 3rd in order and named as one of three *compromissorii* who were to choose six more to add to their number, in the el. of an abp, Reg. G, fo 225ᵛ, Oxford, Bod. Ms Ashmole 794, fo 254ᵛ.

A mazer with his 'sign' *in fundo* is included in a Canterbury college inventory of 1459, Pantin, *Cant. Coll. Ox.*, i, 17 (CCA DCc Cart. Antiq. O.135).

Thomas GUSTON [Euston

occ. 1410 d. 1427

1410, 13 Dec., one of eight prof., *SL*, 185, CCA Lit. Ms D.12, fo 6.

1412, 19 Mar., ord dcn, abp's chapel, Saltwood, Reg. abp Arundel, ii, fo 100ᵛ.

1413, 2 Apr., ord pr., Canterbury cathedral, *ib.*, ii, fo 101ᵛ.

1414, Feb., scholar at Canterbury college, Pantin, *Cant. Coll. Ox.*, iii, 72.

1418, Dec., at Oxford, and brought back to Canterbury the body of John Wy, II, q.v., his fellow student and *socius rasture sue*, *Chron. Stone*, 9.

1427, 18 Apr., at this date 'prope gradum bacularii in theologia', *Chron. Stone*, 13.

1414, 12 Mar., 77th in order at the el. of an abp, *Reg. abp Chichele*, i, 4.

1421, 25 Dec., proposed by the prior and chapter as one of three nominees for the office of penitentiary, *Reg. abp Chichele*, iv, 241.

1427, 18 Apr., preached to the people on Good Friday in the cemetery on the text 'Oblatus est quia voluit' (Isaiah 53, 7) in the presence of the abp, *Chron. Stone*, 13 and CCA Lit. Ms D.12, fo 22 (the latter provides 'in the cemetery' and gives as the date *ultimo die perascheves*.

1427, 7 May, d., *Chron. Stone*, 13; at the time of his d. he was in the second to last place in the upper choir; he was regarded as *vir magne litterature*, *ib.*

GYFFORD

see Thomas Goldwell II

GYLES

see Gylys

John de GYLLYNGHAM [Gely[n]gham

occ. 1349 d. 1361

1349, 9 Oct., one of six prof., *SL*, 181, CCA Lit. Ms D.12, fo 4.

1350, 18 Sept., ord subdcn, Goudhurst, Reg. abp Islip, fo 310.

1351, 24 Sept., ord dcn, chapel of Herne parish church, *ib.*, fo 312.

1353, 21 Dec., ord pr., abp's chapel, Maidstone, *ib.*, fo 314ᵛ.

1361, 22 July, one of 25 monks who d. of the plague between June and Sept., CCA Lit. Ms D.12, fo 17.

Richard GYLLYNGHAM

occ. 1358/9 d. 1376

1370–1376, prior: el. 2 Aug. 1370, and *prefectio* the following day, Reg. abp Wittlesey, fo 31^{v}; d. on or just before 31 Aug. 1376, Lambeth Ms 20, fo 214^{v}, Reg. abp Sudbury, fo 27^{v}.

1358/9, 28 Oct., one of nine prof., *SL*, 181, CCA Lit. Ms D.12, fo 4.
1360, 29 Feb., ord acol., abp's chapel, Otford, Reg. abp Islip, fo 318.
1360, 4 Apr., ord subdcn, abp's chapel, Saltwood, *ib.*, fo 318^{v}.
1361, 18 Dec., ord dcn, Charing, *ib.*, fo 320.
1362, 11 June, ord pr., Mayfield, *ib.*, fo 321^{v}.

1368/9, bartoner, CCA DCc, Bart. acct 44.
1369/70, warden of manors, CCA DCc Hollingbourne acct 42.
Note: as prior he was also warden of manors in 1371, CCA DCc MA2, fo 265.

1370, 18 July, with William Vielston, q.v., sent to the abp for licence to el. a prior, Reg. abp Wittlesey, fo 31^{v}.
[1376], 31 Aug., his obit occ. in BL Ms Arundel 68, fo 40; see above.

His name is attached to item 270, Vitas patrum etc., in the Eastry catalogue, James, *Ancient Libraries*, 47–48; this must be an earlier Richard Gyllyngham, prob. not a monk.

Thomas GYLLYNGHAM [Gillyngham

occ. [1336] d. 1349

[1336], n.d., one of seven adm., *SL*, 180, CCA Lit. Ms D.12, fo 4.
1337, 19 June, one of five of the above seven who, although they had not yet completed their yr of probation were urging the prior to rec. their prof.; the prior therefore consulted the abp as he was afraid that they would, if denied, return to the world, Reg. L, fo 67^{v}. The abp's reply was a firm negative, *ib.*

1348, 30 Aug., named by the three initial *compromissorii* as one of seven *compromissorii* in the el. of an abp, Reg. G, fos 30^{v}, 82.
1349, 21 May, one of four who d. of the plague within little more than a month, CCA Lit. Ms D.12, fo 16^{v}; his obit on 20 May is in BL Ms Arundel 68, fo 28.

I William GYLLYNGHAM D.Th. [Gelyngham, Gillyngham, Gilyngham, Gylyngham

occ. [1369] d. 1410/11

[1369], one of four prof., *SL*, 182, CCA Lit. Ms D.12, fo 4^{v}.
1370, 15 Sept., ord acol., abp's chapel, Saltwood, Reg. abp Wittlesey, fo 166.
1370, 21 Sept., ord subdcn, Saltwood, *ib.*, fo 166^{v}.
1372, 21 Feb., ord dcn, abp's chapel, Croydon, *ib.*, fo 168^{v}.
1372, 13 Mar., ord pr., abp's chapel, Otford, *ib.*, fo 168^{v}.

1382/5, 1385/90, master lector in the cloister, Reg. abp Arundel, i, fo 437^{v}, Reg. G, fos 229^{v}, 239^{v}, 240. In 1388/9 he recd 40s. p.a., from the feretrars; and in 1389/90 20s. from the *custos martyrii*, and 20s. from the feretrars, Lambeth Ms 243, fos 212^{v}, 216^{v}.
1403, 28 June, apptd penitentiary, BL Ms Cotton Faustina C.v., fo 39.

1375/6, scholar at Canterbury college and recd 18s. 8d. from the treasurers for his expenses, Pantin, *Cant. Coll. Ox.*, iv, 186.
1376/7, again recd money *versus Oxoniam*, *ib.*, iv, 187.
1380/1, returning from Oxford he recd 3s. 4d. for harness, *ib.*, iv, 188.
1381, ceased to be a scholar, CCA DCc MA2, fo 298, 313.
1382, or before, B.Th., *BRUO*.
1382/4, [at Oxford] and was pd 20s. each yr by the feretrars, *ib.*, iv, 188, 189.
1395, D.Th., the expenses of his inception feast and that of Thomas Everard, q.v., are in Pantin, *Cant. Coll. Ox.*, iii, 54–56 (CCA DCc Cart. Antiq. O.151.3.6); on 7 Aug. 1396 described as *sacre theologie professor*, Reg. G, fo 234.

1372, the chamberlain bought cloth [for his habit], CCA DCc Chamb. acct 50.
1374, 30 June, 54th in order at the el. of an abp, Reg. G, fos 173^{v}–175^{v}.
1374/5, ill and recd a 'pension' of 6d. from the anniversarian, CCA DCc Anniv. acct 6.
1377, 2 Jan., absent from the visitation because he was at Oxford, Reg. abp Sudbury, fo 32.
1381, 31 July, 40th at the el. of an abp, Reg. G, fo 225^{v}.
1382, 1 July, present in the chapter house to hear the abp examine bp Repingdon and two others on their Wyclifite views, *BRUO*.
1396, 7 Aug., 21st in order at the el. of an abp, Reg. G, fo 234^{v}; he preached the sermon, *ib.*, fo 238 and announced the el. of William Arundel, *ib.*, fo 234.
1410/11, was present in Oxford at the inception of Richard Godmersham and John Langdon, q.v., Oxford, Bod. Ms Tanner 165, fo 147.
1410/11, 28 Mar., d. in his fortieth yr of monastic life, CCA Lit. Ms D.12, fo 19; he was buried in the crypt under a stone 'quem ipse primo preparaverat', *ib.* His obit, on 29 Mar., is in BL Ms Arundel 68, fo 22^{v}.

Reputed, by bp Bale, to be the author of
(1) De rebus Cantuariorum and
(2) a treatise on Benedictine writers, *Scriptorum sui ordinis*, J. Bale, *Catalogus*, i, 505; see Pantin, *Cant. Coll. Ox.*, iv, 221, and Pantin,

'Some Medieval English Treatises on the Origins of Monasticism' in *Medieval Studies presented to Rose Graham*, (Oxford, 1950), 208. See also Sharpe, *Latin Writers*.

His writings were so pleasing to his brethren that they were used as the basis for a series of [wall] paintings on the north side of the choir, Pantin, *Cant. Coll. Ox*, iv, 221.

II William GYLLYNGHAM
occ. 1454 d. 1471/2

1454, 28 Apr., one of eight prof., *SL*, 189, CCA Lit. Ms D.12, fo 7ᵛ.
1455, 5 Apr., ord acol. and subdcn, Canterbury cathedral, *Reg. abp Bourgchier*, 359.
1455, 20 Sept., ord dcn, Canterbury cathedral, *ib.*, 361.
1458, 1 Apr., ord pr., Canterbury cathedral, *ib.*, 369.

n.d., chaplain to the prior, CCA Lit. Ms D.12, fo 26.

1466, 17 Feb., 47th in order in an inventory of *jocalia fratrum* [given by him and/or assigned for his use], Reg. N, fo 233ᵛ.
1471/2, d., CCA DCc Treas. acct 22.

III William GYLLYNGHAM D.Th. [Chyllyngham, Gelyngham, Gillyngham, Gylingham
occ. 1495 occ. 1540

1495, 1 Aug., one of four tonsured, *SL*, 192, CCA Lit. Ms D.12, fo 9ᵛ.
1496, 2 Apr., ord acol., Canterbury cathedral, *Reg. abp Morton*, i, no 445a.
1496, 4 Apr., prof., *SL*, 192, CCA Lit. Ms D.12, fo 9ᵛ.
1497, 25 Mar., ord subdcn, Canterbury cathedral, *Reg. abp Morton*, i, no 446b.
1498, 14 Apr., ord dcn, Canterbury cathedral, *ib.*, i, no 447c.
1499/1500, celebrated his first mass and recd 8d. from the sacrist, Woodruff, 'Sacrist's Rolls', 66 (CCA DCc Sac. acct 60).

c. 1508/11, warden of Canterbury college, Pantin, *Cant. Coll. Ox.*, ii, 249–252.
1516/18, bartoner, CCA DCc MA14, fos 6, 63ᵛ.
1518/21, granator, CCA DCc MA14, fos 72, 107, 140.
1521/33, [1538, 8 Feb., after], 1540, 4 Apr., chamberlain, CCA DCc MA14, fo 199, MA30, fo 131, MA14, fos 255, 273, Lambeth Ms 951/1/34, MA15, fos 40ᵛ, 66ᵛ, 150, 201ᵛ, MA16, fos 33ᵛ, 90ᵛ, 138ᵛ, Pantin, *Cant. Coll. Ox.*, iii, 152, *L and P Henry VIII*, xv, no 452.

c. 1501/2, prob. adm. to Canterbury college, see below.
1505/6, scholar at Canterbury college and in receipt of one of Cardinal Morton's exhibitions, Pantin, *Cant. Coll. Ox.*, iii, 242 (CCA DCc Cart. Antiq. O.151.36, fo4ᵛ).
1509, 30 Jan., adm. B.Th., since he had studied logic, philosophy and theology for eight yrs, Pantin, *ib.*, iii, 250 (Oxford Univ. Archives, Reg. G, fo 68ᵛ).
1511, with Thomas Goldwell II, q.v., studied at the university of Paris, Reg. abp Warham i, fo 35; they recd licence from the prior on 1 May 1511, Pantin, *Cant. Coll. Ox.*, iii, 140–141 (Reg. T, fo 92ᵛ).
1512, [9 April], the two were in Louvain and were addressed as doctors by the prior who ordered them to return because the world was 'so jeobardus', Pantin, *Cant. Coll. Ox.*, iii, 141.

1501, 26 Apr., 52nd in order at the el. of an abp, Reg. R, fo 56ᵛ.
1511, 2 Sept., 35th in order on the visitation certificate but absent in Paris, Wood-Legh, *Visit.*, 3 (Reg. abp Warham, i, fo 35ᵛ).
1534, 12 Dec., acknowledged the Act of Supremacy, *DK 7th Report*, Appndx 2, 282.
[1538, 3 Feb., after], on a list of monks prob. prepared for Thomas Cromwell he was described as a 'symple' man, 66 yrs of age, Pantin, *Cant. Coll. Ox.*, iii, 152.
1540, 4 Apr., awarded £13 6s. 8d., *L and P Henry VIII*, xv, no 452.

Name in Wisbech Museum/Town Library, C.3.8, Epistole Pii secundi, Lyons, A.D. 1497 (printed book).

Stephen GYLYS [Gyles
occ. 1533 occ. 1540

1533, 12 May, one of eight tonsured, *SL*, 196, CCA Lit. Ms D.12, fo 12.
1534, 21 Mar., made his prof. before the prior who had recd the abp's comm., *ib.*

1534, 12 Dec., acknowledged the Act of Supremacy, *DK 7th Report*, Appndx 2, 282.
1537, 28 Jan., one of the monks named by John Waltham III, q.v., in a letter to Cranmer in which he accused them of hearing words spoken vs the king, *L and P Henry VIII*, xii, pt. 1, no 256; see John Stone II.
[1538, 8 Feb., after], in a list of monks prob. prepared for Thomas Cromwell, he was described as 'a good man' and 25 yrs of age, Pantin, *Cant. Coll. Ox.*, iii, 153.
1540, 4 Apr., awarded £3 p.a. and became a scholar in the new foundation, *L and P Henry VIII*, xv, no 452. See *BRUO, 1501–1540*.

H.
occ. 1189/91

1189, Sept., cellarer, *Epist. Cant.*, 308.
1191, May, removed from the office of cellarer by the abp who replaced him by Felix I, q.v., *ib.*, 333.

1189, after 12 Oct., one of three monks sent to the king to offer a gift and gain his support in their dispute with the abp, *Epist. Cant.*, 313. The unnamed monk writer of the letter recounting this event to Geoffrey II, subprior, q.v., describes H. as *cognatum vestrum*, *ib*.

H.
see also Hamo, Henry, Herveus, Hugh

HACHARD
see Acharde

Alexander HA . . . DN
n.d.

n.d., 23 Feb., pr., whose obit occ. in BL Ms Arundel 68, fo 17ᵛ.

I William HADLEGH D.Th. [Hadle, Hadleygh, Hadly, Hadlygh
occ. 1444 d. 1500

1444, 21 Dec., one of four prof., *SL*, 188, CCA Lit. Ms D.12, fo 7ᵛ.
1445, 27 Mar., ord acol., Canterbury cathedral, Reg. abp Stafford, fo 198.
1446, 16 Apr., ord subdcn, Canterbury cathedral, *ib*., fo 199ᵛ.
1448, 23 Mar., ord dcn, Canterbury cathedral, *ib*., fo 202ᵛ.
1450, 3 Apr., ord pr., Canterbury cathedral, *ib*., fo 204ᵛ.

1459/66, warden of Canterbury college; his accts for the yrs 1459/60, 1462/3 are in Pantin, *Cant. Coll. Ox*., ii, 179–184 (CCA DCc Cart. Antiq. O.151.16, 17); he recd a stipend of £13, *ib*.
1468/9, *custos corone*, CCA DCc Prior acct 11.
1471/5, subprior, CCA DCc Sac. accts 51, 53, 56, 57; he was apptd 30 May 1471, Cambridge, Corpus Christi College Ms 417, fo 92, but see William Pettham I regarding the date because Hadlegh was apptd the day after the *prefectio* of the prior acc. to *Chron. Stone*, 116. He prob. continued in office until 1498; see below.
1475, Mar./May, penitentiary, *Lit. Cant*., no 1083 (Reg. S, fo 273ᵛ).

1450/1, 1453/5, 1458/9, scholar at Canterbury college, CCA DCc Chamb. acct 60, Pantin, *Cant. Coll. Ox*., ii, 174, 176 (CCA DCc Cart. Antiq. O.151.15), *ib*., Chamb. acct 62.
1466, 21 Sept., granted licence to study for three yrs at any university, Pantin, iii, 108 (Reg. S, fo 225ᵛ); registered in the theological faculty of the university of Bologna on 14 Mar. 1467, *BRUO*, Pantin, *Cant. Coll. Ox*., iv, 80.
[1467/8], D.Th. Bologna; described as D.Th. in 1468 in Reg. S, fo 231ᵛ.

1454, 18 Apr., did not return for the el. of an abp but named the prior as proxy for him and for Arnold Parmistede and William Sellyng I, q.v, Pantin, *Cant. Coll. Ox*., iii, 105 (Reg. N, fo 185).
1466, 17 Feb., 34th in order in an inventory of *jocalia fratrum* [given by him and/or assigned for his use], Reg. N, fo 232ᵛ.
1474, keeper [*custos*] of the hospital of St James, BL Add.Ms 32098, fo 1.
1484, 25 Aug., present at the visitation and celebrated the mass, *Reg. abp Bourgchier*, 457.
1486, 3 Apr., named by the prior as auditor of causes in the court of Canterbury, *sed. vac*., Reg. R, fos 4, 6–6ᵛ, Reg. N, fo 172.
[1486], Apr. × Oct., one of the monks licensed to preach, Reg. N, fo 172 and possibly as confessor, *ib*.
1500, 19 Jan., d. 'ex diversis infirmitatibus ex rupt' ydropic' strang et de consumpcione', *SL*, 188, CCA Lit. Ms D.12, fo 28; he was buried in the infirmary chapel under the great stone on which the corpses of the brethren used to be laid and close to the burial place of John Langdon I, q.v. who had been 'his novice'. The obituary describes him as 'vir laudabilis vite honeste et religiose conversacionis', *ib*. His obituary is in BL Ms Arundel 68, fo 13ᵛ.

Name in
(1) BL Ms Arundel 155, Psalterium (11th c.) which had been used by John Waltham, q.v., and which he passed on to William Ingram I, q.v; his name is on fo 1ᵛ.
(2) BL Add Ms 32098, a cartulary of St James' hospital, Canterbury which was compiled by him in 1474.

Gave altar frontals *cum floribus saracenorum* and hangings to Canterbury college, Pantin, *Cant. Coll. Ox*., i, 29 (CCA DCc Cart. Antiq. O.137).

II William HADLEGH B.Th. [Hadleigh, Hadleighe, *alias* Hunt
occ. 1502 occ. 1540

1502, 25 Aug., one of eight tonsured, *SL*, 193, CCA Lit. Ms D.12, fo 10.
1503, 4 Apr., made his prof. before the prior, *ib*.
1505, 22 Mar., ord subdcn, Canterbury cathedral, Reg. abp Warham, ii, fo 262.
1506, 11 Apr., ord dcn, Canterbury cathedral, *ib*., ii, fo 262ᵛ.
1511, 19 Apr., ord pr., Canterbury cathedral, *ib*., ii, fo 265ᵛ.
1510/11, celebrated his first mass, CCA DCc Sacrist acct 73; the date was the first Sun. in April 1511, when he recd 4d. from the *custos martyrii*, CCA Lit. Ms C.11, fo 52.

1521/2, warden, Canterbury college, Oxford; his acct is in Pantin, *Cant. Coll. Ox*., ii, 257–259 (CCA DCc Cart. Antiq. O.151.46).
1522, 12 Feb., named penitentiary in the priory, Reg. T, fo 231.
[1538, 8 Feb., after], 1540, 4 Apr., subprior, Pantin, *Cant. Coll. Ox*., iii, 152, *L and P Henry VIII*, xv, no 452.

1508/9, student at Canterbury college and the warden recd £6 10s. for his pension and room, Pantin, *Cant. Coll. Ox*., ii, 250 (CCA DCc Cart. Antiq. O.151.42).
1510/11, at Canterbury college as above, Pantin, *ib*., ii, 253 (CCA DCc Cart. Antiq. O.151.43).

1516/17, at Canterbury college and the warden recd £7 5s., Pantin, *ib.*, ii, 256 (CCA DCc Cart. Antiq.O.151.44).
1517/18, B.Th., Pantin, *ib.*, ii, 273 (CCA DCc DE70).
1521, returned from Oxford to preach on the rogation days, Pantin, Pantin, *ib.*, iv, 206.

1511, 2 Sept., 53rd in order on the visitation certificate, but absent at Oxford, Wood-Legh, *Visit.*, 3 (Reg. abp Warham, i, fo 35^{v}).
1533, c. 25 Sept., with Edward Bockyng, q.v., apprehended because of their connection with Elizabeth Barton, *L and P Henry VIII*, vi, no 1149.
1534, 12 Dec., acknowledged the Act of Supremacy, *DK 7th Report*, Appndx 2, 282.
[1538, 8 Feb., after], in a list of monks prob. prepared for Thomas Cromwell, he was described as a 'good man', 51 yrs old, Pantin, *Cant. Coll. Ox.*, iii, 152.
1540, 4 Apr., became prebendary in the new foundation, *L and P Henry VIII*, xv, no 452; apptd canon of the eighth prebend the following yr, *Fasti 1541–1857*, iii, 30.

Name in Lambeth Ms 159, Vite sanctorum Cantuariensium etc., (early 16th c.) which he gave to John Salisbury III, q.v., and much of which was written by Richard Stone, q.v. On the front flyleaf after his name, the date of his d. has been added: 28 Jan. 1546.

James HAGHE [Hagh', Haghwe, Hawe, Haze
occ. c. 1380 d. 1400

c. 1380, one of four prof., *SL*, 183, CCA Lit. Ms D.12, fo 5.
1380, 24 Mar., ord subdcn, Canterbury cathedral, Reg. abp Sudbury, fo 147^{v}.

1381, 31 July, 60th in order and second to last at the el. of an abp, Reg. G, fo 225^{v}.
1387/8, 1388/9, 1390/1, recd small sums from the prior; in this last yr it was *pro benedictione*, 12d., Lambeth Ms 243, fos 208^{v}, 212^{v}, 220^{v}.
1396, 7 Aug., 32nd in order at the el. of an abp, Reg. G, fo 234^{v}.
1400, 20 Dec., d., CCA Lit. Ms D.12, fo 18.

Thomas HAGHE [Hagh, Haugh, Hawe
occ. 1382 d. 1443

1382, 5 Sept., one of six who were clothed in the monastic habit, *SL*, 183, CCA Lit. Ms D.12, fo 5.
1383, 11 Aug., the prior was comm. to rec. his prof., Reg abp Courtenay, i, fo 42^{v}.
1389, 12 June, ord pr., St Dunstan's church, London, Reg abp Courtenay, i, fo 311^{v}.

1388/9, recd 2s. from the prior, Lambeth Ms 243, fo 212^{v}.
1390/1, recd 12d. from the prior, *ib.*, fo 220^{v}.
1396, 7 Aug., 40th in order at the el. of an abp, Reg. G, fo 234^{v}.
1414, 12 Mar., 11th in order at the el. of an abp, *Reg. abp Chichele*, i, 4.
1443, 31 Jan., d., 'cuius fenis dat' fuerat fratribus minoribus', CCA Lit. Ms D.12, fo 24^{v}. Since, according to *Chron. Stone*, 29–30, he had lived the monastic life for 62 yrs he prob. entered in 1381. His obit in BL Ms Arundel 68, fo 15 is on 1 Feb.

HAIMO
see Hamo

HALDENE
see Richard Holden

John de HALE
occ. 1206

1206, 30 Mar., one of the monks summoned by the pope to Rome to give evidence in the dispute over their el. of Reginald, q.v., as abp. *CPL*, i (1198–1304), 26; while there, they el. Stephen Langton, *Fasti*, ii, 6.

HALFELD
see Hatdfeud

Walter HALSTEDE [Halsted
occ. [1420] d. 1449

[1420], 24 Aug., [*adjunctus*] to five others who had been adm. earlier in the yr, *SL*, 186, CCA Lit. Ms D.12, fo 6^{v}.
1421, 4 Apr., prof., *SL*, 186, CCA Lit. Ms D.12, fo 6^{v}.
1422, 11 Apr., recd his tonsure at an ordination in Canterbury cathedral, *Reg. abp Chichele*, iv, 352.
1422, 6 June, ord subdcn, Canterbury cathedral, *ib.*, iv, 354.
1423, 18 Dec., ord dcn, Rochester cathedral, *ib.*, iv, 358.
1425, 22 Dec., ord pr., Charing, *ib.*, iv, 374.
Note: there is some confusion over this date in that an entry for 1423, 18 Dec. includes his name under the priests ord, but this must surely be an error.

1439, 7 Jan., one of several monks licensed to leave the priory, *pro recreacione*, and he returned on 20 Jan., Chron. Wm Glastynbury, fo 182^{v}/177^{v}.
1449, 10 May, d., *Chron. Stone*, 47 (CCA Lit. Ms D.12, fo 25^{v}); his obit occ. on 11 May in BL Ms Arundel 68, fo 27.

John de HAMME [Humme
occ. 2nd half 13th c.

n.d., name occ. in the list in *SL*, 175, CCA Lit. Ms D.12, fo 2^{v}.

Thomas de HAMME
occ. 1309 d. 1316

1309, 18 Oct., one of nine prof., *SL*, 179, CCA Lit. Ms D.12, fo 3^{v}.

1316, 29 July, d., CCA Lit. Ms D.12, fo 15^{v}; his obit, in BL Ms Arundel 68, fo 36, describes him as a dcn.

I HAMO
occ. early 12th c.

n.d., reported as having taken abp Anselm's girdle to a friend of his who was ill, and the man was miraculously cured, Eadmer, *Vita Anselmi*, 431.

In the *Vita Anselmi*, 431, 450, he is described as the nephew of Eadmer, q.v.

II HAMO [Haymo
occ. 1187 d. 1188

1187, one of three monks vs whom the pope urged abp Baldwin not to bear malice, *Epist. Cant.*, 43; see also M. Edmund and Humphrey.

1187, one of the monks sent to the curia in the appeal vs the abp; his situation was discussed in a letter written by Honorius II, q.v., in July from Soissons, who reported that he had been sent back to Rome because he was not safe without letters of papal protection, *ib.*, 66–67.

1188, ?c. July, his d. abroad was reported by Honorius III, q.v., *ib.*, 254.

Note: the obit of a Haymo on 31 Mar. is in BL Ms Arundel 68, fo 22^{v}.

An inventory of the refectory dated 1328 includes a *ciphus de mirra* [*sic*] 'cum circulo et 3 platis deauratis et barr'. Dart, *Antiq. Cant.*, xxii (BL Ms Cotton Galba E.iv, fo 180).

According to Gervase, when the spirits of everyone were flagging he alone remained resolute in his defence of the convent's rights, *Gervase Cant.*, i, 389.

Note:
(1) These two monks named Hamo are prob. not identical but see Hamo de Thaneto who is prob. the same as Hamo II.
(2) The name occ. in a kalendar, Kalendarium Haymonis, in the fragment of a catalogue c. 1170, James, *Ancient Libraries*, no 176 (p. 11).

Gilbert HAMON
occ. 1st half 13th c.

n.d., name occ. in the *post exilium* list in *SL*, 173, CCA Lit. Ms D.12, fo 1^{v}.

Note: could this be Gilbert II, q.v.?

Edward HAMPTON
occ. 1533/4

1533, 12 May, one of eight who were tonsured, *SL*, 196, CCA Lit. Ms D.12, fo 12.

1534, 21 Mar., the prior was comm. to rec. his prof., *ib.*

1534, 12 Dec., acknowledged the Act of Supremacy, *DK 7th Report*, Appndx 2, 282 (where the name is given as ?Nante).

William de HARDENAY
occ. 1st half 13th c.

n.d., name occ. in the *post exilium* list, *SL*, 172, CCA Lit. Ms D.12, fo 1.

HARDUS
occ. [1096 × 1109]

[1096 × 1109], sent by abp Anselm to count Elias with a letter, *Anselm Letters*, no 466.

Adam de HARDYS
occ. 1st half 13th c.

n.d., name occ. in the *post exilium* list, *SL*, 174, CCA Lit. Ms D.12, fo 1.

Andrew de HARDYS [Hardis, Hardres
occ. 1294 d. 1305

1294, 18 Oct., one of eight prof., *SL*, 178, CCA Lit. Ms D.12, fo 3.

1299, 19 Sept., ord pr., Littlebourne, *Reg. abp Winchelsey*, 931.

1303/4, Sept. to Feb., with Stephen de Faversham, q.v., recd from the treasurers £46 19s. 3d., for their travel and other expenses to Paris, Pantin, *Cant. Coll. Ox.*, iv, 173. See Sullivan, *Benedictine Monks at Paris*, no 319.

1304, 6 Sept., student at the university of Paris with Stephen de Faversham, q.v. As they had run out of money the prior sent a messenger with 10m., and a letter urging them to practise moderation in expenditure, Pantin, *ib.*, iv, 209 (CUL Ms Ee.5.31, fo 101^{v}).

1305, 15 Apr., recalled by the prior, Pantin, *ib.*, iv, 209–210 (Ms Ee.5.31, fo 102^{v}).

1305, 5 July, d., CCA Lit. Ms D.12, fo 15^{v}; obit in BL Ms Arundel 68, fo 32^{v}.

Three volumes of his are listed in the Eastry catalogue, one being a copy of the Summa of Thomas Aquinas, James, *Ancient Libraries*, nos 1621–1623 (p. 134).

A list of vestments, *temp.* prior Eastry, includes a green chasuble and an alb of his [?gift],Legg and Hope, *Inventories*, 52, 59 (BL Ms Cotton Galba E.iv, fo 112^{v}, 115).

John de HARDYS [Hardres, Hardris
occ. [late 1260s] 1291 occ. 1300

[late 1260s], one of five prof., *SL*, 176, CCA Lit. Ms D.12, fo 3.

1291/9, 1300, chaplain to the prior, CCA DCc MA1, fos 173–222, 225.

1293, 24 Feb., one of the monks present at Leighton Buzzard [Lecton] to hear Robert Winchelsey's consent to his el. as abp, *Reg. abp Winchelsey*, 1274.

1294/5, pd a supervisory visit to Meopham, CCA DCc Meopham acct 21.

1296, 19 Oct., apptd proctor for parliament in Bury St Edmunds, *Parl. Writs*, i, 656 (CUL Ms

Ee.5.31, fo 68v). See John de Thaneto, II, q.v.

1297, 1 Mar., apptd proctor to represent the prior and convent in discussions with the king concerning the defence of church and realm, CUL Ms Ee.5.31, fo 71.

1297, *in Caab'* of St Martin, [a date] with Geoffrey de Chilham, q.v., apptd by the prior and chapter to attend convocation in the New Temple, London on 20 Nov., *ib.*, fos 75v–76.

1298, 20 June, again with Chilham, named proctor by the prior and chapter to attend convocation in the same place, *ib.*, fo 77.

A list of missing books dated 1 Mar. 1338, ref. to his Tractatus de x. praeceptis for which Richard de Ikham, q.v., was held responsible, *Lit. Cant.*, no 618 (Reg. L, fo 104); his name was also in Veritas theologica, which Walter de Norwyco, q.v. had borrowed, *ib.*

There are also sixteen items under his name in the Eastry catalogue including the Rule and a treatise on the Rule, the Sentences of Peter Lombard, sermons, meditations and the Excepciones decretorum Gratiani, James, *Ancient Libraries*, nos 1570–1585 (pp.130–131).

Robert de HARDYS [Hardis, Hardres

occ. 1329 d. 1339

1329, 9 Oct., one of eight prof., *SL*, 180, CCA Lit. Ms D.12, fo 3v.

1339, 25 Apr., d., CCA Lit. Ms D.12, fo 16v; his obit is in BL Ms Arundel 68, fo 24v.

Name in Cambridge, Corpus Christi College Ms 288, Alanus prior etc. (12th/13th c.) on fo 3v; see M Alan I.

William de HARDYS [Hardres

occ. [1241] occ. 1254

[1241], name occ. in the list in *SL*, 174, CCA Lit. Ms D.12, fo 2; he was prob. one of the twelve prof. with Richard de Wynchepe, q.v.

1254, 9 Apr., with Walter de Hatfeld, q.v., recd a delegation from Rochester cathedral priory, *Reg. Roff.*, 99.

A W. de Hardres' two *ciphi de murra* are included in an inventory of the refectory dated 1328, Dart, *Antiq. Cant.*, xxi, xxii (BL Ms Cotton Galba E.iv, fos 179, 180).

Simon HARIATTYSHAM [Hariatsham, Harietisham, Hariettisham, Haryatysham, Haryetesham

occ. 1450 d. 1471/2

1450, 25 Jan., one of seven prof., *SL*, 189, CCA Lit. Ms D.12, fo 7v.

1450, 3 Apr. ord acol., Canterbury cathedral, Reg. abp Stafford, fo 204.

1451, 20 Mar., ord subdcn, Canterbury cathedral, Reg. abp Stafford, fo 205v.

1452, 8 Apr., ord dcn, Canterbury cathedral, *ib.*, fo 206v.

1455, 5 Apr., ord pr., chapel within the priory, *Reg. abp Bourgchier*, 360.

[1471/2], feretrar, prob. at the time of his d., CCA Lit. Ms D.12, fo 26.

1466, 17 Feb., 43rd in order in an inventory of *jocalia fratrum* [given by him and/or assigned for his use], Reg. N, fo 233v.

1471/2, d., CCA Lit. Ms D.12, fo 26; his obit on 7 July is in BL Ms Arundel 68, fo 33.

HARLEWINE

see Herlewin I

HARST

see Herst

James HARTEY [Harteye, Harty, Herty

occ. 1500 occ. 1522

1500, 28 July, one of eight tonsured, *SL*, 193, CCA Lit. Ms D.12, fo 10. Each of these novices recd a gold noble worth 6s. 8d. for their labours with regard to the funeral of abp Morton who d. c. 15 Sept. 1500, CCA Lit. Ms D.12, *ib.*

1501, 19 Apr., made his prof. before the prior, *sed. vac.*, *ib.*

1507, 3 Apr., ord pr., Canterbury cathedral, Reg. abp Warham, ii, fo 263. He celebrated his first mass on the third Sunday in Apr. and recd 4d. from the *custos martyrii*, CCA Lit. Ms C.11, fo 49v.

1520, 1521, 1522, all on 25 Mar., named as *custos corone*, CCA Lit. Ms C.11, fos 60v, 61, 61v.

1508/9, student at Canterbury college, to whom the warden pd 1s. *pro pensione*, Pantin, *Cant. Coll. Ox.*, ii, 250 (CCA DCc Cart. Antiq. O.151.42).

1510/11, student, whose 'pension' was £5 15s., Pantin, *ib.*, iii, 253 (Cart. Antiq. O.151.43); he was ill during this yr *ex morbo pestilenciali* and his medical expenses were 5s. 4d., Pantin, *ib.*, ii, 255.

1512, student at Canterbury college for whose 'stuffe' the treasurers pd carriage expenses from Oxford to Canterbury, Pantin, *ib.*, iv, 205.

1501, 24 Apr., 71st and last but one in order on the list of those eligible to take part in the el. of an abp., Reg. R, fo 56.

1511, 2 Sept., 49th in order on the visitation certificate but absent from the visitation on 9 Sept. because he was at Oxford, Wood-Legh, *Visit.*, 3 (Reg. abp Warham, i, fo 35v).

n.d., an undated scrap of paper listing the delinquencies of several monks notes that he 'peius servat claustrum, set melius servatt completorium', Pantin, *Cant. Coll. Ox.*, iii, 143 (CCA DCc Ms Scrap Book B.193).

Name in Lambeth Ms 159, Vite sanctorum Cantuariensium etc. (early 16th c.); *liber*—on front flyleaf, where his name is scratched through and replaced by N. Herst; see also William Hadlegh II, Nicholas Herst II, John Salisbury III, Richard Stone.

I Walter HARTFORDE [Hertfford, Hertforde, Hertteford

occ. 1428 d. 1471

1428, 2 Jan., one of six prof., *SL*, 187, CCA Lit. Ms D.12, fo 7.

[1429, summer], ord acol. and subdcn, place not named, Reg. Langdon (Rochester), fo 74.

1433, 28 Mar., ord pr., Charing, *Reg. abp Chichele*, iv, 378.

1435, third chaplain to the prior, *Chron Wm Glastynbury*, 129.

1441/2, second treasurer, CCA DCc Treas. acct 14.

1446, Sept./Dec., chaplain to the prior, CCA DCc MA4, fo 133.

1446/8, 1449/51, 1452, 30 May, 29 June, bartoner, CCA DCc Caruc. Serg. accts 27, 28, Bart. acct 83, Caruc. Serg. acct 29, *Chron. Stone*, 54.

1452, 30 May and 29 June, 1454, 4 Apr., warden of manors, *Chron. Stone*, 54, 56.

1459/60, 1463/4, 1467/8, bartoner, CCA DCc Bart. acct 87, Caruc. Serg. accts 32, 33; in Oct., 1459 and May 1460, he was described as warden of manors, CCA DCc RE430, RE431.

1468/9, 1471, 10 Mar., subprior, CCA DCc Sac. acct 47, Treas. acct 22; he was apptd on 3 Sept. 1468, *Chron. Stone*, 106.

n.d., also served as subchaplain [to the prior] and subcellarer, *Chron. Stone*, 115.

1452, 30 May, sent with John Waltham, q.v., as proctors to the king for licence to el. an abp, *Chron. Stone*, 54; on 29 June he and Richard Gravene, q.v., returned to the king to announce the el. of John Kemp and they also went to visit the elect, *ib.*

1455/7, served as one of the eight *barones* of the convent exchequer, CCA DCc Prior accts 10, 15.

1466, 17 Feb., 16th in order in an inventory of *jocalia fratrum* [given by him and/or assigned for his use], Reg. N, fo 231. In this yr he gave a tapestry to the altar of St Martin depicting both Sts Dunstan and Martin; his name is inscribed at the bottom. It is now in the possession of the London Vintners' company, N. Ramsay and M. Sparks, *The Image of St Dunstan* (Canterbury, 1988), 32.

1468, 3 Sept., on the day of his apptment as subprior he celebrated the first mass of St Gregory, *Chron. Stone*, 106.

1471, 10 Mar., d., *ex vi pestilencie* and was buried the same day by the *magister mense* in the infirmary chapel; Stone states that he performed 'multa bona . . . in vestiario et in mensa magistrorum' and elsewhere, *Chron. Stone*, 115. His obit is in BL Ms Arundel 68, fo 19^{v}.

II Walter HARTFORDE [Hartford, Hertforth

occ. 1500 occ. 1511

1500, 28 July, one of eight tonsured, *SL*, 193, CCA Lit. Ms D.12, fo 10; each of these novices recd a gold noble worth 6s. 8d. for their labours with regard to the funeral of abp Morton who d. c. 15 Sept. 1500, CCA Lit. Ms D.12, *ib.*

1501, 19 Apr., made his prof. before the prior, *sed. vac.*, *ib.*

1506, 11 Apr., ord pr., Canterbury cathedral, Reg. abp Warham, ii, fo 262^{v}; he recd 4d. from the *custos martyrii* after the celebration of his first mass, CCA Lit. Ms C.11, fo 48^{v}.

1501, 24 Apr., 69th in order of those eligible to take part in the el. of an abp, Reg. R, fo 56.

1511, 2 Sept., 48th on the visitation certificate, Wood-Legh, *Visit.*, 3 (Reg. abp Warham, i, fo 35^{v}).

n.d., 18 Mar., obit occ. in BL Ms Arundel 68, fo 21.

William HARTFORDE [Hertford

occ. 1481 d. 1497

1481, 21 Dec., one of four prof., *SL*, 191, CCA Lit. Ms D.12, fo 8^{v}.

1483, 29 Mar., ord subdcn, Canterbury cathedral, *Reg. abp Bourgchier*, 439.

1484, 17 Apr., ord dcn, Canterbury cathedral, *ib.*, 444.

1496, 2 Apr., ord pr., Canterbury cathedral, *Reg. abp Morton*, i, no 445d.

Note: the extraordinarily long delay before ordination to the priesthood is surprising, but he may have been ill.

1493, 1 May, 42nd in order at the ratification of an agreement, Reg. S, fo 383^{v}; but see John Crosse I.

1497, 14 Feb., d. *ex consumpcione*, CCA Lit. Ms D.12, fo 27^{v}.

HARTFORD

see also Herford

HARTLIP

see Hertlepe

HARYATYSHAM, Haryetesham

see Hariattysham

HASTINGS

see Robert IV

Gregory de HASTYNG

occ. 1st half 13th c.

n.d., name occ. in the list in *SL*, 173, CCA Lit. Ms D.12, fo 1^{v}.

Richard HATFELD [Hathfeld, Hattefeld, *alias* Turpyn

occ. 1356/1362 occ. 1384/5

1356, 28 Oct., one of nine prof., *SL*, 181, CCA Lit. Ms D.12, fo 4, but

1362, 23 Jan., formerly monk of Hatfield Regis, now accepted as a monk of Canterbury because of his devotion to St Thomas and his desire for a stricter life, *Lit. Cant.*, no 881 (Reg. L, fo 51).

Note: it is quite clear from other entries that CCA Lit. Ms D.12 has become confused here and therefore the date 1356 does not apply to him. However, he follows John de Otford I, q.v., in order of seniority.

1368/9, 1370/1, monk *supervisor*, CCA DCc Agney acct 54, Adisham acct 34.

1372/6, warden of manors, CCA DCc MA2 fos 269–294v, Treas. acct 5 (1373/4).

1376/7, bartoner and warden of manors, CCA DCc Bart. acct 54, MA2 fos 294v–311.

1376/80, treasurer with William Woghope, q.v., CCA DCc MA2 fos 313v–323v.

1377/9, 1380/3, bartoner CCA DCc Bart. accts 55–60.

[1383], 1 June, named *primarius*, Reg. abp Courtenay, i, fo 39.

1384/5, third prior, Lambeth Ms 243, fos 192v, 196v.

1386, Sept., sacrist, CCA DCc Arrears acct 117.

1368, [c. 22] Feb., at Canterbury college, Pantin, *Cant. Coll. Ox.*, iii, 18 (Reg. L, fo 98).

1369/70, possibly at Canterbury college, sent with another [?to London] to the chancellor on college affairs, Pantin, *Cant. Coll. Ox.*, iv, 184.

1366, 10 May, present at the el of an abp, Reg. G, fo 147.

1374, 30 June, 23rd in order at the el. of an abp, Reg. G, fos 173v–175v.

1376, Apr., one of ten monks nominated to the committee set up for regulating the infirmary, *Lit. Cant.*, no 945 (CCA DCc Cart. Antiq. c.206).

1381, 31 July, 15th at the el. of an abp and chosen as one of the six *compromissorii*, nom. by the original three *compromissorii* to form the electoral body of nine, Reg. G, fos 225v, 222v, Oxford, Bod. Ms Ashmole 794, fo 254v.

n.d., 2 May, the obit of a Richard Hathfelde occ. in BL Ms Arundel 68, fo 26v.

Walter de HATFELD [Halfeld, Hatdfeud, Hatfeud, Hedfelt

occ. 1244 occ. 1259/60

n.d., name occ. in the list in *SL*, 173, CCA Lit. Ms D.12, fo 1v.

1250/7, chamberlain, CCA DCc MA1, fos 91v–99, Reg. H, fo 186 (1256/7, 3 Mar.).

1244, 4 June, in response to his request the king ordered the sheriff of Suffolk to inquire into the whereabouts of his father Walter, brother William and kinsman Thomas who had been accused in a lawsuit; they were not to be imprisoned and if they were in prison they were to be freed, *CClR, 1242–1247*, 194 (as R. de Hatfeld).

1244 × 1258], *temp.* prior Nicholas de Sandwich, q.v., who sent him with Nicholas de Grantebrygg, q.v., to Anglesey to collect John Chrysostom's De laude apostoli which had been borrowed, *Acta Guala*, no 156.

[1244 × 1258], sent by the prior and chapter, with Andrew de Biham, q.v., to the king to confer with him, CCA DCc Cart. Antiq. B.393(20).

1254, 9 Apr., with William de Hardys, q.v., recd a delegation from Rochester cathedral priory, *Reg. Roff.*, 99 (under Rochester).

1259/60, pd visits to Meopham, CCA DCc Meopham acct. 1.

Robert HATHBRANDE [Athebrand, Hadbrande, Hadebrand, Hathebrand

occ. 1323 d. 1370

1338–1370, prior: el. 11 Sept. 1338, BL Add. Ms 6160, fo 252v; d. 16 July 1370, Reg. abp Wittlesey, fo 31v.

1323, one of six who were [clothed in the monastic habit], CCA Lit. Ms D.12, fo 3v (*SL*, 179).

[1325], 18 Oct., prof. Reg. L, fo 141v.

1331/4, treasurer, CCA DCc MA2, fos 209–229, prob. with Stephen de Tyerne, see CCA DCc DE3, fos 1, 2, 18.

1332/3, subchaplain to the prior, CCA DCc DE3, fo 34.

1332, *magister corone*, CCA DCc MA2, fo 211v.

1335, 1337, subprior CCA DCc DE3, fos 5v, 10.

1335/7, warden of manors, CCA DCc MA2, fos 239–253.

1333, 6 Dec., with M. Andrew de Sapiti apptd proctor to carry letters to the pope concerning the postulation of John Stratford, bp of Winchester as abp, Reg. G, fos xxxvv–xxxvi. On the same day he and Richard de Wylardeseye and Hugh de St Ives, q.v., were authorised to obtain a loan in the curia or elsewhere, Reg. Q, fos 196v–197.

1335, with Adam Murimuth, apptd proctor for the chapter to attend parliament, *Hist. Mss Comm. 9th Report*, Appndx, 82.

[1336], 25 Nov., sent by the prior, Richard Oxenden, q.v., to the abp with a personal message accepting the latter's arbitration in the dissension within the priory, *Lit. Cant.*, no 608 (Reg. L, fo 67).

1338, 1 Mar., in an inventory of missing service books he was held responsible for the ordinal which was kept in the 'painted chamber', *Lit. Cant.*, no 618 (Reg. L, fo 104).

1338, 6 Dec., a *littera excusatoria* to the abp reveals that Richard, bp of Chichester presided at his el. because the abp was abroad and because the bp was the abp's vicar general in spirituals, Reg. L, fos 72ᵛ–73.

1351, 12 Mar., granted papal dispensation to choose his own confessor who was empowered to give plenary remission of sins at d., *CPL*, iii (1342–1362), 376.

1353, 4 June, granted a similar dispensation, *ib.*, 504.

1356, 28 Jan., petitioned the pope for permission to use pontifical insignia such as the prior of Worcester [John de Evesham I, q.v.] had obtained, *Lit. Cant.* no 810 (Reg. L, fo 87ᵛ). Several more petitions followed, which strongly urged that Canterbury's preeminence should be recognized and not outshone by lesser cathedral priors, *ib.*, nos 811–815 (Reg. L, fos 88, 45, 45ᵛ, 46).

1357, 23 July, authorized by the pope to choose, examine and swear in two clerks for the office of notary, *ib.*, 582.

1367, 25 Mar., presided over the enthronement of abp Langham, and the mass celebrated was that of the Trinity, *Reg. abp Langham*, 115–116, Reg G, fo 133ᵛ.

1370, 1 Aug., buried in St Michael's chapel on the south side, Cambridge, Corpus Christi College Ms 298, fo 119, Reg. abp Wittlesey, fo 31ᵛ.

An inventory of his *camera*, dated 1 July 1339, has been printed in Hope, 'Inventories of Priors', 283.

A *procuratorium* (dated 5 Mar. 1361) of an Alice Hathbrande [?his sister] is entered in *Lit. Cant.*, no 883 (Reg. L, fo 52ᵛ), in which she apptd the Christ Church notary and another to act for her.

Parts of his letter book survive in Reg. L, beginning on fo 72ᵛ, which has the heading 'His incipit Registrum litterarum domini Roberti prioris'; then follow two form letters, invitations, in French and Latin, to be sent to unnamed persons to attend his first mass as prior on St Edward's day (?13 Oct.). The leaves of this reg. are no longer in chronological order and so the entries made during his priorate are scattered. There is also a fragment of a register, covering the yrs 1341–1348, in Oxford, Bod. Ms Ashmole 794, fos 207–222. Some of his *acta sed. vac.* are in Reg. Q, beginning on fo 204.

The anonymous Historia Decanorum et Priorum Ecclesiae Christi Cantuariensis printed in *Anglia Sacra*, i, 142, praises him for his many virtues including his piety, competent rule and building achievements; among these last were the stone hall called *mensa magistri* (or Master's Hall, on the north side of the infirmary) and seven adjoining rooms for the sick, and a new kitchen; he was also responsible for two of the bells, Jesus and Dunstan, in the *clocarium*, as well as for the 'great organ'. The writer sympathetically observes that he suffered 'graves et intolerabiles expensas circa dominum regem et reginam et suos', *ib.*, i, 142. The 'Anon. Chron.' (written c. 1414) states that he was tutor to two of the king's sons (?at his own expense) and also praises him for his 'honourable and splendid rule'; but then adds that in the yr of his d. the convent owed the treasurers £990, 56–59. See also the résumé in BL Ms Arundel 68, fo 34ᵛ.

Geoffrey HAVERYNG [Haverynge
occ. 1435 d. 1453

1435, 11 Nov., one of five clothed in the monastic habit, Chron Wm Glastynbury, fo 117ᵛ (*SL*, 188, CCA Lit. Ms D.12, fo 7ᵛ).

1436, 3 Mar., ord acol., infirmary chapel, *Reg. abp Chichele*, iv, 383.

1439, 19 Jan., one of several monks granted licence to leave the priory *pro recreacione*, Chron Wm Glastynbury, fo 182ᵛ/177ᵛ.

1452, 26 Mar., ill and his expenses were 3s. 4d., CCA Lit. Ms E.6, fo 64ᵛ.

1453, 12 Sept., d., *Chron. Stone*, 58; his obit on 13 Sept. is in BL Ms Arundel 68, fo 41ᵛ.

HAUGH, Hawe
see Haghe

HAUKHERST(E)
see Hawkherst

James HAWKHERST [Haukherste, Haukhurst, Hawkerst, Hawkeherst, Hawkehurst
occ. 1444 d. [1489 × 1492]

1444, 21 Dec., one of four prof., *SL*, 188, CCA Lit. Ms D.12, fo 7ᵛ.

1445, 27 Mar., ord acol., Canterbury cathedral, Reg. abp Stafford, fo 198.

1446, 16 Apr., ord subdcn, Canterbury cathedral, *ib.*, fo 199ᵛ.

1447, 8 Apr., ord dcn, Canterbury cathedral, *ib.*, fo 201.

1450, 3 Apr., ord pr., Canterbury cathedral, *ib.*, fo 204ᵛ.

1456/7, subsacrist, CCA DCc, Prior acct 15.

1472/4, chamberlain, CCA DCc, Prior accts 12, 14.

1475, Jan./1476, cellarer, CCA DCc Cell. acct 12, Windsor, St George's chapel, XI.E.4.

1484/5, cellarer, CCA DCc Cell. acct 8.

1486/9, bartoner, CCA DCc, MA7 fos 34ᵛ, 71ᵛ, 95.

1489 × 1492], d., CCA Lit. Ms D.12, fos 27, 31ᵛ; his obit on 20 Apr., is in BL Ms Arundel 68, fo 16ᵛ.

I Thomas HAWKHERST [Haukherste, Hawkerst
occ. [1395] d. 1396

1395], 12 Mar, one of eight prof., *SL*, 184, CCA Lit. Ms D.12, fo 5.

1396, 1 Apr., ord subdcn, Canterbury cathedral, Reg. abp Courtenay ii, fo 186.

1396, 7 Aug., 75th in order at the el. of an abp, Reg. G, fo 236.

1396, d., CCA Lit. Ms D.12, fo 17^{v}.

II Thomas HAWKHERST [Haukherst, Hawkerst, Hawkhurst

occ. 1497 occ. 1529

1497, 28 July, one of nine tonsured, *SL*, 192, CCA Lit. Ms D.12, fo 9^{v}.

1498, 14 Apr., ord acol., Canterbury cathedral, *Reg. abp Morton*, i, no 447a.

1498, 19 Apr., prof., *SL*, 192, CCA Lit. Ms D.12, fo 9^{v}.

1503/4, celebrated his first mass and recd a gift from the sacrist, CCA DCc Sac. acct 61.

1524, 1525, 1526, 1528, all on 25 Mar., warden of St Mary in crypt, CCA Lit. Ms C.11, fos 63, 63^{v}, 64, 65.

1529, 25 Mar., *custos corone*, *ib.*, fo 65^{v}.

1501, 26 Apr., 63rd in order at the el. of an abp, Reg. R, fo 56^{v}.

1511, 2 Sept., 43rd in order on the visitation certificate, Wood-Legh, *Visit.*, 3 (Reg. abp Warham, i, fo 35^{v}).

HAYHORNE

see William de Eythorne

HAYMO

see Hamo

HAYWARD

see Robert de Thaneto

HAZE

see Haghe

HEDE

see Ralph de Hethe

John de HEDECRON [Edecrone, Hedcrone, Hedecrone, Hetecrone

occ. 1330 d. 1361

1330, 9 Oct., one of six prof., *SL*, 180, CCA Lit. Ms D.12, fo 3^{v}.

1337, feretrar, CCA DCc MA2 fo 255.

1342, 12 May, *coronarius*, CCA DCc DE3, fo 49^{v}.

1347/8, 1349/50, almoner, CCA DCc Monkton acct 71, Eastry acct 81.

1353/1354, Aug., 1359/61, Aug., subprior CCA DCc Appledore acct 42, Anniv. acct 5, Copton acct 27, CCA Lit. Ms D.12, fo 17. He had been recommended as the most suitable of the three names sent to the abp on 10 Apr. [1353], Reg. L, fo 85.

1335/6, student at Canterbury college Oxford who was provided with his *capa in panno burneto*, Pantin, *Cant. Coll. Ox.*, iv, 180 (Lambeth Ms 243, fo 65–65^{v}).

1348, 30 Aug., named by three initial *compromissorii* as one of seven *compromissorii* in the el. of an abp, Reg. G, fos 30^{v}, 82; on 3 Sept., with James de Oxney I, q.v., apptd to inform the pope and the elect [Thomas Bradwardine] of the chapter's choice, *ib.*, fo 84.

1349, 4 June, 31st in order and named as one of thirteen *compromissorii* in the el. of an abp, *ib.*, fos 60^{v}, 61^{v}.

1349, 8/9 Sept., 30th at the el. of an abp, and again one of thirteen *compromissorii*, *ib.*, fos 76^{v}, 77.

1350, 5 Apr., apptd proctor with James de Oxney I, q.v., in negotiations to settle the dispute with Dover priory, *Lit. Cant.*, nos 781, 782 (Reg. H, fo 36).

1361, 17 Aug., d. of the plague, CCA Lit. Ms D.12, fo 17.

Gave to Canterbury college 'liber 6us et Clementine cum doctore Digno de regulis juris' which is listed in college inventories in 1443 and 1459, Pantin, *Cant. Coll. Ox.*, i, 4, 13 (CCA DCc Cart. Antiq. O.134, 135).

HEDFELT

see Walter de Hatfeld

John HEEDE

see John Hethe II

HEERNE

see Herne

James HEGHAM [Eyham, Higham

occ. [1369] occ. 1414

1369/70], one of four novices; but he was not clothed with them—'hic solus induebatur', *SL*, 182, CCA Lit. Ms D.12, fo 4^{v}; at the foot of the chamberlain's acct for 1370/1 is a petition requesting an *allocatio* for £8 5s. 7d., 'pro habitu et necessariis ad ingressum' of Hegham, CCA DCc Chamb. acct 53.

1370, 16 Dec., novice, made his prof. with John Aleyn I, q.v., before the prior, Reg. abp Wittlesey, fo 36^{v}.

1371, 20 Dec., ord subdcn, abp's chapel, Otford, *ib.*, fo 168.

1372, 21 Feb., ord dcn, abp's chapel, Croydon *ib.*, fo 168^{v}.

1372, 13 Mar., ord pr., abp's chapel, Otford, *ib.*, fo 168^{v}.

1372/3], subchaplain to the prior, Lambeth Ms 243, fo 151^{v}.

1379, feretrar, CCA DCc MA2 fo 318.

1381/2, *custos martyrii*, *ib.*, fos 325–329^{v}.

1374, 27 June, apptd William de Dover, q.v., his proxy at the el. of an abp because he was absent on *ardua negocia*, Reg. G, fo 172^{v}; however, he is listed as 56th in order in the el. proceedings on 30 June, *ib.*, fos 173^{v}–175^{v}.

1381, 31 July, 42nd at the el. of an abp, *ib.*, fo 225^{v}.

1396, 7 Aug., 22nd at the el. of an abp, *ib.*, fo 234^{v}.
1414, 12 Mar., 3rd at the el. of an abp, *Reg. abp Chichele*, i, 4.

John HEGHAM [Hezgham, Hygham
occ. 1426 d. 1435

1426, 7 May, one of three prof., *SL*, 187, CCA Lit. Ms D.12, fo 7.
[1432], 11 June, ord dcn, place not named, Reg. Langdon (Rochester), fo 74^{v}.
Note: under the date 1430, 23 Dec., at the bp's chapel, Trottiscliffe, his ordination as dcn is also recorded, *ib.*, fo 72x, but Langdon's register is in a state of confusion here.
1435, before 13 Oct., chaplain to the subprior, 'Chron. Wm Glastynbury', 130 (Ms fo 116^{v}); see William Walbroke.
1435, 14 Oct., d., *ex epidemia*, CCA Lit. Ms D.12, fo 23^{v}, where he is described as chaplain as above; his obit on 13 Oct. is in BL Ms Arundel 68, fo 45.

Richard de HEGHAM [Eygham, Hetham, Heygham
occ. 1339 occ. 1375/6

1339, 13 Dec., one of five prof., *SL*, 180, CCA Lit. Ms D.12, fo 4.
1350/1, *custos martyrii*, CCA DCc Treas. acct 27, fo 2^{v}.
1359/60, fourth prior, CCA DCc Anniv. acct 5.
1370/6, granator, CCA DCc Arrears acct 66, MA2, fos 266^{v}–296^{v}.

1349, 4 June, 51st in order at the el. of an abp, Reg. G, fo 60^{v}.
1349, 8/9 Sept., 50th at the el. of an abp, *ib.*, fo 76^{v}.
1359/60, ill [in the infirmary] and the anniversarian pd a 2s. 'pension' toward his expenses, CCA DCc Anniv. acct 5.
1374, 30 June, 8th at the el. of an abp, Reg. G, fos 173^{v}–175^{v}.

HEGHAM
see also Hygham

HELHAM
see Robert de Elham

HELIAS
see Elias I

HELRICUS
n.d.

n.d., 9 Nov., pr., whose obit occ. in BL Ms Arundel 68, fo 47^{v}.

Henry HENFELD B.Th. [Enefeld, Evenfeld, Henefeld, Henfylde, Hevenfeld
occ. 1373 d. 1396

1373, 8 Aug., one of two *clerici*, adm. and clothed by the prior by licence of the abp, Reg. abp Wittlesey, fo 62^{v}; *SL*, 183 and CCA Lit. Ms D.12, fo 4^{v} are confused here.
1374, 27 Apr., one of six novices to make their prof. before the prior by comm. from the abp, Reg. abp Wittlesey, fo 130^{v}.

1380/1, student at Canterbury college and recd 50s. for *capa sua scolastica*, Pantin, *Cant. Coll. Ox.*, iv, 188.
1381/2, 1383/4, at Oxford and recd 5s. from the prior *vs Oxoniam*, Lambeth Ms 243, fos 188, 192^{v}, the latter being printed in Pantin, *ib.*, iv, 189. On 15 Aug. 1383, he was described as B.A. which is prob. a mistake for B.Th., Pantin, *ib.*, iii, 45 (Reg. abp Courtenay, i, fo 43).
1384/5, at Oxford and recd travelling expenses to return to Canterbury, Pantin, *Cant. Coll. Ox.*, iv, 190.
1385/6, at Oxford and recd 5s. from the prior at Christmas, Pantin, *ib.*, iv, 190 (Lambeth Ms 243, fo 200^{v}).
1386/7, recd 5s. *pro benedictione* from the prior *vs Oxoniam*, Pantin, *Cant. Coll. Ox.*, iv, 190 (Lambeth Ms 243, fo 204^{v}).
n.d. (but see above) B.Th., CCA Lit. Ms D.12 17^{v}, which records his death.

1391/2, gave the sacrist 20d. for candles to burn at night before the image of our Lady, CCA DCc Sac. acct 10; also in Woodruff, 'Sacrist's Rolls', 47, but incorrectly dated.
1396, 7 Apr., d., CCA Lit. Ms D.12, fo 17^{v}, where he is described as 'predicator maximus verbi dei'.

John HENFELD, B.Th. [Henefelde, Henffeld, Henfylde, Hentfeld
occ. 1488 occ. 1511

1488, 12 Mar., one of six who were tonsured, *SL*, 191–192, CCA Lit. Ms D.12, fo 9.
1488, 30 Sept., prof., *ib.*
1490, 10 Apr., ord subdcn, Canterbury cathedral, *Reg. abp Morton*, i, no 438b.
1492, 21 Apr., ord dcn, Canterbury cathedral, *ib.*, i, no 441c.
1496, 2 Apr., ord pr., Canterbury cathedral, *ib.*, i, no 445d.
1496, 3 Apr., celebrated his first mass, Pantin, *Cant. Coll. Ox.*, iv, 203; he recd 5s. from the treasurer on 1 May, *ib.*, iv, 204.

1495, 8 Feb., one of six scholars at Canterbury college, Oxford, from whom letters of proxy were obtained at the time of the el. of a prior, Pantin, *Cant. Coll. Ox.*, iv, 203.
1498/1500, student, with a pension of £6 10s. each yr, Pantin, *ib.*, ii, 226, 229 (CCA DCc Cart. Antiq. O.151.30, 31).
1500/1, at Oxford and given travelling expenses between Oxford and Canterbury, Pantin, *ib.*,

iv, 205; he also had the £6 10s. pension, *ib.*, i, 232 (CCA DCc Cart. Antiq. O.151.32).
n.d., B.Th., according to *BRUO* with no ref.

1501, 26 Apr., at Oxford, absent from the el. of an abp, Reg. R, fo 56.
1511, 2 Sept., 24th in order on the visitation certificate, Wood-Legh, *Visit.*, 3 (Reg. abp Warham, i, fo 35).
n.d., licensed by abp Warham to transfer to Battle abbey where he was recd and prof., CCA Lit. Ms D.12, fo 9.

Name in
(1) Cambridge, Corpus Christi College Ms 137, Philosophia monachorum (14th c.); on fo 1 his name occ. twice, upside down below the table of contents.
(2) Hereford Cathedral Library, H.ii.7, Augustine (printed book), Basel, 1489.

Gave silver spoons to Canterbury college, Pantin, *Cant. Coll. Ox.*, i, 37 (CCA DCc Inventory box no 21; date 1501), *ib.*, iv, 148 where a 'Henfelds cup' is also mentioned.

I HENRY
occ. c. 1074 occ. 1096

c. 1074–1096, prior: formerly a monk of Bec, apptd by abp Lanfranc, *HRH*, 33, *Fasti*, ii, 8.
1096, 11 June, el. abbot of Battle, *ib.*

Lanfranc addressed his reform statutes to prior Henry and the monks, D. Knowles, ed., *The Monastic Constitutions of Lanfranc*, London, 1951, 1.

As prior he was the recipient of a number of letters from Anselm, abbot of Bec: *Anselm Letters*, nos 58, 63, 67, 73, 93, 140, 182.

II HENRY
occ. [1139 × 1150]

1139 × 1150], with Gilbert de Clare, q.v., attested a deed of abp Theobald; possibly both were chaplains to the abp, *Theobald Charters*, no 151.

Note: [1163 × 1167], a survey of cathedral holdings in Canterbury compiled in these yrs ref. to a gift of land by a Henry, father of Hamo the reeve, *quando monachatum suscepit*, Urry, *Canterbury*, 242–243.

III HENRY
occ. 1189

1189, occ. at Rheims with Jonas, q.v., *Epist. Cant.*, 282.

IV Henry SACERDOS
occ. 1st half 13th c.
n.d., name occ. in the list in *SL*, 173, CCA Lit. Ms D.12, fo 1ᵛ.

V HENRY
occ. 1276/7 occ. [1281]

1276/7, chaplain to the prior, CCA DCc Cliffe acct 1.
1281], 9 Nov., with W., q.v., bearers of letters between the prior and the abp, *Epist. Pecham*, 245.

HERCLEPE
see Hertlepe

HEREWARDUS
n.d.
n.d., 21 Apr., obit occ. in Lambeth Ms 20, fo 181.

John de HERFORD [Herdford, Hertford
occ. [1222 × 1238] occ. 1239

n.d., name occ. in the *post exilium* list in *SL*, 173, CCA Lit. Ms D.12, fo 1.

1222 × 1238], warden of manors, Reg. B, fo 143.

1239, 4 Jan., one of the group of monks accused of contumacy by the abp after the forgery scandal, *Gervase Cant.*, ii, 144; see Simon de Hertlepe. On 1 Feb. he was among those summoned to appear before the abp after the monks' el. of Roger de La Lee, q.v., as prior, *ib.*, ii, 153.

The Eastry catalogue contains five items formerly his, James, *Ancient Libraries*, nos 1327–1331 (p. 114).

HERFORD
see also Hartforde

HERIATUS
n.d.
n.d., subdcn, whose obit on 30 Jan. occ. in BL Mss Cotton Nero C.ix, fo 4ᵛ and Arundel 68, fo 14ᵛ.

I HERLEWIN [Harlewine, Herlewynus, Herluin
occ. before 1177 occ. 1179

1177–1179, prior: [apptd] prior in 1177; res. 6 Aug. 1179, *HRH*, 34, *Fasti*, ii, 10.

1177, chaplain to the abp, before he became prior, *Fasti*, ii, 10.

1174, Aug. × 1177, autumn] , with Ralph II, q.v., witnessed a confirmation of abp Richard, *Eng. Epis. Acta*, ii, no 58.
[1174 ?Aug. × 1175, Sept.], both again served to witness an archiepiscopal instrument, *ib.*, ii, no 111.
1179, 6 Aug., res. because of old age and blindness, *Gervase Cant.*, i, 293.
n.d., 9 May, obit in BL Ms Arundel 68, fo 26ᵛ.

A letter addressed to him and to Herbert Le Poer, adcn of Canterbury, was written by John of Salisbury while bp of Chartres, *Salisbury Letters*, ii, no 325.

II HERLEWIN [Herelwynus, Leclinensis, Likemens', Likilmensis (i.e. Leighlin)
occ. before 1202

1204, 22 Apr., by this date bp of Leighlin, J. Sayers, 'Papal Privileges for St Alban's Abbey and its Dependencies' in *Law and Records in Medieval England*, London, 1988, 60–61.

n.d., 24 Mar., obit occ. in BL Ms Arundel 68, fo 22, where he is described as bp and monk of 'our congregation', whose anniversary is celebrated in gratitude with an expenditure of 20s. *in refeccione*, and 10s. to the prior, which sums come from his gift of a house that he himself built next to the [Christ Church] cemetery gate; Lambeth Ms 20, fo 175v also has the obit.

III HERLEWIN
occ. 1207 occ. 1225/6

1207 × 1214], name occ. in the list of those who were in exile in *SL*, 172, CCA Lit. Ms D.12, fo 1.
1207, 15 July, sacrist, CCA Lit. Ms D.12, fo 1.
1215, 29 Sept., 1216, 29 Sept., granator, CCA DCc MA1, fos 56v, 58v.
1220, 18 Oct., 1221/6, sacrist; CCA DCc MA1, fos 64, 65–70v, AS1 (1224/5).

IV HERLEWIN [Herlewynus
n.d.

n.d., 1 Sept., acol., whose obit occ. in BL Ms Arundel 68, fo 40.

HERMANNUS
n.d.

n.d., 23 Sept., obit occ. in BL Ms Arundel 68, fo 42v.

HERMERUS
n.d.

n.d., 29 Oct., dcn, whose obit occ. in BL Ms Cotton Nero C.ix, fo 14v.

Roger de HERMODYSWOYT
occ. 2nd half 13th c.

n.d., name occ. in the list in *SL*, 174, CCA Lit. Ms D.12, fo 2.

Hamo de HERNE [Hiern, Hierne, Hirne, Hyerne
occ. 1354 d. 1400

1354, 28 Nov., one of seven prof., *SL*, 181, CCA Lit. Ms D.12, fo 4.
1356, 18 June, ord acol., Hoath chapel in Reculver parish, Reg. abp Islip, fo 316.
1356, 24 Sept., ord subdcn, abp's chapel, Tenham, *ib.*, fo 316.
1358, 22 Sept., ord dcn, Charing, *ib.*, fo 317.
1360, 29 Feb., ord pr., abp's chapel, Otford, *ib.*, fo 318.
1376/7, chaplain to the prior, CCA DCc Elverton acct 38.
1377, feretrar, CCA DCc MA2, fo 312.
1378, 1380/1, chaplain to the prior, CCA DCc MA2, fos 315, 321v–325v.
1381/2, cellarer, CCA DCc MA2 fos 325v–329v; he was already cellarer on 18 June, 1381, Oxford Bod. Ms Ashmole, 794, fo 248v.
1382/4, 1385, chaplain to the prior, CCA DCc Treas. accts 26, fos 2v, 7, MA2, fo 335.
1386/8, third prior, Lambeth Ms 243, fos 204v, 208v.

1366, 10 May, present at the el. of an abp, Reg. G, fo 147.
1374, 30 June, 16th in order at the el. of an abp, *ib.*, fos 173v–175v.
1381, 31 July, 10th at the el. of an abp, *ib.*, fo 225v.
1396, 7 Aug., 4th at the el. of an abp, *ib.*, fo 234v.
1400, 27 June, d. in the 46th yr of his monastic life, CCA Lit. Ms D.12, fo 18.

Thomas HERNE [Heerne
occ. [1388] d. 1433

[1388], adm. as a monk; see below under 1433.
1389, 6 Nov., one of eight prof., *SL*, 184, CCA Lit. Ms D.12, fo 5.
1391, 25 Mar., ord dcn, Canterbury cathedral, Reg. abp Courtenay, i, fo 312.

1396/7, feretrar, CCA DCc Prior acct 4.
1403, 22 Dec., 1410, 13 Dec., *magister ordinis*, *SL*, 185, CCA Lit. Ms D.12, fos 5v, 6.
1410, 13 Dec., *magister ordinis*, *SL*, 185, CCA Lit. Ms D.12, fo 6.
1411/12, chamberlain, CCA DCc Chamb. acct 71; he prob. continued in this office until 23 Feb. 1415 when he was removed *ex certis causis*, *Reg. abp Chichele*, iv, 114–115; 18 May 1416, named again as chamberlain, *ib.*, iv, 151.
1416, 22 June, *magister ordinis*, *SL*, 186, CCA Lit. Ms D.12, fo 6.
1420, 23 July, subprior, *Chron. Stone*, 10.
1422, 30 Apr., apptd sacrist, *Reg. abp Chichele*, iv, 246.
1428, [31] Mar., 1429/30, chamberlain, Oxford, Bod. Ms Tanner 165, fo 6v, CCA DCc Chamb. acct 59.
n.d., treasurer, see below.
1396, 7 Aug., 59th in order at the el. of an abp, Reg. G, fo 234v.
1414, 12 Mar., 23rd at the el. of an abp, *Reg. abp Chichele*, i, 4.
1428, [31] Mar., one of the monks invited to the abp's palace after the *prefectio* of prior William Molassh, q.v., Oxford, Box. Ms Tanner 165, fo 6v.
1433, 20 Jan., d. in the 45th yr of his monastic life; he was laid in the infirmary chapel *nuda facie* during the *commendatio* and the prior celebrated the requiem, CCA Lit. Ms D.12, fo 23v, where it is also stated that he served *honorifice* in a number of offices. *Chron. Stone*, 17, gives his date of d. as 19 Jan. 1434, and also states that he was in the 42nd yr of his prof. Stone gives further details of his office holding: treasurer twice, sacrist and subprior three times, novice master and *gardianus* of Elverton. 'For future

remembrance' he then ref. to Thomas's adm. as a monk and clothing in the habit by prior John Fynch, q.v., in 1378 [a mistake for 1388], *ib.*, 18.

The reason for this lengthy obituary is explained by an inventory of the gifts made by Thomas to Christ Church; these include his spice money for two yrs which he (and others) contributed to the fabric fund, and other sums to the building of the new chapter house and cloister; he also provided new vestments and ornaments, *Chron. Stone*, 18–19. Cambridge, Corpus Christi College Ms 417 gives the date of adm. as 1388 and his yrs of monastic life as 42; it then lists his gifts to Christ Church, fos 17–19.

The above list of gifts mentions two volumes, an antiphoner and 'uno libro conscribendo qui dicitur Racionale divinorum' the cost of which is stated as £9 6s. 8d., Cambridge, Corpus Christi College, Ms 417, fo 18; he drew up a sheet of instructions for his successors in the chamberlain's office to guide them by providing rules and regulations to be followed; this survives as CCA DCc Ms Scrap Book C.112.

HERNOSTUS
see Ernulf, Arnost

I Nicholas HERST [Herste, Hurst
occ. 1439 d. 1485

1439, 4 or 15 Dec. [St Barbara], one of six clothed in the monastic habit, *SL*, 188, CCA Lit. Ms D.12, fo 7ᵛ.

[1440], 8 or 20 July [St Margaret], prof., Chron Wm Glastynbury, fo 119ᵛ.

1444, 11 Apr., ord pr., Canterbury cathedral, Reg. abp Stafford, fo 197.

1460/1, 1463/4, treasurer, CCA DCc Treas. accts 32, 18.

1472/4, chaplain to the prior, CCA DCc, Prior accts 12, 14.

1466, 17 Feb., 27th in order in an inventory of *jocalia fratrum* [given by him and/or assigned for his use], Reg. N, fo 232.

1485, c. 5 Nov., d. of 'le Swete' and was one of nine who succumbed within sixteen days, CCA Lit. Ms D.12, fo 26ᵛ and BL Ms Arundel 68, fo 47ᵛ, where his obit is given on 5 Nov.

II Nicholas HERST [Harste, Herste, Hurste
occ. 1510 occ. 1540

1509, 22 Dec., ord acol., Canterbury cathedral, Reg. abp Warham, ii, fo 264.

1510, 16 June, one of eight tonsured, *SL*, 194, CCA Lit. Ms D.12, fo 11.

1511, 1 Jan., prof., *ib.*

1511, 19 Apr., ord dcn, Canterbury cathedral, Reg. abp Warham, ii, fo 265ᵛ.

1518, 25 Dec., almoner, CCA Lit. Ms C.11, fo 59ᵛ.

1519, 1521, 1525, all on 25 Mar., subalmoner, *ib.*, fos 59ᵛ, 61, 63ᵛ.

1534, 20 Oct.; [1538, 8 Feb., after]; 1540, 4 Apr., penitentiary, Reg. T, fo 32ᵛ; Pantin, *Cant. Coll. Ox.*, iii, 152; *L and P Henry VIII*, xv, no 452.

n.d., his *magister regule* for two yrs was John Garard, q.v., and he *non perfecit*, Pantin, *Cant. Coll. Ox.*, iv, 54 (CCA DCc Ms Scrap Book B.186).

1511, 2 Sept., 76th in order on the visitation certificate, Wood-Legh, *Visit.*, 3 (Reg. abp Warham, i, fo 35ᵛ).

1534, 12 Dec., acknowledged the Act of Supremacy, *DK 7th Report*, Appndx 2, 282.

[1538, 8 Feb., after], in a list of monks prob. prepared for Thomas Cromwell, he was described as a 'good man', 50 yrs old, Pantin, *Cant. Coll. Ox.*, iii, 152.

1540, 4 Apr., awarded £6 13s. 4d. p.a., *L and P Henry VIII*, xv, no 452.

[c. 1514 × 1524], an undated scrap of paper listing the delinquencies of several monks reports that [he] 'dixit pupplice coram iiijo [priore] in loco quando erat proclamatus hec verba: "ego [?non] faciam clamores"; et dixit iiijus prior: "quare"; et respondit: "quia est officium obprobrii"; et sic raro vel nunquam facit clamores, et bene servat horas suas', Pantin, *Cant. Coll. Ox.*, iii, 143 (CCA DCc Ms Scrap Book, B.193).

Name in Lambeth Ms 159, Vite sanctorum Cantuariensum etc., (early 16th c.); *liber* James Hartey q.v., for which name that of N. Herst has been substituted.

HERTFORD
see Hartforde, Herford

John HERTLEPE [Herclepe
occ. [c. 1280] d. 1298

[c. 1280], one of four prof., *SL*, 176, CCA Lit. Ms D.12, fo 3.

1298, 29 Aug., d., CCA Lit. Ms D.12, fo 15.

An inventory of the refectory dated 1328, includes five silver *ciphi* and one *de murra* formerly his, Dart, *Antiq. Cant.*, xix, xxiii (BL Ms Cotton Galba E.iv, fos 178ᵛ, 180).

Simon de HERTLEPE [Herclepe
occ. 1236/7

n.d., name occ. in the list in *SL*, 174, CCA Lit. Ms D.12, fo 1ᵛ.

1236/7, *custos* of the charters, *Gervase Cant.*, ii, 131.

1236/7, accidentally tore the 'charter of St Thomas', and with the connivance of the prior, John de Chatham q.v. and the assistance of Ralph de Orpynton II, q.v. had a copy made to which the original seal was attached, *Gervase Cant.*, ii, 131. He and the prior and Bartholomew de Sandwyco q.v., were summoned by the abp when the forgery became known, and he was provided with a licence to join a stricter order, *ib.*, ii, 133. See Cheney, 'Cant. Forgery', 17–20.

HERTY
see Harty

I HERVEUS [Hervey
occ. [1149 × 1154] occ. 1155

1149 × 1154], chaplain to abp Theobald, and attested an archiepiscopal deed, *Theobald Charters*, 542.
1155, 28 Mar., witnessed a similar deed, *ib.*, 536.

See note below Herveus II; see also the entry under H.

II HERVEUS [Hereveus
occ. 1189 occ. 1207

1189, Oct./Nov., precentor, *Epist. Cant.*, 312, 315.
1193 × 1199, subprior, A.M. Woodcock, *Cartulary of the Priory of St Gregory, Canterbury*, Camden Society, 3rd series, 88 (1956), p. 14, no 17.
1207, cellarer, CCA DCc MA1, fo 59^{v}.

1189, Oct., one of the monks summoned by the bp to cooperate with him in the el. of a prior, but he refused to go; on 5/8 Nov., he was one of the group sent by the convent to confer with the king in London during the course of the dispute with the abp, *ib.*, 312, 315.

Name in CUL Ms Gg.4.17, Peter Cantor etc. (late 12th/early 13th c.); at the top of fo 3, liber— ; see William Brito.

HETECRONE
see Hedecron

HETHAM
see Hegham

I John HETHE [Hethe, Hythe
occ. [1390] occ. 1416

[1390], 28 Sept., one of seven prof., *SL*, 184, CCA Lit. Ms D.12, fo 5.
1394, 18 Apr., ord dcn, Canterbury cathedral, Reg. abp Courtenay ii, fo 185.
1396, 1 Apr., ord pr., Canterbury cathedral, *ib.*, ii, fo 186^{v}.

1404/7, treasurer, CCA DCc, Bailiff of Liberty accts 15, 16, Treas. acct 8.
1407/8, warden of manors, CCA DCc Adisham acct 48.
1407, 21 Aug., apptd cellarer, Reg. abp Arundel, i, fo 448^{v}, Reg. G, fos 240, 290; 1407/8, cellarer, CCA DCc Agney acct 71.

1394, went up to Canterbury college Oxford and was given commons of 18d., Pantin, *Cant. Coll. Ox.*, ii, 136 (CCA DCc Cart. Antiq. O.151.2).
1394/5, at Canterbury college, Pantin, *ib.*, ii, 138 (CCA DCc Cart. Antiq. O.151.3).
1396, 7 Aug., 64th in order at the el. of an abp, Reg. G, fo 234^{v}.
1414, 12 Mar., 26th at the el. of an abp, *Reg. abp Chichele*, i, 4.
1415, 15 Mar., granted a papal dispensation to hold a benefice with or without cure, *CPL*, vi (1404–1415), 466, 467.
1416, recd papal licence, in the 26th yr of his monastic life, to take a living *iuxta* Gravesend where he d. within a few yrs, *Chron. Stone*, 7.

Stone also makes the following comment: 'nullum habens inter nos beneficium spirituale in communi', *Chron. Stone*, 7, and CCA Lit. Ms D.12, fo 20^{v}.

II John HETHE [Heede, Hiethe, Hithe, Hyede
occ. 1468 d. 1487

1468, 12 Oct., one of four to rec. the tonsure, *SL*, 190, CCA Lit. Ms D.12, fo 8 (where 1469 has been added in the margin); *Chron. Stone*, 106, gives the date as 1468, 12 Oct., and adds that he was one of four almonry [school] boys to be clothed on this day.
1469, 1 Apr., ord acol., Canterbury cathedral, *Reg. abp Bourgchier*, 402.
1469, 21 Apr., prof., SL 190 (Cambridge, Corpus Christi College Ms 298).
1470, 21 Apr., ord subdcn, Canterbury cathedral, *Reg. abp Bourgchier*, 406.
1471, 9 Mar., ord dcn, Canterbury cathedral, *Reg. abp Bourgchier*, 405.
1471/2, celebrated his first mass and recd a gift from the sacrist, Woodruff, 'Sacrist's Rolls', 63 (CCA DCc Sac. acct 51).

n.d., sacrist, prob. at the time of d., CCA Lit. Ms D.12, fo 27.

1487, 26 Sept., d., *ex vehementi pestilencia*; he was 39 yrs old and was in the 20th yr of monastic life, CCA Lit. Ms D.12, fo 27. His obit is in BL Ms Arundel 68, fo 43.

Ralph de HETHE [Hede, Heth, Hethe
occ. 1265 d. 1290

n.d., name possibly occ. in *SL*, 175, CCA Lit. Ms D.12, fo 2^{v}, as Radulphus; however, this could also ref. to Ralph de Adesham, q.v.

1265/8, in each yr on 29 Sept., treasurer, CCA DCc MA1, fos 107^{v}, 108^{v}, 110, 111.
1268/9, granator, CCA DCc, AS 21.
1269, 29 Sept., 1270, 29 Sept., treasurer, CCA DCc MA1, fos 112, 113.
1271, 1272, 1273, 1274, 1275, treasurer, CCA DCc MA1, fos 114^{v}, 116, 117^{v}, 119, 120^{v}.
1276, granator, CCA DCc, MA1, fo 123^{v}.
1276/7, 1278, treasurer, Reg. H, fo 216, CCA DCc, fo 127.
1279, anniversarian, CCA DCc MA1, fo 130.
1279, 1280, treasurer, CCA DCc MA1, fos 129^{v}, 131.

1280/3, sacrist, CCA DCc MA1, fos 132v–139v, Treas. acct 1 (1282/3).
1281, treasurer, CCA DCc MA1, fo 134.
1285/90, chamberlain, CCA DCc MA1, fos 144v–165.

1290, 17 Oct., d., CCA Lit. Ms D.12, fo 15.

An inventory of the refectory, dated 1328, includes a silver *ciphus* formerly his, Dart, *Antiq. Cant.*, xix (BL Ms Cotton Galba E.iv, fo 178).

I William de HETHE M.A., D.Th. [Heth
occ. [1329] d. 1347

[1329], 28 Oct., clothed; in a letter to the subprior, dated Sept., the prior requested that M. William who had been adm. should be clothed on 28 Oct., *Lit. Cant.* ,no 383 (Reg. L, fo 11).
1330, 9 Oct., one of six prof., *SL*, 180, CCA Lit. Ms D.12, fo 3v.
1333, 18 Sept., ord subdcn, Malling, *Reg. Hethe* (Rochester), 534, 1114.
1334, 24 Sept., ord dcn, Bromley, *ib.*, 534, 1114.
[c. 1337/47], lector in the claustral school for ten yrs or more, BL Ms Arundel 68, fo 31v; but see John Frome.
1332/3, student at Canterbury college Oxford for three quarters of the yr, Pantin, *Cant. Coll. Ox.*, iv, 178 (Lambeth Ms 243, fo 41).
1333/6, at Canterbury college, Pantin, *ib.*, iv, 179, 180 (Lambeth Ms 243, fos 49v, 57, 57v, 58, 65, 65v).
n.d., D.Th., BL Ms Arundel 68, fo 31v.

1338, 1 Mar., an inventory of missing books included three of Thomas Aquinas and one of Augustine which had been borrowed by him, *Lit. Cant.* no 618 (Reg. L, fo 104).
1347, 22 June, d., CCA Lit. Ms D.12, fo 16v; his obit on 23 June is in BL Ms Arundel 68, fo 31v.

Note: He had previously been a fellow of Merton college and was described as of founder's kin and M.A.; he may also have owned two Merton mss; see *BRUO*, which provides refs.

II William de HETHE [junior
occ. 1336 occ. 1343

1336, 24 July, presented to the abp after having been adm., *Lit. Cant.*, no 630 (Reg. L, fo 68).
1343, 2 Apr., recd the habit of the brothers of Mount Carmel at Sandwich, CCA Lit. Ms D.12, fo 16v.

HETHE
see also Ethe

Roger de HETON
occ. 2nd half 13th c.

n.d., name occ. in the list in *SL*, 176, CCA Lit. Ms D.12, fo 2v.

HEVENFELD
see Henfeld

Oswald/Osward de HEYE
see Eastry

Roger de HEYE
n.d.

n.d., 20 July, obit occ. in BL Ms Arundel 68, fo 35v.

Note: this may be Roger de Eastry, I, q.v.

HEYHORNE
see Eythorne

Simon de HIBERNIA [Hybernn
occ. 1231

n.d., name occ. in the *post exilium* list in *SL*, 172, CCA Lit. Ms D.12, fo 1.

1231, name occ. as one of the acctnts on the Assisa scaccarii acct, CCA DCc AS3.

In the Eastry catalogue are two of his books, James, *Ancient Libraries*, nos 1301, 1302 (p. 112).

HIERNE
see Herne

HIKHAM
see Ikham

HILLARIUS
occ. 1221/2

[1207 × 1214], name in the list of those who were in exile in *SL*, 172, CCA Lit. Ms D.12, fo 1; *SL* thinks this is Hilary de Taneto, q.v.

1221/2, chaplain to the prior, CCA DCc MA1, fos 65–66v.

An inventory of the refectory, dated 1328, includes four *ciphi de murra* of his, or of another Hillarius, Dart, *Antiq. Cant.*, xxi (BL Ms Cotton Galba E.iv, fo 179).

HINGSTON
see Hyngeston

HIRNE
see Herne

HITHE
see Hethe

HO
see Hoo

Gervase de HOGLE
occ. 1st half 13th c.

n.d., name occ. in the *post exilium* list in *SL*, 173, CCA Lit. Ms D.12, fo 1.

Henry HOLDEN [Holdenne
occ. 1439 d. 1488/9

1439, 4 or 15 Dec. [St Barbara], one of six clothed in the monastic habit, *SL*, 188, CCA Lit. Ms D.12, fo 7v.

[1440], 8 or 20 July [St Margaret], made his prof., Chron Wm Glastynbury, fo 119ᵛ.
1444, 11 Apr., ord pr., Canterbury cathedral, Reg. abp Stafford, fo 197.
1465, 4 Apr., *magister ordinis*, *SL*, 190, CCA Lit. Ms D.12, fo 8.
1468/9, chamberlain, CCA DCc Prior acct 11.
1475 Mar./May, penitentiary of Christ Church, with William Thornden, q.v., *Lit. Cant.*, no 1083 (Reg. S, fo 273ᵛ).
1466, 17 Feb., 28th in order in an inventory of *jocalia fratrum* [given by him and/or assigned for his use], Reg. N, fo 232ᵛ.
1488/9, d., CCA DCc Sac. accts 58, 68; his obit is on 3 June in BL Ms Arundel 68, fo 29ᵛ.

In the item above dated 1475 he is described as 'vir in morum probitate et religiosa conversatione satis laudabilis'.

Richard HOLDEN [Haldene, Holdene, Holdenn
occ. [1395] d. 1413

[1395], 12 Mar., one of eight prof., *SL*, 184, CCA Lit. Ms D.12, fo 5ᵛ.
1396, 1 Apr., ord subdcn, Canterbury cathedral, Reg. abp Courtenay ii, fo 186ᵛ.
1401, 2 Apr., ord pr., Canterbury cathedral, Reg. abp Arundel, i, fo 328ᵛ.
1405/6, 1407/10, treasurer, CCA DCc Bailiff of Liberty acct 16, Treas. accts 8–10.
1409/11, warden of manors, CCA DCc Ebony acct 73, Chamb. acct 38.
1413, to 15 June, warden of Canterbury college, CCA Lit. Ms D.12, fo 19ᵛ.
1397/8, student at Canterbury college, one of six who recd money *pro benedictione* from the feretrars, CCA DCc Feret. acct 1; and see below.
1396, 7 Aug., 81st and last in order at the el. of an abp, Reg. G, fo 236.
1413, 15 June, d. *ex pestilencia vehementi* at Monks Risborough [Bucks], one of the Christ Church manors, where he had gone to escape the epidemic in Oxford; he was buried the same day in the parish church of St Dunstan there at the foot of the image of St Dunstan near the high altar. He was in his eighteenth yr of monastic life, CCA Lit. Ms D.12, fo 19ᵛ. His obit is in BL Ms Arundel 68, fo 34ᵛ.

Robert HOLDEN
occ. 1511 d. 1518/19

1511, 1 Sept., one of eight tonsured, *SL*, 194, CCA Lit. Ms D.12, fo 11.
1512, 26 Mar., ord subdcn, Canterbury cathedral, Reg. abp Warham, ii, fo 266ᵛ.
1513, 19 Apr., prof., *SL*, 194, CCA Lit. Ms D.12, fo 11.
1511, 2 Sept., novice, not prof. and 86th and last but two in order on the visitation certificate, Wood-Legh, *Visit.*, 3 (Reg. abp Warham, i, fo 35ᵛ).
[c. 1511 × 1514], had Thomas Goldston V, q.v., as his *magister regule*, Pantin, *Cant. Coll. Ox*, iv, 54 (CCA DCc Ms Scrap Book B.186).
1518/19, ill and spent time in the infirmary, CCA DCc Infirm. acct 1.
1518/19, d., Pantin, *Cant. Coll. Ox.*, iv, 206; his obit on 9 Nov. is in BL Ms Arundel 68, fo 47ᵛ where he is described as *levita*.

Robert de HOLEKUMBE [Olecumbe, Ulcombe
occ. before 1235 d. 1248

n.d., name occ. in the list in *SL*, CCA Lit. Ms D.12, fo 1ᵛ.
1235/48: apptd prior of Dover, by abp Edmund of Abingdon in 1235, Lambeth Ms 241, fo 30ᵛ; d. 14 May 1248, *ib.* There are two obit dates in two kalendars; BL Ms Arundel 68, fo 27ᵛ (14 May) and *ib.* on fo 32 (30 June); similarly in Lambeth Ms 20, fo 187 (14 May), and *ib.* on fo 197 (30 June). See also Eustace de Faversham and John de Chatham.

HOLVARDUS [Hulvardus, Hulwardus
occ. [before 1074]

[1074, before], described as *Hulvardum Anglum, consobrinum domini Osberni* I, q.v., in a letter of [abbot] Anselm, *Anselm Letters*, nos 69, 74. The date is suggested on the grounds that another letter in which he was mentioned was addressed to Henry who was presumably the future prior, *ib.*, no 33 (see Henry I).

I John HOLYNGBORNE [Holyngborn, Holynbourne, Holyngbourne
occ. 1443 d. [1489 × 1492]

1443, 25 Mar., one of six prof., *SL*, 188, CCA Lit. Ms D.12, fo 7ᵛ.
1445, 27 Mar., ord subdcn, Canterbury cathedral, Reg. abp Stafford, fo 198.
1448, 23 Mar., ord dcn, Canterbury cathedral, *ib.*, fo 202ᵛ.
1450, 3 Apr., ord pr., Canterbury cathedral, *ib.*, fo 204ᵛ.
1457/8, Oct., 1459, 14 Oct., 1460/1, 1463/4, 1469, 19 July, treasurer, CCA DCc Treas. acct 17, DE 15C/14, 22, Treas. accts 32, 18, DE13.
1472/4, cellarer, CCA DCc Prior accts 12, 13.
1486/9, until 8 Dec., chamberlain, CCA DCc MA7, fos 36ᵛ, 63ᵛ, 90ᵛ, Reg. N, fo 256.
1444/5, student at Canterbury college who recd a pension of 30s. for one term and three weeks, Pantin, *Cant. Coll. Ox.*, ii, 167 (CCA DCc Cart. Antiq. O.151.13).
1447/8, student who recd travelling expenses *versus Oxoniam*, Pantin, *ib.*, iv, 194.
1449, Mar./June, student, with a pension of 42s. 6d. Pantin, *ib.*, ii, 171 (CCA DCc O.151.14).

1466, 17 Feb., 29th in order in an inventory of *jocalia fratrum* [given by him and/or assigned for his use], Reg. N, fo 232v.

1468, 10 May, apptd proctor for the prior and convent at convocation, Reg. S, fo 230.

1472, 8 Mar., acted as proctor for the priory in negotiations with the king over the manor of Walworth, *Lit. Cant.*, no 1068 (Reg. S, fo 252).

[1489 × 1492], *stationarius*, d., CCA Lit. Ms D.12, fos 27, 31v; his obit. on 11 Dec. is in BL Ms Arundel 68, fo 51v.

In 1474 he commissioned a painting of the martyrdom of St Erasmus now the property of the Society of Antiquaries in London.

II John HOLYNGBORNE [Holyngbourn

occ. 1509 occ. 1534

1509, 22 Dec., ord acol., Canterbury cathedral, Reg. abp Warham, ii, fo 264v.

1510, 16 June, one of eight tonsured, *SL*, 194, CCA Lit. Ms D.12, fo 11.

1511, 1 Jan., prof., *ib.*

1511, 19 Apr., ord dcn, Canterbury cathedral, Reg. abp Warham, ii, fo 265v.

1513, 26 Mar., ord pr., Canterbury cathedral, *ib.*, fo 266v.

n.d., succentor, BL Ms Arundel 68, fo 9v.

1511, 2 Sept., 77th in order on the visitation certificate, Wood-Legh, *Visit.*, 3 (Reg. abp Warham, i, fo 35v).

1534, 12 Dec., acknowledged the Act of Supremacy, *DK 7th Report*, Appndx 2, 282.

n.d., as succentor, responsible for recording the names of members of the Christ Church confraternity, BL Ms Arundel 68, fo 9v.

Name in

(1) BL Ms Cotton Vespasian B.xxv, Solinus etc. (12th c.); *liber—emptus* . . . AD 1503.

(2) Lambeth Ms 558, Psalterium etc. (mainly late 13th c.); his name is at the top of fo 14.

(3) Oxford, Corpus Christi College Ms 189, Constantinus Africanus etc. (12th/13th c.); *de empcione*—on fo 1.

(4) ?Cambridge, Trinity College Ms 829; see John Chillenden.

Note: a John Holyngborne had as his *magister regule* for two yrs, John Salisbury [?II or III] q.v., Pantin, *Cant. Coll. Ox.*, iv, 54 (CCA DCc Ms Scrap Book B.186). Although there is no date for this record it prob. applies to John Salisbury III. Pantin seems to have been confused about the ownership of the books, *ib.*, iv, 223.

On 17 Feb., 1518, his mother, Margery Fuller, was recd into confraternity with Christ Church, BL Ms Arundel 68, fo 11.

Robert HOLYNGBORNE D.Th.
[Holyngboorne, Holyngbourne

occ. 1488 d. [1508]

1488, 30 Sept., one of six tonsured, *SL*, 192, CCA Lit. Ms D.12, fo 9.

1490, 4 Apr., made his prof. before the abp, CCA Lit. Ms D.12, *ib.*; the delay in prof. did not preclude the six from having 'pecunias sicut ceteri fratres cum ebd' servicio et assignacione ad refect' et mensam conventus' by permission of the prior and *magister ordinis*, *ib.*

1491, 2 Apr., ord acol., Canterbury cathedral, *Reg. abp Morton*, i, no 439a.

1492, 21 Apr., ord subdcn, Canterbury cathedral, *ib.*, i, no 441b.

1495, 14 Mar., ord dcn, by *lit. dim.*, Abingdon, Reg. Blythe (Salisbury), fo 104v.

1496, 2 Apr., ord pr., Canterbury cathedral, *Reg. abp Morton*, i, no 445d.

1501/4, warden of Canterbury college whose inventory on entering office in 1501 survives, Pantin, *Cant. Coll. Ox.*, i, 34–44 (CCA DCc Inventory box no 21). There is another inventory of his clothes, books and plate and those of Anthony Wootton, c. 1508, printed in Pantin, *ib.*, i, 84–88 (CCA DCc DE76 and Z204). His accts for 1501/1503, Mar., are also in Pantin, *ib.*, ii, 233–240.

1504, 15 May; 1505, Apr., 1506, 5 May, warden of manors, CCA DCc MA114, MA115, MA116; see also Pantin, *Cant. Coll. Ox.*, ii, 241 (CCA DCc Cart. Antiq. O.151.38) which covers the period 1504/5, Apr. to Mar., and *ib.*, ii, 244 which covers 1505, Mar./1506, Apr. (CCA DCc Cart. Antiq. O.151.38, 39).

1506/7, 1508, warden of Canterbury college; his acct for 1506/7 is in Pantin, *Cant. Coll. Ox.*, ii, 247–249 (CCA DCc Cart. Antiq. O.151.41), and his apptment on 23 June in *ib.*, iii, 139 (Reg. T, fo 52). He was prob. still warden in June 1508, Pantin, *ib.*, ii, 244 (CCA DCc Cart. Antiq. O.138.b).

1493, Apr., student at Canterbury college, Pantin, *Cant. Coll. Ox.*, ii, 274 (CCA DCc RE6).

c. 1495, student, at Canterbury college who was given for his use some fifteen volumes of which an inventory was kept, Pantin, *ib.*, i, 80–81 (CCA DCc Inventory Box no 33).

1496, Mar. to Sept., at Canterbury college and provided with a pension of £4, Pantin, *ib.*, ii, 223 (CCA DCc Cart. Antiq. O.151.29).

1498/1501, at Canterbury college, with a pension of £6 10s. each yr, Pantin, *ib.*, ii, 226, 229, 232 (CCA DCc Cart. Antiq. O.151.30, 31, 32).

1506, 24 Oct., licensed to incept in theology, Pantin, *ib.*, iii, 251 (Oxford Univ. Archives, Reg. G, fo 25); on 4 Dec. he was dispensed from the regency, Pantin, *ib.*, iii, 251 (Univ. Reg. G, fo 28) and incepted on 26 Jan. 1507, Pantin, *ib.*, iii, 252 (Univ. Reg. G, fo 31v).

1501, 26 Apr., at Oxford and absent from the el. of an abp, Reg. R, fo 56.

[1508], d., see above under his wardenship of Canterbury college; his obit on 18 Aug. is in BL Ms Arundel 68, fo 38v.

Name in Oxford, New College Ms 300, Miscellanea theologica (16th c.); libellus manebit (?)—.

A letter from him to the prior, prob. written in 1506 or 1507 is in Pantin, *Cant. Coll. Ox.*, iii, 139–140 and *Christ Church Letters*, i, 58.

Note: Dr Bowers has drawn attention to his concern for liturgical observance at Canterbury college and his introduction of polyphony in the college chapel, 'Cathedral Liturgy and Music', in Collinson, *Canterbury Cathedral*, 425.

Roger de HOLYNGBORNE [Holynborne
occ. 1289 d. 1333

1289, 19 Dec., one of eight prof., *SL*, 177, CCA Lit. Ms D.12, fo 3.
1305, granator, CCA DCc MA1, fo 257v.
1328, 29 Sept., refectorer, Dart, *Antiq. Cant.*, xviii (BL Ms Cotton Galba E.iv, fo 178).
1333, 29 Nov., d., CCA Lit. Ms D.12, fo 16.

An inventory of the vessels [*vasa*] in the refectory was drawn up by him in 1328 and is given in Dart *Antiq. Cant.*, xviii–xxiii (BL Ms Cotton Galba E.iv, fos 178–180v).

Stephen de HOLYNGBORNE [Holynborne
occ. 1st half 13th c.

n.d., name in the *post exilium* list in *SL*, 173, CCA Lit. Ms D.12, fo 1v.

Thomas de HOLYNGBORNE [Holynbourn
occ. 1314 d. 1351

1314, 13 Dec., one of five prof., *SL*, 179, CCA Lit. Ms D.12, fo 3v.
1315, 20 Dec., ord subdcn, Maidstone, Reg. abp Reynolds, fo 173v.
1330, 20 Feb., apptd kitchener by letter of the prior to the subprior in his absence, *Lit. Cant.*, no 298 (Reg. L, fo 170).
1335/7, *custos tumbe*, CCA DCc DE3, fo 37, MA2, fos 250–255.
1326/7, spent four days at Godmersham with Hugh de St Ives, q.v., CCA DCc Godmersham acct 10.
1349, 4 June, 10th in order at the el. of an abp, Reg. G, fo 60v.
1349, 8/9 Sept., 10th at the el. of an abp, *ib.*, fo 76.
1351, 25 Mar., d., CCA Lit. Ms D.12, fo 16v.

William de HOLYNGBORNE [Holingborne, *alias* Thoms
n.d.

n.d., 25 Mar., obit occ. in BL Ms Arundel 68, fo 22.

HOMFREY
see Humfrey

HONICHURCH
see Honychyrche

Simon de HONNE [?Houne, Houve
occ. [1285]

[1285], one of four prof., *SL*, 177, CCA Lit. Ms D.12, fo 3.

I HONORIUS
n.d.

n.d., 21 Apr., obit occ. in BL Ms Arundel 68, fo 24v.

II HONORIUS
occ. [1153 × 1161]

[1153 × 1161], *temp.* abp Theobald and prior Wibert, q.v., precentor, *Theobald Charters*, no 40 (Reg. B, fo 146v).
[1153 × 1161], attested a grant by the prior and convent in response to a request from the abp, *ib.*

III HONORIUS
occ. 1186 d. 1188

1186–1188, prior: apptd 13 July 1186; d. at Velletri or Rome, 21 Oct., 1188, *Fasti*, ii, 10, *HRH*, 34.
1186, before 13 July, described as former cellarer and one time chaplain to abp Baldwin, *Gervase Cant.*, i, 336.
1186, 19/20 Dec., suspended by the abp for involvement in the opposition party in the convent, he left for Rome to appeal vs the abp's proposed foundation at Hackington, *Gervase Cant.*, i, 345; see also *Epist. Cant.*, 23–24, and *Eng. Epis. Acta*, ii, no 250.
1187, c. 1 Mar., with his monk companions appeared before the pope to explain the cause of the dispute, *Gervase Cant.*, i, 356.
1188, 21 Oct., d., as above, one of five monks who died of the pestilence; his obit in BL Ms Arundel 68, fo 46 praises him for his labours on behalf of Christ Church and states that he was buried in the Lateran *in ostio capituli.* See also *Gervase Cant.*, i, 429.

Two volumes of his are listed in the Eastry catalogue, James, *Ancient Libraries*, nos 982–983 (p. 96).

Some of his letters to the subprior, Geoffrey II, q.v. and the monks during his journey to the curia are in *Epist. Cant.*, and report on his itinerary and progress: he landed in Flanders on 22 Dec. (*Epist. Cant.*, 16), reached the curia in Mar. 1187 (*ib.*, 21–22), was successful in obtaining judgement vs the abp in May (*ib.*, 34–35), at Soissons in July (*ib.*, 65), at Verona on 11 Sept. (*ib.*, 100), at Parma in late Nov. (*ib.*, 123), prob. back in Rome in Mar. 1188 (*ib.*, 188–189), prob. in Verona again in Sept. (*ib.*, 258).

Other letters written by him give encouragement to monks at Canterbury, e.g. *ib.*, 41–42, 81–83, 199–200, 210–211.

There is a summary of his achievements in BL Ms Cotton Claudius C.vi, fo 171v. He was eulogized in several short poems by Nigel Wireker, q.v.

IV HONORIUS
occ. 1206

1206, 30 Mar., one of the monks summoned by the pope to Rome to give evidence in the dispute over their el. of Reginald, q.v., as abp, *CPL*, i (1198–1304), 26; while there, they el. Stephen Langton, *Fasti*, ii, 6.

Gilbert HONYCHYRCHE [Honichirch
occ. 1361 occ. 1377

1361, 28 Oct., one of nine prof., *SL*, 182, CCA Lit. Ms D.12, fo 4v.
1363, 23 Sept., ord subdcn, Faversham monastery, Reg. abp Islip, fo 323.
1363, 23 Dec., ord dcn, Charing, *ib.*, fo 324v.

1369/71, treasurer, CCA DCc MA2, fos 265–269.
1373/6, feretrar, CCA DCc Treas. acct 5, MA2, fos 281v–296.
1377, granator, CCA DCc MA2, fo 312.

1366, 10 May, present at the el. of an abp, Reg. G, fo 147.
1369/70, 2 Mar., obtained a papal mandate addressed to lay persons requiring them to restore the goods and chattels of the prior and convent which had been bequeathed to him before he entered the monastery, *CPL*, iv (1362–1404), 80–81.
1374, 30 June, 30th in order at the el. of an abp, Reg. G, fos 173v–175v.

I John de HOO
occ. 1st half 13th c.

n.d., name occ. in the list in *SL*, 174, CCA Lit. Ms D.12, fo 1v.

II John de HOO
occ. 1520/1

1520/1, ill and spent time in the infirmary, CCA DCc Infirm. acct 2.

Note: this monk prob. occ. elsewhere in the list under his patronymic which, however, remains unidentified.

Robert de HOO
occ. [c. 1255]

[c. 1255], name occ. as having been prof. with four others, *SL*, 176, CCA Lit. Ms D.12, fo 2v.

Sampson de HOO
occ. 1st half 13th c.

n.d., name occ. in the *post exilium* list in *SL*, 173, CCA Lit. Ms D.12, fo 1.

William de HOO [Ho
occ. 1239

n.d., name occ. in the list in *SL*, 174, CCA Lit. Ms D.12, fo 1v.

1239, 4 Jan., one of the group of monks accused of contumacy by the abp after the forgery scandal, *Gervase Cant.*, ii, 144; see Simon de Hertlepe. On 1 Feb. he was among those summoned to appear before the abp after the monks' el. of Roger de La Lee, q.v., as prior, *ib.*, ii, 153.

Anthony HORDEN [*alias* Chillenden
occ. 1506 occ. 1511

1506, 21 Mar., one of six tonsured, *SL*, 193, CCA Lit. Ms D.12, fo 10v.
1506, 11 Apr., ord acol., Canterbury cathedral, Reg. abp Warham, ii, fo 262v (as Chillenden).
1506, 30 Sept., prof., *SL*, 193, CCA Lit. Ms D.12, fo 10v.
1508, 22 Apr., ord subdcn, Canterbury cathedral, Reg. abp Warham, ii, fo 263v.
1508/9, student at Canterbury college, Oxford, Pantin, *Cant. Coll. Ox.*, ii, 250 (CCA DCc Cart. Antiq. O.151.42).
1510/11, at Canterbury college, and 12d. in expenses were noted on the warden's acct when he was ill, Pantin, *ib.*, ii, 255 (CCA DCc Cart. Antiq. O.151.43).

1511, 2 Sept., 62nd in order on the visitation certificate, Wood-Legh, *Visit.*, 3 (Reg. abp Warham, i, fo 35v).
n.d., 30 Sept., *levita*, whose obit occ. in BL Ms Arundel 68, fo 43v.

Thomas HORDEN
n.d.

n.d., 22 Apr., obit occ. in BL Ms Arundel 68, fo 24v.

Richard HORE [Hoore
occ. 1444 d. 1457

1444, 21 Dec., one of four prof., *SL*, 188, CCA Lit. Ms D.12, fo 7v.
1445, 27 Mar., ord acol., Canterbury cathedral, Reg. abp Stafford, fo 198.
1446, 16 Apr., ord subdcn, Canterbury cathedral, *ib.*, fo 199v.
1447, 8 Apr., ord dcn, Canterbury cathedral, *ib.*, fo 201.
1450, 3 Apr., ord pr., Canterbury cathedral, *ib.*, fo 204v.

1457, 14 Aug., before, chaplain to the subprior, *Chron. Stone*, 69.

1457, 14 Aug., d., in his twelfth yr of monastic life, *Chron. Stone*, 68–69, CCA Lit. Ms D.12, fo 25v.

Robert HORE [Hoore
occ. 1363 occ. 1383

1363, 6 Aug., ord acol., abp's chapel, Canterbury, Reg. abp Islip, fo 323.
1364, one of eleven prof., *SL*, 182, CCA Lit. Ms D.12, fo 4ᵛ.
1364, 9 Mar., ord subdcn, abp's chapel, Charing, Reg. abp Islip, fo 325.
1365, 29 Mar., ord dcn, abp's chapel, Charing, *ib.*, fo 326.
1367, 18 Sept., ord pr., Lambeth palace chapel, *Reg. abp Langham*, 383.
1367/8, 1371, subchaplain to the prior, CCA DCc Godmersham acct 23, MA2, fo 266ᵛ (where he is *loco capellani*).
1371/2, 1373/4, 1375/6, treasurer, CCA DCc MA2, fo 275, Treas. acct 5, MA2, fo 311.
1376/8, Nov., 1379/80, chaplain to the prior, CCA DCc Arrears acct 40, Prior's Chaplain accts 11, 2, MA2, fos 318–321ᵛ.
1380, 3 July, apptd precentor, Reg. abp Sudbury, fo 63ᵛ; still precentor on 18 June, 1381, Oxford, Bod. Ms Ashmole 794, fo 248ᵛ.
1382, 1383, chamberlain, CCA DCc MA2, fo 329ᵛ, Treas. acct 26, fo 2ᵛ.
1383, 1 Sept., [re]apptd precentor, Reg. abp Courtenay, i, fo 44ᵛ.
1368, Mar., visited Godmersham, CCA DCc Godmersham acct 23 (1367/8).
1374, 30 June, 34th in order at the el. of an abp, Reg. G, fos 173ᵛ–175ᵛ.
1381, 31 July, 24th at the el. of an abp, *ib.*, fo 225ᵛ.
n.d., 13 Aug., obit occ. in BL Ms Arundel 68, fo 38.

[Robert HOUGHE
occ. 1540

1540, 4 Apr., awarded a pension of £3 and became a scholar in the new foundation, *L and P Henry VIII*, xv, no 452; his name appears to have been substituted for Thomas Langdon, q.v. Was he ever a monk?]

HOUNE
see Honne

William HOVERLEY [Hou'ley
occ. 1506
1506, 101 Apr., ord dcn, Canterbury cathedral, Reg abp Warham, ii, fo 262ᵛ.

I HUBERT [grossus
occ. [1207 × 1214]

[1207 × 1214], name occ. in the list of those who were in exile, *SL*, 172, CCA Lit. Ms D.12, fo 1.

II HUBERT
occ. 1218 occ.1229/30

1218, 7 Nov., granator, CCA DCc MA1, fo 60.
1220, 18 Oct., sacrist, CCA DCc MA1, fo 64.
1224/5, 1224/7, 1229/30, bartoner, CCA DCc AS1, MA1, fos 68ᵛ–71, AS2.
1228, 3 Aug., named as one of five *compromissorii* in the el. of an abp; see Walter de Eynesham, *Gervase Cant.*, ii, 120, 121, 123.

Note: the two Huberts may be identical.

I HUGH
occ. [1115 × 1122] occ. [1138 × 1161]
[1115 × 1122], with Theodore I, q.v., attested a charter of abp Ralph d'Escures, Eng. Epis. Acta, Canterbury, 1070–1136, no 47, forthcoming.
[1138 × 1161], along with the prior, accused of contempt by abp Theobald in a letter to the pope, *Salisbury Letters*, i, no 59.
1145, 1 Sept., with Walter [Durdent] prior and Clement I and Reynaldus, q.v., witnessed a [prob. spurious] inspeximus by abp Theobald of a (wholly spurious) charter of bp Gundulf of Rochester, *Theobald Charters*, no 222.

Note: this may be Hugh de Caen, q.v.

II HUGH
occ. 1218 occ. 1244
1218, 7 Nov., granator, CCA DCc MA1, fo 60.
1221/9, 1225, Nov., almoner, CCA DCc MA1, fos 65–72ᵛ, *Langton Acta*, no 78.
1244/5, refectorer, CCA DCc AS1.
1244, 2 Apr., subprior; *CPL*, i (1198–1304), 208.
1244, 2 Apr., mentioned in negotiations concerning the pallium for abp Boniface, *CPL*, i (1198–1304), 208.

Note: there may be two Hughs involved here because there are two contemporary Hughs, Eastry and Geround, q.v., either of whom may be identical with this one.

III HUGH
occ. 1313/14
1313/14, warden of manors, CCA DCc Agney acct 29.

HUGH
see also Caen and the entry under H.

Nicholas HULL [Hulle
occ. 1497 occ. 1511

1497, 28 July, one of nine tonsured, *SL*, 192, CCA Lit. Ms D.12, fo 9ᵛ.
1498, 14 Apr., ord acol., Canterbury cathedral, *Reg. abp Morton*, i, no 447a.
1498, 19 Apr., prof., *SL*, 192, CCA Lit. Ms D.12, fo 9ᵛ.
1501, 26 Apr., dcn and 59th in order at the el. of an abp, Reg. R, fo 56ᵛ.
1508, contributed 9d. toward the repair of books, CCA Lit. Ms C.11, fo 103ᵛ; see William Ingram I.

1511, 2 Sept., 40th on the visitation certificate, Wood-Legh, *Visit.*, 3 (Reg. abp Warham, i, fo 35v).
n.d., 26 May, obit occ. in BL Ms Arundel 68, fo 28v.

HULVARDUS
see Holvardus

Thomas HUMFREY B.Th. [Homfrey, Humfray, Humfry, Umfray, Umfrey, Wmfray
occ. 1459 d. 1494/5

1459, 30 Nov., one of six prof., *SL*, 189, CCA Lit. Ms D.12, fo 8.
1461, 4 Apr., ord dcn, Canterbury cathedral, *Reg. abp Bourgchier*, 378.
1462, 17 Apr., ord pr., Canterbury cathedral, *ib.*, 382.
1475/8, warden of Canterbury college: his accts are in Pantin, *Cant. Coll. Ox.*, ii, 195–203 (CCA DCc Cart. Antiq. O.151.21, 151.4, 151.22a). The prior's undated letter to the abp recommending him for the office is in Pantin, *ib.*, iii, 115.
1478, Apr., Sept.; 1479, Apr., Sept.; 1480, Apr.; 1482, Apr., Sept., warden of manors, CCA DCc Monk Warden accts 12–16, 29, 17.
1482/4, treasurer, Lambeth ED85, CCA DCc Treas. acct 20.
1486, 6 Apr.; 1493, Jan.; 1494, Jan., chaplain to the prior, Cambridge, Corpus Christi College Ms 298, fo 130v; CCA DCc MA8, fo 219; in the 1486 entry it says only chaplain.
n.d., *magister corone*, CCA Lit. Ms D.12, fo 27v; see below.
1467/8, 1469/71, student at Canterbury college for the whole yr (i.e. four terms) and recd £8 each yr, Pantin, *Cant. Coll. Ox.*, ii, 188, 191, 193.
1471/4, evidence of his continued presence at Oxford and travels back and forth between Canterbury and Oxford is in the accts in Pantin, *ib.*, iv, 197, 198.
n.d., B.Th., *BRUO*. In Apr. 1486 he is so described, Cambridge, Corpus Christi College Ms 298, fo 130v.
1486, 6 Apr., with Reginald Goldston I, q.v., was sent to the king for licence to el. an abp, Cambridge, Corpus Christi College Ms 298, fo 130v.
1489, recd 8d. in a bequest from a parishioner of St Martin's, Canterbury, Hussey, 'Kentish Wills', 43.
1493, 1 May, 16th in order at the ratification of an agreement, Reg. S, fo 383v; but see John Crosse I.
1494/5, d., Woodruff, 'Sacrist's Rolls', 65 (CCA DCc Sac. acct 59), CCA Lit. Ms D.12, fo 27v which records that he was chaplain to prior Sellyng before being *magister corone*; his obit, on 4 May, is in BL Ms Arundel 68, fo 26v.

Name in CCA Lit. Ms A.9, Duns Scotus (14th c.); *hic liber constat*—.

Two of his letters written to the prior during his wardenship of Canterbury college have been printed by Pantin, *Cant. Coll. Ox.*, iii, 116, 118–119. In the latter, dated 24 Jan [?1478], he accepted the prior's invitation to preach on Holy Thursday; but he urged the prior not to recall him for good to Canterbury. If he were ordered to return he begged that he might be provided with 'suche stuffe and apparell as y have att Oxford' and an 'honest chambyr', *ib.*, 119.

HUMME
see Hamme

I M. HUMPHREY [Humfridus
occ. 1187 d. 1188

1187, c. 1 Mar., with prior Honorius II, q.v., and others appeared before the pope to explain the cause of the dispute with the abp, *Gervase Cant.*, i, 356. As a result the pope wrote to the abp requiring that he refrain from his hostility to the prior, Humphrey and others because of their opposition to his plans, *Epist. Cant.*, 43; see Hamo, Edmund.
1188, Mar., with prior Honorius, q.v., and others he was at the curia from where he wrote to the monks in Canterbury to encourage them in their tribulations arising out of the strained relations with the abp, *Epist. Cant.*, 177–178, 189–191, 238–239.
Note: However, see also Edmund who wrote similar letters, and their correspondence may have become mixed together and misattributed, as Stubbs suggests, *ib.*, 192, note.
1188, July, one of five monks who d. in Rome, *Epist. Cant.*, 254; his obit on 13 July is in BL Ms Arundel 68, fo 34.

An M. Humphrey [presumably this ?monk], had six vols under his name in the Eastry catalogue, nos 1044–1049; they include Sententie Longobardi and Decreta Graciani, James *Ancient Libraries*, 99; see also *ib.*, no 267 (p. 172).

II HUMPHREY
occ. 1197 occ. 1213

1197/1204, 1207, 1213, 29 Sept., chamberlain, CCA Lit. Ms D.4, fos 2v, 4v, 9, 10v, 12v, 14, 15v, CCA DCc MA1, fos 59, 53.

HUNT
see William Hadlegh II

HURST(E)
see Herst

HWYTE
see Whyte

HWYTSTAPLE
see Witstapla

HYBERNIA
see Hibernia

HYCHAM
see Ikham

HYEDE
see John Hethe II

HYERNE
see Herne

HYGHAM
see John Hegham

Stephen de HYNGESTON [Hingston, Hyngston
occ. 1341 d. 1361

1341, 13 Dec., one of nine prof., SL., 180 (as Kyngston), CCA Lit. Ms D.12, fo 4.

1349, 4 June, 55th in order at the el. of an abp, Reg. G, fo 60^{v}.

1349, 8/9 Sept., 55th at the el. of an abp, *ib.*, fo 76^{v}.

1359/60, ill in the infirmary and recd a 'pension' of 5s. from the anniversarian CCA DCc Anniv. acct 5.

1361, 13 July, one of 25 who d. [of the plague] between June and Sept., CCA Lit. Ms D.12, fo 17.

HYTHE
see John Hethe I

IERAM
see Jerom

Peter de IKHAM [Hikham, Hycham, Yckham
occ. 1270 d. 1295

n.d., name occ. in the list in *SL*, 175, CCA Lit. Ms D.12, fo 2^{v}.

1287/8, *magister corone*, CCA DCc MA1, fo 153^{v}.

1270, 7 Sept., named as one of seven *compromissorii* in the el. of an abp, *Gervase Cant.*, ii, 253; see Adam de Chillenden.

1271, commissary of Geoffrey de Romenal, q.v., who was official of the court of Canterbury, *sed. vac.*, and as such he presided over the court, Selden Soc., *Select Cases Eccles.*, 19; (CCA DCc ES Roll 370 contains his *acta*).

1294, 13 June, comm. by the prior and convent, with Richard de Clyve, q.v., to rec. the purgation of clerics, CUL Ee.5.31, fo 60^{v}.

1295, 4 May, d., CCA Lit. Ms D.12, fo 15; obit in BL Ms Arundel 68, fo 26^{v}.

Ten volumes are listed as his in the Eastry catalogue; these include legal texts (Justinian's Institutes, for example), James, *Ancient Libraries*, nos 1538–1547 (pp.128–129). See also the observations in Selden Soc., *Select Cases Eccles.*, 19, which ref. to the probability of his authorship of several chronicles.

An inventory of the refectory dated 1328 includes two silver *ciphi* of his and four *de murra*, Dart, *Antiq. Cant.*, xix, xxi, xxiii (BL Ms Cotton Galba E.iv, fos 178^{v}, 179^{v}, 180).

Richard de IKHAM [Icham, Ykham
occ. 1302 d. 1344

1302, 19 Oct., one of four prof., *SL*, 178, CCA Lit. Ms D.12, fo 3^{v}; (*SL* has the wrong month and Causton has confused the yr).

1305, 12 June, ord dcn, Smeeth chapel by Aldington, *Reg. abp Winchelsey*, 977.

1320/2, treasurer, CCA DCc MA2, fos 109–117.

1324/6, *custos* of the high altar, CCA DCc MA2, fos 137^{v}–154^{v}.

1327, part yr, granator, CCA DCc MA2, fo 165^{v}, Gran. acct 18; see William de Thrulegh.

1327/9, 1330, 1330/1, warden of manors, CCA DCc MA2, fos 162–182, 190, Elverton acct 19.

Note: in 1329/30 he is described as *custos*, Worcester Cathedral Muniment, C.573 (Great Chart acct); on 20 Feb. 1330 he was apptd 'custos maner' de Waldis' by the absent prior, *Lit. Cant.*, no 298 (Reg. L, fo 170).

1331/2, chaplain to the prior, CCA DCc MA2, fos 202^{v}–212, DE3, fo 1, Lambeth Ms 243, fo 34^{v}.

1333, 1334, warden of manors, CCA DCc MA2, fos 219, 229.

1335/6, 1337, cellarer, CCA DCc AS14, MA2, fo 256; in July [1336] the prior requested the abp to replace him as he was unfit for the office and the subcellarer was doing his work, *Lit. Cant.*, no 599 (Reg. L, fo 65^{v}). See below.

1339/40, 1341/3, infirmarer, CCA DCc Bart. accts 23, 25, 26.

1327, with Geoffrey de Poterel involved in negotiations concerning the el. of an abp, Lambeth Ms 243, fo 5.

1332/3, recd 13s. from the prior for his expenses in going to London to attend the [church] council, CCA DCc DE3, fo 34. This yr, with Edmund de Adesham, q.v., pd a supervisory visit to Godmersham, CCA DCc Godmersham acct 15.

1333, 3 Nov., named by the prior and chapter as one of seven *compromissorii* in the el. of an abp, Reg. G, fos xxxii, xxxvii and Reg. Q, fo 193^{v}; on 7 Nov. he was sent as proctor, with Simon de St Paul, q.v., to inform the king of the chapter's el. of John Stratford as abp, *ib.*, fo 33^{v}.

1334, Apr. × Dec., recd 10s. from the prior for his expenses in petitioning for a royal writ 'pro domo empta Oxon', Pantin, *Cant. Coll. Ox.*, iv, 179 (CCA DCc DE3).

1335, 31 May, was ordered to remove all the servants of the cellarer's household except for about 30 who were named, *Lit. Cant.*, no 572 (Reg. L, fo 109).

1338, 1 Mar., an inventory of missing service books held him responsible for the loss of the diurnale of Lambert de Clyve, q.v., *Lit. Cant.*, no 618 (Reg. L, fo 104).
1344, 9 Mar., d., CCA Lit. Ms D.12, fo 16^{v}.

Robert IKHAM [Ykham
occ. 1462 d. 1478/9

1462, 17 Apr., ord acol., Canterbury cathedral, *Reg. abp Bourgchier*, 381.
[1462], 6 Dec., one of six prof., SL 190, CCA Lit. Ms D.12, fo 8.
Note: this must have been incorrectly dated 1464 in the margin of the ms; 1462 (or 1463) is more likely.
1463, 9 Apr., ord subdcn, Canterbury cathedral, *Reg. abp Bourgchier*, 385.
1464, 31 Mar., ord dcn, Canterbury cathedral, *ib.*, 390.
1464, 22 Dec., ord pr., bp's chapel, Otford, *ib.*, 388.
1473/5, anniversarian with Robert Dene, q.v., CCA DCc, Prior acct 14, Lambeth ED43.
n.d., precentor, prob. at the time of d., see below.
1466, 17 Feb., 71st in order in an inventory of *jocalia fratrum* [given by him and/or assigned for his use], Reg. N, fo 234^{v}.
1478/9, d., CCA Lit. Ms D.12, fo 26, where he is named precentor; his obit on 1 Jan. is in BL Ms Arundel 68, fo 12; also named precentor in the obit in Lambeth Ms 20, fo 157.

Stephen de IKHAM [Icham, Ycham
occ. 1262 d. 1301

n.d., name occ. in the list in *SL*, 175, CCA Lit. Ms D.12, fo 2^{v}.
1262, 1263, 1264/8 on 29 Sept., treasurer, CCA DCc MA1 fos 104^{v}, 105^{v}, 106^{v}, 107^{v}, 108^{v}, 110, 111.
1276/7, warden of manors, Reg. H, fo 209^{v}.
1280/1, cellarer, CCA DCc MA1, fos 132^{v}–135.
1283, bartoner, CCA DCc, fo 139^{v}.
1286, 1294, 1 Jan., bailiff of the liberty, CCA DCc MA1, fo 1^{v}.
1287/96, warden of manors, CCA DCc, fos 150^{v}–200.
1293, 26 Jan., absent from the priory and cited to the el. of an abp, *Reg. abp Winchelsey*, 1261–1262.
1301, 17 Dec., d., CCA Lit. Ms D.12, fo 15^{v}.

Two volumes of his are listed in the Eastry catalogue, James, *Ancient Libraries*, nos 716, 717 (p. 78).

An inventory of the sacrist's office, *temp.* prior Eastry, includes a silk alb and a linen alb, embroidered, Legg and Hope, *Inventories*, 58 (BL Ms Cotton Galba, E.iv, fo 114^{v}).

An inventory of the refectory, dated 1328, includes a silver *ciphus* formerly his, and one *de murra*, Dart, *Antiq. Cant.*, xix (as S. de Icham), xxii (as D. de Icham) (BL Ms Cotton Galba E.iv, fos 178^{v}, 179^{v}).

I Thomas IKHAM
occ. 1423 d. 1457

1423, 30 Sept., one of five prof., *SL*, 187, CCA Lit. Ms D.12, fo 6^{v}.
1425, 22 Dec., ord acol., Charing, *Reg. abp Chichele*, iv, 373.
[1432], 11 June, ord pr., place not named, Reg. Langdon (Rochester), fo 74^{v}.
1435, third cantor, 'Chron. Wm Glastynbury', 129 (Ms fo 117).
1447, 8 Sept., apptd precentor, Reg. abp Stafford, fo 27^{v}, CCA DCc DE121; he was precentor on 7 Dec. 1449 and precentor at the time of his d., see below.
1439, 20 Jan., one of several monks licensed to leave the priory *pro recreacione*, and he returned on 31 Jan., Chron. Wm Glastynbury, fo 182^{v}/177^{v}.
1449, 7 Dec., one of the board of examiners of John Charyng, q.v., *Chron. Stone*, 47.
1457, 30 July, d., in the 33rd yr of his monastic life and was described as precentor, *Chron. Stone*, 67, CCA Lit. Ms D.12, fo 25^{v}; obit in BL Ms Arundel 68, fo 68^{v}.

II Thomas IKHAM [Ykham
occ. 1485 occ. 1520

1485, 12 Mar., one of six tonsured, *SL*, 191, CCA Lit. Ms D.12, fo 8^{v}.
1485, 2 Apr., ord acol., Canterbury cathedral, *Reg. abp Bourgchier*, 450.
1485, 6 Dec., prof., *SL*, 191, CCA Lit. Ms D.12, fo 8^{v}.
1491, 2 Apr., ord pr., Canterbury cathedral, *Reg. abp Morton*, i, no 439d.
1503, 6 July, 1507, 26 Nov., precentor, CCA Lit. Ms C.11, fo 35^{v}, CCA DCc DE61; he was apptd by the abp on 23 Apr. 1502, Reg. T, fo 415^{v}.
1493, 1 May, 49th in order at the ratification of an agreement, Reg. S, fo 383^{v}; but see John Crosse I.
1501, 26 Apr., 33rd at the el. of an abp, Reg. R, fo 56^{v}.
1505/6, repaired two copes [*cappe*], CCA DCc Sac. acct 66.
1511, 2 Sept., 17th in order on the visitation certificate, Wood-Legh, *Visit.*, 3 (Reg. abp Warham, i, fo 35^{v}); on 10 Sept. he was one of six obedientiaries who, with the prior, were apptd to oversee corrections in the priory after the abp's visitation, *ib.*, 5.
1520, apptd prior of Folkestone by the abp; ref. not found.
n.d., obit occ. 11 Jan., Lambeth Ms 20, fo 158^{v}.

III Thomas IKHAM [Hyckham, Ikhame

occ. 1517 occ. 1540

1517, 12 Mar., one of six tonsured, *SL*, 194, CCA Lit. Ms D.12, fo 11–11v.

1517, 29 Sept., made his prof., before the abp on the day on which the new prior, Thomas Goldwell, q.v., celebrated his first pontifical mass, *ib.*

1532, 25 Mar., subalmoner, CCA Lit. Ms C.11, fo 68.

[1538, 8 Feb., after], 1540, 4 Apr., third prior, Pantin, *Cant. Coll. Ox.*, iii, 153, *L and P Henry VIII*, xi, no 452.

1534, 12 Dec., acknowledged the Act of Supremacy, *DK 7th Report*, Appndx 2, 282.

[1538, 8 Feb., after] in a list of monks prob. drawn up for Thomas Cromwell, he was described as 'wytty' and 40 yrs of age, Pantin, *Cant. Coll. Ox.*, iii, 153.

1540, 4 Apr., awarded £3 p.a., *L and P Henry VIII*, xv, no 452.

ILGERIUS

n.d.

n.d., pr. whose obit occ. on 28 Sept. in BL Ms Cotton Nero C.ix, fo 12v.

William INGRAM [Ingramm, Yngham, Yngram

occ. 1483 occ. 1533

1483, 30 Sept., one of six tonsured, *SL*, 191, CCA Lit. Ms D.12, fo 8v.

1484, 10 June, prof., *ib.*

1485, 2 Apr., ord subdcn, Canterbury cathedral, *Reg. abp Bourgchier*, 450.

1485, 24 Sept., ord dcn, Canterbury cathedral, *ib.*, 452.

1503, after 6 July; 1504, 24 June; 1505/10, all on 29 Sept., *custos martyrii*, CCA Lit. Ms C.11, fos 32, 47, 40v, 41v, 42v, 43v, 44v, 45v; his accts for 1503/4 and following yrs are in his reg. (Lit. Ms C.11), fos 38ff.

1511, 7 June, apptd penitentiary by the chapter on the d. of Henry Arundel, q.v., CCA Lit. Ms C.11, beginning on fo 54, and he continued until 1533.

1493, 1 May, 43rd in order at the ratification of an agreement, Reg. S, fo 383v; but see John Crosse I.

1501, before 26 Apr., cited to appear for the el. of an abp on 26 Apr., but was ill in the infirmary and therefore absent, Reg. R, fo 56–56v.

1508, compiled a list of books from the library over the prior's chapel which were repaired, a total of 306 items, each with the incipits on fo 2, James, *Ancient Libraries*, 152–164 (CCA Lit. Ms C.11, fos 95–104). He was ill in the infirmary in Oct of this yr and charged his office 4s. 2d *pro cibariis emptis*, CCA Lit. Ms C.11, fo 117.

1511, 2 Sept., 12th in order on the visitation certificate, Wood-Legh, *Visit.*, 3 (Reg. abp Warham, i, fo 35); on 10 Sept. he was one of six obedientiaries who, with the prior, were apptd to oversee corrections in the priory after the abp's visitation, *ib.*, 5.

1520/1, spent time in the infirmary, CCA DCc Infirm. acct 2.

1533, the date of the final entries in his 'register', see below.

His 'penitentiary's register' has been preserved and remains *in situ* in the cathedral library where it is Lit. Ms C.11; it is his acct book for the period when he served as *custos* of Becket's shrine and, from 1511, as penitentiary in the priory. It also provides interesting details of his activities as revealed by the list of books repaired (see above), a number of inventories and mass rotas, expenses arising from the entertainment of guests, and from the care of servants and of some of the boys of the almonry school whom he may have tutored. See Rooke, 'William Ingram', 30–44. In 1521 and possibly other yrs, he pd the rent for his mother's tenement in the suburbs near Barton mill, CCA Lit. Ms C.11, fo 134v. See also F.A. Gasquet, 'Cant. Claustral School', 225–246.

Name in Canterbury cathedral Mss (CCA):

(1) Lit. Mss E.7 and E.8, two vols, paper; 'iste liber constat—qui erat compositus A.D.1478', on p.1. These two vols are his notebooks containing various treatises on logic etc., with capitals and blank spaces embellished in red and blue and a few elaborate designs. See *MMBL* for further description.

(2) Lit. Ms D.8, Miscellanea jur. (14th c.); on the front flyleaf, *pertinet ad—penitenciar'*, see also William London.

Name also, in BL Mss:

(1) Arundel 155, Psalterium (11th c.); on fo 4 and again on fo 8, 'si quis invenerit restituat—', and the date 1492 in another hand. See also William Hadlegh I.

(2) Harley 1587, Grammatica etc. (1396 to 15th/16th c.); on fo 15 his name and again, on fo 188v with that of Reginald Goldston I, his senior, who passed it on to him [*testante*]; see Gasquet, Cant. Claustral School', 225–246.

II William INGRAM

occ. 1522 occ. 1526/7

1521, [June], an almonry schoolboy, with Christopher Jamys, q.v., CCA Lit. Ms C.11, fo 136.

1522, 11 Feb., one of ten tonsured, *SL*, 195, CCA Lit. Ms D.12, fo 11v.

1522, 24 Nov., prof., *ib.*

1526/7, celebrated his first mass and recd a small gift from the sacrist, Woodruff, 'Sacrist's

Rolls', 72. He also recd a small sum from William Ingram I, CCA Lit. Ms C.22, fo 139v.

1523, Sept./Dec. recd a pair of *heleclowth* from his namesake above, q.v., CCA Lit. Ms C.11, fo 137v.

Note:

(1) some of the mss listed under William Ingram I may have been in this monk's possession.

(2) the obit of a William Ingram occ. on 13 Aug. in BL Ms Arundel 68, fo 38.

IPSWYCH

see Epyswyche

ISAAC

n.d.

n.d., 11 July, cantor, whose obit occ. in BL Ms Arundel 68, fo 34; was he one of the four who d. in Rome on or about this date in 1188? See Edmund II.

John ISLEP [Islop, Yslep

occ. 1376 d. 1401

1376, 14 or 15 Nov., one of seven who were clothed in the monastic habit, CCA Lit. Ms D.12, fo 4v, *SL*, 183.

1380, 24 Mar., ord subdcn, Canterbury cathedral, Reg. abp Sudbury, fo 147v.

1396/7, *custos martyrii*, CCA DCc Prior acct 4.

1381, 31 July, 58th in order at the el. of an abp, Reg. G, fo 225v.

1396, 7 Aug., 30th in order at the el. of an abp, *ib.*, fo 234v.

1401, 26 Jan., d.; on 21 Jan. he was found beside his bed in the dormitory 'super terram in stamino et femoralibus suis semivivus', and was taken to the infirmary where he recd the last rites, CCA Lit. Ms D.12, fo 18.

Simon ISLEP [Islepe, Isleppe, Islyp

occ. 1500 d. 1507

1500, 28 July, one of eight tonsured, *SL*, 193, CCA Lit. Ms D.12, fo 10; each of these novices recd a gold noble worth 6s. 8d. for their labours with regard to the funeral of abp Morton who d. c. 15 Sept., 1500, CCA Lit. Ms D.12, *ib.*

1501, 19 Apr., made his prof. before the prior, *sed. vac.*, *SL*, 193, CCA Lit. Ms D.12, fo 10.

1506/7, student at Canterbury college with a pension of £5, Pantin, *Cant. Coll. Ox.*, ii, 248 (CCA DCc Cart. Antiq. O.151.41).

1501, 24 Apr., 70th on the list of those eligible to participate in the el. of an abp, Reg. R, fo 56.

1507, 4 Oct., d.; his d. is the last entry in CCA Lit. Ms D.12 (fo 36) and he is described there as pr., prof. monk and Oxford scholar who d. at Canterbury college *ex infirmitate consumpcionis* in the 7th yr of his monastic life at the age of 23. The obit in BL Ms Arundel 68, fo 4, however, calls him *levita.*

IUSWYNUS

n.d.

n.d., 16 Feb., pr., whose obit occ. in BL Ms Arundel 68, fo 16v.

Nicholas de IVYNGHOE [Ivengho, Ivynghoe, Ivyngo, Yvingho, Yvingo, Yvyngo

occ. 1307 d. 1334

1307, 10 Aug., one of two prof., *SL*, 179, CCA Lit. Ms D.12, fo 3v.

1315, 25 Oct., 1317, 17 Oct., and 5 Nov., penitentiary, CUL Ms Ee.5.31, fos 161, 181v.

1327, feretrar, CCA DCc MA2, fo 164v.

1329, Mar./Sept., almoner, CCA DCc Eastry acct 55 and Alm. acct 40.

1332/3, feretrar, with Thomas de Greneway, q.v., CCA DCc MA2, fos 211v–221.

1315, 25 Oct., with William de Norwyco, q.v., recd letters of credence in order to confer with the abp 'for the sake of the community's peace and tranquillity', CUL Ms Ee.5.31, fo 161.

1317, 5 Nov., penitentiary and one of three monks who with the prior examined all their brethren as required by the abp in an inquiry over the circulation of letters, containing false and harmful statements, CUL Ms Ee.5.31, fo 181v; see Clement II and Walter de Eastry.

1319, 30 Apr., one of the witnesses who gave evidence at the enquiry into the sanctity of abp Winchelsey, Wilkins, *Concilia*, ii, 487 (CUL Ms Ee.5.31, fos 202v–204v).

1327, 11 Dec., named as one of seven *compromissorii* in the el. of an abp, Reg. Q, fo 123; see also *CPL*, ii (1305–1342), 272.

1331, [Apr.], one of four monks who were sent to consult the abp about the el. of a prior, Lambeth Ms 243, fo 26v.

1332, 22 May, with William de Mondham, q.v., apptd by the abp as two of several examiners of ordinands' papers, *Reg. Hethe*, 520 (Reg. L, fo 20).

1334, 18 Sept., d., CCA Lit. Ms D.12, fo 16.

Name in Lambeth Ms 399, Summa Raymundi etc. (late 13th c.); name on (front flyleaf); he bought it from the *feret' benedicti Thome martyrii* for 10s., fo 238v.

I J.

occ. 1233 occ. 1236/7

1233, 1236/7, precentor, CCA DCc MA1, fo 76, AS5.

II J.

occ. 1240/1

1240/1, subcellarer, CCA DCc MA1, fos 81v–82v.

III J.
occ. 1271/3

1271, subcellarer, CCA DCc MA1, fo 115.
1272/3, cellarer, CCA DCc MA1, fos 116v–118.

I JAMES [Jacobus
n.d.

n.d., 28 July, *levita*, whose obit occ. in BL Ms Arundel 68, fo 36.

II JAMES
occ. [1163 × 1167] occ. 1189

[1163 × 1167], name occ. in a survey of cathedral holdings in Canterbury when his mother, Edieue, gave a *mansura* to Christ Church, Urry, *Canterbury*, 237.
1189, 12 Oct., sent with Elias III q.v. to the king concerning the removal of abp Baldwin's proposed collegiate foundation at Lambeth, *Epist. Cant.*, 312.
1189, 5/8 Nov., one of the party of monks who went to confer with the king in London on this matter, *ib.*, 315.

JAMES [Flandrensis
occ. [?c. 1200]

[?c. 1200], land in All Saints' parish Canterbury, acc. to a survey of cathedral holdings of this date, was given at the time of his entry, Urry, *Canterbury*, 300.

Christopher JAMYS [Jamez
occ. 1524 occ. 1527/8

1521, almonry schoolboy for whom William Ingram I pd for the repair of his *sotular'*; in 1522 he pd 8d. to the grammar master on his behalf, CCA Lit. Ms C.11, fos 135v, 137.
1524, 21/22 July, one of eleven granted adm. [*ingressum*] to Christ Church, fos 11v–12.
1524, 4 Aug., one of eleven tonsured, *SL*, 195, CCA Lit. Ms D.12, fos 11v–12.
1525, 19 Apr., prof., *ib.*
1527/8, celebrated his first mass and recd a small gift from the sacrist, Woodruff, 'Sacrist's Rolls', 72.

Thomas le JAY
occ. 1245 occ. 1261/2

1245/50; 1260, Apr./Sept.; 1260/2, cellarer, CCA DCc MA1, fos 86v–91v; Reg. H, fo 201, 204v; CCA DCc MA1, fos 103v–104v. He was also cellarer in 1252/3 acc. to Reg. H, fo 176.

An inventory of the refectory, dated 1328, includes a silver *ciphus* formerly his, Dart, *Antiq. Cant.*, xix (BL Ms Cotton Galba E.iv, fos 178).

Note: is this Thomas Fay, q.v.?

I JEREMIAH [Jeremias
occ. 1136 occ. c. 1143

1137–c. 1143, prior: el. by the monks, *sed. vac.*, 1137; deposed by the abp c. 1143 but soon reinstated by the papal legate acting on a papal mandate. However, he then res. and became a monk at St. Augustine's, Canterbury, *Fasti*, ii, 9, and see below. See also *Theobald Charters*, 57–58 and Walter Durdent.
1136, led the resistance of Christ Church to the abp's plan to introduce regular canons at Dover priory and in the defence of Canterbury's rights over Dover, *Gervase Cant.*, i, 97–99, ii, 288; he appealed to Rome, *ib.*, ii, 383.
1138, 18 Dec., summoned to the legatine council at Westminster, *ib.*, i, 106.
1143, when the abp deprived him he went to Rome to plead, with success, his own cause; but he then res. to alleviate the abp's continuing wrath vs the monks, *ib.*, ii, 126–127.

See note below Jeremias II.

II JEREMIAS
occ. 1st half 13th c.

n.d., name occ. in the *post exilium* list in *SL*, 173, CCA Lit. Ms D.12, fo 1v.

Note:
(1) the obits of two monks named Jeremias occ. in BL Ms Arundel 68: 21 May (fo 28), 4 Aug. (fo 37).
(2) In the inventory of the refectory, dated 1328, there is a *ciphus de murra* ascribed to Jeremias, Dart, *Antiq. Cant.*, xxii (BL Ms Cotton Galba E.iv, fo 180).

William JEROM [Geram, Ieram, Jerome
occ. 1519 occ. 1537

1519, 6 May, one of nine tonsured, *SL*, 194, CCA Lit. Ms D.12, fo 11v.
1520, 3 Feb., prof., *ib.*
1528/9, student at Canterbury college, Oxford, as Jeronimus, with a pension of £6 10s. pd for him [to the warden], Pantin, *Cant. Coll. Ox.*, ii, 259 (CCA DCc Cart. Antiq. O.151.48).
1530, Nov., supplicated for B.Th., after eight yrs of study; granted, Pantin, *ib.*, iii, 252.
[1534], 24 Mar., presumably at the college because the warden apptd him his proctor and attorney in the collection of debts, Pantin, *ib.*, iii, 269.

1520/1, spent time in the infirmary, CCA DCc Infirm. acct 2.
1537, 20 May,. pr., dispensed to hold a benefice and change his habit [to secular clerical dress]; the fee was waived, Chambers, *Faculty Office Regs*, 98. His enthusiasm for Lutheran views cost him his life three yrs later when he was burned at the stake, *BRUO, 1501–1540*.

JODWYNSTONE
see Joseph Goodnyston

I JOHN
occ. 1154

1154, chaplain to prior Walter de Meri, q.v.

II JOHN [son of Walter de Sartrino
occ. [1157 × 1161]

[1157 × 1161], was made a monk by abp Theobald, and his house and land in Westgate, which belonged to the abp's fee, were made over by the abp to the priory, *Theobald Charters*, no 35, and Urry, *Canterbury*, 398.

III JOHN
occ. 1180

1180, cellarer, apptd prior of Dover, *HRH*, 88.

Note:
(1) see also John Bockyng and John Bremble who may be identical with John II and/or John III.
(2) in a survey of cathedral holdings dated [1163 × 1167] there is ref. to a *mansura* given at the time of the adm. of John, son of Mary, Urry, *Canterbury*, 236.
(3) John, sacrist, appears [1193 × 1199] as a witness to a charter with Herveus II subprior, q.v.

IV JOHN
occ. 1201 occ. 1218

1201/2, almoner, CCA Lit. Ms D.4 fo 12^{v}, and see Robert VI.
1213, 1215, 1216, all on 29 Sept., 1217, 7 Nov., subcellarer, CCA DCc MA1, fos 53^{v}, 56^{v}, 58, 60^{v}.
1218, 7 Nov., granator, CCA DCc MA1, fo 60.

Note: the divisions between John IV, V and VI are arbitrary and it is prob. that John V is made up of entries applying to more than one monk. John VI (and some of John IV) may ref. to John de Chatham, prior, q.v.), but the name is too common for certainty.

V JOHN
occ. 1227/8 occ. 1244/5

1227/30, sacrist, CCA DCc, MA1, fos 71–73^{v}, AS2.
1229/30, Nov. to Sept., granator, CCA DCc, AS2.
1229/30, Dec./Jan., cellarer, *ib.*
1231, granator, CCA DCc MA1, fo 74.
1233/6, cellarer, CCA DCc MA1, fos 76–78^{v}, AS4 (1235, Sept./Dec.)
1234, chamberlain, CCA DCc MA1, fo 77^{v}.
1236, Jan./1244, sacrist, CCA DCc, AS4, AS5, MA1, fos 78^{v}–85^{v}.
1237, May/Sept., 1244/5, granator, CCA DCc AS5, AS16.

See note under John IV.

VI JOHN
occ. 1228

1228, 3 Aug., subprior, *Gervase Cant.*, ii, 121.
1228, 3 Aug., one of five *compromissorii* in the el. of an abp, *ib.*, ii, 120, 121, 123.

James attributes item no 1017 in the Eastry catalogue to this monk, *Ancient Libraries*, 98.

See the notes between John III and IV, and John IV and V.

JOHN
see also Calderum

Andrew JOHN [Andreas Johannes
occ. 1186

1186, 25 Nov., a young dcn [*levita*] to whom abp Thomas Becket appeared and revealed the designs of abp Baldwin, *Gervase Cant.*, i, 338–343, where he is described as 'binomius ex fonte baptismatis et ex professione monachili' (*ib.*, 338); see Honorius II, prior.

JONAS [Jhonas
occ. 1188/9

1188, c.Dec./1189, Jan., one of the monks in the party of those who went with the prior [Honorius II q.v.] to the curia and was acting as a messenger for them, bearing letters, *Epist. Cant.*, 271, 276, 278.
1189, Feb., at Rheims with brother R. I, q.v., *ib.*, 282.
1189, July/Aug., with S[imon], treasurer, q.v., sent by the Christ Church monks to meet the duke, [i.e. Richard I], *ib.*, 306, 307.

Note: the obit of a Jonas occ. on 4 Apr., BL Ms Cotton Nero C.ix, fo 9.

JORDAN
occ. 1219

1219, 1 Nov., granator, CCA MA1, fo 61^{v}.
n.d., 12 Nov., the obit of a Jordan, *levita*, occ. in BL Ms Arundel, 68, fo 48.

The Processionale of a Jordan (who was d.) had been lost by prior Eastry according to an inventory of missing books dated 1 Mar. 1338, *Lit. Cant.*, no 618 (Reg. L, fo 104).

Note: see also Jordan de Roff' who is prob. this monk.

I JOSEPH
occ. [c. 1089 × 1114]

[c. 1089 × 1114], soon after the d. of abp Lanfranc in 1089 he made a pilgrimage to Jerusalem in search of relics of St Andrew for the new cathedral church at Rochester. The acct of his visit to that city and to Constantinople in Ms Vatican Lat. 4950, fo 220, is transcribed in C.H. Haskins, *Studies in*

Mediaeval Culture (Oxford, 1929), 162–163. This 12th c. ms is a Rochester lectionary.

[1096 × 1107], *temp.* prior Ernulf, with Eadmer, q.v., witness to a charter of abp Anselm for Rochester cathedral, *Text Roff.*, ii, fo 179 and cap 93.

[1115 × 1122], *temp.* bp Ernulf [Rochester], with Eadmer, witnessed a charter of abp Ralph also for Rochester, *ib.*, 179v and cap 94.

Note: both of these may be spurious; the latter will be printed in Eng. Epis. Acta Canterbury, 1070–1136, no 37, forthcoming.

n.d. 27 Mar., it is prob. his obit that occ. in Lambeth Ms 20, fo 175v, (and BL Ms Arundel 68, fo 22), on this date acc. to Haskins, *ib.*, 161, n. 2; but see Joseph II.

Name prob. in BL Ms Royal, 5.E.1, Isidorus (12th c.), *per*—. This suggestion by Haskins *ib.*, 161, n. 2, is persuasive, although Ker in *MLGB* assumed that Joseph was a Rochester monk, q.v., under Rochester.

II JOSEPH
occ. 1203/4 occ. 1219

1203/4, cellarer, CCA Lit. Ms D.4, fo 15v.

1213/16, all on 29 Sept., 1217, 7 Nov., 1218 and 1219, 1 Nov., chamberlain, CCA DCc MA1, fos 53v, 54v, 56v, 58, 60, 61v.

1206, 30 Mar., one of the monks summoned by the pope to Rome to give evidence in the dispute over their el. of Reginald, q.v., as abp. *CPL*, i (1198–1304), 26; while there, they el. Stephen Langton, *Fasti*, ii, 6.

Note: is this Joseph de Mallyng, q.v.? See Joseph I.

JOSEPH
see also Goodnyston

JULIAN
occ. [1163 × 1167]

[1163 × 1167], a survey of cathedral holdings in Canterbury of this date ref. to land given with Julian 'our monk', Urry, *Canterbury*, 243.

n.d., 18 June, dcn, whose obit occ. in BL Ms Arundel 68, fo 31.

JUSWYNUS
see Iuswynus

Robert KANIM [?Kamin
occ. [c. 1280]

n.d. [c. 1280], one of four prof., *SL*, 176, CCA Lit. Ms D.12, fo 3.

KARLEMANNUS
n.d.

n.d., *levita*, whose obit occ. on 12 Feb., and who gave Broke [*sic*] at the time of his adm. as a monk, BL Ms Cotton Nero C.ix, fo 5v.

KAUSTON, Kawston, Kauxton
see William Causton

John KEBULL [Kebyl, Kevyle, Keybyl
occ. 1517 occ. 1520

1517, 12 Mar., one of six tonsured, *SL*, 194, CCA Lit. Ms D.12, fo 11–11v.

1517, 29 Sept., prof., *ib.*

1517, and other yrs, he rcd small sums from William Ingram I as recorded in the latter's notebook, CCA Lit. Ms C.11, e.g., 10d. in this yr (fo 129), an ordinal or 6d. towards one in 1520 (fo 131), and in the same yr 4d. for his habit (fo 131v), 12d. *pro cometiva* (fo 133v) and 12d. for making his *froce* and *cuculle* (fo 134).

n.d., 24 Oct., the obit of a John Keybyl, pr., occ in BL Ms Arundel 68, fo 46.

Note: this may be one of the almonry school boys for whom William Ingram I, q.v., had been responsible, CCA Lit. Ms C.11 as above.

John KENERTON [Kenarton
occ. 1470 d. 1470

1470, 25 Jan., one of eight prof., *SL*, 190, CCA Lit. Ms D.12, fo 8.

1470, 21 Apr., ord acol., Canterbury cathedral, *Reg. abp Bourgchier*, 405.

1470, 19 Oct., d., in the sacrist's chamber, *Chron. Stone*, 114; his obit occ. in BL Ms Arundel 68, fo 45v.

William KENERTON [Kenarton, Kennerton, Kenyngton, Kynarton *alias* Chaloner
occ. 1373 d. 1404

1373, 23 Aug., the prior was comm. to adm. and clothe William Chaloner, *clericus*, and another, Reg. abp Wittlesey, fo 62v; he is one of eight [novices] grouped together in *SL*, 183, CCA Lit. Ms D.12, fo 4v, where he is named Kennerton.

1374, 27 Apr., novice whom the prior was comm. to prof., Reg. abp Wittlesey, fo 130v.

1377, 28 Mar., ord pr., Canterbury cathedral, Reg. abp Sudbury, fo 141 (as Kenyngtone).

1389/90, succ. Nicholas Galeye, q.v., in the office of fourth prior, Lambeth Ms 243, fo 216v.

1401, 17 Oct., apptd chamberlain, Reg. abp Arundel, i, fo 437; he prob. continued in this office until d., see below.

1383, 1 Sept., apptd second scholar at Canterbury college, Pantin, *Cant. Coll. Ox.*, iii, 47 (Reg. abp Courtenay, i, fo 44v); he recd a small sum from the prior this yr 'versus Oxoniam *pro benedictione*', Pantin, *ib.*, iv, 188 (Lambeth Ms 243, fo 183v).

1384/5, at Oxford and recd travelling expenses to return to Canterbury, Pantin, *ib.*, iv, 190.

1381, 31 July, 49th in order at the el. of an abp, Reg. G, fo 225^v.
1396, 7 Aug., 25th at the el. of an abp, *ib.*, fo 234^v.
1404, 24 Oct., chamberlain, d., CCA Lit. Ms D.12, fo 18.

Alan KENEVYLE
occ. [1241]

[1241] name occ. in the list in *SL*, 174, CCA Lit. Ms D.12, fo 2; he was possibly one of the twelve prof. with Richard de Wynchepe, q.v.

Reginald KENYNGTON [Kenynton
occ. [1207 × 1214]

n.d. [1207 × 1214], name occ. in the list of those in exile, *SL*, 172, CCA Lit. Ms D.12, fo 1.

n.d., subprior of Dover, *Lit. Cant.*, Appndx, no 34 (CCA DCc Z.D.4, 24).

An inventory of the refectory, dated 1328, includes two *ciphi de murra*, Dart, *Antiq. Cant.*, xxi (BL Ms Cotton Galba E.iv, fos 179).

William KENYNGTONE
see Kenerton

KEVYLE, Keybyl
see Kebull

KILLEY
see Kylley

KINSINUS
n.d.

n.d., dcn, whose obit occ. on 23 Nov. in BL Ms Cotton Nero C.ix, fo 16.

William de KLYNSTEDE [Clynstede
occ. 2nd half 13th c.

n.d., name occ. in the list in *SL*, 175 (as Clynstede), CCA Lit. Ms D.12, fo 2^v.

I William de KNOLTON
d. by 1338

1338, 1 Mar., his antiphoner was missing according to the inventory of service books, and Luke [?II] was held responsible, *Lit. Cant.*, no 618 (Reg. L, fo 104).

Note: this section of the list records books that had belonged to monks deceased before this date.

An inventory of the refectory, dated 1328, includes a *cuppa de murra* of his, Dart, *Antiq. Cant.*, xviii (BL Ms Cotton Galba E.iv, fo 178).

II William KNOLTON
occ. 1376 d. 1395

1376, 14 or 15 Nov., one of seven who were clothed in the monastic habit, CCA Lit. Ms D.12, fo 4^v, *SL*, 183.

1376, 20 Dec., ord acol., Canterbury cathedral, Reg. abp Sudbury, fo 140^v.
1377, 19 Sept., ord subdcn, Lambeth palace chapel, *ib.*, fo 142.
1378, 17 Apr., ord dcn, Canterbury cathedral, *ib.*, fo 145^v.

1381, 31 July, 56th in order at the el. of an abp, Reg. G, fo 225^v.
1388/9, 1390/1, recd small sums from the prior, Lambeth Ms 243, fos 212^v, 220^v.
1392/3, gave the sacrist 13s. 4d., *pro dealbatione chori* and 20d. 'ad sereum ardentem in nocte coram imagine beate Marie virginis', CCA DCc Sac. acct 11.
1395, 11 Apr., d., CCA Lit. Ms D.12, fo 17; obit occ. in BL Ms Arundel 68, fo 23^v.

John de KOMPYS [Compys
occ. 1294 d. 1332

1294, one of eight prof., *SL*, 178, CCA Lit. Ms D.12, fo 3.

1323/6, *custos martyrii*, CCA DCc MA2, fos 128^v–154^v.

1332, 25 Nov., d., CCA Lit. Ms D.12, fo 16.

James KRANBROKE
occ. [c. 1415 × 1445]

[c. 1415 × 1445], Chron Wm Glastynbury, fo 168^v/162^v has the following entry: 'iste apos' venit de Begham et sic assumptus habitum necnon apostavit illic et ibi mansit'.

Ralph KYLL'
n.d.
n.d., 31 Jan., obit occ in BL Ms Arundel 68, fo 15.

Thomas KYLLEY [Killey, Kyllay
occ. [1395] d. 1418

[1395], 12 Mar., one of eight prof., *SL*, 184, CCA Lit. Ms D.12, fo 5.
1396, 1 Apr., ord subdcn, Canterbury cathedral, Reg. abp Courtenay, ii, fo 186^v.
1396, 7 Aug., 74th in order (out of 81) at the el. of an abp, Reg. G, fo 234^v.
1414, 12 Mar., 35th at the el. of an abp, *Reg. abp Chichele*, i, 4.
1418, 14 May (vigil of Pentecost), d., according to CCA Lit. Ms D.12, fo 21, which seems to be copying from *Chron. Stone*, 8, or *vice versa.* However, his obit occ. on 27 May in BL Ms Arundel 68, fo 28^v.

KYNERTON
see Kenerton

Edmund KYNGSTON [Kyngeston
occ. 1401 occ. 1428

1401, 19 Mar., ord acol., Canterbury cathedral, Reg. abp Arundel, i, fo 327^v.

1401, 25 Mar., one of seven prof., *SL*, 185, CCA Lit. Ms D.12, fo 5^v^.
1401, 17 Dec., ord subdcn, Canterbury cathedral, Reg. abp Arundel, i, fo 329.
1403, 14 Apr., ord dcn, Canterbury cathedral, *ib.*, i, fo 331.
1428, *custos martyrii*, who with John Viel, q.v., compiled a customary of the shrine; see below.
1414, 12 Mar., 53rd in order at the el. of an abp, *Reg. abp Chichele*, i, 4.

Name in BL Add. Ms 59616, which contains the customary he compiled; see D.H. Turner, 'The Customary of St Thomas Becket', *Cant. Cath. Chron.*, no 70 (1976), 16–22.

John KYNGSTON [Kyngeston, Kyngiston
occ. 1381 d. 1413

1381, 6 May, one of eight prof., *SL*, 183, CCA Lit. Ms D.12, fo 5.
1385, 23 Dec., ord pr., abp's chapel, Otford, Reg. abp Courtenay, i, fo 308.
[1413], *magister mense*, prob. at the time of d., see below.
1390/1, recd a gift of 12d. from the prior, Lambeth Ms 243, fo 220^v^.
1396, 7 Aug., 38th in order at the el. of an abp, Reg. G, fo 234^v^.
1413, 17 Oct., d., CCA Lit. Ms D.12, fo 19^v^, where he is described as *magister mense*; his obit on 18 Oct. is in Bl Ms Arundel 68, fo 45^v^.

I Richard KYNGSTON [Kyngeston, Kyngiston, Kyngistone
occ. [1406] d. 1460

1406, 21 Oct., one of seven prof., *SL*, 185, CCA Lit. Ms D.12, fo 5^v^.
1407, 26 Mar., ord acol., Canterbury cathedral, Reg. abp Arundel, i, fo 340^v^.
1407, 24 Sept., ord subdcn, collegiate church, Maidstone, *ib.*, i, fo 341.
1410, 22 Mar., ord pr., Canterbury cathedral, *ib.*, ii, fo 98^v^.
1420, subsacrist, *Chron. Stone*, 78.
1430/2, bartoner, CCA DCc, Bart. accts, 90, 91.
1435, feretrar, 'Chron. Wm Glastynbury', 129 (Ms fo 117); see below.
1435, 28 Mar., apptd warden of manors, Chron. Wm Glastynbury, fo 117.
1436/7, cellarer, CCA DCc, Prior acct 7.
1437/8, bartoner, CCA DCc, Bart. acct 94.
1438/9, 1442/3; 1444, Apr., cellarer, Lambeth, ED59, CCA DCc, Prior acct 6; he was relieved of this office in Apr., 1444, Reg. abp Stafford, fo 14^v^.
1445, 20 Apr., 1446, 23 Apr., treasurer, CCA DCc, DE15C/31, 38.
1446, Apr./1448, cellarer; he was apptd on 13 Apr. 1446, Reg. abp Stafford, fo 22, Lambeth, ED74 (1446/7), CCA DCc MA4, fo 174^v^ (1447/8).
1450/1, 1453/4, 1455, 1 Oct., chamberlain, CCA DCc Chamb. accts 60, 66, DE50.
n.d., high [*summus*] chaplain to the prior, and *supervisor novi operis*, *Chron. Stone*, 78–79.
1414, 12 Mar., 53rd in order at the el. of an abp, *Reg. abp Chichele*, i, 4.
1460, 17 Apr., *stacionarius*, d., in the 54th yr of his monastic life, having been blind for over two yrs; the prior and convent said the *commendatio* in the infirmary chapel where he lay on the stone, *Chron. Stone*, 78–79. Stone adds that he served *strenue* in many offices, all of which *laudabiliter gubernavit*, *ib.* His obit is in BL Ms Arundel 68, fo 24^v^.

Canterbury college inventories of 1459 and 1469 include a 'ciphus *de murra* scriptus in fimbria R. Kyngston', Pantin, *Cant. Coll. Ox.*, i, 17 (CCA DCc Cart. Antiq. O.135), 77 (Reg. N, fo 235^v^).

II Richard KYNGSTON [Kyngeston, Kyngiston
occ. 1491 d. 1504

1491, 11 Sept., one of four tonsured, *SL*, 192, CCA Lit. Ms D.12, fo 9.
1492, 12 Apr., ord acol., Canterbury cathedral, *Reg. abp Morton*, i, no 441a.
1493, 6 Apr., ord subdcn, Canterbury cathedral, *ib.*, i, no 442b.
1494, 29 Mar., ord dcn, Canterbury cathedral, *ib.*, i, no 443c.
1497, 25 Mar., ord pr., Canterbury cathedral, *ib.*, i, no 446d.
1496/7, celebrated his first mass and recd 8d. from the sacrist, CCA DCc, Sac. acct 67.
1493, 1 May, 62nd in order at the ratification of an agreement, Reg. S, fo 383^v^; but see John Crosse I.
1501, 26 Apr., 41st in order at the el. of an abp, Reg. R, fo 56^v^.
1504, 25 Sept., d., *ex consumpcione*; he was the *ultimus senior*, 28 and a half yrs old and in his thirteenth yr of monastic life, CCA Lit. Ms D.12, fo 35. His obit on 27 Sept. is in BL Ms Arundel 68, fo 43.

Thomas de KYNGSTON [Kyngeston, *?alias* Bereham
occ. 1355 d. 1361

1355, 30 May, a Thomas Bereham ord subdcn, abp's chapel Maidstone, Reg. abp Islip, fo 315^v^
1355, 19 Sept., ord dcn, abp's chapel, Saltwood, *ib.*, fo 315^v^.
1356, 18 June, ord pr., Hoath chapel, Reculver parish, *ib.*, fo 316.
1361, 29 July, one of c. 25 monks who d. [of the plague] between June and Sept., CCA Lit. Ms D.12, fo 17.

KYNGSTON
see also Hyngeston

M. John KYNTON, B.C.L., B.CnL [Kyngton

occ. 1410 d. 1416

1410, [21 Mar.], *clericus*, clothed in the monastic habit and made his prof. the same day at the high altar in the presence of the abp, *SL*, 185, CCA Lit. Ms D.12, fo 6, *Chron. Stone*, 7.

1414, 12 Mar., 5th in order at the el. of an abp, *Reg. abp Chichele*, i, 4; his insertion into the order of seniority immediately below William Chart I who was adm. in 1370, is worthy of note.

1414, prior to 25 June, had been apptd commissary for the prior and convent, *sed. vac.* [in testamentary causes] and had proved the will of the bp of Coventry and Lichfield, *Reg. abp Chichele*, iv, 6.

1416, 18 Oct., d., and was buried in the infirmary chapel between two columns *versus ostium cimiterii*, *Chron. Stone*, 7 (CCA Lit. Ms D.12, fos 20v–21); his obit, on 19 Oct., is in BL Ms Arundel 68, fo 45v.

Name in

(1) Canterbury Cathedral Ms B.11, Egidius Romanus (15th c.); on a front flyleaf, *liber* M.—, *monachi*. The ownership inscription has been reproduced in pl. 79(c) in Collinson, *Canberbury Cathedral*.

(2) Oxford Bod., Ms Laud misc. 444, Pseudo-Chrysostomus (late 14th c.); on an end flyleaf, *liber iste constat* M.—.

He had previously obtained degrees in canon and civil law and had held a number of canonries and prebends, had been a clerk in chancery, had served as chancellor to the queen, and had been sent on various embassies abroad, *BRUO*, and *Chron. Stone*, 7–8.

Roger de la LEE

see Lee

John de LA LESE

see Lese

John LAMBERHERST [Lambarherst, Lamberherste, Lambherst, Lambyrherst

occ. 1509 occ. 1540

1509, 22 Dec., ord acol., Canterbury cathedral, Reg. abp Warham, ii, fo 264v.

1510, 16 June, one of eight tonsured, *SL*, 194, CCA Lit. Ms D.12, fo 11.

1511, 1 Jan., prof., *ib.*

1511, 19 Apr., ord dcn, Canterbury cathedral, Reg. abp Warham, ii, fo 265v.

1538, 8 Feb., after], 1540, 4 Apr., penitentiary, Pantin, *Cant. Coll. Ox.*, iii, 152, *L and P Henry VIII*, xv, no 452.

1511, 2 Sept., 79th and last but one of the prof., on the visitation certificate, Wood-Legh, *Visit.*, 3 (Reg. abp Warham, i, fo 35v).

1534, 12 Dec., acknowledged the Act of Supremacy, *DK 7th Report*, Appndx 2, 282.

[1538, 8 Feb., after], in a list of monks prob. prepared for Thomas Cromwell, he was described as 'symple' and 56 yrs of age, Pantin, *Cant. Coll. Ox.*, iii, 152.

1540, 4 Apr., awarded £6 13s. 4d. p.a., *L and P Henry VIII*, xv, no 452.

Thomas LAMBERHERST [Lamberherste, Lambyrherst

occ. 1446 d. 1467

1446, 21 Dec., one of seven tonsured, *SL*, 189, CCA Lit. Ms D.12, fo 7v.

1447, 4 Mar., ord acol., Canterbury cathedral, Reg. abp Stafford, fo 199.

1447, 27 Aug., made his prof., with the other six in the presence of the abp, *Chron. Stone*, 41–42.

1447, 23 Dec., ord subdcn, Canterbury cathedral, Reg. abp Stafford, fo 201v.

1448, 17 Feb., ord dcn, Canterbury cathedral, *ib.*, fo 202.

1450, 3 Apr., ord pr., Canterbury cathedral, *ib.*, fo 204v.

1464/5, anniversarian, CCA DCc, U15/24/7.

n.d., subsacrist, CCA Lit. Ms D.12, fo 26.

n.d., feretrar, prob. at the time of d., *Chron. Stone*, 98.

1466, 17 Feb., 39th in order in an inventory of *jocalia fratrum* [given by him and/or assigned for his use], Reg. N, fo 233.

1467, 27 Mar., d., *ex vi pestilencie*, in his 20th yr of monastic life, and was buried immediately, *Chron. Stone*, 98.

LAMBERT

occ. 1258/9 occ. 1278/9

1258, Nov./1260, Apr., subcellarer, Reg. H, fos 198, 201.

1267/9, cellarer, CCA DCc, MA1, fos 110–112.

1269/76, 1278/9, sacrist, CCA DCc MA1, fos 112–123v, 128–130.

1263, accompanied Adam de Chillenden, prior elect q.v., to meet abp Boniface at Amiens, and obtain confirmation of his el., *Gervase Cant.*, ii, 227–228.

Note: this is almost certainly Lambert de Clyve, q.v.

LAMBERT

see also Gargate

William LANE

occ. 1443

1443, 25 Mar., one of six prof., *SL*, 188, CCA Lit. Ms D.12, fo 7v.

n.d., he had been a secular pr. before his adm. and was at an unknown date licensed to transfer to Folkestone, Chron Wm Glastynbury, fo 168v/162v.

I John LANGDON, D.Th. [Langdene, Langdone, Langedon, Longdon
occ. [1399] occ. 1421

[1399], one of four prof., *SL*, 184, CCA Lit. Ms D.12, fo 5v.
1401, 2 Apr., ord subdcn, Canterbury cathedral, Reg. abp Arundel, i, fo 328.
1401, 28 May, ord dcn, Canterbury cathedral, *ib.*, i, fo 328v.
1404, 24 May, ord pr., abp's chapel, Maidstone, *ib.*, i, fo 333.
1410, Sept., apptd warden of Canterbury college, Pantin, *Cant. Coll. Ox.*, iii, 68 (Reg. abp Arundel, ii, fo 125); he was still warden the following Aug., Pantin, *Cant. Coll. Ox.*, iii, 68 (Reg. S, fo 62–62v), and prob. still or again on 21 Feb. 1414, Reg. S, fo 68v; see below.
1412/13, almoner, CCA DCc, Treas. acct 11.
n.d., subprior, BL Ms Arundel 68, fo 43v.

1407/8, went up to Canterbury college, and was provided with his *capa*, Pantin, *Cant. Coll. Ox.*, iv, 191; however, he must have begun his studies at Oxford several yrs earlier in order to be qualified to incept by 1410/11.
1410/11, incepted D.Th., the expenses of the inception of Langdon and of Richard Godmersham I, q.v., are recorded in detail and the total was £118 3s. 5d., Pantin, *ib.*, iii, 63–67 (Oxford, Bod. Ms Tanner 165, fos 146–147v, CCA DCc Prior acct 2).
1411, one of the university committee involved in examining the writings of John Wyclif, Wilkins, *Concilia*, iii, 172; he was apptd by the abp this same yr as one of the commissioners to obtain oaths from all members of the university that they would avoid Wyclif's errors, *BRUO*.
1414, 21 Feb., at Canterbury college [?as warden], Pantin, *Cant. Coll. Ox.*, iii, 72 (Reg. S, fo 68v).

1411, 29 Nov., apptd proctor to attend convocation, Reg. S, fo 63v.
1414, 12 Mar., 34th in order at the el. of an abp and acted as proxy for John Otford, q.v.; he also announced the chapter's choice, *Reg. abp Chichele*, i, 4–5.
1417, 1 Nov., named as one of the members of the English delegation to the council of Constance, Reg. S, fo 77; one of his stated aims was to procure a bull of indulgence for the jubilee of St Thomas in 1420, Pantin, *Cant. Coll. Ox.*, iii, 76, iv, 224 (PRO E36/196, fo 35).
1419, Oct., 1421, 5 May, preached the sermon at convocation, *Reg. abp Chichele*, iii, 51, 63; at the latter he was nominated to a committee which was to examine and report on the orthodoxy of the writings of William Taylor, Wilkins, *Concilia*, iii, 406.
1421, 17 Nov., named bp of Rochester by papal provision, having been unsuccessfully put forward by the king and abp for the see of Lisieux, Pantin, *Cant. Coll. Ox.*, iii, 74–76, 77–78.

See *BRUO* for his episcopal career. His episcopal register, 1421–1434 survives; see the bibliography for Rochester.

II John LANGDON, D.Th. [Langdone, Langedon, London
occ. 1465 d. 1496

1465, 4 Apr., one of seven prof., *SL*, 190, CCA Lit. Ms D.12, fo 8.
1465, 13 Apr., ord subdcn, place not stated, *Reg. abp Bourgchier*, 391.
1469, 1 Apr., ord pr., Canterbury cathedral, *ib.*, 402.
1468/9, celebrated his first mass and recd a gift from the sacrist, CCA DCc, Sac. acct 47.
1478/82, 1486/95, warden of Canterbury college; his accts for 1478/9, 1480/2, 1486/8, 1489/90 survive and are printed by Pantin in *Cant. Coll. Ox.*, ii, 203–223 (CCA DCc Cart. Antiq. O.151.22b, 24, 24a, 26, 27, 28). On 6 Jan. 1495, he, with the monk fellows, was summoned to the el. of a prior, Pantin, *ib.*, iii, 131 (Reg. S, fo 394); on 7 June his belongings were transported back to Canterbury, *ib.*, iv, 203. Two letters in English from him as warden to prior Sellyng are printed in Pantin, *ib.*, iii, 120–121, 128–129.
1486, chancellor of Christ Church, Reg. S, fo 362v.

[1473], Sept., [1474], Sept., [1475], Mar., student at Canterbury college, for whom the warden of manors pd [some of] his stipend, 70s., £4 and £4 respectively. Pantin, *Cant. Coll. Ox.*, ii, 263, 264 (CCA DCc Cart. Antiq. O.151.8). In Oct. 1473 he recd his *capa scolar'*, Pantin, *ib.*, iv, 199.
1475/6, student, who recd £8 p.a. stipend, Pantin, *ib.*, ii, 195 (CCA DCc Cart. Antiq. O.151.21).
[1477], Apr. and Sept., student, receiving a stipend as above, Pantin, *ib.*, ii, 265 (Cart. Antiq. O.151.8).
1486, 23 Apr., B.Th. by this date, Reg. R, fo 14.
1495, 6 Jan., before this date D.Th., Pantin, *Cant. Coll. Ox.*, iii, 131 (Reg. S, fo 394).

c. 1465, as a novice had as his 'tutor' [*magister regule*] William Hadlegh I, q.v., *SL*, 188, CCA Lit. Ms D.12, fo 28v.
1466, 17 Feb., 76th and last in order in an inventory of *jocalia fratrum* [given by him and/or assigned for his use], and he had none, Reg. N, fo 235.
1486, 23 Apr., apptd commissary general with others by the prior and convent, *sed. vac.*, Reg. R, fo 14.
[1486], licensed to preach in Canterbury diocese, Reg. R, fo 8v.
1496, 14 Mar., d., CCA Lit. Ms D.12, fo 31v, where he is described as 'egregius. . . predicator'; he

was buried in the infirmary chapel, *ib.*, see William Hadlegh I.

Name in Manchester, John Rylands University Library Ms Lat. 474 Biblia (13th c.); quondam in custodia—; see William Bonyngton II and John Wodnesburgh III.

Gave to Canterbury college a red *tapetum* for the high altar there and two *tabula depicta*, Pantin, *Cant. Coll. Ox.*, i, 31, 35.

III John LANGDON, B.Th. [Langdown, Langdun

occ. 1497 occ. 1540

1497, 28 July, one of nine tonsured, *SL*, 192, CCA Lit. Ms D.12, fo 9ᵛ.

1498, 14 Apr., ord acol., Canterbury cathedral, *Reg. abp Morton*, i, no 447a.

1498, 19 Apr., prof., *SL*, 192, CCA Lit. Ms D.12, fo 9ᵛ.

1503/4, celebrated his first mass and recd a gift from the sacrist, CCA DCc, Sac. acct, 61.

1514, 25 Mar., 24 June, *custos* of St Mary in crypt, CCA Lit. Ms C.11, fo 56, 56ᵛ.

[1538, 8 Feb., after], 1540, 4 Apr., refectorer, Pantin, *Cant. Coll. Ox.*, iii, 152, *L and P Henry VIII*, xv, no 452.

1501/4, 1508/9, 1510/11, student at Canterbury college Oxford, with a pension varying from 50s. to £4, the latter being the amount for half the yr, Pantin, *Cant. Coll. Ox.*, ii, 234, 236, 239, 250, 253 (CCA DCc Cart. Antiq. O.151.33, 35, 37, 42, 43); in 1505/6 he was at Oxford, Pantin, *ib.*, iii, 242 (CCA DCc Cart. Antiq. O.151.36).

1512, the treasurers pd the expenses of conveying his 'stuffe' from Oxford to Canterbury, Pantin, *ib.*, iv, 205.

[1538, 8 Feb., after], B.Th., by this date, Pantin, *ib.*, iii, 152.

1501, 26 Apr., dcn and 56th in order at the el. of an abp, Reg. R, fo 56ᵛ.

1511, 2 Sept., 38th on the visitation certificate, Wood-Legh, *Visit.*, 3 (Reg. abp Warham, i, fo 35ᵛ).

1516, Sept./Dec., William Ingram I, q.v., pd 8d. *pro capicio* for him, CCA Lit. Ms C.11, fo 128.

1534, 12 Dec., acknowledged the Act of Supremacy, *DK 7th Report*, Appndx 2, 282.

[1538, 8 Feb., after], on a list of monks prob. prepared for Thomas Cromwell he was described as 'symple' and 58 yrs of age, Pantin, *Cant. Coll. Ox.*, iii, 152.

1540, 4 Apr., awarded £10 p.a., *L and P Henry VIII*, xv, no 452.

Note: *BRUO, 1501–1540* suggests that he is the Mr Langdon who, with George Frevell, q.v., is found as a monk of the newly refounded Westminster in c. 1556; see E.H. Pearce, *The Monks of Westminster* (Cambridge, 1916), 215.

Nicholas LANGDON [Langedon

occ. 1406 d. 1420

1406, 21 Oct., one of seven prof., *SL*, 185, CCA Lit. Ms D.12, fo 5ᵛ.

1407, 24 Sept., ord dcn, collegiate church, Maidstone, Reg. abp Arundel, i, fo 341.

1410, 22 Mar., ord pr., Canterbury cathedral, *ib.*, ii, fo 98ᵛ.

1414, 12 Mar., 61st in order at the el. of an abp, *Reg. abp Chichele*, i, 4.

1420, 12 May, d., in the 15th yr of his monastic life, *Chron. Stone*, 10, CCA Lit. Ms D.12, fo 21ᵛ; his obit is in BL Ms Arundel 68, fo 27.

Thomas LANGDON [*alias* Odian

occ. 1533 occ. 1540

1533, 12 May, one of eight tonsured, *SL*, 196, CCA Lit. Ms D.12, fo 12.

1534, 21 Mar., made his prof. before the prior who had been comm. by abp Cranmer, *ib.*

1534, 12 Dec., acknowledged the Act of Supremacy, *DK 7th Report*, Appndx 2, 282.

[1538, 8 Feb., after], in a list of monks prob. prepared for Thomas Cromwell he was described as a 'good man', 25 yrs of age, Pantin, *Cant. Coll. Ox.*, iii, 154.

1540, 4 Apr., name appears on the pension list but is cancelled and replaced by that of Robert Houghe, q.v., *L and P Henry VIII*, xv, no 452.

LANGINUS

n.d.

n.d., pr. whose obit occ. on 6 Feb. in BL Ms Cotton Nero C.ix, fo 5.

I John LANGLE [Langlee, Langeley

occ. [1390] d. 1416

[1390], 28 Sept., one of seven prof., *SL*, 184, CCA Lit. Ms D.12, fo 5.

1394, 18 Apr., ord dcn, Canterbury cathedral, Reg. abp Courtenay ii, fo 184ᵛ.

1407, Apr./1408, June, 1409/10, 1411, Sept., sacrist, CCA DCc, CR90, Sac. acct 16, Prior acct 1.

1390/1, recd 12d. *pro benedictione* from the prior, Lambeth Ms 243, fo 220ᵛ.

1396, 7 Aug., 66th in order at the el. of an abp, Reg. G, fo 234ᵛ.

1414, 12 Mar., 28th at the el. of an abp, *Reg. abp Chichele*, i, 4.

1416, 6 Sept., d., in the 26th yr of his monastic life, *Chron. Stone*, 7; CCA Lit. Ms D.12, fo 20ᵛ, has 5 Sept. and the obit in BL Ms Arundel 68, fo 40ᵛ is on 7 Sept.

II John LANGLE [Langlee, Langley

occ. 1446 d. 1457

1446, 21 Dec., one of seven [tonsured], *SL*, 188–189, CCA Lit. Ms D.12, fo 7ᵛ.

1447, 4 Mar., ord acol., Canterbury cathedral, Reg. abp Stafford, fo 199.
1447, 27 Aug., made his prof., during a mass at which the abp was the celebrant, *Chron. Stone*, 41–42.
1447, 23 Dec., ord subdcn, Canterbury cathedral, Reg. abp Stafford, fo 201v.
1448, 23 Mar., ord dcn, Canterbury cathedral, *ib.*, fo 202v.
1451, 20 Mar., ord pr., Canterbury cathedral, *ib.*, fo 205v.
1457, before 18 Sept., *parvus sacrista*, *Chron. Stone*, 70.
1457, 18 Sept., d., in his tenth yr of monastic life, *Chron. Stone*, 70; the obit is in BL Ms Arundel 68, fo 42.

III John LANGLE
occ. 1465 occ. 1470
1465, 4 Apr., one of seven prof., *SL*, 190, CCA Lit. Ms D.12, fo 8.
1465, 13 Apr., ord subdcn, place not stated, *Reg. abp Bourgchier*, 391.
1468, 12 Mar., ord pr., Canterbury cathedral, *ib.*, 398.
1470, 1 July, *migravit*, CCA Lit. Ms D.12, fo 26; he obtained licence from the prior and convent to transfer to the priory of the Augustinian hermits at Rye, Sussex, Reg. S, fo 244.

Peter LANGLEE [Langlaye, Langley
occ. 1527 occ. 1540
1527, 25 May, one of twelve tonsured, *SL*, 195, CCA Lit. Ms D.12, fo 12.
1528, 2 Mar., prof., *ib.*
[by 1538], student at Canterbury college, Oxford, Pantin, *Cant. Coll. Ox.*, iii, 149–150; and see below.
1534, 12 Dec., acknowledged the Act of Supremacy, *DK 7th Report*, Appndx 2, 282.
[1538, 8 Feb., after], in a list of monks prob. prepared for Thomas Cromwell he was described as a scholar, 'witty', and 30 yrs old, Pantin, *Cant. Coll. Ox.*, iii, 153.
1540, 4 Apr., became scholar in the new foundation, *L and P Henry VIII*, xv, no 452.

LANZO
occ. [1093 × 1109]
[1093 × 1109], novice, mentioned by abp Anselm in a letter to Warner, q.v., whom he tells to share the contents with him, *Anselm Letters*, no 335; he also recd a long letter of advice and encouragement from Anselm; see also *ib.*, no 2 written to him and to Odo, q.v., before they became monks.

I LAURENCE [Laurentius
occ. [1153 × 1161]
[1153 × 1161], *temp.*, abp Theobald and prior Wibert, q.v., almoner, *Theobald Charters*, no 40 (Reg. B, fo 146v).
[1153 × 1161], witnessed a grant by the prior and convent in response to a request of the abp, *ib.*

II LAURENCE
occ. c. 1200
c. 1200, in a survey of cathedral holdings in Canterbury of this date a *mansura* is described as given by Lieuenoth de Northewede *cum Laurencio filio suo*, Urry, *Canterbury*, 259.

III LAURENCE [Laurentius
occ. 1255/6
n.d., name occ. in the list in *SL*, 173, CCA Lit. Ms D.12, fo 1v.
1255, Dec., 1256, Nov., treasurer, CCA DCc MA1, fos 96, 97v.

IV LAURENCE
occ. 2nd half 13th c.
[mid 1260s], one of seven prof., *SL*, 176, CCA Lit. Ms D.12, fo 2v.
Note: the obit of a Laurence occ. on 31 Mar. in BL Ms Arundel 68, fo 22v.
See also Laurence de Marisco.

LAY', Laycestria
see Leycestria

LECLINENSIS
see Herlewin II

I John LEDEBERY
occ. 1289 d. 1291
1289, 19 Dec., one of eight prof., *SL*, 177, CCA Lit. Ms D.12, fo 3.
1291, 27 Sept., d., CCA Lit. Ms D.12, fo 15.

II John LEDEBERY [Lidebery, Lydebery, Lytebery
occ. 1346 occ. 1367
1346, 11 Nov., one of eight prof., *SL*, 181, CCA Lit. Ms D.12, fo 4.
1350, 18 Sept., ord pr., Goudhurst, Reg. abp Islip, fo 310v.
1366, 10 May ,1366/7, cellarer, Reg. G, fo 149, CCA DCc, Ebony acct 62.
1367, 28 Mar., apptd sacrist, *Reg. abp Langham*, 283.
1348/9, ill, and recd a *liberatio* from the anniversarian, CCA DCc Annivers. acct 3.
1359/60, ill and recd a 2s. 'pension' from the anniversarian for his expenses [while in the infirmary], *ib.*, acct 5.
1366, 10 May, named as one of seven *compromissorii* in the el. of an abp, Reg. G, fo 149.

William de LEDEBERY [Ledeberi, Leduburi, Lidebury, Ludeburi, Lydbury
occ. 1295 d. [1328]

1295, 23 Nov., one of five prof., *SL*, 178, CCA Lit. Ms D.12, fo 3.
1299, 19 Sept., ord dcn, Littlebourne, *Reg. abp Winchelsey*, 930.
1300, 4 June, ord pr., Smeeth chapel by Aldington, *ib.*, 936.
1312/14, feretrar, CCA DCc, MA2, fos 37–52.
1315/16, treasurer, CCA DCc, MA2, fo 67.
1316/18, 1319/22, 1323/4, warden of manors, CCA DCc, Charlwood acct 34, Cheam acct 34, Meopham acct 61, Cheam acct 37, Meopham acct 63, MA2, fos 126–135.
1324/8, cellarer, CCA DCc, MA2, fos 138–176v.
n.d., he may have gone to study at Oxford and met John de St Germans there; see below.
1315, 30 Dec., with John de Weston, q.v., apptd parliamentary proctors, *Parl. Writs*, ii, pt 3, 1084 (CUL Ms Ee.5.31, fo 162).
[1317], 5 Dec., with Geoffrey Poterel, q.v., sent to the abp of York, *ib.*, fo 184v.
1318, 15 Jan., he and Edmund de Adesham were given letters of credence to discuss certain matters with the abp, *ib.*, fo 187v; these concerned Robert de Thaneto, q.v., *ib.*, fos 188v–189.
1318, 19 Feb., with John de Valoyns, q.v., apptd proctors for convocation, *ib.*, fo 188.
1319, 10 July, with Robert de Clyve, q.v., sent by the prior and chapter to confer with the abp about their rights over Dover priory, *ib.*, fo 206; he was again involved in these negotiations on 14 Apr. 1320, *ib.*, fo 213.
[1320], seems to have been involved in some unknown way in the disturbance caused by Robert de Aldon, q.v.
1321, 13 July, apptd proctor for the prior and convent to attend parliament at Westminster, *Lit. Cant.*, no 57 (Reg. L, fo 181); see also *Parl. Writs*, ii, pt 3, 1084.
1323, 13/15 May, with William de Coventre, q.v., sent by the prior and convent to negotiate for the purchase of the manor of Wickham, *Lit. Cant.*, nos 108, 109 (Reg. L, fo 125v).
1324, 2 Feb., apptd proctor by the prior and convent to attend parliament at Westminster, *Parl. Writs*, ii, pt 3, 1085 (CUL Ms Ee.5.31 fos 234v–235).
1324, 23 Apr., in a letter from the prior to the chancellor of the university of Oxford there is a ref. to his visiting the priory manors near Oxford on business, *Lit. Cant.*, no 120 (Reg. L, fo 138v).
[1328], 16 Aug., soon after his d. an inventory of silver *cuppe* which had been in his care was drawn up, Reg. L, fo 108 (*Hist. Mss Comm 9th Report*, Appndx, 90). His obit is on 2 Aug. in BL Ms Arundel 68, fo 36v.

Name in Oxford, Bod., Ms Bodley 336, Legenda sanctorum (early 14th c.).

A list of 24 volumes, including the one named above (which is no 1793), is included in the Eastry catalogue, James, *Ancient Libraries*, nos 1773–1795 (pp.140–141); there are writings of Thomas Aquinas, Peter Lombard, Aristotle's Physicorum, Innocencius super decretales, and Liber de legibus Anglie. Two of these turn up in an inventory of books (dated 1443) at Canterbury college, Pantin, *CCO*, i, 12, 14 (CCA DCc Cart. Antiq. O.134); and see *ib.*, iv, 157.

An inventory of missing service books, dated 1 Mar. 1338, includes a psalter of his, which was at this time 'charged out' to John de Valoyns, q.v., *Lit. Cant.*, no 618 (Reg. L, fo 104).

There is a letter copied into Worcester cathedral Ms Q.20, fo 34v., prob. written by John de St Germans, q.v., (under Worcester) to him.

An inventory of vestments acquired *temp.* prior Eastry includes one set of his and of Richard de Rawe, q.v., feretrars, Legg and Hope, *Inventories*, 64 (BL Ms Cotton Galba, E.iv, fo 116v). There are also eight full sets of vestments to which his name only is attached, Legg and Hope, *Inventories*, 67–68 (BL Ms Cotton Galba, E.iv, fo 118–118v).

An inventory of the refectory, dated 1328, includes three silver gilt *cuppe*, eleven silver *ciphi*, some of them enamelled, twenty four silver spoons and three *ciphi de murra*, Dart, *Antiq. Cant.*, xviii, xx, xxiii (BL Ms Cotton Galba E.iv, fos 178, 178v, 180).

I John LEDYS
occ. 1st half 13th c.

n.d., name occ. in the *post exilium* list in *SL*, 174, CCA Lit. Ms D.12, fo 2.

II John LEDYS [Ledes, Ledis
occ. 1428 occ. 1457

1428, 2 Jan., one of six prof., *SL*, 187, CCA Lit. Ms D.12, fo 7.
[1429, summer], ord acol. and subdcn, place not named, Reg. Langdon (Rochester), fo 74 (as Robert).
1433, 28 Mar., ord pr., Charing, *Reg. abp Chichele*, iv, 378.
1435, before 14 July, refectorer, 'Chron. Wm Glastynbury', 129; on 14 July he was replaced by John Newynham, q.v., Chron. Wm Glastynbury, fo 117.
1448/9, fourth prior, CCA DCc, Sac. acct 35.
[1457], 7 Apr., invited to return to Christ Church with the assurance that all was forgiven; he was at this time residing in the household of the count of Montferrat at Casale in Lombardy, *Lit. Cant.*, no 1045 (Reg. N, fo 189v).

Henry LEE [Legh
occ. 1419 d. 1460

1419, 25 Jan., one of four prof., SL 186, CCA Lit. Ms D.12, fo 6v.
1419, 15 Apr., ord acol., chapel in the priory, *Reg. abp Chichele*, i, 192.
1420, 6 Apr., ord subdcn, Canterbury cathedral, *ib.*, iv, 341.
1424, 22 Apr., ord pr., Canterbury cathedral, *ib.*, iv, 360.

1435, before 14 July, subrefectorer, Chron. Wm Glastynbury, fo 117.
[1441] 5 Jan., apptd fourth prior, *ib.*, fo 119v.
n.d., granator, prob. at the time of d., see below.

1435, 24 Oct., one of three monks promoted to the upper choir, Chron. Wm Glastynbury, fo 117v.
1451, 12 Dec., ill and his expenses were 20d., CCA Lit. Ms E.6, fo 64v.
1452, 23 Dec., one of several monks promoted *ad primam mensam*, i.e. one of twenty senior monks, *Chron. Stone*, 56.
1460, 8 Mar., d., in his 40th yr of monastic life, *ib.*, 77 and CCA Lit. Ms D.12, fo 26, which describes him as granator.

James LEE
n.d.

n.d., 16 Feb., obit in BL Ms Arundel 68, fo 16v.

John LEE [Le
occ. 1468 occ. 1520/1

1468, 12 Oct., one of four tonsured, *Chron. Stone*, 106; he was one of four almonry school boys to be clothed on this day, *ib.* (*SL*, 190, CCA Lit. Ms D.12, fo 8, where the date 1469 has been added later).
1469, 1 Apr., ord acol., Canterbury cathedral, *Reg. abp Bourgchier*, 402.
1469, 21 Apr., prof., *SL*, 190 (Cambridge, Corpus Christi College Ms 298).
1470, 21 Apr., ord subdcn, Canterbury cathedral, *Reg abp Bourgchier*, 406.
1471, 9 Mar., ord dcn, Canterbury cathedral, *ib.*, 405.
1473, 13 Mar., ord pr., Canterbury cathedral, *ib.*, 410.

1496/7, *magister ordinis*, CCA DCc MA9, fo 113.
1497/8, July to Apr., third prior and *magister ordinis*, *SL*, 192, CCA Lit. Ms D.12, fo 9v.
1501/4, bartoner, CCA DCc MA1, fos 104, 168, 179.
1506/10, 1510/11, 1 Jan., 1512/13, infirmarer, CCA DCc MA11, fos 5v, 36v, Lambeth ED88, Lambeth Ms 951/1/31, CCA Lit. Ms D.12, fo 11, Lambeth Ms 951/1/32 and CCA DCc Sac. accts 71–73 (1508/11).
1509, Mar., master of novices, CCA Lit. Ms C.11, fo 51.
1508/9, 1510/11, June to Jan., *magister ordinis*, CCA DCc MA11, fo 101, *SL*, 194, and CCA Lit. Ms D.12, fo 11.

1493, 1 May, 25th in order at the ratification of an agreement, Reg. S, fo 383v; but see John Crosse I.
1501, 26 Apr., 14th in order at the el. of an abp, Reg. R, fo 56v.
1511, 2 Sept., 4th in order on the visitation certificate, Wood-Legh, *Visit.*, 3 (Reg. abp Warham, i, fo 35).
1520/1, *stationarius*, CCA DCc Infirm. acct 2.
n.d., 27 May, obit in BL Ms Arundel 68, fo 28v.

Roger de la LEE [de Lega, de La Le, de La le, de Lalehe
occ. before 1214 d. 1258

1239–1244, prior: el. 7 Jan. 1239 by the monks in the absence of the abp and without his approval; the abp withheld his confirmation until his d. in Nov. 1240, despite appeals to the pope; res. 1244 prob. after 9 Oct., *Fasti*, ii, 11.

n.d., name occ. on the list of those in exile in *SL*, 172, CCA Lit. Ms D.12, fo 1.

1239, 4 Jan., one of the monks accused by the abp of contumacy after the forgery scandal and ordered to appear before him, *Gervase Cant.*, ii, 144; see John de Chatham and Simon de Hertlepe.
1239, 7 Jan., named by the chapter as one of five *compromissorii* in the el. of a prior, *ib.*, ii, 146; the chapter was excommunicated in Apr. for the irregular el. of Roger himself, carried out without the abp's presence and scrutiny, *ib.*, ii, 151, 153, 167–168, 171, 175. The subprior was absent at this time in Rome; see Ralph de Westgate.
1244, res., see above.
1258, d., *Gervase Cant.*, ii, 206 prob. on 24 Aug., where his obit as *quondam prior* occ. in BL Ms Arundel 68, fo 39.

His name heads a list of ?18 vols in the Eastry catalogue, nos 584–?600, James, *Ancient Libraries*, 68–69; they include sermons, biblical texts and glosses.

There is a seal of his priorate in CCA DCc Cart. Antiq. no 27 (dated 1243), Hasted, *Kent*, xi, 439 note.

I Thomas LEE
occ. 1435 d. c. 1476

1435, 11 Nov., one of five clothed in the monastic habit, Chron. Wm Glastynbury, fo 117v (*SL*, 188, CCA Lit. Ms D.12, fo 7v).
1436, 3 Mar., ord acol., infirmary chapel, *Reg. abp Chichele*, iv, 383.

1454, 28 Apr., *magister ordinis*, *SL*, 189, CCA Lit. Ms D.12, fo 8.
1457, 13 Aug., fourth prior, *Chron. Stone*, 68.
1459, 30 Nov., [1461], 19 Apr., *magister ordinis*, *SL*, 189, CCA Lit. Ms D.12, fo 8.

1462/5, sacrist, CCA DCc Sac. accts 43–45.
1468/70, warden of manors, CCA DCc MA 156, MA 157.
1471/2, treasurer, CCA DCc, Treas. acct 19.
1476, sacrist, CCA DCc, MA5, fo 45.

1457, 13 Aug., on the committee of monks apptd to examine Richard Godmersham II, q.v., a novice, *de redditu*, *Chron. Stone*, 68.
1466, 17 Feb., 24th in order in an inventory of *jocalia fratrum* [given by him and/or assigned for his use], Reg. N, fo 232^{v}.
c. 1476, d., CCA Lit. Ms D.12, fo 26; his obit on 2 Apr. is in BL Ms Arundel 68, fo 22^{v}.

II Thomas LEE [Leegh, Legh
occ. 1497 d. 1524

1497, 28 July, one of nine tonsured, *SL*, 192, CCA Lit. Ms D.12, fo 9^{v}.
1498, 14 Apr., ord acol., Canterbury cathedral, *Reg. abp Morton*, i, no 447a.
1498, 19 Apr., prof., *SL*, 192, CCA Lit. Ms D.12, fo 9^{v}.
1507, 3 Apr., ord pr., Canterbury cathedral, Reg. abp Warham, ii, fo 263. On the second Sun. in April he celebrated his first mass and recd 4d. from the *custos martyrii*, CCA Lit. Ms C.11, fo 49^{v}.
1519, Aug., chancellor, with Thomas Goldston V, q.v., Reg T, fo 162^{v}.
1517, 29 Sept., 1519, 25 Mar., warden of St Mary in crypt, CCA Lit. Ms C.11, fos 58^{v}, 59^{v}.
1520/1, novice master and chamberlain, CCA DCc, MA14, fos 137, 138.
1521/3, granator, CCA DCc MA14, fos 201, 212^{v}.
1522, Feb./Nov., *magister ordinis*, and chancellor, *SL*, 195, CCA Lit. Ms D.12, fo 11^{v}, CCA DCc Treas. acct 25.
1521/3, 1524, before 11 Aug., granator, CCA DCc, MA14, fos 201, 212^{v}; CCA Lit. Ms D.12, fo 12.
1524, before 11 Aug., *magister ordinis*, *SL*, 195, CCA Lit. Ms D.12, fo 12; he was succ. by John Wodnesburgh V, q.v.

1501/2, student at Canterbury college with a pension of 100s., Pantin, *Cant. Coll. Ox.*, ii, 234 (CCA DCc Cart. Antiq. O.151.33).

1501, 26 Apr., dcn and 61st in order at the el. of an abp, Reg. R, fo 56^{v}.
1511, 2 Sept., 41st on the visitation certificate, Wood-Legh, *Visit.*, 3 (Reg. abp Warham, i, fo 35^{v}).
1524, 11 Aug., d., CCA Lit. Ms D.12, fo 12; his obit is on 17 Aug. in BL Ms Arundel 68, fo 38^{v}.

Roger de LEGA
see Lee

William de LEGA [Lege
occ. 1224/5

n.d., name occ. in the *post exilium* list in *SL*, 173, CCA Lit. Ms D.12, fo 1.

1224/5, warden of manors, CCA DCc, AS1.

LEGH
see Lee

John de LEKEDE
occ. [1316] d. 1349

[1316], 6 Nov., one of five prof., *SL*, 179, CCA Lit. Ms D.12, fo 3^{v}.

1330/3, *custos tumbe*, CCA DCc MA2, fos 192–221, DE3, fos 1–3.
1334/6, bartoner, CCA DCc Arrears acct 5, MA2, fos 241^{v}–250^{v}.
1334/5, *custos* of the vineyard, CCA DCc, MA2, fos 232–241^{v}.

1342, name occ. in CCA DCc DE3, fo 50.
1349, 27 Feb., d., CCA Lit. Ms D.12, fo 16^{v}.

John de LENHAM
occ. 1309 d. 1337

1309, 18 Oct., one of nine prof., SL., 179, CCA Lit. Ms D.12, fo 3^{v}.
1317, 28 May, ord pr., Lambeth palace chapel, Reg. abp Reynolds, fo 178.
1331, Dec./1333, *custos corone/magister corone*, CCA DCc, DE3, fo 1, MA2, fo 211^{v}, DE3, fo 34.
1337, 16 June, d., CCA Lit. Ms D.12, fo 16^{v}; his obit is in BL Ms Arundel 68, fo 31.

LEOFRIC [Lifric
occ. before 1098 × 1108

1098 × 1108, before, on being prof. he gave the church of St Pancras, Soper Lane, London, to Christ Church, Kissan, 'London Deanery', 210.
n.d., 25 July, obit occ. in BL Ms Arundel 68, fo 36.

Marcellus de LESE [de la Lese
occ. [1260] d. 1306

[c. 1260], one of five prof., *SL*, 176, CCA Lit. Ms D.12, fo 2^{v}.

1282, subchamberlain, CCA DCc MA1, fo 137^{v}.
1287/8, *custos martyrii*, CCA DCc MA1, fo 153^{v}.
1289/94, granator, CCA DCc, MA1, fos 158^{v}–190.
1295/9, 1300, warden of manors, CCA DCc, MA1, fos 194–222, 225.
1306, before 21 Apr., subprior, CCA Lit. Ms D.12, fo 15^{v}.

1306, 21 Apr., d., CCA Lit. Ms D.12, fo 15^{v}; his obit is in BL Ms Arundel 68, fo 24^{v}.

The Eastry catalogue lists three of his volumes: Biblia, Casus decretalium, Sententiae, James, *Ancient Libraries*, nos 1624–1626 (p. 134).

An inventory of the sacrist, *temp.* prior Eastry, includes a chasuble [?given by him], Legg and Hope, *Inventories*, 52 (BL Ms Cotton Galba, E.iv, fo 112).

An inventory of the refectory, dated 1328, includes two silver *ciphi* and three *de murra*, Dart,

Antiq. Cant., xx, xxii, xxiii (BL Ms Cotton Galba E.iv, fos 178^{v}, 179^{v}, 180).

Note: see also Marcellus [de Capella] who is prob. the same monk.

Roger de LEU
occ. 1st half 13th c.

n.d., name occ. in the list in *SL*, 174, CCA Lit. Ms D.12, fo 2.

LEVELOND
see Lovelond

Ralph de LEWYS
occ. 2nd half 13th c.

n.d., name occ. in the list in *SL*, 175, CCA Lit. Ms D.12, fo 2.

Nicholas LEYCESTR' [Laycestr'
occ. 2nd half 13th c.

n.d., name occ. in the list in *SL*, 175, CCA Lit. Ms D.12, fo 2^{v}.

Simon de LEYCESTRIA [Laycestr'
occ. 1234 occ. 1239

n.d., name occ. in the list in *SL*, 174, CCA Lit. Ms D.12, fo 1^{v}.

1234, before 2 Apr., brought the pallium from Rome for abp Edmund [Abingdon], Paris, *Chron. Majora*, iii, 272.

1239, before 7 Jan., deputed with John de Maydeston I, q.v., to cite Eustace [de Faversham] q.v., to the el. of a prior, *Gervase Cant.*, ii, 145.

1239, 7 Feb., apptd proctor with Gregory de Audinges, q.v., to convey to the abp a letter informing him of the el. of Roger de la Lee, q.v., as prior, *Gervase Cant.*, ii, 154, 155.

An inventory of missing books, dated 1 Mar. 1338, includes his Digesta vetus which had been lent to a secular person, *Lit. Cant.* ,no 618 (Reg. L, fo 104). It is included, with five other canon law texts, in the Eastry catalogue, James, *Ancient Libraries*, nos 1346–1351 (p. 115).

Thomas de LEYCESTRIA [Laycestre, ?Lay
occ. late 1260s d. 1290

[late 1260s], one of five prof., *SL*, 176, CCA Lit. Ms D.12, fo 3.

1288, ill, and Gervase, *cirurgiko*, was pd 3s. for his services, Lambeth Ms 242, fo 105^{v}.

1290, 5 Dec., d., CCA Lit. Ms D.12, fo 15.

The Eastry catalogue lists three, possibly more, books formerly his, James, *Ancient Libraries*, nos 345, 534–535 (536–540) (pp 52, 63–65).

An inventory of the refectory dated 1328 includes a *ciphus de murra* formerly his, Dart, *Antiq. Cant.*, xxii (BL Ms Cotton Galba E.iv, fo 180).

William de LEYCESTR'
occ. 1st half 13th c.

n.d., name occ. in the *post exilium* list in *SL*, 173, CCA Lit. Ms D.12, fo 1.

LICHFELDE
see Lychfeld

LIDEBERY
see Ledebery

LIFRIC
see Leofric

LIKEMENS', Likilmensis
see Herlewin II

LINESTUDE
see Lynstede

LINTUN
see Lynton

Salamon LITELBOURNE [Salomon Litelburne, Litilborne, Lytilborne, Lytleborne, Lyttelborne, Lyttlebourn, Lytylborne
occ. 1365 d. 1408

1365, one of eight prof., *SL*, 182, CCA Lit. Ms D.12, fo 4^{v}.

1367, 18 Sept., ord subdcn, Lambeth palace chapel, *Reg. abp Langham*, 383.

1368, 4 Mar., ord dcn, Canterbury cathedral, *ib.*, 388.

1368, 25 Mar., ord pr., abp's chapel, Charing, *ib.*, 389.

1380, subchaplain to the prior, CCA DCc, MA2, fo 321^{v}.

1384, 29 Aug., *magister ordinis*, *SL*, 183, CCA Lit. Ms D.12, fo 5.

1385, Jan./Mar., third prior, Lambeth Ms 243, fo 196^{v}.

1374, 30 June, 43rd in order at the el. of an abp, Reg. G, fos 173^{v}–175^{v}.

1381, 31 July, 32nd at the el. of an abp, *ib.*, fo 225^{v}.

1383/4, 1389/90, recd small sums from the prior *pro benedictione*, Lambeth Ms 243, fos 192^{v}, 216^{v}.

1396, 7 Aug., 14th in order at the el. of an abp, Reg. G, fo 234^{v}.

1408, 24 Dec., d., in his 44th yr of monastic life; the subprior conducted a service for him in the infirmary chapel but the other ceremonies were delayed until 26 Dec., CCA Lit. Ms D.12, fo 19.

Thomas LITILBORNE [Lytleborne
occ. [c. 1255]

n.d. [c. 1255], name occ. in the list in *SL*, 176, CCA Lit. Ms D.12, fo 2^{v}.

Thomas LITLE [Litlee, Littill, Little, Lityll', Lytle, Lytyll
occ. [1392] d. 1430

[1392], 21 Nov., one of four prof., *SL*, 184, CCA Lit. Ms D.12, fo 5.
1394, 18 Apr., ord subdcn, Canterbury cathedral, Reg. abp Courtenay ii, fo 184v.
1395, 10 Apr., ord dcn, Canterbury cathedral, *ib.*, ii, fo 185v.
1396, 7 Aug., 67th in order at the el. of an abp, Reg. G, fo 234v.
1414, 12 Mar., 29th at the el. of an abp, *Reg. abp Chichele*, i, 4.
1430, 15 Nov., d. in the 39th yr of his monastic life, *Chron. Stone*, 16, CCA Lit. Ms D.12, fo 23; his obit is in BL Ms Arundel 68, fo 48.

LIVINGUS
occ. before 1087

1087, before, a married pr., who on becoming a monk gave the church of St Mary le Bow, London, to Christ Church, Kissan, 'London Deanery', 210.
n.d., 26 Jan., his obit occ. in BL Ms Cotton Nero C.ix, fo 4v.

LODELAWE
see Ludlow

LOMBARD
see Lumbardus

Alexander LONDON [Lundon *alias* Goodschep
occ. [1394] d. 1451

[1394], 21 Nov., one of six prof., *SL*, 184, CCA Lit. Ms D.12, fo 5.
1395, 10 Apr., ord dcn, Canterbury cathedral, Reg. abp Courtenay, ii, fo 185v (as Goodschep).
1411, one of the chancellors, Reg. S, fo 61v; see Thomas Bungay.
1417/18, third prior, CCA DCc Sac. acct 20 (as Alexander).
1435, *magister mense*, with Richard Crophell, q.v., 'Chron. Wm Glastynbury', 129.
1396, 7 Aug., 71st in order at the el. of an abp, Reg. G, fo 234v.
1414, 12 Mar., 32nd at the el. of an abp, *Reg. abp Chichele*, i, 4.
1451, 23 Feb., d., after almost 60 yrs as a monk, *Chron. Stone*, 51; in CCA Lit. Ms D.12, fo 25v, he is described as *stationarius*.

Geoffrey de LONDON [Londonia
occ. 1300

1300, 4 June, ord subdcn, Smeeth chapel by Aldington, *Reg. abp Winchelsey*, 934.

Note: this is prob. Geoffrey Poterel, q.v.

Girard de LONDON
occ. 1st half 13th c.

n.d., name occ. in the list in *SL*, 174, CCA Lit. Ms D.12, fo 1v.

In the Eastry catalogue one item, containing a miscellaneous collection of treatises and tracts entitled Liber florum is listed under the name of Gerald de Londone, James, Ancient Libraries, no 1359 (p. 116).

I John de LONDON
occ. 1250 occ. 1255/6

n.d., name occ. in the list in *SL*, 173, CCA Lit. Ms D.12, fo 1v.
1250/3, cellarer, CCA DCc, MA1, fos 91v–94.
1253/6, anniversarian, Reg. H, fos 178, 181, 185v.

Note: see the notes below John de London II and III.

II John de LONDON
occ. 1285 d. 1299

n.d. [c. 1283], one of five prof., *SL*, 177, CCA Lit. Ms D.12, fo 3.
1285, 22 Sept., ord pr., collegiate church, South Malling, *Reg. abp Pecham*, i, 222.
1293, subchamberlain, CCA DCc MA1, fos 91v–94.
1285, 5 Jan., one of the monks imprisoned by royal officers for whose release into his charge the abp now gave orders, *Epist. Pecham*, 876–877.
1299, 8 July, d., CCA Lit. Ms D.12, fo 15; obit in BL Ms Arundel 68, fo 34.

An inventory of missing books, dated 1 Mar. 1338, includes his copy of Bryto super Bibliam for which John de Wy, q.v. was held responsible, *Lit. Cant.*, no 618 (Reg. L, fo 104). It is possible that this ref. is to John de London I above.

Note: there are two collections of books in the Eastry catalogue which had been in the hands of John de London I or/and II; one includes the Brito (no 1555) mentioned above. Since there are two separate lists headed John de Londoniis the only problem is which list belongs to which monk, James, *Ancient Libraries*, nos 505–514, 1554–1556 (pp. 61–62, 129).

The same problem as above applies to the silver *ciphus* and the two *ciphi de murra* listed in the 1328 inventory of the refectory, Dart, *Antiq. Cant.*, xix (BL Ms Cotton Galba E.iv, fos 178, 180).

III John LONDON
occ. 1341 d. 1349

1341, 13 Dec., one of nine prof., *SL*, 180, CCA Lit. Ms D.12, fo 4.
1349, 4 June, 56th in order at the el. of an abp, Reg. G, fo 60v.

1349, 7 June, one of four who d. of the plague in May and June, CCA Lit. Ms D.12, fo 16v.

Name in
(1) CUL Ms Ff.3.19, Peter Lombardus (14th c.).
(2) London, College of Arms, Ms Arundel 20, Chronica (14th) c.

Note: a John de London's obit on 12 Jan. occ. in BL Ms Arundel, 68, fo 13; which one is this?

Ralph de LONDON
occ. 1st half 13th c.

n.d., name occ. in the *post exilium* list in *SL*, 173, CCA Lit. Ms D.12, fo 1v.

I Richard de LONDON
occ. 2nd half 13th c.

n.d., name occ. in the list in *SL*, 174, CCA Lit. Ms D.12, fo 2.

A *ciphus de murra* is recorded as his in an inventory of the refectory dated 1328, Dart, *Antiq. Cant.*, xxi (BL Ms Cotton Galba, E.iv, fo 179v).

II Richard LONDON [Lundun, Lundune
occ. 1446 d. 1504

1446, 21 Dec., one of seven tonsured, *SL*, 188, CCA Lit. Ms D.12, fo 7v.
1447, 27 Aug., made his prof., with the other six, during the high mass at which the abp was the celebrant, *Chron. Stone*, 41–42.
1447, 23 Dec., ord subdcn, Canterbury cathedral, Reg. abp Stafford, fo 201v.
1448, 23 Mar., ord dcn, Canterbury cathedral, *ib.*, fo 202v.
1452, 8 Apr., ord pr., Canterbury cathedral, *ib.*, fo 207.
1461, 1468, one of the chancellors, Reg. S, fos 208v, 234; see William Thornden and Simon Tent.
1479/80, anniversarian with James Burton, q.v., CCA DCc Anniv. acct 16.
1490, 6 Feb., *custos martyrii*, Legg and Hope, *Inventories*, 129.
1466, 17 Feb., 36th in order in an inventory of *jocalia fratrum*, [given by him and/or assigned for his use], Reg. N, fo 233.
1493, 1 May, 11th in order at the ratification of an agreement, Reg. S, fo 383v; but see John Crosse I.
1501, 26 Apr., ill in the infirmary and absent from the el. of an abp, Reg. R, fo 56v.
1504, 14 Jan., *stationarius*, d., 'ex infirmitate vocata Empematis, id est Tussus et de la murre', in the 58th yr of his monastic life, at the age of 74, CCA Lit. Ms D.12, fo 34. His obit is one of the later additions to BL Ms Arundel 68, fo 13. See John Browne II.

Robert LONDON
occ. [1392]

[1392], 21 Nov., one of four prof., SL., 184, CCA Lit. Ms D.12, fo 5.

I William de LONDON
occ. 1299 d. 1333

1299, 24 Aug., one of seven prof., *SL*, 178, CCA Lit. Ms D.12, fo 3v.
1300, 4 June, ord subdcn, Smeeth chapel by Aldington, *Reg. abp Winchelsey*, 934.
1321, 3 Nov., subsacrist, Legg and Hope, *Inventories*, 51.
1323, *custos* of abp Winchelsey's tomb and of the high altar, CCA DCc MA2, fo 128v.
1328/9, *custos* of the high altar, CCA DCc MA2, fos 175v–183v.
1321, 3 Nov., with Robert de Dover, q.v., he accepted delivery of the inventory of the *ornamenta, textus* and *reliquie*, Legg and Hope, *Inventories*, 51 (BL Ms Cotton Galba E.iv, fos 112–122).
1333, 28 Aug., d., CCA Lit. Ms D.12, fo 16.

II William LONDON [Lundyn
occ. c. 1389 occ. 1399

c. 1389, 6 Nov., one of eight prof., SL 184, CCA Lit. Ms D.12, fo 5.
1391, 25 Mar., ord dcn, Canterbury cathedral, Reg. abp Courtenay, i, fo 312.
1394, 18 Apr., ord pr., Canterbury cathedral, Reg. abp Courtenay ii, fo 185.
1396, 7 Aug., 57th in order at the el. of an abp, Reg. G, fo 236.
[1398], 8 Jan., was with abp Arundel in exile in Florence, and the abp wrote to the prior and convent begging them not to denounce him, *Lit. Cant.*, no 969 (Reg. S, fos 39v–40).
1399, 29 Jan., [still] in the household of Arundel and now absolved from excommunication for joining the exiled abp at the curia without the prior's licence. He was to be allowed to remain with Arundel and return when he wished, *CPL*, v (1396–1404), 202.

Note: see the note below William London III.

III William LONDON [Londone
occ. 1524 occ. 1540

1524, 21/22 July, one of eleven granted adm. [*ingressum*] to Christ Church, CCA Lit. Ms D.12, fos 11v–12.
1524, 4 Aug., one of eleven tonsured, *SL*, 195, CCA Lit. Ms D.12, fo 11v.
1525, 19 Apr., prof., *ib.*
1527/8, celebrated his first mass and recd a small gift from the sacrist, Woodruff, 'Sacrist's Rolls', 72.
[1538, 8 Feb., after], subcellarer, Pantin, *Cant. Coll. Ox.*, iii, 153.
1534, 12 Dec., acknowledged the Act of Supremacy, *DK 7th Report*, Appndx 2, 282.
[1538], 8 Feb., after], in a list of monks prob. drawn up for Thomas Cromwell he is described as a 'good man', 31 yrs old, Pantin, *Cant. Coll. Ox.*, iii, 153.

1540, 4 Apr., awarded 10m., p.a., *L and P Henry VIII*, xv, no 452.

Name in CCA Lit. Ms D.8, Miscellanea jur. (14th c.); on front flyleaf *liber— ex dono*. See William Ingram I.

Note: this ref. could apply to William London II, q.v.

LONDON
see also William Langdon II

Nigel de LONGCHAMP
see Wireker

LONGDON
see Langdon

William de LONGUEVILLE [Longavilla
occ. 1136/7

1136, before, sacrist, *HRH*, 87.

1136, apptd prior of Dover by the abp, *HRH*, 87.
1137, sent back to Canterbury, *ib.*; and see *Gervase Cant.*, i, 99.

Roger LORENG
occ. 2nd half 13th c.

n.d., name occ. in the list in *SL*, 175, CCA Lit. Ms D.12, fo 2.

William de LOVELL [Lovel
occ. [late 1260s] d. 1311

[late 1260s], one of five prof., *SL*, 176, CCA Lit. Ms D.12, fo 3.

1311, 27 May, d., CCA Lit. Ms D.12, fo 15ᵛ; obit in Ms Arundel 68, fo 28ᵛ.

A stole and maniple *consuta* [*sic*] of his, or made for/by him, are listed in an inventory of the sacrist, *temp.* prior Eastry, Dart, *Antiq. Cant.*, viij (BL Ms Cotton Galba, E.iv, fo 115ᵛ).

Note: Legg and Hope, *Inventories*, 61, treat this as a ref. to K[atherine] Lovell.

Bartholomew de LOVELOND [Levelond
occ. 1362 occ. 1383

1362, 25 Oct., for fourteen yrs an Augustinian canon of Leeds [Kent], and now recd licence to become a monk at Christ Church '. . . propter frugem melioris vite'; *Lit. Cant.* no 896 (Reg. L, fo 98ᵛ).

1364, one of eleven prof., *SL*, 182, CCA Lit. Ms D.12, fo 4ᵛ.

1380, before 26 June, precentor, Reg. abp Sudbury, fo 61ᵛ; on 20 Aug. 1383, the prior and chapter included his name among the three nominees for [reapptment to] this same office, Reg. abp Courtenay, i, fo 43.

1374, 30 June, 33rd in order at the el. of an abp, Reg. G, fos 173ᵛ–175ᵛ.

1381, 31 July, 23rd at the el. of an abp, *ib.*, fo 225ᵛ.

LOWINUS
n.d.

n.d., pr. whose obit occ. on 6 Feb. in BL Ms Cotton Nero C.ix, fo 5.

LUDEBURI
see William de Ledebery

Robert de LUDLOW
occ. 1324 occ. 1339

1324/7, 1330/3, 1337/9, anniversarian, CCA DCc, Godmersham accts 8–10, 13–17.

There is a Digestum vetus under the name R. de Lodelawe in the Eastry catalogue, James, *Ancient Libraries*, no 575 (p. 68). See the ref. to a clerk of Christ Church by this name who occ. in 1252, D. J. Jones, ed., *Saint Richard of Chichester: the sources for his life* (Sussex Record Society 79, 1995), 38.

W. de LUDLOW
occ. 1291/2

1291/2, anniversarian, CCA DCc Godmersham acct 7.

LUDO
n.d.

n.d., pr. whose obit occ. on 11 Feb. in BL Ms Cotton Nero C.ix, fo 5ᵛ.

LUDOWICUS
occ. 1189

1189, Oct., one of the monks whom the abp unsuccessfully ordered to appear before him and to cooperate with him in the el. of a prior, *Epist. Cant.*, 312; see Roger Norreys I.

I LUKE [Lucas
occ. 1214 occ. 1217

1214, 1216, both yrs on 29 Sept., granator, CCA DCc MA1, fos 54ᵛ, 58ᵛ.
1217, 7 Nov., bartoner, CCA DCc MA1, fo 60ᵛ.

See note *re* obits below Luke II.

II LUKE
occ. 1279 occ. 1303

1279, cellarer, CCA DCc MA1, fo 130; in 1286 he was described as 'former cellarer', CCA DCc, Treas. acct 2.
1303, 23 Nov., removed from the office of feretrar after the abp's visitation, *Reg. abp Winchelsey*, 1306.

See Luke de Ospring who is prob. this monk; however it is possible that there are two Lukes in these two entries and that only the one who was feretrar was Luke de Ospring. See the note below.

Note: there are obits for three monks called Luke in BL Ms Arundel 68: 1) a subdcn, 4 Feb. (fo 15); 2) a pr., 17 Feb. (fo 16ᵛ); 3) a pr., 1 Apr. (fo 22ᵛ).

M. Peter LUMBARDUS
occ. ?1240

n.d., name occ. in the list in *SL*, 175, CCA Lit. Ms D.12, fo 2ᵛ.

There are eleven books in the Eastry catalogue under the name of M. Peter Lumbard; they include the Instituta Justiniani and several works of canon law, James, *Ancient Libraries*, nos 564–574 (p. 68).

Note: it is prob. this monk who acted as official of the prior *sed. vac.* after the d. of abp Edmund in 1240, Churchill, *Cant. Admin.*, i, 551.

LUNDUN
see London

LURDINGDEN
see Roger II

William LYCHFELD [Lichfelde, Lychefylde, Lytchefelde, Lytchfylde
occ. 1509 occ. 1540

1509, 22 Dec., ord acol., Canterbury cathedral, Reg. abp Warham, ii, fo 264ᵛ.

1510, 16 June, one of eight tonsured, *SL*, 194, CCA Lit. Ms D.12, fo 11.

1511, 1 Jan., prof., *ib.*

1511, 19 Apr., ord dcn, Canterbury cathedral, Reg. abp Warham, ii, fo 265ᵛ.

1513, 26 Mar., ord pr., Canterbury cathedral, *ib.*, fo 266ᵛ.

1529/30, second sacrist, CCA DCc MA1, fos 159, 160.

1530/4, 1537, 20 Sept., [1538, 8 Feb., after], 1540, 4 Apr., sacrist, CCA DCc MA16, fos 1, 63, Sac. acct 75, DE57B, Cart Antiq. and Miscell. vi, no 136, Pantin, *Cant. Coll. Ox.*, iii, 152, *L and P Henry VIII*, xv, no 452. His apptment on 27 Apr, 1530 is in Reg. T, fo 346.

n.d., had as his *magister regule*, John Shepay II, q.v., Pantin, *Cant. Coll. Ox.*, iv, 54 (CCA DCc Ms Scrap Book B.186).

1511, 2 Sept., 73rd in order on the visitation certificate, Wood-Legh, *Visit.*, 3 (Reg. abp Warham, i, fo 35ᵛ).

1534, 12 Dec., acknowledged the Act of Supremacy, *DK 7th Report*, Appndx 2, 282.

[1538, 8 Feb., after], described on a list of monks, prob. prepared for Thomas Cromwell, as 'wytty' and 50 yrs of age, Pantin, *Cant. Coll. Ox.*, iii, 152.

1540, 4 Apr., awarded a pension of £10 p.a. and became a petty canon in the new foundation, *L and P Henry VIII*, xv, no 452.

Name in Oslo/London, Schøyen Collection, Ms 15, a Bible (late 13th c.) as William Lighfield; see J. Griffiths, 'Manuscripts in the Schøyen Collection Copied or Owned in the British Isles before 1700', *English Manuscript Studies, 1100–1700*, 5, (1995), 37.

A memorandum book compiled by him as sacrist, 1533/4, and containing rentals and accts is preserved in CCA DCc DE57B.

LYDEBERY, Lydebury
see Ledebery

John de LYNDESTEDE
occ. 1304/5

1304/5, granator, CCA DCc MA1, fos 251ᵛ–257ᵛ.

n.d., 3 Jan., pr., whose obit occ. in BL Ms Arundel 68, fo 12; his name is entered immediately before that of William Codelawe, q.v., who d. in 1307.

An inventory of vestments, *temp.* prior Eastry, includes two chasubles and an alb of his [?gift], Legg and Hope, *Inventories*, 52, 60. (BL Ms Cotton Galba E.iv, fos 112ᵛ, 115). In another inventory, this one of the refectory dated 1328, his name is attached to a silver *ciphus* and a *ciphus de murra*, Dart, *Antiq. Cant.*, xxiii (BL Ms Cotton Galba E.iv, fos 178ᵛ, 180).

LYNDESTEDE
see also Lynstede

Robert LYNGEFELD
occ. 1st half 13th c.

n.d., name occ. in the list in *SL*, 174, CCA Lit. Ms D.12, fo 1ᵛ.

Robert LYNSTEDE, B.Th. [Lynsted
occ. 1432 d. 1447

1432, 19 Sept., one of six prof., *SL*, 188, CCA Lit. Ms D.12, fo 7ᵛ.

1434, 13 Mar., ord acol., infirmary chapel, *Reg. abp Chichele*, iv, 378.

1436, 3 Mar., ord pr., [*recte* ?dcn], infirmary chapel, *ib.*, iv, 384.

1439, 28 Feb., novice, ord pr., infirmary chapel, 'Chron. Wm Glastynbury', 132 (Ms fo 118).

1440/1, student at Canterbury college, from Sept. to Mar., with a pension of 100s., Pantin, *Cant. Coll. Ox.*, ii, 160 (CCA DCc Cart. Antiq. O.151.11).

n.d., B.Th., *SL*, 139, without any ref.

1447, 9 Aug., d. at Chartham, and the funeral ceremonies were conducted by the subprior, Thomas Goldston, q.v., in the choir of the cathedral the following day, *Chron. Stone*, 41, CCA Lit. Ms D.12, fo 25ᵛ; the latter notes that he was in the fifteenth yr of his monastic life. His obit on 10 Aug. is in BL Ms Arundel 68, fo 37ᵛ.

1446/7, the prior listed under *obvenciones*, 6s. 8d., recd from [the sale of] his *peculium*, Pantin, *Cant. Coll. Ox.*, iv, 194.

William LYNSTEDE [Linestude
occ. 1267 occ. 1271

n.d., name occ. in the list in *SL*, 175, CCA Lit. Ms D.12, fo 2.

1267/71, chamberlain, CCA DCc, MA1, fos 110–115, AS10 (1268/9).

I Robert LYNTON, B.Th. [Lintun, Lyntone
occ. 1423 d. 1448

1423, 30 Sept., one of five prof., *SL*, 187, CCA Lit. Ms D.12, fo 6v.
1424, 22 Apr., tonsured, Canterbury cathedral, *Reg. abp Chichele*, iv, 359.
1427, 5 Dec., ord subdcn, Trottiscliffe, Reg. Langdon (Rochester), fo 59v.
1428, 3 Apr., ord dcn, Rochester cathedral, *ib.*, fo 65.
[1432], 11 June, ord pr., place not named, *ib.*, fo 74v.
1443/8, warden of Canterbury college, Oxford; an inventory made at the time of his entry into office is printed in Pantin, *Cant. Coll. Ox.*, i, 1–9 (CCA DCc Cart. Antiq. O.134); his accts for 1443/5 are also *ib.*, i, 163–170. He d. in office, see below.
[1435], student at Canterbury college, Chron Wm Glastynbury, fo 116v.
1436, Mar./Sept., 1436/7, student at Canterbury college, Pantin, *Cant. Coll. Ox.*, ii, 147, 153 (CCA DCc Cart. Antiq. O.151.8, 9).
1438, 21 Sept., recd 10s. 'ex gracia speciali versus Oxoniam', Pantin, *ib.*, iv, 192.
1440/1, student and acting as assistant to the warden, Pantin, *ib.*, ii, 160, 162 (CCA DCc Cart. Antiq. O.151.11).
1443, by this date, B.Th., *Chron. Stone*, 31.
1441, 7 May, recd 20s. 'pro expensis suis pro sermone faciendo' [?at Canterbury], Pantin, *Cant. Coll. Ox.*, iv, 193.
1443, 22 Apr., with John Elham II, q.v., sent by the prior and chapter to the king for licence to el. an abp, *Chron. Stone*, 31.
1448, 18 Feb., d. in Oxford, and buried in St Frideswide's priory church in the choir before the high altar, *Chron. Stone*, 43; see William Richemund. His obit is in BL Ms Arundel 68, fo 12.

Three books given by him to Canterbury college are listed in a college inventory of 1459, Pantin, *Cant. Coll. Ox.*, i, 12, 15 (CCA DCc Cart. Antiq. O.135); one of these is a vol. of Wyclif's sermons.

II Robert LYNTON
occ. 1459 occ. 1466

1459, 30 Nov., one of six prof., *SL*, 189, CCA Lit. Ms D.12, fo 8.
1461, 4 Apr., ord dcn, Canterbury cathedral, *Reg. abp Bourgchier*, 378.
1464, 31 Mar., ord pr., Canterbury cathedral, *ib.*, 390.
1463/4, celebrated his first mass and recd a small gift from the sacrist, CCA DCc, Sac. acct 44.
1466, 17 Feb., 61st in order in an inventory of *jocalia fratrum*, [given by him and/or assigned for his use], but he had none, Reg. N, fo 234v.
1466, 8 Oct., obtained licence from the abp to transfer to Dover priory, *Hist. Mss Comm. 9th Report*, Appndx, 104 (Reg. N, fo 199); see also Reg. S, fo 225.

LYOFNOTHUS
n.d.

n.d., pr., whose obit occ. on 30 June in BL Ms Arundel 68, fo 32.

LYTCHEFELDE
see Lychfeld

LYTEBERY
see Ledebery

LYTLE, Lytyll
see Litle

LYTLEBORNE, Lyttelborne, Lytylborne
Litelbourne

MACARIUS [Macharius
n.d.

n.d., 17 Feb., pr., whose obit occ. in BL Ms Arundel 68, fo 16v.

Robert MAFFELDE [Maveld, Mavyld
occ. 1413 d. 1469

1413, 6 Oct., one of six tonsured, *SL*, 186, CCA Lit. Ms D.12, fo 6. That this date ref. to tonsure rather than prof. is shown by the fact that none of the six took part in the el. of abp Chichele on 12 Mar. 1414, *Reg. abp Chichele*, i, 4.
1414, 22 Dec., ord acol. and subdcn, Canterbury cathedral, *Reg. abp Chichele*, iv, 317.
1416, 18 Apr., ord dcn, Canterbury cathedral, *ib.*, iv, 320.
1418, 21 May, ord pr., bp's chapel, Halling, Reg. Young (Rochester), fo 5v.
1435, 12 Nov., apptd *custos martyrii*, Chron. Wm Glastynbury, fo 117.
[1440], before 31 Oct., chaplain [to the prior], *ib.*, fo 119v.
[1440], 31 Oct., apptd third prior to succ. Thomas Wakeryng, q.v., *ib.*, fo 119v.
1451, 20 Mar., *custos tumbe*, *Chron. Stone*, 51.
1451, 20 Mar., present at the ceremony of the blessing of the cathedral bells in St George's tower, *Chron. Stone*, 51.
1466, 17 Feb., 5th in order in an inventory of *jocalia fratrum*, [given by him and/or assigned for his use], Reg. N, fo 230.

1468, 1 Sept., as one of the seniors stood beside the new prior, John de Oxney II, q.v., at his installation, *Chron. Stone*, 106.

1469, 16 Mar., *stationarius*, d. in his 50th yr of monastic life, *Chron. Stone*, 107; there is surely a mistake in the reckoning here! His obit on 18 Mar. is in BL Ms Arundel 68, fo 21. CCA Lit. Ms D.12, fo 26 lacks a date.

John MAGHFELD [Mondfeld, Moundfeld, Mundefelde, Munfeld, Mynfeld

occ. 1386 d. 1408

1386, 28 Oct., one of two clothed in the monastic habit, CCA Lit. Ms D.12, fo 5, *SL*, 183 (as Munfeld).

1389, 12 June, ord dcn, St Dunstan's church, London, Reg. abp Courtenay, i, fo 311v (as Maghfeld).

1391, 25 Mar., ord pr., Canterbury cathedral, *ib.*, i, fo 312 (as Moundfelld).

1388/9, 1389/90, recd small sums from the prior [*pro benedictione*], Lambeth Ms 243, fos 212v, 216v.

1396, 7 Aug., 52nd in order at the el. of an abp, Reg. G, fo 234v.

1408, 25 Sept., d., CCA Lit. Ms D.12, fo 19, [Moundfeld] where he is described as *eximius organista*; his obit occ. in BL Ms Arundel 68, fo 43 [Mundefelde].

MAIDSTONE

see Maydeston

MAINER

occ. [1167/8]

[late 1167/early 1168], mentioned by John of Salisbury, in a letter to Ralph de Arundel, q.v., as involved in intriguing vs the church of Canterbury, i.e., as having turned against the abp [Becket] and made an appeal [?to the curia] to which the cardinals had responded, *Salisbury Letters*, ii, no 246.

John de MALDON [Maldone, Maldune, Malton

occ. 1287 d. 1329

1287, 16 Mar., one of five prof., *SL*, 177, CCA Lit. Ms D.12, fo 3.

1309/11, bartoner, CCA DCc MA2, fos 17v–30.

1312, 11 Sept., apptd sacrist, Reg. abp Reynolds, fo 118v.

1315/16, warden of manors, CCA DCc Chartham acct 10.

1316, 11 Sept., 1317/18, sacrist, CCA DCc EC V/44, MA2, fos 79v–88v; he succ. Richard de Sharstede, q.v., Reg. K, fo 150v.

1318, 10 Oct., 1319, 10 Apr., precentor, CCA DCc EC I/39, CUL Ms Ee.5.31, fo 200.

1324/6, warden of manors, CCA DCc Cheam acct 38, MA2, fos 143–152.

1293, 26 Jan., absent from the monastery and recalled for the el. of an abp, *Reg. abp Winchelsey*, 1261–1262.

1319, 10 Apr., with Walter de Norwyco, q.v., carried letters from the prior and chapter to the king and to the duke of Lancaster concerning the disputed claims over Dover priory, CUL Ms Ee.5.31, fo 200.

1321, 24 Nov., with William de Ledebury, q.v., apptd proctor for convocation, *ib.*, fo 224.

1324, 29 May, as a result of the abp's injunctions after a visitation he and six other monks had been placed on a diet of bread and water, separated from the community and confined to the precincts; the prior and convent now wrote to urge the lightening of their penances, saying that they needed the company of their brethren, CUL Ms Ee.5.31, fo 236v; see also *Lit. Cant.*, no 205 (CCA DCc Cart. Antiq. C.1294a) which has been dated 18 Feb. 1327 by J.B. Sheppard, but surely pertains to this incident and was therefore prob. written earlier, i.e. on 18 Feb. 1325; in it the abp tells the prior to take into acct the 'status quem optinuit [Maldon] in Ecclesia nostra' and to mitigate his penance.

1325, 19 Oct., was alleged to have been involved in the disturbances caused by Robert de Aldon, q.v., because the latter had placed a forged letter on his bed, *Lit. Cant.*, no 156 (Reg. L, fo 142, CCA, DCc Cart. Antiq. C.1294).

[1325], 16 Nov., with Simon de St Peter, q.v., apptd parliamentary proctor by the prior and chapter, CUL Ms Ee.5.31, fo 244.

1329, 14 July, d., CCA Lit. Ms D.12, fo 16; his obit is in BL Ms Arundel 68, fo 34.

According to an inventory of missing service books dated 1 Mar. 1338, he was responsible for the loss of the diurnale of Ralph de Pretelwelle, q.v., *Lit. Cant.*, no 618 (Reg. L, fo 104).

Alexander MALEMYNS

occ. 2nd half 13th c.

n.d., name occ. in the list in *SL*, 176, CCA Lit. Ms D.12, fo 2v.

Joseph de MALLYNG

occ. [1207 × 1214]

n.d., [1207 × 1214], name occ. in the list of those who were in exile, *SL*, 172, CCA Lit. Ms D.12, fo 1.

Nicholas de MALLYNG

occ. 1st half 13th c.

n.d., name occ. in the *post exilium* list in *SL*, 173, CCA Lit. Ms D.12, fo 1v.

Richard de MALLYNG [Mallinge, Mallinges

occ. [1207 × 1214] occ. 1239

[1207 × 1214], name occ. in the list of those who were in exile, *SL*, 172, CCA Lit. Ms D.12, fo 1.

1239, 4 Jan., one of the group of monks accused of contumacy by the abp after the forgery scandal, *Gervase Cant.*, ii, 144; see Simon de Hertlepe. On 1 Feb. he was among those summoned to appear before the abp after the monks' el. of Roger de La Lee, q.v., as prior, *ib.*, ii, 153–154.
n.d., 26 Jan., pr., whose obit occ. in BL Ms Arundel 68, fo 14^{v}.

In the Eastry catalogue, four and possibly more items are listed under his name; they are mainly sermons, and some of Alexander Neckham's writings, James, *Ancient Libraries*, nos 1231–1234, ?1235–1237 (p. 108).

Robert MALLYNG
occ. [1373] occ. 1388/9

[1373], previously prior of [the Augustinian house of] Tonbridge, one of eight prof., *SL*, 183, CCA Lit. Ms D.12, fo 4^{v}.
1383/4, treasurer, CCA DCc MA2, fo 333.
1381, 30 July, 47th in order at the el. of an abp, Reg. G, fo 225^{v}.
1388/9, recd 12d. from the prior [*pro benedictione*], Lambeth Ms 243, fo 212.

Stephen de MALLYNG
occ. 1st half 13th c.

n.d., name occ. in the *post exilium* list in *SL*, 173, CCA Lit. Ms D.12, fo 1.

William de MALLYNG
occ. 1309 d. 1360

1309, 18 Oct., one of nine prof., *SL*, 179, CCA Lit. Ms D.12, fo 3^{v}.
1317, 28 May, ord pr., Lambeth palace chapel, Reg. abp Reynolds, fo 178.
1329, *custos martyrii*, CCA DCc MA2, fo 183^{v}.
1337, *custos tumbe*, CCA DCc MA2, fo 255.
1332/3, visited Godmersham with his *socius*, CCA DCc Godmersham acct 15.
1338, 1 Mar., reported to have lost two service books that had belonged to Henry de Depham, q.v., *Lit. Cant.*, no 618 (Reg. L, fo 104).
1349, 4 June, 8th in order at the el. of an abp, Reg. G, fo 60^{v}.
1349, 8/9 Sept., 8th at the el. of an abp, *ib.*, fo 76.
1360, 13 Mar., d., CCA Lit. Ms D.12, fo 17.

MALTON
see Maldon

MARCELLUS [de Capella
occ. 1282 occ. 1303

1282, subchamberlain, CCA DCc, Treas. acct 1.
1299, *custos de Wald*, Reg. Q, fo 29/43.
1303, 6 Dec., apptd penitentiary, *Reg. abp Winchelsey*, 1306 (Reg. Q, fo 30^{v}/42). He is named as Marcellus only.

Note: was this monk also known as Marcellus de Lese, q.v.?

Edmund MARCHALL
occ 1509 occ. c. 1513

1509, 22 Dec., ord acol., Canterbury cathedral, Reg. abp Warham, ii, fo 264^{v}.
1510, 16 June, one of eight tonsured, *SL*, 194, CCA Lit. Ms D.12, fo 11.
1511, 1 Jan., prof., *ib.*
1511, 19 Apr., ord subdcn, Canterbury cathedral, Reg. abp Warham, ii, fo 265^{v}.
[c. 1512/13], student at Canterbury college with an exhibition from cardinal Morton, Pantin, *Cant. Coll. Ox.*, ii, 273, 274 (CCA DCc Cart. Antiq. O.151.36, part 1).
Note: since he d., still only a subdcn or dcn, his student days were prob. c. 1512/13.
1511, 2 Sept., 78th in order on the visitation certificate, Wood-Legh, *Visit.*, 3 (Reg. abp Warham, i, fo 35^{v}).
n.d., 25 Apr., *levita*, d., BL Ms Arundel 68, fo 24^{v}.

I John MARCHALL
occ. 1401 d. 1445

1401, 25 Mar., previously monk of Dover, now prof. at Christ Church with six others, *SL*, 185, CCA Lit. Ms D.12, fo 5^{v}.
1435, 25 Dec., apptd *magister mense*, Chron. Wm Glastynbury, fo 117^{v}.
[1440], before 27 June, *magister mense*, and now succ. by William Glastynbury, q.v.; on 27 June apptd *magister tumbe* and *magister martyrii ad tumbam* following Robert Smerden, q.v., Chron. Wm Glastynbury, fo 119^{v}.
1445, before 17 Sept., *custos corone*, CCA Lit. Ms D.12, fo 25; in CCA DCc MA4, fo 29^{v} he was *custos* this yr on 11 June and 6 Aug.
1414, 12 Mar., 50th in order at the el. of an abp, *Reg. abp Chichele*, i, 4.
1445, 17 Sept., d., in his 45th yr of monastic life, CCA Lit. Ms D.12, fo 25; this suggests that he had spent barely a yr at Dover. His date of death in *Chron. Stone*, 38, is 16 Sept., but his obit in BL Ms Arundel 68, fo 41^{v} is in accord with CCA Lit. Ms D.12.

Note: see Me. . .sall who may be this monk.

II John MARCHALL
occ. 1497

1497, second treasurer, CCA DCc, Treas. acct 23.
Note: this is prob. a mistake for Richard Marchall I, q.v.

Leonard MARCHALL
occ. 1522

1522, 11 Feb., one of ten tonsured, *SL*, 195, CCA Lit. Ms D.12, fo 11^{v}.
1522, 24 Nov., prof., *ib.*

n.d., 18 July, *levita*, whose obit occ. in BL Ms Arundel 68, fo 35.

I Richard MARCHALL [Marshall
occ. 1470 occ. 1520/1

1470, 25 Jan., one of eight prof., *SL*, 190, CCA Lit. Ms D.12, fo 8.
1470, 21 Apr., ord acol., Canterbury cathedral, *Reg. abp Bourgchier*, 405.
1473, 13 Mar., ord dcn, Canterbury cathedral, *ib.*, 410.
1475, 23 Sept., ord pr., prior's chapel, *ib.*, 419.
1491, 11 Sept., 1493/4, 26 July to 19 Apr., *magister ordinis* and third prior, *SL*, 192, CCA Lit. Ms D.12, fo 9–9v.
1493/4, novice master, CCA DCc Sac. acct 63 and MA9, fo 46.
1495, 1 Aug.; 1496/7; 1497/8, treasurer, CCA DCc DE15A; Pantin, *Cant. Coll. Ox.*, iv, 204; CCA DCc Treas. acct 55; and see John Marchall II above.
1500, 13 May, 1501, 26 Apr., 1502/3, warden of manors, CCA DCc MA112, Reg. R, fo 56v, Pantin, *Cant. Coll. Ox.*, ii, 235.
1503/9; 1511, June; 1516, 25 Mar.; 1516/21, Mar., chamberlain, CCA DCc MA10, fos 177v, 204, MA11, fos 4v, 34v, 73, 100; CCA Lit. Ms C.11, fo 54; *ib.*, fo 57v; MA14, fos 4, 40, 70, 105, Chamb. acct 61, CCA Lit. Ms C.11, fo 61.
1517/18, almoner, CCA DCc DE70.
1493, 1 May, 28th in order at the ratification of an agreement, Reg. S, fo 383v; but see John Crosse I.
1501, 26 Apr., 16th in order at the el. of an abp, Reg. R, fo 56v.
1511, 2 Sept., 5th on the visitation certificate, Wood-Legh, *Visit.*, 3 (Reg. abp Warham, i, fo 35).
1520/1, *stationarius*, CCA DCc Infirm. acct 2.
1521, Mar., possibly d. as his acct as chamberlain ceases at the end of Mar., see above.

II Richard MARCHALL [Marshall
occ. 1533 occ. 1540

1533, 12 May, one of eight tonsured, *SL*, 196, CCA Lit. Ms D.12, fo 12.
1534, 21 Mar., made his prof. before the prior *ex licentia* of abp Cranmer, *ib.*
[1538, 8 Feb., after], dcn, Pantin, *Cant. Coll. Ox.*, iii, 154.
1534, 12 Dec., acknowledged the Act of Supremacy, *DK 7th Report*, Appndx 2, 282.
[1538, 8 Feb., after], in a list of monks prob. prepared for Thomas Cromwell he was described as a dcn, aged 21 and a 'good man', Pantin, *Cant. Coll. Ox.*, iii, 154.
1540, 4 Apr., awarded a pension of £3 and became a scholar in the new foundation, *L and P Henry VIII*, xv, no 452.

Laurence de MARISCO
d. 1286

1286, 7 Apr., d., CCA Lit. Ms D.12, fo 15.

See also Laurence III and IV.

MATTHEW
occ. 1260/1

1260/1, chamberlain, Reg. H, fo 204v.

See also Prekepelse.

MAURITIUS [Maurice
[?1070s]

[?1070s], told by Anselm to read Virgil under Ernulf I if he was not already doing so, *Epist. Anselm*, iii, 180–181.
n.d., the obit of a subdcn by this name occ. on 20 July in BL Ms Arundel 68, fo 35v.

MAURUS
n.d.

n.d., 15 Feb., pr., whose obit occ. in BL Ms Arundel 68, fo 16v.

Note: a monk by this name was subcellarer, *temp.* Eadmer, q.v., and was mentioned by him in his 'De Reliquis sancti' Audoeni et quorundam aliorum Sanctorum quae in Aecclesia domini Salvatoris habentur', transcribed by A. Wilmart in *Revue des Sciences Religieuses'*, t.15 (1935), 368.

MAVELD, Mavyld
see Maffelde

John MAY
occ. 1358/9 d. 1361

1358/9, 28 Oct., one of nine prof., *SL*, 181, CCA Lit. Ms D.12, fo 4.
1360, 29 Feb., ord acol., abp's chapel, Otford, Reg. abp Islip, fo 318.
1360, 4 Apr., ord subdcn, abp's chapel, Saltwood, *ib.*, fo 318v.
Note: the prof. date, from CCA Lit. Ms D.12, has been added in the margin later and is possibly a yr or so out.
1361, 25 July, d., one of c.25 who d. [of the plague] between June and Sept., CCA Lit. Ms D.12, fo 17.

Thomas le MAY

Note: a Thomas le Maij is referred to several times in a memorandum dated 25 July 1333 when several items of plate were given into his care, Hope 'Inventories of Priors', 279–280; possibly not a monk.

See also le Jay

Hugh MAYDESTON [Maideston, Maydston, Maydynston
occ. 1462 d. 1500

1462, 17 Apr., ord acol., Canterbury cathedral, *Reg. abp Bourgchier*, 381.

[1462], 6 Dec., one of six prof., *SL*, 190, CCA Lit. Ms D.12, fo 8.

Note: this must have been incorrectly dated 1464 in the margin of the ms; 1462 (or 1463) is more likely.

1465, 13 Apr., ord dcn, place not stated, *Reg. abp Bourgchier*, 391.

1468, 12 Mar., ord pr., Canterbury cathedral, *ib.*, 398.

1466, 17 Feb., 74th in order in an inventory of *jocalia fratrum*, [given by him and/or assigned for his use], but he had none, Reg. N, fo 235.

1493, 1 May, 20th in order at the ratification of an agreement, Reg. S, fo 383ᵛ; but see John Crosse I.

1500, 28 Jan., *conventualis*, d., *ex infirmitate pluris'*, in the 37th yr of his monastic life and his 53rd yr of age, CCA Lit. Ms D.12, fo 28; his obit is in BL Ms Arundel 68, fo 14ᵛ.

I John de MAYDESTON [Maydestane, Maydestone

occ. 1239

n.d., name occ. in the *post exilium* list in *SL*, 173, CCA Lit. Ms D.12, fo 1ᵛ.

1239, before 7 Jan., deputed with Simon de Leycestria, q.v., to cite Eustace [de Faversham], q.v., to the el. of a prior,. *Gervase Cant.*, ii, 145.

II John MAYDESTON [Maydenstan, Maydenston, Maydyston

occ. [1393] occ. 1405

[1393], 21 Nov., one of six prof., *SL*, 184, CCA Lit. Ms D.12, fo 5.

1394, 18 Apr., ord subdcn, Canterbury cathedral, Reg. abp Courtenay ii, fo 184ᵛ.

1396, 1 Apr., ord dcn, Canterbury cathedral, *ib.*, ii, fo 186ᵛ.

1396, 7 Aug., 72nd in order at the el. of an abp, Reg. G, fo 234ᵛ.

1405, 20 July, recd permission from the abp to 'migrate' to Dover priory, Reg. S, fo 55ᵛ.

Robert de MAYDESTON [Maydyston

occ. 1st half 13th c.

n.d., name occ. in the *post exilium* list in *SL*, 174, CCA Lit. Ms D.12, fo 1ᵛ.

Salmon de MAYDESTON

occ. 1st half 13th c.

n.d., name occ. in the *post exilium* list in *SL*, 173, CCA Lit. Ms D.12, fo 1.

See also Salomon.

Tbomas de MAYDESTON [Maydyston

occ. 2nd half 13th c.

n.d., name occ. in the list in *SL*, 175, CCA Lit. Ms D.12, fo 2.

See Thomas II.

W. de MAYDESTON [Maydenstane

occ. 1327 occ. 1331

1327, 13 June, in need of correction acc. to a letter from the abp to the prior, Reg. abp Reynolds, fo 149ᵛ.

1331, 13 Sept., in a letter directed to the 'barons and *communitas* of Romney' among whom were his friends, the prior said that he had been twice ord acol. through his own ignorance and had gone to Rome to obtain absolution for this sacrilege, Reg. L, fo 10ᵛ.

I Walter or possibly William de MAYDESTON [Maidenston, Maydenstan, Maydenston, senior

occ. 1354 occ. 1385

1354, 28 Nov., one of seven prof., *SL*, 181, CCA Lit. Ms D.12, fo 4.

1356, 18 June, ord acol., Hoath chapel in Reculver parish, Reg. abp Islip, fo 316.

1356, 24 Sept., ord subdcn, abp's chapel, Tenham, *ib.*, fo 316.

1358, 22 Sept., ord dcn, Charing, *ib.*, fo 317.

1361, 18 Dec., ord pr., Charing, *ib.*, fo 320.

1364/5, Mar., chamberlain, CCA DCc Chamb. acct 67.

1368/9, cellarer, CCA DCc Bart. acct 44.

1370, Apr./1372, Mar., chamberlain, CCA DCc, Chamb. accts 49, 53, 52.

1371/2, monk surveyor, CCA DCc, Eastry acct 105; on 13 Apr. 1372 he was dismissed from the office of chamberlain, Reg. abp Wittlesey, fo 52.

[1371/3, chamberlain, CCA DCc MA2, fos 266ᵛ–276ᵛ; but see the entry above].

1372/3, *custos* of abp Islip's sheep, CCA DCc Sheep Warden Acct 1.

1373/7, chaplain to the prior, CCA DCc, MA2, fos 276ᵛ–312, Thes. acct 5 (1373/4).

1373/4, 1375/6, warden of St Mary in crypt, CCA DCc Thes. acct 5, MA2, fos 291–296; see Walter Gabriel.

1378, 8 Oct., absolved from the office of precentor because of serious illness, Reg. abp Sudbury, fo 50ᵛ.

1380, 1381, 1382/4, third prior, Lambeth Ms 243, fos 180ᵛ, 183, 188, 188ᵛ, 192ᵛ.

1385, granator, CCA DCc MA2, fo 335.

1366, 10 May, present at the el. of an abp, Reg. G, fo 147.

1383, 20 Aug., a William Maydeston, *senior*, was one of the three names presented to the abp for the office of subprior, Reg. abp Courtenay, i, fo 43.

See the note below the next entry.

II Walter or possibly William de MAYDESTON [junior

occ. 1368 occ. [1372]

1368, 24 Feb., in response to the prior's request the abbot of Faversham provided a licence for

Walter to transfer to Christ Church '. . . propter frugem melioris vite', Reg. L, fo 98v.
[1372], black cloth for [the habit of] Walter Maydeston *junior* was purchased by the chamberlain, CCA DCc Chamb. acct 50.

Note: there are serious problems here; all that is clear is that there were two Walter or William Maydestons in [1372] and 1383. The numerous offices here listed under Walter I must be divided between them after 1368, but they cannot be assigned without more evidence. See also Walter Gabriel.

John MENYS [Mynnes, Myns, Mynse, *?alias* Frevell

occ. 1485 occ. 1540

1485, 12 Mar., one of six tonsured, *SL*, 191, CCA Lit. Ms D.12, fo 8v.
1485, 6 Dec., prof., *ib.*
1490, 10 Apr., ord pr., Canterbury cathedral, *Reg. abp Morton*, i, no 438d.
1494, 5 Nov., 1500/1, 1503, 21 Feb., 1504, 10 Nov., 1505, 28 Jan., 1508/9, treasurer, CCA DCc RE116, Lambeth ED86, Reg. T, fo 15v, CCA DCc Ms Scrap Book A90d and 90b, Lambeth ED88.
1499, chancellor, with John Goodnyston II, q.v., Reg. S, fo 430v; also in 1500 with William Molassh II, q.v., *ib.*, fo 435v.
1511, 29 Sept.; 1512, June; 1513, May; 1514, 1515, both on 24 June; 1515, 1516, both on 25 Dec.; 1518/25, each yr on 25 Mar.; 1525, 1526, both on 29 Sept.; 1528, 25 Mar.; 1529, 24 June; 1530/3, each yr on 25 Mar., chaplain to the prior, CCA Lit. Ms C.11, fos 54v, 55v, 56v, 57, 57v, 58, 58v, 59v, 60v, 61, 61v, 62, 63, 63v, 64, 65, 65v, 66, 67, 67v, 68.
1493, 1 May, 48th in order at the ratification of an agreement, Reg. S, fo 383v; but see John Crosse I.
1501, 26 Apr., 32nd in order at the el. of an abp, Reg. R, fo 56v.
1503, 25 Jan., apptd proctor for the prior and chapter at convocation at Westminster, Reg. T, fo 439.
1511, 2 Sept., 16th in order on the visitation certificate, Wood-Legh, *Visit.*, 3 (Reg. abp Warham, i, fo 35).
[1526], gave the penitentiary 12d. for a *dirige* and mass for the soul of his sister, CCA Lit. Ms C.11, fo 64.
1534, acknowledged the Act of Supremacy, *DK 7th Report*, Appndx, 2, 282.
[1538, 8 Feb., after], in a list of monks prob. prepared for Thomas Cromwell he was described as 'stacionar' and 'witty', 71 yrs old, Pantin, *Cant. Coll. Ox.*, iii, 152.
1541, 8 Apr., apptd canon of the 6th prebend, *Fasti 1541–1857*, iii, 26, after being named as prebendary of the new foundation on 4 Apr., 1540, *L and P Henry VIII*, xv, no 452.

A letter from him to the prior, dated at the latter's 'place in Southwark' on 6 Nov. [c. 1520] shows him to be conducting business affairs for the prior in London, *Christ Church Letters*, 70–71 (CCA DCc Cart. Antiq. 19).

His sister Johanna Frevell, [*consoror*], gave thee *cappe* and two vestments to Christ Church; her obit on 28 May is in Lambeth Ms 20, fo 190–190v.

Robert MENYS [Mennys, Menysshe, *alias* Nale

occ. 1524 occ. 1535

1524, 21/22 July, one of eleven granted adm. [*ingressum*] to Christ Church, CCA Lit. Ms D.12, fos 11v–12.
1524, 4 Aug., one of eleven tonsured, *SL*, 195, CCA Lit. Ms D.12, fo 11v.
1525, 19 Apr., prof., *ib.*
1527/8, celebrated his first mass and recd a small gift from the sacrist, Woodruff, 'Sacrist's Rolls', 72.
1534, 12 Dec., acknowledged the Act of Supremacy, *DK 7th Report*, Appndx 2, 282.
1535, 27 Nov., dispensed to change his habit and hold a benefice, Chambers, *Faculty Office Regs.*, 36.

Walter de MERI [Moyri, Murri, Murry, *alias* Parvus

occ. [1141 × 1148] occ. 1154

1149–1152, prior: apptd by the abp [after Oct.] 1149; sought to res. because of a controversy with the abp and was deposed in Mar./Apr. 1152 and imprisoned at Gloucester, *Fasti*, ii, 9 and notes, *HRH*, 34.
[1141 × 1148], before his apptment as prior had served as chaplain to abp Theobald and witnessed two confirmation deeds, *Theobald Charters*, nos 164, 165; he also witnessed another archiepiscopal instrument [1141 × 1148], *ib.*, no 146, all of these with Gilbert [de Clare], q.v. See *Gervase Cant.*, i, 141.
1154, c. 28 Feb., his release from prison was ordered by the pope and with his chaplain, John, q.v., he was summoned to Rome, *Theobald Charters*, 61 (quoting from Gervase and Thorne).
n.d., was allowed to return to Christ Church, *Salisbury Letters*, see *Theobald Charters*, 59–62.
n.d., 7 Jan., his obit occ. in BL Ms Arundel 68, fo 12v as *quondam prior*.

Gervase described him as a man of learning but a poor administrator and said that the monks become so concerned about the crisis caused by his incompetence in the management of their estates that they asked the abp to take charge; but soon after he had, with reluctance, accepted this responsibility, controversy arose between him and the chapter which resulted in the abp's decision to depose the prior; see *Theobald Charters*, 59–62, *Gervase Cant.*, i, 143–146. According to Gervase the understanding with the abp was that the prior would resign and would then be restored, but instead he was deposed, *ib.*

Guy MERIWEDIR [Guido

occ. 1350

1350, 18 Sept., ord subdcn, Goudhurst, Reg. Islip, fo 310.

Note: this is prob. Guy de Rydelyngwolde, q.v.

John MERSHAM [Merstham

occ. 1429

[1429, summer], ord acol. and subdcn, place not given, Reg. Langdon (Rochester), fo 74.
1429, before 21 Sept., and before his prof., expelled, *SL*, 187, CCA Lit. Ms D.12, fo 7.

Richard de MERSTHAM [Mersham

occ. 1328 occ. 1374/5

1328, 25 Nov., one of six prof., *SL*, 179, CCA Lit. Ms D.12, fo 3ᵛ.
1350, 28 Dec., apptd chamberlain, Reg. abp Islip, fo 36ᵛ; see also CCA DCc Chamb. acct 73; he continued in office at least until Apr. 1352, *ib.*, Chamb. acct 41; he succ. William de Eythorne, q.v.
1367, 27 Mar., apptd precentor, *Reg. abp Langham*, 282–283.
1338, 1 Mar., an inventory of missing books held him responsible for the Senatoris of Cassiodorus and a Grecissimus, *Lit. Cant.*, no 618 (Reg. L, fo 104).
1349, 4 June, 22nd in order at the el. of an abp, Reg. G, fo 60ᵛ.
1349, 8/9 Sept., 21st at the el. of an abp, *ib.*, fo 76.
1374, 30 June, 4th at the el. of an abp, *ib.*, fos 173ᵛ–175ᵛ.
1374/5, ill and the anniversarian pd a 'pension' of 3s. 6d. toward his medical expenses, CCA DCc, Anniv. acct 6.
n.d., 23 Mar., obit occ. in BL Ms Arundel, 68, fo 21ᵛ.

John ?ME. . .SALL

n.d.

Name in Oxford, Bod. Ms Lyell, 19, Regula S. Benedicti (15th c.), on fo 1; it also contains the rules of Augustine and Basil and is a pocket size vol.

Note: this may be John Marchall I, q.v.

Martin de MEYLOND

occ. [1241]

n.d., name occ. in the list in *SL*, 174, CCA Lit. Ms D.12, fo 2; he was prob. one of the twelve prof. with Richard de Wynchepe, q.v.

MICHAEL

n.d.

n.d., 21 May, obit occ. in Lambeth Ms 20, fo 188 and BL Ms Arundel 68, fo 28.

MIDDLETON

see Myddylton

MIDELTON

see William Milton I

MILES, Milo

see Crispin

MILLYS

see Warham

John MILTON [Mylton

occ. 1430 d. 1450

1430, c. 21 Sept., *adiunctus* in place of John Mersham, q.v., *SL*, 187, CCA Lit. Ms D.12, fo 7.
1431, 4 Apr., prof., *ib.*
1433, 28 Mar., ord dcn, Charing, *Reg. abp Chichele*, iv, 377.
1434, 13 Mar., ord pr., infirmary chapel, *ib.*, iv, 379.
1450, 16 July, d., *Chron. Stone*, 50; obit in BL Ms Arundel 68, fo 34ᵛ.

Thomas MILTON [Mylton

occ. 1514 occ. 1520/1

1514, 1 Sept., one of seven tonsured, *SL*, 194, CCA Lit. Ms D.12, fo 11.
1515, 19 Apr., prof., *ib.*
n.d., had John Garard, q.v., as his *magister regule*, Pantin, *Cant. Coll. Ox.*, iv, 54.
1518/19, 1520/1, spent time in the infirmary, CCA DCc Infirm. accts 1, 2.
[c. 1514 × 1524], an undated scrap of paper listing the delinquencies of several monks noted that 'nichill facit . . . ad regulam beati Benedicti', prob. referring to his failure to learn the Rule by heart, Pantin, *ib.*, iii, 143 (CCA DCc Ms Scrap Book B.193).
n.d., 26 May, obit occ. in BL Ms Arundel 68, fo 28ᵛ.

I William MILTON [Middilton, Midelton

occ. 1376 d. 1398

1376, 14 or 15 Nov., one of seven who were clothed in the monastic habit, CCA Lit. Ms D.12, fo 4ᵛ.
1376, 20 Dec., ord acol., Canterbury cathedral, Reg. abp Sudbury, fo 140ᵛ.
1377, 19 Sept., ord subdcn, Lambeth palace chapel, *ib.*, fo 142.
1378, 17 Apr., ord dcn, Canterbury cathedral, *ib.*, fo 145ᵛ.
1382, 20 Dec., ord pr., abp's chapel, Mayfield, Reg. abp Courtenay, i, fo 305ᵛ.
1385/6, subcellarer, Lambeth Ms 243, fo 200ᵛ.

1391/3, chamberlain, CCA DCc, Chamb. acct 56 (his first yr), Sac. acct 11.
[1392], 21 Nov., *magister ordinis*, *SL*, 184, CCA Lit. Ms D.12, fo 5.
1396/7, 1398, before 8 Nov., granator, CCA DCc Prior acct 4, CCA Lit. Ms D.12, fo 18.

1379/80, student at Canterbury college who recd money for his *capa scolastica*, Pantin, *Cant. Coll. Ox.*, iv, 188.
1382, Dec., *recessit*, [and returned to Canterbury], Pantin, *ib.*, ii, 129.

1377, recd a small sum from the prior *pro benedictione*, Lambeth Ms 243, fo 176.
1381, 31 July, 54th in order at the el. of an abp, Reg. G, fo 225v.
1391/2, 1392/3, gave the sacrist 5s. and 6s. 8d. respectively for candles to burn during the night before the image beate Marie, CCA DCc Sac. accts 10, 11.
1391, c. 25 Jan., with William Stone, q.v., sent to the abp at Croydon to inform him of the d. of prior Fynch, q.v., Reg. abp Courtenay, i, fo 336v.
1396, 7 Aug., 27th at the el. of an abp, Reg. G, fo 234v.
1398, 8 Nov., d., CCA Lit. Ms D.12, fo 18.

II William MILTON [Mylton
occ. [1448] d. 1472/3

[1448], 25 Jan., one of four prof., *SL*, 189, CCA Lit. Ms D.12, fo 7v.
1448, 17 Feb., ord acol., Canterbury cathedral, Reg. abp Stafford, fo 202.
1449, 12 Apr., ord subdcn, Canterbury cathedral, *ib.*, fo 203v.
1450, 3 Apr., ord dcn, Canterbury cathedral, *ib.*, fo 204v.
1452, 8 Apr., ord pr., Canterbury cathedral, *ib.*, fo 207.

1472/3, *magister mense*, at the time of d., CCA Lit. Ms D.12, fo 26.

1466, 17 Feb., 40th in order in an inventory of *jocalia fratrum*, [given by him and/or assigned for his use], Reg. N, fo 233.
1472/3, d., Woodruff, 'Sacrist's Rolls', 64 (CCA DCc Sac. acct 53).

MOHT
see Moth

MOLAND
see Molond

John MOLASSH [Molessch, Molesshe
occ. 1358/9 occ. 1381/2

1358/9, 28 Oct., one of nine prof., *SL*, 181, CCA Lit. Ms D.12, fo 4.
1360, 29 Feb., ord acol., abp's chapel, Otford, Reg. abp Islip, fo 318.
1360, 4 Apr., ord subdcn, abp's chapel, Saltwood, *ib.*, fo 318v.
1361, 18 Dec., ord dcn, Charing, *ib.*, fo 320.
1362, 11 June, ord pr., Mayfield, *ib.*, fo 321v.

1366/7, subchaplain to the prior, CCA DCc Barksore acct 49.
1368, 23 Sept., apptd sacrist, *Reg. abp Langham*, 310.
1369, 22 June, apptd sacrist, Reg. Wittlesey, fo 13.
1369/70, chaplain to the prior, CCA DCc Eastry acct 103.
1370/1, sacrist and chaplain to the prior, CCA DCc MA2, fo 266v; he was also monk *supervisor* this yr, CCA DCc MA2, fo 266v.
Note: it seems unusual for one monk to be both chaplain and sacrist, but he may have shared one or both of these offices with another monk or there may have been a few months of overlapping. As to his acting as *supervisor* at the same time, this too seems surprising.
1371/2, chaplain to the prior, CCA DCc MA2, fos 266v–270v.
1372/4, 1375, warden of manors, CCA DCc Adisham acct 36, Eastry acct 108, MA fo 290.
1373/4, first treasurer (with Robert Hore, q.v.) and had been *custos* of East Kent, CCA DCc Treas. acct 5.
1374/6, treasurer, CCA DCc, MA2, fos 294v–311.
1376, 29 Sept., 1378/9, cellarer, CCA DCc, Arrears acct 40, MA2, fos 315–318.
1381/2, chaplain to the prior, CCA DCc, MA2, fos 325v–329v.

1359/60, ill and recd a 2s. 'pension' [for his medical expenses] from the anniversarian, CCA DCc Anniv. acct 5.
1374, 30 June, 23rd in order at the el. of an abp, Reg. G, fos 173v–175v.
1376, 30 Mar., recd papal dispensation to choose his own confessor, *CPL*, iv (1362–1404), 220.
1376, Apr., one of ten monks nominated to the committee set up to regulate the infirmary, *Lit. Cant.*, no 945 (CCA DCc Cart. Antiq. C.206).
1381, 31 July, 17th in order at the el. of an abp, Reg. G, fo 225v.

Richard MOLASSH [Molasche, Molasshe, Molesche
occ. 1439 occ. 1474

1439, 4 or 15 Dec., [St Barbara], one of six clothed in the monastic habit, *SL*, 188, CCA Lit. Ms D.12, fo 7v.
[1440] 8 or 20 July, [St Margaret], made his prof., Chron. Wm Glastynbury, fo 119v.

[1464], *recessit*, CCA Lit. Ms D.12, fo 26; he then was presented to St John's church in Thanet (Margate), *Hist. Mss Comm. 9th Report*, Appndx, 116–117.
1474, Dec., humbly petitioned the prior to be allowed to return to Christ Church as he deeply regretted his action in seeking and obtaining papal dispensation from his monastic vows; the petition is written in English with

the exception of the last sentence: *Ecclesia nulli resistit gremium*, *ib*. See also the full transcription in *Lit. Cant.*, no 1077 (Reg. S, fos 269ᵛ–270).

I William MOLASSH [Molasch, Molashe, Molesh, Molesshe

occ. 1398 d. 1438

1428–1438, prior: el. [30] Mar., 1428, *prefectio*, by the abp [31] Mar., see below; d. 19 Feb. 1438, *Chron. Stone*, 21.

1398, 13 or 14 Nov., one of four prof., *SL*, 184, CCA Lit. Ms D.12, fo 5ᵛ.

1401, 2 Apr., ord dcn, Canterbury cathedral, Reg. abp Arundel, i, fo 328.

1404, 29 Mar., ord pr., Canterbury cathedral, *ib.*, fo 332ᵛ.

1407/8, third treasurer, CCA DCc Treas. acct 8.

1408/11, treasurer, CCA DCc Treas. accts 9–11; he was second treasurer in 1410.

1410/11, 1412/13, chaplain to the prior, CCA DCc Prior's Chaplain acct 8, Treas. Acct 11.

1413/14, warden of manors and treasurer, CCA DCc London acct 32.

c. 1413/14, warden of Canterbury college, Pantin, *Cant. Coll. Ox.*, iv, 191; he was presumably warden on 25 Feb. 1414 when the prior wrote to summon him and the students to return to Canterbury for the el. of an abp, Pantin, *ib.*, iii, 72 (Reg. S, fo 68ᵛ).

1414/15, warden of manors, CCA DCc, Bocking acct 53.

1414/16, 1417, Apr./Sept., chaplain to the prior, CCA DCc Prior's Chaplain accts 9, 15, 14.

1419/20, almoner, Lambeth ED81 and CCA DCc RE113.

1422/3, warden of manors, CCA DCc Prior acct 5; see John Chart.

1423/Jan. 1424, chaplain to the prior, CCA DCc Prior's Chaplain acct 10.

1425, Mar./Dec., bartoner, with Henry Sutton, q.v., CCA DCc Bart. acct 88.

1425/6, with Henry Sutton, q.v., receivers *bonorum et proventorum* by order of the prior, CCA DCc Receiver acct 1.

1426, 29 Sept., warden of manors, CCA DCc, Ms Scrap Book A.128.

1426/7, 1428, before 31 Mar., almoner, CCA DCc Adisham acct 54, Oxford, Bod. Ms Tanner 165, fo 6ᵛ.

n.d., there are no records of any period of study at Canterbury college before he was apptd warden; see above.

1414, 12 Mar., 39th in order at the el. of an abp, *Reg. abp Chichele*, i, 4.

1421, 24 Sept., apptd general proctor by the prior and convent jointly with a secular cleric, Reg. S, fo 87–87ᵛ,

1424, 3 Oct., appted by the prior and chapter as their proctor for convocation, Reg. S, fos 90ᵛ–91.

1428, 30/31 Mar., the details of the el. proceedings are given at length in the opening folios of his register, now Oxford, Bod. Ms Tanner 165; but, despite the exemplary neatness and clarity of the script, the sequence of events remains somewhat problematical. The community gathered in the chapter house on 30 or 31 Mar., in the presence of the abp who had directed that Thomas Asshe I, q.v. should preach. The abp then proceeded with the customary scrutiny of each monk and recorded the votes. The writer of the acct noted for posterity that never before had an el. been carried out so smoothly and speedily. The following day the abp returned to the chapter house to announce the result, *ib.*, fos 4ᵛ–6ᵛ.

1433, 3 Aug., presided over the laying of the foundation of Bell Harry tower, Woodruff, *Memorials Cant.*, 270.

1438, 19 Feb., d., and the fragment of a mortuary roll sent out by the chapter to announce his death is in John Rylands University Library, Latin Ms 474 and is described by Cheney in 'Mortuary Rolls', 111–114. See also William Bonyngton II.

1438, buried in the crypt with his parents, Cambridge, Corpus Christi College Ms 298, fo 120.

Name in

(1) Oxford, Bod. Ms 648, Miscellanea (15th c.) which contains historical and medical treatises; name—prior on fo 1. See William Bolde.

(2) CCA Lit. Ms C.12, Decretales (late 14th c.); name on flyleaf.

Some of his *acta* are contained in

(1) Oxford, Bod. Ms Tanner 165 which is a collection of miscellaneous items mainly for ref. and cannot be described as a letter book. See Rouse and Mynors, *Reg. Anglie de Libris*, xxx–xxxviii.

(2) Reg. S, fos 98ᵛ–129.

He was responsible for the construction of the chapel of St Michael and 'illam partem atrii ecclesie perfecit', Cambridge, Corpus Christi College Ms 298, fo 120.

Gave a red vestment of gold cloth [embroidered] with winged beasts to Canterbury college, Pantin, *Cant. Coll. Ox.*, i, 2, 10, 29.

See the note below William Molasshe II.

II William MOLASSH [Molasche, Molosch, *alias* Goldsmith

occ. 1483 d. 1532/3

1483, 30 Sept., one of six tonsured, *SL*, 191, CCA Lit. Ms D.12, fo 8ᵛ.

1485, 2 Apr., ord subdcn, Canterbury cathedral, *Reg. abp Bourgchier*, 450.

1486, 25 Mar., ord dcn, Canterbury cathedral, *ib.*, 455.

1488/9, celebrated his first mass and recd a small gift from the sacrist, CCA DCc Sac. acct 58 and 68.

1500/1, infirmarer, CCA DCc MA10, fo 35v.
1500, 1501, 26 Apr., one of the chancellors, Reg. S, fo 435v, Reg. R, fo 56v.
1501/2, third prior, CCA DCc MA10, fo 99.
1517/18, 1520/1, 1529/30, infirmarer, Lambeth ED89, CCA DCc Infirm. acct 2, MA15, fo 163.
n.d., *magister regule*, for Robert Fonteyn, q.v., and Richard Bonyngton, q.v., Pantin, *Cant. Coll. Ox.*, iv, 54 (CCA DCc Ms Scrap Book B.186).

1493, 1 May, 45th in order at the ratification of an agreement, Reg. S, fo 383v; but see John Crosse I.
1501, 26 Apr., 29th in order at the el. of an abp, Reg. R, fo 56v.
1508, contributed 9d. to the repair of books, CCA Lit. Ms C.11, fo 103v; see William Ingram I.
1511, 2 Sept., 14th on the visitation certificate, Wood-Legh, *Visit.*, 3 (Reg. abp Warham, i, fo 35).
1532/3, d., CCA DCc Sac. acct 75.

A George and Agnes Goldsmith of Canterbury, who were members of the Christ Church confraternity left 110m. and *jocalia* to their son William Molassh, BL Ms Arundel 68, fo 46v.

I John MOLOND [Moland, *alias* Chekyr
occ. 1401 d. 1428

1401, 19 Mar., ord acol., Canterbury cathedral, Reg. abp Arundel, i, fo 327v (as Chekyr).
1401, 25 Mar., one of seven prof., *SL*, 185, CCA Lit. Ms D.12, fo 5v.
1401, 17 Dec., ord subdcn, Canterbury cathedral, Reg. abp Arundel, i, fo 329.
1403, 14 Apr., ord dcn, Canterbury cathedral, *ib.*, i, fo 331.
1406, 10 Apr., ord pr., Canterbury cathedral, *ib.*, i, fo 338.
1410/11, *custos* of the high altar, CCA DCc Prior acct 2.
1417/18, warden of manors, CCA DCc Agney acct 73.
1425/6; 1428, [31] Mar., 18 Apr., sacrist, CCA DCc Sac. acct 24; Oxford, Bod. Ms Tanner 165, fo 6v, CCA Lit. Ms D.12, fo 22v.

1414, 12 Mar., 51st in order at the el. of an abp, *Reg. abp Chichele*, i, 4.
1428, [31] Mar., one of the monks invited by the abp to dine with him after the *prefectio* of prior Molassh, q.v., Oxford, Bod. Ms Tanner 165, fo 6v.
1428, 18 Apr., d., in the 28th yr of his monastic life and was buried in the infirmary chapel in front of the altar of St Agnes, CCA Lit. Ms D.12, fo 22v and *Chron. Stone*, 14, which are virtually identical; his obit is in BL Ms Arundel 68, fo 24v.

II John MOLOND [Molande, Mullonde
occ. 1457 d. 1472

1457, 13 Dec., one of six who were clothed in the monastic habit, *Chron. Stone*, 71 (CCA Lit. Ms D.12, fo 8).
1458, 12 Feb., 'venerunt ad parvum servitium' and on 26 Feb., 'ad commune servicium', *Chron. Stone*, 71.
1458, 21 Apr., one of the same six who made their prof., *Reg. abp Bourgchier*, 368.
1459, 24 Mar., ord dcn, Canterbury cathedral, 371.
1460, 12 Apr., ord pr., Canterbury cathedral, *ib.*, 376.
1460, celebrated his first mass and recd 8d. from the chamberlain, CCA DCc Chamb. acct 65.
n.d., [1471/2], anniversarian, CCA Lit. Ms D.12, fo 26.

1466, 17 Feb., 54th in order in an inventory of *jocalia fratrum* [given by him and/or assigned for his use], and reported as having none, Reg. N, fo 234.
1471/2, d., CCA DCc Treas. acct 22; it is very prob. his obit on 10 Aug. in BL Ms Arundel 68, fo 37v. CCA Lit. Ms D.12, fo 26 has no dates.

MONDFELD
see Maghfeld

[M. William de MONDHAM
occ. 1331/2

Note: there is no evidence that this is a monk of Christ Church although *BRUO* has included him as such].

Henry de MONGEHAM [Monygham, Monyngham
occ. 1307 d. 1323

1307, 10 Aug., one of two prof., *SL*, 179, CCA Lit. Ms D.12, fo 3v.

n.d., possibly sacrist or subsacrist before 1315; see the inventory below.

1323, 16 Aug., d., CCA Lit. Ms D.12, fo 16.

In an inventory of vestments, *temp.* prior Eastry, two albs decorated with gold lions are included under his name, Legg and Hope, *Inventories*, 66 (BL Ms Cotton Galba E.iv, fo 117).

Richard de MONGEHAM [Monyngham
occ. 1341 occ. [1357]

1341, 13 Dec., one of nine prof., *SL*, 180, CCA Lit. Ms D.12, fo 4.

1349, 4 June, 54th in order at the el. of an abp, Reg. G, fo 60v.
1349, 8/9 Sept., 52nd at the el. of an abp, Reg. G, fo 76v.

[1357], named on the accts, Lambeth Ms 243, fo 104^{v}.

Stephen de MONGEHAM [Monyngham
occ. 1341 d. 1377

1376–1377, prior: el. 9 Sept. 1376, the abp personally scrutinizing the voting and on 10 Sept. he announced the result, Reg. abp Sudbury, fo 27^{v}; 14 June 1377, d., Lambeth Ms 20, fo 194 (*Fasti*, vi, 6).

1341, 13 Dec., one of nine prof., *SL*, 180, CCA Lit. Ms D.12, fo 4.

1356/7, treasurer, Lambeth Ms 1025/8.

1358/60, 1361/2, 1365/9, 1371/6, warden of manors, CCA DCc Ebony acct 58, Barksore acct 46, Borley accts 6, 7, Illeigh accts 24–26, MA2, fos 265–294^{v}; in 1361/2 he paid a supervisory visit to Lydden, Lydden acct 69.

1372/3, warden of Canterbury college, Pantin, *Cant. Coll. Ox.*, iv, 185. The first and only ref. to his appearance at Oxford is as warden of the college. In this yr [c. 1372, Dec./1373, Feb.], he served as proctor in a dispute with St Frideswide's priory, Pantin, *ib.*, iii, 27–28 (Reg. H, fo 77^{v}).

1349, 4 June, 53rd in order at the el. of an abp, Reg. G, fo 60^{v}.

1349, 8/9 Sept., 51st at the el. of an abp, Reg. G, fo 76^{v}.

1360, 3 Oct., absent from the house but cited to return for the visitation, Reg. H, fo 98.

1366, 10 May, named as one of the three initial *compromissorii* who were to choose seven *compromissorii* for the el. of an abp, Reg. G, fo 149.

1371, 3 June, with John Aleyn I, q.v., apptd as proctors to present the papal bull which required the exclusion of seculars from Canterbury college, *Lit. Cant.* no 939; see Pantin, *Cant. Coll. Ox.*, iv, 34–35.

1374, 30 June, 9th in order at the el. of an abp, Reg. G, fos 173^{v}–175^{v}.

1376, 30 Mar., obtained papal dispensation to choose his own confessor, *CPL*, iv (1362–1404), 220.

1377, 14 June, d., as above.

Stephen MONKETON [Monkenton, Monkton, Munketon, Munketone
occ. 1382 d. 1433

1382, 5 Sept., one of six who were clothed in the monastic habit, SL 183, CCA Lit. Ms D.12, fo 5.

1383, 11 Aug., the prior was comm. to rec. his prof., Reg. abp Courtenay, i, fo 42^{v}.

1397/1405, 1412/13, treasurer, CCA DCc, Bailiff of Liberty accts 8–15, Treas. accts 6, 11.

1415/19, bartoner, CCA DCc, Bart. accts 77–80.

1386/7, 1388/9, 1390/1, recd small sums from the prior, Lambeth Ms 243, fos 204^{v}, 208^{v}, 220^{v}.

1396, 7 Aug., 43rd in order at the el. of an abp, Reg. G, fo 234^{v}.

1414, 12 Mar., 13th at the el. of an abp, *Reg. abp Chichele*, i, 4.

1433, 3 Nov., d., in the 51st yr of his monastic life, 'cuius corpus propter quedam incommoda statim traditum est sepultur' ', CCA Lit. Ms D.12, fo 23^{v}.

MORIS
see Morys

MORRI, Morry
see Meri

I John MORTON
occ. 1354 d. 1361

1354, 28 Nov., one of seven prof., *SL*, 181, CCA Lit. Ms D.12, fo 4.

1356, 18 June, ord acol., Hoath chapel in Reculver parish, Reg. abp Islip, fo 316.

1356, 24 Sept., ord subdcn, abp's chapel, Tenham, *ib.*, fo 316.

1358, 22 Sept., ord dcn, Charing, *ib.*, fo 317.

1361, 7 July, d., one of c. 25 monks who were carried off [by the plague] between June and Sept., CCA Lit. Ms D.12, fo 17.

II John MORTON
occ. 1502 d. 1516/17

1502, 25 Aug., one of eight tonsured, *SL*, 193, CCA Lit. Ms D.12, fo 10.

1505, 22 Mar., ord dcn, Canterbury cathedral, Reg. abp Warham, ii, fo 262.

1507, 3 Apr., ord pr., Canterbury cathedral, *ib.*, ii, fo 263. His first celebration of mass was on the second Sun. in May when he recd 4d. from the *custos martyrii*, CCA Lit. Ms C.11, fo 49^{v}.

c. 1512, student at Canterbury college with an exhibition of 20s., Pantin, *Cant. Coll. Ox.*, ii, 272.

1511, 2 Sept., 56th in order on the visitation certificate, Wood-Legh, *Visit.*, 3 (Reg. abp Warham, i, fo 35^{v}).

1513, a John Marten recd a bequest of a silver spoon from a parishioner of St Clement's, Sandwich, Hussey, 'Kentish Wills', 43.

1516/17, d., Woodruff, 'Sacrist's Rolls', 69; the obit of a John Morton, presumably this one, occ. on 19 Aug. in BL Ms Arundel 68, fo 38^{v}.

III John MORTON
occ. 1519 occ. 1540

1519, 6 May, one of nine tonsured, *SL*, 194, CCA Lit. Ms D.12, fo 11^{v}.

1520, 3 Feb., prof., *ib.*

[1538, 8 Feb., after], *custos corone* with John Salisbury III, q.v., Pantin, *Cant. Coll. Ox.*, iii, 152.

1534, 12 Dec., acknowledged the Act of Supremacy, *DK 7th Report*, Appndx 2, 282.

[1538, 8 Feb., after], in a list of monks prob. prepared for Thomas Cromwell, he was described as a 'good man', 38 yrs old, Pantin, *Cant. Coll. Ox.*, iii, 152.

1540, 4 Apr., awarded £6 p.a., *L and P Henry VIII*, xv, no 452.

Richard MORYS [Moris

occ. 1367 occ. 1374

1367, 11 Nov., one of nine prof., *SL*, 182, CCA Lit. Ms D.12, fo 4ᵛ.

1369, 22 Dec., ord subdcn, abp's chapel, Charing, Reg. abp Wittlesey, fo 165ᵛ.

1370, 21 Sept., ord dcn, Saltwood, *ib.*, fo 166ᵛ.

1371, 20 Dec., ord pr., abp's chapel, Otford, *ib.*, fo 168.

1374, 30 June, 52nd in order at the el. of an abp, Reg. G, fos 173ᵛ–175ᵛ.

I MOSES [Moyses

occ. [1089 × 1092]

[1089 × 1092], described by abbot Anselm in a letter to prior Henry, q.v., as having taken refuge at Bec, *Anselm Letters*, no 140, and as being anxious to return to Canterbury, *ib.*, no 141; this latter was addressed to Gundulf, bp of Rochester, and requested his aid.

Note: the obit of a Moses occ. on 1 Aug. in BL Ms Arundel 68, fo 36ᵛ.

II MOSES [Moises, Moyses

occ. 1183

1183, Jan., chaplain to abp Richard de Dover, q.v., and so prob. a monk of Canterbury; he was el. prior of Coventry in Jan. of this yr, *HRH*, 41. See under Coventry.

His obit on 16 July was remembered at Canterbury, BL Ms Arundel 68, fo 34ᵛ.

Henry MOTH [*dictus* Moht, Mot

occ. [1284] d. 1314

[1283, Sept., a Henry Mot, ord subdcn, Faversham, 'ad titulum patrimonii ut affidenter testatur quod habet sexaginta solidatas et amplius redditus infra libertates domini in suburbis Cantuarie', *Reg. abp Pecham*, i, 205].

[1284], one of four prof., *SL*, 177, CCA Lit. Ms D.12, fo 3.

1301/2, granator, CCA DCc MA1, fos 231ᵛ–237ᵛ.

1305/6, 1307/8, warden of manors, CCA DCc Ebony acct 21, Agney acct 23.

1311, 26 Sept./17 Oct., bartoner, CCA DCc Bart. acct 3.

1307, 11 Mar., with Richard de Clyve, q.v., recd a *procuratorium generale* from the prior and chapter, CUL Ms Ee.5.31, fo 106.

1312, 3 Jan., described as *reprobat[us]* by the subprior and convent who dissociated themselves from any appeals in which he was or might become involved, CUL Ms Ee.v.31, fo 118.

1314, 12 May, d., CCA Lit. Ms D.12, fo 15ᵛ.

An inventory of missing books dated 1 Mar. 1338 includes the Instituta of Peter Lombard for which he was held responsible, *Lit. Cant.*, no 618 (Reg. L, fo 104).

Note: see Henry de Bello who may be the same monk.

MOYRI

see Meri

Stephen de MULIETU

n.d.

n.d., 4 Nov., obit occ. in BL Ms Arundel 68, fo 47.

MULLOND

see Molond

MUNDEFELDE

see Maghfeld

MUNKETON(E)

see Monketon

MURRI, MURRY

see Meri

John de MYDDYLTON [Middleton, Midilton

occ. 1346 d. 1361

1346, 11 Nov., one of eight prof., *SL*, 181, CCA Lit. Ms D.12, fo 4.

1350, 18 Sept., ord pr., Goudhurst, Reg. abp Islip, fo 310.

1361, 13 Aug., d., one of c. 25 monks carried off [by the plague] between June and Oct., CCA Lit. Ms D.12, fo 17.

I Thomas de MYDDYLTON [Middeltone, Midilton

occ. [1284] d. 1323

[1284], n.d., one of four prof., *SL*, CCA Lit. Ms D.12, fo 3.

1299, granator, CAC DCc MA1, fo 222.

1307/11, 1312, July/1314, warden of manors, CCA DCc Agney accts 23, 24, 26–28, Loose acct 29, Agney acct 29.

1314, Mar./Sept., 1315/17, Nov., bartoner, CCA DCc Bart. acct 5, MA2, fos 52–88ᵛ, Bart. accts 6–8.

1319, sacrist, CCA DCc MA2, fo 97; he was sacrist until 28 June this yr, CCA DCc EC V/33.

[1296], included among the juniors whom the abp found to be lax in attendance at divine office and in the performance of other monastic duties, *Reg. abp Winchelsey*, 92.

1308, 6 July, with Richard de Clyve, comm. by the prior and chapter to collect tithes in the parish of Halstow, CUL Ms Ee.5.31, fo 111.

1323, 26 Nov., d., CCA Lit. Ms D.12, fo 16.

A list of missing service books, dated 1 Mar. 1338, includes a diurnal and a psalter for which he was held responsible, *Lit. Cant.* no 618 (Reg. L, fo 104).

In an inventory of vestments, acquired *temp.* prior Eastry, his name heads a short list of vestments, Legg and Hope, *Inventories*, 66 (BL Ms Cotton Galba E.iv, fo 117).

II Thomas MYDDYLTON [Middelton, Middilton, Middleton, Midilton
occ. 1399 d. 1415/16

1399, a former monk of Bermondsey who with John Stanys, q.v., came to Christ Church where they were prof. with four others, *SL*, 185, CCA Lit. Ms D.12, fo 5v.
1400, 3 Apr., ord subdcn, Hoath chapel in Reculver parish, Reg. abp Arundel, i, fo 325.
1401, 2 Apr., ord dcn, Canterbury cathedral, *ib.*, i, fo 328.
1405, 18 Apr., ord pr., Canterbury cathedral, *ib.*, i, fo 334.
1414, 12 Mar., 49th in order at the el. of an abp, *Reg. abp Chichele*, i, 4.
1416, 31 Mar., d., in the fifteenth yr of his monastic life; he was at this time 'primus in inferiori choro', *Chron. Stone*, 7, who has dated his d. a yr later than CCA Lit. Ms D.12, fo 20v.

MYLTON
see Milton

MYNS(E)
see Menys

NALE
see Robert Menys

Henry de NATYNDON [Natindon
occ. 1314 d. 1354

1314, 13 Dec., one of five prof., *SL*, 179, CCA Lit. Ms D.12, fo 3v.
1315, 20 Dec., ord acol., Maidstone, Reg. abp Reynolds, fo 173.
1317, 28 May, ord subdcn, Lambeth palace chapel, Reg. abp Reynolds, fo 176v.
1330/1, treasurer, CCA DCc MA2, fo 199.
1332/3, warden of manors, CCA DCc MA2, fos 209–219.
1334/5, chaplain to the prior, and feretrar, CCA DCc Brook acct 18, MA2, fos 231–241; he may possibly have moved from one office to the other during the yr or he may have held both offices, see also CCA DCc DE3, fos 3, 6v.
1335/6, treasurer, and chaplain to the prior, CCA DCc MA2, fos 248, 241v–250v; see note in the entry above.
1337/8, 1339/40, 1341, Feb./Sept., 1341/5, 1346/50, warden of manors, CCA DCc West Farleigh acct 43, Agney acct 43, Great Chart acct 46, Agney accts 44, 45, Great Chart acct 49, Agney accts 46, 47, Ebony acct 49, Adisham accts 24, 25.
1352, June/Sept., granator, CCA DCc Gran. acct 35.
1348, 30 Aug., named by the three initial *compromissorii* as one of seven *compromissorii* in the el. of an abp, Reg. G, fos 30v, 82.
1349, 4 June, 11th in order at the el. of an abp, and named as one of thirteen *compromissorii*, *ib.*, fo 60v.
1349, 8/9 Sept., again 11th and again chosen as one of thirteen *compromissorii*, *ib.* ,fos 76, 77.
1354, 26 Dec., d., CCA Lit. Ms D.12, fo 16v.

A missal which he may have given to Canterbury college turns up in 15th and 16th c. inventories there, Pantin, *Cant. Coll. Ox.*, i, 12, 30, 52, 58.

Vincent de NATYNDON
occ. 1st half 13th c.
n.d., name occ. in the *post exilium* list in *SL*, 179, CCA Lit. Ms D.12, fo 1v.

NEIREFORD
see Neyrford

NEUSOLE
see Newsole

Roger NEVYLE
occ. 1st half 13th c.

n.d., name occ. in the *post exilium* list in *SL*, 174, CCA Lit. Ms D.12, fo 1v.

I John NEWBERY [Neubery, Newbury, Nwbyry
occ. [1429] d. [c. 1480]

[1429, summer], ord acol. and subdcn, place not given, Reg. Langdon (Rochester), fo 74.
1430, 4 Apr., one of four prof., *SL*, 187, CCA Lit. Ms D.12, fo 7.
1430, 23 Dec., ord acol., bp's chapel, Trottiscliffe, Reg. Langdon (Rochester), fo 72x.
Note: Langdon's register is in a state of confusion here.
1433, 28 Mar., ord pr., Charing, *Reg. abp Chichele*, iv, 378.
1439, 7 Jan. one of several monks licensed to leave the priory *pro recreacione*, and he returned on 20 Jan., Chron. Wm Glastynbury, fo 182v/177v.
[1457, before 26 Aug.], sent with John Newton, q.v. to Salisbury to attend the translation of St Osmund, *Chron. Stone*, 71.
1466, 17 Feb., 17th in order in an inventory of *jocalia fratrum*, [given by him and/or assigned for his use], Reg. N, fo 231.
[c. 1480], *stationarius*, d., CCA Lit. Ms D.12, fo 26; the obit of a John Newbery occ. on 18 Jan., in BL Ms Arundel 68, fo 13v.

II John NEWBERY
occ. 1493

1493, 26 July, one of ten tonsured, *SL*, 192, CCA Lit. Ms D.12, fo 9v, which adds *recessit ante professionem*.

See John Norbury who is no doubt the same monk.

III John NEWBERY [Newberye
occ. 1500 occ. 1540

1500, 28 July, one of eight tonsured, *SL*, 193, CCA Lit. Ms D.12, fo 10; each of these novices recd a gold noble worth 6s. 8d. for their labours with regard to the funeral of abp Morton, who d. c. 15 Sept. 1500, CCA Lit. Ms D.12, *ib.*
1501, 19 Apr., made his prof. before the prior, *sed. vac.*, *ib.*
1506, 11 Apr., ord pr., Canterbury cathedral, Reg. abp Warham, ii, fo 262v; he recd 4d. from the *custos martyrii* after celebrating his first mass on the fourth Sun. of this month, CCA Lit. Ms C.11, fo 48v.

1515, 1516, both on 25 Dec; 1520, 1521, 1523, 1524, all on 25 Mar., feretrar, CCA Lit. Ms C.11, fos 57v, 58, 60v; 61, 62, 63.
1523/5, granator, CCA DCc MA14, fos 250, 282v.
1526, 1527, 1528, 1529 (25 Dec.), 1532, all but 1529 on 25 Mar., treasurer, CCA Lit. Ms C.11, fos 64, 64v, 65, 66, 67.
[1538, 8 Feb. after], 1540, 4 Apr., treasurer, Pantin, *Cant. Coll. Ox.*, iii, 152, *L and P Henry VIII*, xv, no 452.

1501, 26 Apr., 68th in order at the el. of an abp, Reg. R, fo 56v.
1511, 2 Sept., 47th on the visitation certificate, Wood-Legh, *Visit.*, 3 (Reg. abp Warham, i, fo 35v).
1534, 12 Dec., acknowledged the Act of Supremacy, *DK 7th Report*, Appndx 2, 282.
[1538, 8 Feb., after], in a list of monks prob. drawn up for Thomas Cromwell he was described as a 'good man' ['symple' crossed out] and 56 yrs old, Pantin, *Cant. Coll. Ox.*, iii, 152.
1540, 4 Apr., became a petty canon in the new foundation, *L and P Henry VIII*, xv, no 452.

NEWENDEN
see Newynden

NEWENHAM, Newnham
see Newynham

I Thomas de NEWSOLE [Neusole, Newesol
occ. 1235/6

n.d., name occ. in the *post exilium* list in *SL*, 173, CCA Lit. Ms D.12, fo 1v.
1235/6, granator, CCA DCc, AS4.

See the entry below.

II Thomas de NEWSOLE [Newesole
n.d.

n.d., acol., d., on whose anniversary on 1 Dec. the almoner was required to spend 30s. for *refectio* for the convent and 10s. for the poor; every pr. was to sing one mass and the other monks to recite the psalms, BL Ms Arundel 68, fo 50.

Note: an inventory of the refectory dated 1328 includes a *ciphus de murra* [formerly] belonging to a Thomas Newsole, Dart, *Antiq. Cant.*, xxi (BL Ms Cotton Galba E.iv, fo 179).

John NEWTON [Neweton, Newynton, Nutun, Nwtun
occ. 1428 d. 1457

1428, 2 Jan., one of six prof., *SL*, 187, CCA Lit. Ms D.12, fo 7.
[1432], 11 June, ord pr., place not given, Reg. Langdon (Rochester), fo 74v.

1435, subalmoner, 'Chron. Wm Glastynbury', 130 (Ms fo 116v).
1440, 17 Feb., *magister regule* for William Chart II, q.v., Pantin, *Cant. Coll. Ox.*, iv, 53 (Chron. Wm Glastynbury, fo 119).
[1440], 31 Oct., apptd subalmoner, in place of Richard Burden, q.v., Chron Wm Glastynbury, fo 119v.
1443/4, fourth prior, CCA DCc, Sac. acct 31.
1444, 21 Dec., *magister ordinis*, *SL*, 188, CCA Lit. Ms D.12, fo 7v.
1449, 26 Apr., apptd penitentiary, Reg. abp Stafford, fo 32v, and he was penitentiary at the time of d., CCA Lit. Ms D.12, fo 26.
n.d., *magister mense*, *Chron. Stone*, 71.
1448/9, possibly granted a brief stay at Canterbury college under Richard Gravene q.v., Pantin, *Cant. Coll. Ox.*, ii, 173, but the ref. may be to another John Newton not a monk.

1439, 20 Jan., one of several monks licensed to leave the priory *pro recreacione*, and he returned on 31 Jan., Chron. Wm Glastynbury, fo 182v/177v.
1440, 17 Feb., 'proclaimed' William Chart II, q.v., for his examination, Chron. Wm Glastynbury, fo 119.
[1457, before 26 Aug.], with John Newbery I, q.v., sent to Salisbury to attend the translation of St Osmond, *Chron. Stone*, 71.
1457, 26 Aug., d., in his 40th yr of monastic life acc. to *Chron. Stone*, 71, but see above.

Henry NEWYNDEN [Nwynden
occ. 1417 occ. [1435]

1417, 13 Dec., one of five [?clothed/professed] in the monastic habit, *SL*, 186, CCA Lit. Ms D.12, fo 6v; see John Stone I.

1418, 26 Mar., ord acol., Canterbury cathedral, *Reg. abp Chichele*, iv, 332.
1420, 6 Apr., ord subdcn, Canterbury cathedral, *ib.*, iv, 341.
1424, 22 Apr., ord pr., Canterbury cathedral, *ib.*, iv, 360.
[1435], one of the chancellors, 'Chron. Wm Glastynbury', 129 (Ms fo 116v).
n.d., given a *littera migratoria* by the abp and the prior and convent, Reg. S, fo 141.

There is a lengthy note in *SL*, 186, CCA Lit. Ms D.12, fo 6v, summarizing his fall from grace, which was all the more regrettable in that he was 'persona decens et pulcher facie, multum eloquens, hilaris et affabilis'. He served in a number of offices until a certain calamity led him to choose to depart, and the abp and the prior and chapter arranged for him to transfer to the priory of Totnes. The expulsions of Stephen Tygh and Nicholas Westgate, q.v., are attributed here to his false accusations against them.

Robert de NEWYNDEN [Newendenn
occ. 1298 d. 1337

1298, 18 Oct., one of seven prof., *SL*, 178, CCA Lit. Ms D.12, fo 3.
1299, 19 Sept., ord dcn, Littlebourne, *Reg. abp Winchelsey*, 930.
1300, 4 June, ord dcn, Smeeth chapel by Aldington, *ib.*, 935.
Note: the first ord above should prob. be taken as that of subdcn.
1337, 10 June, d., CCA Lit. Ms D.12, fo 16v.

NEWYNDEN
see also Newynton

James NEWYNHAM [Newenhame, Newnham, Newnam, ?*alias* Piers, q.v.
occ. 1527 occ. 1540

1527, 25 May, one of twelve tonsured, *SL*, 195, CCA Lit. Ms D.12, fo 12.
1528, 2 Mar., prof., *ib.*
[1538, 8 Feb., after], one of four subsacrists, [*parvi sacriste*], Pantin, *Cant. Coll. Ox.*, iii, 153.
1534, 12 Dec., acknowledged the Act of Supremacy, *DK 7th Report*, Appndx 2, 282.
[1538, 8 Feb., after], in a list of monks prob. prepared for Thomas Cromwell, he was described as a 'good man', 29 yrs old, Pantin, *Cant. Coll. Ox.*, iii, 153.
1540, 4 Apr., became a scholar in the new foundation, *L and P Henry VIII*, xv, no 452.

See James Piers.

John NEWYNHAM [Neunenam, Newenham, Newnam
occ. 1428 d. 1439

1428, 2 Jan., one of six prof., *SL*, 187, CCA Lit. Ms D.12, fo 7.
[1429, summer], ord acol. and subdcn, place not given, Reg. Langdon (Rochester), fo 74.
1434, 13 Mar., ord pr., infirmary chapel, *Reg. abp Chichele*, iv, 379.
1435, 14 July, apptd refectorer while still *parvus sacrista*, Chron. Wm Glastynbury, fo 117. On 24 Oct. of this yr he was absolved from the latter office, *ib.*, fo 117v.
1439, before 17 Aug., *adiunctus* treasurer, CCA Lit. Ms D.12, fo 24.
1439, 17 Aug., d., in the tenth yr of his monastic life, CCA Lit. Ms D.12, fo 24; *Chron. Stone*, 25; his obit is in BL Ms Arundel 68, fo 38v.

Laurence NEWYNHAM [Neuham, Newman, Newnam, Newnham, Nunam, *alias* Ambrose
occ. 1511 occ. 1521/2

1511, 1 Sept., one of eight tonsured, *SL*, 194, CCA Lit. Ms D.12, fo 11.
1512, 19 Apr., prof., *ib.*
1513, 26 Mar., ord subdcn, Canterbury cathedral, Reg. abp Warham, ii, fo 266v.
1518/19, student at Canterbury college for whom travelling expenses to Oxford were pd, Pantin, *Cant. Coll. Ox.*, iv, 206.
1521/2, student at Canterbury college, provided with a pension of £6 10s., Pantin, *ib.*, ii, 258 (CCA DCc Cart. Antiq. O.151.46).
1511, 2 Sept., 76th in order on the visitation certificate, novice and not prof., Wood-Legh, *Visit.*, 3 and not prof. (Reg. abp Warham, i, fo 35v).
[c. 1511 × 1514], in a report on the behaviour of some monks he was noted as being one of those whose *magister regule* was Thomas Goldstone V, q.v., 'et non perfecerunt, et non est mirium, quia non vult accipere labores', Pantin, *Cant. Coll. Ox.*, iii, 143 (CCA DCc Ms Scrap Book B.193).
n.d., the above entry fits in with another scrap of information to the effect that Thomas Goldston had four young monks in his care of whom Laurence was one, Pantin, *ib.*, iv, 54 (CCA DCc Ms Scrap Book B.186).
n.d., 25 Dec., obit in BL Ms Arundel 68, fo 52.

His brothers John Ambrose senior, John Ambrose junior and Thomas Ambrose, along with several sisters, were recd into confraternity with Christ Church in 1525, BL Ms Arundel 68, fo 11v.

I Richard NEWYNHAM [Newinham
occ. [1461] d. 1485

1461, 4 Apr., ord subdcn, Canterbury cathedral, *Reg. abp Bourgchier*, 377.
[1461], 19 Apr., one of six prof., *SL*, 189, CCA Lit. Ms D.12, fo 8.
1462, 17 Apr., ord dcn, Canterbury cathedral, *Reg. abp Bourgchier*, 381.

1464, 31 Mar., ord pr., Canterbury cathedral, *ib.*, 390.
1463/4, celebrated his first mass and recd a small gift from the sacrist, CCA DCc Sac. acct 44.
1472/3; 1474, 29 Sept.; 1475, Apr.; 1476, Apr., 29 Sept.; 1477, Apr., 29 Sept., warden of manors, CCA DCc MA160, Monk Warden acct 4; Monk Warden acct 5; Monk Warden acct 6; Monk Warden accts 8, 9; Monk Warden accts 10, 11.
1466, 17 Feb., 67th in order in an inventory of *jocalia fratrum*, [given by him and/or assigned for his use], Reg. N, fo 234v.
1485, Oct./Nov., one of nine who d. of 'le Swete' within sixteen days, CCA Lit. Ms D.12, fo 26v; see Nicholas Herst I.

II Richard NEWYNHAM [Newname
occ. 1500 d. 1502

1500, 28 July, one of eight tonsured, *SL*, 193, CCA Lit. Ms D.12, fo 10; each of these novices recd a gold noble worth 6s. 8d., for their labours with regard to the funeral of abp Morton, who d. c. 15 Sept. 1500, CCA Lit. Ms D.12, *ib*.
1501, 19 Apr., made his prof. before the prior, *sed. vac.*, *ib*.
1501, 26 Apr., 66th in order at the el. of an abp, Reg. R, fo 56.
1502, 25 Sept., subdcn, d., *ex consumpcione*, at the age of 20, CCA Lit. Ms D.12, fo 33v; his obit on 27 Sept. is in BL Ms Arundel 68, fo 43.

Robert NEWYNTON [Newenton, Newnton, Newton
occ. 1475 d. 1497

1476, 27 Mar., one of four prof., *SL*, 191, CCA Lit. Ms D.12, fo 8v.
1475, 23 Sept., ord subdcn, prior's chapel, Canterbury, *Reg. abp Bourgchier*, 418.
1476, 21 Sept., ord dcn, Canterbury cathedral, *ib.*, 421.
1497, before 13 Apr., feretrar, CCA Lit. Ms D.12, fo 27v.
1493, 1 May, 32nd in order at the ratification of an agreement, Reg. S, fo 383v; but see John Crosse I.
1497, 13 Apr., d., *ex paralysi*, CCA Lit. Ms D.12, fo 27v; his obit on 15 Apr. is in BL Ms Arundel 68, fo 24.

William NEYRFORD [Neireford, Neyford, Neyreford
occ. 1251 occ. 1257

n.d., name occ. in the list in *SL*, 174, CCA Lit. Ms D.12, fo 1v.
1251/7, granator *exterior*, Reg. H, fos 174, 176v, 179, 182, 185, 186, 187.
n.d., 17 Mar., obit occ. in BL Ms Arundel 68, fo 20v.

One item in the Eastry catalogue is listed under his name: 'Bibblia. In hoc vol. cont: Interpretaciones Ebraicorum nominum', James, *Ancient Libraries*, no 520 (p. 62).

In an inventory of missing service books dated 1 Mar. 1338, his Processionale had been charged out to William de Cantuaria, q.v., *Lit. Cant.*, no 618 (Reg. L, fo 104).

In an inventory of vestments, *temp.* prior Eastry, his name is attached to a cope of red samite, BL Ms Cotton Galba E.iv, fo 113.

An inventory of the refectory, dated 1328, includes a silver *ciphus* formerly his, Dart, *Antiq. Cant.*, xix (BL Ms Cotton Galba E.iv, fos 178).

I NICHOLAS
occ. [1198] occ. 1207

1207, cellarer, CCA DCc MA1, fo 59v.
[1198, Jan.], with S[imon, q.v.] set out for Rome without licence because they believed that the future of the house was at stake and the prior [Geoffrey II, q.v.] (in Gervase's words) had grown lukewarm during the prolonged dispute with the abp; they wrote from Rome to say that they had made their appeal to the pope, *Epist. Cant.*, 377, *Gervase Cant.*, i, 551. They wrote again to say that the pope had recd their letter on 17 Apr., *Epist. Cant.*, 390 and he had given judgement in the chapter's favour. on their return they were excommunicated by the abp because they had gone to the curia without his licence, *Gervase Cant.*, I, 551–552.

Note:
(1) it is possible that the Nicholas who went to Rome may not have later been cellarer. See also the note below Nicholas II.
(2) a schedule of cathedral holdings in Canterbury, dated c. 1206 ref. to John the brother of Nicholas, monk, Urry, *Canterbury*, 350. It may be the same monk who is reported in a rental of about the same date as having bought a wood at Blean, *ib.*, 379.

II NICHOLAS
occ. 1235 occ. 1242

1235, 1238, 1242, chaplain to the prior, CCA DCc MA1 fos 78, 80, 83v.

Note:
(1) Nicholas de Sandwich I, q.v., and Nicholas de Mallyng, q.v., were alive in this period and one or both may be referred to here.
(2) the obit of a Nicholas pr., occ. on 14 Jan. in BL Ms Arundel 68, fo 13.

NICHOLAS
see also Nicholas II under Worcester

NIGEL
n.d.

Note: there are obits for two monks by this name in BL Ms Arundel 68:
(1) 14 Apr. (fo 24).
(2) 13 Aug. (fo 38), this one a pr.

See also Wireker.

Thomas de NONYNTON [?Novynton
n.d.

n.d., 14 Apr., obit occ. in BL Ms Arundel 68, fo 24.

John NORBURY
occ. 1494

1494, 29 Mar., ord acol., Canterbury cathedral, *Reg. abp Morton*, i, no 443.

Note: this is John Newbery II, q.v., who left within a few wks of this ordination.

NORGATE
see Northgate

NORMAN [Normanns
occ. 1089 occ. [1096 × 1102]

1089, assisted Wido, q.v., in quelling the rebellious monks of St Augustine's, 'Acta Lanfranci', 291–292. See also B. Thorpe, ed., *The Anglo-Saxon Chronicle*, Rolls Series, i (1861), 389.

Note:
(1) [1096 × 1102], abp Anselm wrote to Gervinus, bp of Amiens about 'ille Normannus ecclesiae nostrae professus', who had gone overseas without his knowledge and been el. abbot; Anselm now ordered his return, refusing his consent to the election, *Anselm Letters*, no 187. The date is determined by the abp's election and the d. of the bp of Amiens.
(2) there are obits for two monks of this name in BL Ms Cotton Nero C.ix, on 20 Mar. and 24 Mar. on fo 8, and also in Lambeth Ms 20 on the same days, fos 174 and 175 respectively.

I Roger NORREYS [Noreys, Norreis, Norys
occ. 1187 occ. 1190

1189, Oct./Nov., prior: 6 Oct. 1189, apptd by the abp; 30 Nov., removed because of the monks' protests, *Fasti*, ii, 10, *HRH*, 34; see Osbern de Bristol.

n.d., chaplain to the abp. He was so addressed in a letter written to him by a canon of Cirencester, CCA Lit. Ms B.13, insert between fos 67v and 68.

1187, 28 Aug., apptd cellarer by the abp after deposing the current holder of the office and vs the wishes of the prior and chapter, *Gervase Cant.*, i, 380–381 where he is described by Gervase as *aetate juniorem*; he was cellarer in Oct. 1189 at the time of his apptment as prior, *ib.* See also *Epist. Cant.*, 92. The abp later reported that the monks had deposed and imprisoned him, *ib.* 291.

1187, Sept./Oct., the monks on the continent, pursuing their appeal, were told to report, if required, [to the king or abp] that he was ill and confined to the monastic infirmary, *Epist. Cant.*, 98; see Honorius II.

1188, Jan., left the convent under cover of darkness through the sewer [*per cloacam*] and fled to abp Baldwin at Otford to whom, acc. to Gervase I q.v., he revealed the chapter's secrets, *Gervase Cant.*, i, 404.

1189, 5/8 Nov., one of the party of monks sent to London to confer with the king re the dispute with the abp, Epist. Cant, 315.

1189, after 14 Nov., the convent listed him, with no title or office, as one of the party whom they sent to the king and whose deposition they demanded, *Epist. Cant.*, 315–316.

Note: this may be a ref. to Roger Norreys II below, q.v.

1190, before 6 Mar., apptd abbot of Evesham, *HRH*, 48.

His apptment as prior and removal are recorded in great detail by Gervase who speaks without restraint: 'ab adolescentia monachatus sui superbus, elatus, pomposus in verbis, dolosus in factis, cupidus praelationis . . . ad superiores adulator, ad inferiores contemptor . . . incorrigibilis', *Gervase Cant.*, i, 382 (for the quotation), 460, 465, 475, 477, 481 (for the other details).

Name in CCA Lit. Ms B.13 Sermones (early 13th c.) on fo 1; this may be no 1107 in the Eastry catalogue, James, *Ancient Libraries*, 102.

Note: The Eastry catalogue contains an uncertain number of books listed under the name Roger Noreis, James, *Ancient Libraries*, nos 1100–?1110 (p. 102), and assumes that these belonged to Norreys I.

II Roger NORREYS [Norys
occ. [1207 × 1214]

[1207 × 1214], name occ. in the list of those who were in exile, SL 172, CCA Lit. Ms D.12, fo 1.

See notes under Roger Norreys I above.

I John de NORTHBORNE [Northbourn
occ. 1346 d. 1360/1

1346, 11 Nov., one of eight prof., *SL*, 181, CCA Lit. Ms D.12, fo 4.

1350, 18 Sept., ord pr., Goudhurst, Reg. abp Islip, fo 310.

1349/50, chancellor with Thomas de Tilmerstone, q.v., Reg. H, fo 35 ((*Hist. Mss Comm. 8th Report*, Appndx, 341).

1359/60, anniversarian, CCA DCc Anniv. acct 5.

1360/1, d., most prob. c. 25 Apr. 1360; CCA Lit. Ms D.12, fo 17 has 27 Feb. 1361, but there is confusion about the order of entries here and it looks as though 29 Apr. 1360 was intended; the obit in BL Ms Arundel 68, fo 24 is 25 Apr.

II John de NORTHBORNE
occ. 1365/6

1365, one of eight prof., *SL*, 182, CCA Lit. Ms D.12, fo 4v.

1366, 10 May, present at the el. of an abp, Reg. G, fo 147.

John de NORTHFLETE
occ. before 1248 occ. 1263/4

n.d., name occ. in the list in *SL*, 174, CCA Lit. Ms D.12, fo 1v.

1248/51, apptd prior of Dover by the abp after 30 June 1248, Lambeth Ms 241, fo 30v, suspended briefly in 1250 and then restored, but res. in 1251, *ib*.

1262/4, almoner, CCA DCc Eastry acct 2, Godmersham acct 1.

Henry NORTHGATE [Norgate
occ. 1470 occ. 1521

1470, 25 Jan, one of eight prof., *SL*, 190, CCA Lit. Ms D.12, fo 8.

1470, 21 Apr., ord acol., Canterbury cathedral, *Reg. abp Bourgchier*, 405.

1471, 9 Mar., ord subdcn, Canterbury cathedral, *Reg. abp Bourgchier*, 404.

1474, 26 Mar., ord dcn, Canterbury cathedral, *ib*., 417.

1478, 7 Mar., ord pr., Canterbury cathedral, *ib*., 426.

1496/7, anniversarian, Lambeth ED 45.

1518/20, 1521, 25 Mar., bartoner, CCA DCc MA14, fos 74, 108A, CCA Lit. Ms C.11, fo 61.

1493, 1 May, 30th in order at the ratification of an agreement, Reg. S, fo 383v; but see John Crosse I.

1501, 26 Apr., 18th in order at the el. of an abp, Reg. R, fo 56v.

1511, 2 Sept., 6th on the visitation certificate, Wood-Legh, *Visit.*, 3 (Reg. abp Warham, i, fo 35).

1516, Sept./Dec., William Ingram I, q.v., paid 12d. *pro capicio* for him, CCA Lit. Ms C.11, fo 127v.

NORTHWEDE
see Laurence II

Walter de NORWYCO [Northwico, Northwyco
occ. 1289 d. 1328

1289, 19 Dec., one of eight prof., *SL*, 177, CCA Lit. Ms D.12, fo 3.

1302/3, granator, CCA DCc MA1, fos 240v–244v.

1304/6, warden of manors, CCA DCc Lalling acct 4, Middleton acct 21.

1305/6, 1309/10, 1312/13, subprior, CCA DCc Cliffe acct 23, Cheam acct 26, Barksore acct 19. His apptment is in Reg. Q, fo 31/43 on 1 May 1306.

1314/21, cellarer, CCA DCc MA2, fos 52v–112; he was already cellarer in July 1314, CUL Ms Ee.5.31, fo 147v; and at the request of the prior and convent he was released from office on 12 Jan. 1321, Reg. abp Reynolds, fo 100.

1320/1, 1323/8, warden of manors, CCA DCc Illeigh acct 5, MA2, fos 126–182; see below.

1300, 28 Dec., apptd proctor to represent the prior and chapter in all courts of justice, CUL Ms Ee.5.31, fo 84v.

1314, 28 July, with Geoffrey de Poterel, q.v., involved in the negotiations concerning the abp of York's right to carry his staff in the province of Canterbury, CUL Ms Ee.5.31, fo 147–147v; on 21 Aug. they were sent as proctors to the king in this matter, *ib*., fo 147v.

1314, Aug., apptd proctor to attend parliament, *Parl. Writs*, ii, pt 2, 128.

1316, 1 Apr., sent with Stephen de Feversham II, q.v., to inform the abp of the state of affairs concerning Robert de Thaneto, q.v., *ib*., fo 165.

1319, 10 Apr., with John de Maldon, q.v., carried letters from the prior and chapter to the king and to the duke of Lancaster concerning the disputed claims over Dover priory, CUL Ms Ee.5..31, fo 200.

1320/1, Thomas de Hemenhale, q.v., the master of the cellar at Norwich cathedral priory, gave 10s. 6d. in donations to members of his *familia*, NRO DCN 1/1/28.

1325, 26 Feb., apptd proctor for the prior and chapter over the appropriation of the church of Aysshe in Norwich diocese, CUL Ms Ee.5.31, fos 246–246v, 260.

1327, [Nov.], with Simon de St Peter, q.v., sent by the prior and chapter to the king for licence to el. an abp, Lambeth Ms 243, fo 5.

1328, 28 Oct., d., CCA Lit. Ms D.12, fo 16.

Name in CCA Lit. Ms B.9, W. Northwicensis (13th/14th c.), a Latin commentary on Isaiah.

Some nineteen volumes are entered under his name in the Eastry catalogue including works of Aristotle, Peter Lombard, and Aquinas, and several law books, James, *Ancient Libraries*, nos 1804–1822 (p. 141); one of these, his Digestum vetus, turns up in 15th c. inventories of Canterbury college, Pantin, *Cant. Coll. Ox.*, i, 6, 14. Veritas theologica, which he had borrowed, was reported missing in 1338; see John de Hardys.

An inventory of vestments, acquired *temp.* prior Eastry, includes six sets under his name, Legg and Hope, *Inventories*, 64, 68 (BL Ms Cotton Galba E.iv, fos 116ᵛ, 118ᵛ. His name is also attached to a silver gilt chalice and paten and two silver cruets in a similar inventory, Legg and Hope, *Inventories*, 70, 73 (BL Ms Cotton Galba E.vi, fos 119, 120ᵛ).

An inventory of the refectory, dated 1328, includes five silver *ciphi*, three *de murra*, and twelve spoons, Dart, *Antiq. Cant.*, xx, xxiii (BL Ms Cotton Galba E.iv, fos 179, 180ᵛ).

NORYS
see Norreys

NOTWOLD
see Stodwold

Ralph de NOTYNGHAM
d. [1289]

n.d., name occ. in the list in *SL*, 175, CCA Lit. Ms D.12, fo 2ᵛ.

[1289], 10 Nov., d., CCA Lit. Ms D.12, fo 15.

NUTUN
see Newton

NWBYRY
see Newbery

NWTUN
see Newton

O.
occ. 1265

1265, subcellarer, CCA DCc MA1, fo 107ᵛ.

H. de O.
occ. [1285 × 1331]

[1285 × 1331], occ. *temp.* prior Eastry in BL Add. Ms 6159, fo 97.

Thomas ODIAN
see Langdon

I ODO
occ. [1093 × 1109]

[1093 × 1109], with Lanzo, q.v., recd a letter from abp Anselm before becoming monks, *Anselm Letters*, no 2.

Note: this may not be a monk, but with Lanzo, q.v., he was urged by Anselm to enter [Christ Church], *Anselm Letters*, no 95.

II ODO
occ. [1164 × 1167] occ. 1175

1168/9 to 1175, prior: prob. el. between 16 May 1168 and Oct./Nov. 1169; 10 July 1175 el. abbot of Battle, *Fasti*, ii, 10, *HRH*, 29.

1163; 1168, before, subprior, *Materials Becket*, v, no 27; *Fasti*, ii, 10.

1163, appted as his proctor by the abp in an appeal to the pope vs the abp of York, *Materials Becket*, v, no 27.

1172, as a candidate for the abpric, vacant after Becket's murder, he went to Normandy and stood up to the king by demanding that the latter consult the monks over the apptment. He refused to el. the bp of Bayeux, the king's choice; but after protracted negotiations, during which he upheld the chapter's right to free el., he finally agreed on Richard de Dover, q.v., *Gervase Cant.*, i, 240–245. See also Foreville, *Église et Royauté*, 373–377.

1200, d., *HRH*, 29.

There are two letters to him from John of Salisbury:

(1) [1164 × 1167], to prior Wibert, q.v. and Odo, *Salisbury Letters*, ii, no 205.

(2) [1174/5], to Odo and William Brito q.v., and the monks, *ib.*, ii, no 323.

There is also a lengthy letter, dated June 1173, in the same volume ii (no 311) written by Odo to pope Alexander III in which he recites the calamities since the martyrdom and asks support for Richard of Dover, q.v., as abp. See also the letter to a M. Odo (*ib.*, ii, no 271) which may ref. to him.

His writings include biblical commentaries, saints' lives, sermons and letters; these are listed in Sharpe, *Latin Writers* with refs to the printed editions.

An analysis of some of these writings is in J. Leclercq, 'Profession monastique, baptême et pénitence d'après Odon de Cantorbéry', *Studia Anselmiana, Analecta Monastica*, 2ᵐᵉ série, xxxi (1953), 124–140.

The Eastry catalogue in James, *Ancient Libraries*, contains three books belonging to a monk or monks named Odo: an Antidotarium Odonis which is a 'libellus de cura humani corporis', no 456 (p. 57), Expositiones Odonis super vetus testamentum, no 223 (p. 42) and Parabole M. Odonis, no 1542 (p. 129).

III ODO
occ. 1189

1189, [May], one of several monks whom the abp refused to allow to take part in the discussions to settle the dispute between him and the chapter, *Epist. Cant.*, 292; see Roger Norreys I.

Note: the obits of two monks by this name occ. in BL Ms Arundel 68: 14 Jan. (fo 13) and 18 Apr. (fo 24ᵛ).

William de OFFYNTON [Effyngton, Offyngton, Offyntone, Uffington
occ. [1281/2] d. 1317

[1281/2], one of five prof., *SL*, 177, CCA Lit. Ms D.12, fo 3.

1306/7, 1308/13, June, chamberlain, CCA DCc, MA1, fos 264^{v}–271, Chamb. accts 2–6; his apptment in May 1306 followed the dismissal of Richard de Rawe, q.v., Reg. Q, fo 31/43.
1313, 28 May; 1315/16; 1317, 22 Sept; 1317/18, precentor, Reg. Q, fo 61/75; CCA DCc Ickham acct 18; CCA Lit. Ms D.12, fo 16, CCA DCc Adisham acct 4.
1313, 28 May, apptd by the prior and chapter as one of three initial *compromissorii* who were to choose seven *compromissorii* in the el. of an abp, Reg. Q, fo 61/75.
1317, 22 Sept., d., CCA Lit. Ms D.12, fo 16.

In an inventory of the refectory dated 1328 there were two silver *ciphi* [formerly] belonging to W. de Offyngton, Dart, *Antiq. Cant.*, xix (BL Ms Cotton Galba E.iv, fo 178^{v}).

OLECUMBE
see Holekumbe

William OLIVER
occ. 1396

1396, 7 Aug., 44th in order at the el. of an abp, Reg. G, fo 234^{v}.

Note: is this William Elmore, q.v.?

OLYVER [Oliverius
occ. 1338 or before

1338, 1 Mar., an inventory of this date includes a list of missing books owned by monks now dead; among these were his psalter which had been lost by Richard de Selesia, q.v., *Lit. Cant.*, no 618 (Reg. L, fo 104).

[M. OMER
occ. 1278

1278, nominated by the prior and convent for the office of official of Canterbury, *sed. vac.*, but not a monk, as stated in Selden Soc., *Select Cases Eccles.*, 26; see Churchill, *Cant. Admin.*, i, 55, n.5].

ORDWIUS [Ordwy
occ. [c. 1104 × 1105]

[c. 1104 × 1105], was the recipient of two letters from abp Anselm and also a third letter addressed jointly to him and to Farman and Benjamin, q.v., *Anselm Letters*, nos 327, 336, 355.

I ORDWYN [Ordwinus
n.d.

n.d., 9 Aug., subdcn, whose obit occ. in BL Ms Arundel 68, fo 37^{v}.

II ORDWYN [Orwyn
n.d.

n.d., 16 Aug., obit occ. in BL Ms Arundel 68, fo 38.

ORGARUS
n.d.

n.d., 8 Sept., obit occ. in BL Ms Arundel 68, fo 40^{v}.

Alan ORPYNTON
occ. 1st half 13th c.

n.d., name occ. in the list in *SL*, 174, CCA Lit. Ms D.12, fo 1^{v}.

Nicholas ORPYNTON
occ. 1477 d. 1485

1477, 22 Mar., ord subdcn, Canterbury cathedral, *Reg. abp Bourgchier*, 422.
1477, 19 Apr., one of four tonsured, *SL*, 191, CCA Lit. Ms D.12, fo 8^{v}.
1477, 11 Nov., prof., *SL*, 191, Cambridge, Corpus Christi College Ms 298.
1478, 7 Mar., ord dcn, Canterbury cathedral, *Reg. abp Bourgchier*, 425.
1480, 23 Sept., ord pr., Canterbury cathedral, *ib.*, 431.
1485, c. 16 Oct., d., one of nine monks to have d. from 'le Swete' in the space of sixteen days, CCA Lit. Ms D.12, fo 26^{v} and BL Ms Arundel 68, fo 45^{v}, which gives his obit as 16 Oct.

I Ralph de ORPYNTON [Orpintun
occ. [1187] occ. 1198

[1187, c. Apr., with John de Bockyng I, q.v., prob. wardens of the manors, to whom the abp issued orders that they should be deprived of office and forbidden to go out of the cloister, *Eng. Epis. Acta*, ii, no 251, *Epist. Cant.*, 28.
[1187, 23 June × 25 July], both were excommunicated for disobeying the above, *Eng. Epis. Acta*, ii, no 252, *Epist. Cant.*, 60, 64; but they were absolved on reaching the curia where they had gone with the prior, Honorius II, q.v., and other monks to appeal vs the abp, *Epist. Cant.*, 70, 75.
1189, 12 Oct., after, one of three monks sent to the king to offer a gift and gain his support in the dispute with the abp, *Epist. Cant.*, 313.
1189, 5/8 Nov., one of the party of monks sent to confer with the king, in London, *ib.*, 315.
1198, 4 May, with John de Dover I, q.v., apptd proctor in a suit over land, CCA DCc Cart. Antiq. S.231

An inventory of the refectory dated 1328 includes a *ciphus de murra* formerly his, Dart, *Antiq. Cant.*, xxii (BL Ms Cotton Galba E.iv, fo 180); this may ref. to Ralph de Orpynton II, q.v.

II Ralph de ORPYNTON
occ. 1236/7

n.d., name occ. in the *post exilium* list in *SL*, 173, CCA Lit. Ms D.12, fo 1^{v}.

1236/7, was an accomplice of Simon de Hertlepe, q.v., and the prior John de

Chatham, q.v., in the attempt to 'reconstruct' a copy of the 'charter of St Thomas' when the latter was accidentally torn. He was called in by the prior to affix the original seal to the re-written charter, but later confessed his deed to the abp. When the abp set out for Rome in late 1237 he took Orpynton with him as far as St Bertin, but the prior forced his return to Canterbury, from where, after fifteen days' imprisonment, he was transferred to the Cistercian abbey of Melrose. *Gervase Cant.*, ii, 131–132. See C.R. Cheney, 'Cant. Forgery', 17–18.

Note: there may be only one Ralph de Orpynton; but, if he had been a monk for well over fifty yrs, it is difficult to conceive of his being sent on the long journey to Melrose.

ORUNDELL
see Arundell

I OSBERN
occ. [1074 × 1096]

[1074 × 1096], *temp.* prior Henry, q.v., precentor, Gibson, *Lanfranc*, 12.

n.d., 28 Nov., obit occ. in BL Ms Arundel 68, fo 49^v^.

An Englishman by birth, he had been sent by abp Lanfranc to Bec for two yrs to learn the Norman customs. Later, on his return to Christ Church, he wrote a musical treatise and saints' lives. His life of Dunstan has been printed in *Dunstan Memorials*, 69–161 and of Elphege in *Anglia Sacra* ii, 122–147; Sharpe, *Latin Writers*, has further refs. See Southern, *St Anselm* (1963), 248–252, which outlines his career. Dr Gransden notes the mediocrity of his Latin prose and the inaccuracies and limitations of his writing, *Hist. Writing*, i, 127–128. See also J. Rubenstein, 'The Life and Writings of Osbern of Canterbury' in R. Eales and R. Sharpe, eds, *Canterbury and the Norman Conquest*, London, 1995, 27–40.

In the late 12th c. catalogue one item is listed as Musica Osberni in pargameno, James, *Ancient Libraries*, no 41 (p. 8).

Two letters written by Anselm, while still abbot of Bec, express concern for his well being and imply that he [had] spent some time at Bec, *Anselm Letters*, nos 39, 66. Two letters, which he wrote to Anselm, abp el., urging him to accept the office, are preserved in *ib.*, nos 149, 151.

One of his relatives was named Holvardus, q.v.

II OSBERN
occ. 1214

1214, 29 Sept., cellarer, CCA DCc, MA1, fo 54^v^.

OSBERN
see also Bristol

OSBERT [Osbertus
occ. 1213 occ. 1220

1213, 29 Sept., cellarer, CCA DCc MA1, fo 53^v^.

1217, 11 Nov.; 1218, 1 Nov.; 1219, 1 Nov.; 1220, 18 Oct., almoner, CCA DCc MA1, fos 60, 61^v^, 63, 64.

n.d., 5 Jan., the obit of an Osbert, pr., occ. in BL Ms Arundel 68, fo 12.

Note: see Osbern II who may be the same monk.

Philip de OSEWELL
occ. 2nd half 13th c.

n.d., name occ. in the list in *SL*, 175, CCA Lit. Ms D.12, fo 2.

See also Philip II.

John OSFORD
occ. 1399

1399, 20 Dec., ord subdcn, Canterbury cathedral, Reg. abp Arundel, i, fo 325.

Note: this is John Assheforde I, q.v.

OSMUND
n.d.

n.d., 9 Aug., dcn, whose obit occ. in BL Ms Arundel 68, fo 37^v^.

Benedict de OSPRING [Ospringe
occ. [1241] occ. 1259/60

[1241], name occ. in the list in *SL*, 174, CCA Lit. Ms D.12, fo 2; he was possibly one of the twelve prof. with Richard de Wynchepe, q.v.

1245, cellarer, CCA DCc MA1, fo 86^v^.

1259/60, pd a visit to Meopham, CCA DCc Meopham acct 1.

Luke de OSPRING [Osprenge, Ospringe, Ospryng
occ. 1283 d. 1305

n.d., name occ. in the list in *SL*, 176, CCA Lit. Ms D.12, fo 2^v^.

1283/5, cellarer, CCA DCc MA1, fos 139^v^–142.

1305, 23 Oct., d., CCA Lit. Ms D.12, fo 15^v^.

One item in the Eastry catalogue is listed as his: Collectarium de multis, in lingua Gallicana, James, *Ancient Libraries*, no 768 (p. 81).

An inventory of the refectory dated 1328 includes a *ciphus de murra* formerly his, Dart, *Antiq. Cant.*, xxiii (BL Ms Cotton Galba E.iv, fo 180).

Note: see Luke II who is prob. this monk.

Stephen OSPRING [Ospering
occ. 2nd half 13th c.

n.d., name occ. in the list in *SL*, 175, CCA Lit. Ms D.12, fo 2.

Turgitius de OSTEDE
occ. [1241]

[1241], name occ. in the list in *SL*, 174, CCA Lit. Ms D.12, fo 2; he was possibly one of the twelve prof. with Richard de Wynchepe, q.v.

OSWALD
see Eastry

OSWARDUS
occ. 1268/9 occ. 1271/2

1268/9, 1270/2, treasurer with Randulph, q.v, CCA DCc MA1, fos 112, 113, 114^{v}.

Bartholomew OTFORD [Otforde, Ottforde, Ottforth
occ. 1533 occ. 1540

1533, 12 May, one of eight tonsured, *SL*, 196, CCA Lit. Ms D.12, fo 12.

[1538, 8 Feb., after], 'test chaplyn' [?third] to the prior, Pantin, *Cant. Coll. Ox.*, iii, 153.

1534, 12 Dec., acknowledged the Act of Supremacy, *DK 7th Report*, Appndx 2, 282.

[1538, 8 Feb., after], in a list of monks prob. prepared for Thomas Cromwell he was described as 'wytty' and 25 yrs of age, Pantin, *Cant. Coll. Ox.*, iii, 153.

1540, 4 Apr., awarded £3 p.a. and became a petty canon in the new foundation, *L and P Henry VIII*, xv, no 452.

I John de OTFORD [Otforde, Otteford
occ. 1358/9 d. 1413

1358/9, 28 Oct., one of nine prof., *SL*, 181, CCA Lit. Ms D.12, fo 4. He had previously been a secular pr. attached to the almonry chapel, *ib.*, fo 20–20^{v}.

1370, 11 Oct., apptd precentor, Reg. abp Wittlesey, fo 34^{v}; 1371, 25 Jan., absolved from office, *ib.*, fo 37.

1371, *custos tumbe*, CCA DCc MA2, fo 266.

1373/4, *custos martyrii*, CCA DCc MA2, fos 276–281^{v}.

1378/9, *custos* of St Mary in crypt, CCA DCc MA2, fos 314^{v}–318.

1379/80, Mar., bartoner, CCA DCc Bart. acct 57.

1380/1, *custos martyrii*, CCA DCc MA2, fos 318–321^{v}, and see below.

1382, Sept., possibly apptd sacrist, Reg. abp Courtenay, i, fo 22; see John de Guston.

1383/4, bartoner, CCA DCc, Bart. acct 61; he was also *custos martyrii* during this yr, Treas. acct 26, fos 2–6^{v}.

1384/6, bartoner, CCA DCc, Bart. accts 62, 63.

1413, before 6 July, almoner, CCA Lit. Ms D.12, fo 20^{v}.

1366, 10 May, present at the el. of an abp, Reg. G, fo 147.

1374, 30 June, 21st in order at the el. of an abp, *ib.*, fos 173^{v}–175^{v}.

1381, 31 July, 14th at the el. of an abp, *ib.*, fo 225^{v}.

1396, 7 Aug., 7th at the el. of an abp, *ib.*, fo 234^{v}.

1413, 6 July, d., at the age of 'about 88' and in the 57th yr of his monastic life. He is praised by Causton for his service in many offices and for having made an 'ymaginem beate Marie murali et ferrea clausura' and for having paved with *quadratis tegulis* [the tomb of Becket] and the chapel of St John the Baptist, CCA Lit. Ms D.12, fo 20–20^{v}. His obit is in BL Ms Arundel 68, fo 33.

II John OTFORD [Ottford
occ. 1467 d. [1501]

1467, 2 Mar., ord acol., Canterbury cathedral, *Reg. abp Bourgchier*, 399.

1467, 19 Sept., one of six prof., *SL*, 190, CCA Lit. Ms D.12, fo 8.

1468, 12 Mar., ord subdcn, Canterbury cathedral, *Reg. abp Bourgchier*, 398.

1468, 16 Apr., ord dcn, Canterbury cathedral, *ib.*, 400.

1470, 21 Apr., ord pr., Canterbury cathedral, *ib.*, 406.

1469/70, celebrated his first mass and recd a gift of 8d from the sacrist, Woodruff, 'Sacrist's Rolls', 63 (CCA DCc Sac. acct 48).

1488, Mar./Sept., fourth prior and *magister ordinis*, CCA Lit. Ms D.12, fo 8^{v}.

1492, 5 Feb; 1493, 1 May; 1495, 1 Aug.; 1497/8, treasurer, CCA DCc BB60/1; Reg. S, fo 383^{v}; CCA DCc DE15A; Treas. acct 23.

1493, 1 May, 7th in order at the ratification of an agreement, Reg. S, fo 383^{v}; but see John Crosse I.

[1501], 27 July, d., in the 38th yr of monastic life and at the age of 57, CCA Lit. Ms D.12, fo 28^{v}; if these figures are correct he must have entered Christ Church before 1467; since his d. is recorded on the treasurer's acct for 1500/1, Pantin, *Cant. Coll. Ox.*, iv, 205, the yr of d. can be fixed.

Roger OTFORD ?D.Th. [Otforth, Ottforde
occ. 1511 occ. 1528

1511, 1 Sept., one of eight tonsured, *SL*, 194, CCA Lit. Ms D.12, fo 11.

1512, 19 Apr., prof., *ib.*

1513, 26 Mar., ord subdcn, Canterbury cathedral, Reg. abp Warham, ii, fo 266^{v}.

1520/1, celebrated his first mass and recd a small sum of money from the sacrist, Woodruff, 'Sacrist's Rolls' 70 (CCA DCc Sac. acct 74). In the octave of Easter 1521 he celebrated and recd 8d. from William Ingram I, q.v., CCA Lit. Ms C.11, fo 134^{v}.

1514, possibly went up to Oxford; see below.

1516/17, student at Canterbury college Oxford with a £4 exhibition pd for him to the warden, Pantin, *Cant. Coll. Ox.*, ii, 272 (CCA DCc Cart. Antiq. O.151.36, part ii).

1517/18, student, receiving 66s. 8d. from cardinal Morton's bequest, Pantin, *ib.*, ii, 273 (CCA DCc DE70).

1522, 17 Jan., supplicated for B.Th. after eight yrs' study of logic, philosophy and theology; on 14 May this was granted, Pantin, *ib.*, iii, 252–253. On 15 May he was adm. to oppose and on 21 May 'ad lecturam libri sentenciarum', *ib.*, iii, 257.

1528, 29 Feb., supplicated for D.Th., *BRUO*.

1511, 2 Sept., novice, not prof. and 84th in order on the visitation certificate, Wood-Legh, *Visit.*, 3 (as Robert) (Reg. abp Warham, i, fo 35^{v}).

Alstanus OVER
n.d.

n.d., the first monk who d. on or near 18 Feb., Lambeth Ms 20, fo 165^{v}.

Richard de OXENDEN [Oxinden, Oxindenne, Oxyndenn
occ. 1320 d. 1338

1331–1338, prior: 25 Apr. 1331, el. prior and on the following day his *prefectio* was announced by the abp to the chapter, Reg. G, fo 22^{v}; d. 4 Aug. 1338, CCA Lit. Ms D.12, fo 16^{v} (*Fasti*, iv, 6).

1320, 9 Oct., one of five prof., *SL*, 179, CCA Lit. Ms D.12, fo 3^{v}.

1321, 19 Dec., ord acol. by *lit. dim.*, Rochester cathedral, *Reg. Hethe* (Rochester), 101, 1145.

[1323], subdcn, with Peter de Sales, q.v., sent with *lit. dim.*, to the bp of Rochester for ordination, *Lit. Cant.*, no 138 (Reg. L, fo 136^{v}).

1323, 24 Sept., ord dcn by *lit. dim.*, Rochester cathedral, *Reg. Hethe* (Rochester), 128, 1145.

1329/30, feretrar, CCA DCc MA2, fos 183^{v}–192.

1327, 11 Dec., named as one of three charged with the apptment of seven *compromissorii* for the el. of an abp, Reg. Q, fo 123; see also *CPL*, ii (1305–1342), 272.

1338, Aug., buried in St Michael's chapel on the north side, Cambridge, Corpus Christi College Ms 298, fo 119.

n.d., 4 Aug., obit in BL Ms Arundel 68, fo 37.

CCA Lit. Ms E.27 contains inventories of his 'goods' made on 7 and 25 July 1334; they have been printed by Hope in 'Inventories of Priors', 275–282.

Some of his *acta sed. vac.* are in Reg. Q, beginning on fo 178. A memorandum/acct book covering the yrs 1331–1343 provides a record of his priorate, and is now CCA DCc DE3.

The 'Anon. Chron.' summarized his priorate very briefly: 'quid fecerit est ignotum', 56. However, Woodruff has come to his rescue by noting that in 1336 he contributed most of the sum required for the new window in the chapel of SS. Peter and Paul, *ib.*, 57; see Reg. L, fo 107^{v}.

OXENE, Oxeney
see Oxney

Thomas OXFORD [Oxeford, Oxenford, Oxynford
occ. [1390] d. 1416

[1390], 28 Sept., one of seven prof., *SL*, 184, CCA Lit. Ms D.12, fo 5.

1394, 18 Apr., ord dcn, Canterbury cathedral, Reg. abp Courtenay, ii, fo 185.

1404/6, chamberlain, CCA DCc Prior acct 20; he was apptd on 8 Nov. 1404 and dismissed on 14 Sept. 1406, Reg. abp Arundel, i, fo 437, 437^{v}.

1407/13; 1416, 6 Feb. before, granator, CCA DCc Eastry acct 131, Gran. accts 89–91, Eastry acct 135, Treas. acct 11; CCA Lit. Ms D.12, fo 20^{v}.

1393/5, student at Canterbury college, Oxford, Pantin, *Cant. Coll. Ox.*, ii, 136, 138, 140 (CCA DCc Cart. Antiq. O.151.2, 3).

1390/1, recd 12d. *pro benedictione* from the prior, Lambeth Ms, 243, fo 220^{v}.

1396, 7 Aug., 63rd in order at the el. of an abp, Reg. G, fo 234^{v}.

1414, 12 Mar., 25th at the el. of an abp, *Reg. abp Chichele*, i, 4.

1416, 6 Feb., d., CCA Lit. Ms D.12, fo 20^{v}, in the 26th yr of his monastic life, *Chron. Stone*, 7; his obit is in BL Ms Arundel 68, fo 15^{v}.

William OXFORD [Oxeforde, Oxforde, Oxinforde
occ. [1429] occ. 1466

[1429, summer], ord acol. place not given, Reg. Langdon (Rochester), fo 74.

1430, 4 Apr., one of four prof., *SL*, 187, CCA Lit. Ms D.12, fo 7.

1430, 23 Dec., ord subdcn, bp's chapel, Trottiscliffe, Reg. Langdon (Rochester), fo 72x.

1431, 31 Mar., ord pr., Rochester cathedral, Reg. Langdon (Rochester), fo 69x.

Note: Langdon's register is in a state of confusion here.

1452, 14 July, ill and his expenses were 5s., CCA Lit. Ms E.6, fo 64^{v}.

1466, 17 Feb., 18th in order in an inventory of *jocalia fratrum*, [given by him and/or assigned for his use], Reg. N, fo 231^{v}.

1466, 14 Apr., instituted rector of Hawkinge by dispensation, *Reg. abp Bourgchier*, 282.

n.d., *recessit,* and listed among the monks who departed or d. in the mid-1460s, CCA Lit. Ms D.12, fo 26.

n.d., 8 June, his obit occ. in Lambeth Ms 20, fo 192^{v}.

I James de OXNEY, D.Th. [Oxene, Oxeney, Oxine, Oxne, Oxneye
occ. 1328 d. 1361

1328, 25 Nov., one of six prof., *SL*, 179, CCA Lit. Ms D.12, fo 3ᵛ.
1338/40, subprior, CCA DCc Adisham acct 15, Great Chart. acct 45.
1350/1, warden of manors, CCA DCc Appledore acct 40.
[?1360], 26 Sept., penitentiary whom the prior requested the bp to relieve of his office, Reg. L, fo 92.

1331/2, one of three monks who went up to study at Oxford, Pantin, *Cant. Coll. Ox.*, iv, 178 (Lambeth Ms 243, fo 32).
1332/6, student at Oxford, prob. for three quarters of each yr, Pantin, *ib.*, iv, 178–180 (Lambeth Ms 243, fos 41, 49ᵛ, 57, 58, 65, 65ᵛ).
1340, June, 1342, Aug., at Oxford, *Lit. Cant.*, no 691 (Reg. L, fo 75), Pantin, *ib.*, iv, 180.
[1342/3], told by the prior to instruct the son of Hugh Chaumpeneys, a student at Oxford, 'in scientia et in moribus', *Lit. Cant.*, no 763 (Reg. L, fo 78).
1358, by 25 Oct., D.Th., Reg. abp Islip, fo 144; in 1348 he was described as *licentiato in theologia*, Reg. G, fo 86.

1333, 14/16 Oct., with a secular cleric apptd commissaries by the prior and chapter with regard to the chapter's *sed. vac.* jurisdiction, Churchill, *Cant. Admin.*, ii, 229, (Reg. G, fo 26ᵛ, Reg. Q, fo 192).
1333, 3 Nov., one of three initial *compromissorii* named by the prior and chapter to choose seven *compromissorii* in the el. of an abp, Reg. G, fos xxxii, xxxvii (Reg. Q, fos 189ᵛ, 193ᵛ).
1348, 30 Aug., chosen as one of seven *compromissorii* and preached at the el. of an abp to succ. John Stratford, Reg. G, fos 30ᵛ/82; on 3 Sept., he and John de Hedecron, q.v. were apptd to inform the pope and the elect [Thomas Bradwardine] of the chapter's choice, *ib.*, fo 84, Oxney was sent to the curia, [for confirmation], *ib.*, fo 86. (Also Reg. Q, fos 233–239.)
1349, 4 June, 20th in order and one of three who were chosen to name ten additional *compromissorii* for the el. of an abp, Reg. G, fos 60ᵛ–61ᵛ.
1349, 8/9 Sept., 19th in order at the el. of an abp and named as one of thirteen *compromissorii*, *ib.*, fos 76, 77.
1350, 5 Apr., with John de Hedecron, q.v., apptd proctors in negotiations to settle the dispute with Dover priory, *Lit. Cant.*, nos 781, 782 (Reg. H, fo 36).
1358, 25 Oct., apptd penitentiary in the cathedral, city and diocese, including cases usually reserved to the abp, Reg. abp Islip, fo 144.
1359/60, engaged in negotiations on behalf of the prior and chapter, Lambeth Ms 243, fo 112.
1361, 26 July, d., one of c. 25 monks carried off [by the plague] between June and Oct., CCA Lit. Ms D.12, fo 17; his obit is in BL Ms Arundel 68, fo 36.

Name in CCA Lit. Ms A.13, Duns Scotus (14th c.); on fo 5ᵛ '. . . Scotus super primum et tercium Sentenciarum cum collacione eiusdem dni—doctoris sacre pagine'.

II James de OXNEY [Oxene *alias* Stone
occ. 1372

1372, 14 Mar., one of four novices whom the prior was comm. to prof., Reg. abp Wittlesey, fo 52.

Note: This is James Stone II q.v., who was adm. as Oxney but, apart from this entry, remained known as Stone. Neither of these was prob. his patronymic as Stone and Oxney were neighbouring villages.

III James OXNEY [Oxene, Oxne
occ. 1480 d. 1504

1480, 25 Jan., one of six prof., *SL*, 191, CCA Lit. Ms D.12, fo 8ᵛ.
1480, 1 Apr., ord acol., Canterbury cathedral, *Reg. abp Bourgchier*, 430.
1480, 28 Sept., ord subdcn, Canterbury cathedral, *ib.*, 431.
1483, 29 Mar., ord dcn, Canterbury cathedral, *ib.*, 439.
1485, 24 Sept., ord pr., Canterbury cathedral, *ib.*, 452.

1500, 19 May, ceased to be *custos martyrii*, Legg and Hope, *Inventories*, 127 (CCA Lit. Ms C.11, fo 26).
1504, before 13 May, *magister* of St Mary in crypt, CCA Lit. Ms D.12, fo 34ᵛ.

1493, 1 May, 40th in order at the ratification of an agreement, Reg. S, fo 383ᵛ; but see John Crosse I.
1501, 26 Apr., 26th in order at the el. of an abp, Reg. R, fo 56ᵛ.
1504, 13 May, d., in his 25th yr of monastic life, at the age of 44; described as *vir religiosus*, CCA Lit. Ms D.12, fo 34ᵛ.

I John de OXNEY [Oxne, Oxnee
occ. [1336]

[1336], one of seven adm., SL 180, CCA Lit. Ms D.12, fo 4. Five of the seven pressed the prior to obtain permission from the abp for them to be prof. before their yr of probation was up. Although the abp refused, and despite the prior's fear that they would depart, none of them did so; but this monk, who had not been named as one of the petitioners, must have left; see Thomas de Gyllyngham.

II John de OXNEY [Oxne, Oxnee, Oxone
occ. 1423 d. 1471

1468–1471, prior: el. 31 Aug., *prefectio*, 1 Sept. 1468, *Chron. Stone*, 105, Reg. S, fo 234 [*sublimatus*]; d.

2 July 1471, Pantin, *Cant. Coll. Ox.*, iii, 110 (Reg S, fo 248); cf. *Fasti*, iv, 6.

1423, 30 Sept., one of five prof., *SL*, 187, CCA Lit. Ms D.12, fo 6^{v}.
1424, 22 Apr., recd first tonsure, *Reg. abp Chichele*, iv, 359.
1425, 22 Dec., ord subdcn, Charing, *ib.*, iv, 374.
[1432] 11 June, ord pr., place not named, Reg. Langdon (Rochester), fo 74^{v}.
Note: Langdon's register is in a state of confusion here.
1435, 14 July, apptd subrefectorer, Chron. Wm Glastynbury, fo 117.
[1441], 5 Jan, removed from the office of feretrar, *ib.*, fo 119^{v}.
1445, 20 Apr., 1446, 23 Apr., 1446/50, 1451, 20 July, treasurer, CCA DCc DE15C/31, 38, Treas. acct 15, Lambeth ED82, CCA DCc DE15C/28.
1451/2, 1453/4, 1455/7, 1459, 16 Dec., 1461/2, to 16 May, cellarer, CCA Lit. Ms E.6, fo 39^{v}, CCA DCc Prior acct 9, Cell. acct 5, Prior accts 10, 15, DE44, Cell. acct 6.
1462/5, 1467/8, subprior, CCA DCc Sac. accts 43–46; he was apptd on 9 May 1462, *Chron. Stone*, 86 and relieved of the office on 28 June 1468, *ib.*, 103. However, he was still subprior on 6 Aug. at the time of the d. of prior Thomas Goldston I, q.v., *ib.*, 104.
1439, 20 Jan., one of several monks licensed to leave the priory *pro recreacione*, Chron. Wm Glastynbury, fo 182^{v}/177^{v}.
1466, 17 Feb., 11th in order in an inventory of *jocalia fratrum*, [given by him and/or assigned for his use], Reg. N, fo 230^{v}.
1468, 30 Aug./1 Sept., details of the el. *per viam scrutinii* and the *prefectio* are given in *Chron. Stone*, 105–106.
1468, recd 6s. 8d. in a bequest, Hussey, 'Kentish Wills', 37.
1470, 6/8 July, presided with the abp at the celebrations for the jubilee of St Thomas Becket, *ib.*, 111–112.

Some of his *acta* are in Reg. S, fos 234–247^{v}.

III John OXNEY [Oxne
occ. 1505 occ. 1540

1505, 13 Jan., one of six tonsured, *SL*, 193, CCA Lit. Ms D.12, fo 10.
1505, 22 Mar., ord acol., Canterbury cathedral, Reg. abp Warham, ii, fo 262.
1505, 11 July, prof., *SL*, 193, CCA Lit. Ms D.12, fo 10.
1506, 11 Apr., ord subdcn, Canterbury cathedral, Reg. abp Warham, ii, fo 262^{v}.
1507, 3 Apr., ord dcn, Canterbury cathedral, *ib.*, ii, fo 263.
1509, 7 Apr., ord pr., Canterbury cathedral, *ib.*, ii, fo 264.
1508/9, celebrated his first mass and recd a small sum from the sacrist, CCA DCc Sac. acct, 71.
1527, Sept./Dec., 1528/9, anniversarian, CCA DCc Anniv. acct 21, Lambeth ED51.
1529, 29 Sept., feretrar, CCA Lit. Ms C.11, fo 65^{v}.
1530/1, anniversarian, CCA DCc Anniv. acct 19.
1531, 25 Mar., feretrar, CCA Lit. Ms C.11, fo 67.
1531/4, 1535/6, anniversarian, CCA DCc Anniv. accts 2, 1, 18, Lambeth ED52.
1536, 17 Aug., appted penitentiary, CCA DCc Cart. Antiq. A.22.
[1538, 8 Feb., after], 1540, 4 Apr., treasurer, Pantin, *Cant. Coll. Ox.*, iv, 152, *L and P Henry VIII*, xv, no 452.

1511, 2 Sept., 59th in order on the visitation certificate, Wood-Legh, *Visit.*, 3 (Reg. abp Warham, i, fo 35^{v}).
1534, 12 Dec., acknowledged the Act of Supremacy, *DK 7th Report*, Appndx 2, 282.
[1538, 8 Feb., after], on a list of monks, prob. prepared for Thomas Cromwell, he was described as a 'good man', 56 yrs of age, Pantin, *Cant. Coll. Ox.*, iii, 152.
1540, 4 Apr., awarded £10 p.a, *L and P Henry VIII*, xv, no 452.

Peter OXNEY [Oxeney
occ. 1372/3

1372, 14 Nov., a certain Peter was clothed in the monastic habit by the prior after receiving a comm. from the abp, Reg. abp Wittlesey, fo 57^{v}.
1373, 12 Mar., novice, with John Berham, q.v., made his prof. before the prior who had been comm. by the abp, *ib.*, fo 59.

Note: this is Peter Stone, q.v., see also James Oxney II.

William OXNEY [Oxene, Oxenegh
occ. 1365 occ. 1368

1365, one of eight prof., *SL*, 182, CCA Lit. Ms D.12, fo 4^{v}.
1367, 18 Sept., ord subdcn, Lambeth palace chapel, *Reg. abp Langham*, 383.
1368, 4 Mar., ord dcn, Canterbury cathedral, *ib.*, 388.

Alexander de OXON' [?Exon
occ. [1207 × 1214] occ. 1239

[1207 × 1214], last name to occ. on the list of those who were in exile, *SL*, 172, CCA Lit. Ms D.12, fo 1.
1239, 7 Jan., one of five *compromissorii* named by the chapter in the el. of a prior; they were excommunicated by the abp on 15 Jan. for their illegal el. of Roger de La Lee, q.v., without his presence or approval, *Gervase Cant.*, ii, 146, 151.

An inventory of the refectory, dated 1328, includes a silver *ciphus*, formerly his, Dart, *Antiq. Cant.*, xix (BL Ms Cotton Galba E.iv, fos 178^{v}).

OXYNDENN
see Oxenden

OXYNFORD
see Oxford

Alan OYSELL [Oysel
occ. 1289 d. 1337

1289, 19 Dec., one of eight prof., *SL*, 177, CCA Lit. Ms D.12, fo 3.

1303, 23 Nov., removed from the office of subcellarer, *Reg. abp Winchelsey*, 1306 (Reg. Q, fo 30v/42).

1307/11, granator, CCA DCc Gran. accts 1, 67, MA1, fos 11v–30, Gran. accts 2, 3.

1311, Oct./1314, bartoner, CCA DCc Bart. acct 4, MA2, fos 37–44v, Ebony acct 27.

1323, *custos tumbe*, CCA DCc MA2, fo 128v.

1323, 27 July, 1323/4, 1325/7, 1328/9, chamberlain, CCA DCc EC I/27, Chamb. accts 18–21, MA2, fos 138–184v (1324/9).

1335/6, auditor, CCA DCc, Bocking acct 19.

[1296], his failure to attend [i.e. *non cantat*] the night office had been reported at the abp's visitation and the abp ordered that he be watched by his *magister regule* to ensure that he was present, *Reg. abp Winchelsey*, 92.

1337, 4 Aug., d., CCA Lit. Ms D.12, fo 16v; his obit is in BL Ms Arundel 68, fo 37.

P.
occ. 1276/8

1276/8, sacrist, CCA DCc MA1, fos 123v–128.

Note: there are about five possible contemporary contenders for this entry, none as yet known to have been sacrists: Peter Bramblyng', Peter de Ikham, Peter Lumbardus, Philip de Osewell, Peter Sevenoke, q.v.

PAERMESTEDE
see Parmistede

PANCRACIUS
n.d.

n.d., 27 Mar., obit occ. in BL Ms Arundel 68, fo 22. In BL Ms Cotton Nero C.ix, fo 8v the name is Panectus.

PARETT
see William Chartham IV

Arnold PARMISTEDE, B.Th.
[Paermestede, Parmsted, Parmystede, Permistede, Permystede
occ. 1446 d. 1464

1446, 21 Dec., one of seven tonsured, *SL*, 188, CCA Lit. Ms D.12, fo 7v.

1447, 4 Mar., ord acol., Canterbury cathedral, Reg. abp Stafford, fo 199.

1447, 27 Aug., made his prof. before the abp with the other six, *Chron. Stone*, 41–42.

1447, 23 Dec., ord subdcn, Canterbury cathedral, Reg. abp Stafford, fo 201v.

1448, 17 Feb., ord dcn, Canterbury cathedral, *ib.*, fo 202.

1450, 3 Apr., ord pr., Canterbury cathedral, *ib.*, fo 204v.

[1464], chaplain to the prior, prob. at the time of his d., CCA Lit. Ms D.12, fo 26.

1454/5, student at Canterbury college, Oxford, Pantin, *Cant. Coll. Ox.*, ii, 174, 176 (CCA DCc Cart. Antiq. O.151.14). He did not return to Canterbury for the el. of an abp in Apr. 1454, but named the prior as his proxy, Pantin, *Cant. Coll. Ox*, iii, 105 (Reg. N, fo 185).

1459/60, 1462/3, at Canterbury college, with a pension of £8 7s. for the former yr and 41s. 8d. for the first term of the latter, Pantin, *ib.*, ii, 180, 183 (CCA DCc Cart. Antiq. O.151.16, 17).

1459, 1 Dec., supplicated for B.Th., Pantin, *ib.*, iii, 254.

1462, 27 Mar., supplicated for a reduction of grace, Pantin, *ib.*

1464, 18 Sept., d., *Chron. Stone*, 90; his obit on 19 Sept. is in BL Ms Arundel 68, fo 42.

Name in Cambridge (USA), Harvard University, Houghton Library, Ms Typ.3, Biblia (13th c.); *si hic perdatur—restituatur.* See also John Coventre.

Alexander PARTRICH'
see Rydelyngwolde

Walter PARVUS
see Meri

PAULINUS
occ. ?1239

?1239, name in four vols in the Eastry catalogue, nos 1373–1376, James, *Ancient Libraries*, 117, two of which are collections of sermons; the date is suggested by James.

Note: the obit of a pr. of this name occ. on 7 Feb. in BL Ms Arundel 68, fo 115v, and another on 24 May, *ib.*, fo 28.

John de PAXTON
occ. [1336] d. 1352

[1336], n.d., one of seven adm.; *SL*, 180 and CCA Lit. Ms D.12, fo 4 are confused and confusing here, but an entry in Reg. L, fo 67v, makes it clear that the seven were not yet prof. on 19 June 1337. See Thomas Gyllyngham.

1350/2, warden of manors, CCA DCc Appledore acct 40, Ebony acct 52.

1349, 4 June, 40th in order at the el. of an abp, Reg. G, fo 60v.

1349, 8/9 Sept., 39th at the el. of an abp, *ib.*, fo 76v.

1352, 29 Aug., d., CCA Lit. Ms D.12, fo 16v.

PAYNTON
see Peynton

PECHAM
see Peckham, Pettham

Simon de PECHYNG [Pecchynge, Peschynge
occ. [1316] d. 1334

[1316], one of five prof., *SL*, 179, CCA Lit. Ms D.12, fo 3v.

1333, *custos martyrii*, CCA DCc, MA2, fo 221.
1333/4, chamberlain, CCA DCc, Chamb. acct 26.
1334, cellarer, CCA MA2, fo 232, DE3, fo 3; his apptment on [?26 Sept. 1332] to succ. John de Valoyns, q.v., is in CCA DCc DE3, fo 21v.

1326/7, one of several monks who visited Godmersham, CCA DCc Godmersham acct 10.
1331/2, rec. money for his *expenses equitant' in negotiis*, Lambeth Ms 243, fo 35v.
1334, 8 Sept., d., CCA Lit. Ms D.12, fo 16.

William PECKHAM, B.Th. [Peccham, Pecham, Pekham
occ. 1507 occ. 1522

1507, 12 Oct., one of six tonsured, *SL*, 193, CCA Lit. Ms D.12, fo 10v.
1508, 22 Apr., ord acol., Canterbury cathedral, Reg. abp Warham, ii, fo 263v.
1508, 25 Apr., he and the other five novices made their prof. before the abp, *SL*, 194, CCA Lit. Ms D.12, fo 10v.
1509, 7 Apr., ord subdcn, Canterbury cathedral, Reg. abp Warham, ii, fo 264.
1511, 19 Apr., ord dcn, Canterbury cathedral, *ib.*, ii, fo 265v.

1512, student at Canterbury college, who recd travelling expenses from Canterbury to Oxford, Pantin, *Cant. Coll. Ox.*, iv, 205.
1516/17, student whose pension was £6 10s., *ib.*, ii, 256 (CCA DCc Cart. Antiq. O.151.44).
1517/18, student, Pantin, *ib.*, ii, 273 (CCA DCc DE70).
1521, an inventory of the college lists twenty mss in his 'magna cista in cubiculo', Pantin, *ib.*, i, 62 (CCA DCc Cart. Antiq. O.135A). This same yr his expenses were pd to go to Canterbury in order to preach, Pantin, *ib.*, iv, 206.
1521, 8 May, supplicated for B.Th., Pantin, *ib.*, iii, 253.
1521/2, student, with a pension of £8, Pantin, *ib.*, ii, 258 (CCA DCc Cart. Antiq. O.151.46).
1522, 1 Mar., adm. B.Th., Pantin, *ib.*, iii, 254.

1511, 2 Sept., 70th in order on the visitation certificate, Wood-Legh, *Visit.*, 3 (Reg. abp Warham, i, fo 35v).

Note: for his prob. obit see William Pettham II, n. 2.

John PEKHAM [Peccham, Pecham, Pekham
occ. 1414/15 d. 1457

1414/15, one of five tonsured, *SL*, 186, CCA Lit. Ms D.12, fo 6; see next item.
1415, 10 Nov., the prior was comm. to rec. his prof., *Reg. abp Chichele*, iv, 142.
1416, 18 Apr., ord acol., Canterbury cathedral, *Reg. abp Chichele*, iv, 319 (transcribed as Pelham).
1417, 10 Apr., ord subdcn, Canterbury cathedral, *ib.*, iv, 327.
1419, 1 Apr., ord dcn, chapel within the priory, *ib.*, i, 191.

[1440], 29 June, apptd *custos martyrii* in succ. to Robert Smerden, q.v., Chron Wm Glastynbury, fo 119v.
1457, 1/14 July, *magister mense*, CCA Lit. Ms D.12, fo 25v, *Chron. Stone*, 67.

1439, 3 Feb., one of several monks licensed to leave the priory *pro recreacione*, Chron. Wm Glastynbury, fo 182v/177v.
1457, 14 July, d., *Chron. Stone*, 67; obit on 15 July in BL Ms Arundel 68, fo 34.

PEMBLE
see William Arundell II

John PENY
occ. 1333 d. 1361

1333, 9 Oct., one of eleven prof., *SL*, 180, CCA Lit. Ms D.12, fo 4.

1350, *custos corone*, CCA DCc Treas. acct 27, fo 2v.
1354/5, granator, CCA DCc Gran. acct 37.
1361, before 9 June, chamberlain, Reg. abp Islip, fo 174v.

1349, 4 June, 35th in order at the el. of an abp, Reg. G, fo 60v.
1349, 8/9 Sept., 34th at the el. of an abp, *ib.*, fo 76v.
1361, 9 June, d., one of c. 25 monks carried of [by the plague] between June and Oct., CCA Lit. Ms D.12, fo 17.

PERMISTEDE
see Parmistede

PERY
see Pyrye

PESCHYNGE
see Pechyng

I PETER
n.d.

n.d., 18 Dec., subprior, whose obit is in BL Ms Arundel 68, fo 51v.

II PETER
n.d.

n.d., 20 May, dcn, whose obit occ. in BL Ms Arundel 68, fo 28.

Note: there are at least two other Peters whose obits are in Ms Arundel 68, one on 24 Apr. (fo 24^{v}) and the other on 5 July (fo 32^{v}); there is also a Peter who d. at Rome and whose obit occ. on 27 July in *ib.*, fo 36.

III PETER
occ. 1214 occ. 1229/30

1214, 29 Sept., chaplain to the prior, CCA DCc MA1, fo 54^{v}.
1220, 18 Oct., 1221/7, chamberlain, CCA DCc, MA1, fos 64, 65–71, AS1 (1224/5).
1228/30, cellarer, CCA DCc MA1, fos 69^{v}–72, AS2 (1229, Sept./Dec.).

Note: this may possibly be Peter de Dudyngton, St Elphege, or Tang', q.v.

PETER
see also Peynton, Sales

John PETTHAM [Petham
occ. 1491 d. 1508/9

1491, 11 Sept., one of four tonsured, CCA Lit. Ms D.12, fo 9 (*SL*, 192 is incomplete).
1492, 21 Apr., ord acol., Canterbury cathedral, *Reg. abp Morton*, i, no 441a.
1494, 29 Mar., ord subdcn, Canterbury cathedral, *ib.*, i, no 443b.
1495, 18 Apr., ord dcn, Canterbury cathedral, *ib.*, i, no 444c.
1493, 1 May, 63rd in order at the ratification of an agreement, Reg. S, fo 383^{v}; but see John Crosse I.
1501, 26 Apr., 42nd in order at the el. of an abp, Reg. R, fo 56^{v}.
1508/9, d., Woodruff, 'Sacrist's Rolls', 68 (CCA DCc Sac. acct 71).

Thomas PETTHAM [Petham
occ. 1481 d. 1485

1481, 21 Dec., one of four prof., *SL*, 191, CCA Lit. Ms D.12, fo 8^{v}.
1483, 29 Mar., ord acol., Canterbury cathedral, *Reg. abp Bourgchier*, 439.
1484, 17 Apr., ord dcn, Canterbury cathedral, *ib.*, 444.
1485, 24 Sept., ord pr., Canterbury cathedral, *ib.*, 452.
1485, c. 15 Oct., one of four who d. on the same day of 'le Swete', CCA Lit. Ms D.12, fo 26^{v}; their obit on this day is in BL Ms Arundel 68, fo 45.

I William PETTHAM, B.Cn.L [Petham, Petteham
occ. 1439 d. 1472

1471–1472, prior: *prefectio* 13 Aug. 1471, Reg. S, fo 249; d. 19 Aug. 1472, Pantin, *Cant. Coll. Ox.*, iii, 110 (Reg. S, fo 254).

Note: *Chron. Stone*, 116, states, no doubt wrongly, that the abp *prefecit* Pettham on 29 May 1471.

1439, 4 or 15 Dec. [St Barbara], one of six clothed in the monastic habit, *SL*, 188, CCA Lit. Ms D.12, fo 7^{v}.
[1440], 8 or 20 July [St Margaret], prof., Chron. Wm Glastynbury, fo 119^{v}.
1444, 11 Apr., ord pr., Canterbury cathedral, Reg. abp Stafford, fo 197.
1455/6, 1456, 28 Oct., 1457, 4 Jan., 1457/8, 1458, 26 Oct., 1459, 14 Oct., treasurer, CCA DCc Treas. acct 16, DE15C/3, 7, Treas. acct 17, DE15C/14, 22; in 1455/6 he was also one of the eight *barones*, *ib.*, Prior acct 10.
1461, 12 May and 24 Oct., 1462, Apr., warden of manors, CCA DCc RE434 and 435, Monk Warden acct 1.
1462, May/Sept., 1468/9, 1471, 5 Mar., cellarer, CCA DCc Cell. acct 7, Prior acct 11, RE454.
1470, 19 Mar., 1471, Mar./Aug., subprior, CCA DCc, DE78, Sac. acct 50; *Chron. Stone*, 115, reports that he was apptd subprior on 16 Mar. 1471; and *Chron. Stone*, 116 states that William Hadlegh, I, q.v., succ. him on 30 May.

1447/8, student at Canterbury college who recd travelling expenses for the journey to Oxford, Pantin, *Cant. Coll. Ox.*, iv, 194.
1449, Mar./June, student at Canterbury college, with a pension of 42s. 6d., Pantin, *ib.*, ii, 171.
1451, 18 Apr., supplicated for B.Cn.L on the grounds that 'tres anni, tres magne vacaciones cum multis parvis in eodem iure in ista universitate et unus annus in facultate arcium sufficiant', Pantin, *ib.*, iii, 254.
1451/2, at Oxford for three terms, Pantin, *ib.*, iv, 195.

1460, 1 May, apptd by the prior and chapter as proctor for convocation, Reg. S, fo 204^{v}, and he recd a similar apptment on 9 July 1462, *ib*, fos 209^{v}–210.
1468, recd 6s. 8d. in a bequest, Hussey, 'Kentish Wills', 37.
1471, 28 Sept., entertained the king on his visit to Canterbury, *causa indulgencie*, *Chron. Stone*, 117.
1472, enclosed the 'great marsh' at Appledore at a cost of £300, Reg. S, fo 253.
1472, [Aug.], buried in the crypt of Canterbury cathedral before the altar of St Mary Magdalen, Cambridge, Corpus Christi College Ms 298, fo 121. His obit occ. on 20 Aug. in BL Ms Arundel 68, fo 38^{v}.

Gave Canterbury college an alb of red velvet, Pantin, *Cant. Coll. Ox.*, i, 29, 51 (college inventories, CCA DCc Cart. Antiq O.137, 136).

II William PETTHAM [Pecham, Petham
occ. 1511 d. 1518/19

1511, 1 Sept., one of eight tonsured, *SL*, 194, CCA Lit. Ms D.12, fo 11.
1512, 19 Apr., prof., *ib.*

1513, 26 Mar., ord subdcn, Canterbury cathedral, Reg. abp Warham, ii, fo 266^{v}.

1516/17, student at Canterbury college and provided with a pension of £5, Pantin, *Cant. Coll. Ox.*, ii, 256 (CCA DCc Cart. Antiq. O.151.44).

1511, 2 Sept., 83rd in order, novice and not prof., on the visitation certificate, Wood-Legh, *Visit.*, 3 (Reg. abp Warham, i, fo 35^{v}).

1518/19, d., Pantin, *Cant. Coll. Ox.*, iv, 206.

Note:

(1) the obit of a William Pecham, *levita*, occ. on 15 Feb. in BL Ms Arundel 68, fo 16.

(2) the obit of a William Pekham B.Th. occ. on 4 July in Lambeth Ms 20, fo 198; see William Peckham.

Peter PEYNTON [Paynton

occ. 1384 occ. 1407

1384, 29 Aug., one of seven prof., *SL*, 183, CCA Lit. Ms D.12, fo 5.

1388/91, recd small sums from the prior each yr *pro benedictione*, Lambeth Ms 243, fo 212^{v}, 216^{v}, 220^{v}.

1396, 7 Aug., 48th in order at the el. of an abp, Reg. G, fo 234^{v}.

1407, Dec., granted licence by the abp to transfer to Folkestone priory, Reg. S, fo 58.

I PHILIP [Phillippus

occ. 1207

1207, cellarer, CCA DCc MA1, fo 59^{v}.

Note: this may be Philip de Wynchilsee, q.v.

II PHILIP

occ. 1269/70

1269/70, almoner, CCA DCc Alm. acct 2.

Note: this may be Philip de Osewell, q.v.

III PHILIP

occ. 1353/4

1353/4, cellarer, CCA DCc Bart. acct 33.

Note: which Philip is this?

James PIERS

occ. 1540

1540, 12 Oct., described as late monk of Christ Church, *L and P Henry VIII*, xvi, no 146.

See James Newynham.

PIKENOT

see Pykenot

PINKENY

see Pynkeny

PIRRY

see Pyrye

PLACIDUS

n.d.

n.d., *levita*, whose obit occ. on 31 Dec., in BL Ms Cotton Nero C.ix, fo 18^{v}.

Hugh de PLUKELE

occ. [1207 × 1214]

[1207 × 1214], name occ. in the list of those in exile, *SL*, 172, CCA Lit. Ms D.12, fo 1.

The Eastry catalogue contains eight items under his name including a psalter in Latin and French, James, *Ancient Libraries*, nos 1279–1286 (p. 111).

Richard PLUTO [Dorobernensis

d. c. 1181

c. 1181, d., and was buried in the chapter house, Dart, *Antiq. Cant.*, 182.

Contemporary of Alan I, prior, q.v., author of treatises on mathematics, philosophy and history.

The Eastry catalogue lists a volume containing some of his writings: Liber M.R. Plutonis, versifice, de summo bono; liber eiusdem unde malum, v' (versifice); liber eiusdem de gradibus virtutum, v'; liber eiusdem de virginitate; liber eiusdem de bono mortis, v'; liber eiusdem de loco et tempore, James, *Ancient Libraries*, no 101 (pp. 27–28). These and others are also listed in Bale, *Index Brit. Script.*, 356–357; in the entry in his *Catalogus*, i, 220–221, the name is Richard Pluto Dorbernensis. See Sharpe, *Latin Writers*, who lists and comments on all his known writings.

Geoffrey *dictus* POTEREL [?*alias* London, q.v.

occ. 1298 d. 1328

1298, 18 Oct., one of seven prof., *SL*, 178, CCA Lit. Ms D.12, fo 3^{v}.

[1300, 4 June, ord subdcn, Smeeth chapel by Aldington, *Reg. abp Winchelsey*, 934 (as Geoffrey de London).

1314, 25 Apr., 8 Nov., chaplain to the abp, *Lit. Cant.*, no 41 (CCA DCc Cart. Antiq. C.1294h).

1324, 10 Apr., precentor, CCA DCc EC V/46.

1326, July/1328, almoner, CCA DCc Alm. accts 33, 38, Eastry acct 53.

n.d., prob. student at Oxford before going to Paris; see the Worcester letter below.

1305, 15 Apr., sent by the prior to join Stephen de Feversham II, q.v., who was studying at the University of Paris, to be 'in laboris scolastici solatium' and his *socius*, CUL Ms Ee.5.31, fo 102^{v}. For the period from 14 Feb./25 Dec. 1305, the two were provided with £33 19s., and this included Poterel's travel expenses, Pantin, *Cant. Coll. Ox.*, iv, 174; see Andrew de Hardys. See also Sullivan, *Benedictine Monks at Paris*, no 544.

1313, 28 May, apptd by the prior and chapter to be one of seven *compromissorii* in the el. of an abp, Reg. Q, fos 61^{v}–62/75^{v}–76.

1313, 8 July, one of the monks about to set off for the curia in connection with the chapter's el. of Thomas Cobham as abp, but they were stopped in London because of the provision of Walter Reynolds, CUL Ms Ee.5.31, fo 134.

1314, 25 Apr., apptd by the abp to carry out corrections in the priory after his visitation, *Lit. Cant.*, no 41 (CCA DCc Cart. Antiq. C.1294h); see also Reg. abp Reynolds, fo 104.

1314, 28 July, he and Walter de Norwyco, q.v., were involved in negotiations concerning the abp of York's right to carry his staff in the province of Canterbury, CUL Ms Ee.5.31, fo 147–147ᵛ; on 21 Aug. they were sent to the king in this matter, *ib.*, fo 147ᵛ.

[1315], 3 Mar., apptd penitentiary in the city and diocese of Canterbury, Reg. abp Reynolds, fo 113.

1315, 18 Oct., was the source of friction within the community and between the abp and the monks acc. to a letter written by the subprior to the prior, CUL Ms Ee.5.31, fo 161ᵛ.

1317, 13 Oct., penitentiary, apptd with Richard Clyve, q.v., to discuss with the abp the matter of their rights vis-à-vis Dover priory, CUL Ms Ee.5.31, fo 179ᵛ.

1317, 5 Nov., penitentiary, one of three monks who with the prior examined all their brethren as required by the abp in an inquiry over the circulation of letters containing false and harmful statements, *ib.*, fo 181ᵛ; see Clement II.

1324, 28 May, his presence in London for ten days having been requested by the abp, the prior replied that he would willingly allow a monk to remain with the abp constantly acc. to ancient custom but he warned vs placing his trust in this particular monk, *Lit. Cant.*, no 123 (Reg. L, fo 138ᵛ).

1327, 3 Jan., apptd with a secular cleric to represent the prior and chapter in parliament, with the request that he be allowed to return to Canterbury as soon as possible *pro variis negotiis*, *Lit. Cant.*, no 199 (Reg. L, fo 147ᵛ); in fact he was away for six wks at a cost of £8 2s. 9d., CCA DCc, Alm. acct 38.

1327, 11 Dec., named to be one of seven *compromissorii* in the el. of an abp, Reg. Q, fo 123; see also *CPL*, ii (1305–1342), 272.

1328, 8 Sept., d. at Chester, CCA Lit. Ms D.12, fo 16.

A letter copied into Worcester cathedral Ms Q.20, fo 34ᵛ and prob. written by John de St Germans, q.v., (under Worcester) mentions his name; he prob. met St Germans when a student at Oxford, before being sent to Paris.

John POUCYN [Poucin, Pucyn

occ. 1295 d. 1312

1295/6, for his *rastura*, the almoner, Robert Poucyn, q.v., gave 37s. 9d., CCA DCc, Alm. acct 14.

1295, 23 Nov., one of five prof., *SL*, 178, CCA Lit. Ms D.12, fo 3.

1299, 19 Sept., ord dcn, Littlebourne, *Reg. abp Winchelsey*, 930.

1300, 4 June, ord pr., Smeeth chapel by Aldington, *ib.*, 936.

1312, granator, CCA DCc, MA2, fo 37.

n.d., possibly a student at Oxford as he is mentioned in Worcester cathedral Ms Q.20, fo 34ᵛ in a letter prob. written by John de St Germans, q.v., (under Worcester).

1312, 20 May, d., CCA Lit. Ms D.12, fo 15.

An inventory of missing service books dated 1 Mar. 1338, records the loss of his diurnale, *Lit. Cant.*, no 618 (Reg. L, fo 104).

Robert POUCYN [Poucin, Pucyn

occ. 1281 d. 1310

n.d., name occ. in the list in *SL*, 176, CCA Lit. Ms D.12, fo 2ᵛ.

1281/3, chaplain to the prior, CCA DCc MA1, fos 135–139ᵛ, Treas. acct 1.

1287/8, feretrar, CCA DCc MA1, fo 153ᵛ.

1288/90, treasurer, CCA DCc MA1, fos 152–156.

1291, Feb./1300, Feb., almoner, CCA DCc Alm. accts 7, 10–17, Blean acct 1.

1299/1300, 1301/5, subprior, CCA, DCc, Monkton acct 23, Little Chart acct 6, Barksore acct 15, Adisham acct 3, Meopham acct 42; he was first apptd in mid-Nov., 1298, Reg. Q, fo 41. He was absolved from this office as subprior on 15 Nov. 1303 in the wake of the abp's visitation but was reapptd on the 23rd of that month, *Reg. abp Winchelsey*, 1305 (Reg. Q, fo 42).

1305/6, cellarer, CCA DCc MA1, fos 257ᵛ–264ᵛ.

1306, 21 Jan., named penitentiary, Reg. Q, fo 31/43.

1310, penitentiary at the time of his d., Reg. Q, fo 41.

1282, 15 June, censured by the prior and convent for having revealed chapter secrets, but the abp wrote a letter in his defence and denied the charge, *Epist. Pecham*, 372–373.

c. 1289, a letter from Edmund, earl of Cornwall, requested the prior to send him and Robert de Selesia, q.v., to meet the earl in secret in London on St Margaret's day, CCA DCc EC III/86.

1293, 6 Aug., with Richard de Clyve, q.v., apptd general proctors for the prior and chapter, CUL Ee.5.31, fo 47ᵛ. On 10 Aug. he and Clyve recd a comm. from the prior and chapter *sed. vac.* to take charge of the enthronement of the bp of Bath and Wells in default of the adcn of Canterbury, Churchill, *Cant. Admin.*, ii, 224 (CUL Ms Ee.5.31, fo 49ᵛ).

1299, 30 Oct., with Geoffrey de Chilham, q.v., apptd proctors to attend convocation, CUL Ms Ee.5.31, fo 81.

n.d., recd £75 11s. 3d. from the treasurers to cover expenses of a journey to the curia, Lambeth Ms 242, fo 41.

1310, 19 Nov., d., CCA Lit. Ms D12, fo 15v.

The Eastry catalogue contains seven volumes under his name including the Sententie Lombardi, Decretales abbreviate, a Bible and sermons, James, *Ancient Libraries*, nos 1731–1737 (p. 139).

An inventory of vestments, *temp.* prior Eastry, includes four embroidered linen albs identified as his, Legg and Hope *Inventories*, 59 (BL Ms Cotton Galba, E.iv, fo 115).

An inventory of the refectory, dated 1328, includes three silver *ciphi*, Dart, *Antiq. Cant.*, xxii (BL Ms Cotton Galba E.iv, fo 179v).

Note: these two monks named Poucyn were prob. related. The Poucyn family held land in Minster in the early fourteenth century, see W.A. Scott Robertson, 'Powcy's' in *Archaeologia Cantiana*, 12 (1878), 357–360.

William POWNS [Pouns, Powncy, de Sancto Albano

occ. 1422 occ. 1443

1422, 30 Nov., made his prof. before the prior acting on a comm. from the abp, *SL*, 186–187, CCA Lit. Ms D.12, fo 6v. He had previously been a monk of St Albans. According to a lengthy letter written to him by his abbot, he had been enticed by another monk who had left the abbey for Christ Church [Geoffrey Bonde, q.v.] some yrs earlier. The abbot wrote in forceful language denouncing his departure for which, however, he was made to provide a licence on the intervention of abp Chichele, Amundesham, *Annales*, i, 89–97 (where the name is transcribed as Poverse).

1432/3, fourth prior, CCA DCc Sac. acct 27; see below.

1435, 17 Apr., apptd feretrar and removed from the office of fourth prior, Chron. Wm Glastynbury, fo 117.

1439, 3 Feb., one of several monks licensed to leave the priory *pro recreacione*, Chron. Wm Glastynbury, fo 182v/177v.

1441, 2 Aug., dispensed to take a benefice with cure of souls, *CPL*, ix (1431–1447), 206 (as Powas).

1441, 2 Nov., declared apostate because, in the hope of obtaining the above, he had left Christ Church without licence from the prior and had gone to London; however, he returned within a fortnight and was reinstated on acct of his contrition and of favourable words on his behalf from both the abp and the prior. While in London he had gone to stay at the 'convent' of St Martin the Great and the dean there had written on 17 Nov. to urge the prior to take him back as the prodigal son, *Lit. Cant.*, nos 1017, 1018, 1019 (Reg. N, fo 177).

1443, 25 Apr., obtained a letter from the abbot of the Cistercian monastery of Boxley [Kent] granting him adm. to that house and order, *Lit. Cant.*, no 1020 (Reg. N, fo 179). However, he is listed among the monks who were expelled in Chron Wm Glastynbury, fo 168v/162v. See F.D. Logan, *Runaway Religious*, Cambridge, 1996.

Matthew de PREKEPELSE

occ. [1163 × 1167]

[1163 × 1167], a survey of cathedral holdings in Canterbury compiled at this time ref. to land which had belonged to Matthew 'our monk', Urry, *Canterbury*, 227.

Laurence de PRESTON [Prestone

occ. 1330 d. 1352

1330, 9 Oct., one of six prof., *SL*, 180, CCA Lit. Ms D.12, fo 3v.

1349/50, granator, CCA DCc, Gran. acct 34.

1338, 1 Mar., an inventory of missing books held him responsible for the loss of an ordinale cum ymagine de Ascencione, *Lit. Cant.*, no 618 (Reg. L, fo 104).

1349, 4 June, 30th in order at the el. of an abp, Reg. G, fo 60v.

1349, 8/9 Sept., 29th at the el. of an abp, *ib.*, fo 76v.

1352, 9 Apr., d., CCA Lit. Ms D.12, fo 16v.

William PRESTON

occ. 1454 d. 1457

1454, 28 Apr., one of eight prof., *SL*, 189, CCA Lit. Ms D.12, fo 8.

1455, 5 Apr., ord acol., Canterbury cathedral, *Reg. abp Bourgchier*, 359.

1456, 13 Mar., ord subdcn, Canterbury cathedral, *ib.*, 363.

1457, 28 July, dcn, d. in his third yr of monastic life, *Chron. Stone*, 67; his obit, on 29 July, in BL Ms Arundel 68, fo 36, names him subdcn.

Ralph de PRETELWELLE [Pritelwelle, Prytelewelle, Prytewell

occ. 1282/3 occ. 1295

n.d., the name Ralph [Radulphus] occ. in the late 13th c. section of the list in *SL*, 175, CCA Lit. Ms D.12, fo 2v.

1282/3, warden of manors, CCA DCc Cliffe acct 5.

1284/95, treasurer, CCA DCc MA1, fos 141v–193.

1290, 22 Aug., with Richard de Selesia, q.v., recd letters of credence from the prior and convent to present to Cardinal Benedict, CUL Ms Ee.5.31, fo 31v.

1292, 10 Dec., with Richard de Clyve, apptd general proctors to represent the prior and convent in all causes, CUL Ms Ee.5.31, fo 35.

1296, 31 Mar., d., CCA Lit. Ms D.12, fo 15.

The Eastry catalogue contains five volumes under his name, including several works of history, one of these concerning Mohammed and his followers, James, *Ancient Libraries*, nos 711–715 (p. 78).

An inventory of missing service books dated 1 Mar. 1338 records the loss of his Exequiae, *Lit. Cant.*, no 618 (Reg. L, fo 104).

An inventory of vestments, *temp.* prior Eastry, includes a linen chasuble of his, [?gift] and two albs, Legg and Hope, *Inventories*, 52, 59 (BL Mc Cotton Galba E.iv, fos 112ᵛ, 115).

An inventory of the refectory, dated 1328, includes a silver *ciphus* formerly his, and three *ciphi de murra*, Dart, *Antiq. Cant.*, xix, xxi, xxiii (BL Ms Cotton Galba E.iv, fos 178ᵛ, 179ᵛ, 180).

William de PRINKEHAM
occ. 1st half 13th c.

n.d., name occ. in the list in *SL*, 174, CCA Lit. Ms D.12, fo 1ᵛ.

PRUDENTIUS
n.d.

n.d., 16 May, obit occ. in Lambeth Ms 20, fo 187.

PUCYN
see Poucyn

John PYKENOT [Pikenot
occ. 1235/6 occ. 1260

n.d., name occ. in the list in *SL*, 174, CCA Lit. Ms D.12, fo 1ᵛ.

1235/6, refectorer, CCA DCc AS 4.
1236/7, prob. warden of manors with Ralph de Redyng, q.v., CCA DCc AS5 and see below.
1257, Mar./1259, cellarer, Reg. H, fo 187ᵛ, CCA DCc MA1, fos 99–101ᵛ, Reg. H, fo 198.
1260, May/1261, monk carpenter, Reg. H, fo 205.
n.d., sacrist during the rebuilding of the cloister, Woodruff, 'Letters to Eastry', 6.

[1244 × 1258], one of the monks who were carrying out manorial visits and recd a warning letter from prior Nicholas de Sandwyco, q.v., about their absence from Canterbury for long periods, their excessive hospitality on the manors and their failure to alleviate the financial distress of the priory, CCA DCc Cart. Antiq. B.393(23).

Richard PYKENOT [Pikenot, Pykenoth
occ. c. 1275 d. 1308

1279/81, chamberlain, CCA DCc MA1, fos 130–135.
1289/90, bartoner, CCA DCc MA1, fos 158ᵛ–165.
1299, 25 Apr., apptd chamberlain, *Reg. abp Winchelsey*, 337–338; see also CCA DCc MA1, fo 222, Reg. Q, fo 41.
1300/1, chamberlain, CCA DCc MA1, fos 225–231ᵛ.
c. 1275, alleged to have been the ringleader of the rebellious monks vs prior Thomas de Ryngmer, q.v.
[c. 1283], a report of his misdemeanours and those of William de Tonge, q.v., is preserved in CCA DCc DE73; it alludes to a plot to murder Thomas de Stureye I, q.v. in Italy. Pykenot and Tonge must have been the two monks who had gone to Rome with their accusations vs prior Thomas Ryngmer, q.v.
1308, 29 Nov., d., CCA Lit. Ms D.12, fo 15ᵛ.

The name Pykenot ref. to a Canterbury family whose name was given to a lane in the city, Woodruff, 'Letters to Eastry', 6.

An inventory of the refectory, dated 1328, includes two *ciphi de murra* formerly his, Dart, *Antiq. Cant.*, xxii (BL Ms Cotton Galba E.iv, fo 179ᵛ).

Note: if this monk is listed among the adm. and prof. in *SL*, he must be hidden under his toponymic, but the numerous contemporary Richards discourage any attempt at identification.

John PYKYNHERST
occ. 1st half 13th c.

n.d., name occ. in the list in *SL*, 174, CCA Lit. Ms D.12, fo 1ᵛ.

Matthew PYNKENY [Pinkeny, Pynkeney
occ. 1254/5 occ. 1272/3

n.d., name occ. in the list in *SL*, 174, CCA Lit. Ms D.12, fo 1ᵛ.

1254/60, monk carpenter, Reg. H, fos 181, 185ᵛ, 190ᵛ, 198, 201.
1260, Apr./Sept., 1261/2, chamberlain, Reg. H, fo 201, CCA DCc MA1, fos 103ᵛ–104ᵛ.
1271, cellarer, CCA DCc MA1, fo 115.
1271/3, chamberlain, CCA DCc, fos 115–118.

1259/60, pd a visit to Meopham, CCA DCc Meopham acct 1.

In a list of missing service books, dated 1 Mar. 1338, his diurnale is reported lost, *Lit. Cant.*, no 618 (Reg. L, fo 104).

An inventory of the refectory of 1328 includes a *ciphus de murra* formerly his, Dart, *Antiq. Cant.*, xxi (BL Ms Cotton Galba, E.iv, fo 179ᵛ).

John PYRYE [Pery, Pirry
occ. 1435 d. 1449

1435, 11 Nov., one of five clothed in the monastic habit, Chron Wm Glastynbury, fo 117ᵛ (*SL*, 188, CCA Lit. Ms D.12, fo 7ᵛ).
1436, 3 Mar., ord acol., infirmary chapel, *Reg. abp Chichele*, iv, 383.

1449, d., CCA Lit. Ms D.12, fo 25ᵛ.

Richard QUENYNGATE [Quenygate, Quenynggate, Qwenyngate

occ. [1448] d. 1458

[1448], 25 Jan., one of four prof., *SL*, 189, CCA Lit. Ms D.12, fo 7ᵛ.

1448, 17 Feb., ord acol., Canterbury cathedral, Reg. abp Stafford, fo 202.

1449, 12 Apr., ord subdcn, Canterbury cathedral, *ib.*, fo 203ᵛ.

1450, 3 Apr., ord dcn, Canterbury cathedral, *ib.*, fo 204ᵛ.

1458, student, at Canterbury college, Oxford; see below.

1458, 22 July, d. at Oxford in his tenth yr of monastic life and was buried in St Frideswide's priory church, *Chron. Stone*, 75 (CCA Lit. Ms D.12, fo 26). His obit is in BL Ms Arundel 68, fo 35ᵛ.

College inventories of 1459 and 1465 list six silver spoons formerly his, Pantin, *Cant. Coll. Ox.*, i, 16, 77 (CCA DCc Cart. Antiq. O.135, Reg. N, fo 235ᵛ).

I R.

occ. 1189/91

1189, 5/8 Nov., sacrist, *Epist. Cant.*, 315.

1189, Feb., was among the monks who went to the curia in the appeal vs abp Baldwin and wrote a report of his travels and encounters to the monks at home, *Epist. Cant.*, 281–283; he reported meeting J. [?Jonas, q.v.] and H. [?Henry III, q.v.] at Rheims and then travelling to Le Mans to meet the abp and king ,ib., 282.

1189, 5/8 Nov., one of the monks sent to confer with the king, *Epist. Cant.*, 315.

1191, after 20 May, with J[?onas, q.v.] at the curia and recd a letter from Christ Church, *Epist. Cant.*, 333.

See Ralph, Randulph, Ranulf, Reginald, Richard, Robert, Roger; also Eastry and Tumba.

II R.

occ. 1249/50

1249, 27 Oct., subprior, CCA DCc DE1, i.

1249/50, subchamberlain, CCA DCc MA1, fos 90ᵛ–91ᵛ.

RADYNGATE

see Redyngate

I RALPH [Radulfus

occ. before 1175

1175, el. abbot of Shrewsbury, *Gervase Cant.*, i, 256, *HRH*, 71.

II RALPH

occ. [1175 × 1177] d. 1188

[1175 × 1177], subsacrist, Urry, *Canterbury*, 403.

1188, almoner, *Epist. Cant.*, 254.

[1175 × 1177], witnessed a grant of prior Benedict, q.v, Urry, *Canterbury*, 403.

1188, one of five monks who d. at Rome, *Epist. Cant.*, 254.

III RALPH [Radulfus, Radulphus

occ. 1198 occ. 1202

1198/9, cellarer, CCA Lit. Ms D.4, fo 4ᵛ.

1200/1, sacrist, *ib.*, fo 10ᵛ.

1202/3, cellarer, *ib.*, fo 14.

Note: one of the above Ralphs was prob. the monk whose enthusiasm in support of the cult of St Thomas, immediately after the murder, led to his exile to Colchester abbey by his more discreet and sceptical brethren, *Materials Becket*, ii, 51.

IV RALPH

occ. 1225 occ. 1241

1225/8, 1239, 3 Jan., cellarer, CCA DCc MA1, fos 69ᵛ–72, *Gervase Cant.*, ii, 142.

1241, subprior, *Gervase Cant.*, ii, 197.

1228, 3 Aug., named as one of five *compromissorii* in the el. of an abp, *Gervase Cant.*, ii, 121, 123; see Walter de Eynesham.

1239, 3 Jan., with Stephen de Cranebroke, q.v., sent as proctors to the abp, *Gervase Cant.*, ii, 142.

n.d., 9 May, the obit of a Ralph subprior who d. in Rome occ. in BL Ms Arundel 68, fo 27; but see Ralph II, q.v.

Note: this may be Ralph de Redyng or Ralph de Westgate, q.v.

V RALPH

occ. 1286/7 occ. 1296/7

1286/7, chamberlain, CCA DCc Treas. acct 3.

1296/7, bartoner, CCA DCc MA1, fos 200–208.

Note: the assignment of entries for Ralph III, IV and V above is inevitably arbitrary and may actually include more (or less) than three. See also Ralph de Adesham, Ralph de Pretelwelle, who were contemporaries of Ralph V.

RALPH

see also Rodulfus

RANDULPH [Ranulph

occ. 1275/6 occ. 1286/7

1268/9, treasurer with Oswardus, q.v., CCA DCc MA1 fo 112; also treas. prob. continuously through 1270/7, *ib.*, fos 113, 114ᵛ, 116, 117ᵛ, 119, 121ᵛ, 122ᵛ; see also CCA DCc Monkton acct 5 (1275/6).

1285/6, 1287, treasurer, CCA DCc Meopham acct 8, Treas. accts 2, 3. See John de Well I.

RANULPH [Ranulfus

occ. [1197 × 1198]

[1197, 27 July × 1198, Feb.], with M. Roger, q.v., apptd proctors for the prior and chapter in negotiating a settlement concerning Martham with the prior and chapter of Norwich, *Eng. Epis. Acta*, iii, no 558.

Richard de RAWE [Raw, Rowe

occ. [c. 1281] d. 1330

[c. 1281], one of four prof., *SL*, 176, CCA Lit. Ms D.12, fo 3.

1301/6, chamberlain, CCA DCc MA1, fos 231ᵛ–264ᵛ. His dismissal on 4 May, 1306 is in Reg. Q, fo 31/43; see William de Offinton.

1312/14, 1323/6, 1328, 29 Sept., feretrar, CCA DCc MA2, fos 37–52, 128ᵛ–154ᵛ, BL Ms Cotton Galba E.iv, fo 178; see Thomas de Greneway.

1330, 25 Apr., d., CCA Lit. Ms D.12, fo 16 (as Roger); obit occ. in BL Ms Arundel 68, fo 24ᵛ.

An inventory of missing books, dated 1 Mar. 1338, reported that he had lost the psalterium beatae Mariae of William de Cherryng, q.v., *Lit. Cant.*, no 618 (Reg. L, fo 104).

An inventory of vestments, acquired *temp.* prior Eastry, includes one set made at the order of Rawe and of William de Ledebery, q.v., feretrars, Legg and Hope, *Inventories*, 64 (BL Ms Cotton Galba E.iv, fos 116ᵛ). There is also a chasuble ascribed to Rawe and Greneway, Legg and Hope, *Inventories*, 77 (BL Mc Cotton Galba E.iv, fos 122).

An inventory of the refectory, dated 1328, includes a silver gilt *cuppa* and twelve silver *scutelli*, BL Ms Cotton Galba E.iv, fo 178).

Henry RECOLVER [Recolvere, Reculver, Reyculver

occ. 1416 d. 1462

1416, 22 June, one of eight prof., *SL*, 186, CCA Lit. Ms D.12, fo 6.

1418, 26 Mar., ord acol. and subdcn, Canterbury cathedral, *Reg. abp Chichele*, iv, 332.

1419, 1 Apr., ord dcn, chapel within the priory, *ib.*, i, 191.

1461, 10 July, dismissed from the office of *custos tumbe*, *Chron. Stone*, 84.

1462, 3 Nov., d., in his 47th yr of monastic life, *Chron. Stone*, 87; in CCA Lit. Ms D.12, fo 26, he is described as *conventualis*. His obit on 4 Nov. is in BL Ms Arundel 68, fo 47.

Nicholas RECOLVER [Reculut', Reculver

occ. 1475 d. 1503

1475, 27 Mar., one of four prof., *SL*, 191, CCA Lit. Ms D.12, fo 8ᵛ.

1475, 23 Sept., ord subdcn, prior's chapel, Canterbury, *Reg. abp Bourgchier*, 418.

1476, 21 Sept., ord dcn, Canterbury cathedral, *ib.*, 421.

1483, 29 Mar., ord pr., Canterbury cathedral, *ib.*, 440.

1491, succentor, BL Ms Arundel 68, fo 7ᵛ.

1503, before 29 Jan., feretrar, CCA Lit. Ms D.12, fo 33ᵛ.

1491, as succentor, he was in charge of recording the names of those recd into confraternity with Christ Church, BL Ms Arundel 68, fos 7ᵛ, 8,

1493, 1 May, 34th in order at the ratification of an agreement, Reg. S, fo 383ᵛ; but see John Crosse I.

1501, 26 Apr., 21st at the el. of an abp, Reg. R, fo 56ᵛ.

1503, 29 Jan., d., *explicis* [*sic*], aged 45 and in the 33rd yr of monastic life, CCA Lit. Ms D.12, fo 33ᵛ; there is some error here in the calculations or the copying.

Thomas RECOLVER [Reculver, Reyculvere

occ. 1381 occ. 1385

1381, 6 May, one of eight clothed in the monastic habit, CCA Lit. Ms D.12, fo 5, *SL*, 183.

1385, 23 Dec., ord pr., abp's chapel, Otford, Reg. abp Courtenay, i, fo 308.

1383, 15 Aug., and 29 Aug., one of three nominees for the place of second scholar at Canterbury college, Pantin, *Cant. Coll. Ox.*, iii, 45, 47; but the abp turned him down, *ib.*

1383/4, recd a small sum from the prior *pro benedictione*, Lambeth Ms 243, fo 192ᵛ.

n.d., 16 Apr., obit occ. in BL Ms Arundel 68, fo 24.

William RECOLVER [Raculvr, Raycolvre, Reculver, Reculvere, Reycolver

occ. 1361 d. 1408

1361, 28 Oct., one of nine prof., *SL*, 182, CCA Lit. Ms D.12, fo 4ᵛ.

1362, 24 Sept., ord acol., Charing, Reg. abp Islip, fo 322.

1363, 23 Sept., ord dcn, Faversham monastery, Reg. abp Islip, fo 323ᵛ.

1365, 29 Mar., ord pr., abp's chapel, Charing, *ib.*, fo 326ᵛ.

1372, *custos* of the high altar, CCA DCc MA2, fo 270.

1373/4, 1375/9, *custos martyrii*, CCA DCc Treas. acct 5, MA2, fos 291–318.

1380, *custos tumbe*, CCA DCc MA2, fo 321ᵛ.

[1382, Sept.]/1383, 15 Aug., subprior; he was apptd on the former date and dismissed on the latter, Reg. abp Courtenay, i, fos 22, 42ᵛ.

1390/2, granator, CCA DCc Elverton acct 42, Eastry acct 118.

1391, 25 Apr., one of three monk penitentiaries apptd in the priory, Reg abp Courtenay, i, fo 338.

1362/3, student at Canterbury college, Oxford, for whom cloth *de burneto* was bought for his *cappa scolastica*, Pantin, *Cant. Coll. Ox.*, iv, 182.

1374, 30 June, 25th in order at the el. of an abp, Reg. G, fos 173v–175v.
1381, 31 July, 17th at the el. of an abp, *ib.*, fo 225v.
1396, 7 Aug., 8th at the el. of an abp, *ib.*, fo 234v.
1408, 6 Sept., d. in the 48th yr of his monastic life, CCA Lit. Ms D.12, fo 18v.

REDELYNGWELL
see Rydelyngwolde

Geoffrey REDYNG
occ. 1467 d. 1483

1467, 28 Mar., ord acol., Canterbury cathedral, *Reg. abp Bourgchier*, 399.
1467, 19 Sept., one of six prof., *SL*, 190, CCA Lit. Ms D.12, fo 8.
1468, 12 Mar., ord subdcn, Canterbury cathedral, *Reg. abp Bourgchier*, 398.
1468, 16 Apr., ord dcn, Canterbury cathedral, *ib.*, 400.
1471, 9 Mar., ord pr., Canterbury cathedral, *Reg. abp Bourgchier*, 405.
1483, 5 Sept., d. at the age of 36, CCA Lit. Ms D.12, fo 26v; his obit is in BL Ms Arundel 68, fo 40v.

Henry de REDYNG [Reddyng
occ. 1354 d. 1395

1354, 28 Nov., one of seven prof., *SL*, 181, CCA Lit. Ms D.12, fo 4.
1356, 18 June, ord acol., Hoath chapel in Reculver parish, Reg. abp Islip, fo 316.
1356, 24 Sept., ord subdcn, abp's chapel, Tenham, *ib.*, fo 316.
1358, 22 Sept., ord dcn, Charing, *ib.*, fo 317.
1360, 29 Feb., ord pr., abp's chapel, Otford, *ib.*, fo 318.
1367, 11 Nov., *magister ordinis*, *SL*, 182, CCA Lit. Ms D.12, fo 4v.
1379, *custos martyrii*, CCA DCc MA2, fo 318.
1379/82, 1383/4, *custos*, St Mary in crypt, CCA DCc MA2, fos 318–329v, Treas. acct 26, fos 2–6v.
1385, *custos tumbe*, CCA DCc MA2, fo 334v.
1374, 30 June, 19th in order at the el. of an abp, Reg. G, fos 173v–175v.
1381, 31 July, 13th at the el. of an abp, *ib.*, fo 225v.
1395, 28 Feb., d. in his 41st yr of monastic life, CCA Lit. Ms D.12, fo 17.

Ralph de REDYNG [Reding
occ. 1237

n.d., name occ. in the *post exilium* list in *SL*, 173, CCA Lit. Ms D.12, fo 1.
1236/7, name occ. as an acctant, prob. warden of manors with John Pykenot, q.v., on CCA DCc AS5.
Note: See R. II and Ralph IV.

John de REDYNGATE [Radyngate, Redynggate, Ryedyngate
occ. 1339 occ. 1367

1339, 13 Dec., one of five prof., *SL*, 180, CCA Lit. Ms D.12, fo 4.
1350/1, 1353/4, treasurer, CCA DCc Treas. acct 27, Bocking acct 32.
1354/6, warden of manors, CCA DCc Agney acct 50, Ebony acct 55.
1356/60, 1362/7, bartoner, CCA DCc Bart. accts 35–43.
1362/3, 1366/7, also warden of manors, CCA DCc Eastry accts 97, 100.
1367, 31 Mar./22 Apr., warden of Canterbury college, *Reg. abp Langham*, 283–285, Pantin, *Cant. Coll. Ox.*, iii, 14–16, iv, 19.
1349, 4 June, 49th in order at the el. of an abp, Reg. G, fo 60v.
1349, 8/9 Sept., 48th at the el. of an abp, *ib.*, fo 76v.
1355, 10 Feb., granted papal dispensation to choose his own confessor, *CPL*, iii (1342–1362), 578.
1366, 10 May, named as one of seven *compromissorii* at the el. of an abp, Reg. G, fo 148.
1366, 6 July, one of the monks apptd by the prior, *sed. vac.*, to visit St Gregory's priory, Canterbury, Reg. G, fo 127v.
1366, 16 Sept., with James Stone I, q.v., apptd proctor to attend the Black Monk Chapter meeting in Northampton, Pantin, *BMC*, iii, 59.

REFHAM
see Resham

William REGEWEYE [Regway, Riggeway, Rygewey, Ryggeweye
occ. 1401 d. 1427

1401, 19 Mar., ord acol., Canterbury cathedral, Reg. abp Arundel, i, fo 325.
1401, 25 Mar., one of seven prof., *SL*, 185, CCA Lit. Ms D.12, fo 5v.
1401, 17 Dec., ord subdcn, Canterbury cathedral, Reg. abp Arundel, i, fo 329.
1403, 14 Apr., ord dcn, Canterbury cathedral, *ib.*, i, fo 331.
1414, 12 Mar., 52nd in order at the el. of an abp, *Reg. abp Chichele*, i, 4.
1427, 20 June, d., in his 26th yr of monastic life, CCA Lit. Ms D.12, fo 22–22v; his obit on 15 June, is in BL Ms Arundel 68, fo 31.

REGINALD
occ. 1199 occ. 1205

1199/1203, cellarer, CCA Lit. Ms D.4, fos 9, 10v, 12v, 14.
1205, Oct., before, subprior, *Fasti*, ii, 5.
1205, Oct., not later than, el. abp; quashed by the pope before 20 Dec. 1206, *Fasti*, ii, 5 and see *CPL*, i (1198–1304), 23; see below.

n.d., 17 Apr., the obit of a Reginald occ. in BL Ms Arundel 68, fo 24^{v}.

Note: the Canterbury elections of 1205/6 present a complicated and somewhat uncertain sequence of events which both Prof. Knowles and Prof. Christopher Cheney have sought to elucidate in 'Cant. Election', 211–22 and 'A Neglected Record of the Canterbury Election of 1205–1206' *Bulletin of the Institute of Historical Research* (1946–8), 21, 233–258, respectively. These two articles piece together the order of events as far as these can be determined from a variety of somewhat conflicting sources including Gervase (Gesta Regum), Wendover (Flores Historiarum), Cheney (*Letters of Innocent III*, nos 655, 725–727). The suffragan bps in the province of Canterbury tried to assert their right to participate in archiepiscopal elections, but the pope refused to accept their petition. After Hubert Walter's d., the younger monks el. their subprior without waiting for the royal licence, and sent him to Rome for confirmation. The older monks were content with the king's nomination of the bp of Norwich, thus leading to opposing factions in the chapter. The inquiry set up by the pope resulted in Reginald's el. being quashed around Christmas 1206, after sixteen monks had been summoned to Rome in Mar., 1206 to give evidence, *CPL*, i (1198–1304), 26. They proceeded, as *compromissorii* to make a new el. in the papal presence and chose Stephen Langton.

REGINALD
see also Reynaldus

[Ralph REMENSIS [de Sarr', Serris
occ. 1187 d. 1194/5

Gave a large number of volumes, mainly Old Testament texts and biblical commentaries, listed in the Eastry catalogue, James, *Ancient Libraries*, nos 859–896 (pp. 86–88).

Name in
(1) Cambridge, Pembroke College Ms 210, Numeri, glossed (12th c.), possibly identical with no 862 above.
(2) Cambridge, Trinity College Ms 74, Pseudo-Dionysius etc. (12th c.).
(3) Douai, Bibliothèque, mun. 202, John Scotus (12th c.).

Note: he was dean of Rheims who entertained prior Honorius, q.v, in France during the dispute with abp Baldwin, *Gervase Cant*, i, 366. He was granted [the state of] *monachatus* and even if he should d. before having put on the habit he was to be remembered as though he had, Dart, *Antiq. Cant.*, xxviii (BL Ms Cotton Claudius C.vi, fo 172). James, in *Ancient Libraries*, 537, has mistakenly thought that he might have been almoner and have d. in 1188, but provides no refs. See B. Smalley, *The Becket Conflict and the Schools*, (Oxford, 1973), 210–211 for his career and relations with Christ Church.

There are several letters written in 1187/8 to him in *Epist. Cant.*, 13–14, 113, 188, 220, and one written by him to the Christ Church monks prob. in 1187, *ib.*, 88.

Stubbs states that he was an Englishman, educated at Christ Church and d. c. 1194/5, *ib.*, 559.]

REMIGIUS
n.d.

n.d., the obit of a pr. by this name occ. on 9 Jan in BL Ms Cotton Nero C.ix, fo 3^{v} and Lambeth Ms 20, fo 158.

William de RESHAM [?Refham
occ. [1241] d. 1291/2

[1241], name occ. in the list in *SL*, 174, CCA Lit. Ms D.12, fo 2; he was probably one of the twelve prof. with Richard de Wynchepe, q.v.

[1284 × 1289], almoner, CCA DCc ES Roll 364.

1264, 16 Apr., with Thomas de Stureye I, q.v., and by comm. from the abp, installed prior Adam de Chillenden, q.v., *Gervase Cant.*, ii, 229.

1270, 9 Sept., one of seven *compromissorii* named by the prior and chapter in the el. of an abp, *Gervase Cant.*, ii, 252–253; see Adam de Chillenden.

1291/2, 23 Mar., d., CCA Lit. Ms D.12, fo 15; his obit is in BL Ms Arundel 68, fo 21^{v}.

The Eastry catalogue contains an uncertain no of vols beneath his name, possibly over thirty, James, *Ancient Libraries*, nos 1451–?1484 (pp. 123–124).

REYCULVER
see Recolver

REYNALDUS
occ. 1145

1145, 1 Sept., with Walter [Durdent] prior and Clement I and Hugh I, q.v., witnessed a [probably spurious] inspeximus by abp Theobald of a (wholly spurious) charter of bp Gundulf of Rochester, *Theobald Charters*, no 222.

REYNALDUS
see also Reginald

I RICHARD
occ. [1093 × 1109]

[1093 × 1109], possibly chaplain to abp Anselm, later abbot of Chester, M. Chibnall, 'The Relation of St Anselm with the English Dependencies of the Abbey of Bec, 1079–1093' *Spicilegium Beccense*, 1 (1959), 524**.

Note: a Richard, prob. monk of Canterbury, recd a letter from abp Anselm absolving him from a pilgrimage vow, *Anselm Letters*, no 188.

II RICHARD
occ. [1143 × 1148] occ. 1152

[1143 × 1148], with Walter [Durdent] prior, and Hugh de Caen, q.v., witnessed a confirmation by the abp of the possessions of Dover priory, *Theobald Charters*, no 86.

1152, witnessed a purchase of land in Canterbury by prior Wibert, q.v., Urry, *Canterbury*, 392.

Note:
(1) a Richard, who had been chaplain to abp Theobald and presumably a Christ Church monk, was apptd prior of Dover in 1157, *HRH*, 88.
(2) is Richard II, Richard de Dover I, q.v., whom the monks el. abp in 1173? See also Richard de Witstapla.

III R[?ICHARD
occ. 1187

1187, Sept., *quondam* chaplain of Thomas Becket, sent with Alexander de Dover and others to Normandy, to explain their position vis-à-vis the abp to the king, *Epist. Cant.*, 94–95.

In the Eastry catalogue there are four vols under the name Richard *capellanus S. Thome*,, James, *Ancient Libraries*, nos 897–900 (p. 88).

IV RICHARD
occ. 1213 occ. 1238/9

1213, 29 Sept., cellarer, CCA DCc MA1, fo 53v.
1216, 29 Sept., granator, CCA DCc MA1, fo 58v.
1218, 1 Nov., cellarer, CCA DCc MA1, fo 61v; on 7 Nov. he was named as granator, *ib.*, fo 60.
1219, 1 Nov., 1220/1, Dec., cellarer, CCA DCc MA1, fos 62v, 65, 63v, 66v.
1224/5, granator, CCA DCc AS1, MA1, fos 68v–69v.
1230/2, 1238/9, cellarer, CCA DCc AS2, MA1, fos 73v–75v, 80.

See note below Richard VI.

V RICHARD
occ. 1222 occ. 1235/6

1222/4, chaplain to the prior, CCA DCc MA1, fos 66v–68v.
1227, precentor, CCA DCc MA1, fo 71.
1235, sacrist, CCA DCc MA1, fo 78.
1235/6, chaplain to the prior, CCA DCc MA1, fos 78–79.

See note below Richard VI.

VI RICHARD
occ. 1253 occ. 1257

1253/7, cellarer, CCA DCc MA1, fos 94–99.

Note: the assignment of entries to Richards III, IV and V is, to say the least, arbitrary. My decisions have been influenced by a consistency with regard to apptments to office, a consistency which may well have been non-existent at the time. There are at least nine monks of this name who may be intended, e.g. Richard de Berksore, Richard Bryan junior, Richard Bryan senior, Richard de Cruce Signata, Richard Dygon, Richard de Eastry, Richard de Frakynham, Richard de Gravenall, Richard de Mallyng, Richard de Siwell. See also R.

John de RICHEMOND [Richemund, Rychemund
occ. 1333 d. 1361

1333, 9 Oct., one of eleven tonsured, *SL*, 180, CCA Lit. Ms D.12, fo 4.
1358/9, cellarer; he was apptd 8 Oct. 1358 and absolved 14 Sept. 1359, Reg. abp Islip, fos 144, 151–151v.
1349, 4 June, 34th in order at the el. of an abp, Reg. G, fo 60v.
1349, 8/9 Sept., 33rd at the el. of an abp, *ib.*, fo 76v.
1361, 11 Aug., d., one of c.25 monks carried off [by the plague] between June and Oct., CCA Lit. Ms D.12, fo 17.

Ralph de RICHEMOND [Rychemund
occ. 2nd half 13th c.

n.d., name occ. in the list in *SL*, 176, CCA Lit. Ms D.12, fo 2v.

I William RICHEMOND [Richemund, Richmonde, Rychemond, Rychemont, Rychemund
occ. 1354 d. 1406

1354, 28 Nov., one of seven prof., *SL*, 181, CCA Lit. Ms D.12, fo 4.
1356, 18 June, ord subdcn, Hoath chapel in Reculver parish, Reg. abp Islip, fo 316.
1358, 22 Sept., ord dcn, Charing, *ib.*, fo 317.
1360, 29 Feb., ord pr., abp's chapel, Otford, *ib.*, fo 318.
1367, 1 Aug., apptd penitentiary for Christ Church, *Reg. abp Langham*, 289.
1371, 14 Sept., apptd warden of Canterbury college, Pantin, *Cant. Coll. Ox.*, iii, 22. He had been one of three nom. in Apr. [1367], *ib*, iii, 15.
1373, 20 Feb., apptd penitentiary, Reg. abp Wittlesey, fo 58v; he was penitentiary in June 1374, Reg. G, fo 175v.
1381, May/1383, almoner, CCA DCc Alm. accts 19, 54, 3; he was almoner on 18 June, 1381, Oxford Bod. Ms Ashmole 794, fo 248v.
1389/90, *custos martyrii*, Pantin, *Cant. Coll. Ox.*, iv, 190.
1402, 9 Dec., before; 1406, 17 Nov., before, penitentiary, Reg. abp Arundel, i, fo 43v; CCA Lit. Ms D.12, fo 18; see below.

1366, 6 July, one of the monks apptd by the prior, *sed. vac.* to visit St Gregory's priory, Canterbury, Reg. G, fo 127^{v}.
1374, 30, June, 17th in order and one of three *scrutatores* in the el. of an abp, Reg. G, fo 173^{v}–175^{v}.
1376, Apr., one of ten monks nominated to the committee set up for regulating the infirmary, *Lit. Cant.*, no 945 (CCA DCc Cart. Antiq. C.206).
1381, 31 July, 11th at the el. of an abp, Reg. G, fo 225^{v}; he was chosen as one of six *compromissorii* by the three *compromissorii* previously named, Oxford, Bod. Ms Ashmole 794, fo 254^{v}.
1396, 7 Aug., 5th at the el. of an abp, Reg. G, fo 234^{v}.
1406, 17 Nov., d., in his 54th yr of monastic life, having served for many yrs *strenuissime* in the office of penitentiary, CCA Lit. Ms D.12, fo 18.

Name in Paris, Bibliothèque Mazarine Ms 5, Biblia sacra (13th c.); *cujus custos*—.

II William RICHEMOND [Richemont, Richemund, Rychemond, Rychemont, Rychemund
occ. 1432 d. 1448

1432, 19 Sept., one of six prof., *SL*, 188, CCA Lit. Ms D.12, fo 7^{v}.
1434, 13 Mar., ord acol. and subdcn, infirmary chapel, *Reg. abp Chichele*, iv, 378.
1436, 25 Sept., 1437, 6 Oct., scholar at Canterbury college, Oxford, Pantin, *Cant. Coll. Ox.*, iv, 192.
1439/40, at Oxford and recd travelling expenses to Canterbury, Pantin, *ib.*, ii, 154 (CCA DCc Cart. Antiq. O.151.10).
1440/1, student, with a pension of £5 for half the yr, Pantin, *ib.*, ii, 160 (CCA DCc Cart. Antiq., O.151.11).
1443/5, student for the whole yr with a pension of £10, Pantin, *ib.*, ii, 163, 167 (CCA DCc Cart. Antiq., O.151.12, 13); he did not return to Canterbury for the abp's visitation on 30 Mar. 1444, Pantin, *ib.*, iii, 100–101 (Reg. S, fo 159).
1446/7, given travel money to return to Oxford, *ib.*, iv, 194 (CCA DCc MA4, fo 142^{v}).
1448, 19 Feb., d. at Oxford, and was buried in St Frideswide's priory church in the choir before the high altar, *Chron. Stone*, 43.

A letter prob. written to him by a monk of Peterborough on 2 Sept. [?1438] is printed in Pantin, *Cant. Coll. Ox.*, iii, 96–98.

Fifteenth c. college inventories include a book and a silver *pecia* given by him, Pantin, *Cant. Coll. Ox.*, i, 12, 16, 77 (CCA DCc Cart. Antiq. O.135, Reg. N, fo 235^{v}).

RIGGEWAY
see Regeweye

RINGMER
see Ryngemer

I ROBERT
occ. [1103/4]

[1103/4], described in two letters of Anselm as 'the monk in charge of his *domus* and belongings' [at Canterbury], *Anselm Letters*, nos 289, 331.

II ROBERT
occ. [1153 × 1161]

[1153 × 1161], sacrist [*secretarius*], *Theobald Charters*, no 40 (Reg. B, fo 146^{v}).
[1153 × 1161], *temp.* prior Wibert, q.v., witnessed a grant of certain demesne tithes of the priory at the request of abp Theobald, *ib.*

III ROBERT
occ. 1170 occ. 1197

1170, sacrist, *Gervase Cant.*, i, 222.
[1187, 28 Aug. × Sept.], former sacrist, [re]apptd sacrist by the abp vs the monks' wishes, *Eng. Epis. Acta*, ii, no 253; he was sacrist in Feb. 1188, *Epist. Cant.*, 166; see below and Roger Norreys I.
1193, before, subprior, *HRH*, 88.
1170, spring, involved in the chapter's disputes with the abp, *Epist. Cant.*, 92, *Gervase Cant.*, i, 222.
1187, after 11 Aug., directed by prior Honorius, q.v., not to accept office at the hands of the abp, *Epist. Cant.*, 81, 94–95; see also Roger III.
1187, Sept., had been sent, with Roger Norreys I, q.v., and others to the king and abp at Alençon, Normandy, where he now spoke out vs the abp's treatment of the chapter, *Gervase Cant.*, i, 379. He was reinstated as sacrist by the abp by order of the king as part of a proposed agreement with the abp, *ib.*, i, 380–381. The monks refused to accept him as sacrist, and he wrote to the abp to say that he had not understood the import of the negotiations at Alençon and no longer acquiesced in the terms put forward, *Epist. Cant.*, 92.
1188, Feb., refused the king's order to attend a meeting at Northampton as did the subprior [Geoffrey II, q.v.], *Epist. Cant.*, 166.
1189, 5/8 Nov., an R., sacrist was one of the party of monks sent to London to confer with the king over their dispute with the abp, *ib.*, 315.
1193/6, prior of Dover, *HRH*, 88.
1197/1208, abbot of Eynsham, *ib.*, 88, 49.
1208, d., *HRH*, 49; obit occ. 9 Sept., BL Ms Arundel, fo 40^{v}.

There are two letters from John of Salisbury addressed to him as sacrist:
(1) spring 1170, *Salisbury Letters*, ii, no 299.

(2) mid Oct. 1170, urging him and William Brito, q.v., to meet and welcome the returning abp, *ib.*, ii, no 303.

IV ROBERT [de Hastings
occ. 1186

1186, occ. before May, when he was el. abbot of Chester [abbot Robert III], *HRH*, 39.
1194, res., *ib.*; obit 29 June or 25 Sept., *ib.*

V ROBERT
occ. 1197 occ. 1201

1197/1201, sacrist, CCA Lit. Ms D.4, fos 2ᵛ, 4ᵛ, 9, 10ᵛ.

VI ROBERT
occ. 1198 occ. 1207

1198/1204, 1207, almoner, CCA Lit. Ms D.4, fos 4ᵛ, 9, 10ᵛ, 12ᵛ, 14ᵛ, 16, CCA DCc MA1, fo 59ᵛ.

VII ROBERT
occ. 1238/41

1238, chamberlain, CCA DCc MA1, fo 80.
1239/41, subchamberlain, CCA DCc MA1, fos 80ᵛ–82ᵛ.

VIII ROBERT
occ. [1283]

[1283], 25 Oct., sacrist, *Epist. Pecham*, 628.

[1283], 25 Oct., at the curia, acting as proctor for the prior and convent, *ib.*

Note: in a list of missing books dated 1 Mar., 1338 a Bible, formerly in the possession of Robert, Sacrist, or John de Chatham, q.v., had been 'charged out' to John de Wynchelse I, q.v., Lit. Cant., no 618 (Reg. L, fo 104).

IX ROBERT
occ. 1296

1296, 2 Jan., described as monk of Christ Church, apptd bp of Clonfert, *CPL*, i (1198–1304), 561; obtained royal approval to rec. his temporalities on 24 Sept. of this yr, *CPR 1292–1301*, 203.

Note: Robert VIII and Robert IX may be identical.

RODLANDUS
occ. 2nd half 13th c.

n.d., name occ. in the list in *SL*, 175, CCA Lit. Ms D.12, fo 2.

RODULFUS
n.d.

n.d., *conversus*, 'who gave Tincham' and whose obit occ. on 24 Jan. in BL Ms Cotton Nero C.ix, fo 4.

Jordan de ROFF' [Rofa
occ. 1239

n.d., name occ. in the list in *SL*, 172, CCA Lit. Ms D.12, fo 1.

1239, 4 Jan., one of the group of monks accused of contumacy by the abp after the forgery scandal, *Gervase Cant.*, ii, 144; see Simon de Hertlepe. On 1 Feb. he was among those summoned to appear before the abp after the monks' el. of Roger de La Lee, q.v., as prior, *ib.*, ii, 153.
n.d., 7 Jan., pr., whose obit occ. in BL Ms Arundel 68, fo 12ᵛ.

Name in Oxford, Pembroke college Ms 5, T. Wallensis etc. (13th to 15th cs); on fo 114, Interpretaciones hebraicorum nominum secundum Remigium— (genitive).

Three items in the Eastry catalogue are ascribed to Jordan, nos 1303–1305, of which no 1305 is the Pembroke college Ms above, James, *Ancient Libraries*, 112.

Note: see also Jordan.

John de ROFFA
occ. 1221/2

1221/2, cellarer, CCA DCc MA1, fo 66ᵛ.

Note: this may be Jordan de Roff', q.v., above.

I ROGER
occ. [1103]

[1103], named in a letter of abp Anselm to prior Ernulf, q.v., in which the abp stated that he had written to Roger to reprimand him for his neglect in allowing the brethren to be reduced to penury, *Anselm Letters*, no 307. Was he treasurer?

II ROGER
occ. before 1175

1175, became abbot of St Augustine's, *HRH*, 36.
n.d., 21 Oct., obit occ. in BL Mss Cotton Nero C.ix, fo 14 and Arundel 68, fo 46.

Note: he is sometimes called Lurdingden, e.g. by Elmham, C. Hardwick, ed., *Historia monasterii S. Augustini Cantuariensis, by Thomas of Elmham*, Rolls Series (1858), 37.

III ROGER
occ. 1187

1187, Aug./Sept., treasurer, *Epist. Cant.*, 81, 94; he was no longer in this office on 1 Jan. 1188, *ib.*, 126.

1187, after 11 Aug., had been sent with Robert III, sacrist, q.v. and others to confer with the abp in Alençon, Normandy and instructed by the prior, Honorius, q.v., not to accept any office at the hands of the abp, *Epist. Cant.*, 81, 94–95.

IV M. ROGER
occ. [1197 × 1198]

[1197, 27 July × 1198, Feb.], with Ranulf, q.v., apptd proctors for the prior and chapter in negotiating a settlement concerning Martham with the prior and chapter of Norwich, *Eng. Epis. Acta*, iii, no 558.

V ROGER

occ. 1205 occ. 1235

1213/19, Nov., sacrist, CCA DCc MA1, fos 53v–62v.

1219, 1 Nov. ,1220, 18 Oct., subchamberlain, CCA DCc MA1, fos 61v, 64.

1221/2, bartoner, CCA DCc MA1, fos 65–66v.

1230/5, chaplain to the prior, CCA DCc MA1, fos 73v–78.

1205, 11 Dec., one of the monks who appealed to the pope to confirm the chapter's el. of their subprior, Reginald, q.v., as abp, *CPL*, i (1198–1304), 23.

Note: there may be more than one Roger included under Roger V; and possibly some of the entries apply to Roger III and/or Roger IV; see also Roger de La Lee.

VI ROGER

occ. 1254/6

1254, 13 Nov., 1255, 3 Dec., 1256, 15 Nov., treasurer, CCA DCc MA1, fos 95, 96, 97v.

Note: the obit of a Roger dcn occ. on 3 Jan. in BL Ms Arundel 68, fo 12.

ROGER

see also Tumba

Thomas ROKYSLE [Rokesle, Rokysley

occ. 1423 d. 1439

1423, 30 Sept., one of five prof., *SL*, 187, CCA Lit. Ms D.12, fo 6v.

1425, 22 Dec., ord subdcn, Charing, *Reg. abp Chichele*, iv, 374.

[1432] 11 June, ord pr., place not named, Reg. Langdon (Rochester), fo 74v.

1435, 11 Nov., absolved from the office of *parvus sacrista*, Chron. Wm Glastynbury, fo 117v.

1440, 31 Jan., d., *Chron. Stone*, 23.

Stephen ROLLYNG

occ. 1364 d. 1404

1363, 6 Aug., ord acol., abp's chapel, Canterbury, Reg. abp Islip, fo 323.

1364, one of eleven prof., *SL*, 182, CCA Lit. Ms D.12, fo 4v.

1364, 9 Mar., ord subdcn, abp's chapel, Charing, Reg. abp Islip, fo 325.

1365, 29 Mar., ord dcn, abp's chapel, Charing, *ib.*, fo 326.

1367, 18 Sept., ord pr., Lambeth palace chapel, *Reg. abp Langham*, 383.

1371/2, 1373/4, feretrar, CCA DCc MA2, fos 266–270, Treas. acct 5.

1373/4, *custos* of St Mary in crypt, CCA DCc MA2, fos 276–281v.

1375/8, feretrar, CCA DCc MA2, fos 291–314v.

1380/1, treasurer, CCA DCc MA2, fo 328.

c. 1380, *magister ordinis*, *SL*, 183, CCA Lit. Ms D.12, fo 5.

1382, feretrar, CCA DCc MA2, fo 329v.

1382/3, chamberlain, CCA DCc Alm. acct; he was apptd Sept. 1382, Reg. abp Courtenay, i, fo 22, but served only part of the yr; see Robert Hore and William Brygge II.

1383, 25 Aug., apptd cellarer, Reg. abp Courtenay, i, fo 43v, but absolved the following day, *certis de causis*, *ib.*

1383/4, feretrar, CCA DCc Treas. acct 26, fos 2–6v.

1384, chamberlain, CCA DCc Treas. acct 26, fo 7.

1384/5, cellarer, CCA DCc Godmersham acct 27.

1385, feretrar, CCA DCc MA2, fo 334v.

1388/9, third prior, Lambeth Ms 243, fo 212v.

1397/8, n.d., but before 1404, 26 May, subprior, CCA DCc Feret. acct 1, and CCA Lit. Ms D.12, fo 18, where it states that he was twice subprior.

1374, 30 June, 39th in order at the el. of an abp, Reg. G, fos 173v–175v.

1381, 31 July, 27th at the el. of an abp, *ib.*, fo 225v.

1392/3, contributed 12s. to the sacrist *pro dealbacione chori*, Woodruff, 'Sacrist's Rolls', 48 (CCA DCc Sac. acct 11).

1396, 7 Aug., 12th in order at the el. of an abp, Reg. G, fo 234v.

1404, 26 May, d., CCA Lit. Ms D.12, fo 18.

Geoffrey de ROMENAL [Rumenhale

occ. 1270 d. 1301

n.d., name in the list in *SL*, 175, CCA Lit. Ms D.12, fo 2.

1271, 1273, 21 Mar., third prior, Reg. A, fo 332, Lambeth Ms 241, fo 10v.

1283/5, 1288/9, precentor, CCA DCc Meopham accts 4, 5, Merstham acct 7.

1289, 23 June, chamberlain, and was not to be allowed to res. until the abp had consulted the convent, *Reg. abp Pecham*, ii, 242 and CCA DCc EC IV/101.

1293, 13 Feb., 20 and 23 Mar., 26 May; 1294, 14 Oct., precentor, *Reg. abp Winchelsey*, 1262, 1281, 1276, 1279, 5 (where the first name is Galterus).

1270, apptd by the prior and convent to be official of the court of Canterbury, *sed. vac.*, Selden Soc., *Select Cases Eccles.*, 16, 19.

1273, 21 Mar., proctor for the prior and convent in negotiations with Dover priory, Lambeth Ms 241, fo 10v.

1290, served as proctor at the provincial council at Ely, *ib.*, 19, n.1.

1292, 19 Dec., present at the funeral of abp Pecham in Canterbury cathedral, *Reg. abp Winchelsey*, 1258.

1293, 13 Feb., named as one of seven *compromissorii* in the el. of an abp and acted as proxy for William de Codelawe, q.v., *ib.*, 1265, 1262, also Reg. Q, fos 14ᵛ, 19ᵛ.

1293, 20 Mar., with Robert de Selesia, q.v., sent to Rome to obtain confirmation of the el. of the abp, *Reg. abp Winchelsey*, 1281. On 4 Aug. he wrote to the prior from monte Viterbo asking for credit through Italian bankers in London, *ib.*, 1282–1284 (CCA DCc Cart. Antiq. S.380).

1294, 14 Oct., one of the monks present in Siena when abp Winchelsey made an apptment to the see of Llandaff, *Reg. abp Winchelsey*, 5–6.

1294, 26 Oct., in Rome with his *socii*, to whom the prior wrote with news of English affairs and the assurance of the much needed funds, CUL Ms Ee.5.31, fo 63ᵛ; see Richard de Selesia.

1301, 21 Oct., d., CCA Lit. Ms D.12, fo 15ᵛ.

His name heads a list of up to forty-five volumes in the Eastry catalogue; these cover a wide range of subjects including works of history, theology and canon law, James, *Ancient Libraries*, nos 721–?767 (pp. 79–81).

Two volumes, Magister historiarum and Casus Bernardi, formerly his, turn up in 15th and 16th c. Canterbury college inventories the latter being no 748 or no 753 in the Eastry catalogue, Pantin, *Cant. Coll. Ox.*, i, 3, 5, 11, 14, 40, 97.

A list of missing service books dated 1 Mar. 1338, includes his diurnale which had been passed on to Thomas de Myddelton, q.v., *Lit. Cant.*, no 618 (Reg. L, fo 104).

An inventory of the refectory dated 1328 includes a silver gilt *cuppa*, two silver *ciphi* and one *de murra* and six small silver *ciphi*, formerly his, Dart, *Antiq. Cant.*, xviii, xix, xxii (BL Ms Cotton Galba, E.iv, fo 178, 178ᵛ, 180).

Gervase commended him for defending the chapter's *sed. vac.* jurisdiction, vs the inroads of the suffragan bps, *Gervase Cant.*, ii, 251. See also *Reg. Giffard* (Worcester), 47–48, which provides evidence of the suffragans appealing to Rome vs the Canterbury chapter in 1271.

M. Hugh de ROMENAL
occ. 1st half 13th c.

n.d., name occ. in the list in *SL*, 173, CCA Lit. Ms D.12, fo 1.

In the Eastry catalogue item nos 1334, 1335, a Bible and Decretales epistole, are attached to his name, James, *Ancient Libraries*, 114.

Richard de ROMENAL
d. 1301

n.d., name occ. in the list in *SL*, 176, CCA Lit. Ms D.12, fo 2ᵛ.

1301, 30 Jan., d., CCA Lit. Ms D.12, fo 15ᵛ.

Adam de ROMENEY [Romne, Rompney, Rumenay, Rumeney
occ. 1493 d. 1497

1493, 26 July, one of ten tonsured, *SL*, 192, CCA Lit. Ms D.12, fo 9ᵛ.

1494, 29 Mar., ord acol., Canterbury cathedral, *Reg. abp Morton*, i, no 443a.

1494, 19 Apr., prof., *SL*, 192, CCA Lit. Ms D.12, fo 9ᵛ..

1495, 18 Apr., ord subdcn, Canterbury cathedral, *Reg. abp Morton*, i, no 444b.

1496, 2 Apr., ord dcn, Canterbury cathedral, *ib.*, i, no 445c.

1497, 25 Mar., ord pr., Canterbury cathedral, *ib.*, i, no 446d.

1496/7, celebrated his first mass and recd 8d. from the sacrist, CCA DCc Sac. acct 67.

1497, 31 Oct., d., *ex magna consumpcione*; he is described as *frater conventualis*, CCA Lit. Ms D.12, fo 28. His obit occ. in BL Ms Arundel 68, fo 47.

Felix de ROSA [?Rofa
occ. [1189] occ. 1196

[1189/91], cellarer, and then sacrist, *HRH*, 88; *Gervase Cant.*, i, 544, names him sacrist (as Felix).

1196, apptd prior of Dover, *HRH*, 88.

1212, 19 July, d., *ib.*

Note: see also Felix III who is surely this monk.

ROWE
see Rawe

RRENKLE
see Brenkle

Alan RUFUS [Ruffus
occ. 1239

n.d., subprior of Dover, *Lit. Cant.*, iii, Appndx, no 34 (CCA DCc Z D4, 23).

1239, 4 Jan., one of the group of monks accused of contumacy by the abp after the forgery scandal, *Gervase Cant.*, ii, 144; see Simon de Hertlepe. On 1 Feb. he was among those summoned to appear before the abp after the monks' el. of Roger de La Lee, q.v., as prior, *ib.*, ii, 153.

See also Alan III and IV, and Alan de Wy.

RUMENAY, Rumeney
see Romeney

RUMENHALE
see Romenal

Roger RUSSEL
see Buch

Richard RUTON [Rutone, Rutton, Rutyn
occ. [1395] d. 1431

[1395], 12 Mar., one of eight prof., *SL*, 184, CCA Lit. Ms D.12, fo 5ᵛ.
1396, 1 Apr., ord subdcn, Canterbury cathedral, Reg. abp Courtenay, ii, fo 186ᵛ.
1422/3, chamberlain, CCA DCc Chamb. acct 63.
1423, 30 Sept., *magister ordinis*, *SL*, 187, CCA Lit. Ms D.12, fo 6ᵛ.
1396, 7 Aug., 77th in order at the el. of an abp, Reg. G, fo 234ᵛ.
1414, 12 Mar., 36th at the el. of an abp, *Reg. abp Chichele*, i, 4.
1419, 30 Aug., before this date he had vestments embroidered for him by Thomas Selmiston, q.v., *Chron. Stone*, 10.
1431, 17 June, d., in the 36th yr of his monastic life, having been ill in the infirmary for more than four yrs, 'tisis et etise infirmitate detentus', *ib.*, 16.

Walter de RYA
occ. 1st half 13th c.

n.d., name occ. in the *post exilium* list in *SL*, 173, CCA Lit. Ms D.12, fo 1.

RYCHEMOND
see Richemond

Alexander de RYDELYNGWOLDE [Redelyngwell, Rydelyngwealde, Rydelyngweld, *alias* Partrich
occ. 1323 d. 1358

1323, one of six [clothed in the monastic habit] *SL*, 179, CCA Lit. Ms D.12, fo 3ᵛ (where it has been mistakenly entered as Bedelyngwell).
[1325], 18 Oct., prof. Reg. L, fo 141ᵛ.
1331, feretrar, CCA DCc MA2, fo 201ᵛ.
1332, 1333/4, *magister corone*, CCA DCc MA2, fos 211ᵛ, 221–231.
1334/7, feretrar, CCA DCc MA2, fos 231–255.
1337, 26 Feb., absolved from the office of penitentiary in Christ Church, *Lit. Cant.*, no 615 (Reg. L, fo 107).
1350, feretrar, CCA DCc Treas. acct 27, fo 2ᵛ.
[1324], 4 Oct., the prior was comm. to absolve him from perjury, Reg. abp Reynolds, fo 133ᵛ (as Partrich). See also CCA DCc EC I/19.
1348, 30 Aug., one of three initial *compromissorii* nominated to choose seven *compromissorii* in the el. of an abp, Reg. G, fos 31, 82.
1349, 4 June, 17th in order and chosen as one of three initial *compromissorii*, who were to name ten more thus making an electoral body of thirteen in the el. of an abp, Reg. G, fos 60ᵛ–61ᵛ.
1349, 8/9 Sept., 16th and one of three chosen to name ten more *compromissorii* in the el. of an abp, *ib.*, fos 76, 77.
1358, 9 Sept., d., CCA Lit. Ms D.12, fo 16.

Guy de RYDELYNGWOLDE [Redelingwold, *alias* Meriwedir
occ. 1346 d. 1352

1346, 11 Nov., one of eight prof., *SL*, 181, CCA Lit. Ms D.12, fo 4.
1351, 24 Sept., ord dcn, chapel of Herne church, Reg. abp Islip, fo 312.
1352, 6 Sept., d., CCA Lit. Ms D.12, fo 16ᵛ.

See Guy Meriwedir who is prob. the same monk.

RYEDYNGATE
see Redyngate

RYGEWEY, Ryggeweye
see Regeweye

John de RYNGMER [Ryngemer, Ryngemor', Rynggemere, Ryngmere,
occ. [1285] d. 1327

[1285], one of four prof., *SL*, 177, CCA Lit. Ms D.12, fo 3.
[1296], included among the juniors accused of being lax in attendance at divine office, and in the observance of other monastic duties, *Reg. abp Winchelsey*, 92.
[1313 × 1327], 3 July, with Gilbert de Bisshoppiston and Hugh de St Ives, q.v, was released from the penalties imposed by the abp at his visitation, CCA DCc EC V/31.
1320, 17 Aug., granted royal letters of recommendation to the pope, *Calendar of Chancery Warrants*, i (1244–1326), 511.
1327, 27 Dec., d., CCA Lit. Ms D.12, fo 16.

An inventory of vestments, *temp.* prior Eastry, includes a red chasuble of his [?gift], Legg and Hope, *Inventories*, 52 (BL Ms Cotton Galba E.iv, fos 112v).

Thomas de RYNGMER [Ryngmere
occ. 1274 occ. 1300

1274–1285, prior: succ. 19 Sept. 1274; res. 17 Mar. 1285, *Fasti*, ii, 12.
n.d., name occ. in the list in *SL*, 175, CCA Lit. Ms D.12, fo 2ᵛ.
1274, 19 Sept., before, chaplain to the abp, *Gervase Cant.*, ii, 278.
1276, [Oct.], with his consent an ordinance was passed in chapter that All Saints be celebrated as a feast of the first rank, *Gervase Cant.*, ii, 284.
1279, 14 Dec., apptd by the abp as his proctor at convocation, *Reg. abp Pecham*, i, 87–88.
1279, n.d., offered absolution by the abp for his failure to pay the tenth, in preference to an appeal to Rome, *Epist. Pecham*, 28; see also *ib.*, 58–61.
[1281], 5 Jan., recd a letter from the abp saying that he hoped to spend Easter with him, *ib.*, 160.

1282, 7 Feb., present at Lambeth and witnessed the abp's mandate concerning the excommunication of the bp of Hereford, *ib.*, 300.

[1283], 12 May, in a letter to one of the cardinal dcns in Rome the abp reported that two monks were stirring up trouble vs the prior whom he commended as 'bonus homo et honestus, in disciplina rigidus, communem utilitatem amplectens, commoda privata detestans'; he now sent Richard de Selesia, q.v., to Rome on the prior's behalf, *ib.*, 546. See Richard Pykenot and William de Tonge I.

n.d., accusations vs him and his replies had been read by the abp and examined by canon and civil lawyers who said that the charges had been made through 'indiscreet zeal'. The abp had then burned both documents; and he gave an ordinance to the chapter which the monks accepted, but Ryngmer made objection to the restrictions imposed on him, *Reg. abp Pecham*, ii, 242.

1285, 17 Mar., res. after the king had seized the priory for some unknown transgression acc. to *Gervase Cant.*, ii, 292. He went to Beaulieu and seems to have put on the Cistercian habit, without the permission of the abp who wrote to the abbot on 26 Feb. 1286, *Epist. Pecham*, 918.

[1286, Mar.], the abp wrote to the bp of Winchester asking him to intervene in this matter, and the bp dutifully wrote, on 27 Mar., to the abbot of Beaulieu, *Reg. Pontissara* (Winchester), 318.

1292, 5 Oct., his successor, prior Henry Eastry, q.v., sent Geoffrey de Chilham and Thomas Beloyzell, q.v., to him 'ad insinuand' nobis ea que statum vestrum decent et honorem', CUL Ms Ee.5.31, fo 34^{v}.

1292, 26 Oct., the abp sent a mandate to the abbot to apprehend Ryngmer who had been sent to Beaulieu to do penance but had disappeared, *Reg. abp Pecham*, ii, 242; see also Reg. I, fos 168^{v}, 169.

1294, 6 Oct., a papal bull was sent to the abp granting permission for Ryngmer to live as a hermit which he had ?already commenced to do, *Reg. abp Winchelsey*, 496.

n.d., retired to Brookwood in Windsor forest to live as a hermit, Reg. I, fo 143–143^{v}. His departure for Brookwood was 23 July 1289 acc. to *Gervase Cant.*, ii, 295.

1300, 16 Apr., the abp remonstrated with prior Henry Eastry, q.v., over the non-payment of Ryngmer's pension, *Reg. abp Winchelsey*, 1321–1322. See also CCA DCc EC IV/79, EC V/12, the former concerning Ryngmer's welfare, the latter a letter of the abp. See Eastry regarding the possibility of his reconciliation with the chapter.

n.d., 11 May, obit occ. in BL Ms Arundel 68, fo 27.

The Eastry catalogue lists eleven books under his name, most of them being medical treatises, and also Algorismus de signis planetarum, James, *Ancient Libraries*, nos 1440–1450 (pp. 122–123).

Four folios of a register containing letters of the abp to prior Ryngmer and other matters between 1280–1282 are in CCA DCc DE106. A fragment containing details of the accusations vs him is now CCA DCc DE105; and there is also a loose document (DE2) which lists Ryngmer's answers to seventeen charges of maladministration and includes mention of his nephew Robert de Kadamo.

A letter of his (dated c. 1281 × 1284) has been copied on to fo 94 of CCA Lit. Ms D.11.

An inventory of vestments, *temp.* prior Eastry, includes a red chasuble embroidered with gold and silver eagles [?of his gift], Legg and Hope, *Inventories*, 52 (BL Mc Cotton Galba E.iv, fos 112^{v}).

S.

occ. 1189 occ. 1198

1189, 5/8 Nov., treasurer, *Epist. Cant.*, 315; he prob. succ. Roger III, q.v.

1189, c. 3 Aug. sent with Alan II and R. de Cripta, q.v., to appear before the abp at Wingham, *Epist. Cant.*, 298.

1189, 5/8 Nov., one of the party of monks sent to the king in London to discuss their dispute with the abp; at the meeting he and Aaron, q.v. walked out in protest, *Epist. Cant.*, 315, 317.

1198, Jan., with Nicholas, q.v., left the priory without licence in order to continue the chapter's appeal vs the abp's proposed Lambeth foundation at the curia where they delivered a letter to the pope on 17 Apr., *ib.*, 377, 390.

1198, after 6 July, informed by their brethren in Canterbury that the abp had ordered their exclusion from the priory on their return, *ib.*, 408.

1198, after 6 Nov., S. and R. [?Ralph III] reported a favourable judgement by the pope, *ib.*, 457.

Note: is this Salomon I, q.v.?

SACERDOS

see Geoffrey V, Henry III

Vivian de ST ALBANS [Sancto Albano

occ. [1153 × 1161]

[1153 × 1161], *temp.* prior Wibert, q.v., witnessed a grant of certain demesne tithes of the priory at the request of the abp, *Theobald Charters*, no 40.

William de ST ALBANS

see Powns

ST ALPHEGE

see St Elphege

Thomas de ST ANDREW [Sancto Andrea, *alias* Barbor, Barbour, Barbur
occ. 1341 d. 1353

1341, 13 Dec., one of nine prof., *SL*, 180–181, CCA Lit. Ms D.12, fo 4.

1349, 4 June, 58th in order at the el. of an abp, Reg. G, fo 60v.

1349, 8/9 Sept., 57th at the el. of an abp, Reg. G, fo 76v.

1353, 28 Apr., d., CCA Lit. Ms D.12, fo 16v; obit in BL Ms Arundel 68, fo 26.

Peter de ST AUGUSTINE [Sancto Augustino
occ. 2nd half 13th c.

n.d., name occ. in the list in *SL*, 175, CCA Lit. Ms D.12, fo 2.

Robert de ST AUGUSTINE [Sancto Augustino
d. 1291

n.d., name occ. in the list in *SL*, 176, CCA Lit. Ms D.12, fo 2v.

n.d., a letter from a student in Paris to prior Eastry refs to his bringing relics of Becket to the abbot of St Denys, Woodruff, 'Letters to Eastry', 18–20.

Peter de ST ELPHEGE [Alphege, Sancto Alphego, Elphego
occ. [1207 × 1214] occ [1222 × 1237]

[1207 × 1214], name occ. in the list of those who were in exile, *SL*, 172, CCA Lit. Ms D.12, fo 1.

[1222 × 1237], one of several monks apptd by M. Laurence de St Nicholas to arrange for his obit celebrations, *Acta Guala*, no 155.

Roger de ST ELPHEGE [Sancto Elphego
occ. [1241] d. 1263

1258–1263, prior: el. confirmed 12 Nov. 1258; d. 29 Sept. 1263, *Fasti*, ii, 11.

[1241], name occ. in the list in *SL*, 174, CCA Lit. Ms D.12, fo 2; he was prob. one of the twelve prof. with Richard de Wynchepe, q.v.

1257, Mar./Sept., 1257/8, Mar., chamberlain, Reg. H, fos 186, 189v.

1258, before 12 Nov., subprior, *Fasti*, ii, 11.

1259, 13 Dec., achieved a peaceful settlement with abp Boniface over the liberties of the church, *Gervase Cant.*, ii, 209, 226.

1263, c. 29 Sept., d., and was buried on the north side of Becket's chapel, Dart, *Antiq. Cant.*, 183; his obit occ. in BL Ms Arundel 68, fo 43v.

Name occ. in CCA Lit. Ms D.7, Sermones (13th c.), which has as its subtitle Collectio de multis on the front flyleaf before his name; see Sharpe *Latin Writers*.

The Eastry catalogue lists nine volumes under his name including two books of sermons (one of which may be the vol. named above), James, *Ancient Libraries*, nos 576–583 (p. 68).

He is known as the founder and builder of the chapel between the dormitory and the infirmary, Dart, *Antiq. Cant.*, 183. According to Cambridge, Corpus Christi College Ms 298, fo 118v, he introduced the obedientiary office of anniversarian and repaired the prior's chapel.

ST ELPHEGE
see also Elphe

Hugh de ST IVES, D.Th. [Sancto Ivone, Yvone
occ. [1316] d. 1336

[1316], 6 Nov., one of five prof., *SL*, 179, CCA Lit. Ms D.12, fo 3v.

1327/8, 1330/1, 1333, 3 Nov., lector in the cloister who recd *de gracia conventus*, for him and his clerk, 40 s, Pantin, *Cant. Coll. Ox.*, iv, 177–178, Reg. G, fos xxxii, xxxviii.

1336, Aug./Nov., almoner, CCA DCc Eastry acct 61.

1331, 28 Oct., with Roger de Godmersham and James de Oxney, q.v. went to Oxford to the hall (near the church of St Peter in the East) which he had prob. been instrumental in hiring, *Lit. Cant.*, no 380 (Reg. L, fo 10v), Pantin, *Cant. Coll. Ox.*, iv, 5, 178.

1332/3, at Oxford for three quarters of the yr, Pantin, *ib.*, iv, 5, 178.

1332, B.Th., Pantin, *ib.*, iv, 211–212 (Reg. L, fo 13v) who has transcribed the prior's letter to him dated 27 Dec. [1331] in which the latter reported that he was sending two swans and thirty hens for the [*introitus*] feast, as well as much needed cash. Another letter to Hugh, dated 6 Dec. 1331 is also transcribed, *ib.*, iv, 211 (Reg. L, fo 13).

1333, May, invited by the university to incept, but was refused permission by the prior for the time being, Reg. L, fo 32; see below.

[1313 × 1327], 3 July, with Gilbert de Bisshopston and John Ryngmer, q.v., was released from the penalties imposed by the abp at his vistation, CCA DCc EC V/31.

1326/7, spent four days at Godmersham with Thomas de Holyngbourne, q.v., CCA DCc Godmersham acct 10.

1327, 11 Dec., named by the prior and chapter as one of seven *compromissorii* in the el. of an abp, Reg. Q, fo 123; see also *CPL*, ii (1305–1342), 272, which is the papal confirmation.

1331, 13 July, in a letter to the abp, prior Richard Oxenden, q.v., informed him of St Ives' opinion concerning the feast of the translation of St Benedict and described him as 'virum providum et discretum', *Lit. Cant.*, no 359 (Reg. L, fo 8).

1333, 3 Nov., chosen as one of seven *compromissorii* in the el. of an abp, Reg. G, fos xxxii, xxxvii, Reg. Q, fo 193v.

1333, 5 Dec., one of three monks authorized to obtain a loan in the curia or elsewhere, Reg. Q, fos 196ᵛ–197. The other two were Robert Hathbrand and Richard de Wylardeseye, q.v.; Hathbrand had been sent to Avignon for confirmation of the postulation of John Stratford as abp and was prob. accompanied by Wylardeseye and St Ives.

1336/7, ill in the almoner's *camera* and charged his acct 16s. 2d. for medical expenses, CCA DCc Alm. acct 45.

1336, 14 Nov., d., CCA Lit. Ms D.12, fo 16ᵛ; the obit in BL Ms Arundel 68, fo 48, states that he was lector in the cloister for eleven yrs and more, and D.Th.

Stephen de ST LAURENCE [Sancto Laurencio, Sent Laurens, Seynt Laurence

occ. 1384 d. 1416

1384, 29 Aug., one of seven prof., *SL*, 183, CCA Lit. Ms D.12, fo 5.

1386, 21 Apr., ord subdcn, Canterbury cathedral, Reg. abp Courtenay, i, fo 308ᵛ.

1389, 12 June, ord dcn, St Dunstan's church, London, *ib.*, i, fo 311ᵛ.

1391, 25 Mar., ord pr., Canterbury cathedral, *ib.*, i, fo 312.

1395/7, treasurer, CCA DCc, Bailiff of the Liberty accts 6, 7.

1397/1401, cellarer, CCA DCc, Eastry acct 119, Agney acct 63, Adisham acct 41, Agney acct 64.

1400/1, chaplain to the prior, CCA DCc, Eastry acct 123.

1412, Mar./Sept., sacrist, CCA DCc, Sac. acct 17.

1412/13, 1414/16, Nov., cellarer, CCA DCc Treas. acct 11, Adisham accts, 50, 51; he was [re]apptd by abp Chichele on the second day after his enthronement, 1414, *Reg. abp Chichele*, iv, 115.

1389/90, recd 2s. from the prior [*pro benedictione*], Lambeth Ms 243, fo 216ᵛ.

1396, 7 Aug., 49th in order at the el. of an abp, Reg. G, fo 234ᵛ.

1414, 12 Mar., 16th at the el. of an abp, *Reg. abp Chichele*, i, 4.

1416, 11 Nov., d. while cellarer, at Meister Omers' [house in the precincts] in the 33rd yr of his monastic life; he was described as 'iocundus et pluribus acceptus, *Chron. Stone*, 8. His obit is in BL Ms Arundel 68, fo 47ᵛ.

Anselm de ST MARGARET [Sancta Margareta, *alias* Child, Chyld

occ. 1341 d. 1361

1341, 13 Dec., one of nine prof., *SL*, 180, CCA Lit. Ms D.12, fo 4.

1349, 4 June, 54th in order at the el. of an abp, Reg. G, fo 60ᵛ.

1349, 8/9 Sept., 54th at the el. of an abp, *ib.*, fo 76ᵛ.

1361, 23 July, d., one of c.25 monks carried off [by the plague] between June and Oct., CCA Lit. Ms D.12, fo 17.

Denys de ST MARGARET [Dionysius de Sancta Margareta

occ. 1309 occ. 1355

1309, 18 Oct., one of nine prof., *SL*, 179, CCA Lit. Ms D.12, fo 3ᵛ.

1317, 28 May, ord pr., Lambeth palace chapel, Reg. abp Reynolds, fo 178.

1321, 3 Nov.; 1323, 21 Oct.; 1329/31, chaplain to the prior, Legg and Hope, *Inventories*, 51, 78 (BL Ms Cotton Galba E.iv, fos 112, 122); CAC DCc DE84; Worcester Cathedral Muniment, C.573 (Great Chart acct), CCA DCc MA2, fos 193–202ᵛ.

1331, Sept./Dec., 1331/3, Jan., bartoner, CCA DCc Bart. acct 20, MA2, fos 202ᵛ–212, Bart. acct 21; see John Andrew.

1335/6, 1337, 1339/40, cellarer, CCA DCc AS14, MA2, fo 256, AS19.

1340, Feb./Sept., 1341/3, chamberlain, CCA DCc Chamb. accts 34, 36, 37.

1347/8, chaplain to the prior, CCA DCc, Prior's Chaplain acct 17.

1348/9, June, chamberlain, CCA DCc Chamb. acct 38.

1355, 19 Dec., apptd cellarer, Reg. abp Islip, fo 108ᵛ.

n.d., subsacrist, see below.

1349, 4 June, 7th in order at the el. of an abp, Reg. G, fo 60ᵛ.

1349, 8/9 Sept., 7th at the el. of an abp, *ib.*, fo 76.

n.d., 25 Oct., obit occ. in BL Ms Arundel 68, fo 46ᵛ.

Name possibly attached to several vols in the Eastry catalogue, James, *Ancient Libraries*, 117. James names this monk as the Dionysius who may have d. in 1239, *ib.*, 535, but see Denys de Cantuar'.

With the sacrist, his name heads a list of *textus*, *temp.* prior Eastry, Legg and Hope, *Inventories*, 78 (BL Ms Cotton Galba E.iv, fo 122); therefore he was prob. subsacrist.

Hugh de ST MARGARET [Sancta Margareta

occ. 1286 d. 1337

1286, 9 Oct., one of six prof., *SL*, 177, CCA Lit. Ms D.12, fo 3.

1297/1307, 1307/13, treasurer, CCA DCc MA1, fos 212–268ᵛ, MA2, fos 10–42ᵛ.

1316, granator, CCA DCc MA2, fo 70.

1317/18, chaplain to the prior, CCA DCc MA2, fo 79, West Farleigh acct 30.

1317, Oct./1319, Jan., almoner, CCA DCc Alm. accts 5, 4.

1318/21, 1323, subprior, CCA DCc Eastry acct 47, Adisham acct 5, Chartham acct 13, MA2, fo 129.
1323, *custos* of the tomb of abp Robert [Winchelsey], *custos* of St Mary in crypt, MA2, fo 128ᵛ.
1324, Nov./1331, sacrist, CCA DCc MA2, fos 146–202ᵛ; he was apptd on 26 Nov., 1324, Reg. abp Reynolds, fo 134.
1329, Mar./Sept., 1331, Feb./June; [1332], 26 Oct.; 1333, Oct./ Nov., almoner, CCA DCc Monkton accts 61, 63; *Lit. Cant.*, no 477 (Reg. L, fo 25); Reg. G, fos xxviiᵛ, xxxii, xxxvii.
1335, 1336, penitentiary, *Lit. Cant.*, no 587 (Reg. L, fo 107ᵛ, CCA DCc MA2, fo 250ᵛ.

[1296], one of the monks accused of being lax in attendance at divine office, *Reg. abp Winchelsey*, 92.
1313, 28 May, named by the prior and chapter as one of seven *compromissorii* in the el. of an abp, Reg. Q, fos 61ᵛ–62/75ᵛ–76.
1315, 17 Jan., with Gilbert de Bisshoppiston, q.v., apptd proctor to attend parliament at Westminster, CUL Ms Ee.5.31, fo 155ᵛ.
1327, 11 Dec., chosen to be one of seven *compromissorii* in the el. of an abp, Reg. Q, fo 123 (*CPL*, ii (1305–1342), 272, the papal confirmation).
1333, 16 Oct., recd a comm. from the prior to be one of three auditors of causes in the court of Canterbury, *sed. vac.*, Churchill, *Cant. Admin.*, ii, 224–225 (Reg. G, fo xxviᵛ).
1333, 3 Nov., again chosen as one of seven *compromissorii* in the el. of an abp, Reg. G, fos xxxii, xxxviiᵛ and Reg. Q, fo 193ᵛ.
1334, 2 Jan., with another, comm. by the prior, *sed. vac.* to conduct a visitation of St Gregory's priory, Canterbury, Reg. G, fo 46ᵛ.
1337, 30 Jan., d., CCA Lit. Ms D.12, fo 16ᵛ; his obit occ. in BL Ms Arundel 68, fo 14ᵛ.

Richard de ST MARGARET [Sancta Margareta
occ. 2nd half 13th c.

n.d., [mid 1260s], one of seven prof. together, *SL*, 176, CCA Lit. Ms D.12, fo 2ᵛ.

Richard de ST MILDRED [Sancta Mildreda, Mildreth
occ. 1278 occ. 1282/3

n.d., name occ. in the list in *SL*, 175, CCA Lit. Ms D.12, fo 2ᵛ.

1278, granator, CCA DCc MA1, fo 128, Reg. H, fo 209.

1282/3, pd a visit to Meopham, CCA DCc Meopham acct 3.

The Eastry catalogue contains one volume of his, Fretulphus, James, *Ancient Libraries*, no 533 (p. 63).

Thomas de ST NICHOLAS [Sancto Nicolao, Sent Nicholas, Seynt Nycholas
occ. 1413 d. 1420

1413, 6 Oct., one of six tonsured, *SL*, 186, CCA Lit. Ms D.12, fo 6. That this date ref. to tonsure rather than prof. is shown by the fact that none of the six took part in the el. of abp Chichele on 12 Mar. 1414, *Reg. abp Chichele*, i, 4.
1414, 22 Dec., ord acol., Canterbury cathedral, *Reg. abp Chichele*, iv, 317.
1417, 10 Apr., ord dcn, Canterbury cathedral, *ib.*, iv, 327.

c. 1420, possibly student at Canterbury college; see below.

1420, 14 Aug., d., *ex pestilencia*, *Chron. Stone*, 11.

The library of Canterbury college contained two volumes formerly his, both in the section *libri logicales*, Pantin, *Cant. Coll. Ox.*, i, 6, 15, 99 (inventories, CCA DCc Cart. Antiq. O.134, 135).

Simon de ST PAUL [Sancto Paulo
occ. [1284] occ. 1338

[1284], one of four prof., *SL*, 177, CCA Lit. Ms D.12, fo 3.

1300, warden of manors, CCA DCc MA1, fo 225.
1312, 28 Aug., named cellarer by the abp in place of Nicholas de Borne I, q.v., Reg. Q, fo 38/50.
1313, 28 May; 1314/15; 1316, to 6 Jan., subprior, Reg. Q, fos 61–62/75–76; CCA DCc Chartham acct 9; he was removed from this office on 6 Jan. 1316, Reg. abp Reynolds, fo 85, and was succ. by Richard de Clyve, q.v.

1313, 28 May, chosen by the prior and chapter as one of seven *compromissorii* in the el. of an abp, Reg. Q, fos 61–62/75–76.
1313, 8 July, one of the monks about to set off for the curia in connection with the chapter's el. of Thomas Cobham as abp, but they were stopped in London because of the provision of Walter Reynolds, CUL Ms Ee.5.31, fo 134.
1315, 18 Oct., wrote to the prior on behalf of himself and the chapter requesting the prior's return to Canterbury before the abp arrived; the implication is that there were domestic problems to be discussed and resolved within the community, CUL Ms Ee.5.31, fo 161ᵛ.
1333, 7 Nov., with Richard de Ikham, q.v., sent as proctors to the king to inform him of the chapter's el. of John Stratford as abp, Reg. G, fo xxxiiiᵛ.
1338, 1 Mar., an inventory of missing books, lists 'five books of Anselm in one volume' (no 1719 below) and a Digesta vetus (no 1717 below) which were his but had been lost, the former by Thomas de Undyrdown I, q.v. and the latter by a layman, *Lit. Cant.*, no 618 (Reg. L, fo 104).

Note: he must have been alive on this date because there is a separate list of the missing books that had belonged to deceased monks.

n.d., 31 May, obit occ. in BL Ms Arundel 68, fo 29.

The Eastry catalogue includes six volumes under his name, two of which are referred to above, James, *Ancient Libraries*, nos 1715–1720 (p. 138).

An inventory of vestments, *temp.* prior Eastry, include a linen alb embroidered with the story of St Thomas and an amice, Legg and Hope, *Inventories*, 58, 60 (BL Ms Cotton Galba E.iv, fo 114v). There are other vestments and ecclesiastical ornaments listed under his name in Legg and Hope, *Inventories*, 73, 76–77 (BL Ms Cotton Galba E.iv, fos 120v, 121).

An inventory of the refectory, dated 1328, includes three silver *ciphi* formerly his, and one *de murra*, Dart, *Antiq. Cant.*, xx, xxii (BL Ms Cotton Galba E.iv, fo 179–179v).

See Simon V and VI.

Simon de ST PETER [Sancto Petro

occ. 1300 d. 1353

1300, 4 June, ord subdcn, Smeeth chapel by Aldington, *Reg. abp Winchelsey*, 934 (as Thomas).
1303, 29 May, one of two prof., *SL*, 178, CCA Lit. Ms D.12, fo 3v.
1305, 12 June, ord dcn, Smeeth chapel by Aldington, *Reg. abp Winchelsey*, 977.

1325/6, monk *supervisor*, CCA DCc, Cheam acct 39.
1327, *custos* of the high altar, CCA DCc MA2, fo 164v.
1327/8, warden of manors, CCA DCc Ickham acct 26, Lydden acct 47.
1327/9, treasurer, CCA DCc MA2, fos 173–182.
1330/1, warden of manors, CCA DCc MA2, fos 190–199.
1333/4, chaplain to the prior, CCA DCc MA2, fos 222v–232.
1334/5, auditor, CCA DCc Bocking acct 18.
1334/7, warden of manors, CCA DCc MA2, fos 229–253.
1335/6, auditor, CCA DCc Bocking acct 19.
1337/40, warden of manors, CCA DCc Cheam acct 50, Meopham acct 79, Middleton acct 50.
1340/4, subprior, CCA DCc Eastry acct 69, Agney accts 44, 45, Adisham acct 19.

1324, one of the monks subjected to penance after the abp's visitation and the prior on 29 May requested the abp to relax the sentence, CUL Ms Ee.5.31, fo 236v.
1325, 16 Nov., with John de Maldon, q.v,. apptd proctor to attend parliament, CUL Ms Ee.5.31, fo 244 (*Parl. Writs*, ii, pt 3, 1387).
1327, [Nov.], sent with Walter de Norwyco, q.v., to the king to obtain licence to el. an abp, Lambeth Ms 243, fo 5.
1331, [Apr.], one of the monks sent to the abp concerning their el. of a prior, *ib.*, fo 26v.
1333, 15 Oct., named proctor with Richard de Wylardeseye, q.v, to inform the king of the d. of abp Meopham. Reg. G, fos xxvi-xxvii.
1334, Sept., apptd proctor with a secular cleric, to attend convocation, Reg. L, fo 37v.
1349, 4 June, 4th in order at the el. of an abp, Reg. G, fo 60v.
1349, 8/9 Sept., 4th at the el. of an abp, *ib.*, fo 76.
1353, 9 Aug., d., CCA Lit. Ms D.12, fo 16v.

Thomas de ST VALERICO [Waler, Walerico

occ. 1224 occ. 1230

n.d., name occ. among the first of those on the *post exilium* list, *SL*, 172, CCA Lit. Ms D.12, fo 1.

1224/5, warden of manors, CCA DCc AS1.
1229/30, refectorer, CCA DCc AS2.

The Eastry catalogue lists four volumes under his name, including a copy of the Rule, Rubrice de sonitu et consuetudinibus and De usu divini officii of Christ Church, James, *Ancient Libraries*, nos 1297–1300 (p. 112).

An inventory of the refectory, dated 1328, includes a cuppa *de murra cum magnis gemmis* of his and a *ciphus de murra*, Dart, *Antiq. Cant.*, xviii, xxi (BL Ms Cotton Galba E.iv, fos 178, 179v).

Peter de SALES [Salis, Salys

occ. 1320 occ. 1368

1320, 9 Oct., one of five prof., *SL*, 179, CCA Lit. Ms D.12, fo 3v.
[c. 1323/4], subdcn on whose behalf the prior requested the bp of Rochester to confer [dcn's] orders, *Lit. Cant.*, no 138 (Reg. L, fo 136v).

1335/6, 1337, Apr./1342, 1344/7, granator, CCA DCc AS14, Gran. accts 8, 88, 64, Ebony acct 45, Gran. accts 31, 87, 32, 33, 65.
1350/1, chaplain to the prior, CCA DCc Treas. acct 27, fo 3v; see Thomas de Garwynton.
1350/2, 1353/6, bartoner, CCA DCc Bart. accts 106, 32, 33, Ickham acct 42, Bart. acct 34.
1356/7, 1360/5, 1366/8, almoner, CCA DCc Eastry acct 88, Alm. accts 49, 51–53, Lambeth ED 31, CCA DCc Alm. acct 35, Eastry acct 101.

1338, 1 Mar., in an inventory of missing books Thomas de Garwynton, q.v., was reported to have mislaid a psalter of Peter [de Sales] and he himself was held responsible for the loss of the Exequiae of Ralph de Pretelwelle, q.v., *Lit. Cant.*, no 618 (Reg. L, fo 104).
1349, 4 June, 14th in order and named as one of thirteen *compromissorii* at the el. of an abp, Reg. G, fos 60v, 61v
1349, 8/9 Sept., 14th at the el. of an abp, and chosen as one of thirteen *compromissorii*, *ib.*, fos 76, 77.
1366, 10 May, again chosen, this time as one of seven *compromissorii*, at the el. of an abp, *ib.*, fo 148.

Nicholas SALEWS [Salus, Salute, Salutz, Saluz, Saluze

occ. 1443 d. 1472/3

1443, 25 Mar., one of six prof., *SL*, 188, CCA Lit. Ms D.12, fo 7v.

1444, 11 Apr., ord subdcn, Canterbury cathedral, Reg. abp Stafford, fo 197.

1445, 27 Mar., ord dcn, Canterbury cathedral, *ib.*, fo 198v.

1447, 23 Dec., ord pr., Canterbury cathedral, *ib.*, fo 201v.

1463/4, fourth prior, CCA DCc Sac. acct 44.

1467, 19 Sept., *magister ordinis*, *SL*, 190, CCA Lit. Ms D.12, fo 8.

1468, 29 Apr., third prior, *Chron. Stone*, 103.

1470/1, granator, CCA DCc Gran. acct 62.

n.d. [1472/3], *magister mense*, CCA Lit. Ms D.12, fo 26.

1452, July, ill and his expenses were 6s. 8d., CCA Lit. Ms E.6, fo 64v.

1466, 17 Feb., 32nd in order in an inventory of *jocalia fratrum*, [given by him and/or assigned for his use], but he had none, Reg. N, fo 232v.

1468, 29 Apr., stood in for the subprior on the committee examining Robert Dene, q.v., *Chron. Stone*, 103.

1472/3, d., CCA Lit. Ms D.12, fo 26.

I John SALISBURY, D.Th. [Salesbery, Salisburi, Salusbery, Salysbery, Sarisbury, Sarysbury

occ. 1406 d. 1446

1438–1446, prior: el. 1 Mar. 1438, *prefectio*, 9 Mar., *Chron. Stone*, 21; d. 19 Jan. 1446, *ib.*, 38.

1406, 21 Oct., one of seven prof., *SL*, 185, CCA Lit. Ms D.12, fo 5v.

1407, 26 Mar., ord acol., Canterbury cathedral, Reg. abp Arundel, i, fo 340v.

1407, 24 Sept., ord subdcn, collegiate church, Maidstone, *ib.*, i, 341.

1410, 13 Sept., ord pr., abp's chapel, Ford, *ib.*, ii, fo 99.

[1428, 3/4 Mar.], 1428, [31] Mar., warden of Canterbury college, Pantin, *Cant. Coll. Ox.*, iii, 82–83, Oxford Bod. Ms Tanner 165, fo 6v.

1429/30; 1430, 15 Nov.; 1431, 17 June, 9 Aug.; 1433, 3 Jan.; 1435, subprior, CCA DCc Sac. acct 26; *Chron. Stone*, 16, 17; *Lit. Cant.*, no 1011 (Reg. S, fo 112v); 'Chron. Wm Glastynbury', 129.

[1414 × 1430], student at Canterbury college, Oxford, mentioned in an oblique ref. in a piece of satirical writing, Pantin, *Cant. Coll. Ox.*, iii, 72.

[1428, before 7 July or 1429], incepted at the same time as John Wodnesburgh II, q.v.; the total expenditure for both, including various fees, gifts, food and wine was £92 8d, Pantin, *Cant. Coll. Ox.*, iii, 84–87, where the full acct is printed from CCA DCc Cart. Antiq. O.128 A (also found in Oxford, Bod. Ms Tanner 165, fo 149, 149v).

Note: on [31] Mar. 1428 he was addressed as *M[agister]*, Oxford, Bod. Ms Tanner 165, fo 6v.

1414, 12 Mar., 63rd in order at the el. of an abp, *Reg. abp Chichele*, i, 4.

1420, 14 Feb., licensed to preach in all authorized places within the diocese of Canterbury, *ib.*, iv, 201–202.

1428, [31] Mar., one of the monks invited to the abp's palace after the *prefectio* of William Molassh q.v., as prior, Oxford, Bod. Ms Tanner 165, fo 6v.

1431, 16 Feb., 1432, 12 Apr., apptd proctor for the prior and chapter to attend convocation, Reg. S, fos 107, 111.

1432/3, attended the council of Basel; he sailed from Dover on 22 Dec. [1432] with the bp of Norwich and the prior of Norwich [William Worstede, q.v.], Pantin, *Cant. Coll. Ox.*, iv, 91 (Chron. Wm Glastynbury, fo 185v). See also John Fornset under Norwich and *Memorials Bury*, iii, 254–257 (BL Add. Ms 7096, fos 161v–162) where there is a copy of Fornset's letter referring to John Salisbury consorting with 'his father' [the prior of Norwich].

1434, 2 Oct., apptd proctor to attend convocation, Pantin, *ib.*, iv, 226 (Reg. S, fo 118).

1435, 17 Nov., obtained a papal indult to celebrate, or have celebrated, masses in places under interdict, *CPL*, viii (1427–1447), 574.

1438, 4 Oct., obtained an indult to choose his own confessor, *ib.*, viii, 394.

1443, 17 Apr., 20 May, presided at the exequies of abp Chichele and the el. of his successor [John Stafford], *Chron. Stone*, 30–31.

1446, 19 Jan., d. at the manor of Chartham; he was buried in the nave of the cathedral, *Chron. Stone*, 38 (CCA Lit. Ms D.12, fo 25). His obit is in BL Ms Arundel 68, fo 13v.

Canterbury college inventories of the mid fifteenth and sixteenth centuries include silver plate and vestments given by him, Pantin, *Cant. Coll. Ox.*, i, 2, 7, 8, 10, 16, 29, 77.

Some of his *acta* are in Reg. S, fos 130–164.

II John SALISBURY [Sarisbury, Sarusbury

occ. 1477 occ. 1511

1477, 22 Mar., ord subdcn, Canterbury cathedral, *Reg. abp Bourgchier*, 422.

1477, 19 Apr., one of four tonsured, *SL*, 191, CCA Lit. Ms D.12, fo 8v.

1477, 11 Nov., prof., *SL*, 191, Cambridge, Corpus Christi College Ms 298.

1480, 1 Apr., ord dcn, Canterbury cathedral, *Reg. abp Bourgchier*, 430.

1481, 22 Sept., ord pr., Sevenoaks, *ib.*, 433.

1486, c. 15 Apr., third chaplain [?to the prior], Cambridge, Corpus Christi College Ms 298, fo 128v.

1500/1, July to Apr., *magister ordinis* and fourth prior, *SL*, 193, CCA Lit. Ms D.12, fo 10, Lambeth, ED 86.
1503, 21 Feb., penitentiary, Reg. T, fo 15ᵛ.
1511, 10 Sept., *magister mense*, Wood-Legh, *Visit.*, 5.

1493, 1 May, 37th in order at the ratification of an agreement, Reg. S, fo 383ᵛ; but see John Crosse I.
1500, recd a laton basin and laver in a bequest from a parishioner of St Mildred's, Canterbury, Hussey, 'Kentish Wills', 43.
1501, 26 Apr., 24th in order at the el. of an abp, Reg. R, fo 56ᵛ.
1508, 21 May, delegated to celebrate the Sun. mass, CCA Lit. Ms C.11, fo 17ᵛ.
1511, 2 Sept., 10th on the visitation certificate, Wood-Legh, *Visit.*, 3 (Reg. abp Warham, i, fo 35); on 10 Sept., he was one of six obedientiaries apptd with the prior to oversee corrections in the priory, Wood-Legh, *Visit.*, 5.

He gave cloths [*panni*] to hang above the altar of St Michael's chapel, Legg and Hope, *Inventories*, 149.

See note below the next entry.

III John SALISBURY [Salesbury, Sarisbury, Sarusbury, Sarysbery, Sarysbury, Sharysburie

occ. 1511 occ. 1540

1511, 1 Sept., one of eight tonsured, *SL*, 194, CCA Lit. Ms D.12, fo 11.
1512, 19 Apr., prof., *ib.*
1513, 26 Mar., ord subdcn, Canterbury cathedral, Reg. abp Warham, ii, fo 266ᵛ.

1520, 25 Dec., *custos martyrii*, CCA Lit. Ms C.11, fo 61.
1526, 1527, 1528, all on 25 Mar., subalmoner, *ib.*, fos 64, 64ᵛ, 65.
1532, 24 June, [1538, 8 Feb. after], *magister corone*, *ib.*, fo 68 and Pantin, *Cant. Coll. Ox.*, iii, 152.

[c. 1511 × 1514], had Thomas Goldston V, q.v., for his *magister regule*, Pantin, *Cant. Coll. Ox.*, iv, 54 (CCA DCc Ms Scrap Book B.186).
1511, 2 Sept., 85th in order on the visitation certificate, and not prof., Wood-Legh, *Visit.*, 3 (Reg. abp Warham, i, fo 35ᵛ).
[1538, 8 Feb., after], in a list of monks prob. prepared for Thomas Cromwell he was described as 'wytty' and 46 yrs of age, Pantin, *Cant. Coll. Ox.*, iii, 152.
1540, 4 Apr., assigned £3 and became a petty canon in the new foundation, *L and P Henry VIII*, xv, no 452.

Name in
(1) Lambeth Ms 78, Speculum parvulorum (15th c.); name and the date 1520 on a flyleaf; see William Chartham II.
(2) Lambeth Ms 159, Vite sanctorum (early 16th c.); *modo liber—ex dono mag.* William Hadlegh II, q.v.; see also James Hartey and Nicholas Herst II.

Note: A John Salisbury [?II or III] was *magister regule* for a John Holyngbourne [?II], q.v. for two yrs, Pantin, *Cant. Coll. Ox.*, iv, 54 (CCA DCc Ms Scrap Book B.186).

I SALOMON

occ. 1198

1198, [Nov.], met prior Geoffrey II, q.v., at Lucca and had with him the [papal] mandate; the prior retained him because he was worn out and *archiepiscopo odioso* [*sic*], *Epist. Cant.*, 458, see S., and W. precentor.

II SALOMON

occ. 1205 occ. 1213

[1207 × 1214], name occ. in the list of those who were in exile, where he is described as *quondam supprior*, *SL*, 172, CCA Lit. Ms D.12, fo 1.

1213, 29 Sept., subprior, CCA DCc MA1, fo 53.
1205, 11 Dec., one of the monks who appealed to the pope to confirm their el. of Reginald, subprior, q.v., as abp, *CPL*, i (1198–1304), 23, 26.

Name in
(1) Cambridge, Corpus Christi College Ms 51, Eusebius (12th c.).
(2) BL Ms Egerton 3314, Aedthelardus de compoto' etc. (11th/12th cs), with notes added in his hand.

His Cronica Eusebius is included in the Eastry catalogue, James, *Ancient Libraries*, no 282 (p. 49), as well as his Musica (Boethius), no 442 (p. 55) and other works, nos 990–995 (pp. 96–97), and possibly no 1390 (pp. 118–119). His Verbum abbreviatum *ib.*, no 991 (p. 96) is also in the 1508 catalogue of repairs of Wm Ingram I, q.v., *ib.*, no 285 (p. 163).

III SALOMON

occ. 1226

1226, feretrar, CCA DCc MA1, fo 70ᵛ.

Note:
(1) a Salomon, nephew of George, q.v., is named in a schedule of cathedral tenants in Canterbury, where it states that he entered Christ Church with a gift of property, Urry *Canterbury*, 321.
(2) a Salomon, son of William de Hakintun', was 'given' to the monastery by his father with land outside Westgate, *ib*, 321.
(3) the obits of two monks of this name occ. in BL Ms Arundel 68, 31 Mar. (fo 22ᵛ), 10 Aug. (fo 37ᵛ) and three others in Lambeth Ms 20, 12 Jan. (fo 158ᵛ), 3 Feb. (fo 161ᵛ) and 16 Feb. (fo 164).

SALUS, Salute, Saluz

see Salews

SALUSTIUS
n.d.

n.d., pr., whose obit occ. on 4 Oct., in BL Ms Cotton Nero C.ix, fo 13.

SALWIUS
occ. before 1096

[1096, before], in a letter to prior Henry, q.v., abbot Anselm referred to him as *carissimo filio vestro* who was then at Bec, and promised to care for him, *Anselm Letters*, no 58.

SAMPSON [Samson Dorobernensis
occ. [c. 1168/9 × 1175]

[1168/9 × 1175], reputed to have been a noted preacher and writer of tracts and homilies *temp.* prior Odo, q.v., Hasted, *Kent*, xi, 433; see Sharpe, *Latin Writers*.

The late 12th c. catalogue contains Remigius super Donatum, Macrobius, Marcianus Capella and Ovidius epistolarum listed under the name Samson, James, *Ancient Libraries*, no 24 (p. 7), no 58 (p. 8), no 71 (p. 9), no 166 (p. 11).

Note: there are two obits for monks by the name of Sampson: 3 Jan., in BL Ms Arundel 68, fo 12 (designated as pr.) and 10 Mar., in Lambeth Ms 20, fo 171. One of these may be Sampson de Hoo, q.v.

SAMUEL
n.d.

n.d., 3 Nov., *levita*, whose obit occ. in BL Ms Arundel 68, fo 47.

An inventory of the refectory, dated 1328, includes one *ciphus de murra* formerly his, Dart, *Antiq. Cant.*, xxi (BL Ms Cotton Galba E.iv, fos 179).

SAMUEL
see also Suffleton

John SAMUELL
occ. 2nd half 13th c.

n.d., name occ. in the list in *SL*, 175, CCA Lit. Ms D.12, fo 2.

SANCTO ALBANO
see St Albans

SANCTO ALPHEGO, Elphego
see St Elphege

SANCTO ANDREA
see St Andrew

SANCTO AUGUSTINO
see St Augustine

SANCTO IVONE
see St Ives

SANCTO LAURENCIO
see St Laurence

SANCTA MARGARETA
see St Margaret

SANCTA MILDREDA
see St Mildred

SANCTO NICOLAO
see St Nicholas

SANCTO PAULO
see St Paul

SANCTO PETRO
see St Peter

SANCTO VALERICO
see St Valerico

William de SANDFORD [?Standford, Staunford
occ. 1st half 13th c.

n.d., name occ. in the *post exilium* list in *SL*, 173, CCA Lit. Ms D.12, fo 1.

Note: this is prob. William de Staunford who was apptd prior of Dover, to succ. Reginald de Sheppey, q.v., *Lit. Cant.*, iii, Appndx no 34 (CCA DCc Z.D4, 23). In the list of Dover priors, a William de Dover, confessor of the abp, was apptd by the abp on 26 June 1229, Lambeth Ms 241, fo 29, and d., c. 1235, *ib.*, fo 30; see William de Dover II.

Edmund SANDHURST
occ. 1401

1401, 19 Mar., ord acol., Canterbury cathedral, Reg. abp Arundel, i, fo 327^{v}.

Note: this is possibly Edmund Kyngston, q.v., whose ordination as acol. may have been, by mistake, entered once under each name.

Alexander SANDWYCH
see Sandwyco

Hugh SANDWYCHE [Sandwich
occ. 1451 d. 1457

1451, 21 Oct., one of four prof., *SL*, 189, CCA Lit. Ms D.12, fo 7^{v}.

1452, 23 Sept., ord subdcn, Canterbury cathedral, Reg. abp Kemp, fo 254.

1453, 31 Mar., ord dcn, Canterbury cathedral, *ib.*, fo 254^{v}.

1455, 5 Apr., ord pr., chapel in Canterbury cathedral, *Reg. abp Bourgchier*, 360.

1457, 10 Aug., d., in the eighth yr of monastic life, *Chron. Stone*, 68; CCA Lit. Ms D.12, fo 25^{v}, describes him as *conventualis*. His obit is in BL Ms Arundel 68, fo 37^{v}.

I John SANDWYCH [Sandwyco, Sanwych
occ. 1361 occ. 1366

1361, 28 Oct., one of nine prof., *SL*, 181, CCA Lit. Ms D.12, fo 4^v.
1362, 24 Sept., ord acol., Charing, Reg. abp Islip, fo 322.
1363, 23 Sept., ord dcn, Faversham monastery, *ib.*, fo 323^v.
1363, 23 Dec., ord pr., Charing, *ib.*, fo 324^v.
1366, 10 May, present at the el. of an abp, Reg. G, fo 147.

II John SANDWYCH [Sandwich ?*alias* Smyth
occ. 1467 d. 1506

1467, 28 Mar., ord acol., Canterbury cathedral, *Reg. abp Bourgchier*, 399.
1467, 19 Sept., one of six prof., *SL*, 190, CCA Lit. Ms D.12, fo 8.
1468, 12 Mar., ord subdcn, Canterbury cathedral, *Reg. abp Bourgchier*, 398.
1468, 16 Apr., ord dcn, Canterbury cathedral, *ib.*, 400.
1471, 13 Apr., ord pr., Canterbury cathedral, *ib.*, 407.
1493, 1 May, 23rd in order at the ratification of an agreement, Reg. S, fo 383^v; but see John Crosse I.
1501, 26 Apr., 12th in order at the el. of an abp, Reg. R, fo 56^v.
1506, 27 July, d., suddenly *ex pestilencia*, at the age of 57, in his 40th yr of monastic life, CCA Lit. Ms D.12, fo 35^v, which states that he was 'senior de prima mensa et *conventualis*'.
n.d., pd for the expense of embroidering frontals given by Geoffrey Glastynbury, q.v., Legg and Hope, *Inventories*, 127; he also gave white silk hangings for the martyrdom, *ib.*, 128.

Note: the obit of a John Sandwych, prob. this one, occ. on 30 July in BL Ms Arundel 68, fo 36^v.

John SANDWYCH
see also Sandwyco

Simon SANDWYCH
occ. 1424 d. 1489

1424 ,13/14 Nov., one of two clothed in the monastic habit, *SL*, 187, CCA Lit. Ms D.12, fo 6^v–7; that this date ref. to clothing rather than prof. is based on the prof. date of Robert Bynne, q.v. as both *SL* and Causton are confused.
1425, 22 Dec., ord subdcn, Charing, *Reg. abp Chichele*, iv, 374.
1428, 3 Apr., ord dcn, Rochester cathedral, Reg. Langdon (Rochester), fo 65.
1447, 18 Sept., apptd succentor, Chron. Wm Glastynbury, fo 63^v.
1449/50, fourth prior, CCA DCc Sac. acct 36, Gran. acct 56.
1453/4, 1455/6, feretrar, CCA DCc Prior accts 9, 10.
1465/9, anniversarian, CCA DCc U15/24/7, Anniv. acct 20, Lambeth ED42, CCA DCc Prior acct 11.
1439, 7 Jan., one of several monks licensed to leave the priory *pro recreacione*, and he returned on 20 Jan., Chron. Wm Glastynbury, fo 182^v/177^v.
1466, 17 Feb., an inventory of *jocalia fratrum* includes a silver *salsarium* of his and a *nux* which he had repaired, *Hist. Mss Comm. 9th Report*, Appndx, 105; he was 13th in order of seniority on this list, Reg. N, fo 231.
1489, 24 Feb., d., CCA Lit. Ms D.12, fo 27, which describes him as *senior* and *stacionarius* for fourteen yrs; he was in the 74th yr [*recte* ?64] of his monastic life and 98th yr of age and his *veneys* were given to the observant friars in Greenwich, *ib.* The entry is repeated on *ib.*, fo 31^v but the wording is not quite identical.

Note: there is an obit of a Simon Sandwych on 22 Jan. in BL Ms Arundel 68, fo 14.

William SANDWYCH, B.Th. [Sandwyche *alias* Gardiner
occ. 1511 occ. 1540

1511, 1 Sept., one of eight tonsured, *SL*, 194, CCA Lit. Ms D.12, fo 11.
1512, 19 Apr., prof., *ib.*
1513, 26 Mar., ord subdcn, Canterbury cathedral, Reg. abp Warham, ii, fo 266^v.
1520, [Apr.], celebrated his first mass and recd 8d. from William Ingram I, q.v., CCA Lit. Ms C.11, fo 132^v.
1534, [1537, before 19 Aug.], [1538], 17 Mar., 2 Oct., warden of Canterbury college, Pantin, *Cant. Coll. Ox.*, i, 72 (CCA DCc Cart. Antiq. O.151.47); he was apptd on 14 Apr. 1534, Pantin, *ib.*, iii, 148 (Reg. T, fo 10), 151, 154, 155.
1516/17, student at Canterbury college, provided with a pension of £5, Pantin, *Cant. Coll. Ox.*, ii, 256.
1521/2, student, with a pension of £6 10s., Pantin, *ib.*, ii, 258.
1524, 2 May, supplicated for B.Th. after nine yrs of study in logic, philosophy and theology, Pantin, *ib.*, iii, 255.
1527, 22 May, adm. *ad opponendum* and on 4 June 'ad lecturam libri sententiarum', i.e., B.Th., Pantin, *ib.*, iii, 255.
1541, 28 Feb., supplicated for D.Th., *ib.*
1511, 2 Sept., 88th and last in order, novice and not prof., on the visitation certificate, Wood-Legh, *Visit.*, 3 (Reg. abp Warham, i, fo 35^v).
[1537, before 19 Aug.], apptd by Thomas Cromwell to preach at Paul's Cross, Pantin, *Cant. Coll. Ox.*, iii, 151.
[1538, 8 Feb., after], in a list of monks prob. prepared for Cromwell he was described as 'witty' and 42 yrs of age, Pantin, *ib.*, iii, 152.

1538, 17 Mar., abp Cranmer remarked that he was one of the monks who had their sights on the office of prior, *L and P Henry VIII*, xiii, pt 1, no 527; see Richard Thornden.

1538, 2 Oct., as warden of Canterbury college, complained to Cromwell of the poor financial state of the college for which he blamed the prior, *ib.*, xiii, pt i, no 514.

1540, 4 Apr., became a prebendary in the new foundation, *L and P Henry VIII*, xv, no 452; apptd canon of the ninth prebend the following yr, *Fasti, 1541–1857*, iii, 32.

SANDWYCH
see also Sandwyco

Alexander de SANDWYCO [Sandwico
occ. 1289 d. 1326

1289, 19 Dec., one of eight prof., *SL*, 177, CCA Lit. Ms D.12, fo 3.

1311/14, chaplain to the prior, CCA DCc MA2, fos 30–52.

1323/4, warden of manors, CCA DCc MA2, fos 126–135.

1302, 10 May, with Laurence de Cheyham, q.v., witnessed the oath of obedience of a rector in the prior's chapel, CUL Ms Ee.5.31, fo 85.

1311, 28 Nov., apptd proctor for the prior and chapter to attend parliament, *ib.*, fo 117^{v} and *Parl. Writs*, ii, pt 2, 67.

1314, 14 Nov., provided with a letter of credence to the Count of Boulogne, *ib.*, fo 154^{v}.

1315, ordered by the abp to be placed under a 'stricter anathema' as he had taken money and goods belonging to the church for his own use and was to find and return them, Reg. abp Reynolds, fo 69–69^{v}.

1315, 8 Nov., a royal writ was issued vs him for dissipating the goods of his office, with the order that, on the prior's request, he be sent to a stricter house, *Hist. Mss Comm. 9th Report*, Appndx, 74 (Reg. I, fo 439).

Note: this must be the Alexander de Stanwyk named in *CClR (1313–1318)*, 316, where the king ordered the abp to send him to another house.

1324, 29 May, having been subjected to penance by the abp after his visitation, the prior now requested some relaxation, CUL Ms Ee.5.31, fo 236–236^{v}. His absolution is in CCA DCc EC I/46.

1326, 17 Aug., d., CCA Lit. Ms D.12, fo 16.

1326, 19 Sept., the prior wrote to someone whom he believed to have been lent certain goods of Christ Church by the deceased Alexander and asked for their return, *Lit. Cant.*, no 189 (Reg. L, fo 127^{v}).

Four volumes in the Eastry catalogue are listed under his name: Constituciones provinciales, Summa Innocencii, Summa Reymundi and a new missal, James, *Ancient Libraries*, nos 1635–1638 (p. 135).

A list of missing books dated 1 Mar. 1338 charged him with the loss of Bruttus Gallice of Richard Wynchepe, q.v., *Lit. Cant.*, no 618 (Reg. L, fo 104).

Up to seven sets of vestments made, *temp.* prior Eastry, are attached to his name, Legg and Hope, *Inventories*, 64–65 (BL Ms Cotton Galba, E.iv, fo 116^{v}).

An inventory of the refectory, dated 1328, includes three silver *ciphi* and two *de murra* under his name, Dart, *Antiq. Cant.* xx, xxiii (BL Ms Cotton Galba, E.iv, fos 179, 180).

Bartholomew de SANDWYCO
occ. [1207 × 1214] occ. 1238

[1207 × 1214], name occ. in the list of those who were in exile, *SL*, 172, CCA Lit. Ms D.12, fo 1.

1236/7, was involved in the scandal arising out of the forged charter of St Thomas which was produced to replace the torn original; it was reported during the subsequent inquiry in 1238 that he had burnt a papal privilege which had been altered by the prior where the wording was detrimental to the chapter's interests, *Gervase Cant.*, ii, 133, Cheney, 'Cant. Forgery', 19; see Simon de Hertlepe.

1238, was sent to Westminster abbey for an indefinite period, *Gervase Cant.*, ii, 134.

Edmund de SANDWYCO
occ. 2nd half 13th c.

n.d., name occ. in the list in *SL*, 175, CCA Lit. Ms D.12, fo 2.

John de SANDWYCO [Sandwico
occ. 1302 d. 1350

1302, 19 Oct., one of four prof., CCA Lit. Ms D.12, fo 3^{v}, *SL*, 178.

1305, 12 June, ord dcn, Smeeth chapel by Aldington, *Reg. abp Winchelsey*, 977.

1324, Mar./July, 1326/7, subalmoner, CCA DCc Alm. acct 29, Blean acct 2.

1334, 1335, Feb./1337, Apr., chamberlain, CCA DCc Arrears acct 5, Chamb. accts 10, 28,11.

[1344 × 1348], penitentiary whose illness caused the prior to ask the abp to relieve and replace him, *Lit. Cant.*, no 758 (Reg. L, fos 80^{v}–81).

1333, 3 Nov., apptd one of three who were to name seven *compromissorii* in the el. of an abp, Reg. G, fos xxxii, xxxvii, Reg. Q, fo 193.

1348/9, ill and the anniversarian pd 6s. as *liberatio* [for his medical expenses], CCA DCc Anniv. acct 3.

1349, 4 June, 3rd in order at the el. of an abp, Reg. G, fo 60^{v}.

1349, 8/9 Sept., 3rd at the el. of an abp, *ib.*, fo 76.

1350, 17 Nov., d., CCA Lit. Ms D.12, fo 16.

Two sets of vestments are listed under his name in an inventory of those acquired *temp.* prior

Eastry, q.v., Legg and Hope, *Inventories*, 69 (BL Ms Cotton Galba, E.iv, fo 118v).

I Nicholas de SANDWYCO

occ. 1243 occ. 1262

1244–1258, prior: apptd and installed 25/27 Oct. 1244; res. 1258, last occ. 16 July, 1258, *Fasti*, ii, 11; see Roger de St Elphege.

n.d., name occ. in the *post exilium* list in SL 173, CCA Lit. Ms D.12, fo 1v.

1262, apptd precentor by the abp, but soon res. because of objections within the community, *Gervase Cant.*, ii, 217. Dart, *Antiq. Cant.*, 183 states that he was precentor until his d. but he has prob. confused him with Nicholas II below.

1243, [Sept./Oct.], with Richard de Siwell, q.v., sent by the prior and chapter across the channel to meet abp el. Boniface, *Gervase Cant.*, ii, 200.

n.d., as prior wrote to the prior of Anglesey concerning the return of a book; see Walter de Hatfeld.

n.d., 11 Feb., *quondam prior* whose obit occ. in BL Ms Arundel 68, fo 16.

The Eastry catalogue contains seven items below his name covering a variety of subjects, James, *Ancient Libraries*, nos 1383–1389 (p. 118).

An inventory of the refectory, dated 1328, includes a silver *ciphus* formerly his, Dart, *Antiq. Cant.*, xix (BL Ms Cotton Galba E.iv, fo 178).

Some of his correspondence has been preserved in CCA DCc Cart. Antiq. B.393, e.g. item (23), his letter to the monks who were making the rounds of the manors rebuking them for their failure to alleviate the financial plight of the priory and for their prolonged absence and excessive hospitality.
See the note below the next entry.

II Nicholas de SANDWYCO [Sandwico, junior, *minor*

occ. [mid 1260s] d. 1290

[mid-1260s], one of seven prof., *SL*, CCA Lit. Ms D.12, fo 2v.

1290, 19 Sept., d., CCA Lit. Ms D.12, fo 15.

The Eastry catalogue includes an uncertain number of items under his name, prob. five, three of which contain a variety of treatises, *libelli*, etc.; he also had a copy of the Rule, De professione monachorum and De institucione noviciorum, James, *Ancient Libraries*, nos 541–545 (pp. 65–67).

Note: one of the above monks named Nicholas owned Cambridge, Corpus Christi College Ms 288, which contains letters of Alan I, prior, q.v.

An inventory of the refectory, dated 1328, includes a silver *ciphus* formerly his, Dart, *Antiq. Cant.*, xix (BL Ms Cotton Galba E.iv, fos 178v).

Note: there is a letter of a Nicholas de Sandwyco 'our chaplain' in CCA DCc EC III/28.

Peter de SANDWYCO

occ. 2nd half 13th c.

n.d., name occ. in the list in *SL*, 175, CCA Lit. Ms D.12, fo 2.

Stephen de SANDWYCO

occ. [1296]

[1296], one of the monks accused of laxity in attendance at divine office after a visitation, *Reg. abp Winchelsey*, 92.

Thomas de SANDWYCO [Sandwico

occ. 1309 d. 1345

1309, 18 Oct., one of nine prof., *SL*, 179, CCA Lit. Ms D.12, fo 3v.

1317, 28 May, ord pr., Lambeth palace chapel, Reg. abp Reynolds, fo 178.

1330, bartoner, CCA DCc MA2, fo 193; he was apptd on 20 Feb. by the absent prior in a letter to the subprior, *Lit. Cant.*, no 298 (Reg. L, fo 170).

1330/2, 1333/6, granator, CCA DCc Gran. accts 23, 24, 27–29, and prob. from 1331/6, CCA DCc MA2, fos 202v–250v.

1335/6, 1337, chaplain to the prior, CCA DCc AS14, MA2, fo 256.

1338/40, sacrist, CCA DCc Bart. accts 22, 23 and also granator during 1339, CCA DCc DE3, fo 15.

[c. 1320], with Robert de Aldon and Robert de Thaneto, q.v., and other monks involved in a dispute with prior Eastry, q.v., CCA DCc *Cart. Antiq.* C.1294, C.1296, Ms Scrap Book C.146.

1327, May, released from incarceration, and by 11 July he had left the cloister; on 16 July the prior wrote to M. John de Mallyng at the curia, describing him as 'nunc apostata et fugitivus', Reg. L, fo 152; the prior also wrote to the abp explaining the matter in detail and stating that he would be taken back only if he renounced his appeal and returned voluntarily in a state of submission. He would be required to present himself in chapter, with a humble petition for forgiveness and to state his willingness to do penance, Reg. L, fos 152–155; some of the relevant letters and statements are in *Lit. Cant.*, nos 230, 232, 233, 235, 237. One of the prior's letters to the abp, dated 19 Aug. 1327 while Thomas was still holding out vs the prior and convent, is in CUL Ms Ee.5.31, fo 262. See also CCA DCc EC I/48, 66.

[1327], 13 Oct., his return to Christ Church was reported to the abp by the prior, *Lit. Cant.*, no 235 (Reg. L, fo 155v).

1345, 14 Feb., d., CCA Lit. Ms D.12, fo 16v; his obit is in BL Ms Arundel 68, fo 16.

SANDWYCO
see also Sandwych

SARISBURY
see Salisbury

SARR'
see Remensis

SARTRINO
see John II

SARUSBURY
see Salisbury

Richard SARYCH [Sarch, Sarich, Sarygh
occ. [1373] d. 1396

[1373], one of eight prof., *SL*, 183, CCA Lit. Ms D.12, fo 4ᵛ; he had previously been a canon of Christ church, London, *ib.*

1391, 25 Apr., one of three monk penitentiaries apptd in the priory, Reg. abp Courtenay, i, fo 388.

1381, 31 July, 48th in order at the el. of an abp, Reg. G, fo 225ᵛ.

1396, 24 Feb., d., CCA Lit. Ms D.12, fo 17ᵛ.

John SCARLE
occ. 1396/7

1396/7, chancellor, CCA DCc Prior acct 4.

Note: this monk prob. occ. elsewhere in the list under his toponymic.

SCHAMELFORD
see Shamelysford

SCHARSTEDE
see Sharstede

SCHELVESTON
see Selveston

SCHEPEY
see Shepay, Sheppey

SCHORHAM
see Shoreham

SCOLANDUS [Scothlandus
n.d.

n.d., 29 Nov., pr. whose obit occ. in BL Mss Cotton Nero C.ix, fo 16ᵛ and Arundel 68, fo 49ᵛ.

Henry de SCOLDON [Scholdone
occ. 1364 occ. 1372

1364, one of eleven prof., *SL*, 182, CCA Lit. Ms D.12, fo 4ᵛ.

1371, *custos martyrii*, CCA DCc MA2, fo 266.

1372, *custos* of St Mary in crypt, CCA DCc MA2, fo 270.

1366, 10 May, present at the el. of an abp, Reg. G, fo 147.

n.d., 27 Mar., obit occ. in Lambeth Ms 20, fo 175ᵛ.

SCOTINDONE
see Shotyndon

SEFREDUS
see Siefrid

SEGARUS
n.d.

n.d., 21 June, pr., whose obit occ. in BL Ms Arundel 68, fo 31ᵛ.

Gregory de SELDING
occ. [late 13th c.]

[late 13th c.], almoner, Lambeth CM VI/127.

[late 13th c.], named in a lease, *ib.*

Robert de SELESIA [Celeseya, Celeseye, Cheleseye, Seleseye, Selysheye
occ. [c. 1270] occ. 1294

[c. 1270], prof., *SL*, 176, CCA Lit. Ms D.12, fo 3 (as Richard). The groupings of names of monks' professions together break down here because this monk was active in 1272 while the one immediately above him in the same group was not ord pr. until 1285; see Robert de Dover.

1279, 18 Aug., during the vacancy of the see had acted as commissary of the prior in the court of Canterbury, Selden Soc., *Select Cases Eccles.*, 26–27, *Epist. Pecham*, 51. See also Churchill, *Cant. Admin.*, ii, 237.

[1280, July/Nov.], with Henry de Eastry, q.v., involved in the el. of Richard de la More, adn of Winchester as bp of Winchester, BL Ms Arundel 68, fos 54ᵛ–55.

1281, 31 Mar., was in the abp's household at Freckenham, *Epist. Pecham*, 188.

1282, 7 Feb., at Lambeth witnessed the abp's mandate concerning the excommunication of the bp of Hereford, *Epist. Pecham*, 300.

[1283], 12 May, proctor in Rome; he was sent by the abp in connection with the behaviour of two monks and the opposition to prior Thomas Ryngmer, q.v., *Epist. Pecham*, 545–546; see also *ib.*, 550. Between 1280 and 1286 he acted as proctor for Christ Church; Prof Jane Sayers describes him as 'a typical professional monk proctor at the Roman curia, appearing sometimes on behalf of the abp and sometimes on behalf of the prior and convent', 'Cant. Proctors', 323.

1286/7, recd money from the treasurer for the expenses of his return journey from Rome, CCA DCc Treas. acct 3.

1292, 15 Dec., having been apptd by the prior and convent official of the court of

Canterbury, *sed. vac.*, he now began to hear cases in London in the Court of Arches, Selden Soc., *Select Cases Eccles.*, 33; see also Churchill, *Cant. Admin.*, ii, 222, 237, and CCA DCc EC IV/111.

1292, 19 Dec., present at the funeral of abp Pecham, *Reg. abp Winchelsey*, 1258.

1293, 13 Feb., named as one of seven *compromissorii* in the el. of the abp's successor, *ib.*, 1265, 1276–1277.

1293, 20 Mar., with Geoffrey de Romenal, q.v., sent to Rome to obtain confirmation of the el., *ib.*, 1281–1282.

1294, 14 Oct., one of the monks present at Siena when abp Winchelsey made an apptment to the see of Llandaff, *Reg. abp Winchelsey*, 5–6.

In c. 1282 he wrote a letter on behalf of his brother Richard with regard to apptment to a benefice in London, CCA DCc EC II/43.

In the list of missing books, dated 1 Mar. 1338, he was recorded as having been responsible for two service books previously belonging to Robert de Foxhele and Olyver, q.v., *Lit. Cant.*, no 618 (Reg. L, fo 104).

John SELLYNG [Sellynge

occ. 1519 occ. 1534

1519, 6 May, one of nine tonsured, *SL*, 194, CCA Lit. Ms D.12, fo 11v.

1534, 12 Dec., acknowledged the Act of Supremacy, *DK 7th Report*, Appndx 2, 282.

I Richard SELLYNG [Sellynge

occ. 1380/1

c. 1380, one of four prof., *SL*, 183, CCA Lit. Ms D.12, fo 5.

1380, 24 Mar., ord subdcn, Canterbury cathedral, Reg. abp Sudbury, fo 147v.

1380, 1381, recd small sums from the prior, Lambeth Ms 243, fos 180, 188v.

1381, 31 July, 61st in order at the el. of an abp, Reg. G, fo 225v.

II Richard SELLYNG

occ. 1410 d. 1417

1410, 13 Dec., one of eight prof., *SL*, 185, CCA Lit. Ms D.12, fo 6.

1413, 2 Apr., ord dcn, Canterbury cathedral, Reg. abp Arundel, ii, fo 101.

1417, 22 May, dcn, d., in his sixth yr of monastic life, *Chron. Stone*, 8, CCA Lit. Ms D.12, fo 21.

III Richard SELLYNG B.Cn.L [Selling, Sellynge

occ. 1477 occ. 1508

1476, 21 Sept., ord acol., Canterbury cathedral, *Reg. abp Bourgchier*, 420.

1477, 22 Mar., ord subdcn, Canterbury cathedral, *ib.*, 422.

1477, 19 Apr., one of four tonsured, *SL*, 191, CCA Lit. Ms D.12, fo

1477, 11 Nov., prof., *SL*, 191, Cambridge, Corpus Christi College Ms 298.

1480, 1 Apr., ord dcn, Canterbury cathedral, *Reg. abp Bourgchier*, 430.

1483, 24 May, ord pr., Sevenoaks, *ib.*, 440.

1490, 1493/6, 1504, Nov., 1506, Mar., 1508, one of the chancellors, Reg. S, fos 363v, 381v, 389v, 396, 405v, Reg. T, fos 445v, 448.

[c. 1482/3], 14 July, student, wrote to the prior, signing himself 'your chylde of obedyence and novyce' requesting permission to transfer from arts to [?canon] law, Pantin, *Cant. Coll. Ox.*, iii, 126–127; Pantin suggests [1489/90] as an alternative possible date.

[1483, Sept.], student at Canterbury college and recd a gift of 25s. from his mother, Pantin, *ib.*, ii, 267 (CCA DCc Cart. Antiq. O.151.8).

[1489, Sept.], [1490, Apr. and Sept.], student, Pantin, *ib.*, ii, 269, 270 (CCA DCc Cart. Antiq. *ib.*).

1501, 26 Apr., B.Cn.L by this date, Reg. R, fo 56v.

1493, 1 May, 35th in order at the ratification of an agreement, Reg. S, fo 383v; but see John Crosse I.

1501, 26 Apr., 22nd in order at the el. of an abp, Reg. R, fo 56v.

1508, 7 May, delegated to celebrate the Sun. mass, CCA Lit. Ms C.11, fo 17v.

For his mother, see above.

Thomas de SELLYNG

occ. 2nd half 13th c.

n.d., name appears on the list in *SL*, 175, CCA Lit. Ms D.12, fo 2v.

An inventory of the refectory, dated 1328, includes two *ciphi de murra* of his, Dart, *Antiq. Cant.*, xxii (BL Ms Cotton Galba E.iv, fo 180).

I William SELLYNG, D.Th. [Cellyng, Sellingh, Sellynge, *alias* Tillaeus, Tilly, Tyll

occ. [1448] d. 1494

1472–1494, prior: el. and *prefectio* 10 Sept. 1472, Reg. S, fo 254; d. 29 Dec. 1494, *ib.*, fo 393.

[1448], 25 Jan., one of four prof., *SL*, 189, CCA Lit. Ms D.12, fo 7v.

1448, 17 Feb., ord acol., Canterbury cathedral, Reg. abp Stafford, fo 202.

1449, 12 Apr., ord subdcn, Canterbury cathedral, *ib.*, fo 203v.

1450, 3 Apr., ord dcn, Canterbury cathedral, *ib.*, fo 204v.

1456, 18 Sept., ord pr., abp's chapel, Otford, *Reg. abp Bourgchier*, 365.

1456, 26 Sept., celebrated his first mass, and for the whole of the [following] wk was the celebrant at the high mass, *Chron. Stone*, 66.

1470, 1472, one of the chancellors, Reg. S, fos 245^{v}–246.

1471/2, treasurer, CCA DCc Treas. acct 19.

1472, 8 May, monk *supervisor*, CCA DCc RE359.

1454/5, student at Canterbury college provided with £5 pension, Pantin, *Cant. Coll. Ox.*, ii, 174; on 18 Apr. 1454, he and his fellow students at Oxford, Arnold Parmistede and William Hadlegh I, q.v. made the prior their proxy in the el. of an abp, Pantin, *ib.*, iii, 105 (Reg. N, fo 185).

1457/8, student, provided with travelling expenses between Oxford and Canterbury, Pantin, *ib.*, iv, 196.

1458/9, student for three terms, CCA DCc Chamb. acct 62.

1458, 7 Feb., supplicated for B.Th., after studying philosophy for eight yrs and theology for six yrs, Pantin, *ib.*, iv, 255–256.

1459/60, student, receiving £8 7s. for the yr, Pantin, *ib.*, ii, 180.

1462/3, at Canterbury college for the yr, Pantin, *ib.*, ii, 183.

n.d., at Oxford he heard the lectures of an eminent Italian humanist, Stefano Surigone, and prob. met Thomas Chaundler, for both of whom see *BRUO*; and for his contacts with them and others and his possible study of Greek, see Weiss, *Humanism*, 153–154.

1464, 26 Sept., granted licence by the prior and chapter to study [abroad] at any university for three yrs; he went to the university of Bologna, Pantin, *ib.*, iii, 107 (Reg. S, fo 215), Pantin, *ib.*, iv, 80.

1466, 22 Mar., his name appears in the reg. of the theological faculty of Bologna, prob. the date of his adm. to the doctorate, Pantin, *ib.*, iv, 80 and *BRUO*.

1466, 17 Feb., 41st in order in an inventory of *jocalia fratrum* [given by him and/or assigned for his use], Reg. N, fo 233^{v}.

1468, 31 Aug., preached at the el. of a prior on the theme 'Qui ascendit contra Chananeum et erit dux belli' (Judges, 1, 1), *Chron. Stone*, 105.

1469, 19 Mar., read out the articles of belief now repudiated by a heretic at the public ceremony of renunciation and repentance before high mass; he then preached on the text 'Per proprium sanguinem introivit semel in sancta', and proceeded to explain to the assembled throng the falsity of heretical teaching and its dangers, and the necessity of adherence to the sacramental teaching of the church, *ib.*, 108–109.

1469, after Oct., with Reginald Goldston I, q.v., went to Rome to obtain indulgences for Christ Church for the jubilee of St Thomas (1470); he must have used this opportunity to collect Greek and Latin mss, Pantin, *Cant. Coll. Ox.*, iii, 108–109 (CCA DCc Ms Scrap Book C. loose), which is an acct of their expenses; see also, Pantin, *ib.*, iv, 80–81. *Lit. Cant.* no 1058 (Reg. L, fo 237^{v}), dated 30 Oct. 1469, which is the abp's letter of recommendation on their behalf.

1486, 19 Apr., conducted a visitation, *sed. vac.*, of St Gregory's [priory], Canterbury, Cambridge, Corpus Christi College Ms 298, fo 131.

1486, 9 Dec., took the cross of the church of Canterbury to the new abp [Morton] in London and preached before him, *Reg. abp Morton*, i, no 7. Close to this date, c. 15 Oct./24 Nov., he purchased in London for John Langdon II, q.v. 'j boke . . . callyd Perottis gramer xij d', Pantin, *Cant. Coll. Ox.*, i, 109 (CCA DCc DE18).

1487, May, with the bps of Durham and Hereford went on a mission to the pope as envoys for the king, *Hist. Mss Comm. 5th Report*, Appndx, 454, Weiss, *Humanism*, 156. He made use of this opportunity to obtain papal orders to confirm his [the prior's] *sed. vac.* jurisdiction and Christ Church's exemption from attendance at Black Monk chapters, *CPL*, xiv (1484–1492), 193–194, 204–208; he was described as the king's orator, see below.

1490/1, sent on several missions to France to negotiate peace; his first apptment was on 27 Feb., 1490, Rymer, *Foedera*, ii, 431.

1494, 29 Dec., d. and soon afterwards was buried in the martyrdom of the cathedral, Cambridge, Corpus Christi College Ms 298, fo 122^{v} (the northwest transept).

A series of extant letters to him and from him as prior have been transcribed in Pantin, *Cant. Coll. Ox.*, iii, 116–126, 128–129.

Some of his *acta* are in Reg. S, fos 254–393.

He gave an unspecified no of books to Canterbury college in 1481, Pantin, *Cant. Coll. Ox*, ii, 212 (CCA DCc Cart. Antiq. O.135d).

His fine italic handwriting is prob. in Reg. S, fos 245^{v}–246, which are dated 1471/2, during his chancellorship, Pantin, *Cant. Coll. Ox.*, iv, 226.

Sellyng left his mark on Christ Church; he was responsible for the glazing of the south side of the cloister where he put in carrels; he built 'Sellinggate', at the entrance to the Green Court, with a study above; and the work on the central tower of the cathedral was continued and almost completed during his priorate, see Woodruff, *Memorials Cant.*, 206–207. See also Willis, 'Arch. Hist. Christ Church', 45, and the summary of his achievements as prior in BL Ms Arundel 68, fo 4–4^{v}.

There is general agreement that he was prob. the leading classical scholar of his day in England and a champion of Greek studies, Pantin, *Cant. Coll. Ox.*, iv, 83. Weiss, *Humanism*, especially 153–159; see also *DNB*, under Celling. For a discussion of his part in the revival of classical scholarship and his circle of friends see F.A. Gasquet,

The Old English Bible and Other Essays, 2nd edn (London, 1908) 305–318. See also the recent appraisal by R.B. Dobson in 'Canterbury in the Later Middle Ages', in Collinson, *Canterbury Cathedral*, 114–115.

CCA Lit. Ms D.12, fo 27v/31v provides a succinct and sober summary of his career: 'Hic in divinis agendis multum devotus, lingua greca atque latina valde eruditus; necnon Regis embassiatoris extit ad summam pontificem ubi orationem fecit. Ac eciam regi francorum missus qui laudabiliter se habuit'.

II William SELLYNG [Sellynge
occ. 1495 d. 1501

1495, 1 Aug., one of four tonsured, *SL*, 192, CCA Lit. Ms D.12, fo 9v.
1496, 2 Apr., ord acol., Canterbury cathedral, *Reg. abp Morton*, i, no 445a.
1496, 4 Apr., prof., *SL*, 192, CCA Lit. Ms D.12, fo 9v.
1497, 25 Mar., ord subdcn, Canterbury cathedral, *Reg. abp Morton*, i, no 446b.
1498, 14 Apr., ord dcn, Canterbury cathedral, *ib.*, i, no 447c.
1500/1, celebrated his first mass and recd a small gift from the sacrist, CCA DCc Sac. acct 70.
1501, before 12 Sept., chaplain to the subprior, CCA Lit. Ms D.12, fo 28v/33v.
1501, 26 Apr., 54th in order at the el. of an abp, Reg. R, fo 56v.
1501, 12 Sept., d., *ex vehementi pestilencie*; he was at the time of his d. 'juvenis sacerdos inferioris chori ad cursum diaconorum', and was 22 yrs of age, CCA Lit. Ms D.12, fo 28v/33v. His obit on 13 Sept. is in BL Ms Arundel, fo 41v.

III William SELLYNG B.Th. [Sellynge
occ. 1502 d. 1518/19

1502, 25 Aug., one of eight tonsured, *SL*, 193, CCA Lit. Ms D.12, fo 10.
1503, 4 Apr., prof., *ib.*
1510, Apr., celebrated his first mass on the first Sun. of this month and recd 4d. from the *custos martyrii*, CCA Lit. Ms C.11, fo 51v.
1517/18, warden of manors, CCA DCc, Ms DE 70.
1504/6, Easter to Easter, student at Canterbury college and provided with a pension of £5, Pantin, *Cant. Coll. Ox.*, ii, 241, 245 (CCA DCc Cart. Antiq. O.151.38, 39).
1506/7, Easter to Easter, student, with a pension of £6 10s., Pantin, *ib.*, ii, 248 (CCA DCc Cart. Antiq. O.151.41).
1508/9, 1510/11, student, with a pension of £8 and of £6 10s. respectively, Pantin, *ib.*, ii, 250, 252 (CCA DCc Cart. Antiq. O.151.42, 43).
1512, [student], recd travel expenses from Oxford to Canterbury, Pantin, *ib.*, iv, 205.
1513, 28 Apr., supplicated for B.Th., after eight yrs of study in logic, philosophy and theology; adm. *ad opponendum* on 28 May and adm. 'ad lecturam libri sentenciarum' on 16 June, Pantin, *ib.*, iii, 256.
1516, 1 Feb., supplicated for D.Th., after nine yrs of study in logic, philosophy and theology, Pantin, *ib.*, iii, 256–257.
1516/17, student, with a £4 pension, *ib.*, ii, 256.
1511, 2 Sept., 52nd in order on the visitation certificate but reported absent at Oxford, Wood-Legh, *Visit.*, 3 (Reg. abp Warham, i, fo 35v).
1518/19, d., Pantin, *Cant. Coll. Ox.*, iv, 206.

SELSEY
see Selesia

Henry de SELVERTON [Selvertone
occ. [1336] d. 1358

[1336], one of seven adm.; *SL*, 180 and CCA Lit. Ms D.12, fo 4 are not accurate: on 10 Nov. [1336], the prior had agreed to accept him if he passed an examination to be conducted by John de Paxton (not the monk by this name); he was at this time a novice at the Augustinian priory of Kenilworth, *Lit. Cant.*, no 606 (Reg. L, fo 66v). On 19 Dec. [1336] he was one of the five among the seven adm. about whom the prior wrote to the abp to allow them to be prof. before their yr of probation was completed; the abp replied no, Reg. L, fo 67v.
1349, 4 June, 42nd in order at the el. of an abp, Reg. G, fo 60v.
1349, 8/9 Sept., 41st at the el. of an abp, *ib.*, fo 76v.
1356, 22 Mar., d., CCA Lit. Ms D.12, fo 17.

Adam de SELVESTON [Schelveston, Selm'ston, Selvestone, Selvistone
occ. 1298 d. 1332

1298, 18 Oct., one of seven prof., *SL*, 178, CCA Lit. Ms D.12, fo 3.
1299, 19 Sept., ord [sub]dcn, Littlebourne, *Reg. abp Winchelsey*, 930.
1300, 4 June, ord dcn, Smeeth chapel by Aldington, *ib.*, 935.
Note: on both dates he is entered under ord to the diaconate.
1322/3, 1324/7, Mar., granator, CCA DCc Gran. accts 14–17; there are also accts between 1321 and 1326 which name him in this office, CCA DCc MA2, fos 112–155v.
1327/8, *custos martyrii*, CCA DCc MA2, fos 164v–175v.
1329, Mar./Sept., 1329/30, Mar., chamberlain, CCA DCc Chamb. accts 22, 33; he was dismissed from this office on 15 Jan. 1330, Reg. I, fo 432.
[1332], 21 Sept., gravely ill, *Lit. Cant.*, no 468 (Reg. L, fo 23v).
1332, 4 Oct., d., CCA Lit. Ms D.12, fo 16.

Thomas SELVYSTON [Sylveston
occ. 1398 d. 1419

1398, one of four prof., *SL*, 184, CCA Lit. Ms D.12, fo 5v.
1399, 20 Dec., ord dcn, Canterbury cathedral, Reg. abp Arundel, i, fo 325.
1401, 19 Mar., ord pr., Canterbury cathedral, *ib.*, i, fo 328.

1414, 12 Mar., 41st in order at the el. of an abp, and served as proxy for John de Wy II, q.v., *Reg. abp Chichele*, i, 4.
1419, 30 Aug., d. *ex vehementi pestilencia*, *Chron. Stone*, 10, which describes him as 'persona religiosa et honeste conversacionis, decens et pulcra facie set pulchrior fide, a singulis fratribus multumque delectus' and records that he was an expert in the art of embroidery of vestments, *ib.* His obit is in BL Ms Arundel 68, fo 39v.

SERRIS
see Remensis

John SEVENOKE
occ. 1291

n.d., name occ. in the list in *SL*, 176, CCA Lit. Ms D.12, fo 2v.

1291, pd a supervisory visit to Meopham, CCA DCc Meopham acct 15.

Michael de SEVENOKE
occ. [1260]

n.d. [1260], one of five prof., *SL*, 176, CCA Lit. Ms D.12, fo 2v.

Peter SEVENOKE
d. [1287]

n.d., name occ. in the list in *SL*, 175, CCA Lit. Ms D.12, fo 2v.

[1287], 23 Sept., d., CCA Lit. Ms D.12, fo 15.

SEVERIUS
n.d.

n.d., *levita*, whose obit occ. on 18 Apr., in BL Ms Cotton Nero C.ix, fo 10.

SEWOLD
n.d.

n.d., 23 Oct., obit occ. in BL Ms Cotton Nero C.ix, fo 14.

SEWYNUS
n.d.
n.d., 6 May, obit occ. in Lambeth Ms 20, fo 185.

John de SHAMELYSFORD [Schamelford, Schamelsford
occ. [1281] d. 1290

[1281], 9 Nov., mentioned by the abp in a letter, *Epist. Pecham*, 245; see Nicholas de Grantebrygg.
[1285], 5 Jan., one of several monks imprisoned by royal officers whose release into his charge the abp now arranged; he is described as apostate, *Epist. Pecham*, 876–877.
1290, 17 Dec., d., CCA Lit. Ms D.12, fo 15.

Three volumes in the Eastry catalogue come under his name, two containing decretals, James, *Ancient Libraries*, nos 704–706 (p. 77).

Note: this may be Thomas de Chalmysforde, q.v.

Richard de SHARSTEDE [Scharstede, Sharsted
occ. [1260] d. 1316

[1260], one of five prof., *SL*, 176, CCA Lit. Ms D.12, fo 2v.

1295/8, 1298/9, warden of manors, CCA DCc MA1, fos 194–215v, Ickham acct 13.
1307, 1308/9, bartoner, CCA DCc MA1, fo 271, MA2, fos 11v–17v.
1309/10, cellarer, CCA DCc fos 17v–23v; he was removed on 18 Oct. 1310, Reg. Q, fo 41/53; see Nicholas de Borne I.
1313/16, sacrist, CCA DCc MA2, fos 44v–70; he was succ. by Robert de Dover q.v., in Feb. 1316 acc. to Reg. I, fo 343; see below.

1316, 2 Aug., d., CCA Lit. Ms D.12, fo 15.

An inventory of vestments, ornaments, gospel books [*textus*] and relics in the care of the sacrist was drawn up on 2 Feb. 1316 at the end of his term of office, Legg and Hope, *Inventories*, 50–94 (BL Ms Cotton Galba, E.iv, fos 112–127v). In this list there are two embroidered linen albs of his [?gift], Legg and Hope, *Inventories*, 60 (BL Ms Cotton Galba, E.iv, fo 115). See John le Spycer.

I John SHEPAY [Schepey, Shepeye
occ. 1389 d. 1439

1389, 6 Nov., one of eight prof., *SL*, 184, CCA Lit. Ms D.12, fo 5.
1391, 25 Mar., ord dcn, Canterbury cathedral, Reg. abp Courtenay, i, fo 312.
[1404/5], subsacrist, CCA DCc Prior acct 20; he was also *custos* of the high altar, *ib.*
1396, 7 Aug., 56th in order at the el. of an abp, Reg. G, fo 234v.
1414, 12 Mar., 21st at the el. of an abp, *Reg. abp Chichele*, i, 4.
1439, 26/27 Dec., d.; on 27 Dec., before his burial, mass was said in the chapel *de Requiem* (is this the name of the chapel or the mass?), *Chron. Stone*, 26. (CCA Lit. Ms D.12, fo 24). His obit on 26 Dec. is in BL Ms Arundel 68, fo 52.

His portrait may be seen on a boss on the vault of the east walk of the cloister, a photograph of which appears in Collinson, *Canterbury Cathedral*, pl. 21. With his friends he had given £100 toward the cloister building work, R. Griffin, *Friends of Canterbury Cathedral 8th Annual Report*, (1935), 52.

II John SHEPAY [Schepey, Shepey, Sheppey

occ. 1500 occ. 1518/19

1500, 28 July, one of eight tonsured, *SL*, CCA Lit. Ms D.12, fo 10; each of the novices recd a gold noble worth 6s. 8d. for their labours with regard to the funeral of abp Morton who d. c. 15 Sept. 1500, CCA Lit. Ms D.12, *ib.*

1501, 19 Apr., he made his prof. before the prior, *sed. vac.*, *SL*, 193, CCA Lit. Ms D.12, fo 10.

1506, 11 Apr., ord pr., Canterbury cathedral, Reg. abp Warham, ii, fo 262v; he recd 4d. from the *custos martyrii* after celebrating his first mass on the third Sun. of this month, CCA Lit. Ms C.11, fo 48v.

1514, 29 Sept.; 1515, 24 June; 1516, 25 Dec.; 1517, 25 Mar., *custos* of St Mary in crypt, CCA Lit. Ms C.11, fos 56v, 57, 58 bis.

1519, 25 Dec.; 1520/1; 1522, 25 Dec.; 1526, 1527, 1528, all on 25 Mar; 1529, 25 Dec.; 1530, 25 Mar., treasurer, CCA Lit. Ms C.11, fo 60; CCA DCc Treas. acct 25; CCA Lit. Ms C.11, fo 62; *ib.*, fos 64, 64v, 65; *ib.*, fo 66; *ib.*, fo 67v.

n.d., *magister regule* for William Lychfeld and John Asshforde II, q.v., Pantin, *Cant. Coll. Ox.*, iv, 54 (CCA DCc Ms Scrap Book B.186).

1512, student at Canterbury college, Oxford, whose expenses were pd for the transport of his 'stuffe' from Oxford to Canterbury, Pantin, *Cant. Coll. Ox.*, iv, 205.

1501, 26 Apr., 68th in order at the el. of an abp, Reg. R, fo 56.

1511, 2 Sept., 47th on the visitation certificate, Wood-Legh, *Visit.*, 3 (Reg. abp Warham, i, fo 35v).

1518/19, ill in the infirmary, CCA DCc Infirm. acct 1.

Nicholas SHEPAY [Schepey, Shepeye

occ. [1389] d. 1438

[1389], 6 Nov., one of eight prof., *SL*, 184, CCA Lit. Ms D.12, fo 5.

1391, 25 Mar., ord dcn, Canterbury cathedral, Reg. abp Courtenay, i, fo 312.

1400/3, treasurer, CCA DCc Bailiff of Liberty accts 11–13.

1410/11, *custos* of St Mary in crypt, CCA DCc Prior acct 2.

1411/13, cellarer, CCA DCc Eastry acct 135, Treas. acct 11.

1414/15, before, chaplain to the prior, CCA DCc Prior's Chaplain acct 9.

1414/15, bartoner, CCA DCc Bart. acct 76.

1418/19, treasurer, Lambeth ED81.

1419, 3 Oct.; 1421/2; 1424/6, 1427/8, cellarer, *Reg. abp Chichele*, iv, 196–197; CCA DCc Eastry acct where he is also named as warden of manors; CCA DCc Great Chart acct 100, RE134; Eastry acct 154; his apptment to office was on 3 Oct. 1419, as above.

1433/6, 1438, before 23 Feb., granator, CCA DCc Gran. accts 44–46, *Chron. Stone*, 22.

1389/90, recd 12d. from the prior *pro benedictione*, Lambeth Ms 243, fo 216v.

1396, 7 Aug., 55th in order at the el. of an abp, Reg. G, fo 234v.

1410/11, gave the prior a gift of 20s., CCA DCc Prior acct 2.

1414, 12 Mar., 20th in order at the el. of an abp, *Reg. abp Chichele*, i, 4.

1428, [31] Mar., one of the monks invited to the abp's palace after the *prefectio* of William Molassh, q.v., as prior, Oxford, Bod. Ms Tanner 165, fo 6v.

1438, 23 Feb., d., *Chron. Stone*, 22 (CCA Lit. Ms D.12, fo 24, incomplete).

Reginald de SHEPPEY

occ. before 1212

1212, apptd prior of Dover, *HRH*, 88.

1228/9, d., *ib.*, his obit occ. on 1 Feb. in BL Ms Arundel 68, fo 15.

James de SHERDENN

occ. 2nd half 13th c.

n.d., name occ. in the list in *SL*, 176, CCA Lit. Ms D.12, fo 2v.

Robert SHERWODE [Shirewood, Shirwod, Shirwoode, Shyrewode

occ. 1488 occ. 1496

1488, 30 Sept., one of six tonsured, *SL*, 192, CCA Lit. Ms D.12, fo 9.

1490, 4 Apr., made his prof. before the abp, CCA Lit. Ms D.12, *ib.*; the delay in prof. did not preclude the six from having 'pecunias sicut ceteri fratres cum ebd' servicio et assi-gnacione ad refect' et mensam conventus' by permission of the prior and *magister ordinis*, *ib.*

1491, 2 Apr., ord acol., Canterbury cathedral, *Reg. abp Morton*, i, no 439a.

1492, 21 Apr., ord subdcn, Canterbury cathedral, *ib.*, i, no 441b.

1494, 29 Mar., ord dcn, Canterbury cathedral, *ib.*, i, no 443c.

1496, 2 Apr., ord pr., Canterbury cathedral, *ib.*, i, no 445d.

1493, 1 May, 58th in order at the ratification of an agreement, Reg. S, fo 383v; but see John Crosse I.

n.d., *recessit*, *SL*, 192, CCA Lit. Ms D.12, fo 9.

John SHOREHAM [Schorham, Scorham, Shorham

occ. 1364 occ. 1375

1364, n.d., one of eleven prof., *SL*, 182, CCA Lit. Ms D.12, fo 4v.

1364, 9 Mar. ord subdcn, abp's chapel, Charing, Reg. abp Islip, fo 325.

1365, 29 Mar., ord dcn, abp's chapel, Charing, *ib.*, fo 326 (by the bp of Worcester).
1367, 18 Sept., ord pr., Lambeth palace chapel, *Reg. abp Langham*, 383.

1371, *custos* of the high altar, CCA DCc MA2, fo 266.

1373, subchaplain to the prior, CCA DCc MA2, fo 276v.

1373/5, treasurer, CCA DCc MA2, fos 290–294v.

1366, 10 May, present at the el. of an abp, Reg. G, fo 147.

1374, 30 June, 35th in order at the el. of an abp, *ib.*, fos 173v–175v; on 27 June he had been named proxy for William Woghope, q.v., who was unable to be present, *ib.*, fo 172v.

John SHOTYNDON [Shotindune, Shotynden, Sotindune
d. 1239

n.d., name occ. in the *post exilium* list in *SL*, 173, CCA Lit. Ms D.12, fo 1v.

1239, 4 Jan., one of the group of monks accused of contumacy by the abp after the forgery scandal, *Gervase Cant.*, ii, 144; see Simon de Hertlepe. On 1 Feb. he was among those summoned to appear before the abp after the monks' el. of Roger de La Lee, q.v., as prior, *ib.*, ii, 153.
1239, 23 Oct., d., his funeral took place while all the people of Canterbury were under sentence of excommunication, *Gervase Cant.*, ii, 173.

I William de SHOTYNDON [Scotindone, Shotindune, Sotindune
occ. 1239/41 occ. [1262]

n.d., name occ. near the beginning of the *post exilium* list in *SL*, 172, CCA Lit. Ms D.12, fo 1.

1239, 1 Feb., Mar; 1241, 1 Feb., precentor, *Gervase Cant.*, ii, 153, 154, 157, 186, 190.

1239, 4 Jan., one of the group of monks accused of contumacy by the abp after the forgery scandal, *Gervase Cant.*, ii, 144; see Simon de Hertlepe. On 1 Feb. he was among those summoned to appear before the abp after the monks' el. of Roger de La Lee, q.v., as prior, *ib.*, ii, 153.
1239, 5 Feb., Mar., with Stephen Cranbroke, q.v., wrote letters to the abp asking him to explain the reasons for his condemnation of the chapter, *Gervase Cant.*, ii, 154, 157.
1241, 1 Feb., one of the *compromissorii* in the el. of an abp, *ib.*, ii, 186, 190 (as William, precentor).
[1262], d., while precentor and was succ. by Nicholas de Sandwyco I, q.v., *ib.*, ii, 217.

The Eastry catalogue includes eleven volumes of his: a Martilogium novum cotidianum, sermons and several moralia, James, *Ancient Libraries*, nos 293, 1287–1296 (pp. 50, 111—112).

II William SHOTYNDON [Schotynden, Schotyngdon, Shortyndon
occ. 1298 d. 1305

1298, 18 Oct., one of seven prof., *SL*, 178, CCA Lit. Ms D.12, fo 3.
1299, 19 Sept., ord [sub]dcn, Littlebourne, *Reg. abp Winchelsey*, 930.
1300, 4 June, ord dcn, Smeeth chapel by Aldington, *ib.*, 935.
Note: on both dates he is entered under ord to the diaconate.

1305, 16 Jan., d., CCA Lit. Ms D.12, fo 15v.

Note: see the books listed under the preceding entry; they may belong here.

SHYREWODE
see Sherwode

SIDINGEBURNE
see Sittingborne

SIEFRID [Sefredus
occ. [1114 × 1122]

[1114 × 1122], brother of abp Ralph d'Escures, Eadmer, *Hist. Nov.*, 256.

n.d., 7 Oct., the obit of a Sefredus occ. in BL Ms Cotton Nero C.ix, fo 13.

Daniel de SIFFLINGTON [Sifletone, Siflettone, Suffleton
occ. 1280 d. 1307

n.d., name occ. in the list in *SL*, 175, CCA Lit. Ms D.12, fo 2v (as Daniel).

1280, Mar./Sept., 1280/1, granator, CCA DCc Gran. acct AS 25, MA1, fos 132v–135 (as Daniel).
1287/94, monk warden, CCA DCc MA1, fos 150v–190 (as Daniel).
1291/3, chamberlain, CCA DCc MA1, fos 173–185 (as Daniel); he was on the list of names for [reapptment to] this office sent to the abp in Apr. 1299, *Reg. abp Winchelsey*, 337–338.
1303, 23 Nov., removed from the office of penitentiary, *Reg. abp Winchelsey*, 1305 (Reg. Q, fo 30v/42).

1307, 2 Jan., d., CCA Lit. Ms D.12, fo 15v; his obit on 5 Jan. is in BL Ms Arundel 68, fo 12 (as Sufflete).

The Eastry catalogue lists five titles under his name including a Bible and the Sententie of Peter Lombard, James, *Ancient Libraries*, nos 1616–1620 (p. 134).

In the list of missing books dated 1 Mar. 1338, his missale was charged out to John le Spycer, q.v, *Lit. Cant.*, no 618 (Reg. L, fo 104).

An inventory of the refectory, dated 1328, includes two silver *ciphi* and two *de murra* once his, Dart, *Antiq. Cant.*, xx, xxi (BL Ms Cotton Galba E.iv, fos 178v, 179v).

An inventory of vestments, *temp.* prior Eastry, includes two linen chasubles and four albs of his, Legg and Hope, *Inventories*, 52, 60 (BL Ms Cotton Galba, E.iv, fos 112, 115).

SIFFLINGTON
see also Suffleton

SIGARUS
n.d.

n.d., subdcn whose obit occ. on 5 Dec., BL Ms Cotton Nero C.ix, fo 17.

I SILVESTER
occ. [1115 × 1122]

[1115 × 1122], presumably a Christ Church monk who, with the adcn of Canterbury and others, witnessed a grant of abp Ralph d'Escures to Christ Church, Eng. Epis. Acta, Canterbury, 1070–1136, no 37, forthcoming.

II SILVESTER
occ. 1st half 13th c.

n.d., name occ. in the list in *SL*, 173, CCA Lit. Ms D.12, fo 1^v.

An inventory of the refectory dated 1328 includes a *ciphus de murra* prob. of his, Dart, *Antiq. Cant.*, xxii (BL Ms Cotton Galba E.iv, fo 180).

I SIMON [Symon
occ. 1155 d. ?1188

1155, 28 Mar., with William, subprior, q.v., attested a confirmation of abp Theobald, *Theobald Charters*, 536.
?1188, July, one of five monks who d. in Rome, *Epist. Cant.*, 254.

Note: an obit of a Simon occ. in BL Ms Arundel 68, fo 34 and Lambeth Ms 20, fo 201.

II SIMON
occ. 1187/9

1187, 28 Aug., reapptd chamberlain, *Gervase Cant.*, i, 381; he had previously occupied this office, *Eng. Epis. Acta*, ii, no 253, *Epist. Cant.*, 254.
1189, Aug., Nov., treasurer, *Epist. Cant.*, 298, 306, 315 (as S.).
1187, involved in the chapter's dispute with abp Baldwin over the latter's rights in the apptment of obedientiaries; in Sept., both he and Robert III, sacrist, q.v., refused to accept their offices from the abp, *Epist. Cant.*, 92, *Gervase Cant.*, i, 379, 381.
1189, Aug., sent, with Jonas, q.v., to meet the new king, Richard I, *Epist. Cant.*, 306.
1189, Sept., in a letter of Geoffrey II, subprior, q.v., to Alan II, third prior, q.v., he [the subprior] stated his willingness to accept Simon as prior if he were to be el. by the convent, *Epist. Cant.*, 308. On the other hand he does not seem to have been popular among his brethren because another letter recd by the subprior from unnamed monks expressed the fear that he or Roger Norreys I, q.v., would be the next prior, *ib.*, 309.
1189, 9 Nov., was one of the monks who, with Aaron, q.v., walked out in protest during discussions with the king, *ib.*, 317.

Note the presence of two contemporary Simons: one who d. in Rome in July 1188, *Epist. Cant.*, 254; one who was sent back to England in Apr. 1189, *ib.*, 289.

Note: in a survey of cathedral holdings in Canterbury dated c. 1200 there is ref. to Jordan, brother of Symon, 'our monk', Urry, *Canterbury*, 296.

III SIMON
occ. 1198/9 occ. [1207 × 1214]

[1207 × 1214], occ. in the list of those who were in exile, *SL*, 172, CCA Lit. Ms D.12, fo 1.
1198/9, chaplain to the prior, Lit. Ms D.4, fo 4^v.
1201/2, 1203/4, monk carpenter, Lit. Ms D.4, fos 12^v, 16.
[1207 × 1214], described in the *SL* list as *tunc precentor*, see above.
[1193, Nov. × 1195, Apr. or 1198, Feb. × 1205, July], with Walter II, q.v., witnessed a grant of abp Hubert Walter, *Eng. Epis. Acta*, iii, no 399.
1205, 11 Dec., one of the monks who appealed to the pope to confirm the chapter's el. of their subprior, Reginald, q.v., as abp, *CPL*, i (1198–1304), 23, 26.

IV SIMON
occ. 1236/7

1236/7 bartoner, CCA DCc AS5.

V SIMON
occ. 1291/3

1291/3, subalmoner, CCA DCc Eastry accts 19, 20.

VI SIMON [Symon
occ. 1315

1315, 5 Oct., subprior, CUL Ms Ee.5.31, fo 161.
n.d., 25 May, subprior, whose obit occ. in BL Ms Arundel 68, fo 28^v.

Name in CUL Ms Kk.1.28, Isidorus etc. (13th c.).

In the Eastry catalogue the penitenciale of a Symon, subprior is no 229, James, *Ancient Libraries*, (p. 42); and nos 1164 prob. to 1180 (pp. 104–105), also under his name, include a Bible in verse, the Diadema monachorum, Sentencie of Peter Lombard, a concordance of the Old and New Testaments and various treatises and *libelli* including one on herbal remedies.

Note: Simon was a fairly common name in the 12th/13th cs; some of these entries, arbitrarily assigned for lack of evidence, may apply to Simon Eynysforde, Simon Hertlepe, Simon de Hibernia, Simon de Leycestria, Simon de St Paul, q.v. The list of books above has also been arbitrarily assigned.

SINOTHERUS
n.d.

n.d., pr., whose obit occ. on 21 Apr. in BL Ms Cotton Nero C.ix, fo 10.

SIRICUS
n.d.

n.d., pr., whose obit occ. on 9 Oct. in BL Ms Cotton Nero C.ix, fo 13ᵛ.

I M. John de SITTINGBORNE [Sidingeburne, Sydyngborne
occ. [1207 × 1214] d. 1235/8

1222–1235 × 1238, prior: succ. Walter III, q.v., 1222; date of d. uncertain, between Dec. 1235 and 1238, *Fasti*, ii, 11; see below.

[1207 × 1214], name heads the list of those who were in exile, *SL*, 172, CCA Lit. Ms D.12, fo 1.

1228, 3 Aug., presided at the el. of an abp, when Walter de Eynesham was el., *Gervase Cant.*, ii, 116–124.

1232, 16 Mar., el. abp by the chapter, *ib.*, ii, 129 and set off for Rome where he res. on 12 June, *ib.*, and *Fasti*, ii, 6.

His obit on 18 July occ. in BL Ms Arundel 68, fo 35. *Ann. Waverley*, 320, states that he became a Carthusian in 1238 and d. shortly after. Such a move is hardly surprising in the demoralizing dispute between the monks and abp Edmund.

The Eastry catalogue contains an uncertain no of volumes under his name, possibly thirty; these include his own questiones, theological works, sermons, and a volume entitled Concilium Lateranense, James, *Ancient Libraries*, nos 1246–?1275 (pp. 109–111).

It is Gervase who assigned to him the title of *Magister* and described him as 'vir religiosus, literatus et discretus', *Gervase Cant.*, ii, 129.

II John SITTINGBORNE [Sydyngborne, Sydyngbourne
occ. 1414/15 d. 1437

1414/15, n.d., one of five adm., *SL*, 186, CCA Lit. Ms D.12, fo 6; see the next entry.

1415, 10 Nov., one of six whom the prior was comm. to prof., *Reg. abp Chichele*, iv, 142.

1416, 18 Apr., ord acol., Canterbury cathedral, *Reg. abp Chichele*, iv, 319.

1419, 1 Apr., ord dcn, chapel within the priory, *ib.*, i, 191.

1419, 15 Apr., ord pr., chapel within the priory, *ib.*, i, 193.

[1435], 1437, before 30 Oct., one of the chancellors, 'Chron. Wm Glastynbury', 129 (Ms fo 116ᵛ).

1437, 30 Oct., d., Chron. Wm Glastynbury, fo 117; CCA Lit. Ms D.12 reports the d. as caused by an epidemic, fo 24. His obit is in BL Ms Arundel 68, fo 46ᵛ.

Richard de SIWELL [Suthwelle, Suwell, Suwelle
occ. 1239 occ. 1244

n.d., name occ. in the list in *SL*, 173, CCA Lit. Ms D.12, fo 1.

1239, 1 Feb.; 1240, cellarer, *Gervase Cant.*, ii, 153, 176.

1239, 4 Jan., one of the group of monks accused of contumacy by the abp after the forgery scandal, *Gervase Cant.*, ii, 144; see Simon de Hertlepe. On 1 Feb. he was among those summoned to appear before the abp after the monks' el. of Roger de La Lee, q.v., as prior, *ib.*, ii, 153.

1240, [Mar.], sent as proctor to the king, *ib.*, ii, 176.

1241, 1 Feb., chosen to be one of seven *compromissorii* in the el. of an abp, *Gervase Cant.*, ii, 186, 187, 190.

1243, [Sept./Oct.], with Nicholas de Sandwyco, q.v., sent by the chapter to the continent to meet abp el. Boniface, *ib.*, ii, 200.

1244, 20 Mar., royal assent was given to his el. as abbot of Cerne, *CPR (1232–1247)*, 421, 422.

Guy de SMERDEN [Guido de Smerdenne, Smerdeun
occ. [c. 1255] d. 1323

[c. 1255], name occ. in the list in *SL*, 176, CCA Lit. Ms D.12, fo 2ᵛ.

1289/90, bartoner, CCA DCc Bart. B acct 40.

1308/9, 1313, 28 May, 1315, almoner, CCA DCc Alm. acct 21, Reg. Q, fo 61ᵛ/75ᵛ; he was removed by the abp in 1315, Reg. abp Reynolds, fo 69.

1285/6, visited Meopham with prior Henry de Eastry, q.v., CCA DCc Meopham acct 8.

1306, Apr., witnessed the creation of a notary by the prior, Reg. I, fo 266ᵛ.

1307, Oct., apptd proctor to attend parliament at Northampton, *Parl. Writs*, ii, pt 3, 546.

1313, 28 May, appointed one of seven *compromissorii* in the el. of an abp, Reg. Q, fo 61ᵛ/75ᵛ.

1315, n.d., the abp ordered his removal from the office of almoner and from any other office *quod gerit exterius* within eight days; he was not to undertake any office without the abp's licence, Reg. abp Reynolds, fo 69.

1323, 20 Nov., d., CCA Lit. Ms D.12, fo 16.

Robert SMERDEN [Smerdenn
occ. 1403 d. ?1440/1

1403, 22 Dec., one of six prof., *SL*, 185, CCA Lit. Ms D.12, fo 5v.
1404, 29 Mar., ord subdcn, Canterbury cathedral, Reg. abp Arundel, i, fo 332v.
1405, 18 Apr., ord dcn, Canterbury cathedral, *ib.*, i, fo 334.

1417, 13 Dec., *magister ordinis*, *SL*, 186, CCA Lit. Ms D.12, fo 6v.
[1440], 27 June, absolved from the two offices of *magister tumbe* and *magister martyrii ad tumbam*, Chron. Wm Glastynbury, fo 119v.

1425, 5 Nov., granted papal licence to choose his own confessor, *CPL*, vii (1417–1431), 416.
1438, 21 Dec., d., acc. to CCA Lit. Ms D.12, fo 24v. However, acc. to *Chron. Stone*, 28, it was 20 Dec. 1441. Causton (Lit. Ms D.12) agrees with this latter date to the extent that he says that it was the 38th yr of his monastic life; his obit on 20 Dec. is in BL Ms Arundel 68, fo 51v.

SMYTH
see John Sandwych II

Simon de SOLIS [Soles
occ. 1329 d. 1337

1329, 9 Oct., one of eight prof., *SL*, 180, CCA Lit. Ms D.12, fo 3v.

1337, 16 Feb., d., CCA Lit. Ms D.12, fo 16v; his obit is in BL Ms Arundel 68, fo 16v.

In an inventory of missing books dated 1 Mar. 1338, the loss of a psalterium beate Marie was charged vs him, *Lit. Cant.*, no 618 (Reg. L, fo 104).

John SOMERSETT [Somerset, Somersete
occ. 1438 d. 1464

1438, 9 Jan., one of four prof., *SL*, 188, CCA Lit. Ms D.12, fo 7v.

1464, before 6 June, refectorer, CCA Lit. Ms D.12, fo 26.

1464, 6 June, d., *Chron. Stone*, 90 (CCA Lit. Ms D.12, fo 26); the obit, on 8 June, is in BL Ms Arundel 68, fo 30.

SOTHERUS
n.d.

n.d., 22 Aug., *conversus*, whose obit occ. in BL Ms Arundel 68, fo 39.

SOTINDUNE
see Shotyndon

John le SPYCER [le Espicer, *dictus* Spicer
occ. 1298 d. 1336

1298, 18 Oct., one of seven prof., *SL*, 178, CCA Lit. Ms D.12, fo 3.

1299, 19 Sept., ord [sub]dcn, Littlebourne, *Reg. abp Winchelsey*, 930.
1313, 11 May, before, chaplain to abp Winchelsey for two yrs, Wilkins, *Concilia*, ii, 488 (CUL Ms Ee.5.31, fo 203v).
1316, subsacrist, CCA DCc MA2, fo 70; he was still in office in 1321 on 2 Feb., and vacated it on 3 Nov., Legg and Hope, *Inventories*, 50, 51.
1324, June/Sept., fourth prior, CCA DCc DE84.
1330/1, *custos martyrii*, CCA DCc MA2, fos 192–201v.

1316, 2 Feb., with the sacrist, Richard de Sharstede, q.v., drew up an inventory of vestments, ornaments, gospel books [*textus*] and relics, Legg and Hope, *Inventories*, 50–94 (BL Ms Cotton Galba, E.iv, fos 112–127v).
1336, 2 Apr., d., CCA Lit. Ms D.12, fo 16; his obit is in BL Ms Arundel 68, fo 22v.

In an inventory of missing books dated 1 Mar. 1338 he was held responsible for several books including Peter Lombard's Sentences, *Lit. Cant.*, no 618 (Reg. L, fo 104).

Note: is this John de Cantuar', q.v.?

Thomas STABYLGAT'
occ. 1st half 13th c.

n.d., name occ. in the list in *SL*, 174, CCA Lit. Ms D.12, fo 1v.

William de STANDFORD
see Sandford

David STANFORD
occ. 1st half 13th c.

n.d., name occ. in the list in *SL*, 174, CCA Lit. Ms D.12, fo 1v.

[STANWYK
see Alexander de Sandwyco]

John STANYS
occ. 1399 d. 1421

1399, a former monk of Bermondsey who, with Thomas Myddylton II, q.v., came to Christ Church where they were prof. with four others, *SL*, 185, CCA Lit. Ms D.12, fo 5v.

n.d., precentor and *organista precipuus*, *Chron. Stone*, 12.

1414, 12 Mar., 43rd in order at the el. of an abp, *Reg. abp Chichele*, i, 4.
1421, 19 Dec., d.; the *Chron. Stone* summary records that 'Omnem cantum organicum in ecclesia disposuit et gubernavit in magnam laudem et ecclesie honorem', 12 (CCA Lit. Ms D.12, fo 21v). His obit is in BL Ms Arundel 68, fo 51v.

I Alexander STAPLE [Stapill, Stapyll
occ. 1438 d. 1471

1438, 9 Jan., one of four prof., *SL*, 188, CCA Lit. Ms D.12, fo 7v.

1451, 8 Dec., 1454, 21 Oct., treasurer, CCA DCc DE15C/20, 24.
1455/6, chaplain to the prior, CCA DCc Prior acct 10; he was also fourth prior, *ib.*, Treas. acct 17.
1458, chancellor with Nicholas Bertyn, q.v., Reg. S, fo 200.
1462, 6 Dec., *magister ordinis*, *SL*, 190, CCA Lit. Ms D.12, fo 8.
1471, before 14 Dec., *magister mense*, *Chron. Stone*, 115.
1439, 19 Jan., with William Glastynbury, q.v., licensed to leave the priory *pro recreacione*, and they returned on 21 or 28 Jan. [St Agnes], Chron. Wm Glastynbury, fo 182ᵛ/177ᵛ.
1440, 8 or 20 July [St Margaret], declared ready by his *magister* [*regule*], William Glastynbury, q.v. for his final examination [*redditus*], Pantin, *Cant. Coll. Ox.*, iv, 53 (Chron. Wm Glastynbury, fo 119ᵛ).
1466, 17 Feb., 26th in order in an inventory of *jocalia fratrum* [given by him and/or assigned for his use], Reg. N, fo 232.
1471, 14 Dec., d., *Chron. Stone*, 115 (CCA Lit. Ms D.12, fo 26); his obit is in BL Ms Arundel 68, fo 51.

II Alexander STAPLE [Staphill, Stapill, Stapull, Stapyll
occ. 1488 d. 1528/9

1488, 30 Sept., one of six tonsured, *SL*, 192, CCA Lit. Ms D.12, fo 9.
1490, 4 Apr., made his prof. before the abp, CCA Lit. Ms D.12, *ib.*; the delay in prof. did not preclude the six from having 'pecunias sicut ceteri fratres cum ebd' servicio et assignacione ad refect' et mensam conventus' by permission of the prior and *magister ordinis*, *ib.*
1491, 2 Apr., ord acol., Canterbury cathedral, *Reg. abp Morton*, i, no 439a.
1492, 21 Apr., ord subdcn, Canterbury cathedral, *ib.*, i, no 441b.
1493, 6 Apr., ord dcn, Canterbury cathedral, *ib.*, i, no 442c.
1495, 18 Apr., ord pr., Canterbury cathedral, *ib.*, i, no 444d.
1506, Sept., fourth prior, CCA Lit. Ms C.11, fo 49.
1511, June, *custos corone*, CCA Lit. Ms C.11, fo 54.
1511/12, Sept. to Apr., *magister ordinis* and fourth prior, *SL*, 194, CCA Lit. Ms D.12, fo 11.
1513, May, 1514, 29 Sept., *custos corone*, CCA Lit. Ms C.11, fos 55ᵛ, 56ᵛ, 58.
1515/17, 1518/20, *magister regule* for John Cranbroke II, q.v., and kept the acct of expenses for food, drink, candles and oblations up to the time of his first mass, CCA DCc DE62B, 63.
1516/17, novice master, CCA DCc MA14, fo 3.
1517, Mar./Sept., *magister ordinis* and *custos corone*, *SL*, 194, CCA Lit. Ms D.12, fo 11ᵛ.
n.d., *magister regule* for Robert Boxlee, q.v., Pantin, *Cant. Coll. Ox.*, iv, 54 (CCA DCc Ms Scrap Book B.186).
1493, 1 May, 60th in order at the ratification of an agreement, Reg. S, fo 383ᵛ; but see John Crosse I.
1501, 26 Apr., 40th in order at the el. of an abp, Reg. R, fo 56ᵛ.
1511, 2 Sept., 26th on the visitation certificate, Wood-Legh, *Visit.*, 3 (Reg. abp Warham, i, fo 35ᵛ).
1524, 23/24 Sept., conducted the burial rites for John Alyngton, q.v., *SL*, 195.
1528/9, d., Woodruff, 'Sacrist's Rolls', 73; his obit on 25 Dec. occ. in BL Ms Arundel 68, fo 52.

William de STAPLE
occ. 1306 d. 1352

1306, 9 Oct., one of two prof., *SL*, 178, CCA Lit. Ms D.12, fo 3ᵛ.
1328/9, treasurer, CCA DCc MA2, fo 182.
1330, Mar./1331, 1332/3, chamberlain, CCA DCc Chamb. accts 23–25, MA2, fos 193–222ᵛ.
1339/40, 1343/4, precentor, CCA DCc Great Chart acct 45, Adisham acct 19.
1338, 1 Mar., a list of missing books includes a volume of Avicenna for which he was held responsible, *Lit. Cant.*, no 618 (Reg. L, fo 104).
1349, 4 June, 6th in order at the el. of an abp, Reg. G, fo 60ᵛ.
1349, 8/9 Sept., 6th at the el. of an abp, *ib.*, fo 76.
1352, 29 Dec., d., CCA Lit. Ms D.12, fo 16ᵛ.

STAUNFORD
see Sandford

STEDE
see Richard Thornden

I STEPHEN
n.d.

n.d., 25 Apr., obit occ. in BL Ms Arundel 68, fo 24ᵛ.

Note: a Steffanus, monk, appears in a survey of cathedral holdings in Canterbury, compiled c. 1163 × 1167, in a ref. to his nephew, Aaron, who was a cathedral tenant, Urry, *Canterbury*, 240.

II STEPHEN
n.d., 13 July, obit occ. in BL Ms Arundel 68, fo 34.

Note: one of these obits above may refer to Stephen Cranebroke, q.v; see also below.

III STEPHEN
occ. 1292/3

1292/3, subalmoner, CCA DCc Eastry acct 5.

Note: one of the obits under Stephen I and II may apply to this monk who is prob. entered elsewhere in this section under his toponymic, perhaps Stephen de Ikham, q.v.

STEPHEN, subprior
see Cranebroke

Thomas de STODEWOLD [Stodwolde
occ. 1299 d. 1316

1299, 24 Aug., one of seven prof., *SL*, 178, CCA Lit. Ms D.12, fo 3ᵛ.
1300, 4 June, ord subdcn, Smeeth chapel by Aldington, *Reg. abp Winchelsey*, 934.
1316, 13 June, d., if he is Thomas de Notwold in CCA Lit. Ms D.12, fo 15ᵛ; the obit, under Stodwold, occ. on 13 June in BL Ms Arundel 68, fo 30ᵛ and Lambeth Ms 20, fo 194.

Stephen de STOKBERY [Stocbery, Stokeberye, Stokebury, Stokeby
occ. 1341 d. 1361

1341, 13 Dec., one of nine prof., *SL*, 181, CCA Lit. Ms D.12, fo 4.
1356/7, treasurer, Lambeth Ms 1025/8 (as Stokeby).
1349, 4 June, 57th in order at the el. of an abp, Reg. G, fo 60ᵛ.
1349, 8/9 Sept., 56th at the el. of an abp, *ib.*, fo 76ᵛ.
1361, 7 Aug., d., one of c.25 monks carried off [by the plague] between June and Oct., CCA Lit. Ms D.12, fo 17.

William STOKBERY [Stocbury, Stokbury, Stokebery
occ. 1408/9 d. 1461

1408/9, 21 Mar., one of six prof., CCA Lit. Ms D.12, fo 6 (*SL*, 185).
1410, 22 Mar., ord dcn, Canterbury cathedral, Reg. abp Arundel, ii, fo 98ᵛ.
1435, feretrar, 'Chron. Wm Glastynbury', 129.
1436/7, warden of manors, CCA DCc Ickham acct 62.
1438/9, bartoner, Lambeth ED53.
1440/2, treasurer, CCA DCc MA26, Treas. acct 14; he was apptd on 31 Oct. [1440] to succ. William Wynchepe II, q.v., Chron Wm Glastynbury, fo 119ᵛ.
1414, 12 Mar., 71st in order at the el. of an abp, *Reg. abp Chichele*, i, 4.
1444, 15 Oct., apptd proctor by the prior and chapter for convocation, Reg. S, fo 162ᵛ.
1461, 2 Mar., d., in the 53rd yr of monastic life, *Chron. Stone*, 82; his obit is in BL Ms Arundel 68, fo 18ᵛ. He is described by CCA Lit. Ms D.12, fo 26, as 'supervisor manerii de Ikham'.

STOLL
see Stoyl

Richard de STONDON [Stondone
occ. [1241]

[1241], name occ. in the list in *SL*, 174, CCA Lit. Ms D.12, fo 2; he was prob. one of the twelve prof. with Richard de Wynchepe, q.v.

I James de STONE [Stoone, *alias* Oxneye
occ. 1341 occ. 1367

1341, 13 Dec., one of nine prof., *SL*, 180, CCA Lit. Ms D.12, fo 4.
1356/8, chaplain to the prior, Lambeth Ms 1025/8, CCA DCc Barksore acct 45.
1360/1, warden of manors, CCA DCc Great Chart acct 62.
1361/2, sacrist, CCA DCc, Sac. acct 3.
1362/3, cellarer, CCA DCc, Bart. acct 39; acc. to Arrears acct 70 he was [also] chaplain to the prior.
1363/7, warden of manors, CCA DCc Barksore acct 48, Appledore acct 43, Agney acct 53, Appledore acct 44.
n.d., 26 Sept., his dismissal from the office of *primarius* was requested by the prior of the abp, Reg. L, fo 92.
1367, 19 Jan., apptd prior of Dover, *Reg. abp Langham*, 276–278; his profession as prior is recorded in full in Lambeth Ms 241, fo 26–26ᵛ.
1369, 19 Sept., apptd prior, as above, for life, Reg. abp Wittlesey, fo 16.
1349, 4 June, 52nd in order at the el. of an abp, Reg. G, fo 60ᵛ.
1349, 8/9 Sept., 53rd at the el. of an abp, *ib.*, fo 76ᵛ; the slight discrepancy in order is insignificant.
1366, 10 May, chosen as one of seven *compromissorii* in the el. of an abp, *ib.*, fo 148.
1366, 16 Sept., apptd proctor with John de Redyngate, q.v., to attend the Black Monk Chapter meeting in Northampton, Pantin, *BMC*, iii, 59.
c. 1371, d., before 24 May 1371 when his succ. as prior of Dover was apptd, Reg. abp Wittlesey, fo 85ᵛ.

II James de STONE [*alias* Oxene
occ. 1370 occ. 1374

1370, 2/6 June, one of four adm./tonsured, *SL*, 18, CCA Lit. Ms D.12, fo 4ᵛ.
1372, 14 Mar., one of four whose prof. the prior was comm. to rec., Reg. abp Wittlesey, fo 52 (as Oxene, q.v., under James de Oxney II).
1372, 19 Sept., ord acol., abp's chapel, Saltwood, Reg. abp Wittlesey, fo 169ᵛ; however, see Henry Cranbroke I.
1373, 12 Mar., ord subdcn, abp's chapel, Charing, *ib.*, fo 170.
1373, 16 Apr., ord dcn, Canterbury cathedral, *ib.*, fo 170ᵛ.
1374, 30 June, dcn and 60th in order at the el. of an abp,. Reg. G, fos 173ᵛ–175ᵛ.

I John STONE
occ. 1417 d. c. 1480

1417, 13 Dec., one of five [?clothed/professed], *SL*, 186, CCA Lit. Ms D.12, fo 6v.
Note: this entry takes into acct two conflicting statements: 1) *SL* and CCA Lit. Ms D.12 give the date 1417, 13 Dec. without specifying whether this ref. to tonsure, clothing or prof., and 2) *Chron. Stone*, 5, states that this monk, one of the five, was clothed on 13 Dec. 1418.
1418, 26 Mar., ord acol., Canterbury cathedral, *Reg. abp Chichele*, iv, 332.
1419, 1 Apr., ord subdcn, infirmary chapel, *ib.*, i, 191.
1421, 20 Dec., ord pr., St Paul's cathedral, London, *ib.*, iv, 349.

1451, 20 Mar., refectorer, *Chron. Stone*, 51.
1457, 13 Dec., *magister ordinis*, *SL*, 189, CCA Lit. Ms D.12, fo 8, *Chron. Stone*, 71.
1457, n.d., subsacrist, *Chron. Stone*, 71.
1461, 10 July, third prior, *ib.*, 84.

1435, 11 Nov., one of three who were promoted to the upper choir, Chron. Wm Glastynbury, fo 117v.
1451, 20 Mar., present at the blessing of the bells in St George's tower, *Chron. Stone*, 51.
1452, 23 Dec., promoted *ad primam mensam*, *ib.*, 56.
1461, 10 July, in the absence of the subprior, presided in the *scaccarium* over an apptment to the office of *custos tumbe*, *Chron. Stone*, 84.
1466, 17 Feb., 9th in order in an inventory of *jocalia fratrum* [given by him and/or assigned for his use], Reg. N, fo 230v.
1468, 17 Mar., placed by the prior *in capite chori;* this was his 52nd yr of monastic life, *ib.*, 107.
c. 1480, stacionarius, d., CCA Lit. Ms D.12, fo 26.

Name in Cambridge, Corpus Christi College Ms 417, 'liber—quem ex suo magno labore composuit', AD 1457. This is the chronicle cum obituary record of the Christ Church community between 1415 and 1471. The printed version is listed under *SL* in section D.i of the refs.

II John STONE
occ. 1527 occ. 1540

1527, 25 May, one of twelve tonsured, *SL*, 195, CCA Lit. Ms D.12, fo 12.
1528, 2 Mar., prof., *ib.*

1534, 12 Dec., acknowledged the Act of Supremacy, *DK 7th Report*, Appndx 2, 282.
1537, 28 Jan., one of several monks examined in connection with his naming two popes in the reading of the martiloge vs the royal decree, in the presence of Stephen Gylys, q.v., and others; he asked to be pardoned, *L and P Henry VIII*, xii, pt 1, no 256.
[1538, 8 Feb., after], in a list of monks prob. prepared for Thomas Cromwell, he was described as a 'good man', 35 yrs of age, Pantin, *Cant. Coll. Ox.*, iii, 153.
1540, 4 Apr., awarded £6 p.a., *L and P Henry VIII*, xv, no 452.

Peter STONE [*alias* Oxeney
occ. 1372/3

1372, 14 Nov., the prior was comm. to adm. and clothe a 'certain Peter', Reg. abp Wittlesey, fo 57v.
1373, 12 Mar., the prior was comm. to profess Peter Oxeney, novice, *ib.*, fo 59.

Note: in CCA Lit. Ms D.12, fo 4v John Bertram, q.v. and Peter Stone were listed together and in Wittlesey's reg. they were prof. together (*SL*, 182); see Peter Oxeney.

Richard STONE
occ. 1483 d. 1508

1483, 30 Sept., one of six tonsured, *SL*, 191, CCA Lit. Ms D.12, fo 8v.
1484, 10 June, prof., *ib.*
1488/9, celebrated his first mass, CCA DCc Sac. accts 58, 68.

1499/1501, infirmarer, CCA DCc MA10, fos 82v, 35v.

1493, 1 May, 46th in order at the ratification of an agreement, Reg. S, fo 383v; but see John Crosse I.
1501, 26 Apr., 30th in order at the el. of an abp, Reg. R, fo 56v.
1508/9, d., Woodruff, 'Sacrist's Rolls', 68 (CCA DCc Sac. acct 71); his obit on 11 Oct. is in BL Ms Arundel 68, fo 44v where the name is written in red.

Name in
(1) Cambridge, Corpus Christi College Ms 375, Passio S. Katerine etc. (12th/13th c.).
(2) Lambeth Ms 159, Vite sanctorum (early 16th c.); on fo 176 *scriptum per*—AD 1507. James (Lambeth Mss Catalogue, 249) says that most of this paper vol. is in his neat hand, and the Ingram catalogue (James, *Ancient Libraries*, no 304, p.164) Chronica abbreviata refers no doubt to this vol.

There is an undated inventory of the books, clothes, plate, vestments and other items (e.g. three bows and a supply of arrows) found in his *cubiculum* [?in the dormitory or possibly the infirmary] prob. after his d.; apart from service books and Bibles there were about thirty volumes including works of history and grammar and the Passio S. Katerine listed above, Pantin, *Cant. Coll. Ox.*, i, 88–90.

An inventory of the *custos martyrii*, dated 1506, includes a frontal of satin and two *tuellis per fratrem*—, Legg and Hope, *Inventories*, 131.

I William STONE
occ. 1367 d. 1415

1367, 11 Nov., one of nine prof., *SL*, 182, CCA Lit. Ms D.12, fo 4v.
1368, 4 Mar., ord acol., Canterbury cathedral, *Reg. abp Langham*, 387.
1369, 22 Dec., ord subdcn, abp's chapel, Charing, Reg. abp Wittlesey, fo 165v.
1370, 21 Sept., ord dcn, Saltwood, *ib.*, fo 166v.
1371, 20 Dec., ord pr., abp's chapel, Otford, *ib.*, fo 168.
1378/83, treasurer, CCA DCc MA2, fos 320–328, Treas. acct 26.
1383/4, 1385/6, warden of manors and treasurer, CCA DCc Meopham acct 98, MA2, fo 333, Lambeth Ms 243, fo 200v.
1389/91, treasurer, Lambeth Ms 243, fos 215, 217.
1391, June/1393, bartoner, CCA DCc, Bart. acct 65, Eastry acct 118, Monkton acct 103.
1396/7, anniversarian and bartoner, CCA DCc Prior acct 4.
1397/1402, anniversarian, CCA DCc Anniv. acct 7.
1399/1404, granator, CCA DCc Gran. accts 92, 95, Eastry acct 124, Prior acct 3, Eastry acct 127.
1403/4, anniversarian, CCA DCc Anniv. acct 23.
1404/7, 1415, before 12 Nov., granator, CCA DCc, Prior acct 20, Chartham acct 46, Gran. acct 93, *Chron. Stone*, 7.
1376/7, scholar at Canterbury college and recd 66s. 8d. for his *capa scolastica* and for travelling expenses to Oxford, Pantin, *Cant. Coll. Ox.*, iv, 187; for this reason he was absent from the abp's visitation on 2 Jan. 1377, Reg. abp Sudbury, fo 32.
1374, 30 June, 48th in order at the el. of an abp, Reg. G, fos 173v–175v.
1377, 1 Jan., named on the visitation certificate as one of the five monks at Oxford, Reg. abp Sudbury, fo 32.
1381, 31 July, 36th at the el. of an abp, *ib.*, fo 225v.
1391, Jan., with William Milton, q.v., took the news of the d. of prior John Fynch, q.v., to the abp, Reg. abp Courtenay, i, fo 336v.
1396, 7 Aug., 18th at the el. of an abp, Reg. G, fo 235v.
1411/12, the chamberlain spent 11d. in cloth *pro habitu W. Ston'*, CCA DCc Chamb. acct 71.
1415, 12 Nov., d., and was buried in the crypt before the altar of St Catherine and St Mary Magdalen; he was described by John Stone as 'vir decentissimus et magne stature inter omnes quos nostris temporibus vidimus', *Chron. Stone*, 7.

II William STONE
occ. 1485

1485, 24 Sept., ord subdcn, Canterbury cathedral, *Reg. abp Bourgchier*, 452.

Henry STORDY [Sturdi, Sturdy
occ. [1241] occ. 1277

[1241], name occ. in the list in *SL*, 174, CCA Lit. Ms D.12, fo 2; he was prob. one of the twelve prof. with Richard de Wynchepe, q.v.
1252, Mar./1253, monk carpenter, Reg. H, fos 172, 175v.
1260/2, anniversarian, CCA DCc MA1, fos 103v–104v.
1277, treasurer, Reg. H, fo 206.
[1256/7], lent money to a woman who in return mortgaged land to Christ Church, Turner and Coxe, *Charters and Rolls*, 107.
n.d., c.3 Aug., d. in Rome acc. to the obit on this day in BL Ms Arundel 68, fo 37.

John STORDY [Sturrey
occ. 1st half 13th c.

n.d., name occ. in the *post exilium* list in *SL*, 173, CCA Lit. Ms D.12, fo 1v.

John STOREYE [Storey, Stori, Sturrey
occ. 1381 d. 1439

1381, 6 May, one of eight prof., *SL*, 183, CCA Lit. Ms D.12, fo 5.
1386, 17 Mar., ord pr., St Stephen's chapel, Westminster, Reg. abp Courtenay, i, fo 308v.
1398, 13/14 Nov., *magister ordinis*, *SL*, 184, CCA Lit. Ms D.12, fo 5v.
1404/5, *custos tumbe*, CCA DCc, Prior acct 20.
1396, 7 Aug., 37th in order at the el. of an abp, Reg. G, fo 234v.
1414, 12 Mar., 9th at the el. of an abp, *Reg. abp Chichele*, i, 4.
1439, 27 June, d., *Chron. Stone*, 22, CCA Lit. Ms D.12, fo 24; his obit is in BL Ms Arundel 68, fo 32.

Thomas STOYL [Stoll, Stoyle
occ. 1299 d. 1333

1299, 24 Aug., one of seven prof., *SL*, 178, CCA Lit. Ms D.12, fo 3v.
1309/10, possibly feretrar, see below.
1313/20, treasurer, CCA DCc MA2, fos 49v–102.
1321/9, chaplain to the prior, CCA DCc MA2, fos 112–184v.
1328/33, 20 Aug., subprior, CCA DCc Great Chart acct 37, Agney accts 37, 38, Chartham acct 19, Adisham acct 10.
1333, *custos*, St Mary in crypt, CCA DCc MA2, fo 221.
1309/10, pd the lector his annual stipend, Pantin, *Cant. Coll. Ox.*, iv, 175, Lambeth Ms 242, fo 273); he was possibly feretrar.
1313, 28 May, named as one of seven *compromissorii* in the el. of an abp, Reg. Q, fos 61v–62/75v–76.

1327, 11 Dec., again one of seven *compromissorii* in the el. of an abp, *ib.*, fo 123; see also *CPL*, ii (1305–1342), 272.
1333, 20 Aug., d., CCA Lit. Ms D.12, fo 16.

Name in
(1) Cambridge, Corpus Christi College Ms 63, i-iii, Anselm etc. (13th/14th c.); . . . *olim ut videtur peculium*—.
(2) Lambeth Ms 180, Diadema monachorum (14th c.); his name is at the head of the list of contents.

Fifteenth century inventories of Canterbury college include both a volume of Thomas [Aquinas] super 4^m sentenciarum and Templum Domini inscribed as his, Pantin, *Cant. Coll. Ox.*, i, 4, 5, 11, 13; 16th c. inventories list his Questiones Fyschakyr super 3^m sentenciarum, *ib.*, i, 22, 42.

A list of missing books, dated 1 Mar. 1338 includes Summa super librum phisicorum which had been his, *Lit. Cant.*, no 618 (Reg. L, fo 104).

An inventory dated 26 Apr. 1331, lists one 'ymago eburnea sancte marie et filii sui precium xls' in his care [*habet*], Hope, 'Inventories of Priors' 268; there are also refs to his *ciphi* and plate, *ib.*, 277, 278. The inventory dated 25 July 1333, under *lectisternia* in the prior's *camera* reads 'Item lectisternium rubeum fratris Thome Stoyl, i', *ib.*

In a letter written by Robert de Thaneto q.v., he was described as *radix multorum malorum*, acc. to *Hist. Mss Comm. 5th Report*, Appndx, 438.

John STRATFORD [Strafford
occ. 1410 d. 1420

1410, 13 Dec., one of eight prof., *SL*, 185, CCA Lit. Ms D.12, fo 6.
1413, 2 Apr., ord dcn, Canterbury cathedral, Reg. abp Arundel, ii, fo 101.
1416, 18 Apr., ord pr., Canterbury cathedral, *Reg. abp Chichele*, iv, 320.
1420, 23 July, chaplain to the subprior, *Chron. Stone*, 10.
1414, 12 Mar., 79th and last in order at the el. of an abp, *Reg. abp Chichele*, i, 4.
1420, 23 July, d., *in pestilencia*, *Chron. Stone*, 10, CCA Lit. Ms D.12, fo 21^v; the obit is in BL Ms Arundel 68, fo 35^v.

John de STRODE
occ. 2nd half 13th c.

n.d., name occ. in the list in *SL*, 174, CCA Lit. Ms D.12, fo 2.

Radulphus de STRODE
occ. 2nd half 13th c.

n.d., name occ. in the list in *SL*, 175, CCA Lit. Ms D.12, fo 2^v.

Walter de STURA [Sture
occ. 1189

1189, 6 Oct., one of the monks excommunicated by abp Baldwin during the controversy between him and the chapter, *Epist. Cant.*, 311. About 14 Nov. he was sent away from Christ Church by the monks, with Ysaac de Cantuariensis, q.v., after reports that the abp was about to seize them. Unfortunately, he was caught as he was fleeing and was reportedly bound and taken captive to [?the abp's prison at] Tenham, *ib.*, 317–318.

STURDI, Sturdy
see Stordy

I Thomas de STUREYE [Stureya, Sturie, Sturreye, senior
occ. 1264 d. [1272]

n.d., name occ. in the list in *SL*, 174, CCA Lit. Ms D.12, fo 2.

1270, 7 Sept., subprior, *Gervase Cant.*, ii, 252.

1264, 16 Apr., with William de Resham, q.v. installed Adam de Chillenden, q.v. as prior, by comm. from the abp, *Gervase Cant.*, ii, 229.
1270, 7 Sept., one of seven *compromissorii* in the el. of an abp, *ib.*, ii, 252–253; see Adam de Chillenden.
[1272], d. in Rome where he had gone, presumably with Adam de Chillenden, q.v., to obtain papal confirmation of the latter's el. as abp, *ib.*, and BL Ms Arundel 68, fo 37, where the obit is on 7 Aug. Report of a plot to murder him in Italy, in which Richard Pykenot and William de Tonge q.v., were allegedly implicated, came to light later [?1283], CCA DCc DE73.

Name in
(1) Cambridge, Trinity College Ms 98, Postille in Danielem, etc. (late 13th c.); *senior* after his name.
(2) Oxford, Bod. Ms Digby 4, Tractatus super canonem misse etc. (12th/13th c.), which Sharpe, *Latin Writers*, attributes to his authorship.
(3) *ib.*, Ms Laud misc. 160, Postille super xii prophetas (late 13th c.).
(4) *ib.*, Ms Laud misc. 161, Postille super pentateuchum (late 13th c.).
(5) Lincoln cathedral, Ms 139, Sermones et sententiae (late 12th c.).

The Eastry catalogue contains an unknown no of volumes listed under his name, many of them biblical commentaries and writings of Augustine, James, *Ancient Libraries*, nos 907–?965 (pp. 89–94); no 922 survives as no 3) in the above list and no 921 is no 4). For no 616 in this catalogue, see the note below Thomas de Stureye II.

II Thomas de STUREYE [?Storey, Stureya, Stureye, junior
occ. [mid 1260s] d. 1298

[?mid 1260s], name in the list as one of seven prof. in *SL*, 176, CCA Lit. Ms D.12, fo 2v.

1298, bartoner, CCA DCc, MA1, fo 215v (as Storey).

1298, 25 July, d., *SL*, 176, CCA Lit. Ms D.12, fo 15.

Three volumes in the Eastry catalogue are listed beneath his name, including Ysadorus and Hugucius et Bruto, James, *Ancient Libraries*, nos 530–532 (p. 63). The latter turns up in the 15th c. Canterbury college inventories, Pantin, *Cant. Coll. Ox.*, i, 3, 11.

Note: there is also a volume of miscellanea entitled Quedam summa quam habuit T. de Stureya, *ib.*, no 616 (p. 71), which may have belonged to either of the two monks by this name.

Two albs of a Thomas de Stureye 'cum parura de Inde velvet' ' are included in an inventory of vestments, *temp.* prior Eastry, Legg and Hope, *Inventories*, 59 (BL Ms Cotton Galba, E.iv, fo 114v).

STURREY
see Stordy, Storeye

John SUDBURY [Sudbery
occ. 1488 occ. 1518/19

1488, 12 Mar., one of six tonsured, *SL*, 192, CCA Lit. Ms D.12, fo 9.

1490, 10 Apr., ord subdcn, Canterbury cathedral, *Reg. abp Morton*, i, no 438b.

1491, 2 Apr., ord dcn, Canterbury cathedral, *ib.*, i, no 439c.

1494, 29 Mar., ord pr., Canterbury cathedral, *ib.*, i, no 443d.

1493/4, celebrated his first mass and recd a small gift from the sacrist, CCA DCc, Sac. acct 63.

1504, Mar./June, 1505, 13 Jan./11 July, fourth prior and *magister ordinis*, CCA Lit. Ms C.11, fo 48, *SL*, 193, CCA Lit. Ms D.12, fo 10.

1493, 1 May, 52nd in order at the ratification of an agreement, Reg. S, fo 383v; but see John Crosse I.

1501, 26 Apr., 36th in order at the el. of an abp, Reg. R, fo 56v.

1511, 2 Sept., 20th on the visitation certificate, Wood-Legh, *Visit.*, 3 (Reg. abp Warham, i, fo 35).

1518/19, ill in the infirmary, CCA DCc, Infirm. acct 1.

n.d., examined [*audivit*] John Chart II, novice, q.v., Pantin, *Cant. Coll. Ox.*, iv, 54 (CCA DCc Ms Scrap Book B.186).

n.d., 15 Nov., his obit occ. in BL Ms Arundel 68, fo 48.

Name in London, College of Arms, Ms Arundel 20, Chronica (14th c.).

I William SUDBURY
occ. 1522 occ. 1525/6

1522, 11 Feb., one of ten tonsured, *SL*, 195, CCA Lit. Ms D.12, fo 11v.

1522, 24 Nov., prof., *ib.*

1525/6, celebrated his first mass and recd a small sum of money from William Ingram I, CCA Lit. Ms C.11, fo 139v.

n.d., 19 July, obit occ. in BL Ms Arundel 68, fo 35v.

II William SUDBURY [Subbery
occ. 1527 occ. 1540

1527, 25 May, one of ten tonsured, *SL*, 195, CCA Lit. Ms D.12, fo 12.

1528, 2 Mar., prof., *ib.*

[1538, 8 Feb., after], one of four subsacrists [*parvi sacriste*], q.v., Pantin, *Cant. Coll. Ox.*, iii, 153.

1534, 12 Dec., acknowledged the Act of Supremacy, *DK 7th Report*, Appndx 2, 282.

[1538, 8 Feb., after], in a list of monks prob. prepared for Thomas Cromwell he was described as a 'good man', 28 yrs of age, Pantin, *Cant. Coll. Ox.*, iii, 153.

1540, 4 Apr., name occ. on but has been deleted from the surrender list, *L and P Henry VIII*, xv, no 452.

1540, 4 Apr., scholar in the new foundation, *L and P Henry VIII*, xv, no 452.

Note: there is some confusion here between the two contemporary monks by the same name. The obit must belong to the earlier one because the latter survived the dissolution.

Samuel SUFFLETON
d. before 1338

A list of missing service books, belonging to deceased monks and dated 1 Mar. 1338, includes his missale, *Lit. Cant.*, no 618 (Reg. L, fo 104).

See also Samuel.

SUFFLETON
see also Sifflington

Daniel de SUTTON [Suttone
occ. [c. 1255] occ. 1316

[c. 1255], one of five prof., *SL*, 176, CCA Lit. Ms D.12, fo 2v.

1294/1313, treasurer, CCA DCc MA1, fos 193–268v, MA2, fos 10–42v.

1316, 2 Jan., d., CCA Lit. Ms D.12, fo 15v; his obit is in BL Ms Arundel 68, fo 12.

An inventory of vestments, *temp.* prior Eastry, includes a chasuble of red samite under his name, Legg and Hope, *Inventories*, 52 (BL Ms Cotton Galba, E.iv, fo 112v).

An inventory of the refectory, dated 1328, includes a silver *ciphus* of his, Dart, *Antiq. Cant.*, xx (BL Ms Cotton Galba E.iv, fo 179).

Henry SUTTON [Suthon
occ. [1389] d. 1429

[1389], 6 Nov., one of three clothed, CCA Lit. Ms D.12, fo 5; *SL*, 184 is inaccurate.

1410/11, *custos corone*, CCA DCc Prior acct 2.
1412/13, treasurer, CCA DCc Treas. acct 11.
1414, first penitentiary, apptd on the second day after his enthronement, *Reg. abp Chichele*, iv, 115–116.
1416/18, cellarer, CCA DCc Eastry acct 139, Godmersham acct 33.
1419/20, treasurer, with Robert Browning, q.v., Lambeth ED81.
1421/2, cellarer, Eastry acct 146.
1424, Sept./Dec., bartoner, Bart. acct 88.
1425/6, cellarer, and subprior, CCA DCc Adisham acct 53, Great Chart acct 101; he was apptd cellarer on 5 Apr. 1425, *Reg. abp Chichele*, 264. This same yr he and William Molassh I, q.v, were receivers *bonorum et proventorum*, by order of the prior, CCA DCc Receiver acct 1.
1425, Mar./Dec., 1426/7, bartoner, CCA DCc Bart. accts 88, 89; see William Molassh I.
1426, 28 Oct.; 1427, 7 May, 2 Dec.; 1428, [31] Mar., subprior, *Chron. Stone*, 13, 14; Oxford Bod. Ms Tanner 165, fo 6ᵛ; see Thomas Bray.
1429, 26 Aug., almoner, *Reg. abp Chichele*, iv, 264, *Chron. Stone*, 15.

1393/4, student at Canterbury college receiving commons and having money for battels, Pantin, *Cant. Coll. Ox.*, ii, 132, 133, 135, 136.
1394/5, student, *ib.*, ii, 138, 140.

1396, 7 Aug., cited as contumacious for failing to appear at the el. of an abp, Reg. G, fo 238.
1414, 12 Mar., 19th in order at the el. of an abp, *Reg. abp Chichele*, i, 4.
1420, 29 Dec., was sent to the abp with a letter concerning John Langdon I, q.v., *Lit. Cant.*, no 997 (Reg. S, fo 85).
1428, [31] Mar., one of the monks invited to the abp's palace after the *prefectio* of William Molassh, q.v., as prior, Oxford, Bod. Ms Tanner 165, fo 6ᵛ.
1429, 26 Aug., d. and was buried in the infirmary chapel before the altar of St Leonard, *Chron. Stone*, 15; CCA Lit. Ms D.12, fo 22ᵛ, names the altar as that of St Benedict.

James SUTTON
n.d.

n.d., 11 June, obit occ. in BL Ms Arundel 68, fo 30ᵛ.

John SUTTON [Suttone
occ. 1488 d. 1500

1488, 30 Sept., one of six tonsured, *SL*, 192, CCA Lit. Ms D.12, fo 9.
1489, 4 Apr., prof., *ib.*
1491, 2 Apr., ord acol., Canterbury cathedral, *Reg. abp Morton*, i, no 439a.
1492, 21 Apr., ord subdcn, Canterbury cathedral, *ib.*, i, no 441b.
1493, 6 Apr., ord dcn, Canterbury cathedral, *ib.*, i, no 442c.
1494, 29 Mar., ord pr., Canterbury cathedral, *ib.*, i, no 443d.
1493/4, celebrated his first mass and recd 8d. from the sacrist, CCA DCc Sac. acct 69.

1500, before 3 June, third chaplain to the prior, CCA Lit. Ms D.12, fo 33.

1493, 1 May, 59th in order at the ratification of an agreement, Reg. S, fo 383ᵛ; but see John Crosse I.
1500, 3 June, d., *ex infirmitate nigra consumpcione*; he had his seat at this time in the lower choir, and was 26 yrs old, CCA Lit. Ms D.12, fos 32ᵛ–33. His obit is on 11 June in BL Ms Arundel 68, fo 30ᵛ.

I Robert SUTTON
occ. 1408/9 d. 1457

1408/9, 21 Mar., one of six prof., CCA Lit. Ms D.12, fo 6 (*SL*, 185).
1410, 13 Sept., ord dcn, abp's chapel, Ford, Reg. abp Arundel, ii, fo 99.

1429/30, fourth prior, CCA DCc Sac. acct 26.
1440, 17 Feb., absolved from the office of feretrar and apptd treasurer, Chron. Wm Glastynbury, fo 118.
[1440], 31 Oct., apptd bartoner, *ib.*, fo 119ᵛ.
1447/9, warden of manors, CCA DCc MA, 142, 143.
1455/6, one of eight *barones*, CCA DCc Prior acct 10.
1457, before 25 Sept., *magister operum*, CCA Lit. Ms D.12, fo 25ᵛ.

1414, 12 Mar., 70th in order at the el. of an abp, *Reg. abp Chichele*, i, 4.
1438, 23 Aug., was one of the nominees for the wardenship of Canterbury college, Pantin, *Cant. Coll. Ox.*, iii, 95.
1440, 6 Nov., granted one yr's leave of absence from the cloister and provided with a royal licence to accompany the duke of Orleans, who had been released from the Tower of London, to France; he returned on 24 Dec. 1441, 'Chron. Wm Glastynbury', 135–136, *Chron. Stone*, 28.
1457, 25 Sept., d., in the 50th yr of his monastic life, *Chron. Stone*, 70, CCA Lit. Ms D.12, fo 25ᵛ. His obit, on 27 Sept. is in BL Ms Arundel 68, fo 43.

II Robert SUTTON [Suttoon
occ. 1514 d. 1518/19

1514, 1 Sept., one of seven tonsured, *SL*, 194, CCA Lit. Ms D.12, fo 11.

1518/19, d., Pantin, *Cant. Coll. Ox.*, iv, 206. The obit of a Robert Sutton, *levita*, on 21 Sept. occ. in BL Ms Arundel 68, fo 45ᵛ.

William SUTTON
occ. 1416 d. 1468

1416, 22 June, one of eight prof., *SL*, 186, CCA Lit. Ms D.12, fo 6.
1417, 10 Apr., ord acol., Canterbury cathedral, *Reg. abp Chichele*, iv, 327.
1418, 26 Mar., ord subdcn, Canterbury cathedral, *ib.*, iv, 332.
1419, 1 Apr., ord dcn, chapel within priory, *ib.*, i, 191.
1424, 22 Apr., ord pr., Canterbury cathedral, *ib.*, iv, 360.
1437, 30 Oct., apptd chancellor, Chron. Wm Glastynbury, fo 117v.
1437/44, 1446/7, 1450, before 29 Sept., anniversarian, Chron. Wm Glastynbury, fos 145v, 146–151, Lambeth ED74, CCA DCc Anniv. acct 10.

1439, 7 Jan., one of several monks licensed to leave the priory *pro recreacione*, and he returned on 20 Jan., Chron. Wm Glastynbury, fo 182v/177v.
1466, 17 Feb., 7th in order in an inventory of *jocalia fratrum* [given by him and/or assigned for his use], but he had none, Reg. N, fo 230v.
1468, 21 July, *stacionarius*, d., in the 53rd yr of monastic life, *Chron. Stone*, 104; in CCA Lit. Ms D.12, fo 26 he is described as *conventualis*.

SUWELL(E)
see Siwell

SWAWOLDES
n.d.

n.d., 23 Oct., pr., whose obit occ. in BL Ms Arundel 68, fo 46.

SYDYNGBOURNE
see Sittingborne

SYLVESTON
see Selvyston

SYMON
see Simon

SYWARDUS
n.d.

There are obits of two priests by this name in BL Ms Arundel 68: 22 Mar., fo 21v and 19 June, fo 31v.

I T.
occ. 1198

1198, Dec., was already in Rome when Geoffrey II prior, q.v., arrived, *Epist. Cant.*, 478.

II T.
occ. 1284/5

1284/5, chaplain to the prior, CCA DCc MA1, fos 142–144v.

Hilary de TANETO
occ. [1207 × 1214]

[1207 × 1214], as Hillarius, the name occ. in the list of those who were in exile, *SL*, 172, CCA Lit. Ms D.12, fo 1.
n.d., occ. as subprior of Dover, *Lit. Cant.*, iii, Appndx no 34 (CCA DCc Z.D4, 23).

See also Hillarius.

Thomas de TANETO
occ. 1st half 13th c.

n.d., name occ. in the list in *SL*, 174, CCA Lit. Ms D.12, fo 2.

Walter de TANETO
occ. 1st half 13th c.

n.d., name occ. in the list in *SL*, 174, CCA Lit. Ms D.12, fo 1v.

TANETO
see also Tent, Thaneto

Peter de TANG'
occ. 1st half 13th c.

n.d., name occ. in the list in *SL*, 173, CCA Lit. Ms D.12, fo 1v.

William TAYLOR [Taylour
occ. 1497 occ. 1511

1497, 28 July, one of nine tonsured, SL 192, CCA Lit. Ms D.12, fo 9v.
1498, 14 Apr., ord acol., Canterbury cathedral, *Reg. abp Morton*, i, no 447a.
1498, 19 Apr., prof., *SL*, 192, CCA Lit. Ms D.12, fo 9v.
1507, Sept., succentor, CCA Lit. Ms C.11, fo 50.
1501, 26 Apr., 57th in order at the el. of an abp, Reg. R, fo 56v.
1511, 2 Sept., 39th on the visitation certificate, Wood-Legh, *Visit.*, 3 (Reg. abp Warham, i, fo 35v).
n.d., obtained permission from the abp to transfer to the London house of the friars preachers, but he ended up as a secular pr., *SL*, 192, CCA Lit. Ms D.12, fo 9v.

TEGH
see Tygh

John TENHAM [Thenam
occ. 1428 d. 1454

1428, 2 Jan., one of six prof., *SL*, 187, CCA Lit. Ms D.12, fo 7.
[1432] 11 June, ord pr., place not named, Reg. Langdon (Rochester), fo 74v.
1439, 3 Feb., one of several monks licensed to leave the priory *pro recreacione*, Chron. Wm Glastynbury, fo 182v/177v.

1454, 18 Feb., d., 'cuius liberacionem habuerunt fratres Carmelitarum le ?lennam', *Chron. Stone*, 58; his obit is in BL Ms Arundel 68, fo 16^{v}. According to the prior's acct (CCA DCc Prior acct 9), he left 20s. *de peculiis*.

Richard de TENHAM
occ. 2nd half 13th c.

n.d., name occ. in the list in *SL*, 175, CCA Lit. Ms D.12, fo 2^{v}.

Laurence TENT [de Thaneto
occ. 1361 d. 1405

1361, 28 Oct., one of nine prof., *SL*, 181, CCA Lit. Ms D.12, fo 4^{v}.
1362, 24 Sept., ord acol., Charing, Reg. abp Islip, fo 322.
1363, 23 Sept., ord dcn, Faversham monastery, *ib.*, fo 323^{v}.
1363, 23 Dec., ord pr., Charing, *ib.*, fo 324^{v}.
1372, 1376, *custos tumbe*, CCA DCc MA2, fos 270, 296.
1379/82, granator, CCA DCc MA2, fos 318–329^{v}.
1382, 1383/4, 1385, 1396/7, feretrar, CCA DCc MA2, fo 329^{v}, Treas. acct 26, fos 2–6^{v}, MA2, fo 334^{v} Prior acct 4.
1366, 10 May, present at the el. of an abp, Reg. G, fo 147.
1374, 30 June, 26th in order at the el. of an abp, *ib.*, fos 173^{v}–175^{v}.
1381, 31 July, 18th at the el. of an abp, *ib.*, fo 225^{v}.
1396, 7 Aug., 9th at the el. of an abp, *ib.*, fo 234^{v}.
1405, 30 June, d., in the 44th yr of monastic life, CCA Lit. Ms D.12, fo 18.

Robert TENT [Thent
occ. 1382 d. [1436]

1382, 5 Sept., one of six clothed in the monastic habit, *SL*, 183, CCA Lit. Ms D.12, fo 5.
1383, 11 Aug., the prior was comm. to rec. his prof., Reg. abp Courtenay, i, fo 42^{v}.
1385, 23 Dec., ord pr., abp's chapel, Otford, *ib.*, i, fo 308.
1410/11, *custos martyrii*, CCA DCc, Prior acct 2.
1386/9, 1390/1, recd small sums each yr from the prior, Lambeth Ms 243, fos 204^{v}, 208^{v}, 212^{v}, 220^{v}.
1396, 7 Aug., 42nd in order at the el. of an abp, Reg. G, fo 234^{v}.
1414, 12 Mar., 12th at the el. of an abp, *Reg. abp Chichele*, i, 4.
[1436], d., CCA Lit. Ms D.12, fo 24; his obit on 1 Dec. is in BL Ms Arundel 68, fo 49^{v}.

Simon TENT [Tenett
occ. 1443 occ. 1472

1443, 25 Mar., one of six prof., *SL*, 188, CCA Lit. Ms D.12, fo 7^{v}.
1444, 11 Apr., ord subdcn, Canterbury cathedral, Reg. abp Stafford, fo 196^{v}.
1446, 16 Apr., ord dcn, Canterbury cathedral, *ib.*, fo 199^{v}.
1447, 23 Dec., ord pr., Canterbury cathedral, *ib.*, fo 201^{v}.
1468, chancellor, with Richard London II, q.v., Reg. S, fo 234.
1451, Dec., ill on two occasions and his expenses were 6s. 4d., CCA Lit. Ms E.6, fo 64^{v}.
1466, 17 Feb., 30th in order in an inventory of *jocalia fratrum* [given by him and/or assigned for his use], but he had none, Reg. N, fo 232^{v}.
1472, *recessit*, CCA Lit. Ms D.12, fo 26.

Robert TENTYRDEN [Tynterden
occ. 1475 d. [1485]

1475, 27 Mar., one of four prof., *SL*, 191, CCA Lit. Ms D.12, fo 8^{v}.
1475, 23 Sept., ord subdcn, prior's chapel, Canterbury, *Reg. abp Bourgchier*, 418.
1476, 21 Sept., ord dcn, Canterbury cathedral, *ib.*, 421.
1480, 23 Sept., ord pr., Canterbury cathedral, *ib.*, 431.
[1485], he was one of four who d. on the same day of 'le swete', CCA Lit. Ms D.12, fo 26^{v}; and their obit is on 15 Oct. in BL Ms Arundel 68, fo 45.

Stephen TENTYRDEN
occ. 1524 occ. 1527/8

1524, 21/22 July, one of eleven granted adm. [*ingressum*] to Christ Church, CCA Lit. Ms D.12, fos 11^{v}–12.
1524, 4 Aug., one of eleven tonsured, *SL*, 195, CCA Lit. Ms D.12, fo 12.
1525, 19 Apr., prof., *ib.*
1527/8, celebrated his first mass and recd a small gift from the sacrist, Woodruff, 'Sacrist's Rolls', 72.

TERNE
see Tyerne

M. William TERRACII [Terri, Terrici, Turris
occ. 1216 occ. 1249

n.d., name occ. in the *post exilium* list in *SL*, 173, CCA Lit. Ms D.12, fo 1^{v}.
1244, chamberlain, Urry, *Canterbury*, 155 (CCA DCc AS acct 6), *Gervase Cant.*, ii, 144, 153.
1216, acted as collector of money obtained from the sale of wine from the priory's French vineyards, Urry, *Canterbury*, 155 (CCA DCc MA1).
[1222 × 1237], one of the monks named by M. Laurence de St Nicholas to arrange for his obit celebrations, *Acta Guala*, no 155 (as M. William Teric').

1239, 4 Jan., one of the group of monks accused of contumacy by the abp after the forgery scandal, *Gervase Cant.*, ii, 144; see Simon de Hertlepe. On 1 Feb. he was among those summoned to appear before the abp after the monks' el. of Roger de La Lee, q.v., as prior, *ib.*, ii, 153.
1241, 1 Feb., named as one of seven *compromissorii* in the el. of an abp, *Gervase Cant.*, ii, 186, 187, 190.
1249, was *nuncius brevium defunctorum*, Urry, *Canterbury*, 155 (CCA DCc DE1).
n.d., 3 June, his obit occ., together with a record of his father's gifts to Christ Church, in BL Ms Arundel 68, fo 29v.

The Eastry catalogue includes three volumes under W. de Terri, James, *Ancient Libraries*, nos 1320–1322 (p. 113).

An inventory of the refectory, dated 1328, includes a silver gilt *cuppa W. Terri*, BL Ms Cotton Galba E.iv, fo 178.

He was the son of Terric, the goldsmith, who lived in Burgate Street near Christ Church gate in 1200 and d. in 1208 before William became a monk; these and further details of the family are in Urry *Canterbury*, 174–176.

TEWKESBURY
see Alan I

M. Hamo de THANETO
occ. 1187 d. 1188

1187, the monk who took the lead in opposing abp Baldwin, *Gervase Cant.*, i, 389.
1188, was sent to Rome to appeal vs the abp and was one of five who d. there, *Epist. Cant.*, 254; his obit on 7 July is in BL Ms Arundel 68, fo 33.

See Hamo who is surely the same monk.

Helias de THANETO
occ. [1207 × 1214]

[1207 × 1214], one of the monks on the list of those who were in exile, *SL*, 172, CCA Lit. Ms D.12, fo 1.

An inventory of the refectory dated 1328 includes a *ciphus de murra* under his name, Dart, *Antiq. Cant.*, xxii (BL Ms Cotton Galba E.iv, fo 180).

I John de THANETO [Taneto
occ. 1241

n.d., name in the list in *SL*, 175, CCA Lit. Ms D.12, fo 2.

1241, 10 June, with Stephen Cranebroke, and Thomas de Brydlynton, q.v., sent as proctors to Rome to obtain confirmation of the chapter's el. of Boniface of Savoy as abp, *Gervase Cant.*, ii, 187–189, 191; he and Stephen arrived at their destination after many trials, including capture by the Emperor Frederick II, *ib.*, 197–198, but he soon returned on his own, *ib.*, 198.

II John de THANETO [Tanetho, Tanneto, Thanete
occ. [c. 1281] d. 1319

[c. 1281], one of four prof., *SL*, 176, CCA Lit. Ms D.12, fo 3.

1287/8, *custos* of St Mary in crypt, CCA DCc MA1, fo 153v.
1291/6, treasurer, CCA DCc MA1, fos 169v–198.
1297/1300, warden of manors, CCA DCc MA1, fos 208–222, Bocking acct 5.
1301/2, 1303/4, 1306/7, 1309, 20 Jan., 1309/12, 1313, 16 May, precentor, CCA DCc Cliffe acct 20, Adisham acct 3, West Farleigh acct 23, CUL Ms Ee.5.31, fo 110, CCA DCc Copton acct 5, Brook acct 13, Copton acct 7, CUL Ms Ee.5.31, fo 121–121v; he was apptd on 27 Nov. 1299, Reg. Q, fo 29.
1313/14, May, cellarer, CCA DCc Chamb. acct 8.
1313/15, treasurer, CCA DCc MA2, fos 49v–58.
1314, 30 Apr., one of the wardens of manors whose removal the abp ordered, Reg. abp Reynolds, fo 104v and CCA DCc EC V/28.
1292/3, with Geoffrey de Chilham, q.v., visited Meopham *circa comp[otum audiend[um*, CCA DCc Meopham acct 17.
1296, 19 Oct., with John de Hardys, q.v,. named proctors for parliament, CUL Ms Ee.5.31, fo 68v.
1305, 25 Feb., sent by the prior and chapter as their proctor to parliament, CUL Ms Ee.5.31, fo 102.
1309, Mar., witnessed the prior creating a notary, Reg. I, fo 303.
1319, 29 Dec., d., CCA Lit. Ms D.12, fo 16.

According to the somewhat unreliable Dart, *Antiq. Cant.*, 184, as precentor he provided (?composed) musical settings for the services and he also wrote legends of the saints. He also says that he d. on 8 Apr. 1330 at the age of 92 *ib.*

Three vols in the Eastry catalogue are listed beneath the name of John de Taneto nos 1722–1724, James, *Ancient Libraries*, 139.

In the list of missing books dated 1 Mar. 1338, the Exequie belonging to I. de Tanneto was 'charged out' to John le Spycer, q.v., *Lit. Cant.*, no 618 (Reg. L, fo 104v) as also his Miracula b. Marie in lingua Gallicana, which is no 1724 in the Eastry catalogue.

An inventory of vestments, *temp.* prior Eastry, includes a chasuble 'de rubeo sindone de tuly cum rosis brudato' of J. de Taneto, also an alb, Legg and Hope, *Inventories*, 52, 59 (BL Ms Cotton Galba, E.iv, fos 112v, 114v).

An inventory of the refectory, dated 1328, includes a silver *ciphus de murra*, formerly his, Dart, *Antiq. Cant.*, xxii (BL Ms Cotton Galba E.iv, fo 180).

III John de THANETO
occ. 1333 d. 1361

1333, 9 Oct., one of eleven prof., *SL*, 180, CCA Lit. Ms D.12, fo 4.

1361, 25 June, apptd chamberlain, Reg. abp Islip, fo 174^{v}.

1349, 4 June, 37th in order at the el. of an abp, Reg. G, fo 60^{v}.

1349, 8/9 Sept., 36th at the el. of an abp, *ib.*, fo 76^{v}.

1360/1, recd money from the prior for [celebrating] the *magna missa*, Lambeth Ms 243, fo 115.

1361, 3 Aug., d., one of c.25 monks carried off [by the plague] between June and Oct., CCA Lit. Ms D.12, fo 17. His obit is in BL Ms Arundel 68, fo 36^{v}.

Reginald de THANETO [Taneto
occ. [1281/2] d. 1326

[1281/2], one of five prof., *SL*, 177, CCA Lit. Ms D.12, fo 3.

1285, Sept., ord dcn, collegiate church, South Malling, *Reg. abp Pecham*, i, 222.

1326, 6 July, d., CCA Lit. Ms D.12, fo 16; his obit is in BL Ms Arundel 68, fo 16.

An inventory of vestments, *temp.* prior Eastry, includes a set of vestments and a richly decorated chasuble of his, Legg and Hope, *Inventories*, 52–53, 66 (BL Ms Cotton Galba, E.iv, fos 112^{v}, 117–117^{v}).

An inventory of the refectory, dated 1328, includes three silver *ciphi* formerly his, Dart, *Antiq. Cant.*, xx (BL Ms Cotton Galba E.iv, fo 179).

Richard de THANETO
occ. 1329 d. 1343

1329, 9 Oct., one of eight prof., CCA Lit. Ms D.12, fo 3^{v}.

1343, 2 Sept., d., CCA Lit. Ms D.12, fo 16^{v}.

Robert de THANETO [*alias* Hayward
occ. 1306 occ. 1318

1306, 9 Oct., one of two prof., *SL*, 178, CCA Lit. Ms D.12, fo 3^{v}.

1315, among his injunctions [after a visitation] abp Reynolds ordered Thaneto to be sent to Rochester cathedral priory for correction, Reg. abp Reynolds, fo 69–69^{v}.

1315, 5 Oct., his bad behaviour and bad influence on the juniors were reported by Simon VI, subprior, q.v, to the abp, with the information that he had discarded his habit and left the monastery, CUL Ms Ee.5.31, fo 161.

1316, 21 Apr., the subprior and chapter recorded their objection to his appeal vs them as being unseemly for religious, *ib.*, fo 167^{v}.

1317, 18 May, a letter to their representative at the curia was sent by the chapter to explain that he, who had been the cause of much dissension in the house and was now an apostate, was prob. on his way to the pope, *ib.*, fo 176–176^{v}; on 13 July they refused to accept responsibility for any loans in his name, *ib.*, fos 177^{v}–178.

1317 [13 June] prior Eastry warned the public to avoid him, an apostate monk, who had left the cloister for the third time, *Hist. Mss Comm. 5th Report*, Appndx, 437 (transcribed as Baners), (CCA DCc Cart. Antiq. C.1295).

Note: there are further refs concerning the litigation, which his apostasy, his accusations and appeals vs abp and chapter necessitated, in J.R. Wright, *The Church and the English Crown, 1305–1334*, (Toronto, 1980) 325.

1318, 6 Apr., the abp had requested a pension of £10 p.a., for him to which the prior and convent objected, although they were concerned about him and wanted to do what was right in the abp's view; it seems that he had expressed an interest in living at Boxgrave [?Boxgrove], CUL Ms Ee.5.31, fo 190^{v}.

1318, 8 May, in a letter to three Christ Church advisers the prior and chapter summarized the problems he had caused by his insolence and disobedience: he had sown discord in the community, left without permission, returned and undergone correction but continued to be a disturber of the peace. The abp had ordered his separation from the rest of the community until he mended his ways, but he had left again taking books and possessions of Christ Church, *ib.*, fos 191^{v}–192.

1318, 30 Aug., in a letter to the pope the prior and chapter recounted his actions and requested that he be sent to another monastery, *ib.*, fo 193^{v}.

See Robert de Aldon, to whom he wrote several letters from Rome expressing warm friendship, CCA DCc Cart. Antiq. C.1294, and the two appear to have been closely linked.

Note: who is the Robert de Thenet who d. on 1 Jan. 1316, CCA Lit. Ms D.12, fo 15^{v}?

His brother, Peter Hayward of Thanet, expressed his penitence on acct of the goods of Christ Church that he had recd from his deceased brother, and obtained the prior's forgiveness in 1361, *Lit. Cant.*, no 873 (Reg. L, fo 47^{v}).

Roger de THANETO
occ. 1328 d. 1346

1328, 25 Nov., one of six prof., *SL*, 179, CCA Lit. Ms D.12, fo 3^{v}.

1333, July; 1334/5, subchaplain to the prior, Hope, 'Inventories of Priors', 275 (CCA Lit. Ms E.27, insert); CCA DCc Brook acct 18.

1334/7, treasurer, CCA DCc MA2, fos 239–253.

1337/8, 1339/40, chaplain to the prior, CCA DCc West Farleigh acct 43, Eastry acct 67.

1339/40, 1341, Feb./Sept., 1342/4, cellarer, CCA DCc Agney acct 43, Great Chart acct 46, Agney acct 45, West Farleigh acct 48.
1345/6, warden of manors, CCA DCc Bocking accts 27, 28.

1346, 31 Dec., d., CCA Lit. Ms D.12, fo 16v.

Stephen de THANETO [Taneto
occ. 1354 d. 1396

1354, 28 Nov., one of seven prof., *SL*, 181, CCA Lit. Ms D.12, fo 4.
1356, 18 June, ord subdcn, Hoath chapel in Reculver parish, Reg. abp Islip, fo 316.
1358, 22 Sept., ord dcn, Charing, *ib.*, fo 317.
1360, 29 Feb., ord pr., abp's chapel, Otford, *ib.*, fo 318.
1372, Mar./1374, chamberlain, CCA DCc Chamb. accts 50, 51, 46.
1373/5, *custos* of abp Islip's sheep, CCA DCc Sheep Warden accts 2, 3.
1373/5, 1376/7, chamberlain CCA DCc Treas. acct 5, Chamb. accts 54, 55; also 1373/82 acc. to CCA DCc MA2, fos 276v–329v.
1378, granator, CCA DCc MA2, fo 315.
1380/1, *custos* of abp Islip's sheep, Sheep Warden acct 4.
1374, 30 June, 18th in order at the el. of an abp, Reg. G, fos 173v–175v.
1381, 31 July, 12th at the el. of an abp, *ib.*, fo 225v.
1396, 7 Aug., 6th at the el. of an abp, *ib.*, fo 234v.
1396, 8 Aug., d., CCA Lit. Ms D.12, fo 17v; he was described as 'vir sagacis ingenii sed impeditoris lingue', *ib.*

Name possibly in Oxford, Bod. Ms Rawlinson B.191, Polychronicon (14th c.); only Stephen T legible.

Thomas de THANETO
occ. 1st half 13th c.

n.d., name occ. in the list in *SL*, 174, CCA Lit. Ms D.12, fo 2.

I Walter de THANETO [Taneto
occ. 1st half 13th c.

n.d., name occ. in the list in *SL*, 174, CCA Lit. Ms D.12, fo 1v.

II Walter de THANETO
occ. [late 1260s] d. 1297

[late 1260s], one of five prof., *SL*, 176, CCA Lit. Ms D.12, fo 3.

1297, 10 Nov., d., CCA Lit. Ms D.12, fo 15.

William de THANETO
occ. 1323 occ. 1367/8

1323, one of six clothed in the monastic habit, *SL*, 179, CCA Lit. Ms D.12, fo 3v.
[1325], 18 Oct., prof, Reg. L, fo 141v.
1331, 1333, *magister corone*, CCA DCc MA2, fos 201v, 221.
1335/6, 1337/8, June, 1338/46, 347/8, bartoner, CCA DCc MA2, fo 256, Eastry acct 63, Bart. accts 22–30.
1348/54, warden of manors, CCA DCc Ebony acct 50, Agney acct 49, Adisham accts 26–29.
1354/5, monk *supervisor*, CCA DCc Agney acct 50.
1358/62, chaplain to the prior, CCA DCc, Copton acct 26, Ebony acct 59, Prior's Chaplain acct 1, Barksore acct 47.
1361, Nov./1362, monk *supervisor*, CCA DCc Agney acct 52.
1361/2, 1363/5, 1366, 10 May, 1367/8, chaplain to the prior, CCA DCc Lydden acct 69, Great Chart accts 63, 64, Reg. G, fo 149, CCA DCc Godmersham acct 23.
1366/7, monk *supervisor*, CCA DCc Eastry acct 100.

1338, 1 Mar., an inventory of missing books includes a Logica vetus et nova for which he was held responsible, *Lit. Cant.*, no 618 (Reg. L, fo 104).
1349, 4 June, 16th in order at the el. of an abp and named as one of thirteen *compromissorii*, Reg. G, fo 60v.
1349, 8/9 Sept., 15th at the el. of an abp and one of thirteen *compromissorii*, *ib.*, fos 76, 77v.
1366, 10 May, apptd one of three to name seven *compromissorii* in the el. of an abp, *ib.*, fo 149.

THENAM
see Tenham

THENT
see Tent

I THEODORE [Theodericus, Theodoricus, Thiodricus, Thodoricus
occ. [1115 × 1122]

[1115 × 1122], attested a charter of abp Ralph d'Escures, Eng. Epis. Acta, Canterbury, 1070–1136; no 47, forthcoming; he heads the witness list as *Theoder' priore Cantuar'*, but there is no other ref. to his ever holding this office.

He may be the monk of Christ Church who copied [*scripsit*]. Cambridge, Trinity College Ms 111, Augustinus, etc. (12th c.).

One vol. of his verse with the Parabole Salomonis Thodorici are listed in the late 12th c. catalogue and the Eastry catalogue respectively, no 194 of the former and no 105 of the latter, James, *Ancient Libraries*, 12, 28–29

Note: this may also be the Thidricus or Thidircus to whom abp Anselm addressed two affectionate letters, *Anselm Letters*, nos 334, 379; in the latter the abp told him to make corrections in what he had written in order to have an accurate text for future transcription.

II THEODORE
occ. 1199/1201

1199/1201, monk carpenter, CCA Lit. Ms D.4, fos 9, 10v.

THOKYNHAM
see Tokenam

I THOMAS
n.d.

n.d., 14 Jan., pr., whose obit occ. in BL Ms Arundel 68, fo 13.

II THOMAS
occ. [1153 × 1159]

[1153 × 1159], third prior, *Theobald Charters*, no 40 (Reg. B, fo 146v).

[1153 × 1159], witnessed a grant of prior Wibert, q.v. in response to a request of the abp, *ib.*

Note: is this the brother of Gervase, q.v., *Gervase Cant.*, ii, 551? In *ib.*, i, 89 he states that he wrote his chronicle for his brother, Thomas; and in *ib.*, i, 231, he recounts the appearance of abp Thomas [Becket] to a certain brother, a clerk. It is suggested in *DNB*, (under Gervase) that his brother was Thomas de Maydeston, q.v., under Maydeston.

III THOMAS
occ. 1219 occ. 1243/4

1219, 1 Nov., granator, CCA DCc MA1, fo 61v.
1220, 18 Oct., bartoner and granator, CCA DCc MA1, fo 64.
1221/3, granator, CCA DCc MA1, fos 65–67v.
1224, bartoner, CCA DCc MA1, fo 68v.
1229, subchamberlain, CCA DCc MA1, fo 72v.
1229, Oct./1230, 1230/2, sacrist, CCA DCc AS2, MA1, fos 73v–75v.
1236/7, May, granator, CCA DCc AS5.
1242/4, almoner, CCA DCc MA1, fos 83v–85v.

IV THOMAS
occ. [1250 × 1300]

[1250 × 1300], a monk, or more prob., monks by the name of Thomas who served in the office of chancellor, CCA DCc Rental 39.

Note:
(1) a Thomas was proctor for the prior and chapter in 1238, Sayers, 'Cant. Proctors', 325, 327, 337 (CCA DCc Cart. Antiq. A.206).
(2) Thomas I is likely to be identical with one of the other monks of that name listed here above.
(3) Thomas III may well be a conflation of the careers of several monks of this name, as Thomas IV almost certainly is.
(4) among the 13th c. monks to whom these entries may refer are Thomas de Brydlynton, Thomas de Elham, Thomas de Newsole, Thomas de St Valerico, Thomas de Westgate, etc., q.v.

THOMAS
see also Ryngmer

William THOMS
see Holyngborne

THONEBREGG
see Tonbregg'

THORHOLT
see Torolte

Hugh THORNDEN [Thorndon
occ. 1533/4

1533, 12 May, one of eight tonsured, *SL*, 196, CCA Lit. Ms D.12, fo 12.
1534, 21 Mar., prof., *ib.*
1534, 12 Dec., acknowledged the Act of Supremacy, *DK 7th Report*, Appndx 2, 282.

Richard THORNDEN, D.Th. [*alias* le Stede
occ. 1511 occ. 1540

1511, 1 Sept., one of eight tonsured, *SL*, 194, CCA Lit. Ms D.12, fo 11.
1512, 19 Apr., prof., *ib.*
1513, 26 Mar., ord subdcn, Canterbury cathedral, Reg. abp Warham, ii, fo 266v.
1517, celebrated his first mass on the second Sun. in Apr. and recd 4d. from William Ingram I, q.v., CCA Lit. Ms C.11, fo 128v.
1524, warden of Canterbury college; his inventory on entering office is printed in Pantin, *Cant. Coll. Ox.*, i, 65–72 (CCA DCc Cart. Antiq. O.135.C). He was appted on 8 Mar. 1524, Pantin, *ib.*, iii, 146 (Reg. T, fo 231).
1528/9, [1533], 21 Dec., [1534], 28 Jan., warden; his acct for 1528/9 survives and is transcribed in Pantin, *ib.*, ii, 259–261 (CCA DCc Cart. Antiq. O.151.48).
1534, before 14 Apr., [1538, 8 Feb., after], 1540, 4 Apr., warden of manors, Pantin, *Cant. Coll. Ox*, iii, 148, 152, *L and P Henry VIII*, xv, no 452; see also *L and P Henry VIII*, vii, no 33, where this apptment is discussed in a letter from the prior to Cromwell.
1516/18, student at Canterbury college, Pantin, *Cant. Coll. Ox.*, ii, 272, 273; in the latter yr he recd 66s. 8d. *pro sua exhibicione* from cardinal Morton's bequest, *ib.*, ii, 273.
1521, 26 Apr., 1522, 14 May, supplicated for B.Th.; he was adm. ad opponendum on 15 May 1522 and with Roger Otford adm. 'ad lecturam libri sentenciarum' on 21 June, Pantin, *ib.*, iii, 257.
1527, 12 Dec., supplicated for D.Th., after sixteen yrs of study in logic, philosophy and theology, *ib.*, iii, 258.

1528, 29 Feb., 1531, 12 Oct., supplicated for reduction of grace on the grounds of poverty, Pantin, *Cant. Coll. Ox.*, iii, 258, *ib.*, iv, 82. In this yr he preached the university sermon on Ash Wednesday and Ascension day, *ib.*, iv, 226.

1532, 5 Feb., incepted D.Th., *ib.*, iii, 258–259.

1511, 2 Sept., novice, not prof., and 81st in order on the visitation certificate, Wood-Legh, *Visit.*, 3 (Reg. abp Warham, i, fo 35^{v}).

1521, travelled from Oxford to Canterbury to preach, Pantin, *Cant. Coll. Ox.*, iv, 206.

[1534], 26 Jan., it had been reported to Cromwell that the warden of Canterbury college, Oxford, was an enemy of the king's cause, *L and P Henry VIII*, vii, no 101.

[1534], 28 Jan. wrote to Cromwell to inform him that he was sending two books which had belonged to John Dering, q.v., for his examination and requesting Cromwell's support in his apptment to the office of warden of manors and the apptment of William Jerome, q.v. to succ. him as warden of Canterbury college, Pantin, *Cant. Coll. Ox.*, iii, 147–148. He wrote again on 4 Nov. 1538 a letter in which it is clear that he was looking out for his own future, *L and P Henry VIII*, xiii, pt 2, no 749, and see also *ib.*, pt 2, no 465.

[1538, 8 Feb., after], on a list of monks prob. prepared for Thomas Cromwell, he was reported as 46 yrs old, Pantin, *Cant. Coll. Ox.*, iii, 152. In this same yr, Cranmer summed up his character in a letter to Cromwell in which he recommended him for the office of prior; among other good qualities he was 'veray tractable, and . . . redy to sett forwarde hys pryncis causes', *ib.*, iii, 154.

1538, 30 Sept., 4 Nov., addressed two letters to Cromwell concerning the latter's order that the monks must change their habits, *L and P Henry VIII*, xiii, pt. 2 nos 465, 749.

[1541, 8 Apr., named suffragan bp of Dover and canon of the first prebend, *Fasti, 1541–1857*, iii, 17].

Robert THORNDEN [Thorinden

occ. 1491 d. 1510/11

1491, 11 Sept., one of four tonsured, CCA Lit. Ms D.12, fo 9 (*SL*, 192).

1492, 21 Apr., ord acol., Canterbury cathedral, *Reg. abp Morton*, i, no 441a.

1494, 29 Mar., ord subdcn, Canterbury cathedral, *ib.*, i, no 443b.

1495, 18 Apr., ord dcn, Canterbury cathedral, *ib.*, i, no 444c.

1499/1500, celebrated his first mass and recd a small gift from the sacrist, Woodruff, 'Sacrist's Rolls', 66 (CCA DCc Sac. acct 60).

1493, 1 May, 64th in order at the ratification of an agreement, Reg. S, fo 383^{v}; but see John Crosse I.

1501, 26 Apr., 43rd in order at the el. of an abp, Reg. R, fo 56^{v}.

1510/11, d., Woodruff, 'Sacrist's Rolls', 69 (CCA DCc Sac. acct 73); his obit occ. in BL Ms Arundel 68, fo 51^{v} on 19 Dec.

William THORNDEN, D.Th. [Thorndene, Thorndenne, Thorndon, Thornton, Thorynden

occ. 1432 d. 1483

1432, 19 Sept., one of six prof., *SL*, 188, CCA Lit. Ms D.12, fo 7^{v}.

1434, 13 Mar., ord acol. and subdcn, infirmary chapel, *Reg. abp Chichele*, iv, 378.

1435, 2 Apr., ord dcn, infirmary chapel, *ib.*, iv, 389.

1454/5, 1456/7, 1459, warden of Canterbury college, Pantin, *Cant. Coll. Ox.*, ii, 176, iv, 196; his inventory on leaving office in 1459 is in Pantin, *ib.*, i, 9–17; it includes two vols given by him to the college, *ib.*, i, 15, 16. Other vols given are discussed in *ib.*, iv, 159. See below for the new library.

1461, one of the chancellors, Reg. S, fo 208^{v}. See Richard London II.

1462, 26 Dec., penitentiary in the priory, *Lit. Cant.*, no 1051 (Reg. S, fo 199^{v}); see Robert Chelmynton.

1437, Oct., student at Canterbury college, provided with travelling expenses to Oxford, Pantin, *Cant. Coll. Ox.*, iv, 192.

1439/41, student, possibly not for the full yr, Pantin, *ib.*, ii, 154, 160 (CCA DCc Cart. Antiq. O.151.10, 11).

1443/4, student/fellow, receiving a pension of £10, Pantin, *ib.*, ii, 163 (CCA DCc Cart. Antiq. O.151.12); he was therefore absent from the abp's visitation in Canterbury on 30 Mar. 1444, Pantin, *ib.*, iii, 100–101 (Reg. S, fo 159).

1444/5, student for three terms, Pantin, *ib.*, ii, 167 (CCA DCc Cart. Antiq. O.151.13).

1448/9, student, Pantin, *ib.*, ii, 171 (CCA DCc Cart. Antiq. O.151.14).

1450, 13 June, supplicated for B.Th. after eight yrs of philosophy and five yrs of theology, Pantin, *ib.*, ii, 259.

1456, 4 Feb., 1459, 22 Feb., supplicated for D.Th., *ib.*, ii, 259–260; acc. to his obit he did incept, BL Ms Arundel 68, fo 39.

1444, Mar., absent from the abp's visitation because *ad studium generale transmiss'*, Reg. abp Stafford, fo 41.

1454, 23 Apr., preached in Latin in the cathedral, beginning with the words 'Elegit nobis hereditatem suam' (Psalm 46/47, 5), after which the chapter proceeded to postulate Thomas Bourgchier as abp, *Chron. Stone*, 60. He preached again on 22 Aug., on receipt of the papal confirmation of the el., *ib.*, 61.

1454/5, as warden of Canterbury college he was in charge of the building of the new library, Pantin, *Cant. Coll. Ox.*, ii, 176.

1460, 11 Apr., gave the Good Friday sermon in the cathedral nave on the text 'Christus pro nobis mortuus est' (Rom. 5, 8), *Chron. Stone*, 78.
1462, 26 Dec., as penitentiary, signed with the cross a pilgrim who had made a private vow to go to the Holy Land, *Lit. Cant.*, no 1051, (Reg. S, fo 199ᵛ).
1466, 17 Feb., 23rd in order in an inventory of *jocalia fratrum* [given by him and/or assigned for his use], Reg. N, fo 231ᵛ.
1468, 3 Sept., preached to the monks at a requiem mass for prior Thomas Goldston I, q.v., taking as his text 'Salvum faciet in regno suo celesti' (2 Tim. 4, 18), *Chron. Stone*, 106.
1469, 19 Mar., preached to the people in the chapter house at the time of the high mass, on the occasion of the abjuration of a heretic, *ib.*, 109; see William Sellyng.
1469, 31 Dec., pledged a copy of *Duns Scotus Super secundum sententiarum* when he borrowed a vol., *Excepciones ex libris 23 auctorum* etc. (now BL Ms Royal 7, B.xiii), from Rochester cathedral priory, *BRUO*, *MLGB*.
1472/3, preached the sermon [in the cathedral] on Ash Wednesday and recd 6s. 8d., [?because he had to travel from Oxford], Pantin, *Cant. Coll. Ox.*, iv, 198; see William Chichele I.
1475, 5 May, penitentiary in city and diocese, *Lit. Cant.*, no 1083, (Reg. S, fo 274ᵛ).
1483, 22 Aug., d., at the age of 66, CCA Lit. Ms D.12, fo 26ᵛ; his obit on 23 Aug. is in BL Ms Arundel 68, fo 39.

During his term of office as warden of Canterbury college he gave the college some [of his] books, Pantin, *Cant. Coll. Ox.*, i, 15, *ib.*, iv, 159–160.

An inventory of St Michael's chapel dated 1511 includes a red altar hanging of cloth of gold given by him, Legg and Hope, *Inventories*, 149.

THOROLK, Thorolt
see Torolte

THROCKING
see Trokkyng

Hamo THROWLEY [Haymo, Throwle, Throwlegh, Trowhley
occ. 1497 d. 1505

1497, 28 July, one of nine tonsured, CCA Lit. Ms D.12, fo 9, *SL*, 192.
1498, 14 Apr., ord acol., Canterbury cathedral, *Reg. abp Morton*, i, no 447a.
1498, 19 Apr., prof., *ib.*
1501/3, student at Canterbury college with a pension of £5 each yr, Pantin, *Cant. Coll. Ox.*, ii, 234, 236 (CCA DCc Cart. Antiq. O.151.33, 35).
1503/4, student, with a pension of 50s., Pantin, *ib.*, ii, 239 (CCA DCc, Cart. Antiq. O.151.37).
1504/5, Easter to Easter, student, receiving a pension of £6 10s., Pantin, *ib.*, ii, 241 (CCA DCc, Cart. Antiq. O.151.38); he was ill this yr, *laboranti tisica passione*, and his medical expenses were 12s., Pantin, *ib.*, ii, 244.
1501, 26 Apr., dcn, and 60th in order at the el. of an abp, Reg. R, fo 56ᵛ.
1505, 14 Apr., dcn and scholar, d. at the age of 24, *ex consumpcione*, CCA Lit. Ms D.12, fo 35ᵛ. His obit on 15 Apr. is in BL Ms Arundel 68, fo 24.

I John THROWLEY [Drowle, Throwle
occ. 1454 d. [1457]

1454, 28 Apr., one of eight prof., *SL*, 189, CCA Lit. Ms D.12, fo 8.
1455, 5 Apr., ord acol. and subdcn, chapel within the cathedral, *Reg. abp Bourgchier*, 359.
[1457], d., CCA Lit. Ms D.12, fo 25ᵛ; the obit of a John Throwle, dcn, occ. on 12 Aug. in BL Ms Arundel 68, fo 38 and ref. almost certainly to this monk.

II John THROWLEY, B.Th. [Throwlee, Thoroughley, Trwley
occ. 1514 occ. 1540

1514, 1 Sept., one of seven tonsured, *SL*, 194, CCA Lit. Ms D.12, fo 11.
1515, 19 Apr., prof., *ib.*
[1538, 8 Feb., after], 1540, 4 Apr., one of the chancellors, Pantin, *Cant. Coll. Ox.*, iii, 152, *L and P Henry VIII*, xv, no 452.

1516/17, 1521/2, student at Canterbury college, Oxford, with a pension of 50s., the first yr and £6 10s. the second, Pantin, *Cant. Coll. Ox.*, ii, 256, 258 (CCA DCc Cart. Antiq. O.151.44, 46).
1524, 29 July, supplicated for B.Th., after eight yrs of study of logic, philosophy and theology, Pantin, *ib.*, iii, 260.
1527, 14 Nov., supplicated again after ten yrs, *ib.*, iii, 260. He was adm. *ad opponendum* on 16 Nov., and *ad lecturam alicuius libri sentenciarum* on 17 Jan. 1528, *ib.*, iii, 260–261.
1528, 27 May, supplicated for permission to preach by deputy; granted, Pantin, *ib.*, iii, 261.
[1545, adm. to practice in medicine after ten yrs study in the faculty of medicine, Pantin, *ib.*, iii, 261.]

1534, 12 Dec., acknowledged the Act of Supremacy, *DK 7th Report*, Appndx 2, 282.
[1538, 8 Feb., after], in a list of monks prob. prepared for Thomas Cromwell, he was described as witty and 40 yrs of age, Pantin, *Cant. Coll. Ox.*, iii, 152.
1540, 4 Apr., awarded £8 p.a., *L and P Henry VIII*, xv, no 452.

Name in Oxford, Bod. Ms Selden supra 65, Artes dictandi (early 15th c.), formerly in Canterbury college library; name on fo 145. See Pantin, *Cant. Coll. Ox.*, i, 112.

William de THRULEGH [Trule, Trulegh
occ. 1309 d. 1334

1309, 18 Oct., one of nine prof., *SL*, 179, CCA Lit. Ms D.12, fo 3^{v}.
1317, 28 May, ord pr., Lambeth palace chapel, Reg. abp Reynolds, fo 178.
1327, July/1330, granator, CCA DCc Gran. accts 18, 20–22. Worcester Cathedral Muniment, C.573 (Great Chart acct, 1329/30).
1329/30, treasurer, CCA DCc MA2, fo 190.
1330/1, 1332/3, warden of manors, CCA DCc Hadleigh acct 10, MA2, fos 209–219, Middleton acct 43.
1334, 23 Jan., d., CCA Lit. Ms D.12, fo 16; his obit occ. on 24 Jan. in BL Ms Arundel 68, fo 14.

TIERNE
see Tyerne

Thomas de TILMERSTONE [Tilmanstone, Tylmerston
occ. 1346 occ. 1349/50

1346, 11 Nov., one of eight prof., *SL*, 181, CCA Lit. Ms D.12, fo 4.
1350, 18 Sept., ord pr., Goudhurst, Reg. abp Islip, fo 310^{v}.
1349/50, chancellor with John de Northbourne, q.v., Reg. H, fo 35.

Thomas TOKENAM [Thokynham, Tokenham, Tokkinam, Toknam, Tokynham
occ. 1386 d. 1414

1386, 28 Oct., one of two clothed, CCA Lit. Ms D.12, fo 5 (*SL*, 183).
1401, warden of Canterbury college until 2 Aug. of this yr, Pantin, *Cant. Coll. Ox*, iii, 59–60 (Reg. abp Arundel, i, fo 437).
1393/4, student at Canterbury college, Pantin, *Cant. Coll. Ox.*, ii, 132, 133, 135, 136, 138, 140 (CCA DCc Cart. Antiq. O.151.2).
1397/8, one of six at Oxford who recd a small sum from the feretrars *pro benedictione*, CCA DCc Feret. acct 1.
1387/8, recd 5s. from the prior, Lambeth Ms 243, fo 208^{v}.
1396, 7 Aug., 51st in order at the el. of an abp, Reg. G, fo 236.
1414, 12 Mar., sick in the infirmary at the time of the el. of an abp and named Richard Godmersham I, q.v., as his proxy, *Reg. abp Chichele*, i, 4.
1414, 21/22 Mar., d., CCA Lit. Ms D.12, fo 20, where he is described as 'scolaris peritissimus sacre theologie'.

Thomas de TONBREGG' [Thonebregg, Thonebrugg, Tonebrigg
occ. 1353 occ. 1367/8

1353, 27 Sept., one of five prof., *SL*, 181, CCA Lit. Ms D.12, fo 4.
1355, 30 May, ord acol., abp's chapel, Maidstone, Reg. abp Islip, fo 315^{v}.
1355, 19 Sept., ord subdcn, abp's chapel, Saltwood, *ib.*, fo 315^{v}.
1356, 18 June, ord dcn, Hoath chapel in Reculver parish, *ib.*, fo 316.
1356, 24 Sept., ord pr., abp's chapel, Tenham, *ib.*, fo 316.
1366/8, warden of manors, CCA DCc Appledore accts 44, 45.

Richard TONGE
occ. 1500 occ. 1523

1500, 28 July, one of eight tonsured, *SL*, 193, CCA Lit. Ms D.12, fo 10; each of the novices recd a gold noble worth 6s. 8d., for their labours with regard to the funeral of the abp who d. c. 15 Sept., 1500, CCA Lit. Ms D.12, *ib.*
1501, 19 Apr., made his prof. before the prior, *sed. vac.*, *ib.*
1507, 3 Apr., ord pr., Canterbury cathedral, Reg. abp Warham, ii, fo 263. On the fourth Sun. in Apr. he celebrated his first mass and recd 4d. from the *custos martyrii*, CCA Lit. Ms C.11, fo 49^{v}.
1519, 24 June; 1520, 1521, 1522, 1523, all on 25 Mar., *custos* of St Mary in crypt, CCA Lit. Ms C.11, fos 60, 60^{v}, 61, 61^{v}, 62.
1501, 26 Apr., 73rd and last in order at the el. of an abp, Reg. R, fo 56^{v}.
1511, 2 Sept., pr., and 50th on the visitation certificate, Wood-Legh, *Visit.*, 3 (Reg. abp Warham, i, fo 35^{v}).
1516, Sept./Dec., William Ingram I pd 18d. *pro froco et capicio* for him, CCA Lit. Ms C.11, fo 127^{v}.
1518/19, spent time in the infirmary, CCA DCc Infirm. acct 1.

I William de TONGE [Tong, Tonghe
occ. [mid 1260s] occ. [c. 1283]

n.d. [mid 1260s], one of seven prof., *SL*, 176, CCA Lit. Ms D.12, fo 2^{v}.
[c. 1275], with Richard Pykenot, q.v., led the opposition vs prior Thomas Ryngmer, q.v., CCA DCc Cart. Antiq. C.1296, summarized in *Hist. Mss Comm. 5th Report*, Appndx, 438.
[c. 1283], it was later revealed that he and Richard Pykenot, q.v., may have hatched a plot to murder Thomas de Stureye I, q.v., in Italy. These must have been the two monks who had gone to Rome with their accusations vs prior Ryngmer, q.v. For an acct of their misdemeanours see CCA DCc DE73; a frag-

ment containing details of their accusations is preserved in CCA DCc DE105

II William TONGE [Tongge, Toong
occ. 1444 d. 1505

1444, 21 Dec., one of four prof., *SL*, 188, CCA Lit. Ms D.12, fo 7^{v}.
1445, 27 Mar., ord acol., Canterbury cathedral, Reg. abp Stafford, fo 198.
1446, 16 Apr., ord subdcn, Canterbury cathedral, *ib.*, fo 199^{v}.
1447, 8 Apr., ord dcn, Canterbury cathedral, *ib.*, fo 201.
1449, 12 Apr., ord pr., Canterbury cathedral, *ib.*, fo 203^{v}.
1467/75, and prob. from 1465, sacrist, CCA DCc Sac. accts 46–48, 50, 51, 53, 56, 57, MA5, fo 12ff.
1466, 17 Feb., 33rd in order in an inventory of *jocalia fratrum* [given by him and/or assigned for his use], Reg. N, fo 232^{v}.
1488, was to rec. 20s. or a maser from a bequest, Hussey, 'Kentish Wills', 42 (transcribed as Couge).
1493, 1 May, 10th in order at the ratification of an agreement, Reg. S, fo 383^{v}; but see John Crosse I.
1501, 26 Apr., ill in the infirmary and absent from the el. of an abp, Reg. R, fo 56^{v}.
1505, 28 May, *stacionarius*, d., *ex magna consumpcione*; he had been first in choir [*in capite chori*] for twelve yrs and was in his 62nd yr of monastic life and 79 yrs of age, CCA Lit. Ms D.12. fo 35^{v}, where he is described as 'vir bonus, devotus et religiosus and valde maturus in moribus'. His obit is in BL Ms Arundel 68, fo 28^{v}.

Richard TOROLTE [Thorholt, Thorolk, Thorolt, Torold, Turholt
occ 1473 d. [1485]

1473, 12 Mar., ord acol., Canterbury cathedral, *Reg. abp Bourgchier*, 410.
1473, 28 Apr., one of six prof., *SL*, 190 CCA Lit. Ms D.12, fo 8^{v}.
1474, 26 Mar., ord subcn, Canterbury cathedral, *Reg. abp Bourgchier*, 416.
1475, 23 Dec., ord dcn, prior's chapel, Canterbury, *ib.*, 418.
1480, 1 Apr., ord pr., Canterbury cathedral, *ib.*, 430.
[1485], d., CCA Lit. Ms D.12 fo 26^{v}; his obit on 13 Oct occ. in BL Ms Arundel 68, fo 45.

John TRENDLE [Trendele, Trendeley, Trendlee
occ. 1399 d. 1433

1399, n.d., one of six prof., *SL*, 185, CCA Lit. Ms D.12, fo 5^{v}.
1399, 20 Dec., ord subdcn, Canterbury cathedral, Reg. abp Arundel, i, fo 325.
1400, 3 Apr., ord dcn, Hoath chapel in Reculver parish, *ib.*, i, fo 326.
1404, 29 Mar., ord pr., Canterbury cathedral, *ib.*, i, fo 332^{v}.
1433, before 3 May, *magister mense* and infirmarer, CCA Lit. Ms D.12, fo 23^{v}.
1414, 12 Mar., 47th in order at the el. of an abp, *Reg. abp Chichele*, i, 4.
1433, 3 May, d., in his 30th yr of monastic life; 'hic suffocatus erat Apostemate desubtus pulmonem secundum phisicos', CCA Lit. Ms D.12, fo 23^{v}. His obit is in BL Ms Arundel 68, fo 26^{v}.

Name in Oxford, Bod. Ms Digby 92, Astronomica etc. (13th/14th c.); on fo 15 he is referred to as *nuper* monk of Christ Church who drew up the *tabula* mentioned in the treatise.

He was known as an *astronimus egregius*, CCA Lit. Ms D.12, fo 5^{v} and a *subtil' valde . . . et eximius calculator*, who *magnum de vij planetis fecit librum*, *ib.*, fo 23^{v}.

Roger de TROKKYNG [Throcking, Trockinge, Trockyng
occ. 1260/1 d. 1307

n.d., name appears in the list in *SL*, 175, CCA Lit. Ms D.12, fo 2.
1260/1, 1262/75, granator, Reg. H, fo 201^{v}, (*interior*), CCA DCc MA1, fos 104^{v}–121^{v}; AS9 (1263/4).
1274/5, 1276/7, 1278/9, warden of manors, CCA DCc Great Chart acct 2 and Worcester Cathedral Muniment, C.572 (Great Chart acct), Reg. H, fo 209^{v}, Appledore acct 4.
1279/80, granator, CCA DCc MA1, fo 130, AS25.
1272, sent as proctor by the prior and chapter, *sed. vac.*, to ask the bp of Rochester to hold an ordination, *Lit. Cant.*, no 453 (Reg. L, fo 21).
1283, 22 June, his separation from the rest of the community ordered after it was found that he had supported two monks who had left without permission, and had been the source of division in the priory, *Epist. Pecham*, 573–4; see Thomas Ryngmer.
1307, 29 June, d., CCA Lit. Ms D.12, fo 15^{v}; his obit is in BL Ms Arundel 68, fo 32.

The Eastry catalogue includes a copy of Diadema monachorum which had belonged to him, James, *Ancient Libraries*, no 1721 (p. 139).

An inventory of the refectory dated 1328 includes a silver *ciphus* of his, Dart, *Antiq. Cant.*, xix (BL Ms Cotton Galba E.iv, fo 178^{v}).

TROWHLEY, Trwley
see Throwley

TRULE(GH)
see Thrulegh

Andrew de TUMBA
occ. [1207 × 1216]

[1207 × 1214], name in the list of monks who were in exile, *SL*, 172, CCA Lit. Ms D.12, fo 1.

M. O de TUMBA
occ. 1189

1189, after 6 Oct., one of the monks imprisoned by the abp at Tenham when they were sent to him as messengers, *Epist. Cant.*, 311; see Baldwin.

Note: the vol. in the Eastry catalogue which M.R. James attributed to prior Odo II, q.v., may have belonged to this monk.

Roger de TUMBA
occ. 1189 occ. 1206

1189, 5/8 Nov., he and a contingent of monks were sent to London to the king, *Epist. Cant.*, 315–316.

1206, 30 Mar., one of the monks summoned by the pope to Rome to give evidence in the dispute over their el. of Reginald, q.v., as abp. *CPL*, i, (1198–1304), 26; while there, they el. Stephen Langton, *Fasti*, ii, 6.

I TURKILLUS
n.d.

n.d., 28 Aug., *conversus*, whose obit occ. in BL Ms Arundel 68, fo 39v.

II TURKILLUS
n.d.

n.d., 23 Oct., pr., whose obit occ. in BL Ms Arundel 68, fo 46, and in BL Ms Cotton Nero C.ix, fo 14.

Richard TURPYN
see Hatfeld

William TURRIS
see Terracii

Stephen TYE
see Tygh

Stephen de TYERNE [Terne, Therne, Tierne
occ. 1314 d. 1342

1314, 9 Dec., one of five prof., *SL*, 179, CCA Lit. Ms D.12, fo 3v.

1315, 20 Dec., ord subdcn, Maidstone, Reg. abp Reynolds, fo 173v.

1329/35, treasurer, CCA DCc MA2, fos 190–239.

1336/8, warden of manors, CCA DCc MA2, fos 248–253, Adisham acct 14.

1341/2, anniversarian, Lambeth ED37.

1331/2, one of the monks who recd money from the prior for *equitant' in negociis*, Lambeth Ms 243, fo 35v.

1342, 25 Apr., d., CCA Lit. Ms D.12, fo 16v.

William de TYERNE
occ. 2nd half 13th c.

n.d., name in the list in *SL*, 175, CCA Lit. Ms D.12, fo 2.

n.d., 13 Jan., precentor, whose obit follows that of Eadmer, q.v. on this day, BL Ms Arundel 68, fo 13.

An inventory of the refectory, dated 1328, includes a *ciphus de murra* of his, Dart, *Antiq. Cant.*, xxi (BL Ms Cotton Galba E.iv, fo 179v).

Stephen TYGH [Tegh, Tye, Tyghe, Tyre
occ. [1399] occ. 1423

[1399], n.d., one of four prof., *SL*, 184, CCA Lit. Ms D.12, fo 5v.

1399, 20 Dec., ord subdcn, Canterbury cathedral, Reg. abp Arundel, i, fo 325.

1400, 3 Apr., ord dcn, Hoath chapel in Reculver parish, *ib.*, i, fo 326.

1401, 19 Mar., ord pr., Canterbury cathedral, *ib.*, i, fo 328.

1414, 12 Mar., 45th in order at the el. of an abp, *Reg. abp Chichele*, i, 4.

1423, 6 Apr., provided with a licence by the abp to transfer to St Martin's priory, Dover, *ib.*, iv, 247 (Reg. S, fo 88v). Causton's explanation for this decision was delicately worded: 'propter causas non dicendas', CCA Lit. Ms D.12, fo 5v; he had become involved with Henry Newynden, q.v. He later left Dover for Faversham but did not remain there long enough to be prof., *ib.* His obit occ. in BL Ms Arundel 68, fo 47v (as Tyee).

TYLMERSTON
see Tilmerstone

TYNTERDEN
see Tentyrden

ULCOMBE
see Holekumbe

William de UFFINGTON
see Offynton

UMFREY
see Humfrey

John UNDYRDOWN [Underdon, Underdoun, Wndirdown
occ. [1373] occ. 1381

1373, 23 Aug., one of two *clerici*, whom the prior was comm. to adm., Reg. abp Wittlesey, fo 62v; he was prob. one of eight but *SL*, 183, and CCA Lit. Ms D.12, fo 4v are not clear on this point.

1374, 27 Apr., novice, made his prof. before the prior, by comm. from the abp, Reg. abp Wittlesey, fo 130v.

1377, 19 Sept., ord pr., Lambeth palace chapel, Reg. abp Sudbury, fo 141ᵛ.

1374/5, ill in the infirmary and the anniversarian contributed to his medical expenses, CCA DCc Anniv. acct 6.

1380, recd a small sum [*pro benedictione*] from the prior, Lambeth Ms 243, fo 180ᵛ.

1381, 31 July, 50th in order at the el. of an abp, Reg. G, fo 225ᵛ.

I Thomas UNDYRDOWN [senior, Underdoune, Underdune, Undyrdoun, Wndyrdown

occ. 1320 d. 1347

1320, 9 Oct., one of five prof., *SL*, 179, CCA Lit. Ms D.12, fo 3ᵛ.

1338, 1 Mar., had borrowed from the library Brito super prologis, a Bible and five books of Anselm in one volume, which were now reported missing, *Lit. Cant.*, no 618 (Reg. L, fo 104).

1347, 6 Sept., d., CCA Lit. Ms D.12, fo 16ᵛ.

II Thomas UNDYRDOWN [junior, Underdoune, Undyrdoun, Wndirdown

occ. 1333 d. 1361

1333, 9 Oct., one of eleven prof., *SL*, 180, CCA Lit. Ms D.12, fo 4.

1350/1, second feretrar, CCA DCc Treas. acct 27, fo 2ᵛ.

1349, 4 June, 36th in order at the el. of an abp, Reg. G, fo 60ᵛ.

1349, 8/9 Sept., 35th at the el. of an abp, *ib.*, fo 76ᵛ.

1361, 5 Aug., d., one of c. 25 monks carried off [by the plague] between June and Oct., CCA Lit. Ms D.12, fo 17.

Note: BL Ms Arundel 68, fo 15ᵛ, records a monk by this name whose obit occ. on 6 Feb.

URSUS

n.d.

n.d., 9 Nov., obit occ. in BL Ms Arundel 68, fo 47ᵛ.

VACHAN

see Vaughan

John de VALOYNS [Valens, Valeyns, Valoynes, Waleyns, Wayloyns

occ. 1309 d. 1337

1309, 18 Oct., one of nine prof., *SL*, CCA Lit. Ms D.12, fo 3ᵛ.

1317, 28 May, ord pr., Lambeth palace chapel, Reg. abp Reynolds, fo 178.

1329, Feb./May, 1329/31, warden of manors, CCA DCc Illeigh accts 7, 8, MA fos 190–199.

1331/3, cellarer, CCA DCc MA2, fos 202ᵛ–222ᵛ; however, he was removed [?on 12 Sept. 1332] acc. to CCA DCc DE3, fo 21ᵛ.

1335/7, chaplain to the prior, CCA DCc AS14, MA2, fo 256.

1318, 19 Feb., with William de Ledebury, q.v., apptd proctors for convocation, CUL Ms Ee.5.31, fo 188.

1324, 29 May, one of the monks for whom the prior requested a relaxation of the penance imposed by the abp after his visitation, *ib.*, fo 236–236ᵛ.

1325, 19 Oct., the inquisition into the misdeeds of Robert Aldon, q.v., found him implicated in the theft of silver found in Aldon's possession, a fact which he denied, *Lit. Cant.*, no 156 (Reg. L, fo 142–142ᵛ).

[1327], 27 May, the abp ordered his punishment to be remitted by royal command, *Lit. Cant.*, no 215 (CCA DCc Cart. Antiq. C.1294b).

1337, 1 Feb., d., CCA Lit. Ms D.12, fo 16ᵛ; his obit is in BL Ms Arundel 68, fo 15.

Simon de VALOYNS

occ. [c. 1283] occ. 1299

n.d. [c. 1283], one of five prof., *SL*, 177, CCA Lit. Ms D.12, fo 3.

1285, 22 Sept., ord dcn, collegiate church, South Malling, *Reg. abp Pecham*, i, 222.

1299, bartoner, CCA DCc MA1, fos 222, 225.

Note: see Simon de Byford who may be this monk.

A William de Valoynes was sheriff of Kent before 1280, CCA DCc DE15E.

Richard VAUGHAN, D.Cn.L [Vachan, Vaghan, Wachan, Waghan

occ. c. 1352 occ. 1360

[1302/3], name inserted, as Richard Wagham, D.Cn.L, in the list in *SL*, 178, CCA Lit. Ms D.12, fo 3ᵛ. The date is 29 Dec. 1303 in Cambridge, Corpus Christi College Ms 298.

c. 1352, prof., see below.

In 1348 he was adcn of Surrey and acting as counsel for the prior and chapter, *Lit. Cant.*, no 764 (Reg. L, fo 81), and the following yr was granted accommodation in the priory, *ib.*, no 769 (*ib.*, fo 82).

1353, 21 Feb., addressed as *frater* by the abp and apptd by him auditor of causes in the court of Canterbury, Churchill, *Cant. Admin.*, ii, 212–213 (Reg. abp Islip, fo 65).

[1353], composed a petition to the king with regard to the prior's relation to the Black Monk Chapter, *Lit. Cant.*, no 870 (Reg. L, fo 44), where it is dated [1360].

Name in Oxford, New College Ms 207, Liber sextus, but this was never in the Christ Church library; see L. Boyle 'A Study of the Works attributed to William of Pagula, Oxford, D.Phil thesis, 1956, i, 413–414.

His career before he entered Christ Church c. 1351 is summarized in *BRUO*. The reason for the insertion of his name in the adm/prof. list almost fifty yrs earlier suggests:
(1) that he was not a young man when he became a monk.
(2) that his degree and reputation were judged to merit the rank of a senior monk despite his late entry.

John VIEL [Viell, Vyel, Vyell
occ. 1399 d. 1445

1399, n.d., one of six prof., *SL*, 185, CCA Lit. Ms D.12, fo 5ᵛ.
1399, 20 Dec., ord subdcn, Canterbury cathedral, Reg. abp Arundel, i, fo 325.
1401, 2 Apr., ord dcn, Canterbury cathedral, *ib.*, i, fo 328.
1405, 18 Apr., ord pr., Canterbury cathedral, *ib.*, i, fo 334.
1428, 20 July, 1428/30, 1432/3, 1435, 1436/7, sacrist, CCA DCc CR89, Sac. accts 25–27, 'Chron. Wm Glastynbury', 129, CCA DCc Sac. acct 28.
1444, before 4 or 10 Mar., 4 Dec., *custos corone*, CCA Lit. Ms D.12, fo 25, CCA DCc MA4, fo 29ᵛ.
1414, 12 Mar., 48th in order at the el. of an abp, *Reg. abp Chichele*, i, 4.
1428, with Edmund Kyngston, q.v., compiled a customary for Becket's shrine, which is in BL Add. Ms 59616; see D.H. Turner 'The Customary of the Shrine of St Thomas Becket', *Cant. Cath. Chron.*, no 70 (1976), 16–22.
1445, 4 Mar., d., *Chron. Stone*, 36; in CCA Lit. Ms D.12 fo 25, the date is 10 Mar.

William de VIELSTON [Vialeston, Vieleston, Vielleston, Vyeleston, Vyelstone
occ. 1346 occ. 1374/5

1346, 11 Nov., one of eight prof., *SL*, 181, CCA Lit. Ms D.12, fo 4.
1352, 2 June, ord pr., abp's chapel, Mayfield, Reg. abp Islip, fo 312ᵛ.
1366/8, chaplain to the prior, CCA DCc Barksore acct 49, Godmersham acct 23.
1367, 27 Mar., apptd cellarer, *Reg. abp Langham*, 282–283; 1367/8, cellarer and chaplain to the prior, CCA DCc Ebony acct 63, Barksore acct 50.
1368/70, 1371, warden of manors, CCA DCc Adisham acct 33, Eastry acct 103, MA2, fo 265.
1370, 6 Oct., apptd subprior, Reg. abp Wittlesey, fo 34.
1370/1, 1373/4, subprior, CCA DCc Elverton acct 37, Eastry acct 108.
1348/9, ill and recd 18d., *liberatio* from the anniversarian [for his medical expenses], CCA DCc Anniv. act 3.
1368, visited Godmersham in Apr. and in Sept., CCA DCc Godmersham acct 23.
1369/70, stopped at Godmersham with the monk ordinands on their way to Charing and the sergeant charged 13s. 4d. to his acct, CCA DCc Godmersham acct 25.
1370, 18 July, with Richard Gyllyngham, q.v., sent to the abp for licence to el. a prior, Reg. abp Wittlesey, fo 31ᵛ.
1374, 30 June, 10th in order at the el. of an abp, Reg. G, fos 173ᵛ–175ᵛ.
1374/5, ill and recd a 'pension' of 2s. 6d. from the anniversarian, CCA DCc Anniv. acct 6.

VINCENTIUS
n.d.

n.d., 7 June, pr., whose obit occ. in BL Ms Arundel 68, fo 30.

VITALIS
n.d.

n.d., the obits of two priests by this name occ. in BL Ms Arundel 68: 26 Feb (fo 18), 30 May (fo 29).

VIVIAN
see St Alban's

VODENYSBERG'
see John de Wodnesburgh II

William VOWLE [Foule, Fowghell, Fowle, Veuzll, Voule, Vowel, Wowle
occ. 1454 d. 1501

1454, 28 Apr., one of eight prof., *SL*, 189, CCA Lit. Ms D.12, fo 7ᵛ.
1455, 5 Apr., ord acol. and subdcn, chapel within the priory, *Reg. abp Bourgchier*, 359.
1456, 13 Mar., ord dcn, Canterbury cathedral, *ib.*, 363.
1459, 24 Mar., ord pr., Canterbury cathedral, *ib.*, 372.
1458/9, celebrated his first mass and recd 8d. from the chamberlain, CCA DCc Chamb. acct 62.
1469/71, fourth prior, CCA DCc Sac. acct 48, Caruc. Serg. acct 36.
1473, 28 Apr., *magister ordinis*, *SL*, 190, CCA Lit. Ms D.12, fo 8ᵛ.
1486/8, granator, CCA DCc MA7, fo 61ᵛ.
1466, 17 Feb., 48th in order in an inventory of *jocalia fratrum* [given by him and/or assigned for his use], Reg. N, fo 234.
[1486], one of the monks apptd by the prior, *sed. vac.*, as confessors in the diocese, Reg. N, fo 172.
1493, 1 May, 13th in order at the ratification of an agreement, Reg. S, fo 383ᵛ; but see John Crosse I.
1501, 5 Feb., d., *ex infirmitate ydropici et stranguilitate*, in the 50th yr of monastic life at the age of 68,

CCA Lit. Ms D.12, fo 33; he had a special devotion to the Virgin Mary and himself pd for *omnia edificia* in the Lady chapel in the infirmary, CCA Lit. Ms D.12, fos 28v, 33 (repeated with slight changes). His obit is in BL Ms Arundel 68, fo 15v.

VYEL(L)
see Viel

VYELESTON
see Vielston

VYNCH, le Vynch
see Fynch

I W.
occ. 1198 occ. 1205

1198, after 20 Nov., precentor, *Epist. Cant.*, 458.
1198, after 20 Nov., was with the subprior at [Rome and] Lucca and involved in negotiations, *ib.*
1205, 11 Dec., one of the monks who petitioned the pope to confirm the el. of Reginald, q.v., as abp, *CPL*, i, (1198–1304), 23, 26.

II W.
occ. 1271 occ. 1280/1

1271, cellarer, CCA DCc MA1, fo 115.
1280/1, subprior, CCA DCc, Ickham acct 4.
[1281], 9 Nov., with Henry IV, q.v., bearers of letters between the prior and the abp, *Epist. Pecham*, 245.

III W.
n.d.

n.d., treasurer, whose name heads a list of four volumes in the Eastry catalogue, one of these being Liber de legibus et consuetudines Anglie, James, *Ancient Libraries*, nos 1192–1195 (p. 106).

Note: there may be more or less than three monks referred to in the above three entries.

WACHAN
see Vaughan

Laurence WADE [Vade
occ. 1467 d. 1507

1467, 28 Mar., ord acol., Canterbury cathedral, *Reg. abp Bourgchier*, 399.
1467, 19 Sept., one of six prof., *SL*, 190, CCA Lit. Ms D.12, fo 8.
1468, 12 Mar., ord subdcn, Canterbury cathedral, *Reg. abp Bourgchier*, 398.
1468, 16 Apr., ord dcn, Canterbury cathedral, *ib.*, 400.
1471, 13 Apr., ord pr., Canterbury cathedral, *ib.*, 407.
1507, before 19 Aug., refectorer, CCA Lit. Ms D.12, fo 36.
1493, 1 May, 22nd in order at the ratification of an agreement, Reg. S, fo 383v; but see John Crosse I.
1501, 11th in order at the el. of an abp, Reg. R, fo 56v.
1507, 19 Aug., d., *ex infirmitate ydropici* in his 43rd yr of monastic life and at the age of 60, CCA Lit. Ms D.12, fo 36; at the time of his d. he was *de prima mensa*, *ib.* His obit on 20 Aug. occ. in BL Ms Arundel 68, fo 38v.

Name in Cambridge, Corpus Christi College Ms 298, Vita cum actibus Thome [Becket] Cantuariensis archiepiscopi (early 16th c.); on fo 2 a statement to the effect that this was a translation into English verse by Laurence Wade [in 1497].

WAGHAM
see Vaughan

Thomas WAKERYNG [Wakryng
occ. 1410 d. 1466

1410, 13 Dec., one of eight prof., *SL*, 185, CCA Lit. Ms D.12, fo 6.
1414, 22 Dec., ord dcn, Canterbury cathedral, *Reg. abp Chichele*, iv, 318.
1417, 10 Apr., ord pr., Canterbury cathedral, *ib.*, iv, 328.
1435, 1436/7, *custos* of St Mary in crypt, 'Chron. Wm Glastynbury', 129, CCA DCc, Prior acct 7.
1439/40, fourth prior, Lambeth ED34.
[1440], 30 Nov., absolved from the office of third prior, Chron. Wm Glastynbury ,fo 119v.
1444/5, feretrar, CCA DCc MA4, fo 29v.
1445, 8 Oct., 1446/9, *custos corone*, CCA DCc MA4, fo 29v; Lambeth ED74, CCA DCc MA4, fos 174, 216.
1451/2, *custos* of St Mary in crypt, CCA Lit. Ms E.6, fo 38.
1414, 12 Mar., 76th in order at the el. of an abp, *Reg. abp Chichele*, i, 4.
1452, Easter term, ill and his expenses were 20d., CCA Lit. Ms E.6, fo 64v.
1466, 7 Jan., *stacionarius*, d., he was buried the following day in the cemetery in the teeth of a gale of wind and rain, with only the master of the infirmary present to conduct the interment, *Chron. Stone*, 96 (CCA Lit. Ms D.12, fo 26). His obit occ. on 8 Jan. in BL Ms Arundel 68, fo 12v.

William WALBROK [Walbroke
occ. 1429 d. [1455]

1429, n.d., one of two tonsured, CCA Lit. Ms D.12, fo 7 (*SL*, 187 is confused here).
[1429, summer], ord acol. and subdcn, place not given, Reg. Langdon (Rochester), fo 74.
1430, 23 Dec., ord subdcn [?*recte* dcn], bp's chapel, Trottiscliffe, Reg. Langdon (Rochester), fo 72x.

Note: Langdon's register is in a state of confusion here.
1431, 31 Mar., ord pr., Rochester cathedral, Reg. Langdon (Rochester), fo 69x.
1435, 13 Oct., appted to replace John Hegham, q.v., as chaplain to the subprior, Chron, Wm Glastynbury, fo 117.
1451, 12 Dec., ill and his expenses were 2s. 8d., CCA Lit. Ms E.6, fo 64v.
[1455], *conventualis*, d., CCA Lit. Ms D.12, fo 25v; his obit occ. on 19 June in BL Ms Arundel 68, fo 31v.

Guy de WALDA [Guido, Gwydo, Wido, de Walde, Waldo
occ. 1250 occ. ?1260
n.d., name occ. in the *post exilium* list in *SL*, 173, CCA Lit. Ms D.12, fo 1.
n.d., sacrist, *Gervase Cant.*, 204.
1250, Mar., apptd subprior of Dover, by abp Boniface, Lambeth Ms 241, fo 30v; he succ. Walter de Cantuaria, q.v., under Walter V.
c. 1253/60, prior of Dover, apptd 16 Feb. 1253/4 Lambeth Ms 241, fo 31; res. 7 Apr. 1260, *ib.*, fo 33v. He possibly returned to Canterbury.
Note: see also Guido I.

WALER, Walerico
see St Valerico

WALEYNS
see Valoyns

I Ralph WALLER [Wallar, Wallare
occ. 1446 d. 1449
1446, 21 Dec., one of seven tonsured, *SL*, 188, CCA Lit. Ms D.12, fo 7v.
1447, 4 Mar., ord acol., Canterbury cathedral, Reg. abp Stafford, fo 199.
1447, 27 Aug., made his prof. with the other six in the presence of the abp, *Chron. Stone*, 41–42.
1447, 23 Dec., ord subdcn, Canterbury cathedral, Reg. abp Stafford, fo 201v.
1448, 17 Feb., ord dcn, Canterbury cathedral, *ib.*, fo 202.
1449, 29 Jan., d., *Chron. Stone*, 45. According to CCA Lit. Ms D.12, fo 25v, he had been marshal of the hall of Queen Catherine [of Valois] and then marshal of the prior's hall in Canterbury before joining the community *cum magna devotione*; his d. was caused by an illness unknown to the doctors.

II Ralph WALLER [Wallar
occ. 1481 d. [1488 × 1492]
1481, 21 Dec., one of four prof., *SL*, 191, CCA Lit. Ms D.12, fo 8v.
1483, 29 Mar., ord subdcn, Canterbury cathedral, *Reg. abp Bourgchier*, 439.
1484, 17 Apr., ord dcn, Canterbury cathedral, *ib.*, 444 (as Richard).
1488/9, celebrated his first mass and recd a small gift from the sacrist, CCA DCc Sac. accts 58, 68.
[1488 × 1492], *conventualis*, d., CCA Lit. Ms D.12, fos 27 and 31v (repeated); his obit occ. on 18 July in BL Ms Arundel 68, fo 35.

I WALTER [Gauterus, Gualterus
occ. [1150 × 1152]
[1150 × 1152], *temp.* prior Walter [de Meri], q.v., chaplain to the abp, *Theobald Charters*, no 310; see Felix and Miles Crispin.
[1150 × 1152], attested a grant of tithes made by the abp, *ib.*

II WALTER
occ. [1193 × 1205]
[1193, Nov. × 1195, Apr. or 1198, Feb. × 1205, July], with Simon III, q.v., witnessed a grant of abp Hubert Walter, *Eng. Epis. Acta*, ii, no 399.
1205, 11 Dec., one of the monks who appealed to the pope to confirm the chapter's el. of their subprior, Reginald, q.v., as abp, *CPL*, i (1198–1304), 23, 26.
Note: a Walter occ. c. 1180 in a rental of the city of Canterbury, Urry, *Canterbury*, 155 (CCA DCc X.2, fo 4).

III WALTER [Gauterius
occ. c. 1213 d. 1222
1213–1222, prior: prob. el. by the monks, recd temporalities 1 June 1213; d. 1222, *Fasti*, ii, 11, *HRH*, 34.
1220, was granted an indult from the pope to use ring and mitre, Woodruff, *Memorials Cant.*, 267 with no other ref.
n.d., 6 Feb., obit occ. in BL Ms Arundel 68, fo 15v.
Item no 984 in the Eastry catalogue, Biblia, cum interpretacionibus hebraicorum nominum, is listed as having belonged to W. Gauterius prior, James *Ancient Libraries*, 96.
Note: his earlier career may be contained in Walter II.

IV WALTER
occ. 1227
1227, 7 Feb., named, with William VI, q.v., proctor in the dispute with the chapter of Rochester over procedure in the el. of a bp of Rochester, *Langton Acta*, no 100.
Note: Walter II may be identical with Walter IV, but see the note under Walter III.

V WALTER [de Cantuaria
occ. before 1250

1250, Mar., subprior of Dover, suspended by the abp, Lambeth Ms 241, fo 30v; see Guy de Walda.

VI WALTER
occ. 1456/7

1456/7, one of the *barones* of the exchequer, CCA DCc, Prior acct 15.

Note: this is prob. Walter Hartforde I, q.v.

WALTER
see also Ba, Chillenden, Durdent, Gloucestre, Meri

Note: the obits of a number of Walters occ. in BL Ms Arundel 68, e.g.: 29 Mar. (fo 22v), 3 Apr. (fo 23), 25 Apr. (fo 24v), and Walter, *conversus*, 3 Nov. (fo 47).

I John WALTHAM B.Th. [Wautham
occ. 1419 d. 1471

1419, 25 Jan., one of four prof., *SL*, 186, CCA Lit. Ms D.12, fo 6v.
1419, 15 Apr., ord acol., chapel within priory, *Reg. abp Chichele*, i, 192.
1420, 6 Apr., ord subdcn, Canterbury cathedral, *ib.*, iv, 341.
1427, 5 Dec., ord pr., bp's chapel, Trottiscliffe, Reg. Langdon (Rochester), fo 59v, by *lit. dim.*

1438/41, warden of Canterbury college; he was apptd soon after 23 Aug. 1438, Pantin, *Cant. Coll. Ox.*, iii, 95; his accts for 1439/41 survive and are transcribed in Pantin, *ib.*, ii, 154–162 (CCA DCc Cart. Antiq. O.151.10, 11).
1443/4, warden of manors, CCA DCc MA 140.
1444, 6 Nov., apptd penitentiary for Christ Church, Reg. abp Stafford, fo 17.
1453/4, 1455/7, *custos corone*, CCA DCc Prior accts 9, 10, 15.
1458, 16 July, sacrist, CCA DCc BB62/4, ES Roll 327.

1432, prob. at Oxford by this date, Pantin, *Cant. Coll. Ox.*, iii, 87, 91.
1436, Mar./Sept., student at Canterbury college, Pantin, *ib.*, ii, 147 (CCA DCc Cart. Antiq. O.151.8).
1452, 30 May, by this date, B.Th., *Chron. Stone*, 54.

[1419 × 1428], excommunicated by prior John Wodnesburgh, q.v., for being disobedient and rebellious, Reg. N, fo 213v.
1438, c. Feb., sent as proctor to inform the abp of the d. of William Molassh, prior, q.v., Reg. S, fo 129.
1452, 30 May, with Walter Hertforde, q.v., sent to the king for licence to el. an abp, *Chron. Stone*, 54.
1452, 23 Dec., promoted *ad primam mensam*, *ib.*, 56.
1454, 23 Apr., after the chapter's el. of Thomas Bourgchier as abp he preached in the choir on the text, 'Gaudium vestrum impleatur' (John 16, 24), *ib.*, 60; the following day he and William Wynchepe, q.v. were sent to inform the king and the elect, *ib.*, 60.
1466, 17 Feb., 10th in order in an inventory of *jocalia fratrum* [given by him and/or assigned for his use], Reg. N, fo 230v.
1471, 19 Aug., d., *Chron. Stone*, 117; CCA Lit. Ms D.12, ref. to him as *stacionarius* at the time of d., fo 26. His obit is in BL Ms Arundel 68, fo 38v.

An inventory of Canterbury college, Oxford, dated 1459, includes 'commentator Averoys super libros celi et mundi et de anima' given by him, Pantin, *Cant. Coll. Ox.*, i, 15.

William Glastynbury q.v., corresponded with him while he was at Oxford and preserved in his notebook a letter he had recd from Waltham dated 15 Dec. [1432] reminding him of their holiday at Dover priory with the prior, [John Coumbe, q.v.], Pantin, *Cant. Coll. Ox.*, iii, 90 (Chron. Wm Glastynbury, fo 185). His name is also mentioned in other letters written by Glastynbury in this notebook to John Wodnesburgh III, warden of the college, q.v., Pantin, *ib.*, iii, 91, 93.

II John WALTHAM B.Th.
occ. 1483 d. 1525

1483, 30 Sept., one of six tonsured, *SL*, 191, CCA Lit. Ms D.12, fo 8v.
1484, 10 June, prof., *ib.*
1493, 6 Apr., ord pr., Canterbury cathedral, *Reg. abp Morton*, i, no 442d.

1501, 1503, 1504, one of the chancellors, Reg. T, fos 411, 415, 415v, 442, 443, also the *libellus* at the end of Reg. E, fo 1 (*Hist. Mss Comm. 8th Report*, Appndx, 331).
1511, 10 Sept., 1516/18, granator, Wood-Legh, *Visit.*, 5, CCA DCc MA14, fos 8v, 61v.
1519, 9 May; 1520, 7 May, 26 Oct; 1521, 1522, 1523, 1524, 1525, all on 25 Mar., warden of manors, CCA DCc MA117; MA13, fos 15v, 2; CCA Lit. Ms C.11, fos 61, 61v, 62, 63, 63v.

[1490], student at Canterbury college, Oxford, Pantin, *Cant. Coll. Ox.*, ii, 270 (CCA DCc Cart. Antiq. O.151.8).
1492/3, at Canterbury college for half the yr, Pantin, *ib.*, iv, 202.
[1493], student, Pantin, *ib.*, ii, 274 (CCA DCc Cart. Antiq. O.151.8).
1495, 8 Feb., one of six scholars at Canterbury college from whom letters of proxy were obtained at the time of the el. of a prior, Pantin, *ib.*, iv, 203.
1496, Mar./Sept., student with a pension of £4, Pantin, *ib.*, ii, 224 (CCA DCc Cart. Antiq. 0.151.29).

1498, travelled from Oxford to Canterbury in [preparation for] Lent [*erga xl^m*], Pantin *ib.*, iv, 205.
1498/1501, student with a pension of £8 p.a., Pantin, *ib.*, ii, 226, 229, 232 (CCA DCc Cart. Antiq. O.151.30, 31, 32).
n.d., B.Th., see below.
1501, 26 Apr., apparently absent from the el. of an abp although he travelled back and forth in 1500/1 between Canterbury and Oxford, Pantin, *ib.*, iv, 205.
1511, 2 Sept., 15th in order on the visitation certificate, Wood-Legh, *Visit.*, 3 (Reg. abp Warham i, fo 35); on 10 Sept. he was one of six obedientiaries who, with the prior were apptd to oversee corrections in the priory after the abp's visitation, Wood-Legh, *Visit.*, 5.
1524/5, d., Woodruff, 'Sacrist's Rolls', 71; the obit of a John Waltham, B.Th. occ. on 30 June in BL Ms Arundel 68, fo 32.

Name in BL Ms Arundel 155, Psalterium (early 11th c.), given to him by William Hadlegh II, q.v; name on fo 1^v^.

He joined with Roger Benet and John Henfeld, q.v. in giving eight silver spoons to Canterbury college before or in 1501, Pantin, *Cant. Coll. Ox.*, i, 37.

III John WALTHAM
occ. 1527 occ. 1538

1527, 25 May, one of twelve tonsured, *SL*, 195, CCA Lit. Ms D.12, fo 12.
1528, 2 Mar., prof., *ib.*
1534, 12 Dec., prob. student at Canterbury college acc. to Pantin, as his name was not among those who acknowledged the Act of Supremacy, *Cant. Coll. Ox.*, iv, 216, 227; see below.
1537, Jan., wrote to Thomas Cranmer naming the brethren who were continuing to include the popes in the reading of the martiloge, *L and P Henry VIII*, xii pt. 1, no 256; see Stephen Gylys.
[1538, 8 Feb., after], in a list of monks prob. prepared for Thomas Cromwell, he was reported as 'nowe being at Parrys' and as witty and 28 yrs old, Pantin, *Cant. Coll. Ox.*, iii, 153; see also Thomas Wylfrid.

Geoffrey WALTON [Waltune
occ. [c. 1255]

[c. 1255], n.d., one of five prof., *SL*, 176, CCA Lit. Ms D.12, fo 2^v^.
n.d., 13 July, obit occ. in BL Ms Arundel 68, fo 34.

An inventory of missing service books dated 1 Mar. 1338 ref. to the loss of his diurnale by William de Coventre, q.v., *Lit. Cant.*, no 618 (Reg. L, fo 104).

John WARHAM B.Th. [Warrhame, *alias* Millys
occ. 1524 occ. 1540

1524, 21/22 July, one of eleven granted adm. [*ingressum*] to Christ Church, CCA Lit. Ms D.12, fos 11^v^–12.
1524, 4 Aug., one of eleven tonsured, *SL*, 195, CCA Lit. Ms D.12, fo 11^v^.
1525, 19 Apr., prof., *ib.*
1534, 12 Dec., name not included among the signatories of the Act of Supremacy, prob. because he was at Oxford, Pantin, *Cant. Coll. Ox.*, iv, 216, 227.
1537, Nov., supplicated for B.Th., after twelve yrs' study of logic, philosophy and theology; on 16 Jan. 1538 he was adm. *ad opponendum* and on 8 Feb., *ad lectionem libri sententiarum*, Pantin, *ib.*, iii, 261–262.
[1538, 8 Feb., after], in a list of monks, prob. drawn up for Thomas Cromwell, he was described as 'witty' and 30 yrs of age, Pantin, *ib.*, iii, 153.
1540, 4 Apr., apptd prebendary in the new foundation, *L and P Henry VIII*, xv, no 452; the following yr he was named canon of the 10th prebend, *Fasti 1541–1857*, iii, 34.

In an inventory of Canterbury college dated 1534 there is ref. to a missing silver gilt chalice of his which he had lost or sold, Pantin, *Cant. Coll. Ox.*, i, 76.

M. WARIN [Warinus
occ. 1174 d. 1180

1174, cellarer, *HRH*, 88.
1174, apptd prior of Dover, *ib.*
1180, 21 Sept., d., *ib.*; his obit is in BL Ms Arundel 68, fo 42^v^.

The late 12th c. catalogue lists a volume of Priscianus magnus in asseribus, prob. formerly his, James, *Ancient Libraries*, no 4 (p. 7); and in the Eastry catalogue there are five volumes, including Sententie Longobardi, *ib.*, nos 1206–1210 (p. 106–107).

WARNER [Guarnerius, Warnerus
occ. [1105 × 1106] occ. 1125

[1105 × 1106], novice, who wrote to Anselm and recd a grateful and encouraging reply, *Anselm Letters*, no 375. See note below.
1114, one of the monks who was sent to the curia to obtain the pallium for abp Ralph d'Escures, Eadmer, *Hist. Nov.*, 226.
[1116 × 1118], the pope asked the abp to allow him to remain with him for a time, *ib.*, 246.
n.d., witnessed three deeds *temp.* bp Ernulf of Rochester, *Text. Roff*, fo 191^v^ and cap 163, fo 197 and cap 178, fo 199^v^ and cap 183, the first and last with Alban, q.v.
1125, 8 Mar., el. abbot of Battle; in 1138 he retired to Lewes priory, *HRH*, 29.

n.d., 23 Sept., his obit occ. in BL Ms Arundel 68, fo 42^{v}.

Note: this is prob. the monk Warnerus to whom Anselm wrote a letter of encouragement and advice *Anselm Letters*, no 335. See Lanzo.

John WASSHE
occ. 1370/1

1370/1, chaplain to the prior, CCA DCc, Arrears acct 66.

Note: this monk prob. appears elsewhere under his toponymic.

Richard WATYRDOWNE [Waterdon, Watyrdon
occ. 1459 d. 1484

1459, 30 Nov., one of six prof., *SL*, 189, CCA Lit. Ms D.12, fo 8.
1461, 4 Apr., ord dcn, Canterbury cathedral, *Reg. abp Bourgchier*, 378.
1462, 17 Apr., ord pr., Canterbury cathedral, *ib.*, 382.
1466, 17 Feb., 62nd in order in an inventory of *jocalia fratrum* [given by him and/or assigned for his use], but he had none, Reg. N, fo 234^{v}.
1484, 2 Nov., d., CCA Lit. Ms D.12, fo 26^{v}; his obit on 3 Nov. is in BL Ms Arundel 68, fo 47.

WAUTHAM
see Waltham

William de WAYE
occ. [c. 1281]

[c. 1281], one of four prof., *SL*, 176, CCA Lit. Ms D.12, fo 3.

WAYLOYNS
see Valoyns

Adam de WELL [Welles
occ. 1251/2 occ. 1258/9

1251/3, 1257/9, granator, CCA DCc AS7, Reg.H, fos 173^{v}, 177, 192, 197^{v}.

Note: this may be Adam Blasyng' or Adam Ferr', q.v.

I John de WELL [Welles
occ. [mid 1260s] d. 1310

[mid. 1260s], one of seven prof., *SL*, 176, CCA Lit. Ms D.12, fo 2^{v}.

1276/7, 1278, 1279, 1280, 1281, 1282, 1284, 1286, 1287, 1288, treasurer, Reg. H, fo 216, CCA DCc MA1, fos 127, 129^{v}, 131, 134, Treas. acct 1, MA1, fos 141^{v}–152 (1284/8), Treas. accts 2, 3. He was third treasurer with John de Begbroke and prior Henry Eastry, q.v., in 1282 (Treas. acct 1) and second treasurer with Randulph, q.v. in 1286 and 1287 (Treas. accts 2, 3); see note below.
1289/93, 1295/9, 1300/5, cellarer, CCA DCc MA1, fos 158^{v}–185, 194–222, 225–257^{v}. On 12 Apr. 1295 he was apptd to this office, *Reg. abp Winchelsey*, 18–19, absolved on 15 Nov. 1303 and reapptd on 23 Nov. 1303 after the visitation, *ib.*, 1305 (Reg. Q, fo 30^{v}/42^{v}).
1304, 25 Nov., subprior, removed from this office at the abp's command because of infirmity, Reg. Q, *ib.*

Note: he is named as treasurer at Winchelsey's el. on 13 Feb. 1293, and also on 14 Oct. 1294, *Reg. abp Winchelsey*, 1265, 5.

[1285], 5 Jan., one of several imprisoned by royal officers for whose release into his hands the abp now gave orders, *Epist. Pecham*, 876–877.
1293, 13 Feb., named as one of seven *compromissorii* in the el. of an abp, *Reg. abp Winchelsey*, 1265 (Reg. Q, fo 31^{v}).
1293, 23 Mar., with Robert de Elham, q.v. apptd general proctors with regard to the el. of abp Winchelsey, CUL Ms Ee.5.31, fos 42^{v}, 43.
1294, 14 Oct., one of the monks present in Siena when abp Winchelsey made an apptment to the see of Llandaff, *Reg. abp Winchelsey*, 5–6.
1299, 7 Dec., the abp wrote to the prior with regard to his perseverance *in sua vocacione pristina*, CCA DCc EC V/5.
1310, 17 Jan., d., CCA Lit. Ms D.12, fo 15^{v}; his obit on 18 Jan. occ. in BL Ms Arundel, fo 13^{v}.

The Eastry catalogue contains eight volumes under his name including Constituciones Octonis, Octoboni and Bonifacii archiepiscopi, a copy of the Rule and a Collectarium de iure canonico et civile', James, *Ancient Libraries*, nos 1627–1634 (pp.134–135).

An inventory of vestments, *temp.* prior Eastry, includes three linen albs, formerly his, one of which was embroidered with the heads of kings and bps, Legg and Hope, *Inventories*, 59 (BL Ms Cotton Galba, E.iv, fo 115).

An inventory of the refectory, dated 1328, includes three silver *ciphi* formerly his, and two *de murra*, Dart, *Antiq. Cant.*, xx, xxii, (BL Ms Cotton Galba E.iv, fo 179–179^{v}).

II John WELL [Welle
occ. 1367 occ. 1381

1367, 11 Nov., one of nine prof., *SL*, 182, CCA Lit. Ms D.12, fo 4^{v}.
1368, 4 Mar., ord acol., Canterbury cathedral, *Reg. abp Langham*, 387.
1369, 22 Dec., ord subdcn, Charing, Reg. abp Wittlesey, fo 165^{v}.
1370, 21 Sept., ord dcn, Saltwood, *ib.*, fo 166^{v}.
1371, 31 May, ord pr., abp's chapel, Charing, *ib.*, fo 167.
1374, 30 June, 50th in order at the el. of an abp, Reg. G, fos 173^{v}–175^{v}.

1374/5, ill [in the infirmary] and the anniversarian pd a 'pension' of 15s. 6d. [for his medical expenses], CCA DCc Anniv. acct 6.
1377, recd a small sum [*pro benedictione*] from the prior, Lambeth Ms 243, fo 176.
1381, 31 July, 38th at the el. of an abp, Reg. G, fo 225v.

Thomas WELL [Welle, Wellys
occ. 1413 d. 1471

1413, 6 Oct., one of six tonsured, *SL*, 186, CCA Lit. Ms D.12, fo 6. That this date ref. to tonsure rather than prof. is shown by the fact that none of the six took part in the el. of abp Chichele on 12 Mar. 1414, *Reg. abp Chichele*, i, 4.
1414, 22 Dec., ord acol. and subdcn, Canterbury cathedral, *ib.*, iv, 317.
1416, 18 Apr., ord dcn, Canterbury cathedral, *ib.*, iv, 320.
1418, 21 May, ord pr., bp's chapel, Halling, Reg. Yonge (Rochester), fo 5v.
1435, 1436/7, subsacrist, 'Chron. Wm Glastynbury', 129, CCA DCc, Prior acct 7.
1436/7, feretrar, CCA DCc, Prior acct 7.
[1440, 8 Feb.], dismissed from the office of treasurer, Chron. Wm Glastynbury, fo 119.
1441/2, third prior, CCA DCc, Sac. acct 29.
1446/9, 1450, Jan., treasurer, CCA DCc Treas. acct 15, Lambeth, ED 82, CCA DCc DE 15C/8.
1456/7, 1460/1, anniversarian, CCA DCc Prior acct 15, Anniv. acct 12.
1452, 24 June, ill and his expenses were 6s. 8d., CCA Lit. Ms E.6, fo 64v.
1455/7, one of the eight *barones*, CCA DCc Prior accts 10, 15.
1466, 17 Feb., 4th in order in an inventory of *jocalia fratrum* [given by him and/or assigned for his use], Reg. N, fo 230.
1468, 1 Sept., as one of the most senior monks he stood beside John de Oxney II, q.v. at his *prefectio* by the abp as prior, *Chron. Stone*, 106.
1471, *stacionarius*, d., CCA Lit. Ms D.12, fo 26; the obit on 22 Apr. is in BL Ms Arundel 68, fo 24v, the day of his d. acc. to *Chron. Stone*, 115.

William de WELL [Welles
occ. 1330 d. 1361

1330, 9 Oct., one of six prof., *SL*, 180, CCA Lit. Ms D.12, fo 3v.
1346/8, precentor, CCA DCc Godmersham accts 19, 20.
1338, 1 Mar., reported in an inventory of missing service books to have lost the Ordinale, formerly used by John de Bocton, q.v., *Lit. Cant.*, no 618 (Reg. L, fo 104).
1348, 30 Aug., named by three initial *compromissorii* to be one of seven *compromissorii* in the el. of an abp, Reg. G, fos 30v, 82.
1349, 4 June, 27th in order at the el. of an abp and chosen as one of thirteen *compromissorii*, Reg. G, fos 60v, 61v.
1349, 8/9 Sept., 26th at the el. of an abp, *ib.*, fo 76.
1361, 12 Sept., d., one of c. 25 monks carried off [by the plague] between June and Oct., CCA Lit. Ms D.12, fo 17.

WENCHEPE
see Wynchepe

Nicholas de WENDLESTONE
occ. 1305/6

1305/6, bartoner, CCA DCc, Arrears acct 46.

William WENDEVERE [Wendover, Wendovere, Wendovyr
occ. 1403 d. 1416

1403, 22 Dec., one of six prof., *SL*, 185, CCA Lit. Ms D.12, fo 5v.
1404, 29 Mar., ord acol., Canterbury cathedral, Reg. abp Arundel, i, fo 332v.
1405, 18 Apr., ord subdcn, Canterbury cathedral, *ib.*, i, fo 333v.
1407, 26 Mar., ord dcn, Canterbury cathedral, *ib.*, i, fo 340v.
1416, 24 Oct., d. in the twelfth yr of monastic life, after [he] *devote sumpsit omnia sacramenta ecclesie*, *Chron. Stone*, 8, CCA Lit. Ms D.12, fo 21. His obit is in BL Ms Arundel 68, fo 46.

WENTON
see Wynton

William de WERNESELL [Wormesell, Wornesell
occ. 1329 d. 1354

1329, 9 Oct., one of eight prof., *SL*, 179, CCA Lit. Ms D.12, fo 3v.
1344/5, chaplain to the prior, CCA DCc Lalling acct 10.
1348/9, June, warden of manors, CCA DCc Bocking acct 30.
1350/1, 1352/3, cellarer, CCA DCc Treas. acct 27, fo 3, Ebony acct 53; he was ordered to be removed on 18 Jan. 1353, Reg. abp Islip, fo 75v.
1352, before 17 June, granator, CCA DCc Gran. acct 35.
1352/5, warden of manors, CCA DCc Appledore accts 41, 42, Ebony acct 54.
1349, 4 June, 24th in order at the el. of an abp, Reg. G, fo 60v.
1349, 8/9 Sept., 23rd at the el. of an abp and chosen as one of the thirteen *compromissorii*, *ib.*, fos 76, 77.
1354, 30 Aug., d., CCA Lit. Ms D.12, fo 16v.

William de WERTON [?Wenton
occ. 1221

n.d., name occ. in the *post exilium* list in *SL*, 173, CCA Lit. Ms D.12, fo 1.

1221, responsible for the purchase and delivery of wine, *Hist. Mss Comm. 5th Report*, Appndx, 441 (CCA DCc Cart. Antiq. C.165).

John WEST [Weste
occ. 1413 occ. 1433/4

1413, 6 Oct., one of six prof., *SL*, 186, CCA Lit. Ms D.12, fo 6.
1414, 22 Dec., ord acol. and subdcn, Canterbury cathedral, *Reg. abp Chichele*, iv, 317.
1417, 10 Apr., ord dcn, Canterbury cathedral, *ib.*, iv, 327.
1419, 1 Apr., ord pr., chapel within the priory, *ib.*, i, 192.
1433/4, 3 Feb. (St Agatha), granted licence by the prior and chapter with the abp's approval, to join the Augustinian hermits of Canterbury; he is in the list of Wm Glastynbury, q.v., among those who were *expulsi*, Chron. Wm Glastynbury, fo 168ᵛ/162ᵛ.

Edmund WESTGATE
occ. 1364

1364, n.d., one of eleven prof., *SL*, 182, CCA Lit. Ms D.12, fo 4ᵛ.

I John de WESTGATE
occ. 1263 d. [1287]

n.d,. name occ. in the list in *SL*, 174, CCA Lit. Ms D.12, fo 2.
1263, 18 July, subprior, at the time of the agreement made concerning the monks' observance of abp Boniface's anniversary after his d., BL Ms Arundel 68, fo 35.
[c. 1287], 9 Sept., d., CCA Lit. Ms D.12, fo 16.

II John de WESTGATE
occ. [1281/2] occ. 1285

[1281/2], n.d., one of five prof., *SL*, 177, CCA Lit. Ms D.12, fo 3.
1285, 22 Sept., ord pr., collegiate church of South Malling, *Reg. abp Pecham*, i, 222.

III John WESTGATE
occ. 1303 d. 1325

1303, 29 May, one of two prof., *SL*, 178, CCA Lit. Ms D.12, fo 3ᵛ.
1305, 12 June, ord dcn, Smeeth chapel by Aldington, *Reg. abp Winchelsey*, 977.
1324, n.d., apptd third chancellor, the first time a third chancellor had been named, CUL Ms Ee.5.31, fo 234ᵛ.
1325, 14 Sept., d., CCA Lit. Ms D.12, fo 16.
1325, 19 Oct., an inquiry into the misdeeds of Robert Aldon, q.v., revealed that Westgate had been instructed by Aldon to copy several documents which were thus incorporated into what became known as the *littera famosa*, *Lit. Cant.*, no 156 (Reg. L, fo 142).

Three sets of vestments, acquired *temp.* prior Eastry, are listed under this name in an inventory in Legg and Hope, *Inventories*, 65–66 (BL Ms Cotton Galba, E.iv, fo 117).

IV John de WESTGATE
occ. 1401 d. 1406

1401, 19 Mar., ord acol., Canterbury cathedral, Reg. abp Arundel, i, fo 327ᵛ.
1401, 25 Mar., one of seven prof., *SL*, 185, CCA Lit. Ms D.12, fo 5ᵛ.
1401, 17 Dec., ord subdcn, Canterbury cathedral, Reg. abp Arundel, i, fo 329.
1403, 14 Apr., ord dcn, Canterbury cathedral, *ib.*, fo 331.
1405, 18 Apr., ord pr., Canterbury cathedral, *ib.*, fo 334.
1406, 8 June, d., CCA Lit. Ms D.12, fo 18.

V John de WESTGATE
occ. 1414/15 d. 1439

1414/15, one of five adm., *SL*, 186, CCA Lit. Ms D.12, fo 6; see next item below.
1415, 10 Nov., the prior was comm. to rec. his prof., *Reg. abp Chichele*, iv, 142.
1416, 18 Apr., ord acol. and subdcn, Canterbury cathedral, *ib.*, iv, 319.
1417, 10 Apr., ord dcn, Canterbury cathedral, *ib.*, iv, 327.
1418, 21 May, ord pr., bp's chapel, Halling, Reg. Yonge (Rochester), fo 5ᵛ.
1436/7, second anniversarian, CCA DCc Anniv. acct 8; he was anniversarian at the time of his d., CCA Lit. Ms D.12, fo 24.
1439, 24 June, d., *Chron. Stone*, 22; his obit is in BL Ms Arundel 68, fo 31ᵛ.

Nicholas WESTGATE
occ. 1416 occ. 1423

1416, 22 June, one of eight prof., *SL*, 186, CCA Lit. Ms D.12, fo 6.
1417, 10 Apr., ord acol., Canterbury cathedral, *Reg. abp Chichele*, iv, 327.
1418, 26 Mar., ord subdcn, Canterbury cathedral, *ib.*, iv, 332.
1419, 1 Apr., ord dcn, chapel within the priory, *ib.*, i, 191.
1420, 6 Apr., ord pr., Canterbury cathedral, *ib.*, iv, 342.
1423, 6 Apr., provided with a licence by the abp to transfer to Totnes priory, 'quibus de causis melius est sub silencio preterire', CCA Lit. Ms D.12, fo 6; see Henry Newynden and Stephen Tygh. The licence is in *Reg. abp Chichele*, iv, 247, but undated; the date is in Reg. S, fo 88ᵛ.

Ralph de WESTGATE
occ. 1238/9

n.d., name at the head of the *post exilium* list of monks, *SL*, 172, CCA Lit. Ms D.12, fo 1.

1238, subprior, *Gervase Cant.*, ii, 133; see John de Chatham.

1238, with Richard Dygon and William de Dover II, q.v., went to the curia as a result of the forgery crisis and the difficulties with the abp, *Gervase Cant.*, ii, 133.

1239, after 2 Mar., wrote from Rome to tell the monks of the audience with the pope and of the progress of their appeal, *ib.*, ii, 183–185. He and his companions must have been absent from the el. of Roger de La Lee, q.v., as prior on 7 Jan.; but at the time of writing this letter he had recd the news and he now gave his approval, *ib.*

An inventory of vestments, *temp.* prior Eastry, includes two copes of red samite of his [?gift] embroidered with gryphons, Legg and Hope, *Inventories*, 53 (BL Ms Cotton Galba, E.iv, fo 112^{v}).

Thomas de WESTGATE
occ. 1st half 13th c.

n.d., name occ. in the *post exilium* list of monks, *SL*, 173, CCA Lit. Ms D.12, fo 1.

An inventory of the refectory dated 1328 includes a *ciphus de murra*, formerly his, Dart, *Antiq. Cant.*, xxii (BL Ms Cotton Galba E.iv, fo 180).

Ralph de WESTHEDE
occ. 2nd half 13th c.

n.d., name occ. in the list in *SL*, 175, CCA Lit. Ms D.12, fo 2^{v}.

WESTMANNUS [?William Westmannus, Westmennius
n.d.

n.d., 31 Mar., obit occ. in BL Ms Arundel 68, fo 22^{v}. Since his name precedes Salomon I, q.v., on this day he is presumably pre-exile. As Westmennius the obit occ. on the same day in BL Ms Cotton Nero C.ix, fo 8^{v}.

John de WESTON
occ. 1287 d. 1329

1287, 16 Mar., one of five prof., *SL*, 177, CCA Lit. Ms D.12, fo 3.

1324/5, sacrist, CCA DCc MA2, fos 138–146; he was apptd on 23 May 1324, *Lit. Cant.*, no 122 (Reg. L, fo 136).

[1296], included among the junior monks accused at the visitation of being lax in attendance at divine office, and in the performance of other monastic duties, *Reg. abp Winchelsey*, 92.

1315, 30 Dec., with William de Ledebury, q.v., apptd proctor to attend parliament, *Parl. Writs*, ii, pt 3, 1084 (CUL Ms Ee.5.31, fo 162).

1329, 1 Nov., d., CCA Lit. Ms D.12, fo 16.

An inventory of the refectory, dated 1328, includes a silver *olla* for water, formerly his or his gift, BL Ms Cotton Galba E.iv, fo 178).

I John WESTWELL
occ. 1374 occ. 1383/4

1374, 27 Apr., novice, whom the prior was comm. to prof., Reg. abp Wittlesey, fo 130^{v}; in SL 183 and CCA Lit. Ms D.12, fo 4^{v} there are eight grouped together with no date.

1381, 31 July, 51st in order at the el. of an abp, Reg. G, fo 225^{v}.

1383/4, recd a small sum from the prior *pro benedictione*, Lambeth Ms 243, fo 192^{v}.

II John WESTWELL
occ. 1443 d. 1464

1443, 25 Mar., one of six prof., *SL*, 188, CCA Lit. Ms D.12, fo 7^{v}.

1444, 11 Apr., ord subdcn, Canterbury cathedral, Reg. abp Stafford, fo 196^{v}.

1445, 27 Mar., ord dcn, Canterbury cathedral, *ib.*, fo 198^{v}.

1447, 23 Dec., ord pr., Canterbury cathedral, *ib.*, fo 201^{v}.

1464, before 16 Jan., *custos* of St Mary in crypt, *Chron. Stone*, 89.

1452, 14 Mar., ill and his expenses were 3s., CCA Lit. Ms E.6, fo 64^{v}.

1464, 16 Jan., d., *Chron. Stone*, 89, CCA Lit. Ms D.12, fo 26; his obit occ. on 18 Jan. in BL Ms Arundel 68, fo 13^{v}.

Richard WESTWELL
occ. 1382 occ. 1390/1

1382, 5 Sept., one of six clothed in the monastic habit, *SL*, 183, CCA Lit. Ms D.12, fo 5.

1383, 11 Aug., the prior was comm. to rec. his prof., Reg. abp Courtenay, i, fo 42^{v}.

1387, 6 Apr., ord pr., Canterbury cathedral, *ib.*, i, fo 309^{v}.

1388/9, 1390/1, recd small sums from the prior [*pro benedictione*], Lambeth Ms 243, fos 212^{v}, 220^{v}.

William WESTWELL
occ. 1410 d. 1413

1410, 13 Dec., one of eight prof., *SL*, 185, CCA Lit. Ms D.12, fo 6.

1413, 2 Apr., ord subdcn, Canterbury cathedral, Reg. abp Arundel, ii, fo 101.

1413, 10 Nov., subdcn and *ultimus professus*, d. of the plague [*pestilencia*], CCA Lit. Ms D.12, fo 20.

WESYNDEN
see Wysynden

WEYLFRYD
see Wylfryde

WEYNCHEPE
see Richard de Wynchepe

I James WHYTE [Hwyte, le Hwyte
occ. [1336] occ. 1354

[1336], one of seven adm., *SL*, 180 and CCA Lit. Ms D.12, fo 4 are inaccurate; on 19 Dec. [1336] he was one of the five novices among the seven about whom the prior wrote to the bp to allow them to be prof. before their yr of probation was completed; the abp replied no, *Lit. Cant.*, no 621 (Reg. L, fo 67ᵛ).

1349, 4 June, 41st in order at the el. of an abp, Reg. G, fo 60ᵛ.

1349, 8/9 Sept., 40th at the el. of an abp, *ib.*, fo 76ᵛ.

1354, Aug., recd permission to transfer to the Cistercian monastery at Robertsbridge, *Lit. Cant.*, nos 805, 806, 808 (Reg. L, fos 59ᵛ, 60, 87, 87ᵛ); but see the entry below.

II James WHYTE [Hwyte
occ. 1369/70 occ. 1372/3

1369/70, 1371, chaplain to the prior, CCA DCc Godmersham acct 25, MA2, fo 266ᵛ.

1370, Mar./Sept., 1371/3, sacrist, CCA DCc Sac. acct 5, MA2, fos 266ᵛ–276ᵛ.

Note: is this James Whyte I returned from Robertsbridge or is it James Hegham, q.v.?

I WIBERT [Guibertus, Wybertus
occ. 1146 d. 1167

c. 1152–1167, prior: prob. apptd c.Sept. 1152 on the abp's return from exile but his first certain occurrence as prior is 28 Mar. 1155; d. 27 Sept. 1167, *Fasti*, ii, 10.

1148, 1152, subprior, *HRH*, 34; in 1152 he was acting as prior, presumably after the deposition of Walter de Meri, q.v.; see *Gervase Cant.*, i, 48, 146.

1146, soon after 19 Apr., with prior Walter [de Meri], q.v. attested an archiepiscopal deed, *Theobald Charters*, 538.

1162, May, went with the senior monks to London to discuss with the king and the bps the el. of an abp, *Gervase Cant.*, i, 170, *Fasti*, ii, 4.

1167, 27 Sept., d., and was buried in the chapter house, Cambridge, Corpus Christi College, Ms 298, fo 115; his obit is in BL Ms Arundel 68, fo 43.

One volume in the Eastry catalogue, Psalterium glos., secundum Longobardum, is described as his, James, *Ancient Libraries*, no 981 (p. 96)

One of John of Salisbury's letters [dated 1164 × 1167] is addressed to him and to Odo II, q.v., *Salisbury Letters*, ii, no 205. There is another letter to him from pope Alexander, dated 16 Dec. 1163 in *Materials Becket*, v, no 38.

He was described by Gervase as a man of prudence and industry who performed many good works, *Gervase Cant.*, i, 146, 197. He was responsible for building a treasury for the newly created monastic office of treasurer; but the most remarkable of these accomplishments was the waterworks, for which the original plans have been preserved in the Psalter of Eadwine, q.v. They show details of the whole system of water distribution within the precincts from its entrance on the north eastern side, from where it was conveyed to the octagonal water tower south of the infirmary cloister, and thence to all the conventual buildings; at the same time an elaborate drainage system was constructed, prob. all under the personal supervision of Wibert himself. See Willis, 'Arch. Hist. Christ Church', 158–173, John Hayes, 'Prior Wibert's Waterworks', *Cant. Cath. Chron.*, no 71 (1977), 17–26. A summary of his gifts and achievements is given in BL Ms Arundel 68, fo 43 and BL Ms Cotton Claudius C.vi, fo 171ᵛ. His gifts of vestments and ornaments are listd in Legg and Hope, *Inventories*, 44 (Lambeth Ms 20, fo 225ᵛ). See also M. Gibson's chapter in Collinson, *Canterbury Cathedral*, 58–60, for a recent assessment of his achievements.

II WIBERT
[c. 1206]

[c. 1206], a schedule of cathedral tenants in Canterbury of this date ref. to land given *cum Wiberto monacho*, Urry, *Canterbury*, 357.

WICHAM
see Wykham

WIDO
occ. [1089]

[1089], with Norman, q.v., *sed. vac.*, ordered by the [suffragan] bps to quell the unruly monks of St Augustine's, 'Acta Lanfranci', 292.

Note: there seems to have been a Wido, abbot of St Augustine's, vs whom some monks were rebelling as well as a Wido, monk of Canterbury, called in to subdue them.

WIDO
see also Guido, Walda

WIKYNG
see Wykyng

WILFRIDE
see Wylfryde

WILLARDESEYE
see Wylardeseye

I WILLIAM
n.d.

n.d., 5 Jan., *conversus*, whose obit occ. in BL Ms Arundel 68, fo 12.

II WILLIAM
occ. [1093 × 1096]

[1093 × 1096], in a letter to prior Henry, q.v., abp Anselm said that he held William chiefly responsible for the discord in the community, and orderd him to be obedient to the prior, *Anselm Letters*, no 182. He may also be the William referred to in *ib.*, nos 230 and 414.

III WILLIAM
occ. before 1152

1152, became abbot of Winchcombe, *HRH*, 79.

Note: a monk named William witnessed a purchase of land in Canterbury by prior Wibert, q.v, Urry, *Canterbury*, 392.

IV WILLIAM
occ. [1153 × 1161] occ. 1155

[1153 × 1161]; 1155, 28 Mar., subprior, *Theobald Charters*, no 40; p.536.

[1153 × 1161], named with prior Wibert, q.v., in a request made by the abp, and he witnessed the prior's reply, *Theobald Charters*, no 40.

1155, 28 Mar., witnessed an agreement between the monks and a priory tenant, *ib.*, 536.

V WILLIAM
occ. before 1187

1187, c. 17 May, apptd prior of Dover, but d. the following yr, *HRH*, 88.

VI M. WILLIAM
occ. 1188 occ. 1198

1198, Nov., precentor, *Epist. Cant.*, 458 (as W.).

1188, after 18 July, was with prior Honorius, q.v. on their prolonged journey to Rome and both were ill, while five of their number d., *Epist. Cant.*, 254. In mid Sept. with Ralph, *quondam* almoner, q.v., he was still travelling in Italy on negotiations, *ib.*, 258 (as M. William). In Nov. he was reported as being the only survivor among one group of the monks abroad, but still unwell, *ib.*, 269. In Jan. 1189, still ill, he was in Rome, *ib.*, 275 (as M. William).

1189, 6 Oct., one of the monks excommunicated by the abp, *ib.*, 311 (as M. William).

1189, 8 Nov., was spokesman for the group of monks sent to the king to explain their grievance vs abp Baldwin, but the latter tried to send him away as excommunicate, *Epist. Cant.*, 315, 317.

1198, Nov., with prior Geoffrey II, q.v., he was back at the curia in renewed appeals, this time vs abp Hubert Walter, and he was entrusted to carry back a papal mandate, *ib.*, 458.

Note:

(1) this may be the William who was described, in a letter written by John de Bremble, q.v., when they were together in France in Apr. 1189, as 'diligent and faithful in service', *Epist. Cant.*, 286.

(2) it is possible that there are two Williams implicated here; it is also possible that this one is both William de Dover II and William Sandford, q.v.

(3) see also William Cantuariensis.

VII WILLIAM
occ. 1213 occ. 1227

1213, 29 Sept., granator, CCA DCc MA1, fo 53v.

1214, 29 Sept., granator and cellarer, CCA DCc MA1, fo 54v.

1215, 1216, both on 29 Sept.; 1217, 7 Nov., cellarer, CCA DCc MA1, fos 56v, 58; *ib.*, fo 60.

1227, 7 Feb., with Walter IV, q.v., named proctor in the dispute with the chapter of Rochester over procedure in the el. of a bp of Rochester, *Langton Acta*, no 100.

Note: see the note below William de Dover II.

VIII WILLIAM
occ. 1230 occ. 1244

1230, chaplain to the prior, CCA DCc MA1, fo 73v.

1237, Apr./Sept., 1237/8, cellarer, CCA DCc AS 5, MA1, fos 79–80.

1241, 1 Feb., precentor, *Gervase Cant.*, ii, 186, 187, 190.

1241/4, chamberlain, CCA DCc MA1, fos 82v–85v.

1241, 1 Feb., named as one of seven *compromissorii* in the el. of an abp, *Gervase Cant.*, ii, 186, 187, 190.

IX WILLIAM
occ. 1456/7

1456/7, one of the *barones* of the exchequer, CCA DCc Prior acct 15.

Note: the assignment of entries to monks of this name can be no more than arbitrary and some of them are no doubt entered elsewhere under their toponymic or patronymic.

WILLIAM
see also Cantuarensis

WINCHELSEE, WINCHELSEY
see Wynchilsee

WINCHEPE
see Wynchepe

WINGHAM
see Wyngham

Nigel WIREKER [Witeker, or de Longchamp, de Longo Campo
occ. 1189 occ. 1215/16

1215, 1216, (as Nigel) both yrs on 29 Sept., almoner, CCA DCc, MA1, fos 56v, 58v.

1189, 5/8 Nov., one of a party of monks who were sent to London to confer with the king over abp Baldwin's scheme for a collegiate church at Lambeth, *Epist. Cant.*, 315. On 14 Nov. he spoke out at the meeting with the king, *ib.*, 317.

Name in Cambridge, Trinity College Ms 342, Historia Scolastica (Peter Comestor) (12th/13th c.); on the flyleaf Histor[ie manducatoris nigelli; this may be no 1084 in the Eastry catalogue.

By 1443 the Distinctiones Nigelli super psalterium had found its way to the Canterbury college library, Pantin, *Cant. Coll. Ox.*, i, 5, 13, 22, 59.

The Eastry catalogue contains several of the volumes in his possession, including the above Distinctiones, Cronica decani London and a copy of Interpretaciones ebraicorum nominum, James, *Ancient Libraries*, no 278 (p. 48), nos 1084–?1090 (p. 101).

There is a copy of the treatise ascribed to him, Epistole nigelli monachi de eruditione prelatorum, which was addressed to William de Longchamp, bp of Ely in Cambridge, Corpus Christi College Ms 441, pp.253–309; it is no 1354 in the Eastry catalogue, James *Ancient Libraries*, 115; see Gregory de Wynchilse.

One of his works has recently been ed. by J.H. Mozley and R.R. Raymo, *Nigel de Longchamps Speculum Stultorum*, (University of California, 1960). Mozley has also discussed 'The Unprinted Poems of Nigel Wireker' in *Speculum*, 7 (1932), 398–403; several of these sing the praises of Honorius III, q.v. See Sharpe, *Latin Writers*, under Witeker, for further refs. and a list of all his known works with the printed editions.

In a survey of cathedral holdings in Canterbury, [c. 1200], there is ref. to Agatha, sister of Nigel, 'our monk', Urry, *Canterbury*, 296, 297. Dr Urry argues convincingly that this is Wireker, son of Gilbert de Sarnai[s], and that the name Wireker is a misreading of Wetekere or Whiteacre, a village just southwest of Canterbury, and also that the families of Sarnai[s] and Whiteacre were connected, *ib.*, 154. There is another ref. to a purchase of land by Nigel in a schedule of cathedral holdings in Canterbury in c. 1206, *ib.*, 369.

See also Nigel.

WISINDEN
see Wysynden

Richard de WITSTAPLA [Hwytstaple
occ. [1150 × 1161] occ. [1148 × 1182]

[1150 × 1161], with Richard de Clare and Walter de Gloucestre, q.v., witnessed an archiepiscopal instrument, *Theobald Charters*, no 225.

[1153 × 1161], witnessed a grant of prior Wibert, q.v., in response to a request from the abp, *ib.*, no 40.

[1148 × 1182], *temp.* bp Walter of Rochester witnessed an agreement between this bp and the adcn of Rochester, *Reg. Roff.*, 58 (Rochester ref.).

WLFLUINUS [Wlfluvius
n.d.

n.d., 29 Apr., obit occ. in BL Ms Arundel 68, fo 26.

WLFNOTH
n.d.

n.d., 14 July, obit occ. in BL Ms Arundel 68, fo 34.

WLFWYNUS
n.d.

n.d., pr., whose obit occ. on 9 Jan. in BL Ms Arundel 68, fo 12v.

WLMER
n.d.

n.d., pr., whose obit occ. on 22 Apr. in BL Ms Arundel 68, fo 25.

WLNODUS
n.d.

n.d., pr., whose obit occ. on 11 Apr. in BL Ms Arundel 68, fo 23v.

See also Wolnotus.

WLSTANUS
n.d.

n.d., *conversus*, whose obit occ. on 14 Jan. in BL Ms Arundel 68, fo 13.

WMFRAY
see Humfrey

WNDIRDOWN, Wndyrdown
see Undyrdown

John de WODECHYRCHE
occ. 1st half 13th c.

n.d., name occ. in the list in *SL*, 173, CCA Lit. Ms D.12, fo 1v.

An inventory of missing service books dated 1 Mar. 1338 includes a psalterium formerly his, *Lit. Cant.*, no 618 (Reg. L, fo 104).

Roger WODECHYRCHE
occ. 1419 occ. 1424

1419, 25 Jan., one of four prof., *SL*, 186, CCA Lit. Ms D.12, fo 6v.

1419, 15 Apr., ord acol., infirmary chapel, *Reg. abp Chichele*, iv, 192.

1424, 22 Apr., ord pr., Canterbury cathedral, *ib.*, iv, 360.

n.d., left without licence, was declared apostate and d. overseas, CCA Lit. Ms D.12, fo 6v, Chron. Wm Glastynbury, fo 168v/162v.

Stephen WODECHYRCHE
occ. 2nd half 13th c.

n.d., name occ. in the list in *SL*, 175, CCA Lit. Ms D.12, fo 2.

Henry de WODEHULL, D.Th. [Wodell, Wodehulle, Wodhell, Wodhulle
occ. 1361 occ. 1368

1361, 1 Apr., the prior was comm. to adm. and rec. his prof., Reg. abp Islip, fo 170^{v}. He had previously been a monk of Abingdon for 28 yrs and had obtained his D.Th. (see *BRUO*). The letter of acceptance by the prior, dated 24 Mar., is in *Lit. Cant.*, no 937 (Reg. H, fo 82^{v}) and his prof. by the subprior is recorded on 6 Apr. in Reg. H, fo 83 and Reg. abp Islip, fo 171^{v}. The reason given for his desire to transfer was stated in the usual formula as due to his devotion to St Thomas and the other Canterbury saints and would, so he stated, enable him to lead a stricter life [*vitam arciorem*], *Lit. Cant.*, no 937; however, *BRUO* attributes it to a dispute with his abbot at the time of his inception. His name is entered in the Canterbury prof. list in 1333, the yr of his prof., at Abingdon, *SL*, 180, CCA Lit. Ms D.12, fo 3^{v}. See Richard Vaughan.

1363, 19 Mar., apptd warden of Canterbury college, Pantin, *Cant. Coll. Ox.*, iii, 3 (Reg. abp Islip, fo 192^{v}); in Dec. 1365 he was replaced by John Wyclyf, Pantin, *ib.*, iii, 11.

1367, 22 Apr., reapptd warden by the next abp Langham, Pantin, *Cant. Coll. Ox.*, iii (*Reg. abp Langham*, 284–285); however, the secular warden and fellows refused to accept him, and the dispute was taken to the curia where Wodehull was present in person and gave evidence. On 27 May 1370 he was reinstated as rightful warden but was himself soon replaced by John Bydynden, q.v., Pantin, *Cant. Coll. Ox.*, iii, 184–205, where details of the proceedings at the curia are transcribed from Reg. B, fos 368–374 and Lambeth Ms 104, fos 213–219^{v}; see also Pantin, *ib.*, iv, 17–35 *passim*. See also next entry.

1362/3, 1365/6, lector, Pantin, *Cant. Coll. Ox.*, iv, 71, without refs; the master lector recd 40s. in 1362/3, and Wodehull recd 13s. 4d. for the first term acc. to the entry on the same acct immediately below, Pantin, *ib.*, iv, 182 (Lambeth Ms 243, fo 122). There are similar entries for 1365/6, *ib.*, iv, 183 (Lambeth Ms 243, fo 136).

1366, 10 May, preached at the el. of abp Edington, Reg. G, fo 147.

1366, 6 July, one of the monks apptd by the prior to visit St Gregory's priory, Canterbury, *sed. vac.*, *ib.*, fo 127^{v}; on 15 Sept., he was hearing causes, *pro tribunali sedente*, *ib.*, fo 158^{v}.

1368, 24 Feb., spokesman for the chapter in requesting that abp Langham as a Benedictine conduct his visitation of Christ Church without the presence of any secular clerks; the abp conceded, *Reg. abp Langham*, 230.

n.d., 25 Sept., his obit occ. in BL Ms Arundel 68, fo 42^{v}.

A concordantie of his was given to the library of Canterbury college, Pantin, *Cant. Coll. Ox.*, i, 4, 12, 97.

I John de WODNESBURGH [Wodenysbergh
occ. 1323 d. 1331

1323, one of six clothed in the monastic habit, *SL*, 179, CCA Lit. Ms D.12, fo 3^{v}.

[1325], 18 Oct., prof. Reg. L, fo 141^{v}.

1331, 23 Aug., d., CCA Lit. Ms D.12, fo 16.

II John WODNESBURGH [Vodenysberg', Wodenesbergh, Wodenysbergh, Wodnesbergh, Wodnisbury, Wodnysbergh, Wodnysbrough, Wodnysbrowgh, Woodnesborough
occ. 1381 d. 1428

1411–1428, prior: el. 3 Sept. 1411, Reg. abp Arundel, i, fo 132; d. 28 Feb., 1428, *Chron. Stone*, 14.

1381, 6 May, one of eight prof., *SL*, 183, CCA Lit. Ms D.12, fo 5.

1393/1404; 1405/8, warden of manors, CCA DCc Appledore acct 56, Bocking accts 41, 42, Ebony acct 68, Adisham acct 40, Agney acct 63, Bocking acct 44, Agney accts 64, 65, Bocking acct 47, Agney acct 67; Treas. acct 7, Adisham acct 47, Ageny acct 71.

1394/1401, 1405/6, chaplain to the prior, CCA DCc Ickham acct 57, Prior acct 4, Prior's Chaplain accts 3, 4, Eastry accts 122, 123, Prior's Chaplain acct 7.

1400/7; 1408/11, cellarer, CCA DCc Bocking acct 45, Cell. acct 4, Eastry acct 124, Prior acct 3, Adisham accts 44–46, Great Chart acct 90, Agney acct 72, Eastry acct 133, Prior acct 2.

1403/6; 1407/10, bartoner, CCA DCc Bart. accts 102, 70, Chartham acct 46; Bart. accts 71–73.

1405/10, treasurer, CCA DCc, Bailiff of Liberty acct 16, Treas. accts 8–10.

1408, 1 Apr., 1410, almoner, 'Anon. Chron', 76–77, CCA DCc Cart. Antiq. F.158.

Note: there is a remarkable amount of overlapping of office holding here; what is the explanation?

1383/4, 1386/7, recd small sums from the prior *pro benedictione*, Lambeth Ms 243, fos 192^{v}, 204^{v}.

1396, 7 Aug., 33rd in order at the el. of an abp, Reg. G, fo 234^{v}; with Thomas Everard, q.v., carried the news of his postulation as abp to Thomas Arundel, *ib.*, fo 239^{v}.

1408, 1 Apr., given charge of the administration of the priory in the absence of prior Thomas Chillenden, q.v., Anon. Chron., 76–77.

1417, Nov./Dec., along with other cathedral priors at convocation he was appted by the abp to a committee to look into the poverty of university graduates, *Reg. abp Chichele*, iii, 37.

1418, 17 Dec., apptd vicar general, *Reg. abp Chichele*, i, 183; the reg. of his acta during the absence of the abp (until c. Aug. 1420) is in *Reg. abp Chichele*, i, 183–195 and Reg. S, fo 81^{v}.

1423, 29 Mar., with Thomas Brouns appted to act as commissaries for bp Langdon of Rochester during his absence abroad, Reg. Langdon (Rochester), fos 17^{v}–18.

1426, 7 June, because of old age and infirmity his confessor was authorized to permit him to eat meat outside the precincts in Advent, three weeks before Lent and on Wednesdays, *CPL*, vii (1417–1431), 456.

1428, 28 Feb., d., in his chamber called *le gloriet*; buried on the following day, in his priestly robes, with mitre [*mitratus*] and pastoral staff, at the foot of prior Thomas Chillenden, q.v., in the nave. The expenses of his funeral are given as evidence of the honour in which he was held; they include alms to religious and other needy persons, torches, and food and drink for the assembled throng afterwards, and the total was £143 6s. 10d., Oxford, Bod. Ms Tanner 165, fo 4^{v}.

The abp did not arrive in Canterbury until 27 Mar., and brought with him John Langdon q.v. [bp of Rochester], who celebrated a requiem mass on 28 or 29 Mar. at which Richard Godmersham I, q.v, preached on the text 'Transit de morte ad vitam', *ib.*, fo 4–4^{v}.

Some of his *acta* are in Reg. S, fos 61^{v}–98.

A summary of his achievements reveals a high degree of financial acumen since he was able to wipe out debts and liabilities totalling £2811 17s. 9¾d. within the space of three yrs and balance the books, while at the same time continuing work on the new cloister and carrying out repairs on the manors, 'Anon. Chron.', 78–83.

III John WODNESBURGH, D.Cn.L [Wodesbergh, Wodnysborowe, Wodnysbrowgh, Wodnysburgh

occ. 1413 d. 1457

1413, 6 Oct., one of six prof., SL 185–186, CCA Lit. Ms D.12, fo 6.

1416, 18 Apr., ord acol. and subdcn, Canterbury cathedral, *Reg. abp Chichele*, iv, 319.

1417, 10 Apr., ord dcn, Canterbury cathedral, *ib.*, iv, 327.

1428, 3 and 8 Mar.; 1435/7, midsummer; 1441, 25 Mar./1443; 1448, 26 Mar., warden of Canterbury college, Pantin, *Cant. Coll. Ox.*, iii, 82 (Reg. S, fo 97^{v}); Pantin, *ib.*, ii, 147–159 where his accts are printed (from CCA DCc Cart. Antiq. O.151.8, 9) for 1435/7; Pantin, *ib.*, ii, 162, 163; *ib.*, iii, 102 (Reg. abp Stafford, fo 29). He was succ. by Richard Gravene, q.v., in Apr. 1449.

Note: in between the terms of his tenure as warden Pantin has suggested that he may have served as *lector in claustro*, Pantin, *Cant. Coll. Ox.*, iv, 77, n. 7.

1443/5, 1448, 24 Mar., almoner, Reg. abp Stafford, fo 42^{v}, CCA DCc MA4, fo 33^{v}, *Chron. Stone*, 44.

1449, 19 Apr., apptd subprior, *ib.*, 46. He was subprior until Sept. 1449, CCA DCc Sac. acct 35; and also in 1453, 22 Apr., 1454, 25 Aug., 1455, 26 Jan., 1457, 9 Aug., *Chron. Stone*, 46, 57, 61, 63, 68.

[1418], prob. a student at Canterbury college in order to qualify for the first degree by 1422; see William Petham I.

1422, 1 Aug., B.Cn.L by this date, *CPL*, vii (1417–1431), 318.

[1428, before 7 July, or 1429], he and John Salisbury I, q.v., both incepted at the same time and the total expenditure for the two of them, including various fees and gifts, food and wine was £92 8d., Pantin, *Cant. Coll. Ox.*, iii, 84–87, where the full acct is printed from CCA DCc Cart. Antiq. O.128 A (also in Oxford Bod. Ms Tanner 165, fo 149–149^{v}.

1436, 22 Apr., described as *scolaris Oxonie* who recd travelling expenses between Canterbury and Oxford, Pantin, *ib.*, iv, 192.

1422, 1 Aug., obtained papal dispensation to choose his own confessor, *CPL*, vii (1417–1431), 318.

1422/3, was sent as proctor to the general council at Pavia and provided with £20 by the prior, CCA DCc Prior acct 5, Pantin, *Cant. Coll. Ox.*, iv, 191.

1428, 3 and 8 Mar., cited to return to Canterbury for the el. of a prior, Pantin, *ib.*, iii, 82–83 (Reg. S, fo 97^{v}).

1443, 22 May, sent by the prior and chapter with John Elham, q.v. as proctors to inform the king and John Stafford of the latter's el. as abp, *Chron. Stone*, 32.

1444, 4 Sept., conveyed a relic of St Wilfred of York to the bp and cathedral of Chichester, *ib.*, 35.

1454, 25 Aug., preached before the abp elect in his hospice in Holborn; his theme was 'exita potenciam tuam et veni' (Psalm 79/80, 3), *ib.*, 61.

1455/6, one of the *barones*, Prior acct 10.

1457, 9 Aug., d., in the 45th yr of monastic life and was buried in the infirmary chapel before the altar of Ss Agnes and Agatha, *ib.*, 68, CCA Lit. Ms D.12, fo 25^{v}. His obit is in BL Ms Arundel 68, fo 37^{v}.

Name in:

(1) CCA Lit. Ms B.4, John de Aton' [?Acton] super constitucionibus Othonis (14th c.); fo 126 *per I Wodnysbergh colacio fit totalis.*

(2) Manchester, John Rylands University Library, Ms Lat. 474, a Bible (13th c.); see John Langdon II.

Some of his correspondence with William Glastynbury, q.v., c. 1432/3, while Wodnesburgh was at Oxford and possibly warden of Canterbury college, has been preserved in Glastynbury's notebook and printed in Pantin, *Cant. Coll. Ox.*, iii, 88–93 (Chron. Wm Glastynbury, fo 185–185^{v}). In one of the letters he ref. to John Asshe q.v., as *amicus meus specialissimus*, Pantin, *ib.*, iii, 92.

He was a relative of the prior, John Wodnesburgh II, q.v., Pantin, *Cant. Coll. Ox.*, iii, 82 (Reg. S, fo 97^{v}) where he is described as *eiusdem prioris cognato*. His head is believed to be portrayed on a boss on the vault of All Saints' chapel, Collinson, *Canterbury Cathedral*, pl. 19.

IV John WODNESBURGH [Wodnesbourgh, Wodnysborowe, Wodnysburgh, Wonysbergh

occ. 1462 d. [1489 × 1492]

1462, 17 Mar., ord acol., Canterbury cathedral, *Reg. abp Bourgchier*, 381.

[1462], 6 Dec., one of six prof., *SL*, 190, CCA Lit. Ms D.12, fo 8.

Note: this must have been incorrectly dated 1464 in the margin of the ms; 1462 (or 1463) is more likely.

1463, 9 Apr., ord subdcn, Canterbury cathedral, *Reg. abp Bourgchier*, 385.

1464, 31 Mar., ord dcn, Canterbury cathedral, *ib.*, 390.

1465, 13 Apr., ord pr., place not stated, *ib.*, 392.

1481, 21 Dec., c. 1490, *magister ordinis*, *SL*, 191, CCA Lit. Ms D.12, fos 8^{v}, 27, 31^{v}.

1466, 17 Feb., 72nd in order in an inventory of *jocalia fratrum* [given by him and/or assigned for his use], but he had none, Reg. N, fos 234^{v}–235 (name repeated).

[1489 × 1492], d., CCA Lit. Ms D.12, fos 27, 31^{v}; it is prob. his obit that occ. on 16 Dec. in BL Ms Arundel 68, fo 51.

V John WODNESBURGH [Wodenesbergh, Wodnysbrough, Woednysborowe, Wonnysborowe, Woodnysbrough, Wyndisborough

occ. 1497 occ. 1534

1497, 28 July, one of nine tonsured, *SL*, 192, CCA Lit. Ms D.12, fo 9^{v}.

1498, 14 Apr., ord acol., Canterbury cathedral, *Reg. abp Morton*, i, no 447a.

1498, 19 Apr., prof., *SL*, 192, CCA Lit. Ms D.12, fo 9^{v}.

1516/17, anniversarian, Lambeth, ED 48.

1523/4, 1526/7, novice master, CCA DCc MA14, fo 224, MA15, fo 37.

1524, Aug./1525, Apr., 1527, May/1528, Mar., third prior and *magister ordinis*, CCA Lit. Ms D.12, fos 11^{v}, 12.

1534, 20 Oct., penitentiary, Reg. T, fo 32^{v}.

1501, 26 Apr., dcn, 64th and last in order at the el. of an abp, Reg. R, fo 56^{v}.

1511, 2 Sept., 44th on the visitation certificate, Wood-Legh, *Visit.*, 3 (Reg. abp Warham, i, fo 35^{v}).

1516/23, 1524/6, 1527/33, was [one of the] organist[s] acc. to CCA DCc MA4, fos 3, 39, 69, 103^{v}, 136^{v}, 176^{v}; MA30, fo 130^{v}; MA14, fos 224, 281; MA30, fo 153; MA15, fos 4, 53, 103, 163; MA16, fos 3^{v}, 65^{v}, 105. The sacrists' accts for these yrs record small payments to him for his playing: Woodruff, 'Sacrist's Rolls', 69, 71, 72 and CCA DCc Sac. accts 74, 75. On a number of occasions in the 1520s the amount pd was 10s., *ib.*

Robert WODNESBURGH [Wodenesbergh, Wodenisbergh, Wodnysbergh, Wodnysbrowgh, Wodnysburghe

occ. 1450 d. 1457

1450, 25 Jan., one of seven prof., *SL*, 189, CCA Lit. Ms D.12, fo 7^{v}.

1450, 3 Apr., ord acol., Canterbury cathedral, Reg. abp Stafford, fo 204.

1451, 20 Mar., ord subdcn, Canterbury cathedral, *ib.*, fo 205^{v}.

1452, 8 Apr., ord dcn, Canterbury cathedral, *ib.*, fo 206^{v}.

1456, 13 Mar., ord pr., Canterbury cathedral, *Reg. abp Bourgchier*, 363.

1457, before 29 Aug., *parvus sacrista*, *Chron. Stone*, 69.

1457, 29 Aug., d., *Chron. Stone*, 69, CCA Lit. Ms D.12, fo 25^{v}; his obit occ. in BL Ms Arundel 68, fo 39^{v}.

I William WOGHOPE [Woghoope, Wohope, Wozghope

occ. 1364 d. 1397

1363, 6 Aug., ord acol., abp's chapel, Canterbury, Reg. abp Islip, fo 323.

1364, n.d., one of eleven prof., *SL*, 182, CCA Lit. Ms D.12, fo 4^{v}.

1364, 9 Mar., ord subdcn, abp's chapel, Charing, Reg. abp Islip, fo 325.

1365, 29 Mar., ord dcn, abp's chapel, Charing, *ib.*, fo 326.

1367, 18 Sept., ord pr., Lambeth palace chapel, *Reg. abp Langham*, 383.

1376/7, bartoner, with Richard Hatfeld, q.v., CCA DCc Bart. acct 54.

1376/8, treasurer, CCA DCc MA2, fos 313^{v}–316^{v}.

1380/2, 1383/5, 1386/8, 1390/2, warden of manors, CCA DCc MA2, fos 320–328, Treas. acct 26, fos 1–5^{v}, Borley acct 8, Eastry acct 116,

Lalling acct 20, Eastry accts 117, 118; see note below.

1393/4, almoner, CCA DCc Meopham acct 99; prob. almoner in 1397 at the time of his d., CCA Lit. Ms D.12, fo 17v.

Note: CCA Lit. Ms D.12 records that 'diu Gardianus omnium maneriorum ecclesie Christi qui primus omnia maneria simul gubernavit', fo 17v.

1368, 22 Feb., student at Canterbury college, Oxford cited to a visitation, Pantin, *Cant. Coll. Ox.*, iii, 18 (Reg. L, fo 98).

[c. 1372, Dec./1373, Feb.], student, apptd proctor with Stephen Mongeham, q.v., in a dispute with St Frideswide's Oxford, Pantin, *ib.*, iii, 27–28 (Reg. H, fo 77v).

1366, 10 May, present at the el. of an abp, Reg. G, fo 147.

1374, 30 June, 36th in order at the el. of an abp, but was absent and made John Shoreham, q.v., his proxy, *ib.*, fos 173v–175v, 199v.

1374/5, recd £20 13s. for his expenses on his mission to the curia, Pantin, *Cant. Coll. Ox.*, iv, 185; was this related to the controversy about attendance at the Black Monk Chapter?

1376, Apr., one of ten monks nominated to the committee set up for regulating the infirmary, *Lit. Cant.*, no 945 (CCA DCc Cart. Antiq. C.206).

1376, 31 Aug., with William de Dover III, q.v., took news of the d. of prior Richard Gyllyngham, q.v. to the abp, Reg. abp Sudbury, fo 27v.

1381, 31 July, 25th in order at the el. of an abp and named as one of three *compromissorii* deputed to choose an additional six, Reg. G, fo 225v, Oxford, Bod. Ms Ashmole 794, fo 254v.

1396, 7 Aug., 11th in order at the el. of an abp, Reg. G, fo 234v.

1397, 30 Sept., d., CCA Lit. Ms D.12, fo 17v, where he is praised as a 'vir magne discretionis et sapientie mundialis' and for his achievement in having built the chamber called 'heven'. His obit on 1 Oct. is in BL Ms Arundel 68, fo 43v.

II William WOGHOPE [Woghhope, Wohope

occ. 1408/9 d. 1426

1408/9, 21 Mar., one of six prof., *SL*, 185, CCA Lit. Ms D.12, fo 6.

1410, 22 Mar., ord dcn, Canterbury cathedral, Reg. abp Arundel, ii, fo 98v.

1413, 2 Apr., ord pr., Canterbury cathedral, Reg. abp Arundel, ii, fo 101.

1414, 12 Mar., 73rd in order at the el. of an abp, *Reg. abp Chichele*, i, 4.

1426, 28 Oct., d., in his 19th yr of monastic life, *Chron. Stone*, 13, CCA Lit. Ms D.12, fo 22; his obit on 29 Oct. occ. in BL Ms Arundel 68, fo 46v.

WOLNODUS

n.d.

n.d., 15 Apr., obit occ. in Lambeth Ms 20, fo 180.

WOLNOTUS [?Wlnodus

n.d.

n.d., 13 Mar., *conversus*, whose obit occ. in BL Ms Arundel 68, fo 20, which records that he gave the *hospitalis de Blen* [Blean].

WOLNOTUS

see also Wlnodus

Walter WOLTON

occ. 1380/1

c. 1380, one of four prof., *SL*, 183, CCA Lit. Ms D.12, fo 5.

1380, 24 Mar., ord subdcn, Canterbury cathedral, Reg. abp Sudbury, fo 147v.

1381, 31 July, 62nd and last in order at the el. of an abp, Reg. G, fo 225v.

WOLWARDUS

n.d.

n.d., 27 Nov., obit occ. in BL Ms Arundel 68, fo 49v.

WOODTON, Wootton

see Wotton

Robert de WORCLYNG

occ. 2nd half 13th c.

n.d., name occ. in the list in *SL*, 176, CCA Lit. Ms D.12, fo 2v.

WORMEDALE

see Wrmdale

WORNESELL

see Wernesell

Stephen de WORTHE [Wrthe

occ. c. 1286 d. 1310

c. 1286, one of five prof., *SL*, 177, CCA Lit. Ms D.12, fo 3.

1297/9, granator, CCA DCc MA1, fos 208–222.

1299, bartoner, CCA DCc MA1, fo 222.

1306/7, 1308/9, cellarer, CCA DCc MA1, fos 264v–271, MA2, fos 11v–17v; his apptment is dated 21 Jan., 1306, Reg. Q, fo 30v/42v, and his release from this office was requested by the prior and convent on 5 Feb. 1309 on account of the burden of work which was *super vires sui corporis*, CUL Ms Ee.5.31, fo 110v. The abp replied favourably to this request on 13 Feb., *Reg. abp Winchelsey*, 1051.

1300, 1 Nov., with Robert de Elham, q.v., apptd proctors to the curia 'ad contradicendum in audiencia et ad impetrandum privilegia', CUL Ms Ee.5.31, fos 83v–84. They carried with them twelve *cartas* to enable them to contract loans up to 3000 m., *ib.*, fo 84^{v}.

1301, 14 Sept., with John de Thaneto, q.v., sent to the executors of Edmund, earl of Cornwall in order to rec. certain goods from them, *ib.*, fo 86^{v}.

1302, 3 Mar., with Daniel de Sutton, q.v., recd letters of credence in order to confer with the abp, *ib.*, fo 87^{v}.

1302, 25 May, with Guy de Smerden, q.v., named proctors to attend convocation, *ib.*, fo 90^{v}.

1310, 22 Oct., d., CCA Lit. Ms D.12, fo 15^{v}.

An inventory of missing service books dated 1 Mar. 1338 includes his Exequiae, *Lit. Cant.*, no 618 (Reg. L, fo 104).

Two albs are listed under his name in an inventory of linen vestments, *temp.* prior Eastry, Legg and Hope, *Inventories*, 59 (BL Ms Cotton Galba, E.iv, fo 115).

An inventory of the refectory, dated 1328, includes a silver gilt *cuppa* formerly his, and a *ciphus de murra*, Dart, *Antiq. Cant.*, xxiii, (BL Ms Cotton Galba E.iv, fos 178, 180).

John WOTLYNG

occ. 2nd half 13th c.

n.d., name occ. in the list in *SL*, 175, CCA Lit. Ms D.12, fo 2^{v}.

Anthony WOTTON [Woodton, Wootton

occ. 1506 d. c. 1508

1506, 21 Mar., one of six tonsured, *SL*, 193, CCA Lit. Ms D.12, fo 10–10^{v}.

1506, 11 Apr., ord acol., Canterbury cathedral, Reg. abp Warham, ii, fo 262^{v}.

1506, 30 Sept., prof., *SL*, 193, CCA Lit. Ms D.12, fo 10.

1508, 22 Apr., ord subdcn, Canterbury cathedral, Reg. abp Warham, ii, fo 263^{v}.

1508, student at Canterbury college for a brief period before his d., see below.

c. 1508, d., at Oxford, see below; n.d., 18 July, subdcn, whose obit occ. in BL Ms Arundel 68, fo 38^{v}.

An inventory of the books and clothing in his room at Oxford is printed in Pantin, *Cant. Coll. Ox.*, i, 87–88 (CCA DCc DE76); see Robert Holyngbourne who also d. about the same time.

Among his books were Epistole Tulli, Liber Therencii, Burleus super logica (*sic*), Pantin, *ib.*, i, 87 (from CCA DCc DE76, Z.204).

I John WOTTON [Wottone, Wucton

occ. 1398 occ. 1416

1398, 13 or 14 Nov., one of four prof., *SL*, 184, CCA Lit. Ms D.12, fo 5^{v}.

1399, 20 Dec., ord dcn, Canterbury cathedral, Reg. abp Arundel, i, fo 325.

1401, 19 Mar., ord pr., Canterbury cathedral, *ib.*, i, fo 328.

1416, 18 May, apptd penitentiary, but absolved on 22 May, *Reg. abp Chichele*, iv, 150, 151.

1416, before his apptment to Dover, treasurer, CCA Lit. Ms D.12, fo 5^{v}.

1408/9, student at Canterbury college, Oxford, with John Dover II, q.v., Pantin, *Cant. Coll. Ox*, iv, 191 (as Wucton).

1414, 12 Mar., 42nd in order at the el. of an abp, *Reg. abp Chichele*, i, 4.

[1416, Nov.], apptd prior of Dover, *Reg. abp Chichele*, i, 151–152; he succ. Walter Causton, q.v., and the mandate for his installation as prior is dated 11 Nov., *ib.*, i, 152.

II John WOTTON [Wutton

occ. 1425 d. 1443

1425, 20 Mar., dcn and previously a monk of Dover and relative of John Wotton I, q.v.; made his prof. before the abp during the morning mass, *SL*, 187, CCA Lit. Ms D.12, fo 7.

1425, 23 Dec., ord pr., Charing, *Reg. abp Chichele*, iv, 374.

Note: records of his ordinations while at Dover are also in *ib.*, iv, 352, 354, 358.

1432, 19 Sept., *magister ordinis*, *SL*, 188, CCA Lit. Ms D.12, fo 7^{v} (as Robert).

1443, 11 Sept., d., *Chron. Stone*, 33. His *fenis* [?*senis*, ?alms] were given to Robert Pelham, a friar minor after the latter's inception, CCA Lit. Ms D.12, fo 24^{v}.

WOWLE

see Vowle

WOYLFRYD

see Wylfryde

WOZGHOPE

see Woghope

Roger de WRMDALE [Wormedale, Wrmedale, ?Wy[r]nedale

occ. [1207 × 1214] occ. 1228

[1207 × 1214], name occ. in the list of monks who were in exile, *SL*, 172, CCA Lit. Ms D.12, fo 1.

1228, 3 Aug., named as one of five *compromissorii* in the el. of an abp, *Gervase Cant.*, ii, 120, 121, 123.

A *ciphus magnus de murra* of his is listed in an inventory of the refectory dated 1328, Dart, *Antiq. Cant.*, xxii (BL Ms Cotton Galba, E.iv, fo 180).

Note: is this perhaps Roger Nevyle, q.v.?

Roger de WROTHAM [Wroteham

occ. 1254 d. 1298

n.d., name on the list in *SL*, 174, CCA Lit. Ms D.12, fo 2.

1254/7, subsacrist, CCA DCc MA1, fos 96–99, Reg. H, fo 187v (1256, Sept./1257, Mar.).
1260, Dec./1261, Dec., treasurer, one of three this yr, CCA DCc MA1, fos 102v, 103v, Reg. H, fo 203.
1287/8, 1296, 5 Mar., feretrar, CCA DCc MA1, fo 153v, *Reg. abp Winchelsey*, 1304.
1275/6, pd a supervisory visit to Monkton, CCA DCc Monkton acct 5.
1296, before 5 Mar., one of two senior monks who with the prior were examined by the abp on the general state of the convent, *Reg. abp Winchelsey*, 1303–1304; see Martin de Clyve.
1298, 6 Dec., d., CCA Lit. Ms D.12, fo 15.

A silver gilt *ciphus* of his and two *de murra* are listed in an inventory of the refectory dated 1328, Dart, *Antiq. Cant.*, xix, xxiii (BL Ms Cotton Galba E.iv, fos 178, 179v, 180).

WRTHE
see Worthe

WUCTON, Wutton
see Wotton

Alan de WY
occ. [1207 × 1214] occ. 1239

[1207 × 1214], name occ. in the list of those who were in exile, *SL*, 172, CCA Lit. Ms D.12, fo 1.

Note: is this Alan Rufus, q.v.? See also Alan III.

I John de WY
occ. 1285 d. 1302

[c. 1283], one of five prof., *SL*, 177, CCA Lit. Ms D.12, fo 3.
1285, Sept., ord pr., collegiate church, South Malling, *Reg. abp Pecham*, i, 222.
1296, before 5 Mar., 1299, 27 Nov., chaplain to the abp, *Reg. abp Winchelsey*, 1303, Reg. Q, fo 29/41; on the latter occasion the abp refused to let his name stand for precentor.
1291, 15 Dec., apptd general proctor for the prior and convent, CUL Ms Ee.5.31, fo 15v.
1292, 19 Dec., present at abp Pecham's funeral, *Reg. abp Winchelsey*, 1258, and was sent with Walter de Chillenden q.v., on 22 Dec. to Newcastle-on-Tyne to the king for licence to el. his successor, *ib.*
1293, 13 Feb., named as one of seven *compromissorii* at the el. of an abp, *Reg. abp Winchelsey*, 1265.
1293, 24 Feb., one of the monks present at Leighton Buzzard [Lecton] to hear Robert Winchelsey's consent to his el. as abp, *ib.*, 1274.
1296, before 5 Mar., present as the abp's chaplain, during the abp's visitation of the priory, *ib.*, 1303–1304.
1302, 31 Jan., d., CCA Lit. Ms D.12, fo 15v; his obit occ. in BL Ms Arundel 68, fo 15.

The Eastry catalogue includes two volumes under his name: Distinctiones Mauricii and Sermones, James, *Ancient Libraries*, nos 1614, 1615 (p. 133).

An inventory of vestments, *temp.* prior Eastry, includes an alb of his, Legg and Hope, *Inventories*, 59 (BL Ms Cotton Galba, E.iv, fo 115).

An inventory of the refectory, dated 1328, includes three silver *ciphi* formerly his, Dart, *Antiq. Cant.*, xx (BL Ms Cotton Galba E.iv, fo 178v).

II John WY [Wye
occ. 1410 d. 1418

1410, 13 Dec., one of eight prof., *SL*, 186, CCA Lit. Ms D.12, fo 6.
1413, 2 Apr., ord dcn, Canterbury cathedral, Reg. abp Arundel, ii, fo 101v.
1417, 10 Apr., ord pr., Canterbury cathedral, *Reg. abp Chichele*, iv, 328.
1418, student at Canterbury college before his d., see below.
1414, 12 Mar., ill in the infirmary at the time of the el. of the abp and apptd Thomas Selvyston q.v., his proxy, *Reg. abp Chichele*, i, 4.
1418, 7 Dec., d. at Oxford, and his body was returned to Canterbury by the *socium sue rasture*, Thomas Guston, q.v., *Chron. Stone*, 9, where details of the funeral are given; his obit occ. in BL Ms Arundel 68, fo 51.

College inventories of the 15th c. include *j bona* in the chapel which was his, Pantin, *Cant. Coll. Ox.*, i, 3, 11 and two cushions in the warden's chamber, *ib.*, i, 7.

WYCHAM
see Wykham

Richard de WYCUMBE [Wycombe
occ. 1346 d. 1361

1346, 11 Nov., one of eight prof., *SL*, 181, CCA Lit. Ms D.12, fo 4.
1349, 4 June, 59th and last in order at the el. of an abp, Reg. G, fo 60v.
1349, 8/9 Sept., 58th and last at the el. of an abp, *ib.*, fo 76v.
1361, 25 July, d., one of c.25 monks carried off [by the plague] between June and Oct., CCA Lit. Ms D.12, fo 17.

WYDO
see Guido

Richard WYKE
occ. 1358/9 occ. 1360/1

1358/9, 28 Oct., one of nine prof., *SL*, 181, CCA Lit. Ms D.12, fo 4.
1360, 29 Feb., ord acol., abp's chapel, Otford, Reg. abp Islip, fo 318.
1360, 4 Apr., ord subdcn, abp's chapel, Saltwood, *ib.*, fo 318v.

1361, 18 Dec., ord pr., Charing, *ib.*, fo 320.

1360/1, ill and 3s. 6d. spent on medicine, Lambeth Ms 243, fo 115ᵛ.

n.d., 'miserrime recessit et sic [vitam] finivit', CCA Lit. Ms D.12, fo 4ᵛ.

Note: the obit of a Richard Wyke occ. on 29 Mar. in BL Ms Arundel 68, fo 22ᵛ.

I John WYKHAM
occ. 1398 d. 1421

1398, 13/14 Nov., one of four prof., *SL*, 184, CCA Lit. Ms D.12, fo 5ᵛ.

1399, 20 Dec., ord dcn, Canterbury cathedral, Reg. abp Arundel, i, fo 325.

1401, 19 Mar., ord pr., Canterbury cathedral, *ib.*, i, fo 328.

1415, 10 Nov., *magister ordinis*, *SL*, 186, CCA Lit. Ms D.12, fo 6.

1421, before 25 Oct., third prior, CCA Lit. Ms D.12, fo 21ᵛ.

1414, 12 Mar., 40th in order at the el. of an abp, *Reg. abp Chichele*, i, 4.

1421, 25 Oct., d., *ex asmatica passione*, *Chron. Stone*, 11, CCA Lit. Ms D.12, fo 21ᵛ; his obit occ. in BL Ms Arundel 68, fo 46ᵛ.

II John WYKHAM [Wycham
occ. 1446 d. [1492]

1446, 21 Dec., one of seven tonsured, *SL*, 188, CCA Lit. Ms D.12, fo 7ᵛ.

1447, 8 Apr., ord acol., Canterbury cathedral, Reg. abp Stafford, fo 201.

1447, 27 Aug., prof., with the other six, *Chron. Stone*, 41–42.

1447, 23 Dec., ord subdcn, Canterbury cathedral, Reg. abp Stafford, fo 201ᵛ.

1448, 23 Mar., ord dcn, Canterbury cathedral, *ib.*, fo 202ᵛ.

1451, 20 Mar., ord pr., Canterbury cathedral, *ib.*, fo 205ᵛ.

1468/9, Oct. to Apr., fourth prior, *magister noviciorum/magister ordinis*, *Chron. Stone*, 106, *SL*, 190, CCA Lit. Ms D.12, fo 8.

1477/8, second anniversarian, CCA DCc, Anniv. acct 15.

1480, 25 Jan., *magister ordinis*, *SL*, 191, CCA Lit. Ms D.12, fo 8ᵛ.

1486/92, sacrist, CCA DCc MA7, fos 36ᵛ, 67, Sac. acct 58, MA7, fos 148ᵛ, 169ᵛ.

1466, 17 Feb., 38th in order in an inventory of *jocalia fratrum* [given by him and/or assigned for his use], Reg. N, fo 233.

[1492], d., CCA Lit. Ms D.12, fos 27, 31ᵛ (repeated).

III John WYKHAM [Wicham
occ. 1495 occ. 1511

1495, 1 Aug., one of four tonsured, *SL*, 192, CCA Lit. Ms D.12, fo 9ᵛ.

1496, 2 Apr., ord acol., Canterbury cathedral, *Reg. abp Morton*, i, no 445a.

1496, 4 Apr., prof., *SL*, 192, CCA Lit. Ms D.12, fo 9ᵛ.

1497, 25 Mar., ord subdcn, Canterbury cathedral, *ib.*, i, no 446b.

1498, 14 Apr., ord dcn, Canterbury cathedral, *ib.*, i, no 447c.

1500/1, celebrated his first mass and recd a small gift from the sacrist, CCA DCc Sac. acct 70.

1503, 6 July, chaplain to the subprior, CCA Lit. Ms C.11, fo 32.

1501, 26 Apr., pr. and 55th in order and last among the priests at the el. of an abp, Reg. R, fo 56ᵛ.

1511, 2 Sept., 37th on the visitation certificate, Wood-Legh, *Visit.*, 3 (Reg. abp Warham, i, fo 35ᵛ).

n.d., 'recessit in apostasia, et sic complevit dies suos', CCA Lit. Ms D.12, fo 9ᵛ.

Philip de WYKHAM [Wycham
occ. 1333 occ. 1360

1333, 9 Oct., one of eleven prof., *SL*, 180, CCA Lit. Ms D.12, fo 4.

1349/50, bartoner and warden of manors, CCA DCc Bart. acct 31, Meopham acct 87.

1350/1, 1352/3, warden of manors, CCA DCc Lalling acct 12, Meopham acct 90.

1352/3, chaplain to the prior, CCA DCc Bocking acct 31.

1353/4, warden of manors, CCA DCc Bocking acct 32.

1356, Aug./Sept., warden of manors, CCA DCc Chartham acct 34.

1349, 4 June, 32nd in order at the el. of an abp, Reg. G, fo 60ᵛ.

1349, 8/9 Sept., 31st at the el. of an abp, *ib.*, fo 76ᵛ.

1355, 17 Mar., granted papal licence to choose his own confessor, *CPL*, iii (1342–1362), 556.

1360, 3 Oct., absent from the house but cited to return for the visitation, Reg. H, fo 98.

Roger de WYKHAM
occ. 1st half 13th c.

n.d., name occ. in the *post exilium* list, *SL*, 173, CCA Lit. Ms D.12, fo 1.

Thomas WYKYNG [Wikyng, Wykynge, Wykyngge
occ. 1365 d. 1407

1365, n.d., one of six prof., *SL*, 182, CCA Lit. Ms D.12, fo 4ᵛ.

1367, 18 Sept., ord subdcn, Lambeth palace chapel, *Reg. abp Langham*, 383.

1368, 4 Mar., ord dcn, Canterbury cathedral, *ib.*, 388.

1370, 21 Sept., ord pr., Saltwood, Reg. abp Wittlesey, fo 166ᵛ.

1373/4, feretrar, CCA DCc MA2, fos 276–281v.
1377, 2 Jan., prob. warden of Canterbury college. He was absent from the abp's visitation of Christ Church, Reg. abp Sudbury, fo 32.
1381, 6 May, *magister ordinis*, SL 183, CCA Lit. Ms D.12, fo 5.
1381, 18 June, penitentiary, Oxford, Bod. Ms Ashmole 794, fo 248v.
1382, 15 Sept., absolved from the office of penitentiary, Reg. abp Courtenay, i, fo 21v.
1382/3, ?1384, cellarer, CCA DCc Godmersham acct, Treas. acct 26, fo 7; he was apptd in Sept. 1382, Reg. abp Courtenay, i, fo 22 and absolved on 15 Aug. 1383, *ib.*, i, fo 42v.
1384/5, chaplain to the prior, CCA DCc MA2, fo 335.
1386, *magister ordinis* for part of the yr 1386/7, *SL*, 183, CCA Lit. Ms D.12, fo 5; see Walter Gabriel.
1390/2, cellarer, CCA DCc Eastry accts 117, 118; he was dismissed from this office before 29 Apr. 1392 and replaced by Henry Cranbroke I, q.v., Reg. abp Courtenay, ii, fo 224.
1394/5, 1396/7, sacrist, CCA DCc Sac. acct 12, Prior acct 4; he was dismissed from this office 10 Sept. 1399, Reg. abp Arundel, i, fo 391v.
1395, 12 May, *magister ordinum*, *SL*, 184, CCA Lit. Ms D.12, fo 5v.
1401, 6 Aug., warden of Canterbury college, apptd, Pantin, *Cant. Coll. Ox.*, iii, 60 (Reg. abp Arundel, i, fo 437); see Richard Godmersham I, his successor.
n.d., penitentiary twice, sacrist twice, warden of Canterbury college twice, feretrar twice, *coronator* twice, *SL*, 182, CCA Lit. Ms D.12, fo 18v.

1375/6, student at Canterbury college, Pantin, *Cant. Coll. Ox.*, iv, 186.
1397/8, prob. at Oxford and one of six, who recd a small sum *pro benedictone* from the feretrars, CCA DCc Feret. acct 1.

1374, 30 June, 45th in order at the el. of an abp, Reg. G, fos 173v–175v.
1381, 31 July, 33rd at the el. of an abp, *ib.*, fo 225v.
1391/2, gave 6s. 8d. towards the repair of the choir vault, CCA DCc Sac. acct 10.
1396, 7 Aug., 15th at the el. of an abp, Reg. G, fo 234v.
1407, 15 Nov., d., in the 43rd yr of his monastic life in the infirmary, sound in mind, and with the prayer to the blessed Virgin at the end of nocturns on his lips. He served as master and instructor of many of the brethren 'super informationem missarum celebrand' ' and exhorted all of his 'disciples' to include the prayer to the virgin, for whom he had a special devotion, in all their masses, CCA Lit. Ms D.12, fo 18v. The latter goes on to extol his character and personality at some length: 'vir . . . erat honestissimus et purus tam in corpore quam in mente et habitu et venustissime morigeratus ultra omnes qui ad tunc visi fuerant vel diutissime ante eum. Hic fovet sepius pacem et concordiam inter presidentem et confratres nec aliquam molestiam sinebat absque concordia in quantum valuit preterire', *ib.* (*SL*, 182). His obit occ. in BL Ms Arundel 68, fo 48.

Gave [a set of] vestments to Canterbury college, Pantin, *Cant. Coll. Ox.*, i, 10, 29.

Richard de WYLARDESEYE [Willardeseye, Willardishey, Willarsay

occ. 1304 d. 1354

1304, 15 Mar., prof., *SL*, 178, CCA Lit. Ms D.12, fo 3v.
1305, 12 June, ord subdcn, Mayfield, *Reg. abp Winchelsey*, 977.

1334/5, subprior, CCA DCc Barksore acct 34.
1337/9, chamberlain, CCA DCc Chamb. accts 30, 32.

1333, 15 Oct., with Simon de St Peter, q.v., sent to inform the king of the d. of abp Meopham, Reg. G, fos xxvi-xxvii; on 3 Nov., named as one of seven *compromissorii* in the el. of an abp, Reg. G, fos xxxii, xxxvii, Reg. Q, fo 193v.
1333, 6 Dec., with Robert Hathbrand and Hugh de St Ives, q.v., authorized to obtain a loan in the curia or elsewhere, Reg. Q, fos 196v–197. This suggests that the three monks went to Avignon to obtain confirmation of their postulation of John Stratford as abp; see Robert Hathbrand.
1338, 1 Mar., an inventory of missing books charged him with the loss of Vita et miracula beati Thomae, *Lit. Cant.*, no 618 (Reg. L, fo 104).
1348/9, ill and recd a *liberatio* of 4s. from the anniversarian, CCA DCc Anniv. acct 3.
1349, 4 June, 5th in order at the el. of an abp and apptd one of three *compromissorii* who were to choose ten to add to their number, Reg. G, fos 60v–61v.
1349, 8/9 Sept., 5th at the el. of an abp, *ib.*, fo 76.
1354, 9 Jan., d., CCA Lit. Ms D.12, fo 16v; his obit occ. in BL Ms Arundel 68, fo 12v.

I Thomas WYLFRYDE [Weylfryd, Wilfride, Woylfryd

occ. 1507 occ. 1519

1507, 12 Oct., one of six tonsured, *SL*, 193, CCA Lit. Ms D.12, fo 10v.
1508, 22 Apr., ord acol., Canterbury cathedral, Reg. abp Warham, ii, fo 263v.
1508, 25 Apr., he and the other five novices made their prof. before the abp, *SL*, 194, CCA Lit. Ms D.12, fo 10v.
1511, 19 Apr., ord dcn, Canterbury cathedral, Reg. abp Warham, *ib.*, ii, fo 265v.
1511, 2 Sept., 71st in order on the visitation certificate, Wood-Legh, *Visit.*, 3 (Reg. abp Warham, i, fo 35v).

n.d., possibly had as his *magister regule*, John Garard, q.v., for two yrs *et non perfecit*, Pantin, *Cant. Coll. Ox.*, iv, 54 (CCA DCc Ms Scrap Book B.186).

Note: this entry may ref. to Thomas Wylfryde II below.

1519, several members of his family, by the name of Borne, were recd into the Christ Church confaternity, BL Ms Arundel 68, fo 11.

n.d., 27 Aug., pr. by this name whose obit occ. in BL Ms Arundel 68, fo 39ᵛ.

II Thomas WYLFRYDE [Wylfride

occ. 1522 occ. 1540

1522, 11 Feb., one of ten tonsured, *SL*, 195, CCA Lit. Ms D.12, fo 11ᵛ.

1522, 24 Nov., prof., *ib.*

1526/7, celebrated his first mass and recd a small gift from the sacrist, Woodruff, 'Sacrist's Rolls', 72.

[1538, 8 Feb., after], reported to be 'at Parrys at stody', Pantin, *Cant. Coll. Ox.*, iii, 153; see John Waltham.

n.d., possibly had John Garard, q.v. for two yrs as his *magister regule, et non perfecit*, Pantin, *Cant. Coll. Ox.*, iv, 54 (CCA DCc Ms Scrap Book B.186).

Note: this entry may ref. to Thomas Wylfryde I above.

1534, 12 Dec., acknowledged the Act of Supremacy, *DK 7th Report*, Appndx 2, 282.

[1538, 8 Feb., after], in a list of monks prob. drawn up for Cromwell he was described as 'witty' and 34 yrs of age, Pantin, *Cant. Coll. Ox.*, iii, 153.

1540, 4 Apr., apptd scholar in the new foundation, *L and P Henry VIII*, xv, no 452.

WYMBOURNE

see Wynborne

Richard WYMHIS

occ. 1465

1465, 13 Apr., ord subdcn, place not stated, *Reg. abp Bourgchier*, 311.

WYMUNDUS

n.d.

n.d., 21 May, obit occ. in BL Ms Arundel 68, fo 28 and Lambeth Ms 20, fo 188.

William WYNBORNE [Wymbourne

occ. 1339 d. 1349

1339, 13 Dec., one of five prof., *SL*, 180, CCA Lit. Ms D.12, fo 4.

1348/9, ill [in the infirmary] and recd a *liberatio* of 2s. from the anniversarian, CCA DCc Anniv. acct 3.

1349, 6 June, d. of the plague, one of four who succumbed in May and June, CCA Lit. Ms D.12, fo 16ᵛ (where the date is *xiii idus* June, prob. instead of viii).

WYNCH

see Fynch

I John de WYNCHELSE [Winchelese, Wynchelsee, Wyndchelesee

occ. 1299 d. 1328

1299, 24 Aug., one of seven prof., *SL*, 178, CCA Lit. Ms D.12, fo 3ᵛ.

1300, 4 June, ord subdcn, Smeeth chapel by Aldington, *Reg. abp Winchelsey*, 934.

1316/19, treasurer, CCA DCc MA2, fos 76–94.

1320/2, 1323/4, bartoner, CCA DCc Bart. accts 11–13, MA2, fos 112–138 (1321/4).

1328/9, warden of manors, CCA DCc MA2, fo 173ᵛ, Lydden acct 48, but see below.

1328, 11 Sept., d., CCA Lit. Ms D.12, fo 16.

The Eastry catalogue includes three missale and two ordinale under his name and Palladius de agricultura, James, *Ancient Libraries*, nos 1826–1831 (p. 142).

In the list of missing books dated 1 Mar., 1338, he was held responsible for a Bible which had formerly belonged to John de Chatham or Robert VIII, q.v., and for a processionale of Dionisius [?de Cantuar' or St Margaret], *Lit. Cant.*, no 618 (Reg. L, fo 104).

An inventory of vestments, acquired *temp.* prior Eastry, lists two sets of vestments and two albs under his name, Legg and Hope, *Inventories*, 69 (BL Ms Cotton Galba, E.iv, fo 118ᵛ).

An inventory of the refectory, dated 1328, includes three silver *ciphi* formerly his, and three *de murra*, Dart, *Antiq. Cant.*, xxi, xxiii (BL Ms Cotton Galba E.iv, fos 179, 180ᵛ).

II John WYNCHELSE [Wynchylse, Wynchilse

occ. 1505 d. 1532/3

1505, 13 Jan., one of six tonsured, *SL*, 193, CCA Lit. Ms D.12, fo 10.

1505, 11 July, prof., *ib.*,

1508, 22 Apr., ord subdcn, Canterbury cathedral, Reg. abp Warham, ii, fo 263ᵛ.

1513, 26 Mar., ord pr., Canterbury cathedral, *ib.*, ii, fo 266ᵛ.

1511, 2 Sept., 61st in order on the visitation certificate, Wood-Legh, *Visit.*, 3 (Reg. abp Warham, i, fo 35ᵛ).

1518/19, 1520/1, spent time in the infirmary, CCA DCc Infirm. accts 1, 2.

1532/3, d., Woodruff, 'Sacrist's Rolls', 73.

John de WYNCHELSEE

see Fynch

Robert de WYNCHELSE [Wynchilse
occ. 1st half 13th c.

n.d., name occ. in the list in *SL*, 174, CCA Lit. Ms D.12, fo 1v.

n.d., 2 Jan., dcn whose obit occ. in BL Ms Arundel 68, fo 12.

An inventory of missing books dated 1 Mar. 1338 includes Scriptum Thomae super primo et secundo sententiarum et Augustinus super libero arbitrio, formerly his, *Lit. Cant.*, no 618 (Reg. L, fo 104); see William de Hethe I.

I Thomas de WYNCHELSE [Winchelese, Wyncelsee, Wynchelese
occ. c. 1300 occ. 1309

n.d., name occ. in the list in *SL*, 175, CCA Lit. Ms D.12, fo 2.

c. 1300, 1305/6, 1308/9, warden of manors, CCA DCc AS20, West Farleigh acct 22, Meopham act 50.

[1296], one of the monks accused at the visitation of laxity in attendance at divine office, *Reg. abp Winchelsey*, 92.

1309, 25 Apr., with Nicholas de Borne I apptd proctor for parliament, CUL Ms Ee.5.31, fo 111.

1309, 19 Nov., with Nicholas de Borne I, apptd proctor for the provincial council at St Paul's, *ib.*, fo 112.

Note: an inventory, *temp.* prior Eastry includes a chasuble *de panno croceo de Tharse*, described as [?the gift] of a Thomas de Winchelesee, Legg and Hope, *Inventories*, 52 (BL Ms Cotton Galba, E.iv, fo 112v).

An inventory of the refectory, dated 1328, includes a *ciphus de murra*, formerly his, Dart, *Antiq. Cant.*, xxi (BL Ms Cotton Galba E.iv, fo 179v).

II Thomas WYNCHELSE
see Wynchilsee

Richard de WYNCHEPE [Wenchepe, Weynchepe
occ. 1241 occ. 1273

n.d., name occ. in the list in *SL*, 174, CCA Lit. Ms D.12, fo 2.

1241, 1 Dec., one of thirteen prof., *Gervase Cant.*, ii, 192.

1258, Mar./Sept., 1259/60, Apr., chamberlain, Reg. H, fos 189v, 201.

1260, Apr./1261, 1263/4, 1268, sacrist, Reg. H, fos 200v, 204v, CCA DCc AS9, CCA Lit. Ms D.12, fo 2; also CCA DCc MA1, fos 103v–112 (1261/9).

1263, with Adam de Chillenden, q.v., acted as the abp's treasurers, *Gervase Cant.*, ii, 227.

1268, 28 Oct., apptd prior of Dover by the abp, *ib.*, ii, 247.

1268/73, prior of Dover; removed *iniuste* on 9 Mar. 1273, CCA Lit. Ms D.12, fo 2.

1270, Sept., *tanquam monachus*, came to Canterbury to take part in the el. of an abp but despite the prior's support he was refused, *Gervase Cant.*, ii, 253; see Adam de Chillenden, William de Dover II, the latter having also asserted his right in an archiepiscopal el. This same yr he was ordered to come to Canterbury by the prior and convent, *sed. vac.*, but suspecting trouble refused, and departed for Tournai, *ib.*, ii, 254–258.

1271/3, on his return he found himself *persona non grata* with the Dover monks, *Gervase Cant.*, ii, 259–265 and returned to Christ Church where he was recd and forgiven, *ib.*, ii, 266–267. Despite the problems at Dover he seems to have gone back; but the new abp Kilwardby was unable to mediate succesfully and ordered him to return to Canterbury, where he found the doors now closed to him, for fear of establishing a precedent acc. to Gervase. Soon, however, he was readmitted but had to be content with a cell in the guest hall, *ib.*,ii, 274–277, 282–283. See Anselm de Eastry.

1273, was restored as prior of Dover, deposed, and again returned to Christ Church, *Gervase Cant.*, ii, 253–274, 274–276; see Anselm de Eastry.

Name in Cambridge, Corpus Christi College Ms 441, Miscellanea (13th c.); on fo 2v *hic est liber*—. It includes a treatise on the instruction of novices.

The Eastry catalogue contains an uncertain no of volumes listed under his name, one of which (no 1420) is the Ms above, James, *Ancient Libraries*, nos 1416–1420 and possibly nos 1421–1435 (pp.120–122).

A list of missing books dated 1 Mar. 1338 includes his Bruttus Galice which was charged out to Alexander de Sandwyco, q.v., *Lit. Cant.*, no 618, (Reg. L, fo 104).

In an inventory of plate and jewels, *temp.* prior Eastry, his name is attached to one item among the treasures of St Thomas, Legg and Hope, *Inventories*, 72.

In an inventory of the refectory dated 1328 a silver *cuppa*, a silver *ciphus* and two *de murra* of his are listed, Dart, *Antiq. Cant.*, xviii, xix, xxii (BL Ms Cotton Galba E.4, fos 178, 180).

I William de WYNCHEPE
occ. 1244 occ. 1268

n.d., name occ. in the list in *SL*, 174, CCA Lit. Ms D.12, fo 1v.

1244, Sept./Nov., 1244/5, 1256/7, Mar., cellarer, CCA DCc AS16, MA1, fos 85v–86v, Reg. H, fo 187v.

1262, 1263/4, 1265/8, bartoner, CCA DCc MA1, fo 104v, AS9, MA1, fos 107v–111.

Item nos 518 and 519 are listed in the Eastry catalogue under W. Weynchepe, James, *Ancient Libraries*, 62.

An inventory of the refectory, dated 1328, includes a silver gilt *ciphus*, formerly his, Dart, *Antiq. Cant.*, xix (BL Ms Cotton Galba E.iv.14, fo 185).

II William WYNCHEPE
occ. 1414/15 d. 1468/9

1414/15, n.d., one of five adm., *SL*, 186, CCA Lit. Ms D.12, fo 6; see next item below.
1415, 10 Nov., the prior was comm. to hear his prof., *Reg. abp Chichele*, iv, 142.
1416, 18 Apr., ord acol. and subdcn, Canterbury cathedral, *ib.*, iv, 319.
1417, 10 Apr., ord dcn, Canterbury cathedral, *ib.*, iv, fo 327.
1420, 6 Apr., ord pr., Canterbury cathedral, *ib.*, iv, fo 342.

1435, 24 Dec., *magister regule* for John Crosse I, q.v., Chron. Wm Glastynbury, fo 117^{v}.
c. 1437, treasurer, CCA DCc DE15C/21; described as former treasurer on 31 Oct. 1440, Chron. Wm Glastynbury, fo 119^{v}.
1440/1, chaplain to the prior, CCA DCc Ms Scrap Book C.129; he was apptd 31 Oct [1440] to succ. Robert Maffeld, q.v., Chron. Wm Glastynbury, fo 119^{v}.
1450, 25 Jan., *magister ordinis*, *SL*, 189, CCA Lit. Ms D.12, fo 7^{v}.
1451/2, 1453/4, chaplain to the prior, CCA Lit. Ms E.6, fo 41^{v}, CCA DCc Prior acct 9, *Chron. Stone*, 60.
1455/7, 1458/9, chamberlain, CCA DCc Prior accts 10, 15, Chamb. acct 62.
1454, 24 Apr., with John Waltham, q.v., sent as proctors to inform the king and Thomas Bourgchier of the chapter's choice of the latter as abp, *Chron. Stone*, 60.
1456/7, one of the *barones*, Prior acct 15.
c. 1460, spent 20 wks ill in the infirmary, CCA DCc Chamb. acct 65.
1466, 17 Feb., 6th in order in an inventory of *jocalia fratrum* [given by him and/or assigned for his use], Reg. N, fo 230^{v}.
1468/9, d., CCA DCc Sac. acct 47; he is described, not surprisingly, as *stacionarius* in CCA Lit. Ms D.12.

III William WYNCHEPE [Wynchepp
occ. 1470 d. 1485

1470, 25 Jan., one of eight prof., *SL*, 190, CCA Lit. Ms D.12, fo 8.
1470, 21 Apr., ord acol., Canterbury cathedral, *Reg. abp Bourgchier*, 405.
1474, 26 Mar., ord dcn, Canterbury cathedral, *ib.*, 417.
1477, 22 Mar., ord pr., Canterbury cathedral, *ib.*, 422.
1485, [Oct./Nov.], d. of 'le swete', one of nine who d. within sixteen days, CCA Lit. Ms D.12, fo 26^{v}.

Note: there are obits for two William Wynchepes:
(1) 15 Oct. (BL Ms Arundel 68, fo 45) and
(2) 6 Nov. (*ib.*, fo 47^{v}); the question remains, which is which?

IV William WYNCHEPE [Wyncheap, Wynchep, Wynchypp, Wynecheppe
occ. 1493 occ. 1540

1493, 26 July, one of ten tonsured, *SL*, 192, CCA Lit. Ms D.12, fo 9^{v}.
1494, 29 Mar., ord acol., Canterbury cathedral, *Reg. abp Morton*, i, no 443a.
1494, 19 Apr., prof., *SL*, 192, CCA Lit. Ms D.12, fo 9^{v}.
1496, 2 Apr., ord subdcn, Canterbury cathedral, *ib.*, i, no 445b.
1497, 25 Mar., ord dcn, Canterbury cathedral, *ib.*, i, no 446c.

1511, 25 Dec., 1513, 25 Dec., *custos* of St Mary in crypt, CCA Lit. Ms C.11, fos 54, 56.
1514, 1515 on 29 Sept.; 1515, 1516 on 25 Dec.; 1517, 29 Sept.; 1519, 1520, 1521, 1523, 1524, 1525 all on 25 Mar., feretrar, CCA Lit. Ms C.11, fos 56^{v}–58^{v}, 59^{v}, 60^{v}, 61, 62, 63, 63^{v}.
1525/33, 1540, 4 Apr., granator, CCA DCc MA30, fo 154^{v}, MA15, fos 34^{v}, 84, 152^{v}, 193^{v}, MA16, fos 50^{v}, 93^{v}, 145, *L and P Henry VIII*, xv, no 452. He is described as 'garrentar' in [1538, 8 Feb., after], Pantin, *Cant. Coll. Ox.*, iii, 152.
1501, 26 Apr., 51st in order at the el. of an abp, Reg. R, fo 56^{v}.
1511, 2 Sept., 34th on the visitation certificate, Wood-Legh, *Visit.*, 3 (Reg. abp Warham, i, fo 35^{v}).
1534, 12 Dec., acknowledged the Act of Supremacy, *DK 7th Report*, Appndx 2, 282.
[1538, 8 Feb., after], in a list of monks prob. prepared for Thomas Cromwell he was described as a 'good man', 60 yrs of age, Pantin, *Cant. Coll. Ox.*, iii, 152.
1540, 4 Apr., apptd petty canon in the new foundation, *L and P Henry VIII*, xv, no 452.

See Thomas Anselme I concerning books.

Benedict de WYNCHILSEE [Wynchelese, Wyndchelesee
occ. [1285]

n.d. [1285], one of four prof., *SL*, 177, CCA Lit. Ms D.12, fo 3.

1293, 8 Aug., d., CCA Lit. Ms D.12, fo 15.

Gregory WYNCHILSEE [Wynchyllsee
occ. 1502 d. 1503

1502, 25 Aug., one of eight tonsured, *SL*, 193, CCA Lit. Ms D.12, fo 10.
1503, 4 Apr., made his prof. before the prior, *sed. vac.*, *ib.*

1503, 29 July, acol., d., *ex consumpcione* at the age of sixteen, CCA Lit. Ms D.12, fos 29ᵛ, 34.

Nicholas WYNCHILSEE [Wynchelse
occ. 1465 d. 1471

1465, 4 Apr., one of seven prof., *SL*, 190, CCA Lit. Ms D.12, fo 8.

1471, 24 Aug., pr., d., in his 8th yr of monastic life; he was born 'in mare versus Franciam', *Chron. Stone*, 117; CCA Lit. Ms D.12, fo 26 describes him as *conventualis*. His obit is in BL Ms Arundel 68, fo 39.

Philip de WYNCHILSEE [Wynchylse
occ. [1207 × 1214]

[1207 × 1214], name occ. in the list of the monks who were in exile, *SL*, 172, CCA Lit. Ms D.12, fo 1.

Note: see Philip I who is prob. this monk.

Robert WYNCHILSEE
occ. 1374

1374, 27 Apr., one of six novices whom the prior was comm. to prof., Reg. abp Wittlesey, fo 130ᵛ; in *SL*, 183, and CCA Lit. Ms D.12, fo 4ᵛ there are eight grouped together but no date.

I Thomas WYNCHILSEE
see Wynchelse

II Thomas WYNCHILSEE [Wyndchelese
occ. [1285] d. 1314

[1285], one of four prof., *SL*, 177, CCA Lit. Ms D.12, fo 3.

1314, 15 Aug., d., CCA Lit. Ms D.12, fo 15ᵛ.

Note: since Thomas Wynchilsee I and Thomas Wynchilsee II were contemporaries or near contemporaries the entries cannot be assigned with any degree of certainty.

John WYNGHAM
occ. 1367 occ. 1374/5

1367, 11 Nov., one of 9 prof., *SL*, 182, CCA Lit. Ms D.12, fo 4ᵛ.

1369, 22 Dec., ord subdcn, abp's chapel, Charing, Reg. Wittlesey, fo 165ᵛ.

1370, 21 Sept., ord dcn, Saltwood, *ib.*, fo 166ᵛ.

1371, 20 Dec., ord pr., abp's chapel, Otford, *ib.*, fo 168.

1374, 30 June, 51st in order at the el. of an abp, Reg. G, fos 173ᵛ–175ᵛ.

1374/5, ill and the anniversarian pd a 'pension' of 6s. 6d. [for medical expenses], CCA DCc Anniv. acct 6.

I William WYNGHAM [Wingham, Wynghame
occ. 1454 d. 1499

1454, 28 Apr., one of eight prof., *SL*, 189, CCA Lit. Ms D.12, fo 8.

1455, 5 Apr., ord acol. and subdcn, chapel within the priory, *Reg. abp Bourgchier*, 359.

1455, 31 May, ord dcn, abp's chapel, Otford, *ib.*, 361.

1458, 1 Apr., ord pr., Canterbury cathedral, *ib.*, 369.

1472, 8 May, 1475, 29 Sept., monk *supervisor*/warden of manors, CCA DCc, RE359, Monk Warden acct 7.

1499, before 4 Oct./Nov., for fourteen yrs *officiarius et penitenciarius* of the abp, CCA Lit. Ms D.12, fos 28, 32.

1466, 17 Feb., 50th in order in an inventory of *jocalia fratrum* [given by him and/or assigned for his use], but he had none, Reg. N, fo 234.

[1486, Apr. × Oct.], one of the monks apptd by the prior *sed. vac.* to serve as confessors in the diocese, Reg. N, fo 172.

1492, recd one pair of 'my best sheets' in a bequest, Hussey, 'Kentish Wills', 42.

1493, 1 May, 5th in order at the ratification of an agreement, Reg. S, fo 383ᵛ; but see John Crosse I.

1499, 4 Oct., d., 'ex infirmitate qui vocatur fistila in ano', at the age of 66, CCA Lit. Ms D.12, fo 28; the date is 4 Nov. and the age 67, on *ib.*, fos 32, 32ᵛ; in both refs he is described as *vir valde religiosus*. His obit is in BL Ms Arundel 68, fo 44.

II William WYNGHAM
occ. 1505 occ. [1538]

1505, 13 Jan., one of six tonsured, *SL*, 193, CCA Lit. Ms D.12, fo 10.

1505, 22 Mar., ord acol., Canterbury cathedral, Reg. abp Warham, ii, fo 262.

1505, 11 July, prof., *ib.*

1506, 11 Apr., ord subdcn, Canterbury cathedral, Reg. abp Warham, ii, fo 262ᵛ.

1507, 3 Apr., ord dcn, Canterbury cathedral, ib., ii, fo 263.

1509/10, celebrated his first mass and recd a small gift from the sacrist, CCA DCc Sac. acct 72. He celebrated on the first Sun. in Apr. [1510] and recd 4d. from the *custos martyrii*, CCA Lit. Ms C.11, fo 51ᵛ.

1516, 25 Dec., warden of manors, CCA Lit. Ms C.11, fo 58.

1523, 25 Mar.; 1525, 24 June; 1526, 25 Mar., 1528, 25 Mar., *custos corone*, CCA Lit. Ms C.11, fos 62, 63ᵛ, 64, 65.

[1538, 8 Feb., after], 'one of the masters of the table in the halle', Pantin, *Cant. Coll. Ox.*, iii, 152.

n.d., as a novice, had John Garard, q.v., as his *magister regule*, and *perfecit*, Pantin, *Cant. Coll. Ox.*, iv, 54 (CCA DCc Ms Scrap Book B.186).

1511, 2 Sept., 60th in order on the visitation certificate, Wood-Legh, *Visit.*, 3 (Reg. abp Warham, i, fo 35ᵛ).

1534, 12 Dec., acknowledged the Act of Supremacy, *DK 7th Report*, Appndx 2, 282.
[1538, 8 Feb., after], in a list of monks prob. drawn up for Thomas Cromwell he was described as a 'good man', 56 yrs of age, Pantin, *Cant. Coll. Ox.*, iii, 152.

WYNNIDUS
n.d.

n.d., 8 Mar., acol., whose obit occ. in BL Ms Arundel 68, fo 19.

William de WYNTON [Wenton, Wyntonia
occ. 1251/2 occ. 1257/8

n.d., name occ. in the list in *SL*, 174, CCA Lit. Ms D.12, fo 2.
1251/2, Sept. to Mar., monk carpenter, Reg. H, fo 172.
1256/8, anniversarian, *ib.*, fos 189, 190^v.
n.d., 10 Jan., pr., whose obit occ. in BL Ms Arundel 68, fo 12^v.

John WYRCESTRE
n.d.

Name in Cambridge, Corpus Christi College Ms 337, Liber scintillarium (13th c.); name on a fly-leaf, partially erased and only just legible under ultra violet lamp.

Percival WYSYNDEN [Wesynden, Wisinden, Wysinden, Wyssenden
occ. 1454 d. 1503

1454, 28 Apr., one of eight prof., *SL*, 189, CCA Lit. Ms D.12, fo 8.
1455, 5 Apr., ord acol., Canterbury cathedral, *Reg. abp Bourgchier*, 359.
1456, 13 Mar., ord subdcn, Canterbury cathedral, *ib.*, 363.
1458, 1 Apr., ord dcn, Canterbury cathedral, *ib.*, 368.
1461, 4 Apr., ord pr., Canterbury cathedral, *ib.*, 378.
1460/1, celebrated his first mass and recd a small gift from the sacrist, CCA DCc Sac. acct 42.
1475/6, anniversarian with Robert Dene, q.v., Lambeth ED44.
1493, 1 May, 1501, 26 Apr., precentor, Reg. S, fo 383^v, Reg. R, fo 56^v.
1493, 1 May, 4th in order at the ratification of an agreement, Reg. S, fo 383^v; but see John Crosse I.
1466, 17 Feb., 52nd in order in an inventory of *jocalia fratrum* [given by him and/or assigned for his use], Reg. N, fo 234.
1501, 26 Apr., 3rd at the el. of an abp, Reg. R, fo 56^v.
1503, 12 Mar., 'submersit seipsum in fonte in novo orto conventus', CCA Lit. Ms D.12, fo 8.

YCKHAM
see Ikham

Henry de YERDE [Zerde
occ. 1329 d. 1333

1329, 9 Oct., one of eight prof., *SL*, 179, CCA Lit. Ms D.12, fo 3^v.
1333, 20 Sept., d., CCA Lit. Ms D.12, fo 16.

YNGHAM, Yngram
see Ingram

John YONGE [Young, Zounge
occ. [1390] d. 1413

[1390], 28 Sept., pr., one of seven prof., *SL*, 184, CCA Lit. Ms D.12, fo 5; he had previously been a secular pr., *ib.*, fo 19^v.
1406, 21 Oct., *magister ordinis*, *SL*, 185, CCA Lit. Ms D.12, fo 6.
n.d., subprior, acc. to *SL*, 184.
1396, 7 Aug., 61st in order at the el. of an abp, Reg. G, fo 234^v.
1413, 25 Oct., d. 'ex morbo ulceris pestilencial' vocat' carbuncl' ', CCA Lit. Ms D.12, fo 19^v; he was described as 'persona honestissima et in divino officio multum assiduus et devotus', *ib.* His obit occ. in BL Ms Arundel 68, fo 46^v.

Nicholas YONGE [Younge
occ. 1421 d. 1422

1421, 4 Apr., one of six prof., *SL*, 186, CCA Lit. Ms D.12, fo 6^v. Because of illness he made his prof. in a chapel in the infirmary, *Chron. Stone*, 12.

1422, 14 Feb., acol., d., CCA Lit. Ms D.12, fo 21^v; his obit occ. in BL Ms Arundel 68, fo 16, and in Lambeth Ms 20, fo 104, on 16 Feb.

YPESWYCHE
see Epyswyche

YSAAC
see Cantuariensis

YSIDORUS
n.d.

n.d., 12 Feb., obit occ. in BL Ms Arundel 68, fo 16.

YSLEP
see Islep

YVINGHO
see Ivynghoe

ZACHARIAS [Zakarias
occ. 1189/91

1189, 6 Oct., one of the monks whom the abp ordered to cooperate with him in the el. of a prior, but he refused, *Epist. Cant.*, 312.

1191, May, described as 'adverso a via veritatis' by the prior and convent and removed from the chapter, *Epist. Cant.*, 334.

Note: the obit of a monk by this name occ. on 12 May, in BL Ms Arundel 68, fo 27 and another by the same name on 9 Nov., *ib.*, fo 47v.

ZACHEUS
n.d.

n.d., 9 Jan., pr., whose obit occ. in BL Ms Arundel 68, fo 12v.

ZERDE
see Yerde

ZOUNGE
see Yonge

COVENTRY CATHEDRAL PRIORY

INTRODUCTION

The early history of the cathedral church and chapter of St Mary, Coventry, has much in common with that of Bath. However, the monastic community here had a shorter pre-conquest existence since it was founded some time before the mid-eleventh century.[1] The episcopal seat underwent two moves before 1228: from Lichfield to Chester in 1075 and from there, briefly, to Coventry in 1102, presumably because the latter was a larger and more important centre.[2] Finally, in 1228 the continuing claims of Lichfield resulted, as for Bath and Wells, in the combining of the two chapters under the episcopal title of Coventry and Lichfield. Here, too, the settlement was preceded by a lengthy period of controversy, during which the monks became subject to a series of oppressive bishops beginning with Robert de Limesey, whose transfer of the see to Coventry established him and his successors as titular abbots.[3]

The main highlights of these unsettled years can be briefly summarized, with a view to setting forth the circumstantial background of some of the entries in the monks' biographies. Surprisingly, perhaps, one of these oppressive bishops was Walter Durdent (1149–1159), prior of Canterbury (q.v. under Canterbury) before he was elected by the Coventry monks, who, in so doing, ignored the protests of the Lichfield canons and deprived them of any say.[4] The chronicles are unanimous in their depiction of bishop Hugh de Nonant (1188–1198), who provoked the monks into violence, during a synod in 1189, in which he himself sustained injury; this provided him with an excuse to expel the monks and replace them with a secular chapter.[5] The prior, Moses, q.v., another former monk of Canterbury, saw no alternative but to surrender the priory demesne and barony to the bishop and take his case to Rome. The monks were restored by papal mandate in 1197 while the repentant bishop was on his deathbed far away at Bec, the abbot of Bury St Edmunds being one of the prelates commissioned to reinstate them.[6]

Persevering in their claims the canons of Lichfield elected one of themselves as their candidate for the see in 1208, while the monks chose their prior, Joybert, q.v. This impasse occurred in the critical years of king John's quarrel with the monks of Canterbury and his refusal to accept Stephen Langton as archbishop; it lasted almost

[1] Demidowicz, *Coventry's First Cathedral*, 18 (article by R. Morris).

[2] In the last quarter of the 14th c. Coventry ranked as the third largest city in England, coming next after York and Bristol.

[3] Demidowicz, *op. cit.*, 118–138, where M. Franklin delineates the careers of the bishops between c. 1072 and 1208 and concludes with the 'provisional statement' that the period was one of 'almost unremitting oppression of the monks of Coventry', 138.

[4] He may have been archbishop Theobald's nominee, Coss, *Coventry Records*, xviii. See Laurence I.

[5] *Gervase Cant.*, i, 461 (Canterbury reference), *Chron. Devizes*, 387 (Winchester reference); see also Geoffrey I.

[6] *Ann. Winton.*, ii, 67, D. Greenway and J. Sayers, *Jocelin of Brakelond, Chronicle of the Abbey of Bury St Edmunds* (Oxford, 1989), 83–84. Abbot Samson entertained fourteen of the Coventry monks in Oxford where the formal ceremony of repossession took place, *ib.*, 84; had he perhaps given some of the monks refuge during their exile?

six years, during which time the monks received contradictory commands from pope and king; and by electing Joybert in obedience to the former they found themselves victims of the fury of the latter. Finally, both parties agreed to a compromise candidate, William Cornhill, royal clerk and justiciar. On his (resignation and) death in 1223 when the monks once again elected their prior, Geoffrey [I], q.v., and the canons again objected, the pope provided Alexander Stavensby.[7] It was clearly in the interests of both parties to resolve their disputed claims; a series of agreements followed, culminating in that of 1248, which was confirmed in 1255 and granted equal rights in future episcopal elections.[8] This did not end all controversy as indicated by the attempted promotion by the Bath monks of their prior, Henry de Leycester [I], q.v., to the see in 1321; but a gradual change occurred in the status and relationship of the two chapters. The secular bishops tended to reside in and to centre their administrative activities in and around secular Lichfield rather than monastic Coventry so that, while the latter retained authority and prestige within its own environs, it largely lost its significance within the diocese.

There may have been unknown fluctuations in the monastic population of Coventry in between the few dates for which numbers recorded have been preserved. As it stands, however, the evidence suggests that the size of the community showed only slight variation after its probable peak of thirty-six in 1214 followed by a drop to about thirty-one in the mid-thirteenth century.[9] In 1364/5, within the space of nine months, the prior obtained papal authorization to present a total of sixteen monks for ordination to the priesthood while they were still two years under the minimum age; this suggests that, although the Black Death must have caused a serious decline in numbers, there was little delay in filling the vacancies.[10] In 1409 twenty-six monks signed a letter of gratitude to bishop Burghill; a century later twenty-three were present at an episcopal visitation; but there are only thirteen signatures on the surrender deed of January, 1539.[11]

The number of obedientiary offices at Coventry, as at Bath, seems to have been almost as many as the number of monks, but here too there is no evidence of their early growth and development. In the first half of the thirteenth century references occur to a subprior (William de Montpellier, q.v.), a chamberlain (Simon III, q.v.), and a precentor (R., q.v.); in 1256 comes the earliest mention of an almoner (John III, q.v.), and in 1287 a cellarer (Henry de Stratton, q.v.) and a monk gardener (John de Merstone, q.v.). The first known reference to a sacrist appears in 1321 (William de Blaby, q.v.), although there can be no doubt of the presence of this important obedientiary at least a century earlier; the same holds true for the earliest known infirmarer (John de Grenborough, q.v.), who occupied his post for some thirty years from c. 1353, for the first treasurer (John de Tomworth, q.v.), who appears in 1385, and for the pittancer (John de Bromlegh, q.v.), first named c. 1390. A refectorer (John Volney, q.v.), a *custos* of the Lady chapel (Richard Stoke, q.v.), a monk [land] steward (Nicholas

[7] *Langton Acta*, no 61.

[8] *Magnum Reg. Album*, nos 240, 24, 589 and Demidowicz, *op. cit.*, 145 (article by R. Swanson). Between 1242 and 1245 the monks had unsuccessfully tried to put in William de Montpellier, q.v., one of their number, as bishop. See also the summary by J. C. Cox in *VCH Warwickshire*, ii, 54; and note the agreement in operation in later years in the entry under William de Greneburgh.

[9] See John II and *Ann. Burton*, 379.

[10] *CPL*, iv (1362–1402), 39, 47.

[11] Reg. Burghill, fo 207, *Blyth Visit.*, 15–17 (in 1518; six years later, at the next visitation, twenty-one were named, *ib.*, 115–117); Demidowicz, *op. cit.*, 161–2 (article by J. Scarisbrick).

Caldecote, q.v.), and a succentor (Gilbert Newton, q.v.) are identified in 1409, and a third prior (Roger Felford, q.v.) in 1453. However, the remaining offices, those of hostiller (John Eccleshall, q.v.), subsacrist (Thomas Lichfield, q.v.), and subtreasurer (John Deane, q.v.) are not visible until the sixteenth century. To these must be added the office of *aqueductor*, unique to Coventry and, perhaps, an overseer of the water supply for the priory, a position first mentioned when the above John Deane held it in conjunction with his duties as subtreasurer. Since, in the sixteenth century the novices, who were not eligible for office, comprised about a quarter of the community, it is no wonder that John Deane and other senior monks each served in several obediences simultaneously. Thomas Knyghton, q.v., for example, in 1535 was pittancer, refectorer, almoner, and hostiller, while Roger Grene, q.v., in c. 1521 combined the offices of infirmarer, sacrist, and coadjutor, this last position remaining unexplained.

The surviving records of three of bishop Blyth's visitations of the chapter (c. 1518, 1521, 1524) lack the injunctions that presumably would have condemned the plurality of office holding, but the bishop would have been hard pressed to suggest an alternative. As to the appointment of obedientiaries, there is no reference in the episcopal registers to indicate that the bishop had any rights, as did the bishops of Bath and Wells, and of all other cathedral chapters apart from Winchester.[12] The Coventry bishops' visitatorial functions within the chapter receive only passing mention in their registers with the exception of those of Blyth and the archiepiscopal visitation of cardinal Morton, for which the certificate listing all the monks was entered in his register.[13]

The early priors of Coventry are for the most part no more than shadowy figures about whom little is known; in some cases, Bruning and German, q.v., for example, even the dates of their priorate are uncertain. It is fortunate for us that, on the death of a prior, the subprior and chapter were obliged to obtain a licence from the king before proceeding to an election because the patent rolls are one of the main sources of information for the succession of priors. Coventry was the only cathedral priory among the religious houses that had military obligations to the crown as these were retained after the abbey had become the mother church of the see of Coventry. As a tenant-in-chief holding the monastic estates as a barony, the prior was in a position similar to that of the bishop: whenever there was a vacancy the king had to issue a licence to elect and to give his assent to the chapter's choice.[14] The earliest evidence of this process in operation is in 1216 with the election of Geoffrey [II], q.v.; and the act of fealty that was also required is recorded in 1396 after the election of Roger de Coton, q.v. Some of the priors like Moses, Joybert, and Geoffrey, all referred to above, appear to have been men of strength and conviction. In the mid-thirteenth century William de Brythwalton, q.v., was awarded the privilege of wearing the pontifical ring, thereby obtaining the status of a mitred prior. The dates and the very existence of possibly three successive priors between c. 1294 and 1342 remain shrouded in mystery, the facts at odds one with another and their interpretation equally at variance. Since these three (if there were three!) were all named Henry and many of the relevant sources refer only to 'the prior', to 'prior Henry', and to 'prior Henry *dictus* Houwhel', confu-

[12] The Coventry registers are extant from 1296 onwards, but of course that is not to say that they are complete.

[13] *Reg. abp Morton*, ii, no 374.

[14] Chew, *Eng. Eccles. Tenants-in-Chief*, 6, 194. This anomaly also explains the prior's seat in parliament, which was based on his secular status before he was eligible as a mitred prelate.

sion continues to reign; my own contribution to a solution will be found under Henry le ?Irreys and Henry de Leycester I and II. As patrons of the two churches of Ufton Cantoris and Ufton Decani the priors presented to both benefices, which were attached to prebendal stalls in Lichfield cathedral, but these appointments would not have given them any say in Lichfield chapter affairs.[15]

Less than a dozen volumes have been identified as having belonged to the medieval library and cloister of Coventry. A list of some thirty volumes copied by John de Bruges, q.v., monk and scribe c. 1240, includes many service books, a copy of the Rule, Palladius' De agricultura, Generaciones veteris et novi Testamenti and Librum decretalium; none of these sheds any light on the contents or extent of a library that, at the very least, must have included commentaries on scripture, pastoral handbooks, sermon collections, and theological treatises in addition to the one volume of Aquinas that still survives.[16] John de Grenborough, q.v., purchased a copy of Gilbertus Anglicus and added valuable notes of his own in a volume now among the Royal manuscripts; and Robert Shirwood, q.v., produced his own Latin translation from the Hebrew of the Old Testament book of Ecclesiastes. We can be sure, however, that there were a few other monks with literary interests, like prior Geoffrey [II], q.v., for example, who wrote a chronicle about the dramatic events surrounding the 1191 expulsion, and there must have been others who had recourse to the library to pursue their studies.

It may be significant that nine named monks were selected for university studies in the one hundred and twelve years between 1409 and 1521, and that in the former year two and in the latter year as many as four were being maintained as students; these facts prompt the thought that the Coventry chapter gave serious heed to its obligation to provide for one monk student in twenty, for on both dates above the monks were greatly exceeding this quota.[17] Although there is one recorded instance of the chapter's failure to maintain monk students, conclusions cannot be drawn from such meagre evidence; and the loss and destruction of obedientiary and manorial accounts and other records are to be greatly regretted because they would have helped to fill in what will probably continue to be a bleak picture.[18] These lacunae also explain our dearth of information about the almonry school. We may be reasonably confident of its origin at an early though uncertain date; but the tragic loss of all the almoner's account rolls and, indeed, of all but three obedientiary accounts, has removed the vital evidence for this and many other details concerning day-to-day affairs. It was functioning c. 1518 when the prior reported to the bishop that the number of boys had declined and that there was room for more.[19]

[15] See Demidowicz, *op. cit.*, 148 where Dr Swanson points out the incorrect reference to 'collations' in *Fasti*, x, 61–64. See also n. 15 in the Introduction to Bath cathedral priory.

[16] See *MLGB*, *MLGB Suppl.*, and Sharpe, *English Benedictine Libraries*, iv, B23; this last lists the books of Bruges.

[17] The named monks are Thomas Ascheby, Richard Barnacle, Richard Blake, Thomas Clypston, Richard Coventry II, Thomas Knyghton, Robert Shirwood, Nicholas Webster, Thomas Weoford, q.v.; Roger de Walton, q.v., prior in the early 13th c. was also given the title of *magister*. The Black Monk Chapter regulation is to be found in Pantin, *BMC*, ii, 22. Canterbury college, Oxford, which was set up for the use of Christ Church monks, possessed a Coventry chamber before 1490; see Richard Blake, and Pantin, *Cant. Coll. Ox.*, iv, 93.

[18] That is, unless some of the lost archives were not destroyed and still await discovery. The absence of monks at university in 1425/6 is noted in Pantin, *BMC*, ii, 172, 174.

[19] 'Numerus confratrum est completus sed non de pueris in elemosinaria', *Blyth Visit.*, 15. Note that the charitable works of the monks would also have appeared on the almoner's rolls.

The role of the cathedral priory within the diocese may have waned in the later Middle Ages, but not so its prestige and power within the city, for it 'played a key part in Coventry's medieval development'.[20] This was mainly, but not solely, because of the extent of the priory's ownership of urban properties, including the important market place, and its patronage of parish churches and chapels within the city.[21] With so many tenants in the city who paid their rents to the prior or to one of the obedientiaries and who regularly appeared in the priory courts, disputes were to be expected. Indeed, there was a lengthy span of hostilities in the early fourteenth century when the whole of Coventry was effectively under the prior's lordship. Opposition to the prior's alleged oppressive régime led to an armed siege of the priory in 1322 followed by a case brought before the court of king's bench; and in the 1330s the prior's jurisdiction in Coventry was challenged by queen Isabella.[22] Another serious altercation broke out in 1480 during the priorate of Thomas Deram, q.v., who accused the mayor and citizens of many transgressions against priory rights and jurisdiction; the mayor's response and the prior's rebuttal were recorded in full in the city's leet book. Good relations must have been restored before 1487 as prior Richard Coventry [II], q.v., Deram's successor, was at this date a member of one of the city guilds, that of Corpus Christi; later priors, namely William Pollesworth, John Impingham, and John Webbe, q.v., were also members and the last two also had membership in the Trinity guild. With regard to recruitment, if we may judge by their toponymics, most of the monks were of local origin, with names like Coventry, Kenilworth, Leicester, Lichfield, and Nottingham; in most cases, however, next to nothing is known of their family backgrounds, Robert Colman and Henry de Leycester II being two of the few of whom names of relatives have been found in the sources.

Priors Richard Coventry [II] and William Pollesworth must have wielded some considerable influence at the triennial Black Monk Chapters in the 1490s and, again, between 1504 and 1516 when the meetings were held in Coventry cathedral and chapter house rather than in the more usual location in the Cluniac priory at Northampton. Presumably the influx of people into the city on account of these gatherings would have promoted, if only briefly, trade and business among those responsible for providing for the visitors' needs. The mayor and burgesses certainly turned out in strength to participate in these occasions, and especially, no doubt, when the prior played host to the royal court and to parliament. The relative frequency of royal visits may have been one effect of the prior's dual relationship to the king, as mitred prelate among the ecclesiastical lords, and as an ecclesiastical baron or tenant-in-chief. In 1404 the so-called *parliamentum indoctorum* met in Coventry under archbishop Arundel's chancellorship, with prior Richard Crosby, q.v., no doubt playing a prominent role. Prior John Shotteswell, q.v., was host to two sessions of parliament in 1456 and 1459, and prior Thomas Deram, q.v., provided hospitality for the king, queen, and court during the Christmas festivities in 1467.[23] The royal presence with its entourage of ministers, officials, and servants was not the only financial burden

[20] Demidowicz, *op. cit.*, 96 (article by K. Lilley).

[21] For the origin and early history of the priory's dominant position in the city, see Coss, *Coventry Records*, xv–xlii.

[22] See the recent article by J. Röhrkasten, 'Conflict in a Monastic Borough: Coventry in the Reign of Edward II', *Midland History*, 18 (1993), 1–18.

[23] Winchester is the only other cathedral priory that served as a setting for parliament.

imposed by the king; the priory also suffered from a succession of corrodians, retired royal servants, pensioned off by the king at the expense of the house.[24]

In keeping with government policy in the 1530s elections of superiors by monastic chapters were no longer left to free choice. Coventry priory felt the heavy hand of Cromwell in 1538 on the death of prior Thomas Weoford, q.v., who four years previously had stood up to Cromwell by refusing to grant the position of receiver in the priory to one of Cromwell's servants. It was now made known to the monks that the 'preferred' candidate was Thomas Carnswell, q.v. A few months after the 'election', eleven of the monks purchased dispensations from the new faculty office of the archbishop to allow them to 'change their habits' and obtain secular benefices, a sure sign of loss of morale within the community when its members were found seeking individual insurance against an uncertain future.[25] Nevertheless, they all remained in the house to sign the surrender deed in January 1539.

It seems clear that the last twenty years of Coventry cathedral priory were overshadowed by a lack of impetus. Nothing more is heard of the bright young monk students, of whom there were four in 1521 and one overseas in 1524, and numbers declined over the next fifteen years from twenty-one to thirteen.[26] Eight monks who were present at bishop Blyth's visitation in 1524 survived to receive pensions after the dissolution; most of the others had probably died before the surrender, almost half of them having been professed by or before 1504. Of the seven new names occurring in the list of those who applied to the faculty office and/or signed the surrender deed, up to four were probably aliases of monks who had been novices in 1524. If young men did continue to arrive to fill the vacant places of deceased monks, most of them have disappeared without trace. The failure to attract candidates who might have instilled fresh life and vigour into the community reflects the loss of nerve among its members and, consequently, their waning influence in the world outside. The combined presence of these factors in the final years before the dissolution may go a long way toward explaining the tragic loss of the medieval cathedral that no one felt inspired to save.[27]

COVENTRY REFERENCES WITH ABBREVIATIONS

Note: if the particular reference sought does not appear below, turn to the General Bibliography on pp. xv–xix, or the Canterbury section, pp. 58–65.

A. Manuscript Sources

i Episcopal Registers, in Lichfield Joint Record Office (LJRO)

Reg. [Walter] Langton (1296–1321)		B/A/1/1, fos 1–142
Reg. [Roger] Northburgh (1322–1358) 3 vols:	i	B/A/1/1, fos 143–216 (ordinations)
	ii	B/A/1/2
	iii	B/A/1/3
Reg. [Robert] Stretton (1360–1385) 3 vols:	i	B/A/1/4
	ii	B/A/1/5i
	iii	B/A/1/5ii

[24] See *VCH Warwickshire*, ii, 55–56.

[25] Chambers, *Faculty Office Regs*, 175; the date was 20 Oct. 1538.

[26] See Thomas Leeke, who complained of the cost of maintaining the students, and also Thomas Weoford, student. There were twenty-one monks present at the visitation in 1524, *Blyth Visit.*, 115–117.

[27] Demidowicz, *op. cit.*, 161 (article by J. Scarisbrick).

Reg. [Walter] Skirlaw (1386)		B/A/1/6
Reg. [Richard] Scrope (1386–1398)		B/A/1/6
Reg. [John] Burghill (1398–1414)		B/A/1/7
Reg. [John] Catterick (1415–1419)		B/A/1/8
Reg. [William] Heyworth (1420–1447)		B/A/1/9
Reg. [William] Booth (1447–1452)		B/A/1/10
Reg. [Reginald] Boulers (1453–1459)		B/A/1/11
Reg. [John] Hales (1459–1490)		B/A/1/12
Reg. [William] Smith (1493–1496)		B/A/1/13, fos 138–191
Reg. [John] Arundel (1496–1502)		B/A/1/13, fos 200–297
Reg. [Geoffrey] Blyth (1503–1531), 2 vols:	i	B/A/1/14i
	ii	B/A/1/14ii (ordinations only)
Reg. [Rowland] Lee (1534–1543)		B/A/1/14iii
Bishop Blyth's Visitation Book		B/V/1/1

Note: for Hereford episcopal registers, see under Worcester.

ii Priory Registers and Cartularies

BL Add. Ms 32100	Transcripts of charters mainly royal and episcopal.
Gregory Leiger Book	Ms Gregory-Hood, Shakespeare Birthplace Library, Stratford-upon-Avon.
Oxford, Bod. Ms Top. Warwicks C.8	Notes and abstracts from a lost cartulary and other original sources.
Reg. Haloughton	Priory register, 14th/15th c., Public Record Office (PRO), E164/21.

B. Other Manuscript Sources

i Obedientary Accounts

(*a*) Birmingham City Archives (BCA)

Cel.	Cellarer	1502/3	168239 (DV2)
Pit.	Pittancer	1478/9	168237 (DV2)
	ib.	1505/6	168235 (DV2)

Note: extracts from these accts were copied into Oxford, Bod. Ms Top. Warwicks C.8, fos 42v–46v, 102–111v, 113–119v.

(*b*) Lichfield Cathedral Library

Magnum Reg. Album	Magnum Registrum Album, 14th c., earliest register/act book of the cathedral chapter (Ms 28).

(*c*) Lichfield, Joint Record Office (LJRO)

Lichfield, Chapter Act Book	Chapter act book, 14th/15th centuries (D 30/2/1/1).

(*d*) Oxford, Bodleian Library (Oxford, Bod.)

Ms Ashmole 794	Lichfield Chapter Act Book, 14th c.
Ms Charters Northamptonshire	Pittancer accts, nos 127, 135, 145, 156

Note: these are calendared in Turner and Coxe, *Charters and Rolls*; for full reference to this vol. see General References.

C. Printed Sources

i Episcopal Registers (in chronological order)

Reg. Stretton (1907) R. A. Wilson, ed., *The Registers or Act Books of the Bishops of Coventry and Lichfield, Book 4, being the register of the guardians of the spiritualities during the vacancy of the see, and the first register of Bishop Robert de Stretton, 1358–1385: on abstract of the contents*, William Salt Archaeological Society, new series, 10, part 2, 1907.

Reg. Stretton (1905) R. A. Wilson, ed., *The Registers or Act Books of the Bishops of Coventry and Lichfield, Book 5, being the second register of Bishop Robert de Stretton. A.D. 1360–1385: an abstract of the contents*, William Salt Archaeological Society, new series, 8, 1905.

Reg. Catterick R. N. Swanson, ed., *The Register of John Catterick, Bishop of Coventry and Lichfield, 1415–1419*, Canterbury and York Society 77, 1990.

Blyth Visit. Peter Heath, ed., *Bishop Geoffrey Blythe's Visitations c. 1515–1525*, Staffordshire Record Society, 4th series, 7, 1973.

Note: for printed Hereford episcopal registers, see under Worcester.

ii Priory Registers and Cartularies

None in print

D. Other Printed Sources and References

Chew, *Eng. Eccles. Tenants-in-Chief* H. M. Chew, *English Ecclesiastical Tenants-in-Chief and Knight Service*, London, 1932.

Clapham, 'Bede-Rolls' A. Clapham, 'Three Bede-Rolls', *Archaeological Journal*, cvi (1949), supplement, 40–53.

Coss, *Coventry Records* P. R. Coss, ed., *The Early Records of Medieval Coventry*, British Academy, Records of Social and Economic History, new series, xi, 1986.

Demidowicz, *Coventry's First Cathedral* G. Demidowicz, ed., *Coventry's First Cathedral Priory of St Mary*, Papers from the 1993 Anniversary Symposium, Stamford, 1994.

Dugdale, *Coventre* W. Dugdale, *The Antiquities of Coventre,* Coventry 1765, extract from his *Antiquities of Warwickshire* of 1656.

Fasti, x B. Jones, comp., *John Le Neve, Fasti Ecclesiae Anglicanae, Coventry and Lichfield Diocese, 1300–1541*, London, 1964.

Fretton, 'Coventry' W. G. Fretton, 'The Benedictine Monastery and Cathedral of Coventry', *Trans. of the Birmingham and Midland Institute (Archaeological Section)* (1876), 19–38.

A. and E. Gooder, 'Coventry before 1355: Unity or Division? The Importance of the Earl's Half', *Midland History*, 6 (1981), 1–38.

Harris, *Coventry Leet Book* M. Harris, ed., *The Coventry Leet Book or Mayor's Register*, Early English Text Society, four vols in two, 1907–1913.

B. Hobley, 'Excavations at the Cathedral Church and Benedictine Priory of St. Mary, Coventry', *Trans. of the Birmingham and Warwickshire Archaeological Society*, 84 (1971), 45–139.

Lancaster, 'Coventry Forged Charters J. Lancaster, 'The Coventry Forged Charters: a Reconsideration', *Bulletin of the Institute of Historical Research*, 27 (1954), 113–140.

Magnum Reg. Album H. E. Savage, ed., *The Great Register of Lichfield Cathedral known as Magnum Registrum Album*, William Salt Archaeological Society, 3rd series, 1924 (1926).

Röhrkasten, 'Conflict' J. Röhrkasten, 'Conflict in a Monastic Borough: Coventry in the Reign of Edward II', *Midland History*, 18 (1993), 1–18.

COVENTRY CATHEDRAL PRIORY

1102–1539

Richard ABEL [Abbell
occ. 1409 occ. [1414/15]

1410, 17 May, ord subdcn, Eccleshall, Reg. Burghill, fo 229.
1411, 11 Apr., ord dcn, Coventry cathedral, *ib.*, fo 231^{v}.
n.d., [1414/15], ord pr., place not stated, *Reg. abp. Chichele* iii, 329.

1409, 14 Oct., 26th and last in order in a letter of gratitude from the chapter to the bp, Reg. Burghill, fo 207.

I ADAM
occ. 1214

1214 [c. 9 July], 11th in order on the list of monks who assented to the el. of William Cornhill as bp of Coventry, CUL Ms Ee.5.31, fo 240.

II ADAM
occ. 1214

1214 [c. 9 July], 23rd in order on the list as above, *ib.*, fo 240^{v}.

ALAN
occ. 1249

1249, 14 June, with Richard de Greneberg, q.v., sent by the prior and chapter to Stanley to the bp with a letter concerning the prof. of monks; two days later the bp recd the prof. of seventeen monks in the chapter house, *Magnum Reg. Album*, no 422 (fo 196).

Note: rather than a surprising influx of prospective monks at this time, the situation prob. arose out of the delay caused by problems, with regard to rights and procedures concerning profession, that had first to be settled.

John ALDURTON [Alderton, Allerton
occ. 1425 occ. 1453

1425, 2 June, ord subdcn, Coventry cathedral, Reg. Heyworth, fo 212^{v}.
1430, 11 Mar., ord pr., Lichfield cathedral, *ib.*, fo 221^{v}.

1453, 12 Mar., with Thomas Deram, q.v., proctors in the el. proceedings of prior Shotteswell, Reg. abp Kemp, fo 332–332^{v}.

I ALEXANDER [senior
occ. 1293

1293, 1 June, witnessed an act of homage made to the prior, Oxford, Bod. Ms Top. Warwicks C.8, fo 74.

II ALEXANDER
n.d.

n.d., there is a ref. to his obit in Fretton, 'Coventry', 36. Dugdale states that his anniversary occ. in an acct roll in 'Sharp's larger register' (now lost), *Monasticon*, iii, 188; see also Oxford, Bod. Ms Top. Warwicks C. 8, fo 49^{v}.

Note: An Alexander, not designated senior, witnessed an act of homage on 15 May, 1295, *ib.*, fo 74^{v}.

Thomas ALNETON
occ. 1427

1427, 20 Sept., ord dcn, Colwich, Reg. Heyworth, fo 217.

ANSELM
occ. 1214 occ. 1223

1223, almoner, *Langton Acta*, no 61; see also *Magnum Reg. Album*, no 464 (fos 204^{v}–205).

1214 [c. 9 July], 24th on the list of monks who assented to the el. of William Cornhill as bp of Coventry, CUL Ms Ee.5.31, fo 240^{v}.
1223, before 29 Nov., with W. subprior and R. precentor q.v., sent to the abp to inform him of the chapter's el. of Geoffrey, their prior q.v., as bp of Coventry, *Langton Acta*, no 61; see also *Magnum Reg. Album*, no 463 (fos 204^{v}–205).

APESFORD
see Happesford

John de ARDESLEY
occ. 1355

1355, 19 Sept., ord pr., Kenilworth, Reg. Northburgh, i, fo 212.

Thomas ASCHEBY [Assheby
occ. 1401 occ. 1409

1401, 15 Mar., ord subdcn, Eccleshall, Reg. Burghill, fo 220^{v}.
1405, 19 Dec., ord dcn, Eccleshall, *ib.*, fo 223.
1408, 10 Mar., ord pr., Lichfield cathedral, *ib.*, fo 225^{v}.

1409, 14 Oct., described as second scholar [?at Oxford], Reg. Burghill, fo 207.

1409, 21st in order in a letter of gratitude from the chapter to the bp, Reg. Burghill, fo 207.

Henry de ASTON
occ. 1355

1355, 1 May, the prior applied to chancery for a writ *de apostato capiendo* vs Henry, prof. lay brother, [*conversus*], because of his disobedience and unauthorized departure from the monastery, PRO C81/1786/11.

1355, 13 June, the writ was sent, PRO C81/1786/12 and *CPR (1354–1358)*, 289.

John ASTON
occ. 1523/4

1523, 19 Dec., ord subdcn, Lichfield cathedral, Reg. Blyth, ii, fo 161v.

1524, [Dec], ord pr., Lichfield cathedral, *ib.*, ii, fo 169.

Robert de AULA
occ. 1296

1296, 29 Jan., abp Winchelsey wrote to the prior and convent on behalf of Robert who, while still a minor had been forced to become a monk of Coventry; he said that he had been beaten and unjustly accused of theft by the monks and so he had fled; he wanted to return but did not dare ask. The abp urged the prior and convent to take him back, *Reg. abp Winchelsey* i, 71–72.

John AYLEM'
occ. 1295

1295, 15 May, one of the monks who witnessed an act of homage to the prior, Oxford, Bod. Ms Top. Warwicks C. 8, fo 74v.

John BACUN [Bacon
occ. 1294/6

1296, 12 Jan., precentor, *CPR (1292–1301)*, 182.

1294, 16 Jan., recd licence from the king to el. a prior *CPR, (1292–1301)*, 60.

1295, 15 May, one of the monks who witnessed an act of homage to the prior, Oxford, Bod. Ms Top. Warwicks C. 8, fo 74v.

1296, 12 Jan., with Adam de Wolveleye, q.v., recd licence from the king to el. a bp., *CPR, (1292–1301)*, 182.

William BARDON
occ. 1409 occ. 1436

1410, 17 May, ord subdcn, Eccleshall, Reg. Burghill, fo 229.

1411, 11 Apr., ord dcn, Coventry cathedral, *ib.*, fo 231v.

1413, 17 June, ord pr., Colwich, *ib.*, fo 235.

1409, 14 Oct., 23rd in order in a letter of gratitude from the chapter to the bp, Reg. Burghill, fo 207.

1436, 14 Sept., recd royal assent to his el. as abbot of Alcester, *CPR (1436–1441)*, 2.

John de BARESHAM [Barsham
occ. 1329 occ. 1356

1329, 23 Sept., ord subdcn, Southam, Reg. Northburgh, i, fo 156v.

1356, 26 Nov., granted royal pardon, along with the prior and other monks, for all the crimes with which they had been charged, *CPR (1354–1358)*, 474.

Richard BARNACLE, B.Th. [Barnacull, Barnakyll, Bernaculum
occ. 1505 occ. 1539

1505, 17 May, ord dcn, Lichfield cathedral, Reg. Blyth, ii, fo 17.

1506, 6 June, ord pr., Longdon, *ib.*, ii, fo 27.

1539, 15 Jan., subprior, *DK 8th Report*, Appndx 2, 16.

1514, 16 May, at Oxford, and after six yrs' study supplicated for adm. to oppose; on 6 Mar., 1517, this was granted, *BRUO*.

1516, 14 Oct., proctor, sent to the king for licence to el. a prior, *L and P Henry VIII*, ii, pt 1 (1515–1516), no 2489; and see William Hynde.

[1518], 9th to be questioned at the episcopal visitation, and agreed that all was well, *Blyth Visit.*, 16.

[1521], 12 Dec., 9th to be questioned at the episcopal visitation and stated that no mortal could persuade him that the prior [John Webbe, q.v.] loved him. For his part the prior reported that Richard was given to drunkenness and the antipathy was mutual, *Blyth Visit.*, 86.

1524, 16 July, 9th to be questioned at the episcopal visitation and reported that the feast of the translation of St Benedict [11 July] was celebrated with greater solemnity than was prescribed. He was accused by John Pope, q.v., of being disobedient and of conducting a whispering campaign vs the prior, *ib.*, 115–116.

1538, 20 Oct., dispensed to hold a benefice, with change of habit, Chambers, *Faculty Office Regs*, 175.

1539, 15 Jan., signed the deed of surrender, *DK 8th Report*, Appndx 2, 16; he was awarded a pension of £13 6s. 8d. p.a., Dugdale, *Coventre*, 30; (no sum is given in the pension list in *L and P Henry VIII*, xiv, pt 1, p. 601). The original deed reveals a very shaky handwriting, PRO E322/61.

Robert BARNESLEY [Bernysley
occ. 1494 occ. 1524.

1494, 20 Sept., ord subdcn, Coventry cathedral, Reg. Smith, fo 180v.

1495, 14 Mar., ord dcn, Eccleshall, *ib.*, fo 184.

1495, 13 June, ord pr., Coventry cathedral, *ib.*, fo 187.

[1518] precentor, *Blyth Visit.*, 16.

1496, 8 Mar., 15th in order on the visitation certificate, and last in order before the novices, *Reg. abp Morton*, ii, no 374.

[1518], 3rd to be questioned at the episcopal visitation and spoke in glowing terms, *non parva laude*, of the prior [John Webbe, q.v.], *Blyth Visit.*, 16.
[1521], 12 Dec., 3rd to be questioned at the episcopal visitation and again spoke well of the prior [John Webbe, q.v.], who, however, accused Robert of seeking support from members of the marquis of Dorset's household *pro causis suis promovendis*. He reported the poor financial state of the pittancer's office; see John Boodon, *Blyth Visit.*, 86.
1524, 16 July, 5th to be questioned at the visitation, but he was *secundus in ordine*, and stated that the prior [John Webbe, q.v.] had everything under control, *ib.*, 115.

Thomas BARTON
occ. 1427

1427, 14 June, ord pr., Colwich, Reg. Heyworth, fo 217.

William BARTON
occ. 1453/5

1453, 24 Feb., ord subdcn, Lichfield cathedral, Reg. abp Kemp, fo 337 and Reg. Boulers, fo 5.
1453, 22 Sept., ord dcn, Longdon, Reg. Boulers, fo 98^v.
1455, 20 Sept., ord pr., Lichfield cathedral, *ib.*, fo 106.

William BAXSTER
occ. 1481/3

1481, 22 Sept., ord dcn, Lichfield cathedral, Reg. Hales, fo 275.
1483, 24 May, ord pr., Lichfield cathedral, *ib.*, fo 283.

William BEDALE
occ. 1461 occ. 1465

1461, 19 Dec., ord subdcn, Lichfield cathedral, Reg. Hales, fo 185.
1462, 18 Sept., ord dcn, Lichfield cathedral, *ib.*, fo 187v, (as Bedar).
1465, 8 June, ord pr., Lichfield cathedral, *ib.*, fo 195.

Robert de BEKYNGHAM
occ. 1356

1356, 26 Nov., granted royal pardon, along with the prior and other monks, for all the crimes with which they had been charged, *CPR (1354–1358)*, 474.

Geoffrey de BELEGRAVE
occ. 1316/17

1316, 18 Dec., ord subdcn, bp's chapel, Bishops Itchington, Reg. Langton, fo 128.
1317, 2 Apr., ord dcn, Lichfield cathedral, Reg. Langton, fo 129^v.

John BETTE [Brette
occ. 1490 occ. 1496

1490, 18 Sept., ord dcn, Lichfield cathedral, Reg. Hales, fo 231.
1491, 28 May, ord pr., Lichfield cathedral, Reg. Smith, fo 123.
1496, 8 Mar., 11th in order on the visitation certificate, *Reg. abp Morton*, ii, no 374, (transcribed as Belle)

Nicholas BISHOPPE [Bysshop
occ. 1481 occ. 1483

1481, 22 Sept., ord dcn, Lichfield cathedral, Reg. Hales, fo 275.
1483, 24 May, ord pr., Lichfield cathedral, *ib.*, fo 283.

Thomas de BLABY
occ. 1361

1361, 30 June, apptd penitentiary in the diocese, *Reg. Stretton* (1905), 98.
n.d., arrangements for his anniversary are given in PRO E164/21, fo 102^v.

Name possibly in Cambridge, Magdalene College Ms 26, Isidore. De rerum natura (13th c.); on an end flyleaf T. de B. has copied a quitclaim dated 1342 to which the seal of the prior, 'W. de G', was attached. See William Irreys who was prior at this time; could his toponymic have begun with 'G' or did Irreys have alternative spellings, e.g. Gerrys, Jerreys?

William de BLABY
occ. 1321/2

1321, 22 Nov., sacrist *CPR (1321–1324)*, 33.
1321, 22 Nov., one of two monk proctors who, with two canons of Lichfield, recd royal licence to el. a bp, *ib.*; see Simon de Frankeloyn.
1322, described as the prior's steward during the six day siege of the priory by the townsmen, Röhrkasten, 'Conflict', 11; see Henry 'Houwhel'.

Richard BLAKE
occ. 1457 occ. 1475

1457, 17 Dec., ord acol., Lichfield cathedral, Reg. Boulers, fo 111^v.
1458, 23 Dec., ord subdcn, Lichfield cathedral, *ib.*, fo 115^v.
1460, 20 Sept., ord pr., Lichfield cathedral, *ib.*, fo 181.
[c. 1474], scholar at Oxford (Canterbury College), but, owing to his conduct, he was reprehended by his prior and dismissed. The prior wrote on 30 June, to the prior of Christ Church, William Sellyng, q.v., (in Canterbury section), explaining that he had without permission 'sued for a capacite' and had been dis-

missed from their community, *Christ Church Letters*, 29–30, Pantin, *Cant. Coll. Ox.*, iii, 116.

Note: was he perhaps the Coventry monk staying at Canterbury college in 1459/60? Pantin, *Cant. Coll. Ox.*, iii, 179; see Richard Coventry II.

1475, 23 Aug., granted dispensation to rec. and retain a benefice dependent on Coventry or on any other monastery of any order, *CPL*, xiii, (1471–84), 451.

Ankerus de BONEYE [?Boveye
occ. 1322

1322, 5 June, ord pr., by *lit. dim.*, Winchcombe abbey, *Reg. Cobham*, (Worcester), 127.

John BOODON [Boydon, Bowdun
occ. 1514 occ. 1524

1514, 15 June, ord pr., Lichfield cathedral, Reg. Blyth ii, fo 98^{v}.

[1518], novice master, *Blyth Visit.*, 17.

[1521], 12 Dec., pittancer, refectorer and master of the Lady chapel (*magister capelle beate Marie*), *ib.*, 87.

[1518], 13th to be questioned at the episcopal visitation, and agreed with his brethren that all was well, *Blyth Visit.*, 17.

[1521], 12 Dec., 12th to be questioned at the visitation and reported himself in agreement with the depositions of his brethren. The financial state of his office of pittancer was stated as poor by Robert Barnesley, q.v., because of an increase in the number of empty tenements and no blame was attached, *ib.*, 86–87.

1524, 16 July, 13th to be questioned at the visitation, and stated that all was in order, *ib.*, 116.

George BOSWORTH
occ. [1518] occ. 1520

[1518], prof., and still a novice at this date, *Blyth Visit.*, 17.

1520, 2 June, ord subdcn, Lichfield cathedral, Reg. Blyth, ii, fo 135.

1520, 22 Sept., ord dcn, Lichfield cathedral, *ib.*, ii, fo 137.

[1518], first named of six novices at the episcopal visitation who all reported *omnia bono ordine*, *Blyth Visit.*, 17.

BOVEYE
see Boneye

Thomas BRACKELEYE [Brakley
occ. 1387 occ. 1398

1387, 21 Sept., ord subdcn, Colwich, Reg. Scrope, fo 142^{v}.

1389, 18 Sept., ord pr., Colwich, *ib.*, fo 145.

1398, 27 Jan., licensed as penitentiary for one yr., Reg. Burghill, fo 141^{v}.

Robert BRAYMER
occ. 1457 occ. 1460

1457, 17 Dec., ord subdcn, Lichfield cathedral, Reg. Boulers, fo 111^{v}.

1458, 23 Dec., ord dcn, Lichfield cathedral, *ib.*, fo 115^{v}.

1460, 20 Dec., ord pr. Lichfield cathedral, Reg. Hales, fo 181^{v}.

John BREDON
occ. 1433/4

1433, 7 Mar., ord subdcn, Lichfield cathedral, Reg. Heyworth, fo 224^{v}.

1433, 6 June, ord dcn, Colwich, *ib.*, fo 225.

1434, 18 Sept., ord pr., Colwich, *ib.*, fo 227^{v}.

Note: a John Bredon, OFM, in 1445, preached a sermon vs the custom of Coventry cathedral church but afterwards recanted, Lincoln cathedral Ms 108, fo 87–87^{v}.

BRETTE
see Bette

John BRISTOWE [Brystow
occ. 1494 occ. 1496

1494, 20 Sept., ord subdcn, Coventry cathedral, Reg. Smith, fo 180^{v}.

1495, 14 Mar., ord dcn, Eccleshall, *ib.*, fo 184.

n.d., 22 Dec., [*temp.* Henry VII], pittancer, Oxford, Bod. Ms Charters, Northamptonshire, no 156.

1496, 8 Mar., 13th in order on the visitation certificate, *Reg. abp Morton*, ii, 374.

BRITHWAULTON
see Brythwalton

John de BROKHAMPTON
occ. 1313

1313, 10 Mar., ord dcn, Worcester cathedral, *Reg. Reynolds* (Worcester), 137.

John de BROMLEGH [Bromeleye
occ. 1367 occ. 1402

1367, 12 June, ord subdcn, bp's chapel, Heywood, *Reg. Stretton* (1905), 209.

1367, 8 Oct., subdcn, recd *lit. dim.* to all orders, *ib.*, 39.

1368, 4 Mar., ord dcn, *ib.*, 213.

1368, 23 Sept., ord pr., Hartlebury, Reg. Wittlesey (Worcester), 74.

[1390], pittancer, Oxford, Bod. Ms Top. Warwicks C. 8, fo 78.

[1390], one of the monks who witnessed an act of homage made to the prior, *ib.*

1402, 13 June, the bp wrote to the prior to commend the 'good and religious conduct' of John de Napton, William Haloughton, q.v., and Bromlegh, Oxford Bod. Ms Top. Warwicks C. 8, fos 64, 84.

Richard BROMLEY
occ. 1393 occ. 1399

1393, 1 Mar., ord subdcn, Colwich, Reg. Scrope, fo 150v.
1393, 22 Mar., ord dcn, Kenilworth priory, *ib.*
1394, 14 Mar., ord pr., Colwich, *ib.*, fo 152.
1397, 27 Apr., licensed as penitentiary, Reg. Scrope, fo 135.
1399, 22 Apr., licensed as penitentiary during pleasure, Reg. Burghill, fo 142.

I William BROMLEY
occ. 1443

1443, 21 Sept., ord subdcn, Lichfield cathedral, Reg. Heyworth, fo 242v.

II William BROMLEY
occ. [1518] occ. 1526

[1518], novice and prof. by this date, *Blyth Visit.*, 17.
1523, 19 Dec., ord subdcn, Lichfield cathedral, Reg. Blyth, ii, fo 161v.
1524, [Dec.], ord dcn, Lichfield cathedral, *ib.*, ii, fo 168v.
1526, 26 May, ord pr., Lichfield cathedral, *ib.*, ii, fo 180v.

[1518], 5th of six novices at the episcopal visitation who all agreed that *omnia bono ordine*, *Blyth Visit.*, 17.
[1521], 12 Dec., 3rd of four novices at the visitation who all complained of having to do without a change of clothing, *ib.*, 87.
1524, 16 July, 3rd of four novices at the visitation, who all spoke well of the prior [John Webbe, q.v.] and said that they were being taught by a secular chaplain, *ib.*, 117.

Note: it is possible that this monk's patronymic was Buchere or Foster, q.v.

Nicholas BROMYCHE [Bremyshe
occ. 1538/9

1538, 20 Oct., dispensed to hold a benefice and change his habit, Chambers, *Faculty Office Regs*, 175.
1539, 15 Jan., signed the deed of surrender, *DK 8th Report*, Appndx 2, 16; awarded a pension of £5 6s. 8d., p.a., Dugdale, *Coventre*, 30 (transcribed as Brenynth); no sum is given in the pension list in *L and P Henry VIII*, xiv, pt 1, p. 601; the original is PRO E322/61.

Note: is this Nicholas Webster, q.v.?

John de BRUGES [Bruches, ? meaning Brigge
occ. c. 1240

Name in
(1) Oxford, Bod. Ms Digby 104, Bede etc., fos 169–174, (13th c.); on fo 171, is a list of 32 books written by him ad opus Covintr' ecclesie. This includes several missals and benedictionals, a psalter and other service books for prior Roger [de Walton, q.v.] and for the sick brethren, also a psalter for Robert de Honintona, q.v., the office of St Mary, for Walter de Wigornia q.v., a martyrologium, two kalendars listing obits, one of which was kept on the high altar, two books of charters and one of decretals, a copy of the rule of St Benedict and Gregory's Pastoral Care and 'tabulam responsorium corneam quam fecit cum magno labore'. The list has been printed in Hearne, *Antiq. Glastonbury*, 291–293 and Dugdale, *Monasticon*, iii, 186, note b.
(2) Oxford, Bod. Ms Auct. F.5.23, Miscellanea (13th/14th c.), contains the same list on fo 166v.

See Sharpe, *English Benedictine Libraries*, iv, B23.

BRUNING [Burwyng
d. before 1122

[c. 1102 × 1122], first prior, acc. to Joan Lancaster, 'Coventry Forged Charters', 138, but not included in *HRH*. She was quoting from an 1122 bede roll, Clapham, 'Bede-Rolls', 47; see also Delisle, *Rouleaux des Morts*, 313 and Sharp's lost cartulary in Dugdale, *Monasticon*, iii, 182.

BRYSTOW
see Bristowe

William de BRYTHWALTON [Brithwaulton, Brychtwalton
occ. 1249 occ. 1280

1249–1280, prior: royal licence to el., granted on 26 May, 1249, *CPR (1247–1258)*, 42; res. by 9 May, 1280, *CPR (1272–1281)*, 369.
1249 × 1250, purchased the 'Earl's half' of Coventry from Roger de Montalt, Coss, *Coventry Records*, xxlv, 29–30.
1251, ?7 Mar., granted the privilege of wearing the [pontifical] ring without restriction of time or place except while celebrating mass, *CPL*, i (1198–1304), 268.
[1273/4], requested the apptment of a substitue for himself as collector of [dues from] the Jews of Warwick because he was ill, and also because it was not proper that he should act, PRO SC1/7/9.

William BUCHERE
occ. 1539

1539, 15 Jan., signed the deed of surrender, *DK 8th Report*, Appndx 2, 16.

See William Bromley II.

Robert BURNE
occ. 1461 occ. 1465

1461, 19 Dec., ord subdcn, Lichfield cathedral, Reg. Hales, fo 185.

1462, 18 Sept., ord dcn, Lichfield cathedral, *ib.*, fo 187ᵛ.
1465, 8 June, ord pr., Lichfield cathedral, *ib.*, fo 195.

I John BURTON
occ. 1400 occ. 1409

1400, 23 Dec., ord subdcn, Eccleshall, Reg. Burghill, fo 219.
1401, 15 Mar., ord dcn, Eccleshall, *ib.*, fo 220ᵛ.
1405, 19 Dec., ord pr., Eccleshall, *ib.*, fo 223.
1409, 14 Oct., 17th in order in a letter of gratitude from the chapter to the bp, Reg. Burghill, fo 207.

II John BURTON
occ. 1518 occ. 1524

[1518], novice and prof. by this date, *Blyth Visit.*, 17.
1523, 19 Dec., ord subdcn, Lichfield cathedral, Reg. Blyth, ii, fo 161ᵛ.
1524, 12 May, ord dcn, Lichfield cathedral, *ib.*, ii, fo 164ᵛ.
1524, [Dec.], ord pr., Lichfield cathedral, *ib.*, ii, fo 169.
[1518], 3rd of six novices at the episcopal visitation, who all agreed that *omnia bono ordine*, *Blyth Visit.*, 17.
[1521], 12 Dec., 2nd of four novices at the visitation, who all complained of having to do without a change of clothing, *ib.*, 87.
1524, 16 July, 2nd of four novices at the visitation, who all spoke well of the prior [John Webbe, q.v.] and said that they were being taught by a secular chaplain, *ib.*, 117.

William BURTON
occ. [1445] occ. 1453

[1445], with Nicholas Crofte, q.v., present at a sermon given by John Bredon, preaching vs the custom of the cathedral church of Coventry, Lincoln Cathedral Ms 108, fo 87–87ᵛ.
1453, c. 12 Mar., involved in the el. proceedings of prior Shotteswell, Reg. abp Kemp, fo 333.

BURWYNG
see Bruning

Thomas BURY
occ. 1440

1440, 23 Sept., ord dcn, Lichfield cathedral, Reg. Heyworth, fo 239.

Nicholas CALDECOTE [Calcot, Caldekot
occ. 1394 occ. 1419

1394, 19 Sept., ord subdcn, Eccleshall, Reg. Scrope, fo 152ᵛ.
1395, 10 Apr., ord dcn, Kenilworth priory., *ib.*, fo 153ᵛ.
1395, 18 Sept., ord pr., Colwich, *ib.*, fo 154ᵛ.
1409, 14 Oct., monk steward [*senescallus*], Reg. Burghill, fo 207.
1400, 6/7 Nov., exempted from attendance at the visitation *per edictam*, Reg. abp Arundel, i, fo 479ᵛ.
1409, 14 Oct., 12th in order in a letter of gratitude from the chapter to the bp, Reg. Burghill, fo 207.
1414, 20 Dec., given papal licence to choose his confessor, who was authorized to give plenary remission at the hour of d., *CPL*, vi, (1404–1415), 353.
1419 6 June, witness to an agreement, PRO E164/21, fo 75.

John de CALOUNDON [Calfdon, Calwedon
occ. 1362/3

1362, 24 Sept., ord subdcn, Coventry cathedral, *Reg. Stretton* (1905), 177.
1362, 17 Dec., ord dcn, bp's chapel, Heywood, *ib.*, 179.
1363, 25 Feb., ord pr., bp's chapel, Heywood, *ib.*, 181.

Thomas CARNSWELL [Camswell, Caswell
occ. 1538/9

1538–1539, prior: 'el.' by 2/4 Mar., 1538, *Fasti*, x, 5.
Note: a letter to Cromwell dated 4 Jan., 1538 ref. to the bearer of the letter as the monk whom Cromwell preferred to be prior. If this is Carnswell the el. date can be placed closer to the d. of Thomas Weoford, q.v., which seems more likely, *L and P Henry VIII*, xiii, pt. i, no 30. Note that licence to el. was given on 1 Nov. 1537; see Thomas Woolson.
1538 20 Oct., dispensed to hold a benefice with change of habit, Chambers, *Faculty Office Regs*, 175.
1539, 15 Jan., headed the surrender list, *DK 8th Report*, Appndx 2, 16; on 20 Feb. he was awarded a pension of £133 6s. 8d. p.a., *L and P Henry VIII*, xiv, pt 1, p. 601.

After the dissolution a Michael Camswell, prob. his brother, acquired land formerly held by the priory, Oxford, Bod. Ms Top. Warwicks C. 8, fo 58ᵛ; see also the refs in Demidowicz, *Coventry's First Cathedral.* 163, 167.

Note: it is extraordinary that this monk should, at this late date, first make his appearance, and as prior. He is surely lurking somewhere in this register. I suggest that he may be Thomas Coventry or Thomas Woolson, q.v.

John de CATESBY
occ. 1370/1

1370, 8 June, ord subdcn, Sallow, *Reg. Stretton* (1905), 235.

1370, 21 Sept., ord dcn, Colwich, *ib.*, 238.
1371, 20 Dec., ord pr., Colwich, *ib.*, 253.

Winfred CELLAR [?i.e. the cellarer
occ. 1539

1539, 15 Jan., signed the deed of surrender, *DK 8th Report*, Appndx 2, 16 (PRO E322/61).

Note: is this Humphrey Celler, q.v.?

Humphrey CELLER [Celar, Seller, Seler
occ. 1504 occ. 1539

1504, 21 Sept., ord dcn, Eccleshall, Reg. Blyth, ii, fo 10.
1504, 21 Dec., ord pr., Lichfield cathedral, *ib.*, ii, fo 13.
[1518], monk steward [*senescallus*], *Blyth Visit.*, 16.
[1521], 12 Dec., preceptor of novices and almoner, *ib.*, 86.
1524, 16 July, with William Hynde, q.v., *custodes* at St Modwenna, [a chapel at Offchurch], *ib.*, 115.
1517, c. 16 June, 3rd in order on the list of nine monks [?*compromissorii*] who petitioned the king to confirm the el. of John Webbe, q.v., as prior, *L and P Henry VIII*, ii, pt 2 (1517–1518), no 3464.
[1518], 6th to be questioned at the episcopal visitation, and reported that all was well, *Blyth Visit.*, 16.
[1521], 12 Dec., 6th to be questioned at the visitation, but here designated *secundus in ordine*; he supported the statements of the prior [John Webbe, q.v.] and of [Robert] Barnesley, q.v., *ib.*, 86.
1524, 16 July, 3rd to be questioned at the visitation and stated, with William Hynde, q.v., that the prior [John Webbe, q.v.] was 'nonmodo discretum verum etiam optimum patrem', *ib.*, 115.
1538, 20 Oct., dispensed to hold a benefice and change his habit, Chambers, *Faculty Office Regs*, 175.
1539, 15 Jan., awarded a pension of £5 6s. 8d. p.a., Dugdale, *Coventre*, 30; no sum is given in the pension list in *L and P Henry VIII*, xiv, pt 1, p. 601; the original is PRO E322/61.

Thomas CHAMBUR [Chambers
occ. 1538/9

1538, 20 Oct., dispensed to hold a benefice and change his habit, Chambers, *Faculty Office Regs*, 175.
1539, 15 Jan., signed the deed of surrender, *DK 8th Report*, Appndx 2, 16; awarded a pension of £6 13s. 4d. p.a., Dugdale, *Coventre*, 30; no sum is given in the pension list in *L and P Henry VIII*, xiv, pt 1, p. 601); the original is PRO E322/61.

William de CHEUTONE
occ. [1339]

[1339], 11 June, witness to the homage of a tenant, PRO E164/21, fo 50v.

William CHICHESTRE
occ. 1443 occ. 1449

1443, 21 Dec., ord dcn, Coventry cathedral, Reg. Heyworth, fo 243.
1449, 7 June, ord pr., Lichfield cathedral, Reg. Booth, fo 108v.

Thomas de CLIFTON
occ. 1325/7 occ. [1339]

1325, 21 Sept., ord subdcn, Tutbury priory, Reg. Northburgh, i, fo 150v.
1327, 20 Sept., ord pr., Sallow, *ib.*, i, fo 153.
[1339], 11 June, witness to the homage of a tenant, PRO E164/21, fo 50v.

Thomas CLYPSTON
occ. 1399 occ. 1409

1399, 29 Mar., ord subdcn, Trinity church, Coventry, Reg. Burghill, fo 213v.
1400, 23 Dec., ord dcn, Eccleshall, *ib.*, fo 219.
1409, 14 Oct., described as first scholar [?at Oxford], Reg. Burghill, fo 207.
1409, 14 Oct., 16th in order in a letter of gratitude from the chapter to the bp, Reg. Burghill, fo 207.

Robert COLMAN
occ. 1487 occ. 1505/6

1487, 22 Sept., ord subdcn, Lichfield cathedral, Reg. Hales, fo 233v.
1488, 31 May, ord dcn, Lichfield cathedral, *ib.*, fo 239.
1488, 20 Sept., ord pr., Lichfield cathedral, *ib.*, fo 240v.
1496, 8 Mar., cellarer, *Reg. abp Morton*, ii, no 374.
1505/6, pittancer, BCA 168235 (DV2).
1496, 1 Mar., 8th in order on the visitation certificate, *Reg. abp Morton*, ii, no 374.
1496, 30 June, granted papal dispensation to rec. and hold for life one benefice with or without cure of souls, *CPL*, xvi (1492–1498), no 541.
1505/6, bought red herring from his father, Robert Colman, on several occasions, BCA 168235 (DV2).

Family connections, see above.

Robert COMBE [Cumbe
occ. 1518 occ. 1537

[1518], novice and prof. by this date, *Blyth Visit.*, 17.
1523, 19 Dec., ord subdcn, Lichfield cathedral, Reg. Blyth, ii, fo 161v.
1524, [Dec.], ord dcn, Lichfield cathedral, *ib.*, ii, fo 168v.
1526, 26 May, ord pr., Lichfield cathedral, *ib.*, ii, fo 180v.
1535, *senescallus* and cellarer, *Valor Eccles.*, iii, 50, 51.

[1518], last of six novices at the episcopal visitation who all agreed that *omnia bono ordine*, *Blyth Visit.*, 17.
[1521], 12 Dec., last of four novices at the visitation, who all complained of having to do without a change of clothing, *ib.*, 87.
1524, 16 July, last of four novices at the visitation who all spoke well of the prior [John Webbe, q.v.] and said that they were being taught by a secular chaplain, *ib.*, 117.
1537, 1 Nov., one of two monk proctors sent to the king for licence to el. a prior, *L and P Henry VIII*, xii, pt 2, no 1011; see Thomas Woolson.

Note: this may be Robert Wyldy, q.v.

Thomas CORLEY
occ. 1421/2

1421, 15 Feb., ord subdcn, Lichfield cathedral, Reg. Heyworth, fo 205ᵛ.
1421, 20 Sept., ord dcn, Longdon, *ib.*, fo 206ᵛ.
1422, 19 Sept., ord pr., Lichfield cathedral, *ib.*, fo 208.

Roger de COTON
occ. 1380 occ. 1409.

1396–1399, prior: el., 27 June/7 July, 1396 *CPR (1396–1399)*, 4 and *Fasti*, x, 4; res. before 16 Apr., 1399, *Fasti*, x, 4.
[1380], 18 Feb., ord subdcn, Colwich, *Reg. Stretton* (1905) 348.
1380, 22 Sept., ord subdcn, (?*recte* dcn) Colwich, *ib.*, 354.
1396, before 27 June, subprior, *CPR (1396–1399)*, 12.
1396, after his el., made his act of fealty to the king, PRO C.270/25/26.
1404, 31 May, licensed as penitentiary in the diocese, Reg. Burghill, fo 153.
1409, 14 Oct., 3rd in order in a letter of gratitude from the chapter to the bp, Reg. Burghill, fo 207.

I Richard de COVENTRY
occ. 1305

1305, 18 Dec., ord subdcn, Colwich, Reg. Langton, fo 101.

II Richard COVENTRY D.Th. [*alias* Share, Shaw, Shawe
occ. 1459 d. 1501.

1481–1501, prior: el. 19 Apr./14 May, 1481; d. by 6 Feb., 1501, *Fasti*, x, 5.
1460, 20 Sept., ord subdcn, Lichfield cathedral, Reg. Hales, fo 180ᵛ.
1461, 27 Feb., given *lit. dim.*, to all orders, *ib.*, fo 132.
1462, 3 Apr., ord dcn, Downham, by *lit. dim.*, Reg. Grey (Ely), fo 210.
1459, before this date, student at Oxford as he now stated that he had studied there for nine yrs, *CU Grace Bk A*, 25.
Note: in 1455/6 and 1459/60 a Coventry monk, possibly this one, was staying at Canterbury college, Oxford, Pantin, *Cant. Coll. Ox.*, iii, 179; see also Richard Blake.
1459/60, student at Cambridge, and granted grace to oppose in theology, *ib.*
1462, presumably student at Cambridge because of the ord above at Downham.
1486/7, incepted in theology at Cambridge and pd to the university proctors 3s. 4d. for his inception and incorporation *CU Grace Bk A*, 203, and another 10m., *ib.*, 205; he put in six pieces of plate as *caucio* to the same proctors, *ib.*, 205. The details are in *BRUC* (but there is confusion as Coventry has somehow slipped into *BRUO*, without his monastic attribution).
1472, 18 Dec., obtained dispensation to rec. and retain a benefice with or without cure of souls, *CPL*, xiii, (1471–1484), 324.
1487, 1489, member of the guild of Corpus Christi in Coventry, Dugdale, *Monasticon*, iii, 183.
1487, 23 Apr., the king held a council at the priory and the prior pronounced a curse on any who spoke vs the king's right to the throne, Fretton 'Coventry', 31.
1498 c. 2 July, played host to the meeting of the Black Monk Chapter, Pantin, *BMC*, iii, 217 and Harris, *Coventry Leet Book*, ii, 588.
1496, c. 8 Mar., present at the metropolitan visitation, *Reg. abp Morton*, ii, no 374 (name transcribed as Share).
1498, 6/10 Oct., Prince Arthur recd hospitality from the prior and monks, Fretton 'Coventry', 31.

Note: Coventry seems to have been a very youthful monk not in orders when first at Oxford unless there is a case of mistaken identity.

Thomas COVENTRY [Coventre
occ. 1515 occ. 1524

1515, 22 Sept., ord subdcn, Derby, St Peter's church, Reg. Blyth, ii, fo 105ᵛ.
1516, 20 Sept., ord pr., Lichfield cathedral, *ib.*, ii, fo 112ᵛ.
[1521], 12 Dec., succentor, *Blyth Visit.*, 87.
1517, c. 16 June, 8th in order on the list of nine monks [?*compromissorii*] who petitioned the king to confirm the el. of John Webbe, q.v., as prior, *L and P Henry VIII*, ii, pt 2 (1517–1518), no 3464.
[1518], 15th to be questioned at the episcopal visitation and agreed with his brethren that all was well, *Blyth Visit.*, 17.
[1521], 12 Dec., 14th to be questioned at the visitation and said that he agreed with the complaints about the subprior [John Pope, q.v.], *ib.*, 87.

1524, 16 July, 15th to be questioned at the visitation, and complained that he had recd nothing for instructing the novices for almost two yrs when a layman would have recd 26s 8d. He blamed the subprior [John Pope q.v.] that his bed in the dormitory was broken. For his part he was accused by the subprior of disobedience and of conducting a whispering campaign vs the prior [John Webbe, q.v.]. Thomas Leek, q.v., reported Thomas's animosity towards the prior and accused him of saying 'I pray god I may sey deprofundis for his solle or I departe', *ib.*, 115–116.

1524, 17 July, promised before the vicar general and the prior and convent that he would not in future exercise the office of public notary [which had been conferred on him] without licence from the prior, *ib.*, 117. This statement was signed *per me Dompnum Thomam Coventre.*

Note: see Thomas Carnswell.

I William de COVENTRY [Coventre

occ. 1367 occ. 1409

1367, 8 Oct., acol., given *lit. dim.*, for all orders, *Reg. Stretton* (1905) 39.

1368, 4 Mar., ord subdcn, bp's chapel, Heywood, *ib.*, 213.

1370, 8 June, ord pr., Sallow, *ib.*, 236.

1409, 14 Oct., precentor, Reg. Burghill, fo 207.

1409, 14 Oct., 8th in order in a letter of gratitude from the chapter to the bp, Reg. Burghill, fo 207.

1409, 14 Dec., licensed as penitentiary in the diocese, Reg. Burghill, fo 201^v.

II William COVENTRY [Coventre

occ. 1433

1433, 7 Mar., ord subdcn, Lichfield cathedral, Reg. Heyworth, fo 224^v.

1433, 6 June, ord dcn, Colwich, ib., fo 225.

Adam de CRAST [Craft

occ. 1331 occ. 1356

1331, 25 May, ord dcn, St John's church, Chester, Reg. Northburgh, i, fo 163^v.

1332, 13 June, ord pr., Coleshull, *ib.*, i, fo 167^v.

1356, 26 Nov., granted royal pardon, along with the prior and other monks, for all the crimes with which they had been charged, *CPR (1354–1358)*, 474.

CRETELTON

see Curtlyngton

Nicholas CROFTE [?Graffte

occ. 1433 occ. [1445]

1433, 7 Mar., ord subdcn, Lichfield cathedral, Reg. Heyworth, fo 224^v.

[1445], with William Burton, q.v., present at a sermon given by John Bredon, preaching vs the custom of the cathedral church of Coventry, Lincoln Cathedral Ms 108, fo 87–87^v.

Richard CROSBY [Crosseby

occ. 1387 occ. 1437

1399–1437, prior: el. 23 Apr./1 May, 1399, *Fasti*, x, 4; *prefectio*, 10 May, 1399, Reg. Burghill, fo 6v; d. by 5 Apr., 1437, *Fasti, ib.*

1387, 21 Sept., ord subdcn, Colwich, Reg. Scrope, fo 142^v.

1390, 28 May, ord pr., Colwich, *ib.*, fo 146.

1404, 6 Oct., played host to a meeting of parliament at which abp Arundel defended the status of the Church and clergy (the so called *parliamentum indoctorum*); see P. Heath, *Church and Realm, 1272–1461*, London, 1988, 257.

1409, 14 Oct., headed the list of monks who signed a letter of gratitude to the bishop, Reg. Burghill, fo 207.

1410, 13 Oct., at a synod held in the cathedral, the bp declared that the feast of St Osburga, whose shrine was near the high altar should be celebrated througout the adcnry of Coventry. Demidowicz, *Coventry's First Cathedral*, 61, 154 (articles by J. Hunt and R. Swanson).

1412, 20 Oct., granted licence for a portable altar, *CPL*, vi, (1404–15), 382.

1414, 5 Oct., named as one of the executors of the will of bp Burghill, *Reg. abp Chichele*, iv, 15.

1417, Feb., one of those commissioned to act for the abp as defenders of English Cluniac houses, *Reg. abp Chichele*, iv, 48–51.

1417, Nov./Dec., present at convocation, *ib.*, iii, 37–38 and apptd by the abp, along with other cathedral priors, to serve on a committee to look into the poverty of university graduates, *ib.*

1420, 1423, July, present at the Black Monk Chapter in Northampton, Pantin, *BMC*, ii, 96, 137; in 1423 he was named as one of the electors of the future presidents, and apptd to visit Daventry priory on acct of disturbances there, *ib.*, 152, 153.

1424, 30 Nov., deterred from preaching in Trinity Church, Coventry to denounce a Lollard preacher beause of unrest in the city, Harris, *Coventry Leet Book*, ii, 96–97.

1426, July, apptd visitor of Benedictine houses in the diocese of Coventry and Lichfield by the Black Monk Chapter, Pantin, *BMC*, ii, 169.

1429, July, present at the Black Monk Chapter, Northampton, but *quia senex recessit*, *ib.*, ii, 183.

Name in Trinity College, Cambridge, Ms 1088, Bede (12th c.); on fo 2 *ex dono—.*

During his priorate and through his initiative, the eastern arm of the cathedral, which was prob. still largely Romanesque, was remodelled and a new chevet constructed, Demidowicz, *Coventry's First Cathedral*, 63.

Dugdale states that his portrait was in a window in St Mary's hall, Coventry, *Monasticon*, iii, 183.

Nicholas Crosby, a contemporary, who in 1422 held the prebend of Ufton Cantoris in Lichfield cathedral and a chantry in Coventry cathedral (both of which were under the priory's patronage), may have been a relative, Reg. Heyworth, fo 9; see *Fasti*, x, 62.

William CROSSEBY
occ. 1433 occ. 1478/9

1433, 7 Mar., ord subdcn, Lichfield cathedral, Reg. Heyworth, fo 224v.

1478/9, pittancer, BCA 168237 (DV2).

Richard CROYLAND
occ. 1478

1478, 19 Sept., ord dcn, bp's chapel, Beaudesert, Reg. Hales, fo 266.

William de CUKFORD
see Tuckeford

CUMBE
see Combe

Thomas CURTLYNGTON [Cretelton, Kurtylyngton
occ. 1440 occ. ?1478/9

[1440], 24 Sept., ord dcn, Lichfield cathedral, Reg. Heyworth, fo 237v.

1443, 21 Sept., ord pr., Lichfield cathedral, *ib.*, fo 243.

1478/9, former pittancer, BCA 168237 (DV2).

John de DAVENTRE [Davyntre
occ. 1367/8

1367, 8 Oct., acol., given *lit. dim.*, for all orders, *Reg. Stretton* (1905), 39.

1368, 4 Mar., ord subdcn, bp's chapel, Heywood, *ib.*, 213.

[1368], 3 June, ord dcn, Colwich, *ib.*, 216.

1368, 23 Sept., ord pr., Hartlebury, Reg. Wittlesey (Worcester), 74.

John DEANE [Deyn, Deyne
occ. [1518] occ. 1535

[1518], almoner, *Blyth Visit.*, 16.

[1521], 12 Dec., subtreasurer and *aqueductor*, *Blyth Visit.*, 87.

1535, sacrist, *Valor Eccles.* iii, 50.

[1518], 12th to be examined at the episcopal visitation, and agreed that all was well, although he made one complaint vs Thomas Leeke, q.v., *Blyth Visit.*, 16.

[1521], 12 Dec., 11th to be questioned at the visitation, and spoke in generally favourable terms of the state of the house, *ib.*, 87.

1524, 16 July, 10th to be questioned at the visitation, and reported that all was well; however, John Pope q.v., accused him of disobedience and of carrying on a whispering campaign vs the prior [John Webbe, q.v.], *ib.*, 116.

John de DEPYNG
occ. 1324/5

1324, 22 Sept., ord subdcn, Spondon, Reg. Northburgh, i, fo 148v.

1325, 2 Mar., ord dcn, [?Bishops] Tachbrook, *ib.*, i, fo 149v.

Thomas DERAM [Derham
occ. 1452 d. 1481

1461–1481 prior: el. before 5 Nov., 1461 *CPR (1461–1467)*, 85; d., 14 Apr., 1481, *Fasti*, x, 5.

1452, 4 July, monk steward [*senescallus*], *CPL*, xi, (1455–1464), 83.

1461, before 5 Nov., subprior, *CPR (1461–1467)*, 85.

1453, 12 Mar., with John Aldurton, q.v., proctors in the el. proceedings of prior Shotteswell, Reg. abp Kemp, fo 332–332v.

1467, Dec., played host to the king and queen who spent Christmas at the priory, Fretton, 'Coventry', 31.

[c. 1474], wrote to William Sellyng, prior of Christ Church, Canterbury, q.v., (under Canterbury) about Richard Blake, q.v., *Christ Church Letters*, 29–30.

1480, 16 Nov., issued a lengthy list of complaints vs the mayor and citizens, mainly about property rights, rents and jurisdiction in the city, to which the mayor and council replied; the prior then responded with the chapter's objections and no agreement was achieved. The details are recorded in Harris, *Coventry Leet Book*, i, 443–473.

Robert DERBY
occ. 1494 occ. 1496

1494, 20 Sept., ord subdcn, Coventry cathedral, Reg. Smith, fo 180v.

1495, 13 June, ord pr., Coventry cathedral, *ib.*, fo 187.

1496, 8 Mar., 14th in order on the visitation certificate, *Reg. abp Morton*, ii, no 374.

Thomas DERBY
occ. 1409 occ. 1412

1410, 17 May, ord subdcn, Eccleshall, Reg. Burghill, fo 229.

1411, 11 Apr., ord dcn, Coventry cathedral, *ib.*, fo 231v.

[1412], 24 Sept., ord pr., Colwich, *ib.*, fo 234.

1409, 14 Oct., 25th in order in a letter of gratitude from the chapter to the bp, Reg. Burghill, fo 207.

DERHAM
see Deram

John DEYN(E)
see Deane

Richard DROWTE [Drowthe, Drought, Droute
occ. 1467 occ. 1496

1467, 19 Dec., ord subdcn, Coventry cathedral, Reg. Hales, fo 202.
1469, 28 Feb., a papal indult was issued for him, though only in his 22nd year, to be promoted to the orders of dcn and pr., *CPL* xii (1458–1471), 670.
1469, 27 May, ord dcn, Eccleshall, *ib.*, fo 206.
1469, 23 Sept., ord pr., Colwich, *ib.*, fo 206v.
1486, 2 Oct., subprior and pittancer, Oxford, Bod. Ms Charters, Northamptonshire, no 135.
1496, 8 Mar., monk steward, [*senescallus*], *Reg. abp Morton*, ii, no 374.
1475, 23 Aug., granted dispensation to rec. and retain any benefice dependent on Coventry or on any other monastery of any order, *CPL*, xiii, (1471–1484), 413.
1496, 8 Mar., 4th in order on the visitation certificate, *Reg. abp Morton*, ii, no 374.

William de DUNSTABLE [Dunstaple
occ. 1319 d. 1361

1349–1361, prior: el. by 10 Aug., 1349, *Fasti*, x, 4, because royal asent was obtained on this date; *prefectio*, 26 Aug., 1349, Reg. Northburgh ii, fo 49; d. by 2 July, 1361, *CPR (1361–1364)*, 35.
1319, 2 June, ord dcn, Eccleshall, Reg. Langton, fo 136v.
1320, 24 May, ord pr., Southam, *ib.*, fo 139v.
1349, before 10 Aug., sacrist, *CPR (1348–1350)*, 357.
n.d., there is a ref. to William having been cellarer and [monk] steward, *CPR (1354–1358)*, 474.
1342, Apr., one of nine *compromissorii* at the el. of a prior, Reg. Northburgh, ii, fo 38v; see William Irreys.
1356, 26 Nov., granted royal pardon, along with other monks, for all the crimes with which they had been charged, *CPR (1354–1358)*, 474.
1360, 16 Sept., apptd vicar general in spirituals with M. Walter de Chilterne, canon of Lichfield, *Reg. Stretton* (1905), 3; on 26 Nov., acting as such they issued a mandate, *Reg. Stretton* (1907), 105.

John ECCLESHALL [Ecclesall, Eccleshale, Eccleshalle
occ. 1515 occ. 1539

1515, 22 Sept., ord subdcn, St Peter's church, Derby, Reg. Blyth, ii, fo 105v.
1516, 20 Sept., ord pr., Lichfield cathedral, *ib.*, ii, fo 112v.
[1518], hostiller [*hospitularius*], *Blyth Visit.*, 17.
[1518], 14th to be questioned at the episcopal visitation, and concurred with the others that all was well, apart from some difficulty concerning the subprior [John Pope, q.v.], *Blyth Visit.*, 17.
[1521], 12 Dec., 13th to be questioned at the visitation and was critical of the drinking habits of [John Pope, q.v.], the subprior [when carrying out duties] in parish churches and of the way in which the divine office was performed, *ib.*, 87.
1524, 16 July, 14th to be questioned at the visitation, and reported agreement with the statements of the others, *ib.*, 116.
1538, 20 Oct., dispensed to hold a benefice and change his habit, Chambers, *Faculty Office Regs*, 175.
1539, 15 Jan., awarded a pension of £5 6s. 8d. p.a., Dugdale, *Coventre*, 30; no sum is given in the pension list in *L and P Henry VIII*, xiv, pt 1, p. 601; the original is PRO E322/61.

Robert EIRENE
see Grene

Thomas ENNE [?Eure, Yeme
occ. 1467 occ. 1471

1467, 19 Dec., ord subdcn, Coventry cathedral, Reg. Hales, fo 202.
1469, 27 May, ord dcn, Eccleshall, *ib.*, fo 206.
1471, 21 Dec., ord pr., Coventry cathedral, *ib.*, fo 247.

John de ESTON
occ. 1288

1288, 18 May, witnessed an act of homage made to the prior, Oxford, Bod. Ms Top. Warwicks C. 8, fo 73v.

I John de ETONE
occ. 1352 occ. 1358

1352, 2 June, ord dcn, St Catherine's chapel, Hereford, *Reg. Trillek* (Hereford), 583.
1358, 30 Nov., obtained royal licence to el. a bp (with William de Greneburgh, q.v., and two canons of Lichfield), *CPR (1358–1361)*, 122.

II John ETON
occ. 1399 occ. 1409

1399, 29 Mar., ord subdcn, Trinity church, Coventry, Reg. Burghill, fo 213v.
1400, 23 Dec., ord dcn, Eccleshall, *ib.*, fo 219.
1409, 14 Oct., 15th in order in a letter of gratitude from the chapter to the bp., Reg. Burghill, fo 207.

John EVANS [Evance
occ. 1538/9

1538, 20 Oct., dispensed to hold a benefice and change his habit, Chambers, *Faculty Office Regs*, 175.

1539, 15 Jan., signed the deed of surrender, *DK 8th Report*, Appndx 2, 16; he was awarded a pension of £5 6s. 8d. p.a., Dugdale, *Coventre*, 30; no sum is given in the pension list in *L and P Henry VIII*, xiv, pt 1, p. 601); the original is PRO E322/61.

Robert de EVERDON
occ. 1361 occ. 1388

1361, 22 May, ord pr., Alvechurch, by *lit. dim.*, Reg. Bryan (Worcester), i, 122.
[1385], 12 Feb., comm. as penitentiary in the diocese, *Reg. Stretton* (1905), 89.
1388, 27 Jan., comm. as penitentiary, Reg. Scrope, fo 124.

Name in Oxford, Bod. Ms Auct. F.5.23, Miscellanea, (13th/14th c.); *ex dono fratris*—on fo 86, at the end of Exposiciones partium biblie post M. Alexandrum Necham.

William de EVERDON [Everton, Overdon
occ. 1383 occ. 1385

1383, 14 Feb., ord subdcn, Colwich, *Reg. Stretton* (1905), 378.
1383, 19 Sept., ord dcn, Colwich, *ib.*, 384.
[1385], 25 Feb., ord pr., Colwich, *ib.*, 396.

Thomas EYRE [Here
occ. 1500/1

1500, 19 Sept., ord acol., Lichfield cathedral, Reg. Arundel, fo 289^v.
1501, 19 Mar., ord subdcn, Lichfield cathedral, *ib.*, fo 292^v.
1501, 18 Sept., ord dcn, Lichfield cathedral, *ib.*, fo 297^v.

William de EYTON [Eton
occ. 1325 occ. 1327

1325, 21 Sept., ord subdcn, Tutbury priory, Reg. Northburgh, i, fo 150^v.
1327, 19 Sept., ord pr., Sallow, *ib.*, i, fo 153.

Roger FELFORD [? Fifelde
occ. 1425 occ. 1461

1425, 2 June, ord dcn, Coventry cathedral, Reg. Heyworth, fo 212^v, (as Fifelde).
1427, 20 Sept., ord pr., Colwich, *ib.*, fo 217^v.

1444, 3 July, subprior *CPL*, ix, (1431–1447), 424.
1453, 7/15 Mar., third prior at the el. of prior Shotteswell, Reg. abp Kemp, fo 332.
1461, 27 Feb., subprior, Reg. Hales, fo 132.
1461, 27 Feb., licensed as penitentiary, Reg. Hales, fo 132.

Thomas FERBY [Feryby
occ. 1387 occ. 1409

1387, 21 Sept., ord subdcn, Colwich, Reg. Scrope, fo 142^v.
1390, 28 May, ord pr., Colwich, *ib.*, fo 146.
1409, 14 Oct., treasurer, Reg. Burghill, fo 207.
1409, 14 Oct., 9th in order in a letter of gratitude from the chapter to the bp, Reg. Burghill, fo 207.

Roger FIFELDE
see Felford

John FORSTER
occ. 1467 occ. 1471

1467, 19 Dec., ord subdcn, Coventry cathedral, Reg. Hales, fo 202.
1469, 23 Sept., ord dcn, *ib.*, fo 209^v.
1471, 21 Dec., ord pr., Coventry cathedral, *ib.*, fo 247.

William FOSTER
occ. 1538/9

1538, 20 Oct., dispensed to hold a benefice and change his habit, Chambers, *Faculty Office Regs*, 175.
1539, 15 Jan., signed the deed of surrender, *DK 8th Report*, Appndx 2, 17; awarded a pension of £5 6s. 8d. p.a., Dugdale, *Coventre*, 30; no sum is given in the pension list in *L and P Henry VIII*, xiv, pt 1, p. 601); the original is PRO E322/61.

Note: see William Bromley II.

John de FOXTON
occ. 1344 occ. 1346

1344, 18 Sept., ord dcn, Chesterton, Reg. Northburgh, i, fo 197.
1346, 13 Sept., ord pr., by *lit. dim.*, Stow, *Reg. Bransford* (Worcester), no 1073 (p. 261).

John FRANKELOYN [Frankelayne, Frankelyn
occ. 1433/5

1433, 7 Mar., ord subdcn, Lichfield cathedral, Reg. Heyworth, fo 224^v.
1433, 6 June, ord dcn, Colwich, *ib.*, fo 225^v.
1435, Sept., ord pr., Eccleshall, *ib.*, fo 229.

Simon de FRANKELOYN [? Frankelois
occ. 1305 occ. 1321

1305, 18 Dec., ord dcn, Colwich, Reg. Langton, fo 101.
1321, 22 Nov., cellarer, *CPR (1321–1324)*, 33 (transcribed as Franketon).
1321, 22 Nov., one of two monk proctors who, with two canons of Lichfield, recd royal licence to el. a bp, *ib.*, see William de Blaby.

Robert FYSSHER
occ. 1470 occ. 1476

1470, 22 Sept., ord acol., Coventry cathedral, Reg. Hales, fo 209.
1473, 12 June, ord subdcn, Longdon, ib., fo 250.

1475, 18 Feb., ord dcn, Kenilworth, *ib.*, fo 253v.
1476, 9 Mar., ord pr., Lichfield cathedral, *ib.*, fo 256.

I GEOFFREY
occ. 1214

1214, [c. 9 July], 25th on the list of monks who assented to the el. of William Cornhill as bp of Coventry, CUL Ms Ee.5.31, fo 240v; prob. identical with the following entry.

II GEOFFREY
occ. 1216 d. 1235

1216–1235, prior: el. before 7 July, 1216, *HRH*, 41; d., 1235, *VCH Warwicks*, ii, 58; but see Simon. He succ. Joybert, q.v.
1223, 7 June, apptd one of the justiciars on assize in Warwickshire, *CPR (1216–1225)*, 394.
1223, before 29 Nov., el. bp, but the el. was quashed, *Langton Acta*, nos. 61, 64, *Magnum Reg. Album*, no 464 (fos 204v–205).
1227, 4 Aug., recd royal licence to go to the curia, *CPR (1225–1232)*, 137.
1232, suspended by the bp for refusing to allow him on his visitation of the priory to introduce members of another order as visitors; he appealed to Rome, *Ann. Tewkesbury*, 89.
1233, 4 Feb., granted royal protection on the journey to Rome, *CPR (1232–1247)*, 10.
1233, 27 May, one of three who were apptd to settle a long standing dispute between the abbeys of Westminster and Pershore, *CPL*, i (1198–1304), 134.

Author of a lost chronicle that covered the events of 1191 when the bp expelled the monks, Dugdale, *Monasticon*, vi, pt 3, num. VI, 1242–1244, (BL Ms Cotton Ch. xiii, 26). See Sharpe, *Latin Writers*.

Note: see also the preceding entry. *Councils and Synods*, ii, 48 suggests that it was he, as prior, who attended the fourth Lateran council in 1215.

GERMAN
occ. 1139

1139, 18 Apr., occ. as prior, *HRH*, 40; see *Magnum Reg. Album*, no 454 (fo 202–202v). He is not included in the list in Sharp's cartulary, Dugdale, *Monasticon*, iii, 182, where his probable successor Laurence I, q.v., does occ.

GODVINUS [Goduinus
occ. before 1122

1122, d. by this date when he occ. in a mortuary roll of Savigny, Clapham, 'Bede-Rolls', 47.

GRAIE
see Thomas Knyghton

John de GRENBOROUGH
occ. 1353 occ. [1380s]

1353, 21 Sept., ord pr., Colwich, Reg. Northburgh, i, fo 208v.
1353 × 1380s, infirmarer for 30 yrs, BL Ms Royal 12 G.iv, fo 187v.

Name in BL Ms Royal 12 G.iv., Gilbertus Anglicus etc., (early 14th c.); he bought it for the use of the sick and made additions from other treatises of English, Irish, Jewish, Saracen, Lombard and Italian [*Salernitorum*] authorities as he carefully noted on fo 187v, with a cautionary remark that not all the cures he included in the new quires proved successful because some doctors were ignorant and wrote *multa verba et vacua*.

Robert GRENE
occ. 1461 occ. 1496

1461, 19 Dec., ord subdcn, Lichfield cathedral, Reg. Hales, fo 185.
1462, 18 Sept., ord dcn, Lichfield cathedral, *ib.*, fo 187v.
1465, 8 June, ord pr., Lichfield cathedral, *ib.*, fo 195.
1491, 23 Apr., pittancer, Oxford, Bod. Ms Charters, Northamptonshire, no 145.
1491, 23 Apr., acknowledged receipt of rent, Oxford, Bod. Ms Charters, Northamptonshire, no 145.
1496, 8 Mar., penitentiary and 3rd in order on the visitation certificate, *Reg. abp Morton*, ii, no 374 (transcribed as Eirene).

Roger GRENE
occ. 1504 occ. 1524

1504, 21 Sept., ord dcn, Eccleshall, Reg. Blyth, ii, fo 10.
1504, 21 Dec., ord pr., Lichfield cathedral, *ib.*, ii, fo 13.
[1518], refectorer, *Blyth Visit.*, 16.
[1521], 12 Dec., sacrist, infirmarer and coadjutor *ib.*, 87.
1517, c. 16 June, 5th in order on the list of nine monks [?*compromissorii*] who petitioned the king to confirm the el. of John Webbe, q.v., as prior, *L and P Henry VIII*, ii, pt 2 (1517–1518), no 3464.
[1518], 8th to be questioned at the episcopal visitation, and he agreed with all the others especially the prior [John Webbe, q.v.], *Blyth Visit.*, 16.
[1521], 12 Dec., 8th to be questioned at the visitation, and reported that all was well, *ib.*, 87.
1524, 16 July, 8th to be questioned at the visitation, and agreed with Robert Barnesley and Thomas Leeke, q.v., *ib.*, 116.

Richard de GRENEBERG [Greneberge, Greneburg

occ. 1249 occ. 1285/6

1249, 14 June, with Alan, q.v., sent by the prior and chapter to Stanley to the bp with a letter concerning the prof. of monks; two days later the bp recd the prof. of seventeen monks in the chapter house, *Magnum Reg. Album*, no 422 (fo 196).

Note: rather than a surprising influx of prospective monks at this time, the situation prob. arose out of the delay caused by problems, with regard to rights and procedures concerning profession, that had first to be settled.

1280, 9 May, recd royal licence to el. a prior, *CPR (1272–1281)*, 369.

1285/6, aged 70 yrs and was witness to an agreement concerning tithes at Wasperton, BL Add. Ms 32100, fo 46; he had given evidence during the inquiry, *ib.*, fo 104.

William de GRENEBURGH

occ. 1339 d. 1390

1361–1390, prior: el. by 13 July, 1361, when royal assent was given, confirmed by the bp 23 July, *Reg. Stretton* (1907), 20; d. by 12 Sept., 1390, *Fasti*, x, 4.

1339, 18 Dec., ord subdcn, Eccleshall, Reg. Northburgh, i, fo 187.

1353, 10 Aug., given papal licence to choose his confessor, who was authorized to give plenary remission at the hour of d., *CPL*, iii, (1342–1362), 511.

1358, 30 Nov., obtained royal licence to el. a bp, with John de Eton, q.v., and two canons of Lichfield, *CPR (1358–1361)*, 122.

[1363, Sept.], one of the diffinitors at the Black Monk Chapter, Pantin, *BMC*, iii, 33.

1364, 3 Mar., obtained papal permission to present six monks for ordination to the priesthood although under age because of the d. of many monks during the Black Death epidemic, *CPL*, iv, (1363–1395), 39; on 17 Jan., the following yr he obtained a similar dispensation for ten monks, *ib.*, iv, 47.

William le GYNUR

occ. 1285/6

1285/6, aged 40 yrs and witness to an agreement concerning tithes at Wasperton, BL Add. Ms 32100, fo 46; he had given evidence at the inquiry, *ib.*, fo 105^{v}.

Richard HALL

occ. 1526/7

1526, 26 May, ord subdcn, Lichfield cathedral, Reg. Blyth, ii, fo 179.

1527, 15 June, ord dcn, Lichfield cathedral, *ib.*, ii, fo 188.

William HALOUGHTON [Halouton, Halughton

occ. 1393 occ. 1424

1393, 19 Sept., ord subdcn, Eccleshall, Reg. Scrope, fo 152^{v}.

1395, 10 Apr., ord dcn, Kenilworth priory, *ib.*, fo 153^{v}.

1395, 18 Sept., ord pr., Colwich, *ib.*, fo 154^{v}.

1409, 14 Oct., pittancer, Reg. Burghill, fo 207.

1410/11, possibly cellarer and pittancer, as there are rentals for both offices for approximately the same dates in PRO E164/21 fo 137^{v}; however, he may simply have been responsible for compiling the cellarer's rental.

1402, 13 June, the bishop wrote to the prior to commend his 'good and religious conduct' and that of John de Bromlegh and John de Napton, q.v., Oxford, Bod. Ms Top. Warwicks C. 8, fos 64, 84.

1409, 14 Oct., 13th in order in a letter of gratitude from the chapter to the bp, Reg. Burghill, fo 207.

1414, 20 Dec., given papal licence to choose his confessor, who was authorized to give plenary remission at the hour of d., *CPL*, vi, (1404–1415), 353.

1419, 6 June, witness to an agreement, PRO E164/21, fo 75.

1424, 24 June, witness, Reg. Heyworth, fo 202^{v}.

His register, PRO E164/21, includes rentals, surveys and copies of charters etc., 13th to 15th c.; it is dated on fo 1, 1410/11. Also on fo 1, *factum per—*.

Adam HAPPESFORD [Apesford, Happusford

occ. 1387 occ. 1409

1387, 21 Sept., ord subdcn, Colwich, Reg. Scrope, fo 142^{v}.

1390, 28 May, ord pr., Colwich, *ib.*, fo 146.

[1407], 4 Feb., licensed as penitentiary in the diocese, Reg. Burghill, fo 195.

1409, 4 Oct., penitentiary and 10th in order in a letter of gratitude from the chapter to the bp, *ib.*, fo 207.

I HENRY

occ. 1214

1214 [c. 9 July], 10th in order on the list of monks who assented to the el. of William Cornhill as bp of Coventry, CUL Ms Ee.5.31, fo 240.

II HENRY

occ. 1214

1214, [c. 9 July], 21st on the list as above, *ib.*, fo 240^{v}.

III HENRY
occ. 1320

1320, 24 May, ord dcn, Southam, Reg. Langton, fo 138^{v}.

IV HENRY
see Aston

HERBERT
occ. 1214

1214, [c. 9 July] 9th on the list of monks who assented to the el. of William Cornhill as bp of Coventry, CUL Ms Ee. 5.31, fo 240.

Thomas de HERBURBUR' [Herberbur'
occ. 1322/3 occ. 1331

1322, 15 Sept., ord dcn Southam, Reg. Northburgh, i, fo 144^{v}.
1323, 19 Feb., ord pr., Aylwaston, *ib.*, i, fo 146.
1331, 11 Jan., witnessed an act of homage made to the prior, Oxford, Bod. Ms Top. Warwicks C. 8, fo 71.

HERE
see Eyre

Nicholas HERNEYS [? Herveys
occ. 1313

1313, 10 Mar., ord dcn, Worcester cathedral, *Reg. Reynolds* (Worcester), 137.

John HERT
occ. 1457 occ. 1460

1457, 17 Dec., ord subdcn, Lichfield cathedral, Reg. Boulers, fo 111^{v}.
1458, 23 Dec., ord dcn, Lichfield cathedral, *ib.*, fo 115^{v}.
1460, 20 Dec., ord pr., Lichfield cathedral, Reg. Hales, fo 181^{v}.

HERVEY [Herwey
occ. c. 1122

The second prior, alive in 1122, acc. to Joan Lancaster, 'Coventry Forged Charters', 138; Dugdale, *Monasticon*, iii, 182; see also Bruning (the first prior). Not in *HRH*.

John HEYWODE [Hewood
occ. 1470 occ. 1496

1470, 22 Sept., ord acol., Coventry cathedral, Reg. Hales, fo 209.
1473, 12 June, ord subdcn, Longdon, *ib.*, fo 250.
1475, 18 Feb., ord dcn, Kenilworth, *ib.*, fo 253^{v}.
1496, 8 Mar., 5th in order on the visitation certificate, *Reg. abp Morton*, ii, no 374.

John HOLEWEYE
occ. 1295

1295, 15 May, one of the monks who witnessed an act of homage made to the prior, Oxford, Bod. Ms Top. Warwicks C. 8, fo 74^{v}.

John de HOLOND
occ. 1342

1342, 8 Mar., ord pr., Rugeley, Reg. Northburgh, i, fo 193.

Robert de HONINTONA
n.d.

n.d., [?mid 13th c.], prob. a brother monk for whose use John de Bruges, q.v., wrote a psalter, Oxford, Bod. Ms Digby 104, fo 171.

HONINTONA
see also Hunyton

James de HORTON
occ. 1363 d. 1396

1390–1396, prior: el. 12/23 Sept 1390, *Fasti*, x, 4; d., 20 June, 1396, Reg. Scrope, fo 11.
1363, 27 May, ord subdcn, bp's chapel, Bishops Itchington, *Reg. Stretton* (1905), 183.
1363, 21 Dec., ord pr., bp's chapel, Heywood, *ib.*, 194.

Henry dictus 'HOUWHEL' [Howel
occ. 1324

1324, 25 Apr., a mandate was sent by the pope to inquire into simony, perjury and sortilege ascribed to him who is named as prior, *CPL*, ii, (1305–1342), 237.

Note: some months prior to the papal mandate a case before the king's bench revealed an attempt on the part of a group of Coventry burgesses who employed a necromancer to bring about the death of the king, Earl Despenser, the prior and several others who were alleged to be oppressing the townspeople, Selden Society, *Select Cases King's Bench under Edward II*, 74, no 54. Röhrkasten's 'Conflict', 12–18, identifies the prior as Henry Howel and assumes that, from 1302 through the period of prolonged conflict between town and priory leading up to the siege of the priory in 1322, he remained in office. Röhrkasten also suggests that the inquiry concerning Houwhel's necromancy was part of the complex play of power politics in the competition for the controlling influence within the town, *ib.* See Henry de Leycester I and II and Henry le ?Irreys.

John HOWLEE [Houvy
occ. 1525 occ. 1539

1525, 23 Sept., ord pr. Lichfield cathedral, Reg. Blyth, ii, fo 174^{v}.
1539, 15 Jan., signed the deed of surrender, *DK 8th Report*, Appndx 2, 16.

Note: this may be John Kenelworth, q.v.

John HUNTE
occ. 1500 occ. 1503

1500, 19 Sept., ord acol., Lichfield cathedral, Reg. Arundel, fo 289^{v}.

1503, 10 June, ord subdcn, Lichfield cathedral (*sed. vac.*, Canterbury and Coventry/Lichfield), Canterbury, Reg. F, fo 287.

William de HUNYTON [Honintona
occ. 1286

1286, 3 July, chamberlain, Oxford, Bod. Ms Top. Warwicks C. 8, fo 73.

1286, 3 July, witnessed an act of homage made to the prior, *ib*.

William HYNDE [?Wynde
occ. 1496 occ. 1524

1496, 8 Mar., novice, *Reg. abp Morton*, ii, no 374 (transcribed as Wynde).

1498, 22 Sept., ord subdcn, Lichfield cathedral, Reg. Arundel, fo 273^v.

1498, 22 Dec., ord dcn, Lichfield cathedral, *ib.*, fo 276^v.

1499, 23 Feb., ord pr., Lichfield cathedral, *ib.*, fo 278^v.

[1521], 12 Dec., monk steward [*senescallus*] and cellarer, *Blyth Visit.*, 86.

1524, 16 July, with Humphrey Celler, q.v., *custodes* at St Modwenna, [a chapel at Offchurch] *ib.*, 115.

1496, 8 Mar., 17th and last in order on the visitation certificate, *Reg. abp Morton*, ii, no 374.

1516, 14 Oct., apptd proctor, with Richard Barnacle, q.v., to obtain licence from the king to el. a prior, *L and P Henry VIII*, ii, pt 1 (1515–1516), no 2489.

[1518], 4th to be questioned at the episcopal visitation, and reported that all was well, *Blyth Visit.*, 16.

[1521], 12 Dec., 4th to be questioned at the visitation, and stated that all was well, *ib.*, 86.

1524, 16 July, 2nd to be questioned at the visitation and stated, with Humphrey Celler q.v., that the prior [John Webbe, q.v.] was 'nonmodo discretum verum etiam optimum patrem', *ib.*, 115.

John IMPINGHAM [Impyngham, Ympingham
occ. 1493 d. 1517

1516–1517, prior: el. 26/29 Oct./5 Nov., 1516; d. on or by 16 June, 1517, *Fasti*, x, 5, *L and P Henry VIII*, ii, pt 2 (1517–1518), no 3400.

1493, 2 Mar., ord pr., Tutbury priory, Reg. Smith, fo 172.

1516, 14 Oct., subprior, *L and P Henry VIII*, ii, pt 1 (1515–1516), no 2489.

1516, Oct., became a member of both the Trinity and Corpus Christi guilds in Coventry, Dugdale, *Monasticon* iii, 183 (transcribed as Impyngton).

Henry le ?IRREYS [de Irreys, Jerreys, le orde
occ. before 1328

1328 before 12 Sept., prior; on this date arrangements were completed for a chantry, at the altar of the Trinity and St Mary, for Henry *nuper prior* and for [? the present prior's] family, Robert and William de Leicester, canons of Lichfield, and their parents and others, Reg. Northburgh, iii, fo 27. See also Hugh de Rochwell.

Note: None of the evidence for the existence of this monk and prior can be verified from primary sources, but there are enough secondary references to merit attention. For example, Wharton states that he was prior in 1321 when he was el. bp by the Coventry chapter alone, *Anglia Sacra*, i, 464, but he omits Henry de Leycestre, q.v., entirely from his list of priors. Browne Willis names Henry de Leycestre as prior in 1293, and Henry Jerreys as his successor who was el. bp in 1321 (*Mitred Abbies*, i, 71). The revised Dugdale refs to the lost mss of Thomas Sharp, antiquary (1770–1841), whose transcripts mentioned a Henry Irreys, prior in the years 16 and 18 Edward II, Dugdale, *Monasticon*, iii, 183, note. The problem is compounded by the fact that Reg. Northburgh, not only names Henry *nuper prior* above but records the d. of Henry de Leycestre, prior, in 1342. Thus we cannot identify Irreys and Leycestre as one and the same, nor can we safely concur in the conclusion of the antiquarian writers who may have been repeating errors from one another. I suggest the following possible solution:

1294 × ?1321, Henry de Leycester I, prior, q.v.
?1321 × ?1328, Henry le Irreys, prior, who may also have been known as Henry de Leycester
?1328 × 1342, Henry de Leycester II, prior, q.v.

But see also Henry 'Houwhel'.

William IRREYS [Ireys, le Irrois
occ. 1313 d. 1349

1342–1349, prior: el. 1342, before 19 Apr., when the bp confirmed him, Reg. Northburgh, ii, fos 38^v, 39; d. on or by 1 Aug., 1349, *CPR (1348–1350)*, 353.

1313, 10 Mar., ord dcn, Worcester cathedral, *Reg. Reynolds* (Worcester), 137.

[1339], 11 June, witness to the homage of a tenant, PRO E164/21, fo 50^v.

1342, Apr., one of nine *compromissorii* at his own el., Reg. Northburgh, ii, fo 38^v.

Note: see Thomas de Blaby.

I JOHN
occ. 1214

1214, [c. 9 July], 28th on the list of monks who assented to the el. of William Cornhill as bp of Coventry, CUL Ms Ee.5.31, fo 240^v.

II JOHN
occ. 1214

1214, [c. 9 July], 36th and last on the list as above.

III JOHN
occ. 1256

1256, 30 Dec., almoner, obtained a royal licence to el. a bp, *CPR (1247–1258)*, 535.

M. JOYBERT [Josbert, Jocabertus
occ. 1198 d. 1216

1198–1216, prior: previously monk of La Charité; prior of Much Wenlock and Coventry together; 18 Jan., 1198, apptd prior by abp Hubert after the monks' restoration by the pope on this date, Paris, *Chron. Majora*, ii, 445. d., 14 June, 1216; possibly also prior of Daventry and Bermondsey, *HRH*, 41.
Note: all the monasteries named, other than Coventry, were Cluniac and daughter houses of La Charité.

1198, 21 June, read the *postulatio* of the bp, Geoffrey Muschamp, at his consecration at Canterbury. The following day he was one of the monk superiors named as present in the chapter house there who urged the abp to come to an agreement with the Canterbury monks by giving up his project for a collegiate church at Lambeth, *Gervase Cant.*, i, 556.
Note: He was reluctant to read the postulation until the canons of Lichfield had been removed, but the abp replied that the assembly had heard enough of his protestations (but they *were* removed!), Dugdale, *Monasticon*, vi, pt 3, num. VI, 1242. The protracted negotiations with king John over the el. of a bp during the interdict are dramatically recounted in *ib.*, num. VI, pp. 1242–1244; the persistent refusal of the prior with his monk delegates to cooperate by electing one of the king's nominees and to sanction the participation of the Lichfield chapter lasted through a series of confrontations with the king at Tewkesbury and Nottingham and with the papal legate at Oxford and Eton. The legate's mediation finally broke the deadlock in 1214, *ib.*
1214, [c. 9 July], assented to the el. of William Cornhill as bp of Coventry, CUL Ms Ee.5.31, fo 240.

John KEMBERTON [Kembyrton
occ. 1383 occ. 1404

1383, 14 Feb., ord subdcn, Colwich, *Reg. Stretton* (1905), 378.
1383, 19 Sept., ord dcn, Colwich, *ib.*, 384.
1384, 4 June, ord pr., Colwich, *ib.*, 390.

1404, 31 May, licensed as penitentiary in the diocese, Reg. Burghill, fo 153.

John KENELWORTH
occ. 1518 occ. 1524

[1518], novice and prof. by this date, *Blyth Visit.*, 17.
1524, 21 May, ord dcn, Lichfield cathedral, Reg. Blyth, ii, fo 164v.

[1518], 2nd of six novices at the episcopal visitation, who all agreed that omnia bono ordine, *Blyth Visit.*, 17.
[1521], 12 Dec., 1st of four novices at the visitation, who all complained at having to do without a change of clothing, *ib.*, 87.
1524, 16 July, 1st of four novices at the visitation, who all spoke well of the prior [John Webbe, q.v.], and said they were being taught by a secular chaplain, *ib.*, 117.

Thomas de KEREBY
occ. 1313

1313, 10 Mar., ord dcn, Worcester cathedral, *Reg. Reynolds* (Worcester), 137.

William KNYGHTCOTE [Knytecot
occ. 1313 occ. 1342

1313, 10 Mar., ord dcn, Worcester cathedral, *Reg. Reynolds* (Worcester), 137.
1342, April, one of nine *compromissorii* at the el. of a prior, Reg. Northburgh, ii, fo 38v; see William Irreys.

Thomas KNYGHTON, B.Cn.L. [*alias* ?Graie
occ. 1514 occ. 1535

1514, 10 June, ord pr., Lichfield cathedral, Reg. Blyth, ii, fo 98v.

[1518], cellarer, *Blyth Visit.*, 16.
1535, pittancer, almoner, refectorer, and hostiller, *Valor Eccles*, iii, 50.
1523, 26 Apr., student at Oxford, and supplicated for B.Cn.L. after three and a half yrs' study, *BRUO, 1501–1540*.
Note: on the page with his name in the printed book below he is described as scholar.
1517, [c. 16 June], 7th in order on the list of nine monks [?*compromissorii*] who petitioned the king to confirm the el. of John Webbe, q.v., as prior, *L and P Henry VIII*, ii, pt 2 (1517–1518), no 3464.
[1518], 11th to be questioned at the episcopal visitation, and agreed that all was well, *Blyth Visit.*, 16.
[1521], 12 Dec., absent from the visitation, *ib.*, 87.
1524, 16 July, 12th to be questioned at the visitation, and agreed with the accusations made by the subprior, [John Pope, q.v.], concerning Thomas Coventre and others, but he also accused the subprior of failure to comply with certain regulations, *ib.*, 116.

Name in Oxford Bod. 4°V.16(2)Th., M. Vegius (printed book), Paris, AD 1511; at the end of the treatise Dialogii Alithie et Philalithis *frater—est possessor huius libri*; see *MLGB Suppl.*

Robert KYRKEBY
occ. 1400

1400, 13 Mar., ord subdcn, Trinity church, Coventry, Reg. Burghill, fo 215.

Thomas de KYRKEBY
occ. 1324/5

1324, 22 Sept., ord subdcn, Spondon, Reg. Northburgh, i, fo 148v.
1325, 2 Mar., ord dcn, [?Bishops] Tachbrook, *ib.*, i, fo 149v.

Walter LANGLEY [Langley
occ. 1425/7

1425, 2 June, ord dcn, Coventry cathedral, Reg. Heyworth, fo 212v.
1427, 20 Sept., ord pr., Colwich, *ib.*, fo 217v.

I LAURENCE
occ. 1144 d. 1179

c. 1144–1179 prior: occ. 4 May, 1144; d., 29 Jan., 1179, *HRH*, 40–41.
1148/9, journeyed to Rome, after he and the monks had carried out the el. of a bishop at Leicester in the presence of abp Theobald, to obtain confirmation of the chapter's el. of Walter Durdent (q.v., under Canterbury) vs the protestations of the Lichfield chapter, Dugdale, *Monasticon*, iii, item VI, pp. 1242, 1244 (BL Ms Cotton Ch xiii, 26). See Demidowicz *Coventry's First Cathedral*, 129.
1149, 26 Jan., present in Worcester cathedral chapter with abp Theobald and others and attested a general confirmation of Simon, bp of Worcester in favour of his own cathedral priory, *Theobald Charters*, 546.
1152, 14 Feb., called to Rome with the bp in order to settle their differences, *Magnum Reg. Album*, no 262, and see Coss, *Coventry Records*, xviii–xix; the bp had laid claim to some of the priory estates.
n.d., founded the hospital of St John the Baptist, *VCH Warwicks*, ii, 53.

II LAURENCE
occ. 1214 occ. 1223

1214, [c. 9 July], 12th on the list of monks who assented to the el. of William Cornhill as bp of Coventry, CUL Ms Ee.5.31, fo 240.
1223, before 29 Nov., a Laurence is named as proctor in el. proceedings with R. precentor, W. subprior and Anselm, q.v., in *Magnum Reg. Album*, no 463 (fos 205–205v); see Geoffrey II.

LEASSTAN
[?c. 1122 × 1139]

[?c. 1122 × 1139], the third in a list of priors named in Sharp's lost cartulary, *Monasticon*, iii, 182; see also Bruning (the first prior), and Laurence I above. Not in *HRH*.

Reginald de LEEK
occ. 1336

1336, 6 Nov., apptd by Henry [de Leycester], the prior, q.v., to represent him in a suit before the king's council between the queen and the prior [?over the royal right to demand corrodies], *CClR (1333–1337)*, 707; see also William de Sheynton and John de Sutham.

Thomas LEEKE [Lecke, Leke
occ. 1503 occ. 1539

1503, 10 June, ord subdcn, Lichfield cathedral (*sed. vac.*, Canterbury and Coventry/Lichfield), Canterbury Reg. F., fo 287.
1504, 21 Dec., ord dcn, Lichfield cathedral, Reg. Blyth, ii, fo 12.
1505, 15 Feb., ord pr., Lichfield cathedral, *ib.*, ii, fo 15.
[1518], *aqueductor*, *Blyth Visit.*, 16.
1517, c. 16 June, 2nd in order on the list of nine monks [?*compromissorii*] who petitioned the king to confirm the el. of John Webbe, q.v., as prior, *L and P Henry VIII*, ii, pt 2 (1517–1518), no 3464.
[1518], 5th to be questioned at the episcopal visitation; he concurred with the other seniors in praising the rule of the prior [John Webbe q.v.]; however, he was himself accused by John Deane q.v., of causing dissension in the community, *Blyth Visit.*, 16.
[1521], 12 Dec., 5th to be questioned at the visitation, and complained of the heavy expenses laid on the community which was maintaining three scholars in addition to [Robert] Shirwood, q.v., He also complained of the absence from divine office of the subprior [John Pope, q.v.], of his failure to fulfil his responsibilities, of his indebtedness and of his meals more splendid than those of the prior, *ib.*, 86.
1524, 16 July, 6th to be questioned at the visitation and affirmed the hostility between the prior [John Webbe, q.v.] and Thomas Coventre, q.v., *ib.*, 116.
1538, 20 Oct., dispensed to hold a benefice and change his habit, Chambers, *Faculty Office Regs*, 175.
1539, 15 Jan., signed the deed of surrender, *DK 8th Report*, Appndx 2, 16; he was awarded a pension of £6 p.a., Dugdale, *Coventre*, 30; no sum is given in the pension list in *L and P Henry VIII*, xiv, pt 1, p. 601); the original is PRO E322/61.

I Henry de LEYCESTER [Leycestr'
occ. 1290 occ. before 1321

1294 × ?1321, prior: el. 12/27 Jan., 1294, *Fasti*, x, 4; royal assent was granted on 2 Feb., *CPR (1292–1301)*, 61; see Henry le Irreys.

1290, 24 Nov., 1291, 23 Nov.; 1292, Mar., chaplain to the prior, PRO E164/21, fo 50v; Oxford, Bod. Ms Top. Warwicks C. 8, fo 74v; *ib.* fo 74.

1300, 27 Dec., obtained royal protection for two yrs on going overseas, *CPR, (1292–1301)*, 560.

1301, 26 Jan., apptd two [?monk] attorneys in his absence, *ib.*, 562.

1305, 4/7 Nov., granted royal letters of protection before going overseas to Rome and also the right to name two attorneys in his absence, *CPR (1301–1307)*, 393, 395.

1312, one of the cathedral priors summoned to London to meet the papal nuncios, *Councils and Synods*, ii, 1377.

1321, [Nov.], Henry, prior, was el. bp by the Coventry chapter, but the Lichfield chapter objected and Roger de Northburgh was provided, *Fasti*, x, i.

Note: This is prob. Henry le Irreys q.v., but see also Henry 'Houwhel'.

II Henry de LEYCESTER [Leycestr'
occ. 1326 or 1328 d. 1342

?1326 or 1328 × 1342, prior: a Henry de Leycester occ. as prior on 31 Oct., 1326, on 24 Feb., 1329 and on 14 Aug., 1333, Oxford, Bod. Ms Ashmole 794, fos 16v, 29v, 47. On 12 Sept., 1328 a chantry was ordained, at the altar of the Trinity and St Mary, for the souls of Henry *nuper* prior, and for his [i.e. ?the present prior's] family, Robert and William de Leicester, canons of Lichfield and their parents and others, Reg. Northburgh, iii, fo 27; see also Hugh de Rochewell. D. before 2 Feb., 1342, *CClR (1341–1343)*, 391; Reg. Northburgh, i, fo 38v also notes he d. in 1342.

1336, 6 Nov., apptd Reginald de Leek, William de Sheynton and John de Sutham, q.v., to represent him in a suit before the king's council between the queen and himself [?over the royal right to demand corrodies], *CClR (1333–1337*, 707.

Note:
(1) His brother Robert de Leycester gave several grants of land to the priory during his priorate, PRO E164/21 fos 96, 104v, 105.
(2) See Henry le Irreys.

John de LEYCESTER [Leycestre
occ. 1367 occ. 1371

1367, 8 Oct., acol., given *lit. dim.*, for all orders, *Reg. Stretton* (1905), 39.

1368, 4 Mar., ord subdcn, bp's chapel Heywood, *ib.*, 213.

[1368], 3 June, ord dcn, Colwich, *ib.*, 216.

1371, 20 Dec., ord pr., Colwich, *ib.*, 253.

Simon de LEYCESTRE
occ. 1305

1305, 18 Dec., ord dcn, Colwich, Reg. Langton, fo 101.

William de LEYCESTRE
occ. 1342

1342, 8 Mar., ord pr., Rugeley, Reg. Northburgh, i, fo 193.

William LIBARD [de Lymbart, Lybard
occ. 1368 occ. 1409

1368, 4 Mar., ord subdcn, bp's chapel, Heywood, *Reg. Stretton* (1905), 213.

1371, 20 Dec., ord pr., Colwich, *ib.*, 253.

1409, 14 Oct., 7th in order in a letter of gratitude from the chapter to the bp, Reg. Burghill, fo 207.

Thomas LICHFELD [Lichefeld, Lychefeld
occ. 1515 occ 1521

1515, 22 Sept., ord subdcn, St Peter's church, Derby, Reg. Blyth, ii, fo 105v.

1517, before 19 Sept., described as novice before this date when he was ord pr., Lichfield cathedral, *ib.*, ii, fo 120.

[1518], subsacrist, *Blyth Visit.*, 17.

1517, c. 16 June, 9th and last in order on the list of nine monks [?*compromissorii*] who petitioned the king to confirm the el. of John Webbe, q.v., as prior, *L and P Henry VIII*, ii, pt 2 (1517–1518), no 3464.

[1518], 16th to be questioned at the episcopal visitation, and agreed with the other monks that all was well, *Blyth Visit.*, 17.

[1521], 12 Dec., 15th to be questioned at the episcopal visitation and concurred with the report of the prior, [John Webbe, q.v.], *ib.*, 87.

Walter LICHFELD
occ. 1443 occ. 1448

1443, 21 Dec., ord dcn, Coventry cathedral, Reg. Heyworth, fo 243.

1448, 21 Dec., ord pr., Lichfield cathedral, Reg. Booth, fo 107.

Richard de LODBROK
occ. 1305 occ 1342

1305, 18 Dec., ord dcn, Colwich, Reg. Langton, fo 101.

1331, 31 July, sacrist, Reg. Northburgh, iii, fo 24v.

1331, 11 Jan, witnessed an act of homage made to the prior, Oxford, Bod. Ms Top. Warwicks C. 8, fo 71.

1342, Apr., named as one of nine *compromissorii* at the el. of a prior, Reg. Northburgh, ii, fo 38v; see William Irreys.

William de LODBROK
occ. 1342

1342, Apr., named as one of nine *compromissorii* at the el. of a prior, Reg. Northburgh, ii, fo 38v; see William Irreys.

Thomas LONDON
occ. 1416/18

1416, 13 June, ord subdcn, Lichfield cathedral, *Reg. Catterick*, no 224.
1416, 19 Sept., ord subdcn [?*recte* dcn], Coventry cathedral, *ib.*, no 225.
1418, 21 May, ord pr., Lichfield cathedral, *ib.*, no 236.

John de LONGEBRUG'
occ. 1320

1320, 24 May, ord dcn, Southam, Reg. Langton, fo 138v.

Bartholomew de LUDE
occ. 1320

1320, 24 May, ord dcn, Southam, Reg. Langton, fo 138v.

Nicholas LUFF [Louf
occ. 1370/1 occ. 1385

1370, 8 June, ord subdcn, Sallow, *Reg. Stretton* (1905), 235.
1370, 21 Sept., ord dcn, Colwich, *ib.*, 238.
1371, 20 Dec., 1371, ord pr., Colwich, *ib.*, 253.
1385, 4 Apr., subprior, Lichfield Chapter Act Book, fo 3v.
1385, 4 Apr., with John de Tomworth, q.v., appted as proctors in the negotiations with the Lichfield chapter over the el. of a bp, *ib.*, fos 3v–4v.

Richard LUFFE [Luff
occ. 1387 occ. 1414

1387, 21 Sept., ord subdcn, Colwich, Reg. Scrope, fo 142v.
1390, 28 May, ord pr., Colwich, *ib.*, fo 146.
1409, 14 Oct., subprior, Reg. Burghill, fo 207.
1414, 20 Dec., 1419, 6 June, subprior, *CPL*, vi (1404–1415), 353, PRO E164/21, fo 75.
1414, 20 Dec., granted papal licence to choose his confessor who was authorized to give plenary remission at the hour of d., *CPL*, vi, (1404–1415), 353.
Name in Oxford, Bod. Ms Digby 33, Bonaventure etc., (12th to 15th cs), ex dono—on a front flyleaf.

LYCHFELD
see Lichfeld

John LYMBUR
occ. 1514

1514, 10 June, ord pr., Lichfield cathedral, Reg. Blyth, ii, fo 98v.

John LYNBY [Lymby
occ. 1437 occ. 1455

1437, 16 Mar., ord subdcn, Coventry cathedral, Reg. Heyworth, fo 231v.
[1440], 24 Sept., ord pr., Lichfield cathedral, *ib.*, fo 237v.
1455, 6 Nov., the prior requested a royal writ *de apostato capiendo* vs him because of his disobedience and unauthorized departure from the monastery, PRO C81/1786/13.

John LYTYLE [Lylor, Lytlor, Lytle
occ. 1487 occ. 1490

1487, 10 Mar., ord acol., Lichfield cathedral, Reg. Hales, fo 222.
1487, 22 Sept., ord subdcn, Lichfield cathedral, *ib.*, fo 233v.
1488, 31 May, ord dcn, Lichfield cathedral, *ib.*, fo 239.
1490, 18 Sept., ord pr., Lichfield cathedral, *ib.*, fo 231.

MATTHEW
occ. 1214

1214, [c. 9 July], 20th in order on the list of monks who assented to the el. of William Cornhill as bp of Coventry, CUL Ms Ee.5.31, fo 240v.

William MAXSTOK [Maxstoke
occ. 1387 occ. 1409

1387, 21 Sept., ord subdcn, Colwich, Reg. Scrope, fo 142v.
1390, 28 May, ord pr., Colwich, *ib.*, fo 146.
1409, 14 Oct., infirmarer, Reg. Burghill, fo 207.
1405, 5 Jan., licensed as penitentiary, Reg. Burghill, fo 154v.
1409, 14 Oct., 11th in order in a letter of gratitude from the chapter to the bp, Reg. Burshill, fo 207.

John de MERSTONE
occ. 1282 occ. 1286/7

1287, 28 Feb., gardener, Oxford, Bod. Ms Top. Warwicks C. 8, fo 73.
Note: the date may be 26 Sept., 1286, since the feast is only referred to as *Mat' Apl'*.
1282 [Sept./Nov.], acted as attorney for the prior in arranging payment of a fine owed to the king, *CClR (1279–1288)*, 175.
1287, 28 Feb., witnessed an act of homage made to the prior, Oxford, Bod. Ms Top. Warwicks C. 8, fo 73.

William de MERSTONE [Mershton
occ. 1316 occ. 1342

1316, 18 Dec., ord subdcn, bp's chapel, Bishops Itchington, Reg. Langton, fo 128v.
1317, 2 Apr., ord dcn, Lichfield cathedral, *ib.*, fo 129v.

1342, Apr., named as one of nine *compromissorii* at the el. of a prior, Reg. Northburgh, ii, fo 38v; see William Irreys.

Simon de MIDLECOMBE [Mildecombe
occ. 1325 occ. 1352

1325, 2 Mar., ord subdcn, [?Bishops] Tachbrook, Reg. Northburgh, i, fo 149v.
1332, 30 Nov., the pope ordered the reservation of a benefice or dignity for him in the gift of the prior and convent, to the value of 30 m., *CPL*, ii (1305–1342), 371.
1352, 2 Aug., a royal mandate was issued for the arrest of Simon, a vagabond monk in secular dress, *CPR (1350–1354)*, 339; on 5 Aug., the bp comm. the adcn of Coventry to inquire into his apostasy, Reg. Northburgh, iii, fo 129.

William de MONTPELLIER [Monte Pessul'
occ. 1242 occ. 1251

1242, precentor, Paris, *Chron. Majora*, iv, 171–172.
1248; 1250, 19 Aug., subprior, *Magnum Reg. Album*, no 276 (fo 159v); *CPR (1247–1258)*, 72.

1242, 14 Jan., one of two monks who obtained a royal licence to el. a bp, *CPR (1232–1247)*, 270.
1242, was el. bp, Paris, *Chron. Majora*, iv, 171–172; but due to opposition, controversy and the costly lawsuit at the curia he had res. by 13 June, 1245, *ib.*, and see *CPL*, i (1198–1304), 203, 214, 218.
1251, 6 Mar., apptd abbot of Shrewsbury by the bp, but the pope annulled the apptment, *CPL*, i (1198–1304), 269; see also *CPR (1247–1258)*, 72, 94.
Note: see Roger de Walton.

Thomas MORTON
occ. 1401 occ. 1409

1401, 15 Mar., ord subdcn, Eccleshall, Reg. Burghill, fo 220v.
1405, 19 Dec., ord dcn, Eccleshall, *ib.*, fo 223.
1408, 22 Sept., ord pr., Eccleshall, *ib.*, fo 226v.

1409, 14 Oct., 19th in order in a letter of gratitude from the chapter to the bp., Reg. Burghill, fo 207.

MOSES [Moyses
occ. 1183 d. 1198

1183–1198, prior: el. Jan., 1183, expelled by the bp with all the monks 1191; d., prob. 16 July, 1198, at Rome, *HRH*, 41.
Note: the monks had been restored on 18 Jan., 1198, *ib.*; see Joybert.

1183, present at Christ Church, Canterbury when Waleran, bp of Rochester, made his act of fealty to Christ Church, *Gervase Cant.*, i, 306, 328. He was chaplain to the abp before being el. prior of Coventry and prob. therefore a monk of Canterbury, *HRH*, 41. (He attested a number of the abp's charters, *Eng. Epis. Acta*, ii, nos. 64–65, 69–70, 84, 92, 112, 144, 160, 163, 170, 221–222).
1183, 25 Sept., present at the consecration of the bp of [Chester] Coventry, and read the *postulatio*, *Gervase Cant.*, i, 307.
[1183, 25 Sept., × 1184, 16 Feb.], witnessed a confirmation of abp Richard, *Eng. Epis. Acta*, ii, no 54.
1189, under pressure from the bishop, Hugh de Nonant, he surrendered the demesne and barony of the priory at Reading to the bp in the presence of the abp and other bps, Chew, *Eccles. Tenants-in-Chief*, 164.
1191, went to Rome after the expulsion of the monks by the bp, *Gervase Cant.*, i, 489.
n.d., 16 July, obit occ. in BL Ms Arundel 68, fo 34v.

He gave vestments, an alb and amice, to Rochester cathedral priory and was included among the benefactors, *Registrum Roffense*, 123.

N.
occ. 1256

1256, precentor, *Ann. Burton*, 378, Magnum Reg. Album, fo 54.

1256, [?Nov/Dec] sent with a canon of Lichfield to obtain confirmation of the two chapters' el. of a bp from the abp, *Ann. Burton*, 378.

Note: see Nicholas IV.

John de NAPTON
occ. 1363 occ. 1409

1363, 27 May, ord subdcn, bp's chapel, Bishops Itchington, *Reg. Stretton*, (1905), 183.
1364, 21 Dec., ord dcn, bp's chapel, Heywood, *ib.*, 193.
1366, 28 Feb., ord pr., bp's chapel, Heywood, *ib.*, 201, (as Nepton).

1409, 14 Oct., sacrist, Reg. Burghill, fo 207.

1402, 13 June, the bp wrote to the prior to commend his 'good and religious conduct' and that of John de Bromlegh and William Haloughton q.v., Oxford, Bod. Ms Top. Warwicks C. 8, fos 64, 84.
1409, 14 Oct., 5th in order in a letter of gratitude from the chapter to the bp., Reg. Burghill, fo 207.

Gilbert de NEWENHAM
occ. 1313 occ. 1349

1313, 10 Mar., ord dcn, Worcester cathedral, *Reg. Reynolds* (Worcester), 137.

1325, 22 Aug., sacrist, PRO E164/21, fo 104.
1349, 5 Feb., the bp wrote to the prior and convent to choose a suitable monk to replace him as penitentiary as he was old and infirm, Reg. Northburgh, iii, fo 115v.

1325, 22 Aug., land was given to the prior and convent to have masses celebrated at St Catherine's altar in the cathedral for his soul and that of another four times each week, PRO E164/21, fo 104.
1348, 19 May, granted a papal licence to choose his confessor, who was authorised to give plenary remission at the hour of d., *CPL*, iii (1342–1362), 310.

Gilbert NEWTON [Neweton
occ. 1398 occ. 1409

[1398], 15 Mar., ord subdcn, Lichfield cathedral, Reg. Burghill, fo 213v.
1399, 29 Mar., ord dcn, Trinity church, Coventry, *ib.*, fo 213v.
1409, succentor, Reg. Burghill, fo 207.

1409, 14th in order in a letter of gratitude from the chapter to the bp., Reg. Burghill, fo 207.

I ?NICHOLAS
occ. ?1179

?c. 1179, occ. as prior, *HRH*, 41; see Laurence I.

II NICHOLAS
occ. 1214

1214, [c. 9 July], 7th in order on the list of monks who assented to the el. of William Cornhill as bp of Coventry, CUL Ms Ee.5.31, fo 240.

III NICHOLAS
occ. 1214

1214, [c. 9 July], 32nd in order on the list as above, *ib.*, fo 240v.
Note: see the note below Nicholas IV.

IV NICHOLAS
occ. 1249 occ. 1285/6

1249, 26 May, precentor, *CPR (1247–1258)*, 42.
1285/6, precentor, BL Add. Ms 32100, fo 46.

1249, 26 May, obtained royal licence to el. a prior, *CPR (1247–1258)*, 42.
1285/6 aged 70 years and witness to an agreement concerning tithes at Wasperton, BL Add. Ms 32100, fo 46; he had given evidence during the inquiry, *ib.*, fo 104.
Note:
(1) the first entry, dated 1249, may be Nicholas III.
(2) see also N.

Thomas NORBRYGG [Norbrygge, Northbrugg
occ. 1425 occ. 1430

1425, 2 June, ord subdcn, Coventry cathedral, Reg. Heyworth, fo 212v.
1427, 20 Sept., ord dcn, Colwich, *ib.*, fo 217.
1430, 11 Mar., ord pr., Lichfield cathedral, *ib.*, fo 221v.

John NORCROFTE [Norcrofft
occ. 1498/9

1498, 22 Sept., ord subdcn, Lichfield cathedral, Reg. Arundel, fo 274.
1498, 22 Dec., ord dcn, Lichfield cathedral, *ib.*, fo 276v.
1499, 23 Feb., ord pr., Lichfield cathedral, *ib.*, fo 278v.

NORTHBRUGG
see Norbrygg

John NORTHAMPTON
occ. 1416

1416, 13 June, ord subdcn, Lichfield cathedral, *Reg. Catterick*, no 224.
1416, 19 Sept., ord subdcn (?*recte* dcn) Coventry cathedral, *ib.*, no 225.

John de NORTHON [Norton
occ. 1327/9

1327, 19 Sept., ord dcn, Sallow, Reg. Northburgh, i, fo 153.
1329, 23 Sept., ord pr., Southam, *ib.*, i, fo 156v.

NORTON
see Northon

Richard NOTTINGHAM [Notyngham
occ. 1421 d. 1453

1437–1453, prior: el. 9/23 Apr., 1437, and royal assent was given on 28 Apr., *CPR (1436–1441)*, 55; d., 4 Mar., 1453, Reg. abp Kemp, fo 333v.
1421, 15 Feb., ord subdcn, Lichfield cathedral, Reg. Heyworth, fo 205v.
1421, 20 Sept., ord dcn, Longdon, *ib.*, fo 206v.
1423, 18 Sept., ord pr., Colwich, *ib.*, fo 210.
1437, before 9 Apr., subprior, *CPR (1436–1441)*, 18.

[1445], a John Bredon, preached a sermon vs the custom [?and the prior] of the cathedral church, Lincoln cathedral Ms 108, fo 87–87v.
1450, 21/29 Sept., entertained the king who stayed for a week at the priory, Oxford, Bod. Ms Top. Warwicks C. 8, fo 53.

Robert de NOTTINGHAM
occ. 1320

1320, 24 May, ord dcn, Southam, Reg. Langton, fo 138v.

Thomas OKAM
occ. 1425

1425, 2 June, ord dcn, Coventry cathedral, Reg. Heyworth, fo 212v.

Hugh OKY
occ. 1301

1301, 23 Dec., ord subdcn, All Saint's church, Derby, Reg. Langton, fo 95v.

Peter de OPTON
occ. 1305

1305, 18 Dec., ord subdcn, Colwich, Reg. Langton, fo 101.

le ORDE
see Henry le ?Irreys

OSBERN
occ. 1214

1214, [c. 9 July], 35th in order on the list of monks who assented to the el. of William Cornhill as bp of Coventry, CUL Ms Ee.5.31, fo 240v.

OVERDON
see Everdon

OWYNE
occ. [1122 × 1139]

[1122 × 1139], the fourth in a list of priors named in Sharp's lost cartulary, Dugdale, *Monasticon*, iii, 182; see Bruning (the first prior). Not in *HRH*. See Leasstan.

John de OXONIA
occ. 1256

1256, Jan., with William de St Nicholas, q.v., and two canons of Lichfield chosen to be the electors in an episcopal el., *Ann. Burton*, 379.

William de PAKKEWOD
occ. 1322/4

1322, 15 Sept., ord dcn, Southam, Reg. Northburgh, i, fo 144v.
1324, 22 Sept., ord pr., Spondon, *ib.*, i, fo 149.

John de PAKWOD [Pacwode
occ. 1362/4

1362, 24 Sept., ord subdcn, Coventry cathedral, *Reg. Stretton* (1905), 177.
1362, 17 Dec., ord dcn, bp's chapel, Heywood, *ib.*, 178.
1364, 18 May, ord pr., bp's chapel, Heywood, *ib.*, 190.

Thomas PAKYNGTON [Pakynton
occ. 1400 occ. 1409

1400, 23 Dec., ord subdcn, Eccleshall, Reg. Burghill, fo 219.
1401, 15 Mar., ord dcn, Eccleshall, *ib.*, fo 220v.
1405, 19 Dec., ord pr., Eccleshall, *ib.*, fo 223.
1409, 14 Oct., chaplain [to the prior], Reg. Burghill, fo 207.
1409, 14 Oct., 18th in order in a letter of gratitude from the chapter to the bp, Reg. Burghill, fo 207.

Thomas PALMER
occ. 1505/6

1505, 17 May, ord dcn, Lichfield cathedral, Reg. Blyth, ii, fo 17.
1506, 6 June, ord pr., Longdon, *ib.*, ii, fo 27.

PATRICIUS
occ. before 1122

1122, d. by this date when he appears in a mortuary roll of Savigny, Clapham, 'Bede-Rolls', 47.

Thomas de PAVY
occ. 1280 d. 1294

1280–1294, prior: el. between 9/19 May, 1280, *CPR (1272–1281)*, 369–370; d. before 16 Jan., 1294, *CPR (1292–1301)*, 60.
1283, 1 May, reached agreement and signed a composition with the bp concerning visitation procedure, *Magnum Reg. Album*, no 643 (fo 255–255v).
1289, was apptd one of the judges in an appeal over tithes between the abbot of Darley and prior of Dunstable, *Ann. Dunstable*, 285–286.

William PEASALE [Persall
occ. 1481/3

1481, 22 Sept., ord dcn, Lichfield cathedral, Reg. Hales, fo 275.
1483, 224 May, ord pr., Lichfield cathedral, *ib.*, fo 283.

Thomas POLLESWORTH
occ. 1416

1416, 13 June, ord subdcn, Lichfield cathedral, *Reg. Catterick*, no 224.
1416, 19 Sept., ord subdcn, (?*recte* dcn), Coventry cathedral, *ib.*, no 225.

William POLLESWORTH
occ. 1470 d. 1516

1501–1516, prior: el. 6/19 Feb., 1501; d. by 14 Oct., 1516, *Fasti*, x, 5.
1470, 22 Sept., ord acol., Coventry cathedral, Reg. Hales, fo 209.
1473, 12 June, ord subdcn, Longdon, *ib.*, fo 250.
1475, 18 Feb., ord dcn, Kenilworth church, *ib.*, fo 253v.
1476, 9 Mar., ord pr., Lichfield cathedral, *ib.*, fo 256v.
1496, 8 Mar., 1501, before his el., subprior, *Reg. abp Morton*, ii, no 374, *CPR (1494–1509)*, 227.
1496, 8 Mar., 2nd in order on the visitation certificate, *Reg. abp Morton*, ii, no 374.
1504, 1507, 1509, 1510, 1512, [1516], played host to the Black Monk Chapter meetings, Pantin, *BMC*, iii, 218–219.

According to Dugdale, *Monasticon*, iii, 183, he was a member of the guild of Corpus Christi, Coventry.

John POPE [Poope
occ. 1491 occ. 1524

1491, 28 May, ord pr., Lichfield cathedral, Reg. Smith, fo 123.

[1518], subprior, sacrist, pittancer and infirmarer, *Blyth Visit.*, 16. See below.

[1521], 12 Dec., subprior and sacrist, *ib.*, 86.

1524, 16 July, subprior, *ib.*, 115.

1496, 8 Mar., 10th in order on the visitation certificate, *Reg. abp Morton*, ii, no 374.

1517, c. 16 June, first in order on the list of nine monks [?*compromissorii*] who petitioned the king to confirm the el. of John Webbe, q.v., as prior, *L and P Henry VIII*, ii, pt 2 (1517–1518), no 3464. He was prob. subprior.

[1518], 2nd to be questioned at the episcopal visitation and spoke well of the prior [John Webbe, q.v.] and his administration. Thomas Leeke, q.v., reported that the subprior was elderly and often ill and absent from divine office, and he cut short the readings when he was in charge, *Blyth Visit.*, 16.

[1521], 12 Dec., 2nd to be questioned at the visitation and reported himself in agreement with the prior's report, *ib.*, 86. However, there were a number of accusations vs him in the depositions of Thomas Leeke, and of John Eccleshall, q.v.

1524, 16 July, 3rd to be questioned at the visitation and reported that Deane, Barnacle and [Thomas] Coventre q.v., were disobedient and conducting a whispering campaign vs the prior [John Webbe, q.v.]. He in turn was accused of failing to comply with regulations concerning the eating of meat and confession, *ib.*, 115–116.

R.
occ. 1223

1223, precentor, *Magnum Reg. Album*, no 463 (fo 205–205^{v}).

1223, before 29 Nov., with W. subprior and Anselm, almoner, q.v., sent to the abp to inform him of the chapter's el. of Geoffrey II, their prior, q.v., as bp of Coventry, *Langton Acta*, no 61. See also the *Magnum Reg. Album* ref. above.

Philip de RAGGELEY
occ. 1286 occ. 1301

1286, 3 July, 1301, 15 Apr., one of the monks who witnessed acts of homage made to the prior, Oxford, Bod. Ms Top. Warwicks C. 8, fo 73.

John RAMSEY
occ. 1401

1401, 26 Feb., licensed as penitentiary for one yr, Reg. Burghill, fo 144^{v}.

REGINALD
occ. 1285/6

1285/6, subprior, BL Add. Ms 32100, fos 103, 45^{v}.

1285/6 aged 70 yrs, and *dictus medicus*, named as one who gave evidence and was a witness in a dispute over tithes at Wasperton, BL Add. Ms 32100, fos 103, 45^{v}; see also Lancaster, 'Coventry Forged Charters', 128.

There is a ref. to a gift of land in Wasperton for his anniversary in Oxford, Bod. Ms Top. Warwicks C. 8, fo 49, fo 35^{v}–36.

John RESTON
occ. 1539

1539, 15 Jan., signed the deed of surrender, *DK 8th Report*, Appndx 2, 16.

John REVELL [Ryvell
occ. 1422 occ. 1426

1422, 19 Sept., ord subdcn, Lichfield cathedral, Reg. Heyworth, fo 208.

1423, 30 May, ord dcn, Lichfield cathedral, *ib.*, fo 209^{v}.

1426, 21 Dec., ord pr., Eccleshall, *ib.*, fo 215^{v}.

REYNALD
occ. 1214

1214, [c. 9 July], 31st in order on the list of monks who assented to the el. of William Cornhill as bp of Coventry, CUL Ms Ee.5.31, fo 240^{v}.

I RICHARD
occ. [c. 1122 × 1139]

[c. 1122 × 1139], the sixth in a list of priors, named in Sharp's lost cartulary, Dugdale, *Monasticon*, iii, 182; see Bruning (the first prior). Not in *HRH*.

II RICHARD
occ. 1214

1214, [c. 9 July], 13th in order on the list of monks who assented to the el. of William Cornhill as bp of Coventry, CUL Ms Ee.5.31, fo 240.

III RICHARD
occ. 1214

1214, [c. 9 July], 29th in order on the list as above, *ib.*, fo 240^{v}.

IV RICHARD
occ. 1256

1256, 30 Dec., subprior, *CPR (1247–1258)*, 535.

1256, 30 Dec., obtained royal licence to el. a bp, *CPR (1247–1258)*, 535.

I ROBERT
occ. 1214

1214, [c. 9 July], 10th in order on the list of monks who assented to the el. of William

Cornhill as bp of Coventry, CUL Ms Ee.5.31, fo 240.

II ROBERT
occ. 1214

1214, [c. 9 July], 15th in order on the list, as above, fo 240ᵛ.

III ROBERT
occ. 1214

1214, [c. 9 July], 16th in order on the list, as above.

IV ROBERT
occ. 1214

1214, [c. 9 July], 17th in order on the list, as above.

V ROBERT
occ. 1214

1214, [c. 9 July], 18th in order on the list, as above.

VI ROBERT
occ. 1214

1214, [c. 9 July], 33rd in order on the list, as above.

Hugh de ROCHEWELL
occ. 1328 occ. 1342

1328, 12 Sept., mentioned in connection with the chantry of prior Henry [de Leycestre II], q.v., among those to be remembered, Reg. Northburgh, iii, fo 27.

1342, Apr., one of nine *compromissorii* at the el. of a prior, Reg. Northburgh, ii, fo 38v; see William Irreys.

I ROGER
occ. 1214

1214, [c. 9 July], 5th in order on the list of monks who assented to the el. of William Cornhill as bp of Coventry, CUL Ms Ee.5.31, fo 240.

II ROGER
occ. 1214

1214, [c. 9 July], 8th in order on the list, as above.

III ROGER
occ. 1214

1214, [c. 9 July], 27th in order on the list, as above, fo 240ᵛ.

Note: one of these Rogers may be Roger de Walton, q.v.

John ROOS [Rose
occ. 1453/5

1453, 24 Feb., ord subdcn, Lichfield cathedral, Reg. abp Kemp, fo 336v and also Reg. Boulers, fo 5.

1453, 24 Sept., ord dcn, Longdon, Reg. Boulers, fo 98ᵛ.

1455, 20 Sept., ord pr., Lichfield cathdral, *ib.*, fo 106.

Peter RUSSELL
occ. 1433/4

1433, 7 Mar., ord subdcn, Lichfield cathedral, Reg. Heyworth, fo 224ᵛ.

1433, 6 June, ord dcn, Colwich, *ib.*, fo 225ᵛ.

1434, 18 Sept., ord pr., Colwich, *ib.*, fo 227ᵛ.

John RUYTON [Ryton
occ. 1413

1413, 17 June, ord dcn, Colwich, Reg. Burghill, fo 235.

[1414/15] ord pr., place not stated, *Reg. abp Chichele*, iii, 329.

William de ST NICHOLAS [Sancto Nicholao
occ. 1256 OCC. 1280

1256, Jan., with John de Oxonia and two canons of Lichfield, chosen as electors of a bp, *Ann. Burton*, 379.

1280, 9 May, recd royal licence to el. a prior, *CPR (1272–1281)*, 369.

Thomas SAMPSON
occ. [1440] occ. 1461

[1440], 24 Sept., ord dcn, Lichfield cathedral, Reg. Heyworth, fo 237ᵛ.

1461, 27 Feb., licensed as penitentiary, Reg. Hales, fo 132.

SAUTHAM
see John de Southam I

SCALYNTON
see Stalynton

Thomas SCHEFELD [Schefelde
occ. 1425 occ. 1429

1425, 2 June, ord dcn, Coventry cathedral, Reg. Heyworth, fo 212ᵛ.

1429, 19 Feb., ord pr., Lichfield cathedral, *ib.*, fo 219ᵛ.

SCHEPEY
see Shepey

SCHEYNTON
see Sheynton

SCHOTESWELL
see Shotteswell

Thomas de SCRAPETOFT
occ. 1305

1305, 18 Dec., ord subdcn, Colwich, Reg. Langton, fo 101.

Alexander SECOM [Sekom
occ. 1451/3

1451, 19 June, ord subdcn, Eccleshall, Reg. Booth, fo 112v.
1453, 24 Feb., ord dcn, Lichfield cathedral, Reg. abp Kemp, fo 337 and Reg. Boulers, fo 5v.
1453, 20 Sept., ord pr., Lichfield cathedral, Reg. Boulers, fo 106.

SELER, Seller
see Celler

Richard SHARE, Shaw
see Richard Coventry II

John SHEPEY [Schepey
occ. 1481/2 occ. 1485

1481, 9 June, ord acol., Lichfield cathedral, Reg. Hales, fo 273.
1481, 22 Sept., ord subdcn, Lichfield cathedral, *ib.*, fo 275.
1482, 1 June, ord dcn, Lichfield cathedral, *ib.*, fo 279.
1482, 20 Sept., ord pr., Lichfield cathedral, *ib.*, fo 280.
1485, 23 Apr., subprior and pittancer, Oxford, Bod. Ms Charters, Northamptonshire, no 127.
1485, 23 Apr., acknowledged receipt of rent, *ib.*

SHERWOOD
see Shirwood

William de SHEYNTON [Scheynton, Shenkton
occ. 1331 occ. 1356

1331, 25 May, ord subdcn, St John's church, Chester, Reg. Northburgh, i, fo 162v.
1331, 21 Sept., ord dcn, Ladbrooke, *ib.*, i, fo 164v.
1332, 21 Dec., ord pr., Rugeley, *ib.*, i, fo 165v.
1336, 6 Nov., apptd by Henry, the prior, to represent him in a suit before the king's council between the queen and the prior [? over the royal right to demand corrodies], *CClR (1333–1337)*, 707; see also John de Sutham and Reginald de Leek.
1342, Apr., one of nine *compromissorii* at the el. of a prior, Reg. Northburgh, ii, fo 38v; see William Irreys.
1356, 26 Nov., granted royal pardon, along with the prior and other monks, for all the crimes with which they had been charged, *CPR (1354–1358)*, 474.

[Robert] SHIRWOOD [Sherwood
occ. [1521]

[1521], 12 Dec., described as scholar; see below.
[1521], 12 Dec., not present at the episcopal visitation, because he was one of four scholars being maintained by the chapter [at university], *Blyth Visit.*, 86; see Thomas Leeke.

Note: this must be the Robert Sherwood, native of Coventry, 'student at Oxford and at Loraine in Brabant, where he read the Hebrew lecture for a month in 1520', Foster, *Alumni Oxon.*, iv, 1350. See also Wood, *Athenae Oxon.*, i, 58, where he is named as the author of *Liber Hebræorum Concionatoris, seu Ecclesiasten, nuper ad veritatem Hebræicam recognitus, cum nonnullis annotationibus Chaldaicis, et quorundam Rabbinorum sententiis, textus obscuros aliquos literaliter explanantibus*, Oxford Bod. H.12.Th.Selden (printed book) Antwerp, 1523. It is in fact his own translation of Ecclesiastes from the Hebrew into Latin and is printed in parallel columns, the Vulgate Aeditio on the left and his Latin rendering of the Hebraica Veritas on the right. It is dedicated to his prior, John Webbe, q.v.: '. . . hanc lucubratiunculam nostram amoris in te mei monumentum accipe', the date is given as 20 Jan 1523.

John SHOTTESWELL [Shoteswell, Schoteswell
occ. 1425 d. 1461

1453–1461, prior: el. c. 12 Mar., 1453, *via inspirationis*, Reg. abp Kemp, fos 331–335; d., 30 Oct., 1461, *Fasti*, x, 4; see Richard Nottingham.
1425, 2 June, ord subdcn, Coventry cathedral, Reg. Heyworth, fo 212v.
1427, 14 June, ord dcn, Colwich, *ib.*, fo 217.
1429, 19 Feb, ord pr., Lichfield cathedral, *ib.*, fo 219v.
1453, subprior at the time of his el., *CPR (1452–1461)*, 49, Reg. abp Kemp, fo 331v.
1456, Feb/Mar., the king and queen stayed at the priory while parliament was in session, and on 11 Oct., of this yr the king held his court at the priory and gave the great seal to bp Waynflete, Fretton 'Coventry', 30.
1459, Nov/Dec, played host to a session of parliament in the chapter house, Oxford, Bod. Ms Top. Warwicks C. 8, fo 53.

I SIMON
occ. 1214

1214, [c. 9 July], 4th in order on the list of monks who assented to the el. of William Cornhill as bp of Coventry, CUL Ms Ee.5.31, fo 240.

II SIMON
d. 1223

1223, prior, d., *Ann. Wigorn.*, 415.

III SIMON
occ. 1249

1249, 26 May, chamberlain, *CPR (1247–1258)*, 42.
1249, 26 May, obtained royal licence to el. a prior, *ib.*, 42.

Robert de SLOLEYE
occ. 1301

1301, 26 Jan., apptd as one of two [? monk] attorneys by the prior [Henry de Leycestre, q.v.] before going overseas, *CPR (1292–1301)*, 562; see also Thomas de Sutham.

Hugh SMITH [Smyth
occ. 1526/7

1526, 26 May, ord subdcn, Lichfield cathedral, Reg. Blyth, ii, fo 179.
1527, 15 June, ord dcn, Lichfield cathedral, *ib.*, ii, fo 188.

Roger de SOLERS
occ. 1242

1242, 14 Jan., one of two monks who obtained royal licence to el. a bp., *CPR (1232–1247)*, 270.

I John de SOUTHAM [Sautham, Sutham
occ. 1320 occ. ?1399

1320, 24 May, ord subdcn, Southam, Reg. Langton, fo 138v.
1342, Apr., one of nine *compromissorii* at the el. of a prior, Reg. Northburgh, ii, fo 38v; see William Irreys.
1355, 4 May, granted papal licence to choose his own confessor, *CPL*, iii, (1342–1362), 557 and again on 8 Sept., 1355, *ib.*, 559.
1356, 26 Nov., granted royal pardon, along with the prior and other monks, for all the crimes with which they had been charged, *CPR (1354–1358)*, 474.
1360, comm. as penitentiary for the diocese, *Reg. Stretton*, (1905), 92.
1399, 13 Apr., granted papal dispensation to hold a benefice with or without cure of souls, *CPL*, v, (1396–1404), 190.
1399, 29 May, apptd papal chaplain, *ib.*, 218.

Note: these last two entries may refer to John de Southam II, q.v., but he is unlikely to have been apptd a papal chaplain so early in his monastic career. See also John de Sutham who may be this monk.

II John SOUTHAM [Sowtham
occ. 1393 occ. ?1399

1391, 1 Mar., ord subdcn, Colwich, Reg. Scrope, fo 150v.
1393, 22 Mar., ord dcn, Kenilworth priory, ib.
1394, 14 Mar., ord pr., Colwich, *ib.*, fo 152.
1398, 3 Mar., licensed as penitentiary in the cathedral church, Reg. Scrope, fo 136v.
1399, 27 Jan., licensed as penitentiary for one yr, Reg. Burghill, fo 141v.

See also the note below the preceding entry; the last two entries here may refer to John de Southam I.

I Thomas de SOUTHAM
occ. 1363 occ. 1367

1363, 27 May, ord subdcn, bp's chapel, Bishops Itchington, *Reg. Stretton* (1905), 183.
1364, 21 Dec., ord dcn, bp's chapel, Heywood, *ib.*, 193.
1367, 13 Mar., ord pr, bp's chapel, Heywood, *ib.*, 208.

II Thomas SOUTHAM [Sowtham
occ. 1478 occ. 1496

1478, 19 Sept., ord dcn, bp's chapel, Beaudesert, Reg. Hales, fo 266.
1496, 8 Mar., precentor, *Reg. abp Morton*, ii, no 374.
1496, 8 Mar., 6th in order on the visitation certificate, *Reg. abp Morton*, ii, no 374.

SOUTHAM
see also Sutham

Nicholas SPIGURNEL
occ. 1301

1301, 23 Dec., ord subdcn, All Saints' church, Derby, Reg. Langton, fo 95v.

Robert de STALYNTON [Scalynton
occ. 1320

1320, 20 Sept., ord dcn, Darley abbey, Reg. Langton, fo 140.

STANULPH
occ. [c. 1122 × 1139]

[c. 1122 × 1139], the fifth prior named in Sharp's cartulary, Dugdale, *Monasticon*, iii, 182; see Bruning (the first prior). Not in *HRH*.

Thomas STEPHEN [Stephanus
occ. 1478 occ. 1481

1478, 19 Dec., ord subdcn, Lichfield cathedral, Reg. Hales, fo 266v.
1481, 17 Mar., ord pr., Lichfield cathedral, *ib.*, fo 272v.

Richard STOKE [Stokes
occ. 1401 occ. 1422

1401, 15 Mar., ord subdcn, Eccleshall, Reg. Burghill, fo 220v.
1405, 19 Dec., ord dcn, Eccleshall, *ib.*, fo 223.
1407, 24 Sept., ord pr., Eccleshall, *ib.*, fo 225.
1409, 14 Oct., *custos* of the Lady chapel, Reg. Burghill, fo 207.
1422, 15 Jan., precentor, Reg. Heyworth, fo 8.
1409, 14 Oct., 22nd in order in a letter of gratitude from the chapter to the bp, Reg. Burghill, fo 207.

Henry de STRATTON [Stretton
occ. 1286/7 occ. 1294

1287, 28 Feb., cellarer, Oxford, Bod. Ms Top. Warwicks C. 8, fo 73.

Note: the date may be 26 Sept., 1286, since the feast is only referred to as *Mat' Apl'*.

1287, 28 Feb., witnessed an act of homage made to the prior, Oxford, Bod. Ms Top. Warwicks C. 8, fo 73.

1294, 16 Jan., recd licence from the king to el. a prior, *CPR (1292–1301)*, 60.

Thomas de STYNDON
occ. [1390]

[1390], almoner, Oxford, Bod. Ms Top. Warwicks C. 8, fo 78.

[1390], one of the monks who witnessed an act of homage made to the prior, *ib.*

John de SUTHAM
occ. 1336

1336, 6 Nov., apptd by Henry, the prior, to represent him in a suit before the king's council between the queen and the prior [?over the royal right to demand corrodies], *CClR (1333–1337)*, 707; see also William de Sheynton and Reginald de Leek.

Note: this may be John de Southam I, q.v.

Thomas de SUTHAM
occ. 1301

1301, 26 Jan., apptd one of two [?monk] attorneys by the prior [Henry de Leycestre, q.v.] before going overseas. *CPR (1292–1301)*, 562; see also Robert de Sloleye.

SUTHAM
see also Southam

William SUTTON
occ. 1481/3

1481, 24 Sept., ord dcn, Lichfield cathedral, Reg. Hales, fo 275.

1483, 24 May, ord pr., Lichfield cathedral, *ib.*, fo 283.

TAMWORTH
see Tomworth

TEXFORD
see Tuckford

John de TEYNTON
occ. 1344/6

1344, 18 Sept., ord dcn, Chesterton, Reg. Northburgh, i, fo 197.

1346, 23 Sept., ord pr., Stow, by *lit. dim.*, *Reg. Bransford* (Worcester), no 1073 (p. 261).

Richard THOLY [Toly
occ. 1409 occ. 1422

1410, 17 May, ord subdcn, Eccleshall, Reg. Burghill, fo 229.

1411, 11 Apr., ord dcn, Coventry cathedral, *ib.*, fo 231ᵛ.

[1412], 24 Sept., ord pr., Colwich, *ib.*, fo 234.

1422, 15 Jan., subprior, Reg. Heyworth, fo 8.

1409, 14 Oct., 24th in order in a letter of gratitude from the chapter to the bp, Reg. Burghill, fo 207.

I THOMAS
occ. before 1122

1122, d. by this date when he appears in a mortuary roll of Savigny, Clapham, 'Bede-Rolls', 47.

II THOMAS
occ. 1198

1191/8, [after the d. of prior Moses q.v.] he alone stayed on at the papal court and boldly approached Innocent III with his petition for the monks' restoration; he had been refused by popes Clement and Celestine, Innocent's two predecessors, and was willing to wait until there was a pope who would recognize the justice of his cause, Paris, *Chron. Majora*, ii, 444–445; see Joybert. See also Dugdale, *Monasticon*, iii, 180.

III THOMAS
occ. 1214

1214, [c. 9 July], 22nd in order on the list of monks who assented to the el. of William Cornhill as bp of Coventry, CUL Ms Ee.5.31, fo 240v; possibly identical with the entry below.

John de TOMWORTH [Tamworth
occ. 1362 occ. 1385

1362, 24 Sept., ord subdcn, Coventry cathedral, *Reg. Stretton* (1905), 177.

1362, 17 Dec., ord dcn., bp's chapel, Heywood, *ib.*, 179.

1385, 4 Apr., treasurer, Lichfield Chapter Act Book, fo 3ᵛ.

1385, 4 Apr., with Nicholas Luff, q.v., appted as proctors in the negotiations with the Lichfield chapter over the el. of a bp, *ib.*, fos 3ᵛ–4ᵛ.

William TOMWORTH
occ. 1441

1441, 22 Sept., ord subdcn, Lichfield cathedral, Reg. Heyworth, fo 241.

Thomas TOPCLYFFE [Topliffe
occ. 1483 occ. 1487

1483, 20 Sept., ord acol., Lichfield cathedral, Reg. Hales, fo 284ᵛ.

1484, 18 Sept., ord subdcn, Lichfield cathedral, *ib.*, fo 290.

1487, 10 Mar., ord dcn, Lichfield cathedral, *ib.*, fo 222.

1487, 22 Sept., ord pr., Lichfield cathedral, *ib.*, fo 233v.

Thomas TREWBRUGGE [Treubrugge
occ. 1450 occ. 1453

1450, 19 Dec., ord subdcn, Lichfield cathedral, Reg. Booth, fo 111v.
1451, 19 June, ord dcn, Eccleshall, *ib.*, fo 112v.
1453, 26 May, ord pr., Lichfield cathedral, Reg. Boulers, fo 97v.

William TROWTHE [Trowte, Trowt
occ. 1494/6

1494, 20 Sept., ord subdcn, Coventry cathedral, Reg. Smith, fo 180v.
1495, 14 Mar., ord dcn, Eccleshall, *ib.*, fo 184.

1496, 8 Mar., 12th in order on the visitation certificate, *Reg. abp Morton*, ii, no 374.

William de TUCKEFORD [Cukford, Tuckesford, Texford
occ. 1367 occ. 1409

1367, 8 Oct., acol., given *lit. dim.*, for all orders, *Reg. Stretton* (1905), 39.
1368, 4 Mar., ord subdcn, bp's chapel, Heywood, *ib.*, 213.
[1368], 3 June, ord dcn, Colwich, *ib.*, 216.
1376, 20 Dec., ord pr., (as Texford), Colwich, *ib.*, 313.

1409, 14 Oct., 6th in order in a letter of gratitude from the chapter to the bp, Reg. Burghill, fo 207.

John VOLNEY [Wolnes, Wolney
occ. 1401 occ. 1409

1401, 15 Mar., ord subdcn, Eccleshall, Reg. Burghill, fo 220v.
1401, 19 Dec., ord dcn, Eccleshall, *ib.*, fo 223.
1407, 24 Sept., ord pr., Eccleshall, *ib.*, fo 225.
1409, 14 Oct., refectorer, Reg. Burghill, fo 207.

1409, 14 Oct., 20th in order in a letter of gratitude from the chapter to the bp, Reg. Burghill, fo 207.

I W.
occ. 1214 occ. 1223

1214, [c. 9 July], 1223, before 29 Nov., subprior, CUL Ms Ee.5.31, fo 240, *Langton Acta*, no 61.

1214 [c. 9 July] who assented to the el. of William Cornhill as bp of Coventry, CUL Ms Ee.5.31, fo 240.

1223, before 29 Nov., sent to inform the abp of the chapter's el. of prior Geoffrey II, q.v., as bp, *Langton Acta*, no 61; see also Anselm and R.

II W.
occ. 1251

1251, 15 Oct., subprior, *CClR (1247–1251)*, 565.
Note: a W. subprior was proctor at the time of the el. of Roger de Walton, q.v., as prior, *Magnum Reg. Album*, no 712 (fo 277).

W.
see also William VI

Thomas de WALLEFORDE [Walforth, Walford
occ. 1373/5

1373, 18 Mar., ord subdcn, Colwich, *Reg. Stretton* (1905), 280.
1374, 27 May, ord dcn, Colwich, *ib.*, 285.
1375, 17 Mar., ord pr., Worcester cathedral by *lit. dim.*, *Reg. Sed. Vac.* (Worcester), 331.

WALTER
occ. 1214

1214, [c. 9 July], 14th in order on the list of monks who assented to the el. of William Cornhill as bp of Coventry, CUL Ms Ee.5.31, fo 240v.

M. Roger de WALTON [Wootton
occ. 1235 occ. 1249

1235–1249, prior: royal assent to the el., was given on 19 Sept., 1235, *CPR (1232–1247)*, 118; res. before 26 May, 1249, *CPR (1247–1258)*, 42. He succ. Geoffrey II, q.v.
Note: the bp refused to accept his el. *propter certas causas* but then apptd him by his own prerogative [*ex dono*], *Magnum Reg. Album*, no 712 (fo 277).

1235, before his el., penitentiary, *Magnum Reg. Album*, no 712 (fo 277).
1241, 1 June, with the chapter came to an agreement with the bp over the church of St Michael adjacent to the priory, *Magnum Reg. Album*, nos 238, 239 (fos 146v–147). See Coss, *Early Records*, 5–6 which outlines the details of his success in obtaining the appropriation of this church in Apr. 1249.
1242, in the wake of the unsuccessful el. of William de Montpellier, q.v., as bp, the king and the Lichfield canons caused such harassment that the prior and monks were forced to disperse for over a yr, and the prior and some of the monks were given hospitality at St Alban's abbey, Paris, *Chron. Majora*, iv, 172.

John de Bruges, q.v., wrote several service books for him.

Note: there were three monks named Roger, q.v., in 1214; is this one of them?

John WARDE
occ. 1491 occ. 1502/3

1491, 28 May, ord pr., Lichfield cathedral, Reg. Smith, fo 123.

1502/3, cellarer, BCA 168239 (DV2).

1496, 8 Mar., 9th in order on the visitation certificate, *Reg. abp Morton*, ii, no 374.

Walter WAREN [Waryn, Warren
occ. 1504 occ. 1524

1504, 21 Sept., ord subdcn, Eccleshall, Reg. Blyth, ii, fo 9.
1505, 17 May, ord dcn, Lichfield cathedral, *ib.*, ii, fo 17.
1506, 16 June, ord pr., Longdon, *ib.*, ii, fo 27.

[1518], chaplain, [? to the prior], *Blyth Visit.*, 16.
[1521], 12 Dec., chaplain, *ib.*, 87.

1517, c. 16 June, 6th in order on the list of nine monks [?*compromissorii*] who petitioned the king to confirm the el. of John Webbe, q.v., as prior, *L and P Henry VIII*, ii, pt 2 (1517–1518), no 3464.
[1518], 10th to be questioned at the episcopal visitation and said that all was well, *Blyth Visit.*, 16.
[1521], 12 Dec., 10th to be questioned at the visitation and agreed with the prior [John Webbe, q.v.], *ib.*, 87.
1524, 16 July, 11th to be questioned at the visitation and supported the statement made by the subprior [John Pope, q.v.], *ib.*, 116.

Richard de WARR'
occ. 1330 occ. 1335

1330, 29 May, ord subdcn, Ecccleshall, Reg. Northburgh, i, fo 169^v.
1334, 21 May, ord dcn, Aston, *ib.*, i, fo 172^v.
1335, 20 Sept., ord pr., Harbury, *ib.*, i, fo 176.

Richard WARREWYK [Warrewyke
occ. 1361 occ. 1409

1361, 22 May, ord pr., Alvechurch, by *lit. dim.*, Reg. Bryan (Worcester), i, 122.

1402, 1 May, before this date, treasurer and sacrist, Oxford, Bod. Ms Top. Warwicks C. 8, fo 64.
1402, 1 May, an episcopal injunction ordered that he be dismissed from the office of sacrist because no one should hold two offices, *ib.*, fo 64.
1409, 14 Oct., 4th in order in a letter of gratitude from the chapter to the bp, Reg. Burghill, fo 207. (The three who preceded him were the prior, subprior and former prior; thus he was the most senior monk).

John de WARWYK [Warwyc
occ. 1377/8

1377, 23 May, ord subdcn, Colwich, *Reg. Stretton* (1905), 325.
1377, 19 Sept., ord dcn, Colwich, (wrongly described as canon of Coventry), *ib.*, 328.
1378, 18 Sept., ord pr., Colwich, *ib.*, 340.

WARYN
see Waren

John WEBBE [Webe, ?Weedon
occ. 1500 occ. 1527

1517–1527, prior: el. 21/25 June/11 July, 1517; res. by 22 July, 1527, *Fasti*, x, 5, and *L and P Henry VIII*, iv, pt 2 (1526–1528), no 3292.

1500, 19 Sept., ord acol., Lichfield cathedral, Reg. Arundel, fo 289^v.
1501, 19 Mar., ord subdcn, Lichfield cathedral, *ib.*, fo 292^v.
1501, 18 Sept., ord dcn, Lichfield cathedral, *ib.*, fo 297^v.
1503, 10 June, ord pr., Lichfield cathedral, (*sed. vac.*, Canterbury and Coventry/Lichfield), Canterbury Reg. F, fo 187^v.

1517, 16/25 June, subprior, *L and P Henry VIII*, ii, pt 2 (1517–1518), no 3400.
1517, Aug., became a member of the Trinity guild in Coventry, and on 4 Oct., of the same yr, became a member of the Corpus Christi guild, Dugdale *Monasticon*, iii, 183–184; in 1528 his name also occ. in the guilds' accts, ib.
[1518], present at the episcopal visitation and reported that apart from a heavy burden of debt the house was in good order: 'Fratres omnes religioso vivunt in omnibus', *Blyth Visit.*, 15.
[1521], 12 Dec., present at the visitation and reported that he had reduced the debt, but complained of 'frater Barnacle' and 'Barnesley', q.v., and of other obedientiaries whose unseemly behaviour and inefficient administration were reprehensible, *ib.*, 85–86.
1524, 16 July, present at the visitation and reported that the chapter owed £280 to creditors. He complained that the brethren continued to have *arma invasiva*, *ib.*, 115. The debt was in part due to the fact that the priory had made a grant of £333 6s. 8d. to the king, *L and P Henry VIII*, iii, pt 2 (1519–1523), no 2483.
1525, Princess Mary was entertained by the prior for two days while she attended the Coventry plays, Fretton, 'Coventry', 31.

Note:
(1) is this possibly John Weedon I, q.v.?
(2) see Robert Shirwood who dedicated a book to him.

Nicholas WEBSTER
occ. 1515 occ. 1524

1515, 22 Sept., ord subdcn, St Peter's church, Derby, Reg. Blyth, ii, fo 105^v.
1520, 2 June, ord pr., Lichfield cathedral, *ib.*, ii, fo 136.

[1518], scholar, *Blyth Visit.*, 17.
[1521], 21 Dec., scholar, *ib.*, 86.

[1518], 17th [on the list] to be questioned at the episcopal visitation, *Blyth Visit.*, 17; no deposition was entered and so he may have been absent.
[1521], 21 Dec., absent from the visitation, *ib.*, 86.

1524, 16 July, 16th to be questioned at the episcopal visitation and reported agreement with the statements made by others, *ib.*, 117.

Note: this may be Nicholas Bromwych, q.v.

I John WEEDON
occ. 1496 occ. 1503

1496, 8 Mar., novice, *Reg. abp Morton*, ii, no 374.
1503, 10 June, ord pr., Lichfield cathedral, (*sed. vac.*, Canterbury and Coventry/Lichfield), Canterbury Reg. F, fo 187^{v}.

1496, 8 Mar., 16th in order on the visitation certificate, *Reg. abp Morton*, ii, no 374.

II John WEEDON [Wydon, Wedon
occ. 1498/9

1498, 22 Sept., ord subdcn, Lichfield cathedral, Reg. Arundel, fo 273^{v}.
1498, 22 Dec., ord dcn, Lichfield cathedral, *ib.*, fo 276^{v}.
1499, 23 Feb., ord pr., Lichfield cathedral, *ib.*, fo 278^{v}.

Note: this monk is not identical with the preceding, but the entries may have been wrongly divided between them. Dr Heath (*Blyth Visit.*, 15, n. 5) suggests that Weedon I and John Webbe are identical.

WE'ETER
see Winters

John de WELLEFORD
occ. 1325/7

1325, 21 Sept., ord subdcn, Tutbury priory, Reg. Northburgh, i, fo 150^{v}.
1327, 19 Sept., ord pr., Sallow, *ib.*, i, fo 153.

William WELLEFORD [Welford
occ. 1422 occ. 1426

1422, 19 Sept., ord subdcn, Lichfield cathedral, Reg. Heyworth, fo 208.
1426, 21 Dec., ord pr., Eccleshall, *ib.*, fo 215^{v}.

Henry WELLYS [Wells, Wellis
occ. 1485 occ. 1496

1485, 24 Sept., ord acol., Lichfield cathedral, Reg. Hales, fo 213^{v}.
1485, 17 Dec., ord subdcn, Lichfield cathedral, *ib.*, fo 215.
1486, 20 May, ord dcn, Lichfield cathedral, *ib.*, fo 217^{v}.
1487, 22 Sept., ord pr., Lichfield cathedral, *ib.*, fo 233^{v}.

1496, 8 Mar., succentor, *Reg. abp Morton*, ii, no 374.
1496, 8 Mar., 7th in order on the visitation certificate, *Reg. abp Morton*, ii, no 374.

William WELLYS [Wels
occ. 1425 occ. 1430

1425, 2 June, ord subdcn, Coventry cathedral, Reg. Heyworth, fo 212^{v}.
1427, 14 June, ord dcn, Colwich, *ib.*, fo 217.
1430, 11 Mar., ord pr., Lichfield cathedral, *ib.*, fo 221^{v}.

Roger de WENTEBRIGGE [Wentebrigg
occ. 1344 occ. 1361

1344, 18 Sept., ord subdcn, Chesterton, Reg. Northburgh, i, fo 196.
1345, 21 May, ord dcn, Tewkesbury abbey, by *lit. dim.*, *Reg. Bransford* (Worcester), no 1064 (p. 236).
1346, 23 Sept., ord pr., Stow, by *lit. dim.*, *ib.*, no 1073 (p. 261).

1361, 30 June, comm. as penitentiary in the diocese, *Reg. Stretton* (1905), 98.

Thomas WEOFORD [Weyford, Wyford
occ. [1518] d. 1537

1527–1538, prior: el. 22 July/27 Aug., 1527, *Fasti*, x, 5; d., 31 Oct., 1537, *L and P Henry VIII*, xii, pt ii, no 1010.

[1518], novice, prof. by this date, *Blyth Visit.*, 17.
1520, 2 June, ord subdcn, Lichfield cathedral, Reg. Blyth, ii, fo 135.
1525, 23 Sept., ord pr., Lichfield cathedral, *ib.*, ii, fo 174^{v}.

1524, 16 July, student, reported to be [studying] overseas, *Blyth Visit.*, 117.
Note: Dr Heath suggests that since he was absent from the 1521 visitation he may have been one of the four students about whom Thomas Leek, q.v., complained, *ib.*, 117, n.3.

[1518], 4th of six novices at the episcopal visitation who all agreed that *omnia bono ordine*, *Blyth Visit.*, 17.
[1521], 12 Dec., absent from the visitation, *ib.*, 87.
1534, 29 Jan., refused Cromwell's request to grant the receivership of the priory to one of Cromwell's servants, but agreed to try to oblige later if an opening occurred, *L and P Henry VIII*, vii, no 122.

Robert WETHYBROKE
occ. 1400

1400, 23 Dec., ord dcn, Eccleshall, Reg. Burghill, fo 219.

WEYFORD
see Weoford

William de WHESTON
occ. 1307

1307, 16 July, witnessed an act of homage made to the prior, Oxford, Bod. Ms Top. Warwicks C. 8, fo 74^{v}.

WILDE
see Wyldy

Walter de WIGORNIA
occ. mid 13th c.

n.d., John de Bruges, q.v., wrote 'totum officium de sancta Maria per annum ad missam, super missale dompni—'; presumably this ref to a fellow monk, Oxford, Bod. Ms Digby 104, fo 171.

I WILLIAM
occ. 1214

1214, [c. 9 July], 3rd in order on the list of monks who assented to the el. of William Cornhill as bp of Coventry, CUL Ms Ee.5.31, fo 240.

II WILLIAM
occ. 1214

1214, [c. 9 July], 6th in order on the list as above.

III WILLIAM
occ. 1214

1214, [c. 9 July], 26th in order on the list as above, *ib.*, fo 240v.

IV WILLIAM
occ. 1214

1214, [c. 9 July], 30th in order on the list as above.

V WILLIAM
occ. 1214

1214, [c. 9 July], 34th in order on the list as above.

William WINTERS [We'eter, Wynter
occ. 1504 occ. 1539

1504, 21 Sept., ord subdcn, Eccleshall, Reg. Blyth, ii, fo 9.

[1518], *coadiutor magistri capelle beate Marie* and succentor, *Blyth Visit.*, 16.

[1521], 12 Dec., precentor, *ib.*, 86.

1517, c. 16 June, 4th in order on the list of nine monks [?*compromissorii*] who petitioned the king to confirm the el. of John Webbe, q.v., as prior, *L and P Henry VIII*, ii, pt 1 (1515–1516), no 3464.

[1518], 7th to be questioned at the episcopal visitation and agreed with his brethren in regarding the prior [John Webbe, q.v.] as *prudentem, discretum et circumspectum*, *Blyth Visit.*, 16.

[1521], 12 Dec., 7th to be questioned at the visitation and designated tertius in ordine; he supported the statements of the prior and also agreed with the deposition concerning [Richard] Barnacle q.v., *ib.*, 86.

1524, 16 July, 7th to be questioned at the visitation and concurred with [the depositions of] Thomas Leeke, q.v., and the subprior [John Pope, q.v.]; he also stated that the juniors rarely attended divine office, *ib.*, 116.

1538, 20 Oct., dispensed to hold a benefice and change his habit, Chambers, *Faculty Office Regs*, 175.

1539, 15 Jan., signed the deed of surrender, *DK 8th Report*, Appndx 2, 16; he was awarded a pension of £6 13s. 4d. p.a., Dugdale, *Coventre*, 30 (as Thomas Winters); no sum is given in the pension list in *L and P Henry VIII*, xiv, pt 1, p. 601); the original is PRO E322/61.

WIRCETUR
see Worcett'

WLFELE
see Wolveleye

William WODECOTE
occ. 1377/8

1377, 23 May, ord subdcn, Colwich, *Reg. Stretton* (1905), 325.

1377, 19 Sept., ord dcn, Colwich (wrongly described as canon of Coventry), *ib.*, 328.

1378, 18 Sept., ord pr., Colwich, *ib.*, 340.

Roger de WOLASTON
occ. 1330 occ. 1334

1330, 29 May, ord subdcn, Eccleshall, Reg. Northburgh, i, fo 169v.

1333, 18 Sept., ord dcn, bp's chapel, Bishops Itchington, *ib.*, i, fo 170v.

1334, 21 May, ord pr., Aston, *ib.*, i, fo 172.

WOLNES, Wolney
see Volney

Adam de WOLVELEYE [Wlfele, Wolveley, Wulvele
occ. 1286 occ. 1301

1286, 3 July; 1291, 11 July; 1292, Mar.; 1293, 1 June, chaplain to the prior, Oxford, Bod. Ms Top. Warwicks C. 8, fos 73, 74.

1296, 12 Jan., 1301, 15 Apr., subprior, *CPR (1292–1301)*, 182, Oxford, Bod. Ms Top. Warwicks C. 8, fo 73.

1286, proctor for the prior and chapter in a dispute with the prior of Daventry over tithes at Wasperton, BL Add. Ms 32100, fo 92v.

1286, 3 July, witnessed an act of homage made to the prior, Oxford, Bod. Ms Top. Warwicks C. 8, fo 73.

1296, 12 Jan., with John Bacun, q.v., recd licence from the king to el. a bp, *CPR (1292–1301)*, 182.

1301, 15 Apr., witnessed an act of homage made to the prior, Oxford, Bod. Ms Top. Warwicks C. 8, fo 73.

Thomas WOOLSON
occ. 1537

1537, 1 Nov., sent as proctor with Robert Combe, q.v., to obtain licence from the king to el. a prior, *L and P Henry VIII*, xii, pt ii, no 1011.

Note: could this be Thomas Carnswell, q.v.?

WOOTTON
see Walton

Henry WORCETT' [Wircetur
occ. 1483/4

1483, 20 Sept., ord acol., Lichfield cathedral, Reg. Hales, fo 284v.
1484, 18 Sept., ord subdcn, Lichfield cathedral, *ib.*, fo 290.

John de WOTTON
occ. 1344 occ. 1346

1344, 18 Sept., ord subdcn, Chesterton, Reg. Northburgh, i, fo 196.
1345, 21 May, ord dcn, Tewkesbury abbey, by *lit. dim.*, *Reg. Bransford* (Worcester), no 1064 (p. 236).
1346, 23 Sept., ord pr., Stow, by *lit. dim.*, *ib.*, no 1073 (p. 261).

WULVELE
see Wolveleye

Thomas WYFORD
see Weoford

Robert WYLDY [Wilde, Wylde
occ. 1538/9

1538, 20 Oct., dispensed to hold a benefice and change his habit, Chambers, *Faculty Office Regs*, 175.
1539, 15 Jan., signed the deed of surrender, *DK 8th Report*, Appndx 2, 16; he was awarded a pension of £16 6s. 8d. p.a., Dugdale, *Coventre*, 30; no sum is given in the pension list in *L and P Henry VIII*, xiv, pt 1, p. 601); the original is PRO E322/61.

WYNDE
see Hynde

WYNTER
see Winters

YEME
see Enne

YMPINGHAM
see Impingham

ELY CATHEDRAL PRIORY

INTRODUCTION

Like most of the other cathedral priories, that of St Peter and St Etheldreda at Ely had its origin in a pre-conquest abbatial foundation. In 1109 king Henry I removed the county of Cambridge from the vast diocese of Lincoln to form the new see of Ely, with the Norman Hervey, previously bishop of Bangor, as the first bishop and Vincent, q.v., as the first prior. The imposition of a titular abbot *qua* bishop on the former abbey necessitated a number of important changes for the monks, one of which was a division of the monastic estates between bishop and chapter in order to provide income to support two separate households. This was not accomplished at once or without difficulty, partly on account of the civil war in which bishop Hervey's successor, Nigel, became embroiled, and partly because much of East Anglia including Ely was devastated by king Stephen.[1]

Ely was a large establishment in its early days, with a community of seventy-two monks at the time of the transfer to cathedral status; and it probably remained above fifty until the Black Death, when numbers were reduced by half. However, most of the empty places seem to have been filled within a relatively short space of time according to the figures on the account rolls, which record the presence of forty-six or forty-seven monks in the mid-1360s. There followed some fluctuations downward towards the end of the century, but there were about forty-five in 1404/5 and in 1427/8 and forty-two in 1498/9. However, in the year of the passage of the Act of Supremacy numbers were down to thirty-three and by the time of the surrender the total had been reduced to twenty-five.[2]

The rudiments of the so-called 'obedientiary system', or organization of offices within the monastery, probably preceded the change of status, but the earliest known references for the cathedral priory occur in the 1120s and 1130s. Aelfwardus, q.v., who by his name may have been a survivor of pre-conquest days, had been sacrist (*secretarius*) before his death shortly before 1122/3. Aelfstan and Aluricus (?Aelfricus), q.v., were subsacrist and succentor respectively in 1134 and the latter probably went on to become precentor. In 1177 a subprior, Richard, q.v., is named, in 1201 a chamberlain, Robert, q.v. An almoner, Martin, q.v., appears in 1229, an infirmarer, Walter de Walpole, q.v., possibly the following year, and a pittancer, N., q.v., in 1233. Although we have to wait until 1288/9 for the cellarer to be identified (Ralph de Waltham, q.v.) and until the end of the century to encounter a treasurer by name (Hermanus de

[1] Bishop Hervey's charter in which the monks' lands are specified is in *Liber Elien.*, 262–263 and Miller, *Abbey and Bishopric*, 282–283. A similar charter of bishop Nigel is in *Liber Elien.*, 299–301, and other gifts by him in *ib.*, 336–337, 383, 390–391. See also the interventions of archbishop Theobald in the 1150s in *Theobald Charters*, nos 101–103.

[2] These figures, with the exception of the two latest in date, have been drawn from a variety of manuscript sources, the first in chronological order being recorded in *Liber Elien.*, 261. The account rolls of five of the obedientiaries entered their distributions of clothing, pittances of food, and money (the latter sometimes called *gracie*) to specified numbers of monks, and these may be compared at intervals and combined with other references to produce the close approximations I have provided. The final two references, for 1534 and 1539, are to be found in Reg. Goodrich, fo 261 and *L and P Henry VIII*, xiv, pt 2, no 542.

Bredingdon, q.v.), these important offices must all have been functioning for as long as that of the sacrist. There were a range of other offices, some important and others less so; among these there are a few like the *custos roserie*, for example, who occurs only in the 1340s and 1350s (William de Spalding II, q.v.), because in later years the responsibility for (cutting) the rushes was given to a *serviens*. Another office, that of *senescallus forinsecus* (Richard de Newmarket, q.v., in 1260), is probably synonymous with the *senescallus terrarum* or land steward (Alan II, q.v., in 1303/4), but in 1402/3 the former office was held by a layman.[3] There was also a *senescallus hospitii*, or steward in charge of the prior's hospice for important guests, first named in c. 1321 (Richard de Spalding, q.v.). The remaining obediences and their first known incumbents in order of appearance are as follows: gardener (Alan de Soham, q.v., c. 1298), granator or granger (Walter de Hildercle, q.v., 1307), third prior (William de Hoveden, q.v., 1319), kitchener (Richard de Spalding, q.v., 1319), refectorer (John de Ramesey II, q.v., 1323/4), *custos* of the Lady chapel (Ralph de Rysyng, q.v., 1349) who had been preceded by a *custos* of the Lady altar (Alan de Walsingham, q.v., 1318/9), hostiller or guestmaster (Ralph de Hinton, q.v., 1328/9), feretrar (John de Croxton, q.v., 1349/50). This was a complement of nineteen or twenty monk officials, each of whom had at least several clerks and servants under him and some of whom ran a large department employing other monks and numerous clerks and laymen both within the cloister and on the manors. Although the prior, with advice from other senior monks, was free to make appointments to most of these obediences, the bishop's authority as titular abbot was expressed by his right to nominate to the offices of subprior, sacrist, cellarer, and chamberlain.[4]

At Ely many of the obedientiaries had monk assistants or *socii* whose names were sometimes included in the heading of the account roll.[5] In the case of the treasurers and *senescalli terrarum* it would seem that when two names are given at the top of the treasurer's account the second name was probably that of the *senescallus*; this is clearly stated on the 1465/6 account, which specifies that John Ely VII, q.v., was treasurer and Nicholas Derby, q.v., *senescallus*. Again, this time in reverse order, in 1525/6 another John Ely was *senescallus* and William Danyell, q.v., treasurer.[6] The close cooperation of these two obedientiaries in the financial affairs of the house would have rendered it unnecessary for the *senescallus* to produce his own separate account.

For these and many other informative details the obedientiary, and to a lesser extent the manorial, account rolls are our main source because of the survival of a significant collection from about thirteen of the offices and from a number of manors. An approximate total of close to four hundred obedientiary accounts dating from the 1280s survives, many of them fragmentary and in an advanced state of disintegration; and others, illegible or no longer extant, have been preserved in the neat and accurate transcriptions made by James Bentham in the late eighteenth century.[7] These

[3] CUL EDC 5/12/2.

[4] BL Add. Ms 9822, fo 64; one assumes that this was preceded, as elsewhere, by consultation with the prior and senior monks; see Chapman, *Sacrist Rolls*, ii, 167–177.

[5] e.g. Chapman, *Sacrist Rolls*, ii, 160 where Robert de Sutton, q.v., is the sacrist and Thomas de Aldborough, q.v., his *socius* in 1354/5; also, in 1382/3 Peter de Stapleford, q.v., was chamberlain and John de Wormyngton, q.v., his *socius*, CUL Add. Ms. 2957, fo 35. This was in accordance with the statutes of bishop Walpole in 1300, Evans, *Ely Chap. Ord.*, 21.

[6] CUL EDC 5/13/-, 5/13/18; the second John Ely may be John Ely XII, q.v., but see the note attached to the entry. For a discussion of the duties of the *senescallus* see Evans, *Ely Chap. Ord.*, xiii.

[7] See the notes in the Ely References in Section B, i and ii.

annual reports provide the historian with many insights beyond that of the financial state and organization of the house but, of course, their sole purpose was, in modern parlance, to 'balance the books'.[8] All of the obedientiaries who presented accounts at the annual audit received varying amounts of income that had been assigned to their offices and was derived from their manors and churches in the form of rents, dues, and tithes. The largest revenues, making up a common fund, were in the hands of the treasurer(s), who made allocations to the other obedientiaries; for example, about half of the chamberlain's income in 1334/5 came from the treasurer and possibly up to two-thirds of the cellarer's total receipts in the same period.[9] The existence of this common fund shows that a fair degree of centralization was in place, but there are no signs that the independence of the monk accountants was ever curtailed to the extent that archbishop Arundel enjoined in 1403 in an order that would have deprived them of any separate source of revenue.[10] While the prior does not appear to have had his own account, most of his expenses were provided for by the treasurer, and his weekly kitchen accounts and itinerary while visiting the manors were entered on the account of the steward of his hospice.

The sacrist, who was also *custos operum* at Ely, was the only obedientiary other than the treasurer who exercised considerable independence; he administered his own sizeable estate and his income was augmented by the receipts from shrines, notably that of St Etheldreda which amounted to over £90 in 1406/7.[11] There were extensive and prolonged building operations, made necessary by the collapse of the central tower in February 1322, soon after the appointment of Alan de Walsingham, q.v., as sacrist. The *novum opus*, as it was described on his accounts, absorbed his attention as well as vast sums of money during the next twenty years, and culminated in the completion of a stone octagon topped by a timber lantern that are still the glory of Ely. There was also a new Lady chapel under construction at this time under the supervision of John de Wisbech, q.v.; and in addition a new sacristy, prior's chapel, and study were also in progress.[12] Like his counterpart at Worcester, the Ely sacrist was, on at least one occasion, appointed to be the bishop's receiver.[13] It is not surprising that the sacrist's heavy responsibilities for the maintenance of the cathedral fabric and other buildings within the cloister, as well as for the administration of his estate and his involvement in ecclesiastical affairs, resulted in frequent periods of absence from the house. When he was attending diocesan synods, making the rounds of his manors for purposes of inspection and for the receipt of rents and other payments due (*liberatio*

[8] A warning here is essential to emphasize that medieval accounting methods were remote from our own and not easily interpreted without careful study.

[9] CUL EDC 5/3/1, 5/2/2, 5/13/7, although the figures must be treated with caution as the treasurer's allocations varied from year to year and the total receipts often included the arrears from the previous account.

[10] His injunction on this matter is in Evans, *Ely Chap. Ord.*, 52–53; in it he commanded that all moneys were to be paid directly to two treasurers. See also the same author's *The Medieval Estate of the Cathedral Priory of Ely, a Preliminary Survey* (Ely, 1973).

[11] CUL EDC 5/10/26.

[12] See Coldstream, 'Ely Cathedral' and Lindley, 'Ely'; the latter is a thesis which, it is hoped, will soon be available in print. In the meantime, there is a short article by Lindley entitled 'The Fourteenth Century Architectural Programme at Ely', in W. M. Ormrod, ed., *England in the Fourteenth Century, Proceedings of the 1985 Harlaxton Symposium* (Woodbridge, 1986), 119–129.

[13] See John Ely IV. Two other monks, John Cornewaill and William Wells III, q.v., were employed as receivers of the bishopric by a probably absent cardinal Louis de Luxemburg; they were serving in the office of almoner at the time. For Worcester see the Introduction to that section, n. 13.

denariorum), purchasing supplies at the annual fairs or inspecting building materials, his place in the choir was occupied by one of his brethren who was appointed to be his vicar; only one of them, William Burdeleys, q.v., is named on his account although the payments occur frequently in the first half of the fourteenth century.[14]

Enough names have been mentioned above to warrant the conclusion that almost all the Ely monks had their roots in the towns and villages of the surrounding region or in the adjoining counties of East Anglia. Unfortunately, there is no information about their family backgrounds except in a few cases, like those of John Salmon, Alan de Walsingham, William Wells II, and Robert Wells, q.v., all of them priors, and also of the more lowly Robert Iselham, q.v. As many as twenty-five bore the toponymic 'Ely' and were presumably of local origin, although John de Lincoln I, q.v., seems to have laid claim to Ely as well, a reminder that toponymics should be treated with caution. The churches and manors belonging to the prior and chapter could also prove fruitful recruiting grounds as suggested by the fact that there were ten monks named Wisbech and six named Lakyngheth.[15]

There was only one dependent cell attached to the cathedral priory in which three or four monks were probably resident on a temporary basis. This was the former Augustinian priory at Spinney in Wicken that was transferred to Ely in 1449 and dissolved in 1538.[16] Only a few references provide names of priors and monks of Spinney during the period of its subjection to Ely: John Hadnam, q.v., in 1462/3 was described as a former *custos*, Michael Barnyngham, q.v., was the cell's prior in 1530, and Roger Westminster, q.v., while prior of Ely, paid a visit to Spinney.

The early priors of Ely were probably appointed by the bishop until 1271 when bishop Hugh Balsham, q.v., who had previously been subprior, issued a licence giving the right to the chapter to elect; their choice was Henry de Bancs, q.v. The chapter's preference for the *via compromissi* usually resulted in an electoral body of seven or nine monks, but on one occasion the power of nomination was given to a sole *compromissor*, a unique practice as far as I know. (What does this imply about the preliminary negotiations?)[17] One of the early fourteenth-century priors, Robert de Orford, q.v., followed Balsham's progress to the episcopal throne as did John de Ketene, q.v., who was elected while serving as almoner. Although monastic solidarity was no doubt behind four other attempts to promote Ely priors and subpriors to the bishopric, it is unlikely that they stood much chance between the rival candidates put forward by pope and king.[18] Not surprisingly, the later priors displayed marked variation in ability and character, the financial acumen of John de Crauden, q.v., compensating for the incompetence of John de Fresingfeld, q.v., and Crauden and Walsingham collaborating in the building programme that the latter completed after succeeding the former as prior. William Powcher, q.v., acquired the privilege of being numbered among the mitred abbots and priors in a papal bull of 1413; in the same year he obtained papal approval to carry out constitutional reforms within the priory. Robert Colville,

[14] See Chapman, *Sacrist Rolls*, *passim*. The cellarer also had a vicar who appears on a few accounts, CUL EDC 5/2/2, 5/2/16.

[15] The church of Wisbech was appropriated to the monks and Lakenheath was one of their manors.

[16] The papal confirmation of the transfer is dated 12 June 1453, *CPL*, x (1447–1455), 251. See also *VCH Cambridgeshire*, ii, 249–254.

[17] See Nicholas de Copmanford. A similar situation, however, seems to have occurred when prior John de Fresingfeld, q.v., acted as sole *compromissor* in the election of bishop Hotham.

[18] The four were John Salmon, John de Crauden, Alan de Walsingham, and Peter de Ely, q.v.

q.v., who became prior after almost forty years in the cloister, was an accomplished organist and served for a time as precentor. The presence of William Foliot, q.v., as prior c. 1515/16 (according to *Fasti*, iv, 17) is almost certainly a matter of mistaken identity; Foliot's toponymic was Wittlesey and both names seem to have been used interchangeably. Robert Wells, the last prior, will be discussed below.

The episcopal registers at Ely, though incomplete and patchy, provide much valuable information about priory affairs, including ordinations, appointments to office, visitations and visitation injunctions; these last are supplemented by a useful collection of chapter ordinances, many of which have been preserved in two priory registers along with some early statutes and injunctions.[19] Since the form in which this legislation is cast is, for the most part, general rather than personal, it only rarely provides biographical information unless identification is possible by means of the offices to which allusion is made. According to the chronicler Oxenedes, archbishop Pecham ordered the removal of all the major obedientiaries in 1285, but stopped short of the prior, John de Hemmingestone, q.v.; this was probably in the wake of a visitation.[20] When archbishop Reynolds carried out a visitation *sede plena* in 1315 both the bishop and prior (John de Fresingfeld, q.v.) protested against his intrusion, but the monks quietly approved the injunction to build a church for the parishioners who worshipped in the nave and disturbed the monks at their office in the choir.[21] At archbishop Wittlesey's visitation in 1373 the sacrist was singled out on account of his maladministration, and archbishop Arundel brought about the resignation of the prior in 1401.[22] In the fifteenth and sixteenth centuries there are examples of equally vigorous admonitions and action arising out of visitations, such as an injunction addressed to prior Henry Peterborough, q.v., that he treat his monks more kindly and the resignation of prior William Wittlesey, q.v., after his alleged maladministration had been exposed.

One of bishop Fordham's injunctions concerns the periodic blood letting (*minutio[nes]*) of the monks and is known only because of an entry in the treasurer's account of 1389/90. In order to explain a slight increase in his contributions paid to the chamberlain and the precentor he noted, for the auditors' benefit no doubt, that the additional sum was for the monks' *minutiones*; the chamberlain, for his part, recorded the receipt of a sum from the treasurer 'pro minuc[ionibus sepius tenend' ultra prius usual' prout ordinatum est per dominum Episcopum, eo quod dominus prior non tenet minuc' ut solebat'.[23] It seems that Fordham's predecessor Arundel had given a similar directive, but the monks must have continued to complain that the order had not been fully implemented.[24] The Ely rolls contain many references to the *minutiones* because of their importance as welcome rest periods for the monks; these were times when they were able to enjoy several days of relaxation and comfort in the *aula* or *domus minutorum* where their diet was supplemented by more ample and varied fare. A

[19] These are printed in Evans, *Ely Chap. Ord.*, along with records of two archiepiscopal visitations. The earliest injunctions, those of bishops Balsham and Orford, and the statutes of bishop Walpole are in BL Add. Ms 9822 and the others in BL Add. Ms 41612.

[20] *Chron. Oxenedes*, 264.

[21] BL Add. Ms 41612, fo 34, and see also Chapman, *Sacrist Rolls*, i, 117 and ii, 193–194, which is the expense account for building the church in 1359/60, over forty years later! See M. Franklin, 'The Cathedral as Parish Church: The case of Southern England', in D. Abulafia, M. Franklin, M. Rubin, eds, *Church and City 1000–1500, Essays in honour of Christopher Brooke* (Cambridge, 1992), 192–194.

[22] See John de Ely IV and William de Walpole I.

[23] CUL EDC 5/13/8 (treasurer), 5/3/23 (chamberlain).

[24] CUL EDC 5/2/25.

rota system was in operation, traces of which appear from time to time on the accounts as, for example, when the sacrist listed the names of seven *minutorum* in 1341 with his payment of 4s.6¾d. for their (dietary) expenses for the three-day break.[25]

From evidence compiled from disparate sources we can observe the Ely monks fulfilling their responsibilities in the promotion of learning within the cloister. An almonry school was probably functioning in the late thirteenth century, if not before, but first comes into view in a chapter ordinance of 1314; this required the almoner not only to be more generous in the allowances of food distributed to the poor but also to provide meals of better quality for the scholars and their master. It also laid down regulations governing their admission and the length of their stay.[26] Their number and the cost of their board and lodging are entered on the almoner's subsequent account rolls but unfortunately with no names, so that it is not possible to ascertain if any of the almonry boys later entered monastic life at Ely.[27] As to monastic studies within the cloister we are better informed; both Robert de Sutton and Roger de Norwich, q.v., were described as *instructores* in the second half of the fourteenth century and received small sums from several of the obedientiaries for teaching the junior monks. What little remains of the monastic library consists largely of chronicles and service books, with only three surviving volumes of the early fathers and one of Aquinas. As early as c. 1093 there were reported to have been over two hundred volumes in addition to a large number of service books; but there is only one medieval list of less than a dozen and Leland lists only eight.[28] However, there are signs of activity on the precentor's accounts because, as in most Benedictine houses, he was also in charge of the scriptorium and the library. In 1320/1, for example, Walter de Wygenhale, q.v., bought a copy of Adalbert's Speculum Gregorii, and stipends paid to scribes appear regularly on many accounts throughout the fourteenth century.

The claustral instructors prepared some of the more promising junior monks for higher studies at Cambridge. They were often sent within four or five years after their profession and most pursued their courses in theology and canon law on a part-time basis.[29] The Black Monk Chapter decreed in 1363 that one monk in twenty should be maintained at university by each house, an obligation that seems to have been consistently met after prior Crauden, q.v., established a hostel in Cambridge for the Ely monks c. 1340 and possibly before. This is certainly true for most of the years for which there are obedientiary accounts to record student pensions; I have been able to estimate that there were fewer than thirty years during the two centuries before the dissolution when no Ely monk was at Cambridge; and it was frequently the case that two and, on a few known occasions, three were being maintained. A total of thirty-seven monk students are named in this period, twenty of whom obtained degrees, an excellent record when compared with some of the other cathedral priories like

[25] Chapman, *Sacrist Rolls*, ii, 106.

[26] Evans, *Ely Chap. Ord.*, 38–39.

[27] See Evans, 'Ely Almonry Boys and Choristers in the Later Middle Ages', in J. C. Davies, ed., *Studies presented to Sir Hilary Jenkinson* (London, 1957), 155–163.

[28] See *MLGB* and *MLGB Suppl.*; the medieval list is in Lambeth Ms 448, fo 119^{v} and those seen by Leland are in Sharpe, *Eng. Benedictine Libraries*, iv, B27. Another list, that of eleven volumes returned to the library by a borrower, occurs in BL Add. Ms 41612, fo 72; these include works of Aristotle and Avicenna and the Summa [theologica] of Henry of Gent. A letter to the king [in 1331/2] reveals that three stolen volumes, two of them canon law texts, had turned up in Paris, BL Add. Ms 41612, fo 74!

[29] See J. Greatrex, 'Rabbits and Eels', *Proceedings of the 1994 Harlaxton Symposium*, forthcoming.

Winchester.[30] In the 1530s there were four monk students who, if they were not all contemporaries at Cambridge, must have overlapped.[31]

Ely cathedral priory was never at the centre of ecclesiastical or secular affairs beyond the diocese, although the priors sat in parliament from the mid-thirteenth century and played their part in the triennial Black Monk Chapters.[32] One prior, Roger Westminster, q.v., was made a burgess of Ipswich, and Edmund Walsingham, q.v., was consulted about the appointment of a prior for the monk students at Cambridge. Although royal visits to Ely were infrequent, there was intermittent pressure from the king and corresponding protests from the monks over the former's right to impose his servants and officers as corrodians on the priory.[33]

There is some evidence to suggest that Ely continued to be relatively unaffected by outside pressures in the last years before the dissolution. This can be partly explained by the fact that the last prioral election had taken place as far back as 1522 when Robert Wells, q.v., who was probably still a student at Cambridge, was chosen by his fellow monks. He seems to have stood his ground in the 1530s when negotiating with Cromwell and was none the worse off for doing so, as he became dean of the new foundation. In these years it was not only the pursuit of learning that was in a healthy state. Not long before the visitation of bishop Goodrich in 1534 the whole community had been replenished by ten recent admissions, almost a third of the thirty-three monks listed on the visitation certificate.[34] Even though this did not result in an increase of numbers, because they were probably filling places left vacant by deceased brethren, an influx of young men drawn to the monastic life at Ely and professed within a space of only a few years speaks well for its internal regime and its external influence in the surrounding community. Their presence is a strong indication that this house, even though reduced in size from its earlier years, was not in a state of demoralization or decline until the very last days.

ELY REFERENCES WITH ABBREVIATIONS

Note: if the particular reference sought does not appear below, turn to the General Bibliography on pp. xv–xix, or the Canterbury section, p. 58–65.

A. Manuscript Sources

i Episcopal Registers

(*a*) Cambridge University Library (CUL)

Reg. [Simon de] Montacute (1337–1345)	EDR G/1/1, fos 1–101
Reg. [Thomas] de Lisle (1345–1361)	EDR G/1/1/, fos 1–125, second foliation
Reg. [Thomas] Arundel (1374–1388)	EDR G/1/2
Reg. [John] Fordham (1388–1425)	EDR G/1/3
Reg. [Thomas] Bourgchier (1443–1454)	EDR G/1/4

[30] Greatrex, *ib.*; the list of named monks is in the appendix to this article. There were probably other monks not identified by name.

[31] They were Robert Hamond, John Skelsyn, Thomas Wilberton, and William Wisbech, q.v.

[32] *VCH Cambridgeshire*, ii, 208, Pantin, *BMC*, ii, 137, 138, 143 etc.

[33] There are a number of examples in BL Add. Ms 41612, fos 40^{v}, 42, 62, 62^{v}, 77, 77^{v}, 105–105^{v}, CUL EDC 1B/168.

[34] The last ten names on the list, unlike the others, lacked the title *dominus* because they were not yet ordained [?priests], Reg. Goodrich, fo 90^{v}.

Reg. [William] Gray (1454–1478)	EDR G/1/5
Reg. [John] Alcock (1486–1500)	EDR G/1/6
Reg. [Nicholas] West (1515–1533)	EDR G/1/7, fos 1–87v
Reg. [Thomas] Goodrich (1534–1554)	EDR G/1/7, fos 88–283

(*b*) London Guildhall Library (LGL)

Reg. [Robert] Gilbert (1436–1448) Ms 9531/6

ii Priory Registers and Cartularies

(*a*) Cambridge University Library (CUL)

Alm. Cart	Almoner's Cartulary,	EDC 1A/2
Liber B	Priory register, c. 1407–1515, sometimes referred to as Reg. Almack; entries have been numbered.	EDR G/2/3
Liber M	[Prior's] cartulary, compiled *temp.*, prior John Crauden, q.v; paginated.	EDR G/3/28
Liber Quartus	Possibly a supplement to Liber M above.	EDC 1/A/1
Reg. Walsingham	Fragment of the register of prior Edmund Walsingham, q.v.; most entries have been numbered.	EDC 1A/3

(*b*) London, British Library (BL)

Add. Ms 9822	General register, 14th/15th cs, sometimes referred to as Liber A; this contains copies of charters etc., and also the chapter ordinances transcribed and printed by S. J. A. Evans. See Section D. below.
Add. Ms 41612	Priory register c.1273–1366; sometimes referred to as the Leconfield ms. See *Hist Mss Commission, 6th Report*, Appendix, in Section D. below which is a somewhat inaccurate calendar of the contents (pencil foliation followed in my references).
Ms Egerton 3047	General cartulary, in a 15th c. hand of which the second half appears below in ii d); sometimes known as Liber L.
Ms Cotton Vespasian A.vi	Almoner's cartulary, 14th c., fos 90–133; see also ii a) above.

(*c*) London, Lambeth Palace Library (Lambeth)

Ms 448 'Chronica et memoranda Eliensia' as described by M. R. James, 15th/16th cs; pencil foliation followed.

(*d*) Oxford, Bodleian Library (Oxford, Bod.)

Ms Ashmole 801 General cartulary, fos 74–143, of which the first half is now BL Ms Egerton 3047; see ii (*b*) above.

B. Other Manuscript Sources

i Obedientiary Accounts

(*a*) Cambridge University Library (CUL)

Almoner	c.1327/8 to 1473/4	EDC 5/1/-
Cellarer	c.1280s to 1475/6	EDC 5/2/-
Chamberlain	c.1288/9 to 1519/20	EDC 5/3/-
Custos of the Lady Chapel	1318/19 to 1488/9	EDC 5/7/-
Custos of the Rushes [*Roserie*]	1344/5 to 1353/4	EDC 5/6/-
Note: the later accountants were not monks.		
Feretrar	1421 to 1498/9	EDC 5/11/-
Granator	1307 to 1527/8	EDC 5/4/-

Hostiller	1328/9 to 1445/6	EDC 5/5/-
Infirmarer	1458/9	EDC 5/7/1

Note: one account only for this office.

Pittancer	1309 to 1510/11	EDC 5/8/-
Precentor	1300/1 to 1523/4	EDC 5/9/-
Sacrist	c.1293 to 1516/17	EDC 5/10/-;

Note: see also Section D. under Chapman for the printed accounts.

Steward of the Prior's Hospice	1370/1 to 1445/6	EDC 5/12/-
Treasurer(s)	1281/2 to 1475/6	EDC 5/13/-

Note: the treasurer's accts were usually headed by two monks, the first of whom was often named as treasurer and the second as steward of lands [*senescallus terrarum*].

Because there is as yet no printed, definitive list of the above obedientiary accounts some of the numbering remains uncertain or incomplete; however, the dates provided should in most cases be sufficient to enable them to be located.

In addition, there are transcripts of many obedientiary accts, now lost or fragmentary and illegible, which were made by James Bentham (1708–1794). These are found among the Add. Mss in the Cambridge University Library and are identified as such, CUL Add. Mss 2944–2959. There are also the more recent Crosby transcripts in CUL Add. Mss 6382(C)–6391 (C)

(*b*) London, Public Record Office (PRO)

Treasurer(s)	1428/9 to 1466/7	SC6/1257/4–9; six accts only

ii Manorial Accounts and Court Rolls in Cambridge University Library (CUL)

(*a*) Manorial Accounts

Kingston (Suffolk)	EDC 7/14C/-
Lakenheath	EDC 7/15/-
Melbourn	EDC 7/8/-
Melton	EDC 7/16/-
Sutton	EDC 7/3/-
Swaffham Prior	EDC 7/12/-
Wentworth	EDC 7/4/-
Whittlesey	EDC 7/6/-
Winston	EDC 7/17/-
Witcham	EDC 7/7/-

Note: there is as yet no definitive list and some of the numbering is uncertain; however, the name of the manor and the date should provide an adequate reference.

(*b*) Manorial and Miscellaneous Loose Deeds

Note: Only some of these have been numbered and listed as EDC 1B/1–.

iii Chronicles and Miscellaneous Manuscripts

BL Ms Cotton Tiberius A.vi	Collection of privileges of the church of Ely and the Historia Eliensis, 12th c.
BL Ms Cotton Titus A.1	Historia Eliensis, book ii, 12th/13th cs, with charters and some later additions.
Cambridge, Trinity College MS 1105	Liber Eliensis, 12th c., with a kalendar and obits.
Cambridge University Library, CUL EDC 1B/1-	Loose charters and deeds including royal, episcopal, papal, and land grants to the priory.

iv Unpublished Thesis

Lindley, 'Ely' P. Lindley, 'The Monastic Cathedral at Ely c.1320–c.1350, Art and Patronage in Medieval East Anglia', 2 vols, Cambridge, Ph.D., 1985.

C. Printed Sources

i Episcopal Registers

Note: none have appeared in print but J. H. Crosby provided abstracts of some of the contents of the registers in the *Ely Diocesan Remembrancer* between 1889 and 1914; there is an offprint of this by W. M. Palmer in the Cambridge University Library Mss Room, Adv. c.1161.

ii Priory Registers and Cartularies

None on print, but see Section A ii (*b*) above.

D. Other Printed Sources and References

Aston, *Arundel* — M. Aston, *Thomas Arundel, a Study of Church Life in the Reign of Richard II*, Oxford, 1967.

Bentham, *Hist. Ely* — James Bentham, *The History and Antiquities of the Conventual and Cathedral Church of Ely*, 2nd edn, Norwich, 1812.

Bentham Supplement — W. Stevenson, *A Supplement to the First Edition of Mr. Bentham's History and Antiquities of the Cathedral and Conventional Church of Ely*, Norwich, 1817.

Chapman, *Sacrist Rolls* — F. R. Chapman ed., *The Sacrist Rolls of Ely*, 2 vols, Cambridge, 1907, printed for private circulation only; vol ii contains transcriptions of the first fifteen accts.

Chron. Bury — A. Gransden, ed., *The Chronicle of Bury St. Edmunds, 1212–1301*, London, 1964.

Coldstream, 'Ely Cathedral' — N. Coldstream, 'Ely Cathedral: The Fourteenth-Century Work', in British Archaeological Association Conference Transactions, ii, *Medieval Art and Architecture at Ely Cathedral*, 1979, 28–46.

Evans, *Ely Chap. Ord.* — S. J. A. Evans, *Ely Chapter Ordinances and Visitation Records, 1241–1515, Camden Miscellany*, 3rd series, xvii, 1940, 1–74.

Evans, 'Mepal' — S. J. A. Evans, 'The Purchase and Mortification of Mepal by the Prior and Convent of Ely', *English Historical Review*, li (1936), 113–120.

Graham, 'Ely Vacancies' — Rose Graham, 'The Administration of the Diocese of Ely during the Vacancies of the See, 1298–9 and 1302–3', *Transactions of the Royal Historical Society*, 4th series, xii (1929), 49–74.

Greatrex, 'Rabbits and Eels' — J. Greatrex, 'Rabbits and Eels at High Table: Monks of Ely at the University of Cambridge, c. 1337–1539', in B. Thompson, ed., *Proceedings of the 1994 Harlaxton Symposium*, forthcoming.

Hist. Mss Comm. 6th Report — A. J. Horwood, 'Calendar of BL Add. Ms 41612', in *Historical Manuscripts Commission, 6th Report*, Appendix, 1877.

Liber Elien. — E. O. Blake, ed., *Liber Eliensis*, Camden Society, 3rd series, xcii (1962); transcript of early versions of a 12th-c. cartulary *cum* chronicle.

Miller, *Abbey and Bishopric* — E. Miller, *The Abbey and Bishopric of Ely*, Cambridge, 1969.

Stewart, *Arch. Hist. Ely* — D.J. Stewart, *Architectural History of Ely Cathedral*, London, 1868.

ELY CATHEDRAL PRIORY
1109–1539

I ADAM
occ. 1134

1134, 5 Jan., witnessed an inventory of the treasury ordered by bp Nigel, *Liber Elien.*, 289.

II ADAM
occ. 1197 × 1215

1197 × 1215, sacrist, occ. in a charter of bp Eustace, Liber M, 165 *bis.*

AELFRICUS
[?c. 1143]

[?c. 1143], precentor, who gave or had made four albs included in the inventory of the treasury, *Liber Elien.*, 293.

Note:
(1) this is prob. a variation of Aluricus, q.v.
(2) the obit of an Aelfricus, prior, occ. on 10 Aug. in Cambridge, Trinity College Ms 1105, fo k8^{v}.

AELFSTAN [Alstanus
occ. 1134

1134, 5 Jan., subsacrist, *Liber Elien.*, 289.

1134, 5 Jan., witness to an inventory of the treasury, ordered by bp Nigel, *ib.*

AELFWARDUS
occ. before 1122/3

1122/3, before, sacrist [*secretarius*], Delisle, *Rouleaux des Morts*, 339.

1122/3, d. by this date when his name occ. on a mortuary roll of Savigny, *ib.*

AELWINUS
occ. before 1122/3

1122/3, d. by this date when his name occ. on a mortuary roll of Savigny, Delisle, *Rouleaux des Morts*, 339.

Thomas AGARSTON [Hagarston, Harston, Hayardston
occ. 1534 occ. 1539

[1534], 10 Sept., 33rd and last in order on the visitation certificate; he was one of ten not styled *dominus* and therefore recently adm. and not yet in major orders, Reg. Goodrich, fo 90^{v}.
1539, 18 Nov., assigned a pension of £5 6s. 8d. p.a., *L and P Henry VIII*, xiv, pt 2, no 542.

AILESHAM
see Aylesham

I ALAN
n.d.

n.d., 31 Dec., obit occ. in Cambridge, Trinity College Ms 1105, fo k12^{v}

II ALAN [Alanus
occ. 1303/4

1303/4, monk steward [*senescallus*], visited Lakenheath, CUL EDC 7/15/acct.

III ALAN
occ. 1358/9

1358/9, monk steward [*senescallus terrarum*], CUL EDC 7/15/acct.

Note: this may be Alan Sutton or Alan Walsingham the prior, q.v., acting as land steward this yr.

Thomas de ALDBOROUGH [Aldebrugh, Aldeburgh
occ. [1349] d. 1389/90

[1349, Nov.], subdcn, recd *lit. dim.* for orders of dcn and pr., Reg. de Lisle, fo 30.
1350, 18 Dec., ord pr., Ely cathedral, *ib.*, fo 97.

1356/7, 1360/1, granator, CUL EDC 5/4/11, 12.
1369/70, almoner, CUL Add. Ms 2957, fo 11.

1356/7, on the granator's acct a memorandum *de novo furno facto* [?in the brewery] by him, CUL EDC 5/4/11.
1354/5, *socius* of the sacrist, Chapman, *Sacrist Rolls*, ii, 160, (CUL EDC 5/10/13).
1360/1, gave 100s. of his own to alleviate the granator's deficit, CUL EDC 5/4/12.
1361, contributed 40s. towards the purchase of the manor and advowson of Mepal, Evans, 'Mepal', 118 (CUL EDC 1B/box 23).
1379, 8th in order on the clerical poll tax list and gave 3s. 4d., PRO E179/23/1.
1389/90, d., and the chamberlain gave the almoner 5s. CUL EDC 5/3/23.

William de ALDEBY
occ. 1359 occ. 1379

1359, Jan./1361, Dec., *socius* of the precentor, CUL Add. Ms 2957, fo 44, CUL EDC 5/9/3.
1361, contributed 10s. towards the purchase of the manor and advowson of Mepal, Evans, 'Mepal', 118 (CUL EDC 1B/box 23).

1362/3, *socius* of the chamberlain, CUL Add. Ms 2957, fo 28.
1379, 10th in order on the clerical poll tax list and pd 3s. 4d., PRO E179/23/1.

Thomas ALDRED
d. 1516/17

1516/17, one of eight monks who d., and the sacrist sent 5s. for each to the almoner, CUL EDC 5/10/44.

ALESHAM
see Aylesham

I ALEXANDER
occ. [1139/40] occ. c. 1158

1151 × 1152–c. 1158, prior: first occ. as prior Feb. 1151 × June 1152; last occ. c. 1158, *Fasti*, ii, 48, *HRH*, 46.

[1139/40], went to Rome to inform the pope of bp Nigel's deprivation and exile by the king, acc. to *Liber Elien.*, 315–316; however, Dr. Blake shows (*ib.*, 316, n. 2) that the text is inaccurate and that he was a member of the delegation sent by the bp to attend the second Lateran council (1139).
1151, Mar/Apr. × 1152, June, as prior wrote to the pope concerning the dispute with the adcn over the manor of Stetchworth, *Liber Elien.*, 351–352.
1154, responsible for the translation of the relics of the benefactors of Ely *in septentrionalem partem ecclesie*, *ib.*, xlviii (n. 7), 155.
n.d., as prior, witnessed a charter of bp Nigel, Liber M, 158.

Described as 'virum bene religiosum, doctum et eloquentem Latina, Gallicana et lingua Anglica', *Liber Elien.*, 316.

II ALEXANDER
occ. 1281

1281, 11 Oct., sacrist, CUL EDC 1B/113.

1281, 11 Oct., one of the monks who were absolved from excommunication because of irregularities that had occurred over payment of a tenth for the Holy Land, *ib.*

Note: it is possible that Alexander II is Alexander de Ely, q.v.

ALSTANUS
see Aelfstan

ALURICUS [?Aelfric, Aelfricus
occ. 1134 × 1169

1134, 5 Jan., succentor, *Liber Elien.*, 289.
[1134 × 1169], precentor, *temp.* bp Nigel, BL Add. Ms 9822, fo 61.

1134, 5 Jan., witness to an inventory of the treasury ordered by bp Nigel, *Liber Elien*, 289.
n.d., named [as precentor] when bp Nigel gave two churches and tithes for the scriptorium *ad libros faciendos et emendandos*, BL Add. Ms 9822, fo 61.
n.d., 23 Apr., the obit of Aluricus cantor, occ. in Cambridge, Trinity College Ms 1105, fo k4^{v}.

While precentor he made, or more likely, caused to be made a copy of the Gospels, 'textus superargentatus cum ymaginibus sancte Aetheldrede deauratus per totum', *Liber Elien.*, 291.

Note: see also Aelfricus

AUGUSTINE [?Augustus
occ. [1152 × 1158] occ. 1169

1166/9, present with bp Nigel during his last illness, *Liber Elien.*, 384.
[1152 × 1158], with prior Alexander, q.v., witnessed a charter of bp Nigel, Liber M, 158.

Robert de AYLESHAM [Ailesham, Alesham, Daylesham, Haylisham
occ. 1325/6 occ. 1351

1331/3, granator, CUL EDC 5/13/6, 5/4/6; see John de Ely II.
1333/4, *prefectio* as *senescallus terrarum*, CUL EDC 7/16/acct and court; and see below.
1345/6; 1348, 15 Sept.; 1347/8; 1351, 11 Mar., sacrist, CUL EDC 5/10/10; Reg. de Lisle, fo 88; CUL EDC 7/4/1 acct; Reg. de Lisle, fo 87^{v}.

1325/6, occ. on the treasurer's acct, CUL EDC 5/13/1.
1326/7, pd a visit to Lakenheath, CUL EDC 7/15/acct.
1332, 26 Aug., with a secular clerk, apptd proctor for convocation, BL Add. Ms 41612, fo 73.
1331/2, as subcollector of a royal tenth, travelled to London and elsewhere; as granator he spent £19 on supplies of grain [*blad'*], CUL EDC 5/13/6.
1333/4, pd two supervisory visits to Melton, and held court there in Oct. 1334, CUL EDC 7/16/acct and court.
1334, 21 Feb., as subcollector of papal tenths in the city and diocese of Ely turned in his report [*instrumentum*], dated by the collector on this day, see BL Add. Ms 41612, fos 84^{v}–85^{v}. He was also involved with the collection of a royal tenth and fifteenth, 1334/5, *ib.*, fo 86, 86^{v}.
1335, 5 May, apptd, with a secular cleric, as proctors to the parliament at York, BL Add. Ms 41612, fo 73.
1336, 27 Feb., with a secular clerk, apptd proctor to attend convocation at St Paul's and parliament at Westminster, *ib.*, fo 75; the treasurer gave him 105s. 5d., by indenture for his expenses, CUL EDC 5/13/7 (1335/6). He went again to London on 1 May *in brevibus impetratis* and also to Anglesey, Clare and elsewhere on business for the house. In late Aug. he was in London, and he was sent to a council in Nottingham [in Sept.], *ib.*

1338/9, pd a supervisory visit to Melton, CUL EDC 7/16/acct.
1339, 31 Mar., with Alan de Walsingham, q.v., and others, apptd proctors to treat with bp Hotham's executors over certain terms of his will, BL Add. Ms 41612, fo 101.
1341, 25 Oct., apptd proctor to inform the bp of the chapter's choice of a prior, and present on 19 Nov., at the bp's examination of the elect, Reg. Montacute, fo 25, 25v.
1344, 25 July, apptd proctor, with Geoffrey de Sutton, q.v., to act for the prior and chapter in a dispute with Thomas de Stalario, knight, Liber M, 624.
1344, 18 Oct., one of four monks who were cited to appear before the pope for arresting the proctor of the rector of Hadenham while he was in the chapter house reading out a papal letter concerned with disputed claims over Hadenham church, *CPL*, iii (1342–1362), 140–141, 171.
1344/5, with William de Spalding, q.v., visited Lakenheath, CUL EDC 7/15/acct.
1345, 28 June, with John de Hamerton, q.v., recd licence from the king, at Sandwich, to el. a bp, *CPR (1343–1345)*, 486.
1345, 1 Dec., apptd penitentiary, Reg. de Lisle, fo 87v; on 17 Dec., he and William de Spalding, q.v., attended a meeting in which the abbots of Ramsey and Thorney presented their conflicting claims over Kingsdelf, *Cart. Ramsey*, i, 78.
1345/6, visited the fairs at Reach and Stourbridge and attended synod [in Cambridge] in June 1346, Chapman, *Sacrist Rolls*, ii, 134–135 (CUL EDC 5/10/10).
1346, 20 Apr., comm., with another, to rec. the purgation of clerks in prison, Reg. de Lisle, fo 61v.
1348, 15 Sept., retained as penitentiary in the city of Ely *ib.*, fo 88.
1348 or 1349, 9 Feb., one of several monks who witnessed an agreement settling transgressions in Lakenheath and other places, Liber M, 628.
1351, 11 Mar., retained as penitentiary, Reg. de Lisle, fo 87v.
1354/5, the sacrist bought from the prior for 50s. a *byker* (a drinking goblet) with a silver lid which had formerly belonged to him, Chapman, *Sacrist Rolls*, ii, 167 (CUL EDC 5/10/13).

John de AYLINTON
occ. 1265

1265, 30 Aug., with other monks witnessed an acquittance for part of a sum owed to a Florentine merchant by the bp, prior and chapter, CUL EDC 1B/106.

AZO
occ. [1114 × 1130] occ. [1151 × 1158]

[1151 × 1158], sacrist, Oxford, Bod. Ms Ashmole 801, fo 139.
[1114 × 1130], with prior Henry, q.v., witness to a grant of land by the abbot of Ramsey, *Chron. Ramsey*, 250.
[1151 × 1158], witness to a charter, *temp.*, prior Alexander, q.v., Oxford, Bod. Ms Ashmole 801, fo 139.
n.d., 13 Nov., the obit of an Azo, sacrist, occ. in Cambridge, Trinity College Ms 1105, fo k11v.

Note: An Azo, nephew of prior William, q.v., occ. as a witness, Liber M, 158.

AZORIUS
n.d.

n.d., 13 June, obit occ. in Cambridge, Trinity College Ms 1105, fo k6v.

Hugh de BALSHAM
occ. 1256/7

1256, 13 Nov., subprior, *Fasti*, ii, 46.
1256, 13 Nov., el. bp. Both king and abp at first refused assent, but after an appeal to the pope the el. was confirmed, *ib.* He went to Rome in person to pursue his cause, Dugdale, *Monasticon*, i, 464.
1257, 11 Sept., the acct of his visit to the papal court and his examination by the pope are given in Liber M, 37–39; the pope confirmed the el. on 6 Oct., *Fasti*, ii, 46.

Henry de BANCS [Bancis, Bauns
occ. 1271/3

1271–1273, prior: el. 20 Oct. × 11 Nov. 1271; d. 25 Dec. 1273, *Fasti*, ii, 49.
1272, Nov., sat as one of the justices in eyre in the bp's temporal court, Bentham, *Hist. Ely*, 218.

Note: this is the first record of the free el. of the prior.

Simon de BANHAM D.Th. [Banneham
occ. 1347 occ. 1379

1347, 11 Dec., recd *lit. dim.*, for the order of subdcn, Reg. de Lisle, fo 85v.
1348, 14 June, ord dcn, Over, *ib.*, fo 96.
1371/2, 1374/5, feretrar, CUL EDC 5/10/18, 19.
1379, prob. subprior, PRO E179/23/1.
1354/5, student at Cambridge with pension contribution of 10s. 10¾d., from the sacrist, Chapman, *Sacrist Rolls*, ii, 167 (CUL EDC 5/10/13).
1357/8, student, with pension contributions from the chamberlain and sacrist, CUL EDC 5/3/12, Chapman, *Sacrist Rolls*, ii, 178, (CUL EDC 5/10/14).
1358/9, student, with pension contribution from the chamberlain, CUL EDC 5/3/13.
1359/60, student, with pension contribution from the sacrist, Chapman, *Sacrist Rolls*, ii, 190, (CUL EDC 5/10/15).
1360/1, student, with pension contribution from the cellarer, CUL EDC 5/2/16.

1366, incepted in theology; the granator contributed 12 quarters, 4 bushels of wheat and 9 quarters, 4 bushels of malt [toward the feast] on his 1365/6 acct, CUL EDC 5/4/14a; the chamberlain gave 2s. 3d., on his 1366/7 acct, CUL EDC 5/3/15.

1361, contributed 13s. 4d., towards the purchase of the manor and advowson of Mepal, Evans, 'Mepal', 118 (CUL EDC 1B/box 23).

1374, 18 Mar., licenced to hear confessions in the city and diocese, Reg. Arundel, fo 1; another similar licence was issued on 21 Jan. 1375, *ib.*, fo 5ᵛ.

1376, 24 Feb., described as *sacre pagine professori* and comm. as penitentiary in the city and diocese, *ib.*, fo 13.

1379, 2nd in order on the clerical poll tax list and pd 3s. 4d., PRO E179/23/1.

BARBOR, Barbour
see Richard Ely

E. de BARINGTON
occ. 1290/1

1290/1, pd a supervisory visit to Melton, CUL EDC 7/16/2 acct.

Alexander BARKLEY [Barckeley, Barkeley
occ. 1515/16

1515, 15 Apr., 21st in order out of 35 monks on the *sed. vac.*, visitation certificate, Reg. abp Warham, ii, fo 277.

1516, 22 Mar., 16th in order in the chapter which chose 29 Mar. as the date for the el. of a prior, Reg. West, fo 55.

Note: there were five monks senior to him absent from the chapter house on 22 Mar. when the above list was made.

Described as both poet and scholar, he was for a time a secular priest in the college of Ottery St Mary, Devon. At an unknown date he was recd into the Ely community where he wrote his 'Eclogues' and translated a life of St George. He left Ely to join the Franciscans at Canterbury. For his other writings see *DNB* which gives his dates as c. 1475 to 1552.

Warin de BARNTONE [Barton, Beryngton
occ. 1302 d. 1322/3

1302, 14 Apr., almoner, Lambeth Ms 448, fo 49 (for the date), *CPL*, i (1198–1304), 604 (for the name).

1302, 14 Apr., one of the seven *compromissorii* named by the chapter in the el. of a bp, *ib.*, (both refs. above); see Robert de Orford.

1310, 28 Feb., again one of seven *compromissorii* in the el. of a bp, BL Add. Ms 41612, fo 49ᵛ. In this case it appears that they failed to agree and seven others were chosen; see John de Ketene.

1322/3, d. and the sacrist sent 5s. to the almoner, Chapman, *Sacrist Rolls*, ii, 31, (CUL EDC 5/10/3).

Michael BARNYNGHAM [Bernyngham, ?Beryngham
occ. 1514 occ. 1534

1514/15, *custos* of the Lady chapel, Add. Ms 2957, fo 64.

1530, 21 Feb., prior of Spinney, *VCH Cambridgeshire*, ii, 253 (PRO C1/642, no 18, Early Chancery Proceedings).

1535/6, granator, CUL EDC 5/13/-.

1515, 15/16 Apr., 14th in order on the *sed. vac.* visitation certificate, Reg. abp Warham, ii, fo 277.

1516, 22 Mar., 11th in order in the chapter which chose 29 Mar. as the date for the el. of a prior, Reg. West, fo 55.

1534, 8 Sept., 4th in order on the visitation certificate, Reg. Goodrich, fo 90ᵛ.

BARNYNGHAM
see also Berningham

BARTON
see Barntone, Berton

BAUNS
see Bancs

BEDON
see Bredon

John de BEKKLES [Becklys, Beklis, Beklys
occ. 1337/8 d. 1355/6

1349, 2 July, apptd cellarer, by the vicar general present in chapter, Reg. de Lisle, fo 22ᵛ.

1337/8, prob., student at Cambridge, named as J., who with W[alter de Walsoken, q.v.] recd 60s. *pro vestura* from the chamberlain, CUL EDC 5/3/4.

1339/40, Sept. to Mar., prob. student as he recd 12d. with John de Sautre, q.v., *pro generali suo* from the cellarer, CUL EDC 5/2/6.

1340/2, student at Cambridge, with pension contributions from the cellarer and sacrist; the former pd *pro generali suo* for 31 wks from Jan. to Aug. at the rate of 3 ½d. per wk, and an additional 8½d. based on [a levy of] ½d. in the £, CUL EDC 5/2/7, 8, CUL Add. Ms 2957, fo 3. The sacrist contributed 11s. 11d., to him and Walter de Walsoken and 6s. 8d., *ex curialitate*, Chapman, *Sacrist Rolls*, ii, 107 (CUL EDC 5/10/9).

1343, Jan./Sept., prob. still a student with Walter de Walsoken as they occur together under the chamberlain's *liberationes*, CUL EDC 5/3/6a.

1355/6, d., and the precentor gave 5s. to the almoner, CUL Add. Ms 2957, 44.

Robert BELL
d. 1527/8

1527/8, d., and the treasurer gave 5s. to the almoner, CUL Add. Ms 2957, fo 80.
Note: this may be Robert Stuntney, q.v.

I BENEDICT
occ. 1134

1134, 5 Jan., witness to an inventory of the treasury ordered by bp Nigel, *Liber Elien.*, 289.
n.d., the obit of a Benedict occ. in Cambridge, Trinity College Ms 1105, fo k6ᵛ.

II BENEDICT
occ. 1288/9

1288/9, recd 1s. from the chamberlain [*pro vestura*], CUL Add. Ms 2957, fo 16.

Roger de BERGHAM [Bercham, Brigham
occ. 1203 d. 1229

1215–1225 × 1228, prior: occ. as prior before Feb. 1215; still prior 1225 × 1228, *Fasti*, ii, 49, *HRH*, 46.
[1197 × 1215], witnessed two charters of bp Eustace, Liber M, 167 *bis*.
1203, represented the prior in a suit vs the abbot of Bury St Edmunds, *Curia Regis Rolls*, ii, 140.
1229, before 6 Mar., d., *Fasti*, ii, 49.

BERGHAM
see also Brigham

John de BERNEWELL
occ. 1341/2 d. 1368/9

1341/2, subsacrist, Chapman, *Sacrist Rolls*, ii, 120 (CUL EDC 5/10/9b).
1348/9, chamberlain, CUL Add. Ms 2957, fo 25.
1341, Sept./Nov., on the sacrist's list of his *socii* who had two *minutiones*, Chapman, *Sacrist Rolls*, ii, 106 (CUL EDC 5/10/9a).
1345/6, 1349/50, *socius* of the sacrist, *ib.*, 126, 140 (CUL EDC 5/10/10, 11).
1351/4; 1358/9, 1360/1, *socius* of the chamberlain, CUL Add. Ms 2957, fo 27, CUL EDC 5/3/11; CUL EDC 5/3/13, 14.
1361, contributed 13s. 4d., towards the purchase of the manor and advowson of Mepal, which he obtained *pro pecijs argenti furatis*, Evans, 'Mepal', 119 (CUL EDC 1B/box 23).
1368/9, d., and the sacrist gave 5s. to the almoner, CUL EDC 5/10/16.

R. de BERNINGHAM
d. 1315/16
1315/16, one of ten who d.; the chamberlain gave 5s. to the almoner for each, CUL Add. Ms 2957, fo 19.

BERNYNGHAM
see Barnyngham

John de BERTON [Barton, Burton
occ. 1377/8 occ. 1401

1382/3; 1388/9; 1391/2; 1393/4, treasurer, CUL EDC 5/2/23, CUL Add. Ms 2957, fo 5; CUL EDC 5/3/22; CUL EDC 7/17/acct; CUL EDC 5/6/13, 7/16/25.
1377/8, *socius* of the cellarer, CUL EDC 5/2/20.
1379, 27th in order on the clerical poll tax list and pd 3s. 4d., PRO E179/23/1.
1379/80, *socius* of the cellarer, CUL EDC 5/2/21.
1380/1, *socius* of the sacrist, CUL Add. Ms 2956, fo 60.
1381/2, *socius* of the cellarer, CUL EDC 5/2/22.
1382/3, pd a visit to Melton for *liberatio denariorum*, CUL EDC 7/16/23.
1384/6, 1388/9, *socius* of the cellarer, CUL EDC 5/2/26–28; he was also treasurer again during 1388/9 as above.
1391/2, visited Winston, CUL EDC 7/17/acct.
1401, 14 Sept., 8th in order on the metropolitan visitation certificate, Reg. Fordham, fo 131.

Thomas de BERTON
occ. 1337/8

1337, 16 Sept., subdcn, obtained *lit. dim.*, for dcn's orders, Reg. Montacute, fo 96.
1338, 19 Sept., ord dcn, St Mary's church, Ely, *ib.*, fo 101ᵛ.

BERY, Biry
see Bury

BERYNGTONE
see Barntone

Thomas de BOCEKISHAM [Bodekesham, Bodekysham
occ. 1341 occ. 1347/8

1341, Sept./Nov., listed among those who were *socii* of the sacrist and underwent *minutiones* twice, Chapman, *Sacrist Rolls*, ii, 106 (CUL EDC 5/10/9a).
1347/8, pd a [supervisory] visit to Winston, CUL EDC 7/17/acct.

John de BOKENHAM
occ. 1341/3

1341, 24 Mar., ord dcn, Willingham, Reg. Montacute, fo 107ᵛ.
1343, 29 Mar., ord pr., Willingham, *ib.*, fo 111ᵛ (not identified by religious house).

BOKENHAM
see also Buckenham

BOKTON
see Bukton

John de BOROUDIT [?Borondit
occ. 1277

1277, June, with Andrew de Swaffham, q.v., proctor for the prior and convent who obtained a receipt, in London for a pension pd to a papal notary's relative, CUL EDC 1B/115b.

Thomas de BOTILSHAM [Botlesham
occ. 1341 occ. 1347/8

1341, Dec., accompanied the sacrist to Lynn to buy wax and other necessities, Chapman, *Sacrist Rolls*, ii, 120 (CUL EDC 5/10/9b).
1347/8, visited Lakenheath, CUL EDC 7/15/acct.

Simon BOTOLFF [Batoll
occ. 1469/70 occ. 1497/8

1469/70, steward of the prior's hospice, CUL EDC 5/13/-.
1497/8, subprior and *custos communis thesaurarie* CUL EDC 5/13/17.

On the 1497/8 acct above there is ref. to a debt owed to a John Botolff.

Thomas BOXWORTH [Boxwurth
occ. 1463 occ. 1500

1463, 9 Apr., ord acol., bp's [*magna*] chapel, Downham, Reg. Gray, fo 210^{v}.
1466, 5 Apr., ord subdcn, bp's palace chapel, Ely, *ib*., fo 211.
1467, 14 Mar., ord dcn, bp's palace chapel, Ely, *ib*., fo 211^{v}.
1467, 28 Mar., ord pr., bp's palace chapel, Ely, *ib*., fo 212.

1495/6, chamberlain, CUL Add. Ms 2957, fo 32.
1500, 30 Oct., refectorer, Canterbury Reg. R, fo 70.

1473/4, *socius* of the almoner, CUL EDC 5/1/14.
1500, 30 Oct., 8th to be examined at the *sed. vac*., visitation by the commissary of the prior of Christ Church, Canterbury (when the sees of Ely and Canterbury were both vacant); he gave his *omnia bene*, Canterbury Reg. R, fo 70.

Thomas BRABY
see Over

John BRAFFELD [Brasfeld
occ. 1534

1534, 8 Sept., 30th in order on the visitation certificate, Reg. Goodrich, fo 90^{v}; he was one of ten not styled *dominus* and therefore recently adm. and not yet in major orders.

William BRAMICHE [?Braunche
occ. 1534

1534, 8 Sept., 28th in order on the visitation certificate, Reg. Goodrich, fo 90^{v}; he was one of ten not styled *dominus* and therefore recently adm. and not yet in major orders.

Richard de BRAUNFORD [Bramford
occ. 1281 occ. 1302

1302, 29 Oct., prob. the Richard who had been hostiller, *CPL*, i, (1198–1304), 604 and see below.
Note: *CPL* has rendered the Latin into the English 'doorkeeper'.

1281, 11 Oct., one of the monks who were absolved from irregularities that had occurred over payment of a tenth for the Holy Land, CUL EDC 1B/113.
1286, before 8 July, sent as proctor, with William de Brigham and William de Wyght, q.v., to inform the king of the d. of the bp; the king issued the licence in Paris on 8 July, Liber M, 119, CUL Add. Ms 2948, fo 143.
1298, 24 Apr., with Robert de Orford and William de Brigham, q.v., recd royal licence to el. a bp, *CPR (1292–1301)*, 345.
1302, 14 Apr., as Richard, one of seven *compromissorii* named by the chapter in the el. of a bp, BL Ms Harley 258, fo 87^{v}.

Note: see also Richard de Cantebrigge who may have been the hostiller and *compromissorius* in 1302.

Hermannus de BREDINGDON
occ. 1299

1299, Feb./Mar., receiver [*receptor*], CUL EDC 7/14/1 acct.

1299, Feb./Mar., visited Kingston for *liberatio denariorum*, *ib*.

John BREDON [Bedon, Brydon
occ. 1497/8 d. 1526/7

1500, Oct., third prior, Canterbury Reg. R, fo 70, as Bedon.
1505/6, 1509/10, prob. feretrar, CUL Add. Ms 2956, fos 174, 176.

1497/9, *socius* of the feretrar, CUL EDC 5/11/10.
1500, 30 Oct., 14th to be examined at the *sed. vac.* visitation by the commissary of the prior of Christ Church, Canterbury (when the sees of both Ely and Canterbury were vacant). He reported *omnia bene*, Canterbury Reg. R, fo 70^{v}.
1515, 15/16 Apr., 4th in order on the *sed. vac*., visitation certificate, Reg. abp Warham, ii, fo 277.
1516, 22 Mar., 3rd in order in the chapter which chose 29 Mar. as the date for the el. of a prior, Reg. West, fo 55.
1524/5, 1526/7, *socius* of the chamberlain, CUL Add. Ms 2957, fos 33, 34.
1526/7, d., and the chamberlain gave 5s. to the almoner, CUL EDC 5/13/19.

William de BRIGHAM [Bergham
occ. 1286 occ. 1298

1286, before 8 July, sent as proctor, with Richard de Braunford and William de Wyght, q.v., to

inform the king of the d. of the bp; the king issued the licence in Paris on 8 July, Liber M, 119, CUL Add. Ms 2948, fo 143.
1289, 30 June, one of a group of monks and others who sat on a commission to investigate disputed boundaries in Lakenheath, Liber M, 603.
1298, 24 Apr., with Robert de Orford and Richard de Braunford, q.v., recd royal licence to el. a bp, *CPR (1292–1301)*, 345.

BRIGHAM
see also Bergham

BRISMERUS [Brihtmaer
occ. 1134

1134, 5 Jan., witness to an inventory of the treasury ordered by bp Nigel, *Liber Elien.*, 289.
n.d., witness to a miraculous cure by means of the *tunica* of St Etheldreda, *ib.*, 306.

Richard BROKESWURTH [Brekeswurth, Brexeworthe, Brykeswurth, Bryxworth
occ. 1446/7 occ. 1466/7

1446/7, 1448/9, granator, CUL EDC 5/4/36, [56].
1458/9, infirmarer, CUL EDC 5/7/1 (infirmarer acct).
1462/3, steward of the prior's hospice, CUL EDC 5/13/- (noted on 1465/6 acct).
1447/8, 1449/50, *socius* of the cellarer, CUL Add. Ms 2957, fo 6.
1458/9, with ten *socii* spent some time at Quaveney during July, CUL EDC 5/7/1 (infirmarer).
1460, Apr./Sept., recd 3s. 4d., *ad subsidium* of the dormitory from the chamberlain, CUL Add. Ms 2957, fo 32.
1466/7, recd a payment for the excess expenditure on his acct as steward of the hospice PRO SC6/1257/9.

Simon de BROUGHTON [Brockton, Brocton, Brouton
occ. [1349] occ. 1381/2

[1349, Nov.], subdcn, recd *lit. dim.*, for orders of dcn and pr., Reg. de Lisle, fo 30.
1350, 18 Dec., ord pr., Ely cathedral, *ib.*, fo 97.
1354/5, 1357/61, 1362/5, 1366/70, chamberlain, CUL Add. Ms 2957, fos 28, 29, CUL EDC 5/3/12–18.
1361, contributed 10s. towards the purchase of the manor and advowson of Mepal, Evans 'Mepal', 118 (CUL EDC 1B/box 23).
1379, 7th in order on the clerical poll tax list and pd 3s. 4d., PRO E179/23/1.
1381/2, *socius* of the hostiller, CUL EDC 5/5/3, 4.

Walter de BROUGHTON [Brocton
occ. 1346/7

1346, 1 Apr., ord subdcn, Ely cathedral, Reg. de Lisle, fo 92^{v}.
1346, 23 Dec., ord dcn, bp's chapel, Downham, *ib.*, fo 94^{v}.
1347, 17 Mar., ord pr., St Mary's church, Ely, *ib.*, fo 95^{v}.

John de BRUNDIS [?Brundre
occ. 1279

1279, 21 Jan., apptd proctor in a suit over tithes, Oxford, Bod. Ms Ashmole 801, fo 75.

Robert de BRUNDISCH [Brundich
occ. [1310] occ. 1327/8

1326/7, almoner, CUL Add. Ms 2957, fo 8.
[1310], with Amys de Mordone, q.v., accused of withholding a ring which had belonged to the late bp Orford and which ought to have gone to Canterbury, *Reg. abp Winchelsey*, 1071–1072.
1326/7, bought land in the name of the almoner's office, CUL Add. Ms 2957, fo 8.
1327/8, visited Lakenheath with Geoffrey de Carleton and Stephen de Swaffham II, q.v., and their horses were fed, CUL EDC 7/15/acct.

BRYDON
see Bredon

BRYXWORTH
see Brokeswurth

John BUCKENHAM [Buknaham, Buknam
occ. 1496 occ. 1499

1496, 2 Apr., ord subdcn, Ely cathedral, Reg. Alcock, fo 240.
1496, 24 Sept., ord dcn, bp's chapel, Downham, *ib.*, fo 241^{v}.
1499, 21 Sept., ord pr., bp's chapel, Downham, *ib.*, fo 251.
Note: on the latter two ord. lists he is named James.

BUCKENHAM
see also Bokenham

Robert BUCKNAHAM [Buck', Buknam
occ. 1511/12, occ. 1516

1511/12, chamberlain, CUL Add. Ms 2957, fo 32.
1515, 15/16 Apr., 19th in order on the *sed. vac.* visitation certificate, Reg. abp Warham, ii, fo 277.
1516, 22 Mar., 15th in order in the chapter which chose 29 Mar. as the date for the el. of a prior, Reg. West, fo 55.

I John de BUKTON [Bokton, Bucton, Buk', Buketon
occ. 1350 d. 1396

1364–1396, prior: first occ. 24 Sept. 1364, CUL EDC 7/7/2; d. about 21 Oct. 1396, CUL EDC 5/4/19; see William Walpole I and below.

1350, 18 Dec., ord subdcn, Ely cathedral, Reg. de Lisle, fo 96v.

1353, 21 Sept., ord pr., Swavesey, *ib.*, fo 99v.

1355/6, steward of the prior's hospice, part yr, CUL EDC 7/15/acct; see John de Walsingham.

1359/60, treasurer, CUL EDC 5/2/15; see John de St Ives.

1361/2, steward of the prior's hospice, part yr, CUL EDC 7/15/acct; see Henry de Wyke.

1355/6, pd a [supervisory] visit to Lakenheath, CUL EDC 7/15/acct.

1359/60, went to Melton for *liberatio denariorum*, CUL EDC 7/16/acct.

1361, contributed 20s. to the purchase of the manor and advowson of Mepal, Evans, 'Mepal', 118 (CUL EDC 1B/box 23).

1361/2, visited Lakenheath, CUL EDC 7/15/acct.

1364, 24 Sept., made his first visit as prior to Witcham, CUL EDC 7/7/2.

1373, 9 July, present at the metropolitan visitation, *sed. vac.*, Reg. abp Wittlesey, fo 152v.

1375, 28 Oct., present at the consecration of Henry Wakefield [el. of Worcester] by bp Thomas Arundel at Hatfield, Reg. Arundel, fo 10v.

1376, 20 Apr., present at the enthronement of bp Arundel in Ely cathedral, Reg. Arundel, fo 14v.

[1378], 4 Oct., apptd vicar general during the bp's absence, *ib.*, fo 27v.

1379, on the clerical poll tax list and pd £4, PRO E179/23/1.

1389/90, with his council [*concilio*] present at the assizes in Cambridge. He also went to Huntingdon to meet the abp of York and made two trips to Doddington to see the bp of Ely, CUL EDC 5/13/8.

[1393], apptd monastic visitor of Ely and Norwich dioceses for the Black Monk Chapter, Pantin, *BMC*, ii, 94.

1396/7, d., as above. His obit occ. on 21 Oct. in BL Add. Ms 33381, fo 12. The treasurer spent over £28 on the funeral; this included 100s. distributed among the poor, twelve white garments for the poor and 9s. 10d., to those who recited the psalter on the day of his burial, CUL EDC 5/13/10 and CUL Add. Ms 2957, fo 73. The succentor made the mortuary roll or brief and recd 20s. from the treasurer, while the brief bearer was pd 13s. 4d., CUL EDC 5/13/10.

II John de BUKTON [junior, Buckton, Bucktone, Buketon

occ. 1379 occ. 1420

1383/4, *custos* of the Lady chapel, CUL EDC 5/7/8.

1384/8, treasurer, CUL EDC 5/2/25, 5/4/18, 7/14C/33, 5/5/5; he succ. and alternated with John de Berton, q.v.

1388/90, steward of the prior's hospice, CUL EDC 5/13/8.

1392/3, treasurer, CUL EDC 5/13/9.

1396/7, *senescallus forinsec'* with Ralph de Derham, q.v., CUL EDC 5/13/10.

1407/9, treasurer, CUL EDC 5/6/17, 18.

1420, 20 Apr., refectorer, Oxford, Bod. Ms Ashmole 801, fos 138, 141v.

1379, 36th in order on the clerical poll tax list and pd 3s. 4d., PRO E179/23/1.

1384/5, pd a supervisory visit to Lakenheath, CUL EDC 7/15/acct.

1385/7, prob. visited Kingston both yrs, CUL EDC 7/14C/33, 34 accts.

1389/90, went to Lynn and to Cambridge to purchase wine, CUL EDC 5/13/8.

1396/7, [Oct. 1396], sent with William Walpole, q.v., to Hatfield to obtain a licence to el. a prior, CUL EDC 5/13/10.

1398, 16 Nov., acted with other monks as attorneys in taking seisin of a messuage in Ely, BL Ms Egerton 3047, fo 120.

1401, 10 Sept., 14th in order on the certificate for the metropolitan visitation, Reg. Fordham, fo 131.

[1402/3], described as *custos manerii* of Caxton which his namesake, the former prior, q.v., had acquired, CUL Add. Ms 2956, fo 164.

1420, 20 Apr., as refectorer recd a grant, Oxford, Bodley, Ms Ashmole 801, fo 138.

Name in Lambeth Ms 448, Chronica et Memoranda Eliensis (15th c. with later additions); on fo 99v *iste liber pertinet dno—*.

In 1410 he gave to the Ely monk students who were studying canon law at Cambridge a book called Lectura Hostiensis in 2 vols, Lambeth Ms 448, fo 94.

William BURDELEYS [Burdeloys

occ. 1341/2 occ. 1379

1341/2, vicar *in choro* of the sacrist and recd 10s., Chapman, *Sacrist Rolls*, ii, 119 (CUL EDC 5/10/9b).

1361, contributed 13s. 4d., towards the purchase of the manor and advowson of Mepal, Evans, 'Mepal', 118 (CUL EDC 1B/box 23).

1379, 9th in order on the clerical poll tax list and pd 3s. 4d., PRO E179/23/1.

Adam de BURGH [Burgo

occ. 1247/50

1247/50, sacrist, BL Ms Cotton Tiberius B.ii, fos 246–248; CUL Add. Ms 2950, fos 4–6.

1247, Mar./1250, Nov., rendered the acct of the receipts and expenditures of the new presbytery, *ib.*

Henry BURGH

occ. 1460

1460, 10 Apr., apptd cellarer by the bp personally in chapter, Reg. Gray, fo 46v; CUL

EDC 5/2/35 is prob. a fragment of his acct.

Note: this is Henry Peterborough, q.v.

Martin de BURGO
see Pappele

BURTON
see Berton

Alexander de BURY [or de St Edmunds, Sancto Edmundo
occ. 1356 d. 1392/3

1356, 9 Apr., ord subdcn, bp's chapel, Wisbech castle, Reg. de Lisle, fo 101.

1376/7, steward of the prior's hospice, CUL EDC 7/15/acct.
1381, 23 Dec., apptd cellarer, Reg. Arundel, fo 38ᵛ (as Alexander).
1381, Dec./1383, 1384/6, 1388/90, cellarer, CUL EDC 5/2/22–28, 5/13/8.
1376/7, procured 20 rabbits from Lakenheath, CUL EDC 7/15/acct.
1379, 15th in order on the clerical poll tax list and pd 3s. 4d., PRO E179/23/1.
1381/2, went [on business] to Bury [St Edmunds], CUL EDC 5/2/22.
1392/3, d., and the treasurer sent 5s. to the anniversarian, CUL EDC 5/13/9.
n.d., arrangements for the celebration of his anniversary by two junior monks in priests' orders are in Cambridge, Trinity College Ms 1145 fo 3b.

His name was in the old east window of Meldreth church, acc. to S. J. A. Evans.

I John de BURY [Bery or de St Edmunds
occ. [?1315/16] d. 1328/9

[1315/16 or earlier], 1323/5, treasurer, CUL EDC 5/12/-, 5/13/*status prioratus*, CUL Add. Ms 2957, fo 65.
1332/3, referred to as a former *custos gran[arie*, CUL EDC 5/13/6.
1318/19, name occ. on the treasurer's acct, 5/13/3.
1319, 13 July, one of the senior monks [*senes*] who formed an arbitration committee in the *contentio* concerning the authority of the subprior, Lambeth Ms 448, fos 97ᵛ–88.
1325/6, pd a supervisory visit to Lakenheath, CUL EDC 7/15/acct.
1328/9, d., and the chamberlain gave 5s. to the almoner, CUL Add. Ms 2957, fo 20.

II John de BURY
occ. 1379 occ. 1389/90

1379, 40th in order on the clerical poll tax list and pd 3s. 4d., PRO E179/23/1.
1389/90, *socius* of the sacrist, CUL Add. Ms 2956, fo 161.

III John de BURY
occ. 1400 occ. 1428/9

1400, 13 Mar., ord acol., Doddington, Reg. Fordham, fo 240.
1400, 12 June, ord subdcn, Doddington, *ib.*, fo 240ᵛ.
1400, 18 Sept., ord dcn, bp's chapel, Doddington, *ib.*
1400, 18 Dec., ord pr., bp's chapel, Downham, *ib.*, fo 241.
1418/21, granator, CUL EDC 7/12/acct, 7/15/acct, 5/2/30.
1424/6, precentor, CUL EDC 5/11/4a and b.
1427/9, granator, CUL EDC 5/4/28, 29, PRO SC6/1257/4.

1401, 14 Sept., 39th and second to last in order on the metropolitan visitation certificate, Reg. Fordham, fo 131.
1418/19, visited Swaffham Prior for *liberatio denariorum*, CUL EDC 7/12/acct.
1419/20, 1427/8, pd visits to Lakenheath, CUL EDC 7/15/acct.
1423, 5 July, a John Bury was one of two monks described as *hostiarii* at the Black Monk Chapter in Northampton, Pantin, *BMC*, ii, 135.
1425, 10 May, obtained a papal indult to choose his own confessor, *CPL*, vii (1417–1431), 416.

IV John BURY
occ. 1526/7 occ. 1540

1526/7, treasurer, CUL EDC 5/13/19.
1539, 18 Nov., described as a 'good choir man' and assigned a pension of £8 p.a., *L and P Henry VIII*, xiv, pt. 2, no 542.

Robert de BURY
occ. 1361 d. 1409/10

1396/9, chamberlain, CUL EDC 5/13/10, 5/3/24, CUL Add. Ms 2957, fos 36, 29.
1401, 6 Apr., the bp ordered his replacement as chamberlain by Thomas de Ramesey, q.v., Reg. Fordham, fo 192ᵛ.

1361, a *ciphus* of his was sold in aid of the fund for the purchase of the manor and advowson of Mepal, Evans, 'Mepal', 119 (CUL EDC 1B/box 23).
1371/2, *socius* of the precentor, CUL EDC 5/9/4, CUL Add. Ms 2957, fo 44.
1372/4, *socius* of the chamberlain, CUL EDC 5/3/19, 20.
1374/5, *socius* of the sacrist, CUL EDC 5/10/19.
1379, 23rd in order on the clerical poll tax list and pd 3s. 4d., PRO E179/23/1.
1401, 14 Sept., 6th in order on the metropolitan visitation certificate, Reg. Fordham, fo 131.
1409/10, d.; the chamberlain sent 5s. to the almoner, CUL Add. Ms 2957, fo 30.

I William de BURY [Bery, Biry
occ. 1317 d. 1341/2

1317, Feb./Aug., 1320/1 to Aug., pittancer, CUL EDC 5/8/3, 5.

1323/4, with Robert de Saham, q.v., carried out negotiations for the treasurer, CUL EDC 5/13/-.

1328/30, *socius* of the chamberlain, CUL Add. Ms 2957, fos 20, 21.

1339/40, recd 3s. from the chamberlain *pro linea tela*, *ib.*, fo 22.

1341/2, d., and the chamberlain gave 5s. to the almoner, *ib.*, fo 23.

II William de BURY
occ. 1412 occ. 1448/9

1412, 28 May, ord acol., bp's chapel, Downham, Reg. Fordham, fo 261.

1413, 23 Sept., ord subdcn, bp's chapel, Downham, *ib.*, fo 262^{v}.

1413, 23 Dec., ord dcn, bp's chapel, Downham, *ib.*, fo 263.

1414, 3 Mar., ord pr., bp's chapel, Downham, *ib.*, fo 263^{v}.

1448/9, feretrar, CUL EDC 5/10/33.

III William BURY
occ. 1532/3 occ. 1535/6

1535/6, feretrar, CUL Add. Ms 2956, fo 177.

1532/3, *socius* of the chamberlain, CUL Add. Ms 2957, fo 34.

1534, 8 Sept., 16th in order on the visitation certificate, Reg. Goodrich, fo 90^{v}.

BURY
see also St Edmunds [Sancto Edmundo

Thomas de BYTHAM
occ. 1361 occ. 1368/9

1361, gave 20s., *pro pittancia sua* towards the purchase of the manor and advowson of Mepal, Evans, 'Mepal', 119 (CUL EDC 1B/box 23).

1368/9, *socius* of the sacrist, CUL EDC 5/10/16.

Roger de CALTHORP [Calthrop
occ. 1339/40 d. 1344/5

1339/40, Sept. to Mar., with John de Orewell, q.v., recd 12d. from the cellarer *pro generali suo*, prob. when they were absent from the house, CUL EDC 5/2/6.

1339/40, with Nicholas de Copmanford q.v. spent four days in April at Northwold 'pro stauro et statu manerii supervidend' ', CUL Add. Ms 2957, fo 2^{v}.

1344/5, d., and the chamberlain gave the almoner 5s., CUL Add. Ms 2957, fo 24; the almoner pd for the brief bearer's shoes, *ib.*, fo 11.

John CAMBRIG' [Cambryge
occ. 1486/7

1486, 23 Dec., ord dcn, Lady chapel, Ely cathedral, Reg. Alcock, fo 223.

1487, 22 Sept., ord pr., place not recorded *ib.*, fo 224.

Robert CAMBRIG' [Cambryg'
occ. 1492 occ. 1495

1492, 21 Apr., recd first tonsure and/or ord subdcn, Ely cathedral, Reg. Alcock, fo 231^{v} and the tonsure entry was repeated on fo 232^{v}.

1494, 29 Mar., ord dcn, Ely cathedral, *ib.*, fo 235.

1495, 14 Mar., ord pr., bp's chapel, Downham, *ib.*, fo 237.

Roger CAMBRIGGE
occ. 1457

1457, 17 Dec., ord acol., bp's chapel, Downham, Reg. Gray, fo 204^{v}.

Note: this is prob. Roger Westminster, q.v.

William CAMBRIG'
occ. 1498

1498, 14 Apr., ord acol., Ely cathedral, Reg. Alcock, fo 246^{v}.

Note: this monk possibly assumed his patronymic, as became fairly frequent at this time, and he may be entered as such elsewhere in this section of the register, but where?

J. de CANTEBRIG' [Cauntebregg
occ. 1328/9 occ. 1342/3

1328/9, 1330/1, pittancer, CUL EDC 5/8/13, 14; both accts run from July to July.

1331/2, prob. Sept. to July, treasurer, CUL EDC 5/13/6.

1342/3, precentor, succ. by John de Wells I, q.v., CUL Add. Ms 2957, fo 42.

Richard de CANTEBRIGGE
occ. 1289 d. 1315/16

1293/4, chamberlain, CUL Add. Ms 2957, fo 17.

1312, 29 Sept., sacrist, CUL EDC 1/B/333.

1289, 30 June, one of a group of monks and others who sat on a commission to investigate disputed boundaries in Lakenheath, Liber M, 603.

1291/2, recd 3s. from the chamberlain *ex curialitate*, CUL Add. Ms 2957, fo 17.

1310, 28 Feb., named as one of seven *compromissorii* in the el. of a bp, BL Add. Ms 41612, fo 49^{v}. In this case it appears that they failed to agree and seven other *compromissorii* were chosen; see John de Ketene.

1315/16, one of ten who d. this yr; the chamberlain gave 5s. to the almoner for each, CUL Add. Ms 2957, fo 19.

Note: see the note under Richard de Braunford.

CANTOR
see John V

Geoffrey de CARLETON
occ. 1303/4 occ. 1327/8

1303/4, sent to Melton for supervisory duties, CUL EDC 7/16/3 acct.
1327/8, visited Lakenheath with Robert de Brundisch and Stephen de Swaffham II, q.v., and their horses were fed, CUL EDC 7/15/acct.

CAUNTEBREGG
see Cantebrig'

John CAUSTON
occ. 1418 × 1424

Possibly a monk of Ely who had accompanied Thomas Chelmesforthe, q.v., to Walden when the latter went there to be abbot; in Chelmesforthe's letter to the prior [Edmund Walsingham, q.v.], he sent his humble regards, Reg. Walsingham, no 16.

Richard de CAVENHAM
d. 1322/3

1322/3, d. and the sacrist gave 5s. to the almoner, Chapman, *Sacrist Rolls*, ii, 31, (CUL EDC 5/10/3).

CESTRETON, Cettone
see Chestreton

Azo de CHATRIS
occ. 1281

1281, 11 Oct., one of the monks who were absolved from irregularities that had occurred over payment of a tenth for the Holy Land, CUL EDC 1B/113.

John CHATTERIS [Chateres, Chatterys, ?*alias* Skele/Skyle
occ. 1523/4 occ. 1539

1523/4, *socius* of the precentor, CUL EDC 5/9/10.
1534, 8 Sept., 13th in order on the visitation certificate, Reg. Goodrich, fo 90ᵛ.
1539, 18 Nov., assigned a pension of £8 p.a., and described as a 'good choirman', *L and P Henry VIII*, xiv, pt 2, no 542.

Simon de CHATTERIS [Chateris, Chaterich
occ. 1335/6 d. 1344

1335/6, with John de Crishale, q.v., recd 12d. *pro liberatione* on the cellarer's kitchen acct during one wk, CUL EDC 5/2/2.
1339/40, 1341/2, *socius* of the chamberlain, CUL Add. Ms 2957, fo 23; both of these accts run from Mar. to Mar.
1339/40, Sept. to Mar., with John de Jernemuth, q.v., recd 12d. from the cellarer *pro generali suo*, prob. because they were absent from the house, CUL EDC 5/2/6.
1344, Mar./Dec., d., and the chamberlain gave 5s. to the almoner, CUL Add. Ms 2957, fo 23.

John CHELMSFORTH [Chelmesford, Chelmysford
occ. 1389 occ. 1401

1389, 18 Feb., one of three whose prof. the prior was comm. to rec., Reg. Fordham, fo 5ᵛ.
1389, 12 June, ord acol., Doddington, *ib.*, fo 230.
1389, 18 Sept., ord subdcn, Doddington, *ib.*, fo 230ᵛ.
1390, 18 Dec., ord dcn, bp's chapel, Downham, *ib.*, fo 231.
1391, 23 Sept., ord pr., bp's chapel, Downham, *ib.*, 232.
1401, 14 Sept., 26th in order on the metropolitan visitation certificate, Reg. Fordham, fo 131.

Thomas CHELMESFORTHE
occ. c. 1418 × 1424

A letter written by him, [now] abbot of Walden, to the prior [Edmund Walsingham q.v.] implies that he had been a monk at Ely under Walsingham; he said that he longed to see his beloved father [prior Walsingham] but was, for the present, detained by a number of obligations, Reg. Walsingham, no 16; see also John Causton.

John de CHESTRETON [Cestreton, Cettone
occ. 1319 d. 1347

1344/6, granator, CUL EDC 7/15/i/13, EDC 5/4/8.
1319, 13 July, was at the centre of a dispute over the authority of the subprior; this arose after the latter, John de Crishale I, q.v., accused the third prior, William de Hoveden, q.v., of usurping his authority by giving a licence to him and to Richard de Spalding, q.v., to leave the cloister *causa recreationis*, after undergoing *minutiones*, Lambeth Ms 448, fos 97ᵛ, 98.
1323/4, *socius* of the chamberlain, CUL Add. Ms 2957, fo 20.
1337/8, *socius* of the cellarer, CUL EDC 5/2/3A.
1344/5, pd a visit to Lakenheath for supplies of wheat and barley, CUL EDC 7/15/acct.
1347, 9 June, d., and the chamberlain gave 5s. to the almoner, CUL Add. Ms 2957, fo 24.

Simon de CHESTRETON [Chesterton
occ. 1352 d. 1360/1

1352, 24 Mar., ord acol., Swavesey, Reg. de Lisle, fo 98.
1352, 22 Sept., ord subdcn, Over, *ib.*, fo 98ᵛ.
1352, 22 Dec., ord dcn, Downham, *ib.*, fo 98ᵛ.
1353, 21 Sept., ord pr., Swavesey, *ib.*, fo 99ᵛ.

1360/1, d., and the chamberlain gave 5s. to the almoner, CUL EDC 5/3/14, CUL Add. Ms 2957, fo 28.

Stephen de CHESTRETON [Cestreton
occ. 1339/40 d. 1341/2

1339/40, *socius* of the cellarer, CUL Add. Ms 2957, fo 2.
1341/2, a ?. . . de Cestreton d., and the chamberlain sent 5s. to the almoner, CUL Add. Ms 2957, fo 23.

Thomas CHESTRETON [Chesterton
occ. 1515/17

1517, 7 Mar., ord dcn, bp's chapel, Ely, Reg. West, fo 83v.
1515, 15/16 Apr., 35th and last in order on the *sed. vac.* visitation certificate, Reg. abp Warham, ii, fo 277.
1516, 22 Mar., 30th and last in order in the chapter which chose 29 Mar. as the date for the el. of a prior, Reg. West, fo 55v.
Note: there were a number of monks absent on this date.

William de CLARE
occ. 1300 d. 1302/3

1303, prior: el. and d. within the yr, *Fasti*, iv, 16.
Note: since he was el. to succ. Robert de Orford, q.v., whom the monks had el. as bp on 14 Apr., 1302, he may have been el. before the end of the yr. Because the accting yr ran from Michaelmas to Michaelmas he presumably d. before 28 Sept. 1303.
1300, 17 Dec., with Peter de Reche, q.v., apptd proctors for the convent, BL Ms Egerton 3047, fo 246v.
1302, 4 Apr., one of three monks who recd a licence to el. a bp, *CPR (1301–1307)*, 26.
1302/3, d., and the sacrist contributed 8d. to his burial expenses, Chapman, *Sacrist Rolls*, ii, 18 (CUL EDC 5/10/2). See above.

I CLEMENT
n.d.

n.d., 13 May, the obit of a Clement, sacrist, occ. in a kalendar in BL Ms Cotton Vespasian A.vi, fo 133v, BL Add Ms 33381, fo 12 and CUL Add. Ms 2950, fo 13. (The obits of Walter III, prior, and Martin, q.v., occ. on the same day.)
Note:
(1) He was prob. contemporary with or later than Walter II, q.v.
(2) The obit of another Clement occ. on 22 Aug. in Cambridge, Trinity College Ms 1105, fo k8v.

II CLEMENT
see Thetford

John CLEY [Clay
occ. 1428/9 occ. 1444/5

1428/9, celebrated his first mass and recd a gift from the treasurer, PRO SC6/1257/4.
1436/7, 1439/41, granator, CUL EDC 5/4/31, PRO SC6/1257/6, 7, 8, CUL EDC 5/4/32.
1439/40, treasurer, PRO SC6/1257/7, 8.
1441/2, 1443/5, chamberlain, CUL Add. Ms 2957, fo 31.
1443/4, *senescallus terrarum*, CUL EDC 5/4/34, possibly only for the last quarter of the accting yr; see John Somersham.

William CLIFFORD [Clyfford, Clyford
occ. 1515 d. 1519/20

1515, 15/16 Apr., 29th in order on the *sed. vac.* visitation certificate, Reg. abp Warham, ii, fo 277.
1516, 22 Mar., 24th in order in the chapter which chose 29 Mar. as the date for the el. of a prior, Reg. West, fo 55.
1519/20, *socius* of the sacrist, CUL Add. Ms 2956, fo 176.
1519/20, d., and the chamberlain gave 5s. to the almoner, CUL EDC 5/3/[34].

William COLCHESTER [Colcestre
occ. 1457 occ. 1499/1500

1457, 17 Dec., ord acol., bp's chapel, Downham, Reg. Gray, fo 205.
1459, 24 Mar., ord subdcn, bp's chapel, Downham, *ib.*, fo 205v.
1459, 19 May, ord dcn, bp's chapel, Downham, *ib.*, fo 206v.
1466, 5 Apr., ord pr., bp's palace chapel, Ely, *ib.*, fo 211.
1499/1500, *custos* of the Lady chapel, CUL Add. Ms 2957, fo 64.
1459, ill in the infirmary during the summer, CUL EDC 5/7/1 (infirmarer acct).
1500, 30 Oct., at the *sed. vac.* visitation by the commissary of the prior of Christ Church, Canterbury (when the sees of both Ely and Canterbury were vacant), Thomas Drayton, q.v., complained of his failure to return the organ to the Lady chapel, Canterbury Reg. R, fo 70v.

Robert COLVILLE [Colevile, Colevyl, Colevylle, Colwylle
occ. 1465/6 occ. 1516

c. 1500 × 1510, prior: occ. as prior 5 Oct. 1500, CUL EDC 7/17/74; res. before 27 Sept. 1510, *Fasti*, iv, 17; see William Wittlesey I.
1463, 9 Apr., recd first tonsure, [*magna*] chapel, Downham, but not identified as a monk, Reg. Gray, fo 210v;
1466, 5 Apr., ord acol., bp's palace chapel, Ely, *ib.*, fo 211.
1467, 14 Mar., ord subdcn, bp's palace chapel, Ely, *ib.*, fo 211v.

1469, 1 Apr., ord dcn, bp's chapel, Downham, *ib.*, fo 214.

1473, 17 Apr., ord pr., bp's [*magna*] chapel, Downham, *ib.*, fo 215.

1476/7, treasurer, CUL EDC 5/13/16.

1479/80, *custos* of the Lady chapel, CUL Add. Ms 2957, fo 63.

1483/4, precentor, CUL EDC 5/9/9.

1495, 12 Oct., cellarer, CUL Add. Ms 2950, fo 84.

1468/9, student [at Cambridge], recd 20s. from the treasurer, CUL EDC 5/13/-; this is entered on the 1469/70 acct as part payment of his pension for the previous year.

1465/6, recd 2s. from the precentor *ad erudiend' ludere organa*, CUL EDC 5/9/8.

1473/4, recd 26s. 8d., from the treasurer for his organ studies CUL EDC 5/13/-.

1476, 5 Feb., recd papal dispensation to rec. and retain a benefice, including a parish church, *CPL*, xiii (1471–1484), 493.

1495, 12 Oct., apptd proctor with William Wittlesey, q.v., to attend convocation, Liber B, no 239, CUL Add. Ms 2950, fo 84.

1500, 30 Oct., prior, and present at the *sed. vac.* visitation by the prior of Christ Church, Canterbury when the sees of Ely and Canterbury were both vacant. Examined by the prior's commissary, he reported that monastic observance and discipline were duly kept in full by all but the aged and infirm, that the monks were 40 in number and the income of the house amounted to 1800 m., Canterbury Reg. R, fos 69v, 70.

1510, 9 Jan., unable to attend convocation because of illness, CUL Add. Ms 2950, fo 85.

1515, 15/16 Apr., apparently absent from the abp's *sed. vac.* visitation, Reg. abp Wareham, ii, fo 277.

1516, 29 Mar., absent from the el. of a prior to succ. William Foliot, q.v., and declared contumacious, Reg. West, fos 55v–57.

COMBIRTUS
see Theinbert

John de CONINGTON [Cointone, Conigton, Conyngton, Conyton
occ. 1310 d. 1330/1

1315, Aug./1316, June, pittancer, CUL EDC 5/8/2, 9.

1310, 27 Feb., one of the officials apptd for the el. proceedings of a bp, BL Add. Ms 41612, fo 50v; see John de Ketene.

1316, 25 June, one of three *instructores* sent to the abp after the el. of bp Hotham, BL Add. Ms. 41612, fo 40; with Amys de Mordone and John de Orewell, q.v., he was apptd proctor in all matters relating to this el., *ib.*

1319, 13 July, one of the senior monks [*senes*] who formed an arbitration committee in the *contentio* concerning the authority of the subprior John de Crishale I, q.v., Lambeth Ms 448, fos 97v–98.

1320/1, gave [a gift of] 12s. 8d., to the chamberlain, CUL Add. Ms 2957, fo 20.

1323/4, sent by the treasurer to represent the chapter at the court of Canterbury, CUL EDC 5/13/-.

1323, 20 Aug., with William de Hoveden, q.v., apptd proctor to settle accts with bp Ketene's executors, BL Add. Ms 41612, fo 61.

1326/7, pd a [supervisory] visit to Lakenheath, CUL EDC 7/15/acct.

1330/1, d., and the chamberlain gave 5s. to the almoner, CUL Add. Ms 2957, fo 21.

Edmund COOTES, Cootis
see Denver

Nicholas de COPMANFORD [Copaunford, Copmanforth
occ. 1318/19 d. 1344

1320/1, Apr. to Apr., 1323/5, chamberlain, CUL Add. Ms 2957, fo 19, CUL EDC 5/13/-, CUL Add. Ms 2957, fo 20.

1325/7, *senescallus terrarum*, CUL EDC 5/13/1, 7/16/acct, 7/15/acct.

1328/34, Apr., chamberlain, CUL Add. Ms 2957, fos 20, 21; and for 1332/3, CUL EDC 5/13/6.

1332, Apr./Sept., 1335/6, 1337/1340, Mar., cellarer, CUL Add. Ms 2957, fos 1, 2.

1341, 25 Oct., subprior, Reg. Montacute, fo 25.

1341/2, Nov. to Sept., 1343, 7 Nov., sacrist, Chapman, *Sacrist Rolls*, ii, 113–125, (CUL EDC 5/10/9b), *CPP*, i (1342–1404), 28; since this latter date is that on which he recd a papal dispensation to hold the office for life he prob. continued as sacrist until 1344.

1318/19, *socius* of the treasurers, CUL EDC 5/13/3.

1325, 2 June, apptd proctor, with Walter de Ikelyngham, q.v., and others, to take charge of the collection of rents, tithes and offerings in Witcham, BL Add. Ms 41612, fo 75.

1325/6, pd a supervisory visit to Melton, CUL EDC 7/16/acct.

1326/8, pd visits to Lakenheath, CUL EDC 7/15/accts.

1327, 2 Jan., with a secular cleric apptd proctor for parliament; later the same month he was apptd general proctor for the convent, BL Add. Ms 41612, fos 69v, 70. He was also sent, with another, to discuss certain matters concerning the manor of Lakenheath with Elizabeth de Burgh, Lady of Clare, *ib.*, fo 69v.

1327/8, stopped at Lakenheath on a return journey from Suffolk, CUL EDC 7/15/acct.

1330/2, *ex licencia* of the bp and *ex concessione* of the prior he recd 40s., both yrs, *pro camera sua*, CUL Add. Ms 2957, fo 21.

1332, 25 Apr., with a secular cleric apptd proctor in matters concerning the chapter's rights in the church of Witcham, BL Add. Ms 41612, fo 74^{v}. He was still involved in this on 30 May 1333, *ib.*, fo 75.

1333/4, continued to rec. his 40s. clothing allowance, CUL Add. Ms 2957, fo 21.

1334/5, stopped at Lakenheath on his way to pay a supervisory visit to Northwold, CUL EDC 7/15/acct.

1336, 8 Apr., named as their attorney by two chaplains in a dispute over some tenements in London, BL Add. Ms 41612, fo 82^{v}.

1337/8, responsible for the construction of thirteen new shops in Ely, CUL EDC 5/2/4.

1339/40, recd 3s. *pro linea tela* from the chamberlain and the cellarer pd *pro generali suo*, CUL Add. Ms 2957, fo 22, CUL EDC 5/2/8a.

1340/1, Mar. to Mar., spent four days at Northwold 'pro stauro et statu manerii supervidend' ' and went with the cellarer, John de Wisbech, q.v., to confer with the bp at Somersham, CUL Add. Ms 2957, fos 2, 3.

1341, 14 Oct., sent with Philip de Dallyng and Alan de Walsingham, q.v., to obtain licence from the bp to el a prior, Reg. Montacute, fo 25. On 25 Oct., he was el. sole *compromissorius* in the el. of a prior; he named Alan de Walsingham, q.v., *ib.*, fo 25. See also BL Ms Cotton Titus A.i, fo 126.

1341, Dec., went to Lynn for three days to buy wax and other necessities, Chapman, *Sacrist Rolls*, ii, 120 (CUL EDC 5/10/9b); he made another three day visit there in Apr. 1342, both times by water, *ib.*

1342, 27 May, attended the synod [in Cambridge], *ib.* He also went to the fairs at Barnwell and Stourbridge, *ib.*

1342, 16 Mar., took four monks for ordination at Willingham, Chapman, *Sacrist Rolls*, ii, 120 (CUL EDC 5/10/9b); transcribed by Chapman as Wynebrigham.

1343, 7 Nov., obtained licence from the pope to remain in the office of sacrist for life, to avoid being removed at the whim of the bp, *CPP*, i, (1342–1404), 28 and *CPL*, iii (1342–1362), 142 where the date is 1344, 7 Nov.

1344, Jan./Sept., d., and the chamberlain gave 5s. to the almoner, CUL Add. Ms 2957, fo 23; the almoner pd for the brief bearer's shoes, CUL Add. Ms 2957, fo 11.

In 1340/1, a Robert de Copmanford, described as his 'boy', was in his employ and was sent as a messenger to London; a John de Copmanford was also in his service this yr, CUL Add. Ms 2957, fo 2^{v}.

John CORBET [Corbett

occ. 1515 occ. 1539

1516/17, one of the subsacrists [*vestiarius*], CUL EDC 5/10/44.

1515, 15/16 Apr., 24th in order at the *sed. vac.*, visitation, Reg. abp Warham, ii, fo 277.

1516, 22 Mar., 19th in order in the chapter which chose 29 Mar. as the date for the el. of a prior, Reg. West, fo 55.

1534, 8 Sept., 7th on the visitation certificate, Reg. Goodrich, fo 90^{v}.

1539, 18 Nov., assigned a pension of £6 p.a., *L and P Henry VIII*, xiv, pt. 2, no 542.

John CORNEWAILL [Cornewayle, Cornewaylle, Cornwaill

occ. 1419 d. 1439/40

1419, 7 June, ord acol., bp's chapel, Downham, Reg. Fordham, fo 272.

1419, 10 June, ord subdcn, bp's chapel, Downham, *ib.*

1419, 23 Sept., ord dcn, bp's chapel, Downham, *ib.*, fo 272^{v}.

1431/2, granator, CUL EDC 5/4/30; he was also treasurer acc. to the Lakenheath acct, CUL EDC 7/15/acct, and former treasurer by 1434/5, PRO SC6/1257/5.

1432/3, steward of the prior's hospice, CUL EDC 7/17/acct.

1436/7, almoner, CUL Add. Ms 2957, fo 31.

1428/9, sent to London at the treasurer's expense, PRO SC6/1257/4.

1431/2, pd a supervisory visit to Lakenheath, CUL EDC 7/15/acct.

1432/3, visited Winston, CUL EDC 7/17/acct.

1434/5, assisted the treasurers in the collection of tithes, and went for this purpose to Ramsey (by boat), Peterborough, Crowland and Thorney etc., PRO SC6/1257/5; he also celebrated masses for the soul of John Dyngayne and recd 6s. 8d., from the hostiller, CUL EDC 5/5/6.

1436/7, was receiver for the bpric, PRO SC6/1257/6.

1439/40, d., and the chamberlain gave 5s. to the almoner, CUL Add. Ms 2957, fo 31.

John COTTENHAM, B.Cn.L., B.Th. [Cotenham, Cotname, Cottingham, Cotynham

occ. 1488 d. 1522

1516–1522, prior: el. 29 Mar. 1516, Reg. West, fo 55; d. 1522, *Fasti*, iv, 17; see William Wittlesey I.

1488, 5 Apr., ord acol., Ely cathedral, Reg. Alcock, fo 224^{v}.

1488, 20 Sept., ord subdcn, bp's chapel, Downham, *ib.*, fo 225.

1488, 20 Dec., ord dcn, bp's chapel, Downham, *ib.*, fo 225^{v}.

1491, 24 Sept., ord pr., bp's chapel, Downham, *ib.*, fo 230.

1509/10, *senescallus terrarum*, CUL EDC 5/4/50.

1510, 9 Jan., subprior, Liber B, no 429, CUL Add. Ms 2950, fo 85.

[c. 1491], 1501/2, 1505/6, student at Cambridge; he must have begun his university studies about 1491 acc. to the entries in *CU Grace Book B*, i, 212, 216, but was prob. in attendance only part time.

1505/6, granted B.Cn.L., *BRUC*.

1513/14, by this date B.Th.; granted the grace to proceed towards inception in theology, *CU Grace Book Γ*, 4, 35, 36, 120, 163; see *BRUC*.

1510, 9 Jan., apptd proctor with others to represent the chapter at convocation, Liber B, no 429, CUL Add. Ms 2950, fo 85.

1515, 15/16 Apr., 5th in order on the *sed. vac.* visitation certificate, Reg. abp Warham, ii, fo 277.

1516, 22 Mar., 4th in the chapter which chose 29 Mar. as the date for the el. of a prior, Reg. West, fo 55; on 29 Mar. he was himself el. prior, *via spiritus*, *ib.*, fo 57v; the bp confirmed the el. on 1 Apr., *ib.*, fo 59. See Thomas Soham.

1522, d., as above.

William COTTENHAM [Cotenham, Cotnam, Cotname, Cotynham

occ. 1486 occ. 1516

1486, 23 Dec., ord pr., Lady chapel, Ely cathedral, Reg. Alcock, fo 223.

1497/9, feretrar, CUL EDC 5/11/[9].

1500, 30 Oct., subprior, Canterbury Reg. R, fo 70.

1500, 30 Oct., present at the *sed. vac.* visitation by the commissary of the prior of Christ Church, Canterbury, when the sees of Ely and Canterbury were both vacant. When examined, he made a statement similar to that of the prior, Robert Colville, q.v. John Palmer, q.v., deposed that he was to blame for the lack of bread and drink after *minutiones*, Canterbury Reg. R, fo 70–70v.

1515, 15/16 Apr., 3rd in order on the *sed. vac.* visitation certificate, Reg. abp Warham, ii, fo 277.

1516, 29 Mar., absent from the el. of a prior but was represented by Robert Wells, q.v., Reg. West, fo 56.

John de CRAUDEN [Craudone, Crawedene, Crowdene

occ. 1310 d. 1341

1321–1341, prior: 1321, 20 May *suscepit . . . prioratus regimen*, CUL Add. Ms 2957, fo 65; d. 25 Sept. 1341, Reg. Montacute, fo 25.

1310, named as an executor of bp Orford, CUL Add. Ms 2957, fo 68.

1316, 25 June, sent by the chapter with Simon de Westone, q.v., to seek confirmation of the el. of bp Hotham from the abp, BL Add. Ms 41612, fo 40, 40v.

1319, 13 July, one of the monks [*senes*] who formed an arbitration committee in the *contentio* over the authority of the subprior, John de Crishale I, q.v., Lambeth Ms 448, fo 97v.

1322, wrote to Edward II to inform him of the collapse of the central tower *Hist. Mss Comm. 6th Report*, Appndx, 295 (BL Add. Ms 41612, fo 60).

1323/4, visited Lakenheath and the treasurer provided 40s. for expenses CUL EDC 5/13/-.

1325, 18 Sept., presided at the bp's [consistory] court with three justices, CUL EDC 1B/1159.

1325, 29 Sept., a *status prioratus* on the treasurer's acct lists his achievements, during his first four yrs as prior, in paying off the debts of his predecessor and also details of his building programme, CUL Add. Ms 2957, fos 65–68 (and CUL EDC 5/13/unnumbered). The new building containing his chapel and study [*camera*] cost £138 8s. 5d., *ib.*

1326, 13 May, presided again at the bp's court, CUL EDC 1B/1163.

1327/8, made frequent visits to Lakenheath and entertained guests there; the stock and grain supplies consumed were listed on the grange acct, and in addition the sergeant charged 23s. 10d., on his expense acct in an entry headed *Expense domini prioris*, CUL EDC 7/15/acct.

1334, 14 Dec., again presided at the bp's court, CUL EDC 1B/1172, 1173.

1337, 12 Mar., el. bp by the chapter, *via compromissi*, but Simon de Montecute was provided, BL Ms Cotton Titus A.i, fo 124.

1341, 30 Sept., buried, Reg. Montacute fo 25, at the feet of bp Hotham, near the high altar, Lambeth Ms 448 fo 59–59v; the chamberlain sent no money to the almoner [*pro errogacione*] *quia ipse invenit*, CUL Add. Ms 2957, fo 23. His obit occ. on 24 Sept. in Cambridge, Trinity College Ms 1105, fo k9v. However, in BL Add. Ms 33381 his anniversary and that of Alan de Walsingham, q.v., were celebrated on 15 May.

Betweeen 1321 and 1337, with the bp [John de Hotham], and his fellow monks John de Wisbech and Alan de Walsingham, q.v., he was in charge of the building programme, Lindley, 'Ely', 12. See also Coldstream, 'Ely Cathedral', 28–46.

Some of his *acta* are included in BL Add. Ms 41612, fo 33–c. fo 91.

His character and achievements are recorded in Lambeth Ms 448, fo 59–59v where he is described as a monk of fervent spirituality who was to be found frequently at prayer and in meditation in his chapel during the night watches. For his chapel he comm. a beautiful missal and benedictional. He also purchased a house in Cambridge for the use of Ely monk students, Bentham, *Hist. Ely*, 220, and Greatrex, 'Rabbits and Eels', forthcoming.

On the 1325 *status prioratus* there is a ref. to his brother of the same name who provided a loan of 12s., CUL Add. Ms 2950, fo 69.

Note: see J. de Crouden who is prob. this monk; if so, his first occurrence may be dated six to seven yrs earlier.

I John de CRISHALE [Creshale, Crishalle, Crissale, Crosale, Cryshale
occ. 1315 occ. 1335/6

1315, 14 June; 1316, 19 Nov.; 1317, 27 Feb.; 1319, 13 July, subprior, BL Add. Ms 41612, fo 41v; *ib.* fo 26v; *ib.* fo 40v; Lambeth Ms 448, fo 97v.

1316, 19 Nov., with John de Ramesey II, q.v., given, by the prior with the consent of the chapter, custody of four of their churches for one yr from 2 Feb., for purposes of administration of tithes and tenths, BL Add. Ms 41612, fo 27v.

1317, 27 Feb., present at the el. of a bp and pronounced the *monitio* vs all who were not entitled to participate, *ib.*, fo 41v.

1318/19, became ill while in Cambridge and the *custos* of the altar of St Mary gave him 3s., *ex curialitate*, CUL Add. Ms 2957, fo 50.

1319, 13 July, involved in the *contentio* over his authority when the third prior, William Hoveden, q.v., issued a licence to John de Chestreton and Richard de Spaldyng, q.v., to leave the cloister for a holiday [*ad spaciand'*]. He immediately denounced the third prior and demanded the latter's apology for failing to send the monks to him as he had been in the monastery at the time and *causa recreationis in lecto*. His demand for ecclesiastical censures to be placed on Hoveden was not upheld by the arbitration committee because his absence from collation and compline had prob. led the third prior to believe he had gone out of the monastery, Lambeth Ms 448, fos 97v–98. See John de Fresingfeld.

1335/6, with Simon de Chatteris, q.v., recd 12d. *pro liberatione* on the cellarer's kitchen acct during one wk, CUL EDC 5/2/2.

II John de CRISHALE junior [Crishal', Cryshale
occ. 1318/20

1318/19, *socius* of the chamberlain, CUL Add. Ms 2957, fo 19.

1320/1, pd 25s. in partial repayment of a debt owed to the chamberlain, *ib.*

John CROLE
occ. 1413/14 occ. [1415/16]

1413/14, granator, CUL EDC 5/4/25.

[1415/16], keeper of the common treasury [*custos communis thesaurarie*], CUL EDC 5/13/11.

J. de CROUDEN [Crouden'
occ. 1303/4

1303/4, named several times on the grange (dorse) acct of Lakenheath. He was involved in procuring supplies for the cathedral priory and possibly for the prior; thus, he may have been steward of the prior's hospice, CUL EDC 7/15/acct.

Note: see John Crauden who is prob. the same monk.

CROWDENE
see Crauden

Richard CROWLAND [Croyland
occ. 1492 occ. 1516

1492, 21 Apr., recd the tonsure and/or ord subdcn, Ely cathedral, Reg. Alcock, fo 231v, and the tonsure entry is repeated on fo 232v.

1494, 29 Mar., ord dcn, Ely cathedral, *ib.*, fo 235.

1495, 14 Mar., ord pr., bp's chapel, Downham, *ib.*, fo 237.

1515, 15/16 Apr., 7th in order on the *sed. vac.* visitation certificate, Reg. abp Warham, ii, fo 277.

1516, 22 Mar., 6th in order in the chapter which chose 29 Mar. as the date for the el. of a prior, Reg. West, fo 55.

Gilbert CROXTON
occ. 1534

1534, 8 Sept., 29th in order, on the visitation certificate, Reg. Goodrich, fo 90v; he was one of ten not styled *dominus* and therefore recently adm. and not yet in major orders.

John de CROXTON [Croxstone, Croxtone
occ. 1320/1 d. 1353

1337/8, granator, CUL EDC 5/4/7.

1349/50, 1352/3, feretrar, Chapman, *Sacrist Rolls*, ii, 147, 149, (CUL EDC 5/10/11, 12).

1320/1, Apr. to Apr., recd 20s. from the chamberlain for all his clothing supplies apart from *linea tela*, CUL Add. Ms 2957, fo 20.

1336/7, visited Lakenheath, CUL EDC 7/15/acct.

1353, d. His d. was recorded by the sacrist who gave 5s. *pro errogacione* in 1352/3 to the almoner and by the chamberlain who also gave 5s. in 1353/4, Chapman, *Sacrist Rolls*, ii, 157 (CUL EDC 5/10/12), CUL EDC 5/3/11.

CROYLAND
see Crowland

CRYSHALE
see Crishale

John CUST, Custance
see John Ely XII

Philip de DALLYNG [Dallynge, Dalyng
occ. 1320/1 d. 1349

1323/4, chaplain [?to the prior], CUL EDC 5/13/-.

1329/30, 1331/2, *senescallus* [?*terrarum*], CUL EDC 7/17/court, CUL EDC 7/16/7 (acct).

1341, 25 Oct., third prior, Reg. Montacute, fo 25.

1344/5, cellarer, CUL EDC 5/2/10.
1349, sacrist until 9 July, Reg. Lisle, fo 22v and Chapman, *Sacrist Rolls*, i, 83–84 (CUL EDC 5/10/11); see Adam de Lynsted.

1320/4, 1326/7, pd visits to Lakenheath during these yrs [for supervisory purposes] and in 1326/7 held the leet court, CUL EDC 7/15/accts.
1328/9, 1331/2, pd visits to Melton, CUL EDC 7/16/6, 7 accts.
1329/30, held court at Winston in Nov., CUL EDC 7/17/court.
1336/7, visited Lakenheath, CUL EDC 7/15/acct.
1341, Mar./Dec., employed by the cellarer in negotiations concerning Northwold, CUL EDC 5/2/7; sent by the cellarer to Elgey, ib.; this yr he was on the sacrist's lists of those undergoing *minutiones*, Chapman, *Sacrist Rolls*, ii, 106 (CUL EDC 5/10/9).
1341, 14 Oct., with Nicholas de Copmanford and Alan de Walsingham recd from the bp licence to el. a prior, Reg. Montacute, fo 25.
1347/8, stopped at Lakenheath on his way to and from Northfl' [*sic*] and charged the manorial acct 2s. 8d., CUL EDC 7/15/acct.
1349, before 9 July, d., Reg. de Lisle, fo 22v.

William DANYELL
occ. 1515 occ. 1525/6

1525/6, treasurer, CUL EDC 5/13/18.

1515, 15/16 Apr., 32nd in order on the *sed. vac.* visitation certificate, Reg. abp Warham, ii, fo 277.
1516, 22 Mar., 27th in order in the chapter which chose 29 Mar. as the date for the el. of a prior, Reg. West, fo 55.

DAYLESHAM
see Aylesham

John de DENEVER
d. 1325/6

1325/6, d., and the sacrist gave 5s. to the almoner, Chapman, *Sacrist Rolls*, ii, 58 (CUL EDC 5/10/5).

DENNYS
see Denys

Edmund DENVER [*alias* Cootes, Cootis, Coots, Cootys
occ. 1515 occ. 1539

1525/9, almoner, CUL EDC 5/13/18–20, CUL Add. Ms 2957, fo 34.

1515, 15/16 Apr., 26th in order on the *sed. vac.* visitation certificate, Reg. abp Warham, ii, fo 277.
1516, 22 Mar., 20th in order in the chapter which chose 29 Mar. as the date for the el. of a prior, Reg. West, fo 55.
1534, 8 Sept., 9th on the visitation certificate, Reg. Goodrich, fo 90v.
1539, 18 Nov., described as a 'discreet man' and assigned a pension of £8 p.a., *L and P Henry VIII*, xiv, pt. 2, no 542.

Laurence DENVER [Denever
occ. 1475/6 occ. 1500

1483/4, pittancer, CUL EDC 5/4/47, as Laurence only.

1475/6, *socius* of the cellarer, CUL EDC 5/2/32.
1500, 30 Oct., described as *stagiarius* and was 7th to be examined at the *sed. vac.* visitation by the commissary of the prior of Christ Church, Canterbury (when the sees of Ely and Canterbury were both vacant). When questioned, he reported *omnia bene* except for the gate leading into the cloister [Vine Gate] which needed repair and was left open to the public, Canterbury Reg. R, fo 70.

Thomas DENVER [Denever
occ. 1473/4 occ. 1478/9

1473/4, treasurer, CUL EDC 5/13/14, CUL Add. Ms 2957, fo 74.
1478/9, *custos* of the Lady chapel, CUL EDC 5/7/13.

W. DENWER
occ. 1476/7

1476/7, recd 6s. 8d., from the treasurer for saying masses for the soul of Philip Lyle, CUL EDC 5/13//16.

Richard DENYS [Dennys
occ. 1527 occ. 1539

1533/4, 1535/6, steward of the prior's hospice, CUL EDC 5/13/-.

1527, 12 Sept., accused with Robert Derham, q.v., of assaulting a boy going to Ely grammar school, PRO STAC 2/17/223, 383. The prior allegedly refused any recompense to the boy as he denied that any offence had taken place, *ib.*
1534, 8 Sept., 19th in order on the visitation certificate, Reg. Goodrich, fo 90v.
1539, 18 Nov., assigned a pension of £6 p.a., *L and P Henry VIII*, xiv, pt. 2, no 542.

W. de DENYTON
d. 1315/16

1315/16, one of ten monks who d. this yr for each of whom the chamberlain gave the almoner 5s., CUL Add. Ms 2957, fo 19.

Thomas DEPYNG
occ. 1447

1447, 4 Mar., ord subdcn, church of St John the Baptist, Ely, Reg. Bourgchier, fo 47.

Nicholas DERBY [Derbi
occ. 1436/7 d. 1466/7

1436/7, steward of the prior's hospice, PRO SC6/1257/6.
1439/40, former treasurer, PRO SC6/1257/7.
1439/41, chamberlain, CUL Add. Ms 2957, fo 31.
1440/1, 1442/4, *senescallus terrarum*, CUL EDC 5/4/32, CUL EDC 7/15/acct, 7/16/35; he succ. William Wells III, q.v.
1446/7, named as former *custos* of the Lady chapel, CUL Add. Ms 2957, fo 61.
1464/6, *senescallus terrarum*, CUL EDC 5/4/-, 5/13/-.

1442/3, pd a visit to Lakenheath, CUL EDC 7/15/acct.
1443/4, visited Melton, CUL EDC 7/16/35.
1465/6, went to London in Feb. and again in Apr., CUL EDC 5/13/-.
1466/7, d., PRO SC6/1257/9.

Ralph de DERHAM
occ. 1376 d. 1419/20

1376, 29 Mar., ord acol., church of St Mary outside Trumpington gate, Cambridge, Reg. Arundel, fo 117.
1376, 20 Sept., ord subdcn, Lady chapel, Ely cathedral, *ib.*, fo 119.
1377, 14 Mar., ord dcn, Lady chapel, Ely cathedral, *ib.*, fo 121.
1378, 12 June, ord pr., bp's chapel, Ditton, *ib.*, fo 123.

1396/7, former steward of the prior's hospice, CUL EDC 5/13/10.
1396/7, *senescallus forinsecus*, CUL EDC 5/13/10.
1405, 10 Nov., apptd cellarer, Reg. Fordham, fo 201; 1405/6, cellarer, CUL EDC 5/4/22.

1379, 44th in order on the clerical poll tax list and pd 3s. 4d., PRO E179/23/1.
1393/4, pd a visit to Melton, CUL EDC 7/16/25 (acct).
1394/5, visited Lakenheath, CUL EDC 7/15/acct.
1396/7, went to Bury St Edmunds and to Cambridge twice in order to arrange for a loan required by the king; and he spent 24 days in London on negotiations for the treasurer, CUL EDC 5/13/10.
1401, 14 Sept., 20th in order on the certificate for the metropolitan visitation, Reg. Fordham, fo 131.
[1403/4], visited Melton, CUL EDC 7/16/28 acct.
1414/15, pd visits to Melton and Winston, the latter for *liberatio denariorum*, CUL EDC 7/16/29, 7/17/acct.
1419/20, d., and the sacrist gave 5s. to the almoner, CUL EDC 5/10/30.

Richard de DERHAM
occ. 1281

1281, 11 Oct., one of the monks who were absolved from irregularities that had occurred over payment of a tenth for the Holy Land, CUL EDC 1B/113.

Robert DERHAM [Dereham
occ. 1527 occ. 1539

1527, 12 Sept., accused, with Richard Denys, q.v., of assaulting a boy going to Ely grammar school, PRO, STAC 2/17/223, 383. The prior allegedly refused any recompense to the boy as he denied that any offence had taken place, *ib.*
1534, 8 Sept., 18th in order on the visitation certificate, Reg. Goodrich, fo 90v.
1539, 18 Nov., described as a 'good choir man' and assigned a pension of £7 p.a., *L and P Henry VIII*, xiv, pt. 2, no 542.

Note: see Robert Taverham.

Geoffrey de DEYS
occ. 1392/3

1392/3, gave 12s. to the treasurer as part payment of his tithe debt, CUL EDC 5/13/9.

DIONISIUS
occ. 1134

1134, 5 Jan., witnessed an inventory of the treasury, ordered by bp Nigel, *Liber Elien.*, 289.
n.d., 30 Dec., the obit of a Dionisius occ. in Cambridge, Trinity College Ms 1105, fo k12v.

See William II, his nephew.

DODELYNGTON
see Dudlington

I John DOUNHAM senior
occ. 1419 occ. 1458/9

1419, 5 June, ord acol., bp's chapel, Downham, Reg. Fordham, fo 272.
1419, 10 June, ord subdcn, bp's chapel, Downham, *ib.*, fo 272.
1419, 23 Sept., ord dcn, bp's chapel, Downham, *ib.*, fo 272v.

1434/5, steward of the prior's hospice and hostiller, PRO SC6/1257/5, CUL EDC 5/5/6.
1443/4, former *custos* of the Lady chapel, CUL EDC 5/7/9.
1458/9, refectorer and former infirmarer, CUL EDC 5/7/1 (infirmarer acct).

1422/4, *socius* of the precentor, CUL Add. Ms 2957, fo 47.
1444/6, recd 6s. 8d., from the hostiller for celebrating chantry masses, CUL EDC 5/5/7, 8.
1458/9, ill in the infirmary, CUL EDC 5/7/1 (infirmarer acct).

II John DOUNHAM junior [Downham
occ. 1464/5

1464/5, *socius* of the cellarer, CUL Add. Ms 2957, fo 6.

Note: there is a John Dounham junior described as chaplain in 1448 who was apptd to teach grammar to the monks and to five boys in the almonry school for fifteen years, Liber B nos 46, 47, (both items are crossed through).

Richard DOUNHAM [Douneham, Downham *alias* Taylor
occ. 1515 d. 1516/17

1516, 8 Mar., ord pr., Lady chapel, Ely cathedral, *ad titulum eiusdem monasterii*, Reg. West, fo 81.
1515, 15/16 Apr., 34th (and last but one) in order on the *sed. vac.* visitation certificate, Reg. abp Warham, ii, fo 277.
1516, 22 Mar., 29th in order in the chapter which chose 29 Mar. as the date for the el. of a prior, Reg. West, fo 55v.
1516/17, one of eight who d., and the sacrist sent 5s. for each to the almoner, CUL EDC 5/10/44.

I Thomas de DOUNHAM B.Cn.L. [Downham
occ. 1371/2 d. 1402/3

1384/5, 1394/5, 1396/7, almoner, CUL EDC 5/1/11, CUL Add. Ms 2957, fo 13.
1398, 26 June, apptd cellarer, Reg. Fordham, fo 189v; 1401, 4 Jan., removed from this office, *ib.*, fo 192; see Richard Madyngle, his predecessor, and Peter de Ely, his successor.
1371/2, student at Cambridge with John de Hatfeld, q.v., and the precentor contributed 11 3/4d. at the rate of ½d. in the £, CUL Add. Ms 2957, fo 45.
1383, 19 Sept., described as *bacallar' in decretis*, Reg. Arundel, fo 46. Not noted in *BRUC*.
1379, 29th in order on the clerical poll tax list and pd 3s. 4d., PRO E179/23/1.
1383, 19 Sept., comm. as penitentiary in city and diocese and enjoined to consider the circumstances in each case, Reg. Arundel, fo 46.
1398, 10 May, apptd confessor to the nuns of Chatteris, Reg. Fordham, fo 189v.
1402/3, d., and the sacrist gave 5s. to the almoner *pro errogatione*, CUL Add. Ms 2956, fo 165.

II Thomas DOUNHAM
occ. 1463 d. 1505/6

1463, 9 Apr., ord acol., bp's [*magna*] chapel, Downham, Reg. Gray, fo 210v.
1466, 5 Apr., ord subdcn, bp's palace chapel, Ely, *ib.*, fo 211.
1467, 14 Mar., ord dcn, bp's palace chapel, Ely, *ib.*, fo 211v.
1467, 28 Mar., ord pr., bp's palace chapel, Ely, *ib.*, fo 212.
1473/5, 1476/7, 1481/2, steward of the prior's hospice, CUL EDC 5/13/-, 5/13/16, 7/15/acct.
1488/9, *custos* of the Lady chapel, CUL Add. Ms 2957, fo 64.
1481/2, pd a visit to Lakenheath, CUL EDC 7/15/acct.
1505/6, d., and the sacrist gave 5s. to the almoner, CUL EDC 5/10/42.

John DOUNTON
occ. 1445/6

1445/6, *socius* of the cellarer, CUL EDC 5/2/31.

Thomas DRAYTON
occ. 1500

1500, 30 Oct., 10th to be examined at the *sed. vac.*, visitation by the commissary of the prior of Christ Church, Canterbury when the sees of both Ely and Canterbury were vacant. When questioned, he said that all was well, apart from the fact that the former *custos* of the Lady chapel, William Colchester, q.v., had removed the organ from the chapel for repairs and it had not yet been returned, Canterbury Reg. R, fo 70–70v.

Robert de DRINCHESTUNE
occ. 1134

1134, 5 Jan., witnessed an inventory of the treasury ordered by bp Nigel, *Liber Elien.*, 289.

William DUDLINGTON [Dodelyngton, Dudlyngton
occ. 1448/9 d. 1469/70

1448/50, 1451/2, 1455/6, *senescallus terrarum*, CUL EDC 5/4/-, 7/16/36/acct, 7/15/accts, 5/4/39.
1460, 30 Sept., apptd sacrist by the bp personally in chapter, Reg. Gray, fo 47v; he succ. John Soham I, q.v.
1438/9, *socius* of the sacrist, CUL EDC 5/10/32.
1449/50, pd a visit to Melton, CUL EDC 7/16/36 acct.
1451/2, 1455/6, visited Lakenheath, CUL EDC 7/15/accts.
1460, 29 Apr., with Robert Fordham, q.v., apptd to represent the prior and chapter in convocation, Liber B, no 240.
1469/70, d., and the *senescallus terrarum* sent 5s. to the almoner, CUL EDC 5/13/-.

Thomas de DULLYNGHAM
occ. 1379 occ. 1406/7

1379, 41st in order on the clerical poll tax list and pd 3s. 4d., PRO E179/23/1.
1398/9, *socius* of the almoner, CUL Add. Ms 2957, fo 13.
1401, 14 Sept., 17th in order on the metropolitan visitation certificate, Reg. Fordham, fo 131.
1406/7, *socius* of the sacrist, CUL EDC 5/10/26, CUL Add. Ms 2956, fo 166.

William de DUNELM [Dunolm
occ. 1239 × 1240 occ. [1241 × 1254]

1239 × 1240, Oct., acted as prior's attorney in a final concord concerning land, Liber M, 598.

[1241 × 1254], witness to a charter of bp Hugh [Northwold], *temp.* prior Walter, q.v, Liber M, 188. But if this is bp Hugh Balsham the dates would be 1257 × 1259.

Nicholas DUXFER [Duxford
see Ely

EBORARDUS
see Everardus

ELEWYNGTON
see Helvyngton

ELINGHAM, Ellingham
see Elyngham

W. de ELM
occ. c. 1323/5

c. 1323/5, infirmarer, CUL EDC 5/13/*status prioratus.*

Alexander de ELY
occ. 1300/1 d. 1315/16

1300/3, precentor, CUL Add. Ms 2957, fos 38–41; during the yr 1302/3 he was succ. by Robert de Swaffham, q.v.

1302, 14 Apr., one of the seven *compromissorii* chosen to el. a bp, [Robert de Orford, q.v.], Lambeth Ms 448, fo 49 (for the date) and *CPL*, i (1198–1304), 604 (for the name).

1302/3, took monk ordinands to Histon and to Barnwell for ordination, and with Robert de Swaffham, q.v., went to Impington after Michaelmas to estimate the yield. He also visited Walden in connection with the abp's visitation, CUL Add. Ms 2957, fo 41.

1310, 28 Feb., named as one of the seven *compromissorii* for the el. of a bp, but others were later chosen to replace them when they failed to agree, BL Add. Ms 41612, fo 49ᵛ; see John de Ketene.

1315/16, one of ten monks who d.; the chamberlain gave 5s. to the almoner for each, CUL Add. Ms 2957, fo 19.

Note: see Alexander II who is prob. the same monk.

Henry de ELY
see Langham

I John de ELY
occ. 1283

1283, 26 Aug., with the prior, John de Hemmingestone, q.v., and others, accused of breaking into houses and taking goods at Bergham, Suffolk, *CPR (1281–92)*, 99.

John de ELY
see Salmon

II John de ELY [?senior
occ. [1315/16] d. 1346

[1315/16], chamberlain, CUL EDC 5/12/-, (steward of the prior's hospice accts).

1332/4, 1335/6, granator, CUL EDC 5/13/6, 5/4/6, 5/13/7; he succ. Robert de Aylesham, q.v.

1344/5, treasurer, CUL EDC 7/15/acct.

[1323/4], *socius* of the pittancer, CUL EDC 5/8/8.

1327/8, visited Lakenheath with John de Jernemuth, q.v., CUL EDC 7/15/acct.

1329/30, visited Stoke, CUL EDC 7/17 acct.

1344/5, visited Lakenheath, CUL EDC 7/15/acct.

1346, Nov., d., and the chamberlain gave 5s. to the almoner, CUL Add. Ms 2957, fo 24.

III John de ELY junior
occ. 1338/9 occ. ?1358/9

1358/9, possibly treasurer, CUL EDC 5/3/13; but see John de Ely IV below.

1338/9, identified as 'junior' when he recd 2s. from the chamberlain [?for clothing], CUL Add. Ms 2957, fo 22.

IV John de ELY [?*alias* Lincoln
occ. 1350 d. 1385/6

1350, 18 Dec., ord subdcn, Ely cathedral, Reg. de Lisle, fo 96ᵛ.

1351, 2 Apr., ord dcn, St Mary's church, Ely, *ib.*, fo 97.

1353, 21 Sept., ord pr., Swavesey, *ib.*, fo 99ᵛ.

1358/9, possibly treasurer, CUL EDC 5/3/13; but see John de Ely III above.

1364/5, hostiller, CUL EDC 5/4/13.

1369/72; 1373, 9 July; 1374/5; 1376, 21 Sept.; 1380, 4 Mar.; 1380/1, sacrist, CUL EDC 5/10/17–18; Reg. abp Wittlesey, fo 152ᵛ; CUL EDC 5/10/19; Reg. Arundel, fo 19ᵛ; *ib.*, fo 32–32ᵛ; CUL Add. Ms 2956, fo 160. On 23 Dec. 1381 he was removed from this office by the bp *ex causis legitimis*, Reg. Arundel, fo 38ᵛ, and succ. by William de Ely I, q.v.

1376, 22 Nov., a John de Ely was removed from the office of cellarer and was succeeded by William de Ely I, q.v., Reg. Arundel, fo 20ᵛ.

1359/60, prob. *socius* of the sacrist, Chapman, *Sacrist Rolls*, ii, 191 (as Lincoln) (CUL EDC 5/10/15).

Note: he may have been known also as Lincoln, as a *Dom.* by this name with a clerk appears to be working under the sacrist's direction this yr, *ib.*

1371/2, attended the synods held in Oct. and June; went to Stourbridge [fair]; took monk ordinands to Hatfield and Somersham to rec. orders, CUL EDC 5/10/18.

1373, 9 July, present at the metropolitan visitation, *sed. vac.* and denied accusations vs his administration of the office of sacrist, viz of incurring debts and allowing the cathedral fabric to deteriorate, Reg. abp Wittlesey, fo 152ᵛ.

1374/5, again attended the two annual synods; went to Stourbridge [fair]; took a monk for ordination to Beckford, CUL EDC 5/10/19.

1376, 21 Sept., with the bp's official comm. to deal with a criminous clerk, Reg. Arundel, fos 19ᵛ, 20.

1378, 27 Feb., recd another apptment to deal with the purgation of a criminous clerk, Reg. Arundel, fo 26ᵛ.

1378/81, receiver of bp Arundel; in the uprising of 1381 he took refuge at the priory manor of Wentworth as he was the object of the rioters' wrath, prob. on acct of his connection with the bp, Aston, *Arundel*, 141.

1379, 11th in order on the clerical poll tax list and pd 3s. 4d., PRO E179/23/1. He was 'senior' although not so named; see John de Ely V below.

1380, 3 Oct., entertained the bp and his sister, Joan Bohun, Aston, *Arundel*, 172.

1381/2, ill in the infirmary, CUL EDC 5/2/22.

1385/6, d., and the chamberlain gave 5s. to the almoner, CUL Add. Ms 2957, fo 35.

V John de ELY

occ. 1376 d. 1406/7

1376, 29 Mar., ord acol., church of St Mary outside Trumpington gate, Cambridge, Reg. Arundel, fo 117.

1376, 20 Sept., ord subdcn, Lady chapel, Ely cathedral, *ib.*, fo 119.

1377, 14 Mar., ord dcn, Lady chapel, Ely cathedral, *ib.*, fo 121.

1378, 18 Dec., ord pr., Lady chapel, Ely cathedral, *ib.*, fo 124.

1397, May/Sept., granator, CUL EDC 5/4/19.

1399, Dec./1400, *custos* of the Lady chapel, CUL Add. Ms 2957, fo 58; he succ. William de Thetford, q.v.

1379, 43rd in order on the clerical poll tax list and described as 'junior'; he pd 3s. 4d., PRO E179/23/1.

1401, 14 Sept., 19th in order on the metropolitan visitation certificate and now described as 'senior', Reg. Fordham, fo 131.

1406/7, d., and both the precentor and sacrist sent 5s. to the almoner, CUL Add. Ms 2957, fo 47, CUL EDC 5/10/26.

n.d., a letter written by a John de Ely to the prior concerns the disposition of the money and belongings of John Wormyngton, q.v., (d. 1398/9), Reg. Walsingham no 40; this letter also asks for the prior's clarification on certain recent ordinances of the bp concerning the disposition of the money belonging to deceased monks and *officiarii*.

VI John de ELY [junior, Elys

occ. 1397 occ. 1424

1397, 16 June, ord acol., bp's [*maior*] chapel, Downham, Reg. Fordham, fo 238.

1398, 1 June, ord subdcn, Somersham, Lincs., *ib.*, fo 239.

1399, 29 Mar., ord dcn, bp's chapel, Somersham, *ib.*, fo 239.

1400, 13 Mar., ord pr., Doddington, *ib.*, fo 240.

1401, 14 Sept., 33rd in order on the metropolitan visitation certificate, Reg. Fordham, fo 131; he is styled 'junior'.

1408/9, *socius* of the precentor, CUL Add. Ms 2957, fo 47.

1418, 17 Nov., with Peter de Ely I, q.v., involved [as proctors] in a suit over tithes in the court of Canterbury, CUL EDC 1/B/721.

1424, 8 Jan., with Thomas de Elyingham, q.v., given permission by the prior to go to the Holy See on condition that they returned by 24 June, unless they had reasonable cause for delay, Reg. Walsingham, loose fragment. On 15 Jan., the Ferentini bankers were authorized to provide letters of exchange to the value of 100s, payable to them in foreign parts, *CClR (1422–1429)*, 484.

VII John ELY

occ. 1437 occ. 1470

1437, 23 Feb., ord. pr., St Bride's Fleet Street, London, Reg. Robert Gilbert (London), fo 153.

1443/4, chamberlain, CUL EDC 5/3/33.

1444/5, former treasurer and now granator, CUL EDC 5/4/35; 1445/6, granator, CUL EDC 5/2/31.

1465/6, treasurer, CUL EDC 5/13/-.

[1470], 11 Sept., his dismissal from the office of subprior was ordered, Reg. Gray, fo 80ᵛ.

1434/5, *socius* of the hostiller, CUL EDC 5/5/6.

1442/3, *socius* of the precentor, CUL EDC 5/9/12.

1449, 10 Apr., licensed to preach in the diocese, Reg. Bourgchier, fo 21.

VIII John ELY B.Th. [?*alias* Ingram

occ. 1466 occ. 1487/8

1466, 5 Apr., ord acol., bp's palace chapel, Ely, Reg. Gray, fo 211.

1467, 14 Mar., ord subdcn, bp's palace chapel, Ely, *ib.*, fo 211ᵛ; the name is given as John Ingram.

1469, 1 Apr., ord dcn, bp's chapel, Downham, *ib.*, fo 214.

[1470], 11 Sept., a commission was issued for his apptment as cellarer, Reg. Gray, fo 80ᵛ.

1472/4; 1475/7; 1478, 26/28 July, cellarer, CUL Add. Ms 2957, fo 6, CUL EDC 5/13/-, 5/13/16; Lambeth Ms 448, fo 113.

[1462 × 1478], *temp.* prior Henry Peterborough, q.v., described as B.Th., Liber B, no 241, as in *BRUC*.

[1462 × 1478], with Thomas Wells II, q.v., apptd general proctors by the prior and chapter, Liber B, no 241.

Note: the date of the two above entries is prob. 1473/4; see Thomas Wells II.

1473/4, sent with Thomas Wells II, q.v., and with seven horses, to the Black Monk Chapter at Northampton [July 1474] where they stayed for six days; as visitors for the Chapter they spent eleven days visiting several religious houses including Thorney, CUL EDC 5/13/-.

1478, 19 July, accompanied John Soham I, subprior, q.v. and other monks to the bp to discuss arrangements for the pension of the prior, Henry Peterborough, q.v., Lambeth Ms 448, fo 113.

1487/8, described as a 'stager' for whom the sacrist purchased oil for the lamp *ad tria altaria*, CUL Add. Ms 2956, fo 173 (CUL EDC 5/10/40).

IX John ELY

occ. 1475/6

1475, 25 Mar., ord acol., bp's chapel, Doddington, Reg. Gray, fo 215v.

1476, 13 Apr., ord subdcn, bp's palace chapel, Ely, *ib.*, fo 216v.

X John ELY [*alias* Sampson

occ. 1488 occ. 1491

1488, 20 Dec., ord dcn, bp's chapel, Downham, Reg. Alcock, fo 225v.

1491, 24 Sept., ord pr., bp's chapel, Downham, *ib.*, fo 230.

XI John ELY [?*alias* Palmer

occ. 1492 occ. 1495

1492, 21 Apr., ord subdcn, Ely cathedral, Reg. Alcock, fo 231v and again on fo 233.

1495, 14 Mar., ord pr., bp's chapel, Downham, *ib.*, fo 237.

Note: see John Palmer for further entries.

XII John ELY [?*alias* Cust', Custance, Custans

occ. 1496 occ. 1539

1496, 2 Apr., ord subdcn, Ely cathedral, Reg. Alcock, fo 240.

1498, 14 Apr., ord dcn, Ely cathedral, *ib.*, fo 246v.

1539, 18 Nov., *senescallus terrarum*, *L and P Henry VIII*, xiv, pt. 2, no 542, as John Custance.

1539, 18 Nov., he was assigned a pension of £16 p.a., *L and P Henry VIII*, xiv, pt. 2, no 542.

[1541, 10 Sept., apptd canon of the 6th prebend in the new foundation (as Custans), *Fasti 1541–1857*, vii, 24.]

***

Note: Due to some confusion and omissions in the records and to the frequent recurrence of the name John Ely, of whom there were sometimes two, and possibly even three, in the community at the same time, it has proved impossible to disentangle all the details of their individual careers. Some of the entries are prob. misplaced; and for the last three (X, XI, XII) it would be futile to attempt to assign the offices held by those who bore this name. The following entries are therefore given chronologically without attribution:

1511/12, first year as almoner, succeeding John Pate, q.v., CUL EDC 1/C/7, fo 28.

1515, 15/16 Apr., 18th in order on the metropolitan visitation certificate Reg. abp Warham, ii, fo 277.

1516, 22 Mar., 14th in order in the chapter which chose 29 Mar. as the date for the el. of a prior, Reg. West, fo 55.

1517, Mar./Sept., 1518/19, chamberlain, CUL Add. Ms 2957, fo 33.

1519/20, almoner, CUL EDC 5/3/34.

1519/20, prob. feretrar, CUL Add. Ms 2956, fo 176.

1522/3, almoner, CUL EDC 1/C/7, fo 28.

1519/21; 1523/8, chamberlain, CUL EDC 5/3/34, CUL Add. Ms 2957, fo 33, CUL EDC 5/13/19, 20.

1525/8, *senescallus terrarum*, CUL EDC 5/13/18–20, CUL Add. Ms 2957, fos 74, 79, 80.

1528/30, 1532/3, c. 1535/7, chamberlain, CUL Add. Ms 2957, fos 34, 81, 82, CUL EDC 5/13/1.

1534, 8 Sept., 6th in order on the visitation certificate, Reg. Goodrich, fo 90v.

Lancelot ELY

occ. 1534

1534, 8 Sept., 32nd and last but one in order on the visitation certificate, Reg. Goodrich, fo 90v; he was one of ten not styled *dominus* and therefore recently adm. and not yet in major orders.

Nicholas ELY [*alias* Duxfer, Duxfford, Duxford

occ. 1519 occ. 1539

1519, 24 Sept., ord subdcn, Lady chapel, Ely cathedral, Reg. West, fo 87.

1534, 8 Sept., 15th in order on the visitation certificate, Reg. Goodrich, fo 90v.

1539, 18 Nov., described as chaplain and assigned a pension of £6 p.a., *L and P Henry VIII*, xiv, pt. 2, no 542.

I Peter de ELY

occ. 1384 d. 1431/2

1425–?1430, prior: el. by 7 Mar. 1425 (his first yr), CUL EDC 7/7/5 court, 7/17/46 court; d. 1431/2, CUL EDC 5/4/30, between 13 Nov. and 3 July, CUL EDC 7/7/5 court, 7/12/6 court; concerning his prob. res., see below.

1384, 24 Sept., ord acol., bp's chapel, Downham, Reg. Arundel, fo 131ᵛ.
1385, 18 Mar., ord subdcn, Lady chapel, Ely cathedral, *ib.*, fo 132ᵛ.
1385, 27 May, ord dcn, bp's chapel, Downham, *ib.*, fo 132ᵛ.
1388, 23 May, ord pr., bp's chapel, Holborn (London), *ib.*, fo 136.

1394/5, 1396/7, steward of the prior's hospice, CUL EDC 7/15/acct, 5/13/10.
1399/1400, *senescallus terrarum,* CUL EDC 7/16/27 acct.
1401, 4 Jan., the bp comm. his chancellor to put him in as cellarer, Reg. Fordham, fo 192; 1405, 10 Nov., a similar comm. to remove him, *ib.*, fo 201.
1405, 10 Nov., the bp ordered his apptment as subprior, *ib.*, fo 201.
1412/13, sacrist, CUL Add. Ms 2956, fo 167.
1419/20, feretrar, CUL EDC 5/11/1, 5/10/30.
1394/5, visited Lakenheath, CUL EDC 7/15/acct.
1399/1400, visited Melton, CUL EDC 7/16/26, 27 acct.
[1400/1], *socius* of the cellarer, prob. c. Sept./Jan., CUL EDC 5/4/20, 21.
1401, 14 Sept., 25th in order on the metropolitan vistitation certificate, Reg. Fordham, fo 131; on 13 Oct., with Edmund de Totyngton, q.v. as proctors of the subprior and chapter informed William Powcher, q.v., of his postulation as prior, Reg. abp Arundel, i, fo 494ᵛ.
1412, 21 Dec., as sacrist, apptd a public notary as his general proctor, Liber B, no 275, CUL Add. Ms 2950, fos 64–65.
1418, 17 Nov., with John de Ely VI, q.v., involved [as proctors] in a suit over tithes in the court of Canterbury, CUL EDC 1B/721.
1426, 5 Jan., vs the king's wishes el. bp by the chapter, but Philip Morgan was provided, BL Cotton Ms Titus A.i, fo 144ᵛ, Lambeth Ms 448, fo 80ᵛ.
n.d., wrote a letter to the prior denying that he had any connection with the Countess of Hertford, Reg. Walsingham, no 18.
1431/2, d., as above; he seems to have res. before 1 Oct. 1430; see William Wells II.

II Peter ELY
occ. 1443/4 occ. 1469/70

1443/4, treasurer, CUL Add. Ms 2957, fo 31.
1444/6, hostiller, and steward of the prior's hospice, CUL EDC 5/5/7 and 8, 5/12/5 and 6.
[1467], 11 Oct., a comm. was issued for his apptment as chamberlain, Reg. Gray, fo 70; he succ. John Munden, q.v.
[1470], 11 Sept., the bp ordered his dismissal from the office of chamberlain, Reg. Gray, fo 80ᵛ.
1473/4, described as former steward of the prior's hospice, CUL EDC 5/13/-.
1444/5, as hostiller went to Meldreth and Witchford 'pro rectoria supervidend' et denariis recipiend' ', CUL EDC 5/5/7.
1465/6, recd 6s. 8d., from the treasurer for celebrating [chantry] masses for Philip Lyle, CUL EDC 5/13/-.

Note: it is possible that there are two monks conflated here because of the twenty yr gap between 1444 and 1465.

Richard ELY [*alias* Barbor, Barbour
occ. 1454 occ. 1482/3

1454, 15 June, ord dcn, place not stated, Reg. Bourgchier, fo 48.
1467/8, steward of the prior's hospice, CUL EDC 7/15/acct.
1470/1, *custos* of the Lady chapel, CUL EDC 5/7/12, as Barbor and Ely.
1476/7, 1482/3, pittancer, CUL EDC 5/8/16, 5/4/47.
1467/8, pd a visit to Lakenheath, CUL EDC 7/15/acct.

Robert de ELY
occ. [1241 × 1254]

[1241 × 1254], *temp.* prior Walter, q.v., witness to a charter of bp Hugh [de Northwold], Liber M, 188.
Note: if the bp is Hugh [de Balsham] the dates should be revised to 1257 × 1259.
n.d., had been assaulted by men who gave bonds to observe the awards made vs them, CUL EDC 1B/134, 135.

Thomas ELY
occ. 1457 occ. 1487/8

1457, 17 Dec., ord acol., bp's chapel, Downham, Reg. Gray, fo 204ᵛ.
1458, 23 Dec., ord subdcn, bp's chapel, Downham, *ib.*, fo 205.
1459, 24 Mar., ord dcn, bp's chapel, Downham, *ib.*, fo 205ᵛ.
1460, 8 Mar., ord pr., bp's [*magna*] chapel, Downham, *ib.*, fo 208.

1478/9, 1485/6, 1487/8, prob. feretrar, CUL EDC 5/10/36, 38, CUL Add. Ms 2956, fos 172, 173.
1485/6, 1487/8, sacrist, CUL EDC 5/10/38–40.
Note: it seems prob. that the sacrist was also the feretrar here as it was he who turned over to the sacrist the receipts from the shrine of St Etheldreda.
1478/9, *custos* of the manor of Caxton, CUL EDC 5/10/36.
1487/8, went to Cambridge to arrange for parish chaplains and to settle affairs between St Andrew's church and the *aula regia*, CUL EDC 5/10/40.

I William de ELY [?*alias* Powcher
occ. 1369/70 occ. 1389/90

1376, before 22 Nov., chamberlain, Reg. Arundel, fo 20ᵛ.
1376, 22 Nov., apptd cellarer, *ib.*, succ. John de Ely III, q.v.
1377/8, 1379/81, cellarer, CUL EDC 5/2/19–21, CUL Add. Ms 2957, fo 4.
1381, 23 Dec., apptd sacrist (at the request of the prior and convent), Reg. Arundel, fo 38ᵛ, succ. John de Ely IV, q.v.
1386/90, sacrist, CUL Add. Ms 2956, fo 162.

1369/70, *socius* of the chamberlain, CUL EDC 5/3/18.
1379, 20th in order on the clerical poll tax list and pd 3s. 4d., PRO E179/23/1.
1387, Feb./1390, June, as sacrist he was concerned with the new work on the [reredos of the] high altar; the total cost was £167 15s. 10d., CUL EDC 5/10/22, CUL Add. Ms 2956, fo 162.

Note: this is prob. the early career of William Powcher, q.v., who was el. prior in 1401.

II William ELY
occ. 1492/4

1492, 21 Apr., ord subdcn, Ely cathedral, Reg. Alcock, fos 231ᵛ, 233.
1494, 29 Mar., ord pr., Ely cathedral, *ib.*, fo 235ᵛ.

[I Thomas de ELYNGHAM
occ. 1356/7

1356/7, *magister scolar'*, Worceser Cathedral Muniment, C.248.

Note: this is no doubt a cleric but not necessarily a monk; this acct was reported as having been returned to Ely, but is now missing.]

II Thomas de ELYNGHAM [Elingham, Ellyngham
occ. 1392 occ. 1438/9

1392, 19 Oct., one of three whose prof. the prior was comm. to rec., Reg. Fordham, fo 179.
1392, 21 Dec., ord acol., bp's chapel, Doddington, *ib.*, fo 233ᵛ.
1393, 1 Mar., ord subdcn, bp's chapel, Doddington, *ib.*, fo 233ᵛ.
1393, 31 May, ord dcn, bp's [*maior*] chapel, Downham, *ib.*, fo 234.
1393, 20 Sept., ord pr., bp's chapel, Doddington, *ib.*, fo 234ᵛ, [as Elyngton].

1408/9, steward of the prior's hospice, CUL EDC 5/6/18.
1409/10; 1411/12, steward as above and cellarer, CUL EDC 7/15/acct, 5/2/29; 5/4/24.
1413/23, 1425/6, 1438/9, sacrist, CUL EDC 7/4/2 and 3, 5/10/27–32; and see below.

1398, 16 Nov., acted as attorney, with other monks, in taking seisin of a messuage in Ely, BL Ms Egerton 3047, fo 120.
1401, 14 Sept., 28th in order on the metropolitan visitation certificate, Reg. Fordham, fo 131.
1403/4, 1405/6, *socius* of the sacrist, CUL EDC 5/10/24, 25.
1409/10, visited Lakenheath, CUL EDC 7/15/acct.
1413, 20 July, as sacrist, appted a proctor, Liber B, no 277.
1414, 8 Jan., with the prior and in his office of sacrist, apptd Edmund Walsingham and Henry Maddyngle, q.v., his proctors, with three secular clerks, in a case against the bp, Liber B, no 278, CUL Add. Ms 2950, fos 66–69.
1417, under the initiative of prior William Powcher, q.v., built a new hall in the infirmary *pro minutionibus*, Lambeth Ms 448, fo 94.
1420, 10 Oct., with Henry Maddyngle, q.v., apptd proctor by the prior and chapter in a lawsuit, Reg. Walsingham, no 35.
1424, 8 Jan., with John de Ely VI, q.v., given permission by the prior to go to the Holy See on condition that they returned by 24 June, unless prevented by reasonable cause, Reg. Walsingham, loose fragment. On 15 Jan, the Ferentini bankers were authorized to provide letters of exchange to the value of 100s, payable to them in foreign parts, *CClR (1422–1429)*, 484.
1428/9, sent to London on business for the treasurer, PRO SC6/1257/4.
1436, 13 Feb., granted a papal indult permitting him to resign after 24 yrs as sacrist because he was a sexagenarian and desired to give himself to prayer, *CPL*, viii (1427–1447), 553.
1438/9, took four monks to Papworth for ordination, CUL EDC 5/10/32.

Paulinus de ERPINGHAM [Erpyngham, Herpyngham
occ. 1341 [d. 1349]

1341, 24 Mar., ord subdcn, Willingham, Reg. Montacute, fo 107 (no house named).
1343, 29 Mar., ord dcn, Willingham, Reg. Montacute, fo 111.

[1349], 2 July, apptd chamberlain, Reg. de Lisle, fo 22ᵛ; he d. within the week, *ib.*

Walter de ESCHALERS
occ. early 13th c.

Note: the only ref. is that provided by S.J.A. Evans, viz., Muniment 677, which I have not been able to trace.

EVERARDUS [Eboradus, Eborardus
occ. 1251

1251, keeper of the Ely bridge, CUL EDC 1B/150.

John de EXNYNG [Exenyng, Ixenyngis, Ixing, Ixnyngge, Yxing, Yxneng, Yxnyng
occ. 1374 d. 1405/6

1374, 27 May, ord dcn, London, St Paul's cathedral, Reg. Arundel, fo 115.

1375, 17 Mar., ord pr., Dorking, Surrey, *ib.*, fo 115[v].

1392/3, steward of the prior's hospice, CUL EDC 5/13/9.

1392, 9 Oct., the bp ordered his commissaries to make him chamberlain, Reg. Fordham, fo 178[v].

1396/7, to Apr., chamberlain, CUL EDC 5/13/10, CUL Add. Ms 2957, fo 37.

1379, 35th in order on the clerical poll tax list and pd 3s. 4d., PRO E179/23/1.

1401, 14 Sept., 13th on the metropolitan visitation certificate, Reg. Fordham, fo 131.

1405/6, d., the chamberlain and sacrist sent 5s. to the almoner, CUL EDC 5/3/26 (CUL Add. Ms 2957, fo 3), CUL EDC 5/10/25.

John FELTWELL B.Th. [Feltewelle

occ. 1420 occ. 1469/70

1420, 21 Dec., ord dcn, St Mary's church [Ely], Reg. Fordham, fo 108.

1437/40, *senescallus terrarum*, CUL EDC 7/15/acct, 7/16/34 acct, PRO SC6/1257/7.

1439/40, 1446, 1 June, sacrist, CUL Add. Ms 2956, fo 168, CUL Add. Ms 2950, fo 76; and see William Feltwell below.

1457/9, 1460, 10 Apr., sacrist, CUL Add. Ms 2956, fo 168, CUL EDC 5/10/34, Reg. Gray, fo 46[v].

1460, 10 Apr., apptd subprior by the bp personally in chapter, Reg. Gray, fo 46[v].

1423/4, 'third scholar' at Cambridge and recd 37s. 10d., for bread and ale from the treasurer. CUL EDC 5/13/12, CUL Add. Ms 2957, fo 73. The other two were John Sutton II and William Wells II, q.v.

1428/9, student and recd 37s. 10d., from the treasurer, PRO SC6/1257/4.

1436/7, B.Th. [*bacular*], and recd contributions *ad introitum* from the chamberlain and the treasurer, CUL Add. Ms 2957, fo 31, PRO SC6/1257/6; see also John Sutton II.

1428, 5 July, acted as attorney in the collection of a tenth for the king, Oxford, Bod., Ms Laud 647, fo 180.

1430, 1 Oct., apptd as general proctor for the prior and chapter with John Sutton II, q.v., Liber B, no 233; CUL Add. Ms 2950, fo 74.

1434/5, sent by the prior and chapter with John Yaxham, q.v., to visit their churches in Norwich and Bury St Edmunds; they took with them three servants and five horses, PRO SC6/1257/5; he also went to Northampton to the Black Monk Chapter, *ib.*

1435, 27 Oct., named by the prior and chapter, with John Stretham, q.v., and others as proctors for convocation, CUL Add. Ms 2950, fo 75, Liber B, no 74.

1437/8, visited Lakenheath, CUL EDC 7/15/acct.

1438/9, pd visits to Kingston and Melton, CUL EDC 7/14/45 acct, 7/16/34 acct.

1439/40, May, while *senescallus terrarum* spent 5 wks in London on negotiations PRO SC6/1257/7; in 1440 he went on business to see John Tiptoft, *ib.*, 1257/8.

1446, 1 June, acted with John Soham I, q.v., as proctor in a tithe dispute, Liber B, no 234, CUL Add. Ms 2950, fos 76, 77.

1469/70, still alive, CUL EDC 5/13/-.

Richard de FELTWELL

occ. 1286 d. [1336 × 1342]

1286, 11 July, with Robert de Swaffham, q.v., delivered in London the sum of £120 collected for the tenth levied for the Holy Land which had been deposited in the priory, CUL EDC 1B/116.

[1336 × 1342], d., acc. to the Crosby transcripts, CUL Add. Ms 639(C), fo 10.

William FELTWELL

occ. 1447

[1447], 20 Apr., sacrist, Reg. Bourgchier, fo 12[v].

[1447], 20 Apr., licensed to hear confessions, *ib.*

Note: this may be a scribal error and refer to John Feltwell q.v.

FENCHAM, Fincham

see Fyncham

William FOLIOT [Folyott ?*alias* Wittlesey

occ. 1516

1516, by 22 Mar., res. as prior; this must be William Wittlesey I or II, q.v.

Note: acc. to the list of priors entered by Robert Wells, q.v., the last prior, on fo 96[v] of Lambeth Ms 448 there was no prior between William Wittlesey and John Cottenham, q.v. (or if there was, he was for some reason not included). Since Wells was a monk at the time he must have known the facts. It would make more sense to suggest that the two contemporary William Wittleseys, q.v, have confused historians and that the prior accused of maladministration by the abp in Apr. 1515 was one of these.

Richard de FORDHAM

occ. 1341/3

1341, 24 Mar., ord acol., Willingham, Reg. Montacute, fo 106[v].

1342, 16 Mar., ord subdcn, Willingham, *ib.*, fo 108.

1343, 29 Mar., ord dcn, Willingham, *ib.*, fo 111.

Robert FORDHAM [Fordam

occ. 1455 occ. 1476/7

1455, 5 Apr., ord pr., St Mary in the market, Cambridge, Reg. Gray, fo 202[v].

1464/7, 1469/70, cellarer, CUL Add. Ms 2957, fo 6, PRO SC6/1257/9, CUL EDC 5/13/-; on 11

Sept. 1470, the bp ordered his dismissal from this office, Reg. Gray, fo 80ᵛ.
1473/4, named as former *senescallus terrarum*, CUL EDC 5/13/-.

[1459, a Robert Fordam, monk, was granted grace to oppose in theology in his 12th yr at Cambridge; no religious house was named. See *BRUC*.]

1457, 6 Oct., named, with others, as proctor for the chapter in an appropriation, Liber B, no 237, CUL Add. Ms 2950, fo 78.
c. 1460, apptd, with others, proctor in matters arising out of an episcopal visitation, Liber B, no 237a and CUL Add. Ms 2950, fo 79.
1460, 29 Apr., with William Dudlington, q.v., apptd proctor for the prior and convent at convocation, Liber B, no 240.
1470, 6 Oct., apptd by the prior and convent as one of several proctors in an appropriation, Liber B, no 237.
1476/7, apptd by the prior and chapter to attend the Black Monk Chapter [Northampton, 30 June, 1477], CUL EDC 5/13/16.

William de FORDHAM [Ford'
occ. 1320/1 d. 1323/4

[1320/1], *socius* of the pittancer, CUL EDC 5/8/5.
1321/1325, with John de Wisbech, q.v., pd off some of the outstanding debt of prior John de Fresingfeld, q.v., owed to the king, CUL EDC 5/13/*status prioratus*, CUL Add. Ms 2957, fo 66.
1323/4, d., and the sacrist sent 5s. to the almoner *pulsantibus campanas pro anima*, Chapman, *Sacrist Rolls*, ii, 44 (CUL EDC 5/10/4); the treasurer also sent 5s. *pro errogacione pauperum*, CUL EDC 5/13/-.

FREDERICUS
n.d.

n.d., 2 June, obit occ. in Cambridge, Trinity College Ms 1105, fo k6ᵛ.

J. de FRES'
occ. 1332/3

1332/3, *custos gran[arie]*, CUL EDC 5/13/6; but see Robert de Aylesham and also John de Fresingfeld below.

Benedict de FRESINGFELD [Freisingfeld, Fresyngfeld
occ. 1332/3 occ. 1346/7

1332 July/Sept., 1335/6, second treasurer, with John de Orewell, q.v., CUL EDC 5/13/6, 7, CUL Add. Ms 2957, fo 58.
c. 1337/8, hostiller, CUL EDC 5/4/7.
1344, Jan./1347, July, chamberlain, CUL EDC 5/3/6–8.

1335, Mar./Sept., recd 6d. *pro communibus* from the cellarer, CUL EDC 5/2/2.
1345/7, made annual visits to the fairs at St Ives and Stourbridge to purchase cloth and other necessities, CUL EDC 5/3/6, 7.

John de FRESINGFELD [Freisingfeld
occ. 1303 d. 1338

1303–1321, prior: occ. 24 Dec. 1303; res. 16 Feb. 1321, *Fasti*, iv, 16.

1305, 12 Mar., with the approval of the chapter issued a set of ordinances regulating his and the monks' daily life. Those directly applying to him concerned his apptment of monk stewards [*senescalli terrarum* and *hospicii*] and personal chaplain, and required him to take advice before action and to reduce the size of his household, Evans, *Ely Chap. Ord.*, 24–28 (BL Add. Ms 41612, fos 30–33.
1307, 2 Mar., ordered by the bp [Orford, himself a previous prior] after his visitation to reduce the expenses of his household and be kind to his brethren, Evans, *Ely Chap. Ord.*, 32.
1312, one of the cathedral priors summoned to London to meet the papal nuncios, *Councils and Synods*, ii, 1377.
1314, 7 Jan., presided at the bp's [consistory] court with several justices, CUL EDC 1B/920.
1315, June, despite the bp's protest, abp Reynolds visited the priory and the prior explained that there was no place to appeal for help as the papal throne was vacant, and the king was on the side of the abp; 'et sic ob maius malum evitandum minus malum' he made no resistance, Churchill, *Cant. Admin.*, i, 308–310 (BL Ms 41812, fo 33ᵛ).
1316, 14 June, presided at the el. of a bp and given power as sole *compromissarius* by the chapter; he at once rose and announced the choice of John de Hotham, BL Add. Ms 41612, fo 40.
1319, 13 July, absent from the monastery when a *contentio* arose over the authority of the subprior, John de Crishale I, q.v. On his return on 27 July he heard the case, rebuked the subprior for his behaviour and ordered him to move from his presidential seat in the chapter and to go to his stall. He commanded that there be no more rancour, to which the subprior replied that he felt none and he kissed his former adversary, the third prior [William Hoveden, q.v.], Lambeth Ms 448, fos 97ᵛ–98.
1321, 16 Feb., res. because of the accumulation of debts and expensive lawsuits for which he was responsible. Evidence of his incompetence /mismanagement is provided by the *status prioratus* [dated 29 Sept. 1325] of his successor, John de Crauden, q.v., when the sum owed was said to have been £835 19s. 11d., CUL EDC 5/13/ *status prioratus*, CUL Add. Ms 2957, fos 65, 66. His infirmity was also referred to in the acct of the el. of his successor, Lambeth Ms 448, fo 51. See John de Crauden.

1328/32, 1334/5, 1337/8, the chamberlain pd him an annual sum of 40s. *pro habitu*, CUL Add. Ms 2957, fos 20–22, and CUL EDC 5/3/1, 4.
1338, c. 6 Apr. d., as this is the date of his obit in BL Add. Ms 33381, fo 12; see also CUL Add. Ms 2957, fo 22.

Some of his official *acta* may be found in BL Add. Ms 41612 scattered *passim* on folios before fo 62.

Note: the entry under John de Fres' above may ref. to this monk.

Robert de FREYSINGFEUD
occ. 1265

1265, 30 Aug., with other monks witnessed an acquittance for part of a sum owed to a Florentine merchant by the bp and the prior and chapter, CUL EDC 1B/106.

John FYNCHAM [Fyncheham
occ. 1400 occ. 1425

1400, 13 Mar., ord acol., Doddington, Reg. Fordham, fo 240.
1400, 12 June, ord subdcn, Doddington, *ib.*, fo 240ᵛ.
1400, 18 Sept., ord dcn, bp's chapel, Doddington, *ib.*, fo 240ᵛ.
1400, 18 Dec., ord pr., bp's chapel, Downham, *ib.*, fo 241.
1411/12, treasurer and steward of the prior's hospice, CUL EDC 5/4/24; and see Thomas Elyngham.
1413/14, treasurer, CUL EDC 5/4/25.
1414/16, *senescallus terrarum*, CUL EDC 7/16/29 acct, 7/12/acct.
1418, May/Sept., *custos* of the Lady chapel, CUL Add. Ms 2957, fo 59.
1423/4, almoner, CUL EDC 5/13/12.

1409/10, student at Cambridge with Henry Madyngle, with maintenance from the cellarer of c. 23s. *pro interferculis* and 17d. [calculated] at the rate of ½d. in the £, CUL EDC 5/2/29.

1401, 14 Sept., 38th in order on the metropolitan visitation certificate, Reg. Fordham, fo 131.
1410, 2 Nov., with Thomas Ramesey II, q.v., and others, apptd general proctors for the prior and convent, Liber B, no 269.
1414/15, pd visits to Melton and Winston, CUL EDC 7/16/29 acct, 7/17/acct.
1415/16, pd a visit to Swaffham [Prior], CUL EDC 7/12/acct.
1425, 10 May, obtained an indult to choose his own confessor, *CPL*, vii (1417–1431), 416.

Thomas FYNCHAM [Fencham, Fincham
occ. 1412 d. 1453/4

1412, 28 May, ord acol., bp's chapel, Downham, Reg. Fordham, fo 261.
1413, 23 Sept., ord subdcn, bp's chapel, Downham, *ib.*, fo 262ᵛ.
1413, 23 Dec., ord dcn, bp's chapel, Downham, *ib.*, fo 263.
1414, 22 Dec., ord pr., bp's chapel, Downham, *ib.*, fo 264.

1449/50, *socius* of the almoner, CUL EDC 5/1/13.
1453/4, d., and the precentor gave 5s. to the almoner, CUL EDC 5/9/7 and CUL Add. Ms 2957, fo 48.

GERNMUTHA
see Jernemuth

GILBERT
see Lakyngheth

GODMUNDUS
see Guthmund

GODTHINUS [Gozelinus, de Wintonia
occ. before 1122/3

1122/3, d. by this date when his name occ. on a mortuary roll of Savigny, Delisle, *Rouleaux des Morts*, 339.

Note: the Anglo Saxon thorn has been transcribed by Delisle as a 'p', i.e. Godpinus.

Note: he is described as a monk of Winchester (q.v. under Winchester), but listed under Ely monks here; possibly he came from Winchester to Ely with Simeon, prior of Winchester, q.v., who became abbot of Ely in 1082 and who d. in 1093, *HRH*, 45.

Alexander GRAY
d. 1330/1

1330/1, d., and the chamberlain gave 5s. to the almoner, CUL Add. Ms 2957, fo 21.

GREGORY [Gregorius
occ. [1100 × 1135]

Author of a life of St Etheldreda, a copy of which is preserved in Cambridge, Corpus Christi College, Ms 393, Historia Eliensis, (12th c.); see Dr. Blake's comments in *Liber Elien.*, xxx–xxxiv, where he sought to identify passages in *Liber Elien.*, Book I, derived from Gregory.

Thomas GRENEWOD [Grenwod
occ. 1515/17

1515, 15/16 Apr., 30th in order (out of 35) on the *sed. vac.* visitation certificate, Reg. abp Warham, ii, fo 277.
1516, 29 Mar., 25th at the el. of a prior, Reg. West, fo 55.
1516/17, one of eight monks who d., for each of whom the sacrist gave 5s. to the almoner, CUL EDC 5/10/44.

John GROVE
occ. 1396/7 occ. 1420

1396/7, *socius* of the precentor, CUL Add. Ms 2957, fo 45.

1402/3, *socius* of the sacrist, CUL Add. Ms 2956, fo 164.

1406/7, *socius* of the precentor, CUL Add. Ms 2957, fo 47.

1417, 12 Apr., recd a warmly worded letter of recommendation from the prior affirming his good character and conversation, Liber B, nos 213–214. Item no 71 in the same ms is an undated licence permitting him to transfer to Syon, *temp.* William [Powcher] prior, q.v.

1420, 3 Jan., recd a dispensation, in which he, now elderly, was described as anchorite and Ely monk, allowing him to eat meat in his own place of reclusion, *Reg. abp Chichele*, iv, 198.

GUTHMUND [Godmundus, Guthmundus
occ. c. 1143

c. 1143, sacrist, Liber Elien., 290.

In the inventory of treasure ordered by bp Nigel he was described as the maker of two processional crosses, a silver and ivory gospel book, a silver thurible and vestments, *ib.*, 291–293.

Note: the dating is based on *Liber Elien.*, 288, n. 2. However, a Guthmundus, sacrist, [*secretarius*], had presumably d. by 1122/3 when his name occ. on a mortuary roll of Savigny, Delisle, *Rouleaux des Morts*, 339.

Simon de H.
occ. 1350/1

1350/1, one of two *socii* of the sacrist, Chapman, *Sacrist Rolls*, ii, 146, (CUL EDC 5/10/11).

Note: see also Simon, and Simon de Banham (if the H. is a misreading).

I J. de HADENHAM
occ. 1290/1

1290/1, on the Lakenheath acct there is a ref. to a brother J. who d. there, to '*temp.* brother J.', '*temp.* J. de Hadenham', and to 'brother J., *sen[escallus*', CUL EDC 7/15/acct.

?Name in Cambridge, Corpus Christi College Ms 416, Amalarius (12th c.); on fo 140ᵛ the name has been scribbled.

II John HADENHAM
occ. 1534

1534, 8 Sept., 27th in order on the visitation certificate, Reg. Goodrich, fo 90ᵛ; he was one of ten not styled *dominus* and therefore recently adm. and not yet in major orders.

HADENHAM
see also Hadnam

William de HADHAM
occ. 1350 occ. 1361

1350, 18 Dec., ord subdcn, Ely cathedral, Reg. de Lisle, fo 96ᵛ.

1352, 22 Sept., ord dcn, Over, *ib.*, fo 98ᵛ.

1356, 9 Apr., ord pr., Wisbech castle chapel, *ib.*, fo 101.

1361, contributed 6s. towards the purchase of the manor and advowson of Mepal, Evans, 'Mepal', 118 (CUL EDC 1B/box 23).

Richard HADLEY
occ. 1420

1420, 21 Dec., ord dcn, St Mary's church [?Ely], Reg. Fordham, fo 108.

John HADNAM
occ. ?1462/3 occ. ?1467/8

1462/3, described as former *custos* of Spinney, CUL EDC 5/4/40.

1467/8, described as former *custos* of the Lady chapel, CUL EDC 5/7/11, CUL Add. Ms 2957, fo 62; a similar ref. occ. in 1470/1 on the acct of the Lady chapel, CUL EDC 5/7/12.

HAGARSTON, Harston
see Agarston

John HALPENY
occ. 1510/11

1510/11, *socius* of the pittancer, CUL EDC 5/8/17.

Note: this is one of several monks who may possibly be entered twice in this register: by their patronymic, as here, and also by their toponymic elsewhere.

William de HALYWELL
occ. 1374 d. 1402/3

1374/5, and prob. 1375/6, *socius* of the almoner, CUL EDC 5/1/7, 8.

1379, 19th in order on the clerical poll tax list and pd 3s. 4d., PRO E179/23/1.

1402/3, d., and the sacrist sent 5s. to the almoner *pro arrogacione*, CUL Add. Ms 2956, fo 165.

John de HAMERTON [Hamirton
occ. 1332/3 occ. 1345

1332/3, 1335/6, steward of the prior's hospice, CUL EDC 5/13/6, 7.

1335/6, involved with the purchase of hay for the treasurer, CUL EDC 5/13/7, CUL Add. Ms 2957, fo 71.

1337, 3 Mar., with Ralph de Saxmundham, q.v., recd royal licence to el. a bp, *CPR (1334–1338)*, 386; see John de Crauden.

1338, Apr./?Sept., recd 3s. from the chamberlain, *pro linea tela*, CUL Add. Ms 2957, fo 22.

1344, 18 Oct., one of four monks who were cited to appear before the pope for arresting the proctor of the rector of Hadenham while he was in the chapter house reading out a papal letter concerned with the disputed claims over Hadenham church, *CPL*, iii (1342–1362), 140–141, 171.

1345, 28 June, with Robert de Aylesham, q.v., recd licence from the king, at Sandwich, to el. a bp, *CPR (1343–1345)*, 486.

Roger de HAMERTON [Hamertone
occ. 1347 d. 1368/9

1347, 11 Dec., given *lit. dim.* for the order of acol., Reg. de Lisle, fo 85v.
1348, 14 June, ord subdcn, Over, *ib.*, fo 96.
1361, contributed 10s. towards the purchase of the manor and advowson of Mepal, Evans, 'Mepal', 118 (CUL EDC 1B/box 23).
1363/4, *socius* of the cellarer, CUL EDC 5/2/18.
1368/9, d., and the sacrist sent 5s. to the almoner, CUL EDC 5/10/16.

Robert HAMOND [Hamonde
occ. 1528/9 occ. 1539

1539, 15 Nov., subprior, *L and P Henry VIII*, xiv, pt. 2, no 542.
1528/9, student at Cambridge, with John Ward, q.v., and together they recd £7 11s. 8d., from the treasurer, CUL Add. Ms 2957, fo 80.
1532/3, student with John Skelsyn, q.v., and recd support from the treasurer and from the chamberlain, CUL EDC 5/13/-, CUL Add. Ms 2957, fo 34.
[?1534/5], student, who with John Skelsyn, q.v., recd £8 13s. 4d., from the treasurer. His room at Cambridge needed hinges and other materials for the repair of doors and windows, for which the treasurer pd 20d., CUL EDC 5/13/-, CUL Add. Ms 2957, fo 81.
1535/6, one of three students who recd support from the sacrist, CUL EDC 5/10/33; see also Thomas Wilberton, William Wisbech.
1534, 8 Sept., 17th in order on the visitation certificate, Reg. Goodrich, fo 90v.
1539, 18 Nov., assigned a pension of £13 6s. 8d., p.a., *L and P Henry VIII*, xiv, pt. 2, no 542.
[1541, 10 Sept., apptd canon of the 7th prebend in the new foundation, *Fasti 1541–1857*, vii, 26].

William HAND [Hande
occ. 1534 occ. 1539

1534, 8 Sept., 31st in order on the visitation certificate, Reg. Goodrich, fo 90v; he was one of ten not styled *dominus* and therefore recently adm. and not yet in major orders.
1539, 18 Nov., assigned a pension of £6 p.a., *L and P Henry VIII*, xiv, pt. 2, no 542.

Robert HARTE
d. 1516/17

1516/17, one of eight who d., and the sacrist gave 5s. to the almoner for each, CUL EDC 5/10/44.

Thomas de HASTYNG
occ. 1344 d. 1346

1344, 3 Apr., ord subdcn, bp's chapel, Downham, Reg. Montacute, fo 116v.
1345, 21 May, ord pr., Linton, *ib.*, fo 119v.
1346, c. 26 Dec., d., and the chamberlain sent 5s. to the almoner, CUL EDC 5/3/7.

John de HATFELD [Hatfyld, Hathfeld, Hattefeld
occ. 1371/2, d. 1431/2

1389/90, described as former steward of the prior's hospice, CUL EDC 5/13/8.
1396/7, 1398/9, treasurer, CUL EDC 5/13/10, 5/6/14.
1402/3, steward of the prior's hospice, CUL EDC 5/12/2.
1403, 30 Oct., apptd chamberlain, Reg. Fordham, fo 196.
1403/4, 1405/6, 1407/8, 1409/10, 1416/17, chamberlain, CUL EDC 5/3/25–29.
1420/1, 1423/4, *custos* of the Lady chapel, CUL Add. Ms 2957, fos 58v, 59.
1371/2, student at Cambridge, with Thomas Dounham, q.v., and the precentor contributed 8½d., to their maintenance for three quarters of the yr, CUL EDC 5/9/6, CUL Add. Ms 2957, fo 45.
1379, 37th in order on the clerical poll tax list and pd 3s. 4d., PRO E179/23/1.
1401, 14 Sept., 15th on the metropolitan visitation certificate, Reg. Fordham, fo 131.
1403/4, visited Hauxton [Hawkston], CUL EDC 5/3/25.
1405/6, visited Hauxton [Hawkston] for a holiday [*spaciant'*] and also went to Cambridge, CUL EDC 5/3/26.
1409/10, pd three visits to Hauxton [Hawkston] to supervise the work on the rectory; he also visited Waltham, CUL EDC 5/3/28.
1431/2, d., and the chamberlain sent 5s. to the almoner, CUL Add. Ms 2957, fo 30.

William de HATHFIELD
occ. c. 1363/4

c. 1363–1364, prior: preceded John de Bukton I, q.v., acc. to BL Ms Egerton 3047, fo 218v; see Alan de Walsingham.

Note: if Walsingham res. c. July 1363 he might have been prior for about a yr, but if Walsingham d. in May 1364 he would have had only a bare three months in office.

HAYARDSTON
see Agarston

HAYLISHAM
see Aylesham

John HELGAY [Helgey, Helgeye
occ. 1457 occ. 1462

1457, 17 Dec., ord acol., bp's chapel, Downham, Reg. Gray, fo 204v.
1458, 23 Dec., ord subdcn, bp's chapel, Downham, *ib.*, fo 205.

1459, 19 May, ord dcn, bp's chapel, Downham, *ib.*, fo 206ᵛ.
1462, 3 Apr., ord pr., Downham, *ib.*, fo 210.

John HELVYNGTON [Elewyngton, Helweton, Helwyngton
occ. 1420 d. 1443/4

1420, 21 Dec., ord pr., St Mary's church, [? Ely], Reg. Fordham, fo 108.

1434/5, granator, PRO SC6/1257/5.
1436/7, treasurer, PRO SC6/1257/6.

1439/40, *socius* of the sacrist, CUL Add. Ms 2956, fo 168.

1443/4, d., and the chamberlain gave 5s. to the almoner, CUL EDC 5/3/33, CUL Add. Ms 2957, fo 31.

Alan de HEMMINGESTONE [Hemingston, Hemminggeston, Hemmyngestone
occ. 1302 d. 1316

1316, 14 June, almoner, BL Add. Ms 41612, fo 38ᵛ.

1302, Apr./Oct., prob. went to the curia with the bp el., Robert de Orford, q.v., to appeal vs the abp's refusal to confirm the chapter's choice. While there he wrote an informative letter to the prior of Gloucester College, Oxford, *Reg. Sed. Vac.* (Worcester), 31–32 (where the name has been transcribed as Adam).
1310, 10 Feb., with John de Saunford and Stephen de Swaffham II, q.v., recd licence from the king to el. a bp, *CPR (1307–1313)*, 208.
1310, 2 Mar., chosen by the prior and chapter as one of seven *compromissorii* in the el. of a bp, BL Add. Ms 41612, fo 50ᵛ; this was the second set of *compromissorii* as the first had failed to agree; see John de Ketene.
1310, 11 Mar., with Amys de Mordone, q.v., apptd by the prior and chapter to inform the abp of their choice of John de Ketene, q.v., BL Add. Ms 41612 fo 53, and see *Reg. abp Winchelsey*, 1114–1116. The same two proctors also went to the king to obtain his assent to the el., BL Add. Ms 41612, fo 53.
1316, 1 June, with Simon de Westone, q.v., recd licence from the king to el. a bp, *CPR (1313–1317)*, 465; they had been sent on 26 May, BL Add. Ms 41612, fo 37ᵛ; on 14 June the two were sent to obtain the consent of the bp el. and present him to the abp, *ib.*, fo 38ᵛ, and on 25 June, he and John de Crauden, q.v., went to obtain the abp's confirmation, *ib.*, fo 40–40ᵛ.
1316, between 14 June and 29 Sept., d. (one of ten who d. in the yr 1315/16); the chamberlain gave 5s. to the almoner, CUL Add. Ms 2957, fo 19.

John de HEMMINGESTONE [Hemmisgiston
occ. 1273 d. 1288

1273–1288, prior: el. after 27 Dec. 1273; d. c. 9 Nov. 1288, *Fasti*, ii, 49.

1280, 17 Nov., in a letter to the bp, abp Pecham ordered him to stop the prior from advocating the use of a shortened form of the monastic office that had been approved by the Black Monk Chapter, *Epist. Pecham*, 150–151.
1281, 8 Oct., ill and sent Clement de Thetford, q.v., as his proctor to rec. absolution from excommunication for irregularities that had occurred over payment of a tenth for the Holy Land, CUL EDC 1B/112.
1283, 26 Aug., with John de Ely I, q.v., and others, accused of breaking into houses and taking goods at Bergham, Suffolk, *CPR (1281–1292)*, 99.
1285, at his visitation abp Pecham removed all the major obedientiaries except for the prior, *Chron. Oxenedes*, 264.
1287, 8 Sept., wrote to his brethren, following a request from the precentor and almoner, giving permission for the monks to have three nights outside the precincts after *minutio*, (transcribed and translated in) J. Willis Clark, ed., *The Observances in use at the Augustinian Priory of S. Giles and S. Andrew at Barnwell, Cambridgeshire*, Cambridge, 1897, lxv.
[1288], 9 Nov., obit occ. in BL Ms Cotton Vespasian A.vi, fo 130ᵛ and in BL Add. Ms 33381, fo 12.

The new refectory was built during his priorate, Bentham, *Hist. Ely*, 218.

Robert de HEMMINGSTON
occ. [c. 1270]

[c. 1270], almoner, Liber M, 569 (and 1B/517).
[c. 1270], named as recipient in a charter granting land to the almonry, for which he pd 40s., *ib.*

HENRY
occ. c. 1129 occ. 1134

c. 1129–1133, prior: res. before 5 Jan. 1134, *Fasti*, ii, 48, *HRH*, 45.

1134, 5 Jan., former prior and witness to an inventory of the treasury ordered by bp Nigel, *Liber Elien.*, 288.

HERBERT [Herebertus
occ. 1134

1134, 5 Jan., witness to an inventory of the treasury ordered by bp Nigel, *Liber Elien.*, 289.

HERPYNGHAM
see Erpingham

Thomas HETHE [Hith, Hithe, Hyth, Hythe
occ. 1515 d. 1516/17

1515, 15/16 Apr., 27th in order on the *sed. vac.* visitation certificate, Reg. abp Warham, ii, fo 277.
1516, 22 Mar., 21st in order in the chapter which chose 29 Mar. as the date for the el. of a prior, Reg. West, fo 55.
1516/17, *socius* of the sacrist and one of eight who d., CUL EDC 5/10/44; this yr he recd 10s. *pro orologio custod' et attend'*, *ib.*

Walter de HILDERCLE [Hildircle, Hyldircle, Hyldurcle, Hynderkle
occ. 1307 d. 1335/6

1307, Mar./Sept., granator, CUL EDC 5/4/1.
1325/6, treasurer, CUL EDC 5/13/1.
1320/1, Apr. to Apr., *socius* of the chamberlain, CUL Add. Ms 2957, fo 19.
1327/8, pd a visit to Lakenheath, CUL EDC 7/15/acct.
1335/6, d., and the chamberlain sent 5s. to the almoner, CUL Add. Ms 2957, fo 22.

William HILLARD
occ. c. 1418 × 1425

c. 1418 × 1425, was defamed by unknown persons who had accused him of intoxicating some of the monks and writing libels vs the prior, Edmund Walsingham, q.v. The latter ordered that the offenders be found and brought to justice, Reg. Walsingham, nos 33, 34.

Ralph de HINTON [Hyniton, Hynton, Hyntone
occ. 1328/9 occ. 1348/9

1328/9, hostiller, CUL EDC 5/5/1.
1335/6, prob., steward of the prior's hospice, or chaplain to the prior, CUL EDC 5/13/7 and CUL Add. Ms 2957, fo 71; see below.
1348/9, almoner, CUL Add. Ms 2957, fo 25.
1339/40, recd 3s. for *linea tela* from the chamberlain, CUL Add. Ms 2957, fo 22.
1344, 18 Oct., one of four monks cited to appear before the pope for arresting the proctor of the rector of Hadenham while he was in the chapter house publishing papal letters during a dispute over claims to Hadenham church, *CPL*, iii (1342–1362), 140–141, 171.
1344/5, *socius* of the cellarer, CUL EDC 5/2/10 and CUL Add. Ms 2957, fo 2ᵛ.
1348/9, Sept. to June, recd 30s. from the chamberlain for the six brethren who had d., CUL EDC 5/13/7, CUL Add. Ms 2957, fo 25.
1348 or 1349, 9 Feb., one of several monks who witnessed an agreement settling transgressions in Lakenheath and other places, Liber M, 628.

HITHE
see Hethe

William HOLM [Holme
occ. 1457 occ. 1500

1457, 17 Dec., ord acol., bp's chapel, Downham, Reg. Gray, fo 204ᵛ.
1458, 23 Dec., ord subdcn, bp's chapel, Downham, *ib.*, fo 205.
1459, 22 Dec., ord dcn, bp's chapel, Downham, *ib.*, fo 207ᵛ.
1463, 9 Apr., ord pr., bp's [*magna*] chapel, Downham, *ib.*, fo 210ᵛ.
1469/70, treasurer, CUL EDC 5/13/-, CUL Add. Ms 2957, fo 73.
1459, ill during the summer, CUL EDC 5/7/1 (infirmarer acct).
1500, 30 Oct., 11th to be examined at the visitation by the commissary of the prior of Christ Church, Canterbury, (*sed. vac.* both Ely and Canterbury). He reported *omnia bene*, Canterbury Reg. R., fo 70ᵛ.

Peter de HORNYNGSEYE [Horniggeseye, Horningeseye
occ. 1310 d. 1320/1

1310, 2 Mar., named as one of seven *compromissorii* in the el. of a bp, BL Add. Ms 41612, fo 50ᵛ; this was the second set of *compromissorii* as the first had failed to agree; see Adam de Neuton, John de Ketene.
1319, 13 July, one of the senior monks [*senes*] who formed an arbitration committee in the *contentio* over the authority of the subprior, John de Crishale I, q.v., Lambeth Ms 448, fos 97ᵛ–98.
1320/1, d., and the chamberlain and precentor both sent 5s. to the almoner, CUL Add. Ms 2957, fos 20, 42.

William HORNYNGSEYE [Hornsey, Hornyngsey
occ. 1454 d. 1463/4

1454, 15 June, ord dcn, place not stated, Reg. Bourgchier, fo 48.
1458, 23 Dec., ord pr., bp's chapel, Downham, Reg. Gray, fo 205.
1463/4, d., CUL EDC 5/9/7a.

HOROLD
see Robert Iselham

William de HOVEDEN [Hovedene, Huvden
occ. 1319 d. 1334/5

1319, 13 July, third prior, Lambeth Ms 448, fos 97ᵛ–98.
1323, 20 Aug., subprior, BL Add. Ms 41612, fo 61.
1325, 29 Sept., cellarer, CUL EDC 5/13/*status prioratus*, CUL Add. Ms 2957, fo 66.
1319, 13 July, as third prior was responsible for a *contentio* over the authority of the subprior,

John de Crishale I, q.v., by issuing an exeat licence to two monks in the belief that the subprior was absent. The latter denounced him and called for ecclesiastical censures, but on the return of the prior, John de Fresingfeld, q.v., Hoveden was excused and the subprior's authority in this area confirmed, Lambeth Ms 448, fos 97v–98. See John de Chesterton and Richard de Spalding.

1323, 20 Aug., with John de Conington, q.v., apptd proctor to treat with bp Ketene's executors, BL Add. Ms 41612, fo 63.

1334/5, d., and the sacrist pd 5s. to the almoner and 1s. to the bellringer, Chapman, *Sacrist Rolls*, ii, 71 (CUL EDC 5/10/6).

HUGH
occ. c. 1203 × 1208

c. 1203 × 1208, prior: occ. between Jan. 1203 and May 1207/May 1208, *Fasti*, ii, 49, *HRH*, 46.

William de HUNTEDON [?Huntingdon
d. 1291/2

1291/2, d., Chapman, *Sacrist Rolls*, ii, 5 (CUL EDC 5/10/1).

HUVDEN
see Hoveden

HYLDIRCLE, Hyldurcle
see Hildercle

HYNITON, Hynton(e)
see Hinton

HYTHE
see Hethe

Walter de IKELYNGHAM [Iklyngham
occ. 1325 d. 1344/5

[1330s], described on the cellarer's kitchen acct as *cum priore*, possibly as chaplain, CUL EDC 5/2/35.

1325, 2 June, with Nicholas de Copmanford, q.v., responsible for collecting tithes and other offerings at Witcham, BL Add. Ms 41612, fo 75.

1330/2, 1333/8, *socius* of the chamberlain, CUL Add. Ms 2957, fos 21, 22, CUL EDC 5/3/1–4.

1344/5, d.; the chamberlain gave the almoner 5s., and the almoner pd the brief bearer *ad sotular'*, CUL Add. Ms 2957, fos 24, 11.

Ralph de IKELYNTON [Iklyngton
occ. 1352

1352, 24 Mar., ord acol., Swavesey, Reg. de Lisle, fo 98.

IKESWORTH
see Ixworth

John INGRAM
see John Ely VIII

Henry ISELHAM
occ. 1497/8 occ. 1500

1500, 30 Oct., prob. precentor; see below.

1497/8, a monk named Iselham was *socius* of the pittancer, CUL EDC 5/8/-.

1500, 30 Oct., at the visitation by the commissary of the prior of Christ Church, Canterbury (*sed. vac.* both Ely and Canterbury), his absence was referred to by William Whitefote, q.v. The latter complained that divine worship was not being properly performed *propter absenciam domini* Henry, who was prob. precentor, Canterbury Reg. R, fo 70.

Note: this may be Henry Succurman, q.v.

John ISELHAM [Islam
occ. 1400 d. 1423/4

1400, 13 Mar., recd first tonsure and ord as acol., Doddington, Reg. Fordham, fo 240.

1400, 18 Dec., ord subdcn, bp's chapel, Downham, *ib.*, fo 241.

1402, 11 Mar., ord dcn, bp's chapel, Downham, *ib.*, fo 241v.

1403, 9 June, ord pr., bp's chapel, Downham, *ib.*, fo 243.

1419/21, steward of the prior's hospice, CUL EDC 7/15/acct, 5/2/30.

1401, 14 Sept., 37th in order on the metropolitan visitation certificate, Reg. Fordham, fo 131.

1419/20, pd a visit to Lakenheath, CUL EDC 7/15/acct.

1423/4, d., and the precentor and the treasurer both sent 5s. to the almoner, CUL Add. Ms 2957, fo 47, CUL EDC 5/13/12.

Robert ISELHAM [Isleham *alias* Horold
occ. 1355 occ. 1369

1355, 31 May, was 'made a monk', *Cal. Inquis. P.M.*, xii, no 388.

He was the son of Walter Horold who gave testimony on 22 Nov. 1369 that he remembered his son being 'made a monk' at Ely on 31 May 1355, at which time he was fourteen, PRO C135/211/14 (calendared in the printed text above).

Roger de ISELHAM [Isilham, Islam]
occ. 1335/6 occ. 1360/1

1335/6, pittancer, CUL EDC 5/13/7.

1339/40, Mar. to Mar., 1341/2, Mar. to Mar., 1343, Mar./Dec., chamberlain, CUL Add. Ms 2957, fo 23.

1350/3, cellarer, CUL EDC 5/2/11–14.

1335/6, gave 38s. 4d., to the prior, John de Crauden, q.v., whose horses had been destroyed in a fire, CUL EDC 5/13/7.

1338, Apr./1339, recd 3s. from the chamberlain, *pro linea tela*, CUL Add. Ms 2957, fo 22.
1359/61, *socius* of the cellarer, CUL EDC 5/2/15, 16.

Thomas de ISELHAM [Islam, Yselham
occ. 1389 occ. ?1402/3

1389, 18 Feb., one of three whose prof. the prior was comm. to rec., Reg. Fordham, fo 5v.
1389, 12 June, ord acol., Doddington, *ib.*, fo 230.
1389, 18 Sept., ord subdcn, Doddington, *ib.*, fo 230v.
1390, 18 Dec., ord dcn, bp's chapel, Downham, *ib.*, fo 231.
1393, 31 May, ord pr., bp's [*maior*] chapel, Downham, *ib.*, fo 234.
1402/3, former steward of the prior's hospice, CUL EDC 5/12/2.

IXENYNGIS, Ixing, Ixnyng(e)
see Exnyng

I G[eoffrey] de IXWORTH [senior, Ijkesworth, Ixeworth
occ. 1318/19 d. 1328/9

1318/19, July to July, as G. senior, he contributed 15s. towards the cost of a 'jocal' argent . . . pro oleo sancte Marie imponend' ', CUL Add. Ms 2957, fo 50.
1328/9, d., and the chamberlain gave 5s. to the almoner, CUL Add. Ms 2957, fo 20.

Note: all the other entries between 1318/19 and 1328/9 cannot be assigned as they could apply to either monk by this name; they have been arbitrarily placed under Geoffrey de Ixworth II below.

II Geoffrey de IXWORTH [Ikesworth, Ixeworth, Ykisworth
occ. 1320/1 d. 1344/5

1320/1, prob. former precentor, CUL Add. Ms 2957, fo 42; see below.
1325/6, (or 1326/7), 1327/9, granator, CUL EDC 5/4/2–5.
1320/1, his debt [?as precentor] of 20s. to the almoner and treasurer was pd by the precentor, CUL Add. Ms 2957, fo 42.
1327/8, visited Lakenheath, CUL EDC 7/15/acct.
1344/5, d., and the almoner pd the brief bearer *ad sotular'*, while the chamberlain gave 5s. to the almoner, CUL Add. Ms 2957, fos 11, 24.

See note above under G. de Ixworth I.

John de IXWORTH [Ixeworth
occ. 1320/1 occ. 1340/1

1320/4, 1326/7, pd visits to Lakenheath, CUL EDC 7/15/accts.
1340/1, Mar. to Mar., name occ. on the cellarer's acct, CUL EDC 5/2/7.

Richard de IXWORTH [Ixeworth
occ. 1335/6 occ. 1361

1335/6, his nephews recd 10s. from the treasurer, *ad scolam*, CUL Add. Ms 2957, fo 71.
1361, contributed 10s. towards the purchase of the manor and advowson of Mepal, Evans, 'Mepal', 118 (CUL EDC 1B/box 23).

Robert de IXWORTH [Ikesworth, Yxeworth
occ. 1344/5 d. 1367/8

1344, 3 Apr., ord subdcn, bp's chapel, Downham, Reg. Montacute, fo 116v.
1345, 21 May, ord pr., Linton, *ib.*, fo 119v.
1361, contributed 10s. towards the purchase of the manor and advowson of Mepal, Evans, 'Mepal', 118 (CUL EDC 1B/box 23).
1367/8, d., CUL EDC 5/3/16.

William de IXWORTH
see Thorp

John de JERNEMUTH [Gernmutha
occ. 1327/8 occ. 1339/40

1332/3, former treasurer, CUL EDC 5/13/6.
1327/8, with John de Ely II, q.v., visited Lakenheath, CUL EDC 7/15/acct.
1334, Apr./Sept., 1335, *socius* of the cellarer, CUL Add. Ms 2957, fo 1, CUL EDC 5/2/2.
1339/40, Sept. to Mar., with Simon de Chatteris, q.v., recd 12d. *pro generali suo* from the cellarer; they were prob. absent from the house, CUL EDC 5/2/6.

I JOHN
occ. [1109 × 1131]

[1109 × 1131], responsible for the construction of a causeway from Soham to Ely, *temp.* bp Hervey, *Liber Elien.*, 266.

Described as 'natura, verbo, et vultu simplicissimus' who, to the amazement of everyone, built the causeway, *ib.*

II JOHN
see Strateshete

III JOHN
occ. 1302

1302, 14 Apr., subsacrist, *CPL*, i, (1198–1304), 604.
1302, 14 Apr., one of the seven *compromissorii* in the el. of a bp [Robert de Orford, q.v.], *ib.*

IV JOHN
n.d.

n.d., subprior, named in a grant in Bergham, Liber M, 388.

JOHN [Cantor
n.d.

n.d., 12 Jan., obit occ. in Cambridge, Trinity College Ms 1105, fo k1v.

Stephen de KENTEFORD
occ. 1337/8

1337, 16 Sept., granted *lit. dim.*, for the order of pr., Reg. Montacute, fo 96.
1338, 19 Sept., ord pr., St Mary's church, Ely, *ib.*, fo 102.

John de KETENE
occ. 1310

1310, before 2 Mar., almoner, BL Add. Ms 41612, fo 53.

1310, 2 Mar., el. bp by the prior and chapter, *per viam compromissi*, by the second set of *compromissorii* as the first set had failed to agree; see Robert de Swaffham, BL Add. Ms 41612, fo 50v. Concerning the el. see *Reg. abp Winchelsey*, 1114–1116; the abp did not give his confirmation until 10 July, *ib.* See also Amys de Mordone.

Roger de KYRKEHAM
occ. 1233

1233, 11 Sept., witness to an agreement over tithes, Liber M, 319.

Gilbert LAKYNGHETH [Lakingheth, Lakynghethe, Lakynghithe, Lakynheth
occ. 1453/4 occ. 1485/6

1453/4; 1457/61; 1465/6, precentor, CUL EDC 5/9/7; CUL Add. Ms 2957, fos 48, 49; CUL EDC 5/9/8; see William Wotton.
1467/8, prob. former *custos* of the Lady chapel, CUL EDC 5/7/11.
1468/71, 1472/3; 1473/5; 1476/7; 1478/9, 1483/4, 1485/6; granator, CUL EDC 5/4/42–44, 5/4/- (unnumbered); 5/4/45; 5/13/16; 5/4/46–48.

John LAKYNGHETH [Lakynghith, Lakynghithe
occ. 1466 occ. 1473

1466, 5 Apr., recd the tonsure and ord acol., bp's palace chapel, Ely, Reg. Gray, fo 211.
1467, 14 Mar., ord subdcn, bp's palace chapel, Ely, *ib.*, fo 211v.
1473, 17 Apr., ord pr., bp's [*magna*] chapel, Downham, *ib.*, fo 215.

Reginald LAKYNGHETH [Lakenhith, Lakynghithe, Lekynheth
occ. 1488 occ. 1504

1488, 5 Apr., ord subdcn, Ely cathedral, Reg. Alcock, fo 224v.
1490, 10 Apr., ord dcn, Ely cathedral, *ib.*, fo 228.
1492, 21 Apr., ord pr., Ely cathedral, *ib.*, fo 231v.
1502, 7 Feb., 1504, 13 Feb., *senescallus terrarum*, Liber B, nos 381, 386, CUL Add. Ms 2950, fos 84, 85.
1502, 7 Feb., with Richard Swaffham, q.v., and the chancellor of the diocese apptd proctors for convocation, Liber B, no 381, CUL Add. Ms 2950, fos 84, 85.
1504, 13 Feb., with the chancellor, apptd proctors for convocation, Liber B, no 386, CUL Add. Ms 2950, fo 85.

Richard LAKYNGHETH [Lakingheth, Lakynghethe, Lakynghith
occ. c. 1379 d. 1417/18

1399/1400, former *custos* of the Lady chapel, CUL Add. Ms 2957, fo 58.
1379, 34th in order on the clerical poll tax list and pd 3s. 4d., PRO E179/23/1.
1381/2, reported as ill by the cellarer, CUL EDC 5/2/37.
1384/5, 1394/5, *socius* of the almoner, CUL EDC 5/1/11, CUL Add. Ms 2957, fo 13.
1401, 14 Sept., 12th on the metropolitan visitation certificate, Reg. Fordham, fo 131.
1417/18, d., and the chamberlain sent 5s. to the almoner, CUL EDC 5/3/30, CUL Add. Ms 2957, fo 30.

Robert LAKYNGHETH [Lakynghithe
occ. 1419

1419, 10 June, recd the tonsure and ord acol., bp's chapel, Downham, Reg. Fordham, fo 272.
1419, 23 Sept., ord subdcn, bp's chapel, Downham, *ib.*, fo 272v.

Thomas LAKYNGHETH [Lakenheth, Lakynghyth, Lakynhyth
occ. 1509/10 d. 1516/17

1509/10, *socius* of the sacrist, CUL EDC 5/10/43.
1515, 15/16 Apr., 17th in order on the *sed. vac.* visitation certificate, Reg. abp Warham, ii, fo 277.
1516, 22 Mar., 13th in the chapter which chose 29 Mar. as the date for the el. of a prior, Reg. West, fo 55.
1516/17, one of eight who d., and the sacrist sent 5s. for each to the almoner, CUL EDC 5/10/44.

John de LANGELEY [Langele, Langle, Langlee
occ. 1379/80 d. 1396/7

1379/81, *senescallus* [*terrarum*], CUL EDC 7/3/1, 7/15/acct.
1388, 1 July, the bp comm. his official to appt him chamberlain, to succ. Peter de Stapleford, q.v., Reg. Arundel, fo 62v.
1388, July/1391, chamberlain, CUL EDC 5/3/21–23, CUL Add. Ms 2957, fo 36.
1392, 9 Oct., the bp issued a comm. to remove him from the office of chamberlain and make him cellarer, to succ. Robert de Sutton, q.v., Reg. Fordham, fo 178v.
1396/7, described as *quondam* cellarer, CUL EDC 5/13/10.

1379, 21st in order on the clerical poll tax list and pd 3s. 4d., PRO E179/23/1.
1379/80, pd visits to Winston for supervisory purposes, and to Sutton where he held the court and view of frankpledge and added 14s. 6d., to the reeve's acct there, CUL EDC 7/17/acct, 7/3/1.
1380/1, visited Lakenheath, CUL EDC 7/15/acct. On 12 Feb. 1381 he and the prior were accused of seizing the beasts of a villein at Sutton, *CPR (1377–1381)*, 599.
1396/7, d., and the chamberlain sent 5s. to the almoner, CUL Add. Ms 2957, fo 37.

In 1387/8, his brother came to stay as a guest, CUL EDC 5/5/5.

Henry LANGHAM [*alias* Ely
occ. 1400 occ. 1424/5

1400, 13 Mar., ord acol., Doddington, Reg. Fordham, fo 240 (as Henry Ely).
1400, 18 Dec., ord subdcn, bp's chapel, Downham, *ib.*, fo 241 (as Henry Ely).
1401, 24 Sept., ord dcn, Downham, *ib.*, fo 241ᵛ, as Henry Langham, q.v.
1402, 11 Mar., ord pr., bp's chapel, Downham, *ib.*, fo 242 (as Henry Ely).
1414/15, treasurer, CUL EDC 5/6/19.
1418/19, to 22 June, *custos* of the Lady chapel, and succ. by Thomas Ramesey I, q.v., CUL Add. Ms 2957, fo 58.
1424/5, treasurer, CUL EDC 5/4/26.

1401, 14 Sept., 36th in order on the metropolitan visitation certificate, Reg. Fordham, fo 131.
1414/15, pd a visit to Melton, CUL EDC 7/16/29 acct.

LAURENCE
see Denver, Steynton

John de LAVENHAM
occ. 1374 occ. 1379

1374, 27 May, ord pr., London, St Paul's cathedral, Reg. Arundel, fo 115.

1379, 32nd in order on the clerical poll tax list and pd 3s. 4d., PRO E179/23/1.

John de LAXFELD [Laxfelde
occ. 1337/8

1337, 16 Sept., subdcn, obtained *lit. dim.* for dcn's orders, Reg. Montacute, fo 96.
1338, 19 Sept., ord dcn, St Mary's church, Ely, *ib.*, fo 101ᵛ.

LEKYNHETH
see Lakyngheth

LENN(E)
see Lynn

LETTON
see Leyghton

Robert de LEVERINGTON [Leverton
occ. [c. 1247] d. 1271

1261–1271, prior: occ. Jan. 1261; occ. 1 Jan. 1271; d. before 23 Sept., 1271, *Fasti*, ii, 49; see below.
[1241 × 1254], witnessed a charter of bp Hugh [de Northwold], *temp.* prior Walter, concerning the chantry on the green, Liber M, 188 (c. 1247 acc. to S.J.A. Evans). Also, *temp.* Hugh bp, he sat in the bp's temporal court as one of the justices in eyre, Bentham, *Hist. Ely*, 216. See Walter II, prior.
Note: if the ref. is to bp Hugh [de Balsham] q.v., the date cannot be earlier than 1257 nor later than 1259.
1254, 9 Sept., with Robert de Orford and John de Swaffham I, q.v., recd royal licence to el. a bp, *CPR (1247–1258)*, 328.
1256, 9 Nov., with Martin and Richard de Newmarket, q.v., recd, at Windsor, royal licence to el. a bp, *ib.*, 530, Liber M, 118–119.
1271, d.; his obit occ. on 12 Sept., in BL Cotton Vespasian A.vi, fo 130ᵛ.

Thomas LEVERYNGTON [*alias* Tuk'
occ. 1515/16 occ. 1520/1

1520/1, subprior and *[custos] communis thesaurarie*, CUL EDC 5/13/-.

1515, 15/16 Apr., 33rd in order on the *sed. vac.* visitation certificate, Reg. abp Warham, ii, fo 277, as Tuk'.
1516, 22 Mar., 28th in the chapter which chose 29 Mar. as the date for the el. of a prior, Reg. West, fo 55ᵛ.

William de LEYGHTON [Letton
occ. 1229

1229, 10 Jan., chamberlain, *CPR (1225–1232)*, 234–235.
[1229 × 1254], sacrist, *temp.* bp Hugh de Northwold, BL Add. Ms 9822, fo 26ᵛ.

1229, 10 Jan., with Martin, q.v., recd licence from the king to el. a bp, *CPR (1225–1232)*, 234–235.
[1229 × 1254], as sacrist was inducted into a church appropriated by bp Northwold, BL Add. Ms 9822, fo 26ᵛ.

I JOHN DE LINCOLN
see John de Ely IV

II John LINCOLN [Lyncoln
occ. 1514/15 d. 1526/7

1514/15, recd 13s. 4d., from the *custos* of the Lady chapel for celebrating masses for the soul of John Pelham, CUL Add. Ms 2957, fo 64.
1515, 15/16 Apr., 11th in order on the *sed. vac.* visitation certificate, Reg. abp Warham, ii, fo 277.
1516, 22 Mar., 8th in the chapter which chose 29 Mar. as the date for the el. of a prior, Reg. West, fo 55.

1516/17, described as *vestiarius* by the sacrist and was engaged in making communion hosts, CUL EDC 5/10/44.
1526/7, d., and both the chamberlain and treasurer sent 5s. to the almoner, CUL Add. Ms 2957, fo 34, CUL EDC 5/13/19, CUL Add. Ms 2957, fo 79.

Thomas de LINCOLN [Lyncoln
occ. 1341 occ. 1357/8

1341, 24 Mar., ord acol., Willingham, Reg. Montacute, fo 106v.
1342, 16 Mar., ord subdcn, Willingham, *ib.*, fo 108.
1343, 29 Mar., ord dcn, Willingham, *ib.*, fo 111.
1355/7, prob. *senescallus terrarum*, CUL EDC 7/17/acct, 7/15/acct; see below.
1347/8, Sept. to June, student [at Cambridge], with John de Sautre, q.v.; together they recd 46s. from the chamberlain for 'calig', pedul', botis yemalibus et estival', tunic', linea tela, staminis, stragulis et robis' and in addition a contribution of 2s. 3½d., based on the rate of 1d. in the £, CUL EDC 5/3/10, CUL Add. Ms 2957, fo 24.
1355/6, recd rents and payments from Winston, CUL EDC 7/17/acct.
1356/7, visited Kingston, Lakenheath and Melton for *liberatio denariorum*, CUL EDC 7/14c/22 acct, 7/15/acct, 7/16/14 acct.
1357/8, *socius* of the sacrist, Chapman, *Sacrist Rolls*, ii, 172, (CUL EDC 5/10/14).

William LINCOLN
occ. 1498

1498, 14 Apr., ord acol., Ely cathedral, Reg. Alcock, fo 246v.

William de LIVERMERE [Lyvermere
occ. 1310 d. 1315/16

1310, 28 Feb., one of seven *compromissorii* named by the prior and chapter to el. a bp, BL Add. Ms 41612, fo 49v. In this case it appears that they failed to agree and seven others were chosen; see John de Ketene.
[1315/16 or before], name occ. on an acct of the cellarer and on one of the steward of the prior's hospice, CUL EDC 5/2/33a, 5/12/-.
1315/16, one of ten monks who d. this yr and the chamberlain sent 5s. for each to the almoner, CUL Add. Ms 2957, fo 19.

John LOLLEWORTH [Lolworth
occ. 1454 d. 1486/7

1454, 15 June, ord dcn, place not stated, Reg. Bourgchier, fo 48.
1454, 21 Sept., ord pr., Lady chapel, Ely cathedral, Reg. Gray, fo 201.
1486/7, d., and the chamberlain sent 5s. to the almoner, CUL Add. Ms 2957, fo 32.

John de LONDON
occ. 1281

1281, 11 Oct., one of the monks who were absolved from irregularities that had occurred over payment of a tenth for the Holy Land, CUL EDC 1B/113.

Robert de LONGCHAMP [Longfild
occ. 1194 occ. 1197

1194–1197, prior: occ. 3 June 1194; el. abbot of St Mary's, York, 17 Mar. 1197, *Fasti*, ii, 48, *HRH*, 46.

He had prob. been a monk of Caen and was the brother of William de Longchamp, bp of Ely 1189/97, *ib.*, both refs.

William de LOPHAM
occ. 1355/6 occ. 1361

1356, Nov./Dec., 1359/July 1360, *custos* of the Lady chapel, CUL Add. Ms 2957, fo 53.
1360/1, July to July, precentor, CUL Add. Ms 2957, fo 44, CUL EDC 5/9/3.
1355/6, Jan. to Jan., accompanied the precentor, William de Riston, q.v., to Impington to meet the parishioners, make an inventory and grant leases, CUL Add. Ms 2957, fo 44.
1360/1, went to Impington to oversee the inventory; he also went to Pampisford [Pampesworth] and Littlebury to arrange for the sale of tithes, and he twice sent a boy to find out when the bp of Norwich was holding ordinations, *ib.*, fo 44.

LYNCOLN
see Lincoln

Henry de LYNNE [Lynnya
occ. 1382 d. 1406/7

1382, 31 May, ord acol., bp's chapel, Downham, Reg. Arundel, fo 129v.
1382, 20 Sept., ord subdcn, bp's chapel, Downham, *ib.*, fo 129v.
1383, 16 May, ord dcn, bp's chapel, Downham, *ib.*, fo 130v.
1386, 22 Sept., ord pr., bp's chapel, Downham, *ib.*, fo 134.
1396/7, *socius* of the almoner, CUL Add. Ms 2957, fo 13.
1401, 14 Sept., 24th in order on the metropolitan visitation certificate, Reg. Fordham, fo 131.
1406/7, d., and the chamberlain and sacrist both sent 5s. to the almoner, CUL EDC 5/3/26, 5/10/25.

John LYNNE [Lenne
occ. 1450

1450, 26 Oct., granted a licence to visit Rome on condition that he return without delay, Reg. Bourgchier, fo 24v.

Richard LYNNE
occ. 1459 occ. 1487/8

1460, 10 Apr., recd an apptment as chamberlain from the bp personally in chapter, Reg. Gray, fo 46v; 1460, 13 Apr./Sept., chamberlain, CUL Add. Ms 2957, fo 32.
1465/6, almoner, CUL EDC 5/13/-.
1467/8, and prob. 1468/9, *custos* of the Lady chapel, CUL EDC 5/7/11, 12.
1469/70; 1473/4, 1475/7; 1478, 19 July, almoner, CUL EDC 5/13/-, but see William Makeroo; CUL EDC 5/1/14, 5/13–, 5/13/16; Lambeth Ms 448, fo 113.
1459, ill in the infirmary during the summer, CUL EDC 5/7/1 (infirmarer acct).
1469/70, recd 6s. 8d. from the treasurer, for celebrating chantry masses for the soul of Philip Lyle, CUL EDC 5/13/-.
1478, 19 July, accompanied John Soham I, q.v., subprior and other monks, to the bp to discuss arrangements for the pension of the prior, Henry Peterborough, q.v., Lambeth Ms 448, fo 113.
1487/8, 'stager' for whom the sacrist bought oil for the lamp *ad tria altaria*, CUL EDC 5/10/40, CUL Add. Ms 2956, fo 173.

Robert LYNNE
occ. 1473

1473, 17 Apr., ord subdcn, bp's [*magna*] chapel, Downham, Reg. Gray fo 215.

William LYNNE [Lenn, Lenne
occ. 1466/9

1466, 5 Apr., recd the tonsure and ord acol., bp's palace chapel, Ely, Reg. Gray, fo 211.
1469, 1 Apr., ord subdcn, bp's chapel, Downham, *ib.*, fo 213v.

Adam de LYNSTED [Lynstede
occ. 1342 occ. 1361

1342, 16 Mar., ord subdcn, Willingham, Reg. Montacute, fo 108.
1343, 29 Mar., ord pr., Willingham, *ib.*, fo 111.
1349, 9 July, recd his apptment as sacrist from the vicar general, in person in chapter, succ. Philip de Dalling, q.v., Reg. de Lisle, fo 22v.
1349/51, 1352/3, sacrist, Chapman, *Sacrist Rolls*, ii, 140–159, (CUL EDC 5/10/11, 12).
1354/5, possibly feretrar as he turned over to the sacrist the receipts from the shrine of St Etheldreda, Chapman, *Sacrist Rolls*, ii, 160 (CUL EDC 5/10/13).
1356/7, *senescallus* [?*hospicii*], CUL EDC 7/15/acct, 7/16 acct; see John de St Ives who was *senescallus terrarum.*
1359/61, *senescallus* [?*terrarum*], CUL EDC 7/16/15, 16; but see John de St Ives.
[1349], 29 Sept., apptd penitentiary, with Walter de Walsoken, q.v., by the prior, Alan de Walsingham, q.v., acting as vicar general, *nullis casibus exceptis*, Reg. de Lisle, fo 29.
1349/50, attended synods in Oct. and May/June [at Barnwell] and the fairs at St Ives, Reach and Stourbridge, Chapman *Sacrist Rolls*, ii, 145 (CUL EDC 5/10/11).
1352/3, attended both synods, went to several fairs and to Boston and [Saffron] Walden on business, Chapman, *Sacrist Rolls*, ii, 157 (CUL EDC 5/10/12).
1356/7, pd 50s. to the *custos* of the Lady chapel for a debt of the preceding yr [?when he had been custos], CUL Add. Ms 2957, fo 53. This yr he sent 22 rabbits from Lakenheath to the prior in London and 134 to Ely to the prior's hospice; he also pd three visits to Melton, CUL EDC 7/15/acct, 7/16/acct.
1359/60, as *senescallus* [*terrarum*] visited Melton 'pro statu manerii supervid[endo et vis[u fac[iendo', and his expenses were 14s. 3d., CUL EDC 7/16/acct.
1360/1, visited Melton and his expenses were 12s. 8d., CUL EDC 7/16/acct.
1361, contributed £24 11d. *de graciis* towards the purchase of the manor and the advowson of Mepal, Evans, 'Mepal', 118 (CUL EDC 1B/box 23). (This must have been raised by the sale of stock or grain, or possibly a loan arranged in his capacity as *senescallus terrarum.*)

Note: is this Adam de Wisbech, q.v.?

LYVERMERE
see Livermere

M.
occ. 1233

1233, 11 Sept., precentor and witness to an agreement over tithes, Liber M, 319.

Note: this may be Martin, q.v.

MACRO, MACROW
see Makeroo

Henry MADYNGLE B.Th/D.Th. or B.CnL/D.Cn.L [Maddynglee
occ. 1404 d. 1421/2

1404, 19 Nov., one of six whose prof. the prior was comm. to rec., Reg. Fordham, fo 198v.
1404, 20 Dec., ord acol., bp's chapel, Downham, *ib.*, fo 244.
1405, 14 Mar., ord subdcn, bp's chapel, Downham, *ib.*, fo 244.
1405, 18 Apr., ord dcn, Ely cathedral, *ib.*, fo 244v.
1408, 18 Apr., ord pr., bp's chapel, Downham, *ib.*, fo 247.
1419/20, *senescallus terrarum*, CUL EDC 7/15/acct, 5/2/30.
1409/10, student at Cambridge, CUL EDC 5/2/29.
1415, 8 May, at Cambridge and licensed to preach in any church [?in Cambridge]

appropriated to Ely cathedral, *Reg. abp Chichele*, iv, 126–127. See Edmund Walsingham, John Stunteney and John Yaxham.

1416/17, with Edmund Walsingham, q.v. incepted, and the chamberlain contributed 3s. 4d., CUL EDC 5/3/29.

1414, 8 Jan., apptd by the sacrist, Thomas Elyngham, q.v., as proctor, with Edmund Walsingham, q.v., and others in a dispute with the bp, CUL Add. Ms 2950, fos 66–69.

1419/20, visited Kingston and Lakenheath, CUL EDC 7/14c/39 acct, 7/15/acct.

1420, 10 Oct., apptd proctor, with Thomas Elyngham, q.v. in a lawsuit, Reg. Walsingham, no 35.

1421/2, d., and the chamberlain sent 5s. to the almoner, CUL Add. Ms 2957, fo 30.

Richard de MADYNGLE [Maddinglegh, Maddyngley, Madingle, Madynglee

occ. 1376 d. 1422/3

1376, 29 Mar., ord acol., St Mary's church outside Trumpington gate [Cambridge], Reg. Arundel, fo 117.

1376, 20 Sept., ord subdcn, Lady chapel, Ely cathedral, *ib.*, fo 119.

1376, 20 Dec., ord dcn, Lady chapel, Ely cathedral, *ib.*, fo 119v.

1377, 14 Mar., ord pr., Lady chapel, Ely cathedral, *ib.*, fo 121.

1398, 20 Apr., recd an apptment to the office of cellarer, Reg. Fordham, fo 189v, but see Thomas de Downham I who was named to replace him on 26 June [1398], *ib.*, fo 189v.

1398/9, almoner, CUL Add. Ms 2957, fo 13.

1379, 42nd in order on the clerical poll tax list and pd 3s. 4d., PRO E179/23/1.

1401, 14 Sept., 18th on the metropolitan visitation certificate, Reg. Fordham, fo 131.

1422/3, d., and the precentor sent 5s. to the almoner, CUL Add. Ms 2957, fo 47.

In 1387/8, his mother was a guest [in the guest hall], CUL EDC 5/5/5.

William MAKEROO [Macro, Macrow, Makero, Makerowe

occ. 1447 occ. 1500

1447, 4 Mar., ord subdcn, church of St John the Baptist, Ely, Reg. Bourgchier, fo 47.

1448, 21 Dec., ord dcn, no place recorded, *ib.*, fo 47v.

1462/6, granator, CUL EDC 5/4/40,and 41, 5/4/54.

1466/7, 1469/70, almoner, PRO SC6/1257/9, CUL EDC 5/13/-.

[1470], 11 Sept., a comm. was issued for his apptment as chamberlain, Reg. Gray, fo 80v.

1473/5, 1476/7, 1482/3, chamberlain, CUL EDC 5/13/-, 5/13/16, CUL Add. Ms 2957, fo 32; he prob. had been previously cellarer, CUL EDC 5/13/- (1473/4).

1491/2, feretrar, CUL EDC 5/11/9.

1473/4, recd 6s. 8d., from the treasurer for celebrating chantry masses, CUL EDC 5/13/-.

1500, 30 Oct., *stagiarius*, and 3rd to be examined at the *sed. vac.* visitation by the commissary of the prior of Christ Church, Canterbury (*sed. vac.* both Ely and Canterbury). He deposed that the Vine gate entrance to the precincts was no longer locked but was used as a public thoroughfare, Canterbury Reg. R., fo 70.

Thomas de ?MA. . .LE [?Manhale

occ. 1330/1

1330/1, almoner, CUL EDC 5/1/4.

Robert de MALKSHAM [Mawsham

occ. 1291

1291, 29 Oct., appeared in London at St Bartholmew's as proctor on behalf of the prior and chapter, Oxford, Bod. Ms Ashmole 801, fo 136–136v.

[Robert de MARHAM

occ. 1342

1342, obtained a licence to visit the papal curia, acc. to S.J.A. Evans, but the ref. is missing and has not been found.]

MARTIN

occ. 1229 occ. 1256

1229, 10 Jan., almoner, *CPR (1225–1232)*, 234–235.

1242/4, M. sacrist, CUL Add. Ms 2950, fos 2, 3 (BL Ms Cotton Tiberius B ii, fo 246v).

[1241 × 1259], subprior, Liber M, 188.

Note: if this ref. is to bp Hugh [de Balsham], q.v., the dates should be 1257 × 1259.

1256, 9 Nov., sacrist, *CPR (1247–1258)*, 530, and Liber M, 118.

1229, 10 Jan., with William de Leyghton, q.v., recd royal licence to el. a bp, *CPR (1225–1232)*, 234–235.

[1241 × 1259], witnessed a charter of bp Hugh [Northwold], *temp.* prior Walter, q.v., Liber M, 188.

Note: if the ref. is to bp Hugh [de Balsham], the dates would be [1257 × 1259].

1256, 9 Nov., with Robert de Leverington and Richard de Newmarket, q.v., recd licence to el. a bp from the king at Windsor, *CPR (1247–1258)*, 530, Liber M, 118–119.

n.d., 13 May, the obit of a Martin occ. in a kalendar in BL Ms Cotton Vespasian, A.vi, fo 133v, BL Add. Ms 33381, fo 12, and CUL Add. Ms 2950, fo 13; see Clement and Walter III.

MARTIN, Martyn

see William Wells II

John MASSYNGHAM
occ. 1515/17

1515, 15/16 Apr., 22nd in order on the *sed. vac.* visitation certificate, Reg. abp Warham, ii, fo 277.
1516, 22 Mar., 17th in the chapter which chose 29 Mar. as the date for the el. of a prior, Reg. West, fo 55.
1516/17, one of eight who d., and the sacrist sent 5s. for each to the almoner, CUL EDC 5/10/44.

Thomas MAUNDES [Mawnds, Mawnse, Mounds and possibly Maune, Maunt'
occ. 1534 occ. 1539

1534, 8 Sept., 24th in order on the visitation certificate, Reg. Goodrich, fo 90v; he was one of ten not styled *dominus* and therefore recently adm. and not yet in major orders.
1539, 18 Nov., assigned a pension of £5 6s. 8d., p.a., *L and P Henry VIII*, xiv, pt. 2, no 542.

Thomas MEER
occ. 1341

1341, 24 Mar., ord dcn, Willingham, Reg. Montacute, fo 107v.

Thomas MELBOURNE
occ. 1515 occ. 1534

1515, 15/16 Apr., 25th in order on the *sed. vac.* visitation certificate, Reg. abp Warham, ii, fo 277.
1516, 22 Mar., absent when cited to the el. of a prior but present at the el. on 29 Mar., Reg. West, fos 55v, 56.
1519/20, *socius* of the chamberlain from whom he recd 10s., CUL EDC 5/3/[34].
1534, 8 Sept., 8th in order on the visitation certificate, Reg. Goodrich, fo 90v.

MELRE
see John Salmon

[MENDHAM
occ. 1478/9

1478/9, rewarded for singing, on the feast of the translation of St Etheldreda, by the *custos* of the Lady chapel, CUL EDC 5/7/13, CUL Add. Ms 2957, fo 63.

Note: This may not have been a monk.]

Robert de MENDHAM [Mendam
occ. 1345 occ. 1362/3

1345, 21 May, ord acol., Linton, Reg. Montacute, fo 116v.
1346, 1 Apr., ord subdcn, Ely cathedral, Reg. de Lisle, fo 92v.
1346, 23 Dec., ord dcn, bp's chapel, Downham, *ib.*, fo 94v.
1347, 17 Mar., ord pr., St Mary's church, Ely, *ib.*, fo 95v.
1352/3, July to July, former hostiller, CUL EDC 5/5/2.
1361/2, treasurer, CUL EDC 7/15/acct; also named as treasurer on an undated acct of the *custos roserie*, CUL EDC 5/6/23.
1361/2, pd a visit to Lakenheath, CUL EDC 7/15/acct.
1362/3, visited Kingston for *liberatio denariorum*, CUL EDC 7/14c/acct.

Thomas de MENDHAM
occ. 1379 d. 1398

1394, 5 May, the bp issued a comm. to remove him from the office of cellarer, Reg. Fordham, fo 183v, but this may have been rescinded; see below.
1396/7, and until c. 20 Apr. 1398, cellarer, CUL EDC 5/13/10, 5/4/19, Reg. Fordham, fo 189v; see Richard Madyngle who succ. him on his d.

1379, 38th in order on the clerical poll tax list and pd 3s. 4d., PRO E179/23/1.
1394/5, visited Lakenheath, CUL EDC 7/15/acct.
1398, d. just before 20 Apr.; the chamberlain sent 5s. to the almoner *pro errogatione*, CUL EDC 5/3/24, CUL Add. Ms 2957, fo 37.

Amys de MORDONE [Amice, Amysius de Morden, Mourdone, Comes de Mordon
occ. before 1310 d. 1320/1

1310, before, prob. chaplain to the bp; see below.
1315, July 17, 1318/20, Apr., chamberlain, CUL Add. Ms 2957, fos 18, 19.

1310, 2 Mar., chosen by the prior and chapter as one of seven *compromissorii* in the el. of a bp, BL Add. Ms 41612, fo 50v; this was the second set of *compromissorii* as the first had failed to agree; see John de Ketene. On 11 Mar., he and Alan de Hemmingstone, q.v., were sent by the prior and chapter to inform both king and abp of their choice, BL Add. Ms 41612, fos 50v, 53.
1310, 10 July, with Alan de Hemmingstone, q.v., obtained from the abp confirmation of the el., *Reg. abp Winchelsey*, 1114–1116.
1310, with Robert de Brundisch, q.v., was declared contumacious and under sentence of excommunication because they had withheld a ring which had belonged to the late bp Orford and which ought to have gone to Canterbury, *Reg. abp Winchelsey*, 1071–1072. He appeared before the abp and explained that the bp had given it to adorn the shrine of St Edburga while he had been living in the episcopal household as *domesticus* and *commensalis* of the late bp, *ib.*
1316, 25 June, one of three *instructores* at the el. of a bp, BL Add. Ms 41612, fo 40 and sent by the prior and chapter to the abp to seek confirmation of the el., *ib.*; he was named here as

Comes de Mordon. See John de Conington and John de Orewell.

1319, 13 July, one of the senior monks [*senes*] who formed an arbitration committee in the *contentio* concerning the authority of the subprior, John de Crishale I, q.v., Lambeth Ms 448, fos 97v–98.

1320/1, recd 5s. 6d., from the chamberlain [for some of his clothing], also *pro pelic'* 3s., *pro habitu* 5s., CUL Add. Ms 2957, fo 20.

1320/1, d., and the chamberlain and precentor both sent 5s. to the almoner, CUL Add. Ms 2957, fos 20, 42.

John/William MORTON
occ. 1498/9

1498, 14 Apr., ord acol., Ely cathedral, Reg. Alcock, fo 246v, (as John).

1499, 21 Sept., ord subdcn, Downham, *ib.*, fo 250v, (as William).

Note: it is prob. that only one monk is intended here and that the confusion of Christian names is a slip of the scribal pen.

MOUNDS
see Maundes

Edmund MOUNTENEYE
occ. 1404 d. 1438/9

1404, 19 Nov., one of six whose prof. the prior was comm. to rec., Reg. Fordham, fo 198v.

1404, 20 Dec., ord acol., bp's chapel, Downham, *ib.*, fo 244.

1405, 14 Mar., ord subdcn, bp's chapel, Downham, *ib.*, fo 244.

1405, 18 Apr., ord dcn, Ely cathedral, *ib.*, fo 244v.

1406, 10 Apr., ord pr., Ely cathedral, *ib.*, fo 245.

1426/9, precentor, CUL EDC 5/11/5.

1438/9, d., and the sacrist sent 5s. to the almoner, CUL EDC 5/10/32.

John MUNDEN [Mundene
occ. 1453 d. 1487/8

1453, 31 Mar., ord pr., bp's [*parva*] chapel, Downham, Reg. Bourgchier, fo 47v.

1464/5, 1466/7, chamberlain, CUL Add. Ms 2957, fo 32, PRO SC6/1257/9.

[1467], 11 Oct., a comm. was issued for his removal from the office of chamberlain, Reg. Gray, fo 70; he was, however, named on the 1466/7 acct as above.

1487/8, d., and the sacrist gave 5s. to the almoner, CUL EDC 5/10.40.

N.
occ. 1233

1233, 11 Sept., pittancer and witness to an agreement over tithes, Liber M, 319.

Note: see Nicholas, Nigel.

NEEDE
see Weede

Adam de NEUTON [Neutone
occ. 1310 occ. 1327/8

1327/8, possibly steward of the prior's hospice, CUL EDC 7/15/acct.

1310, 2 Mar., chosen by the prior and chapter as one of seven *compromissorii* in the el. of a bp, BL Add. Ms 41612, fo 51v; this was the second set of electors chosen, as the first had failed to agree; however, his place seems to have been taken by Peter de Hornyngseye. See John de Ketene.

1327/8, visited Lakenheath, CUL EDC 7/15/acct.

Richard de NEWMARKET [Novo Mercato
occ. 1252 occ. 1260

1260, 1 Aug., *senescallus forinsecus*, CUL EDC 1B/138.

[1260 × 1271], *temp.* Robert [de Leverington], q.v., prior, infirmarer, Liber M, 417.

1252, 1 July, as proctor for the prior and convent obtained a receipt in London from a merchant of Siena for the sum of 22 marks, CUL EDC 1B/102.

1254, 29 July, obtained a receipt for 18 marks from a Florentine merchant in part payment of a larger sum, CUL EDC 1B/103.

1256, Jan., acted as attorney for the prior and convent in a case before the royal justices in Cambridge, Liber M, 118–119.

1256, 9 Nov., with Robert de Leverington and Martin, q.v., recd licence at Windsor from the king to el. a bp, *CPR (1247–1258)*, 530, Liber M, 118–119.

[1260 × 1271], as infirmarer, he was the recipient of the grant of a messuage in Ely for which he pd 40s., Liber M, 417.

1260, 1 Aug., named as proctor for the prior and charged with contracting a loan of up to £50, CUL EDC 1B/138.

Thomas NEX
see Soham

NICHOLAS
occ. [1261 × 1271]

[1261 × 1271], almoner, *temp.* prior Robert de Leverington, q.v., Liber M, 487.

[1261 × 1271], made many purchases of land, Liber M, 487, 489, 508; see also *Alm. Cart.*, fos 13v, 20, 20v, 21, 21v, 26v, 27v, 28v, 29, 30.

He was the son of Alexander, Liber M, 493.

NIGEL [Nigellus
n.d.

n.d., 25 June, obit occ. in Cambridge, Trinity College Ms 1105, fo k6v.

John de NORWICH [Norwico
occ. 1347/8

1347, 11 Dec., obtained *lit. dim.*, for the order of acol., Reg. de Lisle, fo 85v.
1348, 14 June, ord subdcn, Over, *ib.*, fo 96.

Nicholas de NORWICH [Norwico
occ. 1344/5

1344, 3 Apr., ord subdcn, bp's chapel, Downham, Reg. Montacute, fo 116v.
1345, 21 May, ord pr., Linton, *ib.*, fo 119v.

I Peter de NORWICH [Norwico, Norwyco
occ. 1337 d. 1368/9

1337, 16 Sept., subdcn, obtained *lit. dim.*, for the order of dcn, Reg. Montacute, fo 96.
1338, 19 Sept., ord dcn, St Mary's church, Ely, *ib.*, fo 101v.
1341, 24 Mar., ord pr., Willingham, *ib.*, fo 107v.
1347, July/1348, chamberlain, CUL EDC 5/3/9, 10.
1350/1, granator, CUL EDC 5/4/10.
1351/2, 1353/4, *custos roserie*, CUL EDC 5/6/2, 3.
1368/9, d., and the sacrist sent 5s. to the almoner, CUL EDC 5/10/16.

II Peter de NORWICH, ?D.Th. [Northwyco, Norwych, Norwyco
occ. 1364/5 d. 1403/4

1379/80, 1381, Sept./Dec., *custos* of the Lady chapel, CUL EDC 5/7/6, 7.
1383/4, granator, CUL EDC 5/4/17.
1390, 19 July, chancellor of the chapter, BL Add. Ms 9822, fo 73.

1364/5, a monk named de Northwyco, described as *inceptor* in theology, recd a contribution of 3½d. from the granator, CUL EDC 5/4/13. The sum pd was based on ?1d. in the £, and there can be no doubt that the ref. is to a monk of the house. See the note below Roger de Norwich I.
1373/4, recd 7s. from the precentor *pro labore suo hoc anno* [?lector], CUL EDC 5/3/20, CUL Add. Ms 2957, fo 45.
1377/8, *socius* of the almoner, CUL Add. Ms 2957, fo 12.
1379, 31st in order on the clerical poll tax list and pd 3s. 4d., PRO E179/23/1.
1390, 19 July, chancellor of the chapter with Robert de Sutton II, q.v., and they lent some charters concerning the bpric to bp Fordham, BL Add. Ms 9822, fo 73.
1401, 14 Sept., 11th in order on the metropolitan visitation certificate, Reg. Fordham, fo 131.
1403/4, d., and the chamberlain sent 5s. to the almoner, CUL EDC 5/3/25, CUL Add. Ms 2957, fo 29.

Name in Cambridge, St John's College, Ms 23, Richard Rolle (15th c.); on fo iv, *liber dompni*—, and on the last folio the arms of Robert [Steward] Wells, q.v.

I Roger de NORWICH, D.Th. [Norwyco
occ. 1364/5 occ. 1392/3

1376, 22 Nov., a comm. was issued to remove him from the office of subprior, Reg. Arundel, fo 20v.
1377/8, almoner, CUL EDC 5/1/10, CUL Add. Ms 2957, fo 12.
[1390], 2 June, a comm. was issued for his apptment as sacrist, Reg. Fordham, fo 12; he succ. William Powcher, q.v.
1392/3, sacrist, CUL EDC 5/10/23, CUL Add. Ms 2956, fo 163.

1384/5, student at Cambridge, to whose inception the chamberlain contributed 13s. 4d., and an additional 3s. 4d., in procurations laid down by the Black Monk Chapter at the rate of ½d. in the £ for this yr and the following two years, CUL Add. Ms 2957, fo 35. The cellarer contributed 20s. and also 10s. in *exhennia*, *ib.*, fo 5. For the inception feast 260 rabbits [rabett'] were sent up from Lakenheath, CUL EDC 7/15/acct.
1385/6, recd 2s. 3d., from the chamberlain and 4d. from the granator *pro regencia sua*, CUL Add. Ms 2957, fo 35, CUL EDC 5/4/18.
1388, 3 Nov., described as *sacre pagine professor*, Reg. Fordham, fo 4.
1389/90, [still at Cambridge and] *legens in theologia*, with 36s. 7d., maintenance from the treasurer, CUL EDC 5/13/8.

1364/5, recd 4s. from the *custos* of the Lady chapel *pro informatione juniorum monachorum*, CUL Add. Ms 2957, fo 54.
1379, 16th in order on the clerical poll tax list and pd 3s. 4d., PRO E179/23/1.
1388, 3 Nov., apptd penitentiary within the diocese, Reg. Fordham, fo 4.
1388/9, recd 6½d. from the chamberlain *pro instructione monachorum*, CUL EDC 5/3/21, CUL Add. Ms 2957, fo 36.
1389/90, recd 13d. from the chamberlain *pro instructione monachorum*, CUL EDC 5/3/23; he was also named this yr as proctor for the Black Monk Chapter meeting in Northampton [on 4 July 1390], CUL EDC 5/13/8.
1392, 13 Oct., authorized, with others, to deal with the purgation of a criminous clerk, Reg. Fordham, fo 178v.

Note: there is possibly some confusion between the contemporary Peters de Norwich and Roger I above, but it seems clear, because of the twenty yr gap between inception dates, that both Peter II and Roger I obtained doctorates in theology.

II Roger NORWICH
occ. 1515/16

1515, 15/16 Apr., 20th in order on the *sed. vac.* visitation certificate, Reg. abp Warham, ii, fo 277.

1516, 22 Mar., 23rd in the chapter which chose 29 Mar. as the date for the el. of a prior, Reg. West, fo 55.

Note: the apparent discrepancy in the order of seniority is due to the absence of three monks senior to him at the 1515 visitation.

Matthew NOTYNGHAM
occ. 1414/15 d. 1439/40

1414/15, steward of the prior's hospice, CUL EDC 5/6/19.
1418/19, June, former *custos* of the Lady chapel, CUL Add. Ms 2957, fo 59.
1425, 11 Apr., subprior, Liber B, no 230, CUL Add. Ms 2950, fo 73.
1425, 11 Apr., with the chapter he apptd proctors for convocation, Liber B, no 230.
1439/40, d., and the chamberlain gave 5s. in alms to the almoner, CUL Add. Ms. 2957, fo 31.

NOVO MERCATO
see Newmarket

Thomas de ?OCCLIE [?Occlre, Ocolie
occ. 1281

1281, 11 Oct., one of the monks who were absolved from irregularities that had occurred over payment of a tenth for the Holy Land, CUL EDC 1B/113.

William de OFFORD
d. 1331/2

1331/2, d., and the chamberlain gave 5s. to the almoner, CUL Add. Ms 2957, fo 21.

John de OREWELL
occ. 1310 occ. 1339/40

1325, 29 Sept., named as former *custos roserie*, CUL EDC 5/13/*status prioratus*, CUL Add. Ms 2957, fo 66.
1321, Aug./1323, Aug., and prob. 1323 ?Aug./1324, Aug., pittancer, CUL EDC 5/8/6–8, 5/13/-.
1332/3, 1335/6, 1337/8, treasurer, CUL EDC 5/13/6, 7, 5/2/2, 3a.
1310, 2 Mar., chosen by the prior and chapter as one of seven *compromissorii* in the el. of a bp, BL Add. Ms 41612, fo 50ᵛ; this was the second set of *compromissorii* as the first had failed to agree; see John de Ketene.
1316, 25 June, one of three *instructores* at the el. of a bp, BL Add. Ms 41612, fo 40, and sent by the prior and chapter to the abp as proctors to seek confirmation of the el., *ib.*
1323/4, recd 40s. p.a., from the treasurer *pro vinea fodiend'* CUL EDC 5/13/-.
1332/3, visited Kingston for *liberatio denariorum*, CUL EDC 7/14c/acct.
1339/40, name occ. on the cellarer's acct, as with Roger de Calthorp, q.v., he recd 12d. *pro generali suo*, prob. because they were absent from the house, CUL EDC 5/2/6.

Thomas OREWELL [Orwell, Orwelle
occ. 1404 occ. 1438/9

1404, 19 Nov., one of six whose prof. the prior was comm. to rec., Reg. Fordham, fo 198ᵛ.
1404, 20 Dec., ord acol., bp's chapel, Downham, *ib.*, fo 244.
1405, 14 Mar., ord subdcn, bp's chapel, Downham, *ib.*, fo 244.
1405, 18 Apr., ord dcn, Ely cathedral, *ib.*, fo 244ᵛ.
1405, 13 June, ord pr., bp's chapel, Downham, *ib.*, fo 244ᵛ.

1437/9, treasurer, CUL EDC 7/15/acct, 7/16/acct.

1425, 10 May, granted a papal indult to choose his own confessor, *CPL*, vii (1417–1431), 416.
1437/8, pd a visit to Lakenheath, CUL EDC 7/15/acct.
1438/9, visited Melton, CUL EDC 7/16/acct.

Robert de ORFORD [Oreford
occ. 1254 occ. 1302

1299–1302, prior: el. after 26 Oct. 1299; el. bp 14 Apr. 1302 and consecrated Oct., *Fasti*, ii, 50.

1268, 1 Oct., chamberlain, CUL EDC 1B/107.
1298, 24 Apr., subprior, *CPR (1292–1301)*, 345.
1254, 9 Sept., with Robert de Leverington and John de Swaffham I, q.v., recd licence from the king to el. a bp, *CPR (1247–1258)*, 328.
1268, 1 Oct., with John de St Faith, q.v., proctor for the prior and convent in London where they obtained a receipt from Florentine merchants for a pension owed to Cardinal Jordan, CUL EDC 1B/107.
1298, 24 Apr., with Richard de Braunford and William de Brigham, q.v., recd licence from the king to el. a bp, *CPR (1292–1301)*, 345.
1302, 14 Apr., el. bp by seven *compromissorii* named by the chapter. The abp objected on the grounds of insufficient learning; and the bp el. took his appeal to Rome in person, where he resigned and was then, on 29 Oct., provided by the pope, Lambeth Ms 448, fos 47–49, *CPL*, i, (1198–1304), 604. See Alan de Hemmingestone who prob. accompanied him and gave a vivid record of the proceedings in a letter. See also Graham, 'Ely Vacancies', 67–72.
1301/2, the sacrist contributed £66 13s. 4d., towards the prior's appeal, *in auxilium*, in support of his el. as bp, Chapman, *Sacrist Rolls*, ii, 16, (CUL EDC 5/10/2). The record of this el. has been entered in *Cart. Ramsey*, iii, 30–38.

ORWELL(E)
see Orewell

OUNDLE
see Undele

Thomas OUTLAW
see Wilberton

Thomas OVER [Overi, *alias* Braby
occ. 1534 occ. 1539

1534, 8 Sept., 25th in order on the visitation certificate, Reg. Goodrich, fo 90ᵛ; he was one of ten not styled *dominus* and therefore recently adm. and not yet in major orders.
1535/6, named as *vestiarius*, on the sacrist's acct, CUL EDC 5/10/-.
1539, 18 Nov., assigned a pension of 53s. 4d. p.a., *L and P Henry VIII*, xiv, pt. 2, no 542.

Richard de OVERE
d. 1318/19

1318/19, d. and the chamberlain gave 5s. to the almoner, CUL Add. Ms 2957, fo 19.

Richard OVERTON
occ. 1510/11 occ. 1534

1517/18, 1523/4, precentor, CUL Add. Ms 2957, fo 49, CUL EDC 5/9/10.
1510/11, student [at Cambridge] for one quarter of the yr, and the pittancer contributed 42s. 8d., to his pension and that of Robert Wells, q.v., CUL EDC 5/8/17.
1515, 15/16 Apr., 15th in order on the *sed. vac.* visitation certificate, Reg. abp Warham, ii, fo 277.
1516, 22 Mar., absent from the house when cited to the el. of a prior, but present at the el. on 29 Mar., Reg. West, fos 55ᵛ, 56.
1534, 8 Sept., 5th on the visitation certificate, Reg. Goodrich, fo 90ᵛ.

Thomas OWTWELL
occ. 1454

1454, 21 Sept., ord dcn, Lady chapel, Ely cathedral, Reg. Gray, fo 201.

Thomas OXBOROUGH [Oxborugh, Oxborow, Oxboragh
occ. 1509/10 d. 1528/9

1509/10, granator, CUL EDC 5/4/50.
1510/11, pittancer, CUL EDC 5/8/17.
1516/17, 1519/20, sacrist, CUL EDC 5/10/44, CUL Add. Ms 2956, fo 176.
1525/9, cellarer, CUL EDC 5/13/18–20, CUL Add. Ms 2957, fos 78–80.
1510/11, went to Wisbech and Lynn with his *serviens pro pecuniis recipiend'* and also to Wisbech *pro supervidend' rectoria*, CUL EDC 5/8/17.
1515, 15/16 Apr., 13th in order on the *sed. vac.* visitation certificate, Reg. abp Warham, ii, fo 277.
1516, 22 Mar., 10th in the chapter which chose 29 Mar. as the date for the el. of a prior, Reg. West, fo 55; on 1 Apr., he, with Thomas Soham II and Robert Stunteney went to the bp for confirmation of the el., *ib.*, fo 59. This same yr he travelled by boat to Stourbridge fair, CUL EDC 5/4/50.
1528/9, d., and the chamberlain sent 5s. to the almoner, CUL Add. Ms 2957, fo 34.

John PA. . . [?illegible
d. 1515/16

1515/16, one of eight who d., and the sacrist sent 5s. for each to the almoner, CUL EDC 5/10/44.

Note: if this is John Palmer below, as seems likely, the latter's d. has been recorded.

PAATE
see Pate

John PALMER [Palmar
occ. 1495 ?d. 1516

1495, 14 Mar., ord pr., Downham, Reg. Alcock, fo 237 (as Ely).
1500, 30 Oct., chamberlain, Canterbury Reg. R., fo 70ᵛ.
1500, 30 Oct., 10th to be examined at the visitation by the commissary of the prior of Christ Church, Canterbury (*sed. vac.* both Ely and Canterbury). He reported *omnia bene* apart from the fact that the brethren were not receiving their due allowance of bread and drink in the 'Seyne hall' (where they resorted after *minutiones*) for which he blamed the subprior, William Cottenham, q.v., Canterbury Reg. R., fo 70ᵛ.
1515, 15/16 Apr., 8th in order on the *sed. vac.* visitation certificate, Reg. abp Warham, ii, fo 277.
1516, 22 Mar., absent from the house when cited to the el. of a prior, but present on 29 Mar. at the el., Reg. West, fos 55ᵛ, 56.

Note: see also John Ely XI, and John Pa. . . above.

Martin de PAPPELE [Pappole *alias* de Burgo
occ. 1354 occ. 1368/9

1354, 20 Sept., ord subdcn, bp's chapel, Doddington, Reg. de Lisle, fo 100.
1355, 19 Sept., ord dcn, Doddington church, *ib.*, fo 100ᵛ (as de Burgo).
1356, 9 Apr., ord pr., Wisbech castle chapel, *ib.*, fo 101.
1362/4, 1366/9, *socius* of the chamberlain, CUL EDC 5/3/15–17, CUL Add. Ms 2957, fo 28.

John PATE [Paate
occ. 1511/12 d. 1526

1511/12, relinquished the office of almoner, CUL EDC 1/C/7, fo 28.
1511/12, name occ. [possibly *socius*] on the chamberlain's acct, CUL Add. Ms 2957, fo 33.

1515, 15/16 Apr., 28th in order on the *sed. vac.* visitation certificate, Reg. abp Warham, ii, fo 277.
1516, 22 Mar., 22nd in the chapter which chose 29 Mar. as the date for the el. of a prior, Reg. West, fo 55.
1526, d.; the chamberlain sent 5s. to the almoner, CUL Add. Ms 2957, fo 34 (1526/7), and the treasurer made two payments for the same to the same, CUL EDC 5/13/18 and CUL Add. Ms 2957, fo 78 (1525/6), CUL EDC 5/13/19 and CUL Add. Ms 2957, fo 79 (1526/7).

PAULINUS
see Erpingham

I PETER
occ. 1134

1134, 5 Jan., one of the witnesses to an inventory of the treasury ordered by bp Nigel, *Liber Elien.*, 289.

Note: he is identified as the son of Gaufridus, *constabulus*, *ib.*

II PETER
occ. [?mid-13th c.]

[?mid-13th c.], gave land to the priory at the time of his adm.: 'dedit eis [the prior and convent] inperpetuam [*sic*] elemosinam cum seipso die qua suscepit monachatum in Elyen' Eccl[esia', Liber M, 254. It may be his father Fulco who was a clerk of bp Eustace (1198/1215), Liber M, 167, 253.

PETER
see also Reche

Henry PETERBOROUGH [Burgh, Petyrborough
occ. 1445/6 d. 1480

1462–1478, prior: held his first court at Winston on 14 June 1462, CUL EDC 7/17/court; res. 26 July 1478, *Fasti*, iv, 17.

1447/8, precentor, CUL EDC 5/9/11.
1460, Apr./Sept., cellarer, CUL Add. Ms 2957, fo 6.
1473/5, as prior he administered the office of *senescallus terrarum*, CUL EDC 5/13/-, CUL Add. Ms 2957, fo 74.

1445/6, *socius* of the hostiller, CUL EDC 5/5/8.
1447/8, went to Impington to supervise the refectory and to [Saffron] Walden 'pro scrutinio faciend' super diversis tenementis', CUL EDC 5/9/9.
1465, 9 Jan., present in the Lady chapel, with the subprior and senior monks, when the bp examined a man accused of being a *nigramanticum*, Reg. Gray, fo 133.
1466, 27 May, was personally cautioned by the bp to strive to be loved rather than feared, as the Rule required (quoting from chap. 64, 15), Evans, *Ely Chap. Ord.*, 58.
1469, 12 Feb., granted papal indult to have a confessor of his choice who was authorized to give plenary remission of sins at the hour of his d., *CPL*, xii (1458–1471), 772.
1473/4, with 20 servants he spent two wks in Suffolk in Oct.; he also visited Doddington twice in order to see the bp; he pd visits to Lakenheath, Mildenhall and Whittlesey, and at Whittlesey gave alms to the poor, CUL EDC 5/13/-.
1474/5, rode around visiting and inspecting the Suffolk manors in October; travelled to Lynn in Nov. accompanied by two monks and fourteen servants; he also went to Whittlesey in June and to Doddington to see the bp, CUL EDC 5/13/-.
1476, 20 Dec., sold a number of distant manors in Norfolk and Suffolk and bought others nearer, CUL EDC IB/176.
1478, 14 Feb., became dumb and on 24 June the bp appted John Soham I, q.v., coadjutor. On 18 July John Soham and other monks went to the bp to discuss arrangements for his pension. He res. 26 July and was granted a room in the infirmary and £40 p.a. pension for himself and his *capellanus* and servants, *Anglia Sacra*, i, 672, Lambeth Ms 448, fo 113. It is odd that on the treasurer's acct for 1476/7 he was already described as *nuper prior*, CUL EDC 5/13/16 (unless this acct should be dated 1477/8); see William Tylney.
1480, d., 10 Aug., Lambeth Ms 448, fo 113.

Note: see Henry Burgh who must be the same monk.

Peter PEYNTON [Poynton
occ. 1376 occ. 1381/2

1376, 29 Mar., ord subdcn, St Mary's church outside Trumpington gate, Cambridge, Reg. Arundel, fo 117.
1376, 20 Sept., ord dcn, Lady chapel, Ely cathedral, *ib.*, fo 119.
1380, 22 Dec., ord pr., bp's chapel, Downham, *ib.*, fo 128ᵛ.

1379, 45th in order on the clerical poll tax list and pd 3s. 4d., PRO E179/23/1.
1381/2, Dec. to Aug., reported ill [*firmus*] by the cellarer, who also sent him to Downham to speak with the bp, CUL EDC 5/2/22.
[1381/2], *socius* of the cellarer, CUL EDC 5/2/37.

William PICWORTH [Pikworth
occ. 1388/90

1388, 1 Feb., there is extant a note to the effect that he and bp Fordham had collated a copy of a charter confirmed by Richard II with the original, BL Add. Ms 9822, fo 21; a similar note is in *ib.*, fo 133.
1390, 19 July, soon after, brought back from the

bp a charter which the monks had lent him, *ib.*, fo 73; see Henry de Wyke.

PIKE
see Thomas de Thetford II

William POWCHER [Poucher ?*alias* Ely
occ. 1388 d. ?1418

1401–?1418, prior: the mandate to install him was issued on 24 Sept. 1401, Reg. abp Arundel, i, fo 495; an apptment of proctors by him, which can be dated 1416/18, was copied into CUL Add. Ms 2950, fos 69, 70; see Edmund Walsingham and below.

Note: he was prob. el. on 22 Sept., *via spiritus*; see John de St Ives.

[1390], 2 June, a comm. was issued by the bp for his removal from the office of sacrist, Reg. Fordham, fo 12; see below.

n.d., subprior, CUL EDC 5/12/-, (treasurer's acct).

1388, 7 Dec., nom. by the king as prior of Swavesey which, as an alien priory, was in the king's hands; this proved unsuccessful, *CPR (1388-1392)*, 1; see John Thornton.

[1390], 2 June, his removal from the office of sacrist was due to his el. as abbot of [Saffron] Walden, Reg. Fordham, fo 12.

1401, 22/23 Sept., during the metropolitan visitation, the prior, William Walpole, q.v., res., and Powcher, who was present, was el. *per viam inspirationis* after having been postulated by Walpole, Reg. abp Arundel, i, fos 494, 495.

1405, 25 Feb., apptd by the bp, with the chapter, as collectors of the half tenth required by the king, Reg. Fordham, fos 143^{v}, 145.

1413, 27 Jan., on his petition the pope issued a mandate to the adcn of Norwich to examine the constitutions and ordinances of Ely cathedral priory in order to eliminate those which were mutually contradictory, obscure, ambiguous or unreasonable because out of date, *CPL*, vi (1404–1415), 394, CUL Add. Ms 2947 fos 155–156 and Liber B, no 5.

1413, 19 Feb., a papal bull was issued permitting him and his successors to use the mitre, ring, staff and other pontifical insignia in the cathedral and in churches in their charge, CUL Add. Ms 2950, fo 23 and Liber B no 4.

1417, Nov./Dec., one of a number of cathedral priors who were apptd by the abp to a committee of Convocaton to look into the poverty of university graduates *Reg. abp Chichele*, iii, 37.

1417, 6 Dec., a final agreement [*laudum*] was confirmed between the bp and the prior and chapter after a costly dispute of some 17 yrs over their respective jurisdictions and privileges within the Isle, Bentham, *Hist. Ely*, 167, Appndx *27–*34, *CPR (1416–1422)*, 183–195 dated 20 Apr., where the terms of the agreement are given.

According to *Anglia Sacra*, i, 684, he built the infirmary hall in 1417; see Thomas de Elyngham.

Note: see William de Ely I which prob. provides his early career.

William POWER
occ. 1448 occ. 1478/9

[1448], 23 Mar., ord acol., Lady chapel, Ely cathedral, Reg. Bourgchier, fo 44, where the date is, surely mistakenly, 1452.

1448, 21 Dec., ord subdcn, no place recorded, *ib.*, fo 47^{v}.

1466/7, pittancer, and steward of the prior's hospice, PRO SC6/1257/9.

1459, ill during the summer, CUL EDC 5/7/1 (infirmarer acct).

1474/5, 1476/7, pd by the treasurer for celebrating [chantry] masses for the soul of Philip Lyle, CUL EDC 5/13/-, 5/13/16.

1478/9, named on the sacrist's acct because he owed money, CUL EDC 5/10/36, CUL Add. Ms 2956, fo 170.

In 1432, a Richard Power was the bp's *servitor* and *marescallus*, Liber B, no 96.

POYNTON
see Peynton

John PULHAM
occ. 1392 occ. 1427/8

1392, 19 Oct., one of three whose prof. the prior was comm. to rec., Reg. Fordham, fo 179.

1392, 21 Dec., ord acol., bp's chapel, Doddington, *ib.*, fo 233^{v}.

1393, 1 Mar., ord subdcn, bp's chapel, Doddington, *ib.*, fo 233^{v}.

1393, 31 May, ord dcn, bp's [*maior*] chapel, Downham, *ib.*, fo 234.

1394, 14 Mar., ord pr., bp's chapel, Doddington, *ib.*, fo 235.

1403/7, treasurer, CUL EDC 7/16/28 acct; 5/6/15, 16; 5/3/26; 7/17/acct.

1411/12, 1413/15, 1419/20 part yr, cellarer, CUL EDC 5/4/24, 25, CUL Add. Ms 2957, fos 5^{v}, 6.

1421/2, former chamberlain, CUL Add. Ms 2957, fo 30.

1426/8, cellarer, CUL EDC 5/4/27, 28.

1401, 14 Sept., 29th in order on the metropolitan visitation certificate, Reg. Fordham, fo 131.

[1403/4], pd a visit to Melton, CUL EDC 7/16/28.

1409/10, *socius* of the cellarer, CUL EDC 5/2/29; he visited Kingston, Lakenheath and Winston, CUL EDC 7/14c/38 acct, 7/15/acct, 7/17/acct.

PYKIS
see Thomas de Thetford II

Simon QUAVENEY [Quavenay,
occ. 1458 occ. 1500

1458, 23 Dec., ord subdcn, bp's chapel, Downham, Reg. Gray, fo 205.

1460, 8 Mar., ord pr., bp's [*magna*] chapel, Downham, *ib.*, fo 208.

1500, 30 Oct., cellarer, Canterbury Reg. R., fo 70v.

1500, 30 Oct., 12th to be examined at the visitation by the commissary of the prior of Christ Church, Canterbury (*sed. vac.* both Ely and Canterbury). He gave his *omnia bene* except for the poor service in the 'Seyne hall' of which John Palmer, q.v., had complained, and for the continued absence of the organ in the Lady chapel concerning which Thomas Drayton, q.v., had made a deposition, Canterbury Reg. R, fo 70v.

Note: see the note below Simon Stunteney I.

Laurence de QWYE
occ. 1361

1361, sold his *ciphus* for 13s. 4d., as his contribution towards the purchase of the manor and advowson of Mepal, Evans, 'Mepal', 119 (CUL EDC 1B/box 23).

I RALPH [Radulfus
occ. [1100 × 1135]

[1100 × 1135], *temp.* Henry I, before becoming a monk he had a *batellum in mare de Saham* and one of his servants was cured by St Etheldreda, *Liber Elien.*, 265.

He was the son of Colsaianus, *ib.*

II RALPH
occ. 1134 occ. [1144 × 1151]

[1134 × 1143], sacrist, *Liber Elien.*, 289, 292, 293, 294; also [in 1144 × 1151], *temp.* prior Theinbert, q.v., *ib.*, 340, 386 [*secretarius*].

[c. 1143], made or had made two *baculi*, a cope on which Guthmund, q.v., had worked and other items, *ib.*, 292, 293, 294.

1134, 5 Jan., witnessed an inventory of the treasury ordered by bp Nigel, *ib.*, 289.

III RALPH
occ. [1198 × 1204]

[1198 × 1204], apptd by the pope, with the bp of Ely and prior of Norwich, to visit Westminster Abbey to investigate a dispute, *CPL*, i (1198–1204), 133.

IV RALPH
occ. 1229 occ. 1238

?1229–1238, prior: prob. confirmed c. 25 Mar. 1229; first occ. as prior Aug. 1233; last occ. Apr./May 1238, *Fasti*, ii, 49.

V RALPH
occ. [1229 × 1254]

[1229 × 1254], sacrist, Liber M, 188.

[1229 × 1254], witnessed a charter of bp Hugh [de Northwold], *ib.*

Note: if this ref. is to the later bp Hugh [de Balsham] the dates should read 1257 × 1286.

VI RALPH
occ. 1302

1302, 14 Apr., sacrist, *Anglia Sacra*, i, 604.

1302, 14 Apr., one of the seven *compromissorii* named by the prior and chapter in the el. of a bp [Robert de Orford, q.v.], Lambeth Ms 448, fo 49 (for the date) and *CPL*, i (1198–1304), 604 (for the name).

Note:
(1) this may be Ralph de Saxmundham, q.v.
(2) some of the above Ralphs are almost certainly identical, but which?

I John de RAMESEY [senior
occ. c. 1274/5

c. 1274/5, Sept. to Oct., receiver [?treasurer] with John Schepey, q.v., Lambeth Ms 448, fo 119, CUL Add. Ms 2950, fo 10.

Note:
(1) the two monks are named as receivers of the money collected for the construction of the new refectory, *ib.*
(2) see the note below his namesake immediately below.

II John de RAMESEY [Rameseya, junior
occ. 1307 d. 1328/9

1307, Mar./ Sept., granator, CUL EDC 5/4/1.

1316, *senescallus forinsecus* and almoner, BL Add. Ms 41612, fos 26v, 27v.

1323/4, refectorer, CUL EDC 5/13/-.

1316, 19 Nov., with John de Crishale I, q.v., given by the prior and chapter custody of four of the priory churches for one yr from 2 Feb, for purposes of administration of tithes and tenths, BL Add. Ms 41612, fo 27v.

1320/4, pd visits to Lakenheath, CUL EDC 7/15/accts.

1328/9, d., and the chamberlain sent 5s. to the almoner, CUL Add. Ms 2957, fo 20.

Note: The fact that the above two monks were styled senior and junior implies that they were both members of the community at the same time.

III John RAMESEY [Ramsey
d. 1449/50

1449/50, d., and the almoner recd 5s. from both the chamberlain and the treasurer, CUL EDC 5/1/13.

I Thomas de RAMESEY [Ramsey, Ramysseye
occ. 1382 d. 1419/20

1382, 31 May, ord acol., bp's chapel, Downham, Reg. Arundel, fo 129v.
1382, 20 Sept., ord subdcn, bp's chapel, Downham, *ib.*, fo 129v.
1383, 16 May, ord dcn, bp's chapel, Downham, *ib.*, fo 130v.
1386, 22 Sept., ord pr., bp's chapel, Downham, *ib.*, fo 134.
1399/1400, 1402/3, treasurer, CUL EDC 5/4/20, 7/16/27 acct, 5/12/2.
1401, 6 Apr., a comm. was issued for his appt-ment as chamberlain to succ. Robert de Bury, q.v., Reg. Fordham, fo 192v.
1403, 30 Oct., a comm. for his removal from this office was issued, *ib.*, fo 196 and he was to be replaced by John de Hatfeld, q.v.
1405/6, granator, CUL EDC 5/4/22.
1409/10, *senescallus terrarum*, CUL EDC 7/14c/38 acct (as T. R.).
1419, 22 June/Sept., became *custos* of the Lady chapel, succ. Henry Langham, q.v., CUL Add. Ms 2957, fo 58.
1399/1400, visited Melton, CUL EDC 7/16/27 acct.
1401, 14 Sept., 23rd in order on the metropolitan visitation certificate, Reg. Fordham, fo 131.
1409/10, visited Kingston, CUL EDC 7/14c/38 acct, 7/17 acct.
1410, 13 Feb., apptd, with others, proctor to attend convocation, Liber B, no 266.
1410, 2 Nov., with John Fyncham, q.v., and others apptd general proctors, *ib.*, no 269.
1411, 16 Nov., apptd, with others, proctor for convocation, *ib.* no 274.
1419/20, d., CUL EDC 5/10/30.

In 1387/8, his father spent more than a wk in the guest hall, CUL EDC 5/5/5.

Note: see also Thomas Ramesey II below. It does seem a little surprising that Thomas Ramesey I combined the two offices of treasurer and chamberlain, and so there may be two monks by this name conflated here. If so, the entry for Thomas Ramesey II would ref. to one of them.

II Thomas de RAMESEY
occ. 1426/8

1426/8, almoner, CUL EDC 5/4/27, 28.

III Thomas de RAMESEY [Ramsey
occ. 1466 occ. 1486/7

1466, 5 Apr., ord subdcn, bp's palace chapel, Ely, Reg. Gray, fo 211.
1467, 14 Mar., ord dcn, bp's palace chapel, Ely, *ib.*, fo 211v.
1469, 1 Apr., ord pr., Downham, *ib.*, fo 214.
1486/7, chamberlain, CUL Add. Ms 2957, fo 32.
1476, 5 Feb., granted papal dispensation to rec. and retain a benefice with cure of souls, *CPL*, xiii (1471–1484), 495.

William RAMESEY
occ. 1448

1448, 21 Dec., ord subdcn, no place recorded, Reg. Bourgchier, fo 47v.

A. de RAUELE [?Ranele
d. 1315/16

1315/16, one of ten monks who d., and the chamberlain sent 5s. to the almoner for each, CUL Add. Ms 2957, fo 19.

Peter de RECHE
occ. 1298 d. 1320/1

1302, 4 Apr., subprior, *CPR (1301–1307)*, 26.
1298, 1 July, named as proctor for the subprior and some of the monks on behalf of John Salmon whom they had el. bp, and appeared before the abp at Lambeth, *Reg. abp Winchelsey*, 266.
1300, 17 Dec., with William de Clare, q.v. apptd proctors for the convent, BL Ms Egerton 3047, fo 246v.
1302, 4 Apr., with William de Clare and Stephen de Swaffham recd royal licence to el. a bp, *CPR (1301–1307)*, 26; at the el. on 14 Apr., he was named as one of the seven *compromissorii*, Lambeth Ms 448, fo 49 (for the date) and *CPL*, i (1198–1304), 604 (for the name).
1319, 13 July, one of the senior monks [*senes*] who formed an arbitration committee in the *contentio* concerning the authority of the subprior, John de Crishale I, q.v., Lambeth Ms 448, fos 97v–98.
1320/1, recd 5s. 6d., from the chamberlain *pro strag', stamin', botis estival'* etc., CUL Add. Ms 2957, fo 20.
1320/1, d., and the chamberlain sent 5s. to the almoner, *ib.*

REGINALD
occ. [1133 × 1169]

[1133 × 1169], name occ. in two deeds of gift to the priory, *temp.* bp Nigel, Oxford, Bod. Ms Ashmole 801, fo 74, 74v.
[c. 1160], there is ref. to a monk, Reginald, in a grant made to the monks by Robert II, q.v., *Anglia Sacra*, i, 628–629, *Liber Elien.*, 387–388.

John de REPYNGHALE
occ. 1346

1346, 12 July, apptd penitentiary, Reg. de Lisle, fo 87v.

RIBALDUS
occ. before 1122/3

1122/3, d. by this date when his name occ. on a mortuary roll of Savigny, Delisle, *Rouleaux des Morts*, 339.

I RICHARD
occ. [1133 × 1169] occ. 1189

c. 1177–1189, prior: prob. succeeded Salomon, q.v.; last occ. 2 Dec. 1189, *HRH*, 46, *Fasti*, ii, 48. *HRH* suggests that his priorate may have begun c. 1174, quoting *Chron. Ramsey*, 294.

1177, before this date prob. subprior, *Liber Elien.*, xlvii.

1150/51, went to the papal curia to plead the monks' case in the appeal over their right of possession of Stetchworth, *Liber Elien.*, 347–351, 405–407.

He was a monk writer/historian, *temp.* bp Nigel, [1133 × 1169], who may have been responsible for much of the Liber Eliensis, prob. during Nigel's episcopate; see *Liber Elien.*, xlvii–xlix, where the question of authorship is treated in detail. See also Gransden, *Hist. Writing*, i, 271. He is described as 'historiarum studiosissimi deserti et eloquentissimi viri', *Liber Elien.*, 284; and as 'auctor huius operis et hanc hystoriam' [i.e., the litigation over Stetchworth], *ib.*, 345, xxxviii–xxxix. His work was continued by Thomas, q.v. See also Sharpe, *Latin Writers.*

II RICHARD
occ. [1241 × 1254]

[1241 × 1254], sacrist, Liber M, 188.
n.d., pittancer, Liber M, 467, 472.

[1241 × 1254], witnessed a charter of bp Hugh [Northwold] *temp.* Walter II, prior, q.v., Liber M, 188.
n.d., acquired land in Sutton, *ib.*, 467–468, 472.

Note: it is possible that two Richards are involved here and also that the bp is the later Hugh [de Balsham], q.v., in which case the dates should be 1257 × 1259..

III RICHARD
d. 1331/2

1331/2, d., and the chamberlain sent 5s. to the almoner, CUL Add. Ms 2957, fo 21.

RICHARD
see also Braunford, Cantebrigge

RIKELING, Rikelyng
see Rykelyng

RISING
see Rysyng

William de RISTON [Ristone, Rostone, Rustone, Ryston
occ. 1347 d. 1369/70

1347, 11 Dec., recd *lit. dim.* for the order of subdcn, Reg. de Lisle, fo 85v.
1348, 14 June, ord dcn, Over, *ib.*, fo 96.

1350/1, precentor, CUL Add. Ms 2957, fo 44.
1351, July/Sept., hostiller, CUL EDC 5/5/2.
1355/6, Jan. to Jan; 1359, Jan./July, precentor, CUL Add. Ms 2957, fo 44.
1355/6, *senescallus* [?*terrarum*], CUL EDC 7/15/acct; John de St Ives, q.v., was also a *senescallus* this yr.
1368/9, 1369/70, part yr, sacrist, CUL EDC 5/10/16.

1349/51, one of two *socii* of the sacrist, CUL EDC 5/10/11.
1355/6, went to Impington to meet the parishioners, draw up an inventory and arrange leases [*terras dimittend'*] and was assisted by William de Lopham, q.v., CUL Add. Ms 2957, fo 44; this yr he also pd visits to Lakenheath and Winston, CUL EDC 7/15/acct, 7/17/acct.
1360/1, July to July, accompanied William de Lopham, now precentor, to Impington to draw up the inventory, CUL Add. Ms 2957, fo 44.
1361, contributed 20s. towards the purchase of the manor and advowson of Mepal, Evans, 'Mepal', 118 (CUL EDC 1B/box 23).
1368/9, went to Stourbridge fair, CUL EDC 5/10/16.
1369/70, d. while sacrist, and the almoner recd 5s. from each of the prior, chamberlain, precentor and sacrist, CUL Add. Ms 2957, fo 11; the chamberlain's payment is recorded on CUL EDC 5/3/18.

RISTON
see also Roston

I ROBERT
occ. before 1122/3

1122/3, d. by this date when his name occ. on a mortuary roll of Savigny, Delisle, *Rouleaux des Morts*, 339.

II ROBERT [Rodbertus
occ [c. 1160]

[c. 1160), chamberlain of the Earl of Richmond, he was clothed as a monk on his deathbed and gave the church of Denny and other gifts of land and churches to the prior and chapter, *Anglia Sacra*, i, 628–629, *Liber Elien.*, 387–388.

I ROGER
see Bergham

II ROGER
d. 1460/1

1460/1, d., and the precentor sent 5s. to the almoner, CUL Add. Ms 2957, fo 48.

Note: see Roger Swanton, Roger Wisbech II.

III ROGER
occ. 1467/8

1467/8, granator, CUL EDC 7/15/acct.

1467/8, visited Lakenheath, *ib.*

Note: This may be Roger Westminster, q.v.

John de ROSTON [?Riston
occ. 1393/4

1393/4, treasurer, in his first yr in succ. to Alan de Sutton, q.v., CUL EDC 7/15/acct.

1393/4, pd a visit to Lakenheath, *ib.*

J. RUSSELL
occ. [1291/2]

[1291/2], recd 7d. from the chamberlain, CUL Add. Ms 2957, fo 17.

John de RYKELYNG [Rikeling, Rikelyng
occ. 1337 d. 1339/40

1337, 16 Sept., dcn, given *lit. dim.* for the order of pr., Reg. Montacute, fo 96.
1338, 19 Sept., ord pr., St Mary's church, Ely, *ib.*, fo 102.

1339/40, Mar. to Mar., d., and the chamberlain gave 5s. to the almoner, CUL Add. Ms 2957, fo 23.

Robert de RYKELYNG [Rikeling, Rikelyng
occ. c. 1321 occ. 1351

1325, 29 Sept., named as [former] steward of the prior's hospice under prior John de Fresingfeld, q.v., [i.e. before 16 Feb. 1321], CUL EDC 5/13/*status prioratus*, CUL Add. Ms 2957, fos 66, 67.
1322/3, feretrar, *Anglia Sacra*, i, 645 (as Bykelyng), Lambeth Ms 448, fo 54.
1343, June/Sept., 1344/5, almoner, CUL Add. Ms 2957, fo 10, CUL EDC 5/1/6; he succ. John de Sutton I, q.v.
1351, 11 Mar., prob. subprior, Reg. de Lisle, fo 87v; this is by inference only, see below.
1322/3, sent by the sacrist to London in search of the gold and silver which had been stolen from the shrine of St Etheldreda, Chapman, *Sacrist Rolls*, ii, 31, (CUL EDC 5/10/3).
1345, 1 Dec., apptd *primarius* [penitentiary], Reg. de Lisle, fo 87v.
1348, 15 Sept., retained as general penitentiary, *ib.*, fo 88,
1351, 11 Mar., licence as penitentiary renewed, *ib.*, fo 87v (named only as subprior).

RYSTON
see Riston

Ralph de RYSYNG [Rising
occ. 1337 d. 1355/6

1337, 16 Sept., dcn, obtained *lit. dim.*, for the order of pr., Reg. Montacute, fo 96.
1338, 19 Sept., ord pr., St Mary's church, Ely, *ib.*, fo 102.

c. 1346, either a former granator or about to assume office, CUL EDC 5/4/9.
1349, July/Sept., 1351/5, *custos* of the Lady chapel, CUL Add. Ms 2957, fos 51, 52.
1341, Dec./1342, with the sacrist Nicholas de Copmanford, q.v., escorted four monks to Willingham [transcribed as Wynebrigham] for orders on 16 Mar. [1342], Chapman, *Sacrist Rolls*, ii, 120 (CUL EDC 5/10/9b).
1351, 3 July, apptd by the prior and chapter as proctor in an appropriation, BL Add. Ms 41612, fo 109.
1355/6, d., and the precentor sent 5s. to the almoner, CUL Add. Ms 2957, fo 44.

John de SAHAM
occ. 1327/30

1327, July/1330, July, almoner, CUL EDC 5/1/1–3.

Richard de SAHAM [Same
occ. 1354 ?d. 1361

1354, 20 Sept., ord subdcn, bp's chapel, Doddington, Reg. de Lisle, fo 100.
1355, 19 Sept., ord dcn, Doddington, *ib.*, fo 100v.
1356, 9 Apr., ord pr., Wisbech castle chapel, *ib.*, fo 101.

1361, ?d., his clothes [*vestibus*] were sold for 28s. 5d., and the money was given to the fund for the purchase of the manor and advowson of Mepal, Evans, 'Mepal', 119 (CUL EDC 1B/box 23).

Robert de SAHAM
occ. 1323/4 d. 1339/40

1330, c. July/Sept., treasurer, CUL EDC 5/13/6.
1323/4, with William de Bury I, q.v., carried out negotiations for the treasurer, CUL EDC 5/13/-.
1324/5, *socius* of the treasurer, CUL EDC 5/13/*status prioratus*.
1339/40, d., and the chamberlain and sacrist each sent 5s. to the almoner, CUL Add. Ms 2957, fo 23, Chapman, *Sacrist Rolls*, ii, 94, (CUL EDC 5/10/8).

SAHAM
see also Soham

Alexander de ST EDMUNDS [Sancto Edmundo]
see Bury

H. de ST EDMUNDS [Sancto Edmundo
1258/9

1258/9, chamberlain, CUL Add. Ms 2957, fo 14.

John de ST EDMUNDS [Sancto Edmundo]
see John de Bury I

John de ST FAITH [Sancta Fide
occ. 1268

1268, 1 Oct., with Robert de Orford, q.v., proctor for the prior and convent in London where they obtained a receipt from Florentine merchants for a pension owed to cardinal Jordan, CUL EDC 1B/107.

William de ST FAITH [Sancta Fide
occ. 1347/9

1347, July/1349, June, *socius* of the chamberlain, CUL EDC 5/3/9, 10, CUL Add. Ms 2957, fo 25.

John de ST IVES [Sancto Ivone
occ. 1345 occ. 1401

1345, 21 May, ord acol., Linton, Reg. Montacute, fo 116v.
1346, 1 Apr., ord [subdcn], Ely cathedral, Reg. de Lisle, fo 92v.
1346, 23 Dec., ord dcn, bp's chapel, Downham, *ib.*, fo 94v.
1347, 26 May, ord pr., Willingham, *ib.*, fo 96.
1349, 9 July, apptd chamberlain by the vicar general in person in chapter and succ. Paulinus de Erpingham, q.v., Reg. de Lisle, fo 23; 1349/50, chamberlain, CUL Add. Ms 2957, fo 25.
1355/7, *senescallus* [*terrarum*], CUL EDC 7/15/acct, 7/16/14 acct; but see William de Riston and Adam de Lynstede.
1359/60, treasurer, with John de Bukton I, q.v., CUL EDC 5/2/15.
1361/2, 1364/5, *senescallus terrarum*, CUL EDC 7/15/acct, 7/16/17 acct.
1376, 22 Nov., cellarer, prior to this date, Reg. Arundel, fo 20v.
1376, 22 Nov., apptd subprior, Reg. Arundel, fo 20v; also subprior on 1377, 10 Feb., 1378, 30 Sept., Reg. Arundel, fos 22, 27v.
1355/6, visited Lakenheath, CUL EDC 7/15/acct.
1356/7, pd several visits to Melton, CUL EDC 7/16/14 acct.
1359/61, pd visits to Melton for *liberatio denariorum*, CUL EDC 7/16/15, 16 accts.
1361, contributed 13s. 4d., towards the purchase of the manor and advowson of Mepal, Evans, 'Mepal', 118 (CUL EDC 1B/box 23).
1361/2, stayed at Lakenheath for supervisory purposes, CUL EDC 7/15/acct.
1364/5, went to Lakenheath to hold courts and *pro statu supervidend'* and charged the manorial acct 25s. 10d., CUL EDC 7/15/acct. He also visited Melton and Winston, CUL EDC 7/16/17 acct, 7/17/acct.
1374, 18 Mar., licensed to hear confessions in the diocese, Reg. Arundel, fo 1.
[1377], 10 Feb., licensed to hear confessions in the city and diocese during the bp's absence, *ib.*, fo 22.
1378, 30 Sept., with the bp's commissary and another, apptd to celebrate the synod at Barnwell, Reg. Arundel, fo 27v.
1379, 4th in order on the clerical poll tax list and pd 3s. 4d., PRO E179/23/1.
1401, 14 Sept., 3rd in order on the metropolitan visitation certificate, Reg. Fordham, fo 131.
1401, 22 Sept., was in the infirmary when, during the above visitation, prior William Walpole, q.v., res., did not take part in the el., but his consent to the el. of William Powcher, q.v., was recorded in the presence of the prior of Christ Church, Canterbury [Thomas Chllenden, q.v.], and others in the infirmary chapel, Reg. abp Arundel, i, fo 494. He had been opposed, however, to carrying out the el. *via spiritus*, *ib.*

John SAKEVILLE
d. 1440/1

1440/1, d., and the chamberlain sent 5s. to the almoner, CUL Add. Ms 2957, fo 31.

SALEBANK, Salebrook
see William Wisbech

John SALMON [de Ely, de Melre, Saleman, Salomon
occ. 1291/2 occ. 1299

1292–1299, prior: el. 1292; el. bp of Ely, 19 May 1298 but provided to the see of Norwich by 18 June 1299 although he occ. as prior as late as 26 Oct. of this yr, *Fasti*, ii, 47.
1292, before his el. subprior, *Chron. Bury*, 113.
1291/2, the chamberlain gave 11s. to him at his installation as prior, CUL Add. Ms 2957, fo 17.
1291/2, pd his first visit to Lakenheath as prior, CUL EDC 7/15/acct.
1295, defended the royal authority over the church in a case before the king's bench on the grounds that the king's duty was to 'maintain and defend the rights and inheritances of Holy Church which is always under age', Selden Society, *Select Cases, King's Bench*, iii, xxvi and 203.
1295, summoned to parliament on 1 Aug. at Westminster, *Parl. Writs*, i, 581.
1298, 19 May, el. bp by a majority of the chapter, but a minority el. John de Langeton in accordance with the king's wishes, *Fasti*, ii, 47, Graham, 'Ely Vacancies', 55–59.
1299, 17 Feb., recd letters of protection for his journey to Rome to appeal, *CPR (1292–1301)*, 395.
n.d., witnessed the confirmation of two charters of bp Nigel, Liber M, 157, 159.

His father was Salomon, a goldsmith of Ely, and his brother Simon held land in Stetchworth, and became adcn of Sudbury acc. to Bentham, *Hist. Ely*, 219.

I SALOMON
n.d.

n.d., 10 Dec., the obit of a Salomon occ. in Cambridge, Trinity College Ms 1105, fo k12v.

II SALOMON [Salamon, Solomon
occ. [1151 × 1158] occ. 1176

1163–1176, prior: occ. 1163; el. abbot of Thorney 1176, *HRH*, 75, *Fasti*, ii, 48.

[1151 × 1158], precentor, *Liber. Elien.*, 351, Oxford, Bod. Ms Ashmole 801, fo 139.

[1151 × 1158], witnessed a charter, *ib.*

[1133 × 1169], witnessed a charter of bp Nigel, Liber M, 157, 159.

1174, 6 Oct., present at Canterbury for the consecration of bp Geoffrey Ridel and exercised his right to present the el. (after being unsuccessfully challenged by the adcn of Ely), Bentham, *Hist. Ely*, 216.

SALYBANK
see William Wisbech

SAME
see Saham, Soham

John SAMPSON
see John Ely X

SAMUEL
n.d.

n.d., 11 Dec., obit occ. in Cambridge, Trinity College Ms 1105, fo k12ᵛ.

SANCTO EDMUNDO
see St Edmund

SANCTA FIDE
see St Faith

SANCTO IVONE
see St Ives

SATHEREY
see Sothrey

John de SAUNFORD
occ. 1305 d. 1315/16

1305, June/1306, Sept., chamberlain, CUL Add. Ms 2957, fos 17, 18.

1310, 10 Feb., with Alan de Hemmingestone and Stephen de Swaffham II, q.v., recd licence from the king to el. a bp, *CPR (1307–1313)*, 208.

1315/16, one of ten monks who d., for each of whom the chamberlain pd 5s. to the almoner, CUL Add. Ms 2957, fo 19.

John de SAUTRE [Sautrey, Sautry
occ. 1337 d. ?1349

1337, 16 Sept., dcn, recd *lit. dim.* for the order of pr., Reg. Montacute, fo 96.

1338, 19 Sept., ord pr., St Mary's church, Ely, *ib.*, fo 102.

1349, 25 June, apptd subprior by the vicar general in chapter, *ib.*, fo 22ᵛ; he prob. d. this same yr because Walter de Walsoken, q.v., succ. him.

1339/40, Sept. to Mar., prob. student [at Cambridge] with John de Bekkles, q.v., and during the yr they were given 12d. *pro generali suo* by the cellarer; however, he may have merely been absent from the house, CUL EDC 5/2/6.

1347/8, student [at Cambridge] with Thomas de Lincoln, q.v.; together, they recd from the chamberlain 46s. for 'calig', pedul', botis yemalibus et estival', tunic', linea tela, staminis, stragulis et robis', and in addition a contribution of 2s. 3½d. based on the rate of 1d. in the £, CUL EDC 5/3/10, CUL Add. Ms 2957, fo 24.

1342, Apr., accompanied the sacrist to Lynn, Chapman, *Sacrist Rolls*, ii, 120, (CUL EDC 5/10/9).

SAWELL
see Sewall

Ralph de SAXMUNDHAM [Saxham
occ. 1322/3 d. 1342

1325/6 steward of the prior's hospice, CUL EDC 5/13/*status prioratus*, CUL Add. Ms 2957, fo 67.

1322/3, 1325/6, made the rounds of some of the manors including Lakenheath, CUL EDC 7/15/acct, 5/13/4. The 1325 *status prioratus* records a debt of £21 11s. 8d., owed to him as steward of the prior's hospice, CUL EDC 5/13/*status prioratus.*

1335, 2 Aug., with the prior, John de Crauden, q.v., named in a quitclaim in their favour, BL Ms Egerton 3047, fo 209.

1336/8, Apr. to Apr., recd contributions from the chamberlain *pro stall' [chori] faciend'*, CUL EDC 5/3/3, 4, CUL Add. Ms 2957, fo 22.

1337, 3 Mar., with John de Hamerton, q.v., recd royal licence to el. a bp, *CPR (1334–1338)*, 386; see John de Crauden.

1338/9, under his supervision work on the new choir was begun, Chapman, *Sacrist Rolls*, i, 59, (CUL Add. Ms 2950, fo 11), Lambeth Ms 448, fo 119.

1339/40, recd a contribution of 40s. from the cellarer *ad fabricam novi chori*, CUL EDC 5/2/6; he also recd 3s. from the chamberlain *pro linea tela*, CUL Add. Ms 2957, fo 22.

n.d., recd 20s. from the almoner for the new choir, CUL Add. Ms 2957, fo 10.

1342, 8 Mar., represented the prior and convent in the court of Canterbury in a dispute with the rector of Doddington over tithes, Reg. Montacute, fo 35ᵛ.

1342, between Mar. and Sept., d. and the chamberlain pd 5s. to the almoner, CUL Add. Ms 2957, fo 23; see the entry above.

Note: see Ralph VI who is prob. this monk.

SAYWELL
see Sewall

John de SCHELFORD
occ. [1241 × 1259]

[1241 × 1259], *temp.* Walter II, prior, q.v., witnessed a grant of land to the prior and convent in Newton, as did John de Selford, knight, who may have been a relative, Liber M, 216.

John de SCHEPEY [Schepereth
occ. c. 1274/5

c. 1274/5, Sept. to Oct., receiver [treasurer] with John de Ramesey I, q.v., Lambeth Ms 448, fo 119, CUL Add. Ms 2950, fo 10.

Note:
(1) these two monks were receivers of the money collected for the construction of the new refectory,*ib*.
(2) this must be John de Shepreth, q.v.

John SCRANTON [Stranton
occ. 1404 d. 1449/50

1404, 19 Nov., one of six whose prof. the prior was comm. to rec., Reg. Fordham, fo 198v.
1404, 20 Dec., tonsured and ord acol., bp's chapel, Downham, *ib*., fo 244.
1405, 14 Mar., ord subdcn, bp's chapel, Downham, *ib*., fo 244.
1405, 18 Apr., ord dcn, Ely cathedral, *ib*., fo 244v.
1405, 13 June, ord pr., bp's chapel, Downham, *ib*., fo 244v; as Stanton.
1418/19, steward of the prior's hospice, CUL EDC 7/12/acct.
1421/3, 1429/30 or 1430/1, treasurer, PRO SC6/1257/4, CUL EDC 7/14c/40 acct, PRO SC6/1257/5; (the PRO accts are dated 1428/9 and 1434/5 respectively but ref. to these earlier yrs).
1418/19, went to Swaffham [Prior] for *liberatio denariorum*, CUL EDC 7/12/acct.
1419/20, possibly *socius* of the sacrist, CUL EDC 5/10/30.
1422/3, visited Kingston for *liberatio denariorum*, CUL EDC 7/14c/40 acct.
1429/30, 1433/4, 1439/40, 1445/6, *socius* of the cellarer, CUL Add. Ms 2957, fo 6.
1449/50, d., and the almoner recd 5s. from both the chamberlain and the treasurer, CUL EDC 5/1/13.

H. de S[ELVERTON
occ. 1336/7

1336/7, pittancer, CUL EDC 5/8/10.

SEMERSHAM
see Thomas Somersham II

William SEWALL [Sawell, Saywell, Sewell
occ. 1519 occ. 1539

1519, 24 Sept., ord dcn, Lady chapel, Ely cathedral, Reg. West, fo 87.
1520/1, recd 6s. 8d., from the treasurer for celebrating masses for the soul of John Hundredyer, CUL EDC 5/13/-.
1534, 8 Sept., 11th in order on the visitation certificate, Reg. Goodrich, fo 90v.
1539, 18 Nov., assigned a pension of £8 p.a., and described as a 'good choir man', *L and P Henry VIII*, xiv, pt. 2, no 542.

John de SHEPRETH [Schepereth
occ. 1281 d. 1292

1288–1292, prior: el. after 16 Nov. 1288; d. 22 Apr. 1293, *Fasti*, ii, 49.
1281, 11 Oct., one of the monks who were absolved on acct of irregularities that had arisen over payment of a tenth for the Holy Land, CUL EDC 1B/113.
1288/9, at his installation the chamberlain gave him a gift of 10s. and also 2s. for ale, CUL Add. Ms 2957, fo 15.
1292, d., as above.

Note: see John de Schepey who must be the same monk.

John SHULDHAM
occ. 1394

1394, 16 Feb., one of two whose prof. the prior was comm. to rec., Reg. Fordham, fo 181v.

SIMON
occ. 1354/5

1354/5, treasurer, CUL EDC 7/14c/20 acct.
1354/5, visited Kingston, *ib*.

John SKELSYN [Skeel, Skellyn, Skelsing, Skyle
occ. 1532 occ. 1539

1532/3, student at Cambridge with Robert Hamond, q.v.; they recd support from the chamberlain, who contributed 2s. 4d., and from the treasurer who gave £8 13s. 4d., CUL EDC 5/13/-, CUL Add. Ms 2957, fo 34, CUL Add. Ms 2957, fo 81.
[?1534/5], student, with Hamond, with a pension of £8 13s. 4d., from the treasurer who also pd 7s. 6d., for repairing the windows of his room in Cambridge, CUL EDC 5/13/-.
1534, 8 Sept., 21st in order on the visitation certificate, Reg. Goodrich, fo 90v.
1536, 25 Apr., described as former monk who was now dispensed to become a secular pr., *gratis*, Chambers, *Faculty Office Regs*, 52.
1539, 18 Nov., name on the surrender list as Skyle, CUL Add. Ms 2957, fo 166v; but he is not on the pension list unless he is John Chatteris, q.v.

Name in Oxford Bod. Broxb.30.4, M. Luther, OSA, *Collected Writings and Sermons*, Wittenburgh,

1519; ownership inscription, deleted but legible, on the front leaf. I am grateful to Mr R. J. Roberts, deputy librarian at the Bodleian library for this information.

William de SNETERTON [Snyterton, Snytreton

occ. 1349/50 d. 1390/1

1349/50, 1357/8, *socius* of the chamberlain, CUL Add. Ms 2957, fo 25, CUL EDC 5/3/12.
1361, contributed 10s. to the purchase of the manor and advowson of Mepal, Evans, 'Mepal', 118 (CUL EDC 1B/box 23).
1378/9, pd a visit to Lakenheath, CUL EDC 7/15/acct.
1379, 5th in order on the clerical poll tax list and pd 3s. 4d., PRO E179/23/1.
1390/1, d., and the chamberlain sent 5s. to the almoner, CUL Add. Ms 2957, fo 36.

Alan de SOHAM [Saham

occ. [before 1298]

n.d., gardener, Liber M, 483.
n.d., took possession of a messuage in Ely, on behalf of his office, for which he pd 30s., *ib.*

Note: acc. to S. J. A. Evans, muniment no 494 provides the date, but I have been unable to find this document.

I John SOHAM B.Cn.L. [Saham

occ. 1444/5 d. 1483/4

1444/5, treasurer, CUL EDC 5/12/5.
1449/50, 1451/2, 1455/6, granator, CUL EDC 5/4/37–39.
1460, 10 Apr., apptd sacrist by the bp personally in chapter, Reg. Gray, fo 46ᵛ; on 30 Sept., this same yr, he was removed, *ex certis causis legitimis*, from this office, *ib.*, fo 47ᵛ.
1465/7, infirmarer, CUL EDC 5/13/-, PRO SC6/1257/9.
[1470], 11 Sept., a comm. was issued for his apptment as subprior, Reg. Gray, fo 80ᵛ; he succ. John Ely VII, q.v.
1472, 15 Jan.; 1473, 20 Jan., subprior, Liber B, nos 221, 238, CUL Add. Ms 2950, fos 80, 81.
1473/4, former *senescallus terrarum*, CUL EDC 5/13/-.
1475, 25 Jan.; 1475/6; 1478, 26/28 July, subprior and *custos communis thesaurarie*, CUL EDC 5/13/-; Lambeth Ms 448, fo 113, CUL Add. Ms 2950, fo 81.
1478, 26/28 July, subprior, Lambeth Ms 448, fo 113.

1455, described as *bacularius*, Lambeth Ms 448, fo 98ᵛ.
1472, 15 Jan., described as *in decretis bacalarius*, Liber B, no 221.

1446, 1 June, with John Feltwell, q.v., acted as proctor in a tithe dispute, Liber B, no 234, CUL Add. Ms 2950, fos 76, 77.
1455, made various payments concerning the covering [*coopertorium*] over the shrine of St Etheldreda and the hangings inside [*intus*], Lambeth Ms 448, fo 98ᵛ.
1461/2, visited Melton for *liberatio denariorum*, on the treasurer's behalf, CUL EDC 5/13/14.
1469/70, celebrated masses for the soul of Philip Lyle and recd 6s. 8d., from the treasurer, CUL EDC 5/13/-.
1472, 15 Jan., apptd by the prior and chapter, with Roger Westminster, q.v., as proctor for convocation, Liber B, no 221, CUL Add. Ms 2950, fo 80.
1473, 20 Jan., recd a similar apptment with Alexander Wittlesey, q.v., and others, Liber B, no 238, CUL Add. Ms 2950, fo 81.
1474/5, spent a fortnight in London on business negotiations including the matter of a loan to the king, CUL EDC 5/13/-.
1475, 25 Jan., again apptd by the prior and chapter, one of several proctors for convocation, Liber B, no 222.
1477/8, *custos* of the manor of Caxton, CUL EDC 5/10/35.
1478, 24 June, named coadjutor when prior Henry Peterborough, q.v., became dumb, Lambeth Ms 448, fo 113; on 19 July, he and other senior monks went to the bp to discuss arrangements concerning the prior's pension, *ib.* After obtaining licence to el., he, as subprior, presided over the el. on 28 July, *ib.*, fo 113–113ᵛ. See Roger Westminster.
1483/4, d., and the precentor gave 5s. to the almoner, CUL EDC 5/9/9.

II John SOHAM

occ. 1475 occ. 1539

1475, 25 Mar., ord acol., bp's chapel, Doddington, Reg. Gray, fo 215ᵛ.
1476, 13 Apr., ord subdcn, bp's palace chapel, Ely, *ib.*, fo 216ᵛ.

1539, 18 Nov., 'old and weak' and assigned a pension of £13 6s. 8d., *L and P Henry VIII*, xiv, pt 2, no 542.

Note: he must have been well over 80.

Simon SOHAM

occ. 1419 occ. c. 1443/4

1419, 7 June, ord acol., bp's chapel, Downham, Reg. Fordham, fo 272.
1419, 10 June, ord subdcn, bp's chapel, Downham, *ib.*, fo 272.
1419, 23 Sept., ord dcn, bp's chapel, Downham, *ib.*, fo 272ᵛ.

1434/5, former steward of the prior's hospice, CUL EDC 5/12/3.
1443/4, former *custos* of the Lady chapel, CUL EDC 5/7/9.

1431/2, visited Lakenheath for *liberatio denariorum*, CUL EDC 7/15/acct.

I Thomas de SOHAM
occ. [1315/16]

[1315/16 or earlier], mentioned on the steward of the prior's hospice acct, CUL EDC 5/12/-, with William de Livermere, q.v.

II Thomas SOHAM [Same, Some, Sowm, *alias* Nex
occ. 1492 occ. 1539

1492, 21 Apr., recd tonsure, Ely cathedral, Reg. Alcock, fo 231 and repeated on fo 232v.
1494, 29 Mar., ord dcn, Ely cathedral, *ib.*, fo 235.
1497, 23 Sept., ord pr., Wisbech, *ib.*, 243.

1514/15, 1516/17, granator, CUL EDC 5/4/51, 52.
1532/3, cellarer, CUL EDC 5/12/-, 5/13/-, CUL Add. Ms 2957, fo 81.
1534, 10 Sept., subprior, Reg. Goodrich, fo 90v; see below.
1535/6, cellarer, CUL EDC 5/12/-, (treasurer's acct).

1515, 15/16 Apr., 6th in order on the *sed. vac.* visitation certificate, Reg. abp Warham, ii, fo 277.
1516, 22 Mar., 5th in order in the chapter which chose 29 Mar., as the date for the el. of a prior, Reg. West, fo 55. He recd the licence to el. from the bp on 27 Mar., *ib.*, and was sent as proctor to seek the consent of the el., John Cottenham, q.v., and then to the bp for his confirmation, *ib.*, fos 58, 59. See Thomas Oxborough and Robert Stunteney.
1534, 8 Sept., 2nd in order (and subprior) on the visitation certificate, Reg. Goodrich, fo 90v.
1539, 18 Nov., name on the surrender list, CUL Add. Ms 2957, fo 166v, but not on the pension list in *L and P Henry VIII*, xiv, pt 2, no 542.

SOLOMON
see Salmon and Salomon

John SOMERSHAM
occ. 1440 occ. 1443/4

1442/4, granator, CUL EDC 5/4/33, 34; see John Cley.
1440, May/Sept., 1443/4, steward of the prior's hospice, PRO SC6/1257/8, CUL EDC 5/12/4.
1442/3, visited Lakenheath as granator, CUL EDC 7/15/acct.

I Thomas de SOMERSHAM [Somersom
occ. 1361 d. 1407/8

1364/6, granator, CUL EDC 5/4/13, 14.

1361, contributed 6s. 8d., to the purchase of the manor and advowson of Mepal, Evans, 'Mepal', 118 (CUL EDC 1B/box 23).
1364, Sept./Dec., took charge of the new work *del malthous et zilhous* for which he acctd, CUL EDC 5/4/13.
1373/5, *socius* of the precentor, CUL Add. Ms 2957, fo 45, CUL EDC 5/9/5.
1379, 13th in order on the clerical poll tax list and pd 3s. 4d., PRO E179/23/1.
1401, 14 Sept., 5th on the metropolitan visitation certificate, Reg. Fordham, fo 131.
1407/8, d. and the chamberlain sent 5s. to the almoner, CUL EDC 5/3/27.

II Thomas SOMERSHAM [?Semersham
occ. 1497/8

1497/8, pittancer, CUL EDC 5/8/-.
1497/8, visited Sutton to supervise repairs, CUL EDC 5/8/-.

John SOTHREY [Satherey, Sotherey
occ. 1454 occ. 1500

1454, 21 Sept., ord pr., Lady chapel, Ely cathedral, Reg. Gray, fo 201.

1473/4, 1476/7, precentor, CUL EDC 5/13/-, 5/13/16; in 1473/4 he possibly succ. Thomas Wells II, q.v.

1500, 30 Oct., *stagiarius*, and 7th to be examined at the visitation by the commissary of the prior of Christ Church, Canterbury (*sed. vac.* both Ely and Canterbury). He stated *omnia bene*, but agreed with those who urged that the Vine gate into the cloister should be closed; see Richard Swaffham, Canterbury Reg. R., fo 70.

William SOTHREY
occ. 1498

1498, 14 Apr., ord acol., Ely cathedral, Reg. Alcock, fo 246v.

SOTTON
see Sutton

SOWM
see Soham

Anthony de SPALDING [Spaldyng
d. 1331/2

1331/2, d. and the chamberlain sent 5s. to the almoner, CUL Add. Ms 2957, fo 21.

I John de SPALDING [Spaldyng
occ. 1384 d. 1396/7

1384, 24 Sept., ord acol., bp's chapel, Downham, Reg. Arundel, fo 131v.
1385, 18 Mar., ord subdcn, Lady chapel, Ely cathedral, *ib.*, fo 132v.
1385, 27 May, ord dcn, bp's chapel, Downham, *ib.*, fo 132v.
1388, 23 May, ord pr., bp's chapel, Holborn, London, *ib.*, fo 136.

1396/7, d., and the chamberlain and precentor both sent 5s. to the almoner, CUL Add. Ms 2957, fos 37, 46.

Note: the ordination dates may apply to John de Spalding II below.

II John de SPALDING [Spaldyng
d. 1428/9

1428/9, d. recorded by the treasurer, PRO SC6/1257/4.

Note: see John de Spalding I above.

Richard de SPALDING [Spaldyng
occ. 1318/19 d. 1339/40

1318/19, second of three treasurers, CUL EDC 5/13/3.
1319, 13 July, kitchener, Lambeth Ms 448, fo 97v.
1325, 29 Sept., named as former steward of the prior's hospice under prior John Fresingfeld (res. 1321), q.v., CUL EDC 5/13/*status prioratus*.
1323/4, 1325/6, 1332/3, cellarer, CUL EDC 5/13/-, 5/2/1A, 5/13/6; he was succ. as cellarer by Nicholas de Copmanford, q.v., CUL Add. Ms 2957, fo 1.
1334/8; Apr. to Apr., 1338/9, Apr. to May, chamberlain, CUL EDC 5/3/1–4, CUL Add. Ms 2957, fo 22.

1319, 13 July, was involved in the *contentio* over the authority of the subprior John de Crishale I, q.v., as he had been licensed by the third prior, William de Hoveden, q.v., to leave the monastery with John de Chestreton, q.v., for a period of recreation after *minutio*, Lambeth Ms 448, fo 97v.
1328/9, pd a visit to Melton, CUL EDC 7/16/6 acct.
1335/6, went to the fair at St Ives, CUL EDC 5/3/2.
1337/8, went to the fairs at Stourbridge and St Ives and also to Wisbech to collect rents, CUL EDC 5/3/4.
1339/40, d., and the chamberlain and sacrist each sent 5s. to the almoner, CUL Add. Ms 2957, fo 23, Chapman, *Sacrist Rolls*, ii, 94, (CUL EDC 5/10/8).

I William de SPALDING
n.d.

n.d., witnessed a miracle of St Etheldreda while he was still a secular and related it to his brethren, BL Ms Cotton Titus A.i, fos 122–123 (?*temp.* bp Hotham, 1316–1337).

Note: this may be a ref. to the second William de Spalding below.

II William de SPALDING [Spaldyng
occ. 1344/5 d. 1368/9

1344/5, *custos roserie* and *senescallus* [*terrarum*], CUL EDC 5/6/1, 7/15/acct.
1347/8, 1349/50, *senescallus* [*terrarum*], CUL EDC 7/15/acct, 7/16/11 acct.
1359/61, 1363/4, cellarer, CUL EDC 5/2/15–18.

1344/5, visited Lakenheath where expenses were heavy because of the need to buy off members of the royal household, who were in the vicinity, CUL EDC 7/15/acct.
1345, 17 Dec., with Robert de Aylesham, q.v., attended a meeting in which the abbots of Ramsey and Thorney presented their conflicting claims over Kingsdelf, *Cart. Ramsey*, i, 78.
1347/8, visited Lakenheath and Winston, CUL EDC 7/15/acct, 7/17/acct.
1348 or 1349, 9 Feb., one of several monks who witnessed an agreement settling transgressions in Lakenheath and other places, Liber M, 628.
1349, 6 Nov., was attacked after putting a bond man in the stocks, *CPR (1348–1350)*, 453.
1349/50, visited Melton, CUL EDC 7/16/11, 12 accts.
1361, contributed 13s. 4d., towards the purchase of the manor and advowson of Mepal, Evans, 'Mepal', 118 (CUL EDC 1B/box 23).
1368/9, d., and the sacrist sent 5s. to the almoner, CUL EDC 5/10/16.

Note: see the note under William de Spalding I.

John SPYRARD [Spirard
occ. 1534 occ. 1539

1534, 8 Sept., 20th in order on the visitation certificate, Reg. Goodrich, fo 90v.
1535/6, *socius* of the sacrist, CUL EDC 5/10/33, CUL Add. Ms 2956, fo 177.
1539, 18 Nov., assigned a pension of £5 6s. 8d., p.a., *L and P Henry VIII*, xiv, pt. 2, no 542; there was also a John Spyrard, described as an old, blind servant, who was given a small pension, *ib.*

STANARD
n.d.

n.d., 12 Jan., obit occ. in Cambridge, Trinity College Ms 1105, fo k1v.

James STANTON
occ. 1412 occ. 1421/2

1412, 28 May, ord acol., bp's chapel, Downham, Reg. Fordham, fo 261.
1413, 23 Sept., ord subdcn, bp's chapel, Downham, *ib.*, fo 262v.
1413, 23 Dec., ord dcn, bp's chapel, Downham, *ib.*, fo 263.
1414, 3 Mar., ord pr., bp's chapel, Downham, *ib.*, fo 264.

1421/2, treasurer, CUL EDC 5/13/12.

STANTON
see Scranton, Staundon

Peter de STAPLEFORD [Stapelford, Stapilford, Stapylford
occ. 1367/8 d. 1392/3

1371/2, pittancer, CUL EDC 5/8/15.
1376, 22 Nov., a comm. was issued for his apptment as chamberlain, Reg. Arundel, fo 20v; on 24 May, 1377, another comm. was issued for

his removal from this office, *ib.*, fo 23v. He was succ. by Henry de Wykes, q.v.

1376/9, *senescallus* [*terrarum*], CUL EDC 7/15/acct, (but see William de Wells I), 7/17/acct, 7/16/22 acct.

1382/3, 1384/6, 1387/8, July, chamberlain, CUL Add. Ms 2957, fo 35; 1388, 1 July, a comm. was issued for his removal from office, and for his successor to be John de Langeley, q.v., Reg. Arundel, fo 62v.

1389/90, and prob. 1390/1, steward of the prior's hospice, CUL EDC 5/13/8, 7/17/acct where he is merely *senescallus*.

1367/8, made an *oblatio* of 6s. 8d., to the *custos* of the Lady chapel, CUL Add. Ms 2957, fo 55.

1376/7, visited Lakenheath, CUL EDC 7/15/acct.

1377/8, visited Winston, CUL EDC 7/17/acct.

1378/9, pd visits to Lakenheath and Melton, CUL EDC 7/15/acct, 7/16/22 acct.

1379, 17th in order on the clerical poll tax list and pd 3s. 4d., PRO E179/23/1.

1384/5, visited Lakenheath, CUL EDC 7/15/acct.

1389/90, went by boat to Cambridge, where he was involved in a lawsuit, and attended the assizes, CUL EDC 5/13/8.

1389/91, pd visits to Winston, CUL EDC 7/17/accts.

1392/3, d., and the sacrist sent 5s. to the almoner, CUL EDC 5/10/23, CUL Add. Ms 2956, fo 164.

STASTED
see Stisted

William de STAUNDON [Staundone
occ. 1284/5 d. 1302/3

1284/90, chamberlain, and prob. also 1290/1, CUL Add. Ms 2957, fos 14–17.

1302/3, d., and the chamberlain, precentor and sacrist each sent 5s. to the almoner, CUL Add. Ms 2957, fos 17, 41, Chapman, *Sacrist Rolls*, ii, 18 (CUL EDC 5/10/2).

STEPHEN
see Swaffham

Nicholas STEPHENSON
occ. 1464

1464, 20 Mar., granted papal dispensation to rec. and retain a benefice with cure of souls, including a parish church usually assigned to a secular clerk and in the patronage of a layman, *CPL*, xii (1458–1471), 201.

Nicholas de STETCHWORTH
occ. 1327

1327, 14 Feb., *custos* of the black hostelry i.e. hostiller, BL Ms Egerton 3047, fo 94–94v.

STEWARD
see Robert Wells

Laurence de STEYNTON
occ. 1338/9

1338, Apr./1339, Mar. or Sept., *socius* of the chamberlain, CUL Add. Ms 2957, fo 22.

Ralph de STISTED [Stasted, Stistede, Stythstede
occ. 1318/19 d. 1334/5

1318 or 1319, June/July, cellarer, CUL EDC 5/2/1, as Stasted.

1333, July/Sept., refectorer, CUL EDC 5/13/6.

1334/5, d., and the chamberlain and sacrist sent 5s. to the almoner, CUL EDC 5/3/1, Chapman, *Sacrist Rolls*, ii, 71 (CUL EDC 5/10/6); the sacrist gave 1s. to the bellringer, *ib*; the scribe has written Roger but was surely referring to this monk.

I Thomas de STOKTON
occ. 1340/1 occ. 1375/6

1340/1, treasurer, CUL EDC 7/17/acct.

1349/50, precentor, CUL Add. Ms 2957, fo 43.

1361, subprior, Evans, 'Mepal', 118 (CUL EDC 1B/box 23).

1367/8, ?1371/2, 1372/3, 1375/6, *custos* of the Lady chapel, CUL Add. Ms 2957, fos 55, 56, CUL EDC 5/7/4, 5.

1340/1, pd a visit to Winston, CUL EDC 7/17/acct.

1361, contributed £6 towards the purchase of the manor and advowson of Mepal, *ib.*

Note: The two overlapping Thomas de Stoktons are impossible to distinguish and both may have been treasurer in the 1350s and early 1360s but Thomas I must have d. before 1379. See below.

II Thomas de STOKTON
occ. 1345 d. 1388/9

1345, 21 May, ord pr., Linton, Reg. Montacute, fo 119v.

1351/2, 1353/4, treasurer, CUL Add. Ms 2957, fo 27, CUL EDC 5/3/11.

1363/9, treasurer, CUL EDC 7/14c/26, 5/6/4, 7/16/18, 5/6/5, 7/17/acct, 5/6/6.

1370/1, 1372/80, treasurer, CUL EDC 5/12/1, 5/3/19, 20, 7/14c/32 acct, 5/4/14, 7/15/acct, 5/2/20, 7/15/acct, 5/6/10.

1380/2, treasurer, CUL EDC 7/15/acct, 5/2/22.

1362/3, visited Kingston for *liberatio denariorum*, CUL EDC 7/14c/25 acct.

1363/4, pd a visit to Kingston, CUL EDC 7/14c/26 acct.

1364/5, visited Lakenheath and Melton for *liberatio denariorum* and also pd a visit to Winston, CUL EDC 7/15/acct, 7/16/17 acct, 7/17/acct.

1365/6, pd a visit to Melton CUL EDC 7/16/18 acct.

1367/8, visited Winston for *liberatio denariorum*, CUL EDC 7/17/acct.
1372/3, pd visits to Kingston, and to Melton for *liberatio denariorum*, CUL EDC 7/14c/30 acct, 7/16/19 acct.
1373/4, visited Kingston and Lakenheath, CUL EDC 7/14c/31 acct, 7/15/acct.
1374/5, visited Kingston, CUL EDC 7/14c/32 acct.
1376/7, visited Lakenheath, CUL EDC 7/15/acct.
1377/8, recd *liberatio denariorum* at Winston, CUL EDC 7/17/acct.
1378/9, visited Lakenheath for *liberatio denariorum* and was also at Melton, CUL EDC 7/15/acct, 7/16/31 acct.
1379, 3rd in order on the clerical poll tax list and pd 3s. 4d., PRO E179/23/1.
1379/80, visited Sutton, CUL EDC 7/3/1 acct.
1380/1, went to Lakenheath for *liberatio denariorum*, which included £11 for the sale of rabbits, CUL EDC 5/15/acct.
1388/9, d., and the chamberlain sent the almoner 5s. *pro errogacione*, CUL EDC 5/3/22.

Note: Some of the details in this entry may apply to Thomas de Stokton I above, q.v. However, there is no doubt that Thomas II, ord pr. in 1345 is the Thomas who ranked third in order of seniority in 1379; see Simon de Banham and John de St Ives.

John STONHAM [Stonam, Stoneham
occ. 1515 occ. 1539

1525/9, 1532/3, steward of the prior's hospice, CUL EDC 5/13/18–20, CUL Add. Ms 2957, fos 78–81.
1526/9, 1532/3, granator, CUL EDC 5/13/18, 5/4/53, 5/13/20, CUL Add. Ms 2957, fos 79, 6, 81.
1539, 18 Nov., almoner, *L and P Henry VIII*, xiv, pt 2, no 542.

1515, 15/16 Apr., 31st in order on the *sed. vac.* visitation certificate, Reg. abp Warham, ii, fo 277.
1516, 22 Mar., 26th in the chapter which chose 29 Mar. as the date for the el. of a prior, Reg. West, fo 55.
1534, 8 Sept., 10th on the visitation certificate, Reg. Goodrich, fo 90ᵛ.
1539, 18 Nov., assigned a pension of £10 p.a., *L and P Henry VIII*, xiv, pt 2, no 542.

STONTENEY
see Stunteney

R. de STRADEBROC [Stradbrok
occ. 1240 occ. 1247

1245/7, sacrist, BL Ms Cotton Tiberius B.ii, fo 246, CUL Add. Ms 2950, fo 4; he was succ. by Adam de Burgh, q.v.
1240, 1242/6, *socius* of the sacrist M[artin], q.v., BL Ms Cotton Tiberius B.ii, fo 246ᵛ–247, CUL Add. Ms 2950, fos 2–4.
1240/7, concerned with the construction of the new presbytery, BL Ms Cotton Tiberius B.ii, fo 246, CUL Add. Ms 2950, fos 2–4.

Thomas de STRADEBROK
d. 1315/16

1315/16, one of ten monks who d. this yr, for each of whom the chamberlain sent 5s. to the almoner, CUL Add. Ms 2957, fo 19.

STRANTON
see Scranton

John de ?STRATESHETE [?Stradset, Strager, Stratfeld
occ. [1197] occ. 1200

[1198–?1202] prior: prob. el. Feb. 1198; succ. by prior Hugh, q.v., who occ. Jan. 1203, *Fasti*, ii, 48–49, *HRH*, 46.

1197, John, subprior and witness, BL Ms Egerton 3047, fo 97ᵛ, and CUL 1B/677.
[1198 × 1202], prior, witnessed a charter of Alexander, abbot of Sawtry, Liber M, 222.

Note:
(1) a John subprior occ. with Richard, prior, q.v., in a *placitum* on 2 Dec. 1189, BL Ms Cotton Tiberius B.ii, fo 254.
(2) he was prob. the first prior to have been el. by the monks.

I John STRETHAM
occ. 1412 d. 1442/3

1412, 28 May, ord acol., bp's chapel, Downham, Reg. Fordham, fo 261.
1413, 23 Sept., ord subdcn, bp's chapel, Downham, *ib.*, fo 262ᵛ.
1413, 23 Dec., ord dcn, bp's chapel, Downham, *ib.*, fo 263.
1414, 3 Mar., ord pr., bp's chapel, Downham, *ib.*, fo 263ᵛ.

1423/4, hostiller, CUL EDC 5/13/12.
1427/9, steward of the prior's hospice, CUL EDC 5/3/32, PRO SC6/1257/4.
1430/1, 1432/3, 1434/5, 1436/7, *senescallus terrarum*, CUL EDC 7/17/accts, 5/12/3, PRO SC6/1257/5, 6.
1442/3, almoner, CUL EDC 5/9/12.

1420, Feb./Sept., student at Cambridge with John Swanton, q.v., and with financial support from the cellarer based on an assessment of ½d. in the £ for half the yr; in addition he gave them more *pro interferc[ulis suis*, CUL EDC 5/2/30.
1428, Oct., with William Swanton, q.v., held courts on the Suffolk manors, PRO SC6/1257/4.
1430/1, visited Melton and Winston, CUL EDC 7/16/33, 7/17/acct.

1432/3, stayed at Winston with others of the prior's council in May and Oct., and held courts, supervised the manor and recd payments, CUL EDC 7/17/acct.

1434/5, made trips to London, first for royal licence to el. a bp and then to inform the bp elect, PRO SC6/1257/5; see Thomas Wells I.

1435, 27 Oct., with John Feltwell, q.v., and others apptd proctor for convocation by the prior and chapter, CUL Add. Ms 2950, fo 75, Liber B, no 74.

1442/3, d., and the precentor sent 5s. to the almoner's office, CUL EDC 5/9/12.

Note: There must have been two John Strethams and it seems that one may have followed the other in the office of almoner. Some of the other entries under John I almost certainly pertain to John II, but which?

II John STRETHAM
occ. 1443/4 occ. 1449/50

1443/4, 1446/7, 1448/50, almoner, CUL Add. Ms 2957, fo 31, CUL EDC 5/1/13.

1449/50, spent three days at Foxton for supervisory purposes, CUL EDC 5/1/13.

See the note under John Stretham I above.

STUARD
see Robert Wells

John STUNTENEY [Stonteney, Stonteneye, Stounteneye
occ. 1404 d. 1453/4

1404, 19 Nov., one of six whose prof. the prior was comm. to rec., Reg. Fordham, fo 198v.

1404, 20 Dec., ord acol., bp's chapel, Downham, *ib.*, fo 244.

1405, 14 Mar., ord subdcn, bp's chapel, Downham, *ib.*, fo 244.

1405, 18 Apr., ord dcn, Ely cathedral, *ib.*, fo 244v.

1407, 26 Mar., ord pr., bp's chapel, Downham, *ib.*, fo 245v.

1421/2; 1427/9; 1430/1; 1434/7, chamberlain, CUL Add. Ms 2957, fo 30; CUL EDC 5/3/32, PRO SC6/1257/4; CUL EDC 5/3/31; PRO SC6/1257/5, CUL Add. Ms 2957, fo 31, PRO SC6/1257/6.

1415, 8 May, student at Cambridge and licensed to preach in any church [?in Cambridge] appropriated to Ely cathedral, *Reg. abp Chichele*, iv, 126; see Henry Madyngle, Edmund Walsingham and John Yaxham.

1424, 26 July, the Ferentini bankers were authorized to provide letters of exchange to the value of 10 m. payable to him in foreign parts, *CClR (1422–1429)*, 487.

1425, 17 Apr., granted papal indult to choose his own confessor, *CPL*, vii (1417–1431), 420.

1453/4, d., and the precentor sent 5s. to the almoner CUL EDC 5/9/7, CUL Add. Ms 2957, fo 48.

Robert STUNTENEY [Stonteney, Stuntney
occ. 1496 occ. 1516/17

1496, 2 Apr., ord subdcn, Ely cathedral, Reg. Alcock, fo 240.

1496, 24 Sept., ord dcn, bp's chapel, Downham, *ib.*, fo 241v.

1516, 27 Mar., subprior, Reg. West, fo 55.

1516/17, feretrar, CUL EDC 5/10/44.

1515, 15/16 Apr., 10th in order on the *sed. vac.* visitation certificate, Reg. abp Warham, ii, fo 277.

1516, 29 Mar., presided as subprior, over the el. of a prior, and on 1 Apr. went with the elect to seek the bp's confirmation, Reg. West, fo 59; see John Cottenham and Thomas Oxborough.

I Simon STUNTENEY [Stontenay, Stuntneye
occ. 1457 d. 1460

1457, 17 Dec., ord acol., bp's chapel, Downham, Reg. Gray, fo 205.

1459, 19 May, ord dcn, bp's chapel, Downham, *ib.*, fo 206v.

1460, before 10 Apr., subprior, Reg. Gray, fo 46v.

1460, before 10 Apr., d. and was replaced as subprior by John Feltwell, q.v., *ib.*

Note: The ordination dates of Simon Stunteney I and Simon Quaveney, q.v., fit together in sequence to suggest that they could be the same monk; the remaining evidence, however, contradicts this hypothesis unless the Simon Stunteney, subprior who d. was ordained at an earlier unrecorded date; this does seem possible.

II Simon STUNTENEY
see note above

STYTHSTEDE
see Stisted

STYWARD
see Robert Wells

SUAFFAM, Suafham
see Swaffham

Henry SUCCURMAN
d. 1505/6

1505/6, d. and the sacrist sent 5s. to the almoner, CUL EDC 5/10/42.

Note: see Henry Isleham who is prob. this monk.

Alan de SUTTON
occ. 1379 occ. 1401

1385/6, 1389/90, granator, CUL EDC 5/4/18, 5/13/8.

1392/3, treasurer, CUL EDC 7/14c/36 acct, see John de Riston his successor.
1395, 5 May, a comm. was issued to appt him cellarer, Reg. Fordham, fo 183^{v}.
1396/7, former cellarer, CUL EDC 5/13/10.

1379, 26th in order on the clerical poll tax list and pd 3s. 4d., PRO E179/23/1.
1380/1, *socius* of the cellarer, CUL Add. Ms 2957, fo 4.
1392/3, visited Kingston and Lakenheath, CUL EDC 7/14c/36 acct, 7/15/acct.
1394, 30 May, obtained papal indult to choose his own confessor, *CPL*, iv (1362–1404), 496.
1401, 14 Sept., 7th in order on the metropolitan visitation certificate, Reg. Fordham, fo 131.

Note: an Alan de Sutton occ. on a treasurer's acct of 1428/9 as a former treasurer, PRO SC6/1257/4; could it be this monk reappointed to this office?

Geoffrey de SUTTON
occ. 1344

1344, 25 July, acted as proctor, with Robert de Aylesham, q.v., in arranging a settlement over a disputed tenement, Liber M, 624.

I John de SUTTON
occ. 1316 d. 1343

1316/19, treasurer, CUL EDC 5/13/1–3; in 1318/19, Nicholas de Copmanford and Richard de Spalding, q.v., also shared the office.
1321, 20 Oct., *senescallus* [*?terrarum*], CUL EDC 7/7/court.
1326/7, July to July, 1335/6, 1342/3, June, almoner, CUL Add. Ms 2957, fos 7, 70, 10; also CUL EDC 5/13/7 for 1335/6. He was succ. by Robert de Rykelyng, q.v.

c. 1323/5, travelled to London several times for various 'negotiations' and stayed for lengthy periods at great expense 'pro rotulis de lib[ertate eccl[esie Elyen' scrutand' ' and as proctor attended parliament at Westminster, CUL EDC 5/13/-.
1321, 20 Oct., held the court at Witcham, CUL EDC 7/7/court; he also pd off a creditor by selling him a horse for 100s., CUL Add. Ms 2957, fo 68, CUL EDC 5/13/*status prioratus*.
1326/7, pd a visit to Lakenheath, CUL EDC 7/15/acct.
1335/6, gave £4 11s. 8d., *ex curialitate* to the prior who had lost his horses in a fire, CUL Add. Ms 2957, fo 70, CUL EDC 5/13/7.
1343, June, d., CUL Add. Ms 2957, fo 10; the chamberlain sent 5s. to the almoner, CUL Add. Ms 2957, fo 23.

II John SUTTON D.Th.
occ. 1419 d. 1442/3

1419, 5 June, ord acol., bp's chapel, Downham, Reg. Fordham, fo 272.
1419, 10 June, ord subdcn, bp's chapel, Downham, *ib.*, fo 272.
1419, 23 Sept., ord dcn, bp's chapel, Downham, *ib.*, fo 272^{v}.
1421, 20 Sept., ord pr., Lady chapel, Ely cathedral, *ib.*, fo 109^{v}.

1439/41, almoner, CUL Add. Ms 2957, fo 31, PRO SC6/1257/8 (1440, May/Sept.).

1423/4, student at Cambridge with William Wells II and John Feltwell, q.v., and he and William recd £8 4s. 2d., from the treasurer, CUL EDC 5/13/12.
1428/9, student, with William Wells, for whom the treasurer provided £6 17s. 6d., PRO SC6/1257/4.
1434/5, at Cambridge with John Feltwell and William Wells and they recd together 46s. 8d. through the cellarer, and also £8 4s. 2d., PRO SC6/1257/5.
1435/6, incepted, and the prior ordered the granator to send three quarters of wheat and four quarters of malt [*bras*'] [to Cambridge for the inception feast], CUL EDC 5/4/31.
1436/7, at Cambridge with John Feltwell, PRO SC6/1257/6.
1416/17, *socius* of the sacrist, CUL EDC 5/10/29, CUL Add. Ms 2956, fo 167.
1428, 30 June, with John Yaxham, q.v., apptd proctor by the prior and chapter for convocation, fo 146, CUL Add. Ms 2950, fo 74.
1430, 1 Oct., apptd general proctor for the prior and convent with John Feltwell, q.v., CUL Add. Ms 2950, fo 74; Liber B, no 233.
1437, Mar., sent to London to convocation, PRO SC6/1257/6.
1442/3, d., and the precentor sent 5s. to the almoner, CUL EDC 5/9/12.

I Robert de SUTTON
occ. 1348/9 d. 1367/8

1350, June/Sept., 1351/4, chamberlain, CUL Add. Ms 2957, fos 26, 27, CUL EDC 5/3/11; he succ. John de St Ives, q.v.
1354/5, 1357/8, 1359/60, 1361, 1363, 10 Feb., sacrist, Chapman, *Sacrist Rolls*, ii, 160–196 (CUL EDC 5/10/13–15), Evans, 'Mepal', 118, (CUL EDC 1B/box 23).

1348 or 1349, 9 Feb., one of several monks who witnessed an agreement settling transgressions in Lakenheath and other places, Liber M, 628.
1349/56, with the prior, Alan de Walsingham, q.v., bought three *peciis argent'* from the *custos* of the Lady chapel, Ralph de Rysyng, q.v., CUL Add. Ms 2957, fo 51.
1354/5, attended the synods [at Barnwell] in Oct. and June, went to the fairs at Reach and Stourbridge, visited the bp at Hatfield and went to Wisbech to procure chrism on Maundy Thursday, Chapman, *Sacrist Rolls*, ii, 169 (CUL EDC 5/10/13).

1355, 11 June, because he held the office of sacrist he was granted by the prior the use [*aysementa*] of a chamber between the guest hall and the infirmary which had formerly been used by the brethren to entertain relatives and friends, Oxford, Bod. Ms Ashmole 801, fo 120.
1357/8, attended the synods, visited the fairs and went to Sall, Chapman, *Sacrist Rolls*, ii, 179 (CUL EDC 5/10/14).
1359/60, attended the synods, *ib.*, 191 (CUL EDC 5/10/15); he also went to the fairs and took six monks to Oxney in Lent and two monks to East Dereham in Sept. for ordination, *ib.*
1361, contributed £8 16s. 4d., towards the purchase of the manor and advowson of Mepal, Evans, 'Mepal', 118 (CUL EDC 1B/box 23); he and John de St Ives, q.v., went to London to obtain the charter of mortification, Oxford, Bodley, Ms Ashmole, fo 134.
1367/8, d., CUL EDC 5/3/16.

II Robert de SUTTON
occ. 1367/8 occ. 1418 × 1425
1375/6, former granator, CUL EDC 5/4/14.
1392/3, cellarer, CUL EDC 5/13/9; but on 9 Oct. 1392 a comm. was issued for his removal from this office, Reg. Fordham, fo 178ᵛ; he was succ. by John de Langeley, q.v.
1367/8, 1368/9, *instructor juvenum*; he recd 2d. from the *custos* of the Lady chapel, CUL Add. Ms 2957, fo 56 (1367/8), and 2s. 11¾d., from the sacrist, CUL EDC 5/10/16, CUL Add. Ms 2956, fo 157 (1368/9).
1373, 9 July, gave the sermon at the metropolitan visitation, *sed. vac.*, Reg. abp Wittlesey, fo 152ᵛ.
1379, 18th in order on the clerical poll tax list and pd 3s. 4d., PRO E179/23/1.
1389/90, recd a small sum from the treasurer for saying chantry masses for the soul of Nicholas Stucley, CUL EDC 5/13/8.
1390, 19 July, chancellor of the chapter with Peter de Norwich II, q.v., and they lent some charters concerning the bpric to bp Fordham, BL Add. Ms 9822, fo 73.
1418 × 1425, 2 Sept., wrote a letter to the prior, Edmund Walsingham, q.v, concerning the latter's business appointments, Reg. Walsingham, no 12.

III Robert SUTTON [Sotton
occ. 1496 occ. 1539
1496, 2 Apr., ord subdcn, Ely cathedral, Reg. Alcock, fo 240.
1498, 14 Apr., ord dcn, Ely cathedral, *ib.*, fo 246ᵛ.
1511/12, subprior, CUL EDC 1/C/7, fo 28.
1500, 30 Oct., last but one to be examined at the visitation by the commissary of the prior of Christ Church, Canterbury (*sed. vac.* both Ely and Canterbury). His deposition was recorded as *omnia bene*, Canterbury Reg. R., fo 70ᵛ.
1511/12, present at the inventory of the almoner's office on the apptment of a new obedientiary, CUL EDC 1/C/7, fo 28.
1515, 15/16 Apr. 9th in order on the *sed. vac.* visitation certificate, Reg. abp Warham, ii, fo 277.
1516, 22 Mar., 7th in order in the chapter which chose 29 Mar. as the date for the el. of a prior, Reg. West, fo 55.
1523/4, 1528/30, 1532/3, *socius* of the chamberlain who gave him 10s. p.a., CUL Add. Ms 2957, fos 33, 34.
1534, 8 Sept., 3rd on the visitation certificate, Reg. Goodrich, fo 90ᵛ.
1539, 18 Nov., described as 'aged and very sick' and assigned an annual pension of £10, *L and P Henry VIII*, xiv, pt 2, no 542.

Andrew de SWAFFHAM [Suafham
occ. 1276/7
1276, 24 June, proctor with Clement de Thetford, q.v., when they obtained a receipt for the payment of a pension of 30 m. owed to the nephew of a papal notary, CUL EDC 1B/115a.
1277, June, with John de Boroudit, q.v., obtained a receipt, in London, for a pension pd to the same, CUL EDC 1B/115b.

I John de SWAFFHAM [Suaffam, Suafham, Swafham
occ. 1247 occ. 1276
1265, 30 Aug., subprior, CUL EDC 1B/106.
1276, 4 Aug., sacrist, Liber M, 198.
[1241 × 1254], *temp.* prior Walter and bp Hugh, chaplain to bp Hugh [Northwold] and witnessed an episcopal charter, Liber M, 188.
Note: if this bp is Hugh [de Balsham], the dates would be 1257 × 1259. Dean Evans' notes record a charter dated 1247 with ref. [?Liber] M, 187b in which he was the bp's chaplain, but I have not been able to find it.
1254, 9 Sept., one of the monks who obtained licence from the king to el. a bp, *CPR (1247–1258)*, 328; see Robert de Leverington and Robert de Orford.
1265, 30 Aug., with other monks witnessed an acquittance for part of a sum owed by the bp and the prior and convent to a Florentine merchant, CUL EDC 1B/106.
1276, 4 Aug., involved in a dispute over tithes with the rector of Stretham [Straham], Liber M, 198.

II J[ohn] de SWAFFHAM D.Th. [Suafham
occ. 1289/90
1289/90, recd 4s. from the chamberlain at his inception, CUL Add. Ms 2957, fo 17.

III John de SWAFFHAM [Swafham
occ. 1397 d. 1436/7
1397, 16 June, ord acol., bp's [*maior*] chapel, Downham, Reg. Fordham, fo 238.

1398, 1 June, ord subdcn, Somersham, [Lincs.], *ib.*, fo 239.
1399, 29 Mar., ord dcn, bp's chapel, Somersham, *ib.*, fo 239.
1400, 12 June, ord pr., Doddington, *ib.*, fo 240ᵛ.
1401, 14 Sept., 35th in order on the metropolitan visitation certificate, Reg. Fordham, fo 131.
1416/18, 1427/8, *socius* of the chamberlain, CUL EDC 5/3/29, 30, 32.
1436/7, d. and the chamberlain sent 5s. to the almoner, CUL Add. Ms 2957, fo 31.

IV John SWAFFHAM [Swafham
occ. 1454 occ. 1462

1454, 15 June, ord subdcn, place not stated, Reg. Bourgchier, fo 48.
1457, 17 Dec., ord dcn, bp's chapel, Downham, Reg. Gray, fo 205.
1462, 13 Mar., ord pr., bp's [*magna*] chapel, Downham, *ib.*, fo 209ᵛ.

V John SWAFFHAM
occ. 1519

1519, 24 Sept., recd the tonsure and ord acol., Lady chapel, Ely cathedral, Reg. West, fo 87.

Peter de SWAFFHAM [Swafham
n.d.

n.d., name occ. in a quitclaim by his brother Baldewin, son of Fulk, to the prior and convent: 'illam [virgatam] . . . quam Petrus frater meus dedit eis imperpetuum cum seipso die qua suscepit monachatum in Elyen' ', BL Ms Egerton 3047, fo 195ᵛ, Liber M, 254.

Richard SWAFFHAM D.Th. [Swapham, Swofham
occ. 1473 occ. 1502

1473, 17 Apr., ord subdcn, bp's [*magna*] chapel, Downham, Reg. Gray, fo 215.
1475, 25 Mar., ord pr., bp's chapel, Doddington, *ib.*, fo 215ᵛ.
1484/5, sacrist, CUL Add. Ms 2956, fo 172.
1487/8, 1494/5, prob. feretrar, CUL EDC 5/10/40, CUL Add. Ms 2956, fo 174.
1500, 30 Oct., almoner, Canterbury Reg. R., fo 70.
[1476/6 or before], prob. student [at Cambridge] since his *introitum* was only four yrs later; see below.
1479, 4 Apr., described as a scholar [at Cambridge], CUL EDC 5/10/36.
1480, 18 June, B.Th., and admitted to oppose in theology, *BRUC*.
1486/7, incepted, *ib*; he paid 20d. for his *communia* this yr to the university proctors, *CU Grace Book A*, 203 (as Richard, monk of Ely).
1487/8, described as doctor by the sacrist, CUL EDC 5/10/40, CUL Add. Ms 2956, fo 173.
1500, 30 Oct., described as *sacre theologie professor*, Canterbury Reg. R., fo 70.
1475/6, recd 6s. 8d., for celebrating masses for the soul of John Hundredyer, CUL EDC 5/13/-.
1476/7, sent as proctor to the Black Monk Chapter in Northampton (4 July 1477), CUL EDC 5/13/16.
1478/9, gave the Palm Sunday (4 Apr. 1479) sermon in the cathedral but was not pd because he was a scholar, CUL EDC 5/10/36.
1487/8, preached in the cathedral on both Good Friday and Easter day, CUL EDC 5/10/40.
1500, 30 Oct., fourth to be examined at the visitation by the commissary of the prior of Christ Church, Canterbury (*sed. vac.*, both Ely and Canterbury); he deposed that there had been 48 monks, but numbers were reduced to 40 because of recent deaths, and he also referred to Vine gate which was not kept closed to the public; see William Makeroo, Canterbury Reg. R., fo 70.
1502, 7 Feb., apptd proctor by the prior and chapter, with Reginald Lakyngheth, q.v., to attend convocation, Liber B, no 381, CUL Add. Ms 2950, fos 84, 85.

Robert de SWAFFHAM [Suapham, Swafham
occ. 1286 occ. 1310

1303/4, 1310, 2 Mar., precentor, CUL Add. Ms 2957, fo 41, BL Add. Ms 41612, fo 50; he succ. Alexander de Ely, q.v.
1286, 11 July, with Richard de Feltwell, q.v., delivered the money collected for the tenth levied for the Holy Land to the papal collector in London, CUL EDC 1B/116.
1300, 11 Oct., was denounced as an evil monk by the abp in a letter to the bp because he had been wandering about the country with men at arms in defence of the 'church of Ely' during the dispute over the episcopal el., *Reg. abp Winchelsey*, 721; also *ib.*, 275, and Graham, 'Ely Vacancies', 56.
1303, Sept., went with Alexander de Ely to Impington *pro estimacio[ne bladi*, CUL Add. Ms 2957, fo 41.
1310, 2 Mar., chosen by the prior and chapter as one of seven *compromissorii* in the el. of a bp, BL Add. Ms 41612, fo 50ᵛ; this was the second set of *compromissorii* as the first had failed to agree. He was apptd to announce the result of the el., *ib.* fo 51, and Lambeth Ms 448, fos 49, 50; see John de Ketene.

Simon de SWAFFHAM [Swafham
occ. 1303/4 occ. 1327/8

1303/4, name occ. on the grange acct at Lakenheath, CUL EDC 7/15/acct.
1327/8, visited Lakenheath with Geoffrey de Ixworth, q.v., CUL EDC 7/15/acct.

I Stephen de SWAFFHAM [Suafham
occ. 1315 d. 1316/17

1315, July/1317, *socius* of the chamberlain, CUL Add. Ms 2957, fos 18, 19.
1316/17, recd 10s. from the chamberlain *pro tunica*; he d. this yr and the chamberlain sent 5s. to the almoner.
Note: see note under Stephen de Swaffham II below.

II Stephen de SWAFFHAM [Suafham
occ. 1302 occ. 1327/8

1302, 4 Apr., cellarer, *CPR (1301–1307)*, 26.
1323/4, almoner, CUL EDC 5/13/-.
1326/7, former almoner, CUL EDC 5/13/*status prioratus*, CUL Add. Ms 2957, fo 6v.
1302, 4/14 Apr., with Peter de Reche and William de Clare, q.v., recd royal licence to el. a bp, *CPR (1301–1307)*, 26. On 14 Apr., he was chosen by the prior and chapter as one of seven *compromissorii*, Lambeth Ms 448, fo 49 (for the date) and *CPL*, i (1198–1304), 604 (for the name, Stephen).
1302, 20 July, apptd attorney, with another, by the bp el., Robert de Orford, q.v., during his absence at the curia, *CPR (1301–1307)*, 45, 50.
1310, 10/28 Feb., with Alan de Hemmingestone and John de Saunford, q.v., recd royal licence to el. a bp, *CPR (1307–1313)*, 208. On 28 Feb., he was chosen to be one of seven *compromissorii* in the el. of a bp, BL Add. Ms 41612, fo 49v. In this case it appears that they failed to agree and seven others were chosen; see John de Ketene.
1315/16, *socius* of the pittancer, CUL EDC 5/8/9.
1319, 13 July, one of the senior monks [*senes*] who formed an arbitration committee in the *contentio* concerning the authority of the subprior, John de Crishale I, q.v., Lambeth Ms 448, fos 97v–98.
1327/8, the Lakenheath acct was charged for the provender of two of his horses, CUL EDC 7/15/acct.
Note: There are clearly two Stephens de Swaffham but which of them did what before 1316/17 is impossible to ascertain, and the assignments above are tentative.

William de SWAFFHAM [Swapham
occ. 1340/1

1340/1, *socius* of the cellarer, CUL Add. Ms 2957, fo 2, CUL EDC 5/2/7.
n.d., attested a miracle, Lambeth Ms 448, fo 57v.

John SWANTON
occ. 1420

1420, Feb./Sept., student at Cambridge, with John Stretham, q.v., and with financial support from the cellarer based on an assessment of ½d. in the £ for half the yr; the cellarer also gave them an additional sum *pro interferc[ulis suis*, CUL EDC 5/2/30.

Roger SWANTON
occ. 1460

1460, 10 Apr., removed from the office of cellarer by the bp personally in chapter, Reg. Gray, fo 46v.

William SWANTON
occ. 1412 d. 1460/1

1412, 28 May, ord acol., bp's chapel, Downham, Reg. Fordham, fo 261.
1413, 23 Sept., ord subdcn, bp's chapel, Downham, *ib.*, fo 262v.
1413, 23 Dec., ord dcn, bp's chapel, Downham, *ib.*, fo 263.
1414, 22 Dec., ord pr., bp's chapel, Downham, *ib.*, fo 264.
1423/6, 1428/9, *senescallus terrarum*, CUL EDC 5/13/12, 7/17/acct, 7/16/acct, PRO SC6/1257/4.
1431/2; 1434/5; 1436/7, cellarer, CUL EDC 5/4/30; EDC 5/12/3 and PRO SC6/1257/5; PRO SC6/1257/6.
1439/41, 1443/7, 1449/50, cellarer, PRO SC6/1257/7, 8, CUL Add. Ms 2957, fo 6, CUL EDC 5/4/34, 35, 5/2/31, 5/4/36, 37; also CUL EDC 5/12/5 for 1444/5.
1454/5, 1457/8, 1459/60, Apr., cellarer, CUL Add. Ms 2957, fo 6.
1424/5, visited Winston, CUL EDC 7/17/acct.
1425/6, visited Melton, CUL EDC 7/16/32 acct.
1425, 10 May, obtained papal indult to choose his own confessor, *CPL*, vii (1417–1431), 416.
1427/8, went about holding courts on the Suffolk manors, PRO SC6/1257/4.
1434/5, with John Stretham, I or II, went to London to obtain royal licence to el. a bp, PRO SC6/1257/5.
1438/9, *custos* of the manor of Caxton for the sacrist, CUL EDC 5/10/32.
1460/1, d., prob. in Apr. 1460 and the chamberlain sent 5s. to the almoner *pro anniversario* [?in Apr. 1461], CUL Add. Ms 2957, fo 32.

SWOFHAM
see Swaffham

Robert TAVERHAM [?*alias* Derham
occ. 1539

1539, 18 Nov., name on the surrender list, CUL Add. Ms 2957, fo 166v, but he is not on the pension list unless he is Robert Derham, q.v.

Richard TAYLOR
see Downham

TEFFORD
see Thetford

THEINBERT [Combirtus, Thembert
occ. 1144 occ. before 1151

1144–?1151, prior: references to him occur in *Liber. Elien.*, 335, 337, 340, 386; see *Fasti*, ii, 48, *HRH*, 45.

[1133 × 1169], as prior, *temp.* bp Nigel, witnessed an episcopal charter, Liber M, 151, and *Liber Elien.*, 337.

n.d., in the additions to the inventory of the treasury he is named as having given four albs, an embroidered cope and other vestments, *Liber Elien.*, 293–294.

Note: the obit of a Theinbertus, not named as prior, occ. on 28 June in Cambridge, Trinity College Ms 1105, fo 6k^v^.

Clement de THETFORD [Tefford, Thethford
occ. 1265 occ. 1302/3

1281, 8/11 Oct., chamberlain, CUL EDC 1B/112.
1291/2, sacrist, Chapman, *Sacrist Rolls*, ii, 3–13, (CUL EDC 5/10/1).

1265, 30 Aug., with other monks attested a quittance for a sum owed to a Florentine merchant by the bp and the prior and chapter, CUL EDC 1B/106.

1276, 24 June, with Andrew de Swaffham, q.v., delivered 30 m. by way of a pension to the nephew of a papal notary, CUL EDC 1B/115a.

1281, 8/11 Oct., acted as proctor for the prior John de Hemmingestone, q.v., who was ill and unable to be absolved in person from excommunication for irregularities that had occurred over payment of a tenth for the Holy Land, CUL EDC 1B/112, 113.

1290, 6 Apr, with Robert de Orford and Robert de Swaffham, q.v., sent by the prior and chapter to inform the king of the d. of the bp and recd licence to el, *CPR (1281–1292)*, 349.

1291/2, made two visits to Turbutsey [Tydbury], on the feast of St Withburga after *minutio*, Chapman, *Sacrist Rolls*, ii, 6, 8 (CUL EDC 5/10/1).

1302/3, recd £1 6s. from the sacrist, p.a., Chapman, *Sacrist Rolls*, ii, 16 (CUL EDC 5/10/2).

Note: see Clement I, note 2.

John THETFORD [Thettforthe, Thorford
occ. 1515/16

1515, 15/16 Apr., 23rd in order on the *sed. vac.* visitation certificate, Reg. abp Warham, ii, fo 277.
1516, 22 Mar., 18th in order at the el. of a prior, Reg. West, fo 55.

I Thomas de THETFORD [senior,
occ. 1356 d. 1394/5

1356, 9 Apr., ord acol., bp's chapel, Wisbech castle, Reg. de Lisle, fo 101.

*1381/2, Sept. to Jan., hostiller, CUL EDC 5/5/3.

1379, 14th in order on the clerical poll tax list and pd 3s. 4d., PRO E179/23/1.
*1381/2, reported as ill by the cellarer, CUL EDC 5/2/22, and also ill on 5/2/37 which is close in date but lacks a head.
1394/5, d., and the almoner recd 20s. [from other obedientiaries] *pro errogatione* of Thetford *senior*, CUL Add. Ms 2957, fo 13.

Note: the entries marked * may refer to Thomas de Thetford II below, but the ordination date is correctly assigned by reference to Alexander de Bury, q.v.

II Thomas de THETFORD [junior, Thetford *alias* Pike, Pyk', Pykis
occ. 1371/2 occ. 1388/9

1371/2, 1373/5, 1385/6, 1388/9, precentor, CUL EDC 5/9/4, 6, CUL Add. Ms 2957, fo 45, CUL EDC 5/9/5, CUL Add. Ms 2957, fo 6; in 1373/4 he is named 'junior' and 'Pyk' de Thetford'.

1371/2, pd 40s. to a clerk of Adam de Easton, q.v. (under Norwich), *pro labore suo*, CUL EDC 5/9/6, CUL Add. Ms 2957, fo 45.
1374/5, went to Impington and Littlebury twice, CUL EDC 5/9/5.
1379, 24th in order on the clerical poll tax list and pd 3s. 4d., PRO E179/23/1, as Pykis.
1381/2, reported ill by the cellarer, CUL EDC 5/2/22, as Pike.

Note: see the note under Thomas de Thetford I.

I William de THETFORD [Thefford
occ. 1371/2 d. 1403/4

1381, Dec./1382, 1398/1400, *custos* of the Lady chapel, CUL Add. Ms 2957, fos 57, 58.
1393/4, treasurer, named on a bailiff acct for Ely in *Bentham Supplement*, 67.

1371/2, *socius* of the sacrist, CUL EDC 5/10/18.
1378, 14 Oct., a 'letter of credence' from John, prior of the [Cluniac] priory of Thetford stated that he had been prof. at Thetford, had transferred to Ely and now wanted to return to Thetford if he obtained the consent of the prior of Ely, Reg. Walsingham, no 22.
1379, 30th in order on the clerical poll tax list and pd 3s. 4d., PRO E179/23/1.
1381, Sept./Dec., *socius* of the *custos* of the Lady chapel, CUL EDC 5/7/7.
1401, 14 Sept., 10th in order on the metropolitan visitation certificate, Reg. Fordham, fo 131.
1403/4, d., and the chamberlain sent 5s. to the almoner, CUL Add. Ms 2957, fo 29, CUL EDC 5/3/25.

Note: see also the ref. to an undated letter by a William de Thetford under William de Thetford II.

II William de THETFORD
occ. 1397 occ. 1401

1397, 16 June, ord acol., bp's [*maior*] chapel, Downham, Reg. Fordham, fo 238.
1398, 1 June, ord subdcn, Somersham, [Lincs.], *ib.*, fo 239.
1399, 29 Mar., ord dcn, bp's chapel, Somersham, *ib.*, fo 239.
1400, 18 Sept., ord pr. bp's chapel, Doddington, *ib.*, fo 240v.

1401, 14 Sept., 32nd in order on the metropolitan visitation certificate, Reg. Fordham, fo 131.

Note: a copy of an undated letter written by a William Thetford to the prior concerning a financial matter related to St Peter's College [Cambridge] has been entered in Reg. Walsingham, no 13; see Edmund Walsingham.

THOMAS
[fl. 1175]

n.d., author of a collection of miracles wrought by St Etheldreda of which one is included in *Liber Elien.*, 312–314. He was prob a monk scribe assigned to the scriptorium, *ib.*, 312; see also *ib.*, xlvi–xlvii.

See *DNB*, under Thomas of Ely, which suggests the date fl. 1175; see also Sharpe, *Latin Writers*.

Edmund de THOMESTON [Thomston, Tomeston, Tomestone, Tomston, Tomyston
occ. 1379 d. 1417/18

1379, 24 Sept., ord acol. and subdcn, bp's chapel, Downham, Reg. Arundel, fo 125.
1379, 17 Dec., ord dcn, Lady chapel, Ely cathedral, *ib.*, fo 125v.
1380, 22 Dec., ord pr., bp's chapel, Downham, *ib.*, fo 128v.

1401, 14 Sept., subprior, Reg. Fordham, fo 131; 1405, 10 Nov., a comm. was issued for his dismissal from this office, *ib.*, fo 201.
1406/7, feretrar, CUL EDC 5/10/26.

1389/90, student at Cambridge with Edmund de Totyngton, q.v., with maintenance of £8 4s. 2d., pd by the treasurer, CUL EDC 5/13/8.
1396/7, student, with John de Yaxham, q.v., and together they recd £6 3s. for three quarters of the yr, CUL EDC 5/13/10, CUL Add. Ms 2957, fo 72.

1379, 46th and last but one in order on the clerical poll tax list and pd 3s. 4d., PRO E179/23/1.
1401, 14 Sept., 2nd in order on the metropolitan visitation certificate, Reg. Fordham, fo 131.
1402, 8 Mar., licensed to hear confessions of parishioners within the city and diocese of Ely, *ib.*, fo 193v; on this same day he recd a licence to choose his own confessor, *ib.*, fo 194.
1417/18, d., and the chamberlain sent 5s. to the almoner, CUL EDC 5/3/30, CUL Add. Ms 2957, fo 30.

In 1387/8, his father stayed [in the guest hall] as a guest, CUL EDC 5/5/5.

THORFORD
see John Thetford

John de THORNTON [Thorndon
occ. 1379 occ. 1389

1379, 33rd in order on the clerical poll tax list and pd 3s. 4d., PRO E179/23/1.
1385, 19 Oct., recd dispensation from the bp to be allowed to rec. 6m. each yr for celebrating an anniversary mass in the cathedral; the bp gave as his reason: 'ad relevamen persone tue quam veraciter scimus ere alieno graviter oneratam et ex certis causis et legitimis', Reg. Arundel, fo 53v.
1389, 1 Aug., nominated by the king to be prior of the alien priory of Swavesey, *CPR (1388–1392)*, 88; this is entered a second time on 28 Aug., *ib.*, 109.
1389, 2 Sept., presented to Swavesey by Hugh de la Zouche, lord of Ashby de la Zouche; 5 Sept., licensed by the prior and chapter to accept the priorate; 6 Sept., the comm. was issued for his adm. and induction; n.d., gave his submission to the bp as prior; all of these are given in Reg. Fordham, fo 18–18v. See also *CPR (1388–1392)*, 88, 109.

Note: he occ. as prior of Swavesey in 1396/7, CUL EDC 5/13/10; also 1399, 1 Feb., Reg. Fordham, fo 122.

Godfrey de THORP
d. 1333/4

1333/4, Sept. to Apr., d. and the chamberlain gave 5s. to the almoner, CUL Add. Ms 2957, fo 21.

John de THORP [Thorpe
occ. 1341/3

1341, 24 Mar., ord dcn, Willingham, Reg. Montacute, fo 107v.
1343, 29 Mar., ord pr., Willingham, *ib.*, fo 111v (not identified by religious house).

William de THORP [Thorpe *alias* Ixworth
occ. 1379 occ. 1408/9

1379, 24 Sept., ord acol. and subdcn, bp's chapel, Downham, Reg. Arundel, fo 125 (as Ixworth),
1379, 17 Dec., ord dcn, Lady chapel, Ely cathedral, *ib.*, fo 125v.
1380, 22 Dec., ord pr., bp's chapel, Downham, *ib.*, fo 128v.

1394/5, granator, CUL EDC 7/15/acct.
1396/7, 1406/7, 1408/9, precentor, CUL EDC 5/13/10, CUL Add. Ms 2957, fo 47.

1379, 47th and last in order on the clerical poll tax list and pd 3s. 4d., PRO E179/23/1.
1394/5, pd a visit to Lakenheath, CUL EDC 7/15/acct.
1401, 14 Sept., 21st on the metropolitan visitation certificate, Reg. Fordham, fo 131.

In 1387/8, his mother was a guest in the priory, CUL EDC 5/5/5.

THURSTAN [Turstanus iuvenis
[?1071 × 1134]

[1071/2, monk and reeve [*prepositus*] who may have fought with Hereward, *Liber Elien.*, 182, n. 2, 219 n. 3.]
[1109 × 1131], *temp.* bp Hervey, removed from his office [?as sacrist] through an unjust accusation, *ib.*, 339.
n.d., in the additions to the inventory of the treasury he is named as having given a stole, alb, amice and other vestments, *ib.*, 293–294.
1134, by this date d., *ib.*, 219 n. 3.

TIDDE
see Tydde

TILNEY
see Tylney

TOMESTON, Tomston, Tomyston
see Thomeston

Robert TOPLYFF [?Topclyff
occ. 1476

1476, 5 Feb., granted papal dispensation to rec. and retain a benefice with cure of souls including a parish church, *CPL*, xiii (1471–1484), 493.

Edmund de TOTYNGTON D.Th. [Todyngton
occ. 1382 occ. 1406/7

1382, 31 May, ord acol., bp's chapel, Downham, Reg. Arundel, fo 129ᵛ.
1382, 20 Sept., ord subdcn, bp's chapel, Downham, *ib.*, fo 129ᵛ.
1383, 16 May, ord dcn, bp's chapel, Downham, *ib.*, fo 130ᵛ.
1384, 9 Apr., ord pr., Ely cathedral, *ib.*, fo 131ᵛ, (the scribe has written Tomeston, q.v., (under Thomeston), prob. because he had here confused the two contemporary Edmunds).

1401, 13 Oct., 1402, 1 May, 1403/4, 1405/7, sacrist, Reg. abp Arundel, i, 494ᵛ, *CPL*, v (1396–1404), 506, CUL EDC 5/10/24–26, CUL Add. Ms 2956, fos 165, 166.

1389/90, student at Cambridge, with Edmund de Thomeston, q.v., and with maintenance of £8 4s. 2d., pd by the treasurer, CUL EDC 5/13/8.
1396/7, *in inceptione Biblie*, the precentor contributed two eels, costing 16d., for the inception feast, CUL Add. Ms 2957, fo 46 (not in *BRUC*).
1401, 14 Sept., 22nd in order on the metropolitan visitation certificate, Reg. Fordham, fo 131; on 13 Oct., with Peter de Ely I, q.v., as proctors of the subprior and chapter informed William Powcher, q.v., of his postulation as prior, Reg. abp Arundel, i, fo 494ᵛ.
1402, 1 May, granted papal dispensation to hold a benefice with or without cure of souls, *CPL*, v (1396–1404), 506.
1403, 9 Nov., with the bp's official, recd a comm. to examine a criminous clerk, Reg. Fordham, fo 196.

Thomas TOTYNGTON
occ. 1419 occ. 1430/1

1419, 5 June, ord acol., bp's chapel, Downham, Reg. Fordham, fo 272.
1419, 10 June, ord subdcn, bp's chapel, Downham, *ib.*, fo 272.
1419, 23 Sept., ord dcn, bp's chapel, Downham, *ib.*, fo 272ᵛ.
1423/6; 1427/31, treasurer, CUL EDC 5/13/12, 7/17/acct, 7/16/33 acct; CUL EDC 7/15/acct, PRO SC6/1257/4, CUL EDC 5/6/20, 21.
1424/5, pd a visit to Winston for *liberatio denariorum* and prob. visited Lakenheath, CUL EDC 7/17/acct, 7/15/acct.
1425/6, visited Melton, CUL EDC 7/16/32 acct.
1427/8, visited Lakenheath for *liberatio denariorum*, CUL EDC 7/15/acct.
1430/1, prob. pd visits to Kingston and Winston, CUL EDC 7/14c/41 acct, 7/17/acct.

Thomas TUK'
see Leverygton

Robert TYDDE [Tidde, Tyd
occ. 1463 d. 1499

1463, 9 Apr., ord acol., bp's [*magna*] chapel, Downham, Reg. Gray, fo 210ᵛ.
1466, 5 Apr., ord subdcn, bp's palace chapel, Ely, *ib.*, fo 211.
1467, 28 Mar., ord pr., bp's palace chapel, Ely, *ib.*, fo 212.

1494/5, sacrist, CUL EDC 5/10/41, and prob. in office until 1499; see below.

1477/9, 1483/4, *socius* of the sacrist, CUL EDC 5/10/35, 36; as *socius* in 1478/9 he recd 10s. 'ad attend' et custodiend' le clok'.
1500, 30 Oct., reported as formerly sacrist who d. [before 29 Sept.] 'last yr', Canterbury Reg. R., fos 69ᵛ, 70.

William TYDDE [Tydd *alias* Whitred, Whytred
occ. 1534 occ. 1539

1534, 8 Sept., 14th in order on the visitation certificate, Reg. Goodrich, fo 90ᵛ.
[1535/6, described as *vestiarius* by the sacrist, acc. to S.J.A. Evans without ref., and not traced.]

1539, 18 Nov., assigned a pension of £6 p.a., *L and P Henry VIII*, xiv, pt 2, no 542.

William TYLNEY [Tilney
occ. 1453 occ. 1487/8

1453, 31 Mar., ord pr., bp's [*parva*] chapel, Downham, Reg. Bourgchier, fo 47v.
1464/73, 1474/5, 1476/7, 1477/8, feretrar, CUL EDC 5/11/7, 5/10/35.
1487/8, *custos* of the Lady chapel, CUL EDC 5/7/14, CUL Add. Ms 2957, fo 64.
1464/5, and later yrs, as feretrar, pd himself 40s. 'ex consuetudine pro diligent' attendent' circa officium', CUL EDC 5/11/7.
1478, 26 July, acted for prior Henry Peterborough, q.v., in tendering the latter's resignation, *Anglia Sacra*, i, 672, Lambeth Ms 448, fo 113.

William UNDELE [Undeley
occ. 1486 occ. 1500

1486, 23 Dec., ord dcn, Lady chapel, Ely cathedral, Reg. Alcock, fo 223.
1487, 14 Apr., ord pr., Ely cathedral, *ib.*, fo 223v.
1500, 30 Oct., *senescallus* [?of the prior's hospice] and penitentiary, Canterbury Reg. R., fo 70; see William Wittlesey who was *senescallus terrarum* at this time.
1500, 30 Oct., at the visitation by the commissary of the prior of Christ Church, Canterbury (*sed. vac.*, both Ely and Canterbury), the prior, Robert Colville, q.v., reported that William held the two offices named above because it seemed, to him (the prior) *magis expediens*, Canterbury Reg. R., fo 70.

Peter de VALENEM
occ. [?1198 × ?1202]

[?1198 × ?1202], with prior John [de Strateshete], q.v., witnessed a charter of Alexander, abbot of Sawtry, Liber M, 222.
Note: Alexander occ. as abbot of Sawtrey, 1185 × 1204, *HRH*, 142.

I VINCENT
occ. 1109 × c. 1128

1109 × c. 1128, the first prior: occ. between these dates, *Liber Elien.*, 279, 346; *Fasti*, ii, 47, *HRH*, 45. He must have res. and been succeeded by Henry, q.v., *Liber Elien.*, 279.
1109 × c. 1128, witnessed a charter, Alm. Cart., fo 69v.
n.d., 23 Nov., the obit of a Vincent occ. in Cambridge, Trinity College Ms 1105, fo k11v.

II VINCENT
occ. 1173

1173, sent with a letter concerning the el. of bp Ridel to Rome, Holtzmann, *Papsturkunden*, ii, no 130.

W.
occ. 1233

1233, 11 Sept., subprior and witness to an agreement over tithes, Liber M, 319.
Note: this may be Walter II, q.v.; see also Walter de Walpole.

John WACE [Was, Wassh
occ. 1447 occ. 1473/4

1447, 4 Mar., ord subdcn, church of St John the Baptist, Ely, Reg. Bourgchier, fo 47.
1448, 21 Dec., ord dcn, place not stated, *ib.*, fo 47v.
1473/4, celebrated [chantry] masses for the soul of Philip Lisle and recd 6s. 8d., from the treasurer, CUL EDC 5/13/-.

Richard de WALPOL'
d. 1335/6

1335/6, d. and the treasurer pd 5s. to the almoner, CUL EDC 5/13/7, CUL Add. Ms 2957, fo 70.

Walter de WALPOLE [Walepol
occ. [?1230]

[?1230], infirmarer, Liber M, 424.
[?1230], as infirmarer, pd 22s. in return for a grant of land, *ib.*
See Walter II prior.

I William de WALPOLE [Walpol, Walpoll, Walpool
occ. 1370 occ. 1401

1396/7–1401, prior: occ. 29 Sept. 1397, and there is a ref. to his el. on the 1396/7 treasurer's acct, CUL EDC 5/13/10; res. 22 Sept. 1401 during the metropolitan visitation, Evans, *Ely Chap. Ord.*, 48–49, (Reg. abp Arundel, i, fo 494); he postulated William Powcher, q.v., to succ. him, Evans, *Ely Chap. Ord.*, 50.
1370/1, steward of the prior's hospice, CUL EDC 5/12/1.
1372/6, chamberlain, CUL EDC 5/3/19, 20, CUL Add. Ms 2957, fo 29.
1382, Jan./Sept., 1387/8, hostiller, CUL EDC 5/5/4, 5.
1390/3, *senescallus* [*terrarum*], CUL EDC 7/14c/35 acct, CUL EDC 7/17/acct, 7/14c/36 acct, 5/13/9 (1392/3).
1393, 13 Nov., a comm. was issued for his apptment as sacrist, Reg. Fordham, fo 181.
1396/7, *senescallus* [*terrarum*], CUL EDC 7/15/acct.
1379, 22nd in order on the clerical poll tax list and pd 3s. 6d., PRO E179/23/1.
1387/8, went to Stourbridge fair to purchase provisions including fish and spices, CUL EDC 5/5/5.
1390/1, pd a visit to Kingston, CUL EDC 7/14c/35 acct.

1391/2, visited Winston, CUL EDC 7/17/acct.

1392/3, visited Kingston; journeyed to London *pro negociis* and his expenses were 62s. 8d.,; went to Nottingham to obtain letters patent for the mortification of several manors, CUL EDC 7/14c/36 acct, 5/13/9, CUL Add. Ms 2957, fo 72.

1396/7, sent by the chapter with John de Bukton II, q.v., to the bp at Hatfield for a licence to el. a prior; the el. expenses are on the treasurer's acct and amounted to £22 8s. 9d., CUL EDC 5/13/10; he stayed at Downham rectory on three occasions *tempore electionis*, *ib.*

1398, 21 Mar., recd the *recognitio* at his first appearance at the court at Whittlesey, CUL EDC 7/6/9.

1401, 22 Sept., res. during the visitation of abp Arundel, as above. Two undated letters in Reg. Walsingham (nos 8 and 9) from abp Arundel written shortly after the visitation refer to the inadequate provision assigned for his needs in his retirement and order the monks to give him maintenance befitting his former status. According to a Bury chronicle the abp declared his election to have contravened canon law. The arrangements made for him specified that the manor of Wodeley and its income (assessed at £20 p.a.) were to be assigned to him, together with £10 for his clothing [*cameraria*]; a chamber within the monastery was to be set aside for him and the chaplain of his choice, and food and drink provided for him and his servants, [*de plenis corrodiis quatuor monachorum*] whether he was at the manor or in the priory, *Memorials Bury*, iii, 183–184.

Ely porta, at the south western end of the monastic precincts, was known as Walpole's Gate or Gate House, as its construction was under way in 1396/7, CUL EDC 5/13/10.

See the note below under William Walpole II.

II William WALPOLE

occ. 1419/20

1419/20, visited Lakenheath for *liberatio denariorum*, CUL EDC 7/15/acct.

Note: could this be the retired prior above, still active?

Alan de WALSINGHAM

occ. 1318/19 d. ?1364

1341–1363 or 1364, prior: el. 25 Oct. 1341 by a single *compromissorius*, Nicholas de Copmanford, q.v., whom the chapter had authorized to make the choice, Reg. Montacute, fo 25–25[v], also BL Ms Cotton Titus A.i, fo 126; last occ. 12 July 1363, BL Ms Egerton 3047, fo 224; see below and William de Hathfield. Did Walsingham res. before he d.?

1318/19, July to July, *custos* of the Lady altar, CUL Add. Ms 2957, fo 50.

1321, 16 Feb., apptd subprior and held the office until 21 Dec., *Anglia Sacra*, i, 643; and see Lambeth Ms 448, fo 51–51[v].

1321, 21 Dec./1341, 25 Oct., sacrist, *ib*. Accts survive for the following years: 1322/4, 1325/6, 1334/5, 1336/7, 1339/40, 1341, Sept./Nov., Chapman, *Sacrist Rolls*, ii, 25–110, (CUL EDC 5/10/3–9).

1318/19, with two *socii* spent a fortnight at Quaveney, CUL Add. Ms 2957, fo 50.

1322/42, initiated and completed the construction of the octagon and lantern of the cathedral, the total cost being £2406 6s. 11d., Lambeth Ms 448, fo 119.

1322, Oct., travelled by water to the synod at Barnwell accompanied by his *socius*, Chapman, *Sacrist Rolls*, ii, 31 (CUL EDC 5/10/3); he also went to the synod the following June, *ib.*

1322/3, went to Lynn, Melbourn and Wisbech, *ib.*

1323/4, went to Boston fair to purchase clothing, wax and tallow; attended synods in Oct. and June, also visited Melbourn and Lakenheath, and went to London to speak to the bp, Chapman, *Sacrist Rolls*, ii, 45 (CUL EDC 5/10/4).

1325/6, went to several fairs and the synods, *ib.*, ii, 58 (CUL EDC 5/10/5).

1336/7, attended both synods and several fairs and prob. went to London to obtain licence from the king to el. a bp, *ib.*, 281–282 (CUL EDC 5/10/7).

1338, 29 Mar., with the bp's official apptd to rec. the purgation of criminous clerks, Reg. Montacute, fo 42[v].

1338/9, Apr. to Mar., recd 3s. from the chamberlain *pro linea tela*, CUL Add. Ms 2957, fo 22.

1339, 31 Mar., with Robert de Aylesham, q.v., and others, apptd proctors to treat with bp Hotham's executors over certain terms of his will, BL Add. Ms 41612, fo 101.

1339/40, attended the synods and fairs, Chapman, *Sacrist Rolls*, ii, 94–95 (CUL EDC 5/10/8).

1341, 19 Oct., attended the synod at Barnwell, Chapman, *Sacrist Rolls*, ii, 110, (CUL EDC 5/10/9a).

1341, 20 Nov., installed as prior by the bp in person, Lambeth Ms 448, fo 61, Reg. Montacute, fo 25.

1341, 8 Dec., pd his first visit to Swaffham as prior, CUL EDC 7/12/5 acct.

1345, 7 July, el. bp, BL Cotton Ms Titus A i, fo 128[v], but Thomas de Lisle was provided, *Fasti*, iv, 13–14.

1348, 1 Oct., with four others, apptd vicar general, *coniunctim et divisim*, during the bp's absence abroad, Reg. de Lisle, fo 17; in this capacity some of his acta are recorded, *ib.*, fos 22, 23[v], 24, 25, 28[v], 29.

1349, 9 Apr., named by the bp in a comm. to his vicars general as a substitute if necessary with regard to the provision of heads of religious houses and the examination and confirmation of elections, *ib.*, fo 21.

1361, contributed £66 13s. 4d., towards the purchase of the manor and advowson of Mepal, Evans, 'Mepal', 118 (CUL EDC 1B/box 23).

1363, Feb., acquired property to fund an annual pension of 66s. 8d., 40s. of which was to be distributed by the almoner among the poor and 26s. 8d. to be divided among the monks as pittances on his anniversary and the anniversaries of John de Crauden, q.v., and Adam and Agnes, the parents of the former, CUL EDC 1B/1151.

n.d., 15 May, his anniversary occ. in BL Add. Ms 33381, fo 12, on the same day as John de Crauden, q.v.

Mention must be made of the great building works undertaken during his priorate; these include the Lady chapel, octagon and lantern over the central crossing, and the new buildings for the sacrist's office. They were admired by his brethren and contemporaries and remain a source of inspiration in our own generation. In two of his writings Thomas Walsingham, monk of Bury St Edmunds, reported that as a junior monk he was known to have been a skilled goldsmith, *Hist. Anglicana*, i, 104, and *Gesta Abbatum*, i, 34–35. As sacrist his knowledge and experience in this craft would have been invaluable. In a recent and as yet unpublished study (a doctoral thesis) Dr Philip Lindley has concluded that, although Walsingham was not an architect, he may well have 'played a pivotal role' in the conception of the octagon, Lindley 'Ely' 33; see also *ib.*, 'The Fourteenth Century Architectural Programme at Ely' in W. M. Ormrod, ed., *Proceedings of the 1985 Harlaxton Symposium*, Woodbridge, 1986, 119–129.

Some of his *acta* are in BL Add. Ms 41612, fos 91ᵛ–114ᵛ.

His family connections are given in Walsingham, *Gesta Abbatum*, i, 34–35.

He is believed to be buried between the nave altar and the pulpitum, BL Add. Ms 33381, fo 2, which states *iacet ante chorum* and lists his achievements including the new *turre* and the purchase of Mepal.

Edmund WALSINGHAM B.Th./D.Th. or B.Cn.L./D.Cn.L.

occ. 1400 occ. 1424

1418–1424, prior: occ. 25 July 1418, CUL EDC 7/8/3 court; occ. 7 Nov., 1424, CUL EDC 7/7/5 court; see Peter de Ely I.

1400, 13 Mar., ord subdcn, Doddington, Reg. Fordham, fo 240.

1401, 24 Sept., ord dcn, bp's chapel, Downham, *ib.*, fo 241ᵛ.

1402, 11 Mar., ord pr., bp's chapel, Downham, *ib.*, fo 242.

1415, 8 May, student at Cambridge, with Henry Madyngle, John Stunteney and John Yaxham, q.v., and licensed to preach in any church [?in Cambridge] appropriated to Ely cathedral, *Reg. abp Chichele*, iv, 126–127.

1416/17, the chamberlain gave 3s. 4d., to him and to Henry Madyngle *ad inceptionem*, CUL EDC 5/3/29, CUL Add. Ms 2957, fo 30; the sacrist gave them 20s. *ad introitum*, CUL EDC 5/10/29, CUL Add. Ms 2956, fo 167.

1401, 14 Sept., 40th and last in order on the metropolitan visitation certificate, Reg. Fordham, fo 131.

[1418/20], during his absence in London the vicar general arbitrarily removed the subprior, John de Yaxham, q.v., from office; this led to a dispute lasting six months, during which Walsingham appealed to the Court of Arches, Lambeth Ms 448, fo 85–85ᵛ.

1420, 6 May, carried out a visitation of Bury St Edmunds on behalf of the Black Monk Chapter, Pantin, *BMC*, iii, 238–239.

1420, 8–10 July, was present in person at the Black Monk Chapter in Northampton, *ib.*, ii, 96, where he was named as one of the examiners of the monk proctors, as one of the electors of monk visitors and as one of the electors of the presidents for the next Chapter, *ib.*, ii, 138, 145, 152.

1423, 18 May, carried out a visitation of Ramsey for the Black Monk Chapter, *ib.*, iii, 240–241 (Reg. Walsingham, no 24). On 5 July he and the subprior attended the Black Monk Chapter and on 8 July examined the proctors, Pantin, *BMC*, ii, 137–138.

[1423, Oct.], wrote to the abbot of Bury St Edmunds in reply to the latter's request (dated 19 Oct.) for payment of the contributions owed by the prior and chapter of Ely to the Black Monk Chapter. He apologized that the sum was overdue and was now sending it with the bearer, Pantin, *BMC*, iii, 150, 151 (Reg. Walsingham, nos 28, 29).

[1423 × 1425], 10 Sept., asked by William, abbot of Bury St Edmunds as president of the Black Monk Chapter, to appt a prior for the monk students at Cambridge, Pantin, *BMC*, iii, 102 (Reg. Walsingham, fo 4 and repeated on fo 5ᵛ, no 4). There are two other letters on the same subject from the abbot, *ib.*, nos 10 and 30, which can only be dated by his presidency; however, they were almost certainly directed to prior Edmund Walsingham, a Cambridge graduate, rather than to his successor, Peter de Ely, q.v., and may therefore be placed between Sept. 1423 and Mar. 1425.

Note: see Robert Sutton II.

John de WALSINGHAM [Walsyngham
occ. 1348 d. 1373/4

1348, 14 June, ord acol., Over, Reg. de Lisle, fo 96.
[1349, Nov.], dcn, granted *lit. dim.*, for the order of pr., *ib.*, fo 30.
1355/6, steward of the prior's hospice and granator, CUL EDC 7/15/acct; see John de Bukton I, who was also steward during this yr.
1364/5, *custos* of the Lady chapel, CUL EDC 5/7/3.
1370/1, cellarer, CUL EDC 5/12/1.
1355/6, visited Lakenheath, CUL EDC 7/15/acct.
1361, contributed 13s. 4d., towards the purchase of the manor and advowson of Mepal, Evans, 'Mepal', 118 (CUL EDC 1B/box 23).
1367/8, made an offering [*oblatio*] of 3s. 4d., to the *custos* of the Lady chapel, CUL Add. Ms 2957, fo 55.
1373/4, d., and the chamberlain and precentor sent 5s. to the almoner, CUL EDC 5/3/20, CUL Add. Ms 2957, fos 29, 45.

Stephen WALSINGHAM [Walsyngham
occ. 1397 d. 1446/7

1397, 16 June, ord subdcn, bp's [*maior*] chapel, Downham, Reg. Fordham, fo 238.
1398, 1 June, ord dcn, Somersham, [Lincs.], *ib.*, fo 239.
1400, 18 Sept., ord pr., bp's chapel, Doddington, *ib.* fo 240v.
1418/20, treasurer, CUL EDC 7/12/acct, 7/15/acct.
1426/7, *custos* of the Lady chapel, CUL Add. Ms 2957, fo 59.
1427/9, treasurer, CUL EDC 5/4/28, 29.
1401, 14 Sept., 34th in order on the metropolitan visitation certificate, Reg. Fordham, fo 131.
1418/19, visited Swaffham Prior for *liberatio denariorum*, CUL EDC 7/12/acct.
1419/20, pd visits to Lakenheath and Sutton, CUL EDC 7/15/acct, 7/14c/39 acct. He was *socius* of the cellarer between Feb./Sept. of 1420, CUL EDC 5/2/30.
1423/4, recd 6s. 8d., for saying [chantry] masses for the soul of John Lyle, CUL EDC 5/13/12.
1446/7, d. and the chamberlain pd 5s. to the almoner, CUL Add. Ms 2957, fo 31.

Thomas de WALSINGHAM
occ. 1379 occ. 1402

1379, 39th in order (out of 47) on the clerical poll tax list and pd 3s. 4d., PRO E179/23/1.
1387/8, *socius* of the hostiller, CUL EDC 5/5/5.
1401, 14 Sept., 16th on the metropolitan visitation certificate, Reg. Fordham, fo 131.
1402, 8 Mar., licensed to hear the confessions of parishioners within the city and diocese of Ely, *ib.*, fo 193v.

I William de WALSINGHAM [Walsyngham
occ. 1334/5 occ. 1339/40

1334/5, *socius* of the sacrist, Chapman, *Sacrist Rolls*, ii, 70, (CUL EDC 5/10/6).
1339/40, was sent by the sacrist to Wisbech on negotations, *ib.*, ii, 95 (CUL EDC 5/10/8).

II William WALSINGHAM [Walsyngham
occ. 1513

1513, 20 Mar., pr.; was granted licence by the prior, with the bp's approval, to transfer to St Alban's abbey, Liber B, no 438.

Walter de WALSOKEN [Walsokne
occ. 1337 d. 1352/3

1337, 16 Sept., dcn, granted *lit. dim.*, for the order of pr., Reg. Montacute, fo 96.
1338, 19 Sept., ord pr., St Mary's church, Ely, *ib.*, fo 102.
[1349], 29 Sept., subprior, Reg. de Lisle, fo 29.
1337/8, prob. student at Cambridge with John de Bekkles, q.v., (as J. and W.) who recd 60s. from the chamberlain *pro vestura*, CUL EDC 5/3/4.
1339/40, Sept. to Mar., student at Cambridge for half a yr and recd 8s. 5d., from the cellarer, CUL EDC 5/2/6.
1340/1, student in canon law and recd pension contributions of 8s. 5d., from the cellarer, CUL EDC 5/2/7, CUL Add. Ms 2957, fo 3,; he and John de Bekkles also recd 11s. 11d., from the sacrist, Chapman, *Sacrist Rolls*, ii, 107 (CUL EDC 5/10/9).
1343, Jan./Sept., prob. still a student with John de Bekkles, as they occur together under the chamberlain's *liberationes*, CUL EDC 5/3/6a.
[1349], 29 Sept., licensed as penitentiary, with Adam de Lynstede, q.v., by the prior Alan de Walsingham, q.v., acting as vicar general, *nullis casibus exceptis*, Reg. de Lisle, fo 29.
1352/3, d., and the sacrist sent 5s. to the almoner *pro errogacione*, Chapman, *Sacrist Rolls*, ii, 157, (CUL EDC 5/10/12).

I WALTER
occ. before 1122/3

1122/3, before, as his name occ. on a mortuary roll of Savigny, Delisle, *Rouleaux des Morts*, 339.

II WALTER
occ. [1151 × 1158]

[1151 × 1158], with prior Alexander, q.v., witnessed a charter of bp Nigel, Liber M, 158.
n.d., the obit of a Walter occ. on 7 Jan. in Cambridge, Trinity College Ms 1105, fo k1v.

III WALTER
occ. 1241 occ. 1259

c. 1241–1259, prior: occ. as W. prior, Apr. 1241; occ. 16 Mar. 1259, *Fasti*, ii, 49.

1251, Apr., signed an agreement with David, abbot of Thorney concerning Aldegore marsh, Liber M, 385.
[1241 × 1254], witnessed a charter of bp Hugh [Northwold,] Liber M, 188.
Note: the bp may be the second Hugh [Balsham] in which case these dates would be extended to 1259; see Robert de Leverington.
n.d., 13 May, obit occ. in the kalendars in BL Ms Cotton Vespasian A.vi fo 133^{v}, BL Add. Ms 9822, fo 105, CUL Add. Ms 2950, fo 13, also BL Add. Ms 33381, fo 12.

Chapter ordinances from his priorate are extant and have been printed in Evans, *Ely Chap. Ord.*, 1–3 (from BL Add. Ms 9822, fo 57).

Note: see Walter de Walpole who may be the same monk.

Ralph de WALTHAM [Wautham
occ. 1288/9 occ. 1302/3

1288/9, cellarer, CUL Add. Ms 2957, fo 1.
1302/3, sacrist, Chapman, *Sacrist Rolls*, ii, 14–21, (CUL EDC 5/10/2).

1289, 30 June, one of a group of monks and others who sat on a commission to investigate disputed boundaries in Lakenheath, Liber M, 603.
1290, visited Melton for *liberatio denariorum*, CUL EDC 7/16/2.

John de WALTONE
occ. 1301/2 occ. 1325

1301/2, chamberlain, CUL Add. Ms 2957, fo 17.
1325, 29 Sept., described as cellarer (prob. former cellarer) under prior John de Fresingfeld, q.v., that is, c. 1321, CUL EDC 5/13/*status prioratus*, CUL Add. Ms 2957, fo 66.

1310, 2 Mar., chosen by the prior and chapter as one of seven *compromissorii* in the el. of a bp, BL Add. Ms 41612, fo 50^{v}; this was the second set of *compromissorii* as the first had failed to agree; see John de Ketene.
1319, 13 July, one of the senior monks [*senes*] who formed an arbitration committee in the *contentio* concerning the authority of the subprior, John de Crishale I, q.v., Lambeth Ms 448, fos 97^{v}–98.

John WARD [Warde
occ. 1519 occ. 1539

1519, 24 Sept., ord acol., Lady chapel, Ely cathedral, Reg. West, fo 87.

1535/6, sacrist, CUL Add. Ms 2956, fo 177.

1518/19, student at Cambridge, with maintenance of 2s. 4d., from the chamberlain, CUL EDC 5/3/34.
1523/5, student, with Laurence Wittlesey, q.v. and with 2s. 4d., between them from the chamberlain, CUL Add. Ms 2957, fo 33.
1525/8, student with Laurence Wittlesey, for whom the treasurer provided £8 13s. 4d., each yr, CUL EDC 5/13/18–20, CUL Add. Ms 2957, fos 75, 79, 80.
1528/9, student with Robert Hammond, q.v., for whom the treasurer provided £7 11s. 8d., CUL Add. Ms 2957, fo 80.

1534, 8 Sept., 12th in order on the visitation certificate, Reg. Goodrich, fo 90^{v}.
1536, 14 Feb., pd £8 to be dispensed to wear a secular habit and hold a benefice, Chambers, *Faculty Office Regs*, 46.
1539, 18 Nov., assigned a pension of £8 p.a., *L and P Henry VIII*, xiv, pt 2, no 542.
[1541, 10 Sept., apptd canon of the 8th prebend in the new foundation, *Fasti, 1541–1857*, vii, 27.]

WARIN
see Barntone

WAS
see Wace

WATTON
see Wotton

WAUTHAM
see Waltham

John WEDE [Weede, Neede
occ. 1454 d. 1459

1454, 15 June, ord subdcn, place not given, Reg. Bourgchier, fo 48.
1455, 5 Apr., ord dcn, church of St Mary in the market, Cambridge, Reg. Gray, fo 202, (as Neede).

1459, d., late summer, CUL EDC 5/7/1 (infirmarer's acct).

Geoffrey de WELLINGTON B.Cn.L. [Wellyngton, Welyngton
occ. 1394 occ. 1407/8

1394, 16 Feb., one of two whose prof. the prior was comm. to rec., Reg. Fordham, fo 181^{v}.
1394, 19 Dec., ord acol., bp's [*maior*] chapel, Downham, *ib.*, fo 235^{v}.
1395, 6 Mar., ord subdcn, bp's chapel, Somersham, [Lincs.], *ib.*, fo 236.
1395, 18 Sept., ord dcn, Somersham, *ib.*, fo 236.
1395, 18 Dec., ord pr., bp's chapel, Somersham, *ib.*, fo 236^{v}.

1407/8, student at Cambridge for some yrs prior to this date when the chamberlain gave him 6s. 8d., 'ad introitum in canone', CUL EDC 5/3/27.

1401, 14 Sept., 31st in order on the metropolitan visitation certificate, Reg. Fordham, fo 131.

I John de WELLS [Welle, Wellys
occ. 1340/1 occ. 1361

1341/2, 1343/4, July to July, and prob. to 1349, precentor, Chapman, *Sacrist Rolls*, ii, 115 (CUL

EDC 5/10/9b), CUL Add. Ms 2957, fos, 42, 43; see below.

1349/55, almoner at some time during this period, CUL Add. Ms 2957, fo 51.

1357/8, 1359/60, possibly feretrar, Chapman, *Sacrist Rolls*, ii, 172, 184, (CUL EDC 5/10/14, 15).

1340/1, recd from the cellarer £3 6s. 8d., towards the construction of the new choir, CUL Add. Ms 2957, fo 3.

1341/2, recd contributions for the new choir from the sacrist, Chapman, *Sacrist Rolls*, ii, (CUL EDC 5/10/9).

1349 × 1355, pd the *custos* of the Lady chapel £4 which had been lent to him by a previous *custos*, CUL Add. Ms 2957, fo 51; see John de Wisbech.

1349/50, assisted his successor in the office of precentor, Thomas de Stokton I, q.v., CUL Add. Ms 2957, fo 43.

1361, contributed 40s. towards the purchase of the manor and advowson of Mepal, Evans, 'Mepal', 118 (CUL EDC 1B/box 23).

II John WELLS [Wellys

occ. 1453 d. 1458/9

1453, 31 Mar., ord dcn, bp's [*parva*] chapel, Downham, Reg. Bourgchier, fo 47v.

1455, 5 Apr., ord pr., church of St Mary in the market, Cambridge, Reg. Gray, fo 202v.

1458/9, d., CUL EDC 5/7/1, (infirmarer's acct).

Richard de WELLS [Welle, Welles

occ. 1337/8

1337, 16 Sept., dcn, recd *lit. dim.*, for the order of pr., Reg. Montacute, fo 96.

1338, 19 Sept., ord pr., St Mary's church, Ely, *ib.*, fo 102.

Robert WELLS M.A. [Welles, Wellis, Wellys *alias* Steward, Stuard, Styward

occ. 1510/11 occ. 1539

1522–1539, prior: el. 1522, *Anglia Sacra*, i, 685; res. and apptd dean of the new foundation in 1541, *Fasti*, iv, 17, *Fasti, 1541–1857*, vii, 10.

1510/11, student [at Cambridge] for the entire yr, with Richard Overton, q.v., for 1/4 yr, and the pittancer contributed 42s. 8d., CUL EDC 5/8/17.

1511/12, student at Cambridge to whom the chamberlain contributed 14d., CUL Add. Ms 2957, fo 33.

1516/17, student, with a contribution from the sacrist, CUL EDC 5/10/44; he obtained his B.A. this yr, Venn, *Gonville and Caius*, i, 23–24.

1518/25, a pensioner at Gonville Hall, M.A. 1520, *ib.* This must be inaccurate since he became prior in 1522.

1515, 15/16 Apr., 16th in order on the *sed. vac.* visitation certificate, Reg. abp Warham, ii, fo 277.

1516, 29 Mar., 12th at the el. of a prior, Reg. West, fo 55; he served as proxy for William Cottenham, q.v., who was absent, *ib.*, fo 56.

1525/6, ill, and the treasurer pd 62s. to M. Horwood, *phisico*, who remained eight days in attendance; he also spent 60s. 11d., on medicine, spices and other necessities, CUL EDC 5/13/18.

1527, involved in the Star Chamber case concerning Richard Denys and Robert Derham, q.v., PRO STAC 2/17/223, 383.

[1532/3], visited London in Mar. and Apr. [1533], CUL EDC 5/13/-.

[1533/4], went to West Derham to meet the king's commissioners, to Wisbech to see the bp and to London in Nov. for five wks; he also made a journey to London to speak with 'Mr Crumwell', CUL EDC 5/13/-, CUL Add. Ms 2957, fo 81.

1533, 9 and 18 Oct., wrote two letters to Cromwell concerning the king's claim to the revenues of the bpric during the vacancy of the see to which he objected on the grounds of the privileges granted to the prior and convent by the king's forbears. He appears to have intimated that he would defend these claims against any officials sent by the king even when they produced their royal commission, as one such 'meddling' intruder reported to Cromwell on 3 Dec., *L and P Henry VIII*, vi, nos 1244, 1310, 1494.

1535, 3 Nov., accused by a resident in the county, in a letter to Cromwell, of 'surmising a riot against me', *ib.*, ix, no 754.

1535/6, went to London on 6 Feb. for a month and again on 27 June for 24 days; his expenses were over £15 and £13 respectively, CUL EDC 5/13/-. This yr 'M. Visitator' and queen Catherine d., *ib.*

1536, nom. by the bp of Ely as a candidate for the suffragan-bpric of Colchester, *L and P Henry VIII*, xi, no 519 (19).

1538, 15 Oct., in a letter from Richard Cromwell to [Thomas] Cromwell he was described as 'of a froward sort', *L and P Henry VIII*, xiii, pt 2, no 612.

1539, 18 Nov., awarded a pension of £120 p.a., *L and P Henry VIII*, xiv, pt 2, no 542. See above.

Name in the following mss (all with his armorial insignia):

(1) Cambridge, St John's College, Ms. 23, Richard Rolle (15th c.).

(2) BL Ms Cotton Caligula A.viii, Vite sanctorum (12th c.).

(3) BL Ms Harley 3721, Chronicon Eliense (early 16th c.).

(4) Lambeth Ms 204, Gregorius etc. (10th/11th c.).

(5) Oxford, Bod. Ms Laud misc. 112, a collection of treatises including a copy of the Rule, dated 1522 beside his name on fo 432v.

He is reputed to be the author of the Continuatio Historiae Eliensis (1486–1554) printed in *Anglia Sacra*, i, 675–678; see also *ib*., i, 686 for his genealogy written by himself. *DNB* and Venn, *Alumni Cant.* iv, pt i, 161, q.v. are in disagreement about his degree and pedigree.

He was the son of Nicholas Steward of Wells, Norfolk, Venn, *Gonville and Caius*, i, 23.

I Thomas WELLS [Well, Welles, Wellis

occ. 1404 d. 1459

1404, 19 Nov., one of six whose prof. the prior was comm. to rec., Reg. Fordham, fo 198v.

1404, 20 Dec., ord acol., bp's chapel, Downham, *ib*., fo 244.

1405, 14 Mar., ord subdcn, bp's chapel, Downham, *ib*., fo 244.

1405, 18 Apr., ord dcn, Ely cathedral, *ib*., fo 244v.

1422/4, precentor, CUL EDC 5/11/2, 3.

1426/7, described as former *custos* of the Lady chapel, CUL Add. Ms 2957, fo 60.

1443/4, *custos* of the Lady chapel, CUL EDC 5/7/9, CUL Add. Ms 2957, fo 61.

1443, apptd subprior in the prior's absence by the vicar general of the abp [Louis de Luxemburg], thus causing a lengthy dispute, *Anglia Sacra*, i, 670–671, Lambeth Ms 448, fo 85–85v; see John de Yaxham.

1434/5, with John Stretham I, q.v., sent to London to inform the bp of his postulation, PRO SC6/1257/5.

Note: 1435/6 was the yr of four prospective candidates for the bpric, see *Fasti*, iv, 15.

1458/9, ill, and d. in the summer of 1459, CUL EDC 5/7/1 (infirmarer acct).

II Thomas WELLS B.Cn.L. [Welles, Wellis, Wellys

occ. 1454 occ. 1481/2

1454, 15 June, ord subdcn, place not stated, Reg. Bourgchier, fo 48.

1458, 23 Dec., ord pr., bp's chapel, Downham, Reg. Gray, fo 205.

1462/4, 1466/9, *senescallus terrarum*, CUL EDC 5/4/40, 41, 7/15/acct, 5/4/42; 1466/7 is PRO SC6/1257/9.

1466/7, *custos* of the Lady chapel, CUL Add. Ms 2957, fo 62. In 1467/8 he is named as *custos anni preteriti*, *ib*.

1473/4, precentor, CUL EDC 5/13/-, perhaps only part of the yr; see John Sotherey.

1475/6, feretrar, CUL EDC 5/11/7; see William Tylney who both preceded and succeeded him.

1476/7, 1478/9, 1481/2, *senescallus terrarum*, CUL EDC 5/13/16, 5/10/36, 7/15/acct.

1473/4, recd 5s or 6s. 8d., from the cellarer 'ad introitum suum in universitate Cantab' ', CUL Add. Ms 2957, fo 6; the almoner contributed 6s. 8d., to him 'qui intravit gradum bacularium iuris canonici', CUL EDC 5/1/14.

[1462 × 1478], *temp.* Henry Peterborough, described as *in decretis [bacallariatus]*, Liber B, no 241; see John Ely VIII; the date is prob. 1473 × 1478 because of the entry immediately above.

[1462 × 1478], with John Ely VIII, q.v., appointed general proctors by the prior and chapter, Liber B, no 241; see the entry above.

1467/8, visited Lakenheath, CUL EDC 7/15/acct.

1473/4, with John Ely VIII, q.v., and taking seven horses with them, went to the Black Monk Chapter at Northampton [July 1474] where they stayed six days. As visitors for the Chapter they spent eleven days this yr visiting several religious houses including Thorney; he also went to London on business, CUL EDC 5/13/-.

1476/7, held the Martinmas court at Whittlesey, was in London in Nov. and Jan. on various negotiations, went to the fair at Barnwell and to Northampton, with Richard Swaffham q.v., for the Black Monk Chapter [June 1477], CUL EDC 5/13/16.

1478, 19 July, accompanied the subprior, John Soham I, q.v., and other monks, to the bp to discuss arrangements for the pension of the prior, Henry Peterborough, q.v., Lambeth Ms 448, fo 113. On 8 Aug., with Alexander Wittlesey, q.v., sent as proctors to inform the king [and John Morton] of their election of the latter as bp, Lambeth Ms 448, fo 113v .

1478/9, pd a visit to Melton, CUL EDC 7/16/38 acct.

1481/2, visited Lakenheath, CUL EDC 7/15/acct.

I William de WELLS [Welle, Welles, Wellys

occ. 1350 d. 1406/7

1350, 18 Dec., ord subdcn, Ely cathedral, Reg. de Lisle, fo 96v.

1351, 2 Apr., ord dcn, St Mary's church, Ely, *ib*., fo 96v.

1353, 21 Sept., ord pr., Swavesey, *ib*., fo 99v.

1365/6, 1367/8, 1373/4, 1376/7, 1382/3, *senescallus terrarum*, CUL EDC 7/16/18 acct, 7/17/acct, 7/15/accts, 7/16/23 acct.

1389/90, feretrar, CUL EDC 5/10/22, CUL Add. Ms 2957, fo 161.

1361, contributed 10s. towards the purchase of the manor and advowson of Mepal, Evans, 'Mepal', 118 (CUL EDC 1B/box 23).

1365/6, visited Melton, CUL EDC 7/16/18 acct.

1367/8, held the court at Winston, and also at Lakenheath where the view of frankpledge was included, CUL EDC 7/14/acct, 7/15/acct.

1373/4, pd several visits to Lakenheath to hold courts and supervise the manor which was charged with his expenses of 20s. 8d., CUL EDC 7/15/acct.

1382/3, visited Melton, CUL EDC 7/16/23 acct.
1401, 14 Sept., 4th in order on the metropolitan visitation certificate, Reg. Fordham, fo 131.
1406/7, d., and both the precentor and sacrist sent 5s. to the almoner, CUL Add. Ms 2957, fo 47, CUL EDC 5/10/26.

There is an undated letter from him to the prior, William [?Walpole or Powcher, q.v.] in Reg. Walsingham, no 11; it refers to the d. of John Wormyngton, q.v., and to the sum of money which had belonged to the deceased and was now in his hands.

II William WELLS B.Cn.L. [Welles *alias* Martin, Martyn

occ. 1419 occ. 1461

1430–1461, prior: occ. 1 Oct. 1430, Liber B, no 233; occ. 26 June 1461, Oxford Bod. Ms Ashmole 801, fo 95. See Henry Peterborough.
1419, 7 June, ord acol., bp's chapel, Downham, Reg. Fordham, fo 272.
1419, 10 June, ord subdcn, bp's chapel, Downham, *ib.*, fo 272.
1419, 23 Sept., ord dcn, bp's chapel, Downham, *ib.*, fo 272v.
1423/4, student at Cambridge with John Sutton II, q.v., and provided with £8 4s. 2d., maintenance from the treasurer, CUL EDC 5/13/12.
1428/9, student, with John Sutton; the treasurer pd them £6 17s. 6d., maintenance, PRO SC6/1257/4.
1430/1, a '. . . Wels, monachus de Ely', owed 40s. 'quia non continuavit lecturam suam in iure canonico post admiscionem suam ad gradum bacularitatus in eodem', CUL Cambridge Univ. Reg., 1.2.1. This must be William who did not lecture because he was el. prior.
1459, 2 Jan., addressed by the bp as *in decretis bacal[ariatus]*, Reg. Gray, fo 38.
1426, 1 Apr., named as proctor for the prior and chapter at convocation, fo 146, Liber B, no 231.
1432, 20 May, held the court at Winston, CUL EDC 7/12/6 court; on 20 July he held the court at Witcham, CUL EDC 7/7/5.
1434/5, this yr's manorial itinerary is recorded on the acct of the steward of the prior's hospice; it included visits to Shepey, Oundle and Sutton, and he spent over 35 wks at home in Ely, CUL EDC 5/12/3.
1435, 22 Oct., acting as *custos* of the bpric, *sed. vac.*, Reg. Walsingham, unnumbered fo.
1445/6, entertained Henry VI overnight, CUL EDC 5/12/6.
1447, 27 Mar., present at the installation of the bp, Reg. Bourgchier, fo 12.
1449, 31 July, accepted the transfer of the Augustinian priory of Spinney as a cell of Ely, *VCH Cambridgeshire*, ii, 252 and *CPR (1446–1452)*, 249. On 1 Aug., took possession of Spinney, BL Ms Harley 3721, fo 76.
1459, 2 Jan., recd a comm. from the bp, with another, to look into a violation of the liberty of the church of Ely, Reg. Gray, fo 38.
1461, 26 June, William, prior and the convent confirmed arrangments for masses to be said for his brother, Thomas Martyn of Ely, Liber B, no 3, Oxford, Bod. Ms Ashmole 801, fos 94v–95.

He was buried in Wilburton church with other members of his family (named Martyn), CUL Add. Ms 2947, fo 153. His parent's names were Richard and Idonea Andreas for whom the prior of Spinney was to celebrate an annual mass in Ely cathedral acc. to Lambeth Ms 448, fo 97.

III William WELLS [Welles

occ. 1439/40 occ. 1460

1439/40, *senescallus terrarum*, PRO SC6/1257/7, 8.
1440/1, former *senescallus terrarum*, succ. this yr by Nicholas Derby, q.v., CUL EDC 5/4/32.
1442/3, precentor, CUL EDC 5/9/12.
1444/5, former steward of the prior's hospice, (before 1443/4), CUL EDC 5/12/4.
1446/7, 1448/50, chamberlain, CUL Add. Ms 2957, fos 31, 32.
1460, 10 Apr., removed from the office of chamberlain by the bp personally in chapter, Reg. Gray, fo 46v.
n.d., prior of Spinney, Lambeth Ms 448, fo 97.
1439/40, receiver of the bpric, PRO SC6/1257/8.
1440, July, went to Bury St Edmunds on business affairs for the house, *ib.* He also went to Barnwell fair to purchase stock for the hospice, and made the rounds of a number of manors and visited Cambridge, *ib.*
1458/9, ill in the infirmary, CUL EDC 5/7/1, (infirmarer acct).

Roger WESTMINSTER [Westmenstyr, Westmestr', Westmynster ?*alias* Cambrigge

occ. 1458 occ. 1499

1478–1499, prior: el. 28 July 1478, Lambeth Ms 448, fo 113, and see below; occ. 15 Nov. 1499, Liber B, no 376; see Robert Colville.
1458, 23 Dec., ord subdcn, bp's chapel, Downham, Reg. Gray, fo 205.
1460, 8 Mar., ord dcn, bp's [*magna*] chapel, Downham, *ib.*, fo 208.
1463, 9 Apr., ord pr., bp's [*magna*] chapel, Downham, *ib.*, fo 210v.
Note: for his prob. ord. as acol. in 1457, see Roger Cambrigge, presumably the same monk.
1466/7, second treasurer, with Thomas Wells II, q.v., PRO SC6/1257/9; he was also granator, *ib.*
1469/70, *senescallus terrarum*, CUL EDC 5/13/-, CUL Add. Ms 2957, fo 73.

1470/1, 1472, 15 Jan., 1477/9, sacrist, CUL Add. Ms 2956, fo 168, Liber B, no 221, CUL Add. Ms 2950, fo 80, CUL EDC 5/10/35, 36.
As prior, his name heads the following acct:
1483/4, sacrist; his *socius* was Robert Tyd, q.v., who had previously served in this capacity under him, CUL EDC 5/10/37.

1472, 15 Jan., with John Soham I, q.v., apptd proctor for convocation, Liber B no 221, CUL Add. Ms 2950, fo 80.
1473, 20 Jan., with John Soham I and Alexander Wittlesey, q.v., apptd proctor for convocation, Liber B no 238, CUL Add. Ms 2950, fo 81.
1478, 19 July, accompanied John Soham I, q.v., subprior and other monks, to the bp to discuss arrangements for the pension of the prior, Henry Peterborough, q.v, Lambeth Ms 448, fo 113–113ᵛ.
1478, 28 July, present at the mass preceding the el. of the prior, was Edmund Conynsberg', abp of Armagh. The subprior nom. Westminster and all concurred; the elect assented *cum difficultate*, *ib.* He was examined in the Lady chapel *per diversa argumenta doctorum* on 31 July and was confirmed and installed on 1 Aug., *ib.*
1480, 29 Aug., took part in the ceremony of the installation of bp Morton, BL Ms Harley 3721, fo 64.
1491/2, recd a gift of 2s. 9d., from the feretrar while staying at the cell of Spinney, CUL EDC 5/11/9.
1492, 17 Aug., was the recipient of a grant by the bailiffs of Ipswich to himself and his successors to be a burgess of the city CUL EDC 1B/28/178.
1493, 4 July, comm. by the bp to examine and assign penance to a woman of ill repute, Reg. Alcock, fo 87.
1495, 12 Oct., 1497, 15 Jan., ill and unable to attend convocation, Reg. Alcock, fos 120, 149.

Robert de WESTON
d. 1368/9

1368/9, d., and the sacrist sent 5s. to the almoner, CUL EDC 5/10/16.

Simon de WESTONE
occ. 1309/10 occ. 1316

1309/10, pittancer, CUL EDC 5/8/1.
1316, 14 June, cellarer, BL Add. Ms 41612, fo 38ᵛ.
1319, almoner, BL Cotton Ms Vespasian A vi, fo 114.

1310, 28 Feb., one of seven *compromissorii* named in the el. of a bp, BL Add. Ms 41612, fo 49ᵛ. In this instance it appears that they failed to agree and seven others were chosen; see John de Ketene.
1316, 1 June, with Alan de Hemmingestone, q.v., recd licence from the king to el. a bp, *CPR (1313–1317)*, 465, BL Add. Ms 41612, fo 37ᵛ (they had been sent on 26 May); on 14 June, the two were sent to obtain the consent of the bp el. and to present him to the abp, BL Add. Ms 41612, fo 38ᵛ. On 25 June he and John de Crauden, q.v., were sent by the prior and chapter to obtain confirmation of the el. from the abp, *ib.*, fo 40–40ᵛ.

John WETING [Wetyng
occ. 1492 occ. 1496

1492, 21 Apr., recd first tonsure, Ely cathedral, Reg. Alcock, fo 231ᵛ, and the tonsure entry was repeated on fo 232ᵛ.
1494, 29 Mar., ord dcn, Ely cathedral, *ib.*, fo 235.
1496, 24 Sept., ord pr., Downham, *ib.*, fo 241ᵛ.

John WHITBY [Whitbye, Whytby
occ. 1534 occ. 1539

1534, 8 Sept., 22nd in order on the visitation certificate, Reg. Goodrich, fo 90ᵛ.
1539, 18 Nov., assigned a pension of £5 6s. 8d., p.a., *L and P Henry VIII*, xiv, pt 2, no 542.

William WHITEFOTE
occ. 1500 occ. 1524/5

1500, 30 Oct., granator, Canterbury Reg. R., fo 70.
1500, 30 Oct., 6th to be examined at the visitation by the commissary of the prior of Christ Church, Canterbury (*sed. vac.* both Ely and Canterbury). He stated that divine worship [*divinus cultus*] was not being conducted as it should be, due to the absence of Henry Iselham, q.v. He also complained, along with others, about the precinct gate being left open and the outer wall remaining unrepaired, Canterbury Reg. R., fo 70; see William Wittlesey.
1524/5, presumably holding an obedientiary office as he pd rent to the pittancer, CUL EDC 1/C/7, fo 71ᵛ.

WHITRED
see William Tydde

WHYTBY
see Whitby

Simon de WICHAM [Wyccham, Wycham, ?Wytham
occ. 1389 d. 1428/9

1389, 18 Feb., one of three whose prof. the prior was comm. to rec., Reg. Fordham, fo 5.
1389, 12 June, ord acol., Doddington, *ib.*, fo 230.
1389, 18 Sept., ord subdcn, Doddington, *ib.*, fo 230ᵛ.
1390, 18 Dec., ord dcn, bp's chapel, Downham, *ib.*, fo 231.
[1391], 24 Sept., ord pr., Doddington, *ib.*, fo 231ᵛ.
1399/1401, granator, CUL EDC 5/4/20, 21.
1405/6, steward of the prior's hospice, CUL EDC 5/6/16.

1409/12, 1413/14, granator, CUL EDC 7/15/acct, CUL EDC 5/4/23–25.
1416/18, chamberlain, CUL Add. Ms 2957, fo 30, CUL EDC 5/3/30.
1420, Feb./Sept., cellarer, CUL EDC 5/2/30.
1424/5, 1426/7, granator, CUL EDC 5/4/26, 27.
1428/9, cellarer, PRO SC6/1257/4.

1401, 14 Sept., 27th in order on the metropolitan visitation certificate, Reg. Fordham, fo 131.
1409/10, visited Lakenheath, CUL EDC 7/15/acct.
1428/9, d. while cellarer, PRO SC6/1257/4.

WICHAM
see also Wykham

WIGGENHALL, Wiggenhale
see Wygenhale

WIKES
see Wyke

Thomas WILBERTON [Wylberton *alias* Outlaw, Owtlaw
occ. 1534 occ. 1539

[1535/6], student at Cambridge with William Wisbech for whom the prior authorized repairs costing ?30s. to their rooms there, CUL EDC 5/13/-.
1535/6, student at Cambridge with Robert Hamond and William Wisbech, q.v., and together they recd 15s. from the treasurer, CUL EDC 5/10/33.
1539, 18 Nov., student, see below.

1534, 8 Sept., 23rd in order on the visitation certificae, Reg. Goodrich, fo 90v.
1539, 18 Nov., with William Wisbech, q.v., described as student and assigned a pension of £6 13s. 8d., p.a., *L and P Henry VIII*, xiv, pt 2, no 542.

William WILBERTON [Wylberton
occ. 1505/6 d. 1526/7

1510/11, chamberlain, CUL Add. Ms 2957, fo 32.
1505/6, *socius* of the sacrist, CUL Add. Ms 2956, fo 174.
1514/15, recd 13s. 4d., from the *custos* of the Lady chapel for celebrating masses for the soul of John Pelham, CUL Add. Ms 2957, fo 64.
1515, 15/16 Apr., 12th in order on the *sed. vac.* visitation certificate, Reg. abp Warham, ii, fo 277.
1516, 22 Mar., 9th in order in the chapter which chose 29 Mar. as the date for the el. of a prior, Reg. West, fo 55.
1526/7, d., and the chamberlain and treasurer sent 5s. to the almoner, CUL Add. Ms 2957, 34, CUL EDC 5/13/19.

I WILLIAM
occ. 1133 × 1137 occ. [?1140 × 1142]

1133 × 1134/5 × 1137, prior: apptd between May 1133 and 5 Jan. 1134; deposed between Nov. 1135 and Nov. 1137, *Fasti*, ii, 48, which also ref. to a prior W. [1140 × 1142]; see also *HRH*, 45.

Prob. previously sacrist, *Anglia Sacra*, i, 625; but see William III.

1134, 5 Jan., witnessed an inventory of the treasury ordered by bp Nigel, *Liber Elien.*, 288.
n.d., obit occ. on 29 Jan., in Cambridge, Trinity College Ms 1105, fo k1v.

II WILLIAM, nephew of Dionisius, q.v.
occ. 1134

1134, 5 Jan., witnessed an inventory of the treasury ordered by bp Nigel, *Liber Elien.*, 289.

See also William III below.

III WILLIAM
occ. [c. 1143/4]

[c. 1143/4], sacrist, *Liber Elien.*, 339.

IV WILLIAM
occ. 1281

1281, 11 Oct., precentor, CUL EDC 1B/113.

1281, 11 Oct., one of the monks who were absolved from excommunication on acct of irregularities over payment of the tenth for the Holy Land, *ib.*

Robert WILTON [Wylton
occ. 1457 occ. 1469/70

1457, 17 Dec., ord acol., bp's chapel, Downham, Reg. Gray, fo 205.
1458, 23 Dec., ord subdcn, bp's chapel, Downham, *ib.*, fo 205.
1459, 22 Dec., ord dcn, bp's chapel, Downham, *ib.*, fo 207v.
1462, 13 Mar., ord pr., bp's [*magna*] chapel, Downham, *ib.*, fo 209v.

1469/70, name occ. on the treasurer's acct, CUL EDC 5/13/-.

WIMERUS
occ. before 1122/3

1122/3, d. by this date when his name occ. on a mortuary roll of Savigny, Delisle, *Rouleaux des Morts*, 339.

WINTONIA
see Godthinus

Adam de WISBECH [Wysebech
occ. 1341

1341, 24 Mar., ord acol., Willingham, Reg. Montacute, fo 106v.

Note: see Adam de Lynsted who may be the same monk.

Alan de WISBECH [Wysebech
occ. 1233

1233, 11 Sept., witness to an agreement over tithes, Liber M, 319.

Geoffrey de WISBECH [Wysbeche, Wysebech

occ. 1379 occ. 1401 and ?1428/9

1389/90, 1394/5, treasurer, CUL EDC 5/13/8, 7/15/acct.

1396/7, Sept. to June, granator, CUL EDC 5/4/19, he is also named as cellarer and as *senescallus* [?*terrarum*] during this yr, CUL EDC 5/13/10.

1428/9, described as former treasurer, PRO SC6/1257/4; and prob. still living.

1379, 28th in order on the clerical poll tax list and pd 3s. 4d., PRO E179/23/1.

1382/3, *socius* of the cellarer, CUL EDC 5/2/23.

1389/90, visited Winston, CUL EDC 7/17/acct.

1394/5, visited Lakenheath, CUL EDC 7/15/acct.

1401, 14 Sept., 9th on the metropolitan visitation certificate, Reg. Fordham, fo 131.

In 1388 his brother came to stay in the guest hall during Easter wk, CUL EDC 5/5/5.

John de WISBECH

occ. 1321 d. 1349

1340, Mar./1341, Dec., cellarer, CUL EDC 5/2/7.

1321, Mar./1349, in charge of the construction of the Lady chapel on the east side of the north transept running east, parallel to the presbytery. He is described as a *simplici monacho*, a man of faith and perseverance, who, while digging on the site of the foundations of the chapel, uncovered an urn full of coins which he used to pay the wages of the labourers. For 28 yrs he supervised the building and collected the necessary funds, without being ashamed to beg for more, *Anglia Sacra*, i, 651–652, Lambeth Ms 448, fos 61v–62, 119.

1329/30, visited Stoke, CUL EDC 7/17/acct; he also accompanied Nicholas de Copmanford, q.v., to confer with the bp at Somersham, CUL Add. Ms 2957, fo 3.

1340/1, travelled to London and Norwich on business affairs, CUL EDC 5/2/7; he also accompanied Nicholas de Copmanford, q.v., to confer with the bp at Somersham [Lincs.], CUL Add. Ms 2957, fo 3.

1344, 18 Oct., one of four monks cited to appear before the pope for arresting the proctor of the rector of Hadenham while he was in the chapter house publishing papal letters during a dispute over claims to the church there, *CPL*, iii (1342–1362), 140–141, 171.

1349, 16 June, d., and was buried at the entrance to the Lady chapel, CUL Add. Ms 2947, fo 175v.

Reginald de WISBECH [Wysebech, Wysbech

occ. 1310 d. 1320/1

1310, 28 Feb., named by the prior and chapter as one of seven *compromissorii* in the el. of a bp, BL Add. Ms 41612, fo 49v. In this case it appears that they failed to agree and seven others were chosen; see John de Ketene.

1320/1, Apr. to Apr., recd from the chamberlain 5s. 6d., *pro stragul', stamin' botis estival'* etc., CUL Add. Ms 2957, fo 20; he d. this year and the chamberlain sent 5s. to the almoner, *ib.*

Richard WISBECH [Wisbich

d. 1527/8

1527/8, d., and the treasurer sent 5s. to the almoner, CUL EDC 5/13/20, CUL Add. Ms 2957, fo 80.

Robert de WISBECH

occ. 1338

1338, 19 Sept., ord dcn, St Mary's church, Ely, Reg. Montacute, fo 101v.

I Roger de WISBECH [Wysebech

occ. 1347/8

1347, 11 Dec., obtained *lit. dim.*, for the order of subdcn, Reg. de Lisle, fo 85v.

1348, 14 June, ord dcn, Over, *ib.*, fo 96.

II Roger WISBECH [Wisebech, Wysebech

occ. 1419 occ. 1454/5

1419, 10 June, ord subdcn, bp's chapel, Downham, Reg. Fordham, fo 272.

1419, 23 Sept., ord dcn, bp's chapel, Downham, *ib.*, fo 272v.

1446/7, 1452/5, *custos* of the Lady chapel, CUL Add. Ms 2957, fos 60, 61, CUL EDC 5/7/10 (for 1453/4).

William WISBECH [Wisbeche, Wysbich *alias* Salebank, Salebrook, Salybank

occ. 1534 occ. 1539

1534, 8 Sept., he was one of ten not styled *dominus* and therefore recently adm. and not yet in major orders, Reg Goodrich, fo 90v.

[1535/6], student at Cambridge with Thomas Wilburton q.v., for whom the prior authorized repairs costing ?c. 30s. to their rooms there, CUL EDC 5/13/-.

1535/6, student at Cambridge with Robert Hamond and Thomas Wilberton, q.v., and together they recd 15s. from the sacrist, CUL EDC 5/10/33.

1539, 18 Nov., student, see below.

1534, 8 Sept., 26th in order on the visitation certificate, Reg. Goodrich, fo 90v.

1539, 18 Nov., described as student and assigned a pension of £6 13s. 8d., *L and P Henry VIII*, xiv, pt 2, no 542.

Alexander WITTLESEY [Witelesey, Witlesey, Wythlesey, Wytlesey

occ. 1457 occ. 1489/90

1457, 17 Dec., ord acol., bp's chapel, Downham, Reg. Gray, fo 204v.

1458, 23 Dec., ord subdcn, bp's chapel, Downham, *ib.*, fo 205.
1459, 24 Mar., ord dcn, bp's chapel, Downham, *ib.*, fo 205^v.
1462, 13 Mar., ord pr., bp's [*magna*] chapel, Downham, *ib.*, fo 209^v.

1472/3, *senescallus terrarum*, CUL EDC 5/4/55.
1476/7, 1478/9, precentor, CUL EDC 5/13/16, Lambeth Ms 448, fo 113^v.
1487/8, 1489/90, *senescallus terrarum*, CUL EDC 7/15/acct, 5/4/49.

1473, 20 Jan., with John Soham I, q.v., and others, apptd proctor for the prior and chapter in convocation, Liber B, no 238, CUL Add. Ms 2950, fo 81.
1478, 8 Aug., sent with Thomas Wells II, q.v., as proctors to inform the king and John Morton that they had elected the latter as bp, Lambeth Ms 448, fo 113^v.

John WITTLESEY [Wytlesey
occ. 1485/6

1485/6, broke a cross *deaurat'* and the sacrist pd the cost of repair, CUL EDC 5/10/38, CUL Add. Ms 2956, fo 172.

Laurence WITTLESEY [Witleseye, Wytlesey
occ. 1519 d. 1527/8

1519, 24 Sept., ord subdcn, Lady chapel, Ely cathedral, Reg. West, fo 87.

1523/5, student at Cambridge, with John Ward, q.v., and together they recd 2s. 4d., from the chamberlain, CUL Add. Ms 2957, fo 33.
1525/8, student with John Ward, for whom the treasurer provided £8 13s. 4d., each yr, CUL EDC 5/13/18–20, CUL Add. Ms 2957, fos 75, 79, 80; the chamberlain also made a contribution to them in 1526/7, CUL Add. Ms 2957, fo 34.

1527/8, d., and the treasurer sent 5s. to the almoner, CUL EDC 5/13/20.

I William WITTLESEY [Witlese, Witlesey, Wittilsey, Wytlesey, Wyttilsey *alias* Foliot, Folyott
occ. 1475 occ. 1516

c. 1510–1516, prior: occ. 27 Sept. 1510, Liber B, no 435; res. before 22 Mar., 1516, Reg. West, fo 55, where he is named William Folyott (Foliot, q.v.).

Note: because it seems almost certain that there were two contemporary William Wittleseys their respective biographical details cannot, in some cases, be safely assigned. Some of the entries below may ref. to William II, q.v.

1475, 25 Mar., ord acol., bp's chapel, Doddington, Reg. Gray, fo 215^v.
1476, 13 Apr., ord subdcn, bp's palace chapel [Ely], *ib.*, fo 216^v.

1489/90, granator, CUL EDC 5/4/49.
1500, 30 Oct., *senescallus terrarum*, Canterbury Reg. R., fo 70.
1504/6, 1509/10, sacrist, CUL EDC 7/4/5 acct, CUL Add. Ms 2956, fos 174–176, CUL EDC 5/10/42, 43.

1495, 12 Oct., named as proctor, with Robert Colville, q.v., for convocation, Liber B, no 239, CUL Add. Ms 2950, fo 83.
1497, 15 Jan., with Robert Colville and another he was named proctor for convocation, Liber B, no 350, CUL Add. Ms 2950, fo 84.
1500, 30 Oct., 5th to be examined at the visitation by the commissary of the prior of Christ Church, Canterbury (*sed. vac.* both Ely and Canterbury). He reported *omnia bene* apart from the fact that the cloister door [Vine gate] remained open to the public and the precinct wall was in a ruinous state, matters of which several other monks had complained, e.g., Richard Swaffham, q.v., Canterbury Reg. R., fo 70.
1504/5, prob. visited Sutton, CUL EDC 7/4/5 acct.
1505/6, went to Boston to see tenants there and rec. rents and also to Bowden with four of his brethren and others who were to rec. orders, CUL EDC 5/10/42.
1509/10, conducted four monks, with nine horses, to Norwich for orders; they were away for three and a half days and three nights, for which the sacrist's acct was charged 34s. 7d. He also went to Stourbridge [fair] for two days, CUL EDC 5/10/43.
1515, 16 Apr., present at the *sed. vac* visitation at which the abp recd reports of his maladministration, Reg. abp Warham, ii, fo 277; see Evans, *Ely Chap. Ord.*, 65–66, where, however, the date is wrong. On 26 June he replied to the accusations and the visitation was concluded in peace, Reg. abp Warham, ii, fo 277–277^v.
1516, before 22 Mar., he had res; see John Cottenham.

See William Wittlesey II below, and William Foliot (*alias* Wittlesey).

II William WITTLESEY [Wittilsey
occ. 1515 occ. 1524/5

1520/1, 1523/5, *senescallus terrarum*, CUL Add. Ms 2957, fo 33.

1515, 15/16 Apr., 2nd in order on the *sed. vac.* visitation certificate, Reg. abp Warham, ii, fo 277.
1516, 22 Mar., 2nd in order (the subprior, Robert Stunteney, q.v., being first) in the chapter which chose 29 Mar. as the date for the el. of a prior, Reg. West, fo 55. With Thomas Soham, q.v., he had been sent by the chapter to the bp for licence to el., and went to the prior elect, John Cottenham, q.v., to seek his consent, *ib.*, fo 58–58^v.

John WOODE
occ. 1458/9

1458/9, spent part of the summer quarter of 1459 in the infirmary and d., CUL EDC 5/7/1 (infirmarer's acct).

John WORMYNGTON [Wyrmington, Wyrmyngton
occ. 1374/5 occ. 1398/9

1374/6, 1377, May/Sept., 1377/80, *socius* of the chamberlain, CUL Add. Ms 2957, fos 29, 34, 35.

1379, 25th in order on the clerical poll tax list and pd 3s. 4d., PRO E179/23/1.

1382/3, 1384/6, 1387/91, 1396/9, *socius* of the chamberlain, CUL Add. Ms 2957, fos 35, 36, CUL EDC 5/3/21–23, CUL Add. Ms 2957, fo 36, CUL EDC 5/3/24, CUL Add. Ms 2957, fo 37.

1398/9, d., and the chamberlain sent 5s. to the almoner, CUL Add. Ms 2957, fo 37.

There are two undated letters concerning him written after his d:

(1) from William de Wells I, q.v., to William [?Walpole] prior, concerning a sum of 14 m. which Wormyngton had placed in his keeping and of which he had used 10 m. to pay a debt, Reg. Walsingham, no 11.

(2) from John de Ely V or VI, q.v., to the prior concerning the disposition of his money and belongings. The writer reported that his clothes had been distributed by the subprior, the almoner and himself, and the sum of 65s. 4d., remained in his custody until the prior gave his instructions, *ib.*, no 40.

William WOTTON [Watton, Wutton
occ. 1463/4 d. 1483/4

1463/5, precentor, CUL EDC 5/9/7a, 5/13/-; he succ. Gilbert Lakyngheth, q.v., and was succ. by him.

1476/7, name occ. on the pittancer's acct, CUL EDC 5/8/16.

1483/4, d. and the precentor sent 5s. to the almoner, ED 5/9/9.

John WRAUBY [Wraunby, Wrawby, Wrayby
occ. 1427/8 d. 1443/4

1434/6, treasurer, CUL EDC 5/12/3, PRO SC6/1257/5, CUL EDC 7/14c/43 acct.

1440/1, named as former pittancer, CUL EDC 5/4/32.

1427/8, recd 20s. as a gift, *de mandato* of the prior, *pro factur'*, CUL EDC 5/11/5; this yr the feretrar recorded that he was engaged in binding a book of chronicles, *ib.*

1434, 1435/6, visited Kingston, CUL EDC 7/14c/43 acct.

1443/4, d. and the chamberlain sent 5s. to the almoner, CUL EDC 5/3/33, CUL Add. Ms 2957, fo 31.

WYCCHAM, Wycham
see Wicham

Richard de WYGENHALE
occ. 1318/19 d. 1345/6

1318/19, July to July, recd a sum of money from the *custos* of the Lady altar, 66s. 8d., CUL Add. Ms 2957, fo 50, (the verb is *liberat*).

1345/6, d., and the chamberlain gave 5s. to the almoner, CUL EDC 5/3/6, CUL Add. Ms 2957, fo 24.

See the entry below.

Walter de WYGENHALE [Wygenale
occ. 1320/1 occ. 1343/4

1320/1, 1329/30, Sept. to July, precentor, CUL Add. Ms 2957, fo 42, CUL EDC 5/9/1; the heading on the acct itself is barely legible and could be Richard de Wygenhale above.

1320/1, bought a copy of [Adalbert's] Speculum Gregor[ii for 2s., CUL Add. Ms 2957, fo 42.

1329/30, went to Balsham *pro libris ibidem querend'*, *ib.*

1343/4, name occ. on the precentor's acct concerning unpd rents in Cattemere and Huntedon between 1339/41, *ib.*

William de WYGHT [Wyht
occ. 1286

1286, before 8 July, sent, with Richard de Braunford and William de Brigham, q.v., by the prior and chapter as proctors to the king to obtain a licence to el. a bp; the king issued the licence in Paris on 8 July, Liber M, 119, CUL Add. Ms 2948, fo 143.

Henry de WYKE [Wikes, Wykes
occ. 1347 d. 1392/3

1347, 11 Dec., obtained *lit. dim.*, for the order of subdcn, Reg. de Lisle, fo 85^{v}.

1348, 14 June, ord dcn, Over, *ib.*, fo 96.

1361/2, steward of the prior's hospice for part of the yr, succ. John de Bukton I, q.v., CUL EDC 7/15/acct.

1374/6, almoner, CUL EDC 5/1/7, 8.

1376, May/Sept., 1377/80, chamberlain, CUL Add. Ms 2957, fos 29, 34, 35; the comm. for his apptment was issued on 24 May [1376], Reg. Arundel, fo 23^{v}.

1390, 19 July, subprior, BL Add. Ms 9822, fo 73.

1371/2, visited Winston *pro statu manerii supervidend'*, CUL EDC 7/17/acct.

1379, 6th in order on the clerical poll tax list and pd 3s. 4d., PRO E179/23/1.

1390, 19 July, with other monks delivered a charter to the bp for his examination, BL Add. Ms 9822, fo 73; see William de Picworth.

1392/3, d., and the treasurer sent 5s. to the anniversarian, CUL EDC 5/13/9.

Peter de WYKHAM
occ. 1348

1348, 14 June, ord subdcn, Over, Reg. de Lisle, fo 96.

WYKHAM
see also Wicham

George WYKYN
occ. 1473 occ. 1487/8

1473, 17 Apr., ord subdcn, bp's [*magna*] chapel, Downham, Reg. Gray, fo 215.
1475, 25 Mar., ord pr., bp's chapel, Doddington, *ib.*, fo 215ᵛ.
1485/6, 1487/8, *socius* of the sacrist, CUL EDC 5/10/38–40, CUL Add. Ms 2956, fo 162.

WYLBERTON
see Wilberton

WYLTON
see Wilton

WYRMINGTON
see Wormington

WYSBECH(E), Wysebech
see Wisbech

WYTHLESEY, Wytlesey, Wyttilsey
see Wittlesey

Roger de WYVELINGHAM [Wyvilyngham
occ. 1309/10 d. 1315/16

1309/10, *socius* of the pittancer, CUL EDC 5/8/1.
1315/16, d., and the chamberlain sent 5s. to the almoner, CUL Add. Ms 2957, fo 19.

R. de YAKESHAM
occ. 1321/3

1321/3, [Aug.] to Aug., *socius* of the pittancer, CUL EDC 5/8/6.

John de YAXHAM B.Cn.L. [Yaxsam, Yoxham, Zaxham, Yoxham
occ. 1392 occ. 1443

1392, 19 Oct., one of three whose prof. the prior was comm. to rec., Reg. Fordham, fo 179.
1392, 21 Dec., ord acol., bp's chapel, Doddington, *ib.*, fo 233ᵛ.
1393, 1 Mar., ord subdcn, bp's chapel, Doddington, *ib.*, fo 233ᵛ.
1393, 31 May, ord dcn, bp's [*maior*] chapel, Downham, *ib.*, fo 234.
1394, 19 Dec., ord pr., bp's [*maior*] chapel, Downham, *ib.*, fo 235ᵛ.

1411/12, almoner, CUL EDC 5/4/24.
1421, June/Sept., 1422/9, feretrar, CUL EDC 5/11/1–5.
1443, subprior and *custos communis thesaurarie*, CUL EDC 5/13/11; see below.

1396/7, student at Cambridge for three quarters of the yr with Edmund de Thomeston, q.v., and recd £6 3s. from the treasurer, and for the fourth quarter the treasurer gave him 20s. 6d., CUL EDC 5/13/10, CUL Add. Ms 2957, fo 72.
1415, 8 May, student, licensed to preach in any church [?in Cambridge], appropriated to Ely cathedral, *Reg. abp Chichele*, iv, 126–127.
n.d., described as *in decretis bachalar'*, Liber B, no 232a.

1401, 14 Sept., 30th in order on the metropolitan visitation certificate, Reg. Fordham, fo 131.
1428, 30 June, with John Sutton II, q.v., and others, apptd proctor for the prior and chapter in convocation, fo 146, Liber B, no 232.
1428/9, rode to Northampton to attend the Black Monk Chapter (4 July 1429), and also to Bardney to conduct a visitation there on behalf of the Black Monk Chapter, PRO SC6/1257/4.
1434/5, with John Feltwell, q.v., sent by the prior and chapter to visit their churches in Norwich and Bury St Edmunds; they took with them three servants and five horses, PRO SC6/1257/5.
n.d., while feretrar he acctd for expenses in the construction of a new *camera* of stone between the Lady chapel and the cathedral, CUL EDC 5/11/6.
1443, was removed from the office of subprior by the vicar general of the abp, while the prior was absent in London, without any reference to the prior and chapter, and Thomas Wells I, q.v., was apptd in his place. Both monks claimed the office and the community was divided in its allegiance while the prior appealed to the Court of Arches; the controversy lasted over six months, *Anglia Sacra*, i, 670–671, Lambeth Ms 448, fo 85–85ᵛ.

YSELHAM
see Thomas Iselham

YXEWORTH
see Robert Ixworth

YXNING, Yxneng, Yxnyng
see Exnyng

NORWICH CATHEDRAL PRIORY

INTRODUCTION

The cathedral priory of the Holy Trinity at Norwich came into being when bishop Herbert de Losinga, formerly abbot of Ramsey, transferred his see from Thetford to Norwich c.1095. His aim was to have a cathedral chapter of sixty monks, a complement which he apparently soon achieved;[1] at the same time he established the small dependency of St Leonard's on the outskirts of Norwich and accommodated some of the monks there while the claustral buildings across the river were being completed. St Leonard's continued to function as a cell for seven or eight monks and was soon to be one of four founded by the same bishop, the others being at Aldeby (St Mary's), King's Lynn (St Margaret's), and Yarmouth (St Nicholas'); these last were intended for three or four monks each who were given charge of the nearby parish churches. In 1130 the chapel of St Edmund at Hoxne, Suffolk, became the fifth cell attached to Norwich with a complement of seven to eight monks.[2] Every monk was professed in the cathedral priory and was a full member of the monastic chapter no matter where he was resident at any given time, and all appointments to the cells were made by the prior of Norwich.

Statistics of the monastic population at Norwich begin to appear on the obedientiary accounts on the eve of the Black Death and continue at fairly frequent intervals for the next two centuries.[3] In 1348 there were about sixty-five monks in all, half of whom died in the plague the following year; by the mid-1360s there were over fifty, and in 1389/90 this upward trend reached fifty-nine. Half a century later the total was about fifty-five, while in 1503/4 there were fifty monks. Since this last figure appears to refer only to Norwich, the total would have to be raised in order to include those members of the community who were residing in the cells but whose numbers are unknown. Twenty years on, numbers on the accounts stood at only forty-two; thirty-seven occur in the year that saw the Act of Supremacy come into force, and only eighteen names are to be found on the surrender deed. These figures must be interpreted with an awareness of their underlying ambiguities, namely that many of the later totals, probably, and the surrender deed itself, certainly, apply only to the cathedral community, which saw a mass exodus of about fourteen monks in the spring of 1538.[4]

References to some of the obedientiary offices occur in records dating from the early

[1] Dodwell, 'The Foundation of Norwich Cathedral', 12, and Fernie, *Arch. Hist. Norwich*, 13–15. The bishop had been a monk of Fécamp and decreed that the cathedral priory should follow the customs of that house; see Tolhurst, *Customary*, which is a transcription of a 13thc. manuscript, now Cambridge, Corpus Christi College Ms 465.

[2] Knowles and Hadcock, *MRH*, 58, Dodwell, *op. cit.*, 10, *MRH*, 68. Durham was the only cathedral priory with more dependencies but some of them were later acquisitions.

[3] The extensive collection of close to 1,500 rolls begins as early as 1263/4. Because many of these exist in duplicate and many rolls consist of consecutive years attached together, the numbering of the accounts does not follow in strict chronological sequence as one might, unless warned, expect.

Most of my figures are drawn from the accounts of St Leonard's priory which recorded annual payments to all the monks residing in the cathedral community; thus, another twelve to fifteen, full members of the Norwich chapter, are probably not accounted for in these calculations. For further statistical details see Greatrex in 'Norwich Monk Students', 559–560, and in 'Statistics', 183–185.

[4] The circumstances surrounding the surrender will be discussed more fully below.

to mid-twelfth century; sacrists (Giulfus, William III, q.v.), subpriors (William de Turba, Richard de Ferreres, q.v.), a precentor (William de Turba), and a cellarer (Elias I, q.v.). The first known almoner appears c.1200 (Roger Tancre, q.v.) and a master of St Paul's hospital (M. Simon III, q.v.) at about the same time;[5] a chamberlain soon follows in the 1260s (Richer de Baldeswell, q.v.). The remaining offices, though assuredly functioning at a much earlier date, have no names of their occupants until they show up on the headings of their accounts, the earliest survivals of which date from the 1260s. Thus, the first known master of the cellar is Frebertus de ?Basel, q.v., 1263/4, who was the equivalent of the treasurer, bursar, or receiver at other monastic establishments; he also had the responsibilities of the obedientiary known elsewhere as the granator or granger. The communar/pittancer (W. de Sweynesthrop, q.v.) comes on the scene in 1282/13 and combined the two offices with his two accounts on the same roll; the first refectorer known by name (Reyner de Lakenham, q.v.) heads an account of 1288/9; the earliest account of an infirmarer (Geoffrey de Totyngton, q.v.) is dated 1312/3; that of the hostiller (William de Hadesto, q.v.) is 1319/20; and the first monk gardener's account (headed John de Clipesby, q.v.) bears the date 1329/30. A succentor (Benedict de Lenn, q.v.) is named in 1293/4, and a master of the high altar (William de Martham, q.v.) in 1315. It seems clear, however, that this latter office and that of the *custos* of the Lady chapel were usually the responsibility of chaplains or clerks paid by the sacrist.[6] The earliest prior of any of the cells is probably Herveus II, q.v., though of unknown date, at Hoxne, followed by Robert [II], q.v., at [King's] Lynn in 1178/9, Ralph de Elingham, q.v., at Yarmouth in 1291/2, and, in the mid-fourteenth century, John de Bedingfeld at Aldeby and John de Hengham [I], q.v., at St Leonard's. There is a late thirteenth-century reference to a third prior, but we have to wait until the sixteenth century for one to be named (John Shelton, q.v.) and for that of a fourth prior (Thomas Morton, q.v.) and a fifth prior (Robert Stanton II, q.v.). At Norwich the bishop had the right of appointment to the offices of prior of all the cells except St Leonard's, of subprior, sacrist, cellarer, precentor, chamberlain, and master of St Paul's hospital. The prior and seniors presented their nomination and the bishop made the appointment; dismissal from office was also the bishop's prerogative usually on the convent's request.[7]

An inquiry of 1257 found that the Norwich chapter possessed the right of free election of a prior upon receipt of an episcopal licence.[8] Thus, it is probable that Roger de Skerning, q.v., may have been the first prior chosen by the monks; he was also only the second to be elected bishop, William de Turba, q.v., having preceded him over a century earlier. Alexander de Totyngton, q.v., was the only other Norwich monk bishop before the 1530s, and he succeeded only after some months spent in prison at Windsor, suffering from the king's displeasure at the monks' persistence in opposing the royal will.[9] Although several registers of the priors' *acta* survive, none contains

[5] The hospital or Normanspital in Norwich was in the care of the monks and provided a home for twenty poor men; there are a few 15th-c. accounts.

[6] NRO DCN 1/4/14, 1/4/36, 1/4/37, etc. The Lady chapel, an eastern extension behind the high altar, was built in the mid-13th c.

[7] At Canterbury three nominations were the custom, from whom the archbishop selected and appointed one. See below for further discussion.

[8] *CClR, 1256–1259*, 66, 137–138.

[9] William Repps, q.v., became bishop in 1536. John Salmon, prior of Ely, q.v., had been provided to Norwich in 1299. Thomas de Hemenhale, q.v., who had been an unsuccessful candidate for the episcopate at Norwich, was provided to the see of Worcester in 1337, and Thomas Brinton, q.v., to Rochester in 1373.

details of the proceedings of episcopal or prioral elections.[10] In fact, the episcopal registers, though the series is unbroken from 1299, have been sadly depleted of so much of their original contents that they have become known as institution books, an apt description of most of what survives. Thus, the formal appointment [*prefectio*] and commission for installation of priors and obedientiaries may be found, but little more.

These lacunae also extend to ordination lists, which, at Norwich, with only a few exceptions, are confined to secular clergy; ordinations of religious must have been recorded separately and have not survived. It follows that for the Norwich monks we are in most cases deprived of their exact admission, profession, and ordination dates; however, the fairly frequent occurrence of two other entries, both recorded on obedientiary account rolls, provides a probably close approximation. The first of these is the purchase of a *ciphus*, a drinking cup or bowl, one of the items listed among the equipment to be provided by or for the novice at the time of his entry into the monastery.[11] Frequently, so it seems at Norwich, the young novice purchased one from the refectorer, whose supply was constantly being replenished by the *ciphi* of deceased monks and by bequests.[12] The second date, probably occurring soon after admission because it is often the earliest record of the monk's presence in the community, is an entry concerning his illness. It is fortunate that the infirmarer's accounts are more numerous for Norwich than for other cathedral priories, and that those of the refectorer are even more plentiful.[13] The mid-fifteenth-century mass rotas preserved in Ms 142 of Emmanuel College, Cambridge, are also informative in providing lists of monks assigned to celebrate chantry masses and also of those who were to be celebrants at the high mass on Sundays on specified dates; apart from a few undated fragments at Canterbury these records are unique.

Various distributions, known as pittances, were made to the monks at Norwich, as elsewhere, during the course of the year, usually on festivals and the commemoration of anniversaries. One of these commonly referred to as 'le O', is mentioned in a few entries in this section of the Register when obedientiaries made contributions to the fund. The 'O' payments were associated with the Advent antiphons, eight ancient hymns sung in praise and expectancy during the week preceding the Christmas feast, all of which began with 'O'.[14] At Norwich these payments were occasionally diverted to relieve a financial crisis brought on by a costly building programme as, for example, in 1316/17.[15] Individual monks also contributed to the reconstruction of the cloister throughout the lengthy period during which it was under way (Hugh de Bradewelle, q.v., in 1348/9, Alexander Denton, q.v., in 1421/2, being two who were generous). No rota of the monks undergoing the periodic blood letting, or *minutio*,

[10] For this reason there are no lists of monks in order of seniority before the 1490s when visitation records of bishop Goldwell and archbishop Morton remedy this deficiency. Negotiations over the unsuccessful attempt of the prior and convent to have Robert de Baldock, chancellor, as their bishop in 1325 are entered in (Priory) Reg. IX, fos 42–62^{v} *passim.* Expenses relating to elections make frequent appearances on the obedientiary accounts, for example see under Hemenhale.

[11] Such a list is printed in Stewart, *Arch. Hist. Ely*, 232 from Lambeth Ms 448, fo 106^{v}, and another from Canterbury in Pantin, *Cant. Coll. Ox.*, iv, 118; see William Glastynbury (Canterbury).

[12] The sums paid varied but 6s. 8d. was an average price; see, for example, John Donemowe, Adam Elye, Simon Harpele, and John Stowe I (who paid 10s.).

[13] There are thirty-eight rolls of the infirmarer and 119 of the refectorer. The Durham infirmarer's accounts are the one exception in exceeding those of Norwich in number.

[14] The prior, for example, contributed 26s. 8d. in 1378/9 and the gardener gave the same amount in 1400/1, NRO DCN 1/9/17, 1/11/3.

[15] See Ralph de Betele I, Peter de Dereham, and Geoffrey de Wroxham.

exists but there are frequent references to contributions of wine and spices on these occasions by obedientiaries: for example, in the 1370s the precentor (William de Thetford, q.v.) recorded his payment *pro minucionibus et aliis recreacionibus.*[16] It was common practice for monks to be deputed to celebrate special anniversary and other private masses, and to receive a small remuneration, although details of the arrangements are comparatively rare survivals. At Norwich there is one fragmentary record for a brief period in the 1440s that lists the monks deputed to say weekday and chantry masses in the cathedral and those on duty for the Sunday mass, for example both the monks named Denton, q.v. (whom one is tempted to think were not only brothers but possibly twins). Many entries record the obedientiaries and monks visiting their manors for supervisory purposes, for holding courts and for the periodic receiving of rents and other dues, the *liberatio denariorum*; they were often accompanied by the *senescallus* or land steward, who was a layman at Norwich receiving his fee from the master of the cellar.[17] Whenever the chamberlain entered the alms of a monk on his account, under the heading 'foreign receipts', he was in fact recording that monk's death. The 'alms' may have been in the form of money found among the deceased monk's belongings or, as at Worcester, money obtained from the sale of the monk's clothing, bedding, and riding equipment.[18] Only a glance through the monks' names is required in order to observe that the toponymics are invariably of local origin, Norwich, Yarmouth, and Lenn [Lynn] being among the most frequent; there is a marked insularity here.

Surviving sources give the impression that the prior and chapter of Norwich actively resisted any attempt to challenge what they regarded as pertaining to their rights and jurisdiction. Their procedure on these occasions is dramatically illustrated in the dispute with archbishop Reynolds over the *sede vacante* administration of the diocese and with bishop Despenser over his right of intervention in chapter affairs; both of these cases were taken to the curia. The first arose on the death of bishop Salmon in 1325 when archbishop Reynolds asserted his right of spiritual jurisdiction in the diocese and announced his intention to hold a visitation *jure metropolitico*. The monks responded with their claim to exercise spiritual jurisdiction during a vacancy. The visitation did not take place, but the prior and chapter wasted no time in sending a delegation to Avignon to appeal against the archbishop; John de Mari, q.v., set out in October 1325 and Richard de Hecham [II] and Roger de Eston, q.v., were there in 1329/30. Priory Reg. X, fos 8–34 resembles a somewhat jumbled and incomplete log-book of the progress of the hearings at Avignon between the spring of 1326 and January 1328.[19] The case continued for another three years after Reynolds' death in November 1327, until a final agreement was achieved between his successor, Simon de Meopham, and prior William Claxton, q.v., and the chapter. The terms provided for a monk official, *visitator*, whose authority during a vacancy was restricted to the power of visitation in the cathedral, city, and diocese, i.e. 'excepted jurisdiction', while the archbishop's

[16] NRO DCN 1/9/16, 1/9/13.

[17] John Berney was *senescallus* between c. 1337 and 1369, NRO DCN 1/1/34–51, and Robert Caille succeeded him, *ib.*, 1/1/53.

[18] The fact that it was the chamberlain who dealt with this matter strongly suggests that the Worcester practice also applied here. To indicate that the disposition of these gifts was not specifically willed by the giver in the usual way, I have used quotation marks for 'alms'.

[19] See also *Lit. Cant.*, nos 159, 160 (Canterbury ref.), which are extracts from Canterbury Reg. L, fos 168–168^{v}.

appointed official was in charge of the other spheres of *sede vacante* administration. Moreover, the prior and chapter were to provide three names as suitable candidates for the post of *visitator*, leaving only the final selection to the archbishop.[20]

Every obedientiary contributed from the funds pertaining to his office in order to meet the cost of litigation against bishop Despenser in the 1390s.[21] The dispute arose over conflicting claims concerning the bishop's rights in his cathedral chapter, including those of visitation, correction, and the appointment of certain obedientiaries. It is not clear what arguments must have led to open hostility because the little surviving evidence suggests that relations had been amicable in the two preceding decades. Prior Nicholas de Hoo, q.v., was on several occasions appointed vicar-general for the often absent bishop, and the appointment and removal of obedientiaries appears to have been running smoothly, with the bishop's commissaries consulting with the prior and senior monks over the selection of worthy candidates for office.[22] Tension may have developed at the time of the episcopal visitation in 1393, as an inhibition from the court of Canterbury states that the bishop had overstepped the prior's rights at that time.[23] The suit was certainly pending in Rome before 4 April 1395 and continued for seven years through a succession of papal ordinances, commissions, and mandates, some of them directed to the archbishop. The papal judgement, issued in December 1402, more or less restored the *status quo ante*, with the result that the bishop retained his rights as patron but was warned to exercise them promptly within six days.[24] Finally, in 1411, archbishop Arundel drew up a conclusive settlement in which all the terms were clearly spelled out, the formalities of episcopal appointments to office being retained, for example, but the single nomination put forward by the chapter was not to be overruled.[25]

An examination of the evidence for intellectual interests and the pursuit of learning proves beyond doubt that these ranked high on the monastic agenda at Norwich. An almonry school was certainly being maintained before 1272, and the monks themselves believed that it dated back to their founder, bishop Losinga, who himself had donated books for the library.[26] There are many references to the almonry boys, some of them children of poor families and others fee-paying, on the almoner's accounts; but apart from this obedientiary's obvious involvement there is no mention of monks acting as instructors. While it is worth noting that one of the John de Strattons, q.v., had in his possession a copy of Vincent de Beauvais' De puerorum nobilium eruditione, there is only a possibility that he put its contents into practical use.[27] The educational programme for the young novices, none of whom are known to have been almonry boys, can only be conjectured in general terms on the basis of what is known from, for example, Canterbury sources, and also by an examination of the monastic library at Norwich. William Courtenay's remark that, in the fourteenth century, Norwich was a flourishing centre of learning, with black monks and friars combining their resources

[20] Churchill, *Cant. Admin.*, i, 194–198 (Canterbury ref.).

[21] NRO DCN 2/1/20 (Lynn, 1393/4 to 1396/7), NRO DCN 1/2/31 (cellarer, 1397/8), NRO DCN 1/6/26, 27 (almoner, 1396/7, 1397/8), and others.

[22] Reg. Despenser, fos 89–89^{v}, 90^{v}.

[23] NRO DCN 42/2/12; see Thomas de Tunstale. Alexander de Totyngton, q.v., had succeeded as prior.

[24] *CPL*, iv (1362–1402), 525, *CPL*, v (1396–1404), 11–12, 273–274, 318–319, 380, 526–527; see also NRO DCN 42/2/24–26.

[25] NRO DCN 42/2/29 and (Priory) Reg. I, fos 267–270; it has been transcribed, somewhat indifferently, in E. H. Carter, *Studies in Norwich Cathedral History* (Norwich, 1935), 46–59.

[26] Greatrex, 'Almonry School', 169–171, Cotton, *Historia*, 391.

[27] Greatrex, *ib.*, 175–177, 181.

and working together, should also be borne in mind.[28] Over a hundred volumes from the medieval library have survived, most of them now in the university and college libraries of Cambridge, while others are known from medieval book lists and from references in the accounts of several of the obedientiaries. Richard Sharpe's forthcoming guide to English Benedictine medieval library catalogues discusses all of these and reproduces the lists of books donated by prior Simon Bozoun, q.v., the inventories of books in two of the cells, and the relevant extracts from the account rolls.[29] Aside from bibles and service books the collection contained works of theology, including Aquinas and Peter Lombard, of the Fathers, including Augustine and Gregory, canon law texts, handbooks for preachers, and a surprising number of chronicles and other historical writings.[30] Two sets of entries on the precentor's accounts between 1476/7 and 1480/1 may show the studious side of some of the young novices. Their names first occur in entries concerning books, one probably relating to the borrowing of books and the other to the production of a new book catalogue [*pro libris in cathologo*] or possibly a new subject index [*pro intabulacione librorum*]. In both cases small sums of money were paid to the precentor. The press mark and titles of the books supposedly borrowed are included in the entry. Was this a display of youthful enthusiasm for the written word or simply obedience to new regulations, or possibly both?[31]

In the above context the consistently high number of Norwich monk students selected for university study causes no surprise. The total number known by name over about two and a half centuries (1290–1540) is eighty-six, a ratio of one in seven of the monks who have entries in the Register; about twenty-three of these obtained degrees in theology and six in canon law. Two, Hervey de Swafham and John de Mari, q.v., were regent masters at Oxford, the preferred *studium* until the late fifteenth century when Cambridge came into its own. There does not appear to have been any reduction in the numbers of monks sent up to university in the sixteenth century: four are known to have taken degrees at Cambridge and three attended Oxford; of these, four were students in the 1520s. A sizeable proportion of them, on their return, were appointed to the office of prior of one of the outlying cells, a preference or policy also followed at Durham.[32]

The profile of the monastic community that was presented to the world outside the gate can be glimpsed as its members went about the regular supervisory rounds of their properties administering justice and charity and also, in the rarer but more dramatic moments, when violent clashes erupted between them and the citizens of Norwich. The account rolls afford abundant evidence of frequent almsgiving on the part of all the obedientiaries; these took the form of distributions of food, clothing, and cash not only at the monastery gate but also to the poor on their manors and in the

[28] W. J. Courtenay, *Schools and Scholars in Fourteenth-Century England* (Princeton, 1987), 107.

[29] Sharpe, *Eng. Benedictine Libraries*, iv, B57–B64. See also the entry under Adam de Easton, one of whose books was a Hebrew text.

[30] See Dodwell, 'History and Norwich Monks', *passim.*

[31] The borrowers, whose first recorded appearance in the monastery is in these entries, are Nicholas Bardney, John Colchestre, Thomas Hoo, q.v. Of course, it is possible that they were merely contributing to the repair of the specified book. Those who are first heard of when giving some of their pocket money to help pay for a new catalogue are John Atelburgh, Nicholas Bedingham, Walter Burnham, John Hempstede, John Hervy, John Stowe II, John Sybly, q.v. There are also references to the compilation of an earlier catalogue; see Richard Hecham II and Robert Swanton; see also Greatrex, 'Norwich Monk Students', 575–576.

[32] Greatrex, *ib.*, 570, 579–583.

parishes in their charge, to lepers at the city gates, to prisoners in Norwich castle, and to friars and anchorites. The prior's expenditures were entered on the account of the master of the cellar, and in the fourteenth century provide ample detail including named but otherwise unknown persons. These entries were clearly distinguished from those under the heading of gifts [*dona* and *exennia*].[33] There was also the hospital of St Paul within the city, whose master was a monk of the cathedral chapter who kept accounts like the other obedientiaries; his total receipts in 1422/3 amounted to approximately £80, almost all of which was spent in the care of the twenty poor inmates and the upkeep of the buildings. Details are omitted and sums decrease in later years, but it would be a mistake to attribute the reduction solely to a decline in generosity and to neglect other factors such as a change in accounting methods.[34]

Disputes between monks and citizens centred on their respective liberties granted and confirmed in a succession of royal charters. Several outbreaks of violence occurred during the thirteenth century, most notably that of 1272 when the cathedral church and other buildings in the precinct were badly damaged by fire; royal intervention was necessary and offenders on both sides, including the prior William Burnham, q.v., punished. Another riot in the mid-fifteenth century may have been fomented by the presence of a contentious mayor and an offensive prior, John Heverlond, q.v. Once again the king deprived the city of its liberties until peace was restored and fines paid.[35]

There are no signs of serious weakness or incompetence on the part of the priors, with the possible exception of William Burnham, q.v., whose role in the 1272 affray cannot be determined from the partisan accounts.[36] Many of them, like Henry de Lakenham, q.v., who attended the council of Lyons in 1274 and Simon Bozoun, q.v., whose book collection enriched the library, appear to have been both learned and adept rulers. Yet another, William Worstede, D.Th., q.v., played a prominent role in the Black Monk Chapter and was one of the delegates appointed to represent the English Benedictines at the council of Basel. From 1295 the priors were summoned to parliament and either attended in person or sent proctors, although they did not become mitred prelates until 1519.[37] The fourteenth-century episcopal and archiepiscopal visitation injunctions reveal little beyond the usual problems arising out of laxity in discipline and in the conduct of daily affairs. Not until the sixteenth century do we find reports of internal disharmony, and then only because of the survival of the personal depositions of individual monks given in private to the bishop's official examiners; this evidence needs to be treated with caution. Even so, although there were some complaints and accusations levied in 1514 and 1520, none of these denounced the prior, Robert Catton [I], q.v., apart from hearsay reports of an instance of illicit use of the common seal.[38] Behind the 1526 visitation it is possible to sense more overt signs of growing discord, with ten juniors complaining against some of the basic reg-

[33] NRO DCN 1/1/11, 14, 17, 18, 42, 46, etc.

[34] See Barbara Harvey's perceptive conclusions on monastic charity in *Living and Dying in England, 1100–1540: The Monastic Experience* (Oxford, 1993), 33.

[35] There is a summary of these disputes in *VCH Warwickshire*, ii, 319–321; see also Fernie, *Arch. Hist. Norwich*, 211–212 for a transcription of the account of the 1272 riot as given by Cotton and another by a London chronicle from an opposing view; also Tanner, *Church in Norwich*, 149–151 for the account relating to the riot in the 1440s.

[36] *VCH Warwickshire*, ii, 319.

[37] Beeching and James, 'Norwich Library', 80 n.

[38] Jessopp, *Visit.*, 74, 75 (in 1514).

ulations in response to which the senior monks accused them of disobedience; and the prior was blamed for his uneven treatment in meting out punishment.[39] Six years later, the bishop's commissary encountered an atmosphere of malaise although six monks gave their *omnia bene* under examination. Those accused of being the instigators of dissension were reported to be in touch with the former prior, now abbot of St Albans, with a view to obtaining his support in their agitation for reform.[40] Depositions of some of the monks contradicted those of others; for example, five monks complained of the failure to send monks to university as was required, while others accused the two monks who were described as *scolares* of being contemptuous of their brethren.[41]

There is no evidence of any royal or episcopal interference at the time of the election of William Castleton, q.v., in 1529; those pressures had already been felt at Bath in 1525 and would be experienced at Worcester and elsewhere in the 1530s. However, this last prior appears as an enigmatic figure, possibly a 'yes man' in favour of the new regime, as he was appointed dean of the new foundation in 1538; on the other hand, his resignation the following year suggests that either he or Cromwell had had second thoughts. There is no way of reconstructing what went on behind the scenes within the cloister during Castleton's priorate, apart from the fact that he and twenty-four monks were dispensed to hold canonries in April 1538 and about twelve of these stayed on to sign the surrender. The remaining six signatories of this final deed used their family names and may have been recent admissions not previously recorded; or, it is possible that some of them are entered in the Register under their toponymics. With insufficient evidence no connecting links between entries can be made. Further confusion arises in that there are seventeen monks' names first occurring in 1520 or later; and about half of these do not appear until 1532 or later. Yet none of these are on the two final lists, unless, here again, the aliases cause the problem; and in at least four cases the commonplace Christian names will not permit any links to be made between alias and toponymic. A tentative but reasonably safe conclusion would suggest that there continued to be a few entrants to the monastery in the 1530s, some of whom were probably brief sojourners; but the very movement of monastic personnel in both directions is a sign that there was life and hope in the Norwich community until the end.

NORWICH REFERENCES WITH ABBREVIATIONS

Note: if the particular reference sought does not appear below, turn to the General Bibliography on pp. xv–xix, or the Canterbury section, pp. 58–65.

A. Manuscript Sources

i Episcopal Registers, in Norfolk Record Office (NRO)

Reg. [John] Salmon (1299–1325)	DN Reg/1/1
Reg. [William] Ayermine (1325–1336)	DN Reg/1/2
Reg. [Anthony] Bek (1337–1343)	DN Reg/1/3
Reg. [William] Bateman (1344–1355)	DN Reg/2/4
Reg. [Thomas] Percy (1356–1369)	DN Reg/2/5

[39] *Ib.*, 198, 201. [40] See Richard Lopham. [41] See Richard Norwich and Thomas Morton.

Reg. [Henry] Despenser (1370–1406)	DN Reg/3/6
Reg. [Alexander] Totyington (1407–1413)	DN Reg/4/7, fos 1–71.
Reg. [Richard] Courtenay (1413–1415)	bound with the above, fos 72–104.
Reg. [John] Wakeryng (1416–1425)	DN Reg/4/8
Reg. [William] Alnwick (1426–1436)	DN Reg/5/9
Reg. [Thomas] Brouns (1436–1445)	DN Reg/5/10
Reg. [Walter] Lyhert (1446–1472)	DN Reg/6/11
Reg. [James] Goldwell (1472–1499)	DN Reg/7/12
[Reg. [Thomas] Jane] (1499–1500)	DN Reg/8/13, ?on fo 13]
Reg. [Richard] Nikke (1501–1535), parts of 5 vols	DN Regs/8/13, 9/14, 9/15, 10/16, 11/17.
Reg. [William] Repps (1535–1550), parts of 2 vols	DN Regs/10/16, 11/17.

Note: Regs 10/16, 11/17 lack any semblance of chronological order; see D.M. Smith, *Guide to Bishops' Registers of England and Wales*, Royal Historical Society, 1981, 156–157. There is also an Ordination Reg., DN ORR/1/1 that covers the years 1530–1561.

ii Priory Registers and Cartularies in Norfolk Record Office (NRO)

Reg. I	Registrum Primum, cartulary of the master of the cellar written c.1306, with a short history of the priory; see *N. Cath. Charters*, i, xxv; DCN 40/1. See also Saunders in Section C.ii below.
Reg. II, i	Almoner's Register, mainly 14th c., sometimes referred to as Registrum Secundum i; see *N. Cath. Charters*, i, xxvij; DCN 40/2/1.
Reg. II, ii	Similar to and probably a copy of Reg. I, sometimes referred to as Registrum Secundum ii; see *N. Cath. Charters*, i, xxviij; DCN 40/2/2.
Reg. III	Register of royal grants, compiled c. mid-15th c.; see *N. Cath. Charters*, i, xxx; DCN 40/3.
Reg. IV	Register of episcopal grants, similar to the above and also of approximately the same date; see *N. Cath. Charters*, i, xxxij; DCN 40/4.
Reg. V	Cellarer's Register begun in 1282; see *N. Cath. Charters*, i, xxxiij; DCN 40/5.
Reg. VI	Chamberlain's Register, 14th c.; see *N. Cath. Charters*, i, xxxiv; DCN 40/6.
Reg. VII	Cartulary of the master of the cellar, late 13th c.; see *N. Cath. Charters*, i, xxxvj; DCN 40/7.
Reg. IX	Register or letter-book, early 14th c.; DCN 40/9.
Reg. X	Register of priory acta, 14th c.; DCN 40/10.
Reg. XI	Sacrist's Register with a kalendar, 13th/14th cs; see *N. Cath. Charters*, i, xxxvij; DCN 40/11.
Reg. XII	Inventory of muniments, early 14th c.; see *N. Cath. Charters*, i, xxxix; DCN 40/12.
Reg. XIII	'Proficuum' of the priory manors, 14th c.; DCN 40/13.

B. Other Manuscript Sources

i Obedientiary Accounts

(*a*) Norfolk Record Office (NRO)

Almoner	1275/6 to 1532/3	DCN 1/6/-
Cellarer	1284/5 to 1530/1	DCN 1/2/-
Chamberlain	1291/2 to 1535/6	DCN 1/5/-
Communar and Pittancer	1282 to 1536	DCN 1/12/-
Note: see also below under *Comm. Rolls* in Section D.		
Gardener	1339/40 to 1529/30	DCN 1/11/-
Note: see also below under (*b*).		
Hostiller	1319/20 to 1534/5	DCN 1/7/-
Infirmarer	1312/13 to 1529/30	DCN 1/10/-
Master of the Cellar	1263/4 to 1535/6	DCN 1/1/-

Precentor	1282/3 to 1532/3	DCN 1/9/-
Refectorer	1288/9 to 1534/5	DCN 1/8/-
Sacrist	1272/3 to 1535/6	DCN 1/4/-

(*b*) Canterbury Cathedral Archives (CCA DCc)

Gardener 1329/30

ii Accounts of Priors of the Cells

(*a*) Norfolk Record Office (NRO)

Aldeby	1380/1 to 1525/6	DCN 2/2/-
Hoxne	1394/5 to 1534/5	DCN 2/6/-
See also under (*b*)		
Lynn	1370/1 to 1535/6	DCN 2/1/-
St Leonard's	1347/8 to 1535/6	DCN 2/3/-
St Paul's Hospital	1422/3 to 1509/10	DCN 2/5/-
Yarmouth	1355/6 to 1528/9	DCN 2/4/-

(*b*) Cell Accounts in Windsor, St George's chapel

Hoxne	?1330s to 1509/10	I.C.1–37
Yarmouth	four 15th c. rolls	XV.55.75–78

Note: the gardener acct for 1389/90 is also here, XI. E. 18.

(*c*) Obedientiary Accounts in Oxford, Bod. Ms Charters and Rolls, Norfolk

These include a few accts of the master of the cellar (1491/2), the precentor (1324/5), and the refectorer (1339/40 to 1506/7, six accounts only).

Note: these are included among the Norfolk Charters and Rolls which are calendared in Turner and Coxe, *Charters and Rolls*; the full reference of this volume is given in General References.

iii Manorial Accounts in Norfolk Record Office (NRO)

Catton	DCN 60/4/-
Denham	DCN 60/7/-
Henley	DCN 60/16/-
Hindolveston	DCN 60/18/-
Hindringham	DCN 60/20/-
Martham	DCN 60/23/-
Plumstead	DCN 60/29/-
Sedgeford	DCN 60/33/-

iv Miscellaneous Manuscripts

Note: these are grouped by location.

(*a*) Cambridge, Emmanuel College

Cambridge, Emm. Coll. Ms 142 Concilium Basiliense and miscellaneous notes and lists, 15th c.

(*b*) London, British Library (BL)

Ms Cotton Nero C.v	contains the chronicle of Bartholomew Cotton, fos 162–285.
Ms Harley 3950	a psalter containing a Norwich kalendar and obits, 14th c.
Ms Royal, 14 C.i	contains the chronicle of Bartholomew Cotton, fos 20–137.

(*c*) London, Lambeth Palace Library (Lambeth)

Ms 368 a psalter with kalendar, late 13th/early 14th c.

(*d*) Norfolk Record Office (NRO)

Loose Documents, Inventories, Episcopal Instruments and Charters.

These are listed as DCN 3/- to DCN 95/-; there are also rentals of the cellarer, DCN 1/3/- and several rolls headed 'status obedientiariorum', DCN 1/13/-.

(*e*) Oxford, Bodleian Library (Oxford, Bod.)

Ms Charters and Rolls, Norfolk	see Section B.ii (*c*) above.
Ms Tanner 100	contains late 15th-c. episcopal visitations, transcribed by Jessopp; see Section D below.
Ms Tanner 132	contains early 16th-c. episcopal visitations, also transcribed as above.
Ms Tanner 210	contains more early 16th-c. visitations transcribed as above.
Ms Tanner 342	extracts from a Norwich register on fos 105–110, identified by Pantin.

v Unpublished Theses

B. Burnham 'The Episcopal Administration of the Diocese of Norwich in the Later Middle Ages', Oxford, B.Litt., 1971.

L. J. Macfarlane 'The Life and Writings of Adam Easton, OSB', 2 vols, London, Ph.D., 1955.

C. Printed Sources

i Episcopal Registers

None

ii Priory Registers

Saunders, Reg. I H. W. Saunders, *The first Register of Norwich Cathedral Priory*, Norfolk Record Society, xi, 1939; transcript and translation of the 13th-c. chronicle contained in Reg. I.

D. Other Printed Sources and References

Anstruther, *Epist. Losinga* R. Anstruther, ed., *Epistolae Herberti de Losinga, Primi Episcopi Norwicensis, Osberti de Clara et Elmeri Prioris Cantuariensis*, Brussels, 1846.

Beeching and James, 'Norwich Library' H. C. Beeching and M. R. James, 'The Library of the Cathedral Church of Norwich with an Appendix of Priory Manuscripts now in English Libraries', *Norfolk Archaeology*, xix (1917), 67–116.

Bensly, 'St Leonard's' W. T. Bensly, 'St Leonard's Priory, Norwich', *Norfolk Archaeology*, xii (1895), 190–227; includes a transcription of inventories of 1424 and 1452/3.

Blomefield, *Norfolk* F. Blomefield and C. Parkin, *An Essay towards a Topographical History of the County of Norfolk*, 11 vols, London, 1805–10.

Cheney, 'Norwich Cath. Priory' C. R. Cheney, 'Norwich Cathedral Priory in the Fourteenth Century', *Bulletin of the John Rylands Library*, 20 (1936), 93–120.

Comm. Rolls E. C. Fernie and A. B. Whittingham, eds, *The Early Communar and Pitancer Rolls of Norwich Cathedral Priory with an Account of the Building of the Cloister*, Norfolk Record Society, 41, 1972.

Cotton, *Historia*	H. R. Luard, ed., *Bartholomaei de Cotton, monachi Norwicensis, historia Anglicana (A.D. 449–1298), necnon eiusdem liber de archiepiscopis et episcopis Angliae*, Rolls Series, 1859.
Davis, *Paston Letters*	Norman Davis ed., *Paston Letters and Papers of the Fifteenth Century*, 2 vols., Oxford, 1971, 1976.
	M. A. Devlin, ed., *The Sermons of Thomas Brinton, Bishop of Rochester (1373–1389)* Camden 3rd series, 85 and 86, 1954.
Dodwell, 'The Foundation of Norwich Cathedral'	B. Dodwell, 'The Foundation of Norwich Cathedral', *Transactions of the Royal Historical Society*, 5th series, 7 (1957), 1–18.
Dodwell, 'History and Norwich Monks'	B. Dodwell, 'History and the Monks of Norwich Cathedral Priory', *Reading Medieval Studies*, 5 (1979), 38–56.
Eng. Epis. Acta, vi	C. Harper-Bill, ed., *English Episcopal Acta*, vi, *Norwich, 1070–1214*, British Academy, Oxford, 1990.
Fernie, *Arch. Hist.Norwich*	E. Fernie, *An Architectural History of Norwich Cathedral*, Oxford, 1993.
Gairdner, *Paston Letters*	James Gairdner, ed., *The Paston Letters, 1422–1509 AD*, 3 vols., Edinburgh, 1910.
Greatrex, 'Almonry School'	J. Greatrex, 'The Almonry School of Norwich Cathedral Priory in the Thirteenth and Fourteenth Centuries', *Studies in Church History*, 31 (1994), 169–182.
Greatrex, 'Norwich Monk Students'	J. Greatrex, 'Monk Students from Norwich Cathedral Priory at Oxford and Cambridge, c. 1300 to 1530', *English Historical Review*, 106 (1991), 555–583.
Hudson, 'Camera Roll'	W. Hudson, 'The Camera Roll of the Prior of Norwich in 1283 compiled by Bartholomew de Cotton', *Norfolk and Norwich Archaeological Society, Original Papers*, 19 (1917), 268–313.
Jessopp, *Visit.*	A. Jessopp, ed., *Visitations of the Diocese of Norwich, A.D. 1492–1532*, Camden Society, new series, 43, 1888.
Jessopp and James, *St. William*	A. Jessopp and M. R. James, eds, *The Life and Miracles of St. William of Norwich by Thomas of Monmouth*, Cambridge, 1896; transcribed from CUL Add. Ms 3037.
Ker, 'Norwich Cathedral Mss'	N. R. Ker, 'Medieval Manuscripts from Norwich Cathedral Priory', in *Transactions of the Cambridge Bibliographical Society*, 1 (1949–53), 1–28 and reprinted in A. G. Watson, ed., N. R. Ker, *Books, Collectors and Libraries, Studies in the Medieval Heritage*, London, 1985, 243–272; references are to the reprinted article.
N. Cath. Charters i and ii	B. Dodwell, ed., *The Charters of Norwich Cathedral Priory*, Pipe Roll Society, new series, xl (1965–66), i, new series, xlvi (1978–80), ii.
Owen, *King's Lynn*	D. M. Owen, ed., *The Making of King's Lynn, a Documentary Survey*, British Academy, London, 1985.
St Benet Holme Cart.	J. R. West, ed., *The Register of the Abbey of St. Benet of Holme*, 2 vols, Norfolk Record Society, 1932.
Saunders, *Obed. Rolls*	H. W. Saunders, *An Introduction to the Obedientiary and Manor Rolls of Norwich Cathedral Priory*, London, 1930.
Tanner, *Church in Norwich*	N. Tanner, *The Church in late medieval Norwich, 1370–1532*, Toronto, 1984.
Tolhurst, *Customary*	J. Tolhurst, ed., *The Customary of the Cathedral Priory of Norwich*, Henry Bradshaw Society, 1948.

NORWICH CATHEDRAL PRIORY

1096 × 1101–1538/9

Edmund de ACLE [Ocle
occ. 1347/8

1347/8, ill and 4d. was spent by the infirmarer on medicine, NRO DCN 1/10/6.

William de ACLE [Akel, Hocle
occ. [1278/9] occ. 1282/3

n.d., prior of Hoxne, Blomefield, *Norfolk*, iii, 609–10.

[1278/9], almoner, *Cal. Inq. Misc.*, ii, no 1260.

1282/3, the almoner pd a £9 debt for him, and £5 to his nephew (?because he was a previous almoner), NRO DCN 1/6/5.

John ACRE
occ. 1419 d. 1425/6

1419, Dec./1424, Sept., refectorer, NRO DCN 1/8/67–71.

1422/3, gave 6s. 8d. to the office of refectorer *de dono et devocione*, NRO DCN 1/8/70.

1425/6, d., and the chamberlain recd 'alms' of 26s. 8d.

ADAM
n.d.

n.d., 2 Aug., name occ. in the Canterbury obit list, BL Ms Arundel 68, fo 36v.

AIRYCH
see Ayrych

William de AKEFORD
occ. 1255/6

1255/6, sacrist and visited [North] Elmham, NRO DCN 60/10/1.

AKEL
see Acle

ALAN
occ. 1313/14 occ. 1322/3

1313/14, 1322/3, chamberlain, NRO DCN 1/1/23; DCN 60/20/21.

1322/3, visited Hindringham, NRO DCN 60/20/21.

Adam de ALDEBY [Audeby
occ. 1314/15 occ. 1346/7

1314/15, gave 20s. to the master of the cellar *ad negotia domus*, NRO DCN 1/1/23.

1318/19, gave a gift of 60s. to the cellarer, NRO DCN 1/2/12; and the cellarer pd 18d. for Adam and two other monks [?in negotiations on their behalf], *ib.*

1345/6, ill, 4d. was spent by the infirmarer on medicine, NRO DCN 1/10/4.

1346/7, again ill, 4d. spent on medicine, NRO DCN 1/10/5.

Note: in 1348 the refectorer gave 1d. as a gift to a M. Adam de Aldeby, NRO DCN 1/8/37; this may be another man, his namesake.

Name in Norwich, Castle Museum Ms 99.20, Liber glosarum (late 13th c.); on fo 1 *liber*—. See *MLGB* and Ker 'Norwich Cathedral Mss', 257.

John de ALDEBY [Aldby
occ. 1356/7 occ. 1367/8

1356/7, bought a *ciphus* for 13s. 4d. from the refectorer, prob. soon after adm. NRO DCN 1/8/40.

1361/2, refectorer, NRO DCN 1/8/41.

1365/6 and 1367/8, master of the cellar, NRO DCN 1/1/49 and 50; and see Joseph de Martham who seems to have relinquished office during 1365/6 and resumed it in 1368/9.

1361/2, charged his office (above) 13s. 4d. for the medical treatment he required when ill, NRO DCN 1/8/41.

Richard ALDEBY
occ. and d. 1455/6

1455/6, ill, 8s. were spent by the infirmarer on medicine, NRO DCN 1/10/24; he d. the same yr and the chamberlain received 'alms' of 5s. 10d., NRO DCN 1/5/87.

ALDELM
n.d.

n.d., 20 July, his obit occ. in the kalendar in Reg. XI, fo 5.

Roger de ALDERFORD
occ. 1288/9

1288/9, named by the communar with Bartholomew de Cotton, q.v., in connection with arrangements for the sale of wood, *Comm. Rolls*, 51 (NRO DCN 1/12/2).

I ALEXANDER
n.d.

n.d., 26 Sept., precentor, occ. in the Canterbury obit list, BL Ms Arundel 68, fo 43.

II ALEXANDER
occ. [1150 × 1159]

[1150 × 1159], witness to the confirmation of a charter in favour of the prior and convent, *N. Cath. Charters* i, no 134, and also in *Eng. Epis. Acta*, vi, no 128.

III ALEXANDER
occ. 1245

1245, 12 June, occ. as 'prior of St Margaret's', possibly Lynn, C. W. Foster, ed., *Final Concords of the County of Lincoln from the Feet of Fines preserved in the Public Record Office, AD 1244–1272*, ii (Lincoln Record Society, 1920), 18 (no 57).

IV ALEXANDER
occ. c. 1367

c. 1367, communar, NRO DCN 2/3/6, possibly a reference to Alexander de Totyngton, q.v.

Note: acc. to Blomefield, *Norfolk*, viii, 495, an Alexander was prior of Lynn in 1381.

ALEXANDER
see also Hikling, Totyngton

John ATELBURGH [Atleburgh, Attilborough, Attleborough, Attleburgh, Attylburgh
occ. 1480/1   d. 1505/6

1490/2, communar/pittancer, NRO DCN 1/12/78 and 79.
1492/3, 1493/4, 1495/8, 1498/1500, prior of Hoxne, NRO DCN 2/6/30; Windsor, St George's chapel, I.C.29; NRO DCN 2/6/31–33; Windsor, St George's chapel, I.C.30,31.
1500, 26 Sept., subprior, Canterbury Reg. R, fo 46.
1501/2, 1504/5, prior of Yarmouth, NRO DCN 2/4/19 and 20.
1497/1500, pensioner at Gonville Hall, Cambridge, *BRUC* and Venn, *Gonville and Caius*, i, 14.
Note: It is unusual to find a monk being sent to university after at least seventeen yrs in the cathedral priory; this may be the toponymic of another monk.
1480/1, gave the precentor 3d. *pro intabulacione librorum*, NRO DCN 1/9/78.
1491/2, ill and charged his office 8s. for medicine, NRO DCN 1/12/79
1492, 7 Sept., the bp replied to the prior's letter requesting his apptment as prior of Hoxne, Reg. Goldwell, fo 159v; see above.
1492, 5/8 Oct., 19th in order at the visitation of bp Goldwell, Jessopp, *Visit.*, 8.
1499, 6 Apr., 13th on the metropolitan visitation certificate, *Reg. abp Morton*, iii, no 258.
1500, 26 Sept., one of three monks nominated by the prior and chapter for the office of *visitator, sed. vac.* Norwich, Canterbury Reg. R, fo 46.
1505/6, d., NRO DCN 1/4/109.

Name in Durham University Library, Ms Cosin V.u.12, Dares Phrygius etc. (15th c.), *in custodia*—; see Ker, 'Norwich Cathedral Mss', 265.

Francis ATMERE
see Norwich

Nicholas ATTILBURGH [Attleburgh, Attylborogh, Attilburghe *alias* Thurkill
occ. 1520   occ. 1538

1520, 3 Sept., succentor, Jessopp, *Visit.*, 193.
1532, 3 June; 1534/5, prior of Hoxne, Jessopp, *Visit.*, 264; NRO DCN 2/6/45; and Windsor, St George's chapel, I.C.39.
1520, 3 Sept., present at the visitation of bp Nikke, Jessopp, *Visit.*, 193.
1532, 3 June, at the visitation of bp Nikke and admonished for laxity in dress against the Rule, Jessopp, *Visit.*, 263.
1534, 28 July, subscribed to the Act of Supremacy, *DK 7th Report*, Appndx 2, 295.
1538, 30 Apr., paid a fee to be dispensed to wear the habit of a secular pr. and hold a canonry and prebend in the cathedral and any other benefice, and be non resident, Chambers, *Faculty Office Regs*, 137 (as Nicholas Thurkyll).
1538, 2 May, apptd canon of the 5th prebend in the new foundation, *Fasti 1541–1857*, vii, 57.

Note: see also William Thirkell.

AUDEBY
see Aldeby

Geoffrey AYLESHAM [Aylsham, Aylysham
occ. 1492   occ. 1502/3

1497/8, student, first year at Cambridge, NRO DCN 1/10/33.
1500/1, student, with pension contributions from the almoner, cellarer, chamberlain and the priors of Aldeby and Hoxne, NRO DCN 1/6/113; 1/2/86; 1/5/126; 2/2/27; Windsor, St George's chapel, I.C.32.
1501/2, student, with pension contributions from the hostiller and master of the cellar, NRO DCN 1/7/124; 1/1/100.
1502/3, student, with contributions from the cellarer and the prior of Hoxne, NRO DCN 1/2/88; Windsor, St George's chapel, I.C.34.
See also Venn, *Gonville and Caius*, i, 15, where he is listed as a pensioner in 1503.
1492, 5/8 Oct., 40th in order (out of 46) at the visitation of bp Goldwell, Jessopp, *Visit.*, 8.

1499, 6 Apr., 32nd on the visitation certificate, *Reg. abp Morton*, iii, no 258.

Nicholas AYLESHAM
occ. 1414

1414, 14 Oct., one of six whose prof. the bp comm. the prior to rec., Reg. Courtenay, fo 102v.

Robert de AYLESHAM
occ. 1376/7

1376/7, the precentor reported the receipt of a legacy *per fratrum*—, NRO DCN 1/9/15.

Simon de AYLESHAM
occ. 1345

1345 (between 6 Jan. and 2 July), ill and the infirmarer pd for medicine, NRO DCN 1/10/2.

Nicholas AYRICH [Airych, Ayrych, Ilyrich
occ. 1426 d. 1480/1

1427, 4 Jan., one of seven whose prof. the bp solemnized in chapter, Reg. Alnwick, fo 97, after the prior's written request of 31 Dec. 1426, *ib.*

1442/5, communar, NRO DCN 1/12/58.
1451/2, cellarer, NRO DCN 1/2/60 [as Ilyrich].
1457/60, refectorer, NRO DCN 1/8/91 and 92.
1471, 1472/5, 1476/9, prior of St Leonard's, NRO DCN 2/3/80–89.

1427/8, ill and the infirmarer pd 2s. 8d. for medicine, NRO DCN 1/10/15.
1446, name occ. on the rough list of those assigned to celebrate weekday and chantry masses, Cambridge, Emm. Coll. Ms 142, fo 68; he was also on another similar list (prob. 1446/7) for the Bateman, Wakering and Erpingham chantries, *ib.*, fo 77v.
1454/5, ill and 12d. spent on medicine, NRO DCN 1/10/24.
1480/1, d., and the chamberlain recd 5s. 'alms', NRO DCN 1/5/109.

Thomas BAA
see Elsyng

I William BAKONESTHORP [Bakunsthorp, Bakynesthorp
occ. 1414 d. 1448/9

1414, 14 Oct., one of six whose prof. the bp comm. the prior to rec., Reg Courtenay, fo 102v.

1426/7, gave the refectorer 10s. *pro cipho*, NRO DCN 1/8/73.
1443/4, came from the cell of Lynn to Norwich to preach on Ash Wednesday, NRO DCN 1/12/58.
1446, name occ. on a rough list of those assigned to celebrate weekday and chantry masses, Cambridge, Emm. Coll. Ms 142, fo 68; also on another similar list (prob. 1446/7) for the Totyngton and Wakering chantries, *ib.*, fo 77v.
1448/9, d., and the chamberlain recd 'alms' of 23s. 8d., NRO DCN 1/5/80–81.

II William BAKONESTHORP [Baconthorpe, Bakensthorp, Bakonnesthorpe, Bakunesthorp, Bakunysthorp
occ. 1487 d. 1503/4

1503–1504, prior: licence to el. was granted on 16 Nov. 1503, *Fasti*, iv, 26; d. within the yr., NRO DCN 1/2/89.

1487, 26 Nov., confirmed in the office of cellarer by the bp, Reg. Goldwell, fo 130.
1487/91, 1497/8, 1499/1503 cellarer, NRO DCN 1/2/81–88.
1493/5, almoner, NRO DCN 1/6/109,110.
1495/6, 1498/1501, chamberlain, NRO DCN 1/5/123–127.
1500/1, prior of Aldeby, NRO DCN 2/2/27.

1492, 5/8 Oct., 20th in order at the visitation of bp Goldwell, Jessopp, *Visit.*, 8.
1493, 18 Jan., apptd penitentiary, Reg. Goldwell, fo 163v.
1499, 6 Apr., 14th on the visitation certificate, *Reg. abp Morton*, iii, no 258.
1500, 26 Sept., one of three monks nominated by the prior and chapter for the office of *visitator, sed. vac.* Norwich, Canterbury Reg. R, fo 46.

Note: according to Blomefield, *Norfolk*, iii, 605, he d. 23 Sept. 1504 and was buried in the south transept.

Richer de BALDESWELL [Baldwelle
occ. 1263/4

1263/4, before, prob. chamberlain, NRO DCN 1/1/1.

1263/4, pardoned a debt which he had owed *super compotum camer[ar]ie quando recessit*, this suggests that he had previously been chamberlain, *ib.*

Alan de BANHAM
occ. [1321 × 1323] occ. 1348/9

[1321 × 1323], the prior asked the bp to approve and bless him as he had been accepted as a monk, Reg. IX, fo 35v.

1337/44, cellarer, NRO DCN 1/2/101 and 102.
1348/9, chamberlain, NRO DCN 1/12/27.

1337/8, went to Martham for *liberatio denariorum*, NRO DCN 60/23/24.
1341, ill and charged his office *contra infirmitate* 4s. 10d., NRO DCN 1/2/102.
1348/9, gave the pittancer 37s. 9d. for 151 *ped' de magnis voussuris*, NRO DCN 1/12/27; (these are prob. mouldings for the cloister vaults, see *Comm. Rolls*, 108, where the word is *petiis*).

Geoffrey de BANHAM
occ. 1263/4

1263/4, subprior, and went to London, NRO DCN 1/1/1.

Nicholas BARDNEY [Barney, Berdenay, Berdeney
occ. 1476 occ. 1499

1476/7, 1478/80, hostiller, NRO DCN 1/7/109–112.
1480/2, 1483/5, prior of Hoxne, NRO DCN 2/6/24–27.
1485/8, sacrist, NRO DCN 1/4/100–103.
1489/90, 1493/4, 1497/9, prior of Lynn, NRO DCN 2/1/74–77; his office was confirmed by the bp on 7 Feb. 1489, Reg. Goldwell, fo 136.

1477/8, pd the precentor for Summa Hugucionis [Hugutio of Pisa] super grammatica, press mark dxxxiiij, 5d. [?borrowed from the library], NRO DCN 1/9/76; see Greatrex 'Norwich Monk Students', 575–576.
1478/9, gave the precentor 4d. *pro intabulacione librorum* (see Greatrex 'Norwich Monk Students', *ib.*), NRO DCN 1/9/77.
1483/4, sent to London [as proctor] to attend convocation, NRO DCN 1/12/73.
1484/5, sent by the communar to London [to the bp] *pro confirmacione officiariorum*, NRO DCN 1/12/74.
1492, 5/8 Oct., 9th in order at the visitation of bp Goldwell, Jessopp, *Visit.*, 8.
1499, 6 Apr., 7th on the visitation certificate *Reg. abp Morton*, iii, no 258.

George BARETT [Baret
occ. 1499 d. 1511/12

1499, 30 Mar., ord subdcn, Norwich, *Reg. abp Morton*, iii, no 53.

1506/8, almoner, NRO DCN 1/6/116 and 117.
1510/11, hostiller, NRO DCN 1/7/131.
1511/12, sacrist, NRO DCN 1/4/111.

1499, 6 Apr., 47th in order on the visitation certificate, *Reg. abp Morton*, iii, no 258.
1511/12, d. as sacrist, NRO DCN 1/4/111.

Adam BARKER
see Sloley

BARTHOLOMEW
see Cotton, Scrowtby

William [BARYDITM]
see Haridaunce

BASEL'
see Frebertus

George BAWCHAM
see Hanworth

William BAYFELD
occ. 1427

1427, 7 Jan., One of four *clerici* adm. *ad osculum et benedictionem* by the bp after acceptance by the chapter as a monk, Reg. Alnwick, fo 97^{v}.

Alexander de BECLES [Beclis
occ. ?1258/9 occ. 1273/4

1272/4, master of the cellar with John de Fuldon, q.v., NRO DCN 1/1/2, DCN 60/39/1.

[?1258/9] visited Denham, NRO DCN 60/7/1.
1272/3, visited Catton, Hemsby, Hindolveston, Hindringham, Martham, [North] Elmham and Sedgeford, in most cases with John Fuldon and for *liberatio denariorum*, NRO DCN 60/4/2; 60/15/2; 60/18/5; 60/20/4; 60/23/4; 60/10/4; 60/33/4.
1273/4, visited Gnatingdon, Hindolveston, Newton, [North] Elmham, Sedgeford, Taverham and Worstead, NRO DCN 60/14/5; 60/18/6; 60/28/1; 60/10/5; 60/20/4; 60/35/7; 60/39/1.
1273/4, with Walter de Walpole, q.v., recd £132 15s. 8d. from the master of the cellar [?for payment of tenths] NRO DCN 1/1/3.

Richard de BECCLES
occ. 1339/40 occ. 1366

1344/6, refectorer, NRO DCN 1/8/36.

1339/40, 2s. 6d. were spent by the refectorer on mending his *ciphus*, Oxford, Bod. Ms Rolls, Norfolk, no 48.
1366, 20 June, residing at the cell of Yarmouth and summoned to a Black Monk Chapter visitation (as Ricardus de B.) Pantin, *BMC*, iii, 55.

T. de BECCLES
occ. 1220

[1220, 15 May], acted as proctor in a dispute over land, *N. Cath. Charters*, ii, no 75.

John de BEDINGFELD [Bedinfeld
occ. 1331/2 occ [1352 × 1357]

[1352 × 1357], prior of Aldeby, Reg IX, fo 20.

1331/2, pd 2s. to the refectorer for a spoon (*coclear'*), NRO DCN 1/8/30.

Adam de BEDINGHAM
occ. 1308 occ. 1319

1308/17, cellarer, NRO DCN 1/2/8–10.

[1314 × 1318], sent as proctor to the lord chancellor about the chapter's right of presentation to Chalk church, Reg. IX, fo 9.
1319, 23 Feb., ordered by the prior to remain in the cell of Aldeby to maintain daily offices, and not to return to Norwich for the episcopal visitation, Reg. IX, fo 5^{v}. (The reference is to 'Ad. de B.', and so this may be Adam de Belagh, q.v.)

Nicholas BEDINGHAM [Bedyngham
occ. 1478/9 occ. 1520

1506/8, hostiller, NRO DCN 1/7/127 and 128.
1511/12, 1513/14, 1515/16, 1517/18, infirmarer, NRO DCN 1/10/34–37, Jessopp, *Visit.*, 74.
1520, 3 Sept., subprior, *ib.*, 192, and described as *senex et surdus* by Thomas Walsham, q.v., *ib.*, 193.
1478/9, gave the precentor 8d. *pro intabulacione librorum* (see Greatrex 'Norwich Monk Students', 575–576), NRO DCN 1/9/77.
1492, 5/8 Oct., 21st in order at the visitation of bp Goldwell, Jessopp, *Visit.*, 8.
1499, 6 Apr., 15th on the visitation certificate, *Reg. abp Morton*, iii, no 258.
1505, 14 Feb., named among the list of pilgrims staying at the English hospice in Rome, B. Newns, 'The Hospice of St Thomas and the English Crown, 1474–1538', *The English Hospice in Rome* (The Venerabile), vol. xxi (1962), 125.
1520, 3 Sept., present at the visitation of bp Nikke and remarked on the decline in nos in the almonry school, Jessopp, *Visit.*, 192.

Adam de BELAGH [Belhawe
occ. 1309/10 occ. 1318/19

1312/16, master of the cellar, NRO DCN 60/33/18, NRO DCN 1/1/23–25; he succ. William de Haddesto, q.v., NRO DCN 60/15/9.
1309/10, mentioned, NRO DCN 1/1/19.
1312/13, visited the manors of Catton, Denham, Hindolveston, Hindringham, [North] Elmham and Sedgeford, NRO DCN 60/4/21; 60/7/6; 60/18/18; 60/20/17; 60/10/15; 60/33/18; he also stopped at Hemsby with his *socius* on his return journey from Aldeby and pd a second visit there for *liberatio denariorum*, NRO DCN 60/15/9.
1313/14, visited Hindolveston NRO DCN 60/18/19.
1313/15, collected tenths with Nicholas de Hyndolveston, q.v., NRO DCN 1/1/23,24.
1317, 17 July, one of two monk proctors apptd to answer charges of non-payment of tenths for which he was a collector, Reg. IX, fo 1; see Nicholas de Hindolveston.
1318/19, visited Hindolveston and Hindringham, NRO DCN 60/18/21; 60/20/19.
[1318/19], 14 Dec., apptd by the prior, who was named as visitor of Benedictine houses in Lincoln diocese, to visit the monks of Ramsey, Pantin, *BMC*, i, 177, 178.

Note: see the ref. under Adam de Bedingham dated 1319, 23 Feb.

Robert BELAWE
occ. 1467/8

1467/8, ill and 18d. was spent by the infirmarer on medicine, NRO DCN 1/10/27.

Simon de BELHAGHE
occ. 1395/6

1395/6, d., and the chamberlain recd 'alms', NRO DCN 1/5/27.

BELLAFAGO
see Richard I

Thomas BELTAM
occ. 1427 occ. 1428/9

1427, 7 Jan., One of four *clerici* adm. *ad osculum et benedictionem* by the bp after acceptance by the chapter as a monk, Reg. Alnwick, fo 97^{v}.
1428/9, ill, and 16d. was spent by the infirmarer on medicine, NRO DCN 1/10/16.

James BELTON
d. 1505/6

1505/6, d., and the sacrist pd 8d. for candles, NRO DCN 1/4/109.

Robert BENNYS, Benneys
see Robert Catton II

BERDENAY
see Bardney

John BERGERSH [de Bergh'
occ. 1403 d. 1445/6

1403, Jan. to June; 1406, Feb. to ?Nov., gardener, NRO DCN 1/11/5,7,8.
1406/Jan. 1409, communar/pittancer, NRO DCN 1/12/40–42.
1408/10, hostiller, NRO DCN 1/7/56/57.
1410/11, refectorer, NRO DCN 1/8/55 and 56.
1411/13, precentor, NRO DCN 1/9/30/31.
1421/4, Nov., prior of St Leonard's, NRO DCN 2/3/37–39, 41,42; see Richard de Helyngton.
1403/4, went to Rome and the hostiller gave him a loan of 10s., NRO DCN 1/7/53.
1407/9, visited the curia [?a second visit], and charged his office with some of his expenses, NRO DCN 1/12/40–42; he set out in late May according to NRO DCN 1/12/40.
1412/13, gave 24s. 2 1/2d. to the office of precentor, NRO DCN 1/9/32.
1427/8, 1428/9 ill, and 20d. was spent by the infirmarer on medicine on each occasion, NRO DCN 1/10/15,16.
1429/30, gave 20d. to St Leonard's cell, NRO DCN 2/3/46.
1430/1, ill and 2s. 11d. spent on medicine, NRO DCN 1/10/18.
1431/2, ill and pd 4s. 8d. for his own medicine, NRO DCN 1/10/19.
1440/1, ill and 18d. spent by the infirmarer on medicine, NRO DCN 1/10/22.
1445/6, d., and the chamberlain recd 'alms' of 31s. 6d, NRO DCN 1/5/77.

John de BERNEY
d. by 1393/4

1393/4 in the refectorer's inventory John de Hoo, q.v., was reported to have the *ciphus* formerly used by him, NRO DCN 1/8/48.

Note: A John de Berney was lay steward of the priory between c. 1337/8 and 1369/70 (NRO DCN 1/1/34–51), prob. a relative; it is possible that the monk and steward are identical, but the context supports the existence of two separate individuals.

For a Walter de Berney (d. 1379) see *Comm. Rolls*, 39–40.

John de BERTON
occ. 1345/6 occ. 1348/9

1345/6, responsible for funds for the reconstruction of the cloister, NRO DCN 1/12/25.
1347/8, ill, and 21d. was spent by the infirmarer on medicine, NRO DCN 1/10/6.
1348/9, gave 100s. to the pittancer for building work, NRO DCN 1/12/27.

BERTON
see also Burton

John de BETELE ?D.Th. [Betle, Betyle
occ. 1336/7 occ. 1346/7

1336/7, one of four students at Oxford who received money from the cellarer, NRO DCN 1/2/101. See Thomas de Runhale, John de Stukle, Robert Sturmyn.
1343/4, the communar pd 6s. for transport of books and other necessities to Oxford, NRO DCN 1/12/23.
1344/5, the communar pd travelling expenses of 13s. 4d. to Oxford and 17s. 2d. for transport of clothing and books, NRO DCN 1/12/24.
1344/5, at least two monks incepted, one of whom was John Stukele, q.v.; the other was almost certainly Betele: the infirmarer gave a total of 40s. to *confratribus pro inceptione eorum*, NRO DCN 1/10/2.
1345/6, the communar pd 26s. 8d. for transport of his possessions to Oxford, NRO DCN 1/12/25.
1346/7, sick and 21d. was spent by the infirmarer on medicine, NRO DCN 1/10/5.

I Ralph de BETELE [Betelee
he or they occ. between 1311/12 and 1369/70

1316/17, prob. infirmarer, see below.
1322/8, chamberlain, NRO DCN 1/5/7.
1335/7, subprior in charge of the cloister work, NRO DCN 1/12/19.
Note: he may also have been subprior in 1329/30, NRO DCN 1/4/24, and filling in for the sacrist while the latter was at the curia (see Richard Hecham)].

1311/12, visited Hindolveston manor, NRO DCN 60/18/17.
1316/17, pd the communar £1 6s. 8d. for the 'O' of the infirmarer, *Comm. Rolls*, 88.
1346/7, ill and the infirmarer spent 4d. on medicine, NRO DCN 1/10/5.

II Ralph de BETELE
1369/70 refectorer, NRO DCN 1/8/43.

Note: it is probable that there are two monks by the same name or initial R., covering this lengthy span of over 55 yrs; but there is no way of distinguishing between the entries, some of which are given as R. de Betele.

William BEXWELL [Boxwell
occ. 1492 d. 1515/16

1505/6, prior of Aldeby, NRO DCN 2/2/28.
1514, 27 Apr., subprior, Jessopp, *Visit.*, 75.

1492, 5/8 Oct., 34th in order at the visitation of bp Goldwell, Jessopp, *Visit.*, 8.
1499, 6 Apr., 26th on the visitation certificate, *Reg. abp Morton*, iii, no 258.
1514, 27 Apr., present at the visitation of bp Nikke and complained of obedientiaries not rendering their accts, of general laxity and incomptence and of the promiscuity of Richard Worsted, q.v., Jessopp, *Visit.*, 75.
1515/16, d., and the sacrist pd for four *cereis ardentibus* for his funeral, NRO DCN 1/4/116.

John BILNEYE
see Tilney

Richard de BILNEYE [Bulneye, Bylneye
occ. 1366 occ. 1395

1366/7, precentor, NRO DCN 1/9/9.
[1375], 29 Oct., confirmed as sacrist, Reg Despenser, fo 38.
1376, 31 May and 23 June, master of St Paul's hospital, NRO DCN 45/31/20,21.
1376/8, prior of Hoxne, Windsor, St George's chapel, I.C.4.
1382/5, precentor, NRO DCN 1/9/20–22.
1383/4, gave the chamberlain 9s. 7d. [for robes for the officials and servants working in the precentor's office], NRO DCN 1/5/18.
1395, 4 Apr., the pope ordered an inquiry into his excommunication by the prior for disobedience and other 'excesses' and into the reason for the bp's interference in the matter by providing absolution, *CPL*, i, (1362–1402), 525.

Note: there may have been two monks by this name because of the entries covering the yrs 1375/6, but frequent changes of office were not unusual.

BILNEYE
see also Bylney, Tilney and Tylney

William de BLAFELD [Blafeud
occ. 1313/14 occ. 1315/16

1313/14, recd a gift of 2s. from the master of the cellar, NRO DCN 1/1/23.
1314/15, the master of the cellar pd him *pro labore suo*, NRO DCN 1/1/24.
[?c. 1315], one of the two monks apptd as parliamentary proctors, Reg. IX, fo 8; see William de Martham.
1315/16, bought grain and carried out other business negotiations for the master of the cellar, NRO DCN 1/1/25.

John BLAKENEYE [Blakneye
occ. 1426 occ. 1446

1427, 4 Jan., one of seven whose prof. the bp solemnized in chapter, after the prior's written request of 31 Dec. 1426, Reg. Alnwick, fo 97.
1427/8, ill and 2s. 1d. were spent by the infirmarer on medicine, NRO DCN 1/10/15.
1446, name occ. on a rough list of those assigned to celebrate weekday and chantry masses, Cambridge, Emm. Coll. Ms 142, fo 68, and on another similar list (prob. also c. 1446/7), for the Tye, Bateman, Totyngton, Wakering and Erpingham chantries, *ib.*, fo 77^{v}.

Richard de BLAKENEYE [Blakene, Blakenee
occ. 1376 d. 1405

1381/3, Oct., chamberlain, NRO DCN 1/5/15–17, Windsor, St George's chapel, XI.E.17; see Thomas de Tunstale.
1386/1405, 5 Feb., prior of St Leonard's except for several months between Sept. and Feb. 1390/91, NRO DCN 2/3/9–22; see Thomas de Tunstale.
1376, 18 Nov., named in an agreement with the Carmelites of Norwich, Reg. I, fo 261.
1390, 20 Sept., granted royal licence to go overseas, taking three hackneys, *CClR, 1389–1392*, 571; on the same day financial arrangements for payment of 100s. to him were concluded with an Italian banker, Angelus Christofori, *CClR, 1392–1396*, 541 (supplement).
1397/9, acted as proctor during the controversy with bp Despenser, NRO DCN 42/2/19.
1405, d. before 1 Sept. and the chamberlain recd 16s. in 'alms', NRO DCN 1/5/35; his obit on 4 Aug. is in Reg. XI, fo 5^{v}.

Ralph de BLICLINGG [Bliclyngg, Blichyngg
occ. 1347/8 d. by 1393/4

1353/4, before this date, almoner (as in this year he was described as *quondam*, leaving debts), NRO DCN 1/6/16.
1347/8, ill and 5s. 6d. were spent by the infirmarer on medicine, NRO DCN 1/10/6.
1353, 14 May, recd a papal licence to choose his confessor, *CPL*, iii, (1342–1362), 506.
1393/4, d. by this date, because the refectorer stated that John de Claxton, q.v., was now using the *ciphus* formerly belonging to him, NRO DCN 1/8/48.

Roger de BLIKLING [Bliclingge, Blikkelyng, Blykelyng
occ. 1313 d. by 1376/7

1313/14, with Harvey de Hapesburgh, q.v., contributed 26s. 8d. *ad negotia domus* to the master of the cellar, NRO DCN 1/1/23.
1376/7, d. by this date, as his *ciphus* was bought by Bartholomew [de Scrowtby], q.v., from the refectorer for 13s. 4d., NRO DCN 1/8/45.

Name in CUL Ms Ii.4.12, Summa Ricardi de Wetherset, G. Monemutensis etc., (14th c.); see Ker, 'Norwich Cathedral Mss', 257 and Dodwell 'History and Norwich Monks', 48. His name is on p. 7.

Richard BLYCLYNG [Blychlyng
occ. 1427/8

1427/8 [d.] the infirmarer pd 5s. 2d. to tenants and other poor persons on his behalf, NRO DCN 1/10/15; and the chamberlain recd his 'alms' of 18s. 9d., NRO DCN 1/5/54.

Richard de BOCEKISHAM [?Botekisham
occ. 1356/7

1356/7, Sept. to Mar., refectorer, NRO DCN 1/8/40.

I John de BOKENHAM
occ. 1345/6 occ. 1357

1357, Mar./Sept., refectorer, NRO DCN 1/8/40.
1345/6, ill, and 10d. was spent by the infirmarer on medicine, NRO DCN 1/10/4.
1345/6, d., and the pittancer recd 20s. from him *de dono, ad opus claustri*, NRO DCN 1/12/25.

II John BOKENHAM [Bukkenham
occ. 1446 d. 1450/1

1446, name occ. on a rough list of those assigned to celebrate weekday and chantry masses, Cambridge, Emm. Coll. Ms 142, fo 68; also, the name Bokenham occ. on a Sunday mass list for the following dates: 1446, 18 Dec.; 1447, 9 Apr., 30 July, 19 Nov.; 1448, 10 Mar., 30 June, 20 Oct.; 1449, 16 Feb.; also J. Bokenham on another list (prob. 1446/7) for the chantries of Bateman, Totyngton, Wakering, Tye and Erpingham, *ib.*, fo 77^{v}; also a Bokenham was assigned to a *magna missa* prob. in this same period *ib*.
1450/1, d., and 'alms' of 20s. were recd by the chamberlain, NRO DCN 1/5/83.

Note: the Sunday masses and the *magna missa* may apply to either John Bokenham II or William Bokenham, q.v., or to both of them.

William BOKENHAM [Bokynham
occ. 1428/9 occ. 1460/1

1447, 14 June, prior of Yarmouth, (and witness to the will of Sir John Fastolf), Davis, *Paston Letters*, no 54.
1454, Feb./Sept.; 1460/61, prior of Hoxne, NRO DCN 2/6/17; Windsor, St George's chapel, I.C. 19.
1428/9, ill, and the infirmarer spent 4d. on medicine, NRO DCN 1/10/16.
1429/30, ill, and the infirmarer spent 10d. on medicine, NRO DCN 1/10/17.
1438/9, his expenses were pd by the almoner when he celebrated masses at Wicklewood for twelve days, NRO DCN 1/6/64.
1446, name occ. on a rough list of those assigned to celebrate weekday and chantry masses, Cambridge, Emm. Coll. Ms 142, fo 68; also prob. some of the Sunday masses 1446 to 1449 noted in the entry under John Bokenham II, q.v.; also on another list (prob. 1446/7) for the Bateman, Totyngton, Wakering, Tye and Erpingham chantries, *ib.*, fo 77^v.
Name in two medical treatises in Wellcome Institute for the History of Medicine, Ms. 408, fos 4-13, that were compiled by him.

BOKENHAM
see also Bukenham

John BONWELL B.Th. [Bonewell
occ. 1443 d. 1488

1480–1488 prior: el. confirmed by the bp. at Hoxne, 23 Apr. 1480, Reg. Goldwell, fo 163^v; d. before 22 Dec. 1488, *Fasti*, ii, 26; see William Spynk.
1443, 1 Nov., one of two *clerici*, adm. *ad osculum et benedictionem* by the bp in his parlour at Thorpe after their acceptance by the chapter as monks, Reg. Brouns, fo 109^v.
1469/70, prior of Yarmouth, NRO DCN 2/4/14.
1471/2, 1473/5, 1476/7, prior of Lynn, NRO DCN 2/1/64–68.
1452/3, student, at university with pension contributions from the chamberlain, master of the cellar, sacrist and master of St Paul's hospital, NRO DCN 1/5/85; 1/1/88; 1/4/83; 2/5/6.
1453/4, student, with contributions from the chamberlain, infirmarer, and master of the cellar, NRO DCN 1/5/86; 1/10/23; 1/1/89.
1454/5, student, with contributions from the chamberlain and infirmarer, NRO DCN 1/5/87; 1/10/24.
1455/6, student, with contributions from the cellarer, chamberlain and refectorer, NRO DCN 1/2/61A; 1/5/88; 1/8/91.
1459, 9 Oct., supplicated for B.Th. at Oxford; see *BRUO* and *BRUC* as he studied at both Oxford and Cambridge.
1458/9, responsible for the accts of the Wakering and Erpingham chantries, NRO DCN 4/8.
1488/9, d.; the chamberlain recd only 9s. 4d., 'alms' because 6s. 8d. was pd to the bearer of the brief soliciting prayers for his soul, NRO DCN 1/5/117.
Among the Paston correspondence is a letter written by Bonwell in 1486/7 concerning William Paston's chantry in the cathedral, Davis, *Paston Letters*, no 962.

Martin BOONE
occ. 1520

3 Sept. 1520, subdcn and present at the visitation of bp Nikke, Jessopp, *Visit.*, 193; he reported *omnia bene.*

BOOTON
see Boton(e)

BOSCO
see Richard I

BOSONII
See Bozoun

Reginald BOSTON
occ. 1492 occ. 1509/10

1501/2, communar, NRO DCN 1/12/85.
1505/6, prior of Hoxne, Windsor, St George's chapel, I.C. 36.
1492, 5/8 Oct., 32nd in order at the visitation of bp Goldwell, Jessopp, *Visit.*, 8.
1493/4, pd by the master of the cellar, *pro expensis in equitand'* (added in margin of acct), NRO DCN 1/1/97.
1499, 6 Apr., 24th on the visitation certificate. *Reg. abp Morton*, iii, no 258.
1509/10, pd 10d. [?a debt] to the prior of Hoxne, Windsor, St George's chapel, I.C. 37.

BOTEKISHAM
see Bocekisham

John BOTON
occ. 1419/20

1419/20, d., and the chamberlain recd 'alms', NRO DCN 1/5/47.

Roger de BOTONE [Booton
n.d.

Name in CUL Ms Kk.2.13, Isidore etc., (13th/14th c.) on fo 1.

Robert BOWGYN
see Worsted

Thomas BOWYR [Boure, Bowre
occ. 1486 occ. 1499

1486/9; 1491/3; 1494/6, refectorer, NRO DCN 1/8/99–101; Oxford, Bod. Ms Rolls, Norfolk, no 51, NRO DCN 1/8/102; Oxford, Bod. Ms Rolls, Norfolk, no 52, NRO DCN 1/8/103.

1492, 5/8 Oct., 5th in order at the visitation of bp Goldwell, Jessopp, *Visit.*, 8.

1499, 6 Apr., 5th on the visitation certificate, *Reg. abp Morton*, iii, no 258.

BOXWELL
see Bexwell

Robert BOYS [Boyce
occ. 1491/2 occ. 1499

1491/2, gave the hostiller 4d. toward the new great window in the *hostillaria*, NRO DCN 1/7/120.

1492, 5/8 Oct., 35th in order at the visitaton of bp Goldwell, Jessopp, *Visit.*, 8.

1499, 6 Apr., 27th on the visitation certificate, *Reg. abp Morton*, iii, no 258.

Simon BOZOUN [Bosonii
occ. 1326 occ. 1352

1344–1352 prior: el. confirmed [*prefectio*] by the vicar general of the bp, 25 Aug. 1344, Reg. Bateman, fo 45^{v}; res. by 24 Apr. 1352, *ib.*, fo 138^{v}; see Laurence de Leck.

1326/7, hostiller, NRO DCN 1/7/2, as Simon Bo[?zoun].

1339/40, hostiller, NRO DCN 1/7/6.

1352, 30 Aug., apptd prior of St Leonard's, Reg. X, fo 40.

1351, 1 Feb., recd papal licence to choose his confessor *CPL*, iii, (1342–1362), 408.

1351, 26 May, with John Peche and William de Witton, q.v., involved in a dispute about the chapter's rights over the passage of St Olave between Norwich and Great Yarmouth, *CPR (1350–1354)*, 155.

A list of Bozoun's books, printed from BL Ms Royal 14 C. xiii, fo 13v is in *Giraldi Cambrensis Opera*, v, p. xxxix n; see also Sharpe, *Eng. Benedictine Libraries*, iv, B58 where the 31 items with their respective prices are recorded.

Name in

(1) Cambridge, Corpus Christi College Ms 264, Bede etc. (14th c.); on fo 1 liber—.

(2) *Ib.*, Ms 407, Itineraria, Liber Secreti Secretorum etc. (14th c.); on fo 1 *liber*—.

(3) BL Ms Royal 14 C.xiii, Polychronicon etc. (14th c.); on fo 14 *liber*—.

(4) Oxford, Bod. Ms Fairfax 20, Flores historiarum (14 c.).

1393/4, Richard Midelton q.v,. was reported as having Bozoun's cedar *ciphus*, NRO DCN 1/8/48.

There were Bozouns at Taverham in 1349/50 and 1351/2, NRO DCN 60/35/30,31; in 1349/50 this was John Bozoun of Whissonsett.

Thomas BOZOUN D.Cn.L.
occ. 1440/1 d. 1480

1471–1480, prior: el. confirmed [*prefectio*] by the bp, 8 June 1471; d. by 23 Apr. 1480, *Fasti*, iv, 26. See John Bonwell.

1460/1, hostiller, NRO DCN 1/7/196.

1462/4, 1465/9, prior of Lynn, NRO DCN 2/1/58–63.

1454/7, student and recd pension contributions from the chamberlain, NRO DCN 1/5/87–89; in 1455/6 the communar contributed to his pension, NRO DCN 1/12/66.

1456/8, student, and recd a contribution from the refectorer, NRO DCN 1/8/91, 92.

1456/7, student with a contribution from the cellarer, NRO DCN 1/2/62.

1457/8, student to whose expenses the almoner, hostiller, sacrist and prior of St Leonard's contributed *pro gradu bacalariatus suscipiendo*, NRO DCN 1/6/72; 1/7/94; 1/4/86; 2/3/69; and see *BRUC*. There is no evidence that he was ever at Oxford.

1463/4, incepted D.Cn.L. Cambridge, *BRUC*.

1440/1, ill, and the infirmarer spent 12d. on medicine, NRO DCN 1/10/22.

1474/5, granted a grace by the university of Cambridge to wear a cap [*pilium*] while preaching *propter quandam infirmitatem in capite*, *CU Grace Book A*, 107.

Dugdale states that the Bozoun family came from Whissonsett and that his monument was placed in St Luke's chapel in the cathedral, Dugdale, Monasticon, iv, 7, (prob. quoting Blomefield, *Norfolk*, iii, 604). See also Simon Bozoun.

Hugh de BRADEWELLE
occ. 1346/7 occ. 1348/9

1346/7, ill, and 8d. was spent by the infirmarer on medicine, NRO DCN 1/10/5.

1348/9, gave the pittancer 20s. for [the reconstruction of] the cloister, NRO DCN 1/12/27.

Richard BRADLE [Bradley
occ. 1426 occ. 1448/9

1427, 4 Jan., one of seven whose prof. the bp solemnized in chapter after the prior's request in a letter of 31 Dec. 1426, Reg. Alnwick, fo 97.

1441/5, hostiller, NRO DCN 1/7/81.

1448/9, prior of Aldeby, NRO DCN 2/2/17.

1427/8, ill and 10d. was spent by the infirmarer on medicine, NRO DCN 1/10/15.

1446, name occ. on a rough list of those assigned to celebrate weekday and chantry masses, Cambridge, Emm. Coll. Ms 142, fo 68; also on a similar list (prob. 1446/7) for the Totyngton, Wakering and Erpingham chantries, *ib.*, fo 77^{v}.

Nicholas de BRAMERTONE [Brampton
occ. 1266 d. 1269

1266–1269, prior: el. confirmed 18 Apr. 1266; d. 19 Feb. 1269, *Fasti*, ii, 61. Blomefield, *Norfolk*, iii, 601, gives the el. date as 3 Jan 1265/6.

Several charters are extant from his short priorate, see *N. Cath. Charters*, ii, nos 5, 170, 175.

Richard de BRAMPTON
occ. c. 1274

c. 1274, sent as proctor to Rome, Dugdale, *Monasticon*, iv, 4; see Gerard de Fordham.

Robert BRASYR [Brasere
occ. 1453/4 d. 1471/2

1453/4, ill, and the infirmarer spent 6s. 8d. on medicine, NRO DCN 1/10/23.
1464/5, ill, and the infirmarer spent 6d. on medicine, NRO DCN 1/10/26.
1471/2, d., and the sacrist pd for the funeral tapers, NRO DCN 1/4/93.

Roger de BRAUNFELD
occ. 1347/8

1347/8, ill and the infirmarer spent 6d. on medicine, NRO DCN 1/10/6.

Bartholomew de BRETENHAM [Brethenham
occ. 1414/15 occ. 1446

1419/20, gardener, NRO DCN 1/11/9.

1414/15, contributed 20d. to the precentor for a chancel window in Plumstead church, NRO DCN 1/9/31.
1434/5, ill, and 2s. were spent by the infirmarer on medicine, NRO DCN 1/10/21.
1446, name occ. on a rough list of those assigned to celebrate weekday and chantry masses, Cambridge, Emm. Coll. Ms 142, fo 68; also the name Bretenham occ. on a Sunday mass list for the following dates:
1447, 1 Jan., 23 Apr., 13 Aug., 3 Dec.; 1448, 24 Mar., 14 July, 3 Nov; a Bretenham was assigned to a *magna missa* and a *parva missa*, prob. during this period, *ib.*, fo 77^{v}.

Note: the Sunday masses and the *magna* and *parva* masses may apply to either Bartholomew or Robert Bretenham, q.v., or to both of them.

Robert BRETENHAM [Brethenham
occ. 1421/2 d. 1468/9

1438/42, 1446/9, communar/pittancer, NRO DCN 1/12/57–60.
1440/1, hostiller, NRO DCN 1/7/81; at the foot of the acct. *non me sed tua voluntas fiat.*
1442/3, cellarer, NRO DCN 1/2/56.
1450/1, gardener, NRO DCN 1/11/19.
1450/1, 1452/3, and 1454/5, master of St Paul's Hospital, NRO DCN 2/5/5 and 6 and see below.
1458/9, prior of Hoxne, Windsor, St George's chapel, I.C. 18; according to Blomefield, *Norfolk*, iii, 432, he was [?still] prior in 1470.
1421/2, ill, and the infirmarer spent 3d. on medicine, NRO DCN 1/10/14.
1426/7, gave a 2s. gift to the cellarer's office, NRO DCN 1/2/45.
1429/30, ill, and the infirmarer spent 2s. on medicine, NRO DCN 1/10/17.
1446, name occ. on a rough list of those assigned to celebrate weekday and chantry masses Cambridge, Emm. Coll. Ms 142, fo 68; also prob. some of the Sunday and other masses 1446 to 1448 noted in the entry under Bartholomew Bretenham, q.v.; also on another list (prob. 1446/7) for the chantries of Tottington, Wakering and Erpingham, *ib.*, fo 77^{v}.
1452/3, contributed 13s. 4d. to the precentor for the *portiforium* of Thomas Crane, q.v., NRO DCN 1/9/66.
1454/5, the prior and convent sent a letter (pd for by the communar/ pittancer) to the bp to request his removal from the mastership of St Paul's hospital, NRO DCN 1/12/65; in the same yr he gave 10s. toward the repair of the *domus necessariorum* in the infirmary, NRO DCN 1/10/24.
1468/9, d., and the sacrist pd for funeral tapers, NRO DCN 1/4/91.

BRICE
see Cam

John de BRINTON
occ. 1345/6 occ. 1348/9

1345/6, ill and 4d. was spent by the infirmarer on medicine, NRO DCN 1/10/4.
1347/8, ill and the same amount spent, NRO DCN 1/10/6.
1348/9, ill again, NRO DCN 1/10/7.

Thomas de BRINTON D.Cn.L. [Brunton, Brompton, Brynton
occ. 1352/3 occ. 1373

1352/3, prob. student at Cambridge, NRO DCN 1/1/44 (now dated 1353/4) and M.A. Devlin, ed., *The Sermons of Thomas Brinton, Bishop of Rochester (1373–1389)*, Camden 3rd series (1954) (vol) i, xi.
1356, student; came home, probably from Oxford, to preach on Good Friday, and returned to his studies, NRO DCN 1/12/29. See the prior's letter concerning his decision to keep Adam de Easton, q.v., at home rather than to recall Brinton, Pantin, *BMC*, iii, 29.
1363/4, his inception, to which the sacrist contributed, NRO DCN 1/4/35.

1364/5, student, with a pension from the refectorer, NRO DCN 1/8/42.
1366, 25 Nov., described as D.Cn.L., *CPL*, iv (1362–1404), 25.
?1363, visited the curia with prior Nicholas de Hoo, q.v., Pantin *BMC*, iii, 61 n.
1364, 31 Jan., apptd proctor at the curia by the Black Monk Chapter, Pantin, *BMC*, iii, 52–53.
1366, 25 Nov., described as papal penitentiary and nuncio, *CPL*, iv (1362–1404), 25.
1373, 31 Jan., bp of Rochester by papal provision, *Fasti*, iv, 38. He was consecrated at Avignon on 6 Feb., *ib.*

Note: for later biographical details and a bibliography, see *BRUO*, and for his writings, Sharpe, *Latin Writers*.

BROC(K)
see Brok

John BRODYCH [Broktdyssh
occ. 1533 occ. 1535

1533, 20 Sept., ord exorcist and acol., Norwich cathedral, NRO DN ORR/1/1, fo 16v.
1535, [Sept./Dec.] ord subdcn, place uncertain, *ib.*, fo 26v.

1534, 28 July, subscribed to the Act of Supremacy, *DK 7th Report*, Appndx 2, 295.

Since this name occ. only here it is fairly certain he went more often under the name of his 'home town'; and so he is probably to be found twice in this list, but where?

Robert de BROK [Broc, Brock
occ. 1290/1 occ. 1318/19

1297/1301, 1301/2, 1302/4, 1305/6, 1307/8, master of the cellar, NRO DCN 1/1/13–18; 60/28/4 (1301/2); 60/7/5 (1302/4); 60/35/14 (1305/6).
1309/10, master of St Paul's hospital, NRO DCN 1/1/21.

1290/1, 1291/2, performed duties for the master of the cellar, including the purchase of books and journeys to Oxford and London, NRO DCN 1/1/10 and 11.
1297/8, held courts with the steward at Hindringham and Hindolveston, NRO DCN 60/20/12; 60/18/13; also stayed at [North] Elmham, NRO DCN 60/10/10.
1297/9, pd visits to Plumstead, NRO DCN 60/29/12 and 13.
1299/1300 and 1305/6, pd visits to Catton, NRO DCN 60/4/13, 16.
1305/6, visited Gnatingdon and [North] Elmham, for *liberatio denariorum*, NRO DCN 60/14/12; 60/10/11.
1311/12, involved in the collection of tenths, NRO DCN 1/1/22.
1317/19, pd visits to Hindolveston, NRO DCN 60/18/20,21.

Thomas de BROK [Broc
occ. 1310/11 occ. 1336/7

1331/2, 1333/5, 1336/7, refectorer, NRO DCN 1/8/30–35.

1310/11, pd the refectorer 13s. 4d. for a *ciphus cum pede*, NRO DCN 1/8/21.

John de BROMHOLM [Bromeholme
occ. 1282/3 d. 1321/2

1297/8, cellarer, NRO DCN 1/2/3.
1310, 5 Feb., 1313, 24 July, prior of Lynn, Reg. Salmon, fo 35, *CPR (1313–1317)*, 57; possibly d. as prior, NRO DCN 1/5/6.

1282/3, visited Taverham for *liberatio denariorum*, NRO DCN 60/35/9.
1283/4, performed duties for the master of the cellar NRO DCN 1/1/7.
1284/5, took money to Oxford, *ad scolas*, NRO DCN 1/1/8.
1287/8, visited Catton, [North] Elmham, Plumstead, Sedgeford and Taverham, prob. making the rounds of these manors with the steward (who is named on the Sedgeford acct), NRO DCN 60/4/9; 60/10/7; 60/29/5; 60/33/8; 60/35/10.
1288, 10 Oct., sent, with Guy de St Edmund, q.v., to the king for the licence to el. a bp, *N. Cath. Charters*, i, no 55.
1288/9, visited Newton for *liberatio denariorum*, NRO DCN 60/28/2.
1298, June, John Celerarii went to London on business with Robert de Langele, q.v., *Comm. Rolls*, 71.
1313, 24 July, named among the mob alleged to have assaulted the lord of Bishop's Lynn, *CPR (1313–1317)*, 57.
1321/2, d., NRO DCN 1/5/6.

Note: see also John de Celar' who may be the same monk.

BROMPTON
see Thomas de Brinton

Robert BRONDE
see Robert Catton I

John de BRUNHAM
occ. ?1352/3

1352/3, d. by this date when the chamberlain recd £4 for his *portiforium*, NRO DCN 1/5/13.

BRUNHAM
see also Burnham

John de BRUNSTED [Brunstede
occ. 1397/8 occ. 1414/15

1397/8, 1399/1400, prior of Aldeby, NRO DCN 2/2/2,3.
1405/6, 1407/9, prior of St Leonard's, NRO DCN 2/3/22–25.

1412, 15 July, confirmed as subprior [*prefectio*] by the bp, Reg. Totyngton, fo 50.
1414/15, prior of Yarmouth, Windsor, St George's chapel, XV.55.75.

BRUNTON, Brynton
see Thomas de Brinton

Ed[mund] de BUKENHAM
occ. 1362/3

1362/3, *commonachus*, given a robe costing 26s. 8d. by the master of the cellar, NRO DCN 1/1/48.

BUKENHAM
see also Bokenham

Nicholas BURGATE
occ. 1413/14 occ. 1453/4

1413/17, master of the cellar, NRO DCN 1/1/73.
1418, 23 Apr., took office as chamberlain, NRO DCN 1/5/45 after the prior's formal request to the bp on 8 Apr., Reg Wakering, fo 32v.
1418/20, chamberlain, NRO DCN 1/5/45–47.
1420/Nov. 1424, precentor, NRO DCN 1/9/31–37.
1424 Nov./1426, 1427/9, 1430/7, chamberlain, NRO DCN 1/5/52–67.
1437/9, 1444/8, refectorer, NRO DCN 1/8/76, 77, 82–85.
1440, Apr. to July, prior of St Leonard's, NRO DCN 2/3/54.
1443, 7 Oct., at request of the prior (dated 5 Oct.) removed by the bp from the office of subprior, Reg. Brouns, fo 109.
1453/4, infirmarer, NRO DCN 1/10/23.

1421/3, pd visits to Plumstead and Kimberley, NRO DCN 1/9/37.
1440, gave three *laton' basown'* brought from London to hang before the altar at St Leonard's, NRO DCN 2/3/54.
1446, name occ. on a rough list of those assigned to celebrate weekday and chantry masses, Cambridge, Emm. Coll. Ms 142, fo 68; also on the Sunday mass list for the following dates:
1447, 15 Jan.; 7 May.; 3 Sept.; 24 or 25 Dec; 1448, 21 Apr., 4 Aug., *ib.*

Robert de BURNHAM [Brunham
occ. 1391 occ. 1427

1407–1427, prior: el. 23 Nov. 1407, Reg. XI, fo 7; el. confirmed 20 Dec., Reg. Totyngton, fo 3v; res. by 14 Sept. 1427, Reg. Alnwick, fo 97v.
1391, May/Sept., 1393/4, 1398/9, communar/ pittancer, NRO DCN 1/12/35–37.
1399/1400, recd 40s. from the chamberlain *pro perditione decimarum*, NRO DCN 1/5/31.
1399, 18 Mar., involved as proctor for the chapter in their dispute with bp Despenser, and present with the prior and other monks in the Star Chamber to hear the abp's *decretum*, NRO DCN 42/1/21.
1399, 20 Mar., present, as one of the proctors, in St James' church Garlickhithe, London, in appeal vs. the above, NRO DCN 42/1/22.
1414/15, contributed 6s. 8d. to the precentor's expenses in repairing a chancel window at Plumstead, NRO DCN 1/9/31.
1417, 27 Feb., apptd as one of the conservators of Cluniac privileges in England, *Reg. abp Chichele*, iv, 48–51.
1417, Nov./Dec., attended convocation and, with other cathedral priors, was apptd to a committee set up by the abp to consider ways of alleviating the impecunious state of Oxford and Cambridge graduates, *Reg. abp Chichele*, iii, 36–37.
1420, 8 July, attended the Black Monk Chapter at Northampton, Pantin, *BMC*, ii, 96.

Walter BURNHAM
occ. 1478/9 occ. 1499

1478/9, gave the precentor 5d. *pro intabulacione librorum*, NRO DCN, 1/9/77; see Greatrex, 'Norwich Monk Students', 575–576.
1492, 5/8 Oct., 23rd in order at the visitation of bp Goldwell, Jessopp, *Visit.*, 8.
1499, 6 Apr., 16th on the visitation certificate, *Reg. abp Morton*, iii, no 258.

William de BURNHAM [Brunham
occ. [1268/9] d. 1273

[1268/9]-1272, prior: 1269, before 25 Mar., succ. as prior; c. 1272, 23 Sept., the priory was taken into the king's hands after the dispute between the monks and the town and the resulting conflagration within the precincts. Acc. to Bartholomew Cotton, the prior had fled to Yarmouth but returned with armed men, and false rumours accused him of causing the fire, *Historia*, 143, 148–149. On 27 Sept., he res., *Fasti*, ii, 61.

1273, 13 Feb., d., Cotton, *Historia*, 150.

BURNHAM
see also Brunham

John BURTON B.Th.
occ. 1440/1 d. 1463/4

1454/5, 1456/61, 1463/4, prior of Lynn, NRO DCN 2/1/50–57; 1/5/93.
1443/5, student [at Oxford in 1443/4] with pension contributions from the precentor and refectorer, NRO DCN 1/9/57,58; 1/8/81,82.
1445/6, student, with contributions from the chamberlain, master of the cellar and refectorer, NRO DCN 1/5/77; 1/1/87; 1/8/83.
1446/8, student, with contributions from the cellarer and chamberlain, NRO DCN 1/2/57,58; 1/5/78,79.
1447/9, student, with contributions from the almoner, precentor and refectorer, NRO DCN 1/6/68,69; 1/9/61,62; 1/8/85,86.

1449/50, student with contributions from the cellarer, chamberlain, precentor and refectorer, NRO DCN 1/2/59; 1/5/82; 1/9/63; 1/8/87.
1450, 8 May, supplicated for B.Th.; see *BRUO* where the name, but not the religious house is given.
1450/1, student, with contributions from the master of St Paul's hospital, NRO DCN 2/5/5.
1451/2, student, with contributions from the almoner and cellarer, NRO DCN 1/6/70; 1/2/60.
1452/3, student, with contributions from the chamberlain, master of the cellar and sacrist, NRO DCN 1/5/85; 1/1/88; 1/4/83; the prior gave Burton's servant at Oxford 3s. 4d., NRO DCN 1/1/88.
1453/4, student, with contributions from the chamberlain, infirmarer, and master of the cellar, NRO DCN 1/5/86; 1/10/23; 1/1/89.
1440/1, ill and 12d. was spent by the infirmarer on medicine, NRO DCN 1/10/22.
1463/4, d. while prior of Lynn and the chamberlain recd 'alms' of 20s., NRO DCN 1/5/93.

William BURTON
occ. 1520 occ. 1526

1520, 3 Sept., 22nd to be questioned at the visitation of bp Nikke and was nineteen yrs of age; he did not understand what he was ordered to read and lacked instruction in grammar, according to the bp's *comperta*, Jessopp, *Visit.*, 193.
1526, 7 June, present at the visitation of bp Nikke; he was one of the younger monks who complained vs. the seniors, Jessopp, *Visit.*, 198, and who in turn was condemned as incorrigible, 'est indocilis nec vult erudiri et est suscitator brigarum', *ib.*, 202. He was told to move to a lower stall and after questioning was imprisoned to await punishment, *ib.*, 202–203. The bp ordered him to have the lowest seat in choir and at table until he could recite the psalter, and to occupy the lowest seat among the professed, *ib.*, 205–206.

J. de BURY
occ. 1410

1410, occ. in the refectorer's inventory as having once ?owned three covers for *ciphi* given to the refectorer by Robert de Lakenham, q.v., NRO DCN 1/8/56.

Simon BYLNEY
occ. 1469/70 occ. 1499

1469/70, mentioned by the sacrist, NRO DCN 1/4/92.
1476/7, gave the precentor 3s. 4d. *pro libris in cathologo*, NRO DCN 1/9/75; and see Greatrex, 'Norwich Monk Students', 575–6.
1492, 5/8 Oct., 11th in order at the visitation of bp Goldwell, Jessopp, *Visit.*, 8.
1499, 6 Apr., 8th on the visitation certificate, *Reg. abp Morton*, iii, no 258.

BYLNEY
see also Bilneye, Tilney, Tylney

John BYNTR' [Byntre
adm. 1427 occ. 1453/4

1427, 7 Jan., one of four *clerici* adm. *ad osculum et benedictionem* by the bp after acceptance by the chapter as a monk, Reg. Alnwick, fo 97v.
1428/9, ill, and 2s. were spent by the infirmarer on medicine, NRO DCN 1/10/16.
1440/1, ill and 20d. spent on medicine, NRO DCN 1/10/22.
1446, name occ. on a rough list of those assigned to celebrate weekday and chantry masses, Cambridge, Emm. Coll. Ms 142, fo 68; also on a similar list (prob. 1446/7) for the Totyngton, Wakering, Tye, and Erpingham chantries, *ib.*, fo 77v.
1451/2, served as one of the chaplains at Plumstead, NRO DCN 1/9/65.
1453/4, ill, and 2s. were spent by the infirmarer on medicine, NRO DCN 1/10/23.

CAAM
see Cam

Peter de CALNA [Calne
occ. 1236

1236, 22 Aug., sacrist, and recd from the king licence to el. a bp, *CPR (1232–1247)*, 156.

William CALY
occ. 1477/8 occ. 1492

1477/8, pd the precentor for a *portiforium*, press mark Bxlv, 6d., NRO DCN 1/9/76, which he was prob. borrowing; and see Greatrex, 'Norwich Monk Students', 575–576.
1492, 5/8 Oct., 12th in order at the visitation of bp Goldwell, Jessopp, *Visit.*, 8.

Brice de CAM
occ. 1345 occ. 1347/8

1345, reported as ill by the infirmarer, NRO DCN 1/10/2.
1346/7, ill and the infirmarer spent 11d. on medicine, NRO DCN 1/10/5.
1347/8, ill and 2s. 10d. spent on medicine, NRO DCN 1/10/6.

Robert de CAM [Caam, Kaam
occ. 1330/1 occ. 1347/8

1330/1, involved in business transactions for the master of the cellar, NRO DCN 1/1/31.
1345/6, ill, and the infirmarer spent 10d. on medicine, NRO DCN 1/10/4.

1346/7, ill, and the infirmarer spent 4d. on medicine, NRO DCN 1/10/5.
1347/8, ill, and 5s. 4d. spent on medicine, NRO DCN 1/10/6.

[Theobald de CAMBRIDGE
occ. 1144
1144, said to be a converted Jew and monk of Norwich, see Jessopp and James, *St William*, lxxix, 93.]

CAMBRIDGE
see also Cawmbridge and Cawmbrygg(e)

CANTABRYGGE
see Cawmbridge

William de CANTEBRIG'
occ. 1263/4
1263/4, with Nicholas de Kirkeby, q.v., *custodes commune*, NRO DCN 1/1/1.

George CANTLY [Canteley
occ. 1533 occ. 1535
1533, 20 Sept., ord exorcist and acol., Norwich cathedral, NRO DN ORR/1/1, fo 16ᵛ.
1535, [Sept./Dec.] ord subdcn, place uncertain, *ib.*, fo 26ᵛ.
1534, 28 July, subscribed to the Act of Supremacy, *DK 7th Report*, Appndx 2, 295.
See note under John Brodych.

Thomas CANTYRBERY
occ. 1477/8
1477/8, the sacrist [Wm. Fode, q.v.] went to see the bp in London with regard to the confirmation of his reception and that of two others as monks, NRO DCN 1/12/70.
Note: possibly identical with Thomas Davy, q.v.

John de CARLETON [Carltone
occ. 1382 occ. 1398
1382/3, 1384/5, 1386/7, 1388/9, 1390/1, cellarer, NRO DCN 1/2/25- 29.
1391, sacrist for part of the yr., NRO DCN 1/4/39.
1393/8, prior of Lynn, NRO DCN 2/1/20–21.
1384/5, bought arms and armour for the defence of the monastery, NRO DCN 1/2/26.

Richard de CARLETON
occ. 1373 d. 1382/3
1373, 5 July, inducted as rector of Sprowston by mandate of the bp, NRO DCN 35/5, (the prior and convent had recd a licence to appropriate the church at Sprowston in 1361).
1382/3, d., and the chamberlain pd 6s. 8d. to the brief bearer, NRO DCN 1/5/16; see William Thetford.

William CASTLEACRE
occ. 1491/2 occ. 1499
1491/2, gave the hostiller 8d. towards the great window in the *hostillaria*, NRO DCN 1/7/120.
1492, 5/8 Oct., 26th in order at the visitation of bp Goldwell, Jessopp, *Visit*, 8.
1499, 6 Apr., 19th on the visitation certificate, *Reg. abp Morton*, iii, no 258.

William CASTLETON [Castleten, Castilton, Castylten
occ. 1499 occ. 1538
1529–1538, prior: el. after ?Nov. 1529, NRO DCN 1/4/121; 2 May 1538 became dean of the new foundation, *L and P Henry VIII*, xiii, pt 1, no 1115(4). Res. by Aug. 20, 1539, *Fasti*, vii, 42.
While prior he also held the office of master of the cellar 1531, Mar./Sept., 1532/3, 1534/6, NRO DCN 1/1/105–108.
1499, 30 Mar., ord subdcn in Norwich cathedral, *Reg. abp Morton*, iii, no 53.
1504/6, 1508/9, hostiller, NRO DCN 1/7/125,126,129; Blomefield, *Norfolk*, iii, 432 states that 'Castelyn' was master of St Paul's hospital in 1504.
1510/11, sacrist, NRO DCN 1/4/110.
1499, 6 Apr., 45th in order at the visitation, *Reg. abp Morton*, iii, no 258.
1532, 3 June, present at the episcopal visitation and reported the house to be 100m. in debt, Jessopp, *Visit.*, 268.
1534, 28 July, subscribed to the Act of Supremacy, *DK 7th Report*, Appndx 2, 295.
1535, 10 July, with four other monks, obtained archiepiscopal dispensation to eat meat in private and in public, Chambers, *Faculty Office Regs*, 34.
1538, 30 Apr., pd. £20 to be dispensed to become a secular pr., and hold the office of dean of the cathedral, *ib.*, 137. The charter setting up the new foundation of dean and chapter is dated 2 May 1538, *L and P Henry VIII*, xiii, pt 1, no 1115(4).

Alexander de CASTRE
occ. 1345/6 occ. 1375/6
?1350 × 1355, prob. refectorer, NRO DCN 1/8/39.
1359/60, cellarer, NRO DCN 1/2/21.
1375/6, prior of Hoxne, Windsor, St George's chapel, I.C. 4.
1345/6, ill and 10d. was spent by the the infirmarer on medicine, NRO DCN 1/10/4.
1348/9, the infirmarer on assuming office recd from him in gold and silver £27 10s. including counterfeit money [*cum fals' moneta*], NRO DCN 1/10/7; this may mean that he had been infirmarer.

William de CASTRE
occ. 1291 occ. 1296

1291/2, 1294/5, master of the cellar. NRO DCN 1/1/11,12.

1291/2, 1293/6, pd frequent visits to Sedgeford for *liberatio denariorum*, often with the steward, NRO DCN 60/33/9–12.

1291/3, 1294/5, visited Hindringham for *liberatio denariorum*, NRO DCN 60/20/8–10; in 1292/3, he made three visits to Taverham with the steward, NRO DCN 60/35/12.

1293/4, went to Plumstead, NRO DCN 60/29/7.

1294/6, pd visits to Catton, Gnatingdon and Hemsby, NRO DCN 60/4/10,12; 60/14/7,8; 60/15/4,5.

1294/5, pd four visits with the steward to Hindolveston, NRO DCN 60/18/11.

1295/6, pd four visits with the steward to Hindringham; also visited [North] Elmham and Taverham, NRO DCN 60/20/11; 60/10/9; 60/35/13.

John CATTON
d. 1473/4

1473/4, d., and the sacrist pd 8d. for candles for the funeral, NRO DCN 1/4/94.

I Robert CATTON *alias* Bronde
occ. 1492 occ. 1529

1504-?1529, prior: el. 1504, date uncertain, ?Sept./Oct., *Fasti*, iv, 26; ?res. by Nov. 1529, *ib.*; abbot of St Albans, royal assent given 14 Mar. 1531, *L and P Henry VIII*, v, no 166 (28).

1499, 30 Mar., ord subdcn in Norwich cathedral, *Reg. abp Morton*, iii, no 53.

While prior he also held the following offices:

(1) sacrist, 1504/6, 1511/12, 1517/18, 1522/3, 1525/6, NRO DCN 1/4/108, 109, 111, 114, 117, 118.
(2) cellarer, 1511/14, NRO DCN 1/2/91–93.
(3) prior of St Leonard's, 1512/13, 1517/18, NRO DCN 2/3/115,116.
(4) master of the cellar, 1519/20, 1523/4, 1527/9, and 1530/1 from 29 Sept. to 25 Mar. This last was the first year of Castleton's priorate, q.v., and it would seem that Catton briefly continued on as master of the cellar, prob. until he had received royal assent to his el. to St Albans.

1494/5, student at Cambridge with pension contributions from the almoner, chamberlain, hostiller, refectorer, sacrist, and prior of St Leonard's, NRO DCN 1/6/110; 1/5/122; 1/7/120; Oxford, Bod. Ms Rolls, Norfolk, no 52; NRO DCN 1/4/107; 2/3/99.

1495/6, student, with contributions from the chamberlain, hostiller, master of the cellar, refectorer, and the priors of St Leonard's and Hoxne, NRO DCN 1/5/123; 1/7/120; 1/1/98; 1/8/103; 2/3/100; 2/6/31.

1496/7, student, with contributions from the refectorer and the prior of Hoxne, NRO DCN 1/8/104; 2/6/32.

1497/8, student, with contributions from the hostiller, infirmarer, and the prior of Hoxne, NRO DCN 1/7/120; 1/10/33; 2/6/33.

1498/9, student, with contributions from the chamberlain, hostiller, and the prior of Lynn, NRO DCN 1/5/124; 1/7/120; 2/1/77.

1499/1500, student, with contribution from the chamberlain, NRO DCN 1/5/125.

1500/1, student, with contributions from the almoner, cellarer, chamberlain and the priors of Aldeby and Hoxne, NRO DCN 1/6/113; 1/2/86; 1/5/126; 2/2/27; Windsor, St George's chapel, I.C. 32.

1501/2, student, with contributions from the hostiller, master of the cellar, priors of St Leonard's and Yarmouth, NRO DCN 1/7/124; 1/1/100; 2/3/102; 2/4/19.

1502/3, student, with contribution from the cellarer and the prior of Hoxne, NRO DCN 1/2/88; Windsor, St George's chapel, I.C. 34.

See also *BRUC*; and Venn, *Gonville and Caius*, i, 15, where he is listed as a pensioner in 1502/3.

1492, 5/8 Oct., 44th in order at the visitation of bp Goldwell, Jessopp, *Visit.*, 8.

1499, 6 Apr., 36th on the visitation certificate, *Reg. abp Morton*, iii, no 258.

1514, 27 Apr., at the episcopal visitation was accused by Ralph Sybly, q.v., of misuse of the common seal, Jessopp, *Visit.*, 74.

1519, mitred in this yr acc. to Beeching and James, 'Norwich Library', 80 n.; Dugdale states that the east window in St Mary in the Marsh had his effigy, mitred, with the date 1528, *Monasticon*, iv, 7.

1526/8, vicar of St Mary in the Marsh, Blomefield, *Norfolk*, iv, 51.

Note: this may ref. to Robert Catton II.

1526, 11 Feb., as prior he was apptd to the commission of the peace in Norfolk, *L and P Henry VIII*, iv, no 2002(11).

1526, 7 June, at the episcopal vistation was accused of uneven treatment in punishing those who did not obey orders, Jessopp, *Visit.*, 201.

Note: the name Robert Catton is in four Cambridge University Library Mss; see the note below Robert Catton II.

II Robert CATTON [*alias* Bennys
occ. 1520 occ. 1538

1526, 7 June, fourth prior, Jessopp, *Visit.*, 202.

1531/2, communar, NRO DCN 1/12/107.

1532, 3 June, master of St Paul's hospital, Jessopp, *Visit.*, 268, but see Henry Manuel.

1532, 12 Aug., master of St Paul's hospital, NRO DCN 45/31/34.

1533/4, communar, NRO DCN 1/12/108.
1520/1, student at Oxford, with pension contributions from the almoner, chamberlain, refectorer and prior of Lynn, NRO DCN 1/6/126; 1/5/138; 1/8/114; 2/1/82.
1521/2, student, with contributions from the chamberlain, hostiller, refectorer, sacrist and prior of Lynn, NRO DCN 1/5/139; 1/7/141; 1/8/114; 1/4/116; 2/1/82.

1526, 7 June, present at the visitation of bp Nikke, and stated that religion was in a perilous state because the juniors were not observing the solemnities (ceremonias) and the seniors were failing to instruct by example, Jessopp, *Visit.*, 202.
1526/8, the entry under Robert Catton I, q.v., seems more applicable to this monk.
1532, 3 June, present at the visitation and stated that all was well, Jessopp, *Visit.*, 268.
1534, 28 July, subscribed to the Act of Supremacy, *DK 7th Report*, Appndx 2, 295.
1538, 30 Apr., dispensed to wear the habit of a secular pr. and hold a canonry and prebend in the cathedral and any other benefice and be non-resident, Chambers, *Faculty Office Regs*, 137.
1538, 2 May, licensed as a secular canon, *L and P Henry VIII*, xiii, pt 1, no 1115(4).

Note: the name Catton is in six CUL Mss:
(1) Ii.4.2 Bonaventura (late 13th c.); name R. Catton on fo 1^{v}; see also Henry Langrake and Henry de Lakenham.
(2) Ii.4.15, Liber eruditionis religiosorum (14th c.); name R. Catton on fo 5; see also Henry de Lakenham.
(3) Ii.4.37, Egidius Romanus (14th/15th c.); name R. Catton on fos 1 and 3.
(4) Ii.2.7, Constitutiones etc. (14th c.); name on p. 9.
(5) Ii.1.30, Januensis tabula (15th c.); see also Henry Langrake.
(6) Ii.1.20, Jacobus de Losano (14th c.); name on fo 1.

Name also in NRO DCL/2, Boccaccio etc. (15th c.); see Ker, 'Norwich Cathedral Mss', 259. Also in BL Ms Cotton Claudius E. viii, Flos historiarum, comm. by bp Despenser, the name is on fo 1.

CAUSTON
see Cawston

John CAWMBRIDGE [Cambregge, Caumbrig', Cauntibrigge
occ. 1497/8 occ. 1514

1514, 27 Apr., refectorer, Jessopp, *Visit.*, 74.

1497/8, first year as student at Cambridge, NRO DCN 1/10/33.
1500/1, student at Cambridge with pension contributions from the almoner, cellarer, chamberlain, and the priors of Aldeby and Hoxne, NRO DCN 1/6/113; 1/2/86; 1/5/126; 2/2/27; Windsor, St George's chapel, I.C. 32.
1500/3, pensioner at Gonville Hall, see Venn, *Gonville and Caius*, i,15, and *BRUC*.
1501/2, student with contributions from the hostiller, master of the cellar and the prior of Yarmouth, NRO DCN 1/7/124; 1/1/100; 2/4/19.
1502/3, student with contribution from the cellarer and the prior of Hoxne, NRO DCN 1/2/88; Windsor, St George's chapel, I.C. 34.

1499, 6 Apr., 42nd on the visitation certificate, *Reg. abp Morton*, iii, no 258.

I Thomas CAWMBRIDGE [Cantabrygge, Caumbryg, Cauntybrygge
occ. 1411/12 d. 1437/8

1411/12, communar/pittancer, NRO DCN 1/12/43.
1413/1419, Dec., precentor, NRO DCN 1/9/31.
1419, Dec./1420, 1421/31, almoner, NRO DCN 1/6/46–61.

1413/14, ill and the precentor's acct was charged 2s. for medicine, NRO DCN 1/9/31.
1425/6, gave 10d. to the chamberlain towards a new barn at Lakenham, NRO DCN 1/5/53.
1427, 8 Oct., one of the proctors in the el. negotiations of prior William Worstede, q.v., Reg. Alnwick, fo 8.
1431/2, pd the refectorer 6s. 8d. *pro uno cipho cedrino*, NRO DCN 1/8/74.
1437/8, d., and the chamberlain recd 'alms', NRO DCN 1/5/68.

Note: As there are two contemporary monks by this name, some of the biographical details may have been incorrectly assigned. It may well be, for instance, that one of them was the infirmarer while the other was on the sick list; see below.

II Thomas CAWMBRYGGE
occ. 1413/14 occ. 1434/5

1413/14, novice and pd 6s. 8d. to the refectorer for a *ciphus*, NRO DCN 1/8/59.

1427/33, 1434/5, infirmarer, NRO DCN 1/10/15–21; also in 1433/4, 1/4/73.

1428/9, ill and spent 4d. for his medicine, NRO DCN 1/10/16.
1431, ill and spent 12d. for his medicine, NRO DCN 1/10/19.
1434/5, ill and spent 22d. for his medicine, NRO DCN 1/10/21.
1430/1, gave 3s. 4d. to the gardener to repair the wall *vs Holmstrete*, NRO DCN 1/11/14.

Note: one of the monks by this name gave a red damask chasuble to St Leonard's which appears in the inventory of 1452/3, Bensly, 'St Leonard's' 212–213; he also gave a new 'pecia belleschap cum cooperculo et corona in summitate', *ib.*, 216–217.

William de CAWMBRYGG' [Caumbrugg', Caumbryg', Cawmbrigge
occ. 1418 occ. 1440/1

1418, 20 Apr., one of four *clerici* whom the prior requested the bp to rec. and bless as they had been examined and adm. by the chapter and were about to be clothed, Reg. Wakering, fo 32ᵛ.

1428/9, gardener, NRO DCN 1/11/10–12.
1436/7, almoner, NRO DCN 1/6/62.
1440/1, prior of Hoxne, Windsor, St George's chapel, I.C. 13.

1425/6, gave 20d. to the chamberlain towards a new barn at Lakenham, NRO DCN 1/5/53.
1432/3, recd 6s. 8d. from the infirmarer on setting out to join prior William Worstede, q.v., at the Council of Basel, NRO DCN 1/10/20; the chamberlain referred to the departure for Basel and contributed 6s. 8d., NRO DCN 1/5/59.

John de CAWSTON [Causton, Caustone
occ. [1276/7] occ. 1295/6

1284/5, master of the cellar, NRO DCN 1/1/8.
1291/3, chamberlain, NRO DCN 1/5/1,2.

[1276/7, a John de Causton gave 57s. 8d. to the sacrist, NRO DCN 1/4/3].
[1278, 21 Sept.], acted as proctor for the prior and chapter in a dispute, *N. Cath. Charters*, i, no 231.
1285/6, visited Sedgeford with the steward, NRO DCN 60/33/7, and also visited Catton for *liberatio denariorum*, NRO DCN 60/4/8.
?1286/7, visited Denham, NRO DCN 60/7/3.
1287/8, went to Hindolveston for *liberatio denariorum*, NRO DCN 60/18/9; stopped at Hemsby, NRO DCN 60/15/3.
1288/9, visited Plumstead with the steward, NRO DCN 60/29/6.
1291/2, 1293/6, visited Sedgeford to hold courts and for *liberatio denariorum*, NRO DCN 60/33/9–12.

Name in Oxford, Magdalen Coll. Ms 180, Vincent of Beauvais, Speculum historiale (14th c.).

Robert de CAWSTON [Causton
occ. 1418 d. 1430/1

1418, 20 Apr., one of four *clerici* whom the prior requested the bp to rec. and bless as they had been examined and adm. by the chapter and were about to be clothed, Reg. Wakering, fo 32ᵛ.

1421/2, ill, and 4d. was spent by the infirmarer on medicine, NRO DCN 1/10/14.
1427/8, ill, and 3s. spent on medicine, NRO DCN 1/10/15.
1428/9, ill, and 3s. 4d. spent on medicine, NRO DCN 1/10/16.
1429/30, ill, and 15s. 4d. spent on medicine, NRO DCN 1/10/17.
1430/1, d., and the chamberlain pd for the brief, NRO DCN 1/5/57.

John de CELAR' [Celerarius
occ. 1265/6 occ. ?1290/1

1267/8 or 1290/1, master of the cellar, NRO DCN 1/1/9.

1265/6, visited Catton, Monks Grange, Plumstead and Taverham for *liberatio denariorum*, NRO DCN 60/4/1; 60/26/3; 60/29/2; 60/35/4.
[1273/4], visited Denham for *liberatio denariorum*, NRO DCN 60/7/2.

Note: see also John de Bromholm who may be identical with this monk.

CHAMPENEYS
see Chaumpeneys

CHATEGRAVE
see Chattegrove

Richard CHATERIS [Chaterys, Chatres, Chatris, ?Chathouse
occ. 1492 d. 1517/18

1508/9, 1512/13, communar, NRO DCN 1/12/88,90.
1513/14, almoner and communar, NRO DCN 1/6/119; 1/12/92.
1514/15, almoner and chamberlain, NRO DCN 1/6/120, 1/5/133.
1515/16, almoner, chamberlain and hostiller, NRO DCN 1/6/121, 1/5/135, 1/7/137.

1492, 5/8 Oct., 46th and last in order at the visitation of bp Goldwell, Jessopp, *Visit.*, 8.
1499, 6 Apr., 38th on the visitation certificate, *Reg. abp Morton*, iii, no 258.
1514, 27 Apr., present at the visitation of bp Nikke and complained that divine service was perfunctorily performed, especially by the subprior and third prior, Jessopp, *Visit.*, 74.
1517/18, d., and the sacrist pd 16d. for four candles for the funeral, NRO DCN 1/4/114.

Robert de CHATTEGROVE [Chategrave
occ. [1319/20] occ. 1346

[1319/20], one of two *clerici* whom the prior sent to the bp bearing a letter requesting him to rec. [and bless] them, Reg. IX, fo 26.

1343/4, 1345/6, hostiller, NRO DCN 1/7/7,8.

John de CHAUMPENEYS [Champeneys, Chummpeneys, Chawmpeneys
occ. 1432/3 d. 1485/6

1456/7, 1462/3, precentor, NRO DCN 1/9/67,68.
1467/8, prior of Aldeby, NRO DCN 2/2/21.
Note: the precentor's accounts between 1457 and 1462 are missing, as are those of Aldeby for the immediate years before and after 1467/8.

1439/40, student at [Oxford] university, with pension contributions from the master of the cellar, sacrist and the priors of Aldeby and St Leonard's, NRO DCN 1/1/84; 1/4/78; 2/2/13; 2/3/54.

1440/1, student, with contributions from the almoner, cellarer, hostiller, master of the cellar, precentor and prior of Aldeby, NRO DCN 1/6/65; 1/2/54; 1/7/81;1/1/85; 1/9/55; 2/2/14.

1441/2, student, with contributions from all of the 1440/1 list apart from the precentor, NRO DCN 1/6/66; 1/2/55; 1/7/81; 1/1/86; 2/2/15.

1442/3, student, with contributions from the almoner and hostiller, NRO DCN 1/6/67; 1/7/81.

1432/3, ill, and 2s. were spent by the infirmarer on medicine, NRO DCN 1/10/20.

1438/9, gave 12d. towards building operations in the cloister, NRO DCN 1/12/57.

1440/1, the infirmarer pd a 12d. contribution to Chaumpeneys *pro parliamento* [?at Reading in Jan. 1440, which would have been an easy journey from Oxford], NRO DCN 1/10/22.

1446/9, name occ. on a rough list of those assigned to celebrate Sunday masses as follows:

1446, 25 Dec.; 1447, 19 Mar., 6 Aug., 26 Nov.; 1448, 17 Mar., 7 July, 27 Oct.; 1449, 9 Feb., Cambridge, Emm. Coll. Ms 142, fo 68.

1485/6 d., and the chamberlain recd 6s. 8d. 'alms', NRO DCN 1/5/115.

Name in CUL Ms Ii.3.31, Ludolphus, Vita Christi, (15th c.), which he gave to the convent library, see Ker, 'Norwich Cathedral Mss', 259.

CHRISTOFER

occ. 1502 occ. c. 1504

1502, 23 June, one of four *clerici* whom the bp comm. the prior to adm. [*monachand'*], Reg. Nikke (8/13), fo 13ᵛ.

[c. 1504], a Christofer, along with six other priests, (Christian names only given) made their prof.; this is recorded on an inserted leaf (prob. of rough notes) between fos 27ᵛ and 28 in Reg. Nikke (9/14).

CIPRIANUS

occ. [1121 × 1135]

[1121, 12 June × 1135], witnessed the confirmation of a charter with Elias the cellarer, q.v., *Eng. Epis. Acta*, vi, no 49.

n.d., 17 July, obit occ. in the kalendar in Reg. XI, fo 5.

John de CLAXTON

occ. 1393/4 d. 1396/7

1393/4, was currently using the *ciphus* of cedar which had formerly belonged to Ralph de Bliclingg, q.v., NRO DCN 1/8/48.

1396/7, d., and the chamberlain recd his 'alms', NRO DCN 1/5/28.

William de CLAXTON [Clackiston, Clasthun, Claston, Claxisthon

occ. 1313 d. 1344

1326–1344, prior: el. confirmed 4 Sept. 1326, Reg. Ayermine, fo 9; d. before 25 Aug. 1344, Reg. Bateman, fo 45ᵛ, *Fasti*, iv, 25; see Simon Bozoun.

1326, 1 Jan., prior of Yarmouth, Reg. Ayermine, fo 79.

1313/14, student at Oxford, with pension contribution from the master of the cellar, NRO DCN 1/1/23.

1314/16, student, with contributions from the master of the cellar and the refectorer, NRO DCN 1/1/24, 25; 1/8/23.

1317/19, student, with contribution from the master of the cellar, NRO DCN 1/1/26, 27.

1315, 20 Sept., attended the Black Monk Chapter meeting at Northampton, Pantin, *BMC*, i, 280 n. 2 and NRO DCN 1/1/25.

[1313 × 1320], the prior informed the bp that he would be the preacher instead of Robert de Ely, q.v.; this prob. refers to an impending visitation by bp Salmon, either that of Jan. 1314 or, more likely, Mar. 1319. However, it could also refer to a later visitation c. 1323. All the relevant sources are in the priory register IX (in which there is only a semblance of chronological order), on fos 5,29,39ᵛ.

1320/1, stayed at Hindolveston, NRO DCN 60/18/22; he recd a 2s. gift from the hostiller this yr, NRO DCN 1/7/1.

1326, 1 Jan., authorized by the bp to hear confessions in the parish church of Yarmouth, Reg. Ayermine, fo 79.

1326, 4/5 Sept., installed as prior by Hervey de Swafham, q.v., *ib.*, fo 9ᵛ.

1330, 14 Aug., reached agreement with abp Meopham over jurisdiction rights *sede vacante*, NRO DCN 42/2/4.

1335/6, attended parliament, NRO DCN 1/1/33.

1337, 8 Apr., apptd vicar general, with the adcn of Suffolk, Reg. Bek, fo 1.

1344, 17 Feb., ordered by the king to appear before him at Westminster to discuss urgent matters concerning the crown and the state; he had failed to appear on the first summons, *CClR, 1343–1346*, 353.

1344, 12 Mar., again apptd vicar general, Reg. Bateman, fo 41ᵛ.

1344, d. between 12 Mar. and 25 Aug. (The chamberlain records his d. on the 1343/4 acct, NRO DCN 1/5/12).

Priory registers IX and X (NRO DCN 40/9 and 10) contain copies of his wide ranging correspondence.

CLEMENT
n.d.

n.d., 13 Aug., obit occ. in the kalendar in Reg. XI, fo 5v.

John de CLIPESBY [Clepysby, Clipesbi, Clipysby
occ. 1317/18 occ. 1347/8

1319/20 or 1320/1, chaplain to bp Salmon, NRO DCN 1/1/27.
1329/30, gardener, NRO DCN 1/11/1A.
1345, before, infirmarer, NRO DCN 1/10/4.
1345/6, subprior, NRO DCN 1/12/25.

1317/18, prob. student at Oxford, with pension contribution from the master of the cellar, NRO DCN 1/1/26.
1319/20, student, with contributions from the cellarer and hostiller, NRO DCN 1/2/12; 1/7/1; and see *BRUO* and Greatrex, 'Norwich Monk Students', 582.
1320/21, 1322/3, recd 12d. gifts from the refectorer, prob. still a student, NRO DCN 1/8/25,26; see below.
Note: these dates correct and supplement those in Greatrex, 'Norwich Monk Students', 582.

1319/20, stopped at [North] Elmham [prob. on his way to or from Oxford; see John de Mari], NRO DCN 60/10/17.
1321, 13 July, one of the two convent proctors for parliament Reg. IX, fo 31.
1321/2, various small sums were pd to him by the master of the cellar; he went to London twice; his boy was given 6d., NRO DCN 1/1/28.
1322/3, stopped at [North] Elmham [prob. on his way to or from Oxford, as above], NRO DCN 60/10/19.
1323/4, again in London and the communar contributed 13s. 4d. *Comm. Rolls*, 94.
1324/5, bought part of a Bible from the precentor and pd 10s., NRO DCN 1/9/4.
1346/7, ill and 11d. was spent by the infirmarer on medicine, NRO DCN 1/10/5.
1347/8, ill and 13d. spent on medicine, NRO DCN 1/10/6.

John de COLCHESTRE [Colchestyr
occ. 1477/8 occ. 1493/4

1493/4, student, with pension contributions from the almoner, hostiller, master of the cellar, sacrist and prior of St Leonard's; all but the last specify either half pension or pension for half a yr. NRO DCN 1/6/109; 1/7/120; 1/1/97; 1/4/106; 2/3/97.
Note: The entry in *BRUO* refers to this monk but must have confused him with another who went on to graduate. In fact, *Reg. Univ. Oxon.*, i, 39,293, the *BRUO* ref., does not name the monastery. This monk had prob. been a student for some yrs before this date, unless there are two monks by the same name conflated here.

1477/8, pd the precentor 12d. for [?the loan of] Brito super biblia, press-mark Cxxxij, NRO DCN 1/9/76.
1492, 5/8 Oct., 22nd in order at the visitation of bp Goldwell, Jessopp, *Visit.*, 8.

Peter CORNELYS
occ. 1534

1534, 28 July, subscribed to the Act of Supremacy, *DK 7th Report*, Appndx 2, 295.

John de CORPSTY [Corpesty
occ. 1377/8 d. 1399/1400

c. 1377/8, prob. entered when he bought a *ciphus* from the refectorer, NRO DCN 1/8/46.
1388, June/1391, Jan., communar/pittancer, NRO DCN 1/12/33–35; 1391/2, 1399/1400, master of the cellar, NRO DCN 1/1/66, 67 (note, the accts between these dates are missing).
1399/1400, d., and the chamberlain recd 'alms', NRO DCN 1/5/31.

Richard CORPSTY [Corpusty
occ. 1414/15 d. 1423/4

1414/17, hostiller, NRO DCN 1/7/60–62.
1418, 8 Apr., the prior requested the bp to confer the office of master of St Paul's hospital on him, Reg. Wakering, fo 32v.
1422/3, master of St Paul's hospital, NRO DCN 2/5/1.
1423/4, gave 100s. to St Leonard's, NRO DCN 2/3/39.
1423/4, d., and the chamberlain recd 'alms' of 19s. NRO DCN 1/5/50.

Thomas de CORPSTY [Corpesty, Corpisty, Corpysty
occ. 1403 d. 1435/6

1403, Aug./1404, 1405/6, Feb., gardener, NRO DCN 1/11/5–7.
1433/4, described as formerly infirmarer, NRO DCN 1/4/73.
1412/13, gave 6s. 8d. to the office of refectorer, NRO DCN 1/8/58.
1414/15, gave 6s. 8d. to [repairs in] the church of St Etheldreda in Norwich (for which the refectorer was responsible), NRO DCN 1/8/60.
1429/30, ill and the infirmarer spent 6d. on medicine, NRO DCN 1/10/17.
1435/6, d., and 'alms' of 27s. 4d. were recd by the chamberlain, NRO DCN 1/5/64.

Bartholomew de COTTON [Cottun
occ. 1282/3 d. 1321/2

1282/4, master of the cellar, NRO DCN 1/1/6,7 (the 1282/3 acct has been transl. and ed. by the Rev. W. Hudson in *Norfolk and Norwich Archaeological Society*, 19 (1917) 268–313).

1282/3, visited Catton and [North] Elmham for *liberatio denariorum*, NRO DCN 60/4/7; 60/10/6.

1288/9, with Adam de Schipdam and Roger de Alderford, q.v., named on the communar's acct in connection wtih arrangements for the sale of wood, *Comm. Rolls*, 51 (NRO DCN 1/12/2).

1321/2, d., and the chamberlain pd the brief bearer, NRO DCN 1/5/6.

His own writings, viz., Historia Anglicana (AD 449–1298) and Liber de archiepiscopis et episcopis Angliae, have been ed. by H.R. Luard in the Rolls Series, no 16 (1859). For an analysis and commentary see Gransden, *Hist. Writing*, i, 440–448; see also Sharpe, *Latin Writers*.

Note:

(1) in Gransden and elsewhere it is assumed that he d. in 1298, as the above reference had not been noted.

(2) Ker doubts that Chronicon Anglie (13th c.) (Norwich Cathedral Ms 1, now NRO DCL/1) was compiled by Cotton, *MMBL*, iii, 527. See Ralph de Fretenham.

John COWLYNGE

occ. 1464/5

1464/5, ill and 12d. was spent by the infirmarer on medicine, NRO DCN 1/10/26.

Thomas CRANE B.Th. [Krane

occ. 1437/8 occ. 1466

1452/3, precentor, NRO DCN 1/9/66.

1458, Sept./Dec., cellarer, NRO DCN 1/2/64.

1465, Feb./Sept. 1466, hostiller, NRO DCN 1/7/99–100.

1437/8, student at [Oxford] university, with pension contributions from the chamberlain and prior of St Leonard's, NRO DCN 1/5/68; 2/3/52.

1438/39, student, with contributions from the almoner, master of the cellar, refectorer and sacrist, NRO DCN 1/6/64; 1/1/83; 1/8/77; 1/4/76.

1439/40, student, with contributions from the master of the cellar, sacrist and prior of Aldeby, NRO DCN 1/1/84; 1/4/78; 2/2/13.

1440/1, student, with contributions from the almoner, cellarer, hostiller, master of the cellar, precentor, refectorer and prior of Aldeby, NRO DCN 1/6/65; 1/2/54; 1/7/81; 1/1/85; 1/9/55; 1/8/78; 2/2/14.

1441/2, student, with contributions from the almoner, cellarer, hostiller, master of the cellar, refectorer and prior of Aldeby, NRO DCN 1/6/66; 1/2/55; 1/7/81; 1/1/86; 1/8/79; 2/2/15.

1443/5, student, with contributions from the precentor, NRO DCN 1/9/57–58.

1446/7, student, with contributions from the cellarer, chamberlain, hostiller, precentor and refectorer, NRO DCN 1/2/57; 1/5/78; 1/7/81; 1/9/60; 1/8/84.

1447/8, student, with contributions from the almoner, cellarer, hostiller, precentor, refectorer and prior of St Leonard's, NRO DCN 1/6/68; 1/2/58; 1/7/81; 1/9/61; 1/8/85; 2/3/54.

1448/9, student, with contributions from the almoner, hostiller, precentor, refectorer and prior of Aldeby, NRO DCN 1/6/69; 1/7/81; 1/9/62; 1/8/86; 2/2/17.

1449/50, student with contributions from the cellarer, chamberlain, precentor and refectorer, NRO DCN 1/2/59; 1/5/82; 1/9/63; 1/2/59; 1/8/87.

Note: a number of these entries are specified as half pensions or pensions for half a year; this prob. indicates that his residence at university, though over a long period, was not continuous.

1450, Mar., supplicated at Oxford for B.Th; see *Reg. Univ. Oxon.* i, 9 and *BRUO*.

1452/3, recd from four of his brethren for his own *portiforium* 13s. 4d., NRO DCN 1/9/66. Note that this is on his own acct as precentor; was he having a sale of books? See Robert Brethenham, Thomas Fulmerston, Edmund Sall, William Stonhalle.

The d. of his mother, Margaret Crane, has been added to the kalendar in Lambeth Ms 368, fo 9v.

William CROMER

occ. 1480/2

1480/1, gave the precentor 4d. *pro intabulacione librorum*, NRO DCN 1/9/78; see Greatrex, 'Norwich Monk Students', 525–526.

1482, 2 Jan., described as pr. and given papal dispensation to rec. and retain a benefice. *CPL*, xiii, (1471–1484), 802.

Walter CROWMER, B.Cn.L. [Cromer *alias* Grime, Gryme

occ. ?1504 occ. 1538

[1504], a Walter, along with six other priests (Christian names only given) made his prof.; this is recorded on an inserted leaf (prob. of rough notes) between fos 27v and 28 in Reg Nikke (9/14).

1511/14, hostiller, NRO DCN 1/7/132–136.

1526, 7 June, prior of Yarmouth, Jessopp, *Visit.*, 197.

1529/32, sacrist, NRO DCN 1/4/120–122.

1532, 3 June, subprior, Jessopp, *Visit.*, 265.

1534/6, sacrist NRO DCN 1/4/123–125.

1538, before 2 May, subprior, *Fasti, 1541–1857*, vii, 51.

1503, pensioner at Gonville Hall, Venn, *Gonville and Caius*, i,18.

1509/10, pensioner at Gonville Hall, obtained B.Cn.L., Venn, *Alumni*, i, 421.

1526, 7 June, present at the visitation of bp Nikke, Jessopp, *Visit.*, 197, and complained of the plumbing in the cloister, *ib.*
1532, 3 June, present at the visitation of bp Nikke, *ib.*, 265, and stated that all was well; but the bp said that although he was both subprior and sacrist he needed only one servant not two, *ib.*, 269.
1534, 28 July, subscribed to the Act of Supremacy, *DK 7th Report*, Appndx 2, 295.
1538, 30 Apr., dispensed to wear the habit of a secular pr. and hold a canonry and benefice in the cathedral and any other benefices and be non-resident; this cost him £10, Chambers, *Faculty Office Regs*, 137.
1538, 2 May, apptd canon of the 1st prebend in the new foundation, *Fasti, 1541–1857*, vii, 51. See also *L and P Henry VIII*, xiii, pt 1, no 1115(4).

John DALLYNG
d. 1412/13

1412/13, d., and the chamberlain recd 'alms' of 14s. 6d., NRO DCN 1/5/42.

William DALLYNG
occ. 1454/5 occ. 1464/5

1464/5, Sept. to Feb., cellarer, NRO DCN 1/2/65.
1466/7, ref. on the chamberlain's acct to his debt, NRO DCN 1/5/97, (therefore prob. formerly chamberlain).
1454/5, ill and the infirmarer spent 2s. on medicine, NRO DCN 1/10/24.
1463, 26 July, described as pr., given papal dispensation to rec. and retain a benefice, *CPL*, xii, (1458–1471), 190.

Stephen DARSHAM [Darseham, Derseham, Dersham, *alias* Roper
occ. 1514 occ. 1538

1520, 3 Sept., *custos cellarie*, Jessopp, *Visit.*, 192.
1520/1, hostiller, NRO DCN 1/7/140.
1522, Mar./Sept., 1523/4, 1529/31, prior of Hoxne NRO DCN 2/6/41–44, and Windsor, St George's chapel, I.C. 38; also, on 7 June 1526, prior of Hoxne, Jessopp, *Visit.*, 203.
1532, 3 June, prior of Yarmouth, *ib.*, 265.
1514, 27 Apr., present at the visitation of bp Nikke and accused of not applying himself *ad scolas sed utitur aliis artibus*, and also of not wearing his habit, Jessopp, *Visit.*, 74, 77.
1520, 3 Sept., present at the visitation of bp Nikke, and said *omnia bene*, *ib.*, 192.
1526, 7 June, present at the visitation of bp Nikke and stated that he was ignorant of internal affairs in Norwich because he was at Hoxne, *ib.*, 203.
1532, 3 June, present at the visitation of bp Nikke and complained of the insolent and dissolute behaviour of some of the monks placed under his charge at Yarmouth, *ib.*, 265.
1534, 28 July, subscribed to the Act of Supremacy, *DK 7th Report*, Appndx 2, 295.
1538, 30 Apr., dispensed to wear the habit of a secular pr. and hold a canonry and benefice in the cathedral and any other benefice and be non-resident; Chambers, *Faculty Office Regs*, 137.
1538, 2 May, licensed as a secular canon, *L and P Henry VIII*, xiii, pt 1, no 1115(4).

John DAVENTRE [Dauntre
occ. 1394 d. 1407

1394, succentor, NRO DCN 42/2/13.
1400, June/Dec. hostiller, NRO DCN 1/7/9,50.
1401/5, almoner, NRO DCN 1/6/29–33.
1394, accused by the bp at his visitation of mismanagement in the office of succentor, NRO DCN 42/2/13.
1395, 4 Apr., as a result of the bp's interference in the correction of monks and the appeal of the prior and chapter vs him, the pope ordered an inquiry into accusations vs Daventre, *CPL*, iv, (1362–1402), 525; see also John de Kirkeby and Thomas de Tunstale.
1407, 25 Nov., obit occ. in Reg XI, fo 7.

Thomas DAVY
occ. 1477

1477, 4 Nov., one of three *clerici* whom the prior requested the bp to rec. and bless, Reg. Goldwell, fo 9; on 8 Nov. the bp comm. the prior to perform the ceremony, *ib.*

DEERHAM
see Dereham, Derham

[William DENBURY
occ. 1431/2

1431/2, gave 5s. to the office of chamberlain, NRO DCN 1/5/58, but he may have been a lay official.]

Alexander DENTON [Dentone
occ. 1414 occ. 1449

1414, 14 Oct., one of six whose prof. the bp comm. the prior to rec., Reg. Courtenay, fo 102ᵛ.
1421/2, gave 20d. to [building operations in] the cloister, NRO DCN 1/12/49.
1429/30, gave 4d. to St Leonard's cell, NRO DCN 2/3/46.
1446, both Dentons (see following entry) occ. on a rough list of those assigned to celebrate weekday and chantry masses, Cambridge, Emm. Coll. Ms 142, fo 68. Denton (no initial) also occ. on a similar list for Sunday masses on the following dates: 1447, 26 Feb., 11 June, 1 Oct.; 1448, 14 Jan., 19 May, 1 Sept.; 1449, 19 Jan.

Thomas DENTON
occ. 1414 occ. 1466/7

1414, 14 Oct., one of six whose prof. the bp comm. the prior to rec., Reg. Courtenay, fo 102ᵛ.
1438/41, 1442/52, precentor, NRO DCN 1/9/53–65.
1465/6 gardener, NRO DCN 1/11/20.
1466/7, refectorer, NRO DCN 1/8/94.
1446, both Dentons (see preceding entry) occ. on a rough list of those assigned to celebrate weekday and chantry masses, Cambridge, Emm. Coll. Ms 142, fo 68.
1446, 23 Oct., T. Denton is also on a similar list for the Sunday masses on one date only, namely 23 Oct.; Denton (no initial) is on this list for other Sundays 1447–1449 as in the previous entry.
1459/60, may have given money for repairs to the nave; the amount was £13 which makes it fairly certain that the sum would have been in fact a contribution from the [unknown] office wich he held that yr, NRO DCN 1/4/87.

Thomas de DEPEDALE [Deppedale
occ. 1345 occ. 1347/8

1345, ill and the infirmarer pd for medicine, NRO DCN 1/10/2.
1345/6, ill and 3s. 5d. spent on medicine, NRO DCN 1/10/4.
1346/7, ill and 15d. spent on medicine, NRO DCN 1/10/5.
1347/8, ill and 4s. spent on medicine, NRO DCN 1/10/6.
1346/7, under 'foreign expenses' the almoner gave 4s. to him and his *socius*, NRO DCN 1/6/14. Could he have been given a short spell at university?

G. or J. de DEPHAM
occ. 1272/3

1272/3, there are refs to his presence at Catton and Martham, NRO DCN 60/4/4 (tithe acct), 60/23/4.

William DEPHAM
occ. 1400 d. 1412/13

1400/3, prior of Aldeby, NRO DCN 2/2/3.
1406/7, gardener, NRO DCN 1/11/8.
1412, 29 June/Sept., prior of St Leonard's, NRO DCN 2/3/28; the office of prior had two other occupants in 1411/12, see John de Ely and Richard de Midelton.
1412, before 15 July, subprior, Reg. Totyngton, fo 50; on this date removed from office, *ib.*
1412/13, d., and the chamberlain recd 16s. 'alms', NRO DCN 1/5/42.

Edmund DEREHAM [Derham
occ. 1471/2 occ. 1502/3

1471/4, communar/pittancer, NRO DCN 1/12/70.
1476/7, cellarer, NRO DCN 1/2/73.
1483/4, communar/pittancer, NRO DCN 1/12/73.
1485/7, almoner, NRO DCN 1/6/100–101.
1487, 26 Nov., the bp confirmed his appt as chamberlain, Reg. Goldwell, fo 130.
1487/93, 1494/5, chamberlain, NRO DCN 1/5/116–122.
1489, 7 Feb., the bp confirmed his appt as sacrist, Reg. Goldwell, fo 135ᵛ.
1491/4, sacrist, NRO DCN 1/4/104–106.
1492, 7 Sept., the bp replied unfavourably to the request of the prior and chapter to approve his removal from the office of sacrist and to appt William Spynk, prior, q.v., to take his place, Reg Goldwell, fo 159ᵛ.
1494, 27 Sept., removed from the office of sacrist, Reg. Goldwell, fo 180.
1493/6, Jan., prior of St Leonard's, NRO DCN 2/3/97–100; see William Spynk.
1478/9, reported by his successor in the cellarer's office as having alienated a silver salt cellar [*salsarius*] now redeemed, NRO DCN 1/2/74.
1483/4, responsible for the accts of the Wakering and Erpingham chantries, NRO DCN 4/10.
1492, 5/8 Oct., 6th in order at the visitation of bp Goldwell, Jessopp, *Visit.*, 8.
1502/3, the refectorer spent 12d. *pro materia fratris Edmundi*, 1/8/109; the prior of Hoxne also contributed this year and in 1500/1, Windsor, St George's chapel, I.C. 32, 34.

John de DEREHAM, D.Th. [Derham
occ. 1393/4 d. 1449/50

1402/4, hostiller, NRO DCN 1/7/52–53.
1408, Jan./June, almoner, NRO DCN 1/6/38.
1410/12, hostiller, NRO DCN 1/7/57–58.
1414/16, 1417/20, prior of St Leonard's, NRO DCN 2/3/31–36.
1423/4, 1426/7, 1428/30, 1431/3, 1434/6, prior of Lynn, NRO DCN 2/1/22–31; also prior on 21 Apr. 1425, *Reg. abp Chichele*, iii, 468.
1393/4, student at Oxford where he had the *ciphus* with a silver base, which had belonged to Peter de Dereham, q.v., NRO DCN 1/8/48.
1415, 1 Oct., decribed as B.Th., *Reg abp Chichele*, iii, 351.
1419/20, recd 4s. 4d. from the prior of St Leonard's towards the expenses of his inception, NRO DCN 2/3/36; the sacrist gave M. John and Robert Gedge, q.v., 15s., NRO DCN 1/4/55.
1421, by this date, D.Th., Pantin *BMC*, ii, 97 and 121, where he is named *Magister*.
Note: Dereham's university career has almost failed to be recorded on the obedientiary accts, which in this period continue to include regular payments to students but rarely give names.

1411/12, gave 2s. 6d. to [the reconstruction of] the cloiser, NRO DCN 1/12/43.
1415, 1 Oct., one of three monks nominated by the prior and chapter for the office of *visitator, sed. vac.* Norwich, *Reg. abp Chichele*, iii, 351–352.
1420, 8 July, apptd diffinitor for the Black Monk Chapter meeting at Northampton, Pantin, *BMC*, ii, 97, and was assigned to preach in the vulgar tongue at the next assembly in 1423, *ib*.
1422, member of the committee apptd to reply to the king's articles on the reformation of the Benedictines, Pantin, *BMC* ii, 121 ff; see also William Worstede. For more details see Pantin, *BMC* iii, 319.
1421/2, received some of the books of Thomas Hevyngham, q.v., who had d., NRO DCN 1/9/37.
1423, 5–7 July, attended the Black Monk Chapter, where he was apptd to the committee to el. the presidents for the 1426 meeting, Pantin, *BMC*, ii, 152; he preached to the clergy and people *famosissime*, and was addressed as *sacre theologie doctor*, *ib*., 155.
1425, 8 Apr., one of three monks, named by the chapter for the office of *visitator*, *sed. vac.* Norwich, *Reg. abp Chichele*, iii, 468.
1427, 8 Oct., one of the proctors in the el. proceedings of William Worstede, q.v., as prior, Reg. Alnwick, fo 8.
1427, 17 Oct., comm. by the vicar general to install Worstede, Reg. Alnwick, fo 8.
1430, 23 Sept., apptd penitentiary at Lynn and described as *sacre paginis professori*, Reg. Alnwick, fo 102.
1449/50, d., and the chamberlain recd 'alms' of 18s., NRO DCN 1/5/82.

The 1424 inventory of St Leonard's records his gift of an ivory pyx, Bensly, 'St Leonard's', 198–199; see also *ib*, 212–213.

It was prob. he, when prior of Lynn and as such in charge of the parish there, who was praised by Margery Kempe for his valiant stand in a dispute among the parishoners, B. Windeatt, ed., *The Book of Margery Kempe,* Penguin Books, 1985, 95, 311.

Peter de DEREHAM [Deerham, Derham

occ. 1378/9 d. 1392/3

1378/9, almoner, NRO DCN 1/6/18–19.
1379/81, 1383/7, 1389/90, master of the cellar, NRO DCN 1/1/57–65.
1391/2, cellarer, 1/2/29.

1379/80, went twice to London to negotiate the exchange of the churches of Chalk (Kent) and Martham, NRO DCN 1/1/57.
1386/7, went to London [on negotiations] with John de Kirkeby, q.v., and recd 'O' money to help with their expenses, NRO DCN 1/1/64.
1387/8, gave 6s. 8d. for [construction in] the cloister, NRO DCN 1/12/33.
1389/90, ill and the infirmarer spent 12s. in medicine, NRO DCN 1/1/65.
1390, 17 Sept., granted royal licence to go overseas, *CClR, 1389–1392*, 571.
1392/3, d., and the chamberlain recd 'alms' of 6s. 8d. and pd the same amount to the brief bearer. NRO DCN 1/5/24.
1393/4, his *ciphus* was reported to be at Oxford, see John de Dereham.
1410, the refectorer's inventory lists three knives and a sheath which had been given by him, NRO DCN 1/8/56.

Name in and portrait possibly in Oxford, Bod. Ms 316 on the first fo next to the initial; Ker suggests that this copy of a portion of the Polychronicon may have originated in the Norwich scriptorium although it was not a cathedral ms, see Ker, 'Norwich Cathedral Mss', 262, where he acknowledges Prof. Karl Leyser's intuition about the portrait. Paris, Bibliothèque Nationale, Ms lat. 4922 is another contemporary copy of the Polychronicon which has similar decorations in the same hand and the scroll held by the monk is inscribed 'celorum munus petro det trinus et unus'; the Oxford scroll lacks the inscription.

Robert DERHAM

occ. 1453/4 d. 1456/7

1453/4, ill and 12d. was spent by the infirmarer on medicine, NRO DCN 1/10/23.
1454/5, ill and 20d. spent on medicine, NRO DCN 1/10/24.
1456/7, d., and the chamberlain recd 'alms' of 12s. 6d., NRO DCN 1/5/89.

Thomas de DERHAM

occ. 1384/5 d. 1386/7

1384/5, pd the master of the cellarer for the meals of a man named Silkman who worked for him for 30 weeks, NRO DCN 1/1/61; this suggests that he was an obedientiary, possibly sacrist.
1386/7, d., and the chamberlain recd 'alms', NRO DCN 1/5/19.

DERSEHAM, Dersham

see Darsham

William de DERSINGHAM [Dersyngham

occ. 1345/6 occ. 1358

1346/7, master of the cellar, NRO DCN 1/1/42.
1348/June 1349, communar/pittancer, NRO DCN 1/12/27.
1350/1, cellarer, NRO DCN 1/2/19.
1353/6, communar/pittancer, NRO DCN 1/12/29.
1356/7, precentor, NRO DCN 1/9/8.

1345/6, ill and 6d. spent by the infirmarer on medicine, NRO DCN 1/10/4.
1351, 20 Nov., given papal licence to choose his confessor, who would be authorized to give

plenary remission of sins at d., *CPL* 3 (1342–1362), 452.

1356/7, ill and 29s. 10d. charged to the precentor's acct; the clerks who worked day and night while he was ill recd payment, as did the clerk who cared for him during his convalescence, NRO DCN 1/9/8.

1358, 1 Jan., one of three monks licensed to hear confessions in the cathedral, Reg. Percy, fo 23v.

DIONISIUS
see Dyonisius

I John de DISCE [Dysse
occ. 1366 occ. 1369

1366, student [at university], and the prior of St Leonard's contributed 8s. 8d., NRO DCN 2/3/7.

1369, 17 Aug., apptd official [*visitator*] for excepted jurisdiction on nomination of the prior and chapter, *sed. vac.* Norwich, Churchill, *Cant. Admin.*, ii, 251; this was accompanied by a comm. to visit the prior and chapter on behalf of the abp, Reg. abp Wittlesey, fo 140.

II John de DISCE [Disse, Dysce, Dysse
occ. 1425/6 d. 1432/3

1425/6, gave 12d. to the chamberlain towards a new barn at Lakenham, NRO DCN 1/5/53.

1429/30, ill, and 2s. were spent by the infirmarer on medicine, NRO DCN 1/10/17.

1432/3, ill and 2s. 2d. were spent on medicine, NRO DCN 1/10/20.

1432/3, d., and the chamberlain recd 'alms' of 17s. 8d., NRO DCN 1/5/59.

Stephen de DISCE [Diss, Disse
occ. 1371 d. 1397/8

1371/Jan. 1378, hostiller, NRO DCN 1/7/28–34.

1397/8, d., and the chamberlain recd 'alms', NRO DCN 1/5/29.

Robert de DOCKING
occ. 1367

1367, 26 May, master of St Paul's hospital, NRO DCN 45/31/17.

1367, 26 May, as master he negotiated a lease, *ib.*

DOFR'
see Dorobina

John DONEMOWE [Donmow, Dunmowe
occ. 1425/6 occ. 1467/8

1425/6, the refectorer recd from him 6s. 8d. for a small, worn *ciphus*, NRO DCN 1/8/72; this prob. denotes his adm. into the community.

1437/8 hostiller, and communar/pittancer, NRO DCN 1/7/78, 1/12/57.

1439/42, master of the cellar, NRO DCN 1/1/84–86.

1445/6, prior of Aldeby, NRO DCN 2/2/16.

1446/51, chamberlain, NRO DCN 1/5/78–84.

1452/4, master of the cellar, NRO DCN 1/1/88–89.

1452/7, 1459/61, 1463/4, chamberlain, NRO DCN 1/5/78–84, 91–93.

1457/64, 1465/6, 1467/8, prior of St Leonard's, NRO DCN 2/3/69–78.

Note: were there two monks, contemporaries, by this name? It is unlikely that one monk could serve as chamberlain at Norwich and prior of St Leonard's at the same time although they were within a mile of each other.

1431/2, ill and 22d. was spent by the infirmarer on medicine, NRO DCN 1/10/19.

1446, name occ. on a rough list of those assigned to celebrate weekday and chantry masses, Cambridge, Emm. Coll. Ms 142, fo 68; also on a similar list (prob. 1446/7) for the Wakering and Erpingham chantries, *ib.*, fo 77v.

Peter de DONEWICH [Donewico, Doneqyco
occ. 1334 occ. 1346/7

1334/5, ?before, prob. prior of Hoxne as Robert de Ormesby, q.v., pd his debts, Windsor, St George's chapel, I.C.1.

1334/5, hostiller, NRO DCN 1/7/5.

1339/40, gardener, NRO DCN 1/11/1.

1341/2, communar, NRO DCN 1/12/22 and master of the cellar from Nov. 1341, NRO DCN 1/1/39, succeeding Robert de Donewich, q.v.

1342/3, master of the cellarer, NRO DCN 1/1/40; 60/35/28.

1343/4, communar, NRO DCN 1/12/23, and possibly master of the cellar, NRO DCN 60/4/43.

1344/Jan. 1345, master of the cellar, NRO DCN 1/1/41.

1345, Jan./July, infirmarer, NRO DCN 1/10/12.

1342/3, visited Taverham, NRO DCN 60/35/28.

1345, ill and the infirmarer pd for medicine, NRO DCN 1/10/2.

1346/7, ill and the infirmarer spent 12d. on medicine, NRO DCN 1/10/5.

Robert de DONEWICH [Donewico, Donewyco
occ. 1329/30 occ. 1344

1331/3, hostiller, NRO DCN 1/7/3–4.

1333/41 Nov., master of the cellar, NRO DCN 1/1/33–39; succ. by Peter de Donewich, q.v.

1341, Sept./Nov., communar, NRO DCN 1/12/22; *Comm. Rolls*, 37.

1341/4, chamberlain, NRO DCN 1/5/12.

1329/30, was sent to London to buy 'colours' for the new [Bauchun] chapel (of which the decoration cost over £13), NRO DCN 1/1/30.

1330, sent by the sacrist, Richard de Hecham, q.v., to London to arrange a loan of 100s. to help with the travel expenses of the monks and officials who had been comm. by the chapter to pursue the chapter's case vs the abp at the papal curia, NRO DCN 1/1/30, 1/4/24; see also Roger de Eston.

1333/4, apptd proctor by the prior for parliament in London and allowed 23s. 4d. for his expenses, NRO DCN 1/1/38.

1334/5, visited Catton, Martham and Plumstead for *liberatio denariorum*, NRO DCN 60/4/34; 60/23/23; 60/29/24.

1337/8, attended parliament *pro priore*, NRO DCN 1/1/34.

1338/9, spent £14 9s. 6d for arms for the defence of the monastery, NRO DCN 1/1/36.

1341, at the end of the parchment book which contains his accts as master of the cellar 1333/41, he provided a memorandum listing his achievements: he had greatly reduced the debt which he had inherited from his predecessor in office, he left more in the granary than when he took over, he had spent £77 in purchasing land, and had incurred heavy expenses in entertaining the king and queen, NRO DCN 1/1/38.

1343/4, charged his office 40d. for the expense of being treated by M. Galfridus, *medicus*, and another 40d. for medicine, NRO DCN 1/5/12.

Name in CUL Ms Kk.2.21, Bernardus Cassinensis, (14th c.), liber fratris—- on flyleaf; see Ker 'Norwich Cathedral Mss', 260. This vol. containes an *expositio* on the Rule.

Roger de DOROBINA [Doufr', Dofr'

occ. 1290/1 occ. 1298/9

1290/2, 1293/4 or 1294/5, 1296/9, with Elias de Hoxne, q.v., communar/pittancer, NRO DCN 1/12/3–8 and *Comm. Rolls*, 9, 57–75.

1291/2, recd money from the master of the cellar *ad opus cementar'*, NRO DCN 1/1/10 and 11.

1293/4, visited Sedgeford, NRO DCN 60/33/10.

1294/5, given 4d. by the master of the cellar *ad picturam ymag'*, NRO DCN 1/1/12.

1296/7, went to London and Yarmouth, *Comm. Rolls*, 68 (NRO DCN 1/12/6).

Edmund DRAKE

see Norwich

DUNMOWE

see Donemowe

DYONISIUS

n.d.

n.d., 19 Mar., obit occ. in the kalendar in Reg XI, fo 3.

DYSCE, Dysse

see Disce

Adam de EASTON D.Th., [Eston

occ. 1352 d. 1397

[1352], student at Oxford; the bp ordered his immediate return and that of 'Jo.' [possibly Betele or Stukle, q.v.] from university to Norwich, for 'certain reasons' and they were to bring with them the books and valuable plate which belonged to the priory, D.M. Owen, ed., *John Lydford's Book*, Devon and Cornwall Record Soc., no 19 (Hist. Mss Commission no 22), 1974, no 201.

1352, 5 June, Easton replied that he had the prior's permission to remain at Oxford until 12 June, that he had not been summoned to Laurence de Leck's el. as prior, q.v., and that he had appealed to the pope vs the subprior [on this acct] and vs the bp, *ib.*, no 202.

1355/6, student at Oxford and returned to Norwich to preach on the vigil of the feast of the Assumption [14 August 1356] NRO DCN 1/12/29.

[1357 × 1363], the prior informed the prior of students at Oxford that he was not sending Adam back to incept for the present as his presence was required in Norwich in order to preach true doctrine and confound the friars, Pantin, *BMC* iii, 28–29 (from Oxford, Bod. Ms 692, fo 116).

1363/4, the communar pd for his travel expenses to Oxford on two occasions, once with all his belongings, and the total cost was 154s. 8d., NRO DCN 1/12/30.

1363/4, the sacrist contributed to his inception, NRO DCN 1/4/35.

1364/5, the refectorer contributed to his inception, NRO DCN 1/8/42.

1365/6, the master of the cellar gave 30s. to him, 'master of divinity', NRO DCN 1/1/49.

1366, 20 Sept., *prior studentium* at Oxford, Pantin, *BMC*, iii, 60.

1371/2, Thomas Pykis, precentor of Ely, q.v. (under Ely), pd 40s. to one of Easton's clerks, *pro labore suo*, CUL EDC 5/9/6, CUL Add. Ms 2957, fo 45.

Note: his later career, as ?secretary to Cardinal Langham and at Avignon, where he was promoted to the cardinalate and became actively involved in many of the ecclesiastical and theological controversies of the day, are summarised in *BRUO*, with a bibliography of his writings. He may never have returned to Norwich, but there are four late references to him on the Norwich accts:

(1) 1389/90, the master of the cellar pd 48s. 7d. for the transport of Easton's books from Flanders to Norwich, NRO DCN 1/1/65.

(2) 1389/90, the almoner pd 10s. *pro cariagio librorum domini cardinalis*, NRO DCN 1/6/23.

(3) 1389/90, the prior of Lynn also contributed towards the expenses *circa libros domini Ade de Eston*, 20s., NRO DCN 2/1/17. Why were these books being returned to Norwich at this

time? Was he possibly planning to return himself?

(4) 1393/4, Thomas de Walton, q.v., had a *ciphus* of oak which had formerly belonged to him.

1397, 15 or 20 Sept., d. at Rome, *BRUO*.

1407, [Oct./Nov.], the king ordered the six barrels of books, brought to London from Rome, to be delivered to Norwich, *CClR, 1405–1409*, 299.

In 1407/8, six barrels of his books reached Norwich, and the communar/pittancer pd 12s. carrying charges (NRO DCN 1/12/41); this was in accordance with Easton's will, but only five volumes have been traced:

(1) Avignon, Bibl. de la ville, 996, B. de Gordonio etc., (14th c.).
(2) Cambridge, Corpus Christi College Ms 74, Berengarius Biterrensis (early 14th c.); on fo 1, *per magistrum*—.
(3) *Ib.*, Ms 180, Richardus Armachanus (14th c.); on fo 88, *liber*—-.
(4) *Ib.*, Ms 347, Almanacs etc. (early 14th c.); on p. 163 an exposition of astrological terms *quos scripsit*—, with marginal notes ?possibly in his hand.
(5) Oxford, Bod. Ms 151, William de S. Amore (14th c); see Ker, 'Norwich Cathedral Mss', 260–261.

Oxford, Bod. Ms 692, fo 21 contains 'questiones disputata in vesperiis domini Ade' dated 1363/4 and Worcester Cathedral Ms F. 65 also includes his Questiones disputata et determinatio. Among the surviving works to be ascribed to him are the Defensorium ecclesiastice potestatis in which there is evidence of his knowledge of Hebrew and of a translation of the Old Testament from Hebrew to Latin by him. His other known writings and his stand on Wyclifism and on the election of Urban VI are set out by Leslie Macfarlane in the *Dictionnaire de Spiritualité ascétique et mystique, doctrine et histoire*, iv (Paris, 1960). See also Sharpe, *Latin Writers*.

There is also an undated letter to him in Cambridge Corpus Christi College Ms 358, fos 91–93 and another letter, dated only 31 Mar., that concerns one of his acts at the curia on behalf of the English Benedictines. He had been instrumental in procuring a bull from Urban VI which contained 'quasdam constituciones et ordinaciones statum, regimen et utilitatem nostri ordinis consernentes' for the reform of their order. Unfortunately, the bull had been stolen from the bearer on arrival in England 'in non modicum preiudicium et gravamen ordinis predicte ac contemptum sedis apostolice', Pantin *BMC*, iii, 81–82, where it is assigned a date c. 1384–1389. The original is in Reg. Walsingham no 15 (see under Ely priory registers).

Note:

(1) Dr Margaret Harvey has informed me that she has found no ref to his being Langham's secretary but he was described as his *socius*.
(2) In 'Norwich Cathedral Mss', p. 254 n. 4, Ker has assigned five more Norwich vols to Easton on the strength of a Norwich press mark peculiar to his books. One of these is David Kimchi's Book of Roots (now Cambridge, St John's College MS 218), a Hebrew text.

EASTON
see also Eston

John de ECLES
occ. 1311/12

1311/12, the refectorer pd 19s. 8d. to have a cover made for his *ciphus*, NRO DCN 1/8/21.

EDMUND Junior
occ. 1146 × 1172

1146 × 1172, troubled by a toothache and cured by touching St William's sepulchre, Jessopp and James, *St William*, 129.

I John EGLINGTON [Eglyngton
occ. 1417/18 d. 1444

1417/Jan 1418, communar/pittancer, NRO DCN 1/12/46.

1428/Feb. 1429, 1430/1, 1433/4, 1435/6, prior of Hoxne, NRO DCN 2/6/9; Windsor, St George's chapel, I.C. 10; NRO DCN 2/6/11; Windsor, St George's chapel, I.C. 12.

1430, 4 Oct., prior of Hoxne, apptd penitentiary there, Reg. Alnwick, fo 102^{v}.

1437/9, master of the cellar, NRO DCN 1/1/82–83.

1441, 6 Apr., refectorer, Reg. Brouns, fo 108.

1443, 7 Oct., confirmed as prior of Yarmouth *ib.*, fo 109.

1441, 6 Apr., witnessed an agreement between the bp and prior [John Heverlond, q.v], regarding their relationship, Reg. Brouns, fo 108.

1443, 9 Oct., apptd to hear confessions in the parish church of Yarmouth, *ib.*, fo 109.

1444, d. at Yarmouth, by 11 Oct., *ib.*, fo 111^{v}. His funeral expenses came to 29s. 8d., NRO DCN 2/4/8.

Note: there were two monks by this name who are not distinguished in the records; my assignment of offices is therefore not necessarily correct and may require rearrangement if more information comes to light; see next entry.

II John EGLINGTON [Eglyngton
occ. 1437/8 occ. 1446

1437/8, cellarer and precentor, NRO DCN 1/2/53; 1/9/52.

1440/3, refectorer, NRO DCN 1/8/78–80.

1442/3, gave 13s. 4d. to the chamberlain, NRO DCN 1/5/75; and bought four glazed windows from Nicholas de Randworth, q.v., NRO DCN 1/8/80.

1446, name occ. on a rough list of those assigned to celebrate weekday and chantry masses, Cambridge, Emm. Coll. Ms 142, fo 68.

Name on the flyleaf of priory Reg. III.

See note in preceding entry.

William ELGER
occ. 1453/4 d. 1473/4

1472, Mar./1474, precentor, NRO DCN 1/9/70–72.

1453/4, ill and the infirmarer pd 12d. for medicine, NRO DCN 1/10/23.

1464/5, ill and 12d. spent on medicine, NRO DCN 1/10/26.

1473/4, d., and the sacrist pd 8d. for candles at the funeral, NRO DCN 1/4/94.

I ELIAS [Helias
occ. [1121 × 1135]

[1121, 12 June × 1135], cellarer, witnessed the confirmation of a charter with Ciprianus, q.v., *Eng. Epis. Acta*, vi, no 49.

II ELIAS [Elyas, Helyas
occ. c. 1146 d. 1150

c. 1146–1150, prior: occ. 1146; d. 22 Oct. 1150, *Fasti*, ii, 59, *HRH*, 57.

[1146 × late spring 1147], served as witness in a grant to St Benet of Hulme, *Eng. Epis. Acta*, vi, no 94.

[c.1150, before 22 Oct.], witnessed an episcopal grant, *ib*, vi, no 79, also another grant, *ib.*, vi, no 97.

[1150], 22 Oct., obit occ. in the kalendar in Reg XI, fo 6ᵛ and BL Ms Harley 3950, fo 7ᵛ; see also Jessop and James, *St William*, 166. He was not keen on the promotion of the cult of St William, *ib.*, 127, 139–140.

Note: perhaps identical with the preceding entry.

ELIAS
see also under Hoxne

[George ELINGHAM
occ. 1509/10

1509/10, prior of Lynn acc. to Blomefield, *Norfolk*, viii, 497.]

I John de ELINGHAM
occ. 1277/8

1277/8, visited Taverham for *liberatio denariorum*, NRO DCN 60/35/8.

II John de ELINGHAM [Elyngham
occ. 1355/6 occ. 1362/3

1356/7, 1359/60, 1361/3, master of the cellar, NRO DCN 1/1/45–48.

1355/6, gave 66s. 8d. to the communar [?for the construction of the cloister], NRO DCN 1/12/29.

1355/6, visited Catton, NRO DCN 60/4/51.

III John ELINGHAM [Elyngham
occ. 1418 d. 1454/5

1418, Jan. to Sept., 1419/22, communar/pittancer, NRO DCN 1/12/46–49.

1422/1 Nov. 1424, chamberlain, NRO DCN 1/5/48–50; (the NRO list dates these three accts one yr behind because of inconsistencies in dating which occur in this period).

1424, 18 Oct./1425, 1426/7, cellarer, NRO DCN 1/2/44–45.

1433/5, 1436/7, master of St Paul's hospital, NRO DCN 2/5/2–4.

1436/7, 1438/40, sacrist, NRO DCN 1/4/75–78.

1440, Mar./1450, 1451/2, prior of St Leonard's, NRO DCN 2/3/54–65.

1418, 9 Apr., delivered three letters to the bp at Thorpe, Reg. Wakering, fo 32, 32ᵛ; on 20 Apr., the prior requested the bp to rec. four *clerici* and bless them before they were clothed in the monastic habit by Elingham, *ib.*, fo 32ᵛ.

1420/1, ill and charged his office 2s. for doctors and medicine, NRO DCN 1/12/48; he also contribued to the cloister fund, *ib*.

1421/2, ill and 9d. was spent by the infirmarer on medicine, NRO DCN 1/10/14.

1425, 8 Apr., one of three monks nominated by the prior and chapter for the office of *visitator*, for excepted jurisdiction *sed. vac.* Norwich, *Reg. abp Chichele*, iii, 468.

1430, 23 Sept., apptd pentientiary in the cathedral, Reg. Alnwick, fo 101ᵛ.

1431/2, went to London with the prior, NRO DCN 1/1/80, and the sacrist contributed to his expenses, NRO DCN 1/4/70, as did the cellarer, hostiller, infirmarer and refectorer; NRO DCN 1/2/48; 1/7/73; 1/10/19; 1/8/74; the precentor also contributed *pro causa monasterii*, 1/9/46; and see William Worstede.

1436/7, gave a gift of 6s. 8d. to the chamberlain, NRO DCN 1/5/66.

1441, 6 Apr., witnessed an agreement between the bp and prior [John Heverload, q.v], regarding their relationship, Reg. Brouns, fo 108.

1449/50, gave 3s. 4d. to the precentor because of his financial difficulties, NRO DCN 1/9/63.

1451/2, gave 6s. 8d. to the hostiller for lead to repair a *fontis* (prob. a well), NRO DCN 1/7/89.

1454/5, ill and 4s. spent; [?after a stay in the infirmary], he gave 13s. 4d. towards the repair of the *domus necessariorum* there, NRO DCN 1/10/24.

1454/5, d., and the chamberlain recd 'alms' of 36s. 10d., NRO DCN 1/5/87.

1455/6, the chamberlain records receipt of 40s. left by Elingham towards repairs at the manor of Arminghall, NRO DCN 1/5/88.

1469/70, there is ref. to his gift of a piece of silver plate to the cellarer's office, NRO DCN 1/2/68.

Name in Oxford, Bod. Ms 787, Bernardus de Parantinis (15th c); *ex dono*—-; and see John Marton.

The 1424 inventory of St Leonard's records his gift of a silver gilt paxborde and a cover for the cup of St Leonard, Bensly, 'St Leonard's', 198–199; 204–205.

Ralph de ELINGHAM [Elyngham
occ. 1278/9 occ. [1306/7]

1278/80, master of the cellar [*custos celarii*], NRO DCN 1/1/4–5.
1282/5, cellarer, NRO DCN 1/2/1.
1291/2, prior [*custos*] of Yarmouth, *Comm. Rolls*, 61.
[1306/7], sacrist *N. Cath. Charters*, ii, no 335.
1278/9, visited Sedgeford with the steward, NRO DCN 60/33/6.
1279/80, spent over a month in London and appeared before the king with regard to the collection of a fifteenth; his expenses were over £5, NRO DCN 1/1/5.
1291/2, contributed £1 to the communar's building operations, *Comm. Rolls*, 61.
1298/9, went with Thomas de Plumsted to ?Elurent [*sic*] on business for the communar. *Comm. Rolls*, 74.
1303/4, visited Henley for *liberatio denariorum*, NRO DCN 60/16/3.
[1306/7], as sacrist arranged a lease, *N. Cath. Charters*, ii, no 335.

Name in Aberystwyth, National Library of Wales, Ms 21878 E, a Bible, (late 13th c.), *MLGB* suppl.

While cellarer he compiled priory Reg. V., see *N. Cath. Charters*, i, xxxiii.

Robert de ELINGHAM [Elyngham
occ. 1338/40

1338/40, refectorer, Oxford, Bod. Ms Rolls, Norfolk, no 48, which is incorrectly listed in Turner and Coxe, *Charters and Rolls*, under Clyngham.

Simon de ELINGHAM [Elyngham
occ. 1363/4 d. 1396/7

1368, Feb./1370, hostiller, NRO DCN 1/7/24–27.
1387/8, prior of Aldeby, NRO DCN 1/12/33.
1363/4, student [at Oxford] with pension contribution from the communar, NRO DCN 1/12/30.
1387/8, gave 3s. 4d. to the cloister work, NRO DCN 1/12/33.
1396/7, d., and the chamberlain recd 'alms', NRO DCN 1/5/28.

H. de ELMHAM
occ. and d. 1317/18

[?1317], prob. prior of Hoxne, as suggested by a letter of the prior of Norwich to a member of a confraternity there, Reg. IX, fo 9ᵛ.
1317/18, d., and the chamberlain pd the brief bearer, NRO DCN 1/5/5.

I John ELMHAM
occ. 1427/8 d. 1482/3

1435/6, gardener, NRO DCN 1/11/18.
1438/9, prior of Hoxne, NRO DCN 2/6/12.
1445/6, communar/pittancer, NRO DCN 1/12/58.
1445/8, hostiller, NRO DCN 1/7/81.
1427/8, ill and 3s. were spent by the infirmarer on medicine, NRO DCN 1/10/15.
1446/8, name occ. on a rough list of those assigned to celebrate weekday and chantry masses, Cambridge, Emm. Coll. Ms 142, fo 68; also on a similar list for Sunday masses on the following dates: 1446, 18 Oct; 1447, 19 Feb., 18 June, 8 Oct.; 1448, 28 Jan., 12 May, 8 Sept., *ib.*, fo 77ᵛ. Name also on another list (prob. 1446/7) for masses for the Totyngton, Wakering and Erpingham chantries, *ib.*
1482/3, d., and the chamberlain recd 'alms' of 6s. 8d., NRO DCN 1/5/112.

II John ELMHAM [Elmeham
occ. 1532

1532, 3 June, present at the visitation of bp Nikke and complained of the fifth prior's favouritism, and of the subsacrist's tardiness in ringing the bell for matins. Jessopp, *Visit.*, 268.

I Simon de ELMHAM [Helmham
occ. 1235 occ. 1257

1235–1257, prior: occ. 4 Sept. 1235; d. 8 June 1257, *Fasti*, ii, 60.
Note: a Sedgeford acct of 1255/6 is headed *Anno Simonis xxij*, NRO DCN 60/33/1.
1236, before 9 Nov. el. as bp, but despite an appeal to the pope the el. was quashed by 17 Jan. 1239, see *Fasti*, ii, 57.
[1257], obit occ. on 8 June, in BL Ms Harley 3950, fo 5ᵛ.

Name in CUL Ms Ff.5.28, J. Beleth. Summa etc. (13th c.); on front flyleaf—*emit librum istum*. See Ker, 'Norwich Cathedral Mss', 256; but see also the entry below.

In the words of Matthew Paris he was *vir magnae sanctitatis et eminentis literaturae*, *Chron. Majora*, v, 643.

A large number of charters survive from his priorate and are included in *N. Cath. Charters*, i, and ii, *passim*.

II Simon de ELMHAM [Helmham
occ. 1295/6

1295/6, recd a *capa* from the refectorer, NRO DCN 1/8/7.

Note: the ms listed under Simon de Elmham I could have belonged to this monk.

W. de ELMHAM
occ. 1292/4

1292/4, refectorer, NRO DCN 1/8/6.

ELRICUS [H'ercicus
d. 1172

1172, prior: he d. this year, *Fasti*, ii, 59, *HRH*, 58; see Ranulph and John II.

[1172], 11 June, obit occ. in BL Ms Harley 3950, fo 5v, and in the kalendar in Reg XI, fo 4v.

Thomas BAA DE ELSYNG [Elsyngge
occ. 1364/5 d. 1395/6

1364/5, 1366/7, hostiller, NRO DCN 1/7/22,23.
1370/2, possibly precentor, NRO DCN 1/9/11,12.
1373/4, 1374, Apr./1375, Nov. master of the cellar, NRO DCN 60/35/42; 1/1/52–54.
1378, Jan./July, hostiller, NRO DCN 1/7/35.
1381/2, 1385/6, 1387/Mar. 1388, communar/pittancer, NRO DCN 1/12/31–33.
1385/6, 1389/91, 1393/4, 1395/1396, Nov., sacrist, NRO DCN 1/4/37–41.

1387/8, gave 8s. 8d. to the cloister work, NRO DCN 1/12/33; ill, this yr and charged the communar's office 5s. for medicine; *ib*.
1393/4, ill and charged the sacrist's office 5s. 8d. for medicine, NRO DCN 1/4/40.
1393/4, the refectorer referred in his inventory to a *ciphus* of wood given by him, NRO DCN 1/8/48.
1395/6, d., and the chamberlain recd 'alms', NRO DCN 1/5/27.

Name in CUL Ms Kk. 3.25, Gregorius, Homilie in Evangelia (14th c.); on flyleaf liber—. See Ker, 'Norwich Cathedral Mss', 260.

ELY
see Elias

Adam ELYE [Elys
occ. 1422/3 d. 1436/7

1422/3, pd the refectorer for a *ciphus*, 6s. 8d., NRO DCN 1/8/70.

1427, 4 Jan., one of seven whose prof. the bp solemnized in chapter, after the prior's request in a letter of 31 Dec. 1426, Reg. Alnwick, fo 97.

1436/7, d., and the chamberlain recd 'alms' of 21s. 3d., NRO DCN 1/5/66.

Note: there is an unusually long gap here between adm. and prof.; perhaps he entered at an exceptionally early age. Was he a boy in the almonry school?

John de ELY [Elys
occ. 1405/6 d. 1419/20

1405/6, hostiller, NRO DCN 1/7/54.
1407, Aug./1408, Jan., prior of Lynn, NRO DCN 2/1/21; Blomefield, *Norfolk*, viii, 495, says that he was prior in 1403.
1411, Sept./Nov; 1412, Sept./1414, Oct., prior of St Leonard's, NRO DCN 2/3/28–30.
1400 × 1418, former cellarer, NRO DCN 1/2/100.

1413/14, gave a gift of 100s. *ex gratia* to the cellarer, NRO DCN 1/2/36.
1419/20 d., and the chamberlain recd 'alms', NRO DCN 1/5/47.
1449/50, Geoffrey Sall, q.v., bought his *ciphus* from the refectorer, NRO DCN 1/8/87.

Robert de ELY [Eli
occ. 1317/18 occ. 1337/8

1323/5, precentor, NRO DCN 1/9/4, Oxford, Bod. Ms Rolls, Norfolk, no 55.
1333, June/1337, cellarer, NRO DCN 1/2/101.

1317/18, [student] with 8s. contribution for him and John de Clipesby, q.v., from the master of the cellar, NRO DCN 1/1/26.
1318/19, student at Oxford with William de Kenighale, q.v., and recd a contribution from the refectorer, NRO DCN 1/8/24.
1320/1, student, and with John de Mari and John de Clipesby, q.v., recd small sums from the hostiller, NRO DCN 1/7/1.

[?1320], the prior referred in a letter to the bp that he could not preach as he had not been well, Reg. IX, fo 29.
1321/2, recd a gift of 3s. from the master of the cellar, NRO DCN 1/1/28.
[1324/5], the bp wrote to the prior concerning him, whose services in some negotiations he requested, Reg. IX, fo 55.
1325, 8 July, proctor, sent to the king for licence to el. a bp, Reg. IX, fo 42; 13 July, recd royal licence, *CPR (1324–1327)*, 150.
1334, 3 Apr., one of two proctors who obtained royal licence to el. a bp, *CPR (1334–1338)*, 244; see John de Hengham I.
1336, 4 Mar., one of three proctors sent to parliament by both the prior and the monks, Reg. X, fo 7v.
1337/8, visited Martham for *liberatio denariorum*, NRO DCN 60/23/24.

I William de ELY
occ. 1346/8

1346/7, ill and 14d. was spent by the infirmarer on medicine, NRO DCN 1/10/5.
1347/8, ill and 9d. spent on medicine, NRO DCN 1/10/6.

II William ELY [Elye
occ. 1514 occ. 1520

1514, 27 Apr., present at the visitation of bp Nikke and complained of non payment of the

accustomed pensions. Jessopp *Visit.*, 73 (where the name is incorrectly given as Eby).
1520, 3 Sept., present at the visitation of bp Nikke and stated that reform was in progress, but the sick required more care, *ib.*, 193.

ELYNGHAM
see Elingham

Richard ELYNGTON
occ. before 1433/4
1433/4, described as formerly sacrist, NRO DCN 1/4/73.
Note: see Richard de Helyngton who is prob. this monk.

Adam de ERPINGHAM
occ. 1345/6
1345, ill and required medicine, NRO DCN 1/10/2.
1345/6, ill and 2s. 2d. were spent by the infirmarer on medicine, NRO DCN 1/10/4.
Note: almost a contemporary of Sir Thomas Erpingham, but there is no evidence of any family relationship.

John ESTON
occ. 1418 occ. 1469/70
1418, 20 Apr., one of four *clerici* whom the prior requested the bp to rec. and bless as they had been examined and adm. by the chapter and were about to be clothed, Reg. Wakering fo 32v.
1431/3, 1434/7, hostiller, NRO DCN 1/7/73–77.
1441/2, prior of Hoxne, Windsor, St George's chapel, I.C. 14; apptd 1 Nov. 1441, Reg. Brouns, fo 108.
1443/4, 1445/6, 1447/9, prior of Hoxne, NRO DCN 2/6/13 and Windsor, St George's chapel, I.C. 15; NRO DCN 2/6/14; 2/6/15,16.
1451/2, 1454/5, 1455/6, prior of Hoxne, Windsor, St George's chapel, I.C. 16; NRO DCN 2/6/18; Windsor, St George's chapel, I.C. 17. See Robert Gatele.
1463/6, 1467/8, 1469/70, prior of Hoxne, Windsor, St George's chapel, I.C. 20; NRO DCN 2/6/19; Windsor, St George's chapel, I.C. 21,22; NRO DCN 2/6/20.
Note: there are several periods between 1453 and 1460 when other monks served as priors of Hoxne; see, for example, William Bokenham.
1441, 21 Nov., licensed by the bp to hear confessions in the chapel at Hoxne, Reg. Brouns, fo 108.
1446, name occ. on a rough list of those assigned to celebrate weekday and chantry masses, Cambridge, Emm. Coll. Ms 142, fo 68; also on a similar list (prob. 1446/7) for the Totyngton, Wakering and Erpingham chantries, *ib.*, fo 77v.

Roger de ESTON*
occ. 1323 occ. [1348/9]
1339/40, 1342/3, sacrist, NRO DCN 1/4/32,34.
1323, student at Oxford with John de Mari, q.v., and recd pension contribution from the refectorer, NRO DCN 1/8/27.
1324/5, the communar pd travelling expenses for de Mari and Eston returning from Oxford, *Comm. Rolls*, 98.
1325, 10 July, the prior recalled Eston and de Mari from Oxford on the d. of the bp [for an el.], Reg. IX, fo 61v.
1326/7, the communar pd travelling expenses to Oxford, *Comm. Rolls*, 102.
1329, travelled with the sacrist, Richard de Hecham, q.v., to Avignon to further their cause vs the abp [Reynolds]. Details of the journey are given and expenses for their travel and eleven week stay at the papal court, NRO DCN 1/4/24.
1335/6, gave 5s. to the master of the cellar *ad ostium claustri* NRO DCN 1/1/38.
1344, 25 Aug., comm. by the vicar general to install prior Simon Bozoun, which he did on 27 Aug., Reg. Bateman, fo 46.
1348/9, Roger de Sacristaria ill; since there are no surviving accts between 1342/3 and 1363/4 it is reasonable to suggest that this may refer to Eston, NRO DCN 1/10/7; but see Roger de Jernemuth.

* *BRUO* has two entries for this monk, the second one being under de Oxonia; this is a misreading of the communar's acct of 1324/5 on which John de Mari and Roger [returned] *de Oxonia*.

ESTON
see also Easton

EUSTACE
occ. [1121 × 1143]
[1121 × 1143], with William de Turba, q.v., witness to an episcopal charter, *Eng. Epis. Acta*, vi, no 36.
n.d., 20 July, obit occ. in the kalendar in Reg. XI, fo 5.
Note: it is possible that the obit refers to another monk of the same name.

I EVERARD
n.d.
n.d., 14 Mar., obit occ. in the kalendar in Reg. XI, fo 3.

II EVERARD
occ. 1288
1288, 27 July, a letter was addressed to him (?precentor) and to the prior and convent from the prior of Canterbury concerning Hugh II, q.v., CUL Ms Ee.5.31, fo 28v.

EVERARDUS
see II Gerard

EWDO
n.d.

n.d., 19 Mar., pr. and monk whose name occ. in the Canterbury obit lists, BL Ms Arundel 68, fo 21, and Lambeth Ms 20, fo 174.

Richard de EYE
occ. 1421/2 d. 1449/50

1421/6; 1430, 23 Sept., prior of Aldeby, NRO DCN 2/2/7–11; Reg. Alnwick, fo 102v.
1435/7, precentor, NRO DCN 1/9/50–51.
1430, 23 Sept., apptd penitentiary at Aldeby, Reg. Alnwick, fo 102v.
1446, name occ. on a rough list of those assigned to celebrate weekday and chantry masses, Cambridge, Emm. Coll. Ms 142, fo 68; also on other fragmentary lists (prob. of similar date) concerning the *magna missa*, *parva missa* and the Bateman, Tye and Wakering chantries, *ib.*, fo 77v.
1449/50, d., and the chamberlain recd 'alms' of 12s. 4d., NRO DCN 1/5/82.

John FAKENHAM
d. 1465/6

1465/6, d., and the sacrist pd for funeral tapers, NRO DCN 1/4/90.

Thomas de FAKENHAM
occ. 1331/2

1331/2, gave the refectorer 10s. for a *ciphus*, NRO DCN 1/8/30; (one of three monks who purchased *ciphi* this year, probably soon after adm.; see also Robert Sturmyn).

FELIX
n.d.

n.d. 20 July, obit occ. in the kalendar in Reg. XI, fo 5.

Note: several of bp Losinga's letters were addressed to a Felix who was prob. a monk; see Anstruther, *Epist. Losinga*, nos 23, 43, ?46.

John FELMYNGHAM
occ. 1492 occ. 1499

1492, 5/8 Oct., 33rd in order at the visitation of bp Goldwell, Jessopp, *Visit.*, 8.
1499, 6 Apr., 25th on the visitation certificate, *Reg. abp Morton*, iii, no 258.

Thomas de FELTHORP
occ. 1358 occ. ?1393/4

1358, 1 Jan., one of three monks licensed to hear confesssions of religious and laity who came to the cathedral church, Reg. Percy, fo 23v.
1393/4, an inventory of some of the items lodged in the infirmary, for which the refectorer was responsible, includes one *pec[ia]* with a lid *ex dono*—, NRO DCN 1/8/48.

Simon FELTWELL [Feltwelle
occ. 1438/9 occ. 1460/1

1438/9, purchased a *ciphus* for 13s. 4d. from the refectorer, prob. soon after adm., NRO DCN 1/8/77.
1456/7, hostiller, NRO DCN 1/7/93.
1469/70, prob. former cellarer, because of the ref. to a debt owed by him, NRO DCN 1/2/68.
1440/1, ill and the infirmarer spent 4d. on medicine, NRO DCN 1/10/22 (as Simon only).
1448/9, a monk named Feltwell appears on a rough list of those assigned to celebrate Sunday masses on the following dates: 1448, 21 Jan., 5 May, 25 Aug.; 1449, 12 Jan., Cambridge, Emm. Coll. Ms 142, fo 68.
1456/7, made a gift of 3s. 4d. to the precentor, NRO DCN 1/9/67.
1460/1, sold one 'barwewhel' to the master of the cellar for 5d., NRO DCN 1/1/90.

William FELTWELL
occ. 1471/2

1471, June/Sept., gardener, NRO DCN 1/11/21.
1471/2, d., and the sacrist pd for funeral tapers, NRO DCN 1/4/93.
Note: see the preceding entry under 1448/9.

Stephen FEROUR
occ. 1425/6

1425/6, gave 5d. to the chamberlain towards the cost of a new barn at Lakenham, NRO DCN 1/5/53.

Richard de FERRERES [Ferrariis, Ferreris
occ. ?1146 d. 1158

c. 1150–1158 prior: el. before 25 Dec. 1150; d. 1158, *Fasti*, ii, 59, *HRH*, 57.
n.d., prob. subprior previously, Jessopp and James, *St William*, 133.
[1146 × 1150, 25 Dec.,] witness to charters concerning St Benet of Hulme, *Eng. Epis. Acta*, vi, nos 95, 96.
[c. 1150, before 22 Oct,] with Elias II, prior, q.v., witness to a charter, *ib.*, no 79.
1154, 19 Dec. × 1158, 16 May, prior and witness to charters, *ib.*, nos 72, 73.
Note: another charter relating to his priorate occ. in *N. Cath. Charters*, ii, no 84.
n.d., 16 May, obit occ. in BL Ms Harley 3950, fo 5.

As prior he was an ardent supporter of the cult of St William, Jessopp and James, *St William*, xii.

Note: Jessopp and James state that he was a grandson of the Norman baron Hermer de

Ferrariis who held many estates in Norfolk and that his elder brother, also Hermer, was a benefactor of the priory during his priorate, *St William*, 142 n. His uncle and aunt, Alan and Muriel de Setchy, are also referred to in *St William*, 133. His nephew, also Hermer, of Wormegay, gave 20s. in rent to the priory in 1158 after his death for the celebration of his, the prior's anniversary, *N. Cath. Charters*, ii, nos 492, 493.

[?M.] Ralph de FILBY [Fylby

occ. 1364 occ. 1370

1364/5, refectorer, NRO DCN 1/8/42.

1370, 3 Apr./11 Aug., master of St Paul's hospital, NRO DCN 45/31/18,19; Blomefield states that he was master in 1398, *Norfolk*, iii, 432.

1361/2, a M. Ralph Fylb', monk, stayed one night at Hindolveston, NRO DCN 60/18/38.

William FODE [Foode

occ. 1440/1 d. by 25 Mar. 1484

1454/6, communar/pittancer, NRO DCN 1/12/65, 66.

1464/5, a reference on the infirmarer's acct suggests that he had previously been infirmarer, NRO DCN 1/10/26.

1464/6, 1468/70, 1471/2, 1473/5, 1477/8, 1481/2, 1483/4, Mar., sacrist, NRO DCN 1/4/89–98.

1440/1, ill, prob. twice, and the infirmarer spent 20d., and 15d. on medicine, NRO DCN 1/10/22.

1446, name occ. on a rough list of those assigned to celebrate weekday and chantry masses. Cambridge, Emm. Coll. Ms 142, fo 68; also on a similar list for Sunday masses on the following dates: 1446, 20 Nov.; 1447, 12 Mar., 2 July, 22 Oct; 1448, 11 Feb., 16 June, 22 Sept., 24 Nov. Name on another list (prob. also 1446/7) for masses in the Bateman, Totyngton, Wakering, Tye and Erpingham chantries, *ib.*, fo 77ᵛ.

1456/7, 1457/8, 1461/2, recd 20s. from the sacrist *in regardo* on each of these accts, and in 1459/60 he recd 13s. 4d., NRO DCN 1/4/85–88 (prob. because of the item immediately below).

1457/8, responsible for the accts of the Wakering and Erpingham chantries, NRO DCN 4/7.

1469, 7 Sept., apptd confessor to the nuns at Carrow, Reg. Lyhart, fo 277ᵛ.

1473, gave 67s. 3d. to St Leonard's cell, NRO DCN 2/3/82.

1477, 4 Nov., conveyed a letter from the prior and convent to the bp, requesting him to receive two *clerici* they had recently adm., Reg. Goldwell, fo 9.

1477/8, went to the bp in London with the chapter seal *pro monachand'* John Stanfelde, Thomas Cantyrbery and Thomas More, q.v., NRO DCN 1/12/70.

1478/9, recd payment from the cellarer for redeeming a black *ciphus*, NRO DCN 1/2/74, 75.

1481/2, sent to London for 'negotiations' on behalf of the chapter, NRO DCN 1/12/72.

1484, before 25 Mar., d. while sacrist, and the office accounted for 8d. for wax tapers for his funeral. NRO DCN 1/4/98; the chamberlain recd 'alms', NRO DCN 1/5/114; the communar/pittancer sent letters to the cells announcing his d., NRO DCN 1/12/73.

Simon FOLCARD [Folkarde

occ. 1472/3 d. ?1501

1472/3, 1474/5, 1477/8, 1478/80, prior of Hoxne, Windsor, St George's chapel, I.C. 23; NRO DCN 2/6/22, NRO DCN 2/6/23 and Windsor, St George's chapel, I.C. 24–26.

1480/2, precentor, NRO DCN 1/9/78, 79.

1483/4, master of the cellar, NRO DCN 1/1/94.

1487/90, 1491/2, prior of St Leonard's, NRO DCN 2/3/93–96.

1493, 18 Jan., apptd prior of Yarmouth, Reg. Goldwell, fo 163ᵛ.

1495/7, prior of Yarmouth, Windsor, St George's chapel, XV.55.77 and 78.

1500, Sept., prior of Lynn, Canterbury Reg. R, fo 46.

1492, 5/8 Oct., 7th in order at the visitation of bp Goldwell, Jessopp, *Visit.*, 8.

1499, 6 Apr., 6th on the visitation certificate, *Reg. abp Morton*, iii, no 258.

1500, 1 Oct., apptd official [*visitator*] by the prior of Canterbury for excepted jurisdiction, *sed. vac.* Norwich and Canterbury, after nomination by the prior and chapter of Norwich, Canterbury Reg. R, fo 46 (and Churchill, *Cant. Admin.*, 2, 253 as Folkland).

1501, d. according to Blomefield, *Norfolk*, iv, 18, and was buried in the south transept of the cathedral.

In the 1430s a John Folcard pd rent to the hostiller for a tenement in St Cuthbert's parish in the city of Norwich, NRO DCN 1/7/73; in [1464] prob. the same John, alderman of Norwich, d., and his will is entered in the consistory court records in the Guildhall, Norwich City Records, NCC Brosyard, vol. 350.

John FOLSHAM, B.Th.

occ. 1420/1 d. 1457

1438/40, hostiller, NRO DCN 1/7/78.

1444, 11 Oct., the prior requested the bp to confirm his apptment as prior of Yarmouth, Reg. Brouns, fo 111ᵛ.

1444/7, 1450/1, 1452/3, prior of Yarmouth, NRO DCN 2/4/9–13.

1456/7, Nov. to July, prior of St Leonard's, NRO DCN 2/3/68.

1426/7, student [prob. at Oxford] with pension contribution from the almoner, NRO DCN 1/6/57, 58.

1427/9, student, with contributions from the almoner and chamberlain, NRO DCN 1/6/59; 1/5/54, 55.

1429/30, student, with contributions from the almoner, infirmarer and master of the cellar, NRO DCN 1/6/59; 1/10/17; 1/1/79.

1431/2, student, with contributions from the chamberlain and master of the cellar, NRO DCN 1/5/58; 1/1/80.

1432/3, student, with contributions from the chamberlain and infirmarer, NRO DCN 1/5/59; 1/10/20.

1433/4, student, with contributions from the cellarer and chamberlain, NRO DCN 1/2/50; 1/5/60, 61.

1434/5, student, with contributions from the cellarer, chamberlain and infirmarer, NRO DCN 1/2/51; 1/5/62/63; 1/10/21.

1435/6, student, with contribution from the chamberlain, NRO DCN 1/5/64, 65.

1436/7, student, with contributions from the cellarer, chamberlain and the priors of Lynn and St Leonard's, NRO DCN 1/2/52; 1/5/66, 67; 2/1/32; 2/3/51.

1437/8, student, with contributions from the almoner, cellarer, hostiller, master of the cellar, precentor, refectorer and the priors of Aldeby and St Leonard's, NRO DCN 1/6/63; 1/2/53; 1/7/78; 1/1/82; 1/9/52; 1/8/77; 2/2/12; 2/3/52. The prior of Aldeby noted that his contribution was towards the expenses *pro introitu*, and the cellarer *pro gradu baculariato*. There is a ref. to the *introitus* of a 'J.F.' in Cambridge, Emm. Coll. Ms 142, fo 123[v] followed by *questiones*. However, this may be John de Fornsete. q.v.

1438/9, student, with contributions from the hostiller and prior of St Leonard's, NRO DCN 1/7/78; 2/3/53.

1439/40, student, with contributions from the chamberlain and hostiller, NRO DCN 1/5/71; 1/7/78.

Note: there is a brief entry in *BRUO*.

1420/1, purchased a *ciphus* from the refectorer for 13s. 4d., prob. soon after adm., NRO DCN 1/8/68.

1441, 1 Nov., licensed by the bp to hear confessions in city and diocese, and addressed as S.T.B., Reg. Brouns, fo 108[v].

1444, 13 Oct., recd a comm. from the bp to hear confessions at Yarmouth, Reg. Brouns, fo 112.

1445, Dec., one of three monks nominated by the prior and chapter for the office of *visitator* for excepted jurisdiction, *sed. vac.* Norwich. Reg. abp. Stafford, fo 57.

c. 1446/7, name occ. on a rough list of those assigned to celebrate masses in the Bateman, Totyngton, Wakering and Erpingham chantries, Cambridge, Emm. Coll. Ms 142, fo 77[v].

1457, July to Sept., ill at St Leonard's and a servant was pd. 3s. to care for him, NRO DCN 2/3/68.

1457, d., and the the chamberlain recd 'alms' of 8s. 10d., NRO DCN 1/5/89.

Name in CUL Ms Ii.3.22 Sermones etc. (15th c.), *ex dono*—on fo 7; a collection of sermons of well known preachers.

There is also a 15th c. sermon collection in Worcester Cathedral Library, Ms F.10, in which the name 'Folsam' occ. on fos 54 and 57[v]; see under John de Fordham in the Worcester section.

Richard de FOLSHAM

occ. 1398 occ. 1407

1398/1407, prior of Lynn, NRO DCN 2/1/21.

1399, 18 Mar., present in the Star Chamber before abp Walden as one of the proctors for the chapter in the dispute with bp Despenser, NRO DCN 42/1/21; two days later he was present in the church of St James, Garlickhithe, London, when the prior and convent made a formal protest against the abp's decree, 42/1/22.

1406, 29 Aug., apptd official, [*visitator*] for excepted jurisdiction by the abp after nomination by the prior and chapter, *sed. vac.* Norwich, Churchill, *Cant. Admin.*, ii, 252.

Blomefield states that he was 'a great favourite of Thomas Arundel, Archbishop . . . [and] was much in the pope's court at Rome, and very conversant with John XXIII to whom he wrote many epistles', *Norfolk*, iii, 616.

FOODE

see Fode

Gerard de FORDHAM [Fordam

occ. 1272/4

1272/3, sacrist, NRO DCN 60/15/2.

1272/3, cellarer, apptd in Aug. 1272, NRO DCN 1/1/2; he followed Walter de Walpole, q.v.

1273/4, cellarer, NRO DCN 60/20/5.

1272/3, visited Gnatingdon and Hindringham with other monks for *liberatio denariorum*, NRO DCN 60/14/4; 60/20/4; also visited Sedgeford for the same purpose, 60/33/4; stopped at Hindolveston, 60/18/5, and visited Hemsby with the steward, NRO DCN 60/15/2.

1273/4, visited Hindringham, NRO DCN 60/20/5.

c. 1274, sent as proctor to Rome, Dugdale, *Monasticon*, iv, 4 (as Gervase); see Richard de Brampton. But see Adam de Hilleye.

John de FORNSETE D.Th. [Fornecete, Fornesete, Fornsett, Forneshete

occ. 1415 occ. 1454/5

1415, 10 June, one of four whom the prior requested the bp to rec. *ad osculum et benedic-*

tionem as he had been adm. by the prior and chapter, Reg. Courtenay, fo 103v.
1418, 8 Apr., one of four whose prof. the prior requested the bp to rec.; the bp replied by sending a comm. to the prior, authorizing him to do so, Reg. Wakering, fo 32v.
Note: this is an unusually long period of probation, perhaps because they had entered at an early age.

1436/43, 1444/52, prior of Lynn. NRO DCN 2/1/32–49.
1454/5, infirmarer, NRO DCN 1/10/24.

1424/5, student [at Oxford] with pension contribution from the chamberlain, NRO DCN 1/5/51, 52.
1425/6, student, with contributions from the almoner and chamberlain, NRO DCN 1/6/55, 56; 1/5/53.
1426/7, student, with contribution from the almoner, NRO DCN 1/6/57, 58.
1427/9, student, with contributions from the almoner and infirmarer NRO DCN 1/6/59; 1/10/15, 16; and in 1428/9, also from the chamberlain, 1/5/55.
1429/31, student, with contribution from the infirmarer, NRO DCN 1/10/17, 18.
1431/2, student, with contributions from the cellarer, chamberlain, infirmarer, master of the cellar and the prior of Lynn, NRO DCN 1/2/48; 1/5/58; 1/10/19; 1/1/80; 2/1/27. The infirmarer gave an additional sum *pro bachilariatu*; and the cellarer's account and that of Lynn recorded payment *pro oppositione sua in teologia*. See John Folsham.
1434/5, student, with contributions from the chamberlain and infirmarer, NRO DCN 1/5/62, 63; 1/10/21.
1435/6, student, with contribution from the chamberlain, NRO DCN 1/5/64.
1445, 14 Dec., addressed as S.T.P. (i.e., D.Th.), Churchill, *Cant. Admin.*, ii, 253; and see *BRUO*.

1428/9, 1429/30, ill, and the infirmarer spent 8d. on medicine on each occasion, NRO DCN 1/10/16, 17.
1431/2, ill, and 3s. 6d. were spent on medicine, NRO DCN 1/10/18.
1431/2, gave 6s. 3d. to the chamberlain's office, NRO DCN 1/5/58.
1433/5, accompanied the prior to the Council of Basel, *Memorials Bury*, iii, 254–257; and see under William Worstede.
1440/1, ill at Lynn and £3 were pd for medicine, NRO DCN 2/1/36.
1445, 14 Dec., apptd official [*visitator*] by the abp for excepted jurisdiction, *sed vac.* Norwich, after nomination by the prior and chapter, Churchill. *Cant. Admin.*, ii, 253.
c. 1445, 14 Dec., abp Stafford comm. him and the prior *sed. vac.* to make a visitation of the cathedral priory, Reg. abp Stafford, fo 57v.

Two of his letters are extant:

(1) a letter from Fornsete to Abbot Curteys of Bury St Edmunds, printed in *Memorials Bury*, iii, 254–257 (from BL Add. Ms 7096, fo 161v). This furnishes a firsthand acct of proceedings at the Council of Basel after the arrival of the Abbot of Cîteaux in 1435.
(2) a letter addressed to Fornsete as prior of Lynn, on the verso of which there is a list of papal privileges granted to the friars; this is in Cambridge, Emm. Coll. Ms 142, fo 69, the volume which is inscribed with the name of John Stowe I, q.v.

He was a friend of the Paston family, Davis, *Paston Letters*, no 962.

FOULDON
see Fuldon

Robert FRAMYNGHAM [Frammyngham
occ. 1520 occ. 1534

1520, 3 Sept., present at the visitation of bp Nikke and stated that *omnia bene*, Jessopp, *Visit.*, 193.
1526, 7 June, residing at Yarmouth but present at the visitation of bp Nikke and repeated *omnia bene*, *ib.*, 197.
1534, 28 July, subscribed to the Act of Supremacy, *DK 7th Report*, Appndx 2, 295.

Roger FRAMYNGHAM, D.Th.
occ. 1453/4 occ. 1499

1455/6, a ref. to his ordination, NRO DCN 1/12/66.

1470/1, prior of Hoxne, NRO DCN 2/6/21.
1471/2, almoner, NRO DCN 1/6/84.
1483, 25 Mar./1485, Sept., sacrist, NRO DCN 1/4/98,99.
1492, 5/8 Oct., 1494/5, subprior, Jessopp, *Visit.*, 2; NRO DCN 1/4/107.

[c. 1446], began his university studies at Cambridge; see below.
1458/9, student, with pension contributions from the almoner, cellarer, hostiller, refectorer and prior of St Leonard's, NRO DCN 1/6/73; 1/2/64; 1/7/95; 1/8/92; 2/3/70.
1459, Apr., in his thirteenth yr of study, he now recd grace to oppose in theology, *CU Grace Book A*, 15.
1459/60, student, with contributions from the almoner, chamberlain, refectorer, sacrist and prior of St Leonard's, NRO DCN 1/6/74; 1/5/91; 1/8/92; 1/4/87; 2/3/71, 72.
1460/1, student ,with contributions from the almoner, chamberlain, hostiller, infirmarer, master of the cellar, and prior of Hoxne, NRO DCN 1/6/75, 76; 1/5/92; 1/7/96; 1/10/25; 1/1/90; Windsor, St George's chapel, I.C. 19.
1461/2, student, with contributions from the almoner, sacrist and prior of St Leonard's, NRO DCN 1/6/77; 1/4/88; 2/3/74.
1462/63, student, with contributions from the almoner, hostiller, master of the cellar and

precentor, NRO DCN 1/6/78; 1/7/97; 1/1/91; 1/9/68.

1463/4, student, with contributions from the almoner, chamberlain, hostiller and the priors of Lynn and St Leonard's, NRO DCN 1/6/79; 1/5/93; 1/7/98; 2/1/59; 2/3/76.

[1464/9, during these years most of the money allocated for student pensions was requisitioned for the repair and reconstruction work of the cathedral, NRO DCN 1/4/89, 90; 2/1/62,63].

1471/2, student, with contributions from the almoner, chamberlain, hostiller, precentor, refectorer, sacrist and prior of Hoxne, NRO DCN 1/6/84, 85; 1/5/100; 1/7/106; 1/9/70; 1/8/95; 1/4/93; 2/6/21.

1472/3, student, with contributions from the almoner, precentor and prior of St Leonard's, NRO DCN 1/6/86; 1/9/71; 2/3/82.

1473/4, student [at Oxford, NRO DCN 1/12/70], with contributions from the almoner, hostiller, communar/pittancer, sacrist and prior of St Leonard's, NRO DCN 1/6/87, 88; 1/7/107; 1/12/70; 1/4/94; 2/3/83.

1474/5, student [at Oxford, NRO DCN 1/2/71], with contributions from the cellarer, chamberlain and sacrist, NRO DCN 1/2/71; 1/5/101; 1/4/95.

1475/6, student [at Oxford, NRO DCN 1/12/70], with contributions from the almoner, chamberlain, communar/pittancer, and hostiller, NRO DCN 1/6/90, 91; 1/5/102, 103; 1/12/70; 1/7/108.

1476/7, student, with contributions from the almoner, cellarer, chamberlain, hostiller, precentor and refectorer, NRO DCN 1/6/93; 1/2/73; 1/5/104; 1/7/109; 1/9/75; 1/8/96. The almoner's acct refers to 'doctor' Roger Framyngham.

Note: *BRUO* and *BRUC* both include entries for this monk, but the refs are incomplete.

1453/4, ill and 3s. 4d. were spent on medicine by the infirmarer, NRO DCN 1/10/23.

1481, one of three monks at Aldeby in 1481 according to *VCH, Norfolk*, ii, 328 (no ref.).

1492, 5/8 Oct., 3rd in order at the visitation of bp Goldwell, and subprior; he preached the opening sermon, Jessopp, *Visit.*, 2, 8.

1499, 5 Mar., apptd by the abp official [*visitator*] for excepted jurisdiction on nomination of the prior and chapter, *sed. vac.* Norwich, Churchill, *Cant. Admin.*, ii, 253.

1499, 11 Mar., styling himself Roger Framyngham, S.T.P., and visitor of the diocese, apptd two commissaries, *Reg. abp Morton*, iii, nos 253–254.

1499, 6 Apr., 3rd in order on the visitation certificate, *Reg. abp Morton*, iii, no 258.

1494/5, Agnes Goscelyn, mother of Roger, subprior, gave a gift to the sacrist, NRO DCN 1/4/107.

Hugh FRAUNCEYS
see Norwich

Nicholas FRAUNSHAM
occ. 1526

1526, 7 June, one of the group of junior monks, present at the visitation of bp Nikke, who complained that they were required by the seniors to memorize the psalter, and the antiphons and responses etc., which they considered a waste of time, Jessopp, *Visit.*, 198. He also made several depositions, among which were harsh treatment when he was ill, neglect in the observance of the regulations concerning eating in the refectory and failure to provide adequate food for visiting parents, *ib.*, 204.

Thomas de FRAUNSHAM [Fransham, Frawnsham
occ. 1409 d. 1415/16

1409, Jan./Sept., 1410/11, communar/pittancer, NRO DCN 1/12/42,43.

1414, 14 Oct., the bp comm. the prior to appt him prior of Aldeby, Reg. Courtenay, fo 102^v.

1414/15, prior of Aldeby, NRO DCN 2/2/6.

1415/16, d., and 'alms' of 17s. were recd by the chamberlain, NRO DCN 1/5/44.

1417/18, the refectorer recd 6s. 8d. from a novice who purchased the *ciphus* [formerly] belonging to him, NRO DCN 1/8/63.

FREBERTUS [de ?Basel'
occ. 1263/4 occ. 1272/3

1263/4, ?master of the cellar, NRO DCN 1/1/1 (the roll is almost illegible).

1263/4, visited Gnatingdon, Martham and Sedgeford with the steward, NRO DCN 60/14/2; 60/23/2; 60/33/2.

1272/3, visited Hindolveston, NRO DCN 60/18/5.

FREDENHAM
see Fretenham

Geoffrey de FREKENHAM
occ. 1425 d. 1433/4

1425/7, 1430/1, refectorer, NRO DCN 1/8/72, 73, Oxford, Bod. Ms Rolls, Norfolk, no 50.

1433/4, d., and 'alms' of 18s. 5d. were recd by the chamberlain, NRO DCN 1/5/60.

FREKENHAM
see also Fretenham

Thomas FRENG [Freeng, Frenge
occ. 1429/30 d. 1452/3

1429/32, gardener, NRO DCN 1/11/13–15.

1434/5, ill, and the infirmarer spent 2s. on medicine, NRO DCN 1/10/21.

1446, name occ. on a rough list of those assigned to celebrate weekday and chantry masses, Cambridge, Emm. Coll. Ms 142, fo 68; also on fragmentary lists, prob. of similar date, for the *magna missa* and *parva missa* (as Freeng), *ib.*, fo 77^{v}.

1452/3, d., and the chamberlain recd 'alms' of 16s. 4d., NRO DCN 1/5/85.

William FRESYNGFELD [Fresynfeld
d. 1476/7

1476/7, d., and the chamberlain recd 7s. 7d. in 'alms', NRO DCN 1/5/104.

Ralph de FRETENHAM [Fredenham, ?Frekenham, Fretinham
occ. 1273/4

1273/4, master of the cellar, NRO DCN 1/1/3.

1273/4, visited Gnatingdon for *liberatio denariorum*, NRO DCN 60/14/5.

He used and possessed a number of mss:

(1) NRO DCL/1, Chronicle of Bartholomew Cotton, q.v. (late 13th c.), on fo 1; Ker states that he wrote this copy, *MLGB*, 285. In the more recent *MMBL*, iii, 527, he notes that fos 1–32^{v} and 45–53 are in Fretenham's hand because it is identical with the hand of the writer of NRO DCN 1/1/3 which is headed *per manus*; but should this phrase be understood literally?

(2) CUL Ms Kk.4.20, Summa Raymundi etc. (late 13th c.) name on fo 1.

(3) BL Add. Ms 30079, Topographia Insule Anglicane (13th c.); see Dodwell, 'History and Norwich Monks', 45.

These are described in Ker, 'Norwich Cathedral Mss', 256.

John de FULDON [Fouldon, Fuldone, Fuldune, Fulgdune
occ. 1272/3 occ. 1303/4

1272/3, master of the cellar with Alexander de Becles, q.v., NRO DCN 1/1/2.

1289/91, 1293, 1296/7, 1299/1301, 1303/4, sacrist, NRO DCN 1/4/9–15.

1272/3, with Becles made the rounds of a number of manors for *liberatio denariorum*, viz., Catton, Hemsby, Hindolveston, Hindringham, Martham, [North] Elmham, Plumstead, Sedgeford, and Taverham NRO DCN 60/4/4; 60/15/2; 60/18/5; 60/20/4; 60/23/4; 60/10/4; 60/29/3; 60/33/4; 60/35/6.

1273/4, with Becles visited Catton, Newton, [North] Elmham and Taverham, NRO DCN 60/4/5; 60/28/1; 60/10/5; 60/35/6.

1278, 11 Feb., proctor, recd licence from the king to el. a bp *N. Cath. Charters*, i, no 54; see Walter de Walpole.

1291/2, sent as proctor to London to the [church] council, and bought two books for which the prior pd him 24s., NRO DCN 1/1/11.

1303/4, visited Henley for *liberatio denariorum*, NRO DCN 60/16/3.

Ralph de FULDON
occ. 1236

1236, 22 Aug., proctor, with Peter de Calna, q.v., and recd licence from the king to el. a bp, *CPR (1232–1247)*, 156.

Thomas FULMERSTON [Folmerston, Fulmoderston
occ. 1452/3 d. 1485/6

1465, June/1467; 1468/9; 1471/2, chamberlain, NRO DCN 1/5/94–98, 100.

1465/6, communar/pittancer, NRO DCN 1/12/67.

1466/8, hostiller, NRO DCN 1/7/101, 102.

1468/9, master of the cellar, NRO DCN 1/1/92.

1472/8, almoner, NRO DCN 1/6/86–95.

1474/6, cellarer, NRO DCN 1/2/71, 72.

1480/2, 1483/5, almoner, NRO DCN 1/6/96–99.

1481/2, 1484/1485, June, hostiller, NRO DCN 1/7/113, 114.

1452/3, one of several monks who gave the precentor small sums for the *portiforium* of Thomas Crane, q.v., NRO DCN 1/9/66.

1479/80, 1483/4, some of the money remaining from the accts of the Wakering and Erpingham chantries was in his keeping, NRO DCN 4/9,10.

1485/6, d., and the chamberlain recd 'alms' of 6s. 8d., NRO DCN 1/5/115.

Note: this seems to be a rare and extreme example of plurality of office and of frequent change of office. There appears to have been a decrease in numbers on several recorded occasions in the late 1460s and early 1470s, as well as the mid 1480s, and this may have caused a shortage of competent office holders. (Statistics derived from accts of St Leonard's). It is possible that there are two contemporary monks here.

FYLBY
see Filby

GALFRIDUS
see Geoffrey

GALIENUS
n.d.

n.d., 20 June, name occ in a Canterbury obit list, BL Ms Arundel 68, fo 31^{v}.

William GARDENER
occ. 1532

1532, 3 June, resident at Lynn, but present at the visitation of bp Nikke, and complained of the poor financial state of the cell, [*aere alieno*], Jessopp, *Visit.*, 267.

John de GATELE
occ. 1329/30

1329/30, the master of the cellar made a gift of 3d. to his boy [*garcioni*], NRO DCN 1/1/30.

Robert GATELE [Gatlee
occ. 1430 occ. 1458/9

1453, Sept./1454, Mar., prior of Hoxne, NRO DCN 2/6/17.
1458, Dec./1459, cellarer, NRO DCN 1/2/64.
1430/1, ill, and the infirmarer spent 2s. 6d. on medicine, NRO DCN 1/10/18.
1432/3, ill, and 12d. spent on medicine, NRO DCN 1/10/20.
1446, name occ. on a rough list of those assigned to celebrate weekday and chantry masses, Cambridge, Emm. Coll. Ms 142, fo 68; name also on a similar list (prob. also c. 1446/7) for the Bateman, Totyngton, Wakering, Tye and Erpingham chantries, *ib.*, fo 77^{v}.
1453/4, ill, and 6d. was spent on medicine, NRO DCN 1/10/23.

GAYTUN
see Geyton

Robert GEDGE [Geegh, Gegh, Geggham
occ. 1418/19 occ. 1423/4

1418/19, student [at Oxford], with pension contributions from the cellarer, precentor and refectorer, NRO DCN 1/2/39; 1/9/31; 1/8/64, 65.
1419/20, student, with contributions from the chamberlain, master of the cellar and precentor, NRO DCN 1/5/47; 1/1/74; 1/9/31, 36. See also John de Dereham.
1420/1, student, with contributions from the almoner, cellarer, hostiller and precentor, NRO DCN 1/6/47; 1/2/41; 1/7/65; 1/9/31.
1421/2, student, with contributions from the almoner, chamberlain, hostiller and precentor, NRO DCN 1/6/48, 49; 1/5/48; 1/7/66; 1/9/37; the chamberlain recorded that he was at Oxford.
1422/3, student with contributions from the hostiller and precentor, NRO DCN 1/7/67; 1/9/37.
1423/4, student, with contributions from the almoner, chamberlain, precentor and prior of Aldeby, NRO DCN 1/6/52, 53; 1/5/50; 1/9/39; 2/2/9.

In the years 1418/21 the cellarer, chamberlain and precentor noted that they had contributed only a half pension because of the debt of his father, NRO DCN 1/2/41; 1/5/47; 1/9/31 and 36.

Note: this monk is not in *BRUO* or *BRUC*.

William GEDNEY [Gedeney
occ. 1481/2 occ. 1486/7

1481/7, student [at Oxford], with pension contributions for the entire six years from the precentor, NRO DCN 1/9/79–84. In addition:
1481/2, student, with contributions from the almoner, cellarer, hostiller, and sacrist, NRO DCN 1/6/97; 1/2/76; 1/7/113; 1/4/97.
1482/3, student, with contributions from the chamberlain and infirmarer, NRO DCN 1/5/112; 1/10/30.
1483/4, student, with contributions from the infirmarer, master of the cellar, refectorer and prior of St Leonard's, NRO DCN 1/10/31; 1/1/94; 1/8/98; 2/3/90. The infirmarer noted that he was at Oxford.
1484/5, student, with contributions from the almoner, hostiller, sacrist and the priors of Hoxne and Yarmouth, NRO DCN 1/6/99; 1/7/114; 1/4/98; 2/6/26; 2/4/16; the prior of Aldeby noted that he was at Oxford.
1485/6, student, with contributions from the almoner, communar, hostiller, sacrist and the priors of Aldeby and Hoxne, NRO DCN 1/6/100; 1/12/75; 1/7/115; 1/4/99,100; 2/2/24; 2/6/27.
1486/7, student, with contributions from the almoner, hostiller, refectorer and sacrist, NRO DCN 1/6/101; 1/7/116; 1/8/99; 1/4/101.

Note: this monk is not in *BRUO* or *BRUC*.

In 1446/7 a John Gedney leased a tenement in the city parish of St Michael Coslany from the refectorer, NRO DCN 1/8/84.

GEEGH, Geggham, Gegh
see Gedge

I GEOFFREY [Galfridus
n.d.

n.d., 3 Aug., name occ. in a Canterbury obit list, BL Ms Arundel 68, fo 37.

II GEOFFREY [Galfridus
occ. ?1190

Blomefield, *Norfolk*, iii, 432, has a Geoffrey as master of St Paul's hospital in 1190.

GEOFFREY
see also Stowe

I GERARD
occ. [1134 × 1140]

n.d., [1134 x1140] witnessed a charter in favour of the monks of St Benet of Hulme, *St Benet Holme Cart.*, no 139.

II GERARD [Everardus, Girard
occ. 1174/5 occ. 1202

c. 1175–1202, prior: succ. [?el.] 1175; last occ. 1 Aug. 1202, *Fasti*, ii, 60, *HRH* 58; see William de Walsham.

c. 1174/5, possibly cellarer, *Fasti*, ii, 60.

1182, one of the royal justices according to Dugdale, *Monasticon*, iv, 7.

n.d., 17 Dec., obit occ. in BL Ms Harley 3950, fo 8v.

Several charters dated during his priorate have been calendared in *N. Cath. Charters*, i, nos 321, 327, 330; two others are printed in *ib.*, ii, nos 264, 413. See also *Eng. Epis. Acta*, vi, nos 304 (a copy of no 264 above), 217, 260, 287, 291, 310A.

He was one of the correspondents of John of Salisbury who wrote to him [in 1167/8], *Salisbury Letters*, ii, no 251.

III GERARD
n.d.

n.d., 31 Oct., name occ. in a Canterbury obit list, BL Ms Arundel 68, fo 47.

Richard GERNUN [?Germin
occ. 1266

c. 1266, 18/19 Apr., chamberlain, Cotton, *Historia*, 141.

1266, 18/19 Apr., comm. by the bp to install prior Nicholas de Bramertone, q.v., *ib.*, 141.

Nicholas GEYTON [Gaytun
occ. 1390 occ. 1399

1390, June/ 1391; 1393/4, hostiller, NRO DCN 1/7/43–45.

1394, 1395/7, 1398/9, almoner, NRO DCN 1/6/25–28.

1394/5, deputy of the prior of Hoxne, NRO DCN 2/6/1.

GIDO [Guydo
occ. 1272 occ. 1292

1272/3, chaplain of the prior, NRO DCN 1/1/2.

1291/2, prior of Lynn, *Comm. Rolls*, 61.

1291/2, gave a ring [*anulum*] to the communar, worth 2s., *Comm. Rolls*, 61.

Note: this is prob. Guy de St Edmund, q.v.

GILBERT
n.d.

n.d., 13 June, name occ. in a Canterbury obit list. BL Ms Arundel 68, fo 30v.

Note: a Gilbert, monk, prob. of Norwich, appeared as a witness to a charter [1161 × 1168] of bp William de Turba, *Eng. Epis. Acta*, vi, no 131.

GISC, Gist
see Gys

GIULFUS
occ. 1150s

1150s, sacrist, Jessopp and James, *St William*, 186, 213–214.

1151, 2 July, assisted Thomas de Monmouth, q.v., in moving the body of St William from the chapter house to the cathedral; but he was later reluctant to heed the instructions of the saint given in a dream to a young girl of Norwich, *ib.*

GOCELINUS
n.d.

n.d, 2 July, obit occ. in the kalendar in Reg. XI, fo 5.

GODESMANUS
n.d.

n.d., 30 Jan., name occ. in a Canterbury obit list, BL Ms Arundel 68, fo 15.

Note: a person, very possibly a monk, by this name went to Cambridge in 1282/3 to attend the installation of the chancellor, Hudson, 'Camera Roll', 289 (NRO DCN 1/1/6).

GODEWYNUS
n.d.

n.d., 10 Mar., obit occ. in a kalendar in Reg. XI, fo 3.

Thomas GOLDINGE
occ. 1526

1526, 7 June, one of the group of junior monks, present at the visition of bp Nikke, who complained that they were required by the seniors to memorize the psalter, and the antiphons and responses etc. which they considered a waste of time, Jessopp, *Visit.*, 198. He also complained of the food served to the sick monks and to the parents who came to visit, *ib.*, 204.

GOSFRIDUS
occ. [?1107]

[?1107], with Ingulph, Macarius and Stannard, q.v., witnessed a final concord of the bp, *Eng. Epis. Acta*, vi, no 5.

n.d., recd a letter from bp Losinga, Anstruther, *Epist. Losinga*, no 16.

Thomas GRAFTON
occ. 1520

1520, 3 Sept., acol., present at the visitation of bp Nikke and made depositions vs Thomas Pellis and John Lakenham, q.v., Jessopp, *Visit.*, 193.

Robert GRENE
see Trows

Walter GRIME
see Crowmer

Thomas GROWTE
occ. 1502

1502, 23 June, one of four *clerici* whom the bp comm. the prior to adm. [*monachand'*], Reg. Nikke (8/13), fo 13v.

Note: this is prob. Thomas Sall, q.v.

GUIDO, GUY
see Gido, Guy de St Edmund

Robert GUNTON
occ. 1440/1 d. 1459/60

1440/1, ill and 8d. was spent by the infirmarer on medicine, NRO DCN 1/10/22.
1446, name occ. on a rough list of those assigned to celebrate weekday and chantry masses, Cambridge, Emm. Coll. Ms 142, fo 68.
1447/8, also on a similar list for Sunday masses on the following dates: 1447, 29 Jan., 27 Aug., 17 Dec.; 1448, 7 Apr., 28 July, 17 Nov., *ib.* Also on another list (prob. of similar date) for masses for the Bateman, Totyngton, Wakering, Tye and Erpingham chantries, *ib.*, fo 77v.
1453/4, ill and 2s. were spent on medicine, NRO DCN 1/10/23.
1459/60, d., and the chamberlain recd 'alms', NRO DCN 1/5/91.

William de GUNTON
occ. 1387 d. 1398/9

1387, Aug./Sept., refectorer, NRO DCN 1/8/47.
1398/9, d., and the chamberlain recd 'alms', NRO DCN 1/5/30.

GUYDO
see Gido, Guy de St Edmund

Nicholas GYS [Gisc, Gist
occ. 1363/4 occ. ?1393/4

1363/4, ref. to his taking monks to an ordination at Holt, NRO DCN 1/12/30.
1393/4, an inventory of the refectorer lists one *pecia* with a cover made of glass and an *aquaria* given by him for the *camera minutorum* in the infirmary, and also his *ciphus* of cedar now being used by the prior [Alexander de Totyngton, q.v.], NRO DCN 1/8/48.
1410, an inventory of the refectorer includes the *ciphus* of cedar formerly belonging to him, and now kept in the prior's chamber, NRO DCN 1/8/56.

William GYSSYNGE
occ. 1440/1 d. 1452/3

1440/1, ill and 20d. were spent by the infirmarer on medicine, NRO DCN 1/10/22.
1452/3, d., and the chamberlain recd 'alms' of 10s. 6d., NRO DCN 1/5/85.

Roger de HADESTO [Hadisto
occ. 1350 occ. 1357

1350, Jan./1351, hostiller, NRO DCN 1/7/13–16.
1352/4, almoner, NRO DCN 1/6/16, 17.
1355/6, cellarer, NRO DCN 1/2/20.
1357, 14 Dec., in compliance with the bp's comm., he sent a certificate to say that he had installed the new prior, [Nicholas de Hoo, q.v.], Reg. Percy, fo 23–23v.

William de HADESTO [Haddestho, Haddesto
occ. 1309 occ. 1324

1310, July/1311, 1311/13, master of the cellar, NRO DCN 1/1/21,22; 60/33/16 and 18; he was followed by Adam de Belagh, q.v., NRO DCN 60/15/9.
1319/20, hostiller, NRO DCN 1/7/1.
1323/4, July to July, refectorer, NRO DCN 1/8, 26, 27.
1309/10, visited Hindolveston, NRO DCN 60/18/16.
1310/11, a pair of *parures* [?ecclesiastical apparel] was bought for him, NRO DCN 1/1/22.
1311/12, visited Gnatingdon, Hindringham and [North] Elmham, NRO DCN 60/14/14; 60/20/16; 60/10/13.
1311/13, pd visits to Hindolveston, Martham and Sedgeford. NRO DCN 60/18/17, 18; 60/23/13, 14; 60/33/16, 18.
1312/13, visited Gnatingdon, Hemsby and Taverham, NRO DCN 60/14/15; 60/15/9; 60/35/17.

[J. HAKENEY
An incorrect entry in *BRUO* has resulted from a misreading of the master of the cellar's acct for 1346/7 (NRO DCN 1/1/42), which records the expense '. . . in j hakeney pro scolar' v' Oxon' conducto iij s. iiij d.'].

HAMO
occ. 1302/3

1302/3, accompanied the prior to the Black Monk Chapter in London, *Comm. Rolls*, 83, and Pantin, *BMC* i, 279.

George HANWORTH [Hanwurth *alias* Bawcham, Beawchyn
occ. 1526 occ. 1538

1526, 7 June, one of the group of junior monks, present at the visitation of bp Nikke, who complained that they were required by the seniors to memorize the psalter, and the antiphons and responses etc., which they considered a waste of time, Jessopp, *Visit.*, 198; he was detained for punishment with Robert Twaytes, q.v., *ib.*, 203.
1534, 28 July, subscribed to the Act of Supremacy, *DK 7th Report*, Appndx 2, 295.

1538, 30 Apr., paid a fee to be dispensed to wear the habit of a secular pr. and hold a canonry and prebend in the cathedral and any other benefice and be non resident, Chambers, *Faculty Office Regs*, 137.

1538, 2 May, licensed as a secular canon *L and P Henry VIII*, xiii, pt 1, no 1115(4).

Harvey de HAPESBURGH [Hapesburch, Hapisburg

occ. 1313/14 occ. 1316/17

1313/14, with Roger de Blikling, q.v., gave 26s. 8d. *ad negotia domus*, NRO DCN 1/1/23.

1316/17, made a gift of 10s. to the communar [towards the building operations], *Comm. Rolls*, 89.

John de HAPISBURGH [Happisburgh, Hasbourgh

occ. 1333/4 d. 1386/7

1347, Feb./1339, June, hostiller, NRO DCN 1/7/10–12.

1349, Mar./Sept., refectorer, NRO DCN 1/8/37.

1350/1351, Feb., precentor, NRO DCN 1/9/5.

1351/5, chamberlain, NRO DCN 1/5/13,14.

1368/76, prior of St Leonard's, NRO DCN 2/3/6–8.

1333/4, pd the refectorer for a *ciphus*, NRO DCN 1/8/31; prob. this was soon after adm.

1386/7, d., and the chamberlain recd 'alms', NRO DCN 1/5/19, 20.

1393/4, on the refectorer's inventory there is mention of a cedar *ciphus* formerly his, which William de Penteney, q.v., was now using, NRO DCN 1/8/48.

Robert HARDWYK [Hardewyk, Herdwik, Herdwyk

occ. 1415 d. ?1447

1415, 10 June, one of four whom the prior requested the bp to rec. *ad osculum et benedictionem* as he had been adm. by the prior and chapter, Reg. Courtenay, fo 103ᵛ.

1418, 8 Apr., one of four whose prof. the prior requested the bp to rec.; in reply the bp comm. the prior to do so, Reg. Wakering, fo 32ᵛ.

Note: this is an unusually long period of probation; perhaps they had entered at an early age.

1427/8, ill and the infirmarer spent 12d. on medicine, NRO DCN 1/10/15.

1440/1, ill and 21d. was spent on medicine, NRO DCN 1/10/22.

1446, name occ. on a rough list of those assigned to celebrate weekday and chantry masses, Cambridge, Emm. Coll. Ms 142, fo 68.

1446/7, name also on another list, for Sunday masses, viz., for 12 Feb. 1447, but no more; and so one may assume he d., *ib.*, fo 68. Name on another list of those assigned to celebrate masses in the Erpingham chantry, *ib.*, fo 77ᵛ.

1446/7, the refectorer recd 7s. 4d. from the chamberlain for his *ciphus in excambio*, NRO DCN 1/8/84.

1447, ?d., prob. soon after 12 Feb., as above.

William HARIDAUNCE [Harridaunce, Harridans, Harydans, incorrectly Baryditm

occ. 1501 occ. 1538

1514, 27 Apr., chaplain to the prior, and also subcellarer, Jessopp, *Visit.*, 77.

1514, 27 Apr.; 1518/19; 1520, 3 Sept.; 1525/7, 1529/31; 1532, 3 June; 1538, before 2 May, cellarer, Jessopp, *Visit.*, 77; NRO DCN 1/2/94; Jessopp, *Visit.*, 192; NRO DCN 1/2/96–97; NRO DCN 1/2/98–99; Jessopp, *Visit.*, 267; *Fasti, 1541–1857*, vii, 52.

1520/9, 1530/6, prior of St Leonard's, NRO DCN 2/3/119–140.

1501, 11 Nov., the prior of Lynn contributed the sum of 17s. 1d. to him [?on adm., to help with the purchase of necessary articles like the *ciphus*], NRO DCN 2/1/78.

1514, 27 Apr., present at the visitation of bp Nikke; named in the *comperta* as above, and also as *custos cervisiarii, et minus debite exercet officia cellerarii*, Jessopp, *Visit.*, 77.

1520, 3 Sept., present at the visitation of bp Nikke and reported *omnia bene*, Jessopp, *Visit.*, 192.

1526, 7 June, present at the visitation of bp Nikke and described as a senior monk; he made depositions vs. the subprior, sacrist, precentor and the junior monk priests, Jessopp, *Visit.*, 202–203.

1532, 3 June, present at the visitation of bp Nikke and reported that the junior monks were allowed too much freedom, Jessopp, *Visit.*, 267.

1534, 28 July, subscribed to the Act of Supremacy, *DK 7th Report*, Appndx 2, 295 (where the name is given as Baryditm).

1538, 30 Apr., paid £10 to be dispensed to wear the habit of a secular pr. and hold a canonry and prebend in the cathedral and any other benefice and be non resident, Chambers, *Faculty Office Regs*, 137.

1538, 2 May, apptd canon of the 2nd prebend of the new foundation, *Fasti, 1541–1857*, vii, 52. See also *L and P Henry VIII*, xiii, pt 1, no 1115(4).

A contemporary, Robert Harydaunc', was a Norwich citizen and alderman, NRO DCN 1/12/90.

Simon HARPELE [Harpelee, Harple, Harpole

occ 1376/7 d. 1398/9

1387/8, 1387/8, gardener, NRO DCN 1/11/2/.

1376/7, bought a *ciphus* for 6s. 8d. from the refectorer, prob. soon after his adm., NRO DCN

1/8/44; since a similar entry occurs on the acct for 1377/8 (1/8/46), he may have pd in two instalments.
1385/6, gave 2s. 2d. to the building work in the cloister, NRO DCN 1/12/32.
1398/9, d., and the chamberlain recd 6s. 8d. as 'alms', NRO DCN 1/5/30.

HARRIDANS, Harridaunce
see Haridaunce

HARVEY
see Herveus

HASBOURGH
see Hapisburgh

John HASYNGHAM [Hasingham
occ. 1408 occ. 1418

1408, June/Sept., almoner, NRO DCN 1/6/38.
1410, 28 Apr., master of St Paul's hospital, NRO DCN 45/31/24; Blomefield, *Norfolk*, iii, 432, says that he was master in 1418.
1418, before 8 Apr., subprior, Reg. Wakering, fo 32.
1418, 8 Apr., the prior requested the bp to dismiss him from the office of subprior, Reg. Wakering fo 32.

HATERSET
see Hedirset

John HAYLE, B.Th. [Hayles
occ. 1510/11 occ. ?1521

1510/11, student [at Cambridge] with pension contributions from the hostiller and sacrist. NRO DCN 1/7/131; 1/4/110.
1511/12, student, with contribution from the hostiller, NRO DCN 1/7/132.
1514/21, pensioner at Gonville Hall, and prob. B.Th., 1520, Venn, *Gonville and Caius*, i, 22.

I Richard de HECHAM
occ. [1235 × 1257]

[1235 × 1257, 8 June], almoner, mentioned in a gift of land, *N. Cath. Charters*, ii, no 444.

II Richard de HECHAM [Heccham
occ. 1305/6 occ. 1335/6

1310/15, precentor, NRO DCN 1/9/3.
1317/18, chamberlain, NRO DCN 1/5/5.
1322/3, 1324/5, 1328/31, 1333/6, sacrist, NRO DCN 1/4/21–26, 29–31.

1305/6, visited Sedgeford, NRO DCN 60/33/14.
1307/8, recd £10 for his expenses from the master of the cellar for a quitclaim [which he presumably had negotiated], NRO DCN 1/1/18; this same yr both he and Hervey de Swafham, q.v., are listed together as receiving a gift of 4s. from the communar, *Comm. Rolls*, 87. It is possible that, since Swaffham was a student at Oxford at this time Hecham also was at the university.
1308/9, another gift to him, this time of 10s. from the master of the cellar, NRO DCN 1/1/19.
1312/13, visited Plumstead, for *liberatio denariorum*, NRO DCN 60/29/17.
Note: the church at Plumstead provided the main source of income for the precentor's office.
[1314/15], sent to the lord chancellor concerning the presentation to Chalk church and provided with a letter of credence, Reg. IX, fo 8v. He also bought skins for a [book] catalogue this yr, NRO DCN 1/9/3.
[1316, Sept.], named as one of the monk proctors to go to St Paul's cathedral on 11 Oct., for convocation, Reg. IX, fo 11.
[?1318], sent by the prior with a letter to Walter de Norwich, baron of the Exchequer with a letter from the prior, Reg. IX, fo 5.
Note: in the three missions above he was accompanied by Ralph de Monesle, q.v.
1325, 10 July, sent to the king for licence to el. a bp., Reg. IX, fo 62.
[c. 1326, 15 Dec.], bp Ayermine sent a letter in reply to the prior's letter, for both of which he served as one of the bearers and as ambassador, Reg. IX, fo 51v.
1329/30, as sacrist accounted for the travelling expenses for [?himself and] Roger de Eston, q.v., to Avignon, NRO DCN 1/4/24.

Note: it may be that there are two monks by this name (or the initial 'R') whom I have failed to disentangle. However, since none of the details are mutually contradictory, the fact that some entries refer to R. and others to Richard seems insufficient evidence on which to try to reconstruct two biographies. See the following entry.?

T. de HECHAM
occ. 1291/2

1291/2, ref. to ?T. under expenses incurred at St Botulph's fair, NRO DCN 1/1/11.

Note: could this be identical with the preceding?

John de HEDIRSET [Haterset, Hedersett, Hedirsete, Hedyrsete, Hetersete, Hetirsete, Hoderset
occ. 1326/7 occ. 1356/7

1326/7, 1329/31, 1331/2, 1332/3, master of the cellar, NRO DCN 1/1/29–32; 60/26/23 (1331/2).
1339/40, 1345/7, 1348/9, almoner, NRO DCN 1/6/12–15.
1349, July/1350, Dec., infirmarer, NRO DCN 1/10/7,8.
1350/1, communar/pittancer, NRO DCN 1/12/28.
1353/7, prior of St Leonard's, NRO DCN 2/3/2–5.

1331/2, visited Plumstead for *liberatio denariorum*, NRO DCN 60/29/23.
1353, 18 Jan., given papal licence to choose his own confessor, *CPL*, iii, (1342–1362), 492.

In 1320/1 a Simon de Hederset was the *senescallus* [land steward] for the priory, possibly a relative, NRO DCN 1/1/26.

John HELGEY [Helgay, Helzey
occ. 1475/6 occ. 1486/7

1475/6, student at Oxford, with pension contribution from the almoner, NRO DCN 1/6/90, 91.
1476/7, student with contribution from the communar/pittancer, NRO DCN 1/12/70.
1477/8, student, with contributions from the almoner, chamberlain, sacrist and prior of St Leonard's, NRO DCN 1/6/95; 1/5/105; 1/4/96; 2/3/87.
1478/9, student at Oxford (NRO DCN 1/12/70), with contributions from the chamberlain, communar/pittancer and hostiller, NRO DCN 1/5/106, 107; 1/12/70; 1/7/110.
1479/80, student, with contributions from the chamberlain, communar/pittancer, infirmarer, and refectorer, NRO DCN 1/5/108; 1/12/71; 1/10/29; 1/8/97. He returned [from Oxford] to take part in the el. of a prior, NRO DCN 1/12/71.
1480/1, student, with contributions from the almoner, chamberlain and precentor, NRO DCN 1/6/96; 1/5/109; 1/9/78.
1481/2, student, with contributions from the almoner, cellarer, chamberlain, hostiller, precentor and sacrist, NRO DCN 1/6/97; 1/2/76; 1/5/110,111; 1/7/113; 1/9/79; 1/4/97.
1482/3, student, with contributions from the chamberlain, infirmarer and precentor, NRO DCN 1/5/112,113; 1/10/30; 1/9/80.
1483/4, student at Oxford (NRO DCN 1/10/31), with contributions from the almoner, infirmarer, master of the cellar, precentor, refectorer, sacrist and prior of St Leonard's, 1/6/98; 1/10/31; 1/1/94; 1/9/81; 1/8/98; 1/4/98; 2/3/90.
1484/5, student with contributions from the almoner, hostiller, precentor, sacrist, and the priors of Hoxne and Yarmouth, NRO DCN 1/6/99; 1/7/114; 1/9/82; 1/4/99; 2/6/26; 2/4/16.
1485/6, student, with contributions from the almoner, communar/pittancer, hostiller, precentor, sacrist and prior of Aldeby, NRO DCN 1/6/100; 1/12/75; 1/7/115; 1/9/83; 1/4/100; 2/2/24.
1486/7, student, with contributions from the almoner, hostiller, precentor, refectorer, and sacrist, NRO DCN 1/6/101; 1/7/116, 117; 1/9/84; 1/8/99; 1/4/101.

Note: there is no evidence to substantiate the entry in *BRUC*, and there is no entry in *BRUO*.

HELIAS
see Elias

HELINGTON
see Helyngton

HELMHAM
see Elmham

Richard de HELYNGTON [Helington
occ. 1406 d. 1424/5

1406, Sept./Nov., communar/pittancer, NRO DCN 1/12/40.
1409/10, almoner, NRO DCN 1/6/39, 40.
1410/11, 1412/13, master of the cellar, NRO DCN 1/1/70, 71.
1414/15, and up to 8 Apr. 1418, sacrist, NRO DCN 1/4/51; the prior requested the bp to remove him, Reg. Wakering, fo 32.
1424, Nov./1425, prior of St Leonard's, NRO DCN 2/3/40, with an inventory dated 1424 when John Bergersh, q.v., took over the office from him, NRO DCN 2/3/41.
1408/9, went to Hoxne, with expenses pd by the communar/ pittancer, NRO DCN 1/12/42.
1420/2, the almoner fed his nephew for 10 wks the first yr and 48 wks the second, NRO DCN 1/6/47, 48; this almost certainly means that the nephew was one of the boys in the almonry school.
1424/5, d., and the chamberlain recd 20s. 'alms', NRO DCN 1/5/51.

The first inventory of St Leonard's (dated 1424) includes his gift of a *pecia deaurata cum cooperculo*, Bensly, 'St Leonard's', 204–205. The 1452/3 inventory mentions one *pecia magna chalyschap deaurata* which is prob. the same item, *ib.*, 216–217. A *chronica noviter scripta* is also listed in this later inventory as his gift, *ib.*, 224–225. See also Sharpe, *Eng. Benedictine Libraries*, iv, B62 and B63 which list the books found in the two inventories above.

Family conections, see above.

Note: see Richard Elyngton who is prob. the same monk.

HELZEY
see Helgey

Thomas de HEMENHALE [Hemnhall
occ. 1314 occ. 1337

1319/21, 1322/3, 1324/6, master of the cellar, NRO DCN 1/1/28; 60/4/24; 60/20/21; 60/35/21; 60/33/25.
1314/15, prob. student, with pension contribution from the refectorer, NRO DCN 1/8/23.
1315/16, student at Oxford, with contribution from the master of the cellar, NRO DCN 1/1/25.

1319/20, pd visits to Gnatingdon, Martham, [North] Elmham, Plumstead and Sedgeford, NRO DCN 60/14/8; 60/23/17; 60/10/17; 60/29/18; 60/33/21, usually for *liberatio denariorum* as often stated on these and the following accts.
1320/1, pd visits to Gnatingdon, Hindolveston, Hindringham, Martham, [North] Elmham, Plumstead and Sedgeford, NRO DCN 60/14/19; 60/18/22; 60/20/20; 60/23/18; 60/10/18; 60/29/19; 60/33/22.
1322/3, pd visits to Gnatingdon, Hemsby, Hindringham, Martham, and [North] Elmham, NRO DCN 60/14/20; 60/15/13; 60/20/21; 60/23/19; 60/10/19.
1324/5, visited Gnatingdon and Martham, NRO DCN 60/14/21; 60/23/20.
1325, 10 July, one of the monk proctors sent to the king for licence to el. a bp, Reg. IX, fo 62.
1325/6, visited Hindolveston, Martham, [North] Elmham and Sedgeford, NRO DCN 60/18,25; 60/23/21; 60/10/21; 60/33/23.
1327, 8 Feb., appeared before the dean of St Paul's in London as proctor for the chapter in an appeal vs the abp, Reg. X, fo 26ᵛ.
1330/1, supervised grain supplies for the master of the cellar, NRO DCN 1/1/31.
1336, 6 Apr., el. bp by the prior and chapter, Reg. Ayermine, fo 77, but res. by 14 Mar. 1337, as the pope had reserved the bpric and provided Anthony Bek, *CPL*, ii, (1305–1342), 541.
1337, 14 Mar., provided to the see of Worcester, *ib.*, 541.
1336/7, the refectorer contributed 40s. towards the el. expenses, NRO DCN 1/8/34; and the master of the cellar pd £20 towards expenses of the 'bp of Worcester', NRO DCN 1/1/38.
[1338, 21 Dec. d., and the obit occ. in BL Ms Harley 3950, fo 8ᵛ.]

Blomefield states that he was a monk of Eye before transferring to Norwich, *Norfolk*, iii, 504.

Geoffrey de HEMESBY [Hemmysby
occ. 1453/4 occ. 1471

1453/4, ill and the infirmarer spent 6s. 8d. on medicine, NRO DCN 1/10/23.
1454/5, ill and 2s. spent on medicine, NRO DCN 1/10/24.
1456/7, name linked with Thomas Bozoun and Edmund Sall, q.v., who recd pension contributions as students from the chamberlain; he is not described as a scholar, but was given 3s. 4d. *ex gratia*, NRO DCN 1/5/89. In this same yr the prior of St Leonard's also gave him a gift of 4s., NRO DCN 2/3/68. It is permissible to wonder if he was pursuing studies in the cloister and being rewarded for good work.
1471, 12 Oct., given a papal dispensation to rec. and retain any benefice, *CPL*, xiii, (1471–1484), 290.

Richard de HEMESBY
occ. 1334/5

1334/5, procured a *ciphus* from the refectorer for 13s. 4d., *de licencia prioris* [?because it was more than the usual amount pd by a novice], NRO DCN 1/8/32.

John de HEMMESBY
occ. 1345/6

1345/6, the communar/pittancer pd his travelling expenses to Oxford with those of John de Saham, q.v., NRO DCN 1/12/25, as in *BRUO*. They were both students at the same time as John Stukle, q.v., and possibly his *socii*.

HEMNHALL
see Hemenhale

John HEMPSTEDE [Hempsted, Hemstede
occ. 1476/7 d. 1512

1488/9, or 1489/90, hostiller, NRO DCN 1/7/120.
1489/90, communar, NRO DCN 1/12/77.
1490/4, master of the cellar, NRO DCN 1/1/95; Oxford, Bod. Ms Rolls, Norfolk, no 54; NRO DCN 1/1/96, 97.
1500/1, prior of Yarmouth, NRO DCN 2/4/20.
1501/3, refectorer, NRO DCN 1/8/108,109.
1504/5, prior of Lynn, NRO DCN 2/1/80.
1506/7, 1508/10, prior of St Leonard's, NRO DCN 2/3/109,110.
1508/9, almoner, NRO DCN 1/6/118.
1511/12, prior of St Leonard's, NRO DCN 2/3/111.

1476/7, gave the precentor 6d. *pro libris in cathologo*, [?for a new book list], NRO DCN 1/9/75; see Greatrex, 'Norwich Monk Students', 575.
1480/1, gave the precentor 20d. *pro intabulacione librorum*, NRO DCN 1/9/78 and Greatrex, *ib*; this monk was no doubt concerned about the monastic library.
1492, 5/8 Oct., 17th in order at the visitation of bp Goldwell, Jessopp, *Visit.*, 8.
1499, 6 Apr., 12th on the visitation certificate, *Reg. abp Morton*, iii, no 258.
1512, d. by 29 Sept., NRO DCN 2/3/112; the infirmarer gave 2s. 8d. *pro magna missa* of *Johannis nostri confratris*, NRO DCN 1/10/34.

Richard de HEMPSTEDE [Hemstede
occ. 1374/5 d. 1390

1374/5, 1376/8, refectorer, Oxford, Bod. Ms Rolls, Norfolk, no 49; NRO DCN 1/8/44, 45.
1380, June/1381, precentor, NRO DCN 1/9/18, 19.
1389/June 1390, hostiller, NRO DCN 1/7/43.
1390, d. before 24 June, and the chamberlain pd 6s. 8d. to the brief bearer, NRO DCN 1/5/23.

George HENGHAM [Hingham, Hyngham
occ. 1492 d. 1534

1497/9, hostiller, NRO DCN 1/7/120.
1501/4, prior of Hoxne, Windsor, St George's chapel, I.C. 33–35; NRO DCN 2/6/34.
1503/5, 1507/8, cellarer, NRO DCN 1/2/89; 2/4/20; 1/2/90.
1504/5, 1507/10, chamberlain, NRO DCN 1/5/128–132.
1505/22, 1523/5, 7 June 1526, 1528/32, prior of Lynn, NRO DCN 2/1/81, 82; Jessopp, *Visit.*, 198; NRO DCN 2/1/82–90. He prob. d. at Lynn as prior; see below.

1492, 5/8 Oct., 41st in order at the visitation of bp Goldwell, Jessopp, *Visit.*, 8.
1499, 6 Apr., 33rd on the visitation certificate, *Reg. abp Morton*, iii, no 258.
1514, 27 Apr., present at the visitation of bp Nikke and stated that he knew little about the state of the community at Norwich [because he was prior at Lynn]. Jessopp, *Visit.*, 73.
1526, 7 June, present at the visitation of bp Nikke and reported that the junior monks played games of dice and cards, a disgrace to religion, and that the brethren addressed the prior [of Norwich] as 'my lord' [*dominus*], and not as 'father prior' in accordance with custom, Jessopp, *Visit.*, 198. As to the state of the cell at Lynn he reported the house to be in *mediocri statu*, *ib.*, 196–198.
1534, 7 June, date entered for his commemoration, where he is described as prior of Lynn, BL Ms Harley 3950, fo 5v.

I John de HENGHAM [Hingham
occ. 1317/18 occ. 1348/9

1317/18, chaplain to the prior, NRO DCN 60/33/19.
1318 × 1320, communar/pittancer, *Comm. Rolls*, 20, n. 1, 107–109; he followed Nicholas de Hindolveston, q.v.
1328/9, almoner, NRO DCN 1/6/10.
1329, Nov./1333, June, cellarer, NRO DCN 1/2/16, 101.
1348, prior of St Leonard's, NRO DCN 2/3/7.
1317/18, visited Sedgeford, NRO DCN 60/33/19.
1322/3, 1323/4, responsible for the collection of tenths or tithes, NRO DCN 1/8/27; *Comm. Rolls*, 94.
[1325], 4 Oct., sent to the prior of Ipswich to urge him to resist the abp's projected intrusion [*sed. vac.* Norwich] as the prior and chapter of Norwich intended to do, Reg. IX, fo 45v.
1328/9, gave 20s. to his nephew, Thomas, who was about to enter Colchester abbey, NRO DCN 1/6/10.
1329/30, one of several monks who went to London concerning a lawsuit between the prior and chapter and the abp, NRO DCN 1/4/24.
1336, 3 Apr., one of two proctors who obtained royal licence to el. a bp, *CPR (1334–1338)*, 244; see Robert de Ely.
1348/9, gave to the pittancer 66s. 8d. as a personal contribution (?for repairs in the dormitory and *schola* which were under way, or perhaps towards the completion of the work in the cloister), NRO DCN 1/12/27.

Family connections, see above.

II John de HENGHAM
occ. 1410/11

1410/11, pd the refectorer 13s. 4d. for a *ciphus*, (and therefore prob. a novice), NRO DCN 1/8/55.

R. de HENGHAM
d. 1317/18

1317/18, d., and the chamberlain pd the brief bearer, NRO DCN 1/5/5.

I Thomas HENGHAM [Ingham, Yngham
occ. 1420/1 d. 1463/4

1420/1, pd the refectorer 13s. 4d. for a *ciphus* (and therefore prob. a novice), NRO DCN 1/8/68.
1425/6, returned from Hoxne and the precentor pd for his travelling expenses by horse, NRO DCN 1/9/37.
1438/9, gave 20d. to the communar for the cloister work, and the communar gave him 16d. for his help with the pictures on the windows [*pro historiis fenestr'*] in the cloister, NRO DCN 1/12/57.
1446, name occ. on a rough list of those assigned to celebrate weekday and chantry masses, Cambridge, Emm. Coll. Ms 142, fo 68.
1446/8, also on a similar list for Sunday masses for the following dates: 1446, 27 Nov.; 1447, 16 Apr., 9 July, 29 Oct.; 1448, 18 Feb., 9 June, 29 Sept., 1 Dec. *ib.*; also on another list (prob. of similar date) for masses in the Bateman, Totyngton, Wakering, Tye and Erpingham chantries, *ib.*, fo 77v.
1463/4, d., and the chamberlain recd 'alms' of 22s. 4d., NRO DCN 1/5/93.

II Thomas HENGHAM [Ingham, Yngham
occ. 1463/4 occ. 1467/8

1467, 19 Sept., ord dcn, Downham, by *lit. dim.*, Reg. Grey (Ely), fo 212v.

1463/4, student, with pension contribution from the chamberlain, NRO DCN 1/5/93.
1466/7, student, with contributions from the chamberlain, hostiller, refectorer and the prior of Lynn, NRO DCN 1/5/97; 1/7/101; 1/8/94; 2/1/61.
1467/8, student, with contributions from the hostiller, infirmarer and the priors of Aldeby, Lynn and St Leonard's, NRO DCN 1/7/102; 1/10/27; 2/2/21; 2/1/62; 2/3/78.

Note: although there is an entry in *BRUC*, no reference to either university has come to light; however, the fact of his ordination by the bp of Ely while he was a student points to Cambridge.

Name in

(1) CUL Ms Ii.3.10, Sermones Johannis Pape xxii (14th c.); the date after his name on fo 1 may be 1462; see Ker, 'Norwich Cathedral Mss', 258.

(2) Edinburgh, National Library of Scotland, Ms 6125 (14th c.), Cronica anglie ad annum 1317, *liber*—; see Ker, *ib.*, 271, n.

Henry de HENHAM

occ. 1273/4

1273/4, went with a *socius* to the papal court in Rome, NRO DCN 1/1/3.

I HENRY

n.d.

n.d., 22 May, name occ. in Canterbury obit lists, BL Ms Arundel 68, fo 28 and Lambeth Ms 20, fo 188.

II HENRY

occ. c. 1504

c. 1504, Henry, along with six other priests, (Christian names only given) made his prof.; this is recorded on an inserted leaf (prob. of rough notes) between fos 27ᵛ and 28 in Reg. Nikke (9/14).

Note: this may be Henry Manuel.

HERDEWIK, Herdwyk

see Hardwyk

Nicholas HERRE

occ. 1379/80

1379/80, recd a *pellicia* from the precentor costing 3s. 4d., NRO DCN 1/9/18.

I HERVEUS

n.d.

n.d., 24 May, obit occ. in the kalendar in Reg. XI, fo 4; this is prob. not Hervey Swafham, q.v.

II HERVEUS

n.d.

n.d., prior of Hoxne acc. to Blomefield, *Norfolk*, iii, 609.

John HERVY [Herwy

occ. 1476/7 occ. 1486

1476/7, gave the precentor 5d. *pro libris in cathologo*, NRO DCN 1/9/75.

1478/9, gave the precentor 16d. *pro intabulacione librorum*, NRO DCN 1/9/77.

Note: this was a monk who was concerned about the monastic library and its contents; see Greatrex, 'Norwich Monk Students', 575–576.

1486, 29 July, given papal dispensation to receive and retain a benefice, *CPL*, xv (1484–1492), 59, (no. 113).

Thomas HERWARD

occ. 1421/2 d. 1453/4

1421/2, ill and the infirmarer spent 14d. on medicine, NRO DCN 1/10/14.

1427/8, ill and 8d. was spent on medicine, NRO DCN 1/10/15.

1428/9, 1429/30, 1430/1, 1431/2, 1432/3, 1434/5, ill and 20d., 3s. 8d., 9d., 2s. 18d., and 25s. 6d. were spent respectively, NRO DCN 1/10/16–21.

1440/1, ill on two occasions and 8d. and 20d. were spent on medicine, NRO DCN 1/10/22.

1446, name occ. on a rough list of those assigned to celebrate weekday and chantry masses, Cambridge, Emm. Coll. Ms 142, fo 68; name on a similar list (prob. c. 1446/7) for masses in the Bateman, Totyngton, Wakering, Tye and Erpingham chantries, *ib.*, fo 77ᵛ.

1453/4, d., and the chamberlain recd 'alms' of 13s 4d., NRO DCN 1/5/86.

Thomas HETHYL [Hethyll

occ. 1432/3 d. 1463/4

1455/6, 1458/9, 1462/4, prior of Aldeby, NRO DCN 2/2/18–20; 1/5/93.

1462/3, master of the cellar, NRO DCN 1/1/91.

1432/3, ill, and the infirmarer spent 8d. on medicine, NRO DCN 1/10/20.

1434/5, ill, and 2s. were spent on medicine, NRO DCN 1/10/21.

1446, name occ. on a rough list of those assigned to celebrate weekday and chantry masses, Cambridge, Emm. Coll. Ms 142, fo 68.

1446/7, name on a similar list for Sundays masses for the following days: 1446, 30 Oct.; 1447, 21 May, 24 Sept. (this last was the dedication feast) *ib.*; name on another list (prob. also 1446/7) for masses in the Bateman, Totyngton, Wakering, Tye and Erpingham chantries, *ib.*, fo 77ᵛ.

1463/4, d. as prior of Aldeby and the chamberlain recd 15s. 'alms', NRO DCN 1/5/93.

John HEVERLOND [Heverynglond, Hevyrlond

occ. 1420/1 d. 1453/4

1436–1454, prior: *prefectio*, 12 Oct. 1436, Reg. Alnwick fo 87ᵛ; d. before 20 Jan. 1454, Reg. Lyhart, fo 31ᵛ; see John Molet.

1423/4, communar/pittancer, NRO DCN 1/12/50.

1430, 23 Sept., prior of Yarmouth, Reg. Alnwick, fo 102.

As prior he also held the following offices:

1437/9, 1440/3, almoner, NRO DCN 1/6/63–67.

1443/4, prior of Yarmouth, NRO DCN 2/4/8.

1420/1, student [prob. at Oxford], with pension contributions from the almoner, cellarer, hostiller, master of the cellar and precentor, NRO DCN 1/6/47; 1/2/41; 1/7/65; 1/1/75; 1/9/31.

1430, 23 Sept., apptd penitentiary at Yarmouth, Reg. Alnwick, fo 102.

1439, 8 May, given papal licence to choose his own confessor, *CPL*, 8 (1427–1447), 392.

1440/1, visited Hoxne, and the expenses charged to the Hoxne acct were 8s. 4d., Windsor, St George's chapel, I.C.13. In this year he and others were accused of resorting to violence vs the mayor and sheriffs of Norwich as a result of disputes with the city government over various rights, Tanner, *Church in Norwich*, 146–148; see also Richard Walsham and John Wichyngham.

1441, 6 Apr., came to an agreement with the bp over the *reverentie* that the later claimed as his due, Reg. Brouns, fo 108; this did not end the friction, see below.

1444, 14 Dec., a long standing dispute with bp Brouns over precedence and status was resolved by a compromise, and the prior and he exchanged the kiss of peace at the high altar during the liturgy, Reg. Brouns, fos 101, 102, 108–111. See Tanner, *Church in Norwich*, 160–161; see also Richard de Walsham under 1443, Jan.

1449/50, the communar/pittancer provided him with £6 for his expenses in riding up to London, NRO DCN 1/12/58.

1452/3, ill, and the master of the cellar spent 20s. on medicine, NRO DCN 1/1/88.

1453/4, d., and the chamberlain received 53s. 4d. in 'alms' *patris nostri defuncti*, NRO DCN 1/5/86.

He was a friend of the Paston family, Davis, *Paston Letters*, no 962.

On the basis of his manifest lack of hesitation in taking on both bp and city when rights and status were at stake he has been described as 'an aggressive man', in Tanner, *Church in Norwich*, 146. He showed little restraint in becoming inolved in city politics and in actively taking sides with a former mayor and some of the country magnates who had grievances vs the citizenry, *ib.*, 146–152.

Thomas de HEVYNGHAM [Hevingham
occ. 1402 d. 1421/2

1402, Sept., 1403/7, sacrist, NRO DCN 1/4/46–49.

1421/2 [in and prob. before] prior of Lynn before his d., NRO DCN 1/9/37.

1407, 3 Nov., recd licence from the bp to el. a prior, Reg. Totyngton, fo 3v.

1412, mentioned on St Leonard's acct in connection with the receipts of offerings at the shrine there, *pro tempore fratris*—, as though he had been prior, NRO DCN 2/3/28; however, the names of the priors at St Leonard's between 1401/12 are all known and he does not occur.

1415, 1 Oct., one of the three monks nominated by the prior and chapter as *visitator* for excepted jurisdiction, *sed. vac.* Norwich, *Reg. abp Chichele*, iii, 351–352.

1421/2, d., and the precentor received 7s. 8d. when his books [having been brought back from Lynn] were assigned to other monks, including John Dereham and William Worstede, q.v., NRO DCN 1/9/37; the chamberlain recd 22s. in 'alms', NRO DCN 1/5/48.

1422/3, the precentor also recd 2s. for his tunic, NRO DCN 1/9/37.

Name possibly in CUL Ms Gg.1.33, Nicholas de Gorran, Distinctiones (13th/14th cs); but only Thomas is clearly legible on fo 3 and the rest is at best a calculated guess; see Thomas V.

In the inventory of 1424 of St Leonard's one of the items is a red vestment described as his gift, Bensly, 'St Leonard's', 196–197; see also *ib.*, 212–213.

There is an undated ref. to him as prior of Lynn in *The Book of Margery Kempe*, 178 (ref. under John de Derham).

Richard de HEYDON
occ. 1347/8

1347/8, ill and the infirmarer spent 12d. on medicine, NRO DCN 1/10/6.

Alexander de HIKLING B.Th. [Hik', Hykelingge, Ikkeling
occ. 1326/7 d. 1343/4

1326/7, student, with pension contribution from the master of the cellar and a 20s. gift from the prior, NRO DCN 1/1/29.

1329/30, student at Oxford, with contribution from the master of the cellar, and travelling expenses pd by the communar, NRO DCN 1/1/30; 1/12/18.

1331/2, student, with contributions from the cellarer, hostiller and refectorer, NRO DCN 1/2/101; 1/7/3; 1/8/30.

1332/3, student, with contributions from the master of the cellar and the sacrist, NRO DCN 1/1/32; 1/4/27, 28.

1333/4, student, with contributions from the refectorer, NRO DCN 1/8/31.

1334/5, student, with contributions from the master of the cellar, and the refectorer, NRO DCN 1/1/38; 1/8/32.

1340, 13 Sept., the presidents of the Black Monk Chapter were asked to write to the prior of Norwich, urging him to send Alexander to Oxford to incept in theology, Pantin, *BMC*, ii, 16; and see John de Mari and John de Whyteley.

[?1335 × 1340], travelled to the papal curia bearing letters concerning the lawsuit between the prior and chapter and the abp of Canterbury; he stopped at Fécamp to solicit the support of the abbot and convent there, with whom the Norwich monks had been in confraternity since their foundation, Reg. X, fos 34v–35v. He is described here as B.Th., a fact not noted in *BRUO*.

1343/4, d., and the chamberlain pd the brief bearer, NRO DCN 1/5/12.

Adam de HILLEYE

occ. 1273/4

1273/4, cellarer, see below.

1273/4, recd 10s. from the master of the cellar towards his travelling expenses to [?the Council of] Lyons, NRO DCN 1/1/3; there is also ref. to a payment of 44s. to the cellarer and sacrist for the return journey on this same acct. The sacrist was Henry de Lakenham, q.v., and so Adam must have been cellarer. But see Gerard de Fordham.

Denys de HINDOLVESTON [Hindolpheston, Hyldolveston, Hyndolveston

occ. 1471/2 occ. 1492

1475/6, hostiller, NRO DCN 1/7/108.
1476/9, precentor, NRO DCN 1/9/75–77.
1476/80, communar/pittancer, NRO DCN 1/12/70, 71; see below.
1484/5, prior of Yarmouth, NRO DCN 2/4/16.
1489/92, almoner, NRO DCN 1/6/104–108; see below.
1492, acc. to Blomefield, *Norfolk*, iii, 432, master of St Paul's hospital, and see below.

1471/2, student at Oxford (NRO DCN 1/4/93), with pension contributions from the almoner, chamberlain, hostiller, precentor, refectorer, sacrist and the prior of Lynn. NRO DCN 1/6/84, 85; 1/5/100; 1/7/106; 1/9/70; 1/8/95; 1/4/93; 2/1/64.
1472/3, student, with contributions from the almoner, precentor and prior of St Leonard's, NRO DCN 1/6/86; 1/9/71; 2/3/82.
1473/4, student, with contributions from the almoner, hostiller, sacrist and prior of St Leonard's, NRO DCN 1/6/87, 88; 1/7/107; 1/4/94; 2/3/83.
Note: there is no evidence of his presence at Cambridge as indicated in *BRUC*.

1479/80, responsible for the accts of the Wakering and Erpingham chantries, NRO DCN 4/9.
1480, 25 Oct., granted a general pardon by the king and described as *alias* Hyldyrston, *CPR (1476–1485)*, 221.
1483/4, some of the money remaining from the accts of these two chantries was in his keeping, NRO DCN 4/10.
1492, 5/8 Oct., 8th in order at the visitation of bp Goldwell, Jessopp, *Visit.*, 8; it was reported that he was holding simultaneously a number of obedientiary offices, viz., those of communar, almoner, infirmarer, pittancer and the mastership of St Paul's hospital, and also that he had appropriated the convent herb garden for his own personal use in which saffron [*crocus*] was grown, *ib.*, 3–4.

Nicholas de HINDOLVESTON [Hildolveston, Hyndolfston, Hyndolveston, Hyndolwston

occ. 1296/7 occ. 1317

1313/14, 1316/17, communar, *Comm. Rolls*, 20, n. 1, 107, 89.

1296/7, gave the sacrist 16s. 7d. [for the building of the tower], NRO DCN 1/4/12.
1302/3, went to London with Thomas Celararii, [Thomas de Plumsted, q.v.] on business for the communar, *Comm. Rolls*, 83.
1309/10, visited Hindolveston, NRO DCN 60/18/16.
1309/10, with Hervey de Swafham, q.v., proctor, apptd by the prior and chapter to attend the Black Monk Chapter at Westminster, NRO DCN 1/1/21, and Pantin, *BMC*, i, 166–167 (from Reg. IX, fo 12).
1312/13, visited Hindolveston with his *socius*, NRO DCN 60/18/18.
1313/14, 1314/15, with Adam de Belagh, q.v., apptd to collect tenths, NRO DCN 1/1/23, 24.
1314/15, 1315/16, collector of tenths, NRO DCN 1/8/23.
1316/17, ill and spent 3s. 6d. in *infirmitate nostro*, *Comm. Rolls*, 90.
1313/14, 1316/17, as communar involved with building operations, *Comm. Rolls*, 89–93, 107–112.
1317, 17 July, one of two monk proctors apptd by the chapter to appear before the sheriff who had recd a royal writ to distrain over non payment of tenths, Reg. IX, fo 1; see Adam de Belagh.

HINGHAM

see Hengham, Ingham

HO

see William de Hoo

HOCLE

see Acle

HODERSET

see Hedirset

[Richard HODGE

Incorrectly identified as a monk (through a misreading of the original text) in *CClR, 1485–1500*, no 832].

HOLM

see Hulme

Thomas HOLT
occ. 1499 d. 1518/19

1499, 30 Mar., ord subdcn, Norwich cathedral, *Reg. abp Morton*, iii, no 53.

1499, 6 Apr., 46th in order on the visitation certificate, *Reg. abp Morton*, iii, no 258.

1511/12, rewarded by the infirmarer for celebrating masses at St Peter's, Parmentergate, one of the churches in Norwich for which the infirmarer was responsible, NRO DCN 1/10/34.

1518/19, d., and the sacrist pd for two tapers at his funeral, NRO DCN 1/4/115.

John de HOO D.Th.
occ. 1363/4 d. 1413/4

1386/7, 1387/8, 1400/1, 1404/6, prior of Yarmouth, NRO DCN 2/4/2–4; Windsor, St George's chapel, XV.55.76.

1363/4, student [at Oxford], with pension contribution from the communar/pittancer, NRO DCN 1/12/30.

1377/8, incepted in theology at Oxford, (NRO DCN 1/1/55), and recd money for his expenses from the hostiller, master of the cellar, precentor and refectorer, NRO DCN 1/7/34; 1/1/55; 1/9/16; 1/8/46.

1387/8, as prior of Yarmouth, gave 6s. 8d. to the pittancer towards the cloister work, NRO DCN 1/12/33.

1393/4, the refectorer's inventory notes that he now had the cedar *ciphus* formerly in the custody of John de Berney, q.v., NRO DCN 1/8/48.

1407, 20 Nov., with William de Thetford, q.v., installed Alexander de Totyngton, q.v., as bp., Blomefield, *Norfolk*, iii, 526.

1413/14, d., and 'alms' of 8s. were recd by the chamberlain, NRO DCN 1/5/43.

1418/19, the refectorer recorded that William Metyngham, q.v., had pd for the repair of the *ciphus*, formerly belonging to M. John Hoo, NRO DCN 1/8/64; it is described as of silver gilt.

Name in
(1) CUL Ms Kk.2.15, Augustine, Sermones (14th c.); on fo 1, *tradatur*—.
(2) CUL Ms Mm.3.16, Avicenna (13th/14th c.); *libri*—; see Ker, 'Norwich Cathedral Mss', 259, 261.

His *portiforium magnum* (press mark D.xxv) was at Yarmouth priory; see Beeching and James, 'Norwich Cathedral Library', 78, and Sharpe, *Eng. Benedictine Libraries*, iv, B64.27.

The 1424 inventory of St Leonard's records his gift of glosses in the gospels of Mark and Luke, Bensly, 'St Leonard's' 210–211, Sharpe, *Eng. Benedictine Libraries*, iv, B62.45.

Nicholas de HOO
occ. 1352 occ. 1381

1357–1381, prior: 12 Dec. 1357, *prefectio*, by the bp at Bures, Reg. Percy, fo 23v; res. before 24 June 1381, NRO DCN 1/6/20.

c. 1350/2, prob. refectorer, NRO DCN 1/8/39; also Windsor, St George's chapel, XI.E.13.

1352, Apr./Sept., 1353/4, master of the cellar, NRO DCN 60/29/27; 60/4/47; 1/1/44; (he took over from Roger de Wolterton, q.v.)

1359, 27 June, with the official, apptd as special commissaries of the bp, Reg. Percy, fo 32v.

1360/1, ill and the master of the cellar pd William Rugham, *medicus* 2s. for his services, NRO DCN 1/1/47.

1361, 2 July, with two others apptd as the bp's special commissaries, Reg. Percy, fo 45.

1363, visited the curia where he obtained at least five indults including indulgences for penitents visiting the cathedral and giving alms, licences to dispense ten monks in their 20th yr to be ord pr., to create three notaries and to be granted plenary remission of his own sins at the hour of his death, all dated 31 July, *CPP*, i, (1342–1419), 445. See also under William Watyr.

1365, 11 July, apptd sole vicar general [in spirituals] by the bp, Reg. Percy, fo 65.

1366/7, spent some time at Newton and his expenses amounted to 15s. in cash, in addition to milk, butter, eggs, and other products of the manor, NRO DCN 60/28/6.

1367/8, ill, and drugs and cordials [*species and lectuar'*], costing 8s. 7d. were purchased for his treatment, NRO DCN 1/1/50.

1368, [8] July, apptd commissary by the bp, Reg. Percy, fo 82.

1370, 22 July, with the official, comm. as vicars general, Reg. Despenser, fo 1; he prob. continued to act, usually with the official, until the beginning of Aug. 1372, when the bp returned, *ib.*, fos 1–15v.

1373/4, ill and the prior of St Leonard's pd for medicine, prob. because he was staying there, NRO DCN 2/3/6.

1374, 13 June, another comm. as vicar general, again a joint apptment with another, Reg. Despenser, fo 26v

1375, 4 Aug., 5 Dec. 1375, 26 Dec. 1376, 17 Oct. 1378, are the other dates on which the bp comm. him to act as one of usually two vicars general, *ib.*, fos 35, 41, 49, 60; in this last instance the word commissary is substituted for vicar general.

1379/80, a coadjutor was provided for him, to whom the master of the cellar gave a gift or gifts, NRO DCN 1/1/58.

1381, 2 May, with John de Lenn I, q.v., and others acted as executors of a will, *CPR (1377–1381)*, 593.

1381, June/Sept., the almoner pd him as [former] prior a pension of 10s. for two terms (St

John the Baptist and Michaelmas), NRO DCN 1/6/20; prob. he d. around the end of this yr.

Some of his correspondence may be found in Reg. X, e.g. on fos 41–44v.

Thomas HOO B.Cn.L.
occ. 1473/4 d. 1493

1473/4, master of the cellar, NRO DCN 1/1/93.
1475/6, 1478/9, prior of Aldeby, NRO DCN 2/2/22, 23.
1488/90, and prob. until 1493, prior of Yarmouth, NRO DCN 2/4/17, 18, and see below.
1482/3, grace for entering in canon law at Cambridge granted.
1485/6, B.Cn.L., adm., incepted in canon law.
Note: these entries are given in *BRUC* (from *CU Grace Book A*). Hoo's is clearly an unusual case. He must have entered the monastery some years prior to his appointment to the important office of master of the cellar, and he must also have been pursuing his studies for some eight to ten years before obtaining a degree. Since there is no early reference to him in the Norwich accts, or in any other Norwich records, he may have sought adm. after an initial period of study as a secular clerk.
1477/8, pd the precentor 20d. *pro M[agistro] historiarum*, a library volume with the press-mark l.xxvij, which he was presumably borrowing, NRO DCN 1/9/76; see Greatrex, 'Norwich Monk Students', 575–576.
1492, 5/8 Oct., 16th in order at the visitation of bp Goldwell, Jessopp, *Visit.*, 8.
1493, 18 Jan., d. by this date when his successor as prior of Yarmouth was apptd, Reg. Goldwell, fo 163v; he is described here as B.Cn.L.

William de HOO [Ho
occ. 1272 [occ. 1277/8]

1272, 2 Oct., precentor, Cotton, *Historia*, 149.
[1277/8], almoner, NRO DCN 45/32/1.

1272, 2 Oct., installed William Kirkeby, q.v., as prior, Cotton, *Historia*, 149.

Note: Dr Gransden suggested that William transferred to the Abbey of Bury St Edmunds where he became sacrist and was responsible for the continuation of the Bury chronicle. The latter vividly describes the Norwich city riot vs the monks in 1272 and the burning of the cathedral and some of the monastic buildings, an acct which could well have come from the pen of a monk who witnessed these events; see her *Hist. Writing*, i, 399–400. However, the dating of a title deed in which he is named as almoner at Norwich after his supposed transfer and a recent discovery of his presence at Bury in 1262 render this hypothesis unlikely.

John de HOVYNG [Hovynge
occ. 1320/1 occ. 1346/7

1320/1, purchased a *ciphus* from the refectorer, prob. soon after adm., NRO DCN 1/8/25.

1339/40, the refectorer pd 9d. for mending his *ciphus*, Oxford, Bod. Ms Rolls, Norfolk, no 48.
1346/7, ill and the infirmarer spent 4d. on medicine, NRO DCN 1/10/5.

John HOWCHON
occ. 1494

1494, 20 Nov., one of two *clerici* whom the bp comm. the prior to rec. on his behalf, [*monachand'*], Reg. Goldwell, fo 181v.

Note: see John Walsham II, who may be this monk.

Elyas de HOXNE
occ. 1290 occ. 1302/3

1290/2, 1293/4 or 1294/5, 1296/9, with Roger de Dorobina, q.v., communar/pittancer, NRO DCN 1/12/3–8 and *Comm. Rolls*, 57–75; also in 1299/1300, Oxford, Bod. Ms Charters, Norfolk, no 269.
1300/3, communar/pittancer on his own, NRO DCN 1/12/9–11 and *Comm. Rolls*, 76–86.

1292, recd money [for pittances] from the master of the cellar for the anniversary of prior [William de] Kirkeby, q.v., NRO DCN 1/1/10.
1295/6, visited Catton for *liberatio denariorum*, NRO DCN 60/4/11.

Richard de HOXNE
n.d.

n.d., [*temp.* prior William] prior of Hoxne, Suffolk Record Office, HD 1538/265/1, p. 10 (fragment of a Hoxne cartulary). See also *HRH*, 92.
n.d., as prior witnessed a grant to the chapel of Hoxne, with Walter, q.v., *ib.*, p. 14.

Note: there are four early priors named William between 1205 and 1289; see William de Walsham, William son of Odo, William de Burnham, William de Kirkeby.

[I HUGH
occ. 1158

1158, called 'dapifer monachorum' which Dugdale interpreted as cellarer, *Monasticon*, iv, 8].

II HUGH
occ. 1288

1288, described as 'in theologia et aliis scientiis excellenter expertus', who considered himself to have been under 'obligation' to Christ Church, Canterbury. In a letter to Everard, q.v., and to the prior and convent of Norwich in reply to their inquiries, prior Henry de Eastry (q.v. Canterbury), assured them that he was not in any way bound to Christ Church and was free to make his prof. at Norwich. The letter concluded by saying that in the event that Hugh should desire to visit Canterbury he would be welcome, CUL Ms Ee.5.31, fo 28v.

Thomas ?HU—HSON
occ. 1535

1535 [Sept./Dec.] ord subdcn, place uncertain, NRO DN ORR/1/1, fo 26v.

Ralph de HULME [Holm
occ. c. 1319/20 d. c. 1349

[1319/20], one of two *clerici* whom the prior sent to the bp bearing a letter requesting him to rec. [and bless] them, Reg. IX, fo 26.

1329/30, chaplain to the prior, NRO DCN 1/4/24.

1349, part yr, refectorer, his first year, NRO DCN 1/8/37.

1320/1, pd the refectorer for a *ciphus*, NRO DCN 1/8/25.

1329/30, one of the monks involved in the financial arrangements in preparation for the lawsuit at the curia; see Richard de Hecham, NRO DCN 1/4/24.

1349, Sept., prob. d. as he was replaced as refectorer by Roger de Thurstone, q.v.

John HUNTYNGDON
occ. 1478/80

1478/80, student at Cambridge, with travelling expenses pd by the communar/pittancer, NRO DCN 1/12/70, 71.

1479/80, returned [from Cambridge] for the el of a prior, NRO DCN 1/12/71.

HWAPLOD
see Waplode

HYKELINGGE
see Hikling

HYLDOLVESTON
see Hindolveston

Thomas de HYNDRINGHAM [Hyndryngham
occ. 1400 occ. 1434/5

1400, 4 Sept.; 1411/12; 1413/15; 28 Aug. 1417, almoner, NRO DCN 45/33/65; 1/6/41–45; Reg. II, i, fo 92.

1417, Oct./1418, Apr., sacrist, NRO DCN 1/4/52.

1422, Jan./Sept., infirmarer, NRO DCN 1/10/14.

1420/1, gave 20s. to the building work in the cloister, NRO DCN 1/12/48.

1425/6, gave the chamberlain 3s. 4d. towards the expense of a new barn at Lakenham, NRO DCN 1/5/53.

1427/8, ill and the infirmarer spent 2s. 6d. on medicine, NRO DCN 1/10/15.

1430/1, gave the gardener 3d. to help with the repair of the wall *vs Holmstrete*, NRO DCN 1/11/14.

1431/2, ill and 2s. were spent on medicine, NRO DCN 1/10/19.

1432/3, ill and 6d. spent on medicine, NRO DCN 1/10/20.

1434/5, ill and 20d. spent on medicine, NRO DCN 1/10/21.

Name in CUL Ms Kk.2.20, Haymo super epistolas Pauli etc. (14th c.), with an index to Haymo (fos 4–9v), *tabula scripta per*—on fo 9v, and his name also occ. on fo 276, *liber*—; see Ker, 'Norwich Cathedral Mss', 259.

W. de HYNDRINGHAM
occ. 1299/1300

1299/1300, stayed one night at Hindolveston for which the manorial acct was charged 4d., NRO DCN 60/18/14.

HYNGHAM
see Hengham

IKKELING
see Hikling

ILYRICH
see Ayrich

Robert de INGHAM
occ. 1383/4

1383/4, d., and the chamberlain pd the brief bearer, NRO DCN 1/5/17.

INGHAM
see also Hengham

INGULPH [Ingulfus
occ. [1106/1107] occ. c. 1136

[1106 × 1107]–c. 1136 prior: first occ. [1106 × 1107] and last occ. after 1136, *Fasti*, ii, 58–59, *HRH*, 57.

[?1107], as a monk, presumably of Norwich, with Gosfridus, Macarius and Stannard, q.v., witnessed a final concord of the bp, *Eng. Epis. Acta*, vi, no 5.

[1107 × 1119, 1 Mar.], as prior, witness to an episcopal agreement concerning Hoxne, *ib.*, vi, no 19.

1119, 10 Nov., made a grant to the hospital of St Paul, *N. Cath. Charters*, ii, no 496.

[1121 × 1136], witnessed a number of episcopal *acta*, *Eng. Epis. Acta.*, vi, nos 30, 35; nos 51 and 52.

n.d., 16 Jan. obit occ. in BL Ms Harley 3950, fo 3.

n.d., received a number of letters from bp Losinga which are printed in Anstruther, *Epist. Losinga*:
(1) before he became prior, no 14.
(2) while prior, nos 15, 17, 51, 52.

JAK'
occ. 1290/1

1290/1, the following entry occ. in *Comm. Rolls*, 60 (NRO DCN 1/12/3): *pro panno fratris Jak'*, 13s. 4d.

William de JAXHAM [Jakisham, Yaxham
occ. 1314/15 d. 1345/6

1317/18, 1319/20, 1321/2, refectorer, NRO DCN 1/8/24–26.
1345/6, and possibly before, prior of St Leonard's, see below.

1314/15, recd 18d. from the refectorer prob. because he was at Oxford with Thomas de Hemenhale, q.v., to whom the refectorer also gave a small sum in the same section of his acct, NRO DCN 1/8/23.
Note: the entry in *BRUO*, taken from Saunders, *Obed. Rolls*, 185, n.1, has not been found, and it is likely that it is a misreading or misprint for the above.
1345/6, d. at St Leonard's and the pittancer acknowledged a contribution of £10 for the building work in the cloister, NRO DCN 1/12/25.

John de JERNMUTH [Zernemuth
occ. 1384/5 d. 1418/19

1384/5, hostiller, NRO DCN 1/7/42.
1394/9, *custos* of Hoxne, NRO DCN 2/6/1–5; in his first yr he was assisted by Nicholas de Geyton, q.v.
1402/3, refectorer, NRO DCN 1/8/49.
1418/19, d., and the chamberlain recd 'alms' of 13s. 4d., NRO DCN 1/5/46.

Nicholas de JERNEMUTH
occ. 1357

1357, 28 Sept., master of St Paul's hospital and arranged a lease, NRO DCN 45/31/15.

I Robert de JERNMUTH [Jernemuth
occ. 1339/40 occ. 1358

1339/40, recd 5s. from the refectorer for his *ciphus*, Oxford, Bod. Ms Rolls, Norfolk, no 48, (possibly because he had himself pd to have it mended).
1345, ill and the infirmarer cared for him, NRO DCN 1/10/2.
1346/7, 1347/8 and possibly 1348/9, ill, and the infirmarer spent 14d., 21d., and pd for a cordial respectively; in 1348/9 the initial R. only is given and so the ref. may be to Roger de Jernmuth, q.v.
1349/50, the prior of St Leonard's pd him £5 3s. 6d. *pro quodam vestimento*, NRO DCN 2/3/2.
1353, 14 May, granted a papal indult to choose his confessor, *CPL*, iii, (1342–1362), 506.
[1350 × 1355], apptd by the prior and chapter as proctor to go to the abbot of Gloucester concerning payment of a pension, Reg. X, fo 38v.
1358, 1 Jan., comm. by the bp to hear confessions of monks and of others in the cathedral church, Reg. Percy, fo 23v.

II Robert de JERNMUTH [Iernemuth, Yarnemuth, Yermuth, Zermode
occ. 1411/12 d. 1459/60

1418/23, and prob. to Nov. 1424, hostiller, NRO DCN 1/7/63–68.
1440/1, infirmarer, NRO DCN 1/10/22.
1443/4, refectorer, NRO DCN 1/8/81.

1411/12, student at Oxford, and recd a contribution of 46s. 3d. from the chamberlain, NRO DCN 1/5/41.
1430, 23 Sept., licensed as penitentiary [in the cathedral church], Reg. Alnwick, fo 102.
1430/1, gave the gardener 20d. to help with the repair of the wall *vs Holmstrete*, NRO DCN 1/11/14.
1440/1, ill, while infirmarer and spent 2s. 10d. on medicine for himself, NRO DCN 1/10/22.
1443, 31 Oct., with the prior and the bp served at the pontifical mass at the high altar, Reg. Brouns, fo 109; see John Heverlond.
1445, Dec., one of three monks nominated by the prior and chapter for the office of *visitator* for excepted jurisdiction, *sed. vac.* Norwich, Reg. abp. Stafford, fo 57.
1448, 15 Dec., name occ. on a rough list of those assigned to celebrate Sunday masses, but occ. only on this one occasion, Cambridge, Emm. Coll. Ms 142, fo 68.
1459/60, d., and the chamberlain recd 'alms', NRO DCN 1/5/91.

See note in next entry.

III Robert JERNMUTH [Jernemuth, Yermuth, Yernemuth
occ. 1490/1 d. 1505/6

1490/94, hostiller, NRO DCN 1/7/119, 120.
1494/5, sacrist, NRO DCN 1/4/107; apptment confirmed by the bp., 27 Sept. 1494, Reg. Goldwell, fo 180.
1496/1502, 1503/4, prior of St Leonard's, NRO DCN 2/3/102–108.

1492, 5/8 Oct., 27th in order at the visitation of bp Goldwell, Jessopp, *Visit.*, 8.
1499, 6 Apr., 20th on the visitation certificate, *Reg. abp Morton*, iii, no 258.
1505/6, d., and the sacrist pd 16d. for tapers for his funeral, NRO DCN 1/4/109; the ordinary monk had only 8d. worth of tapers, but he

prob. d. while prior of St Leonard's and therefore ranked higher.

Name in two mss:
(1) NRO DCL/2, John Boccatius etc. (15th c.); on fo 22^{v} *per dompnum*—.
(2) Oxford, Bod. Ms Canonici misc. 110, Anticlaudianus, etc. (early 15th c.).

Note: one or both of these mss could have been in the possession of Robert de Jernemuth II above.

Roger de JERNEMUTH [Zernemuth
occ. 1345/6 occ. 1348/9

1348/9, student at Oxford and the communar pd for his travel expenses and for the transporting of his books and other necessities, 24s.; he also pd for the expenses of the return journey for him and his *socius*, 25s. 6d., NRO DCN 1/12/27.

1345/6, ill and the infirmarer spent 13s. on medicine, NRO DCN 1/10/4.

1346/7, 1347/8, ill, and the infirmarer spent 12d., and 7d. respectively on medicine, NRO DCN 1/10/5, 6.

1348/9, an R. de Jernemuth ill, and was given a cordial by the infirmarer, NRO DCN 1/10/7; however, this may ref. to Robert de Jernemuth I, q.v.; also a Roger de Sacristaria was ill this year, who was prob. either this monk or Roger de Eston, q.v.

Thomas JERNEMUTH [Zermowth
d. 1450/1

1450/1, d., and the chamberlain recd 'alms' of 16s. 8d., NRO DCN 1/5/83.

1450/1, his *ciphus* was purchased from the refectorer by Henry de Stokysby, q.v., NRO DCN 1/8/88.

I JOHN
n.d.

n.d., 28 Aug., name occ. in a Canterbury obit list, BL Ms Arundel 68, fo 39^{v}.

II JOHN [?de Oxonia
occ. [1153 × 1168] occ. [1168 × 1174]

[1153 × 1168], prior: he also occ. [1168 × 1174], *Fasti*, ii, 59, *HRH*, 57–88. See Richard de Ferreres his predecessor and Elricus and Ranulph, one of whom was prob. his successor.

[c. 1157], recd a visit from John of Salisbury who reported a kind welcome, *Salisbury Letters*, i, no 39; he is named by Salisbury only as John the monk and so this may be another monk.

[1168] recd a letter from John of Salisbury concerning his experiences in exile with abp Anselm, *ib.*, ii, no 252.

n.d., 6 Apr. the obit of John de Oxon' occ. in the kalendar in Reg. XI, fo 5^{v}.

III JOHN
occ. c. 1504

c. 1504, a John, along with six other priests, (Christian names only given) made his prof.; this is recorded on an inserted leaf (prob. of rough notes) between fos 27^{v} and 28 in Reg. Nikke (9/14).

IV JOHN
occ. c. 1504

c. 1504, another John, along with two other dcns (Christian names only given) made his prof.; this is recorded on an inserted leaf (prob. of rough notes) between fos 27^{v} and 28 in Reg. Nikke (9/14).

Note: see John Orwell.

Thomas JOLY [Jolye
occ. 1526, occ. 1538

1526, 7 June, one of a group of younger monks present at the visitation of bp Nikke, who complained that they were required by the seniors to memorize the psalter, and the antiphons and responses etc., which they considered a waste of time, Jessopp, *Visit.*, 198.

1534, 28 July, subscribed to the Act of Supremacy, *DK 7th Report*, Appndx 2, 295.

1538, 30 Apr., dispensed to wear the habit of a secular pr. and hold a canonry and prebend in the cathedral and any other benefice, and be non resident, Chambers, *Faculty Office Regs*, 137.

1538, 2 May, licensed as a secular canon, *L and P Henry VIII*, xiii, pt 1, no 1115(4).

JORDAN
n.d.

n.d., 26 Apr., obit occ. in the kalendar in Reg. XI, fo 3^{v}.

KAAM
see Cam

J. de KANT'
occ. 1278/9

1278/9, recd a *capa* from the prior, NRO DCN 1/1/4.

William KEGELL
see William London II

Nicholas de KELFELD [Kelfeeld
occ. 1424 d. 1452/3

1424, prior of Hoxne, acc. to Blomefield, *Norfolk*, iii, 609.

1424/7, 1428/35, precentor, NRO DCN 1/9/37–49.

1436, 1437/8, prior of Aldeby, NRO DCN 2/2/12 and see below.

1436, 22 Jan., apptd by the bp as penitentiary at Aldeby, Reg. Alnwick, fo 103^{v}.

1446, name occ. on a rough list of those assigned to celebrate weekday and chantry masses, Cambridge, Emm. Coll. Ms 142, fo 68; also on a similar list (prob. of similar date) for the *magna missa*, *ib.*, fo 77v.
1452/3, d., and the chamberlain recd 'alms' of 20s., NRO DCN 1/5/85.
1454/5, the refectorer spent 4d. in repairing his *ciphus*, NRO DCN 1/8/91.

[Richard KEMP
1339/40, communar or pittancer, acc. to Saunders, *Obed. Rolls*, 195; he gives no further ref.
Note: there is an R.K., whom the prior recommended for ordination, c.1319 in Reg. IX, fo 22v; but he was not then a monk. See John de Worstede.]

W. de KENIGHALE [Kenighal, Kenynghale
occ. 1312/13 occ. 1318/19
1312/13, was given a *capa* by the infirmarer, NRO DCN 1/10/1; he also recd a small sum from the refectorer and therefore may have been a student as below, NRO DCN 1/8/22.
1314, possibly a student at Oxford like Hervey de Swafham and Alexander de Sprowston, q.v., NRO DCN 1/8/22.
1315/16, with other monks given a small sum under 'donations' by the master of the cellar, NRO DCN 1/1/25.
1318/19, possibly a student at Oxford as he and Robert de Ely, q.v., together recd 4s. from the refectorer, NRO DCN 1/8/24.

John de KIMBURLE
occ. 1297/8
1297/8, was pd expenses by the master of the cellar for a journey to Salisbury, NRO DCN 1/1/13.

John KING
occ. 1532
1532, 3 June, present at the visitation of bp Nikke and said that he had been 'incarcerated' for disobedience, Jessopp, *Visit.*, 267.

John KIRBY [Kyrby, *alias* Sherene, ?Shereve, Sherve
occ. 1526 occ. 1538
1532, 3 June, succentor, Jessopp, *Visit.*, 267.
1526, 7 June, one of a group of younger monks, present at the visitation of bp Nikke, who complained that they were required by the seniors to memorize the psalter and the antiphons and responses etc., which they considered a waste of time, Jessopp, *Visit.*, 198; he also deposed that the cloister and dormitory doors remained open at night allowing access to intruders, and that the novices were clothed at the expense of the junior monks instead of the seniors according to custom, *ib.*, 203.
1532, 3 June, present at the visitation of bp Nikke and was accused of being one of a group of monks who caused discord in the community and were in correspondence with Robert Catton I, q.v. (who had left not long before to become abbot of St Alban's), seeking support from him for their 'reform measures', Jessopp, *Visit.*, 265. He himself reported that all was well, apart from the lack of students at university, *ib.*, 267. (Note: as to this last statement see under Thomas Morton and Richard Norwich.
1538, 30 Apr., dispensed to wear the habit of a secular pr. and hold a canonry and prebend in the cathedral and any other benefice, and be non resident, Chambers, *Faculty Office Regs*, 137.
1538, 2 May, licensed as a secular canon, *L and P Henry VIII*, xiii, pt 1, no 1115(4).

John de KIRKEBY [Kyrkeby
occ. 1380/1 d. 1413/14
1380/1, prior of Aldeby, NRO DCN 2/2/1.
1387/8, 1393/4, 25 Mar., infirmarer, NRO DCN 1/12/33; 1/10/9.
1408, June/1409, infirmarer, NRO DCN 1/10/12, 13.
1384/5, concerned with negotiations for the master of the cellar, NRO DCN 1/1/61.
1386/7, accompanied the master of the cellar to London, NRO DCN 1/1/64.
1387/8, infirmarer and gave 20s. to the communar towards the building operations in the cloister, NRO DCN 1/12/33.
1394, 1 Jan., proctor for the prior and chapter in their case vs. bp Despenser arising out of his visitation, NRO DCN 42/2/12; he was one of several monks deposed by the bp for mismanagement in office, NRO DCN 42/2/13; see Thomas de Tunstale.
1395, 4 Apr., mentioned in a papal comm. addressed to the abp of Canterbury and bp of Hereford who were apptd to adjudicate in the above dispute, *CPL*, iv, (1362–1402), 525.
1397, 30 Nov., the king ordered his immediate return from Rome, where he was speaking and acting against the king's interests, *CClR, 1396–1399*, 278.
1400, 13 Oct., proctor of the prior and chapter [?in Rome], NRO DCN 42/2/16.
1413/14, d., and the chamberlain recd 'alms' of 18s., NRO DCN 1/5/43.

I Nicholas de KIRKEBY [Kyrkeby
occ. 1263/4 occ. 1272/3
1263/4, with William de Cantebrig', q.v., named as *custodes commune*, NRO DCN 1/1/1.
1272/3, visited Hemsby for *liberatio denariorum*, NRO DCN 60/15/2.

II Nicholas de KIRKEBY [Kyrkeby
occ. 1306/7 occ. 1312/13

1306/7, bought a *ciphus* from the refectorer for 8s., NRO DCN 1/8/18.
1312/13, ill, and the infirmarer cared for him, NRO DCN 1/10/1.

Note: the allocation of biographical details to these two monks is arbitrary and there may only be one individual rather than two over an exceptionally long span of time.

William de KIRKEBY [Kirkby
occ. 1272 d. 1289

1272–1289, prior: el. 1 Oct. 1272, Cotton, *Historia*, 149, see William de Hoo; d. 9 Mar. 1289, *ib.*, 170; and see *Fasti*, ii, 61.
1272/3, visited Gnatingdon for *liberatio denariorum*, NRO DCN 60/14/4; visited [North] Elmham, NRO DCN 60/10/4.
1273/4, went to the coronation of Edward I, for which his expenses were £13 4s. 4d., NRO DCN 1/1/3; also he went to confer with the king about the attack on the priory by the citizens of Norwich [in 1272], and his expenses for this visit were £13 5s. 2d., *ib.*
1279, invited to abp Peckham's enthronement which took place 8 Oct. 1279, *Fasti*, ii, 7; the invitation is also in *Epist. Pecham* i, 38.
1282/3, pd visits to Thetford, Sedgeford, Hindolveston, Ipswich and Cambridge, Hudson, 'Camera Roll', 281 (NRO DCN 1/1/6).
1289, 9 Mar., obit occ. in BL Ms Harley 3950, fo 4.

Some of his official acts as prior are recorded in a number of charters printed in *N. Cath. Charters*, i, nos 230, 362–369, 374–380 and others in *ib.*, ii, *passim.* A series of ordinances made during his priorate to regulate the almonry school have come to light at Worcester, WCM B.680; see Greatrex, 'Almonry School', 171.

John KNOWTE
occ. 1477

1477, 8 Nov. one of three *clerici* whom the prior requested the bp to rec. and bless, Reg. Goldwell, fo 9; on 8 Nov., the bp comm. the prior to perform the ceremony, *ib.*

KRANE
see Crane

Edmund KYNESTEDE
see Ryngsted

KYRBY
see Kirby

KYRKEBY
see Kirkeby

M. Henry de LAKENHAM
occ. [1266] d. 1310

1289–1310, prior: occ. as prior 27 June 1289; res. by 5 Feb. 1310, *Fasti*, ii, 61. The date of his res. is given as 17 Jan. in the kalendar in Lambeth Ms 368, fo 4.
[1266, 28 Nov.], apptd dean of the manors by the bp and designated *magister*, *confrater noster capituli' nostri monachus*, *N. Cath. Charters*, i, no 225. See Cheney, 'Norwich Cath. Priory', 98–99.

Note: he is the only monk known to have held this office.

1272/86, sacrist, and almost certainly sacrist until his el. as prior in c. 1289, NRO DCN 1/4/1–7; he continued as sacrist for a short time after his el., i.e until July 1289, NRO DCN 1/4/8.
1273/4, the master of the cellar recorded 44s. in expenses for him and the cellarer returning from the 'papal council' [at Lyons], NRO DCN 1/1/3; see Adam de Hilleye.
1290/1, attended the Black Monk Chapter at which there were discussions about the newly opened house of study for monks at Oxford, Pantin, *BMC*, i, 129–131.
1291/2, went to London *in anniversarium Regine* [?Eleanor of Castile] and his expenses were £7 13. 9d., NRO DCN 1/1/11.
1295, summoned to parliament at Westminster on 1 Aug., *Parl. Writs*, i, 763; he was also summoned on 30 Sept. 1297, *ib.*
1295/6, spent Christmas at Hindolveston, NRO DCN 60/18/12.
1297/8, stayed at [North] Elmham during the fair there, NRO DCN 60/10/10.
1299/1300, visited Denham, and his falcon was fed from the poultry stock at the manor, NRO DCN 60/7/4.
1303/4, ill, and 9s. 3d. were spent on medical treatment, NRO DCN 1/1/17.
1307/8, stipends were pd to workers on the prior's tomb; there were also more medical expenses, NRO DCN 1/1/18.
1308/10, *triasandali* and other cordials were purchased for his treatment, NRO DCN 1/1/19, 21.
1309/10, gave £40 *ad faciend' campanile*, NRO DCN 1/1/21.
1309/10, [after his resignation], stopped at Hindolveston where his horse was given fodder, NRO DCN 60/18/16.
1310/11, d., and on the day of his burial, £21 3s. were distributed *in usus pauperum*, NRO DCN 1/1/22.
[1310] 21/22 Oct., in BL Ms Harley 3950, fo 7v he is commemorated on 21 Oct.; this suggests that he d. on 21 Oct. 1310; in the kalendar in Reg. XI, fo 6v, the obit date is 22 Oct.

Name in four CUL Mss:
(1) Ii.1.32, Flores Bernardi etc. (14th c.) name on fo 3.

(2) Ii.4.2, Bonaventura (late 13th c.); [*liber*]—on fo 5; see also Henry Langrake and Robert Catton I.
(3) Ii.4.15, Liber eruditionis religiosorum (14th c.); see also Robert Catton II.
(4) Ii.4.35, Hugo de Folieto (13th/14th c.); name on fo 3.

Miss Dodwell has recently estimated that he may have possessed at least seventeen volumes; see also her 'History and Norwich Monks', 41.

Some of his official acts are recorded in the charters printed in *N. Cath. Charters*, i, nos 57, 233, 237, 371 and *ib.*, ii, *passim* (indexed under his name).

John LAKENHAM

occ. 1492 occ. 1520

1494/5, 1497/8, 1499/1501, communar, NRO DCN 1/12/80, 82–84.
1501/2, 1503/4, prior of Lynn, NRO DCN 2/1/78,79.
1514, 27 Apr., prior of Aldeby, Jessopp, *Visit.*, 72.
1492, 5/8 Oct., 25th in order at the visitation of bp Goldwell, Jessopp, *Visit.*, 8.
1495/6, recd 9d. from the hostiller *in nomine subsidii*, NRO DCN 1/7/120.
1499, 6 Apr., 18th in order on the visitation certificate, *Reg. abp Morton*, iii, no 258.
1506, 3 Dec., obtained papal dispensation to rec. and retain any benefice with or without cure of souls, *CPL*, xviii (1503–1513), no 699.
1514, 27 Apr., present at the visitation of bp Nikke and stated that he knew little of the community affairs at Norwich as he was prior of Aldeby; he adm. that he had failed to render his acct for the previous yr but it was now ready for inspection, and the cell was £10 in debt, Jessopp, *Visit.*, 72–73, where there are additional details.
1520, 3 Sept., absent from the visitation of bp Nikke, and it was reported that he was in charge of the church at Martham [*deservit curae de Martham*]. *ib.*, 193.

Reyner de LAKENHAM

occ. 1282/3 occ. 1288/9

1282/6, almoner, NRO DCN 1/6/5–7.
1288/9, refectorer and prob. pittancer, as both accts are on the same roll, NRO DCN 1/8/1.

Note: see Reyner I, II and III, especially III.

Richard de LAKENHAM [R. de Lak'

occ. 1305/6 ?occ. 1342/3

1308/10, master of the cellar, NRO DCN 1/1/19–21; he was followed by William de Hadesto, q.v., in July 1310.
1327/8, master of the cellar, NRO DCN 60/4/33; 60/20/23; 60/35/24; 60/26/22.
*1328/40, chamberlain, NRO DCN 1/5/8–11.
*1320/1, R. de Lak' vs. Oxford recd 18d. from the master of the cellar under *donationes*, and in the same section Ric. de Lak' was given 3s., NRO DCN 1/1/28; there are other named university students receiving small sums under this same heading on this acct.
1305/6, visited Sedgeford, NRO DCN 60/33/14.
1308/9, pd a supervisory visit to Catton, NRO DCN 60/4/17.
1309/10, pd supervisory visits to Catton, Hindolveston, Hindringham, [North] Elmham and Sedgeford, NRO DCN 60/4/18; 60/18/16; 60/20/15; 60/10/12; 60/33/15. These manorial visits give the name as R. or Ric' de Lak'; visited Gnatingdon [as R. de Lakenham] for *liberatio denariorum*, NRO DCN 60/14/13.
*1329/30, handed over [*per manum*] £10 to the communar for the building expenses of the Bauchun chapel in the cathedral, *Comm. Rolls*, 117.
**1340/1, recd 2s. from the master of the cellar for a saddle, NRO DCN 1/1/37.
**1342/3, a Richard de Lakenham was responsible for swans, NRO DCN 1/1/40.

Note: there is some uncertainty here, which can be dealt with in several ways. I have decided to enter the facts as though they all concern only one monk; however, the unmarked entries could refer to one individual, while those marked by * could be treated as a second monk of the same name who early in his monastic life spent a brief period at Oxford. The two last entries marked by ** may not be a monk, but are included in the hope that they may help to shed light on this matter if new information becomes available. See also R. de Lok'.

Robert de LAKENHAM

d. 1404/5

1404/5, d., and the chamberlain recd 'alms' of 15s., NRO DCN 1/5/35.
1410, the refectorer's inventory refers to a *pecia ex dono* Robert, and to three covers for *ciphi*, NRO DCN 1/8/56; see also J. de Bury.
n.d., 20 July, obit occ. in the kalendar in Reg. XI, fo 5.

Name in a *magnum portiforium* listed among the books of the chapel of St. Leonard's in the 1424 inventory, *de dono*—; in the second inventory of 1452/3 it was described as *novum et magnum*, Bensly, 'St Leonard's', 206–207, 216–217. See also Sharpe, *Eng. Benedictine Libraries*, iv, B62.6, B63.7.

Richard de LANGELE

occ. 1345/6 d. 1383/4

1345/6, ill, and 20d. was spent by the infirmarer on medicine, NRO DCN 1/10/4.
1347/8, ill and 17d. spent on medicine, NRO DCN 1/10/6.
1383/4, d., and the chamberlain pd for the brief, NRO DCN 1/5/18.

Robert de LANGELE [Langle
occ. 1290/1 occ. 1326

1310–1326, prior: el. 29 Jan., 1310, Lambeth Ms 368, fo 4, el. confirmed [*prefectio*] by the bp at Spinney, 5 Feb., Reg. Salmon, fo 35; res. before 4 Sept. 1326, Reg. Ayermine, fo 9; see William de Claxton.

1310, before his el., subprior, Reg. Salmon, fo 35.

1290/1, 1291/2, gave small sums to the communar for the building work, *Comm. Rolls*, 57, 61.

1297/8, with Thomas Stokton, q.v., attended the Black Monk Chapter at Northampton, NRO DCN 1/12/7 and printed in Pantin, *BMC*, i, 279 [where it is dated 1298/9]. This same year he went to London with John Celararii, q.v., in June, *Comm. Rolls*, 71.

1302/3, with Hamo, q.v., attended the Black Monk Chapter in London, NRO DCN 1/12/11, and Pantin, *BMC*, i, 279 [dated 1303/4]. Note: these entries are also found in the more recent *Comm. Rolls*, 71, 83 (dated as here).

1310, 5 Feb., bp comm. John de Bromholm, q.v., to install him as prior, Reg. Salmon, fo 35. (Installed 28 Feb., Reg. IX, fo 22; there are copies of invitations to the ceremony sent to the abbot of Dereham and the priors of Bromholm and Toft Monks in this priory Reg. on fos 21, 22).

1311, in London from Easter to Pentecost and his expenses were over £43, NRO DCN 1/1/22.

1312, one of the cathedral priors summonned to meet the papal nuncios in London, *Councils and Synods*, ii, 1377.

Note: due to uncertainties and discrepancies in the dating of accts the 1311 entry immediately above may be a yr out and so may refer to this meeting.

1317, 13 Oct., the king comm. the prior to take the oath of John Howard, earl of Norfolk and Suffolk, whom the king had apptd custodian of Norwich Castle, Reg. IX, fo 1v.

1318/19, comm. the copying of a Ms of Cassiodorus, see below.

1324, 28 Nov., apptd vicar general in spirituals by the bp during his absence, Reg. Salmon, fo 111v; his *acta* are in the bp's register, beginning on fo 115.

1325, Lent, visited Hindolveston, NRO DCN 60/18/24.

1325, 16 Aug., apptd vicar general by the bp el., Robert Baldock, Reg. Baldock, fo 1, (that is, fo 1 of Reg. Ayermine).

n.d., 25 Aug., obit occ. in BL Ms Harley 3950, fo 6v.

Reg. IX contains a large collection of his correspondence, both official and personal.

Note: although there are no extant mss known to have been in his possession, Miss Dodwell remarks on his interest in obtaining books in 'History and Norwich Monks', 49, where she notes that he must have sanctioned the copying of a ms of Cassiodorus in 1318/19 for which the scribe was pd 50s., NRO DCN 1/1/27.

In 1322/3, his nephew, also Robert, stopped at [North] Elmham on his way back from Oxford, NRO DCN 60/10/19.

Roger de LANGELE [Langgele
occ. 1291/2 occ. 1346/7

1291/2, the master of the cellar bought rushes (under the heading 'Mariscus') from him, NRO DCN 1/1/11.

1337/8, recd a gift of 2s. from the master of the cellar, NRO DCN 1/1/34.

1346/7, ill and the infirmarer spent 5d. on medicine, NRO DCN 1/10/5.

Thomas de LANGELE
occ. 1330/1

1330/1, the master of the cellar bought rushes from him, (under the heading 'Mariscus'), NRO DCN 1/1/31.

LANGHAM
see Longham

Henry LANGRAKE [Lanrake
occ. 1492 occ. 1516/17

1514, 27 Apr., prior of Yarmouth, Jessopp, *Visit.*, 72.

1516/17, sacrist, NRO DCN 1/4/113.

1493/4, student [prob. at Cambridge], with pension contributions from the almoner, hostiller, master of the cellar, and the priors of Lynn and St Leonard's, NRO DCN 1/6/109; 1/7/120; 1/1/97; 2/1/75; 2/3/97/98.

1494/5, student, with contributions from the almoner, hostiller, refectorer, sacrist and the prior of St Leonard's, NRO DCN 1/6/110; 1/7/120; Oxford, Bod. Ms Rolls, Norfolk, no 52; 1/4/107; 2/3/99.

1495/6, student, with contributions from the chamberlain, hostiller, master of the cellar, refectorer, and the priors of Hoxne and St Leonard's, NRO DCN 1/5/123; 1/7/120; 1/1/98; 1/8/103; 2/6/31; 2/3/100, 101.

1496/7, student, with contributions from the refectorer and the prior of Hoxne, NRO DCN 1/8/104; 2/6/32.

1497/8, student, with contributions from the infirmarer and the prior of Hoxne, NRO DCN 1/10/33; 2/6/33.

1498/9, student, with contributions from the chamberlain, hostiller and the prior of Lynn, NRO DCN 1/5/124; 1/7/120; 2/1/77.

1499/1500, student, with contributions from the chamberlain, NRO DCN 1/5/125.

1501/2, student, with contributions from the hostiller and the priors of Yarmouth and St Leonard's, NRO DCN 1/7/124; 2/4/19; 2/3/102.

1502/3, student, with contribution from the cellarer and the prior of Hoxne, NRO DCN 1/2/88; Windsor, St George's chapel, I.C.34. Venn, *Gonville and Caius*, i, 16, lists him as a pensioner in 1503.

1492, 5/8 Oct., 45th in order at the visitation of bp Goldwell, Jessopp, *Visit.*, 8 (and last but one).

1499, 6 Apr., 37th in order on the visitation certificate, *Reg. abp Morton*, iii, no 258.

Name in two CUL Mss:

(1) Ii.1.30, Januensis Tabula (15th c.), which he purchased for 3s. 4d; see Robert Catton II.

(2) Ii.4.2, Bonaventura (late 13th c.); name on fo 1ᵛ; see also Robert Catton II.

LAURENCE

occ. c. 1504

c. 1504, a Laurence, along with six other priests, (Christian names only given) made their prof.; this is recorded on an inserted leaf (prob. of rough notes) between fos 27ᵛ and 28 in Reg. Nikke (9/14).

LAVERINGTON

see Leverington

Laurence de LECK [Lek, Leke

occ. 1315/16 d. 1357

1352–1357, prior: el. confirmed [*prefectio*] 24 Apr. 1352, Reg. Bateman, fo 138ᵛ; d. before 12 Dec. 1357, *Fasti*, iv, 25.

1315/16, the precentor bought a *ciphus* from the refectorer for 10s. *ad opus confratris nostri Laurentii*, prob. at the time of or shortly after adm., NRO DCN 1/8/23.

1329/30, prob. student, as the communar pd £1 5s. for him to go to Oxford, *Comm. Rolls*, 113; this entry comes under 'contributions' and in between two similar payments to John de Mari and Alexander de Hikling, q.v., both students at the time.

1352, 24 Apr., when examining the el. proceedings the bp found that they contravened conciliar regulations and so he pronounced the el. null and void and exercised his right of provision in this case; he then provided Laurence, Reg. Bateman, fo 138ᵛ.

1353, 11 Feb., comm. by the bp, with the adcn of Norwich, as vicar general in spirituals, Reg. Bateman, fo 145ᵛ; there is a second comm. issued at Dover on 13 Nov., *ib.*, fo 149.

1355, 12 × 18 Apr., the bp el. comm. the prior as one of two vicars general, Reg. Percy, fo 9.

1356, 3 Jan., the bp apptd the prior as one of two vicars general, the apptment to take effect on 25 Mar. 1356, Reg. Percy, fo 14.

Some of his correspondence is found in Reg. IX, e.g. on fos 17, 20, and Reg. X, fos 39 and 40.

He wrote a eulogy at the head of the obituary roll of bp Bateman: 'Historiola de vita et morte Reverendi domini Willelmi Bateman Norwicensis episcopi,' which is printed in F. Peck, *Desiderata Curiosa*, 2 vols in one (London, 1774), vii, 239–242.

Thomas LEMAN

occ. 1514 occ. 1538

1520, 3 Sept., master of the Lady altar, Jessopp, *Visit.*, 192.

1521/7, 1528/9, hostiller, NRO DCN 1/7/141–145.

1526, Dec./1527, 1528/9, communar, NRO DCN 1/12/102, 105.

1529/30, 1531/3, almoner, NRO DCN 1/6/134–137; in 1529/30 there are two names on the head of the acct of which the other name is illegible.

1531/2, 1533/6, chamberlain, NRO DCN 1/5/146–151. See Henry Manuel, also almoner and chamberlain.

1514, 14 Apr., present at the visitation of bp Nikke where it was reported that he did not regularly wear his habit, Jessopp, *Visit.*, 74.

1520, 3 Sept., when questioned at the visitation of bp Nikke he said that 'omnia debite fiunt tam in spiritualibus quam in temporalibus', *ib.*, 192.

1526, 7 June, present at the visitation of bp Nikke and complained that silence was not observed in accordance with the Rule, *ib.*, 201.

1532, 3 June, present at the visitation of bp Nikke and, as both almoner and chamberlain, reported *omnia bene*, *ib.*, 266.

1534, 28 July, subscribed to the Act of Supremacy, *DK 7th Report*, Appndx 2, 295.

1538, 30 Apr., dispensed to wear the habit of a secular pr. and hold a canonry and prebend in the cathedral and any other benefice, and be non resident, Chambers, *Faculty Office Regs*, 137.

1538, 2 May, licensed as a secular canon, *L and P Henry VIII*, xiii, pt 1, no 1115(4).

A contemporary, Stephen Leman, was pd by the convent as a barber [*rasor*], NRO DCN 1/12/90.

Benedict de LENN

occ. 1287/8 occ. 1298

1293/4, before Apr., succentor, NRO DCN 1/9/2.

1294, Apr./Sept., 1296/8, precentor, NRO DCN 1/9/2; *Comm. Rolls*, 68, 71.

1287/8, stopped at Hindolveston, NRO DCN 60/18/9.

1293/4, while succentor, recd 3s. 4d. 'oblations' from the precentor, NRO DCN 1/9/2.

1293, as precentor, went to Lynn, NRO DCN 1/9/2.

1296/7, 1297/8, with Thomas de Plumstede, q.v., made journeys to London at the expense of the communar, who charged his acct £3 7s.

7¾d., and £2 15s. 7¾d. respectively; they were prob. assisting with matters relating to the building operations in the cloister, *Comm. Rolls*, 68, 71.

I John de LENN
occ. 1345/6 d. 1394/5

1379/81, 1383/4, 1389/91, almoner, NRO DCN 1/6/19–21, 23, 24; he was also almoner in 1388, NRO DCN 1/12/33.

1345/6, ill, and the infirmarer spent 2s. 3d. on medicine, NRO DCN 1/10/4.
1381, 2 May, acted with the prior [Nicholas de Hoo, q.v.] and others as executors of a will, *CPR 1377–1381*, 593.
1388, gave 20s. [?from the office of almoner] to the communar for the building work in the cloister, NRO DCN 1/12/33.
1394/5, d., and the chamberlain recd 6s. 8d. as 'alms', NRO DCN 1/5/26.

II John de LENN [Linne, Lynne
occ. 1425/6 occ. 1464/5

1427, 4 Jan., one of seven whose prof. was solemnized by the bp in chapter after the prior had written to him on 31 Dec. 1426, Reg. Alnwick, fo 97.
1442/3, 1445/6, 1448/9, master of the cellar, NRO DCN 60/20/42; 1/1/87; 60/20/43.
1449/53, communar/pittancer, NRO DCN 1/12/58, 63, 64.
1450/3, refectorer, NRO DCN 1/8/88–90.
1455/7, cellarer, NRO DCN 1/2/61, 62.
1464/5, infirmarer, NRO DCN 1/10/26.

1425/6, gave 8d. to the chamberlain towards the expense of a new barn at Lakenham, NRO DCN 1/5/53.
1432/3, ill and the infirmarer spent 16d. on medicine, NRO DCN 1/10/20.
1446, the name Lenne occ. on the rough list of those assigned to celebrate weekday and chantry masses, Cambridge, Emm. Coll. Ms 142, fo 68; the name [J. Lynne] is also on a similar list (prob. of similar date) for masses in the Totyngton, Wakering and Erpingham chantries, *ib.*, fo 77ᵛ.

I Simon de LENN
occ. 1272/4

1272/3, was in London after Christmas on priory affairs, NRO DCN 1/1/2; and see William de Kirkeby.
1273/4, sent by the master of the cellar on business to London and to Thetford, NRO DCN 1/1/3; one of his responsibilities was to present a gift [*exennia*] of £20 to the king [Edward I, because of the coronation], *ib.*

II Simon LENN [Lenne, Lynne
occ. 1453/4 d. 1505/6

1453/4, novice and the infirmarer gave him 10s., *ex gratia*; a monk named Simon was also ill and cost the infirmarer 4d. in medicine, NRO DCN 1/10/23.

1493/7, master of St Paul's hospital acc. to Blomefield, *Norfolk*, iii, 432.
1496/7, infirmarer, NRO DCN 1/10/32.

1492, 5/8 Oct., 4th in order at the visitation of bp Goldwell, Jessopp, *Visit.*, 8.
1499, 6 Apr., 4th on the visitation certificate, *Reg. abp Morton*, iii, no 258.
1503/4, to the relief of the acct of the cell of Hoxne he gave £20 *de sua mera elemosina*, Windsor, St George's chapel, I.C.35.
1505/6, d., and the sacrist pd 8d. for funeral tapers, NRO DCN 1/4/109.

Thomas de LENN [Lenne, Lynne
occ. 1390/1 occ. 1410/11

1390/1, part yr., prior of St Leonard's, NRO DCN 2/3/9;see Richard de Blakeneye.
1395, 4 Apr., master of St Paul's hospital; *CPL*, iv, (1362–1402), 525. Blomefield, *Norfolk*, iii, 432, lists him as master in 1411.
1407, 2 Nov., subprior, Reg. Totyngton, fo 3ᵛ.
1409/11, prior of St Leonard's, NRO DCN 2/3/26, 27.
1395, 4 Apr., as a result of the bp's interference in the correction of monks after a visitation, and of the appeal of the prior and chapter vs him, the pope ordered an inquiry into the accusations vs him and other monks in the performance of their offices which had led to their condemnation, *CPL*, iv (1362–1402), 525; see also John Daventre and John de Kirkeby.
1399, 4 Jan., granted a papal indult to choose his own confessor who was authorized to absolve him from excommunication and interdict even in reserved cases, *CPL*, v (1396–1404), 216.
1407, 14 Sept., pronounced the chapter's choice of Alexander de Totyngton, q.v., as bp, Blomefield, *Norfolk*, iii, 525.

I William de LENN [Lynne
occ. 1345 occ. 1368/9

[1343 × 1351], prior of Hoxne, Reg. X, fo 38.

1345, on the infirmarer's sick list, NRO DCN 1/10/2.
1345/6, 1346/7, ill and the infirmarer spent 7d., and 4d. respectively, NRO DCN 1/10/4, 5.
1348/9, ill, and the infirmarer charged his acct for various purchases of cordials and other items including *indeliteriz* and one *emplaistr'*, NRO DCN 1/10/7.
[1343 × 1351], prior of Hoxne about whose dismissal from office the prior wrote to the bp; no specific mention of illness, but of the heavy burden of office ['onerosa custodia tam corporis quam anime'], Reg. X, fo 38.
1348/9, gave the pittancer £6 13s. 4d., prob. for building work, and the large sum suggests that

it came from the funds of Hoxne or of an unknown office which he held at the time, NRO DCN 1/12/27.

1360/1, 1365/6, 1368/9, named on the acct of the master of the cellar as being concerned with the monks' annual pensions from the church at Fring [Frenze] [in accordance with bp Bateman's will, Reg. X, fo 46v], NRO DCN 1/1/47, 49, 51.

II William LENNE [Lynne

occ. 1474/5 occ. 1492

1474/6, communar/pittancer, NRO DCN 1/12/70.

1474/6, precentor, NRO DCN 1/9/73, 74.

1476/7, 1479/80, refectorer, NRO DCN 1/8/96, 97.

1481/2, again communar/pittancer, NRO DCN 1/12/72 (but not in the intervening years).

1484/May to Sept., infirmarer ,NRO DCN 1/10/31.

1485/8, prior of Aldeby, NRO DCN 2/2/24–26.

1476/7, gave 20d. to the precentor *pro libris in cathologo*, NRO DCN 1/9/75; possibly a new book list, see Greatrex, 'Norwich Monk Students', 575–576.

1483/4, some of the money remaining from the accts of the Wakering and Erpingham chantries was in his keeping, NRO DCN 4/10.

1492, 5/8 Oct., 10th in order at the visitation of bp Goldwell, Jessopp, *Visit.*, 8.

LENNE

see also Lunna

R. de LETTIMER [?Leccimer, ?Lettun'

occ. 1282/3

1282/3, a monk from whom the almoner recd 24s., NRO DCN 1/6/5.

John de LEVERINGTON [Laverington

occ. 1345/8

1345/6, 1346/7, 1347/8, ill during each of these yrs. and the infirmarer bought medicines costing 18d., 4s. 11d., and 11d. respectively, NRO DCN 1/10/4–6.

R. de LOK' [?Lak'

Name in Cambridge, Corpus Christi College Ms 465, Ordinale fratris R. de Lok (late 13th c.); this has been ed. by Tolhurst, *Customary*, (see the References).

Note: there is no more evidence to identify this monk. Could he be R[ichard] de Lak[enham], q.v.?

I William LONDON

occ. 1492 d. 1505/6

1504/5, sacrist, d. in office, NRO DCN 1/4/108.

1492, 5/8 Oct., 39th in order at the visitation of bp Goldwell, Jessopp, *Visit.*, 8.

1499, 6 Apr., 31st on the visitation certificate, *Reg. abp Morton*, iii, no 258.

1505/6, d., and the sacrist's office pd 8d. for funeral tapers, NRO DCN 1/4/109.

A William London, alderman of Norwich, who d. in 1493 mentioned his son William, monk, in his will, PRO Prob/11/10 (Reg. Vox, 1493–1496), fo 5 (London).

II William LONDON [*alias* Kegell

occ. 1526 occ. 1538

1526, 7 June, one of a group of younger monks, present at the visitation of bp Nikke, who complained that they were required by the seniors to memorize the psalter and the antiphons and responses etc., which they considered a waste of time, Jessopp, *Visit.*, 198; when questioned he remarked on the severity of Thomas Sall, q.v., *ib.*, 204.

1532, 3 June, present at the visitation of bp Nikke and was accused of being one of a group of monks who caused discord in the community and were in correspondence with Robert Catton I, q.v., (who had left not long before to become abbot of St Alban's), seeking support from him for their 'reform measures', Jessopp, *Visit.*, 265. The prior of Yarmouth [Stephen Darsham, q.v.] accused London, when residing in that cell, of murmuring vs his authority and of wanting to implement reforms there while not himself refraining from games of dice, *ib.* When questioned he complained of inadequate care of the sick and of the failure to send monks to university, *ib.*, 267. He was also accused of being *indebitatus multis et omnino indoctus*, *ib.*, 268. See, however, Thomas Morton, Richard Norwich and Robert Catton I.

1534, 28 July, subscribed to the Act of Supremacy, *DK 7th Report*, appndx 2, 295.

1538, 30 Apr., dispensed to wear the habit of a secular pr. and hold a canonry and prebend in the cathedral and any other benefice, and be non resident, Chambers, *Faculty Office Regs*, 137.

1538, 2 May, licensed as a secular canon, *L and P Henry VIII*, xiii, pt 1, no 1115(4).

John LONGHAM [Langham

occ. 1413/14 d. 1445/6

1415/16, communar/pittancer, NRO DCN 1/12/45.

1417, for a few weeks, sacrist, NRO DCN 1/4/52.

1417/21, 1422/4, 1425/6, 1427/9, master of the cellar, NRO DCN 60/35/47–51; 1/1/74–76; 60/33/31; 60/20/38–40; 1/1/77,78.

1428/9, cellarer, NRO DCN 1/2/46, 47.

1413/14, pd the refectorer 13s. 4d. for a *ciphus*, NRO DCN 1/8/59.

1414/15, gave the precentor 20d. towards the cost of the chancel window at Plumstead, NRO DCN 1/9/31.

1417/21, pd annual visits to Taverham, NRO DCN 60/35/47–51.

1419/20, pd the refectorer 13s. 4d. for a *ciphus*, a second time, NRO DCN 1/8/67.

1422/3, 1425/6, 1427/8, visited Hindringham, NRO DCN 60/20/38–40.

1423/4, visited Sedgeford, NRO DCN 60/33/31.

1436/7, gave a gift of 20d. to the chamberlain, NRO DCN 1/5/66.

1446, the name Longham occ. on a rough list of those assigned to celebrate weekday and chantry masses, Cambridge, Emm. Coll. Ms 142, fo 68.

1445/6, [my dating], d., NRO DCN 1/5/76; but the NRO list dates this one yr earlier, which contradicts the preceding entry, unless there are two contemporary monks of this name. In the latter case the purchase of the two *ciphi* might be explained.

Richard LOPHAM [*alias* Underwood, Undrewod

occ. 1526 occ. 1536

1526, 7 June, one of a group of younger monks, present at the visitation of bp Nikke, who complained that they were required by the seniors to memorize the psalter and the antiphons and responses etc., which they considered a waste of time, Jessopp, *Visit.*, 198; he also objected to the behaviour of the precentor and the third prior. [John Sall II and Thomas Sall, q.v.]; *ib.*, 203.

1532, 3 June, present at the visitation of bp Nikke and was accused of being one of a group of monks who caused discord in the community and were in correspondence with Robert Catton I, q.v., (who had left not long before to become abbot of St Alban's), seeking support from him for their 'reform measures', Jessopp, *Visit.*, 265. The prior of Yarmouth [Stephen Darsham, q.v.] accused Lopham, when residing in that cell, of murmuring vs his authority and of wanting to implement reforms there while not himself refraining from games of dice, *ib.* When questioned he complained of inadequate care of the sick and of the failure to send monks to university, *ib.*, 267. See, however, Thomas Morton, Richard Norwich.

1536, 17 July, stated that he had been prof. 'in childhood before his 24th yr'; after paying 40s., by royal decree he was now permitted to become a secular pr., Chambers, *Faculty Office Regs*, 63.

Note: the entry in the Ms Faculty Office Reg. (Lambeth) reads '24th yr' which must surely be an error (for ?14th).

Richard de LUNNA [Lynne

occ. [c. 1150]

[c. 1150], before the d. of prior Elias, q.v., he fell ill, saw visions while praying at the tomb of St William, but failed to carry out all the instructions he had recd and consequently d., according to Thomas de Monmouth, q.v., Jessopp and James, *St William*, 137–144.

John LYHERT

occ. 1468/9

1468/9, d., and the sacrist pd for funeral tapers, NRO DCN 1/4/91.

There is also a John Lyhert mentioned in the arrangements made concerning the chantry of bp Walter Lyhart, but this latter John was not a monk as the *CClR, 1484–1500*, no 832, states through a misreading of the original text.

LYNNE

see Lenn, Lunna

MACARIUS [Macharius

[?1107]

[?1107], with Gosfridus, Ingulph and Stannard, q.v., witnessed a final concord of the bp, *Eng. Epis. Acta*, vi, no 5.

n.d., 11 July, the obit of a Macarius occ. in the kalendar in Reg. XI, fo 5.

John MANFELD

occ. 1535

1535 [Sept./Dec.] ord subdcn, place uncertain, NRO DN ORR/1/1, fo 26v.

Henry MANUEL [Manuell

occ. 1502 occ. 1538

1502, 23 June, one of four whom the bp comm. the prior to adm., [*monachand'*], Reg. Nikke (8/13), fo 13v; see Henry II for his prob. prof.

1520, 3 Sept., chaplain to the prior, Jessopp, *Visit.*, 194.

1520/2, refectorer, NRO DCN 1/8/114.

1525/7, 1528/9, almoner and chamberlain, NRO DCN 1/6/130, 131, 133; 1/5/142–145; almoner also in 1527/8, NRO DCN 1/6/132.

1526, 7 June; 1529/30, infirmarer, Jessopp, *Visit.*, 197; NRO DCN 1/10/38.

1532, 3 June, master of St Paul's hospital, Jessopp, *Visit.*, 266.

1538, precentor, NRO DCN 29/3, fo 136v.

1520, 3 Sept., present at the visitation of bp Nikke, and reported *omnia bene*, Jessopp, *Visit.*, 194.

1526, 7 June, present at the visitation of bp Nikke, and accused of holding three offices simultaneously, *ib.*, 197; he was described as one of the senior brethren, *ib.*, 202- 203; when questioned he said that the prior was implementing reform and the state of the monastery was good, *ib.*, 197.

1532, 3 June, present at the visitation of bp Nikke, and reported that the cathedral church was in need of repair, *ib.*, 266.

1534, 28 July, subscribed to the Act of Supremacy, *DK 7th Report*, Appndx 2, 295.
1538, spent 4s. on books *pro erudicione puerorum*, NRO DCN 29/3, fo 136v.
1538, 30 Apr., dispensed to wear the habit of a secular pr. and hold a canonry and prebend in the cathedral and any other benefice, and be non resident, Chambers, *Faculty Office Regs*, 137.
1538, 2 May, appted canon of the 3rd prebend in the new foundation, *Fasti, 1541–1857*, vii, 54. See also *L and P Henry VIII*, xiii, pt 1, no 1115(4).

William MANUEL [Manuell
occ. 1492 occ. 1504/5

1494/7, hostiller, NRO DCN 1/7/120.
1497/1504, master of St Paul's hospital acc. to Blomefield, *Norfolk*, iii, 432.
1500/1, refectorer, NRO DCN 1/8/107.
1504/5, pittancer, NRO DCN 1/12/86.

1492, 5/8 Oct., 28th in order at the visitation of bp Goldwell, Jessopp, *Visit.*, 8.
1499, 6 Apr., 21st on the visitation certificate, *Reg. abp Morton*, iii, no 258.

William MANYNGTON [Manynton
occ. 1414 d. 1438/9

1414, 14 Oct., before, prior of Aldeby; on this date the bp comm. the prior to remove him from this office, Reg Courtenay, fo 102v; there is also a ref. to him on the Aldeby acct of his successor, NRO DCN 2/2/6.
1420/1, with Clement [Thornage, q.v.] he assisted the precentor by performing various services in the parish and church of Plumstead during a vacancy there, NRO DCN 1/9/31, 1/9/37.
1425/6, pd by the sacrist *pro pargamino libri de pensionibus*, NRO DCN 1/4/59, 60; see note below.
1427/8, gave 6s. 8d. gift *ad opus claustri*, NRO DCN 1/12/52.
1428/9, 1429/30, 1430/1, ill each yr and the sums spent on medicine by the infirmarer were 20d., 8d., and 16d. respectively, NRO DCN 1/10/16–18.
1431/2, ill, and the infirmarer spent 5s. 4d. on surgery [*cirurgia*] and medicine, NRO DCN 1/10/19.
1432/3, 1434/5, more illness, which cost the infirmarer 2s. 3d., and 8d. respectively, NRO DCN 1/10/20, 21.
1438/9, d., and the chamberlain recd 'alms', NRO DCN 1/5/69.

Note: a ref. from Thomas Searl, a 17th century registrar of the cathedral, states that Manyngton wrote a 'magnum registrum ecclesiae Norwicensis'judged by Luard to be the copy of the volume of Bartholomew Cotton, q.v., which he transcribed in the Rolls Series; see p. xxiv of the latter work.

John de MARI D.Th. [Mare, Marry, Mer
occ. [1317/18] d. 1343/4

1342, 27 Sept., prior of Lynn, Reg. Bek, fo 61v.

[1317/18], student [at Oxford], with pension contribution from the master of the cellar, NRO DCN 1/1/26.
1319/20, one of four students receiving contributions from the hostiller, NRO DCN 1/7/1.
1320/1, student, with contribution from the master of the cellar, NRO DCN 1/1/28.
1322/3, student, with contribution from the refectorer, NRO DCN 1/8/26; stopped at [North] Elmham [prob. on his way to or from Oxford], NRO DCN 60/10/19.
1324/5, student at Oxford with travelling expenses pd by the communar, *Comm. Rolls*, 98.
1327/8, stopped at [North] Elmham with his *socius* on 3 July [prob. en route to or from Oxford], NRO DCN 60/10/22.
1329/30, student at Oxford, with contributions from the communar and the master of the cellar, *Comm. Rolls*, 113; NRO DCN 1/1/30; the communar referred to his inception. See also below.

1320, 15 Sept., apptd proctor to the Black Monk Chapter meeting in Northampton on 21 Sept., Pantin, *BMC*, i, 201 (from Reg. IX, fo 28v).
1322/3, stopped at Hindolveston, NRO DCN 60/18/23.
1325/6, sent to the curia, and the sacrist sold him a horse for £4 *in transfretatione sua*, NRO DCN 1/4/23, Reg. X, fo 8v.
1325, 1 Oct., took letters to Robert Baldock, the chancellor, who had been el. as bp, but had res. 3 Sept., because of the papal provision of Ayermine, Reg. IX, fo 45.
1325, 4 Oct., the prior provided him with two letters for the journey to the curia:
(1) a letter of reference [*littere commendatorie*], Reg. IX, fo 48v.
(2) a letter of credit [*littere obligatorie*] for a loan of up to 30 marks, *ib.*, fo 49.
Note: other entries in this section of the Reg. make it clear that the *ardua negocia* with which he was entrusted concerned *sed. vac.* jurisdiction.
1336, 13 May, apptd by the abp [as *visitator*] for excepted jurisdiction, *sed. vac.* Norwich, he wrote to the prior of Dodnash that he intended to visit the chapter there, NRO DCN 42/1/16; he is described as *sacre pagine professor*. See also R.M. Haines, *Archbishop John Stratford, Political Revolutionary and Champion of the English Church, ca. 1275/80–1348*, Toronto, 1986, 67 n. 72.
1335/6, pd the master of the cellar 62s. which he had received from the above visitation, NRO DCN 1/1/38, 38.
1337/8, attended the Black Monk Chapter, NRO DCN 1/1/34, where he was among those cho-

sen to el. the presidents and was named as a diffinitor, Pantin, *BMC*, ii, 8, 9, 12. The meeting was held at Northampton, 10–13 June 1338, Pantin, *ib.*, ii, 5.

1340, 11–15 Sept., attended the Black Monk Chapter where he was assigned to preach *in lingua materna* at the next meeting in 1343, if the prior of Shrewsbury was prevented from doing so, Pantin, *BMC*, ii, 15; see also the entries under Alexander de Hikling and John de Whyteley.

[1340 × 1343], 8 Jan., the president of the Black Monk Chapter wrote to the prior asking him to allow de Mari to return to Oxford as regent, Pantin, *BMC*, iii, 19–21 (from Reg. X, fo 34).

[1340 × 1343], 8 June, the prior wrote an affirmative reply to the above request stating that he would go to Oxford around Michaelmas, *ib.*

1342, 27 Sept., informed the bp that he had confirmed the el. of the prioress of [the Augustinian convent of] Crabhouse and had installed her, *Reg. Bek*, fo 61v.

1343/4, d., and the chamberlain pd the brief bearer, NRO DCN 1/5/12.

There are two letters, undated, concerning his scholastic progress, and a third ordering his return from Oxford to Norwich in July 1325:

(1) from prior Langley to John and to Martin de Middleton, q.v., in reply to their request to stay on at Oxford during the autumn term.

(2) from the prior to John; this makes it clear that de Mari was seeking permission to begin his lectures on the Sentences, and thus provides evidence that he had just taken a first degree. Both letters are in Reg IX fo 30, and have been transcribed by V.H. Galbraith in *Snappe's Formulary*, 377–378; Pantin dates 2) to c. 1321 in *BMC*, iii, 321.

(3) 10 July 1325, the prior wrote to de Mari and Roger [de Eston, q.v.] four days after bp Salmon's death; although he did not give details he was without doubt recalling them for the el. of a successor, Reg. IX, fo 61v; see also the 1324/5 entry above in which the communar pd travelling expenses.

See *BRUO* for bp Bale's ref. to de Mari's Lectura Sententiarum and Sermones varii.

There were de Maris in Scratby in the last quarter of the 13th c., *N. Cath. Charters*, ii, nos 316–331.

Richard MARSHAM

occ. 1453/4 d. 1483/4

1461/5, 1466/7, 1468/71, almoner, NRO DCN 1/6/77–83.

1468/71, hostiller, NRO DCN 1/7/103–105.

1474/5, 1479/80, 1482/4, May, infirmarer, NRO DCN 1/10/28–31.

1453/4, 1454/5, ill in both yrs and the infirmarer spent 3s. 4d. and 20d. respectively, NRO DCN 1/10/23, 24.

1477/8, gave the precentor 13d., *pro portiforio, Bxxx*, NRO DCN 1/9/76; perhaps a borrowing fee or a fine; see Greatrex, 'Norwich Monk Students', 575.

1483/4, d. before 3 May and the chamberlain recd 'alms', NRO DCN 1/5/114; the communar/pittancer sent letters to the cells announcing his d., NRO DCN 1/12/73.

Joseph de MARTHAM [Marcham

occ. 1355/6 d. 1395/6

1355/6, hostiller, NRO DCN 1/7/17.

1365/6, 1368/9, 1370/2, master of the cellar, NRO DCN 60/35/35; 1/1/51; 60/35/39, 40; and see John de Aldeby.

1395/6, subprior, NRO DCN 1/4/41; 1/5/27; Blomefield says he succ. William de Thetford, q.v., on 27 June 1383, *Norfolk*, iii, 603.

1393/4, the refectorer's inventory lists two *nuces de buglo* given by him and a *ciphus* of cedar which was in his possession, NRO DCN 1/8/48.

1395/6, d., and the sacrist pd 12s. *pro factura sepulcri*, NRO DCN 1/4/41; the chamberlain recd 'alms', NRO DCN 1/5/27, and also pd the brief bearer, *ib.*

1410, on the refectorer's inventory of the *camera prioris* a *ciphus cedrinus quondam* his, NRO DCN 1/8/56.

Ralph de MARTHAM

occ. 1362 d. 1393

1362, 24 Sept., ord pr., Chelmsford, Reg. Sudbury (London), ii, 11.

1372/3, 1375/6, 1377, 5 Feb., 1379/93, Jan., prior of Lynn, NRO DCN 2/1/2–20; D. Owen, *King's Lynn*, 122, no 6 (1375/6), *ib.*, 149, no 162 (1377).

1371/2, visited Taverham, NRO DCN 60/35/40.

1393, by 25 Jan., d. at Lynn and his body and books were carried back to Norwich; the total cost, including *le enterment* and the travelling expenses of the monks going from Lynn to Norwich and back was over £6, NRO DCN 2/1/20.

1393/4, the refectorer lists in his inventory a *pecia* with a cover shaped like a dish, *ex dono*—-, NRO DCN 1/8/48.

1410, the refectorer's inventory lists the same gift, NRO DCN 1/8/56.

Note: Blomefield calls him William Ralflede Markham, prob. mistakenly.

William de MARTHAM

occ. 1312/13 occ. 1316/17

1315, 18 Feb., described as *magister magni altaris*, Reg. IX, fo 8v; see below.

1312/13, possibly a student [at Oxford], as he recd a small sum from the refectorer along with several others known to have been students at this time, NRO DCN 1/8/22.

1315/16, possibly a student as he recd small sums as *donationes* from the master of the cellar, along with other possible students, NRO DCN 1/1/25.

[?c. 1315], one of two monks apptd as parliamentary proctors, Reg. IX, fo 8; see William de Blafeld.

1315, 18 Feb., conveyed a letter from the prior to the bp thanking him for the gift of a *tabula* for the high altar of which he was *magister*, Reg. IX, fo 8^v.

1316/17, the communar pd 2s. for his *capa* and lent him 1s., *Comm. Rolls*, 90.

John MARTON [Marten, Martyn, Merton
occ. 1499 occ. 1526

1499, 30 Mar., ord subdcn, Norwich cathedral, *Reg. abp Morton*, iii, no 53.

1517/19, hostiller, NRO DCN 1/7/138, 139.

1518/20, prior of St Leonard's, NRO DCN 2/3/117, 118.

1518/19, 1520, 3 Sept., 1521/2, sacrist, NRO DCN 1/4/115, Jessopp, *Visit.*, 192; NRO DCN 1/4/116.

1499, 6 Apr., 48th and last in order on the visitation certificate, *Reg. abp Morton*, iii, no 258.

1514, 27 Apr., present at the visitation of bp Nikke and complained of another monk's unchaste behaviour and reported the poor financial state [*aere alieno*] of the monastery, Jessopp, *Visit.*, 74. See Robert Worsted.

1520, 3 Sept., sacrist and prior of St Leonard's, present at the visitation of bp Nikke and reported that the prior was implementing reform measures, Jessopp, *Visit.*, 192.

1526, 7 June, present at the visitation of bp Nikke and complained of the failures of both John Sall and Thomas Sall, q.v., and of the general laxity in discipline in the community, *ib.*, 199–200. He in turn was accused of lack of charity and severity in meting out punishment, *ib.*, 201.

Name in

(1) Oxford, Bod. Ms 787, Bernardus de Parantinis (15th c.); on fo 113^v, *Explicit J. Marton, monachus N.*, and on an end leaf this is repeated. On fo 113^v, above the signature, an interesting passage is inserted outlining the best method of copying the ms in order to avoid confusion and misunderstanding on the part of the reader. This Ms was *ex dono* John Elingham III, q.v.

(2) CUL Ms Ii.1.22, Hugh de S. Victore etc. (13th c.); name on two front flyleaves; see also Robert de Rothewelle.

Robert de MASSYNGHAM
d. 1382/3

1382/3, d., and the chamberlain pd the brief bearer, NRO DCN 1/5/16.

Thomas MAWTSBY
d. 1513/14

1513/14, d., and the sacrist pd for funeral tapers, NRO DCN 1/4/112.

Bartholomew de MENDELSHAM [Mendisham
occ. 1313/14

1313/14, gave 20s. to the master of the cellar *ad negotia domus*, NRO DCN 1/1/23.

1318/19, a *dominus* de Mendlesham gave £6 to the cellarer, NRO DCN 1/2/12.

[Note: this may not be a monk, but if he had been an obedientiary he could have given this large sum to help the cellarer who was some £280 in the red.]

Adam de MEPHAM
occ. 1255/6

1255/6, visited Taverham for *liberatio denariorum*, NRO DCN 60/35/1.

MER
see Mari

MERTON
see Marton

John METHAM
occ. 1438/9 occ. 1499

1438/9, gave the refectorer 10s. for a *ciphus*, prob. soon after adm., NRO DCN 1/8/77.

1471, June/1472, 1473/4, hostiller, NRO DCN 1/7/105–107.

1480/1, 1483/4, gardener, NRO DCN 1/11/22–23.

1440/1, ill, and the infirmarer spent 2s. and later 12d. on medicine, NRO DCN 1/10/22.

1453/4, ill, and 8d. spent on medicine, NRO DCN 1/10/23.

1492, 5/8 Oct., 2nd in order at the visitation of bp Goldwell, Jessopp, *Visit.*, 8.

1499, 6 Apr., 2nd in order on the visitation certificate, *Reg. abp Morton*, iii, no 258.

William de METYNGHAM [Metynham
occ. 1418/19 occ. 1446

1419, Sept./Dec., almoner, NRO DCN 1/6/46.

1427/8, Mar., gardener, NRO DCN 1/11/10, 11.

1429, June/1430, prior of Hoxne, NRO DCN 2/6/9, 10.

1431/2, 1435/6, refectorer, NRO DCN 1/8/74, 75.

1437/42, chamberlain, NRO DCN 1/5/68–74.

1418/19, gave the refectorer 6s. 8d. for the repair of the *ciphus* of M. John Hoo, q.v., because has own *ciphus* was broken, NRO DCN 1/8/64.

1420/1, gave the communar 3s. 4d. for the cloister work, NRO DCN 1/12/48.

1422/3, gave the refectorer 13s. 4d. for a *ciphus*, NRO DCN 1/8/70.

1442/3, on leaving office as chamberlain he 'gave' £22 to the office, NRO DCN 1/5/75.
1446, name occ. on a rough list of those assigned to celebrate weekday and chantry masses, Cambridge, Emm. Coll. Ms 142, fo 68; also on a similar list for the *magna missa* and *parva missa* (prob. of similar date), *ib.*, fo 77ᵛ, and possibly for the Totyngton and Bateman chantries, *ib.*

MICHAEL
n.d.
n.d., 27 Aug., obit occ. in the kalendar in Reg. XI, fo 5ᵛ.

John de MIDDLETON [Midelton
d. 1397/8
1397/8, d., and the chamberlain recd 6s. 8d. in 'alms', NRO DCN 1/5/29.

Martin de MIDDLETON, ?B.CnL.
occ. 1320 occ. 1323/4
1320/1, student [at Oxford], with pension contribution from the master of the cellar, NRO DCN 1/1/28.
There are also two letters, undated, but prob. c. 1321, which concern his scholastic progress:
(1) from prior Langley to both John de Mari, q.v., and Martin in reply to their request to stay on at Oxford during the autumn term.
(2) from the prior to Martin granting permission for him to go on to commence his lectures on the decretals; this indicates that he had taken his first degree and was hoping to begin his public lectures in canon law. See the references under John de Mari.
1323/4, the precentor recd 20s. from him, from which the precentor was to pay 16s. on his behalf to a certain man in Cambridge; but he did not know who the man was, Oxford, Bod. Ms Rolls, Norfolk, no 55.

Richard de MIDELTON [Middeltone, Midilton, Mydeltone
occ. 1393/4 d. 1437/8
1400, Apr./Sept., 1400/1, 1402/3, master of the cellar, NRO DCN 1/1/67–69.
1411/12, Nov. to June, prior of St Leonard's, NRO DCN 2/3/28; see John de Ely and William Depham.
1420/1, 1422/3, 1424/35, and prob. until 1436, sacrist, NRO DCN 1/4/56–75.
1393/4, the refectorer noted in his inventory that Midelton had the *ciphus* of cedar formerly belonging to Simon Bozoun, q.v., NRO DCN 1/8/48.
1410, another inventory of the refectorer stated that Midelton was now using the *parvus ciphus* with silver base which had formerly belonged to William Pekeworth, q.v., NRO DCN 1/8/56.
1412, 21 Apr., given papal dispensation to hold any benefice, with or without cure of souls, *CPL*, 6 (1404–1415), 282; this grant is also entered in Reg. Wakering, fo 160.
1412, 9 May, papal affirmation that he, now rector of Marsham, was in good standing and accusations of apostasy were unfounded, *CPL*, vi (1404–1415), 380.
[1413], 9 May, in Wakering's reg., however, a papal cancellation of the above occ., carrying the same date (?or could it be the same day but a year later) and stating that the dispensation was null and void because he had not sought or obtained a licence from his superior and was therefore apostate, Reg. Wakering, fo 160.
1413/14, the cellarer recd from him 24s. *pro mensa sua*; why? NRO DCN 1/2/36.
1437/8, d., and the chamberlain recd 'alms', NRO DCN 1/5/68.

Name in the Norwich Cathedral Ms called the 'Norwich Domesday';—'me dedit sacristarie ecclesie Trinitatis'.

The 1424 inventory of St Leonard's includes two small kitchen pots given by him, Bensly, 'St Leonard's', 202–203.

Walter de MINTLYNG [Mintlinge, Mintlingham
occ. 1307/8 occ. 1329/30
1307/8, pd the refectorer 13s. 4d. for a *ciphus sine pede*, prob. soon after adm., NRO DCN 1/8/19.
1326/30, cellarer, NRO DCN 1/2/14–16.
1319/20, possibly student at Oxford, as he and John de Clipesby, q.v., stopped at [North] Elmham [?en route], NRO DCN 60/10/17; and see John de Mari under the same date.
1324/5, visited Hindolveston, NRO DCN 60/18/24.

John MOLET D.Th. [Mollett
occ. 1437/8 d. 1471
1454–1471, prior: el. confirmed [*prefectio*] by the vicar general of the bp, 29 Jan. 1454, Reg. Lyhart fo 31ᵛ; d. before 8 June 1471; *ib.*, fo 179.
1425, 2 June, ord acol. in the chapel of the bp's palace, Norwich, *Reg. abp Chichele*, iii, 477; he is not distinguished as a monk.
1441/3, prior of Yarmouth, NRO DCN 2/4/6, 7.
1443, 7 Oct., the prior requested the bp to confirm him as subprior, Reg. Brouns, fo 109.
1446/8, 1449/50, cellarer, NRO DCN 1/2/57–59.
1447/9, 1451/2, almoner, NRO DCN 1/6/68–70.
1452/3, sacrist, NRO DCN 1/4/83.
As prior he held the following offices:
1454/5, 1457/61, almoner, NRO DCN 1/6/71–76.

1454/5, 1456/8, 1459/60, 1461/2, sacrist, NRO DCN 1/4/84–88.
1457, part yr, prior of St Leonard's, NRO DCN 2/3/65; see John Folsham.
1468/9, prior of St Leonard's, NRO DCN 2/3/79.
1469/70, chamberlain, NRO DCN 1/5/99.

1437/8, student [prob. at Oxford] with pension contributions from the almoner, cellarer, chamberlain, hostiller, master of the cellar and the priors of Lynn and St Leonard's, NRO DCN 1/6/63; 1/2/53; 1/5/68; 1/7/78; 1/1/82; 2/1/33; 2/3/52.
1438/9, student, with contributions from the almoner, master of the cellar, and sacrist, NRO DCN 1/6/64; 1/1/83; 1/4/76.
1440/1, student, with contributions toward the cost of inception from the infirmarer and the master of the cellar, NRO DCN 1/10/22; 1/1/85.
1441/2, the prior of Lynn's acct records a contribution toward inception, NRO DCN 2/1/37.
Note: these entries suggest that Molet may have entered the monastery after the commencement of a career at the university since there are no references on the accts before 1437/8, and he could not have incepted within four years without a minimum of four or five years of previous study. On 21 Nov., 1441 he was described as *sacre pagine professor*. Reg. Brouns, fo 108.

1438/9, went to London to request the bp's confirmation of the apptment of new penitentiaries, NRO DCN 1/12/57.
1441, 21 Nov., apptd to hear confessions at Yarmouth, Reg. Brouns, fo 108.
1444, 13 Jan., comm. by the bp as penitentiary in the city and diocese in response to the prior's request, Reg. Brouns, fo 109v.
1446, name occ. on a rough list of those assigned to celebrate weekday and chantry masses, Cambridge, Emm. Coll Ms 142, fo 68.
1453/4, repairs to the [new] prior's quarters [*camere*] cost £9, NRO DCN 1/1/89.
1455/6, visited Newton (manor) and St Leonard's, and his expenses were pd by the communar, NRO DCN 1/12/66.
1462/3, went to London in order to exonerate himself 'de crimine falso intoxicat' Johannis Burton sibi imposito', and his expenses were 11s., NRO DCN 1/1/91. Is this John Burton, the monk, q.v.?
1467, 5 Mar., as a result of his appeal to the pope because the bp threatened to depose him—although he was canonically elected and had been prior for some years—an inquiry was ordered, *CPL*, xii (1458–1471), 560.

Name in CUL Mss:
(1) Ii.3.29. J. Waldeby (14th c.); *ex dono*—on fo 2.
(2) Ii.4.37., Egidius Romanus (14th/15th c.); *possessio*—.

There is no doubt that members of the Paston family were good friends of the Norwich community as a letter of Prior Bonwell, q.v., makes clear; but both James Gairdner and Norman Davis have confused John Mowght, a Franciscan friar, (see *BRUC*), with Molet in their editions of the Paston letters. In the Davis edition, four of the letters make reference to Molet: no 926 (as Molet) and nos 512, 530, 893 (as prior).

Ralph de MONESLE [Moneslee, Munesle, Mundesley

occ. 1307 occ. 1332

1307/8, communar, *Comm. Rolls*, 9, 87 [as Mundesley].
1309/11, almoner, NRO DCN 1/6/9.
1318/20, cellarer, NRO DCN 1/2/11, 12.
1325, 3 Sept., subprior, Reg. IX, fo 62v.
1332, 7 Sept., prior of Lynn, Reg. Ayermine, fo 53.

1309/10, visited Hindringham, NRO DCN 60/25/15.
[1314/15], given a letter of credence to the lord chancellor with details concerning the church of Chalk, Reg. IX, fo 8v.
[1316, Sept.], named as one of two monk proctors to attend Convocation at St Paul's on 11 Oct., Reg. IX, fo 11.
[?1318], sent to Walter de Norwich, baron of the Exchequer, with a letter from the prior, Reg. IX, fo 5.
Note: in these three missions he was accompanied by Richard de Hecham, q.v.
1321, 13 July, named as one of two monk proctors to represent the chapter at the council at Westminster, Reg. IX, fo 31.
1325, 3 Sept., sent by the prior and chapter to Robert Baldock, whom they had el. as bp, to discuss certain matters with him, Reg. IX, fo 62v.
[Note: Baldock res. on 3 Sept. because the pope had provided William de Ayermine.]

Thomas de MONMOUTH [Monemutensis

occ. c. 1146/1172

n.d., sacrist, Jessopp and James, *St William*, 139.
n.d., precentor, *ib.*, 214.

c. 1172, wrote the life of St William, Jessopp and James, *St William*, liii.

According to Jessopp he must have pursued scholarly studies in his youth and was well read in the Latin poets as well as the lives of of the saints, *ib.*, ix–x. He was apptd sacrist of the shrine, perhaps by bp Turba, *ib.*, xxi–xxii.
The single remaining copy of the Ms which has been ed. by Jessopp and James is CUL Add. Ms 3037.

Thomas MORE [Moore
occ. 1477 occ. 1499

1477, c. 4 Nov., the sacrist [Wm. Fode, q.v.] went to see the bp in London with regard to the confirmation of the reception of three *clerici* as monks, NRO DCN 1/12/70.
1477, 4 Nov., one of three *clerici* whom the prior requested the bp to rec. and bless, Reg. Goldwell, fo 9; on 8 Nov. the bp comm. the prior to perform the ceremony, *ib.*

1492, 5/8 Oct., 30th in order at the visitation of bp Goldwell, Jessopp, *Visit.*, 8.
1499, 6 Apr., 23rd on the visitation certificate, *Reg. abp Morton*, iii, no 258.

MORETON
see Morton

John MORLEE
d. 1471/2

1471/2, d., and the sacrist pd for funeral tapers, NRO DCN 1/4/93.

J. de ?MORTIMER
occ. 1287/8

1287/8, almoner, NRO DCN 1/6/8.

Note: see R. de Lettimer.

Thomas MORTON [Moreton, Mortun
occ. 1520 d. 1535

1520, 3 Sept., in subdcn's orders, Jessopp, *Visit.*, 193.
1532, 3 June, fourth prior and gardener, Jessopp, *Visit.*, 266.

1526/7, student at Oxford, with pension contributions from the almoner, cellarer, chamberlain, pittancer, and precentor, NRO DCN 1/6/131; 1/2/97; 1/5/143,144; 1/12/103,104; 1/9/94,95.
1527/8, student, with contributions from the almoner and refectorer, NRO DCN 1/6/132; 1/8/116.
1528/9, student, with contributions from the almoner, chamberlain, hostiller and the prior of Lynn, NRO DCN 1/6/133; 1/5/145; 1/7/145; 2/1/82.
1529/30, student, with contributions from the almoner, hostiller, infirmarer and the prior of Lynn, NRO DCN 1/6/134; 1/7/146; 1/10/38; 2/1/82.
1530/1, student, with contributions from the cellarer, hostiller, refectorer and the prior of Lynn, NRO DCN 1/2/99; 1/7/147; 1/8/117; 2/1/82; returned [from Oxford] for the el. of a prior, NRO DCN 1/12/106.
1532, 3 June, described as scholar, see below.
1520, 3 Sept., subdcn, present at the visitation of bp Nikke, and when questioned he stated *omnia bene*, Jessopp, *Visit.*, 193.
1532, 3 June, present at the visitation of bp Nikke, described as 'scholar' and accused of putting on airs and sowing discord in the community, Jessopp, *Visit.*, 264; when questioned he reported that sick monks were receiving inadequate care, *ib.*, 266.
1535, 22 Apr., committed suicide, [*occidit se*], BL Ms Harley 3950, fo 4v.

Name in Oxford, Bod. Vet. E.l.f.134, J. Faber Stapulensis, (printed book), Paris, 1521.

MUNDESLEY, Munesle
see Monesle

Robert MUTFORD [Motforth, Motsforth, Mutforth
occ. 1489/90 occ. ?1510/11

1506/8, refectorer, Oxford, Bod. Ms Rolls, Norfolk, no 53; NRO DCN 1/8/110.
1511/12, before, infirmarer, NRO DCN 1/10/34.
1489/90, student [at Cambridge], with pension contributions from the almoner, chamberlain, gardener, precentor and the prior of St Leonard's, NRO DCN 1/6/104–106; 1/5/118; 1/11/26; 1/9/87; 2/3/95.
1490/91, student with contributions from the almoner, cellarer, chamberlain, hostiller, master of the cellar and the prior of Hoxne, NRO DCN 1/6/107; 1/2/83; 1/5/119; 1/7/119; 1/1/95; 2/6/28.
1491/2, student, with contributions from the hostiller, master of the cellar, refectorer, sacrist and the prior of Hoxne, NRO DCN 1/7/120; Oxford, Bod. Ms Rolls Norfolk, no 54; Oxford, Bod. Ms Rolls Norfolk, no 51; NRO DCN 1/4/104; NRO DCN 2/6/29.
In Venn, *Gonville and Caius*, i, 14, he is listed as a pensioner in 1490/1 (as 'Yutforth'); see *BRUC*.
1492, 5/8 Oct., 38th in order at the visitation of bp Goldwell, Jessopp, *Visit.*, 8.
1499, 6 Apr., 30th on the visitation certificate, *Reg. abp Morton*, iii, no 258.

MYDELTONE
see Midelton

Peter de MYNTELYNG [Myntelynge
occ. 1388 d. 1393/4

1388, Mar./June, communar/pittancer, NRO DCN 1/12/33.
1393/4, d., and the chamberlain pd the brief bearer, NRO DCN 1/5/25.

MYNTELYNG
See also Mintlyng

William MYNTING
occ. 1532/4

1532, [13] Mar., ord dcn, St Mary's chapel, Norwich cathedral, NRO DN ORR/1/1, fo 2.

1533, 29 Mar., ord pr., St Mary's chapel, Norwich cathedral, *ib.*, fo 12v.

1532, 3 June, present at the visitation of bp Nikke and reported *omnia bene*, but was accused of being one of the favourites of Adam Sloley, the fifth prior, q.v., Jessopp, *Visit.*, 268.

1534, 28 July, subscribed to the Act of Supremacy, *DK 7th Report*, Appndx 2, 295.

I NICHOLAS
occ. 1255/6

1255/6, visited [North] Elmham, NRO DCN 60/10/1.

II NICHOLAS
occ. 1374

1374, 25 Mar., prior of Lynn, D. Owen, *King's Lynn*, 87, no 53.

III NICHOLAS
occ. c. 1504

c. 1504, a Nicholas, along with six other priests, (Christian names only given) made their prof.; this is recorded on an inserted leaf (prob. of rough notes) between fos 27v and 28 in Reg. Nikke (9/14).

NORMAN
n.d.

n.d., acc. to Blomefield he was the first master of St Paul's hospital, Norwich; hence Norman's spital, *Norfolk*, iii, 482.

NORTHWOLD
see Norwold

Richard NORTWYCKE
occ. 1387

1387, 2 Mar., ord pr., Hartlebury church, by *lit. dim.*, *Reg. Wakefield* (Worcester), no 913g.

Andrew NORWICHE
occ. 1526

1526, 7 June, one of a group of younger monks, present at the visitation of bp Nikke, who complained that they were required by the seniors to memorize the psalter and the antiphons and responses etc., which they considered a waste of time, Jessopp, *Visit.*, 198.

Note: this is the only record of a monk by this name, who may also have been known by his family name; see under Andrew Tooke for possible later references.

Edmund NORWICH, B.Cn.L. [*alias* Drake
occ. 1510 occ. 1538

1523/4, 1525/6, 1532, 3 June, prior of Aldeby, NRO DCN 2/2/29/30, Jessopp, *Visit.*, 263.

1535/6, prior of Lynn, NRO DCN 2/1/91.

1538, before 2 May, prior of Aldeby, *Fasti, 1541–1857*, vii, 55.

1510, pensioner at Gonville Hall, Cambridge, Venn, *Gonville and Caius* i, 19.

1511/12, student at Cambridge, with pension contributions from the hostiller, infirmarer, sacrist and prior of St Leonard's, 1/7/132; 1/10/34; 1/4/111; 2/3/111.

1514/18, at Gonville Hall, Venn, *Gonville and Caius*, i, 19.

1520, B.Cn.L., Venn, *ib.*

1520/1, student at Oxford, with contributions from the almoner, chamberlain, refectorer and the priors of Lynn and St Leonard's, NRO DCN 1/6/126; 1/5/138; 1/8/114; 2/1/82; 2/3/119.

1521/2, student [at Oxford], with contributions from the almoner, chamberlain, hostiller, refectorer, sacrist, and the prior of Lynn, NRO DCN 1/6/127; 1/5/139; 1/7/141; 1/8/114; 1/4/116; 2/1/82.

1526, 7 June, present at the visitation of bp Nikke and complained of the practice of sending difficult monks to the cells, and of the lack of consultation of the brethren before important decisions were made; he also accused the prior of holding on to the office of sacrist, Jessopp, *Visit.*, 197.

1532, 3 June, present at the visitation of bp Nikke and stated that being resident at Aldeby he knew little of the state of the Norwich community, but he went on to report on some laxity in discipline; on the whole he considered that 'omnia debite et commode fiunt juxta vires', Jessopp, *Visit.*, 263.

1534, 28 July, subscribed to the Act of Supremacy, *DK 7th Report*, Appndx 2, 295.

1538, 30 Apr., dispensed to wear the habit of a secular pr. and hold a canonry and prebend in the cathedral and any other benefice, and be non resident, Chambers, *Faculty Office Regs*, 137.

1538, 2 May, apptd canon of the 4th prebend in the new foundation, *Fasti 1541–1857*, vii, 55. See also *L and P Henry VIII*, xiii, pt 1, no 1115(4).

Francis NORWICH [*alias* Atmere
occ. 1514 occ. 1538

1514, 27 Apr., present at the visitation of bp Nikke and accused of disobedience and of instigating disputes among the monks, Jessopp, *Visit.*, 74, 77.

1520, 3 Sept., present at the visitation of bp Nikke and accused the third prior, Thomas Pellys, q.v., of showing favouritism, *ib.*, 193.

1532, 3 June, present at the visitation of bp Nikke and reported *omnia bene*, *ib.*, 267.

1534, 28 July, subscribed to the Act of Supremacy, *DK 7th Report*, Appndx 2, 295.

1538, 30 Apr., dispensed to wear the habit of a secular pr. and hold a canonry and prebend in

the cathedral and any other benefice, and be non resident, Chambers, *Faculty Office Regs*, 137.
1538, 2 May, licensed as a secular canon, *L and P Henry VIII*, xiii, pt 1, no 1115(4).

Geoffrey de NORWICH
occ. 1400/1 d. 1419/20

1400/Feb. 1402, gardener, NRO DCN 1/11/3, 4.
1407/9, 1409/10, 1410/11, 1413/15, 1416/18, prior of Hoxne, NRO DCN 2/6/6, 7; Windsor, St George's chapel, I.C.5; NRO DCN 2/6/8; Windsor, St George's chapel, I.C. 6–9.

1419/20, d., and the chamberlain recd 'alms', NRO DCN 1/5/47.

Hugh NORWICH [Norwych *alias* Fraunceys
occ. 1494 occ. 1520

1494, 20 Nov., one of two *clerici* whom the bp comm. the prior to receive on his behalf, [*monachand'*], Reg. Goldwell, fo 181v.

1514, 27 Apr., succentor, Jessopp, *Visit.*, 74.
1515/17, gardener, NRO DCN 1/11/28–30.
1520, 3 Sept., master of the high altar [*magister summi altaris*], Jessopp, *Visit.*, 192.

1499, 6 Apr., 44th in order on the visitation certificate, *Reg. abp Morton*, iii, no 258.
1511/12, the infirmarer pd for two cartloads of faggots for him [?living in the infirmary on acct of age or ill health], NRO DCN 1/10/34.
1514, 27 Apr., present at the visitation of bp Nikke and complained that, even when ill in the infirmary, monks were ordered to celebrate mass [*summas missas celebrare*], Jessopp, *Visit.*, 74.
1520, 3 Sept., present at the visitation of bp Nikke and reported *omnia bene*, *ib.*, 192.

I John NORWICH, B.Th. [Norwych
occ. 1438/9 d. 1452/3

1438/9, pd the refectorer 10s. for a *ciphus*, prob. soon after adm., NRO DCN 1/8/77.

1443/4, 1444/5, student, with pension contributions from the precentor and refectorer, NRO DCN 1/9/57,58; 1/8/81,82.
1445/6, student, with contributions from the chamberlain, master of the cellar and refectorer, NRO DCN 1/5/77; 1/1/87; 1/8/83.
1446/7, student, with contributions from the cellarer and chamberlain, NRO DCN 1/2/57; 1/5/78.
1447/8, student, with contributions from the almoner cellarer, chamberlain, precentor and refectorer, NRO DCN 1/6/68; 1/2/58; 1/5/79; 1/9/61; 1/8/85.
1448/9, student, with contributions from the almoner, precentor and refectorer, NRO DCN 1/6/69; 1/9/62; 1/8/86.
1450, 14 Mar., supplicated at Oxford for B.Th., after two and a half years of study at Cambridge and six at Oxford, *Reg. Univ. Oxon.*, i, 9.
1450/1, student, with contribution from the master of St Paul's hospital, NRO DCN 2/5/5.
1451/2, student, with contributions from the almoner, cellarer and refectorer, NRO DCN 1/6/70; 1/2/60; 1/8/89.
1452/3, student, with contributions from the chamberlain, master of the cellar, refectorer, sacrist and the master of St Paul's hospital, NRO DCN 1/5/85; 1/1/88; 1/8/90; 1/4/83; 2/5/6.

1452/3, d., and the chamberlain recd 6s. in 'alms', NRO DCN 1/5/85; the communar/pittancer sent letters to the cells announcing his d., NRO DCN 1/12/63.

II John NORWICH
occ. 1491/2

1491/2, gave the hostiller 2s. towards the expense of the construction of the great window in the *hostillaria* [*ad novam facturam magne fenestre*], NRO DCN 1/7/120.
1492, 5/8 Oct., 31st in order at the visitation of bp Goldwell, Jessopp, *Visit.*, 8.

I Richard NORWICH
occ. 1492

1492, 5/8 Oct., 15th in order at the visitation of bp Goldwell, Jessopp, *Visit.*, 8.

II Richard NORWICH [*alias* Skyp, Skyppe
occ. 1524/5 occ. 1532

1532, 3 June, third prior and pittancer, Jessopp, *Visit.*, 266.

1526/7, student at Oxford, with pension contributions from almoner, cellarer, chamberlain, pittancer and precentor, NRO DCN 1/6/131; 1/2/97; 1/5/143,144; 1/12/103,104; 1/9/94.
1527/8, student, with contributions from the almoner and refectorer, NRO DCN 1/6/132; 1/8/116.
1528/9, student, with contributions from the almoner, chamberlain, hostiller and the prior of Lynn, NRO DCN 1/6/133; 1/5/145; 1/7/145; 2/1/82.
1529/30, student, with contributions from the almoner, cellarer, hostiller, infirmarer and the prior of Lynn, NRO DCN 1/6/134; 1/2/98; 1/7/146; 1/10/38; 2/1/82.
1530/1, student, with contributions from the cellarer, hostiller, refectorer, and the prior of Lynn, NRO DCN 1/2/99; 1/7/147; 1/8/117; 2/1/82; returned [from Oxford] for the el. of a prior, NRO DCN 1/12/106.
1532, 3 June, described as scholar, Jessopp, *Visit.*, 266.

1524/5, the precentor gave him a 'reward' for repairing choir books, NRO DCN 1/9/93.

1532, 3 June, present at the visitation of bp Nikke and reported that reforms were under way [*omnia reformantur*], Jessopp, *Visit.*, 262. He preached in Latin at the opening ceremonies on the theme 'Be ye therefore perfect as your heavenly Father is perfect (Math., 5, 48); but later, during the proceedings, was accused [with Thomas Morton, q.v.] of snubbing his brethren and sowing discord, *ib.*, 262, 264.

Simon NORWICH [Norwych
occ. 1467/8 occ. 1501/2

1482/90, precentor, NRO DCN 1/9/80–87.
1483/4, refectorer, NRO DCN 1/8/98.
1486/7, 1488/90, gardener, NRO DCN 1/11/24–26.
1501/2, hostiller, NRO DCN 1/7/124.

1467/8, ill and the infirmarer spent 2s. 4d. on medicine, NRO DCN 1/10/27.
1477/8, gave 4d. to the precentor for 'Hylton V lxxix' (i.e. a volume, which he may have been borrowing), NRO DCN 1/9/76; see Greatrex, 'Norwich Monk Students', 575–576.
1492, 5/8 Oct., 13th in order at the visitation of bp Goldwell, Jessopp, *Visit.*, 8.
1499, 6 Apr., 9th on the visitation certificate, *Reg. abp Morton*, iii, no 258.

I William de NORWICO
occ. 1257

1257, 28 May, sacrist, *CPR (1247–1258)*, 557.

1257, 28 May, with Roger de Skerning, q.v., as proctors for the prior and chapter, recd royal licence to el. a bp, *ib.*

II William de NORWICO
see William Worstede

John de NORWODE
occ. 1336/7

1336/7, gave the refectorer 12s. for a *ciphus*, with the prior's permission, NRO DCN 1/8/34.

Henry de NORWOLD [Northwold
occ. before 1310/11

n.d., almoner, Reg. II (Almoner's Reg.), fo 84^{v}.
1310/11, mentioned on the almoner's acct, as though a former almoner, NRO DCN 1/6/9; an undated almoner's acct, NRO DCN 1/6/138, has his name on the head and states that it was his eighth yr in office.

Robert NOSTELL [Notell, Nottell
occ. before 1520 occ. 1537

1526, 7 June, present at the visitation of bp Nikke and linked with accusations vs John Sall, q.v., Jessopp, *Visit.*, 199. (Jessopp has read 'Nottell' here and below).
1532, 3 June, present at the visitation of bp Nikke and reported that monks were not being sent to university (but see under Thomas Morton and Richard Norwich II); Jessopp, *Visit.*, 267.
1537, 31 Jan., pd £8 to obtain dispensation to hold a benefice, wth the prior's consent, and to wear the habit of his order under that of a secular pr., Chambers, *Faculty Office Regs*, 85.

A John Notell, alderman of Norwich, who d. in Aug. 1520, mentioned in his will Robert his son, a monk, who was to sing for 'my soul and my friends' souls at the university of Cambridge or Oxford for one year', Norwich, Norwich Consistory Court Records, Robinson, 131.

OCLE
see Acle

ODO
occ. 1339/40

1339/40, the chamberlain pd 6s. 8d. to Odo, and to John de Stukle q.v., who were then at Oxford, for their *pellicia*; he was prob. Stukle's *socius*, NRO DCN 1/5/11.

Walter ONY
occ. 1427 d. ?1438/9

1427, 7 Jan., one of four *clerici* adm. *ad osculum et benedictionem* by the bp after acceptance by the chapter as a monk, Reg. Alnwick, fo 97^{v}.
1438/9, a Walter d., and the chamberlain recd 20s. in 'alms', NRO DCN 1/5/69; see also Walter Redenhale.

OREWELL
see Orwell

Robert de ORMESBY
occ. 1330s

?1336, before, prior of Hoxne for at least two yrs, Windsor, St George's chapel, I.C.1.
1336/7, given 66s. 8d. by the communar *ad opus elect'* [i.e., Thomas de Hemenhale, q.v.], NRO DCN 1/12/20. This suggests that he may have been subprior, as the holder of this office is known to have been responsible for the collection and distribution of certain funds, see Greatrex, 'Norwich Monk Students', 566, and below.

Name in Oxford, Bod. Ms Douce 366 (13th/14th c.), 'Psalterium fr Roberti de Ormesby monachi Norwyc' per eundem assignationem choro ecclesie sancte Trinitatis Norwici ad iacendum coram Suppriorem qui pro tempore fuerit in perpetuum'; see Ker, 'Norwich Cathedral Mss', 255.

Note: Sidney Cockerell noted that a gift of such magnitude as this beautiful, illuminated psalter presupposes a donor of some wealth and social standing. He therefore suggested that Robert prob. belonged to the family who held the lordship of Ormesby and that he may have purchased the volume before he entered the cathedral priory. A contemporary secular cleric, William de Ormesby, possibly his brother, was rector of St Mary in the Marsh (in the cathedral precincts) and gave a glossed 13th c. Bible to the monks (now CUL Ms Kk. 4.3). See S. Cockerell, *Two East Anglian Psalters at the Bodleian Library, Oxford*, Oxford, 1926, 36–37. Could the inscription reference to the subprior imply that Robert himself occupied this position?

Walter de ORMESBY [Ormisby
occ. 1377 ?occ. 1418/19

1377/Dec. 1382, hostiller, NRO DCN 1/7/36–41.
1397/8, for a few months only, prior of Lynn, NRO DCN 2/1/21; see John de Carleton.

1418/19, ?d. by this date; the refectorer recd 10s. for his *ciphus*, which he had put out on loan, or possibly exchanged [*mutato*], NRO DCN 1/8/64 and 66; the latter acct does not mention a loan but simply records the receipt of 10s. for the *ciphus*, *ad opus refectorarii*, a useful phrase!

John ORWELL [Orewell
occ. 1502

1502, 23 June, one of four *clerici* whom the bp comm. the prior to clothe [*monachand'*] Reg. Nikke (8/13), fo 13^{v}.

See also John III or IV for his prob. prof.

OTHO
n.d.

n.d., 14 Mar., obit occ. in the kalendar in Reg. XI, fo 3.

John OVERTON
occ. 1421/4

1421/2, contributed 20d. to the communar's fund for the cloister work, NRO DCN 1/12/49.
1423/4, d., and the chamberlain recd 16s. in 'alms', NRO DCN 1/5/50.

John de OXNEGG
occ. 1309/10 occ. 1314/15

1314, Mar./1315, refectorer, NRO DCN 1/8/22, 23.
1309/10, visited Hindringham, [North] Elmham, and Sedgeford, NRO DCN 60/20/15; 60/10/12; 60/33/15.

John de OXONIA
see John II

John PALGRAVE
occ. 1429/30 d. 1475/6

1429/30, novice, NRO DCN 1/10/17.

1448/53, 1454/5, hostiller, NRO DCN 1/7/81–92.
1460/1, infirmarer, NRO DCN 1/10/25.
1462/3, Sept./June, hostiller, NRO DCN 1/7/97.
1429/30, 1430/1, ill both years and the chamberlain spent 8d. and 10d. respectively on medicine, NRO DCN 1/10/17,18.
1446, name occ. on a rough list of those assigned to celebrate weekday and chantry masses, Cambridge, Emm. Coll. Ms, 142, fo 68.
1449, 26 Jan., name also occ. on a Sunday mass rota for this date, *ib.*; also on lists (prob. also during these years) for masses in the Bateman, Totyngton, Wakering, Tye and Erpingham chantries, *ib.*, fo 77^{v}.
1475/6, d., and the chamberlain recd 17s. 8d. in 'alms', NRO DCN 1/5/102.

Reginald de PANKESFORD
n.d.

n.d., [?1st half 13th c.], master of St Paul's hospital acc. to Blomefield, *Norfolk*, iii, 432.

Botulph PARKER
occ. 1532 occ. 1538

1532, 3 June, present at the visitation of bp Nikke, although at that time he was a member of the community at Yarmouth; he reported *omnia bene* as far as he knew, Jessopp, *Visit.*, 266.
1530/1, pd by the precentor for binding the 'great Bible' in the refectory, NRO DCN 1/9/97; and see William Thirkell.
1534, 28 July, subscribed to the Act of Supremacy, *DK 7th Report*, Appndx 2, 295.
1538, 30 Apr., dispensed to wear the habit of a secular pr. and hold a canonry and prebend in the cathedral and any other benefice, and be non resident, Chambers, *Faculty Office Regs*, 137.
1538, 2 May, licensed as a secular canon, *L and P Henry VIII*, xiii, pt 1, no 1115(4).

Robert PARKER [Parkeer
occ. 1419/20

1419, Dec./1420, precentor, NRO DCN 1/9/31.

1419/20, d., and the chamberlain recd 'alms', NRO DCN 1/5/47.

PAUL
occ. [c. 1146 × 1172]

Said by Thomas de Monmouth, q.v., to have been one of his brethren, who was related to Hildebrand of Norwich, founder of a hospital called after him, Jessopp and James, *St William*, 159.

John PECHE [Pecche
occ. 1345 occ. 1351

1345, between Jan. and July, on the infirmarer's sick list, NRO DCN 1/10/2.
1345/6, 1346/7, ill both years and the infirmarer spent 3d. and 4d. respectively on medicine, NRO DCN 1/10/4, 5.
1351, 26 May., with the prior, Simon Bozoun, and William de Witton, q.v., involved in a

dispute about the chapter's rights over the passage of St Olave between Norwich and Great Yarmouth, *CPR (1350–1354)*, 155.

William PEKEWORTH
occ. before 1410/11

1410, on the refectorer's inventory, Richard de Midelton, q.v., was reported to be using the *parvus ciphus* which had belonged to him, NRO DCN 1/8/56.

Thomas PELLYS
occ. 1492 occ. 1520

1509/10, 1511/12, 1514, 27 Apr., prior of Hoxne, Windsor, St George's chapel, I.C.37, NRO DCN 2/6/35; Jessopp, *Visit.*, 73.
1520, 3 Sept., third prior, Jessopp, *Visit.*, 192.

1492, 5/8 Oct., 42nd in order at the visitation of bp Goldwell, Jessopp, *Visit.*, 8.
1499, 6 Apr., 34th on the visitation certificate, *Reg. abp Morton*, iii, no 258.
1505/6, pd by the almoner for certain expenses pertaining to this office, NRO DCN 1/6/115.
1514, 27 Apr., present at the visitation of bp Nikke, and stated that although he was often away from Norwich [at Hoxne] he thought the community was in a fair state with respect to religious observance, but the financial state was poor [*aere alieno*]; he also reported that he did not pay any pension to Norwich because of the large sum required [from Hoxne] for the monk students, Jessopp, *Visit.*, 73.
1520, 3 Sept., present at the visitation of bp Nikke and reported *omnia bene*, *ib.*, 192; a young acol. accused him of being malicious and of showing favouritism (see Robert Grafton), *ib.*, 193.

Note: not to be confused with another Thomas Pellys, a secular cleric and LL D.; both Blomefield and Venn have made this mistake.

John de PENESTORP
occ. 1320/1

1320/1, one of the monks who may have been briefly among the Oxford group, as the refectorer pd him a small sum along with others who were students, NRO DCN 1/8/24.

William de PENTENEY [Penteneye
occ. 1385 d. 1408/9

1385, June/Sept., 1386/7, 1394/5, precentor, NRO DCN 1/9/22–24.

1393/4, in the refectorer's inventory he was listed as having had the *ciphus* of cedar which had belonged to John de Hapisburgh, q.v., NRO DCN 1/8/48.
1394/5, ill, and his expenses in the infirmary, the *camera minutorum* and at St Leonard's were, 7s. 3d., in addition to 6d. for medicine, NRO DCN 1/9/24.
1408/9, d., and the chamberlain recd 'alms' of 11s. 8d., NRO DCN 1/5/39.

PETER
n.d.

n.d., 16 Sept., name occ. in the Canterbury obit list, BL Ms Arundel 68, fo 41^{v}.

Peter PEVERELL
occ. [c. 1146 × 1172]

Contemporary of Thomas de Monmouth, q.v., who says that he had previously been in the privy chamber of Henry II, and who reports a vision which, during an illness, he had had of St William, and his cure wrought by the saint, Jessopp and James, *St William*, 129–131; 211–212.

Jessopp and James, *ib.*, 129 n., state that his brother was Sir Matthew Peverell, who had an estate at Great Melton and gave lands to the cathedral priory on condition that the chapter recd Peter as a monk; see NRO DCN 44/80/1 and Reg. V, fo 45^{v}.

Henry de PLUMSTED
occ. 1357 occ. 1363/4

1358/61, hostiller, NRO DCN 1/7/18–21.
1363/4, communar/pittancer, NRO DCN 1/12/30.

1357, bought a *ciphus* for 13s. from the refectorer, NRO DCN 1/8/40.

John de PLUMSTEDE
occ. [1270 × 1300]

[1270 × 1300], warden of St Paul's hospital, concerned with a land transaction, *N. Cath. Charters*, ii, no 507.

Thomas de PLUMSTED [Plumpsted, Plumpstede, Plumstede
occ. 1288/9 ?d. 1323

1302/8, cellarer, NRO DCN 1/2/4–7.
1321/3 Mar., sacrist, NRO DCN 1/4/21,22.

1288/9, one of the monks whose expenses in connection with the confirmation of the el. [of Ralph de Walpole as bp] were pd by the communar, *Comm. Rolls*, 56.
[1292], allocations were pd to him by the master of the cellar because of many losses [*amissionibus*], NRO DCN 1/1/10.
1296/7, accompanied the cellarer to Bury St Edmunds on business and the expenses were pd by the communar; he also made two journeys to London which cost the communar £4 17s., *Comm. Rolls*, 68.
1297/8, made two journeys to London for the communar, one costing over £3 and the other £2 15s., *Comm. Rolls*, 71.
1298/9, made two further business trips for the communar, *Comm. Rolls*, 74; these, too, were expensive.
1302/3, another journey to London for the communar, *Comm. Rolls*, 83.

Note: Most of these journeys were prob. related to the cloister building programme.
1323, prob. d. in Mar. as the refectorer pd for repairing the *ciphus quondam Thome*, NRO DCN 1/8/27, and note the date under the sacrist above.

Name in Oxford, Magdalen College, Ms lat. 53, pp. 169–98, Annales Norwicenses, etc., (late 13th c.); see Ker, 'Norwich Cathedral Mss', 258.

QWAPLODE
see Waplode

RADULFUS
n.d.

n.d., 3 Sept., name occ. in a Canterbury obit list, BL Ms Arundel 68, fo 40.

I RALPH, son of Eborard
occ. early 13th c.

[early 13th c.], name mentioned in NRO DCN 45/33/1, a loose deed connected with St Peter Mancroft.

II RALPH
occ. 1304 occ. 1306/7

1304, sacrist, following John Fuldon, q.v., NRO DCN 1/4/15; and prob. in 1306/7 as R., NRO DCN 1/4/17.

See Ralph de Elingham.

John de RANDWORTH [Randeworth
occ. 1413/14 d. 1421/2

1413/4, communar/pittancer, NRO DCN 1/12/44.
1414/15, gave the precentor 12d. towards the cost of a window in the chancel at Plumstead, NRO DCN 1/9/31.
1421/2, ill and the infirmarer spent 3s. 4d. on medicine, NRO DCN 1/10/14.
1421/2, d., and the chamberlain recd 17s. in 'alms', NRO DCN 1/5/48.

Nicholas de RANDWORTH [Randeworth
occ. 1401/2 d. 1448/9

1411/1419, Dec., refectorer, NRO DCN 1/8/57–66.
1424/1427, Jan., hostiller, NRO DCN 1/7/69–72.
1426, before 31 Dec., master of St Paul's hospital; the prior wrote to the bp requesting his removal on this date, Reg. Alnwick, fo 97.
1426, 31 Dec., his apptment as subprior was requested by the prior in the letter referred to above.

1401/2, student [at Oxford] during the term of St John the Baptist with a contribution from the hostiller, NRO DCN 1/7/51.

1426, 31 Dec., his apptment as penitentiary was requested by the prior, Reg. Alnwick, fo 97.
1430, 23 Sept., apptd penitentiary in the cathedral church, Reg. Alnwick, fo 101v.
1430/1, gave 6s. 8d. to the gardener towards the repair of the wall *vs Holmstrete*, NRO DCN 1/11/14.
1442/3, sold four glazed windows to John Eglington, q.v., NRO DCN 1/8/80.
1444, 13 Jan., the prior requested the bp to remove him from the office of penitentiary in the cathedral because he was *grandevus et senio confractus*, Reg. Brouns, fo 109v.
1446, name heads a rough list of those assigned to celebrate weekday and chantry masses, Cambridge, Emm. Coll. Ms 142, fo 68; also a memorandum to the effect that the new cursus of weekday masses began with him on 5 June [?1447], *ib.*, 77v; his name also occ. on other fragmentary lists for chantry masses on fo 77v.
1448/9, d., and the chamberlain recd 28s. 10d. in 'alms', NRO DCN 1/5/80.

I RANULPH
occ. [?1161 × 1174]

[?1161 × 1174], prior: the dating is so uncertain that he may have occ. before or after John II, q.v.

[1161 × 1168, prob. 1163 autumn], witnessed an episcopal charter, *Eng. Epis. Acta*, vi, no 114.
n.d., 29 May, obit occ. in BL Ms Harley 3950, fo 5; it occ. on 28 May in Reg. XI, fo 4.

II M. RANULPH
occ. [1195 × 1198]

[1195 × 1198], with John [de Oxford] bp and M. Roger, q.v., appeared before the abp at Lambeth in a dispute over the church of Martham between the bp and the chapter, *N. Cath. Charters*, i, no 263.

Walter REDENHALE
occ. 1430/1 d. 1438/9

1430/1, ill, and the infirmarer spent 5s. on medicine, NRO DCN 1/10/18.
1438/9, a Walter d., and the chamberlain recd 20s. in 'alms', NRO DCN 1/5/69; see also Walter Ony.

Henry de REDING
occ. 1292/3

1292/3, the refectorer pd 2s. 3d. for the repair of his *ciphus*, NRO DCN 1/8/5.

REGINALDUS
n.d.

n.d., 7 Apr., name occ. in a Canterbury obit list, BL Ms Arundel 68, fo 23.

REINALDUS
occ. [?1146 or c. 1149]

[?1146 or c. 1149], witness to a charter in favour of the prior and convent, *N. Cath. Charters* i, no 129.

Note: possibly identical with Reginaldus, q.v., above, but possibly a monk of St Benet of Hulme.

William REPPS, D.Th. [Reppis, Reppys, Roppez *alias* Rugg'
occ. 1510/11 occ. 1530

1513/14, sacrist, NRO DCN 1/4/112.
1514/15, prior of St Leonard's, NRO DCN 2/3/114.
1520, 3 Sept., prior of Yarmouth, Jessopp, *Visit.*, 192.
1526, 7 June, subprior, *ib.*, 203.
1528/9, prior of Yarmouth, NRO DCN 2/4/21.

1510/11, student at Cambridge, and B.Th., with pension contributions from the hostiller and sacrist, NRO DCN 1/7/131; 1/4/110.
1511/12, student at Cambridge, with contributions from the infirmarer, sacrist and prior of St Leonard's, NRO DCN 1/10/34; 1/4/111; 2/3/111.
1513/14, 1514/15, described as S.T.P., and D.Th. on his obedientiary acct rolls, NRO DCN 1/4/112; 2/3/114.
Note: Venn's entry, in *Gonville and Caius*, i, 18, states that he was a pensioner 1509/13; B.A. 1504/5; M.A. 1508; B.Th. 1509; D.Th. 1513. See also *CU Grace Book Γ*, 66, 74, 109.
1513, 24 May, the prior informed the chancellor of the university that he would allow William, B.Th., who aspired to the doctorate, to take the oath required of an inceptor, CUL Archives, Luard 153.
1514, 27 Apr., present at the visitation of bp Nikke and preached in Latin on the text, 'Cast out the old leaven' (1 Co. 5, 7), Jessopp, *Visit.*, 71.
1520, 3 Sept., present at the visitation of bp Nikke and reported that, as far as he knew [residing at Yarmouth], all was well, *ib.*, 192.
1526, 7 June, present at the visitation of bp Nikke, at which there were several depositions vs him, *ib.*, 199, 200. He himself had nothing to report, but was ordered to cease from annulling the third, fourth and fifth priors' decisions concerning punishment [of disobedient monks], the implication being that he was 'easygoing' [*facilis*], *ib.*, 202–203.
1530, 12 Apr., abbot of St Benet of Hulme, royal assent obtained to his el., *L and P Henry VIII*, iv, pt 3, no 6331.
1536/50, bp of Norwich, *Fasti*, iv, 25, and *Fasti, 1541–1857*, vii, 37.

One of the authors of the Institution of a Christian Man acc. to Venn, *Gonville and Caius*, i, 18.

Described by Leland as *theologus ad unguem doctus*, Dugdale, *Monasticon*, iii, 65.

Venn, *Gonville and Caius*, i, 18, states that he was the son of William Rugg of Northrepps, Norfolk. For details of his later career see *DNB* under Rugg.

Thomas de RESHAM
occ. 1345/6.

1345/6, ill, and the infirmarer spent 4d. on medicine, NRO DCN 1/10/4.

I REYNER
n.d.

n.d., 18 Apr., name occ. in a Canterbury obit list, BL Ms Arundel 68, fo 24^v.

II REYNER
n.d.

n.d., 29 Apr., name occ. in a Canterbury obit list, BL Ms Arundel 68, fo 25^v, and Lambeth Ms 20, fo 184.

III REYNER
occ. 1288/9

1288/9, pittancer, from whom the communar recd £6 12s. 7¾d. but his name does not occur on the pittancer's section of the joint acct, NRO DCN 1/12/2; also named as refectorer this yr, NRO DCN 1/8/1.

Perhaps identical with Reyner I or II above, and/or Reyner de Lakenham, q.v.

REYNER
see also under Lakenham

John de REYNHAM
occ. 1347/8

1347/8, ill, and the infirmarer spent 12d. on medicine, NRO DCN 1/10/6.

Name in Cambridge, Corpus Christi College, Ms 252, which contains an exposition of the Rule as well as a life of St Helen and the liber de stimulo amoris divini (early 14th c.); on fo 183^v 'liber Johannis de Reynham monachi Norwici quem ipse in parte scripsit et in parte scribi fecit'; on fos 7 and 14, 'God is al my love'.

I RICHARD
occ. [1096 × 1119]

[1096 × 1119], *temp* bp Losinga, son of Agnes de Bellafago, was one of the earliest to be recd into the priory, Reg. I, fo 55; de Bosco as in the Ms is an error according to B. Dodwell.

He was prob. of the same family as William de Bello Fago, bp Losinga's predecessor in the see (Elmham/Thetford).

II RICHARD
n.d.

n.d., 15 Dec., subprior, name occ. in a Canterbury obit list, BL Ms Arundel 68, fo 51.

III RICHARD
n.d.

n.d., 15 Sept., name occ. in a Canterbury obit list, BL Ms Arundel 68, fo 41v.

Note: in [1146 × 1149], with Wimer, q.v., a Richard witnessed a grant of rent in Coslany to the monks of St Benet of Hulme, *St Benet Holme Cart.*, no 154.

IV RICHARD
n.d.

n.d., 26 Apr., name occ. in a Canterbury obit list, BL Ms Arundel 68, fo 25v.

Richard II, III or IV may have acted as witness, with Wimer, q.v.; one of the obits may ref. to Richard I.

RICHARD [?Ickens
see Wikens

RINGLANDE
see Ryngland

I ROBERT
occ. [c. 1146 × 1172]

Brother of St William, previously a clerk, prob. from Haveringland, see Jessopp and James, *St William*, 38, 91 and 296 note.

II ROBERT
occ. [1178 × 1179]

[1178 × 1179], prior of Lynn, *HRH*, 93 (BL Ms Harley 2110, fo 81–81v).

III ROBERT
n.d.

n.d., 8 Oct., name occ. in a Canterbury obit list, BL Ms Arundel 68, fo 44v.

IV ROBERT
occ. c. 1504

c. 1504, a Robert, along with six other priests, (Christian names only given) made their prof.; this is recorded on an inserted leaf (prob. of rough notes) between fos 27v and 28 in Reg. Nikke (9/14).

V ROBERT
occ. c. 1504

c. 1504, a Robert, along with two other dcns, (Christian names only given) made their prof.; this is recorded on an inserted leaf (prob. of rough notes) between fos 27v and 28 in Reg. Nikke (9/14).

I M. ROGER
occ. [1195 × 1198]

[1195 × 1198], with John [de Oxford] bp and M. Ranulph II, q.v., appeared before the abp at Lambeth in a dispute over the church of Martham between the bp and the chapter, *N. Cath. Charters*, i, no 263.

II ROGER
occ. before ?1278/9

?1278/9, before, prior of Hoxne, possibly between Richard de Hoxne, q.v. and William de Acle, q.v., acc. to Blomefield, *Norfolk*, iii, 609.

III ROGER
occ. 1282/3

1282/3, the communar pd 1s. 4d. for his *sotularibus* and 6d. *in ligatura libri fratris*—-, *Comm. Rolls*, 46, 47 (NRO DCN 1/12/1).

Note: is this a young Roger de Eston, q.v.?

[John de la ROKELE
occ. 1332/3

1332/3, incepted [at Oxford] and the master of the cellar contributed 13s. 4d., under *donationes*, NRO DCN 1/1/32; but he was prob. a friend or protégé and not a monk as *BRUO* assumed.]

ROLAND
n.d.

n.d., 14 July, obit occ. in the kalendar in Reg. XI, fo 5.

Stephen ROPER
see Darsham

ROPPEZ
see Repps

Robert de ROTHEWELL [Rothewelle
n.d.

Name in CUL Ms Ii.1.22, Hugh de St Victore etc. (13th c.) on fo 4; see Ker, 'Norwich Cathedral Mss', 257; see also John Marton.

RUGG'
see Repps

Thomas de RUGHTON [Rouchton, Roughton, Ructon, Rugthon
occ. 1402 d. 1419/20

1402, Feb/1403, Jan., gardener, NRO DCN 1/11/4, 5.

1404/5, communar/pittancer, NRO DCN 1/12/39.

1406/8, Jan., almoner, NRO DCN 1/6/35–37.

1408/10, 1411/14, 1415/16, 1417/18, Apr., chamberlain, NRO DCN 1/5/39–45.

1418, 8 Apr., the prior requested that he be removed from the office of chamberlain and be confirmed as subprior, Reg. Wakering, fo 32.

1408/9, went to Hoxne, with expenses pd by the communar/ pittancer, NRO DCN 1/12/42.

1419/20, d., and the chamberlain recd 'alms', NRO DCN 1/5/47.

Thomas de RUNHALE
occ. 1335/6 d. 1343/4

1335/6, student [at Oxford], with pension contribution from the master of the cellar, NRO DCN 1/1/38.
1336/7, one of four students at Oxford; his travel expenses were pd by the communar with a contribution from the cellarer, NRO DCN 1/12/20; 1/2/101. See John de Betele, John de Stukle, Robert Sturmyn.
1343/4, d., and the chamberlain pd the brief bearer, NRO DCN 1/5/12.

William de RYKINGHALE [Rykynghal'
occ. 1345/6 occ. 1369

1351, Mar./1354, precentor, NRO DCN 1/9/5–7.
1358/66, 1369, prior of St Leonard's, NRO DCN 2/3/6, 7.
1345/6, ill, on the infirmarer's sick list, NRO DCN 1/10/4.
1347/8, ill, and the infirmarer spent 4d. on medicine, NRO DCN 1/10/6.
1351, ill and charged his own office of precentor 12d. for a cordial, NRO DCN 1/9/5.
1354, ill in the infirmary and the precentor's office bore the cost, NRO DCN 1/9/71.

Andrew RYNGLAND [Ringlonde
occ. 1514 occ. 1526

1520, 3 Sept., fifth prior and subsacrist, Jessopp, *Visit.*, 193.
1526, 7 June, succentor, *ib.*, 203.
1514, 27 Apr., present at the visitation of bp Nikke, Jessopp, *Visit.*, 73; he made three factual depositions:
(1) that there were only 38 monks instead of the prescribed 60.
(2) that the chantries were not being served in accordance with their foundation statutes.
(3) that there was no schoolmaster [*ludi litterarii magistrum*].
As to (1) the master of the cellar's acct confirms that there was a marked drop in numbers between 1501/2 and 1523/4; in 1519/20 there were only 35, but numbers stood at 42 on the other two dates (NRO DCN 1/1/100–102). However, these statistics (and his statement) must be treated with caution since it is unclear whether absent brethren are counted, including those residing in the cells. As to (2) the ref. is to a grammar master for the monks; the *comperta* reveal that a master came to give instruction twice a wk, Jessopp, *Visit.*, 77.
1520, 3 Sept., present at the visitation of bp Nikke and concurred that all was in good order, *ib.*, 193.
1526, 7 June, present at the visitation of bp Nikke and reported that noise and levity had replaced silence in the cloister, *ib.*, 203.
Note: although there were three contemporary Andrews in the 1520s and 1530s, the other two being Norwich and Tooke, q.v., it is probable that these last are one and the same.

Edmund RYNGSTED [Ryngstede, ?Kynestede
acc. 1414 d. 1473/4

1414, 14 Oct., one of six whose prof. the bp comm. the prior to rec., Reg. Courtenay, fo 102v [as Kynestede].
1446, name occ. on a rough list of those assigned to celebrate weekday and chantry masses, Cambridge, Emm. Coll. Ms 142, fo 68; also on a similar list (prob. of similar date) for masses in the Bateman, Totyngton, Wakering, Tye and Erpingham chantries, *ib.*, 77v.
1473/4, d., and the sacrist pd for the funeral tapers, NRO DCN 1/4/94.
Note: Edmund Kynestede and/or Ryngsted[e] may possibly be two monks, rather than one who would have been at least a septuagenarian.

John de SAHAM
occ. 1345/6

1345/6, student at Oxford, and the communar pd for his travel expenses and for the transport of his belongings, NRO DCN 1/12/25.

William de SAHAM
occ. c. 1310/11

[1310/11], given a letter of credence by the prior, and described as monk and *nuncius*, Reg. IX, fo 7.

Guy de ST EDMUND [Sancto Edmundo
occ. 1288

1288, 10 Oct., with John de Bromholm, q.v., sent by the prior and chapter to the king to procure a licence to el. a bp, *N. Cath. Charters*, i, no 55.
Note: this is prob. the monk Gido [Guydo], q.v.

Hugh de ST EDMUND [Sancto Edmundo
occ. 1312/13

1312/13, ill, in the infirmary, and cured of his ailment, NRO DCN 1/10/1.

Edmund SALL [Salle
occ. 1452/3 d. 1471/2

1466/7, 1469/71, communar/pittancer, NRO DCN 1/12/68–70.
1470/Mar. 1472, precentor, NRO DCN 1/9/69,70.
1455/6, student [at Cambridge], with pension contribution from the cellarer and the chamberlain, NRO DCN 1/2/61A; 1/5/88.

1456/7, student, with contributions from the cellarer, chamberlain and sacrist, NRO DCN 1/2/62; 1/5/89,90; 1/4/85.

1457/8, student, with contributions from the almoner, hostiller, refectorer and sacrist, NRO DCN 1/6/72; 1/7/94; 1/8/92; 1/4/86.

1458/9, student, with contributions from the almoner, cellarer, hostiller, refectorer and the prior of St Leonard's, NRO DCN 1/6/73; 1/2/64; 1/7/95; 1/8/92; 2/3/70.

1459, Apr., grace to oppose in theology granted, in his 13th yr, *BRUC* (quoting *CU Grace Book A*).

1459/60, student, with contributions from the almoner, chamberlain, refectorer, sacrist and the prior of St Leonard's. NRO DCN 1/6/74; 1/5/91; 1/8/92; 1/4/87; 2/3/71.

1460/1, student, with contributions from the chamberlain, hostiller, infirmarer, master of the cellar, and prior of Hoxne, NRO DCN 1/5/92; 1/7/96; 1/10/25; 1/1/90; Windsor, St George's chapel, I.C.19.

1461/2, student, with contributions from the almoner, sacrist, and the prior of St Leonard's, NRO DCN 1/6/77; 1/4/88; 2/3/74.

1462/3, student, with contributions from the almoner, hostiller, master of the cellar, precentor and the priors of Aldeby and Lynn, NRO DCN 1/6/78; 1/7/97; 1/1/91; 1/9/68; 2/2/20; 2/1/58.

1463/4, student, with contributions from the almoner, chamberlain, hostiller, and the priors of Lynn and St Leonard's, NRO DCN 1/6/79; 1/5/93; 1/7/98; 2/1/59; 2/3/76.

See also the entry in Venn, *Alumni*, pt I, iv, 8.

1452/3, contributed 4d. to the precentor for the *portiforium* of Thomas Crane, q.v., NRO DCN 1/9/66.

1453/4, 1454/5, ill, both yrs and the infirmarer spent 3s. 4d. on each occasion, NRO DCN 1/10/23,24.

1471/2, d., and the sacrist pd for funeral tapers, NRO DCN 1/4/93.

Geoffrey SALL [Salle

occ. 1415 d. 1454/5

1415, 10 June, one of four whom the prior requested the bp to rec. *ad osculum et benedictionem* as he had been adm. by the prior and chapter, Reg. Courtenay, fo 103v.

1418, 8 Apr., one of four whose prof. the prior requested the bp to solemnize; the bp replied by commissioning the prior to do so, Reg. Wakering, fo 32v.

Note: this is an unusually long period of probation; perhaps they had entered at an early age.

1448/50, refectorer, NRO DCN 1/8/86,87.

1430/1, gave 12d. to the gardener towards the repair of the wall *vs Holmstrete*, NRO DCN 1/11/14.

1436/7, gave 20d. as a gift to the chamberlain's office, NRO DCN 1/5/66.

1440/1, ill, and the infirmarer spent 10d. on medicine, NRO DCN 1/10/22.

1446, name occ. on a rough list of those assigned to celebrate weekday and chantry masses, Cambridge, Emm. Coll. Ms 142, fo 68.

1448, 22 Dec., name occ. on a Sunday mass rota for this date, *ib.*, also on another list (prob. of similar date) for masses in the Totyngton chantry, *ib.*, fo 77v.

1449/50, pd 16s. 4d. to the office of refectorer for the *ciphus* which had belonged to John Tylney, q.v., and afterwards to John de Ely, q.v., NRO DCN 1/8/87.

1454/5, d., and the chamberlain recd 'alms' of 13s. 4d., NRO DCN 1/5/87.

I John SALL [Salle

occ. 1418 d. 1424/5

1418, 20 Apr., one of four *clerici* who had been examined and adm. by the prior and chapter; the prior now requested the bp to rec. and bless them before their clothing, Reg. Wakering, fo 32v.

1420/1, contributed 22d. to the communar for the construction work in the cloister, NRO DCN 1/12/48.

1421/2, ill, and the infirmarer spent 3s. on medicine, NRO DCN 1/10/14.

1424/5, d., and the chamberlain recd 21s. 6d. in 'alms', NRO DCN 1/5/51.

II John SALL [Salle

occ. 1513/14 occ. 1534

1513/15, 1519/20, 1524/5, 1526, 7 June, precentor, NRO DCN 1/9/90–93; Jessopp, *Visit.*, 199.

1522/5; 1526, 7 June; 1526, Sept./Dec., communar, NRO DCN 1/12/96–99; Jessopp, *Visit.*, 199; NRO DCN 1/12/101.

1526/7, 1528/9, 1530/1, 1532/3, precentor, NRO DCN 1/9/94–98.

1514, 27 Apr., present at the visitation of bp Nikke and made a number of depositions including reports of incompetence and rumours of scandal among the brethren; Jessopp, *Visit.*, 74–75. He was accused of failing to pay the customary 'pensions' from the precentor's office to the community, *ib.*, 77.

1520, 3 Sept., present at the visitation of bp Nikke and reported *omnia bene*, Jessopp, *Visit.*, 192.

1526, 7 June, present at the visitation of bp Nikke; there were many complaints vs his behaviour, incompetence, his personal choice of clothing as if he were a layman and his failure to attend mass and divine office, while he complained of the urgent need of repairs to the monastic buildings and urged the imposition of an injunction concerning stricter accting procedures by the obedientiaries, Jessopp, *Visit.*, 197–201, 205. An injunction was issued that he be removed from the office of communar, *ib.*, 206.

1532, 3 June, present at the visitation of bp Nikke and was the object of many accusations, but confined his own depositions to the need for repairs to the chapel of St Anne and the Jesus chapel, and the inadequate care of the monks in the infirmary. Jessopp, *Visit.*, 263–269.
1534, 28 July, subscribed to the Act of Supremacy, *DK 7th Report*, Appndx 2, 295.

Thomas SALL [Salle *alias* Growte
occ. 1526 occ. 1537

1526, 7 June, third prior, Jessopp, *Visit.*, 197.
1527/8, 1530/1, 1534/5, refectorer, NRO DCN 1/8/116–118.
1532, 3 June, infirmarer and penitentiary, Jessopp, *Visit.*, 265; but see Ralph Sybly.

1526, 7 June, present at the visitation of bp Nikke and was accused of putting on secular dress and going into the town, of being severe [in his treatment of the juniors], of disobedience to the subprior, and of being one who caused dissension in the community, Jessopp, *Visit.*, 197–205; he denounced William Reppes' behaviour and the prior's mismanagement on one of the manors, *ib.*, 200.
1526/7, 1528/9, pd. by the precentor for repairing books, in the former year choir books and in the latter a *portiforium* and a primer [*primarius*] *cum scriptura et ligatura eorundem*, NRO DCN 1/9/94–96.
1532, 3 June, present at the visitation of bp Nikke and accused some of the younger monks of causing trouble (see Richard Lopham) and of not attending to their studies, Jessopp, *Visit.*, 265–266. He was again condemned for his behaviour and his failure to be present at divine office, *ib.*, 267, and also for wearing *calceis* vs the Rule, *ib.*, 263.
1534, 28 July, subscribed to the Act of Supremacy, *DK 7th Report*, Appndx 2, 295.
1537, 1 Dec., obtained gratis, a dispensation to wear his habit under that of a secular pr., Chambers, *Faculty Office Regs*, 116.

William SALLE
occ. 1492 occ. 1499

1492, 5/8 Oct., 14th in order at the visitation of bp Goldwell, Jessopp, *Visit.*, 8.
1499, 6 Apr., 10th on the visitation certificate, *Reg. abp Morton*, iii, no 258.

Richard SALTHOUS [Salthows, Salthowse
occ. 1443 d. 1487

1443, 1 Nov., one of two *clerici* adm. *ad osculum et benedictionem* by the bp in his parlour at Thorpe, after their acceptance by the chapter as monks [*monachand'*], Reg. Brouns, fo 109v.
1457/9, hostiller, NRO DCN 1/7/94, 95.
1460/1, part yr, master of the cellar, NRO DCN 1/1/90.
1464, Mar./Sept., 1464/5, hostiller, NRO DCN 1/7/98,99.
1464/5, Sept. to June, chamberlain, NRO DCN 1/5/94.
1465/6, cellarer, NRO DCN 1/2/66.
1467/8, infirmarer, NRO DCN 1/10/27.
1468/70, 1471/2, cellarer, NRO DCN 1/2/67,68.70.
1470/1, Sept. to June, gardener, NRO DCN 1/11/21.
1474/84, 1485/6, chamberlain, NRO DCN 1/5/101–115, and until Nov. 1487; see below.
1478/9, 1481/2, 1483/6, and until Nov. 1487, cellarer, NRO DCN 1/2/74–80, and see below.
1483/4, 1485/7, prior of St Leonard's, NRO DCN 2/3/90–92.

1454/5, recd 6s. 8d. from the almoner, John Molet, q.v., (who had been el. prior in Jan. 1454 but continued on as almoner for some yrs); it is clear from this payment that he was doing some, prob. most, of Molet's work, NRO DCN 1/6/71.
1478/9, as cellarer redeemed a silver salt cellar [*salsarium*] alienated by his predecessor Edmund Dereham, q.v., NRO DCN 1/2/74.
1487, 26 Nov., d. before this date, when a new chamberlain and a new cellarer were apptd because of his d., Reg. Goldwell, fo 130.

Name in CUL Ms Ii.4.12, G. Monemutensis (?14th c.); Richard Salthowus on p. 3. See also Roger de Blikling.

John SALUS [Salys
occ. 1476/7 occ. 1483/4

1476/7, gave the precentor 4d. *pro libris in cathologo*, NRO DCN 1/9/75, [?a new library catalogue]; see Greatrex, 'Norwich Monk Students', 575–576.
1483/4, ill, and the communar/pittancer pd 22d. for medicine, NRO DCN 1/12/73.

SANCTO EDMUNDO
see St Edmund

SCHELLTON, Schelton
see Shelton

SCHERNINGE
see Skerning(e)

Adam de SCHIPDAM [Schipedham, Schypidham, Scypydam, Sipett'
occ. 1263/4 occ. 1292/3

1285, prior of Lynn acc. to Dugdale, *Monasticon*, vi, 463; and also later acc. to Blomefield, *Norfolk*, vii, 495.

1263/4, attended the Black Monk Chapter in Oxford, NRO DCN 1/1/1; this single entry is noted by Pantin in *BMC*, i, 278; he also went to London at the master of the cellar's expense this same yr, *ib.*

1288/9, gave 6s. 8d. to the communar for the cloister construction work, *Comm. Rolls*, 51; and with Bartholomew de Cotton, q.v., arranged for the sale of wood on behalf of the communar, *ib.*
1292/3, d., and the chamberlain pd the brief bearer, NRO DCN 1/5/2.

Andrew de SCRIFFORD [?Strifford
occ. 1309/11

1390/10, with other monk students recd payment from the master of the cellar, NRO DCN 1/1/21.
1310/11, a similar payment to 'our brothers', Andrew and Robert de Swanton, q.v., 20s., NRO DCN 1/1/22; Swanton was at Oxford at this time.

Bartholonew de SCROWTBY [Skrowt'
occ. 1376/7 d. 1386/7

1386, Sept./1387, Aug., refectorer, NRO DCN 1/8/47.
1376/7, pd the refectorer 13s. 4d. for a *ciphus* which had formerly belonged to Roger de Blikling, q.v., NRO DCN 1/8/44.
1386/7, d., and the chamberlain recd 'alms', NRO DCN 1/5/19.

Roger de SCURSTON [Sturston
occ. 1345/6

1345, 1345/6, listed among the monks who were ill on both of these infirmarer's accts, and 2s. 4d. was spent on the second occasion, NRO DCN 1/10/2,4.

Note: could this be an alternative spelling for Thurston [Turston], q.v.?

SCYPYDAM
see Schipdam

[R. de SECHEFORD
occ. 1263/4

1263/4, pd a visit to Sedgeford and dined on goose, NRO DCN 60/33/2.

Note: this may be a priory official who was a *clericus* rather than a monk.]

Alan SEFUL [?Sesul
occ. 1307/8

1307/8, prob. d. by this date when his *ciphus* was sold by the refectorer to Nicholas de Kirkeby II, q.v., NRO DCN 1/8/18.

John SEGRYM
d. 1417/18

1417/18, d., and the chamberlain recd 10s. 8d. in 'alms', NRO DCN 1/5/45.

Note: a former mayor of Norwich named Ralph Segrum d. in 1478/9, Tanner, *Church in Norwich*, 216–217; this may be a family connection.

John de SHAMELISFORD
n.d.

n.d., acc. as prior of Hoxne, somewhere between William de Acle, q.v., and Geoffrey de Norwich, q.v., acc. to Blomefield, *Norfolk*, iii, 609.

John SHELTON [Schellton, Schelton, Shilton
occ. 1499 occ. 1526

1514, 27 Apr., third prior, Jessopp, *Visit.*, 76.
1518/24, almoner, NRO DCN 1/6/123–129.
1518/23, 1524/5, chamberlain, NRO DCN 1/5/136–141.

1499, 6 Apr., 39th in order on the visitation certificate, *Reg. abp Morton*, iii, no 258.
1514, 27 Apr., present at the visitation of bp Nikke, and reported that the priory was in debt, and that both sheep and women had free access to the cloister, Jessopp, *Visit.*, 76.
1520, 3 Sept., present at the visitation of bp Nikke and reported *omnia bene* except for the sheep in the cloister, *ib.*, 192.
1526, 7 June, present at the visitation of bp Nikke; he was accused of being a bad example, his sins were described as unmentionable [*nephanda*] and, when sent to Yarmouth for disciplining, his behaviour had been even worse, and the office of chamberlain had suffered during his charge, *ib.*, 200–201.

John SHERENE, ?Shereve
see Kirby

John SHREWISBURY [Shrewesberr'
occ. 1499 d. 1513/14

1499, 6 Apr., 40th in order on the visitation certificate, *Reg. abp Morton*, iii, no 258.
1513/14, d., and the sacrist pd for funeral tapers, NRO DCN 1/4/112.

SIBLI, Siblye
see Sybly

William de SILTON [Schilton, Shilton, Sylton
occ. 1412/13 d. 1438/9

1412/13, prior of Yarmouth, NRO DCN 2/4/5.
1418, Apr., before, master of St Paul's hospital, Reg. Wakering, fo 32, 32^{v}.
1418, 8 Apr., the prior requested the bp to confirm his apptment as sacrist, *ib.*
1418, 10 Apr./Sept.; 1419/20, Oct., sacrist, NRO DCN 1/52–55.

1413, 6 May, apptd official [*visitator*] by the abp for excepted jurisdiction, *sed. vac.* Norwich, after nomination by the prior and chapter, Churchill, *Cant. Admin*, ii, 252 (as Shilton).
1413, 18 June, as commissary for the abp. *sed. vac.*, held a visitation at Beccles, P.Brown, ed.,

Sibton Abbey Cartularies, 4 vols, Suffolk Records Society (1985–1988), iv, no 1171.

1415, 5 Oct., again apptd official [*visitator*] as above, *ib.*, 253 (as Sylton). These apptments are in *Reg. abp Chichele*, iii, 351–354 with further details including the abp's comm. to Silton to visit, with the prior, the cathedral priory, the city and the diocese, and to appt penitentiaries. He took his oath of office on 14 Oct. in the church at Lynn, *ib.*, 354.

1420/1, contributed 6s. 8d. to the cloister building work, NRO DCN 1/12/48.

1429/30, ill, and the infirmarer spent 9d. on medicine, NRO DCN 1/10/17.

1434/5, ill, and 6d. spent on medicine, NRO DCN 1/10/21.

1438/9, made another gift, of 12d., to the cloister, NRO DCN 1/12/57; this same yr the communar spent 4s. in repairing Silton's window, *ib.*

1438/9, d., and the chamberlain recd 'alms', NRO DCN 1/5/69.

Name in CUL Mss:

(1) Ii.1.31, Bernardus etc. (15th c.); *liber*—on fo 1.

(2) Ii.2.27, Walter Wiburn etc. (14th c.); *liber*—on fo 4 (the top has been shaved off and the name partially removed). See Ker, 'Norwich Cathedral Mss', 260.

I SIMON [Symon

n.d.

n.d., 4 Jan., name occ. in the Canterbury obit list, BL Ms Arundel 68, fo 12.

II SIMON

n.d.

n.d., 24 June, name occ. in the Canterbury obit list, BL Ms Arundel 68, fo 31v.

III M. SIMON [Symon

occ. [early 13th c.]

[early 13th c.], *procurator* or *custos* of St Paul's hospital, and described as M., *N. Cath. Charters*, ii, no 497.

n.d., [as above], acquired land for the hospital, *ib.*

IV SIMON

occ. [1245]

[1245, 7 May], acted for the prior in a land dispute, *N. Cath. Charters*, i, no 349.

[1245, 26 May], acting again as above, *ib.*, no 335.

Note: Simon III and IV may be identical.

SIPETT'

see Schipdam

Richard de SKERNINGE [Scherninge

occ. [c. 1277 × 1300]

[c. 1277 × 1300], *custos* of St Paul's hospital and involved in a land transaction, *N. Cath. Charters*, ii, no 510.

Roger de SKERNING

occ. 1257 occ. 1266

1257–1266, prior: el. between 23 June and 9 Dec. 1257; bp of Norwich, el. 23 Jan. 1266; d. 22 Jan. 1278, *Fasti*, ii, 61.

Note: he was prob. the first prior to have been freely elected, *ib.*

1257, 28 May, as proctor of the prior and chapter with William de Norwico I, q.v., recd royal licence to el. a bp, *CPR (1247–1258)*, 557.

1263/4, stayed at Sedgeford and the manorial acct records expenses of 15s. 7d., NRO DCN 60/33/2.

Many of his official *acta* are printed in *N. Cath. Charters*, ii, *passim*, (indexed under Scarning).

SKROWT'

see Scrowtby

Richard SKYPPE

see Richard Norwich II

Adam SLOLEY [*alias* Barker

occ. 1532 occ. 1538

1532, 3 June, fifth prior and subsacrist, Jessopp, *Visit*, 266.

1532, 3 June, present at the visitation of bp Nikke and accused of being one of a group of reforming monks who caused discord in the community and were in correspondence with Robert Catton I, q.v. (who had left not long before to become abbot of St Alban's), seeking support from him for their 'reform measures', Jessopp, *Visit.*, 265. He was also accused of levity, and of being unworthy of the office of subsacrist, *ib.*, 266. When questioned, he complained of the failure to send monks to the university, *ib.*, 267.

1538, 30 Apr., dispensed to wear the habit of a secular pr. and hold a canonry and prebend in the cathedral and any other benefice, and be non resident, Chambers, *Faculty Office Regs*, 137.

1538, 2 May, licensed as a secular canon, *L and P Henry VIII*, xiii, pt 1, no 1115(4).

Geoffrey de SMALBERGH

n.d.

Name in BL Ms Cotton Nero C.v, (13th/14th c.), a copy of the chronicle of Bartholomew Cotton which, with BL Ms Royal 14 C.i, formed a single vol; the name is in the former on fo 285v, see Ker 'Norwich Cathedral Mss', 258.

Robert SMYTH [Smythe

occ. 1532 occ. 1538

1533, 20 Sept., ord subdcn, Norwich cathedral, NRO DN ORR/1/1, fo 16v.

1533, 20 Dec., ord dcn, Norwich cathedral, *ib.*, fo 17v.

1534, 9 Sept., ord pr., Norwich cathedral, *ib.*, fo 23.
1532, 3 June, present at the visitation of bp Nikke and stated that all was in good order, Jessopp, *Visit.*, 268.
1534, 28 July, subscribed to the Act of Supremacy, *DK 7th Report*, Appndx 2, 295.
1538, 30 Apr., paid £4 for licence to wear the habit of a secular pr. and hold a canonry and prebend in the cathedral and any other benefice, and be non resident, Chambers, *Faculty Office Regs*, 137.

William de SNITERLE
occ. [1318 × 1322]

[1318 × 1322], communar/pittancer, *Comm. Rolls*, 20, n.1., 107–109; he followed John de Hengham I, q.v., and was involved in the cloister building operations, *ib.*

SOUFFHAM
see Swafham

John SPOO'
d. 1471/2

1471/2, d., and the sacrist pd for funeral tapers, NRO DCN 1/4/93.

Alexander de SPROWSTON [Sprouston, Sproustone
occ. 1304/5 occ. 1313/14

1304/5, student at Oxford, with pension contribution from the refectorer and sacrist, NRO DCN 1/8/17; 1/4/16.
1306/7, [student], with the gift of a *capa* from the sacrist, NRO DCN 1/4/17.
1308/9, student at Oxford, with contributions from the chamberlain, master of the cellar and refectorer, NRO DCN 1/5/4; 1/1/19; 1/8/20; his *armiger* was given 2s. this year, 1/1/20.
1309/10, student, with contributions from the master of the cellar, NRO DCN 1/1/21.
1311/12, with his *socius*, stopped at [North] Elmham and had two fowl [prob. on their way to or from Oxford; see John de Mari], NRO DCN 60/10/13.
1313/14, student, with contributions from the master of the cellar and refectorer, NRO DCN 1/1/23; 1/8/22; the 'boy' of Sprowston and of William de Claxton, q.v., recd 6d., 1/1/23.

Name in
(1) CUL Ms Kk.4.11, Augustine (14th c.); name on fo 4[v].
(2) Worcester Cathedral Library, Ms F. 101, Thomas Aquinas (early 14th c.); this has an inscription to the effect that it was [to be] handed over to 'domino Alexandro monacho vel alicui socio de Nortwych, Oxon' commoranti'; see Little and Pelster, *Oxford Theology*, 241; and see the section of Worcester monks under Richard de Bromwych.

William SPYNK, D.Th. [Spynke
occ. 1458/9 d. 1503

1488–1503, prior: 22 Dec. 1488, el. confirmed by the bp at Hoxne, Reg. Goldwell, fo 135[v]; d. 1503, before 16 Nov., see William Baconthorpe II.

1471/2, prior of Yarmouth, NRO DCN 2/4/15.
1479/82, 1483/9, Mar., prior of Lynn, NRO DCN 2/1/69–73.
While prior he also held the following offices:
1495/7, master of the cellar, NRO DCN 1/1/98,99.
1496, Jan./Sept., prior of St Leonard's, succeeding Edmund Dereham, q.v., NRO DCN 2/3/100,101.
1458/9, student [at Cambridge], with pension contributions from the almoner, cellarer, hostiller, refectorer, and the prior of St Leonard's, NRO DCN 1/6/73; 1/2/64; 1/7/95; 1/8/92; 2/3/70.
1459/60, student, with contributions from the almoner, chamberlain, refectorer, sacrist and the prior of St Leonard's, NRO DCN 1/6/74; 1/5/91; 1/8/92; 1/4/87; 2/3/71; in this, his 13th yr he was granted grace to oppose in theology (*BRUC*, quoting from *CU Grace Book A*).
1460/1, student, with contributions from the almoner, chamberlain, hostiller, infirmarer, and prior of Hoxne, NRO DCN 1/6/75,76; 1/5/92; 1/7/96; 1/10/25; Windsor, St George's chapel, I.C.19.
1461/2, student, with contributions from the almoner, sacrist and the prior of St Leonard's, NRO DCN 1/6/77; 1/4/88; 2/3/74.
1462/3, student, with contributions from the almoner, hostiller, master of the cellar and precentor, NRO DCN 1/6/78; 1/7/97; 1/1/91; 1/9/68.
1466/7, the communar gave him 12d. for [?coming back from university and] preaching, NRO DCN 1/12/68.
1479/80, the communar contributed to the expenses involved in 'taking' his B.Th., NRO DCN 1/12/71. This must refer to his inception, i.e. D.Th; see *BRUC*.

1492, 7 Sept., the bp refused the request of the prior and chapter to approve the apptment of the prior to the office of sacrist, because it would be 'harmful to the cathedral church and a betrayal of his own conscience', Reg. Goldwell, fo 159[v].
1499, 6 Apr., name headed the list on the visitation certificate, *Reg. abp Morton*, iii, no 258; thus he was present at the abp's visitation, *sed. vac.* Norwich.

Name in Manchester, J. Rylands R. 32528, A. de Rampegollis, (printed 1487, Cologne); this was part of *ib.*, R. 32548, T. Anguilbertus (n.d., Louvain). See *MLGB*, and *BRUC*.

A William Spynk of Weston was in arrears of rent to the pittancer in 1496/7, NRO DCN 1/12/81.

Robert STALHAM [Staleham
occ. 1492 occ. 1499

1492, 5/8 Oct., 37th in order at the visitation of bp Goldwell, Jessopp, *Visit.*, 8.
1499, 6 Apr., 29th on the visitation certificate, *Reg. abp Morton*, iii, no 258.

John STANFELDE
occ. 1477/8

1477/8, the sacrist [Wm. Fode, q.v.] went to see the bp in London with regard to the confirmation of his reception and that of two others as monks, NRO DCN 1/12/70; see Thomas More.

Thomas de STANFEUD
occ. [1257 × 1266]

[1257, June × 1266, Jan.], almoner, *N. Cath. Charters*, ii, no 445.

[1257 × 1266, Jan.], recd a grant of land, made to his office, *ib.*

Thomas STANHOWE
d. 1424/5

1424/5, d., and the chamberlain recd 'alms' of 18s. 4d., NRO DCN 1/5/51.

STANNARD [Steinardus, ?Stanus
[occ. 1096 × 1119]

[occ. 1096 × 1119], *temp.* bp Losinga carried letters of the bp to queen Matilda and to the abbot of Fécamp, Anstruther, *Epist. Losinga*, nos 25, 34.
[1096 × 1106], with Ingulph and William, q.v., recd a letter from bp Losinga, Anstruther, *ib.*, no 14, where the name is Stanus.
[?1107], a monk named Steinardus witnessed an episcopal agreement, *Eng. Epis. Acta*, vi, no 5; see Ingulph.

His name indicates that he was prob. English and possibly recruited locally.

I Robert STANTON
d. 1505/6

1505/6, d., and the sacrist spent 8d. for funeral tapers, NRO DCN 1/4/109.

II Robert STANTON [Staunton
occ. 1526 occ. 1538

1526, 7 June, fifth prior, Jessopp, *Visit.*, 202.
1529/31, hostiller, NRO DCN 1/7/146,147.
1532, 3 June, chaplain to the prior, Jessopp, *Visit.*, 266.
1534, an inventory of the hostiller ref. to him *in adventu* [*suo*]; thus he had either a second term in the office of hostiller or was chaplain to the prior at the same time, NRO DCN 1/7/148.
1526, 7 June, present at the visitation of bp Nikke and reported that no reforms were required, but accused William Burton, q.v., of being unwilling to learn and of instigating disputes, Jessopp, *Visit.*, 202.
1532, 3 June, present at the visitation of bp Nikke and condemned Adam Slolely and both John Sall II and Thomas Sall, q.v., Jessopp, *ib.*, 266–267.
1534, 28 July, subscribed to the Act of Supremacy, *DK 7th Report*, Appndx 2, 295.
1538, 30 Apr., dispensed to wear the habit of a secular pr. and hold a canonry and prebend in the cathedral and any other benefice, and be non resident, Chambers, *Faculty Office Regs*, 137.
1538, 2 May, licensed as a secular canon, *L and P Henry VIII*, xiii, pt 1, no 1115(4).

STEPHEN
n.d.

n.d., 17 July, obit occ. in the kalendar in Reg. XI, fo 5.

J. de STOCTON
occ. c. 1321 × 1326

c. 1321 × 1326, addressed as prior of Lynn by the prior Robert [de Langele, q.v.], writing on behalf of a nephew of John de Bromholm, q.v., after the latter's death, Reg. IX, fo 32.

Thomas de STOCTON [Stokthune, Stokton
occ. 1295/6 occ. 1318/19

1295/6, chamberlain, NRO DCN 1/5/3.
1295/6, spent £4 16s. 9d. *in armis* for the convent, NRO DCN 1/5/3.
1297/8, with Thomas de Plumsted, q.v., went to London at the expense of the communar; the cost was over £3 and was prob. connected with the cloister building programme, *Comm. Rolls*, 71.
1297/8, one of the monk proctors sent to the Black Monk Chapter meeting in Northampton, *Comm. Rolls*, 71, and Pantin, *BMC*, i, 279 (where the name is transcribed as 'Scotton').
1318/19, he, with other monks, recd a small sum from the cellarer, NRO DCN 1/2/12.

STOCTON
see also Stokton

STOGHE
see Stowe

STOKE(S)
see Stokis

Robert de STOKESBY
occ. [?mid 13th c.]

[?mid 13th c.], master of St. Paul's hospital before John de Plumstede, q.v., acc. to Blomefield, *Norfolk*, iii, 342.

STOKESBY
see also Stokysby

Richard STOKIS [Stoke, Stokes, Stokys
occ. 1426/7 d. 1456/7

1426/7, gave a gift of 3s. 4d. to the cellarer's office, NRO DCN 1/2/45.
1434/5, 1440/1, ill during both yrs, and 2s. were spent on medicine by the infirmarer on the second occasion, NRO DCN 1/10/21, 22.
1446, name occ. on a rough list of those assigned to celebrate weekday and chantry masses, Cambridge, Emm. Coll. Ms 142, fo. 68; also on a similar list (prob. of similar date) for masses in the Totyngton, Wakering and Erpingham chantries, *ib.*, fo 77v.
1453/4, ill, and 2s. spent by the infirmarer on medicine, NRO DCN 1/10/23.
1456/7, d., and the chamberlain recd 'alms' of 25s. 4d., NRO DCN 1/5/89.

Walter de STOKTON [Stoktone
occ. 1341/2 occ. 1354/5

1349/50, prior of St Leonard's, NRO DCN 2/3/1.
1341/2, student at Oxford, with travelling expenses pd by the communar, NRO DCN 1/12/22.
1343/4, student at Oxford, and the communar pd for the expense of bringing back his books and belongings, NRO DCN 1/12/23.
1343/4, apptd proctor of the convent for the council called by the abp, NRO DCN 1/12/23.
1345, ill, and his treatment was charged to the infirmarer, NRO DCN 1/10/2.
1347/8, ill, and the infirmarer spent 6d. on medicine, NRO DCN 1/10/6.
1348/9, contributed 66s. 8d. to the cloister work, NRO DCN 1/12/27.
1354/5, pd 18s. to the chamberlain for timber, NRO DCN 1/5/14.

STOKTON
see also Stocton

Henry STOKYSBY [Stokesby
occ. 1450/1 occ. 1464/5

1450/1, pd the refectorer 13s. 4d. for the *ciphus* which had formerly belonged to Thomas Jernemuth, q.v., NRO DCN 1/8/88.
1453/4, ill, and the infirmarer spent 3s. 4d. on medicine, NRO DCN 1/10/23.
1464/5, ill, and 18d. was spent on medical treatment, NRO DCN 1/10/26.

STOKYSBY
see also Stokesby

William STONHALL
occ. 1452/3 d. 1454/5

1452/3, one of several monks who gave money to the precentor, Thomas Crane, q.v., for the latter's *portiforium*; he contributed 4d., NRO DCN 1/9/66.
1454/5, ill, and the infirmarer pd 16s. 8d. for treatment, NRO DCN 1/10/24.
1454/5, d., and the chamberlain recd 8s. in 'alms', NRO DCN 1/5/87.

[Robert de STONNE
occ. 1263/4

1263/4, pd a visit to Sedgeford and dined on goose, NRO DCN 60/33/2.

Note: this may be a priory official who was a *clericus* rather than a monk.]

Geoffrey de STOWE
occ. 1291 occ. before 1308/9

1291, part yr, master of the cellar, NRO DCN 1/1/10.
1308/9, before, a Geoffrey was chamberlain, preceding John de Stratton II, q.v., NRO DCN 1/5/4.

I John STOWE ?D.Th. [Stoghe
occ. 1423/4 occ. 1454/5

1423/4, bought a *ciphus* from the refectorer for 10s. probably soon after adm., NRO DCN 1/8/71.
1439/42, prior of Aldeby, NRO DCN 2/2/13–15.
1429/30, student [at Oxford], with pension contributions from the almoner, infirmarer and master of the cellar, NRO DCN 1/6/59; 1/10/17; 1/1/79.
1430/1, student, with contributions from the chamberlain, infirmarer and master of the cellar, NRO DCN 1/5/56,57; 1/10/18; 1/1/80.
1431/3, student, with contribution for both years from the infirmarer, NRO DCN 1/10/19,20; and for 1431/2 from the chamberlain, NRO DCN 1/5/58.
Note: *BRUO*, q.v., notes that Bale describes him as D.Th. of Oxford and author of Collectiones variae; see below.
1432/3, ill, and the infirmarer spent 12d. on medicine, NRO DCN 1/10/20.
1446/9, name occ. on a rough list of those assigned to celebrate Sunday masses on the following dates: 1446, 4 Dec.; 1447, 26 Mar., 16 July, 5 Nov; 1448, 25 Feb., 2 June, 6 Oct.; 1449, 23 Feb., Cambridge, Emm. Coll. Ms 142, fo 68.
1454/5, ill, and the infirmarer spent 12d. on medicine, NRO DCN 1/10/24.

Name in Cambridge, Emm. Coll. Ms 142, Collectiones variae, which includes, among its contents, Acta Concilii Basiliensis; the inscription 'hic liber est Johannis Stowe monachi Norwicensis' seems to be the sole basis for Bale's attribution of authorship in *Index Brit. Script.*, 258. It is possible that Stowe accompanied his fellow monks, prior William Worstede, John Fornsete and William Cawmbrygg', q.v., to Basel. Dugdale states that he was in Basel in 1432, *Monasticon*, iv, 9; his prob. source was Blomefield, *Norfolk*, iii, 616.

II John STOWE
occ. 1476/7 occ. 1488/9

1484/6, 1487/8, communar/pittancer, NRO DCN 1/12/74–76.
1487/8, hostiller, NRO DCN 1/7/118.
1488/9, almoner, NRO DCN 1/6/102,103.

1476/7, contributed 2d. to the precentor *pro libris in cathologo*, NRO DCN 1/9/75 [?a new library catalogue]; see Greatrex 'Norwich Monk Students', 575–576.

III John STOWE
occ. 1489/90 occ. 1491/2

1489/90, student [at Cambridge], with pension contributions from the almoner, chamberlain, gardener, precentor and the prior of St Leonard's, NRO DCN 1/6/104–106; 1/5/118; 1/11/26; 1/9/87; 2/3/95.
1490/1, student, with contributions from the cellarer, chamberlain, hostiller, master of the cellar and the prior of Hoxne, NRO DCN 1/2/83; 1/5/119; 1/7/119; 1/1/95; 2/6/28.
1491/2, student, with contributions from the almoner, chamberlain, hostiller, master of the cellar, refectorer, sacrist and the prior of Hoxne, NRO DCN 1/6/108; 1/5/120; 1/7/120; Oxford, Bod. Ms Rolls, Norfolk, no 54; Oxford, Bod. Ms Rolls, Norfolk, no 51; NRO DCN 1/4/104; 2/6/29.
1489/92, pensioner at Gonville Hall, Venn, *Gonville and Caius*, i, 13, 14.

Note: there are confused and misleading entries about John Stowe II and III in both *BRUO* and *BRUC*, based on errors in Saunders, *Obed. Rolls*. The details of office holding, which were incorrectly dated, have been assigned here to John Stowe II, q.v., as it is unlikely that a monk would go up to university after some years in office.

I John de STRATTON [Strattone senior
occ. 1278/9

1278/9, visited Sedgeford, NRO DCN 60/33/6.

Name in Cambridge, Corpus Christi College Ms 325, Vincent de Beauvais, De puerorum nobilium eruditione, etc. (13th/14th c.). Because this volume has a medieval press-mark denoting its Norwich cathedral provenance, it may be presumed that Stratton was a Norwich monk; see Ker, 'Norwich Cathedral Mss', 258. It is possible that he may have made practical use of this vol. if he had been assigned to teach the boys in the almonry school, see Greatrex, 'Almonry School', 181.

See also the entry below; the visit to Sedgeford may apply to John de Stratton II.

II John de STRATTON [Strattone
occ. 1308/9 occ. 1345/6

1308/9, chamberlain, NRO DCN 1/5/4, his first yr.
1313/14, 1319/20, 1321, Sept./Dec., sacrist, NRO DCN 1/4/19–21.
1326, 19 Feb., prior of Lynn, Reg. Ayermine, fo 79v.

1326, 19 Feb., as prior of Lynn, recd licence to hear confessions in the parish church and deanery there, Reg. Ayermine, fo 79v.
1345/6, ill, and the infirmarer spent 6d. on medicine, NRO DCN 1/10/4; he prob. d. this same yr because among the pittancer's receipts is an entry for 20s. which had been his but had been temporarily misplaced, and was now found and added to the cloister fund, NRO DCN 1/12/25.

Note: some of the entries here may apply to John Stratton I above, and *vice versa*.

STRIFFORD
see Scrifford

John de STRUMHAST
occ. 1302/3

1302/3, student at Oxford, and the communar pd 14s. 10d. for his travelling expenses *cum libris*, *Comm. Rolls*, 83; also mentioned by B. Dodwell in 'History and Norwich Monks', 41.

John de STUKLE, D.Th. [Stucle, Stuckelee, Stukelee
occ. 1333/4 occ. 1346/7

1333/4, student [at Oxford], with pension contribution from the refectorer, NRO DCN 1/8/31.
1334/5, student, with contributions from the master of the cellar and the refectorer, NRO DCN 1/1/38; 1/8/32,33.
1335/6, student, with contributions from the master of the cellar and the sacrist, NRO DCN 1/1/33,38; 1/4/31.
1336/7, student, with contributions from the cellarer and the master of the cellar, NRO DCN 1/2/101; 1/1/38. He was one of four students this yr, see John de Betele, Thomas de Runhale, Robert Sturmyn.
1337/8, student, with contributions as in the previous yr, NRO DCN 1/2/101; 1/1/34,38.
1339/40, student, for whom the chamberlain provided a *pellic'*, (as also for Odo, q.v.), as well as making a contribution to 'our brothers at Oxford', NRO DCN 1/5/11.
1342/3, attended the Black Monk Chapter meeting, NRO DCN 1/1/40.
1340/4, it is worth noting that although Stukle's name does not appear on any extant accts, there were regular contributions by the obedientiaries to the monk students.

1344/5, student, and the communar pd for travelling expenses from Oxford and back to Oxford as well as for a messenger conveying a letter to him, NRO DCN 1/12/24.

1345, the infirmarer's contribution of the large sum of 40s. was entered as *confratribus pro inceptione eorum*; it is almost certain that the ref. is to Stukle and John de Betele, q.v., NRO DCN 1/10/2.

1345/6, student, whose travelling expenses between Oxford and Norwich were pd by the communar, NRO DCN 1/12/25.

1346/7, student, for whom the communar pd the expenses of transporting his books [from Oxford to Norwich or *vice versa*], NRO DCN 1/12/26.

One ms written by Stukle survives at Clairvaux, namely, part of a commentary on the Sentences; see W.J. Courtenay, 'The "Sentences"—Commentary of Stukle: a New Source for Oxford Theology in the Fourteenth Century', *Traditio*, 34 (1978), 435–438, and by the same author, *Schools and Scholars in Fourteenth Century England* (Princeton, 1987), 275, 329–330, 347. On p. 329 Prof. Courtenay suggests that Stukle was lecturing in Oxford in the 1340s and that his commentary prob. dates from c. 1340 or shortly after; these observations are in agreement with the evidence provided by the Norwich accts. There is also a ref. to Stukle in J. A. Weisheipl, 'Ockham and the Mertonians', in Catto, *Hist. Univ. Oxford*, i, 650, and in the chapter by Courtenay, 'Theology and Theologians from Ockham to Wyclif', in *ib.*, ii, 29–31.

Dugdale refers to a John Meare, and Blomefield to a John Meare of Stukey, who wrote commentaries on the Sentences, Dugdale, *Monasticon*, iv, 9; Blomefield, *Norfolk*, iii, 616–617 adds that he also wrote a book of sermons. This may be John de Mari, q.v.

Robert STURMYN [Sturmyng
occ. 1331/2 occ. 1336/7

1331/2, bought a *ciphus* for 20s. from the refectorer, NRO DCN 1/8/30.

1336/7, student, at Oxford, who with three other monks (Thomas de Runhale, John de Betele and John de Stukle, q.v.) recd financial support from the cellarer, NRO DCN 1/2/101.

STURSTON
see Scurston

Roger STYWARD
occ. 1413/14 d. 1415/16

1413/14, hostiller, NRO DCN 1/7/59.

1415/16, d., and the chamberlain recd 'alms' of 10s., NRO DCN 1/5/44.

Stephen SUTTON
occ. 1484/5 occ. 1512/13

1508/9, gardener, NRO DCN 1/11/27.

1509/10, 1512/13, refectorer, NRO DCN 1/8/111–113.

1484/5, student, and the almoner contributed 9s. *in exhibitione*, NRO DCN 1/6/99.

1492, 5/8 Oct., 36th in order at the visitation of bp Goldwell, Jessopp, *Visit.*, 8.

1499, 6 Apr., 28th on the visitation certificate, *Reg. abp Morton*, iii, no 258.

Hervey de SWAFHAM, D.Th. [Swafam, Souffham
occ. 1297/8 occ. 1326

1297/8, student at Oxford, with travelling expenses pd by the communar, *Comm. Rolls*, 71.

1298/9, student, with the expenses for transporting his books pd by the communar, *Comm. Rolls*, 74.

1300/1, student, with a *capa* given by the sacrist, NRO DCN 1/4/14.

1302/3, student, with contribution from the communar, *Comm. Rolls*, 83.

1303/4, student, with contribution from the master of the cellar, NRO DCN 1/1/17.

1306/7, [student], made a journey to Cambridge, NRO DCN 1/4/17.

1307/8, student, with contribution from the communar, *Comm. Rolls*, 87.

1309/10, student, with contribution from the master of the cellar, who also pd for him to attend the Black Monk Chapter, NRO DCN 1/1/21, (and see Nicholas de Hindolveston).

1310/11, student, with contributions from the almoner, master of the cellar and refectorer, NRO DCN 1/6/9; 1/1/22; 1/8/21.

1312/13, student, with contribution from the refectorer, NRO DCN 1/8/22.

1313/14, student, with contributions from the master of the cellar and sacrist, NRO DCN 1/1/23; 1/4/19. The master of the cellar gave an additional sum of £20 15s. 8d., which he sent through a merchant to pay inception expenses, and the sacrist contributed £4.

1314/15, still at Oxford and with contributions from the master of the cellar and the refectorer, NRO DCN 1/1/24; 1/8/23.

1315/16, at Oxford with contribution from the master of the cellar, NRO DCN 1/1/25; and in 1316 from the precentor, NRO DCN 1/9/3.

1318/19, [at Oxford], with contributions from the cellarer, master of the cellar and refectorer, NRO DCN 1/2/12; 1/1/27; 1/8/24. The refectorer seems a little late with his contribution towards the inception: to M. Hervey, 'causa inceptionis monachi sancti Benedicti'. Apart from the refectorer's entry the other two may have been simply gifts.

1319/20, recd. 2s. from the hostiller, NRO DCN 1/7/1.

1320/1, the master of the cellar gave 'M. Hervey' 6s. 8d., NRO DCN 1/1/28.

Note: Pantin, *BMC*, iii, 323, states that c. 1314/16 he was regent at Oxford. There appears to be no clear evidence of this in the accts, although the fact that he continued to stay on for at least two yrs after his inception does suggest that this may have been so; see below. See also *BRUO*, which does not refer to the regency.

1313/14, his expenses during a stopover at Hindolveston (which were charged to the manorial acct), were 7d. and 2 bushels of oats for his horse, NRO DCN 60/18/19.

1314, Feb., he was one of the doctors of divinity [*regentes in theologia*] at Oxford who condemned a number of articles as heretical; see Anstey, *Munimenta Acad.*, i, 101.

1324/5, contributed £2 to the communar for the cloister construction, *Comm. Rolls*, 100.

1326, 4 Sept., comm. by the bp to install William Claxton, q.v., as prior, Reg. Ayermine, fo 9ᵛ; replied on 5 Sept. that he had done so, *ib.*

n.d., 9 Jan., obit occ. in BL Ms Harley 3950, fo 3.

Name in CUL Ms Kk.4.12, Egidius Romanus etc., (early 14th c.); on fo 2, *liber*—.

In 1315/16, his nephew recd 4s. from the master of the cellar, NRO DCN 1/1/25.

Thomas SWAFHAM
occ. 1475/6 occ. 1499

1485/7, 1487/8, 1490/2, prior of Hoxne, Windsor, St George's chapel, I.C.27, 28; I.C.11; NRO DCN 2/6/28, 29. On 7 Sept. 1492, the bp acceded to the prior's request to approve his removal from Hoxne, Reg. Goldwell, fo 159ᵛ.

1497/8, infirmarer, NRO DCN 1/10/33.

1475/6, recd. 3s. 4d. from the precentor for looking after St James' church, Plumstead, from Michaelmas to Christmas, NRO DCN 1/9/74.

1476/7, gave the precentor 12d., *pro libris in cathologo*, NRO DCN 1/9/75.

1478/9, gave the precentor 4d. *pro intabulatione librorum*, NRO DCN 1/9/77; these entries may refer to a new catalogue or subject index for the library; see Greatrex, 'Norwich Monk Students', 575–576.

1492, 5/8 Oct., 18th in order at the visitation of bp Goldwell, Jessopp, *Visit.*, 8.

1499, 6 Apr., 11th on the visitation certificate; *Reg. abp Morton*, iii, no 258.

Alexander de SWANTON [Swantune
occ. 1307/8

1307/8, [student]; the communar pd 7s. 'in cariagio pannorum Alexandre Swantun' de Oxonia', NRO DCN 1/12/12; did he die there? *Comm. Rolls*, 87 (mistakenly transcribed as Swanam).

John de SWANTON
occ. 1365/6

1365/6, concerned in some way with the monks' pensions from Fring [Frenze], NRO DCN 1/1/49; see William de Lenn I.

Ralph de SWANTON
occ. 1309/10 occ. 1347/8

1345/9, infirmarer, NRO DCN 1/10/3–7.

1309/10, [?student at Oxford], receiving money from the master of the cellar, and named along with Hervey de Swafham, q.v., who was then a student, NRO DCN 1/1/21.

*1310/11, prob. at Oxford as he, along with Hervey de Swafham and William de Witton, q.v., recd money from the almoner, NRO DCN 1/6/9.

*1318/19, an R. de Swanton gave the refectorer 6s. 8d., for a *ciphus*, at the prior's wish [*ex voluntate prioris*], NRO DCN 1/8/24.

1345/6, 1346/7, 1347/8, while infirmarer he was ill each yr and charged his office for medicine 17d., 7 1/2d., and 7d. respectively, NRO DCN 1/10/4–6.

* The asterisk indicates that this detail may apply to Robert de Swanton below.

Robert de SWANTON
occ. 1309/10 d. 1336/7

1315/16, precentor, NRO DCN 1/9/3.

1309/10, [?student at Oxford], receiving money from the master of the cellar and named along with Hervey de Swafham, q.v., who was then a student, NRO DCN 1/1/21.

1312/13, possibly a student with William de Martham, q.v., as they both recd small sums from the refectorer, NRO DCN 1/8/22.

*1310/11, with Andrew Scrifford, q.v., R. recd 20s. from the master of the cellar, NRO DCN 1/1/22.

*1311/12, R. visited Hindolveston, NRO DCN 60/18/17.

*1312/13, the infirmarer gave R. a small sum for spices, NRO DCN 1/10/1.

1312/3, visited Plumstead with the precentor [Richard de Hecham II, q.v.], NRO DCN 60/29/17.

*1313/14, R., together with William de Martham, q.v., recd 2s. from the refectorer, NRO DCN 1/8/22.

1315/6, spent 12d. *in factura catologi*, NRO DCN 1/9/3; see Richard de Hecham II.

[c. 1326], 15 Dec., bp Ayermine replied to the prior's letter which had been delivered by Robert and Richard de Hecham II, q.v., Reg. IX, fo 51ᵛ.

1336/7, d., and the chamberlain pd the brief bearer, NRO DCN 1/5/10.

Note: the entry in *BRUO*, under Ralph de Swanton, has confused and combined the details of both Robert and Ralph.

* The asterisk indicates that, since only the initial 'R' is given, the entry may refer to Ralph de Swanton above.

W. de SWEYNESTHROP [Swenysthorp, Sweynstorp
occ. 1282/3 occ. 1293/4

1282/3, 1288/9, communar/pittancer, *Comm. Rolls*, 45–56.
1289/94, precentor, NRO DCN 1/9/2.

John SYBLY [Sybelyce, Sybelye, Syblye
occ. 1478/9 occ. 1514

1498/9, 1500/1, almoner, NRO DCN 1/6/111–113.
1509/10, master of St Paul's hospital, NRO DCN 2/5/7.
1513/14, prior of St Leonard's, NRO DCN 2/3/113.
1513/14, before, gardener, see below.

1478/9, gave 3d. to the precentor *pro intabulacione librorum*, NRO DCN 1/9/77; possibly a new book catalogue, see Greatrex, 'Norwich Monk Students', 575–576.
1492, 5/8 Oct., 24th in order at the visitation of bp Goldwell, Jessopp, *Visit.*, 8.
1499, 6 Apr., 17th on the visitation certificate, *Reg. abp Morton*, iii, no 258.
1514, 27 Apr., present at the visitation of bp Nikke and was reported to have failed to render accts for St Paul's hospital, and should also be held responsible for many problems at St Leonard's, Jessopp, *Visit.*, 75. As a former gardener he had allowed sheep and other animals into the precincts, *ib.*, 76.
1514, 5 Dec., the bp's injunctions ordered his removal from the office of prior of St Leonard's and prohibited him from holding any office, *ib.*, 79.

Ralph SYBLY [Sibli, Siblye, Syblis
occ. 1492 d. 1534

1505/6, pittancer, NRO DCN 1/12/87.
1507/8, 1508/9, 1511/12, precentor, NRO DCN MC 136/2; 1/9/88,89.
1510/11, 1512/13, pittancer, NRO DCN 1/12/89,91; and in 1512/13, Richard Chateris, q.v., was communar.
1514/19, prior of Hoxne, NRO DCN 2/6/36–40.
1522/4; 1526, 7 June, refectorer, NRO DCN 1/8/115; Jessopp, *Visit.*, 201.
1527/8, 1529/30, gardener, NRO DCN 1/11/32,33.
1532, 3 June, infirmarer, Jessopp, *Visit.*, 264; see also Thomas Sall. Oxford, Bod. Ms Tanner fos 132, 124–125, the original record of this visitation, names both these monks as infirmarer, but in Sybly's case it is probable that this was a scribal error for 'infirm', which is more likely at the age of 62.

1492, 5/8 Oct., 43rd in order at the visitation of bp Goldwell, Jessopp, *Visit.*, 8.
1499, 6 Apr., 35th on the visitation certificate, *Reg. abp Morton*, iii, no 258.
1514, 27 Apr., present at the visitation of bp Nikke, made accusations vs the prior's use of the common seal and was quoted by others in their accusations vs the prior; he was reported to have been himself disobedient to the prior, Jessopp, *Visit.*, 74–75.
1526, 7 June, present at the visitation of bp Nikke, and reported *omnia bene*, *ib.*, 201.
1532, 3 June, present at the visitation of bp Nikke, and stated that he was 62 yrs old; he complained that there were so many dogs being fed within the priory that the poor were receiving less than their due, *ib.*, 264.
1534, 29 June, d., BL Ms Harley 3950, fo 5^v.

SYLTON
see Silton

SYMON
see Simon

Hugh de TACKLESTON
occ. 1314/15

1314/15, the refectorer pd for the repair of the *ciphus* formerly belonging to him, and now kept in the 'lower infirmary', thus he may have recently died, NRO DCN 1/8/23.

Roger TANCRE
occ. [c. 1200]

[c. 1200], almoner, *N. Cath. Charters*, ii, nos 482, 483.
[c. 1200], Roger, almoner, and prob. the same monk, occ. in three similar gifts of land in ib., nos 258, 262, 263; nos 482 and 483 above are also concerned with gifts of land.

TANCRED [Tancretus
occ. c. 1172 d. 1175

c. 1172–1175, prior: occ. before Jan. 1174; d. 1175, *Fasti*, ii, 60, *HRH*, 58.
[1172 × 1174, 17 Jan.], confirmed a grant in favour of Castle Acre priory, *Eng. Epis. Acta*, vi, no 78.
n.d., 15 June, obit occ. in BL Ms Harley 3950, fo 5^v.

A note concerning the manor of Postwick *temp.* Tancred is given in *N. Cath. Charters*, ii, no 230; see also *Eng. Epis. Acta*, vi, no 131A.

John de TATERSET [Tatersete, Tatirsete
occ. 1345/6 d. ?1351

1345/6, and prob. until 1350, cellarer, NRO DCN 1/2/102.
1351, precentor, from 2 Feb. to 25 Mar. only; there were three precentors during the course of the yr, NRO DCN 1/9/5; see John de Hapisburgh, William de Rykinghale.

John de THETFORD [Thetforthe
occ. 1426 occ. 1465/6

1427, 4 Jan., one of seven whose prof. the bp solemnized in chapter after the prior's request of 31 Dec. 1426, Reg. Alnwick, fo 97.
1436/7, gave a 2s. gift to the chamberlain, NRO DCN 1/5/66.
1446, name occ. on a rough list of those assigned to celebrate weekday and chantry masses, Cambridge, Emm. Coll. Ms 142, fo 68; also on a similar list (prob. of similar date) for masses in the Bateman, Totyngton, Wakering, Tye and Erpingham chantries, *ib.*, fo 77v.
1465/6, gave 10s. towards the rebuilding of the cathedral church, NRO DCN 1/4/90.

William de THETFORD [Thedforth, Thedforde, Thefford
occ. 1374/5 d. 1413/14

1374/80, precentor, NRO DCN 1/9/13–18.
1383, before 27 June, subprior, when the prior requested the bp to approve his dismissal from this office, Reg. Despenser, fo 90v.
1393/1394, June, refectorer, NRO DCN 1/8/48.
1394, Mar./Sept., infirmarer, NRO DCN 1/10/9, described as *custos*.
1395/6, sacrist, NRO DCN 1/4/41.
1398/9, infirmarer, NRO DCN 1/10/10, (*custos*).
1399, Sept./Nov. only, sacrist, NRO DCN 1/4/42.
1400/1, infirmarer, NRO DCN 1/10/11, (*custos*).
1400/2, sacrist, NRO DCN 1/4/44.
1407/1408, June, infirmarer, NRO DCN 1/10/12.
Note: there are several instances here of plurality in office holding, but some of these may perhaps be best described as an overlapping.
1383, given charge of the church at Sprowston, Blomefield, *Norfolk*, iii, 603; see Richard de Carleton.
1383/4, 1386/7, 1388/9, one of seven monks, the others being obedientiaries and not named, who did not rec. the usual clothing allowance from the chamberlain; the latter's office was deeply in debt and he was thus being temporarily relieved of some of his annual payments, NRO DCN 1/5/18, 19, 22.
1407, 20 Nov., with John de Hoo, q.v., installed Alexander de Totyngton as bp, Blomefield, *Norfolk*, iii, 526.
1413/14, d., and the chamberlain recd 'alms' of 12s., NRO DCN 1/5/43.

William THIRKELL [Thyrkyll, Thurkyll
occ. 1532/3 occ. ?1538

1532, 3 June, present at the visitation of bp Nikke and stated that monks were not being sent to Oxford and the hall there, which was built for them, was prob. falling into a ruinous state, Jessopp, *Visit.*, 266; but see Thomas Morton..
1532/3, pd by the precentor for binding the 'great Bible' in the refectory, also an antiphoner and *pro factura foliorum organorum*, NRO DCN 1/9/98; see Botulph Parker.
1538, 2 May, a Nicholas Thurkyll *alias* Attleburgh, occ. as canon of the new foundation, *Fasti 1541–1857*, vii, 57; see also *L and P Henry VIII*, xiii, pt 1, no 1115(4).

Note: see Nicholas Attilburgh.

I THOMAS
n.d.

n.d., 6 Jan., name occ. in the Canterbury obit list, BL Ms Arundel 68, fo 12.

II THOMAS
n.d.

n.d., 14 Apr., name occ. in the Canterbury obit list, BL Ms Arundel 68, fo 24.

III THOMAS
occ. [c. 1146 × 1172]

Described as the eldest of the monks, who was ill and unable to sleep until he prayed to St William, Jessopp and James, *St William*, 134–135.

IV THOMAS
occ. [c. 1146 × 1172]

Described as cantor [precentor], Jessopp and James, *St William*, 214.

V THOMAS
occ. [1257 × 1266]

[1257 × 1266], almoner, *temp.*, prior Roger de Skernyng, q.v., NRO DCN 45/40/48.

VI THOMAS
occ. 15th c.

n.d., name in CUL Ms Gg.1.33, Nicholas de Gorram, Distinctiones (13th/14th cs); on fo 2v, *in custodia—*.

Note: this may be Thomas de Hevyngham, q.v., but the surname is illegible.

Clement THORNAGE [Thornege
occ. 1409/10 d. 1453/4

1409/10, novice and bought a *ciphus* from the refectorer for 13s. 4d., NRO DCN 1/8/53.
1425/6, 1427/9, 1430/1, 1433/5, 1436/7, communar/pittancer, NRO DCN 1/12/51–57.
1420/1, with William Manyngton, q.v., assisted the precentor by performing various services in the parish and church of Plumstead during a vacancy there, NRO DCN 1/9/31, 37.
1426, 6 Jan., conveyed to the bp the request to admit *ad osculum et benedictionem* four *clerici* who had been accepted by the prior and convent, *Reg. Alnwick*, fo 97v.
1427, 31 Dec., sent by the prior to convey a letter to the bp, Reg. Alnwick, fo 97; and again on 6 Jan. 1428, *ib.*, 97v.

1446, name occ. on a rough list of those assigned to celebrate weekday and chantry masses, Cambridge, Emm. Coll. Ms 142, fo 68; also on another list (prob. of similar date) for the Totyngton chantry, *ib.*, fo 77v.
1453/4, d., and the chamberlain recd 'alms' of 16s. 8d., NRO DCN 1/5/86.

John de THORP
d. 1419/20

1419/20, d., and the chamberlain recd 'alms', NRO DCN 1/5/47.

Walter de THORP
occ. 1360/1

1360/1, the hostiller makes mention [of] *fratris nostri*, NRO DCN 1/7/20.

THOTYNGTON
see Totyngton

John de THURGARTON [Thurgerton, Thurgeton
occ. 1384/5 occ. 1401

1384/5, chaplain to the prior, NRO DCN 1/1/61.
1396/9, hostiller, NRO DCN 1/7/46–48.
1401/2, chamberlain, NRO DCN 1/5/32.
1403, May/1410, prior of Aldeby, NRO DCN 2/2/4, 5.
1411/12, sacrist, NRO DCN 1/4/50.
1399, 18 Mar., present in the Star Chamber before abp Walden as one of the proctors for the chapter to hear the abp's judgement in the dispute between the chapter and bp Despenser, NRO DCN 42/1/21; two days later he was present in the church of St James, Garlickhithe, London, when the prior and convent made a formal protest vs the abp's decree, NRO DCN 42/1/22.
1401, apptd proctor in the chapter's appeal to Rome in the above case, NRO DCN 42/2/25.

William THURKELL, Thurkyll
see Thirkell

Nicholas THURKILL
see Nicholas Attilburgh

Roger de THURSTON [Thurstone, Thurton, Turston, Turton
occ. 1309/10 occ. 1368/9

1349/50, refectorer, first yr., NRO DCN 1/8/38.
1351/2, prior of Hoxne, Windsor, St George's chapel, I.C.3; there is a letter [dated 1343 × 1351] of the prior to bp William [Bateman] requesting his apptment, Reg. X, fo 2v; he replaced John de Worstede, q.v.
1363/4, 1366/7, 1368/9, sacrist, NRO DCN 1/4/35; NRO DCN MC 136/1; NRO DCN 1/4/36.
1309/10, given a winter tunic by the prior, NRO DCN 1/1/21.
1310/11, recd a pair of *parures* [?ecclesiastical apparel] from the master of the cellar, NRO DCN 1/1/22.
1347/8, ill, and the infirmarer spent 10d. on medicine, NRO DCN 1/10/6.
1355, 8 Feb., apptd *visitator* by the abp for excepted jurisdiction on the nomination of the prior and chapter, *sed. vac.* Norwich, Reg. abp Islip fo 334, and printed in Churchill, *Cant. Admin.*, ii, 251; this is followed by a comm. addressed to him, on the same day, requiring him to visit the chapter and other religious houses in the city and diocese, Reg. abp Islip, fo 334.

Note: Because of the long time span there may be two monks by this name included in this one entry.

THWAITES
see Twaytes

THYRKYLL
see Thirkell

John de TILNEY [Tylney, Tylneye, or possibly Bilneye
occ. 1384/5 d. 1399/1400

1384/5, chaplain to the prior, NRO DCN 1/1/61.

1400, 31 Mar., obtained the privilege of apptment as a papal chaplain, *CPL*, 4 (1362–1404), 310.
1399/1400, d., and the chamberlain recd 'alms' of 3s. 4d., NRO DCN 1/5/31.
1449/50, his *ciphus* was bought from the refectorer by Geoffrey Sall, q.v., which had recently been in the possession of John de Ely, q.v., NRO DCN 1/8/87.

TILNEY
see also Bilneye, Bylney, Tylney

William de TITLESHALE
occ. [1257 × 1264]

[1257 × 1264], visited [North] Elmham, NRO DCN 60/10/2.

Robert de TOFTES
occ. 1345/6 ?occ. 1366

1345/6 and 1346/7, ill during both years and the infirmarer spent 8d., and 10d. respectively on medicine, NRO DCN 1/10/4,5.
1366, 20 June, a 'Robert de T.' who was residing at Yarmouth was recalled to Norwich by the prior for a Black Monk Chapter visitation, Pantin, *BMC*, iii, 55.

John TOLLER
see John Well'

Andrew TOOKE [Toke
occ. 1532 occ. 1538

1532, 3 June, residing at Lynn but was present at the visitation of bp Nikke, and reported *omnia bene* as far as he knew, Jessopp, *Visit.*, 264.
1534, 28 July, subscribed to the Act of Supremacy, *DK 7th Report*, Appndx 2, 295.
1538, 30 Apr., dispensed to wear the habit of a secular pr. and hold a canonry and prebend in the cathedral and any other benefice, and be non-resident, Chambers, *Faculty Office Regs*, 137.
1538, 2 May, licensed as a secular canon, *L and P Henry VIII*, xiii, pt 1, no 1115(4).
Note: this monk was possibly also known as Andrew Norwich, q.v.

Alexander de TOTYNGTON [Thotyngton, Tottington
occ. 1369/70 occ. 1406/7

1381–1406, prior: el. Mar./June 1381 (NRO DCN 1/6/20, and see under Nicholas de Hoo); el. bp 14 Sept. 1406, acc. to *Anglia Sacra* i, 415, which also ref. to the king's refusal to accept the chapter's choice and to Totyngton's imprisonment at Windsor, *ib.*, 416; provided to the see, 19 Jan. 1407, *Fasti*, iv, 24.
1369/72, cellarer, NRO DCN 1/2/22–24.
1375/6, 1377/9, master of the cellar, NRO DCN 1/1/54–56.
While prior he also held the following office :
1396/9, cellarer, NRO DCN 1/2/30–32.
1377/8, spent two wks in London, while negotiations over the farm of the manor of Chalk were proceeding; he also made excuses, on behalf of the prior and chapter, for turning down the king's request for a loan, NRO DCN 1/1/55. His expenses were 76s. 2d. This yr he was ill and charged the office 10s. for medicine and the services of a doctor, *ib.*
1380/1, went to London with the master of the cellar, [Peter de Dereham, q.v.], over the exchange between Chalk church and the manor of Martham, NRO DCN 1/1/58.
1382/3, entertained the king and queen, NRO DCN 1/9/20.
1391/2, the prior and master of the cellar were both ill and the latter's office was charged 12s. 6d., NRO DCN 1/1/66.
1393/4, the prior was using a *ciphus* of cedar which had belonged to Nicholas Gys, q.v., NRO DCN 1/8/48.
1397, 20 Oct., granted papal licence to choose his confessor and have plenary remission of his sins as often as desired, *CPL*, v (1396–1404), 47.
1399, 18 Mar., present in the Star Chamber before abp Walden, together with three monk proctors, to hear the abp's judgement in the dispute between the chapter and bp Despenser, NRO DCN 42/2/18; see John de Thurgarton.
1402/3, stayed at Hindolveston *pro captione corporis nativi*; his visit cost the manor 68s. 6d., NRO DCN 60/18/54.
1406/7, the chamberlain contributed 20s. to his el. expenses as bp, NRO DCN 1/5/38.
1407, between 19 Jan., and 23 Oct., the king wrote to the abp of Canterbury to express his annoyance that the prior of Norwich had asked the abp to give him livery of the spiritualities of the see on the strength of papal bulls in his favour; the prior was to be told to relinquish this claim, *CSL Henry IV and V*, no 943.
1407, 20 Nov., the enthronement ceremony was performed by John de Hoo and William de Thetford, q.v., Blomefield, *Norfolk*, iii, 526.
In Totyngton's will provision was made for every professed monk to take it in turn to say mass daily, on a weekly rotation, in the chapel of St Mary, i.e. his chantry mass, Reg. abp Arundel ii, fos 165v–166 and mentioned in Tanner, *Church in Norwich*, 214.

Geoffrey de TOTYNGTON [Tuttington, Tuttynton
occ. 1295/6 occ. 1312/13

1309/10, 1312/13, infirmarer, NRO DCN 1/1/19, 1/10/1.
1295/6, student at Oxford, with pension contribution from the master of the cellar, NRO DCN 1/1/12.
1300/1, sent as proctor to the Black Monk Chapter meeting [either in Oxford on 21 Sept. 1300, or in Northampton on 21 Sept. 1301, Pantin, *BMC*, i, 141, 145]; monk students were usually selected to attend these Chapters, *Comm. Rolls*, 76.
1302/3, the communar pd for the transport of his books and clothing from Oxford to Norwich, *Comm. Rolls*, 83; the communar also pd for iron bars or fittings [*ferramentis*] for the windows in his chamber, *ib.*
1309/10, took money to Oxford to the monk students there [but prob. not himself a student], NRO DCN 1/1/21.

[W. de TOTYNGTON [Tutyngton
occ. 1299/1300

1299/1300, stayed at Hindolveston, NRO DCN 60/18/14.
Note: it is possible that this was a clerical official rather than a monk.]

Henry TROWS
occ. 1463/5

1463, June/1464, Mar., hostiller, NRO DCN 1/7/97, 98.
1464/5, ill and the infirmarer spent 12d. on medicine, NRO DCN 1/10/26.

Robert TROWS [*alias* Grene
occ. 1520 occ. 1538

1520, 5 Sept., subcellarer, Jessopp, *Visit.*, 193.
1526, 7 June, chaplain to the prior, *ib.*, 203.
1534, Sept., hostiller before this date, NRO DCN 1/7/148.

1520, 5 Sept., present at the visitiaton of bp Nikke, was described as pr., and reported *omnia bene*, Jessopp, *Visit.*, 193.
1526, 7 June, present at the visitation of bp Nikke, and stated that he knew of nothing in need of reform, *ib.*, 203.
1534, 28 July, subscribed to the Act of Supremacy, *DK 7th Report*, Appndx 2, 295.
1538, 30 Apr., dispensed to wear the habit of a secular pr. and hold a canonry and prebend in the cathedral and any other benefice, and be non resident, Chambers, *Faculty Office Regs*, 137.
1538, 2 May, licensed as a secular canon, *L and P Henry VIII*, xiii, pt 1, no 1115(4).

Laurence de TUNSTALE [Tunstall
occ. 1343/4 occ. 1366

1361, 7 Dec., prior of Lynn, D. Owen, *King's Lynn*, 116, no 87.
1366, 20 June, prob. prior of Yarmouth, Pantin, *BMC*, iii, 55–56.

1343/4, student at Oxford, and the communar pd for the transport of his books from Norwich to Oxford, NRO DCN 1/12/23.

1366, 20 June, the prior wrote to 'Laurence de T.', prior of Yarmouth, requesting his return for a Black Monk Chapter visitation; there can be little doubt that this ref. to Tunstale, Pantin, *BMC*, iii, 55–56.

Thomas de TUNSTALE
occ. 1381/2 occ. 1399/1400

1383/4, 1386/90, 1392/1400, chamberlain, NRO DCN 1/5/18–31.

1381/2, visited Plumstead, accompanying the master of the cellar [Peter de Dereham, q.v.] as his *socius*, NRO DCN 60/29/35.
1394, 1 Jan., mentioned in the inhibition sent by the official of the Court of Canterbury to the bp who had been accused by the prior and chapter of exceeding his prerogative during his visitation, when he had deposed Tunstale from office, NRO DCN 42/2/12; as a result, this same yr the bp was cited to the papal curia in the above matter in which he and two other monks were the centre of controversy, all having been accused by the bp of incompetence and mismanagement in office, NRO DCN 42/2/13; see also John Daventre, John de Kirkeby.
1395, 4 Apr., mentioned in a papal comm. addressed to the abp of Canterbury and the bp of Hereford, requiring them to adjudicate in the above dispute, *CPL*, iv (1362–1402), 525.
1398, 16 Apr., granted papal licence to choose his confessor, *CPL*, v (1396–1404), 147.
1399/1400, gave a gift of 50s. to the chamberlain's office, NRO DCN 1/5/31.

William de TURBA [Turbe
occ. 1130s occ. 1146/7

c. 1136 × 1143–1146 × 1147, prior: succ. Ingulph, q.v., sometime after 1136 and before 1143; el. bp in 1146 or 1147, *Fasti*, ii, 59, 56; *HRH*, 57.

c. 1136, before, subprior, *Eng. Epis. Acta*, vi, xxxiii and no 51.
1136, after, prob. precentor, *Fasti*, ii, 59, but see *Eng. Epis. Acta*, vi, no 51, note j.

[1121 × 1135], as monk, witnessed a number of charters of bp Everard, *Eng. Epis. Acta*, vi, nos 30, 49, 50; also [1121 × 1143], *ib.*, vi, no 36.
[1136 × 1145], as monk, witnessed charters of bp Everard, *Eng. Epis. Acta*, vi, nos 51, 52.
[1136 × 1143], as prior, witnessed the confirmation of two charters in favour of Stoke by Clare priory, *ib.*, vi, nos 46, 47.
[1136 × 1145], as prior, witnessed grants, *ib.*, vi, nos 32, 43; the former of the monks, the latter of the bp. No 32 is also in *N. Cath. Charters*, ii, no 83.

Two letters addressed to him by bp Losinga are printed in Anstruther, *Epist. Losinga*, nos 41, 42.

Details of his career, including his probable Norman origin and early entry as an oblate into the cathedral priory, where he was educated, are given in C. Harper-Bill, 'Bishop William Turbe and the Diocese of Norwich, 1146–1174', *Anglo-Norman Studies*, vii (Woodbridge, 1985), 142–160.

His niece, Alda Cattus, appears in a gift of land to her and her husband from the bp, c. 1150, *Eng. Epis. Acta*, vi, no 79.

TURSTON, Turton
see Thurston

TUTTINGTON
see Totyngton

Robert TWAYTES [Thwaites, Tweits, Twhaytt', Twhaytys
occ. 1520 occ. 1538

1520, 3 Sept., refectorer, Jessopp, *Visit.*, 192.

1520, 3 Sept., present at the visitation of bp Nikke and concurred with other obedientiaries that all was well, Jessopp, *Visit.*, 192.
1526, 7 June, present at the visitation of bp Nikke and was detained for punishment on acct of his incriminating remarks and his behaviour, *ib.*, 203.
1534, 28 July, subscribed to the Act of Supremacy, *DK 7th Report*, Appndx 2, 295.
1538, 30 Apr., paid £6 13s. 4d, to be dispensed to wear the habit of a secular pr. and hold a canonry and prebend in the cathedral and any

other benefice, and be non resident, Chambers, *Faculty Office Regs*, 137.
1538, 2 May, licensed as a secular canon, *L and P Henry VIII*, xiii, pt 1, no 1115(4).

Thomas de TYLNEYE
d. 1419/20

1419/20, d., and the chamberlain recd 'alms', NRO DCN 1/5/47.

TYLNEYE
see also Bilney, Bylneye, Tilney

UNDERWOOD
see Lopham

Walter de WALPOLE [Walepol, Walpol
occ. 1263/4 occ. 1278

1272, cellarer, before Gerard de Fordham, q.v.; he took over in Aug., NRO DCN 1/1/2.
1265/6, visited Sedgeford, NRO DCN 60/33/5.
[1266], visited Denham, NRO DCN 60/7/1.
1263/4, mentioned on the master of the cellar's acct, NRO DCN 1/1/1.
1271/2, the master of the cellar pd him, the cellarer, returning from Rome, 100s., NRO DCN 1/1/2.
1272/3, visited Catton and [North] Elmham for *liberatio denariorum*, NRO DCN 60/4/2; 60/10/4.
1273/4, sent on business to London by the master of the cellar who gave him £19 [?for expenses, or to make certain payments; see Alexander de Becles], NRO DCN 1/1/3.
1278, 11 Feb., proctor, sent to the king for licence to el. a bp, *N. Cath. Charters*, i, no 54; see John de Fuldon.

William de WALPOLE [Walpool, Wolpol
occ. 1415 d. 1421/2

1415, 10 June, one of four whom the prior requested the bp to adm. *ad osculum et benedictionem*, Reg. Courtenay, fo 103v.
1418, 8 Apr., one of four whose prof. the prior requested the bp to solemnize, or to comm. himself to do so; in reply the bp comm. the prior, Reg. Wakering, fo 32v.
Note: this seems an unusually long period of probation; perhaps he had entered at an early age.
1421/2, d., and the chamberlain recd 9s. 2d. in 'alms', NRO DCN 1/5/48.

I John de WALSHAM
occ. 1407/8 d. 1439/40

1407/8, hostiller, NRO DCN 1/7/55.
1407/8, 1409/11, 1413/16, 1418/21, 1422/4, cellarer, NRO DCN 1/2/33–43.
1425/8, 1429/30, 1431/3, 1434/40, prior of St Leonard's, NRO DCN 2/3/43–54.
1425/6, gave 6d. to the chamberlain towards a new barn at Lakenham, NRO DCN 1/5/53.
1439/40, d., and the chamberlain recd 15s. in 'alms', NRO DCN 1/5/71.
1440/1, the hostiller records that Walsham was owed £6 by the hostiller's office, NRO DCN 1/7/81.
1449/50, Thomas Hethyll, q.v., bought his *ciphus* for 10s. from the refectorer, NRO DCN 1/8/87.

The 1452/3 inventory of St Leonard's lists one old spoon for the use of the sick given by him, Bensly, 'St Leonard's', 218–219.

II John WALSHAM, [or ?Howchon
occ. 1494 occ. 1499

1494, 20 Nov., one of two *clerici* whom the bp comm the prior to adm., [*monachand'*] ?as John Howchon, q.v., Reg. Goldwell, fo 181v.
1499, 6 Apr., 43rd in order on the visitation certificate, *Reg. abp Morton*, iii no 258.

I Nicholas de WALSHAM
occ. 1289/90 occ. 1292/3

1289/93, refectorer, NRO DCN 1/8/2–5; his first yr in office was 1289/90.

II Nicholas WALSHAM
d. 1471/2

1471/2, d. at Yarmouth, NRO DCN 2/4/15.

Richard de WALSHAM
occ. 1410/11 occ. 1456

1410/11, novice, gave the refectorer 13s. 4d. [for a *ciphus*], NRO DCN 1/8/55.
1426, 31 Dec., the prior requested the bp to approve his apptment as penitentiary [in the priory], Reg. Alnwick, fo 97.
1427, 31 Dec., the prior requested the bp to approve his apptment as master of St Paul's hospital, Reg. Alnwick, fo 97.
1429, 18 June, master of St Paul's hospital, Reg. Alnwick, fo 33v.
1429/30, 1431/2, 1433/4, 1436/7, master of the cellar, NRO DCN 1/1/79, 80; 60/33/32; 1/1/81.
1440/2, 1451/2, sacrist, NRO DCN 1/4/79–82.
1445, 21 Jan., the prior requested the bp to confirm his apptment as penitentiary [in the priory], Reg. Brouns, fo 112; he did so on 25 Jan., *ib*.
1452/30 Nov. 1455, prior of St Leonard's, NRO DCN 2/3/66, 67.
1426, 25 Jan., acted (with another) as commissary for the bp in a visitation of the priory of Redlingfield, Reg. Alnwick, fo 104.
1428, 8 Feb., ref. made to the sum of £10 owed to him by a Lombard banker, Ubertinus de Bardes, *CClR (1429–1435)*, 376.
1430/1, gave the gardener 3s. 4d. towards the repair of the wall *vs Holmstrete*, NRO DCN 1/11/14.

1436/7, pd a visit to Hindringham, NRO DCN 60/20/44.
1439, 8 May, obtained papal licence to choose his confessor, *CPL*, viii (1427–1447), 392.
1441, 6 Apr., sacrist, and witness to an agreement intended to settle the dispute between the bp and the prior [John Heverland, q.v.], regarding their relationship, Reg. Brouns, fo 108.
1441/2, sent to London [as proctor] to attend Convocation, NRO DCN 1/12/70.
1443, 9 Jan., he and the bp's registrar together were comm. to deal with probates in the bp's consistory court, Reg. Brouns, fo 108ᵛ. Also this month, with John Wichyngham, q.v., stemmed the insurrection of the citizens of Norwich and their assault on the priory gates by relinquishing a document which furnished evidence of an earlier agreement between the city and the priory, Tanner, *Church in Norwich*, 150.
1446/7, the hostiller acknowledged a gift of timber from him, from the wood at Archewellethorp, NRO DCN 1/7/81.
1451/2, ill, and charged 10s. to his acct (as sacrist) for medicine, NRO DCN 1/4/82.
1456, 15 Jan., the prior made a formal provision for him to lead a solitary life at St Leonard's in a newly constructed dwelling lying between the priory and kitchen and the great entrance gates there. He was to have the use of the cook's garden to grow his own vegetables; and wood faggots and other necessities were to be provided for him and his servant. The reason for this arrangement was that he had contracted leprosy, was *in ultima etate . . . constitutus* and had borne the burden of many offices; none of the doctors and surgeons who had been consulted had been able to cure him, NRO DCN 35/7.

Name in CUL Ms Ll.5.21. Cyrillus episcopus etc. (15th c.); on fo 3, *liber*—.

He was a friend of the Paston family, Davis, *Paston Letters*, no 926.

Thomas WALSHAM
occ. 1514 occ. 1520

1514, 27 Apr., present at the visitation of bp Nikke and accused the third prior [John Shilton, q.v.] of partiality in correcting the brethren; he also complained of the lack of [time for] recreation, Jessopp, *Visit.*, 73.
1520, 3 Sept., present at the visitation of bp Nikke and complained of the subprior's unsuitability to hold office because of age and deafness [see Nicholas Bedingham], *ib.*, 193.

William de WALSHAM
occ. 1201 × 1205 d. ?1217

1205-?1217, prior: succ. Gerard I, q.v., possibly as early as 1201 (Cotton, *Historia*, 92), but first occ. 10 Feb., 1205, *Fasti*, ii, 60, *HRH*, 58; d. 1217 according to Cotton, *Historia*, 109, his last occurrence being 1212 × 1214, *Fasti*, ii, 60, *HRH*, 58. See Ranulf de Wareham.
1205, 17 May, as prior, reached agreement with the bp in an exchange of lands, *Eng. Epis. Acta*, vi, no 383; on 28 May he and the bp resolved their difficulties over their respective rights with regard to presentation to a number of churches, *ib.*, vi, no 390. These agreements are also in *N. Cath. Charters*, i, nos 175, 177.
1211, 3 Nov., a new agreement was reached between bp and prior, to replace no 390 above, *Eng. Apis. Acta*, vi, no 409, also in *N. Cath. Chapters*, i, no 179.
n.d., 23 Feb., obit occ. in BL Ms Harley 3950, fo 3ᵛ.

I Robert de WALSINGHAM
occ. 1345 occ. 1347/8

1345, ill, and cared for by the infirmarer, NRO DCN 1/10/2.
1346/7, 1347/8, ill during both yrs and the infirmarer's medical expenses were 9d. and 3s. 6d. respectively, NRO DCN 1/10/5, 6.

II Robert WALSINGHAM [Walsyngham
occ. 1492 occ. 1499/1500

1496/7, pittancer, NRO DCN 1/12/81.
1496/7, 1499/1500, refectorer, NRO DCN 1/8/104–106.

1492, 5/8 Oct., 29th in order at the visitation of bp Goldwell, Jessopp, *Visit.*, 8.
1499, 6 Apr., 22nd on the visitation certificate, *Reg. abp Morton*, iii, no 258.

William WALSINGHAM
occ. 1520

1520, 3 Sept., in dcn's orders, present at the visitation of bp Nikke and reported *omnia bono statu*, Jessopp, *Visit.*, 194.

John de WALSOKEN [Walsokene
occ. 1388/9 occ. 1397/8

1388/9, gave 3s. 4d. to the communar towards the cloister building work, NRO DCN 1/12/34.
1397/8, d., and the chamberlain recd 'alms', NRO DCN 1/5/29.

I WALTER
n.d.

n.d., witnessed a grant to the chapel of Hoxne, with prior Richard de Hoxne, q.v., Suffolk Record Office, HD 1538/265/1, p. 14 (fragment of a Hoxne cartulary).

II WALTER
occ. c. 1504

c. 1504, a Walter, along with six other priests, (Christian names only given) made their prof.;

this is recorded on an inserted leaf (prob. of rough notes) between fos 27v and 28 in Reg. Nikke (9/14).

Note: this may be Walter Crowmer, q.v.

I Roger de WALTON
occ. 1344/5 occ. 1364/5

1344/7, communar/pittancer, NRO DCN 1/12/24–26.
1348/9, part yr, master of the cellar, NRO DCN 60/4/45.

1364/5, had in his possession 3s. 4d. belonging to the refectorer, NRO DCN 1/8/42.

II Roger de WALTON
occ. 1394 occ. 1414/15

1394, June/Sept., 1404/5, 1407/10, refectorer, NRO DCN 1/8/48–54.
c. 1400 × 1420, subprior, NRO DCN 1/2/100.

1411/12, gave a small sum to his successor in the office of refectorer towards the *opus camere* of St Etheldreda's church, NRO DCN 1/8/57; this church in Norwich was in the hands of the refectorer.
1414/15, made another gift, this time of 100s., for the same purpose, NRO DCN 1/8/60.

Thomas de WALTON
occ. 1393/4 d. 1408/9

1399/1400 Nov., sacrist, NRO DCN 1/4/42–44.
1400, Dec./1402, hostiller, NRO DCN 1/7/50, 51.
1402/3, 1404/8, chamberlain, NRO DCN 1/5/33–38, Windsor, St George's chapel, XI.E.19.

1393/4, had a *ciphus* made of oak which had formerly belonged to Adam de Easton, q.v., NRO DCN 1/8/48.
1408/9, d., and the chamberlain recd 'alms' of 12s. 9d., NRO DCN 1/5/39.

WALTYRTON
see Wolterton

Alan de WAPLODE [Hwaplod', Qwaplode, Qwhaplode, Wappelod, Whaplode
occ. 1393/4 occ. 1410/11

1404/5, 1407/11, precentor, Oxford, Bod. Ms Charters, Norfolk, no 288, NRO DCN 1/9/26–29.

1393/4, the refectorer's inventory included a *ciphus* of cedar with silver gilt bands [*ligaminibus*] which was at this time in his possession, NRO DCN 1/8/48.
1410, another inventory listed a *ciphus* of cedar, *quondam* his, which Richard de Midelton, q.v., now had, NRO DCN 1/8/56. He may have d. during this year.

M. Ranulph de WAREHAM [Warham
occ. 1202 occ. 1217

?1215–1217, prior: first occ. after 28 Sep. 1215 when he was described as monk and official [of the bp of Norwich]; prior and still official when el. bp of Chichester before 17 Dec., 1217, *Fasti*, ii, 60; see also *HRH*, 58, which provides many refs. He succ. William de Walsham, q.v.
1202, Easter, official of the bp, *Fasti*, ii, 60.
[1211 × 1214], still, or again, official of the bp, *Eng. Epis. Acta*, vi, nos 336, 365.

Robert WATFELD
occ. 1499 occ. [1508 × 1511]

[1508 × 1511], cellarer, NRO DCN 1/2/91.

1499, 6 Apr., 41st in order on the visitation certificate, *Reg. abp Morton*, iii, no 258.

William WATYR [Wat'
occ. 1362/3 occ. 1385/6

1362/3, the master of the cellar entered expenses *querent'* Watyr, NRO DCN 1/1/48.
[1363], 4 Aug., a dispute between prior Nicholas de Hoo, q.v, and him was in process at the papal court in Avignon according to a letter in a fragment from a letter book. The unknown writer in Avignon informed a friend [prob. the bp of Norwich] of the progress of the case in the effort to reach agreement between the two parties. It would seem that prior Nicholas was present in person, as well as William, and other evidence (see the entry under Hoo) also lends support to this conjecture. Reconciliation and a public instrument recording the agreement were the successful outcome, and the writer urged the person whom he was addressing to rec. Watyr kindly, Oxford, Bod. Ms Tanner 342, fo 109v.
1383/4, in the chamberlain's distribution of the clothing allowances, he recd only 3s. 4d., while the other monks recd 10s., NRO DCN 1/5/18.
1385/6, he and the priors of four of the cells were excluded from receiving the monastic pensions pd each yr out of the income from Chalk church; the entry concerning the four priors occ. regularly, but his name, for some unknown reason, was added this yr, NRO DCN 1/1/62.

WECHYNGHAM
see Wichyngham

WECLEWODE
see Wiclewode

John WELL' [Wellis *alias* Toller
occ. 1532 occ. 1538

1532, [13] Mar., ord dcn, St Mary's chapel, Norwich cathedral, NRO DN ORR/1/1, fo 2.
1532, 25 May, ord pr., Norwich cathedral, *ib.*, fo 5v.

1532, 3 June, present at the visitation of bp Nikke and reported *omnia bene*, Jessopp, *Visit.*, 268. He was named as being one of the favourites of Adam Sloley, the fifth prior, q.v., *ib.*

1534, 28 July, subscribed to the Act of Supremacy, *DK 7th Report*, Appndx 2, 295.

1538, 30 Apr., paid £4 to be dispensed to wear the habit of a secular pr. and hold a canonry and prebend in the cathedral and any other benefice, and be non resident, Chambers, *Faculty Office Regs*, 137.

Stephen WELL [Welle

occ. 1453/4 d. 1480/1

1471/2, refectorer, NRO DCN 1/8/95.
1471/3, gardener, NRO DCN 1/11/21.

1453/4, ill, and the infirmarer spent 2s. on medicine, NRO DCN 1/10/23.

1480/1, d., and the chamberlain recd 8s. in 'alms', NRO DCN 1/5/109.

Richard WEYBREDE

?d. 1417/18

1417/18, ?d.; the refectorer recd 6s. 8d. for his *ciphus* which another monk [*confrater*] bought from him; this suggests that Weybrede had possibly d., NRO DCN 1/8/63.

WHYTE

see Wyght

John de WHYTELEY

occ. 1340

1340, 14 Sept., the Black Monk Chapter, meeting at Northampton, requested the presidents to write to the prior of Norwich on behalf of Whyteley, described as a canonist, to allow him to go to Oxford to study, Pantin, *BMC*, ii, 16; see also under Alexander de Hikling and John de Mari.

Richard ?WIKENS

occ. 1410

1410, the refectorer lists a *cuppa ex dono*—, NRO DCN 1/8/56.

WICHEMAN [Wickman

occ. [c. 1146]

[c. 1146], apptd prob. first by bp Everard, and later by William de Turba, q.v., his successor, to hear confessions of penitents who came to St William's shrine, Jessopp and James, *St William*, 30, 84.

John WICHYNGHAM [Wechyngham, Wicchyngham, Wychingham, Wychyngham, Wythingham

occ. 1414 occ. 1456/7

1414, 14 Oct., one of six whose prof the bp comm. the pr to rec., Reg. Courtenay, fo 102^{v}.

1431/7, cellarer, NRO DCN 1/2/48–52.
1432/4, gardener, NRO DCN 1/11/16, 17.
1437/8, 1440/2, cellarer, NRO DCN 1/6/63; 1/2/54, 55.
1442/3, 1444/6, chamberlain, NRO DCN 1/5/75–77.
1454/7, refectorer, NRO DCN 1/8/91.

1443, Jan., with Richard Walsham, q.v., stemmed the insurrection of the citizens of Norwich and their assault on the priory gates by relinquishing a document which furnished evidence of an earlier agreement between the city and the priory, Tanner, *Church in Norwich*, 150.

1447/8, name occ. on a rough list of those assigned to celebrate Sunday masses on the following dates: 1447, 22 Jan., 4 June, 10 Sept.; 1448, 1 Jan., 14 Apr., 11 Aug., 29 Dec., Cambridge, Emm. Coll. Ms 142, fo 68.

He was a friend of the Paston family, Davis, *Paston Letters*, no 962.

Richard de WICLEWODE [Weclewode, Wyclewode

occ. 1310/11 occ. 1324/5

1315/16, refectorer, NRO DCN 1/8/23.
1316/17, prob. subprior, responsible for money contributions to be sent to the university of Oxford, NRO DCN 1/1/25; and see Greatrex, 'Norwich Monk Students', 566.
1317/19, master of the cellar, NRO DCN 60/20/18; 60/18/21; 60/35/18, 19.
1322/3, 1324/5, refectorer, NRO DCN 1/8/27–29.

1310/11, sent to London on business by the master of the cellar, NRO DCN 1/1/22.

1313/14, recd 11s. 9d. from the master of the cellar, *ad negotia domus*, NRO DCN 1/1/23.

1315/16, employed by the master of the cellar in more 'negotiations', NRO DCN 1/1/25.

1317/18, pd visits to Hemsby, Hindringham, Martham and Sedgeford, NRO DCN 60/15/10; 60/20/18; 60/23/15; 60/33/19.

1318/19, visited Catton, Gnatingdon, Hindolveston and Sedgeford, NRO DCN 60/4/23; 60/14/17; 60/18/21; 60/33/20.

WICTTON

see Wytton

I WILLIAM

n.d.

n.d., 1 July, name occ. in a Canterbury obit list, BL Ms Arundel 68, fo 32^{v}.

Note: a William occ. with Wimer, q.v., as witness to an episcopal confirmation [1121, 12 June × 1122, 19 Oct.], *Eng. Epis. Acta*, vi, no 45.

II WILLIAM

n.d.

n.d., 29 Dec., name occ. in a Canterbury obit list, BL Ms Arundel 68, fo 52^{v}.

Note: a William, cantor, possibly occ. as witness [1136 × 1145] with Ingulph prior and William de Turba, q.v., but this may ref. to Turba, *Eng. Epis. Acta*, vi, no 51, note j.

III WILLIAM
occ. [?1140s]

[?1140s], sacrist, who became ill, was partially cured through prayer to St William, but died after breaking a vow, Jessopp and James, St William, 145–147, 174–177.

IV WILLIAM
occ. 1182

1182, 21 July, prior of Lynn, *HRH*, 93.

Note: see also the notes under William II and III.

V WILLIAM
occ. c. 1504

c. 1504, a William, along with two other dcns, (Christian names only given) made their prof.; this is recorded on an inserted leaf (prob. of rough notes) between fos 27v and 28 in Reg. Nikke (9/14).

WILLIAM, son of ODO of Norwich
occ. c. 1219 occ. 1235

c. 1220 × 1235, prior: possibly installed 1219, and prob. d. 1235, *Fasti*, ii, 60; see Simon de Elmham.

[1235] d., commemorated 12 Apr. [as William II], BL Ms Harley 3950, fo 40v.

Note: the designation William II denotes that he was the second prior by this name; see William de Walsham; there is also William de Turba, q.v., who was prob. remembered as bp.

Charters dated during his priorate are in *N. Cath. Charters*, i, nos 40, 42, 334, 338, 340, 342, 344, 352, 357 and ii, nos 90, 265, (where he is designated William *secundus prior*), 295, 296.

WIMER [Winemerus
occ. [1121 × 1149]

[1121, June, × 1122, c. 19 Oct.], occ. as witness with William I, q.v., monk, of an episcopal confirmation, *Eng. Epis. Acta*, vi, no 45.

[1135 × 1141], again, a witness in an episcopal confirmation, *ib.*, vi, no 48.

[1146 × 1149], with Richard III, q.v., witnessed a grant of rent in Coslany to the monks of St Benet of Hulme, *St Benet Holme Cart.*, no 154.

WINKFELD
see Wyngfeld

WIRLY
see Worly

WIRSTEDE
see Worstede

Robert WITTFELDE
occ. 1505/6

1505/6, almoner, NRO DCN 1/6/114, 115.

WITTFELDE
see also Watfeld

William de WITTON [Wittun, Wytton, Wyttone
occ. 1309/10 occ. 1351

1336/7, communar/pittancer, NRO DCN 1/12/20.

1309/10, student [at Oxford], with pension contribution from the prior and the master of the cellar, NRO DCN 1/1/21.

1310/11, student, with contributions from the almoner, master of the cellar and refectorer, NRO DCN 1/6/9; 1/1/22; 1/8/21.

1312/13, stopped at [North] Elmham [prob. en route to or from Oxford; see John de Clipesby and John de Mari], NRO DCN 60/10/15.

1344/5, the pittancer recorded the receipt of £12 from him *ad opus claustri*, NRO DCN 1/12/24.

1345/6, another sum, £6 13s. 4d., from him was given to the pittancer for the cloister, NRO DCN 1/12/25.

Note: this suggests that he was in charge of an obedientiary office unless he was collecting donations from outside the monastery.

1347/8, ill, and the infirmarer spent 4d. on medicine, NRO DCN 1/10/6.

1350/1, gave the cellarer 12d. de *quodam sibi cons-ess'*, NRO DCN 1/2/19.

1351, 26 May, with Simon Bozoun and John Peche, q.v., involved in a dispute about the chapter's rights over the passage of St Olave between Norwich and Great Yarmouth, *CPR (1350–1354)*, 155.

WITTON
see also Wytton

William WODHOWSE [Wodows, Woodhus
occ. 1532 occ. 1538

1533, 20 Dec., ord subdcn, Norwich cathedral, NRO DN ORR/1/1, fo 18.

1534, 4 Apr., ord dcn, Norwich cathedral, *ib.*, fo 20v.

1532, 3 June, acol., present at the visitation of bp Nikke and stated that the care of the sick monks was inadequate, Jessopp, *Visit.*, 268.

1534, 28 July, subscribed to the Act of Supremacy, *DK 7th Report*, Appndx 2, 295.

1538, 30 Apr., paid £4 to be dispensed to wear the habit of a secular pr. and hold a canonry and prebend in the cathedral and any other benefice, and be non resident, Chambers, *Faculty Office Regs*, 137.

WOLPOL
see Walpole

Roger de WOLTERTON [Waltyrton, Wlterton
occ. 1344/5 occ. 1364/5

1344/7, communar/pittancer, NRO DCN 1/12/24–26.
1348/50, 1351/Apr. 1352, master of the cellar, NRO DCN 60/4/45–47; 1/1/43; in 1348/9, he succ. Roger de Walton I, q.v., NRO DCN 60/4/45.
1350/6, prior of Yarmouth, NRO DCN 2/4/1.
Note: it would be difficult to hold the offices of master of the cellar and prior of the distant cell of Yarmouth concurrently, but it should be remembered that the ravages of the plague had reduced the community to about half of its former size (Greatrex, 'Norwich Monk Students', 559).
1350s, prob. subprior, NRO DCN 1/2/100.
1345/6, ill, and the infirmarer spent 4d. on medicine, NRO DCN 1/10/4.
1349/50, visited Gnatingdon and Martham, NRO DCN 60/14/25; 60/23/25.
1351/2, as master of the cellar visited Hindolveston, Hindringham and Plumstead, NRO DCN 60/18/34; 60/20/28; 60/29/27.
1355, 31 Jan., apptd one of the proctors for negotiating the farm of the church of East Chalk, Reg. IX, fo 53v.
1364/5, mentioned on the refectorer's acct as having 3s. 4d. of the excess, NRO DCN 1/8/42.

WOODHUS
see Wodhowse

WOORSTED
see Worsted

Geoffrey WORLY [Wirly, Wowly
occ. 1425 d. 1446/7

1425, 2 June, ord acol. in the chapel of the bp's palace, Norwich, *Reg. abp Chichele*, iii, 477.
1427, 4 Jan., one of seven whose prof. the bp solemnized in chapter, after the prior's request of 31 Dec., 1426, Reg. Alnwick, fo 97.
Note: it was unusual to remain unprofessed for more than a yr, and so this is prob. a case of entry at an early age.
1434/5, ill and 4s. spent by the infirmarer on medicine, NRO DCN 1/10/21.
[1446/7], name occ. on a rough list of those assigned to celebrate masses in the Bateman, Totyngton, Wakering, Tye and Erpingham chantries, Cambridge, Emm. Coll. Ms 142, fo 77v.
1446/7, d., and the chamberlain recd 6s. 8d. in 'alms', NRO DCN 1/5/78.

John de WORSTEDE [Worthsted, Wrstede, Wurthestede
occ. 1322/3 occ. 1351

1322/31, communar/pittancer, NRO DCN 1/12/14–18 and *Comm. Rolls*, 94–118.
1335/6, pittancer, NRO DCN 1/12/112.
1338/40, communar/pittancer, NRO DCN 1/12/21; 1/1/38.
[1343 × 1351], prior of Hoxne, removed at the prior's request, in a letter to the bp, Reg. X, fo 2v; see Roger de Thurston.
1320s and 1330s, as communar, in charge of the cloister construction, which as his accts record, brought a heavy burden of responsibility and led to criticism from his own brethren 'quia . . . scandalizatus sum ex guorundam dictis de multiplici dampno facto conventui per me', *Comm. Rolls*, 109. There is a detailed discussion of his supervision of the building programme during these years in *Comm. Rolls*, 34–38.
1338/9, visited Catton, NRO DCN 60/4/36.
1341, 12 Nov., royal protection was granted until Easter to him and his household; he had been in London since the feast of St Dunstan and was informing the king 'of matters specially concerning his [the king's] profit and advantage', *CPR 1340–1343*, 345.
1346/7, recd 5s. from the communar [for supervising the quarrying] at Pickworth, NRO DCN 1/12/26.
1351, 4 May, obtained a papal licence to choose his confessor, *CPL*, iii (1342–1352), 411.

Robert WORSTED [Woorsted, Wursted, alias Bowgyn
occ. 1514 occ. 1538

1530/1, communar, NRO DCN 1/2/106.
1514, 27 Apr., present at the visitation of bp Nikke, when the subprior [William Bexwell, q.v.] reported that he had fathered a child, Jessopp, *Visit.*, 76. John Marton, q.v., made the same accusation vs him, *ib.*, 74.
1526, 7 June, present at the visitation of bp Nikke, and made a lengthy deposition in which he made accusations vs several of his brethren including the prior, John Sall and John Shelton, q.v., *ib.*, 200–201.
1534, 28 July, subscribed to the Act of Supremacy. *DK 7th Report*, Appndx 2, 295.
1538, 30 Apr., dispensed to wear the habit of a secular pr. and hold a canonry and prebend in the cathedral and any other benefice, and be non resident, Chambers, *Faculty Office Regs*, 137.
1538, 2 May, licensed as a secular canon, *L and P Henry VIII*, xiii, pt 1, no 1115(4).

William WORSTEDE D.Th., [Wirstede, Worsted, or de Norwico
occ. [?1412] d. 1436

1427–1436, prior: el. before 8 Oct. 1427, Reg. Alnwick, fo 8; *prefectio*, 17 Oct., *ib.*, fo 27v; d. prob. before 29 Sept. 1436 (see below).

1425, 8 Apr., subprior, *Reg. abp Chichele*, iii, 467–468.

[?1412], prob. a student at Oxford because of his inception below. His preaching assignment below, in 1416/17, suggests that he had been a student for several years.

1422/3, student [at Oxford] for whose inception this yr some of the obedientiaries recorded their contributions: the almoner, cellarer, chamberlain, hostiller, master of the cellar, precentor, sacrist and the prior of St Leonard's, NRO DCN 1/6/50; 1/2/42; 1/5/49; 1/7/67; 1/1/76; 1/9/37; 1/4/57; 2/3/38. The almoner and the master of the cellar listed two separate payments, the other one being their student pension contribution; the refectorer entered only the sum allocated for the pension, NRO DCN 1/8/70; the hostiller noted that a total of £10 had been voted by the chapter for the inception expenses of which his share amounted to 15d. The chamberlain made two separate payments and gave an additional 20s. as a gift, NRO DCN 1/5/49.

1423, at the same time, the accts of the two presidents of the Black Monk Chapter allocated a sum of £25 for his inception in theology, Pantin, *BMC*, iii, 190.

Note: although there are no references to him as a member of the community before 1416/17, he was no doubt one of the unnamed scholars receiving regular pensions from the various obedientiaries in the 8 to 10 yrs prior to his inception.

1416/17, pd 3s. 4d. by the precentor *pro labore suo et predicatione*, NRO DCN 1/9/31.

1421/2, ill, and the infirmarer spent 11s. 1d. on medicine, NRO DCN 1/10/14; this same yr he was given for his use some boots of Thomas Hevyngham, q.v., who had d., NRO DCN 1/9/37.

1422, named, with John Dereham, q.v., as a member of the committee which criticized the king's proposals for the reform of the Black Monks, Pantin, *BMC*, ii, 121.

1423, 5–7 July, present at the Black Monk Chapter and named as diffinitor, Pantin, *BMC*, ii, 145; apptd to the committee to el. the presidents for the next [1426] chapter, *ib.*, 152; also one of those chosen to preach a sermon in English at the 1426 chapter, *ib.*, 156.

1425, 21 Apr., apptd official [*visitator*] by the abp for excepted jurisdiction, *sed. vac.* Norwich, after nomination by the prior and chapter, Churchill, *Cant. Admin.*, ii, 253; he took the oath of office on 30th Apr., see *Reg. abp Chichele*, iii, 468–469.

1426, 6–8 July, present at the Black Monk Chapter and served as diffinitor, Pantin, *BMC*, ii, 163, 174–175; he was apptd again to the committee to el. the presidents for the next [1429] meeting, *ib.*, 173, 175; he preached to the clergy and people *commendabiliter*, *ib.*, 180.

1427/8, the master of the cellar contributed £8 13s. 4d. to his el. expenses, NRO DCN 1/1/77.

1427, 17 Oct., installed as prior by John Dereham, q.v., who had been comm. by the bp, Reg. Alnwick, fo 27v.

1430, the date of the completion of the rebuilding of the cloister over a period of one hundred and thirty-three yrs, Fernie, *Arch. Hist. Norwich*, 166–167, from Reg. I, fo 266v.

1430/1, gave 6s. 8d. to the gardener to help with the repair of the wall *vs. Holmstrete*, NRO DCN 1/11/14.

1431/2, went to London, with John Elyngham, q.v., at the expense of the infirmarer, NRO DCN 1/10/19; the refectorer also contributed, NRO DCN 1/8/74.

1432, 31 Dec., chosen as one of the delegates to represent the English Benedictines at the Council of Basel, Pantin, *BMC*, iii, 105; this apptment was renewed on 12 Jan 1435, *ib.*

Contributions from the obedientiaries to the Council and to the prior's expenses and those of his associates, who included William de Cawmbrygg, John Fornsete and possibly John Stowe I, q.v., are entered on the accts: in 1431/2 the master of the cellar gave £4 17s. 3d., NRO DCN 1/1/80, and the refectorer contributed a small sum 'to the ambassadors to Basel', NRO DCN 1/8/74; in 1433/4 a contribution of £20 was sent by the cellarer to the prior in Basel, NRO DCN 1/2/50.

Note: see also *BRUO* which names him as one of the English ambassadors to Basel apptd by Henry VI, and as one of the Council members named to concern themselves with the reformation of religion and with peace with France. As ambassador he made a protest on behalf of the English delegation, Oxford, Bod. Ms Tanner, 165 fos 139v–140.

1435/6, d., and the chamberlain recd 67s. 8d. *de elemosina patris nostri*, NRO DCN 1/5/64.

1436/7, the precentor pd for the brief announcing his d., NRO DCN 1/9/51.

Note: since the accts ran from Michaelmas to Michaelmas he prob. d. before 29 Sept., 1436 to enable the chamberlain to enter the receipt of money from the 'late prior'.

H. de WORT'

occ. 1273/4

1273/4, visited Sedgeford *pro liberatione denariorum*, NRO DCN 60/33/5.

WOWLY

see Worly

Geoffrey de WROXHAM [Wrexham, Wrokesham

occ. 1310/11 d. 1321/2

1310/11, 1312/Mar. 1313, refectorer, NRO DCN 1/8/21, 22.

1316/17, gardener, *Comm. Rolls*, 89 [transcribed as D. de Wrokesham].

1316/17, gave the communar his 'O' money towards the cloister construction, *Comm. Rolls*, 89.
1321/2, d., and the chamberlain pd the brief bearer, NRO DCN 1/5/6.

Name in Cambridge, Trinity Coll. Ms 883, Rule for nuns, with commentary on the Rule in French (13th/14th c.); see Ker, 'Norwich Cathedral Mss', 258.

John WROXHAM
occ. 1420/1 occ. 1446

1420/1, bought a *ciphus* from the refectorer for 10s., prob. soon after adm., NRO DCN 1/8/68.
1427/8, recd 3s. 9d. 'pro ligatur' ij librorum cum evidenc' monasterii', NRO DCN 1/1/77.
1428/9, ill and the infirmarer spent 12d. on medicine, NRO DCN 1/10/16.
1446, name occ. on a rough list of those assigned to celebrate wkday and chantry masses, Cambridge, Emm. Coll. Ms 142, fo 68; also on a similar list (prob. of similar date) for the Bateman, Totyngton, Wakering, Tye and Erpingham chantries, *ib.*, fo 77ᵛ.

WRSTEDE
see Worstede

John WULRYNGHAM
occ. 1428

1428, Jan./Sept., hostiller, NRO DCN 1/7/72.

WURSTED, Wurthestede
see Worstede

[John WYCHAM
Name in Oxford, Bod. Ms Jones 46, Horae (early 15th c.), the name is on fo 107; monk or scribe or monk/scribe?]

WYCHINGHAM
see Wichyngham

WYCLEWODE
see Wiclewode

John de WYGENHALE
d. 1406/7

1406/7, d., and the chamberlain recd 20s. in 'alms', NRO DCN 1/5/38.
n.d., 20 Apr., the obit of a monk by this name occ. in the kalendar in Reg. XI, fo 3ᵛ; does this ref. to the same person?

James WYGHTT [Whyte
occ. 1534 d. 1535

1534, 28 July, subscribed to the Act of Supremacy, *DK 7th Report*, Appndx 2, 295.
1535, 27 May, d., his obit occ. in BL Ms Harley 3950, fo 5.

Richard WYKHAM
occ. 1532

1532, 3 June, pr., present at the visitation of bp Nikke and stated that everything was in good order, Jessopp, *Visit.*, 268.

John WYLLYS
d. 1471/2

1471/2, d., and the sacrist pd for funeral tapers, NRO DCN 1/4/93.

John de WYMONDHAM
occ. 1291/2 occ. 1298/9

1291/2, the master of the cellar pd him and Robert de Brok', q.v., *ad unum librum*, 6s., NRO DCN 1/1/11.
1295/6, the refectorer pd 4d. for repairs to his *ciphus*, NRO DCN 1/8/7.
1298/9, ill, and the prior spent 5s. 5d. in medical treatment on his behalf, NRO DCN 1/1/14.

Robert de WYMONDHAM
occ. 1335/6 d. 1336/7

1335/6, mentioned performing a task for the master of the cellar, NRO DCN 1/1/33.
1336/7, d., and the chamberlain pd the brief bearer, NRO DCN 1/5/10.

Thomas WYNFYLD [Wyngfeldt
occ. 1533/5

1533, 20 Sept., ord exorcist and acol., Norwich cathedral, NRO DN ORR/1/1, fo 16ᵛ.
1535, [Sept./Dec.] ord subdcn, place uncertain, *ib.*, fo 26ᵛ.
1534, 28 July, subscribed to the Act of Supremacy, *DK 7th Report*, Appndx 2, 295.

William WYNGFELD [Winkfeld
occ. 1514 d. 1525/6

1525/6, *magister summi altaris*, NRO DCN 1/4/118.
1514, 27 Apr., present at the visitation of bp Nikke, and criticized the prior of St Leonard's, John Sybly, q.v.; he also expressed concern that the number in the community had decreased from 60 monks to 40, Jessopp, *Visit.*, 75. On the size of the community see Greatrex, 'Norwich Monk Students', 558–560.
1525/6, d., and the sacrist pd for funeral tapers, NRO DCN 1/4/118.

Thomas de WYSEBECHE
occ. 1345/6

1345/6, ill on two occasions, and the infirmarer spent 8d. on medicine the second time, NRO DCN 1/10/2, 4.

WYTHINGHAM
see Wichyngham

R[alph] de WYTTON [Wictton, Wycton, Wyton
occ. 1265/6 occ. 1318/19

1318/19, master of the cellar, NRO DCN 60/18/21.

1265/6, visited Taverham for *liberatio denariorum*, NRO DCN 60/35/5.
1309/10, visited Hindringham, NRO DCN 60/20/15.
1312/13, ill, and the infirmarer spent 3s. 4d. on 'his cure', NRO DCN 1/10/1.
1318/19, visited Hindolveston, NRO DCN 60/18/21.

Note: The full name Ralph is given only on the Taverham acct; there may be two monks here.

WYTTON
see also Witton

YARMOUTH, Yarnemuth
see Jernmuth

YAXHAM
see Jaxham

Francis YAXLEY
occ. 1525/6 occ. 1538

1525/6, celebrated his first mass, NRO DCN 1/4/118.
1532, 3 June, subcellarer, Jessopp, *Visit.*, 267.
1525/6, the sacrist recd the offerings at his first mass, NRO DCN 1/4/118.
1526, 7 June, one of a group of younger monks, present at the visitation of bp Nikke, who complained that they were required by the seniors to memorize the psalter and the antiphons and responses etc., which they considered a waste of time, Jessopp, *Visit.*, 198; he also deposed that the obedientiaries were failing to render their accts, *ib.*, 203.
1532, 7 June, present at the visitation of bp Nikke and reported that the sacrist had allowed one of the buildings [in the precincts] to become ruinous, *ib.*, 267.
1534, 28 July, subscribed to the Act of Supremacy, *DK 7th Report*, Appndx 2, 295.
1538, 30 Apr., dispensed to wear the habit of a secular pr. and hold a canonry and prebend in the cathedral and any other benefice, and be non resident, Chambers, *Faculty Office Regs*, 137.
1538, 2 May, licensed as a secular canon, *L and P Henry VIII*, xiii, pt 1, no 1115(4).

Edmund YELVERTON [Zelverton
d. 1423/4

1423/4, d., and the chamberlain recd 'alms' of 11s. 2d., NRO DCN 1/5/50.

John YELVERTON
occ. 1477/80

1477/8, gave the precentor 2d. *pro libris in cathologo*, NRO DCN 1/9/76; possibly a new book list, see Greatrex 'Norwich Monk Students', 575–576.
1480, 10 Jan., the pope ordered the bp to absolve him and give him penance, in response to his petition to the pope; although he had been declared apostate and excommunicate he was repentant and anxious to return. He was also to be dispensed so that he might hold a benefice, *CPL*, xiii (1471–1484), 714.

YERMUTH
see Jernmuth

YNGHAM
see Hengham

ZERMODE, Zernemuth
see Jernmuth

ZERMOWTH
see Jernemuth

ROCHESTER CATHEDRAL PRIORY

INTRODUCTION

It is difficult to present a balanced historical survey of Rochester cathedral priory over the whole four and a half centuries of its existence. The problem lies with the capriciousness of the survival of the sources on which all study must inevitably be based; these implicitly, if not overtly, give a misleading impression because the scales are tipped in favour of the early years. No doubt the fourteenth- and fifteenth-century Rochester monks tended to look back on the past achievements of their monastic predecessors in the community with some degree of nostalgia, but they saw themselves as their heirs and descendants in a direct line of continuity.

Although the cathedral, dedicated to St Andrew, and the diocese of Rochester had their origins in the early seventh century, the monastic chapter did not arrive until the appointment of archbishop Lanfranc's close friend, Gundulf, as bishop in 1077. The canons were replaced in 1083 by twenty-two monks, many of whom were probably, like Gundulf himself, former monks of Caen; at the time of his death in 1108 this small band had increased in numbers to over sixty.[1] For several reasons the diocese and its cathedral were unique among their medieval counterparts in England and Wales. The diocese itself, one of two in the single county of Kent, was diminutive in size, and its bishop stood in a peculiar relationship with the archbishop of Canterbury that probably derived from pre-conquest times: on the one hand the former was directly subservient to the latter rather than, like other bishops, to the crown; at the same time the former functioned as the latter's deputy on the frequent occasions when the archbishop was required to conduct affairs outside Canterbury diocese.[2] Provision for the support of the bishop and the growing monastic community at Rochester was made by gifts of land from many benefactors, royal, ecclesiastical, and lay, in a series of grants and charters, and royal and archiepiscopal confirmations of charters, many of which are recorded in the *Textus Roffensis*. However, it is essential for the historian to distinguish the genuine grants from those which were later attempts to supply documents believed to have been among the Rochester muniments but, in the moment of need, found to be missing.[3] Some of these early donations accompanied the admission of a relative to the monastery, as in the case of Aethelnoth and of Geroldus and Peter, q.v. In Gundulf's lifetime there was no real problem over the division of the newly augmented cathedral estates between the episcopal and monastic households, but later, especially when secular clerks rather than monks occupied the see, this became a controversial issue.[4]

[1] The second prior, Ralph [I], q.v., for example, had come originally from Caen, and other monks may have been former members of the Bec community where Gundulf had begun his monastic life. References to numbers are in Knowles and Hadcock, *MRH*, 74 and *Text. Roff.*, ii, fo 172; Thomson, *Gundulf*, 40.

[2] Churchill, *Cant. Admin.*, i, 279–285, discusses both of these anomalies with supporting evidence from the Reg. Temp[oralium].

[3] Brett, 'Forgery at Rochester', 401–406 and *passim.*

[4] See Dr Brett's chapter in Yates, *Rochester Cathedral*, forthcoming.

Names of obedientiaries and their offices at Rochester occur from an early period in charters and manuscripts.[5] Before c. 1108 a subprior (Ordwinus and William I, q.v.), a cellarer (William IV, q.v.), a chamberlain (Ralph III, q.v.), and a cantor or precentor (Baldwin II, q.v.) appear; in the mid-twelfth century a sacrist (Rainaldus, q.v.) is mentioned, and by or before the end of the century possibly a granator or granger (Elias II or III, q.v.).[6] The early thirteenth-century records produce an infirmarer (Richard de Eastgate, q.v.); an almoner (Adam II, q.v.) shows himself in 1250, and the *custodes maneriorum*, unnamed, occur in the injunctions of archbishop Winchelsey dated 1299, the only reference to this office known to date.[7] The 1333 prioral election brings a few more monk officials to light: the third prior (William de Maydeston II, q.v.), the refectorer (William de Bradebourne, q.v.), the succentor (John de Reynham II, q.v.), subsacrist (John de Shepey II, q.v.), and subchamberlain (Henry de Hengseye, q.v.). The first reference to a *hostiarius*, or master of the hospice for guests, is in 1317 (Walter de Rawe, q.v.), and in 1345 comes the one and only reference to a receiver.[8] Two final additions in the sixteenth century, both of them almost certainly in existence much earlier, are the subcellarer (Robert Smyth, q.v.) and the *custos* of the Lady chapel (John Rye, q.v.). Over this array of offices the prior, with his senior monk advisers, had the sole right of appointment, with the exception of those of subprior, cellarer, precentor, sacrist, and chamberlain. These five were appointed by the bishop after nomination by the prior and chapter.[9]

In line with the subjection of Rochester to Canterbury the bishops who succeeded Gundulf were appointed by the archbishop until 1238, when the right of free election was judged by the pope to belong to the monks, as long as they had obtained an archiepiscopal licence.[10] However, on most occasions royal and archiepiscopal nominations to the see and papal provisions continued to thwart the monks in their choice. They were successful in promoting to the episcopate four members of their community: John de Bradefeld, q.v., in 1278, Thomas de Wouldham, prior, q.v., in 1291, Hamo de Hethe, prior, q.v., in 1317 and his successor both as prior and bishop, John de Shepey II, q.v.[11] There are a number of dramatic episodes in the relations between

[5] This is an example of the vagaries of the survival of records.

[6] I take *primicerius* to be precentor on the advice of Dr Brett. There is also a cook/kitchener named Reginald [I], c. 1055 × 1107, if *archimagrinus* is a variation of *archimagirus*; Reginald was also *oeconomus*, a word not encountered elsewhere in this context.

[7] *Reg. abp Winchelsey*, 840; were the later *custodes* or *senescalli* laymen as at Winchester and Worcester? There were earlier monk *custodes* of individual manors, e.g. Clement I, Robert de Hecham, q.v.

[8] No name is given but he is mentioned with the cellarer as sharing the charge of temporal affairs in the monastery during the prior's absence: 'celerarius et receptor pecunie in temporalibus negociis custodiam seu administracionem . . . exerceant', *Reg. Hethe*, 741 (fo 213^{v}). It is true that archbishop Pecham had ordered the appointment of three monk treasurers at Rochester in 1283 in order to centralize the financial administration, *Epist. Pecham*, 622–623 (Canterbury reference), but it is doubtful that he succeeded; see Brown, 'Financial System of Rochester', 116–120.

[9] It seems unusual that a memorandum in bishop Langdon's register (fo 81^{v}) dated 1432 lists the five over which the bishop has the right of *prefectio*, followed by a list of those pertaining to the prior and chapter, without any mention of a treasurer or receiver, who was surely a monk. The second list consists of the almoner, subcellarer, three subsacrists, subchamberlain, and master of the hospice; it is surely incomplete, but for what reason? Ann Brown's conclusion, in 'Financial System of Rochester', 118, that the prior was, and continued to be, the treasurer except when he was away in 1345 is convincing; see Walter Boxley, prior and treasurer in 1535.

[10] *Reg. Roff.*, 95–98.

[11] For assessments of Hethe's episcopal career see the two recent articles by R. M. Haines, 'The Episcopate of a Benedictine Monk: Hamo de Hethe, Bishop of Rochester (1317–1352)', *Revue Bénédictine*, cii (1992), 192–207 and 'Bishops and Politics in the Reign of Edward II: Hamo de Hethe, Henry Wharton and

bishop and chapter recounted by the Rochester chroniclers, some of which appear in the biographical entries that follow. These were mainly centred on disputed rights and obligations concerning the internal affairs of the priory, and also the lands and churches claimed by the monks but frequently, so it seems, seized by the bishops for their own use. The foundation of the hospital of St Mary at Strood in 1192/3 by bishop Gilbert de Glanville is a case in point, and led to the chronicler's damning verdict that he was *inter fundatores confundator*.[12] Another source of contention was the matter of the appointment of lay servants in the priory, a custom that may have originated before the separation of the episcopal and monastic households.[13] Both Glanville and Hamo de Hethe were offenders in this *cause célèbre* according to the monks who complained to the archbishop on his visitation in 1330 that Hethe had named twenty priory servants; archbishop Islip reduced the number to ten in 1360.[14] There were also the unique arrangements provided for the annual celebration of the patronal feast of St Andrew, commonly referred to as the *exennium* (gift). On this occasion certain gifts of produce from the priory manors were delivered to the bishop as a contribution towards his hospitality for the festivities. The practice probably goes back to Gundulf's episcopate; but only later did it become necessary to draw up precise regulations, when argument arose over such matters as the procedure in the event of the bishop's absence from Rochester at the time of the feast. Prior Hamo de Hethe, q.v., went to bishop Wouldham as the latter lay dying and effected a reconciliation over the *exennium* controversy between chapter and bishop, only later to be himself accused as bishop, before archbishop Meopham, of the same charge of neglecting the episcopal obligations at the feast.[15]

Only a few of the archiepiscopal and episcopal visitation proceedings and injunctions for Rochester prove informative. John de Reynham, q.v., was removed as prior in 1283 by archbishop Pecham, but once he had obtained dispensation for illegitimacy he was returned for a second term. Winchelsey's injunctions in 1299 are cast in general terms and throw no light on named individuals; Meopham's 1330 *sede plena* visitation of the bishop and chapter has been mentioned above, and Chichele in 1418 recorded merely that nothing serious was amiss. From archbishop Morton's visitation in 1496 we have only one useful record: the visitation certificate that lists the monks present in order of seniority.[16]

Election records of priors are more abundant and more informative in their details. From 1239 the Rochester chapter exercised their right to free election, William de Hoo, q.v., being possibly the first chosen by the monks themselves, probably by

the "Historia Roffensis"', *Journal of Ecclesiastical History*, 44 (1993), 586–609. Other monk bishops of Rochester were Ascelin, prior of Dover (1142–1148), Thomas Brinton, q.v., of Norwich cathedral priory (1373–1389), John Langdon [I], q.v., of Christ Church, Canterbury (1421–1434), and William Wells, abbot of St Mary's, York (1436–1444).

[12] *Flores Hist.*, ii, 150. For the support of the hospital bishop Gilbert had appropriated two of the priory churches. A lengthy account of the diverse and complex causes that lay behind the monks' grievances has survived in a Canterbury manuscript and is printed in Selden Society, *Select Cases Eccles.*, 41–46 (from Canterbury Cart. Antiq., R.70 a, b).

[13] *Cust. Roff.*, 32.

[14] *Reg. Hethe*, 425, Reg. abp Islip, fo 223^v. The entry under Robert de Leuesham, q.v., provides an example of an episcopal commission to induct one of these servants. Bishops Ingoldisthorpe and Wouldham also incurred the monks' wrath over these appointments.

[15] *Anglia Sacra*, i, 357, *Reg. Hethe*, 425, 427.

[16] *Reg. abp Winchelsey*, 838–842, Churchill, *Cant. Admin.*, i, 342, quoting from Chichele's register, *Reg. abp Morton*, ii, no 446.

scrutiny, in the presence of the bishop, following the custom at Canterbury.[17] The entry for a certain Wynand de Dryland, alleged to have occurred as prior c. 1294, requires a few words of explanation. The name appeared on a scrap of paper, written in an unidentifiable hand, possibly attempting to simulate printing, that fell out of my copy of *Fasti*, ii, several years ago; the only reference provided was 'not in *Fasti*'! My *Fasti* is never taken out of my study and, therefore, the enigma of the arrival of the scrap of paper cannot be connected with a borrower. No amount of searching through my memory or through the records has produced any clue. In case this is the admittedly mysterious but possibly genuine desire of a ghostly figure to be rescued from oblivion, I insert his name and circumstances here, along with the warning that it may not be a message from Wynand himself but one of my contemporaries playing a practical joke. If so, I dare the culprit to confess!

There are few recorded details about many of the later priors. Hamo de Hethe, q.v., was in office only for three years before his election as bishop, but his lengthy episcopal career revealed that he was a man of many talents. His predecessor, John de Grenestrete, q.v., had been deposed by archbishop Reynolds because of his incompetent rule; his successor, John de Westerham, q.v., was a senior monk who strove to bring order to manorial administration through the compilation of a custumal for all the manors and their tenants. The election of John de Shepey II, q.v., in 1333 is entered in the register of Hethe, who presided at the proceedings and scrutinized the votes.[18] Like the bishop, prior Shepey had been caught up in worldly affairs beyond the diocese but had expected to resign after twenty years in office until a new career opened when he succeeded Hethe in the see. It was Richard Pecham, q.v., who, in 1463, acquired for himself and his successors a confirmation and extension of the papal grant of pontificalia, on the grounds of previous grants for which, however, no evidence has been found. William Fresell, q.v., a monk of St Alban's, was appointed by the archbishop in 1509 because of a disagreement between bishop Fisher and the prior and chapter over the election of a prior; this was resolved when both parties devolved their rights on their metropolitan.

It is necessary to draw attention to the preponderance of entries recording admissions, professions, and ordinations at Rochester and of appointments to obedientiary office. The explanation lies in the survival of most of the episcopal registers, which have not been tampered with as at Norwich; there are also two priory registers, those of the second prior John de Shepey [III], q.v., and of priors William Wode II, q.v., and Thomas Bourne, q.v., though the latter is only a fragmentary record of their *acta*. Many of the other details of the monks' activities have disappeared with the loss of all but about ten of the obedientiary accounts and a few rolls of the manors and courts. There is some slight compensation in a rough thirteenth/fourteenth-century list inserted in a miscellaneous register (now BL Ms Cotton Vespasian A. xxii) that enables us to be more precise in dating the monks there named; they were the ones delegated

[17] However, the chronicler, Edmund de Hadenham, q.v., says that Hoo's predecessor, Richard de Darente, q.v., was elected. There is uncertainty about a few of the later 13th-c. priors about whose elections (or appointments) nothing is known; see Simon de Clyve and John de Reynham.

Rochester seems to have had no customs of its own but to have followed those of Canterbury as exemplified in the *via scrutinii* for prioral elections. It is worth noting that the first Rochester library catalogue included a copy of archbishop Lanfranc's customs for Canterbury bound with a copy of the Rule, *Text. Roff.*, ii, fo 229.

[18] This election provides a list of monks in order of seniority and also records their nominations.

to say mass daily for the first month after the death of one of their brethren: the phrase is *ad tricennale celebrandum*. Fortunately for us, the names of the deceased are also given.

Apart from the early monks with only Christian names, who appear on charter witness lists, most of the names are toponymic and as such give some, not necessarily completely reliable, information about the monks' family origins. The clear indication is that the great majority came to Rochester from the towns and villages of Kent; for example, there were nine from Maidstone and nine from Canterbury, eight from Tonbridge and the same number from [the Isle of] Sheppey. There were also thirteen from London, one of whom, Thomas de London I, q.v., was ordained, with letters dimissory, at St Paul's cathedral. The prior Alexander de Glanville, q.v., was probably a descendant of the Norman family of that name which had provided Gilbert to the see of Rochester and Ranulf to the justiciarship several generations earlier; also, the monk named Pelegrini, q.v., was very likely related to the papal nuncio of that name. However, these are rare exceptions to the local background of most members of the monastic community at Rochester.

The one dependent cell in Suffolk at Felixstowe, or Walton St Felix, originated in a gift of land to the prior and convent before 1100; here, from c. 1177 there were usually two or three monks in residence.[19] The earliest known priors are Aufredus, q.v., who may have been the first; Fulk, q.v., who followed soon after c. 1180; and Robert de Waletone, q.v., a scholar, who was in charge there before 1202.[20] At the time of the episcopal election of 1291, John III, q.v., prior, was appointed one of the five electors [*compromissorii*], but in 1333 on the occasion of the prioral election it was recorded that the monks at Felixstowe were not allowed to participate.[21] The single surviving account roll for the cell, that of prior William Waterford, q.v., for 1496/7, reports the payment of debts of [?the late] Richard Pecham, q.v., who may have retired to Felixstowe, probably as its prior, after resigning as prior of Rochester c. 1468. The cell was suppressed in 1528 to provide support for cardinal Wolsey's short-lived foundation of a college at Ipswich.[22] There was also a small dependency at Darenth after 1195 for an unknown length of time. Richard de Darente, q.v., was probably prior there at the time of his election as prior of Rochester in 1225, and Ralph IV, q.v., was its prior sometime before 1311.

There can be no doubt that during the first century after the foundation of the cathedral priory intellectual endeavour at Rochester was unflagging, and the scriptorium was employing some thirty scribes up to c. 1150.[23] The extraordinarily prolific output in these early years was at least partly due to the influence and inspiration of its Norman founder and his scholarly formation and experience both at Bec and later, under Lanfranc, at Canterbury. The earliest library catalogue, dated 1122/3, includes almost one hundred items, many containing several texts. There are many patristic writings as well as works of Lanfranc and Anselm, and historical works of Eusebius, Josephus, Paul the Deacon, and Bede. In the 1202 list of books there are about two hundred and forty volumes including a number of duplicate copies and also Latin

[19] Knowles and Hadcock, *MRH*, 66, state that there were three monks in 1381.

[20] For Waletone's books see the entry in the Register, and Sharpe, *Eng. Benedictine Libraries*, iv, B79, at the end of the section.

[21] BL Ms Cotton Faustina B.v, fo 66, printed in *Anglia Sacra*, i, 371–372.

[22] *L and P Henry VIII*, iv, pt 2, nos 4673, 4755; the prior, Richard Faversham, and two unnamed monks signed the surrender.

[23] Waller, 'Library', 134; at least some of the scribes were monks.

grammars, classical texts, and medical treatises besides biblical texts and commentaries and sermon collections. These and the other medieval catalogues of Rochester, including the one compiled by Alexander II, q.v., the precentor, and the list of books given by Hamo de Hethe, q.v., are printed *in extenso* in *English Benedictine Libraries*, vol. iv, edited by Richard Sharpe.[24] An extensive collection such as this was intended for the use of the community to provide its members with the essential tools for monastic study within the cloister. Intellectual as well as manual labour was recommended by the Black Monk Chapter statutes of 1343, and it is scarcely credible that the Rochester community failed to take advantage of the treasures of learning provided for them by their predecessors.[25] The problem is that our judgement is adversely affected by the lack of evidence of scholarly pursuits in the later Middle Ages after the initial outburst of creative activity in building up the library. Unless there are tangible results intellectual endeavour remains unseen and unknown in monastic anonymity.

At least one industrious monk was making use of some fifteen or sixteen volumes, about half of which are listed in the early catalogues, while he was a student at Oxford in the 1460s. His name was Thomas Wybarn, q.v., and from the inscription in many of them it seems that he was a bibliophile as well as a scholar. Unfortunately, among Rochester monks at Oxford, evidence of his working collection of texts is a unique survival. Of the other thirteen monk students known to have gone to Oxford there is scant information: at least three obtained degrees in theology and two in canon law; and John de Shepey II, q.v., after his inception in theology may have been regent master at Gloucester Hall. The lack of sources leaves us with the impression that Rochester monks made a poor showing at university, but on the other hand they do not appear on any of the surviving 'black lists' of monastic houses that failed to maintain their quota of students at Oxford or Cambridge.[26]

The presence of an almonry school in 1299 is attested by an injunction of archbishop Winchelsey. He ordered the almoner to feed and provide for poor scholars in the almonry *sicut antiquitus consuevit fieri*; this suggests that the priory was in line with Canterbury and other cathedral priories in establishing a school for young boys within the cloister.[27] The name M. Hamo [?Kok'], which is attached to two volumes in the earliest catalogue, possibly identifies one of the twelfth-century masters who may have been employed to teach both boys and novices.[28] Two monks are known to have received their early education in the school, John de Bradefeld and John de Shepey II, q.v.; the former's subsequent election by his brethren to the bishopric was soon regretted because it seems to have turned his head, but the latter, who also became bishop, was remembered for his many achievements.[29]

The Rochester monks, mostly in the person of their priors, made some impact on the urban community outside the precincts. One location in which there was frequent, if not daily, encounter between the community and the townspeople was within the

24 There is a lengthy general introduction full of informative detail that summarizes the present state of scholarship, followed by Professor A. G. Watson's introductions for each list; the lists are numbered B77–83.

25 Pantin, *BMC*, ii, 51.

26 These monitions directed to the delinquent houses are transcribed in *ib.*, ii, *passim.* The Chapter wrote to the prior in 1340 to urge him to allow John de Whytefeld, q.v., to return to Oxford to incept in theology. Had more obedientiary accounts survived, other names and details would have come to light.

27 *Reg. abp Winchelsey*, 841.

28 Waller, 'Library', 65. In 1430/1 the almoner purchased candles, fish, and parchment for the boys, CKS DRc/F11.

29 Shepey's episcopal register has survived and is listed in the References.

nave of the cathedral which, as at Ely, served as the parish church. The constant comings and goings of the laity to pray and to worship at the nave altar of St Nicholas disturbed the monks, who restricted times of entry and caused increasing friction between the community and the parishioners. Bishop Hethe tried to conclude an agreement by requiring the monks to provide a chapel in the north-west corner of the nave, but separate from it, which would be accessible from the outside at all hours. The satisfaction of both parties was not achieved, however, until a new church was constructed and completed in 1423, when the vicar and parishioners renounced their rights in the nave.[30] Almsgiving to the poor on the death or anniversaries of monks and bishops and also to poor parishioners occurs as a regular entry on the few extant obedientiary accounts, which also refer to expenses for the entertainment of guests.[31] The priors were on occasion involved with city and castle defences by royal command, and in the absence of the bishop several of them, like John Shepey III and William Tonebregg II, q.v., were appointed to act as his vicars-general in the diocese.[32]

The reduced population of the house in the 1530s was not the result of a recent or a gradual decline, since a substantial decrease in numbers had taken place even before the mid-fourteenth-century epidemic of the Black Death. In 1317 there were thirty-five monks present at Hamo de Hethe's election to the bishopric, and thirty-four at the prioral election in 1333.[33] The chamberlain gave supplies of clothing to twenty-four on his three surviving accounts for the years 1385/6, 1396/7, and 1415/16, thus indicating that losses from the plague had not been made up.[34] Only nineteen were cited to appear at cardinal Morton's visitation in 1496,[35] but none of the sixteenth-century figures are below twenty.

The last years of the monastic community at Rochester remain clouded by uncertainty for us, as they must have been for the monks. Nevertheless, there continued to be a sizeable intake that resulted in a total of twenty-two between 1514 and 1527.[36] At the election of prior Laurence Mereworth, q.v., in 1532, twenty-three monks cast their votes, eleven of whom had entered within the previous ten years. All of the eleven, together with the prior and eight senior monks, appended their names to the Act of Supremacy two years later;[37] but, the following year, a few months after the execution of their bishop, John Fisher, five of the younger monks and one of the older ones obtained dispensations to become secular priests and left the monastery.[38]

30 CKS DRc/L7 and *Reg. Hethe*, 604 relate to the first agreement and *Reg. Roff.*, 568, 571 (Reg. Langdon, fo 45^{v}) to the second; see, for example, John Clyve II. Dr M. Franklin has discussed these points in 'The Cathedral as Parish Church: The case of southern England' in D. Abulafia, M. Franklin, M. Rubin, eds, *Church and City 1000–1500: Essays in honour of Christopher Brooke* (Cambridge, 1992), 178–182.

31 The obedientiary accounts are listed in the References, Section B.i (*a*).

32 See John de Shepey III and also John de Hertlepe II, who was put in charge of the sea defences at Gravesend.

33 *Reg. Hethe*, 533–534.

34 CKS DRc/F13, 14, 15. It is to be noted that all of these statistics probably apply only to the cathedral priory and do not include the cell.

35 *Reg. abp Morton*, ii, no 446.

36 Seven or eight were professed together in 1514, 1522, and 1527; see Walter Boxley, John Chechestre, and William Canturbury. Owen Oxford, q.v., was clothed as late as 1537.

37 There was actually one monk, Richard Chatham, q.v., who failed to be included in 1534 but was still in the priory in 1540.

38 These details are, of course, in the appropriate entries and all derive from Chambers, *Faculty Office Regs*, 35, 36, 37. Some monks at Norwich who obtained similar dispensations did not leave until the priory was dissolved.

Mereworth's resignation as prior in July 1538 was probably the result of governmental pressure, for the bishop, John Hilsey, wrote to Cromwell to urge him to order his reinstatement. In the letter he reported that the internal state of the priory had deteriorated since the departure of his 'poor monk'.[39] It is uncertain when or how Mereworth's successor, Walter Boxley, q.v., came to office, but there is no doubt that he was in favour of, and with, the royal authority since he became the first dean of the new foundation.[40]

A summing up, by way of conclusion, should not fail to draw attention to the continuing attraction of Benedictine life in Rochester cathedral priory until at least the late 1520s. However, increasing unease must have followed upon the passage of the Act of Supremacy, the execution of Fisher, and the resignation of prior Mereworth; the latter departed or died before the final surrender and the same manner of exit applies to about three or four others, for there were only thirteen names on the pension list.[41] Like the monks, the library volumes were also put out of their home by the king, who seized a large number of them for himself. In this way, however, unlike the monks, they were able to remain together and have been preserved as part of the Royal Collection in the British Library.

ROCHESTER REFERENCES WITH ABBREVIATIONS

Note: if the particular reference sought does not appear below, turn to the General Bibliography on pp. xv–xix, or the Canterbury section, pp. 58–65.

A. Manuscript Sources

Note: The episcopal registers and other episcopal archives (DRb) are currently deposited in Maidstone, while the dean and chapter records are at the Rochester upon Medway Studies Centre, Strood (DRc); the prefix CKS applies to both.

i Episcopal Registers

(*a*) The Centre for Kentish Studies (CKS)

Reg. [Hamo de] Hethe (1319–1352)	DRb Ar1/1
Reg. [John] Shepey (1353–1360)	DRb Ar1/2
Reg. [William] Wittlesey (1362–1364)	DRb Ar1/3
Reg. [Thomas] Trillek (1364–1372)	DRb Ar1/4
Reg. William Bottlesham (1389–1400)	DRb Ar1/5
Reg. John Bottlesham (1400–1404)	DRb Ar1/6
Reg. [Richard] Young (1404–1418)	DRb Ar1/7
Reg. [John] Langdon (1422–1434)	DRb Ar1/8
Reg. [Thomas] Brouns (1435–1436)	DRb Ar1/9
Reg. [William] Wells (1437–1444)	DRb Ar1/10
Reg. [John] Lowe (1444–1467)	DRb Ar1/11
Reg. [Thomas] Savage (1493–1496)	DRb Ar1/12
Reg. [Richard] Fitzjames (1497–1503)	DRb Ar1/13; fos 18–36, 39
Reg. [John] Fisher (1504–1535)	DRb Ar1/13; fos 40–182
Reg. [John] Hilsey (1535–1539)	DRb Ar1/14

[39] *L and P Henry VIII*, xiii, pt 1, no 1391. Hilsey was a Dominican friar.

[40] None of the monks became prebendaries.

[41] *L and P Henry VIII*, xv, 196–197. Owen Oxford, q.v., the young novice, appears here.

(*b*) London, Guildhall Library (GL)

Reg. [Simon] Sudbury (1362–1375)	Ms 9531/2
Reg. [Robert] Braybroke (1382–1404)	Ms 9531/3
Reg. [Richard] Clifford (1407–1421)	Ms 9531/4
Reg. [Robert] Gilbert (1436–1448)	Ms 9531/6
Reg. [John] Stokesley (1530–1539)	Ms 9531/11

ii Priory Registers, Cartularies and Custumals

BL Ms Cotton Domitian A.x	Cartulary, early 13th c., fos 90–208.
BL Ms Cotton Vespasian A.xxii	Miscellaneous register, with rentals, custumals, etc., 13th c., fos 60–129; see Benedict II.
Cust. Roff.	Custumal, 14th c., CKS DRc/R2. See also Section C.ii below.
Reg. Temp.	Liber temporalium, register and a miscellaneous collection of documents, CKS DRb/Ar2.
Reg. prior Shepey	Register of *acta*, 1379–1417, of prior John Shepey II, BL Ms Cotton Faustina C.v.
Reg. Wode/Bourne	Fragment of a register, mainly *temp.* priors William Wode and Thomas Bourne, c. 1478–1504; often referred to as 'Primum Registrum' because it is bound in with the first register of the dean and chapter, 20 fos only, CKS DRc/Elb 1A.
Text. Roff.	Textus Roffensis, early 12th c., cartulary with additions of other material, CKS DRc/R1; see both Hearne and Sawyer under *Text. Roff.*, Section C.ii below.

B. Other Manuscript Sources

i Accounts

(*a*) Obedientiary Accounts, Centre for Kentish Studies (CKS)

Almoner	1430/1	DRc/F11
Cellarer	1383/4	DRc/F12
Chamberlain	1385/6, 1396/7, 1415/16	DRc/F13–15
Composite Account	1511/12	DRc/F17
Infirmarer	1424/5	DRc/F16
Sacrist	1511/12	DRc/M7

Note: one acct of the cell of Felixstowe for 1497/8 is in Dugdale, *Monasticon*, iv, 563–565.

(*b*) Manorial Accounts and Court Rolls, Centre for Kentish Studies (CKS)

Note: there are only a few of these; they are listed with the obedientiary accounts under DRc/F-.

ii Chronicles

BL Ms Cotton Faustina B.v	Historia Roffensis, chronicle attributed to William Dene, c. 1315–c. 1350; printed in *Anglia Sacra*, i, 356–377.
BL Ms Cotton Nero D.ii	Chronicle attributed to Edmund de Hadenham, q.v., up to 1307; printed in *Anglia Sacra*, i, 341–355. See also *Flores Hist.* in Section D below.

iii Charters and Loose Deeds and Fragments

(*a*) Centre for Kentish Studies (CKS)

Note: these have been listed as DRc/L (legal instruments) and DRc/T (title deeds); there is also a 12th-c. book list, DRc/Z18/1–2.

(*b*) Oxford, Bodleian Library (Oxford, Bod.)

Note: these include a number of charters relating to Kent and Suffolk estates and to the cell at Felixstowe (Walton St Felix); they have been calendared in Turner and Coxe, *Charters and Rolls* (see General References).

iv Unpublished Theses

Mifsud, 'John Shepey' — G. Mifsud, 'John Sheppey, Bishop of Rochester as Preacher and Collector of Sermons', Oxford, B. Litt., 1953.

Waller, 'Library' — K. Waller, 'The Library, Scriptorium and Community of Rochester Cathedral Priory c. 1080–c. 1150', Liverpool, Ph.D., 1981.

C. Printed Sources

i Episcopal Registers

(*a*) Rochester

Reg. Hethe — C. Johnson, ed., *Registrum Hamonis Hethe, Diocesis Roffensis, AD 1319–1352*, 2 vols, Canterbury and York Society 48, 49, 1948; continuous pagination; vol ii begins on p. 593.

(*b*) London

Reg. Sudbury — R. C. Fowler and C. Jenkins, eds, *Registrum Simonis de Sudbiria, diocesis Londoniensis, A.D. 1362–1375*, 2 vols, Canterbury and York Society 34, 38, 1927, 1938.

ii Priory Registers and Cartularies and Custumals

Cust. Roff. — J. Thorpe, ed., *Custumale Roffense*, 1788; this contains, on pp. 1–37, a transcript of the Custumale in Section A.ii above.

Reg. Roff. — J. Thorpe, ed., *Registrum Roffense*, London, 1769, a collection of records and documents.

Text. Roff. — T. Hearne, ed., *Textus Roffensis*, Oxford, 1720; this was transcribed, not directly from the Textus but, from BL Ms Harley 6523. References are indicated by 'cap' or 'caps' (*capitulus, capituli*).

Text. Roff., i and ii — P. Sawyer, ed., *Textus Roffensis, Early English Manuscripts in Facsimile*, 2 vols, Copenhagen, vii (i) 1957, xi (ii) 1962.

D. Other Printed Sources and References

Arch. Cant., iii — W. Rye, 'Catalogue of the Library of the Priory of St. Andrew, Rochester, A.D. 1202', *Archaeologia Cantiana*, iii (1860), 47–64.

Arch. Cant., vi — R. Coates, 'Catalogue of the Library of the Priory of St. Andrew, Rochester, from the Textus Roffensis', *Archaeologia Cantiana*, vi (1864/5), 120–128.

D. Bethell, 'The Miracles of St Ithamar', *Analecta Bolandiana*, 89 (1971), 421–437.

Brett, 'Forgery at Rochester' — M. Brett, 'Forgery at Rochester', *Falschungen im Mittelalter Monumenta Germaniae Historica Schriften*, 33 (1988), iv, 397–412.

Brown, 'Financial System of Rochester' — A. Brown, 'The Financial System of Rochester Cathedral Priory: A Reconsideration', *Bulletin of the Institute of Historical Research*, 50 (1977), 115–120.

Eng. Epis. Acta, Rochester, 1075–1235 — M. Blount, and M. Brett, eds, *English Episcopal Acta*, Rochester, 1075–1235, British Academy, Oxford, forthcoming.

Flores Hist. — H. R. Luard, ed., *Flores Historiarum*, Rolls Series, 3 vols, 1890.

Hope, *Arch. Hist. Rochester*	W. St. John Hope, *The Architectural History of the Cathedral Church and Monastery of St. Andrew at Rochester*, London, 1900.
Richards, 'Texts'	M. P. Richards, 'Texts and their Traditions in the Medieval Library of Rochester Cathedral Priory', *Transactions of the American Philosophical Society*, lxxviii/3 (1988).
Thomson, *Gundulf*,	R. Thomson, ed., *The Life of Gundulf Bishop of Rochester*, Toronto Medieval Latin Texts, 1977.
Vita Malchi	L. R. Lind, 'The Vita Sancti Malchi of Reginald of Canterbury', *Illinois Studies in Language and Literature*, xxvii, no 3 (1942).
Yates, *Rochester Cathedral*	W. N. Yates, ed., *A History of Rochester Cathedral*, forthcoming.

Note: Some of the printed sources and references under Canterbury, Section D, are also relevant for Rochester.

ROCHESTER CATHEDRAL PRIORY
1083–1540

I A.
occ ?late 12th c.

n.d., prior; see (1) Alfred, (2) Alexander de Glanville.

Name in two Mss:
(1) BL Royal Ms 3 B.i, Isidorus etc. (12th c.); this vol. appears in the library catalogue of 1122/3 in *Text. Roff.*, ii, fos 224–230, and in that of 1202 in BL Ms Royal 5 B.xii, fo 2; these are printed in Sharpe, *Eng. Benedictine Libraries*, iv, where the refs are B77.52 and B79.93.
(2) BL Royal Ms 5 E.x, Prosper, Vita contemplativa etc. (12th c.); this vol. appears in the library catalogue of 1122/3 in *Text. Roff.*, ii, fos 224–230, and in that of 1202 in BL Ms Royal 5 B.xii, fo 2; these are printed in Sharpe, *Eng. Benedictine Libraries*, iv, where the refs are B77.23 and B79.80.

Note: The date ascribed to these Mss suggests that prior Alfred was prob. responsible for their acquisition.

II A.
occ. ?early 13th c.

n.d., precentor, BL Ms Royal 10 C.iv, fo 1.

Name in BL Ms Royal 10 C.iv, Omnibonus (early 13th c.); the volume was acquired through him, *per*—on fo 1. See Alexander, precentor; this vol. appears in the 1202 library catalogue in BL Ms Royal 5 B.xii, fo 2, printed in Sharpe, *Eng. Benedictine Libraries*, iv, B79.236.

John ABBAS
occ. 1454 occ. 1462

1454, 20 Dec., ord acol. and subdcn, Rochester, Reg. Lowe, fo 27v.
1455, 20 Sept., ord dcn, bp's chapel, Halling, *ib.*, fo 28v.
1462, 18 Dec., ord pr., bp's chapel, Halling, *ib.*, fo 38.

Thomas ABBOT
see London

I ADAM
occ. [1148 × 1182]

[1148 × 1182], *temp.* bp Walter, witness to two episcopal instruments, *Reg. Roff.*, 169, 666. He is not identified as a monk of Rochester but heads the witness list of the episcopal confirmation and may have been in the bp's household. See Robert VI.

Note: The date of the episcopal confirmation in *Reg. Roff*, 169 can be narrowed down by the presence of Gilbert Foliot, bp of London, i.e., not earlier than 1167.

II ADAM
occ. c. 1250 occ. 1254

c. 1250, almoner, CKS DRc/T215; see also Thomas de Mepeham.
1254, 9 Apr., sacrist, *Reg. Roff.*, 99.
1254, 9 Apr., with Samson, q.v., came to Canterbury to present the bp's protests vs the abp's holding back of certain payments due to them, *Reg. Roff.*, 99–100.

III ADAM
see Cobeham

Laurence de ADYNGTON
occ. 1354 occ. 1361

1354, 20 Dec., ord subdcn, Malling abbey, Reg. Shepey, fo 7.
1355, 22 Dec., ord dcn, Rochester cathedral, *ib.*, fo 12.
1361, 20 Feb., ord pr., Strood, *ib.*, fo 32.

AELDING
see Ealding

Adam de AELHAM [?Selham
occ. c. 1303

[c. 1303], one of four monks who were assigned *ad tricennale celebrandum* for John Pantoum, q.v., BL Ms Cotton Vespasian A.xxii, fo 127.

AETHELNOTH, son of
n.d.

n.d. was made a monk, when his father, a *probus homo regis* of Hoo gave a marsh, *Text Roff.*, ii, fo 182v, and cap 102.

Ralph de AILESBURI [Ailesberi, Eylesburi
occ. ?late 13th c.

Name in
(1) Edinburgh, Ms N.L., Adv. 18.5.18. Boethius, etc., (13th c.).
(2) BL Ms Royal 2 F.iv, Evangelia glossata (late 13th c.); on fo 3, *Liber de claustro Roffensi*—.

ALAN
occ. 1217 occ. 1223

1217, 31 Mar., 1223, occ. as prior of Felixstowe [Walton St Felix], *Reg. Roff.*, 381, CKS DRc/BZ1.

1217, 31 Mar., as prior of Felixstowe, witness to an episcopal instrument at Felixstowe, *Reg. Roff.*, 381.

Richard ALBERTSON
see Chatham

William ALBON
occ. 1517 occ. 1540

1517, 11 Apr., ord subdcn, bp's palace chapel, Rochester, Reg. Fisher, fo 59^{v}.

1526, 20 Jan., apptd chamberlain, Reg. Fisher, fo 116.

1534, 10 June, subscribed to the Act of Supremacy, *DK 7th Report*, Appndx 2, 299.

1540, 8 Apr., assigned a pension of £10 p.a., *L and P Henry VIII*, xv, no 474.

Note: see also William St Albans who is the same monk.

ALDYNG
see Ealding

I ALEXANDER
n.d.

n.d., son of Elias [I], q.v., grandson of Kenstanus, entered with his father and brother Stephen, q.v.; they gave land outside Eastgate and were numbered among the benefactors, *Reg. Roff.*, 119.

II ALEXANDER
occ. before 1202

1202, described as *quondam cantor*, *Arch. Cant.*, iii, 60 (BL Ms Royal 5 B.xii, fo 3).

1202, compiled a library catalogue which is in BL Ms Royal 5 B.xii, Augustinus (12th c.) on fo 2 and printed in Sharpe, *Eng. Benedictine Libraries*, iv, B80.

Name also in BL Ms Royal 10 A.xii, Collectanea theologice (early 13th c.); on fo 111^{v} 'Hos libros vel scripsit vel acquisivit Alexander' followed by a list which includes biblical texts, sermons, works of Seneca, Plato, Boethius, Gratian, Aelred and others. It has recently been suggested that he prob. himself gave two volumes of sermons and the letters of Sidonius Apollinaris included in this list, which also notes that *scripsit tertiam partem novi bibli* stored in one of the book cupboards; see Richards, 'Texts', 17, 18 and the list itself in Sharpe, *Eng. Benedictine Libraries*, iv, B79, where his medical books are listed at 216–235. See also *ib.*, B79.85, 115.

III ALEXANDER, prior
see Glanville

IV ALEXANDER
occ. 1235

1235, 18 Aug., with Robert VII, q.v., sent by the prior and chapter to the curia to appeal vs the abp's refusal to confirm the bp el., *CPL*, i (1198–1304), 148; see also Reg. Temp., fo 114.

V ALEXANDER
occ. 1296 occ. c. 1298

1296, one of four monks who were assigned *ad tricennale celebrandum* for Osbern de Stoke, q.v., BL Ms Cotton Vespasian A.xxii, fo 126^{v}.

[c. 1298], one of four assigned to celebrate as above for John de Maydestane and Robert de Leuesham, q.v., *ib.*

ALFRED [Alured
occ. c. 1182/6

c. 1182–1186, prior: prob. succ. Richard II, q.v.; became abbot of Abingdon 1186, *Fasti*, ii, 79, *HRH*, 25, 64.

n.d., listed among the benefactors: gave a *capam optimam* and had a window constructed in the dormitory *ultra lectum prioris*, *Reg. Roff.*, 121.

Note: see Aufredus who may be the same monk.

ALKEWINUS
occ. ?12th c.

Name in Cambridge, Corpus Christi College Ms 62, fo 209. Beda (early 12th c.). This vol. appears in the early 12th c. fragment of a library catalogue in CKS DRc/Z18/1–2 and the catalogue of 1202 in BL Ms Royal 5 B.xii, fo 2; these are printed in Sharpe, *Eng. Benedictine Libraries*, iv, where the refs are B78.31 and B79.148.

ANCELLIN
see Auncell

ANDREAS
occ. ?12th c.

Name in

(1) BL Ms Royal 6 B.vi, Ambrosius, etc. (12th c.), on fo 2 Liber de claustro Roffense *per—monachum*. This vol. appears in the library catalogue of 1122/3 in *Text. Roff.*, ii, fos 224–230, and in that of 1202 in BL Ms Royal 5 B.xii, fo 2; these are printed in Sharpe, *Eng. Benedictine Libraries*, iv, where the refs are B77.44 and B79.30.

(2) a book borrowed by the bp and the rector of Southfleet on 1 June 1390: 'Item, exposicionem beati Jero'. . . cum ali[is] in uno volumine Andree monachi', Reg. prior Shepey, fo 50^{v}. This may ref. to a later Andrew.

ANFRIDUS
see Aufredus

ANSELM
see Betlescumbe

ANSGOTUS [de Roucestria
occ. 1083 × 1108

n.d., *temp.* bp Gundulf, gave all his tithes from Deltsa [Delce] and elsewhere and also land within and outside the monastic enclosure. In return 'iuxta peticionem suam [monachi] dederunt ei pannos monachicos in articulo mortis suae, et fecerunt servitium pro eo sicuti pro monacho', *Text. Roff.*, ii, fo 197v and cap 180.

Nicholas ARNOLD
see Speldhurst

I ARNULFUS
occ. 1107 × 1108

1107 × 1108, chaplain to bp Gundulf, *temp.* Ordwinus, prior, q.v., *Text. Roff.*, ii, fo 198, and cap 181.

II ARNULFUS
see Ernulph

William ASCHEFORDE
occ. 1522

1522, 19 Jan., one of seven who made their solemn prof. before the bp, Reg. Fisher, fo 91.

ASKETILLUS [Ansketill
occ. ?late 11th/early 12th cs.

n.d., listed among the benefactors: gave a chasuble kept in the prior's chapel, and other vestments, *Reg. Roff.*, 124.

[1095 × 1107], one of the monks greeted by Reginald, monk of St Augustine's, Canterbury, in his preface to his *Vita Malchi* by the phrase *de quo gaudent angeli*, 38; and see also *ib.*, 12 and 11 for the prob. dating which has been followed here.

Name in three BL Royal Mss:

(1) 5 A.vii, Paschasius Radbertus, etc. (12th c.); this vol. appears in the library catalogue of 1122/3 in *Text. Roff.*, ii, fos 224–230, and in that of 1202 in BL Ms Royal 5 B.xii, fo 2; these are printed in Sharpe, *Eng. Benedictine Libraries*, iv, where the refs are B77.39 and B79.83.

(2) 5 B.vii, Augustinus etc. (12th c.), *per*—; this vol. appears in three library catalogues; that of 1122/3 in *Text Roff.*, ii, fos 224–230, the fragments in CKS DRc/Z18/1–2 of similar date, and that of 1202 in BL Ms Royal 5 B.xii, fo 2; these are printed in Sharpe, *Eng. Benedictine Libraries*, iv, where the refs are B77.8, B78.6 and B79.15 respectively.

(3) 6 A.xii, J. Chrysostomus, etc. (12th c.); this vol. appears in the library catalogue of 1122/3 in *Text. Roff.*, ii, fos 224–230, and in that of 1202 in BL Ms Royal 5 B.xii, fo 2; these are printed in Sharpe, *Eng. Benedictine Libraries*, iv, where the refs are B77.59 and B79.76.

AUFREDUS [Anfridus
occ. [1174 × 1181]

[1174, Aug., × 1181, Sept.], prior of Felixstowe, *Eng. Epis Acta*, ii, no 190, *Reg. Roff.*, 410–411; see also BL Ms Cotton Domitian A.x, fo 184. He was prior on 15 May 1177; see note 2) below.

[1174, Aug., × 1181, Sept.], with Osbert the chamberlain, q.v., involved in a dispute over tithes, *Eng. Epis Acta*, ii, no 190.

1177, 15 May, prior, named with Osbert, q.v., as convent proctors during a legal process, prob. the above dispute, CKS DRc/L17; see note (2) below.

Note:

(1) he may later have been prior of Rochester and abbot of Abingdon, *ib.*

(2) the charter in which he is named as prior of Felixstowe on 15 May 1177 (*Reg. Roff.*, 410–411) is spurious; see *Eng. Epis. Acta*, ii, no 194, note.

(3) see Alfred who may be this monk.

John AUNCELL [Ancellin, Awncell
occ. [1465] occ. 1517

[1465], 30 Mar., recd tonsure and ord acol., bp's chapel, Halling, Reg. Lowe, fo 43v.

1465, 21 Dec., ord subdcn, bp's chapel, Halling, *ib.*, fo 45v.

1466, 20 Dec., ord dcn, bp's chapel, Halling, *ib.*, fo 47v.

1494, 18 May, apptd subprior, succeeding John Novyn, q.v., Reg. Savage, fo 7v.

1496, 4 Nov., subprior, *Reg. abp Morton*, ii, no 446.

1509, 11 Sept., as president of the chapter, presumably subprior; see below.

1511/12 subprior, CKS DRc/F17.

[1517], 17 Dec., removed from the office of subprior, Reg. Fisher, fo 59v; see Anthony London.

1494, 14 Apr., presided at the el. of a prior, Reg. Savage, fo 7.

1496, 4 Nov., 2nd in order on the visitation certificate, *Reg. abp Morton*, ii, no 446.

1509, 11 Sept., as president of the chapter involved in a controversy with the bp over the method of el. of a prior and both parties appealed to the abp, Reg. abp Warham, ii, fo 337 and *Reg. Roff.*, 139–140; see William Fresell.

1511/12, recd 5s. from the treasurer for celebrating the mass of St Laurence, CKS DRc/F17.

William AUNCELLE [Ancellin, Awncell, Awnsell
occ. 1461 d. 1501

1461, 19 Sept., ord subdcn, bp's chapel, Halling, Reg. Lowe, fo 35v.

1462, 3 Apr., ord dcn, place not named, *ib.*, fo 36v.
[1465], 30 Mar., ord pr., bp's chapel, Halling, *ib.*, fo 43v.
1496, 4 Nov., also before 1501, 12 Feb., precentor, *Reg. abp Morton*, ii, no 446, Reg. Fitzjames, fo 9.
1480, 14 June, present in chapter when William Leicestre, q.v., was released from his obedience in order to transfer, Reg. Wode/Bourne, fo 6, *Reg. Roff.*, 139.
1496, 4 Nov., 3rd in order on the visitation certificate, *Reg. abp Morton*, ii, no 446.
1501, c. 12 Feb., d., Reg. Fitzjames, fo 9.

B.
occ. ?12th c.

n.d., chamberlain, BL Cotton Ms Royal 12 C.i, fo 3.

Name in the above Ms, Miscellanea theologica (12th c.), which occ. in the library catalogue of 1122/3 in *Text. Roff.*, ii, fo 229v, and in that of 1202 in BL Ms Royal 5 B.xii, fo 2; these are printed in Sharpe, *Eng. Benedictine Libraries*, iv, where the refs are B77.80 and B79.99.

John BAGG
occ. 1505

1505, 8 Mar., ord dcn, chapel of St Blaise, bp's manor, Bromley, Reg. Fisher, fo 24.

William BAKER
see Qwenburgh

BALDELAWE
see Bledlawe

I BALDWIN [Baldeuuinus
occ. [1093 × 1108]

[1093 × 1108] *temp.* abp Anselm, with Guido, q.v., attested a grant to bp Gundulf and the monks, *Text. Roff.*, ii, fo 185v and cap 121.

A Baldwin, monk, had a brother Adeloldus of Chelsfield, a minor tenant of the priory who gave tithes and other gifts at his d., *Text. Roff.*, ii, fos 184v, 185v, 196, and caps 114, 118, 121, 176.

II BALDWIN
occ. [1095 × 1107]

[1095 × 1107], described as *primicerius* [?prior] and greeted by Reginald, monk of St Augustine's, Canterbury, in his preface to his life of Malchus, a copy of which he sent to Baldwin, *Vita Malchi*, 37; and see *ib.*, 12, and 11 for the prob. dating which has been followed here.

Note:
(1) the two Baldwins may be identical.
(2) the obit of a Baldwin occ. on 22 Oct. in BL Ms Arundel 68, fo 46.

Richard BAMBURGH
occ. 1459

1459, 18 Oct., apptd chamberlain, Reg. Lowe, fo 32v.

Nicholas de BECHESHANGRE
occ. [c. 1306]

[c. 1306], one of four monks who were assigned *ad tricennale celebrandum* for Elias [IV], q.v., BL Ms Cotton Vespasian A.xxii, fo 127.

Note: see also Nicholas III who is prob. the same monk.

I BENEDICT [Benedictus
n.d.

n.d., listed as a benefactor of the priory who gave land at the time of his entry, *Reg. Roff.*, 118.

II BENEDICT [Benedictus
occ. ?early 13th c.

Name in BL Ms Cotton Vespasian A.xxii, miscellaneous register, chronica, etc. (early 13th c.); it was prob. acquired by [*per*] him.

Note: These two entries may refer to the same monk.

John BENET
occ. 1505

1505, 8 Mar., ord dcn, chapel of St Blaise, bp's manor, Bromley, Reg. Fisher, fo 24.

Thomas BENEYT
occ. 1322 occ. 1333

1322, 27 Mar., ord subdcn, bp's chapel, Trottiscliffe, Reg. Hethe, fo 55v (p. 110).
1323, 24 Sept., ord pr., Rochester cathedral, *ib.*, fo 61 (p. 1060).
1333, 19 Aug., 15th in order at the el. of a prior and voted for John de Shepey II, q.v., Reg. Hethe fo 157 (p. 534).

Anselm de BETLESCUMBE
n.d.

n.d., listed among the benefactors as having given a 3s. rent, *Reg. Roff.*, 124.

John de BEVERLE
occ. 1294 d. [c. 1301]

1294, one of four monks who were assigned *ad tricennale celebrandum* for prior John de Reynham, q.v., Bl Ms Cotton Vespasian A.xxii, fo 126v.
1297, one of four monks who were assigned to celebrate as above on behalf of Ralph de Estone, q.v., *ib.*
[c. 1301], d., and four of the brethren were assigned to celebrate for him, *ib.*

James de BEYERSSE
d. [c. 1302]

[c. 1302], d., and four monks were assigned *ad tricennale celebrandum* for him, BL Ms Cotton Vespasian A.xxii, fo 126v.

Note: the name is close to Reyersh and its variants but the initial letter cannot be read as an 'R'.

Note: see also James who is prob. the same monk.

Nicholas BIGTON [Bygton of Ossory, Ireland
occ. 1461/2

1461, 19 Sept., ord subdcn, no place stated, Reg. Lowe, fo 36v.
1462, 18 Dec., ord dcn, bp's chapel, Halling, *ib.*, fo 38.

William BISSHOPE B.Cn.L [Bischopp, Bysshope, *alias* Leynham
occ. 1480 occ. 1509

1494–1509, prior: el. 14 Apr. 1494, Reg. Savage, fo 7; res. by 30 July 1509, Reg. Fisher, fo 36.
1494, before, student at university, see below.
1480, 14 June, present in chapter when William de Leicestre, q.v., was released from his obedience in order to transfer, Reg. Wode/Bourne, fo 6, *Reg. Roff.*, 139.
1494, 14 Apr., named as prior by the bp, *via scrutinii*, and described here as B.Cn.L, Reg. Savage, fo 7.
1496, 23 Mar., gave a bond to the bp for £100 to be pd by Easter, *ib.*, fo 15.
1496, 21 Nov., present at the metropolitan visitation, *Reg. abp Morton*, ii, no 446.
1502, 5 Nov., granted papal dispensation to receive and hold *in commendam* with the priorship a benefice with or without cure of souls, *CPL*, xvii (1495–1503), pt 1, no 882.

His brother, John, d. in 1497 and was buried in the cathedral before the image of our Lady of grace, Hope, *Arch. Hist. Rochester*, 95, quoting a will.

Richard de BLEDLAWE [Baldelawe, Bledelowe, Bledlowe, Bledewale
occ. 1314 occ. 1333

1314, 21 Dec., ord acol., Lambeth palace chapel, Reg. abp Reynolds, fo 13.
1315, 17 May, ord subdcn, Croydon by *lit dim*, *ib.*, fo 170v.
1315, 20 Dec., ord dcn, Maidstone, by *lit dim*, *ib.*, fo 173v.
1317, 28 May, ord pr., Lambeth palace chapel, *ib.*, fo 177v.
1333, 19 Aug., cellarer, Reg. Hethe, fo 157 (p. 534).
1333, 19 Aug., one of the five monks who nom. William de Reyersh, q.v., for the office of prior, *ib.*

John de BORDEN [Bordene, Bordenne, Bordon
occ. 1335 occ. 1359

1335, 23 Sept., ord subdcn, Malling, Reg. Hethe, fo 165 (p. 1065).
1336, 25 May, ord dcn, bp's chapel, Halling, *ib.*, fo 166 (p. 1065).
1337, 15 Mar., ord pr., bp's chapel, Halling, *ib.*, fo 169v (p. 1065).
1344, 2 Mar., 10 Oct., 30 Oct.; 1345, 4 Mar., 10 Dec.; 1346, 13 Feb., 30 Apr.; 1347, 16 Jan., 21 Sept., 23 Nov.; 1349, 14 Mar., 5 Apr., 15 Sept., 11 Oct., present in the bp's household [as chaplain], *Reg. Hethe*, pp. 725, 733, 735; 746, 762; 766, 781 and 783; 797, 833, 837; 858, 860, 889, 896.
1346, 30 Apr., witness to gifts including books made by the bp to the monks, *Reg. Roff.*, 128, and Reg. Hethe, fo 223 (pp. 781–783).
1348, 14 Mar., present with the bp at Trottiscliffe at the institution of the vicar of St Nicholas' parish in Rochester cathedral, Reg. Hethe, fo 257.
1349, 23 July, present at the el. of the abbess of Malling and assigned to read the prayers at the high altar there, *Reg. Hethe*, p. 893.
1349, 15 Sept., witnessed the oath of obedience of a canon of Leeds as incumbent of a parish, Reg. Hethe, fo 267 (p. 889).
1352, 9 June, granted papal dispensation to choose his own confessor who was empowered to give plenary remission at the hour of d., *CPL*, iii (1342–1362), 474.
1359, 15 Nov., recd a bequest of 20s. from the rector of Rotherfield, Reg. Shepey, fo 25; see also John de Ledes II.

William de BORSTALL [Borstalle
occ. c. 1160 × 1180

c. 1160 × 1180, prior: after prior Reginald and before prior Silvester, q.v., *Fasti*, ii, 79, *HRH*, 64.

n.d., cellarer, before being apptd prior, *Reg. Roff.*, 121.

n.d., listed among the benefactors as he bought vestments for the monastery, *ib.*

Note: see also William VIII.

John BOSTON
occ. 1512 occ. 1516

1512, 10 Apr., ord acol., bp's palace chapel, Rochester, Reg. Fisher, fo 42.
1516, 22 Mar., ord dcn, Rochester cathedral, *ib.*, fo 56v.

Thomas BOURNE [Bourn
occ. 1459 occ. 1494

c. 1480–1494, prior: first ref. as prior, 14 June 1480, *Reg. Roff.*, 138; res. by 14 Apr. 1494, *Fasti*, iv, 40.

1459, 24 Mar., ord acol., Rochester cathedral, Reg. Lowe, fo 32.
1460, 12 Apr., ord subdcn, Rochester cathedral, *ib.*, fo 33.
1461, 19 Sept., ord dcn, bp's chapel, Halling *ib.*, fo 35ᵛ.
1462, 3 Apr., ord pr., place unnamed, *ib.*, fo 36ᵛ.
1492, 22 June, conducted a visitation of Westminster abbey for the Black Monk Chapter, Pantin, *BMC*, iii, 244.

A few of his *acta* as prior are to be found in Reg. Wode/Bourne, e.g. the release of William de Leicestre, q.v., from his obedience.

Walter BOXLEY [*alias* Philip, Phylypp
occ. 1514 occ. 1540

1538–1540, prior: occ. as prior 1538, CKS DRc/T164; see below.
1514, 26 Nov., one of seven who made their prof. before the bp, Reg. Fisher, fo 55.
1522, 20 Dec., ord dcn, bp's palace chapel, Rochester, *ib.*, fo 92.
1535, cellarer, *Valor Eccles.*, i, 102.
1532, 21 Oct., 11th at the el. of a prior, Reg. Fisher, fo 156.
1534, 10 June, subscribed to the Act of Supremacy, *DK 7th Report*, Appndx 2, 299.
1540, 8 Apr., designated to be dean of the new foundation, *L and P Henry VIII*, xv, no 474; the date of his apptment was 18 June 1541, *Fasti, 1541–1857*, iii, 54.

Name in Cambridge, Corpus Christi College Ms 62, Vita S. Bernardi etc., (12th c.); on a leaf stuck in behind fo 212, *Universi pubi Roffensis ludi literarii*—. See also Alkewinus, Paulinus I.

William de BRADEBOURNE
occ. 1315/16 occ. 1333

1333, 19 Aug., refectorer, Reg. Hethe, fo 157 (pp. 533–534).
1315/16, pd a visit to Wouldham for *liberatio denariorum*, WCM C.834.
1333, 19 Aug., 6th in order at the el. of a prior and voted for John de Shepey, q.v., Reg. Hethe, fo 157 (pp. 533–534).

John de BRADEFELD
occ. 1278

1278, before, precentor, *Fasti*, ii, 77.
1278, el. bp; chosen by his fellow monks because of his humility and peaceable nature, and they believed that he would follow in the footsteps of bp Gundulf; *sed mutatus in virum alium, Flores Hist.*, iii, 50–51 (*Anglia Sacra*, i, 352). Acc. to *Flores Hist.*, *ib.*, he had been educated in the monastery school.

Richard BRADFELDE [*alias* Revell
occ. 1529 occ. 1532

1529, 1 Aug., made his prof. before the bp, Reg. Fisher, fo 134.
1532, 21 Oct., 23rd and last in order at the el. of a prior, Reg. Fisher, fo 156.

Note: see Richard Revell who is prob. the same monk.

Henry BRIDD
see Southflete

BRIEN [Brienus
occ. 1142 × 1148

c. 1145–?1148, prior: occ. 1 Sept. 1145 and *temp.* bp Ascelin, i.e., before 24 Jan. 1148, *Fasti*, ii, 79, 77, *HRH*, 64.
[1142 × 1148], *temp.* bp Ascelin witnessed, as prior, an episcopal grant to the monks, *Reg. Roff.*, 10.
1145, 1 Sept., attested abp Theobald's confirmation of bp Gundulf's charter (which is spurious), *Theobald Charters*, no 222; the confirmation is also prob. spurious. See also CKS DRc T57.
n.d., 5 Dec., his obit occ. in BL Ms Arundel 68, fo 50; see other refs in *Fasti*, ii, 79 and *HRH*, 64.

John de BROKHULL [Brokhelle
occ. 1341/3

1341, 2 June, ord acol., bp's chapel, Halling, Reg. Hethe, fo 195 (p. 1069).
1342, 16 Mar., ord subdcn, Trottiscliffe, *ib.*, fo 196ᵛ (p. 1069).
1343, 7 June ord dcn, bp's chapel, Halling, *ib.*, fo 206 (p. 1069).

William de BROMFELD [Brumfeld
occ. c. 1307 occ. 1346

1333, 19 Aug., chamberlain, Reg. Hethe, fo 157 (p. 534).
1336, 17 May, replaced as chamberlain by Richard de Tonnbregg, q.v., *ib.*, fo 166 (p. 559).
1338, 27 Sept., dismissed from the office of subprior and replaced by Henry de Hengseye, q.v., Reg. Hethe, fo 173ᵛ (p. 585).
1338, 27 Sept., succ. Richard de Cantuaria, q.v., as cellarer, *ib.*, fo 173ᵛ (p. 585).
1339, 28 Sept., replaced as cellarer by Ralph de Cantuaria, q.v., *ib.*, fo 175 (p. 590).
1341, 29 Sept., reapppointed chamberlain to succeed Richard de Tonnbregg, *ib.*, fo 195ᵛ (p. 672).
1346, 19 Aug., chamberlain, *ib.*, fo 223ᵛ (p. 790).
[c. 1307], one of four monks who were assigned *ad tricennale celebrandum* for John Pouncz q.v., BL Ms Cotton Vespasian A.xxii, fo 127.

1333, 19 Aug., 12th in order at the el. of a prior and voted for John de Shepey II, q.v., Reg. Hethe, fo 157 (p. 534).

1342, 24 Apr., comm. to induct into his office a sergeant, whom the bp had apptd for the priory, *ib.*, fo 197 (p. 679).

1346, 19 Aug., comm. to induct into his office a tailor for the *sartoria*, *ib.*, fo 223^{v} (p. 790).

Thomas BROUN [Bruyn

occ. 1384 occ. 1412

1400, 11 Oct., the prior was comm. to install him into the office of subprior, Reg. J. Bottlesham, fo 3.

1400 × 1412, subprior, refs in Reg. prior Shepey, e.g., fos 103^{v}, 123^{v}; for 1409 see below.

1384, 16 Oct., 17th in order in chapter for the apptment of a proctor in the curia, Reg. prior Shepey, fo 21.

1400, 11 Oct., comm. as *primarius* in the city and diocese, Reg. J. Bottlesham, fo 3, 3^{v}.

1409, 20 Nov., [prob. as subprior] presided in chapter at the apptment of a proctor in a lawsuit, Reg. prior Shepey, fo 120.

Anthony BROWN

see London

BRUMFELD

see Bromfeld

Richard BRUTIN, brother of

n.d.

n.d., became a monk at the time of his brother's gift of tithes to the priory, *Text. Roff.*, fo 191 and cap 159.

Thomas BRUYN

occ. 1347

1347, 23 May, granted *lit. dim.* for the order of dcn, Reg. Hethe, fo 229^{v} (p. 820).

1347, 26 May, ord subdcn, bp's chapel, Southwark, *Reg. Edington* (Winchester) ii, no 733.

Name in BL Cotton Ms 9 C.iv, T. Aquinas (14th c.); [acquired] *per*—.

BRUYN

see also Broun

John de BURGHAM

occ. 1335 occ. 1341

1335, 23 Sept., ord acol., Malling, Reg. Hethe, fo 165 (p. 1071).

1336, 25 May, ord subdcn, bp's chapel, Halling, *ib.*, fo 166 (p. 1071).

1338, 19 Sept., ord dcn, Wouldham, *ib.*, fo 173^{v} (p. 1071).

1341, 2 June, ord pr., bp's chapel, Halling, *ib.*, fo 195 (p. 1071).

BYGTON

see Bigton

BYSSHOPE

see Bisshope

CAEN

see Ralph I

John CAMBRIDGE [Cambreg

occ. 1512 occ. 1518

1512, 10 Apr., ord acol., bp's palace chapel, Rochester, Reg. Fisher, fo 42.

1516, 22 Mar., ord subdcn, Rochester cathedral, *ib.*, fo 56^{v}.

1518, 28 Feb., ord pr., bp's palace chapel, Rochester, *ib.*, fo 60.

I John de CANTUAR' [Cant

occ. 1296 d. 1297/8

1296, one of four monks who were assigned *ad tricennale celebrandum* for Osbern de Stoke, q.v., BL Ms Cotton Vespasian A.xxii, fo 126^{v}.

1297/8, d., and four monks were assigned *ad tricennale celebrandum* for him, *ib.*

II John de CANTUARIA

occ. 1326 occ. 1335

1326, 8 Mar., ord subdcn, Wouldham, Reg. Hethe, fo 71 (p. 1074).

1328, 2 Apr., ord dcn, Malling, *ib.*, fo 126 (p. 1074).

1333, 19 Aug., 21st in order at the el. of a prior among those who voted for John de Shepey II, q.v., Reg. Hethe, fo 157 (p. 534).

1335, 16 Sept., present in the bp's household as witness [and possibly chaplain], *ib.*, fo 178 (p. 607).

Ralph de CANTUARIA [Canterbirs

occ. 1329 occ. 1351

1329, 8 Apr., ord subdcn, Wouldham, Reg. Hethe, fo 128 (p. 1074).

1330, 22 Sept., ord pr., Aylesford, *ib.*, fo 134 (p. 1074).

1338, 27 Sept., replaced in the office of cellarer by William de Bromfeld, q.v., Reg. Hethe, fo 173^{v} (p. 585).

1333, 19 Aug., 22nd in order at the el. of a prior among those who voted for John de Shepey II, q.v., Reg. Hethe, fo 157 (p. 534).

1351, 18 Aug., one of the monks who, with the prior, Robert de Southflete II, q.v., witnessed a grant, *CClR (1349–1354)*, 379.

Richard de CANTUARIA [Cantuar'

occ. 1347 occ. 1353

1347, 1 July, ord acol., bp's small chapel, Halling, Reg. Hethe, fo 230^{v} (p. 824).

1348, 14 June, ord subdcn, bp's chapel, Halling, *ib.*, fo 237^{v} (p. 1074).

1349, 7 Mar., ord dcn, bp's chapel, Trottiscliffe, *ib.*, fo 242 (p. 1074).
1353, 23 Mar., ord pr., Rochester cathedral, Reg. Shepey, fo 2.

William de CANTUARIA
occ. 1320 occ. 1333
1320, 24 May, ord subdcn, Rochester cathedral, Reg. Hethe, fo 44^{v} (p. 71).
1321, 6 Mar., ord dcn, Rochester cathedral, *ib.*, fo 51 (p. 96).
1323, 24 Sept., ord pr., Rochester cathedral, *ib.*, fo 61 (p. 1075).

1333, 19 Aug., voted for John de Shepey II, q.v., as prior, Reg. Hethe, fo 157 (p. 534).

William CANTURBURY [Canterberi, Caunterbury, *alias* Lamb
occ. 1527 occ. 1540
1527, 22 Dec., one of eight monks who made their prof. before the bp, Reg. Fisher, fo 121^{v}.
1532, 21 Oct., 18th in order at the el. of a prior, Reg. Fisher, fo 156.
1534, 10 June, subscribed to the Act of Supremacy, *DK 7th Report*, Appndx 2, 299.
1540, 8 Apr., assigned a pension of £5 p.a., *L and P Henry VIII*, xv, no 474.

John CARDON
see John Clyve II

John CAUNTURBERY
occ. 1448 occ. 1452
1448, 21 Sept., ord [acol.], Rochester cathedral, Reg. Lowe, fo 16^{v}.
1449, 7 June, ord subdcn, Rochester cathedral, *ib.*, fo 21^{v}.
1452, 3 June, ord pr., bp's chapel, Halling, *ib.*, fo 26; he was presented by Bertram London, q.v.

Richard CAUNTURBERY [Caunterbery
occ. 1450 occ. 1454
1450, 19 Sept., ord acol. Rochester cathedral, Reg. Lowe, fo 21^{v}.
1451, 19 June, ord subdcn, Halling, *ib.*, fo 22.
1452, 3 June, ord dcn, bp's chapel, Halling, *ib.*, fo 23^{v}; he was presented by Bertram London, q.v.
1454, 15 June, ord pr., Halling, *ib.*, fo 26.

William CAUNTYRBERY [Caunterbury
occ. 1423 occ. 1455
1423, 18 Dec., ord acol., Rochester cathedral, *ib.*, fo 26^{v}.
1425, 22 Sept., ord dcn, bp's chapel, Trottiscliffe, *ib.*, fo 48^{v}.

1455, 12 Oct., apptd precentor, Reg. Lowe, fo 28.

John CAUSTON [Cawston
occ. 1440 occ. 1466
1440, 3 Mar., one of two whom the prior was comm. to rec. and clothe as a novice; the bp had examined and approved of them, and ordered that they rec. instruction, [*habitum imponat' et instruat'. . .*], Reg. Wells, fo 33.
1440, 24 Sept., ord subdcn, Rochester cathedral, *ib.*, fo 36.
1443, 22 Sept., ord dcn, Rochester cathedral, *ib.*, fo 70.
1444, 19 Sept., ord pr., Southfleet, Reg. Lowe, fo 2.
1465, 11 Oct., apptd precentor after nomination by the prior and chapter, Reg. Lowe, fo 45^{v}.
1466, 10 Oct., apptd chamberlain and was succ. as precentor by John Sunnyng, q.v., *ib.*, fo 47^{v}.

William [CAYNOK]
see Evynok

Simon de CHALKE
occ. 1345 d. 1361
1345, 21 May, ord dcn, bp's chapel, Trottiscliffe, Reg. Hethe, fo 216, (p. 1076).
1361, before 15 June, sacrist, Reg. abp Islip, fo 225.
1351, 18 Aug., one of the monks who, with the prior, Robert de Southflete II, q.v., witnessed a grant, *CClR (1349–1354)*, 379.
1361, by 15 June, d., Reg. abp Islip, fo 225.

Robert CHAMBERLAYN
see London

William CHARNOCK [Charnell, Charnok
occ. 1514 occ. 1532
1514, 2 Dec., apptd cellarer in place of Laurence Mereworth, q.v., Reg. Fisher, fo 55^{v}.
1518, 12 Nov., released from the cellarer's office and succ. by Laurence Mereworth, q.v., *ib.*, fo 60^{v}.
1511/12, named at the head of a composite obedientiary acct roll as one of four monk auditors in conjunction with one of the king's auditors, CKS DRc/F17.
1532, 21 Oct., 2nd in order at the el. of a prior, Reg. Fisher, fo 156.

Richard CHATHAM [Chetham *alias* Albertson
occ. 1527 occ. 1540
1527, 22 Dec., one of eight who made their prof. before the bp, Reg. Fisher, fo 121^{v}.
1532, 21 Oct., 21st in order at the el. of a prior, Reg. Fisher, fo 156.
1540, 8 Apr., assigned a pension of £5 p.a., *L and P Henry VIII*, xv, no 474.

CHATHAM
see also Chetham

John CHECHESTRE
occ. 1522 occ. 1525
1522, 19 Jan., one of seven whose prof was solemnized by the bp, Reg. Fisher, fo 91.

1522, 20 Dec., ord subdcn, bp's palace chapel, Rochester, *ib.*, fo 92.
1525, 6 June, [dcn], recd *lit. dim.* for priest's orders, *ib.*, fo 112^v.

Roger de CHELESHAM
d. 1295

1295, d., and four monks were assigned *ad tricennale celebrandum* for him, BL Ms Cotton Vespasian A.xxii, fo 126^v.

John CHETHAM
occ. 1415 occ. 1419

1415, 12 June, one of three whose prof. the prior was comm. by the bp to rec., Reg. prior Shepey, fo 116.

1419, 31 Aug., 18th in order at the el. of a prior, *Reg. abp Chichele*, i, 62.

Nicholas de CHETHAM
occ. 1329 occ. 1349

1329, 8 Apr., ord subdcn, Wouldham, Reg. Hethe, fo 128 (p. 1077).
1330, 22 Sept., ord dcn, Aylesford, *ib.*, fo 134 (p. 1077).
1331, 21 Sept., ord pr., Rochester cathedral, *ib.*, fo 145^v (p. 1077).
1349, 15 May, chamberlain, Reg. Hethe, fo 260^v (p. 868).
1333, 19 Aug., present at the el. of a prior and nom. William de Reyersh, q.v., Reg. Hethe, fo 157 (p. 534).
1349, 15 May, comm. to induct a *cissor* into his office [in the *sartoria*], *ib.*, fo 260^v, (p. 868).

CHETHAM
see also Chatham

Richard de CLAUDEVILLA [Clovilla
occ. late 11th/early 12th cs.

n.d., when he entered his father gave tithes, *Text. Roff.*, ii, fo 186 and cap 123; also *Cust. Roff.*, 12.
[?1137 × 1143] witnessed an episcopal instrument of bp John [II], as Ricard de Clovilla, *Reg. Roff.*, 370, 413. Robert Pullen was also a witness as adcn of Rochester; hence the suggested dating in line with *Fasti*, ii, 81. (Dates of his adcnry uncertain).
[1095 × 1107], greeted by Reginald, monk of St Augustine's, Canterbury, in his preface to the *Vita Malchi*, 38; see *ib.*, 12 and 11 for the prob. dating which has been followed here.

His father William was a tenant of Godfrey Talbot in Oakleigh, *Text. Roff.*, ii, fo 186 and cap 123. Dr Brett suggests that the family were French.

Note: a Richard de Clovilla witnessed a grant to the monastery dated 1143, *Text. Roff.*, ii, fo 230^v, and cap 220.

I CLEMENT [Clemens
occ. [1108 × 1114]

n.d., for a time as a monk *habuit custodiam de Hedenham*, *Reg. Roff.*, 119.
[1108 × 1114], with Martin I and Humphrey q.v., witness to an agreement *temp.* Ralph, bp and Ordwinus prior, q.v., *Cust. Roff.*, 35, *Text. Roff.*, ii, fo 193^v, and cap 170.
n.d., with Martin I, q.v., attested a grant, *Text Roff.*, ii, fo 195^v and cap 175.

He is listed among the benefactors, as he gave vestments and a silver crucifix, *Reg. Roff.*, 119.

II CLEMENT [Clemens
occ. 1143

1143, his *cognatus* Robert occ. as a witness to a charter, *Reg. Roff.*, 653.

Note: it is uncertain how many monks in this period were named Clement.

CLEVE
see Clyve

I John CLIVE
occ. [c. 1307]

[c. 1307], one of four monks who were assigned *ad tricennale celebrandum* for John Pouncz q.v., BL Ms Cotton Vespasian A.xxii, fo 127.

CLOVILLA
see Claudevilla

CLYFF
see Ralph London

II John CLYVE [Cleve, *alias* Cardon
occ. 1399 d. 1460

1445–1460, prior: el. 14 May 1445, *Fasti*, iv, 40; d. by 10 Sept. 1460, Reg. Lowe, fo 34^v.

1399, 30 Aug., one of three whose prof. the prior was comm. to rec., Reg. prior Shepey, fo 89^v.
1401, 16 Feb., acol., granted *lit. dim. ad omnes*, Reg. prior Shepey, fo 111.
1402, 23 Sept., ord subdcn, bp's chapel Trottiscliffe, Reg. John Bottlesham, fo 33^v.
1403, 22 Sept., ord dcn, bp's chapel Trottiscliffe, *ib.*, fo 38^v.
1404, 29 Mar., ord pr., bp's chapel Trottiscliffe, *ib.*, fo 46^v.

1423, 18 Dec., 1425, 23 May, cellarer, *Reg. Roff.*, 568, 571, (Reg. Langdon, fo 30^v, 45^v).

1409, 20 Nov., 19th in order of those present in chapter to appt a proctor in a lawsuit, Reg. prior Shepey, fo 120.
1419, 31 Aug., 11th in order at the el. of a prior, *Reg. abp Chichele*, i, 61–62 (transcribed as Clyne).
1423, 18 Dec., present at the renunciation of their rights, with regard to St Nicholas' altar in the cathedral nave, by the vicar and parishioners

who worshipped there, *Reg. Roff.*, 568, (Reg. Langdon, fo 30v).

1425, 23 May, present in the chapel at the east end of the great hall when the bp gave his decision on the annual rent to be pd by the vicar of the newly built parish church of St Nicholas close to the cathedral, *Reg. Roff.*, 571 (Reg. Langdon, fo 45v).

1445, 14 May, el. prior *per viam scrutinii* in the bp's presence by the *maior et sanior pars* and installed the same day, Reg. Lowe, fo 4v.

Simon de CLYVE

occ. 1236 occ. 1262

1252–1262, prior: succ. 5 × 25 Mar., 1252; res. 1262, *Fasti*, ii, 80.

1252, before Mar., sacrist, *Flores Hist.*, ii, 377 (*Anglia Sacra*, i, 350).

1236/7, with Alexander de Glanville, q.v., sent by the prior and chapter to the curia to appeal vs the abp's refusal to confirm Richard de Wendene as bp, *Flores Hist.*, ii, 219, (*Anglia Sacra* i, 348); they stayed at the curia for a yr as their return journey was impeded by the war between the pope and the emperor, *Flores Hist.*, ii, 223–224.

1262, res. because of illness, [*debilitato*], *Flores Hist.*, ii, 478, (*Anglia Sacra*, i, 351, 393).

Described as *virum pacificum et modestum*, *Flores Hist.*, ii, 377, (*Anglia Sacra*, i, 350).

John COBB

see Stapelhurst

Henry de COBBEHAM

occ. 1297 d. [c. 1300]

1297, one of four monks who were assigned *ad tricennale celebrandum* for John Sauvage, q.v., BL Ms Cotton Vespasian A.xxii, fo 126v.

[c. 1299], one of four assigned to celebrate as above for Richard de Waledene, q.v., *ib.*

[c. 1300], d., and four monks were assigned to celebrate as above for him, *ib.*

Adam de COBEHAM

n.d.

n.d., son of Ralph, priest, who gave land at the time of Adam's adm. as a monk. The father was thus listed among the benefactors, *Reg. Roff.*, 118.

Name in Chronica Ade de Cobeham which appears in the 1202 library catalogue in BL Ms Royal 5 B.xii, fo 2, printed in Sharpe, *Eng. Benedictine Libraries*, iv, B79.164; this entry was added later.

I John COBHAM

occ. 1443/4

1443, 18 Apr., one of four adm. by the bp in person at his London house in Queenshithe, Reg. Wells fo 67; see Richard de Oxenford.

1443, 24 Oct., the prior was comm. to rec. his prof., Reg. Wells, fo 71.

1444, 7 Mar., ord acol., Rochester cathedral, Reg. abp Stafford, fo 196.

1444, 19 Dec., ord subdcn, chapel within the rectory of Southfleet, Reg. Lowe, fo 4.

II John COBHAM [*alias* Stace

occ. 1514 occ. 1534

1514, 26 Nov., one of seven who made their prof. before the bp, Reg. Fisher, fo 55.

1516, 22 Mar., ord subdcn, Rochester cathedral, *ib.*, fo 56v.

1517, 11 Apr., ord dcn, bp's palace chapel, Rochester, *ib.*, fo 57v.

1518, 28 Feb., ord pr., bp's palace chapel, Rochester, *ib.*, fo 60.

1532, 21 Oct., 9th in order at the el. of a prior, Reg. Fisher, fo 156.

1534, 10 June, subscribed to the Act of Supremacy, *DK 7th Report*, Appndx 2, 299.

Thomas COKK [Cox, Coxe

occ. 1527 occ. 1540

1527, 22 Dec., one of eight who made their prof. before the bp, Reg. Fisher fo 121v.

1532, 21 Oct., 22nd at the el. of a prior, Reg. Fisher, fo 156.

1534, 10 June, subscribed to the Act of Supremacy, *DK 7th Report*, Appndx 2, 299.

1540, 8 Apr., assigned a pension of 40s. p.a., in addition to his apptment as 'epistoler', *L and P Henry VIII*, xv, no 474.

Thomas COLCHESTRE

occ. 1407/9

1407, 15 Aug., one of two whose prof. the prior was comm. to rec., Reg. prior Shepey, fo 116.

1407, 24 Sept., ord acol., collegiate church of All Saints, Maidstone, Reg. abp Arundel, i, fo 341, (named here as monk of Canterbury).

1408, 22 Dec., ord dcn, Lambeth palace chapel, *ib.*, i, fo 343v.

1409, 21 Sept., ord pr., abp's chapel Maidstone *ib.*, ii, fo 96v.

1409, 20 Nov., 22nd in order and last of those present in chapter to appt a proctor in a lawsuit, Reg. prior Shepey, fo 120.

Thomas de COLVERDENE [Colverdenn

occ. 1314 occ. 1317

1314, 21 Dec., ord acol., Lambeth palace chapel, Reg. abp Reynolds, fo 13.

1315, 17 May, ord subdcn, Croydon, by *lit. dim.*, *ib.*, fo 170v.

1315, 20 Dec., ord dcn, Maidstone, by *lit. dim.*, *ib.*, fo 173v.

1317, 28 May, ord pr., Lambeth palace chapel, *ib.*, fo 177v.

COMLYNE
see Tomlyne

COOSTE
see Thomas Stoke

John de CORF [Corfe, Coorf
occ. 1367 occ. 1384

1367, 12 June, ord acol. Rochester cathedral, Reg. Trillek, fo 9v.
1370, 9 Mar., ord subdcn, St Paul's cathedral, London, *Reg. Sudbury*, (London), ii, 77.
1370, 8 June, ord dcn, St Paul's, London, *ib.*, ii, 86.
1370, 20 June, dcn, granted *lit. dim.* [for the order of pr.], Reg. Trillek, fo 24v.
1371, 1 Mar., ord pr., St Paul's cathedral, London, *Reg. Sudbury* (London), ii, 100.
1384, 16 Oct., 12th in order in chapter for the apptment of a proctor in the curia, Reg. prior Shepey, fo 21.

William de CORNUBIA
d. 1296

n.d., one of the monks, with Roger de Saunford, q.v., *in dispersione* at Westminster; on their return they enriched the altar of St Edward with ornaments and an image of the saint because of their devotion to that saint,and were listed among the benefactors, *Reg. Roff.*, 125, (BL Ms Cotton Vespasian A.xxii, fo 91v).
1296, d., and four monks were assigned *ad tricennale celebrandum* for him, BL Ms Cotton Vespasian A.xxii, fo 126v.

Name in Cambridge, Corpus Christi College Ms 318, Vite sanctorum (12th c.), on fo 1, *per*—-.

COSTE
see Thomas Stoke

Eilwinus COTERE
n.d.

n.d., gave land in Strood and other gifts when he was recd as a monk [*dedit secum*], and was listed among the benefactors, *Reg. Roff.*, 119.

COX(E)
see Cokk

John CRAY [Craye, Creye
occ. 1387 occ. 1403

1387, 15 Aug., accepted by the prior of the London Charterhouse for a yr's probation before prof., Reg. prior Shepey, fo 34v.
1387, 18 Aug., granted licence by the prior to transfer to the Carthusian order *causa frugis vite arcioris*, *ib.*
1387, 3 Oct., renewed his obedience on his return from the London Charterhouse as 'probam me dicti ordinis non posse sufferr' rigorem', *ib.*, fos 34v-35.
1393, 6 Aug., the prior of the Coventry Charterhouse wrote to the prior and chapter to say that since he aspired 'ad frugem vite melioris seu arcioris' he would be admitted, Reg. prior Shepey, fo 67, 67v.
1393, 13 Dec., accepted by the Friars Minor of Cambridge, *ib.*, fo 70–70v.
1393, 20 Dec., granted licence by the prior to transfer *causa frugis vite melioris*, *ib.*, fo 70.
1394, 28 Aug., the prior recd a letter from the abbot of Glastonbury, president of the Black Monk Chapter, reporting that he had encountered *quemdam de confratibus vestris* without companion, money or an office book and urging the prior to recall and discipline him, Pantin, *BMC*, iii, 84–85 (Reg. prior Shepey, fo 73).
[1394], 8 Sept., the prior's reply stated that after his return from the Carthusians, this restless, inconstant monk had obtained permission to join the Cluniac priory at Bermondsey but had soon left. He was discovered by the lord of Cobham and brought back to Rochester. He next asked permission to become a Franciscan friar at Cambridge and produced letters of acceptance from the guardian of the house which were assumed to be valid. But he went to Rome and not to Cambridge and returned from there with letters from the papal penitentiary to the bp requiring that he be restored to his former position in chapter without any correction. At the time of writing Cray was reportedly wandering about awaiting the expected invitation to return on his terms. The prior and chapter were willing to have him back on condition that he submit to correction, Pantin, *BMC*, iii, 85–87 (Reg. prior Shepey fos 73v, 74).
1401, 9 Apr., obtained licence from the bp who noted that 'ubi spiritus dei est ibi libertas' but added a warning that change should not be made lightly and should be 'ad frugem melioris vite et ordinem arciorem'. He was to have six months in which to find a suitable order, Reg. prior Shepey, fo 102.
1403, 25 Apr., provided with a licence from the bp to present to the abbot or prior of the house he wished to enter and confirm that he had the bp's approval, Reg. John Bottlesham, fo 35.

Richard CROWMER
occ. 1437 occ. 1465

1437, 21 Dec., ord acol., Rochester cathedral, Reg. Wells, fo 7.
1440, 24 Sept., ord subdcn, Rochester cathedral, *ib.*, fo 36.
1441, 10 June, ord dcn, Trottiscliffe, *ib.*, fo 40.
1465, 11 Oct., apptd sacrist at the nomination of the prior and chapter, Reg. Lowe, fo 45v.

Peter DANCASTRE
occ. 1369/71

[1369], 20 Sept., had recd first tonsure and now granted *lit. dim.* to all minor orders, Reg. Trillek, fo 20.
1370, 9 Mar., ord acol., St Paul's cathedral, London, *Reg. Sudbury* (London), ii, 76.
1370, 8 June, ord subdcn, St Paul's, *ib.*, ii, 84.
1371, 1 Mar., ord dcn, St Paul's, *ib.*, ii, 99.

John DANE
see John de Hertlepe II

Laurence DANN
see Mereworth

M. Richard de DARENTE [Derente
occ. c. 1225 × 1238

c. 1225–1238, prior: el. c. 26 May 1225; last occ. 30 Nov. 1238, *Fasti*, ii, 80.
Note: 'Ricardus dictus prior de Derente electus est in priorem Roffensem', *Flores Hist.*, ii, 183. Abp Hubert gave the manor of Darenth to the prior and convent in 1195 and there was a cell there for a time, prob. until 1255, Knowles and Hadcock, *MRH* and *CPL*, i (1198–1304), 325; but see Ralph IV.
1227, described as *magistrum Ricardum priorem*, sent with W. sacrist and J. chamberlain q.v., to the abp to announce the el. of Henry de Saunford, as bp, *Flores Hist.*, ii, 190.
1238, 30 Nov., present at the installation of Richard de Wendene as bp, whom he had postulated [as bp], *ib.*, ii, 226, 230.

DARENTE
see also Derenth

Nicholas DARSYNGHAM [Dersyngham
occ. 1512 occ. 1521

1512, 10 Apr., ord acol., bp's palace chapel, Rochester, Reg. Fisher, fo 42.
1516, 22 Mar., ord pr., Rochester cathedral, *ib.*, fo 56ᵛ.
1521, 12 Nov., apptd precentor to succ. Thomas Hemysby, q.v., Reg. Fisher, fo 91.

John DARTFORD [Dertford
occ. 1496 occ. 1518

1514, 2 Dec., apptd precentor, succ. John Maideston IV, q.v., Reg. Fisher, fo 55ᵛ.
[1516/17], 8 Jan., apptd chamberlain, having prob. been precentor until this date when Thomas Hemysby, q.v., was named to the office, *ib.*, fo 56ᵛ.
1518, 12 Nov., res. from the chamberlain's office and was succ. by John Pecham q.v., *ib.*, fo 60ᵛ.
1496, 4 Nov., 8th in order on the visitation certificate, *Reg. abp Morton*, ii, no 446.
1496/7, there is a ref. to his *camera* at Felixstowe, Dugdale, *Monasticon*, iv, 564.

Gausfridus de DELTSA, son of [Delsa
n.d.
n.d., at the time of adm., his father gave land, *Text. Roff.*, ii, fos 194ᵛ, 195 and caps 173, 175.

DERENTE
see Darente

Geoffrey de DERENTH
n.d.

n.d., named in a list of monk benefactors between William de Hoo and Simon de Clyve, CKS DRc/Z14, dorse.

Thomas DERHAM [Doreham, Dorham
occ. 1458/60

1458, 24 Sept., ord acol., bp's chapel, Halling, Reg. Lowe, fo 32.
1459, 24 Mar., ord subdcn, Rochester cathedral, *ib.*, fo 32.
1460, 12 Apr., ord dcn, Rochester cathedral, *ib.*, fo 33.
1460, 7 June, ord pr., bp's chapel, Halling, *ib.*, fo 33.

DERSYNGHAM
see Darsyngham

John de DOVOR [Dovoria, Dovorria
occ. 1327 occ. 1333

1327, 11 Apr., ord pr., Trottiscliffe, Reg. Hethe, fo 76 (p. 1093).
1333, 19 Aug., present at the el. of a prior and was one of three who nom. Robert de Southflete II, q.v., Reg. Hethe, fo 157 (p. 534).

Simon de DOVOR
occ. 1348 occ. 1361

1348, 14 June, ord dcn, bp's chapel, Halling, Reg. Hethe, fo 237ᵛ (p. 1092).
1353, 23 Mar., ord pr., Rochester cathedral, Reg. Shepey, fo 2.
1361, 15 June, the prior and chapter requested the abp [*sed. vac.*], to appt him sacrist in place of Simon de Chalke, q.v., Reg. abp Islip, fo 225; the abp sent his *prefectio* on 19 June, *ib.*

Thomas de DOVORR [Dovoria
occ. 1347 occ. 1386

1347, 1 July, ord acol., bp's small chapel, Halling, Reg. Hethe, fo 230ᵛ, (p. 824).
1348, 14 June, ord dcn, bp's chapel, Halling, *ib.*, fo 237ᵛ (p. 1092).
1349, 7 Mar., ord pr., bp's chapel, Trottiscliffe, *ib.*, fo 242 (p. 1092).
[1367], 3 Nov., apptd cellarer, Reg. Trillek, fo 11ᵛ.
1372, 27 Dec., the prior and chapter requested the abp [*sed. vac.*] to appt him sacrist in place of John Morel, q.v.; and he sent the required *admissio*, Reg. abp Wittlesey, fos 137ᵛ, 138.

1384, 29/30 Mar., at the request of the prior and chapter, apptd precentor by the bp in succ. to John de Speldhurst II, Reg. prior Shepey, fos 22, 13^{v}.
1384, 18 Sept., the prior and chapter requested the bp to dismiss him from this office; the bp sent the comm. on 19 Dec., *ib.*, fo 20^{v}; see John de Speldhurst II.
1385, 29 Mar., the prior and chapter requested his [re]apptment as precentor, *ib.*, fo 22.
1386, 17 Apr., 'absolved' again from the office of precentor, *ib.*, fo 23; see John Pleme.

1384, 16 Oct., 8th in order among those present in chapter for the apptment of a proctor in the curia, Reg. prior Shepey, fo 21.

John DRYE
occ. 1522

1522, 20 Dec., ord dcn, bp's palace chapel, Rochester, Reg. Fisher, fo 92.

DRYKE
see William Mayfelde II

[Wynand de DRYLAND
see Introduction, p. 000.

DUNSTAN [Dunstanus
n.d.

n.d., ordered by Paulinus, q.v., to complete and perfect a hanging [cortina] which had been given by the wife of Ansfrid the sheriff, *Reg. Roff.*, 118.
Note: Ansfrid, sheriff, may be dated 1131 × 1136 acc. to Dr M. Brett; see J. A. Green, *English Sheriffs to A.D. 1154* (Public Record Office handbook 24, 1990), p. 51.
[1095 × 1107], one of the monks greeted by Reginald, monk of St Augustine's, Canterbury, in his preface to his *Vita Malchi*, 38; see *ib.*, 12 and 11 for the prob. dating which has been followed here.

EADMER, son of
n.d.

n.d., his father, described as Eadmer of Darenth, gave tithes at the time of his adm., *Text. Roff.*, ii, fos 183–184, and cap 106.

EADMUND [Eadmundus
n.d.

n.d., son of Godfrey the merchant; gave a messuage, was clothed in the monastic habit just before his d. [*ad succurrendum*] and is listed among the benefactors, *Reg. Roff.*, 122.

EADMUND
see also Edmund

John de EALDING B.Th [Aelding, Aldyng, Ealdyng, Eldyng, Eldyngh, Yalding
occ. 1384 d. 1439

1384, 16 Oct., prof. by this date; see below.
1388, 23 May, ord dcn, bp's chapel, Holborn, Reg. Arundel (Ely), fo 136.
1391, 20 Sept., the prior wrote to the bp of London on his behalf, requesting that he be ord [pr.], and stating that he had been provided with *lit. dim.* by the bp, Reg. prior Shepey, fo 47^{v}.
1391, 23 Sept., ord pr., St Paul's cathedral, London, Reg. Braybrooke (London), fo 27^{v}.

1402, 18 Sept., recd apptment as precentor from the bp in place of Robert de Strode, q.v., Reg. prior Shepey, fo 101^{v}.
1405, 1/2 July, replaced as precentor by Thomas de London, at the request of the prior and chapter, *ib.*, fo 110–110^{v}.
1412, 26 Oct., prior of Felixstowe before this date when he was replaced by John de Sutton, q.v., *ib.*, fo 129.
1425, 23 May, precentor, Reg. Langdon, fo 45^{v}.
1432, 7 Oct., apptd to succ. John de Shepton, q.v. as precentor, *ib.*, fo 72^{v}.
1439, 22 Apr., precentor before this date; see below.

1387, 9 Oct., with Roger de Stapelhurst, q.v., granted licence by the prior to go to study at Oxford, Reg. prior Shepey, fos 35^{v}–36.
1393, 1 July, student at Oxford, Reg. prior Shepey, fo 64; see the entry under the same date below.
1402, 30 June, still at Oxford and described as B.Th., *ib.*, fo 106.

1384, 16 Oct., 23rd in order in chapter [and one may assume prof. by this date] to appt a proctor in the curia, Reg. prior Shepey, fo 21.
1387, 13 Mar., present in the prior's chapel for a renunciation and a renewal of obedience by William de Reynham, q.v., Reg. prior Shepey, fo 95–95^{v}.
1387, 1 Sept., one of ten monks, and on the same day one of eight monks, who with four clerks were apptd general proctors, Reg. prior Shepey, fos 58^{v}, 68.
1393, 13 June, with John de Speldhurst, q.v., apptd by the prior to carry out Black Monk Chapter visitations of Faversham, St Augustine's Canterbury and St Martin's, Dover, Pantin, *BMC*, iii, 248, (Reg. prior Shepey, fo 62^{v}). On 1 July, he was apptd by the prior to attend the Black Monk Chapter in Northampton, Pantin, *BMC*, iii, 212–213.
1397, 14 May, one of eight monks and four clerks apptd general proctors, prob. on acct of an impending metropolitan visitation, Reg. prior Shepey, fos 81, 81^{v}, 83.
1402, 30 June, apptd proctor to attend the Black Monk Chapter in Northampton, Pantin, *BMC*, iii, 212 (Reg. prior Shepey, fo 106).

1418, 24 May, acted as proctor for the prior and chapter in an appeal vs the bp's ordinance concerning the construction of a parish church to replace the nave church of St Nicholas, *Reg. Roff.*, 561–562.

1418, 4 June, acted as proctor for the prior and chapter in an appeal concerning tithes, Reg. Young, fo 6^{v}.

1419, 23 May, sent by the subprior, William Marchaunt, q.v., to the abp to announce the d. of prior John Shepey III, q.v., *Reg. abp Chichele*, i, 60.

1419, 31 Aug., 4th in order at the el. of a prior and preached the sermon, *ib.*, i, 61–62.

1425, 23 May, present in the chapel at the east end of the great hall when the bp gave his decision on the annual rent to be pd by the vicar of the newly built parish church of St Nicholas close to the cathedral, *Reg. Roff.*, 571 (Reg. Langdon, fo 45^{v}).

1434, Trinity term, with Walter Rochestre, q.v., appeared in chancery to explain the non payment of the stipend of the chaplain of Shepey's chantry, *CClR (1429–1435)*, 324–325.

1439, 22 Apr., was d. by this date, when Richard de Oxenford, q.v., was apptd to replace him as precentor, Reg. Wells, fo 22.

Thomas de EALDING [Ealdyng

occ. 1391 occ. 1425

1391, 13 June, one of three monks whose prof. the prior was comm. to rec., Reg. prior Shepey, fo 50.

1392, 9 Mar., ord acol., St Paul's cathedral, London, Reg. Braybrooke (London), fo 28^{v}.

1394, 14 Mar., ord dcn, Maidstone, by *lit. dim.*, Reg. abp Courtenay, ii, fo 184.

1397, 15 Sept., granted *lit. dim.* to all orders, by the bp, Reg. prior Shepey, fo 97.

1401, 30 Oct., the prior was comm. to induct him as chamberlain to succ. Nicholas de Frendesbury, q.v., Reg. John Bottlesham, fos 18^{v}-19.

1415/16, chamberlain, CKS DRc/F15.

1423, 18 Dec.; 1425, 22 Apr., 23 May, sacrist, *Reg. Roff.*, 568 (Reg. Langdon, fo 30^{v}), *Reg. Roff.*, 571 (Reg. Langdon, fo 45^{v}).

1397, 14 May, one of eight monks and four clerks apptd general proctors, prob. on acct of an impending metropolitan visitation, Reg. prior Shepey, fos 81, 81^{v}, 83.

1409, 20 Nov., 11th in order among those present in chapter to appt a proctor in a lawsuit, Reg. prior Shepey, fo 121^{v}.

1419, 31 Aug., 6th in order at the el. of a prior, *Reg. abp Chichele*, i, 61.

1423, 18 Dec., present at the renunciation of their rights, with regard to St Nicholas' altar in the cathedral nave, by the vicar and parishioners who worshipped there, *Reg. Roff.*, 568 (Reg. Langdon, fo 30^{v}).

1425, 22 Apr., present at Malling abbey for the prof. of nuns, Reg. Langdon, fo 46^{v}.

1425, 23 May, present in the chapel at the east end of the great hall when the bp gave his decision on the annual rent to be pd by the vicar of the newly built parish church of St Nicholas close to the cathedral, *Reg. Roff.*, 571 (Reg. Langdon, fo 45^{v}).

Richard de EASTGATE [Estgate]

occ. [?1227 × 1240]

n.d., infirmarer before becoming sacrist, CKS DRc/Z14, dorse.

[?1227 × 1240], sacrist, who began construction of the north *ala*, *Reg. Roff.*, 125; this is a ref. to the north west transept and not to the north aisle acc. to Hope, who provides the date, *Arch. Hist. Rochester*, 47; see William de Hoo.

n.d., listed among monk benefactors, CKS DRc/Z14, dorse.

William de EBOR'

see York

EDMUND

occ. 1294 occ. [c. 1303]

1294, one of four monks who were assigned *ad tricennale celebrandum* for prior John de Reynham I, q.v., BL Ms Cotton Vespasian A.xxii, fo 126^{v}.

1297, one of four assigned to celebrate as above on behalf of John Sauvage, q.v., *ib.*

[c. 1303], one of four assigned as above on behalf of John Pantoum, q.v., *ib.*, fo 127.

Note: this may be Edmund de Hadenham, q.v.

I ELIAS [Elyas, Helyas

n.d.

n.d., son of Hamo, son of Kenstanus, gave land with himself and his sons, Alexander and Stephen, q.v., and was listed among the benefactors, *Reg. Roff.*, 119; see also CKS DRc/T302.

II ELIAS [Elyas

occ. ?12th c.

n.d., precentor, BL Ms Royal 5 C.i.

Name in BL Ms Royal 5 C.i, Augustinus (12th c.); on fo 1, *liber Elye precentoris*; this vol. appears in the 1202 library catalogue in BL Ms Royal 5 B.xii, fo 2, printed in Sharpe, *Eng. Benedictine Libraries*, iv, B79.20.

Note: an Elias, prob. monk of Rochester, occ. as witness in a confirmation of bp Walter in favour of the monks of Stoke by Clare, C. Harper-Bill and R. Mortimer, eds, *Stoke by Clare Cartulary*, Suffolk Records Society, 3 vols (1982–1984), i, no 101 where it is dated 1152 × 1179.

III ELIAS [Elyas, Helyas
occ. 1203 × 1217

c. 1214–1217, prior: occ. 1 Nov. 1214; occ. 1217, *Fasti*, ii, 79–80, *HRH*, 64.

1203, Jan., prob. sacrist, *Fasti*, ii, 79.

As prior he is listed among the benefactors on acct of his many gifts and achievements among which were the acquisition of vestments and ornaments, the roofing of that part of the cloister *versus dormitorium*, the construction of a *lavatorium* and a new refectory door; as sacrist he made contributions of never less than £20 for the new work on the church. He also commissioned the copying of William of Malmesbury's Historia Regum and Historia Episcoporum, *Reg. Roff.*, 122–123; see Sharpe, *Eng. Benedictine Libraries*, iv, B81.

A brief statement of his character occ. *Reg. Roff.*, 123,: he was 'ad necessitatem primus qui dixit ego dabo, vel faciam, vel ibo'.

IV ELIAS [Elya
d. c. 1306

[c. 1306], d., and four monks were assigned *ad tricennale celebrandum* for him, BL Ms Cotton Vespasian A.xxii, fo 127.

Note: it is uncertain how many monks called Elias occur in this period.

I ERNULPH [Arnulf, Ernulphus
occ. before 1107 d. by 1113

1107, before, prior: evidence that he had been prior is found in Delisle, *Rouleaux des Morts*, 203, where he was being prayed for in 1113; cf. BL Ms Royal 5 B.xvi, fo 187 and the spurious CKS DRc/T49. See Ralph I, his successor, and *HRH*, 63.

The name M. Ernulf, prior, is attached to a vol. of verse De conflictu vitiorum et virtutum, in the 1202 catalogue in BL Ms Royal 5 B.xii, fo 2, prob. as author; see Sharpe, *Eng. Benedictine Libraries*, iv, where the ref is B79.165 (an entry added later).

II ERNULPH [Arnulfus, Ernulphus
occ. [1104 × 1108]

[1104, before 29 Sept.], greeted as chaplain by abp Anselm in a letter to bp Gundulf, *Anselm Letters*, v, no 330.

[1107 × 1108], chaplain to bp Gundulf, who, with prior Ordwinus, q.v., witnessed an oath of fidelity to the bp, *Text. Roff.*, ii, fo 198, 198ᵛ and cap 181.

John de ESHE [Esshe
occ. 1291

1291, during an altercation with some of the brothers of Strood hospital, at the time of a procession and prayers for rain that took place at Frindsbury, he was seized and thrown into a dung heap, *Flores Hist.*, iii, 73 (*Anglia Sacra*, i, 353).

Adam de ESSEX
occ. 1250/[1]

1250, 13/14 Nov., with Alexander de Glanville and Osbern de Stoke, q.v., set out for the curia where they stayed for 21 wks, and returned on 8 Apr. [1251] having successfully obtained papal confirmation for their choice of Laurence de St Martin as bp, *Flores Hist.*, ii, 369 (*Anglia Sacra*, i, 350).

ESTGATE
see Eastgate

Ralph de ESTONE
d. 1297

1297, d., and four monks were assigned *ad tricennale celebrandum* for him, BL Ms Cotton Vespasian A.xxii, fo 126ᵛ.

William de ETERHAMME [?Etesham
occ. [1093 × 1108]

n.d., gave a silver-gilt ampulla and his mother gave an alb, and he is listed among the benefactors, *Reg. Roff.*, 123.

[1093 × 1108], witnessed a grant of land *temp.* bp Gundulf and abp Anselm, *Text. Roff.*, ii, fo 185ᵛ and cap 121 [as Etesham].

Note: There may be two monks conflated here.

EUSTACHIUS
n.d.

n.d., a gift of land was made at the time of his adm. and so he is included among the benefactors, *Reg. Roff.*, 118.

Note: the entry reads '[terra] data fuit cum Ricardo de Wldeham et Eustachio monachis'; see Wouldham.

William EVYNOK
occ. 1496

1496, 4 Nov., 7th in order on the visitation certificate, *Reg. abp Morton*, ii, no 446 (where it has been transcribed as 'Caynok').

EWER
see St Clare

EYLESBURY
Ailesburi

William de FARINDONE [Farindon, Farndone
occ. 1349/50

1349, 13 Sept., ord acol., bp's oratory, Halling, Reg. Hethe, fo 267 (p. 888).

1349, 19 Sept., ord subdcn, Rochester cathedral, *ib.*, fo 268ᵛ.

1350, 20 Feb., ord dcn, Maidstone, Reg. abp Islip, fo 308.

1350, 18 Dec., ord pr., Maidstone, *ib.*, fo 311.

1350, 28 Mar., was allegedly assaulted by John de Mepham, q.v., Reg. Hethe, fo 272 (pp. 906–907).

William FARLEY [*alias* Harvy
occ. 1514 occ. 1518

1514, 26 Nov., one of seven who made their prof. before the bp, Reg. Fisher, fo 55.
1517, 11 Apr., ord subdcn, bp's palace chapel, Rochester, *ib.*, fo 57^v.
1518, 28 Feb., ord dcn, bp's palace chapel, Rochester, *ib.*, fo 59^v.

FARNDONE
see Farindone

I John de FAVERSHAM [Faveresham, Feversham
occ. 1318 occ. 1332

1318, 23 Dec., ord subdcn, Maidstone, Reg. abp Reynolds, fo 182.
1320, 24 May, ord pr., Rochester cathedral, Reg. Hethe, fo 44^v (p. 71).

1321, Jan., 22 Mar., 3 Apr., 3 May, 10 June, 5 Oct.; 1322, 13 Feb, 5 and 23 June, 19 Aug., 25 Sept., 18 Dec.; 1323, 13 July; 1324, 29 Feb., 15 June, 23 Oct., 12 Dec.; 1325, 6 Sept., present in the bp's household and prob. chaplain as is specified in Jan. 1321, on 18 Dec. 1322 and 12 Dec. 1324, BL Ms Cotton Faustina B.v., fo 33, *Reg. Hethe*, 97–99, 213; 108, 111, 113, 116 (bis), 105; 124; 129, 131, 145, 147; 155.

1322, 5 June, present at an ordination in the cathedral, Reg. Hethe, fo 56 (p. 111).
1324, 15 June, present with John de Ledes, q.v., as witness to an episcopal instrument at Bromley, Reg. Hethe, fo 62 (p. 131); on 23 Oct., he performed the same service at Lambeth, *ib.*, fo 65 (p. 145).
1325, 6 Sept., with three other monks witnessed an episcopal instrument at Halling, *ib.*, fo 68 (p. 155).
1326, 29 Oct., served as proctor for the prior and chapter in a dispute with a vicar, *ib.*, fo 87 (p. 231).
1332, 1 June, present, with the prior and William Reyersh, q.v., and others in the prior's *camera* for the reading of a comm. sent to the bp from the abp, Reg. Hethe, fo 151 (p. 516); and see Robert de Gelham.

His brother was Thomas de le Hore of Wrotham, BL Ms Cotton Faustina, B.v., fo 33.

II John de FAVERSHAM [Feversham, Fevyrsham, *alias* Wells
occ. 1443 occ. 1449

1443, 18 Apr., as Wells, one of four adm. as monks by the bp in person at his London house at Queenshithe, Reg. Wells, fo 67; see Richard Oxenford.
1443, 24 Oct., the prior was comm. to rec. his prof., *ib.*, fo 71^v.
1444, 7 Mar., ord acol., Rochester cathedral, Reg. abp Stafford, fo 196.
1444, 19 Dec., ord subdcn, chapel within the rectory of Southfleet, Reg. Lowe, fo 4.
1445, 18 Sept., ord dcn, bp's chapel, Halling, Reg. Lowe, fo 5^v.
1449, 7 June, ord pr., Rochester cathedral, *ib.*, fo 21^v.

Richard FAVERSHAM
occ. 1528

1528, prior of Felixstowe, PRO SP1/50/p. 119.

1528, with two unnamed monks surrendered the priory [cell] to cardinal Wolsey, *ib.* See also *L and P Henry VIII*, iv, pt 2, no 4755.

Note: this monk prob. entered and was ord between 1468 and 1492, a period for which no episcopal regs have survived.

FLEPLEME
see Pleme

Thomas FLERE [*alias* Maynard, Mayner
occ. 1527 occ. 1535

1527, 22 Dec., one of eight who made their prof. before the bp, Reg. Fisher, fo 121^v.
1533, 20 Dec., ord pr., bp's palace chapel [Rochester], *ib.*, fo 163^v.

1532, 21 Oct., 17th in order at the el. of a prior, Reg. Fisher, fo 156.
1534, 10 June, subscribed to the Act of Supremacy, *DK 7th Report*, Appndx 2, 299.
1535, 4 Dec., dispensed to change his habit and hold a benefice for which he pd £8, Chambers, *Faculty Office Regs*, 37.

Benedict de FOLKESTON [Folkestane, Fulkestane
occ. 1347/9

1347, 1 July, ord acol., bp's small chapel, Halling, Reg. Hethe, fo 230^v (p. 824).
1348, 14 June, ord dcn, bp's chapel, Halling, *ib.*, fo 253^v (p. 1099).
1349, 7 Mar., ord pr., bp's chapel, Trottiscliffe, *ib.*, fo 258 (p. 1099).

Robert FORMAN
see Maydeston

John de FREND' [?Frendesbury
occ. [?early 14th c.]

n.d., pd visits [to ?Frindsbury], for supervisory purposes, CKS DRc/F7.

John de FRENDESBURY
occ. 1283

1283, 29 Apr., with William de Schotindon, q.v., recd licence from the abp to el. a bp, *Reg. abp Pecham*, ii, 195–196.

Note: the above two entries may refer to the same monk.

Nicholas de FRENDESBURY [Frendesbyry, Fryndesbury
occ. 1366 d. 1415/16

1366, 30 May, ord dcn, Malling, Reg. Wittlesey, fo 7v.

1367, 13 Mar., ord pr., abp's chapel, Otford, by *lit. dim.*, *Reg. abp Langham*, 379.

1385/6, the prior was comm. to appt him chamberlain on 2 Oct. 1385, Reg. prior Shepey, fo 14; his acct for this yr is CKS DRc/F13.

1390, 20 Apr., requested to be relieved of the office of chamberlain and the prior and chapter wrote to the bp to this effect, Reg. prior Shepey, fo 43; see John Pleme.

1393, 26 June, the prior wrote to him granting his request to be relieved of the office of prior/*custos* of Felixstowe, Reg. prior Shepey, fo 64v.

1393, 27 June, the prior and convent requested the bp that he be relieved of the office of prior/*custos* of Felixstowe and replaced by Thomas de Hariettisham, q.v., *ib.*, fo 64–64v.

1394, 7 Feb., the prior and chapter requested the bp to reappt him as chamberlain, Reg. William Bottlesham, fo 45v and Reg. prior Shepey, fo 68.

1396, 7 Oct., the bp approved his dismissal from this office and the apptment of Roger de Stapelhurst, q.v., after the prior and convent had sent him their letter of request, Reg. William Bottlesham, fo 92, Reg. prior Shepey, fos 77, 81 and CKS DRc/F14.

1398, 30 June, in response to the request of the prior and chapter reapptd chamberlain by the bp, Reg. William Bottlesham, fo 86v.

1401, 30 Oct., the bp approved his dismissal from this office and the apptment of Thomas de Ealding, q.v., after rec. a request from the prior and chapter written on 22 Oct., Reg. John Bottlesham, fos 18v-19, Reg. prior Shepey, fo 105.

1382, 13 Nov., apptd by the prior and chapter as proctor for convocation, Reg. prior Shepey, fos 14v–15.

1384, 16 Oct., 10th in order in chapter, for the apptment of a proctor in the curia, *ib.*, fo 21.

1387, 1 Sept., one of ten monks, and on the same day one of eight monks, who with four clerks were apptd general proctors, Reg. prior Shepey, fos 58v, 68.

1389, 29 Apr., prob. the monk named Nicholas, who had been a former chaplain to bp Thomas Brinton, and who was bequeathed 40s. in the latter's will, Reg. abp Courtenay, i, fo 231; see John Swan I.

1396/7, gave the chamberlain 10s. for the new latrine, CKS DRc/F14.

1397, 14 May, one of eight monks and five clerks apptd by the prior and chapter as general proctors prob. on acct of an impending metropolitan visitation, Reg. prior Shepey, fos 81, 81v, 83.

1397, 1 Sept., one of eight monks and four clerks apptd as general proctors, *ib.*, fo 68.

1409, 20 Nov., 4th in order of those in chapter to appoint a proctor in a lawsuit, Reg. prior Shepey, fo 121v.

1415/16, d. and the chamberlain gave 1s. to the poor on the day of his burial, CKS DRc/F15.

I Thomas de FRENDESBURY
occ. 1348/9

1348, 14 June, ord dcn, bp's chapel, Halling, Reg. Hethe, fo 253v (p. 1101).

1349, 7 Mar., ord pr., bp's chapel, Trottiscliffe, *ib.*, fo 258 (p. 1101).

II Thomas FRENDESBURY [Frendysbery
occ. 1431 occ. 1444

1431, 31 Mar., ord subdcn, Rochester cathedral, Reg. Langdon, fo 69x.

1431, 5 Apr., ord dcn, Malling, *ib.*, fo 70xv.

1434, 23 May, ord pr., bp's London chapel, Queenshithe, *ib.*, fo 71xv.

1444, 3 Mar., sent as proctor to the abp for licence to el. a bp, Reg. abp Stafford, fo 43–43v.

Thomas FRESELL
occ. 1512

1512, 10 Apr., ord acol., bp's palace chapel, Rochester, Reg. Fisher, fo 42.

William FRESELL [Fressel, Frysell
occ. 1509 d. 1532

1509–1532 prior: apptd by the abp by right of devolution, 11 Sept. 1509, Reg. abp Warham, ii, fo 337; d. 18 Oct. 1532, Reg. Fisher, fo 156.

Note: because of the disagreement between the bp and convent over the el. of a prior, on this occasion both parties relinquished their claims in favour of the abp.

1511/12, with his servants he spent four days in London in Dec. and the cost was 42s. 2d.; after Easter he went to Hadenham and his expenses there were £4, CKS DRc/F17.

1519, 28 Oct., appted by Wolsey coadjutor to Thomas, abbot of St Alban's who was old and infirm, *L and P Henry VIII*, iii, pt 1, no 487.

Previously a monk of St Alban's and prior of its dependent cell at Binham, Norfolk, Reg. Fisher, fo 36.

Acc. to W. B. Rye, he was highly commended as a 'distinguished judge and encourager of critical literature', *Arch. Cant.*, iii, 53.

FULK
occ. [c. 1180]

[c. 1180], occ. as prior of Felixstowe, in a grant to the church and monks there, Oxford, Bod. Ms Charters, Suffolk, no 240; dated by Turner and Coxe, *Charters and Rolls*, 536.

FULKESTANE
see Folkeston

I G.
n.d.

Name in Oxford, Bod. Ms 387, Augustinus etc., (early 12th c.); *per*—. This vol. appears in three library catalogues; that of 1122/3 in *Text Roff.*, ii, fos 224–230, the fragments in CKS DRc/Z18/1–2 of similar date, and that of 1202 in BL Ms Royal 5 B.xii, fo 2; these are printed in Sharpe, *Eng. Benedictine Libraries*, iv, where the refs are B77.30, B78.12 and B79.45 respectively.

II G.
occ. before 1202

n.d., cellarer, see below.

Name in BL Ms Royal 12 C.iv, Hyginus etc., (astronomical and historical treatises), (13th c.); on fo 1 *per*—, *celerarium*. This vol. appears in the library catalogue of 1122/3 in *Text. Roff.*, ii, fos 224–230, and in that of 1202 in BL Ms Royal 5 B.xii, fo 2; these are printed in Sharpe, *Eng. Benedictine Libraries*, iv, where the refs are B77.73 and B79.92.

III G.
n.d.

n.d., subprior, see below.

Name occ. in BL Ms Royal 12 F.i, Aristoteles etc. (late 13th c.); *liber—suppriors.*

IV G.
occ. before 1202

n.d., chamberlain, see below.

Name in Cambridge, Trinity College Ms 1238, Jeronimus (12th c.), *per*—. This vol. appears in three library catalogues; that of 1122/3 in *Text Roff.*, ii, fos 224–230, the fragments in CKS DRc/Z18/1–2 of similar date, and that of 1202 in BL Ms Royal 5 B.xii, fo 2; these are printed in Sharpe, *Eng. Benedictine Libraries*, iv, where the refs are B77.29, B78.11 and B79.46 respectively.

Note:
(1) four separate G.s but possibly less than four monks. There is also ref. to a G. who accompanied L., q.v., to Boxley [1198 × 1205].
(2) two monks, G. and L., q.v., were sent to Boxley when the church there was vacant, and they were molested by the bp's henchmen, Selden Society, *Select Cases Eccles.*, 44. See Ralph de Ros.

Robert de GELHAM
occ. 1295 occ. 1333

1329, 9 Feb; 1333, 19 Aug., almoner, Reg. Hethe, fos 149ᵛ, 157 (pp. 510, 533).

1295, one of four monks who were assigned *ad tricennale celebrandum* for William de Schotingdon, q.v., BL Ms Cotton Vespasian A.xxii, fo 126ᵛ.
1297/8, one of four assigned as above to celebrate for John de Cantuaria and William de Tonnbregg I, *ib.*
[c. 1301], one of four assigned as above to celebrate for John de Beverle, q.v., *ib.*
[c. 1304], one of four assigned as above to celebrate for Thomas Payn, q.v., *ib.*, fo 127.
1317, [18 Oct.], named as proctor in the appeal over the el. of Hamo de Hethe, q.v. as bp; he was among those sent to Durham to confer with cardinals there and later went, as arranged, to meet the cardinals in London, c. 18 Oct., BL Ms Cotton Faustina B.v., fo 4.
1323, 12 Mar., acted as one of two examiners of ordinands for the bp at Halling, Reg. Hethe, fo 59 (p. 122).
1329, 9 Feb., took part in the el. proceedings of the prioress of Higham, Reg. Hethe, fos 87ᵛ, 149ᵛ (pp. 241, 510).
1332, 22 May, present with the prior and monks in chapter and accepted on their behalf a comm. sent to the bp from the abp, Reg. Hethe, fo 151 (p. 517).
1333, 19 Aug., 3rd in order at the el. of a prior among those who voted for John de Shepey II, q.v., Reg. Hethe, fo 157 (p. 533).

Name in
(1) BL Ms Royal 2 C.v, Nicholas de Gorran (13th/14th c.); on fo 1, *per*—.
(2) BL Ms Royal 6 C.iv, Ambrosius (12th c.), *per*—. This vol. appears in the library catalogue of 1122/3 in *Text. Roff.*, ii, fos 224–230, and in that of 1202 in BL Ms Royal 5 B.xii, fo 2; these are printed in Sharpe, *Eng. Benedictine Libraries*, iv, where the refs are B77.42 and B79.31.
(3) BL Ms Royal 3 B.i, Isidorus (12th c.); 'Robertus de Gelham est bonus puer', in the margin of fo 84. See entry for the monk A.I (1) under Mss.

GERARDUS [Ierardus
n.d.

Name in
(1) BL Ms Royal 12 F.viii, J. Saresburiensis (12th/13th cs); on fo 1, *per*—. This vol. appears in the 1202 library catalogue in BL Ms Royal 5 B.xii, fo 2, printed in Sharpe, *Eng. Benedictine Libraries,* iv, B79.239. See also Robert de Waletone.

(2) BL Ms Royal 15 C.x, Statius (later 10th c.); on fo 1^{v}, *per*—. This vol. appears in the 1202 library catalogue in BL Ms Royal 5 B.xii, fo 2, printed in Sharpe, *Eng. Benedictine Libraries*, iv, B79.197.

GEROLDUS, Hamo the sheriff's man, son of

n.d.

n.d., at the time of his adm. as a monk his father gave tithes worth 20s. p.a., *Text. Roff.*, ii, fo 185 and cap 117.

GILBERTUS [Gillebertus

n.d.

Name in BL Ms Royal 2 E.vii, Gilbert Foliot (early 13th c.); on fo 4, *per*—. This vol. appears in the 1202 library catalogue in BL Ms Royal 5 B.xii, fo 2, printed in Sharpe, *Eng. Benedictine Libraries*, iv, B79.240.

Simon GILLYNGHAM [Gylyngham

occ. 1391 occ. 1396

1391, 13 June, one of three monks whose prof. the prior was comm. by the bp to rec., Reg. prior Shepey, fo 50.

1392, 9 Mar., ord acol., St Paul's cathedral, London, Reg. Braybrooke (London), fo 28^{v}.

1393, 31 May, ord subdcn, abp's chapel Croydon, Reg. abp Courtenay, ii, fo 182.

1396, 26 Feb., ord pr., collegiate church of All Saints, Maidstone, *ib.*, ii, fo 186^{v}.

GISLEBERTUS

occ. [1083 × 1100]

[1083 × 1100], *temp.* bp Gundulf and William II, entered the priory at the time when the bp acquired the manor of Aston Subedge [Easton], Gloucestershire which was held by his son Ralph and Osmund, his relative, [*generis*], *Text. Roff.*, ii, fos 213^{v}–214 and cap 208.

Alexander de GLANVILL [Glanville, Granvilla

occ. 1236 d. 1252

1242–1252, prior: el. 5 Nov. 1242; d. 5 Mar. 1252, *Fasti*, ii, 80.

1236/7, with Simon de Clyve, q.v., sent by the prior and chapter to the curia to appeal vs the abp's refusal to confirm Richard de Wendene as bp, *Flores Hist.*, ii, 219 (*Anglia Sacra*, i, 348); they stayed at the curia for a yr as their return journey was impeded by the war between the pope and the emperor, *Flores Hist.*, ii, 223–224.

1242, 5 Nov., Richard bp and Richard subprior, q.v., scrutinized the votes at his el., *Flores Hist.*, ii, 256.

1250, 13/14 Nov., with Adam de Essex and Osbern de Stoke, q.v., set out for the curia where they stayed for 21 wks, and returned on 8 Apr. [1251] having successfully obtained papal confirmation for their choice of Laurence de St Martin as bp, *Flores Hist.*, ii, 369, (*Anglia Sacra*, i, 350).

1252, 5 Mar., d. from disappointment and shock when he discovered that the bp, with whom he had been on affectionate terms before the bp's el., had completely changed character and had begun to make encroachments on the chapter's rights and possessions, *Flores Hist.*, ii, 376–377.

Name in the following Mss:

A. as Alexander prior

(1) Cambridge, St John's College, Ms 89, Epistles of St Paul (12th c.); on fo 1 at the foot, *Alexandri prioris.*

(2) BL Harley 261, William of Malmesbury (12th/13th cs); this vol. appears in the 1202 library catalogue in BL Ms Royal 5 B.xii, fo 2, printed in Sharpe, *Eng. Benedictine Libraries*, iv, B?79.120.

(3) BL Royal 3 C.vii, Zach. Chrysopolitanus (13th c.); on fo 7, *per*—; this vol. appears in the 1202 library catalogue in BL Ms Royal 5 B.xii, fo 2, printed in Sharpe, *Eng. Benedictine Libraries*, iv, B79.241. See Robert de Waletone.

(4) BL Royal 6 C.x, Gregorius (12th c); *per*—; this vol. appears in three library catalogues; that of 1122/3 in *Text Roff.*, ii, fos 224–230, the fragments in CKS DRc/Z18/1–2 of similar date, and that of 1202 in BL Ms Royal 5 B.xii, fo 2; these are printed in Sharpe, *Eng. Benedictine Libraries*, iv, where the refs are B77.48, B78.17 and B79.29 respectively.

B. as Alexander de Glanville, prior

(5) and (6) BL Royal 7 C.xiii, and xiv, Peter de Cornubia (early 13th c.), on fos 2 and 7, *per*—.

(7) BL Royal 7 E.viii, Peter de Cornubia (early 13th c.); on fo 4, *Alexander prior de Glanvilla.*

John GLASTONBURY [Glastingbury

occ. 1389 occ. 1409

1389, 6 Aug., the prior was granted licence by the abp, *sed. vac.*, to rec. the prof. of John, pr., and novice, Reg. prior Shepey, fo 42^{v}.

1409, 20 Nov., 9th in order of those present in chapter to appt a proctor in a lawsuit, Reg. prior Shepey, fo 121^{v}.

GODFREY [Godfridus

occ. [c. 1123]

Name in Oxford, Bodley Ms 387, Opuscula Hieronimi et Augustini (not later than 1123); on fo 1, *per*—. This vol. appears in three library catalogues; that of 1122/3 in *Text Roff.*, ii, fos 225^{v}–226, the fragments in CKS DRc/Z18/1–2 of similar date, and that of 1202 in BL Ms Royal 5 B.xii, fo 2; these are printed in Sharpe, *Eng. Benedictine Libraries*, iv, where the refs are B77.30,

B78.12 and B79.45 respectively. The date has been assigned by Watson in *Dated and Datable Mss*, i, no 82.

GOGNOSTUS
n.d.

n.d., precentor, BL Ms Royal 6 A.i, fo 1.

Name in BL Ms Royal 6 A.i, Ambrosius (12th c.) on fo 1. This vol. appears in the library catalogue of 1122/3 in *Text. Roff.*, ii, fos 224–230, and in that of 1202 in BL Ms Royal 5 B.xii, fo 2; these are printed in Sharpe, *Eng. Benedictine Libraries*, iv, where the refs are B77.37 and B79.34. (BL Ms Royal 7A.xi, fos 17–24 is also part of this ms.)

Thomas GOLDFYNCH
occ. 1370 occ. 1384

1370, 24 Feb., precentor, Reg. Trillek, fo 23v.

1370, 24 Feb., comm. by the bp to 'induct' two of the lay *seriantes* whom the bp had apptd for the priory, Reg. Trillek, fo 23v.

1377, 27 June, served as witness to the confirmation of an appropriation by the prior and chapter, *Reg. Roff.*, 266.

1384, 16 Oct., 7th in order in chapter for the apptment of a proctor in the curia, Reg. prior Shepey, fo 21.

William GOLDSMITH [Goldsmyth
occ. 1447 occ. 1455

1447, 23 Dec., 1455, 20 Sept., presented the Rochester monks for ordination, Reg. Lowe, fos 15, 28v.

I GOLDWINUS, son of
n.d.

n.d., at the time of his son's entry, Goldwinus son of Edith gave half a *mansus*, *Text. Roff.*, ii, fo 192v and cap 167.

II GOLDWINUS Grecus, son of
n.d.

n.d., at the time of his adm., his father gave the monks two hays in Rochester, *Text. Roff.*, ii, fo 191v and cap 164.

See Peter and Richard III.

John de GOUTHERST
occ. 1367

1367, 13 Mar., ord acol., abp's chapel, Otford, by *lit. dim.*, *Reg. abp Langham*, 378.

GRANVILLA
see Glanvill

GRAYE
see Hemysby

I GREGORY [Gregorius
occ. [1226 × 1235]

[1226 × 1235], *temp.* bp Henry de Sandford, witnessed an appropriation, *Reg. Roff.*, 186 (BL Ms Campbell xiv.3).

II GREGORY
n.d.

n.d., *socius* of Peter, precentor, q.v., gave an alb and is listed among the benefactors, *Reg. Roff.*, 124.

Note: the above two entries may refer to the same monk.

John de GRENESTRETE [Greenstrete, Grenstrete
occ. 1291 d. 1321

1301–1314, prior: el. Feb. 1301, *Flores Hist.*, iii, 110; removed before 8 May 1314, *Fasti*, iv, 40.

1291, 6 June, named as one of five *compromissorii* in the el. of a bp, Oxford, Bod. Ms Charters, Suffolk, no 1384.

1292 × 1301, for seven yrs during this period served as chaplain to bp Thomas de Wouldham, former prior, q.v., *Anglia Sacra*, i, 356–357.

1297, one of four monks who were assigned *ad tricennale celebrandum* for Ralph de Estone, q.v., BL Ms Cotton Vespasian A.xxii, fo 126v.

[c. 1299], one of four assigned to celebrate as above for Richard de Waledene, q.v., *ib.*

1314, deposed because of incompetence; commissaries of the abp visited the prior and chapter and discovered rebellious monks and £500 of debts. The chronicler remarked that because he had been the bp's chaplain he had vainly hoped for episcopal support, *Anglia Sacra*, i, 356–357.

[1301/2], with the convent issued a charter granting a lease, *Reg. Roff.*, 693.

1321, 18 Dec., buried by bp Hethe, *Anglia Sacra*, i, 362.

Name possibly in BL Ms Royal 12 G.ii, Aristoteles (late 13th c.); on fo 1v, *per Johannem priorem*, which, however, may refer to John de Reynham I, q.v.

GREY
see Hemysby

GRIM
occ. [1077 × 1108]

[1077 × 1108], monk and long [*diu*] reeve of Freckenham, *temp.* bp Gundulf, who gave testimony in a dispute over land, *Text. Roff.*, ii, fos 175v-176v, and cap 91.

GRUER
see St Clare

GUIDO [Wido
occ. [1093 × 1108]

[1093 × 1108], *temp.* abp Anselm and bp Gundulf, attested a grant of Hamo son of Vitalis to the bp and monks, *Text. Roff.*, ii, fo 185ᵛ and cap 121.

Thomas de GULEFORD
occ. ?early 14th c.

n.d., visited Frindsbury for *liberatio denariorum*, CKS DRc/F7.

GYLYNGHAM
see Gillyngham

John GYNNETT
occ. 1496

1496, 4 Nov., 11th in order on the visitation certificate *Reg. abp Morton*, ii, no 446.

I H.
n.d.

Name in BL Ms Royal 6 A.xi, Honorius Augustodunensis etc., (12th c.); on fo 1 a 14th c. inscription, *liber—monachi.*

Note: an H. *monachus* also occ. in BL Ms Cotton Domitian A.x, a 13th c. cartulary; on fo 90 'Liber iii de consue[tudinibus et copia cart[arum per—'.

II H.
n.d.

n.d., precentor, see below.

Name in BL Ms Royal 6 B.ii, Gregorius (13th c.); on fo 1 a 14th c. inscription, *per—cantorem.*

See Hubert I who may be this monk.

Edmund de HADENHAM [Hedenham
occ. [c. 1300]

[c. 1300], one of four monks who were assigned *ad tricennale celebrandum* for Henry de Cobbeham, q.v., BL Ms Cotton Vespasian A.xxii, fo 126ᵛ.

The reputed author of the Annales Ecclesie Roffense to 1307 in BL Ms Cotton Nero D.ii, extracts of which are interpolated into *Flores Hist.*, ii and iii, and printed in *Anglia Sacra*, i, 341–355. See Sharpe, *Latin Writers*.

Note: see also Edmund.

Geoffrey de HADENHAM
n.d.

n.d., in one day pd to creditors 1700 marks which was owed *pro prosecucione juris eleccionis*; he also gave gifts of money and of brocade and was listed among the benefactors, *Reg. Roff.*, 125.
n.d., bought land at Darenth; made or had made the altar of St Edmund in the crypt to which he assigned the rents from Darenth; *habuit Darente sicut Hadenham*, BL Ms Cotton Vespasian A.xxii, fo 91ᵛ.

Richard de HADENHAM
occ. 1370/2

1370, 8 June, ord acol., St Paul's cathedral, London, *Reg. Sudbury* (London), ii, 83.
1371, 1 Mar., ord subdcn, St Paul's cathedral, *ib.*, ii, 97.
1372, 21 Feb., ord dcn, St Paul's cathedral, *ib.*, ii, 111.

HADENHAM
see also Hedenham

William de HADLO [Haudlo, Haudloo
occ. 1331 occ. 1351

1331, 21 Sept., ord acol., Rochester cathedral, Reg. Hethe, fo 145ᵛ (p. 1109).
1333, 18 Dec., ord subdcn, bp's chapel, Halling, *ib.*, fo 159 (p. 1109).
1338, 19 Sept., ord pr., Wouldham, *ib.*, fo 173ᵛ (p. 1109).
1333, 19 Aug., 23rd in order at the el. of a prior and voted for John de Shepey, II, q.v., Reg. Hethe, fo 157 (p. 534).
1351, 18 Aug., one of the monks who, with the prior, Robert de Southflete II, q.v., witnessed a grant, *CClR (1349–1354)*, 379.

Simon HAKE
occ. 1445

1445, 18 Sept., ord dcn, bp's chapel, Halling, Reg. Lowe, fo 5ᵛ.

Hamo de HAKYNTONE [Hakynton
occ. [c. 1302] occ. [c. 1305]

[c. 1302], one of four monks who were assigned *ad tricennale celebrandum* for James de Beyersse, q.v., BL Ms Cotton Vespasian A.xxii, fo 126ᵛ.
[c. 1305], one of four assigned to celebrate, as above, for Geoffrey de London, q.v., *ib.*, fo 127.

Thomas de HAKYNTONE [Hakintone
occ. 1291 d. c. 1301

1291, 6 June, named as one of five *compromissorii* in the el. of a bp, Oxford, Bod. Ms Charters, Suffolk, no 1384.
[c. 1300], one of four monks who were assigned *ad tricennale celebrandum* for Henry de Cobbeham, q.v., BL Ms Cotton Vespasian A.xxii, fo 126ᵛ.

John HALIWELL [Halywell
occ. 1370/2

1370, 8 June, ord acol., St Paul's cathedral, London, *Reg. Sudbury* (London), ii, 83.
1371, 1 Mar., ord subdcn, St Paul's cathedral, *ib.*, ii, 97 (as Haltwell).
1372, 21 Feb., ord dcn, St Paul's cathedral, *ib.*, ii, 111.

Richard de HALSTEDE [Halsted, ?Halstode
occ. [c. 1304] occ. 1317

[c. 1304], one of four monks who were assigned *ad tricennale celebrandum* for Adam de Hoo, q.v., BL Ms Cotton Vespasian A.xxii, fo 127.
1317, 18 Mar., with John de Westerham and John de Marchia, q.v., supervised the voting [*via scrutinii*] at the el. of Hamo de Hethe, q.v., as bp, BL Ms Cotton Faustina B.v fo 8; this is recounted also in *CPL*, ii (1305–1342) 189, and Reg. Temp., fos 118ᵛ-119.

HAMO [Fitzvitalis, brother of
nd., became a monk when Hamo gave a church and land to the prior and convent, *Text. Roff.*, ii, fo 185ᵛ and cap 121.

Walter HARENG
d. [c. 1300]

[c. 1300], d., and four monks were assigned *ad tricennale celebrandum* for him, BL Ms Cotton Vespasian A.xxii, fo 126ᵛ.

Note: see also Walter who is prob. the same monk.

Thomas de HARIETTISHAM [Harryetsham, Herietesham, Heriettisham, Heriotsham, Heryettysham
occ. 1361 occ. 1397

1361, 18 Sept., ord acol., abp's chapel, Otford, Reg. abp Islip, fo 319ᵛ.
1362, 11 June, ord subdcn, Mayfield, *ib.*, fo 321 (by the bp of Rochester).
1362, 17 Dec., ord dcn, Rochester cathedral, Reg. Wittlesey, fo 8.
1363, 18 Mar., ord pr., abp's chapel Mayfield, Reg. abp Islip, fo 322ᵛ.
1384/5, chamberlain, CKS DRc/F13.
1385, 20 Oct., dismissed from this office as requested by the prior and chapter and replaced by Nicholas de Frendesbury, q.v., Reg. prior Shepey, fo 14.
1388, 9 Apr., apptd prior of Felixstowe in succession to Henry Raundes, q.v., *ib.*, fo 36.
1393, 27 June, apptd *custos* of Felixstowe to succ. Nicholas de Frendesbury, q.v., *ib.*, fo 64–64ᵛ.

1377, 27 June, acted as witness to the confirmation of an appropriation by the prior and chapter, *Reg. Roff.*, 266.
1384, 27 Nov., recd an apptment as proctor for the subprior and chapter to represent them at convocation; on the same day he recd a second apptment as proctor for the prior also, Reg. prior Shepey, fos 21ᵛ, 22.
1387, 1 Sept., one of ten monks, and one the same day, one of eight monks, who with four clerks were apptd general proctors, *ib.*, fos 58ᵛ, 68.
1397, 14 May, one of eight monks and five clerks apptd general proctors, prob. on acct of an impending metropolitan visit., *ib.*, fos 81, 81ᵛ, 83.

HARROKE
see Rye

HARTLEPE
see Hertlepe

John HARVEY
see John Maideston IV

Robert HARVY
occ. 1514

1514, 31 Mar., apptd precentor, Reg. Fisher, fo 42; but see John Maideston IV, *alias* Harvy.

Note: this is prob. a slip for John Harvy.

William HARVY
see Farley

Edmund HATFELD [Hatfelde
occ. 1466 d. c. 1510/11

1466, 20 Dec., recd tonsure and ord acol., bp's chapel, Halling, Reg. Lowe, fo 47ᵛ.

1480, 14 June, 1483, 18 Feb., subprior, *Reg. Roff.*, 139, *CPL*, xiii (1471–1484), 830.
[1500/1], 27 Feb., apptd cellarer to succ. John Pecham, q.v., Reg. Fitzjames, fo 9ᵛ.

1480, 14 June, present in chapter when William Leicestre, q.v., was released from his obedience in order to transfer, Reg. Wode/Bourne, fo 6, *Reg. Roff.*, 139.
1483, 18 Feb., granted papal dispensation to rec. and retain in commendation for life, in conjunction with any office including the priorate, any benefice with or without cure which belonged to his order, *CPL*, xiii (1471–1484), 830.
1496, 4 Nov., 5th in order on the visitation certificate, *Reg. abp Morton*, ii, no 446 (transcribed as Hertfeld).
1510/11, prob. d., as reported *nuper defunct'* in 1511/12; the chamberlain contributed 10s. and the treasurer 6s. 8d. for his anniversary, CKS DRc/F17.

Note: acc. to W.B. Rye, he translated a poem about St Ursula at the request of Henry VII's mother, Margaret Beaufort, and this was printed by Wynkyn de Worde, *Arch. Cant.*, iii, 53.

HAUDLO(O)
see Hadlo

Robert de HECHAM
occ. [1185 × 1214]

[1185 × 1214], described as a monk who was *custos* of the manor of Southfleet, *temp.* bp Glanville, BL Ms Cotton Vespasian, A.xxii, fo 127.
n.d., gave many gifts including vestments, money for windows *in fronte versus majus altare* and at

the altar of St Catherine, and a volume of Isidore's Etymologies which he placed in the cloister cupboard, *Reg. Roff.*, 123, also Sharpe, *Eng. Benedictine Libraries*, iv, B79.110.

Name in Ysidorus Ethimologia in the 1202 library catalogue in BL Ms Royal 5 B.xii, fo 2, printed in Sharpe, *Eng. Benedictine Libraries*, iv, as above.

Note: there may be two Robert de Hechams conflated here.

Reginald de HEDENHAM
n.d.

n.d., subprior, CKS DRc/Z14, dorse.
n.d., listed among monk benefactors, *ib.*

HEDENHAM
see also Hadenham

John HEGHAM
occ. 1399 occ. 1404

1399, 30 Aug., one of three whose prof. the prior was comm. to rec., Reg. prior Shepey, fo 89ᵛ.
1400, 18 Dec., ord acol., Malling, Reg. John Bottlesham, fo 8.
1401, 16 Feb., granted *lit. dim.*, ad omnes, Reg. prior Shepey, fo 111.
1402, 23 Sept., ord subdcn, bp's chapel, Trottiscliffe, Reg. John Bottlehsam, fo 33ᵛ.
1403, 22 Sept., ord dcn, bp's chapel, Trottiscliffe, *ib.*, fo 38ᵛ.
1404, 29 Mar., ord pr., bp's chapel, Trottiscliffe, *ib.*, fo 46ᵛ.

HELYAS
see Elias

Thomas HEMYSBY [Hemisby, Hemsby, Hempsty, *alias* Gray, Graye, Grey
occ. 1496 occ. 1540

1501, 12 Feb., apptd precentor in place of William Auncelle, q.v., Reg. Fitzjames, fo 9, as Graye.
[1510], 8 Nov., released from the office of precentor and succ. by John Noble, q.v., Reg. Fisher, fo 38.
[1516/17], 8 Jan., reapptd precentor, *ib.*, fo 56ᵛ (as Graye).
1521, 12 Nov., replaced as precentor by Nicholas Dersyngham, q.v., *ib.*, fo 91.
1523, 20 Aug., apptd sacrist, succ. John Noble, q.v., *ib.*, fo 93ᵛ.
1530, 9 Oct., removed from the above office and succ. by Robert Rochestre, q.v., *ib.*, fo 142ᵛ.
1535, 1 Dec., reapptd precentor in place of William Mayfeld II, q.v., Reg. Hilsey, fo 2ᵛ.

1496, 4 Nov., 12th in order on the visitation certificate, *Reg. abp Morton*, ii, no 446.
1497/8, was residing at Felixstowe and sent to Rochester [on business], Dugdale, *Monasticon*, iv, 564.

Note: some of the debts of Richard Pecham, q.v., were owed to him, *ib.*
1532, 21 Oct., 3rd at the el. of a prior, Reg. Fisher, fo 156.
1534, 20 June, subscribed to the Act of Supremacy, *DK 7th Report*, Appndx 2, 299.
1540, 8 Apr., assigned a pension of 40s. p.a. and apptd gospeller in the new foundation, *L and P Henry VIII*, xv, no 474.

Note: it seems surprising to find a monk who had been well over 40 yrs in the community (since he was 12th as early as 1496) with a strong enough voice to be named gospeller. The alternatives are that there were two monks named Thomas Hemysby/Gray: the name Gray occ. first in 1502, without Hemysby; Hemysby only in 1510; Gray only in 1517; Gray only in 1521; Hempsty only in 1523 and 1532; and Grey in 1540.

Henry de HENGSEYE [Hengeseye, Henxeye, Heynexeye, Hingeseye
occ. [c. 1302] occ. 1345

1333, 19 Aug., subchamberlain, Reg. Hethe, fo 157 (p. 534).
1338, 27 Sept., apptd subprior in place of William de Bromfeld, q.v., *ib.*, fo 173ᵛ (p. 585).
1342, 24 Mar., apptd precentor to succeed John de Reynham II, q.v., *ib.*, fo 197 (p. 677).
1345, 18 Nov., released from the above office and replaced by John de Mepham, q.v., *ib.*, fo 218 (p. 759).

[c. 1302], one of four monks who were assigned *ad tricennale celebrandum* for William de Ledes, q.v., BL Ms Cotton Vespasian A.xxii, fo 127.
[c. 1306], one of four assigned to celebrate, as above, for Elias IV, q.v., *ib.*
1330, 10 Feb., reported as unjustly treated by the bp who refused to rec. his purgation until he had appealed to the abp, Reg. Hethe, fo 130ᵛ (p. 427) and BL Ms Cotton Faustina B.v, fo 54; see also Robert de Morton and John de Oxonia.
1333, 19 Aug., 7th in order at the el. of a prior among those who cast their vote for John de Shepey II, q.v., Reg. Hethe, fo 157 (p. 534).

I HENRY
occ. [1149 × 1161]

[1149 × 1161], attested a charter of abp Theobald, *Theobald Charters*, no 225, *Reg. Roff.*, 58.

II HENRY
occ. [1148 × 1182]

[1148 × 1182], chaplain to bp Walter, *Reg. Roff.*, 124.
[1148 × 1182], *temp.* bp Walter, gave an alb and was listed among the benefactors, *ib.*
[1148 × 1182], possibly one of the witnesses to a charter of bp Walter, *ib.*, 666.

III HENRY
occ. 1242

1242, 1 Dec., witnessed an appropriation, *Reg. Roff.*, 597.

HENXEYE
see Hengseye

HERIETESHAM, Heriotsham
see Hariettisham

I John de HERTLEPE [Hertilepe
occ. 1348 occ. 1385/6

1361–1380, prior: el. 6 Aug. 1361; res. 6 Nov. 1380, *Fasti*, iv, 40.

1348, 14 June, ord dcn, bp's chapel, Halling, Reg. Hethe, fo 253ᵛ (p. 1111).

1361, before this date, prior of Felixstowe, *Anglia Sacra*, i, 394 (BL Ms Cotton Vespasian A.xxii, fo 34).

[1363, Sept.], one of the diffinitors at the Black Monk Chapter, Pantin, *BMC*, iii, 33.

1368, 11 Jan., apptd by the king chief master of the [building] works at Rochester castle, *CPR (1367–1370)*, 43.

1371, 23 Jan., acted as controller of the king's works at Gravesend and responsible for repairs to the king's manor there, *CClR (1369–1374)*, 167.

1372, 27 Dec., el. bp, but Thomas Brinton was provided, Reg. abp Wittlesey, fo 138.

1376, 18 June, prior to this date had been chief master of the king's works at Rochester castle as well as in charge of [repairs to] the king's manor at Gravesend, *CClR (1369–1374)*, 321.

1385/6, recd 40s. for his clothing allowance from the chamberlain, CKS DRc/F13.

II John de HERTLEPE [Herstlep, Hertelepe, Hertlep, *alias* Dane
occ. 1360 occ. 1384

1361, 20 Feb., ord acol., Strood, Reg. Shepey, fo 32ᵛ.

1361, 18 Sept., ord subdcn, abp's chapel, Otford, Reg. abp Islip, fo 319ᵛ.

1362, 11 June, ord dcn, Mayfield, *ib.*, fo 321ᵛ (by the bp of Rochester).

1362, 17 Dec., ord pr., Rochester cathedral, Reg. Wittlesey, fo 8.

1383/4, 1384, 16 Oct., cellarer, CKS DRc/F12, Reg. prior Shepey, fo 21.

1384, 16 Oct., 3rd in order of those present in chapter to appt a proctor in the curia, Reg. prior Shepey, fo 21 (as Dane).

Hamo de HETHE
occ. c. 1302 occ. 1317

1314–1317, prior: el. 8 May 1314; el. bp 18 Mar. 1317, by way of scrutiny, *Fasti*, iv, 40, 37. A lengthy controversy ensued because, although the abp and king supported his el. as bp, the queen espoused the cause of John de Puteolis, her confessor, who had been provided on 19 Mar. Hethe travelled to Avignon to pursue his claim, arriving on 27 Jan. 1319, and his el. was confirmed on 21 July, *Anglia Sacra*, i, 357–361. He had recd 26 out of 35 votes and one of the two other nominees renounced his nomination by seven of the monks, *CPL*, ii (1305–1342), 188–189; see also Reg. Temp., fos 118ᵛ-120.

[c. 1302], one of four monks who were assigned *ad tricennale celebrandum* for William de Ledes, q.v., BL Ms Cotton Vespasian A.xxii, fo 127.

1307/14, was a member of the household of bp Wouldham, *Reg. Hethe*, x.

1315/16, stayed at Malling [abbey], and went to Leybourne to speak with the abp, Worcester Cathedral Muniment C.834.

1317, 27 Feb., went to the bp who was on his deathbed and obtained a reconciliation which brought to an end a controversy that had begun during the priorate of John de Grenestrete over the *exennium* of St Andrew, *Anglia Sacra*, i, 357.

As a child he had lived with his parents, Gilbert and Alice Noble, in St Leonard's parish, Hythe, Reg. Hethe, fos 121ᵛ, 184 (pp.393, 635). In 1328 his brother William Noble d., *Anglia Sacra*, i, 368. Other details of his family connections are provided in *Reg. Hethe*, ix-xi, where his brother John and nephew John are named. He was said to have been over 80 in 1353, *CPL*, ii, (1342–1362).

Although his name does not occ. in any extant mss it is to be noted that he gave to the monastic library a sizeable collection of books, including texts of canon law and of English provincial constitutions, biblical texts, theological works and spiritual treatises and a book on grammar. These were to be kept in a chest and to be available for the use of secular clergy [*curatis et penitenciariis*], *Reg. Roff.*, 127; see also Sharpe, *Eng. Benedictine Libraries*, iv, B82.

Peter de HETHE [Heth
occ. 1323 occ. 1333

1323, 24 Sept., ord acol., Rochester cathedral, Reg. Hethe, fo 60ᵛ (p. 1114).

1324, 14 Apr., ord subdcn, bp's chapel, Halling, *ib.*, fo 61ᵛ (p. 1114).

1324, 22 Sept., ord dcn, bp's chapel, Halling, *ib.*, fo 64 (p. 1114).

1325, 21 Sept., ord pr., Wouldham, *ib.*, fo 70 (p. 1114).

1330, 9 Nov., chaplain to the bp and witness, Reg. Hethe, fo 134ᵛ (p. 439).

1333, 19 Aug., present at the el. of a prior and was one of three who nom. Robert de Southflete I, q.v., Reg. Hethe, fo 157, (p. 534).

HINGESEYE
see Hengseye

HNESSINDENE
see Thomas II

HO
see Hoo

John de HOLYNGBOURNE [Holingbourne, Holingburne
occ. 1382 occ. 1419

1382, 20 Dec., ord subdcn, bp's chapel, Highclere by *lit. dim.*, *Reg. Wykeham* (Winchester), i, 303.
1383, 2 Feb., provided with a *littera testimonialis* for orders addressed to bps of Canterbury province and stating that he was a professed monk who had been sent to study at Oxford, Reg. prior Shepey, fo 16.
1383, 16 May, ord dcn, bp's chapel, Esher, by *lit. dim.*, *Reg. Wykeham* (Winchester), i, 305.

1392, 1 June, on request of the prior and chapter apptd subprior to succ. John Morel, q.v., Reg. William Bottlesham, fos 26^v-27 and Reg. prior Shepey, fo 55^v.
1400, 8 Oct., the prior was comm. to induct him into the office of cellarer to succ. John Swan, q.v., Reg. John Bottlesham, fo 2^v.
1400, 11 Oct., his removal from the office of subprior and replacement by Thomas Broun, q.v., approved by the bp, Reg. John Bottlesham, fo 3; the prior and chapter had written to the bp on 10 Oct., Reg. prior Shepey, fo 103^v.

1382, 9 Oct., recd licence from the prior and chapter to study at Oxford, Reg. prior Shepey, fo 12^v.
1383, 2 Feb., student at Oxford as stated in *lit. dim.*, Reg. prior Shepey, fo 16; his pension from the cellarer for 1383/4 was 57s, CKS DRc/F12.
1384, 28 June, student, Reg. prior Shepey, fo 20.
1387, 28 June, student, *ib.*, fo 33.

1382, 12 Nov., apptd proctor for the chapter to meet with the abp at St Frideswide's, Oxford, in order to discuss affairs of church and state, Reg. prior Shepey, fo 15.
1384, 28 June, apptd proctor to attend the Black Monk Chapter in Northampton, Pantin, *BMC*, iii, 210 (Reg. prior Shepey, fo 20).

1387, 28 June, apptd proctor to represent the chapter at the Black Monk Chapter, *BMC*, iii, 210 (Reg. prior Shepey, fo 33, 33^v).
1390, 10 June, apptd commissary for the prior to visit Battle abbey on behalf of the Black Monk Chapter, Pantin, *BMC*, iii, 248 (Reg. prior Shepey, fo 41^v).
1390, 30 June, with John Morel, q.v., apptd proctor to attend the Black Monk Chapter in Northampton, *ib.*, iii, 212 (Reg. prior Shepey, fo 42).
1409, 20 Nov., 7th in order of those present in chapter to appt a proctor in a lawsuit, Reg. prior Shepey, fo 121^v.
1419, 31 Aug., 3rd in order at the el. of a prior, *Reg. abp Chichele*, i, 61.

Adam de HOO [Ho
occ. 1296 d.c. 1304

1296, precentor, BL Ms Cotton Vespasian A.xxii, fo 126^v.

1296, one of four monks who were assigned *ad tricennale celebrandum* for William de Cornubia, q.v., BL Ms Cotton Vespasian A.xxii, fo 126^v.
[c. 1298], one of four assigned to celebrate as above for John de Maydestane and Robert de Leuesham, q.v., *ib.*
[c. 1300], one of four assigned to celebrate as above for Henry de Cobbeham, q.v., *ib.*
[c. 1304], d. and four monks were assigned to celebrate as above for him, *ib.*, fo 127.

I Robert de HOO
n.d.

n.d., gave eleven albs and other gifts and was listed among the benefactors, *Reg. Roff.*, 125.

II Robert de HOO
occ. 1296 d.c. 1303/4

1296, one of four monks who were assigned *ad tricennale celebrandum* for William de Cornubia, q.v., BL Ms Cotton Vespasian A.xxii, fo 126^v.
[c. 1298], one of four assigned to celebrate as above for John de Maydestan and Robert de Leuesham, q.v., *ib.*
[c. 1303/4], was not assigned to celebrate as above because of illness, *ib.*, fo 127; he d. within the yr and four monks were assigned to celebrate for him, *ib.*

Simon de HOO [*alias* Stevyn
occ. 1443 occ. 1449

1443, 18 Apr., one of four adm. as monks by the bp in person, in his London house at Queenshithe, Reg. Wells, fo 67 (as Stevyn); see Richard de Oxenford.
1443, 24 Oct., the prior was comm. to rec. his prof. Reg. Wells, fo 71^v.
1444, 7 Mar., ord acol., Rochester cathedral, Reg. abp Stafford, fo 196.
1444, 19 Dec., ord subdcn, chapel within the rectory of Southfleet, Reg. Lowe, fo 4.
1449, 21 Sept., ord pr., bp's chapel, Halling, *ib.*, fo 21.

Stephen HOO [*alias* Millet
occ. 1507/9

1507, 18 Dec., ord dcn, bp's chapel of St Blaise, Bromley, Reg. Fisher, fo 31.
1509, 22 Dec., ord pr., Bromley, *ib.*, fo 36^v.

I William de HOO
occ. before 1239 occ. 1242

1239–1242, prior: el. 25 June 1239 in the presence of the bp, *Flores Hist.*, ii, 235; res. between

June/Nov. 1242 and left to become a Cistercian at Woburn, *Fasti*, ii, 80.

Before 1239, 12 June, sacrist, *Reg. Roff.*, 125; Hope concludes that he was sacrist before 1226, *Arch. Hist. Rochester*, 48.

As sacrist he was responsible for the construction of the choir east of the transepts, for which he used the offerings to St William, *Reg. Roff.*, 125; see also Hope, *Arch. Hist. Rochester*, 47–48.

As prior he was condemned for refusing to sell the wood at Chattenden and Frindsbury and res.: 'nimia persecucione persecutus, mutato habitu aput Wobbourne', *ib.*

Name in Edinburgh, National Library of Scotland, Advocates' Mss 18.3.9. Hegesippus (early 12th c.) as [?] H. de Hoo prior. This vol. appears in the library catalogue of 1122/3 in *Text. Roff.*, ii, fos 224–230, and in that of 1202 in BL Ms Royal 5 B.xii, fo 2; these are printed in Sharpe, *Eng. Benedictine Libraries*, iv, where the refs are B77.53 and B79.74.

Note: see also William VIII.

II William de HOO
occ. 1295 occ. [c. 1304]

1295, one of four monks who were assigned *ad tricennale celebrandum* for Roger de Chelesham, q.v., BL Ms Cotton Vespasian A.xxii, fo 126v.
1297/8, one of four assigned to celebrate as above for John de Cantuar' and William de Tonebregg I, q.v., *ib.*
[c. 1301], one of four assigned to celebrate as above for John de Waltham, *ib.*
[c. 1304], one of four assigned to celebrate as above for Adam de Hoo, q.v., *ib.*, fo 127.

William HORNEY
see St Albans

John HOROLD
see Roffa

Thomas de HORSTED [Horstede
occ. 1331 occ. 1333

1331, 21 Sept., ord subdcn, Rochester cathedral, Reg. Hethe, fo 145v (p. 1117).
1332, 4 Apr., ord dcn, Wouldham, *ib.*, fo 150v (p. 1117).
1333, 18 Dec., ord pr., bp's chapel, Halling, fo 159 (p. 1117).

n.d., precentor; see below.

1333, 19 Aug., 24th in order at the el. of a prior and voted for John de Shepey II, q.v., Reg. Hethe, fo 157 (p. 534).

Name in the following BL Mss in the Royal collection:
(1) 4 E.v, Concordancie biblie (14th c.); *per*—
(2) 5 A.x, Flores Bernardi etc (12th/14th c.); on fo 1, *per*—with a request for prayers for his soul.
(3) 6 D.vii, Gregorius (14th c.); on fo 1, *per*—, and see Thomas Wybarn II; he wrote the *tabula* to the Moralia in this vol. (fos 268–296).
(4) 7 E.iv, J. de Bromyard (late 14th c.); on fo 10 *per—precentorem.*
(5) 7 F.iv, P. de Cornubia (late 13th c.); on fo 1, *per*—.

Name also in two other Mss:
1390, 1 June, the prior and convent lent a number of their books to the bp and to the rector of Southfleet, and among these were 'concordancias pulchras in magno volumine fratris Thome de Horstede', and 'librum Augustini de civitate dei fratris Thomas de Horstede', Reg. prior Shepey, fo 50–50v.

I HUBERT [Hubertus
n.d.

n.d., precentor, see below.

Name in BL Ms Harley 3680, Beda (12th c.); this vol. appears in the library catalogue of 1122/3 in *Text. Roff.*, ii, fos 224–230, and in that of 1202 in BL Ms Royal 5 B.xii, fo 2; these are printed in Sharpe, *Eng. Benedictine Libraries*, iv, where the refs are B77.65 and B79.50.

Note: this monk may be identical with H. II, q.v.

II HUBERT
occ. [before 1126]

[1126, before], described as *ministrans* under Hugh de Trottiscliffe, q.v., who was remembered for his improvements to the priory lands and buildings and was responsible for the marling of all the demesne lands; he was named with Hugh among the benefactors, *Reg. Roff.*, 119.

I HUGH [Hugo
occ. [1114 × 1122]

[1114 × 1122], *temp.* bp Ernulf with Silvester I, q.v., witnessed a charter, possibly spurious of abp Ralph, *Text. Roff.*, ii, fo 179v, and cap 94; this will appear in *Eng. Epis. Acta*, Canterbury, 1070–1161, no 51, forthcoming, where it is dated [1115 Dec. × 1116, Sept., or 1120, Jan. × 1122, Oct.].

II HUGH
n.d.

n.d., sacrist, *Cust. Roff.*, 13.

Note: c. 1200, a Hugh sacrist appears as witness on a title deed, CKS DRc/T27b.

HUMPHREY [Humfridus, Hunfridus
occ. [1083 × 1125]

n.d., precentor, BL Ms Royal 5 B.iv; see below.

[1083 × 1108], attested a grant *temp.* bp Gundulf, *Text. Roff.*, ii, fo 184 and cap 107.

[1108 × 1114], witnessed an agreement, *temp.* bp Ralph and prior Ordwinus, q.v., with Clement

I and Martin I, q.v., *Text. Roff.*, ii, fo 193ᵛ and cap 170; also *Cust. Roff.*, 35.

[1114 × 1124], with Martin I, Robert V and William III, q.v., witnessed an agreement, *temp.* bp Ernulf, *Text. Roff.*, ii, fo 199ᵛ and cap 183.

[1114 × 1124], attested a grant with Robert V and Richard I, q.v., *temp.* bp Ernulf, *Text. Roff.*, ii, fo 191ᵛ and cap 163.

[1114 × 1125], with Martin I, q.v., attested a grant, *temp.* Hervey adcn (*Fasti*, ii, 81) and Warner, q.v., (under Canterbury), *Text. Roff.*, ii, fo 195ᵛ and cap 175.

Name in

(1) BL Ms Royal 5 B.iv, Augustinus (12th c.), which acc. to a 13th c. inscription 'in eodem claustro scripsit—precentor'. This vol. appears in three library catalogues; that of 1122/3 in *Text Roff.*, ii, fos 224–230, the fragments in CKS DRc/Z18/1–2 of similar date, and that of 1202 in BL Ms Royal 5 B.xii, fo 2; these are printed in Sharpe, *Eng. Benedictine Libraries*, iv, where the refs are B77.7, B78.2 and B79.2 respectively.

(2) BL Ms Royal 5 B.xii, Augustinus (12th c.); on fo 4ᵛ, *memoriale—precentoris.* On fo 2 there is a list of books dated 1202 by Alexander *quondam cantor*, q.v. Peter Sawyer notes that the 13th c. inscription should not be taken literally and that the *memoriale* means that Humphrey used the Ms as a pledge, *Text. Roff.*, i, 13. This is also found in the earlier catalogue, *Text. Roff.*, ii, fo 224ᵛ (de doctrina Christiana); also in Sharpe, *Eng. Benedictine Libraries*, iv, where the refs are B77.10 and B79.11.

John HUNFREY
see Umfray

John HWYTEFELD
see Whytefeld

IERARDUS
see Gerardus

John ILSTOKE [Ipstok
occ. 1522

1522, 19 Jan., one of seven whose prof., was solemnized by the bp, Reg. Fisher, fo 91.

1522, 20 Dec., ord dcn, bp's palace chapel, Rochester, *ib.*, fo 92.

I J.
n.d.

Name in BL Ms Royal 7 F.x, Sermones (later 12th c.); *per I priorem.*

Note: this is prob. John de Reynham I, q.v., the only known J. who was prior before 1301; see also John I.

II J.
occ. 1227

1227, chamberlain, *Flores Hist.*, ii, 190.

1227, with Richard de Darente and W., q.v., sent to the abp to announce the el. of Henry de Saunford as bp, *ib.*, ii, 190.

JAMES
occ. 1297 occ. c. 1300

1297, one of four monks who were assigned *ad tricennale celebrandum* for Ralph de Estone, q.v., BL Ms Cotton Vespasian A.xxii, fo 126ᵛ.

[c. 1299], one of four assigned to celebrate as above for Richard de Waledene, q.v., *ib.*

[c. 1300/1], excused from celebrating as above for Henry de Cobbeham *propter missam S . . .* [illegible], *ib.*, but he was one of four named to celebrate for John de Waltham, q.v., *ib.*

Note: see James de Beyersse who is prob. the same monk.

I JOHN
n.d.

n.d., prior; see below.

Name John, prior, in the following Mss:

(1) BL Ms Royal 1 B.iv, Parabole etc., (early 13th c.); on fo 5, *per—priorem.*

(2) BL Ms Royal 12 G.ii and iii, Aristoteles (late 13th c.); in 12 G.ii, on fo 1ᵛ, *per—priorem*, and notes by Henry de Renham, a scribe/student at Oxford.

(3) Rochester Cathedral Library Ms P. Lombard (late 13th c.); *per—.*

Note: these Mss may have been in the possession of prior John de Reynham and/or prior John de Grenestrete, q.v.

II JOHN
occ. 1217/18

1218, 4 Oct., chaplain to bp Benedict, *Reg. Roff.*, 380, *Reg. Hethe*, 24.

1217, 22 Mar., witnessed an episcopal instrument at Walton [Felixstowe] with Alan, q.v., prior of Felixstowe, and therefore perhaps resident in the cell, *ib.*, 381, or possibly serving as the bp's chaplain as above, *ib.*, 381. See also CKS DRc/BZ1.

1218, 4 Oct., witnessed an inspeximus, *Reg. Roff.*, 380.

III JOHN
occ. 1291

1291, 6 June, *custos*/prior of Felixstowe, Oxford, Bod. Ms Charters, Suffolk, no 1384.

1291, 6 June, named by the prior and chapter to be one of five *compromissorii* for the el. of a bp, *ib.*

Note: The number of monks involved in the entries under J. and John remains uncertain.

JOHN
see also London

JOHNSON
see Oxford

JORDANUS
n.d.

n.d., subprior, *Cust. Roff.*, 30.
n.d., ref. to the land of Jordanus, monk, from which tithes were obtained, *Cust. Roff.*, 32.
His brother Eilredus was employed in the brewhouse, *ib.*, 30.

JOSEPH
n.d.

Name in BL Ms Royal 5 E.i, Isidorus etc., (12th c.); on fo 2, *per—monachum*. This vol. appears in the 1202 library catalogue in BL Ms Royal 5 B.xii, fo 2, printed in Sharpe, *Eng. Benedictine Libraries*, iv, B79.81.

William KEBLE
see Saxton

Richard KUKKILSTON
occ. 1381

1381, 10 Oct., with another, apptd general proctors, Reg. prior Shepey, fo 6v.

William KYRTON
occ. 1446 occ. 1449

1446, 7 Sept., one of three whose prof. the prior was comm. to rec., Reg. Lowe, fo 9v.
1446, 17 Dec., ord acol. and subdcn, bp's chapel, Halling, *ib.*, fo 11.
1447, 23 Dec., ord [dcn], bp's chapel, Halling, *ib.*, fo 15.
1449, 7 June, ord pr., Rochester cathedral, *ib.*, fo 21v.

L.
occ. [?1198 × 1205]

[?1198 × 1205], sent with G.IV, q.v., to Boxley when the church there was vacant, and they were molested by the bp's henchmen, Selden Society, *Select Cases Eccles.*, 44. See Ralph de Ros.

L.
see also Leonard, Luke

William LAMB
see Canturbury

Peter de LAMBURNE [Lamburn
occ. 1322 occ. 1333

1322, 27 Mar., ord subdcn, bp's chapel, Trottiscliffe, Reg. Hethe, fo 55v (p. 110).
1323, 24 Sept., ord pr., Rochester cathedral, *ib.*, fo 61 (p. 1060).
1333, 19 Aug., subcellarer, Reg. Hethe, fo 157 (p. 534).
1333, 19 Aug., present at the el. of a prior and was one of five who nom. William de Reyersh, q.v., Reg. Hethe, fo 157 (p. 534).

Robert de LANGERECHE
n.d.

n.d., gave land at the time of his entry, *Reg. Roff.*, 118.
n.d., he also gave a chalice, chasuble and other gifts to the crypt altar of St Catherine and was numbered among the benefactors, *ib.*, 123.

LECESTRE
see Leicestre

I John de LEDES
occ. 1295 occ. 1325

1295, one of four monks who were assigned *ad tricennale celebrandum* for William de Schotindon, q.v., BL Ms Cotton Vespasian A.xxii, fo 126v.
1297/8, one of four assigned to celebrate as above for John de Cantuar' and William de Tonebregg I, q.v., *ib.*
[c. 1301], one of four assigned to celebrate as above for John de Beverle, q.v., *ib.*
[c. 1304], one of four assigned to celebrate as above for Adam de Hoo, q.v., *ib.*, fo 127.
1325, 6 Sept., present in the bp's household at Halling and acted as witness, Reg. Hethe, fo 68 (p. 155).

II John de LEDES [Leedes
occ. 1345 occ. 1359

1345, 21 May, ord dcn, bp's chapel, Trottiscliffe, Reg. Hethe, fo 216 (p. 1127).
1347, 24 May, granted *lit. dim.*, for pr.'s orders, *ib.*, fo 229v (p. 820).
1351, 18 Aug., one of the monks who, with the prior, Robert de Southflete II, q.v., witnessed a grant, *CClR (1349–1354)*, 379.
1353, 5 June, granted papal dispensation to choose his own confessor who was empowered to give plenary remission of sins at the hour of d., *CPL*, iii (1342–1362), 510.
1359, 15 Nov., recd 40s as a bequest from the rector of Rotherfield, Reg. Shepey, fo 25; see also John de Borden.

Thomas de LEDES [Ledis, Ledys
occ. [1361] occ. 1390

[1361 18 Sept., ord acol., abp's chapel, Otford, Reg. abp Islip, fo 319v.]
[1362, 11 June, ord subdcn, Mayfield, Reg. abp Islip, fo 321 (by the bp of Rochester)].
1362, 17 Dec., ord dcn, Rochester cathedral, Reg. Wittlesey, fo 8.
1364, 18 May, ord pr., Wye, Reg. abp Islip, fo 325v.
1384, 16 Oct., 9th in order in chapter for the apptment of a proctor at the curia, Reg. prior Shepey, fo 21.

1390, 30 Sept., obtained licence to go to the curia '. . . ad visitandum et consulendum sacrosanctam sedem apostolicam inter certas et arduas causas anime sue salutem et consciencie serenacionem concernentes'. The licence included a request for hospitality on the part of those whom he encountered en route and specified a time limit: 'presentibus ultra quadraginta septimanas minime valituris', *ib.*, fo 42ᵛ.

William de LEDES
occ. 1296 d. [c. 1302]

1296, ill and therefore he was not assigned *ad tricennale celebrandum* for Osbern de Stoke, q.v., BL Ms Cotton Vespasian A.xxii, fo 126ᵛ.
[c. 1298], one of four assigned to celebrate as above for John de Maydestan and Robert de Leuesham, q.v., *ib.*
n.d., pd a supervisory visit [to Frindsbury], CKS DRc/F7.
[c. 1302], d., and four monks were assigned to celebrate for him, BL Ms Cotton Vespasian, A.xxii, fo 127.

Walter LEE
occ. 1415 occ. 1422

1415, 12 June, one of three whose prof. the prior was comm. by the bp to rec., Reg. prior Shepey, fo 116.
1419, 23 Sept., ord dcn, Fulham, London, Reg. Clifford (London), fo 88ᵛ.
1422, 7 Mar., ord pr., Rochester cathedral, *Reg. abp Chichele*, iv, 352.
1419, 31 Aug., 20th in order at the el. of a prior, *Reg. abp Chichele*, i, 62.

William LEICESTRE [Lecestre
occ. 1480

1480, 14 June, in the presence of the bp and prior requested and obtained absolution from his obedience in order that he might transfer his obedience to prior Hugh Lempster of the priory of St Giles, Canwell, Coventry and Lichfield diocese. Placing both hands between the hands of prior Hugh he made his promise, *more professionis*, *Reg. Roff.*, 138–139 (Reg. Wode/Bourne, fo 6).

LEICESTRE
see also Leycestria.

LEONARD [Leonardus
n.d.

Name in
(1) BL Ms Royal 5 E.xx, Anselmus etc, (12th c.); on fo 3, *per*—.
(2) Oxford, Bod. Ms Laud misc. 40, Reginald, monk of St Augustine's, Canterbury, Vita Malchi, etc, (12th c.), *per*—; this is 'the oldest and most neatly written of the Mss containing the complete Vita', Lind, *Vita Malchi*, 21.

This vol. appears in the 1202 library catalogue in BL Ms Royal 5 B.xii, fo 2, printed in Sharpe, *Eng. Benedictine Libraries*, iv, B79.144.

Robert de LEUESHAM
occ. 1287 d. [c. 1298]

1287, 9 July, appeared as proctor for the prior and convent before the abp at Otford in an inquiry about the bp's right of apptment to office within the priory, *Reg. Roff.*, 90–91.
1291, proctor for the convent in [?continuing] negotiations with the bp over the apptment of servants in the priory, Reg. Temp., fo 113.
1296, one of four monks who were assigned *ad tricennale celebrandum* for Osbern de Stoke, q.v., BL Ms Cotton Vespasian A.xxii, fo 126ᵛ.
[c. 1298], d. and four monks were assigned to celebrate as above for him, *ib.*

R. de LEWIS
occ. 1262

1262, with the bp's official, was placed in charge of the voting by scrutiny at the el. of John de Reynham, q.v., as prior, *Flores Hist.*, ii, 477–478, (*Anglia Sacra*, i, 351).
Note: this monk may be identical with Robert de Leuesham above.

Robert de LEYBURNE
occ. 1295

1295, 8 June, witnessed a charter concerning Strood hospital, *Reg. Roff.*, 260.

John de LEYCESTRIA [Leycestr'
occ. c. 1305 occ. 1333

[c. 1305], one of four monks who were assigned *ad tricennale celebrandum* for Geoffrey de London, q.v., BL Ms Cotton Vespasian A.xxii, fo 127.
1333, 19 Aug., *magister hospicii*, Reg. Hethe, fo 157 (p. 533), 4th in order at the el. of a prior and voted for John de Shepey II, q.v., Reg. Hethe, fo 157 (p. 533).

LEYCESTRIA
see also Leicestre

LEYNHAM
see Bisshope

Thomas LINCOLN
see Thomas London II

LODDESDON
see Ludesdon

Anthony LONDON [*alias* Brown
occ. 1508 occ. 1540

1508, 8 Apr., ord acol., bp's palace chapel, Rochester, Reg. Fisher, fo 33.
1509, 22 Dec., ord subdcn, Bromley, *ib.*, fo 36ᵛ.

1510, 30 Mar., ord dcn, bp's palace chapel Rochester, *ib.*, fo 37.
1511, 19 Apr., ord pr., Rochester cathedral, *ib.*, fo 38ᵛ.
1514, 2 Dec., apptd chamberlain to succeed William Waterford, q.v., Reg. Fisher, fo 55ᵛ.
1517, 17 Dec., apptment as subprior confirmed, succ. John Auncell, *ib.*, fo 59ᵛ.
1526, 5 Oct., res. from the above office and was apptd cellarer, *ib.*, fo 117ᵛ; he succ. Laurence Mereworth, q.v.
1532, 12 Nov., his apptment as sacrist was approved, *ib.*, fo 157; he was also sacrist in 1535, *Valor Eccles.*, i, 103.
1540, 8 Apr., cellarer, *L and P Henry VIII*, xv, no 474.

1511/12, student at Oxford and recd a £10 pension, CKS DRc/F17.

1532, 21 Oct., 7th in order at the el. of a prior, Reg. Fisher, fo 156.
1534, 10 June, subscribed to the Act of Supremacy, *DK 7th Report*, Appndx 2, 299.
1540, 8 Apr., assigned a pension of £10 p.a., *L and P Henry VIII*, xv, no 474.

Bertram LONDON [Bertrandus
occ. 1437 occ. 1459

1437, 21 Dec., ord acol., Rochester cathedral, Reg. Wells, fo 7.
1440, 24 Sept., ord subdcn, Rochester cathedral, *ib.*, fo 36.
1441, 10 June, ord dcn, Trottiscliffe, *ib.*, fo 40.
1444, 19 Dec., ord pr., chapel within the rectory of Southfleet, Reg. Lowe, fo 4.

1452, 3 June, precentor, Reg. Lowe, fo 23ᵛ.
1459, 1 Dec., released from the office of precentor and succ. by William Maydeston II, q.v., Reg. Lowe, fo 32ᵛ.

1452, 3 June, presented the ordination candidates at Halling, Reg. Lowe, fo 23ᵛ.

Geoffrey de LONDON
occ. [c. 1301] d. [c. 1305]

[c. 1301], one of four monks who were assigned *ad tricennale celebrandum* for Thomas de Hakyntone, q.v., BL Ms Cotton Vespasian A.xxii, fo 126ᵛ.
[c. 1305], d., and four monks were assigned to celebrate as above for him, *ib.*, fo 127.

I John de LONDON
n.d.

n.d., gave rents in London worth half a mark [?at the time of his adm.] and was listed among the benefactors, *Reg. Roff.*, 124.

II John de LONDON
occ. 1325 occ. 1333

1325, 2 Mar., ord acol., Trottiscliffe, Reg. Hethe, fo 67ᵛ.
1326, 8 Mar., ord subdcn, Wouldham, *ib.*, fo 71.
1328, 2 Apr., ord dcn, Malling, *ib.*, fo 126.

1333, 19 Aug., 20th in order at the el. of a prior and voted for John de Shepey II, q.v., Reg. Hethe, fo 157 (p. 534).

III John de LONDON
occ. 1395

1395, 6 Mar., ord pr., Rochester cathedral, Reg. William Bottlesham, fo 149.

Note: this may be a mistake for Thomas de London I, q.v.

IV John LONDON [Lundon
occ. 1431

1431, 31 Mar., ord subdcn, Rochester cathedral, Reg. Langdon, fo 69x.
1431, 5 Apr., ord dcn, Malling, Reg. Langdon, fo 70xᵛ.

Ralph LONDON [*alias* Clyff, Clyfh
occ. 1459 occ. 1464

1459, 24 Mar., ord acol., Rochester cathedral, Reg. Lowe, fo 32.
1462, 18 Dec., ord subdcn, bp's chapel, Halling, *ib.*, fo 37ᵛ.
1464, 22 Dec., ord dcn, bp's chapel, Halling, *ib.*, fo 44 (as Clyff).

Robert LONDON [*alias* Chamberlayn, Chamberleyn
occ. 1527 occ. 1535

1527, 22 Dec., one of eight who made their prof. before the bp, Reg. Fisher, fo 121ᵛ.
1532, 25 May, ord pr., bp's palace chapel, Rochester, *ib.*, fo 147.
1532, 21 Oct., 16th in order at the el. of a prior, Reg. Fisher, fo 156.
1534, 10 June, subscribed to the Act of Supremacy, *DK 7th Report*, Appndx 2, 299.
1535, 14 Nov., dispensed to change his habit and hold a benefice, for which he paid £4, Chambers, *Faculty Office Regs*, 35.

I Thomas de LONDON [*alias* Abbot
occ. 1389 occ. 1391

1389, 6 Aug., one of two *clerici* whom the prior was comm. by the abp to adm. and clothe as a monk (as Abbot), Reg. prior Shepey, fo 42ᵛ.
1390, 26 Feb., ord acol., St Paul's cathedral, London, Reg. Braybrooke (London), fo 21.
1391, 16 Feb., granted *littera testimonialis* for him, a prof. monk, for holy orders not yet recd, Reg. prior Shepey, fo 43ᵛ.
1391, 18 Feb., ord subdcn, St Paul's, London, Reg. Braybrooke (London), fo 24ᵛ.
1391, 20 Sept., the prior wrote to the bp of London to request ordination as dcn, Reg. prior Shepey, fo 47ᵛ.

1391, 23 Sept., ord dcn, St Paul's, London, Reg. Braybrooke, (London), fo 27.

II Thomas LONDON [*alias* Lincoll', Lincoln
occ. 1443 occ. 1480

1443, 18 Apr., one of four adm. as monks by the bp in person in his London house at Queenshithe, Reg. Wells, fo 67 (as Lincoln); see Richard de Oxenford.
1443, 24 Oct., the prior was comm. to rec. his prof. *ib.*, fo 71ᵛ.
1444, 7 Mar., ord subdcn, Rochester cathedral, Reg. abp Stafford, fo 196.
1444, 19 Dec., ord dcn, chapel within the rectory of Southfleet, Reg. Lowe, fo 4.
1446, 17 Dec., ord pr., bp's chapel, Halling, *ib.*, fo 11.
1480, 14 June, present in chapter when William Leicestre, q.v., was released from his obedience in order to transfer, Reg. Wode/Bourne, fo 6, *Reg. Roff.*, 139 (as Lincoll').

I William de LONDON
occ. 1384 d. 1396/7

1384, 16 Oct., 20th in order of those present in chapter to appt a proctor in the curia, Reg. prior Shepey, fo 21.
1396/7, d; the chamberlain pd 8d to 'diversis vigilantibus cum fratre . . . tempore mortis sue', CKS DRc/F14.

II William de LONDON
occ. [1440] occ. 1458

[1440], novice, and the prior, as vicar general, was comm. to rec his prof., Reg. Wells, fo 37.
1440, 24 Sept., ord subdcn, Rochester cathedral, *ib.*, fo 36.
1441, 10 June, ord dcn, Trottiscliffe, *ib.*, fo 40.
[1443, 18 Apr.], granted *lit. dim.* for pr's orders, *ib.*, fo 67.
1458, 14 Dec., apptd cellarer in place of John Snell, q.v., and the prior was comm. to induct him into this office, Reg. Lowe, fo 32ᵛ.

William LORKYN
occ. 1422 occ. 1455

1422, 7 Mar., ord acol., Rochester cathedral, *Reg. abp Chichele*, iv, 350.
1423, 18 Dec., ord subdcn, Rochester cathedral, Reg. Langdon, fo 26ᵛ.
1424, 22 Apr., ord dcn, Rochester cathedral, *ib.*, fo 28.
1426, 7 Mar., ord pr., Rochester cathedral, *ib.*, fo 44ᵛ.
1455, 12 Oct., apptd chamberlain in place of William Shepey, q.v., Reg. Lowe, fo 28.

William de LOSE
occ. 1294 occ. [c. 1304]

1294, one of four monks who were assigned *ad tricennale celebrandum* for prior John de Reynham, q.v., BL Ms Cotton Vespasian, A.xxii, fo 126ᵛ.
1297, one of four monks who were assigned to celebrate as above for John Sauvage, q.v., *ib.*
[c. 1304], one of four assigned to celebrate as above for Adam de Hoo, q.v., *ib.*, fo 127.

John de LUDESDON [Loddesdon
occ. 1353 occ. 1358

1353, [18 May], ord dcn, Halling, Reg. Shepey, fo 3ᵛ.
1358, 22 Dec., ord pr., Rochester cathedral, *ib.*, fo 23.

John LUK [Luke
occ. 1454

1454, 15 June, ord acol. and subdcn, bp's chapel, Halling, Reg. Lowe, fo 26.
1454, 20 Dec., ord dcn, bp's palace chapel, Rochester, *ib.*, fo 27ᵛ.

LUKE [Lucas
n.d.

n.d., cellarer, *Reg. Roff.*, 118.
n.d., he acquired rents in Southgate and Sittingbourne, *ib*; he was, as cellarer, responsible for the building of the main gatehouse [*porta*], and was listed among the benefactors, *ib.*

William LUNT [Lunte, Lunto
occ. 1496 occ. 1532

1496, 4th Nov., 15th in order on the visitation certificate, *Reg. abp Morton*, ii, no 446.
1532, 21 Oct., 5th at the el. of a prior, Reg. Fisher, fo 156.

Thomas LYNTON [*alias* Maye
occ. 1514

1514, 26 Nov., one of seven monks who made their prof. before the bp, Reg. Fisher, fo 55.

MAFELD, Maffeld
see Mayfelde

MAGHFELD
see Mawfeld

MAGNUS
n.d.

n.d., precentor for 35 yrs, CKS DRc/Z14, dorse.
n.d., while precentor wrote many books, *ib.*

I John de MAIDENSTAN [Maydestan
occ. 1345 occ. 1348

1345, 21 May, ord subdcn, bp's chapel, Trottiscliffe, Reg. Hethe, fo 216 (p. 1132).

1345, 24 Sept., ord dcn, bp's chapel, Halling, *ib.*, fo 217 (p. 755 but on p.1132, incorrectly 22 Sept.).

II John de MAIDESTON [Maydenstan, Maydestan
occ. 1362 occ. 1367

1362, 17 Dec., ord acol., Rochester cathedral, Reg. Wittlesey, fo 8.
1363, 23 Sept., ord subdcn, Faversham convent, Reg. abp Islip, fo 323^{v}.
1367, 12 June, ord pr., Rochester cathedral, Reg. Trillek, fo 9^{v}.

III John MAIDESTON [Maydeston
occ. 1458 occ. 1465

1458, 24 Sept., ord acol., bp's chapel, Halling, Reg. Lowe, fo 32.
1459, 24 Mar., ord subdcn, Rochester cathedral, *ib.*, fo 32.
1460, 12 Apr., ord dcn, Rochester cathedral, *ib.*, fo 33.
1465, 11 Oct., apptd subprior, Reg. Lowe, fo 45^{v}.

IV John MAIDESTON [Madeston *alias* Harvey, Harvy, Harvye
occ. 1508 d. 1521

1508, 8 Apr., ord acol., bp's palace chapel, Rochester, Reg. Fisher, fo 33.
1509, 22 Dec., ord subdcn, Bromley, *ib.*, fo 36^{v}.
1510, 30 Mar., ord dcn, bp's palace chapel, Rochester, *ib.*, fo 37 (as Harvy).
1511, 19 Apr., ord pr., Rochester cathedral, *ib.*, fo 38^{v}.
1514, 31 Mar., apptd precentor, succeeding Thomas Stoke, q.v., Reg. Fisher, fo 54 (if he is Robert Harvy, q.v.).
1514, 2 Dec., res. the above office, *ib.*, fo 55^{v}, and was succ. by John Dartford, q.v.
1518, 20 Nov., apptd sacrist to succ. Laurence Mereworth, q.v., *ib.*, fo 60^{v}; see below.
1521, 26 Nov., d. by this date while serving as sacrist, Reg. Fisher, fo 91.

MAIDESTON
see also Maydenstone, Maydestane, Maydeston

John de MALLYNG [Mallinges, Mallingges
occ. 1384 occ. 1388
1384, 16 Oct., 16th in order among those present in chapter to appt a proctor in the curia, Reg. prior Shepey, fo 21.
1387, 10 Oct., sentence of excommunication pronounced vs him in chapter because he had left the monastery without permission and had taken a gold chalice, *ib.*, fo 35, 35^{v}.
1388, 2 Mar., the king wrote to the mayor and bailiffs of Bristol in response to an undated letter of the prior to the chancellor concerning John, apostate; he was reported to have been seen in Bristol and the mayor was ordered to find and restore the plate and vestments (valued by the prior at £100) which he had stolen from the priory, *ib.*, fos 49 (an insert), 50, also *CClR (1385–1389)*, 371.

Name in BL Ms Royal 12 F.xiii, Bestiarium etc. (early 13th c.); on fo 149, *iste liber reparatum* [sic] *fuit per—*.

Robert de MALLING [Mallinge
occ. [c. 1301] occ. [c. 1304]

[c. 1301], one of four monks who were assigned *ad tricennale celebrandum* for John de Beverle, q.v., BL Ms Cotton Vespasian A.xxii, fo 126^{v}.
[c. 1304], one of four assigned to celebrate as above for Thomas Payn, q.v., *ib.*, fo 127.

William de MALLING
occ. 1296 occ. [c. 1299]

1296, one of four monks who were assigned *ad tricennale celebrandum* for Osbern de Stoke, q.v., BL Ms Cotton Vespasian A.xxii, fo 126^{v}.
[c. 1299], one of four assigned to celebrate as above for Richard de Waledene, q.v., *ib.*

William MARCHAUNT, B.Cn.L
occ. 1393 occ. 1446

1393, 1 Sept., one of three whose prof. the prior was comm. to rec., Reg. William Bottlesham, fo 43 and Reg. prior Shepey, fo 66.
1395, 6 Mar., ord subdcn, Rochester cathedral, Reg. William Bottlesham, fo 148^{v}.
1396, 26 Feb., ord dcn, collegiate church of All Saints, Maidstone, by *lit. dim.*, Reg. abp Courtenay ii, fo 186.
1397, 15 Sept., granted *lit. dim.*, by the bp [for pr.'s orders], Reg. prior Shepey, fo 97.
1419, 23 and 25 Aug., subprior, *Reg. abp Chichele*, i, 60–61.
1423, 18 Dec.; [1425, Jan.], 1425, 7 Apr., subprior, *Reg. Roff.*, 568; Reg. Langdon, fo 30, *Reg. Roff.*, 587–588
1446, 6 Oct., at the request of the prior and chapter, released from the office of subprior and succ. by Richard de Oxenford, q.v., Reg. Lowe, fo 10.

1423, 18 Dec., described as B.Cn.L, *Reg. Roff.*, 568 (Reg. Langdon, fo 30^{v}, where he is John.)
1419, 31 Aug., presided at the el. of a prior, *Reg. abp Chichele*, i, 61–62.
1423, 18 Dec., 2nd in order of those present at the renunciation of their rights, with regard to St Nicholas' altar in the cathedral nave, by the vicar and parishioners who worshipped there, *Reg. Roff.*, 568 (Reg. Langdon, fo 30^{v}).
1425, 7 Apr., witnessed an episcopal instrument, *Reg. Roff.*, 588.
[1425, Jan.], with secular clerks, comm. by the bp to denounce convicted clerks, Reg. Langdon, fo 30.

1445, 14 May, gave the sermon at the el. of a prior, Reg. Lowe, fo 4^{v}; see John Clyve II.

John de MARCHIA [?Marham
occ. 1295 occ. 1317

1295, one of four monks who were assigned *ad tricennale celebrandum* for Roger de Chelesham, q.v., BL Ms Cotton Vespasian, A.xxii, fo 126^{v}.
1317, 18 Mar., with Richard de Halstede and John de Westerham, q.v., supervised [by scrutiny] the voting in the episcopal el., BL Ms Cotton Faustina B.v, fo 8; this is also noted in *CPL*, ii (1305–1342), 189. See also Reg. Temp., fos 118^{v}-119.

I MARTIN [Martinus
occ. [?1108 × 1124]

[1114 × 1125], cellarer, *temp.* Hervey adcn (*Fasti*, ii, 81) and Warner, q.v., (under Canterbury), *Text. Roff.*, ii, fo 195^{v} and cap 175.
[1108 × 1114], witness to an agreement with Clement I and Humphrey, q.v., *temp.* Ralph, bp and Ordwinus, prior, q.v., *Cust. Roff.*, 35, *Text. Roff.*, ii, fo 193^{v} and cap 170.
[1114 × 1124], with Humphrey, Robert V and William III, witnessed an agreement, *temp.* bp Ernulf, *Text. Roff.*, ii, fo 199^{v} and cap 183.
[1114 × 1125], with Humphrey attested a grant, *Text Roff*, ii, fo 195^{v} and cap 175.
n.d., with Clement I, q.v., attested a grant, *Text. Roff.*, ii, fo 195^{v} and cap 175.
Note: see note below Martin II.

II MARTIN
n.d.

n.d., chamberlain, *Reg. Roff.*, 119.
n.d., was the first [*primo*] to construct a mill below Rochester castle; he also gave vestments and was listed among the benefactors, *Reg. Roff.*, 119.
Note: these two Martins may be one and the same monk.

MAUNCOY
see Monkoy

MAUR' [Maurus
n.d.

n.d., Name in Oxford, Bod. Ms Wood B. 3, Juvenalis (11th c.); on fo 1, *De claustro Roff'— mo'.*

I William de MAWFELD [Maghfeld, Maufeld, Mawghfeld
occ. 1396 occ. 1419

1396, 20 Sept., one of three whose prof. the prior was comm. by the bp to rec., Reg. prior Shepey, fo 78–78^{v}.
1396, 24 Sept., ord acol., Rochester cathedral, Reg. William Bottlesham, fo 149^{v}.
1397, 15 Sept., granted *lit. dim.*, by the bp *ad omnes ordines*, Reg. prior Shepey, fo 97.
1398, 21 Dec., ord subdcn, Rochester cathedral, Reg. William Bottlesham, fo 150.
1400, 18 Dec., ord dcn, Malling, Reg. John Bottlesham, fo 8^{v}.
1402, 18 Feb., ord pr., chapel of the bp of Worcester in [the Strand], London, by *lit. dim.*, Reg. Clifford (London), fo 59. The *lit. dim.* were issued on 16 Feb., Reg. prior Shepey, fo 111.
1409, 20 Nov., 16th in order of those present in chapter to appt a proctor in a lawsuit, Reg. prior Shepey, fo 121^{v}.
1419, 31 Aug., 10th at the el. of a prior, *Reg. abp Chichele*, i, 61–62.

II William MAWFELD
see Mayfelde

I William de MAYDENSTONE [Maidenst', Maydenstan
occ. 1318 occ. 1333

1318, 23 Dec., ord subdcn, Maidstone, Reg. abp Reynolds, fo 182.
1320, 24 May, ord pr., Rochester cathedral, Reg. Hethe, fo 44^{v} (p. 71).
1333, 19 Aug., third prior, Reg. Hethe, fo 157 (p. 534).
1333, 19 Aug., 14th in order at the el. of a prior among those who voted for John de Shepey II, q.v., Reg. Hethe, fo 157 (p. 534).

II and III William de MAYDENSTONE
see Maydeston

John de MAYDESTANE
occ. 1295 d. [c. 1298]

1295, one of four monks who were assigned *ad tricennale celebrandum* for William de Schotindon, q.v., BL Ms Cotton Vespasian, A.xxii, fo 126^{v}.
1297, one of four monks who were assigned to celebrate as above for Ralph de Estone, q.v., *ib.*
[c. 1298], d., and four monks were assigned to celebrate for him, *ib.*

Robert MAYDESTON [Madeston, Maydston *alias* Forman
occ. 1514 occ. 1535

1514, 26 Nov., one of seven monks who made their prof. before the bp, Reg. Fisher, fo 55.
1517, 11 Apr., ord subdcn, bp's palace chapel, Rochester, *ib.*, fo 57^{v}.
1518, 27 Feb., ord dcn, bp's palace chapel, Rochester, *ib.*, fo 59^{v} (as Forman).
[1524, 16 Feb.], apptd chamberlain in place of John Peckham, q.v., Reg. Fisher, fo 94.
1525, 20 Sept., res. from this office, *ib.*, fo 113^{v}; see John Noble.

1530, 30 Sept., apptd precentor, *ib.*, fo 142; see William Mayfeld II, q.v; he was also precentor in 1535, *Valor Eccles.*, i, 103.
1532, 11 Nov., 10th in order at the el. of a prior, Reg. Fisher, fo 156.
1534, 10 June, subscribed to the Act of Supremacy, *DK 7th Report*, Appndx 2, 299.
1535, 10 Nov., dispensed to change his habit and hold any benefice with cure of souls, for which he pd £4, Chambers, *Faculty Office Regs*, 35.

I William de MAYDESTON
see Maydenstone

II William de MAYDESTON [Maidestan, Maydenston
occ. 1362/4
1362, 17 Dec., ord acol., Rochester cathedral, Reg. Wittlesey, fo 8.
1363, 23 Sept., ord subdcn, Faversham convent, Reg. abp Islip, fo 323^v.
1364, 18 May, ord dcn (by the bp of Rochester), Wye, *ib.*, fo 325.
1366, 30 May, ord pr., Malling, Reg. Trillek, fo 7^v.

III William MAYDESTON
occ. 1437 occ. 1459
1437, 21 Dec., ord acol., Rochester cathedral, Reg. Wells, fo 7.
1439, 4 Apr., ord subdcn, chapel *prope infirmariam* (within the monastery), *ib.*, fo 22.
1440, 24 Sept., ord dcn, Rochester cathedral, *ib.*, fo 36.
1444, 7 Mar., ord pr., Rochester cathedral, Reg. abp Stafford, fo 196^v.
1459, 1 Dec., apptd precentor to succ. Bertram London, q.v., Reg. Lowe, fo 32^v.

Thomas MAYE
see Lynton

I William MAYFELDE
see I William de Mawfeld

II William MAYFELDE [Mafelde, Maffeld, *alias* Dryke
occ. 1522 occ. 1535
1522, 19 Jan., one of seven who made their prof. before the bp, Reg. Fisher, fo 91.
1525, 6 June, [dcn], recd *lit. dim.* for pr's orders, *ib.*, fo 112^v.
1525, 28 July, apptd precentor, *ib.*, Reg. Fisher, fo 113.
1530, 30 Sept., res. the above office and was succ. by Robert Maydeston, q.v., *ib.*, fo 142.
1535, 1 Dec., replaced as precentor by Thomas Hemysby, q.v., Reg. Hilsey, fo 2^v.
1532, 21 Oct., 13th in order at the el. of a prior, Reg. Fisher, fo 156.
1534, 10 June, subscribed to the Act of Supremacy, *DK 7th Report*, Appndx 2, 299.
1535, 26 Nov., dispensed to change his habit and hold a benefice, for which he pd £8, Chambers, *Faculty Office Regs*, 36.

MAYNARD, MAYNER
see Flere

Laurence MELFORD
occ. 1419
1419, 23 Sept., ord pr., Fulham, London, Reg. Clifford (London), fo 89.
1419, 31 Aug., 16th in order at the el. of a prior, *Reg. abp Chichele*, i, 62.

Geoffrey de MEPEHAM [Meapham
occ. [c. 1301] occ. 1317
1317, 18 Mar., sacrist, *Anglia Sacra*, i, 357, (BL Ms Cotton Faustina B. v, fo 3^v).
[c. 1301], one of four monks who were assigned *ad tricennale celebrandum* for Thomas de Hakyntone, q.v., BL Ms Cotton Vespasian, A.xxii, fo 126^v.
[c. 1305], one of four assigned to celebrate as above for Geoffrey de London, q.v., *ib.*, fo 127.
1315/16, with the prior, Hamo de Hethe, q.v, stayed at Malling in order that the prior could speak with the abp at Leybourne, Worcester Cathedral Muniment C.834 (acct of the sergeant of Wouldham).
1317, 19 Apr., with John de Westerham, q.v., appeared at Lambeth to present to the abp the details of the el. of their prior, Hamo de Hethe, as bp, *Anglia Sacra*, i, 357 (BL Ms Cotton Faustina B.v, fo 3^v).
1317, May, sent, with another, by the bp el., to the curia to appeal vs the claims of a rival candidate; they set out on 7 May and arrived on the 24th, *Anglia Sacra*, i, 358. See Hamo de Hethe.

Henry de MEPEHAM [Mepham
occ. [c. 1303] occ. 1317
[c. 1303], one of four monks who were assigned *ad tricennale celebrandum* for John Pantoum, q.v., BL Ms Cotton Vespasian A.xxii, fo 127.
1317, 27 Feb., recd 20s. as a bequest from bp Wouldham, *Reg. Roff.*, 113.
Name in
(1) BL Ms Royal 4 B.ii, Epistole Pauli etc., (12th c.); on fo 6, *per*—.
(2) BL Ms Royal 10 B.ii, W. Peraldus (theological treatises), (13th c.); *per*—.

I John de MEPEHAM [Mepham
occ. [c. 1303] occ. [c. 1307]
[c. 1303], one of four monks who were assigned *ad tricennale celebrandum* for John Pantoum, q.v., BL Ms Cotton Vespasian A.xxii, fo 127.

[c. 1307], one of four assigned to celebrate as above for John Pouncz q.v., *ib.*

II John de MEPEHAM

occ. 1319 occ. 1351

1328, Easter, prior of Felixstowe, *Index of Placita de Banco*, pt 2, 614.

1333, 19 Aug., precentor, Reg. Hethe, fo 157 (p. 534).

1345, 18 Nov., apptd precentor in place of Henry de Hengseye, q.v., Reg. Hethe, fo 218 (p. 759); on 12 Sept., 1348, he was still or again precentor, *ib.*, fo 254^{v} (p. 848).

1319, 20 Dec.; 1323, 31 Mar., present in the bp's household and prob. serving as chaplain, Reg. Hethe, fo 41; fo 59^{v} (p. 58; p.123).

1333, 19 Aug., 10th in order at the el. of a prior among those who voted for John de Shepey II, q.v., Reg. Hethe, fo 157 (p. 534).

1334, 5 Jan., present in London at the presentation of the acct of a royal and papal tenth for the diocese of Rochester, Reg. Hethe, fo 159^{v} (p. 537).

1348, 12 Sept., present in London to pay procurations owed to the cardinal nuncios by the bp and prior, Reg. Hethe, fo 254^{v} (p. 849).

[1349], 1 Jan., present as witness at the oath of obedience of a canon of Leeds as incumbent of a parish, *ib.*, fo 267 (p. 889).

[1350], 30 Apr., provisionally absolved from excommunication incurred because he had assaulted William de Farindon, q.v., on Easter day; the inquiry into the incident had been held on 20 Apr., and he had confessed his guilt, *ib.*, fos 271^{v}-272 (pp. 906–907, 908).

1351, 18 Aug., one of the monks who, with the prior, Robert de Southflete II, q.v., witnessed a grant, *CClR (1349–1354)*, 379.

Thomas de MEPEHAM

occ. [?c. 1250]

[?c. 1250], almoner, CKS DRc/T205, 208; see also Adam II.

n.d., almost completd the north *ala* [i.e. transept, see Richard de Eastgate], and was included among the benefactors, *Reg. Roff.*, 125. The building of these transepts is assigned by Hope to the yrs 1227/1240, *Arch. Hist. Rochester*, 47.

Laurence MEREWORTH [*alias* Dan, Dann

occ. 1505 occ. 1538

1532–1538, prior: el. 21 Oct. 1532, Reg. Fisher, fo 156; res. before 16 July 1538, see below.

1505, 8 Mar., ord dcn, bp's chapel of St Blaise, Bromley, Reg. Fisher, fo 24 (as Dann).

1514, 2 Dec., replaced as cellarer by William Charnock, q.v., and was apptd sacrist in place of Robert Smyth, q.v., Reg. Fisher, fo 55^{v}.

1518, 12 Nov., reapptd cellarer in place of William Charnock, q.v., *ib.*, fo 60^{v}; 1518/19, cellarer, *Reg. Roff.*, 607, (CKS DRc/F17).

1518, 20 Nov., replaced as sacrist by John Maideston IV, q.v., Reg. Fisher, fo 60^{v}.

1522, 22 Oct., reapptd cellarer, *ib.*, fo 91^{v}.

1526, 5 Oct., apptd subprior in place of Anthony London, q.v., *ib.*, fo 117^{v}.

1532, 21 Oct., subprior, *ib.*, fo 156.

1535, acting as treasurer, *Valor Eccles.*, i, 101.

1511/12, went to London *pro necessar' monasterii* at a cost of 5s; he also bought linen for tablecloths, CKS DRc/F17.

1532, 21 Oct., as subprior, presided at the el. of a prior, Reg. Fisher, fos 156–157; he was himself elected, *ib.*

1534, 10 June, subscribed to the Act of Supremacy, *DK 7th Report*, Appndx 2, 299.

1538, [16 July], the bp wrote to Cromwell to urge him to command 'my poor monk' to return to his office of prior as the state of the priory had greatly deteriorated since his resignation, *L and P Henry VIII*, xiii, pt 1, no 1391.

John de MESEHALE [Mosehale

occ. 1347/9

1347, 24 May, granted *lit. dim.*, for the order of acol., Reg. Hethe, fo 229^{v} (p. 820).

1349, 7 Mar., ord pr., bp's chapel, Trottiscliffe, *ib.*, fo 258 (p. 1140).

Stephen MILLET

see Hoo

Thomas MONKOY [Mauncoy, Mounchey, Mouncoy

occ. 1341/3

1341, 2 June, ord acol., bp's chapel Halling, Reg. Hethe, fo 195 (p. 1139 where the date is incorrect; see *ib.*, p. 671).

1342, 16 Mar., ord subdcn, Trottiscliffe, *ib.*, fo 196^{v} (p. 1139).

1343, 7 June, ord dcn, bp's chapel, Halling, *ib.*, fo 206 (p. 1139).

John MOREL [Morell

occ. 1344 occ. 1392

1344, 29 May, recd first tonsure, Reg. Hethe, fo 210^{v} (p 1139).

1355, 22 Dec., ord pr., Rochester cathedral, Reg. Shepey, fo 12.

[1368], 23 Dec., apptd subprior, Reg. Trillek, fo 14.

1372, 27 Dec., in response to the request of the prior and chapter, absolved from the office of sacrist, *propter alias occupationes sibi assignatas*, Reg. abp Wittlesey, fos 137^{v}-138.

[1382], 17 May, *custos* of Felixstowe, Reg. prior Shepey, fo 10^{v}.

1382, 30 Nov., apptd subprior, *ib.*, fo 15.

1384, 16 Oct.; 1390, 10 and 30 June; 1392, before 1 June, subprior, Reg. prior Shepey, *ib.*, fos 21; 41v, 42; Reg. William Bottlesham, fos 26v-27.

1372, 27 Dec., with Richard de Shorn, q.v., sent to the abp for a licence to el. a bp, Reg. abp Wittlesey, fo 137v.

[1382], 17 May, the prior wrote to him concerning Henry Raundes, q.v., who conveyed the letter to Felixstowe, Reg. prior Shepey, fo 10v.

1384, 16 Oct., present in chapter for the apptment of a proctor at the curia, *ib.*, fo 21.

1387, 13 Mar., present in the prior's chapel for a renunciation and a renewal of obedience of William de Reynham, q.v., Reg. prior Shepey, fo 95, 95v.

1390, 10 June, comm. by the prior, with John de Holyngbourne, q.v., to visit Battle abbey on behalf of the Black Monk Chapter, Pantin, *BMC*, iii, 248 (Reg. prior Shepey, fo 41v).

1390, 30 June, comm. by the prior, with John de Holyngbourne, q.v., to attend the Black Monk Chapter at Northampton, Pantin, *BMC*, iii, 212, (Reg. prior Shepey fo 42).

1392, 1 June, had d. by this date, and was replaced as subprior by John de Holyngbourne, Reg. William Bottlesham, fos 26v-27.

Name in a Ms that was among those lent to the bp and the rector of Southfleet on 1 June 1390: 'Item, Petrum de Tarentasio cum tabul' super epistolas jero[nimi cuius ij folium incipit efficacior simpl[iciter fratris Johannis Morell', Reg. prior Shepey, fo 50v.

Robert de MORTON [Mortone
occ. 1315 occ. 1351

1315, 17 May, ord subdcn, Croydon, by *lit. dim.*, Reg. abp Reynolds, fo 170v.

1315, 20 Dec., ord dcn, Maidstone, by *lit. dim.*, *ib.*, fo 173v.

1320, 24 May, ord pr., Rochester cathedral, Reg. Hethe, fo 44v (p. 71).

1327, 6 July, wrongly accused of adultery by a laywoman, Reg. Hethe, fo 87 (p. 233).

1330, 10 Feb., reported as unjustly treated by the bp who refused to rec. his purgation until he had appealed to the abp, Reg. Hethe, fo 130v (p. 427) (BL Ms Cotton Faustina B.v, fo 54); see Henry de Hengseye and John de Oxonia.

1333, 19 Aug., present at the el. of a prior and was one of five who nom. William de Reyersh, q.v., *ib.*, fo 157, (p. 534).

1351, 18 Aug., one of the monks who, with the prior, Robert de Southflete II, q.v., witnessed a grant, *CClR (1349–1354)*, 379.

MOSEHALE
see Mesehale

MOUNCHEY, Mouncoy
see Monkoy

N.
n.d.

n.d., cellarer, *Cust. Roff.*, 13.

Thomas NEVELL [Nevill, Nevylle
occ. 1508 occ. 1540

1508, 8 Apr., ord acol., bp's palace chapel, Rochester, Reg. Fisher, fo 33.

1509, 22 Dec., ord subdcn, Bromley, *ib.*, fo 36v.

1510, 30 Mar., ord dcn, bp's palace chapel, Rochester, *ib.*, fo 37.

1511, 19 Apr., ord pr., Rochester cathedral, *ib.*, fo 38v.

1530, 9 Oct., apptd chamberlain, succ. William Albon, q.v., Reg. Fisher, fo 142v; he was also chamberlain in 1535, *Valor Eccles.*, i, 103.

1532, 21 Oct., 8th in order at the el. of a prior, *ib.*, fo 156.

1534, 10 June, subscribed to the Act of Supremacy, *DK 7th Report*, Appndx 2, 299.

1540, 8 Apr., assigned a pension of £6 13s. 4d. p.a., *L and P Henry VIII*, xv, no 474.

In 1506/7, a John Nevyll, *fratre cenobii Rofensis* may have been a student residing at Canterbury college, Oxford, because he pd 5s. 'pro camera subter cameram de ly Wynchester pro dimidio anno et non plus quia vacavit', Pantin, *Cant. Coll. Ox.*, ii, 247.

Thomas NEWYNGTON
occ. 1500/1

1500/1, student at Oxford and resident in Canterbury College; possibly monk of Rochester, Pantin, *Cant. Col. Ox.*, ii, 231.

I NICHOLAS
occ. [?c. 1200]

n.d., cellarer, CKS DRc/T105/1.

n.d., as cellarer, provided vestments and is listed among monk benefactors, CKS DRc/Z14, dorse.

Note: see also N.

II NICHOLAS
n.d.

n.d., his sister, Elviva of Winchester, gave vestments and was listed among the benefactors, *Reg. Roff.*, 123.

Note: the above two entries may refer to one monk.

III NICHOLAS
occ. [c. 1303]

[c. 1303], was not assigned *ad tricennale celebrandum* because he was absent from the house, BL Ms Cotton Vespasian, A.xxii, fo 127.

[c. 1303/4], one of four monks who were assigned to celebrate as above for Robert de Hoo, q.v., *ib.*

Note: see also Nicholas de Becheshangre who is prob. this monk.

NICHOLAS
see also Nicholas de Frendesbury

William NICOLL
occ. 1496

1496, 4 Nov., was living as an apostate acc. to the certificate in reply to the abp's visitation notice, *Reg. abp Morton*, ii, no 446.

NIGEL [Nigellus
n.d.

n.d., precentor, gave vestments and was included among the benefactors, *Reg. Roff.*, 123.

John NOBLE
occ. 1496 d. 1526

[1510], 8 Nov., apptd precentor to succeed Thomas Hemysby, q.v., Reg. Fisher, fo 38.
1521, 26 Nov., apptd sacrist in place of John Maideston IV, *ib.*, fo 91.
1523, 20 Aug., replaced as sacrist by Thomas Hemysby, q.v., *ib.*, fo 93^{v}.
1525, 20 Sept., apptd chamberlain in place of Robert Maydeston, *ib.*, fo 113.

1496, 4 Nov., 14th in order on the visitation certificate, *Reg. abp Morton*, ii, no 446.
1526, d. by 20 Jan., Reg. Fisher, fo 116; see William Albon.

Name in
(1) BL IA, 3420, Augustinus, (printed book), n.d.
(2) Messrs Maggs, Ludolphus Carthus, (printed book), Paris, 1506.
In both cases his name is preceded or followed by *pertinet*.

John NOVYN [Nodyn
occ. [1465] occ. 1496

[1465], 30 Mar., recd the tonsure and ord acol., bp's chapel, Halling, Reg. Lowe, fo 43^{v}.
1465, 21 Dec., ord subdcn, bp's chapel, Halling, *ib.*, fo 45^{v}.
1466, 20 Dec., ord dcn, bp's chapel, Halling, *ib.*, fo 47^{v}.

1494, 18 May, removed from the office of subprior and replaced by John Auncell, q.v., Reg. Savage, fo 7^{v}.

1496, 4 Nov., 4th in order on the visitation certificate, *Reg. abp Morton*, ii, no 446.

William ?OLISTONIB' [?Oliscomb'
occ. 1389

1389, 6 Aug., one of two *clerici* whom the prior was comm. by the abp, *sed. vac.*, to rec. and clothe, Reg. prior Shepey, fo 42^{v}.

OMFRAY, Omfrey
see Umfrey

OPCHERCH, Oppechurche
see Upcherch

ORDWINUS [Orduuinus,
occ. [1095 × 1107] occ. 1107/8 × 1125

1107 × 1108–1125, prior: occ. 1107 × 1108; occ. after May 1125, *Fasti*, ii, 78; see also *HRH*, 64, n.1 for a discussion of the dating problems.

[1095 × 1107], described as *prothoprior* and greeted by Reginald, monk of St Augustine's, Canterbury, in his preface to his life of Malchus, *Vita Malchi*, 38; see Baldwin II.
[1107 × 1108], attested bp Gundulf's so called great but prob. spurious charter, CKS DRc/T47; see Brett, 'Forgery at Rochester', 403–404.
[1107 × 1108], as prior, *temp.* bp Gundulf, witnessed the oath of obedience of the abbess of Malling, *Text. Roff.*, ii, fo 198 and cap 181.
[1108 × 1114], as prior witnessed an agreement *temp.* bp Ralph, *Cust. Roff.*, 35, *Text. Roff.*, ii, fo 193^{v} and cap 170.
[1114 × 1124], as prior, witnessed a grant of bp Ernulf, *Text. Roff.*, fo 196^{v} and cap 177.
[1125], as prior, *temp.* bp John [I], witnessed a grant, *Reg. Roff.*, 8; see also BL Ms Cotton Domitian A.x, fo 122^{v}.

Note: it is possible that he, like his two predecessors, Ernulph and Ralph I, q.v., may have been a monk of Canterbury, *Fasti*, ii, 78–79; see Orwius under Canterbury.

OSBERN
see Shepey, Strode

OSBERT [Osbertus
occ. [1174 × 1181]

[1174, Aug. × 1181, Sept.], chamberlain, *Eng. Epis. Acta*, ii, no 190. He was chamberlain on 15 May 1177, see below.

[1174, Aug. × 1181, Sept.], with Aufredus, prior of Felixstowe, q.v., acted for the priory in a dispute over tithes, *ib.*
1177, 15 May, with Aufredus, q.v., acted as proctors for the chapter in a process, prob. the above dispute, CKS DRc/L17; see also BL Ms Cotton Domitian A.x, fos 184, 207 (this latter charter is, however, spurious).

OSSORY
see Bigton

OWEN
see Oxford

Richard de OXENFORD [Oxeford, Oxinforde
occ. 1407 occ. 1446

1407, 15 Aug., one of two whose prof. the prior was comm. to rec., Reg. prior Shepey, fo 116.
1407, 24 Sept., ord acol., collegiate church of All

Saints, Maidstone, Reg. abp Arundel, i, fo 341 (named as monk of Canterbury).
1408, 22 Dec., ord dcn, Lambeth palace chapel, *ib.*, i, fo 343^{v}.
1409, 21 Sept., ord pr., abp's chapel, Maidstone, ib., ii, fo 96^{v}.
1439, 22 Apr., apptment as precentor to succeed John Ealding, q.v., confirmed by the bp, Reg. Wells, fo 22.
1445, 29 May, precentor; see below.
1446, 6 Oct., released from the offices of precentor and sacrist and apptd subprior in place of William Marchaunt, q.v., Reg. Lowe, fo 10.
1409, 20 Nov., 21st in order of those present in chapter to appt a proctor in a lawsuit, Reg. prior Shepey, fo 121^{v}.
1419, 31 Aug., 13th in order at the el. of a prior, *Reg. abp Chichele*, i, 62.
1443, 18 Apr., presented four candidates for adm. to the priory to the bp at his house in Queenshithe, London, Reg. Wells, fo 67.
1444, 19 Dec., presented five monks for ordination at Southfleet, Reg. Lowe, fo 4.
1445, 29 May, [as precentor] presented a candidate for ordination in the bp's chapel at Halling, Reg. Lowe, fo 4^{v}.

Owen OXFORD [*alias* Johnson
occ. 1537/40

1537, 12 Mar., recd the tonsure and clothed as a monk, Reg. Hilsey, fo 11.

1540, 8 Apr., awarded no pension because apptd 'under-sexton' in the new foundation, *L and P Henry VIII*, xv, no 474 (as Owen Oxforde).

John de OXONIA
occ. [c. 1302] occ. 1342

1342, 4 Jan., apptd subpr., in place of John Whytefeld, q.v., Reg. Hethe, fo 196^{v} (p. 676).

[c. 1302], one of four monks who were assigned *ad tricennale celebrandum* for William de Ledes, q.v., BL Ms Cotton Vespasian, A.xxii, fo 127.
1330, 10 Feb., reported as unjustly treated by the bp who refused to rec. his purgation until he had appealed to the abp, Reg. Hethe, fo 130^{v} (p. 427) (BL Ms Cotton Faustina B.v, fo 54); see also Henry de Hengseye and Robert de Morton.
1333, 19 Aug., 8th in order at the el. of a prior among those who voted for John de Shepey II, q.v., Reg Hethe, fo 157 (p. 534).

PAEN
see Payn

John PAGE
occ. 1496

1496, 4 Nov., 13th in order on the visitation certificate, *Reg. abp Morton*, ii, no 446.

John PANTOUM [?Pantoun
d. [c. 1303]

[c. 1303], d., and four monks were assigned *ad tricennale celebrandum* for him, BL Ms Cotton Vespasian, A.xxii, fo 127.

PAUL [Paulus
n.d.

Name in BL Ms Royal 2 F.vi, Esaias (13th c.); *per Paulum priorem.*

Note: see the entry below.

I PAULINUS
n.d.

Name in Cambridge, Corpus Christi College Ms 62 which contains Vita S. Bernardi (12th c.); on fo 49 *per paulin[um priorem.* On fo 1, which is the beginning of Parabole etc, and is 13th C., *per Paulum priorem.* The Vita S. Bernardi is in the 1202 library catalogue in BL Ms Royal 5 B.xii, fo 2, printed in Sharpe, *Eng. Benedictine Libraries*, iv, B79.104.

Note: who are these priors Paul and Paulinus?

II PAULINUS
occ. [1095 × 1107]

n.d., sacrist, see below.
n.d., as sacrist, built the first church at Frindsbury and provided it with books, vestments and candelabra and was listed among the benefactors, *Reg. Roff.*, 118; see Dunstan.
[1095 × 1107], sacrist, greeted by Reginald, monk of St Augustine's, Canterbury, in his preface to his life of Malchus, *Vita Malchi*, 38; and see *ib.*, 12 and 11 for the prob. dating which has been followed here.
[1107 × 1108], *secretarius*, with Ordwinus, prior, q.v., and others witnessed the oath of obedience of the abbess of Malling to bp Gundulf, *Text. Roff.*, ii, fo 198 and cap 181.

Note: see the note above under Paulinus I.

Thomas PAYN [Paen
occ. [c. 1302] d. [c. 1304]

[c. 1302], one of four monks who were assigned *ad tricennale celebrandum* for James de Beyersse, q.v., BL Ms Cotton Vespasian, A.xxii, fo 127.
[c. 1304], d. and four monks were assigned to celebrate as above for him, *ib.*

I John de PECHAM
occ. [c. 1301]

[c. 1301], one of four monks who were assigned *ad tricennale celebrandum* for Thomas de Hakyntone, q.v., Bl Ms Cotton Vespasian, A.xxii, fo 126^{v}.

II John PECHAM [Peckham
occ. 1496 [d. 1524]

[1500/1], 27 Feb., dismissed from the office of cellarer and succ. by Edmund Hatfield, q.v., Reg. Fitzjames, fo 9^{v}.

1518, 12 Nov., apptd chamberlain in place of John Dartford, q.v., Reg. Fisher, fo 60^{v}.
[1524, 16 Feb.], chamberlain before this date when replaced by Robert Maydeston, q.v., *ib.*, fo 94.

1496, 4 Nov., 9th in order on the visitation certificate, *Reg. abp Morton*, ii, no 446.
[1524, by 16 Feb.], d., Reg. Fisher, fo 94.

Richard PECHAM [Peccham, Pekham
occ. 1446 ?d. 1496/7

1460–?1468, prior: el. by scrutiny in the presence of the bp, 24 Sept. 1460, Reg. Lowe, fo 33^{v}; prior 1463, CKS DRc/T336; see William Wode.

1446, 7 Sept., one of three whose prof. the prior was comm. to rec., Reg. Lowe, fo 9^{v}.
1446, 17 Dec., ord acol., and subdcn, bp's chapel, Halling, *ib.*, fo 11.
1447, 23 Dec., ord [dcn], bp's chapel, Halling, *ib.*, fo 15.
1450, 19 Sept., ord pr., Rochester cathedral, *ib.*, fo 21^{v}.

1463, after, prob. prior of Felixstowe, Dugdale, *Monasticon*, iv, 564.

1463, 7 May, obtained papal confirmaton of earlier grants (of which there appears to be no evidence in the extant papal regs) of the privilege of using the mitre, ring and other insignia, including staff and almuce reported to have been previously omitted. This was to apply under the usual conditions, i.e., when no bp or papal legate was present, *CPL*, xi, (1455–1464), 645.
1471, 12 Oct., granted papal licence to rec. and retain for life any benefice with or without cure of souls, *CPL*, xiii, (1471–1484), 290 (transcribed as Percham). He is described merely as monk.
1496/7, there are several refs to the payment of his debts (amounting to c. £10) on the Felixstowe acct for this yr, Dugdale, *Monasticon*, iv, 564; prob. he had recently d.

Robert PECHAM
occ. 1534

1534, 10 June, subscribed to the Act of Supremacy, *DK 7th Report*, Appndx 2, 299.

William PECHAM [Peckam, Pekham
occ. 1399 occ. 1430

1399, 30 Aug., one of three whose prof. the prior was comm. to rec., Reg. prior Shepey, fo 89^{v}.
1400, 18 Dec., ord acol., Malling, Reg. John Bottlesham, fo 8.
1402, 16 Feb., acol., granted *lit. dim.*, to all orders, Reg. prior Shepey, fo 111.
1402, 23 Sept., ord subdcn, bp's chapel, Trottiscliffe, Reg. John Bottlesham, fo 33^{v}.
1403, 22 Sept., ord dcn, bp's chapel, Trottiscliffe, *ib.*, fo 38^{v}.
1404, 29 Mar., ord pr., bp's chapel, Trottiscliffe, *ib.*, fo 46^{v}.

1429/30, almoner, CKS DRc/F11.

1409, 20 Nov., 18th in order among those present in chapter to appt a proctor in a lawsuit, Reg. prior Shepey, fo 121^{v}.

Raymond PELEGRINI [?Pelegrim
occ. 1358 occ. 1361

1358, 22 Dec., ord subdcn, Rochester cathedral, Reg. Shepey, fo 23.
1361, 20 Feb., ord dcn, Strood, *ib.*, fo 32^{v}.
1361, 18 Sep., ord pr., abp's chapel Otford, Reg. abp Islip, fo 320.

Note: On 1 July 1358, the bp authorized M. Hugh Pelegrini, [papal nuncio and collector; see *BRUO*] treasurer of Lichfield cathedral, to visit *limina apostolorum Petri et Pauli*, Reg. Shepey, fo 19^{v}. Are these two perhaps relatives?

William PEPER [Pepir
occ. 1333 occ. 1342

1333, 18 Dec., ord dcn, bp's chapel, Halling, Reg. Hethe, fo 159 (p. 1148).

1333, 19 Aug., 25th and last in order at the el. of a prior among those who voted for John de Shepey II, q.v., Reg. Hethe, fo 157 (p. 534).
1340, 11 Oct.; 1341, 6 May; 1342, 1 May, 8 Oct., present in the bp's household and prob. chaplain, Reg. Hethe, fos 183^{v}, 195, 197^{v}, 199 (pp. 631, 670, 679, 685).

Note: see William de St Radegund who is prob. the same monk.

William de PEREWICH [Perewych, Perewyco, Perwico
occ. [c. 1301] occ. 1325

1322, 5 June, 18 Dec., precentor, Reg. Hethe, fos 56, 54^{v} (pp. 111, 105).
1325, 12 Oct., granted release from the office of subprior in which he had served *laudabiliter* and *per diuturna tempora*, *ib.*, fo 113 (p. 353).

[c. 1301], one of four monks who were assigned *ad tricennale celebrandum* for John de Beverle, q.v., BL Ms Cotton Vespasian, A.xxii, fo 126^{v}.
[c. 1304], one of four assigned to celebrate, as above, for Thomas Payn, q.v., *ib.*, fo 127.
1322, 5 June, present at an ordination in Rochester cathedral, Reg. Hethe, fo 56 (p. 111).
1322, 18 Dec., comm. by the bp to have oversight, with others, of the financial affairs of Strood hospital, Reg. Hethe, fo 54^{v} (p. 105).

PETER [Petrus
n.d.

n.d., precentor, *Reg. Roff.*, 123.

n.d., at the time of his adm., his father Goldwinus Grecus gave land and his mother gave eight albs, *Text. Roff.*, ii, fo 191^{v}-192, and cap 183, *Reg. Roff.*, 118–119. His sister Goda, of London, also gave vestments, *ib.*, 123. His own benefactions, as precentor, included the construction of a cupboard for the graduals and psalters. His generous gifts of money *ad novum opus ecclesie* were never less than 20s., *ib.*, 124.

Name in

(1) BL Ms Cotton Otho A.xv, Acta Pontificum which was burnt in 1731; this vol. appears in the 1202 library catalogue in BL Ms Royal 5 B.xii, fo 2, printed in Sharpe, *Eng. Benedictine Libraries*, iv, B79.135; see *MLGB*, 161.

(2) BL Ms Royal 5 B.xvi, Augustinus, (12th c.); on fo 3,—*precentoris*. This vol. appears in the library catalogue of 1122/3 in *Text. Roff.*, ii, fos 224–230, and in that of 1202 in BL Ms Royal 5 B.xii, fo 2; these are printed in Sharpe, *Eng. Benedictine Libraries*, iv, where the refs are B77.15 and B79.21.

Note: see Goldwinus I and II; one of these may ref. to Peter. See also Richard III.

PHILIP
see St Clare

Walter PHILIP
see Boxley

Robert PILTON
see Rochestre

John PLEME [Flepleme
occ. [1369] d. 1394

[1369], 20 Sept., had recd first tonsure and now given *lit. dim.* for all minor orders, Reg. Trillek, fo 20.

1370, 9 Mar., ord acol., St Paul's cathedral, London, *Reg. Sudbury* (London), ii, 76.

1370, 8 June, ord subdcn, St Paul's, London, *ib.*, 84.

1371, 1 Mar., ord dcn, St Paul's, London, *ib.*, 99.

1386, 17 Apr., apptd precentor in place of Thomas de Dovor, q.v., Reg. prior Shepey, fo 23.

1390, 20 Apr., request by the prior and chapter on his behalf to release him from the precentor's office and appt him chamberlain in place of Nicholas de Frendesbury, q.v., *ib.*, fo 43; the bp confirmed this on the following day, *ib.*, fo 68^{v}.

1394, 7 Feb., chamberlain up to this date, *ib.*, fo 68.

1384, 16 Oct., 12th in order of those present in chapter to appt a proctor in the curia, Reg. prior Shepey, fo 21.

1387, 13 Mar., present in the prior's chapel for the renunciation and renewal of obedience of William de Reynham, q.v., Reg. prior Shepey, fo 95–95^{v}.

1387, 1 Sept., one of ten monks and four clerks apptd general proctors, Reg. prior Shepey, fo 58^{v}.

1394, 7 Feb., d. by this date, *ib.*, fo 68.

John POUNCZ [Pountz
d. [c. 1307]

[c. 1307], d. and four monks were assigned *ad tricennale celebrandum* for him, BL Ms Cotton Vespasian A.xxii, fo 127.

John QUYNTLOK
occ. 1496

1496, 4 Nov., 10th in order on the visitation certificate, *Reg. abp Morton*, ii, no 446.

William QWENBURGH [*alias* Baker and Shepey
occ. 1450/2

1450, 19 Sept., recd the tonsure and ord acol., Rochester cathedral, Reg. Lowe, fo 21^{v}.

1451, 19 June, ord subdcn, Halling, *ib.*, fo 22, as Shepey.

1452, 3 June, ord dcn, Halling, *ib.*, fo 23^{v}.

R
n.d.

n.d., precentor; see below.

Name in

(1) BL Ms Royal 3 C.iv, Gregorius (12th c.); *per—precentorem*. This vol. appears in the library catalogue of 1122/3 in *Text. Roff.*, ii, fos 224–230, and in that of 1202 in BL Ms Royal 5 B.xii, fo 2; these are printed in Sharpe, *Eng. Benedictine Libraries*, iv, where the refs are B77.45 and B79.24.

(2) BL Ms Royal 12 F.xiii, Bestiarium etc. (early 13th c.),—*precentoris*.

RAINALDUS
occ. 1143

1143, *secretarius*, witness to a grant to the priory, *Text. Roff.*, ii, fo 230^{v} and cap 220.

I RALPH [Radulfus, Radulphus
occ. before 1107

1107, before, prior: previously monk of Caen and then of Christ Church Canterbury (q.v., under Canterbury); 1 Aug. 1107, el. abbot of Battle, *Fasti*, ii, 78, *HRH*, 63.

1107 × 1108, as abbot of Battle, witnessed the oath of obedience of the abbess of Malling, *Text. Roff.*, ii, fo 198 and cap 181; see also CKS DRc/T47.

While at Rochester he wrote a number of theological treatises and meditations showing the influence of Anselm so strongly that they were for long considered Anslelm's, Southern, *Anselm*, (1990), 372–376; and see E. Searle, ed., *The*

Chronicle of Battle Abbey, (Oxford, 1980), for his career and writings, 116, 118, 130, 132.

II RALPH
mid-12th c.

mid-12th c., brother of Ansfridus the sheriff; previously *custos* of the manor of Lambeth and brought vestments, ornaments and plate with him and was listed among the benefactors *Reg. Roff.*, 119.

Note: Ansfrid, sheriff, may be dated 1131 × 1136 acc. to Dr M. Brett; see J. A. Green, *English Sheriffs to A.D. 1154* (Public Record Office handbook 24, 1990), p. 51.

III RALPH
occ. [1093 × 1108]

[1093 × 1108], chamberlain, *Text. Roff.*, ii, fo 185^v and cap 121.

[1093 × 1108], with Baldwin and Wido, q.v., witnessed a grant to the priory *temp.* bp Gundulf and abp Anselm, *ib.*

Note: see also Ralph de Ros.

IV RALPH
occ. [before 1311]

[1311, before], prior of Darenth, C. Cotton, 'A Kentish Chartulary of the Order of St John of Jerusalem', *Kent Archaological Society Records Branch*, xi, (1930), 124. See Richard de Darente.

[1311, before], prior at the time of an agreement between the Templars and the prior of Darenth and others, *ib.*

Note: see Ralph de Stoke who may be this monk.

RALPH, prior
see also Ros

Henry RAUNDES
occ. 1382 occ. 1388

1382, 30 Nov., apptd *custos* of Felixstowe in place of John Morel, q.v., Reg. prior Shepey, fo 15.

1388, 9 Apr., released from this office because 'nequit ibidem diutius commode ministrare', and Thomas de Hariettisham, q.v., was to be sent in his place, *ib.*, fo 36.

1382, 26 Mar., prof. obedience, 'de novo prestita . . . Iuro pure, sponte quod de cetero ero obediens vobis domino .. priori', Reg. prior Shepey, fo 9^v.

1382, 17 May, sent by the prior to Felixstowe with a letter to the *custos* containing the order that he was to remain there for a time; the letter requested the *custos* of the cell to watch Raundes' behavour to ensure that he observed the Rule and was obedient, *ib.*, fo 10^v.

1382, 27 Sept., reminded of his above promise of obedience and of the penalties of imprisonment and excommunication, *ib.*, fo 11. (This entry is headed *iniunctio.*)

Walter de RAWE
occ. 1317

1317, *quondam hostiar'*, BL Ms Cotton Faustina B.v, fo 4.

1317, one of the monks involved in the appeal after their el. of Hamo de Hethe as bp, *ib.*

I REGINALD
occ. [1095 × 1107]

[1095 × 1107], described as *oeconomus et archimagrinus* when greeted by Reginald, monk of St Augustine's, Canterbury, in his preface to his life of Malchus, *Vita Malchi*, 38; see *ib.*, 12 and 11 for the prob. dating of this ms which has been followed here.

II REGINALD
occ. 1155 occ. 1160

1155, 1160, prior: occ. 8 Mar. 1155, Nov. × Dec. 1160, *Fasti*, ii, 79, *HRH*, 64.

n.d., had two bells made and placed in the great tower [*majori turri*], *Reg. Roff.*, 118.

REINER [Reinerius
n.d.

n.d., *nauta* and *monachus ad succurrendum*; gave his ship which was sold for 40s., and was named among the benefactors, *Reg. Roff.*, 122.

Note: see also Reynerius.

RENHAM, Rensham
see Reynham

Richard REVELL
see Bradfelde

William REVILL
occ. 1534

1534, 10 June, subscribed to the Act of Supremacy, *DK 7th Report*, Appndx 2, 299.

William de REYERSH [Reyersse, Reyersshe, Reyherche, Rierssh, Ryarsh, Ryerhs
occ. [c. 1303/4] occ. 1333

1326, 10 Mar., possibly chaplain to the bp, Reg. Hethe, fo 71^v (p. 163); see below.

1326, 17 Sept., the prior and chapter requested his apptment as chamberlain in place of Robert de Southflete, q.v., *ib.*, fo 118^v (pp. 380–381).

1328, 14 May, chamberlain, Reg. Hethe, fo 119^v (p. 385).

1333, 19 Aug., sacrist, and candidate for the office of prior, *ib.*, fo 157 (p. 534); see below.

[c. 1303/4], one of four monks who were assigned *ad tricennale celebrandum* for Robert de

Hoo, q.v., BL Ms Cotton Vespasian, A.xxii, fo 127.

1321, 6 Feb., apptd proctor by the prior and chapter in a case of non payment of pension, Reg. Hethe, fo 83v (pp. 211–212).

1322, 5 June, present at an ordination in Rochester cathedral, Reg. Hethe, fo 56 (p. 111).

1326, 10 Mar., in attendance on the bp at Halling, *ib.*, 71v, (p. 163).

1328, 15 May, comm. by the bp to rec. the prof. of two worthy clerks seeking adm. to St Mary's, Strood, *ib.*, fo 119v (p. 385).

1332, 1 June, present in the prior's *camera* with the prior and John de Faversham I, q.v., and others for the reading of a comm. sent to the bp from the abp, Reg. Hethe, fo 151 (p. 516).

1333, 1 Jan., named as proctor of the prior and chapter who were subcollectors of a royal and papal tenth in the city and diocese of Rochester, Reg. Hethe, fo 159v, (pp. 537–538).

1333, 19 Aug., 13th in order at the el. of a prior among the majority who nom. John de Shepey II, q.v.; there were also five monks who nom. him for this office, *ib.*, fo 157 (p. 534).

Name in BL Ms Royal 9 E.xi, Alexander de Hales (13th/14th c.); on fo 1 *per fratrem—*.

REYERSH
see also Beyersse

REYNERIUS
n.d.

n.d., name in BL Ms Royal 11 B.xv, Instituta (Justinian) etc., (13th c.); on fo 1, *per— monachum.*

REYNERIUS
see also Reiner

I John de REYNHAM [Renham, Rensham, Reyneham
occ. 1262 d. 1294

1262–1283, 1292–1294, prior: succ. 1262, res. because of illegitimacy before 24 Dec. 1283. Succ. 7 Jan. 1292 for a second term, having recd a dispensation for illegitimacy; d. 1294, *Fasti*, ii, 80. See Thomas de Wouldham.

[1272 × 1280], involved as one of the judges in an appeal by the abbey of Bec vs its English cell at St Neots, Pantin, *BMC*, i, 119; iii, 273.

1283, 3 Dec., the abp ordered his deprivation, *Epist. Pecham*, no 499.

1286, 13 June, the pope granted him a dispensation for having held the office of prior with an uneasy conscience, although he had previously recd papal dispensation as the son of a priest, before being ord, *CPL*, i (1198–1304), 487. *Anglia Sacra* records that he was deposed because the abp learned during a visitation that he was suspected of having procured the el. of John [de Bradefeld, q.v.] as bp by dishonest means, and of financial mismanagement and simony, *ib.*, i, 394, (Reg. abp Pecham, fo 87v, *Epist. Pecham*, no 486).

Name possibly in BL Ms Royal 12 G.ii, Aristotles (late 13th c.); on fo 1v, *per Johannem priorem*, which could also refer to John de Greenstrete, q.v.

II John de REYNHAM [Renham
occ. 1322 occ. 1342

1322, 27 Mar., ord acol., bp's chapel, Trottiscliffe, Reg. Hethe, fo 55v (p. 110).

1322, 5 June, ord subdcn, Rochester cathedral, *ib.*, fo 56 (p. 1152).

1322, 18 Sept., ord dcn, bp's chapel, Trottiscliffe, *ib.*, fo 57v (p. 1152).

1323, 24 Sept., ord pr., Rochester cathedral, *ib.*, fo 61 (p. 1152).

1333, 19 Aug., succentor, Reg. Hethe, fo 157 (p. 534).

1339, 13 Aug., apptd precentor, *ib.*, fo 174v (p. 589).

1342, 24 Mar., the prior and chapter requested his removal from the office of precentor and his apptment as cellarer to succ. Richard de Tonnbregg, q.v.; on 26 Mar. the bp complied, *ib.*, fo 197 (pp. 677–678).

1333, 19 Aug., 17th in order at the el. of a prior among those who nom. John de Shepey II, q.v., Reg. Hethe, fo 157 (p. 534).

1338, 27 Sept., present at the apptment of William de Bromfeld, q.v., as cellarer, *ib.*, fo 173v (pp. 585–586).

III John REYNHAM
occ. 1384

1384, 16 Oct., 21st in order of those present in chapter to appt a proctor in a lawsuit, Reg. prior Shepey, fo 21.

Thomas de REYNHAM
occ. 1361

1361, 20 Feb., ord pr., Strood, Reg. Shepey, fo 32v.

William de REYNHAM
occ. 1384 occ. 1409

1384, 16 Oct., 18th in order of those present in chapter to appt a proctor in a lawsuit, Reg. prior Shepey, fo 21.

1387, 13 Mar., in the prior's chapel in the presence of the prior made a renunciation and a renewal of obedience: 'Ego Willelmus dico . . . quod licet mihi nuper fuerit quoddam privilegium ab apostolica sede indultum quod forem ab obediencia superiorum meorum Episcopi et Prioris Roffen[se] ac quorumque aliorum ordinariorum absolutus pariter et exemptus'. He was thus directly answerable only to the pope or to the papal chaplains.

However, he had now changed his mind and decided that he desired to remain in the monastery 'sub obediencia venerabilium patrum Dominorum Episcopi et Prioris', *ib.*, fo 95, 95v.

1409, 20 Nov., 5th in order of those assembled in chapter to appt a proctor in a lawsuit, *ib.*, fo 121v.

I RICHARD
occ. [1114 × 1124]

[1114 × 1124], with Humphrey and Robert V, q.v, witnessed a grant of Hugh son of Fulk to the priory, *Text. Roff.*, ii, fo 191v and cap 163.

II RICHARD [Ricardus
occ. 1181/2

1181–1182, prior: occ. after Nov. 1181; became abbot of Burton c. 1182, *Fasti*, ii, 79, *HRH*, 31, 64.

n.d., as prior listed among the benefactors for his gift of two copes [*cappas*], *Reg. Roff.*, 121.

III RICHARD
n.d.

n.d., at the time of his adm. his father, Goldwin the priest gave a messuage, *Text. Roff.*, ii, fos 199v-200 and cap 184. Goldwin attested bp Gundulf's prob. spurious charter of 1107 × 1108, CKS DRc/T47.

IV RICHARD
n.d.

Name in Cambridge, Corpus Christi College Ms 184, Eusebius (12th c.), on fo 1, *per*—. This vol. appears in the library catalogue of 1122/3 in *Text. Roff.*, ii, fos 224–230, and in that of 1202 in BL Ms Royal 5 B.xii, fo 2; these are printed in Sharpe, *Eng. Benedictine Libraries*, iv, where the refs are B77.55 and B79.96.

V RICHARD
occ. [1185 × 1214]

[1185 × 1214], witnessed a charter of bp Gilbert de Glanville, *Reg. Roff.*, 688. See also CKS DRc/T572/5, T572/7.

VI RICHARD
occ. 1242

1242, 5 Nov., subprior, *Flores Hist*, ii, 256.

1242, 5 Nov., with the bp acted as *scrutator* in the el. of a prior [Alexander de Glanville, q.v.], *ib.*

VII RICHARD
occ. [1389 × 1400]

[1389 × 1400], witnessed a charter of bp William Bottlesham concerning Strood hospital, *Reg. Roff.*, 399.

Note: Seven Richards as entered above, but how many monks are involved?

See also Richard de Waledene.

RIERSSH
see Reyersh

I ROBERT [Robertus
n.d.

n.d., priest and later a monk who gave land in Sutgate and was named among the benefactors, *Reg. Roff.*, 118.

II ROBERT
n.d.

n.d., *vinitarius*, gave a 4s. rent and was listed among the benefactors, *Reg. Roff.*, 124.

III ROBERT
n.d.

n.d., *susfache*, gave vestments and was listed among the benefactors, *Reg. Roff.*, 123.

IV ROBERT
occ. [c. 1109 × 1114]

[c. 1109 × 1114], 'assiduus in servitio Radulfi Rofensis episcopi' and therefore prob. the bp's chaplain, Eadmer, *Vita Anselmi* 147–8.

[c. 1109 × 1114], had an accident on London Bridge and lost his horse and baggage which, however, were safely recovered, *ib.* The event is reported as occurring after abp Anselm's d.

V ROBERT [Robertus, Rodbertus
occ. [1114 × 1124]

[1114 × 1124], *temp.* bp Ernulf, with Humphrey and Richard I, q.v., witnessed a grant of Hugh son of Fulk to the priory, *Text. Roff.*, ii, fo 191v and cap 163.

[1114 × 1124], witnessed an agreement, with Humphrey, Martin I and William III, q.v., *ib.*, ii, fo 199v, and cap 183.

Note: Robert III, IV and V may be identical.

VI ROBERT [Rodbertus
occ. [1148 × 1182]

[1148 × 1182], chamberlain, *Reg. Roff.*, 169.

[1148 × 1182], with Adam I, q.v., attested a confirmation of bp Walter, *ib.*

VII ROBERT
occ. 1235 d. c. 1240

1235, 18 Aug., with Alexander IV, q.v., sent by the prior and chapter to the curia to appeal vs the abp's refusal to confirm the bp el. [Richard de Wendene], *CPL*, i (1198–1304), 148.

1240, sent by the prior and convent to the curia in their appeal vs the abp over the church of Northfleet and other negotiations; he d. while at the curia, *Flores Hist.*, ii, 243–244 (*Anglia Sacra*, i, 349).

Note: some of these entries under Robert may overlap; the question remains, how many monks are involved? One of them may be the M. Robert, who gave a copy of Priscian to the monastic library; see also Robert de Waletone.

John ROCHESTER [*alias* Watts
occ. 1527 occ. 1534

1527, 22 Dec., one of eight who made their prof. before the bp, Reg. Fisher, fo 121v.

1534, 10 June, subscribed to the Act of Supremacy, *DK 7th Report*, Appndx 2, 299.

Robert ROCHESTRE [*alias* Pilton, Pylton
occ. 1496 occ. 1540

1511, 20 Sept., apptd sacrist, Reg. Fisher, fo 40v; 1511/12, sacrist, CKS DRc/F17.
1514, 31 Mar., released from the above office, Reg. Fisher, fo 54 (as Pilton).
1530, 9 Oct., reapptd sacrist, *ib.*, fo 142v.
1531, 12 Apr., referred to as former prior of Felixstowe, *L and P Henry VIII*, v, no 220(11).
Note: this would have been before 9 Sept., 1528 when the priory was suppressed, *ib.*, iv, pt 2, no 4673.
1532, 12 Nov., released from the office of sacrist as requested by the prior and chapter on 11 Nov., *ib.*, fo 157.
1534, 10 June, subprior, *DK 7th Report*, Appndx 2, 299.
1535, almoner, *Valor Eccles.*, i, 104.
1540, 8 Apr., prob. subprior, see below.

1496, 4 Nov., student at Oxford, *Reg. abp Morton*, ii, no 446.

1496, 4 Nov., 17th in order on the visitation certificate, *Reg. abp Morton*, ii, no 446.
1511/12, named at the head of a composite obedientiary acct roll as one of four monk auditors in conjunction with one of the king's auditors, CKS DRc/F17.
1532, 21 Oct., 4th at the el. of a prior, Reg. Fisher, fo 156.
1534, 10 June, subscribed to the Act of Supremacy, *DK 7th Report*, Appndx 2, 299.
1540, 8 Apr., prob. subprior as he heads the list of pensions and was assigned £10 p.a., *L and P Henry VIII*, xv, no 476.

Walter ROCHESTRE [Roffchestre, Rouchestre
occ. 1393 occ. 1434

1393, 1 Sept., one of three whose prof. the prior was comm. to rec., Reg. William Bottlesham, fo 43 and Reg. prior Shepey, fo 66.
1395, 6 Mar., ord subdcn, Rochester cathedral, Reg. William Bottlesham, fo 148v.
1396, 26 Feb., ord dcn, collegiate church of All Saints, Maidstone, by *lit. dim.*, Reg. abp Courtenay ii, fo 186.
1397, 15 Sept., granted *lit. dim.*, by the bp for [priest's] orders, Reg. prior Shepey fo 97.
1398, 2 Mar., ord pr., Holy Trinity friary, London, Reg. Braybrooke (London), fo 48.
1423, 18 Dec., chamberlain, *Reg. Roff.*, 568 (Reg. Langdon, fo 30v).
1432, 7 Oct., released from the above office and was succ. by John Shepton, q.v., Reg. Langdon, fo 72v.

1409, 20 Nov., 13th in order among those present in chapter to appt a proctor in a lawsuit, Reg. prior Shepey, fo 121v.
1419, 31 Aug., 8th at the el. of a prior, *Reg. abp Chichele*, i, 61.
1423, 18 Dec., present at the renunciation of the rights of the vicar and parishioners of St Nicholas' altar in the cathedral nave where they had been accustomed to worship, *Reg. Roff.*, 568 (Reg. Langdon, fo 30v).
1434, Trinity term, with John de Ealding, q.v, appeared in chancery to explain the non payment of the stipend of the chaplain of Shepey's chantry, *CClR (1429–1435)*, 324–325.

ROCHESTRE
see also Roffa, Rouchestre

I John de ROFFA [*alias* Horold
occ. 1345/7

1345, 15 May, ord acol., bp's small chapel, Trottiscliffe, Reg. Hethe, fo 215v (p. 751) (as Horold).
1345, 21 May, ord subdcn, bp's chapel, Trottiscliffe, *ib.*, fo 216 (p. 1156).
1345, 24 Sept., ord dcn, bp's chapel, Halling, *ib.*, fo 217 (p. 1156).
1347, 24 May, granted *lit. dim.*, for the order of pr., *ib.*, fo 229v (p. 820).
1347, 26 May, ord pr., bp's chapel, Southwark, *Reg. Edington* (Winchester), ii, no 735 (transcribed as Resa).

II John de ROFFA
occ. 1353

1353, [18 May], ord dcn, Halling, Reg. Shepey, fo 3v.

ROFFCHESTRE
see Rochestre

Ralph de ROS
occ. before 1193 occ. 1203 × ?1208

c. 1193–1203, prior: occ. before 14 Aug. 1193; occ. Jan. 1203 and perhaps later, until before 18 May 1208, *Fasti*, ii, 79, *HRH* 64.

1193, before 14 Aug, sacrist, *Reg. Roff.*, 122.

[1198 × 1205], with the convent involved in a dispute with the bp [Gilbert de Glanville] over his appropriation of some of their rights and revenues, Selden Society, *Select Cases Eccles.*, 40–48. Dr Brett has determined the date as c. 1203; see Brett, 'Forgery at Rochester', 399, n. 9.
[1185 × 1214], as prior, *temp.* bp Glanville, named in a grant in the cartulary now BL Ms Cotton

Domitian A.x, fo 176ᵛ, and again, *temp.* abp Hubert Walter, *ib.*, fos 208ᵛ-209.
n.d., 20 Apr., commemorated, *Cust. Roff.*, 37.

As sacrist he was responsible for the forging of a new bell which was named Bretun after the donor, *Reg. Roff.*, 122.

As prior he undertook various building works including a greater and a lesser chamber for the prior's use, a hostelry, brewhouse and several granges; and after the d. of Richard de Wouldham, q.v, he undertook the custody of Hadenham. He also wrote or had written two missals, and is numbered among the benefactors, *ib.* See Sharpe, *Eng. Benedictine Libraries*, iv, B81.

Name in BL Ms Royal 3 C.ix, Leviticus etc (late 12th c.); *per*—. This vol. appears in the 1202 library catalogue in BL Ms Royal 5 B.xii, fo 2, printed in Sharpe, *Eng. Benedictine Libraries*, iv, B79.49.

John ROUCHESTRE [Roffa, Rouchester
occ. 1423/5

1423, 18 Dec., ord acol., Rochester cathedral, Reg. Langdon, fo 26ᵛ.
1425, 22 Sept., ord subdcn, bp's chapel, Trottiscliffe, *ib.*, fo 48ᵛ.

William de ROUCHESTRE [Roffa
occ. 1384 occ. 1432

1399, 2 Oct., the bp confirmed his nomination by the prior and chapter to the office of sacrist in place of Richard Shorn, q.v., Reg. prior Shepey, fo 90.
[1412], removed from the office of cellarer and prob. replaced by William Tonebregg II, q.v., Reg. prior Shepey, fos 124ᵛ-125.
1425, 23 May, subprior, *Reg. Roff.*, 571 (Reg. Langdon, fo 45ᵛ).
1432, 7 Oct., replaced as chamberlain by John Shepton, q.v., Reg. Langdon, fo 72ᵛ.

1384, 16 Oct., 19th in order among those present in chapter to appt a proctor in the curia, Reg. prior Shepey, fo 21.
1388, 10 Oct., apptd proctor for the subprior and chapter in convocation, *ib.*, fo 38ᵛ.
1409, 20 Nov., 6th among those present in chapter to appt a proctor in a lawsuit, *ib.*, fo 121ᵛ.
1419, 31 Aug., 2nd in order at the el. of a prior, *Reg. abp Chichele*, i, 61–62; see William Marchaunt who was subprior.
1425, 23 May, present in the chapel at the east end of the great hall when the bp gave his decision on the annual rent to be pd by the vicar of the newly built parish church of St Nicholas close to the cathedral, *Reg. Roff.*, 571 (Reg. Langdon, fo 45ᵛ).

RYARSH
see Reyersh

John RYE [Ry *alias* Harroke
occ. 1522 occ. 1535

1522, 19 Jan., one of seven who made their prof. before the bp, Reg. Fisher, fo 91.
1522, 20 Dec., ord dcn, bp's palace chapel, Rochester, *ib.*, fo 92.

1535, *custos* of the Lady chapel, *Valor Eccles.*, i, 104.

1532, 21 Oct., 14th in order at the el. of a prior, Reg. Fisher, fo 156.
1534, 10 June, subscribed to the Act of Supremacy, *DK 7th Report*, Appndx 2, 299.
1535, 13 Nov., dispensed to change his habit and hold a benefice, for which he pd £4, Chambers, *Faculty Office Regs*, 36.

RYERHS
see Reyersh

William ST ALBANS [*alias* Horney
occ. 1514 occ. 1532

1514, 26 Nov., one of seven who made their prof. before the bp, Reg. Fisher, fo 55 (as William Horney sancti Albani).
1518, 28 Feb., ord subdcn, bp's palace chapel, Rochester, *ib.*, fo 59ᵛ (as Albon).

1526, 20 Jan., apptd chamberlain, Reg. Fisher, fo 116 (as Albon).
[1530], 9 Oct., dismissed from this office, *ib.*, fo 142ᵛ (as Albon).

1532, 21 Oct., 12th in order at the el. of a prior, Reg. Fisher, fo 156 (as Albon).

Note: see William Albon who is prob. the same monk.

Philip EWER de ST CLARE [Gruer de St Clare
occ. [?1137 × 1143]

[?1137 × 1143], witnessed two episcopal instruments of bp John ?II with Richard de Claudevilla, q.v., *Reg. Roff.*, 370, 413, both of which had a connection with the St Clare family, Robert Pullen was also a witness as adcn of Rochester; hence the suggested dating in line with *Fasti*, ii, 81.
n.d., possibly the Philip commemorated at Christ Church, Canterbury on 27 Oct., Dart, *Antiq. Cant.*, Appndx, xxxviii (BL Ms Cotton Nero C.ix, fo 20).

William de ST LUPUS [Sancto Lupo
occ. 1185 × 1214

[1185 × 1214], precentor, *temp.* bp Gilbert de Glanville, *Reg. Roff.*, 687.

[1185 × 1214], one of his tenants or lay officials gave land to the precentor's office, *ib.* (BL Ms Cotton Domitian A.x, fos 174ᵛ, 180).

William de ST RADEGUND [?*alias* Peper, q.v.
occ. 1333/5

1333, 20 Mar., ord subdcn, Strood, Reg. Hethe, fo 154^{v} (p. 1159).
1335, 23 Sept., ord pr., Malling, Reg. Hethe, fo 165^{v} (p. 1159).

SAMSON
occ. 1254

1254, 9 Apr., chaplain to the bp, *Reg .Roff.*, 49.
1254, 9 Apr., with Adam II, q.v., came to Canterbury to present the bp's protests vs the abp's holding back of certain payments due to them, *ib.*, 99–100.

William de SANDWYCH [Sandwyco
occ. 1314 occ. 1328

1314, 21 Dec., ord acol., Lambeth palace chapel, Reg. abp Reynolds, fo 13.
1315, 17 May, ord subdcn, abp's chapel Croydon, by *lit. dim.*, *ib.*, fo 170^{v}.
1315, 20 Dec., ord dcn, Maidstone, by *lit. dim.*, *ib.*, fo 173^{v}.
1317, 28 May, ord pr., Lambeth palace chapel, *ib.*, fo 177^{v}.
1328, 24 Mar., present in the bp's household at Trottiscliffe, Reg. Hethe, fo 78^{v} (p. 183).

Simon SAUCIER
n.d.

n.d., described as *claudus*; gave ten albs and was included among the benefactors, *Reg. Roff.*, 125.

Roger de SAUNFORD [Sanford
occ. 1263

n.d., cellarer, *Reg. Roff.*, 125.
1263, 1 July, acted as attorney in a final concord, CKS DRc/T358/2.
n.d., with William de Cornubia, q.v. (d. 1296), *in dispersione* at Westminster; on their return they enriched the altar of St Edward with ornaments and an image of the saint because of their devotion to him and were listed among the benefactors, *Reg. Roff.*, 125 (BL Ms Cotton Vespasian A.xxii, fo 91^{v}).

As cellarer he built a stone brewery, *Reg. Roff.*, 125, which acc. to Hope must have replaced the earlier structure of prior Ralph de Ros, q.v., *Arch. Hist. Rochester*, 188.

John SAUVAGE
d. 1297

1297, d., and four monks were assigned *ad tricennale celebrandum* for him, BL MS Cotton Vespasian A.xxii, fo 126^{v}.

William SAXTON [*alias* Keble
occ. 1527

1527, 22 Dec., one of eight who made their prof. before the bp, Reg. Fisher, fo 121^{v}.

SCAPEIA, Scapeya, Schepeye
see Shepey

SCHEPTON
see Shepton

SCHORN, Schorna
see Shorne

William de SCHOTINDON [Schetingdone, Schotingdone, Shotindon, Shotingdon, Sotyndun
occ. 1283 d. 1295

1283, 29 Apr., 30 Nov., precentor, *Reg. abp Pecham*, ii, 195–196, CKS DRc/T341/1.
1284, 29 Sept., almoner, CKS DRc/T270.
1291, 6 June, sacrist, Oxford, Bod. Ms Charters, Suffolk, no 1384.

1283, 29 Apr., with John de Frendesbury, q.v., recd licence from the abp to el. a bp, *Reg. abp Pecham*, ii, 195–196.
1284, 29 Sept., as almoner, involved in a lease pertaining to his office, CKS DRc/T270.
1291, 6 June, named as one of the five *compromissorii* in the el. of a bp, Oxford, Bod. Ms Charters, Suffolk, no 1384.
1295, d., and four monks were assigned *ad tricennale celebrandum*, BL Ms Cotton Vespasian, A.xxii, fo 126^{v}.

SEDYNGBORNE
see Sydyngbourne

SELEFORDE
see Shelford

SELHAM
see Aelham

Thomas SELLING
occ. 1448/9

1448, 21 Sept., ord [acol.], Rochester cathedral, Reg. Lowe, fo 16^{v}.
1449, 7 June, ord subdcn, Rochester cathedral, *ib.*, fo 21^{v}.
1449, 21 Sept., ord dcn, bp's chapel, Halling, *ib.*, fo 21.

Thomas de SHELFORD [Seleforde, Shileford
occ. 1294 occ. 1301/2

1294–1301 or 1302; prior: succ. 1294; res. because of illness [c. 2 Feb.], 1301/2, *Fasti*, ii, 80.
1295, 19 June, granted dispensation to retain the priorate despite illegitimacy, *ib.*

I John de SHEPEY [Scapeya
occ. [1301] occ. 1333

1333, 19 Aug., subsacrist, Reg Hethe, fo 157 (p. 533).

[c. 1301], one of four monks who were assigned *ad tricennale celebrandum* for Thomas de Hakyntone, q.v., BL Ms Cotton Vespasian, A.xxii, fo 126v.

[c. 1305], one of four assigned to celebrate, as above, for Geoffrey de London, q.v., *ib.*, fo 127.

1333, 19 Aug., present at the el. of John de Shepey II and was 5th in order among those who voted for his namesake, q.v., Reg. Hethe, fo 157 (p. 534).

II John de SHEPEY, D.Th [Scapeia, Scapey, Scapeya, Schepeye, Shepeya, junior; (Prior I)
occ. 1318 occ. 1352

1333–1352, prior: el. 12 or 19 Aug. 1333; res. c. 1 Feb. 1350, see below; papal provision to the bpric 22 Oct. 1352, *Fasti*, iv, 40, 37. See also Reg. abp Islip, fo 65–65v.

1318, 17 June, ord dcn, Maidstone, Reg. abp Reynolds, fo 181.

[c. 1322/32], student at Oxford; recd licence to incept in theology from the prior and convent, 2 June 1332, Reg. Hethe, fo 151 (p. 515).

1333, 5 Jan., possibly regent master at Gloucester Hall, Oxford, Pantin, *Cant. Coll. Ox.*, iv, 218.

*1325, 6 Sept., present, with other monks, in the bp's household at Halling, Reg. Hethe, fo 68 (p. 155).

*1327, [?Jan.], warned the bp to stay away from Rochester during the unrest of the last days of Edward II, *Anglia Sacra*, i, 366.

1333, 12 or 19 Aug., as John Shepey junior, present at the el. of a prior and was one of three who nom. Robert de Southflete I, q.v. for the position; the el. was carried out acc. to custom, *per viam scrutinii*; he recd 25 out of 33 votes, Reg. Hethe, fo 157 (pp. 533–534).

Note: the bp presided over the el. and prob. confirmed [*prefecit*] the elect on the same day that he accepted the res. of John de Speldhurst I, q.v., but he may have recd it a wk earlier which would acct for the two dates.

1336, 9 Sept., present at the episcopal visitation at which John de Whytefeld, q.v, challenged the bp's authority. A disagreement ensued between the prior and the bp, but it was short-lived as the prime concern of both was the church of Rochester, *Anglia Sacra*, i, 373.

1338, 15 May, the king ordered the presidents of the Black Monk Chapter to excuse him from attendance, as he was needed at home in Rochester to watch the coastal defences in case of a French invasion, Pantin, *BMC*, iii, 15.

c. 1345, instrumental in the foundation of a loan-chest at Oxford, *BRUO*.

1345, 13 Jan., the king wrote to the pope to recommend the prior who was going to the curia on his behalf and that of the church, Reg. Hethe, fo 212v (pp. 736–737). By about 20 Jan., a second letter of recommendation was sent from the bp to the pope stating that the bp had approved the prior's visit to the curia and would himself look after the monastery in his absence. He also said that the prior had recd his early education in the priory before being adm. as a monk and had later shown such ability that he had been sent to university to study theology where 'infra breve compendium . . . cathedram ascendit magistralem'. The bp also expressed his wish that the prior should succ. him as bp. The abbot of St Alban's, one of the presidents of the Black Monk Chapter, also wrote a commendatory letter to the pope *ib.*, fos 212v, 213 (pp. 737–740).

1345, July, appted by the king to the regency council under his son Lionel, *CClR (1346–1349)*, 157. He was in Aquitaine when the king apptd him to go to Castile to make arrangements for the marriage of Edward III's daughter to the son of Alfonso XI, and he proceeded from there to Avignon, BL Ms Cotton Faustina B.v, fo 90v, *Reg. Hethe*, 737–739, *CClR (1343–1346)*, 492.

1347, 12 Oct., comm. to visit the cathedral chapter and the clergy and people of Rochester on behalf of the bp, *Reg. Hethe*, 834–835.

1348, between 12 Mar. and 1350, 23 Nov., involved, with the abps, bps and others, in peace negotiations initiated by the pope between the kings of England and France, *CPL*, iii (1342–1362), 47–48.

1349, designated by both the monks and the king as bp to succeed Hamo do Hethe q.v., whose resignation, however, was not accepted by the pope, acc. to *Anglia Sacra*, i, 378, but not otherwise verified.

1349, 6 May, comm. by the bp to preside at the el. of an abbess at Malling, Reg. Hethe, fo 261.

1349/50, 10 Mar., sent on another diplomatic mission, this time to Calais, concerning arrangements for a truce with France, Rymer, *Foedera*, iii, pt 1, 48 (BL Ms Cotton Faustina B.v, fo 100).

1350, 1 Feb., granted licence by the pope to res. as prior and have an annual pension of £40. In addition he was to have the rents and profits of lands and tenements to be given him by the prior, subprior, cellarer and sacrist, to be allowed to live with the monks or elsewhere with a monk companion, and to retain the use of his possessions during his lifetime. The petition to the pope rehearsed his achievements during his sixteen yrs as prior; these included removing the burden of debt incurred by his predecessors, supervising building works and repairs within the enclosure and acquiring lands and rents to augment the income, *CPP*, i (1342–1419), 192. On this same day the prior of Christ Church, Canterbury, was instructed to rec. the res., *CPL*, iii (1342–1362), 319, *CPP*, i (1342–1419), 192.

1350, 29 May, granted papal licence to have a portable altar, *CPL*, iii (1342–1362), 400.

1351, 21 Feb., the king gave his licence for the above pension, *CPR (1350–1354)*, 41.

1351, 14 July, granted papal dispensation to choose his own confessor, and with his fellow monk, in whatever university they were staying, to eat meat in Septuagesima week, *CPL*, iii (1342–1362), 430. On the same day he also obtained dispensation for his confessor to grant plenary remission at the time of his d., *ib.*, 437. Slightly different versions of the 1351 papal grants occ. in *CPP*, i (1342–1419), 217; these make it clear that he was given licence to pursue study at any university accompanied by a monk of his own choosing and that [some of] his financial support came from an arrangement whereby 'professed religious' were authorized to 'let to him at a yearly cess churches appropriated to them or their monasteries', to provide him with income from the revenues of these churches, *ib.*

1352, 22 Oct., bp el. by this date as this is the date of his papal apptment to the see, *CPL*, iii (1342–1362), 469.

Name in BL Ms Royal 12 D.xiv, Aristoteles etc. (late 13th c.); on fo 1 *per mag[istrum—priorem* and on fo 1^{v} *Ioh. Roffensis monachi prec.[ium] xvi s.*

For his [mainly episcopal] sermons, preserved in Oxford, Merton College, Ms B.1.6 and *ib.*, New College, Ms 92, see refs in *BRUO*.

The joint achievements of prior Shepey and bp Hethe included the foundation of a new refectory in 1336, and a new belfry with four bells in 1344, BL Ms Cotton Faustina B.v, fos 78^{v}, 90^{v}. He himself improved the financial state of the priory and was also responsible for the building of the refectory, hospice and vestibule of the church and for repairs to the dormitory, infirmary and other buildings, *Reg. Roff.*, 551–552, *CPP*, i (1342–1419), 192.

In his will there is ref. to his sister, Alice, and his nephew, Peter, Reg. abp Islip, fos 169^{v}-170.

Note: the items marked * could apply to John de Shepey I.

III John de SHEPEY [Shepaye (Prior II)

occ. 1366 d. 1419

1380–1419, prior: el. 14 Dec. 1380; d. 2 Aug 1419, *Fasti*, iv, 40.

1366, 30 May, ord subdcn, Malling, Reg. Trillek, fo 7^{v}.

1367, 13 Mar., ord dcn, abp's chapel Otford, *Reg. abp Langham*, 378.

1367, 19 Sept., ord pr., Rochester cathedral, Reg. Trillek, fo 10^{v}.

1380, before, chaplain to the bp and receiver of the bpric, Reg. prior Shepey, fo 19.

1380, before 14 Dec., subprior, BL Cotton Vespasian, A.xxii, fo 34.

1380, 14 Dec., the bp came to the chapter house and scrutinized the vote of every monk and pronounced him prior, Reg. prior Shepey, fo 19.

1382, 29 Sept., recd an acquittance from the bp for the time when he was chaplain to the bp and receiver of the bpric, Reg. prior Shepey, fo 19.

1386, 28 Sept., with three others made responsible for the fortifications of Rochester including repair of the walls and gates, *CPR (1385–1389)*, 215.

1390, 30 June, reported to the presidents of the Black Monk Chapter that he was unwell and overburdened with work and could not attend the meeting in Northampton, Reg. prior Shepey, fo 42; see John Morel and John Holyngbourne.

1395, 6 Apr., apptd controller of [the works of] Rochester castle, *CPR (1391–1396)*, 569.

1401, 2 Nov., with the bp's official comm. as vicar general, Reg. John Bottlesham, fo 19.

1403, 23, granted papal indult for the confessor of his choice to give him plenary remission of his sins as often as required, *CPL*, v (1396–1404), 564.

1406, 9 Aug., was acting as collector of the royal tenth in the diocese, *CPR (1405–1408)*, 215.

1417, Nov./Dec., one of the cathedral priors apptd by the abp to look into the poverty of university graduates, *Reg. abp Chichele*, iii, 36–37.

His letter book or register of *acta* survives in BL Ms Cotton Faustina C.v, referred to here as Reg. prior Shepey. For his patience and understanding, in dealing with a troublesome monk, which required a lengthy and time consuming correspondence, see under John Cray.

IV John SHEPEY

occ. 1437/40

1437, 21 Dec., ord acol., Rochester cathedral, Reg. Wells, fo 7.

1439, 4 Apr., ord subdcn, chapel *prope infirmariam* (within the monastery), *ib.*, fo 22.

1440, 24 Sept., ord dcn, Rochester cathedral, *ib.*, fo 36.

Osbern de SHEPEY [Scapeia, ?Osbert

occ. 1189/90

1189–1190, prior: O., prior, occ. 1189 Sept. × 1190 Sept., *Fasti*, ii, 79, *HRH*, 64.

Note: if he is the prior referred to in the record of the dispute between his successor Ralph de Ros, q.v., with the chapter, and the bp, the implication is that he res. after an unsuccessful attempt to reach a settlement and after encountering opposition from some of his monks and menacing remarks from the bp, Selden Society, *Select Cases Eccles.*, 45 and note; see also *Flores Hist.*, ii, 149, and for further refs see *Eng. Epis. Acta*, ii, no 244.

n.d., sacrist, *Anglia Sacra*, i, 393.

He did 'great works' for the house before and during his priorate and was numbered among the benefactors. These include the addition of books to the library and a *camera* for the prior beside the infirmary. Among the books which he completed [*perfecit*] were 'historias magistri Petri, et breviarium de capella infirmitorii, et Ysaiam glosatum Ascelini episcopi . . . et librum de claustro anime', *Reg. Roff.*, 121; Sharpe, *Eng. Benedictine Libraries*, iv, B81.

The lady Cecilia de Scapeia [?his mother or sister] gave gifts and is mentioned with him among the benefactors, *ib.*

Walter SHEPEY [Shepeye

occ. 1419 occ. 1430/1

1430/1, almoner, CKS DRc/F11.

1419, 31 Aug., 14th in order at the el. of a prior, *Reg. abp Chichele*, i, 62.

I William SHEPEY [Shepeye

occ. 1423 occ. 1455

1423, 18 Dec., ord acol., Rochester cathedral, Reg. Langdon, fo 26^v^.

1424, 22 Apr., ord subdcn, Rochester cathedral, *ib.*, fo 28.

1426, 7 Mar., ord dcn, Rochester cathedral, *ib.*, fo 44^v^.

1427, 5 Apr., ord pr., Rochester cathedral, *ib.*, fo 60.

1455, 12 Oct., dismissed from the office of chamberlain and replaced by William Lorkyn, q.v., Reg. Lowe, fo 28.

II William SHEPEY

see Qwenburgh

John SHEPTON [Schepton, Sheptone

occ. 1411 occ. 1446

1411, 5 Aug., the prior was comm. by the bp to rec. his prof., Reg. prior Shepey, fo 116.

1432, 7 Oct., dismissed from the office of precentor and apptd chamberlain to succ. William Rouchestre, q.v., Reg. Langdon, fo 72^v^.

1446, 6 Oct., apptd sacrist to succ. Richard Oxenford, q.v., Reg. Lowe, fo 10.

1415/16, student [at Oxford], and recd a pension of 17s. for clothing from the chamberlain, CKS DRc/F15.

SHILEFORD

see Shelford

I John de SHORNE [Schorna, Schorne

occ. 1345/7

1345, 21 May, ord dcn, bp's chapel, Trottiscliffe, Reg. Hethe, fo 216 (p. 1164).

1347, 24 May, granted *lit. dim.*, for the order of pr., *ib.*, fo 229^v^ (p. 820).

1347, 26 May, ord pr., bp's chapel, Southwark, *Reg. Edington* (Winchester), ii, no 735.

II John SHORNE

occ. 1419/20

1420, 21 Dec., ord pr., St Paul's cathedral, London, Reg. Clifford (London), fo 95.

1419, 31 Aug., 15th in order at the el. of a prior, *Reg. abp Chichele*, i, 62.

Richard de SHORNE [Schorn

occ. 1353 occ. 1409

1353, 23 Mar., ord dcn, Rochester cathedral, Reg. Shepey, fo 2.

1355, 22 Dec., ord pr., Rochester cathedral, *ib.*, fo 12.

1384, 16 Oct., sacrist, Reg. prior Shepey, fo 21.

1399, 2 Oct., released from the office of sacrist and succ. by William de Rouchestre, q.v., *ib.*, fo 90.

1372, 27 Dec., with John Morel, q.v., apptd proctor to obtain a licence from the abp to el. a bp, Reg. abp Wittlesey, fo 137^v^.

1383, 24 Nov., apptd proctor by the subprior and chapter for convocation, Reg. prior Shepey, fo 18.

1384, 16 Oct., 3rd in order among those present in chapter to appt a proctor in the curia, *ib.*, fo 21.

1387, 13 Mar., witnessed a renunciation and a prof. of obedience by William de Reynham, q.v., *ib.*, fo 95.

1387, 1 Sept., one of ten monks and four clerks, and on the same day one of eight monks, apptd as general proctors by the prior and chapter, *ib.*, fos 58^v^, 68.

1389, 4 May, with Roger de Stapelhurst, q.v., sent by the prior and chapter to obtain from the abp of Canterbury licence to el. a bp, *ib.*, fo 51.

1397, 14 May, one of eight monks and five clerks apptd by the prior and chapter as general proctors, prob. on acct of an impending metropolitan visitation, *ib.*, fos 81, 81^v^, 83.

1398, 6 May, with a secular clerk, apptd by the prior as proctor to meet with the abp [in convocation] to discuss the state of the kingdom, *ib.*, fo 84.

1409, 20 Nov., second in order among those present with the subprior to appt a proctor in a lawsuit, *ib.*, fo 121^v^.

Note: there is no evidence that two monks are conflated in this entry but the active career covers a remarkably long span of 56 yrs.

Robert SHORNE [Schorn, Schorne
occ. 1391 occ. 1426

1391, 13 June, one of three whose prof. the prior was comm. to rec., Reg. prior Shepey, fo 50.
1392, 9 Mar., ord subdcn, St Paul's cathedral, London, Reg. Braybrooke (London), fo 29.
1392, 19 Sept., subdcn, granted by the prior a *littera testimonialis* for dcn's orders, which was accompanied by the bp's licence, Reg. prior Shepey, fo 57v.
1393, 31 May, ord pr., Maidstone, by *lit. dim.*, Reg. abp Courtenay ii, fo 182v.
1426, 22 Mar., granted papal indult to have a portable altar, *CPL*, vii (1417–1431), 430.

SHOTINGDON
see Schotindon

[I SILVESTER
occ. [1114 × 1122]

[1114 × 1122], *temp.* bp Ernulf with Hugh I, q.v., witnessed a charter, possibly spurious of abp Ralph, *Text. Roff.*, ii, fo 179v, and cap 94; this will appear in *Eng. Epis. Acta*, Canterbury, 1070–1161, no 51, forthcoming, where it is dated [1115 Dec. × 1116, Sept., or 1120, Jan. × 1122, Oct.].
Note: it is not clear that this is a monk of Rochester.]

II SILVESTER
occ. c. 1177 × 1180

c. 1177 × 1180, prior: occ. as S., prior, 15 May 1177; occ. 8 Apr. 1180, *Fasti*, ii, 79, *HRH*, 64.
Note: the deed dated 15 May 1177 is, however, spurious, *Eng. Epis. Acta*, ii, no 194, note.
n.d., possibly cellarer before 1177, *Fasti*, ii, 79; a Silvester, cellarer had a sister who married the under baker, *Cust. Roff.*, 28.
As prior he carried out notable works in the priory including the construction of the refectory and dormitory and also the *hostelerium* at Felixstowe; he also installed three windows at the east end of the chapter house. He was numbered among the benefactors, *Reg. Roff.*, 121.
n.d., 23 Oct., commemorated, *Cust. Roff.*, 37.
Name in:
(1) BL Ms Royal 8 D.xvi, J. Cassianus (12th c.); on fo 1 *Silvestri prioris* in a much later hand. This vol. appears in the library catalogue of 1122/3 in *Text. Roff.*, ii, fos 224–230, and in that of 1202 in BL Ms Royal 5 B.xii, fo 2; these are printed in Sharpe, *Eng. Benedictine Libraries*, iv, where the refs are B77.72 and B79.91.
(2) BL Ms Royal App. 10, P. Riga (13th c.), one fo only remains; prob the first leaf of Ms Royal 15 A.xix.

III SILVESTER
occ. 1294 occ. 1333

1333, 19 Aug., subprior, Reg. Hethe, fo 157 (p. 533).
1294, one of four monks who were assigned *ad tricennale celebrandum* for John de Reynham I, q.v., BL Ms Cotton Vespasian A.xxii, fo 126v.
[c. 1300], one of four assigned to celebrate as above for Walter Hareng, q.v., *ib.*
[c. 1301], one of four assigned to celebrate as above for John de Waltham, q.v., *ib.*, fo 127.
[c. 1303/4], one of four assigned to celebrate as above for Robert de Hoo, q.v., *ib.*
1333, 19 Aug., 2nd in order at the el. of a prior among those who voted for John de Shepey II, q.v., Reg. Hethe, fo 157 (p. 533).
Note: the monk priest celebrating masses in 1294 and [c. 1300] may be a fourth Silvester.

SITTON
see Sutton

Robert SMYTH [Smythe
occ. 1496 occ. 1540

1511/12, subcellarer, CKS DRc/F17.
1514, 31 Mar., appt sacrist to succ. Robert Rochestre, Reg. Fisher, fo 54.
1514, 2 Dec., replaced as sacrist by Laurence Mereworth, q.v., *ib.*, fo 55v.
1496, 4 Nov., 16th in order on the visitation certificate, *Reg. abp Morton*, ii, no 446.
1511/12, named at the head of a composite obedientiary acct roll as one of four monk auditors in conjunction with one of the king's auditors, CKS DRc/F17.
1532, 21 Oct., 6th in order at the el. of a prior, Reg. Fisher, fo 156.
1540, 8 Apr., described as impotent and no pension assigned, *L and P Henry VIII*, xv, no 474.

John SNELL [Snel
occ. 1415 d. 1458

1415, 12 June, one of three whose prof. the prior was comm. to rec., Reg. prior Shepey, fo 116.
1419, 11 Mar., ord dcn, St Bride's, Fleet Street, London, Reg. Clifford (London), fo 85v.
1421, 20 Dec., ord pr., St Paul's cathedral, London, *Reg. abp Chichele*, iv, 349.
1444, 19 Sept., prob. precentor, Reg. Lowe, fo 2; see below.
1446, 8 Jan., cellarer, *ib.*, fo 7v.
[1455], 23 June, cellarer, *ib.*, fo 27v.
1458, 14 Dec., cellarer up to this date, *ib.*, fo 32v; see William de London, II.
1419, 31 Aug., 19th in order at the el. of a prior, *Reg. abp Chichele*, i, 62.

1444, 3 Mar., sent as proctor to the abp for licence to el. a bp, Reg. abp Stafford fo 43–43v.
1444, 19 Sept., presented a monk for ordination at Southfleet, Reg. Lowe, fo 2.
1446, 8 Jan., comm. to induct a servant into the office assigned to him in the brewery, *ib.*, fo 7v.
1449, 21 Sept., presented the ordination candidates at Halling, *ib.*, fo 21.
[1455], 23 June, with John Tonnbregg, q.v., comm. to induct the gatekeeper [*janitor*] into his office, *ib.*, fo 27v.
1458, 14 Dec., d. by this date when he was replaced as cellarer by William de London II, q.v., Reg. Lowe, fo 32v.

Nicholas SNOTELONDE [Snodelond
occ. 1405/7
1405, 2 July, one of two whose prof. the prior was comm. to rec., Reg. prior Shepey, fo 105v.
1407, 24 Sept., ord acol., collegiate church of All Saints, Maidstone, Reg. abp Arundel, i, fo 341, where he is listed among the Canterbury monks.

SONNYNG
see Sunnyng

SOTTONE
see Sutton

Henry SOUTHFLETE [*alias* Bridd
occ. 1514 occ. 1518
1514, 26 Nov., one of seven monks who made their prof. before the bp, Reg. Fisher, fo 55.
1517, 11 Apr., ord subdcn bp's palace chapel, Rochester, *ib.*, fo 57v.
1518, 28 Feb., ord dcn, bp's palace chapel, Rochester, *ib.*, fo 59v.

I Robert de SOUTHFLETE [Suthflete
occ. [c. 1307] occ. 1326
1326, 17 Sept., res. as chamberlain, Reg. Hethe, fo 118v (pp. 380–381).
[c. 1307], one of four monks who were assigned *ad tricennale celebrandum* for John Pouncz, q.v., BL Ms Cotton Vespasian, A.xxii, fo 127.

II Robert de SOUTHFLETE [Suthflet, Suthflete senior
occ. 1325 d. 1361
1350–1361, prior: el. before 18 Aug. 1351, *CClR (1349–1354)*, 379; d. before 6 Aug. 1361, *Fasti*, iv, 40.
Note: prior John de Shepey II, q.v., res. c. 1 Feb. 1350 and so one may presume that Southflete's el. followed soon after that date. See Reg. abp Islip, fo 65–65v.
1325, 21 Sept., ord subdcn, Wouldham, Reg. Hethe, fo 69v (p. 1166).
1326, 8 Mar., ord dcn, Wouldham, *ib.*, fo 71 (p. 1166).
1327, 11 Apr., ord pr., Trottiscliffe, *ib.*, fo 76 (p. 1166).
1349, 23 Apr., cellarer, Reg. Hethe, fo 258v.
n.d., but before 1352, 22 Oct., *custos* of Felixstowe, *Anglia Sacra*, i, 394 (BL Ms Cotton Vespasian A.xxii, fo 34).
1329, 27 May, served as a witness in a case before the bp. Reg. Hethe, fo 88 (pp. 241–242).
1333, 19 Aug., 11th in order at the el. of a prior among those who voted for John de Shepey II, q.v., and himself was nom. by three monks, Reg. Hethe, fo 157 (p. 534). It is possible, however, that it was Robert de Southflete III (junior), q.v., who was nom.
1336, 19 Nov., served as proctor for the vicar of St Nicholas' altar (in the cathedral nave), Reg. Hethe, fo 177v (p. 604).
1349, 23 Apr., as cellarer, commanded to induct a new pottinger [*serianc[iam potagiarii*], Reg. Hethe, fo 258v.
1359, 15 Nov., recd a silver cup with cover as a bequest from the rector of Rotherfield, Reg. Shepey, fo 25.

III Robert de SOUTHFLETE [Southflet, Suthflete junior
occ. 1328 occ. 1344
1328, 6 July; 1329, 30 Apr., 1330, 13 Feb., present in the bp's household, and prob. chaplain, Reg. Hethe, fo 126 (p. 403, as junior); fo 128 (p. 413); fo 132v (p. 434, as junior); and see below.
1330, 3 Mar., present at an ordination in the bp's chapel at Halling and acted as witness to the petition of one candidate, *ib.*, fo 132v.
1333, 19 Aug., 18th in order at the el. of a prior among those who voted for John de Shepey II, q.v., *ib.*, fo 157 (p. 534). One of the two monks by this name was nominated by three of the brethren; see Robert de Southflete II.
1344, 29 Feb., acted as witness [?and chaplain] in the bp's household at Halling, *ib.*, fo 209v (p. 725, as junior).
Note: Robert de Southflete II and III overlap, but their order of seniority serves to avoid some of the ambiguity.

Thomas de SOUTHFLETE
see Wouldham

I John de SPELDHURST [Spelderhurst, Speldherst
occ. [c. 1300] occ. 1333
1321–1333, prior: el. 30 Jan. 1321, *Anglia Sacra*, i, 362 and 20 Jan. *ib.*, 394 (31 Jan. in *Fasti*, iv, 40); res. 19 Aug. 1333, Reg. Hethe, fo 157 (p. 531), but 12 Aug., in *Anglia Sacra*, i, 394 (BL Ms Cotton Faustina B.v, fo 66). See John de Shepey II.
1321, before 30 Jan., cellarer, *Anglia Sacra*, i, 362.

[c. 1300], one of four monks who were assigned *ad tricennale celebrandum* for Henry de Cobbeham, q.v., BL Ms Cotton Vespasian A.xxii, fo 126ᵛ.
[c. 1306], one of four monks who were assigned to celebrate, as above, for Elias IV, *ib.*, fo 127.
[1327, Nov.], acted as commissary for the bp in the appropriation of Westerham to the prior and chapter of Canterbury, *Lit. Cant.*, no 246.
1329, Nov., an accusation of illegitimacy came to light during the abp's visitation, and the bp was denounced for ignoring this fact when he named him prior, *Anglia Sacra*, i, 369.
1333, 19 Aug., present at the el. of his successor and was one of the majority who voted for John de Shepey II, q.v., Reg. Hethe, fo 157 (p. 533).

II John de SPELDHURST [Speldhyrst
occ. 1362 occ. 1397

1362, 17 Dec., ord acol., Rochester cathedral, Reg. Wittlesey, fo 8.
1363, 18 Mar., ord subdcn, abp's chapel, Mayfield, Reg. abp Islip. fo 322.
1363, 23 Sept., ord dcn, Faversham convent, *ib.*, fo 323ᵛ.
1384, 30 Mar., on receipt of a request from the prior and chapter on 29 Mar., the bp dismissed him from the office of precentor and apptd Thomas de Dovorr, q.v., Reg. prior Shepey, fos 22, 13v.
1384, 18 Sept., the prior and chapter requested his apptment as precentor in place of Thomas de Dovorr, q.v., Reg. prior Shepey, fo 20ᵛ; the bp sent the comm. to the prior on 19 Dec., but he was already named as precentor on 16 Oct., *ib.*, fo 21.
1384, 16 Oct., 5th in order among those present in chapter to appt a proctor in the curia, Reg. Shepey, fo 21.
1387, 13 Mar., present in the prior's chapel for a renunciation and a renewal of obedience of William de Reynham, q.v., *ib.*, fo 95, 95ᵛ.
1387, 1 Sept., one of ten monks and four clerks, and on the same day one of eight monks, apptd as general proctors, *ib.*, fos 58ᵛ, 68.
1393, 13 June, with John de Ealding, q.v., apptd by the prior to carry out Black Monk Chapter visitations of Faversham, St Augustine's, Canterbury, and St Martin's, Dover, Pantin, *BMC*, iii, 248 (Reg. prior Shepey, fo 62ᵛ).
1397, 1 Sept., one of eight monks and five clerks apptd as general proctors, Reg. prior Shepey, fo 68.

Nicholas SPELDHURST [Spelherste, Spelhurst *alias* Arnold
occ. 1522 occ. 1540

1522, 19 Jan., his prof. and that of six others was solemnized by the bp, Reg. Fisher, fo 91.
1532, 21 Oct., 15th in order at the el. of a prior, Reg. Fisher, fo 156.
1534, 10 June, siged the Act of Supremacy, *DK 7th Report*, Appndx 2, 299.
1535, 20 Nov., dispensed to change his habit and hold a benefice, for which he pd £8, Chambers, *Faculty Office Regs*, 36.
1540, 8 Apr., apptd 'high sexton' in the new foundation and in addition awarded a pension of 40s. p.a., *L and P Henry VIII*, xv, no 474.

STACE
see Cobham

John STAPELHURST [Stapelherst, Staplehurste, *alias* Cobb
occ. 1527 occ. 1534

1527, 22 Dec., one of eight who made their prof. before the bp, Reg. Fisher, fo 121ᵛ.
1532, 21 Oct., 20th in order at the el. of a prior, Reg. Fisher, fo 156.
1534, 10 June, subscribed to the Act of Supremacy, *DK 7th Report*, Appndx 2, 299.

Roger de STAPELHURST [Stapelherste, Stapilherst, Stapulherst
occ. 1387 occ. 1398

1392, 13 Apr., apptd precentor in place of Robert de Strode, q.v., Reg. prior Shepey, fo 54 and Reg. William Bottlesham, fo 26.
1394, 28 July, in response to the request of the prior and chapter, dismissed from the office of precentor and replaced by Robert de Strode, q.v., Reg. William Bottlesham, fo 52.
1396, 7 Oct., the prior and chapter requested his apptment as chamberlain in place of Nicholas de Frendesbury, q.v., Reg. prior Shepey, fo 77; a comm. to the prior followed the same day, *ib.*, fo 81. This apptment is also in Reg. William Bottlesham, fo 92. His acct for 1396/7 reports that he built a new latrine at a cost of £9 7s. 7d., CKS DRc/F14.
1398, 30 June, released from the office of chamberlain and replaced by Nicholas de Frendesbury, Reg. prior Shepey, fo 86ᵛ, and Reg. William Bottlesham, fo 120.
1387, 9 Oct., with John de Ealding, q.v., granted licence by the prior and chapter to go to study at Oxford, Reg. prior Shepey, fo 35ᵛ.
c. 1393, at Oxford, *BRUO*, quoting *The Life and Times of Anthony Wood*, Oxford Historical Society, iv (1895), 108.
1387, 1 Sept., one of ten monks and four clerks, and on the same day one of eight monks, apptd as general proctors, Reg. prior Shepey, fos 58ᵛ, 68.
1389, 4 May, with Richard Shorne, q.v., sent by the prior and chapter to obtain from the abp licence to el. a bp. Reg. prior Shepey, fo 51.
1397, 18 Feb., apptd proctor by the prior to attend convocation, Reg. prior Shepey, fo 80, 80ᵛ.
1397, 14 May, one of eight monks and five clerks apptd as general proctors, prob. on acct of an

impending metropolitan visitation, *ib.*, fos 81, 81^v, 83.
1397, 1 Sept., one of eight monks, and four clerks apptd as general proctors, Reg. prior Shepey, fo 68.
n.d., [29 Sept.], involved in difficulties over the collection of a half tenth, *ib.*, fo 69.

STEPHEN [Stephanus
n.d.
n.d., son of Elias I, q.v., grandson of Kenstanus, entered the priory with his father and brother Alexander, q.v.; they gave land outside Eastgate and were numbered among the benefactors, *Reg. Roff.*, 119.

Simon STEVYN
see Hoo

Henry STOKE
occ. 1396 occ. 1409
1396, 9 May, one of two whose prof. the prior was comm. by the bp to rec., Reg. prior Shepey, fo 77^v.
1396, 24 Sept., ord acol., Rochester cathedral, Reg. William Bottlesham, fo 149^v.
1397, 15 Sept., recd licence from the bp to proceed *ad omnes ordines*, Reg. prior Shepey, fo 97.
1398, 21 Dec., ord subdcn, Rochester cathedral, Reg. William Bottlesham, fo 150.
1400, 18 Dec., ord pr., Malling, Reg. John Bottlesham, fo 8^v.
1409, 20 Nov., 15th in order among those present in chapter to appt a proctor in a lawsuit, Reg. prior Shepey, fo 121^v.

Osbern de STOKE [Stokys
occ. 1250/1 d. 1296
1250, 13/14 Nov., with Adam de Essex and Alexander de Glanville, q.v., set out for the curia where they stayed for 21 wks, and returned on 8 Apr. [1251] having successfully obtained papal confirmation for their choice of Laurence de St Martin as bp, *Flores Hist.*, ii, 369 (*Anglia Sacra*, i, 350).
1296, d., and four monks were assigned *ad tricennale celebrandum* for him, BL Ms Cotton Vespasian, A.xxii, fo 126^v (as Osbert).

Ralph de STOKE
n.d.
Name in BL Ms Royal 2 C.i, P. Comestor (13th c.); on fo 1, *per*—in a 13th c. hand.

Thomas STOKE [*alias* Cooste, Coste
occ. 1508 occ. 1514
1508, 8 Apr., ord acol., bp's palace chapel, Rochester, Reg. Fisher, fo 33.
1509, 22 Dec., ord subdcn, Bromley, *ib.*, fo 36^v.
1510, 30 Mar., ord dcn., bp's palace chapel, Rochester, *ib.*, fo 37.
1511, 19 Apr., ord pr., Rochester cathedral, *ib.*, fo 38^v.
1511, 1 Oct., apptd precentor, Reg. Fisher, fo 40^v (as Coste); 1511/12 precentor, CKS DRc/F17.
1514, 31 Mar., succ. as precentor by John Maideston IV, q.v., Reg. Fisher, fo 54.
1514, 31 Mar., d. by this date; Reg. Fisher, fo 54, see John Maideston IV.

John STOKEBURY [Stokbery
occ. 1405 occ. 1426
1405, 2 July, one of two whose prof. the prior was comm. to rec., Reg. prior Shepey, fo 105^v.
1407, 24 Sept., ord acol., collegiate church of All Saints Maidstone, Reg. abp Arundel, i, fo 341 (listed among the Canterbury monks).
1409, 20 Nov., 20th in order among those present in chapter to appt a proctor in a lawsuit, Reg. prior Shepey, fo 121^v.
1419, 31 Aug., 12th at the el. of a prior, *Reg. abp Chichele*, i, 62.
1426, 22 Mar., granted an indult to have a portable altar, *CPL*, vii (1417–1431), 430.

M. G. de STRATTON [Strattone
n.d.
Name in
(1) BL Ms Royal 2 D.vi, Flores psalterii etc. (13th c.); *per—monachum.*
(2) BL Ms Royal 4 D.xiii, Esaias etc. (13th c.); on fo 2 *per*—.
(3) Cambridge, Trinity College Ms 1128, Grammatica etc. (early 12th c.); on fo 1. *per magistrum*—. This vol. appears in three library catalogues; that of 1122/3 in *Text Roff.*, ii, fo 229 (Alcuinus), the fragments in CKS DRc/Z18/1–2 of similar date, and that of 1202 in BL Ms Royal 5 B.xii, fo 2; these are printed in Sharpe, *Eng. Benedictine Libraries*, iv, where the refs are B77.67 (crossed out), B78.20 and B79.98 respectively.

Osbern de STRODE [Strodes
n.d.
n.d., at the time of his adm. gave rents in Strood and was listed among the benefactors, *Reg. Roff.*, 124.

Robert de STRODE
occ. 1384 occ. 1402
1390, 20 Apr., the prior and chapter requested his apptment as precentor to succ. John Pleme, q.v., and the bp issued his comm. the following day, Reg. prior Shepey, fos 43, 68v.
1392, 13 Apr., released from the office of precentor and succ. by Roger Stapelhurst, q.v., Reg. prior Shepey, fo 54, and Reg. William Bottlesham, fo 26.
1394, 28 July, [re]apptd precentor on the request of the prior and chapter, Reg. William Bottlesham, fo 52.

1400, 10 Oct., the prior and chapter requested the bp to release him from the office of precentor and to appt John Swan I in his place; he did so on 11 Oct., Reg. prior Shepey, fo 103v, 107, and Reg. John Bottlesham, fo 3.
1401, 1 Apr., apptd precentor to replace John Swan I, q.v, Reg. prior Shepey, fo 101v, and Reg. John Bottlesham, fo 12.
1402, 18 Sept., dismissed from the office of precentor and succ. by John de Ealding, q.v., Reg. prior Shepey, fo 101v.

1384, 16 Oct., 14th in order of those present in chapter to appt a proctor in the curia, Reg. prior Shepey, fo 21.

Thomas STRODE
occ. 1419

1419, 31 Aug., 17th in order at the el. of a prior, *Reg. abp Chichele*, i, 62.

I William de STRODE [Stroude
occ. 1348 occ. 1353

1348, 14 June, ord acol., bp's chapel, Halling, Reg. Hethe, fo 253v.
1349, 19 Sept., ord subdcn, Rochester cathedral, *ib.*, fo 268v.
1350, 18 Dec., ord dcn, Maidstone, by *lit. dim.*, Reg. abp Islip, fo 310v.
1353, 23 Mar., ord pr., Rochester cathedral, Reg. Shepey, fo 2.

II William STRODE
occ. 1459

1459, 24 Mar., ord acol., Rochester cathedral, Reg. Lowe, fo 32.

Thomas de SULEFORD
occ. late 13th c.

late 13th c., visited [Frindsbury] for *liberatio denariorum, temp.* William Ledes and John de Frendesbury, q.v., CKS DRc/F7.

John SUNNYNG [Sonnyng, Sunyng
occ. 1454 occ. 1466

1454, 20 Dec., ord acol., and subdcn, bp's palace chapel, Rochester, Reg. Lowe, fo 27v.
1455, 20 Sept., ord dcn, bp's chapel, Halling, *ib.*, fo 28v.
1457, June (no day given), ord pr., bp's chapel, Halling, *ib.*, fo 29.
1466, 10 Oct., apptd precentor in place of John Causton, q.v., Reg. Lowe, fo 47v.

Robert SUSFACHE
see Robert III

SUTHFLET(E)
see Southflete

Thomas de SUTHGATE
occ. 1335/7

1335, 23 Sept., ord subdcn, Malling, Reg. Hethe, fo 165 (p. 1167).
1336, 26 May, ord dcn, bp's chapel, Halling, *ib.*, fo 166 (pp. 560, 1167).
1337, 15 Mar., ord pr., bp's chapel, Halling, *ib.*, fo 169v (p. 1167).

John SUTTON [Sitton, Sottone
occ. 1387 occ. 1426

1387, 20 Sept., subdcn, granted *lit. dim.*, for dcn's orders, Reg. prior Shepey, fo 35.
1387, 21 Sept., ord dcn, chapel in Tunbridge castle, by *lit. dim.*, Reg. abp Courtenay, i, fo 310.
1391, 28 Feb., given *littere testimoniales* by the prior addressed to all bps in Canterbury province for the order of pr., Reg. prior Shepey, fo 43; on 22 Mar. the prior wrote to the abp requesting that he be ordained pr., *ib.*, fo 45.
1391, 25 Mar., ord pr., Canterbury cathedral, by *lit. dim.*, Reg. abp Courtenay, i, fo 312.

1412, 26 Oct., apptd *custos* of Felixstowe, Reg. prior Shepey, fo 129.

1389, 11 Oct., given licence to study at Oxford, Reg. prior Shepey, fo 42.
1391, 28 Feb., student at Oxford, *ib.*, fo 43.

1387, 1 Sept., one of ten monks and four clerks, and onthe same day one of eight monks, named as general proctors, Reg. prior Shepey, fos 58v, 68.
1397, 14 May, one of eight monks and four clerks named as general proctors, prob. on acct of an impending metropolitan visitation, Reg. prior Shepey, fos 81, 81v, 83.
1409, 20 Nov., 8th among those present in chapter to appt a proctor in a lawsuit, *ib.*, fo 121v.
1419, 31 Aug., 5th in order at the el. of a prior, *Reg. abp Chichele*, i, 61.
1426, 22 Mar., granted papal licence to have a portable altar, *CPL*, vii (1417–1431), 430.

Name in BL Ms Royal 7 A.v, H. de Folieto (late 13th c.); on fo 2, *liber . . . fratris*—.

Reginald de SUTTON
occ. 1345/7

1345, 15 May, ord acol., bp's small chapel, Trottiscliffe, Reg. Hethe fo 215v (p. 751).
1345, 21 May, ord subdcn, bp's chapel, Trottiscliffe, *ib.*, fo 216 (p. 1171).
1345, 24 Sept., ord dcn, bp's chapel, Halling, *ib.*, fo 217 (p. 1171).
1347, 24 May, granted *lit. dim.*, for the order of pr., *ib.*, fo 229v (p. 820).
1347, 26 May, ord pr., bp's chapel, Southwark, *Reg. Edington*, (Winchester), ii, no 735.

I John SWAN
occ. 1384 occ. 1401

1398, 28 Sept., the prior and chapter requested the bp to appt him to the office of cellarer; the bp did so on the following day, Reg. prior Shepey, fos 89v-90.

1400, 8 Oct., at the request of the prior and chapter on 7 Oct. released from the office of cellarer and replaced by John Holyngbourne, q.v., *ib.*, fos 115, 112v, and Reg. John Bottlesham, fo 2v.

1400, 10 Oct., apptment as precentor requested in place of Robert Strode, q.v., Reg. prior Shepey, fo 103v; the bp responded the following day, *ib.*, fo 107 and Reg. John Bottlesham, fo 3.

1401, 1 Apr., 'absolved' from the office of precentor and succ. by Robert Strode, q.v., Reg. prior Shepey, fo 101v, and Reg. John Bottlesham, fo 12.

1384, 16 Oct., 21st in order of those present in chapter to appt a proctor in the curia, Reg. prior Shepey, fo 21.

1387, 1 Sept., one of ten monks and four clerks, and on the same day one of eight monks named as general proctors, *ib.*, fos 58v, 68.

1389, 29 Apr., chaplain to bp Brinton who bequeathed 40s. to him and his *optimam robam*, Reg. abp Courtenay, i, fo 231; see also Nicholas de Frendesbury.

1397, 14 May, one of eight monks and five clerks apptd by the prior and chapter as general proctors prob. on acct of an impending metropolitan visitation, Reg. prior Shepey, fos 81, 81v, 83.

1400, 22 July, apptd papal chaplain 'gratis de mandato domini nostri pape', *CPL*, iv (1362–1402), 311.

II John SWAN
occ. 1464/5

1464, 22 Dec., ord acol. and subdcn, bp's chapel, Halling, Reg. Lowe, fo 44.

1465, 30 Mar., ord dcn, bp's chapel, Halling, *ib.*, fo 43v.

John de SYDYNGBORNE [Sydyngebourne
occ. [c. 1302] occ. [c. 1306]

[c. 1302], one of four monks who were assigned *ad tricennale celebrandum* for James de Beyersse, q.v., BL Ms Cotton Vespasian, A.xxii, fo 127.

[c. 1306], one of four assigned to celebrate as above for Elias [IV] q.v., *ib.*

William SYDYNGBOURNE [Sedyngborne, Sydingborne, Sythingborn
occ. 1390 d. 1415/16

1390, 26 Feb., ord acol., St Paul's cathedral, London, Reg. Braybrooke (London), fo 21.

1391, 18 Feb., ord subdcn, St Paul's, London, *ib.*, fo 24v; the prior had provided a *littera testimonialis*, for orders not yet recd on 16 Feb., and the bp had issued a *lit. dim.*, Reg. prior Shepey, fo 43v.

1391, 22 Mar., the prior sent a *littera testimonialis* to the abp on his behalf requesting ordination as dcn, *ib.*, fo 45.

1391, 25 Mar., ord dcn, Canterbury cathedral by *lit. dim.*, Reg. abp Courtenay, i, fo 312.

1391, 23 Sept., ord pr., St Paul's cathedral, London, Reg. Braybrooke (London), fo 27v; on 20 Sept. he had obtained *littera testimonialis* from the prior addressed to the bp of London and had recd from the bp [of Rochester] his *lit. dim.*, Reg. prior Shepey, fo 47v.

1409, 20 Nov., 17th in order among those in chapter to appt a proctor in a lawsuit, Reg. prior Shepey, fo 121v.

1415/16, d., and the chamberlain gave 1s. to the poor on the day of his burial, CKS DRc/F15.

TERRITIUS
n.d.

n.d., infirmarer, see below.

Name in BL Ms Royal 4 B.vii, Flores psalterii etc. (13th c.); on fo 2, *.X. Territii infirmarii.*

THALEBOT
n.d.

n.d., sacrist, responsible for the construction of the old *lavatorium*, the 'great' cross, the great clock which to that day was ref. to as his ['usque in hodiernum diem optinet nomen predicti Thaleboti'] and other gifts; he was listed among the benefactors, *Reg. Roff.*, 121.

I THEODERICUS
n.d.

Name in BL Ms Royal 10 A.xii, Collectanea theologice (early 13th c.); on fo 8, *liber— . . . monachi super Ioel de claustro Roffen'.* See Alexander II.

Note: this monk may possibly be the author or donor of this section of the vol., and he may also be the monk below.

II THEODERICUS
n.d.

n.d., responsible for securing a gift from a woman of Halling which enabled him to provide a window, vestments and other furnishings for the crypt altar of St Mary Magdalen; his name was placed among the benefactors, *Reg. Roff.*, 124.

I THOMAS
occ. [c. 1128 × 1137]

[c. 1128 × 1137], prior, *Fasti*, ii, 79, *HRH*, 64.

Note: the dating, contribued by Dr M. Brett, ref. to the dedication of Thorney abbey and the d. of bp John [I].

II THOMAS, son of, son of Scotland de Hnessindene (i.e. ?grandson)
n.d.

n.d., at the time of his adm. as a monk his father, Thomas, gave land in Sheppey and a message in Rochester, *Reg. Roff.*, 282.

Thomas THOMLEN
occ. 1510/11

1510, 30 Mar., ord dcn., bp's palace chapel, Rochester, Reg. Fisher, fo 37.
1511, 19 Apr., ord pr., Rochester cathedral, *ib.*, fo 38^{v}.

THOMLEN
see also Tomlyne

Richard THORNHAM
occ. 1393 occ. 1424/5

1393, 1 Sept., one of three whose prof. the prior was comm. to rec., Reg. William Bottlesham, fo 43 and Reg. prior Shepey, fo 66.
1394, 14 Mar., ord dcn, Maidstone, Reg. abp Courtenay ii, fo 184.
1396, 24 Sept., ord pr., Rochester cathedral, Reg. William Bottlesham, fo 149^{v}.

1424/5, infirmarer, CKS DRc/F16.

1397, 14 May, one of eight monks and five clerks apptd as general proctors prob. on acct of an impending metropolitan visitation, Reg. prior Shepey, fos 81, 81^{v}, 83.
1409, 20 Nov., 12th in order among those present in chapter to appt a proctor in a lawsuit, *ib.*, fo 121^{v}.
1419, 31 Aug., 7th at the el. of a prior, *Reg. abp Chichele*, i, 61.

William de THORNHAM [Thorneham
occ. 1367 occ. 1390

1367, 13 Mar, ord acol., abp's chapel, Otford, by *lit. dim.*, *Reg. abp Langham*, 378.
1367, 12 June, ord subdcn, Rochester cathedral, Reg. Trillek, fo 9^{v}.
1367, 19 Sept., ord dcn, Rochester cathedral, *ib.*, fo 10^{v}.
[1369], 20 Sept., dcn., granted *lit. dim.* for orders of pr., *ib.*, fo 20.
1370, 9 Mar., ord pr., St Paul's cathedral, London, *Reg. Sudbury* (London), ii, 79.

1384, 16 Oct., 10th in order among those present in chapter to appt a proctor in the curia, Reg. prior Shepey, fo 21.
1387, 1 Sept., one of ten monks and four clerks apptd as general proctors, Reg. prior Shepey, fo 58^{v}.
1390, 7 Mar., royal licence granted to a Lombard banker to issue a letter of exchange for 8 m. payable to him, *CClR (1392–1396)*, 523.

THURSTAN [Turstinus
occ. [?1083 × 1108]

[?1083 × 1108], son of Geroldus, *Text. Roff.*, ii, fo 189^{v} and cap 145; Ulgerius the nephew of Geroldus occ. in this and in another grant in *Text. Roff.*, ii, fo 196 and cap 176, the latter an ordinance explicitly said to be dated *temp.* bp Gundulf.

Roger de TICHESEIE
n.d.

n.d., gave 'the best chasuble' to St Mary's altar and was named among the benefactors, *Reg. Roff.*, 124.

Thomas TOMLYNE
occ. 1496

1496, 4 Nov., 17th in order on the visitation certificate and reported as ill, *Reg. abp Morton*, ii, no 446 [transcribed as Comlyne].

I William de TONEBREGG [Tonbregg
occ. 1295 d. 1297/8

1295, one of four monks who were assigned *ad tricennale celebrandum* for Roger de Chelesham, q.v., BL Ms Cotton Vespasian, A.xxii, fo 126^{v}.
1297/8, d. and four monks were assigned to celebrate, as above, for him, *ib.*

II William TONEBREGG [Tonnbreg, Tounbregge, Tunbrygge
occ. 1396 d. 1445

1419–1445, prior: el. 31 Aug. 1419; d. before 14 May 1445, see below.

1396, 9 May, one of two whose prof. the prior was comm. to rec., Reg. prior Shepey, fo 77^{v}.
1396, 24 Sept., ord acol., Rochester cathedral, Reg. Williamm Bottlesham, fo 149^{v}.
1397, 15 Sept., obtained licence *ad omnes ordines* from the bp, Reg. prior Shepey, fo 97.
1398, 21 Dec., ord subdcn, Rochester cathedral, Reg. William Bottlesham, fo 150.
1400, 18 Dec., ord pr., Malling, Reg. John Bottlesham, fo 8^{v}.

[1412], apptment as cellarer requested by the prior and chapter to succ. William Rouchestre, q.v., Reg. prior Shepey, fos 124^{v}-125.

1409, 20 Nov., 14th in order among those present in chapter to appt a proctor in a lawsuit, Reg. prior Shepey, fo 121^{v}.
1419, 31 Aug., 9th in order at the el. of a prior; the abp supervised the proceedings *sed. vac.*, and he was el. by the monks, *Reg. abp Chichele*, i, 61–62.
1420, 8 July, attended the Black Monk Chapter at Northampton, Pantin, *BMC*, ii, 96.
1423, 24 Mar., comm. by the bp to confer [all] offices *infra claustura* during the bp's absence abroad, Reg. Langdon, fo 19.
1423, 10 July, appted to visit Westminster abbey on behalf of the Black Monk Chapter, Pantin, *BMC*, ii, 148.
1423, 18 Dec., present at the renunciation of the rights of the vicar and parishioners with regard to St Nicholas' altar in the cathedral nave, which had been their accustomed place of worship, *Reg. Roff.*, 568 (Reg. Langdon, fo 30^{v}).

1425, 23 May, present in the chapel at the east end of the great hall when the bp gave his decision on the annual rent to be pd by the vicar of the newly built parish church of St Nicholas close to the cathedral, *Reg. Roff.*, 571 (Reg. Langdon, fo 45v).
1435, 24 July, appted by the bp to a comm. to investigate heretics, Reg. Brouns, fo 1v.
1440, 29 Apr., comm. as one of two vicars general, Reg. Wells, fo 34v; acting as vicar general 18 Oct. [1441], *ib.*, fo 60.
1444, 7 Feb., was bequeathed 13s. 4d. by the bp, William Wells, with the request that he pray for his soul, Reg. abp Stafford, fo 122v.
1445, d. shortly before 14 May, Reg. Lowe, fo 4v; see John Clyve who was el. to succ. him on that day.

TONEBREGG
see also Tunebregg

John TONNBREGG [Tounbregg, Tonnbrig
occ. 1431 occ. [1455]

1431, 31 Mar., ord subdcn, Rochester cathedral, Reg. Langdon, fo 69x.
1431, 5 Apr., ord dcn, Malling, *ib.*, fo 70x.
1437, 21 Sept., ord pr., St Paul's cathedral, London, Reg. Gilbert (London), fo 155.
[1455], 23 June, subprior, Reg. Lowe, fo 27v.
[1455], 23 June, with John Snell, q.v., comm. to induct a gatekeeper [*janitor*] for the priory, Reg. Lowe, fo 27v.

Richard de TONNBREGG [Thonebregg, Thonebrugg, Tonebregge
occ. 1324 d. 1342

1324, 25 June, the prior was comm. to rec. his prof., Reg. Hethe, fo 62 (p. 132).
1324, 22 Sept., ord subdcn, bp's chapel, Halling, Reg. Hethe, fo 64 (p. 1176).
1324, 22 Dec., ord dcn, bp's chapel, Halling, *ib.*, fo 66 (p. 1176).
1325, 2 Mar., ord pr., Trottiscliffe, *ib.*, fo 67v (p. 1176).
1336, 17 May, apptd chamberlain to succ. William de Bromfeld, q.v., Reg. Hethe, fo 166 (p. 559).
1336, 20 July, res. the above office and was succ. by John de Werburgh, q.v., *ib.*, fo 129v (pp. 420–421).
1341, 6 May, chamberlain, *ib.*, fo 195 (p. 671).
1341, 29 Sept., apptd cellarer in place of Ralph de Cantuaria, q.v., *ib.*, fo 195v (p. 672); he d. in office, see below.
1333, 19 Aug., 18th in order at the el. of a prior among those who voted for John de Shepey II, q.v., Reg. Hethe, fo 157 (p. 534).
1342, 24 Mar., d. by this date when he was succ. as chamberlain by John de Reynham II, q.v., *ib.*, fo 197 (p. 677).

I Thomas TONNBREGG [Tonbregg, Tunbregg', Tunbrygg
occ. 1422 occ. 1427

1422, 7 Mar., ord acol., Rochester cathedral, *Reg. abp Chichele*, iv, 350.
1423, 18 Dec., ord subdcn, Rochester cathedral, Reg. Langdon, fo 26v.
1426, 7 Mar., ord dcn, Rochester cathedral, *ib.*, fo 44v.
1427, 14 June, ord pr., bp's chapel, Trottiscliffe, fo 62v.

II Thomas TONNBREGG [*alias* Ware
occ. 1512

1512, 10 Apr., ord acol. and subdcn, bp's palace chapel, Rochester, Reg. Fisher, fo 42.

TONNEBREGG
see Tunebregge

Hugh de TROTTISCLIFFE [Trotesclive
occ. before 1126

n.d., a notable improver of the priory estates and benefactor who gave vestments; he also built the infirmary chapel which he furnished with the 'best' psalter, and the church of St Bartholomew for lepers, *Reg. Roff.*, 119. See Hubert II.
[1114 × 1122], sent by abp Ralph to claim the manor of Mucheberdesham [*sic*] for Christ Church, *Theobald Charters*, 536–537.
1126, became abbot of St Augustine's, Canterbury, *HRH*, 36.

Geoffrey de TUNEBREGGE
n.d.

n.d., precentor, made vestments used for major feasts and was listed among the benefactors, *Reg. Roff.*, 121.

Heymeric de TUNEBREGGE
occ. [c. 1193/1203]

[1193 × 1203], was responsible for building the 'cloister towards the infirmary', *Reg. Roff.*, 123. Hope interprets this to mean in the garden between the dorter and infirmary which was surrounded by covered walks between buildings, *Arch. Hist. Rochester*, 190; he also suggests that this construction was in progress *temp.* prior Ralph de Ros, q.v., *ib.*, 192. He was remembered among the benefactors as having provided windows for the crypt altars of the Trinity and of St Michael as well as for gifts of furnishings for these altars, *Reg. Roff.*, 123; see also Sharpe, *Eng. Benedictine Libraries*, iv, B81.

TUNEBREGGE
see also Tonebregg, Tonnbregg

John UMFREY [Hunfrey, Omfray, Omfrey
occ. 1367 occ. 1382

1367, 13 Mar., ord acol., abp's chapel, Otford, by *lit. dim.*, *Reg. abp Langham*, 378.
1367, 12 June, ord subdcn, Rochester cathedral, Reg. Trillek, fo 9^v.
[1369], 20 Sept., subdcn, granted *lit. dim.* for dcn's orders, *ib.*, fo 20.
1370, 9 Mar., ord dcn, St Paul's cathedral, London, *Reg. Sudbury*, (London), ii, 79.
1370, 8 June, ord pr., St Paul's cathedral, *ib.*, ii, 88.

1382, 12 Nov., third prior, Reg. prior Shepey, fo 15.
1382, 12 Nov., wrote to the abp concerning the chapter's apptment of John Holyngbourne, q.v., as their proctor for convocation, Reg. prior Shepey, fo 15.

John de UPCHERCH [Opcherch, Oppechurche, Uppecherche
occ. 1335 occ. 1341

1335, 23 Sept., ord acol., Malling, Reg. Hethe, fo 165 (p. 1178).
1336, 26 May, ord subdcn, bp's chapel, Halling, *ib.*, fo 166 (p. 1178).
1338, 19 Sept., ord dcn, Wouldham, *ib.*, fo 173^v (p. 1178).
1341, 2 June, ord pr., bp's chapel, Halling, *ib.*, fo 195 (p. 1178).

I William de UPCHERCH [Upcherche, Upchirche
occ. 1361/2

1361, 20 Feb., ord acol., Strood, Reg. Shepey, fo 32^v.
1361, 18 Sept., ord subdcn, abp's chapel, Otford, Reg. abp Islip, fo 319^v.
1362, 11 June, ord dcn, Mayfield, *ib.*, fo 321^v, by the bp of Rochester.
1362, 17 Dec., ord pr., Rochester cathedral, Reg. Wittlesey, fo 8.

II William de UPCHERCH [Upcherche
occ. [1369] occ. 1384

[1369], 20 Sept., had recd first tonsure and now granted *lit. dim.* for all minor orders, Reg. Trillek, fo 20.
1370, 9 Mar., ord acol., St Paul's cathedral, London, *Reg. Sudbury* (London), ii, 76.
1370, 8 June, ord subdcn, St Paul's cathedral, *ib.*, ii, 84.
1371, 1 Mar., ord dcn, St Paul's cathedral, *ib.*, ii, 99.
1372, 21 Feb., ord pr., St Paul's cathedral, *ib.*, ii, 111.
1384, 16 Oct., 13th in order among those present in chapter to appt a proctor in the curia, Reg. prior Shepey, fo 21. There can be no doubt that this is a ref. to William de Upcherch II because of his position in relation to John Pleme, q.v.

Robert VINITARIUS
see Robert II

W.
occ. 1227

1227, sacrist, *Flores Hist.*, ii, 190.
1227, with Roger de Darente and J. II, q.v., was sent to the abp to announce the el. of Henry de Saunford as bp, *ib.*

Henry WADE
see Ward

William WADEHURST [Watherst
occ. 1419

1419, 11 Mar., ord dcn, St Bride's, Fleet Street, London, Reg. Clifford (London), fo 85^v.
1419, 1 Apr., ord pr., Canterbury cathedral, *Reg. abp Chichele*, i, 192.

1419, 31 Aug., 21st and last in order at the el. of a prior, *ib.*, i, 62.

William WALBROKE [Walbrok
occ. 1446 occ. 1453

1446, 7 Sept., one of three whose prof. the prior was comm. to rec., Reg. Lowe, fo 9^v.
1446, 17 Dec., ord acol., bp's chapel, Halling, *ib.*, fo 11.
1449, 7 June, ord subdcn, Rochester cathedral, *ib.*, fo 21^v.
1450, 19 Sept., ord dcn, Rochester cathedral, *ib.*, fo 21^v.
1453, 22 Sept., ord pr., bp's chapel, Halling, *ib.*, fo 27.

Richard de WALEDENE
occ. 1296 d. [c. 1299]

n.d., sacrist, *Reg. Roff.*, 125.
1296, one of four monks who were assigned *ad tricennale celebrandum* for William de Cornubia, q.v., BL Ms Cotton Vespasian, A.xxii, fo 126^v.
n.d., responsible for the making of the bell called Andrew which cost 80 m. and with his own hands made the beam over the high altar carved with the apostles and with St Andrew standing above. He also provided a cupboard for relics and many books and supervised the construction of the south west transept [*ala*] towards the curia, *Reg. Roff.*, 125; see William de Hoo. The dating of the rebuilding of the south west transept is considered to be the latter part of the 13th c., Hope, *Arch. Hist. Rochester*, 52.
[c. 1299], d., and four monks were assigned *ad tricennale celebrandum* for him, BL Ms Cotton Vespasian, A.xxii, fo 126^v.

Robert de WALETONE [Waletune
n.d.

n.d., prior of Felixstowe; see below.

n.d., a supplement to the 1202 library catalogue in BL Ms Royal 5 B.xiii, fo 3, lists six volumes donated by him at least four of which have survived, but none have his name. These were with him at the cell of Felixstowe and are now BL Mss Royal:

(1) 10 C.iv, Omnibonus (early 13th c.). This vol. appears in the 1202 library catalogue in BL Ms Royal 5 B.xii, fo 2, printed in Sharpe, *Eng. Benedictine Libraries*, iv, B79.236.

(2) 2 E.vii, G. Foliot (early 13th c.). This vol. appears in the 1202 library catalogue in BL Ms Royal 5 B.xii, fo 2, printed in Sharpe, *Eng. Benedictine Libraries*, iv, B79.240.

(3) 2 F.xi, Flores psalterii (12th/13th c.); this has *per Laurentium episcopum* (1250–1274) on fo 1. This vol. appears in the 1202 library catalogue in BL Ms Royal 5 B.xii, fo 2, printed in Sharpe, *Eng. Benedictine Libraries*, iv, B79.237.

(4) 12 F.viii, Joh. Saresburiensis (12th/13th c.); this has *per Ierardum monachum* on fo 1 (see Gerard). This vol. appears in the 1202 library catalogue in BL Ms Royal 5 B.xii, fo 2, printed in Sharpe, *Eng. Benedictine Libraries*, iv, B79.239.

The other two vols named were a Compendium novi et veteris testamenti and Unum ex quatuor of Zacharias Chrysopolitanus (Ms Royal 3 C.vii, possibly a later copy), see Sharpe, *Eng. Benedictine Libraries*, iv, B79.238, B79.241. See also Richards, 'Texts', 18, 41, where it is suggested that M. Robert, q.v., who gave a fifth copy of Priscian, may be the same monk (*ib.*, B79.174).

WALTER
occ. 1295

1295, one of four monks who were assigned *ad tricennale celebrandum* for William de Schotindon, q.v., BL Ms Cotton Vespasian, A.xxii, fo 126^v.

John de WALTHAM [Wautham
occ. 1283 d. [c. 1301]

1283, 19 June, sent as proctor, with Thomas de Wouldham, q.v., to the abp for licence to el. a bp, *Epist. Pecham*, no 443.

1296, one of four monks who were assigned *ad tricennale celebrandum* for William de Cornubia, q.v., BL Ms Cotton Vespasian, A.xxii, fo 126^v.

[c. 1301], d., and four monks were assigned to celebrate, as above, for him, *ib.*

Henry WARDE [Wade, Ward
occ. [1459] occ. 1466

[1459, 24 Mar.], ord acol., Rochester cathedral, Reg. Lowe, fo 32.

1462, 3 Apr., ord subdcn, place not recorded, *ib.*, fo 36^v.

1462, 8 Dec., ord dcn, bp's chapel, Halling, *ib.*, fo 38.

1466, 20 Dec., ord pr., bp's chapel, Halling, *ib.*, fo 47^v.

Thomas WARE
see Thomas Tonnbregg II

William WATERFORD
occ. 1486 occ. 1514

1497/8, *custos*, of Felixstowe, Dugdale, *Monasticon*, iv, 563–565 (a transcript of his acct).

1511, 1 Oct., apptd chamberlain, Reg. Fisher, fo 40^v.

1514, 2 Dec., was succeeded as chamberlain by Anthony London, q.v., *ib.*, fo 55^v.

1486, 25 Apr., named as proctor for the prior and chapter in a union of two parish churches, *Reg. Roff.*, 165.

1496, 4 Nov., 6th in order on the visitation certificate, *Reg. abp Morton*, ii, no 446 (transcribed as Watford).

1511/12, named at the head of a composite obedientiary acct roll as one of four monk auditors in conjunction with one of the king's auditors, CKS DRC/F17. This same yr he was sent to Otford to see the abp, *ib.*

WATHERST
see Wadehurst

John WATTS
see John Rochester

WAUTHAM
see Waltham

William WELDE
occ. 1334

1334, 11 Mar., ord dcn, bp's chapel, Halling, Reg. Hethe, fo 163^v (not in the printed vol.).

John WELLS
see John Faversham II

John de WERBURGH [Warburgh, Wereburgh
occ. 1326 occ. 1351

1326, 20 Dec., ord subdcn, Wouldham, Reg. Hethe, fo 74 (p. 1181).

1327, 11 Apr., ord dcn, Trottiscliffe, *ib.*, fo 76 (p. 1181).

1327, 19 Dec., ord pr., Wouldham, *ib.*, fo 125 (p. 1181).

1336, 20 July, apptment as chamberlain requested in place of Richard de Tonnbregg, q.v., Reg. Hethe, fo 129^v (pp. 420–421).

1350, 3 May, apptd precentor, Reg. Hethe fo 272 (p. 909).

1333, 19 Aug., present at the el. of a prior and was one of five who nom. William de Reyersh, q.v., Reg. Hethe, fo 157 (p. 534).
1351, 18 Aug., one of the monks who, with the prior, Robert de Southflete II, q.v., witnessed a grant, *CClR (1349–1354)*, 379.

John de WESTERHAM
occ. 1291 d. 1321

1320–1321, prior: el. 14 Jan. 1320, *Fasti*, iv, 40; buried 30 Jan. 1321, *Anglia Sacra*, i, 394.
1291, 6 June, named as one of five *compromissorii* in the el. of a bp, Oxford, Bod. Ms Charters, Suffolk, no 1384.
1295, one of four monks who were assigned *ad tricennale celebrandum* for John de Chelesham, q.v., BL Ms Cotton Vespasian, A.xxii, fo 126[v].
1297, one of four assigned to celebrate, as above, for John Sauvage, *ib.*
[c. 1301], one of four assigned to celebrate, as above, for John de Waltham, *ib.*
[c. 1303/4], one of four assigned to celebrate, as above, for Robert de Hoo, q.v., *ib.*, fo 127.
1317, 18 Mar., named as proctor, with Geoffrey de Mepeham, q.v., at the el. of a bp, BL Ms Cotton Faustina B. v, fo 3[v]; with Richard de Halstede and John de Marchia, q.v., he supervised the voting [*per viam scrutinii*] and he and Geoffrey de Mepeham went to Lambeth to inform the abp of the result, *ib.*, fo 8, *Anglia Sacra*, i, 357. See also Reg. Temp., fo 118[v]-120.

Name in BL Ms Royal 11 C.i, Peter Lombard (early 14th c.); on fo 1, *per fratrem—quondam priorem.*

He was prob. responsible for the compilation of the Custumale Roffense, a record 'quarumdam consuetudinum, maneriorum et tenencium ecclesie Roffensis', before he became prior, *Cust. Roff.*, 1.

John de WHYTEFELD ?D.Th [Hwitfeld, Hwytefeld, Whitfeld, Whitefeld
occ. 1322 occ. 1342

1322, 27 Mar., ord acol., bp's chapel, Trottiscliffe, Reg. Hethe, fo 55[v] (p. 110).
1322, 5 June, ord dcn, Rochester cathedral, *ib.*, fo 56 (p. 1185).
1322, 7 June, ord pr., bp's chapel, Trottiscliffe, *ib.*, fo 57[v] (p. 1185).
1342, 4 Jan., dismissed from the office of subprior and succ. by John de Oxonia, q.v., Reg. Hethe, fo 196[v] (p. 676).
[?1322 × 1335], student at Oxford; see below.
1340, 14 Sept., the Black Monk chapter requested the presidents to write to the prior of Rochester to urge him to send Whytefeld to Oxford *ad incipiendum in theologia*, Pantin, *BMC*, ii, 16.
Note: see also John de Ikkelyng in the Norwich section.

1333, 19 Aug., 15th in order at the el. of a prior among those who voted for John de Shepey II, q.v., Reg. Hethe, fo 157 (p. 534).
1336, 9 Sept., preached at the episcopal visitation on the text, *Fratres tuos visitabis* (1 Kings 17, 8). He asserted that the bp [Hamo de Hethe] was visiting the chapter *ut fratres* and not *ut . . . subditos* because he had been *creatus et promotus* by the chapter; he also noted the contrast with the bp of Norwich, John Salmon (q.v., under Ely) who had preached to the Norwich chapter, 'Non vos me elegistis, sed ego elegi vos'. The chronicler's explanation for this disparaging outburst was that he had previously been put up to it by some of the brethren who had plied him with a gallon of wine. At the end of the sermon the bp made a statement in the form of a reply: he had come to visit them *ut filii*; he denounced those who having promoted him now found fault with him and said that in *nullo monachis tenebatur*, *Anglia Sacra*, i, 373 (BL Ms Cotton Faustina B.v, fo 78[v]).

Name in
(1) BL Ms Royal 4 A.xv, N. de Lyra (late 14th c.); on fo 5, *per*—. Ker's judgement as to date seems a trifle late in this case.
(2) Oxford, Bod. Ms Hatton 54, W. Malmesburiensis (early 14th c.); on fo 250 *liber—monachi de Roucestria*, rubricated; fos 1–86 were transcribed by him acc. to *BRUO*.

WIDO
see Guido

I WILLIAM [Guillelmus, Willelmus
occ. [1095 × 1107]

[1095 × 1107], subprior, *Vita Malchi*, 38, *Text. Roff.*, ii, fo 198 and cap 181; in the *Vita Malchi* he is *ippoprior.*

[1095 × 1107], greeted by Reginald (q.v. under Canterbury) in his preface to his life of Malchus. *Vita Malchi*, 38, and see *ib.*, 12 and 11 for the prob. dating which has been followed here.
[1107 × 1108], witness, *temp.* bp Gundulf and prior Ordwinus, q.v., to the oath of obedience of the abbess of Malling, *Text. Roff.*, ii, fo 198 and cap 181; see also Ralph I, Paulinus.

II WILLIAM
occ. [1083 × 1100] occ. [1114 × 1124]

[1083 × 1100], *temp.* bp Gundulf and king William II, described as reeve of Hadenham, now given by the bp charge [*curam*] of the manor of Aston Subedge [Easton], Gloucestershire, recently acquired by the bp, *Text. Roff.*, ii, fo 214[v] and cap 208; see Gislebertus.
[1114 × 1124], *temp.* bp Ernulf, with Humphrey, Martin I and Robert V, witnessed an agreement, *Text. Roff.*, ii, fo 199[v] and cap 183.

III WILLIAM
occ. [?1137 × 1143]

[?1137 × 1143], witnessed an episcopal instrument of bp John II, *Reg. Roff.*, 370, 413.

IV WILLIAM
occ. [1083 × 1108]

n.d., cellarer, *Cust. Roff.*, 28.

[1083 × 1108], *temp.* bp Gundulf who sent Wlfricus to him to be trained as the monastery baker, *ib.*

V WILLIAM
occ. [c. 1150]

n.d., son of Ernulf de Strodes, CKS DRc/T191/1, 2.

VI WILLIAM
n.d.

n.d., sacrist, see below.

n.d., as sacrist bought land in Frindsbury from a soapmaker, *Cust. Roff.*, 13.

VII WILLIAM
occ. 1219

1219, 12 Sept., chaplain to bp Benedict and witness to a final concord, *Reg. Roff.*, 437.

VIII WILLIAM
occ. 1218 occ. 1222

c. 1218–1222, prior: occ. 6 Oct. 1218; occ. Apr. 1222, *Fasti*, ii, 88, 80.

n.d., there is ref. to a William, prior, in a grant of rents in Wouldham, *Reg. Roff.*, 691.

Note: this last entry may refer to William de Borstall or William de Hoo, q.v.

IX WILLIAM
occ. 1293

1293, 4 Aug., prior, named in an agreement concerning lands in Elham, Oxford, Bod. Ms Charters, Kent, no 214.

Not otherwise known; see John de Reynham and Wynand de Dryland.

Note: It is not possible to make a clear distinction between some of the above Williams.

WINCHESTRE
see Wynchestre

WLDEHAM
see Wouldham

I William at WOD
occ. 1377

1377, 27 June, witnessed the confirmation of an appropriation by the prior and chapter, *Reg. Roff.*, 266.

II William WODE [Wod, Wodd, Wold, Woode
occ. 1440 occ. 1475

?1468 × 1475, prior: he succ. Richard Pecham, q.v., and was prior on 20 Oct. 1468; occ. 18 June [1470], 20 Jan [1472], 8 Oct. 1475, CKS DRc/T301, T288, T281.

1440, 3 Mar., one of two whom the prior was comm. to rec. and clothe as a novice; the bp had examined and approved of them, and ordered that they rec. instruction, [*habitum imponat' et instruat'. . .*], Reg. Wells, fo 33.

1461, 10 Sept., adm. to the office of subprior by the bp, *sed vac.*, priory, Reg. Lowe, fo 34^{v}.

A few of his *acta* as prior occ. in Reg. Wode/Bourne.

John de WODESTOK [Wodestoke
occ. [c. 1302] occ. 1333

1333, 19 Aug., infirmarer, Reg. Hethe, fo 157 (p. 534).

[c. 1302], one of four monks who were assigned *ad tricennale celebrandum* for William de Ledes, q.v., BL Ms Cotton Vepasian, A.xxii, fo 127.

1329, Nov., had been accused of incontinence at the abp's visitation, and the bp was denounced for failing to discipline him, *Anglia Sacra*, i, 369–370.

1330, 10 Feb., reported in the abp's injunctions as dwelling in the cell at Felixstowe, Reg. Hethe, fo 130^{v} (pp. 425–426) and BL Ms Cotton Faustina B.v, fo 54.

1333, 19 Aug., 9th in order at the el. of a prior among those who voted for John de Shepey II, q.v., Reg. Hethe, fo 157 (p. 534).

Richard de WOULDHAM [Wldeham
n.d.

n.d., land outside the precinct wall to the north was given with him and with Eustace, q.v., i.e., at the time of his entry, and he was listed among the benefactors, *Reg. Roff.*, 118. See Ralph de Ros.

Thomas de WOULDHAM [Wldham, Woldeham, *alias* Southflete
occ. 1283 occ. 1291

1283–1291, prior: succ. 24 Dec. 1283; el. bp [for the second time] 6 June 1291, *Gervase Cant.*, ii, 297 (*Fasti*, ii, 80, 78); see below.

1283, 19 June, with John de Waltham, q.v., sent by the prior and chapter to the abp for licence to el. a bp, *Epist. Pecham*, no 443.

Early in his priorate he and the chapter became involved in a controversy with the newly el. bp over several issues including the latter's apptments to offices within the priory vs their advice and request; the abp came to investigate and denounced the bp for his behaviour vs the rights and customs of the church of

Rochester, *Flores Hist.*, iii, 59 (*Anglia Sacra*, i, 353).

1291, el. bp, but renounced the el. because of *injurias . . . irrogatas* vs him by the clerks of the abp; the monks obtained a second licence from the abp and reelected him; see above.

Thomas WROTHAM

occ. 1454

1454, 15 June, ord acol. and subdcn, bp's chapel, Halling, Reg. Lowe, fo 26.

Thomas WYBARN, B.Th

occ. 1458 occ. 1470/1

1458, [1] Apr., ord subdcn, Reg. Lowe, fo 32.

1458, 24 Sept., ord dcn, bp's chapel, Halling, *ib.*, fo 32.

1459, 24 Mar., ord pr., Rochester cathedral, *ib.*, fo 32.

[1464], 2 Feb., apptd subprior, Reg. Lowe, fo 43ᵛ.

Note: this apptment may seem surprising for a monk (prob. less than 10 yrs professed), who was presumably at Oxford for part of the yr since he obtained a degree in 1467; however, he may have served only temporarily as a replacement.

1470/1, almoner, first yr, acc. to a note on the dorse of CKS DRc/F11 (an almoner's acct for 1430/1; see Walter Shepey).

1467/8, student at Oxford and placed a book in the Chichele chest as caution for a loan, 20 Aug. 1467, 20 Aug. 1468; see below 1). In this year an unnamed monk of Rochester pd 10s. for a room in Canterbury college, Pantin, *Cant. Coll. Ox.*, ii, 188.

1467, described as B.Th.; see below, (9) and (15).

Name and notes in the following Mss in the BL Royal collection:

(1) 2 C.i, P. Comestor (13th c.); on fo 2* a note that the book was pledged for the price of Duns Scotus' Sententiae on 20 Aug. 1467; on fo 166 a note states that it was pledged, exactly a yr later, for 26s. 8d. See Ralph de Stoke.

(2) 2 E.vii, G. Foliot (early 13th c.); on fo 3ᵛ, written by him: 'Qui servare libris preciosis nescit honorem. Illius a manibus sit procul iste liber'. This vol. appears in the 1202 library catalogue in BL Ms Royal 5 B.xii, fo 2, printed in Sharpe, *Eng. Benedictine Libraries*, iv, B79.240. It also contains the name Gilbertus, q.v., and appears in the list of Robert de Waletone, q.v.

(3) 4 A.xv, N. de Lyra (late 14th c.); on fo 5 the first line of the verse in 2) appears and the name John de Whytefeld, q.v., who also made use of this volume.

(4) 4 B.vii, Flores psalterii etc. (13th c.); on fo 1ᵛ, the verse as above. The name Territius, q.v., is on fo 2.

(5) 5 B.iv, Augustinus (12th c.); on fo 2ᵛ, *Orate pro eo quod* [Thomas] Wybarn. This vol. appears in three library catalogues; that of 1122/3 in *Text Roff.*, ii, fos 224–230, the fragments in CKS DRc/Z18/1–2 of similar date, and that of 1202 in BL Ms Royal 5 B.xii, fo 2; these are printed in Sharpe, *Eng. Benedictine Libraries*, iv, where the refs are B77.7, B78.2 and B79.2 respectively. See also Humphrey, precentor.

(6) 5 B.xii, Augustinus (12th c.); on fo 3ᵛ a note by Wybarn. This vol. appears in the library catalogue of 1122/3 in *Text. Roff.*, ii, fos 224–230, and in that of 1202 in BL Ms Royal 5 B.xii, fo 2; these are printed in Sharpe, *Eng. Benedictine Libraries*, iv, where the refs are B77.10 and B79.11. See also Alexander II and Humphrey, precentors, where further refs are given.

(7) 5 C.viii, Augustinus (De verbo Domini) (12th c.); on fo 250, the verse, as above and his name; this vol. appears in the 1202 library catalogue in BL Ms Royal 5 B.xii, fo 2, printed in Sharpe, *Eng. Benedictine Libraries*, iv, B79.5.

(8) 5 D.ix, Augustinus (12th c.); on fos 1 and 259 the verse, name and other notes in his hand. This vol. appears in the library catalogue of 1122/3 in *Text. Roff.*, ii, fo 224 (De civitate Dei), and in that of 1202 in BL Ms Royal 5 B.xii, fo 2; these are printed in Sharpe, *Eng. Benedictine Libraries*, iv, where the refs are B77.2 and B79.1.

(9) 6 D.ii, Jeronimus (12th c.); on fo 1 the verse in Wybarn's hand as above and on a flyleaf 'Iste liber ligatus erat Oxonii in Catstrete ad instantiam reverendi—in sacra theologia bacalarii . . . 1467'. This flyleaf, now lost, was copied by an 18th c. librarian. This vol. appears in the library catalogue of 1122/3 in *Text. Roff.*, ii, fos 224–230, and in that of 1202 in BL Ms Royal 5 B.xii, fo 2; these are printed in Sharpe, *Eng. Benedictine Libraries*, iv, where the refs are B77.19 and B79.37.

(10) 6 D.vii, Gregorius (14th c.); on fo 1, the verse and a prayer for Thomas de Horstede, q.v.

(11) 9 E.xi, Alexander de Hales (13th/14th c.); on fo 2, the verse and name; on fo 1, William de Reyershe, q.v.

(12) 10 C.xii, Bonaventura etc. (early 14th c.); on fo 1ᵛ the verse and name.

(13) 12 F.viii, Johannes Saresberiensis (12th/13th c.); on fo 114ᵛ, a prayer and a few lines of verse in his hand. This vol. appears in the 1202 library catalogue in BL Ms Royal 5 B.xii, fo 2, printed in Sharpe, *Eng. Benedictine Libraries*, iv, B79.239. See also Ierardus (Gerardus) and Robert de Waletone.

(14) 15 A.xxii, Solinus etc. (12th c.); on fo 1ᵛ the couplet (as in no 2) and his name and title

subprior. This ms and BL Ms Cotton Vespasian D.xxi, fos 1–17, is B77.91 in Sharpe, *Eng. Benedictine Libraries*, iv, and one of the two books entered at B79.100.

Other manuscripts:

(15) Cambridge, Trinity College, Ms 1128, Grammatica etc. (early 12th c.); on fo xv^{v}, the verse, name and title *bacallarius*. This vol. appears in three library catalogues; that of 1122/3 in *Text Roff.*, ii, fos 224–230, the fragments in CKS DRc/Z18/1–2 of similar date, and that of 1202 in BL Ms Royal 5 B.xii, fo 2; these are printed in Sharpe, *Eng. Benedictine Libraries*, iv, where the refs are B77.67 (entry deleted), B78.20 and B79.98 respectively. See G. de Stratton.

[(16) Cambridge, Trinity College, Ms 610, Lucanus (early 12th c.); on fo 5^{v} a portion of the verse which suggests his possible ownership]. This vol. appears in the 1202 library catalogue in BL Ms Royal 5 B.xii, fo 2, printed in Sharpe, *Eng. Benedictine Libraries*, iv, presumably one of the three Lucans entered at B79.186.

Robert de WYLMYNTON

occ. [c. 1304]

[c. 1304], one of four monks who were assigned *ad tricennale celebrandum* for Thomas Payn, q.v., BL Ms Cotton Vespasian, A.xxii, fo 127.

Valentine WYNCHESTRE

occ. 1522

1522, 19 Jan., one of seven who made their prof. before the bp, Reg. Fisher, fo 91.

1522, 20 Dec., ord subdcn, bp's palace chapel, Rochester, *ib.*, fo 92.

YALDING

see Ealding

William de YORK [Yorke, Ebor'

occ. 1392 occ. 1397

1392, 18 Sept., the prior and chapter informed the abbot and convent of St Osyth, London diocese, that they would accept William, canon, on probation as he had expressed the desire to lead a more rigorous life as a Benedictine at Rochester, Reg. prior Shepey, fo 57.

1392, 24 Sept., obtained his licence to transfer from St Osyth, *ib.*, fo 57–57^{v}.

1392, 9 Nov., the prior was comm. by the bp to rec. his prof., Reg. prior Shepey, fo 59.

1393, 31 May, ord acol., abp's chapel, Croydon by *lit. dim.*, Reg. abp Courtenay, ii, fo 182.

1394, 14 Mar., ord dcn, Maidstone, *ib.*, ii, fo 184.

1396, 26 Feb., ord pr., collegiate church of All Saints, Maidstone, *ib.*, ii, fo 186^{v}.

1397, 18 Sept., the abbot of Westminster asked the prior for a licence permitting him to transfer to Westminster, Reg. prior Shepey, fo 83^{v}; the prior and chapter and the bp sent the required permission on 19 Sept., *ib.*, fo 84.

ZACARIAS [Zacharia

n.d.

n.d., precentor, Cambridge, St John's College Ms 70, fo 1.

n.d., son of Eilevinus, clerk, who gave land with his son to the priory and is listed among the benefactors, *Reg. Roff.*, 118.

Name in Cambridge, St John's College, Ms 70, Epistolae Pauli (12th c.); on fo 1 *per—precentorem.*

WINCHESTER CATHEDRAL PRIORY

INTRODUCTION

A monastic connection with Winchester cathedral can be traced back to the seventh century, when it already had its threefold dedication to the Holy Trinity and Saints Peter and Paul. Some time after the death of the ninth-century bishop Swithun, his name was added, and from that date onward this single dedication was the one commonly used. The continuous presence of Benedictine monks can be dated from the arrival of the reforming bishop Aethelwold in 964 who introduced a group of monks from Abingdon to replace the married clergy then occupying the monastery.[1] When the Norman abbot Lanfranc was appointed archbishop of Canterbury by William I in 1070 he initiated another wave of monastic renewal, beginning with his monastic chapter at Canterbury and spreading to other cathedral monasteries including Rochester, Worcester, and, probably, Winchester.[2] Unfortunately, the first post-conquest bishop, Walkelin, was not a monk, unlike his episcopal colleagues at Canterbury, Rochester, and Worcester, but a secular canon of Rouen, whose presence as titular abbot of a monastic chapter proved a strain to all concerned.[3] Relations improved, however, with the installation of his brother, Simeon, q.v., a monk of Saint-Ouen, as prior; and an ambitious building programme for a new cathedral church was soon launched by the bishop with the co-operation of the monks.[4]

At Winchester the priors continued to be appointed by the bishops until the late thirteenth century; nominations to the obedientiary offices were also claimed as pertaining to the episcopal prerogative by Aymer de Valence in 1256 and by John de Pontissara in 1284; on the latter date Edward I intervened to settle what had been a long-standing dispute about this and other matters between the monastic chapter and a succession of bishops. The resulting agreement provided for free election of the prior on receipt of an episcopal licence, and free appointment and dismissal of all obedientiaries, the latter privilege being one that none of the other southern cathedral priories ever acquired.[5] Episcopal interference in the internal affairs of the priory was thus greatly reduced, and the bishop was compensated by the relinquishment to him of several priory manors.[6] The priorate of William de Basyng I, q.v., straddled this transition from appointment to free election; his resignation, which took place at about the

[1] Aethelwold collaborated with bishop Oswald of Worcester and archbishop Dunstan in providing the *Regularis Concordia* (ed. by T. Symons, London, 1953) as a basic guide for the implementation of reform in English monastic houses.

[2] See D. Knowles, ed., *The Monastic Constitutions of Lanfranc* (London, 1951), and his *MO*, 619–622.

[3] Walkelin had at first considered removing the monks in favour of secular canons but was prevented from doing so by Lanfranc.

[4] Simeon went on to become the abbot of Ely. For details of the construction of the Norman cathedral see J. Crook, 'Bishop Walkelin's Cathedral', in Crook, *Winchester Cathedral*, 21–36.

[5] For Valence see *Ann. Waverley*, 349. The terms of the settlement are in *Reg. Pont.*, 426–430. In the northern province, Durham cathedral chapter had obtained the right of free appointment of obedientiaries in 1229 in a composition known as *le convenit*; it is printed in W. Greenwell, ed., *Feodarium Prioratus Dunelmensis* (Surtees Society, 1872), 212–217.

[6] The charter of this transfer is in *Reg. Pont.*, 430–431.

same time as the signing of the agreement, seems to have been in order to pave the way for the chapter to exercise their rights for the first time.

There were usually about twenty obedientiary offices at Winchester, but some, like those of the gardener and the *speciarius*, occur only occasionally and were possibly responsibilities sometimes assigned to secular clerks or lay officials.[7] The names of a few obedientiaries are known in the late eleventh and early twelfth centuries: Nigel, q.v., sacrist before 1094, for example, Wlnoth, q.v., precentor c. 1107, Geoffrey II, q.v., hordarian, before 1111, and Edmund, q.v., subprior in the 1140s. The office of hordarian was unique to St Swithun's and was probably similar to that of cellarer where the latter was in charge of the provision and distribution of food supplies for the monks and their secular officials and servants working within the precincts. At Winchester, however, the hordarian's income appears to have been greater than his counterpart at Ely and Norwich and the monk kitchener and monk curtarian/cellarer were both subordinate to him.[8] A *custos* of the Lady altar, Adam de Wyg', q.v., occurs in 1223; and in the 1230s, during vacancies of both the see and the priory, a chamberlain (Anselm, q.v.), bartoner (John de Basyng I, q.v.), *custos operum* (Simon II, q.v.), hostiller (John de Dureville, q.v.), infirmarer (Thomas de Henton, q.v.), and refectorer (Philip I, q.v.) all come into view because of royal interventions in priory appointments. An anniversarian (Philip Trenchefoil, q.v.) turns up in the mid-thirteenth century; it was he who made distributions to the poor on the commemoration days of patrons and benefactors and gave pittances to the monks on such occasions.[9] The earliest known almoner (Hugh Langover, q.v.) and the first receivers (Henry Aurifaber and Gilbert de Froyle, q.v.) occur in the 1260s, the latter usually in pairs and one or both of them indifferently referred to also as treasurers. Finally, there was a monastic official at Winchester who came to be known as the *depositarius* and was first appointed in 1286 to be in charge of any surplus funds for distribution to the monks as treats or pittances; his equivalent at other monasteries like Worcester and Ely was the pittancer.[10]

As a major cathedral, the seat of one of the most senior bishops, with royal connections stretching back to the late seventh century, and located in a city that boasted a royal residence and provided a centre of government for the early Norman kings, Winchester played a significant role in the history of the medieval English church and state. It is disappointing that the sources from which this history could be reconstructed have been sadly depleted over the intervening centuries; what remains, while impressive, is a patchwork with many holes that can be filled in only tentatively through comparison with parallel developments in other cathedral priories. Apart from one lengthy gap, the bishops' registers are complete from 1282, but the loss of the second volume of bishop, later cardinal, Beaufort's register in the sixteenth century has left a thirty-year blank which is evident in many of the entries where, for

[7] The records provide the names of five monk gardeners in the 14th and 15th cs, the earliest being Robert de Basyng, q.v.; only three *speciarii* are known, John Andever, John Thurston, and Nicholas Salisbury, q.v. In this summary of obedientiaries I have not referred to the third and fourth priors, both of whom occur at Winchester.

[8] The earliest known kitchener is Robert de Godeshulle, q.v., in 1311 and the first curtarian to be named is Henry Byset, q.v., in 1239. It is likely that the cellarer and curtarian were always one and the same obedientiary, probably performing two closely related jobs; see J. Greatrex, 'St. Swithun's Priory in the Later Middle Ages', in Crook, *Winchester Cathedral*, 149.

[9] His income was chiefly derived from the Wiltshire manor of Bishopstone—today Bushton—where he was frequently found making supervisory visits.

[10] He was first called *custos espernii* or *custos depositi*. See Greatrex, 'St. Swithun's Priory' (n. 8 above), 150.

example, ordination dates are missing. The earliest priory register has only a few entries before 1400, and the two sixteenth-century registers contain little beyond leases, appointments of lay officials, and confirmations of episcopal *acta*. Some seventy of the one hundred and twenty-five extant account rolls of obedientiaries were competently transcribed *in extenso* by Dean Kitchin over a century ago, but only nine of the obedientiary offices are included.[11] Since his day other accounts, including the only two pertaining to the infirmarer, have been found. The losses are partially compensated for by some impressive runs of manorial accounts and some early composite rolls of fifteen to twenty membranes each, resembling exchequer 'pipe roll' accounts; these latter begin in 1248. Among the former a few are available in the typescript transcripts and translations of J. S. Drew.[12]

St Swithun's was probably intended to house a community of some sixty to seventy monks. The earliest reference to numbers is in the *Annales de Wintonia* where it is stated that there were sixty-one present at the episcopal election in 1262; in 1325 another list of sixty-four monks provides us with the earliest record of names in order of seniority.[13] The Black Death had an adverse effect on the monastic population of St Swithun's from which recovery was still incomplete almost half a century later for, in 1387, bishop Wykeham noted that there were only some forty brethren whereas there had previously been eighty.[14] Six years later, with a seemingly greater concern for accuracy, he gave these numbers as forty-six and sixty, the former being the precise number at the time.[15] In the first half of the fifteenth century, while numbers fluctuated between thirty-five and forty, the number of *juvenes* was on several occasions as high as five or more, thus suggesting that there was no lack of young men seeking admission.[16] During the last century of its existence, however, with the exception of the final decade, numbers do not appear to have totalled more than thirty-five;[17] it is surprising, therefore, to find forty-five monks being accounted for by both the anniversarian (in 1530/1) and the hordarian (in 1532/3) and the former distinguishes eighteen as being *non domini capellani*, presumably implying that they were not yet priests.[18] Further details of the closing years will be discussed in the final paragraphs below.

The St Swithun's chapter rarely had any influence in the choice of their bishop. The holder of the see of Winchester was almost invariably an important figure in public affairs, frequently as a minister of state; as such his selection could not be left to the local monastic community whose claim to the right to elect their titular abbot retained little weight or meaning. However, the monks continued to go through the

[11] See Section C.ii of the References. There are no surviving rolls for the precentor or hostiller.

[12] Details are provided in Section B. v (*a*) of the References.

[13] *Ann. Winton.*, 99 (1262); the 1325 list is a later insertion on a blank leaf in *Reg. Pont.*, 556–557. The house count was probably similar when, in 1342, the monks refused to accept a candidate proposed by the king because their numbers were complete, *Winch. Cart.*, nos 121–123.

[14] BL Ms Harley 328, fo 7.

[15] *Ib.*, fo 18.

[16] There were actually forty-two monks at the election of prior Thomas Nevyle, q.v., as bishop in 1404, *Reg. Common Seal*, no 68. In 1409/10 the hordarian's account reported five *juvenes*; in 1422/3 the chamberlain provided for seven in one term on his account and five in another, and in 1432/3 he accounted for six in two of the four terms and five in another. These accounts are all in the Cathedral Library and can be located by date.

[17] In 1498 there were thirty-two at the election of prior Thomas Silkstede, q.v., of whom there were seven not yet in priest's orders, Reg. Langton, fo 73; in 1524 thirty monks took part in the election of Henry Broke, q.v., Reg. Fox, v, fos 74–83ᵛ.

[18] These accounts are also in the Cathedral library. Unfortunately there are no ordinations of St Swithun's monks after 1528.

formalities of an election and sometimes held out against royal objections, as in the case of bishop William de Ralegh in 1240/1, in this instance successfully because of papal support.[19] In 1280, after the pope had quashed the first election of Robert Burnell, an ecclesiastical careerist high in the royal favour, the monks proceeded to choose the archdeacon of Winchester, Richard de la More; this gained royal assent but aroused papal disapproval on the grounds of pluralism. The prior, Adam de Farnham, q.v., and other monks suffered a brief spell of excommunication after this unfortunate episode.[20] Papal provision was decisive in several disputed elections where monks had been put forward. In 1261 for example, when Andrew de London, q.v., the prior, and William de Taunton, q.v., a former prior, were both candidates the pope stepped in to quash the election and provide John of Exeter. The king and pope supported different candidates in the 1319 election: when the monks put forward Adam de Wynton II, q.v., one of their number, against the king's wishes, the pope responded by providing his choice, Rigaud de Asserio, his chaplain. Having chosen one of their brethren, John le Devenish, q.v., in 1345 the monks again incurred the royal displeasure, with the result that prior Alexander de Heriard, q.v., and other monks had to petition for a royal pardon, from which Devenish was excluded. The last unsuccessful attempt to promote one of the brethren to the episcopate was in 1404 when the monks elected their prior Thomas Nevyle, q.v.; he stood no chance against the king's nomination of his half-brother Henry Beaufort. Two letters survive to show that royal *congés d'élire* were probably often accompanied by a directive containing the royal nomination.[21] The one success story was Henry Woodlock, q.v., whose election in 1305 was approved by both king and archbishop without hesitation or delay.

The year 1305 was memorable as the year of three visitations of St Swithun's priory. Archbishop Winchelsey arrived in January soon after the death of bishop Pontissara, and he came a second time, *sede plena*, in early November only a few weeks after Woodlock had completed his first visitation of the chapter.[22] No injunctions survive for these visits, but Woodlock's injunctions of 1308 follow the standard oft-repeated form, with admonitions to the prior N[icholas de Tarente, q.v.] to present the required annual financial statements to the chapter, to appoint competent lay stewards for supervision of the priory estates, to consult his senior monk advisers in important affairs, and so on. The 1315 injunctions were also similar on many points and warned prior Richard de Enford, q.v., not to show any favouritism at the time of recreation, nor to use the common seal without consultation; in addition there were a number of practical requirements laid upon the prior and obedientiaries for the well-being and orderly running of the house.[23] An earlier visitation by bishop Pontissara in 1286 had resulted in more specific injunctions with the intention of removing the cause of a dispute that had arisen between prior William Basyng I, q.v., and his chapter because the prior had reduced the amount spent on the monks' pittances in order to alleviate the monastery's debt. Through the bishop's mediation a satisfactory compromise was agreed by which all members of the community including the prior accepted some reductions in their food rations, the new amounts and arrangements

[19] *Fasti*, ii, 86.

[20] *Ib.*, ii, 87.

[21] One letter refers to the king's wish to have John de Sandale elected bishop in 1316, *Reg. Sandale*, 335; the other names William Waynflete as the royal choice in 1447, *Reg. Common Seal*, no 314.

[22] For the archbishop see *Reg. abp Winchelsey*, xviii–xix, 496–497, and for the bishop, *Reg. Woodlock*, 48; Winchelsey's second visit is also referred to in *Reg. Woodlock*, 52.

[23] *Reg. Woodlock*, 507–509 (1308), 747–751 (1315).

being precisely laid down.[24] The injunctions sent to the chapter after bishop John Stratford's visitation in February 1326 aroused such indignation that the monks objected to their strict enforcement; they insisted that some of the measures were in contravention of the Rule and would severely hamper the prior and obedientiaries in their administration. Stratford's register provides a full record of this visitation including the *comperta*, negotiations between convent and visitor and the injunctions, issued in July; to the last of these, censures were attached but their implementation delayed. Some seven months later the bishop wrote to express his continued dissatisfaction with their conduct and the negligent governance of prior Enford. However, in July 1327 both parties made public renunciations, the bishop withdrawing his censures and the monks the appeal they had initiated against him in the court of Canterbury.[25] When Stratford was removed by translation to Canterbury in 1333, the monks addressed him in the friendliest of terms, although not entirely free from self-interest.[26]

There was another dramatic episode arising out of Wykeham's visitatorial activities in 1387 and 1392. It would appear that on the former occasion the bishop prohibited the monks from continuing to receive money in lieu of pittances and of some items of clothing, and he, too, imposed *penas et censuras*. However, on the second occasion he removed the censures and agreed that they could be allowed their cash payments, yielding to the monks' claim to 'an ancient custom' of their church. His volte-face was, in reality, due to the monks' intransigence in refusing to have any share in his building programme for the repair and restoration of the cathedral fabric so long as he refused them their pocket-money. By the terms of the agreement of 1 August 1393 the monks pledged themselves to a substantial financial contribution over a seven-year period and to other measures of practical assistance.[27] Depositions survive from only two later *sede vacante* visitations by Canterbury, those of archbishop Morton through his vicar-general in October 1492 and of the prior of Christ church, *sede vacante* Canterbury, through the latter's commissary in 1500. The tenor of both of these reports was that, despite continuing complaints about such matters as the quality and quantity of food provided, the inadequate care of the sick, and the inevitable irritations and aggravations that beset a closely knit community, nothing ever changed.[28] Depositions, however, cannot be treated *per se* as a true reflection of the internal state of a monastic community because they must surely have more often been spontaneous expressions of dissatisfaction than reasoned statements prepared in advance.[29]

As far as is known there were few remarkable priors of Winchester, but there were several able administrators; there were also some colourful characters who were at the centre of controversies both within and beyond the priory. Andrew I, q.v., for example, was undaunted by excommunication and used violence to subdue monks opposed to his rule. William of Taunton, q.v., who in 1254 obtained the right to use pontifical

[24] *Winch. Cart.*, no 111.

[25] Reg. Stratford, fos 171^{v}–178; notification of the appeal to the court of Canterbury in March 1327 is in *Winch. Cart.*, no 250, and the bishop's letter to the convent in June after learning of their renewed zeal and obedience is *ib.*, no 251.

[26] They expressed gratitude for his successful efforts in obtaining royal confirmation of their charters, *Winch. Cart.*, no 276.

[27] Greatrex, 'Injunction Book', 245–246, based on BL Ms Harley 328, fos 12–27^{v}.

[28] *Reg. abp Morton*, ii, no 127 and Canterbury Reg. R, fos 114^{v}–115^{v}; the Christ Church prior was the second Thomas Goldston, q.v.

[29] The question arises as to what extent and by what date had visitation proceedings become a formality?

regalia, was expelled the next year but continued to have wide support in the community and was put forward as a candidate for the bishopric. His successor, another Andrew [de London], q.v., aroused opposition within the community both in and out of office for over twenty years, and the career of prior Valentine, q.v., was equally stormy both before and after his deprivation in 1276. Among fourteenth-century priors, Alexander de Heriard, q.v., seems to have experienced both denunciation and approbation by the chapter over his administration in the 1330s, and it was he and the chapter who had to seek a royal pardon for their defiance of the royal will in the election of John le Devenish, q.v. The priorate of Thomas Nevyle, q.v., referred to above and, indeed, his origins and family background remain overshadowed by mystery. He was elected prior in 1395 soon after completing his doctorate, was called in by the king to give advice during the papal schism, was a joint president of the Black Monk Chapter in 1404, and the following year was elected bishop by a unanimous chapter. On the papal provision of Henry Beaufort he resumed his office as prior until, in August 1415, he was imprisoned in the Tower of London. The records are silent as to his alleged crime, but it has been suggested that he may have had some connection with the conspirators in the Southampton plot. It is also possible that strained relations with the all-powerful bishop may have been a factor and, if he had influential family links whose loyalties were uncertain, this could have made him appear as a liability in a time of political tension and instability. The last two priors of St Swithun's will be considered in the final paragraphs concerning events leading up to the dissolution.

The monks were generally known by their toponymics, which serve as indicators of their family origins, though they are not always reliable. Nevertheless, we are probably safe in assuming that most of the fifteen or so monks named Basing (and its variations) came from the parish of that name, now Basingstoke, and similarly for those named Sarum or Salisbury. At least sixteen were probably members of Winchester families, one of these being John le Devenish [de Winton], q.v., who probably retained his patronymic because of his prominent family connections. Others came from priory manors such as Alton, Chilbolton, Enford, and Stockton, these last two being in Wiltshire. About 1409/10 Ralph Mascal, q.v., whose father, a *nativus*, had been farmer at Stockton, was admitted as a monk; his father was later manumitted, and in retirement was the recipient of a corrody within the priory. Higher up on the social scale were monks whose family names were Brokas and Gilers, q.v., and possibly Haywode, q.v.[30]

That an almonry school for boys existed at Winchester is beyond doubt. Many of the references, however, are resistant to unambiguous interpretation, but it is clear that the frequently mentioned *juvenes in scola* are not boys but young monks who received small sums from the almoner and from several other obedientiaries from about 1386/7 on.[31] A month before his death in 1404, bishop Wykeham secured an agreement with the monks to provide for the services he desired in his chantry chapel in the cathedral nave; in this document the *pueri elemosinarie* were to sing the antiphon and recite the psalm each evening.[32] On the eve of the dissolution the appointment of a grammar

30 A Walter Haywode was the lay steward of St Swithun's in 1380/1, WCL Wootton account roll.

31 Kitchin, *SS*, no 51, p. 413 (1386/7).

32 *Reg. Common Seal*, no 63; see also *ib.*, no 53, and R. Bowers, 'The Lady Chapel and its Musicians, c. 1210–1559', in Crook, *Winchester Cathedral*, 249–250.

master specifies three groups of boys whom he was to teach: the juniors, the 'chyldern of the chapell', and the 'chyldern of the almery', thus at this late date clarifying what had probably been in existence for more than a century.[33] Rarely are the junior monks named and nothing more is known of the education they received in their early years as novices or juniors.[34] There are no medieval book lists or catalogues of the library over which the precentor presided, although the scriptorium produced splendid work in the tenth and eleventh centuries as attested by the Winchester Bible, still surviving *in situ*. Only about eighty volumes have been traced and a third of these are pre-conquest.[35] It is hardly credible that the book collection at Winchester was inferior to those at Rochester or Worcester, and it must have been adequate for those monks who were being prepared for Oxford.

Here again, however, the records prove disappointing. Although St Swithun's must have been concerned with the setting up of Gloucester Hall in the 1290s as a house of studies for Benedictines at Oxford, the earliest known monk student is Philip de Lusteshall, q.v., who may have first gone up in 1306.[36] Between this date and 1539 only twenty-eight other monks are known to have spent some time at Oxford; but the proportion of those who stayed long enough to obtain degrees is impressive in totalling fifteen.[37] Most of the Winchester monks would have stayed at Gloucester Hall, although there was a Winchester chamber at Canterbury college where the Christ Church monks from time to time accommodated a few of their brethren from St Swithun's.[38] One *prior studentium* at Oxford in the mid-fifteenth century was a Winchester monk, William Wroughton, q.v., and William Basyng IV, q.v., was the university preacher on Easter day in 1528. When bishop Fox reprimanded the chapter for their failure to maintain monk students at Oxford in 1521, John Avynton had just obtained his doctorate in theology after a lengthy period of study there, William Basyng IV must have been in the middle of his university career, William Manydowne had just successfully completed a first degree, and Richard Petersfeld supplicated for a B.Th. that very year; how are we to interpret the relevance of the bishop's complaint?[39]

The monks of St Swithun's were in frequent, if not daily, contact with the world outside the monastery. Among pastoral responsibilities the bishop regularly licensed one or two of them as penitentiaries or confessors within the city and diocese.[40]

[33] Reg. iii, fo 83^{v}.

[34] See Richard Dummer, Nicholas Warner, and John Bowlond. There is a single reference to the master who instructed the juniors *in cantu* in the 1430s, *Reg. Common Seal*, no 236.

[35] See *MLGB* and Sharpe, *Eng. Benedictine Libraries*, iv, where an early 16th-c.book list of some twelve volumes is printed as B111. It is interesting to note that one Winchester manuscript, now Oxford Ms Bod. 58, contains a lengthy treatise on the game of chess [*super ludo scachorum*], fos 52–128^{v}, including both its history and a detailed explanation of the rules; it is attributed to the Dominican, James de Cessolis.

[36] This interest, if not initial direct participation, is surely reflected by the entries concerning the foundation of Gloucester Hall in *Winch. Cart.*, nos 61–66.

[37] Six obtained a first degree in theology and one in canon law; seven achieved a doctorate in theology and one in canon law. It is worth noting that a number of manorial accounts are useful in recording the names of monk students who broke their journeys to and from Oxford by stopping for a meal and a bed, e.g. Whitchurch and Hurstbourne. Food supplies were sometimes sent up to Oxford from Woolstone; see, for example, Thomas Nevyle and Ralph de Basyng.

[38] James Dorsett, John Hampton, and Thomas Tystede, q.v., were three of these. Prior Thomas Silkstede, q.v., visited Canterbury college in 1510/11.

[39] Reg. Fox, iv, fo 67–67^{v}.

[40] See Philip de Avinton, Richard de Merewell I, and Ralph Basyng, to name three among many.

Records of monks preaching to the laity are few, but the prior was among those whom bishop Edington instructed to explain to the faithful the teaching of the Church concerning the resurrection; this was in the context of the epidemic of 1349 and the disruption of a funeral.[41] John Hyde and Thomas de Stoke, q.v., who served as hostillers in the 1370s, were both commissioned by bishop Wykeham to administer the sacraments at Littleton, the manor of which provided most of the income of their obedientiary office.[42] Although further evidence is wanting, we may presume that homilies were included in these parish duties and probably in some of the supervisory visits of monks to their manors.[43] It was the hostiller and the almoner who were concerned with the welfare of guests, pilgrims, and the poor; the former accommodated visitors to the monastery in the pilgrims' hall and the latter was in charge of the hospital known as the Sustern Spital that was situated just outside the South Gate. Almost half of the almoner's income was spent in 1316/17 in providing for the spiritual and physical requirements of its twenty or so needy inmates.[44] The burden of obligatory hospitality was a heavy one for St Swithun's because of frequent royal visits. Although accommodation was not required because of the proximity of the castle, entertainment in the form of banquets and expensive gifts were obligations not to be ignored at such times as the marriage of Henry IV and Joan of Navarre in 1403 and the baptism of prince Arthur in 1486.

There were periods of strained relations between monks and citizens and, during one outbreak of violence in 1264, Kingsgate and buildings within and close to the precinct walls were burned.[45] Disputes followed as to responsibilities for the repair of this gate and Southgate until prior Valentine, q.v., came to an agreement with the mayor and commonalty. On three occasions in the fourteenth century parliament was held in Winchester, in 1330, 1371, and 1393, all of which the prior probably attended in person; on other occasions he might send his proctor both to parliament and to convocation.[46] Several priors played a prominent role as one of the joint presidents of the Black Monk Chapter, Thomas Nevyle as already mentioned, and his two immediate successors, Thomas Shirebourne and William Alton, q.v.

The events of the years immediately preceding the dissolution cannot be satisfactorily reconstructed. Doubts remain as to the identity and movement of monastic personnel at Winchester, and the puzzling list of monks that has turned up among the Selden manuscripts in the Bodleian Library has increased rather than diminished the uncertainties.[47] The reason for this list of thirty-one monks, inserted without Christian names in a thirteenth-century astronomical work, is unclear, as is the way the names have been grouped in columns; however, all but one, Wolindr', q.v., can be identified and, from internal evidence, the dates 1528 × 1539 assigned.[48] At the election of Henry Broke, q.v., in 1524, thirty monks cast their votes, giving reasons for their choice that

[41] *Reg. Edington*, ii, no 201. The disruption had turned into violent assault on some of the monks present in the cemetery, and the bishop took the mayor and commonalty to court over their unlawful invasion of the monastic precincts, *VCH Hampshire*, v, 35.

[42] See also John Mideltone.

[43] Evidence for parish preaching exists at Worcester; see Richard de Bromwych.

[44] Kitchin, *SS*, no 24, p. 403 which is, in fact, the duplicate of *SS*, no 23, pp. 400–403.

[45] *Ann. Winton.*, 101; see also *VCH Hampshire*, v, 34.

[46] Prior Thomas Hunton and John Hampton, q.v., together attended convocation in 1472.

[47] Oxford, Bod. Ms Selden supra 76, fo 46v.

[48] Had there been any record of monks' deaths in this period it would have been possible to be more precise.

have been preserved in the bishop's register, a record unique for this particular detail. No acknowledgement of the Act of Supremacy by the Winchester monks has survived, but within a year or two a few monks, including Richard Canterbury *alias* Myllys, John Hubbard, and Henry Kyngeston, q.v., departed. In compliance with the new regime Myllys had complained to Thomas Cromwell of the prior's unjust treatment. The royal visitation in September 1535 was carried out by Cromwell in person; and this same year, as a result of the imposition of restrictive injunctions, the prior found himself obliged to write to Mr Secretary for permission for his 'curtear' [?curtarian] to leave the monastery in order to accompany the steward on his rounds of the manors.[49] The following March, under protest Broke resigned, leaving the priory in debt according to his successor, William Basyng [IV], q.v., *alias* Kingsmill. The latter had already begun to curry favour by the promise of a large sum and there can be little doubt that the 'election', like the one at Worcester this same year, was rigged. The number of monks who participated is not recorded; it would be interesting to know how many joined the ex-prior in being 'unavoidably' absent.[50] The surrender list, which includes thirty-three names, with the pension assigned to each, has two or three new names, presumably recent arrivals in the monastery; one of these, Thomas Eston, q.v., whose *alias* may be Fygge, was included among the four described as priest students at Oxford.[51] Most of the eighteen referred to earlier as not yet in priest's orders in 1530/1 can be tentatively identified and some must have left; but, in order to account for the drop in numbers from forty-five in that year to about thirty-three in 1539, we need to bear in mind that an unknown number of older monks must have died. These few statistics allow us to observe that, despite the uncertain future after prior Broke's departure, almost all the monks remained with their community. The fact that two or three were being received and four university students being maintained on the eve of the dissolution suggests that St Swithun's, although undoubtedly weakened by internal divisions like other religious houses, had not yet succumbed to what would soon prove to be the inevitable.

WINCHESTER REFERENCES WITH ABBREVIATIONS

Note: if the particular reference sought does not appear below, turn to the General Bibliography on pp. xv–xix, or the Canterbury section, pp. 58–65.

A. Manuscript Sources

i Episcopal Registers

(*a*) Hampshire Record Office (HRO)

Reg. [John de] Pontissara/Pontoise (1282–1304)	21M65/A1/1
Reg. [Henry] Woodlock (1305–1316)	21M65/A1/2
Reg. [John] Sandale (1316–1319)	21M65/A1/3

[49] Knowles, *RO*, iii, 476, *L and P Henry VIII*, ix, no 1093.

[50] It would seem that at least two, John Avynton and Richard Petersfeld, q.v., had drawn the commissioners' condemnation down upon themselves for some unspecified reason; perhaps they had challenged the new procedures.

[51] The other recent admissions were Rowland Kingeston and Roger Pratt, q.v., and the other students were James Dorsett, Peter Wareham, and Thomas Tystede, q.v. If Eston is Fygge, q.v., all four would have entered the monastery in 1527/8.

Reg. [Rigaud de] Asserio/Assier (1320–1323)	21M65/A1/4
Reg. [John de] Stratford (1323–1333)	21M65/A1/5
Reg. [Adam de] Orleton (1333–1345)	21M65/A1/6, 7
Reg. [William de] Edington (1346–1366)	21M65/A1/8, 9
Reg. [William de] Wykeham (1367–1404)	21M65/A1/10, 11
Reg. [Henry] Beaufort (1405–1447)	21M65/A1/; only one vol. extant for 1405–1418.
Reg. [William] Waynflete (1447–1486)	21M65/A1/13 and 14
Reg. [Peter] Courtenay (1487–1492)	21M65/A1/15
Reg. [Thomas] Langton (1493–1501)	21M65/A1/16
Reg. [Richard] Fox (1501–1528)	21M65/A1/17–21
Reg. [Thomas] Wolsey (1529–1530)	21M65/A1/22
Reg. [Stephen] Gardiner (1531–1551)	21M65/A1/23

(*b*) Wiltshire Record Office (WRO)

Reg. Mitford (Salisbury) no class number

ii Priory Registers, Cartularies, and Custumals

(*a*) Winchester Cathedral Library (WCL)

Basyng Libellus	Libellus Willelmi Basyng, hordarian's register, dated 1535.
Reg. i	Common seal register, i, 1345–1497; see also under *Reg. Common Seal* in Section C.ii below.
Reg. ii	Common seal register, ii, 1496–1533.
Reg. iii	Common seal register, iii, 1533–1538.
Winch. Cart.	Cartularium prioratus Sancti Swithuni Wynton, now in three ms volumes; miscellaneous register, mainly 14th c. See also under *Winch. Cart.* in Section C.ii below.
Winch. Cust.	Rentale et custumale prioratus Sancti Swithuni, 13th c. See also under Hanna in Section B.iv below.

(*b*) London, British Library (BL)

BL Add. Ms 15350	Cartulary, 12th/13th c., often known as the codex Wintoniensis.
BL Add. Ms 29436	Cartulary, 11th/13th c.; also contains *consuetudines elemosine* (fos 72–80).

B. Other Manuscript Sources

i Obedientiary Accounts

(*a*) Winchester Cathedral Library (WCL)

Almoner	1309 to 1522/3
Anniversarian	1394/5 to 1535/6
Chamberlain	1399/1400 to 1482/3
Curtarian/Cellarer	1411/12 to 1497/8
Custos of the Lady Altar	1529/30
Custos Operum	1408/9 to 1522/3
Hordarian	1327 to 1532/3
Infirmarer	1399/1400
Receiver	1280/1 to 1355/6
Sacrist	1536/7
Also two diet rolls	1492/3, ?1514/15

Note: Most of the above are printed in full in Kitchin's volume; see Section D below. They are here denoted by the numbers he assigned to them followed by the page reference; the sacrist's single account is printed by Kitchin and Madge (Section D), and the earliest receiver's account by Dom A. Watkin (Section D). A definitive list of these accounts and of the manorial and court rolls is currently being prepared, but for the present the originals are easily located by date.

(*b*) Other Locations

Worcester Cathedral Muniments	Anniversarian, 1369/70 to 1476
BL Add. Roll 26872	Anniversarian, 1534/5
Lambeth ED68, ED69	Hordarian, 1311/12, 1391/2
Lambeth ED70	Infirmarer, 1402/3

ii Manorial Accounts and Court Rolls

(*a*) Winchester Cathedral Library (WCL)

These are referred to by manor and date.

(*b*) London, British Library (BL)

Rot. Harl.	Enford account and court rolls
Add. Rolls	Mapledurham account and court rolls
Add. Rolls	Stockton account and court rolls

(*c*) London, Public Record Office (PRO)

SC2/ and SC6/ Woolstone account and court rolls

(*d*) Trowbridge, Wiltshire Record Office

Stockton account and court rolls

(*e*) Worcester, Cathedral Muniments (WCM)

C.866, 867 Chilbolton account rolls

iii Chronicles and Miscellaneous Manuscripts

(*a*) Winchester Cathedral Library (WCL)

Cath. Records, i, ii, iii	Scrapbooks into which have been pasted miscellaneous instruments and deeds.

(*b*) Hampshire Record Office (HRO)

Pipe rolls of the bishopric

(*c*) Cambridge, Corpus Christi College

Ms 110 Chronica cenobii S. Swithuni Winton; see the entry under John de Exeter I.

(*d*) London, British Library (BL)

Ms Cotton Domitian A. xiii	Annales Monasterii de Wintonia, 519–1277; see *Ann. Winton.* in Section D below.
Ms Cotton Nero A. xvii	Chronicon Thomae Rudborne; see the entry under Rudborne.
Ms Harley 328	Injunctions of bishop Wykeham; see also under Greatrex in Section D below.

(*e*) London, Lambeth Palace Library (Lambeth)

Ms 183 Thomas Rudborne, Historia maior; printed in *Anglia Sacra*, i, 179–285 (General References).

(*f*) London, Public Record Office (PRO)

E315/494 Surrender deed, 1539

(*g*) Oxford, Bodleian Library (Oxford, Bod.)

Ms Jones 4 Chronicles and documents including Liber historialis of John of Exeter, q.v.

(*h*) Spain, Simancas, Spanish National Archive

Ms E.593 Deposition of an inquiry in Bruges, 1585.

iv Unpublished Theses

Davis, 'William Waynflete' V. Davis, 'The Life and Career of William Waynflete, Bishop of Winchester, 1447–1486', Trinity College, Dublin, Ph.D., 1985.

J. Greatrex, 'Winchester Cathedral Priory in the Time of Cardinal Beaufort', Ottawa, Ph.D., 1973; copies in the Institute of Historical Research, London, and Winchester Cathedral Library.

K. Hanna, 'The Winchester Cathedral Custumal', 2 vols, Southampton, MA, 1954.

v Unpublished Typescripts by J.S. Drew

(*a*) London, Institute of Historical Research

Account and court rolls of manors transcribed and translated:

Chilbolton	1248–1331	2 vols (1945)
Houghton	1248–1331	(1943)
Michelmersh	1238–1331	(1943)
Silkstead	1267–1399	(1947)
Thurmond	1325–1428	(1941–1942)

(*b*) Winchester Cathedral Library (WCL)

Houghton, Michelmersh, Silkstead, and Thurmond as above, with additions to Silkstead accounts from 1404 onwards.

C. Printed Sources

i Episcopal Registers (in chronological order)

Reg. Pont. C. Deedes, ed., *Registrum Johannis de Pontissara, episcopi Wintoniensis, A.D. MCCLXXXII–MCCCIV*, Canterbury and York Society, 2 vols, 19, 30, 1915–1924. Pagination continuous throughout.

Reg. Woodlock A. W. Goodman, ed., *Registrum Henrici Woodlock, diocesis Wintoniensis, A.D. 1305–1316*, Canterbury and York Society, 2 vols, 43, 44, 1940–1941. Pagination continuous throughout.

Reg. Sandale
Reg. Asserio F. Baigent, ed., *The Registers of John de Sandale and Rigaud de Asserio, Bishops of Winchester (A.D. 1316–1323) with an Appendix of Contemporaneous and Other Illustrative Documents*, Hampshire Record Society, 1897.

Reg. Edington S. Hockey, ed., *The Register of William Edington, Bishop of Winchester, 1346–1366*, Hampshire Record Series, 2 vols, 1986–1987.

Reg. Wykeham T. F. Kirby, ed., *Wykeham's Register*, Hampshire Record Society, 2 vols, 1896–1899.

Reg. Wolsey F. Madge and H. Chitty, eds, *Registrum Thome Wolsey, cardinalis ecclesie Wintoniensis administratoris*, Canterbury and York Society 32, 1926.

Reg. Gardiner H. Malden and H. Chitty, eds, *Registra Stephani Gardiner et Johannis Poynet, episcoporum Wintoniensium*, Canterbury and York Society, 37, 1930.

ii Priory Accounts, Registers, and Cartularies

Kitchin, *SS*	G. W. Kitchin, ed., *Compotus Rolls of the Obedientiaries of St. Swithun's Priory, Winchester*, Hampshire Record Society, 1892.
Reg. Common Seal	J. Greatrex, ed., *The Register of the Common Seal of the Priory of St. Swithun, Winchester, 1345–1497*, Hampshire Record Series, 1978; summary of all the items in Reg. i (Section A. ii (*a*) above).
Winch. Cart.	A. W. Goodman, ed., *Chartulary of Winchester Cathedral*, Winchester, 1927 (see Section A.ii (*a*) above).

D. Other Printed Sources and References

Ann. Waverley *Ann. Winton.*	H. Luard, ed., *Annales Monastici*, Rolls Series, 5 vols, 1864–1869, ii, 1865.
Baigent, *Crondal*	F. Baigent, ed., *A Collection of Records and Records Documents relating to the Hundred and Manor of Crondal in the County of Southampton*, Hampshire Record Society, 1891.
Birch, *Hyde Liber Vitae*	W. de Gray Birch, ed., *Liber Vitae: Register and Martyrology of New Minster and Hyde Abbey, Winchester*, Hampshire Record Society, 1892.
Bird, *Black Book*	W. Bird, ed., *The Black Book of Winchester*, Winchester, 1925.
Chron. Devizes	J. Appleby, ed., *Chronicon Ricardi Divisiensis de tempore Ricardi primi*, Medieval Texts, London, 1963.
Crook, *Winchester Cathedral*	J. Crook, ed., *Winchester Cathedral, Nine Hundred Years, 1093–1993*, Chichester, 1993.
Eng. Epis. Acta, viii	M. Franklin, ed., *English Episcopal Acta*, viii. *Winchester, 1070–1204*, British Academy, London, 1993.
Eng. Epis. Acta, ix	N. Vincent, ed., *English Episcopal Acta*, ix. *Winchester, 1205–1238*, British Academy, London, 1994.
Fasti, 1541–1857, iii	J. Horn, comp., *John Le Neve Fasti Ecclesiae Anglicanae, 1541–1857*, iii. *Canterbury, Rochester, Winchester Dioceses*, London, 1974.
Greatrex, 'Injunction Book'	J. Greatrex, 'A Fourteenth-Century Injunction Book from Winchester', *Bulletin of the Institute of Historical Research*, 50 (1977), 242–246.
Harriss, *Beaufort*	G. L. Harriss, *Cardinal Beaufort, a Study of Lancastrian Ascendancy and Decline*, Oxford, 1988.
Kitchin, *Manydown*	G. W. Kitchin, ed., *The Manor of Manydown*, Hampshire Record Society, 1895.
Kitchin and Madge, *Documents*	G. W. Kitchin and F. T. Madge, eds, *Documents relating to the Foundation of the Chapter of Winchester*, Hampshire Record Society, 1889; includes a transcription of the sacrist's account for 1536/7 (*SS*, no 64, pp. 19–31).
Watkin, 'Rec. Acct.'	A. Watkin, ed., 'Fragment of a Thirteenth Century Receiver's Roll from Winchester Cathedral Priory', *English Historical Review*, 61 (1946), 89–105.
Wilson, 'Hord. Acct.'	J. M. Wilson, ed., *Accounts of the Priory of Worcester for the Year 13–14 Henry VIII, A.D. 1521/2*, Worcester Historical Society, 1907, Appndx vii, 58–61 (a Winchester hordarian's acct).
Winch. Cath. Record	*Winchester Cathedral Record*, annual publication of Winchester Cathedral.

WINCHESTER CATHEDRAL PRIORY
1066–1539

I A.
occ. 1270

1270, Oct., a prior A. apptd a steward [*senescallus*] of all lands in five counties, BL Add. Ms 29436, fo 40.

Note: could this be Andrew de London, q.v., claiming to be the rightful prior?

II A.
occ. [1224]

[1224], 1 May, chaplain, occ. as witness in a land dispute, *Eng. Epis. Acta*, ix, no 6.

ADAM
occ. 1326

1326, 8 July, precentor, WCL Basyng, Libellus, fo 4.

Note: this is probably Adam de Sarum, q.v.

ADAM
see also Donyton, Farnham, Wyg', Wynton

J. de ALBO EQUO
occ. before 1305 occ. 1311

[1295 × 1304], temp. prior Henry [Woodlock], q.v., apptd proctor with regard to the payment of a pension to cardinal Luke, *Winch. Cart.*, 238.

1304/5, stopped at Stockton (Wilts.) with the steward [*senescallus*] on the way to Salisbury for trailbaston and the manorial acct was charged 9s. 1d., for their expenses as well as provender for the horses, WCL acct.

1307/8, 1308/9, 1310/11, visited Chilbolton, WCL acct.

1308/9, visited Hurstbourne, WCL acct.

William ALBON
occ. 1465/6

1465, 21 Sept., ord acol., Hyde abbey, Reg. Waynflete, i, fo I*.

1466, 20 Sept., ord subdcn, Winchester cathedral, *ib.*, i, fo K*^{v}.

ALEN
see William London

I ALEXANDER
occ. 1266/7 occ. 1276

1269/70, curtarian, Wonston, WCL acct.

1276, subprior, removed from office by the bp, *Ann. Winton.*, 123.

1266/7, visited Overton, WCL acct.

1269/70, visited Wonston, WCL acct.

1272/3, an M. Alexander spent one night at Hurstbourne on his way to Oxford, WCL acct.

Note: see also Alexander Berthonarius, Alexander de Wyncestre and de Wynton.

II ALEXANDER
occ. 1308/9 occ. 1311

1310/11, curtarian, Chilbolton, WCL acct.

1308/9, 1310/11, pd visits to Chilbolton, WCL accts.

Note: on many accts in the 1280s an Alexander occ., and some of these refs are to Alexander de Wigornia and de Wynton, q.v., who were more or less contemporaries. For this reason the above two Alexanders cannot be more precisely identified. See also Alexander de Heriard and the note above.

Ralph de ?ALEXUS [?Arexiis
occ. 1266/7

1266/7, chaplain to the prior, Chilbolton, WCL acct.

1266/7, visited Chilbolton, *ib.*

ALEYN
see William London

ALMARUS
d. by 1122/3

1122/3, name occ. in a mortuary roll of Savigny following that of Godfrey, prior, q.v., but not distinguished as a monk, Delisle, *Rouleaux des Morts*, 336.

Simon ALTON
occ. 1513 occ. 1524

1513, 26 Mar., ord subdcn, Winchester cathedral, Reg. Fox, iii, fo 53.

1524, 2 Dec., 20th in order at the el. of a prior, Reg. Fox, v, fo 75; he nom. John Avynton, q.v., *ib.*, v, fo 77^{v}.

Thomas ALTON
occ. c. 1528 occ. 1539

[1528 × 1539], surname occ. in a list of monks copied on to a blank fo in Oxford, Bod. Ms. Selden supra 76, fo 46^{v}; no Christian names are given.

1539, 14 Nov., 24th on the surrender list, among the commoners, and assigned a pension of £5 p.a., *L and P Henry VIII*, xiv, pt 2, no 520 (PRO E315/494).

See Thomas Fygge

William ALTON [Altone, Aulton, Aultone

occ. 1393 d. 1450

1435–1450, prior: first occ. as prior, 23 July 1434, Reg. i, fo 53v (*Reg. Common Seal*, no 234); d. 10 Nov., 1450, Reg. Waynflete, i, fo 29; see Thomas Shirebourne.

Note: *Reg. Common Seal*, no 289, n. 2 is now out of date in two senses of the term!

1393, 1 Mar., ord subdcn, bp's chapel, Farnham, *Reg. Wykeham*, i, 328.

1393, 21 Sept., ord dcn, bp's chapel, Esher, *ib.*, i, 329.

1394, 14 Mar., ord pr., bp's chapel, Marwell, *ib.*, i, 332.

[1393/4], celebrated first mass, WCL, fragment of a chamberlain's acct.

1408/9, apptd subprior, Kitchin, *SS* no 11, p. 213.

1410/11; 1413/14; 1415, 26 Aug.; 1417/18; 1420/1; 1429, 12 Feb., subprior, BL Add. Rolls 28078, 28081; *Reg. Common Seal*, no 158; WCL Crondall acct; BL Add. Roll 28089; *CPL*, viii (1427–1447), 133.

1393, 21/22 Aug., 41st in order (out of 43) to sign the composition with bp Wykeham; BL Ms Harley 328, fo 24v; see Robert de Rodebourne.

1404, 16 Oct., 25th at the el. of a bp, *Reg. Common Seal*, no 68.

1408/9, recd a gift of wine from the *custos operum* on his apptment as subprior, Kitchin, *SS* no 11, p. 213.

1410/11, 1413/14, pd visits to Mapledurham, BL Add. Rolls 28078, 28081.

1415, 26 Aug., present as witness to the resignation of Thomas Nevyle, q.v., *Reg. Common Seal*, no 158.

1415, 24/27 Sept., presided over the el. of a new prior and was himself one of the *compromissorii*, *ib.*, nos 161–164.

1417/18, visited Crondall, and the expense to the manor was 20d, WCL acct.

1420/1, visited Mapledurham, BL Add. Roll 28089.

1429, 12 Feb., granted papal indult to choose his confessor, *CPL*, viii (1427–1447), 133.

1442; 1 Sept.; 1445, 24 Apr., one of the joint presidents of the Black Monk Chapter, Pantin, *BMC*, iii, 108, 110; he may also have continued in office to 26 Sept. 1446, *ib.*, 110.

1445, 15 Apr., presided at the el. of a bp, *via spiritus sancti*, *Reg. Common Seal*, no 316.

1447, 14 Apr., with another, recd a comm. from the abp to prove cardinal Beaufort's will, Reg. abp Stafford, fos 113v–114.

ALTON

see also Aulton

ALURED

d. by 1122/3

1122/3, name occ. in a mortuary roll of Savigny following that of Godfrey, prior, q.v., but not distinguished as a monk, Delisle, *Rouleaux des Morts*, 336.

ALURICUS

d. by 1122/3

1122/3, name occ. in a mortuary roll of Savigny following that of Godfrey, prior, q.v., but not distinguished as a monk, Delisle, *Rouleaux des Morts*, 336.

ALWINUS

d. by 1122/3

1122/3, name occ. in a mortuary roll of Savigny following that of Godfrey, prior, q.v., but not distinguished as a monk, Delisle, *Rouleaux des Morts*, 336.

John de AMBRESBURY

occ. 1345

1345, 28 July, one of nine *compromissorii* chosen to el. a bp, *Reg. Common Seal*, no 5.

John AMBREWYK [Ambrewyke

occ. 1406 occ. 1409/10

1406, 19 Feb., ord acol., Winchester cathedral, Reg. Beaufort, fo A.

1408, 9 June, ord subdcn, Winchester cathedral, *ib.*, fo Bv.

1409, 23 Mar., ord dcn, Winchester cathedral, *ib.*, fo Cv.

1409, 21 Sept., ord pr., Winchester cathedral, *ib.*, fo D.

1409/10, one of five who celebrated their first mass and the hordarian sent gifts, Kitchin, *SS* no 57, p. 290.

AMICELLI, Anceline, Ancelme

see Auncell

John ANDEVER [Andevere, Andevor

occ. 1513 occ. 1539

1513, 26 Mar., ord subdcn, Winchester cathedral, Reg. Fox, iii, fo 53.

1521, 30 Mar., ord pr., Lady chapel, Winchester cathedral, *ib.*, iv, fo 72.

1535, *speciarius*, *Valor Eccles.*, ii, 2.

1524, 2 Dec., 19th in order at the el. of a prior, Reg. Fox, v, fo 75; he nom. Henry Broke, q.v., 'propter eius prudentiam et bonam religionem', *ib.* v, fo 77v.

[1528 × 1539], surname occ. in a list of monks copied on to a blank fo in Oxford, Bod. Ms. Selden supra 76, fo 46v; no Christian names are given.

1539, 14 Nov., 15th on the surrender list, among the commoners, and assigned a pension of £5 p.a., *L and P Henry VIII*, xiv, pt 2, no 520 (PRO E135/494).

I ANDREW
occ. 1239 d. 1243

1239–1243, prior: apptd by the king, *sed. vac.*, 23 Nov. 1239 vs the wishes of the majority of the monks, *Ann. Waverley*, 323–4.; d. 18/26 Dec. 1243, *Fasti*, ii, 89.

1239, before 23 Nov., third prior, *Fasti*, ii, 89; see Ralph de Aremes.

1240, before Nov., excommunicated by the abp of Canterbury, *Fasti*, ii, 89.

1243, 26 Sept., a papal mandate was issued for an investigation by the prior of Rochester [Alexander de Glanville, q.v.] and the prior of Holy Trinity, London, because, with the help of the adcns he had tried to regain control of the priory and had imprisoned some of the monks, *CPL*, i (1198–1304), 200.

n.d., 27 Dec., obit occ. in BL Add. Ms 29436, fo 44.

II ANDREW
occ. 1250

1250, 13 Oct., chamberlain, *CPR (1247–1258)*, 75.

1250, 13 Oct., one of four monks who recd a licence from the king to el. a bp, *ib.*

Note: this is prob. Andrew de London, q.v.

ANSCHETILL'
n.d.

n.d., named as a monk benefactor in a late 12th/early 13th c. fragment of a customary which prescribed the food to be served on his anniversary, BL Add. Ms 29436, fos 75^{v}, 78.

ANSELM
occ. 1238

1238, 11 July, chamberlain, *CPR (1232–1247)*, 226.

1238, 11 July, one of four monks who with the adcns recd a licence from the king to el. a bp, *ib.*

ANTHONY
occ. c. 1111 × 1143

c. 1111, carried relics of St Ethelwold to Thorney abbey, Orderic, *Eccl. Hist.*, iii, 218, n. 1 (Oxford, St John's College Ms 17, fo 29^{v}).

[1114 × 1143], visited the abbey of Saint Évroul, Normandy, and showed Orderic Vitalis a copy of a life of St William, Orderic *Eccl. Hist.*, iii, 218–219.

Note: Mrs Chibnall notes in the vol. above that it is prob. this monk who was commemorated in the Liber vitae of Saint Évroul (Bib. nat. Ms lat. 10092, fo 79^{v}) *ib.*, 218, n. 1.

Ralph de AREMES
occ. 1239

1239, 21 Nov., apptd third prior, *sed. vac.*, by order of the king, *CClR (1237–1242)*, 158; see Andrew I.

Note: this may be Ralph de Dreyms, q.v.

AREXIIS
see Alexus

Richard ARUNDELL
occ. 1492

1492, 29 Oct., 15th to be questioned at the *sed. vac.* visitation and complained about the food, *Reg. abp Morton*, ii, no 127.

Note: this entry should prob. belong to the entry below; the name of the monk immediately preceding was Richard and this prob. explains the scribal slip.

William ARUNDELL
occ. 1475 occ. 1498

1475, 23 Sept., ord acol., Winchester cathedral, Reg. Waynflete, ii, fo 174^{v}.

1481, 16 June, ord subdcn, Winchester cathedral, *ib.*, ii, fo 187.

1481, 22 Dec., ord dcn, Winchester cathedral, *ib.*, ii, fo 187^{v}.

1482, 21 Sept., ord pr., Winchester cathedral, *ib.*, ii, fo 189^{v}.

1498, 23 Apr., refectorer, Reg. Langton, fo 73^{v}.

1486, 7 Dec., 17th in order at the el. of a bp, *Reg. Common Seal*, no 434.

1498, 23 Apr., 5th in order at the el. of a prior, Reg. Langton, fo 73^{v}.

Note: see the note in the entry above under Richard Arundell.

Edward AULTON [Aultone
occ. 1461 occ. 1466

1461, 4 Apr., ord acol., Winchester cathedral, Reg. Waynflete, i, fo Y.

1462, 18 Sept., ord subdcn, Winchester cathedral, *ib.*, i, fo B*^{v}.

1464, 26 May, ord dcn, Winchester cathedral, *ib.*, i, fo F*^{v}.

1466, 20 Dec., ord pr., bp's chapel, [Bishops] Waltham, *ib.*, i, fo K*^{v}.

AULTON
see also Alton

Richard AUNCELL [Amicelli, Anceline, Ancelme, Anselme, Auncelle
occ. 1476 occ. 1501

1476, 9 Mar., ord acol., Winchester cathedral, Reg. Waynflete, ii, fo 175^{v}.

1477, 20 Sept., ord subdcn, no place stated, *ib.*, ii, fo 178^{v}.

1479, 6 Mar., ord dcn, Winchester cathedral, *ib.*, ii, fo 182^{v}.

1482, 21 Sept., ord pr., Winchester cathedral, *ib.*, ii, fo 189ᵛ.

1484/5, curtarian, Kitchin, *SS* no 9, pp. 380–386.

1486, 7 Dec.; 1492, 29 Oct.; 1501, 28 Feb., sacrist, *Reg. Common Seal*, no 434; *Reg. abp Morton*, ii, no 127; Canterbury Reg. R, fo 114ᵛ.

1486, 7 Dec., 18th in order at the el. of a bp, *Reg. Common Seal*, no 434.

1492, 29 Oct., 12th to be questioned at the *sed. vac.* visitation, and complained of the poor food provided for the sick, *Reg. abp Morton*, ii, no 127; he in turn was denounced by John Fetypas and by Thomas Knyght, q.v., *ib.*; see also Thomas Gardiner.

1498, 23 Apr., 6th in order at the el. of a prior, Reg. Langton, fo 73ᵛ.

1501, 27 Feb., 5th at the visitation (*sed. vac.* both Canterbury and Winchester) by the commissary of the prior of Christ Church Canterbury; he reported that the common seal was kept in the library behind two doors and twelve [locks and] keys, and the sick were well cared for; Canterbury Reg. R, fo 114ᵛ.

DE AUNDELY
see Daundele

de AUREVILL'
see Dureville

Blacheman AURIFABER
occ. [1070 × 1098]

[1070 × 1198], a monk in the household of bp Walkelin who allegedly forged a charter and stole a book of St Aethelwold but is not named as a St Swithun's monk, *Winch. Cart.* no 41.

Henry AURIFABER
occ. 1266/7

1267, with Gilbert de Froyle, q.v., receiver, WCL Sutton pipe roll acct.

1266/7, visited Whitchurch for *liberatio denariorum* from the borough there, WCL pipe roll acct.

1266/7, pd visits to Littleton, Patney and Sutton, WCL pipe roll accts.

Philip de AVINTON [Avintone, Avintune
occ. 1269/70 d. c. 1307/8

1269/70, pd two visits to Stockton (Wilts.), WCL acct.

1278, 20 July, ordered by the arbitrators of the dispute between the bp and the monks to be sent, with a secular clerk, to recall Andrew de London, q.v., and all other proctors [of the chapter] in the curia and elsewhere, *Reg. Pontissara*, 647.

1279/80, visited Crondall for *liberatio denariorum*, WCL pipe roll acct.

1281, Mar., went to Wiltshire to hold hock courts and his expenses of 22d. were pd by the receiver, Watkin, 'Rec. Acct', 96. In July of this yr he was sent, with John Gys, John de Ichille, and Peter Mareschall, q.v., to London by the receiver on business for the house, *ib.*, 100; on 20 Oct. he presided at a court at Crondall, Baigent, *Crondal Records*, i, 142.

1281/2, pd visits to Chilbolton and Hurstbourne for *liberatio denariorum*; he also visited Crondall on his way to London to parliament, WCL pipe roll accts.

1282, 7 Aug., proctor for the monks and among those who sought absolution as a result of their involvement in irregularities in the el. of Richard de la More as bp, *Reg. abp Pecham*, i, 188–189; see Adam de Farnham.

1304/5, pd a visit to Stockton (Wilts.), WCL acct.

1305, 1 Apr., apptd penitentiary for the diocese, with the right to name Nicholas de Ham, q.v., as his substitute when necessary, *Reg. Woodlock*, 7.

1305, 29 July/7 Aug., one of the *instructores* in the examination of the el. proceedings of prior Nicholas de Tarente, q.v., *ib.*, 34.

1307, 13 Sept., still penitentiary but overburdened by 'negotiations' on behalf of the priory and so an additional penitentiary was named, *ib.*, 203.

c. 1307/8, was collector, during the first yr, for cardinals' procurations due, but d., *ib.*, 391.

John AVYNTON D.Th. [Avyngdon, Avyngtone, Avyntone *alias* Dean
occ. 1514/15 occ. 1539

1524, 30 Nov., *magister operum*, Reg. Fox, v, fo 75.

1528/39, subprior, *BRUO*.

1535, 1536, 10 Mar., 16 Mar., subprior, *Valor Eccles.*, ii, 2, Reg. iii, fo 27, *L and P Henry VIII*, x, no 480.

1514, 28 May, B.Th., after 13 yrs' study in logic, philosophy and theology, *BRUO*.

1514/15, student at Oxford, with William Manydown, q.v., and each recd an 'exhibition' of 6s. 8d., from the almoner, Kitchin, *SS* no 44, p. 460.

1516/17, student, with Manydown, and both recd the 'exhibition' as above, Kitchin, *SS* no 45, p. 464.

1519, 28 Feb., D.Th.; see *BRUO*.

1520, 14 Feb., described as *sacre theologie professorem* and one of five monks apptd by the prior to attend the Black Monk chapter summoned by cardinal Wolsey at Westminster, Pantin, *BMC*, iii, 120 (Reg. ii, fo 23ᵛ).

1522, [1 May], recd money from the manumission payments of two *nativi* at Stockton (Wilts.), and named as doctor Aldyngton, WRO 906/SC/18 (court roll).

1524, 2 Dec., 2nd in order at the el. of a prior, Reg. Fox, v, fo 75; he voted for John Meone II, q.v., *propter eius virtutes*, *ib.*, fo 77, and he himself was nom. by five, *ib.*

1536, 16 Mar., after visiting the priory Thomas Parry wrote to Cromwell that Avynton and Richard Petersfeld, q.v. 'were chief committers of the sacrilege', prob. implying that they were the only learned monks, *L and P Henry VIII*, × no 480.

1539, 30 July, with Richard Petersfeld, q.v., serving as chaplain in bp Fox's chantry chapel, Oxford, Corpus Christi College A.1 cap 2 (evidence a) 4.

1539, 14 Nov., third name on the surrender list and described as 'doctor of divinite and Reader of the same'; he was assigned a pension of £20 p.a., *L and P Henry VIII*, xiv, pt 2, no 520 (PRO E315/494).

[1541, apptd canon of the 3rd prebend in the new foundation, *Fasti, 1541–1845*, iii, 92.]

Name in the following printed books:

(1) CUL Sel. 3.28–29, Duns Scotus, 2 vols (Venice, 1506), 'ex sumptibus—monachi ac etiam scholaris et baccularii'.
(2) Edinburgh University Library, *E.15.24, N. de Tudeschis etc. (Lyon, 1516); 'ex emptione et salario mag.—doctoris sacre theologie', and the date is 1519.
(3) London, Westminster Abbey, CC. 44, J. Lathbury (Oxford, 1482); 'ex emptione dom—monachi necnon scholaris et baccalarii W. ac nunc sacre theologie professor'.

Dr Angela Smith suggests that he prob. 'oversaw the construction of the presbytery screens. . .and was responsible for commissioning a fine triptych [*sic*] with scenes of the Betrayal, Resurrection and Ascension, which now hangs in the private chapel of Lord Sackville at Knole', 'The Chantry Chapel of Bishop Fox', *Winch. Cath. Record*, no 57 (1988), 32.

Henry BACUN [Bacon

occ. 1295

1295, 6 June, one of seven *compromissorii* chosen by the chapter for the el. of a prior, *Reg. Pontissara*, 73–76.

Thomas BALAM [Balon

occ. 1455 occ. 1462

1455, 20 Sept., ord acol., bp's chapel, Wolvesey, Reg. Waynflete, i, fo K^{v}.

1456, 18 Sept., ord subdcn, bp's chapel, Wolvesey, *ib.*, i, fo M.

1461, 4 Apr., ord dcn, Winchester cathedral, *ib.*, i, fo Y^{v}.

1462, 13 Mar., ord pr., Winchester cathedral, *ib.*, i, fo A*^{v}.

William de BANNEBIRIA

occ. 1282

1282, 7 Aug., one of the monks who sought and obtained absolution as a result of his involvement in irregularities in the el. of Richard de la More as bp, *Reg. abp Pecham*, i, 188–189; the comm. for absolution is dated 10 Aug., *ib.*, ii, 50. See Adam de Farnham.

BARTHOLOMEW [Bartholomeus

occ. 1307/8 d. 1315/16

1307/8, pd a visit to Chilbolton, WCL acct.

1315/16, d., and the almoner gave 6s. 8d., in pittances to the monks on the day of his burial, Kitchin, *SS* no 20, p. 396.

Note: see Bartholomew Pershore and Bartholomew de Wynton.

BARTON, Bartonarius

see Berthonarius, Bertonarius, Bertone

BASINGSTOKE

see William de Basyng I

Hugh de BASYNG [Basynge

occ. 1346 d. 1384

1362–1384, prior: apptd by the bp 11/14 Feb. 1362, after setting aside the el. of William Thudden, q.v., *Reg. Edington*, i, nos 1491, 1493, 1494 (the ms mistakenly reads William); d. 26 Sept. 1384, *Reg. Wykeham*, i, 149.

1346, 1 Dec., acol., given *lit. dim.* for the order of subdcn, *Reg. Edington*, ii, no 712.

1347, 24 Feb., ord subdcn, bp's chapel, Southwark, *ib.*, ii, no 722.

1347, 22 Sept., ord dcn, South Waltham, *ib.*, ii, no 739.

1347, 12 Dec., given *lit. dim*, for the order of pr., *ib.*, ii, no 742.

1349, 7 Mar., ord pr., Cobham, *ib.*, ii, no 772.

1352; 1355/6; 1357; 1360 and 1361, receiver, WCL Wonston acct; WCL SS no 68 (not included in Kitchin, *Obed. Rolls*); WCL Whitchurch acct; WCL Littleton acct.

1351/2, pd a visit to Wonston to rec. rents and dues, WCL acct.

1355/6, visited Hannington for the same purpose, WCL acct.

1356/7, visited Whitchurch for the same purpose, WCL acct.

1359/60, pd visits to Littleton and Whitchurch for the same purpose, WCL acct.

1360/1, pd a visit to Littleton for the same purpose, WCL acct.

1368, 9 July, present at the bp's enthronement, *Reg. Wykeham*, ii, 1.

1369, 1 June, with the abbot of Hyde and the sheriff, comm. by the king to supervise the repair of the city walls, *CPR (1367–1370)*, 250–251.

1373, 3 Dec., with the abbot of Hyde and others, apptd to survey Winchester castle and estimate the necessary repairs, *CPR (1370–1374)*, 398.

1377, 12 Dec., with the prior of Twynham responsible for collecting a royal tenth in the adcnry of Winchester, Reg. Wykeham, ii, fo 161^{v}.

1381/2, visited Crondall and the reeve charged 103s 5d to his acct, WCL acct.
1384, 26 July, was again made responsible for the collection of a tenth, Reg. Wykeham, ii, fo 204v.

J. de BASYNG [Basynge
d. 1314/15

1314/15, d., and the almoner contributed 6s. 8d., towards pittances to the convent on the day of his burial, Kitchin, *SS* no 21, p. 395.

James de BASYNG
occ. 1239 occ. 1250

1239, 21 Nov., by order of the king, *sed. vac.*, apptd *cobōr'* [*sic*], PRO C54/50, m. 20 (*CClR (1237–1242)*, 158).
1240, 1 May, one of four monks who, at Abingdon, recd licence from the king to el. a bp, BL Add. Ms 29436, fo 37v.
1250, 13 Oct., one of four monks who recd licence from the king to el. a bp, *CPR (1247–1258)*, 75.

I John de BASYNG
occ. 1238

1238, 4 Oct., before this date bartoner, *CClR (1237–1242)*, 107.
1238, 4 Oct., reported as having gone to Rome and as guilty of disobedience and of behaving as a layman; the king ordered a successor in the office to be apptd, *sed. vac.*, *CClR (1237–1242)*, 107.

II John de BASYNG
occ. c. 1382

c. 1382, visited Ham (Wilts.), WCL acct.

III John BASYNG D.Th. [Basynge
occ. 1468 occ. 1529

1468, 17 Dec., ord acol., Winchester cathedral, Reg. Waynflete, i, fo M*v.
1469, 23 Sept., ord subdcn, Winchester cathedral, *ib.*, i, fo O*.
1470, 22 Dec., ord dcn, Winchester cathedral, *ib.*, ii, fo 166.
1473, 18 Sept., ord pr., Winchester cathedral, *ib.*, ii, fo 170v.
1476/7, apptd fourth prior, Kitchin, *SS* no 43, p. 456.
1477/8, 1482/3, chamberlain, the former is WCL unnumbered acct, the latter is Kitchin, *SS* no 8, pp. 377–380; see also WCL Ham acct.
1476/7, student at Oxford with John Pynchebeke, q.v., and recd 6s. 8d., *in exhibitione* from the almoner, Kitchin, *SS* no 43, p. 456.
1529, 11 Apr., described as D.Th., *Reg. Wolsey*, 8.
1529, 11 Apr., preached at the enthronement of cardinal Wolsey by proxy as administrator of the see; his theme was 'Pascite qui in vobis est gregem Dei' (1 Pet. 5, 2), *Reg. Wolsey*, 8.

Note: in 1529 this monk must have been at least in his late 70s; are there possibly two monks here? It is more likely that William Basyng IV, q.v., is intended.

Peter de BASYNG [Basynge, Basynges, Basyngge
occ. 1307/8 occ. 1332/3

1307/8; 1308/9; 1310/11; 1311/12; receiver, Kitchin, *SS* no 65, p. 469, with Thomas de Marleburgh, q.v.; WCL Hurstbourne acct; WCL Chilbolton acct; WCL Hurstbourne acct (as P.).
1327, named as former hordarian, Kitchin, *SS* no 47, p. 256.
1307/8, visited Barton and Chilbolton, WCL accts, as receiver.
1308/9, visited Chilbolton, WCL acct with Thomas de Marleburgh, q.v., and Hurstbourne, WCL acct twice with his *socius*.
1309, c. 25 Aug., one of four monks who acted as *instructores* in the examination of the el. of Richard de Enford, q.v. as prior, *Reg. Woodlock*, 385.
1310/11, visited Chilbolton, WCL acct.
1311/12, visited Hurstbourne, WCL acct.
1325, 9 Oct., 23rd in order of seniority, *Reg. Pontissara*, 556.
1328, 7 July, one of three monks who acted as instructores at the examination of the el. of Alexander de Heriard, q.v, as prior, Reg. Stratford, fo 107v.
1328/29, visited Wonston with his *socius*, WCL acct.
1332, 17 May, brought charges vs Alexander de Heriard, prior, q.v., recorded in an instrument drawn up by a notary in St Thomas' chapel in the cathedral. He accused the prior of taking over some of the obedientiary offices, of misuse of the common seal, misappropriation of revenues and other offences. The prior made a written reply on 25 May in which he accused Basyng of leaving the monastery [on 21 May] without permission, *Winch. Cart.*, nos 176 and 200.
[1332/3], accused of apostasy in a letter written by the prior to the pope. He had left the monastery taking with him a gold pyx and other valuables worth over £200 in silver, and was reported to have gone to the curia. The prior asked the pope to have him arrested and returned to Winchester, *ib.*, no 197. The prior also wrote three other letters to persons in the curia to inform them of his offences and seek their assistance. He had been denounced at an episcopal visitation and had fled rather then undergo the discipline of correction; the bp had found upon inquiry that no one in the monastery supported his appeal vs the prior, *ib.*, nos 199, 200.

Note: In Kitchin, *Obed. Rolls*, 98 and 469 he is mistakenly called Philip.

Ralph de BASYNG D.Cn.L. [Basyngge

occ. 1358 d. 1404/5

1358, 2 Oct., granted *lit. dim.*, for all orders, *Reg. Edington*, ii, no 897.

1360, 13 Sept., acol., granted *lit. dim.*, from prior John de Merlawe [I], q.v., acting as vicar general, for the order of subdcn, *ib.*, ii, no 915.

1361, 7 Apr., subdcn, granted *lit. dim.*, for the order of pr., *ib.*, ii, no 916.

1378/9, succ. Ralph de Popham as hordarian, PRO SC6/757/6; 1379/80, 1381/2, 1383/4, 1385/8, 1389/90, 1391/5, 1396/8, 1399/1401, 1401/2, 1404/5, hordarian, SC6/757/7–21; the accts for 1381/2 and 1400/1 are Kitchin, *SS* nos 54 and 55, pp. 279–284, and for 1401/2 there are two copies, WCL unnumbered accts. See John Langreod who succ. him in 1404/5.

1367/8, student at Oxford and stopped at Whitchurch on his way to and from Oxford, WCL acct; see also under 1360/1 below.

1370/1, carts were sent from Whitchurch to Oxford with 'divers' victual' ad opus R. Basyng', and he himself stopped there on his way back from Oxford, WCL acct. See John de Oxystede and Anthony de Saulton.

1374/5, student at Oxford and styled 'Magister'; twelve capons were sent from Woolstone to Oxford for him, prob. because of his inception, PRO SC6/757/2. Not in *BRUO*.

1390, 20 May, described as doctor of decrees, *Reg. Common Seal*, no 18.

1360/1, visited Woolstone, possibly on his way to Oxford, PRO SC6/756/17.

1381/2, ill and charged 21s. *in medicis et medicinis* to the hordarian's acct, SC6/757/8.

1390, 20 May, with John Langreod, q.v., and two secular clerks, apptd general proctors for the prior and chapter, *Reg. Common Seal*, no 18.

1393, 1 Aug., apptd confessor to the nuns of Wherwell, *Reg. Wykeham*, ii, 440.

1393, 21/22 Aug., 3rd to sign the composition with bp Wykeham, BL Ms Harley 328, fo 24; see Robert de Rodebourne.

1395, 28 Jan., sent with John de Bristowe, q.v., as proctors to request from the bp a licence to el a prior, *Reg. Wykeham*, i, fo 242v; they recd it at Southwark on 3 Feb., *ib.*, i, fo 243v.

1396, [Sept.], apptd confessor (one of three) to the nuns of Romsey, *Reg. Wykeham*, ii, 469.

1398, 15 Feb., comm., with Robert de Walyngforde II, q.v., as penitentiaries in the diocese, *ib.*, ii, 477.

1399, 19 May, one of four monks and four seculars apptd as proctors by the prior and chapter in lawsuits over their churches in Salisbury diocese, *Reg. Common Seal*, no 33.

1401/2, as hordarian, sent John de Bristowe, q.v., a gift of wine on the latter's apptment as third prior, WCL unnumbered hordarian's acct.

1404, 16 Oct., third in order at the el. of a bp which was carried out *via inspirationis*, and he was the spokesman who, in the name of the community, elected Thomas Nevyle, the prior, q.v. He was also one of the proctors apptd to announce to the bp el., the chapter's choice. After a second visit to Nevyle on 17 Oct., he obtained the latter's reluctant consent, *Reg. Common Seal*, no 68.

1404/5, d., and the almoner distributed 10s. worth of bread to the poor on the day of his burial, Kitchin, *SS* no 32, p. 427.

A Thomas atte Brygge of Basing[stoke], his brother, left 66s. 8d., in 1408/9, in his will to the office of *custos operum* [for the cathedral fabric], Kitchin, *SS* no 11, p. 210. Earlier refs to a man by this same name supervising stock occ. on the Woolstone accts in the 1380's, PRO SC6/757/6, 7.

Robert de BASYNG [Basynges

occ. 1325 occ. 1334/5

1334/5, *custos gardini*, Kitchin, *SS* no 62, p. 237.

1325, 9 Oct., 8th in order of seniority, *Reg. Pontissara*, 556.

1334/5, recd 41s. from the receiver for hay and pasture, Kitchin, *SS* no 62, p. 237.

Thomas BASYNG

occ. 1501

1501, 27 Feb., acol., and 28th in order at the visitation (*sed. vac.* both Canterbury and Winchester) by the commissary of the prior of Christ Church Canterbury; he deposed that the sick in the infirmary were not being given proper care, Canterbury Reg. R, fo 115.

I William de BASYNG [Basinges, Basingstoke (Prior I)

occ. 1279/80 d. 1295

1283 × 1284–1294 × 1295, prior: ?apptd by order of the bp between 13 Feb. and 9 Apr. 1283, *Reg. Pontissara*, 246; see Adam de Farnham; occ. as prior 4 June 1284, *ib.*, 281; by 13 July 1284 he had res., *ib.*, 284–286, and see Nicholas de Merewell; the bp's licence for an el. was granted 20 July, *ib.*, 286 where a 'fresh el.' is mentioned, possibly implying a previous el.; by 25 Aug. his [?re]el. was confirmed, *ib.*, 294; last occ. 4 Nov. 1294, *Winch. Cart.*, no 442; d. by 30 May 1295, *Reg. Pontissara*, 71–72.

Note: his was prob. the first free el. by the chapter.

1279/80, visited Chilbolton, Crondall, Hurstbourne and Whitchurch borough, WCL pipe roll accts, this last for *liberationes*.

1281, 7 Jan., sent by the chapter to the bp el. [Richard de la More], Watkin, 'Rec. Acct', 95;

this suggests a journey to Rome; see *Ann. Waverley*, 399.

1282, 31 July, with the prior, Adam de Farnham, q.v., absolved from excommunication incurred because of their part in the el. of Richard de la More as bp, *Reg. abp Pecham*, i, 188; he is also named in the comm. for absolution dated 10 Aug., *ib.*, ii, 51.

1284, 4 June, given authority by the bp to dispose of all the obedientiary offices as he saw fit, *Reg. Pontissara*, 281–282; see also *CChR*, ii (1257–1300), 287–289. Details of the point by point settlement of the dispute between the bp and the prior and convent before the king at Aberconway on 11 June this yr are given in BL Add. Ms 29436, fos 56–61.

1284, 20 July, in granting the chapter a licence to el. a prior the bp made it clear that Basyng's res. was not 'pro criminis vel defectus consciencia set humilitatis causa et religionis fervore', *ib.*, 286.

[1284/6], wrote to John de Kyrkby, adcn of Coventry and treasurer about the contention of the adcns that they had the right to take part in elections of priors, PRO SC1/48/124.

1286, 12/13 Mar., at the episcopal visitation complained that the burden of debt had reduced the amount of money available for the monks' pittances and had caused dissension within the community; the abp arranged for a settlement of the differences between the two parties, and the prior for his part was ordered to pay an annual sum from his own income toward the support of ten lepers in the hospital of St Mary Magdalene and to accept a reduced allowance from the chamberlain for his clothing and bedding, *Winch. Cart.*, no 111.

1292, 23 Sept., with Edmund de Winchester and Robert de Hakeborne, q.v., present in the chapter house at Salisbury for the ordination of the vicarage of Enford, Winchester College Muniment 8182.

1292, 10 Dec., he and the convent apptd a *senescallus* of all their lands in five counties, BL Add. Ms 29436, fo 41^{v}.

His tomb was formerly situated in the south transept; what remains now lies in the retrochoir between the Fox and Beaufort chantries, R. N. Quirk, 'The Monuments of Prior Basyng and the "Old Bishop in Marble" ', *Winch. Cath. Record*, no 23 (1954), 12–17.

II William de BASYNG [Basynges

occ. 1325 occ. 1349

1332, 18 Oct., curtarian, *Winch. Cart.*, no 180.

1349, 21/23 Mar., subprior, *Reg. Edington*, i, nos 558, 560.

1325, 9 Oct., 38th in order of seniority, *Reg. Pontissara*, 556.

1332, 25 May, with Edmund de Bolesdon, q.v., attested an instrument setting forth the charges made by Peter de Basyng, q.v., vs the prior and the prior's reply, *Winch. Cart.*, no 176; on 31 May, with Nicholas de Haywode, q.v., witnessed the prior's appointment of proctors in the curia in the above appeal, *ib.*, no 177.

1332, 18 Oct., present in the prior's chapel at the reading of ordinances, drawn up by the chapter following discussions about the debts of two of the obedientiary offices, which prescribed new financial arrangements to alleviate the crisis, *ib.*, no 180; see Alexander de Heriard.

1337/38, one of a number of monks who visited Chilbolton, Worcester Cathedral Muniment, C.866.

III William BASYNG, B.Th.

occ. 1442 occ. 1457

1447, 15 Apr.; 1449, 15 July; 1450, 11 Dec., sacrist, *Reg. Common Seal*, no 316; Reg. Waynflete, i, fo 50*^{v}; *ib.*, i, fo 30^{v}.

1457, 18 Apr., 25 Apr., 15 May, subprior, *Reg. Common Seal*, nos 332, 334, Reg. Waynflete, i, fo 85.

1449, 15 July, designated as B.Th., Reg. Waynflete, i, fo 50*^{v}; see the entry under 1442 below.

1442, visited Manydown, as did William Clement [?on the way to Oxford], WCL acct.

1447, 15 Apr., 16th in order at the el. of a bp, *Reg. Common Seal*, no 316.

1449, 15 July, with Robert Puryton, q.v., and others apptd proctor in the negotiations over the appropriation of Fordingbridge church, Reg. Waynflete, i, fo 50*^{v}.

1450, 11 Dec., 12th in order at the el. of a prior and named by the chapter as one of seven *compromissorii*, *ib.*, i, fo 30^{v}; with William Clement, q.v., acted as proctor in the el. proceedings, *ib.*, i, fo 32^{v}.

1457, 15 May, presided at the el. of a prior, *ib.*, i, fos 85–86.

Name in BL Ms Harley 539, fos 114–116, a copy of the foundation chronicle later copied by John Stowe (d. 1605); see Gransden, *Hist. Writing*, ii, 494 n.

IV William BASYNG D.Th. [*alias* Kingsmill, Kyngesmylle (Prior II)

occ. 1513 occ. 1539

1536–1539, prior: 16/31 Mar. 1536, 'el.', *L and P Henry VIII*, x, nos 480, 588; apptd dean of the new foundation 1541, *Fasti*, iv, 48, *Fasti, 1541–1857*, iii, 83.

1513, prof. in this yr, WCL Basyng Libellus, fo 1.

1521, 30 Mar., ord dcn, Lady chapel, Winchester cathedral, Reg. Fox, iv, fo 71^{v}.

1522, 20 Sept., ord pr., Lady chapel, Winchester cathedral, *ib.*, v, fo 30 (as Kyngesmylle).

1522/3, celebrated his first mass and recd a small gift of money from the almoner, WCL almoner acct SS 45* (not in Kitchin *Obed. Rolls*).

1535, 24 Dec., 1536, 10 Mar., hordarian, WCL Basyng Libellus, fo 1 (see below); Reg. iii, fo 27. In 1535 he was also kitchener, *Valor Eccles.*, ii, 2.

1522/3, student at Oxford with Richard Petersfeld with an exhibition of 3s. 4d. each from the almoner, WCL almoner acct SS 45* (not in Kitchin *Obed. Rolls*).

1524, 2 Dec., student [*scholasticus*] at Oxford, Reg. Fox, v, fo 77v.

1526, 1 June, after twelve yrs of study in logic, philosophy and theology, adm. B.Th., *BRUO 1501–1540*.

1528, 12 Apr., university preacher on Easter day, *ib.*

1529, 15 Mar., D.Th., *ib.*

1524, 2 Dec., 22nd in order at the el. of a prior, Reg. Fox, v, fo 75; he voted for Henry Broke 'propter ipsius sapientiam et experientiam in spiritualibus et temporalibus', *ib.*, v, fo 77v.

[1528 × 1539], surname occ. in a list of monks copied on to a blank fo in Oxford Bod. Ms Selden supra 76, fo 46v; no Christian names are given.

1532, 15 Nov., with Richard Petersfeld, q.v., serving as chaplain in bp Fox's chantry, Oxford, Corpus Christi College A.1 cap 2 (evidence a) 4; an attached inventory states that he had given cushions, altar cloths and a crucifix to the chapel.

1536, 16 Mar., described as a man of learning by Thomas Parry in a letter to Cromwell and was prepared to give £500 to gain favour, *L and P Henry VIII*, x, nos 480, 485; being unable to send the whole sum at once, because Henry Broke, q.v., had left the priory in debt, he sent £100 to Cromwell on 31 Mar., *ib.* no 588.

1538, 22 Dec., sent Cromwell £50, promising future payments, *L and P Henry VIII*, xiii, pt 2, no 1121.

1539, 14 Nov., assigned a pension of £200 p.a., PRO E315/494; this was cancelled *quia decanus electus*, *L and Henry VIII*, xiv, pt 2, no 520.

Name in

(1) BL Ms Sloane 418, Medical treatises, fos 189–352 (15th c.), on fo 352v, in an agreement with the bp dated 1525.

(2) Winchester College B. 32, Bruno Carthusianus, (printed book) Paris 1523.

(3) WCL, the Libellus mentioned above; this ms, now of only seven fos, was compiled by him as hordarian in 1535 and contains twelve items: copies of charters, confirmations and compositions from the 12th to the 15th c. It is prob. a fragment of a larger work.

His mother Alice Tetrydge of Basingstoke, widow, was given the lease of the manor of Silkstead [c. 1538] for 51 yrs, Reg. iii, fo 28.

Some of his *acta* are in Reg. iii, beginning on fo 27.

BEAUMOND

see Bemond

Robert BECHE

occ. 1353 occ. 1358

1353, 22 Aug., recd *lit. dim.*, for subdcn's orders, *Reg. Edington*, ii, no 845.

1355, 17 Sept., recd *lit. dim.*, for dcn's orders, *ib.*, ii, no 866.

1356, 10 Apr., ord dcn, bp's chapel, Esher, *ib.*, ii, no 872.

1358, 2 Oct., recd *lit. dim.*, for pr.'s orders, *ib.*, ii, no 897.

Richard BECKE [Beeke

occ. 1412 d. 1418/19

1412, 27 Feb., ord subdcn, Winchester cathedral, Reg. Beaufort, fo Fv.

1412, 28 Mar., ord dcn, Winchester cathedral, *ib.*, fo Gv.

1418/19, d., and the almoner distributed 10s. worth of bread to the poor, Kitchin, *SS* no 38, p. 441 (transcribed as Reeke).

Thomas BEMOND [Beaumond, Beaumound

occ. 1389 occ. 1418

1389, 17 Apr., ord acol., Winchester cathedral, *Reg. Wykeham*, i, 319.

1392, 9 Mar., ord subdcn, bp's chapel, Marwell, *ib.*, i, 325.

1392, 13 Apr., ord dcn, Winchester cathedral, *ib.*, i, 326.

1393, 21 Sept., ord pr., bp's chapel, Esher, *ib.*, i, 329.

1411/12, 1414/15, curtarian/cellarer, WCL unnumbered obedientiary accts.

1393, 21/22 Aug., 38th to sign the composition with bp Wykeham, BL Ms Harley 328, fo 24v; see Robert de Rodebourne.

1404, 16 Oct., 23rd in order at the el. of a bp, *Reg. Common Seal*, no 68.

1410/11, pd a visit to Wonston after the sheep shearing [*ultra tonsuram*] WCL acct.

1411/12, visited Silkstead, WCL acct.

1415, 24 Sept., absent from the chapter called to fix the el. date for a prior, *Reg. Common Seal*, no 161.

1415/16, visited Chilbolton to supervise the shearing, WCL acct.

1417/18, stopped at Whitchurch for supervisory purposes *ultra tonsuram*, WCL acct.

John BERE

occ. 1528

1528, 11 Apr., one of six not yet prof. but ord exorcist and acol., Lady chapel, Winchester cathedral, Reg. Fox v, fo 38–38v.

BERITON
see Buriton

BERNARD
d. by 1122/3

1122/3, name occ. in a mortuary roll of Savigny following that of Godfrey, prior, q.v., but not distinguished as a monk, Delisle, *Rouleaux des Morts*, 336.

Alexander BERTHONARIUS
occ. 1272/3

1272/3, pd a visit to Chilbolton, WCL acct.

Note: see Alexander I who may be identical with this monk.

BERTHONE
see Bertone

I John BERTONARIUS
occ. [1205]

[1205], 15 Oct., appeared as witness in Rome to the confirmation of an episcopal grant, *Eng. Epis. Acta*, ix, no 81; he was prob. one of the election committee sent by the monks on behalf of the bp el., Peter des Roches. See also Germanus and Walter III.

II John BERTONARIUS
occ. 1238

1238, 11 July, bartoner, see below; he was prob. succ. by Adam de Neubir', q.v; and see John de Basyng I.

1238, 11 July, one of four monks who, with the adcns, recd a licence from the king to el. a bp, *CPR (1232–1247)*, 226.

Note: it is possible that the above two entries refer to the same monk.

Thomas de BERTONE [Berthone
occ. 1325 occ. 1349

1326, 15 Feb., ord acol. and subdcn, Winchester cathedral, Reg. Stratford, fo 143v.
1326, 20 Sept., ord dcn, Kingsclere, *ib.*, fo 144v.
1328, 19 Mar., ord pr., Crawley [Hants.], *ib.*, fo 148.

1325, 9 Oct., 54th in order of seniority, *Reg. Pontissara*, 557.
1344/5, pd a visit to Woolstone, PRO SC6/756/11.
1345, 28 July, named by the prior and chapter as one of nine *compromissorii* in the el. of a bp, *Reg. Common Seal*, no 5.
1346, 24 Feb., apptd to hear the confessions of his brethren and others within the diocese, *Reg. Edington*, i, no 21.
1347, 10 Feb., licensed, with Richard de Merewell I, q.v., as penitentiaries, *ib.*, ii, no 55.
1349, 5 Mar., apptd proctor, with Robert de Popham, q.v., to request from the bp licence to el. a prior, *ib.*, i, no 556.

John BERWIK
occ. 1444/5

1444/5, celebrated his first mass and recd 8d. from the almoner, Kitchin, *SS* no 64, p. 447.

Robert BERY [Bury
occ. 1492 occ. 1498

[1493], ord subdcn, no place given, Reg. Langton, fo 23.
[1493], 21 Sept., ord dcn, Hyde abbey, *ib.*, fo 23v.
1492, 29 Oct., 26th and second to last to be examined at the *sed. vac.* visitation; he made no deposition, *Reg. abp Morton*, ii, no 127.
1498, 23 Apr., pr., and 21st in order at the el. of a prior, Reg. Langton, fo 73v.

John BEST [Beste
occ. 1479 occ. 1501

1479, 18 Dec., ord acol., Winchester cathedral, Reg. Waynflete, ii, fo 184.
1484, 18 Sept., ord subdcn, Winchester cathedral, *ib.*, ii, fo 195v.
1485, 28 May, ord dcn, Winchester cathedral, *ib.*, ii, fo 198.
1485, 24 Sept., ord pr., Winchester cathedral, *ib.*, ii, fo 199v.
1501, 27 Feb., hostiller, Canterbury Reg. R, fo 115.

1486, 7 Dec., 24th in order at the el. of a bp, *Reg. Common Seal*, no 434.
1492, 29 Oct., 21st to be examined at the *sed. vac.* visitation and reported that the altar vessels and cloths were not properly cared for, *Reg. abp Morton*, ii, no 127.
1498, 23 Apr., 12th in order at the el. of a prior, Reg. Langton, fo 73v.
1501, 27 Feb., 10th to be examined at the visitation (*sed. vac.* both Canterbury and Winchester), by the commissary of the prior of Christ Church, Canterbury; he deposed that all was well apart from the poor administration of the infirmary, Canterbury Reg. R, fo 115.

William BETTE
occ. 1385 occ. 1404

1385, 23 Dec., ord acol., bp's chapel, Farnham, *Reg. Wykeham*, i, 310.
1387, 23 Mar., ord subdcn, bp's chapel, Marwell, *ib.*, i, 314.
1387, 21 Sept., ord dcn, bp's chapel, Marwell, *ib.*, i, 316.
1390, 24 Sept., ord pr., bp's chapel, Esher, *ib.*, i, 322.

1402/3, infirmarer, first yr, Lambeth ED 70.

1393, 21/22 Aug., 33rd to sign the composition with bp Wykeham, BL Ms Harley 328, fo 24v; see Robert de Rodebourne.
1404, 16 Oct., 19th at the el. of a bp, *Reg. Common Seal*, no 68.

John de BEVERSTON [Bevereston, Beverstone, Beverstan
occ. 1288 d. 1334/5

1288, 13 Mar., ord subdcn, Reading abbey, Reg. Swinfield (Hereford), fo 48; in *Reg. Swinfield*, 549 (transcribed as Deverston).

1325, 9 Oct., 7th in order of seniority, *Reg. Pontissara*, 556.

1334/5, d., and the receiver distributed 20s. worth of bread on the day of his d., Kitchin, *SS* no 62, p. 232.

BIRITONE
see Buriton

BOKLOND
see Bouklond

Edmund de BOLESDON [Bolusdone, Bolustone
occ. 1325 occ. ?1372

1332, 18 Oct., anniversarian, *Winch. Cart.*, no 180.
1372, sometime before this date, hordarian, PRO SC2/154/79.

1325, 9 Oct., 50th in order of seniority, *Reg. Pontissara*, 557.

1332, 25 May, with William de Basyng [II], q.v., attested an instrument setting forth the charges made by Peter de Basyng, q.v., vs the prior and the prior's reply, *Winch. Cart.*, no 176.

1332, 18 Oct., present in the prior's chapel at the reading of ordinances, drawn up by the chapter following discussions about the debts of two of the obedientiary offices, which prescribed new financial arrangements to alleviate the crisis, *ib.*, no 180; see Alexander de Heriard.

1334/5, sent by the prior and chapter twice to the royal chancery at York to obtain confirmation of various charters and carry out other negotiations; the receiver pd his expenses of £17 6d., Kitchin, *SS* no 62, p. 240.

[1334], 16 Sept., sent with John de Forde, q.v., to the abp of Canterbury to solicit his help in furthering several causes, including the confirmation of the liberties of the cathedral church, *Winch. Cart.*, no 255.

[?1335], 17 May, in a letter to one of the chapter's clerks, the prior requested his favour for E. whom the chapter had sent to the abp of Canterbury, *ib.*, no 266.

1337 [?May/Sept.], sent to London by the chapter to render the acct of the biennial tenth, Kitchin, *SS* no 63, p. 252. He also visited Whitchurch this yr, WCL acct.

1349, 23 Mar., sent by the chapter, with Robert de Popham, q.v., to request the bp to confirm their el. of John de Merlawe, q.v., as prior, *Reg. Edington*, i, no 560. On 31 Mar., he was present with others for the judicial process in which the el. proceedings were examined, *ib.*, i, no 563.

1361/2, visited Whitchurch, WCL acct.

Hugh de BOLRE
occ. 1282

1282, 7 Aug., one of the monks who sought and recd absolution from excommunication incurred on acct of irregularities during the el. of Richard de la More as bp, *Reg. abp Pecham*, i, 188–189; the comm. for absolution is dated 10 Aug., *ib.*, ii, 50. See Adam de Farnham.

John de BOLTESHAM
occ. 1363 occ. 1369/70

1363, 28 Dec., granted *lit. dim*, for minor orders, *Reg. Edington*, ii, no 936.

1365, 20 Sept., ord acol., bp's chapel, Sutton, *ib.*, ii, no 945.

1365, 15 Dec., granted *lit. dim*, for subdcn's orders, *ib.*, ii, no 447.

1366, 28 Feb., ord subdcn, St Elizabeth's chapel near Winchester, *ib.*, ii, no 949.

1368, 4 Mar., ord dcn, Winchester cathedral, *Reg. Wykeham*, i, 253.

1369, 22 Sept., ord pr., Winchester cathedral, *ib.*, i, 257.

1369/70, celebrated his first mass and the anniversarian gave a gift of 6d., Worcester Cathedral Muniment, C.531.

BOLUSDONE, Bolustone
see Bolesdon

BOORNE
see Bourne

BOORTON
see Burton

William BORLOND [Berlond, Beulond
occ. 1417 occ. 1450

1417, 18 Dec., ord acol. and subdcn, Winchester cathedral, Reg. Beaufort, fo O.

1450, 11 Dec., one of two *depositarii*, Reg. Waynflete, i, fo 30^{v}; see William Romsey II.

1447, 15 Apr., 14th in order at the el. of a bp, *Reg. Common Seal*, no 316.

1450, 11 Dec., 10th at the el. of a prior, Reg. Waynflete, i, fo 30^{v}.

I William de BOUKLOND [Boklond, Bouklonde
occ. 1325 occ. 1337/8

1325, 9 Oct., 36th in order of seniority, *Reg. Pontissara*, 556.

1337/8, visited Chilbolton, Worcester Cathedral Muniment, C.866.

II William BOUKLOND [Bokelond, Boklond, Bouclond, Boukelond, Bouklonde

occ. 1363 d. 1389/90

1363, 1 Jan., ord acol., bp's chapel, Farnham castle, *Reg. Edington*, ii, no 933.
1363, 28 May, ord subdcn, bp's chapel, Highclere, *ib.*, ii, 934.
1368, 4 Mar., ord dcn, [Winchester cathedral], *Reg. Wykeham*, i, 253.
1369, 22 Sept., ord pr., Winchester cathedral, *ib.*, i, 257.
1369/70, celebrated his first mass and the anniversarian gave a gift of 6d., Worcester Cathedral Muniment, C.531.
1384/7, anniversarian, Worcester Cathedral Muniment, C.534, C.534a, C.533.
1389/90, d., and the almoner distributed 10s. worth of bread to the poor on the day of his burial, Kitchin, *SS* no 28, p. 417.

Peter BOURNE [Boorne

occ. 1415 occ. 1450

1415, 25 May, ord pr., Winchester cathedral, Reg. Beaufort, fo M.
1447, 15 Apr., 10th in order at the el. of a bp, *Reg. Common Seal*, no 316.
1450, 11 Dec., 8th at the el. of a prior, Reg. Waynflete, i, fo 30ᵛ.

John BOWLOND [Bowelonde

occ. 1447 d. 1476/7

1447, 15 Apr., prof. by this date and one of three *juvenes*, *Reg. Common Seal*, no 316.
1448, 18 May, ord subdcn, Winchester cathedral, Reg. Waynflete, i, fo Aᵛ.
1448, 21 Sept., ord dcn, bp's chapel, Marwell, *ib.*, i, fo B.
1447, 15 Apr., 39th and last in order at the el. of a bp, *Reg. Common Seal*, no 316.
1450, 11 Dec., pr.; 35th and last at the el. of a prior, Reg. Waynflete, i, fo 31.
1476/7, d., and the almoner distributed 10s. worth of bread to the poor on the day of his burial, Kitchin, *SS* no 43, p. 456.

John BOWYER

occ. 1406 occ. 1450

1406, 12 Mar., ord pr., Winchester cathedral, Reg. Beaufort, fo Aᵛ.
1432/3, third prior, his first yr, Kitchin, *SS* no 7, p. 376.
1440/1, anniversarian, Worcester Cathedral Muniment, C.537.
1447, 15 Apr., third prior, *Reg. Common Seal*, no 316.
1450, 11 Dec., subprior, Reg. Waynflete, i, fo 30ᵛ.
1425/6, visited Crondall with Henry Bradele, q.v., WCL acct.
1432/3, recd 18d. worth of bread and wine from the chamberlain on his *creatio*, as third prior, Kitchin, *SS* no 7, p. 376.
1440/1, visited Bishopstone [Bushton, Wilts.], Worcester Cathedral Muniment, C.537.
1447, 15 Apr., 7th in order at the el. of a bp, *Reg. Common Seal*, no 316.
1450, 11 Dec., presided at the el. of a prior, Reg. Waynflete, i, fos 29ᵛ–34.

Henry BRADELE [Bradelegh, Bradeley, Bradle

occ. 1403 occ. 1469/70

1403, 22 Sept., ord subdcn, [?Bishops] Waltham, *Reg. Wykeham*, i, 356.
1404, 23 Feb., ord dcn, [?Bishops] Waltham, *ib.*, i, 357.
1406, 5 May, ord pr., Winchester cathedral, Reg. Beaufort, fo B.
1405/6, celebrated his first mass; the almoner sent 8d. for wine and the hordarian sent 18d. for bread and wine [for the feast], Kitchin, *SS* no 33, 430, *SS* no 56, p. 286.
1411, Eastertide, *custos* of the Lady altar, BL Add. Roll 24362.
1404, 16 Oct., 41st and 2nd to last in order at the el. of a bp, where he is included among the priests, *Reg. Common Seal*, no 68.
1412/13, pd a visit to Wootton, WCL acct.
1415, 24 Sept., absent from the chapter which decided on the date for the el. of a prior, *Reg. Common Seal*, no 161.
1425/6, visited Crondall with John Bowyer, q.v., WCL acct.
1447, 15 Apr., 5th in order at the el. of a bp, *Reg. Common Seal*, no 316.
1450, 11 Dec., 3rd in order and in *senio constitutus* at the el. of a prior; he was named as one of seven *compromissorii*, Reg. Waynflete, i, fos 30ᵛ, 31.
1469/70, from Sept. to June, by order of the prior and convent, the hordarian pd him 13d. per wk, prob. because he had a corrody in the infirmary, Kitchin, *SS* no 58, p. 295.

BRAESFELD, Braisfelde

see Braysfeld

John de BRANDESBURGH [Brandesbury

occ. 1350 occ. 1356

1350, 5 Sept., ord acol., bp's chapel, South Waltham, *Reg. Edington*, ii, no 817.
1350, 18 Sept., ord subdcn, bp's chapel, Highclere, Reg. Edington, ii, fo Y (*Reg. Edington*, ii, no 814 as Grandesburgh).
1351, 23 May, granted *lit. dim* to dcn's orders, Reg. Edington, ii, fo AA.
1353, 22 Aug. obtained *lit. dim* for dcn's orders, *Reg. Edington*, ii, no 845.
1354, 20 Dec., ord dcn, bp's chapel, [?Bishops] Waltham, *Reg. Edington*, ii, no 852.

1355, 17 Sept., obtained *lit. dim*, for pr.'s orders, *ib.*, ii, no 866.
1356, 10 Apr., ord pr., bp's chapel Esher, *ib.*, ii, no 871.

Walter de BRAYE
occ. 1358 occ. 1361

1358, 2 Oct., acol., granted *lit. dim*, to all orders, *Reg. Edington*, ii, no 897 (Reg. Edington, ii, fo LL^{v}).
1360, 13 Sept., obtained *lit. dim*, from prior John Merlawe, q.v., acting as vicar general, for subdcn's orders, *ib.*, ii, no 915.
1361, 7 Apr., dcn, granted *lit. dim*, for pr.'s orders, *ib.*, ii, no 916.

Roger de BRAYSFELD [Braesfeld, Braisfelde, Braysfeyld
occ. 1306/7 occ. 1332

1306/7, 1308/9, pd visits to Chilbolton, WCL accts.
1325, 9 Oct., 12th in order of seniority, *Reg. Pontissara*, 556.
1332, 18 Oct., present in the prior's chapel at the reading of ordinances, drawn up by the chapter following discussions about the debts of two obedientiary offices, which prescribed new financial arrangements to alleviate the crisis, *Winch. Cart.* no 180; see Alexander de Heriard.

John de BREVILL [Brevell, Brevile
occ. 1266/7 occ. 1272/3

n.d., chamberlain, WCL West Meon Custumal Roll; a J., chamberlain, visited Hurstbourne in 1272/3, WCL acct.
1266/7, 1272/3, pd visits to Chilbolton, WCL accts.
n.d., while in his second yr as chamberlain he had a custumal made for West Meon which is WCL West Meon Custumal Roll.

A *dominus* Robert de Brevill also visited Chilbolton in 1272/3, WCL acct.

George de BRISTOWE [Bristoll'
occ. 1360

1360, 11 Mar., granted *lit. dim*, for subdcn's orders, *Reg. Edington*, ii, no 904.
1360, 8 Sept., subdcn, granted *lit. dim*, for dcn's orders, *ib.*, ii, no 915.

John de BRISTOWE [Bristow, Brustowe, Brystowe
occ. 1366 occ. 1415

1366, 28 Feb., ord acol., St Elizabeth's chapel near Winchester, *Reg. Edington*, ii, no 948.
1368, 4 Mar., ord subdcn, Winchester cathedral, *Reg. Wykeham*, i, 252.
1369, 22 Sept., ord pr., Winchester cathedral, *ib.*, i, 257.
1369/70, celebrated his first mass and recd 6d. from the anniversarian, Worcester Cathedral Muniment, C.531.

1393, 21/22 Aug., 1398/9, precentor, BL Ms Harley 328, fo 24^{v}, and Whitchurch and Crondall, WCL accts.
1401/2, apptd third prior, WCL unnumbered hordarian's acct.

1390/1, stayed at Hurstbourne and the manor was charged 13d. for his expenses, WCL acct.
1392/3, visited Whitchurch, WCL acct.
1393, 21/22 Aug., 14th to sign the composition with bp Wykeham, BL Ms Harley 328, fo 24^{v}; see Robert de Rodebourne.
1398/9, took five monks to Farnham [for ordination] and stopped at Crondall on both the outward and return journeys, WCL Crondall acct; he also visited Whitchurch this yr and the manor charged 4d. on the acct as well as one capon and provender for the horse[s], WCL acct.
1399, 19 May, one of four monks and four seculars apptd proctors by the prior and chapter in lawsuits over their churches in Salisbury diocese, *Reg. Common Seal*, no 33.
1401/2, recd 9d worth of wine on his appointment as third prior, WCL unnumbered hordarian's acct.
1404, 16 Oct., 9th in order at the el. of a bp, *Reg. Common Seal*, no 68.
1415, 24/27 Sept., absent from the chapter meeting on 24 Sept., but present at the el. on 27 Sept. and named as one of nine *compromissorii* to choose the new prior, *Reg. Common Seal*, nos 161, 163.

BRISTOWE
see also Brystowe

BROCKHURST
see Brokhurst

Robert le BRODE
occ. 1337

1337, former collector of a fifteenth in the Isle of Wight, Kitchin, *SS* no 63, p. 245.

Note: this could be Robert de Godeshulle, q.v., sent on a mission to his place of origin if this is the Godshill on the Isle of Wight.

William BROKAS [?Broke, Brokeys
occ. 1479 occ. 1483

1479, 18 Dec., ord acol., Winchester cathedral, Reg. Waynflete, ii, fo 184 (as Broke).
1481, 16 June, ord subdcn, Winchester cathedral, *ib.*, ii, fo 187 (as Brokeys).
1482, 21 Sept., ord dcn, Winchester cathedral, *ib.*, ii, fo 189^{v}, (as Brokas).
1483, 20 Dec., ord pr., Winchester cathedral, *ib.*, ii, fo 193.

A Bernard Brocas, armiger, was apptd bailiff of Highclere by the bp in 1486, *Reg. Common Seal*, no 416.

Henry BROKE, B.Th. [Brook
occ. 1496 occ. 1536

1524–1536, prior: el. 2 Dec. 1524, Reg. Fox, v, fos 77–78ᵛ; res. 16 Mar. 1536, *Fasti*, iv, 48.

1496, 24 Sept., ord acol., Hyde abbey, Reg. Langton, fo 29ᵛ.
1498, 10 Mar., ord subdcn, St Laurence's church, Winchester, *ib.*, fo 32.
1499, 21 Sept., ord dcn, bp's chapel, Marwell, *ib.*, fo 34ᵛ.
1499, 21 Dec., ord pr., Winchester cathedral, *ib.*, fo 35.
1501, 27 Feb., fourth prior, Canterbury Reg. R, fo 115.
[c. 1515, Apr.], apptd subprior, Kitchin, *SS* no 14, p. 345; see William Broke.
1524, 2 Dec., subprior at the time of his el., Reg. Fox, v, fos 75–77.

1507, 13 Dec., supplicated for B.Th., *Reg. Univ. Oxon.*, i, 56.
1516, before Dec., had been student [at Oxford], as by this date he was B.Th., Reg. ii, fo 94.

1498, 23 Apr., subdcn, 31st and last in order at the el. of a prior, Reg. Langton, fo 73ᵛ.
1501, 27 Feb., 20th to be examined at the visitation (*sed. vac.* both Canterbury and Winchester), by the commissary of the prior of Christ Church, Canterbury; he deposed that the sick in the infirmary were not well cared for and that the subprior showed favouritism with regard to correction, Canterbury Reg. R, fo 115.
1520, 16 Feb., one of five monk proctors apptd by the prior to attend a Black Monk Chapter summoned by Cardinal Wolsey at Westminster, Pantin, *BMC*, iii, 122 (Reg. ii, fo 23).
1524, 2 Dec., cast his vote for William Manydown as prior *propter scientiam et vite honestatem*, but was himself el. by 15 out of 27 votes, Reg. Fox, v, fos 77–78ᵛ; the monks who had nom. others consenting, the bp confirmed the el. on 3 Dec., *ib.*, v, fo 82.
1535, was the focus of accusations by Richard Myllys, q.v., in a letter to Cromwell, *L and P Henry VIII*, ix, no 1129.
1535, 15 Sept., the priory was visited by Cromwell in person, Knowles, *RO*, iii, 476; on 25 Sept. the prior and convent granted Cromwell an annuity of £10, *L and P Henry VIII*, ix, no 438.
1536, 16 Mar., res. after the visitation by Dr. Legh, *L and P Henry VIII*, x, no 480. In the letter dated 21 Mar. of this yr he complained to Cromwell that he had been forced to res. by Dr. Legh's threat to remove him, and he now asked for a pension, *ib.*, no 511. See William Basyng IV.
1536, 27 May, granted an annual pension of £40 by the prior and chapter from the manor of Eston for himself and his two knights, and also the lease of a house near the bakehouse [in the precincts] which belonged to the chamberlain's office, Reg. iii, fo 51.

Some of his *acta* are in Reg. ii, fos 89 on, and Reg. iii, fos 1–26.

Walter BROKE
see Frost

William BROKE B.Th.
occ. 1520

1520, 14 Feb., subprior, Pantin, *BMC*, iii, 120 (Reg. ii, fo 23ᵛ).

Note: this is an error for Henry Broke, q.v.; *BRUO* has entries for both.

Thomas de BROKHURST [Brockhurst
occ. 1346/8

1346, 1 Dec., acol., recd *lit. dim*, for subdcn's orders, *Reg. Edington*, ii, no 712.
1347, 24 Feb., ord subdcn, bp's chapel, Southwark, *ib.*, ii, no 722.
1347, 22 Sept., ord dcn, South Waltham, *ib.*, ii, no 739.
1348, 2 June, granted *lit. dim*, for pr.'s orders, *ib.*, ii, no 742.

William de la BROME
occ. 1270 occ. 1276

1269/70, receiver, with Adam de Morton, q.v., WCL Havant acct.
1269/70, visited Havant and Hurstbourne, WCL accts.
1276, 26 Mar., apptd proctor by the prior and chapter to inform the bp [Nicholas de Ely] of their appeal to Rome vs his statutes, *Reg. Pontissara*, 645; see Andrew de London.

Henry de BROMLE [Bromly
d. 1311/12

1311/12, d.; the almoner gave [a pittance of] 6s. 8d., to the convent on the day of his burial and distributed 13s. 4d., worth of bread among the poor, Kitchin, *SS* no 18, p. 392, *SS* no 18*, p. 399.

I John de BROMLE [Bromlee, Bromleigh, Bromley
occ. 1373 occ. 1401/2

1373, 12 Mar., ord acol., Winchester cathedral, *Reg. Wykeham*, i, 269.
1374, 25 Feb., ord subdcn, Winchester cathedral, *ib.*, i, 273.
1376, 8 Mar., ord dcn, bp's chapel, Highclere, *ib.*, 279.

1376, 20 Sept., ord pr., bp's chapel, Farnham castle, *ib.*, 281.
1390, 24 Oct., *custos* of the Lady altar, BL Add. Roll 24349.
1393, 21/22 Aug., cellarer, BL Ms Harley 328, fo 24v.
1389, with the prior and other monks and laity, accused of hunting in the bp's warrens, Oxford, New College Ms 9819.
1390, 24 Oct., prob. held the court at Stockton (Wilts.), BL Add. Roll 24349.
1393, 21/22 Aug., 22nd to sign the composition with bp Wykeham, BL Ms Harley, fo 24v; see Robert de Rodebourne.
1401/2, spent a wk in the infirmary and the hordarian pd 6d. [for his needs], WCL, unnumbered obedientiary acct.

II J. de BROMLY
occ. 1310/11

1310/11, visited Chilbolton, WCL acct.

BROOK
see Broke

BRUSTOWE
see Bristowe

John de BRUTONE [Bruiton, Bruyton, Burtone
occ. 1350 occ. 1355

1350, 5 Sept., ord acol., bp's chapel, South Waltham, *Reg. Edington*, ii, no 817.
1350, 18 Sept., ord subdcn, bp's chapel, Highclere, *ib.*, ii, no 814.
1351, 23 May, granted *lit. dim*, for dcn's orders, Reg. Edington, ii, fo AA.
1353, 22 Aug., subdcn, granted *lit. dim*, for dcn's orders, *Reg. Edington*, ii, no 845.
1354, 20 Sept., ord dcn, bp's chapel [Bishops] Waltham, *Reg. Edington*, ii, no 850.
1355, 17 Sept., granted *lit. dim*, for pr.'s orders, *ib.*, ii, no 866.

John BRYNSTONE [Brymstone, Brynstane
occ. 1520 occ. 1524

1520, 22 Dec., ord dcn, Lady chapel, Winchester cathedral, Reg. Fox. iv, fo 71.
1523, 21 Mar., ord pr., Lady chapel, Winchester cathedral, *ib.*, v, fo 31v.
1522/3, celeb. his first mass and recd a small gift from the almoner, WCL unnumbered obedientiary acct.

n.d., sacrist acc. to *MLGB Suppl.*, 112.
1524, 2 Dec., 25th in order at the el. of a prior, Reg. Fox, v, fo 75; he voted for John Avynton, q.v., 'propter eius virtuosam vitam scientiam et experientiam in temporalibus' *ib.*, v, fo 78.

Name in BL Add. Ms 60577, Miscellanea, (15th/16th c.); 'y bowthe hym of brynstane cost me 3s. 4d'; this was written by John Buryton, q.v.

John BRYSTOWE
occ. 1472

1472, 19 Dec., ord acol., Winchester cathedral, Reg. Waynflete, ii, fo 169v.

BUKINGHAM
occ. c. 1528

[1528 × 1539], surname occ. in a list of monks copied on to a blank fo in Oxford, Bod. Ms Selden supra 76, fo 46v; no Christian names are given.

Note: this monk possibly appears elsewhere in this section under his patronymic.

Alan de BUNGEY
d. 1311/12

1311/12, d., and the almoner gave the monks [a pittance] of 6s. 8d, on the day of his burial and distributed 13s. 4d., worth of bread to the poor, Kitchin, *SS* no 18, p. 392, *SS* no 18*, p. 399.

I John de BURGHILDESBURY [Burghildebury, Burtlebury, Burtilburi
occ. 1347 occ. ?1356

1352, 5 Feb., apptd [*ordinatus*] precentor, Oxford, Bod. Ms 767, fo ii.
n.d., [c. ?1356], sacrist, *Winch. Cart.*, nos 384–386.
1347, 22 July, with other people, granted plenary remission on the petition of John le Devenish, q.v., at the curia, *CPP*, i (1342–1404), 335, and *CPL*, iii (1342–1362), 248.
n.d., [?c. 1356], sent by the prior and convent to the bp to complain of the wrongs done to him and to his office as sacrist; two other letters were sent to others asking for advice and help in this matter, *Winch. Cart.*, nos 384–386.

II John de BURGHILDESBURY [Burghildebury
occ. 1358

1358, 2 Oct., acol., granted *lit. dim*, for all orders, *Reg. Edington*, ii, no 897 (Reg. Edington, ii, fo LLv).

John BURITON [Beriton, Buritone, Buryton
occ. 1524 occ. 1539

1524, 2 Dec., master of the Lady chapel, Reg. Fox, v, fo 77v.
1535, *custos* of the Lady chapel, *Valor Eccles.*, ii, 2 (transcribed as Burton).
1536/7, sacrist, first yr, Kitchin and Madge, *Documents*, *SS* no 64, pp. 13–31.
1539, 14 Nov., sacrist [sexten], PRO E315/494.
1524, 2 Dec., 15th in order at the el. of a prior, Reg. Fox, v, fo 75; he nom. John Meone II,

q.v., 'propter eius bonam religionem et honestatem', *ib.*, v, fo 77^{v}.

1539, 14 Nov., 9th on the surrender list, among the seniors, and awarded an annual pension of £10, PRO E315/494.

Name in BL Add. Ms 60577, Miscellanea (15th/16th c.); 'y bowthe hym of brynstane [q.v.] cost me 3s. 4d.'

Richard BURITON [Biritone, Birytone, Buryton, Byritone, Byrytone
occ. 1392 occ. 1419

1392, 13 Apr., ord acol., Winchester cathedral, *Reg. Wykeham*, i, 326.

1393, 1 Mar., ord subdcn, bp's chapel, Farnham castle, *ib.*, i, 328.

1393, 21 Sept., ord dcn, bp's chapel, Esher, *ib.*, i, 329.

1395, 6 Mar., ord pr., bp's chapel, Marwell, *ib.*, i, 336.

1394/5, celebrated his first mass, and the anniversarian gave 6d. [for the feast], Kitchin, *SS* no 1, p. 205.

1413/14, 1415/17, hordarian, PRO SC6/758/2–4.

1393, 21/22 Aug., 43rd and last to sign the composition with bp Wykeham, BL Ms Harley 328, fo 24^{v}; see Robert de Rodebourne.

1400/1, pd a visit to Stockton (Wilts.), BL Add. Roll 24396.

1404, 16 Oct., 27th in order at the el. of a bp, *Reg. Common Seal*, no 68.

1403/4, stayed at Mapledurham *ultra facturam. . .cisere*, BL Add. Roll 28070.

1413/14, visited Woolstone, PRO SC6/758/2.

1414/15, stopped at Crondall, WCL acct.

1415, 27 Sept., named as one of nine *compromissorii* in the el. of a prior, *Reg. Common Seal*, no 163; on 28 Sept., with John Hurst, q.v., he was apptd proctor to obtain the consent of Thomas Shirebourne, q.v., to his el., *ib.*, no 164.

1415/17, pd visits to Woolstone, PRO SC6/758/3, 4.

1419, 1 Sept., with Roland Hoke, q.v., and other seculars, apptd by the prior and chapter proctors for all matters pertaining to their rights in their churches within the diocese of Salisbury, *Reg. Common Seal*, no 186.

BURTLEBURY
see Burghildesbury

I John de BURTONE
occ. 1349

1349, 19 Sept., ord dcn, bp's chapel, [Bishops] Waltham, *Reg. Edington*, ii, 788.

II John BURTON
occ. 1451 occ. 1459

1451, 18 Dec., ord acol., Winchester cathedral, Reg. Waynflete, i, fo D^{v}.

1453, 22 Sept., ord subdcn, Winchester cathedral, *ib.*, i, fo G.

1455, 20 Sept., ord dcn, bp's chapel, Wolvesey, *ib.*, i, fo K^{v}.

1459, 17 Feb., ord pr., Winchester cathedral, *ib.*, i, fo R^{v}.

1458/9, celebrated his first mass and the *custos operum* sent 8d. for wine [for the feast], WCL unnumbered obedientiary acct.

Walter BURTON [Boorton
occ. 1437/8 occ. 1450

1447, 15 Apr., fourth prior, *Reg. Common Seal*, no 316.

1450, 11 Dec., third prior, Reg. Waynflete, i, fos 30^{v}, 31^{v}.

1437/8, stayed at Manydown, 'pro ferma ad opus domini capiend'' and the reeve entered the expense of his visit as 9s., WCL acct.

1447, 15 Apr., 19th in order at the el. of a bp, *Reg. Common Seal*, no 316.

1450, 11 Dec., 15th in order at the el. of a prior and named by the chapter as one of seven *compromissorii*, Reg. Waynflete, i, fo 31^{v}.

BURTON(E)
see also Bruton

BURY
see Bery

BURYTON
see Buriton

BUSSHOPESTONE, Bussupeston
see Bysshopestone

Nicholas de BYKFORD
see Wykford

BYRITONE
see Buriton

Henry BYSET
occ. 1239 occ. 1243

1239, 21 Nov., apptd curtarian by order of the king, *sed. vac.*, *CClR (1237–1242)*, 158.

1243, 4 Oct., possibly anniversarian, see below.

1240, 1 Nov., requested the king to pardon Richard de Wik who had by accident killed a man; the king acceded, *CClR (1237–1242)*, 246.

1243, 4 Oct., the king ordered two oaks to be sent to him to furnish timber for the repair of buildings pertaining to the anniversarian's office, *CClR (1242–1247)*, 47.

Nicholas de BYSSHOPESTONE [Busshopestone, Bussupeston
occ. 1403/4

1403, 22 Sept., ord acol., Waltham, *Reg. Wykeham*, i, 356.

1404, 23 Feb., ord subdcn, Waltham, *ib.*, i, 357.
[1404], 21 May, granted *lit. dim*, for all orders, *ib.*, ii, 556.
1404, 24 May, ord dcn, Sherborne, Reg. Mitford (Salisbury), fo 176.
1404, 20 Sept., ord pr., Waltham, *Reg. Wykeham*, i, 359.
1404, 16 Oct., 37th in order at the el. of a bp, *Reg. Common Seal*, no 68.

Note: in 1402, he was a scholar of Winchester College and described as being from Salisbury, T. F. Kirby, *Winchester Scholars*, London, 1888, 28.

John de CADYNGTONE
occ. 1381/2

1381/2, ill in the infirmary for three wks and recd 18d. from the hordarian, Kitchin, *SS* no 20, p. 279.

CALCETO
see Cauz

Ralph de CALNE [Canne, Caone, Caune
occ. 1295 occ. 1321

1305, 28 Mar., 10 May; 1306, 15 Mar., 21 Sept.; 1307, 3 Mar., 5 Apr., 8 Nov.; 1308, 23/25 Mar., precentor, *Reg. Woodlock*, 7, 22; *ib.*, 115, 143; *ib.*, 166, 173, 219; *ib.*, 255–257.
1310, 17 May, subprior, *ib.*, 444.
1316, 22 Mar., 8 and 27 July; 1317, 13 Mar.; 1321, 10 July, precentor, *ib.*, 668, 335, 337; *Reg. Sandale*, 30; *Reg. Asserio*, 398.
1295, 6 June, apptd proctor by the subprior and chapter to inform the bp of their el. of Henry Woodlock, q.v., as prior and obtain his confirmation, *Reg. Pontissara*, 73.
1305, 28 Mar., recd a comm. from the bp el. [Henry Woodlock] in an ecclesiastical cause, *Reg. Woodlock*, 7; on 10 May the bp issued another similar comm. to him and to his official in the same affair, *ib.*, 22–23.
1305, 13 June, one of three monk proctors who recd from the bp licence to el. a prior and acted as proctor in the process leading up to the confirmation of Nicholas de Tarente, q.v., on 7 Aug., *ib.*, 32–34.
1306, 15 Mar., comm. by the bp to act with the official in an ecclesiastical cause, *ib.*, 115.
1306, 21 Sept., with the official and subprior comm. to rec. the compurgation of a pr., *ib.*, 143.
1307, 3 Mar., comm. by the bp to act with the official in collecting procurations for the cardinals in the adcnry of Winchester, *ib.*, 166–168; on 8 Nov. the two were still involved in the collection, *ib.*, 219.
1307, 5 Apr., with the official comm. to arrange for the papal provision of a poor clerk, *ib.*, 173.
1308, 23 Mar., with the official comm. to hear a suit concerning a rectory, *ib.*, 255. On 24 Mar., he acted as commissary of the official in another dispute, and was involved in a third case with the official the following day, *ib.*, 257–259.
1308, 24 Aug., acted as proctor for the prior and chapter in a dispute about rights of pasturage in West Meon, *ib.*, 300; he also visited Chilbolton this yr, WCL acct.
1309, 25 Aug., with Roger de Entingham, q.v., appeared as proctor before the bp with the prior el., Richard de Enford, q.v., to obtain confirmation of the el., *Reg. Woodlock*, 385.
1310, 17 May, comm. with another to admit a canon of Christchurch by means of a papal provision, *ib.*, 444.
1310/11, visited Chilbolton, WCL acct.
1316, 22 Mar., apptd, with the commissary general, to examine candidates for holy orders, *Reg. Woodlock*, 668.
1316, 8 July with Philip de Lusteshall, q.v., recd licence from the king at Windsor to el. a bp, *Reg. Sandale*, 335; on 27 July he was sent by the prior and chapter to inform the king of the result of the el., *ib.*, 337.
1317, 13 Mar., apptd penitentiary, with a secular pr., in the adcnry of Winchester, *Reg. Sandale*, 30; on 15 Mar. he witnessed the oath of a rector at Wolvesey, *Reg. Sandale*, 233.
1321, 10 June, apptd penitentiary in the diocese, *Reg. Asserio*, 398.

CAMBRAI
see Godfrey I

William de CAMEL
occ. 1325 occ. 1361

1328, 19 Mar., ord subdcn, Crawley [Hants], Reg. Stratford, fo 148.
1329, 18 Mar., ord pr., Chertsey abbey, *ib.*, fo 150.
1338/9, hordarian, and prob. succ. by Geoffrey de Guldeford, q.v., during this yr, PRO SC6/756/9.
1352, 5 Feb., apptd third prior [*ordinatus*], Oxford, Bod. Ms 767, fo ii.
1361, 9 Dec., third prior, Reg. Edington, fo 114^{v}.
1325, 9 Oct., 62nd (out of 64) in order of seniority, *Reg. Pontissara*, 557.
1337/8, sent as proctor to the Black Monk Chapter, and stopped at Whitchurch, WCL acct.
1338/9, visited Woolstone, PRO SC6/756/9.
1361, 9 Dec., president of the chapter in the process before the bp at Southwark concerning the el. of William Thudden, q.v., as prior, Reg. Edington, i, fos 113^{v}–114.

Richard de CANIGG' [Kanigg'
occ. 1272/3 occ. 1281/2

1272/3, one of many monks who visited Chilbolton, WCL acct.
1281/2, visited Crondall, WCL pipe roll acct.

CANNE
see Calne

Richard CANTERBURY [Canterburie, Caunterbury
occ. 1520 occ. 1528

1520, 22 Dec., ord subdcn, Lady chapel, Winchester cathedral, Reg. Fox, iv, fo 71.
1527, 16 Mar., ord dcn, Lady chapel, Winchester cathedral, *ib.*, v, fo 36.
1528, 11 Apr., ord pr., Lady chapel, Winchester cathedral, *ib.*, v, fo 38v.

1524, 2 Dec., student [*scholasticus*] at Oxford, Reg. Fox, v, fo 78.

1524, 2 Dec., subdcn and 28th in order at the el. of a prior, Reg. Fox, v, fo 75v; he voted for John Avynton, q.v., 'propter eius bonam religionem et doctrinam', *ib.*, v, fo 78.

Note: this is prob. Richard Myllys, q.v.

J. de CANTIA
n.d. [early 14th c.]

At her *sponsalia* his sister was given 13s. 4d., by the almoner, Kitchin, *SS* no 46, p. 466.

Note: this acct is only a fragment and the date has gone; see the entry below.

John de CANTUARIA
occ. 1307/8 occ. 1327/8

1307/8, 1308/9, 1310/11, pd visits to Chilbolton, WCL accts.
1311/12, his sister recd 6d. from the almoner, Kitchin, *SS* no 18*, p. 398.
1325, 9 Oct., 14th in order of seniority, *Reg. Pontissara*, 556.
1326, 3 Feb., ill in the infirmary when the bp made his visitation, Reg. Stratford, fo 171v.
1327/8, visited Ham (Wilts.), to rec. moneys due, WCL acct.

Note: this monk is almost certainly identical with J. de Cantia above.

CAONE
see Calne

John CARPENTER
occ. 1539

1539, 14 Nov., assigned a pension of £5 p.a., *L and P Henry VIII*, xiv, pt 2, no 520.

Note: this is prob. the family name of John Guldeford II, q.v. or possibly John Puryton, q.v.; see PRO E315/494.

Romanus CARTER
occ. 1513

1513, 26 Mar., ord acol., Winchester cathedral, Reg. Fox, iii, fo 53.

Richard de CASTELL'
occ. 1239

1239, 21 Nov., apptd *custos operum* by order of the king, *sed. vac.*, *CClR (1237–1242)*, 158.

CAUNE
see Calne

CAUNTERBURY
see Canterbury, Cantuaria

John de CAUZ [Calceto, Caux
occ. 1239 occ. 1250

1243–1244, 1247–1250, prior: apptd by the king, *sed. vac.*, 26 Dec. 1243; deposed by the bp c. 29 Aug. 1244. Again [reapptd] prior after Walter III, q.v., soon after 3 Apr. 1247, until his el. as abbot of Peterborough between 27 Dec. 1249 and 15 Jan. 1250, *Fasti*, ii, 89.

1239, 21 Nov., apptd chamberlain by order of the king, *sed. vac.*, *CClR (1237–1242)*, 158.

William ?CAWTE
d. 1415/16

1415/16, d., and the almoner distributed 10s. worth of bread [to the poor] on the day of his burial, Kitchin, *SS* no 37, p. 439.

CEELER
see Seler

I John CERNE [Serne
occ. 1466 occ. 1486

1466, 20 Sept., ord acol., Winchester cathedral, Reg. Waynflete, i, fo K*v.
1470, 16 June, ord dcn, Winchester cathedral, *ib.*, i, fo Q*.
1471, 30 Mar., ord pr., Winchester cathedral, *ib.*, ii, fo 167.

1486, 19 Nov., granted a letter of transfer by the prior addressed to the abbot of Cerne (Dorset) which arranged for him to stay at Cerne until Henry VII's mother [Lady Margaret Beaufort] or another friend of his made provision for him, *Reg. Common Seal*, no 431. Reasons for these arrangements are obscure.

II John CERNE [Serne
occ. 1501 d. 1522/3

1501, 27 Feb., first *depositarius*, Canterbury Reg. R, fo 115.

1501, 27 Feb., 11th to be examined at the visitation (*sed. vac.* both Canterbury and Winchester) by the commissary of the prior of Christ Church, Canterbury; he said that the needs of the sick in the infirmary were not being provided, Canterbury Reg. R, fo 115.
1522/3, d., and the almoner gave 10s. worth of bread to the poor on the day of his burial, WCL unnumbered almoner acct.

William CHAMBERLAYNE [Chamberleyne, Chaumberleyn
occ. 1392 occ. 1404

1392, 13 Apr., ord acol., bp's chapel, Marwell, *Reg. Wykeham*, i, 326.
1393, 1 Mar., ord subdcn, bp's chapel, Farnham castle, *ib.*, i, 328.
1394, 19 Dec., ord dcn, bp's chapel, Farnham castle, *ib.*, i, 335.
1395, 6 Mar., ord pr., bp's chapel, Marwell, *ib.*, i, 336.
1394/5, celebrated his first mass and the anniversarian gave him 6d., Kitchin, *SS* no 1, p. 205.

1393, 21/22 Aug., 40th to sign the composition with bp Wykeham, BL Ms Harley, fo 24^{v}; see Robert de Rodebourne.
1404, 16 Oct., 24th at the el. of a bp, *Reg. Common Seal*, no 68.

CHELBOURNE
see Ichelbourne

Thomas CHERTESEY B.Th. [Chertesay, Chirtesey
occ. 1498 occ. 1524

1498, 10 Mar., ord acol., St Laurence's church, Winchester, Reg. Langton, fo 32.
1498, 14 Apr., ord subdcn, Winchester cathedral, *ib.*, fo 32^{v}.
1499, 21 Dec., ord dcn, Winchester cathedral, *ib.*, fo 35.

1525, 2 Dec., third prior, Reg. Fox, v, fo 77.

1524, 2 Dec., described as B.Th., Reg. Fox, v, fo 76.

1498, 23 Apr., 30th and last but one in order at the el. of a prior, Reg. Langton, fo 73^{v}.
1501, 27 Feb., dcn and 25th to be examined at the visitation (*sed. vac.* both Canterbury and Winchester) by the commissary of the prior of Christ Church, Canterbury; he reported *omnia bene*, Canterbury Reg. R, fo 115.
1524, 2 Dec., 9th in order and named as one of three *scrutatores* in the el. of a prior, Reg. Fox, v, fos 75–77. He also wrote up the official account of the proceedings of the el. which were addressed to the bp and entered in his reg., *ib.*, v, fos 75–81.

John CHICHESTRE [Chechestre
occ. 1465 occ. 1492

1465, 21 Sept., ord acol., Hyde abbey, Reg. Waynflete, i, fo I*.
1466, 20 Sept., ord subdcn, Winchester cathedral, *ib.*, i, fo K*^{v}.
1467, 19 Sept., ord dcn, Winchester cathedral, *ib.*, i, fo L*^{v}.
1470, 16 June, ord pr., Winchester cathedral, *ib.*, i, fo Q*.

1486, 7 Dec., hostiller, *Reg. Common Seal*, no 434.

1486, 7 Dec., 7th in order at the el. of a bp, *Reg. Common Seal*, no 434.
1492, 29 Oct., 6th to be examined at the *sed. vac.* visitation and made several depositions: the quality of the food was poor; the chapter had no inventory of the jewels and ornaments; the question of reformation was often discussed but with little practical result, *Reg. abp Morton*, ii, no 127.

Robert CHICHESTRE [Chychester, Chychestre
occ. 1366 d. 1411

1366, 28 Feb., ord subdcn, St Elizabeth's chapel near Winchester, *Reg. Edington*, ii, no 949.
1368, 4 Mar., ord dcn, Winchester cathedral, *Reg. Wykeham*, ii, 253 (as Richard).
1370, 21 Sept., ord pr., bp's chapel, Highclere, *ib.*, ii, 261.
1370/1, celebrated his first mass and the anniversarian gave him 6d., WCL unnumbered obedientiary acct.

1371/2, the anniversarian hired a horse for him, Worcester Cathedral Muniment, C.532.
1393, 21/22 Aug., 13th to sign the composition with bp Wykeham, BL Ms Harley 328, fo 24^{v}; see Robert de Rodebourne.
1404, 16 Oct., 8th at the el. of a bp, *Reg. Common Seal*, no 68.
1411, between Apr. and Sept., d., and the almoner distributed 10s. worth of bread to the poor on the day of his burial, Kitchin, *SS* no 35, p. 434.

I Thomas de CHILBOLTON [Chilbalton, Chilbaltone
occ. 1388 occ. 1404

1388, 19 Dec., ord subdcn, bp's chapel, Farnham castle, *Reg. Wykeham*, i, 317.
1389, 13 Mar., ord dcn, bp's chapel, Farnham castle, *ib.*, 318.
1390, 24 Sept., ord pr., bp's chapel, Esher, *ib.*, 322.

[1392/3], student at Oxford, and stopped at Hurstbourne en route, WCL acct.
[1393/4], prob. student, as he stopped at Whitchurch four times [four tallies] with Thomas Shirebourne, q.v., WCL acct.
Note: neither he nor the other two students, William Rodebourne and Thomas Shirebourne, q.v., were present at Winchester to sign the composition with bp Wykeham in Aug. 1393, prob. because they were all at Oxford; see Greatrex, 'Injunction Book', 245.

1394/5, visited Hurstbourne and Whitchurch, Worcester Cathedral Muniment C.867, WCL Whitchurch acct.
1404, 16 Oct., 22nd at the el. of a bp, *Reg. Common Seal*, no 68.

II Thomas CHILBOLTON
occ. 1498 d. 1522/3

1498, 10 Mar., ord acol., St Laurence's church, Winchester, Reg. Langton, fo 32.
1498, 14 Apr., ord subdcn, Winchester cathedral, *ib.*, fo 32v.
1499, 21 Dec., ord dcn, Winchester cathedral, *ib.*, fo 35.

1498, 23 Apr., 28th in order at the el. of a prior, Reg. Langton, fo 73v.
1501, 27 Feb., dcn and 23rd to be examined at the visitation (*sed. vac.* both Canterbury and Winchester) by the commissary of the prior of Christ Church, Canterbury; he reported *omnia bene*, Canterbury Reg. R, fo 115.
1522/3, d., and the almoner gave 10s. worth of bread to the poor on the day of his burial, WCL unnumbered obedientiary acct.

CHIRTESEY
see Chertesey

CHYCHESTRE
see Chichestre

Thomas de CHYNHAM
occ. 1345

1345, 15 Aug., one of the monks found guilty of proceeding with the el. of a bp vs the king's orders, *CPR (1343–1345)*, 581, see John le Devenish.

Richard de CLAVERLYE [Claverle
occ. 1325 occ. 1332

1332, 18 Oct., gardener, *Winch. Cart.*, no 180.

1325, 9 Oct., 10th in order of seniority, *Reg. Pontissara*, 556.
1332, 18 Oct., present in the prior's chapel at the reading of ordinances, drawn up by the chapter following discussions about the debts of two of the obedientiary offices, which prescribed new financial arrangements to alleviate the crisis, *Winch. Cart.*, no 180; see Alexander de Heriard.

William CLEMENT B.Cn.L. [Clemente
occ. 1441/2 occ. 1478

1447, 15 Apr., *custos* of St Mary's altar, *Reg. Common Seal*, no 316.
1450, 11 Dec., infirmarer, Reg. Waynflete, i, fo 30v.
1471/2, 1476/7, almoner, Kitchin, *SS* nos 42 and 43, pp. 451–457.

1441/2, student at Oxford and stopped at Manydown on his way there, WCL acct; see William Basyng III.
1450, 11 Dec., described as *in decretis bacallarius*, Reg. Wayneflete, i, fo 30v.

1447, 15 Apr., 18th in order at the el. of a bp, *Reg. Common Seal*, no 316.
1450, 11 Dec., 14th at the el. of a prior and named as one of seven *compromissorii*, Reg. Waynflete, i, fo 31.
1462, 6 July, apptd by the chapter as their representative at convocation, Reg. Waynflete, i, fo 78*.
1468, 10 May, with the prior, Robert [Westgate, q.v.] named as proctor for convocation, *ib.*, i, fo 94*v.
1470, 26 July, again, with prior Robert, named proctor for convocation, *ib.*, ii, fo 142.
Note: the prior d. before 31 Mar. this yr and so the entry in Waynflete's register is out of date; however, in *Reg. Common Seal*, no 363, an undated entry states that the subprior, John Huntley, q.v., and convent named William Clement as their proctor for this convocation.
1478, 1 Mar., with John Hursley, q.v., apptd proctor to represent the prior and chapter in the ecclesiastical court in Salisbury diocese, *Reg. Common Seal*, no 372.

Name in Oxford, Bod. Ms Rawlinson C.489, Proprium Sanctorum (A.D. 1424); name on fo 25v.

He may have been a relative of M. Vincent Clement, adcn of Winchester, 1459/75, *Fasti*, iv, 51.

William de CLERE
occ. 1325

1325, 9 Oct., 39th in order of seniority, *Reg. Pontissara*, 556.

John de CLIFFORD [Clyfforde
occ. 1323/4 occ. 1346

1332, 18 Oct., *custos operum*, *Winch. Cart.*, no 180.

1323/4, stayed at Whitchurch, Worcester Cathedral Muniment, C.523.
1325, 9 Oct., 41st in order of seniority, *Reg. Pontissara*, 557.
1332, 18 Oct., present in the prior's chapel at the reading of ordinances, drawn up by the chapter following discussions about the debts of two of the obedientiary offices, which prescribed new financial arrangements to alleviate the crisis, *Winch. Cart.*, no 180; see Alexander de Heriard.
1346, 4 Mar., apptd confessor for the monks and others in the diocese, *Reg. Edington*, i, no 21.

John COBBE
see Estgate

John de COMBE [Coumbe
occ. 1317 occ. 1325

1317, 13 Mar., apptd penitentiary in the adcnry of Winchester, *Reg. Sandale*, 30.
1325, 9 Oct., 5th in order of seniority, *Reg. Pontissara*, 556.

Henry CORHAM [Corbin, Corbyn
occ. 1239 occ. 1260/1

1239, 21 Nov., the king ordered his apptment as hordarian *sed. vac.*, *CClR (1237–1242)*, 158; 1240, 20 May, hordarian, *ib.*, 192.

1260/1, curtarian, WCL Alton acct.

1240, 20 May, recd a gift from the king of 60 beech poles to repair a weir [*gurges*], *CClR (1237–1242)*, 192.

1260/1, visited Alton and Wonston, WCL accts.

Richard ?CORRYN
occ. 1394/5

1394/5, with Thomas de Chilbolton I, q.v., visited Hurstbourne, Worcester Cathedral Muniment, C.867.

Walter COTEL
occ. 1308/10

1308/9, visited Chilbolton, WCL acct.

1309/10, d., and on the day of his burial the almoner gave 6s. 8d., in pittances to the convent, Kitchin, *SS* no 15, p. 391.

COUMBE
see Combe

Peter CRANBOURNE [Cranborne
occ. 1406 occ. 1432/3

1406, 19 Feb., ord subdcn, Winchester cathedral, Reg. Beaufort, fo A.

1406, 12 Mar., ord dcn, Winchester cathedral, *ib.*, fo A^{v}.

1415, 26 Aug., chamberlain, *Reg. Common Seal*, no 158.

1428/33, receiver, WCL Hannington and Westwood accts, BL Add. Roll 28106 (1428/30); WCL Silkstead acct (1430/1); WCL Hannington acct, BL Add. Roll 28107, BL Harley Roll X.8, BL Add. Roll 28112 (1431/3). In 1429/30 on the Mapledurham acct (BL Add. Roll 28106) he is named as receiver and as treasurer; he was succ. by Robert Puryton, q.v.

1409/10, visited Hannington *ultra tonsuram*, WCL acct.

1415, 26 Aug., one of the monks who witnessed the resignation of prior Thomas Nevyle, q.v., *Reg. Common Seal*, no 158.

1428/29, visited Hannington, WCL acct.

1429/30, visited Mapledurham, Silkstead and Westwood, BL Add. Roll 28106, WCL accts.

1430/31, visited Silkstead, WCL acct, and also visited Stockton (Wilts.), with Robert Puryton, q.v., for *liberatio denariorum*, BL Add. Roll 24412.

1431/2, visited Hannington for *liberatio denariorum*, and also Manydown where he recd money from the sale of wool, WCL accts.

1432/3, pd visits to Compton, Whitchurch and Enford, WCL accts, BL Harley Roll X.8.

A *dominus* Robert Cranbourne gave to the cathedral priory Cambridge, Trinity College Ms 338, Legenda aurea (14th c.).

John de CRISTCHIRCHE [Cristechirche
occ. 1360 occ. 1363

1360, 8 Sept., subdcn, granted *lit. dim.*, for dcn's orders, *Reg. Edington*, ii, no 915.

1363, 28 May, ord pr., bp's chapel, Highclere, *ib.*, ii, no 934.

John CROCHE
occ. 1282

1282, 7 Aug., one of the monks who sought and recd absolution from excommunication imposed because of irregularities during the el. of Richard de la More as bp, *Reg. abp Pecham*, i, 188–189; the comm. for absolution is dated 10 Aug., *ib.*, ii, 50. See Adam de Farnham.

Thomas CROKER
occ. 1528

1528, 11 Apr., one of six not yet prof., but ord exorcist and acol., Lady chapel, Winchester cathedral, Reg. Fox, v, fo 38–38^{v}.

Gilbert de CRUNDEL [Crundal
occ. 1240

1240, 11 Jan., named proctor, with Robert de Leycestria, q.v., by the prior and chapter who were petitioning the pope to restore their right to el. their bps, *CPL*, i (1198–1304), 185.

DALAREW, Dalaru
see Delarew

R. DAUNDELE [Daundely, Daungdely
occ. 1308/9 occ. 1310/11

1308/9, visited Hurstbourne with Simon Daundele, q.v., and Philip de Lusteshall, q.v., and their horses were fed, WCL acct.

1310/11, visited Chilbolton, WCL acct.

Simon DAUNDELE [Daundely
occ. 1308/9 occ. 1321/2

1308/9, visited Chilbolton, and also Hurstbourne as in the entry above, WCL accts.

1321/2, visited Houghton, WCL acct.

Note: there is a Walter Daundely or de Aundely, knight, on two witness lists dated 1259 in *Winch. Cart.*, nos 208, 209.

DEAN
see John Avynton

Elizaeus DELAREW [Helezaeus Dalarew, Dalaru, de la Rew, Delerewe, de le Rewe, Useus Dularu
occ. [1493] occ. 1501

[1493], ord subdcn, no place named, Reg. Langton, fo 23.

[1493], 21 Sept., ord dcn, Hyde abbey, *ib.*, fo 23^{v}.

1496, 24 Sept., ord pr., Hyde abbey, *ib.*, fo 30.

1498, 23 Apr., 20th in order at the el. of a prior, Reg. Langton, fo 73^{v}.

1501, 27 Feb., 15th to be examined at the visitation (*sed. vac.* both Canterbury and Winchester) by the commissary of the prior of Christ Church, Canterbury; he gave his *omnia bene*, Canterbury Reg. R, fo 115.

John le DEVENISH [de Veneys, Devenissch, Devenys, Devenysh, de Devone, Devonia

occ. 1325 d. 1348

1336, 16 Feb., 19 July, precentor, Reg. Orleton, i, fos 32, 40v; he was also precentor on 7 June, 12 July [1335], *Winch. Cart.*, nos 267, 268.

1338, 17 Apr., subprior, Reg. Orleton, i, fo 58.

1325, 9 Oct., 50th in order of seniority, *Reg. Pontissara*, 557.

[1335], 7 June, sent as proctor, with Richard de Merewell I, q.v., to the bp to discuss certain matters with him, *Winch. Cart.*, no 267; on 12 July the bp wrote to the prior concerning a recent discussion with Devenish about an appropriation, *ib.*, no 268.

1336, 16 Feb., with Richard de Merewell I, q.v., apptd to act as confessors for the monks and for others in the city and diocese, Reg. Orleton, i, fo 32; on 19 July both monks were licensed to hear confessions even in reserved cases in the absence of the bp, *ib.*, i, fo 40v. On 17 Apr. 1338 this license was reconfirmed, *ib.*, i, fo 58.

1338/9, pd a visit to Woolstone, where he dined with his *socius* on goose, PRO SC6/756/9.

1345, 28 July, named by the prior and chapter as one of nine *compromissorii* in the el. of a bp, *Reg. Common Seal*, no 5. He was el. bp vs the king's wish as the king had revoked the licence to el. that had been issued in his name on 26 July, [*sic*] *CClR (1343–1346)*, 590, 639; and he was not included in the royal pardon issued to the monks on 5 Nov., *CPR (1343–1345)*, 569. See John de Fourde.

1346, 13 Sept., formerly bp el., granted papal dispensation to choose his own confessor who was empowered to give plenary remission of sins, *CPL*, iii (1342–1362), 222.

1346, provided to the abbacy of St Augustine's, Canterbury, despite the monks' el. of one of their own number; the king objected and withheld the temporalities. He proceeded to the curia to try to get the provision changed into an el., Twysden, *Hist. Angl. Script.* (from William Thorn's chronicle), ii, col. 2082–2084. See William de Sparsholte who accompanied him.

1348, d. at the curia, *ib*; this fact is given only in the index of Twysden.

He came from a prominent Winchester family one of whom, also John, was mayor in 1318 and 1335, *Winch. Cart.*, nos 112, 145, 149; and Nicholas was mayor in 1339, *CPR (1338–1342)*, 212, 281. While at the curia he obtained a dispensation for his sister Agnes de Cormayls of Schottesden to hear divine office in her chapel, *CPP*, i (1342–1419), 117; and at the same time (13 Sept. 1346) he obtained a dispensation for Nicholas Devenysh to choose a confessor, who would have authority to give plenary remission, *CPL*, iii (1342–1362), 222. The Devenish family chantry was formerly at the altar of the Holy Cross on the north side of the cathedral nave on the site of what is now Bishop Morley's tomb, B. Carpenter Turner, 'A Forgotten Chantry in the Cathedral', *Winch. Cath. Record*, no 60 (1991), 16–17; it was founded in 1335, *Winch. Cart.*, no 265.

Richard de DEVIZES [Divisiensis

occ. 1192 × 1198

Known because of his historical writing in the form of a Chronicon de Tempore Regis Richardi Primi, translated and ed most recently by J. T. Appleby in *Chron. Devizes* (see refs). He visited his former prior, Robert III, q.v., who had resigned the priorate in 1191 to become a Carthusian at Witham, Somerset, and wrote the chronicle at his request because the latter was anxious to keep in touch with current affairs. For a detailed assessment of his literary achievement, his place among the 12th c. monastic historians and a discussion of his possible authorship of a portion of the *Ann. Winton.*, see Gransden, *Hist. Writing*, ii, 247–254.

Name in the ms, which contains his chronicle and is now Cambridge, Corpus Christi College Ms 339 (?12th/13th c.).

DEVONE, Devonia

see Devenish

[Thomas DOLMESBOURNE

Note: in Kitchin, *Obed. Rolls*, 103, the name occ., but is a mistaken transcription of Ichelbourne, q.v.]

DOMMER

see Dummere

W. de DONKELONDE

occ. 1336/7

1336/7, acting with the receiver who was also hordarian and visited Woolstone and ate goose; see John de Merlawe, PRO SC6/756/7.

John de DONKETONE [Donogheton, Dunketon

occ. 1298/9 occ. 1329 × 1332

1298/9, receiver, WCL Chilbolton acct.

1324/5; 1326, 8 July; 1326/8, hordarian, PRO SC6/756/4; Basyng, Libellus, fo 4; Kitchin, *SS* no 47, 253–256, *SS* no 48, 258 (where the yr is wrongly transcribed as 1329/30); he was succ. by John de Merlawe, q.v.

1298/9, visited Chilbolton, WCL acct.
1305, 13 June, with Ralph de Calne and William de Somborne, q.v., as proctors for the chapter, recd licence to el. a prior, *Reg. Woodlock*, 32. On 6 Aug. he with other monks gave evidence to the bp's deputies concerning the proceedings of the el. of Nicholas de Tarente, q.v. as prior, *ib.*, 34.
1307/9, 1310/11, pd visits to Chilbolton, WCL accts; in 1308/9 he visited Hurstbourne and his horse was given oats, WCL acct.
1311, 20 Aug., with William de Marlburgh, q.v., acted as proctors for the prior and chapter at Southwark in a case vs the adcns who claimed the right to participate in the el. of a prior, Winchester College Muniment 1013.
1319, 24 Nov., with Richard de Merewell I, q.v., proctors for the prior and chapter, and recd licence to el a bp from the king, at York, *Reg. Sandale*, 285 (appndx).
1324/5, visited Woolstone, PRO SC6/756/4.
1325, 9 Oct., 3rd in order of seniority, *Reg. Pontissara*, 556.
1328/9, the hordarian spent 16s. 6d., 'in pannis lineis et laneis et ceteris necessariis emptis pro fratre J.'; he also recd 40s. *per talliam* from the hordarian, Kitchin, *SS* no 48, p. 260.
1332, 18 Oct., there is ref. to the debt on his last acct as hordarian but he was not present at the proceedings concerning the priory's financial crisis, *Winch. Cart.*, no 180; see Alexander de Heriard. He is not, however, referred to as d.

Adam de DONYTONE [Donyntone
occ. 1325 occ. 1332

1332, 18 Oct., infirmarer, *Winch. Cart.*, no 180.
1325, 9 Oct., 11th in order of seniority, *Reg. Pontissara*, 556.
1332, 18 Oct., present in the prior's chapel at the reading of ordinances, drawn up by the chapter following discussions about the debts of two of the obedientiary offices, which prescribed new financial arrangements to alleviate the crisis, *Winch. Cart.*, no 180; see Alexander de Heriard.

Gilbert DORSETT
occ. 1461

1461, 4 Apr., ord acol., Winchester cathedral, Reg. Waynflete, i, fo Y.

James DORSETT [Dorset
occ. 1527 occ. 1539

1527, 20 Apr., recd tonsure and ord exorcist and acol., Reg. Fox, v, fo 36^v.
1528, 11 Apr., ord subdcn, Lady chapel, Winchester cathedral, *ib.*, v, fo 38^v.
1532/4, student at Oxford with Thomas Tistede, q.v., and recd 10s. *in exhibitione* from the hordarian as well as 2s. *in curialitate*, Kitchin, *SS* no 61, p. 304. He also recd 5s. from the *custos operum*, *ib.*, *SS* no 12, p. 223; he stayed at Canterbury college and was charged with breach of the peace in Aug. 1534, see *BRUO, 1501–1540*.
1536/7, prob. student but no names are given, Kitchin, *SS* no 64, p. 24.
1539, 14 Nov., student at Oxford, PRO E315/494; see also Thomas Eston, Thomas Tistede, Peter Warham.
1539, 14 Nov., pr., 29th and last to be named on the surrender list, *L and P Henry VIII*, xiv, pt 2, no 520; he was assigned a pension of £10 p.a. (PRO E315/494).

John DORSETT [Dorset
occ. 1468 d. 1513/14

1468, 17 Dec., ord subdcn, Winchester cathedral, Reg. Waynflete, i, fo M*^{v}.
1469, 23 Sept., ord dcn, Winchester cathedral, *ib.*, i, fo O*.
1471, 21 Dec., ord pr., bp's chapel, Waltham, *ib.*, ii, fo 168.
1471/2, celebrated his first mass and the almoner sent 8d. for wine [for the feast], Kitchin, *SS* no 42, 453.
1476/7, anniversarian, Worcester Cathedral Muniment, C.2; his first yr, *ib.*
1486, 7 Dec.; 1498, 23 Apr.; 1501, 28 Feb.; third prior, *Reg. Common Seal*, no 434; Reg. Langton, fo 73^v; Canterbury Reg. R, fo 114^v.
1486, 7 Dec., 9th in order at the el. of a bp, *Reg. Common Seal*, no 434.
1492, 29 Oct., 7th to be examined at the *sed. vac.* visitation and agreed with other deponents that the quality and quantity of food was inadequate and that despite past depositions calling for correction, as John Chichestre, q.v., had also reported, nothing had yet been done, *Reg. abp Morton*, ii, no 127.
1498, 23 Apr., 2nd in order at the el. of a prior, Reg. Langton, fo 73^v.
1501, 27 Feb., 3rd to be examined at the visitation (*sed. vac.* both Canterbury and Winchester) by the commissary of the prior of Christ Church, Canterbury; he reported *omnia bene*, Canterbury Reg. R, fo 114^v.
1513/14, d., and the almoner distributed 10s. worth of bread on the day of his burial, Kitchin, *SS* no 44 (acct for 1514/15), p. 460.

George DOWNTON [Dounton
occ. 1447 occ. 1450

1447, 15 Apr., pr., and prof. and 33rd in order at the el. of a bp, *Reg. Common Seal*, no 316.
1450, 11 Dec., 29th at the el. of a prior, Reg. Waynflete, i, fo 31.

John de DRAYTON [Draytone
occ. [1283] occ. 1307

[1283], one of four monks apptd proctors, with the prior and Valentine [de Wherewell], q.v., in an appeal to the king because of the chapter's dispute with the bp, *Reg. Pontissara*, 662–663 where the date is c. 1276; but see *ib.*, 399–400. See also PRO E135/3/39b, dated 12 Jan 1283 when these proctors were summoned to meet the king and bp concerning the reform of the convent.

1305, 6 Aug., one of four monks who gave evidence to the bp's deputies concerning the proceedings of the el. of Nicholas de Tarente, q.v., as prior, *Reg. Woodlock*, 34.

1307, 20 June, witness to the absolution of a vicar by the bp, *ib.*, 186.

Name in CUL Ms Gg.2.18, J. de Voragine, Aurea legenda (13th/4th cs); 'Memoriale—monachi cuius anime propicietur deus amen', on fo 1.

Richard de DRAYTON
occ. 1345

1345, 28 July, apptd by the prior and chapter as one of nine *compromissorii* in the el. of a bp, *Reg. Common Seal*, no 5.

Ralph de DREYMS [Dreins, de Reyns, ?*alias* Worstone
occ. 1272/3 occ. 1279/80

1272/3, visited Chilbolton, WCL acct.

1275, 10 Apr., was staying at the abbey of St Peter, Gloucester acc. to a letter of the bp of Worcester to the bp of Winchester; the Worcester bp requested his recall because the monasteries in his diocese were hardly able to maintain their own brethren, *Reg. Giffard* (Worcester), 71.

1279/80, stopped at Hurstbourne, with W de Hamelton and William de Hoo, q.v., WCL pipe roll acct.

Note: see Ralph de Aremes who may be the same monk.

DULARU
see Delarew

Richard DUMMERE [Dommer, Dummer
occ. 1447 occ. 1452

1448, 18 May, ord subdcn, Winchester cathedral, Reg. Waynflete, i, fo A^v^.

1448, 21 Sept., ord dcn, bp's chapel, Marwell, *ib.*, i, fo B.

1452, 23 Sept., ord pr., bp's chapel, Waltham, *ib.*, i, fo F.

1450, 11 Dec., student at Oxford, Reg. Waynflete, i, fo 30^v^.

1447, 15 Apr., present at the el. of a prior, was 37th in order out of 39 prof. monks, and was one of the three described as *juvenes*, *Reg. Common Seal*, no 316.

1450, 11 Dec., 33rd at the el. of a prior, Reg. Waynflete, fo 30^v^.

DUNKETON
see Donketone

Walter DURAUNT [Durant
occ. 1353 d. 1389/90

1353, 22 Aug., issued with *lit. dim*, for subdcn's orders, *Reg. Edington*, ii, no 845.

1354, 20 Dec., ord subdcn, bp's chapel [Bishops] Waltham, *ib.*, ii, no 851.

1355, 17 Sept., issued with *lit. dim* for dcn's orders, *ib.*, ii, no 866.

1356, 10 Apr., ord dcn, bp's chapel, Esher, *ib.*, ii, no 872.

1356, 13 June, issued with *lit. dim*, for pr.'s orders, *ib.*, ii, no 874.

1376, Oct., John Talmache left money in his will to this monk, Cath. Records, ii, no 73, fo 81.

1381/2, spent a wk in the infirmary for which the hordarian charged 6d. on his acct, Kitchin, *SS* no 54, p. 279.

1384, 26 Oct., with John de London I, q.v., sent by the prior el., Robert de Rodebourne, q.v., and the chapter to obtain the bp's confirmation of the el., *Reg. Wykeham*, i, 149.

1389/90, d., and the almoner distributed 10s. worth of bread to the poor on the day of his burial, Kitchin, *SS* no 28, p. 417.

John de DUREVILLE [de Aurevill', de Ureville, Durvilla, Wrevil
occ. 1239 d. ?1278/9

1276–1278/9, prior: apptd by the bp, and installed 3 Dec. 1276; d. or res. by Jan. 1279, *Fasti*, ii, 90.

1239, 21 Nov., by order of the king, *sed. vac.*, apptd hostiller, *CClR (1237–1242)*, 158.

1261, 14 June, prior to this date chamberlain, *CPR (1258–1266)*, 159; see Ralph Russel.

n.d., almoner, *CPR (1232–47)*, 413–14.

1276, 13 Mar., formerly subprior, *Reg. Pontissara*, 643 (transcribed as Vrenill).

1240, 16 Aug., was at the curia, with Robert de Walyngford I, q.v., *pro negociis* concerning St Swithun's, and the king ordered his proctors there to allow them to have a loan of up to 100m., *CClR (1237–1242)*, 215.

1243, 16 Dec., apptd with others by the king in his appeal vs William Raleigh's translation from the see of Norwich to that of Winchester, *CPR (1232–1247)*, 412.

1260, 11 Aug., was transferred to St Peter's abbey, Gloucester, until the priory had recovered sufficiently to support all the community, *CClR (1259–1261)*, 195; see Andrew de London.

1276, 13 Mar., acc. to the injunctions of bp Nicholas de Ely he was required to answer for the money collected at the tomb of bp Aymer [de Lusignan] and for other ornaments and utensils while he was subprior, *Reg. Pontissara*, 643.

1278, 22 June, agreement was reached with bp Nicholas de Ely that on Dureville's d., the chapter would have free el. of the prior to succ. him, *ib.*, 649–650.

Note: he is described as a Norman in *Ann. Winton.*, 123.

Robert de DUREVILLE [de Urvilla
occ. 1260 occ. 1279/80

1260, 11 Aug., was transferred to Ramsey abbey until the priory had recovered sufficiently to support all the community, *CClR (1259–1261)*, 195; see Andrew de London.
1279/80, visited Michelmersh, WCL pipe roll acct.

Note: the above two monks are presumably relatives.

Simon de DYMARS
occ. 1282 occ. 1305

1282, 7 Aug., one of the monks who sought and recd absolution from excommunication incurred as a result of irregularities in the el. of Richard de la More as bp, *Reg. abp Pecham*, i, 188–189; the comm. for absolution is dated 10 Aug., *ib.*, ii, 51. See Adam de Farnham.
1305, 6 Aug., one of four monks who gave evidence to the bp's deputies concerning the proceedings of the el. of Nicholas de Tarente, q.v., as prior, *Reg. Woodlock*, 34.

A Richard Dymars of Wroughton [Worstone] was a priory tenant in 1259, and in 1261 × 1265 bailiff of the priory manor of Helbantone, [?Elingdon, Wroughton] *Winch. Cart.*, nos 207, 209.

EADWULF
see Edulfus

EASTGATE
see Estgate

John EDE [Edee, Eode
occ. 1410 occ. 1450

1410, 15 Feb., ord pr., Winchester cathedral, Reg. Beaufort, fo D^v^.
1409/10, one of five who celebrated their first mass, and the hordarian gave 6s. 6d., for their feast, Kitchin, *SS* no 57, 290.
1437/8, 1444/5, almoner, Kitchin, *SS* nos 39 and 40, pp. 442–448.
1437/8, 1444/5, pd visits to Hinton [Ampner], Kitchin, *SS* nos 39 and 40, pp. 444, 447.
1447, 15 Apr., 9th in order at the el. of a bp, *Reg. Common Seal*, no 316.
1450, 11 Dec., 5th at the el. of a prior, Reg. Waynflete, i, fo 31.

Stephen EDE
occ. 1461 occ. 1467

1461, 4 Apr., ord acol., Winchester cathedral, Reg. Waynflete, i, fo Y.
1463, 17 Dec., ord subdcn, Winchester cathedral, *ib.*, i, fo E*.
1464, 26 May, ord dcn, Winchester cathedral, *ib.*, i, fo F*.
1467, 23 May, ord pr., bp's chapel, Waltham, *ib.*, i, fo L*.

EDMUND
occ. [?1142 × 1143]

[1142 × 1143], subprior, *Winch. Cart.*, no 10, and *Eng. Epis. Acta*, viii, no 126.
[1142 × 1143], with Geoffrey III, prior, q.v., witness to an episcopal grant, *ib*, (both refs).

EDULFUS [Eadwulf
occ. 1106

1106, sacrist, *HRH*, 55.
1106, went to Malmesbury as abbot, *ib.*

John de EGGEBURY
occ. 1284

1284, 18/20 July, one of three monk proctors sent by the chapter to obtain from the bp licence to el. a prior, *Reg. Pontissara*, 285–286.

John ELPHEGE [Elfege, Ellfage
occ. 1520 occ. 1539

1520, 22 Dec., ord dcn, Lady chapel, Winchester cathedral, Reg. Fox, iv, fo 71.
1523, 21 Mar., ord pr., Lady chapel, Winchester cathedral, *ib.*, v, fo 31^v^.
1522/3, celebrated his first mass and recd a small gift from the almoner, WCL unnumbered obedientiary acct.
1524, 2 Dec., 26th in order at the el. of a prior, Reg. Fox, v, fo 75; he voted for John Avynton, q.v., 'propter eius probitatem et experientiam in temporalibus', *ib.*, v, fo 78.
[1528 × 1539], surname occ. in a list of monks copied on to a blank fo in Oxford, Bod. Ms Selden supra 76, fo 46^v^; no Christian names are given.
1539, 14 Nov., 14th named on the surrender list, among the 'commoners', and assigned a pension of £5 p.a., *L and P Henry VIII*, xiv, pt 2, no 520 (PRO E315/494).

William de ELY [?Elyngham
occ. 1363 d. 1411

1363, 28 Dec., granted *lit. dim* for minor orders, *Reg. Edington*, ii, no 936.
1365, 20 Sept., ord acol., bp's chapel, Sutton, *ib.*, ii, no 945.
1365, 15 Dec., granted *lit. dim*, for subdcn's orders, *ib.*, ii, no 947.
1368, 4 Mar., ord dcn, Winchester cathedral, *Reg. Wykeham*, i, 253.
1369, 22 Sept., ord pr., Winchester cathedral, *ib.*, i, 257.

1369/70, celebrated his first mass and the anniversarian contributed 6d. toward the feast, Worcester Cathedral Muniment, C.531.
1389, with the prior and other monks and laymen, accused of hunting in the bp's warrens, Oxford, New College Ms 9819.
1393, 21/22 Aug., 11th to sign the composition with bp Wykeham; BL Ms Harley 328, fo 24^{v}; see Robert de Rodebourne.
1400/1, spent two wks in the infirmary and the hordarian pd 12d. for his expenses, Kitchin, *SS* no 55, p. 283.
1404, 16 Oct., 6th in order at the el. of a prior, *Reg. Common Seal*, no 68.
1405/6, spent six wks in the infirmary at a charge of 3s. to the hordarian, *ib.*, Kitchin, *SS* no 56, p. 286.
1411, between Apr. and Sept. d., and the almoner distributed 10s. worth of bread among the poor on the day of his burial, *ib.*, *SS* no 35, p. 434.

I John ENFORD
occ. 1409/11

1409, 23 Mar., ord acol., Winchester cathedral, Reg. Beaufort, fo C^{v}.
1409, 21 Sept., ord subdcn, Winchester cathedral, *ib.*, fo D.
1410, 15 Feb., ord dcn, Winchester cathedral, *ib.*, fo D^{v}.
1411, 6 June, ord pr., Winchester cathedral, *ib.*, fo E^{v}.

II John ENFORD [Endforde, Enedforde
occ. 1444/5 occ. 1450

1444/5, celebrated his first mass and the almoner gave 8d. worth of wine [for the feast], Kitchin, *SS* no 40, p. 447.
1447, 15 Apr., 30th in order at the el. of a bp, *Reg. Common Seal*, no 316.
1450, 11 Dec., 26th at the el. of a prior, Reg. Waynflete, i, fo 30^{v}.

Nicholas de ENFORD [Enedford, Eneforde
occ. 1325 occ. 1338/9

1336/7, precentor, WCL Whitchurch acct.
1325, 9 Oct., 45th in order of seniority, *Reg. Pontissara*, 557.
1332, 17 May, attested an instrument containing charges vs prior Alexander [Heriard] q.v., *Winch. Cart.*, no 176.
1336/7, stopped at Whitchurch *versus ordines cum juvenibus*, WCL acct.
1338/9, visited Woolstone, PRO SC6/756/9.

Richard de ENFORD [Enedford, Eneford
occ. 1304/5 d. 1337

1309–1328, prior: el. after 18 June 1309, and the el. was confirmed 25 Aug., *Reg. Woodlock*, 369, 384–385; res. 25 June, 1328, Reg. Stratford, fo 107. *Fasti*, iv, 47, mistakenly gives the name as Robert.
1304/5, pd two visits to Stockton (Wilts.), WCL acct.
1305, 29 July, with Ralph de Calne, q.v., acted as proctor for the chapter in presenting the prior el., Nicholas de Tarente, q.v., to the bp, *Reg. Woodlock*, 33.
1306/9, pd visits to Chilbolton, WCL accts.
1310, before 25 Dec., invited by the bp to join him at Wolvesey for Christmas to help entertain his guests, *Reg. Woodlock*, 695–696.
1310, 21 July, 1316, 22 Mar., carried out specific commissions for the bp in the diocese, *ib.*, 479–80, 667.
1312, one of the cathedral priors summoned to London to meet the papal nuncios, *Councils and Synods*, ii, 1377.
1315, 9 June, in the bp's injunctions after visitation he was ordered not to show favouritism [*non sit acceptor personarum*] at times of recreation, nor to make use of the common seal without consultation, *Reg. Woodlock*, 750.
1327, 25 Mar., accused by the bp of negligence in failing to implement the corrections prescribed after his visitation, *Reg. Stratford*, fo 177^{v}.
1332, 29 Jan., recd royal pardon for accepting game taken by John de Fourde and Robert de Godeshulle, q.v., from Bere forest, *CPR (1330–1334)*, 251.
1334/5, was in rec. of a pension of £20 from the receiver who also provided him with £30 8s. 4d., *pro ferculis coquine*, Kitchin, *SS* no 62, p. 233. Dean Kitchin thought (ib.) that the sum pertaining to the kitchen suggests that he was acting as kitchener; this seems most unlikely, although £30 is a large amount for his personal needs and those of his servants.
1337, d. between Apr. and Sept., and the receiver pd the brief bearer 10s., 'quia nichil reperiebatur in custodia sua per quod fieri potuit', *ib.*, *SS* no 63, p. 247.

Walter ENFORD [Henford, Inford
occ. 1520 occ. c. 1528

1520, 22 Dec., ord dcn, Lady chapel, Winchester cathedral, Reg. Fox, iv, fo 71 (as Elford).
1523, 21 Mar., ord pr., Lady chapel, Winchester cathedral, *ib.*, v, fo 31^{v}.
1522/3, celebrated his first mass and recd a small gift from the almoner. WCL unnumbered obedientiary acct (as Henforde).
1524, 2 Dec., 24th in order at the el. of a prior, Reg. Fox, v, fo 75; he voted for Henry Broke, q.v., 'propter eius bonam vitam . . . et conscientiam', *ib.*, v, fo 78.
[1528 × 1539], surname occ. in a list of monks copied on to a blank fo in Oxford, Bod. Ms Selden supra 76, fo 46^{v}; no Christian names are given.

Note: see Walter Moryce who is possibly this monk.

Roger de ENTYNGHAM [Entingham, Entingeham

occ. 1295 occ. 1311/12

1308/9, 1311/12, Aug., hordarian, PRO SC6/756/3, Lambeth ED 68.

1311/12, subprior, first yr, Kitchin, *SS* no 18, p. 398; his apptment was prob. in Aug., 1312 as above.

1295, 6 June, acted as one of seven *compromissorii* in the el. of a prior, *Reg. Pontissara*, 73; he was named to announce their choice, *ib.*, 74–76.

1299, 16 May, as proctor of the prior and convent, was inducted as rector of Wotton, recently appropriated to the cathedral priory, *ib.*, 85; an *inspeximus* in *Reg. abp Morton*, i, no 252f repeats this induction.

1308/9, visited Woolstone where he held the court, PRO SC6/756/3.

1311/12, recd a gift of bread and wine from the almoner on his *creatio* as subprior, Kitchin, *SS* no 18, p. 398.

1312, 6 Jan., went to Reading because of a lawsuit, and his travelling expenses were 32s. 6d., Lambeth ED 68.

EODE

see Ede

John ERBURY [Erbery

occ. 1483

1483, 20 Dec., ord acol., Winchester cathedral, Reg. Waynflete, ii, fo 192ᵛ.

Godfrey de ESSEX [Exsex

occ. 1282

1282, 7 Aug., third prior, *Reg. abp Pecham*, i, 189.

1282, 7 Aug., one of the monks who sought and obtained absolution from excommunication incurred on acct of irregularities during their el. of Richard de la More as bp, *Reg. abp Pecham*, i, 188–189; the comm. for absolution is dated 10 Aug., *ib.*, ii, 50; see also Adam de Farnham.

John ESTGATE [Estyate *alias* Cobbe, ?Goble

occ. 1496 occ. 1539

1496, 24 Sept., ord subdcn, Hyde abbey, Reg. Langton, fo 29ᵛ.

1499, 21 Sept., ord dcn, Bishop's chapel, Marwell, *ib.*, fo 34ᵛ.

1524, 2 Dec., 1532/3, hordarian, Reg. Fox, v, fo 75, Kitchin, *SS* no 61, pp. 302–305.

1535, *custos operum*, *Valor Eccles.*, ii, 2.

1498, 23 Apr., 26th in order at the el. of a prior, Reg. Langton, fo 73ᵛ.

1501, 27 Feb., dcn, and 21st to be examined at the visitation (*sed. vac.* both Canterbury and Winchester) by the commissary of the prior of Christ Church, Canterbury; he reported *omnia bene*, Canterbury Reg. R, fo 115.

1524, 2 Dec., 7th in order at the el. of a prior, Reg. Fox, v, fo 75; he voted for John Meone II 'propter eius sapientiam et virtutes', *ib.*, v, fo 77ᵛ.

[1528 × 1539], surname occ. in a list of monks copied on to a blank fo in Oxford, Bod. Ms Selden supra 76, fo 46ᵛ; no Christian names are given.

1539, 14 Nov., 7th on the surrender list, among the seniors, and assigned a pension of £6 13s. 4d., p.a., *L and P Henry VIII*, xiv, pt 2, no 520 (as *alias* Goble) (PRO E315/494). The more likely variation Cobbe occ. in *L and P Henry VIII*, xvi, 719.

Thomas ESTON

occ. 1539

1539, 14 Nov., one of four pr. students at Oxford and assigned a pension of £10 p.a., PRO E315/494; see James Dorsett, Thomas Tistede, Peter Warham.

I John de EXETER

?occ. 1431

There are several copies of a brief chronicle to which this monk's name is attached:

Oxford, Bod. Ms Jones 4.

Oxford, All Souls College Ms 114.

Cambridge, Corpus Christi College Ms 110.

They contain a short history of the cathedral priory and its bps which ends at about 1429 with bp Beaufort in his prime. Although the date of composition is given as 1531, it seems surprising that the chronicle closes abruptly a century earlier; but the copyist may have been careless or may have inserted the date, misleadingly as it has turned out, of his own work.

Furthermore, the later John Exeter below was almost certainly too young and immature to have written the chronicle, as he had entered the monastery only about 1528; see Nicholas Godfrey, who was 22nd in order and immediately above him on the surrender list.

For a discussion of the possible attribution of some of the writings of Thomas Rudborne, q.v., to Exeter, see Gransden, *Hist. Writing*, ii, 395 n. 30.

II John EXETER [Excetor, Excett'

occ. 1539

[1528 × 1539], surname occ. in a list of monks copied on to a blank fo in Oxford, Bod. Ms Selden supra 76, fo 46ᵛ; no Christian names are given.

1539, 14 Nov., 23rd on the surrender list, numbered among the 'commoners', and assigned a pension of £5 p.a., *L and P Henry VIII*, xiv, pt 2, no 520 (PRO E315/494).

Note: there is a problem here, and I have suggested a solution by means of two monks with the same toponymic whose dates are separated by almost exactly a century; see John de Exeter I. See also John Carpenter.

EXSEX
see Essex

Thomas de EYNESTONE
occ. 1363

1363, 23 Sept., ord acol., Lydney, Reg. Lewis Charlton (Hereford), fo 41 (p. 86 in the printed reg).

Philip de FARHAM [?Farnham
occ. 1346/7

1346, 1 Dec., dcn, granted *lit. dim*, for pr.'s orders, *Reg. Edington*, ii, no 712.
1347, 24 Feb., ord pr., bp's chapel, Southwark, *ib.*, no 724.

Adam de FARNHAM
occ. 1279 occ. 1283

1279–1283, prior: apptd by the bp 1279, after 1 Mar., and possibly before 4 Apr.; last occ. 14 Dec. 1282, and prob. res. c. 13 Feb. 1283, *Fasti*, ii, 90–91.
1279/80, made the rounds of some of the manors including Crondall where he recd 102s. 11d., WCL pipe roll acct (as Adam).
1282, 31 July, was excommunicated with the subprior, William de Basyng I, q.v., and other monks because of irregularities in their el. of Richard de la More as bp, *Reg. abp Pecham*, i, 188; the comm. for absolution is dated 10 Aug., *ib.*, ii, 50.
n.d., 14 Dec., with the chapter sent a petition to the bp to come to their aid and relieve the miserable state of the priory, *Reg. Pontissara*, 240.
1283, 12 Jan., with other monks met the king and bp to discuss the reform of the convent, PRO E135/3/39b. See Nicholas de Merewell.
1283, 21 Jan./13 Feb., the bp apptd his treasurer to rec. Adam's resignation and ring of office and to confer the office and bestow the ring on the person he deemed most worthy, *ib.*, 245–246; see William de Basyng I. On 12 Jan. he had been summoned, with other monks, to meet with the king and bp concerning the reform of the house, PRO E135/3/39b.

W. de FARNHAM
occ. 1260/1 occ. 1266/7

1266/7, curtarian/cellarer, WCL Silkstead pipe roll acct.

1260/1, visited Alton, WCL acct.
1266/7, visited Silkstead, WCL pipe roll acct.

Walter FARNHULL [Farnhulle, Franhull
occ. 1361 occ. 1399

1361, 7 Apr., acol., granted *lit. dim*, for subdcn's orders, *Reg. Edington*, ii, no 916.
1362, 26 Feb., subdcn, granted *lit. dim*, for dcn's orders, *ib.*, ii, no 922.
1363, 28 May, ord dcn, bp's chapel, Highclere, *ib.*, ii, no 934.
1363, 28 Dec., granted *lit. dim* for orders of pr., *ib.*, ii, no 936.
1364, 9 Mar., ord pr., bp's chapel, South Waltham, *ib.*, ii, no 937.
1376/7, 1385/6, almoner, WCL Hinton Ampner acct, Kitchin, *SS* no 27, p. 414.
1389/90, named as former chamberlain, Kitchin, *SS* no 28, p. 418; the entry suggests that he was chamberlain before becoming almoner.
1391/3, anniversarian, WCL unnumbered obedientiary acct, Worcester Cathedral Muniment, C.535.
1376/7, pd several visits to Hinton Ampner 'pro manerio et stauro supervidendo' and charged the manorial acct 14s.; he also held courts there, WCL acct.
1386/7, stopped at Crondall on his way to and from London on 'negotiations' for the prior; the manorial acct recorded expenses of 2s. 3d., WCL acct.
1392/3, held court at Hinton Ampner and dined on fowl, WCL acct.
1393, 21/22 Aug., 7th to sign the composition with bp Wykeham, BL Ms Harley 328, fo 24^v; see Robert de Rodebourne.
1395/6, pd a visit to Chilbolton, WCL acct.
1399, 19 May, one of four monks and four seculars apptd proctors by the prior and chapter in lawsuits over their churches in Salisbury diocese, *Reg. Common Seal*, no 33.

John FARYNGDON [Faryngdone
occ. 1451 occ. 1455

1451, 24 Apr., ord acol. and subdcn, Winchester cathedral, Reg. Waynflete, i, fo C^v.
1451, 18 Dec., ord dcn, Winchester cathedral, *ib.*, i, fo E.
1455, 20 Sept., ord pr., bp's chapel, Wolvesey, *ib.*, i, fo K^v.

FELIX
d. by 1122/3

1122/3, name occ. in a mortuary roll of Savigny following that of Godfrey, prior, q.v., but not distinguished as a monk, Delisle, *Rouleaux des Morts*, 336.

John FETYPAS [Feteplace, Fetipase, Fetiplace, Fetteplace, Fetyplace
occ. 1474 occ. 1492

1474, 17 Dec., ord acol., Winchester cathedral, Reg. Waynflete, ii, fo 172v (as Ferplate).

1475, 18 Feb., ord subdcn, Winchester cathedral, *ib.*, ii, fo 173.
1477, 22 Mar., ord dcn, Romsey abbey, *ib.*, ii, fo 177.
1482, 6 Apr., ord pr., Mottisfont abbey, *ib.*, ii, fo 189.
1486, 7 Dec., chamberlain, *Reg. Common Seal*, no 434.
1492, 29 Oct., treasurer, *Reg. abp Morton*, ii, no 127.
1486, 7 Dec., 15th in order at the el. of a bp, *Reg. Common Seal*, no 434.
1490, with Richard Lacy, q.v., apptd proctor to act for the prior and chapter in defending their rights to the *sed. vac.* custody of spirituals in two of their parishes vs the abp of Canterbury, *ib.*, no 508.
1492, 29 Oct., 10th to be examined at the *sed. vac.* visitation, and deposed that the sacrist [Richard Auncell, q.v.] had not made an inventory of 'the goods of the church', *Reg. abp Morton*, ii, no 127.

FIGG
see Fygge

John FLOURE [Flour, Flower
occ. 1451 occ. 1492

1451, 24 Apr., ord acol., and subdcn, Winchester cathedral, Reg. Waynflete, i, fos C[v], D.
1451, 18 Dec., ord dcn, Winchester cathedral, *ib.*, i, fo E.
1452, 23 Sept., ord pr., bp's chapel, Waltham, *ib.*, i, fo F.
1486, 7 Dec., infirmarer, *Reg. Common Seal*, no 434.
1486, 7 Dec., 5th in order at the el. of a bp, *Reg. Common Seal*, no 434.
1492, 29 Oct., 4th to be examined at the *sed. vac.* visitation and stated his agreement with the subprior, William Silkstede, q.v., that all was in order, *Reg. abp Morton*, ii, no 127.

John le FOON [Foun
occ. 1310/11 occ. 1334/5

[1308/9, an ?R. Foun visited Chilbolton, WCL acct.]
1310/11, visited Chilbolton, WCL acct.
1325, 9 Oct., 19th in order of seniority, *Reg. Pontissara*, 556.
1334/5, with Richard de Foxham and John Turpyn, q.v., sent by the receiver to London with regard to a lawsuit between the bp [Orleton] and the adcn of Surrey, Kitchin, *SS* no 62, p. 242.

Richard de FORDE
occ. 1344

1344, 27 May, granted *lit. dim*, for orders, which were addressed to the bp of Bath and Wells, Reg. Orleton, i, fo 125[v].

Thomas de FORDE
occ. 1320/1

1320/1, receiver, with William de Wynhale, q.v., WCL Whitchurch acct.

FOUN
see Foon

Elias de FOURDE [or Helias
occ. 1320/1 occ. 1325

1321/2, receiver, WCL Wonston acct; he succ. Richard de Wollop, q.v.
1320/1, pd a visit to Whitchurch, WCL acct.
1321/2, visited Houghton with Richard de Wollop, q.v., collecting money from the sale of wool, WCL acct; he, and prob. they, also visited Wonston, WCL acct.
1325, 9 Oct., 43rd in order of seniority, *Reg. Pontissara*, 557.

John de FOURDE [Forde
occ. 1308 occ. 1352

1308, 21 Sept., ord dcn, Farnham, *Reg. Woodlock*, 814.
1332, 18 Oct.; 1334, 22 Mar., 16 Sept.; subprior, *Winch. Cart.*, no 180; Reg. Orleton, fo 1, *Winch. Cart.*, nos 258, 259.
1345, 22 July, almoner, *CPR (1343–1345)*, 526.
1352, 5 Feb., *ordinatus fuit* subprior, Oxford, Bod. Ms 767, fo ii.
1325, 5 Mar., apptd, with Alexander de Heriard, q.v., as proctor for the priory in a tithe dispute, *Winch. Cart.*, no 323; see below.
1325, 9 Oct., 29th in order of seniority, *Reg. Pontissara*, 556.
1328, 23 Jan., with Alexander de Heriard, q.v., acted as proctors for the prior and chapter in a tithe dispute, *Winch. Cart.*, no 323.
1332, 29 Jan., with Robert de Godeshulle, q.v., and others recd royal pardon for taking game in Bere forest, *CPR (1330–1334)*, 251.
1332, 18 Oct., present in the prior's chapel at the reading of ordinances, drawn up by the chapter following discussions about the debts of two of the obedientiary offices, which prescribed new financial arrangements to alleviate the crisis, *Winch. Cart.*, no 180; see Alexander de Heriard.
1334, 16 Sept., with a secular clerk, apptd by the prior and chapter as proctor for convocation, *ib.*, no 258; on the same day he and Nicholas de Haywode, q.v., were apptd to represent the prior and chapter in parliament meeting the same wk, *ib.*, no 259. The prior and chapter wrote, prob. on this same day to the abp for his help in several matters including the confirmation of the liberties of their church; and they sent the letter by him and Edmund de Bolesdon, q.v., *ib.*, no 255.
1344, 18 June, recd royal pardon for taking game in the New Forest, *CPR (1343–1345)*, 272.

1345, 22 July, with John de Stokebrugge II, q.v., as proctors, recd from the king licence to el. a bp, *CPR (1343–1345)*, 526.

1345, 29 July, with the prior [Alexander de Heriard, q.v.] ordered to appear in chancery on 2 Aug. to answer for their contempt in proceeding to el. John le Devenish, q.v., as bp vs the king's orders *CClR (1343–1346)*, 590. On 31 Aug. he was in prison in the Tower of London, *ib.*, 604, but was pardoned on 5 Nov., *CPR (1343–1345)*, 569.

Richard de FOXHAM [Foxam
occ. 1307/8 d. 1334/5

1307/9, 1310/11, pd visits to Chilbolton, WCL acct.

1325, 9 Oct., 20th in order of seniority, *Reg. Pontissara*, 556.

1326, 3 Feb., ill in the infirmary when the bp made his visitation, Reg. Stratford, fo 171v.

1332, 18 Oct., present in the prior's chapel at the reading of ordinances, drawn up by the chapter following discussions about the debts of two of the obedientiary offices, which prescribed new financial arrangements to alleviate the crisis, *Winch. Cart.*, no 180; see Alexander de Heriard.

1334/5, with John le Foon and John Turpyn, q.v., sent by the receiver to London with regard to a lawsuit between the bp [Orleton] and the adcn of Surrey, Kitchin, *SS* no 62, p. 242.

1334/5, d., and the receiver spent 20s. on bread for the poor on the day of his d., *ib.*, no 62, p. 232.

FRANHULL
see Farnhull

Thomas FROMUND [Fromond
occ. 1325 occ. 1337/8

1326, 15 Feb., ord acol. and subdcn, Winchester cathedral, Reg. Stratford, fo 143v.

1326, 20 Sept., ord dcn, Kingsclere, *ib.*, fo 144v.

1328, 19 Mar., ord pr., Crawley [Hants.], *ib.*, fo 148.

1325, 9 Oct., 56th (out of 64) in order of seniority, *Reg. Pontissara*, 557.

1332, 17 May, attested an instrument containing charges vs prior Alexander [Heriard], q.v., *Winch. Cart.*, no 176.

1337/8, visited Wootton, Kitchin, *Manydown*, 149.

A Richard Fromond occ. frequently as a witness to priory deeds between 1316 and 1341, *Winch. Cart.*, nos 278, 281, 338, 415, 465, 475, 482; in *ib.*, no 465 he is described as 'of Sparsholte' and may have been in the employ of the priory as the receiver gave him a gift of 20s. in 1334/5, Kitchin, *SS* no 62, p. 238. A later Fromond was steward of the manors of Winchester College, see *Reg. Common Seal*, no 153, n. 3.

Walter FROST [Froste *alias* Broke
occ. 1498 occ. 1539

1498, 10 Mar., ord acol., St Laurence's church, Winchester, Reg. Langton, fo 32.

1524, 2 Dec., curtarian, Reg. Fox, v, fo 75.

1532/3, *custos operum*, Kitchin, *SS* no 12, pp. 215–223.

1534/5, apptd third prior, BL Add. Roll 26872.

1539, 14 Nov., 'chaunter', i.e., precentor, *L and P Henry VIII*, xiv, pt 2, no 520 (PRO E315/494).

1501, 27 Feb., subdcn and 26th to be examined at the visitation (*sed. vac.*, both Canterbury and Winchester) by the commissary of the prior of Christ Church, Canterbury; he reported *omnia bene*, Canterbury Reg. R, fo 115.

1524, 2 Dec., 11th in order at the el. of a prior, Reg. Fox, v, fo 75; he voted for Henry Broke, *ib.*, v, fo 77v.

[1528 × 1539], surname occ. in a list of monks copied on to a blank fo in Oxford, Bod. Ms Selden supra 76, fo 46v; no Christian names are given.

1529, was bequeathed property by his cousin Walter Froste of West Ham, London, Kitchin, *Obed. Rolls*, 215, n. 1.

1534/5, recd a gift of 8d. from the anniversarian on his apptment as third prior, BL Add. Roll 26872, and visited Bishopstone [Bushton, Wilts.] to hold courts and supervise the manor.

1539, 14 Nov., 5th among the seniors on the surrender list and assigned a pension of £10 p.a., *L and P Henry VIII*, xiv, pt 2, no 520 (PRO E315/494).

A William Froste, acc. to Kitchin (*Obed. Rolls*, 215, n. 1) was steward to bp Fox and involved with the new work on the choir screen; see also the ref. to his cousin above.

Gilbert de FROYLE
occ. 1266/7 occ. 1276

1276, ?May, apptd subprior by the bp in place of Alexander I, q.v., whom the bp had removed, *Ann. Winton.*, 123.

1266/7, visited Littleton, Patney and prob. Sutton with Henry Aurifaber, q.v., WCL pipe roll acct.

Note: see also G.[?ilbert]

Thomas FYGGE [Figg
occ. 1528 occ. 1541

c. 1509, born, Archivo General de Simancas, Estado 593.

1528, 11 Apr., one of six not yet prof., but ord exorcist and acol., Lady chapel, Winchester cathedral,, Reg. Fox, v, fo 38–38v.

1541, 28 Apr., although his name does not occ. as Fygge on the surrender list of 1539, he remained to become one of the twelve petty canons employed to sing, Kitchin and Madge, *Documents*, 55.

According to a deposition made on 3 Sept. 1585 in the cathedral at Bruges he had recd his education in the priory at Winchester before being prof. as a monk there. He had served as one of three custodians of the relics before the dissolution but fled to the continent after the d. of Queen Mary, and eventually joined the Benedictine community of St Andrew in Bruges; see P. Bogan, 'Dom Thomas Figg and the Foot of St Philip', *Winch. Cath. Record*, no 61 (1992), 22–26.
Note: it may be that this is Thomas Eston, q.v., but we cannot rule out Thomas Alton, q.v.

W. de FYNDON
occ. 1328/9

1328/9, sent by the prior and chapter, with Geoffrey de Guldeford, q.v., as proctor to the Black Monk Chapter at Abingdon (which assembled on 31 Mar. 1329, Pantin, *BMC*, i, 207); they stopped at Wonston and enjoyed a capon, WCL acct.

G.[?ilbert
occ. 1266/7 occ. 1272/3

1266/7, precentor, pipe roll acct, prob. under Littleton; see Henry Aurifaber.
1269/70, precentor, WCL Hurstbourne acct.
1269/70, 1272/3, hordarian, WCL Hurstbourne acct.
1266/7, visited Whitchurch borough, WCL pipe roll acct; also Chilbolton, (as Gilbert), WCL pipe roll acct.
1269/70, pd two visits to Hurstbourne, WCL acct.
1272/3, stopped at Hurstbourne, WCL acct.

Note: see Gilbert de Froyle

Thomas GARDINER [Gardener, Gardinar, Gardyner
occ. 1455 occ. 1492

1455, 20 Sept., ord acol., bp's chapel, Wolvesey, Reg. Waynflete, ii, fo Kv.
1456, 18 Sept., ord subdcn, bp's chapel, Wolvesey, *ib.*, ii, fo M.
1459, 17 Feb., ord dcn, Winchester cathedral, *ib.*, fo Rv.
1462, 18 Dec., ord pr., Winchester cathedral, *ib.*, fo C*.

1486, 7 Dec., gardener, *Reg. Common Seal*, no 434.

1486, 7 Dec., 6th in order at the el. of a bp, *Reg. Common Seal*, no 434.

1492, 29 Oct., 5th to be examined at the *sed. vac.* visitation. He agreed with others that there should be an inventory of the ornaments and other church goods to prevent further losses of valuables and also reported that the prior [Thomas Hunton, q.v.] kept in his own hands the offices of almoner, anniversarian and third prior, *Reg. abp Morton*, ii, no 127; see also John Chichestre, John Dorsett and John Fetypas.

I GEOFFREY [Gaufridus (Prior I)
occ. 1107 occ. 1111

1107–1111, prior: succ. Godfrey, q.v. in 1107; deposed by the bp 1111 and became abbot of Burton in 1114, *Fasti*, ii, 88, *HRH*, 31, 80.

II GEOFFREY [Gaufridus (Prior II)
occ. 1111 d. 1126

1111–1126, prior: succ. Geoffrey I, q.v., apptd by the bp with the monks' assent; d. 1126, *Fasti*, ii, 88.

1111, before being made prior, hordarian, *Ann. Winton.*, 43.

III GEOFFREY (Prior III)
occ. 1139 × 1153

1139 × 1153, prior: occ. as prior in *Winch. Cart.*, nos 5 (1139 × 1153), 10 (1142 × 1147); see *Fasti*, ii, 88, *HRH*, 80; see also *Eng. Epis. Acta*, viii, nos 24, 44, 54, 125, 126.
Note: he prob. succ. Robert I, q.v. after 1130.

[?1144 × 1148], recd a letter from Gilbert Foliot, abbot of Gloucester, with regard to support for a relative, *Foliot Letters*, no 30.

I GERALD [d'Avranches
occ. before 1086 occ. after 1109

1086, apptd abbot of Cranborne, and in 1102 abbot of Tewkesbury, *Ann. Winton.*, 34, *HRH*, 87, 73.
1109, returned to Winchester, 'regis animum nolens nec valens saturare muneribus', *Ann. Winton.*, 43.

Note: he was thought to have been the son of Reginald de Breone, a Norman, and to have come to England when he became chaplain to Earl Hugh of Chester, Orderic, *Eccles. Hist.*, iii, 216–217; acc. to Orderic he became ill at Winchester while on his way to become a monk at Saint-Évroul, and when death seemed imminent took the habit at the Old Minster, *ib*, iii, 226–227.

II GERALD [Giraldus
occ. [1142 × 1143]

[1142 × 1143], witness, with prior Geoffrey III, q.v., to a grant of bp Henry de Blois to the prior and chapter, *Winch. Cart.*, no 10, *Eng. Epis. Acta*, viii, no 126.

GERMANUS
occ. [1205]

[1205], 15 Oct., appeared as witness in Rome to the confirmation of an episcopal grant, *Eng. Epis. Acta*, ix, no 81; he was prob. one of the election committee sent by the monks on behalf of the bp el., Peter des Roches. See also John Bertonarius I and Walter III.

GERVASE
occ. [1205 × 1238]

[1205 × 1238], *temp.* bp des Roches, made his monastic prof. 'in presentia domini Petri episcopi', *Eng. Epis. Acta*, ix, liv, n. 4 (from Cambridge, Gonville and Caius College Ms 123/60 (Formulary) fo 96v).

I GILBERT
d. c. 1113

Name occ. on a mortuary roll of Matilda, abbess of Caen, following that of Godfrey, prior, q.v., but not named as a monk, Delisle, *Rouleaux des Morts*, 186.

II GILBERT
occ 1266/7

1266/7, with H.I, q.v., visited Chilbolton for *liberatio denariorum*, WCL pipe roll acct.

Note: see G. and Gilbert de Froyle

Arnold GILBERT [Arnulf Gilbard, Gilberd, Gylbart, Glybert
occ. 1489 occ. 1501/2

1489, 14 Mar., ord acol. and subdcn, Winchester cathedral, Reg. Courtenay, fo 14.
1489, 4 Apr., ord dcn, Winchester cathedral, *ib.*, fo 15.

1497/Mar. 1498, curtarian/cellarer; Kitchin, *SS* no 10, pp. 386–389; see Walter Wode, cellarer.
1499/1502, chamberlain, WCL Ham acct; 1501, 27 Feb., chamberlain, Canterbury Reg. R, fo 115.

1492, 29 Oct., 25th to be examined at the *sed. vac.* visitation but made no deposition, *Reg. abp Morton*, ii, no 127.
1498, 23 Apr., 18th in order at the el. of a prior, Reg. Langton, fo 73v.
1501, 27 Feb., 14th to be examined at the visitation (*sed.vac.* both Canterbury and Winchester) by the commissary of the prior of Christ Church, Canterbury; he deposed that every sick monk in the infirmary recd 2d. every day from the bequest of William Talmach, q.v., former hordarian, and that this was in addition to the usual allowance, Canterbury Reg. R, fo 115.

William GILERS [Gylers, Julers/de Nydecgen
occ. 1377 occ. 1390

1377, 19 Dec., ord acol., bp's chapel, Farnham castle, *Reg. Wykeham*, i, 285.
1378, 13 Mar., ord subdcn, Winchester cathedral, *ib.*, 287.
1388, 19 Dec., ord dcn, bp's chapel, Farnham castle, *ib.*, 318.
1389, 13 Mar., ord pr., bp's chapel, Farnham castle, *ib.*, 319.

1390, 30 Nov., apptd papal chaplain, *registrata gratis*, and described as kinsman of the dukes of Gueldres (Gelrie), Juliers and Berg (Montensis), *CPL*, iv (1362–1404), 281.

There are two refs to Elizabeth Juliers, Countess of Kent, dated 1369 and 1377 in *Reg. Wykeham*, ii, 100, 273.

GILFORDE
see Guldeford

John de GLASTYNGBURY
occ. 1347/9

1347, 22 Sept., ord acol., South Waltham, *Reg. Edington*, ii, no 737.
1348, 2 June, granted *lit. dim* for subdcn's orders, *ib.*, ii, no 742.
1349, 7 Mar., ord subdcn, Cobham, *ib.*, no 770.

William GLUAIS
occ. 1283

1283, 25 Oct., previously cellarer but d. by this date and replaced by John de Northwolde, q.v., *Reg. Pontissara*, 9; see also Geoffrey de Meone.

GLYBERT
see Gilbert

GOBLE
see Estgate

Robert de GODESHULLE
occ. 1311/12 occ. 1325

[1311/12], Aug., kitchener, Lambeth ED 68.

1325, 9 Oct., 13th in order of seniority, *Reg. Pontissara*, 556.

Note: see Robert le Brode

I GODFREY [Godefridus de Cambrai
occ. 1082 d. 1107

1082–1107, prior: succ. 1082; d. 1107, *HRH*, 80, *Fasti*, ii, 88.

1096, before 27 Dec., consulted by bp Walkelin concerning the el. of Malchus, q.v., as bp of Waterford, *Anselm Letters*, iv, no 203.

Name entered on the mortuary roll of Matilda, abbess of Caen, dated c. 1113 and on that of Savigny dated 1122/3, Delisle, *Rouleaux des Morts*, 186, 336.

Author of Epigrammatica, Epigrammatica Historica and Epigrammatica Miscellanea printed in Wright, *Satirical Poets*, ii, 103–162. For further refs. and commentary on his writings, see *DNB*. See also Sharpe, *Latin Writers*.

He may also be the author of a poem in praise of bp Wulstan of Worcester; it has been printed in J. Stevenson, ed., *Scalachronica*, Maitland Club, Edinburgh, 1836. See also Hardy, *Catalogue* ii, no 106.

II GODFREY
occ. [before 1107]

[1107, before], sacrist, named in a grant of bp Giffard, *temp.* prior Hugh, q.v., *Eng. Epis. Acta*, viii, no 19.

J. GODFREY [Godefridus
occ. 1269/70

1269/70, visited Hurstbourne with William de la Brome, q.v., WCL acct.

Nicholas GODFREY [Godefrey
occ. 1528 occ. 1539

1528, 11 Apr., one of six not yet prof. but ord exorcist and acol., Lady chapel, Winchester cathedral, Reg. Fox, v, fo 38–38v.

[1528 × 1539], surname occ. in a list of monks copied on to a blank fo in Oxford, Bod. Ms Selden supra 76, fo 46v; no Christian names are given.

1539, 14 Nov., 22nd in order, among the 'commoners' on the surrender list, with an annual pension of £5 assigned, *L and P Henry VIII*, xiv, pt 2, no 520 (PRO E315/494).

GODRIC [Godericus
occ. before 1082

1082, accompanied prior Simeon, q.v., when the latter went to Ely as abbot; he was described as *vir magne sanctitatis*, *Lib. Elien.*, 208–209.

William GOLDWELL [Goldewell
occ. 1524 occ. 1539

1534/5, fourth prior, first yr, BL Add. Charter 26872.

1524, 2 Dec., subdcn and 29th in order at the el. of a prior, Reg. Fox, v, fo 75v; he voted for Henry Broke, q.v., 'propter eius bonam Religionem et doctrinam', *ib.*, v, fo 78.

[1528 × 1539], surname occ. in a list of monks copied on to a blank fo in Oxford, Bod. Ms Selden supra 76, fo 46v; no Christian names are given.

1534/5, recd an 8d. gift from the anniversarian on his *electio* and *creatio* as fourth prior, BL Add. Roll 26872.

1539, 14 Nov., 16th in order, among the 'commoners', on the surrender list with an annual pension of £5 assigned, *L and P Henry VIII*, xiv, pt 2, no 520 (PRO E315/494).

Roger de GORLIE
occ. [c. 1295]

[c. 1295], an insert in bp Pontissara's register referring to the management of the priory manors recommends that the stock [*instaurum*] be kept or sold in accordance with the *visum* of Roger, who was authorized by the bp to remain in charge as before, *Reg. Pontissara*, 529–530.

GOZELINUS
d. by 1122/3

1122/3, name occ. in a mortuary roll of Savigny following that of Godfrey, prior, q.v., but not distinguished as a monk, Delisle, *Rouleaux des Morts*, 336.

Note: it is presumably this monk who also occ. on the same mortuary roll among the Ely monks, *ib.*, 339, where the name is written with a thorn, i.e., Godthinus. See under Ely.

William GRENE
occ. 1476 occ. 1482

1476, 9 Mar., ord acol., Winchester cathedral, Reg. Waynflete, ii, fo 175v.

1478, 19 Sept., ord subdcn, Winchester cathedral, *ib.*, ii, fo 181v.

1479, 6 Mar., ord dcn, Winchester cathedral, *ib.*, ii, fo 182v.

1482, 1 June, ord pr., Winchester cathedral, *ib.*, ii, fo 189v.

Nicholas de GRENHAM
occ. 1269/70 occ. 1282/3

[1259, Apr., a Nicholas de Grenham, clerk, witnessed a grant made by the prior and convent, *Winch. Cart.*, no 207.]

1269/70, with Adam de Morton, q.v., visited Wonston for *liberatio denariorum*, WCL acct.

1270/1, visited Houghton and Patney for the same purpose, WCL accts.

1271/2, visited Whitchurch to rec. *recognitio* (in wax) and *liberatio*, WCL borough acct.

1272/3, pd a visit to Little Hinton [Hiniton] for *liberatio denariorum*, WCL acct.

1281/2, visited Whitchurch borough for *liberatio denariorum*, and Hurstbourne for the same purpose; he also visited Chilbolton, WCL pipe roll acct.

1282/3, with Geoffrey de Meone, q.v., visited Whitchurch for *liberatio denariorum*, WCL pipe roll acct.

Note: it seems reasonably safe to assume that we have here an example of a young clerk, prob. in the employ of the priory, who decided to enter the monastery and who later may have been apptd to the office of receiver, or as an assistant to the receiver.

Geoffrey de GULDEFORD [Guldeforde
occ. 1308/9 occ. 1341/2

1332, 18 Oct., hostiller, *Winch. Cart.*, no 180.

1338/9, 1341/2, hordarian; he prob. succ. William de Camel, q.v., Woolstone accts, PRO SC6/756/9, 10.

1308/9, 1310/11, visited Chilbolton, WCL acct.
1325, 9 Oct., 25th in order of seniority, *Reg. Pontissara*, 556.
1328/9, sent by the prior and chapter, with W. de Fyndon, q.v., as proctor to the Black Monk Chapter at Abingdon (which assembled on 31 Mar. 1329, Pantin, *BMC*, i, 207); they stopped at Wonston and enjoyed a capon, WCL acct.
1332, 18 Oct., present in the prior's chapel at the reading of ordinances, drawn up by the chapter following discussions about the debts of two of the obedientiary offices, which prescribed new financial arrangements to alleviate the crisis, *Winch. Cart.*, no 180; see Alexander de Heriard.
1336/7, named on the receiver's acct with another as responsible for collecting a biennial tenth, Kitchin, *SS* no 63, p. 245.
1337/8, visited Wootton, Kitchin, *Manydown*, 149.
1338/9, 1341/2, visited Woolstone, PRO SC6/756/9, 10.

I John de GULDEFORD
occ. 1347 occ. 1362

1347, 22 Sept., ord acol., South Waltham, *Reg. Edington*, ii, no 737.
1349, 19 Sept., ord pr., bp's chapel, [Bishops] Waltham, *ib.*, ii, no 789.
1362, 17 Jan., succ Richard de Merewell I, q.v., as proctor for the chapter in the proceedings following the el. of William de Thudden', q.v., as prior, when there were objections raised in a process before the bp, *Reg. Edington*, i, no 1490.

Note: a John de Guldeford wrote [*scripsit*] the Custumal, WCL Winchester Custumal, fo 11^{v}.

II John GULDEFORD [Gilforde, Guldeforde, Gylford
occ. 1520 occ. 1539

1520, 22 Dec., ord dcn, Lady chapel, Winchester cathedral, Reg. Fox, iv, fo 71.
1523, 21 Mar., ord pr., Lady chapel, Winchester cathedral, *ib.*, v, fo 31^{v}.
1522/3, celebrated his first mass and recd a small gift from the almoner, WCL unnumbered obedientiary acct.

1534/6, anniversarian (1534/5 was his first yr), BL Add. Roll 26872 (Bussheton in margin), WCL unnumbered obedientiary acct.

1524, 2 Dec., 23rd in order at the el. of a prior, Reg. Fox, v, fo 75; he nom. Henry Broke 'propter eius sapientiam et experientiam in spiritualibus et temporalibus', *ib.*, v, fo 77^{v}–78.
1534/5, rode to Bisshopiston (Bushton, Wilts.) to hold court and *pro manerio et boscis supervidend'*, BL Add. Roll, 26872.
1539, 14 Nov., one of four described as 'late religious' on the surrender list and the only one of the four who was prof., PRO E315/494.

Note: see John Carpenter who may be this monk.

Richard GULDEFORD [Guldford
occ. 1447 occ. 1450

1447, 15 Apr., 25th in order at the el. of a bp, *Reg. Common Seal*, no 316.
1450, 11 Dec., pr., and 21st at the el. of a prior, *Reg. Waynflete*, i, fo 30^{v}.

Robert de GULDEFORD
occ. 1309 occ. 1318/19

1309, 18 June, with William de Romeseye, q.v., sent by the chapter as proctor to request from the bp licence to el. a prior, *Reg. Woodlock*, 369.
1308/9, 1310/11, visited Chilbolton, WCL accts.
1318/19, d., and the almoner spent 13s. 4d., for bread to distribute among the poor on the day of his burial, Kitchin, *SS* no 25, p. 406.

Thomas GYAN
occ. 1477 occ. 1501

1477, 1 Mar., ord acol., Winchester cathedral, Reg. Waynflete, ii, fo 177.
1478, 19 Sept., ord subdcn, Winchester cathedral, *ib.*, ii, fo 181^{v}.
1479, 18 Dec., ord dcn, Winchester cathedral, *ib.*, ii, fo 184.
1483, 20 Dec., ord pr., Winchester cathedral, *ib.*, ii, fo 193.

c. 1495/6, 1498, 23 Apr., almoner, WCL Hinton Ampner acct, Reg. Langton, fo 73^{v}.
1501, 27 Feb., hordarian, Canterbury Reg. R, fo 114^{v}.

1486, 7 Dec., 20th in order at the el. of a bp, *Reg. Common Seal*, no 434.
c. 1495/6, visited Hinton Ampner, WCL acct.
1497, 3 Aug., one of four monks, who with two others, were apptd to act for the prior and convent as proctors in their dispute with the abp of Canterbury, *Reg. abp Morton*, i, no 248.
1498, 23 Apr., 8th in order at the el. of a prior, Reg. Langton, fo 73^{v}.
1501, 27 Feb., 7th to be examined at the visitation (*sed. vac.* both Canterbury and Winchester) by the commissary of the prior of Christ Church, Canterbury, he reported that there ought to be 40 monks but there had only been 35 of late, Canterbury Reg. R, fo 114^{v}.

A Thomas Gyan was treasurer of Wolvesey in the 1460's and 1470's, *Reg. Common Seal*, no 360 and V. Davis, 'William Waynflete', 403 and *passim.*

GYLBART
see Gilbert

GYLERS
see Gilers

GYLFORD
see Guldeford

John GYS
occ. 1280/1

1280/1, Dec. to Sept., receiver, Watkin, 'Rec. Acct', 105.

1281, 13/19 July, with Philip de Avinton, John de Ichulle and Peter Mareschall, q.v., spent six days in London at a cost of 15s. 9 1/2d., Watkin, 'Rec. Acct', 100.

I H.
occ. 1266/7

1266/7, visited Chilbolton with Gilbert II, q.v, for *liberatio denariorum*, WCL pipe roll acct.

II H.
occ. 1357/8

1357/8, receiver, WCL Barton, beadle's acct.

Robert de HAKEBORNE
occ. 1292

1292, 23 Sept., with the prior [William de Basyng I] and Edmund de Winchester, q.v., present in the chapter house at Salisbury for the ordination of the vicarage of Enford, Winchester College Muniment, 8182.

Thomas HALL
occ. 1498 [occ. ?1506]

1498, 14 Apr., ord dcn, Winchester cathedral, Reg. Langton, fo 32^{v}.

1498, 23 Apr., 24th in order at the el. of a prior, Reg. Langton, fo 73^{v}.

[1506, 3 Feb., a Benedictine by this name was B.Th., on this date and supplicated for D.Th.; see *BRUO*].

Nicholas de HAM [Hame, Hamme
occ. 1272/3 occ. 1305

1279/80, 1282, 7 Aug., subprior, WCL Michelmersh acct, *Reg. abp Pecham*, i, 188–90; see also *Winch. Cart.*, no 141.

1272/3, visited Chilbolton, WCL acct.

1279/80, pd a visit to Hurstbourne, Sutton and Michelmersh, WCL pipe roll acct.

1280, 18 Feb., with Geoffrey le Noreys and Philip de Oxonia, q.v., recd a royal licence to el. a bp, *CPR (1272–1281)*, 363.

1282, 7 Aug., with other monks sought and obtained absolution from excommunication incurred because of irregularities in their el. of Richard de la More as bp, *Reg. abp Pecham*, i, 188–189; the comm. for absolution is dated 10 Aug., *ib.*, ii, 50; see also Adam de Farnham.

1305, 1 Apr., named as a penitentiary in the diocese empowered to substitute for Philip de Avinton, q.v., when necessary, *Reg. Woodlock*, 7.

[W. de HAMELETON
occ. 1279/80

1279/80, pd a visit to Hurstbourne, WCL pipe roll acct.

Note: this may not be a monk]

Fochus HAMPTON [Focus Hamptone
occ. 1501 d. 1513/14

1501, 27 Feb., 30th and last to be examined at the visitation (*sed. vac.* both Canterbury and Winchester) by the commissary of the prior of Christ Church, Canterbury; he stated that he was 18 yrs old, had been prof. for about three wks and had not yet been tonsured, but otherwise all was well, Canterbury Reg. R, fo 115.

1513/4, d., and the almoner spent 10s. on bread for the poor on the day of his burial, Kitchin, *SS* no 44, p. 460 (acct for 1514/15).

John HAMPTON [Hamptone
occ. 1451 d. 1472

1451, 18 Dec., ord acol., Winchester cathedral, Reg. Waynflete, i, fo D^{v}.

1453, 22 Sept., ord subdcn, Winchester cathedral, *ib.*, i, fo G.

1455, 20 Sept., ord dcn, bp's chapel, Wolvesey, *ib.*, i, fo K^{v}.

1457, 2 Mar., granted *lit. dim*, for pr.'s orders, *ib.*, i, fo M^{v}.

n.d., prob. student at Oxford, residing at Canterbury College, Pantin, *Cant. Coll. Ox.*, iv, 150; there were two unnamed students at Oxford in 1459/60, Kitchin, *SS* no 65, p. 450. See below.

1472, 26 Jan., with the prior attended convocation, Reg. Waynflete, ii, fo 150^{v}.

n.d., gave an alabaster image of our Lady to Canterbury College, Oxford, which first appears in a 1501 college inventory, Pantin, *Cant. Coll. Ox.*, i, 28, 55.

1472, d., and the almoner spent 10s. on bread for distribution to the poor on the day of his burial, Kitchin, *SS* no 42, p. 453.

Richard HAMPTON
occ. 1405 occ. 1450

1405, 19 Dec., ord acol., Winchester cathedral, Reg. Beaufort, fo A.

1409, 23 Mar., ord dcn, Winchester cathedral, *ib.*, fo C^{v}.

1410, 19 Dec., ord pr., Winchester cathedral, *ib.*, fo E.

1447, 15 Apr., 1450, 11 Dec., precentor, *Reg. Common Seal*, no 316, Reg. Waynflete, i, fo 30^{v}.

1447, 15 Apr., 9th in order at the el. of a bp, *Reg. Common Seal*, no 316.

1450, 11 Dec., 6th in order at the el. of a prior, Reg. Waynflete, i, fo 30^{v}; he was named by the chapter as one of seven *compromissorii*, *ib.*, i, fo 32.

HARDING
d. c. 1113

Name occ. on a mortuary roll of Matilda, abbess of Caen following that of Godfrey, prior, q.v., although not distinguished as a monk, Delisle, *Rouleaux des Morts*, 186; also on a similar roll of Savigny dated 1122/3, p. 336.

John de HAREWELL
occ. 1255

1255, 3 Jan., named with William de Kingate and Philip de Osna, q.v., as proctors for the prior and chapter in connection with the contraction of a loan, *CPL*, i (1198–1304), 309.

Henry de HARWEDON [Harwedone
occ. 1339/40 occ. 1361

1339/40, visited Crondall, WCL acct.

1361, 9/10 Dec., with Richard de Merewell II, q.v., and others, called upon as a witness to the proceedings of the el. of William de Thudden, q.v., as prior; they declared that his el. had been unopposed, contrary to the allegations of others, *Reg. Edington*, i, no 1490.

Note: a William de Harewedone was the treasurer of Wolvesey (bpric) in 1327/8, HRO 11M59/B1/81 (pipe roll).

Simon de HASELDENE [Hasuldene
occ. 1372 d. 1393/4

1372, 18 Sept., ord acol., Winchester cathedral, *Reg. Wykeham*, i, 268.

1373, 12 Mar., ord subdcn, Winchester cathedral, *ib.*, i, 269.

1373, 11 June, ord dcn, bp's chapel, Marwell, *ib.*, i, 271.

1373, 24 Sept., ord pr., bp's chapel, Farnham castle, *ib.*, i, 272.

1393, 21/22 Aug., chamberlain, BL Ms Harley 328, fo 24^{v}.

1393, 21/22 Aug., 20th to sign the composition with bp Wykeham, BL Ms Harley 328, fo 24^{v}; see Robert de Rodebourne.

1393/4, d. and the chamberlain's acct records the receipt of 3d., WCL unnumbered fragment of an obedientiary acct.

John de HASELWODE [Hasilwode
occ. 1362 occ. 1365

1362, 26 Feb., recd first tonsure at Hursley and *lit. dim.*, for minor orders, *Reg. Edington*, ii, no 922 (ms fo QQ).

1363, 1 Jan., ord acol., bp's chapel, Farnham castle, ib, ii, no 933.

1363, 28 May, ord subdcn, bp's chapel, Highclere, *ib.*, ii, no 934.

1363, 28 Dec., granted *lit. dim*, for dcn's and pr.'s orders, *ib.*, ii, no 936.

1364, 9 Mar., ord dcn, bp's chapel, South Waltham, *ib.*, ii, no 937.

1365, 15 Dec., granted *lit. dim*, for pr.'s orders, *ib.*, ii, no 947.

John HAYCROFT [Hethcroft, Heycroft, Meycroft
occ. 1498 occ. 1539

1498, 10 Mar., ord acol., St Laurence's church, Winchester Reg. Langton, fo 32 (as Hethcroft).

1524, 2 Dec., hostiller, Reg. Fox, v, fo 75.

1535, gardener, *Valor Eccles*, ii, 3.

1524, 2 Dec., 10th in order at the el. of a prior, Reg. Fox, v, fo 75; he voted for Henry Broke' propter eius scientiam et bonam vitam', *ib.*, v, fo 77^{v}.

[1528 × 1539], surname occ. in a list of monks copied on to a blank fo in Oxford, Bod. Ms Selden supra 76, fo 46^{v} (as Meycroft); no Christian names are given.

1539, 14 Nov., assigned a pension of £6 p.a., *L and P Henry VIII* xiv, pt 2, no 520; the original in the PRO gives the name Hultofte and he comes 13th in order and last among the seniors, PRO E315/494.

Note: The variations in this name are unusually diverse, but there is a high degree of certainty that they all ref. to the same monk, who was ordained with Walter Frost and John Morton, q.v.

HAYNO(U)
see Heynow

John de HAYWOODE
occ. 1363 occ. 1400/1

1363, 28 Dec., granted *lit. dim*, for minor orders, *Reg. Edington*, ii, no 936.

1365, 15 Dec., granted *lit. dim*, for the order of subdcn, *ib.*, ii, no 947.

1366, 28 Feb., ord subdcn, St Elizabeth's chapel, near Winchester, *ib.*, ii, no 949.

1368, 4 Mar., ord dcn, Winchester cathedral, *Reg. Wykeham*, i, 253.

1369, 22 Sept., ord pr., Winchester cathedral, *ib.*, i, 257.

1369/70, celebrated his first mass and the anniversarian gave a gift of 6d., Worcester Cathedral Muniment, C.531.

1393, 21/22 Aug., senior chaplain [to the prior], BL Ms Harley 328, fo 24.

1393, 21/22 Aug., 10th to sign the composition with bp Wykeham, BL Ms Harley 328, fo 24; see Robert de Rodebourne.

1400/1, ill in the infirmary for 32 wks and the hordarian charged his acct 16s., Kitchin, *SS* no 55, p. 283.

I Nicholas de HAYWODE
occ. 1325 occ. 1359

1326, 15 Feb., ord acol. and subdcn, Winchester cathedral, Reg. Stratford, fo 143^{v}.

1326, 20 Sept., ord dcn, Kingsclere, *ib.*, fo 144v.
1328, 19 Mar., ord pr., Crawley [Hants.], *ib.*, fo 148.
1332, 18 Oct., chaplain to the prior, *Winch. Cart.*, no 180.
1337, May/Sept., receiver, Kitchin, *SS* no 63, 244–253; he followed and was succ. by John de Merlawe I, q.v.
1351/2, 1353/5, c. 1356, 1358/9, hordarian, PRO SC6/756/12–14, *Winch. Cart.*, no 356, PRO SC6/756/16; see Roger Marmyon.
1325, 9 Oct., 57th (out of 64) in order of seniority, *Reg. Pontissara*, 557.
1332, 31 May, witnessed the prior's apptment of proctors to be sent to the curia, *Winch. Cart.*, no 177; see William de Basyng II.
1332, 18 Oct., present in the prior's chapel at the reading of ordinances, drawn up by the chapter following discussions about the debts of two of the obedientiary offices, which prescribed new financial arrangements to alleviate the crisis, *Winch. Cart.*, no 180; see Alexander de Heriard.
1334, 16 Sept., with John de Fourde, q.v., apptd by the prior and chapter as proctor in parliament, *Winch. Cart.*, no 259.
1336/7, visited Whitchurch, WCL acct.
1337/8, visited Wootton and Chilbolton and was sent to the bp at Highclere, Kitchin, *Manydown*, 149, WCL acct, Kitchin, *Manydown*, *ib.*
1351/2, pd visits to Woolstone, PRO SC6/756/12.
[?c. 1356], wrote to the bp in response to the latter's letter requesting him, as hordarian, to arrange a certain lease; he replied that he would have to consult the prior and chapter before taking any action, *Winch. Cart.*, no 356.

II Nicholas de HAYWODE
occ. 1377 occ. 1393

1377, 19 Dec., ord acol., bp's chapel, Farnham castle, *Reg. Wykeham*, i, 285.
1378, 13 Mar., ord subdcn, Winchester cathedral, *ib.*, i, 287.
1379, 26 Mar., ord dcn, Winchester cathedral, *ib.*, i, 291.
1389, 17 Apr., ord pr., Winchester cathedral, *ib.*, i, 319.
1381/2, spent two wks in the infirmary for which the hordarian pd 12d., Kitchin, *SS* no 54, 279.
1389, with the prior and other monks and laymen accused of hunting in the bp's warrens, Oxford, New College Ms 9819.
1393, 21/22 Aug., 23rd to sign the composition with bp Wykeham, BL Ms Harley, 328, fo 24v; see Robert de Rodebourne.

HEGHTERBURI, Hegtelburie
see Heytesbury

HELYS
n.d.

n.d., acc. to Thomas Wright, *Biographia Britannica Literaria*, ii (London, 1846), 123–129, he was the author of a metrical translation into Anglo-Norman of the Disticha of Dionysius Cato of which one ms copy is in Cambridge, Corpus Christi College Ms 405.

HENRY
occ. 1250

1250, 13 Oct., precentor, *CPR (1247–1258)*, 75.
1250, 13 Oct., one of four monks who recd licence from the king to el. a bp, *ib.*

Note: This is probably Henry de St Cross, q.v.

HENFORD
see Walter Enford

Thomas de HENTON
occ. 1239

1239, 21 Nov., apptd infirmarer by order of the king, *sed. vac.*, *CClR (1237–1242)*, 158.

HENTON
see also Hyntone

HERBERT
occ. [1142 × 1143]

[1142 × 1143], precentor, *Winch. Cart.*, no 10 (Goodman's dating).
[1142 × 1143], named in the bp's charter *temp.* prior Geoffrey III, q.v., in which the church of Elingdon [Wroughton, Wilts.] was restored to the precentor's office for the writing of books and repair of organs, *ib.*; this charter is also in *Eng. Epis. Acta*, viii, no 126.

Alexander de HERIARD [Herierd, Herierde, Heryerd
occ. 1325 occ. 1349

1328–1349, prior: el. *per viam scrutinii* 29 June/7 July, Reg. Stratford, fos 107, 108; d. by 5 Mar. 1349, *Reg. Edington*, i, no 556.
1326, 8 July, curtarian, WCL Basyng Libellus, fo 4.
1329/37, as prior, he took on the office of hordarian (and that of chamberlain), Kitchin, *SS* nos 49–53, pp. 257–278; see below and also John de Merlawe I.
1325, 9 Oct., 40th in order of seniority, *Reg. Pontissara*, 557.
1327, 26 June, named as proctor in the bp's letter to the prior and chapter in reply to their letter of compliance and obedience after a visitation the previous yr, followed by injunctions vs which the chapter had appealed; he had delivered the letter to the bp and talked with him in person about the future relations between bp and chapter as they had withdrawn their appeal vs his injunctions, *Winch. Cart.*, no 251.
1328, 23 Jan., with John de Fourde, q.v., proctor, who appeared for the prior and chapter before

the bp in a tithes dispute; they had recd their mandate in chapter two yrs earlier, on 5 Mar. 1325/6 *ib.*, *Winch. Cart.*, no 323.
1330, 25 Sept., named as the subcollector of a papal tenth in the adcnry of Winchester, Reg. Stratford, fo 49.
1331, 1 Apr., with Robert de Stratford, apptd vicar general while the bp was away in France, Reg. Stratford, fo 122.
1332, 2 Mar., with the bp's official, comm. to go to Wherwell and appt a prioress, *ib.*, fo 66.
1332, 25 May, heard the accusations vs him by Peter de Basyng, q.v.; these included taking obedientiary offices into his own hands, diverting revenues to himself and withholding payments due to the convent, misuse of the common seal, selling provisions intended for the monks' needy parents and obtaining money for himself through the sale of corrodies and chantries, *Winch. Cart.*, no 176.
1332, 31 May, apptd proctors to act for him in the curia, *Winch. Cart.*, no 177.
1332, 1 Aug., exhibited an inspeximus of the bull of Innocent IV, dated 7 Sept. 1254, granting the prior's right to the use of pontifical regalia, *Winch. Cart.*, no 178; see William de Taunton.
1332, 18 Oct., present in his chapel at the reading of ordinances in which the chapter requested him to take the offices of hordarian and cellarer into his own hands for six yrs to alleviate the financial crisis, and to make certain regular payments towards the monks' food and clothing, *Winch. Cart.*, no 180. (It appears that the hordarian's office was already in his hands in 1329/32, Kitchin, *SS* nos 11 and 12, pp. 260–264.)
Note: a ms recently acquired by WCL is a lengthy roll written mainly in French and described in the heading as the 'bienfaits e notorie amendements que le Priour Alissaundre adz fait ad diverses offices de sa eglise'. Among these is the record that he had kept the office of hordarian in his hands, at the request of the convent, for six yrs and had freed it of debt.
[1332/3], wrote to the pope, to a cardinal and to friends at the curia about his runaway monk, Peter de Basyng, q.v., *Winch. Cart.*, nos 197–200.
1333, 7 Feb., with the bp's chancellor was apptd vicar general, Reg Stratford, fo 77; some of his *acta* are in *Winch. Cart.*, nos 156–163, 167–170 (in no 170 he styled himself official), 174, all dated between Mar. and July.
1334/5, visited Chilbolton, Hurstbourne, Silkstead and other manors; the receiver entered expenses of £8 4s. 8d.; he also pd out 10s. 4d., *in medicinis et plastris* for the prior, Kitchin, *SS* no 62, pp. 236, 237.
1335, 14 Feb., comm., with the bp's official to hold an inquiry concerning an appropriation, *Winch. Cart.*, no 414; nos 415–418 provide details of the inquiry. See also Reg. Orleton, i, fo 15.
[1335], 14 May, with the bp's official apptd vicar general during the bp's absence, Reg. Orleton, i, fo 19.
1337, 4 Apr., reached an agreement with the subprior and chapter to settle disputed claims about the allocation of revenues and promised to augment the offices of the hordarian and chamberlain by annual payments from the treasury; he gave the chapter acquittances for the debts of these offices which he had settled while he had had them in his hands; the subprior and chapter for their part withdrew all complaints vs him, *Winch. Cart.*, no 104. He visited Wootton this yr and charged the manor 22s. 9d. (two tallies), Kitchin, *Manydown*, 149.
1339, 4 Feb., with Richard, earl of Arundel, comm. to ascertain the amount of repairs necessary for Winchester castle, *CPR (1338–1340)*, 272.
1340, 24 Aug., with the bp responsible for the collection of taxes for the king, *CPR (1340–1343)*, 25, 66.
1341, 24 June, wrote letters to religious superiors in the adcnry of Winchester on behalf of a clerk who had taken up their cause successfully in a case of unjust exaction of a ninth and he now requested them to follow his example in paying the clerk for his efforts, *Winch. Cart.*, no 523.
1342, 4 July, with the abbot of Hyde apptd keepers of Southampton which was threatened by invasion from overseas, *CPR (1340–1343)*, 476.
c. 1344, exchanged letters with the prior of Christ Church, Canterbury; see William de Sparsholt.
1345, 5 Nov., with the chapter recd a royal pardon for carrying out an episcopal el. in defiance of the king's inhibition, *CPR (1343–1345)*, 569; see John le Devenish.

John de HERIERD
occ. 1347/8

1347, 22 Sept., ord acol., South Waltham, *Reg. Edington*, ii, no 737.
1348, 2 June, granted *lit. dim*, for subdcn's orders, *ib.*, ii, no 742.

HETHCROFT, Heycroft
see Haycroft

William de HEYNOW [Hayno, Haynou, Heyno, Heynou
occ. 1325 occ. 1328

1326, 15 Feb., ord subdcn, Winchester cathedral, Reg. Stratford, fo 143ᵛ.
1326, 20 Sept., ord dcn, Kingsclere, *ib.*, fo 144ᵛ.
1328, 19 Mar., ord pr., Crawley [Hants], *ib.*, fo 148.
1325, 9 Oct., 55th (out of 64) in order of seniority, *Reg. Pontissara*, 557.

Nicholas de HEYTESBURY D.Th. [Heghterburi, Heghterbury, Heghtesbury, Heghtrebury, Hegtelburie,

occ. 1309 d. 1334/5

1326, 8 July, subprior, WCL Basyng Libellus, fo 4.

[1311/12], with Philip de Lusteshall, q.v., students at Oxford and they stopped at Hurstbourne several times on their travels back and forth, at a cost of 3s. 6d., to the manorial acct, WCL acct.

1324, 23 Feb., described as professor of sacred theology and therefore D.Th. by this date, *Winch. Cart.*, no 249.

1309, 25 Aug., one of four monk *instructores* who presented the newly el. prior, Richard de Enford, q.v, to the bp for confirmation, *Reg. Woodlock*, 385.

1324, 23 Feb., apptd penitentiary in the diocese in all reserved cases except perjury, *Winch. Cart.*, no 249, Reg. Stratford, fo 1.

1325, 9 Oct., 22nd in order of seniority, *Reg. Pontissara*, 556.

1334/5, d. and the receiver distributed 20s. worth of bread to the poor on the day of his burial, Kitchin, *SS* no 62, p. 232.

Hugh de HIDA

occ. 1280

1280, 25 Sept., with Valentine [de Wherewell] and Peter de Wynton, q.v., obtained licence from the king to el. a bp, *CPR (1272–1281)*, 398.

HIDA

see also Hyda, Hyde

Walter HILLE [Hyll, Hylle

occ. 1479 occ. [1528 × 1539]

1479, 18 Dec., ord acol., Winchester cathedral, Reg. Waynflete, ii, fo 184.

1480, 23 Dec., ord subdcn, Winchester cathedral, *ib.*, ii, fo 185v.

1481, 16 June, ord dcn, Winchester cathedral, *ib.*, ii, fo 187.

1483, 20 Dec., ord pr. Winchester cathedral, *ib.*, ii, fo 193.

1501, 27 Feb., infirmarer, Canterbury Reg. R, fo 114v.

1524, 2 Dec., infirmarer, Reg. Fox, v, fo 75.

1502, 18 July, [student] at Oxford and agreed to testify on 1 Aug., that William Alston, q.v. (under Worcester), had broken a glass vessel containing aqua vitae in the chamber of a Richard Marsche, *Reg. Cancell. Oxon, 1498–1506*, 128–129.

1486, 7 Dec., 23rd in order at the el. of a bp, *Reg. Common Seal*, no 434.

1492, 29 Oct., 20th to be examined at the *sed. vac.* visitation and deposed that almsgiving had been diminished because of payments to persons known to some of the monks, *Reg. abp Morton*, ii, no 127.

1498, 23 Apr., 11th in order at the el. of a prior, Reg. Langton, fo 73v.

1501, 27th Feb., 9th to be examined at the visitation (*sed. vac.* both Canterbury and Winchester), by the commissary of the prior of Christ Church Canterbury; he complained that some of the silver plate bequeathed by Cardinal Beaufort had been used as security for a loan and that the infirmary had been in a dilapidated state for twelve yrs for which he blamed the *custos operum*, Canterbury Reg. R, fos 114v, 115.

1524, 2 Dec., 3rd in order at the el. of a prior, Reg. Fox, v, fo 75 and voted for Henry Broke, *propter zelum bone religionis*, *ib.*, v, fo 77.

[1528 × 1539], surname occ. in a list of monks copied on to a blank fo in Oxford, Bod. Ms Selden supra 76, fo 46v; no Christian names are given.

HO(E)

see Hoo

Roland HOKE [Hook, Hooke

occ. 1403 occ. 1419

1403, 22 Sept., ord acol., Waltham, *Reg. Wykeham*, i, 356.

1404, 21 May, acol., granted *lit. dim*, *ib.*, ii, 556.

1404, 24 May, ord subdcn, Sherborne, Reg. Mitford (Salisbury), fo 176.

1404, 20 Sept., ord dcn, Waltham, *ib.*, i, 359.

1403/4, [before 24 May, 1404; see above] on his way to Sherborne with other monks stopped overnight at Stockton (Wilts.), BL Add. Roll 24399.

1404, 16 Oct., prof., and 39th in order at the el. of a prior, *Reg. Common Seal*, no 68.

1415, 27 Sept., apptd by the chapter as one of nine *compromissorii* in the el. of a prior, *Reg. Common Seal*, no 163; on 29 Sept. he was sent, with John Hurst, q.v., to present the el. to the bp and on 4 Oct. he was named proctor in all negotiations concerning the el., *ib.*, nos 166, 167.

1415/16, stopped at Whitchurch on his way to Oxford, WCL acct.

1417/18, pd a visit to Whitchurch, WCL acct.

1419, 1 Sept., with Richard Buriton, q.v., and several seculars, apptd proctors for the prior and chapter in all matters pertaining to their rights in their churches within the diocese of Salisbury, *Reg. Common Seal*, no 186.

John HOLEWEY [Holway, Holwey

occ. 1468 occ. 1474/5

1468, 17 Dec., ord subdcn, Winchester cathedral, Reg. Waynflete, i, fo M*v.

1469, 23 Dec., ord dcn, Winchester cathedral, *ib.*, i, fo O*.

1474, 17 Dec., ord pr., Winchester cathedral, *ib.*, ii, fo 173.
1474/5, celebrated his first mass and recd a contribution [for the feast] from the anniversarian, Worcester Cathedral Muniment, C.1.

William de HOO [Ho, Hoe, Hou
occ. 1266/7 occ. 1295

1279/80, curtarian, WCL Hurstbourne pipe roll acct; prob. also 1280/2, but only as W. on Hurstbourne accts. In this former yr he and Peter de Mareschall, q.v., held the hundred courts at Crondall, *ib.*

1266/7, pd a visit to Chilbolton, with Adam de Wynton, q.v., and they ate three fowl, WCL pipe roll acct.
1279/80, visited Chilbolton and Hurstbourne, WCL pipe roll accts.
1281/2, visited Chilbolton with the steward [*senescallus*] on his way to visit the queen, and again on his return journey, WCL acct.
1282, 7 Aug., one of the monks who sought and obtained absolution from excommunication incurred through irregularities in their el. of Richard de la More as bp, *Reg. abp Pecham*, i, 188–189; the comm. for absolution is dated 10 Aug., *ib.*, ii, 50. See Adam de Farnham.
1295, 6 June, named as one of seven *compromissorii* in the el. of a prior, *Reg. Pontissara*, 73.

HOOK(E)
see Hoke

Thomas HORTON
occ. 1407/8 occ. 1414/15

1407/8, chamberlain, BL Add. Roll 28074.

1407/8, 1410/11, stayed at Mapledurham, and in the latter yr he was there *in negocio domini*, BL Add. Rolls 28074, 28078.
1414/15, stayed at Crondall for 'negotiations', WCL acct.

John de HOSTILLARIA
see John III

HOU
see Hoo

John HUBBARD [Hubberde
occ. [1537]

[1537], recd a letter of recommendation in which he was described as pr. and former monk, Reg. Common Seal, iii, fo 70.

Note: there is prob. another entry for this monk under his toponymic, but I cannot trace it. He returned as one of the twelve singing petty canons in 1541, Kitchin and Madge, *Documents*, 60.

I HUGH
occ. before 1100

1100, left to become abbot of New Minster (Hyde), *Ann. Winton.*, 40, *HRH*, 82.

II HUGH
occ. before 1107

1107, left to become abbot of Chertsey, *Ann. Winton.*, 42, *HRH*, 38.

Note: there is ref. to a Hugh, former prior, in a grant of bp Giffard [1120 × 1129] *Eng. Epis. Acta*, viii, no 19.

Richard HUNTLEY [Huntly
occ. 1496 occ. [1528 × 1539]

1496, 24 Sept., ord subdcn, Hyde abbey, Reg. Langton, fo 29ᵛ.
1499, 21 Sept., ord dcn, bp's chapel, Marwell, *ib.*, fo 34ᵛ.

1514/15, almoner, Kitchin, *SS* no 44, pp. 457–461.

1498, 23 Apr., 27th in order at the el. of a prior, Reg. Langton, fo 73ᵛ.
1501, 27 Feb., 18th to be examined at the visitation (*sed. vac.* both Canterbury and Winchester) by the commissary of the prior of Christ Church, Canterbury; he reported *omnia bene*, Canterbury Reg. R, fo 115.
1524, 2 Dec., 9th in order at the el. of a prior, Reg. Fox, v, fo 75.
[1528 × 1539], surname occ. in a list of monks copied on to a blank fo in Oxford, Bod. Ms Selden supra 76, fo 46ᵛ; no Christian names are given.

Thomas HUNTON
occ. 1447 d. 1498

1470–1498, prior: el. on or just before 30 Mar. 1470, and confirmed by the bp, 9 Apr., Reg. Waynflete ii, fo 2; d. 21 Apr. 1498, Reg. Langton, fo 73.

1448, 18 May, ord pr., Winchester cathedral, Reg. Waynflete i, fo Aᵛ.

1447, 16 Apr., prof., and 35th in order at the el. of a bp, *Reg. Common Seal*, no 316.
1450, 11 Dec., 31st at the el. of a prior, Reg. Waynflete, i, fo 30ᵛ.
1470, 5 Apr., with his proctors Nicholas Mersch and William Shirebourne, q.v., came before the bp to be examined prior to obtaining confirmation of his el. as prior, Reg. Waynflete, ii, fo 1ᵛ.
1472, 26 Jan., with John Hampton, q.v., attended convocation, Reg. Waynflete ii, fo 150ᵛ.
1473, Feb., attended convocation, *ib.*, ii, fo 156ᵛ.
1486, recd a bequest from bp Waynflete of a 'ciphum honestam deauratum et coopertum' and 40s., Richard Chandler, *The Life of William Waynflete, Bishop of Winchester* (London, 1811), 380.
1486, 7 Dec., presided at the el. of a bp, *Reg. Common Seal*, no 434.
1492, 29 Oct., present at the *sed. vac.* visitation and said that all was in order; however, there were complaints made vs him by Thomas

Gardiner, Thomas Knyght and Peter Marlowe, q.v., *Reg. abp Morton*, ii, no 127.

Many of his *acta* as prior are entered in *Reg. Common Seal*, nos 361–519.

For his architectural achievements in the reconstruction of the Lady chapel, see Crook, *Winchester Cathedral*, 239, 257–258.

John HURSELEY [Hurslegh, Hursley
occ. 1455 occ. 1478

1455, 20 Sept., ord acol., bp's chapel, Wolvesey, Reg. Waynflete, i, fo K^{v}.
1458, 5 Feb., ord subdcn, Winchester cathedral, *ib.*, i, fo O.
1460, 1 Mar., ord dcn, Hyde abbey, *ib.*, i fo V^{v}.
1466, 22 Mar., ord pr., St Mary Overy, Southwark, *ib.*, i, I*^{v}.
1470, [30 Mar./8 Apr.], 1478, 1 Mar. subprior, *Reg. Common Seal*, nos 363, 372. On the other hand, he was third prior on Apr. 1470, acc. to Reg. Waynflete, ii, fo 1^{v}.
1470, [before 27 July], as subprior and with the chapter apptd proctors for convocation; the date refs to the day on which the first session occ.; the prior must have been absent from the house, *Reg. Common Seal*, no 363.
1478, 1 Mar., with William Clement, q.v. and two canon lawyers apptd proctors for the prior and convent in all causes pertaining to their rights in their churches in Salisbury diocese, *Reg. Common Seal*, no 372.

John HURST [Hurste
occ. 1392 occ. 1415

1392, 13 Apr., ord acol., Winchester cathedral, *Reg. Wykeham*, i, 326.
1393, 1 Mar., ord subdcn, bp's chapel, Farnham castle, *ib.*, i, 328.
1393, 21 Sept., ord dcn, bp's chapel, Esher, *ib.*, i, 329.
1395, 6 Mar., ord pr., bp's chapel, Marwell, ib,. i, 336.
1394/5, celebrated his first mass and the anniversarian contributed 6d. for wine [toward the feast], Kitchin, *SS* no 1, p. 205.
1405/6, almoner, first yr., Kitchin, *SS* no 33, pp. 428–430.
1408/9, *custos operum*, *ib.*, *SS* no 11, pp. 209–214.
1415, 26 Aug., sacrist, *Reg. Common Seal*, no 158.
1393, 21/22 Aug., 42nd and last but one to sign the composition with bp Wykeham, BL Ms Harley 328, fo 24^{v}; see also Robert de Rodebourne.
1404, 16 Oct., 26th at the el. of a bp, *Reg. Common Seal*, no 68.
1404/5, sent wine to the prior *et ad dignum in refectorio* to celebrate his apptment as almoner, Kitchin, *SS* no 33, p. 429; in this yr he visited Hinton [Ampner] several times and Quidhampton twice, *ib.*, 430.
1415, 26 Aug., witnessed the resignation of Thomas Nevyle, prior, q.v., *Reg. Common Seal*, no 158; on 31 Aug., he was apptd, with Thomas Shirebourne, q.v., to request from the bp licence to el. a prior, *ib.*, no 159.
1415, 27 Sept., named as one of nine *compromissorii* in the el. of a prior; the following day, with Richard Buryton, q.v., he was apptd to inform Thomas Shirebourne, q.v., of his el.; on the 29th Sept., with Roland Hoke, q.v., he was sent to the bp, to present the elect and request his confirmation as prior, *ib.*, nos 163, 164, 166.

Adam de HYDA
occ. 1282 occ. 1325

1309/19, almoner, Kitchin, *SS* nos 15–25, pp. 389–407.
1282, 15 June, named as having been one of seven *compromissorii* in the second el. of a bp (transcribed as Lyda) after the pope had quashed the previous el., *CPL*, i, (1198–1304), 466. This el. too was quashed and the pope provided John de Pontissara, *ib.*
Note: the *compromissorii* consisted of the adcn of Winchester and six monks, *ib.*
1284, 18 July, one of three monk proctors apptd by the chapter to request from the bp licence to el. a prior, *Reg. Pontissara*, 286.
1295, 30 May, one of three proctors apptd to obtain licence from the bp to el. a prior, *ib.*, 71–72; on 6 June he was one of seven *compromissorii* chosen for the el., *ib.*, 73.
1311/12, ill in the infirmary and charged his own office 15s., Kitchin, *SS* no 18*, p. 398; he went to Overton this yr to be present at a *dies amoris*, *ib.*, 399.
1316/17, again spent time in the infirmary and charged his office 9s. for medicines, *ib.*, *SS* no 23, p. 401.
1318/19, again in the infirmary and his medicines cost him 13s. 4d., *ib.*, *SS* no 25, p. 406.
1325, 9 Oct., 2nd in order (the most senior monk) of seniority, *Reg. Pontissara*, 556.

John HYDE
occ. 1360 occ. 1393

1360, 13 Sept., granted *lit. dim*, for dcn's orders by the prior acting as vicar general, *Reg. Edington*, ii, no 915 (transcribed as Byde); see John de Merlawe I.
1373, 15 Mar., 1375, 19 Apr., hostiller, *Reg. Wykeham*, ii, 186, Reg. Wykeham, ii, fo 126.
1390, June, 'nominated' third prior, Kitchin, *SS* no 52, p. 417.
1393, 21/22 Aug., third prior, BL Ms Harley 328, fo 24.
1373, 15 Mar., licensed to administer the sacraments at Littleton during Lent and Easter because of insufficient funds for a chaplain, *Reg. Wykeham*, ii, 186.

1375, 19 Apr., the above licence was renewed, Reg. Wykeham, ii, fo 126.
1390, June, recd a gift of wine from the almoner on his apptment as third prior, Kitchin, *SS* no 52, 417.
1393, 21/2 Aug., 6th to sign the composition with bp Wykeham, BL Ms Harley 328, fo 24; see also Robert de Rodebourne.

John de HYLDESLYE [Ildeslye
occ. 1325 occ. 1337/8

1325, 9 Oct., 42nd in order of seniority, *Reg. Pontissara*, 557.
1337/8, with other monks visited Chilbolton, Worcester Cathedral Muniment, C.866.

Robert HYLDESLYE [Hildesey, Hyldesley, Illesley
occ. 1465 occ. 1486

1465, 21 Sept., ord acol., Hyde abbey, Reg. Waynflete, i, fo I*.
1466, 20 Sept., ord subdcn, Winchester cathedral, *ib.*, i, fo K*v.
1486, 7 Dec., 8th in order at the el. of a bp, *Reg. Common Seal*, no 434.

HYLL(E)
see Hille

John HYNTONE [Henton, Hentone
occ. 1520 occ. 1527

1520, 22 Dec., ord subdcn, Lady chapel, Winchester cathedral, Reg. Fox, iv, fo 71.
1522, 20 Sept., ord dcn, Lady chapel, Winchester cathedral, *ib.*, v, fo 30.
1527, 20 Apr., ord pr. Lady chapel, Winchester cathedral, *ib.*, v, fo 36v.
1524, 2 Dec., dcn and 27th in order at the el. of a prior, Reg. Fox, v, fo 75; he voted for John Meone II, q.v., 'propter eius virtutes et bonas cond. . .ones' [this last word is partially illegible], *ib.*, v, fo 78.

Thomas ICHELBOURNE [Chelbourne, Ichelebourne, Ichilbourne, Ichenebourne, Ychebourne, Ychenesbourne
occ. 1396 occ. 1415

1396, 25 Feb., ord acol., bp's chapel, Waltham, *Reg. Wykeham*, i, 339 (as Chelbourne).
1396, 23 Sept., ord subdcn, bp's chapel, Waltham, *ib.*, i, 340.
1398, 21 Dec., ord dcn, bp's chapel, Farnham castle, *ib.*, i, 346.
1399, 22 Feb., ord pr., bp's chapel, Farnham castle, *ib.*, i, 348.
1400/1, spent two wks in the infirmary for which the hordarian pd 12d., Kitchin, *SS* no 55, p. 283.
1404, 16 Oct., 30th in order at the el. of a bp, *Reg. Common Seal*, no 68.
1415, 27 Sept., one of nine *compromissorii* chosen by the chapter to el. a prior, *ib.*, no 163.

John de ICHULLE
occ. 1281/2

1281, July, with Philip de Avinton, John Gys and Peter Mareschall, q.v., was sent to London by the receiver on business for the house, Watkin, 'Rec. Acct', 100.
1281/2, visited Crondall, WCL pipe roll acct.

ILDESLYE, Illesley
see Hyldeslye

Henry IMBERT [Imbard, Imberd
occ. 1346 occ. 1372

1346, 1 Dec., dcn, granted *lit. dim*, for pr.'s orders, *Reg. Edington*, ii, no 712.
1347, 24 Feb., ord pr., bp's chapel, Southwark, *ib.*, ii, no 724.
1369/72, anniversarian, Worcester Cathedral Muniment, C.531, WCL unnumbered obedientiary acct, Worcester Cathedral Muniment, C.532.
1369/72, pd visits to Bishopstone [Bushton, Wilts.], Worcester Cathedral Muniment, C.531, WCL unnumbered obedientiary acct, Worcester Cathedral Muniment, C.532.

INFORD
see Enford

INGULPH
occ. c. 1126 occ. 1130

c. 1126–1130, prior: first occ. 1128 though possibly earlier, see Geoffrey II; el. abbot of Abingdon, 8 June 1130, *Fasti*, ii, 88, *HRH*, 80.
1128, c. 24 Nov., × 1129, 25 Jan.], witnessed a grant of the bp to the monks of Waverley, *Eng. Epis. Acta*, viii, no 16.

William de INSULA [?de Lisle
occ. 1304/5 occ. 1325

1321, 4 July, sacrist, *Reg. Asserio*, 449–450.
1304/5, stopped at Stockton (Wilts.), WCL acct.
1321, 4 July, named as patron of the church of St Mary *in atrio sancti Swithuni*, to which he had presented a rector, *Reg. Asserio*, 449–450.
1325, 9 Oct., 6th in order of seniority, *Reg. Pontissara*, 556.

I J.
occ. 1215/16

1215/16, brought letters patent to the bp at Brightwell and recd 12d., *Eng. Epis. Acta*, ix, no 175 (citing the bp's pipe rolls).

II J.
occ. 1247

1247, 12 May [Ascension day], was almost flattened by the weather vane which fell from the tower just as the bells were ringing for vespers, *Ann. Winton.*, 91.

Note: these two Js may be one and the same monk.

III J.
occ. 1308/9

1308/9, curtarian, WCL Hurstbourne acct.

1308/9, visited Hurstbourne, *ib.*

IV J.
occ. 1337/8

1337/8, receiver, Worcester Cathedral Muniment, C.866.

1337/8, stopped at Chilbolton with others on their way to and from Wilts., *ib.*

Note: this is prob. John de Merlawe I, q.v.

J.
see also Brevill

JAMES
occ. 1269/70

1269/70, visited Hurstbourne, WCL acct.

Note: this may be James de Basyng, q.v.

I JOHN
occ. 1185 d. 1187

1185–1187, prior: occ. Apr. 1185 (see Walter I); d. 1187, *Fasti*, ii, 89, *HRH* 80.

II JOHN
n.d.

n.d. [2nd yr of prior Andrew, xxvj], chamberlain, WCL Wyke iuxta Portland acct.

Note: there are two priors named Andrew, q.v., entered under Andrew I and London. If the 'xxvj' on the heading of the acct denotes the regnal yr, it may be 1242 and thus ref. to Andrew I, q.v.

III JOHN [de Ostillaria
occ. 1282

1282, 7 Aug., one of the monks who sought and recd absolution from excommunication incurred because of irregularities in the el. of Richard de la More as bp, *Reg. abp Pecham*, i, 188–189; the comm. for absolution is dated 10 Aug., *ib.*, ii, 50. See Adam de Farnham.

JULERS
see Gilers

KANIGG'
see Canigg'

Richard KANNER [Kannere
occ. and d. 1413/14

1414, 18 Sept., ord pr., Winchester cathedral, Reg. Beaufort, fo I^v^.

1413/14, d., and the almoner bought 10s. worth of bread to distribute among the poor on the day of his burial, Kitchin, *SS* no 36, p. 436. He prob. d. between 18 and 28 Sept. 1414.

John KATERINGTON [Kateryngton, Kateryngtone
occ. 1366 occ. 1404

1366, 28 Feb., ord acol., St Elizabeth's chapel, near Winchester, *Reg. Edington*, ii, no 948.

1368, 4 Mar., ord subdcn, Winchester cathedral, *Reg. Wykeham*, i, 252.

1369, 22 Sept., ord dcn, Winchester cathedral, *ib.*, i, 257.

1370, 21 Sept., ord pr., bp's chapel, Highclere, *ib.*, i, 261.

1370/1, celebrated his first mass and recd 6d. from the anniversarian, WCL unnumbered obedientiary acct.

1399/1400, infirmarer, WCL obedientiary acct.

1389, with the prior, Robert Rodebourne, q.v., and other monks and laymen accused of hunting in the bp's warrens, Oxford, New College Ms 9819.

1393, 21/22 Aug., 12th to sign the composition with bp Wykeham, BL Ms Harley 328, fo 24^v^; see also Robert de Rodebourne.

1404, 16 Oct., 7th in order at the el. of a bp, *Reg. Common Seal*, no 68.

Thomas KENT
occ. 1451 occ. 1456

1451, 24 Apr., ord acol. and subdcn, Winchester cathedral, Reg. Waynflete, i, fos C^v^, D.

1451, 19 June, ord dcn, Winchester cathedral, *ib.*, i, fo D.

1456, 18 Sept., ord pr., bp's palace, Wolvesey, *ib.*, i, fo M^v^.

Robert de KEYNGEHAM
occ. 1238

1238, 11 July, one of four monks who, with the adcns, recd royal licence to el. a bp, *CPR (1232–1247)*, 226.

William de KINGATE [Kingat, Kingesiat or Portroyal, Porta Regia
occ. 1250 occ. 1258

1250, 13 Oct., one of four monks, who recd royal licence to el. a bp, *CPR (1247–1258)*, 75.

1255, 5 Jan., with Philip de Osna, q.v., involved in contracting a loan on behalf of the prior and chapter, *CPL*, i (1198–1304), 309.

1257, 28 Oct., papal chaplain and the subject of a papal injunction to the king to provide royal protection because he had been apptd bp of Connor, *ib.*, i, 352.

1258, 7 Jan., obtained royal confirmation of his apptment as bp, *CPR (1247–1258)*, 610.

KINGESTON
see also Kyngston

Rowland KINGESTON
occ. 1539

1539, 14 Nov., one of four monks described as 'late religious' on the surrender list and not yet prof.; he was assigned a pension of 40s. p.a., *L and P Henry VIII*, xiv, pt 2, no 520 (transcribed as Kympeston) (PRO E315/494).

William KINGSMILL
see William Basyng IV

KINGSTON
see also Kyngston

KIPING
d. by 1122/3

1122/3, name occ. in a mortuary roll of Savigny following that of Godfrey, prior, q.v., but not distinguished as a monk, Delisle, *Rouleaux des Morts*, 336.

Thomas KNYGHT [Knygth
occ. 1481 occ. 1498

1481, 22 Dec., ord acol., Winchester cathedral, Reg. Waynflete, ii, fo 187^{v}.
1483, 24 May, ord subdcn, Winchester cathedral, *ib.*, ii, fo 192.
1485, 17 Dec., ord dcn, Winchester cathedral, *ib.*, ii, fo 200.
[1490], 18 Sept., ord pr., church of St John the Baptist in the Soke, Winchester, Reg. Courtenay, fo 17.
1498, 23 Apr., sacrist, Reg. Langton, fo 73^{v}.

1486, 7 Dec., 27th in order at the el. of a bp, *Reg. Common Seal*, no 434.
1492, 29 Oct., 22nd to be examined at the *sed. vac.* visitation and made several depositions. He agreed with John Best, q.v., and in addition reported that Robert Auncell, sacrist, q.v., had not pd the monks for celebrating the second mass; he also requested that the prior, Thomas Hunton, q.v., improve his behaviour towards his brethren, and that all should watch their manner of speaking, *Reg. abp Morton*, ii, no 127.
1497, 3 Aug., with three of his brethren and two others, recd a comm. to act for the prior and convent in their dispute with the abp of Canterbury; and on 19 Oct. with one of the monks, William Manwode, q.v., and others was apptd proctor in the same case, *Reg. abp Morton*, i, nos 248, 250, 255.
1498, 23 Apr., 15th in order at the el. of a prior, Reg. Langton, fo 73^{v}; he and Manwode had been sent to the bp to inform him of the d. of the prior, *ib.*, fo 73.

William KYNGESMYLLE
see William Basyng IV

Henry KYNGSTON [Kyngestone, Kyngiston, *alias* Webbe
occ. 1521 occ. 1536

1521, 30 Mar., ord pr. Lady chapel, Winchester cathedral, Reg. Fox, iv, fo 72.
1529/30, *custos* of the Lady altar, WCL obedientiary acct, incorrectly numbered SS no 23; not in Kitchin *Obed. Rolls*, whose *SS* no 23 is an almoner's acct.
1535, precentor, *Valor Eccles.*, ii, 2.

1524, 2 Dec., 21st in order at the el. of a prior, Reg. Fox, v, fo 75; he nom. Henry Broke, q.v., 'quia novit eum plurimum Instruentem fratres suos in Religionem', *ib.*, v, fo 77^{v}.
[1528 × 1539], surname occ. in a list of monks copied on to a blank fo in Oxford, Bod. Ms Selden supra 76, fo 46^{v}; no Christian names are given.
1536, 6 Apr., dispensed to wear the habit of his order under that of a secular pr., if the prior consented; he pd £4 for this licence, Chambers, *Faculty Office Regs*, 49.

KYNGSTON
see also Kingeston

Richard LACY [Lasy
occ. 1476 occ. 1498

1476, 21 Dec., ord acol., Winchester cathedral, Reg. Waynflete, ii, fo 176^{v}.
1478, 19 Sept., ord subdcn, Winchester cathedral, *ib.*, ii, fo 181^{v}.
1481, 16 June, ord dcn, Winchester cathedral, *ib.*, ii, fo 187.
1483, 20 Dec., ord pr., Winchester cathedral, *ib.*, ii, fo 193.

1486, 7 Dec., precentor, *Reg. Common Seal*, no 434.
1492, 14 Oct., *custos operum*, *ib.*, no 502.
1498, 23 Apr., again precentor, Reg. Langton, fo 73^{v}.

1486, 7 Dec., 21st in order at the el. of a bp, and preached the sermon in Latin on the theme "choose the better [man] and him who will be pleasing to you from among the sons of our Lord and place him on the throne of his father", *Reg. Common Seal*, no 434.
1490, with John Fetypas, q.v., apptd proctor by the prior and chapter in their dispute with the abp of Canterbury over *sed. vac.* jurisdiction, *ib.*, no 508.
1492, 29 Oct., 14th to be examined at the *sed. vac.* visitation; he, like several others, reported the lack of an inventory [of church goods], requested that a monk be sent away for further study and that delinquent brethren should rec. correction acc. to the Rule, *Reg. abp Morton*, ii, no 127.
1497, 3 Aug., one of four monk proctors and two civil lawyers apptd by the prior and chapter in their dispute with the abp of Canterbury, as above, *ib.*, i, no 248.

1498, 23 Apr., 9th in order at the el. of a prior, Reg. Langton, fo 73v.

Thomas LAMB [Lambe
occ. 1528 occ. 1539

1528, 11 Apr., one of six not yet prof., and ord exorcist and acol., Lady chapel, Winchester cathedral, Reg. Fox, v, fo 38–38v.

[1528 × 1539], surname occ. in a list of monks copied on to a blank fo in Oxford, Bod. Ms Selden supra 76, fo 46v; no Christian names are given.

1539, 14 Nov., one of four monks described on the surrender list as 'late religious' and also, prob. mistakenly, as not prof.; he was assigned an annual pension of 60s., *L and P Henry VIII*, xiv, pt 2, no 520 (PRO E315/494).

William LANE
occ. 1393 d. 1405/6

1393, 21/22 Aug., gardener, BL Ms Harley 328, fo 24v.

1393, 21/22 Aug., 18th to sign the composition with bp Wykeham, BL Ms Harley 328, fo 24v; see Robert de Rodebourne.

1404, 16 Oct., 10th at the el. of a bp, *Reg. Common Seal*, no 68.

1405/6, d., and the almoner distributed 10s. worth of bread among the poor on the day of his burial, Kitchin, *SS* no 33, p. 429.

[W. de LANGELEY
occ. 1266/7 occ. 1269/70

1266/7, pd a visit to Chilbolton, WCL pipe roll acct.

1269/70, visited Hurstbourne, WCL acct.

Note: this may not be a monk.]

LANGELEY
see also Langley

John de LANGESTOKE
d. 1310/11

1310/11, d., and the almoner gave a pittance of 6s. 8d. to the convent on the day of his burial, Kitchin, *SS* no 16, p. 391.

Walter de LANGESTOKE [Langestok, Langgestock
occ. 1321/2 occ. 1328/9

1321/2, with Richard de Pek, q.v., visited Houghton and dined on capon, WCL acct.

1325, 9 Oct., 35th in order of seniority, *Reg. Pontissara*, 556.

1328, 7 July, with Adam de Sarum, q.v., sent by the subprior and convent to inform the bp of their el. of Alexander Heriard, q.v., as prior; he was also named as one of three *instructores* in the examination of the el. proceedings, Reg. Stratford, fo 107, 107v.

1327/9, pd visits to Silkstead, WCL accts.

Note: his namesake, M. Walter de Langestoke, *medicus*, occ. on the receiver's acct for 1334/5, Kitchin, *SS* no 62, p. 233; his biographical details are in *BRUO*.

William LANGLEY
occ. 1475 occ. 1486

1475, 23 Sept., ord acol., Winchester cathedral, Reg. Waynflete, ii, fo 174v.

1476, 21 Dec., ord subdcn, Winchester cathedral, *ib.*, ii, fo 176v.

1477, 20 Sept., ord dcn, place not named, *ib.*, ii, fo 178v.

1484, 17 Apr., ord pr., Mottisfont priory, *ib.*, ii, fo 194v.

1486, 15 Aug., 7 Dec., subprior, *Reg. Common Seal*, nos 433, 434.

1484/5, student at Oxford, with a contribution of 2s. from the hordarian, Kitchin, *SS* no 59, p. 298.

1486, 15 Aug., sent, with Thomas Silkstede, q.v., as proctors to obtain licence from the king to el. a bp, *Reg. Common Seal*, no 433.

1486, 7 Dec., as subprior, 2nd in order at the el. of a bp, *ib.*, no 434.

Hugh LANGOVER
occ. 1266/7

1266/7, almoner, WCL Chilbolton pipe roll acct.

1266/7, visited Chilbolton for *liberatio denariorum*, and partook of a manorial cheese, *ib.*

John LANGREOD [Langerud, Langred', Langrud'
occ. 1363 occ. 1405/6

1363, 28 Dec., granted *lit. dim* for minor orders, *Reg. Edington*, ii, no 936.

1364, 9 Mar., ord acol., bp's chapel South Waltham, Reg. Edington, ii, fo UU.

1365, 20 Sept., ord dcn, bp's chapel, Sutton, *Reg. Edington*, ii, no 945.

1365, 15 Dec., granted *lit. dim*, for pr.'s orders, *ib.*, ii, no 947.

1382/3, treasurer [*thesaurarius* and *scaccarius*] WCL Compton and Sparsholt; accts, also, 1384/5, *ib.*, Barton [receiver], Hannington and Whitchurch accts; 1385/6, *ib.*, Thurmonds and Whitchurch accts; 1386/7, *ib.*, Hannington, Silkstead and Wonston accts; 1387/8, *ib.*, Silkstead and Wonston accts; 1389/90, *ib.*, Whitchurch and Wootton accts; 1390/1, *ib.*, Hurstbourne, Littleton and Silkstead accts; 1391/2, *ib.*, Chilbolton, Whitchurch and Wootton accts. He followed John Wayte I, q.v., and was succ. by Thomas Ware, q.v.

1394/6, anniversarian, Kitchin, *SS* nos 1 and 3, pp. 201–207.

1397/9, 1402/3, 1404/5, almoner, Kitchin, *SS* nos 30–32, pp. 420–427.
1404/6, hordarian, PRO SC6/757/21, 22, Kitchin, *SS* no 56, pp. 285–289; he took over from Ralph de Basyng, q.v.
1384, 14 Nov., with Thomas Nevyle, q.v., acted as *instructores* after the el. of Robert Rodebourne, q.v., to inform the bp of the details of the proceedings, *Reg. Wykeham*, i, 150.
1384/5, visited Hannington, Whitchurch and Wootton, WCL accts.
1385/6, visited Littleton, Silkstead, Whitchurch and Wonston, WCL accts.
1386/7, visited Crondall, Hannington, Silkstead and Wonston, WCL accts.
1389, with the prior and other monks and laymen accused of hunting in the bp's warrens, Oxford, New College Ms 9819.
1389/90, visited Crondall, Whitchurch and Wootton, WCL accts.
1390, 20 May, with Ralph de Basyng, q.v., and two others, comm. as one of four general proctors for the prior and chapter, *Reg. Common Seal*, no 18.
1390/1, visited Hannington, Hurstbourne, Littleton and Silkstead, WCL accts; he was at Hurstbourne *pro fermo capiendo*, and at Silkstead he recd money from the sale of lambs.
1391/2, visited Chilbolton, Hannington, Whitchurch and Wootton, WCL accts.
1392, 15 July, granted by the prior a corrody because of his age (having passed his 50th birthday) and infirmity and in gratitude for his services to the house; this was to be in the form of a room in the infirmary for the rest of his life with the customary allowances of food and pittances, a portion from the prior's table, bread from the pantry, ale from the cellar and other food from the kitchen, WCL fragment of a loose deed, printed in Kitchin, *Obed. Rolls*, 164–166; see below.
1393, 21/22 Aug., 9th to sign the composition with bp Wykeham, BL Ms Harley 328, fo 24; see Robert de Rodebourne.
1394, 25 Apr., in response to Langreod's petition a papal mandate was addressed to the dean of St Paul's to ascertain who was responsible for harassing him in his tenure of the corrody and at the same time the grant itself was reinforced by papal ratification. On 16 Oct. the dean issued a public *monitio* requiring the offenders to be apprehended and the bp to punish by excommunication if necessary, Kitchin, *Obed. Rolls*, 163–169. It appears that Langreod was being 'vexed' and 'molested' from some of the, probably envious, members of his community on acct of his preferential treatment. For a similar case, which does not seem to have caused ill feeling, see Simon Crompe in the Worcester section.
1399, 19 May, with three of his brethren and four seculars apptd by the prior and chapter as proctors in lawsuits over their churches in Salisbury diocese, *Reg. Common Seal*, no 33.
1404, 16 Oct., 5th in order at the el. of a bp, *Reg. Common Seal*, no 68.
1405/6, spent 10s. on three hangings for the hordarian's exchequer on which were depicted the five joys of Mary, Kitchin, *SS* no 56, p. 288. He was at Woolstone this yr, to hold courts and his horse had his due of oats, PRO SC6/757/22.

LASY
see Lacy

John LAUNSON [Launeson, Lawnsone, Lawnston, Lawsone
occ. 1471 occ. 1492

1471, 21 Dec., ord acol., bp's chapel, Waltham, Reg. Waynflete, ii, fo 168.
1472, 14 Mar., ord subdcn, Winchester cathedral, *ib.*, ii, fo 168^v.
1472, 23 May, ord dcn, Winchester cathedral, *ib.*, ii, fo 169.
1475, 5 Mar., ord pr., Mottisfont priory, *ib.*, ii, fo 174.
1474/5, celebrated his first mass and recd a gift from the anniversarian, Worcester Cathedral Muniment, C.1.
1486, 7 Dec., 13th in order at the el. of a bp, *Reg. Common Seal*, no 434.
1492, 29 Oct., 9th to be examined at the *sed. vac.* visitation and made a lengthy deposition. Among his complaints were the following: the poor condition of the dormitory and the infirmary, the dilapidated state of some of the church ornaments and the loss of others, the lack of free access to the books in the library and the misuse of funds by the treasurer, Philip [Yonge] q.v., *Reg. abp Morton*, ii, no 127.

John de LECFORD
occ. 1283

1283, 2 Apr., released from his apptment as confessor to the nuns of Nunnaminster because of ill health, *Reg. Pontissara*, 251; see John de Shipesdon'.

LEMYNGTON
see Lymyngton(e)

LENNE
see Lynne

William de LEPISCOMBE [Lupescombe
occ. 1400/1

1400, 18 Sept., ord acol., bp's chapel, Waltham, *Reg. Wykeham*, i, 351.
1400/1, spent three wks in the infirmary for which the hordarian pd 18d., Kitchin, *SS* no 55, p. 283.

LEUS
see Lues

Robert de LEWES
see Robert I

Richard de LEYCESTRIA
occ. 1240

1240, 11 Jan., with Gilbert de Crundel, q.v., apptd proctors by the prior and chapter who were petitioning the pope to restore their right to el. their bps, *CPL*, i (1198–1304), 185.

William LICHFELD [Lychfelde
occ. 1509 occ. 1513

1509, 24 Mar., ord subdcn, bp's chapel, Esher, Reg. Fox, ii, fo 24.
1513, 26 Mar., ord pr., Winchester cathedral, *ib.*, iii, fo 53.

LISLE
see Insula

Andrew de LONDON [de sancto Martino, St Martin
occ. 1255 occ. 1276

1255–1261, prior: first occ. 20 July 1255, possibly intruded by the bp el., Aymer de Valence; deprived 1261, *Fasti*, ii, 90, and see below.
1257/9, three of his prioral *acta* occ. in *Winch. Cart.*, nos 94, 207, 328; see also BL Add. Ms 29436, fo 39v.
1258, 12 July, res. as prior, but was re-el. the same day and was himself one of the seven *compromissorii* whose choice was unanimous, *Winch. Cart.*, no 22. On 21 Aug. he recd confirmation of the [re]-el. from the abp, *ib.*, no 24.
1258, 11 Dec., granted papal indult stating that he had been dispensed for illegitimacy and was eligible to hold a bpric, *CPL*, i (1198–1304), 361.
1259, 20 Aug., apptd papal chaplain, *ib.*, i, 366.
1261, 3 Feb., with William de Taunton, q.v., a contender for the bpric, but recd only a minority vote (of seven) *Ann. Winton.*, 98–9; cf. *CPL*, i (1198–1304), 378. Later this yr he was deprived of the priorate by the abp, and he appealed to the pope on both matters *sed in vacuum laboravit*, *Ann. Winton.*, 99.
1262, imprisoned at Hyde abbey by the (papally provided) new bp, John [of Exeter], from which he escaped *per cautelam et fraudem*, although he ascribed his escape to the merits of St Thomas Becket, *ib.*, 100.
1264, 9 Sept., in Rome and authorized to contract a loan for £100 for his expenses in his appeal to the apostolic see; he is here described as prior, *CPL*, i (1198–1304), 418.
1268, 13 Jan., on his deathbed the bp confessed his mistake in depriving Andrew of the priorate, removed his sentence of excommunication and restored him to his former position, *Winch. Cart.*, no 23. This restoration promise proved to be a dead letter; see Valentine.
1274, 16 Jan., returned from [?a second journey to] Rome he persisted in his appeal and the case was heard by papal judges delegate *CClR (1272–1279)*, 66. On 29 Jan. he made an abortive attempt to enter the cathedral but was excommunicated together with all those monks and others who continued to support him, *Ann. Winton.*, 116.
1276, after 13 Mar., among the bp's injunctions following a visitation was an order that the monks were not to give him communion nor to have anything to do with him, *Reg. Pontissara*, 643 (which contains the injunctions of bp Nicholas de Ely).
1276, 26 Mar., in reply the presidents of the chapter of St Swithun's gave formal notice to the bp of their appeal to Rome or Canterbury vs his injunctions especially with regard to Andrew whom they judged to have been working for the rights and liberties of their church and was therefore unjustly excommunicate, *ib.*, 644–6.

Note: see also Andrew II who is prob. the same monk, and if so this entry should show his first appearance to have been five yrs earlier.

Other members of his family were his contemporaries M. Laurence de St Martin, bp of Rochester, and M. William, the bp's brother, who was adcn of Rochester and who came to Winchester in Jan. 1274 to support Andrew in his abortive attempt to regain office, *CClR (1272–1279)*, 72, *Ann. Winton*, 117; see the entry under Laurence in the (forthcoming) *New DNB*.

I John de LONDON
occ. 1384

1384, 26 Oct., with Walter Duraunt, q.v., sent by the pr. el. and the chapter to obtain the bp's confirmation of the el. *Reg. Wykeham*, i, 149; see Robert de Rodebourne.

II John LONDON
occ. 1447 occ. 1450

1447, 15 Apr., pr., prof., and 29th in order at the el. of a bp, *Reg. Common Seal*, no 316.
1450, 11 Dec., 25th at the el. of a prior, Reg. Waynflete, i, fo 30v.

Richard de LONDON [Londonia
occ. 1325 d. 1334/5

1325, 9 Oct., 18th in order of seniority, *Reg. Pontissara*, 556.
1334/5, d., and the receiver distributed 20s. worth of bread to the poor on the day of his d., Kitchin, *SS* no 62, 232.

Thomas de LONDON
occ. 1373 occ. 1384

1373, 12 Mar., ord acol., Winchester cathedral, *Reg. Wykeham*, i, 269.
1376, 8 Mar., ord subdcn, bp's chapel, Highclere, *ib.*, i, 279.
1378, 18 Sept., ord dcn, bp's chapel, Farnham castle, *ib.*, i, 288.
1380, 19 May, ord pr., bp's chapel, Farnham castle, *ib.*, i, 296.
1384, 26 Oct., sent by the subprior and chapter, with Walter Duraunt, q.v., to obtain confirmation from the bp of their el. of Robert de Rodebourne, q.v., as prior, *Reg. Wykeham*, i, 149.

William LONDON [*alias* Alen, Aleyn
occ. 1527 occ. 1539

1527, 20 Apr., ord pr., Lady chapel, Winchester cathedral, Reg. Fox, v, fo 76v.
1529/30, *custos* of the Lady altar, WCL obedientiary acct, incorrectly numbered *SS* no 23; not in Kitchin whose *SS* no 23 is an almoner's acct.
[1528 × 1539], surname occ. in a list of monks copied on to a blank fo in Oxford, Bod. Ms Selden supra 76, fo 46v; no Christian names are given.
1539, 14 Nov., 20th to be named on the surrender list, among the commoners, and assigned an annual pension of £5 p.a., *L and P Henry VIII*, xiv, pt 2, no 520 (PRO E315/494).
Note: he appears as William Aleyn, gospeller, in the new foundation of 1541, Kitchin and Madge, *Documents*, 55, and was a musician and possibly composer; see Roger Bowers; 'The Musicians of the Lady Chapel of Winchester Cathedral Priory 1402–1539', *Journal of Ecclesiastical History*, xlv (1994), 229, n. 57.

LOUSTRESHULLE
see Lusteshall

Thomas LOVYNGTONE
occ. 1400/1

1400/1, spent 50 wks in the infirmary for which the hordarian pd 3d. per wk (while those who stayed for shorter periods were allowed 6d.), Kitchin, *SS* no 55, p. 283.

Henry de LUCEGER [Lucegershale
occ. 1272/3

1272/3, one of many monks who visited Chilbolton, WCL acct.

LUCI
see Stephen

Nicholas LUES [Leus
occ. 1350/1

1350, 5 Sept., ord acol., bp's chapel, South Waltham, *Reg. Edington*, ii, no 817 (transcribed as Lenf).
1351, 23 May, granted *lit. dim* for dcn's orders, Reg. Edington, ii, fo AA.
1351, 30 Nov., granted *lit. dim* for pr.'s orders, *ib.*, fo AAv.

LUPESCOMBE
see Lepiscombe

Philip de LUSTESHALL [Loustreshulle, Lusteshulle, Lustushulle
occ. 1306/7 d. 1316/17

1306/9, 1310/11, prob. student at Oxford since he stopped at Chilbolton each yr with *socii* on the way to Oxford, WCL accts.
[1311/12], with Nicholas de Heytesbury, q.v., students at Oxford and they stopped at Hurstbourne several times on their journeys back and forth, at a cost of 3s. 6d. on the manorial acct, WCL acct.
1308/9, visited Hurstbourne with R. Daundele and Simon Daundele, q.v., and their horses were fed, WCL acct.
1309, 25 Aug., one of four monks apptd by the chapter who appeared before the bp at his examination of the el. proceedings of prior Richard de Enford, *Reg. Woodlock*, 385.
1316, 8 July, with Ralph de Calne, q.v., recd licence from the king, at Windsor, to el. a bp, *Reg. Sandale*, 335.
1316/17, recd a loan of 4s. from the almoner; he d. this yr and the almoner distributed bread costing 13s. 4d. among the poor on the day of his burial, Kitchin, *SS* nos 23 and 24, 401 and 403; these accts are both 1316/17.

Name in Oxford, Bod. Ms 442, Hilary of Poitiers, Contra Arrianos etc. (12th c.), which he obtained [*exposuit*] from Richard de Bromwych, q.v., (under Worcester), 'pro uno parvo libello distinctionum super psalterium et tabula super originalibus sancti Augustini' (on front flyleaf).

LYCHFELDE
see Lichfeld

LYDA
see Hyda

W. de LYE
occ. 1279/80

1279/80, pd a visit to Chilbolton, WCL pipe roll acct.

Nicholas LYMYNGTONE [Lemyngtone, Lemyntone
occ. 1406 occ. 1415

1406, 19 Feb., ord acol., Winchester cathedral, Reg. Beaufort, fo A.
1408, 9 June, ord subdcn, Winchester cathedral, *ib.*, fo Bv.
1409, 23 Mar., ord dcn, Winchester cathedral, *ib.*, fo Cv.

1410, 15 Feb., ord pr., Winchester cathedral, *ib.*, fo D[v].

1409/10, one of five monks who celebrated their first mass and recd a small sum from the hordarian, Kitchin, *SS* no 57, p. 290.

1415, 26 Aug., one of the monks who witnessed the resignation of prior Thomas Nevyle, q.v., *Reg. Common Seal*, no 158.

Thomas de LYMYNGTON [Lemyngton, Lemynton
occ. 1362 occ. 1401/2

1362, 26 Feb., recd first tonsure at Hursley and *lit. dim* for minor orders, Reg. Edington, ii, fo QQ; cf. *Reg. Edington*, ii, no 922.

1363, 1 Jan., ord acol., bp's chapel, Farnham castle, *Reg. Edington*, ii, no 933.

1363, 28 May, ord subdcn, bp's chapel, Highclere, *ib.*, ii, no 934.

1363, 28 Dec., granted *lit. dim*, for orders of dcn and pr., *ib.*, ii, no 936.

1364, 9 Mar., ord dcn, bp's chapel, South Waltham, *ib.*, ii, no 937.

1393, 21/22 Aug., 8th to sign the composition with bp Wykeham, BL Ms Harley 328, fo 24; see Robert de Rodebourne.

1398, 17 July, obtained a papal mandate to transfer to Glastonbury in order to lead a stricter life, *CPL*, v (1396–1404), 154.

1401/2, spent 29 wks in the infirmary for which the hordarian pd 3d. per wk; the 10s. ordered by the bp at his visitation had not been pd *quia offic' impotens*, WCL unnumbered obedientiary acct.

Ralph LYNNE [Lenne
occ. 1412 occ. 1418

1412, 27 Feb., ord acol., Winchester cathedral, Reg. Beaufort, fo F[v].

1414, 18 Mar., ord subdcn, Winchester cathedral, *ib.*,fo I.

1415, 16 Mar., ord dcn, Winchester cathedral, *ib.*, fo L[v].

1418, 16 May, ord pr., place not named, *ib.*, fo O[v].

LYWINGUS
d. by 1122/3

1122/3, name occ. in a mortuary roll of Savigny following that of Godfrey, prior, q.v., but not distinguished as a monk, Delisle, *Rouleaux des Morts*, 336.

Geoffrey de MALA TERRA
occ. before 1085

1085, left to become abbot of Burton until 1094 when he was expelled, *HRH*, 31; he was succ. by Nigel, another monk of Winchester, q.v.

MALCHUS
occ. before 1096

1096, 27 Dec., consecrated by abp Anselm as the first bp of Waterford, *HBC*, 376.

1096, before 27 Dec., there are two letters addressed to abp Anselm: (1) from the clergy and people of Waterford and (2) from bp Walkelin (of Winchester) concerning his el. and consecration, *Anselm Letters*, iv, nos 201, 202.

MANHOD(E)
see Manwode

MANIDOWNE
see Manydowne

William de MANNEBURY [?Maunebury
d. 1313/14

1313/14, d., and the almoner gave the brethren a pittance of 6s. 8d., on the day of his burial, Kitchin, *SS* no 19, p. 394.

William MANWODE [Manhod, Manhode, Manwood
occ. 1481 occ. c. 1528

1481, 22 Dec., ord acol., Winchester cathedral, Reg. Waynflete, ii, fo 187[v].

1483, 24 May, ord subdcn, Winchester cathedral, *ib.*, ii, fo 192.

[1491], 28 May, ord pr., bp's chapel, Wolvesey, Reg. Courtenay, fo 18[v].

1493/6, 1498, 23 Apr., hordarian, Kitchin, *SS* no 60, pp. 299–302, Reg. Langton, fo 73[v].

1501, 27 Feb., subprior, Canterbury Reg. R, fo 114[v].

1486, 7 Dec., 26th in order at the el. of a bp, *Reg. Common Seal*, no 434.

1492, 29 Oct., 19th to be examined at the *sed. vac.* visitation and made no deposition, *Reg. abp Morton*, ii, no 127.

1495, 2 Dec., apptd proctor for the prior and chapter in their lawsuit vs the abp over *sed. vac.* jurisdiction, *ib.*, i, nos 229, 236; he recd another letter of apptment on 10 Dec., *ib.*, i, no 242. More details of this lengthy case and of Manwode's participation in the hearings are in *ib.*, i, nos 244, 247–50, 255 (dated 17 Oct. 1497 when tempers flared on both sides and Manwode's manner was reported as insulting), *ib.*, i, 257.

1498, 23 Apr., 14th in order at the el. of a prior, Reg. Langton, fo 73[v]; with Thomas Knyght, q.v., he had been sent to the bp to announce the d. of Thomas Hunton, q.v., the prior, *ib.*, fo 73.

1501, 27 Feb., 2nd to be examined at the visitation (*sed. vac.*, both Canterbury and Winchester) by the commissary of the prior of Christ Church, Canterbury; he reported that all the brethren lived in obedience to the prior and subprior in accordance with their Rule, that the priory was in debt [*oneratum ere alieno*] but he did not know the amount. Henry Broke, prior, q.v., complained of his display of favouritism as subprior, and Philip Yong, q.v., blamed him for the inadequate provision of food and medicine in the infirmary, Canterbury Reg. R, fo 114^{v}.

[1528 × 1539], surname in occ. a list of monks copied on to a blank fo in Oxford, Bod. Ms Selden supra 76, fo 46^{v}; no Christian names are given.

Name occ. in Oxford, Bod., Ms Digby 31, Jacobus de Cessolis (15th c.); this ms contains two treatises: (1) De ludo scacharum by Cessolis (fos 1–72^{v}) and (2) De regimine sanitatis of Bartholomew (fos 73–86). It also contains a list of c. thirteen books which were at New College in 1489 (on fo 88). On the otherwise blank fo 87^{v}, his name in full occ. opposite the list of books.

William MANYDOWNE B.Th. [Manidowne, Manydoune, Manydowen, Manyndowne

occ. 1501 occ. [1528 × 1539]

1519/23, 1524, 30 Nov., 2 Dec., almoner, WCL unnumbered obedientiary acct, Reg. Fox, v, fos 75, 77.

1514/15, 1516/17, student at Oxford with John Avynton, q.v., and they each recd *in exhibicione* from the almoner, 6s. 8d., Kitchin, *SS* no 44, p. 460 and no 45, p. 464.

1518, 27 Nov., supplicated for B.Th., *BRUO, 1501–1540*.

1520, by 14 Feb., B.Th., Pantin, *BMC*, iii, 120.

1501, 27 Feb., sixteen yrs of age and the last to be examined at the visitation (*sed. vac.* both Canterbury and Winchester) by the commissary of the prior of Christ Church, Canterbury; he reported that he had been prof. a little more than three wks earlier but had not yet been tonsured. Apart from this all was well, Canterbury Reg. R, fo 115.

1520, 14/16 Feb., one of five monks apptd to appear at a Black Monk Chapter summoned by cardinal Wolsey to Westminster, Pantin, *BMC*, iii, 120–122 (Reg. ii, fo 23, 23^{v}).

1524, 2 Dec., preached at the el. of a prior and was 12th in order, Reg. Fox, v, fos 75–77. He also was named as one of three *scrutatores*, *ib.* See Henry Broke who cast his vote for Manydowne and was the only one to do so, *ib.*, v, fo 77.

[1528 × 1539], surname occ. in a list of monks copied on to a blank fo in Oxford, Bod. Ms Selden supra 76, fo 46^{v}; no Christian names are given.

William MARCHALL

occ. 1459 occ. 1465

1459, 17 Feb., ord acol., Winchester cathedral, Reg. Waynflete, i, fo R.

1465, 8 June, ord subdcn, Winchester cathedral, *ib.*, i, fo H*^{v}.

Peter MARESCHALL [le Marescal, Marescall, Marescallus

occ. 1279/80 d. 1314/15

1280/1, prob. cellarer, Watkin, 'Rec. Acct', 100.

1279/80, pd visits to Crondall, Eston and Little Hinton [Hiniton], WCL pipe roll accts.

1280/1, recd 8d. from the receiver for [supervising the] winnowing at Mardon; he was also sent, on two occasions, with others to London on business on behalf of the receiver, and appeared before the justices in Southampton, Watkin, 'Rec. Acct', 97, 100, 103.

1314/15, d., and the almoner gave a pittance of 6s. 8d., to the convent on the day of his burial, Kitchin, *SS* no 21, p. 395.

William MARESCHALL [Mareschal, Marschal, Mascal, Maschal

occ. 1361 occ. 1364

1361, 7 Apr., acol. granted *lit. dim* for subdcn's orders, Reg Edington, ii, fo OO^{v}.

1362, 26 Feb., [subdcn], granted *lit. dim.* for dcn's orders, *Reg. Edington*, ii, no 922.

1363, 28 May, ord dcn, bp's chapel, Highclere, *ib.*, ii, no 934.

1363, 28 Dec., granted *lit. dim* for pr.'s orders, *ib.*, ii, no 936 (transcribed as Yascal, sc. Mascal).

1364, 9 Mar., ord pr., bp's chapel, South Waltham, *ib.*, ii, no 937.

MARESCHALL

see also Mascal

John MARLBOROWE

occ. 1492

1492, 29 Oct., 11th to be examined at the *sed. vac.* visitation. He deposed, in line with a number of his brethren, that the sick were not receiving adequate care, that there was no inventory of church goods and that annual accts were not being provided by the obedientiaries, *Reg. abp Morton*, ii, no 127.

Note: this is prob. a slip of the copyist's pen for Richard; see Richard Marleburgh II.

I Richard MARLEBURGH [Marlebergh, Marleburghe

occ. 1403 d. 1457

1450–1457, prior: el. 11 Dec. 1450, Reg. Waynflete, i, fos 29^{v}–34; d. 13 Apr. 1457, *Reg. Common Seal*, no 332.

1403, 22 Sept., ord acol., Waltham, *Reg. Wykeham*, i, 356.

1404, 23 Feb., ord subdcn, Waltham, *ib.*, i, 357.

1404, 21 May, subdcn, granted *lit. dim* to all orders , *ib.*, ii, 556.

1404, 20 Sept., ord dcn, Waltham, *ib.*, i, 358.

1416/17, 1422/3, chamberlain, Kitchin, *SS* nos 4, 5, pp. 363–372.

1423/4, hordarian, PRO SC6/758/5.

1427/8, chamberlain, Kitchin, *SS* no 6, pp. 372–375.
1429/30, hordarian, PRO SC6/758/7.
1432/3, chamberlain, Kitchin, *SS* no 7, pp. 375–376.
1433/5; 1447, 12/17 Apr.; 1450, 11 Dec., hordarian, PRO SC6/758/8 and 9; *Reg. Common Seal*, nos 313, 316, 317; Reg. Waynflete, i, fo 30^{v}.
Note: this seems an unusual pattern of office holding.

1404, 16 Oct., 40th and third from last in order at the el. of a bp; he is described as prof. and in pr.'s orders, but see Henry Bradle.
1409/10, visited Crondall and the manorial acct was charged 12d. for his expenses, WCL acct.
1422/3, pd several visits to Ham (Wilts.) to hold courts, Kitchin, *SS* no 5, p. 371.
1423/4, visited Woolstone, PRO SC6/758/5.
1427/8, held courts at Ham, Kitchin, *SS* no 6, p. 373,
1432/3, pd several visits to Ham, *ib.*, *SS* no 7, p. 376.
1447, 15 Apr., 6th in order at the el. of a bp, *Reg. Common Seal*, no 316; on 12 Apr., he and Robert Puryton, q.v., had been sent by the prior and chapter to the king for licence to el., and on 17 Apr., the same two were sent to obtain royal consent to the el. of Waynflete, *ib.*, nos 313, 317.
1450, 11 Dec., 4th in order at his el. as prior and was named as one of seven *compromissorii*, Reg. Waynflete, i, fos 30^{v}, 31.
1453, [Jan/Feb.], listed on the bp's certificate as intending to appear in person at convocation, Reg. Waynflete, i, fo 20*.

A few of his *acta* as prior are entered in *Reg. Common Seal*, nos 322, 327, 330, 331.

II Richard MARLEBURGH

occ. 1475 occ. 1498

1475, 23 Sept., ord acol., Winchester cathedral, Reg. Waynflete, ii, fo 174^{v}.
1476, 21 Dec., ord subdcn, Winchester cathedral, *ib.*, ii, fo 176^{v}.
1477, 1 Mar., ord dcn, Winchester cathedral, *ib.*, ii, fo 177.

1498, 23 Apr., fourth prior, Reg. Langton, fo 73^{v}.

1486, 7 Dec., 16th in order at the el. of a bp, *Reg. Common Seal*, no 434.
1498, 23 Apr., 4th in order at the el. of a prior, Reg. Langton, fo 73^{v}.

Note: see John Marlborowe who is prob. the same monk.

Thomas de MARLEBURGH [Marleburghe

occ. 1304/5 occ. 1307/8

1307/8, one of two receivers, Kitchin, *SS* no 65, p. 469 and possibly *ib.*, pp. 467–468; see Peter de Basyng.
1304/5, visited Stockton (Wilts.) and Patney, WCL accts; from Patney he took the pound of cumin that had been recd as recognizance.
1307/8, with Peter de Basyng, q.v., visited Chilbolton, WCL acct.

William de MARLEBURGH [Marleberge, Marleburge

occ. 1309 occ. 1325

1309, c. 25 Aug., one of four monks who acted as *instructores* in the el. of a prior, *Reg. Woodlock*, 385.
1311, 20 Aug., named, with John de Donketone, q.v., as proctor for the prior and chapter in a case vs the adcns who claimed the right to participate in the el. of a prior, Winchester College Muniment 1013.
1325, 9 Oct., 21st in order of seniority, *Reg. Pontissara*, 556.

MARLEBURGH

see also Merleburg

Peter MARLOW [Marlowe, Morlowe

occ. 1483 occ. 1501

1483, 24 May, ord acol., Winchester cathedral, Reg. Waynflete, ii, fo 192.
1485, 17 Dec., ord subdcn, Winchester cathedral, *ib.*, ii, fo 200.
1491, 16 June, ord pr., church of St John the Baptist in the Soke, Winchester, Reg. Courtenay, fo 19^{v}.

1498, 23 Apr., hostiller, Reg. Langton, fo 73^{v}.
1501, 27 Feb., precentor, Canterbury Reg. R, fo 115.

1486, 7 Dec., 29th and second to last in order at the el. of a bp, *Reg. Common Seal*, no 434.
1492, 29 Oct., 24th to be examined at the *sed. vac.* visitation and complained of the 'dishonourable words' used by the prior, Thomas Hunton, q.v., to the monks, and of the inadequate care given to the sick, *Reg. abp Morton*, ii, no 127.
1498, 23 Apr., 17th in order at the el. of a prior, Reg. Langton, fo 73^{v}.
1501, 27 Feb., 13th to be examined at the visitation (*sed. vac.* both Canterbury and Winchester) by the commissary of the prior of Christ Church, Canterbury; he deposed that despite the funds provided for the sick they were not being adequately provided for, Canterbury Reg. R, fo 115.

MARLOW

see also Merlawe

Roger de MARMYON

occ. 1325 occ. 1360/1

1351/2, curtarian, WCL Wonston acct.
1358/9, 1360/61, hordarian, PRO SC6/756/16, 17, succ. Nicholas Haywode, q.v; he was followed by William de Thudden, q.v.

1325, 9 Oct., 46th in order of seniority, *Reg. Pontissara*, 556.
1338/9, visited Woolstone for supervisory purposes [*supervidend'*], PRO SC6/756/9.
1345, 28 July, named as one of nine *compromissorii* in the el. of a bp, *Reg. Common Seal*, no 5.
1345, 15 Aug., one of the monks found guilty of proceeding to el. a bp vs the king's command, *CPR (1343–1345)*, 581; see John le Devenish.
1354/5, named as *custos* of the manor of Silkstead, WCL acct.
1358/9, visited Woolstone, PRO SC6/756/16.

A Philip Marmyon was bailiff of Whitchurch in 1329/30, WCL acct.

John MARWELL [Merwell
occ. 1509 occ. 1524
1509, 24 Mar., ord subdcn, bp's chapel, Esher, Reg. Fox, ii, fo 24.
1524, 2 Dec., 17th in order at the el. of a prior, Reg. Fox, v, fo 75; he nom. John Meone II, q.v., 'propter eius bonam religionem et circumspectionem', *ib.*, v, fo 77v.

Ralph MASCAL [Marchall, Marechal, Marschal, Mascall, Maschal
occ. 1412 occ. 1447
1412, 27 Feb., ord acol., Winchester cathedral, Reg. Beaufort, fo Fv.
1414, 18 Mar., ord subdcn, Winchester cathedral, *ib.*, fo I.
1414, 18 Sept., ord dcn, Winchester cathedral, *ib.*, fo Iv.
1415, 2 June, ord pr., Winchester cathedral, *ib.*, fo Kv.
1415/16, celebrated his first mass and was given 8d. by the almoner, Kitchin, *SS* no 37, p. 439.
1423/4, 1425/6, curtarian/cellarer, WCL Chilbolton and Crondall accts.
1447, 15 Apr., infirmarer, *Reg. Common Seal*, no 316.
1423/4, visited Chilbolton at the time of shearing, WCL acct.
1425/6, stayed at Crondall *pro piscibus*, WCL acct.
1431, 18 Apr., granted a plenary indulgence, *CPL*, viii (1427–1447), 363; on 18 June he was granted an indult to choose his confessor, *ib.*, 361.
1447, 15 Apr., 11th in order at the el. of a bp, *Reg. Common Seal*, no 316.

His father was John Mascal of Stockton (Wilts.), *nativus*, who was manumitted on 3 Nov. 1417, *Reg. Common Seal*, no 178, and who served as farmer of the priory manor there in 1399/1400, BL Add. Roll 24395. In 1420 he was granted a corrody, which was charged to the Stockton acct, in the priory at Winchester and which included board, lodging and clothing such as were provided for the prior's *valecti*, *Reg. Common Seal*, no 188. In 1409/10 he had pd a fine to the prior of £13 6s. 8d., BL Add. Roll 24404; could this have been for the freedom of his son? Other relatives occ. at Stockton (Wilts.) in 1462, *Reg. Common Seal*, no 351.

MASCAL
see also Mareschall

Roger MATHEU [Mathew
occ. 1496 occ. 1501
1496, 24 Sept., ord subdcn, Hyde abbey, Reg. Langton, fo 29v.
1497, 11 Mar., ord dcn, St Laurence's church, Winchester, *ib.*, fo 31.
1499, 21 Dec., ord pr., Winchester cathedral, *ib.*, fo 35.
1498, 23 Apr., dcn and 25th in order at the el. of a prior, Reg. Langton, fo 73v.
1501, 27 Feb., 19th to be examined at the visitation (*sed. vac.* both Canterbury and Winchester) by the commissary of the prior of Christ Church, Canterbury; he reported *omnia bene*, Canterbury Reg. R, fo 115.

MAUNEBERY
see Mannebury

John MAYNYSFORD [Mayngsforde
occ. 1461
1461, 30 May, ord acol., Romsey, Reg. Waynflete, i, fo Yv.

Note: in Sept. 1465, he was ord dcn as a canon of Southwark, *ib.*, i, I*, and so either he transferred or the above entry was incorrect.

MEANE
see Meone

Robert de MELUN [Melum
occ. 1187 occ. 1189/90
1187, before, subprior, *Ann. Winton.*, 63, where his el. as abbot of Malmesbury is entered under this yr.
1189/90, el. abbot of Malmesbury, *HRH*, 56.

Geoffrey de MEONE [Mene, Menes, Meynes, Munes
occ. 1279/80 d. 1313/14
1283/4, possibly curtarian/[cellarer], WCL Wonston acct; see John de Northwolde.
1279/80, visited Hurstbourne, WCL pipe roll acct. He also was sent to the king with part repayment of a loan made in aid of the monks to the lay official in charge of the priory *sed. vac.*, *CPR (1272–1281)*, 304.
[1282 Sept.], bp Pontissara wrote to an unnamed monk urging him to persuade Geoffrey to return from the curia where he was campaigning vs the abp, *Reg. Pontissara*, 261 (transcribed as Munes).

[1282], 7 Sept., the abp wrote to the prior and convent ordering them to recall him from the curia where he was seeking papal absolution from the abp's excommunication [over alleged irregularities in the recent episcopal el.]. *Epist. Pecham*, ii, 413.

[c. 1282], wrote a letter to John de Kyrkeby seeking advice, PRO SC1/48/79.

1282/3, with Nicholas de Grenham, q.v., visited Whitchurch for *liberatio denariorum*, WCL borough acct.

1283/4, cheese from Wonston was delivered to him at St Swithun's, WCL acct.

1284, 1 Apr., with the *senescallus*, appted by the prior and chapter to look into their interests in the manor of ?Swainston, Isle of Wight, PRO E42/482.

1313/14, d., and the almoner gave 6s. 8d. in pittances to the convent, Kitchin, *SS* no 19, p. 394.

I John de MEONE [Moene
occ. 1385 d. 1418/19

1385, 23 Dec., ord acol., bp's chapel, Farnham castle, *Reg. Wykeham*, i, 310.

1387, 23 Mar., ord subdcn, bp's chapel, Marwell, *ib.*, i, 314.

1387, 21 Sept., ord dcn, bp's chapel, Marwell, *ib.*, i, 316.

1388, 19 Dec., ord pr., bp's chapel, Farnham castle, *ib.*, i, 318.

1393, 21/22 Aug., 32nd to sign the composition with bp Wykeham, BL Ms Harley 328, fo 24^{v}; see Robert de Rodebourne.

1404, 16 Oct., 18th at the el. of a bp, *Reg. Common Seal*, no 68.

1418/19, d., and the almoner distributed 10s. worth of bread [among the poor] on the day of his burial, Kitchin, *SS* no 38, p. 441.

II John MEONE [Mean, Meane, Mene *alias* Rynge
occ. 1492 occ. 1539

[1493, 21 Sept.], ord acol, Hyde abbey, Reg. Langton, fo 23^{v}.

1520, 14/16 Feb.; 1524, 2 Dec.; [1525], sacrist, Pantin, *BMC*, iii, 120–122 (Reg. ii, fo 23, 23^{v}); Reg. Fox, v, fo 75; BL Add. Ms 29436, fo 352^{v}.

1535, almoner, *Valor Eccles.*, ii, 2.

1492, 29 Oct., 27th and last to be examined at the *sed. vac.* visitation and made no deposition, *Reg. abp Morton*, ii, no 127.

1498, 23 Apr., dcn and 22nd in order at the el. of a prior, Reg. Langton, fo 73^{v}.

1520, 14/16 Feb., one of five Winchester monks apptd to appear at a Black Monk Chapter summoned by cardinal Wolsey to Westminster, Pantin, *BMC*, iii, 120–122 (Reg. ii, fo 23, 23^{v}).

1524, 2 Dec., 5th in order at the el. of a prior and one of three *scrutatores*, Reg. Fox, v, fos 75–78; he was himself nom. by six, *ib.*

[1528 × 1539], surname occ. in a list of monks copied on to a blank folio in Oxford, Bod. Ms Selden supra 76, fo 46^{v}; no Christian names are given.

1539, 14 Nov., 6th in order, among the seniors, in the surrender list and awarded an annual pension of £8, p.a., *L and P Henry VIII*, xiv, pt 2, no 520 (PRO E315/494).

Name in BL Ms Sloane 418, Medical treatises, fos 189–352 (15th c.); on a receipt copied on fo 352^{v} where he is described as sacrist.

Philip de MEONE [Menes
occ. 1325 occ. 1332

1325, 9 Oct., 4th in order of seniority, *Reg. Pontissara*, 556.

1332, 18 Oct., present in the prior's chapel at the reading of ordinances, drawn up by the chapter following discussions about the debts of two of the obedientiary offices, which prescribed new financial arrangements to alleviate the crisis, *Winch. Cart.*, no 180; see Alexander de Heriard.

Thomas MERE [Meere, More, Moure
occ. 1363/5

1363, 28 Dec., obtained *lit. dim.*, for the orders of dcn and pr., *Reg. Edington*, ii, no 936.

1364, 9 Mar., ord dcn, bp's chapel, South Waltham, *ib.*, ii, no 937.

1365, 20 Sept., ord pr., bp's chapel, Sutton, *ib.*, ii, no 945.

Henry de MEREWELL
see Woodlock

Nicholas de MEREWELL [Merewelle
occ. 1260 occ. 1295

1284, 13 July, confirmed by the bp as subprior after having been chosen unanimously by the monks, *sed. vac.*; he was authorized to have full custody of both spirituals and temporals until a prior was el., *Reg. Pontissara*, 284.

1295, 30 May, 6 June, subprior, *ib.*, 71, 73.

1260, 28 Dec., one of three monks who recd a licence to el. a bp from the king at Windsor, *CPR (1258–66)*, 132.

[1270/1], visited Crondall, WCL acct.

1280/1, recd 7d. from the receiver for the expenses of his journey to the Isle of Wight and also 66s. 8d. for him to purchase spices for the convent, Watkin, 'Rec. Acct', 95, 97.

1282, 10 Aug., one of the monks absolved from excommunication incurred because of irregularities in their el. of Richard de la More as bp, *Reg. abp Pecham*, ii, 51; see Adam de Farnham.

1283, 12 Jan., one of the monks apptd to serve with the prior [Adam de Farnham, q.v.] as proctors to meet with the king and bp concerning the reform of the convent, PRO E135/3/39b.

[1283], one of four monks apptd with the prior and Valentine [de Wherewell], q.v., as proctors in an appeal to the king because of the chapter's dispute with the bp, *Reg. Pontissara*, 662–663 (where the date is given as c. 1276; but see *ib.*, 399–400).
1284, 18 July, with the convent applied to the bp for a licence to el. a prior, *Reg. Pontissara*, 284.
1295, 30 May/7 June, presided over the el. of a prior, *ib.*, 71–77.

He is believed to have been the uncle of Henry Woodlock, q.v., Watkin, 'Rec. Acct', 95 n. 8.

I Richard de MEREWELL [Merewelle, Merwell

occ. 1307/8 occ. 1349

1318, Apr.; 1319, 24 Nov., subprior, BL Add. Ms 29436 fo 81; *Reg. Sandale*, 285 and *CPR (1317–1321)*, 402.
1332, 18 Oct.; [1335], 7 June; 1336, 16 Feb., 19 July; 1338, 17 Apr.; 1340, 22 June, 28 Sept.; 1345, 28 July, sacrist, *Winch. Cart.*, no 180; *ib.*, no 267; Reg. Orleton, i, fos 32, 40^{v}; *ib.*, ii, fo 84, i, fo 97; *Reg. Common Seal*, no 5.
1307/9, pd visits to Chilbolton, WCL accts.
1314, 13 Aug., at Waltham, with Adam de Sarum, q.v., witness to an episcopal instrument, *Reg. Woodlock*, 633.
1319, 24 Nov., with John de Donketone, q.v., proctors for the prior and chapter, recd licence to el. a bp from the king, at York, *Reg. Sandale*, 285 (appndx).
1325, 9 Oct., 24th in order of seniority, *Reg. Pontissara*, 556.
1328, 27 June, with Adam de Sarum, q.v., sent by the subprior and chapter to obtain the bp's licence to el. a prior, Reg. Stratford, fo 107.
1330, 8 Jan., with Richard de Pek, q.v., acted as proctors for the prior and chapter in drawing up an agreement over burial rights with the college of St Elizabeth, near Wolvesey, *Winch. Cart.*, no 148.
1332, 18 Oct., joined the monks in urging the prior to agree to the petition presented to him by the chapter in the financial crisis faced by the community, *Winch. Cart.*, no 180; see Alexander de Heriard.
[1335], 7 June, sent as proctor, with John le Devenish, q.v., to discuss certain matters with the bp, *Winch. Cart.*, no 267.
1336, 16 Feb., with John le Devenish, q.v., apptd to act as confessors to the monks and others in the city and diocese, Reg. Orleton, i, fo 32; on 19 July both monks were licensed to hear confessions even in reserved cases during the bp's absence, *ib.*, i, fo 40^{v}.
1338, 17 Apr., the licence to act as penitentiary was reconfirmed, *ib.*, i, fo 58.
1340, 22 June, as sacrist and patron of St Mary *in atrio* [of the cathedral] instituted a new rector, *ib.*, ii, fo 84.
1340, 28 Sept., addressed by the bp as 'our *primarius*', *ib.*, i, fo 97.
1345, 28 July, apptd as one of nine *compromissorii* in the el. of a bp, *Reg. Common Seal*, no 5.
1347, 10 Feb., having been previously apptd penitentiary by the bp el., he was now licensed as such by the bp, *Reg. Edington*, ii, no 55.
1348, 19 Sept., licensed as confessor to the nuns at Romsey at their request, *ib.*, ii, no 162.
1349, 31 Mar., with William de Sparsholt, q.v., acted as *instructores* in the examination of the el. proceedings of prior John de Merlawe, q.v., *Reg. Edington*, i, no 563.

II Richard de MEREWELL [Merewelle, Merwell

occ. 1350 occ. 1361

1350, 5 Sept., ord acol., bp's chapel, South Waltham, *Reg. Edington*, ii, no 817.
1350, 18 Sept., ord subdcn, bp's chapel, Highclere, *ib.*, ii, no 814.
1353, 22 Aug., recd *lit. dim*, for pr.'s orders, *ib.*, ii, no 845.
1354, 20 Dec., ord pr., bp's chapel [Bishops] Waltham, *ib.*, ii, no 852.
1361, 9 Dec., one of the monks who vouched for the unanimity of the el. as prior of William de Thudden at the judicial proceedings before the bp, but on 17 Jan. 1362 he was replaced at the inquiry by John de Guldeford I, q.v., *Reg. Edington*, i, no 1490.

III Richard MEREWELL [Merewelle

occ. 1398 occ. 1402

1398, 21 Dec., ord acol., bp's chapel, Farnham castle, *Reg. Wykeham*, i, 346.
1400, 18 Sept., ord subdcn, bp's chapel, Waltham, *ib.*, i, 351.
1402, 18 Feb., ord dcn, bp's chapel, Waltham, *ib.*, i, 353.

Robert de MEREWELL [Merewelle, Morewelle

occ. 1368 occ. 1393

1368, 4 Mar., ord acol., Winchester cathedral, *Reg. Wykeham*, i, 252.
1368, 23 Dec., ord subdcn, bp's chapel, Farnham castle, *ib.*, i, 255.
1369, 22 Sept., ord dcn, Winchester cathedral, *ib.*, i, 257.
1370, 21 Sept., ord pr., bp's chapel, Highclere, *ib.*, i, 261.
1370/1, celebrated his first mass and recd 6d. from the anniversarian, WCL unnumbered obedientiary acct.
1387, 7 Aug., 1393, 21/2 Aug., sacrist, *Reg. Wykeham*, i, 162, BL Ms Harley 328, fo 24^{v}.
1393, 21/22 Aug., 17th to sign the composition with bp Wykeham, BL Ms Harley 328, fo 24^{v}; see Robert de Rodebourne.

MEREWELL
see also Marwell

John MERKE [Merk
occ. 1399 d. 1422/3

1399, 22 Feb., ord acol., bp's chapel, Farnham castle, *Reg. Wykeham*, i, 347.
1401, 28 May, ord subdcn, bp's chapel, Waltham, *ib.*, i, 352.
1402, 18 Feb., ord dcn, bp's chapel, Waltham, *ib.*, i, 353.
1402, 20 May, ord pr., bp's chapel, Waltham, *ib.*, i, 354.
1404, 16 Oct., 33rd in order at the el. of a bp, *Reg. Common Seal*, no 68.
1422/3, d., and the chamberlain pd the brief bearer 10s., Kitchin, *SS* no 5, p. 370.

I John de MERLAWE
occ. 1325 d. 1361

1349–1361, prior: el. on or by 21 Mar. 1349, *Reg. Edington*, i, no 558; d. before 9 Dec. 1361, *ib.*, i, no 1490.
1325/6, 1328/30, receiver, WCL Chilbolton, Wonston and Whitchurch accts.
1328/9, hordarian, Kitchin, *SS* no 48, pp. 257–260 (where the date is given as 1329/30).
1330/7, receiver, *ib.*, *SS* nos 48–53, pp. 257–278 and no 62, pp. 224–244; during these yrs he also acctd for the hordarian's office which was *in manibus domini prioris*; see the petition below.
1337/40; 1341/4, receiver, WCL Whitchurch, Wonston, Barton accts; Wonston accts.
1344/5, hordarian, PRO SC6/756/11.
1354/5, hordarian, PRO SC6/756/15.
1325, 9 Oct., 37th in order of seniority, *Reg. Pontissara*, 556.
1325/6, visited Chilbolton, WCL acct.
1327/8, visited Silkstead and recd *liberatio denariorum*, for wool, WCL acct.
1328/9, visited Wonston, WCL acct.
1329/30, visited Silkstead and Whitchurch, WCL accts.
1330/2, pd visits to Silkstead as above, WCL accts; he was also at Wonston in 1331/2, WCL acct.
1332, 18 Oct., present in the prior's chapel at the reading of ordinances, drawn up by the chapter following discussions about the debts of two of the obedientiary offices, which prescribed new financial arrangements to alleviate the crisis, *Winch. Cart.*, no 180; see Alexander de Heriard.
1333/4, visited Whitchurch, WCL acct; it was prob. during this yr that he was named proctor for the prior and convent with regard to the *sed. vac.* possession of two of their churches, *ib.*, *Winch. Cart.*, nos 424–427.
1334/5, pd visits to Littleton and Wonston, WCL accts, and also to Woolstone, PRO SC6/756/6.
1335/6, pd visits to Wonston and Woolstone, WCL acct, PRO SC6/756/7; at Woolstone he and his clerk dined on fowl and goose, *ib.*
1336/7, visited Chilbolton, Whitchurch and Woolstone, WCL accts, PRO SC6/756/8.
1337/8, stopped at Chilbolton on his journey to and from Wiltshire where he was involved in a *die amoris* with the prior of St Margaret's, Marlborough, Worcester Cathedral Muniment, C.866; he also visited Wootton for *liberatio denariorum*, Kitchin, *Manydown*, 149.
1338/9, pd several visits to Silkstead, visited Barton and Wonston and also went to Chilbolton for *liberatio denariorum*, WCL accts.
1341/4, made visits to Wonston, WCL accts; in 1343/4 he was at Silkstead for *liberatio denariorum*, WCL acct.
1344/5, pd a visit to Woolstone, PRO SC6/756/11.
1349, 5/31 Mar., details of some of the el. proceedings from the request for the episcopal licence to el. a prior to the episcopal confirmation of the prior elect are in *Reg. Edington*, i, nos 556–565. The subprior and chapter requested the bp, on the grounds that the choice was unanimous, to confirm the el. immediately; the bp refused until he had examined the proceedings.
1351, 24 Sept., on the authority of papal letters, examined a clerk and adm. him to the office of notary, *Winch. Cart.*, no 365.
1354/5, with his palfrey, pd a visit to Woolstone, PRO SC6/756/15.
1355, 10 Nov., comm. by the king to administer the oath of office to the new sheriff and warden of Winchester castle, *Winch. Cart.*, no 347; on 16 Nov., he was comm. to do the same to the mayor of the wool staple, *Winch. Cart.*, no 352.
1356, 14 Feb. comm. by the king to personally inspect the castle and bridge at Winchester and the royal manor at Wolmer [*sic*] in order to examine the repairs carried out and the expense accts; he reported that all was in order, *Winch. Cart.*, nos 357, 358.
1356, 9 Apr., examined and adm. another clerk to the office of notary on papal authority, *Winch. Cart.*, no 366.
1360, 24 Aug., with the chancellor of the diocese, apptd vicar general during the bp's absence in Calais, *Reg. Edington*, i, no 1227; see Ralph de Basyng, Walter de Bray, John Hyde, Robert de Walyngford.

II John MERLAWE [Marlowe, Merelawe, Merlaghe
occ. 1372 d. 1415/16

1372, 18 Sept., ord acol., Winchester cathedral, *Reg. Wykeham*, i, 268.
1373, 12 Mar., ord subdcn, Winchester cathedral, *ib.*, i, 269.
1376, 8 Mar., ord dcn, bp's chapel, Highclere, *ib.*, i, 279.

1377, 19 Dec., ord pr., bp's chapel, Farnham castle, *ib.*, i, 286.

1393, 21/22 Aug., 21st to sign the composition with bp Wykeham, BL Ms Harley 328, fo 24v; see Robert de Rodebourne.

1404, 16 Oct., 12th at the el. of a bp, *Reg. Common Seal*, no 68.

1415, 4 Oct., with Ralph Southam, q.v., apptd instructores to inform the bp of the el. proceedings of Thomas Shirebourne as prior, *Reg. Common Seal*, no 168.

1415/16, d., and the almoner distributed 10s. worth of bread to the poor, Kitchin, *SS* no 37, p. 439.

H. de MERLEBURG
n.d.

Name in Leyden University Library, Voss lat. F. 93, Macrobius etc. (early 13th c.); *contulit*—.

MERLEBURG
see also Marlborowe, Marlburgh

Nicholas MERSCH [Mersh, Merssh
occ. 1447 occ. 1470

1447, 15 Apr., 1450/1, 1458/9, *custos operum*, *Reg. Common Seal*, no 316, WCL unnumbered obedientiary acct fragments.

1458/70, chamberlain, WCL Ham acct for 1469/70.

1447, 15 Apr., 15th in order at the el. of a bp, *Reg. Common Seal*, no 316.

1449/50, pd visits to Enford and Mapledurham, BL Harley Roll X.11, BL Add. Roll 28129.

1450, 11 Dec., 11th at the el. of a prior, Reg. Waynflete, i, fo 30v.

1450/1, visited Stockton (Wilts.) for *liberatio denariorum*, BL Add. Roll 24417.

1457, 18 Apr., with William Wroughton, q.v., apptd proctors to obtain an episcopal licence to el. a prior; *Reg. Common Seal*, no 332; on 15 May the same two were sent to the bp to request his confirmation of the el. of Robert Westgate, q.v., *ib.*, no 336, and two days later they recd an apptment as proctors for the subprior and convent in all matters concerning the el., *ib.*, no 337.

1458/70, pd regular visits to Ham (Wilts.) to hold courts and receive payments due, WCL acct for 1469/70.

1470, 5 Apr., with William Shirebourne, q.v., named as proctors of Thomas Hunton, q.v., prior el., and presented him to the bp seeking confirmation, Reg. Waynflete, ii, fo 1v.

MERTON
see Morton

MERWELL
see Marwell, Merewell

?MEYCROFTE
occ. [1528 × 1539]

[1528 × 1539], surname occ. in a list of monks copied on to a blank fo in Oxford, Bod. Ms Selden supra 76, fo 46v; no Christian names are given. This is almost certainly John Haycroft, q.v., although it is written as above in this manuscript.

MEYNES
see Meone

Robert de MICHELDEVERE [Mucheldevere
occ. 1325 occ. 1337/8

1325, 9 Oct., 52nd in order of seniority, *Reg. Pontissara*, 557.

1337/8, visited Wootton, Kitchin, *Manydown*, 149.

Note: two clerks with this name were given their first tonsure by bp Woodlock on 10 Mar. 1313, *Reg. Woodlock*, 853.

John MIDELTONE [Middultone, Mydelton, Mydeltone
occ. 1368 occ. 1404

1368, 23 Dec., ord subdcn, bp's chapel, Farnham castle, *Reg. Wykeham*, i, 255.

1369, 22 Sept., ord dcn, Winchester cathedral, *ib.*, i, 257.

1370, 21 Sept., ord pr., bp's chapel, Highclere, *ib.*, i, 261.

1370/1, celebrated his first mass and the anniversarian gave him 6d., WCL unnumbered acct.

1400, 10 Dec., [1402], 7 Mar., hostiller, Reg. Wykeham, ii, fos 329, 344.

1393, 21/22 Aug., 19th to sign the composition with by Wykeham, BL Ms Harley 328, fo 24v; see Robert de Rodebourne.

1395/6, visited Chilbolton and dined on capon, WCL acct.

1398/9, visited Crondall, WCL acct.

1400, 10 Dec., as hostiller, licensed to administer the sacraments at Littleton [because of insufficient funds for a chaplain; see John Hyde], for one yr, Reg. Wykeham, ii, fo 324.

[1402], 7 Mar., given another licence for Littleton as above, *ib.*, ii, fo 344.

1404, 16 Oct., 11th in order at the el. of a bp, *Reg. Common Seal*, no 68.

Peter MILYNGTON [Millyngtone
occ. 1471/2

1471, 21 Dec., ord pr., bp's chapel, Waltham, Reg. Waynflete, ii, fo 168.

1471/2, celebrated his first mass and the almoner sent wine for the feast, Kitchin, *SS* no 42, p. 453.

Note: this is prob. Peter Morton, q.v.

Alexander de MONTIBUS
occ. 1279/80 occ. 1282

1279/80, visited Whitchurch borough and, with William de Basyng I and Peter de Wynton, q.v., recd *liberatio denariorum*; he also visited Chilbolton, Houghton and Hurstbourne, WCL pipe roll acct.
1282, 15 June, one of the monks absolved from excommunication for contempt of mandates concerning an episcopal el., *Reg. abp Pecham*, ii, 161–162; he is also named n the comm. for absolution issued 10 Aug., *ib.*, ii, 51.

See also Alexander I and II.

MORE
see Mere

MOREWELL
see Robert de Merewell

MORLOWE
see Marlow

Adam de MORTON [Mortoun
occ. 1266/7 occ. 1269/70

1269/70, prob. receiver, with William de la Brome, q.v., WCL Havant acct.
1266/7, with Walter de Oxonia, q.v., visited Patney, *supervenien[tes ad scaccarium*, Michelmersh and Whitchurch for *liberatio denariorum*, WCL pipe roll acct.
1267/8, with Walter de Oxonia visited Barton for *liberatio denariorum*, WCL acct.
1269/70, pd a visit to Havant, with William de la Brome and also to Hurstbourne for the same reason, WCL accts.

I John de MORTON [Mortune
occ. 1272/3 occ. 1282

1272/3, visited Chilbolton, WCL acct.
1282, 7 Aug., one of the monks who sought absolution from excommunication for irregularities of procedure in their el. of Richard de la More as bp, *Reg. abp Pecham*, i, 188–189; the comm. for absolution is dated 10 Aug., *ib.*, ii, 51. See Adam de Farnham.

II John MORTON [Merton, Mortun'
occ. 1496 occ. 1539

1496, 24 Sept., ord acol., Hyde abbey, Reg. Langton, fo 29v.
1498, 10 Mar., ord subdcn, St Laurence's church, Winchester, *ib.*, fo 32.
1499, 21 Sept., ord dcn, bp's chapel, Marwell, *ib.*, fo 34v.
1520, 14/16 Feb., 1524, 2 Dec., precentor, Pantin, *BMC*, iii, 120–122, Reg. Fox, v, fo 75.
1535, chamberlain, *Valor Eccles.*, ii, 2.

1498, 23 Apr., subdcn and 29th in order at the el. of a prior, Reg. Langton, fo 73v.
1501, 27 Feb., dcn and 23rd to be examined at the visitation (*sed. vac.* both Canterbury and Winchester) by the commissary of the prior of Christ Church, Canterbury; he reported *omnia bene*, Canterbury Reg. R, fo 115.
1520, 14/16 Feb., one of five Winchester monks named to appear at a Black Monk Chapter summoned by cardinal Wolsey to Westminster, Pantin, *BMC*, iii, 120–122 (Reg. ii, fo 23, 23v).
1524, 30 Nov., with William Manydowne sent to the bp for licence to el. a prior, Reg. Fox, v, fo 75.
1524, 2 Dec., 8th in order at the el. of a prior, Reg. Fox, v, fo 75; he voted for John Meone II, being moved by the latter's, 'zelo bonorum morum et sincere consciencie', *ib.*, v, fo 77v.
[1528 × 1539], surname occ. in a list of monks copied on to a blank fo in Oxford, Bod. Ms Selden supra 76, fo 46v; no Christian names are given.
1539, 14 Nov., 8th on the surrender list, among the seniors, and assigned a pension of £6 13s. 4d. p.a., *L and P Henry VIII*, xiv, pt 2, no 520 (PRO E315/494).

Name in
(1) Cambridge, St John's College S. 5.24, *Pupilla oculi*, Paris, A.D. 1510 (printed book); *ex provisione*—. A.D. 1518.
(2) BL Ms Harley 328, Injunctiones, W. Wykham (14th/15th c.); on fo 1,—*possessor*.

Peter MORTON
occ. 1468/9

1468, 17 Dec., ord subdcn, Winchester cathedral, Reg. Waynflete, i, fo M*v.
1469, 23 Sept., ord dcn, Winchester cathedral, *ib.*, i, fo O*.

Note: this is prob. Peter Milyngton, q.v.

William MORTON
occ. 1459 occ. 1465

1459, 17 Feb., ord acol., Winchester cathedral, Reg. Waynflete, i, fo R.
1460, 1 Mar., ord subdcn, Hyde abbey, *ib.*, i, fo vv.
1462, 18 Sept., ord dcn, Winchester cathedral, *ib.*, i, fo B*v.
1465, 9 Mar., ord pr., All Saints' church, Southampton, *ib.*, i, fo G*v.

D. de MORTUO MARI
occ. 1279/80

1279/80, visited Hurstbourne, WCL pipe roll acct.

Walter MORYCE [Morice
occ. 1539

1539, 14 Nov., described as 'styward', PRO E315/494.

1539, 14 Nov., 4th among the seniors on the surrender list and assigned a pension of £13 6s.

8d. p.a., *L and P Henry VIII*, xiv, pt 2, no 520, (PRO E315/494).

Note: is this perhaps Walter Enford, q.v.?

MOURE
see Mere

MUCHELDEVERE
see Micheldevere

Roger de MULLEFORDE
occ. 1325

1325, 9 Oct., 44th in order of seniority, *Reg. Pontissara*, 557.

MULLYNGTON
see Milyngton

MUNES
see Meon

MYDELTON(E)
see Mideltone

Richard MYLLYS [Myll
occ. 1535

1535, described himself as, until recently, a monk of Winchester in two letters to Thomas Cromwell in which he requested an exhibition to enable him to go to Oxford. He complained of the prior's ill will toward him because he spoke out vs veneration of saints, fasting, pilgrimages and the Rule and of the prior's refusal to grant him an exhibition; *L and P Henry VIII*, ix, nos 1128, 1129.

Note: is this perhaps Richard Canterbury, q.v.?

Jerome NASSHE [Jeronimus
occ. 1528

1528, 11 Apr., one of six not yet prof., and ord exorcist and acol., Lady chapel, Winchester cathedral, Reg. Fox, v, fo 38–38^{v}.

Adam de NEUBIR'
occ. 1239

1239, 21 Nov., by order of the king to the keepers of the bpric, *sed. vac.*, he was to be apptd bartoner, *CClR (1237–1242)*, 158.

NEUBIR'
see also Newbury, Nywbury, Nywebury

NEUMAN
see Newman

NEUTON
see Newton

Thomas NEVYLE D.Th. [Nevile
occ. 1377 d. 1415/16

1395–1415, prior: el. 3/11 Feb. 1395, Reg. Wykeham, i, fos 243, 244; res. 26 Aug. 1415, *Reg. Common Seal*, no 158.

1377, 19 Dec., ord acol., bp's chapel, Farnham castle, *Reg. Wykeham*, i, 285.

1378, 13 Mar., ord subdcn, Winchester cathedral, *ib.*, i, 286.

1378, 18 Sept., ord dcn, bp's chapel, Farnham castle, *ib.*, i, 288.

1378, 18 Dec., ord pr., bp's chapel, Highclere, *ib.*, i, 289.

1389/90, 1393, 21/22 Aug., almoner, Kitchin, *SS* no 28, pp. 415–418, BL Ms Harley 328, fo 24.

c. 1383, prob. student at Oxford, see below.

1389/90, [student at Oxford] with William Rodebourne and Thomas Shirebourne, q.v., and they stopped at Whitchurch on their way *versus Oxon*, WCL hundred acct; this same yr he was described as *magister*, WCL Crondall acct.

1390, 16 Apr., student at Oxford with Thomas Shirebourne, q.v., *Reg. Common Seal*, no 17.

[1390/1], named as *magister*, WCL Hurstbourne acct.

1395, 9 Mar., 1405, 12 June, named as professor of theology [*sacre pagine professor*], Reg. Wykeham, ii, fo 280^{v}, *Reg. Common Seal*, no 77.

1381/2, spent five weeks in the infirmary for which the hordarian pd 2s. 6d., Kitchin, *SS* no 54, p. 279.

1382/3, pd a visit to Wootton for which the clerk entered 12d. in expenses on the manorial acct, WCL acct.

1384, 14 Nov., with John Langreod, q.v., at Southwark, acted as *instructores*, to inform the bp of the proceedings in the el. of Robert Rodebourne as prior, *Reg. Wykeham*, i, 150.

1385/6, visited Whitchurch, WCL hundred acct.

1389/90, stopped at Crondall on his way to London and, with Thomas Shirebourne, q.v., visited Whitchurch [?en route to or from Oxford], WCL accts.

1390, 16 Apr., listed as absent from the house on the Black Monk Chapter visitation certificate, because he was at Oxford, *Reg. Common Seal*, no 17.

1390/1, visited Hurstbourne and the reeve recorded 11d. expenses, WCL acct.

1393, 21/22 Aug., 4th to sign the composition with bp Wykeham, BL Ms Harley 328, fo 24; see Robert de Rodebourne.

1395, between 3 and 11 Feb., el. prior *per inspiracionem*, Reg. Wykeham, i, fo 244^{v}.

1395, 9 Mar., licensed as penitentiary to hear confessions in the diocese, *Reg. Wykeham*, ii, 458.

1398, 17 Dec., obtained [confirmation of] a papal grant to use the mitre, staff, ring and other pontifical insignia, *CPL*, v (1396–1404), 194; see William de Taunton.

1398/9, pd three visits to Crondall for which the manorial acct was charged 54s. 11d., WCL acct.

1399, 27 Jan., called by the king to a council at Oxford to discuss the papal schism and advise the king, *CClR (1396–1399)*, 367–368.
1399, with the abbot of St Augustine's, Canterbury, shared the presidency of the Black Monk Chapter, Pantin, *BMC*, iii, 146.
1403, president of the Black Monk Chapter and arranged for the apptment and payment of proctors for the order at the curia, Pantin, *BMC*, iii, 148.
1404, 16 Oct., el. bp by the unanimous choice of the chapter; on 17 Oct., he gave his 'reluctant' consent: 'Domine, si propellatus sum necessarius non recuso. . .', Reg. Common Seal, fo 21ᵛ (no 68); this el. was set aside by the papal mandate dated 19 Nov. to adm. Henry Beaufort by right of papal reservation and provision, *Reg. Common Seal*, no 76.
1415, 20 Aug., the king (?or bp Beaufort) at Farnham issued a commission to John and Henry Popham to arrest Nevyle and deliver him to the constable of the Tower of London, *CPR (1413–1416)*, 409.
1415, 26 Aug., in the presence of the subprior, William Aulton, q.v., and three other monks and several others including the bailiff of the Soke, in 'a certain ground floor chamber within the infirmary signed his resignation: 'non vi vel metu coactus neque dolo inductus aut aliter quovismodo circumventus set pure, sponte et absolute ex mea certa scientia ac animo deliberato propter grandevam etatem ac corporis mei imbecillitatem et impotenciam. . .', *Reg. Common Seal*, no 158.
1415/16, d., and the almoner distributed 10s. worth of bread among the poor *pro sepultura* and also gave a pittance of bread and wine to the monks *die sepulture*, Kitchin, *SS* no 37, p. 439. It is not known whether his body was returned for burial; and it is to be noted that the almoner made no ref. to his being the former prior but simply included him with the other two brethren who had also d. during the year.

Name in Winchester College, Chas Blackstone's Ms Reg. of Benefactors, 26, as having given a missal to the College.

Some of his *acta* as prior are recorded in *Reg. Common Seal*, nos 21–158.

Note: the reasons for his unfortunate end are unknown, but it seems likely that he was implicated, or, alleged to have been implicated, in the Southampton plot, as Dr G. L. Harriss suggested in *Beaufort*, 81.

Robert NEWBURY
occ. 1447 occ. 1450

1447, 15 Apr., hostiller, *Reg. Common Seal*, no 316.
1447, 15 Apr., 17th in order at the el. of a bp, *Reg. Common Seal*, no 316.
1450, 11 Dec., 13th at the el. of a prior, Reg. Waynflete, i, fo 30ᵛ.

NEWBURY
see also Neubir', Nywbury, Nywebury

Robert NEWMAN
occ. 1432/3

1432/3, celebrated his first mass and the chamberlain spent 18d. on bread and wine for his feast, Kitchin, *SS* no 7, p. 376.

Thomas NEWMAN [Neuman
occ. 1468 occ. 1473

1468, 17 Dec., ord acol., Winchester cathedral, Reg. Waynflete, i, fo M*ᵛ.
1472, 19 Dec., ord subdcn, Winchester cathedral, *ib.*, ii, fo 169ᵛ.
1473, 13 Mar., ord dcn, Winchester cathedral, *ib.*, ii, fo 170.

William NEWPORT [Newporte
occ. 1501 occ. 1514/15

1514/15, fourth prior, first yr, Kitchin, *SS* no 44, p. 459.

1501, 27 Feb., acol., and 27th to be examined at the visitation [*sed. vac.* both Canterbury and Winchester] by the commissary of the prior of Christ Church, Canterbury; he reported *omnia bene*, Canterbury Reg. R, fo 115.
1514/15, on his apptment as fourth prior the almoner sent a gift of wine costing 8d., Kitchin, *SS* no 44, p. 459.

Thomas NEWTON [Neutone, Newetone, Nutone
occ. 1377 occ. 1409/10

1377, 19 Dec., ord subdcn, bp's chapel, Farnham castle, *Reg. Wykeham*, i, 286.
1378, 13 Mar., ord dcn, Winchester cathedral, *ib.*, i, 287.
1378, 17 Apr., ord pr., Winchester cathedral, *ib.*, i, 288.

1393, 21/22 Aug., kitchener, BL Ms Harley 328, fo 24ᵛ.
1399/1400, chamberlain, WCL unnumbered obedientiary acct.

1393, 21/22 Aug., 24th to sign the composition with bp Wykeham, BL Ms Harley 328, fo 24ᵛ; see Robert de Rodebourne.
1404, 16 Oct., 13th in order at the el. of a bp, *Reg. Common Seal*, no 68.
1409/10, ill in the infirmary for three wks for which the hordarian pd 18d., Kitchin, *SS* no 57, p. 290.

John NICHOL [Nicole
occ. 1348/9

1348, 2 June, prof., and given *lit. dim.*, for subdcn's orders, *Reg. Edington*, ii, no 742.

1349, 7 Mar., ord subdcn, Cobham, *ib.*, ii, no 770.
1349, 6 June, ord dcn, chapel of St Mary's hospital, Sandown, *ib.*, ii, no 783.

NICHOLAS
occ. [1279 × 1283]

[1279 × 1283], named as subprior in an indenture *temp.* prior Adam de Farnham, q.v., *Winch. Cart.*, no 143.

Note: this may be Nicholas de Tarente, q.v.

William NICOLL
occ. [1416]

[1416], 14 Mar., ord acol. and subdcn, Winchester cathedral, Reg. Beaufort, fo M[v].

NIEUBURY, Niewbury
see Nywebury

NIGEL
occ. before 1094

1094, before his apptment as abbot of Burton, sacrist, *HRH*, 31; see Geoffrey de Mala Terra.

NIWEBURY
see Nywbury

John NORBERY [Nogthbury, Northbury
occ. 1483 occ. 1486

1483, 20 Dec., ord acol., Winchester cathedral, Reg. Waynflete, ii, fo 192[v].
1485, 28 May, ord subdcn, Winchester cathedral, *ib.*, ii, fo 198.
1486, 7 Dec., 30th in order and last at the el. of a bp, *Reg. Common Seal*, no 434.

Geoffrey le NOREYS [Norais, Norays, Norreys
occ. 1266/7 occ. 1284

1266/7, pd visits to Michelmersh and Silkstead; and with John de Brevill, q.v., at Silkstead they dined on goose, WCL pipe roll acct.
1279/80, visited Chilbolton, Crondall, Sutton, and Michelmersh, WCL pipe roll acct.
1280, 18 Feb., with Nicholas de Ham and Philip de Oxonia, q.v., received a royal licence to el. a bp, *CPR (1272–1281)*, 363.
1281/2, visited Chilbolton for *liberatio denariorum*, and the prior gave him a cask of cider, WCL acct.
1282, 7 Aug., one of the monks who sought and obtained absolution from excommunication incurred because of irregularities in their el. of Richard de la More as bp, *Reg. abp Pecham*, i, 188–189; the comm. for absolution is dated 10 Aug., *ib.*, ii, 50. See Adam de Farnham.
1284, 18/20 July, one of three monk proctors sent by the chapter to request from the bp licence to el. a prior, *Reg. Pontissara*, 285–286.

John de NORTHWOLDE
occ. 1283

1283, 25 Oct., collated to the office of cellarer by the bp on the d. of William Gluais, q.v., *Reg. Pontissara*, 9.

Philip de NUTLEY [Nottele, Nuthelegh, Nuthelye, Nutlig', Nuttligh
occ. 1325 occ. 1338/9

1326, 15 Feb., ord acol. and subdcn, Winchester cathedral, Reg. Stratford, fo 143[v].
1326, 20 Sept., ord dcn, Kingsclere, *ib.*, fo 144[v]; the scribe has written 'Thomas' by mistake.
1328, 19 Mar., ord pr., Crawley [Hants], *ib.*, fo 148.
1325, 9 Oct., 53rd in order of seniority (out of 64), *Reg. Pontissara*, 557.
1338/9, with Hugh de Wyly, q.v., visited Chilbolton and had five fowl during their stay, WCL acct.

NUTONE
see Newton

NYDECGEN
see Gilers

John de NYWBURY [Neweburie, Niwebury
occ. 1308 occ. 1325

1308, 21 Sept., ord dcn, Farnham, *Reg. Woodlock*, 814.
1308/9, visited Chilbolton, WCL acct.
1325, 9 Oct., 30th in order of seniority, *Reg. Pontissara*, 556.

Thomas NYWEBURY [Nieubury, Niewbury
occ. 1377 occ. 1393

1377, 19 Dec., ord acol., bp's chapel, Farnham, *Reg. Wykeham*, i, 285.
1378, 13 Mar., ord subdcn, Winchester cathedral, *ib.*, i, 287.
1378, 18 Sept., ord dcn, bp's chapel, Farnham, *ib.*, i, 288.
1380, 19 May, ord pr., bp's chapel, Farnham, *ib.*, i, 296.
1393, 21/22 Aug., 25th to sign the composition with bp Wykeham, BL Ms Harley 328, fo 24[v]; see Robert de Rodebourne.

Simon de OPERATIONIBUS
see Simon II

ORDMARUS
d. by 1122/3

1122/3, name occ. in a mortuary roll of Savigny following that of Godfrey, prior, q.v., but not distinguished as a monk, Delisle, *Rouleaux des Morts*, 336.

Note: is this Geoffrey I, q.v.?

Philip de OSNA
occ. 1255

1255, 5 Jan., with William de Kingate, q.v., involved in contracting a loan on behalf of the prior and chapter, *CPL*, i (1198–1304), 309.

John de OSTILLARIA
see John III

John de OVERTON
occ. 1279/80 occ. 1282

1279/80, visited Chilbolton, WCL acct.
1282, 7 Aug., one of the monks who sought and obtained absolution from excommunication incurred because of irregularities in their el. of Richard de la More as bp, *Reg. abp Pecham*, i, 188–189; the comm. for absolution is dated 10 Aug., *ib.*, ii, 50. See Adam de Farnham.

Matthew OVERTON
occ. 1528

1528, 11 Apr., ord dcn, Lady chapel, Winchester cathedral, Reg. Fox, v, fo 38v.

Nicholas de OXENFORD [Oxenforde
occ. 1385 occ. 1415

1385, 23 Dec., ord subdcn, bp's chapel, Farnham castle, *Reg. Wykeham*, i, 310.
1387, 21 Sept., ord dcn, bp's chapel, Marwell, *ib.*, i, 316.
1388, 19 Dec., ord pr., bp's chapel, Farnham castle, *ib.*, i, 318.
1393, 21/22 Aug., 31st to sign the composition with bp Wykeham, BL Ms Harley 328, fo 24v; see Robert de Rodebourne.
1395/6, pd a visit to Chilbolton and dined on fowl, WCL acct.
1404, 16 Oct., 17th in order at the el. of a bp, *Reg. Common Seal*, no 68.
1415, 27 Sept., named at the el. of a prior as having been in charge of the process of selecting the *compromissorii*, *ib.*, no 163.

Peter de OXENFORDE [Oxeneforde, Oxon', Oxonia
occ. 1345/6 occ. 1371

1345/8, receiver, WCL Wonston and Chilbolton accts.
1345/6, visited Wonston, WCL acct.
1346/8, pd visits to Chilbolton and Silkstead for *liberatio denariorum*, WCL accts.
1351, 5 Oct., with two vicars apptd proctors for the prior and convent in all matters pertaining to two of their churches in Salisbury diocese, *Reg. Common Seal*, no 6.
1370, 9 Mar., one of three monks apptd as penitentiaries within the diocese, *Reg. Wykeham*, ii, 107; see Richard de Pek and Nicholas de Wykford.
1371, 26 Mar., still penitentiary and comm. to hear the confession of a named individual and to absolve him and assign penance, *ib.*, ii, 159.

Adam de OXONIA
occ. 1239

1239, 21 Nov., apptment as almoner by royal order to the keepers of the bpric, *sed. vac.*, *CClR (1237–1242)*, 158.

Philip de OXONIA [Oxon'
occ. 1272/3 occ. 1282

1272/3, visited Chilbolton with William de Salford on 3 May [1273] and they shared a capon, WCL acct.
1279/80, returning from an ordination in Hungerford with seven monks he and they stopped at Hurstbourne, WCL pipe roll acct.
1280, 18 Feb., with Nicholas de Ham and Geoffrey le Noreys, q.v., recd a royal licence to el. a bp *CPR (1272–1281)*, 363.
1282, 7 Aug., one of the monks who sought and obtained absolution from excommunication incurred because irregularities in the el. of Richard de la More as bp, *Reg. abp Pecham*, i, 188–189; the comm. for absolution is dated 10 Aug., *ib.*, ii, 50. See Adam de Farnham.

Walter de OXONIA [Oxon'
occ. 1260 occ. 1269/70

1260, 28 Dec., one of three monks who recd licence to el. a bp from the king at Windsor, *CPR (1258–1266)*, 132; see Nicholas de Merewell, Ralph Russell.
1266/7, went to Michelmersh and Whitchurch with Adam de Morton, q.v., for *liberatio denariorum*; they also performed the same duty at Patney, WCL pipe roll acct.
1267/8, the same two were at Barton for the same purpose, WCL acct.
1269/70, visited Michelmersh with M. de Porland, q.v., for [*contra*] the feast of St Andrew [30 Nov. 1269], WCL acct.

John de OXYSTEDE
occ. 1370/1

1370/1, student at Oxford with Ralph de Basyng and Anthony de Saulton, q.v. and stopped at Whitchurch on his journeys back and forth, WCL acct.

Ralph de PAMPILOU [?Pampilon
occ. 1362

1362, 11 Feb., had succ. John de Guldeford as proctor for the chapter in the proceedings following the disputed el. of William de Thudden, q.v.; and on this date he requested that the prior elect be pronounced contumacious, *Reg. Edington*, i, no 1490.

Robert PAYN [Payne
occ. [1416] occ. 1450

[1416], 14 Mar., ord acol. and subdcn, Winchester cathedral, Reg. Beaufort, fo M^{v}.

1447, 15 Apr., 13th in order at the el. of a bp, *Reg. Common Seal*, no 316.

1450, 11 Dec., 9th at the el. of a prior, Reg. Waynflete, i, fo 30^{v}.

Richard de PEK [le Pek, Peckis, Peek, Pekis
occ. 1321/2 occ. 1370

1321/2, with Walter de Langestoke, q.v., visited Houghton and dined on capon, WCL acct.

1325, 9 Oct., 49th in order of seniority, *Reg. Pontissara*, 557.

1330, 8 Jan., with Richard de Merewell I, q.v., acted as proctors for the prior and chapter in drawing up an agreement over burial rights with the college of St Elizabeth, near Wolvesey, *Winch. Cart.*, no 148.

[?1330's], celebrated a ?daily mass at the nave altar of our Lady which the young William Wykeham regularly attended; this was referred to as 'Pekismass', G. H. Moberly, *Life of William Wykeham*, 2nd edition, Winchester, 1893, 10 (based on Winchester College Ms Aylward 2).

1339/40, visited Crondall, WCL acct.

1345, 15 Aug., one of the monks found guilty of proceeding to el. a bp in defiance of the king's orders, *CPR (1343–1345)*, 561; see John le Devenish.

1370, 9 Mar., apptd one of three monk penitentiaries [in the diocese], *Reg. Wykeham*, ii, 107 (transcribed as Pechy).

Bartholomew de PERSHORE
occ. 1310/11

1310/11, visited Chilbolton with Walter de Selebourne, q.v., WCL acct.

Note: Bartholomew de Wynton, q.v., also visited Chilbolton in 1310/11, and a Bartholomew, q.v., occ. in this period; the question remains: how many monks are involved?

PETER
occ. before 1198

1198, 8 May, late *monachus conversus* whose body was transferred by his son, Geoffrey fitzPeter, from the monks' cemetery into the church, *Ann. Winton.*, 67. Later this same yr the son became justiciar, *ib.*, 69.

Note: this is an example of a man who had taken the habit just before d., that is, *ad succurrendum*.

Richard PETERSFELD B.Th. [Petersfelde, Petersfyld
occ. [c. 1512/13] occ. 1539

1535/6, sacrist, *Valor Eccles*, ii, 2; 1536, 16 Mar., sacrist, *L and P Henry VIII*, x, no 480.

1539, 14 Nov., subprior, PRO E315/494.

[c. 1512/13, prob. student at Oxford; see below].

1521, 7 Dec., supplicated to proceed to B.Th. after eight yrs of study in logic, philosophy and theology; adm. 1522, 21 June, *BRUO 1501–1540*.

1522/3, student at Oxford, with support from the almoner, WCL unnumbered obedientiary acct.

1524, 2 Dec., 18th in order at the el. of a prior, Reg. Fox, v, fo 75; he nom. Henry Broke *propter ipsius plurima merita*, *ib.*, v, fo 77^{v}.

1532, 15 Nov., with William Basyng IV, q.v., was serving as chaplain in bp Fox's chantry, Oxford, Corpus Christi College A. 1 cap. 2 (evidence a) 4.

1536, 16 Mar., after a visitation of St Swithun's, Thomas Parry wrote to Cromwell that John Avynton, q.v., and Petersfeld 'were chief committers of the sacrilege', prob. implying that they were the only learned monks, *L and P Henry VIII*, x, no 480.

1539, 30 July, with John Avynton, q.v., was serving as chaplain in bp Fox's chantry, Oxford, Corpus Christi College A. 1 cap. 2 (evidence a) 4.

1539, 14 Nov., as subprior on the surrender list assigned a pension of £20 p.a., *L and P Henry VIII*, xiv, pt 2, no 520 (PRO E315/494).

John PEUESEY
occ. 1417/18

1417, 18 Dec., ord acol. and subdcn, Winchester cathedral, Reg. Beaufort, fo O.

1418, 21 May, ord dcn, place not given, *ib.*, fo O^{v}.

Thomas de PEUESEYE
occ. 1356

1356, 19 Mar., ord pr., bp's chapel, Southwark, *Reg. Edington*, ii, no 870.

I PHILIP
occ. 1239

1239, 21 Nov., refectorer, and by an order of the king addressed to the keepers of the bpric, *sed. vac.*, to be apptd anniversarian as well, *CClR (1237–1242)*, 158.

II PHILIP
occ. 1262

1262, 28 Nov., subprior, *Winch. Cart.*, no 142.

1262, 28 Nov., during the vacancy of the priory issued a lease under the subprior's seal, *ib.*, *Winch. Cart.*, no 142.

PHILIP
see also Avynton, Lusteshall, Yonge

PICHEBEKE
see Pynchbeke

John de PONYNTONE
occ. 1325 occ. 1344/5

1325, 9 Oct., 48th in order of seniority, *Reg. Pontissara.*
1344/5, pd a visit to Hinton Ampner, WCL acct, printed in Kitchin, *Obed. Rolls*, 150.

Robert de POPHAM
occ. 1326 occ. 1381/2

1326, 15 Feb., ord acol., Winchester cathedral, Reg. Stratford, fo 143v (as Ralph).
1328, 19 Mar., ord subdcn, Crawley, [Hants.], *ib.*, fo 148.
1329, 18 Mar., ord dcn, Chertsey abbey, *ib.*, fo 149v.
1337/8, prob., chaplain to the prior, Kitchin, *SS* no 63, p. 248; see below.
[1360], 21 May, chamberlain, Winchester College Muniment 3533.
1363/4, 1365/6, 1367/8, 1369/70, 1371/3, 1374/8, hordarian, PRO SC6/756/19, 21–24, SC6/757/1–5.
1337/8, distributed the prior's alms, Kitchin, *SS* no 63, p. 248.
1349, 5 Mar., with Thomas de Berton, q.v., sent by the subprior and chapter to obtain a licence from the bp to el. a prior, *Reg. Edington*, i, no 556; after the el. sent again to the bp [on 21 Mar.] to ask for immediate confirmation of their choice of John de Merlawe, q.v., but the bp refused and sent him back with the letter, *ib.*, no 559; on 23 Mar. he was again sent to the bp, with Edmund de Bolesdone, q.v., with a second request for confirmation, *ib.*, no 560.
1360/1, visited Woolstone, PRO SC6/756/17.
1363 × 1378, made regular visits to Woolstone as hordarian; some of these were fairly long visits as, for instance in 1375/6 the manorial acct was charged 20s. for his expenses and the following yr it was 15s., PRO SC6/756/19, 21–24, SC6/757/1–5; 1375/6 (SC6/757/3), 1376/7 (*ib.*, 757/4).
1366, 10 Oct., one of two monks sent by the prior and chapter to obtain licence from the king to el. a bp, PRO C84/29/36.
1381/2, spent 32 wks in the infirmary at a cost of 16s. to the hordarian, Kitchin, *SS* no 54, p. 279.

[M. de PORLAND [Portland
occ. 1269/70 occ. 1279/80

1269/70, with Walter de Oxonia, q.v., visited Michelmersh for [*contra*] the feast of St Andrew [30 Nov. 1269] and also paid a visit to Hurstbourne, WCL pipe roll acct.
1279/80, paid a visit to Hurstbourne, WCL pipe roll acct.

Note: possibly not a monk.]

William de PORTA REGIA or PORT ROYAL
see Kingate

POYLL [?Poytl
occ. [1528 × 1539]

[1528 × 1539], surname occ. in a list of monks entered on a blank fo in Oxford, Bod. Ms Selden supra 76, fo 46v; no Christian names are given.

Note: this monk may be entered elsewhere under his toponymic.

Roger PRATTE
occ. 1539

1539, 14 Nov., one of four not yet prof., described as 'late religious' on the surrender list and assigned a pension of 53s. 4d. p.a., *L and P Henry VIII*, xiv, pt 2, no 520 (PRO E315/494).

PURITON
see Puryton

I John PURY [Purye
occ. 1375 d. 1389/90

1375, 5 Mar., with Robert de Walyngford, q.v., licensed as penitentiary in the adcnry of Winchester, *Reg. Wykeham*, ii, 232.
1389/90, d., and the almoner distributed 10s. worth of bread to the poor on the day of his burial, Kitchin, *SS* no 28, p. 417.

II John PURY [Purye, Pyrie, Pyrye
occ. 1387 occ. 1404

1387, 21 Sept., ord acol., bp's chapel, Marwell, *Reg. Wykeham*, i, 315.
1388, 19 Dec., ord subdcn, bp's chapel, Farnham castle, *ib.*, i, 317.
1389, 13 Mar., ord dcn, bp's chapel, Farnham castle, *ib.*, i, 318.
1389, 17 Apr., ord pr., Winchester cathedral, *ib.*, i, 319.
1393, 21/22 Aug., 35th to sign the composition with bp Wykeham, BL Ms Harley 328, fo 24v; see Robert de Rodebourne.
1404, 16 Oct., 20th in order at the el. of a bp, *Reg. Common Seal*, no 68.

III John PURY [Pery, Purye, Pyry
occ. 1469 d. 1522/3

1469, 23 Sept., ord subdcn, Winchester cathedral, Reg. Waynflete, i, fo O*.
1470, 22 Dec., ord dcn, Winchester cathedral, *ib.*, ii, fo 166.
1471, 30 Mar., ord pr., Winchester cathedral, *ib.*, ii, fo 167.
1498, 23 Apr., *custos* of the Lady chapel, Reg. Langton, fo 73v.
1501, 27 Feb., gardener, Canterbury Reg. R, fo 114v.
1486, 7 Dec., 11th in order at the el. of a bp, *Reg. Common Seal*, no 434.
1492, 29 Oct., 8th to be examined at the *sed. vac.* visitation; he deposed that the quality and

preparation of the food were inadequate and some necessities like wax were no longer being provided acc. to custom, *Reg. abp Morton*, ii, no 127.

1498, 23 Apr., 3rd in order at the el. of a prior, Reg. Langton, fo 73v.

1501, 27 Feb., 4th to be examined at the visitation (*sed. vac.*, both Canterbury and Winchester) by the commissary of the prior of Christ Church, Canterbury; he reported that the brethren were obedient and silence was observed as required, but he knew nothing of the financial state of the house, Canterbury Reg. R, fo 114v.

1522/3, d., and the almoner distributed 10s. worth of bread to the poor on the day of his burial, WCL unnumbered obedientiary acct.

John PURYTON [Puriton

occ. 1536/7 occ. 1539

1536/7, celebrated his first mass and the sacrist bought 18d. worth of wine for the feast, Kitchin and Madge, *Documents*, 25 (*SS* no 64).

[1528 × 1539], surname occ. in a list of monks copied on to a blank folio in Oxford, Bod. Ms Selden supra 76, fo 46v; no Christian names are given.

1539, 14 Nov., 25th on the surrender list and last among the commoners; he was assigned a pension of 100s. p.a., *L and P Henry VIII*, xiv, pt 2, no 520 (PRO E315/494).

Note: see John Carpenter.

Robert PURYTON D.Th. [Puriton, Purytone

occ. 1406 occ. 1449

1406, 19 Feb., ord acol., Winchester cathedral, Reg. Beaufort, fo A.

1408, 9 June, ord subdcn, Winchester cathedral, *ib.*, fo Bv.

1409, 23 Mar., ord dcn, Winchester cathedral, *ib.*, fo Cv.

1410, 15 Feb., ord pr., Winchester cathedral, *ib.*, fo Dv.

1409/10, one of five monks who celebrated their first mass and recd gifts from the hordarian, Kitchin, *SS* no 57, p. 290.

1422/3, almoner, WCL Hinton Ampner acct.

1433/4, receiver, WCL Wonston acct, BL Add. Roll 28112.

1436/8; 1442, 1 Sept.; 1442/3; 1444/6; 1447, 15 Apr., subprior, WCL Crondall acct, Kitchin, *SS* no 39, 445; Pantin, *BMC*, iii, 108; BL Harley Roll X.9; Kitchin, *SS* no 40, p. 448, WCL Whitchurch acct; *Reg. Common Seal*, no 316.

[?1410 × 1420], prob. student and prob. at Oxford; see below.

1428, 24 Oct., addressed as B.Th., *CPL*, viii (1427–1447), 36; but by July 1426 he may have attained the degree, Pantin, *BMC*, ii, 159.

1444, 6 July, included among the doctors of theology in the statutes drawn up by the Black Monk Chapter, Pantin, *BMC*, ii, 188.

Note: in 1449 he was described as B.Cn.L, Reg. Waynflete, i, fo 50*v.

1413/14, pd a visit to Whitchurch [?on his way to/from Oxford] and the manorial acct recorded expenses of 10d., WCL acct.

1414/15, visited Chilbolton, WCL acct.

1415, 27 Sept., named by the chapter as one of nine *compromissorii* in the el. of a prior, *Reg. Common Seal*, no 163.

1425/6, stopped at Crondall on his way to and from London to attend convocation (which met 15–27 Apr. 1426), WCL acct.

1426, 1/6 July, present at the Black Monk Chapter, and named as one of the examiners of the proctors, Pantin, *BMC*, ii, 161.

1427/8, stopped at Crondall on his way to and from London to attend convocation (which met in July and Nov./Dec. 1428), WCL acct.

1428, 24 Oct., obtained papal dispensation to choose his own confessor, *CPL*, viii (1427–1447), 36.

1430/1, with Peter Cranbourne, q.v., visited Stockton (Wilts.) for *liberatio denariorum*, BL Add. Roll 24412.

[1430/47], acted as confessor to bp Beaufort, *CPL*, x (1447–1455), 5; see below.

1433/4, stopped at Crondall [on his way to London] with others, WCL acct.

1436/7, visited Crondall and the reeve recorded his expenses as 22d., WCL acct.

1437/8, as subprior, recd money allocated to him from the almoner's acct, Kitchin, *SS* no 39, p. 445.

1442, 1 Sept., deputized for the prior as one of the presidents of the Black Monk Chapter, Pantin, *BMC*, iii, 108.

1442/3, visited Enford *pro tractatu* with a William Barell', BL Harley Roll X.10.

1444, 6 July, attended the Black Monk Chapter with William Wroughton, q.v., and both were apptd to a committee which was to draw up a new code of statutes for the order. The committee met on 15 Sept. in Oxford; and both were members of a three man team which prepared the final draft and presented it at the end of Sept., Pantin, *BMC*, ii, 188–189. See also William Alton.

1444/5, again/still in rec. of money assigned to him from the almoner's acct, Kitchin, *SS* no 40, p. 448.

1445, 24 Apr., recd licence from the prior, who was president of the Black Monk Chapter, to go to the shrine of St James [Compostela] for the Jubilee, *Reg. Common Seal*, no 289.

1445, 31 May, the cathedral chapter at Compostela wrote to the king of England to thank him for his offering to the shrine which had been brought by Puryton, they had celebrated a thanksgiving mass at which he and other English pilgrims had been present, *Reg. Common Seal*, no 290.

1445/6, stayed at Whitchurch to arrange for a lease of the park and chase at Hurstbourne, WCL Whitchurch acct.

1447, 12 Apr., with Richard Marleburgh, sent by the prior and chapel to obtain royal licence to el. a bp, *ib.*, no 313; on 15 Apr. he participated in the el., *ib.*, no 316, and on 17 Apr., the same two went to the king to obtain royal approval, *ib.*, no 317.

1447, 26 Sept., on the strength of his having been bp Beaufort's confessor for about seventeen years and at the request of bp Waynflete and of himself, he was granted a papal indult to rec. and hold *in commendam* any benefice with cure of souls and still retain his stall in the cathedral and all his former rights and privileges, *CPL*, x (1447–1455), 5.

1449, 15 July, with William Basyng III, q.v., and others apptd proctors in the negotiations over the appropriation of Fordingbridge church, Reg. Waynflete, i, fo 50*ᵛ.

John PYNCHBEKE [Pichebeke, Pynchbek, Pynchebeke

occ. 1476 occ. 1481

1476, 9 Mar., ord acol., Winchester cathedral, Reg. Waynflete, ii, fo 175ᵛ.

1476, 21 Dec., ord subdcn, Winchester cathedral, *ib.*, ii, fo 176ᵛ.

1477, 20 Sept., ord dcn, no place given, *ib.*, ii, fo 178ᵛ.

1481, 22 Dec., ord pr., Winchester cathedral, *ib.*, fo 187ᵛ.

1476/7, student at Oxford with John Basyng III, q.v., and together they recd an exhibition of 13s. 4d. from the almoner, Kitchin, *SS* no 43, p. 456.

PYRY(E)

see Pury

R.

occ. 1355/6

1355/6, curtarian, WCL SS no 68 (receiver's acct) not printed.

1355/6, incurred expenses at Hampton and elsewhere which were pd by the receiver, *ib.*

Henry de RADECLIFF [Radeclyve

occ. 1337/8 occ. 1346/7

1337/8, visited Wootton, Kitchin, *Manydown*, 149.

1345, 15 Aug., one of the monks found guilty of proceeding with the el. of a bp vs the king's orders, *CPR (1343–1345)*, 581.

1346/7, visited Chilbolton and dined on capon, WCL acct.

I RALPH

occ. before 1191

1191, before this date, sacrist, but left with prior Robert III, q.v., to go to the Charterhouse at Witham, Somerset, D. L. Douie and D. H. Farmer eds, *Magna Vita Sancti Hugonis*, 2 vols, Oxford Medieval Texts, 1985, i, 88–89.

II RALPH

see Alexus

RALPH

see also Russel

I John REDE [Reede,

occ. 1396 d. 1432/3

1396, 23 Sept., ord pr., bp's chapel, Waltham, *Reg. Wykeham*, i, 340.

1395/6, celebrated his first mass and recd a gift of wine from the anniversarian, Kitchin, *SS* no 3, p. 207.

1427/8, anniversarian, Worcester Cathedral Muniment, C.536.

1404, 16 Oct., 28th in order at the el. of a bp, *Reg. Common Seal*, no 68.

1427/8, visited Bishopstone [Bushton, Wilts.], as *custos*, Worcester Cathedral Muniment, C.536.

1432/3, d., and the chamberlain pd 10s. to the brief bearer, Kitchin, *SS* no 7, p. 376.

II John REDE

occ. 1509

1509, 24 Mar., ord subdcn, bp's chapel, Esher, Reg. Fox, ii, fo 24.

REDE

see also Reed

I John REDYNG [Redynge

occ. 1406

1406, 19 Feb., ord pr., Winchester cathedral, Reg. Beaufort, fo Aᵛ.

II John REDYNG [Redynge

occ. 1447 occ. 1474/5

1447, 15 Apr., subalmoner, *Reg. Common Seal*, no 316.

1450, 11 Dec., refectorer, Reg. Waynflete, i, fo 30ᵛ.

1474/5, anniversarian, Worcester Cathedral Muniment, C.1.

n.d., chamberlain, WCL Ham acct.

1447, 15 Apr., 24th in order at the el. of a bp, *Reg. Common Seal*, no 316.

1450, 11 Dec., 20th at the el. of a prior, Reg. Waynflete, i, fo 30ᵛ.

1474/5, prob. visited Bishopstone [Bushton, Wilts.], as *custos*, Worcester Cathedral Muniment, C.1.

Note: a John Redyng visited Stockton (Wilts.) in 1438/9 and brought back £4 to the *scaccarium*, WRO 906/SC/10. Some of the dates for these two John Redyngs may have been incorrectly assigned.

John REDYNGTONE [Redyngtune
occ. 1429

1429, 30 Nov., almoner, WCL Hinton Ampner court roll.

Richard REED
occ. 1513

1513, 26 Mar., ord acol., Winchester cathedral, Reg. Fox, iii, fo 53.

REED
see also Rede

REINALD [Reinhald
occ. [?c. 1150]

[?c. 1150], reputed to have been taught in the monastery school and to have travelled to Stavanger, Norway, taking with him a relic of St Swithun and to have become the first bishop there; but firm evidence for this is lacking, C. Hohler, 'The Cathedral Church of Stavanger in the Twelfth Century', *Journal of the British Archaeological Association*, 3rd series, 27/28 (1964), 92–118.

William de RETHERWYKE
occ. 1372 occ. 1375

1372, 13 Mar., ord subdcn, Waltham, *Reg. Wykeham*, i, 266.
1372, 18 Sept., ord dcn, Winchester cathedral, *ib.*, i, 268.
1375, 22 Sept., ord pr., bp's chapel, Esher, *ib.*, i, 277.

Ralph de REYNS
see Aremes, Dreyms

I RICHARD
d. c. 1113

Name occ. on a mortuary roll of Matilda, abbess of Caen following that of Godfrey, prior, q.v., although not distinguished as a monk, Delisle, *Rouleaux des Morts*, 186; also on a similar roll of Savigny dated 1122/3, *ib.*, p. 336.

II RICHARD
occ. 1311/12 occ. 1313/14

1311/12, 1313/14, receiver, WCL Whitchurch accts.

RICHER
occ. [1142 × 1143]

[1142 × 1143], with Geoffrey III, prior, q.v., witness to an episcopal grant, *Winch. Cart.*, no 10, and *Eng. Epis. Acta*, viii, no 126.

I ROBERT [?de Lewes (Prior I)
occ. 1130

1130, before Sept., prior in succession to Ingulph, q.v., and prob. followed by Geoffrey III, q.v., *Fasti*, ii, 88 and *HRH*, 80.

Note: *HRH*, 80 finds no evidence that this prior is to be identified with Robert Lewes who became bp of Bath in 1136; *Eng. Epis. Acta*, viii, seems to assume that they are one and the same, no 24, n. and index, although doubt is expressed in *ib.*, no 125, n.

[II ROBERT
occ. before 1150

1150, occ. as abbot of Burton and possibly previously a monk of Winchester, *HRH*, 31.]

III ROBERT (Prior II)
occ. 1165 occ. 1173

1165–1173, prior: occ. 19 July 1165; el. abbot of Glastonbury 1173, *Fasti*, ii, 88, *HRH*, 80, 52.

1165, 19 July, with the convent confirmed and increased the gift to the monks of Hamble made by his predecessor, William I, q.v., *Winch. Cart.* no 75.

Note: alleged to be the author of De actibus Willelmi et Henrici episcoporum Wintonie, *DNB*.

IV M. ROBERT son of Henry (Prior III)
occ. 1187 res. 1191

1187–1191, prior: became prior 1187; res. to become a Carthusian at Witham, Somerset, 1191, *HRH*, 80, *Fasti* ii, 89; see also D. L. Douie and D. H. Farmer eds, *Magna Vita Sancti Hugonis*, 2 vols, Oxford Medieval Texts, 1985, i, 88–89.

Richard de Devizes, q.v., wrote a chronicle at his request after he had retired to Witham.

V ROBERT
see Melun

William ROBUS, ?B.Th. [Robis, Robys
occ. 1447 occ. 1462

1452, 23 Sept., ord pr., bp's chapel, Waltham, Reg. Waynflete, i, fo F; but see below.

[1448/60], student at Oxford; in Mar. 1460 he supplicated for B.Th., on the grounds that he had studied philosophy for seven yrs and theology for five yrs, *BRUO*. On 11 Dec. 1450 Richard Dummere and Robert Westgate were the only two students at Oxford acc. to the el. list in Reg. Waynflete, i, fo 30ᵛ; did he pursue his studies initially in the cloister and also perhaps only intermittently at Oxford?

1462, 17 July, described as B.Th., *Reg. Common Seal*, no 352.

1447, 15 Apr., 36th (out of 39) in order at the el. of a bp; he is described as prof. and as the most junior among the priests, but this may be a slip of the pen, *Reg. Common Seal*, no 316.

1450, 11 Dec., 32nd at the el. of a prior and again described as a pr., Reg. Waynflete, i, fo 30ᵛ.

1460, Sept., with Robert Westgate, prior, q.v., named to represent the chapter at convocation, Reg. Waynflete, i, fo 63*.
1462, 17 July, again chosen to attend convocation, on this occasion with a secular clerk, *Reg. Common Seal*, no 352.

Robert de RODEBOURNE, B.Th./D.Th. [Rodeborne, Rudborn, Rudborne, Rudbourne, Rudebourne
occ. 1363 d. 1395

1384–1395, prior: el. 5/26 Oct. 1384, *Reg. Wykeham*, i, 149 and see below; d. 20 Jan., 1395, *ib.*, i, 194.
1363, 1 Jan., ord acol., bp's chapel, Farnham castle, *Reg. Edington*, ii, no 933.
1363, 28 May, ord subdcn, bp's chapel, Highclere, *ib.*, ii, no 934.
1363, 28 Dec., granted *lit. dim.*, for the orders of dcn and pr., *ib.*, ii, no 936.
1364, 9 Mar., ord dcn, bp's chapel, South Waltham, *ib.*, ii, no 937.
1365, 20 Sept., ord pr., bp's chapel, Sutton, *ib.*, ii, no 945.
1367/8, [student at Oxford and] stopped at Whitchurch on his travels back and forth, WCL acct.
1384, 26 Oct., described as B.Th., *Reg. Wykeham*, i, 149.
Note: *BRUO* has entered him as D.Th., but has given no ref.
1384/5, pd a visit to Crondall at a charge of 8d. to the acct, WCL acct.
1384, 14/16 Nov., the bp in his chapel at Southwark examined the el. proceedings; on 16 Nov. he confirmed the el. and the new prior made his oath of canonical obedience, *Reg. Wykeham*, i, 149–152.
1387, 20 Aug., comm. jointly with the official to induct the adcn of Winchester, *Reg. Wykeham*, i, 164.
1389/90, visited Crondall and the reeve recorded expenses of 117s. 9d., WCL acct.
1389, with six other monks accused of hunting in the bp's warrens, Oxford, New College Ms 9819.
1393, 21/22 Aug., was instrumental in resolving a six year dispute with the bp through the signing of an agreement by which the prior and chapter bound themselves to provide financial support for the bp's programme of repair and reconstruction of the cathedral fabric; in return the bp lifted the ecclesiastical censures he had imposed because of the monks' infringement of the Benedictine statute forbidding money payments to monks, BL Harley Ms 328. Oxford, New College Ms 3691; see also Greatrex, 'Injunction Book', 242–246.

A few of his *acta* have been preserved in *Reg. Common Seal*, nos 14–20, 38.

William RODEBOURNE
occ. 1389/90 occ. 1394/5

1389/90, [prob. student at Oxford and] stopped at Whitchurch on his return journey from Oxford, WCL acct.
1390/1, 1392/3, [student] with Thomas Shirebourne, q.v., and stopped at Hurstbourne several times on the way back and forth between Oxford and Winchester, WCL accts; see also Thomas Chilbolton.
1393/4, [prob. student], with Thomas Chilbolton and Thomas Shirebourne, q.v., stopped at Whitchurch [on the way to or from Oxford], WCL acct; he is recorded as stopping twice.
Note: none of these three monks signed the composition with bp Wykeham in Aug. 1393, prob. because they were not recalled from Oxford; see Greatrex, 'Injunction Book', 245.
1394/5, pd a visit to Hurstbourne, possibly on his way to or from Oxford, Worcester Cathedral Muniment, C.867.

RODEBOURNE
see also Rudbourne

ROGER
d. by 1122/3

1122/3, name occ. in a mortuary roll of Savigny following that of Godfrey, prior, q.v., but not distinguished as a monk, Delisle, *Rouleaux des Morts*, 336.

John ROMSEY [Rumsey
occ. 1451 occ. 1456

1451, 18 Dec., ord acol., Winchester cathedral, Reg. Waynflete, i, fo D^{v}.
1453, 22 Sept., ord subdcn, Winchester cathedral, *ib.*, i, fo G.
1455, 20 Sept., ord dcn, bp's chapel, Wolvesey, *ib.*, i, fo K^{v}.
1456, 18 Sept., ord pr., bp's chapel, Wolvesey, *ib.*, i, fo M^{v}.

I William de ROMSEY [Romeseye, Romesy
occ. 1309 d. 1315/16

1311/12, third prior, first yr, Kitchin, *SS* no 18*, p. 398.
1309, 18 June, with Robert de Guldeford, q.v., recd licence from the bp to el. a prior, *Reg. Woodlock*, 369.
1311/12, recd a gift of ale from the almoner on his apptment as third prior, Kitchin, *SS* no 18*, p. 398.
1315/16, d., and the almoner gave a pittance of 6s. 8d. to the convent on the day of his burial, Kitchin, *SS* no 20, p. 396.

II William ROMSEY [Romesey
occ. 1447 occ. 1450

1450, 11 Dec., one of two *depositarii*, Reg. Waynflete, i, fo 30^{v}; see William Borlond.

1447, 15 Apr., 26th in order at the el. of a bp, *Reg. Common Seal*, no 316.
1450, 11 Dec., 22nd at the el. of a prior, Reg. Waynflete, i, fo 30^{v}.

Richard de ROSSELL
occ. 1325

1325, 9 Oct., 31st in order of seniority, *Reg. Pontissara*, 556.

ROSSELL
see also Russel

Thomas RUDBORNE [Rudbourne
occ. 1447 occ. 1450

1450, 11 Dec., fourth prior, Reg. Waynflete, i, fo 30^{v}.
1447, 15 Apr., 20th in order at the el. of a bp, *Reg. Common Seal*, no 316.
1450, 11 Dec., 16th at the el. of a prior and preached the sermon, Reg. Waynflete, i, fos 30^{v}, 31.

Author of the Historia Major de Fundatione Ecclesiae et Successionis Episcoporum ejusdem ad Annum 1138, which has been printed by Wharton in *Anglia Sacra*, i, 179–286 from Lambeth Ms 183. He may also have written several other chronicles:
(1) Historia Minor, in BL Ms Nero A. xvii; this covers the period from Brutus to A.D. 1234.
(2) Epitome Historiae Majoris, which relates historical events in England, with frequent ref. to Winchester, from Brutus to Henry VI. This is found in Oxford, All Souls College Ms 114, and in Cambridge, Corpus Christi College Ms 110 which is a copy of the All Souls ms; these and other imperfect copies are described in Gransden, *Hist. Writing*, ii, 394–395.
(3) a short history of Durham covering the period to 1083 comm. by bp Neville of Durham; this is also described by Gransden, *ib.*, ii, 395.

One of Rudborne's contemporaries, John Rous, who was also a historian and author of a life of Richard Beauchamp, visited St Swithun's and talked with him. In Rous's words Rudborne was 'the most learned man of his times in the chronicles of the English', Thomas Hearne, ed., *Joannis Rossi Antiquarii Warwicensis Historia Regum Anglie*, (Oxford, 1716), 73.

The possibility that Rudborne annotated the Codex Wintoniensis (BL Add. Ms 15350), and that the Epitome may have been written by John of Exeter are discussed in Gransden, *ib.*, ii, 494, n. 1. If, as I suggest, there were two Johns of Exeter, q.v., this will alter the perspective. Dr. Gransden provides a detailed analysis of Rudborne's writings, including his use of sources and his interest in monastic origins, and she assesses the literary and historical merits of his work, *ib.*, ii, 394–398. His ecumenical interests are discussed in Greatrex, 'Thomas Rudborne, Monk of Winchester, and the Council of Florence', in *Studies in Church History*, 9 (1972), 171–176.

RUDBORNE
see also Rodebourne

Walter RUFUS [*dictus* Rufus
occ. 1262

1262 × 1265, prior: apptd by the bp in place of the deposed Andrew de London, q.v., soon after 25 Dec. 1262; succ. by Ralph Russel, q.v., c. 1265, *Fasti*, ii, 90.
1262, before 25 Dec., hordarian, *Gervase, Cant.*, ii, 219.

RUMSEY
see Romsey

John RUSSEL
occ. 1308

1308, 21 Sept., ord dcn, Farnham, *Reg. Woodlock*, 814.

Note: unless this monk d. prematurely he may well occ. elsewhere under his toponymic.

Ralph RUSSEL [Russell
occ. 1260 d. 1265

[?1261 × 1265], prior: occ. as prior in *Winch. Cart.*, nos 209, 299, 302, tentatively dated 1261 × 1265, and in 1265 in the cartulary of Christchurch, Twynham, *Fasti*, ii, 90; d. 8 July, 1265, *Ann. Winton.*, 102. See Walter Rufus and Andrew de London his predecessors.
1260, 28 Dec., with Nicholas de Merewell and Walter de Oxonia, q.v., recd from the king, at Windsor, licence to el. a bp, *CPR (1258–1266)*, 132.
n.d., as prior, recd a grant of land in Westwood from Jordan Bulbeck, BL Add. Ms 29436, fo 40^{v}.

Robert RUSSEL
occ. 1350/1

1350, 5 Sept., ord acol., bp's chapel, South Waltham, *Reg. Edington*, ii, no 817.
1350, 18 Sept., ord subdcn, bp's chapel, Highclere, *ib.*, ii, no 814.
1351, 28 May, granted *lit. dim.*, for dcn's orders, Reg. Edington, ii, fo AA.
1351, 30 Nov., granted *lit. dim.*, for pr.'s orders, *Reg. Edington*, ii, no 830.

William RYKENERE [Rykener,
occ. 1377 occ. 1381/2

1377, 19 Dec., ord acol., bp's chapel, Farnham castle, *Reg. Wykeham*, i, 285.

1378, 13 Mar., ord subdcn, Winchester cathedral, *ib.*, i, 287.
1378, 18 Sept., ord dcn, bp's chapel, Farnham castle, *ib.*, i, 288.
1378, 18 Dec., ord pr., bp's chapel, Highclere, *ib.*, i, 289.

1381/2, spent two wks in the infirmary for which the hordarian pd 12d., Kitchin, *SS* no 54, p. 279.

John RYNGE
see John Meone II

Henry de ST CROSS [Sancta Cruce
occ. 1238/9

1238, 31 Aug., sacrist, *CPR (1232–1247)*, 231 (as Henry).
1239, 21 Nov., [?re]apptd sacrist by order of the king, *sed. vac.*, *CClR (1237–1242)*, 158.

1238, 31 Aug., named as one of the guardians of the 30th of the bpric and ordered to pay the king's almoner's expenses, *CPR (1232–1247)*, 231.

Andrew de ST MARTIN [Sancto Martino
see London

Robert de ST OMER [Sancto Omero, Seintomere
occ. 1325 occ. 1344

1325, 9 Oct., 47th in order of seniority, *Reg. Pontissara*, 557.
1339/40, pd a visit to Crondall, WCL acct.
1344, 3 Dec., acted as attorney for prior Alexander de Heriard, q.v., in a dispute with Southwick priory over a tenement in Winchester, K. A. Hanna, ed., *The Cartularies of Southwick Priory*, Hampshire Record Series, ix (1988), no I 192.

SALDFORD
see Saltford

John SALESBURY [Salisbury, Salusbury
occ. 1399/1400 occ. 1404

1400, 18 Sept., ord acol., bp's chapel, Waltham, *Reg. Wykeham*, i, 351.
1401, 28 May, ord subdcn, bp's chapel, Waltham, *ib.*, i, 352.
1402, 18 Feb., ord dcn, bp's chapel, Waltham, *ib.*, i, 353.
[1404], 21 May, granted *lit. dim*, for the order of pr., *ib.*, ii, 556.
1404, 24 May, ord pr., Sherborne, Reg. Mitford (Salisbury), fo 176.

1399/1400, the chamberlain purchased black cloth, costing 5s. 6d., for his frock or cowl [*flosco*], WCL unnumbered obedientiary acct.
1401/2, spent five wks in the infirmary at a cost of 6d. per wk to the hordarian, WCL unnumbered obedientiary acct.
1404, 16 Oct., 34th in order at the el. of a bp, *Reg. Common Seal*, no 68.

Robert de SALESBURY [Salysbury, Sarum
occ. 1369 occ. 1393

1369, 22 Sept., ord subdcn, Winchester cathedral, *Reg. Wykeham*, i, 257.
1372, 18 Sept., ord dcn, Winchester cathedral, *ib.*, i, 268.
1375, 22 Sept., ord pr., bp's chapel, Esher, *ib.*, i, 278.

1393, 21/2 Aug., *custos* of St Mary's altar, BL Ms Harley 328, fo 24^{v}.

1389, with the prior and other monks and laity accused of hunting in the bp's warrens, Oxford, New College Ms 9819.
1393, 21/22 Aug., 15th to sign the composition with bp Wykeham, BL Ms Harley 328, fo 24^{v}; Robert de Rodebourne.

I Nicholas SALISBURY [Salysbury, Sarisbury, Sarum, Sarysburg
occ. 1432/3 occ. 1450

1432/3, celebrated his first mass and recd from the chamberlain 18d. worth of bread and wine for the feast, Kitchin, *SS* no 7, p. 376.

1447, 15 Apr., *speciarius*, *Reg. Common Seal*, no 316.
1450, 11 Dec., gardener, Reg. Waynflete, i, fo 30^{v}.

1447, 15 Apr., 23rd in order at the el. of a bp, *Reg. Common Seal*, no 316.
1450, 11 Dec., 19th at the el. of a prior, Reg. Waynflete, i, fo 30^{v}.

II Nicholas SALISBURY [Salysbury, Sarum
occ. 1466 occ. 1474/5

1466, 20 Sept., ord acol., Winchester cathedral, Reg. Waynflete, i, fo K*^{v}.
1474, 24 Sept., ord subdcn, Winchester cathedral, *ib.*, ii, fo 172.
1474, 17 Dec., ord dcn, Winchester cathedral, *ib.*, ii, fo 172^{v}.
1475, 18 Feb., ord pr., Winchester cathedral, *ib.*, ii, fo 173.
1474/5, celebrated his first mass, and recd a gift of wine from the anniversarian, Worcester Cathedral Muniment, C.1.

SALISBURY
see also Sarum

William de SALTFORD [Saldford, Salford
occ. 1272/3 occ. 1283

1272/3, visited Chilbolton, WCL acct.
1279/80, pd visits to Chilbolton, Hurstbourne and Stockton (Wilts.), WCL accts.
[1283], one of four monks who, with the prior and Valentine [de Wherewell], q.v., were

apptd proctors in an appeal to the king because of the chapter's dispute with the bp, *Reg. Pontissara*, 662–663, where the date is given as c. 1276; see, however, *ib.*, 399–400. See also PRO E135/3/39b, dated 12 Jan 1283 when these proctors were summoned to meet the king and bp concerning the reform of the convent.

SANCTA CRUCE
see St Cross

SANCTO MARTINO
see St Martin

SANCTO OMERO
see St Omer

Adam de SARUM [Saresberia, Saresbiriensis
occ. 1308 occ. 1328

1328, 7 July, precentor, Reg. Stratford, fo 107.
1308, 25/30 Nov., with a monk of Hyde acted as commissary for the bp to convey his injunctions to Tandridge priory, *Reg. Woodlock*, 321, 315–316.
1308/9, visited Michelmersh, WCL acct.
1314, 13 Aug., at Waltham, with Richard de Merewell I, q.v., witnessed an episcopal instrument, *Reg. Woodlock*, 633.
1314, 27 Sept., was apptd attorney for Laurence, prior of Boxgrove while the latter travelled overseas, *CPR (1313–1317)*, 182.
1317/18, visited Michelmersh, WCL acct.
1325, 9 Oct., 27th in order of seniority, *Reg. Pontissara*, 556.
1328, 27 June, with Richard de Merewell I, sent by the subprior and chapter to obtain the bp's licence to el. a prior, Reg. Stratford, fo 107.
Note: see also Adam who is prob. this monk.

Philip de SARUM
occ. 1344
1344, 29 May, granted *lit. dim*, for orders which were addressed to the bp of Bath and Wells, Reg. Orleton, i, fo 125v.

SARUM
see also Salisbury

Anthony de SAULTON
occ. 1370/1
1370/1, student at Oxford with Ralph de Basyng, and John de Oxystede, q.v., and stopped at Whitchurch on his way back and forth, WCL acct.

SCHALDEN
see Shalden

SCHIRBOURNE
see Shirebourne

Walter de SELEBOURNE [Seleborn, Seleburn, Soulbourne
occ. 1308 occ. 1345
1308, 21 Sept., ord dcn, Farnham, *Reg. Woodlock*, 814.
1308/9, 1310/11, pd visits to Chilbolton, WCL accts.
1325, 9 Oct., 32nd in order of seniority, *Reg. Pontissara*, 556.
1327/8, visited Ham (Wilts.), where he partook of capons and cheese, WCL acct.
1345, 15 Aug., one of the monks found guilty of disobeying the king's inhibition by proceeding to el. a bp, *CPR (1343–1345)* 581; see John le Devenish.

Richard SELER [Ceeler, Celer
occ. 1404 occ. 1450
1404, 16 Oct., 38th in order at the el. of a bp, *Reg. Common Seal*, no 68.
1447, 15 Apr., 4th at the el. of a bp, *ib.*, no 316.
1450, 11 Dec., 2nd in order [and the most senior monk] at the el. of a prior, Reg. Waynflete, i, fo 30v.

Thomas SELES
occ. 1362
1362, 26 Feb., recd first tonsure at Hursley and *lit. dim.*, for minor orders, *Reg. Edington*, ii, no 922 (ms fo QQ).
Note: this is prob. Thomas Mere, q.v.

SELKESTEDE
see Silkstede

SELLWODE
occ. [1528 × 1539]
[1528 × 1539], surname occ. in a list of monks entered on a blank fo in Oxford, Bod. Ms Selden supra 76, fo 46v; no Christian names are given.

SERNE
see Cerne

R. de SEWWELL
occ. 1308/9
1308/9, with his *socius*, visited Chilbolton, WCL acct.

William de SEYNTE
occ. 1260
1260, 11 Aug., by order of the king transferred to Malmesbury abbey until St Swithun's had recovered from its 'afflictions and adversities', *CClR (1259–1261)*, 195.

John SHALDEN [Schalden, Shaldene
occ. 1410 occ. 1416/17
1410, 19 Dec., ord acol., Winchester cathedral, Reg. Beaufort, fo E.

1412, 27 Feb., ord subdcn, Winchester cathedral, *ib.*, fo F[v].
1412, 28 Mar., ord dcn, Winchester cathedral, *ib.*, fo G[v].
1416, 18 Apr., ord pr., Winchester cathedral, *ib.*, fo N.
1416/17, celebrated his first mass, and the almoner sent a gift of 8d. worth of bread and wine, Kitchin, *SS* no 34, p. 432 (where the date is incorrectly given as 1409/10); the chamberlain sent him a gift of 12d., *ib.*, *SS* no 4, p. 366.

John de SHIPESDON' [Shyperthon, Shypesdon', Shypesthon', Sibbesdon, Sibesdone, Silbeston, Sillesdon, Sipesdene, Siwesdon
occ. 1279/80 occ. c. 1283

1283, 2 Apr., infirmarer, *Reg. Pontissara*, 251.

1279/80, pd visits to Chilbolton, Crondall and Sutton, WCL accts.
1280/1, sent by the receiver on business to London in Mar., and again in July; on the second journey he was accompanied by Peter Mareschall, q.v., Watkin, 'Rec. Acct', 96, 97.
1282/3, visited Whitchurch, WCL pipe roll acct.
1283, 2 Apr., apptd confessor to the nuns at Nunnaminster in succession to John de Lecford, q.v.; he was to go to them when required but they were not to come to him, *Reg. Pontissara*, 251.
[1283], one of four monks who, with the prior and Valentine [de Wherewell], q.v., were apptd proctors in an appeal to the king because of the chapter's dispute with the bp, *ib.*, 662–663, where the date is given as c. 1276; see, however, *ib.*, 399–400. See also PRO E135/3/39b, dated 12 Jan 1283 when these proctors were summoned to meet the king and bp concerning the reform of the convent.

John SHIRBOURNE [Shyrborne
occ. 1524 occ. 1539

1524, 2 Dec., 16th in order at the el. of a prior, Reg. Fox, v, fo 75.
[1528 × 1539], surname occ. in a list of monks entered on a blank fo in Oxford, Bod. Ms Selden supra 76, fo 46[v]; no Christian names are given.
1539, 14 Nov., 10th on the surrender list, among the seniors, and assigned an annual pension of £6, *L and P Henry VIII*, xiv, pt 2, no 520 (PRO E315/494).

Thomas SHIREBOURNE [Schirbourne, Schyrburn, Schyrebourne, Shirbourne, Shyrbourne
occ. 1381 occ. 1433/4

1415–1433 × 1434, prior: el. 27 Sept. 1415, *Reg. Common Seal*, no 161; occ. on 20 May 1433 in Reg. i, fo 53 (*Reg. Common Seal*, no 231) and on 20 June of this yr in *CClR (1429–1435)*, 289; he must have res. or d. between 20 June 1433 and 23 July 1434 when William Alton first occ. as prior in Reg. i, fo 53[v] (*Reg. Common Seal*, no 234).
Note: the printed text of this first priory reg. unfortunately omitted to name the priors in item nos 231 and 234.

1381, 21 Dec., ord acol., bp's chapel, Highclere, *Reg. Wykeham*, i, 300.
1382, 22 Mar., ord subdcn, Winchester cathedral, *ib.*, i, 301.
1383, 19 Sept., ord dcn, Waltham, *ib.*, i, 305.
1386, 17 Mar., ord pr., bp's chapel, Esher, *ib.*, i, 311.
1385/6, celebrated his first mass and recd a gift of wine costing 8d. from the anniversarian, Worcester Cathedral Muniment, C.533.

1400/1, treasurer, WCL Westwood acct.
1406, Nov., *custos operum*, WCL Nursling and Millbrook court roll.
1407/12, hordarian, PRO SC6/757/23–26, SC6/758/1; his acct for 1409/10 is in Kitchin, *SS* no 57, 290–292. He was prob. succ. by Richard Buriton, q.v.
1415, 26 Aug., again *custos* [*magister*] *operum*, *Reg. Common Seal*, no 158.

1389/90, [student at Oxford] with Thomas Nevyle and William Rodebourne, q.v., stopped at Whitchurch [en route], WCL hundred acct.
1390, 16 Apr., student at Oxford with Thomas Nevyle, *Reg. Common Seal*, no 17, Pantin, *BMC*, iii, 222.
1390/1, student, and stopped at Hurstbourne four times [four tallies] on his way to and from Oxford, WCL acct.
[1392/3], [student], with Thomas Chilbolton, q.v., stopped at Hurstbourne versus Oxon, WCL acct.
[1393/4], [student], with Thomas Chilbolton, stopped four times [four tallies] at Whitchurch en route to and from Oxford, WCL acct. See note under Thomas Chilbolton.

1394/5, visited Hurstbourne, Worcester Cathedral Muniment, C.867.
1398, 17 Dec., was granted papal licence to choose his confessor, *CPL*, v (1396–1404), 216.
1398/9, stopped at Crondall on his way to and from Chertsey and the reeve entered his expenses as 2s. 7d., WCL acct.
1404, 16 Oct., 15th in order at the el. of a bp, *Reg. Common Seal*, no 68; on 17 Oct., he was sent by the chapter, with Ralph Southam, q.v., to obtain the king's consent to their choice of Thomas Nevyle, q.v., *ib.*, no 69.
1415, 26 Aug., one of the monks who witnessed the resignation of Thomas Nevyle as prior, *Reg. Common Seal*, no 158; on 31 Aug., he was apptd, with John Hurst, q.v., to request from the bp licence to el. a prior, *ib.*, no 159.
1415, 27 Sept., named by the chapter as one of nine *compromissorii* to el. a prior, *ib.*, no 163. On

28 Sept., he was officially informed of his el., *ib.*, no 164; his consent is undated, *ib.*, no 165. His confirmation by the bp took place on or shortly after 4 Oct., *ib.*, nos 167–169.

1417, Nov./Dec., at convocation, with other cathedral priors, he was apptd by the abp to a committee to look into the poverty of university graduates, *Reg. abp Chichele*, iii, 37.

1420, 5/8 July, present at the Black Monk Chapter at Northampton, Pantin, *BMC*, ii, 96.

1426, 2 July, named by the Black Monk Chapter as visitor of the Benedictine houses in the diocese of Winchester, *ib.*, ii, 169.

Some of his *acta* are preserved in *Reg. Common Seal*, nos 169–171, 173–232.

His brother, John Shirebourne, was a member of bp Beaufort's household and styled 'servitour', acc. to Harriss, *Beaufort*, 81, where the footnote refs fail to provide the source for this statement.

William SHIREBOURNE [Shirbourne, Shyrborne

occ. 1447 d. 1476/7

1447, 15 Apr., 1450, 11 Dec., curtarian, *Reg. Common Seal*, no 316, Reg. Waynflete, i, fo 30ᵛ.

1459/60, almoner, Kitchin, *SS* no 41, pp. 448–451.

1469/70, hordarian, *ib.*, *SS* no 58, pp. 293–295.

1447, 15 Apr., 21st in order at the el. of a bp, *Reg. Common Seal*, no 316.

1450, 11 Dec., 17th at the el. of a prior, Reg. Waynflete, i, fo 30ᵛ.

1459/60, pd four visits to Hinton Ampner, Kitchin, *SS* no 41, p. 450.

1470, 5 Apr., with Nicholas Mersch, q.v., as proctors, presented Thomas Hunton, q.v., prior el., to the bp in order to obtain his confirmation, Reg. Waynflete, ii, fo 1ᵛ.

1476/7, d., and the almoner distributed 10s. worth of bread among the poor on the day of his burial, Kitchin, *SS* no 43, p. 456.

SHYRBO(U)RNE

see Shir(e)bourne

SIBBESDON, Silbeston

see Shipesdon'

Thomas SILKSTEDE [Selkestede, Silkested, Silkstead, Sylkestede, Sylkstede

occ. 1468 d. 1524

1498–1524, prior: el. 23/24 Apr. 1498, Reg. Langton, fo 73ᵛ; d. 30 Nov. 1524, Reg. Fox, v, fo 75.

1468, 17 Dec., ord subdcn, Winchester cathedral, Reg. Waynflete, i, fo M*ᵛ.

1469, 23 Sept., ord dcn, Winchester cathedral, *ib.*, i, fo O*.

1472, 14 Mar., ord pr., Winchester cathedral, *ib.*, ii, fo 168ᵛ.

1471/2, celebrated his first mass and the almoner sent a gift of 8d. worth of wine for the feast, Kitchin, *SS* no 42, p. 453.

1486, 7 Dec., hordarian, *Reg. Common Seal*, no 434.

1492, 14 and 28 Oct., subprior, *Reg. Common Seal*, no 502, *Reg. abp Morton*, ii, no 127.

1498, 23/24 Apr., still or again subprior, Reg. Langton, fo 73ᵛ. As prior he also took charge of the following office:

1516/17, almoner, Kitchin, *SS* no 45, pp. 462–465.

1486, 15 Aug., with William Langley, q.v., sent by the prior and convent to obtain a royal licence to el. a bp, *Reg. Common Seal*, no 433.

1486, 7 Dec., 10th in order at the el. of a bp, *Reg. Common Seal*, no 434.

1492, 14 Oct., with Richard Lacy, q.v., sent by the prior and convent to obtain a royal licence to el. a bp, *ib.*, no 502.

1492, 28 Oct., second to be examined at the *sed. vac.* visitation and reported on the poor quality of the food, especially the beef and mutton, *Reg. abp Morton*, ii, no 127 (where the name has been entered as William).

1498, 23/24 Apr., as subprior presided at the el. of a prior, Reg. Langton, fo 73ᵛ.

1501, 27 Feb., present at the visitation (*sed. vac.* both Canterbury and Winchester) by the commissary of the prior of Christ Church, Canterbury; he was examined first and at length and stated that all was in good order with regard to the administration of the house and to monastic discipline, that the £100 debt was the result of a lawsuit between the chapter and the deceased abp and that there were 36 monks rather than 40 as previously, Canterbury Reg. R, fo 114–114ᵛ.

1510/11, visited Canterbury College, Oxford, Pantin, *Cant. Coll. Ox*, ii, 253, iv, 101.

1521, 23 Sept., recd the bp who came for an official visitation which was followed up by injunctions the following Feb., Reg. Fox, iv, 68–68ᵛ.

Name in Winchester Cathedral Ms 15, Theodolus etc. (including Promptorium Parvulorum) (15th c.); name on flyleaf and the price 13s. 4d.; also, in a different ink and hand, the date 1493. On fo 228ᵛ *constat—, suppriori*.

Some of his *acta* are found in Reg. ii, fos 1–89; but see also *Reg. Common Seal*, no 462.

His work in the Lady chapel and the canopied seats against the west and south walls of the south transept which bear his initials and device have recently been described in Crook, *Winchester Cathedral*, 239–240, 260–263.

SIMEON [Symeon

occ. before 1081/2

1081/2, before, prior: became abbot of Ely in 1081/2, *Fasti*, ii, 88, *HRH*, 80.

Described as a *vir virtutis amator*, he was the brother of bp Walkelin and a former monk of St Ouen, Rouen; he reformed the monks' diet by substituting deliciously prepared fish in place of their meat dishes, and they were thus persuaded to abstain from meat entirely, *Ann. Winton.*, 33.

I SIMON
d. c. 1113

Name occ. on a mortuary roll of Matilda, abbess of Caen following that of Godfrey, prior, q.v., although not distinguished as a monk, Delisle, *Rouleaux des Morts*, 186.

II SIMON
occ. 1240

1240, 6 Mar., restored, by royal order, to his former position of *custos operum*, *CClR (1237–1242)*, 179.

Note: the king had previously removed him *de operationibus*, *sed. vac.*, *ib.*

SIPESDENE, Siwesdon
see Shipesdon'

William SKYLLYNG [Skellynge, Skillyng
occ. 1347 occ. 1384/5

1347, 22 Sept., ord acol., South Waltham, *Reg. Edington*, ii, no 737.
1348, 2 June, granted *lit. dim* for the order of subdcn, *ib.*, ii, no 742.
1349, 7 Mar., ord subdcn, Cobham, *ib.*, ii, no 770.
1349, 6 June, ord dcn, chapel of the hospital of St Mary Sandown, *ib.*, ii, no 783.
1349, 19 Sept., ord pr., bp's chapel, [Bishops] Waltham, *ib.*, ii, no 789.
1355/6, prob. chaplain to the prior, see below.
1361/5, 1367/8, 1370/1, receiver, WCL Whitchurch accts;
1371/4, receiver, WCL Alton, Whitchurch and Littleton accts respectively; in 1372/3 he is named both receiver and treasurer alternately, and in 1373/4 as treasurer.
1376/83, receiver, WCL Whitchurch acct (1376/7), Hannington (1377/8), Whitchurch (1378/9), Silkstead (1379/80), Wootton (1380/1), Silkstead (1381/3) accts.
Note: he is named receiver during these yrs on a number of other manorial accts; he prob. visited those named above on his regular inspections and for *liberatio denariorum*.
1355/6, responsible for paying some of the prior's 'foreign expenses', receiver's acct, SS, no 68 but not printed in Kitchin, *Obed. Rolls*.
1363/4, stopped at Woolstone on his way to Oxford, PRO SC6/756/19.
1364/5, prob. visited Westwood, WCL acct.
1365/6, visited Chilbolton for *liberatio denariorum* and his expenses there were 9s. 3d., Oxford, Bod. Ms Rolls, Hampshire, 3.
1373/4, while staying at Littleton, dined on capon, WCL acct.
1377/8, pd a visit to Hannington, WCL acct.
1380/1, visited Wootton on three occasions (three tallies), WCL acct.
1381/2, pd two visits (two tallies) to Crondall which cost the reeve 9s. 3d., WCL acct.
1384/5, prob. still alive as named as former receiver, WCL Hannington acct.

Geoffrey de SOMBORNE [Sombourn
occ. 1325 occ. 1337/8

1325, 9 Oct., 34th in order of seniority, *Reg. Pontissara*, 556.
1337/8, pd a visit to Chilbolton with other monks, Worcester Cathedral Muniment, C.866.

William de SOMBORNE [Sumborne
occ. 1283/4 d. 1315/16

1283/4, recd money *super scaccarium* from the reeve of Wonston, WCL Wonston acct.
1305, 15 June, with Ralph de Calne and John de Donketone, q.v., sent as proctors by the chapter to obtain licence from the bp to el. a prior, *Reg. Woodlock*, 32.
1308/9, 1311/12, pd visits to Hurstbourne, WCL accts; he also visited Chilbolton in 1308/9, WCL acct.
1315/16, d., and the almoner gave a pittance of 6s. 8d. to the convent on the day of his burial, Kitchin, *SS* no 20, p. 396.

Thomas SOMERSET [Somersett
occ. [1493] occ. [1528 × 1539]

[1493], 21 Sept., ord acol., Hyde abbey, Reg. Langton, fo 23v.
1499, 21 Dec., ord pr., Winchester cathedral, *ib.*, fo 35.
1498, 23 Apr., 23rd in order and in dcn's orders, at the el. of a prior, Reg. Langton, fo 73v.
1501, 27 Feb., 16th to be examined at the visitation (*sed. vac.* both Canterbury and Winchester) by the commissary of the prior of Christ Church, Canterbury; he reported *omnia bene*, Canterbury Reg. R, fo 115.
1524, 2 Dec., 6th in order at the el. of a prior, Reg. Fox, v, fo 75; he voted for Henry Broke 'propter eius experientiam in spiritualibus et temporalibus', *ib.*, v, fo 77.
[1528 × 1539], surname occ. in a list of monks entered on a blank fo in Oxford, Bod. Ms Selden supra 76, fo 46v; no Christian names are given.

SOULBOURNE
see Selebourne

Ralph de SOUTHAM [Southame, Sutham
occ. 1378 occ. 1418/19

1378, 13 Mar., ord acol., Winchester cathedral, *Reg. Wykeham*, i, 287.

1381, 21 Dec., ord subdcn, bp's chapel, Highclere, *ib.*, i, 300.
1382, 22 Mar., ord dcn, Winchester cathedral, *ib.*, i, 301.
1383, 16 May, ord pr., bp's chapel, Esher, *ib.*, i, 305.
1384/5, celebrated his first mass and recd a gift of 8d. towards his feast from the anniversarian, Worcester Cathedral Muniment, C.534.
1411, Apr./Sept., 1413/14, 1415/17, 1418/19, almoner, Kitchin, *SS* nos 35–37, 34, 38, pp. 430–441; no 34 has been misdated by Kitchin.
1393, 21/22 Aug., 26th to sign the composition with bp Wykeham, BL Ms Harley 328, fo 24ᵛ; see Robert de Rodebourne.
1395/6, visited Chilbolton and dined on capon, WCL acct.
1401/2, visited Mapledurham for *liberatio denariorum*, BL Add. Roll 34934.
1404, 16 Oct., 14th in order at the el. of a bp, *Reg. Common Seal*, no 68.
1408/9, pd a visit to Whitchurch, WCL acct.
1411, Apr./Sept., 1413/14, 1415/17, 1418/19, pd regular visits to Hinton Ampner, Kitchin, *SS* nos 35–37, no 34, no 38, pp. 434, 436, 439, 432, 441.
1415, 27 Sept., named as one of nine *compromissorii* in the el. of a prior, *Reg. Common Seal*, no 163.

William de SPARSHOLT [Sparsholte, Spersholt, Spersolde
occ. c. 1344 occ. 1360/1

1352, May/1353, Sept., almoner, Kitchin, *SS* no 26, pp. 409–412.
c. 1344, carried a letter from the prior [Alexander de Heriard, q.v.,] to the prior of Christ Church, Canterbury whose reply stated that he, [Sparsholt], 'causa devotionis ad sanctum Thomam ex nostri licencia accedit', Canterbury Reg. L., fo 79, summarized in Sheppard, *Hist. Mss Comm., 9th Report*, Appndx (1883), 87.
1344/5, visited Woolstone, PRO SC6/756/11.
1346, accompanied John le Devenish, q.v., to the curia where on 1 Dec. he obtained the privilege of choosing his own confessor who was empowered to grant plenary remission of sins, *CPL*, iii (1342–1362), 118.
1347, 22 July, on the petition of John le Devenish, q.v., granted papal licence to study theology for seven yrs, and to rec. a pension 'when one is void'; the prior and chapter had previously selected him as a university scholar to be supported with a yearly pension, *CPP*, i (1342–1404), 335.
1349, 31 Mar., with Richard de Merewell I, q.v., acted as witnesses at the judicial process of examining the el. as prior of John de Merlawe, q.v., in Farnham; they are described as *instructores*, *Reg. Edington*, i, no 563, and Reg. Edington, i, fo 50ᵛ.
1360/1, pd a visit to Woolstone, PRO SC6/756/17.

Ralph de STANTON [Stancton, Staunton
occ. 1325 occ. 1349

1326, 15 Feb., ord acol. Winchester cathedral, Reg. Stratford, fo 143ᵛ.
1328, 19 Mar., ord subdcn, Crawley, [Hants], *ib.*, fo 148.
1329, 18 Mar., ord dcn, Chertsey abbey, *ib.*, fo 149ᵛ.
1325, 9 Oct., 60th (out of 64) in order of seniority, *Reg. Pontissara*, 557.
1349, 22 Jan., the bp ordered the denunciation and excommunication of those who had assaulted him when he was officiating at a funeral in the cemetery at Winchester [?of someone who had d. of the plague], *Reg. Edington*, ii, no 201.

STEPHEN [de Luci, Lucy
occ. 1201 occ. 1214

1201–1214, prior: first occ. Oct. 1201, but possibly in Mar. and Sept. 1199; el. abbot of Burton before 23 Jan. 1214, *Fasti*, ii, 89, *HRH*, 80, 31.
1200 × 1214, a grant to the prior and convent ref. to Robert de Luci, brother of prior Stephen, *Winch. Cart.*, no 301.

John STOCKETON [Stoughton, Stowghton, Stowgton, Stowton
occ. 1479 occ. 1501

1479, 18 Dec., ord acol., Winchester cathedral, Reg. Waynflete, ii, fo 184.
1480, 23 Dec., ord subdcn, Winchester cathedral, *ib.*, ii, fo 185ᵛ.
1481, 16 June, ord dcn, Winchester cathedral, *ib.*, ii, fo 187.
1498, 23 Apr., chamberlain, Reg. Langton, fo 73ᵛ.
1501, 27 Feb., *magister operum*, Canterbury Reg. R, fo 114ᵛ.
1486, 7 Dec., 22nd in order at the el. of a bp, *Reg. Common Seal*, no 434.
1492, 29 Oct., 16th to be examined at the *sed. vac.* visitation and made no deposition, *Reg. abp Morton*, ii, no 127.
1498, 23 Apr., 10th in order at the el. of a prior, Reg. Langton, fo 73ᵛ.
1501, 27 Feb., 8th to be examined at the visitation (*sed. vac.* both Canterbury and Winchester) by the commissary of the prior of Christ Church, Canterbury; he reported that the prior made no distinctions among the brethren when he made corrections, Canterbury Reg. R, fo 114ᵛ.

STOCKETON
see also Stokton

STOKBRUGGE
see Stokebrugg(e)

Henry de STOKE [Stokes
d. 1312/13

1312/13, d., and the almoner gave a pittance of 6s. 8d. on the day of his burial, Kitchin, *SS* no 22, p. 393.

John STOKE
occ. 1409 occ. 1433/4

1409, 23 Mar., ord acol., Winchester cathedral, Reg. Beaufort, fo C[v].
1409, 21 Sept., ord subdcn, Winchester cathedral, *ib.*, fo D.
1410, 15 Feb., ord dcn, Winchester cathedral, *ib.*, fo D[v].
1414, 18 Sept., ord pr., Winchester cathedral, *ib.*, fo I[v].

1427/8, curtarian, WCL Barton and Littleton accts.

1425/6, visited Crondall *pro piscibus*, WCL acct (possibly because he was arranging for food supplies for the priory, or to go fishing himself).
1427/8, stayed at Littleton *ultra tonsuram* and had one capon, WCL acct.
1428, 24 Oct., granted a papal indult to choose his own confessor, *CPL*, viii (1427–1447), 36.
1433/4, stayed at Crondall *causa infirmitatis sue*, WCL acct.

Thomas de STOKE [Stokes
occ. 1365 d. 1389/90

1365, 20 Sept., ord acol., bp's chapel, Sutton, *Reg. Edington*, ii, no 945.
1365, 15 Dec., granted *lit. dim* for subdcn's orders, *ib.*, ii, no 947.
1368, 4 Mar., ord dcn, Winchester cathedral, *Reg. Wykeham*, i, 253.
1369, 22 Sept., ord pr., Winchester cathedral, *ib.*, i, 257.
1369/70, celebrated his first mass and recd a 6d. gift from the anniversarian, Worcester Cathedral Muniment, C.531.

1378, 13 Mar., 1379, 31 Mar., 1387, 8 Apr., hostiller, Reg. Wykeham, ii, fos 165, 172, 228[v].

1378, 13 Mar., granted licence to administer the sacraments at Littleton [a manor belonging to the office of hostiller]; this was prob. because of insufficient funds to provide for a chaplain, Reg. Wykeham, ii, fo 165; see John de Hyde.
1379, 31 Mar., 1387, 8 Apr., the above licence renewed, *ib.*, ii, fos 172, 228[v].
1389/90, d., and the almoner bought 10s. worth of bread to distribute among the poor on the day of his burial, Kitchin, *SS* no 28, p. 417.

I John de STOKEBRUGG' [Stokbrugge
occ. 1308

1308, 21 Sept., ord acol., Farnham, *Reg. Woodlock*, 811.

II John de STOKEBRUGGE [Stokbrugge
occ. 1325 occ. 1345

1332, 18 Oct., a J. de S. was precentor, *Winch. Cart.*, no 180; note that there was no other J. de S. in the 1325 list on which he was the most junior, see below.
1325, 9 Oct., 64th and last in order of seniority, *Reg. Pontissara*, 557.
1345, 22 July, with John de Fourde, q.v, acted as proctors for the prior and convent and recd royal licence to el. a bp, *CPR (1343–1345)*, 526. On 28 July, named as one of nine *compromissorii* in the el. of a bp, *Reg. Common Seal*, no 5.

Thomas STOKTON
occ. 1447 occ. 1450

1447, 15 Apr., 28th in order at the el. of a bp, *Reg. Common Seal*, no 316.
1450, 11 Dec., 24th at the el. of a prior, Reg. Waynflete, i, fo 30[v].

Robert de STOUDLY
occ. 1345

1345, 15 Aug., one of the monks found guilty of proceeding to el. a bp vs the king's orders, *CPR (1343–1345)*, 581; see John le Devenish.

Robert de STOURTON [Stortone, Stourtone
occ. 1368 occ. 1371/2

1368, 4 Mar., ord acol., Winchester cathedral, *Reg. Wykeham*, i, 252.
1369, 22 Sept., ord subdcn, Winchester cathedral, *ib.*, i, 257.
1370, 21 Sept., ord dcn, bp's chapel, Highclere, *ib.*, i, 261.
1371, 20 Sept., ord pr., Waltham, *ib.*, i, 263.
1371/2, celebrated his first mass and the anniversarian gave a 6d. gift, Worcester Cathedral Muniment, C.532.

William de SUDBURY
occ. 1288

1288, 13 Mar., ord subdcn, Reading abbey, *Reg. Swinfield* (Hereford), 549 (Reg. Swinfield, fo 48).

SUMBORNE
see Somborne

SUTHAM
see Southam

Thomas SUTTON
occ. 1524 occ. 1539

1524, 2 Dec., subdcn, 30th and last in order at the el. of a prior, Reg. Fox, v, fo 75[v]; he nom.

Henry Broke *propter eius bonam religionem*, *ib.*, v, fo 78.
[1528 × 1539], surname occ. in a list of monks copied on to a blank folio in Oxford, Bod. Ms Selden supra 76, fo 46v; no Christian names are given.
1539, 14 Nov., 17th on the surrender list under the commoners and assigned a pension of £5 p.a., *L and P Henry VIII*, xiv, pt 2, no 520 (PRO E315/494).

SYLKESTEDE
see Silkstede

William TALMACH
n.d.

n.d., described by Arnold Gylbert, q.v., as 'quondam' hordarian who gave 2d. per day in his will to provide for the sick in the infirmary; Gylbert was being questioned at a visitation in Feb. 1501 and criticized the state of the infirmary, Canterbury Reg. R, fo 115.

A John and Joanna Talmache were benefactors of St Swithun's, and the hordarian remembered their anniversary with yearly payments to the *custos* of the Lady altar and pittances to the convent, Kitchin, *SS* nos 56 (1405/6), 57 (1409/10), 58 (1469/70), pp. 286–287, 291, 293–294, and later yrs.

Nicholas de TARENTE [Tarrant
occ. 1295 d. 1309

1305–1309, prior: el. on or shortly before 29 July 1305, *Reg. Woodlock*, 32–33; d. before 18 June 1309, *ib.*, 369; see Richard de Enford.
1295, 30 May, one of three monk proctors sent by the chapter to obtain from the bp a licence to el. a prior, *Reg. Pontissara*, 71–72; on 6 June named as one of seven *compromissorii* chosen for the el., *ib.*, 73.
1305, 29 July, appeared before the bp at Marwell as prior el., with two monk proctors, Ralph de Calne and Richard de Enford, q.v., *Reg. Woodlock*, 33. On 7 Aug., after all the formalities of examining the el., he was confirmed as prior, *ib.*, 33–34.
[1306/7], wrote to thank the bp for enabling him to be excused from attending the parliament at Carlisle [on 20 Jan. 1307], *Winch. Cart.*, no 532.
[1308, June], reported by the bp to have fallen from his horse and was therefore unfit to travel; the bp asked the new royal treasurer, Walter Reynolds, bp of Worcester, to postpone the prior's meeting with him until Michaelmas, *Reg. Woodlock*, 679–680. This request was granted on 11 July, *ib.*, 680.
1308, 5 July, in the bp's injunctions after visitation he was ordered to present annual financial statements to the chapter, appoint competent lay stewards to supervise the manors, and consult the senior monks in matters of importance. *Reg. Woodlock*, 509.

Name in BL Ms Harley 315, Versus etc. (13th/14th c.), two loose fos numbered 46, 47; on fo 46, *de dono*—.

William de TAUNTON
occ. 1250 occ. 1262

1250–1255, prior: succ. 12 Feb. 1250 acc. to *Ann. Winton.*, 91, apptd by Aymer de Valence bp el. acc. to *Flores Hist.*, ii, 470–471; expelled before 5 Feb. 1255, but continued to claim the priorate, *Fasti*, ii, 90. See Andrew de London.
1253, because of the monks' dispute with the bp, set out for the curia, *Ann. Winton.*, 94; the quarrel had arisen when the bp deprived the prior and obedientiaries from office because they refused to render their accts to him, *ib.*, 95; see also *Flores Hist.*, ii, 404, Paris, *Chron. Majora*, v, 468–469.
1254, 7 Sept., obtained from the pope the right to use pontifical regalia including mitre, ring, tunic, dalmatic, gloves and sandals, also to bless chalices and other church ornaments, to give first tonsure and confer the minor orders of janitor and lector and to pronounce solemn benediction at divine office and table, *CPL*, i (1198–1304), 305, *Winch. Cart.*, no 53.
1255, 5 Oct., recd papal grant of protection, in which he was named as papal chaplain; this grant covered him and his monk companions in their journey to and from Rome over the dispute with the bp, *CPL*, i (1198–1304), 323, 326. While at Rome, acc. to Matthew Paris, he made extravagant gifts of money to the pope, but failed to obtain reinstatement as prior; on his return he was provided with a manor for his support, Paris, *Chron. Majora*, v, 576, 591.
1256, 6 Dec., recd royal assent to his el. as abbot of Milton, Dorset, *CPR (1247–1258)*, 532.
1261, 3 Feb., el. bp by 54 votes out of 64, while 10 monks voted for Andrew de London, q.v., but M. John Gervais of Exeter was provided, *CPL*, i (1198–1304), 378, *Ann. Winton.*, 98–99.
1262, 6 July, was dispensed for illegitimacy, *Fasti*, ii, 87.

TEZUS
d. c. 1113

Name occ. on a mortuary roll of Matilda, abbess of Caen following that of Godfrey, prior, q.v., although not distinguished as a monk, Delisle, *Rouleaux des Morts*, 186.

Arnold THORNEBERY
occ. 1483

1483, 20 Dec., ord acol., Winchester cathedral, Reg. Waynflete, ii, fo 192v.

William de THUDDEN [Thuddene
occ. 1351/2 occ. 1362

[1361–1362, prior: el. before 9 Dec., 1361, *Reg. Edington*, i, no 1490; el. nullified 11/14 Feb., 1362, because it was 'uncanonical', *ib.*, i, nos 1491, 1493].

1355/6, cellarer, WCL receiver's acct numbered SS 68 but not printed in Kitchin, *Obed. Rolls*.

1360/1, hordarian, prob. succ. Roger Marmyon, q.v., PRO SC6/756/17.

1351/2, 1360/1, pd visits to Woolstone, PRO SC6/756/12, 17.

1361, 9 Dec., the judicial process following the el. revealed irregularities in the el. proceedings, and on 17 Jan., 1362 the prior el. appeared before the bp in Southwark and again on 19 Jan., *Reg. Edington*, i, no 1490.

1362, 14 Feb., after a judicial inquiry had revealed that the el. had not been conducted acc. to the form laid down by the general council it was declared void, *ib.*, i, no 1491; see Hugh de Basyng.

A Walter de Thuddene, knight, is named on the receiver's acct for 1334/5, Kitchin, *SS* no 62, p. 243. Prob. the same Walter de Thuddene visited Wootton in 1337/8 with Nicholas de Haywode, q.v., Kitchin, *Manydown*, 149; a John de Thudden was the bp's marshal in 1330/1, HRO 11M59/B1/84 (pipe roll).

Robert THURSTAYN [Thursteyn
occ. 1350/1

1350, 5 Sept., ord acol., bp's chapel, South Waltham, *Reg. Edington*, ii, no 817.

1350, 18 Sept., ord subdcn, bp's chapel, Highclere, *ib.*, ii, no 814.

1351, 23 May, obtained *lit. dim* for dcn's orders, Reg. Edington, ii, fo Y^{v}.

1351, 30 Nov., obtained *lit. dim* for pr.'s orders, *Reg. Edington*, no 830.

John THURSTON [Thrustan, Thrustone, Thurstane
occ. 1381 d. 1395/6

1381, 21 Dec., ord acol., bp's chapel, Highclere, *Reg. Wykeham*, i, 300.

1382, 22 Mar., ord subdcn, Winchester cathedral, *ib.*, i, 301.

1383, 16 May, ord dcn, bp's chapel, Esher, *ib.*, i, 305.

1383, 19 Sept., ord pr., Waltham, *ib.*, i, 306.

1393, 21/22 Aug., *speciarius*, BL Ms Harley 328, fo 24^{v}.

1394/5, with Thomas Ware, q.v., visited Hurstbourne *pro manerio supervidendo*, Worcester Cathedral Muniment, C.867; this yr they were also at Silkstead and Wootton for the same purpose, WCL accts.

1393, 21/22 Aug., 30th to sign the composition with bp Wykeham, BL Ms Harley 328, fo 24^{v}; see Robert de Rodebourne.

1395/6, d., and the almoner distributed 10s. [worth of bread] among the poor, Kitchin, *SS* no 29, p. 419.

TICHEBURN
see Tychebourne

TICHFELD
see Tychefelde

TIGALE, Tighale
see Tygale

TINCTOR
see Tynctor

TISTEDE
see Tystede

TORPYN
see Turpin

Philip TRENCHEFOIL [Trenchefoille
occ. 1250 occ. 1259

1250, 14 Nov., anniversarian, *CClR (1247–1251)*, 377.

1250, 14 Nov., recd royal grant of free cheminage in Savernake forest for the manors in his charge, *CClR (1247–1251)*, 377.

Note: the manor of Bishopstone [Bushton, Wilts.], provided the major source of income for the anniversarian's office.

1259, 14 Aug., recd royal confirmation as abbot of Tavistock, *CPR (1258–1266)*, 39.

There are other contemporary Trenchefoils named in the Close Rolls of this period; in *CClR (1227–1231)*, 285, a William Trenchfoil is described as a Norman with land in Essex. In 1282, John Trenchfoyl was one of the free tenants named in the custumal, WCL, Winchester Custumal, fo 10.

M. Richard de TRIVERI
occ. 1243

1243, 26 Sept., one of the monks who was seized and bound by Andrew de London, q.v., when he attempted to regain his position as prior and entered the monastery by force, *CPL*, i (1198–1304), 200.

H. TRUWERY
occ. 1240

1240, 1 May, one of four monks who appeared with the two adcns before the king at Abingdon to request a licence to el. a bp, BL Add. Ms 29436, fo 37^{v}; see James de Basyng Thomas de Winton, Richard de Worston.

John TURPYN [Torpyn, Turpin
occ. 1307/8 occ. 1334/5

1307/9, 1310/11, pd visits to Chilbolton, WCL accts.
1325, 9 Oct., 17th in order of seniority, *Reg. Pontissara*, 556.
1332, 18 Oct., at the request of the prior, Alexander de Heriard, q.v., and chapter, he read in their presence the ordinances, drawn up after discussions concerning the debts of two of the obedientiary offices, which prescribed new financial arrangements to alleviate the crisis, *Winch. Cart.*, no 180.
1334/5, with Robert de Foxham and John le Foon, q.v., sent by the receiver on negotiations to London; Kitchin, *SS* no 62, p. 242.

John de TYCHEBOURNE [Ychenesbourne
occ. 1387 occ. 1404

1387, 21 Sept., ord acol., bp's chapel, Marwell, *Reg. Wykeham*, i, 315.
1388, 19 Dec., ord subdcn, bp's chapel, Farnham castle, *ib.*, i, 317.
1389, 13 Mar., ord dcn, bp's chapel, Farnham castle, *ib.*, i, 318.
1390, 24 Sept., ord pr., bp's chapel, Esher, *ib.*, i, 322.
1393, 21/22 Aug., 36th to sign the composition with bp Wykeham, BL Ms Harley 328, fo 24v; see Robert de Rodebourne.
1404, 3 Apr., granted papel licence to choose his own confessor, *CPL*, v (1396–1404), 606.
1404, 16 Oct., 30th in order at the el. of a bp, *Reg. Common Seal*, no 68.

Thomas TYCHEBOURNE [Ticheburn
occ. 1447 occ. 1450

1447, 15 Apr., 22nd in order at the el. of a bp, *Reg. Common Seal*, no 316.
1450, 11 Dec., 18th at the el. of a prior, Reg. Waynflete, i, fo 30v.

John TYCHEFELDE [Tichfeld, Tycchfeld, Tychefeld
occ. 1468 occ. 1486

1468, 17 Dec., ord acol., Winchester cathedral, Reg. Waynflete, i, fo M*v.
1470, 16 June, ord subdcn, Winchester cathedral, *ib.*, i, fo P*v.
1476, celebrated his first mass and recd a gift of 8d. from the anniversarian, Worcester Cathedral Muniment, C.2.
1486, 7 Dec., 12th in order at the el. of a bp, *Reg. Common Seal*, no 434.

William TYCHEFELDE [Tichfield, Tychefeld
occ. 1398 occ. 1404

1398, 21 Dec., ord acol., bp's chapel, Farnham castle, *Reg. Wykeham*, i, 346.
1399, 22 Feb., ord subdcn, bp's chapel, Farnham castle, *ib.*, i, 347.
1401, 28 May, ord dcn, bp's chapel, Waltham, *ib.*, i, 353.
1402, 20 May, ord pr., bp's chapel, Waltham, *ib.*, i, 354.
1404, 16 Oct., 32nd in order at the el. of a bp, *Reg. Common Seal*, no 68.

Laurence TYGALE [Tigale, Tighale, Tygeale, Tyghale
occ. 1381 occ. 1404

1381, 21 Dec., ord acol., bp's chapel, Highclere, *Reg. Wykeham*, i, 300.
1382, 22 Mar., ord subdcn, Winchester cathedral, *ib.*, i, 301.
1384, 4 June, ord dcn, bp's chapel, Highclere, *ib.*, i, 307.
1386, 17 Mar., ord pr., bp's chapel, Esher, *ib.*, i, 311.
1385/6, celebrated his first mass and recd an 8d. gift from the anniversarian, Worcester Cathedral Muniment, C.533.
1393, 21/22 Aug., hostiller, BL Ms Harley 328, fo 24v.
1401/2, curtarian/cellarer, WCL Barton acct.
1393, 21/22 Aug., 27th to sign the composition with bp Wykeham, BL Ms Harley 328, fo 24v; see Robert de Rodebourne.
1404, 16 Oct., 16th in order at the el. of a bp, *Reg. Common Seal*, no 68.

John TYMPANY
occ. 1481 occ. 1501

1481, 22 Dec., ord acol., Winchester cathedral, Reg. Waynflete, ii, fo 187v.
1485, 28 May, ord subdcn, Winchester cathedral, *ib.*, ii, fo 198.
1485, 17 Dec., ord dcn, Winchester cathedral, *ib.*, ii, fo 200.
1488, 9 June, ord pr., Winchester cathedral, Reg. Courtenay, fo 13.
1501, 27 Feb., second *depositarius*, Canterbury Reg. R, fo 115.
1486, 7 Dec. 25th in order at the el. of a bp, *Reg. Common Seal*, no 434.
1492, 29 Oct., 17th to be examined at the *sed. vac.*, visitation and made no deposition, *Reg. abp Morton*, ii, no 127 (transcribed as Gympany).
1498, 23 Apr., 13th in order at the el. of a prior, Reg. Langton, fo 73v.
1501, 27 Feb., 22nd to be examined at the visitation (*sed. vac.*, both Canterbury and Winchester) by the commissary of the prior of Christ Church, Canterbury; he reported *omnia bene*, Canterbury Reg. R, fo 115.

A William Tympany was chaplain to bp Waynflete, V. Davis, 'William Waynflete', 133, and rector of St Bartholomew's, Hyde, in 1474/6, *BRUO*.

John TYNCTOR [Tinctor
occ. 1311/12 occ. 1338/9

1311/12, recd 7s. 2d. *in curialitate* from the almoner at the time of his adm. to the monastery, Kitchin, *SS* no 18*, p. 399.

1325, 9 Oct., 33rd in order of seniority, *Reg. Pontissara*, 556.

1338/9, visited Chilbolton and dined on capon, WCL acct.

Richard TYSTEDE [Tisted, Tistede
occ. 1468 d. 1471/2

1468, 17 Dec., ord subdcn, Winchester cathedral, Reg. Waynflete, i, fo M*ᵛ.

1469, 23 Sept., ord dcn, Winchester cathedral, *ib.*, i, fo O*.

1471/2, d., and the almoner distributed 10s. worth of bread among the poor on the day of his burial, Kitchin, *SS* no 42, p. 453 (misread as Tifoede).

Thomas TYSTEDE [Tistede
occ. 1528 occ. 1539

1528, 11 Apr., ord dcn, Lady chapel, Winchester cathedral, Reg. Fox, v, fo 38ᵛ.

1532/3, student at Oxford with James Dorsett, q.v., with 2s. each *in curialitate* from the hordarian as well as an exhibition of 10s. each, Kitchin, *SS* no 61, p. 304; they also recd 5s. each from the *custos operum* this yr, *ib.*, *SS* no 12, p. 223.

[c. 1535–8], still at Oxford, staying at Canterbury College, and recd a letter from Nicholas Bennet, q.v. (under Canterbury), Pantin, *Cant. Coll. Ox*, iii, 149–150.

1539, 14 Nov., one of the four named on the surrender list who were described as pr. students at Oxford, and assigned pensions of £10 p.a., PRO E315/494.

Robert UPHAM
occ. 1400 d. 1437/8

1400, 18 Sept., ord subdcn, bp's chapel, Waltham, *Reg. Wykeham*, i, 351.

1401, 28 May, ord dcn, bp's chapel, Waltham, *ib.*, i, 353.

1402, 20 May, ord pr., bp's chapel, Waltham, *ib.*, i, 354.

1404, 16 Oct., 35th in order at the el. of a bp, *Reg. Common Seal*, no 68.

1415/16, stopped at Whitchurch and the reeve entered expenses of 2s. 4d. for his stay, WCL acct.

1437/8, d., and the almoner distributed 10s. worth of bread on the day of his burial, Kitchin, *SS* no 39, p. 443.

de UREVILLE, URVILLA
see Dureville

VALENTINE [de Wherewell, Werewell, Werewelle,
occ. 1264 occ. 1289

1265–1267, 1268–1276, prior: succ. 21 July 1265, *Ann. Winton.*, 102 and apptd by the bp acc. to *Winch. Cart.*, no 23; he res. 7 Aug. 1267, *Ann. Winton.*, 105, but was restored 3 July 1268, *ib.*, 107, both acts at the instigation of the papal legate Ottobono. He res. again c. 19 May 1276, *sinistro ductus consilio* as the former prior, Andrew de London, q.v., had swayed many of the monks to his side, *ib.*, 122; he was restored 1 Aug. of this yr, *ib.*, 123 but deprived by the bp before 3 Dec., *ib.* See John de Dureville.

1264, 2 Apr., hordarian, *Winch. Cart.*, no 547a.

1272/3, visited Little Hinton [Hiniton], and made seven visits to Chilbolton (seven tallies), WCL accts.

A few of his *acta* have been preserved and printed in Goodman, *Winch. Cart.*, nos 212d, 219, 248, 312, 316, 332, 404, 550, 552. Of these no 316 marks the restoration of peace between St Swithun's and the mayor and commonalty of Winchester on 16 Nov. 1266; this agreement achieved a settlement of the dispute over the repair and maintenance of both Kingsgate and Southgate.

After his final deprivation he remained a monk of Winchester as the following details show:

1279/80, pd visits to Hurstbourne and Sutton, WCL acct; the reeve of Sutton purchased a horse for 53s. 4d. for him and his *socii* who were setting out *versus curiam Romanam*, *ib.* Their journey must have taken place after the monks' el. of Richard de la More, adcn of Winchester in Nov. 1280, see the entry below.

1280, 25 Sept., named with Hugh de Hida and Peter de Wynton, q.v., as obtaining from the king licence to el. a bp, *CPR (1272–1281)*, 398.

1281/2, visited Hurstbourne, WCL pipe roll acct.

1282, 7 Aug., one of the monks named as seeking and receiving absolution from excommunication arising out of irregularities in their el. of Richard de la More as bp, Reg. *abp Pecham*, 188–189; the comm. for absolution is dated 10 Aug., *ib.*, ii, 50. See Adam de Farnham.

1282, 17 Dec., a royal writ to the prior [?Adam de Farnham, q.v.,] ordered him to appear before the king with four other monks and Valentine in order to settle their dispute with the bp, *Reg. Pontissara*, 400.

1282/3, visited Michelmersh, where his horse(s) recd provender, WCL pipe roll acct.

[1283], the chapter replied to the above writ and named the four monks whom they had chosen to accompany the prior and Valentine to appear before the king as required, *ib.*, 662–663, where it has been dated c. 1273. See also PRO E135/3/39b, dated 12 Jan 1283 when these proctors were summoned to meet the king and bp concerning the reform of the convent.

1284, 16 Aug., denounced and excommunicated by the abp, after a visitation, for behaving like an apostate; he had found Valentine living in a room adjoining the infirmary which he had taken over for himself, although he had been removed by the former bp Nicholas [de Ely], and now was again ordered to be removed by the abp because of his behaviour, 'quodipsum in eadem camera contra beati Benedicti regulam vitam egisse carnalem non sine proprietatis vicio'. The abp ordered him to be separated from the rest of the community until he showed signs of repentance; and the bp was required to report on this matter to the abp, *Reg Pontissara*, 290–292, and *Epist.Pecham*, iii, 806–808 (where the date is 11 Aug.); the abp wrote again on 3 Nov, *ib.*, iii, 837–838.

1289, 8 Oct., still living under excommunication but obtained papal dispensation to celebrate divine office, *Fasti*, ii, 90.

Note: This confused and perplexing acct requires a brief comment. Valentine's priorate was complicated by the fact that it coincided with the episcopate of Nicholas de Ely, with whom the chapter was at odds, and that it was marred by the continuing machinations of Andrew de London, q.v., a former prior, who was intent upon his own reinstatement. The latter was successful in gaining support among many of the monks, thus making Valentine's position untenable. By the time of Valentine's second restoration in 1276 the bp had become determined to assert his prerogative and settle the problem by depriving him once and for all and appting his own nominees, first John de Dureville, q.v., and then Adam de Farnham, q.v.

VENEYS

see Devenish

William VINCENT [Wyncent

occ. 1416 occ. 1424

[1416], 14 Mar., ord acol. and subdcn, Winchester cathedral, Reg. Beaufort, fo M^{v}.

1416, 18 Apr., ord dcn, Winchester cathedral, *ib.*, fo N.

1418, 16 May, ord pr., no place named, *ib.*, fo O^{v}.

Name in Oxford, Bod. Ms Rawlinson, C.489, Proprium sanctorum, dated A.D. 1424, on fo 25^{v}; this contains his own *portiforium* and diurnale which he had comm. and in which he had written his name and this description and date. He also recorded that after he d. it was for the use of the sacrist or another monk of the sacrist's nomination.

William de WALLOP

occ. 1295

1295, 6 June, chosen by the subprior and chapter as one of seven *compromissorii* in the el. of a prior, *Reg. Pontissara*, 73–75.

WALLOP

see also Wollope

WALLYNGFORD

see Walyngford

Edmund de WALRAND [Walraund

occ. 1325 occ. 1328

1326, 15 Feb., ord acol. and subdcn, Winchester cathedral, Reg. Stratford, fo 143^{v}.

1326, 20 Sept., ord dcn, Kingsclere, *ib.*, fo 144^{v}.

1328, 19 Mar., ord pr., Crawley [Hants.], *ib.*, fo 148.

1325, 9 Oct., 59th in order of seniority (out of 64), *Reg. Pontissara*, 557 (as Edward).

I WALTER

occ. before 1154

c. 1154, became abbot of Tavistock, *HRH*, 72.

II WALTER (Prior I)

occ. c. 1173 occ. 1175/6

c. 1173–1175/6, prior: res. to become abbot of Westminster, *Fasti*, ii, 89, *HRH*, 77, 80; see Robert I.

III WALTER (Prior II)

occ. 1215/16 d. 1239

1215/16–1238/9, prior: first occ. c. 1216 but prob. in office by 7 Mar. 1215, *Fasti*, ii, 89; last occ. after 11 July, 1238, *Winch. Cart.*, no 310 and *Ann. Winton.*, 87; d. 1239, *Ann. Waverley*, 323, prob. 10 Nov., Lambeth Ms 20, fo 237^{v}, BL Ms Arundel 68, fo 47^{v}.

Some of his *acta* are in *Winch. Cart.*, nos 144, 300, 304, 308, 310, 321, 329, 331, 333, 398–400, 460, 479, 545b.

Note: this may be the Walter who appeared as witness in Rome in [1205], 15 Oct., *Eng. Epis. Acta*, ix, no 81; see Germanus.

IV WALTER (Prior III)

occ. 1238 occ. 1247

1244/5–1247, prior: possibly apptd by the bp because of a papal mandate of 22 Dec. 1244; occ. 18 Apr. 1245, *Fasti*, ii, 89; d. 3 Apr. 1247, *Ann. Winton.*, 90.

1238, 11 July, hordarian, *CPR (1232–1247)*, 226.

1238, 11 July, one of four monks who, with the two adcns, rec. the royal licence to el. a bp, *CPR (1232–1247)*, 226.

1245, 19 Apr., with the chapter, he confirmed a charter of bp William Ralegh [in favour of Rochester cathedral], *Reg. Roff*, 13. (See Rochester reference list).

V WALTER

occ. 1355/6

1355/6, chamberlain, WCL receiver's acct, SS no 68, but not printed in Kitchin, *Obed. Rolls*.

VI WALTER
occ. 1402/3

1402/3, precentor, Lambeth ED 70.

Note: this may be Walter Farnhull, q.v., who may have followed John de Bristowe, q.v., as precentor.

WALTER
see also Rufus

I Robert de WALYNGFORD
occ. 1240

1240, 16 Aug., had accompanied John de Dureville, q.v., to Rome 'on negotiations' on behalf of St Swithun's and the king now authorized them to have a loan of up to 100m., *CClR (1237–1242)*, 215.

II Robert de WALYNGFORD [Wallyngford, Walyngforth
occ. 1358 occ. 1404

1358, 2 Oct., acol., recd *lit. dim*, for all orders, Reg. Edington, ii, fo LL[v] (ii, no 897).
1360, 13 Sept., recd *lit. dim*, from the prior, acting as vicar general, for subdcn's orders, *Reg. Edington*, ii, no 915; see John de Merlawe I.
1361, 7 Apr., dcn, recd *lit. dim*, for pr.'s orders, Reg. Edington, ii, fo OO[v] (no 916, which has omitted dcn).
1370/2, third prior, WCL unnumbered anniversarian acct, Worcester Cathedral Muniment, C.532.
1391/2; 1393, 21/22 Aug.; 1398, 15 Feb., subprior, WCL Chilbolton acct; BL Ms Harley 328, fo 24; *Reg. Wykeham*, ii, 477.
1404, 16/17 Oct., subprior, *Reg. Common Seal*, nos 68, 69.
1370/1, recd 8d. from the anniversarian on his apptment as third prior, WCL unnumbered obedientiary acct.
1371/2, he and Henry Imbard, q.v., made several journeys to Bishopstone [Bushton, Wilts.] during the yr, and he spent three wks there ill, at a cost of 21s. 1d. to the manor, Worcester Cathedral Muniment, C.532.
1375, 5 Mar., with John Pury, q.v., apptd penitentiary in Winchester adcnry, *Reg. Wykeham*, ii, 232.
1391/2, pd a visit to Chilbolton, WCL acct.
1393, 21/22 Aug., 2nd to sign the composition with bp Wykeham, BL Ms Harley 328, fo 24; see Robert de Rodebourne.
1398, 15 Feb., licensed as penitentiary, with Ralph Basyng, q.v., for the diocese, *Reg. Wykeham*, ii, 477.
1404, 16 Oct., 2nd in order at the el. of a bp, *Reg. Common Seal*, no 68.

WARANNE
see William Wareham

Thomas WARE
occ. 1381 occ. 1397/8

1381, 21 Dec., ord acol., bp's chapel, Highclere, *Reg. Wykeham*, i, 300.
1382, 22 Mar., ord subdcn, Winchester cathedral, *ib.*, i, 301.
1384, 4 June, ord dcn, bp's chapel, Highclere, *ib.*, i, 307.
1386, 17 Mar., ord pr., bp's chapel, Esher, *ib.*, i, 311.
1385/6, celebrated his first mass and recd an 8d. gift from the anniversarian, Worcester Cathedral Muniment, C.533.
1392/4, treasurer, WCL Hannington and Wootton accts.
1392/3, visited Chilbolton, Hannington, Sutton, Whitchurch, Wonston and Wootton, WCL accts.
1393, 21/22 Aug., 29th to sign the composition with bp Wykeham, BL Ms Harley 328, fo 24[v], where is named *scaccarius*; see Robert de Rodebourne.
1394/5, visited Hurstbourne with John Thurston, q.v., *pro manerio supervidendo*, Worcester Cathedral Muniment, C.867; this yr they were also at Silkstead and Wootton for the same purpose, WCL accts.
1397/8, pd a visit to Whitchurch, WCL acct.

Peter WAREHAM [Warham
occ. 1527 occ. 1539

1527, 20 Apr., ord subdcn, Lady chapel, Winchester cathedral, Reg Fox, v, fo 36[v].
1539, 14 Nov., one of four monk students at Oxford, PRO E315/494.
[1528 × 1539], surname occ. in a list of monks entered on a blank fo in Oxford, Bod. Ms Selden supra 76, fo 46[v]; no Christian names are given.
1539, 14 Nov., on the surrender list with the other monk students and assigned a pension of £10 p.a., *L and P Henry VIII*, xiv, pt 2, no 520 (PRO E315/494).

William WAREHAM [Waranne, Warham
occ. 1476 occ. 1479

1476, 9 Mar., ord acol., Winchester cathedral, Reg. Waynflete, ii, fo 175[v].
1477, 31 May, ord subdcn, Winchester cathedral, *ib.*, ii, fo 178.
1479, 6 Mar., ord dcn, Winchester cathedral, *ib.*, ii, fo 182[v].

Thomas WARMYNSTRE
occ. 1524

1524, 2 Dec., chamberlain, Reg. Fox, v, fo 75.
1524, 2 Dec., 13th in order at the el. of a prior, Reg. Fox, v, fo 75; he voted for John Avynton, q.v., 'propter eius scientiam et circumspectionem in temporalibus', *ib.*, v, fo 77[v].

WARMYNSTRE
see also Wermynstre

Nicholas WARNERE [Warner, Warynnere
occ. 1447 occ. 1486

1448, 18 May, ord subdcn, Winchester cathedral, Reg. Waynflete, i, fo A[v].
1448, 21 Sept., ord dcn, bp's chapel, Marwell, *ib.*, i, fo B.
1451, 24 Apr., ord pr., Winchester cathedral, *ib.*, i, fo D.
1450/1, celebrated his first mass and the *custos operum* sent wine for the feast, WCL unnumbered obedientiary acct.

1447, 15 Apr., 38th in order, out of 39 at the el. of a bp., and described as one of three *juvenes* who were prof., *Reg. Common Seal*, no 316.
1450, 11 Dec., 34th in order at the el. of a prior, Reg. Waynflete, i, fo 30[v].
1486, 7 Dec., 4th at the el. of a bp, *Reg. Common Seal*, no 434.

In 1426/7, a Nicholas Warenner was one of the bailiffs of the city of Winchester, Bird, *Black Book*, 195.

John WARYN
occ. 1447 occ. 1457

1447, 15 Apr., 34th in order at the el. of a bp, *Reg. Common Seal*, no 316.
1450, 11 Dec., 30th at the el. of a prior, Reg. Waynflete, i, fo 30[v].
1457, 15 May, apptd by the subprior, William Basyng, q.v., to be responsible for citing the monks to the el. [of a prior], and he was required to turn in a report of his actions in carrying out this assignment, *Reg. Common Seal*, no 335.

Peter WARYN
occ. 1412/14

1412, 27 Feb., ord acol., Winchester cathedral, Reg. Beaufort, fo F[v].
1414, 18 Sept., ord dcn, Winchester cathedral, *ib.*, fo I[v].

Hugh WATFORD [Watforde
occ. 1398 occ. 1447

1398, 21 Dec., ord acol., bp's chapel, Farnham castle, *Reg. Wykeham*, i, 346.
1399, 22 Feb., ord subdcn, bp's chapel, Farnham castle, *ib.*, i, 347.
1400, 18 Sept., ord dcn, bp's chapel, Waltham, *ib.*, i, 351.
1402, 18 Feb., ord pr., bp's chapel, Waltham, *ib.*, i, 354.

1404, 16 Oct., 31st in order at the el. of a bp, *Reg. Common Seal*, no 68.
1447, 15 Apr., 3rd in order [and therefore the most senior monk] at the el. of a bp, *ib.*, no 316.

John WATFORD
occ. 1363

1363, 23 Sept., ord acol., Lydney, Reg. Lewis Charlton (Hereford), fo 41 (p. 86 in the printed reg.).

William WATFORD [Watforde
occ. 1350 occ. 1409/10

1350, 5 Sept., ord acol., bp's chapel, South Waltham, *Reg. Edington*, ii, no 817.
1350, 18 Sept., ord subdcn, bp's chapel, Highclere, *ib.*, ii, no 814.
1351, 23 May, granted *lit. dim*, for dcn's orders, Reg. Edington, ii, fo AA.
1353, 22 Aug., dcn, granted *lit. dim*, for pr.'s orders, *Reg. Edington*, ii, no 845.
1354, 20 Dec., ord pr., bp's chapel, [Bishops] Waltham, *ib.*, ii, no 852.

1393, 21/22 Aug., infirmarer, BL Ms Harley 328, fo 24.

1393, 21/22 Aug., 5th to sign the composition with bp Wykeham, BL Ms Harley 328, fo 24; see Robert de Rodebourne.
1400/2, resident in the infirmary for 50 wks in 1400/1 and for the whole of the following yr, the expense of which was borne by the hordarian at the rate of 3d. per wk (only half of what was pd for short periods of illness), Kitchin, *SS* no 55, p. 283, WCL unnumbered hordarian's acct.
1404, 16 Oct., 4th in order at the el. of a bp, *Reg. Common Seal*, no 68.
1405/6, 1409/10, resident in the infirmary for the whole of both yrs, supported by 3d. per wk from the hordarian, Kitchin, *SS* nos 56 and 57, pp. 286, 290.

I John WAYTE
occ. 1368 occ. 1395/6

1368, 4 Mar., ord acol., Winchester cathedral, *Reg. Wykeham*, i, 252.
1368, 23 Dec., ord subdcn, bp's chapel, Farnham castle, *ib.*, i, 255.
1369, 22 Sept., ord dcn, Winchester cathedral, *ib.*, i, 257.
1370, 21 Sept., ord pr., bp's chapel, Highclere, *ib.*, i, 261.
1370/1, celebrated his first mass and recd a 6d. gift from the anniversarian, WCL unnumbered obedientiary acct.

1382/4, receiver/treasurer, WCL Wootton, Sparsholt (1382/3), Crondall, Silkstead (1383/4) accts; in 1382/3 at Wootton it appears that he took over from William Skylling, q.v., and he was prob. succ. by John Langreod, q.v.
1386/7, almoner, Kitchin, *SS* no 27, pp. 412–415.
1393, 21/22 Aug., *magister operum novorum*, BL Ms Harley 328, fo 24[v]; see below.
1395/6, almoner, Kitchin, *SS* no 29, pp. 418–419.

1382/3, went to Wonston *pro uno preposito ordinando*, WCL acct.
1383/4, prob. visited Crondall and Silkstead, WCL accts.
1393, 21/22 Aug., 16th to sign the composition with bp Wykeham which specified the agreed terms between bp and chapter concerning the new building programme initiated by the former, BL Ms Harley 328, fo 24v. Presumably he was at the time master of the works and therefore of the 'new works' now being undertaken; see Robert de Rodebourne.

II John WAYTE
occ. 1396 occ. 1404

1396, 25 Feb., ord acol., bp's chapel, Waltham, *Reg. Wykeham*, i, 339.
1396, 23 Sept., ord subdcn, bp's chapel, Waltham, *ib.*, i, 340.
1398, 21 Dec., ord dcn, bp's chapel, Farnham castle, *ib.*, i, 346.
1399, 22 Feb., ord pr., bp's chapel, Farnham castle, *ib.*, i, 348.
1404, 16 Oct., 29th in order at the el. of a bp, *Reg. Common Seal*, no 68.

WEBBE
see Kyngston

Richard WELLE [Well
occ. 1410/12

1410, 19 Dec., ord acol., Winchester cathedral, Reg. Beaufort, fo E.
1412, 27 Feb., ord subdcn, Winchester cathedral, *ib.*, fo Fv.
1412, 28 Mar., ord dcn, Winchester cathedral, *ib.*, fo Gv.

John WELLES [Wellys
occ. 1451 occ. 1456

1451, 18 Dec., ord acol., Winchester cathedral, Reg. Waynflete, i, fo Dv.
1453, 22 Sept., ord subdcn, Winchester cathedral, *ib.*, i, fo G.
1455, 20 Sept., ord dcn, bp's chapel, Wolvesey, *ib.*, i, fo Kv.
1456, 18 Sept., ord pr., bp's chapel, Wolvesey, *ib.*, i, fo Mv.

Reginald WELLS
occ. 1540

1540, 12 Jan., described as pr. and former monk in a letter of commendation written by the prior, Reg. iii, fo 30.
Note: is this Reginald Wroughton, q.v.?

Richard WERDMAN [Werdeman, Werdiman
occ. 1403 occ. 1410

1403, 22 Sept., ord acol., Waltham, *Reg. Wykeham*, i, 356.
1404, 23 Feb., ord subdcn, Waltham, *ib.*, i, 357.
1404, 21 May, given *lit. dim*, for dcn's orders, *ib.*, ii, 556.
1410, 15 Feb., ord pr., Winchester cathedral, Reg. Beaufort, fo Dv.
1409/10, celebrated his first mass and recd a gift from the hordarian, Kitchin, *SS* no 57, 290.
1404, 16 Oct., 42nd and last in order at the el. of a bp, *Reg. Common Seal*, no 68.

William WERDMAN
occ. 1405/6

1405/6, ill in the infirmary for two wks and the hordarian pd his expenses of 6d. per wk, Kitchin, *SS* no 56, p. 286.
Note: this is prob. a mistake for Richard Werdman above; the entry on the hordarian's roll names first William Ely, q.v., and then William Werdman immediately following—a slip of the pen perhaps?

Valentine de WEREWELL[E]
see Valentine

John WERMYNSTRE [Wermenstre, Wermestre, Wermystre
occ. 1400 occ. 1404

1400, 18 Sept., ord acol., bp's chapel, Waltham, *Reg. Wykeham*, i, 351.
1401, 28 May, ord subdcn, bp's chapel, Waltham, *ib.*, i, 352.
1402, 20 May, ord dcn, bp's chapel, Waltham, *ib.*, i, 354.
[1404], 21 May, dcn, granted *lit. dim*, for pr.'s orders, *ib.*, ii, 556.
1404, 20 Sept., ord pr., Waltham, *ib.*, i, 359.
1404, 16 Oct., 36th in order at the el. of a bp, *Reg. Common Seal*, no 68.

WERMYNSTRE
see also Warmynstre

WESBURY
see Westbury

Richard WESTBROKE
occ. 1527 occ. 1539

1527, 20 Apr., recd the tonsure and ord acol., Lady chapel, Winchester cathedral, Reg. Fox, v, fo 36v.
1528, 11 Apr., ord subdcn, Lady chapel, Winchester cathedral, *ib.*, v, fo 38v.
[1528 × 1539], surname occ. in a list of monks copied on to a blank fo in Oxford, Bod. Ms Selden supra 76, fo 46v; no Christian names are given.
1539, 14 Nov., 21st on the surrender list, under commoners, and assigned a pension of £5 p.a., *L and P Henry VIII*, xiv, pt 2, no 520 (PRO E315/494).

John WESTBURY [Wesbury, Westebury
occ. 1488 occ. 1501

1488, 20 Dec., ord acol., chapel of St John the Baptist, Winchester cathedral, Reg. Courtenay, fo 14.
[1490], 18 Sept., ord subdcn, church of St John the Baptist in the Soke, Winchester, *ib.*, fo 17.
1491, 16 June, ord dcn, church of St John the Baptist in the Soke, Winchester, *ib.*, fo 19ᵛ.
1495, 19 Sept., ord pr., Winchester cathedral, Reg. Langton, fo 26ᵛ.
1495/6, celebrated his first mass and the hordarian sent 18d. worth of wine for the feast, Kitchin, *SS* no 60, p. 301.

1501, 27 Feb., curtarian, Canterbury Reg. R, fo 115.

1492, 29 Oct., 23rd to be examined at the *sed. vac.* visitation; he deposed that the bells for matins and other offices were not rung at the proper times and that the preparation of food was inadequate, *Reg. abp Morton*, ii, no 127.
1498, 23 Apr., 19th in order at the el. of a prior, Reg. Langton, fo 73ᵛ.
1501, 27 Feb., 17th to be examined at the visitation (*sed. vac.* both Canterbury and Winchester) by the commissary of the prior of Christ Church, Canterbury; he reported *omnia bene*, Canterbury Reg. R, fo 115.

Edward WESTGATE
occ. 1524 occ. 1539

1524, 2 Dec., gardener, Reg. Fox, v, fo 75.
1530/1, anniversarian, WCL unnumbered obedientiary acct.
1535, hostiller, *Valor Eccles.*, ii, 3.

1524, 2 Dec., 14th in order at the el. of a prior, Reg. Fox, v, fo 75; he voted for Henry Broke *propter eius multipliciter virtutes*, *ib.*, v, fo 77ᵛ.
[1528 × 1539], surname occ. in a list of monks copied on to a blank fo in Oxford, Bod. Ms Selden supra 76, fo 46ᵛ; no Christian names are given.
1539, 14 Nov., 11th on the surrender list, among the seniors, and assigned a pension of £6 p.a., *L and P Henry VIII*, xiv, pt 2, no 520 (PRO E315/494).

Robert WESTGATE [Westgat
occ. 1447 d. 1470

1457–1470, prior: el. 15 May 1457, Reg. Waynflete, i, fos 85ᵛ–87ᵛ; d. or possibly res. before 30 Mar. 1470, *ib.*, ii, fo 1; see Thomas Hunton.

1450, 11 Dec., with Richard Dummere, q.v., student at Oxford, Reg. Waynflete, i, fo 30ᵛ. *BRUO* states that he prob. lodged in Canterbury College but gives no ref.; payments for the Winchester chamber of the college occ. frequently in Pantin, *Cant. Coll. Ox.*, ii, e.g., 175 (1454/5), 179 (1455/6).

1447, 15 Apr., prof. and in pr.'s orders and 32nd in order (out of 39) at the el. of a bp, *Reg. Common Seal*, no 316.
1450, 11 Dec., 28th in order at the el. of a prior, Reg. Waynflete, i, fo 30ᵛ.
1457, 28 Mar., licensed as penitentiary in the diocese, *ib.*, i, fo 41*.
1457, 15 May, el. prior *per viam scrutinii*, Reg. Waynflete, i, fo 85ᵛ and presented to the bp the same day, *Reg. Common Seal*, no 336.
1460, Sept., with William Robus, q.v., attended convocation, in person, Reg. Waynflete, i, fo 63*.
1462, 6 July, with William Clement, q.v., named in certificate as proctors for convocation, *ib.*, i, fos 77*-78*.
1468, 12 May, with William Clement again present at convocation, *ib.*, i, fos 93*ᵛ–94*ᵛ.
1468, 13 June, named as one of the examiners in a divorce case, *ib.*, i, fo 94*ᵛ.
1470, 26 July, named in the certificate, with William Clement, as proctors for convocation, *ib.*, ii, fo 142; but he is reported to have d. in Mar.! Perhaps he had merely res.

Some of his *acta* are found in *Reg. Common Seal*, nos 324, 338–360, 396–397.

Valentine de WHEREWELL
see Valentine

Simon WHITESTON [Whitston
occ. 1459 occ. 1462

1459, 17 Feb., ord acol., Winchester cathedral, Reg. Waynflete, i, fo R.
1460, 1 Mar., ord subdcn, Hyde abbey, *ib.*, i, fo vᵛ.
1462, 18 Sept., ord dcn, Winchester cathedral, *ib.*, i, fo B*ᵛ.

Alexander de WIGORNIA [Worcestr', Wygorn'
occ. 1307/8 occ. 1345

1307/9, 1310/11, pd visits to Chilbolton, WCL accts.

1325, 9 Oct., 28th in order of seniority, *Reg. Pontissara*, 556.
1345, 28 July, apptd one of nine *compromissorii* in the el. of a bp, *Reg. Common Seal*, no 5.

WIKEHAM
see Wykham

W. de WILLEHALE
occ. 1304/5

1304/5, pd a visit to Stockton (Wilts.) with Richard de Enford, q.v., WCL acct.

Note: this is prob. William de Wynhale, q.v.

I WILLIAM
occ. [1165]

[1165, before 19 July], prior: he was prob. succ. by Robert II, q.v., *Winch. Cart.*, no 75 which contains the only ref. to this prior and is itself not entirely clear; see *HRH*, 80.

1165, 19 July, d., ,*Winch. Cart.*, no 75.

II WILLIAM
occ. [early 14th c.]

[early 14th c.], kitchener, [*coquinarius*], Kitchin, *SS* no 46, p. 466.

[early 14th c.], the almoner gave him a gift because he had broken his shin bone [*tibia*] *ib.*

WILY
see Wyly

Edmund de WINCHESTER
occ. 1292

1292, 23 Sept., with the prior [William de Basyng I] and Robert de Hakeborne, q.v., was present in the chapter house at Salisbury for the ordination of the vicarage of Enford, Winchester College Muniment 8182.

Edward WINCHESTER [Wynchester
occ. 1509 occ. 1513

1509, 24 Mar., ord subdcn, bp's chapel, Esher, Reg. Fox, ii, fo 24.
1513, 26 Mar., ord pr., Winchester cathedral, *ib.*, iii, fo 53.

WINCHESTER
see also Wynchestre

Thomas de WINTON
occ. 1240

1240, 1 May, appeared before the king at Abingdon, with J[ames] de Basyng, H. Truwery, Richard de Worston, q.v., and the adcns, and recd licence to el. a bp, BL Add. Ms 29436, fos 37^{v}–38.

WINTON
see also Wynton

WLNOTH
occ. [1107]

[1107], precentor, temp. bp Giffard and prior Godfrey, *Winch. Cart.*, no 9 and *Eng. Epis. Acta*, viii, no 17.

[1107], as precentor recd the bp's grant of the church of Ellendone (Elingdon, Wroughton, Wilts.) for the scriptorium, *ib.*

WODDISON
see Wodson

Walter WODE
occ. 1497/8

1498, Mar./Sept., cellarer, succeeding Arnold Gilbert, q.v., Kitchin, *SS* no 10, p. 389.

WODE
see also Woode

[John WODELOK
occ. 1349

1349, 19 Sept., ord pr., bp's chapel [Bishops] Waltham, *Reg. Edington*, ii, no 789.

Note: this monk has prob. been misplaced in the ordination lists, as he (or, conceivably, his namesake) occ. in three previous lists as a monk of Hyde, *ib.*, ii, nos 737, 763, 776. Unless he transferred?]

WODELOK
see also Woodlock

John WODSON [Woddison, Woddson, Wodesun, Woodeson
occ. 1492 occ. 1539

1501, 27 Feb., ?*speciorum custos*, Canterbury Reg. R, fo 115.
1524, 2 Dec., anniversarian, Reg. Fox, v, fo 75.
1535, infirmarer, *Valor Eccles.*, ii, 3.

1492, 29 Oct., 18th to be examined at the *sed. vac.* visitation and made no deposition, *Reg. abp Morton*, ii, no 127.
1501, 27 Feb., 12th to be examined at the visitation (*sed. vac.* both Canterbury and Winchester) by the commissary of the prior of Christ Church, Canterbury; he reported *omnia bene*, Canterbury Reg. R, fo 115.
1524, 2 Dec., 4th in order at the el. of a prior, Reg. Fox, v, fo 75; he voted for Henry Broke *propter eius discretionem*, *ib.*, v, fo 77.
[1528 × 1539], surname occ. in a list of monks entered on a blank fo in Oxford, Bod. Ms Selden supra 76, fo 46^{v}; no Christian names are given.
1539, 14 Nov., 12th on the surrender list, among the seniors, and assigned a pension of £6 p.a., *L and P Henry VIII*, xiv, pt 2, no 520 (PRO E315/494).

Note: this monk and John Woode II, q.v., may be identical; see also John Wydonson.

WOLINDR' [?Welindr'
occ. [1528 × 1539]

[1528 × 1539], surname occ. in a list of monks copied on to a blank fo in Oxford, Bod. Ms Selden supra 76, fo 46^{v}; no Christian names are given.

Richard de WOLLOP [Wollope, Wullup
occ. 1307/8 occ. 1325

1310/12; 1318/19; 1321/2, part yr, receiver, WCL Chilbolton and Hannington accts; WCL Littleton acct; WCL Houghton and Wonston accts where Elias de Fourde, q.v., is also named as receiver.

1307/9, pd several visits to Chilbolton both yrs, WCL accts.

1310/11, visited Chilbolton, WCL acct.

1311/12, pd visits to Easton, Hannington and prob. Hurstbourne, WCL accts.

1321/2, visited Houghton and Wonston, WCL accts.

1323/4, pd visits to Wonston, and to Whitchurch for *liberatio denariorum*, WCL acct, Worcester Cathedral Muniment, C.523.

1325, 9 Oct., 15th in order of seniority, *Reg. Pontissara*, 556.

WOLLOP
see also Wallop

William WOLVELE
occ. 1388 occ. 1393

1388, 19 Dec., ord acol., bp's chapel, Farnham castle, *Reg. Wykeham*, i, 317.

1389, 17 Apr., ord subdcn, Winchester cathedral, *ib.*, i, 319.

1392, 9 Mar., ord dcn, bp's chapel, Marwell, *ib.*, i, 326.

1392, 13 Apr., ord pr., Winchester cathedral, *ib.*, i, 327.

1391/2, celebrated his first mass and recd 8d. [worth of wine] from the anniversarian, WCL unnumbered acct (Bishopstone, now Bushton, Wilts.); he also received a gift from the hordarian, Lambeth ED 69.

1393, 21/22 Aug., 37th to sign the composition with bp Wykeham, BL Ms Harley 328, fo 24^{v}; see Robert de Rodebourne.

Osbert de WOLVESEYE
occ. [c. 1173 × 1191]

[c. 1173 × 1191], *temp.* Reginald, bp of Bath, witnessed a grant by the bp to St Swithun's, *Winch. Cart.*, no 313.

Note: although not named as a monk of St Swithun's he prob. was.

John WONSTON [Wonstone
occ. 1528 occ. 1539

1528, 11 Apr., ord dcn, Lady chapel, Winchester cathedral, Reg. Fox, v, fo 38^{v}.

1539, 14 Nov., 19th on the surrender list, among the commoners, and assigned a pension of £5 p.a., *L and P Henry VIII*, xiv, pt 2, no 520 (PRO E315/494).

Note: the surname of one of the two Wonstons, prob. this one, occ. in a list of monks [1528 × 1539], copied on to a blank folio in Oxford, Bod. Ms Selden supra 76, fo 46^{v}; no Christian names are given. See also John Carpenter.

William WONSTON
occ. 1511

1511, 20 Sept., ord dcn, bp's chapel [Bishops] Waltham, Reg. Fox, iii, fo 51.

Note: see the note above, under John Wonston.

I John WOODE [senior
occ. 1447 occ. 1492

1447, 15 Apr., 31st in order at the el. of a bp, *Reg. Common Seal*, no 316.

1450, 11 Dec., 27th at the el. of a prior, Reg. Waynflete, i, fo 30^{v}.

1486, 7 Dec., 3rd in order at the el. of a bp, *Reg. Common Seal*, no 434, where he is designated 'senior'.

1492, 29 Oct., 3rd to be examined at the *sed. vac.* visitation and reported that to his knowledge all was well, *Reg. abp Morton*, ii, no 127.

II John WOODE [Wode, Wood, junior
occ. 1483 occ. 1498

1483, 24 May, ord acol., Winchester cathedral, Reg. Waynflete, ii, fo 192.

1484, 18 Sept., ord subdcn, Winchester cathedral, *ib.*, ii, fo 195^{v}.

Note: see John Wydonson, ord pr. in 1490.

1486, 7 Dec., 28th in order (out of 30) at the el. of a bp, *Reg. Common Seal*, no 434, where he is designated 'junior'.

1498, 23 Apr., 16th at the el. of a prior, Reg. Langton, fo 73^{v}.

Note: see John Wodson; there is some confusion here.

John WOODESON, Woodesone
see John Wodson

Henry WOODLOCK [Wodelok de Merewell
occ. 1293 occ. 1304/5

1295–1304/5, prior: el. prior, 6 June 1295, *Reg. Pontissara*, 73–77; el. bp, 1304; see below.

1293, 21 Oct., acted as proctor for the prior and chapter in a a lawsuit between St Swithun's and the rector of Chilcombe, *Winch. Cart.*, no 39.

1295, 6 June, chosen by the chapter as one of seven *compromissorii* in the el. of a prior, *Reg. Pontissara*, 73–74, was himself el. the same day and gave his assent, *ib.*, 74–75. On the following day the bp confirmed the el., *ib.*, 77.

1295, summoned to parliament at Westminster on 1 Aug. *Parl. Writs*, i, pt 2, 908.

1295, 17 Dec., with the bp's official, the treasurer of Wolvesey and others, apptd vicars in spirituals during the bp's absence, *ib.*, 779–780.

1296, 3 Mar., with the official, the treasurer and others, acting as vicar general, *Reg. Pontissara*, 801–802; there is also an undated instruction on 803.

1296, 19 Oct., with the official and others addressed by the absent bp as his commissaries and directed to carry out the induction of a clerk, *ib.*, 640; on 17 Dec., the bp addressed them as keepers of spirituals and sent them further instructions, *ib.*, 833–834.
1298/9, visited Chilbolton frequently (nine tallies) and he and his *familia* consumed pottage, lambs, cheese, geese and capons; he also pd several visits to Michelmersh (five tallies).
1304, 23 Dec., × 1305, 29 Jan., el. bp, *Fasti*, iv, 45.
1304/5, made the rounds of the Wiltshire manors, *Reg. Pontissara*, vii.
1305, 30 May was set as the day of his consecration [at Canterbury], acc. to *Reg. Woodlock*, 21; but see *Fasti*, iv, 45.
1305, 10 Oct., was enthroned in the cathedral, *Reg. Woodlock*, 45.

The Woodlock family were landed gentry and long time tenants of the bp at Marwell; Nicholas de Merewell, q.v., was prob. an older relative of Henry, see *Reg. Woodlock*, vi. There is also a paragraph on his domestic activities as prior in *ib.*, vii.

WORCESTER
see Wigornia

Richard de WORSTON [?Wrpton, Wrston
occ. 1240 occ. 1254

1247/8, prob. curtarian, see below under the same date.

1240, 1 May, appeared before the king at Abingdon, with J[ames de Basyng, H. Truwery, Thomas de Winton, q.v., and the adcns, and recd licence to el. a bp, BL Add. Ms 29436, fos 37ᵛ–38 (the initial here resembles S rather than R).
1247/8, visited Whitchurch and other manors for *liberatio denariorum*, WCL pipe roll acct; thus he may have been curtarian.
1254, 5 July, addressed as pr., and given papal dispensation to minister as such and also to accept abbatial and other offices despite illegitimacy, *CPL*, i (1198–1304), 304.

WORSTON
see also Dreyms

Romanus WOTTONE
d. 1513/14

1513/14, d., and the almoner spent 10s. on bread for the poor on the day of his burial, Kitchin, *SS* no 44, p. 460 (acct for 1514/15).

WREVIL
see Dureville

Reginald WROUGHTON [Wrosston, Wrowghton
occ. 1527 occ. 1539

1527, 20 Apr., ord dcn, Lady chapel, Winchester cathedral, Reg. Fox, v, fo 36ᵛ.

[1528 × 1539], surname [Wrosston] occ. in a list of monks copied on to a blank folio in Oxford, Bod. Ms Selden supra 76, fo 46ᵛ; no Christian names are given.
1539, 14 Nov., 18th to sign the surrender list, among the 'commoners' and assigned a pension of £5 p.a., *L and P Henry VIII*, xiv, pt 2, no 520 (PRO E315/494).

Note: is this Reginald Wells, q.v.?

William WROUGHTON D.Th. [Wroghton, Wroston, Wrowghton
occ. 1444 occ. 1462

1447, 15 Apr., almoner, *Reg. Common Seal*, no 316.
1451/2, hordarian, first yr, WCL unnumbered obedientiary acct.

[c. 1435 × 1444], student at Oxford because by 6 July, 1444 he was M.A. and B.Th., Pantin, *BMC*, ii, 188 (BL Ms Egerton 3316, fo 1, 1ᵛ).
1446, Apr., *prior studentium* at Oxford, *Reg. Cancell. Oxon*, i, 130.
1450, 11 Dec., named as *sacre pagine professor*, Reg. Waynflete, i, fo 30ᵛ.

1444, 6 July, with the subprior, Robert Puryton, q.v., attended the Black Monk Chapter, and both were apptd to a committee which was to draw up a new code of statutes for the order. The committee met on 15 Sept. in Oxford; and both were members of a three man team which prepared the final draft and presented it at the end of Sept., Pantin, *BMC*, ii, 188–189.
1447, 15 Apr., 12th in order at the el. of a bp, *Reg. Common Seal*, no 316.
1450, 11 Dec., 7th at the el. of a prior and was named as one of seven *compromissorii*, Reg. Waynflete, i, fos 30ᵛ, 31.
1457, 18/20 Apr., with Nicholas Mersch, q.v., apptd proctors to request from the bp a licence to el. a prior, and they obtained it from him at Esher, *Reg. Common Seal*, nos 332, 333. On 15 May he and Mersch were deputed to seek the bp's confirmation of the chapter's choice of Robert Westgate, q.v., *ib.*, no 336; on 19 May they were also apptd to present the el. to the bp and provide him with details of the proceedings, *ib.*, no 337.
1461, 13 Aug., a Bible of his was sequestered by the chancellor of the university of Oxford because of an unpd debt owed to John Stacionarius, *Reg. Cancell. Oxon, 1434–1469*, ii, 44–45; the second fo began 'ON.AOOEN'.
1462, 7 Jan., comm. by the bp to conduct a visitation of Chertsey abbey which resulted in the deposition of the abbot, Reg. Waynflete, i, fo 69*ᵛ.
1462, 20 Mar., recd royal assent to his el. as abbot of Chertsey, *CPR (1461–1467)*, 180, 185 (where the date is 12 May).

Note: he was deprived of the abbacy on 6 Feb. 1465, *CPR (1461–1467)*, 512–513; *BRUO* suggests that he may have obtained papal dispensation to hold a benefice, and may be the William Wroghton who was rector of Clandon, Surrey in 1471.

WRPTON, Wrston
see Worston

WULLOP
see Wallop, Wollope

WYCFORD
see Wykford

John WYDONSON
occ. [1490]

[1490], 18 Sept., ord pr., church of St John the Baptist in the Soke, Winchester, Reg. Courtenay, fo 17.

Note: could this be John Woode II, q.v.?

Adam de WYG'
occ. 1223

1223, *custos* of the altar of St Mary, Cath. Records, ii, no 5 (fo 2).

1223, as *custos* recd a gift of land for the purchase of lights and ornaments for the altar, *ib.*.

WYGORNIA
see Wigornia

Nicholas de WYKFORD [Wycford, Wycforde, Wychford, Wykforde
occ. 1347 occ. 1377

1347, 24 Feb., ord dcn, bp's chapel, Southwark, *Reg. Edington*, ii, no 723.
1347, 22 Sept., ord pr., South Waltham, *ib.*, ii, no 740.

1350/1, receiver, WCL Wonston acct.

1348/9, visited Wonston for *liberatio denariorum*, WCL acct.
1355/6, employed by the receiver from whom he recd 6s. 8d. by order of the prior, and his clerk was pd 3s. 4d. by the receiver, WCL, SS no 68 (not printed in Kitchin, *Obed. Rolls*).
1356/7, his clerk visited Whitchurch, WCL acct.
1370, 9 Mar., with Peter de Oxenford and Richard de Pek q.v., apptd penitentiaries in the diocese, *Reg. Wykeham*, ii, 107.
1377, 11 Jan., granted licence by the prior to be absent from the priory in order to accompany his brother Robert to Dublin. The latter had been provided to the abpric there in 1375 and had also been apptd chancellor of Ireland, *Reg. Wykeham*, ii, 277; for Robert Wykford see *BRUO* (under Wikeford).

A Robert Wykeford at Oxford recd cheese as a gift from the hordarian in 1351/2, PRO SC6/756/12; this was prob. his brother who was adcn of Winchester in 1361–1372, *Fasti*, iv, 50.

Richard WYKHAM [Wikeham, Wykam
occ. 1472 occ. 1486

1472, 19 Dec., ord acol., Winchester cathedral, Reg. Waynflete, ii, fo 169^{v}.
1474, 17 Dec., ord subdcn, Winchester cathedral, *ib.*, ii, fo 172^{v}.
1475, 18 Feb., ord dcn, Winchester cathedral, *ib.*, ii, fo 173.
1475, 5 Mar., ord pr., Mottisfont priory, *ib.*, ii, fo 174.
1474/5, celebrated his first mass and recd a gift from the anniversarian, Worcester Cathedral Muniment, C.1.
1486, 7 Dec., 14th in order at the el. of a bp, *Reg. Common Seal*, no 434.

WYLENHALE
see Willehale, Wynhale

Thomas de WYLTONE
occ. 1325

1325, 9 Oct., 63rd and second to last in order of seniority, *Reg. Pontissara*, 557.

Hugh de WYLY [Wily, Wyli
occ. 1326 occ. 1346/7

1326, 15 Feb., ord acol. and subdcn, Winchester cathedral, Reg. Stratford, fo 143^{v}.
1326, 20 Sept., ord dcn, Kingsclere, *ib.*, fo 144^{v}.
1328, 19 Mar., ord pr., Crawley (Hants), *ib.*, fo 148.

1325, 9 Oct., 58th in order of seniority, *Reg. Pontissara*, 557.
1338/9, visited Chilbolton with Philip de Nutley, q.v., and had five fowl during their stay, WCL acct.
1346/7, visited Chilbolton and dined on capon, WCL acct.

Peter WYMBORNE [Wymbourne
occ. 1385 occ. 1400/1

1385, 23 Dec., ord subdcn, bp's chapel, Farnham castle, *Reg. Wykeham*, i, 310.
1387, 21 Sept., ord dcn, bp's chapel, Marwell, *ib.*, i, 316.
1389, 17 Apr., ord pr., Winchester cathedral, *ib.*, i, 319.

1393, 21/22 Aug., 34th to sign the composition with bp Wykeham, BL Ms Harley 328, fo 24^{v}; see Robert de Rodebourne.
1400/1, spent one wk in the infirmary at a cost of 6d. to the infirmarer, Kitchin, *SS* no 55, p. 283.

WYNCENT
see Vincent

Alexander de WYNCESTRE
occ. 1338/9

1338/9, visited Chilbolton and dined on goose, WCL acct.

Note: this may be Alexander de Wynton, q.v., or a second monk by the same name.

WYNCHESTER
see Winchester

Henry de WYNCHESTRE [Wynchester
occ. 1381 d. 1402/3

1381, 21 Dec., ord acol., bp's chapel, Highclere, *Reg. Wykeham*, i, 300.
1382, 22 Mar., ord subdcn, Winchester cathedral, *ib.*, i, 301.
1383, 19 Sept., ord dcn, Waltham, *ib.*, i, 305.
1386, 17 Mar., ord pr., bp's chapel, Esher, *ib.*, i, 311.
1385/6, celebrated his first mass and recd a gift of 8d. from the anniversarian, Worcester Cathedral Muniment, C.533.
1393, 21/22 Aug., refectorer, BL Ms Harley 328, fo 24v.
1393, 21/22 Aug., 28th to sign the composition with bp Wykeham, BL Ms Harley 328, fo 24v; see Robert de Rodebourne.
1401/2, spent a wk in the infirmary at a cost of 6d. to the hordarian, WCL unnumbered obedientiary acct.
1402/3, d., and the almoner distributed 10s. worth of bread among the poor on the day of his burial, Kitchin, *SS* no 31, p. 424.

John WYNCHESTRE
occ. 1466 occ. 1470

1466, 20 Sept., ord acol., Winchester cathedral, Reg. Waynflete, i, fo K*v.
1470, 22 Dec., ord dcn, Winchester cathedral, *ib.*, ii, fo 166.

Richard WYNCHESTRE
occ. 1461 occ. 1464

1461, 4 Apr., ord acol., Winchester cathedral, Reg. Waynflete, i, fo Y.
1462, 18 Sept., ord subdcn, Winchester cathedral, *ib.*, i, fo B*v.
1464, 26 May, ord dcn, Winchester cathedral, *ib.*, i, fo F*.

Thomas WYNCHESTRE
occ. 1447 occ. 1450

1447, 15 Apr., pr., prof. and 27th in order at the el. of a bp, *Reg. Common Seal*, no 316.
1450, 11 Dec., 23rd at the el. of a prior, Reg. Waynflete, i, fo 30v.

Anthony WYNDESOR [Wynsore
occ. 1527/[8]

1527, 20 Apr., recd the tonsure and ord acol., Lady chapel, Winchester cathedral, Reg. Fox, v, fo 36v.
[1528 × 1539], surname occ. in a list of monks copied on to a blank folio in Oxford, Bod. Ms Selden supra 76, fo 46v; no Christian names are given.

Richard WYNHALE [Wylenhale
occ. 1392/3

1392, 9 Mar., ord subdcn, bp's chapel, Marwell, *Reg. Wykeham*, i, 325.
1392, 13 Apr., ord dcn, Winchester cathedral, *ib.*, i, 326.
1393, 21 Sept., ord pr., bp's chapel, Esher, *ib.*, i, 329.
1393, 21/22 Aug., 39th to sign the composition with bp Wykeham, BL Ms Harley 328, fo 24v; see Robert de Rodebourne.

William de WYNHALE [Wylehale, Wynnehale
occ. 1320/1 occ. 1332

1320/1, receiver, WCL Whitchurch acct.
1315/16, visited Michelmersh, WCL acct.
1320/1, pd a visit to Whitchurch, WCL acct.
1325, 9 Oct., 9th in order of seniority, *Reg. Pontissara*, 556.
1327/8, visited Ham (Wilts.), and the cost to the manor was 5½d., WCL acct.
1332, 18 Oct., present in the prior's chapel at the reading of ordinances, drawn up by the chapter following discussions about the debts of two of the obedientiary offices, which prescribed new financial arrangements to alleviate the crisis, *Winch. Cart.*, no 180; see Alexander de Heriard.

I Adam de WYNTON
occ. 1266/7

1266/7, visited Chilbolton with William de Hoo, q.v., and they dined on three fowl, WCL pipe roll acct.

II Adam de WYNTON [Wyntonia
occ. 1319 occ. 1323/4

1319, 24 Nov./26 Dec., el. bp, *Reg. Sandale*, 285 (appndx) and *CPR (1317–1321)*, 402, 406, but Rigaud de Asserio was provided, *Fasti*, iv, 45. According to Baigent, the monks had 'postulated [Adam] through their prior, on the 30th of November, 1319, to the Bishoprick', *Reg. Asserio*, xxvii, but he provides no ref.
1322, 7th July, had gone to the papal court at Avignon, to appeal for another promotion; by this date his shortage of funds aroused the sympathy of the successful bp, then at Avignon, to write to the prior and chapter to give him financial assistance, *Winch. Cart.*, no 244 and *Reg. Asserio*, 579.
1322, 19 Aug., the reply of the prior and chapter stated that they had already sent £40 but were too hard pressed to send more for the present; they asked the bp to use his influence on Adam's behalf, *Winch. Cart.*, no 245 and *Reg. Asserio*, 580.

1322, 10 Sept., obtained papal reservation of any office within the Benedictine order in the province of Canterbury which became vacant, his promotion having been supported by both the French and English kings; he accepted the priorate of Lewes but within c. four years was removed; see *Reg. Asserio*, xxvii-xxviii.
1323/4, with Richard de Wollop, q.v., visited Whitchurch for *liberatio denariorum*, Worcester Cathedral Muniment, C.523.

Note: this last entry above (1323/4) may possibly ref. to a third Adam de Wynton, but no one by this name appears in the 1325 list of monks.

Described by John de Trokelowe as a 'virum quidem eminentis litteratura, multarumque virtutum insigniis redimitum' who was unanimously el. bp, *Chron. St Alban's*, 105.

Alexander de WYNTON [Winton, Wyntonia
occ. 1279/80 occ. 1325

1279/80, described as *custos* of the [?vacant] priory and visited Stockton (Wilts.) where he ate capon, WCL pipe roll acct. He also visited Michelmersh, *ib*.
1308/9, 1310/11, visited Chilbolton, and in 1308/9 dined on capon, WCL accts.
1317/18, visited Michelmersh, WCL acct.
1325, 9 Oct., 16th in order of seniority, *Reg. Pontissara*, 556.

Note: see also Alexander II, and Alexander de Wyncestre.

Bartholomew de WYNTON
occ. 1310/11

1310/11, visited Chilbolton, WCL acct.

Note: there are two Bartholomews who visited Chilbolton on this acct, both accompanied by Walter de Selebourne, q.v.; one is Pershore, q.v., and the other de Wynton; are they one and the same? See also Bartholomew.

John de WYNTON'
see Devenish

Peter de WYNTON [Winton
occ. 1279/80 occ. 1295

1279/80, pd visits to Chilbolton, Crondall, Houghton, Hurstbourne and Whitchurch manor and borough, WCL pipe roll accts.
1280, 25 Sept., with Hugh de Hida and Valentine [de Wherewell], q.v., recd licence from the king, at Pickering, to el. another bp on the grounds that the pope had quashed their previous el., *CPR (1272–1281)*, 398.
1281, [Jan.], was sent to Reading to a meeting of Benedictine abbots, and the receiver pd his expenses of 8s. 6d., Watkin, 'Rec. Acct', 95.
1281/2, visited Chilbolton and Hurstbourne, the former for *liberatio denariorum*, WCL pipe roll accts.
1282/3, stopped at Whitchurch on his return journey from Northampton, WCL pipe roll acct.
1295, 4 Nov., with the steward held the court at Michelmersh, WCL (composite) court roll.

Richard de WYNTON [Wyntonia
occ. 1316/17 occ. 1345

1345, 28 July, precentor, *Reg. Common Seal*, no 5.
1316/17, recd 12d. from the almoner *ad placitum suum*, Kitchin, *SS* no 24, p. 404.
1345, 28 July, named as one of nine *compromissorii* in the el. of a bp, *Reg. Common Seal*, no 5.

YCHENESBOURNE
see Ichelbourne, Tychebourne

Philip YONG [Yonge, Yoong
occ. 1476 occ. 1501/2

1476, 21 Dec., ord acol., Winchester cathedral, Reg. Waynflete, ii, fo 176v.
1477, 1 Mar., ord subdcn, Winchester cathedral, *ib.*, ii, fo 177.
1478, 19 Sept., ord dcn, Winchester cathedral, *ib.*, ii, fo 181v.
1481, 22 Dec., ord pr., Winchester cathedral, *ib.*, ii, fo 187v.
1498, 23 Apr., infirmarer, Reg. Langton, fo 73v.
1498/1502, almoner, WCL Hinton Ampner accts.
1486, 7 Dec., 19th in order at the el. of a bp, *Reg. Common Seal*, no 434.
1492, 29 Oct., 13th to be examined at the *sed. vac.* visitation; he complained of the method of distribution of offices among the monks and especially of plurality of office holding, and of the arrangement and the state of disrepair of the refectory seats, *Reg. abp Morton*, ii, no 127.
1498, 23 Apr., 7th in order at the el. of a prior, Reg. Langton, fo 73v.
1498/1502, pd regular visits to Hinton Ampner, WCL accts.
1501, 27 Feb., 6th to be examined at the visitation (*sed. vac.* both Canterbury and Winchester) by the commissary of the prior of Christ Church, Canterbury; he said that none of the brethren was a *proprietarius* and that the prior 'corrected' faults as soon as they came to his attention and always in accordance with Benedictine statutes and customs; however, he blamed the subprior [William Manwode, q.v.] for his failure to provide adequate food and medicine for the sick, Canterbury Reg. R, fo 114v.

WORCESTER CATHEDRAL PRIORY

INTRODUCTION

The see of Worcester has the unique distinction of being the only one to survive the Conquest without losing its diocesan. Wulstan, who had been prior of St Mary's cathedral priory before his election as bishop in 1062, remained in his episcopal office for more than thirty years and guided both his monastic chapter and his clergy and people through the difficult years of transition to Norman rule. Worcester was one of the tenth-century monastic foundations that came under the influence of the reforms led by archbishop Dunstan and implemented there by his episcopal colleague Oswald; and it was the latter who began to build a new cathedral. Bishop Wulstan also continued the building programme in his day, the results of which in the crypt, with its forest of slender columns, remain to inspire the beholder a millennium later.[1]

We are fortunate in the survival of a list of some sixty Worcester monks, dated c. 1104 and preserved in the Durham Liber Vitae because the two monasteries were linked together in confraternity.[2] One of the interesting features of this unusually early, and presumably complete, record is the blend of Anglo-Saxon English and Norman French names, about thirty including Wulstan belonging to the former group, eight, including prior Thomas [I], q.v., clearly to the latter, and over twenty names with scriptural, patristic, and classical connotations that could pertain to either group.[3] Numbers must have fallen by or before 1312 when the prior and convent lamented that their income was no longer sufficient to support fifty monks and provide hospitality for guests and pilgrims.[4] The accuracy of this statement is verified only five years later when, in the earliest record of the proceedings of the election of a prior, forty-seven were named.[5] In the wake of the Black Death the chamberlain accounted for only thirty-four monks in his annual contribution to pittances, and numbers were still below forty in 1381/2; however, by the end of the century the total had risen to its earlier height of just under fifty.[6] Despite the loss of eleven monks in what must have been an epidemic, probably a recurrence of the plague, in 1419/20, the community had again recovered and increased in size to forty-five by the mid-1440s.[7] This seems to have remained a fairly stable optimum for almost a century since forty-one monks subscribed to the Act of Supremacy in 1534.[8]

Although Worcester was not ranked among the major episcopal sees, royal influence seems to have been dominant before 1300 as most of the incumbents were royal clerks. Only two priors, Randulph de Evesham and Silvester, also de Evesham, q.v.,

[1] See R. Gem, 'Bishop Wulfstan and the Romanesque Cathedral Church of Worcester', in *Medieval Art and Architecture at Worcester*, the British Archaeological Association Conference Transactions for the year 1975, 15–37.

[2] See the introduction to *Durham Liber Vitae* and the article (in two parts) by Atkins, 'Church of Worcs', ii, 218–220.

[3] See Mason, *Wulfstan*, 222.

[4] Liber Albus, fo 54^v; this may have been intended to justify a petition for an appropriation.

[5] *Ib.*, fos 83–84; the prior elected was Wulstan de Bransford, q.v.

[6] WCM C.11, C.14, C.23.

[7] WCM C.32, C.333.

[8] *DK 7th Report*, Appendix 2, 305.

were elected by the monks in the thirteenth century, but the former found his promotion quashed, while the latter, though unopposed, died in 1218 after only two years on the episcopal throne. This suggests that, even when the formalities of an election were observed, the results were usually predetermined.[9] In the fourteenth and fifteenth centuries the Worcester monks made a number of valiant attempts to assert their independence by electing members of their own community: John de St Germans, q.v., unsuccessfully in 1302, prior Wulstan de Bransford, q.v., also unsuccessfully in 1327, but successfully twelve years later; priors John de Evesham (in 1349), Walter de Legh (in 1373), and John Grene (in 1395), q.v., were all three elected, again without success because of royal and papal pressure. The titular abbot of Worcester cathedral priory was therefore, except on rare occasions, an outsider and usually a secular rather than a monastic bishop.[10]

As in other cathedral priories, the early priors after the Conquest were probably appointed by the bishop rather than elected by the chapter; but a composition was reached in 1224 after several periods of dissension between the two parties.[11] The settlement continued in force until the dissolution and was unique in its making provision for the initiative of each of the participants in turn: the chapter began the process by nominating seven candidates whom they agreed to be suitable for the office of prior; the bishop then examined them and selected one. William de Bedeforde, q.v., in 1224, was probably the first monk to be elected in this way, and Richard de Feckenham, q.v., in 1274, and his successors certainly were; but evidence is lacking for the four priors occurring in between.[12]

At Worcester appointments to all obedientiary offices were at the disposal of the prior and his monk advisers, with the exception of those of the sacrist and of one of the two tomb keepers [*tumbarii*], or *custodes* of the shrines of Saints Oswald and Wulstan.[13] The bishop regularly appointed the sacrist, who at times found himself seconded to act as receiver in the episcopal household in addition to his responsibilities in the cathedral church. Whether or not he was employed in the episcopal administration, his was always a divided loyalty.

Fourteen obedientiary offices at Worcester were required to present annual accounts, including that of the prior himself, whose income was substantial and derived in part from the manors allocated to him and in part from the cellarer's

[9] See *Fasti*, ii, 99–102.

[10] The exceptions are Baldwin, the Cistercian and former abbot of Forde (1180–1184) who left Worcester for Canterbury and found the Christ Church monks very tiresome (see the Canterbury Introduction p. 000), Henry de Soilli (1193/4), who had been abbot of Glastonbury, Thomas de Hemenhale (1337/8), monk of Norwich, q.v., and Tideman de Winchcombe (1395/1401), a Cistercian and bishop of Llandaff before his provision to Worcester. There was also the Franciscan William de Gainsborough and the Carmelite Thomas Peverel, both ecclesiastical careerists.

[11] See William Norman, and for the composition, *Worcs. Cart.*, nos 437, 540.

[12] That is Richard de Gundicote, Thomas III, Richard de Dumbleton, and William de Cirencester I, q.v. The last prior, whose election was a farce, will be discussed below.

[13] When Nicholas de Bradefeld, q.v., was appointed *tumbarius* by bishop Cobham in 1318 the prior and chapter raised objections to the bishop's rights in the matter; however, Richard de Haddeleye, q.v., in 1344 and Richard de Henkeseye, q.v., in 1351 were also episcopal appointments. By the time of the earliest account for this office, that of 1375/6, and from that date onwards, only one name is given on the heading of the roll. But the bishop had not relinquished his claim, because he appointed J. Thwartoner', q.v., as *tumbarius* in October 1388; the name on the account roll for 1388/9 is, however, John de Teukesbury I, q.v., who must have been the prior and chapter's appointment.

It should be noted also that Thomas IV and John de St Briavel, q.v., were two monks who served as receivers to the bishopric.

regular contributions toward some of his expenses.[14] The cellarer was in fact the bursar—equivalent to the receiver or treasurer elsewhere—although the title of bursar was used only on the earliest accounts of the late thirteenth century.[15] The *custos capelle*, or keeper of the Lady chapel, was sometimes described as *magister capelle*, hence the variations in some of the entries. There was no accounting *magister operum* as at Winchester, but there is reference from time to time to a monk bearing this designation who was responsible to the cellarer, the latter being the obedientiary who, with the sacrist, was in charge of any building work and of repairs to the fabric. The only *conversus*, or lay brother, known by name in the fourteenth-century cathedral chapters is the monk mason John, q.v., at Worcester who probably held this office during the construction of the *nova porta*, or Edgar gate, in the mid-fourteenth century.[16] It was the pittancer's task to distribute wine and spices to the monks on certain festivals throughout the year; but in the week before Christmas he was assisted by contributions from seven of the other obedientiaries when, on eight successive days in Advent, the great 'O' antiphons were sung at the office of vespers.[17] Some of the obedientiaries in question were assigned to sing the antiphon most appropriate to their office: the prior began with 'O sapientia', followed by the precentor with 'O Adonai', the kitchener with 'O radix', the cellarer with 'O clavis David', and so on.[18] The instructions for this procedure form a marginal gloss in a fourteenth-century hand on fos 10^{v}–11 of Ms F. 160, the thirteenth-century Antiphoner, which is one of the treasures of Worcester cathedral still reposing in its original home.

A chamberlain, Godricus, a sacrist, Alferius, and a precentor, Uhtred, q.v., are named in bishop Wulstan's day and a subprior, Heming, q.v., in 1104. However, for references to most of the remaining offices we are dependent for information on the earliest episcopal register, which begins in 1268, and on the obedientiary accounts beginning in the 1290s.[19] In addition to the registers, which are virtually complete, and the obedientiary rolls, which total well over five hundred, there are an impressive number of priory registers; these include the massive Liber Albus that covers the years 1301 to 1489 and the *sede vacante* register of the priors' *acta* during the voidances of the see.[20] Taken together, these records provide a wealth of biographical information about the Worcester monks. Dates of admission and profession are available because it was customary for the bishop or his deputy to examine the applicants; and his presence (to receive the profession) or his commission to the prior (to do so on his behalf) was necessary before the ceremony could be performed, usually within twelve months of admission. Since most of the ordination lists are to be found in the bishops' regis-

[14] His total receipts in 1444/5 were slightly over £145, WCM C.396.

[15] Three of these have been transcribed in Wilson, *Early Comp. Rolls*, 8–32.

[16] He is entered under John [Conversus]; John de Preston I, q.v., also held this office.

[17] That is, from 16 to 23 Dec. inclusive, before and after the Magnificat; more recently the final 'O' has been dropped with the result that the antiphons today begin on 17 Dec.

[18] The others were the sacrist who sang 'O oriens', the subcellarer, 'O Rex Gentium', the chamberlain 'O Emmanuel', and the pittancer 'O Virgo'.

[19] At Worcester there is frequent reference to the prior's chaplain, who acted as his secretary in recording his *acta*; though not, strictly speaking, an obedientiary this position has been included among the obedientiary offices. There was also a *magister communis cene* probably similar to the *magister mense* at Canterbury; his accounts for 1521/2 are printed by Wilson in *Accts Henry VIII*, 28–29.

[20] The first 162 folios of the Liber Albus (out of close to 500 folios) have been briefly calendared by Canon Wilson; see the full reference in Section C.ii of the References under *Liber Albus*. The manuscript volume has recently been expertly restitched and rebound in two handsome volumes to facilitate its preservation and use. The *sede vacante register* has been translated and edited and its full reference is given in the same Section, C.ii under *Reg. Sed. Vac.*

ters, important stages in the early years of monastic life of many of the monks are available for scrutiny. The year of death is also frequently recorded because of entries in either the receipts or expenses section of the chamberlain's accounts. The deceased monk's bedding, clothing, and riding gear were returned to him for redistribution or sale, and in the event of the latter the money obtained was described as 'alms' received; on other occasions, the chamberlain reported his payment for the brief announcing their names for circulation among Benedictine houses.

Surviving election and visitation records furnish us from time to time with the names of monks in their order of seniority, episcopal elections being entered in the *sede vacante* register and those of the prior in the Liber Albus or one of its sequels.[21] Copies of only two certificates presented to the visiting archbishops, those of 1498 and 1521, survive to provide the names of the monks on these dates. An earlier archiepiscopal visitation, the one conducted by Robert Winchelsey in 1301, had proved traumatic both for the aged and bedridden bishop Giffard and for the entire chapter. The Worcester chronicler described it as *dies tribulationis et increpationis* because the archbishop deposed six of the obedientiaries and confined several of them to the cloister for a year.[22] A few months later the prior, Simon de Wyre, q.v., resigned, ostensibly because of age and infirmity but possibly also as a result of the stress of archiepiscopal scrutiny when convent debts and laxity in discipline were laid bare.[23] One aspect of this visitation and its immediate aftermath took the form of a clash between the bishop in his role as titular abbot and the primate, who had overruled him with regard to the appointment and dismissal of the sacrist; Gilbert de Madley, Nicholas de Norton, and later, John Lawerne I, q.v., and others also found to their confusion and cost that they were pawns in the game of rival claims on their obedience.[24] Notices of episcopal visitation of the cathedral priory make a frequent appearance in the records but information about the actual proceedings is invariably incomplete. It would probably have been otherwise had there been serious or prolonged confrontation between bishop and chapter arising out of these occasions.[25]

Visitatorial rights were, however, one element in a bitter dispute between prior John de Evesham, q.v., and bishop Reginald Bryan in the 1350s when the bishop highhandedly announced his intention to visit by apostolic authority. He had already drawn out the mettle of the prior at the time of his previous visitation by challenging Evesham's acquisition of the mitre and other pontifical regalia. He had also paid no heed to the prior's advice against conferring the office of sacrist on John de Powik, q.v. There is no doubt that Evesham was one of Worcester's most distinguished priors but by no means in a class by himself.[26] Three of his close successors, John Grene,

[21] These lists are supplied in the episcopal elections of 1373, 1401, 1419, and 1433, and in the prioral elections of 1317, 1370, 1388, and 1536; the last is in Reg. A.6 (iii), fo 1.

[22] *Ann. Wigorn.*, 549. This episode is described by Rose Graham in 'Visitation', 338–344; she also discusses the monks' complaints against the bishop, whom they held in part responsible for their financial difficulties, *ib.*, 351–353.

[23] Among Worcester priors after 1300 his was the sole resignation until William More, q.v., in 1536. For his successor, John de Wyke, see Wilson's article 'John de Wyke'.

[24] Greatrex, *Monastic or Episcopal Obedience*, 6–8. Injunctions were also issued by cardinal Wolsey and archbishop Cranmer and the latter will be referred to later.

[25] See, in contrast, details of bishop Stratford's visitation of St Swithun's in the Winchester Introduction, p. 655.

[26] His achievements during a lengthy rule bear comparison with those of prior Henry Eastry, q.v., at Canterbury. See Greatrex, 'Prior Evesham', *passim*. The details of these controversies are in the Liber Albus, fos 215–218, 236–245.

John de Fordham, and Thomas Ledbury, q.v., were doctors in theology, and Fordham and Ledbury were members of the English delegation at the council of Constance. Three priors, Wulstan de Bransford, John de Evesham, and John de Fordham, q.v., are known to have acted as vicars general for absent bishops on several occasions. However, the priors of Worcester came into their own during the intervals between the departure or death of one bishop and the arrival of his successor. The prior's *sede vacante* register covers fifteen of the twenty vacancies between 1301 and 1435 all of which intervals were governed by the Boniface composition of 1268.[27] By this agreement, unique to Worcester, the prior obtained the right to exercise episcopal jurisdiction in the diocese during the interregnum and was therefore, as his title made clear, 'by authority of the court of Canterbury, official and administrator of the spiritualities in the city and diocese of Worcester'.[28] On assuming this office the prior immediately issued citations for a visitation of the several deaneries and of the religious houses, and, unless he intended to conduct the visitations in person, he usually appointed one or two of the monks as his official visitors. The cathedral chapter was itself subject to this procedure although it is difficult to believe that it was more than a formality. John de Malverne [II], q.v., as prior, twice performed this function in person, and he went on to visit the clergy and people of the city and deanery of Worcester by summoning them to appear before him in the cathedral. In 1401 John de Dudley I and Thomas de Broghton, q.v., were two of the prior's commissaries in other parts of the diocese, and in 1407 the prior employed John de Fordham and John de Hatfeld, q.v., for a similar purpose.

The priory of Little Malvern was founded sometime before 1150; at this date it was stated to be a cell of the cathedral priory.[29] Bishop Giffard appointed its priors, two of whom were former monks of Worcester;[30] Richard de Wenlok, q.v., was also licensed by the bishop in 1379 to become prior there, but other priors, though episcopal appointments, had no connection with Worcester. Little Malvern's affiliation with and subjection to the cathedral priory have therefore been exaggerated.

The consistently prominent role played by the Worcester monks in the Black Monk Chapter suggests that for more than two centuries they were active in upholding the community fellowship among English Benedictines and in promoting common interests and common goals. Among the latter probably the most important was the aim to provide for monastic studies at the university, a project to which the Worcester chapter was committed from the beginning; moreover, they continued to support it by sending a regular succession of their monks to Oxford, usually in twos or threes, until the dissolution.[31] As early as 1291/2 there were two monk students, John de Arundel and William de Grymeley, q.v., pursuing their studies there and receiving pensions from the cellarer. Between then and 1531/2 fifty-one monks known by name studied theology at Oxford, some for only a year or two, others for periods of ten to

[27] The record of Worcester's succession of bishops from St Wulstan to Latimer shows it to have had one of the most frequent episcopal 'turnovers' through death or translation in all of England and Wales.

[28] *Reg. Sed. Vac.*, 408. See also Churchill, *Cant. Admin.*, i, 184–187.

[29] *Worcs. Cart.*, nos 61a, 77. Apart from the inaccurate foundation date and imputed close ties to Worcester, there is an adequate summary of the priory's subsequent history in *VCH Worcestershire*, ii, 143–147.

[30] See William de Bradewas II, who was probably the monk named, and John de Dumbelton.

[31] Prior Aubyn, q.v., attended in person the meetings of the Chapter in 1290 and 1291 in which the house of studies at Oxford was high on the agenda, Pantin, *BMC*, i, 129–131.

fifteen years and more, undoubtedly on a part-time basis.[32] Twenty of these obtained degrees and three of them were appointed to the position of *prior studentium*.[33] The monk students who were selected for university study had already received several years of instruction with their brother novices in the cloister during which time they would have been introduced to the library and taught how to make use of its contents.[34] Worcester is fortunate in the survival of some three hundred and seventy volumes, of which about two hundred and fifty remain *in situ* in the cathedral. The total would have been over four hundred before the dissolution; and prior William More, q.v., purchased a further seventy-nine, noting the titles in his Journal.[35] Evidence for the use of the library by those monks whose studies did not extend beyond the cloister is provided by notes and 'ownership' inscriptions in some of the volumes; over thirty names have been found to date.[36]

The monastic presence and influence extended beyond the cathedral precincts when the monks encountered the secular clergy and the laity in their spiritual and pastoral assignments as preachers, teachers, and confessors. There is more evidence for these responsibilities being undertaken by monks at Worcester than elsewhere.[37] In 1289/90 the prior and convent received a papal licence to preach in public in Worcester and in the churches in their patronage; and there is reference in 1305 to public lectures in theology given by Worcester monks.[38] Monk scholars at Oxford were often recalled to preach in Worcester on the greater festivals, and they sometimes preached in the parishes in their care, possibly while making supervisory rounds of the manors.[39] Public lectures in theology were given in the chapter house by John de Preston II and John Lawerne I, q.v., in the mid fourteenth and mid-fifteenth centuries respectively and by Roger Neckham, q.v., in the carnary chapel in the 1520s and 1530s.[40] From time to time episcopal licences were issued to many of the monks to act as penitentiaries or confessors in the city and diocese, sometimes three being appointed simultaneously.[41]

Relations with the citizens of Worcester were strained at times, especially during the fourteenth century when a number of clashes occurred, several of these caused by breaches of sanctuary. In the most serious affray, in 1348, the city bailiffs, followed by

[32] See John de Fordham, who may have spent time at Oxford over a period of twenty years.

[33] All the degrees were in theology, evenly divided between bachelors and doctors; unlike monks of Ely and Canterbury, no Worcester monk read canon law. The three *priores studentium* were John de Fordham, Thomas Ledbury, and Humphrey Webley, q.v.

[34] Some of the novices may have received their early education in the almonry school, but no evidence has come to light. Indeed, there is little information about the school apart from a few late 14th- and late 15th-c. references on the almoner's accounts, WCM C.184, C.209, C.210, and in the Liber Albus, fo 384^{v} (in 1396).

[35] See Sharpe, *Eng. Benedictine Libraries*, iv, B114; the books that John Lawerne I, q.v., took to Oxford are listed in *ib.*, iv, B113.

[36] These volumes are listed in the entries in the final section following 'Name in . . .'. The word 'ownership', though in common use, is misleading in a monastic context since private property was forbidden by the Rule; 'user' or 'borrower' would be preferable.

[37] See Greatrex, 'Benedictine Monk Scholars', which discusses the evidence for the teaching and preaching activities of Worcester monks.

[38] *CPL*, i (1198–1304), 510, Bloom, *Liber Ecclesiae*, 17.

[39] See e.g. John Lawerne I, Isaac Ledbury, John Wodeward, Oxford students, and also Richard de Bromwych, who preached at King's Norton in 1335.

[40] The monastic library had at least fifteen volumes of sermon collections as well as a number of biblical commentaries and handbooks for the use of preachers.

[41] In July 1337 Henry Fouke, Simon Crompe, and Nicholas de Stanlake were commissioned for the archdeaconry of Worcester, Reg. Hemenhale, 12.

a large mob, broke into the precincts to claim the body of a townsman who had been killed in the churchyard and buried there. Prior John de Evesham, q.v., and the monks were pursued with bows and arrows, and the monastery narrowly escaped burning, according to the contemporary account related in the prior's successful plea before the justices.[42] However, mutual respect and good will surely lie behind the fact that the sons of at least fifteen Worcester city families are known to have entered the priory, three of whom went on to become priors.[43] To judge by the toponymics most of the other monks hailed from towns and villages in the surrounding countryside, and some from manors and parishes belonging to the priory; there are three from the manor and parish of Bromsgrove, for example, four from Cropthorne, and five from Broadwas.[44] In the case of one monk, who came from further afield in the county of Somerset, an exceptional amount of detail about his family background and early education has been preserved in the Liber Albus; this is Robert de Weston, q.v., whose father was a tenant on a Glastonbury abbey estate.

Royal visits to and demands upon the Worcester chapter were both frequent and costly. The tomb of king John and the shrine of the two saintly bishops, Oswald and Wulstan, were undoubtedly the main attraction for John's descendants, some of whom, like Edward I, had a special affection for St Wulstan.[45] Henry III spent Christmas at Worcester in 1232, and Edward I held parliament in the city in 1282 on his way to subjugate the Welsh.[46] Edward I returned on several other occasions bearing gifts for Wulstan's shrine but, at the same time, imposing a heavy burden upon his monastic hosts who had to accommodate the royal visitor and his entourage. Some of the expenses involved are itemized on obedientiary accounts, chiefly those of the cellarer; but the *tumbarius* felt obliged to explain his extra expenditure on wax for the shrine in 1397/8 as due to the king's presence.[47] There were also frequent demands made on the priory to supply arms and equipment for the king's Welsh and Scottish campaigns to which the monastic response was on occasion a firm negative, as in c. 1322 when Robert de Morton, q.v., conveyed the prior's excuses to the king.

The royal demand for corrodies and pensions for retainers and servants was a recurring source of aggravation which the monks could ill afford either to accept or to reject. There were over fifty of these demands sent during the reign of Edward II on behalf of his clerks, and a similar number of letters were exchanged with regard to the lady-in-waiting, Alice Conan.[48] Corrodies initiated by the prior and convent to provide for their own officials and employees, or granted to others, who paid a lump sum in advance in order to be assured of board and sometimes lodging in retirement, could prove a financial burden in times of stress; the cash received from the last group brought only temporary respite.[49] At Worcester the word 'corrody' was also applied to the daily food allowance, or its cash equivalent, of a deceased monk that was set aside for distribution to the poor during a period of up to a year after his death.

[42] A summary of this and other confrontations is in *VCH Worcestershire*, ii, 106.

[43] These were Philip Aubyn, Simon de Wyre, and Simon Crompe, q.v.

[44] This last is entered as Bradewas.

[45] *Ann. Wigorn.*, 488.

[46] *Ib.*, 484.

[47] WCM C.462.

[48] Many of the letters occur in the Liber Albus *passim*, and extracts of those referring to Alice Conan are in J. M. Wilson and E. C. Jones, eds, *Corrodies at Worcester in the Fourteenth Century*, Worcestershire Historical Society, 1917.

[49] For a detailed examination of the different kinds of corrodies granted by monks see B. Harvey, *Living and Dying in England, the Monastic Experience* (Oxford, 1993), 179–209.

Sometimes the sum, usually reckoned at 9d. or 12d. per week, was allocated to other purposes when money was tight. It was the almoner who recorded the receipt of the money for a named monk, and who occasionally noted that the money came from the cellarer. In 1355/6 he described the corrody of Robert de Clifton II, q.v., as *vendito hoc anno* for twenty-three weeks; but for the corrodies of John de Gloucestre III and John de Kyderminstre I, q.v., in 1380/1 he reported that he received nothing because the money, or perhaps its equivalent in food and clothing, was distributed among the poor for the good of the deceaseds' souls.[50]

In the 1530s the effects of prior More's lax and incompetent rule were exposed to public view. In 1534, in the same week that the forty-one monks subscribed to the Act of Supremacy, they underwent a visitation, *sede plena*, by archbishop Cranmer in person. The injunctions, which were issued the following February, strongly rebuked the prior's failure to treat his brethren with gentleness and kindness, and his lack of concern for the sick members of the community. His slack approach to administration was also singled out for censure, and reform measures were prescribed. In addition, all the monks were ordered to refrain from castigating Thomas Blockeley, q.v., for past misdeeds and from inhibiting Thomas Sudbury, q.v., in his office of cellarer.[51] Cranmer must also have ordered the monks to bypass the prior and send reports about any internal problems directly to him, or to Thomas Cromwell; that they followed his instruction is clear from the letters subsequently written by William Fordham, Roger Neckham, John Musard, q.v., and others. These reveal a divided community in which the individual self-interest that was replacing fraternal solidarity was now being exploited by the newly supreme royal authority; an inner reformation of mind and heart had become impossible.

It was not surprising that the ineffectual prior More was deprived, but the 'election' of his successor in March 1536 made no pretence of legitimacy: the 'elect', Henry Holbech, q.v., had been chosen beforehand; the king's emissary usurped the place of the subprior in presiding over the proceedings; of the four *compromissorii* only two were monks.[52] This same year there was an exodus of some fifteen monks in addition to the two who left prior to the 'election', and several more were lost to sight soon after.[53] In his first visitation in 1537 bishop Latimer, himself no friend of monks, encountered an already depleted chapter whose ignorance and negligence he condemned as 'intollerable'.[54] Only seventeen or eighteen remained to sign the deed of surrender in January 1540; the soul of Worcester cathedral priory had departed before the body was removed.[55]

[50] The first example seems to suggest that, as at Westminster, corrodies were sometimes sold by the cellarer to an outsider, Harvey, *op. cit.*, 191; the corrody of Marmaduke de Pirie, q.v., however, was spent *in expenses domus*. Worcester is the only cathedral priory in the southern province where I have found evidence for this practice. I am grateful to Miss Harvey for her advice concerning these Worcester corrodies.

[51] The injunctions are transcribed in Wilson, 'Visitations', 364–367 from Reg. A.12, fos 144–145 and A.6 (ii), fos 187–188. The royal commissioner, Dr Legh, also visited in July 1535.

[52] Reg. A.6 (iii), fos 1–2; the two compliant monks were John Lawerne II and Roger Neckham, q.v., both of whom became prebendaries in the new foundation.

[53] It is to be hoped that Dr Peter Cunich's research will provide information on the subsequent careers of these and other ex-religious when his Biographical Register (covering the dates c. 1530–1603) has been completed.

[54] Noake, *Worcs. Cathedral*, 227, from Reg. Latimer, fo 17v.

[55] The surrender deed is missing but the names are provided by the pension lists in *L and P Henry VIII*, xv, nos 81, 868, 869.

WORCESTER REFERENCES WITH ABBREVIATIONS

Note: if the particular reference sought does not appear below, turn to the General Bibliography on p. xv–xix, or the Canterbury section, p. 58–65.

A. Manuscript Sources

i Episcopal Registers

(*a*) Worcester Record Office (HWRO)

Note: these have been paginated in pencil.

Reg. [Godfrey] Giffard (1268–1302)	b.716.093–BA.2648/1 (i)
Reg. [William de] Gainsborough (1303–1307)	b.716.093–BA.2648/1 (ii)
Reg. [Walter] Reynolds (1308–1313)	b.716.093–BA.2648/1 (iii)
Reg. [Walter de] Maidstone (1313–1317)	b.716.093–BA.2648/1 (iv)
Reg. [Thomas de] Cobham (1317–1327)	b.716.093–BA.2648/2 (i)
Reg. [Adam de] Orleton (1327–1333)	b.716.093–BA.2648/2 (ii)
Reg. [Simon de] Montacute (1334–1337)	b.716.093–BA.2648/2 (iii)
Reg. [Thomas de] Hemenhale (1337–1338)	b.716.093–BA.2648/2 (iv)
Reg. [Wulstan de] Bransford (1339–1349)	b.716.093–BA.2648/3 (i)
Reg. [John] Thoresby (1350–1352)	b.716.093–BA.2648/3 (ii)
Reg. [Reginald] Bryan (1353–1361)	b.716.093–BA.2648/3, iii (vol i) and iv (vol ii)
Reg. [John] Barnet (1362–1363)	b.716.093–BA.2648/4 (i)
Reg. [William] Wittlesey (1364–1368)	b.716.093–BA.2648/4 (ii)
Reg. [William] Lynn (1369–1373)	b.716.093–BA.2648/4 (iii)
Reg. [Henry] Wakefield (1375–1395)	b.716.093–BA.2648/4 (iv)
Reg. [Tideman de] Winchcombe (1395–1401)	b.716.093–BA.2648/4 (v)
Reg. [Richard] Clifford (1401–1407)	b.716.093–BA.2648/5 (i)
Reg. [Thomas] Peverel (1407–1419)	b.716.093–BA.2648/5 (ii)
Reg. [Philip] Morgan (1419–1426)	b.716.093–BA.2648/5 (iii)
Reg. [Thomas] Polton (1426–1433)	b.716.093–BA.2648/5 (iv)
Reg. [Thomas] Bourgchier (1435–1443)	b.716.093–BA.2648/6 (i)
Reg. [John] Carpenter (1444–1476)	b.716.093–BA.2648/6, ii (vol i) and iii (vol ii)
Reg. [John] Alcock (1476–1486)	b.716.093–BA.2648/7 (i)
Reg. [Robert] Morton (1487–1497)	b.716.093–BA.2648/7 (ii), 1–162; bound with Ghinucci below
Reg. G.[iovanni] de Gigli (1497–1498)	b.716.093–BA.2648/7 (iii)
Reg. S.[ilvestro] de Gigli (1499–1521)	b.716.093–BA.2648/8 (i)
Reg. [Giulio de] Medici (1521–1522)	b.716.093–BA.2648/9 (i), 22–25
Reg. [Geronimo] Ghinucci (1522–1535)	b.716.093–BA.2648/7 (ii), ordinations, 163–174 b.716.093–BA.2648/8 (ii), 28–90 b.716.093–BA.2648/9 (i), 26–159, 182–186
Reg. [Hugh] Latimer (1535–1539)	b.716.093–BA.2648/9 (ii)
Reg. [John] Bell (1539–1543)	b.716.093–BA.2648/9 (iii)

(*b*) Hereford Record Office (HWRO)

Reg. [Richard de] Swinfield (1283–1317)	AL 19/2
Reg. [Adam de] Orleton (1317–1327)	AL 19/3
Reg. [John de] Trillek (1344–1360)	AL 19/5
Reg. Lewis [de] Charlton (1361–1369)	AL 19/6
Reg. [John] Gilbert (1375–1389)	AL 19/6
Reg. [John] Trefnant (1389–1404)	AL 19/7
Reg. [Thomas] Spofford (1422–1448)	AL 19/9

Reg. [John] Stanbury (1453–1474)	AL 19/11
Reg. [Thomas] Milling (1474–1492)	AL 19/11
Reg. [Charles] Booth (1516–1535)	AL 19/13

(*c*) Lincoln Archives Office (LAO)

Reg. William Smith (1494–1514)	Episcopal Register XXIII

ii Priory Registers, and Cartularies, and Customaries

(*a*) Worcester Cathedral Muniments (WCM)

Reg. Sed. Vac. (A.1)	Registrum sede vacante, 1301–1435; see also Section C.ii below.
Reg. A.2	Registrum prioratus, 14th c., mainly rentals and customaries and some charters; see also Section C.ii below.
Liber Pensionum (A.3)	Register of spiritualities, 15th c.; see also Section C. ii below.
Worcs. Cart. (A.4)	General cartulary, 13th c.; see also Section C.ii below.
Liber Albus (A.5)	Priory register, 1301–1454, 2 vols; see also Section C.ii below.
Reg. A.6 (i)	Priory register, 1458–1498
Reg. A.6 (ii)	Priory register, 1499–1534
Reg. A.6 (iii)	Priory register, 1535–1540
Reg. A.8	Cartulary, 16th c.; see Reg. A.10 below.
Reg. Almoner (A.9)	Cartulary of the almoner, 14th c.; see also Section C.ii below.
Reg. A.10	Cartulary, 16th c.; with Reg. A.8 above, possibly fragments of a larger whole.
Jnl More (A.11)	Journal of prior William More, q.v.; see also Section C.ii below.
Reg. A.12	Miscellaneous register, known as the 'Book marked +'.
Reg. A.17	Obedientiary accounts, 1520/5; see Sections B.i (*a*) and D below (under Wilson, *Accts Henry VIII*). Note: this ms has been paginated.
Reg. A.22	Cartulary, 15th c., with inventories of St. Oswald's shrine; see under Blake in Section D below.

(*b*) London, Public Record Office (PRO)

Liber Ecclesiae Wigorniensis	Letter-book, 13th/14th cs; see also Bloom, *Liber Ecclesiae* in Section C.ii below (E315/63).

B. Other Manuscript Sources

i Obedientiary Accounts

(*a*) Worcester Cathedral Muniments (WCM)

Almoner	1341/2 to 1506/7	C.170–C.212
Cellarer/Bursar	[1291/2] to 1506/7	C.51–C.106; also ten others between C.476 and C.846
Chamberlain	[1312/13] to 1503/4	C.8–C.50; also C.497
Custos/Magister Capelle	1356/7 to 1503/4	C.248–C.291; also C.838, 839
Hostiller	[1286/7 or 1320/1] to 1507/8	C.213–C.240; also C.478, C.494, C.499
Infirmarer	1378/9 to 1412	C.241–C.247; C.328
Kitchener	1326/7 to 1503/4	C.107–C.169; C.489
Magister Communis Cene	1520/1 to 1523/4	Reg. A.17, 66, 134, 212, 277
Pittancer	1318/19 to 1501/2	C.292–C.350; C.484
Precentor	1346/7 to 1510/11	C.351–C.394; C.495a
Prior	1341/2 to 1533/4	C.395–C.415
Refectorer	1393/4 to 1501/2	C.416–C.424
Sacrist	1423/4 to 1522/3	C.425–C.430; C.498

Subcellarer	1326 to 1493/4	C.431–C.452
Tumbarius	1375/6 to 1475/6	C.453–C.472

Note: see also Reg. A.17 in Section A.ii (*a*) above, and under Hamilton and Wilson in Section D below for accounts in print.

(*b*) Windsor Castle (Windsor, St George's Chapel)

Cellarer	[c.1348/9]	XI.E.37
Subcellarer	1333/4	XI.E.36 (duplicate)

ii Manorial Accounts in Worcester Cathedral Muniments (WCM)

These are included in the C. class of muniments beginning with C.500 where they are grouped according to place; they are identified in the text by both number and name of manor.

iii Manorial Court Rolls in Worcester Cathedral Muniments (WCM)

These have been assigned to the E. class of muniments, and are identified in the text by both number and name of manor.

iv Loose Deeds and Charters in Worcester Cathedral Muniments (WCM)

About two thousand of these have been listed to date in the B. class of muniments.

v Other Manuscript Sources

Oxford, Bod. Ms 692 Notebook of John Lawerne [I], q.v.

Note: there are also a number of manuscripts in Worcester cathedral library written by Worcester monks; these are identified in the relevant entries.

vi Unpublished Theses

	S. L. Forte 'A study of some Oxford Schoolmen of the Middle of the Fourteenth Century with special Reference to Worcester Cathedral Ms F.65', Oxford, B.Litt., 1947.
McIntyre, 'Early 12th c. Worcester Cathedral Priory'	E. McIntyre, 'Early Twelfth Century Worcester Cathedral Priory with special Reference to the Mss Written there', Oxford, D.Phil., 1978.

C. Printed Sources

i Episcopal Registers (in chronological order)

(*a*) Worcester

Note: in most cases the printed texts make use of the earlier foliation and not the later pagination.

Reg. Giffard	J. W. Willis Bund, ed., *Episcopal Registers, Diocese of Worcester: Register of Bishop Godfrey Giffard, September 23rd 1268 to August 15th 1301*, Worcestershire Historical Society, 2 vols, 1902; continuous pagination.
Reg. Gainsborough	J. W. Willis Bund, ed., *The Register of William de Geynesburgh, Bishop of Worcester, 1302–1307*, Worcestershire Historical Society, 1907.
Reg. Reynolds	R. A. Wilson, ed., *The Register of Walter Reynolds, Bishop of Worcester, 1308–1313*, Worcestershire Historical Society, 1927.
Reg. Cobham	E. H. Pearce, ed., *The Register of Thomas de Cobham, Bishop of Worcester, 1317–1327* Worcestershire Historical Society, 1930.
Reg. Orleton	R. Haines, ed., *Calendar of the Register of Adam de Orleton, Bishop of Worcester, 1327–1333*, Worcestershire Historical Society, new series, and Historical Manuscripts Commission Joint Publication, 1980.

Reg. Bransford R. Haines, ed., *A Calendar of the Register of Wolstan de Bransford, Bishop of Worcester, 1339–49*, Worcestershire Historical Society, new series, and Historical Manuscripts Commission Joint Publication, 1966.

Reg. Wakefield W. Marett, ed., *A Calendar of the Register of Henry Wakefield, Bishop of Worcester, 1375–95*, Worcestershire Historical Society, new series, 1972.

Reg. Clifford W. E. L. Smith, *The Register of Richard Clifford, Bishop of Worcester, 1401–1407: a Calendar*, Pontifical Institute of Mediaeval Studies, Toronto (Subsidia Mediaevalia), 1976.

(*b*) Hereford

Reg. Swinfield W. Capes, ed., *Registrum Ricardi de Swinfield, episcopi Herefordensis, A.D. MCCLXXXIII–MCCCXVII*, Canterbury and York Society 6 (and Cantiplupe Society), 1908.

Reg. Orleton A. T. Bannister, ed., *Registrum Ade de Orleton, episcopi Herefordensis, A.D. MCCCXVII–MCCCXXVII*, Canterbury and York Society, 5, 1908 (and Cantilupe Society, 1907).

Reg. Trillek J. H. Parry, ed., *Registrum Johannis de Trillek, episcopi Herefordensis, A.D. MCCCXLIV–MCCCLXI*, Canterbury and York Society 8, 1912 (and Cantilupe Society, 1910).

Reg. Lewis Charlton J. H. Parry, ed., *Registrum Ludowici de Charltone, episcopi Herefordensis, A.D. MCCCLXI–MCCCLXX*, Canterbury and York Society, 14, 1914 (and Cantilupe Society, 1913).

Reg. Gilbert J. H. Parry, ed., *Registrum Johannis Gilbert, episcopi Herefordensis, A.D. MCCCLXXV–MCCCLXXXIX*, Canterbury and York Society, 18, 1915 (and Cantilupe Society, 1913).

Reg. Trefnant W. W. Capes, ed., *Registrum Johannis Trefnant, episcopi Herefordensis, A.D. MCCCLXXXIX–MCCCCIV*, Canterbury and York Society, 20, 1916 (and Cantilupe Society, 1914).

Reg. Spofford A. T. Bannister, ed., *Registrum Thome Spofford, episcopi Herefordensis, A.D. MCCCCXXII–MCCCCXLVIII*, Canterbury and York Society, 23, 1919 (and Cantilupe Society, 1917).

Reg. Stanbury A. T. Bannister and J. H. Parry, eds, *Registrum Johannis Stanbury, episcopi Herefordensis, A.D. MCCCCLIII–MCCCCLXXIV*, Canterbury and York Society, 25, 1919 (and Cantilupe Society, 1918). This is one of three registers in one volume in the Canterbury and York Society, but the Cantilupe Society registers are separate volumes.

Reg. Milling A. T. Bannister, ed., *Registrum Thome Myllyng, episcopi Herefordensis, A.D. MCCCCLXXIV–MCCCCXCII*, Canterbury and York Society, 26 (and Cantilupe Society), 1920.

Reg. Booth A. T. Bannister, ed., *Registrum Caroli Bothe, episcopi Herefordensis, A.D. MDXVI–MDXXXV*, Canterbury and York Society, 28 (and Cantilupe Society), 1921.

ii Priory Registers and Cartularies

Bloom, *Liber Ecclesiae* J. Bloom, *Liber Ecclesiae Wigorniensis: a Letter Book of the Priors of Worcester*, Worcestershire Historical Society, 1912; see Section A.ii (*b*) above.

Bloom, *Original Charters* J. Bloom, ed., *Original Charters relating to the City of Worcester in Possession of the Dean and Chapter*, Worcestershire Historical Society, 1909.

Heming, Chart. T. Hearne, ed., *Hemingi Chartularium Ecclesiae Wigorniensis*, 2 vols, Oxford, 1723.

Jnl. More E. Fagan, ed., *Journal of Prior William More*, Worcestershire Historical Society, 1914; see Section A.ii (*a*) above.

Liber Albus J. M. Wilson, ed., *The Liber Albus of the Priory of Worcester, Parts 1 and 2*,

Priors John de Wyke, 1301–1317, and Wulstan de Bransford, 1317–1339, folios 1–162, Worcestershire Historical Society, 1919; see Section A.ii (*a*) above.

Liber Pensionum — C. Price, ed., *Liber Pensionum Prioratus Wigorn*, Worcestershire Historical Society, 1925; see Section A.ii (*a*) above.

Reg. Almoner — J. Bloom, ed., *Liber Elemosinarii: the Almoner's Book of the Priory of Worcester*, Worcestershire Historical Society, 1911; see Section A.ii (*a*) above.

Reg. Prioratus — W. Hale Hale, ed., *Registrum sive Liber Irrotulatus et Consuetudinarius Prioratus beate Marie Wigorniensis*, Camden Society, old series, 91, 1865; see Section A.ii (*a*) above.

Reg. Sed. Vac. — J. Willis Bund, ed., *The Register of the Diocese of Worcester during the Vacancy of the See, usually called Registrum Sede Vacante, 1301–1435*, Worcestershire Historical Society, 1893–97; see Section A.ii (*a*) above.

Worcs. Cart. — R. Darlington, ed., *The Cartulary of Worcester Cathedral Priory*, Publications of the Pipe Roll Society, new series, 38, 1968; see Section A. ii (*a*) above.

D. Other Printed Sources and References

Ann. Tewkes.
Ann. Wigorn. — H. Luard, ed., *Annales Monastici*, Rolls Series, 5 vols, 1864–1869; vol. 1, includes Tewkesbury; vol. iv, Worcester.

Ann. Winch. — R. Darlington, ed., 'Winchcombe Annals 1049–1181', in P. Barnes and C. Slade, eds, *A Medieval Miscellany for Doris Mary Stenton*, Pipe Roll Society, 76, 1962, 111–137.

Atkins, 'Church of Worcs' — Ivor Atkins, 'The Church of Worcester from the Eighth to the Twelfth Century', *Antiquaries Journal*, 17 (1937), 371–391 (pt i) and 20 (1940), 1–38 and 203–228 (pt ii).

J. Blake, 'Two Inventories in the Library of Worcester Cathedral', *Journal of the British Archaeological Association*, new series, 38 (1932), 158–171; from Reg. A.22.

Brett, 'John of Worcester' — M. Brett, 'John of Worcester and his Contemporaries', in R. H. C. Davis and J. Wallace-Hadrill, eds, *The Writing of History in the Middle Ages, Essays presented to R. W. Southern*, Oxford, 1981, 101–126.

Cheney, *Bp Roger* — M. Cheney, *Roger, Bishop of Worcester, 1164–1179*, Oxford, 1980.

Chron. John of Worcester — J. R. H. Weaver, *The Chronicle of John of Worcester, 1118–1140*, Anecdota Oxoniensa, Oxford, 1908.

Darlington, *Vita Wulfstani* — R. Darlington, ed., *The Vita Wulfstani of William of Malmesbury, to which are added the extant Abridgement of this Work, and the Miracles and Translation of St. Wulfstan*, Camden Society, 3rd series, 1928.

Durham Liber Vitae — A. Hamilton Thompson, ed., *Liber Vitae Ecclesiae Dunelmensis. A Collotype Facsimile of the original Manuscript, with introductory Essays and Notes*, Surtees Society, 136, 1923.

Floyer, *Catalogue of Worcs. Mss* — J. K. Floyer and S. G. Hamilton, eds, *Catalogue of Manuscripts preserved in the Chapter Library of Worcester Cathedral*, Worcester Historical Society, 1906.

Graham, 'Visitation' — R. Graham, 'The Metropolitical Visitation of the Diocese of Worcester in 1301', *Transactions of the Royal Historical Society*, 4th series, ii (1919), 59–93, reprinted in R. Graham, *English Ecclesiastical Studies*, London, 1929, 330–359. My references are from the latter.

Greatrex, 'Benedictine Monk Scholars' — J. Greatrex, 'Benedictine Monk Scholars as Teachers and Preachers in the Later Middle Ages: Evidence from Worcester Cathedral Priory', *Monastic Studies*, ii (1991), 213–225.

Greatrex, *Monastic or Episcopal Obedience* — J. Greatrex, *Monastic or Episcopal Obedience, the Problem of the Sacrists of Worcester*, Worcestershire Historical Society, Occasional Publications, 3 (1980).

Greatrex, 'Prior Evesham' — J. Greatrex, 'Prior John de Evesham of Worcester: One of St Benedict's Worthy Stewards?', in V. King and A. Horton, eds, *From Buckfast to Borneo, Essays presented to Father Robert Nicholl on the 85th anniversary of his birth, 27 March 1995*, Centre for South-East Asian Studies, University of Hull, 1995, 64–76.

Haines, *Administration of Worcs.* — R. Haines, *The Administration of the Diocese of Worcester in the First Half of the Fourteenth Century*, London, 1965.

Hamilton, *Comp. Rolls* — S. G. Hamilton, ed., *Compotus Rolls of the Priory of Worcester of the 14th and 15th Centuries*, Worcestershire Historical Society, 1910.

Leach, *Education in Worcs.* — A. Leach, ed., *Documents Illustrating early Education in Worcester*, Worcester Historical Society, 1913.

Marett, 'Pontificalia' — P. Marett, 'The Use of Pontificalia by the Priors of Worcester in the Fourteenth Century', *Transactions of the Worcestershire Archaeological Society*, 3rd series, iii (1970–1972), 61–62.

Mason, *Wulfstan* — E. Mason, *St. Wulfstan of Worcester, c. 1008–1095*, Oxford, 1990.

Noake, *Worcs. Cathedral* — J. Noake, *The Monastery and Cathedral of Worcester*, London, 1866.

Turner, *Worcs. Mss.* — C. H. Turner, ed., *Early Worcester Manuscripts, Fragments of Four Books and a Charter of the Eighth Century belonging to Worcester Cathedral*, Oxford, 1916.

Wilson, *Accts Henry VIII* — J. M. Wilson, ed., *Accounts of the Priory of Worcester for the Year 13–14 Henry VIII, A.D. 1521–2*, Worcestershire Historical Society, 1907; part of Reg. A.17 in Section A.ii (*a*) above.

Wilson, *Early Comp. Rolls* — J. M. Wilson and C. Gordon, eds, *Early Compotus Rolls of the Priory of Worcester*, Worcestershire Historical Society, 1908.

Wilson, 'John de Wyke' — J. M. Wilson, 'John de Wyke, Prior of Worcester, 1301–1317. Some glimpses of the early years of his Priorate from the "Liber Albus" ', *Associated Architectural Societies' Reports and Papers*, 34 (1917–18), pt 1, 131–152.

Wilson, 'Visitations' — J. M. Wilson, 'The Visitations and Injunctions of Cardinal Wolsey and Archbishop Cranmer to the Priory of Worcester in 1526 and 1534 respectively', *Associated Architectural Societies' Reports and Papers*, 36 (1921–22), 356–371.

WORCESTER CATHEDRAL PRIORY
1066–1540

AARON
occ. c. 1104

Name occ in the list of monks in *Durham Liber Vitae*, fo 22.

ABEL
occ. 1206

1206, May, sacrist, and d., *Ann. Wigorn.*, 394.

ADAM
see Amisii

ADRIANUS
occ. c. 1104

Name occ. in the list of monks in *Durham Liber Vitae*, fo 22.

AEGELMARUS
occ. c. 1104

Name occ. in the list of monks in *Durham Liber Vitae*, fo 22; see also Atkins, 'Church of Worcs', pt ii, 222 with refs.

AEGELREDUS [Ethelred
occ. [1062 × 1095] occ. [after 1104]

Mentioned by Eadmer, monk of Canterbury, q.v., Dunstan, *Memorials*, 163–164; he was educated in the household of bp Wulstan who sent him to Canterbury for further training. After serving as precentor and subprior there, he returned to Worcester and prob. became prior under the name of Nicholas II, q.v. See also Darlington, *Vita Wulfstani*, xxxviii, n. 2.

Dr Gransden suggests that he was one of Eadmer's informants for his Life of St Dunstan, *Hist. Writing*, i, 129; for Eadmer, see under Canterbury.

AEGELRICUS [Agelric, Egelric, Eilmer
occ. 1092 d. by 1122

1092, present at bp Wulstan's synod, and member of a comm. to investigate a parochial dispute, *Worcs. Cart.*, no 52.

Name occ. in the list of monks in *Durham Liber Vitae*, fo 22.

Name also occ. in the Savigny mortuary roll dated c. 1122/3, Delisle, *Rouleau Mortuaire*, pl. xxv, tit. 87.

See also Darlington, *Vita Wulfstani*, 31, Mason, *Wulfstan*, 179 and Atkins, 'Church of Worcs.', pt ii, 222 with refs; this last names him as adcn.

AEGELUVINUS [Ageluvinus
occ. c. 1104

Name occ. in the list of monks in *Durham Liber Vitae*, fo 22.

AELFGEARDUS
occ. c. 1104

Name occ. in the list of monks in *Durham Liber Vitae*, fo 22.

AELFSTAN [Alfstanus
occ. c. 1062 occ. c. 1077

c. 1062–1077, prior, *Fasti*, ii, 102, *HRH*, 83.

[1066 × 1080] named in a confirmation charter of William I to the cathedral priory, *Worcs. Cart*, no 2.

Brother of bp Wulfstan and prob. succ. him as prior; see Mason, *Wulfstan*, 90, 130.

AELFUVINUS [Aelfwinus
occ. c. 1104

Name occ. in the list of monks in *Durham Liber Vitae*, fo 22; see also Atkins, 'Church of Worcs.', pt ii, 222 with refs.

AELUREDUS
occ. c. 1104

Name occ. in the list of monks in *Durham Liber Vitae*, fo 22; see also Atkins, 'Church of Worcs.', pt ii, 222 with refs.

AERNALIS
occ. 1245

1245, chamberlain, d., *Ann. Wigorn.*, 437.

AERNALIS
see also Ernulf

John de ALCESTER [Alcestre, Alcetr', Alyncestr'
occ. 1400 d. 1420

[1400], 20 May, one of two whom the prior was comm. to prof., Reg. Winchcombe, 97.

1401, 24 June, subdcn, *Reg. Sed. Vac.*, 373.

1404, 20 Sept., ord. pr., Llanthony priory, Gloucester, *Reg. Clifford*, no 122, p. 87.

1404/5, celebrated his first mass; gifts were sent from the cellarer and almoner, WCM C.50, C.187.

1401, 24 June, 44th and last in order at the episcopal el., *Reg. Sed. Vac.*, 373.
1419, 14 Apr., 17th in order at the episcopal el., *Reg. Sed. Vac.*, 407.
1420, d. by 29 Sept., and the chamberlain recd nothing [from the sale of his clothing], WCM C.32.

Richard ALCESTER [Alcetre, Alcetur, Alincester, Alincestr'
occ. 1459/60 d. 1486/7

1460, 20 Dec., ord. subdcn, Worcester cathedral, Reg. Carpenter i, 554.
1461, 28 Feb., ord. dcn, Worcester cathedral, *ib.*, i, 555.
1461, 19 Sept., ord. pr., [North] Claines, *ib.*, i, 555.
1461/2, celebrated his first mass, and recd a gift of 2s. 6d. from the almoner, WCM C.201a.

1477/9, chaplain/secretary to the prior, Reg. A.6(i), fos 72, 81.
1479, 27 Sept., apptd sacrist, Reg. Alcock, 24.
1459/60, was owed 22d. by the cellarer, WCM C.491.
1478, 14 Sept., witness to the homage of a priory tenant, Reg. A.6(i), fo 73v.
1480, 15 Apr., in charge of the image of the Virgin Mary which was *superposita et pendentia* in the [Lady] chapel, Reg. Alcock, 36.
1486/7, d. and 2s. 6d. in alms were distributed [to the poor], WCM C.207.

ALCHURCH
see Alvechurch

Thomas ALDERTON [Aldurton
occ. 1408 d. 1439/40

1408, 14 Apr., ord. acol., Dominican convent, Worcester, Reg. Peverel, 173.
1408, 22 Dec., ord. subdcn, Worcester cathedral, *ib.*, 176.
1409, 2 Mar., ord. dcn, Worcester cathedral, *ib.*, 178.
1410, 20 Sept., ord. pr., Llanthony priory, Gloucester, *ib.*, 185.
1409/10, celebrated his first mass; the hostiller provided bread and ale and the almoner also sent *exennia*, WCM C.219, C.189.

1420, June/1423, kitchener, WCM C.134, C.140–142.
[1423/4], probably kitchener, WCM C.489.
1427/8, subcellarer, WCM C.617.

1419, 14 Apr., 21st in order at the episcopal el., *Reg. Sed. Vac.*, 407.
1427/8, visited the quarry at Ombersley, WCM C.85a.
1433, 9 Dec., 9th in order at the episcopal el., *Reg. Sed. Vac.*, 432.
1439/40, d., and his *harnes'* were sold by the chamberlain for 15s., WCM C.39.

ALDREDUS
occ. c. 1104

Name occ. in the list of monks in *Durham Liber Vitae*, fo 22.
1139 × 48, possibly the chaplain to the monks mentioned in *Worcs. Cart.*, no 252. See also Atkins 'Church of Worcs.', pt ii, 222 with refs.

Note: a monk of this name was sent by bp Wulstan to his new foundation at Westbury, Atkins, 'Church of Worcs.', pt ii, 207, 222; see Mauricius and Coleman.

ALDUVINUS [Aldwin
occ. c. 1104

Name occ. in the list of monks in *Durham Liber Vitae*, fo 22.

Became a hermit at Malvern; see Darlington, *Vita Wulfstani*, 26 and Mason, *Wulfstan*, 167–168.

ALFERIUS [Aelfhere, Alfere
occ. 1092 occ. c. 1104

1092, sacrist [*secretarius*], present at bp Wulstan's synod, and member of a commission to investigate the parochial rights of the cathedral church, *Worcs. Cart.*, no 52; see Thomas I.
c. 1104, name occ. in the list of monks in *Durham Liber Vitae*, fo 22.

ALFUVIUS
occ. c. 1104

Name occ. in the list of monks in *Durham Liber Vitae*, fo 22.

ALINCESTR'
see Alcester

ALLCHURCHE
see Alvechurch

ALSIUS
occ. c. 1104

Name occ. in the list of monks in *Durham Liber Vitae*, fo 22.

William ALSTON, B.Th. [Allston
occ. 1497 occ. 1508

1497, 23 Sept., ord. acol., Oxford, St Frideswide's priory, Reg. William Smith (Lincoln), fo 9.
1497, 23 Dec., ord. subdcn, Winchester cathedral, Reg. Langton (Winchester), fo 31v.
1498, 31 Mar., ord. dcn, Osney abbey, Reg. Smith (Lincoln), fo 12.

1507, 2 June, hostiller, Pantin, *BMC*, iii, 218 (from Reg. A.6(ii) fo 44v).

1498, 25 Oct., scholar at Oxford, *Reg. abp Morton*, ii, no 458.
1502, 2 May, summoned on acct of a debt to appear before [an Oxford] magistrate, *Reg. Cancell. Oxon, 1498–1506*, 122.

1502, 18 July, at Oxford where he was accused of breaking a glass vessel containing *aqua vitae* belonging to a Richard Marsche, *ib.*, 129.
1504, before 4 Oct., at Oxford and had indicted an Alice Browne on a charge of suspected felony which, on 4 Oct., he withdrew and promised to have her released from prison, *ib.*, 85, 87, 235, 236.
1507, 23 Jan., adm. to oppose for B.Th., *Reg. Univ. Ox.*, i, 49, as in *BRUO* under John Alston.

1498, 25 Oct., 34th in order on the visitation certificate, *Reg. abp Morton*, ii, no 458.
1507, 2 June, apptd proctor for the Black Monk Chapter meeting at Coventry, Pantin, *BMC*, iii, 218.
1508, 5 Aug., the prior issued a *dimissio* to William Alston B.Th., allowing him to go to Blyth priory, York diocese as prior, Reg. A.6(ii) fo 58v. There are three entries related to the transfer, which intimate that there had been tension between William and prior Wednesbury, q.v. At Blyth he succ. Thomas Gardyner, monk of Westminster, whom he had probably met at Oxford. However, he may not have taken up the position as there is ref. to a John Baynebrig as Gardyner's successor at Blyth in 1511, Borthwick Reg. 26 (abp Bainbridge, York) fo 22v.

ALURICUS
occ. c. 1104

Name occ. in the list of monks in *Durham Liber Vitae*, fo 22.

Robert ALVECHURCH [Alvechurche, Alchurche, Allchurche
occ. 1483 d. 1532

1483, 20 Sept., ord. acol., carnary chapel by Worcester cathedral, Reg. Alcock, 274.
1488, 20 Sept., ord. pr., Worcester cathedral, Reg. Morton, 142.

1497, 21 Mar., *custos* of the Lady chapel, WCM B.1677b; also on 25 Oct. 1498, *Reg. abp Morton*, ii, no 458; 21 July 1499, Reg. A.6(ii) fo 2; 30 Sept. 1499, WCM C.852.
1501/2, subprior, WCM C.167.
1504, 6 Nov., infirmarer, Reg. A.6(ii), fo 32.
1505/6, chamberlain, WCM C.427.
1507, 10 Sept., subprior, Reg. A.6(ii), fo 25v.
1507/8, sacrist, first yr, WCM C.428; also
1513, 26 Mar., 22 Sept., Reg. S. Gigli, 171, 261; also
1515/17, Reg. A.12, fo 35, WCM C.429; also
1518, 27 Sept., Reg. A.6(ii), fo 113; also
1521, 4 Mar., 22 July, *Jnl More*, 127, Reg. abp Warham ii, fo 293v.
1521/2, subprior and hostiller, Wilson, *Accts Henry VIII*, 26 and WCM C.412; 15 Nov. 1522, subprior, Reg. A.6(ii), fo 133.
1522, 5 Dec., apptd sacrist by the prior, *sed. vac.*, Reg. A.6(ii), fo 135v.
1522/4, sacrist, WCM C.430, C.413.
1523, 10 Mar., as sacrist made his oath of obedience to the new bp's vicar general promising, as required, to render to the bp an annual account of his administration as sacrist, Reg. Ghinucci 8(ii), 26–28.
1529, 7 May, sacrist, and obtained exemption from Cardinal Morton from the necessity of accounting to the bp for his administration, Reg. A.12, fos 127–128.
1531/2, sacrist, Reg. A.12, fo 135.

1498, 25 Oct., 22nd in order on the visitation certificate, *Reg. abp Morton*, ii, no 458.
1499, 21 July, one of two monk proctors apptd to present the seven nominees for the priorate to the bp, Reg. S. Gigli, 343; they met Richard Fox, bp of Durham, acting for Gigli at Southwark on 2 Sept., Reg. A.6(ii), fo 1v.
1503/4, recd 6s. 8d. from the master of the Lady chapel *in emptione organorum*, WCM C.291.
1507, 10 Sept., one of the seven nominees for the priorate, Reg. S. Gigli, 352.
1518, 27 Sept., again one of the seven nominees for the priorate, Reg. A.6(ii), fo 113; they were presented to bp Fox (Winchester), prob at Southwark, where he named William More, q.v., *ib.*
1520, 27 Feb., apptd with Roger Neckham, q.v., to act as *scrutatores* with oversight of all tenements pertaining to the obedientiary offices, and the responsibilty of checking and itemizing all the plate, bedding, books etc., in the house in order to produce an inventory to be read in chapter annually on the first Mon. in Lent, *Jnl More*, 127.
1521, 22 July, 3rd in order on the visitation certificate, Reg. abp Warham ii, fo 293v.
1531/2, 4th in order on the clerical subsidy list and as sacrist pd. £12 plus 3s. 4d. commons, Reg. A.12, fo 135.
1532, 10 Dec., d. while sacrist and was buried under a 'blewe stone before our Ladye Chapel in ye boke of ye church', *Jnl More*, 360; a monk was apptd to say masses for him and was pd 10s. each quarter by the prior; see Thomas Wulstan.
n.d., a 16th c. inventory of plate belonging to some of the obedientiary offices (unspecified) includes a long list to which his name is attached, Reg. A.12, fo 172v.

ALYNCESTR'
see Alcester

Adam AMISII
d. 1218

1218, d., *Ann. Wigorn.*, 410.

AMFRIDUS
occ. ?1146 × 1189

[?1146 × 1189], witnessed a charter of prior R[?alph de Bedeford, q.v.], *Worcs. Cart.*, no 489.

John de ANCREDAM
occ. 1317

1317, 9 Dec., *clericus* and one of four to be examined by the bp's commissary, Liber Albus, fo 84^v; the candidates are described as *vestiendos*. See John de Westbury.

ANCREDAM
see also Ankerdam, Ankerdom

ANDREAS
occ. c. 1104

Name occ. in the list of monks in *Durham Liber Vitae*, fo 22.

Note: an Andreas witnessed a charter, prob. temp. prior R [?alph de Bedeford] (1146 × 1189), *Worcs. Cart.*, no 489.

Thomas ANKERDAM
occ. 1504

1504, 6 Apr., ord. acol., carnary chapel by Worcester cathedral, Reg. S. Gigli, 287.
1504, 21 Dec., ord. subdcn, hospital of St Wulstan, Worcester, *ib.*, 291.

John de ANKERDOM [Ancredam, Onkerdom, Ankerden
occ. 1317 occ. 1341/2

1317, 9 Dec., in response to the prior's request the bp apptd a commissary to examine him and three other clerks before clothing, Liber Albus, fo 84^v.
1318, 24 Mar., recd the monastic habit, Liber Albus, fo 85.
1318, 17 Nov., one of three whom the bp authorized the prior to prof., as the yr of probation had been completed, *Liber Albus*, no 809, and *Reg. Cobham*, 13.
1319, 7 Apr., ord. subdcn, bp's chapel Kempsey, *Reg. Cobham*, 58.
1319, 22 Dec., ord. dcn, St Nicholas' church, Worcester, *ib.*, 68.
1338/9, referred to as former cellarer, WCM C.58.
1341/2, the almoner was pd *pro hospicio* of his mother, WCM C.170.

Henry de ANNOCHIA [Antiochia
occ. [1286/7] occ. 1319

[1286/7], hostiller, WCM C.499. The dating of the heading on this acct is uncertain beyond 14/15 Edward, and so it could be Edward II and 1320/1.
[1292], almoner, *Reg. Giffard*, 412.
1302, 25 Mar. and 29 Oct., infirmarer, as below.
[1319, Nov.], subprior, *Reg. Cobham*, 21 (but see Henry Fouke).
[1292], as proctor for the prior and convent appealed to the bp in a cause concerning the almonry, *Reg. Giffard*, 412.
1302, 25 Mar., one of seven electors of John de St Germans q.v., as bp, *Reg. Sed. Vac.*, 1.
1307, 17 Nov., as pr. and monk, certified proceedings in the el. of a bp, *Reg. Sed. Vac.*, 110.
1317, 20 Oct., in the infirmary and absent from the el. of a prior, Liber Albus, fo 83.
[1319, Nov.], apptd penitentiary, *Reg. Cobham*, 21.

ANNOCHIA
see also Cokesey, Wyrmintone

ANSELM
occ. 1184

1184, 31 Oct., wrote an Epistola de ... planetarum conjunctiòne in which he described the predictions of an illiterate lay brother who fell into a trance and, while lying prostrate before an altar recited a poem and d. within ten days, *Chron. Hovedene*, ii, 293–295, also Worcs. Ms F.114.

ARNULFUS
occ. c. 1104

Name occ. in the list of monks in *Durham Liber Vitae*, fo 22; see also Atkins, 'Church of Worcs.', pt ii, 223.

John de ARUNDEL
occ. 1291 occ. 1294/5

1291/2, student at Oxford with William de Grymeley, q.v.; the cellarer pd them 20s. *versus Oxon*' and also 2m., WCM C.51 and Wilson, *Early Comp. Rolls*, 13, 14.
1294/5, student, with a pension from the cellarer, WCM C.52 and Wilson, *ib.*, 30. See *BRUO*.

Robert de ASCHERUGG [Asschruge, Asserugge
occ. 1317 occ. 1329/30

1317, 20 Oct., 17th in order at the el. of a prior, Liber Albus, fo 83^v.
1324, 29 Mar., witness to an incumbent's oath of office (for a city parish), Liber Albus, fo 115.
1326/7, performed supervisory duties at Bromsgrove, WCM C.544.
1329/30, with the cellarer made two visits to Cleeve Prior, WCM C.557.

Thomas ASTELEY
occ. 1497 occ. 1528

1497, 14 Apr., ord. dcn, carnary chapel by Worcester cathedral, Reg. G. Gigli, 25.
1498, 14 Apr., ord. pr., carnary chapel, *ib.*, 26.
1498, 25 Oct., subsacrist, *Reg. abp Morton*, ii, no 458.
1506/7, subcellarer, WCM C.668, C.783.
1509, chaplain to the prior, Reg. A.6(ii), fo 75.
1516, *magister communis cene*, Reg. A.12, fo 46.
1518, Oct., chaplain to the prior, Reg. A.6(ii), fo 112.
1520/1, hostiller, Reg. A.17, 65.

1521/4, pittancer, WCM C.412, C.413, Reg. A.17, 206.

1498, 25 Oct., 37th in order on the visitation certificate, *Reg. abp Morton*, ii, no 458.
1506/7, visited Newnham and Sedgeberrow as subcellarer, WCM C.668, C.783.
1521, 22 July, 11th in order on the visitation certificate, Reg. abp Warham ii, fo 293v.
[1528], recd small sums as 'rewards' from the prior, *Jnl More*, 277.
1528, 6 Mar., transferred to Abergavenny priory, Reg. A.6(ii), fo 157, *Jnl More*, 265.

Henry de ASTON
occ. 1328

1328, 24 Sept., ord. dcn, St Mary's church at the gate of Gloucester abbey, *Reg. Orleton*, no 9 (p. 12).
1329, 23 Dec., ord. pr., Dodderhill, *ib.*, no 19 (p. 28).

John de ASTON [Astone
occ. 1294/5, occ. 1319

1295, cellarer, Worcs. Ms Q.13.
1300, 19 Aug., *tumbarius*, *Reg. Giffard*, 530.

1294/5, student at Oxford and recd 20s. from the cellarer *ad libros*, Wilson, *Early Comp. Rolls*, 30 (WCM C.52); and see *BRUO*.

1296, 11 July, one of the seven nominees for the priorate, *Reg. Giffard*, 480.
1300, 19 Aug., one of the monks apptd by the bp to assist Nicholas de Norton, q.v., in conducting a visitation in *spiritualibus* of the prior and chapter, *Reg. Giffard*, 530.
1301, 18 July, one of the seven nominees for the priorate, *Reg. Giffard*, 547.
1304, 10 Feb., penitentiary, and ordered by the bp to refrain from dealing with certain reserved cases, *Reg. Gainsborough*, 5.
[1307/8], as penitentiary gave letters of absolution to two clerks, *Reg. Sed. Vac.*, 90.
[1308, Nov.], apptd penitentiary, *Reg. Reynolds*, 2.
1312, 15 Sept., present at the installation of an adcn of Worcester by proxy, Liber Albus fo 57v.
1314, 4 Mar., apptd penitentiary in the diocese, Reg. Maidstone, 4; and again 1 Sept. 1314, *ib.*, 31.
1317, 20 Oct., 10th in order at the el. of a prior, Liber Albus, fo 83v.
[1319, Nov.], apptd penitentiary, *Reg. Cobham*, 21.

Name in two Worcs. Mss:
(1) Q.13, P. Cornubiensis etc. (late 13th c.), which contains Questiones libri physicorum 'notate a J. de Aston post Magistrum ?Nicolaum Clive'.
(2) Q.33, a commentary on the Sentences (late 13th c.), name on [original] vellum cover.

See Little and Pelster, *Oxford Theology*, 78, 258, also *BRUO*.

ATHELELMUS
occ. c. 1104

Name occ. in the list of monks in *Durham Liber Vitae*, fo 22.

ATTE FELDE
see Hatfeld

Philip AUBYN [Obyn *alias* Worcester
occ. 1272 d. 1296

1287–1296, prior: chosen by the bp from the seven nominees, 7 Jan. 1287; d. 7 July 1296, *Fasti*, ii, 104.

n.d., possibly precentor; see below.
1272, 21 Dec., subprior, *Reg. Giffard*, 50.
1274, 21 Sept., subprior, *ib.*, 62.
1287, 2 Jan., subprior, *ib.*, 304.

1272, 21 Dec., one of the seven nominees for the priorate, *Reg. Giffard*, 50.
1274, 21 Sept., one of the seven nominees for the priorate, *ib.*, 62.
1287, 2 Jan., one of the seven nominees for the priorate, *ib.*, 304.
1287/8, 23 Dec., pending the appeal to the court of Canterbury vs the bp's plan to refound Westbury as a collegiate church, he insisted that the bp had no right to enter the chapter for the purpose of exercising his authority to correct, or to rec. the prof. of monks, *Ann. Wigorn.*, 496; see Stephen de Witton.
1290, involved in a dispute with the Worcester Franciscans over the right to bury a certain man named H. Poche, *Ann. Wigorn.*, 502–504.
1290, 11 July, attended the Black Monk Chapter meeting at Abingdon where plans for a house of study at Oxford were discussed, Pantin, *BMC*, i, 129–130.
1290, 7 Nov., at an episcopal visitation, while the bp was in consultation with the subprior Simon [de Wyre, q.v.] and two other monks, he entered the chapter house accompanied by protesting monks and others, and was among those who were excommunicated by the bp, *Reg. Giffard*, 380.
1291, 11 Sept., attended a second meeting at Salisbury for the same purpose as above, *ib.*, i, 129–131.
1294, 21 Nov., celebrated mass before the king, *Ann. Wigorn.*, 517.
1295, summoned to parliament at Westminster on 1 Aug., *Parl. Writs*, i, 912.
n.d., an entry on a flyleaf of Worcs.Ms Q.4 states that those who listened to a sermon of Philip Aubyn would rec. 295 days' indulgence.
1296, 10 July, interred in front of the altar of the Holy Cross, and the abbot of Evesham presided at his burial, *Ann. Wigorn.*, 527 and *Reg. Giffard*, 480. His death and bequest to the convent in 1296 are in *Ann. Wigorn.*, 511.

Name in Worcs. Ms F.167, Bonaventura (late 13th c.) . . . *quem frater—eiusdem* [i.e. Worcester] *monachus scribi fecit.* Was he perhaps at this time precentor?

Prob. related to James *dictus* Aubyn, citizen of Worcester, mentioned in *Reg. Giffard*, 284.

AUGUSTINUS
occ. c. 1104

Name occ. in the list of monks in *Durham Liber Vitae*, fo 22.

Robert AYLESBURY [Aylysbyry, Eylisbury *alias* Blount
occ. 1456 occ. 1478

1456, 27 March, ord acol., chapel of bp's palace, Worcester, Reg. Carptenter i, 541.
1457, 16 Apr., ord subdcn, chapel of bp's palace, Worcester, *ib.*, i, 543.
1458, 23 Sept., ord dcn, Worcester cathedral, *ib.*, i, 547.
1460, 7 June, ord pr., Hereford cathedral, *Reg. Stanbury* (Hereford), 146.
1459/60, celebrated his first mass; the kitchener and prior gave *exennia*, WCM C.149, C.400.
1463/5, *custos* of the Lady chapel, WCM C.492a, C.95.
1466/7, refectorer, WCM C.421.
1462/3 and 1463/4, gave a small sum in alms to the almoner, WCM C.201a, C.201.
1478, 6 Oct., given papal dispensation to rec. and retain a benefice, *CPL*, xiii (1471–1484), 674. (The *alias* Blount occurs here.)

Laurence de BADMINTON
occ. 1271 occ. 1291/2

1271, 21 Dec., one of the two monk proctors who presented the seven nominees for the priorate to the bp, *Reg. Giffard*, 50; see Robert de Wick.
1291/2, turned over to the cellarer the offerings from the shrines (and therefore possibly *tumbarius*), Wilson, *Early Comp. Rolls*, 11 (WCM C.51), as Laurence.

Name on the last flyleaf of Worcs. Ms Q.42, Distinctiones Mauricii (late 13th c.), as one of the eleven monks who contributed to its purchase, in his case 6[?d].

Thomas de BALLESCOT [Balescot or ?Balescoc
occ. [1262/3] occ. ?1270

[1262/3], pd a visit to Hardwick, WCM E.4(2). There are two other undated refs in WCM E.4, (2) and (9); in (6) he and Walter Hallow, q.v., were *itinerant' versus Oxon'.*
1270, named again on the Hardwick acct roll, WCM E.4(3), and also on the Tibberton acct roll undated fragment E.4(11).

Note: he may have been cellarer, *ib.*, E.4(6).

John BARBOUR
occ. 1523/4

1523/4, ill for ten weeks and the infirmarer spent 11s. 8d. on his needs, Reg. A.17, 280 and WCM C.413.

BARDNEY
see Berdney

John BARNDESLEY
occ. 1404

1404/5, mentioned by the cellarer, WCM C.78.

Richard BARNDESLEY [Barndysley, Barnysley, Barundesley, Brandel'
occ. 1412 d. 1446/7

1412, 17 Dec., ord. acol., Worcester cathedral, Reg. Peverel, 193, and subdcn the same day, *ib.*, 194.
1413, 8 Apr., ord. dcn, Worcester cathedral, *ib.*, 195.
1416, 13 June, ord. pr., chapel of [?the Guild of] the Holy Trinity, Worcester, *ib.*, 209.
1415/16, celebrated his first mass, with gifts from the chamberlain and pittancer, WCM C.31, C.323.
[1444/5], 1445/6, infirmarer, WCM C.493, C.842.
1419, 24 Apr., student at Oxford, *Reg. Sed. Vac.*, 407.
1419/20, student at Oxford, pd. by the precentor to return in order to preach, and stayed eight days; came back again to preach on the feast of the Assumption, WCM C.375.
1421/2, rode from Oxford to consult with the prior, WCM C.84a (note: *BRUO* has incorrectly read 'Brameley').
1422/3, student at Oxford, again returning to preach, WCM C.376.
1419, 24 Apr., 29th in order at the el. of a bp, *Reg. Sed. Vac.*, 407.
1433, 9 Dec., 14th in order at the el. of a bp, *ib.*, 432.
1438, 12 Feb., preached at the el. of the seven nominees for the priorate, Reg. Bourgchier, 84.
1446/7, d. and the cellarer gave alms to the Worcester friars [to pray for his soul], WCM C.90.

Name in Worcs. Ms F.86, Walter Burley (15th c.).

I Thomas de BARNDESLEY [Barndeslegh, Barndisle, Brandisle
occ. 1343 occ. 1358

1343, 20 Sept., ord pr., Bishops Cleeve, *Reg. Bransford*, no 1054 (p. 219).
1350, Mar./Sept., cellarer, WCM C.692, succ. Robert de Weston, q.v.
1350/2, cellarer, WCM C.53, C.53a, C.801.

1350, 17 June, apptd proctor for the prior and convent in a dispute, WCM B. 1641.
1357/8, pd a [supervisory] visit to Overbury, WCM C.706.
1358, 6 July, granted papal licence to choose his own confessor, *CPL*, iii (1342–1362), 600.

II Thomas de BARNDESLEY [Barndley
occ. 1388 d. 1409/10

1388, 7 Sept., one of two whom the prior was comm. to prof, Reg. Wakefield, 239 (the entry in the printed register, item no 794, has not distinguished between adm. and prof.).
1389/90, celebrated his first mass and received gifts from the pittancer and the precentor, WCM C.314, C.367 (1390/1).
1392/3, described by the chamberlain as novice, WCM C.20.
1404/5, gave the almoner 12s. or more likely, 12d. as alms, WCM C.187.
1409/10, d. and the almoner bought bread [to distribute among the poor] after his funeral, WCM C.189.

William BARNESLEY B.Th., [Barnisley, Bernesley
occ. 1497 occ. 1508

1497, 23 Sept., ord. acol., St Frideswide's priory, Oxford, Reg. William Smith (Lincoln), fo 9.
1498, 31 Mar., ord. dcn, Osney abbey, Oxford, *ib.*, fo 12.
[1506/7], chamberlain, WCM C.490.
1507, 2 June, fourth prior, Pantin, *BMC*, iii, 218.
1507, 10 Sept., hostiller, Reg. S. Gigli, 349.
1497, 23 Sept.; 1498, 31 Mar., 25 Oct., student at Oxford as shown by the place of ordination above and by the visitation certificate below.
1508, Dec., supplicated for B.Th., as in *BRUO*.
1498, 25 Oct., 33rd in order on the visitation certificate, *Reg. abp Morton*, ii, no 458.

BAROW
see Berrowe

I BARTHOLOMEW
d. 1226

1226, d., *Ann. Wigorn.*, 419.

II BARTHOLOMEW
occ. 1232

1232, cellarer; el. abbot of Alcester. He gave the sacrist of Worcester a cope, *Ann. Wigorn.*, 424.

Roger BATENHALL [Batnal, Battnall, Batynhall
occ. 1521 occ. 1540

1524/5, celebrated his first mass and the almoner gave a pittance, WCM C.414.
1531/2, subchamberlain, Reg. A.12, fo 135v.
1535, subsacrist, *L and P Henry VIII*, ix, no 653.
1521, 22 July, 40th in order on the visitation certificate, Reg. abp Warham ii, fo 293v.
1525/6, 31st on the clerical subsidy list and pd. 3s. 4d., Reg. A.12, fo 125.
1531/2, 31st on the second subsidy list, and as subchamberlain pd. 20d. as well as 3s. 4d. commons, *ib.*, fo 135v.
1534, 17 Aug., subscribed to the Act of Supremacy, *DK 7th Report*, Appndx 2, 305.
1535, signed the petition vs the reinstatement of William Fordham, q.v., as cellarer, *L and P Henry VIII*, ix, no 653.
1536, 13 Mar., 22nd in order at the 'el.' of Henry Holbech, q.v., as prior, Reg. A.6(iii), fo 1.
1540, 18 Jan., assigned a pension of £6 p.a., *L and P Henry VIII*, xv, no 81.

Ralph de BATHONIA
occ. 1142 d. 1143

1142–1143, prior, *Fasti*, ii, 102, *HRH*, 83.

Roger de BATHONIA
occ. 1219

1219, cellarer, and witness to the homage of a tenant, *Ann. Wigorn.*, 411.

BATNAL, Batynhall
see Batenhall

BEAUDLEY
see Bewdeley

Ralph de BEDEFORD [Bedford
occ. 1146 d. 1189

1146–1189, prior: succ. after 26 Jan. 1146, d., c. 23 July 1189, *Fasti*, ii, 103, *HRH*, 83.
[1166/7], recd a letter from John of Salisbury in exile with abp Anselm, *Salisbury Letters*, ii, no 197.
His nephew, M. Godfrey, endowed a chantry for him, details of which were drawn up in an agreement with prior Senatus, q.v., Bloom, *Original Charters*, 172.

M. William de BEDEFORD
occ. 1224 d. 1242

1224–1242 prior: previously monk of St Alban's and physician, Talbot and Hammond *Medical Practitioners*, 131, 384–385, and also prior of Tynemouth; prob. nom. 3 Oct. 1224 and was thus the first prior to be chosen in accordance with the agreement reached between bp and chapter on this date; d., 29 Oct. 1242, *Fasti*, ii, 103. See William Norman.
1225, supervised the building of a new house and offices for the prior, *Ann. Wigorn.*, 418.
1232, 21 Oct., present at the reinterment of King John, *Ann Tewkes.*, 84.

John de BEDWARDINE [Pedewardyn
occ. 1305 occ. 1317

1305, 5 Jan., one of two *clerici* presented to the bp at the time of their adm., *Reg. Gainsborough*, 15.

1317, 20 Oct., 32nd in order at the el. of a prior, Liber Albus, fo 83.

I BENEDICT [Benedictus
occ. c. 1104

Name occ. in the list of monks in *Durham Liber Vitae*, fo 22.

II BENEDICT
occ. before 1095 occ. 1124

1124, a monk who had been trained and ord by bp Wulstan and was now el. abbot of Tewkesbury.

Note: the two Benedicts may be identical.

John BENET [Benett
occ. 1470 d. 1482/3

1470, 17 Mar., ord acol., Lady chapel, Worcester cathedral, Reg. Carpenter i, 575.
[1471] acol., given *lit. dim. ad omnes*, *ib.* ii, 42.
1472, 19 Dec., ord dcn, carnary chapel by Worcester cathedral, *ib.*, ii, 189.
1474, 5 Mar., ord pr., carnary chapel, *ib.* ii, 195.
1473/4, celebrated his first mass; the almoner gave 2s. 3d., the hostiller gave a pittance of bread and wine, and the kitchener gave 2s. 3d. in *exennia*, WCM C.203, C.236, C.157.

1482, student at Oxford, when he placed a Bible in the Chichele chest as caution for a loan; see below.

1482/3, d., and the chamberlain sold his *harnesia* for 22s. 10d., WCM C.47; the precentor pd for the brief announcing his d., WCM C.386; the almoner recd money from the cellarer to pay for his corrody, WCM C.206.

Name in
(1) Worcs. Ms F.118, Logicalia quedam etc. (14th/15th c.); see John Broghton, Thomas More II and Edward Wynchecombe.
(2) Oxford, Bod. Ms Auct. D. infra 2.4, Biblia (13th c.), placed in the Chichele chest in 1482.

William BENET [Bennett
occ. 1520/1 occ. 1536

1520/1, celebrated his first mass; recd a 2s. pittance from the almoner and 1s. from the prior, Reg. A.17, 54, *Jnl More*, 139.

1525/6, subchamberlain, Reg. A.12, fo 125.
1531/2, *magister communis cene*, Reg. A.12, fo 135, WCM C.414c.

1521, 22 July, 36th in order on the visitation certificate, Reg. abp Warham ii, fo 293v.
1525/6, 27th on the clerical subsidy list and pd 5s. Reg. A.12, fo 125.
1531/2, 27th on the second subsidy list and as *magister communis cene*, pd 10s. plus 3s. 4d. commons, *ib.*, fo 135.
1534, 17 Aug., subscribed to the Act of Supremacy, *DK 7th Report*, Appndx 2, 305.
1535, signed the petition vs the reinstatement of William Fordham, q.v., as cellarer, *L and P Henry VIII*, ix, no 653.
1536, 13 Mar., 19th at the 'el.' of Henry Holbech, q.v. as prior, Reg. A.6(iii), fo 1.

Thomas BERDNEY
occ. 1426

1426, 8 Sept., one of two whose prof. the prior was comm. to rec. Reg. Polton, 13.

BERNESLEY
see Barnesley

John BERROWE [Barow, Berowe
occ. 1504 occ. 1540

1504, 6 Apr., ord acol., carnary chapel by Worcester cathedral, Reg. S. Gigli, 287.
1504, 21 Sept., ord subdcn, carnary chapel, *ib.*, 289.
1504, 21 Dec., ord dcn, hospital of St Wulstan, Worcester, ib, 291.
1507/8, celebrated his first mass; the hostiller gave 2s., WCM C.240.
1520/1, refectorer and precentor, Reg. A.17, 67, 63.
1529/30, precentor, WCM C.414a.
1530/2, refectorer, WCM C.414b, C.414c.

1521, 22 July, 16th in order on the visitation certificate, Reg. abp Warham ii, fo 293v.
1523/4, ill for 20 wks and 23s. 4d. charged to the infirmarer's acct, Reg. A.17, 280.
1525/6, 17th on the clerical subsidy list and pd 3s. 4d., Reg. A.12, fo 125.
1530, 1 Jan., gave a gift of two capons to the prior, *Jnl More*, 302.
1531/2, 15th on the second subsidy list and as refectorer pd 6s. 8d. plus 3s. 4d. commons, *ib.*, fo 135.
1534, 17 Aug., subscribed to the Act of Supremacy, *DK 7th Report*, Appndx 2, 305.
1535, did not sign the petition vs the reinstatement of William Fordham, q.v., *L and P Henry VIII*, ix, no 653.
1536, 13 Mar., 9th in order at the 'el.' of Henry Holbech, q.v. as prior, Reg. A.6(iii), fo 1.
1540, 18 Jan., assigned a pension of £6 p.a., *L and P Henry VIII*, xv, no 81.

Ernaldus de BEVERBURNE
occ. 1219

1219, witness to the homage of a tenant, *Ann. Wigorn.*, 411.

John BEWDELEY [Beaudley, Beudeley
occ. 1425 occ. 1430/1

1425, 24 Mar., ord. acol., Worcester cathedral, Reg. Morgan, 207 (as Weudeley).
1425, 21 Sept., ord dcn, Worcester cathedral, *ib.*, 210.
1430/1, celebrated his first mass; a pittance was given by the kitchener, WCM C.144.

Roger BEWDELEY [Beaudley, Beudley, Beydylley
occ. 1516 occ. 1536

1516, 17 May, ord acol., carnary chapel by Worcester cathedral, Reg. S. Gigli, 330.
1520/1, celebrated his first mass; recd a 2s. pittance from the almoner and 1s. from the prior, Reg. A.17, 54; *Jnl More*, 139.
1523/5, subcellarer, WCM C.413, C.414, Reg. A.17, 257.
1529/30, steward of the prior's hospice, *Jnl More*, 301, 309, 314.
1531/2, 1535, chaplain to the prior, Reg. A.12, fo 135, *L and P Henry VIII*, ix, no 653.
1521, 22 July, 33rd in order on the visitation certificate, Reg. abp Warham ii, fo 293v.
1531/2, 25th on the clerical subsidy list and pd 20d. as chaplain to the prior and 3s. 4d. commons, Reg. A.12, fo 135.
1534, 17 Aug., subscribed to the Act of Supremacy, *DK 7th Report*, Appndx 2, 305.
1535, signed the petition vs the reinstatement of William Fordham, q.v., as cellarer, *L and P Henry VIII*, ix, no 653.
1536, 13 Mar., 18th in order at the 'el.' of Henry Holbech, q.v., as prior, Reg. A.6(iii), fo 1.

Nicholas de BEYCIN [Beysin, Boysin
occ. 1314 occ. 1318

1314, 21 Dec., ord. acol., Worcester cathedral, Reg. Maidstone, 38.
1315, 14 Sept., one of three whose prof. the prior was comm. to rec., Reg. Maidstone, 74.
1317, 15 Sept., the bp gave *lit. dim.* for subdcn's orders, *ib.*, 106.
1318, 21 Jan., the bp gave *lit. dim.* to Nicholas, subdcn, for the remaining orders, Liber Albus, fo 87v.
1317, 20 Oct., in the infirmary and absent from the el. of a prior, Liber Albus, fo 83.

William de BIRLINGHAM [Birlyngham
occ. 1336/7 occ. 1340

1336/7, student at Oxford for 45 wks from the end of Sept. to 10 Aug. and was pd 16d. per wk by the cellarer, WCM C.57; see also John de Evesham and John de Preston I.
1338/9, student at Oxford for 48 wks and was pd at the same rate, WCM C.58; listed in *BRUO*.
1339, 12 Apr., one of the seven nominees for the priorate, *Reg. Bransford*, no 38.
1340, 21 Apr., one of the seven nominees for the priorate, *ib.*, no 290.

John BISHAMPTON [Byssampton, Bysshampton
occ. 1447 occ. 1468/9

1447, 8 Apr., ord acol., Worcester cathedral, Reg. Carpenter i, 512.
1448, 17 Feb., ord subdcn, bp's chapel Alvechurch, *ib.*, 517.
1449, 12 Apr., ord dcn, carnary chapel by Worcester cathedral, *ib.*, 524.
1453, 31 Mar., ord pr., carnary chapel, *ib.*, 535.
1452/3, celebrated his first mass; recd *exennia* from the chamberlain and almoner, WCM C.42, C.200c.
1463/5, 1466/9, 1472/3, pittancer, WCM C.337, C.603, C.735, C.736 and E.71, C.697, C.338.
1464/5, visited Hallow, WCM C.603.
1467/8 and 1468/9, visited Overbury, WCM C.736, C.97.

William de BISSELEYE [Buschel'
occ. 1317 occ. 1318/19

1317, 20 Oct., 11th in order at the el. of a prior, Liber Albus, fo 83.
1318/19, recd from the pittancer his two allowances of wine between Michaelmas and Friday after Epiphany, when he d. During this period he had also undergone two *minutiones*, WCM C.294.

John BLACKWELL [Blakewell
occ. 1525 occ. 1540

1525, 23 Dec., ord acol., Bromyard, *Reg. Booth* (Hereford), 320.
1530/1, celebrated his first mass; recd a pittance from the hostiller, WCM C.414b.
1525/6, student [at Oxford], Reg. A.12, fo 125.
[1530], went off to Oxford after Candlemas, after being ill, *Jnl More*, 304, 305.
1531/2, student, Reg. A.12, fo 135v; and see *BRUO 1501–1540*.
1525/6, 34th on the clerical subsidy list and pd 2s., Reg. A.12, fo 125.
1530, ill and the prior pd M. Harry 23s. 4d. for making him 'hoole', *Jnl More*, 304.
1531/2, 35th on the second subsidy list and pd 20d., Reg. A.12, fo 135v.
1534, 17 Aug., subscribed to the Act of Supremacy, *DK 7th Report*, Appndx 2, 305.
1540, 18 Jan., assigned a pension of £10 p.a., *L and P Henry VIII*, xv, no 868.

Note: absent from the 'el.' of a prior, 13 Mar. 1536.

I Thomas BLACKWELL [Blacwelle, Blakwell
occ. 1411 d. 1452/3

1411, 28 Mar., ord dcn., Worcester cathedral, Reg. Peverel, 188.

1412, 24 Sept., ord pr., Llanthony priory, Gloucester, *ib.*, 193.
1412/13, celebrated his first mass; recd [money for] bread and ale from the hostiller, WCM C.222.

1419, 24 Apr., fourth prior, *Reg. Sed. Vac.*, 407.
1420/1, 1422/3, subcellarer, WCM C.720, C.21; he took over from Thomas Musard, q.v.
1429/30, subcellarer, WCM C.771.
1432/4, chamberlain, WCM C.37, C.38.
1434/5, pittancer and chamberlain, WCM C.330, C.87.
1438/40, 1441/3, pittancer, WCM C.725–728.
1445/6, chamberlain, WCM C.40.
1451, chamberlain, WCM C.448.

1419, 24 Apr., 28th in order at the el. of a bp, *Reg. Sed. Vac.*, 407.
1420/1, 1422/3, pd supervisory visits to Overbury, WCM C.720, C.721.
1429/30, pd a supervisory visit to Sedgeberrow, WCM C.771.
1433, 9 Dec., 13th at the el. of a bp, *Reg. Sed. Vac.*, 432.
1438/40, 1441/3, visited Overbury, WCM C.725–728.
1452/3, d. before 24 June; the chamberlain sold his *harnesia*, WCM C.42; the almoner pd the orator of the city of Worcester *pro obitu*, WCM C.200c.

II Thomas BLACKWELL
occ. 1527

1527, 6 Apr., ord dcn, carnary chapel by Worcester cathedral, Reg. Ghinucci 7(ii), fo 163.

Richard BLAKET
occ. 1341 occ. 1343

1341, 11 Oct., one of two *clerici* adm. to the monastic habit by the bp, *Reg. Bransford*, no 1024.
1342, 15 Oct., prof. by the prior on comm. by the bp, Liber Albus, fo 180v.
1342, 21 Dec., ord acol., Hartlebury, *Reg. Bransford*, no 1049.
1343, 20 Dec., ord subdcn, Hartlebury, *ib.*, no 1055.

Thomas BLOCKELEY [Blockley, Blocley, Blokeleye
occ. 1516 occ. 1540

1516, 17 May, ord acol., carnary chapel by Worcester cathedral, Reg. S. Gigli, 330.
1516, 20 Sept., ord subdcn, carnary chapel, *ib.*, 333.
1517, 7 Mar., ord dcn., carnary chapel, *ib.*, 332.
1518, Oct., 'secretary' to the prior and pd 12d. when be began to work on the prior's reg., *Jnl More*, 74.
1527, chaplain to prior More, Reg. A.6(ii) fo 155.
1536, chaplain to prior Holbech, Reg. A.6(iii) fo 9.
1521, 22 July, 27th in order on the visitation certificate, Reg. abp Warham ii, fo 293v.
1531/2, 22nd on the clerical subsidy list and pd 3s. 4d. commons, Reg. A.12, fo 135.
1534, 17 Aug., subscribed to the Act of Supremacy, *DK 7th Report*, Appndx 2, 305.
1535, 22 Feb., one of abp Cranmer's injunctions sent to the prior and chapter after visitation warned the monks against harbouring in their minds the *abjuratis* of Blockeley and continuing to cast aspersion on him on account of past behaviour, Wilson, 'Visitations' 367. This same yr he was accused by John Musard, q.v., of stealing a letter from the latter's cell, *L and P Henry VIII*, ix, no 497; he also signed the petition vs the reinstatement of William Fordham, q.v., as cellarer, *ib.*, no 653.
1536, 13 Mar., 15th in order at the 'el.' of Henry Holbech, q.v., as prior, Reg. A.6(iii), fo 1.
1540, assigned a pension of £8 p.a., *L and P Henry VIII*, xv, no 869.

William BLOUNT [Blounte
occ. 1423 occ. 1441/2

1423, 20 Mar., ord acol., Worcester cathedral, Reg. Morgan, 198.
1423, 3 Apr., ord. subdcn, Worcester cathedral, *ib.*, 200.
1425, 24 Mar., ord dcn, Worcester cathedral, *ib.*, 208.
1429/30, celebrated his first mass; *exennia* from the hostiller, WCM C.231.

1433, 9 Dec., 30th in order at the el. of a bp, *Reg. Sed. Vac.*, 432.
1441/2, gave small sum in alms to the almoner, WCM C.199.

BLOUNT
See also Aylesbury

John BOKENHULL [Bokenyll, Bokynhull
occ. 1425 d. 1452

1425, 24 Mar., ord subdcn, Worcester cathedral, Reg. Morgan, 208.
1425, 21 Sept., ord pr., Worcester cathedral, *ib.*, 211.
1425/6, celebrated his first mass; recd 2s. 6d. from the almoner and also from the precentor, WCM C.228, C.377.

1433, 9 Dec., 32nd in order at the el. of a bp, *Reg. Sed. Vac.*, 432.
1452/3, d. before 8 Dec.; the chamberlain sold his *harnesia* and the almoner pd the orator of the city of Worcester *pro obitu*, WCM C.42, C.200c.

Richard BORDESLEY
occ. 1483 occ. 1488/9

1483, 20 Sept., ord acol., carnary chapel by Worcester cathedral, Reg. Alcock, 274.

1488/9, subcellarer, WCM C.747, C.779.

1488/9, pd supervisory visits to Overbury and Sedgeberrow, WCM C.747, C.779.

William BORDESLEY [Bordysley, Borsley, Broddysley
occ. 1516 occ. 1540

1516, 17 May, ord acol., carnary chapel by Worcester cathedral, Reg. S. Gigli, 330.
1529/31, subcellarer, WCM C.414a, C.414b.
1530/2, *custos* of the Lady chapel, WCM C.414b, C.414c.
1532, 1533/4, chamberlain, *Jnl More*, 62, WCM C.415.
1540, 'steward', see below.

1521, 22 July, 29th in order on the visitation certificate, Reg. abp Warham ii, fo 293v.
1531/2, 23rd on the clerical subsidy list and, as *custos* of the Lady chapel, pd 53s. 4d. plus 3s. 4d. commons, Reg. A.12, fo 135.
1534, 17 Aug., subscribed to the Act of Supremacy, *DK 7th Report*, Appndx 2, 305.
1536, 13 Mar., 16th in order at the 'el.' of Henry Holbech, q.v., as prior, Reg. A.6(iii), fo 1.
1540, described on the pension list as 'steward of the household' and awarded £13 6s. 8d. p.a., *L and P Henry VIII*, xv, no 869.

BORTON
see Burton

Roger de BOSBURY [Bosebury
occ. 1337 occ. 1346/7

1337, 5 Apr., ord subdcn, Worcester cathedral Reg. Montacute, 108.
1337, 20 Sept., ord dcn, King's Norton chapel, Reg. Hemenhale, 36.
1337, 20 Dec., ord pr., Ombersley, *ib.*, 44.

1342, chaplain to the prior, Liber Albus, fo 175.

1338/9, student at Oxford for 48 wks, from Michaelmas to 10 Aug. and recd 64s. from the cellarer, WCM C.58.
1346/7, prob. student; the cellarer pd travelling expenses for him and for Stephen Tetbury, q.v., WCM C.61.
Note: The two cellarer's accts in the intervening years ref. to Oxford students but omit names.

1339, 12 Apr., one of the seven nominees for the the priorate, *Reg. Bransford*, no 38.

Thomas BOTELER [Botelar
occ. 1414/15

1414, 3 Mar., ord. acol., Worcester cathedral, Reg. Peverel, 198.
1415, 23 Mar., ord. subdcn, Dominican convent, Worcester, *ib.*, 203.
1415, 21 Sept., ord. dcn, Hartlebury, *ib.*, 206.

Simon le BOTILER [Botiller, Botyler
occ. 1302 d. 1339

1339 prior: apptd by the bp 12/13 Apr. *Reg. Bransford*, nos 38–40; d. 28 Oct., WCM C.298.

1302, 22 Sept., ord. dcn, [Worcester cathedral], *Reg. Sed. Vac.*, 24.

Before 1317, pittancer, WCM C.294.
1317, 20 Oct., 1320/1, kitchener, Liber Albus, fo 83, WCM C.55.
1322/3, prob. cellarer, with or after Roger de Styvynton, q.v., WCM C.545.
1333/4, cellarer, WCM C.799.
1339, 12 Apr., hostiller, *Reg. Bransford*, no 38.

1317, 20 Oct., 23rd in order at the el. of a prior; one of seven *compromissorii* chosen to nom. the seven candidates for the priorate, and one of the seven nom., Liber Albus, fo 83, 83v.
1317, 18 Nov., as one of the seven nominees for the priorate he was presented to the bp in Dartford parish church, Liber Albus, fos 83,84.
1319/20, stopped at King's Norton on his way back from St Botolph's fair, WCM C.693.
1319, 2 Nov., present with the prior to hear the accusation of the sacrist that the prior had alienated property in Shipston, WCM B.753.
1320/1, sent to buy cloth at St Botulph's fair, WCM C.55.
1338/9, went to London and was one of the monks involved in negotiations concerning the el. of Wulstan de Bransford, q.v. to the see, WCM C.58.
1339, 12 Apr., one of the seven nominees for the priorate, *Reg. Bransford*, no 38. The day of his installation as prior the cellarer pd for minstrels, WCM C.58.
1339, 28 Oct., d., WCM C.298.

Robert BOTER
occ. 1337 d.1339

1337, 5 Apr., ord. pr., Worcester cathedral, Reg. Montacute, 111.

1339, 29 Oct., d., WCM C.298.

John BOYDON
occ. 1423

1423, 3 Apr., ord. dcn, Worcester cathedral, Reg. Morgan, 201; possibly identical with John Clyfton, q.v.

BOYSIN
see Beycin

Bogo le BRACY
occ. 1317

1317, 20 Oct., 24th in order at the el. of a prior, Liber Albus, fo 83v.

John de BRADEFELD [Bratfeld
occ. 1371 d.1404/5

1371, 20 Dec., ord. acol., Worcester cathedral, Reg. Lynn, 54.
1377, 19 Sept., ord. pr., Tewkesbury abbey, *Reg. Wakefield*, no 873h.

1373, 4 Dec., 31st and last in order at the el. of a bp, *Reg. Sed. Vac.*, 290.
1388, 21 Aug., 26th at the el. of a prior, Liber Albus, fo 334^v.
1401, 24 June, 20th at the el. of a bp, *Reg. Sed. Vac.*, 373.
1404/5, d., and the chamberlain sold his *panni* and pd for the brief announcing his d., WCM C.50.

Nicholas de BRADEFELD [Bradisfeld
occ. 1314/15 occ. 1324

1314/15, pittancer, WCM C.581, C.296.
1318, 5 Dec., apptd *tumbarius*, *Reg. Cobham*, 13–14; the prior and chapter objected to the bp's right to make such an apptment, *ib.*
1317, 20 Oct., 19th in order at the el. of a prior, Liber Albus, fo 83^v.
1324, 29 Mar., witness to an incumbent's oath of office (for a parish church in Worcester), *ib.*, fo 115.

Thomas BRADEWAS [Bradwas, Bradwayes, Brodwas
occ. 1527 occ. 1536

1527, 6 Apr., ord. acol., carnary chapel by Worcester cathedral, Reg. Ghinucci 7(ii), 163.
1527, 19 Sept., ord. subdcn, Gloucester abbey, *ib.*, 7(ii), 167.
1532, 16 Mar., ord. dcn, carnary chapel by Worcester cathedral, *ib.*, 7(ii), 172.
1531/2, celebrated his first mass; received a pittance from the almoner, WCM C.414c.
1535, succentor, *L and P Henry VIII*, ix, no 653.
1525/6, 37th on the clerical subsidy list and pd 2s., Reg. A.12, fo 125.
1531/2, 37th on the second subsidy list, not a pr., and pd 2s., *ib.*, fo 135^v.
1534, 17 Aug., subscribed to the Act of Supremacy, *DK 7th Report*, Appndx 2, 305.
1535, signed the petition vs the reinstatement of William Fordham, q.v., as cellarer, *L and P Henry VIII*, ix, no 653.
1536, 13 Mar., 26th in order at the 'el.' of Henry Holbech, q.v. as prior, Reg. A.6(iii), fo 1.

W. de BRADEWAS
occ. 1218 occ. 1220

1218, apptd sacrist by the bp, *Ann. Wigorn.*, 410.
1221, removed from this office, *ib.*, 414; see Osbert.
1220, responsible for new bells which were consecrated by the bp, *Ann. Wigorn.*, 412.
Note: W. may be identical with Walter or William I below.

Walter de BRADEWAS
occ. 1202 occ. 1218

1202, went to Rome with Randulf de Evesham, q.v., to urge the canonization of bp Wulstan, *Ann. Wigorn.*, 391.
1218, 24 July, one of two monk proctors who recd from the king a licence to el. a bp, *CPR (1216–1225)*, 163; see Thomas de Lychfeld.

I William de BRADEWAS
occ. 1216

1216, prob. subprior (as William only), *Ann. Wigorn.*, 407.
1216, el. abbot of Alcester but the bp refused his consent; he then gave up his office of subprior in order to serve the bp [*ut adhaeret ei*] but became ill, *ib.*

II William de BRADEWAS [Bradeweie, Bradeweya
occ. 1266 [occ. 1269]

1266, 28 Feb., apptd proctor in the event that an appeal to Rome became necessary, Bloom, *Original Charters*, 175.
1267, [6 Mar.], one of the proctors for the chapter sent to the official of Canterbury concerning *sed. vac.* jurisdiction, WCM B.1614, and printed in Bloom, *Original Charters*, 176–177.
1268, [4 May], acting in the above appeal, *ib.*, WCM B.1619.
1268, 5 Aug., acting as proctor as above, *ib.*, WCM B.1639.
[1269], 18 Apr., apptd prior of Little Malvern by the bp, *Reg. Giffard*, 7.
Note: the prior of Little Malvern by this name may not have previously been a monk of Worcester, but the odds are in favour.

BRADISFELD
see Bradefeld

BRADEL', Brandisle
see Barndesley

Wulstan de BRANSFORD [Branesford, Braunceford
occ. 1310 occ. 1339

1317–1339, prior: chosen by the bp 21/23 Nov. 1317, Liber Albus, fo 84, 84^v (*Fasti*, iv, 59), el. bp 3/4 Jan. 1339; see below.
[1308, Jan.], the prior provided letters testimonial for Wulstan, clerk, son of John de Braunceford, former citizen of Worcester, *Reg. Sed. Vac.*, 88.
1308, 23 Nov., dcn, provided with *lit. dim.* for priest's orders, *Reg. Reynolds*, 92.
1310, 20 Sept., one of two whose prof. the bp [Walter Reynolds] recd on the day of his enthronement as bp, Liber Albus, fo 45^v.
1313, 5 Apr., chaplain to the prior, Liber Albus, fo 58.
1313/14, went to London on chapter business with John de Stratforde I, q.v., and their expenses were pd by the cellarer, WCM C.482.

1317, 20 Oct., 34th in order at the el. of a prior and one of the seven nominees for the priorate, Liber Albus, fo 83v. On 18 Nov., he was one of the seven candidates presented to the bp at Dartford in the parish church, *ib.*, fo 84.
1318/19, stayed at Grimley on ?eight occasions [*per viij billa*], and the manorial acct was charged 10s. 5d., WCM C.583.
1319/20, visited King's Norton, WCM C.693.
1319, 4 Nov., accused by the sacrist of alienating property in Shipston, WCM B.753.
1327/8, visited Stoke [Prior], and in 1327 King's Norton, WCM C.546a, C.693b.
1327, between 31 Aug. and 8 Sept., el. bp, but Adam Orleton was provided; see *Fasti*, iv, 56.
1328/9, went to Tibberton, where a new ordinance of the prior and auditors concerning the supply of animal stock was inserted in the bailiff's acct, WCM C.798.
1329/30, visited Cleeve Prior, WCM C.557.
1331/2, visited King's Norton, WCM C.694.
1334, 11 Mar, apptd vicar general by the bp, Reg. Montacute, 3.
1334/5, pd two visits to Tibberton, [*ij billa*], WCM C.564.
1336/7, visited Moor [Lindridge], WCM C.646.
1337, 3 Apr., apptd as one of three vicars general, Reg. Hemenhale, 5.
1337, 10 July, licensed, with other monks, to hear confessions within the adcnry of Worcester, Reg. Hemenhale, 12.
1337/8, visited Bromsgrove, WCM C.547.
1339, [5 Jan], on the octave of the Holy Innocents, el. bp, Worcs. Ms F.141; see below. Acc. to *Reg. Sed. Vac.* 259, 268, the date was 4 Jan.

Name in Worcs. Ms F.141, Guido de Baysio etc. (14th c.), on the inside of the back cover of which there is a letter describing his el. as bp on 5 Jan. 1339; the writer was Henry Fouke, q.v.

His *acta* are preserved in the Liber Albus, fos 83–162v.

Family connections, see above.

BRAVONIUS
see Senatus

BREERHULL, Brerhill
see Bryorhull

BREMESGRAVE, Bremesgrove
see Bromesgrove

BREMWYK
see Bromwych

Richard de BRETHENE
d. 1219

1219, d., *Ann. Wigorn.*, 411.

BREVEL
see Saint Briavel

John de BRIERA [Bruera
occ. 1296 occ. 1317

1314, 29 Mar., removed from the office of *tumbarius*, Reg. Maidstone, 5.
1296, 11 July, one of the seven nominees for the priorate, *Reg. Giffard*, 480.
1317, 20 Oct., 4th in order at the el. of a prior, Liber Albus fo 83v.

Richard BRIGGE [Brugg'
occ. 1404 d. 1409/10

1404, 20 Sept., ord dcn, Llanthony priory, Gloucester, *Reg. Clifford*, no 122, p. 86.
1405, 19 Sept., ord pr., Cirencester abbey, *ib.*, no 126, p. 94.
1404/5, celebrated his first mass; received ale from the cellarer, *exennia* from the almoner and a pittance from the precentor, WCM C.78, C.187, C.372 (1405/6).
1409/10, d., and the almoner bought bread [for the poor] on the day of his funeral, WCM C.189.

William BRISTOW
occ. 1430

?1430, 22 Sept., ord acol., Withington, Reg. Polton, 234; the date reads 1431.
1430, 23 Dec., ord subdcn, Alvechurch, *ib.*, 215; in both cases he was presented by John Hembury, q.v.

BROCTON
see Broghton

BRODDYSLEY
see Bordesley

BRODUWAS
see Bradewas

John BROGHTON [Brocton, Broghtone, Broughton, Browhgton
occ. 1428 d. 1449

1428, 28 Sept., ord acol., Worcester [cathedral], Reg. Polton, 100.
1429/30, celebrated his first mass; received *exennia* from the hostiller, WCM C.231.
1432, Oct./1435, Oct., chaplain to the prior, Liber Albus, fo 440.
1444/5, steward of the prior's hospice, WCM C.493; see also William Hodynton II.
1435/6, student at Oxford, and the cellarer pd for the transporting of his bedding and books there and back, and for the maintenance of two monk students £12, WCM C.88; see Hugh Leyntewardine.
1438, 14 Feb., student at Oxford, Reg. Bourgchier, 84.
[1444/5], the cellarer pd the expenses of his return from Oxford with his belongings, WCM C.493; on this acct there is ref. to

'materie pend' inter fratrem J. Broughton [q.v.] et Kanturmaynes'; see Thomas Hosyntre.

1431, recd 3s. 3d. for *minutiones* from the cellarer, WCM, c. 86a.

1433, 9 Dec., 40th in order at the el. of a bp, *Reg. Sed. Vac.*, 432.

1438, 13 Feb., comm. as proctor to present the seven nominees for the priorate to the bp, Liber Albus, fo 457; on the following day he and Thomas Lylleshull, q.v., presented them to the bp at Alvechurch, Reg. Bourgchier, 84.

1438, 11 Apr., comm as proctor for convocation, *ib.*, fo 457v.

1444, 15/16 Jan., one of two proctors who presented the seven nominees for the priorate to the bp, Reg. Bourgchier, 193–195; see Richard Tyberton.

1449, before Easter, d., and the cellarer pd the almoner 26s. for his corrody for half the yr, WCM C.91; the almoner also distributed 12d. worth of bread to the poor on the day of his d. or burial, *ib.*, and the precentor pd for the brief announcing his d., WCM C.379 (1449/50).

Name in Worcs. Mss:

(1) F.86, Walter Burley etc. (15th c.) on the first flyleaf; see Richard Barndesley.

(2) F.118, Logicalia quedam etc. (14th/15th c.), on fo 111; I owe this information to Prof. Rodney Thomson who suggests that Broghton may have himself written fos 108–111. See John Benet and Thomas More II.

(3) Q.27, J. Wallensis (14th c.); on fo 2 there is a list of 30 vols which John Lawerne I, q.v., prob. had with him at Oxford. There are two other monks' names heading the list, one being Isaac Ledbury, q.v., and the other almost certainly this monk, but the writing is only partly legible. It is worth noting that a copy of Walter Burley, very likely Ms F.86, is one of the titles on the list.

Thomas de BROGHTON [Brocton, Brokton, Brouhton, Browhton

occ. 1391 occ. 1412

1391, 22 Feb., one of two whose prof. the prior was comm. to rec., *Reg. Wakefield*, no 580.

1391, 20 May, ord acol. and subdcn, Bredon, *ib.*, no 958b and d.

1391/2, was prob. one of three poor novices to whom the almoner gave 20s. *in primo ingressu*, WCM C.181.

1392, 9 Mar., ord dcn, bp's chapel, Hartlebury, *ib.*, no 971c; 1392, 19 May, given *lit. dim.* for pr's orders, *ib.*, no 966.

1392, 8 June, ord pr., Bromyard, *Reg. Trefnant* (Hereford), 201; also WCM C.76.

1391/2, celebrated his first mass; recd *exennia* from the almoner and hostiller, WCM C.181, C.215.

1392/3, described by the chamberlain as a novice, WCM C.20.

1401, 24 June, chaplain [to the prior], *Reg. Sed. Vac.*, 373.

1401/3, subcellarer, WCM C.681, C.712 (entered as T.B.).

1408, June/1410, kitchener, WCM C.135, C.135a, C.612.

1411, June/1412, precentor, WCM C.373, C.374.

1401, 24 June, 34th in order at the el of a bp, *Reg. Sed. Vac.*, 373.

1401, 4 July, as commissary of the prior, with a secular clerk, visited the deanery of Kidderminster, *sed. vac.*, *ib.*, 383. On 22 Aug. he was witness to an exchange of churches, *ib.*, 379.

Name in Worcs. Ms F.125, Summa Ranfredi (14th c.), *tradatur* [to]—precentor.

BROGHTON

see also Broughton

Philip de la BROKE [Brock

occ. 1332 occ. 1344/5

1332, 18 Apr., ord dcn, Beckford, *Reg. Orleton*, no 25 (p.40).

1343/5, subcellarer, WCM C.434, C.584, C.648.

1343/4, pd a supervisory visit to Grimley, WCM C.584.

1344/5, pd supervisory visit to Moor [Lindridge], WCM C.648.

BROKTON

see Broughton

John de BROMESGROVE [Bremesgrove, Bromesgrave

occ. 1298/9 occ. 1306

1298/9, attended the abp's council [in London] and the Black Monk Chapter, Northampton, WCM C.54; see also Gilbert de Madley and William de Grymeley.

1302, 30 Jan., apptd by the prior and conv., *sed. vac.*, with a secular clerk, general proctors, *Liber Albus*, no 73.

1302, 18 Feb., the abp authorized the prior at his discretion to remove the penance imposed by the abp on Bromesgrove, during his recent visitation, if there were signs of amendment, Liber Albus, fo 11v.

1302, 17/19 Feb., acted as proctor for the prior in obtaining from the abp the prior's apptment as official *sed. vac.*, WCM B.1621a, printed in Haines, *Administration of Worcs.*, 346.

1302, 2 Mar., apptd by the prior to visit Alvechurch, *sed. vac.*, *Liber Albus*, no 104.

1302, 3 Nov., witness to a bond, *Reg. Sed. Vac.*, 29.

1302, 23 Dec., on the submission of the prior to the bp's ordinance, he renounced, in the name of the chapter, all appeals vs. the [new] bp's rights especially any for which he, himself

might have been or might be responsible, *Reg. Gainsborough*, 3.
Note: John de Saint Germans, q.v., had been unsuccessfully el. bp by the monks; see also Gilbert de Madley.
1303, 30 May, apptd proctor, with another, to acct to the abp for the revenues of the diocese during the vacancy, *Reg. Sed. Vac.*, 52.
1304, 16 Sept., apptd proctor, with another monk, to attend the Black Monk Chapter, Westminster, Pantin, *BMC*, i, 162.
1305, 14 Feb., apptd by the prior as proctor in parliament for the adcn of Worcester (an absentee Italian cardinal), *Liber Albus*, no 284. Prob. this same yr he was apptd to act with Gilbert de Madley, q.v., in negotiations concerning the appropriation of the church of Dodderhill, *Liber Albus*, no 286.
1306, 13 May, apptd proctor in the protest vs. the new abbot of Gloucester, Liber Albus, fo 26; see Nicholas de Coderugge.

Richard BROMESGROVE [Bromysgrave
occ. 1448 d. 1500/1

1448, 14 Sept., one of six whose prof. the prior was comm. to rec., Reg. Carpenter, i, 132.
1449, 12 Apr., ord acol. and subdcn, carnary chapel by Worcester cathedral, *ib.*, i, 524.
1450, 4 Apr., ord dcn, bp's chapel, Hartlebury, *ib.*
1453, 31 Mar., ord pr., carnary chapel, *ib.*, i, 535.
1452/3, celebrated his first mass; the chamberlain and almoner sent gifts, WCM C.42, C.200c.

1456/7, subcellarer, WCM C.732.
1459,60, 1461/2, pittancer, WCM C.491, C.731, C.733; in 1461/2 he may have been acting with or for John Webley q.v.

1456/7, pd a supervisory visit to Overbury, WCM C.732.
1478/9, gave 6s. 4d. in alms to the almoner, WCM C.204.
1481/2, given 5s. by the precentor for the binding of five psalters and of *lib[ri] magistri histor[iarum]*, WCM C.385.
1498, 25 Oct., 5th in order on the visitation certificate, *Reg. abp Morton*, ii, no 458.
1500/1, d. and the almoner gave small sums to the friars [to pray] for his soul, WCM C.210.

Hugh BROMSGROVE [Bromisgrove, Bromysgrove
c. 1524/5 occ. 1535

1524/5, celebrated his first mass; recd pittances from the almoner and precentor, WCM C.414.

1531/2, succentor, Reg. A.12, fo 135.

1521, 22 July, 38th in order on the visitation certificate, Reg. abp Warham ii, fo 293v.
1525/6, 29th on the clerical subsidy list and pd 3s. 4d., Reg. A.12, fo 125.
1531/2, 29th on the second subsidy list, and as succentor (*subpresentor*), pd 20d. plus 3s. 4d. commons, *ib.*, fo 135.
*c.*1532, Feb., recd a letter from Robert Joseph, monk of Evesham, H. Aveling and W. Pantin, eds, *The letter Book of Robert Joseph, Monk-Scholar of Evesham and Gloucester College, Oxford, 1530–3* Oxford 1967, no 164.
1534, 17 Aug., subscribed to the Act of Supremacy, *DK 7th Report*, Appndx 2, 305.
1535, 11 Nov., sought permission to leave the monastery and obtain a benefice in the gift of the chapter; Roger Neckham, q.v, wrote to Cromwell to ask his advice, *L and P Henry VIII*, ix, no 807.

John de BROMWYCH
occ. [1369] d. [1370/1]

[1369], 1 Oct., one of seven whose prof. the precentor was comm. to rec., Reg. Lynn, 89.
1370, 21 Dec., ord subdcn, Hartlebury, *ib.*, 53.

[1370/1], d. and the chamberlain sold his *panni*, WCM C.497.

Richard de BROMWYCH D.Th. [Bremwyk, Bromwico
occ. 1301 occ. 1337 ?1349

1317, c. 20 Apr., precentor, *Reg. Sed. Vac.*, 179–180; and on 20 Oct., Liber Albus, fo 83.
1317/18, lector at Worcester, see below.
1320, 2 June, precentor, *Reg. Cobham*, 25.

1302, late, or early 1303, prob. student at Oxford when he sent news to the prior of the resignation of John de Saint Germans bp. el. (q.v.) in Rome and of the provision of William de Gainsborough, *Reg. Sed. Vac.*, 31–32.
c.1305, before, prob. at Oxford as he now obtained his first degree and lectured on the Sentences; see Little and Pelster, *Oxford Theology*, 240–246, where it is noted (on 246) that he had prob. studied at Paris with his fellow monk Saint Germans (q.v.). See also J. I. Catto, *The History of the University of Oxford*, i. *The Early Oxford Schools*, (Oxford, 1984), 513, for a brief summary of his theological views.
1305 × 1312, D.Th., Little and Pelster, *Oxford Theology*, *ib.*; see *BRUO* for further refs.
1301, 18 July, one of the seven nominees for the priorate, *Reg. Giffard*, 547.
1302, 25 Mar., one of seven *compromissorii* in the el. of a bp., and also acted, on 29 Mar. as one of several proctors in announcing the el., *Reg. Sed. Vac.*, 1–2.
1307, 15 Nov., apptd with two other monks to inform Walter Reynolds that the chapter had el. him bp, *Reg. Sed. Vac.*, 108.
1313/14, visited Dore abbey and gave the abbot a saddle, Wilson, *Early Comp. Rolls*, 38, 39 (WCM C.482); he also journeyed to Ludlow this yr with John de Stratford I, q.v., *ib.*
1314, 24 Jan., addressed as 'professor of sacred

theology' and apptd by the prior, *sed. vac.*, to visit in the diocese, *Reg. Sed. Vac.*, 142, 169.

1315, 16 Sept., named as proctor to attend the Black Monk Chapter, Northampton, *Liber Albus*, no 660.

c. 1317/18 and possibly earlier, lecturing to the monks (?and others) at Worcester; see Pantin, *BMC*, i, 181–4, and under Ranulph de Calthrop below.

1317, 20 Oct., 13th in order at the el. of a prior, and one of seven *compromissorii* to select the seven nominees for the priorate, Liber Albus, fo 83. On 18 Nov., he was one of the seven candidates presented to the bp at Dartford in the parish church, *ib.*, fo 84.

1318/19, apptd by the Black Monk Chapter as monastic visitor of Benedictine houses, and he requested the presidents to provide for his travelling expenses, Pantin, *BMC*, i, 186 (*Liber Albus*, no 848).

1319/20, pd two visits to King's Norton, WCM C.693.

1320, 4 Oct., licensed by the prior to become prior of Abergavenny in place of a dissolute prior, and absolved from his obedience to Worcester, Liber Albus, fo 98.

1325, the prior and chapter requested his return as he was urgently required as lecturer; they offered generous terms to him and a corrody for his brother Henry to come to serve his needs, Liber Albus, fo 123v.

1327, 1331/2, pd visits to King's Norton, WCM C.693b, C.694.

1334/5, pd two visits to King's Norton and preached there on the first Sunday in Lent, WCM C.695.

1337, May/Sept., visited Tibberton and ate goose, WCM C.832.

Name in a number of Mss:

(1) Oxford, Bod. Ms 442, Hilary of Poitiers (12th c.); he passed it on to Philip de Lusteshall, q.v. (under Winchester); on the front flyleaf: 'pro uno parvo libello distinctionum super psalterium, et tabula super originalibus sancti Augustini'.

(2) Worcs. Ms F.62, Summa confessorum (early 14th c.), which was sold to Henry Fouke, q.v.

(3) Worcs. Ms F.63, Aristoteles (13th/14th c.); there is a *caucio* at the end: 1305, *tradatur*—and a later *caucio* ref. to John de Westbury, q.v.

(4) Worcs. Ms F.79, Henry of Ghent (13th/14th c.).

(5) Worcs. Ms F.101, Thomas Aquinas (early 14th c.), see also Alexander de Sprowston in the Norwich section.

(6) Worcs. Ms F.139, 'lectura quam fecit fr.—et scripsit manu sua super quatuor libros sententiarum antequam legit librum sentenciarum, Oxon'. [On fo 8v there is an insertion which suggests that Ranulph de Calthorp, q.v., incepted under Bromwych; see Little and Pelster, Oxford Theology, 239]. He passed this volume on to Henry Fouke, q.v., for 20s.; see Sharpe, *Latin Writers*.

(7) Worcs. Ms F.156, Tabula juris (14th c.), a ms which *fecit scribere*; see *MLGB*.

A Richard de Bromwych was one of bp Bransford's executors in 1349, Reg. Thoresby, 11.

?T. de Whateleye, possibly his father, is mentioned in Liber Albus, fo 88.

William BROUGHTON [Brokton, Browhcton, Browhgton

occ. 1419 d. 1432/3

1420, Apr./1429, *custos* of the Lady chapel, WCM C.271–277.

1430/31, kitchener, WCM C.144.

1419, 24 Apr., 24th in order at the el. of a bp, *Reg. Sed. Vac.*, 407.

1432/3, d. and the chamberlain sold *diversis rebus* of his, WCM C.37.

BROUGHTON

see also Broghton

BRUERA

see Briera

BRUGG

see Brigg

Alexander de BRYORHULL [Breerhull, Brerhill]

occ. 1305 occ. 1327

1305, 4 Jan., one of four *clerici* presented to the bp at the time of his adm., *Reg. Gainsborough*, 14.

1308, 25 Oct., given *lit. dim.* for dcn's orders, Reg. Reynolds, 92.

1309, 24 May, ord dcn, Cirencester, *ib.*, 111.

1309, 3 Dec., given *lit. dim.* for pr.'s orders, *ib.*, 93.

n.d. former subcellarer, WCM E.16, item 5.

1317, 20 Oct., 33rd in order at the el. of a prior, and with John de Saint Briavel (q.v.) visited monks in the infirmary beforehand to ascertain whether or not they would be present, Liber Albus, fo 83.

1326/7, 1328/9, pd visits to Bromsgrove and his expenses were charged to the acct there [?perhaps as subcellarer], WCM C.544, C.546.

1327, stopped at King's Norton, WCM C.693b.

John BURTONE

occ. 1429

1429, 26 Mar., ord dcn, carnary chapel by Worcester cathedral, Reg. Polton, 125.

William BURTON [Borton

occ. 1498

1498, 14 Apr., ord subdcn, carnary chapel by Worcester cathedral, Reg. G. Gigli, 26.

1498/9, celebrated his first mass; received a pittance from the hostiller, WCM C.238.

1498, 25 Oct., 39th in order on the visitation certificate, *Reg. abp Morton*, ii, no 458.

BUSCHEL'
see Bisseleye

Thomas BYLFORD
occ. 1482/3

1482/3, celebrated his first mass; received *exennia* from the precentor, WCM C.386.

BYSSHAMPTON
see Bishampton

Richard CALAMAN [Kalaman
occ. 1504 occ. 1540

1504, 6 Apr., ord acol., carnary chapel by Worcester cathedral, Reg. S. Gigli, 287.
1504, 21 Sept., ord subdcn, carnary chapel, *ib.*, 289.
1504, 21 Dec., ord dcn, hospital of St Wulstan, Worcester, *ib.*, 291.
1508, 17 June, ord pr., carnary chapel, *ib.*, 299.
1508, before 29 Sept., celebrated his first mass; recd a pittance of 2s. from the hostiller, WCM C.240.

1516, refectorer, Reg. A.12, fo 46v.
1520/1, *tumbarius*, Reg. A.17, 64, Reg. abp Warham, ii, fo 293v.
1521, 22 July, chaplain [to the prior], *ib.*, ii, fo 293v.
1521/5, 1529/32, chamberlain, WCM C.412; Reg. A.17, 203; WCM C.413 and Reg. A.17, 268; WCM E.265; WCM C.414a; C.414b; 414c. *Jnl More*, 30–44 implies that he was 'chamberer' more or less continuously between 1523 and 1527.
1530/1, *magister communis cene*, WCM C.414b.
1531/2, kitchener, WCM C.414c.
1533, [Oct.], 'tyse' [third] prior, *Jnl More*, 376.

1521, 22 July, 13th in order on the visitation certificate, Reg. abp Warham ii, fo 293v.
1531/2, 13th on the clerical subsidy list and pd £5 [as chamberlain] and 3s. 4d. 'commons', Reg. A.12, fo 135.
1534, 17 Aug., subscribed to the Act of Supremacy, *DK 7th Report*, Appndx 2, 305.
1535, did not sign the petition vs the reinstatement of William Fordham, q.v., *L and P Henry VIII*, ix, no 653.
1536, 13 Mar., 7th in order at the 'el.' of Henry Holbech, q.v. as prior, Reg. A.6(iii), fo 1.
1540, 18 Jan., assigned a pension of £6 p.a., L *and P Henry VIII*, xv, no 81.

Ranulph de CALTHROP, D.Th.
[Calthorpe, Cathrop *alias* Scot
occ. 1301 occ. [1321]

1301, 1 Mar., a testimonial letter on behalf of Ranulph de Calthorp, monk of Worcester, was issued by the bp of Lincoln at the request of his friends. It stated that, as the result of an inquiry, it had been established that he was both free and legitimate, the son of Thomas *dictus* Scot and his wife Custanc' of Calthorpe [Oxfordshire], Little and Pelster, *Oxford Theology*, 238–239 (from the reg. of bp Dalderby, Lincoln).

[1321], apptd sacrist by the bp to succeed Roger de Hervyngton, q.v., *Reg. Cobham*, 112.

1304, 20 Aug., the bp urged the prior to send him away to study and offered [financial] assistance, *Liber Albus*, no 253.
1312/13, prob. student at Oxford, and with John de Saint Germans, q.v., recd a pension from the chamberlain, WCM C.8. The cellarer contributed £4 for debts arising out of the cost of his inception, C.482.
1312, 30 Sept., the prior gave permission for him to take the oath required at the time of inception, *Liber Albus*, no 552, and transcribed in full in Leach, *Education in Worcs.*, 35. See also the note under Worcs. Ms F.139 in the entry under Richard de Bromwych who may have prepared him for his inception.
1308, Jan., with John de Stratford I, q.v. apptd by the prior as his commissaries, *sed. vac.*, to visit St Augustine's abbey, Bristol, *Reg. Sed. Vac.*, 117.
1317, 20 Oct., 14th in order at the el. and one of seven *compromissorii* chosen to name the seven candidates for the office of prior, Liber Albus, fo 83; he is described as *sacre theologie professor*.
1318, Dec., recalled by the prior from Ramsey abbey where he had been lector in theology; the correspondence between the abbot of Ramsey and the prior concerning his return and expressing the abbot's irritation has been printed in Pantin, *BMC*, i, 181–186 (from the Liber Albus, fo 91).
1319/20, pd two [supervisory] visits to King's Norton, WCM C.693.
[1321], as sacrist, recd a comm. from the bp to be one of two officials to examine a case of adultery, *Reg. Cobham*, 112.

Name in two Worcs. Mss:
(1) F.124, Interpretatio nominum hebraicorum etc. (13th/14th c.), which he gave to Henry Fouke q.v. acc. to a note on fo 60 where an unnamed treatise begins.
(2) F.139 as above, under Richard de Bromwych.

Details of his family background are given above.

CALYS
see Colys

CANTOR
see William III

Nicholas CASSY
occ. 1361 occ. 1364

1361, 13 Mar., ord acol., Hartlebury, Reg. Bryan i, 121.

1361, 22 May, ord subdcn, Alvechurch, *ib.*
1361, 18 Sept., ord dcn., Alvechurch, *ib.*, 123.
1364, 26 Dec., ord pr. by *lit. dim.*, Bromyard, *Reg. Lewis Charlton* (Hereford), 93.

Nicholas CASTEL
see Clanefeld

CATHROP
see Calthrop

Ralph ?CAUR'
[?1260 × 1270]
[?1260 × 1270], prob. subcellarer, WCM E.4(6).

Richard CAYNHAM
occ. 1363
1363, 23 Sept., ord subdcn, Lydney, *Reg. Lewis Charlton* (Hereford), 87.

Walter de CESTR'
occ. 1274
1274, 20 Sept., one of five monks chosen by the chapter as *compromissorii* for the purpose of selecting the seven candidates for the office of prior, *Reg. Giffard*, 62.

CESTR'
see also Chester

Thomas de CHELTENHAM [Chiltenham
occ. 1302 occ. 1317
1302, 20 Jan., the bp informed the prior that, although he had been unjustly accused of incontinence at the recent visitation, he had been cleared, Liber Albus, fo 13.
1317, 20 Oct., 8th in order at the el. of a prior, Liber Albus, fo 83^{v}.

Henry CHESTER [Chestor, Chestre, Chestur
occ. 1488 occ. 1519
1488, 5 Apr., ord subdcn, Worcester cathedral, Reg. Morton, 139.
1492, 22 Sept., ord pr., carnary chapel by Worcester cathedral, *ib.*, 157.
1493/4, 1495/6, subcellarer, WCM C.452, C.626.
1495/6, kitchener, WCM C.165.
1496/7, prob. cellarer, WCM C.669.
1497/8, cellarer, WCM C.667, C.781.
1498/9, one of two cellarers, WCM C.627; see John Stratford III.
1516, infirmarer, Reg. A.12, fo 42.
[1492 × 1499], the prior recorded complaints vs him and two other monks (Edmund Ledbury and Thomas Stafford, q.v.) accusing them of being involved in an unlawful assembly with a William Budon, WCM D.336.
1493/4, pd a visit to Grimley, WCM C.588.
1496/7, visited Newnham for *liberatio denariorum*, WCM C.669.
1497/8, visited Newnham and Sedgeberrow, WCM C.667, C.781.
1498, 27 June, sent as proctor to the Black Monk Chapter meeting at Coventry, Pantin, *BMC*, iii, 217 (from Reg. A.6(i) fo 122).
1498, 2 Oct., present in court to hear a case between the king and the prior, William Wenlok, q.v., WCM B.1063.
1498, 25 Oct., 26th in order on the visitation certificate, *Reg. abp Morton*, ii, no 458.
1498/9, visited Harvington, WCM C.627.
1519, 31 Jan., the prior addressed a letter to the bp of Llandaff concerning his transfer [*migratio*] to Chepstow, Reg. A.6(ii), fo 115.

John CICESTRE [Ciscetr', Cisetur, Syssetter
occ. 1481 d. 1500/1
1481, 16 June, ord acol., Whitbourne, *Reg. Milling* (Hereford), 163.
1481, 22 Sept., ord. subdcn, Whitbourne, *ib.*, 164.
1481, 22 Dec., ord dcn, Hartlebury, Reg. Alcock, 265.
1498, 25 Oct., 16th in order on the visitation certificate, *Reg. abp Morton*, ii, no 458 (transcribed as Sylsetter).
1500/1, d., and the almoner gave the [Worcester] Dominicans 20s. [to say mass] for his soul, WCM C.210.

Adam de CIRENCESTER [Cyrencestre, Cyrencestria, alias Dymhok
occ. 1302 occ. 1317
Between 1302 and 1305, chaplain to the prior as follows: 1302, [25 Mar], *Reg. Sed. Vac.*, 79; also 1303, 12 Feb., *ib.*, 38; 1303 (no month) *ib.*, 43; also 1304 and 1305, *Liber Albus*, in the headings above nos. 171 and 358.
1302, 3 Nov., witness to a bond, *Reg. Sed. Vac.*, 29.
[1303], 12 Feb., present in the prior's chamber at the reading of the abp's letter concerning the new bp, *Reg. Sed. Vac.*, 38.
1304, wrote to the abbot of Cirencester to thank him for lessening his sorrow by honouring his father with *solempnes exequias*, Liber Albus, fo 18^{v}; see below. The prior also wrote to thank the abbot, *ib.*
1315, 27 May, present on the occasion of the prior's *creatio* of a notary, Liber Albus, fo 66^{v}.
1317, 20 Oct., 20th in order at the el. of a prior, Liber Albus, fo 83^{v}.

In 1303, on 27 Dec., His father, Robert Dymhok of Cirencester, d., *Liber Albus*, no 147.

I William de CIRENCESTER [Cirencestr', Cyrencestr'
occ. 1266 d. 1274
1272–1274, prior: apptd by the bp, 21 Dec. 1272; d. by 20 Sept. 1274, *Fasti*, ii, 104.
1266, 21 Feb., precentor, *CPR (1258–1266)*, 559.

1272, before 21 Dec., sacrist, *Reg. Giffard*, 50.

1266, 21 Feb., one of three convent proctors who recd licence to el. a bp from the king at Westminster, *CPR (1258–1266)*, 559.

1272, before 21 Dec., one of the seven candidates for the office of prior, *Reg. Giffard*, 51.

II William de CIRENCESTER [Circestr', Cirencestr'

occ. 1343 occ. 1346/7

1343, 20 Sept., ord pr., Bishops Cleeve, *Reg. Bransford*, no 1054.

1346/7, visited Overbury, WCM C.699.

CIRENCESTER

see also Sircestr'

CISETUR

see Cicestre

Nicholas de CLANEFELD [Clanfeld ?alias Castel

occ. 1337 occ. 1361

1337, 5 Apr., ord subdcn, Worcester cathedral, Reg. Montacute, 108.

1337, 20 Sept., ord dcn, King's Norton chapel, Reg. Hemenhale, 36.

1337, 20 Dec., ord pr., Ombersley, *ib.*, 44.

1340, chaplain to the prior, Liber Albus, fo 164.

1344/5, 1346/7, Nov. to Nov., kitchener, WCM C.59, C.112.

1349/50, pittancer, WCM C.292, and during the year he was again assigned to the office of kitchener, succeeding 'R' [who may have d. of the plague], WCM C.692.

1351/2, pittancer, WCM C.293.

1341, [Sept.], apptd by the prior and chapter as one of two proctors and attorneys responsible for the collection and payment of tenths, Liber Albus, fo 171v.

1347/8, visited Harvington for *liberatio denariorum*, WCM C.607.

1349, 10 Sept., as one of two commissaries apptd by the prior, *sed. vac.*, visited clergy and people in the deanery of Kidderminster; on 11 Sept. they visited the deanery of Wych; on 14 Sept. they visited the monastery and deanery of Pershore; on 17 Sept. they visited the abbey at Alcester, and they continued their visitation in the deaneries of Warwick and Kington, followed by the hospitals of St Oswald and St Wulstan in Worcester, and, finally, the priory of Little Malvern on 28 Sept., *Reg. Sed. Vac.*, 250–251.

1349/50, pd a [supervisory] visit to Harvington, WCM C.692.

1350, 10 Dec., with Robert de Weston and Walter de Wynforton, q.v., given letters of attorney by the prior, John de Evesham I, q.v., prob. because the prior was going to Avignon, Bloom, *Liber Ecclesiae*, 51 where the yr is 1351 in both printed calendar and ms (PRO E315/63, fo 58v–59); but see John de Evesham I, under 1350 and 1351.

1351/2, with Robert de Morton, q.v., visited the Hermitage of Little Packington, Warwickshire (which was acctd for by the pittancer), to collect tenths, WCM C.293.

1351, 23 Jan., granted papal licence to choose his own confessor, *CPL*, iii (1342–1362), 452.

1354, 24 Feb., apptd proctor for the prior and chapter in their dispute with the bp over his choice of John de Powick, q.v., as sacrist, Liber Albus, fo 237v; during the course of this controversy one of the legal instruments was issued by Nicholas Castel, proctor, *ib.*, fo 239.

1356/7, visited Overbury for *liberatio denariorum*, WCM C.705; he also went to Gloucester and Newnham for 'negotiations', and to London where he spent nine days *circa tractat[us] inter episcopum et priorem*, WCM C.63. See John de Evesham I.

1358/9, with Thomas Talbot, q.v., stopped at Dodderhill on his way to [?Great] Hampton [?Lucy], WCM C.835.

1360, 16 Aug., comm. by the bp to raise and collect procurations for the cardinals, Reg. Bryan, i, 213.

1361, 9 Mar., went to Alvechurch to present two clerks to the bp for adm. as monks, *ib.*, i, 136.

Simon CLARE

occ. 1464 d. 1486/7

1464, 8 June, one of six whose prof. the bp comm. the prior to rec., Reg. A.6(i), fo 34.

1465, 9 Mar., ord subdcn, St Nicholas' church, Worcester, Reg. Carpenter, i, 562.

1465, 21 Dec., ord dcn, bp's chapel, Alvechurch, *ib.*, i, 564.

1468, 17 Dec., ord pr., St Nicholas' church, *ib.*, i, 573.

1468/9, celebrated his first mass; recd gifts from both the almoner and the kitchener, WCM C.202, C.154.

1486/7, d. and the almoner distributed 2s. 6d. in alms to the poor, WCM C.207.

Richard CLARELEYE [Clarel', Claresley

occ. 1378 occ. 1392/3

1378, 26 Aug., one of two novices whose prof. [*vota*] the bp comm. the prior to rec., Liber Albus, fo 274.

1379, 26 Mar., ord acol., Kidderminster, *Reg. Wakefield*, no 876b.

1380, 19 May, ord subdcn, Bromyard, *Reg. Gilbert* (Hereford), 145.

1382, 19 Sept., recd *lit. dim.*, from the bp for the order of pr., *Reg. Wakefield*, no 896.

1382, 20 Sept., ord pr. Bromyard, *Reg. Gilbert* (Hereford), 152 (misread as 'Garley).

1382/3, celebrated his first mass; the prior gave twelve gallons of ale and the almoner 3s.

towards the celebration of this event, WCM C.70, C.177.

1388, 21 Aug., 33rd in order at the el. of a prior, Liber Albus, fo 334[v].

1392, 29 Sept., owed 6s. 8d. by the cellarer, WCM C.75.

1392/3, ?d. or was absent, as the pittancer's allowance pd to him was less than to the others *quia . . . nullum habuit de termino Michaelmas*, WCM C.316.

CLEMENS [Clement

occ. c. 1104

Name occ. in the list of monks in *Durham Liber Vitae*, fo 22.

Dr Mason suggests that his father was Saulf (or Saewulf, Siword) monk and *conversus*, *Wulfstan*, 188; see Saeuvard.

Thomas CLENT

occ. 1420

1420, 2 Mar., ord acol., Worcester cathedral, Reg. Morgan, 59.

1420, between 2 Mar. and 29 Sept., d., and the chamberlain sold his bedding/clothing [*pannis*], WCM C.32.

John de CLEVE [Cliva, Clyffe, Clyve

occ. 1387 d. 1436/7

1387, 2 Mar., ord dcn, Hartlebury, *Reg. Wakefield*, no 913e.

1388, 7 Sept., granted *lit. dim.*, for priest's orders, *ib.*, no 934.

1388, 19 Sept., ord pr., Hereford cathedral, Reg. Gilbert (Hereford), fo 96[v]; the printed reg. has transcribed the name as Clone (182).

1392, 4 Mar., apptd chaplain to the prior, Liber Albus, fo 359.

1395, 12 Mar. and 19 Sept., cellarer, *Reg. Sed. Vac.*, 353 and Liber Albus, fo 380[v]; see William Power.

1397/8, bursar/[cellarer], prob. for only part of the yr as several others were also named (initials only), WCM C.767.

1401, Apr./1402, Feb., precentor, WCM C.370, C.371.

1405/6, prob. pittancer as he is named on the pittancer's acct of 1406/7 as *nuper pitanciarius*, WCM C.320.

1406, 28 May; 1407, 20 June, sacrist, *Reg. Clifford*, no 316; Liber Albus, fo 431[v].

1408, Jan./1409, Oct., cellarer, WCM C.80–81a.

1408/15, hostiller, WCM C.219–224, C.226a.

1415/16; 1419, 9 Mar. and 14 Apr.; 1420/3; 1423/4, sacrist, WCM C.138; *Reg. Sed. Vac.*, 391 (misread as Elene), 407; WCM C.140–142; WCM C.425.

1424, 15 Nov., sacrist (and therefore prob. 1424/5), Reg. Morgan, 132.

1426, 19 May, apptd sacrist [by the new bp], Reg. Polton, 6.

1428, 16 Oct.; 1429/30, sacrist, Reg. Polton, 104; WCM C.86. See also below under [1435 or 1436].

1388, 21 Aug., 39th in order at the el. of a prior and one of three *scrutatores*, Liber Albus, fos 334[v], 335.

1395, 12 Mar., one of two monk proctors sent by the chapter to the king for licence to el. a bp, *Reg. Sed. Vac.*, 353.

1395, 16 Sept., one of two monks sent to the [new] bp to present the seven candidates chosen by the chapter for the office of prior, Liber Albus, fo 380.

1401, 15 June, one of two monk proctors sent to the king for licence to el. a bp, *Reg. Sed. Vac.*, 372; 24 June, 27th in order at the el., *ib.*, 373 (misread as 'Olyve'); 28 June, one of two monks sent to London to inform Richard Clifford of his el., *ib.*, 374; see William Owston.

1401, 21 July, the prior comm. him and the dean of Worcester to deal with a prisoner who had been abducted from the cathedral churchyard where he had sought sanctuary, *Reg. Sed. Vac.*, 382.

1407, 20 June, as proctor for the prior and convent he made an official protest and an appeal to the pope because the ringing of the cathedral bells on the bp's arrival had not been intended as an act of disobedience, Liber Albus, fo 431[v].

1411, 15 June, granted papal licence to hold a benefice, with or without cure of souls, *CPL*, vi (1404–1415), 275.

1419, 9 Mar., one of two monk proctors sent to the king for licence to el. a bp, *Reg. Sed. Vac.*, 391; 24 Apr., 9th in order at the el., *ib.*, 407.

1420, 8 July, a John Cleve was apptd one of the auditors of accts at the Black Monk Chapter meeting, Pantin, *BMC*, ii, 96 (however, the name John Clyve/Cleve is not uncommon).

1423, 5 Jul, a John Clyve/Cleve again apptd an auditor of accts, as above, Pantin, *BMC*, ii, 139.

1423/4, went to Oxford to be present at the inception of Thomas Ledbury, q.v., and charged his expenses to his acct as sacrist; he also journeyed to London to confer with the bp, Hamilton, *Comp. Rolls*, 68 (WCM C.425).

1425, 15 Nov., as sacrist, asserted his right of presentation to St Michael's church (on the north side of the cathedral), Reg. Morgan, 132.

1426, 6 July, and again a John Clyve was apptd an auditor of accts, Pantin, *BMC*, ii, 161.

1428, 3 Sept., granted papal licence extending the previous one by defining 'cure of souls' to include any parish church, *CPL*, viii (1427–1447), 54.

1428, 16 Oct., obtained licence from the bp to go on pilgrimage to St James, Compostela to fulfil a vow; in his absence, Thomas Ledbury, q.v., subprior was to be responsible for his office (of sacrist), Reg. Polton, 104.

1430, 23 Aug., granted a papal licence to choose his own confessor, *CPL*, viii (1427–1447), 185.
1433, 9 Dec., 6th in order at the el. of a bp, *Reg. Sed. Vac.*, 432.
[1435 or 1436], 1 July, acted as one of two monk proctors in a dispute with the preceptor of St Oswald's hospital, Liber Albus, fo 449; this concerned money owed to the sacrist, and so he may have still held this office.
1436/7, d. recorded by the pittancer, WCM C.332, and the precentor who pd 11d. for the brief, C.378.

Name in the opening initial of Oxford, Bod. Ms Hatton 11, Regimen animarum etc. (?A.D. 1404); Ker suggests that this was written in his own hand, *MLGB*, 318. This might be capable of verification if the Liber Albus, fo 359 et seq., was actually written by him as chaplain to the prior (see above) and not by a scribe in his employ. However, on fo 105 of the Hatton ms there is the following note: 'Explicit liber qui vocatur Regimen animarum compilatus, A.D. 1383'; thus, this section at least appears to antedate Cleve's presence in the priory. Prof. Watson noted his name in the initial on fo 4 and suggested the dates 1412 or 1413 in *Dated and Datable Mss*, i, no 516.

Richard CLEVE [Clyve
occ. 1509 occ. 1540

1509, 22 Dec., ord pr., carnary chapel by Worcester cathedral, Reg. S. Gigli, 301.
1519/20, chaplain to the prior, Reg. A.6(ii), fos 121, 122.
1521/2, *magister communis cene*, first yr, Wilson, *Accts Henry VIII*, 28 (from WCM C.412).
1521, 22 July, 18th in order on the visitation certificate, Reg. abp Warham, ii, fo 293v.
1524, 24 Apr., granted a licence [*dimissio*] to transfer to the Cluniac priory of Dudley, after having been recd there on 9 Apr., Reg. A.6(ii), fo 143v.
Note: it seems that he soon returned, unless there are two monks by the same name who were contemporaries; there is no evidence to support this latter possibility.
1525/6, 20th in order on the first clerical subsidy list and pd 3s. 4d. commons, Reg. A.12, fo 125.
1531/2, 16th on the second subsidy list and pd 3s. 4d. again, Reg. A.12, fo 135.
1532, 1533, pd by the prior for saying the ten o'clock mass, *Jnl More*, 360, 365, 369 (he recd payment for each quarter that he was on duty, and his name occurs on three occasions during these two yrs).
1534, 17 Aug., subscribed to the Act of Supremacy, *DK 7th Report*, Appndx 2, 305.
1535, [29–31 July], during the visitation by the royal commissioners it came to light that he had said 'it was as lawful to appeal to the weathercock as to the Chancery in accordance with the Act of Parliament', that he had denounced the king and his new queen, Anne, and had affirmed his support for Queen Catherine and for papal authority, *L and P Henry VIII*, ix, no 52.2 (ii). John Musard, q.v., had reported these treasonable remarks to the subprior [John Lawerne II, q.v.], and William Fordham q.v., had quoted his actual words to Cromwell. It is possible that he was detained with the prior, William More I, q.v.
1536, 13 Mar., his name does not occ. at the irregular 'el.' proceedings which preceded the advent of Henry Holbech, q.v. as prior, Reg. A.6(iii), fo 1.
1540, 18 Jan., assigned a pension of £6 p.a., *L and P Henry VIII*, xv, no 81.

Robert CLEVE [Clyve
occ. 1437 d. 1482/3

[1434, 21 May, a Robert Clyve ord acol., carnary chapel by Worcester cathedral, *Reg. Sed. Vac.*, 443.]
1437, 1 Sept., ord subdcn, bp's chapel, Alvechurch, Reg. Bourgchier, 61.
1439/40, 'took [?dcn's] orders' at Wigmore abbey; the cellarer records expenses of 12s. 6d. and 3s. for horses, WCM C.89.
Note: the ordination was on 19 Sept. [1440], but there is only a blank space in the register where the scribe failed to fill in the names, Reg. Spofford (Hereford), fo 45.
1441/2, celebrated his first mass; recd gifts from the almoner and pittancer for bread and ale, WCM C.199, C.484.
1472/3, precentor, WCM C.338.
1473/4, hostiller, WCM C.236.
1448/9, 1449/50, one of many monks on the cellarer's list of creditors, WCM C.91, C.92.
1482/3, d., and the precentor sent out the brief, WCM C.386; the almoner recd payment for his corrody from the cellarer, WCM C.206.

Note: the lengthy and inexplicable gaps in this entry suggest that two monks' lives have been conflated; but there is no evidence that there were two contemporaries of this name, and the Worcs. ordination records are full and prob. complete, or nearly so.

William de CLEVE [Clyve
occ. 1322 occ. 1347

1322, 23 Oct., the prior was comm. to rec. his prof., *Liber Albus*, no 954.
1323, 12 Mar., ord subdcn, bp's chapel, Hartlebury, *Reg. Cobham*, 148.
1323, 17 Dec., ord dcn, Cropthorne, *ib.*, 167.
1326, 15 Feb., ord pr., bp's chapel, Hartlebury, *ib.*, 194.
1333/4, 1336/7, 1339/40, kitchener, WCM C.110, C.57, C.647.
1340/7, pittancer, WCM C.299–302 (on this last a note that he was in his seventh yr of office);

note that the pittancer's acct for 1339/40 (C.298) describes him as a former pittancer.

1334 (Oct./Nov.), visited Sedgeberrow, WCM C.755.
1339/40, visited Bromsgrove and Moor [Lindridge], WCM C.552, 647.

Laurence CLIFFORD [Clyfford
occ. 1483 occ. 1498

1483, 20 Sept., ord acol., carnary chapel by Worcester cathedral, Reg. Alcock, 274.
1487, 22 Sept., ord. pr., Ledbury, *Reg. Milling* (Hereford), 174.
1498, 25 Oct., 21st in order on the visitation certificate, *Reg. abp Morton*, ii, no 458.

Richard CLIFFORD [Clyfford
occ. 1447 d. 1482/3

1447, 8 Apr., ord acol. and subdcn, Worcester cathedral, Reg. Carpenter, i, 512.
1448, 17 Feb., ord dcn, bp's chapel, Alvechurch, *ib.*, i, 517.
1450, 4 Apr., ord pr., bp's chapel, Hartlebury, *ib.*, i, 526; also WCM C.92.
1449/50, celebrated his first mass; gifts were recd from the cellarer and precentor, WCM C.92, C.379; but see below where the cellarer owed him money.
1471/4, kitchener, WCM C.155–157.
1481/2, *tumbarius*, WCM C.100.
1449/50, one of many monks on the cellarer's list of creditors, WCM C.92.
1453/4, recd 3s. from the cellarer in part resolution of the above debt, WCM C.94.
1472/3, 1475/6, pd visits to Hallow, WCM C.618, C.604.
1480/1, he had debts which were pd by the cellarer, WCM C.99.
1482/3, d., and the precentor pd for the parchment, paper and the ink for the briefs, Hamilton, *Comp. Rolls*, 49 (WCM C.386); the almoner was pd by the cellarer for his corrody on his 1481/2 acct, WCM C.205.

John CLIFTON [Clyfton
occ. 1422 occ. 1453/4

1422, 7 Mar., ord subdcn, Worcester cathedral, Reg. Morgan, 190.
1424, 24 Mar., ord pr., Worcester cathedral, *ib.*, 209.
1423/4, celebrated his first mass; the hostiller and sacrist gave gifts, the latter specifying bread and ale, WCM C.227 (1424/5), C.425.
1446/7, 1448/50, master of the Lady chapel, WCM C.90–92.
1453/4, kitchener, WCM C.148.
1433, 9 Dec., 26th in order at the el. of a bp, *Reg. Sed. Vac.*, 432.
1449/50, was among the cellarer's many creditors, WCM C.92.

Richard CLIFTON [Clyfton
occ. [1400] occ. 1408/9

[1400], 20 May, one of two whose prof. the prior was comm. to rec., Reg. Winchcombe, 97.
1408, 22 Dec., ord pr., Worcester cathedral, Reg. Peverel, 176.
1408/9, celebrated his first mass; recd gifts of bread, ale and wine from the cellarer and hostiller, WCM C.81, C.218.
1408, Jan./Sept., student at Oxford, and the cellarer pd 5s. 8d. for the transport of *tocius apparatus*, WCM C.80.
1408/9, returned from Oxford with Thomas Ledbury, q.v., for the funeral of prior John de Malverne I, q.v., and the el. and installation of the new prior [John de Fordham, q.v.], WCM C.81; he may also have been present for the bp's visitation, ib, and WCM C.81a.

I Robert de CLIFTON [Cliftone, Clyfton
occ. 1310 occ. 1318

[1312], precentor, *Liber Albus*, no 558.
1313/[14], chamberlain, WCM E.200.
1314/15, 1317/18, cellarer, WCM E.6, E.7, E.8; also possibly part of 1318/19, C.583.
1318, 13 Sept., the bp ordered his removal from the office of sacrist, *Reg. Cobham*, 11; the prior and Clifton had both previously approached the bp on this matter as Clifton had been in charge of both the cellarer's and the sacrist's offices, as noted in *Liber Albus*, nos 782, 783.
1310, 6 Mar., apptd proctor by the prior for the Black Monk Chapter at Westminster, Pantin, *BMC*, i, 167 (*Liber Albus*, no 472).
1311, 4 Aug., apptd proctor by the convent [for convocation] *Liber Albus*, no 533, and again on 25 Nov., *ib.*, no 539. On the second occasion he is named as the prior's representative, *ib.*, no 540; see John de St Briavel.
[1312], acted with John de St Briavel, q.v., regarding the appropriation of Dodderhil, *Liber Albus*, no 558.
1313/14, travelled to London and Canterbury, with expenses of 100s. pd by the cellarer, Wilson, *Early Comp. Rolls*, 39 (WCM C.482).
1314/15, held courts at Hallow and Overbury, WCM E.7.
1317, 20 Oct., 15th in order at el. of a prior and one of the seven *compromissorii* chosen to name the seven candidates, Liber Albus, fo 83; on 17 Nov., with Adam de Theukesbury, q.v., he appeared before the bp at Strood with the official instruments concerning the el., *ib.*, fo 83^v. On the following day at Dartford, they presented the seven candidates to the bp, *ib.*, fo 84.

See note below next entry.

II Robert de CLIFTON [Clyfton
occ. 1325 ?d. 1355/6

1325, 13 May, precentor, Liber Albus, fo 118^v.

1327, 31 Aug., precentor, *CPR (1327–1330)*, 159 (PRO C66/168 m. 26); (transcribed as Oliston).
1328, 30 Mar., sacrist, *Reg. Orleton* (Hereford), 377.
1329, 18 Feb., 18 Mar., sacrist, *Reg. Orleton* (Worcester), nos 82, 599.
1335, 17 Jan.; 1339, Jan./Apr., precentor, Reg. A.8 fo 11; *Reg. Sed. Vac.*, 259, 265–272, *passim.*
1346/7, chamberlain, WCM C.10.

1325, 13 May, comm. by the prior and chapter to institute a clerk to a prebend at Westbury, Liber Albus, fo 118v.
1326, 7 Oct., apptd by the convent as their proctor for the abp's council, *Liber Albus*, no 1111.
1326/7, pd a visit to Bromsgrove, WCM C.544.
1327, 31 Aug., recd licence from the king to el. a bp, *CPR (1327–1330)*, 159.
1327/8, accompanied the cellarer to Bromsgrove, WCM C.546a; and in 1327 he spent a fortnight at King's Norton, WCM C.693b.
1328, 30 Mar., as sacrist, handed over to the new bp [Orleton] at Beaumes a mitre and other episcopal regalia, *Reg. Orleton* (Hereford), 377.
1329, 18 Feb. as sacrist presented a pr. to Sodbury vicarage, *Reg. Orleton*, no 82.
1329, 18 Mar., apptd, with the bp's official, to arrange for the purgation of a criminous clerk, *ib.*, no 599.
1336, 16 Sept., witness to the homage of a priory tenant, Liber Albus, fo 146v.
1339, 4 Jan., apptd by the prior and chapter to order the departure from the chapter house of all who were not eligible to participate in the el. of a bp, *Reg. Sed. Vac.*, 267; on the previous day he had been ordered to cite all absent monks to the el., *ib.*, 259.
1339, 6 Jan., one of four monks apptd by the prior, *sed. vac.*, to perform visitations in the diocese, *Reg. Sed. Vac.*, 265–272.
1339, 12 Apr., the first named of seven candidates chosen by the chapter for the office of prior, *Reg. Bransford*, no 38.
1355/6, the almoner recd 17s. 3d. for the sale of his corrody, from 8 Nov. to 25 Apr. at 9d. per week, WCM C.172; presumably he d. around the former date.

Note: there is no obvious reason to support the case for two Robert de Cliftons, but I have been influenced by the apparent gap in office holding (between 1318 and 1325) and the fact that in both cases the same offices recur.

William CLIFTON [Clyfton
occ. 1475 occ. 1504

1475, 23 Dec., ord subdcn, carnary chapel by Worcester cathedral, Reg. Carpenter, ii, 205.
1476, 8 June, ord dcn, carnary chapel, *ib.*, 207.
1477, 5 Apr., ord pr., Worcester cathedral, Reg. Alcock, 246.
1476/7, celebrated his first mass; recd gifts from the kitchener and precentor, WCM C.158, C.383.
1481/2, subcellarer, WCM C.743.
1484/6, kitchener, WCM C.624, C.200a.
[1490], 25 Mar., sacrist, WCM B.1112a.
1498/9, former chamberlain, WCM C.48.
1503/4; 1504, 6 Nov., master of the Lady chapel, WCM C.291; Reg. A.6(ii), fo 32.

1481/2, visited Overbury, WCM C.743.
1484/5, visited Harvington, WCM C.624.
[1490], 25 Mar., arranged for a lease, WCM B.1112a.
1498, 25 Oct., 9th in order on the visitation certificate, *Reg. abp Morton*, ii, no 458.

CLIVA, Clive, Clyve
see Cleve

CLYFFORD
see Clifford

CLYFTON
see Clifton

Nicholas de CODERUGGE
occ. 1303 occ. 1306

[1303], 5 May, kitchener, *Reg. Sed. Vac.*, 48.
[1305], 28 Feb., cellarer, WCM B.1553.

[1303], 5 May, sent to the abp of Canterbury with a letter from the prior concerning the right of presentation to the church of Dodderhill, *Reg. Sed. Vac.*, 48, 49.
1303, 15 Aug., following his [undated] apptment as proctor in the chapter's appeal to the curia vs the abp's claim to the church of Dodderhill (above), he now announced the withdrawal of the appeal, *ib.*, 58.
1306, 13 May, one of two monk proctors apptd in the protest vs the new abbot of Gloucester, Liber Albus, fo 26; see John de Bromesgrove.

COKE
see Stanford

Henry de COKESEY
occ. 1321

1321, [Aug.], subprior, Liber Albus, fo 103.
1321, [Aug.], witness at the installation of the adcn of Worcester by proxy, Liber Albus, fo 103.

Note: see Henry Fouke with whom he may have been identical.

COLEMAN [Colemannus
occ. 1089 d. 1113

1089, 20 May, chancellor of bp Wulstan, *Worcs. Cart.*, no 3.
n.d., chaplain of bp Wulstan for fifteen yrs, Darlington, *Vita Wulfstani*, 2.
1093, sent to be prior of the bp's new monastic foundation at Westbury-on-Trym, which was intended to be a daughter house of Worcester, Darlington, *Vita Wulfstani*, xxxix–xl. (He

returned to Worcester when Westbury was closed by Wulstan's successor.) See also Maurice I.

n.d., chosen by the bp to preach on peace in the latter's old age and infirmity, Darlington, *Vita Wulfstani*, 40, 88.

1095 × 1113, wrote a Life of bp Wulfstan in Old English, which William of Malmesbury later translated into Latin (ed. by Darlington). A copy of this was sent to Innocent III to promote Wulstan's canonization, Darlington, *Vita Wulfstani*, xlvii.

1113, d., *Ann. Wigorn.*, 375.

Ker has deduced that Coleman's hand appears in a number of marginal headings in Worcs. Ms F.48, Vitas patrum (11th c.); this is stated in a handwritten note attached to the Ms See also 'Old English Notes signed "Coleman"' in Ker, Books, Collectors, Libraries, 27–30. Dr McIntyre has also noted his hand in Worcs. Ms Q.21, 'Early 12th c. Worceser Cathedral Priory', 40–45, where she refers to other mss containing notes written by him, e.g. CUL Ms Kk.3.18, which has the hand of Heming, q.v. as well. See her discussion in *ib.*, 129–149, and also Watson, *Dated and Datable Mss*, i, no 520.

See also Mason, *Wulfstan*, 158, 169, 270, 286, 289.

COLINZ

see Colys

COLUMBANUS

occ. c. 1104

Name occ. in the list of monks in *Durham Liber Vitae*, fo 22.

Thomas COLWALL [Colewell, Collewell, Colwell

occ. 1405/6 occ. 1454/5

1405/6, went to Bromyard to rec. [subdcn's] orders, WCM C.372.

1407, 21 May, ord dcn, Blockley, *Reg. Clifford*, no 132, p. 104.

1411, (not 1410), 28 Mar., ord pr., Worcester cathedral, Reg. Peverel, 188.

1410/11, celebrated his first mass; recd gifts from the chamberlain and hostiller, WCM C.29, C.220a.

1415/17, pittancer, WCM C.323, C.324.

1419, 24 Apr., third prior, *Reg. Sed. Vac.*, 407.

1419, June to Sept., *custos* of the Lady chapel, WCM C.270.

1420/4, 1426/7, chamberlain, WCM C.540a, C.33–36.

1427/9, kitchener, WCM C.617, C.143; in 1427/8 he shared the office with Richard Tyberton, q.v., and in 1428/9 with Richard Cowarn, q.v.

1429/30, bursar, WCM C.86; and on C.771, cellarer.

1432, Aug. to Sept.; 1433/4; 1434/6; 1436/7, part yr (see also William Hertilbury), cellarer, WCM C.86a; C.492; C.87, C.88; C.724, C.772.

1438, 12 Feb.; 1439/40, 1441/4, [1444/5], almoner, Reg. Bourgchier, 84; WCM C.726–729, C.773, C.493.

1446/7; 1448, 14 Sept.; 1449/50, subprior, WCM C.90; Reg. Carpenter, i, 132; WCM C.92.

1419, 24 Apr., 19th in order at the el. of a bp, *Reg. Sed. Vac*, 407.

1420/1, pd visit to Broadwas, WCM C.540a.

1422/3, visited Overbury, WCM C.721.

1427/8, visited Harvington, and the quarry at Ombersley, WCM C.617, C.85a.

1429/30, went to Shrewsbury in order to arrange a *compositio* with the abbot, and also to Evesham to confer with the bp, WCM C.86.

1432, between Aug. and Sept., visited Shrewsbury, Overbury and Teddington, WCM C.86a.

1433, 9 Dec., 7th in order at the el. of a bp, *Reg. Sed. Vac.*, 432.

1434/5, went to Himbleton with the steward, WCM C.87.

1435/6, with his servant(s) went to London for convocation and other business, WCM C.88.

1436/7, visited Overbury, WCM C.724.

1438, 12 Feb., chosen by the chapter as one of the seven nominees for the office of prior, Reg. Bourgchier, 84, and Liber Albus, fo 457v (13 Feb.).

1439/40, visited Bevere and Overbury, WCM C.89, C.726.

1441/4, pd visits to Overbury, WCM C.727–729, and in 1443/4 also to Sedgeberrow, C.773.

1444, 15 Jan., again one of the seven nominees for the office of prior, Reg. Bourgchier, 193.

1454/5, one of the monks on the cellarer's list of creditors and therefore presumably still alive, WCM C.480.

Richard COLYS de WIGORN' [Calys, Colinz, Colis

occ. 1321 occ. 1351

1321, 9 Dec., one of three whose prof. the prior was authorized by the bp to rec., Liber Albus, fo 103.

1321, 19 Dec., ord subdcn, Kidderminster, *Reg. Cobham*, 113.

1322, 18 Dec., ord dcn, Ombersley, *ib.*, 143.

1323, 17 Dec., ord pr., Cropthorne, *ib.*, 167.

1331/6, subcellarer, WCM C.694, C.432, C.799, C.695, C.593.

1339, 15 Nov., apptd sacrist, *Reg. Bransford*, no 231.

1340, 14 Feb., sacrist, *Liber Pensionum*, no 154.

1343, 7 Mar.; 1349, 24 May, 6 July, sacrist, *Reg. Bransford*, pp. 375; 407, 417.

1350, 5 Feb., apptd sacrist, Reg. Thoresby, 11; and on 2 Apr., made receiver for the bpric, *ib.*, 19.

1331/2, visited King's Norton, WCM C.694.

1333/4, visited Hallow and Tibberton, WCM C.591, C.799; in Oct./Nov. 1334, he was also at Sedgeberrow, C.755.
1334/5, while at King's Norton arranged for five quarters of oats to be sent to the bp [?at Alvechurch] for Christmas, WCM C.695.
1335/6, visited Hallow, WCM C.593.
1337, 21 July, witness in the prior's chapel when an accused was presented, Reg. Hemenhale, 13.
1340, 14 Feb., as a result of his complaints concerning the heavy expenses imposed on the sacrist's office, the chapter agreed to provide extra funds, *Liber Pensionum*, no 154.
1340, before 6 Apr., witness, with John Newentone, q.v., WCM B.1638.
1343, 7 Mar., 1349, 24 May and 6 July, as sacrist he was reponsible for institutions to several churches; these are entered in Reg. Bransford, pp. 375, 407, 417.
1351, 21 Jan., granted papal licence to choose his own confessor, *CPL*, iii (1342–1362), 406.

CONDICOTE
see Gundicote

COPTHORNE
see Cropthorn(e)

CORKE
see Stanford

John de COULESDON [Coulusd', Cowlesdon
occ. 1396 d. 1419/20

1396, 1 Apr., ord subdcn, Worcester cathedral, Reg. Winchcombe, 125.
1398/9, celebrated his first mass and the chamberlain gave bread and wine for the celebration afterwards, WCM C.24.

1402, 14 Feb., apptd chaplain to the prior, Liber Albus, fo 409.
1408/9, subcellarer, WCM C.81.
1412/13, kitchener, WCM C.136, C.860.
1413/14, cellarer, WCM E.64.
1419/20, Sept. to Apr., *custos* of the Lady chapel, WCM C.270, C.271a.

1401, 27 June, 40th in order at the el. of a bp, *Reg. Sed. Vac.*, 373.
1401/2, recd money from the chamberlain to pay for his *cucullus*, WCM C.26.
1419, 24 Apr., 15th in order at the el. of a bp, *Reg. Sed. Vac.*, 407.
1419/20, d., but the chamberlain reported that he recd nothing for [the sale of] his *panni*, WCM C.32.

Nicholas de COULESDON [Coules', Coulesdone
occ. 1273 occ. 1294/5

1274, 20 Sept., named by the chapter as one of five *compromissorii* to select the seven candidates for the office of prior, *Reg. Giffard*, 62.
1294/5, pd to the cellarer £15 4s. 8d. [?acquired through business transactions on behalf of the chapter], Wilson, *Early Comp. Rolls*, 27 (WCM C.52).

Name in Worcs. Ms Q.42, Distinctiones Mauricii (late 13th c.). On the last flyleaf he is listed as one of eleven monks who contributed to the purchase of the book; and he gave 28[?d.].

Richard COWARN [Cowarne, Cowern
occ. 1404 d. 1449/50

1404, 24 May, ord acol., bp's chapel, Hillingdon, *Reg. Clifford*, no 121.
1404, 20 Sept., ord. subdcn, Llanthony Priory, Gloucester, *Reg. Clifford*, no 122, p. 87.
1405, 19 Sept., ord dcn, Cirencester abbey, *ib*, no 126, p. 93.
1407, 24 Sept., ord pr., Blockley, *ib.*, no 133, p. 107.
1407/8, Sept. to Jan., celebrated his first mass and the cellarer provided ale, WCM C.79.

1419, 24 Apr., 1420/2, pittancer, *Reg. Sed. Vac.*, 407; WCM C.84, 325.
1424/8, hostiller, WCM C.227–230.
1428/9, kitchener with Thomas Colwall, q.v., WCM C.143.
1429/31, hostiller, WCM C.231, C.232.

1419, 24 Apr., 20th in order at the el. of a bp, *Reg. Sed. Vac.*, 407.
1433, 9 Dec., 8th at the el. of a bp, *ib.*, 432.
1438, 12 Feb., one of the seven nominees for the office of prior, Reg. Bourgchier, 84 (also entered in Liber Albus fo 457^{v} and dated 13 Feb.).
1449/50, d., and the precentor pd for the briefs; the following yr he charged 6d. to his acct for parchment for the briefs for him, WCM C.379, C.380.
1453/4, the cellarer pd off a debt of 7s. of his, WCM C.94.

Roger CRATEFORD
Name in Worcester Cath. Ms F.169, Aristoteles (early 14th c.), *traditus ad usum*—in a 15th/16th c. hand.

Note: this is Roger Neckham, q.v.

A M. Hugh Cratford was master of the boys [of the almonry school] in 1501/2, WCM C.167.

CROLLE
see Crowle

Simon CROMPE de WIGORN' [Cromp, Crumpe
occ. 1310 d. 1340

1339–1340, prior: his letter of apptment, dated 6 Nov. 1339, is in *Reg. Bransford*, nos. 229, 230, and he was installed on 7 Nov., WCM C.298; d. 10 Apr. 1340, *Reg. Bransford*, no 290.

1310, 20 Sept., one of two whose prof. was recd by the new bp [Walter Reynolds] at the latter's installation, Liber Albus, fo 45^{v} (as Wygorn').

1311, 21 Feb., recd *lit. dim.* for all orders, *Reg. Reynolds*, 95.

1312, 6 Mar., ord dcn, Worcester cathedral, *Reg. Reynolds*, 131.

1318/19, pittancer, prob. first yr., succeeding William de Stanweye q.v., WCM C.294.

1328, 26 July ,precentor, *Reg. Orleton*, nos 51, 675.

1334, 26 Jan., the bp, claiming his right to appt the sacrist, chose him, *Liber Albus*, no 1266; on 26 July the apptment occ. in Reg. Montacute, 61, 141.

1335, 17 Feb., apptd cellarer by the prior and chapter, *Liber Albus*, no 1282; the bp refused to relieve him of the sacrist's office, but gave permission for him to retain both obediences for the time being, *ib.*, no 1283 (18 Feb.).

1337, 10 July, [re]apptd sacrist by the [new] bp, Reg. Hemenhale, 12; he was sacrist on 13 Mar. 1337, Reg. Orleton (Winchester), ii, fo 58.

1339, 29 May, sacrist, *Reg. Bransford*, p.358.

1320/1, student at Oxford; the cellarer gave 46s. 8d. for his maintenance, WCM C.55.

1317, 20 Oct., 35th in order at the el. of a prior, Liber Albus, fo 83^{v}.

1318, 5 June, present at the installation of the adcn of Gloucester by proxy, Liber Albus, fo 90.

1319/20, visited King's Norton, WCM C.693.

1326/7, pd visits to Bromsgrove, and King's Norton (in 1327), WCM C.544, C.693b.

1328/9, stayed at Tibberton, WCM C.798.

1329/30, visited Cleeve Prior, WCM C.557.

1333, 10 Jan., obtained permission to be released from some of his duties and was provided with a clerk (named as 'Robert de Warnesleye, or another') to minister to him. The prior and chapter granted this dispensation to him 'who has gone so far as to put his life at risk in serving the community, especially by travelling to the Roman curia on their behalf'. The relaxation allowed him '. . . mitigationem aliqualem super onere tabulari. Ita videlicet quod ad missas omnes ponatur in tabula sicut alius de conventu set ad matutinas scribatur in tabula in festis caparum dumtaxat', Liber Albus, fos 151^{v}–152.

[1334, Mar.], one of three monks comm. by the bp as penitentiary, Reg. Montacute, 4.

1334, 3 Nov., a second comm. to him and two other monks to act as penitentiaries, *ib.*, 151.

1337, 13 Mar., recd a letter from bp Orleton (Winchester) regarding an exchange between the adcns of Wincheser and Worcester, Reg. Orleton (Winchester), ii, fo 58.

1337, 10 July, licensed by the bp to hear confessions in the adcnry of Worcester, Reg. Hemenhale, 12.

1338, 24 Dec., one of two proctors sent to the king to obtain a licence to el. a bp, *Reg. Sed. Vac.*, 257. He was recorded as absent on lawful business when the monks were cited to the el., *ib.*, 259; and see John de Westbury.

1339/40, visited Moor [Lindridge], WCM C.647.

1339, 4/5 Jan., chosen by the chapter as one of five *compromissorii* at the episcopal el., Worcs. Ms F.141; see note under Wulstan de Bransford.

1339, 6 Jan., one of the monks comm. by the prior, *sed. vac.*, to carry out visitations in the diocese, *Reg. Sed. Vac.*, 265; on 29 Jan. he and John de Westbury, q.v., visited Tewkesbury abbey, *ib.*, 273.

1339, 16 Feb., with John de Westbury and two clerks comm. by the bp elect to rec. the canonical obedience of all clergy in the diocese, *Reg. Bransford*, no 6.

1339/40, there is a ref. to his burial on the acct of the reeve of Hallow, WCM C.594. See above.

Name (as Simon de Wygorn') in Worcs.Ms F.105, Thomas Aquinas (14th c.), fo 205.

A John Crumpe, public notary was one of the witnesses at the 1317 el. of a prior, Liber Albus, fo 83^{v}.

CROOS
see Cros

John CROPTHORN [Copthorne, Cropthorne
occ. 1533 occ. 1540

1533, 20 Sept., ord subdcn, carnary chapel by Worcester cathedral, Reg. Ghinucci 7(ii), 174.

1536, 13 Mar., prof. before this date but not yet a pr., Reg. A.6(iii), fo 1.

1534, 17 Aug., subscribed to the Act of Supremacy, *DK 7th Report*, Appndx 2, 305.

1535, signed the petition vs the reinstatement of William Fordham, q.v., as cellarer, *L and P Henry VIII*, ix, no 653.

1536, 13 Mar., 33rd (of 34) in order at the 'el.' of Henry Holbech, q.v., as prior, Reg. A.6(iii), fo 1.

1540, 18 Jan., awarded a pension of £6 p.a., *L and P Henry VIII*, xv, no 81.

Richard CROPTHORNE [Croppethorne, Croppthorn
occ. 1464 d. 1479

1464, 8 June, one of six whose prof. the prior was comm. by the bp to rec., Reg. A.6(i), fo 34.

1465, 21 Dec., ord subdcn, bp's chapel, Alvechurch, Reg. Carpenter, i, 564.

1470, 17 Mar., ord. pr., Lady chapel, Worcester cathedral, *ib.*, 576.

1475/6; 1478, 14 Sept.; 1478/9, pittancer, WCM C.339; Reg. A.6(i), fo 73^{v}; WCM C.340.

1479, 7 Aug., apptd sacrist on the d. of Nicholas Hambury, q.v., Reg. Alcock, 23.

1478, 14 Sept., witness to the homage of a priory tenant, Reg. A.6(i), fo 73[v].
1479, 13 Sept., d., by this date when he was succ. as sacrist by Roger Kyngeslonde, q.v., Reg. Alcock, 24.
1478/9, the almoner recd nothing for his corrody *quia perdonavitur*, WCM C.204.

Thomas CROPTHORN [Croppthorne, Croxthorn, *alias* Fyscher
occ. 1479 occ. 1518

1479, 18 Dec., ord pr., carnary chapel by Worcester cathedral, Reg. Alcock, 260.
1479/80, celebrated his first mass and recd 2s. 6d. from the kitchener [for the feast afterwards], WCM C.160.
1490/2, kitchener, WCM C.163, C.164.
1498/9, hostiller, first yr., WCM C.238.
1515, 20 Sept., 1516, 20 Aug., *tumbarius*, WCM B.1122, C.1172; for 1516 also, Reg. A.12, fo 41[v] (which is an acct).
1498, 25 Oct., 10th in order on the visitation certificate, *Reg. abp Morton*, ii, no 458 (as Croxthorn).
1501/2, one of the monks to whom the kitchener was in debt, WCM C.167.
1504, 16 Nov., obtained papal dispensation to rec. and retain a benefice with or without cure of souls, *CPL*, xviii (1503–1513), no 404.
1518, 27 Sept., one of the two monk proctors apptd to present the seven nominees for the priorate to bp Fox (Winchester), prob. at Southwark, Reg. A.6(ii), fo 113; see William More I.
n.d., a 16th c. inventory of plate belonging to some of the obedientiary offices (unspecified) includes a short list of items to which his name is attached, Reg. A.12, fo 172[v].

William CROPTHORNE [Croppethorne, Croppthorn
occ. 1379 occ. 1433

[1379], 14 Mar., one of two *clerici* presented to the bp by the precentor, John de Malverne I, q.v., and adm. as a monk, *Reg. Wakefield*, no 127.
1380, 19 May, ord acol., Bromyard, *Reg. Gilbert* (Hereford), 145.
1381, 20 Feb., 1381, novice and the prior was comm. by the bp to rec. his prof., Liber Albus, fo 307.
1382, 1 Mar., ord dcn, Kidderminster, *Reg. Wakefield*, no 893f.
1387, [1 June], ord pr., Cirencester abbey, WCM C.73, *Reg. Wakefield*, no 923. Although his name is not in Wakefield's register, the cellarer (whose acct is dated 1387, Feb. to Sept.) named the ordinands and recorded the expenses of the journey to Cirencester, and also the gift of money for bread and wine after their first mass.
1386/7, the hostiller also gave a small sum to two of the newly ordained, one being Cropthorne (on their first mass), and described them as juniors and priests (or, perhaps, junior priests), Hamilon, *Comp. Rolls*, 56 (WCM C.213); see John de Fordham.
1401, 24 June, subsacrist, *Reg. Sed. Vac.*, 373.
1411/16, 1417/June 1418, *custos* of the Lady chapel, WCM C.263–269.
1419, 24 Apr., 1426/7, infirmarer, *Reg. Sed. Vac.*, 407, WCM C.328.
1388, 21 Aug., 35th in order at the el. of a prior, Liber Albus, fo 334[v].
1391/2, owed 13s. 4d. by the cellarer, WCM C.74, C.75.
1401, 24 June, 29th in order at the episcopal el., *Reg. Sed. Vac.*, 373.
1419, 24 Apr., 8th at the episcopal el., *ib.*, 407.
1433, 9 Dec., 5th at the episcopal el., *ib.*, 432.

Thomas CROS [Croos, Crosse, Crus
occ. 1348 occ. 1365/6

1348, 20 Dec., ord acol., bp's chapel, Hartlebury, *Reg. Bransford*, no 1108.
1349, 19 Sept., ord subdcn, Hereford cathedral, by *lit. dim.*, *Reg. Trillek* (Hereford), 500.
1350, 18 Dec., ord dcn, chapel of Prestbury manor, by *lit. dim.* from the vicar general, *ib.*, 548.
1353, 21 Dec., ord pr., Ombersley, Reg. Bryan, i, 14.
1357/8, student at Oxford, with maintenance of 100s. [*liberatio*] pd for him and for Nicholas Morton by the cellarer, WCM C.64; see below and Nicholas Morton.
1359/60, student, recd pension from the cellarer at 16d. per wk, WCM C.65; the total (on the acct covering 58 wks) makes it clear that he was at Oxford for over 50 wks.
1365/6, [student], for whom the precentor pd travelling expenses from Oxford to Worcester, WCM C.359a. Not in *BRUO*.
1358, 14 Oct., absent [at Oxford] from chapter at the reading of the bp's mandate for his impending visitation, Liber Albus, fo 217; his absence is also noted on 15 Oct. in the bp's register, Reg. Bryan, i, 176.
1360/1, recd 12d. for [?travelling] expenses [?as student] from the precentor, WCM C.357.
1363, Jan. to Sept., recd money [for pittances] from the pittancer and for *minutiones*; and, with Thomas Talbot, q.v., was listed separately from the other monks, prob. because he was at Oxford, WCM C.306.

John CROWLE [Crolle, Crowlle of Saye
occ. 1521 occ. 1540

1524/5, celebrated his first mass; recd a gift of 2s. from the almoner, WCM C.414.
1521, 22 July, 39th in order on the visitation certificate, Reg. abp Warham, ii, fo 293[v].

1523/4, ill for ten wks, and the infirmarer spent 11s. 8d. for medical treatment, WCM C.413; also noted in Reg. A.17, 280.
1525/6, 30th on the clerical subsidy list and pd 3s. 4d. commons, Reg. A.12, fo 125.
1528, 5 Apr., the prior gave a 'collation' of 8s. 10d. to 'Dan John Crowle of Saye', *Jnl More*, 268.
1530/1, spent three wks in the infirmary for which the infirmarer charged his acct 3s. 6d., WCM C.414b.
1531/2, again 30th on the clerical subsidy list and pd. 3s. 4d. commons, Reg. A.12, fo 135.
1534, 17 Aug., subscribed to the Act of Supremacy, *DK 7th Report*, Appndx 2, 305. In Oct. the prior pd him 20s. 'upon a rykynyng', *Jnl More*, 395.
1535, signed the petition vs the reinstatement of William Fordham, q.v., as cellarer, *L and P Henry VIII*, ix, no 653.
1536, 13 Mar., 21st in order at the 'el.' of Henry Holbech, q.v., as prior, Reg. A.6(iii), fo 1.
1540, 18 Jan., awarded a pension of £6 p.a., *L and P Henry VIII*, xv, no 81.

William de CROWLE [Croule
occ. 1350 d. 1397/8
1350, 15 May, ord acol., by a Franciscan suffragan bp in the [Franciscan] convent, Worcester, Reg. Thoresby, 30.
1350, 18 Dec., ord. subdcn, chapel of Prestbury manor by *lit. dim.* of the vicar general, *Reg. Trillek* (Hereford), 548.
1353, 21 Dec., ord pr., Ombersley, Reg. Bryan, i, 13.
1370, 3 Apr., succentor, Liber Albus, fo 246.
1370, 3 Apr., 6th in order at the el. of a prior, Liber Albus, fo 246.
1373, 7 Dec., 5th in order at the episcopal el., *Reg. Sed. Vac.*, 290.
1380/1, ill, and the infirmarer spent 12d. on treatment, WCM C.242.
1388, 21 Aug., 3rd in order at el. of a prior, Liber Albus, fo 334v.
1397/8, on the infirmary sick list, WCM C.246.
1397/8, d., and the chamberlain recd 38s. 6d. for the sale of *divers' pertinent' ad officium camer'*, prob. his clothing and bedding; he recd 8s. 10d. for selling more of them the following yr, WCM C.23, C.24.
1398, between 25 Mar. and 29 Sept., the almoner distributed 12d. worth of bread *die obitus*, WCM C.184.

CRUMP
see Crompe

CRUS
see Cros

CYRENCESTRE
see Cirencster

I DAVID
occ. c. 1104
Name occ. in the list of monks in *Durham Liber Vitae*, fo 22.

II DAVID
occ. 1143 occ. 1145
1143–1145, prior: succ. 1143, before 28 Dec; deposed by the bp 1145, *Fasti*, ii, 102, *HRH*, 83.
n.d., on the grounds that the prior had been uncanonically removed, the abp [Theobald] ordered the bp to restore him at least temporarily, vs the wishes of the monks, *Theobald Charters*, 86.

John de DAYL' [?Daylesford]
occ. 1345
1345, 19 Feb., ord subdcn, Hartlebury, *Reg. Bransford*, no 1060.

DEAN(E)
see Dene

Simon de DEFFORD
occ. 1307 d. 1340
1307, 13 Nov., refused to take part in the episcopal el., *Reg. Sed. Vac.*, 107 (misread as Besford).
[1317, c. Aug.], the prior had asked the abbot of Gloucester to rec. him to undergo penance at Gloucester abbey, and now issued the *emissio* in which he described him as a disturber of the peace, and a bad example to the other monks, who showed no sign of amendment of life. The prior laid down regulations with respect to his treatment at Gloucester, which included confinement within the cloister and constant supervision, Pantin, *BMC*, i, 178–180 (from Liber Albus, fo 81).
1317, 24 Aug., the abbot of Gloucester replied that he would accept him and care for him until he improved his conduct and could be sent back to Worcester, *ib.*, 180–181 (Liber Albus fo 81v).
There are two further letters concerning this monk, both undated as to the yr:
(1) the prior wrote to the abbot to recall him and enclosed 40s. to cover the expenses of his stay at Gloucester, Liber Albus, fo 85v.
(2) the abbot replied, giving a good report of his behaviour stating that he was *honeste religionis* and 'decentis conversationis . . . [et] in diurnis et nocturnis officiis tam devote quam obedienter'. He also returned the money sent by the prior, *ib.* The letter is dated 23 Dec. and the bearer was John de Harleye, q.v.
1317, 20 Oct., 27th in order at the el. of a prior, Liber Albus, fo 83v.
[1317], 23 Dec., his recall was ordered by the prior, Liber Albus, fo 85v; see John de Harleye.

1339/40, recd 8d. from the pittancer for *minutiones*, and no more, because he d. c. 25 Mar. 1340, WCM C.298.

Note: if he were actually present at the Oct. el. above he must have been allowed a few days off from his confinement at Gloucester.

Thomas DENE

occ. 1365 occ. 1411/12

1365, 14 Sept., one of three whose prof. the prior was comm. by the vicar general to rec., Liber Albus, fo 229v.

1368, 4 Mar., ord dcn, Hartlebury, Reg. Wittlesey, 72.

1373, 7 Dec., kitchener, *Reg. Sed. Vac.*, 290.

1379/80, subcellarer with William Merston, q.v., WCM C.864.

1381/2, continued as subcellarer for part of the yr, WCM C.598, C.760.

1382, Feb./Sept., chamberlain, first yr, WCM C.540.

1388, 21 Aug.; 1388/9; 1392, Mar./1393, chamberlain, Liber Albus, fo 334v; WCM C.15, C19, C.20.

1388/90, cellarer, WCM C.763, E.35.

1390/2, cellarer from whom William Power, q.v., took over in Mar. 1392, WCM C.766, C.764, C.74.

1395, 15 Sept.; 1395/6; 1397/Mar. 1398, almoner, Liber Albus, fo 380, WCM C.182, C.183.

1397/1400; 1400/1, cellarer, WCM C.679, C.716 (where the term bursar is also used), 476; WCM E.41. On WCM E.39 it appears that he may not have resumed this office until Apr. 1398; see William Power.

1402/3; 1404, Jan.; 1404/5; 1406/7; 1407/Jan. 1408, cellarer, WCM C.611; C.650; C.78; C.813; C.79.

1412, 21–29 Sept., infirmarer, WCM C.247.

1370, 3 Apr., 21st in order at the el. of a prior, Liber Albus, fo 246.

1373, 7 Dec., 18th at the episcopal el., *Reg. Sed. Vac.*, 290.

1379/80, visited Harvington, WCM C.864.

1381/2, pd visits to Broadwas, Hallow and Sedgeberrow, WCM C.540, 598, 760.

1388, 21 Aug., 14th at the el. of a prior and chosen by the chapter as one of the three *scrutatores* of votes, and as one of the seven candidates for the office, Liber Albus, fo 334v, 335.

1388, 22 Aug., the seven were presented to the bp in the hall of the priory, *Reg. Wakefield*, no 788; see Walter de Legh.

1388/9, 1390/1, 1391/2, visited Sedgeberrow, WCM C.763, C.766, C.764.

1395, 15 Sept., chosen by the chapter as one of the seven nominees for the office of prior, Liber Albus, fo 380.

1397/8, visited Leopard Grange, WCM C.679.

1398/9, pd visits to Harvington, Moor [Lindridge] and Tibberton, WCM C.716, C.649, C.810.

1399/1400, visited Newnham, WCM C.657.

1401, 24 June, 10th in order at the episcopal el., *Reg. Sed. Vac.*, 372.

1402/3, pd visits to Harvington and Overbury, WCM C.611, C.712.

1404/5, pd visits to Leopard Grange, Moor [Lindridge], Newnham and Tibberton, WCM C.679, C.650, C.661, C.810.

1406/7, visited Tibberton, WCM C.813.

1411/12, recd 6s. 8d. from the chamberlain for his habit, WCM C.30.

William DENE [Dean, Deane, Deen

occ. 1458 d. 1498/9

1458, 23 Sept., ord acol. and subdcn, Worcester cathedral, Reg. Carpenter, i, 547.

1460, 7 June, ord dcn., Hereford cathedral, *Reg. Stanbury* (Hereford), 146.

1461, 19 Sept., ord pr., [North] Claines, Reg. Carpenter, i, 555.

1461/2, celebrated his first mass, and the almoner contributed 2s. 6d. to the celebration afterwards, WCM C.201a.

1467, chaplain to the prior, Reg. A.6(i), fo 44.

1474/6; 1478, 14 Sept.; 1479/81; 1483/4; 1488/9, master of the Lady chapel, WCM C.283, C.284; Reg. A.6(i), fo 73v; WCM C.285, C.285a; C.286; C.287.

1487, 22 July, subprior, Reg. Morton, 40.

1492, 23/24 June, almoner, Reg. Morton, 91 and Reg. A.6(i), fo 107v.

1492/3, described as *nuper* cellarer, WCM C.104.

1498, 12 Apr., subprior, Reg. G. Gigli, 9.

1467/8, one of three monks who recd gifts from the master of the Lady chapel for singing, WCM C.281.

1478, 14 Sept., witness to the homage of a priory tenant, Reg. A.6(i), fo 73v.

1486/7, with Roger Kingeslonde, q.v., staying in the almonry and recd pennies from the almoner to distribute to the poor, WCM C.207; he also held a court at Bredicot this yr, *ib.*

1487, 22 July, acted as commissary for the abp at the installation of the bp [Morton, by proxy], Reg. Morton, 40.

1489/90, mentioned by the almoner as though he had 20s. for Dene's corrody [?in the almonry], WCM C.208.

1492, 23/24 June, named by the chapter as one of the seven candidates for the office of prior, Reg. Morton, 91 and Reg. A.6(i), fo 107v.

1498, 12 Apr., subprior, [?presided] at the installation of the bp and took the oath of obedience to the vicar general, Reg. G. Gigli, 9.

1498/9, d. and the chamberlain sold his bedding, viz., two coverlets, one mattress, one bolster, for 10s., WCM C.48. The precentor records an extra payment to servants in the kitchen and brewery after his d. and that of two other monks, one of whom was prior William Wenlok, q.v., WCM C.391.

Richard de DERSYNTON [Dersinton
occ. 1311 occ. 1329/30

1311, 17 Nov., one of two whose prof. the prior was comm. to rec., *Reg. Reynolds*, 27 and *Liber Albus*, no 536; on 25 Nov. he made his prof. in the Lady chapel, Liber Albus, fo 50.
1311, 9 Dec., recd *lit. dim.* for all orders, *Reg. Reynolds*, 96.
1312, 6 Mar., ord subdcn, Worcester cathedral, *ib.*, 129.
1314, 21 Dec., ord. pr., Worcester cathedral, Reg. Maidstone, 41.
1326/7, kitchener, WCM C.107.
1318, June/1319, responsible for keeping acct of the priory sheep [*bidentes*], WCM E.16.
1329/30, visited Cleeve Prior, WCM C.557.

Note: this monk was prob. also known as Richard de Winchecumbe, q.v.

Robert de DICLESDONE [Dicledisdone, Diclesdene, Dikklesdon, Duclesdon, Ducleston
occ. 1300 occ. 1317

1300, 19 Aug., almoner, *Reg. Giffard*, 530.
1300, 19 Aug., one of the monks apptd by the bp to assist Nicholas de Norton, q.v., in conducting a visitation in *spiritualibus* of the prior and chapter, *ib.*
[1308], licensed by the bp to hear confessions 'of our subjects', *Reg. Reynolds*, 2.
1312, 15 Sept., present at the installation by proxy of the adcn of Worcester, Liber Albus, fo 57v.
1314, 4 Mar., licensed by the bp to hear confessions in the diocese, Reg. Maidstone, 4.
1314, 1 Sept., given another licence to hear confessions *parochianorum episcopatus*, *ib.*, 31.
1317, 20 Oct., 2nd in order at the el. of a prior, Liber Albus, fo 83.

Name in Cambridge, Peterhouse Ms 71, Peter Lombard (13th/14th c.), *memoriale fratris*—.

Note: Wilson's suggestion that 'R. de D'. in *Liber Albus*, no 422 (dated c. 1307/8) refers to this monk is prob. incorrect, as he would hardly need a character ref. long after entering the priory.

DIZARE
see Dyere

John de DODDEFORD
occ. 1274

1274, 20 Sept., one of five *compromissorii* in the el. of a prior, Reg. Giffard, 62.
n.d. mentioned on a reeve's acct, WCM E.16.

DODDELEYE
see Dudley

Gilbert de DODYNHAM [Dodenham
occ. 1272 occ. 1274

1272, 21 Dec., almoner, *Reg. Giffard*, 50–51.
1272, 21 Dec., chosen by the chapter as one of the seven candidates for the office of prior, *Reg. Giffard*, 50.
1274, 21 Sept., again chosen as one of the seven for the office of prior, *ib.*, 62.

Name in Worcs. Ms Q.42, Distinctiones Mauricii (late 13th c.). On the last flyleaf there is a list of eleven monks who contributed to the purchase of this volume; he pd 12[?d.].

DOMBLETON
see Dumbelton

Roger DON
see Kyngeslonde, Kyngislonde

Robert DONCLENT [Donkelent, ?Douclent, Dunklent
occ. 1353 occ. 1358/9

1353, 26 Nov., one of three *clerici* whom the prior was com. to examine for adm. to the priory, Reg. Bryan, i, 10.
1354, 20 Dec., ord acol., Hartlebury, *ib.*, i, 88.
1355, 10 Mar., ord subdcn, Hartlebury, *ib.*, i, 101.
1356, 17 Dec., ord dcn., Alvechurch, *ib.*, i, 104.
1358, 26 Mar., ord pr., Hartlebury, *ib.*, i, 115.
1358/9, celebrated his first mass, and the precentor gave *exennia*, WCM C.356.

In 1343, a M. Thomas Dunclent was apptd proctor by the prior and chapter, Liber Albus, fo 189, and in 1354/5, the cellarer pd a J. Donclent, notary, for transacting business affairs for the house, WCM C.62.

DORMESTON
see Annochia

DUCLESDON
see Diclesdone

I John de DUDLEY, D.Th [Doddeleye, Dodel', Dodeleie, Dodeleye, Duddeleye, Dudeleye
occ. 1375 occ. 1423

1375, 16 June, ord subdcn, Worcester cathedral, *Reg. Sed. Vac.*, 343.
1377, 19 Sept., ord pr., Tewkesbury abbey, *Reg. Wakefield*, no 873h.
1395/6; 1396, May/1399; 1399/1402, infirmarer, WCM C.21; C.244–246a; C.839, C.256, C.257.
1409, 2 Jan., 1419, 24 Apr., [1420/3], subprior, Wilkins *Concilia*, iii, 326, *Reg. Sed. Vac.*, 407, WCM C.84, C.84a, Pantin, *BMC*, iii, 189.
1379, student at Oxford to whom the chamberlain gave money for clothing, WCM C.12.
1382/3, student, to whom the cellarer gave money *tempore convocationis cleri* [in Oxford,

18/26 Nov. 1382], WCM C.70. On this acct a payment of £12 p.a. is entered for the two Oxford students; see also John de Hatfeld.

1383/4, student, for whom the precentor procured horses for his journeys from Oxford to Worcester and back, WCM C.363.

1384/5, student, and made several journeys back and forth between Worcester and Oxford, WCM C.364.

1388, 22 Aug., described as a scholar of Oxford in the el. of a prior, *Reg. Wakefield*, no 788; and see below.

1389, [student], recd money from the chamberlain [for clothing] for the three months July/Sept., WCM C.16.

1390/1, student, and recd a gift of 3s. 4d. from the precentor, WCM C.367.

1392, c. 25 Mar., student; returned to Worcester for the episcopal visitation and the cellarer pd expenses for travel from and back to Oxford, WCM C.75, Liber Albus fo 359.

1392/3, recd 20s. from the prior for his inception and the cellarer sent the long cart to Oxford [?for his belongings]; he also went as proctor to the Black Monk Chapter at Northampton [on 6 July, 1393, Pantin, *BMC*, iii, 213] and the cellarer pd his expenses of 17s. 6d., WCM C.76, C.76a. The chamberlain gave him [for clothing] 7s. 6d., at Oxford between June and Sept. [1393], WCM C.20.

1393/4, returned from Oxford to preach and his expenses were pd by the precentor, WCM C.368. On the acct of the kitchener for this yr is a payment to him for [food for] one yr and nineteen wks at 8d. per wk, a total of 47s. 4d., WCM C.124.

There are also four letters in the Liber Albus, undated but prob. written c. 1392, concerning his desire to complete his studies by obtaining his doctorate:

(1) from the duke of Gloucester [Thomas of Woodstock], written in London, 25 Mar., in French. He requested the prior to support Dudley, who had already recd encouragement from the bp of Worcester, in his desire to 'commence in theology' since he had completed all the requirements; however, he had expressed reluctance to burden his brethren with the expense, fo 359. This surely refers to his desire to incept.

(2) from the duchess of Gloucester, and almost a repetition of her husband's words, written 26 Mar., in French, fo 359^{v}.

(3) from the duke, a second letter, dated 17 May, and repeating his previous request, fo 360.

(4) from the prior to the duke, written 11 June, in French, giving a vague but generally favourable response to the duke's *desir et commandement*, *ib*.

[1393], it appears that the Black Monk Chapter agreed to contribute an unknown sum towards the expense of his inception, but this was still unpd in 1399 when one of the presidents of the Chapter issued a reminder, Pantin, *BMC*, iii, 146–147.

See also *BRUO*, which, however, is incomplete.

1379/80, ill in the infirmary and the almoner gave 2s. to him and other sick brethren, WCM C.175.

1388, 21 Aug., 31st in order at the el. of a prior, and chosen as one of the seven nominees for the priorate, Liber Albus, fos 334^{v}, 335.

1393, 3 Oct., with Prior John Grene, q.v., acted as an assessor at the trial of Walter Brut, lollard, and present at his abjuration, *Reg. Trefnant* (Hereford), 359.

1395, 15 Sept., one of the seven nominees for the priorate, Liber Albus, fo 380.

1399, 28 May, apptd by the prior as his commmissary to conduct a visitation of Shrewsbury abbey for the Black Monk Chapter, Pantin, *BMC*, iii, 248–249; at the July Chapter in Northampton to which he was sent as proctor (apptd 26 June, *ib*., 212), it was decreed that he be pd 20s. for the office of diffinitor (*ib*., 146). (The first two of these items are transcribed from the Liber Albus fos 399, 411.)

1401, 24 June, 8th in order at the episcopal el. and gave the sermon, *Reg. Sed. Vac*., 372, 373. On 4 July he and another, as the prior's commissaries, *sed. vac*., conducted a visitation of Pershore abbey and went on to carry out visitations in the deaneries of Wych and Warwick and religious houses there and elsewhere, *Reg. Sed. Vac*., 383.

1401/2, recd payment from the chamberlain for preaching, WCM C.26.

1402, 30 June, apptd by the prior as proctor for the Black Monk Chapter meeting at Northampton, Pantin, *BMC*, iii, 212 (Liber Albus, fo 399).

1404/5, recd from the cellarer 49s. 10d. for his expenses in carrying out visitations for the Black Monk Chapter, WCM C.78.

1407/8, with John Fordham, q.v., went to Gloucester to confer with the king and the abp [of Canterbury], and then to Oxford 'causa opinnonum divers' herietic erranc' in fide destruend' ' [*sic*]; the cellarer entered their expenses of £4 12s. 9d. under 'negotiations', WCM C.79.

1409, 2 Jan., present at the trial of John Badby, heretic, in the carnary chapel, Worcester, Wilkins, *Concilia*, iii, 326 (Reg. abp Arundel, ii, fo 17).

1419, 24 Apr., as subprior, second in order at the episcopal el., *Reg. Sed. Vac*., 407.

1420, [8 July], present at the Black Monk Chapter in Northampton and named as an elector of future presidents, Pantin, *BMC*, ii, 97 (as subprior, name not given).

1420, 23 Aug., apptd by Prior Fordham, vicar general, q.v., to rec. the purgation of a heretic, Reg. Morgan, 37–38.

Name in Worcs. Ms Q.50, Alexander Nequam, etc. (13th c.), on fo 49; this could refer to John Dudley II, q.v., but the hand suggests the earlier of the two by this name.

Note: the name Dudley is also in the margin of Cambridge, St John's College Ms 103, Stephen Patrington (early 15th c.), fo 133; this vol. is a copy of the notebook of Patrington, a Carmelite and a contemporary of Dudley at Oxford in the 1380s who incepted three years before Dudley. It consists of a series of theological questions and answers, the reference to Dudley probably relating to the latter's opinion on a certain point.

II John DUDLEY [Duddeley
occ. 1483 d. 1531/2

1483, 20 Sept., ord. acol., carnary chapel by Worcester cathedral, Reg. Alcock, 274.
1487, 22 Sept., ord. pr., Ledbury, *Reg. Milling* (Hereford), 174.

1506, chaplain to the prior, Reg. A.6(ii), fo 35.
1510, 2 Feb., 8 May, 29 Nov; 1512, 29 Sept.; 1514, 23 Mar; 1516; 1519, 29 Sept.; 1520, 14 Feb.; master of the Lady chapel, WCM B.1160, B.1171, B.1165; B.1580; B.1167; Reg. A.12, fo 40v; B.978; B.1581.
1520/1, [still] master of the Lady chapel, and his last yr, Reg. A.17, 55; see John Multon, who succ. him.
1523/5, *magister communis cene*, WCM C.413, C.414; 1523/4, was his first yr, Reg. A.17, 277.
1529/31, infirmarer, WCM C.414a, C.414b.

1498, 25 Oct., 19th in order on the visitation certificate, *Reg. abp Morton*, ii, no 458.
1501/2, was owed 2s. 6d. by the kitchener, WCM C.167.
1510, 1512, 1514, 1519, 1520, as master of the Lady chapel and on dates given above, negotiated and witnessed leases.
1521, 22 July, 6th in order on the visitation certificate, Reg. abp Warham, ii, fo 293v.
1521/4, gave alms of 20d. each yr to the almoner, Wilson, *Accts Henry VIII*, 10, (Reg. A.17, 197, 262).
1531/2, 7th on the clerical subsidy list and as celebrant of the 10 o'clock mass he pd 2s., and also for 'commons' 3s. 4d., Reg. A.12, fo 135. Also, the prior pd him for regularly singing this mass during most of the yr, at 10s. a quarter, *Jnl More*, 340, 345, 351, 356; he succ. Richard Hallow, q.v.
1531/2, d., and the chamberlain recd 10s. from the sale of his clothing [*vestimentorum*], WCM C.414c.

See note concerning Worcs. Ms Q.50 in the previous entry.

Richard DUDLEY [Doddely, Duddeleye
occ. 1382 occ. ?1435/6

1382, 18 Apr., made his prof., Liber Albus, fo 454.
1384, 24 sept., ord acol., Alvechurch, *Reg. Wakefield*, no 906a.
1385, 25 Feb., ord subdcn, Cirencester abbey, *ib.*, no 908d.
1389, 13 Mar., ord pr., Alvechurch, *ib.*, no 935g.
1388/9, celebrated his first mass; recd gifts from the hostiller and the precentor, WCM C.214, C.366; this second acct runs only from 30 Sept to 21 Nov. 1388 and so the ordination date above should prob. be Mar. 1388.

1396, June/1399, infirmarer, WCM C.244a-246a.
1398/1400, kitchener, WCM C.127–128; there are many revisions and adjustments on the 1398/9 acct in the section of weekly expenditures on food, and the total spent has been reduced from £252 to c. £195. According to WCM C.657 (1399/1400), he was succ. in the fourth quarter (i.e. summer 1400) by Thomas Ruydyng, q.v.
1410/11, *custos* of the Lady chapel, WCM C.262.

1388, 21 Aug., 37th in order at the el. of a prior, Liber Albus, fo 334v.
1396, 9 Dec., granted papal licence to choose his own confessor, *CPL*, v (1396–1404), 48.
1401, 24 June, 30th at the episcopal el., *Reg. Sed. Vac.*, 373.
1408/9, sent on 'negotiations' by the cellarer, WCM C.81.
[1435/6], there is an unusual entry in the Liber Albus in the form of a brief and laudatory résumé of his monastic life and career. It is headed *Licencia concedenda . . . ad recipiend' sacros ordines*, but this appears to have been added in a different, and later, hand and is surely an incorrect interpretation of the document, which may have been a copy of the brief sent out at the time of his d. It begins by giving the date of his prof. and states that he went on to receive the orders of subdcn, dcn and pr. He celebrated mass, participated in the divine office and 'officium sacerdotale in dicta nostra ecclesia exercuit laudabili[ter] et honeste boneque fame et oppinionis illese omni tempore suo existens regularem vitam et modestam a tempore professionis sue huiusque prout humana fragilitas cognoscere potuit duxit laudabilem pariter et honestam', Liber Albus, fo 454.

James DUMBELTON [Dombleton, Dumbulton, Dumbylton
occ. 1475 d. 1478/9

1475, 7/8 Jan., one of four who were presented to the bp by two of the monks and the following day were examined by the bp's chancellor in the prior's chamber, in the presence of the prior, precentor and others; he was one of the three adm. for the yr of probation, Reg. Carpenter, ii, 135.
1476, 8 June, ord acol., carnary chapel by Worcester cathedral, *ib.*, ii, 207.

1478/9, d.; the almoner pd the brief bearer and the precentor pd for the briefs, WCM C.204, C.384; the almoner recd nothing for his corrody *quia pardonavitur*, WCM C.204.

John de DUMBELTON [Dombelton, Dombletone

occ. 1288 occ. 1324

1288/9, sacrist, apptd 10 Apr. 1288, *Reg. Giffard*, 320; 'absolved' from office, 9 Dec. 1290, *ib.*, 366; see Nicholas de Norton.

1299, 3 Nov./1300, Dec., prior of Little Malvern, apptd by the bp, *Reg. Giffard*, 515, *Reg. Sed. Vac.*, 2–3, *Ann. Wigorn.*, 542.

[1290], prob. student at Oxford; see Little and Pelster, *Oxford Theology*, 152.

1298/9, prob. at Oxford for part of the yr; recd a stipend of 26s. 8d. from the cellarer, and this entry follows the record of payment of monk scholars at Oxford, WCM C.54.

1301/3, prob. at Oxford from c. Oct. 1301 to Mar. 1303, acc. to the reconstruction of events by Little and Pelster, *ib.*, 237.

1301, Sept./Oct., the prior and chapter wrote to abp Winchelsey, who had performed a visitation of the priory a few months before (see Graham, 'Visitation', 334–344). They stated that he was the centre and cause of controversy in their midst. He, for his part, complained of having been excluded from the community, claimed to have been released from obedience to the prior and to have transferred to a house of another order and desired to have his monastic status in their house annulled. They now sought the abp's advice and were prepared to submit to the final decision of the presidents of the Black Monk Chapter, Pantin, *BMC*, i, 145–146 (*Liber Albus*, no 9).

1301, Sept./Nov., the abp's reply requested the prior and convent to assist him with an allowance pending the decision of the Chapter, *ib.*, 151 (*Liber Albus*, no 36).

1301, Sept./Oct., the presidents of the Black Monk Chapter wrote to the prior and convent asking them to provide him with 5m. before 1 Nov. so that he might have the means to support himself at Oxford or in a Benedictine house elsewhere, *ib.*, 148–149 (*Liber Albus*, no 13).

1301/2, Oct./Jan., letters were sent to the prior from both presidents of the Black Monk Chapter concerning Dumbelton. The abbot of Westminster was concerned that the 5m. had not been pd, *ib.*, 150–151 (*Liber Albus*, no 26); and the abbot of Malmesbury wrote in the same vein and implied that he was possibly at Oxford or was intending to go there 'ad studendum cum ceteris confratribus nostris', *ib.*, 154 (*Liber Albus*, no 60). The reply of the prior to the abbot of Westminster explained that although he and the chapter had searched for Dumbelton at Gloucester, Reading and Malvern they had been unable to find him in order to provide him with funds, *ib.*, 153–154 (*Liber Albus*, no 55).

1302, 25 Mar., he issued a public instrument in which he renounced his right to participate in the el. of a bp (to succeed bp Giffard), giving as his reason the fact that he had been apptd prior of Little Malvern and *ob alias causas multas*. He also stated that he was staying *in scolis Oxonie* at the expense of the prior and convent until the Black Monk Chapter met and decided his future, *ib.*, 155–156 (*Reg. Sed. Vac.*, 2–3).

1302, 22 Dec., the chapter wrote to the prior and convent requiring them to reinstate him in his former status as a full member of the community, *ib.*, 157–158 (*Reg. Sed. Vac.*, 35).

1303, 4 Jan., the prior and convent readmitted him as a member of the chapter, *Reg. Sed. Vac.*, 36. There is a later entry in this register giving the date as 10 Mar., *Reg. Sed. Vac.*, 44 (Pantin, *BMC*, i, 159–160). The latter is the official instrument certified by two representatives of the Black Monk Chapter.

1303, 10 Sept., two further letters concerning him conclude this affair: the abbot of Winchcombe wrote to the prior criticizing, so it appears, the way in which Dumbelton was being treated, and the prior replied that his methods were based on monastic observance which prescribed the application of the *vinum correccionis . . . ad medelam*, Pantin, *BMC*, i, 161 (*Liber Albus*, no 134a, and Liber Albus, fo 16).

1306, 26 Sept., the bp's visitation on this date produced a series of injunctions including one which ordered all members of the chapter to treat Dumbelton *in omnibus et per omnia, fraterna caritate*, Reg. Montacute, 223. (Note: Gainsborough's injunctions are found in this register.)

1317, 20 Oct., 6th in order at the el. of a prior, Liber Albus, fo 83.

1324, 29 Mar., present as witness when an incumbent of a city church took his oath of office, Liber Albus, fo 115.

Name in two Worcs.Mss:

(1) Q.42 Distinctiones Mauricii (late 13th c.). On the last flyleaf there is a list of eleven monks who contributed to the purchase of this volume; his share was 12[?d.].

(2) Q.46, Reportationes J. de Dombletone (late 13th c.) contains notes and sermons prob. copied [in his own hand] while at Oxford; see Little and Pelster, *Oxford Theology*, 152–154 for an analysis of its contents.

Note: Worcs. Ms F.6, which has been assigned in Floyer, *Catalogue of Mss*, to this monk has been shown by Little and Pelster, *ib.*, 237–238, to have been the work of M. John de Dumbelton, a fellow of Merton. See *BRUO*.

Richard de DUMBELTON
occ. 1260 d. 1272

1260–1272, prior: installed 24 Dec. 1260; d. before 21 Dec. 1272, *Fasti*, ii, 104.

1260, before becoming prior, cellarer, *Ann. Wigorn.*, 446.

1272, there is ref. to his d. in Reg. Giffard, 50–51; buried in the cloister, *Ann. Wigorn.*, 462.

Described as *Deo et hominibus amabilis*, *Ann. Wigorn.*, 462.

DUNKLENT
see Donclent

William de DURSLEYE
occ. 1337
1337, 5 Apr., ord. pr., Worcester cathedral, Reg. Montacute, 111.

Reginald DYERE [Dizare, Dyare
occ. 1374 ?d. 1407

1374, 25 Feb., ord subdcn, Worcester cathedral, *Reg. Sed. Vac.*, 300.

1401, 24 June, succentor, *Reg. Sed. Vac.*, 373.
1387/8, recd a *curialitas* from the precentor for helping with the binding and repair of books, WCM C.365.
1388, 21 Aug., 27th in order at the el. of a prior, Liber Albus, fo 334v.
1392/3, recd 3s. 4d. from the cellarer for being his *socius in choro* for half of the previous yr, and another 3s. 4d. described as *oblatio*, WCM C.76,.
1400/1, an indenture attached to the precentor's acct states that the knife [*cultellus*] 'ad planand' libros cum aliis parvis instrumentis' were in his custody, WCM C.370.
1401, 24 June, 22nd in order at the el. of a bp, *Reg. Sed. Vac.*, 373.
1405/6, recd 22d. from the precentor for binding one psalter and one *libr' v passional'*, WCM C.372.
1406/7, recd his share [*porcio*] of pittances, i.e. 5s., which covered the period up to 25 Mar., and so he prob. d., WCM C.320.

DYMHOK
see Adam de Cirencester

EDREDUS
occ. c. 1104

Name occ. in the list of monks in *Durham Liber Vitae*, fo 22.

Note: this may be Ethelred, q.v.

EDWINUS
occ. c. 1104

Name occ. in the list of monks in *Durham Liber Vitae*, fo 22.

I EDRICUS [Edric
occ. c. 1104 occ. 1125 × 1139

c. 1104, name occ. in the list of monks in *Durham Liber Vitae*, fo 22.
1125 × 1139, mentioned in a grant of land to the prior and chapter by bp Simon, *Worcs. Cart.*, no 87.
23 Nov., obit occ. in Oxford Bod. Mss Hatton 113 and 114, Wulstan's Homiliary, where he is described as monk and priest who wrote this acct [*compotum*], Atkins, 'Church of Worcs.', pt ii, 29; see also Watson, *Dated and Datable Mss*, i, no 520.

II EDRICUS
occ. *temp.* St Wulstan

An Edricus described in the *Vita Wulfstani* sang the night office with the bp; Darlington, *Vita Wulfstani*, 47, 95. Is this monk identical with Edricus I?

EGELREDUS
see Aegelredus

EGELRICUS
see Aegelricus

Richard de ?ELLENTRA or OLLENTRA
occ. late 13th c.

Name on a reeve's acct, *temp.* John de Doddeford, Thomas de Wych, Robert de Wych, q.v., WCM E.16.

W. de EPORT
d. 1220

Described as formerly sacrist, *Ann. Wigorn.*, 412.

EPORT
see also Newport

Thomas de ERDINTONE
d. 1218

1218, 20 Mar., d., *Ann. Wigorn.*, 410.

He is described as *sapientissimus et facundissimus* and was clothed as a monk [*cucullatus*] before his d., *ib.*

ERNULF [Aernald
occ. 1236

1236, 24 Aug., one of two monk proctors who recd from the king licence to el. a bp, *CPR (1232–1247)*, 157; see Thomas III.
See also Aernalis.

John ESBURY
occ. 1412 d. 1422/3

1412, 17 Dec., ord acol., Worcester cathedral, Reg. Peverel, 193.
1413 ,8 Apr., ord subdcn, Worcester cathedral, *ib.*, 195.

1413, 23 Sept., ord dcn, Winchcombe abbey, *ib.*, 197.
1414, 22 Sept., ord pr., Stratford, *ib.*, 202.
1413/14, celebrated his first mass; recd *exennia* from the almoner, WCM C.190; the hostiller and pittancer also contributed, but on their accts for 1414/15, WCM C.224, 322.
1419, 24 Apr., 31st in order at the el. of a bp. *Reg. Sed. Vac.*, 407.
1422/3, d. and the chamberlain sold his *vestimenta*, WCM C.34.

Thomas ESBURY
occ. 1379

1379, hostiller, WCM C.597.
1379, visited Hallow, WCM C.597.

Walter de ESTOVER
occ. 1274

1274, 20 Sept., chosen as one of five *compromissorii* in the el. of a prior, *Reg. Giffard*, 62.

ETHELRED
see Aegelredus

EUSTONE
see Owston

I John de EVESHAM, B.Th.
occ. 1323 d. 1370

1340–1370, prior: installed 22 Apr. 1340; d. 27 Mar. 1370, see below for details.
1323, 11 Nov., one of three *clerici* whom the bp comm. his sequestrator to examine at the time of their adm. to the priory, Liber Albus, fo 113^{v}.
1325, 23 Feb., ord subdcn, bp's chapel, Kempsey, *Reg. Cobham*, 178.
1326, 15 Feb., ord dcn, bp's chapel, Hartlebury, *ib.*, 194.
1333/4, student at Oxford, and recd 31s. 8d. p.a. from the kitchener, WCM C.110.
1336/7, student during 45 wks from the end of Sept. to 10 Aug., and recd 16d. per wk from the cellarer, WCM C.57; he was one of three students, see also William de Birlingham and John de Prestone I.
1338/9, student during 48 wks and recd maintenance at the same rate from the cellarer, WCM C.58; see also Thomas de Legh and William de Birlingham.
1340, 21 Apr., described as B.Th., at the el. of a prior, *Reg. Bransford*, no 290.
1339, 4 Jan., named as one of five *compromissorii* at the el. of a bp, Worcs. Ms F.141, inside of back cover; he also travelled to London, with Henry de Fouke and Robert de Weston, q.v., [in connection with their el. of Wulstan de Bransford, q.v.], and returned *in familia Electi*, WCM C.58. It is to be noted, however, that acc. to *Reg. Sed. Vac.*, 267, there were only three *compromissorii*, whose names are not given, merely initials which do not tally with any of the names in Fouke's letter.
1339, 12 Apr., one of the monk proctors sent to the bp to present the seven nominees for the priorate, *Reg. Bransford*, no 38.
1340, 21 Apr., one of the seven candidates nom. for the priorate, *ib.*, no 290.
1340, 22 Apr., the bp comm. the official of the adcn of Worcester to instal him as prior, *ib.*, no 294.
1340, between Apr. and Sept., pd a visit to Moor [Lindridge] after his el. as prior, WCM C.647.
1340, 8 July, apptd to replace William de Beauchamp in setting up the inquiry in the county of Worcester for the reorganization of the ninth granted by the clergy and commons, *CPR (1338–1340)*, 503.
1340, 11 Sept., attended the Black Monk Chapter at Northampton and was assigned to preach the Latin sermon at the 1343 meeting, Pantin, *BMC*, ii, 15.
1342, 3 Oct., apptd Robert de Weston, q.v., and the adcn of Worcester as his proctors for convocation; but his chaplain, Roger de Bosbury, q.v., added a memorandum that this apptment did not take effect *quia prior personaliter fuit ibidem*, Liber Albus, fo 180^{v}.
1342, 13 Oct., comm. by the bp to carry out a papal comm. to find and provide benefices for certain poor clerks in the diocese; his *acta* in this matter are in the Liber Albus, fos 199–201^{v}. The heading is impressive: 'Incipiunt acta et processus provisorum Domini Clementis pape sexti coram fratre . . . prioris'.
1343, 9–11 Sept., attended the Black Monk Chapter and preached on the theme *Consilium quid agere debeamus*; he was nom. as one of the electors of the future presidents, Pantin, *BMC*, ii, 20, 22.
1344/5, went to London for negotiations involving Thomas de Legh, q.v., and matters concerned with others who were going to the curia, [?because of an appeal vs. the abbot of St Albans], WCM C.59.
1346, 25 Sept., attended the Black Monk Chapter in Northampton, with expenses of £6 6s. pd by the cellarer, WCM C.60; the date is in Pantin, *BMC*, iii, 210.
1346/7, went to London and charged the cellarer's acct £10, WCM C.61; he also pd £100 *pro merbur'*, ib; he was present for the tourn at Overbury, WCM C.699.
1347/8, visited Sedgeberrow with the cellarer, WCM C.757.
1348, Sept., he and the monks were threatened by a mob who broke down the gates and entered the monastic precincts following a dispute over a corpse that had been interred in the churchyard adjoining the cathedral, *CPR*

(1348–1350), 245, 249 and Noake, *Worcs. Cathedral*, 97–101.

1349, 25 Aug., royal assent granted to his el. as bp, *CPR (1348–1350)*, 362, (but John de Thoresby was provided, *Fasti*, iv, 56).

1350, 15 July, obtained papal licence to choose his own confessor, *CPL*, iii (1342–1362), 369.

1350, 30 Sept., obtained from the king letters appting two attorneys for one yr to act during his absence on the king's service and on pilgrimage overseas, *CPR (1348–1350)*, 570; was this connected with the papal jubilee? See Nicholas de Clanefeld, Robert de Weston and Walter de Wynforton.

1350/1, the precentor noted that he had been on a visit to Avignon this yr when he recorded payment of his 'O' pittance *in recessu suo de curia*, WCM C.354.

1351, 8 Jan., granted papal indult by Clement VI for the use of pontificals, viz., mitre, ring, staff, dalmatic and tunicle; also to give the solemn blessing at mass and at table in the absence of a papal legate or bishop, *CPL*, iii (1342–1362), 382; on the same day he and the subprior were given papal permission to reconcile the cathedral church and cemetery, and other churches and cemeteries of their patronage, when required, *ib.*, 383. A copy of the former bull is in the Liber Pensionum, fo 51, and Reg. abp Courtenay, fo 69^{v} (printed in Dugdale, *Monasticon*, i, 618), and of the latter bull in Reg. A.12, fo 137; see also *CPL*, iii (1342–1362), 382, 383. In addition, on this same day he obtained indults to celebrate mass before daybreak and to have a portable altar, *CPL*, iii (1342–1362), 400.

1351, 17 Jan., authorized by the pope to examine two clerks for the office of notary and to 'create' them, *ib.*, 399.

1351, 10 Dec., present in chapter where he apptd Nicholas de Clanefeld, Robert de Weston and Walter de Wynforton, q.v., as his attorneys, Bloom *Liber Ecclesiae*, 51 (PRO E315/63 fos 58^{v}–59).

Note: it seems more likely that the yr was 1350, unless this was a reapptment on his return.

1353, 3 July, the new bp [Reginald Bryan] chose John de Powik, q.v. as sacrist, Liber Albus, fo 236; this apptment was strongly opposed by the prior and chapter and was one of several causes of dissension between the monks and the bp, another being (in the bp's view) the scandalous depreciation of episcopal authority resulting from the prior's use of pontifical regalia, which rivalled his own in splendour. During the course of the dispute the bp went so far as to cast doubt on the prior's character and reputation and to question the competence of his administration and even the legality of his status as prior. Lawsuits and appeals to Canterbury and to the papal curia were the inevitable outcome, Liber Albus, fos 236–245. A summary and chronological sequence of the prior's activities can be partially reconstructed:

1354, 21 Apr., the prior asserted his right to pontificals granted by Clement VI, and in face of the bp's opposition he appealed to the pope, Liber Albus, fo 239^{v}.

1354/5, Walter de Wynforton, cellarer, q.v., went to London to obtain the necessary legal instruments for the prior *versus curia Romana*, WCM C.62. A sum of £28 12s. was provided for the prior about to set out for Avignon, *ib.*, and at an unknown date the prior named the subprior John de Legh, Robert de Weston and Walter de Wynforton, q.v., his *vices gerentes* during his absence, Liber Albus, fo 214^{v}. He also visited Moor [Lindridge], and he went to London, WCM C.62.

1355, 22 May, the prior was in chapter at the reading of the legal instrument [*procuratio ad appellandum*] which contains a detailed statement of the prior's privileges acquired in the *bulla privilegiorum originalis* and which on 5 Feb. had been 'unjustly' reduced by Innocent VI on the petition of the bp, Liber Albus fos 241–242^{v}. The amendments are summarized in *CPL*, iii (1342–1362), 571.

Note: on 28 Jan. of this yr, prior Robert Hathbrand, q.v. (under Canterbury) had petitoned the pope for the right to use pontifical regalia, and in a second petition shortly after had pointed out that Worcester was subject to Canterbury, the primatial see, *Lit. Cant.*, nos 810, 811.

1355, 17 July, the subprior and chapter informed the bp that the prior had been absent for some days *pro arduis . . . negociis in remotis agente*, *ib.*, fo 244.

1355, 7 Sept., obtained a permit to go to the curia on business with six members of his household, *CPR (1354–1358)*, 279; on 28 Nov. he apptd two attorneys to act for him in England for one yr. These entries suggest that although he left Worcester in July he did not cross the Channel before Sept. and perhaps not before late November.

1356/7, the cellarer went to London to arrange for money to be sent to the prior and his officials in Avignon, and pd a bearer bringing letters from the prior, WCM C.63.

1357, 23 Sept., the prior was still *in remotis*, Liber Albus, fo 214^{v}.

1357/8, the cellarer pd a messenger bringing news of the prior and another bringing letters from Avignon; he made several visits to London concerning the resolution of the dispute, WCM C.64.

1358, 8 Sept., the prior had returned by this date and entertained guests on this feast, WCM C.64.

1360/1, visited Overbury, WCM C.707.

1362, 14 Apr., comm. by bp [Barnet] to act as collector of tenths, Reg. Barnet, 18.

1363, 13 Feb., comm. by the bp to be vicar general in spirituals during his absence, *ib.*, 47.

1364, 11 Apr., made a visitation of the chapter, *sed. vac.*, in person, and on 12 Apr., visited the clergy and deanery of Powick in the parish church there, *Reg. Sed. Vac.*, 219.

1365, 14 Feb., obtained a grant from Urban V which restored in part some of the privileges obtained in 1351, Reg. Wittlesey, 5 and *CPL*, iv (1362–1404), 48. It was a compromise which was not acceptable to Evesham's successors, Walter de Legh and John Grene, q.v. See Marett, 'Pontificalia', 61–62.

1366, 23 Jan., obtained, on request, a comm. from the pope for the subprior to have the authority to absolve his fellow monks, *conversi*, secular priests and clerks from a number of specified sins which included drinking, gambling, shedding blood and putting off the monastic habit; this is prob. equivalent to the licence commissioning a papal penitentiary, WCM B.1642.

Note: on the basis of a misreading of this document, John Noake has unwittingly brought Evesham's name into disrepute. He thought that the subprior was empowered to absolve the prior, whose sins were enumerated in the list referred to above, *Worcs. Cathedral*, 101–102.

1367, Feb./Sept., visited Newnham, WCM C.654.

1370, 27 Mar., d., acc. to *Anglia Sacra*, i, 549.

1369/70, the cellarer recorded details of expenses *circa sepulturam* which included a ?cloth [*osta*] in which to wrap the body, costing 2s. 3d., food for the mourners and alms for the poor; the total was £23, WCM C.66.

1421/2 and yrs following, the almoner recorded payments *die obitus*, WCM C.191, C.192; in 1504 the sum of £1 p.a. was allocated for this purpose, Reg. A.6(ii), fo 32v.

Fos 175 to 245v of the priory register, the Liber Albus, cover the yrs of his priorate; the entries were made by his chaplains, Roger de Bosbury, John de Hodynton, John de Troubrugg, John de Malverne I, William Power, John de Hatfeld, q.v.

His register of *acta* during several vacancies of the see is found in *Reg. Sed. Vac.*, 191–222.

During his priorate the *nova porta*, almost certainly the Edgar tower/gate, was under construction (i.e., between 1346 and 1353). There were also repairs to the prior's lodgings in 1357/8, WCM C.61, Windsor, St George's Chapel, XI.E.37, WCM C.64; see John *conversus*.

According to Thomas Habington (d. 1647) his effigy was to be seen in the north choir aisle and depicted him with two mitres, one on his head and the other in his left hand, with the inscription 'Johannes de Evesham, prior, privilegiu[m de mitra . . . impetravit, ecclesiam de Overbury et Warrenam . . .', John Amphlett, ed., *A Survey of Worcestershire by Thomas Habington*, Worcestershire Historical Society, 2 vols (1895–1899), ii, 381. The appropriation of Overbury recd papal approval, c. 1347, *Liber Pensionum*, 18–19.

Further details of his career and achievements may be found in Greatrex, 'Prior Evesham', 64–76.

II John EVESHAM

occ. 1425 d. 1457/8

1425, 24 Mar., ord acol., Worcester cathedral, Reg. Morgan, 207.

1426, 30 Mar., ord subdcn, Worcester cathedral, *ib.*, 211.

1428, 28 Sept., ord dcn, Worcester [?cathedral], Reg. Polton, 101.

1429/30, celebrated his first mass, and was one of eight priests who each recd 2s. 8d. from the hostiller, WCM C.231.

1433, 9 Dec., 36th in order at the episcopal el., *Reg. Sed. Vac.*, 432.

1457/8, d. and the chamberlain recd 4s. for his *harnesia*, WCM C.44.

III John EVESHAM [Ewysham

occ. 1497/1500

1497, 14 Apr., ord dcn, carnary chapel by Worcester cathedral, Reg. G. Gigli, 25.

1500, 19 Apr., ord pr., carnary chapel, Reg. S. Gigli, 399.

1498, 25 Oct., 40th in order on the visitation certificate, *Reg. abp Morton*, ii, no 458.

Randulph de EVESHAM, [Hevesham

occ. 1203 occ. 1214

1203–1214, prior: succ. 24 Dec. 1203; el. abbot of Evesham 20 Jan. 1214, *Fasti*, ii, 103, *HRH*, 48.

Before 1203, monk of Evesham, *ib.*

1202, went to Rome to promote the canonization of Wulstan, *Ann. Wigorn*, 391; see Walter de Bradwas.

1213, 2 Dec., el. bp of Worcester, but the election was quashed, *Fasti*, ii, 100, 103.

Reginald EVESHAM

occ. 1490/2

1490, 6 Mar., ord acol., carnary chapel by Worcester cathedral, Reg. Morton, 143.

1490, 10 Apr., ord subdcn, carnary chapel, *ib.*, 145.

1492, 22 Sept., ord dcn, carnary chapel, *ib.*, 157.

Roger de EVESHAM

occ. [1369] d. 1439/40

[1369], 1 Oct., one of seven whose prof. the bp comm. the precentor to rec., Reg. Lynn, 89.

1370, 13 Apr., ord acol., [Worcester cathedral], *ib.*, 50.

1370, 21 Dec., ord subdcn, Hartlebury, *ib.*, 53.

1372, 18 Sept., ord pr., [Worcester cathedral], 60.
1396, Feb./Sept., refectorer, WCM C.417.
1420/2, hostiller, WCM C.225, C.226.

1373, 4 Dec., 26th in order at the episcopal el., *Reg. Sed. Vac.*, 290.
1380/1, ill, and the infirmarer provided medicine, WCM C.242.
1388, 21 Aug., 22nd in order at the el. of a prior, Liber Albus, fo 334v.
1392/3, in the infirmary and was one of those for whom the cellarer provided six chickens, WCM C.76.
1401, 24 June, 16th at the episcopal el., *Reg. Sed. Vac.*, 373.
1408/9, was owed 4s. 8d. by the cellarer, WCM C.81.
1419, 24 Apr., 4th at the episcopal el., *Reg. Sed. Vac.*, 407.
1429/30, was owed 53s. 4d. by the cellarer, WCM C.86.
1433, 9 Dec., [again] 4th in order, at the episcopal el., *ib.*, 432.
1439/40, d. and the chamberlain sold his *harnesia* for 23s., WCM C.39.

Note: it seems clear that we have here one monk who must have rejoiced in 70 years of profession; if he was 25 at his ordination to the priesthood, then he was a nonagenarian. The fact that he was fourth in order on two occasions, fourteen yrs apart is prob. explained by some discrepancy or alteration in the order of seniority of the top four.

Silvester de EVESHAM
occ. 1214/16

1214/15–1216, prior: el. 21 Jan. 1214/15; el. bp of Worcester 3 Apr. 1216, *Fasti*, ii, 103, *HRH*, 84.
1215, as prior he was summoned to and attended the fourth Lateran council in 1215, but before his return he was el. bp by the monks, consecrated at Perugia on 3 July 1216 by the pope and enthroned [in Worcester] on 8 Sept., *Ann. Wigorn.*, 405. The royal letters of protection for him while attending the council are dated 1218 and address him as bp., *CPR (1216–1225)*, 144. See also *Councils and Synods*, ii, 1377.

William EVESHAM
occ. 1419 d. 1419/20

1419, 1 Apr., ord dcn, Worcester cathedral, *Reg. Sed. Vac.*, 392.
1419, 24 Apr., a prof. monk and 38th in order at the episcopal el., *ib.*, 407.
1419/20, d., and the chamberlain sold his *panni*, WCM C.32.

Walter EWYAS [Evyace, Eweas, Ewyars
occ. 1425 d. 1452/3

1425, 21 Sept., ord subdcn, Worcester cathedral, Reg. Morgan, 210.
1427, 15 Mar., ord dcn, Worcester cathedral, Reg. Polton, 209.
1429/30, celebrated his first mass and was one of eight priests who each recd 2s. 8d. *exennia* from the hostiller, WCM C.231.

1433, 9 Dec., 27th in order at the episcopal el., *Reg. Sed. Vac.*, 432.
1448/9, 1449/50, was one of a number of monks on the cellarer's list of creditors, WCM C.91, C.92.
1452/3, d.; the chamberlain recd nothing [for his clothing], WCM C.42.

EWYSHAM
see Evesham

EYLISBURY
see Aylesbury

Richard de FECKENHAM [Fecham
occ. 1272 d. 1286

1274–1286, prior: apptd by the bp 25 Sept. 1274; d. 29 Sept. 1286, *Fasti*, ii, 104.

1272, 21 Dec.; 1274, 21 Sept., chamberlain, *Reg. Giffard*, 50, 62.

1272, 21 Dec., one of the seven nominees for the priorate, *ib.*, 50.
1274, 21 Sept., one of the seven nominees for the priorate, *ib.*, 62.
1282, presumably played host when the king held parliament in Worcester this yr, *Ann. Wigorn.*, 484.
n.d. occ. on an undated acct roll, WCM E.4 (9).

Henry de FEKERHAM [?Fokerham
occ. 1302

1302, 22 Sept., ord subdcn, Worcester [cathedral], *Reg. Sed. Vac.*, 24, (ms fo 11).

FILKYNS
see Fylkes

FLORENCE [Florentius
occ. c. 1104 d. 1118

c. 1104, name occ. in the list of monks in *Durham Liber Vitae*, fo 22.
1118, 7 July, d., *Chron. John of Worcs.*, 13.

Name in the Savigny mortuary roll of c. 1122/3, Delisle, *Rouleau Mortuaire*, pl. xxv, tit. 87.

He was prob. not the author of the Worceser chronicle known as the Chronicon ex Chronicis, but materials which he had compiled were used by John I, q.v. For discussion of the relationship between Florence and John, see Gransden, *Hist. Writing*, i, 143–144.

John de FORDHAM D.Th. [Fordam, Fortham
occ. 1382 d. 1438

1409–1438, prior: installed before 29 Sept. 1409, WCM C.81; d. by 12 Feb. 1438, Reg. Bourgchier, 84, 85.

1382, 1 Mar., ord acol., Kidderminster, *Reg. Wakefield*, no 893b.
1382, 19 Sept., obtained *lit. dim.*, for all orders, *ib.*, no 896.
1384, 24 Sept., ord dcn, Alvechurch, *ib.*, no 906f.
1387, 2 Mar., ord pr., Hartlebury, *ib.*, no 913g.
1387, Feb./Sept., celebrated his first mass; the prior and cellarer contributed bread and wine for the celebratory feast, WCM C.73. The hostiller's 1386/7 acct records payments to two juniors, priests, one of them being Fordham, Hamilton *Comp. Rolls*, 56 (WCM C.213); see William Cropthorne.

1398, Mar./Sept., 1399/1401, 3 Apr., almoner, WCM C.184–186.

1387, Feb./Sept., student at Oxford; came back to Worcester for his ordination (above) and returned to Oxford, WCM C.73.
1389, May/Sept., student, to whom the chamberlain sent money [for clothing] for the three months July/Sept.; he also bought cloth from the chamberlain for one *cucullus* and one *stamen*, WCM C.16.
1390/1, student; the precentor hired two horses to bring him back at Easter and to provide for his return journey to Oxford; this cost him 5s. 6d. and he also gave Fordham 18d. WCM C.367.
1392, c. 25 Mar., student; returned to Worcester for the episcopal visitation and the cellarer pd expenses for travel from and back to Oxford, WCM C.75, Liber Albus, fo 359.
1395/6, the kitchener pd 9s. less than usual to the Oxford scholars because he was at the curia for part of the yr (see below), WCM C.126.
1396/7, [student], to whom the cellarer pd 'for his expenses at Oxford 30s.', WCM C.479.
1401 × 1407, apptd *prior studentium* at Oxford, Pantin, *BMC*, iii, 87; Pantin notes the undated letter to him as *prior studentium* in Oxford, Bod. Ms 692, fo 116, Pantin, *BMC*, iii, 320 and Pantin, *Cant. Coll. Ox.*, iii, 61–62.
c. 1407, D.Th., yr of inception uncertain; *BRUO* suggests this date. He is described as Magister in 1407, *Reg. Sed. Vac.*, 389.
1408, Jan./Sept., took books and clothing to Oxford for which the cellarer pd 13s. 8d., WCM C.80; he also attended the Black Monk Chapter in Northampton, where his expenses were 46s. 8d., *ib.*

1388, 21 Aug., 36th at the el. of a prior, Liber Albus, fo 334v.
1395/6, was owed £10 by the cellarer for obtaining a writ [?connected with the prior's right to pontifical regalia or with the el. of Prior Grene, q.v., as bp]; he went to Nottingham to speak with the king concerning the prior's [pontifical] privileges, WCM C.77; he went to the curia and was away for half the yr which included the time of the death of Prior Grene, q.v., in Sept. 1395, WCM C.126, Liber Albus, fo 380.
1396, 11 Nov., obtained papal licence to choose his own confessor, *CPL*, v (1396–1404), 48.
1401, 24 June, 21st in order at the el. of a bp, *Reg. Sed. Vac.*, 373.
1401/2, recd from the chamberlain 26s. 8d. p.a., [?for clothing, because he was away and prob. at Oxford], WCM C.26.
1407, Oct./Nov., comm. by the prior to conduct *sed. vac.* visitations with a secular clerk in the deaneries of Kidderminster, Wych, Warwick and Stow, *Reg. Sed. Vac.*, 389.
1407/8, accompanied John Dudley I, q.v. to Gloucester to confer with the king and the abp [of Canterbury], and then they went to Oxford 'causa opinnonum divers' herietic' erranc' in fide destruend' ' [*sic*]; the cellarer recorded expenses of £4 12s. 9d. under 'negotiations', WCM C.79.
1408/9, the cellarer pd for the books 'of our lord prior' to be brought back from Oxford; he was therefore presumably nom. by the monks, selected by the bp and installed before 29 Sept. 1409, WCM C.81, where the expenses of his installation were also entered.
c. 1414 × 1417, was a member of the English delegation at the Council of Constance and one of the representatives sent by the Black Monk Chapter, Pantin, *BMC*, iii, 166, 167, 177; see also Thomas Ledbury.
1415, 15 Jan., obtained papal licence to have a portable altar, *CPL*, vi (1404–1415), 357; on 10 Mar. he recd an indult for himself and his monks that the confessors of their choice could grant plenary remission at the hour of d., *ib.*, 355.
1417, Nov./Dec. attended convocation and with other cathedral priors apptd to a committee set up by the abp to consider ways of alleviating the impecunious state of Oxford and Cambridge graduates, *Reg. abp Chichele*, iii, 36–37.
1419, 16 Mar., carried out a *sed. vac.* visitation of the chapter in person, *Reg. Sed. Vac.*, 396.
1419, 16 Sept./1421, c. 22 July, acted as vicar general for the bp, Reg. Morgan, 3–58.
1420/6, one of the presidents of the Black Monk Chapter, Pantin, *BMC*, ii, 95, 106, 134, 157; but he was absent from the 1426 Chapter, *ib.*, 160.
1421, 5 (or 7) May, one of six monks present at the extraordinary meeting of Black Monks summoned by the king to Westminster to discuss reform of the English Benedictines, Pantin, *BMC*, ii, 98–134.
1425, 11 Oct., witness to the abjuration of a heretic, Reg. Morgan, 132.
[1427], 30 Mar., comm. by the bp to hear confessions in reserved cases until 'the close of Easter next', Reg. Polton, 81.
1430, 10 June, presented monk ordinands at Alvechurch, Reg. Polton, 212; on 23 Sept., he did the same in the carnary chapel by Worcester cathedral, *ib.*, 213.

1432, 20 Sept., again present at the ordinations in the carnary chapel, and presented the candidates, Reg. Polton, 222.
1438, d. by 12 Feb., Reg. Bourgchier, 84, 85.
Possibly the author of a treatise on Lamentations; see Bale, *Index Brit. Script.*, 203 and Sharpe, *Latin Writers*.

Name in two Worcs. Mss:
(1) F.10, a collection of sermons (15th c.), one of which (fo 130) is headed *sermo M.J. Ford' in capitulo generali.*
(2) F.128, Distinctiones Cistrensis monachi etc. (late 14th c.), inside front cover . . . *quem contulit.*

Note: see John Folsham under Norwich.

Some of his *acta* are recorded in the Liber Albus, fos 438–457 by his chaplains, Richard Tendebury and Thomas Welford, q.v. For his *sed. vac. acta* see *Reg. Sed. Vac.*, 390–446.

William FORDHAM [Fordam, Fordeham
occ. 1504 occ. 1545/6

1504, 6 Apr., ord acol., carnary chapel by Worcester cathedral, Reg. S. Gigli, 287.
1504, 21 Sept., ord subdcn, carnary chapel, *ib.*, 289.
1504, 21 Dec., ord dcn, hospital of St Wulstan, Worcester, *ib.*, 291.
1506/7, recd pittance from the almoner, possibly at the time of his first mass, WCM C.212.
1516, pittancer, Reg. A.12, fo 43.
1520/1, chamberlain, Reg. A.17, 6.
1521/2, refectorer, WCM C.412.
1521/5; 1527/8, cellarer, Reg. A.17, 117, 196, 261, WCM C.412–414; WCM E.98; also on 28 Sept. 1527, WCM B.448.
1518, 27 Sept., on the election day he was apptd one of two proctors who were to present the seven nominees for the priorate to bp Fox (Winchester), prob. at Southwark, Reg. A.6(ii), fo 113; see William More I.
1520, recd 11s. from the prior for a maser, *Jnl More*, 120.
1521, 22 July, 15th in order on the metropolitan visitation certificate, Reg. abp Warham, ii, fo 293[v].
1525, 9 Feb., as he had left the priory and was wandering about the pr. requested the king to declare him apostate, Reg. A.6(ii), fo 139[v].
1529, 18 Apr., the prior made a second and similar request, *ib.*, fo 162; had he absconded a second time? See above, where he was cellarer in 1527/8.
1531/2, 14th on the clerical subsidy list and pd commons of 3s. 4d., Reg. A.12, fo 135. This yr the cellarer recorded payment to 'various persons' for a debt of Fordham, WCM C.414c. He was ill this yr and spent nine wks in the infirmary, at a cost of 10s. 6d., *ib.*; and the prior provided remedies for his 'disease' between May 1531 and Jan. 1532, *Jnl More*, 328, 329.
1534, 17 Aug., subscribed to the Act of Supremacy, *DK 7th Report*, Appndx 2, 305.
1535, 1 Aug., wrote to Thomas Cromwell with regard to his dismissal from the office of cellarer [several yrs previously; see Thomas Sudbury] claiming that he had the support of his brethren and offering 100m. if Cromwell would restore him, *L and P Henry VIII*, ix, no 6. He wrote again on 29 Aug. professing his loyalty to Cromwell, the 'devoted minister of the king', pledging his unfailing service and relying on his favour to be reinstated. He also stated that he had sent a report on Richard Cleve, q.v., *ib.*, no 204. See also John Musard.
[1535] n.d., a petition, signed by the subprior and 26 monks (out of a total of c. 35) was sent to Cromwell condemning Fordham as a 'troublesome person' who had run up debts of £280 and had borrowed money for his own use. They said that he was a sick man 'infected with the pox' who, if returned to office 'will be the ruin of our house,' *ib.*, no 653.
1536, 13 Mar., 8th in order at the 'el.' of Henry Holbech, q.v. as prior, Reg. A.6(iii), fo 1.
1545/6, 23 Mar., granted the status of denizen in Scotland as he had been a monk of Dunfermline for six yrs, *Register of the Privy Seal of Scotland* (H.M.S.O), iii, no 1599.

John FOREST [Foreste
occ. 1348/9

1348, 20 Dec., ord acol., bp's chapel, Hartlebury, *Reg. Bransford*, no 1108.
1349, 28 Mar., ord subdcn, bp's chapel, Hartlebury, *ib.*, no 1110.

FORTHAM
see Fordham

Henry FOUKE [Fouck, Fowke, Fuke
occ. 1303 occ. 1340/1

1303, 4 Feb., made his prof. in the Lady chapel before the prior, *Reg. Sed. Vac.*, 37; the form of prof. is entered in full in the Ms *Reg. Sed. Vac.* (A.1, fo 15). The prof. is also in *Ann. Wigorn.*, 554.
1317, 20 Oct., subsacrist, Liber Albus, fo 83.
1324, 29 Mar., subprior, Liber Albus, fo 115.
1326/7, cellarer, WCM C.544.
1332, 27 Sept.; 1337, May/Sept.; 1339, 12 Apr., 12 Aug.; 1340, 21 Apr., infirmarer, WCM B.1414; C.832; *Reg. Bransford*, nos 38, 79; *ib.*, no 290.
1317, 20 Oct., 25th in order at the el. of a prior and one of the seven *compromissorii* chosen to el. the seven candidates for the priorate; also one of the seven so named, Liber Albus, fo 83. On 18 Nov., as one of the nominees for the priorate he was presented to the bp in Dartford parish church, *ib.*, fos 83, 84.

1324, 29 Mar., present as witness when an incumbent of a city parish took his oath of office, Liber Albus, fo 115.
1326/7, pd a visit to Bromsgrove, WCM C.544.
[1334, Mar.], one of three monks comm. by the bp as penitentiaries, Reg. Montacute, 4.
1336, 25 Aug., apptd, with Nicholas Maurice, q.v., as proctor to go to the curia, *Liber Albus*, no 1202.
1337, 10 July, licensed by the bp to hear confessions in the adcnry of Worcester, Reg. Hemenhale, 13; between May and Sept. visited Tibberton, WCM C.832.
1338, 25 Mar. (more likely 1339 when the priory was vacant), wrote to bp Hemenhale, q.v., and described himself as penitentiary and *vicem gerens*, Worcs.Ms F.62, inside first flyleaf; see below.
1338/39, went to London with John de Evesham and Robert de Weston, q.v. [concerning the el. of Bransford] and returned *in familia Electi*, WCM C.58.
1339, 4/5 Jan., wrote a letter to Adam Orleton, former bp of Worcester now translated to Hereford, about the el. of Wulstan de Bransford, q.v. as bp; and see below.
1339, 9 Jan., present when the abbot of Cirencester prof. canonical obedience to the subprior, *sed. vac.*, *Reg. Sed. Vac.*, 269.
1339, 12 Apr., one of the seven nominees for the priorate, *Reg. Bransford*, no 38.
1339, 12 Aug., with Nicholas Maurice, q.v., comm. by the bp to rec. the prof. of a nun of Whiston, *Reg. Bransford*, no 79.
1340, 21 Apr., one of the seven nominees for the priorate, *ib.*, no 290.
1340/1, visited Bromsgrove, WCM C.548.

Name in five Worcs. Mss:
(1) F.62, Summa confessorum of J. de Friburgo (early 14th c.). This contains, as above, his letter to Thomas Hemenhale; and on the second flyleaf '. . . quem emit de mag. Ricardo de Bromwych, quondam priorem Bergeveneie pro xx s'. See Richard de Bromwych.
(2) F.77, G. de Tornaco (14th c.), *precium* 4s. 6d., and he bought it from R[obert] de Morton, q.v., *pro quodam iocali eburneo.*
(3) F.124, Interpretatio nominum hebraicorum etc. (13th/14th c.), which he obtained from Ranulph de Calthrop, q.v.; his name is on fo 60 at the beginning of a new section.
(4) F.131, Speculum juris canonici vocatum summa summarum (canon law) (14th c.), for which he pd 50s. Inside the back cover is a letter of his to the Provincial of the Augustinians concerning William de Heatone, *serviente meo.* Floyer conjectures that the tabula [of contents] on fos 399–401 may be in his hand, *Catalogue of Worcs. Mss*, 68.
(5) F.139, R. de Bromwych, q.v., on the Sentences, which he acquired from Bromwych for 20s.

Name also in Oxford, Bod. Ms Rawlinson c. 428, Liber sextus decretalium etc. (early 14th c.).

Note that there are three extant letters written by him, preserved in Worcs.Mss F.62 and F.131 described above, and also F.141 referred to above but described under Wulstan de Bransford, q.v.

See Henry de Cokesey who may be the same monk.

Humphrey FOWNYS
occ. 1529/31

1529/31, pittancer, WCM C.414a, C.414b.

Note: prob. identical with Humphrey Grafton, q.v.

Walter FRAUNCEYS [Fraunces, Frawncesse
occ. 1442 occ. 1483/4

1442, 22 Dec., ord acol. and subdcn, bp's chapel, Alvechurch, Reg. Bourgchier, 201, 202.
1443, 21 Sept., ord pr., carnary chapel by Worcester cathedral, *ib.*, 208.
1443/4, celebrated his first mass; recd a 2s. 3d. gift from the kitchener, WCM C.147.

1455/6, kitchener, WCM C.541.
1459/61; 1463/4; 1466, 20 Sept.; 1469, 14 Aug., chamberlain, WCM E.242; C.45; B.1552b; Reg. A.6(i), fo 60v.
1465/6, precentor, WCM C.96, C.381.
1470/1, cellarer, WCM C.404.
1478, 14 Sept., infirmarer and third prior, Reg. A.6(i), fo 73v.
1478/1481, almoner, WCM C.741, C.742, C.851; since Robert Multon q.v., heads the almoner's acct for 1478/9 and 1481/2, there may have been a change over during the yr, or the bailiff of Overbury may have been in error.
1481/2, subprior, WCM C.100.

1448/9, 1449/50, on the cellarer's list of creditors, WCM C.91, C.92.
1455/6, visited Broadwas, WCM C.541.
1459/60, carried out negotiations with the cellarer, WCM C.491.
1465, 21 Dec., as precentor took five monks of the priory, ordination candidates, to the chapel of the bp's manor at Alvechurch to present them, Reg. Carpenter, i, 564.
1466, 20 Sept., negotiated a lease as chamberlain, WCM B.1552b.
1466/7, stopped at Overbury, WCM C.735.
1469, 14 Aug., one of the seven nominees for the priorate, Reg. A.6(i), fo 60v and Reg. Carpenter, ii, 13–16.
1475, 7 Jan., went as proctor to the bp concerning the adm. and clothing of monks, *ib.*, ii, 135.
1478/9, 1479/80, pd visits to Overbury, WCM C.741, C.742.
1483/4, recd the money owed to him by the cellarer, WCM C.101.

I FREAUVINUS [Frewin
occ. [1093] occ. c. 1104

[1093], occ. as a witness to an episcopal confirmation where he is described as a *clericus* of the bp, *Heming Chart.*, ii, 424.

Name occ. in the list of monks in *Durham Liber Vitae*, fo 22.

II FREAUVINUS [Frewin
occ. c. 1104

Name occ. in the list of monks in *Durham Liber Vitae*, fo 22.

Note:
(1) the two monks by this name are numbered i and ii in the Durham ms.
(2) see Mason, *Wulfstan*, 181–182, where it is suggested that a Frewin began his career in the bp's household before becoming a monk; perhaps he may have been a source for some of the anecdotes recounted by Coleman, q.v., *ib.*, 293.

Richard FREND [Frene
occ. 1301 d. 1303

1303, 26 July, kitchener, *Ann. Wigorn*, 557.
1301, 18 July, one of the seven nominees for the priorate, *Reg. Giffard*, 547.
1303, 26 July, d., *Ann. Wigorn*, 557.

Nicholas de FROMTON [Frompton
occ. 1365 occ. 1368

1365, 7 June, ord subdcn, Winchcombe abbey, Reg. Whittlesey, 39.
1366, 21 Mar., ord dcn, Kidderminster, *ib.*, 41.
1368, 23 Sept., ord pr., Hartlebury, *ib.*, 74.

Walter de FROUCESTRE [Frocester, Froucester, Froucestr'
occ. 1347 d. 1402/3

1347, 19 June, one of two whose prof. the prior was comm. to rec., *Reg. Bransford*, no 832.

1351/2; 1352/4; 1356, Dec./1360, June, subcellarer, WCM C.801 (with John de Troubrugg, q.v.); C.438, C.550; C.440–443.
1360, June/Sept.; 1360/Nov. 1361; 1363, May/1364, kitchener, WCM C.65; C.629 (initial only), C.115; C.117, C.118.
1370, 3 Apr.; 1373, 7 Dec., subprior, Liber Albus, fo 246; *Reg. Sed. Vac.*, 290.
1382/3; 1388, 21 Aug., subprior, WCM C.119; Liber Albus, fo 334v.
1401, 24 June, third prior, *Reg. Sed. Vac.*, 370.

1351, 8 Jan., obtained papal licence to choose his own confessor, *CPL*, iii (1342–1362), 380.
1351/2, pd a visit to Tibberton, WCM C.801.
1352/3, visited Henwick, WCM C.634.
1353/4, visited Bromsgrove, WCM C.550.
1356/7, visited Overbury and Tibberton, WCM C.705, C.803.
1358/9, visited Dodderhill, Harvington, Leopard Grange, Newnham and Woodhall, WCM C.835, C.608, C.676, C.652, C.833a.
1360/1, visited Himbleton, WCM C.629.
1370, 3 Apr., presided at the el. of a prior and was chosen as one of the seven nominees for the priorate, Liber Albus, fo 246, 246v and Reg. Bryan, ii, 15 (in which this record has been bound). See also Reg. Lynn, 46.
1388, 21 Aug., presided at the el. of a prior and was again one of the seven nominees for the priorate, Liber Albus, fo 334v, 335.
1402/3, d., and the chamberlain sold his *panni*, WCM C.26a.

FUKE
see Fouke

Ralph FYLKES [Filkyns, Fylken, Fylkyn, Phylkes
occ. 1392/3 occ. 1420/1

1392/3, novice, WCM C.316.
1393, 4 Jan., one of three whose prof. the pr. was comm. to rec., Liber Albus, fo 363v; the date is 5 Jan in *Reg. Wakefield*, no 723.
1393, 1 Mar., ord acol., and subdcn, Alvechurch, *Reg. Wakefield*, no 982b and d (misread as 'Fywyn' here and above); on his 1392/3 acct the cellarer pd the precentor expenses of 3s. 5d. to take three ordinands to Alvechurch, WCM C.76.
1396/7, celebrated his first mass, and recd eight gallons of wine from the prior and cellarer, WCM C.479.

1419, 24 Apr., *tumbarius*, *Reg. Sed. Vac.*, 407.

1395/6, student at Oxford, going up for the first time; the cellarer pd his travel expenses and also provided £6 p.a. for maintenance, WCM C.77, C.77a.
1396/7, student; Robert, the prior's palfreyman, was twice sent to find him in Oxford, once after Easter, WCM C.479. (Two unnamed scholars were pd the full maintenance of £12, *ib.*)
1401, 24 June, described as scholar, *Reg. Sed. Vac.*, 373.

1392/3, had six *minutiones* and recd 3s. from the pittancer, WCM C.316.
1401, 24 June, 35th in order at the el. of a bp, *Reg. Sed. Vac.*, 373.
1415, 8 Mar., obtained papal licence for a portable altar, *CPL*, vi (1404–1415), 498 (transcribed as Fillem).
1419, 24 Apr., 11th at the el. of a bp, *Reg. Sed. Vac.*, 407.
1420/1, recd 3s. 2d. from the pittancer, WCM C.225.

Thomas FYSCHER
see Cropthorne

John GEORGE [Jeorge, Joorge, Jorge
occ. 1412 occ. 1469

1412, 17 Dec., ord acol. and subdcn, Worcester cathedral, Reg. Peverel, 193, 194.
1413, 8 Apr., ord dcn, Worcester cathedral, *ib.*, 195.
1416, 13 June, ord pr., chapel of the [Guild of the] Holy Trinity, Worcester, *ib.*, 209.
1415/16, celebrated his first mass; the chamberlain and pittancer gave money for bread and wine for the feast afterwards, WCM C.31, C.323.
1431/2, refectorer, Hamilton, *Comp. Rolls*, 56 (WCM C.418).
1450/1, precentor, WCM C.380.
1419, 24 Apr., 30th in order at the el. of a bp, *Reg. Sed. Vac.*, 407.
1433, 9 Dec., 17th at the el. of a bp, *ib.*, 432.
1438, 12 Feb., one of the seven nominees for the priorate, Reg. Bourgchier, 84, and Liber Albus, fo 457v.
1469, 14 Aug., one of the seven nominees for the priorate, Reg. Carpenter, ii, 13–16 and Reg. A.6(i), fo 60v.

GERMANUS
occ. c. 1104

Name occ. in the list of monks in *Durham Liber Vitae*, fo 22, possibly added in a slightly later hand.

John GERMEYN
n.d.

n.d., 3 Nov., name occ. in a Canterbury obit list, BL Ms Arundel 68, fo 47.

Note: prob. identical with John de St Germans, q.v.

GERVASE
occ. c. 1175

1175, 9 Apr., 9 Nov., chamberlain, *Worcs. Cart.*, no 165, WCM B.306a.

1175, 9 Nov., present at an inspeximus of charters, *ib.*, and witness to an episcopal charter on the same date, Reg. A.8, fo 34.

Note: a Gervase, chamberlain, witnessed an undated charter, [?1146 × 1189], *Worcs. Cart.*, no 489.

GILBERT
see Dodynham and Madley

GILEBERTUS
occ. c. 1104

Name occ. in the list of monks in *Durham Liber Vitae*, fo 22.

GILES
see Holywell

Robert de GLASTYNGBURY
occ. 1323

1323, 11 Nov., one of three *clerici* whom the bp comm. his sequestrator to examine at the time of his adm. to the priory, Liber Albus, fo 113v; this is Robert de Weston, q.v., who came from the environs of Glastonbury.

I John de GLOUCESTRE [Gloucestria
occ. 1217

1217, 26 Apr., he and other monks saw two suns, *Ann. Wigorn.*, 408.

II John de GLOUCESTRE [Gloucestr', Gloucestur
occ. 1298/9 d. ?1314

1298/9, kitchener, WCM C.54.
1307, cellarer, WCM E.4, and possibly for several succeeding yrs as he is named *nuper cellerarius* in 1314/15, WCM E.7; see Robert de Clifton I.
1302, 20 Jan., cleared of accusations of incontinence incurred at the metropolitan visitation, Liber Albus, fo 13.
1312, 25 Dec., gaol delivery ordered by the king for him and John de Wyke, prior, q.v., who had been imprisoned in Worcester castle on a charge of robbery, *CPR (1307–1313)*, 546. On 4 Jan. 1313, the bp issued a comm. to the subprior, precentor and others to the same effect, *Reg. Reynolds*, 58.
1314, 6 May, with John de Stratford I, q.v., apptd proctor and attorney by the prior for *sed. vac.* administration of spiritualities in the city and diocese, WCM B.1630.
1314/15, held court at Harvington, WCM E.7.
1314, 29 May, d.; see below.

Name in Worcs. Ms F.75, Caesarius Arelatensis etc. (late 13th c.), [obtained] *per*—, who d. on 29 May, 1314; his name is written large in fancy script on a front flyleaf at the top, and his date of d.

III John de GLOUCESTRE [Gloucester, Gloucestr', Gloucestur
occ. 1335 d. 1380/1

1335, 10 June, ord subdcn, Ombersley, Reg. Montacute, 87.
1335, 23 Sept., ord dcn, Chaddesley [Corbett], *ib.*, 92.
1336, 21 Sept., ord pr., bp's chapel, Hartlebury, *ib.*, 103.

1341, June/Sept., and prob. 1342/3, subcellarer, WCM C.548, C.756; he succ. John de Legh I, q.v., in June 1341.
1345/6, kitchener, WCM C.60.
1351/2, chamberlain, WCM C.11.
1370, 3 Apr., third prior, Liber Albus, fo 246.
1373, 7 Dec.; 1374/5, 1377/8, almoner, *Reg. Sed. Vac.*, 290; WCM C.173, C.174.
1378/9, infirmarer, Hamilton, *Comp. Rolls*, 58

(WCM C.241); it appears that John Grene I, q.v., took over on 30 Mar. acc. to the attached inventory, but the heading on the acct is in John de Gloucestr's name for the full yr.
1337/8, visited Bromsgrove, WCM C.547.
1346/7, visited Overbury, WCM C.699.
1349/50, visited Harvington, WCM C.692.
1370, 3 Apr., 3rd in order at the el. of a prior and chosen as one of the seven nominees for the office, Liber Albus, fo 246.
1373, 3 Dec., 7 Dec., 3rd at the el. of a bp, *Reg. Sed. Vac.*, 290.
1380/1, d.; the almoner gave bread to the poor on the *die obit'* but recd nothing for his corrody because it too was distributed among the poor for the good of his soul, WCM C.176. The chamberlain recd 65s. 6d. for the sale of his *panni*, WCM C.13.

IV John GLOUCESTRE [Gloucestr', Glowcestr'

occ. 1473 occ. 1489/90

1473, 10 May, one of four whom the prior and the bp's chancellor were to examine and if they were suitable they were to be adm., Reg. A.6(i), fo 77; a similar entry occ. in Reg. Carpenter, ii, 94, under 12 May.
1475, 23 Dec., ord subdcn, carnary chapel by Worcester cathedral, Reg. Carpenter, ii, 205.
1476, 8 June, ord dcn, carnary chapel, *ib.*, ii, 207.
1477, 5 Apr., ord pr., Worcester cathedral, Reg. Alcock, 246.
1476/7, celebrated his first mass and recd *exennia* from the precentor, WCM C.383.
1484/6, subcellarer, WCM C.450, C.746 and C.843.
1489/90, *custos* of the Lady chapel, first yr, WCM C.288.
1484/5, 1485/6, pd visits to Overbury, WCM C.745, C.746.

I Richard de GLOUCESTRE [Gloucestr'

occ. [1396] d. 1409/10

[1396], 1 July, one of three novices whose prof. the prior was comm. to rec., Reg. Winchcombe, 32.
1397, 6 June, ord acol., Worcester cathedral, *ib.*, 135.
1400/1, ord [pr.], Alvechurch where he was taken and presented by the precentor, WCM C.370.
1400/1, celebrated his first mass; recd *exennia* of 18d. from each of the chamberlain, hostiller and precentor, WCM C.25, C.216, C.370.
1401, 24 June, 42nd in order at the el. of a bp, *Reg. Sed. Vac.*, 373.
1409/10, d., WCM C.28, and the chamberlain recd 29s. 10d. for the sale of his *panni*; the almoner distributed bread to the poor on the day of his funeral, WCM C.189.

II Richard GLOUCESTRE

occ. 1430

1430, 23 Dec., ord dcn, Alvechurch, and presented by John de Hembury, q.v., precentor, Reg. Polton, 215.

Robert de GLOUCESTRE

occ. 1328 d. 1339

1328, 24 Sept., ord dcn, St Mary at the gate of Gloucester abbey, *Reg. Orleton*, no 9 (p. 12).
1329, 23 Dec., ord pr., Dodderhill, *ib.*, no 19 (p. 28).
1339, 4 Nov., d.; the pittancer gave him pittances after two *minuciones* before his d., WCM C.298.

Thomas GLOUCESTRE [Gloucester, Glowcetter

occ. 1497 occ. 1507/8

1497, 14 Apr., ord dcn, carnary chapel by Worcester cathedral, Reg. G. Gigli, 25.
1500, 19 Apr., ord pr., carnary chapel, Reg. S. Gigli, 399.
1507/8, subsacrist, WCM C.428.
1498, 25 Oct., 42nd in order on the visitation certificate, *Reg. abp Morton*, ii, no 458.
1507/8, responsible for collecting the money left by pilgrims *in pixide beate Marie*, WCM C.428.

GODRICUS [Pirl, Wirl, Godricpirl

occ. 1092 occ. c. 1104

1092, chamberlain, *Worcs. Cart.*, no 52.
1092, present at bp Wulstan's synod and member of a comm. to investigate the parochial rights of the cathedral church, *Worcs. Cart.*, no 52; see Thomas I.
c. 1104, name occ. in a list of monks in *Durham Liber Vitae*, fo 22.
n.d., as a young monk, named as a witness to the devil's attacks on bp Wulstan, *Vita Wulfstani*, 10, 72.

GODWINUS

occ. c. 1104

Name occ. in the list of monks in *Durham Liber Vitae*, fo 22.

Humphrey GRAFTON [*alias* Fones, Fownys

occ. 1490 occ. 1540

1490, 6 Mar., ord dcn, carnary chapel by Worcester cathedral, Reg. Morton, 144.
1493, 1 June, ord pr., carnary chapel, *ib.*, 160.
1496, June/Sept.; 1498/9; 1499/1500, kitchener, WCM C.626, C.165a; C.166, C.627; C.542.
1504, 6 Nov., chamberlain, Reg. A.6(ii), fo 32.
1506/7, kitchener; took over from Thomas Morton, q.v., WCM C.490 (as Fones).
1518, kitchener, Reg. A.6(ii), fo 113.

1520/1, pittancer, transferred to office of kitchener, Reg. A.17, 6, 23, 31.
1521/4, kitchener, Wilson, *Accts Henry VIII*, 32, and Reg. A.17, 216, 281.
1529/31, pittancer, WCM C.414a, C.414b (as Fownys); in 1530 he is named in *Jnl More*, 50, as Fones and pittancer (the index is correct, but the text has changed it to Jones).
1531/2; 1532, 1534; 1535, pittancer, Reg. A.12, fo 135; *Jnl More*, 64, 68; *L and P Henry VIII*, ix, no 653.

1498, 25 Oct., 25th in order on the visitation certificate, *Reg. abp Morton*, ii, no 458.
1518, 27 Sept., one of the seven nominees for the priorate, Reg. A.6(ii), fo 113; they were presented to bp Fox (Winchester), prob. at Southwark, and he named William More I, q.v., *ib.*
1521, 22 July, 7th in order on the visitation certificate, Reg. abp Warham, ii, fo 293v.
1525/6, 16th on the clerical subsidy list and pd 3s. 4d. as commons, Reg. A.12, fo 125.
1528/9, pd by the prior for singing the ten o'clock mass in the summer quarter of 1528, and the spring and summer of 1529, *Jnl More*, 284, 291, 295.
1531/2, 8th on the second subsidy list and pd £3 as pittancer and 3s. 4d. as commons, Reg. A.12, fo 135.
1534, 17 Aug., subscribed to the Act of Supremacy, *DK 7th Report*, Appndx 2, 305.
1535, signed the petition vs the reinstatement of William Fordham, q.v., as cellarer, *L and P Henry VIII*, ix, no 653.
1536, 13 Mar., 5th at the 'el.' of Henry Holbech, q.v. as prior, Reg. A.6(iii), fo 1.
1540, assigned a pension of £8 p.a., *L and P Henry VIII*, xv, 869.

Richard de GRAFTON [Graftone
occ. [1369] d. 1409/10

[1369], 1 Oct., one of seven whose prof. the bp comm. the precentor to rec., Reg. Lynn, 89.

1373, 4 Dec., 22nd in order at the el. of a bp, *Reg. Sed. Vac.*, 290.
1378/9, ill twice and the infirmarer spent 8s. 10d. on 'potions and cordials', WCM C.241.
1380/1, ill, and 4d. spent on medicine, WCM C.242.
1388, 21 Aug., 19th in order at the el. of a prior, Liber Albus, fo 334v.
1396, 11 Nov., obtained papal licence to choose his own confessor, *CPL*, v (1396–1404), 48.
1401, 24 June, 13th at the el. of a bp, *Reg. Sed. Vac.*, 373.
1409/10, d., and the almoner bought bread [for the poor] on the day of his funeral, WCM C.189; the chamberlain recd 32s. 4d. for the sale of his *panni*, WCM C.28.

GREEN
see Grene

GREGORIUS
occ. c. 1104

Name occ. in the list of monks in *Durham Liber Vitae*, fo 22.

Robert GREGORY [Gregori
occ. 1533 occ. 1536

1533, 20 Sept., ord subdcn, carnary chapel by Worcester cathedral, Reg. Ghinucci 7(ii), 174.
1536, 13 Mar., prof. but not a pr., Reg. A.6(iii), fo 1.

1534, 17 Aug., subscribed to the Act of Supremacy, *DK 7th Report*, Appndx 2, 305.
1535, signed the petition vs the reinstatement of William Fordham, q.v., as cellarer, *L and P Henry VIII*, ix, no 653.
1536, 13 Mar., 31st at the 'el.' of Henry Holbech, q.v. as prior, Reg. A.6(iii), fo 1.

William GREGORY
occ. 1529

1529, 21/22 May, ord dcn, Gloucester abbey, Reg. Ghinucci 7(ii), 170.

I John GRENE, D.Th. [Green
occ. c. 1370 d. 1395

1388–1395, prior: nom. 21 Aug. 1388, apptd 22 Aug., Liber Albus, fos 335, 336, and *Reg. Wakefield*, nos 790, 791; buried on 15 Sept. 1395, Liber Albus, fo 380.

1379, Mar./1381; 1388, 21 Aug., infirmarer, WCM C.241, C.242; *Reg. Wakefield*, no 788 and Liber Albus, fo 335.

1374/5, student at Oxford; the precentor pd his travel expenses from Oxford to Worcester and back, WCM C.361.
1375/6, [student], to whom the pittancer gave 10s. *ex precepto domini prioris*, Hamilton, *Comp. Rolls*, 36, where the name Cirencester has been mistakenly substituted for Grene (see WCM C.310).
1376/7, student, with full maintenance of £6 for the yr provided by the cellarer, WCM C.69; the precentor pd travel expenses to and from Oxford for him and for John de Hatfeld, q.v., WCM C.361a.
1377/8, [student], to whom the almoner gave 10s., WCM C.174.
1379/80, student; the almoner gave 6s. 8d. for him and his *socius*, WCM C.175; the chamberlain provided 30s. [for clothing] for him and for John de Dudley I, q.v., WCM C.12; the precentor pd his expenses to return from Oxford for Easter, WCM C.362.
1381, 3 July, described as *sacre theologie professor*, Pantin, *BMC*, iii, 205.

1373, 4 Dec., 19th in order at the el. of a bp, and preached the sermon, *Reg. Sed. Vac.*, 290.
1376/7, the cellarer gave 6s. 8d. gift to him and to John de Hatfeld, q.v., going to London [?to convocation], WCM C.69.

1381, 5 July, apptd proctor to attend the Black Monk Chapter in Northampton, Pantin, *BMC*, iii, 205.
1387, 19 Apr., the bp requested to have him preach at his impending visitation, Liber Albus, fo 318ᵛ.
1387, 5 July, apptd proctor for the Black Monk Chapter, *ib.*, fo 320ᵛ, and WCM C.73.
1388, 21 Aug., at the el. of a prior he was next to the subprior in order, Liber Albus, fo 334ᵛ.
Note: he must have been given some seniority in order to be placed above those who entered c. 1350; see e.g. John de Lyndeseye.
1391, 1 July, 13 Nov.; 1392, 5 Feb., a series of notarial instruments in *Reg. Wakefield*, nos 680, 681, 683, show that the controversy over pontifical regalia had not been finally settled in the time of Prior Evesham, or of his successor, Walter de Legh, q.v. The agreement of 1392, reached after much discussion and consultation, was a compromise, sufficiently imprecise to satisfy both sides. See also John de Malverne I.
1393, 3 Oct., with John de Dudley I, q.v., acted as an assessor at the trial of Walter Brut, lollard, and present at his abjuration, *Reg. Trefnant* (Hereford), 359; prob. this same yr he was apptd one of the diffinitors at the Black Monk Chapter for the next meeting, Pantin, *BMC*, iii, 90.
1395, between 3 Apr. and 4 May, el. bp, but Tideman de Winchcombe was provided, *Fasti*, iv, 57.
1395/6, d., the almoner recd 52s. for his corrody [?from the cellarer], WCM C.182. This was the sum prescribed for the full yr after his d. On the same acct the almoner had pd William, the chaplain, during three quarters of the yr to celebrate [masses] for his soul.

Name in Worcs. Mss F.25–28, Nicholaus de Lyra (biblical commentary) in four volumes (late 14th c.). In F.27 a note records that this book was obtained by him, 'doctorem theologie . . . ad communem utilitatem claustralium' in AD 1386; as all four volumes were written at the same time and appear to be in the same hand, one may presume that he was also responsible for acquiring the other three. W. A. Pantin suggested that his handwriting may be found in the notes in Worcs. Ms F.65; see the ref. under John de Malverne I.

For his career before entering the monastery *BRUO* provides a summary: he was at Oxford in 1365 and was ord subdcn at Ledbury in Sept. 1368 and dcn five months later, *Reg. Lewis Charleton* (Hereford), 116, 119. On the basis of his order of seniority in 1373 he must have been adm. soon after his ordination in 1369.

II John GRENE
occ. 1426/7 occ. 1449/50

1449/50, sacrist, WCM C.92; only for part of the yr, as Thomas Musard, q.v. was also sacrist.
1426/7, visited Sandwell [?priory, Staffs.], WCM C.328.
1449/50, listed among the cellarer's creditors, and he was pd by the cellarer for the debts of Thomas Hosyntre, q.v., WCM C.92.

Note: It is surprising to find so few refs to this monk and none to any ordination dates; this suggests that he went by two names, 'Grene' and his toponymic; and he may therefore occ. elsewhere in this register under the latter.

Thomas GRENE
occ. 1504 occ. 1523/4

1504, 6 Apr., ord acol., carnary chapel by Worcester cathedral, Reg. S. Gigli, 287.
1505, 20 Sept., ord subdcn, carnary chapel, *ib.*, 293.
1507/8, celebrated his first mass, with a 2s. gift from the hostiller, WCM C.240.

1520/1, kitchener, until at least 22 July 1521, but see Humphrey Grafton, Reg. A.17, 6; Reg. abp Warham, ii, fo 293ᵛ.
1522/3, apptd *magister communis cene*, Reg. A.17, 212; for one yr only, see John Dudley II.

1521, 22 July, 14th in order on the visitation certificate, Reg. abp Warham, ii, fo 293ᵛ
1523/4, ill in the infirmary for six wks for which the infirmarer recorded 7s. spent in treatment, Reg. A.17, 280.

Name in Worcs. Ms Q.17, Sermons (13th/14th c.), on the end flyleaf.

Thomas GRYMELEY [Grymleye
occ. 1521 occ. 1536

1522, 20 Dec., ord pr., carnary chapel by Worcester cathedral, Reg. A.6(ii), fo 134ᵛ.
1522/3, celebrated his first mass, with gifts of 2s. from each of the chamberlain, hostiller, pittancer, precentor and sacrist, Reg. A.17, 205, 211, 206, 209, WCM C.430. The chamberlain explained the donation as pittances for the convent at the time of his first mass.

1525/6, subsacrist, Reg. A.12, fo 125.
1531/2, fourth prior, *ib.*, fo 135.

1521, 22 July, 37th in order on the visitation certificate, Reg. Warham, ii, fo 293ᵛ.
1525/6, 28th on the clerical subsidy list and pd 5s. as subsacrist, Reg. A.12, fo 125.
1531/2, 28th on the second subsidy list and pd 3s. 4d. commons, *ib.*, fo 135.
1534, 17 Aug., subscribed to the Act of Supremacy, Dk 7th Report, Appndx 2, 305.
1535, signed the petition vs the reinstatement of William Fordham, q.v. as cellarer, *L and P Henry VIII*, ix, no 653.
1536, 13 Mar., 20th in order at the 'el.' of Henry Holbech, q.v., as prior, Reg. A.6(iii), fo 1.

William de GRYMELEY [Grimele, Grimleye, Grymele
occ. 1283 occ. 1308

[?1282, 19 Sept., ord dcn, Worcester cathedral, *Reg. Giffard*, 160].
1283, 12 June, ord pr., [?Chipping] Campden, *ib.*, 208.
Note: in neither of the above entries is he named as a monk, for no details other than the ordinands' names are provided. The heading of the 1282 ordination list states that it includes only seculars.

1302, 29 Mar., 29 Oct; 1303, 30 May, precentor, *Reg. Sed. Vac.*, 2, *CPL*, i (1198–1204), 604; *Reg. Sed. Vac.*, 55.

1292, Michaelmas term, student at Oxford with John de Arundel, q.v.; the cellarer pd them 20s. *versus Oxon'*, and also 2m., Wilson, *Early Comp. Rolls*, 13, 14 (WCM C.51).
See below for the attribution of the title M.

1298/9, attended the Black Monk Chapter at Northampton, WCM C.54.
1300, 21 Sept., apptd by the Black Monk Chapter to visit the houses of the order in the dioceses of Bath and Wells, Exeter and Salisbury; by 28 July 1301, he had not carried out this comm., as the abbot of Westminster wrote to urge the prior of Worcester to attend to the matter and provide for his expenses, Pantin, *BMC*, i, 143–144 (Liber Albus, fo 2).
1301, 18 July, one of the seven nominees for the priorate, *Reg. Giffard*, 547.
1302, 29 Mar., one of seven *compromissorii* chosen to el. a bp, and one of the proctors sent to the abp to inform him of their el. of John de St Germans, q.v., *Reg. Sed. Vac.*, 2.
1303, 30 May, the prior wrote to the new bp [Gainsborough] to ask that Grymeley, as precentor, be apptd to announce, acc. to custom, the names of the candidates at his impending ordination, *Reg. Sed. Vac.*, 55.
1308, 27/29 Mar., one of the prior's commissaries in the *sed. vac.* visitation of the abbeys of Tewkesbury and Winchcombe, *Reg. Sed. Vac.*, 122.
1308, 1 July, present at the el. of a prioress of Whiston and made the public announcement of the result, *Reg. Sed. Vac.*, 112.

Name in Worcs. Ms Q.5, Beda etc. (late 10th c.); on the inside of the back cover 'Memo quod M. W. de Grimeley recepit dimidum marcum super librum istum et metafisicam'. Is the M. William this monk or the Franciscan, William de Grimele, who is not known to have had a degree? See *BRUO*.

Richard de GUNDICOTE [?Condicote
occ. 1242 d. 1252

1242–1252, prior: apptd by the bp and installed on 19 Nov. 1242; d. 29 Sept. 1252, *Fasti*, ii, 103.
1242, before, 19 Nov., sacrist, *Ann. Wigorn*, 434.

Richard de HADDELEYE [Hadleye
occ. 1337 occ. 1349

1337, 5 Apr., ord subdcn, Worcester cathedral, Reg. Montacute, 108.
1337, 20 Sept., ord dcn, King's Norton chapel, Reg. Hemenhale, 36.
1337, 20 Dec., ord pr., Ombersley, *ib.*, 44. (The date is given as 13 kal. Jan. 1336, surely an error.)

1344, 19 Feb., apptd *tumbarius* by the bp, *Reg. Bransford*, no 599.

1349, 15 Apr., apptd to hear confessions in the diocese with power to absolve even in reserved cases, *ib.*, no 998.

John HALIS [Hales, Halez, Halys
occ. 1477 d. 1506/7

1477, 5 Apr., ord acol., Worcester cathedral, Reg. Alcock, 245.
1478, 16 May, ord subdcn, carnary chapel by Worcester cathedral, *ib.*, 251.
1478, 19 Sept., ord dcn, carnary chapel, *ib.*, 252.
1479, 18 Dec., ord pr., carnary chapel, *ib.*, 260.
1479/80, celebrated his first mass; the kitchener contributed 2s. 6d. for the feast afterwards, WCM C.160.

1500, chaplain to the prior, Reg. A.6(ii), fo 9.
1501/2, refectorer, WCM C.424.
1503/4, hostiller, WCM C.239; also on 30 Nov. 1504, Reg. A.6(ii), fo 32.
1498, 25 Oct., 13th in order on the visitation certificate, *Reg. abp Morton*, ii, no 458.
1506/7, d., and the almoner distributed 2s. 6d. worth of bread to the poor, WCM C.212.

Richard HALIS [Hales, Halys, Hayles, Haylis
occ. 1510 occ. 1519

1510, 21 Sept., ord acol., carnary chapel by Worcester cathedral, Reg. S. Gigli, 304.
1511, 14 June, ord subdcn, carnary chapel, *ib.*, 308.
1512, 27 Mar., ord dcn, carnary chapel, *ib.*, 312.
1513, 24 Sept., ord pr., carnary chapel, *ib.*, 321.

1519, 4 Nov., the prior issued a *dimissio* for his transfer to Monmouth priory, Reg. A.6(ii), fo 120^{v}; the prior also gave him 15s. when he left, *Jnl More*, 92.
1521, the prior entered a 'reward' of 20d. to 'dan Richard Hales' in his acct book, *ib.*, 125; had he come back for a visit?

Richard HALLOWE [Halow, *?alias* Lisle
occ. 1521 occ. 1536

1525, 23 Dec., ord dcn, Bromyard, *Reg. Booth* (Hereford), 321.

1531/2, subsacrist, Reg. A.12, fo 135^{v}.

1521, 22 July, 41st in order on the visitation certificate, Reg. abp Warham ii, fo 293v.
1523/4, ill for eight wks and the infirmarer spent 9s. 4d. for his cure, WCM C.413.
1525/6, 31st on the clerical subsidy list and pd 3s. 4d. commons, Reg. A.12, fo 125.
1529, recd 10s. per quarter from the prior for saying the 10 o'clock mass, *Jnl More*, 301.
1529/31, from the autumn of 1529 through to the late autumn of 1531, recd payments from the prior for the 10 o'clock mass, *Jnl More*, 301, 309, 314, 319, 325, 330, 335, 336.
1530/1, a John Hallow was ill for three wks and cost the infirmarer 3s. 10d., WCM C.414b; prob. a slip of the pen for Richard.
1531/2, 32nd on the second subsidy list and pd 20d. as subsacrist and 3s. 4d. commons, Reg. A.12, fo 135v.
1533/4, recd 40s. for celebrating the 10 o'clock mass at the altar of St Cross, WCM C.415.
1534, 17 Aug., subscribed to the Act of Supremacy, *DK 7th Report*, Appndx 2, 305.
1536, 13 Mar., 23rd in order at the 'el.' of Henry Holbech, q.v., as prior, Reg. A.6(iii), fo 1.
?1540, acc. to Noake, a Richard Lisle had a prebendal stall, *Worcs. Cathedral*, 528; who is this?

Name in Worcs. Ms F.36, G. de Thornaco (13th/14th c.); on fo 200—*habet librum sermonum.*

Walter de HALLOWE [Hallawe
occ. 1274

1274, 20 Sept., one of five *compromissorii* chosen to el. the seven nominees for the priorate, *Reg. Giffard*, 62.
n.d., a Walter de Hall' occ. on an undated acct roll, WCM E.4 (6) where he and Thomas de Ballescot, q.v., were *itinerant' versus Oxon'.*

John de HAMBURY [Hambury, Hanbury
occ. 1396 d. 1420

1396, 1 Apr., ord acol., Worcester cathedral, Reg. Winchcombe, 125.
1401, 24 June, named as a dcn, *Reg. Sed. Vac.*, 373.
1404, 20 Sept., ord pr., Llanthony Priory, Gloucester, *Reg. Clifford*, no 122, p. 87.
1404/5, celebrated his first mass and recd *exennia* from the almoner and chamberlain, WCM C.187, C.50.
1404, 9 Dec., apptd chaplain to the prior, Liber Albus, fo 419v.
1410; 1413/14; 1416/17; 1418/19; 1419/20, to 10 June, cellarer, WCM C.82; C.190; C.614 (as J.H); C.718 (as J.H); C.559, C.83 and E.48.
1401, 24 June, 38th in order at the el. of a bp, *Reg. Sed. Vac.*, 373.
1415, 12 Feb., obtained a papal indult to have a portable altar, *CPL*, vi (1404–1415), 361; on 10 Mar. he was granted a licence to choose his own confessor, *ib.*, 499.
1419, 9 Mar., one of two monk proctors sent to the king for licence to el. a bp, *Reg. Sed. Vac.*, 391.
1419, 24 Apr., 14th in order at the above el., *ib.*, 407.
1419/20, d., prob. around 10 June; the chamberlain sold his *panni*, WCM C.32.

See also John de Hembury.

Nicholas HAMBURY B.Th. [Hambery, Handebury, Hembury
occ. 1448 d. 1479

1448, 14 Sept., one of six whose prof. the prior was comm. to rec., Reg. Carpenter, i, 132.
1449, 12 Apr., ord acol., carnary chapel by Worcester cathedral, *ib.*, i, 524.
1453, 31 Mar., ord subdcn, carnary chapel, *ib.*, i, 535.
1456, 27 Mar., ord dcn, chapel in bp's palace, Worcester, *ib.*, i, 541.
[1465/6], chaplain to the prior, Reg. A.6(i), fo 44.
1473/4; 1475/7; 1478/9, cellarer, WCM C.4; C.604, C.778, C.578, C.740; C.741; see Richard Upton.
1478, took the oath of office as sacrist, Reg. A.6(i), fo 81; sacrist at the time of d. in Aug. 1479, Reg. Alcock, 23.
1462; 1464, 17 Dec.; 1465, Jan. 1467, student at Oxford when he put BL Harley Ms 3066 in the Selton chest as caution for a loan; see *BRUO* which does not include his degree. He described himself as *bachilarium sacre theologie*; see below.
1469, 16 Aug., one of the monk proctors apptd to present the seven nominees for the priorate to the bp, Reg. A.6(i), fo 60v and Reg. Carpenter, ii, 13–16.
1478/9, as cellarer, made the rounds of the manors, WCM C.488.
1479, Aug., d. before 7 Aug., when the bp apptd Richard Cropthorne, q.v., to succeed him as sacrist, Reg. Alcock, 23. The almoner recd nothing for his corrody *quia pardonavitur*, WCM C.204, but he pd the brief bearer, *ib.*, and the chamberlain sold his *vestimenta*, WCM C.46.

Name in
(1) Worcs. Ms F.130. Distinctiones theologie (14th c.); on the first flyleaf: *per dominum—bachilarium sacre theologie.*
(2) BL Harley Ms 3066, Augustine, Enchiridion (early 12th c.), on the end folio; see above.

Note:
(1) this is the only Worcester monk student who was at Oxford and never mentioned by name as such on the acct rolls; regular payments to two or an unspecified number of monk scholars are recorded during the 1460s, and he must have been one of these.
(2) Another unusual feature in this biographical record is the seven yr gap between the orders of acol. and dcn which may have been due to his adm. at an exceptionally early age.

Robert de HAMBURY [Hambory, Hanbury, Hembury
occ. 1365 d. 1410/11

1365, 14 Sept., one of three whose prof. the prior was comm. by the vicar general to rec., Liber Albus, fo 229v.
1368, 4 Mar., ord subdcn, Hartlebury, Reg. Whittlesey, 72.
1369, 22 Sept., ord dcn, Kidderminster, Reg. Lynn, 49.
1372, 18 Sept., ord pr., [Worcester cathedral], *ib.*, 60.
1379/81, 1382/4, 1387/8, 1389/90, 1391/2, almoner, WCM C.175–181; the heading on the 1383/4 acct is so faded as to be unverifiable.
1395, 15 Sept./1396, June, chamberlain, Liber Albus, fo 380, WCM C.21; he may have succ. Thomas Dene, q.v., in 1393.
1396/7; 1401, 24 June, subprior, WCM C.479; *Reg. Sed. Vac.*, 372.
1370, 3 Apr., 19th in order at the el. of a prior, Liber Albus, fo 246.
1373, 7 Dec., 16th at the el. of a bp, *Reg. Sed. Vac.*, 290.
1374, 22 Jan., with a secular clerk, apptd general proctor for the prior and chapter, Liber Albus, fo 269; on 22 Feb. he witnessed the pronouncement of a sentence of excommunication by the prior, *sed. vac.*, *Reg. Sed. Vac.*, 304.
1388, 21 Aug., 13th at the el. of a prior, and chosen as one of the seven nominees for the priorate, Liber Albus, fos 334v, 335.
1395, 15 Sept., present at the el. and was one of the seven nominees for the priorate, Liber Albus, fo 380.
1396/7, ref. to his turn in the rota for *minutiones*, WCM C.479.
1401, 24 June, second in order at the el. of a bp. *Reg. Sed. Vac.*, 372.
1404/5, 1406/7, 1409/10, gave the almoner, in alms, 5s. p.a., WCM C.187–189.
1410/11, d., and the chamberlain sold his *panni*, WCM C.29.

William HAMBURY [Hambere, Hamberye, Hanbure, Hanbury
occ. 1516 occ. 1539

1516, 17 May, ord acol., carnary chapel by Worcester cathedral, Reg. S. Gigli, 330.
1516, 20 Sept., ord subdcn, carnary chapel, *ib.*, 333.
1517, 7 Mar., ord dcn, carnary chapel, *ib.*, 332.
1523, chaplain to the prior, Reg. A.6(ii), fo 140.
1525/6, not named on the 1525/6 clerical subsidy list and was threfore prob. chaplain, subcellarer or third prior who were listed but unnamed, Reg. A.12, fo 125.
1529/32, hostiller, WCM C.414a, C.414b, C.414c.
1535, 29 Sept.; 1538, 25 Mar.; 1539, 11 May, *custos* of the Lady chapel, WCM B.1125, B.1126; B.979; B.1176.
1521, 22 July, 24th in order on the metropolitan visitation certificate, Reg. abp Warham, ii, fo 293v.
1525/6, recd payment from the prior for celebrating the ten o'clock mass, *Jnl More*, 232, 237.
1531/2, 21st on the clerical subsidy list and pd 13s. 4d. as hostiller and 3s. 4d. commons, Reg. A.12, fo 135.
1534, 17 Aug., subscribed to the Act of Supremacy, *DK 7th Report*, Appndx 2, 305.
1535, signed the petition vs the reinstatement of William Fordham, q.v., as cellarer, *L and P Henry VIII*, ix, no 653.
1536, 13 Mar., 14th in order at the 'el.' of Henry Holbech, q.v., as prior, Reg. A.6(iii), fo 1.

HAMBURY
see also Hembury

John HAMPTON
occ. 1508/9

1508, 18 Mar., ord subdcn, carnary chapel by Worcester cathedral, Reg. S. Gigli 297.
1509, 22 Dec., ord pr., carnary chapel, *ib.*, 301.

John de HANLEY
occ. 1420 occ. 1437

1420, 2 Mar., ord acol. and subdcn, Worcester cathedral, Reg. Morgan, 59.
1420, 21 Dec., ord dcn, chapel of [the Guild of] the Holy Trinity, Worcester, *ib.*, 68.
1422/3, celebrated his first mass; the precentor contributed bread and ale for the feast, WCM C.376; the hostiller gave *exennia*, C.226a.
1433/5, possibly *magister operum*, WCM C.492, C.87; see below.
1435/7, pittancer, WCM C.331, C.332, C.724.
1433, 9 Dec., 23rd in order at the el. of a bp, *Reg. Sed. Vac.*, 432.
1433/4, sold a *tribul'* [prob. a digging tool used in quarrying] to the cellarer 'for doors and windows etc.', WCM C.492.
1434/5, the cellarer charged his acct with the expenses of J. and of Peter q.v., *circa mundacionem* of the quarry at Ombersley and also for the cutting of stone there, WCM C.87.
Note: these two entries suggest that he was performing tasks usually assigned to the *magister operum* who, at Worcester, was responsible to the cellarer; see also John [*Conversus*] and John Preston II.
1435/6, the cellarer contributed to the expenses of a lawsuit in which he and John de Hertilbury, q.v., were involved [on behalf of the chapter], WCM C.88.

Richard HANLEY
occ. 1476 d. 1478/9

1476, 8 June, ord acol., carnary chapel by Worcester cathedral, Reg. Carpenter, ii, 207.

1478/9, d., and the almoner pd 2s. to the brief bearer, WCM C.204, but recd nothing for his corrody *quia pardonavitur*, *ib*.

Robert HANUS
see Stanes

I John HARDEWYK [Hardewick, Hardwyke, Herdewyk
occ. 1481 occ. 1502

1481, 16 June, ord acol., Whitbourne, *Reg. Milling* (Hereford), 163.
1481, 22 Sept., ord subdcn, Whitbourne, *ib*., 164.
1482, 21 Dec., ord dcn, carnary chapel by Worcester cathedral, Reg. Alcock, 270.
1489/90; 1493/7; 1498, 25 Oct., pittancer, WCM C.345; C.588; C.346–348, *Reg. abp Morton*, ii, no 458.
1500/2, *custos* of the Lady chapel, WCM C.290, C.605.
1498, 25 Oct., 17th in order on the visitation certificate, *Reg. abp Morton*, ii, no 458.
1499/1500, visited Overbury for *liberatio denariorum*, WCM C.723.

II John HARDWYKE [Hardewyke, Hardwyck, Herdewyk
occ. 1525/6 occ. 1536

1527, 19 Sept., ord subdcn, Gloucester abbey, Reg. Ghinucci 7(ii), 167.
1532, 16 Mar., ord dcn, carnary chapel by Worcester cathedral, *ib*., 172.
[1532, before 29 Sept.], ord pr., see below.
1531/2, celebrated his first mass; recd pittances of 2s. from each of the almoner, cellarer, kitchener and pittancer, WCM C.414c.
1525/6, 40th and last on the clerical subsidy list and pd 2s. as commons, Reg. A.12, fo 125.
1531/2, 40th and last on the second subsidy list; not yet a pr., and pd 2s. as commons, *ib*., fo 135^{v}.
1534, 17 Aug., subscribed to the Act of Supremacy, *DK 7th Report*, Appndx 2, 305.
1535, signed the petition vs the reinstatement of William Fordham, q.v., as cellarer, *L and P Henry VIII*, ix, no 653.
1536, 29th in order at the 'el.' of Henry Holbech, q.v., as prior, and the most junior of the priests, Reg. A.6(iii), fo 1.

John de HARLEYE [Hareleye
occ. 1277 occ. 1317

1277, 31 Oct., recd the monastic habit, with John de Wyke, q.v., *Ann. Wigorn*, 473.
1303, 22 June, cellarer, *Liber Albus*, no 749.
1303, 25 Nov., apptd sacrist by the bp, *Reg. Gainsborough*, 24.
1305, 21 July, removed from the office of sacrist by the bp, *Liber Albus*, no 319.
1283, at the time of his blessing as abbot of Gloucester John de Gamages gave 100s. as a pittance to the prior and chapter *per fratrem* John de Harleye, *Ann. Wigorn*., 489.
1296, 11 July, one of the seven nominees for the priorate, Reg. Giffard, 480.
1302, 20 Feb., one of two monk proctors who recd a licence from the king to el. a bp, *CPR (1301–1307)*, 17, and *Reg. Sed. Vac*., 2; see also Gilbert de Madley.
1303, 22 June, the abp wrote to reprove the prior because he had learned that since his visitation some of the monks had made accusations vs Harleye and Gilbert de Madley, q.v., *Liber Albus*, no 749.
[1304], wrote to the abbot of Malmesbury, requesting him to admit as monks the two bearers of his letter, *Liber Albus*, no 176.
1308, 3 Apr., as commissary of the prior, with John de St Briavel, q.v., conducted a *sed. vac.* visitation of Little Malvern priory, *Reg. Sed. Vac*., 121.
1317, 9 Apr., sent as one of two proctors to the king to obtain a licence to el. a bp., *Reg. Sed. Vac*., 179; see Gilbert de Madley.
[1317, Aug.], sent with a letter to the abbot of Gloucester concerning Simon de Defford, q.v., doing penance at Gloucester, Pantin, *BMC*, i, 178–181.
1317, 20 Oct., 9th in order at the el. of a prior and one of the seven nominees, Liber Albus, fo 83–83^{v}. On 18 Nov., as one of the nominees, he was presented to the bp in Dartford church, *ib*, fos 83–84.
[1317], 23 Dec., took the letter of the prior recalling Simon de Defford, q.v., to the abbot of Gloucester, Liber Albus, fo 85^{v}.

Name in Worcs. Ms Q.42, Distinctiones Mauricii (late 13th c.); on the last flyleaf he is listed as one of eleven monks who contributed to the purchase of the book; he pd 8 [?d.].

Family connections are recounted in *Ann. Wigorn*, 480: there were six brothers, sons of Henry, lord of Harley, who all became monks in different houses and of whom this monk was the eldest.

There are also two undated letters written (c. 1317/18) by him and preserved in the Liber Albus:
(1) to his brother Roger, who was a member of the Cistercian house at Netley, Hants., and who had left the monastery but had been persuaded to return by an understanding and fatherly prior; he urged his brother that 'in ea vocatione qua iam vocati estis, domino disponente, in ipsa permaneatis constanter', fo 86.
(2) to the prior of Netley thanking him for displaying loving concern for his brother and requesting him to guide and instruct him in the way of salvation, *ib*.

A translation of both letters may be found in J.M. Wilson, *The Worcester Liber Albus* (London, 1920), 169–170.

HARTILBURY, Hartlebury, Hartylbury
see Hertilbury

HARVYNGTON
see Hervynton

John de HATFELD B.Th. [atte Felde
occ. 1365 d. 1419/20

1365, 7 June, ord subdcn, Winchcombe abbey, Reg. Whittlesey, 39.
[1366], 21 Mar., ord dcn, Kidderminster, *ib.*, 41.
1368, 23 Sept., ord pr., Hartlebury, *ib.*, 74.
1369, [Oct.], apptd chaplain to the prior, Liber Albus, fo 234v; 1370, 3 Apr., still chaplain, *ib.*, fo 246.
1386/7; 1388, 22 Aug., hostiller, Hamilton, *Comp. Rolls*, 54, (WCM C.213); *Reg. Wakefield*, no 788.
1388, 21 Dec., precentor, took over from John de Malverne I, q.v., Hamilton, *Comp. Rolls*, 44 (WCM C.366).
1388/9; 1390/1; 1392, Mar. to Sept.; 1393/6; 1397, 6 June; 1400/01, 3 Apr., precentor, an acct roll last seen in Norwich as NRO DCN obedientiary acct no 886; WCM C.367; WCM C.75; WCM C.368, C.369, C.77; *Reg. Trefnant* (Hereford), 144; WCM C.370.
1394/5, one of two bursars (as J.H.) with William Owston, q.v., WCM C.762.
1401, 3 Apr. to Sept., 1404/5, 1406/7, 1409/10, 1413/14, almoner, succ. John de Fordham, q.v., WCM C.186–190.
1371/2, student at Oxford, from Dec. to Sept., with £4 10s. maintenance pd by the cellarer, WCM C.67.
1372/3, [student], on whose behalf the cellarer rec. 14s. for bread and ale [?from the kitchener] for twelve wks at 14d. per wk; the cellarer also records payment to him of 60s. for the period between Sept. and mid-Apr., WCM C.68.
1376/7, student, for three quarters of the yr and half [of a quarter] with 105s. maintenance from the cellarer, WCM C.69; see John Grene who recd £6 for the full yr. The precentor pd travelling expenses for both to return home and go back to Oxford, c. 361a.
1382/3, student; the cellarer gave 13s. 4d. to him and to John de Dudley I, q.v., *tempore convocacionis cleri* [in Oxford, 18/26 Nov. 1382], WCM C.70. On this acct a payment of £12, p.a. is entered for [these] two Oxford scholars; see below.
1383/4, student, whose travelling expenses back and forth between Oxford and Worcester were pd by the precentor, WCM C.363.
1407, 2 Nov., referred to as M., *Reg. Sed. Vac.*, 389.

1370, 3 Apr., 16th in order at the el. of a prior and chosen as proctor to present the nominees to the bp, Liber Albus, fo 246 and Reg. Lynn, 46 (4 Apr.).
1373, 7 Dec., 14th at the el. of a bp, *Reg. Sed. Vac.*, 290; this same month he was comm. by the prior as one of two visitors, *sed. vac.*, for the deaneries of Kidderminster and Warwick, *ib.*, 312.
1376/7, with John Grene I, q.v., sent by the cellarer to London, WCM C.69.
1382, 13 Nov., apptd by the prior and chapter (with the adcn of Worcester) as proctor to attend convocation at St Frideswide's priory, Oxford, Liber Albus, fo 280.
1388, 21 Aug., 9th in order at the el. of a prior, and preached the opening sermon, Liber Albus, fos 334v, 335; he was also apptd as one of the proctors to present the seven nominees to the bp, *Reg. Wakefield*, no 789.
1391/2, sent, with William Power, q.v., to confer with the bp, WCM C.74.
1395, 20 May, comm. by the prior to carry out *sed. vac.*, visitations of Gloucester, Tewkesbury and other abbeys in the diocese, *Reg. Sed. Vac.*, 359.
1395, 15 Sept., one of the seven nominees for the priorate, Liber Albus, fo 380.
1397, 6 June, comm. by the bp of Hereford to absolve a penitent heretic, *Reg. Trefnant* (Hereford), 144.
1401, 24 June, 7th in order at the el. of a bp, *Reg. Sed. Vac.*, 372.
1401, 4/5 July, with a secular clerk, by comm. from the prior, carried out *sed. vac.* visitations of religious houses and parish churches in the diocese, *ib.*, 384–385.
1403, 25 Apr., granted papal licence to choose his own confessor, *CPL*, v (1396–1404), 563.
1407, 2/15 Nov., with a secular clerk performed *sed. vac.* visitations as above, *Reg. Sed. Vac.*, 389–390.
1409/10, went to Iccomb to hold courts, WCM C.189.
1419, 17 Mar., with a secular clerk carried out *sed. vac.* visitations of Whiston priory and St Oswald's hospital, Worcester, *Reg. Sed Vac.*, 396.
1419, 24 Apr., 3rd in order at the el. of a bp, *ib.*, 407.
1419/20, d. and the chamberlain sold his *panni*, WCM C.32.

Name in
(1) Worcs. Ms F.43, Robert Kilwardby, (on the Sentences) (late 13th c.); on fo 17v, *liber fratris*—. See also Thomas Ledbury.
(2) Birmingham University Library, Ms.11/v/10. Medica (14th c.); *iste liber est*—.

Note: it has been suggested that Worcs. Ms F.65, a collection of scholastic exercises and disputations in theology at Oxford, may have been compiled by him or by John de Malverne I, q.v., S.L. Forte, 'A Study of some Oxford Schoolmen of the Middle of the Fourteenth Century, with special ref. to Worcs. Cath. Ms F.65', Oxford, Bod., Ms B.Litt., c.10–11, 2 vols, 1947, i, 10–11.

Richard HAWERDYN
occ. 1458

1458, 23 Sept., ord acol., Worcester cathedral, Reg. Carpenter, i, 547.

Thomas HAY
occ. 1391 d. 1396

1391/2, was one of three poor novices to whom the almoner gave 20s. *in primo ingressu*, WCM C.181.
1391, 22 Feb., one of two whose prof the prior was comm. to rec., *Reg. Wakefield*, no 580.
1391, 20 May, ord acol. and subdcn, Bredon, *ib.*, no 958b, 958d.
1392, 9 Mar., ord dcn, bp's chapel, Hartlebury, *ib.*, 971c.
1395, 19 Mar., student at Oxford, *Reg. Sed. Vac.*, 354.
1396, June, d.; the precentor records buying parchment, on which to write the brief announcing the death, on his 1394/5 acct, WCM C.369; but the cellarer pd the brief bearer on his 1395/6 acct, WCM C.21. The almoner recd 38s. for his corrody for 38 wks between Michaelmas and the nativity of St John the Baptist, WCM C.182.

HAYLES
see Halis

HELYNGTON
see Hylynton

John de HEMBURY
occ. 1430/1

1430, 23 Dec., presented the monks for ordination at Alvechurch, Reg. Polton, 215; prob. he was precentor.
1431, 22 Sept., presented the monks for ordination at Withington, *ib.*, 234; see William Bristow.

Note: This cannot be the John de Hambury, q.v., who d. in 1419/20; however, any of the other entries under the former could apply to this monk.

HEMBURY
see also Hambury

HEMING [Hemming
occ. *temp.* bp Wulstan occ. c. 1104

n.d., subprior, Darlington, *Vita Wulfstani*, 7, 70.

c. 1104, name occ. on a list of monks in *Durham Liber Vitae*, fo 22.

Name in BL Ms Cotton Tiberius, A.xiii, a cartulary which he is alleged to have compiled at bp Wulstan's command, but recent research has concluded that there is no evidence to support this statement; see *Heming Chart.*, 282–286. The section prob. written in his hand ends before 1100, acc. to Darlington, *Vita Wulfstani*, xliii. See 'Hemming's Cartulary: a Description of the two Worcester Cartularies in Cotton Tiberius A.xiii' in Ker, *Books, Collectors, Libraries*, 31–59. See also McIntyre, 'Early 12th c. Worcester Cathedral Priory', 150–171. His hand and that of Coleman, q.v., are found in CUL Ms Kk.3.18.

Richard de HENKSEYE [Hengesheye, Hengsceseye, Hengseye, Henkeseye, Henxeye
occ. 1340 occ. 1365/6

1340, 28 Nov., one of three *clerici* whom the prior was comm. to examine and adm. after presenting them to the bp, *Reg. Bransford*, no 377.
1343, 20 Sept., ord pr., Bishops Cleeve, *ib.*, no 1054.
1351, 27 Feb., apptd *tumbarius*, Reg. Thoresby, 58.
1355/6, subcellarer, WCM C.439.
1361/3, 1365/6, precentor, WCM C.358–359a.
1350/1, recd 2s. from the precentor for his 'o' payment; this was the usual share for each monk, but he is named separately which suggests that he may have been absent from the community, WCM C.354.
1355/6, visited Tibberton, WCM C.802.
1364, Apr. and May., as commissary of the prior, with a secular clerk, carried out visitations *sed. vac.* in the deaneries of Pershore and Kidderminster, *Reg. Sed. Vac.*, 219–220.

Roger de HENLEY [Henleye
occ. 1315 d. 1341/2

1315, 14 Sept., one of three whose prof. the prior was comm. to rec., Reg. Maidstone, 74.
1317, 15 Sept., recd *lit. dim.*, for subdcn's orders, *ib.*, 106.
1318, 21 Jan., subdcn, recd *lit. dim.*, for orders of dcn and pr., Liber Albus, fo 87v.
1319, 4 Nov., present at an appeal concerning tithes, WCM B.753.
1341/2, d. and his corrody was sold for 47s. 6d. by the almoner, WCM C.170.

HENRICUS
occ. c. 1104

Name occ. in the list of monks in *Durham Liber Vitae*, fo 22.

Note: it is prob. the same monk who occ. on the Savigny mortuary roll dated c.1122/3, Delisle, *Rouleau Mortuaire*, pl. xxv, tit. 87.

HENXEYE
see Henkseye

HERDEWYK
see Hardewyk

John de HEREFORD
occ. 1337 occ. 1340

1337, 5 Apr., ord subdcn, Worcester cathedral, Reg. Montacute, 108.

1337, 20 Sept., ord dcn, King's Norton chapel, Reg. Hemenhale, 36.
1340, 15 Apr., ord pr., Alvechurch, *Reg. Bransford*, no 1010.

Roger de HEREFORD [Herford
occ. 1343

1343, 20 Sept., ord pr., Bishops Cleeve, *Reg. Bransford*, no 1054.

John HERFORD [Hereford, Hertford *alias* Smaw/?Small
occ. 1458 occ. 1469

1458, 23 Sept., ord acol. and subdcn, Worcester cathedral, Reg. Carpenter, i, 547.
1460, 7 June, ord dcn, Hereford cathedral, *Reg. Stanbury* (Hereford), 146.
1460, 20 Dec., ord pr., Worcester cathedral, Reg. Carpenter, i, 554.
1459/60, celebrated his first mass and recd *exennia* of 2s. 3d. from the kitchener, WCM C.149; there seems to be a slight discrepancy here either in the date or in the kitchener's accts.
1466/7, the cellarer purchased *harness*' for him and also noted that he, along with Richard Lodelowe and William Walweyn, q.v. did not rec. the full sum for their *minutio* pittances because *steterunt extra per unum quaternum anni*, WCM C.97.
1467, 12 Oct., the prior requested a writ *de apostatis capiendis* vs the three absentees, PRO C81/1786/55.
1469, 6 June, granted papal dispensation (as John Smaw) to hold a benefice with cure of souls, *CPL*, xii (1458–1471), 675.

Clement HERTILBURY [Hartillesbury, Hartylbury, Hertelbury, Hertylbury
occ. 1497 d. 1533/4

1497, 14 Apr., ord dcn, carnary chapel by Worcester cathedral, Reg. G. Gigli (7iii), 25.
1498, 14 Apr., ord pr., carnary chapel, *ib.*, 26.
1498, 25 Oct., infirmarer, with Robert Myston, q.v., *Reg. abp Morton*, ii, no 458.
1501/2, subcellarer, WCM C.628.
1520/1, *magister communis cene*, Reg. A.17, 66; prob. also in 1519, see below.
1522/5; 1529/30, hostiller, Reg. A.17, 211, WCM C.413, C.414; C.414a.
1524, former subprior, *Jnl More*, 206.
1533, infirmarer, *Jnl More*, 66.

1498, 25 Oct., 35th in order on the visitation certificate, *Reg. abp Morton*, ii, no 458.
1519, recd 'brekefast' money from the prior, *Jnl More*, 83, 93; he may have been *magister communis cene.*
1521, 22 July, 10th on the metropolitan visitation certificate, Reg. abp Warham, ii, 293v.
1524/5, pd by the prior for saying the ten o'clock mass at the rate of 10s. per quarter, *Jnl More*, 202, 206, 212, 216.
1531/2, 11th on the clerical subsidy list and pd 3s. 4d. as commons, Reg. A.12, fo 135.
1533/4, d., and the chamberlain sold his *vestimenta*, WCM C.415.

John HERTILBURY [Hartylbury, Hertelbury, Hertulbury, Hertylbury
occ. 1425 d. 1457/8

1444–1457/8, prior: one of the seven nom. by the chapter 15 Jan. 1444, apptd by the bp 16 Jan., Reg. Bourgchier, 193–195; d. 1457/8, WCM C.44.

1425, 24 Mar., ord acol., Worcester cathedral, Reg. Morgan, 207.
1426, 8 Sept., recd *lit. dim.* for all orders, Reg. Polton, 13.
1426, 22 Sept., ord subdcn, Bromyard, *Reg. Spofford* (Hereford), 300; the precentor recorded the travelling expenses, WCM C. 377.
1428, 28 Feb., ord dcn, Worcester cathedral Reg. Polton, 236.
1430, 10 June, ord pr., Alvechurch, where he was presented by the prior, Reg. Polton, 212, WCM C.86.
1429/30, celebrated his first mass; the hostiller sent *exennia* of 2s. 8d. to him and seven other newly ord priests, WCM C.231.

1444, 15 Jan., subprior, Reg. Bourgchier, 193.
1429/30, prob. student at Oxford as the cellarer pd for his coming home to rec. orders, WCM C.86; William Hertilbury, q.v. was also at Oxford this yr. He may have been one of the unnamed students who recd maintenance and other expenses on the accts in the early 1430s, as he seems not to have been involved in any administrative tasks or offices.
1433, 9 Dec., 33rd in order at the el. of a bp, *Reg. Sed. Vac.*, 432.
1435/6, with John Hanley, q.v., involved in a lawsuit [on behalf of the chapter], WCM C.88.
1444, 15 Jan., one of the seven nominees for the priorate as above.
1445, 27 Mar., presented John Whetyll, q.v., for ord. in Worcester cathedral, Reg. Carpenter, i, 501.
1449/50, went to the Black Monk Chapter at Northampton, accompanied by John Lawerne I, q.v.; their expenses were £12 4s., WCM C.92.
1457/8, d., and the chamberlain recd £4 for the sale of his *harnecia*, WCM C.44.

Some of his *acta* are recorded in the Liber Albus by his chaplains: fos 475–477 by William Hodynton II, q.v., fos 477–478 by John Morton, q.v., fos 478–486, 489 by Robert Multon, q.v., fo 487v by John Smethwyk, q.v., fo 488 by Hugh Knyghton, q.v.

I Thomas de HERTILBURY [Hartilbury, Hertulbury
occ. 1374 d. 1419/20

1374, 25 Feb., ord subdcn, Worcester cathedral, *Reg. Sed. Vac.*, 300.
1377, 23 May, ord pr., Colwich, *Reg. Stretton* (1905) (Coventry/Lichfield), 326.

1380, 15 Dec., subsacrist, Liber Albus, fo 309v.
1381/4, subcellarer, WCM C.540, C.761, C.553.
1384/5, 1386/7, 1390/2, 1393/5, kitchener, WCM C.120–125.
1401, 24 June, sacrist, *Reg. Sed. Vac.*, 373.
1404/7, kitchener, WCM C.131–133.
1414, June/Sept., kitchener, WCM C.137.
1417/18; 1419, 24 Apr., hostiller, WCM C.224a; *Reg. Sed. Vac.*, 407.

1380, 15 Dec., present at the induction of the adcn of Gloucester, Liber Albus, fo 309v.
1381/2, visited Broadwas, Hallow and Sedgeberrow, WCM C.540, 598, 760; he also visited Dodderhill while subcellarer, WCM C.477 (undated).
1382/3, visited Sedgeberrow, WCM C.761.
1383/4, visited Bromsgrove and Newnham, WCM C.553, C.655a.
1388, 21 Aug., 28th in order at the el. of a prior, Liber Albus, fo 334v.
1408/9, one of the cellarer's creditors, WCM C.81.
1419/20, d., and the chamberlain sold his clothing, WCM C.32.

II Thomas HERTILBURY [Hartilbury, Hartlebury, Hertulbury
occ. 1483 d. [1488/9]

1483, 20 Sept., ord acol., carnary chapel by Worcester cathedral, Reg. Alcock, 274.
1487, 22 Sept., ord pr., Ledbury, *Reg. Milling* (Hereford), 174.

[1488/9], d., and the prior [Robert Multon, q.v.], holding the office of almoner, recd payment from the cellarer for a corrody for him, for three quarters of the yr, WCM C.488.

William HERTILBURY B.Th. [Hertelbury, Hertlebury, Hertulbury, Hertylbury
occ. 1414 occ. 1439/40

1414, 3 Mar., ord acol., Worcester cathedral, Reg. Peverel, 198.
1415, 25 Mar., ord subdcn, Dominican convent, Worcester, *ib.*, 203.
1415, 21 Sept., ord dcn, Hartlebury, *ib.*, 206.
1417/18, celebrated his first mass; the hostiller gave 2s. 6d. in *exennia* and the pittancer gave 2s. 8d. for bread and ale, WCM C.224a, C.324.

1431, Aug./Sept., described as former bursar, WCM C.86a.
1431/5, 1436/7, almoner, WCM C.194–198.
1439/40, sacrist, WCM C.89.

1419/20, student at Oxford, recd 20s. [?for clothing allowance] from the chamberlain, WCM C.32.
1425/6, student, and the precentor hired two horses so that he could return to Worcester in order to preach, WCM C.377.
1429/30, [student]; the cellarer pd his expenses 'coming home' from Oxford, WCM C.86.
1433, 31 Oct., described as *in theologia bacallarius*, Liber Albus, fo 438.
Note: the above entries correct and supplement *BRUO*.

1419, 24 Apr., 35th in order at the el. of a bp, *Reg. Sed. Vac.*, 407.
1421/2, recd a 'reward' of 6s. at the time of his *minutio*, WCM C.84a.
1427/8, sent to London for negotiations and to attend convocation, WCM C.85a.
1432, Aug./Sept., went to Hanley [?Castle] to confer with the Earl of Warwick on business affairs of the house, WCM C.86a.
1433, 31 Oct., apptd with Thomas Ledbury, q.v., as proctor for convocation on 7 Nov., Liber Albus, fo 438.
1433, Oct./Nov., with a secular clerk performed visitations, *sed. vac.*, in churches and religious houses in the adcnry of Gloucester as commissaries of the prior, *Reg. Sed. Vac.*, 429–31.
1433, 8 Nov., sent as proctor, again with Thomas Ledbury, to the king for licence to el. a bp, *ib.*, fo 438v.
1433, 9 Dec., 15th in order at the el., and with Thomas Ledbury was sent to the bp el. [Thomas Bourgchier] in London to inform him of the chapter's choice, *Reg. Sed. Vac.*, 432–435. These two proctors also presented Bourgchier to the king, *ib.*
1433/4, made another journey with Ledbury for another convocation, and their expenses were £4 14s. 4d., WCM C.492.
1434/5, took Hugh Knyghton, q.v., to rec. orders at Bromyard, WCM C.87
1435, 4 July, sent as proctor to the Black Monk Chapter in Northampton, WCM C.87.

Roger de HERVYNTON [Herwintone, Herwynton
occ. 1305 d. 1339/40

1305, 4 Jan., one of four *clerici* presented to the bp at the time of their adm., *Reg. Gainsborough*, 14.
1308, 25 Oct., recd *lit. dim.* for dcn's orders, *Reg. Reynolds*, 92.
1309, 24 May, ord dcn, Cirencester, *ib.*, 111.
1309, 3 Dec., recd *lit. dim.* for orders of pr., *ib.*, 93.

1318, 13 Sept., apptd sacrist by the bp, *Reg. Cobham*, 11; [1321] released from office, *ib.*, 112; see Ranulph de Calthrop.

1317, 20 Oct., 31st in order at the el. of a prior, Liber Albus, fo 83.

1319, 4 Nov., made an appeal to the apostolic see vs the prior for his alienation of convent property, WCM B.753.

1319, 18 Nov., because of building works which he, as sacrist, was currently supervising, the bp granted a slight delay in the payment of money owed to him from the offerings at the shrine and head of St Wulstan, *Reg. Cobham*, 21.

[1319], after his visitation the bp ordered an inventory of the valuables to be drawn up and the items which Hervynton had alienated and used as guarantees for loans were to be recovered, Reg. Montacute, 223 (in which Cobham's injunctions have been bound).

[1321], in his letter announcing the apptment of Hervynton's successor as sacrist the bp stated that he desired 'ut liberius deo et sibi vacare valeat', *Reg. Cobham*, 112.

1322/3, visited Bromsgrove, WCM C.545.

1340, c. 25 Mar., d., as the pittancer gave him less than his usual yearly allowance of pittances during the periodic *minutiones*, WCM C.298.

John de HETHE [de la Heth

occ. 1305 occ. 1316

1305, 28 Feb., almoner, WCM B.1553.

1313, 16 Oct., former *tumbarius*, *Reg. Reynolds*, 77.

1305, 28 Feb., recd a gift of land to the almoner's office, WCM B.1553.

1316, 16 Oct., ordered by the bp to render his acct while *tumbarius* to a named official, *Reg. Reynolds*, 77.

HEVESHAM

see Evesham

HILARIUS

see Hylarius

Henry HIMBLETON [Hymalton, Hymmulton, Hymulton, Hymylton

occ. 1525/6 occ. 1536

1527, 19 Sept., ord subdcn, Gloucester abbey, Reg. Ghinucci 7(ii), 167.

1532, 16 Mar., ord dcn, carnary chapel by Worcester cathedral, *ib.*, 172.

1531/2, celebrated his first mass; recd gifts of 2s. from each of the almoner, cellarer and kitchener, WCM C.414c.

1525/6, 39th on the clerical subsidy list and pd 2s. commons, Reg. A.12, fos 173–125.

1531/2, 39th on the second subsidy list, and pd 2s., *ib.*, fo 135v.

1534, 17 Aug., subscribed to the Act of Supremacy, *DK 7th Report*, Appndx 2, 305.

1535, signed the petition vs the reinstatement of William Fordham q.v. as cellarer, *L and P Henry VIII*, ix, no 653.

1536, 13 Mar., 28th in order at the 'el.' of Henry Holbech, q.v., as prior, Reg. A.6(iii), fo 1.

William HINCKLEY [Hincley, Hinkeley, Hynkeley

occ. 1468 d. 1483/4

1468, 17 Dec., ord pr., St Nicholas' church, Worcester, Reg. Carpenter, i, 573.

1468/9, celebrated his first mass; the almoner contributed 2s. 3d. for the celebratory feast as did the kitchener, WCM C.202, C.154.

1476/7, subcellarer, WCM C.740.

1479/83, pittancer, WCM C.341 and C.742, C.342, C.743, C.744.

1476/7, visited Overbury, WCM C.740.

1483/4, d., and the chamberlain sold his *harnesia* for 16s. 11d., WCM C.47.

Thomas de HINDELEP' [Hindelep', Hyndelep, Hyndelepp

occ. 1280 occ. 1295

1280, 24 Aug., apptd sacrist by the bp, *Reg. Giffard*, 123; he succ. Nicholas de Norton, q.v.

1287, 2 Jan., one of two monk proctors apptd to present the seven nominees for the priorate to the bp, *Reg. Giffard*, 304, 325.

1293/4, went with John de Landaven', q.v., to Stolton [*sic*] *pro transgressione*, Wilson, *Early Comp. Rolls*, 20 (WCM C.51a).

1295, 8 Jan., with Thomas de Wych. appeared before the bp, who was ill in bed at Hartlebury, and announced the renewal of the chapter's appeal vs the bp's collegiate church at Westbury, *Ann. Wigorn*, 518.

John de HODYNTON [Hodinton

occ. 1330 occ. 1342

1330, 11 Aug., one of four whose prof. the prior was comm. to rec., *Reg. Orleton*, no 335.

1331, 25 May, ord subdcn, [?Chipping] Camden, *ib.*, no 21 (p. 35).

1332, 18 Apr., ord pr., Beckford, *ib.*, no 25 (p. 41).

1336/40, subcellarer, WCM C.646, C.547, C.647a, C.647.

1340/1, kitchener, WCM C.111 and C.169; extracts of this latter are printed in Wilson, *Accts Henry VIII*, Appndx vi, 53–57.

[1342], chaplain to the prior, Liber Albus, fo 181v; date of apptment uncertain, but he occ. on 21 Dec., *ib.*, fo 181.

1336/7, visited Moor [Lindridge], and Tibberton, WCM C.646, C.832.

1337/8, visited Bromsgrove for *receptio bladorum*, WCM C.547.

1338/9, visited Moor [Lindridge], WCM C.647a.

1339/40, visited Hallow and Moor [Lindridge], WCM C.594, C.646.

[1336 × 1340], while subcellarer visited Sedgeberrow, WCM C.486a.

1342, 21 Dec., served as witness to the homage of a priory tenant, Liber Albus, fo 181.

Nicholas de HODYNTON [Hodyngton
occ. 1353 d. 1387/8

1353, 26 Nov., one of three *clerici* whom the prior was comm. to examine as suitable candidates for adm., Reg. Bryan, i, 10.
1355, 19 Mar., ord dcn, Hartlebury, *ib.*, i, 101.
1356/7, celebrated his first mass; the cellarer gave 3s. 4d. *pro exeniis* from himself and the prior and 12d. for mead, WCM C.63.

1361/2, kitchener, WCM C.116.
1370, 3 Apr., pittancer, Liber Albus, fo 246.

1358/9, with the chamberlain and Richard Moreys, q.v., visited Dodderhill, WCM C.835.
1370, 3 Apr., 10th in order at the el. of a prior and one of the seven nominees for the priorate, Liber Albus, fo 246, 246v.
1373, 4/7 Dec., 9th at the el. of a bp, *Reg. Sed. Vac.*, 290.
1376/7, ill in the infirmary and the cellarer spent 5s. in *diversis* for him, WCM C.69.
1387/8, d., and the precentor bought parchment for the brief announcing his obit, WCM C.365.

I William HODYNTON [Huddynton
occ. 1408 occ. 1449/50

1408, 22 Dec., ord acol., Worcester cathedral, Reg. Peverel, 175.
1411, 28 Mar., ord dcn, Worcester cathedral, *ib.*, 188 (the scribe has written 1410 in error).
1413, 23 Sept., ord pr., Winchcombe abbey, *ib.*, 197.
1413/14, celebrated his first mass, and recd *exennia* from the almoner and hostiller, WCM C.190, C.223.

1419, 24 Apr., subsacrist, *Reg. Sed. Vac.*, 407.
1423/4; 1425/31; cellarer, WCM C.721 (where he took over from Richard Tyberton, q.v. in the spring of 1423); WCM E.51; C.585 (as W.H.), C.85, 85a, 689, 86 (with Thomas Colwall, q.v., bursar), C.722 (where he is named as both cellarer and bursar).
1432/3, 1438, 12 Feb., kitchener, WCM C.145, Reg. Bourgchier, 84.
1439/40, 1441/2, again cellarer, WCM C.89, 727 (as W.H.)
1442/5, kitchener, WCM C.728 (and C.823 for 1442/3, as W.H.), C.147, C.493.
1444, chaplain to the prior, Liber Albus, fo 475; but see William Hodynton II.
1445/8, almoner, WCM C.842, C.90, E.175.
1448/50, infirmarer, WCM C.91, C.92.

1419, 24 Apr., 27th in order at the el. of a bp, *Reg. Sed. Vac.*, 407.
1426/7, visited Dodderhill with the steward 'pro bladis decenniis vidend' et denar' levand' ', WCM C.85; they also went to Stoke [?Prior] twice to hold the view of frankpledge, *ib.*
1432, Aug./Sept., went to Warwick and Coventry on negotiations, WCM C.86a.
1433, 9 Dec., 12th at the el. of a bp, *Reg. Sed. Vac.*, 432.
1438, 12 Feb., one of the seven nominees for the priorate, Reg. Bourgchier, 84.
1439/40, with the [lay] steward went to Blackwell and Shipston to hold courts and also to Hardwick for the same purpose, WCM C.89.
1444, 16 Jan., one of the seven nominees for the priorate, Reg. Bourgchier, 193–195.
1448/9, 1449/50, one of the creditors of the cellarer, WCM C.91, C.92.

II William HODYNTON
occ. 1419 occ. 1469

1444, chaplain to the prior, Liber Albus, fo 475.
1444/5, steward of the prior's hospice WCM C.493.
1451/2, kitchener, part yr, WCM C.601; succ. by John Smethwyk, q.v.
1452/7, cellarer, WCM C.842a, C.94, C.480, C.541, C.732.
1458/9, almoner, WCM C.685.
1459/60, almoner and cellarer, WCM C.94a, C.400; in this yr John Smethwyk, q.v., took over as cellarer, *ib.*
1460/6, almoner, WCM C.94a, C.733, C.734, C.201, C.95, C.96.
1462/3, 1464/5, 1466/9, kitchener, WCM C.602, C.95, C.152–154.

1419, 24 Apr., 27th in order at the el. of a bp, *Reg. Sed. Vac.*, 407.
1432, Aug./Sept., went to Warwick on negotiations, WCM C.86a.
1433, 9 Dec., 12th at the el. of a bp, *Reg. Sed. Vac.*, 432.
1438, 12 Feb., one of the seven nominees for the priorate, Reg. Bourgchier, 84.
1444, 16 Jan., one of the seven nominees for the priorate, *ib.*, 193–195
1448/9, 1449/50, one of the creditors of the cellarer, WCM C.91, C.92.
1469, 14 Aug., one of the seven nominees for the priorate, Reg. Carpenter, ii, 13–16 and Reg. A.6(i), fo 60v.

Note: there must be two monks, contemporaries, by the same name, but they never occ. together and were never distinguished one from the other. My division of biographical details is purely arbitrary and based on the fact that priors often chose their chaplains from the recently ordained, and this was therefore the first office to which many monks were assigned.

III William HODYNTON [Hodyngton
occ. 1481 occ. 1540

1481, 16 June, ord acol., Whitbourne, *Reg. Milling* (Hereford), 163.
1481, 22 Sept., ord subdcn, Whitbourne, *ib.*, 164.
1481, 22 Dec., ord dcn, Hartlebury, Reg. Alcock, 265.

1487/9, kitchener, WCM C.161, C.162.
1491/2, subcellarer, WCM C.751.
1498, 25 Oct., refectorer, *Reg. abp Morton*, ii, no 458.
1499, 21 July, almoner, Reg. A.6(ii), fo 1^v.
1504, 6 Nov.; 1505/6, pittancer, Reg. A.6(ii), fo 32; WCM C.427.
1507, 10 Sept., subprior, Reg. S. Gigli, 349.
On the following dates between 1515/16 and 1536, almoner: 1515/17, WCM E.182; 1518, 27 Sept., Reg. A.6(ii), fo 113; 1520/1, Reg. A.17, 29; 1521/2, Wilson, *Accts Henry VIII*, 9; 1522/3, Reg. A.17, 197; 1523/4, Reg. A.17, 262; 1524/5, WCM C.414; 1526, WCM E.183; 1527, *Jnl More*, 44; 1529/32, WCM C.414a, C.414b, C.414c; 1534, 17 Aug., *DK 7th Report*, Appndx 2, 305 (as Bodynton); 1535, *L and P Henry VIII*, ix, no 653; 1536, 13 Mar., Reg. A.6(iii), fo 1.

1492, 27 June, one of two proctors apptd to present the seven nominees for the priorate to the bp, Reg. Morton, 90; they did so on 30 June, *ib.*, 91.
1498, 25 Oct., 15th in order on the visitation certificate, *Reg. abp Morton*, ii, no 458.
1499, 21 July, one of the seven nominees for the priorate, Reg. A.6(ii), fo 1^v, Reg. S Gigli, 343; they were presented to bp Fox (Durham) at Southwark on 2 Sept., Reg. A.6(ii), fo 1^v.
1507, 10 Sept., one of the seven nominees for the priorate, Reg. S. Gigli, 349.
1518, 27 Sept., one of the seven nominees for the priorate, Reg. A.6(ii), fo 113; they were presented to bp Fox (Winchester), prob. at Southwark, and he named William More I, q.v., *ib.*
1521, 22 July, 4th in order on the visitation certificate, Reg. abp Warham, ii, fo 293^v.
1531/2, 5th on the clerical subsidy list and pd. £5 as almoner and 3s. 4d. commons, Reg. A.12, fo 135.
1534, 17 Aug., subscribed to the Act of Supremacy, *DK 7th Report*, Appndx 2, 305.
1535, with John Lawerne II and Roger Neckham, q.v., he turned a blind eye on the denunciations made by Thomas Musard, q.v., *L and P Henry VIII*, ix, no 52.2(i); he also signed the petition vs the reinstatement of William Fordham, q.v., as cellarer, *ib.*, no 653.
1536, 13 Mar., 3rd in order at the 'el.' of Henry Holbech, q.v., Reg. A.6(iii), fo 1.
1540, assigned a pension of £8 p.a., *L and P Henry VIII*, xv, no 869.
1540/1, three items of plate are listed as his in an inventory, Reg. A.12, fo 173.

Note: do we again have two monks here? If so, the fourth William Hodynton is prob. the one who was almoner during the twenty years between 1515/16 and 1536; however, there is no evidence that points to two, and so we may assume that William III lived to celebrate the sixtieth anniversary of his prof., prob. on the eve of the dissolution.

Nicholas de HOGSSHAWE [Hoggesschawe

occ. 1328 occ. 1349

1328, 24 Sept., ord subdcn, St Mary's church at the gate of Gloucester abbey, *Reg. Orleton*, no 9 (p. 9).
1329, 17 June, ord dcn, Tewkesbury abbey, *ib.*, no 14 (p. 15).
[1330], 9 Nov., granted *lit. dim.* for orders of pr., *ib.*, no 250.
1349, 11 May, apptd *tumbarius* by the bp, *Reg. Bransford*, no 1001.

Henry HOLBECH, D.Th. [Holbeche *alias* Rands

occ. 1536 occ. 1540

1536–1540, prior: 'el.' 13 Mar. 1536, Reg. A.6(iii) fos 1–2; apptd dean of the new foundation 18 Jan., 1540, *Fasti*, iv, 60.
Before 1536, he was a monk of Crowland and prior of the Benedictine monk students at Cambridge; see *DNB*. The 'el.' was a farce; the proceedings were directed by M. John Tregonwell as the king's emissary, and only two of the four *compromissorii*, who were delegated to choose a prior, were monks. See *L and P Henry VIII*, x, no 56 and *ib.*, ix, no 97.
1537/9, named as holding the office of almoner, WCM E.185.
1540, 18 Jan., on the surrender list, *L and P Henry VIII*, xv, 435.
Some of his *acta* are recorded in Reg. A.6(iii), fos 1–50 by his chaplain, Thomas Blockeley, q.v.

William de HOLTE

occ. 1339

1339, 27 Mar., ord subdcn, Kempsey, *Reg. Bransford*, no 1004.

Giles HOLYWELL [Holewell, Holiwell, Olywell

occ. 1423 occ. 1433

1423, 20 Mar., ord acol., Worcester cathedral, Reg. Morgan, 198.
1424, 18 Mar., ord acol., Worcester cathedral, *ib.*, 202.
Note: this entry occ. twice with different dates.
1426, 30 Mar., ord subdcn, Worcester cathedral, *ib.*, 211.
1429, 26 Mar., ord dcn, carnary chapel by Worcester cathedral, Reg. Polton, 125.
1429/30, celebrated his first mass; and recd 2s. 8d. in *exennia* from the hostiller, WCM C.231.
1433, 9 Dec., 28th in order at the el. of a bp, *Reg. Sed. Vac.*, 432.

Thomas HOSYNTRE [Hosuntre, Osyntre, Osyntree *alias* Parlor
occ. 1437 d. 1444/5

1434, 21 May, a Thomas Parlor *alias* Hosyntre, ord acol., carnary chapel by Worcester cathedral, *Reg. Sed. Vac.*, 443; he had not yet entered the monastery.
1437, 1 Sept., ord subdcn, bp's chapel, Alvechurch, Reg. Bourgchier, 61.
1439/40, went to Wigmore for ord. [as dcn], and the expenses totalled 15s. 6d., WCM C.89. The ordination was in Wigmore abbey on 19 Sept. 1439, but the scribe, who entered the details in the bp's register, had only begun to fill in the names and had left a space which remains incomplete, Reg. Spofford (Hereford), fo 45.
[1441], 22 Sept., ord pr., Lichfield cathedral, Reg. Heyworth (Coventry/Lichfield), fo 241.
1444/5, student at Gloucester College, Oxford and d. there; it cost the cellarer 35s. to transport his body from Oxford to Worcester, WCM C.493. This acct also ref. to his travelling back from Oxford [earlier] during the yr. 'causa Novic' materie pend' inter fratrem J. Broughton [q.v.] et Kanturmaynes'.
1444/5, the cellarer pd 9d. to a man *in factura sepultura . . . in claustro*, WCM C.493.
1444/5, the cellarer pd a debt of 23s. 4d. to the butler [*pincerna*] at Gloucester College, WCM C.493.
1446/7, more of his debts were pd off: 6s. 8d. to John Smyth of Oxford; also 10s. was distributed to the Worcester Dominicans and Franciscans to pray for his soul, and the money came from the corrody fund [*nomine corodii*] which presumably would have been allocated for him, WCM C.90.
1448/9, more debts were pd off: 12s. to Richard Maii of Oxford, WCM C.91.
1449/50, debts of 8d. pd; also of 13s. 4d. to John Grene II, q.v., WCM C.92.
1453/4, the cellarer recorded the final payment of all outstanding debts incurred by him and two other monk students; the sum was over £20 and the other students were Hugh Leyntwardine and John Preston II, q.v., WCM C.94.

HUDDYNTON
see Hodynton

John de HUDSEYO
occ. 1358

1358, 28 June, obtained a papal licence to choose his own confessor, *CPL*, iii (1342–1362), 599.

Note: there is little doubt that this is an error, prob. of the papal scribe, but the Rev. Dr Leonard Boyle, Prefect of the Vatican Library, has kindly verified that this is the correct reading of the original.

HUGH
occ. 1271 occ. 1274

1271, 21 Dec.; 1274, 21 Sept., precentor, *Reg. Giffard*, 51, 62.
1271, 21 Dec., one of the seven nominees for the priorate, *Reg. Giffard*, 51.
1274, 21 Sept., again one of the seven nominees for the priorate, *ib.*, 62.

Note: this is prob. Hugh de Inceberg, q.v.

William de HULTON
occ. 1360/1

1360, 30 Apr., one of three whose prof. the prior was comm. to rec., Reg. Bryan, i, 135; the following day the prior did so, Liber Albus, fo 226^{v}.
1361, 13 Mar., ord. acol., Hartlebury, Reg. Bryan, i, 121.

Note: see William de Shrovesbury.

M. W. HURREL
occ. 1330

1330, 11 Aug., one of four *clerici* to be examined by two officials appted by the bp and recd *ad monachalem ordinem Reg. Orleton*, no 776.

William de HYDESHALE [Ideshall, Idsale, Ydenhale, Ydeshall, Ydushale
occ. 1388 occ. 1406/7

1388, 7 Sept., one of two whom the prior was comm. to prof., Reg. Wakefield, 239.

Note: the entry in the printed register, item no 794, has not distinguished between adm and prof.

1389, 13 Mar., ord dcn, Alvechurch, *Reg. Orleton*, no 935e.
1389/90, celebrated his first mass; the almoner, chamberlain, pittancer and subcellarer sent *exennia*, WCM C.180, C.17, C.314, C.445.
1392/3, described as a novice by the chamberlain who gave him a *pellicia*, costing 4s., WCM C.20; when he was ill in the infirmary this yr, the cellarer sent him two chickens, WCM C.76.
1401, 24 June, 33rd in order at the el. of a bp, *Reg. Sed. Vac.*, 373.
1404/5, 1406/7, gave 2s. to the almoner both yrs as alms, WCM C.187, C.188.

HYLARIUS
d. 1222

1222, d., *Ann. Wigorn*, 415.

Ralph HYLYNTON [Helyngton, Hyllyngton
occ. 1497/9

1497, 14 Apr., ord dcn., carnary chapel by Worcester cathedral, Reg. G. Gigli (7iii), 25.
1498/9, celebrated his first mass; recd a 2s. gift from the hostiller, WCM C.238.

1498, 25 Oct., 36th in order on the visitation certificate, *Reg. abp Morton*, ii, no 258.

HYMALTON, Hymbleton, Hymulton
see Himbleton

HYNCEBERG
see Inceberg

HYNDELEP'
see Hindelep

HYNKELEY
see Hinckley

IDESHALL, Idsale
see Hydeshale

Hugh de INCEBERG [Hynceberg, Inceberge, Inteberg
occ. 1287 occ. 1294/5

1287, 11 Aug., almoner, WCM B.42.
1291/2, 1293/5, cellarer and bursar, Wilson, *Early Comp. Rolls*, 8–32 (WCM C.51, C.51a, C.52).

1287, 11 Aug., involved in negotiations concerning a loan, WCM B.42.

Name on the last flyleaf of Worcs. Ms Q.42, Distinctiones Mauricii (late 12th c.) as one of the eleven monks who contributed to its purchase, in his case 16[?d.].

See also Hugh with whom this monk may be identical.

William de INCEBERG [Ingteberg, Inteberge
occ. 1297 occ. 1319

1297, 29 June, almoner, WCM B.1552a.
1297, 29 June, recd a gift of land to the almoner's office, WCM B.1552a.
1306, 26 Sept., after his visitation, bp Gainsborough required of him and of Stephen [de Wytton q.v.], the sacrist, under pain of imprisonment, 'quod decetero se mutuo diligant ut tenentur'. Reg. Montacute, 223 (in which these injunctions have been bound).
1317, 20 Oct., 5th in order at the el. of a prior, Liber Albus, fo 83^{v}.
1319, 4 Nov., witness to the reading of the sacrist's appeal vs the prior, WCM B.753; see Roger de Hervynton.

John JEORGE
see George

I JOHN [of Worcester
occ. before 1095 occ. c. 1140

c. 1104, name occ. in a list of monks in *Durham Liber Vitae*, fo 22.

Prob. the writer/compiler of the Worcester Chronicle (Chronicon ex chronicis), both the earlier part that has been attributed to Florence, q.v., and the continuation known as his. The evidence is set forth in Gransden, *Historical Writing*, i, 143–145.

He may have been ordered by bp Wulstan to continue the chronicle of Marianus Scotus (who had d. in 1082/3), Mason, *Wulfstan*, 296–297. For a time he was at Winchcombe abbey but he had returned to Worcester by 1139, *John of Worcester, Chronicle*, 57. Dr. Mason suggests (*ib.*, 144) that he had been a member of the Worcester community since boyhood, and that he was in touch with fellow monk historians at Canterbury, Durham and Malmesbury. He may have entertained Orderic Vitalis who came to visit Worcester, and was impressed by John's 'venerable character and learning' as well as by his chronicle, Gransden, *ib.*, 155–156 (quoting Orderic). The 12th c. ms, Florentius Wigorniensis, now Oxford, Corpus Christi College Ms 157, prob. contains his autograph, see *MLGB*, 209 n.4. The Chronicle is in the process of being edited for Oxford Medieval Texts by P. McGurk and the second vol. has just appeared (1995).

His hand occ. in Dublin, Trinity College Ms 503, one of the Chronicon mss, and in several other mss which are discussed by Dr McIntyre in 'Early 12th C. Worcester Cathedral Priory', 45–49. See Watson, *Dated and Datable Mss*, i, no 50, where he suggests that John's hand may be in Oxford Bod. Auct. F.1.9 and Cambridge, Corpus Christi College Ms 157. See also Thomas Streynsham.

For a recent assessment of John's place among 12th-c. monastic historians, see M. Brett:
(1) 'John of Worcester and his Contemporaries', in R. H. C. Davis and J. M. Wallace-Hadrill, *The Writing of History in the Middle Ages, Essays presented to Richard William Southern* (Oxford, 1981), 101–126.
(2) 'The Use of Universal Chronicle at Worcester', in *L'Historiographie Médiévale en Europe*, Éditions du CNRS (Paris, 1991), 277–285.

II JOHN
occ. 1274

1274, 21 Sept., hostiller, *Reg. Giffard*, 62.
1274, 21 Sept., one of the seven nominees for the priorate, *Reg. Giffard*, 62.

Note: could this be John de Wyke, q.v.?

III JOHN
occ. 1313/14

[1313/14], cellarer, Wilson, *Early Comp. Rolls*, 33 (WCM C.482).

JOHN [Conversus, *alias* Mason, *Latomus*
occ. 1339/40 occ. 1360/1

1344/5 × 1359/60, for some of this period prob. *magister operum*, an office which was dependent on the cellarer; see below, and also under John de Preston I.

1339/41, 1343/5, 1346/7, 1349/50, 1351/2, 1355/7, 1360/1, regularly recd pittances from the pittancer when his turn came round for *minuciones*, at the time of the 'o' celebrations in Advent, and when there were other distributions. He was always listed separately by name as 'brother John, *conversus*', and his share, when the amount is stated, was less than the other professed monks, WCM C.298–302, C.292, C.293, C.303–305.

1341/2, 1345/6, 1355/6, recd pittances from the almoner on Maundy Thursday [*pro mandato*] and mentioned by name each time, WCM C.170–172.

1344/7, 1354/5, 1356/8, 1359/60, recd small sums of money for *minuciones* and the 'O' feasts distributed by the cellarer; and again named on each acct, WCM C.59–65.

1346/7, under the heading *Custus nove porte* the cellarer recorded payment of the salaries of masons as noted in the schedule of John, WCM C.61.

[1348/9], under the same heading as above . . . *per vis[um] fratris Johannis cementar[ii]*, Windsor, St George's Chapel, XI.E.37.

1351, 8 Jan., obtained a papal indult [as John Mason, *latomus, conversus*], to choose his own confessor, *CPL*, iii (1342–1362), 380.

1356/7, the cellarer pd the expenses of John, *existent' ad quareram* [?at Ombersley], WCM C.63.

1357/8, work was in progress on the prior's hall for which the cellarer pd *preter opus fratris J. conversi*, WCM C.64.

Note: this is the only known instance of a monk of the mid-fourteenth century in this register remaining a lay brother, although the term *conversus*, was also, occasionally, used to denote a monk not yet in priests's orders; see Henry de Lawerne. He may have been an experienced mason before he entered, as his supervision of the construction of the *nova porta* (?great gate, Edgar tower) seems to indicate.

JORDAN
occ. late 12th c.

n.d., occ. on an acct of Tibberton when he visited there, *temp.* Thomas de Ballescot, q.v., WCM E.4(10).

KALAMAN
see Calaman

KAROLUS
occ. c. 1104

Name occ. in the list of monks in *Durham Liber Vitae*, fo 22.

KEDERMINSTR'
see Kidremistre, Kyderminstre

John KENT
occ. 1473 occ. 1476/7

1473, 10 May, one of four whom the prior and the bp's chancellor were comm. to examine and admit, Reg. A.6(i), fo 77, Reg. Carpenter, ii, 94 (as William, and on 12 May in the latter).

1476/7, celebrated his first mass and the kitchener gave 2s. 3d., WCM C.158.

Walter de KERSWELL [Kereswell, Kereswelle
occ. 1305 occ. 1318

1305, 4 Jan., one of four *clerici* presented to the bp at the time of their adm., *Reg. Gainsborough*, 14.

1306, 31 Mar., the bp recd his prof. in the Lady chapel of the cathedral, *Liber Albus*, no 359.

1317, 20 Oct., 28th in order at the el. of a prior, Liber Albus, fo 83.

1318, before June, kept acct of the priory sheep, WCM E.16.

John KIDREMISTER [Kederminstr', Kedyrmystr', Kedyrmystur
occ. 1490 occ. 1506/7

1490, 6 Mar., ord acol., carnary chapel by Worcester cathedral, Reg. Morton, 143.

1490, 10 Apr., ord subdcn, carnary chapel, *ib.*, 145.

1492, 22 Sept., ord dcn., carnary chapel, *ib.*, 157.

1494, 24 May, ord pr., carnary chapel, *ib.*, 162.

1498, 25 Oct., subalmoner, *Reg. abp Morton*, ii, no 258.

1503, chaplain to the prior, Reg. A.6(ii), fo 26.

1504, 6 Nov., 'chadentter' (?chanter or precentor), Reg. A.6(ii), fo 32.

1506/7, steward of the prior's hospice, WCM C.668.

1498, 25 Oct., 31st in order on the visitation certificate, *Reg. abp Morton*, ii, no 258.

1506/7, visited Newnham, WCM C.668.

See also Kyderminstre.

KINGESLONDE
see Kyngeslonde, Kyngislond

Walter de KIRKEBY [Kyrkeby
occ. [1369] d. 1405/6

[1369], 1 Oct., one of seven whose prof. the bp comm. the precentor to rec., Reg. Lynn, 89.

1370, 13 Apr., ord acol., [Worcester cathedral], *ib.*, 50.

1377, 19 Sept., ord dcn, Tewkesbury abbey, *Reg. Wakefield*, no 873f.

1378, 13 Mar., ord pr., Kidderminster, *ib.*, no 874g.

[1388/8], 1391/2, 1400/1, 1403/4, hostiller, WCM C.214–217.

1373, 4 Dec., 23rd in order at the el. of a bp, *Reg. Sed. Vac.*, 290.
1388, 21 Aug., 20th at the el. of a prior, Liber Albus, fo 334v.
1392/3, ill in the infirmary and recd two chickens from the cellarer, WCM C.76.
1401, 24 June, 14th at the el. of a bp, *Reg. Sed. Vac.*, 373.
1405/6, d., and the precentor pd for the parchment used for the brief, WCM C.372.

Hugh de KNYGHTON [Knyghtone, Knyhton, Knyzton
occ. 1430 d. 1481/2

1430, 23 Sept., ord acol., carnary chapel by Worcester cathedral, and presented by the prior, Reg. Polton, 213.
1432, 15 Mar., ord subdcn, carnary chapel, and presented by Richard Lichfeld, q.v., *ib.*, 218.
1433, 19 Dec., ord dcn, carnary chapel, *Reg. Sed. Vac.*, 419.
1435, 24 Sept., ord pr., Bromyard, *Reg. Spofford* (Hereford), 320; on his 1434/5 acct the cellarer recorded expenses for him and for William Hertilbury, q.v., who presented him, for the journey to Bromyard, WCM C.87.
1446/7, pittancer, WCM C.90.
145[3/4], chaplain to the prior, Liber Albus, fo 488.
1455/7, subcellarer, WCM C.541, 732.

1433, 9 Dec., 45th and last in order at the el. of a bp, *Reg. Sed. Vac.*, 432.
1448/9, 1449/50, 1453, on the cellarer's list of creditors, WCM C.91–93.
1455/6, pd a visit to Broadwas, WCM C.541.
1456/7, visited Overbury, WCM C.732.
1480/1, the cellarer pd part of a debt owed by him, WCM C.99.
1481/2, d., and the brief bearer was pd by the almoner, WCM C.205.

Giles KYDERMINSTRE [Kydermestre, Kydermystr', Kydurmynstre
occ. 1423 occ. 1433

1423, 20 Mar., ord dcn, Worcester cathedral, Reg. Morgan, 199.
1426, 8 Sept., dcn, recd *lit. dim.*, for 'all orders', Reg. Polton, 13.
1426, 22 Sept., ord pr., Bromyard, *Reg. Spofford* (Hereford), 301.
1425/6, celebrated his first mass; *exennia* recd from the hostiller, pittancer and precentor who each gave 2s. 6d. for bread and ale, WCM C.229 (acct for 1426/7), C.377, 377. The precentor also pd the travelling expenses to Bromyard, C.377.

1433, 9 Dec., 29th in order at the el. of a bp, *Reg. Sed. Vac.*, 432.

I John de KYDERMINSTRE [Kederminstre
occ. [1367] d. 1380/1, or possibly 1370; see below

[1367, Aug.], one of two whose prof. the prior was comm. to rec., (bound in) Reg. Bryan, ii, 28.
* 1372, 13 Mar., ord subdcn, Worcester cathedral, Reg. Lynn, 55.
* 1372, 18 Sept., ord dcn, [Worcester cathedral], *ib.*,
* [1374, Dec.], dcn, and the prior sent *lit. dim.* for orders to the bp of Hereford, *Reg. Sed. Vac.*, 322.
* 1374/5, celebrated his first mass; the almoner contributed 3s. 4d., and the precentor 2s., WCM C.173, 361.

1370, 3 Apr., 18th in order at the el. of a prior, Liber Albus, fo 246.
* 1380/1, ill and the infirmarer cared for him and bought medicine, charging 20d. on his acct, WCM C.242.
* 1380/1, d., the almoner recd nothing for his corrody because it was distributed among the poor 'for his soul', WCM C.176.

* See note in the entry below.

II John de KYDERMINSTRE
occ. [?1370/1]

1373, 4/7 Dec., 29th in order at the el. of a bp, *Reg. Sed. Vac.*, 290.

Note: it seems clear that John de Kyderminstre I and II cannot be disentangled, and the items in the previous entry (marked *) may belong to either. The order of seniority, however, by comparison with other monks ranking next in order, is correctly assigned. Kyderminstre II prob. entered in 1370/1; and so the gap of four yrs between prof. and receiving subdcn's orders, as entered under Kyderminstre I, suggests the possibility that the latter d. just before the former entered, i.e. soon after the el. on 3 Apr. 1370.

III John KYDERMINSTRE [Kedermyster
occ. 1448 occ. 1475

1448, 14 Sept., one of six whose prof. the prior was comm. to rec., Reg. Carpenter, i, 132.
1449, 12 Apr., ord acol., carnary chapel by Worcester cathedral, *ib.*, i, 524.
1452, 8 Apr., ord subdcn, carnary chapel, *ib.*, i, 532.
1453, 31 Mar., ord dcn, carnary chapel, *ib.*, i, 535.
1466, 20 Dec.; 1467/8; 1468, 17 Dec.; 1469, 1 Apr.; 1470, 17 Mar., precentor, Reg. Carpenter, i, 566; WCM C.382; Reg. Carpenter, i, 573; *ib.*, i, 574; *ib.*, i, 575.
1471, 16 Feb., apptd sacrist, Reg. Carpenter, ii, 48; 1475, Jan., sacrist, *ib.*, ii, 136.

1452/3, the prior gave a gift of 3s. 4d. each to him and to Isaac Ledbury, q.v., WCM C.399 a.

1459/60, included in the cellarer's list of creditors, WCM C.491.
1466, 20 Dec., 1467, 19 Dec., presented the monk ordinands at ordinations in the carnary chapel, Reg. Carpenter, i, 566, 569.
1467/8, handed over 20s. 11d. to the *custos* of the Lady chapel which was the gift of Hugh Lempster, q.v., WCM C.281.
1468, 17 Dec., 1469, 1 Apr., presented the monk ordinands, Reg. Carpenter, i, 573, 574.
1469, 16 Aug., one of the proctors apptd to present the seven nominees for the priorate to the bp, Reg. Carpenter, ii, 13–16 and Reg. A.6(i), fo 60^{v}.
1470, 17 Mar., presented the monk ordinands, Reg. Carpenter, i, 575.
1475, Jan., as sacrist presented a candidate for apptment to the carnary chapel and library, Reg. Carpenter, ii, 136.

Richard de KYDERMINSTRE [Kidirminstre, Kydermenstre
occ. 1359 occ. ?1378/9

1359, 8 Mar., apptd penitentiary in the city and adcnry of Worcester, Reg. Bryan, i, 190.
1361, 5 Feb., apptd *primarius* (penitentiary), *ib.*, i, 220.
1378/9, an inventory of the infirmarer includes one *coopertorium de dono* (of his), Hamilton, *Comp. Rolls*, 59 (WCM C.241); there is nothing to suggest that he had d.

KYDERMINSTRE
see Kidremister

[Morgan KYNGSLAND
occ. 1509

1508, 18 Mar., ord acol., carnary chapel by Worcester cathedral, Reg. S. Gigli, 297.

Note: the entry in the ord. list has been carelessly copied into the register and this name may be out of place and refer to a monk of another house.]

Roger KYNGESLONDE [Kingeslonde, Kingislond, Kyngislond, *alias* Don
occ. 1458 d. [1488/9]

1458, 23 Sept., ord acol., and subdcn, Worcester cathedral, Reg. Carpenter, i, 547.
1460, 20 Dec., ord dcn, Worcester cathedral, *ib.*, i, 554.
1462, 18 Sept., ord pr., Alvechurch, *ib.*, i, 557.
1465/6, the kitchener gave him 2s. 6d. for his first mass, WCM C.151; it would surely have been several yrs late!
1475/6, *tumbarius*, Hamilton, *Comp. Rolls*, 77 (WCM C.472).
1478/9, chamberlain, Hamilton, *Comp. Rolls*, 6 (WCM C.46).
1479, 13 Sept., apptd sacrist by the bp, Reg. Alcock, 24 (Richard Cropthorn, q.v. had d.); by 27 Sept., he had been dismissed from this office (see Richard Alcester) as the prior and chapter had el. him to be cellarer.
1479/86, cellarer, WCM C.98–100, C.744, C.101, C.102, C.746.
[1485/6], possibly almoner, WCM C.200 a.
1478/86, prob. made regular visits to Overbury as his name is on all the surviving accts between these dates: WCM C.741–746.
1482, 18 Apr., obtained papal dispensation on acct of illegitimacy so that there would be no impediment to his being el. abbot of any Benedictine house, *CPL*, xiii (1471–1484), 748. The name Don occ. here.
1486/7, was staying in the almonry, WCM C.207.
[1488/9], d. and the cellarer pd the almoner 30s. for his corrody for three quarters of the yr, WCM C.488.

Thomas KYNGISLOND [Kyngslond
occ. 1516 occ. 1523

1516, 17 May, ord acol., carnary chapel by Worcester cathedral, Reg. S. Gigli, 330.
1521, 22 July, 31st in order on the visitation certificate, Reg. abp Warham, ii, fo 293^{v}.
1523, 31 Oct., obtained a *dimissio* from the prior to transfer to Chepstow priory, *ob anime sue salutem*, Reg. A.6(ii), fo 139. He was officially recd at Chepstow on 20 Nov., *ib.*
1523, recd 3s. 4d. from the prior when he left for Chepstow *Jnl More*, 181.

KYRKEBY
see Kirkeby

John de LANDAVEN' [Landaf
occ. 1290 occ. 1293/4

1290, 7 Nov., one of the monks who joined with the prior, [Philip Aubyn, q.v.], to interrupt and delay the proceedings during the bp's visitation, and they were excommunicated as a result, *Reg. Giffard*, 380.
1293/4, travelled with Thomas de Hindelep', q.v., to Stolton [*sic*], *pro transgressione*, Wilson, *Early Comp. Rolls*, 20 (WCM C.51a).

John LANGLEY [Langeley, Lanley, Longeley, Longley
occ. 1430/1 d. 1465/6

1430/1, celebrated his first mass; the hostiller contributed 2s. 6d. to the feast, WCM C.232 and the almoner sent 2s. 6d., WCM C.194 (acct for 1431/2).
1444/6, pittancer, WCM C.493, 333.
1433, 9 Dec., 35th in order at the el. of a bp, *Reg. Sed. Vac.*, 432.
1441/2, gave a small sum as alms to the almoner, WCM C.199.
1448/9, was owed 3s. 4d. by the cellarer, WCM C.91; gave 2s. as alms to the almoner, WCM C.200.

1449/50, listed as one of the cellarer's creditors, WCM C.92.
1465/6, d.; the precentor pd for parchment used for the brief, WCM C.381.

LAUGHERN
see Lawerne

LAURENCE
see Badminton

LAURENTIUS
occ. c. 1104

Name occ. in the list of monks in *Durham Liber Vitae*, fo 22.

Henry de LAWERNE [Lawarn
occ. [1350] occ. 1371/2

[1350], 13 Sept., one of two *clerici* whom the prior was comm. to adm., Reg. Thoresby, 24.
1351/2, the pittancer reported that he was not yet prof., Wilson, *Early Comp. Rolls*, 68 (WCM C.293).
1352, 22 Dec., ord dcn, Bromyard, *Reg. Trillek* (Hereford), 590.
[1353, Feb.], given *lit. dim.*, for orders of pr., *Reg. Sed. Vac.*, 201.
1353, 16 Feb., ord pr., Bromyard, *Reg. Trillek* (Hereford), 594.
1358/9, 1360/1, precentor, WCM C.356, C.357.
1371/2, ref. to him as former cellarer, WCM C.67; an 'H' was cellarer in 1363, Sept./Nov., and 1368/9, WCM C.708, C.710.
1351, 8 Jan., obtained a papal licence to choose his own confessor and described as *conversus*, *CPL*, iii (1342–1362), 380.
1355, 22 May, one of four monk proctors apptd and given a general mandate to act for the chapter in all causes pertaining to the status of their church, including matters which could arise during a visitation, Liber Albus, fo 241; see John de Evesham I's problems at this time.
1363, Sept./Nov., visited Overbury, WCM C.708.
1366, 10 Mar., acted as proctor for the convent in the ordination of a vicarage, *Liber Pensionum*, no 63.
1368/9, prob. visited Overbury, WCM C.710.

I John LAWERNE D.Th. [Laughern, Lawarne
occ. 1428 d. 1481/2

1428, 28 Sept., ord acol., Reg. Polton, 100.
1432, 15 Mar., ord subdcn, carnary chapel by Worcester cathedral and was presented by Richard Lichefeld, q.v., *ib.*, 218.
1432, 20 Sept., ord dcn, carnary chapel, *ib.*, 222.
1434, 18 Sept., ord pr., carnary chapel, *Reg. Sed. Vac.*, 443.
1434/5, celebrated his first mass; the cellarer sent *exennia*, WCM C.87.
1448/55, 1456, 21 Sept., almoner, WCM C.91, 92, 334, 41, 200c, 43, 335, B.1256.
1458, 10 Sept., apptd sacrist by the bp, Reg. Carpenter, i, 303.
1469, 12 Sept., replaced as sacrist by John Smethwyk, q.v., *ib.*, i, 493.
1474, 29 June, subprior, Pantin, *BMC*, iii, 216 (Reg. A.6(i), fo 80v).
1478, 14 Sept., subprior, Reg. A.6(i), fo 73v.
1432/3, student at Oxford, with 13s. 4d. allowance from the chamberlain [?for clothing], WCM C.37.
1433/4, came from Oxford for the el. of a bp (prob. Thomas Bourgchier, in ?Dec. 1433) and the cellarer pd for his travelling expenses to Worcester and back again to Oxford, WCM C.492; and see Hugh Leyntewardyne.
1436/7, the precentor pd for him to return from Oxford to preach on the eve of the feast of the Assumption (14 Aug.) and charged his acct 8s. 7d., WCM C.378.
1445, by 6 Oct., B.Th., Oxford, Bod. Ms 692, fo 119.
1447/8, he and Isaac Ledbury, q.v., both recd gifts from the prior and are both given the title of 'magister', WCM C.398.
1448/9, described himself as *sacre pagine professor*, Oxford, Bod. Ms 692, fo 163. In this yr he delivered a series of lectures at Oxford; see below. He gave public lectures at Worcester as well, Bod. Ms 692, fo 119; see also Greatrex, 'Benedictine Monk Scholars', 217, n. 22 and below, under 1445.
1445, 6 Oct., began lecturing on the Sentences [of Peter Lombard] in the presence of the bp and the convent and many others and therefore prob. in the chapter house at Worcester, Oxford, Bod. Ms 692, fo 119; see also John de Preston II.
1448, 3 Sept., attended the trial of M. Thomas Taylor, heretic, Reg. Carpenter, i, 63.
1449/50, accompanied the prior [John Hertilbury, q.v.] to the Black Monk Chapter at Northampton, at a cost of £12 4s. WCM C.92. This meeting was on 1 June 1450, Pantin, *BMC*, iii, 214.
1453/4, recd 6s. from the chamberlain [?for clothing], WCM C.43.
1454/5, recd 20d. from the pittancer, *pro elemosina sua*, WCM C.335.
1455/6, prob. visited Broadwas, WCM C.541.
1459, 27 June, one of three monks sent by the prior as proctors to the Black Monk Chapter, Pantin, *BMC*, iii, 214; the other two were John Smethwyk and William Walweyn, q.v.
1461, 22 Sept., preached in the cathedral at the commencement of a visitation; his text was *Qui est misit me ad vos*, Reg. Carpenter, i, 344.
1464, 7 Feb., a letter from the prior to John Sudbury, subprior, q.v., implies that he had in some way disgraced himself by involvement in a 'conspiracy'; the prior ordered the subprior

to rec. his purgation as he had declared his innocence; the name has been carefully scratched out in two places but the words 'professor' and 'sacrist' leave no room for doubt, Reg. A.6(i), fo 36.

1464, 30 July, one of three monk proctors apptd by the prior and chapter for the diocesan synod, Reg. A.6(i), fo 34v.

1465, 20 June, one of the [same three] proctors [as above] sent to the Black Monk Chapter, Pantin, *BMC*, iii, 214.

1469, 14/16 Aug., one of the seven nominees for the priorate, Reg. Carpenter, ii, 13–16, and Reg. A.6(i), fo 60v.

1474, 29 June, one of two proctors sent to the Black Monk Chapter, Pantin, *BMC*, iii, 216.

1478, 14 Sept., witness to the homage of a priory tenant, Reg. A.6(i), fo 73v.

1481/2, d., and the almoner recd payment [from the cellarer] for his corrody, WCM C.205.

Name in five Worcs. Mss:

(1) F.13, Brito (13th/14th c.); on last flyleaf *iste liber constat—*.

(2) F.19, Tractatus de vitiis et virtutibus etc. (early 15th c.); inside flyleaf *Liber—*.

(3) Q.22, Speculum sacerdotum (late 14th c.); inside frontj cover Liber M.I. Lawerne.

(4) Q.27, J. Wallensis etc. (14th c.); on the second folio a list of thirty volumes, above which is written 'Isti sunt libri pertinentes [ad dom[inum Johannem Lawarne] . . . [Isaac] Ledbury, *dompnus* [*sic*] *Joh*[annes Br[oghton]', q.v. This list, acc. to Ker, *MLGB*, 205, is in Lawarne's hand; and it may have been a record of the volumes which he or they had at Oxford. It includes biblical texts and commentaries, Ms F.19 (above), Peter of Tarentaise on the Sentences, Boethius, De Consolatione and a collection of sermons of St Bernard and others. The complete list is printed by Sharpe in *Eng. Benedictine Libraries*, iv at B113.

(5) Q.89, a sermon collection (late 13th c.); on fo 30v his name and that of Thomas Sudbury, q.v., occ., and on fo 1 there is a note that 'tradatur iste liber fratribus minoribus Wygorn'.

Name also in Oxford, Bod. Ms 692 which is his notebook containing theological lectures, sermons and a miscellaneous collection of letters, some copied from a much earlier source or sources for no apparent reason, others related to Gloucester college and to university affairs, and some of his own personal correspondence. Included among these last are several letters between him and bp Carpenter concerning his position as sacrist and the question of his divided loyalty (between bp and prior); see Greatrex, *Monastic or Episcopal Obedience*, 14.

II John LAWERNE, B.Th. [Laughern, Lawarn, Lawghern, Lawren *alias* Pecock

occ. 1510 [occ. 1540]

1510, 21 Sept., ord acol., carnary chapel by Worcester cathedral, Reg. S. Gigli, 304.

1511, 20 Mar., ord subdcn, carnary chapel, *ib.*, 307.

1512, 27 Mar., ord dcn, carnary chapel, *ib.*, 312.

1515, 22 Sept., ord pr., carnary chapel, *ib.*, 328.

1524/5, *custos* of the Lady chapel, WCM C.414.

1534, 17 Aug.; 1535, n.d., and 8 Sept.; 1536, 13 Mar., subprior, *DK 7th Report*, Appndx 2, 305; *L and P Henry VIII*, ix, nos 52(2), 304; Reg. A.6(iii), fo 1.

1521, 22 July, student at Oxford, Reg. abp Warham ii, fo 293v.

1526, Jan./Feb., after eight yrs of study supplicated to oppose for the degree of B.Th (*BRUO*), and adm. 3 July 1526, *ib.*

1526, the prior contributed 40s. for him 'to be bacheler of divinite' at Oxford, *Jnl More*, 232.

1521, 22 July, 25th in order on the visitation certificate, Reg. abp Warham, ii, fo 293v.

1527, sent to London on business with Thomas Sudbury, q.v., *Jnl More*, 250.

1534, 17 Aug., subscribed to the Act of Supremacy, *DK 7th Report*, Appndx 2, 305.

1535, Feb./Mar., approached a Worcestershire J.P. at the request of the prior [William More I, q.v.] to report that there were two seditious monks in their community [?Richard Cleve, John Musard, q.v.] and was advised to keep them in custody, *L and P Henry VIII*, ix, no 108.

1535, signed the petition vs the reinstatement of William Fordham, q.v. as cellarer, *L and P Henry VIII*, ix, no 653. In this same yr it was claimed by John Musard, q.v., that he had taken action vs Musard rather than vs Cleve when Musard had accused Cleve of treason, *ib.*, no 52.2 (i).

1536, 13 Mar., subprior at the 'el.' of Henry Holbech, q.v., Reg. A.6(iii), fo 1; he participated as one of the four *compromissorii*, only two of whom were monks; the other being Roger Neckham, q.v., *ib.*, fo 1v.

[1542, 24 Jan., canon of the 7th prebend in the new foundation, *Fasti, 1541–1857*, vii, 127.]

Robert de LAWERNE [Lawarne *alias* Mullewurd

occ. 1408 occ. 1430/1

1408, 14 Apr., ord acol., Dominican convent, Worcester, Reg. Peverel, 173.

1408, 22 Dec., ord subdcn, Worcester cathedral, *ib.*, 176.

1409, 2 Mar., ord dcn, Worcester cathedral, *ib.*, 178.

1412, 24 Sept., ord pr., Llanthony priory, Gloucester, *ib.*, 193; the 1411/12 acct of the precentor gives the travelling expenses to Gloucester, WCM C.374.

1412/13, celebrated his first mass and the hostiller gave money for bread and ale, WCM C.222.

1423/4, 1425/6, pittancer, WCM C.326, 327; in 1426/7 Richard Tyberton, q.v., succ. him.

1426/7, 1429/30, kitchener, WCM C.85, 86.

1430/1, steward of the prior's hospice, WCM C.144.

1419, 24 Apr., 23rd in order at the el. of a bp, *Reg. Sed. Vac.*, 407.

1421/2, 1426/7, 1429/30, included in the cellarer's list of creditors, WCM C.84a, 85, 86.

His brother, Richard Mullewurd, is mentioned by the cellarer in 1429/30, WCM C.86.

I Edmund LEDBURY [Leddebury

occ. 1483 occ. 1507

1483, 20 Sept., ord acol., carnary chapel by Worcester cathedral, Reg. Alcock, 274.

1487, 22 Sept., ord pr., Ledbury, *Reg. Milling* (Hereford), 174.

1494/6, precentor, WCM C.389, 390.

1495, 29 June, third prior, Pantin, *BMC*, iii, 216 (Reg. A.6(i), fo 104).

1497; 1498, 25 Oct., chaplain to the prior, Reg. A.6(i), fo 115, *Reg. abp Morton*, ii, no 258; see also John Lechfeld.

1500/2, precentor, WCM C.392, 393 (see William Worcetur who held this office in 1498/9).

1504, 6 Nov., *tumbarius*, Reg. A.6(ii), fo 32.

1507, 10 Sept., chamberlain, Reg. S. Gigli, 349.

1487/8, with Thomas Mildenham, q.v., recd from the kitchener 20s., *pro tempore vacacionis*, WCM C.161; were they students at Oxford?

1492, 27 June, one of two proctors apptd by the chapter to present the seven nominees for the priorate to the bp, Reg. Morton, 90, Reg. A.6(i), fo 107ᵛ; they did so on 30 June, Reg. Morton, 91.

[1492 × 1499], the prior recorded complaints vs him and two other monks (Henry Chester and Thomas Stafford, q.v.), accusing them of being involved in an unlawful assembly with a William Budon, WCM D.336.

1495, 29 June, apptd as one of the monk proctors to attend the Black Monk Chapter in Northampton (see also Thomas Mildenham and John Stratford), Pantin, *BMC*, iii, 216.

1498, 25 Oct., 20th in order on the visitation certificate, *Reg. abp Morton*, ii, no 258.

1507, 10 Sept., one of the seven nominees for the priorate, Reg. S. Gigli, 349.

II Edmund LEDBURY [Ladbery, Ledburi, Ledburye

occ. 1516 occ. 1536

1516, 17 May, ord acol., carnary chapel by Worcester cathedral, Reg. S. Gigli, 330.

1531/2, subalmoner, Reg. A.12, fo 135.

1535, hostiller, *L and P Henry VIII*, ix, no 653.

1521, 22 July, 30th in order on the metropolitan visitation certificate, Reg. abp Warham, ii, fo 293ᵛ.

1531/2, 24th on the clerical subsidy list and pd 20d. for his office and 3s. 4d. commons, Reg. A.12, fo 135.

1534, 17 Aug., subscribed to the Act of Supremacy, *DK 7th Report*, Appndx 2, 305.

1535, signed the petition vs. the reinstatement of William Fordham, q.v., as cellarer, *L and P Henry VIII*, ix, no 653.

1536, 13 Mar., 17th in order at the 'el.' of Henry Holbech, q.v., as prior, Reg. A.6(iii), fo 1.

Roger de LEDEBURY

see Tendebury

Isaac LEDBURY, D.Th. [Isack, Ysaac Letbury, Lydesbury

occ. 1430 occ. 1458

1430, 23 Sept., ord acol., carnary chapel by Worcester cathedral, and was presented by the prior [John Fordham, q.v.], Reg. Polton, 213.

1432, 15 Mar., ord subdcn, carnary chapel, presented by Richard Lichfeld, q.v., *ib.*, 218.

1433, 9 Dec., listed as dcn, *Reg. Sed. Vac.*, 432.

1434, 18 Sept., ord pr., carnary chapel, *ib.*, 443.

1434/5, celebrated his first mass; recd a gift from the cellarer, WCM C.87.

1446/7, infirmarer, WCM C.90.

1447/50, cellarer, WCM C.665, 91, 92.

1456/8, almoner, WCM C.732, 44.

1436/7, student [at Oxford], to whom the almoner gave 6s. 8d. at the prior's request, WCM C.198.

1439/40, student at Oxford, with £4 6s. 8d. *pro liberatione* in bread and ale for the yr, WCM C.89.

1446/7, [student], sent as proctor to the Black Monk Chapter in Northampton for which the cellarer pd him 40s., WCM C.90; on the same acct the sum of 9s. was pd for the transporting of [the books and possessions of] his from Oxford to Worcester.

1447/8, the prior gave *exennia* amounting to 23s. to M. John Lawerne, q.v., and M. Isaac, WCM C.398.

1448, 9 Apr., D.Th., Oxford, Bod. Ms 692, fos 36, 163ᵛ; on 2 Apr., 'Dr Isaac' had taken into his employ Thomas Trelyffe for 40s. p.a., *Reg. Cancell Oxon.*, i, 155.

1433, 9 Dec., 43rd in order at the el. of a bp, *Reg. Sed. Vac.*, 432.

1439/40, on the cellarer's list of creditors, WCM C.89.

1447/8, visited Newnham, WCM C.665.

1448, 3 Sept., attended the heresy trial of Thomas Taylor in the bp's palace, Reg. Carpenter, i, 133.

1448/9, visited Tibberton, for *liberatio denariorum*, WCM C.824.

1449/50, one of the brethren who recd small sums from the precentor for preaching in Advent, WCM C.379; he prob. visited Hallow this yr, WCM C.600a.
1452/3, recd a gift of 3s. 4d. from the prior, WCM C.399a.
1453, 3 Feb., apptd by the prior and chapter as proctor (with a secular clerk) to convocation, Liber Albus, fo 486.

Name in two Worcs. Mss:
(1) F.39, Duns Scotus (14th c.); it was lent by Dr Isack *monacho* to Thomas Jolyffe who was rector of a number of parishes in Worcester diocese in the 1460s, see *BRUO*.
(2) Q.27, where his name follows that of John Lawerne I, q.v.

Thomas LEDBURY, D.Th. [Ludbury
occ. 1396 d. 1444

1438–1444, prior: apptd 15 Feb. 1438; d. before 15 Jan. 1444; see below.
[1396], 1 July, one of three novices whose prof. the prior was comm. to rec., Reg. Winchcombe, 32.
1397, 6 June, ord acol., Worcester cathedral, *ib.*, 135.
1401, 24 June, listed as dcn at el., *Reg. Sed. Vac.*, 373.
1402, 28 June, obtained *lit. dim.* to rec. priest's orders, Reg. Clifford, 105.
[1401/2], celebrated his first mass; the pittancer gave 3s. for bread and ale, WCM C.315.
1428, 16 Oct., subprior, comm. by the bp to perform the duties of sacrist in the absence of John Cleve, q.v., Reg. Polton, 104.
1433/4, sacrist, WCM C.492.
1435, 4 Aug., apptd sacrist by the [new] bp, Reg. Bourgchier, 19.
1438, 14 Feb., sacrist, *ib.*, 84.
1405/6, student at Oxford for three terms, receiving 26s. 8d. from the kitchener, WCM C.132; there were two other unnamed students, *ib.*
1406/7, one of three students (and the only one named), with 34s. 8d. maintenance from the kitchener, i.e. for the whole yr, WCM C.133.
1408/9, with Richard Clifton, q.v., returned from Oxford for the funeral of prior John de Malverne I, q.v., and the el. and installation of the new prior [John Fordham, q.v.]; he may also have been present for the bp's visitation, WCM C.81, 81a.
1413/14, recd a gift of 3s. 4d. from the almoner, as did two other [unnamed] monk students at Oxford, WCM C.190.
c. 1417 × 1423, *prior studentium*, Oxford, Pantin, *BMC*, iii, 321, with a series of refs; and see below.
1419, 16 Mar., described as B.Th., *Reg. Sed. Vac.*, 396.
1420/1, returned from Oxford to confer with the prior, WCM C.84a.
1423/4, D.Th., the sacrist, John Cleve, q.v., went to Oxford for the inception and gave the new 'doctor' 40s., WCM C.425.

1401, 24 June, 43rd in order at the el. of a bp, *Reg. Sed. Vac.*, 373.
[1414 × 1418], accompanied prior John Fordham, q.v., to the Council of Constance, and the Black Monk Chapter granted him £10 for his travelling expenses, Pantin, *BMC*, iii, 185. (Because of his other activities I suggest a slightly earlier date than Pantin.)
1419, 16 Mar., comm. by the prior to carry out, with others, visitations sed. vac in the diocese, *Reg. Sed. Vac.*, 396.
1419, 24 Apr., 10th in order at the el. of a bp and preached the opening sermon, *ib.*, 405, 407.
1420, 8 July, apptd one of the diffinitors at the Black Monk Chapter, and assigned to preach in English [at the next chapter], Pantin, *BMC*, ii, 97.
1421/2, made a trip to London *pro generali consilio*, WCM C.84a.
1423, 5/7 July, attended the Black Monk Chapter and played an active role, especially with respect to university matters about which he spoke at length as *prior studentium* at Oxford, Pantin, *BMC*, ii, 149–151. He was named an elector of the future presidents, *ib.*, 152, and also as one of the preachers (in Latin) and one of the diffinitors for the next chapter, *ib.*, 153. In response to his request he was allocated funds for the construction of a kitchen and three adjoining rooms for the monk students, *ib.*, iii, 189.
1425, 11 Oct., present at the abjuration of a heretic, Reg. Morgan, 170.
1426, 30 June, one of the members of a university delegation apptd to request support from the Black Monk Chapter for the building of the divinity school, Anstey, *Epistolae Oxon.*, i, 21.
1426, 1/3 July, attended the Black Monk Chapter and was again involved in discussions concerning the university, Pantin, *BMC*, ii, 169–170; he was also reapptd to the committee which elected the future presidents, *ib.*, 173, nom. as one of the diffinitors for 1429 and as one of the preachers in English, *ib.*, 179.
1429/30, recd 49s. from the cellarer in payment of a debt, WCM C.86.
1431/2, recd 13s. 4d. p.a. from the almoner [?for, or instead of, a corrody], WCM C.194.
1432, 22 Jan., licensed as penitentiary in the diocese, Reg. Polton, 248.
1432, Aug./Sept., went to Pershore to speak with members of the prior's council and also to London to convocation, WCM C.86a.
1432/3, the kitchener reported having recd nothing from the weir and the *superiori manso* at Bevere 'quia signatur fratri . . . pro sua pitancia', WCM C.145.

1433, 19/29 Oct., with a secular clerk, carried out *sed. vac.* visitations in several deaneries of the diocese as commissaries of the prior, *Reg. Sed. Vac.*, 428–429.

1433, 31 Oct., with William Hertilbury, q.v., named as proctors to convocation on 7 Nov., Liber Albus, fo 438; on 8 Nov., the same two were sent to the king for a [second] licence to el. a bp [as royal assent to the first el. had been refused], *ib.*, fo 438v. The cellarer pd their expenses and also for other trips to London for them during the yr 1433/4 for another convocation and for negotiations concerning the el., WCM C.492.

1433, 9 Dec., 3rd in order at the el. of a bp, was apptd proctor by the convent to announce the name of the elect to the public, and sent, with William Hertilbury, to inform the elect and present him to the king, *Reg. Sed. Vac.*, 432–435.

1433/4, recd 15s. from the chamberlain *pro vestura*, WCM C.38.

1434/5, attended the Black Monk Chapter in Northampton with William Hertilbury [on 4 July 1435] and also pd visits to the abbots of Pershore and Alcester, WCM C.87.

1438, 12/15 Feb., one of the seven nominees for the priorate chosen on 13 Feb., presented to the bp on 14 Feb. and apptd prior on 15 Feb., Liber Albus fo 457v and Reg. Bourgchier, 84–86. The seven were chosen *via scrutinii*.

1444, 15 Jan., d. before this date when the el. took place of the seven candidates for the priorate, Reg. Bourgchier, 193; see John Hertilbury.

A few of his *acta* are preserved in the Liber Albus, fos 457v–474v by his chaplains: Thomas Welford, Hugh Leyntewardyne, Robert Multon, William Walweyn, q.v.

Five letters survive:

(1) In Oxford, Bodley Ms 692, fo 148v, and printed in Pantin, *BMC*, iii, 98–99 where it is dated c. 1417/19. It was copied by John Lawerne, q.v., into his Oxford notebook, and, although the names of both writer and recipient are missing, Pantin has deduced from internal evidence that the former was Ledbury, and the latter the abbot of Bury St Edmunds. In the letter Ledbury informed the abbot that he was sending him a devotional treatise composed by himself and he requested the £5 which was the abbot's share of the sum allocated by the Black Monk Chapter for his expenses incurred in travelling to Constance (see above under [1414 × 1418].

(2) In the Liber Albus, fo 451, sent from him to Edmund Lacy, bp of Exeter and dated 24 Nov. 1435. It is a letter of confraternity informing the bp that his name would be entered in the convent's *martilogium* and on his d. the sacrist would arrange for a mass to be said at St Edmund's altar. The entry is headed 'Littera directa . . . ex labore magistri Thome Ledbury'. Did they meet at Oxford or perhaps when Lacy was bp of Hereford?

(3) In BL Add. Ms 7096 fos 163v–164, sent from him to William Curteys, abbot of Bury St Edmunds (1429–1446) and undated. In it he thanked the abbot for many gifts and kindnesses to him and his brethren [at Gloucester college] and especially for the spiritual benefits of confraternity. He referred to his regency and the burden of heavy responsibility which resulted in sleepless nights and illness.

(4) In *Reg. Whethamstede*, ii, 416–417, a letter sent to Thomas, *prior scolarium*, from John [Whethamstede], abbot of St Albans (1420–1440 and 1452–1465), undated; this concerns the new chapel under construction at Gloucester college. He seems to have become disheartened by criticism which, the abbot insisted, should not deter him from finishing the work as it was a divinely apptd task and he would receive his reward.

(5) In *ib.*, 431–432, another letter sent from abbot Whethamstede to M. Thomas, *studentium priori*, undated, and urging him to bring to completion the building works [at Gloucester college] which had been under way for eighty years.

Name in Worcs. Ms F.43, Robert Kilwardby (on the Sentences) (late 13th c.), *liber—- in custodia*; see also John Hatfeld.

John Lawerne I, q.v., copied the verse carved on Ledbury's tomb into his notebook, Oxford, Bod. Ms 692, fo 38v.

Robert de la LEE [de Lee

occ. 1340

1340, 28 Nov., one of three *clerici* whom the prior was comm. to examine and adm. after presenting them to the bp, *Reg. Bransford*, no 377.

Note: Richard de Henkseye, q.v., was examined and adm. at the same time; since there are no later refs to Lee, he must have left or d.

Thomas de la LEE

occ. 1330 occ. 1344/5

1330, 11 Aug., one of four whose prof. the prior was authorized to rec., *Reg. Orleton*, no 335.

[1330], 9 Nov., recd *lit. dim.*, for all orders, *ib.*, no 250.

1331, 25 May, ord subdcn, [Chipping] Campden, *ib.*, no 21 (p. 35).

1338/9, student at Oxford with John de Evesham I, q.v., for the entire yr less four wks, and supported at the rate of 16d. per wk, WCM C. 58.

1341, 2 Sept., witness to an episcopal instrument at Withington, *Reg. Bransford*, no 432.

1343, Nov., apptd by the prior, with Nicholas de Stanlake, q.v., to ascertain the truth in a lawsuit, Liber Albus, fo 191.

1344/5, the prior went to London *pro negociis tangent' fratrem Thomam*, WCM C.59. Since the entry on the cellarer's acct continues 'cum expensis Johannis Oxon vs curia Romana pro eisdem', £14, there appears to be a connection between him and a journey to the curia.

I John de LEGH [Leye, Leygh

occ. 1328 occ. [1355/7]

1328, 24 Sept., ord dcn, St Mary's church at the gate of Gloucester abbey, *Reg. Orleton*, no 9 (p. 12).

1329, 17 June, ord pr., Tewkesbury abbey, *ib.*, no 14 (p. 22).

1339/40, pittancer, WCM C.298.

1340/1, subcellarer, WCM C.800; see also John de Gloucestr' III.

1346/7, 1348/Apr. 1349, precentor, WCM C.351, 352.

1349, 30 Aug. and 10 Oct.; [1355/7], subprior, *CPR (1348–1350)*, 380, *Reg. Sed. Vac.*, 254; Liber Albus, fo 214v.

1339, 12 Apr., one of the seven nominees for the priorate, *Reg. Bransford*, no 38.

1340, 21 Apr., again one of the seven nominees for the priorate, *ib.*, no 290.

1340/1, pd visits to Bromsgrove and Tibberton, WCM C.548, 800.

1349, 30 Aug., comm. by the prior, *sed. vac.*, to confirm the el. of the abbot of Pershore, *CPR (1348–1350)*, 380.

1349, 10 Oct., one of three monk proctors concerned with a *sed. vac.* controversy concerning visitation rights at Cirencester abbey, *Reg. Sed. Vac.*, 254.

1351, 21 Jan., obtained papal licence to choose his own confessor, *CPL*, iii (1342–1362), 407.

[1355/7], apptd one of three *vicegerentes* during the absence of prior John de Evesham, q.v., Liber Albus, fo 214v; see also Robert de Weston and Walter de Wynforton.

II John de LEGH [Lye, Lygh

occ. 1392/3 d. 1419/20

1392/3, novice, WCM C.316.

1393, 4 Jan., one of three whose prof. the prior was comm. to rec., WCM C.316; Liber Albus, fo 363v; dated 5 Jan. in *Reg. Wakefield*, no 723.

1393, 1 Mar., ord dcn, Alvechurch, *Reg. Wakefield*, no 982f; the precentor took the ordinands [and presented them], WCM C.76.

1393, 31 May, ord pr., Worcester cathedral, *ib.*, no 984h.

1392/3, celebrated his first mass, i.e. between 31 May and 29 Sept.; the cellarer and the prior each gave him four gallons of wine for the feast afterwards, WCM C.76; the chamberlain contributed 3s. 8d., WCM C.20.

1401, 24 June, fourth prior, *Reg. Sed. Vac.*, 373 (as Bye).

1419, 24 Apr., refectorer, *ib.*, 407.

1393, Jan./Sept., while novice had six *minutiones* for which the pittancer pd 3s., WCM C.316.

1401, 24 June, 37th in order at the el. of a bp, *Reg. Sed. Vac.*, 373.

1406/7, gave 2s. 4d. in alms to the almoner, WCM C.188.

1419, 24 Apr., 13th at the el. of a bp, *Reg. Sed. Vac.*, 407.

1419/20, d., and the chamberlain sold his *panni*, WCM C.32.

Walter de LEGH [Leye, Leygh, Lye, Lygh

occ. 1350 d. 1388

1370–1388, prior: one of the seven candidates el. 2/3 Apr. 1370, apptd by the bp 4 Apr., Liber Albus, fo 246v–247; installed by the official on 5 Apr., *ib.*, fo 247v; d. c. 15 Aug. 1388, WCM C.179, and the funeral was on 22 Aug., *Reg. Wakefield*, no 788 (the day after the chapter had el. the seven nominees for the priorate, see John Grene).

Note: the *prefectio* is also in Reg. Lynn, 46.

1350, 18 Dec., ord subdcn, chapel of the manor of Prestbury, by *lit. dim.* from the vicar general, *Reg. Trillek* (Hereford), 548.

1354, 20 Sept., ord pr., Tewkesbury abbey, Reg. Bryan, i, 88.

1360/2; 1363, Sept./Nov.; 1364/5; 1366/9, subcellarer, WCM C.862, 610; C.708; C.758a; C.709, 759a, 710.

1370, 3 Apr., almoner, Liber Albus, fo 246.

1360/1, visited Bromsgrove, WCM C.862.

1361/2, visited Harvington, and between July/Sept. 1362, Newnham WCM C.610, 653.

1363, Sept./Nov., visited Overbury, WCM C.708.

1364/5, visited Sedgeberrow, WCM C.758a.

1366/7, visited Overbury and, between Feb./Sept. 1367, Newnham, WCM C.709, 654.

1367/8, visited Sedgeberrow, WCM C.759a.

1368/9, visited Overbury, WCM C.710.

1370, 2/3 Apr., 5th in order at the el. of a prior, and one of the seven nominees for the priorate, Liber Albus, fo 246–246v; the seven were presented to the bp on 4 Apr., Reg. Lynn, 46.

1370, Apr./Sept., recd 53s. 4d. from the cellarer, *in primo ingressu*; he also recd £40 later, and £17 for expenses to go to London.

1373, 7 Dec., el. bp unanimously by the chapter, *Reg. Sed. Vac.*, 291; royal assent obtained 24 Dec., *ib.*, 283 and *CPR (1370–1374)*, 381; however, Henry de Wakefield was provided, 12 Sept. 1375, *Fasti*, iv, 57. The *Reg. Sed. Vac.*, 282–353, records the prior's *acta* as keeper of the spiritualities during this period of almost two yrs. He was never addressed as bp el., and there is no record of his appealing to the pope.

1381, 5 July, apptd John Grene, q.v., as proctor to represent him at the Black Monk Chapter; in his letter of apptment he referred to disturbances amongst the priory tenants, influenced by the Peasants' Revolt, as in part the cause of his non-attendance, Pantin, *BMC*, iii, 204–205 (Liber Albus, fo 316^v).

1382, embellished the altar of St Cecilia with alabaster images, this being the place in the cathedral where he desired to be buried, Reg. A.12, fo 77^v.

1387, 10 Jan., obtained the abp's confirmation of the bulls of Clement VI and Urban V, granting pontifical regalia, Dugdale, *Monasticon*, i, 618 (Reg. abp Courtenay, i fo 69^v); see John de Evesham I.

1387, 5 July, was prevented from attending the Black Monk Chapter by 'infirmitate quadam gravi [et] variis et arduis negotiis', Liber Albus, fos 320^v–321; he again sent John Grene, *ib.*

1388, c. 15 Aug. d., and the almoner recd nothing for his corrody from the Assumption to Michaelmas *quia expend' in elemosina*, WCM C.179.

Some of his *acta* are preserved in the Liber Albus fos 246–333 by his chaplains: John de Hatfeld, William Owston, John Severne, q.v.. See above for his *acta*, *sed. vac.*

In 1377/8, 1380/1, 1382/3 and 1387/8, the corrody of St Wulstan was assigned to a kinsman [*cognatus*] of the prior, WCM C.174, C.176, C.177, C.179.

I John de LEMENSTRE [Lemenstere, Lempster, Lemynstr', Leomustr'

occ. 1335 occ. 1359/60

1335, 15 Apr., ord acol., bp's chapel, Hartlebury, Reg. Montacute, 83.

1335, 10 June, ord subdcn, Ombersley, *ib.*, 87.

1335, 23 Sept., ord dcn, Chaddesley [?Corbett], *ib.*, 92.

1340, 15 Apr., ord pr., Alvechurch, *Reg. Bransford*, no 1010.

1349/51; 1354, Mar./1355, May, precentor, WCM C.353–355; also on 24 Sept. 1349 and on 19 Feb. 1354, *Reg. Sed. Vac.*, 252, Liber Albus, fo 237.

1345, 12 Oct., the bp had recd a papal privilege allowing him to choose two able monks of the cathedral priory, and to send them for a period of study in the schools, during which time they were to be supported from episcopal revenues; he now wrote to Lemenstre to say that he was sending him to a *studium*, *Reg. Bransford*, no 828, and *CPL*, iii (1342–1362), 70.

1345/6, student at Oxford to whom the cellarer sent a messenger, WCM C.60.

1346/7, student, with a gift of 2s., from the chamberlain, WCM C.10; the precentor sent a boy to Oxford for him *?ad Pasch* and gave him a *curialitas* of 12d., WCM C.351.

1349, 2 July, was apptd penitentiary and given licence to preach publicly within the diocese, *Reg. Bransford*, no 1333.

1349, c. 12 Aug., issued letters of appeal concerning the spiritual jurisdiction of the prior, *sed. vac.*, *Reg. Sed. Vac.*, 225.

1349, 24 Sept./16 Oct., as one of the prior's commissaries carried out *sed. vac.* visitations in several deaneries in the diocese, *ib.*, 252–253; on 12 Oct., he was one of the proctors named by the prior to represent him in a dispute over his visitation rights at Cirencester abbey, *ib.*, 254.

1351, 8 Jan., obtained papal licence to choose his own confessor, *CPL*, iii (1342–1362), 407.

1353, 15/28 Feb., acting as commissary of the prior with a secular clerk conducted *sed. vac.* visitations in several deaneries in the diocese, *Reg. Sed. Vac.*, 201–202.

1354, 17 Feb., became involved in the dispute over the bp's apptment of John de Powik, q.v., as sacrist to which the prior and chapter strongly objected; on 6 June he was apptd proctor in the appeal vs the bp on acct of this and other matters in dispute between chapter and bp, Liber Albus, fos 236^v, 240; see also John de Evesham I.

1355, 9 Mar., licensed as a penitentiary, Reg. Bryan, i, 127.

1355, 22 May, one of four monk proctors named by the prior and chapter *in omnibus causis* concerning the status of their church and including matters which could arise during a visitation, Liber Albus, fo 241; see John de Evesham I.

1356, 9 July, in a mandate to the prior and chapter concerning his intention to have a public procession and mass the bp addressed all the monks *fratre J. de Lemenstre dumtaxat excepto*, Liber Albus, fo 243^v; why?

1359/60, given £15 by the cellarer on 16 Aug. 1360, but did not rec. his usual pittance for the 'O' payments made by the cellarer, WCM C.65; this suggests that he was absent on business affairs of the house.

Name in Worcs. Ms F.68, Aristoteles (later 14th c.); at the end 'papirum, ecclesie cathedralis Wygornie scriptum quondam Avinion' per—. Ker states (*MLGB*, 319 n.) that the scribe who wrote this ms was French, and it is conceivable that it was obtained by Lemenstre (or John de Evesham I, q.v.) during a possible visit to the papal court in 1352.

II John de LEMENSTRE [Leomestre, Leominstr', Lemynstr'

occ. 1375 occ. 1401

1375, 16 June, ord subdcn, Worcester cathedral, *Reg. Sed. Vac.*, 343.

1377, 19 Sept., ord dcn, Tewkesbury abbey, *Reg. Wakefield*, no 873f (as Kemynstr').
1380, 22 Sept., ord pr., bp's chapel, Highnam, *Reg. Gilbert* (Hereford), 147.
1380, May/Sept., celebrated his first mass and the pittancer sent money for bread and ale, WCM C.311; the almoner and infirmarer also contributed, acc. to their 1380/81 accts, WCM C.176, C.242.
1378/9, ill, and the infirmarer spent 3s. 4d. on treatment, WCM C.241.
1388, 21 Aug., 29th in order at the el. of a prior, Liber Albus, fo 334[v].
1396, 9 Dec., granted papal licence to choose his own confessor, *CPL*, v (1396–1404), 48.
1400/1, recd 3s. 4d. for his *cucullus* from the chamberlain, WCM C.25.
1401, 24 June, 25th at the el. of a bp, *Reg. Sed. Vac.*, 373.

III John LEMENSTRE [Lemystre
occ. 1498

1498, 25 Oct., subcellarer, *Reg. abp Morton*, ii, no 458.
1498, 25 Oct., 30th in order on the visitation certificate, *ib.*

Note: this is prob. a scribal error for William Lemster II, q.v.

Hugh LEMSTER [Lempster, Lemstre, Leomstere
occ. 1458 occ. 1467

1458, 23 Sept., ord acol., Worcester cathedral, Reg. Carpenter, i, 547.
1460, 7 June, ord subdcn, Hereford cathedral, *Reg. Stanbury* (Hereford), 145.
1460, 20 Dec., ord dcn, Worcester cathedral, Reg. Carpenter, i, 554.
1462, 18 Sept., ord pr., Alvechurch, *ib.*, i, 557.
1466/7, subcellarer, WCM C.97; and see Thomas Straynesham who succ. him this yr.
1466/7, visited Overbury, WCM C.735; and the cellarer bought *harness'* for him, C.97.
1467, 26 July, recd licence from the prior to 'migrate' to Sandwell priory, Staffs.
1467/8, the master of the Lady chapel recd two gifts from him, through two monks after he had left, *ad usum officii*; the sum was 52s. 7d., WCM C.281.

I William LEMSTER [Lemstre, Lymster, senior
occ. 1448 d. 1501/2

1448, 14 Sept., one of six whose prof. the prior was comm. to rec., Reg. Carpenter, i, 132.
1449, 12 Apr., ord acol. and subdcn, carnary chapel by Worcester cathedral, *ib.*, i, 524.
1450, 4 Apr., ord dcn, bp's chapel, Hartlebury, *ib.*, i, 526.
1453, 31 Mar., ord pr., carnary chapel, *ib.*, i, 535.
1452/3, celebrated his first mass; the almoner and chamberlain sent gifts, WCM C.200c, C.42.
1500/1, prob. succentor; see below.
1461, 19 Jan., granted licence by the prior to 'migrate' to Alcester abbey, Reg. A.6(i), fo 20. However, in 1465 there were no monks there except the abbot, and the monastery became a cell of Evesham, Knowles and Hadcock, *MRH*, 58. He returned, although prob. not immediately.
1498, 25 Oct., described as *maior* and 8th in order on the visitation certificate, *Reg. abp Morton*, ii, no 458.
1500/1, recd a 'reward' of 12d. from the precentor for looking after the keys of the [book] cupboard in the cloister, WCM C.392; he was prob. succentor (see John Weddesbury).
1501/2, d.; the cellarer pd [the almoner] for his corrody, WCM C.106c; the chamberlain sold his bedding and described him as 'senior', WCM C.49.

II William LEMSTER [Lempstyr, Lemstyr, Lemyster, Lymster
occ. 1490 occ. 1540

1490, 6 Mar., ord acol., carnary chapel by Worcester cathedral, Reg. Morton, 143.
1490, 10 Apr., ord subdcn, carnary chapel, *ib.*, 145.
1492, 22 Sept., ord dcn, carnary chapel, *ib.*, 157.
1494, 24 May, ord pr., carnary chapel, *ib.*, 162.
1497/9, subcellarer, WCM C.627, 667, 781; see John Lemenstre III above.
1508, chaplain to the prior, Reg. A.6(ii), fo 61.
1521/4, infirmarer, Wilson, *Accts Henry VIII*, 30 (WCM C.412); Reg. A.17, fo 214; WCM C.413.
1521, 22 July; 1531/2, third prior, Reg. abp Warham, ii, fo 293[v]; Reg. A.12, fo 135.
1498, 25 Oct., 30th in order on the visitation certificate, incorrectly named John, *Reg. abp Morton*, ii, no 458.
1521, 22 July, 9th on the visitation certificate, Reg. abp Warham, ii, fo 293[v].
1530, 1 Jan., gave a gift of two capons to the prior, *Jnl More*, 302.
1531/2, 10th on the clerical subsidy list and pd 20d. as third prior, and for mass celebrated *in mane*, at the sixth hour 2s. and commons 3s. 4d., Reg. A.12, fo 135.
1534, 17 Aug., subscribed to the Act of Supremacy, *DK 7th Report*, Appndx 2, 305.
1535, 1st after the subprior to sign the petition vs. the reinstatement of William Fordham, q.v., as cellarer, *L and P Henry VIII*, ix, no 653.
1536, 13 Mar., 34th and last to be named at the 'el.' of Henry Holbech, q.v., as prior; he was not present in person but by proxy, prob. on acct of his age; this may be the reason that, though one of the most senior monks, he was relegated to the bottom of the list. Reg. A.6(iii), fo 1.

1540, 18 Jan., assigned a pension of £6 13s. 4d. p.a., *L and P Henry VIII*, xv, no 81.

Note: although William Lemster I, q.v, was listed as *maior* in 1498 William II was not distinguished as *minor* or *junior* in the eleven yrs when they overlapped.

William LENCH [Lenche
occ. 1460 d. 1478/9

1460, 20 Dec., ord acol., Worcester cathedral, Reg. Carpenter, i, 554.
1465, 21 Dec., ord dcn, bp's chapel, Alvechurch, *ib.*, i, 564.
1469, 1 Apr., ord pr., St Nicholas' church, Worcester, *ib.*, i, 574.
1468/9, one of six who celebrated their first mass; recd 2s. 3d. from the almoner and a similar amount from the kitchener, WCM C.202, 154.
1459/60, on the list of the cellarer's creditors, for 22d., WCM C.491.
[1467 × 1469], recd final payment for the debt owed by the cellerar, WCM C.846.
1478/9, d.; the chamberlain sold his *vestimenta* and used some of the money to pay off a debt owed by him, WCM C.46. The precentor prepared the brief and the almoner pd the brief bearer, WCM C.384, 204; the almoner also recd money [from the cellarer] for his corrody, WCM C.204.

LEOMINSTR', Leomstere
see Lemenstre, Lemster

LEOURICUS
occ. c. 1104

Name occ. in the list of monks in *Durham Liber Vitae*, fo 22.

LEYE, Leygh
see Legh

Roger LEYNTALL
n.d.

Name in Worcs. Ms F.45, J. de Voragine (early 14th c.); on one of the end flyleaves *iste liber constat—monacho Wigorn'*. Underneath is a list of people who owed him money.

Hugh LEYNTEWARDYNE [Lentewardyn, Lenthwardine, Lentwardyne
occ. 1426 d. 1448/9

1426, 1 Dec., ord subdcn, Worcester cathedral, Reg. Polton, 207.
1427, 15 Mar., ord dcn, Worcester cathedral, *ib.*, 209.
1426/7, celebrated his first mass; recd 2s. 3d. *exennia* from the almoner and 2s. 6d. from the hostiller, WCM C.193, 229.
1438, 29 Sept./1441, 10 Nov., chaplain to the prior, Liber Albus, fos 459[v], 465.
1441/2, chamberlain, WCM C.199.
1433/4, student at Oxford with John Lawerne I, q.v., and returned to Worcester for the el. of a bp, at a cost of 22s. 8d. [for both of them for the 'round trip'] to the cellarer, WCM C.492.
1435/6, student, for whom the cellarer pd the expenses of bringing his books and bedding back from Oxford to Worcester, WCM C.88.
1429/30, recd 13s. 4d. from the cellarer which he had been owed, WCM C.86.
1434/5, with Thomas Ledbury, q.v., visited the abbots of Pershore and Alcester, WCM C.87.
1441/2, gave 6s. in alms to the almoner, WCM C.199.
1448/9, d., and the cellarer pd 13s. to the almoner for his corrody, WCM C.91.
1449/50, 1453/4, there were debts owed by him which the cellarer pd in instalments; in 1453/4, he recorded the final payment of his debts and those of Thomas Hosyntre and John Preston II, q.v., also dead, WCM C.92. The total sum owed was over £20 and the other two had also been at Oxford.

LICHFELD
see Lychefeld

Peter de LINDESEY
occ. 1352/3

1352/3, celebrated his first mass and the subcellarer sent a small contribution to the feast, WCM C.438.

Robert LINDSEY [Lyndesey, Lynnesey, Lynsey
occ. 1476 d. 1524/5

1476, 8 June, ord acol., carnary chapel by Worcester cathedral, Reg. Carpenter, ii, 207.
1477, 5 Apr., ord subdcn, Worcester cathedral, Reg. Alcock, 245.
1478, 7 Mar., ord dcn, carnary chapel by Worcester cathedral, *ib.*, 250.
1479, 18 Dec., ord pr., carnary chapel, *ib.*, 260.
1479/80, celebrated his first mass; the kitchener sent a gift of 2s. 6d., WCM C.160.
1499, from Sept., chaplain to the prior, Reg. A.6(ii), fo 1.
1501/2, infirmarer, WCM C.167.
1504, 6 Nov.; 1505/7, almoner, Reg. A.6(ii), fo 32; WCM E.180, C.212.
1507, 10 Sept., precentor, Reg. S. Gigli, 349–352.
1492, 23/24 June, one of the seven nominees for the priorate, Reg. A.6(i), fo 107[v], Reg. Morton, 91.
1498, 25 Oct., 11th in order on the visitation certificate, *Reg. abp Morton*, ii, no 458.
1499, 21 July, one of the seven nominees for the priorate, Reg. A.6(ii), fo 1[v], Reg. S. Gigli, 343; they were presented to bp Fox (Durham) acting for Gigli at Southwark on 2 Sept., Reg. A.6(ii), fo 1[v].

1507, 10 Sept., one of the seven nominees for the priorate, Reg. S. Gigli, 349–352.
1521, 22 July, 5th in order on the visitation certificate, Reg. abp Warham ii, fo 293.
1524/5, d., and the almoner distributed 2s. 6d. [to the poor], WCM C.414.

See Robert Payn.

LINDSEY
see also Lyndeseye

LILSHILL, LILSULL
see Lylleshull

William de LINGEDEN
occ. 1296

1296, 11 July, one of two proctors apptd to present the seven nominees for the priorate to the bp, *Reg. Giffard*, 480.

Richard LISLE
see Hallowe

John de LODELOWE
occ. 1341 occ. 1359/60

1341, 11 Oct., one of two *clerici* adm. to the monastic habit by the bp, *Reg. Bransford*, no 1024.
1342, 15 Oct., the prior was comm. by the bp to rec. his prof., Liber Albus, fo 180v.
1342, 21 Dec., ord acol., Hartlebury, *Reg. Bransford*, no 1049.
1343, 20 Dec., ord subdcn, Hartlebury, *ib.*, no 1055.
1351, 8 Jan., granted papal licence to choose his own confessor, *CPL*, iii (1342–1362), 380.
1359/60, named with John de Lemenstre I, q.v., as not being given his usual pittance for the 'O' payments made by the cellarer, WCM C.65; were they absent from the house?

Richard LODELOWE [Luddelowe
occ. 1448 d. 1473/4

1448, 14 Sept., one of six whose prof. the prior was comm. to rec., Reg. Carpenter, i, 132.
1449, 12 Apr., ord acol., carnary chapel by Worcester cathedral, *ib.*, i, 524.
1453, 31 Mar., ord subdcn, carnary chapel, *ib.*, i, 535.
1456, 27 Mar., ord dcn, in bp's palace chapel, Worcester, *ib.*, i, 541.
1458, 23 Sept., ord pr., Worcester cathedral, *ib.*, i, 547.
1466/7, recd less money [for pittances] after *minutiones* because he had stayed outside the priory for a quarter of the yr, WCM C.91; see also John Herford and William Walweyn.
1467, 12 Oct., the prior requested a royal writ *de apostatis capiendis* vs the three monks, PRO C81/1786/55.
1473/4, d., and the almoner recd 33s. 4d. for his corrody [from the cellarer], WCM C.203.

I William de LODELOWE [Lodlow, Lodlowe
occ. 1384 d. 1400/1

1384, 24 Sept., ord subdcn, Alvechurch, *Reg. Wakefield*, no 906d.
1385, 25 Feb., ord dcn, Cirencester abbey, *ib.*, no 908f.
1389/90, celebrated his first mass; recd 3s. 8d. from the almoner, 2s. 2d. from the chamberlain, 2s. 1d. from the pittancer and 1s. 4d. (for wine) from the subcellarer, WCM C.180, C.17, C.314, C.445.
1388, 21 Aug., 38th in order at the el. of a prior, Liber Albus, fo 334v.
1399, 23 Oct., obtained the title of papal chaplain *CPL*, iv (1362–1404), 308; this entry is repeated in *ib.*, v (1396–1404), 213, with the additional phrase 'with privileges'.
1400/1, d., and the chamberlain sold some of his bedding and clothing which included one mattress, one cloth blanket and one *par' de langele* for which he recd a total of 9s., WCM C.25.

II William LODELOWE [Lodlowe, Ludlow
occ. 1422 occ. 1444

1422, 7 Mar., ord subdcn, Worcester cathedral, Reg. Morgan, 190.
1425, 24 Mar., ord pr., Worcester cathedral, *ib.*, 209.
1424/5, celebrated his first mass; recd 2s. 6d. from both the hostiller and the sacrist, WCM C.227, 425 (dated 1423/4; there is a discrepancy in dating here).
1434/7, *custos* of the Lady chapel, WCM C.279–280.
1433, 9 Dec., 25th in order at the el. of a bp, *Reg. Sed. Vac.*, 432.
1444, 15 Jan., one of the seven nominees for the priorate, Reg. Bourgchier, 193.

William de LONDON
occ. 1293/4 occ. 1324

1293/5, prob. *tumbarius*, Wilson, *Early Comp. Rolls*, 17, 27 (WCM C.51a, 52).
1310/11, 1312/13, chamberlain, WCM C.198, C.8.
1293/4, 1294/5, the cellarer recd the money collected from the shrines *per manus* [*suas*], Wilson, *Early Comp. Rolls*, 17, 27.
1307, 14 Oct., sent with Gilbert de Madley, q.v., to the king for a licence to el. a bp, *Reg. Sed. Vac.*, 103.
1317, 20 Oct., 3rd in order at the el. of a prior, Liber Albus, fo 83.
1324, 29 Mar., witness to an incumbent taking his oath, *ib.*, fo 115.

LONGLEY
see Langley

LUDBURY
see Ledbury

LUDLOW
see Lodelowe

LULLESHULL, Lulsull
see Lylleshull

John LYCHEFELD [Lechifeld, Lychefeyld, Lychefyld
occ. 1483 occ. 1507

1483, 20 Sept., ord acol., carnary chapel by Worcester cathedral, Reg. Alcock, 274.
1487, 22 Sept., ord dcn, Ledbury, *Reg. Milling* (Hereford), 174.
1488/9, celebrated his first mass and the precentor gave a 2s. gift, WCM C.387.
1498/1500, chamberlain, WCM C.48, 542.
1500/1, and prob. for part of 1502, almoner, WCM C.210, E.179.
1501/2, kitchener, succ. William More, q.v., for the last term, WCM C.628.
1505/6, precentor, WCM C.427.

1498, 25 Oct., 23rd in order on the visitation certificate, *Reg. abp Morton*, ii, no 458.
1507, 31 Mar., given a *dimissio* by the prior to transfer to Chepstow priory, Reg. A.6(ii), fo 42^{v}.

Richard LYCHEFELD [Lichefeld, Lycheffeld
occ. 1412 occ. 1433

1412, 17 Dec., ord acol. and subdcn, Worcester cathedral, Reg. Peverel, 193, 194.
1413, 8 Apr., ord dcn, Worcester cathedral, *ib.*, 195.
1416/17, celebrated his first mass; the pittancer gave 2s. 8d. for bread and ale, WCM C.324.

1432, 15 Mar., precentor, Reg. Polton, 218.

1419, 24 Apr., 33rd in order at the el. of a bp, *Reg. Sed. Vac.*, 407.
1421/2, on the cellarer's list of creditors who were being pd off, WCM C.84a.
1432, 15 Mar., as precentor, presented the monk ordinands in the carnary chapel next to Worcester cathedral, Reg. Polton, 218.
1433, 9 Dec., 18th at the el. of a bp, *Reg. Sed. Vac.*, 432.

Name in Worcs. Ms F.61, W. Brito etc. (14th c.), on one of the end flyleaves which are actually old accts reused for binding purposes and on which several different hands have written odd words and phrases, including the name Richard Lychefeld. It is therefore possible that he had no connection with this ms.

Richard LYLLESHULL [Lylshill, Lylshyll, Lylsill, Lylsulle, Lyllyshull
occ. 1464 occ. 1478

1464, 8 June, one of six whose prof. the prior was comm. to rec., Reg. A.6(i), fo 34.
1465, 9 Mar., ord subdcn, St Nicholas' church, Worcester, Reg. Carpenter, i, 562.
1466, 1 Mar., ord dcn, St Nicholas' church, *ib.*, i, 564.
1469, 1 Apr., ord pr., St Nicholas' church, *ib.*, i, 574.

1478, 14 Sept., kitchener, Reg. A.6(i), fo 73^{v}.

1478, 14 Sept., present as witness to the homage of a priory tenant, *ib.*

Thomas LYLLESHULL [Lilsull, Lulleshull, Lulsull, Lullushull, Lylleshall, Lyllesull, Lyllushall
occ. 1419 occ. 1446/7

1419, 1 Apr., ord dcn, Worcester cathedral, *Reg. Sed. Vac.*, 392.
1422, 19 Sept., ord pr., Gloucester abbey, Reg. Morgan, 196.
1422, celebrated his first mass; the almoner, pittancer and precentor each gave 2s. 6d., and the last two specified 'for bread and ale', WCM C.192 (1422/3), C.325 (1421/2), C.376 (1422/3).
1431/2, pittancer, WCM C.329.
1436/7, 1442/3, precentor, WCM C.378, 728 (as T.L).
1438, 13 Feb., third prior, Liber Albus, fo 457 and Reg. Bourgchier, 84.
1443/5, subcellarer, WCM C.729, 600.
1446/7, possibly *magister operum*, WCM C.90; see below.

1419, 24 Apr., 39th in order at the el. of a bp, *Reg. Sed. Vac.*, 407.
1426/7, 1427/8, gave a small sum in alms to the almoner, WCM C.193, 193a.
1433, 9 Dec., 21st at the el. of a bp, *Reg. Sed. Vac.*, 432.
1438, 13 Feb., comm. as proctor to present the seven nominees for the priorate to the bp, Liber Albus, fo 457; the following day he and John Broghton, q.v., presented them to the bp at Alvechurch, Reg. Bourgchier, 84.
1443/4, visited Overbury and Sedgeberrow, WCM C.729, 773.
1444, 15 Jan., chosen as one of the seven nominees for the priorate who were presented to the bp on 16 Jan., Reg. Bourgchier, 193–195.
1444/5, visited Hallow, WCM C.600, and during the absence of the cellarer [John Sudbury II, q.v.] he made the necessary purchases for the house, WCM C.493.
1446/7, recd 4s. 'reward' from the cellarer for labour and for the supervision of the construction of *odi' calcis* at Crowle, WCM C.90. This suggests that he may have been *magister*

operum like John [Conversus] q.v., an office which was subservient to that of the cellarer.

William LYLLESHULL [Lilshille, Lyllesylle, Lyllsull, Lylsull, Lylsyll, Lynsyll
occ. 1490 d. 1533/4

1490, 6 Mar., ord acol., carnary chapel by Worcester cathedral, Reg. Morton, 143.
1490, 10 Apr., ord subdcn, carnary chapel, *ib.*, 145.
1492, 22 Sept., ord dcn, carnary chapel, *ib.*, 157.
1493, 1 June, ord pr., carnary chapel, *ib.*, 160.

1501/2, 1505/6, subsacrist, WCM C.426, 427.
1510/11; 1516; 1521/4, precentor, WCM C.394; Reg. A.12, fo 44v; Wilson, *Accts Henry VIII*, 23 (C.412), Reg. A.17, 209 and 274.
[1526/7], prob. chaplain to the prior, *Jnl More*, 244, 249; see below.
1529/30, refectorer, WCM C.414a.

1498, 25 Oct., 29th in order on the visitation certificate, *Reg. abp Morton*, ii, no 458.
1521, 22 July, 8th on the metropolitan visitation certificate, Reg. abp Warham, ii, fo 293v.
[1526/7], pd by the prior 10s. a quarter for saying the ten o'clock mass, *Jnl More*, 244, 249.
1531/2, 9th on the clerical subsidy list and pd 3s. 4d. commons, Reg. A.12, fo 135.
1533/4, d., and the chamberlain sold his *vestimenta*, WCM C.415.

LYMSTER
see Lemster

John de LYNDESEYE [Lyndsey
occ. 1350 d. 1404/5

1350, 18 Dec., ord subdcn, chapel of the manor of Prestbury by *lit. dim.* of the vicar general, *Reg. Trillek* (Hereford), 548.
1352, 22 Sept., ord pr., St Catherine's chapel, Hereford by *lit. dim.*, *ib.*, 588.

1370, 3 Apr., chamberlain, Liber Albus, fo 246.
1372/81; 1383, until 16 Sept., sacrist, Reg. A.12, fo 77v; on 16 Sept. removed from office, *Reg. Wakefield*, no 296.
1387, 26 June; 1388, 21 Aug., again sacrist, *Reg. Wakefield*, no 397, Liber Albus, fo 334v.
1391/2, 1395/6, infirmarer, WCM C.243, C.244.
1396/7, possibly sacrist, WCM C.461; see below.

1358/9, the subcellarer noted his gift of four strikes of grain, WCM C.442.
1361/2, recd 26s. 8d. from the kitchener in payment of a debt, WCM C.116.
1370, 3 Apr., 7th in order at the el. of a prior, Liber Albus, fo 246; he was chosen as one of the seven nominees for the priorate, *ib.*, fo 246v.
1372/81, as sacrist he supervised a building programme which is summarized in Reg. A.12, fo 77v; this included a new bell tower, a new dormitory, new vaulting in the nave of the cathedral, a water gate on the Severn, new choir stalls and building work on several of the manors. William Power, cellarer, q.v., was also in charge of some of the operations.
1373, 4 Dec., 6th at the el. of a bp, *Reg. Sed. Vac.*, 290.
1379, 8 Feb., apptd penitentiary in the deanery of Powick, *Reg. Wakefield*, no 834.
1384, 10 Jan., as sacrist, instituted a pr. to St Michael's church, Worcester, *ib.*, no 261.
1387, 26 June, as sacrist, involved in an exchange relating to a church of which he was patron, *ib.*, no 397.
1388, 21 Aug., 4th in order at the el. of a prior, and chosen as one of the seven nominees for the priorate, Liber Albus, fos 334v, 335.
1391/2, a writ of distraint had been issued vs the prior and sacrist on acct of the gold pieces to the value of 300m. which they had found [and not reported]. They were now called upon to explain to the king the details of the gold coins which Lyndeseye had found about seventeen years earlier when digging in the ground in the cemetery within the priory precincts. He had taken them to a goldsmith, not knowing of what metal they were made nor of what value they might be; the goldsmith had given him £86, which he had used for the building operations then in progress. For a fine of £50 to be pd into the royal exchequer, the matter was resolved, Liber Albus fo 371 and repeated on fo 392.
1392/3, 1394/5, 1396/7, building was continuing during these yrs, prob. under him, as sacrist as other obedientiaries were buying from and selling to him timber and other materials; see William Merstone, William Owston, William Power.
1401, 24 June, 4th in order at the el. of a bp, *Reg. Sed. Vac.*, 372.
1404/5, d., and the chamberlain sold his *panni*, WCM C.50.

LYNDESEYE
see also Lindesey, Lindsey

LYNSYLL
see Lylleshull

Gilbert de MADLEY [Maddeleya, Maddeleye, Madeleye, Magdeleye
occ. 1291/2 occ. 1324

1295, 29 Sept., a G. named as cellarer in *Ann. Wigorn*, 523.
1301, 20 Mar., apptd sacrist by abp Winchelsey during his visitation of the chapter and on the recommendation of the monks, *Reg. abp Winchelsey*, 424, and Graham, 'Visitation', 74–75; see also Nicholas de Norton.
1301, 6 Sept., removed from the office of sacrist by the bp, on the grounds that he was also cellarer, *Liber Albus*, no 6. Fearing as much the

abp had written to the bp on 5 Sept. to order him not to interfere, *Reg. abp Winchelsey*, 750–752; and on 20/21 Sept. he wrote to the prior ordering him to demand the immediate resignation of Nicholas de Norton whom the bp had reapptd, *ib.*, 752–753 and *Liber Albus*, no 7. On 7 Nov. the abp wrote again to the prior and monks to insist that they respect him in the sacrist's office and support him vs those of the brethren who continued to oppose him, *Reg. abp Winchelsey*, 424–425, *Liber Albus*, no 37; and see below.

1302, 10 Jan.; 7 Feb., 25 Mar.; 29 Oct., sacrist, *Reg. abp Winchelsey*, 761; *Reg. Sed. Vac.*, 37, 1; *CPL*, i (1198–1304), 604.

1303, 22 June, sacrist, *Liber Albus*, no 745.

1303, 28 Aug., reapptd sacrist by the new bp despite his recent resignation, *Reg. Gainsborough*, 64 and *Liber Albus*, no 131.

1303, 15 Nov., resigned from the office of sacrist, *Reg. Gainsborough*, 80.

[1305, Feb.]; [1308]; [1315]; 1317, 20 Oct., subprior, *Liber Albus*, no 285; *Reg. Sed. Vac.*, 88, 94; *Liber Albus*, no 662; Liber Albus, fo 83v.

1319/21, 1323; 1324, 29 Mar., chamberlain, WCM E.203, 204; Liber Albus, fo 115; also for 1320/1, Wilson, *Early Comp. Rolls*, 4–7 (WCM C.9).

1291/2, visited Blackwell, Wilson, *Early Comp. Rolls*, 18 (WCM 51).

1293/4, sent to London twice on convent business, with expenses totalling 76s. 10d. pd by the cellarer, Wilson, *Early Comp. Rolls*, 19, 21 (WCM C.51a).

1296, 11 July, one of two proctors apptd to present the seven nominees for the priorate to the bp, *Reg. Giffard*, 480.

1298/9, sent, with John de Bromesgrove, q.v., to attend the abp's council [in London], WCM C.54.

1300, 19 Aug., one of the monks apptd by the bp to assist Nicholas de Norton, q.v., in conducting a visitation *in spiritualibus* of the prior and chapter, *Reg. Giffard*, 530 (as Middel).

1302, 10 Jan., the abp wrote to the prior and to Madley as sacrist to move the position of the bp's tomb from the right side of the high altar near St Oswald's shrine to a lower place, *Reg. abp Winchelsey*, 761–762, *Liber Albus*, no 58.

1302, [27/31 Jan.] sent by the chapter, with John de Harleye, q.v., as proctor to obtain a licence from the king to el. a bp, *Liber Albus*, no 68; he recd the licence on 20 Feb., *CPR (1301–1307)*, 17, *Liber Albus*, no 105, *Reg. Sed. Vac.*, 2.

1302, 25 Mar., apptd proctor, with Stephen de Wytton, q.v., to obtain from the deceased bp's executors his seal, registers etc., *Liber Albus*, no 64.

1302, 25 Mar., chosen by the chapter as one of seven *compromissorii* to el. a bp, *Reg. Sed. Vac.*, 1; John de St Germans, q.v., was their choice, and Madley was apptd with Stephen de Wytton, q.v., on 29 Mar., as proctors to inform both the king and the abp, *ib.*, 2.

1302, 27 May, apptd by the prior to appear before the dean of St Paul's as his proctor concerning the collection of a subsidy for the Holy Land, *ib.*, 7.

1302, 1 July, apptd by the prior one of two proctors to negotiate a loan of £100, *ib.*, 29.

1302, 23 Dec., the chapter renounced all appeals which infringed the [new] bp's rights, especially any for which Madley might have been or might be responsible, *Reg. Gainsborough*, 3; see also John de Bromesgrove.

1303, 22 June, the abp again reproved the prior for continuing to allow him and John de Harleye, q.v., to be falsely denounced by some of their brethren, *Liber Albus*, no 749.

[1305], entrusted by the prior, with John de Bromesgrove, q.v., with financial arrangements concerning the appropriation of the church of Dodderhill, *Liber Albus*, no 286; he was also sent to London with John de St Briavel on the same matter, *ib.*, no 342.

Note: acc. to an entry dated 10 May 1303 (in *Ann. Wigorn.*, 557), the abp had deprived the monks of this church.

1307, 15 Oct., apptd proctor, with William de London to obtain a licence from the king to el. a bp, *Reg. Sed. Vac.*, 103; on 17 Oct. they obtained it, *CPR (1307–1313)*, 8.

1307, 15 Nov., sent to inform Walter Reynolds of his el.; there is a detailed acct of the meeting in London with Reynolds, of the latter's delay in accepting, of Madley's return to Worcester and his second journey to London a fortnight later, in order to obtain the consent of the bp el., *Reg. Sed. Vac.*, 108–109. Also on 16 Nov. he was provided with a letter to inform the king of the result of the el. and another letter to inform the administrators of the province of Canterbury, *ib.*, 110.

1308, 5 Mar., comm. by the prior, *sed. vac.*, along with a fellow monk, John de Stratford I, q.v., and two clerks to deal with a purgation, *ib.*, 94.

[1315], apptd, with another, to act for the prior in certain disciplinary matters, *Liber Albus*, no 662.

1317, 9 Apr., sent as proctor, with John de Harleye, q.v. to obtain a licence from the king to el. a bp, *Reg. Sed. Vac.*, 179.

1317, 20 Oct., as subprior presided at the el. of a prior, Liber Albus, fo 83v.

1324, 29 Mar., present on the occasion of an incumbent of a city church taking his oath of office, Liber Albus, fo 115.

MAISEMORE

see Maysemore

I John de MALVERNE [Malvern

occ. 1356 d. 1409

1395–1409, prior: *prefectio*, 19 Sept. 1395, *Reg. Sed. Vac.*, 290–291; d. 1409, as below.

1356, 3 Nov., one of two accepted by the prior and chapter but refused adm. as monks by the bp because of failure to present the correct documents, Reg. Bryan, i, 42.
1358, 22 Sept., ord acol., Tewkesbury abbey, *ib.*, i, 113.
1359, 26 Mar., ord subdcn, bp's chapel, Hartlebury, *ib.*, i, 114.
1359, 6 Apr., ord dcn, bp's chapel, Hartlebury, *ib.*, i, 116.
1359, 15 June, ord pr., Alvechurch, *ib.*, i, 117.
1358/9, celebrated his first mass and recd *exennia* from the precentor, WCM C.356.

1363, [chaplain to the prior]: *hic . . . incepit registrum*, Liber Albus, fo 228v.
1369/70, before, *custos* of the office of sacrist, WCM C.66.
1370, 3 Apr.; 1371, 29 Dec.; 1373, Sept./Dec.; 1375/7; 1378, 25 Apr.; 1379, 16 Mar.; and 1379/80, Sept./May, precentor, Liber Albus, fo 246; *ib.*, fo 259; WCM C.360; WCM C.361, 361a; Liber Albus, fo 270; *Reg. Wakefield*, no 127; WCM C.362.
1379, Feb./Sept., 1380, 12 June; 1380/2, Feb., chamberlain, WCM C.12; Liber Albus, fo 307; WCM C.13, 14.
1384, 16/17 Sept., apptd sacrist, *Reg. Wakefield*, no 296.
1386, 9 Feb., sacrist, *Reg. Wakefield*, no 342.
1387/1388, Dec., precentor, WCM C.365, 366; he seems to have taken over from Robert Stanes, q.v., on 6 Nov. 1385 acc. to an inventory on the acct, Hamilton, *Comp. Rolls*, 42 (WCM C.364).
[1392, 25 May]; 1395, 15 Sept., sacrist, WCM B.1579; Liber Albus, fo 380.

1369/70, student at Oxford from Feb. to Easter, and recd 20s. from the cellarer, WCM C.66.
1371/2, [student], from Dec. to June, and was pd 60s. by the cellarer, Leach, *Education in Worcs.*, 52 (WCM C.67); he is not described as student but as existent' in Oxford. The cellarer also gave him 16s. *pro emend[acione] domus Oxon'*, *ib.*

1369, 25 Nov., apptd proctor by the prior and chapter to represent them at the synod summoned by the bp to be held in the cathedral, Liber Albus, fo 235.
1370, 3 Apr., 11th in order at the el. of a prior, and chosen as one of the seven nominees for the office, *ib.*, fo 246–246v.
1371, 5 Jan., recd two *procuratoria* from the chapter, one an apptment as 'general proctor and special envoy' and the other as proctor in charge of the collection of tenths in the adcnry of Worcester and of presenting the acct at the exchequer, *ib.*, fo 251v.
1371, 29 Dec., apptd proctor by the prior and chapter in matters arising out of an episcopal visitation in which the bp was not satisfied that their muniments, charters and deeds were in order, *ib.*, fos 258v, 259.
1371/2, actively engaged in the business affairs of the house under the cellarer's direction for whom he both pd out and recd sums of money. He was given 40s. for the expenses of a journey to London where he pd 20s. to the chapter's advocate in the Court of Arches; and he recd another 109s. 7d. for making various purchases for the prior, WCM C.67.
1372, 17 Sept., apptd proctor to attend the Black Monk Chapter in Northampton on 27 Sept., Pantin, *BMC*, iii, 210 (Liber Albus, fo 266).
1373, Nov., sent with Richard Wenlok, q.v. to obtain the king's licence to el. a bp, *Reg. Sed. Vac.*, 282.
1373, 4/7 Dec., 10th in order at the el. of a bp, and was proctor, with Richard Wenlok, apptd to inform the prior [Walter de Legh, q.v.] of his el., *Reg. Sed. Vac.*, 291; on 12 Dec. he and two seculars were named to inform the pope, *ib.*, 292.
1375/6, went to the general chapter of the Hospitallers *pro firma Cladon querenda* and recd 10s. from the pittancer and 3s. 2d. in addition *pro labore*, Hamilton, *Comp. Rolls.*, 36 (WCM C.310).
1378, 25 Apr., one of three proctors apptd *pro tempore visitacionis* of the bp, Liber Albus, fo 270; see William Power.
1379, 8 Feb., apptd penitentiary in Worcester, *Reg. Wakefield*, no 834.
1379, 14 Mar., presented two clerks for adm. to the priory to the bp, *ib.*, no 127.
1380, 11 Feb., one of three monks named to represent the chapter in a dispute over tithes, Liber Albus, fo 311v. On 12 June he and the same monks were issued a *procuratorium generale*, prob. in the same case, *ib.*, fo 307; see also William de Owston and William Power.
1380, 15 Dec., present at the induction of the adcn of Gloucester, Liber Albus, fo 309v.
1386, 9 Feb., as sacrist presented a pr. to St Michael's church, Worcester, *Reg. Wakefield*, no 342.
1387, [1 June], took the monk ordinands to Cirencester [abbey], WCM C.73 and *Reg. Wakefield*, no 923.
1388, 21 Aug., 6th in order at the el. of a prior, Liber Albus, fo 334v.
1395, 5 Apr., comm. by the prior to induct a brother into the hospital of St Oswald, *Reg. Sed. Vac.*, 361.
1395, 15/16 Sept., present at the el. of a prior and one of the seven nominees presented to the bp; *prefectio* by the bp on 19 Sept., Liber Albus, fo 380, 380v.
1396, 11 Nov., granted papal licence to choose his own confessor, *CPL*, v (1396–1404), 47.
1396, 11 Dec., ratification obtained from the pope, on the prior's petition, resolving the contradictions in earlier papal indults granted to prior John Evesham, q.v., and later partially withdrawn on acct of the protests which bp Bryan had 'untruly suggested to Innocent VI'.

The prior and subprior were also authorized, with reference to both past and future, to reconcile the cathedral church and cemetery in the absence of the bp and *sed. vac.*, and this authorization applied to churches subject to them, *CPL*, v (1396–1404), 7. See also John Grene I, Walter de Legh.

1398/9, pd a visit to Moor [Lindridge], WCM C.649.

1401, 13 June, his *sed. vac.* register began on this date and is found in *Reg. Sed. Vac.*, 371–390.

1401, 23/25 June, performed in person a visitation, *sed. vac.*, of the cathedral priory, of the clergy and people of the city and deanery of Worcester and of the deanery of Powick, *Reg. Sed. Vac.*, 382.

1401, 24 June, presided at the el. of a bp, *Reg. Sed. Vac.*, 372–374.

1402, 30 June, excused himself from attendance at the Black Monk Chapter because of a Welsh insurrection, Pantin, *BMC*, iii, 209 (Liber Albus, fo 411); see John Dudley.

1405/6, visited Winchcombe [abbey], WCM C.372.

1407, 24/25 Oct., performed in person a visitation, *sed. vac.*, as in 1401 above, *Reg. Sed. Vac.*, 388–389.

1409, 2 Jan., present at the trial of John Badby, heretic, in Worcester carnary chapel, Wilkins, *Concilia*, iii, 326, Reg. abp Arundel, ii, fo 17.

1409, between 2 Jan. and 29 Sept., d., WCM C.81 (where there is ref. to his funeral).

Wrote a continuation of Ranulf Higden's *Polychronicon*, covering the yrs 1348–1377; see Gransden, *Hist. Writing*, ii, 56.

Although his name does not appear as possessor or borrower of any surviving mss, W. A. Pantin and S. L. Forte have both suggested that some of the notes on theological disputations in the university of Oxford which are contained in Worcs. Ms F.65 may be in his hand; see Floyer, *Catalogue of Worcs. Mss*, note added to the entry under F.65 in the interleaved copy of the catalogue in Worcs. Cath. Library and S. L. Forte, 'A Study of some Oxford Schoolmen of the Middle of the Fourteenth Century, with special reference to Worcester Cathedral Manuscript F.65', Oxford, Bod. Ms B.Litt., c. 10–11, 2 vols, 1947, i, 11. Pantin also suggested that the hand could be that of John Grene I, q.v., and Forte suggested that of John Hatfeld, q.v. It is also worth noting that during Malverne's several turns in the office of precentor there are regular entries on his accts which refer to the annual updating of a chronicle which was kept [on a stand] in the cathedral for public reading; see J. Greatrex, 'The English Cathedral Priories and the Pursuit of Learning in the Later Middle Ages', in *The Journal of Ecclesiastical History*, 45 (1994), 405.

Some of his *acta* are found in the Liber Albus, fos 380–c. 432, entered by his chaplains: John Coulesdon, John Hambury, q.v. His *sed. vac. acta* are noted above.

II John MALVERNE [Malvern

occ. 1420 occ. 1478

1420, 2 Mar., ord acol., Worcester cathedral, Reg. Morgan, 59.

1420, 21 Dec., ord subdcn, chapel [of the guild] of the Trinity, Worcester, *ib.*, 68.

1424, 23 Sept., ord pr., Bromyard, *Reg. Spofford* (Hereford), 296.

1423/4, celebrated his first mass, and recd gifts from the chamberlain and pittancer, WCM C.35, 326.

1448/9, *tumbarius*, WCM C.91.

1456/8, hostiller, WCM C.233, 234.

1459/61, precentor, WCM C.491.

1469/70, master of the Lady chapel, WCM C.282.

1478, 19 Dec., possibly precentor; see below.

1433, 9 Dec., 24th in order at the el. of a bp, *Reg. Sed. Vac.*, 432.

1441/2, gave a small sum in alms to the almoner, WCM C.199.

1444/5, sent by the prior to Hatfield to confer with the bp of Ely [Thomas Bourgchier who had been translated from Worcester in 1443] *pro diversis causis pertinent' domino priori*, WCM C.396.

1446/7, sent by the cellarer to Pershore for 'negotiations', WCM C.90.

1448/9, had incurred a debt of £6 to Richard Roo which the cellarer pd, WCM C.91.

1453, Feb./Sept., was obliged to pay a fine *in curia regis* and the cellarer sent the sum, WCM C.93; he was also on the cellarer's list of creditors this yr, *ib.*

1459/60, as precentor took seven brethren to Hereford for ordination, WCM C.491.

1461, 19 Sept., presented monk ordinands at the ordination at Claines, Reg. Carpenter, i, 555.

1469, 14 Aug., one of the seven nominees for the priorate, Reg. Carpenter, ii, 13–16 and Reg. A.6(i), fo 60^v.

1478, 19 Dec., took the monk ordinands to Cirencester abbey for ordination, Reg. Alcock, 253.

III John MALVERNE [Malvorn

occ. 1508 occ. 1511

1508, 18 Mar., ord subdcn, carnary chapel by Worcester cathedral, Reg. S. Gigli, 297.

1511, 20 Sept., ord pr., carnary chapel, *ib.*, 310.

1510/11, celebrated his first mass, and the precentor gave a 2s. pittance, WCM C.394.

IV John MALVERNE [Malvern

occ. 1516 occ. 1521

1516, 17 May, ord acol., carnary chapel by Worcester cathedral, Reg. S. Gigli, 330.

1520/1, celebrated his first mass, and recd 2s. from the almoner and 1s. from the prior, Reg. A.17, 54, *Jnl More*, 139.

1521, 22 July, 32nd in order on the visitation certificate, Reg. abp Warham ii, fo 293v.

Note: this entry has been assigned to John Malverne IV on the basis of the order of seniority; Malverne III could not have been 32nd at this date and so must have d. or departed.

Robert MALVERNE [Malvern
occ. 1504/5

1504, 6 Apr., ord acol., carnary chapel by Worcester cathedral, Reg. S. Gigli, 287.
1504, 21 Dec., ord subdcn, chapel of St Wulstan's hospital, Worcester, *ib.*, 291.
1504/5, d., and the almoner gave 2s. 6d. in alms in bread for the poor, WCM C.211.

Philip MANGAUNT
occ. 1330

1330, 11 Aug., one of four *clerici* to be examined by two officials of the bp and recd *ad monachalem ordinem, Reg. Orleton*, no 776.

Richard de MARCLE
occ. 1339/40

1339/40, recd 4d. from the pittancer after *minutiones* and prob. d., WCM C.298.

MAREYS
see Moreys

MARMADUKE
see Pirie

MARSEMOR
see Maysemore

MARTINUS
occ. c. 1104
Name occ. in the list of monks in *Durham Liber Vitae*, fo 22.

John MASON
see John [Conversus]

MATHEUS
occ. c. 1104
Name occ. in the list of monks in *Durham Liber Vitae*, fo 22.

I MAURICE [Mauricius
occ. before 1093 occ. c. 1104

Name occ. in the list of monks dated c. 1104 in *Durham Liber Vitae*, fo 22. He left Worcester before 1093 to go to bp Wulstan's new foundaton at Westbury, Atkins, 'Church of Worcs.', pt ii, 207; see Coleman.

II MAURICE
occ. before 1216

1216, el. abbot of Alcester, *Ann. Wigorn.*, 407; he returned to attend the dedication of the cathedral the following yr, *ib.*, 409.

MAURICE
see also Moreys, Morice

MAURUS
occ. c. 1104
Name occ. in the list of monks in *Durham Liber Vitae*, fo 22.

Note: it is prob. this monk whose name is recorded in the Savigny mortuary roll of c. 1122/3, Delisle, *Rouleau Mortuaire*, pl. xxv, tit. 87.

John de MAXSTOKE
occ. 1370

1370, 13 Apr., ord acol. [Worcester cathedral], Reg. Lynn, 50.

John de MAYDEWELL
occ. 1330/2

1330, 11 Aug., one of four whose prof. the prior was authorized to rec., *Reg. Orleton*, no 335.
[1330], 9 Nov., obtained *lit. dim.* for all minor and holy orders, *ib.*, no 250.
1331, 25 May, ord subdcn, Campden, *ib.*, no 21 (p. 35).
1332, 18 Apr., ord pr., Beckford, *ib.*, no 25 (p. 41).

William MAYSEMORE [Maisemore, Marsemor, Mayesmor
occ. 1387 d. 1402/3

1387, 2 Mar., ord acol., Hartlebury, *Reg. Wakefield*, no 913a.
1387, between Mar. and Sept., taken to Cirencester by John Malverne, q.v., precentor, for ordination [as subdcn], WCM C.73.
1388, 7 Sept., obtained *lit. dim.*, for dcn's orders, *Reg. Wakefield*, no 934.
1388, 19 Sept., ord dcn, Hereford cathedral, Reg. Gilbert (Hereford), fo 96v.
1390, 24 Sept., ord pr., bp's chapel, Hartlebury, *ib.*, no 947e.
1389/90, celebrated his first mass, and recd gifts from the pittancer and precentor, WCM C.314, 367 (1390/1).
1388, 21 Aug., 40th and last in order at the el. of a prior, Liber Albus, fo 334v.
1401, 24 June, 31st at the el. of a bp, *Reg. Sed. Vac.*, 373.
1402/3, d., and the chamberlain pd for the brief, WCM C.26a.

MELDENHAM
see Mildenham

John de MENSTREWORTH
occ. [1354]

[1354], 19 Feb., delivered a letter from the prior and chapter to the bp, Liber Albus, fo 236.

Note: this is prob. a scribal slip of the pen for Roger de Minstreworth, q.v.

William MEODE [Mede

occ. 1429/30

1429/30, one of the monks on the cellarer's list of creditors, WCM C.86.

Note: this monk may occ. elsewhere in this reg. under another name, but if so, where?

William de MERSTON [Mersshton, Merstone

occ. 1370 occ. 1411/12

1370, 13 Apr., ord subdcn, [Worcester cathedral], Reg. Lynn, 50.

1370, 21 Sept., ord dcn, Westbury collegiate church, *ib.*, 51.

1372, 18 Sept., ord pr., [Worcester cathedral], *ib.*, 60.

1379/80, subcellarer, WCM C.444, 597; prob. with Thomas Dene, q.v., WCM 864.

1381/3, kitchener, WCM C.70, 119.

1387/8; 1389/90; 1391/2; 1392/4, pittancer, WCM C.313; 314; 74; 316, 317.

1394, Dec./1404, *tumbarius*, WCM C.459a-468.

1406/7, 1411/12, 1414/15, pittancer, WCM C.320–322; and also prob. for part of 1401/2, C.315.

1373, 4 Dec., 21st in order at the el. of a bp, *Reg. Sed. Vac.*, 290.

1379/80, pd visits to Hallow and Harvington, WCM C.597, 864.

1388, 21 Aug., 18th in order at the el. of a prior, Liber Albus, fo 334v.

1391/2, was owed £6 10s. 5d. [?for 'O' pittance] by the cellarer, WCM C.74.

1395/6, recd a new *cucullus* from the cellarer as recompense *pro . . . assiduo labore . . . circa pipam* [which carried water from Henwick to the priory], WCM C.77, 77a.

1399/1400, was employed by the cellarer on various 'negotiations', WCM C.476.

1401, 24 June, 12th in order at the el. of a bp, *Reg. Sed. Vac.*, 373.

1411/12, recd 6s. 8d. from the chamberlain for his habit, WCM C.30.

Thomas MILDENHAM [Meldenham, Myldenham

occ. 1475 d. 1507

1499–1507, prior: one of the seven nominees for the priorate, chosen on 21 July 1499, Reg. S. Gigli, 343; they were presented to bp Fox (of Durham, acting for the bp of Worcester) in Southwark; the bp chose him on 2 Sept. 1499, and placed the pontifical ring on his finger, Reg. A.6(ii), fos 1v–3; d. before 10 Sept. 1507; see below.

1475, 5 Apr., ord acol., Worcester cathedral, Reg. Alcock, 245.

1479, 18 Dec., ord subdcn, carnary chapel by Worcester cathedral, *ib.*, 260.

1481, 16 June, ord dcn, Whitbourne, *Reg. Milling* (Hereford), 163.

1491/2, precentor, first yr, WCM C.388.

1495, 22 Feb., 29 June; 1497, 13 May; 1498, 22 Jan., 3 Apr., 27 June, 25 Oct.; 1499, 21 July, sacrist, Reg. A.6(i), fo 104, Reg. Morton, 113; *Reg. Sed. Vac.*, 227; *CPL*, xvi (1492–1498), 594, WCM B. 1651, Reg. A.6(i), fo 122, *Reg. abp Morton*, ii, no 458; Reg. S. Gigli, 343.

1487/8, recd from the kitchener, with Edmund Ledbury, q.v., 20s. *pro tempore vacacionis*; were they students?, WCM C.161.

1492, 23/24 June, one of the seven nominees for the priorate, Reg. Morton, 91 and Reg. A.6(i), fo 107v.

1495, 29 June, apptd proctor to attend the Black Monk Chapter in Northampton, Pantin, *BMC*, iii, 216 (Reg. A.6(i), fo 104).

1497, 13 May, with John Stratford III, q.v., sent as proctor to the abp to obtain the prior's comm. for *sed. vac.* jurisdiction, *Reg. Sed. Vac.*, 227.

1498, 22 Jan., granted dispensation to hold a benefice for life with or without cure of souls and to remain in the monastery as a full member of the chapter, *CPL*, xvi (1492–1498), no 880.

1498, 27 June, again named as proctor to attend the Black Monk Chapter, Pantin, *BMC*, iii, 216 (Reg. A.6(i), fo 122).

1498, 25 Oct., 12th in order on the visitation certificate, *Reg. abp Morton*, ii, no 458.

1499, 3 Apr., comm. by the abp with the prior, William Wenlok, q.v., to install S. de Gigli as bp, Bloom, *Original Charters*, 162.

1499, 21 July, chosen by the chapter as one of the seven nominees for the priorate, Reg. A.6(ii), fo 1v, Reg. S. Gigli, 343.

1506/7, visited Newnham, WCM C.668.

1507/8, went to Ludlow to confer with the king, WCM C.490; one of those comm. by the king as justices of the peace in Worcestershire, *Liber Pensionum*, no 164.

1507, d. before 10 Sept., Reg. S. Gigli, 349–352. The cellarer recorded expenses of £9 11s. 5d. *pro sepultura*, WCM C.490. The subprior, Robert Alvechurch, q.v., summed up his achievements: he pd off the debts of the prior's office amounting to £723 17s. within his first three years and he recovered jewels that had been pawned for a sum totalling £193 6s. 8d. He also founded a chantry in which he provided for a daily mass in the Jesus chapel to be said by a monk chaplain for his soul and for the souls of relatives and benefactors. On the anniversary of his death he decreed that the subprior was to give pittances to the prior, obedientiaries and other monks, Reg. A.6(ii), fo 25v.

Name in Worcs. Ms F.10, Sermones (15th c.), some of which are in English; on one of the end fly leaves *constat*—; see John More II.

Some of his *acta* have been recorded in Reg. A.6(ii), fos 1–48v by his chaplains, among whom was John Kidremister, q.v.

MILDENHAM
see also Myldenham

Roger de MINSTREWORTH [Menstreworth, Munstreworth, Munstruworth
occ. 1339 occ. 1355/6

1339, 27 Mar., ord subdcn, Kempsey, *Reg. Bransford*, no 1004.
1351/2, described as former pittancer, i.e., prob. in 1350/1, WCM C.293.
1355/6, almoner, WCM C.172.
1350/1, recd 10s. from the precentor *in tritur' bladorum . . . per vices*, WCM C.354.
1351, 21 Jan., granted papal licence to choose his own confessor who was empowered to give plenary remission at d., *CPL*, iii (1342–1362), 406.

Note: see John de Menstreworth who is prob. the same monk.

MISTON
see Myston

William MIYTHE
occ. 1509/10

1509, 22 Dec., ord dcn., carnary chapel by Worcester cathedral, Reg. S. Gigli, 301.
1510, 21 Sept., ord pr., carnary chapel, *ib.*, 304.

MOCHELNEYE
see Muchelneye

MOLTON
see Multon

I John MORE
occ. c. 1381 × 1384

1381 × 1384, visited Dodderhill (when Thomas de Hertilbury I, q.v., was subcellarer), WCM C.477.

II John MORE [Moore, ?Moreton
occ. 1534/6

1534, 17 Aug., subscribed to the Act of Supremacy, *DK 7th Report*, Appndx 2, 305.
1535, signed the petition vs the reinstatement of William Fordham, q.v., as cellarer, *L and P Henry VIII*, ix, no 653.
1536, 13 Mar., 32nd in order at the 'el.' of Henry Holbech, q.v., as prior, Reg. A.6(iii), fo 1; he is described as professed but not in pr.'s orders.

Name in Worcs. Ms F.10, Sermones (15th c.), some of which are in English; on one of the end fly leaves *constat*; see Thomas Mildenham.

See also John Moreton.

I Thomas atte MORE [Moor, Mor'
occ. 1371 occ. 1409/10

1371, 20 Dec., ord acol., Worcester cathedral, *Reg. Lynn*, 54.
1373, Dec., subdcn, recd from the prior *lit. dim.*, addressed to the bp of Hereford for [dcn's] orders, *Reg. Sed. Vac.*, 322.
1377, 23 May, ord pr., Colwich, *Reg. Stretton* (1905) (Coventry/ Lichfield), 326.
1393/4, refectorer, WCM C.416.
1396/9; 1399/1400; 1400/3, chamberlain, WCM C.22–24a; E.223 (court rolls for the yrs 1397/1400); C.25–26a.
1404/5, 1409/10, *tumbarius*, WCM C.469, 470.
1373, 4 Dec., 30th in order at the el. of a bp, *Reg. Sed. Vac.*, 290.
1381 × 1384, visited Dodderhill (when Thomas de Hertilbury I, q.v. was subcellarer), WCM C.477.
1388, 21 Aug., 25th at the el. of a prior, Liber Albus, fo 334v.
1396, Sept., visited Stoke Prior, WCM C.789b and c.
1401, 24 June, 19th at the el. of a bp, *Reg. Sed. Vac.*, 373.
1404/5, one of several monks sent to Winchcombe to confer with the abbot, WCM C.78.
1409/10, pd a supervisory visit to Loxley [Locksley] at the behest of the chamberlain, WCM C.28.

Name in
(1) Worcs. Ms Q.54, W. Milverley etc. (15th c.), *ex procuracione* —.
(2) Gloucester Cathedral Ms 25, Medica (13th c.); *exlibris*—on fo iii in a 15th c. hand.

Note: it is uncertain to which of the two monks named Thomas More these mss should be assigned; the hand in the Worcester inscription points to the later Thomas.

His mother was owed £20 by the cellarer in 1395/6, WCM C.77.

II Thomas MORE [Moor, Moore
occ. [1471] d. 1486/7

[1471], acol., recd *lit. dim.* to all orders, Reg. Carpenter ii, 42.
1472, 19 Dec., ord dcn, carnary chapel by Worcester cathedral, *ib.*, ii, 189.
1474, 5 Mar., ord pr., carnary chapel, *ib.*, ii, 195.
1473/4, celebrated his first mass; the almoner gave 2s. 4d., the hostiller provided pittances of bread and ale and the kitchener gave *exennia* of 2s. 3d., WCM C.203, C.236, C.157.
1479 × 1482, ?student at Oxford acc. to an entry in Worcs.Ms F.118; see below.
1486/7, d., and the almoner distributed alms [to the poor], WCM C.207.

Name in
(1) Worcester Cath. Ms F.118, Logicalia quedam (14th/15th c.). Since the three names 'More, Bennett, Waren scolares Oxon' occ. together on a flyleaf it is reasonable to assume that

they were contemporaries at Oxford. A John Benet, q.v., is known to have been there in 1482 and Edward Waren [de Wynchecombe, q.v.] was there in 1479/80. This suggests that the More in question is not William More I as *BRUO* states but Thomas More II. For Waren see Edward Wynchecombe.

(2) See the first manuscript entry under Thomas More I and the note.

I William MORE [Moore *alias* Pears, Peers, Peres

occ. 1488 occ. 1535/6

1518–1536, prior: one of the seven nominees chosen by the chapter on 27 Sept. 1518; they were presented to bp Fox (of Winchester) prob. at Southwark, and he apptd More, Reg. A.6(ii), fo 113. (See Thomas Mildenham). Deprived by 8 Jan. 1536, Reg. A.6(iii), fo 1.

1488, 17 June, adm. as a monk, aged 16., *Jnl More*, 3.
1490, 6 Mar., ord acol., carnary chapel by Worcester cathedral, Reg. Morton, 143.
1490, 10 Apr., ord subdcn, carnary chapel, *ib.*, 145.
1492, 22 Sept., ord dcn., carnary chapel, *ib.*, 157.
1494/5, celebrated his first mass and the pittancer sent bread and ale, WCM C.346.

1498, 25 Oct., fourth prior, *Reg. abp Morton*, ii, no 458.
1499/1500, subcellarer, WCM C.542.
1501/2, third prior, WCM C.831.
1501/2; 1503/4; 1504, 6 Nov; kitchener, apptd Sept. 1501, but succ. by John Lychefeld, q.v., for the last quarter of 1502, Reg. A.12, fo 117, WCM C.167; C.168a, 628; Reg. A.6(ii), fo 32.
1507, 10 Sept.; 1509/10; 1511; 1515, cellarer, Reg. S. Gigli, 349; WCM C.788; C.872; Reg. A.12, fo 31^v.
1516, subcellarer, Reg. A.12, fo 48.
1518, 27 Mar., 27 Sept., subprior, Reg. A.6(ii), fos 108, 113.

?c. 1494, student at Oxford, Worcs.Ms F.118, as in *BRUO*; this is unlikely, see Thomas More II.

1498, 25 Oct., 32nd in order on the metropolitan visitation certificate, *Reg. abp Morton*, ii, no 458.
1499/1500, pd a visit to Broadwas, WCM C.542.
1501/2, visited Harvington and Tibberton, WCM C.628, 831.
1508, 23 Nov., sent to London as proctor in the matter of the bp's appropriation of Tredington to Westminster abbey, Reg. A.6(ii), fo 68^v. John Musard, q.v., accused him of extravagance on this acct.
1509, before 7 June, went to London, to the bp's house in the Strand in order to obtain holy water for the reconciliation of the cathedral cemetery by the prior on the feast of Corpus Christi, Reg. A.6(ii), fo 66.
1518, 27 Mar., authorized to act for the prior [John Wednesbury, q.v.] in his absence, Reg. A.6(ii), fo 108.
1519, 24 Nov., summoned to a special chapter of Benedictines called by cardinal Wolsey to Westminster, to discuss measures for the reform of the order, Pantin, *BMC*, iii, 119–120 (Reg. A.6(ii), fo 121); the meeting was in Feb., and his *Journal* entries, 96 and 101, make it clear that he was present.
1521, c. 22 July, present at the metropolitan visitation, Reg. abp Warham ii, fo 293^v.
1522, 15 Nov., announced to the subprior [Robert Alvechurch, q.v.], his intention to carry out a *sed. vac.*, visitation of the chapter, Reg. A.6(ii), fo 133.
1522/3, bought a new mitre for £50 and a pastoral staff valued at £28 15s., Wilson, *Accts Henry VIII*, 3 (Reg. A. 17, 116). Further details and a description of these two items, which were made in London by John Crancks, goldsmith, are given in *Jnl More*, 144, 163–164.
1523/5, acted as supervisor of the bp's estates and made tours of inspection with the bp's steward, *Jnl More*, 189–190, 207; see also C. Dyer, *Lords and Peasants in a Changing Society: the Estates of the Bishopric of Worcester, 680–1540* (Cambridge, 1980), 155, 158, 161.
1524/35, was accustomed to spend half the yr or more away from Worcester, residing chiefly at the manors of Batenhall, Crowle and Grimley. His personal acct book or journal (printed as *Jnl More*, q.v.) provides a wkly record of his household receipts and expenditures and much informative detail; they reveal a kind-hearted and hospitable person enjoying a comfortable existence. His attention centred on repairing and improving his dwellings and their neighbouring churches, entertaining guests, giving generous gifts to relatives, servants and others, and also constantly adding to his collection of books, *Jnl More*, 192–406; Reg. A.12 contains inventories of the furnishings and equipment at these three manors, fos 1–12, which are printed in *Jnl More*, 416–425.
1525, Aug./Sept., spent six weeks in London during which he supervised work on the burial stone he had planned for himself which was to be placed before 'John's Awter', *Jnl More*, 211, 217; it was brought to Worcester in July 1528, *ib.*, 273; the total cost was over £12 including carriage, *ib.*
1526, 19 Jan. (St Wulstan), 1 Apr. (Easter) and 15 Aug. (Assumption) sang mass at the high altar in the presence of the Princess Mary who had recently been styled princess of Wales and who stayed with him from mid Jan. to Easter at Worcester and at Batenhall. She was then only ten years of age but had been sent to Ludlow as representative of her father and overseer of the royal administration in Wales, *Jnl More*, 37, 38, 224–229 and *DNB* under

Mary. More seems to have been considered as a guardian of the princess, *Jnl More*, iv.

1528, had a list drawn up of his book collecton, Reg. A.12, fo 3 and see below.

1529, 30 Apr., obtained a privilege from cardinal Wolsey appting him the cardinal's special commissary with complete and absolute authority over the monks, Reg. A.6(ii), fo 163. But see Robert Alvechurch.

1532, Feb., apptd to serve as a justice of the peace for Worcestershire, *L and P Henry VIII*, v (1531–1532), no 838, (12).

1532, Nov., carried out a visitation of the chapter, *sed. vac.*, Reg. A.6(ii), fo 133.

1534, 17 Aug., subscribed to the Act of Supremacy, *DK 7th Report*, Appndx 2, 305, the day on which abp Cranmer arrived to conduct a visitation, *Jnl More*, 391.

1535, 22 Feb., several of abp Cranmer's injunctions after his visitation were addressed specifically to the prior and throw light on his character and administration as viewed by his fellow monks: he was to provide a resident grammar master, to show kindness and gentleness towards his brethren, to ensure an adequate supply of wholesome food, to employ two attendants for the sick in the infirmary and he was not to alienate property nor to encourage the lay servants to be critical of the monks, Wilson, 'Visitations', 366–367 (Reg. A.6(ii), fo 187, 187v).

1535, 1 Aug., wrote to Thomas Cromwell concerning a meeting that had been arranged between More, with three of his brethren, and the royal commissioner who, in July, had recently conducted a visitation of the priory, *L and P Henry VIII*, ix, no 5. At the visitation he had been accused by some of the monks of ill treatment and unjust dismissal of obedientiaries, *ib.*, nos 51, 52 (2); see William Fordham, John Musard, Roger Neckham.

1535, 14 Aug., the lord chancellor sent Cromwell a commission of oyer and determiner against him and Richard Cleve, q.v. whose treasonable statements vs the king More had failed to denounce, *L and P Henry VIII*, ix, no 90.

1535, 21 Oct., from a letter of Lady Margery Sandys to Cromwell on his behalf it appears that he was being detained in Gloucester [?abbey], *L and P Henry VIII*, ix, no 656. He may have been detained by 8 Sept. when the subprior [Roger Neckham] and cellarer replied to Cromwell's order to send £7 to the prior, *ib.*, no 304. It is prob. that because of his influential friends and connections he was never brought to trial. See Roger Neckham.

1536, by 8 Jan., he had been deprived; the bp [Latimer] wrote to Cromwell on this date advising him not to restore 'that simple man' who had been incompetent in office even when young, *L and P Henry VIII*, x, no 56. Cromwell recd further charges vs him from John Musard who condemned his extravagance and his partiality to relatives and servants, *ib.*, no 216 (dated 31 Jan.).

1536, 11 Feb., returned from Gloucester to Worcester; from 13 to 17 Feb., visited his manors and chambers and removed money, books and other belongings. He was given £20 and horses by the subprior who made this report in a letter to Cromwell (dated 17 Feb.) which implies that More was on his way to appear before Cromwell, *ib.*, no 311.

n.d., wrote to Cromwell asking to have the manor house at Grimley for himself and his household, and desiring that his pension be pd quarterly, *L and P Henry VIII*, x (1536), no 1272.

1558, d. and was buried at Alveston, F. Hutchinson comp., 'A Record of the Monumental Inscriptions and Burials in the Cathedral Church of Christ and the Blessed Mary the Virgin, Worcester', Oxford, 1944, typescript in Worcester Cathedral Library, 381.

The effigy under which he had hoped to lie in the cathedral has been identified in I. Atkins, 'The Effigy at the Back of the Great Altar Screen in Worcester Cathedral', *Trans. Worcs. Archaeol. Soc.*, 28, NS (1951), 14–22.

Name in

(1) Camb. Univ. Library, Add. Ms 6688, (late 14th c.), a missal, which he gave to Bromsgrove church in 1521 (inscription on fo 372v).

(2) Oxford, Merton College, B.8.G.17, Antonius Andreas, *Super tota arte veteri Aristotelis* (printed book), Venice, A.D.1496.

(3) Duns Scotus, *Super universalibus* (printed book), Venice, 1496; see *BRUO*.

(4) ?Worcs. Mss; these are almost impossible to identify with any degree of certainty. Miss Fegan has listed all More's purchases between 1518 and 1533 which he recorded in his Journal; there are 69 items including both mss and printed books covering a wide range of subjects: theology, history, canon law, spiritual treatises and saints' lives, sermons, parliamentary statutes and four copies of the Rule of St Benedict in English, perhaps the translation of bp Fox (see J. Greatrex, 'On Ministering to 'Certayne Devoute and Religiouse Women': Bishop Fox and the Benedictine Nuns of Winchester Diocese on the Eve of the Dissolution', *Studies in Church History*, 27 (1990), 226–227. Miss Fegan has also tentatively tried to match More's purchases with extant volumes in the cathedral library, an exercise which can be undertaken more definitively only after the mss catalogue has been revised, *Jnl More*, 409–415.

A list of books drawn up in 1528 in Reg. A.12, fo 3 is printed by J. M. Wilson in 'The Library of Printed Books in Worcester Cathedral', *The*

Library, 3rd series, ii (1911), 30–31. See also the more recent Sharpe, *Eng. Benedictine Libraries*, iv, B114.

In addition to his Journal there is an official record of some of his *acta* in Reg. A.6(ii), fos 112v–189v, entered by his chaplains, Thomas Asteley, Richard Cleve, John Musard, William Hambury, Thomas Blockeley, Thomas Wulstan, q.v.

His parents were Richard and Ann Pears whose names occ. frequently in the *Journal* as do those of his brother Robert of Bristol, from whom he regularly purchased wine, and of his sister Alice Parsons. A Richard Pears, his nephew, seems to have acquired his uncle's Journal as he has written his name and right of ownership on several folios.

II William MORE [Moore

occ. 1521 occ. 1530/1

1521, 22 July., prof. before this date, *Reg. abp Warham*, ii, fo 293v.

1525, 23 Dec., ord dcn, Bromyard. *Reg. Booth* (Hereford), 321.

1530/1, kitchener, WCM C.414b.

1521, 22 July., 42nd in order and last on the metropolitan visitation certificate, Reg. abp Warham, ii, fo 293v.

1523/4, ill for nine wks, and 10s. 6d. were spent on his cure, by the infirmarer, Reg. A.17, 280, and WCM C.413.

1529/30, ill for six days, and the infirmarer recorded 12d. in expenses, WCM C.414a.

John MORETON

occ. 1533

1533, 20 Sept., ord subdcn, carnary chapel by Worcester cathedral, Reg. Ghinucci 7(ii), 174.

Note: this monk is prob. identical with John More II, q.v.

Richard MOREYS [Mareys

occ. 1347 occ. 1358/9

1347, 19 June., one of two whose prof. the prior was comm. by the bp to rec., *Reg. Bransford*, no 832.

1351, 8 Jan., obtained licence to choose his own confessor, who could give plenary remission at d., *CPL*, iii (1342–1362), 380.

1358/9 visited Dodderhill with the chamberlain and Nicholas de Hodynton, q.v., WCM C.835.

Nicholas MORICE [Mauricii de Wygornia, Moritz, Moryce

occ. 1311 occ. 1344

1311, 25 Nov., one of two whose prof. was recd by the prior in the Lady chapel, *Liber Albus*, no 537, after the bp had sent his comm. on 17 Nov., Liber Albus, fo 50v.

1311, 9 Dec., obtained *lit. dim.*, for all orders, *Reg. Reynolds*, 96.

1312, 6 Mar., ord acol., Worcester cathedral, *ib.*, 130.

1314, 21 Dec., ord pr. [as *dictus Morice*], Reg. Maidstone, 41.

1336, 25 Aug.; 1339, Jan., Feb., and 12 Aug.; 1340, 21 Apr.; 1344, 22 Nov., subprior, *Liber Albus*, no 1202; *Reg. Sed. Vac.*, 258–268, *Reg. Bransford*, no 79; *ib.*, no 290; *ib.*, no 673.

1317, 20 Oct., 37th in order at the el. of a prior, Liber Albus, fo 83v.

1319, 4 Nov., present with the prior [Wulstan de Bransford, q.v.] when the latter was accused of alienating property, WCM B.753.

1322/3, visited Bromsgrove and dined on fowl, WCM C.545.

1336, 25 Aug., apptd by the chapter, with Henry Fouke. q.v., to go to the curia, *Liber Albus*, no 1202.

1339, 6 Jan., one of four monks apptd by the prior to conduct a *sed. vac.* visitation in the diocese, *Reg. Sed. Vac.*, 265; on 9 Jan., the abbot of Cirencester made his canonical obedience to Morice, commissary general of the prior, *ib.*, 269; on 11 Jan., he acted as official of the prior, *sed. vac.*, in a summons to contumacious persons, *ib.*, 258–9. As subprior and commissary of the prior he performed other similar comm., *ib.*, 262–269.

There are three loose deeds, dated 13 and 16 Jan., and 15 Feb., 1339, which describe him as the prior's commissary in the administration of the spiritualities in the city and diocese during the vacancy of the see, WCM B.793, B.393, B.269a.

1339, 12 Aug., with Henry Fouke. q.v. comm. by the bp to rec. the prof. of a nun of Whiston, *Reg. Bransford*, no 79.

1340, 21 Apr., one of seven nominees for the office of prior, *ib.*, no 290.

1344, 22 Nov., comm. by the bp to rec. the prof. of a nun of Whiston, *ib.*, no 673.

John MORTON [Moorton, Mortun, Mourtone

occ. 1423 d. 1465/6

1423, 20 Mar., ord acol., Worcester cathedral, Reg. Morgan, 198.

1424, 18 Mar., ord subdcn, Worcester cathedral, *ib.*, 203.

1424, 23 Sept., ord dcn, Bromyard, *Reg. Spofford* (Hereford), 296.

1427, 15 Mar., ord pr., Worcester cathedral, Reg. Polton, 210.

1426/7, celebrated his first mass and recd *exennia* from the almoner (2s. 4d.), hostiller (2s. 6d.), and pittancer (2s. 3d.), WCM C.193, 229, 328.

1439/42, subcellarer, WCM C.89, 447, 727.

1445/6, from at least 16 Oct. 1445 to 25 Mar. 1446, chaplain [to the prior] and therefore

responsible for the register viz. Liber Albus, fos 477 to 478v.
1446/7, steward of the prior's hospice [*senescallus hospicii*]. WCM C.397; he prob. continued in this office in 1447/8 and 1448/9, (see entries below).
1451, Mar./Sept., subcellarer, WCM C.448.
1451/4, 1455/6, chamberlain, WCM C.41–43, 541.
1458/60, kitchener, WCM C.685, 149, 491.
1462, Mar./Sept., hostiller, WCM C.235.

1431, Aug./Sept., recd 3s. 3d. [pittance money] for his *minutio*, WCM C.86a.
1439.40, one of the monks on the cellarer's list of creditors, WCM C.89.
1441/2, visited Overbury, WCM C.727.
1446/7, recd sums from the cellarer for his *minutiones* owed from the previous yr and also for his 'O' pittances [?also overdue], WCM C.90.
1447/8, involved in negotiations for the prior, WCM C.398.
1448/9, cited as witness on the almoner's acct regarding the purchase of cloth for hose [*calig'*] for the prior's servants, WCM C.200.
1449/50, again on the cellarer's list of creditors, WCM C.92.
1455/6, visited Broadwas, WCM C.541.
1457/8, went twice to Stoke [?Prior] and stayed for six days, and his expenses of 10s. 6d. were pd by the chamberlain who also sent him on other negotiations WCM C.44, 94b.
1458/9, visited Harvington, WCM C.685.
1459/60, was owed £6 14s. by the cellarer [to his office of kitchener for this yr], WCM C.491.
1463/4, 1464/5, the cellarer recd 33s. 4d. *de communibus* [*suis*] and 18s. 4d. the following yr, WCM C.492a, C.95. He prob. gave up these sums to relieve the cellarer's debt; see John Preston III.
1465/6, d., and the precentor provided the parchment on which to write the brief, WCM C.381.
1466/7, the cellarer reported that his debt had been pd., WCM C.97.

Nicholas de MORTON [Mortone, Mourton
occ. [1350] occ. 1359/60

[1350], 13 Sept., one of two *clerici* whom the prior was comm. to adm., Reg. Thoresby, 24.
1351, 8 Jan., described as *conversus*, *CPL*, iii (1342–1362), 380.
1352, 29 Sept., not yet prof., WCM C.293.
1352, 22 Dec., ord dcn, Bromyard, *Reg. Trillek* (Hereford), 590.
1357, 23 Sept., ord pr., Bredon, Reg. Bryan, i, 108.
1357/8, celebrated his first mass and recd *exennia* from the prior and the cellarer, WCM C.64.

1354/5, student [at Oxford] with Roger de Tendebury, q.v., and the cellarer pd them 104s. *pro liberatione*, WCM C.62.
1357/8, student, with Thomas Cros, q.v., and their maintenance of 100s. was pd by the cellarer, WCM C.64.
1359/60, student, and recd pension from the cellarer at 16d per wk, WCM C.65.

1351, 8 Jan., granted a papal indult to choose his own confessor, who could give plenary remission at d., *CPL*, iii (1342–1362), 380.

Robert de MORTON [Mortone
occ. 1317 occ. 1351/2

1317, 15 Sept., dcn, granted *lit. dim.*, for pr's orders, Reg. Maidstone, 106.
1322/3, subcellarer, WCM C.545; and see John de Wynchcumbe.
1324, Feb./1326, Sept.; 1328, May/Sept., 1328/9, pittancer, WCM C.295, C.296, E.10; C.297; C.297a.
1329/30, subcellarer, WCM C.632.
1330/1331, June; 1334, Sept./Nov., kitchener, WCM C.109, C.109a; C.755.
1345/8, subcellarer, WCM C.551, C.576; C.552, C.791; C.607, C.757.

1317, 20 Oct., 38th in order at the el. of a prior, Liber Albus, fo 83v (as Ourton).
[1322], sent to the king to explain the chapter's impoverished state and inability to send arms to the Welsh marches, *Liber Albus*, nos 938, 939.
1322/3, pd a visit to Bromsgrove, WCM C.545.
1326/7, pd visits to Bromsgrove and Kings's Norton, WCM C.544, C.693b.
1328, May/Sept., sent on negotiations to Leicester, Coventry and Eton, WCM C.297.
1329/30, visited Henwick, WCM C.632.
1331/2, visited King's Norton, WCM C.694.
1340/1 visited Bromsgrove, WCM C.548.
1345/6, visited Bromsgrove and Dodderhill, WCM C.551, C.576.
1346/7, visited Bromsgrove and Tibberton, WCM C.552, C.791.
1347/8, visited Harvington and Sedgeberrow WCM C.607, C.757.
1351, 21 Jan., granted papal licence to choose his own confessor who could give plenary remission at d., *CPL*, iii (1342–1362), 406.
1351/2, accompanied Nicholas de Clanefeld pittancer, q.v., to the Hermitage of Little Packington, Warwickshire., Wilson, *Early Comp. Rolls*, 68 (WCM C.293).

Name in Worcs. Ms F.77, G. de Tornaco (14th c.) which he sold to Henry Fouke, q.v. *pro quodam iocali eburneo*, valued at 4s. 6d.

Thomas MORTON
occ. 1497 occ. 1506/7

1497, 14 Apr., ord subdcn, carnary chapel by Worcester cathedral, Reg. G. Gigli, 25.
1501, 18 Sept., ord pr. carnary chapel, Reg. S. Gigli, 401.

1500/1, celebrated his first mass, and recd 2s. in *exennia* from each of the pittancer and precentor, WCM C.349, 392.

[1506/7], kitchener, WCM C.490; succ. by Humphrey Grafton, q.v.

1498, 25 Oct., 37th in order on the visitation certificate, *Reg. abp Morton*, ii, no 458.

1501/2, listed as one of the creditors of the kitchener, WCM C.167.

W. MORTON

occ. 1467 × 1469

1467 × 1469, celebrated his first mass and the cellarer gave 2s. 6d., WCM C.846.

Robert MOSE

occ. 1313/14

1313, 19 July., one of two whose prof. the prior was comm. to rec., *Liber Albus*, no 593 (mistakenly recorded as adm.), *Reg. Reynolds*, 68.

1314, [2 Mar.,], ord subdcn, Worcester cathedral, *Reg. Sed. Vac.*, 159.

Note: a William de la Mose occ. in Bishops Frome in 1311/12, *Reg. Almoner*, 9.

William MOSE [de Wigornia

occ. 1305 d. 1344/5

1305, 4 Jan., one of four *clerici* presented to the bp at the time of his adm., *Reg. Gainsborough*, 14.

1340, 23 Sept; 1343, 18 Jan., one of the *two tumbarii*, Reg. A.22, fos 17^v, 18; see Roger de Stivynton.

1344, 19 Feb., replaced as *tumbarius* by Richard de Haddeleye, q.v., because of age, *Reg. Bransford*, no 599.

1315, 27 May., present at a ceremony in which the prior created a notary [public], Liber Albus, fo 66^v.

1317, 20 Oct., 29th in order at the el. of a prior, Liber Albus, fo 83^v.

1322/3, pd a visit to Bromsgrove, WCM C.545.

1329/30, visited Cleeve Prior, WCM C.557.

1340, 23 Sept., 1343, 18 Jan., the two *tumbarii* drew up leases, Reg. A.22, fos 17^v, 18.

1344/5, underwent only four *minutiones* before his d. for which the pittancer gave him 8d., WCM C.301; the cellarer also ref. to his d. after four *minutiones* for which the cellarer had contributed 16d., WCM C.59.

Walter MOTLOWE [Motelowe, Muttelowe

occ. 1412 d. 1415/16

1412, 17 Dec., ord acol., and subdcn, Worcester cathedral, Reg. Peverel, 193, 194.

1413, 8 Apr., ord dcn, Worcester cathedral, *ib.*, 195.

1414, 3 Mar., ord pr., Worcester cathedral, *ib.*, 199.

1413/14, celebrated his first mass; the almoner sent *exennia* and the hostiller pd 3s. 8d. for bread and wine, WCM C.190, 223.

1415/16, d., and the chamberlain sold his *panni*, WCM C.31.

MOURTON

see Morton

MOYSES

occ. c. 1104

Name occ. in the list of monks in *Durham Liber Vitae*, fo 22.

John de MUCHELNEYE [Mochelneye, Muchelneie, Mucheney, Muchilneye

occ. 1330 occ. 1370

1330, 11 Aug., one of four *clerici* to be examined and recd *ad monachalem ordinem* by two officials apptd by the bp, *Reg. Orleton*, no 776.

1332, 18 Apr., ord dcn, Beckford, *ib.*, no 25 (p. 40).

1332, 11 Nov., obtained *lit. dim.*, for the order of pr., *ib.*, no 472.

1341/2, 1345/6, June, almoner, WCM C.170, Hamilton, *Comp. Rolls*, 49–54, (WCM C.171).

1360/1, 1370, 3 Apr., infirmarer, WCM C.862, Liber Albus, fo 246.

1338, [Dec.], as general proctor of the prior and chapter petitioned for confirmation, from the apostolic see, of the prior's sed.vac., jurisdiction, *Reg. Sed. Vac.*, 257.

1339, 12 Apr., apptd proctor, with John de Evesham I, q.v., in the el. of a prior, *Reg. Bransford*, no 38.

1351, 21 Jan., granted papal licence to choose his own confessor, who was empowered to give plenary remission at d., *CPL*, iii (1342–1362), 406.

1355, 9 Mar., apptd penitentiary, Reg. Bryan, i, 127.

1360/1, visited Bromsgrove, WCM C.862.

1363, 7 Feb., re-apptd penitentiary in the city and diocese for one yr, Reg. Barnet, 44.

1364, 13 Apr., with a secular clerk as commissary of the prior conducted *sed. vac.*, visitations of the clergy and people of the city and deanery of Worcester in the cathedral church, *Reg. Sed. Vac.*, 219.

1370, 3 Apr., 2nd in order, and the most senior monk, at the el. of a prior, Liber Albus, fo 246; only the subprior was placed ahead of him.

MULLEWURD

see Robert de Lawerne

John MULTON [Molton

occ. 1508 occ. 1536

1508, 18 Mar., ord acol., carnary chapel by Worcester cathedral, Reg. S. Gigli, 297.

1510, 21 Sept., ord dcn., carnary chapel, *ib.*, 305.

1512, 27 Mar., ord pr., carnary chapel, *ib.*, 315.

1520/1, subcellarer, Reg. A.17, 9 and 48, part yr; see Thomas Sudbury.

1521/4, master of the Lady chapel, WCM C.412, Reg. A.17, 200, WCM C.413.

1524/5; 1526, 1527, precentor, WCM C.414; *Jnl More*, 44.

1529/30, *magister communis cene*, WCM C.414a.

1530/2; 1536, 13 Mar., precentor, WCM C.414b, 414c; Reg. A.6(iii), fo 1.

1521, 22 July, 20th in order on the visitation certificate, Reg. abp Warham ii, fo 293v.

1531/2, 18th on the clerical subsidy list and pd 13s. 4d. as precentor and 3s. 4d. commons, Reg. A.12, fo 135.

1534, 17 Aug., subscribed to the Act of Supremacy, *DK 7th Report*, Appndx 2, 305.

1536, 13 Mar., 11th in order at the 'el.' of Henry Holbech, q.v., as prior, Reg. A.6(iii), fo 1.

Robert MULTON [Molton

occ. 1437 d. 1492

1469–1492, prior: 1469, 14 Aug., one of seven nominees el. by the chapter; 18 Aug., presented to the bp at Westbury [on Trym], Reg. Carpenter, ii, 13–16; 19 Aug., apptd by the bp, Reg. A.6(i), 60v; d. before 23 June 1492, which was the day of his burial, Reg. Morton, 91.

[1434, 21 May, a Robert Pete *alias* Molton ord acol., carnary chapel by Worcester cathedral, *Reg. Sed. Vac.*, 443.]

1437, 1 Sept., ord subdcn, bp's chapel, Alvechurch, Reg. Bourgchier, 61.

1439,/40, took [?dcn's] orders at Wigmore [abbey] and the cellarer recorded expenses of 12s. 6d. and 3s. for horses, WCM C.89.

1440, 20 Feb., ord pr., Hereford cathedral, *Reg. Spofford* (Hereford), 333.

1441, from 11 Nov., chaplain to the prior [Thomas Ledbury. q.v.], Liber Albus, fo 465.

1446, from 25 Mar., chaplain to the new prior [John Hertilbury. q.v.], *ib.*, fo 478v.

1446/7, kitchener, WCM C.90.

1448/9, part yr (see Thomas Wych), 1449/50, subcellarer, WCM C.91, 600a.

1451, 1454, chaplain to the prior, Liber Albus, fos 484, 489.

1460/3; 1463/6, subcellarer, WCM C.731, C.733, C.734; C.492a, C.95, C.666.

1466/7, 1468/9, cellarer, WCM C.97, C.623.

Note: During his priorate he also held an obedientiary office: 1477/8, 1478/9, 1481/3, 1486/7 [1488/9], almoner, WCM C.340, C.204–207, C.488.

1442/3, collected rents at Tibberton, WCM C.823.

1448/9, was owed 31s. 6d. by the cellarer, WCM C.91.

1449/50, visited Hallow, WCM C.600a.

1453, on the cellarer's list of creditors, WCM C.93.

1460/3, pd visits to Overbury each yr, WCM C.731, C.733, C.734.

[1463/4], recd 6s. 8d. from the cellarer *pro bona industria sua* in the office of subcellarer, WCM C.492a.

1464/5, visited Hallow and Harvington, WCM C.603, C.622, and recd 6s. 8d. from the cellarer *pro sua bona industria* as subcellarer, WCM C.95.

1465/6, visited Harvington and Newnham, WCM C.686, C.666.

1466/7, visited Overbury and Sedgeberrow, WCM C.735, C.769.

1467/8, visited Overbury, WCM C.736.

1468/9, visited Harvington and Overbury, WCM C.623, C.697.

1486/7, suffered a lengthy illness and had several doctors in attendance. His expenses are listed on his acct under *Empcio medicarum* and include payment to a M. Feysye 20s. and to M. Lenche 20s. plus £4 *in regardo*. (William' Lenche or Lynche, fellow of Oriel College, Oxford, was one of the physicians whose professional services were in demand by Henry VII; see *BRUO*.) William Rice, apothecary of Worcester, also provided medicines. The total costs were £5 12s. 8d., WCM C.409.

1488/9, M. Lenche was sent for from Oxford in order to provide medicine and 'ad supervidend' et custodiend' se in bono statu'; the *custus fusicorum* was 79s. 11d., WCM C.410.

1490/1, once again Lench was in attendance *pro conservacione sanitatis*, and he charged 68s. 8d., WCM C.411.

1491/2, the cellarer pd off a debt of £10 owed by the prior and recorded the prior's d.

Some of his *acta* are entered in Reg. A.6(i), fos 60–106 by his chaplains, Thomas Streynsham, Richard Alcester and Edward Wynchecombe, q.v.

One of his relatives, unnamed, was described as a *sitheredarius*, and was given 12d. by the cellarer in [1463/4], WCM C.492a.

MUNSTREWORTH

see Minstreworth

John MUSARD [Musart, Myssard *alias* Walker

occ. 1504 occ. 1538

1504, 6 Apr., ord acol., carnary chapel by Worcester cathedral, Reg. S. Gigli, 287.

1504, 21 Sept., ord subdcn, carnary chapel, *ib.*, 289.

1504, 21 Dec., ord dcn, hospital of St Wulstan, Worcester, *ib.*, 291.

1508, 17 June, ord pr., carnary chapel. *ib.*, 299.

1507/8, celebrated his first mass, and the hostiller sent 2s. for his feast, WCM C.240.

1521, chaplain to the prior, Reg. A.6(ii), fo 126v.

1521, 22 July, 17th in order on the visitation certificate, Reg. abp Warham, ii, fo 293v.

1525/6, 18th on the clerical subsidy list and pd 3s. 4d. commons, Reg. A.12, fo 125.
1527/8, employed in repairing books in the library and rewarded with small sums of money from the prior, *Jnl More*, 259–262.
1531, Feb./Aug., purchased materials for 'dressing' library books, *ib.*, 322, 324.
1531, July, arrested and imprisoned for theft. He was caught at Overbury after allegedly robbing the prior of 'certen plate and other things', and the prior paid 6s. 8d. to have him brought back. *Jnl More*, 330–331.
1534, 17 Aug., subscribed to the Act of Supremacy, *DK 7th Report*, Appndx 2, 305.
1535, [after the visitation of Thomas Legh, royal commissioner, 29–31 July] wrote directly to the king because, so he alleged, the prior had influenced one of the royal visitors against him and as a result he had been imprisoned. This was because he had reported the treasonable words of Richard Cleve, q.v. He reminded the king of the faithful service rendered to the king's father by his father and uncles in Wales [before 1485], *L and P Henry VIII*, ix, no 52.
1535, 8 Aug., wrote to Cromwell from prison denouncing the false charges made to the visitor, Dr Legh, *ib.*, no 51.
1535, there are four undated papers and petitions concerning this affair, all penned by Musard:
(1) a statement to the effect that he had openly accused Cleve before John Lawerne, subprior, Roger Neckham and William Hodynton III, [the three most senior monks, q.v.] and a complaint against the prior's malpractices and unjust removal of Neckham from the office of subprior and of William Fordham q.v. from that of cellarer, *ib.*, no 52.2(i).
(2) another petition to the king condemning Cleve, *ib.*, no 52.2 (ii).
(3) a memorandum to the president of the king's council [in the Marches] with further complaints of sixteen yrs' oppression under prior More and a reference to having been imprisoned on 2 Mar., by the opposition party in the convent because he had appealed to the abp's visitation [in Aug., 1534], *ib.*, no 52.2(iii).
(4) a report to Cromwell about his exclusion from the el. of the bp [Hugh Latimer, 9/11 Aug] on the grounds that he was excommunicate, after which he was clapped in prison. He also accused Thomas Blockley, q.v. of stealing 'the letter of treason', in which he had denounced Cleve, from his cell, *ib.*, no 497.
1536, 31 Jan., wrote a paper which he sent to Cromwell entitled 'The decays of your honourable Lordship's monastery at Worcester and the occasion thereof'. He complained of being in prison, and he asked to be transferred to Westminster [Abbey], *ib.*, x (1536), no 216. The original of this is in BL Ms Cotton Cleopatra E.iv, fo 98 and is his holograph.
1538, 20 May, recd archiepiscopal dispensation to change his habit; no fee charged *quia pauper*, Chambers, *Faculty Office Regs*, 133.

Thomas MUSARD

occ. 1408 d. 1469

1457/8–1469, prior: apptd by the bp after the d. of John Hertilbury q.v; he appears as prior on 30 Sept., 1458, Reg. Carpenter i, 357–358, and the bp had apptd a new sacrist John Lawerne I, q.v., on 10 Sept., to replace him, *ib.*, 303. D. before 14 Aug., 1469, *Fasti*, iv, 59.

1408, 22 Dec., ord acol., Worcester cathedral, Reg. Peverel, 175.
1411, 28 Mar., ord dcn Worcester cathedral, *ib.*, 188; the scribe has written '1410', almost certainly in error.
1414, 3 Mar., ord pr., Worcester cathedral, *ib.*, 199.
1413/14, celebrated his first mass and recd *exennia* from the almoner and hostiller, WCM C.190, 223; the latter specified 'for bread and wine'.
1419, 14 Apr., chaplain [to the prior], *Reg. Sed. Vac.*, 407.
1420/1, subcellarer, part yr, WCM C.720; see Thomas Blackwell.
1421/3, 1426/8, almoner, WCM C.191–193a.
1429/30; 1433, 9 Dec.; 1438, 12 Feb.; 1439/40, subprior, WCM C.86; *Reg. Sed. Vac.*, 432; Reg. Bourgchier, 84; WCM C.726 (as T.M).
1444/5, sacrist, WCM C.493; 1445, 20 Jan., [re]apptd by the new bp, Reg. Carpenter, i, 25.
1448/9; 1449/50; 1451/2; 1453/4; 1456/8, sacrist, WCM C.91; C.92, part yr because John Grene II, q.v., is also named sacrist on this acct, WCM C.601; C.94; C.233, C.234.

1419, 16 Mar., comm. by the prior, with Thomas Ledbury and two secular clerks, to carry out a *sed. vac.* visitation in the diocese, *Reg. Sed. Vac.*, 396. A record of their visitations in several religious houses and deaneries is in *ib.*, 397–398.
1419, 14 Apr., 25th in order at the el. of a bp, *Reg. Sed. Vac.*, 407.
1420/1, visited Overbury, WCM C.720.
1429/30, one of the monks on the cellarer's list of creditors, WCM C.86.
1433, 9 Dec., present at the el. of a bp, *Reg. Sed. Vac.*, 432.
1438, 12 Feb., one of the seven nominees for the priorate, Reg. Bourgchier, 84.
1439/40, pd a visit to Overbury, WCM C.726.
1444, 15 Jan., again one of the seven nominees for the priorate, Reg. Bourgchier, 193.
1449/50, was owed money by the cellarer, WCM C.92; he visited Hallow, c. 600a.
1451/2, pd a visit to Hallow, WCM C.601.
1453, again on the list of the cellarer's creditors, WCM C.93.

1458/9, excused himself from attendance at the Black Monk Chapter on acct of infirmity and old age as well as urgent business at home, Reg. A.6(i), fo 7^{v}.
1461, 21 Sept., absent from the episcopal visitation on acct of illness, Reg. Carpenter, i, 344.
1465, 20 June, repeated the above excuses for his non-attendance at the Black Monk Chapter, Reg. A.6(i), fo 37.
1466, 23 Oct., ill and unable to attend the bp's visitation, Reg. Carpenter, i, 442.
[1467], in a letter to the abbot of Abingdon concerning the problems caused by William Walweyn, q.v., he described himself as old and infirm, Reg. A.6(i), fo 45.

Some of his *acta* are recorded in Reg. A.6(i), fos 1–59 by his chaplains, Thomas Streynsham, Nicholas Hambury, William Dene, and William Wenlok, q.v.

MUTTELOWE
see Motlowe

William MYLDENHAM
occ. 1472/3

1472/3, apparently one of the obedientiaries who failed to pay his annual contribution to the pittancer for the 'O' fund; he was pardoned the 10s. *ex elemosina* of the prior, *causa paupertatis*, WCM C.338.

MYLDENHAM
see also Mildenham

MYSSARD
see Musard

Richard MYSTON [Miston, Mynstone, Mystone
occ. 1456 d. 1500/1

1456, 27 Mar., ord acol., chapel of bp's palace, Worcester, Reg. Carpenter, i, 541.
1457, 16 Apr., ord acol., chapel of bp's palace, Worcester, *ib.*, i, 543.
1458, 23 Sept., ord dcn, Worcester cathedral, *ib.*, i, 547.
1460, 7 June, ord pr., Hereford cathedral, *Reg. Stanbury* (Hereford), 146.
1459/60, celebrated his first mass, and the prior sent *exennia*, WCM C.400.

1475, 8 Jan., 23 Dec; 1476, 8 June, 1476/7; 1478/80; 1481/2; 1488/9, precentor, Reg. Carpenter, ii, 135, 205; *ib.*, ii, 207, WCM C.383; C.384, C.98; C.100; C.387.
1492, 23/24 June, subprior, Reg. Morton, 91 and Reg. A.6(i), fo 107^{v}.
1498, 25 Oct.; 1499, 21 July, infirmarer, *Reg. abp Morton*, ii, no 458; Reg. A.6(ii), fo 1^{v} and Reg. S. Gigli, 343.

1467/8, one of three monks rewarded for their singing by the master of the Lady chapel, WCM C.281. See also William Dene, Thomas Streynsham.
1475, 8 Jan., present in the prior's chamber at the examination by the bp's chancellor of four who sought adm. to the priory, Reg. Carpenter ii, 135.
1475, 23 Dec., as precentor, presented the monk candidates for ordination in the carnary chapel next to the cathedral, *ib.*, ii, 205.
1476, 8 June, presented the ordination candidates as above, *ib.*, ii, 207.
1477, 5 Apr., again presented the ordination candidates, Reg. Alcock, 245.
1478, acted as one of the witnesses when Robert Alvechurch, q.v., took his oath of office, Reg. A.6(ii), 81.
1479, 18 Dec., presented the ordination candidates in the carnary chapel, Reg. Alcock, 260.
1492, 23/24 June, one of the seven nominees for the priorate, Reg. Morton, 90–92 and Reg. A.6(i), fo 107^{v}.
1498, 25 Oct., 5th in order on the visitation certificate, *Reg. abp Morton*, ii, no 458.
1499, 21 July, one of the seven nominees for the priorate, Reg. A.6(ii), fo 1^{v} and Reg. S. Gigli, 343; they were presented to bp Fox (Durham), acting for Gigli, at Southwark on 2 Sept., Reg. A.6(ii), fo 1^{v}.
1500/1, d., and the almoner gave 20s. to the Dominicans to say masses for him, WCM C.210.

His mother, Johanna Myston, was a tenant of the priory living at Hallow in 1491/2, WCM C.103.

Roger NECKHAM, D.Th [Nechkam, Neckam, Neckeham, Nekham *alias* Cratford
occ. 1504 occ. 1536

1504, 6 Apr., ord acol., carnary chapel by Worcester cathedral, Reg. S. Gigli, 287.
1504, 21 Sept., ord subdcn, carnary chapel, *ib.*, 289.
1504, 21 Dec., ord dcn, hospital of St Wulstan, Worcester, *ib.*, 291.
1506/7, ?celebrated his first mass; recd a 2s. pittance from the almoner, WCM C.212.

1518, 27 Sept., precentor, Reg. A.6(ii), fo 113.
1521, 18 Feb., 22 July, subprior, *Jnl More*, 127, Reg. abp Warham, ii, fo 293^{v}.
1522, Sept/1523 Feb., sacrist, *Jnl More*, 3, 7; and on 30 Nov., 1522, WCM B.1311.
1523, 3 June, subprior, Reg. A.6(ii), fo 138^{v}.
1531/2, infirmarer, WCM C.414c.
1535, removed from the office of subprior by the prior, presumably before the visitation of the royal commissioners, *L and P Henry VIII*, ix, no 52.2; and see John Lawerne II.

[before 1504] student at Oxford; see below.
1511, student at Oxford, where, on 21 June, he supplicated to oppose for B.Th., having

studied for ten yrs in logic, philosophy and theology, *Reg. Univ. Oxon*, i, 78.
1515, 7 June, adm. B.Th.
1519, 28 Feb., D.Th; see *BRUO, 1501–1540*, with refs.
1519, Feb., recd a 'reward' of 42s. from the prior 'to be Doctor of Divinite', *Jnl More*, 79.
1518, 27 Sept., one of the seven nominees for the priorate, Reg. A.6(ii), fo 113; they were presented to bp Fox (Winchester), acting for bp Gigli, prob. at Southwark, and he named William More, q.v., *ib.*
1521, 18 Feb., with Robert Alvechurch, q.v., apptd to act as *scrutatores*, with oversight of all tenements pertaining to the obedientiary offices and the responsibility of checking and itemizing all the plate, bedding and books etc, in the house in order to produce an inventory to be read in chapter annually on the first Mon. in Lent, *Jnl More*, 127.
1521, 22 July, second in order on the visitation certificate, Reg. abp Warham ii, fo 293^{v}.
1522, Sept/1523, Feb., with a secular clerk carried out *sed. vac.* visitations of religious houses in the diocese, *Jnl More*, 3, 7.
1523, 3 June, acted for the prior [William More I, q.v.], who was *in remotis*, concerning a proposed visitation by the bp, Reg. A.6(ii), fo 138^{v}.
1528, 30 Sept., apptd warden or perpetual chaplain of the carnary chapel [on the north side of the cathedral]; this position included the responsibility for a [public] library which was housed there and the obligation to lecture on the New Testament every wk, Reg. Ghinucci 9(i), 82. See Greatrex, 'Benedictine Monk Scholars', 223.
1531/2, 3rd in order on the clerical subsidy list and pd 15s. as infirmarer and 3s. 4d. commons. Reg. A.12, fo 135.
1533, 1 Jan., gave the prior a gift of two capons, *Jnl More*, 361.
1533/4, *custos* of the carnary, recd from the sacrist [who was patron of the carnary] £11 and a *toga*, WCM C.415.
1534, 21 Feb., obtained a licence from the bp *ad proponend' et publice predicand' verbum Dei*, Reg. S. Gigli, 81; a second licence was issued on 11 Mar., *ib.*, 81. These prescribe sermons in both Latin and English to the clergy and people in churches and other places in the city and diocese. Another copy of the earlier licence is in Reg. Ghinucci 9(i), 145; there must have been confusion in the Italian bps' chancery!
1534, 17 Aug., subscribed to the Act of Supremacy, *DK 7th Report*, Appndx 2, 305.
[Note: 1535, 29–31 July, were the dates of the visitation by the royal commissioners.]
1535, 14 Oct., wrote to Cromwell to refute attacks vs his name reported to Cromwell by the cellarer [Thomas Sudbury, q.v.], and stating that the latter was negligent and partial to his friends, *L and P Henry VIII*, ix, no 609. On the same day he wrote to Sir Francis Brian, asking to be recommended to 'Mr Secretary' and referring to the 'litigious' cellarer who was clinging to his office. He spoke as though he had been given charge of the priory, *ib.*, no 610; see below. Brian sent the letter to Cromwell and put in a favourable comment, *ib.*, no 639.
1535, 21 Oct., in a letter to Cromwell Lady Margery Sandys called the prior [William More, q.v.] a true monk and named Neckham as his accuser, *ib.*, no 656. It is clear that Neckham was now officially in control as Thomas Sudbury q.v., wrote to Cromwell on this same day to complain of the new regime, *ib.*, no 654.
1535, 3 Nov., wrote to Cromwell to affirm that he and his brethren were keeping the injunctions left by the royal visitors for 'the king's monastery', *ib.*, no 755.
1535, 11 Nov., wrote to Cromwell concerning the petition of Hugh Bromsgrove, q.v., to be allowed to rec. a benefice, *ib.*, no 807.
1535, 20 Dec., described as *presidens sive provisor* of the priory in the absence of the prior by the authority of Thomas Cromwell, visitor general of the king, Reg. A.6(ii), fo 188.
1536, 19 Jan., in another letter to Cromwell he ref. to various domestic affairs including the troublesome cellarer, *L and P Henry VIII*, x, no 132. On 19 Feb., he reported the return of the prior to clear up his affairs. Neckham also mentioned his difficulties in alleviating the fears of the priory tenants to whom he was proclaiming the king's virtues and need of their support. He added that he intended in future 'to leave Martha's part, and to follow Mary's', *ib.*, no 311.
1536, 13 Mar., 2nd in order at the 'el.' of Henry Holbech as prior, and with John Lawerne II, q.v., participated as *compromissorii* along with two seculars, Reg. A.6(iii), fo 1.
[1542, 24 Jan., canon of the 6th prebend in the new foundation, *Fasti, 1541–1857*, vii, 125.]

Thomas NETHERTON [Nedurton
occ. 1477/8

1477/8, 5 Apr., ord acol., Worcester cathedral, Reg. Alcock, 245.
1478, 16 May, ord subdcn, carnary chapel by Worcester cathedral, *ib.*, 251.
1478, 19 Sept., ord dcn, carnary chapel, *ib.*, 252.

John NEWENHAM [Newham, Newnam, Newneham, Newnhame
occ. 1525/6 occ. 1540

1527, 19 Sept., ord subdcn, Gloucester abbey, Reg. Ghinucci (7ii), 167.
1532, 16 Mar., ord dcn, carnary chapel by Worcester cathedral, *ib.*, 172.
1531/2, celebrated his first mass and recd pittances from the almoner, cellarer, kitchener and pittancer, 2s. in each case, WCM C.414c.

1525/6, 38th in order on the clerical subsidy list and pd 2s. commons, Reg. A.12, fo 125.
1531/2, 38th on the second subsidy list and pd 2s., *ib.*, fo 135v.
1534, 17 Aug., subscribed to the Act of Supremacy, *DK 7th Report*, Appndx 2, 305.
1535, signed the petition vs the reinstatement of William Fordham, q.v., as cellarer, *L and P Henry VIII*, ix, no 653.
1536, 13 Mar., 27th in order at the 'el.' of Henry Holbech, q.v., as prior, Reg. A.6(iii), fo 1.
1540, 18 Jan., assigned £6 p.a., *L and P Henry VIII*, xv, no 81.

Thomas NEWENHAM [Newen', Newman
occ. 1477/8 d. [1488/9]

1477, 5 Apr., ord acol., Worcester cathedral, Reg. Alcock, 245.
1478, 16 May, ord subdcn, carnary chapel by Worcester cathedral, *ib.*, 251.
1478, 19 Sept., ord dcn, carnary chapel, *ib.*, 252.
1478, 19 Dec., ord pr., Cirencester abbey, *ib.*, 253, in the Trinity chapel; he was presented by John Malverne II, q.v.
1478/9, celebrated his first mass; the almoner and precentor both gave 2s. 6d., WCM C.204, 384.
[1488/9], d., and the almoner recd 20s for his corrody for half a yr, WCM C.488.

I John de NEWENTONE
occ. 1225 d. 1225

1225, d. *Ann. Wigorn.*, 418.

II John de NEWENTON [Neuwentone, Newentone, Newynton
occ. 1313 d. 1340

1313, 19 July, one of two whose prof. the prior was comm. by the bp to rec., *Liber Albus*, no 593 (mistakenly recorded as adm.); *Reg. Reynolds*, 68.
1314, [2 Mar.,], ord subdcn, Worcester cathedral, *Reg. Sed. Vac.*, 159.
1317, 15 Sept., dcn, obtained *lit. dim.*, to pr.'s orders, Reg. Maidstone, 106.
1317, 20 Oct., 39th in order at the el. of a prior, Liber Albus, fo 83v.
1327, Jan/Sept., one of many monks who visited King's Norton, WCM C.693b.
1337, 21 July, witness in the prior's chapel at the presentation of an accused, Reg. Hemenhale, 13.
1339/40, recd 8d. from the pittancer for *minutiones*, WCM C.298.
[1340], witness to a deed, WCM B.1638.
1340, 9 Apr., d., WCM C.298.

William de NEWENTON
occ. 1350

1350, 15 May, ord acol., by a Franciscan suffragan bp in the [Franciscan] convent, Worcester, Reg. Thoresby, 30.

See also Newyntone.

Thomas NEWES
occ. 1505/6

1505/6, hostiller, WCM C.427.

Thomas NEWMAN
see Newenham

I John de NEWPORT [Eport, Neuport
occ. [1369] d. 1374

[1369], 1 Oct., one of seven whose prof. the precentor was comm. to rec., Reg. Lynn, 89.
1370, 13 Apr., ord acol. [Worcester cathedral], *ib.*, 50.
1370, 21 Dec., ord subdcn, Hartlebury, *ib.*, 53.
1372, 18 Sept., ord pr. [Worcester cathedral], *ib.*, 60.
1373, 4 Dec., 25th in order at the el. of a bp, *Reg. Sed. Vac.*, 290.
1374, Aug., d., and the almoner recd nothing for his corrody because half of it was assigned to the clerks of the chapel and the other half to the friars minor and friars preachers, WCM C.173. The precentor bought parchment for the briefs, WCM C.361.

II John NEWPORT [Eport
occ. 1448 occ. 1470/1

1448, 14 Sept., one of six whose prof. the prior was comm. to rec., Reg. Carpenter, i, 132.
1449, 12 Apr., ord acol., carnary chapel by Worcester cathedral. *ib.*, i, 524.
1452, 8 Apr., ord subdcn, carnary chapel, *ib.*, i, 532.
1453, 31 Mar., ord dcn, carnary chapel, *ib.*, i, 535.
1465/6, *tumbarius*, WCM C.666.
1470/1, subcellarer, WCM C.587.
1464/5, one of several monks who were owed money by the cellarer and was repaid, WCM C.95.
1465/6, visited Newnham, WCM C.666.
1470/1, visited Grimley, WCM C.587.

John NEWTON [Newtone, Newtowne
occ. 1460 d. 1498/9

1460, 20 Dec., ord acol., Worcester cathedral, Reg. Carpenter, i, 554.
1464, 31 Mar., ord [acol. and] subdcn, carnary chapel by Worcester cathedral, *ib.*, 560; the second ord acol. is no doubt a scribal error.
1465, 21 Dec., ord dcn, bp's chapel, Alvechurch, *ib.*, 564.
1468, 17 Dec., ord pr., St Nicholas' church, Worcester, *ib.*, 573.
1468/9, celebrated his first mass and recd pittances of 2s. 3d. from both the almoner and the kitchener, WCM C.202, C.154.
1478/80, subcellarer, WCM C.741, C.742.

1481/3, precentor, WCM C.385, Hamilton, *Comp. Rolls*, 47–49 (C.386).
1483/4; 1484/6; 1486/7, pittancer, Hamilton, *Comp. Rolls*, 36–40 (WCM C.343); WCM C.745, C.746; C.344, E.76.
1489/90, almoner, WCM C.208.

1459/60, already one of the cellarer's creditors, but the amount was only 22d., WCM C.491.
1478/80, pd visits to Overbury, WCM C.741, C.742.
1481, 22 Dec., 1482, 6 Apr., as precentor presented the monks who were to be ordained, at Hartlebury parish church and at the Dominican convent Worcester respectively, Reg. Alcock, 265, 269.
1484/6, pd visits to Overbury, WCM C.745, C.746.
1498/9, d., and the almoner distributed money to the Dominicans and Franciscans to say masses for his soul, WCM C.209. The precentor rewarded the servants in the kitchen and brewery *pro laboribus post mortem* of Newton and two other monks, WCM C.391.

Henry de NEWYNTON
occ. 1293/4 occ. 1299

1293/5, kitchener, Wilson, *Early Comp. Rolls*, 22, 30 (WCM C.51, C.52).
1293/5, the cellarer pd his debts in the above office, *ib.*, 22, 30.
1299, 7 Dec., apptd proctor to go to Rome to collect the books and other belongings of Thomas de Segesbarowe, q.v., *Ann. Wigorn.*, 543.

I NICHOLAS [Nicholaus
occ. c. 1104

Name occ. in the list of monks in *Durham Liber Vitae*, fo 22.

II NICHOLAS [Nicholaus, ?Aegelredus, Ethelred
occ. by c. 1080 d. 1124

c. 1116–1124, prior: apptd before 15 Aug., 1116; d. 24 June 1124, *Fasti*, ii, 102, *HRH*, 83.
n.d., prob. sent by bp Wulstan to Christ Church, Canterbury to be trained in the new monastic discipline introduced by Lanfranc, Darlington, *Vita Wulfstani*, 56–57. If Ethelred, q.v., was his English name and not another contemporary monk at (or possibly sent to) Canterbury, he served in the offices of precentor and subprior while there, Dunstan, *Memorials*, 163–164 (as Aegelredus, q.v.).
1123, as prior he exerted his influence and authority to enable the chapter to have free el. of a successor to bp Theulf; the dispute and its unsuccessful outcome are described in D. Bethell, 'English Black Monks and Episcopal Elections in the 1120s', *English Historical Review*, 84 (1969), 673–698, esp. 681–684, 694–698.

Eadmer, q.v. (under Canterbury), and the monastic historian, William of Malmesbury, were personal friends to whom he supplied information for their historical writings, Dunstan, *Memorials*, 422–424 and Brett, 'John of Worcester', 113. It was prob. during William's visit to prior Nicholas that the latter recounted many personal anecdotes about bp Wulstan which were incorporated into William's life, Darlington, *Vita Wulfstani*, 51, 52, 54, 56–57. A letter of advice to Eadmer at the time of the latter's el. to the see of St Andrews (1120/1) reveals that he was well versed in the complex historical background to the claims to primacy in Scotland by York; this is printed in *Anglia Sacra*, ii, 234, and see Brett, *ib.*

William of Malmesbury informs us of his noble English birth and of his parents' close relationship with bp Wulstan, who baptised him and described him as his special foster child, Darlington *Vita Wulfstani*, 56–57, William of Malmesbury, *Gest. Pont.*, 287. Dr Mason speculates that he may have been connected with the family of Earl Leofric of Mercia, or possibly, as Ethelred, a son of Harold Godwinson, *Wulfstan*, 219–221.

Dr Gransden describes Ethelred and Nicholas as two monks, the former having been a Canterbury monk before transferring to Worcester in the time of bp Wulstan, and the latter this prior, *Hist. Writing*, i, 129.

Dr Mason puts forward the suggestion that he may have been one of the monks responsible for the forgery of the charter *Altitonantis* recording the monastic foundation of Worcester in 964, but prob. dated close to 1092, *ib.*, 216–217.

See also McIntyre, 'Early 12th c. Worcester Cathedral Priory', 112.

Note: these two monks named Nicholas may be one and the same.

William NORMAN
occ. 1222/4

1222–1224, prior: prior of Malvern before his apptment to Worcester by the bp; the chapter objected and after a protracted dispute he resigned, 3 Oct., 1224, *Fasti*, ii, 103, summarizing *Ann. Wigorn.*, 415–417. This controversy followed upon the bp's deposition of the prior [Simon Pimme, q.v.] which the monks refused to accept. An agreement between bp and chapter was reached by which the monks were to elect seven suitable candidates from whom the bp was to make his choice, a compromise to which both parties adhered until the dissolution.

Nicholas de NORTON
occ. 1280 occ. 1317

1280, 24 Aug., had res. as sacrist by this date when Thomas de Hindelep', q.v., was apptd, *Reg. Giffard*, 123.

1280, 20 Sept., ?sacrist, *ib.*, 124; this is the date of an induction to a church of which the sacrist was patron, and the actual apptment may have preceded his res. above.
1281, sacrist, *Ann. Wigorn.*, 480.
1288, 10 Apr., 'absolved' from the office of sacrist and John de Dumbleton, q.v., was apptd, *Reg. Giffard*, 320.
1289, 9 Dec., reapptd sacrist, *ib.*, 366.
1290, 26 Feb., 8 Nov., sacrist, *ib.*, 368, 380.
1292, 5 July, sacrist, *Ann. Wigorn.*, 510.
1300, 24 Feb., 19/20 Aug., sacrist, *ib.*, 524, 528, 530.
1301, 20 Mar., during his visitation the abp deposed several obedientiaries and suspended him and several others, *Ann. Wigorn.*, 548–549.
1301, 5 and 20 Sept., two letters from the abp to the bp explain the reasons for his removal from office; these included 'dilapidation' [of buildings etc.], disobedience, *proprietas* and his claim to have the right to remain in office for life, which was against all regulations and monastic observance. The abp had heard reports that he had been reapptd sacrist by the bp and told the prior on 20 Sept., to order that, if this were true, he was to be removed immediately and Gilbert de Madley, q.v., reinstated, *Reg. abp Winchelsey*, 421, 750–753. On 6 Sept., before his rec. of the abp's letter, the bp had written to the prior and reapptd Norton sacrist, *Liber Albus*, no 6. See Graham, 'Visitation', 74, 75.
1301, [Sept/Nov.], the prior informed the abp that Norton had resigned voluntarily, *Liber Albus*, no 8.
1302, 15 Mar., chaplain to the prior, *Reg. Sed. Vac.*, 71.

1281, as sacrist, recd 60 marks from the legacy of bp Nicholas de Ely to be used for the rebuilding of the tower, *Ann. Wigorn.*, 480.
1290, 26 Feb., presented a chaplain to a parish church of which the sacrist was patron, *Reg. Giffard*, 368.
1290, 8 Nov., present, with the subprior Simon [de Wyre, q.v.] and another monk, in consultation with the bp during a visitation, when they were interrupted by the arrival in the chapter house of the prior [Philip Aubyn, q.v.] accompanied by a group of monks and others in a noisy protest, *Reg. Giffard*, 380.
1292, 5 July, placed new pictures [*tabulas*] on either side of the image of the Mother of God, *Ann. Wigorn.*, 510.
1300, 24 Feb., made another presentation to a parish church, *Reg. Giffard*, 524.
1300, 19/20 Aug., comm. by the bp, with the bp's chancellor, to visit the prior and chapter, and was himself with the prior given powers of correction *in spiritualibus*, *ib.*, 528, 530. However, on 31 Aug., the bp revoked the comm. to the prior and Norton 'on acct of certain information', *ib.*, 529.
1301, 5 Apr., following his visitation the abp wrote to the prior requiring a report of his administration as sacrist, *Liber Albus*, no 5.
1302, 15 Mar., comm. by the prior to recall all absent brethren for the impending episcopal el., *Reg. Sed. Vac.*, 71; at the el. on 25 Mar., he was named one of seven *compromissorii* [who chose John de St Germans, q.v.], *ib.*, 1.
1305, 14 Feb., with Gilbert de Madley, q.v., apptd proctor to attend parliament, *Liber Albus*, no 282. This yr he wrote a letter of recommendation to the prior of Great Malvern for a clerk wishing to be adm. there, *ib.*, no 338.
1307, 2 Apr., at the Earl of Warwick's request the prince of Wales wrote to the prior asking that he be given a corrody in the monastery as a reward for his good service, *ib.*, no 382. On 8 June the prince thanked the prior for his favourable reply but asked for a letter of confirmation under the convent seal, *ib.*, no 384. The letter was duly sent on 20 June and specified that the corrody included the provision of two servants and two horses, *ib.*, no 385. This corrody was prob. in the tailor's quarters [*sarteria*] to which a mason was later assigned. Liber Albus, fo 76.
1317, 20 Oct., ill in the infirmary and absent from the el. of a prior, Liber Albus, fo 83.
1324, 15 July, another ref. to a corrody in 'the painted chamber' which Norton had formerly occupied, *Liber Albus*, no 1039.

H. R. Luard suggests that, while sacrist, he may have been one of the compilers of the Annales de Wigornia, *Ann. Wigorn.*, xlii.

Thomas NORTON
occ. 1481 d. 1498/9

1481, 16 June, ord acol., Whitbourne, *Reg. Milling* (Hereford), 163.
1481, 22 Sept., ord subdcn, Whitbourne, *ib.*, 164.
1481, 22 Dec., ord dcn, Hartlebury, Reg. Alcock, 265.
1486/7, recd from the almoner 15d. *pro custod' de le Almery*, WCM C.207.
1498/9, d., and the almoner distributed money to the Dominicans and Franciscans to say masses for his soul, WCM C.209.

William NORTON
occ. 1456 occ. 1466/7

1456, 27 Mar., ord acol., chapel of bp's palace, Worcester, Reg. Carpenter, i, 541.
1457, 16 Apr., ord subdcn, bp's palace, Worcester, *ib.*, i, 543.
1458, 23 Sept., ord dcn, Worcester cathedral, *ib.*, i, 547.
1461, 30 May, ord pr., St Oswald's church, outside the walls, Worcester, *ib.*, i, 555.
1466/7, the cellarer purchased *harness'* for him, WCM C.97.

OBIRLEY
see Wolverley

OBYN
see Aubyn

OLISTON
see Robert de Clifton

OLLENTRA
see Ellentra

OLYWELL
see Holywell

John de OMBERSLEYE [Ombresley, Ombrisley, Ombursley
occ. 1443 occ. 1498

1443, 21 Sept., ord acol., carnary chapel by Worcester cathedral, Reg. Bourgchier, 206.
1447, 8 Apr., ord subdcn, Worcester cathedral, Reg. Carpenter, i, 512.
1448, 17 Feb., ord dcn, bp's chapel, Alvechurch, *ib.*, 517.
1450, 4 Apr., ord pr., bp's chapel, Hartlebury, *ib.*, 526; the cellarer [Isaac Ledbury. q.v.] escorted him to the ordination, WCM C.92.
1449/50, celebrated his first mass; the precentor gave 2s. 4d. as pittance, and the cellarer also contributed, but see below, WCM C.92.
1449/50, one of many monks on the cellarer's list of creditors, WCM C.92.
1467/8, handed over a donation from Hugh Lemster, q.v., to the master of the Lady chapel, WCM C.281.
1492, 23/4 June, one of the seven nominees for the priorate, Reg. Morton, 91 and Reg. A.6(i), fo 107v.
1498, 25 Oct., 4th in order on the visitation certificate, *Reg. abp Morton*, ii, no 458.

ONKERDOM
see Ancredam, Ankerdam, Ankerdom

OPTON
see Uptone

ORDGARUS
occ. c. 1104

Name occ. in the list of monks in *Durham Liber Vitae*, fo 22.

I ORDRICUS
occ. c. 1104

Name occ. in the list of monks in *Durham Liber Vitae*, fo 22.

II ORDRICUS
occ. c. 1104

Name occ. in the list of monks in *Durham Liber Vitae*, fo 22.

I OSBERT
occ. 1145/6

1145–1146, prior, *Fasti*, ii, 102, *HRH*, 83; see David, Ralph de Bedeford.

II OSBERT
occ. 1221 d. 1222

1221, apptd sacrist by the bp, *Ann. Wigorn.*, 414.
1222, d., *ib.*, 415.

OSWALDUS
occ. c. 1104

Name occ. in the list of monks in *Durham Liber Vitae*, fo 22.

Ralph OSWALD
occ. 1521 d. 1523/4

1521, 22 July, 34th in order on the visitation certificate, Reg. abp Warham, ii, fo 293v.
1523/4, d., reported by the almoner, WCM C.413.

Thomas OSWALD
occ. 1534/6

1536, 13 Mar., prof. but not pr., Reg. A.6(iii), fo 1.
1534, 17 Aug., last on the list of those who subscribed to the Act of Supremacy, *DK 7th Report*, Appndx 2, 305.
1536, 13 Mar., 30th in order at the 'el.' of Henry Holbech, q.v., as prior, Reg. A.6(iii), fo 1.

OSYNTRE
see Hosyntre

Robert OURTON
see Morton

OUSTON
see Owston

William OVERBURY
occ. 1522 occ. 1527

1522, 20 Dec., ord acol., carnary chapel by Worcester cathedral, Reg. A.6(ii), fo 134.
1527, 15 June, ord pr., Gloucester abbey, Reg. Ghinucci 7(ii), 164.
1527, Feb., recd a reward of 4s. 6d. from the prior, *Jnl More*, 241.
1527, 6 Nov., obtained licence from the cardinal [Wolsey, who had conducted a visitation in 1525] to 'migrate' to Winchcombe abbey 'to serve the most High more freely and quietly', Reg. A.6(ii), fo 158.

OVIRLEY
see Wolverley

William OWSTON [Ouston, Owstone, Eustone
occ. 1375 occ. 1407

1375, 16 June, ord subdcn, Worcester cathedral, *Reg. Sed. Vac.*, 343.
1377, 23 May, ord pr., Colwich, *Reg. Stretton* (1905) (Coventry/Lichfield), p. 326.

1378/80, chaplain to the prior, Liber Albus, fos 270, 275v, 276, 305v; in the heading on fo 270 his name is rubricated.
1386/7; 1388/9 cellarer, prob. only from Feb., to Sept., 1387 (see William Power), WCM C.72, C.73, C.555, C.808; also only part yr 1388/9 (see Thomas Dene), WCM C.763.
1392, Mar./1393, 1394/5, master of the Lady chapel, WCM C.250–252.
1394/5, bursar, with J[ohn] H[atfeld], q.v., WCM C.762.
1395/6, kitchener, WCM C.126.
1401, Apr./Sept., pittancer, WCM C.319.
1401, Dec./1403, kitchener, WCM C.129, C.130.

1379, 31 July, apptd by the prior as his attorney to render the acct for him of the royal subsidy for which the prior was collector in the adcnry of Worcester, Liber Albus, fo 301.
1380, 12 Feb., one of three monk proctors apptd by the prior and chapter in a tithe dispute; see John de Malverne I and William Power, Liber Albus, fo 311v; on 12 June, the same three, with two secular clerks, recd a comm. as general proctors [?in the same case], Liber Albus, fo 307.
1380, 15 Dec., present as witness at the installation of the adcn of Gloucester by the prior, *ib.*, fo 309v.
1384, 20 Nov., one of three proctors, the others being seculars [*iurisperiti*], apptd to deal with visitation procedures related to the documents concerning churches, portions and pensions etc. for the abp's inspection, Liber Albus, fo 287.
1385/6, visited London, on business for the house, WCM C.71.
1386/7, visited Hallow, WCM C.808.
1387, ill in the infirmary and charged his own office [cellarer] 2s. for his expenses, WCM C.73.
1388/9, visited Sedgeberrow, WCM C.763.
1392, 3 Mar., on succeeding John de Stratford, q.v., as master of the Lady chapel he recd the inventory of vestments and plate, WCM B.1870; this has been printed in *Hist. Mss Comm. 14th Report*, Appndx, 8 (1895), 198–199 where Owston has been mistakenly rendered as Dutton.
1392, Mar./Sept., pd visits to Bromsgrove, Kidderminster and Nottingham, WCM C.75.
1393, 12 Aug., recd another apptment from the prior and chapter as general proctor, Liber Albus, fo 368.
1394/5, visited Sedgeberrow, WCM C.762.
1395, 28 Mar., comm. by the prior, *sed. vac.*, with a secular clerk, to rec. canonical obedience from the clergy in the adcnries of Worcester and Gloucester, and also to carry out visitations in several specified deaneries *Reg. Sed. Vac.*, 357.
1395, 15/16 Sept., apptd proctor in the el. negotiations and sent with John Cleve, q.v., to the bp at Windsor to present the seven nominees for the priorate to the bp, Liber Albus, fo 380.
1396, 26 Sept., sent as proctor, with William Power, q.v., to take possession of the appropriated church of Himbleton on the resignation of the vicar, Liber Albus, fo 384.
1401, 24 June, 24th in order at the el. of a bp, and on 28 June apptd proctor, with John Cleve, q.v., to go to London to inform Richard Clifford of his el., *Reg. Sed. Vac.*, 373, 374.
1404/5, recd 3s. 4d. from the chamberlain for his *frocc'*, WCM C.50.
1407, 25 Mar., recd his *portio* from the pittancer, WCM C.320.

PARLOR
see Hosyntre

PATRICIUS
occ. before 1174

Name occ. in the list of monks in *Durham Liber Vitae*, fo 22.

Dr Mason identifies him with Gilla Patraic who was bp of Dublin 1074–1084, *Wulfstan*, 250; see also A. Gwyn ed. and transl., *The writings of Bishop Patrick 1074–1084* (1955), 56–124. See also Sharpe, *Latin Writers*.

Robert PAYN
occ. 1475

1475, 7/8 Jan., one of four who were presented to the bp by two of the monks and the following day were examined by the bp's chancellor in the prior's chamber, in the presence of the prior, precentor and others; he was one of three accepted for the yr of probation, Reg. Carpenter, ii, 135.

Note: he may be identical with either Robert Sudbury or Robert Lindsey, q.v.

PEARS
see William More I

John PECOCK
see John Lawerne II

PEDEWARDYN
see Bedwardine

PERES
see William More I

Edmund PERSHORE [Persshore
?occ. 1426 occ. 1452/3

1426, 1 Dec., ord acol., Worcester cathedral, Reg. Polton, 207.
1427, 15 Mar., ord dcn, Worcester cathedral, *ib.*, 209.
Note: none of the monks ordained on these two dates are identified by their houses.

1452/3, recd *dona* of 6s. 8d. from the prior in the same entry as gifts to Isaac Ledbury and John Kyderminstre, q.v., WCM C.399a.

John de PERSORE
occ. 1272

1272, 21 Dec., cellarer, *Reg. Giffard*, 51.

1272, 21 Dec., one of the seven nominees for the priorate, *Reg. Giffard*, 51.

Roger de PERSOR'
occ. 1262/3 occ. ?1270

1262/3, *custos pitancie*, WCM E.4(2).

1262/3, visited Hardwick, WCM E.4(2).
?1270, prob. visited Hardwick, WCM E.4(3).

I PETER
occ. 1196 d. 1204

1196–1203, prior: succ. 1196, after 20 Nov; deposed 24 Dec. 1203, *Fasti*, ii, 103, *HRH*, 84.

1204, d., *ib.*

[II PETER
occ. 1216

1216, became abbot of Tewkesbury; however, although sometimes described as Peter de Worcester, there is no evidence that he was ever a monk of Worcester; see *HRH*, 73.]

III PETER
occ. 1231

1231, cellarer, *Ann. Wigorn.*, 423.

IV PETER
occ. 1434/5

1434/5, assisted John Hanley, q.v., *circa mundacionem* of the quarry at Ombersley and in cutting stone there, their expenses being charged to the cellarer, WCM C.87.

William de PEYTO
occ. 1321 occ. 1328/9

1321, 9 Dec., one of three whose prof. the prior was comm. to rec., Liber Albus, fo 103; this is not adm. as in *Liber Albus*, no 925.
1321, 19 Dec., ord subdcn, Kidderminster, *Reg. Cobham*, 113.
1322, 18 Dec., ord dcn, Ombersley, *ib.*, 143.
1323, 17 Dec., ord pr., Cropthorne, *ib.*, 167.

1326, Jan/Sept., subcellarer, first yr, Hamilton, *Comp. Rolls*, 69–74 (WCM C.431).
1326/9, subcellarer, WCM C.544, C.546a, C.546; in 1328/9 William de Tony, q.v., was also subcellarer.

1326/7, pd visits to Bromsgrove and Tibberton, WCM C.544, C.796.
1327/8, visited Bromsgrove, Hallow, King's Norton (1327) and Tibberton, WCM C.546a, C.592, C.693b, C.797.
1328/9, visited Bromsgrove, Henwick and Tibberton, WCM C.546, C.940, C.798.

PHILIP
see Aubyn, Pirebroke

PHILIPPUS
occ. c. 1104

Name occ. in the list of monks in *Durham Liber Vitae*, fo 22.

PHYLKES
see Fylkes

Simon PIMME
occ. 1216 d. 1223

1216–1222, prior: el. Oct. 1216; the bp tried to depose him 1220; suspended by the pope before 22 Mar. 1222 and deposed by the bp; d. in Rome, while trying to vindicate himself, *Fasti*, ii, 103, and see below.

1216, before his el., chamberlain, *Ann. Wigorn.*, 407.
1219, the bp tried to depose the prior on the strength of a disgruntled minority, *Ann. Wigorn.*, 411.
1221, despite a papal indult that the prior could not be dismissed without being brought before papal judges delegate, the bp remained unmoved and the prior left for Rome on 2 Nov., taking letters of credit for 200m. and 40m. for his expenses. Suspended by the pope 'on false charges' he was deposed by the bp on his return. The abp absolved him but he renewed his appeal vs the bp, *Ann. Wigorn.*, 414–415; and see William Norman.
1222, returned to Rome where he d. in 1223, *ib.*, 415.

Philip de PIREBROKE [Pirybrook, Pyrebrok, Pyribroke
occ. 1320 occ. 1331

1320, 20 Feb., one of two whose prof. the pr. was comm. to rec., *Reg. Cobham*, 22; this is entered in the Liber Albus under 23 Feb., fo 94v. On 9 Mar., the prior did so, *ib.* In *Liber Albus*, nos 869 and 870, this is given as adm.
1320, 24 May, ord subdcn, Worcester cathedral, *Reg. Cobham*, 84.

1331, one of the *tumbarii*, Reg. A.22, fo 18.

[1324], prob. the monk Philip, who was assaulted while delivering a mandate to a church in the deanery of Campden, *Reg. Cobham*, 181.

1331, with Ralph de Scalleby, q.v., recd the gift of a gold and sapphire ring at St Wulstan's shrine, Reg. A22, fo 18.

John de PIRIA [Pirie
occ. 1287 occ. 1317

1287, 2 Jan., one of the seven nominees for the priorate, *Reg. Giffard*, 304, 325.
1317, 20 Oct., absent from the el. of a prior because he was ill in the infirmary, Liber Albus, fo 83.

Marmaduke de PIRIE [Pyrye
occ. 1297 occ. 1355/6

1297, 18 Oct., the youngest of four monks who made their prof. before the prior, *Ann. Wigorn.*, 534.
1328, before 5 Aug., one of the *tumbarii*, Reg. Orleton, no 549.
1317, 20 Oct., 18th in order at the el. of a prior, Liber Albus, fo 83v.
1326, delivered one quarter of wheat [*frumenti*] to the subcellarer from the cellarer, Hamilton, *Comp. Rolls*, 70 (WCM C.431).
1352, 23 Jan., granted a papal licence to choose his own confessor who was authorized to give plenary remission at d., *CPL*, iii (1342–1362), 452.
1355/6, d., and the money for his corrody was spent *in expensis domus*, WCM C.172.

In Jan 1303 a *liberatio* was sold for £50 to Adam de Pirie, citizen and bailiff of Worcester, and Gunnilda his wife, *Ann. Wigorn.*, 553, 554.

PIRL
see Godricus

POIWYKE
see Powik

Richard POLE
occ. 1442 d. 1451/2

1442, 22 Dec., ord acol., and subdcn, bp's chapel, Alvechurch, Reg. Bourgchier, 201, 202.
1446, 11 June, ord pr., bp's chapel, Hartlebury, Reg. Carpenter, i, 508.
1445/6, celebrated his first mass and recd 2s. 3d. from the pittancer, WCM C.333.
1448/9, and 1449/50, one of many monks on the cellarer's list of creditors, WCM C.91, C.92.
1451/2, d., and the chamberlain sold his *harnesia*, WCM C.41.

William POWER [Pouwer
occ. 1361 d. 1398

1361, 9 Mar., one of two *clerici* presented by Nicholas de Clanefeld, q.v., to the bp at Alvechurch and adm. as a monk, Reg. Bryan i, 136.
1362, 17 Dec., ord subdcn, bp's chapel, Hartlebury, Reg. Barnet, 38.
1363, 23 Sept., ord dcn, Lydney, *Reg. Lewis Charlton* (Hereford), 87.

1366, chaplain [and secretary] to the prior; *hic incipit—registr'*, Liber Albus, fo 231.
1368/70, subcellarer, WCM C.710, C.66.
1370/1, cellarer, first yr, WCM C.66; 1371/2, WCM C.67, and on C.596 Richard Wenlok and he are both described as cellarers and treasurers this yr; 1372/3, WCM C.68.
1374/5, precentor, *habens custodiam*, WCM C.361.
1376/7; 1378, 25 Apr.; 1379; 1380, 12 June; 1381/3; 1384, 11 Jan.; 1384/Feb. 1387, cellarer, WCM C.69, C.806; Liber Albus, fo 270; WCM C.597; Liber Albus, fo 307; WCM C.598, C.70; C.525; C.599, C.71, C.72; and see William Owston.
1388, 21 Aug., third prior, Liber Albus, fo 334.
1389, May/Sept., 1389/90; 1391/1392 Mar., chamberlain, WCM C.16–18.
1392, Mar./Sept., and 1392/4; 1395/7; possibly until 18 Apr., 1398, cellarer, WCM C.76, C.76a, C.539; C.77, C.77a, C.479; WCM E.39 (and see Thomas Dene).
Note: see John de Cleve who is named as cellarer on 12 Mar., and 19 Sept 1395.

1368/9, pd a visit to Overbury, WCM C.710.
1369/70, visited Harvington (between Sept/Nov., 1369), and Sedgeberrow, WCM C.609, C.785.
1370, 3 Apr., 13th in order at the el. of a prior and one of the seven nominees for the priorate, Liber Albus, fo 246, 246v.
1371/2, visited Hallow and Tibberton, WCM C.596, C.806.
1373, 1 Dec., comm. by the prior, with a secular clerk, to rec. the canonical obedience of all the clergy in the adcnry or Gloucester, *sed. vac.*, and also to carry out visitations in a number of specified deaneries and religious houses, *Reg. Sed. Vac.*, 268. He was legitimately absent from the meeting of the chapter on 4 Dec., but present for the el. [of a bp] on 7 Dec., [and was 12th in order], *ib.*, 290.
1374, 19 Jan., sent to the abp with a letter from the prior and chapter asking him to request the king to give his assent to the el., *ib.*, 293.
1374, 22 Apr., and 1375, 6 Apr., acted as deputy or commissary of the prior, *sed. vac.*, in a case of the deprivation of a vicar and of probate of a will, *ib.*, 303, 329.
1376, between Sept./Nov., went to London for ten days on convent business and his expenses were 48s. 10d., WCM C.69.
1377/9, His part in the building programme began in Aug. 1377 when he supervised the completion of the new dormitory, begun by the sacrist, John Lyndeseye, q.v., and of the treasury and library; the following year he completed the water gate 'over the Severn'; and in 1379 he had a shaving room constructed in the infirmary, Reg. A.12, fo 77v.

1378, 25 Apr., apptd, with John de Malverne I, q.v., and a secular clerk as proctor for the prior and chapter in matters concerning the bp's visitation, Liber Albus, fo 270.
1379, visited Hallow, WCM C.597.
1380, 11 Feb., apptd, with John de Malverne I and William Owston, q.v., as proctors for the convent in a dispute over tithes, Liber Albus, fo 311[v], and again on 12 June, with the same two monks and two secular clerks, as general proctors, *ib.*, fo 307.
1381/2, went to London to attend convocation and also to Ludlow, WCM C.70; he also visited Hallow and Sedgeberrow, WCM C.598, C.760.
1386/7, pd a visit to Tibberton, WCM C.808.
1388, 21 Aug., 8th in order at the el. of a prior and one of the seven nominees for the priorate, Liber Albus, fos 334[v], 335.
[1389], apptd proctor by the prior and chapter to take possession of the church of Stoke [Prior] with a view to its appropriation, Liber Albus, fo 348 v.
1391/2, went, with John Hatfeld, q.v., to confer with the bp, WCM C.74; he also visited Sedgeberrow, WCM C.764.
1392/4, visited Henwick both years and Overbury in 1392/3, WCM C.636, C.635, C.752.
1394/5, visited Sedgeberrow, WCM C.764.
1395, 12 Mar., sent as proctor with John de Cleve to obtain from the king a licence to el. a bp, *Reg. Sed. Vac.*, 353; on 19 Mar., the two were reported absent on business. *ib.*, 354.
1395, 16 Sept., one of the seven nominees for the priorate, Liber Albus, fo 380.
1396, 26 Sept., apptd proctor, with William Owston, q.v., to take possession of Himbleton church with a view to its appropriation, Liber Albus, fo 384; on 21 July [1397] a papal instrument was addressed to him as proctor in this same affair, *ib.*, fo 385[v].
1397/8, ill in the infirmary, WCM C.246.
1398, d., prob. c. 18 Apr., WCM E.39; the chamberlain sold *diversis*; which belonged to the chamberlain's office, as he explained on the acct, and from which he recd 55s. 11d., WCM C.23.

John de POWIK [Poiwyke, Poywik, Poywyk
occ. 1339 occ. 1355

1339, 27 Mar., ord subdcn, Kempsey, *Reg. Bransford*, no 1004.
1340, 15 Apr., ord pr., Alvechurch, *ib.*, no 1010.
1353, before 3 July, third prior and before that *tumbarius*, Liber Albus fos 236, 237.
1353, 3 July, apptd sacrist, *ib.*, fo 236, and Reg. Bryan, i, 8.

The above apptment was one of the causes of a prolonged and bitter dispute between the bp [Reginald Bryan] and the prior [John de Evesham I, q.v.] and chapter, which is reported at great length in the Liber Albus, fos 236–245[v]. The 'Powik affair' comes to light on 15 Feb., 1354 when the subprior and chapter wrote to the bp in support of the prior's request for the removal of Powik from office as he was *non solum inhabilem sed inutilem* (fo 236). The arguments, frequently repeated in the exchange of letters and legal instruments which followed were in mutual contradiction: acc. to the bp Powik had discharged his responsibilities in offices previously held in a praiseworthy manner, and, what was incontrovertible, the bp had the right to appt the sacrist; acc. to the chapter he had made a disastrous choice, since Powick was guilty of disobedience, simony, misappropriation of goods in his charge, association with people of ill repute and incontinence. Moreover, the prior had attempted to restrain and discipline him, but to no avail; and his continuation in the office of sacrist was becoming a public scandal. The abp of Canterbury urged the bp to moderate his stance (fo 240[v]), and arbitrators were proposed to discuss terms which would be acceptable to both parties. But the case went before the Court of Canterbury and was, not surprisingly, added to the other grievances over the prior's status and pontifical privileges vis-a-vis the bp, about which the prior himself, q.v., went to the curia.

He was still in office on 11 Aug., 1355 when the bp issued a mandate for the discovery and capture of the armed gang who had forcibly entered the sacrist's dwelling within the cemetery [on the north side of the cathedral], had assaulted and dragged him off and had taken muniments, books, jewels and other goods (fo 245[v]).

Finally, on 27 Sept., the bp ordered the abbots of Gloucester and Tewkesbury to locate him and make sure that he was removed from office since his incontinence had been proved; Reg. Bryan, i, 29.

Nicholas de POWIK
occ. 1218/9

1218/9, d., *Ann. Wigorn.*, 410.

David de PRESTHEMEDE
occ. 1303

1303, 4 Feb., one of four who made their prof. before the prior in the Lady chapel, *Reg. Sed. Vac.*, 37.

I John de PRESTON [Prestone
occ. 1324/5 occ. 1338/9 and later

1324/5, subcellarer, WCM C.675, 796; and see John de Stratford I.
1328/9, July to Mar., kitchener, WCM C.108.
1338/9, *magister operum*, WCM C.58.
Note: there is a John de Prestone in the ordination lists in *Reg. Cobham*, (52, 61, 69) whose dates fit in very well with this monk, who

could have entered after receiving pr.'s orders in Dec., 1319.

1324/5, visited Leopard Grange and Tibberton, WCM C.675, 795.

1328/9, visited Tibberton, WCM C.798.

Note: since John de Preston II, q.v. was described as 'junior' in 1340 and even later, when lecturing at Worcester, this monk must have been still alive.

II John de PRESTON [Prestone de Somersete, or Preston junior

occ. 1335 occ. 1349

1335, 15 Apr., ord acol., bp's chapel, Hartlebury, Reg. Montacute, 83.

1335, 10 June, ord subdcn, Ombersley, *ib.*, 87.

1335, 23 Sept., ord dcn, Chaddesley [?Corbett], *ib.*, 92.

1336, 21 Sept., ord pr., bp's chapel, Hartlebury, *ib.*, 103.

1336/7, student at Oxford, with John de Evesham I and William de Birlingham, q.v. from Sept., to Aug., i.e., for 45 wks, and recd 16d. per wk from the cellarer, WCM C.57.

There is no evidence as to the length of his period of study at Oxford, but there were two monk scholars being supported by the cellarer in the yrs 1344/7. He must have been considered sufficiently trained when he was apptd to deliver a course of public lectures on the Sentences in the chapter house at Worcester beginning on 24 Nov., 13 [blank, *sic*], preceding which he made the usual formal declaration retracting in advance any unwitting lapse from doctrinal orthodoxy. When John Lawerne I, q.v., made a similar declaration before commencing his lectures on the Sentences he had already obtained his B.Th.; and it seems likely that John de Preston had recd or had supplicated for his first degree. The two declarations are to be found in Oxford Bod. Ms 692, fos 99ᵛ, 119, which is Lawerne's notebook. See also J. Greatrex, 'Benedictine Monk Scholars', 217, where the date is suggested as prob. soon after the el of John de Evesham as prior, i.e. the early 1340s.

1340, 21 Apr., apptd proctor, with Nicholas de Stanlake, q.v., to present the seven nominees for the priorate to the bp, *Reg. Bransford*, no 290, where he is called 'junior'.

1349, 15 Apr., apptd penitentiary in the diocese, with power to absolve even in reserved cases, *ib.*, no 998.

Name in

(1) Worcs. Ms F.11, Augustinus (14th c.), *procuravit* in 1348; some of the notes in the margins and at the end may be in his hand.

(2) Cambridge, Corpus Christi College Ms 24, Bradwardine (14th c.), also obtained by him in 1348.

III John PRESTON

occ. 1437 occ. 1464/5

1437, 1 Sept., ord acol., and subdcn, bp's chapel, Alvechurch, Reg. Bourgchier, 61.

1440, 20 Feb., ord dcn, Hereford cathedral, *Reg. Spofford* (Hereford), 333.

1441/2, celebrated his first mass, and the almoner gave 3s. 2d. as pittance and the pittancer a similar amount for bread and ale, WCM C.199, 484.

1459/60, master of the [Lady] chapel, WCM C.491.

1444/5, student at Oxford; the cellarer spent 12s. 4d. for the travelling expenses of Preston and John Broghton, q.v., returning from Oxford with their possessions, and 5s. for Preston going back to Oxford, with an additional 4s. 7d. for his *vestimenta*, WCM C.493.

1447/8, recd 6s. 8d. as a gift from the prior, prob. as pocket money for Oxford, WCM C.398.

1449/50, student, and owed 33s. 4d. and another 20s. for books which he had had to put in one of the university chests as pledge for a loan. The cellarer pd off these debts and also another 5s. to a chaplain of the countess of Warwick, WCM C.92. The debts incurred by him at Oxford were only pd off in 1453/4, but it is not clear that he was then still at Oxford; see below.

1448/9, one of many monks on the cellarer's list of creditors but only 12d. was at stake, WCM C.91.

1453, again on the cellarer's list of creditors, WCM C.93.

1453/4, he was also in financial difficulty for which the cellarer was held responsible, and so he gave 12s. 10d. to the cellarer out of his commons (i.e. money distributed as pittances). The cellarer pd a total of £20 4s. 8d. for the combined debts of Hugh Leyntwardine, Thomas Hosyntre, q.v., and Preston, all of whom had incurred debts as students and the former two had d., WCM C.94.

1464, 11 Jan., recd the sign of the cross *mor' peregrini ut dicitur*, Reg. Carpenter, i, 375.

1463/4 and 1464/5, gave or perhaps gave up 7s. 4d. of his money for commons to the cellarer who recorded it under 'foreign receipts': WCM C.492a, C.95; see also John Morton.

Roger PRIDE

occ. 1328/9

1328, 24 Sept., ord subdcn, St Mary's church at the gate of Gloucester abbey, *Reg. Orleton*, no 9 (p. 9).

1329, 17 June, ord dcn, Tewkesbury abbey, *ib.*, no 14 (p. 15).

Robert PROCTOUR [Proctur

occ. 1475 occ. 1479/80

1475, 7/8 Jan., one of four presented to the bp and the next day examined by the chancellor

of the bp in the prior's chamber in the presence of the prior, and the precentor [Robert Myston, q.v.]; he was accepted for a yr of probation, Reg. Carpenter, ii, 135.
1479/80, celebrated his first mass; the kitchener sent *exennia* of 2s. 6d., WCM C.160.

Richard PULLAN
occ. 1426
1426, 8 Sept., one of two whose prof. the prior was comm. to rec., Reg. Polton, 13.
Note: is this perhaps Richard Gloucester II, q.v.?

PYREBROK
see Pirebroke

PYRYE
see Pirie

RAD'
occ. [c. 1270]
[c.1270], many refs occ. to a *frater Rad'* on the acct of William III, q.v.; he may have been granator, WCM E.4(6).

RALPH
see Fylkes

RALPH, prior
see Bath, Bedeford

RANDS
see Holbech

RANDULPH
see Evesham

RANULF
see Calthrop

William de REDBOURN [Rodebourne
occ. 1356 occ. 1359
1356, 3 Nov., one of two accepted by the prior and chaplain, but refused adm. as monks by the bp because of the failure to present the correct documents, Reg. Bryan, i, 42.
1358, 22 Sept., ord acol., Tewkesbury abbey, *ib.*, i, 113.
1359, 26 Mar., ord subdcn, Hartlebury, *ib.*, i, 114.
1359, 6 Apr., ord dcn, Hartlebury, *ib.*, i, 116.
1359, 15 June, ord pr., Alvechurch, *ib.*, i, 117.
1358/9, celebrated his first mass and the precentor gave *exennia*, WCM C.356.

RICHARD
occ. [1236 × 1266]
[1236 × 1266], *temp.* bp Walter de Cantilupe, sacrist, and involved in the negotiation of a lease, WCM B.929a and b.

ROBERT le Pitauncer
occ. 1316/17
1316/17, pittancer, WCM B.1480.

RODEBOURNE
see Redbourn

Thomas de RODDELEYE [Rodeleye
occ. 1346 occ. 1359/60
1346, 11 Mar., ord dcn, Hartlebury, *Reg. Bransford*, no 1069; no religious house is named.
1349, 19 Dec., ord pr., Ledbury, by *lit. dim.* from the prior, Reg. Trillek (Hereford), fo 212 (the printed reg. has Bodeley).
1349/50, celebrated his first mass, and the precentor sent *exennia* of 2s. 6d., WCM C.353.
1356/7, 1359/60 part yr, kitchener, WCM C.114, C.65; he was succ. by Walter Froucester, q.v.

I ROGER [Rogerius
occ. c. 1104
Name occ. in the list of monks in *Durham Liber Vitae*, fo 22. This entry may be in a slightly later hand.

II ROGER
occ. [?mid-13th c.]
[?mid-13th c.], cellarer, in a lease of saltpans, *Reg. Prioratus*, 95b.

Hugh de ROMESEYE
occ. 1274
1274, 21 Sept., chosen by the chapter as one of the seven nominees for the priorate, *Reg. Giffard*, 62.

Thomas de RUDYNG [Ruydinge, Ruydynge
occ. 1378 d. 1419/20
1378, 26 Aug., one of two novices whose prof. [*vota*] the prior was comm. to rec., Liber Albus, fo 274.
1379, 26 Mar., ord acol., Kidderminster *Reg. Wakefield*, no 876b (as Budyng).
1380, 19 May, ord subdcn, Bromyard, *Reg. Gilbert* (Hereford), 145.
1382, 19 Sept., [dcn], recd *lit. dim.* for pr.'s orders, *Reg. Wakefield*, no 896.
1382, 20 Sept., ord pr., Bromyard, *Reg. Gilbert* (Hereford), 152.
1382/3, celebrated his first mass; the prior gave 12 gallons of ale for the festivities, and the almoner 3s., WCM C.70, 177.
1391/7; 1398/1400, subcellarer, WCM C.764, C.636, C.635, C.762, C.613, C.446; C.649, C.476.
1400/Dec. 1401, kitchener, WCM C.128,129.
1404/Oct. 1405, subcellarer, WCM C.78.
1408/9, hostiller, WCM C.218.
1411/14, subcellarer, WCM C.565, C.659, C.658.
1414, June/Sept; 1415/17; 1419, 14 Apr., kitchener, WCM C.137; C.138, C.139; *Reg. Sed. Vac.*, 407.

1388, 21 Aug., 32nd in order at the el. of a prior, Liber Albus, fo 334v.
1391/2, visited Sedgeberrow, WCM C.764.
1392/3, pd visits to Henwick and Overbury, WCM C.636, C.752.
1393/4, visited Henwick, WCM C.635.
1394/5, visited Sedgeberrow, WCM C.762.
1395/6, visited Harvington; and he recd a *cucullus* from the cellarer as recompense *pro . . . assiduo labore . . . circa pipam* [which carried water from Henwick to the priory], WCM C.613, C.77.
1396/97, was responsible for the construction of a new mill at Mildenham, WCM C.446.
1396, 9 Dec., obtained a papal licence to choose his own confessor, *CPL*, v (1396–1404), 48.
1398/9, visited Moor [Lindridge], WCM C.649.
1401, 24 June, 28th in order at the el. of a bp, *Reg. Sed. Vac.*, 373.
1401/2, an inventory of the precentor's office lists one uter in his care, Hamilton, *Comp. Rolls*, 47 (WCM C.371).
1408/9, was owed 44s. 1d. by the cellarer, WCM C.81.
1411/12, pd a visit to Cropthorne, WCM C.565.
1412/14, pd visits to Newnham, WCM C.659, C.658.
1419, 24 Apr., 7th in order at the el. of a bp, *Reg. Sed. Vac.*, 407.
1419/20, d., but nothing was returned to the chamberlain, WCM C.32.

Note: Most of the entries on the accts give 'T.R.' only, but there can be no doubt as to his identity.

SAEUVARD [?Siward/Saulf
occ. [1062 × 1095]

[1062 × 1095], *temp.* bp Wulstan, became a monk [*conversus*] prob. on his deathbed Mason, *Wulfstan*, 188 and Atkins, 'Church of Worcs.', pt ii, 32.

Note: this may be the father of Clemens, q.v.

See also Sewulf.

SAEWOLDUS
occ. c. 1104.

Name occ. in the list of monks in *Durham Liber Vitae*, fo 22.

John de ST BRIAVEL [Brevel, Briavell, Sancto Brevello, Sancto Briavello
occ. 1300 d. 1324

1305, 5 Jan., prob. precentor; see under this date below.
1307, 13 Nov., precentor, *Reg. Sed. Vac.*, 107.
1308, 14 May, apptd sacrist, *Liber Albus*, no 402; in *Reg. Reynolds*, 2, there is a similar apptment dated 27 Oct., 1308.
1310, 18 Mar; 1311, 13 Feb; 1313, 13 July, 12 Sept., sacrist, *Reg. Reynolds*, 16–17; *ib.*, 20; *Reg. Reynolds*, 68, 72 (also Liber Albus fo 57v).
1314, 29 Mar., apptd sacrist, Reg. Maidstone, 5. An undated letter from the bp to the prior and convent refers to past dissension between the [?former] bp and the monks and to his removal from the office of sacrist vs his will; the bp expressed his willingness to put him back in his former position if this would bring an end to the discord even though he had apptd another, *Liber Ecclesiae*, 35; it would appear that he did reappt him.
1315, 12 Nov., sacrist, *Liber Pensionum*, no 153.
1319, 24 Mar., precentor, *Reg. Cobham*, 58.
1322/3, cellarer, WCM C.545, E.3.

He also served as receiver for the bp [while he was sacrist]:
1310, 24 Feb., comm. as receiver of the income of both spiritualities and temporalities, *Reg. Reynolds*, 14.
1311, 27 Aug., recd another similar comm., *ib.*, 25.
1313, 13 July, 5 Oct., receiver, *ib.*, 68, 73.
1314, 23 Dec., again comm. by the new bp as his receiver, Reg. Maidstone, 41.

1300, 5 July, apptd by the prior as proctor (prob. relating to the bp's impending visitation); on 19 Aug. he was one of six monks comm. to assist the sacrist in visiting the chapter; he was described as 'the least of the monks' in the comm., *Reg. Giffard*, 529, 530. See Nicholas de Norton.
1301, 14 Sept., apptd proctor to attend the Black Monk Chapter in Northampton, Pantin, *BMC*, i, 144 and *Liber Albus*, no 17.
1302, 24 Oct., while in London as proctor for the convent he apptd T. de W. as his substitute, *Reg. Sed. Vac.*, 32; back in Worcester on 3 Nov., he witnessed a bond, *ib.*, 29.
1304, 17 Sept., named as proctor to attend the Black Monk Chapter, Pantin, *BMC*, i, 162 (Liber Albus, fo 21v).
1305, 4/5 Jan., presented six *clerici* to the bp at Hartlebury, before their adm. as monks; he was therefore prob. precentor, *Reg. Gainsborough*, 15.
[1305], went to London with Gilbert de Madley, q.v., over the appropriation of Dodderhill and other business, *Liber Albus*, no 342.
1307, Jan., was present at the parliament in Carlisle in Jan., 1307, representing the prior and convent, *Parl. Writs*, i, 912.
1307, 16 Oct., comm. by the prior, with a clerk, to hear causes, *sed. vac.*, in the consistory courts and elsewhere, *Reg. Sed. Vac.*, 81.
1307, 13 Nov., apptd by the chapter to cite all the monks to the el. of a bp; he reported that this had been done two days later, *ib.*, 107. On 16 Nov., he was apptd an 'instructor', with Richard de Bromwych, q.v., to inform Walter Reynolds of the chapter's choice, *ib.*, 108, 110.
1308, 5 Jan., apptd by the prior, with John de

Stratford I, q.v., to be collectors of the fifteenth in the adcnry of Worcester, *Reg. Sed. Vac.*, 130.

1308, Jan./Apr., comm. by the prior, along with others, to visit religious houses and clergy and people in several deaneries, *sed. vac.*, *ib.*, 121. He also acted as proctor for the prior in rendering the accts to the abp for the administration of the spiritualities of the see during the vacancy, *ib.*, 132–134.

1309, 24 Mar., present in Hereford cathedral as witness to a collation to Knightwick, *Liber Albus*, no 449.

1309, 19 Oct., apptd proctor, with John de Stratford I, q.v., to attend a provincial council concerning the Templars, *Councils and Synods*, ii, 1254; *Liber Albus*, no 469; on 4 Dec., he was apptd to attend the abp's council, *ib.*, no 474.

[1309], wrote to Michael de Berham, chancellor of the abp, about the chapter's concern that the bp was going beyond his rights in certain matters especially with regard to the office of sacrist. At his visitation the abp had decreed that the bp had no control over the sacrist beyond that of apptment, Liber Albus, fo 36^{v}; the prior [John de Wyke, q.v.] also wrote on this matter to Berham.

1310, 21 Dec., sent by the bp, with the official, to investigate complaints about the warden of St Wulstan's hospital, *Reg. Reynolds*, 19.

1311, 13 Feb., 7 Dec., comm. by the bp to adm. monks at Little Malvern, *ib.*, 20, 30.

1311, 4 Aug., apptd as proctor to represent the prior in parliament; the convent sent Robert de Clifton I, q.v., *Liber Albus*, no 533.

1312/13, many entries in the register of bp Reynolds record his activities as receiver, e.g., making payments for provisions of wine and fish, and accting for various other financial transactions, *Reg. Reynolds*, 32, 33, 35, 51, 53, 58, 60, 68, 73.

[1312], authorized by the prior to contract a loan of £100, *in utilitatem et commodum ecclesie*, Liber Albus, fo 54.

1312, 15 Sept., present at the installation of the adn of Worcester, Liber Albus, fo 57^{v}.

[1313], comm., with the bp's official to oversee the removal of tombs in the cemetery that were impeding the repair of the [cathedral] fabric, *Reg. Reynolds*, 16–17.

1313, ?Jan./Mar., sent by the prior to seek assistance from the bp on a certain matter; his approach was successful, for the chapter sent the bp a letter of thanks in Mar., *Liber Albus*, nos 563, 567.

1313, 4 Aug., apptd as proctor to attend parliament, Liber Albus, fo 40^{v}.

1313, 13 Sept., ordered by the bp to investigate reports of misappropriation of income and other abuses on the part of his predecessors in the office of sacrist, *Reg. Reynolds*, 72.

1313, 12 Nov., apptd proctor to go to the [former] bp [Reynolds] to rec. from him the vestments and other ornaments which they had given him for his use while he was bp [he had been translated to Canterbury on 1 Oct.], *Liber Albus*, no 604; on 24 Nov. he was sent by the prior to obtain the latter's *sed. vac.* comm. from the prior of Christ Church [Henry de Eastry, q.v.] *Reg. Sed. Vac.*, 137.

1313/14, the cellarer pd his expenses in London (43s. 8d.) and *in partibus transmarinis* (£10 16s.); he was also given money on two occasions *pro consilio*, one of which cost £7. He may have gone to Paris, if John de St Germans q.v., was there at the time, because on this same acct he delivered 40s. to St Germans, Wilson, *Early Comp. Rolls*, 39, 41 (WCM C.482).

1314, 24 Aug., acted as proctor in *sed. vac.* administration, WCM B.1632b.

1315, 12 Nov., a grant was made by William Calle (Colle), citizen of Worcester, for the provision of a chaplain to say a mass daily for the soul of the grantor and of St Briavel [who was sacrist], and others at the altar of the blessed Virgin at the 'Rededore', *Liber Pensionum*, no 153 (WCM B.1232).

1317, 8 Apr., apptd proctor to go to the abp to obtain the prior's *sed. vac.* comm., *Reg. Sed. Vac.*, 177; he also was sent to the former bp's late official to obtain the [episcopal] seal of office, *ib.*, 178.

1317, 20 Oct., 12th in order at the el. of a prior; with Alexander de Bryorhull, q.v., he visited the sick monks in the infirmary to ascertain whether or not they could attend the proceedings, Liber Albus, fo 83–83^{v}.

1318, 14 Jan., apptd proctor to go to present the accts of first fruits to Rigaud [?de Asserio, the papal collector], *Liber Albus*, no 810; he also acted as proctor in paying dues to the cardinals, *ib.*, no 811 (n.d.). On 2 Feb., he was named proctor for the prior and chapter at convocation, *ib.*, no 814.

1319, 25 Jan., was responsible for rendering acct of the tenth collected in the adnry of Worcester, *ib.* no 865.

1319, 24 Mar., sponsored a secular clerk from York diocese for ord as subdcn, *Reg. Cobham*, 58; the phrase is *ad instanciam* [*suam*]. He continued to support him on 2 June 1319 at the time of his ordination to the diaconate, *ib.*, 62.

1319/20, pd a visit to King's Norton, WCM C.693.

[1320], the bp ordered the prior to lighten his penance, imposed at the recent visitation (by the bp's commissaries), and he also wrote to him to say that the requests of his friends and the humility he had shown in undergoing his penance had caused the bp to remit it, *Reg. Cobham*, 23.

1322/3, visited Bromsgrove, WCM C.545.

1324, Feb./Sept., d., and so the pittancer pd him

only a portion of his pittance money, WCM C.295.

John de ST GERMANS, D.Th. [Sancto Germano, Germeyn

occ. 1298 occ. 1317

1298, Sept./1302, Jan., student at Oxford, and prob. earlier, P. Glorieux, 'Jean de Saint-Germain, maître de Paris et copiste de Worcester' in *Mélanges Auguste Pelzer* (Louvain, 1947), 529. If he obtained his B.Th., there, as seems likely, he must have been at Oxford several yrs earlier; see below under the mss.

1310/12, student in theology at the university of Paris and lectured on the Sentences; see below and *BRUO*.

1312, 31 Mar., student at Paris; the prior gave permission for him to rec. and use at his discretion a sum of money (in florins) which had been left to him by his brother, *Liber Albus*, no 542 (fo 51^{v}). See Sullivan, *Benedictine Monks at Paris*, no 602.

1312/13, [student], recd an allowance from the chamberlain, Wilson, *Early Comp. Rolls*, 2 (WCM C.8); in 1312 incepted, D.Th., *BRUO*, and see below.

1313/14, [student], recd 40s. from the cellarer *per manus* John de St Briavel, q.v., who was prob. on a visit to Paris, Wilson, *Early Comp. Rolls*, 41 (WCM C.482).

1312/15, regent, as noted in the letter, dated 22 June 1315, to the prior from the masters and scholars of the university of Paris in which he is named as doctor and regent in theology. This is a letter of recommendation in which the words of praise and affection seem to go beyond conventional phrases and to express the respect and warmth of feeling shared by the writers. They described his presence among them as that of one who 'inter nos velut stella coruscans sine macula diu fulsit' and his personality as 'personam nobis perambilem et dilectam'. The letter makes clear that the prior had ordered his return, Leach, *Education in Worcs.*, 35–37 (Liber Albus, fo 67^{v}).

1301, 18 July, one of the seven nominees for the priorate, *Reg. Giffard*, 547.

1302, 25 Mar., one of the seven *compromissorii* in the el. of a bp, *Reg. Sed. Vac.*, 1; he was himself chosen as bp and the el. was confirmed by the king on 8 Apr., *CPR (1301–1307)*, 26. However, the abp had doubts about the legality of the el. and delayed his confirmation. On 2 May he wrote to the chapter to ask if there were any who had opposed the el., and if so they were to appear before him, *Reg. Sed. Vac.*, 4. On 19 July he wrote to the pope for advice on the question of the validity of the el. because the votes of the *compromissorii* had failed to produce a majority until the second round. He had discovered this by questioning one of the proctors, although it had been announced as a unanimous choice, *Reg. abp Winchelsey*, 631–634; a similar but shorter letter to the pope, dated 17 July is in *Reg. Sed. Vac.*, 12. See also *Ann. Wigorn.*, 551, 555.

1302, [June], acting as bp el., issued letters of credence, *Reg. Sed. Vac.*, 10.

1302, 15 Aug., obtained licence from the king to go to Rome, *CPR (1296–1302)*, 550.

1302, [July/Aug.], he wrote three letters to the prior, recounting his movements and plans and seeking advice and permission to proceed; they are given in *Reg. Sed. Vac.*, 14–15:

(1) he had consulted a legal expert in London but had been unable to obtain from the abp a statement of his case [*consultatio*]; an appeal to the curia was necessary but he was concerned about the expense that this would entail for the prior and convent and therefore he asked for licence to go himself in order to reduce the cost.

(2) he thanked the prior for sending the licence and gave his views of the importance of pursuing his case: it would be because of his intention to continue with the building of the cathedral church and to improve the monks' diet.

(3) he requested the chapter to send a proctor, or two instructors, to the pope with authority to el. another bp if his el. were to be quashed, and noted that these men would need to be supplied with funds for their food and lodging. If the chapter could not manage to do this, he asked for a letter of excuse to be sent.

1302, 1 Sept., the prior and chapter wrote to the cardinal who was adcn of Worcester in Rome, *Reg. Sed. Vac.*, 18; they also wrote to the pope, n.d., stating that St Germans was on his way, *ib.*, 15.

1302, 13 Oct., arrived in Rome, acc. to a letter written from there which was shown to Richard de Bromwych, q.v., in Oxford, *ib.*, 31–32.

1302, 17 Oct., res., in the presence of the pope, *ib.*, 32, and *Ann. Wigorn.*, 554.

1303, 22 June, the abp wrote to the prior to explain his refusal to confirm St Germans' el. as bp., Liber Albus, insert at fo 82^{v}.

1308/10, lector in theology at St Augustine's abbey, Canterbury. The prior gave permission after the abbot's request, dated 20 Apr., 1308, *Liber Albus*, no 397,399; the abbot wrote a second letter urging him to come immediately after 24 June, *ib.*, no 400.

1310, 22 Dec., the abbot asked the prior to assist him and his chapter in sending St Germans to study *ad scolas* [in Paris], *ib.*, no 514; a vague and offhand reply was sent by the prior on 14 Jan. 1311 to the effect that he and his chapter had provided him 'with the necessary means' and would continue to do so, *ib.*, no 515.

1317, 20 Oct., first on the list of those absent from

the el. of a prior, in his case *per literas suas excusante*, Liber Albus, fo 83.

?1320, at the request of the abbot of St Augustine's abbey, Canterbury he prob. returned there for a time as lector; in his letter the abbot remarked on his *doctrine claritas et conversationis honestas*, the memory of which from his previous stay remained vivid, Leach, *Education in Worcs.*, 39–41 and *Liber Ecclesiae*, 36. The assigning of the date, 1320, to this letter appears purely arbitrary; he may have been at Canterbury in 1317 and hence absent legitimately from the el. above.

n.d., 3 Nov., prob. the date of his d. as the obit of a John Germeyn occ. on this day in the Canterbury obits in BL Ms Arundel 68, fo 47.

Name in three Worcs. Mss:

(1) F.4, fos 168–234, Aristoteles (13th c.), 'caucio—impignoratus in cista communi pro duobus solidis, A.D. 1295'.

(2) F.8, P. Lombardus (13th c.), 'caucio—exposita communi ciste magistri Luce pro quadraginta solidis, A.D. 1314.'

(3) Q.64, Reportationes Januensis (13th/14th c.), 'et hoc manu magistri—theologi et monachi Wygornie'; see Henry Fouke.

Note: One other ms at Worcester, Q.99, Disputationes theologie (13th/14th c.), has been attributed to St Germans by P. Glorieux in the article mentioned above (513–529). He produces evidence to show that its contents were compiled in Paris rather than Oxford and thus he disagrees with A. G. Little's suggestion that it was prob. the work of Richard de Bromwych, q.v., at Oxford (*Oxford Theology*, 219–236, 244–246). Glorieux likens St Germans to a scribe-reporter going around the Paris schools, listening to the discussions and jotting down in this, his notebook, the points that interested him, *ib.*, 521. See Sharpe, *Latin Writers*.

William de ST JOHN [Sancto Johanne
occ. [late 13th c.]

[Late 13th c.], cellarer, WCM B.1454.

Described in a grant as the brother of Simon the weaver of Bedwardine, *ib.*

Richard de ST MARTIN [Sancto Martino
d. 1220

1220, subprior and d., *Ann. Wigorn.*, 412, where he is described as junior.

Stephen de ST WOLSTAN [Sancto Wolstano
occ. 1287 occ. 1300

1287, 2/7 Jan., subcellarer, *Reg. Giffard*, 304, 325.

1287, 2 Jan., one of the seven nominees for the priorate, *Reg. Giffard*, 304, 325.

1290, 7 Nov., at an episcopal visitation, while the bp was in consultation with the subprior, Simon [de Wyre, q.v.], Stephen and other monks entered the chapter house accompanied by the prior Philip [Aubyn, q.v.] and some seculars; they interrupted the proceedings by noisy protestations and were excommunicated, *ib.*, 380.

1292/3, recd from the cellarer £10 for the tithes from Grimley and Hallow, Wilson, *Early Comp. Rolls*, 14 (WCM C.51), named as Stephen.

1293/4, went to London to pay the twentieth to the king, *ib.*, 21 (WCM C.51a); named only as Stephen, see Stephen de Wytton.

1300, 19 Aug., one of the monks comm. by the bp to assist the sacrist, Nicholas de Norton, q.v., in the *sed. vac.*, visitation of the prior and chapter, *Reg. Giffard*, 530.

SALOP, SALOPIA
see Shrovesbury

Richard de SALTEFORD [Saltford
occ. 1305 occ. 1317

1305, 5 Jan., one of two *clerici* presented to the bp at the time of their adm., *Reg. Gainsborough*, 15.

1308, 25 Oct., granted *lit. dim.*, for dcn's orders, *Reg. Reynolds*, 92.

1309, 24 May, ord dcn, Cirencester, *ib.*, 111.

1309, 3 Dec., granted *lit. dim.*, for pr.'s orders, *ib.*, 93.

1317, 20 Oct., 30th in order at the el. of a prior, Liber Albus, fo 83v.

SAMSON
occ. c. 1104

Name occ. in the list of monks in *Durham Liber Vitae*, fo 22.

SAMUEL
occ. c. 1104

Name occ. in the list of monks in *Durham Liber Vitae*, fo 22.

Roger SANDFORD
see Stanford

William SAPY
d. 1486/7

1486/7, the almoner distributed alms to the poor at the time of his death and pd the brief bearer, WCM C.207.

SAY
see John Crowle

Ralph de SCALLEBY [Scaldeby, Scalloby, Scallub'
occ. 1317 d. 1340

1331, one of the two *tumbarii*, Reg. A.22, fo 18.

1317, 20 Oct., ill in the infirmary and absent from the el. of a prior, Liber Albus, fo 83.

1329/30, stopped at Cleeve Prior on his way to and from Whitchurch, WCM C.557.

1339/40, recd his pittances for *minutiones* until he d. on ?4 Apr., WCM C.298.

Thomas SCHELDESLEY [Scheldysley, Schellesley, Sheldesley, Shellisley
occ. 1464 occ. 1471/2

1464, 8 June, one of six whose prof. the prior was comm. to rec., Reg. A.6(i), fo 34.
1466, 1 Mar., ord subdcn, St Nicholas church, Worcester, Reg. Carpenter, i, 564.
1467, 19 Dec., ord dcn, carnary chapel by Worcester cathedral, *ib.*, i, 569.
[1471], dcn, granted *lit. dim.* for pr.'s orders, *ib.*, ii, 42.
1471, 21 Sept., ord pr., Whitbourne, *Reg. Stanbury* (Hereford), 167.
1471/2, celebrated his first mass and recd 2s. 3d. from the kitchener, WCM C.155.

Name in CUL Ms Mm. 1.19, P. Comestor (12th/13th c.); in large letters *Iste liber constat*—, at the foot of the index on fo 2; it also contains Regula monachorum and Lanfrancus de officio monachorum.

Richard de SCHEVINDON [Schemudon
occ. 1301/2

1302, 20 Jan., had been accused of incontinence at the abp's visitation but he had cleared himself, and the abp wrote to the prior to ensure that he suffered no more from the censures of his brethren, Liber Albus, fo 13.

SCHIPSTON
see Shippiston

SCHROSBURY, Schrovesbury
see Shrovesbury

SCOT
see Calthrop

SEEVARNE
see Severne

Thomas de SEGESBAROWE [Seggesberewe, Seggesbergh, Seggesberue, Seggesberwe, Seggesboruwe, Seggesbure
occ. 1287 d. 1299

1287, 7 Jan., prob. one of the monk proctors apptd to present the seven nominees for the priorate to the bp, *Reg. Giffard*, 325; but he is absent from what is essentially the same entry in *ib.*, 304.
1294/5, recd 35s. 4d. from the cellarer for his expenses while in London to attend parliament/convocation around 21 Sept., Wilson, *Early Comp. Rolls*, 23 (WCM C.51a).
1296, 15 Sept., set out for Rome taking with him £20 from the monks' pittances of the previous yr, *Ann. Wigorn.*, 528.
1299, 2 Feb., the abp wrote to him, proctor in Rome, requesting him to deliver the abp's documents, which had been in his custody, to a new proctor, *Reg. abp Winchelsey*, 550.
1299, 24 Sept., d. in Rome and was buried at the convent of the Dominicans at Anagni; Henry de Newynton, q.v., was sent to retrieve his books and possessions, *Ann. Wigorn.*, 543.

Name in Worcs. Mss:
(1) F.37, P. Comestor (13th/14th c.), *per fratres—et Johannem de Wyke*, q.v.
(2) F.102, T. Aquinas (late 13th c.), Summa, *procurata per*—.

M. SENATUS [Senatus Bravonius
occ. 1175 d. 1207

1189–1196; prior: succ. 1189; res. 20 Nov. 1196, *Fasti*, ii, 103, *HRH*, 84.
1175, 9 Apr., precentor, *Worcs. Cart.*, no 165.
[1186 × 1189], chamberlain, Birmingham City Archives, Ms 473632.
n.d. described himself as *bibliothecarius*, Turner, Worcs. Mss, xlv.
1196, styled *magister* and *theologus*, *Ann. Wigorn.*, 388.
n.d., apptd penitentiary by the bp, M. Cheney, *Roger, Bishop of Worcester, 1164–1179* (Oxford, 1980), 58.
1175, 9 Apr., witness to an inspeximus of a charter, *Worcs. Cart.*; no 165.
[1186 × 1189], witnessed a charter, Birmingham City Archives, Ms 473632.
[1189 × 1196], as prior, witnessed a number of grants, charters, and other deeds, *Worcs. Cart.*, nos 303, 334, 444.
1207, d., *Ann. Wigorn.*, 395.

Name occ. in a no of mss as author:
(1) Oxford, Bod. Ms 633, fos 199v–231 (late 12th and early 13th c.) a collection of six letters, several of which are theological treatises written at the request of bp Roger; see Cheney, *Roger* (as above), 58–66, where two of these are discussed in detail and other refs listed. See also Turner, *Worcs. Mss*, who has transcribed in full one of the letters which was addressed to a monk, M. Aeluredus, and was concerned with the application of the Eusebian canons to the study of the Gospels, xlv–li. See also T. Holland, 'The University of Oxford in the Twelfth Century', in *Collectanea*, ii, Oxford Historical Society (1890), 180–182 where two letters from the Bodleian ms are transcribed.
(2) Durham Cathedral Library Ms B.IV.39B, Vita S. Oswaldi and Vita S. Wulfstani (early 13th c.); see the letter addressed to bp Roger in which he stated that he had written a life of St Oswald and an abridged life of St Wulfstan, Oxford Bod. Ms 633, fo 197v. There are other copies of the lives, but this is

the earliest surviving text; for a comparative description of these mss see Mason, *Wulfstan*, 298–300.

In addition, Senatus claimed that he had sent 22 sermons to bp Roger who had commanded him to preach as well as to write, Cheney, *Roger*, 66.

In his lecture 'English Learning in the late Twelfth Century', *Transactions of the Royal Historical Society*, 4th series, 19 (1936), R. W. Hunt placed Senatus among the scholars of the older tradition who were not enthusiastic about the new learning and methods that were gaining popularity in the schools (pp. 29–30). However, Mrs Cheney has pointed out that the monk and the bp were in fact 'debating large issues, in the light of the changing needs and opinions of their time'; she also remarked on the breadth of his theological training and suggested that his unusual name may indicate a continental origin for both his upbringing and education (*Roger*, 64).

See P. Delhaye, 'Deux textes de Senatus de Worcester sur la pénitence', *Recherches de Théologie ancienne et médiévale*, 19 (1952), 203–224. See also Sharpe, *Latin Writers.*

John SERNE
occ. 1353

1353, 21 Dec., ord acol., Ombersley, Reg. Bryan, i, 13.

Note: this may be John de Teukesbury I, q.v.

John SEVERNE [Seevarne, Sevar, Sevarne
occ. 1379 occ. 1400 [?1426/7]

1379, 14 Mar., one of two *clerici*, presented to the bp by the precentor, John de Malverne I, q.v., and adm. as a monk, *Reg. Wakefield*, no 127.

1380, 9 May, ord subdcn, Bromyard, Reg. Gilbert (Hereford), fo 81^{v} (the printed reg. has Semere).

1380, 22 Sept., ord dcn Highnam chapel, *ib.*, fo 82, where the scribe has written 'Wygemore' instead of 'Wyg' or 'Wygorn'.

1381, 20 Feb., novice whom the prior was comm. by the bp to prof., Liber Albus, fo 307.

n.d. ord. pr., no place stated, *Reg. Wakefield*, no 885h.

1380/1, celebrated his first mass and recd *exennia* from the almoner and infirmarer, WCM C.176, C.242.

1387, chaplain to the prior, Liber Albus, fo 318.

1395/6, pittancer, WCM C.318.

1383/4, ill in the infirmary and recd a small gift from the almoner, WCM C.178.

1388, 21 Aug., 34th in order at the el. of a prior, Liber Albus, fo 334^{v}.

1391, 25 Mar., comm. by the bp to induct the new vicar of Hallow church, *Reg. Wakefield*, no 586.

1395/6, returning from the curia he recd 100s. from the cellarer, who may have been a yr behind in his payment, WCM C.77.

1396/7, sold 4000 tiles to the *tumbarius*, for [the repair of] his tenements *extra foregate*, WCM C.461.

1398, 30 Nov., obtained an apptment as a papal chaplain, *CPL*, iv (1362–1404), 305; on the same day another similar apptment was entered in the papal register, *ib.*, v (1396–1404), 212, prob. duplicate entries.

1398, 12 Dec., named as papal chaplain and dispensed to hold a benefice with or without cure of souls, *ib.*, v (1396–1401), 194.

[1399], 22 Apr., the bp issued a mandate forbidding him, who was wandering about in the world, to preach, Reg. Winchcombe, 73.

1399, 5 July, the pope ordered the bp to see that Severne, who claimed to be a papal chaplain and to have a dispensation to hold a benefice, was made to return to the monastery and to obey the Rule, *CPL*, v (1396–1404), 207.

1400, 13 Jan., the bp wrote to the prior and chapter, and especially to Severne, and also to all concerned, to the effect that he had recd the letter above which had revoked his privileges so that he would not bring religion into disrepute by his wandering about in the world and leading a dissolute life. The bp went on to denounce him and order him to return to the priory within fifteen days on pain of excommunication, Liber Albus, fos 400^{v}–401.

[1426/7, a John Sev' visited Overbury, WCM C.717].

SEWULF [Saewulf, ?Saulf
occ. [1062 × 1095]

[1062 × 1095], *temp.* bp Wulstan, occ. in William of Malmesbury, *Gest. Pont.*, 286–287, as a merchant who had St Wulstan as his confessor and who eventually followed the bp's advice and became a monk. Dr Mason suggests that it is more likely he entered the Worcester community than that of Malmesbury and she goes on to postulate that because of the variable spellings of Anglo Saxon names he may be identical with either Saulf *alias* Saeward, q.v., or another Siward who was a *conversus*, *Wulfstan*, 187–188.

Nicholas SHIPPISTON [Schipston, Schypystun, Shipston
occ. 1525 occ. 1536

1525, 23 Dec., ord acol., Bromyard, *Reg. Booth* (Hereford), 320.

1527, 6 Apr., ord dcn, carnary chapel by Worcester cathedral, Reg. Ghinucci 7(ii), 163.

1527, 19 Sept., ord pr., Gloucester abbey, *ib.*, 7(ii), 167.

1528, Sept., recd 2s. as a pr.'s pittance from the prior, i.e., celebrated his first mass, *Jnl More*, 278.

1525/6, 35th on the clerical subsidy list and pd 2s. as commons, Reg. A.12, fo 125.
1531/2, 34th on the second subsidy list and pd 3s. 4d. commons, *ib.*, fo 135v.
1534, 17 Aug., subscribed to the Act of Supremacy, *DK 7th Report*,
Appndx 2, 305.
1535, signed the petition vs the reinstatement of William Fordham. q.v., as cellarer, *L and P Henry VIII*, ix, no 653.
1536, 13 Mar., 24th in order at the 'el' of Henry Holbech, q.v., as prior, Reg. A.6(iii), fo 1.

Robert SHROVESBURY [Schrosbury, Schrovesbury, Shrosbury, Shrovesbury
occ. 1414 d. 1421/2

1414, 3 Mar., ord acol., Worcester cathedral, Reg. Peverel, 198.
1415, 22 Mar., ord subdcn, Dominican convent, Worcester, *ib.*, 203.
1415, 21 Sept., ord dcn, Hartlebury, *ib.*, 206.
1419, 24 Apr., 34th in order at the el. of a bp, *Reg. Sed. Vac.*, 407.
1421/2, d., and the chamberlain sold his *vestimenta*, WCM C.33; the cost of the brief was put on the chamberlain's acct for 1422/3, C.34.

Roger de SHROVESBURY [Salopia, Scrousbury, Scrovesbury, Shrosbury
occ. 1370 d. 1411/12

1370, 13 Apr., ord subdcn, [Worcester cathedral], Reg. Lynn, 50.
1372, 18 Sept., ord pr., [Worcester cathedral], *ib.*, 60.
1395, 15 Sept., third prior, Liber Albus, fo 380.
1402, Feb; 1405/6, precentor, succeeding John de Cleve, q.v., WCM C.371, C.372; the inventory marking the change of office is printed in Hamilton, *Comp. Rolls*, 46–47. See below under 1411.
1373, 4 Dec., 20th in order at the el. of a bp, *Reg. Sed. Vac.*, 290.
1378/9, ill and the infirmarer pd 2s. for his treatment, WCM C.241.
1383/4, ill in the infirmary and the almoner sent a small gift, WCM C.178.
1388, 21 Aug., 17th in order at the el. of a prior; he was one of the three *scrutatores* apptd by the chapter, and he announced the names of the seven candidiates selected for presentation to the bp, Liber Albus, fo 335.
1395, 15 Sept., one of the seven nominees for the priorate, Liber Albus, fo 380.
1395/6, was owed 26s. 8d. [?in clothing allowance] by the chamberlain, WCM C.21.
1401, 24 June, 11th in order at the el. of a bp, *Reg. Sed. Vac.*, 373.
1411, June/Sept., sold a new ordinal [*libro de ordine*] to the [?new] precentor for 6s. 8d., WCM C.373. This suggests that he remained in office as precentor from at least 1405/6 to 1411; see Thomas de Broghton.
1411/12, d., and the chamberlain sold his *vestimenta*, WCM C.30.

William de SHROVESBURY [Salop', Schrovesbury
occ. 1361/3

1361, 22 May, ord subdcn, Alvechurch, Reg. Bryan, i, 121.
1361, 18 Sept., ord dcn, Alvechurch, *ib.*, i, 123.
1362, 17 Dec., ord pr., bp's chapel, Hartlebury, Reg. Barnet, 39.
1362/3, celebrated his first mass and recd a gift of 2s. 2d. from the precentor, WCM C.359.

Note: A William de Hulton, q.v., was ord acol., in Mar. 1361 with two other monks and this William was ord subdcn with the same two on 22 May 1361, as above; both entries may thus refer to the same monk.

SIDBERYE, Sidbury
see Sudbury

SILVESTER
see Evesham

SIMEON [Symeon
occ. c. 1104

Name occ. in the list of monks in *Durham Liber Vitae*, fo 22; his name also occ. in a mortuary roll of Savigny dated c. 1122/3, Delisle, *Rouleau Mortuaire*, pl. xxv, tit. 87.

SIMON
see Pimme, Wyre

John SIRCESTR'
occ. 1428

1428, 28 Sept., ord dcn, Worcester [*sic*], Reg. Polton, 101.

SIWARD
occ. [?1062 × 1095]

[?1062 × 1095], *temp.* bp Wulstan, *conversus*, possibly to be identified with Sewulf, q.v. His obit is given as 25 Nov., Mason, *Wulfstan*, 188.

John SMALL [Smaw
see Herford

John SMETHWYK [Smethewike, Smethewyke
occ. 1441 occ. 1468/9

1441, 24 Sept., ord subdcn, Bromyard, *Reg. Spofford* (Hereford), 337.
1443, 30 Mar., ord dcn, bp's chapel, Hartlebury, Reg. Bourgchier, 204; the scribe has written 1442 and may have been correct though his entries are out of order!
1443, 21 Sept., ord pr., carnary chapel by Worcester cathedral, *ib.*, 208.

1443/4, celebrated his first mass; the kitchener contributed 2s. 3d. to the feast, WCM C.147.

1449/51, pittancer, WCM C.92, C.334.
1451/2, kitchener, part yr succeeding William Hodynton II, q.v., WCM C.601.
1453, chaplain to the prior, Liber Albus, fo 487v.
1453/5, 1456/7, pittancer, WCM C.94, C.335, C.732.
1457/8, chamberlain, WCM C.44.
1458/66, cellarer, WCM C.685, C.491, C.731, C.733, C.734, C.492a, C.95, C.96; for 1463/5, also WCM E.68, E.69.
1462, Mar./Sept., kitchener, WCM C.150.
1465/6, 1467/8, master of the Lady chapel, WCM C.96, C.281.
1466/7, 1468/9, subprior, WCM C.421, C.697.

1448/50, one of the monks on the cellarer's list of creditors, WCM C.91, C.92.
1449/50, 1451/2, pd visits to Hallow, WCM C.600a, C.601.
1453/4, sent by the prior to Evesham to confer with the abbot about John Worcestre, q.v.; his expenses of 2s. were pd by the cellarer, WCM C.94.
1454/5, visited Cleeve [Prior], Cropthorne, Moor [Lindridge], Newnham and Teddington to rec. rents [on behalf of the cellarer], WCM C.335.
1456/7, pd a visit to Overbury, WCM C.732.
1457/8, visited Stoke, WCM C.44.
1458/9, visited Harvington, WCM C.685.
1459, 27 June, one of three monks apptd as proctors to the Black Monk Chapter in Northampton, Pantin, *BMC*, iii, 214 (Reg. A.6(i), fo 7v).
1459/60, prob. visited Sedgebarrow, NRO DCN 60/33/34. (This acct was mistaken for Sedgeford, Norfolk, and has ended up among the archives of the Norwich Dean and Chapter.)
1460/2, pd visits to Overbury, WCM C.731, C.733.
1462/3, visited Hallow and Overbury, WCM C.602, C.734.
[1463/4], with the kitchener and lay steward visited Blackwell, Shipston, Alston [Alveston] and Stratford *tempore cur[iarum post Pasch'*, at a cost of 20s. to his acct as cellarer, WCM C.492a; he was also at Cropthorne during the second wk of Lent *in negociis* and on several occasions later in the yr for supervisory purposes, *ib.*
1464, 30 July, one of three monk proctors apptd by the prior and chapter for the diocesan synod, Reg. A.6(i), fo 34v.
1464/5, visited Hallow and Harvington, WCM C.603, C.622.
1465, 20 June, one of three monk proctors apptd to represent the prior and chapter at the Black Monk Chapter in Northampton, Pantin, *BMC*, iii, 214 (Reg. A.6(i), fo 37).
1465/6, visited Harvington and Newnham, WCM C.686, C.666.
1466, 15 July, obtained a dispensation, because of his illegitimate birth, to enable him to be elected to any administrative office in his order and to rec. and retain a benefice with or without cure of souls which it was customary for Benedictine monks to hold, *CPL*, xii (1458–1471), 541.

SOBBURYE
see Sudbury

SOCKELEGH, Sockeleye
see Suckeley(e)

John SODELEIE
see John Dudley I

Note: Hamilton, *Comp. Rolls*, 42 and *BRUO* following suit have not realized that the clerk who wrote up the acct had written 'D' and not 'S'.

Simon de SOLERS
occ. 1303

1303, 4 Feb., made his prof. before the prior in the Lady chapel, *Reg. Sed. Vac.*, 37.

Thomas de SOLIHULL [Solyhull, Solyhulle
occ. 1323 occ. 1337/8

1323, 11 Nov., one of three *clerici* whom the bp comm. his sequestrator to examine on their adm. to the priory, Liber Albus, fo 113v.
1326/7, visited Bromsgrove with Robert de Morton, q.v., WCM C.544.
1334/5, stopped at King's Norton on his way to Solihull and he and his horse were fed, WCM C.695.
1337/8, visited Bromsgrove, WCM C.547.

J. de STAFFORD
occ. 1326/7

1326/7, one of a number of monks who visited Bromsgrove, WCM C.544.

I John STAFFORD
occ. 1408 d. 1441/2

1408, 14 Apr., ord acol., Dominican convent, Worcester, Reg. Peverel, 173.
1408, 22 Dec., ord subdcn, Worcester cathedral, *ib.*, 176.
1409, 2 Mar., ord dcn, Worcester cathedral, *ib.*, 178.
1411, 28 Mar., ord pr., Worcester cathedral, *ib.*, 188; (the date actually given is 1410, but is almost certainly wrong).
1410/11, celebrated his first mass and recd *exennia* from the chamberlain and hostiller, the latter giving [?money for] bread and wine, WCM C.29 (1410/11), C.220a (1411).

1419, 24 Apr., 40th and last in order at the el. of a prior, *Reg. Sed. Vac.*, 407.

1421/2, one of the monks to whom the cellarer was in debt, WCM C.84a.
1427/8, gave a small sum in alms to the almoner, WCM C.193a.
1433, 9 Dec., 11th in order at the el. of a bp, *Reg. Sed. Vac.*, 432.
1441/2, d., and the almoner gave 12d. for bread for the poor, WCM C.199.

Ralph STAFFORD
occ. 1447/8

1447/8, recd 6s. 8d. from the prior, along with John Lawerne I and John Preston III, q.v., two monk students at Oxford, WCM C.398.

Thomas STAFFORD [Stafforde
occ. 1487 occ. 1518

1487, 22 Sept., ord subdcn, Ledbury, *Reg. Milling* (Hereford), 173.
1488, 5 Apr., ord dcn, Worcester cathedral, Reg. Morton, 140.
1489/90, celebrated his first mass; the pittancer contributed 2s. worth of bread and ale for the feast, and the precentor gave *exennia* of 2s., WCM C.345, 387 (1488/9).
1490/1, subcellarer, WCM C.451.
1498, 25 Oct.; 1499, 21 July, third prior, *Reg. abp Morton*, ii, no 458; Reg. A.6(ii), fo 2v.
1499/1503; 1504, 6 Nov.; 1506/7, cellarer, WCM C.542, C.106; Reg. A.6(ii), fo 32; WCM C.668.
1507, 10 Sept., infirmarer, Reg. S. Gigli, 349.
1515/16, 1518, 27 Sept., chamberlain, Reg. A.12, fo 39, Reg. A.6(ii), fo 113.
1490/1, visited Overbury, WCM C.748.
[1492 × 1499], the prior recorded complaints vs him, and two other monks (Henry Chester and Edmund Ledbury, q.v.), accusing them of being involved in an unlawful assembly with a William Budon, WCM D.336.
1498, 25 Oct., 24th in order on the visitation certificate. *Reg. abp Morton*, ii, no 458.
1499, 21 July, one of two monk proctors apptd to present the seven nominees for the priorate to the bp, Reg. S. Gigli, 343; they met bp Fox (Durham) acting for Gigli at Southwark on 2 Sept., Reg. A.6(ii), fo 1v.
1499/1500, prob. pd visits to Broadwas and Overbury, WCM C.542, C.723.
1501/2, visited Hallow, Harvington adn Tibberton, WCM C.605, C.628, C.831.
1506/7, visited Newnham and Sedgeberrow, WCM C.668, C.783.
1507, 10 Sept., one of the two proctors apptd to present the seven nominees for the priorate to the bp, Reg. S. Gigli, 349.
1518, 27 Sept., one of the seven nominees for the priorate, Reg. A.6(ii), fo 113; they were presented to bp Fox (Winchester), prob. at Southwark, and he named William More I, q.v., *ib.*

Robert STANES [Stanis, Stanus, Stany, Stanys
occ. [1367] d. 1391/2

[1367, Aug.], one of two whose prof. the prior was comm. to rec., Reg. Bryan, ii, 28 (bound here).
1368, 4 Mar., ord dcn, Hartlebury, Reg. Whittlesey, 72.
1368, 23 Sept., ord pr., Hartlebury, *ib.*, 74; his ord as pr. is also entered in Reg. Lynn, 49, on 22 Sept. 1369 at Kidderminster.
1374/5, subcellarer, WCM C.621.
1375/6, pittancer, Hamilton, *Comp. Rolls*, 33–36 (WCM C.310).
1383/5, precentor, WCM C.363, 364.
1370, 3 Apr., 17th in order at the el. of a prior, Liber Albus, fo 246.
1373, 7 Dec., 15th at the el. of a bp, *Reg. Sed. Vac.*, 290 (as Hanus).
1374/5, visited Hallow and Harvington, WCM C.856, 621.
1388, 21 Aug., 11th in order at the el. of a prior, Liber Albus, fo 334v.
1391/2, d. and the almoner spent 2s. on bread for the poor *die obitus*, WCM C.181; in 1393/4 the precentor sent out a second brief announcing his d., WCM C.368.

John STANFORD [Staunford
occ. 1464 d. 1501/2

1464, 8 June, one of six whose prof. the prior was comm. by the bp to rec., Reg. A.6(i), fo 34.
1465, 9 Mar., ord subdcn, St Nicholas' church, Worcester, Reg. Carpenter, i, 562.
1466, 1 Mar., ord dcn, St Nicholas' church, *ib.*, i, 564.
1469, 1 Apr., ord pr., St Nicholas' church, *ib.*, i, 574.
1468/9, celebrated his first mass and the almoner and kitchener both gave gifts of 2s. 3d., WCM C.202, C.154.
1501/2, d., and the cellarer pd [the almoner] for his corrody, WCM C.106c.

Roger STANFORD B.Th [Sandford, Standford, Stanforde, Stawnforde, *alias* Coke, Corke
occ. 1497 occ. 1540

1497, 14 Apr., ord acol., carnary chapel by Worcester cathedral, Reg. G. Gigli, 25.
1500, 19 Apr., ord subdcn, carnary chapel, Reg. S. Gigli, 399.
1504, 21 Sept., ord dcn, carnary chapel, *ib.*, 289.
1505, 15 Feb., ord pr., carnary chapel, *ib.*, 292.
1504/5, celebrated his first mass, and the almoner gave *exennia* of 2s., WCM C.211.
1518, 27 Sept., *tumbarius*, Reg. A.6(ii), fo 113.
1520/1, infirmarer Reg. A.17, 68.
1521/5; 1529/32; 1533, Sept.; 1534, 30 Nov., *tumbarius*, WCM C.412, Reg. A.17, 210, WCM

C.413, C.414; WCM C.414a, C.414b, C.414c; *Jnl More*, 65; WCM B.1123. The acct for 1521/2 is printed in Wilson, *Accts Henry VIII*, 24–26.

1535, chamberlain, *L and P Henry VIII*, ix, no 653.

1510, student at Oxford, prob. from 1507; see below.

1515, 19 May, obtained B.Th., after eight yrs' study of logic, philosophy and theology, *BRUO, 1501–1540*.

1498, 25 Oct., 44th and last in order on the visitation certificate, *Reg. abp Morton*, ii, no 458.

1518, 27 Sept., one of the seven nominees for the priorate, Reg. A.6(ii), fo 113; they were presented to bp Fox (Winchester) prob. at Southwark, and he named William More I, *ib.*

1521, 22 July, 12th in order on the visitation certificate, Reg. abp Warham, ii, fo 293^{v}.

1531/2, 12th on the clerical subsidy list and pd 16s. 8d. [as *tumbarius*] and 3s. 4d., commons, Reg. A.12, fo 135.

1534, 17 Aug., subscribed to the Act of Supremacy, *DK 7th Report*, Appndx 2, 305.

1535, n.d. signed the petition vs the reinstatement of William Fordham, q.v., as cellarer, *L and P Henry VIII*, ix, no 653.

1536, 20 Feb., pd £4 for archiepiscopal dispensation to wear the habit of his order under that of a secular priest and to hold a benefice, Chambers, *Faculty Office Regs*, 45.

1536, 13 Mar., 6th in order at the 'el.' of Henry Holbech, q.v., Reg. A.6(iii), fo 1.

[1542, 24 Jan., canon of the 8th prebend in the new foundation, see *Fasti, 1541–1857*, vii, 128.]

Nicholas de STANLAKE [Stanlack, Stanlak'

occ. 1328 occ. 1346/7

1329, 25 Apr., the prior was authorized to rec. his prof., as he had completed his yr of probation, Liber Albus, fo 134^{v}.

1329, 17 June, ord subdcn, Tewkesbury abbey, *Reg. Orleton*, no 14 (p. 18).

[1330], 9 Nov., recd *lit. dim.* from the bp for the orders of dcn and pr., *ib.*, no 250.

1331, 25 May, ord pr., [?Chipping] Campden *ib.*, no 21 (p. 37).

[1334], 17 Dec., apptd *tumbarius* of the shrines of Sts Oswald and Wulstan, Reg. Montacute, 151.

1339, 4 Jan., pittancer, Worcs. Ms F.141; see below.

Note: during the episcopate of Wulstan de Bransford, q.v., was in frequent attendance upon the bp, prob. serving as his chaplain:

1340, 15 May; 1341, 13 Feb., 2 Sept.; 1343, 8 Nov.; 1346, 29 Jan., witnessed the bp's *acta*, *Reg. Bransford*, nos 244; 3,432; 521; 755; see also below.

1334, Sept./Nov., visited Sedgeberrow, WCM C.755.

1334, 3 Nov., comm. by the bp as penitentiary, Reg. Montacute, 151; this entry, undated, also occ. on p.4 of the register.

1337, 10 July, apptd as penitentiary in the adcnry of Worcester, Reg. Hemenhale, 13.

1339, 4 Jan., acc. to a letter of Henry Fouke found in Worcs.Ms F.141, he was one of the five *compromissorii* chosen as electors of a new prior, but he is not named in the acct entered in *Reg. Sed. Vac.*, 267–268.

1339, 9 Jan., witnessed the oath of canonical obedience made by the abbot of Cirencester to the prior's deputy, *sed. vac.*, *ib.*, 269. On 21 Jan., he was comm. by the prior to visit the hospitals of Sts Oswald and Wulstan and several religious houses, *ib.*, 273.

1340, 21 Apr., with John de Preston II, q.v., apptd proctor by the chapter to present the seven nominees for the priorate to the bp, *Reg. Bransford*, no 290.

1341, 13 Feb., described as the bp's penitentiary and witness to a matrimonial settlement at Hartlebury, *ib.*, no 3.

1343, Nov., apptd by the prior, with Thomas de la Lee, q.v., to ascertain the truth in a lawsuit, Liber Albus, fo 191.

1346/7, described as *comorant' cum episcopo* and recd 26s. 8d. from the chamberlain [for clothing], WCM C.10.

John de STANLEYE

occ. 1361 d. 1399

1361, 9 Mar., one of two *clerici*, presented by Nicholas de Clanefeld, q.v., to the bp at Alvechurch, and they were adm. as monks, Reg. Bryan, i, 136.

1362, 17 Dec., ord acol., bp's chapel, Hartlebury, Reg. Barnet, 38.

1363, 23 Sept., ord subdcn, Lydney, *Reg. Lewis Charlton*, (Hereford), 87.

1370, 3 Apr., 14th in order at the el. of a prior, Liber Albus, fo 246.

1373, 4/7 Dec., 12th at the el. of a bp, *Reg. Sed. Vac.*, 290.

1388, 21 Aug., 9th at the el. of a prior, Liber Albus, fo 334^{v}.

1398/9, recd 6s. 8d. from the chamberlain for his habit; but he d. this year and the chamberlain sold his clothing for 58s. 10d., and pd the brief bearer, WCM C.24. The almoner's acct for 1399/1400 records the sum of 6s. 8d. distributed to the Dominicans and Franciscans to pray for his soul, 12d. distributed among the poor, and the sale of his corrody, WCM C.185.

William de STANWEYE [Staneweye

occ. 1301 occ. 1331/2

1317/18, pittancer, WCM C.294.

1301, 3 Oct., the abbot of Malmesbury, one of the presidents of the Black Monk Chapter, relaxed the penance imposed on him by the abp during his recent visitation, as far as lay within his power, Pantin, *BMC*, i, 149–150; on 8 Oct., the abbot of Westminster, the other president, did the same, *ib.*, 150. Soon afterwards [?Nov] the prior and convent wrote to the abp requesting him to release Stanweye from undergoing further penance, and in Nov./Dec., the abbot of Westminster made a similar request to the prior on behalf of Stanweye, *carcerali custodie mancipati*, who ought to be freed and shown mercy, *ib.*, 152–153 (Liber Albus, fos 1^{v}, 2, 4, 4^{v}).

1317, 20 Oct., 16th in order at the el. of a prior, Liber Albus, fo 83^{v}.

1324, 29 Mar., witnessed the swearing in of a new incumbent of a parish church in Worcester, Liber Albus, fo 115.

1326/7, with his *socius*, visited Bromsgrove, WCM C.544.

1331/2, visited King's Norton, WCM C.694.

Richard STAPYLL [Stapull

occ. 1475

1475, 7/8 Jan., one of four who were presented to the bp by two of the monks and the following day were examined by the bp's chancellor in the prior's chamber, in the presence of the prior, precentor and others; he was one of the three adm. for the yr of probation, Reg. Carpenter, ii, 135.

Note: he may be identical with Richard Hanley, q.v.

Roger de STEVINTONE [Stevynton, Stivynton, Styvynton

occ. [1302] occ. 1343/4

1302, adm. by the prior and chapter at the request of queen Margaret who explained that he was a relative of the king's physician, Liber Albus, fo 4^{v}.

1303, 4 Feb., the prior recd his prof., *Reg. Sed. Vac.*, 37.

1314, 29 Mar., apptd *tumbarius* by the bp, Reg. Maidstone, 5.

1317, 20 Oct., pittancer, Liber Albus, fo 83.

1319/1321, Mar.; 1322/3, cellarer, WCM E.8, 9, C.55; C.545.

1323, May, almoner, WCM B.522.

1334, 8 Oct., pittancer, WCM B.184.

1340/1, 1343/4, with William Mose, q.v., *tumbarius*, Reg. A22, fos 17^{v}, 18.

1317, 20 Oct., 26th in order at the el. of a prior, was chosen as one of seven *compromissorii* to decide on the seven candidates for the office, and was himself put forward as one of the seven nominees, Liber Albus, fo 83, 83^{v}.

1320/1, held courts at Cleeve [Prior] and Sedgeberrow, WCM E.9.

[1321, Aug.], witnessed the installation of the adcn of Worcester, Liber Albus, fo 103.

1322/3, visited Bromsgrove, WCM C.545; and in May 1323 he apptd a chief miller at Laughern [Lawarne], WCM B.522.

1329/30, visited Cleeve Prior, WCM C.557.

1334, 8 Oct., negotiated a lease, WCM B.184.

1331/2, visited King's Norton, WCM C.694.

1337/8, visited Bromsgrove, WCM C.547.

John STODLEY [Stodeley

occ. 1419 occ. 1454/5

1425/6, precentor, WCM C.377; there is a gap of ten yrs (1426 to 1436) in the precentor's accts and so he may have held this office for longer.

1419, 24 Apr., 37th in order at the el. of a bp, *Reg. Sed. Vac.*, 407.

1433, 9 Dec., 20th at the el. of a bp, *ib.*, 432.

1454/5, d., and therefore did not rec. all his *porciones* from the pittancer, WCM C.335.

Bartholomew STOKE

occ. 1525/6 occ. 1540

1527, 6 Apr., possibly ord acol., carnary chapel by Worcester cathedral, Reg. Ghinucci 7(ii), 163, but the name is partly illegible.

1528 × 1533, 14 Dec., obtained *lit. dim.* to rec. orders, Reg. Ghinucci 8(ii), 65.

1532, 21 Dec., ord dcn, Reg. Stokesley (London), fo 128^{v}.

1533/4, celebrated his first mass and the sacrist gave a pittance of 2s. to the convent, WCM C.415.

1529/32, student at Oxford and the prior contributed to his maintenance, which he described as his exhibition on two occasions; in 1531/2 he gave £7 *in regardo . . . in partem exhibicionis sui*, *Jnl More*, 356 and WCM C.414c, but for the other two years only 20s. was entered, WCM C.414a, *Jnl More*, 315, 335 (where the prior adds *ex benevolo animo meo*).

1525/6, 36th in order on the clerical subsidy list and pd 2s. commons, Reg. A.12, fo 125.

1531/2, 36th on the second subsidy list and pd nothing because he was a scholar, Reg. A.12, fo 135.

1534, 17 Aug., subscribed to the Act of Supremacy, *DK 7th Report*, Appndx 2, 305.

Note: he did not sign the petition vs the reinstatement of William Fordham, q.v., as cellarer (1535), and he was absent from the 'el.' of Henry Holbech, q.v., as prior.

1540, assigned a pension of £10 p.a., *L and P Henry VIII*, xv, no 869.

William de STOKE

occ. 1189

1189, became abbot of Sherborne, *Ann. Wigorn.*, 386, *HRH*, 70.

John STOKES [Stokis, Stokys, Stookes
occ. 1481 occ. 1507

1481, 16 June, ord acol., Whitbourne, *Reg. Milling* (Hereford), 163.
1481, 22 Sept., ord subdcn, Whitbourne, *ib.*, 164.
1482, 21 Dec., ord dcn, carnary chapel by Worcester cathedral, Reg. Alcock, 270.

1488/9, subcellarer, WCM C.625.
1498, 25 Oct., 1499, 21 July, *tumbarius*, *Reg. abp Morton*, ii, no 458; Reg. A.6(ii) fo 1v.
1500/2, pittancer, WCM C.349, 350; he was apptd in Sept. 1500.
1502/5, 1507/8, prob. almoner, WCM E.180; on 10 Sept. 1507 he held this office, Reg. S. Gigli, 349.
1504, 6 Nov.; 1505/6, subprior, Reg. A.6(ii), fo 32; WCM C.427.

1488/9, visited Harvington, WCM C.625.
1498, 25 Oct., 18th in order on the visitation certificate, *Reg. abp Morton*, ii, no 458.
1499, 21 July, one of the seven nominees for the priorate, Reg. A.6(ii), fo 1v and Reg. S. Gigli, 343; they were presented to bp Fox (Durham) at Southwark on 2 Sept., Reg. A.6(ii), fo 1v.
[1506], 10 Mar., wrote a letter to the bp in English concerning the privileges of the prior and chapter, Reg. A.6(ii), fo 41.
1507, 10 Sept., one of the seven nominees for the priorate, Reg. S. Gigli, 349.

Richard de STOKTON
occ. 1411 d. 1419/20

1411, 28 Mar., ord dcn, Worcester cathedral, Reg. Peverel, 188; the date was entered as 1410 by the scribe.
1412, 24 Sept., ord pr., Llanthony priory, Gloucester, *ib.*, 193; the precentor went with the ord candidates and charged his acct for expenses of 16d., WCM C.374.
1412/13, celebrated his first mass; the hostiller gave 3s. 6d. for bread and ale for the feast, WCM C.222.

1419, 24 Apr., 26th in order at the el. of a bp, *Reg. Sed. Vac.*, 407 (as Stoolton).
1419/20, d., and the chamberlain sold his clothing, WCM C.32.

John de STONE
occ. 1393 d. 1421/2

1393, 4 Jan., one of three novices whose prof. the prior was comm. to rec., Liber Albus fo 363v; dated 5 Jan. in *Reg. Wakefield*, no 723.
1393, 1 Mar., ord acol. and subdcn, Alvechurch, *Reg. Wakefield*, no 982 b and d.
1393, 31 May, ord dcn, Worcester cathedral, *ib.*, no 984f.
1392/3, the precentor escorted the ord candidates to Alvechurch, WCM C.76.
1392/3, celebrated his first mass and the cellarer and prior each sent four gallons of wine for the feast, WCM C.76.

1401, 24 June, subchamberlain, *Reg. Sed. Vac.*, 373.

1393, Jan./Sept., had six *minutiones* and recd 3s. in pittances from the pittancer, WCM C.316.
1401, 24 June, 36th in order at the el. of a bp, *Reg. Sed. Vac.*, 373.
1419, 24 Apr., 12th at the el. of a bp, *ib.*, 407.
1421/2, d., and the chamberlain sold his clothing, WCM C.33; the brief was entered on the following yr's acct, C.34. The almoner distributed bread to the poor *pro anima*, WCM C.191.

STOOKES
see Stokes

Thomas STOWREBRUGGE [Storbrige, Sturbrig', Sturbrigge, Sturbryge, Sturbyrg
occ. 1510 occ. 1540

1510, 21 Sept., ord acol., carnary chapel by Worcester cathedral, Reg. S. Gigli, 304.
1512, 27 Mar., ord subdcn, carnary chapel, *ib.*, 314.
1515, 22 Sept., ord dcn, carnary chapel, *ib.*, 328.

1523/4, refectorer, first yr, WCM C.413.

1521, 22 July, 23rd in order on the visitation certificate, Reg. abp Warham, ii, fo 293v.
1525/6, 21st on the clerical subsidy list and pd 3s. 4d. commons, Reg. A.12, fo 125.
1531/2, 19th on the second subsidy list and pd 3s. 4d. commons, *ib.*, fo 135.
1534, 17 Aug., subscribed to the Act of Supremacy, *DK 7th Report*, Appndx 2, 305.
1535, signed the petition vs the reinstatement of William Fordham, q.v., as cellarer, *L and P Henry VIII*, ix, no 653.
1536, 13 Mar., 12th in order at the 'el.' of Henry Holbech, q.v., as prior, Reg. A.6(iii), fo 1.
1540, 18 Jan., assigned a pension of £6 per annum, *L and P Henry VIII*, xv, no 81.

STRAINSHAM
see Streynsham

I John de STRATFORD [Stratforde
occ. 1307 occ. 1327

1307, chaplain to the prior, *Liber Albus*, insert between nos 368 and 369.
1317, 20 Oct., almoner, Liber Albus, fo 83.
1323/5, subcellarer, WCM C.794, 795; and see John de Preston I.

1308, 5 Jan., with John de St Briavel, q.v., apptd by the prior to collect the royal subsidy of a half fifteenth, *Reg. Sed. Vac.*, 130; also in Jan. apptd by the prior, with Ranulph de Calthrop, q.v., to carry out a *sed. vac.*, visitation of St Augustine's abbey, Bristol. They were refused entry there but went on to visit other religious houses and deaneries. *Reg. Sed. Vac.*, 117. On 3 Mar. he and Gilbert de Madley, q.v., with two clerks, were comm. by the prior to deal with a case of purgation, *ib.*, 94.

1309, 21 July, presented the acct of the fifteenth granted by the clergy at the exchequer, *Reg. Sed. Vac.*, 132.

1309, 19 Oct., with John de St Briavel, q.v., apptd proctor to attend a provincial council concerning the Templars, *Councils and Synods*, ii, 1254, *Liber Albus*, no 469.

1313/14, sent on business affairs of the house to Ludlow, with Richard de Bromwich, q.v., and to London with Wulstan de Bransford, q.v., Wilson, *Early Comp. Rolls*, 39 (WCM C.482).

1314, 6 May, comm. by the prior, with John de Gloucestre II, q.v., as his proctors with regard to the administration of the spiritualities in the city and diocese of Worcester, *sed. vac.*, and also named as attorneys, in all causes, WCM B.1630.

1317, 20 Oct., 22nd in order at the el. of a prior and chosen as one of the seven nominees for the office, Liber Albus, fo 83–83ᵛ.

1318, 8 Jan., apptd general proctor, with another, i.e., in all causes, for the prior and convent, *Liber Albus*, no 813. Prob. this same yr he visited the prior of Kenilworth to discuss business affairs, *ib.*, no 771.

[1321, c. 6 Aug], present at the installation of the adcn of Worcester, Liber Albus, fo 103.

1323/4, pd a visit to Tibberton, WCM C.794.

1324/5, visited Leopard Grange and Tibberton, WCM C.675, 795.

1327, Jan./Sept., visited King's Norton, WCM C.693b.

II John de STRATFORD [Stretforde

occ. 1375 occ. 1401

1375, 16 June, ord subdcn, Worcester cathedral, *Reg. Sed. Vac.*, 343.

1377, 23 May, ord pr., Colwich, *Reg. Stretton* (1905) (Coventry /Lichfield), 326.

1391/2, Aug. to Mar., *custos* of the [Lady] chapel, WCM C.289, C.250; the inventory of vestments and plate which he handed over to William Owston, q.v., on 3 Mar., has been printed in *Hist. Mss Comm. 14th Report*, Appndx 8 (1895), 198–199 (WCM B.1870).

1401, 24 June, refectorer, *Reg. Sed. Vac.*, 373.

1388, 21 Aug., 30th in order at the el. of a prior, Liber Albus, fo 334ᵛ.

1401, 24 June, 26th at the el. of a bp, *Reg. Sed. Vac.*, 373.

III John STRATFORD [Stratteford, Stretford

occ. 1466 d. 1501/2

1466, 20 Dec., ord acol. and subdcn, carnary chapel by Worcester cathedral, Reg. Carpenter, i, 566.

[1471], dcn, recd *lit. dim.* for pr.'s orders, *ib.*, ii, 42.

1471, 21 Sept., ord pr., Whitbourne, *Reg. Stanbury* (Hereford), 167.

1471/2, celebrated his first mass and recd *exennia* of 2s. 3d. from the kitchener, WCM C.155.

1478/82, kitchener, WCM C.741, C.160, C.99, C.100.

1485/6; 1489/94; 1495, 29 June; 1495/6; 1499, 21 July; 1500, 5 May, cellarer, WCM C.488; C.208, C.748, C.103, C.104, C.588; Reg. A.6(i), fo 104; WCM C.626; Reg. A.6(ii), fo 1ᵛ; WCM B.883. Henry Chester, q.v., and he may have been joint cellarers in 1498/9, WCM C.627.

1496/9, almoner, WCM E.178, C.209, C.209a.

1478/9, visited Overbury, WCM C.741.

1490/1, 1491/2, pd visits to Overbury, WCM C.748, C.751.

1492, 23/24 June, one of the seven nominees for the priorate, Reg. A.6(i), fo 107ᵛ, and Reg. Morton, 91.

1493/4, visited Grimley, WCM C.588.

1495, 29 June, one of three proctors apptd by the prior and convent to attend the Black Monk Chapter, Pantin, *BMC*, iii, 216 (Reg. A.6(i), fo 104).

1495/6, visited Harvington, WCM C.626.

1497, 13 May, sent by the prior, with Thomas Mildenham, q.v., to the abp to obtain the prior's comm. for *sed. vac.* jurisdiction, *Reg. Sed. Vac.*, 227.

1498, 25 Oct., 7th in order on the visitation certificate, *Reg. abp Morton*, ii, no 458.

1498/9, visited Harvington, WCM C.627.

1499, 21 July, one of the seven nominees for the priorate, Reg. A.6(ii), fo 1ᵛ and Reg. S. Gigli, 343; they were presented to bp Fox (Durham) acting for Gigli at Southwark on 2 Sept., Reg. A.6(ii), fo 1ᵛ.

1501/2, d., and the chamberlain sold his bedding, WCM C.49.

IV John STRATFORD [Stretford

occ. 1508/10

1508, 18 Mar., ord acol., carnary chapel by Worcester cathedral, Reg. S. Gigli, 297.

1509, 22 Dec., ord dcn, carnary chapel, *ib.*, 301.

1510, 21 Sept., ord pr., carnary chapel, *ib.*, 305.

[Robert de STRATTONE

occ. 1342 occ. 1346/7

1342, 21 Dec., ord dcn, Hartlebury, *Reg. Bransford*, no 1049, with John Troubrugg, q.v., but no house is specified.

1346/7, visited Bromsgrove twice, WCM C.552.

Note: these entries are uncertain; they may not ref. to a monk of Worcester.]

Richard de STRENGESHAM

occ. 1345 occ. 1351

1345, 19 Feb., ord subdcn, Hartlebury, *Reg. Bransford*, no 1060.

1346, 11 Mar., ord dcn, Hartlebury, *ib.*, no 1069; no house is specified.

1351, 8 June, granted a papal licence to choose his own confessor, who was empowered to give plenary remission at d., *CPL*, iii (1342–1362), 380.

STRETFORD(E)
see Stratford

Thomas STREYNSHAM [Strainsham, Straynnesham, Straynsham, Straynysham, Streynesham
occ. 1458 d. 1486/7

1458, 23 Sept., ord acol. and subdcn, Worcester cathedral, Reg. Carpenter, i, 547.
1460, 7 June, ord dcn, Hereford cathedral, Reg. Stanbury (Hereford), fo 118v (in the printed text it appears as Swaynesham).
1460, 20 Dec., ord pr., Worcester cathedral, Reg. Carpenter, i, 554.
1459/60, celebrated his first mass and the kitchener gave *exennia* of 2s. 3d. The slight discrepancy in the dating may be due to a delay in making up the acct.
1462/3, 1465/6, chaplain to the prior, Reg. A.6(i), fo 24, WCM C.96.
1466/9, subcellarer, WCM C.735, C.736, C. 697.
1472, chaplain again, Reg. A.6(i), fo 74.
1478, 14 Sept., hostiller, *ib.*, fo 73v; also *ib.*, fo 81 dated 1478.
1480/4, chamberlain, WCM C.99, C.100, C.47, E.248.

1466/7, pd visits to Overbury and Sedgeberrow, WCM C.735, C.769.
1467/8, one of three monks who were rewarded by the master of the Lady chapel for singing, WCM C.281; see William Dene and Robert Myston. He also visited Overbury, WCM C.736.
1468/9, visited Harvington and Overbury, WCM C.623, C.697.
1475, 7 Jan., sent with Walter Fraunceys, q.v., to arrange for the adm. of monks to the priory, and on the following day he was present at the examination of the candidates in the prior's chamber, Reg. Carpenter, ii, 135.
1478, present as witness when the sacrist, Nicholas Hambury, q.v., took his oath of office, Reg. A.6(i), fo 81.
1486/7, d., and the almoner pd the brief bearer, WCM C.207.

Name in Oxford, Corpus Christi College Ms 157, Florentius Wigorniensis etc., (early 12th c.), 'memorandum quod—deliberavit hoc librum fr Thome Powycke monacho majoris Malvernie et ipse deliberavit predicto—librum vocatum Guido de bello Trojano, A.D. 1480'.

STURBRIG(GE), Sturbyrg
see Stowrebrugge

STYVYNTON
see Stevintone

John SUCKELEY [Sucley
occ. 1458 occ. 1466/7

1458, 23 Sept., ord acol., Worcester cathedral, Reg. Carpenter, i, 547.
1461, 19 Sept., ord subdcn, Claines, *ib.*, i, 555.
1465, 21 Dec., ord pr., bp's chapel, Alvechurch, *ib.*, i, 564.
1465/6, celebrated his first mass and recd 2s. 3d. from both the precentor and the kitchener, WCM C.381, C.152 (dated 1466/7).

Name in Worcs. Ms Q.30, Porphyrius etc. (13th c.); name occ. twice on the flyleaves.

Name also in Hereford Cathedral Ms P.VI.4, a Bible (13th c.); on fo. 313v—*Monachus Wygornie.*

Robert de SUCKELEYE [Sockelegh, Sockeleye, Sukeleg', Sukkelegg
occ. 1274 occ. 1296

1287, 2 Jan., cellarer, *Reg. Giffard*, 304, 325; in 1292/3, described as former cellarer, Wilson, *Early Comp. Rolls*, 14 (WCM C.51).
1296, 11 July, chamberlain, *ib.*, 480.

1274, 21 Sept., with Thomas de Wych, q.v., apptd proctor to present the seven nominees for the priorate to the bp, *Reg. Giffard*, 62. Here the name is transcribed as 'Strickeley'.
[1283], the bp wrote to him and to Thomas de Wych concerning tithes in the parish of St John, Worcester, *ib.*, 176.
1287, 2 Jan., one of the seven nominees for the priorate, *ib.*, 304, 325.
1290, 10 Apr., the prior [Philip Aubyn, q.v.] pd a heavy fine for himself, Suckeleye, former cellarer, and others for trespass in Feckenham forest, *CPR (1281–1292)*, 350.
1296, 11 July, one of the seven nominees for the priorate, *ib.*, 480.

I John SUDBURY [Subdebury, Suddebury
occ. 1404 d. [by 1419]

1404, 20 Sept., ord acol., Llanthony priory, Gloucester, *Reg. Clifford*, no 122, p. 85.
1405, 19 Sept., ord dcn, Cirencester abbey *Reg. Clifford*, no 126, p. 93; on his 1404/5 acct the cellarer records the expenses of the precentor and ordinands going to Cirencester, WCM C.78.
1407, 24 Sept., ord pr., Blockley, *Reg. Clifford*, no 133, p. 107.

[by 1419, d.; there is only one monk by this name on the 1419 el. list. See below.]

II John SUDBURY
occ. ?1419 occ. ?1476/7

1419, 1 Apr., ord pr., Worcester cathedral, *Reg. Sed. Vac.*, 392.
1423/4, prob. subsacrist, or possibly *tumbarius*, WCM C.425.

1438, 12/13 Feb., chamberlain, Liber Albus, fo 457ᵛ.
1438/9, kitchener, WCM C.146.
1441/3, bursar [cellarer], WCM C.727, C.728.
1443/8, cellarer, WCM C.729 (as J.S.), C.493, C.730, C.90, C.665.
1448/50, precentor, WCM C.824, C.379.
1454/5, *tumbarius*, WCM C.471.
1464/5, [1467 × 1469], subprior, WCM C.95, C.846.
1466/7; 1468/9; 1473/7, almoner WCM C.97; C.202; C.203, C.237, C.472, C.740.

1419, 24 Apr., 36th (out of 40) in order at the el. of a bp, *Reg. Sed. Vac.*, 407.
1433, 9 Dec., 19th at the el. of a bp, *ib.*, 432.
1435/6, 1 July, apptd proctor, with John Cleve, q.v., in a dispute with the preceptor of St Oswald's hospital, Liber Albus, fo 449.
1438, 12 Feb., one of the seven nominees for the priorate, Reg. Bourgchier, 84.
1442/3, pd a visit to Overbury, WCM C.728.
1443/4, visited Overbury and Sedgeberrow, WCM C.729, C.773.
1444, 15 Jan., one of the seven nominees for the priorate, Reg. Bourgchier, 193.
1445/6, visited Overbury, WCM C.730.
1447/8, visited Newnham, WCM C.665.
1448/9, visited Tibberton to rec. rents, WCM C.824.
1451/2, visited Hallow, WCM C.601.
[1464], 30 July, with John Lawerne I and John Smethwyk, q.v., apptd proctors for the diocesan synod, Reg. A.6(i), fo 34ᵛ.
1466/8, pd visits to Overbury, WCM C.735, C.736.
1468/9, visited Harvington and Overbury, WCM C.623, C.697.
1469, 14 Aug., one of the seven nominees for the priorate, Reg. Carpenter, ii, 13–16; also in Reg. A.6(i), fo 60ᵛ (dated 16 Aug.).
1471/3, pd visits to Overbury, WCM C.738, C.739.
1475/6, visited Sedgeberrow, WCM C.778.
1476/7, visited Overbury, WCM C.740.

Note: there is obviously a problem here! I have been guided by the fact that there is no indication of there ever having been two John Sudburys in the house at the same time. It is most unfortunate that the ordination lists fail us here, as do the accts which usually include the death notices. There is a noticeable gap in the second John Sudbury's career between 1454/64 but nothing to suggest that the entries in the later 1460s and the 1470s apply to yet another John Sudbury; it is impossible to draw even an arbitrary line in this case.

III John SUDBURY [Sobburye, Subburye
occ. 1490 d. 1501/2

1490, 6 Mar., ord acol., carnary chapel by Worcester cathedral, Reg. Morton, 143.
1490, 10 Apr., ord subdcn, carnary chapel, *ib.*, 145.
1492, 22 Sept., ord dcn, carnary chapel, *ib.*, 157.
1494, 24 May, ord pr., carnary chapel, *ib.*, 162.

1498, 25 Oct., 27th in order on the visitation certificate, *Reg. abp Morton*, ii, no 458.
1501/2, d., and the chamberlain sold his bedding, WCM C.49.

Robert SUDBURY
occ. 1476 occ. 1482/3

1476, 8 June, ord acol., carnary chapel by Worcester cathedral, Reg. Carpenter, ii, 207.
1477, 5 Apr., ord subdcn, Worcester cathedral, Reg. Alcock, 245.
1478, 7 Mar., ord dcn, carnary chapel, *ib.*, 250.
1479, 18 Dec., ord pr., carnary chapel, *ib.*, 260.

1482/3, subcellarer, WCM C.744.

1482/3, pd a visit to Overbury, WCM C.744.

Thomas SUDBURY [Sidberye, Sidbury, Sudburi, Sudburye
occ. 1510 occ. 1540

1510, 21 Sept., ord acol., carnary chapel by Worcester cathedral, Reg. S. Gigli, 304.
1512, 27 Mar., ord subdcn, carnary chapel, *ib.*, 314.
1515, 22 Sept., ord dcn, carnary chapel, *ib.*, 328.

1520/3, subcellarer; he succ. John Multon, q.v., and was de *novo electo*, Reg. A.17, 9, 27; Wilson, *Accts Henry VIII*, 6–9 (WCM C.412); Reg. A.17, 193.
1527, [Aug.], steward [of the prior's hospice], *Jnl More*, 251.
1527/8, Nov. to Mar., pittancer, *Jnl More*, 44.
1529/32; 1534, 17 Aug.; 1535, 22 Feb.; 1536, 13 Mar., cellarer, WCM C.414a, C.414b, C.414c; *DK 7th Report*, Appndx 2, 305; Reg. A.6(ii), fo 187ᵛ; Reg. A.6(iii), fo 1.

1520, Feb./Mar., went to London to 'general chapter' with prior William More, q.v., *Jnl More*, 101.
1521, 22 July, 22nd in order on the visitation certificate, Reg. abp Warham, ii, fo 293ᵛ.
1527, sent, with John Lawerne II, q.v., to London on business at the prior's expense, *Jnl More*, 250.
1529, went to London during Eastertide on business for the prior, *ib.*, 291.
1530, 1 Jan., gave a gift of two capons to the prior, *Jnl More*, 302.
1531/2, 6th in order on the clerical subsidy list and pd over £26 as cellarer and 3s. 4d. commons, Reg. A.12, fo 135.
1534, 17 Aug., subscribed to the Act of Supremacy, *DK 7th Report*, Appndx 2, 305.
1535, 22 Feb., abp Cranmer issued an injunction that Sudbury, cellarer, was not to be prevented from having his new stall in choir, Wilson, 'Visitations', 367 (Reg. A.6(ii), fos 187,

187^{v} for the injunctions, and Reg. A.12, fo 145 for the items concerning Thomas Blockley, q.v., and Sudbury).

1535, n.d., the petition signed by the subprior [John Lawerne II, q.v.] and many other monks vs the reinstatement of William Fordham, q.v., as cellarer, commended Sudbury as a competent cellarer who had taken in hand reparations on the manors and in the monastery precincts and was also paying off the debts incurred by Fordham, *L and P Henry VIII*, ix, no 653.

1535, 14 Oct., in a letter to Cromwell, Roger Neckham, q.v., declared that Sudbury was negligent and favoured his friends; and in both this and another letter written the same day he accused him of challenging his authority in the house. In the second letter he described Sudbury as quarrelsome and as having asserted his right to remain cellarer, *ib.*, nos 609, 610.

1535, 21 Oct., wrote to Cromwell and denied the above charges, *ib.*, no 654.

1535, 4 Nov., wrote again to Cromwell to deny the accusations of incompetence which he attributed to malice. He said he was willing to resign as long as a 'discreet and provident' monk was apptd in his place, *ib.*, no 764.

1536, 19 Jan., Roger Neckham complained to Cromwell that Sudbury continued to be undecided about whether to remain in office or to resign and had not yet produced his accts for audit which he said he would prefer to show to Cromwell than to Neckham, *L and P Henry VIII*, x, no 132.

1536, 13 Mar., 4th in order at the 'el.' of Henry Holbech, q.v., Reg. A.6(iii), fo 1.

1540, 18 Jan., was assigned a pension of £6 13s. 4d., *ib.*, xv, no 81.

Name in Worcs. Ms Q.89, Sermones etc. (later 13th c.); on fo 30^{v} his name and that of John Lawerne I, q.v., appear and on fo 1 *tradatur iste liber fratribus minoribus Wygorn'*.

As a New Year's gift to the prior in 1530 his mother gave a 'chese', *Jnl More*, 302.

SYSSETTER
see Cicestre

SYMON
d. by 1122/3

1122/3, d. by this date, because his name occ. in a Savigny mortuary roll of the above date, Delisle, *Rouleau Mortuaire*, pl. xxv, tit. 87.

Note: this may be Simeon, q.v.

Thomas TALBOT
occ. 1352 occ. 1366

1352, 24 Sept., one of two whom the prior was comm. by the bp to adm., Liber Albus, fo 210^{v}.

1353, 23 July, the prior was comm. to rec. his prof., *ib.*, fo 213.

1353, 21 Dec., ord acol., Ombersley, Reg. Bryan, i, 13.

1354, 20 Sept., ord subdcn, Tewkesbury abbey, *ib.*, i, 88.

1355, 19 Mar., ord dcn, Hartlebury, *ib.*, i, 101.

1357, 23 Sept., ord pr., Bredon, *ib.*, i, 108.

1357/8, celebrated his first mass; the cellarer and prior gave *exennia*, WCM C.64.

1363, Jan./Sept., prob. student at Oxford with Thomas Cros, q.v., because the pittancer listed them separately on his acct indicating that their share of allowances had to be pd by some means other than the usual procedure, e.g., in their absence. Cros was almost certainly at Oxford and Talbot may have been his *socius* this yr, WCM C.306.

1358/9, with Nicholas Clanefield, q.v., stopped at Dodderhill on the way to [?Great] Hampton [?Lucy], WCM C.835.

1366, 17 Sept., apptd as proctor to attend the Black Monk Chapter in Northampton, Pantin, *BMC*, iii, 203 (Liber Albus, fo 232).

TEDYNHAM
see Tudenham

John TENDEBURY [Temdebury, Temedebury, Tendebury
occ. [1396] occ. 1421/2

[1396], 1 July, one of three novices whose prof. the prior was comm. to rec., Reg. Winchcombe, 32.

1397, 6 June, ord acol., Worcester cathedral, *ib.*, 135.

1399/1400, was taken to Alcester for ord. [pr.] and the cellarer pd the expenses; he also bought bread and wine for Tendebury's celebrations after his first mass, WCM C.476. The almoner sent *exennia* of 3s., WCM C.185.

1419, 24 Apr.; 1419/20, 1422/3, precentor, *Reg. Sed. Vac.*, 407; WCM C.375, C.376.

1401, 24 June, 41st in order at the el. of a bp, *Reg. Sed. Vac.*, 373.

1415, 8 Mar., granted papal licence to have a portable altar, *CPL*, vi (1404–1415), 498.

1419, 24 Apr., 16th at the el. of a bp, *Reg. Sed. Vac.*, 407.

1421/2, on the cellarer's list of creditors, WCM C.84a.

Richard TENDEBURY [Temdebury
occ. 1426 occ. 1457/8

1426, 1 Dec., ord acol., Worcester cathedral, Reg. Polton, 207.

[?1430, Dec.], ord pr., no place named, *ib.*, 231.

1430/1, celebrated his first mass and recd 2s. 6d. *exennia* from each of the almoner, hostiller and kitchener, WCM C.194 (1431/2, a yr late stated), C.232, C.144.

1435/7, chaplain to the prior, and on 8 Oct. 1435 began to make entries in the Liber Albus, fo 448; Thomas Welford, q.v., made his first entry on 15 Aug. 1437, *ib.*, fo 455.

1426/7, ill, and the infirmarer spent 6s. 8d. on medical treatment, WCM C.328.

1433, 9 Dec., 38th in order at the el. of a bp, *Reg. Sed. Vac.*, 432.

1453, Feb./Sept., on the cellarer's list of creditors, WCM C.93.

1457/8, mentioned on the chamberlain's acct with regard to the purchase of cloth [?for his habit], WCM C.44.

Roger de TENDEBURY [Temedebury, Temedbiry, Temedbury

occ. 1348 occ. 1369

1348, 20 Dec., ord acol., bp's chapel, Hartlebury, *Reg. Bransford*, no 1108.

1349, 28 Mar., ord subdcn, bp's chapel, Hartlebury, *ib.*, no 1110.

1349, 6 June, ord dcn, bp's chapel, Hartlebury, *ib.*, no 1341 (p. 342), transcribed as Ledebury.

1349, 19 Sept., ord pr., Hereford cathedral, *Reg. Trillek* (Hereford), 503.

1354/5, student at Oxford, with Nicholas de Morton, q.v., and they recd 104s. for maintenance from the cellarer, WCM C.62.

1351, 8 Jan., granted papal licence to choose his own confessor who was authorized to give plenary remission at d., *CPL*, iii (1342–1362), 380.

1359, 8 Mar., apptd penitentiary in the city and adcnry of Worcester, Reg. Bryan, i, 190.

1361, 5 Feb., another apptment as penitentiary, *ib.*, i, 220.

1363, 7 Feb., apptd penitentiary in the city of Worcester for one yr, Reg. Barnet, 44.

[1364], Apr. and May, with a secular clerk acted as commissary of the prior in conducting *sed. vac.* visitations of the abbeys of Tewkesbury, Gloucester and Cirencester and of several deaneries *Reg. Sed. Vac.*, 220–221.

1369, 2 July, comm. by the bp, with another to deal with criminous clerks, Reg. Lynn, 85.

Name in Worcs. Ms F.56, G. de Fontibus etc., (late 13th c.); contains lectures on the Sentences, *tradatur*—on fo 2.

Stephen de TETBURY [Tettebury

occ. 1345/7

1345, 19 Feb., ord acol., Hartlebury, *Reg. Bransford*, no 1060 (entered as John).

1346, 11 Mar., ord dcn, Hartlebury, *Reg. Bransford*, no 1069.

1346/7, student at Oxford; the cellarer recorded his expenses *vs Oxon'* 30s., and of the hire of two horses for him and for Roger de Bosbury, q.v., 4s. 1d. He also entered a further 3s. 4d. *in expensis eorundem*, and 20s. from the prior for his habit, WCM C.61.

I John de TEUKESBURY [Teukusbury, Theukesbury

occ. 1352 d. 1394/5

1352, 24 Sept., one of two whom the prior was comm. by the bp to adm., Liber Albus, fo 210ᵛ.

1353, 23 July, the prior was comm. by the bp to rec. his prof., *ib.*, fo 213.

1354, 20 Sept., ord subdcn, Tewkesbury abbey, Reg. Bryan, i, 88.

1355, 19 Mar., ord dcn, Hartlebury, *ib.*, 101.

[1359], 26 Mar., ord pr., Hartlebury, *ib.*, 115 (the yr is given as 1358).

1358/9, one of five who celebrated their first mass and the precentor gave *exennia*, WCM C.356.

1370, 3 Apr., kitchener, Liber Albus, fo 246.

1388/91, 1392/3, 1394, Sept./Dec., *tumbarius*, WCM C.455–459.

1373, 4/7 Dec., 7th in order at the el. of a bp, *Reg. Sed. Vac.*, 290.

1378/9, ill, and the infirmarer spent 3s. for medicines, WCM C.241.

1388, 21 Aug., 5th in order at the el. of a prior, Liber Albus, fo 334ᵛ.

1394/5, d., and the precentor bought parchment for the brief, WCM C.369.

II John TEUKESBURY [Teukysbury, Tewkesbury

occ. 1456 occ. 1468/9

1456, 27 Mar., ord acol., chapel of the bp's palace, Worcester, Reg. Carpenter, i, 541.

1457, 16 Apr., ord subdcn, bp's chapel, Worcester, *ib.*, i, 543.

1458, 23 Sept., ord dcn, Worcester cathedral, *ib.*, i, 547.

1460, 7 June, ord pr., Hereford cathedral, *Reg. Stanbury* (Hereford), 146.

1459/60, celebrated his first mass and recd *exennia* from the prior and the kitchener, WCM C.400, C.149.

1468/9, gave a small sum as alms to the almoner, WCM C.202.

Adam de THEUKESBURY [Theokesbur'

occ. 1300 occ. 1317

1300, 17 Dec., ord dcn, Worcester, *Reg. Giffard*, 522; no house specified.

1317, 20 Oct., 21st in order at the el. of a prior, Liber Albus, fo 83ᵛ.

1317, 17 Nov., with Robert de Clifton I appeared before the bp at Strood with the instruments concerning the el., and on 18 Nov. they presented the seven candidates to the bp at Dartford, *ib.*, fos 83ᵛ, 84.

I THOMAS (Prior I)

occ. 1080 d. 1113

1080–1113 prior: succ. Aelfstan q.v., and first occ. 1080; d. 4 Oct. 1113, *Fasti*, ii, 102, *HRH*, 83.

1089, 20 May, as prior witnessed a grant of land by the bp to the monks, *Worcs. Cart.*, no 3.
1092, ordered by bp Wulstan to lead an inquiry into the parochial rights of the cathedral church and of all the other churches in the city of Worcester, *ib.*, no 52.
c. 1104, name occ. in the list of monks in *Durham Liber Vitae*, fo 22; his name also occ. in a mortuary roll of Savigny dated c. 1122/3, Delisle, *Rouleaux des Morts*, 313.

Dr Mason suggests that he may have been of French origin, *Wulfstan*, 170.

II THOMAS
occ. 1175

1175, 9 Apr., subprior, *Worcs. Cart.*, no 165.
1175, 9 Apr., witness to an inspeximus and to an agreement concerning an advowson, *ib.*, nos 165, 177, 178.

III THOMAS (Prior II)
occ. c. 1220 d. 1260

1252–1260, prior: succ. 1 Nov. 1252; d. by Dec. 1260, *Fasti*, ii, 104.
1220/52, subprior, *Ann. Wigorn.*, 441.
1236, 24 Aug., with Ernulf, q.v., recd a royal licence to el. a bp, *CPR (1232–1247)*, 157.
1251, sent by the bp, with the third prior of Gloucester to visit the monks of Tewkesbury in order to find out if they were adhering to his new constitutions, *Ann. Tewkes.*, 146–147.
1252, Sept., excused himself from attendance at the Black Monk Chapter at Osney, *eo quod infirmatur*, Bloom *Original Charters*, 173.
1256, 16 Apr., installed the adcn of Gloucester, *Ann. Wigorn.*, 443; however, the adcn occ. as such the previous yr, *Fasti*, ii, 108.
1258, 12 May, made an agreement with the abbot of Reading, granting land, *Worcs. Cart.*, no 466.

In Reg. A.4, fo 88ᵛ there is a 15th c. copy of an ordinance issued by him in 1253 in the form of a 'relaxatio servicii quod non tanget regulam, de consensu conventu . . . ut divinum servicium protraxius pungtacius honestius et sine tedio fiat'. In return 'dicet conventus cotidie particulatim totum psalterium per porciones cuilibet assignatas', printed in *Worcs. Cart.*, no 552.

IV THOMAS
occ. 1242 occ. 1246/7

1242, chaplain to the bp, *CClR (1237–1242)*, 418.
1246/7, sacrist and at the same time receiver of the bpric, C. Dyer, *Lords and Peasants in a Changing Society: the Estates of the Bishopric of Worcester, 680–1540* (Cambridge, 1980), 380 (Oxford, Bod. Ms Rolls, Worcestershire no 4).
1242, Apr., sent by the prior and chapter to deliver 30m. to the king in aid of his expedition to Gascony, *CClR (1237–1242)*, 418.

V THOMAS
occ. 1292

1292, 16 June, returned after a six yr stay at the curia and was *debilitatus* and *gravatus* because the Roman see was vacant and his stay had been a waste of time, *Ann. Wigorn.*, 512.

VI THOMAS
occ. [1307 × 1313]

[1307 × 1313], sacrist *temp.* bp Walter Reynolds, WCM B.1683.
[1307 × 1313], witnessed a grant, *ib.*

Note: the sacrist's seal is attached to this grant.

THOUN(E)Y
see Tony

THURKILLUS
occ. c. 1104

Name occ. in the list of monks in *Durham Liber Vitae*, fo 22.

J. THWARTONER' [Twharton'
occ. 1388/90

1388, 27 Oct., apptd *tumbarius*, *Reg. Wakefield*, no 795 (as Thwartoneys).
1389/90, the chamberlain bought hide or leather [*emptio pellium*] for making boots for him, WCM C.17.

TIBURTON
see Tyberton

William de TONY [Thouney, Thouny, Toney, Touny
occ. 1321 occ. 1328/9

1321, 9 Dec., one of three whose prof. the prior was comm. to rec., Liber Albus, fo 103 (not adm. as in *Liber Albus*, no 925).
1321, 19 Dec., ord subdcn, Kidderminster, *Reg. Cobham*, 113 (as Tonny).
1322, 18 Dec., ord dcn, Ombersley, *ib.*, 143.
1323, 17 Dec., ord pr., Cropthorne, *ib.*, 167.
1328/9, subcellarer, WCM C.546; and see William de Peyto.
1328/9, visited Bromsgrove and Henwick, WCM C.546, C.940.

John de TREDYNTON [Tredinton, Tredyngtone, Tredyntone
occ. 1360 d. 1401/2

1360, 30 Apr., one of three whose prof. the prior was comm. to rec., Liber Albus, fo 226ᵛ, Reg. Bryan, i, 135.
1361, 22 May, ord acol., and subdcn Alvechurch, Reg. Bryan, i, 121.
1361, 18 Sept., ord dcn, Alvechurch, *ib.*, i, 123.
1362, 17 Dec., ord pr., bp's chapel, Hartlebury, Reg. Barnet, 39.

1362/3, celebrated his first mass and the precentor gave *exennia* of 2s. 2d., WCM C.359.

1370, 3 Apr., subsacrist, Liber Albus, fo 246; and see below.

1370, [Apr.]/1372, subcellarer, taking over from William Power, q.v., WCM C.785, C.805, C.806.

1373, 4 Dec., hostiller, *Reg. Sed. Vac.*, 290.

[1378], precentor, Liber Albus, fo 274 (as J. de T.).

1395/6, 1398/9, prob. subprior, WCM C.496; see below.

1369/70, visited Sedgeberrow, WCM C.785.

1370, 3 Apr., 12th in order at the el. of a prior, Liber Albus, fo 246.

1370/1, visited Tibberton, WCM C.805.

1371/2, visited Hallow and Tibberton, WCM C.596, C.806.

1373, 4/7 Dec., 11th at the el. of a bp *Reg. Sed. Vac.*, 290.

1375/6, had in his custody the 100s. remaining from the acct of the *tumbarius* and may therefore have been subsacrist, Hamilton, *Comp. Rolls*, 75 (WCM C.453).

1376, [Nov./Dec.], present in the dormitory and witnessed the surrender of a lease, WCM E.27.

[1378], apptd proctor, with a secular clerk, in matters relating to an episcopal visitation, Liber Albus, fo 274 (as J. de T.).

1388, 21 Aug., 7th in order at the el. of a prior, Liber Albus, fo 334v.

1395/6, named on the cellarer's acct on the rota for *minutiones*, WCM C.77.

1398/9, a similar ref. on the pittancer's acct, WCM C.496; these entries suggest that he may have been subprior (or possibly precentor) to judge by the format under *minutio* on other accounts.

1398/9, 1400/1, recd 6s. 8d., during both of these yrs from the chamberlain for his habit, WCM C.24, C.25.

1401, 24 June, 5th in order at the el. of a bp, *Reg. Sed. Vac.*, 372.

1401/2, d., and the chamberlain pd the brief bearer, WCM C.26.

John de TROUBRUGG [Troubrugge
occ. 1340 occ. 1356

1340, 28 Nov., one of three *clerici* whom the prior was comm. to examine and adm. after having presented them to the bp, *Reg. Bransford*, no 377.

1342, 21 Dec., ord dcn, Hartlebury, *Reg. Bransford*, no 1049.

1345, chaplain to the prior, Liber Albus, fo 195.

1349/52, subcellarer, WCM C.436, C.590, C.437; see Walter de Froucestre.

1345/6, one of the monks who were employed to pay the manorial reeves *pro messione bladorum*, WCM C.60.

1349/50, pd visits to Harvington and Overbury, WCM C.692, C.700.

1350/1, visited Hallow and Henwick, WCM C.590, C.633.

1351, 8 Jan., granted papal licence to choose his own confessor who was authorized to give plenary remission at d., *CPL*, iii (1349–1362), 380.

1351/2, visited Tibberton, WCM C.801.

1356, 3 Nov., presented two candidates to the bp for adm. as monks, but the bp turned them down because the necessary documents were lacking, Reg. Bryan, i, 42; see John de Malverne I and William de Redbourn.

Walter de TUDENHAM [Tedynham
occ. 1370 d. [1370/1]

1370, 13 Apr., ord subdcn, [Worcester cathedral], Reg. Lynn, 50.

1370, 21 Sept., ord dcn, Westbury collegiate church, *ib.*, 51.

[1370/1], d. and the chamberlain sold his *panni*, WCM C.497.

John TYBERTON [Tiburton, Tyburton
occ. 1510/12

1510, 21 Sept., ord acol., carnary chapel by Worcester cathedral, Reg. S. Gigli, 304.

1510, 21 Dec., ord subdcn, carnary chapel, *ib.*, 305.

1511, 14 June, ord dcn, carnary chapel, *ib.*, 308.

1512, 27 Mar., ord pr., carnary chapel, *ib.*, 315.

Richard TYBERTON [Tiberton, Tyborton, Tyburton
occ. 1407 d. 1457/8

1407, 24 Sept., ord acol. and subdcn, Blockley, *Reg. Clifford*, no 133.

1408, 14 Apr., ord dcn, Dominican convent, Worcester, Reg. Peverel, 173.

1409, 2 Mar., ord pr., Worcester cathedral, *ib.*, 178.

1408/9, celebrated his first mass; the cellarer contributed wine to the festivities and the hostiller, bread, wine and ale, WCM C.81, C.218.

1419, 24 Apr., subcellarer, *Reg. Sed. Vac.*, 407.

1419/20, chamberlain, WCM C.32.

1420, June/1423, spring, cellarer, WCM C.83–84a, C.721; see John Hambury whom he succ. and William Hodynton I who followed.

1426/8, kitchener, WCM C.859 (with Robert Lawerne, q.v.), C.617 (with Thomas Colwall, q.v.).

1439/40, refectorer, WCM C.419.

1415, 4 Mar., obtained a papal licence to choose his own confessor and another licence on 8 Mar. to have a portable altar, *CPL*, vi (1404–1415), 364, 498.

1419, 24 Apr., 22nd in order at the el. of a bp, *Reg. Sed. Vac.*, 407.

1420/1, 1422/3, pd visits to Overbury, WCM C.720, C.721.

1426/7, visited Harvington, WCM C.859.
1433, 9 Dec., 10th at the el. of a bp, *Reg. Sed. Vac.*, 432.
1439/40, visited Bevere with Thomas Colwall, q.v., WCM C.89.
1440/1, on the subcellarer's acct, assisting with *recept' bladorum*, WCM C.447.
1444, 15/16 Jan., proctor, with John Broghton, q.v., apptd to present the seven nominees for the priorate to the bp, Reg. Bourgchier, 193–195.
1453, Feb./Sept., on the cellarer's list of creditors, WCM C.93.
1457/8, d., and the chamberlain sold *divers' harnec'* for which he recd 16s., WCM C.44.

UHTRED [Uhtredus
occ. 1092 d. 1132

1092, precentor, *Worcs. Cart.*, no 52; John of Worcester says that he held this office for many years, see below.
1092, present at bp Wulstan's synod and a member of the comm. set up to investigate the parochial rights of the cathedral church, *Worcs. Cart.*, no 52; see Thomas I.
c. 1104, name occ. in Durham Liber Vitae, fo 22.
1132, 2 Apr., d. after collapsing during mass while John I of Worcester, q.v., was standing beside him; John of Worcester, *Chronicle*, 36. The latter describes him with warm affection as a humble and faithful monk who was old and partially paralysed at the time of his d., *ib.*
Name in Cambridge, Corpus Christi College Ms 367, pt ii, Miscellanea (?11th c.), on fo 52 of which there is a letter addressed to prior Warin, q.v. and to Uhtred *cantor* from the abbot and prior of Westminster concerning a monk of [Great] Malvern.

ULF
occ. c. 1104
Name occ. in the list of monks in *Durham Liber Vitae*, fo 22.

John de UPTONE [Opton
occ. [1369] occ. 1404/5

[1369], 1 Oct., one of seven whom the precentor was comm. to prof., Reg. Lynn, 89.
1370, 21 Dec., ord subdcn, Hartlebury, *ib.*, 53.
1371, 20 Dec., ord pr., Worcester cathedral, *ib.*, 55.
1372/3, the cellarer charged his acct, a yr late, for wine for the festivities after the celebration of Uptone's first mass, WCM C.68.
1389/91, subcellarer, WCM C.445, C.766.
1401, 24 June, third prior, *Reg. Sed. Vac.*, 373.
1373, 4 Dec., 27th in order at the el. of a prior, *Reg. Sed. Vac.*, 290.
1380/1, ill and the infirmarer spent 12d. on medicine, WCM C.242.
1388, 21 Aug., 23rd in order at the el. of a prior, Liber Albus, fo 334v.
1389/90, the chamberlain bought leather or hide [*pell'*] for his boots, WCM C.17.
1390/1, pd a visit to Sedgeberrow, WCM C.766.
1391/2, ill, and the infirmarer charged 4s. 1d. to his acct for treatment, WCM C.243; he was one of the cellarer's creditors, prob. in connection with the subcellarer's office which he had just relinquished, WCM C.74.
1401, 24 June, 17th in order at the el. of a prior, *Reg. Sed. Vac.*, 373.
1404/5, gave 10d. as alms to the almoner, WCM C.187.

Richard UPTON
occ. 1468/9 d. 1479

1468/9, one of six who celebrated their first mass; recd *exennia* from the almoner and kitchener, WCM C.202, C.154.
Note: the other five monks occ. in the ordination lists, and so it seems likely that he entered later, when he was already a dcn. The fact that there was no delay before his apptment to a responsible obedientiary office suggests that he was already a man of maturity and experience.
1471/3; 1474, 29 June; 1475/6, subcellarer, WCM C.738, C.449; Reg. A.6(i), fo 80v; WCM C.778.
1474/5, hostiller, WCM C.237.
1476/8, kitchener, WCM C.158, C.159 (the latter is printed in Hamilton, *Comp. Rolls*, 27–31).
1478/9, acting cellarer on the d. of Nicholas Hambury, q.v., WCM C.741.
1478, third prior, Reg. A.6(i), fo 81.
1471/2, visited Overbury, WCM C.738.
1472/3, visited Harvington and Overbury, WCM C.618, C.739.
1474, 29 June, apptd proctor to attend the Black Monk Chapter, Pantin, *BMC*, iii, 216 (Reg. A.6(i), fo 80v).
1475/6, visited Sedgeberrow, WCM C.778.
1478, one of the witnesses to the sacrist's oath of office, Reg. A.6(i), fo 81.
1478/9, d. and the almoner recd money [from the cellarer] for his corrody and pd the brief bearer, WCM C.204; the chamberlain sold his *vestimenta*, WCM C.46.
1479/80, visited Overbury, WCM C.742; this entry makes it clear that he d. in 1479, prob. in Sept.

I William UPTON
d. 1487

1487, 8/14 Apr. [Passion wk], d., and the almoner distributed 2s. 6d. to the poor [who in return would pray for his soul], WCM C.207.

II William UPTON
occ. 1497 d. 1501/2

1497, 14 Apr., ord acol., carnary chapel by Worcester cathedral, Reg. G. Gigli, 25.

1498, 14 Apr., ord subdcn, carnary chapel, *ib.*, 26.
1499, 25 May, ord pr., carnary chapel, Reg. S. Gigli, 399.
1498/9, celebrated his first mass; the hostiller gave a gift of 2s., WCM C.238.
1498, 25 Oct., 43rd and second to last in order on the visitation certificate, *Reg. abp Morton*, ii, no 458.
1501/2, d.; the chamberlain sold his bedding, WCM C.49.

URBAN
occ. [1090s]
Dr Mason describes him as prob. a monk in the final yrs of bp Wulstan. He had been sent to be educated in the cathedral priory and went on to become bp of Llandaff in 1107 at the age of 32, *Wulfstan*, 247–248.

VICHO
see Wich, Wych

VINCENTIUS
occ. c. 1104
Name occ. in the list of monks in *Durham Liber Vitae*, fo 22.

W. [Cantor
occ. c. 1270
c. 1270, returned from the curia, WCM E.4(7). See William III.

William WALESHALE [Walssale
occ. and d. 1420
1420, 2 Mar., ord acol., Worcester cathedral, Reg. Morgan, 59.
1419/20, [i.e. 1420 after 2 Mar.] d., and the chamberlain sold his *panni*, WCM C.32.

WALEWEN
see Walweyn

John de WALEYS [Walys, and le Waleys
occ. 1308 occ. 1323
1308, 25 Oct., obtained *lit. dim.* for dcn's orders, *Reg. Reynolds*, 92.
1309, 24 May, ord dcn, Cirencester *ib.*, 111.
1309, 3 Dec. obtained *lit. dim.* for pr.'s orders, *ib.*, 93.
1323, 6 Dec., at the request of Richard de Bromwych, q.v., prior of Abergavenny, the prior gave a licence for him to go there for as long as it suited the two of them, Liber Albus, fo 114.

WALKER
see Musard

Robert de WALTON
occ. 1219
1219, chamberlain [*chamberlango*], *Ann. Wigorn.*, 411.
1219, recd a *cappa* from a tenant who performed his act of homage, *ib.*

Richard WALWEYN
occ. 1441
1441, Sept., ord subdcn, Bromyard, *Reg. Spofford* (Hereford), 337.
Note: this is prob. a mistake for William Walweyn below.

William WALWEYN, B.Th., [Walewen, Wallewen, Walwayn, Walwen, Walwyn, Wawen
occ. 1442 occ. 1469
1442, 30 Mar., ord dcn, bp's chapel, Hartlebury, Reg. Bourgchier, 204.
1442, 26 May, ord pr., Ross, *Reg. Spofford* (Hereford), 339.
1441/2, celebrated his first mass, and recd a 2s. 3d. pittance from the almoner and the same amount from the pittancer in bread and ale, WCM C.199, 484.
1442, Oct./1443, Nov. chaplain to the prior, Liber Albus, fo 471.
1464/5, infirmarer, WCM C.498.
1448/9, prob. student at Oxford because the cellarer gave him 6s. 8d. for his expenses, *venient' ab Oxon'*; the cellarer noted that this payment was *ex precepto . . . prioris*, WCM C.91.
1454, 25 Jan., supplicated for B.Th.; see *BRUO*, and below.
1442/3, visited Overbury, WCM C.728.
1447, 27 Apr., obtained a *littera testimonialis* allowing an extension in time of two months on his pilgrimage, with royal licence and episcopal approval, Liber Albus, fo 480.
1453, on the cellarer's list of creditors, WCM C.93.
1459, 27 June, described as B.Th., and apptd one of three proctors to attend the Black Monk Chapter, Pantin, *BMC*, iii, 214 (Reg. A.6(i), fo 7ᵛ); the cellarer ref. to his carrying out 'negotiations' during the yr (1459/60), WCM C.491.
1462, 12 Mar., apptd abbot of Wenlock, but on or by 29 May this apptment had been cancelled and he was given a royal pardon for contravening the statute of provisors, *CPR (1461–1467)*, 180, 187, 192.
1464/5, on the cellarer's list of creditors, WCM C.95; on 20 June, 1465, apptd one of three proctors to attend the Black Monk Chapter, Pantin, *BMC*, iii, 214 (Reg. A.6(i), fo 37).
1465/6, the cellarer ref. to his *malicia* and to the repayment of his debts, WCM C.96.
1466/7, reported as being absent from the house for three months, WCM C.97; see also John Herford and Richard Lodelowe.
[1467], 10 May, the prior wrote to the abbot of Abingdon, on the suggestion of the bp, and asked him to take Walweyn for correction. He

described him as of 'froward dysposicion contrary to hys Relygyon' who had over a long time caused trouble by his 'subtyll and fraudelent' behaviour. The prior also enumerated his misdeeds and failings which included incontinence and apostasy. At Abingdon he was to be kept within the cloister and not allowed any contact with Oxford students. Any expense incurred would be met by the Worcester chapter who would contribute 2d. per day for his keep in accordance with the rules laid down by the Black Monk Chapter, Pantin, *BMC*, iii, 112–115 (Reg. A.6(i), fo 45, 45^v).

1467, 12 Oct., the prior requested a writ *de apostatis capiendis* for Walweyn and the other two named above, PRO C.81/1786/55.

1468, 8 Oct., recd a licence from the prior *ad scolatizand' Oxonie vel Cantabrigie*, at the chapter's expense, in order to pursue his study of theology, Reg. A.6(i), fo 55.

1469, 7 Feb., the prior and convent revoked the above licence, *ib.*; this was no doubt the prelude to his departure:

(1) on 22 Feb., the abbot of Eynsham wrote to the prior *pro dimissione*.

(2) on 25 Feb., the prior gave his consent.

(3) on 4 Mar., the abbot informed the prior that he had been recd, *ib.*, fos 55, 55^v, 57^v.

1469, 15 Oct., as abbot of Eynsham recd the bp's blessing, H. E. Salter, *Eynsham Cartulary*, 2 vols, Oxford Historical Society (1907), i, xxx (quoting from Reg. John Chedworth, Lincoln).

I WARINUS

occ. c. 1104

Name occ. in the list of monks in *Durham Liber Vitae*, fo 22.

Note: it is possible, but prob. unlikely, that this monk is identical with the prior below.

II WARINUS [Warin

occ. [1124] occ. 1140

1133 × 1140, prior: these are the dates of his first and last occurrence as prior, *Fasti*, ii, 102; however, if he succ. prior Nicholas, q.v., without delay and if his successor, Ralph of Bath, q.v., followed immediately, his priorate would have been 1124–1142, *HRH*, 83. See below.

It was he who comm. William of Malmesbury to rewrite Coleman's *Vita Wulfstani* for the monastic community at Worcester, Mason, *Wulfstan*, 196, Darlington, *Vita Wulfstani*, 1–3. Dr. Mason suggests that he may also have been concerned to promote the cult and attract pilgrims, *Wulfstan*, 275, 290. His name prob. indicates that he was of French origin, *ib.*, 274.

Name in Cambridge, Corpus Christi College Ms 367, pt ii, Miscellanea (?11th c.), some of which is in English; on fo 52 there is a letter addressed to him as prior, and to Uhtred, q.v. from the abbot and prior of Westminster concerning a monk of [Great] Malvern. It must have been written before 1132 when Uhtred d.

Edward WARYN

see Wynchecombe

WAWEN

see Walweyn

Humphrey WEBLEY, B.Th. [Webbeley, Webbley, Weble

occ. 1516 occ. 1540

1516, 17 May, ord acol., carnary chapel by Worcester cathedral, Reg. S. Gigli, 330.

1516, 20 Sept., ord subdcn, carnary chapel, *ib.*, 333.

1517, 7 Mar., ord dcn, carnary chapel, *ib.*, 332.

1529/30, kitchener, and master of the Lady chapel, WCM C.414a; the following yr he held neither office.

1533/4; 1534, 11 Nov.; 1535; 1536, 13 Mar.; 1537, 10 July, sacrist, WCM C.415; Reg. Ghinucci 8(ii), 88; *L and P Henry VIII*, ix, no 653; Reg. A.6(iii), fo 1; WCM B.1419.

1520, Mar., 1521, 1525/7, student at Oxford; recd small sums as 'rewards' from the prior, *Jnl More*, 101, 203, 208, 241. At the abp's visitation in July 1521 he was listed as a student, Reg. abp Warham, ii, fo 293^v.

1525/6, student, Reg. A.12, fo 125.

1529, Apr., recd 22s. 6d. from the prior towards his 'commensment to be bacheler of divinite', *Jnl More*, 292. *BRUO* states that he supplicated for the degree in 1522, after nine yrs' study and was adm. 20 Feb. 1529.

1530, 16 June (Corpus Christi), was the university preacher, *BRUO*.

1531/2, *prior studentium*, Reg. A.12, fo 135.

1521, 22 July, 26th in order on the visitation certificate, Reg. abp Warham, ii, fo 293^v.

1525/6, 22nd on the clerical subsidy list and pd 20d. as a scholar, Reg. A.12, fo 125.

1529, [Aug], went to London on the prior's behalf, *Jnl More*, 298.

1531/2, 20th on the second subsidy list and pd 3s. 4d., commons, Reg. A.12, fo 135.

1534, 17 Aug., subscribed to the Act of Supremacy, *DK 7th Report*, Appndx 2, 305.

1535, signed the petition vs the reinstatement of William Fordham, q.v., cellarer, *L and P Henry VIII*, ix, no 653.

1536, 13 Mar., 13th in order at the 'el.' of Henry Holbech, q.v., and was apptd proctor to go to inform Holbech, Reg. A.6(iii), fo 1, 1^v.

[1542, canon of the 9th prebend in the new foundation, *Fasti, 1541–1857*, vii, 130.]

Name in:

(1) London, Mr. A. Ehrman, R.255, Rupertus Tuitionis (printed book), Cologne, AD 1527.

(2) Oxford, Bod. 8° M.122 Th (fly leaves),

Erasmus, *Encomium Moriae* (printed book), Antwerp, AD 1512.

I John WEBLEY [Webbeley
occ. 1428 occ. 1483/4

1428, 28 Sept., ord acol., Worcester [cathedral], Reg. Polton, 100.
1429, 26 Mar., ord dcn, carnary chapel by Worcester cathedral, *ib.*, 125.
1429/30, one of eight who celebrated their first mass and recd 2s. 8d., from the hostiller, WCM C.231.

1443/4, pittancer, WCM C.729.
1448/9, kitchener, WCM C.91.
1449/50, hostiller, WCM C.92.
1458/9, 1460/1, subcellarer, WCM C.685, C.731; in the latter yr Robert Multon, q.v., was also cellarer.
1461/3, pittancer again, WCM C.336, C.602 (he took over in 1461/2 from Richard Bromesgrove, q.v.).
1475, chamberlain, WCM E.210.

1433, 9 Dec., 39th in order at the el. of a bp, *Reg. Sed. Vac.*, 432.
1441, 9 Apr., permitted by the prior to go on pilgrimage *ad . . . apostolorum limina sacrosancta*; he was to return within one yr and one month and not leave the country without a licence from the bp and the king, Liber Albus, fo 467.
1443/4, visited Overbury, WCM C.729.
1446/7, recd sums from the cellarer for his *minutiones* owed from the previous yr, and also for his 'O' pittances [?also overdue], WCM C.90
1458/9, visited Harvington, WCM C.685.
1460/1, visited Overbury, WCM C.731.
1462/3, pd visits to Hallow and Overbury, WCM C.602, C.734.
[1463/4], the cellarer ref. on his acct to a debt of £8 *pro pleg'* owed to him from about five yrs before [?when he was subcellarer], WCM C.492a.
1483/4, ref. to a debt owed to him by the cellarer and now pd, WCM C.101.

Name in Worcs. Ms F.75, Caesarius Arelatensis etc. (late 13th c.); *constat*—on a front flyleaf where the name of John de Gloucestr' II also appears. It is possible that John Webley II below is intended.

II John WEBLEY [Webbeley, Webleye
occ. 1490 occ. 1501/2

1490, 6 Mar., ord acol., carnary chapel by Worcester cathedral, Reg. Morton, 143.
1490, 10 Apr., ord subdcn, carnary chapel, *ib.*, 145.
1492, 22 Sept., ord dcn, carnary chapel, *ib.*, 157.

1498, 25 Oct., subchamberlain, *Reg. abp Morton*, ii, no 458.

1498, 25 Oct., 27th in order on the visitation certificate, *Reg. abp Morton*, ii, no 458.
In 1501/2 the sacrist ref. to the burial of his mother, WCM C.426.

?Name in Worcs. Ms F.75; see John Webley I.

William WEBLEY
occ. 1527

1527, 6 Apr., ord pr., carnary chapel by Worcester cathedral, Reg. Ghinucci 7(ii), 163.

John WEDNESBURY [Weddesbury, Weddysbury, Wodnesbury
occ. 1487 d. 1518

1507–1518, prior: one of the seven nominees chosen by the chapter on 10 Sept. 1507, and apptd by bp Fox (Winchester) in Southwark, acting for bp S. Gigli, on 13 Sept., Reg. S. Gigli, 349–352; d. before 27 Sept. 1518, Reg. A.6(ii), fo 113.

1487, 22 Sept., ord subdcn, Ledbury, *Reg. Milling* (Hereford), 173.
1487, 22 Dec., ord dcn, carnary chapel by Worcester cathedral, Reg. Morton, 138.
1488, 5 Apr., ord pr., Worcester cathedral, *ib.*, 140 (at the age of 23; see below).

1498, 27 June, third prior, Pantin, *BMC*, iii, 216 (Reg. A.6(i), fo 122).
1498, 25 Oct., 1499, 21 July, subprior, *Reg. abp Morton*, ii, no 458; Reg. A.6(ii), fo 1v.
1500, 18 Mar., apptd sacrist, Reg. S. Gigli, 24.
1504, 6 Nov., 1507, 2 June, 10 Sept., sacrist, Reg. A.6(ii), fo 32; *ib.*, fo 44v, Reg. S. Gigli, 349–352.

1498, 27 June, apptd one of three monk proctors to attend the Black Monk Chapter, Pantin, *BMC*, iii, 216 (Reg. A.6(i), fo 122).
1498, 25 Oct., second (as subprior) in order on the visitation certificate, *Reg. abp Morton*, ii, no 458.
1499, 21 July, one of the seven nominees for the priorate, Reg. A.6(ii), fo 1v and Reg. S. Gigli, 343; they were presented to bp Fox (Durham), acting for Gigli, at Southwark on 2 Sept., Reg. A.6(ii), fo 1v.
1507, 2 June, apptd one of three monk proctors for the Black Monk Chapter, Pantin, *BMC*, iii, 218 (Reg. A.6(ii), fo 44v).
1507, Sept., prob. visited Newnham after his apptment to the priorate, WCM C.668 (1506/7).
1513, 22 Sept., gave his age as 48 yrs, Reg. S. Gigli, 261.
1518, 27 Mar., authorized the subprior, William More, q.v., to act for him while he went on pilgrimage to the *limina Apostolorum* and other holy places, Reg. A.6(ii), fo 108.
1518, d., possibly in Rome, see below.

An entry in *Jnl More*, 173, dated c. Mar., 1523 suggests (1) that he may have had a degree [master priurs weddesbury], and (2) that he went to Rome where he left his breviary [*portuos*] which had been returned and rebound. Noake, *Worcs.*

Cathedral, 131, states that the prior had gone to Rome to see bp Gigli.

Some of his *acta* are recorded in Reg. A.6(ii), fos 48v–112v by his chaplains, John Wellys, William Lemster II, and Thomas Asteley, q.v.

Thomas WELFORD [Welleford

occ. 1430 occ. 1438

1430, 23 Sept., ord subdcn, carnary chapel by Worcester cathedral, and was presented by the prior, Reg. Polton, 213.

1432, 20 Sept., ord pr., carnary chapel, *ib.*, 223.

1431/2, celebrated his first mass; both the almoner and the pittancer contributed 2s. 6d. for the feast, WCM C.194, 329.

1437, 15 Aug., apptd chaplain to the prior, Liber Albus, fo 455.

1438, 15 Feb., apptd chaplain by the new prior, *ib.*, fo 457.

1433, 9 Dec., 41st in order at the el. of a bp, *Reg. Sed. Vac.*, 432.

John WELLYS

occ. 1497 occ. 1507

1497, 14 Apr., ord dcn, carnary chapel by Worcester cathedral, Reg. G. Gigli, 25.

1498, 14 Apr., ord pr., carnary chapel, *ib.*, 26.

1507, [prob. in Sept.], apptd chaplain to the [new] prior, Reg. A.6(ii), fo 49v.

1498, 25 Oct., 40th in order on the visitation certificate, *Reg. abp Morton*, ii, no 458.

Richard WELLYS [Welles

occ. 1426/7 occ. 1433

1426/7, kitchener, WCM C.85; he was succ. by Robert Lawerne, q.v.

1429/30, master of the [Lady] chapel, WCM C.278.

1433, 9 Dec., 22nd in order at the el. of a bp, *Reg. Sed. Vac.*, 432.

Richard de WENLOK [Wenlac, Wenlak, Wenlock, Wenloke

occ. 1349 occ. 1379

1349, 6 June, ord pr., bp's chapel, Hartlebury, *Reg. Bransford*, no 1341 (p.343).

1352/3, Dec. to Dec., kitchener, WCM C.113.

1355/7, June to June, 1360/1, pittancer, WCM C.303–305.

1369/70, cellarer, WCM C.66.

1370/1, Dec. to Sept., pittancer, WCM C.308.

1371/2, associated with William Power, q.v. as cellarer and treasurer, WCM C,596.

1373, c. 19 Nov., 7 Dec.; 1375/6, cellarer, *Reg. Sed. Vac.*, 282, 290; Reg. A.12, fo 77v.

1376, Nov./Dec., chamberlain, WCM E.27.

1351, 8 Jan., obtained papal licence to choose his own confessor who was authorized to grant plenary remission at d., *CPL*, iii (1342–1362), 380.

1357/8, accompanied the cellarer [Walter de Wynforton, q.v.] to London on business, WCM C.64.

1370, 3 Apr., 4th in order at the el. of a prior and apptd, with John Hatfeld, q.v., proctor to present the seven nominees to the bp, Liber Albus, fo 246–246v.

1371/2, visited Hallow, WCM C.596; he was reimbursed by the cellarer, William Power, q.v., in the form of one horse and 12m., WCM C.67.

1373, c. 19 Nov., sent by the chapter, with John de Malverne I, q.v. to obtain the royal licence to el. a bp, *Reg. Sed. Vac.*, 282.

1373, 7 Dec., 4th in order at the el. and sent by the subprior and chapter to ask the prior, Walter de Legh, q.v., to accept the bpric, *ib.*, 291.

1375/6, as cellarer, began the construction of the new dormitory, Reg. A.12, fo 77v.

1376, Nov./Dec., present in the dormitory at the surrender of a lease, WCM E.27.

1379, 16 Feb., given a licence by the bp to go to Little Malvern, as prior 'in order to relieve the priory now bereft', Liber Albus, fo 271–271v; the prior and chapter gave their consent the following day, *ib.*, fo 271v.

Note: in 1392 (24 Oct.) he res. as prior but prob. remained at Little Malvern, *Reg. Wakefield*, no 708.

Thomas WENLOK [Wenlock, Wenloke

occ. 1519/21

1519/21, cellarer, WCM E.96, Wilson, *Accts Henry VIII*, 5, 44 (Reg. A.17, 3).

1521, 22 July, 21st in order on the visitation certificate, Reg. abp Warham, ii, fo 293v.

William WENLOK [Wenlake, Wenlocke, Wenloke

occ. 1460 d. 1499

1492–1499, prior: 24 June, 1492, el. one of the seven candidates for the office, and apptd by the bp 2 July, Reg. Morton, 90–93; d. before 21 July 1499, Reg. S. Gigli, 343.

1460, 20 Dec., ord acol. and subdcn, Worcester cathedral, Reg. Carpenter, i, 554.

1461, 19 Sept., ord dcn, Claines, *ib.*, i, 555.

1464, 31 Mar., ord pr., carnary chapel by Worcester cathedral, *ib.*, i, 561.

1463/4, celebrated his first mass and the pittancer sent a gift of 2s. 2d., WCM C.337; the kitchener gave 2s. 6d. and the precentor 2s. 3d., and both charged their 1465/6 accts, WCM C.151, C.381.

1467, chaplain to the prior, Reg. A.6(i), fo 48.

1471/3, cellarer, WCM C.738, C.739.

1488/9, cellarer, WCM C.625.

1489, 10 Mar.; 1492, 24 June, sacrist, Reg. Morton, 57; *ib.*, 91.

1459/60, was owed 22d. by the cellarer, WCM C.491.

1471/2, visited Overbury, WCM C.738.

1472/3, pd visits to Harvington and Overbury, WCM C.618, C.739.

1480, 9 Dec., obtained a papal dispensation to receive and retain a benefice, *CPL*, xiii (1473–1484), 726.

1488/9, visited Harvington, Overbury and Sedgeberrow, WCM C.625, C.747, C.779.

1489, 10 Mar., as sacrist and patron of Sodbury, instituted an incumbent, Reg. Morton, 57.

1492, 23/24 June, one of the seven nominees for the priorate, Reg. A.6(i), fo 107v and Reg. Morton, 91.

1498, 2 Oct., present in court to hear the case between himself and the king because of a writ of summons vs him and other monks accused of transgressions and riots, WCM B.1063.

1499, 3 Apr., comm. by the bp to install S. de Gigli as bp, Bloom, *Original Charters*, 162 (with Thomas Mildenham, q.v.).

1499, d.; the 1498/9 accts of several obedientiaries made entries:

(1) the chamberlain sold some of his bedding, viz., one bolster, one mattress and two blankets for 6s. 8d., WCM C.48.

(2) the almoner distributed money to the Franciscans and Dominicans to say masses for his soul, WCM C.209.

(3) the precentor rewarded the servants in the kitchen and brewery *pro laboribus post mortem* of William, prior, and two other monks, WCM C.391.

Some of his *acta* were recorded in Reg. A.6(ii), fos 107–152 by his chaplains among whom was Edmund Ledbury I, q.v.

John de WESTBURY

occ. 1317 d. 1340/1

1317, 9 Dec., *clericus* and one of four to be examined by the bp's commissary, Liber Albus, fo 84v; the candidates are described as *vestiendos.*

1318, 24 Mar., clothed [*vestiti*], *ib.*, fo 85.

1318, 17 Nov., one of three whose prof. the prior was comm. to rec., *Reg. Cobham*, 13, and *Liber Albus*, no 809.

1319, 7 Apr., ord subdcn, bp's chapel Kempsey, *Reg. Cobham*, 58.

1319, 22 Dec., ord dcn, St Nicholas' church, Worcester, *ib.*, 68.

1333/4, cellarer, WCM C.799, with Simon le Botiler, q.v.

1340, 21 Apr., precentor, *Reg. Bransford*, no 290.

1320 × 1330, he may have been at Oxford during this period, see below.

1332, 29 Aug., apptd by the prior and chapter as proctor to go to St Paul's cathedral for a meeting on 4 Sept. with the abp and the Roman legate, Liber Albus, fo 117v (insert).

1333/4, pd visits to Hallow and Tibberton, WCM C.591, C.799.

1337/8, visited Bromsgrove, WCM C.547.

1338, 24 Dec., absent from the monastery on lawful business when summoned to the episcopal el.; he had been sent as proctor (with Simon Crompe, q.v.) to obtain the royal licence to el., *Reg. Sed. Vac.*, 259, 257.

1339, 4/5 Jan., chosen by the chapter as one of five *compromissorii*, at the el., Worcs.Ms F.141; see Henry Fouke. In *Reg. Sed. Vac.*, 268, three unnamed *compromissorii* are specified, see Reg. Bransford, xiii.

1339, 9 Jan., present as witness when the abbot of Cirencester's proxy made his oath of obedience, *sed. vac.*, to the prior, *Reg. Sed. Vac.*, 269. On 29 Jan. as commissary of the prior, *sed. vac.*, with Simon Crompe, q.v., visited Tewkesbury abbey and went on to Winchcombe and Gloucester abbeys and elsewhere, *ib.*, 273–274. He also carried out further visitations for the prior, with a secular clerk, in a number of specified deaneries in Jan. and Feb. At St Mark de Billeswyck [hospital], Bristol, the master of the house gave 2s. as procuration, but Westbury insisted on returning ½m. because he and his clerks and servants had been fed as guests rather than as official visitors, *ib.*, 274–275.

1339, 12 Apr., one of the seven nominees for the priorate, *ib.*, no 290.

1340, 21 Apr., again one of the seven nominees for the priorate, *ib.*, no 290.

1340/1, d., after having recd only 12d. for *minutio* pittances, *quia tunc obiit*, WCM C.299.

Name in Worcs. Ms F.63, Aristoteles (13th/14th c.); this has a *caucio* of Richard de Bromwych, q.v., which mentions the university chest; beneath, there is another *caucio* dated 7 July 1325, *tradatur eidem* [Bromwych or Adam de Wygornia, q.v.] *vel domino*—. This suggests that he spent at least a short time at Oxford.

Robert de WESTON [Westone

occ. 1323 occ. 1362

1323, 11 Nov., *clericus* adm. with two others after examination by the bp' commissary. He arrived with letters of recommendation from John de Wygorn', precentor of Glastonbury, where he had been taught by Master Edward, and the monk scholars there who all reported well of him. He had shown promise in singing, and everyone spoke highly of his character and behaviour, Liber Albus, fo 113v; and see below.

1325, 23 Feb., ord subdcn, bp's chapel, Kempsey, *Reg. Cobham*, 178.

1326, 15 Feb., ord dcn, bp's chapel, Hartlebury, *ib.*, 194.

1336/9; 1340, 21 Apr.; 1341/2, 1342, 21 Dec.; 1344/8; 1349/50, for two terms, cellarer, WCM C.57, C.606, C.58; *Reg. Bransford*, no 290; WCM C.395 (as R.); Liber Albus, fo 181; WCM C.59–61, C.607; C.700, and see Thomas de Barndesley I.

1350, 14 Apr.; 1354/5, almoner, Reg. Thoresby, 24; WCM C.172.

1351/2, cellarer, Windsor, St George's chapel, XI.E.37.

1362, 2 June, apptd sacrist, Reg. Barnet, 20.

1334, Sept./Nov., visited Sedgeberrow, WCM C.755.

1336, 16 Sept., witness, with Robert de Clyfton, q.v., to the homage of a tenant, Liber Albus, fo 146v.

1337, May/Sept., prob. visited Tibberton, WCM C.832.

1338/9, went to London on business, with Henry Fouke and John de Evesham I, q.v., concerning the el. of Wulstan de Bransford as bp, WCM C.58.

1339, 4/5 Jan., chosen by the chapter as one of five *compromissorii* at the el. of a bp, Worcs.Ms F.141; see Henry Fouke. In *Reg. Sed. Vac.*, 268, only three unnamed *compromissorii* are specified. On 9 Jan. he was present as a witness when the abbot of Cirencester's proxy made his oath of obedience, *sed. vac.*, to the prior, *Reg. Sed. Vac.*, 269.

1340, 21 Apr., one of the seven nominees for the priorate, *Reg. Bransford*, no 290.

1342, 3 Oct., apptd proctor for the chapter, with a secular clerk, to attend convocation, Liber Albus, fo 179v; he was also apptd proctor to represent the prior [John de Evesham, q.v.], but the prior [changed his mind and] went himself, *ib.*, fo 180v. On 21 Dec., he witnessed the homage of a tenant, *ib.*, fo 181.

1344/5, went to Bath and to Wells on business affairs, and also to London, WCM C.59.

1345/6, travelled to Leicester on business, WCM C.60.

1349, 10 Oct., one of four monk proctors apptd to deal with the matters arising out of the visitation of Cirencester abbey which had met with resistance, *Reg. Sed. Vac.*, 254.

1350, 14 Apr., a mandate was issued by the bp because Robert, almoner, was robbed in the almonry, situated within the cemetery of the church, and the thieves were to be tracked down, Reg. Thoresby, 24.

1350, 10 Dec., with Nicholas de Clanefeld and Walter de Wynforton given letters of attorney by the prior, John de Evesham I, q.v., prob. because the prior was going to Avignon, Bloom, *Liber Ecclesiae*, 51. The yr is given as 1351 in both printed calendar and ms (PRO E315/63, fos 58v–59), but see John de Evesham I under 1350 and 1351.

1351, 21 Jan., granted papal licence to choose his own confessor who was authorized to give plenary remission at d., *CPL*, iii (1342–1362), 406.

1354, 21 Apr., served as witness to the prior's declaration of his rights concerning the use of pontifical regalia, Liber Albus, fo 239v; see John de Evesham I.

1355, 22 May, one of four monk proctors apptd and given a general mandate to act for the chapter in all causes pertaining to the status of their church, including matters which could arise during a visitation, Liber Albus, fo 241.

1357, 23 Sept., one of three *vices gerentes* apptd by the prior [John de Evesham I, q.v.] during his absence, Liber Albus, fo 214v; see Walter de Legh and Walter de Wynforton.

1358, [15] Oct., one of three monk proctors apptd in all matters concerning the bp's proposed visitation 'by apostolic authority', Liber Albus, fo 217 (initials, R. de W.; the two others N. de G. and W. de S. cannot be identified).

The letters of recommendation which he brought with him from Glastonbury explained that his father was a tenant of the abbey, who held land by free tenure in Weston, Liber Albus, fo 113v. When he first arrived at Worcester he was known as Robert de Glastyngbury, q.v.

William de WESTON

occ. 1301/2

1302, 20 Jan. had been unjustly accused of incontinence at the abp's visitation; he had cleared himself and the abp wrote to the prior to this effect, Liber Albus, fo 13.

WEYK

see Wyke

John WHETHILL [Whetyll, Whytehull

occ. 1443/5

1443, 21 Sept., ord acol. and subdcn, carnary chapel by Worcester cathedral, Reg. Bourgchier, 206, 207.

1445, 27 Mar., ord dcn, Worcester cathedral, Reg. Carpenter, i, 501; he was presented by the prior.

WHITCHURCH

see Whytchurche

John WHITINGTON [Whytentton, Whytynton, Wythyngton

occ. 1414 d. 1454/5

1414, 3 Mar., ord acol., Worcester cathedral, Reg. Peverel, 198.

1415, 21 Sept., ord subdcn, Hartlebury, *ib.*, 206.

1419, 10 June, ord pr., Worcester cathedral, *Reg. Sed. Vac.*, 402; no house named.

1419, 24 Apr., 32nd in order at the el. of a bp, *Reg. Sed. Vac.*, 407.

1433, 9 Dec., 16th at the el. of a bp, *ib.*, 432.

1441, 21 Mar., granted a licence by the prior to

go on pilgrimage to Rome [*sacra limina apostolorum*] on condition that he obtain approval from the bp and a licence from the king and return within the year, Liber Albus, fo 465v.
1454/5, d., WCM C.480; the pittancer recorded that he d. during this yr and so did not rec. his full share of *porciones*, WCM C.335.

John de WHYCHE
occ. 1350

1350, 15 May, ord acol., Franciscan convent, Worcester, Reg. Thoresby, 30.

WHYCHE
see also Wich, Wych

John de WHYTCHURCHE [Whitchurch, Whytechurch, Wytchurche, Wythchurch, Wyttechirch
occ. [1369] occ. 1401/2

[1369], 1 Oct., one of seven whose prof. the precentor was comm. to rec., Reg. Lynn 89.
1370, 13 Apr., ord acol., [Worcester cathedral], *ib.*, 50.
1370, 21 Dec., ord subdcn Hartlebury, *ib.*, 53.
1371, 20 Dec., ord pr., Worcester cathedral, *ib.*, 55.
1372/3, celebrated his first mass; the cellarer charged his acct, a yr late, for wine for the festivities after the mass, WCM C.68.
1406/9, *custos* of the [Lady] chapel, Hamilton, *Comp. Rolls*, 60–62 (WCM C.259), WCM C.260, C.261.
1373, 4 Dec., 24th in order at the el. of a bp, *Reg. Sed. Vac.*, 290.
1380/1, ill and the infirmarer provided medicine, WCM C.242.
1388, 21 Aug., 21st at the el. of a prior, Liber Albus, fo 334v.
1392/3, 1395/7, *socius in choro* of the cellarer and recd 6s. 8d. each yr, WCM C.76, C.77, C.479.
1401, 24 June, 15th at the el. of a bp, *Reg. Sed. Vac.*, 373.
1401/2, recd money from the chamberlain for his *cucullus*, WCM C.26.

WHYTEHULL
see Whethill

WHYTENTTON
see Whitington

Robert de WICH [Vicho, Wichio, Wych, Wychio
occ. 1271 occ. 1287

1271, 21 Dec., apptd proctor, with Laurence de Badminton, q.v., to present the seven nominees for the priorate to the bp, *Reg. Giffard*, 50.
[late 13th c.], apptd proctor by the prior and chapter in a dispute, WCM B.1640.
1287, 2 Jan., chosen as one of the seven nominees for the priorate, *Reg. Giffard*, 304 (as Richard, prob. in error), 325.

Name in Worcs. Ms Q.42, Distinctiones Mauricii (late 13th c.); on the last flyleaf he is listed as one of eleven monks who contributed to the purchase of the book; he pd 6[?d.].

WICH
see also Whyche, Wych

WIGORN'
see Colys, Crompe

John de WIGORNIA
see John de Worcestre III

William WIGORNIENSIS
n.d.

n.d., granted a letter of confraternity by the Canterbury monks, Dart, *Antiq. Cant.*, xxix (BL Ms Cotton Claudius C.vi, fo 172).

WIKES
see Wyke

I WILLIAM [Willelmus
occ. c. 1104

Name occ. in the list of monks in *Durham Liber Vitae*, fo 22.

II WILLIAM [Willelmus
occ. 1216

1216, Oct., subprior, *Ann. Wigorn.*, 407.
Note: this is prob. William de Bradewas, q.v.

III WILLIAM [Cantor
[?1260 × 1270]

[?1260 × 1270], returned from Rome, WCM E.4(6). See W. [Cantor.

WILLIAM
see also Wigorniensis

Richard de WINCHECUMBE
occ. 1317

1317, 20 Oct., 36th in order at the el. of a prior, Liber Albus, fo 83v.

Note: see Richard de Dersynton who must be the same monk.

WINCHECUMBE
see also Wynchecombe, Wynchecumbe

Raienald de WIRCESTRE
occ. 1377

1377, 23 May, ord pr., Colwich, *Reg. Stretton* (1905) (Coventry/ Lichfield), 326.

WIRECESTRE
see also Wyre

WIRL
see Godricus

WITTENEYE
see Wytteneye

WITTONE
see Wytton

WLSTAN
see Wulstan

Robert WODALL [Wodehall
occ. 1510/12

1510, 21 Sept., ord acol., carnary chapel by Worcester cathedral, Reg. S. Gigli, 304.
1511, 14 June, ord subdcn, carnary chapel, *ib.*, 308.
1512, 27 Mar., ord dcn, carnary chapel, *ib.*, 312.

John WODEWARD
occ. 1396 occ. 1405/6

1396, 1 Apr., ord acol., Worcester cathedral, Reg. Winchcombe, 125.
1397, 6 June, ord subdcn, Worcester cathedral, *ib.*, 135.
1401, 24 June, listed as dcn, *Reg. Sed. Vac.*, 373.
1401, 24 Sept., ord pr., Worcester cathedral, *ib.*, 374.
1400/1, celebrated his first mass and the chamberlain gave *exennia*, WCM C.25.

1401, 24 June, student [at Oxford], *Reg. Sed. Vac.*, 373.
1405/6, rode back from Oxford to preach on Christmas eve and returned there, at a cost of 9s. to the precentor. He came back to Worcester again to preach on Good Friday, and half of his expenses for the return journey were on this occasion charged to the prior's acct, WCM C.372.

1401, 24 June, 39th in order at the el. of a bp, *Reg. Sed. Vac.*, 373.

Name in a letter-sequence in BL Ms Harley 5398, fos 128–131v and Oxford, Bod. Ms Bodley 832, fos 172v–173v. I owe this information to James Clarke who suggests that Wodeward acquired a reputation as a *dictator* and rhetorician and that some of the sermons in Worcester Ms F.10 may have been written by him.

WODNESBURY
see Wednesbury

WOKEWONE
see Wykewane

WOLSTAN
see Wulstan

William WOLVERLEY [?Obirley, Ovirley
occ. 1522 occ. 1536

1522, 20 Dec., ord acol., carnary chapel by Worcester cathedral, Reg. A.6(ii), fo 134.
1525, 23 Dec., ord. subdcn, Bromyard, *Reg. Booth* (Hereford), 320; the scribe in the reg. (fo 227v) has written Richard.
1525/6, 33rd on the clerical subsidy list and pd 3s. 4d. as commons, Reg. A.12, fo 135.
1532, 7/13 Apr., [the wk after Easter], recd 3s. 4d. from the prior for 'pryckyng of v exaltavit of v parts', *Jnl More*, 347.
?1532, 19/25 May [the wk after Whitsunday], recd 2s. from the prior for three 'exultavit of v parts', *ib.*, 350.
1534, 17 Aug., subscribed to the Act of Supremacy, *DK 7th Report*, Appndx 2, 305.
1536, 13 Mar., 25th in order at the 'el.' of Henry Holbech, q.v., Reg. A6(iii), fo 1 (as Obirley).

Florence of WORCESTER
see Florence

George WORCESTRE [Worcestr', Worceter, Worcettur, Wourcettur
occ. 1516 occ. 1530

1516, 17 May, ord acol., carnary chapel by Worcester cathedral, Reg. S. Gigli, 330.
1517, 7 Mar., ord subdcn, carnary chapel, *ib.*, 331.
1521, 22 July, 28th in order on the metropolitan visitation certificate, Reg. abp Warham, ii, fo 293v.
1529/30, ill for three wks in the infirmary and the infirmarer spent 3s. 6d. on his cure, WCM 414a.
1530, 4 Aug., was recd at Abergavenny and his licence to transfer [*migracio*] was sent by the prior from Worcester on 6 Aug., Reg. A.6(ii), 169.
1530, Aug., given 3s. 4d. by the prior on his departure, *Jnl More*, 311.
1534, summer, visited the prior at Grimley, *Jnl More*, 390.

I John de WORCESTRE, John of WORCESTER
see John

II John de WORCESTRE [Wyrcester
occ. 1367

1367, 18 Sept., ord acol., Kidderminster, Reg. Wittlesey, 44.

III John de WORCESTRE [Wigornia, Wircestre, Worcett', Wyrcestr', Wyrcetre
occ. 1371 occ. 1419

1371, 20 Dec., ord acol., Worcester cathedral, Reg. Lynn, 54.
[1374], subdcn, given *lit. dim.*, by the prior, *sed. vac.*, for the bp of Hereford to confer orders, *Reg. Sed. Vac.*, 322 (as Wigornia).
1377, 19 Sept., ord pr., Tewkesbury abbey, *Reg. Wakefield*, no 873h.
1395/1403, *custos* of the [Lady] chapel, WCM C.253–255, C.838, C.839, C.256–258.

1403/5; 1408/12; 1415, Feb.; 1415/16, 1419, 24 Apr., chamberlain, WCM C.27, C.50; WCM E.224, WCM C.28–30; C.789a; C.31; *Reg. Sed. Vac.*, 407.
1373, 4 Dec., 28th in order at the el. of a bp, *Reg. Sed. Vac.*, 290.
1388, 21 Aug., 24th at the el. of a prior, Liber Albus, fo 334v.
1398/9, 1401/2, recd 3s. 4d. from the chamberlain for his *cucullus*, WCM C.24, C.26.
1401, 24 June, 18th in order at the el. of a bp, *Reg. Sed. Vac.*, 373.
1419, 24 Apr., 5th at the el. of a bp., *ib.*, 407.

IV John de WORCESTRE [Worsetur, Wyrcetre
occ. 1425 occ. 1453/4
1425, 24 Mar., ord acol., Worcester cathedral, Reg. Morgan, 207.
1426, 8 Sept., recd *lit. dim.*, for all orders, Reg. Polton, 13.
1426, 22 Sept., ord subdcn, Bromyard, *Reg. Spofford* (Hereford), 300; the precentor pd the expenses for the journey, WCM C.377.
1430, 10 June, ord pr., Alvechurch, and was presented by the prior, Reg. Polton, 212.
1429/30, celebrated his first mass; the hostiller sent *exennia* of 2s. 8d. to him and to seven other newly ord priests, WCM C.231.
1436/7, 1438/9, subcellarer, WCM C.724, C.725.
1432, Aug./Sept., sent to London with Thomas Ledbury, q.v., to attend convocation, WCM C.86a.
1433, 9 Dec., 34th in order at the el. of a bp, *Reg. Sed. Vac.*, 432.
1436/7, pd visits to Overbury and Sedgeberrow, WCM C.724, C.772.
1438/9, visited Overbury, WCM C.725.
1444/5, one of the cellarer's creditors and was now repd, WCM C.493.
1453/4, the prior sent John Smethwyk, q.v., to confer with the abbot of Evesham *penes fratrem [Johannem]*, WCM C.94.

V John WORCESTRE [Worcestr', Worcet'
occ. 1510 occ. 1513
1510, 21 Sept., ord acol., carnary chapel by Worcester cathedral, Reg. S. Gigli, 304.
1511, 20 Mar., ord subdcn, carnary chapel, *ib.*, 307.
1512, 27 Mar., ord dcn, carnary chapel, *ib.*, 314.
1513, 24 Sept., ord pr., carnary chapel, *ib.*, 321.

PHILIP DE WORCESTRE
see Aubyn

I Richard de WORCESTRE [Worcestr', Worcesttr', Wygorn', Wyrcestre, Wyrcetre
occ. 1365 d. 1402/3
1365, 7 June, ord pr., Winchcombe abbey, Reg. Wittlesey, 39.
1370, 3 Apr., 15th at the el. of a prior, Liber Albus fo 246.
1373, 4/7 Dec., 13th at the el. of a bp, *Reg. Sed. Vac.*, 290.
1380/1, ill and the infirmarer spent 7s. 6d. on his cure, WCM C.242.
1383/4, spent time in the infirmary and the almoner gave 3s. 4d. to him and two other sick monks, WCM C.178.
1388, 21 Aug., 12th in order at the el. of a prior, Liber Albus, fo 334v.
1391/2, ill and the infirmarer spent 3s. on medicine, WCM C.243.
1401, 24 June, 6th in order at the el. of a bp, *Reg. Sed. Vac.*, 372.
1401/2, recd 6s. 8d. from the chamberlain for his habit, WCM C.26.
1402/3, d., and the chamberlain sold his *panni* and pd the brief bearer, WCM C.26a.

II Richard WORCESTRE [Worcetur, Wyrcetr'
occ. 1405/6 occ. 1422/3
1405/6, was taken by the precentor [Roger Shrovesbury, q.v.] to Bromyard, for ordination, WCM C.372.
1407, 21 May, ord dcn, Blockley, *Reg. Clifford*, no 132, p. 104.
1410, 20 Sept., ord pr., Llanthony priory, Gloucester, Reg. Peverel, 185.
1409/10, celebrated his first mass and recd 2s. 8d. from the almoner and also a small sum from the chamberlain; the hostiller gave 2s. 8d. for bread and ale, WCM C.189, 28, 220 (1410/11).
1419, 24 Apr., succentor, *Reg. Sed. Vac.*, 407.
1419, 24 Apr., 18th in order at the el. of a bp, *Reg. Sed. Vac.*, 407.
1421/2, one of the monks on the cellarer's list of creditors, WCM C.84a.
1422/3, gave a small sum in alms to the almoner, WCM C.192.

I William WORCESTRE [Worcestr', Worcetter, Worcetur
occ. 1464/6
1464, 8 June, one of six whose prof. the prior was comm. to rec, Reg. A.6(i), fo 34.
1465, 9 Mar., ord subdcn, St Nicholas' church, Worcester, and was presented by the chamberlain, Reg. Carpenter, i, 562.
1466, 1 Mar., ord dcn, St Nicholas' church, *ib.*, i, 564.

II William WORCESTRE [Worcetter, Worcettur
occ. 1481 occ. 1499/1500
1481, 16 June, ord acol., Whitbourne *Reg. Milling* (Hereford), 163.
1481, 22 Sept., ord subdcn, Whitbourne, *ib.*, 164.
1481, 22 Dec., ord dcn, Hartlebury, Reg. Alcock, 265.

1481/2, celebrated his first mass; recd *exennia* of 2s. 3d. from the almoner and 20d. from the precentor, WCM C.205, C.385.

1496/7, subcellarer, WCM C.669.
1498/9, precentor, WCM C.391.
1499/1500, refectorer, WCM C.423.
1496/7, visited Newnham, WCM C.669.
1498, 25 Oct., 14th in order on the visitation certificate, *Reg. abp Morton*, ii, no 458.

Roger de WORFELD [Worfold
occ. 1330 occ. 1344/5

1330, 11 Aug., one of four whose prof. the prior wsa comm. to rec., *Reg. Orleton*, no 335.
1331, 25 May, ord subdcn, [?Chipping] Campden, *ib.*, no 21 (p. 35).
1339, 10 Nov., the pope sent a mandate to the abbot of Bordesley and others to execute the ordinances concerning apostate monks, in this case Worfeld, who asked to be reconciled, *CPL*, ii (1305–1342), 547; this is repeated, *ib.*, 549, but dated 22 Dec.
1343, 24 Oct., the prior wrote to the abbot of Ramsey concerning the proposal to send him to Ramsey for discipline and treatment. His apostasy, incontinence and diabolical behaviour are mentioned and the details of his daily routine at Ramsey spelled out. He was not to participate in solemn masses unless he showed signs of contrition and made his confession; in all else he was to be treated as one of the juniors, and his place in the order was to be after the unprofessed novices, the most junior of the priests. Sufficient money to cover his expenses for a yr was sent with the bearer of the letter, Liber Albus, fo 191.
1344/5, recd a *dona* of 20s. from the cellarer, WCM C.59.

Thomas WOTTON
occ. 1430

1430, 23 Sept., ord acol., carnary chapel by Worcester cathedral, and was presented by the prior, Reg. Polton, 213.

Note: this may be Thomas Wych, q.v.

WOYCH
see Wyche

I WULFSTAN [Wulstan
occ. before 1062 d. 1095

As he was prior before the Conquest, and bp from 1062, he is not included in this register. For the most recent account of his life and career see Mason, *Wulfstan.*

II WULSTAN
see Bransford

Thomas WULSTAN [Wlstan, Wlstane, Wolstan, Wulstane
occ. 1521 occ. 1535

1524/5, celebrated his first mass and recd a 2s. pittance from the almoner, WCM C.414.

1525/6, fourth prior, Reg. A.12, fo 125.
1529, chaplain to the prior, Reg. A.6(ii), fo 164, and perhaps earlier, see below.
1529/30, steward of the prior's hospice, WCM C.414a.
1531/2, subcellarer, WCM C.414c and *Jnl More*, 319.
1533/4, master of the [Lady] chapel, WCM C.415.
1534, [Oct.], third [tysse, tyce] prior, *Jnl More*, 69, 395.

1521, 22 July, 35th in order on the metropolitan visitation certificate, Reg. abp Warham, ii, fo 293v.
1525/6, 26th on the clerical subsidy list and pd 3s. 4d. as commons, Reg. A.12, fo 125.
1527/8, recd 10s. per quarter for singing the ten o'clock mass, *Jnl More*, 252, 266, 278, 272.
1530, 1 Jan., gave a pair of 'kyt gloves' as a New Year's gift to the prior, *ib.*, 302.
1531/2, 26th on the second subsidy list and pd 20d. as subcellarer and 3s. 4d. commons, Reg. A.12, fo 135.
1533, 1 Jan., gave a peacock to the prior as a New Year's gift, *Jnl More*, 361.
1533/4, pd by the prior 10s. per quarter for saying masses for Robert Alvechurch, q.v., who d. in Dec. 1532, *ib.*, 365, 373, 374, 383, 389; and in the spring of 1533 he was given 10s. for 'ye sexten mass, *ib.*, 369.
1534, 17 Aug., subscribed to the Act of Supremacy, *DK 7th Report*, Appndx 2, 305.
1535, signed the petition against the reinstatement of William Fordham as cellarer, *L and P Henry VIII*, ix, no 653.

II Nicholas de WYCH* (see note on p. 901)
occ. 1360 occ. 1363

1360, 30 Apr., one of three novices whose prof. the prior was comm. to rec., which he did on 1 May, Liber Albus, fo 226v; the commission is also in Reg. Bryan, i, 135.
1363, Jan./Sept., celebrated his first mass and the pittancer gave 2s. 6d. *exennia*, WCM C.306.

Richard WYCH [Wyche
occ. 1497 d. 1498/9

1497, 14 Apr., ord subdcn, carnary chapel by Worcester cathedral, Reg. G. Gigli 7(iii), 25.

1498/9, d., and the almoner distributed money to the Dominicans and Franciscans to say masses for his soul, WCM C.209.

I Thomas de WYCH [Wiche, Wychio
occ. 1274 occ. 1296

1288; 1290, 7 Nov.; 1296, 11 July, precentor, *Ann. Wigorn.*, 495; *Reg. Giffard*, 380; *ib.*, 480.

1274, 21 Sept., with Robert de Suckeleye, q.v., apptd proctor to present the seven nominees for the priorate to the bp, *Reg. Giffard*, 62.
[1283], the bp wrote to him and to Robert de Suckeleye, q.v., concerning tithes in the parish of St John, Worcester, *ib.*, 176.
1287, 1 Jan., with Thomas de Hindelep, q.v., apptd proctor to present the seven nominees for the priorate to the bp, *ib.*, 304, 325.
1288, 18 Sept., became involved in a dispute with the bp concerning his right as precentor to call out the names of the ordination candidates at an ordination ceremony at Westbury; the adcn of Gloucester, nephew of the bp, also claimed the right and the prior and chapter launched an appeal, *Ann. Wigorn.*, 495. The following yr on 4 June, he was again refused his right at the ordination in Bromsgrove, *ib.*, 498.
1290, 7 Nov., at an episcopal visitation, while the bp was in consultation with the subprior Simon [de Wyre, q.v.], he was one of the monks who entered the chapter house accompanied by the prior, Philip [Aubyn, q.v.] and others; they interrupted the proceedings by noisy protestations and were excommunicated, Reg. Giffard, 380.
1293/4, sent by the chapter [on business] to Oxford and also to London *cum carta libertatis*; the cellarer pd his expenses of 19s. 6d., Wilson, *Early Comp. Rolls*, 20, 21 (WCM 51a).
1295, 8 Jan., with Thomas de Hindelep, q.v., appeared before the bp, who was ill in bed at Hartlebury, and announced the renewal of the chapter's appeal vs his collegiate church at Westbury, *Ann. Wigorn.*, 518.
1296, 11 July, chosen by the chapter as one of the seven nominees for the priorate, *Reg. Giffard*, 480.

Name in Worcs. Mss:
(1) Q.42, Distinctiones Mauricii (late 13th c.); on the last flyleaf he is listed as one of eleven monks who contributed to the purchase of this book; he pd 12[?d.].
(2) F.88, P. Lombard (13th c.); on the last flyleaf there is an epitaph for *dominus* Thomas de Ferrariis [?of Hanbury] composed by him.

II Thomas WYCH [Wiche, Wyche
occ. 1432 d. 1489/90

1432, 15 Mar., ord subdcn, carnary chapel by Worcester cathedral, and presented by Richard Lychefeld, q.v., precentor, Reg. Polton, 218.
1433, 9 Dec., in dcn's orders, *Reg. Sed. Vac.*, 432.
1434, 18 Sept., ord pr., carnary chapel, *ib.*, 443.
1434/5, celebrated his first mass and recd *exennia* from the cellarer, WCM C.87.
1445/6, 1448/9, part yr, subcellarer, WCM C.730, 91 (see Robert Multon).
1448/9, pittancer, WCM C.91.
1449/50, kitchener, WCM C.92.
1454/5, refectorer, WCM C.420.

1433, 9 Dec., 44th in order at the el. of a bp, *Reg. Sed. Vac.*, 432.
1445/6, visited Overbury, WCM C.730.
1449/50, visited Hallow, WCM C.600a; he was one of the monks on the cellarer's list of creditors this yr, WCM C.92.
1489/90, d., and the almoner recd payment for his corrody from the cellarer, WCM C.208.

I William de WYCH
occ. 1317

1317, 20 Oct., 7th in order at the el. of a prior and was chosen as one of seven *compromissorii* to name the seven candidates for the priorate, Liber Albus, fo 83–83^{v}.

II William WYCHE [Wiche, Woych
occ. 1521 occ. 1540

1522/3, refectorer, Reg. A.17, 213, succeeding William Fordham, q.v.

1521, 22 July, 19th in order on the visitation certificate, Reg. abp Warham, ii, fo 293^{v}.
1523/4, ill for eleven wks in the infirmary at a cost of 12s. 10d. to the infirmarer, WCM C.413.
1525/6, 19th on the clerical subsidy list and pd 3s. 4d. as commons, Reg. A.12, fo 125.
1531/2, 17th on the second subsidy list and pd as above, *ib.*, 135.
1534, 17 Aug., subscribed to the Act of Supremacy, *DK 7th Report*, Appndx 2, 305.
1536, 13 Mar., 10th in order at the 'el.' of Henry Holbech, q.v., as prior, Reg. A.6(iii), fo 1.
1540, 18 Jan., assigned a pension of £6 p.a., *L and P Henry VIII*, xv, no 81.

WYCHE
see also Whyche, Wich

Simon de WYGORN'
see Crompe

John de WYKE [Wikes, Wyk', Wykes
occ. 1277 d. 1317

1301–1317, prior: apptd by the bp, 18 July 1301, *Reg. Giffard*, 547, in *Ann. Wigorn.*, 550, 17 July; d., 5 Oct., 1317, Liber Albus, fo 83. See *Fasti*, iv, 59.

1277, 31 Oct., was clothed in the monastic habit, with John de Harleye, q.v., *Ann. Wigorn.*, 473.

1298/9, Feb. to Feb.; 1300, 19 Aug., bursar and cellarer, WCM C.54; *Reg. Giffard*, 530.
1301, 18 July, before, subprior, *Ann. Wigorn.*, 549.

1287, 2 Jan., one of the seven nominees for the priorate el. by the chapter, *Reg. Giffard*, 304, 325.

1294/5, Sept. to July, employed by the cellarer in collecting fines on the manors and recd payment for a debt owed to him, Wilson, *Early Comp. Rolls*, 32, 30 (WCM C.52).
1296, 11 July, one of the seven nominees for the priorate el. by the chapter, *Reg. Giffard*, 480.
1300, 19 Aug., one of several monks apptd to assist the sacrist, Nicholas de Norton, q.v., to carry out a *sed. vac.* visitation of the priory *in spiritualibus*, *ib.*, 530.
1301, 18 July, [one of the seven nominees for the third time and] named prior by the bp, *ib.*, 547; on 19 July he went to visit the abp, who was in the vicinity, and the following day he was installed, *Ann. Wigorn.*, 550.
1303, 22 Dec., submitted to the bp's ordinance concerning the status of Stephen de Wytton, q.v., and certain rights of the bp, *Reg. Gainsborough*, 3.
[1308, Nov.] one of four monks apptd to hear confessions 'of our subjects', *Reg. Reynolds*, 2.
1312, 17 July, comm., with the official of the bp, to hear and determine certain cases involving criminous clerks, *Reg. Reynolds*, 51.
1312, 25 Dec., gaol delivery ordered by the king for the prior and for John de Gloucester II, q.v., who had been imprisoned in Worcester castle on a charge of robbery, *CPR (1307–1313)*, 546. On 4 Jan. 1313, the bp issued a comm. to the subprior, precentor and others for the same purpose, *Reg. Reynolds*, 58.
1314, 4 Mar., licensed to hear confessions in the diocese, Reg. Maidstone, 4; another entry dated 1 Sept. repeats or renews the licence, *ib.*, 31.
1315, 20 May, comm. by the bp to carry out corrections and mete out punishments to the monks who had been found guilty of misdemeanours during the bp's visitation, *ib.*, 53.
1315, 27 May, created a notary [public] in the prior's hall, *Liber Albus*, no 653.
1314/15, visited Grimley five times during the yr, WCM C.581.

Name in Worcs. Ms Q.42, Distinctiones Mauricii (late 13th c.); on the last flyleaf he is listed as one of the eleven monks who contributed to the purchase of this book; he pd 12[?d.].

His *acta* are preserved in the Liber Albus, fos 1–82v and his *acta* during four vacancies are in *Reg. Sed. Vac.*, 1–191.

For his correspondence concerning a troublesome monk see John de Dumbelton. See also J.M. Wilson, 'Some Correspondence between the Abbot of St Augustine's, Bristol, and the Prior of Worcester in the Year 1311', *Transactions of the Bristol and Gloucester Archaeological Society*, 41 (1918–1919), 37–47.

His brother, Walter de Wikes, acted as messenger in bearing a letter and a gift of £20 to the new bp, Gainsborough, by way of response to the latter's letter to the prior and chapter written on 5 Feb. 1303, *Reg. Sed. Vac.*, 37–38.

Thomas de WYKE [Weyk, Wyk'
occ. 1353 d. 1381/2

1353, 26 Nov., one of three *clerici* whom the prior was comm. to examine as suitable candidates for adm., Reg. Bryan, i, 10.
1354, 20 Dec., ord acol., Hartlebury, *ib.*, i, 88.
1355, 19 Mar., ord subdcn, Hartlebury, *ib.*, i, 101.
1356, 17 Dec., ord dcn, Alvechurch, *ib.*, i, 104.
1359, 26 Mar., ord pr., Hartlebury, *ib.*, i, 115.
1358/9, one of five who celebrated their first mass and the precentor sent them all *exennia*, WCM C.356.
1363, Jan./1364, June, pittancer, WCM C.306, C.307.
1370, 3 Apr., *tumbarius*, Liber Albus, fo 246.
1357/8, pd by the cellarer for procuring *diversa necessaria* for the subprior who was ill, WCM C.64.
1370, 3 Apr., 9th in order at the el. of a prior, Liber Albus, fo 246.
1373, 4/7 Dec., 8th at the el. of a bp, *Reg. Sed. Vac.*, 290.
[1374], described as apostate because he had left the priory without licence, and the prior issued a mandate for his return, by force if necessary, *ib.*, 321.
1381/2, between Sept. and Feb., d., and the chamberlain recd 12d. from the sale of a pair of *botes* which had been his, WCM C.14.

William de WYKEWANE [Wokewone, Wyckewane
occ. 1315 occ. 1329/30

1315, 14 Sept., one of three whose prof. the prior was comm. to rec., Reg. Maidstone, 74.
1317, 15 Sept., obtained *lit. dim.*, for the order of subdcn, *ib.*, 106.
1318, 21 Jan., subdcn, granted *lit. dim.* for the orders of dcn and pr., Liber Albus, fo 87v.
1317, 20 Oct., 41st and last in order of the professed monks at the el. of a prior, Liber Albus, fo 83v.
1329/30, accompanied the cellarer to Cleeve Prior, WCM C.557.

[Adam WYNCHECOMBE
occ. 1508

1508, 18 Mar., ord acol., carnary chapel by Worcester cathedral, Reg. S. Gigli, 297.

Note: the ordination entries are very disordered on this folio and although he is named as a monk of Worcester, this may be an error.]

Edward WYNCHECOMBE [Wynchcombe *alias* Waren, Waryn
occ. 1473 d. 1486/7

1473, 10 May, one of four whom the prior, with the bp's chancellor, was comm. to examine before adm., Reg. A.6(i), fo 77 and Reg. Carpenter, ii, 94 (12 May).

1475, 23 Dec., ord subdcn, carnary chapel by Worcester cathedral, *ib.*, ii, 205.
1476, 8 June, ord dcn, carnary chapel, *ib.*, ii, 207.
1479, 6 Mar., ord pr., carnary chapel, Reg. Alcock, 255.
1478/9, celebrated his first mass; both the almoner and precentor sent *exennia* of 2s. 6d., WCM C.204, C.384.

1479, chaplain to the prior, Reg. A.6(i), fo 89.

1479/80, student at Oxford; was given 40s., 'pro parte exhibicionis sue ex speciali elemosina domini prioris', WCM C.406a.
1481/2, the above entry on the prior's acct is repeated, WCM C.407.

1486/7, d., and the almoner pd the brief bearer, WCM C.207.

Name in Worcs. Ms F.118, Logicalia quedam etc. (14th/15th c.), on an outer vellum leaf as Waren; see John Benet, John Broghton and Thomas More II.

John de WYNCHECUMBE [Wynchecoumbe
occ. 1317 occ. 1322/3

1317, 9 Dec., one of four whom the bp apptd his commissary to examine; they are described as *vestiendos* and were clothed on 24 Mar., 1318, Liber Albus, fos 84ᵛ–85.
1318, 17 Nov., the prior was comm. to rec. his prof., *Reg. Cobham*, 13 and *Liber Albus*, no 809.
1319, 7 Apr., ord subdcn, bp's chapel, Kempsey, *Reg. Cobham*, 58.
1319, 22 Dec., ord dcn, St Nicholas' church, Worcester, *ib.*, 68.
1322/3, subcellarer, WCM C.545; and see Robert de Morton.

Note: there is another entry for the bp's comm. to prof. a John de Wynchecumbe on 20 Feb. 1320, in *Reg Cobham*, and for the prior's receiving it on 9 Mar. in Liber Albus, fo 94ᵛ. Who is this?

WYNCHECOMBE
see also Winchecumbe

Walter de WYNFORTON [Wyneferton, Wynfertone, Wynfreton
occ. 1339 occ. 1360

1339, 27 Mar., ord acol., Kempsey, *Reg. Bransford*, no 1004.
1339, 22 May, ord subdcn, Tewkesbury abbey, *ib.*, no 1008 (p. 185).

1353/5, 1356/8, 1359/61, cellarer, WCM E.5, C.62–65, 629; the last yr he is named only as W. and was succ. by J.

1345/6, employed by the cellarer in paying manorial reeves *pro messione*; sent to Northampton with money for the prior [John de Evesham I, q.v.] at the Black Monk Chapter, WCM C.60.
1350, 27 July, had been sent to the curia in Avignon on behalf of the chapter and had afterwards proceeded, without permission, to Rome for the jubilee; he had therefore been declared apostate and now sought reconciliation. The pope, on this date, issued a mandate to the bp of Hereford and others to take charge of the required procedures, *CPL*, iii (1342–1362), 388.
1350, 10 Dec., with Nicholas de Clanefeld and Robert de Weston, q.v., given letters of attorney by the prior, John de Evesham I, q.v., prob. because the prior had gone to Avignon, Bloom, *Liber Ecclesiae*, 51. The yr is given as 1351 in both printed, calendar and ms [PRO E315/63, fos 58ᵛ–59]; but see John de Evesham I, under 1350 and 1351.
1350/1, his absence from the priory can be inferred from the fact that the precentor pd his 'O' pittance separately and the cellarer excluded him from the list of those receiving pittances for their *minutiones*, WCM C.354, C.53; see John de Evesham I under this date.
1352, 23 Jan., obtained papal licence to choose his confessor who was empowered to grant plenary remission at d., *CPL*, iii (1342–1362), 452.
1354/5, journeyed to Bristol and made several trips to London concerning a law suit in process and also to make arrangements for the prior's departure for Avignon, WCM C.62; see John de Evesham I.
1355, 22 May, one of four monk proctors apptd by, and given a general mandate to act for, the chapter in all causes pertaining to the status of their church, including matters which could arise during a visitation, Liber Albus, fo 241; see John de Evesham I.
1356/7, went to Reading and Abingdon on business and also spent some time in London in negotiations related to the appeal of the prior and convent vs the bp; he also sent money to the prior in Avignon, WCM C.63.
1357, 23 Sept., with John de Legh and Robert de Weston together acting as the prior's vice gerents during his absence, Liber Albus, fo 214ᵛ.
1360, 20 Nov., his apptment by the bp as abbot of Winchcombe recd royal assent, *CPR (1358–1361)*, 493, 497.

Adam de WYNTON
occ. [?late 13th c.]

[?late 13th c.], sacrist, WCM B.1662 (a lease).

Note: an Adam de Wyntone, who may have been a monk, assisted the cellarer in the collection of tithes in 1338/9, WCM C.58.

Simon de WYNTON [Wyntonia
occ. 1330 occ. 1352

1330, 11 Aug., one of four *clerici* to be examined by two officials of the bp and to be recd *ad monachalem ordinem*, *Reg. Orleton*, no 776.
1332, 18 Apr., ord subdcn, Beckford, *ib.*, no 24.

1335, 19 Sept., ord pr., Chaddesley [?Corbett], Reg. Montacute, 92.

1352, 23 Jan., granted papal licence to choose his own confessor who was authorized to give plenary remission at d., *CPL*, iii (1342–1362), 452.

WYRCESTR', Wyrcetre
see Worcestre

Simon de WYRE [*alias* Wirecestre
occ. 1272 occ. 1301

1296–1301, prior: one of the seven candidates elected on 11 July 1296 and apptd prior by the bp on 13 July; res. before 18 July, 1301; see below.

1277/8, possibly subcellarer, as Symon only on a Newnham acct, CCA DCc MBL (Canterbury).
1282, 6 Apr; 1287, 2 Jan., precentor, *Ann. Wigorn.*, 483; *Reg. Giffard*, 305, 324.
1296, 11 July, subprior, *Reg. Giffard*, 480.

1272, 21 Dec., chosen as one of the seven nominees for the priorate, *Reg. Giffard*, 51.
1274, 21 Sept., again chosen as one of the seven nominees for the priorate, *ib.*, 62.
1282, 6 Apr., set out for Rome, *Ann. Wigorn.*, 483.
1287, 2 Jan., one of the seven nominees for the priorate, *Reg. Giffard*, 305, 324.
1288/9, [Dec./Jan.], challenged the bp, when he entered the chapter house to correct *excessus cotidianos*, on the grounds that an appeal was pending. It was a dramatic moment when the bp said 'Nonne facitis mihi professionem?' and the prior replied 'Non; sed Deo et ecclesie', *Ann. Wigorn.*, 496.
1296, 11 July, again one of the seven nominees and this time successful, and apptd prior 13 July, *Reg. Giffard*, 480, 481; installed 23 Sept., by the official of the adcn, *Ann. Wigorn.*, 528.
1298/9, went to a special meeting of the Black Monk Chapter in Oxford [concerning the house of studies for monks there], WCM C.54.
1299, 17 Nov., comm. by the bp to install John de Dumbelton, q.v., as prior of Little Malvern, *Reg. Giffard*, 513.
1300, 27 Aug., comm. by the bp, with Nicholas de Norton, q.v., to see to corrections in the monastery after the visitation, *ib.*, 528.
1301, before 18 July, gave his resignation first to the abp and then to the bp on the grounds of age and infirmity, *ib.*, 547. However, it must also be borne in mind that this was in the wake of the abp's visitation; see the Introduction, p. 0000.

Name in Worcs. Ms Q.42, Distinctiones Mauricii (late 13th c.); on the last flyleaf he is listed as one of eleven monks who contributed to the purchase of this book; he pd 36[?d.], the largest sum.

Henry de WYRMINTONE
occ. *temp.* Simon de Wyre above

Name in Worcs.Ms Q.42, as above; he contributed 12[?d.].

Note: this is prob. Henry de Annochia, q.v.

John de WYTTENEY [Witteneye, Wyttheney
occ. 1365 d. 1415/16

1365, 14 Sept., one of three whose prof. the prior was comm. to rec., Liber Albus, fo 229v.
1368, 4 Mar., ord dcn, Hartlebury, Reg. Wittlesey, 72.
1369, 22 Sept., ord pr., Kidderminster, Reg. Lynn, 49.

1375/8, *tumbarius*, WCM C.453, 454; the 1375/7 accts are printed in Hamilton, *Comp. Rolls*, 75–76.
1380, May/1381, Feb., pittancer, WCM C.311, 312.

1370, 3 Apr., 20th in order at the el. of a prior, Liber Albus, fo 246.
1373, 4/7 Dec., 17th at the el. of a bp, *Reg. Sed. Vac.*, 290.
1388, 21 Aug., 15th at the el. of a prior, Liber Albus, fo 334v.
1389/90, the chamberlain pd for leather [?for his boots] and for those of Wytteney and other monks, WCM C.17.
1392/3, reported by the *custos* of the Lady chapel as 'licenciatus a domino priore ad conferend' de elemosina sua in sustentacione' of J. Defford in place of the clerk; it seems that he had been assisting with the expenses of feeding a clerk who was prob. in the employ of the *custos*, WCM C.251.
1396, 11 Nov., granted papal licence to choose his own confessor, *CPL*, v (1396–1404), 47.
1401, 24 June, 9th at the el. of a bp, *Reg. Sed. Vac.*, 372.
1415/16, d., and the chamberlain sold his *panni*, WCM C.31.

Stephen de WYTTON [Wittone
occ. 1288 occ. 1305

1302, 27 Jan., 25 Mar.; 1303, 2 Apr., subprior, *Liber Albus*, no 64, *Reg. Sed. Vac.*, 1; *ib.*, 45.
1305, 21 July, apptd sacrist in place of John de Harleye, q.v., *Liber Albus*, no 319, and *Reg. Gainsborough*, 22; on 24 July the prior and convent wrote to the bp to request him to appt another sacrist, *Liber Albus*, no 318.

1288, 23 Dec., delivered letters of inhibition to the bp while the chapter's dispute with him [over the right of the precentor to call out names of the ordination candidates at an ordination ceremony] was pending in the court of Canterbury. He proceeded to appeal to Rome at this time, *Ann. Wigorn.*, 496; see Simon de Wyre.

1293/4, went to London to pay the twentieth to the king, Wilson, *Early Comp. Rolls*, 21 (WCM C.51a); named only as Stephen, see Stephen de St Wulstan.

1301, 18 July, chosen as one of the seven nominees for the priorate, *Reg. Giffard*, 547.

1302, 27 Jan., with Gilbert de Madley, q.v., apptd proctor to obtain from the deceased bp's executors his seal, registers etc, Liber Albus, fo 7^{v}.

[1302, Feb./Mar.], with John de Bromesgrove, q.v., apptd proctor by the prior in all causes, *Liber Albus*, no 81.

1302, 18 Feb., the prior authorized by the abp to relax or remit the penance imposed on him as a result of the abp's visitation, Liber Albus, fo 11^{v}; see John de Wyke.

1302, 25 Mar., named as one of seven *compromissorii*, in the el. of a bp, and apptd proctor on 29 Mar. to inform the king of the chapter's choice, *Reg. Sed. Vac.*, 1–2; see John de St Germans.

[1302], 13 Dec., left the monastery without licence, and the prior appealed to the bp to use his influence to bring him back; he returned on 20 Jan. 1303, *Liber Albus*, nos 153, 154.

1303, 2 Apr., given letters of credence to go to the bp to discuss certain matters with him on behalf of the prior and convent, *Reg. Sed. Vac.*, 45.

1303, 22 Dec., the prior, John de Wyke, q.v., submitted to the bp with regard to the position of Wytton, *Reg. Gainsborough*, 3 and Liber Albus, fo 17.

YDENHALE, Ydeshall
see Hydeshale

T. de YEDDESEN [Zedemyn, Yeddenen, Yeddenon, Zeddesen
occ. 1382 d. 1387/8

1382, 1 Mar., ord acol., Kidderminster, *Reg. Wakefield*, no 893b.

1382, 19 Sept., given *lit. dim.*, for all orders, *ib.*, no 896.

1384, 24 Sept., ord dcn, Alvechurch, *ib.*, no 906f.

1385, 25 Feb., ord pr., Cirencester abbey, *ib.*, no 908h.

1384/5, celebrated his first mass and the precentor sent *exennia* of 2s. 2d., WCM C.364.

1387/8, d., and the precentor procured parchment for the brief, WCM C.365.

*As this volume goes to press, an earlier monk by this name has been discovered:

I Nicholas Wych
occ. 1307

1307, 13 July, priest and present in St Paul's cathedral, London, as one of the witnesses at the official inquiry preceding the canonization of Thomas Cantilupe. He gave his age as about 55 yrs and stated that he had been Cantilupe's clerk of the chapel for five yrs before Cantilupe's apptment as bp of Hereford, *Acta Sanctorum Bollandiana Octobris* (Antwerp, 1765), i, 592.

APPENDIX

ARCHBISHOPS, BISHOPS, AND PRIORS IN CHRONOLOGICAL ORDER

Note: Square brackets denote disputed and unsuccessful elections.

I BATH [WELLS]

i Bishops

John de Villula, 1088–1122
Godfrey, 1123–1135
Robert, 1136–1166
Reginald Fitzjocelin, 1173–1191
Savaric, 1191–1205
Jocelin of Wells, 1206–1242
Roger of Salisbury, 1244–1247
William Bitton I, 1248–1264
Walter Giffard, 1264–1266
William Bitton II, 1267–1274
Robert Burnell, 1275–1292
William of March, 1293–1302
Walter Haselshaw, 1302–1308
John Drokensford, 1309–1329
Ralph Shrewsbury, 1329–1363
John Barnet, 1363–1366
John Harewell, 1367–1386
Walter Skirlaw, 1386–1388
Ralph Erghum, 1388–1400
Henry Bowett, 1401–1407
Nicholas Bubwith, 1407–1424
John Stafford, 1424–1443
Thomas Bekynton, 1443–1465
Robert Stillington, 1465–1491
Richard Fox, 1492–1494
Oliver King, 1496–1503
Adriano de Castello, 1504–1518
Thomas Wolsey, 1518–1523
John Clerk, 1523–

ii Priors

John, 1106 × 1109, 1122
Benedict, 1136 × 1157
Peter, 1157 × [1175]
Hugh, 1174 × *c.*1184
Walter, *c.*1184
Robert de Bath, *c.*1198–1223
Thomas, *c.*1223–1261
Walter de Anno, 1261–1290
Thomas de Winton, 1290–1301
Robert de Clopcote, 1301–1332
Robert de Sutton, 1332
Thomas Crist, 1332–1340
John de Iforde, 1340–1359
John de Berewyk, *c.*1362–1379
John de Dunster I, *c.*1397–1412
John Telesford, 1412–1424
William Southbroke, ?1425–1447
Thomas Lacok, 1447–?1467
John Dunster II, *c.*1468–1480
Peter [Twiverton], 1482
John Cantlow, ?1489–1499
William Birde, 1499–1525
William Holleway, 1525–1539

II CANTERBURY

i Archbishops

Lanfranc, 1070–1089
Anselm, 1093–1109
Ralph d'Escures, 1114–1122
William de Corbeil, 1123–1136
Theobald, 1139–1161
Thomas Becket, 1162–1170
Richard of Dover, 1173–1184, monk of Christ Church, q.v.
Baldwin, 1184–1190
[Reginald Fitzjocelin, 1191; see the entry under Bath]
Hubert Walter, 1193–1205
[Reginald, 1205–1206, monk of Christ Church, q.v.]
[John de Grey, 1205–1206]
Stephen Langton, 1206–1228
[Walter de Eynsham, 1228–1229, monk of Christ Church]

Richard Le Grant *alias* Weathershed, 1229–1231
[Ralph de Neville, 1231]
[John de Sittingborne, 1232, monk of Christ Church]
[John Le Blund, 1232–1233]
Edmund of Abingdon, 1233–1240
Boniface of Savoy, 1240–1270
[Adam de Chillenden, 1270–1272, monk of Christ Church]
Robert de Kilwardby, 1272–1278
[Robert Burnell, 1278–1279]
John Pecham, 1279–1292
Robert Winchelsey, 1293–1313
[Thomas de Cobham, 1313]
Walter Reynolds, 1313–1327
Simon de Meopham, 1327–1333
John de Stratford, 1333–1348
[Thomas de Bradwardine, 1348]
John de Offord, 1348–1349
Thomas de Bradwardine, again, 1349
Simon Islip, 1349–1366
[William de Edington, 1366]
Simon Langham, 1366–1368
William Wittlesey, 1368–1374
[Simon Langham, again, 1374]
Simon de Sudbury, 1375–1381
William Courtenay, 1381–1396
Thomas Arundel, 1396–1397
Roger de Walden, 1397–1399
Thomas Arundel, restored, 1399–1414
Henry Chichele, 1414–1443
John Stafford, 1443–1452
John Kempe, 1452–1454
Thomas Bourgchier, 1454–1486
John Morton, 1486–1500
[Thomas Langton, 1501]
Henry Deane, 1501–1503
William Warham, 1503–1532
William Cranmer, 1533–

ii Priors

Godric, before 1070
Henry, 1074–1096
Ernulph, *c.*1096–1107
Conrad, 1108 × 1109–1125 × 1126
Geoffrey I, 1125–1128
Elmer, 1130–1137
Jeremiah, 1137–*c.*1143
Walter Durdent, *c.*1143 × 1149
Walter de Meri *alias* Parvus, 1149–1152
Wibert, 1152–1167
Odo, 1168 × 1169–1175
Benedict, 1175–1177
Herlewin, 1177–1179
Alan, 1179–1186
Honorius, 1186–1188
Roger Norreys, 1189
Osbern de Bristol, 1191
Geoffrey II, 1191–1213
Walter, *c.*1213–1222
John de Sittingborne, 1222–1235 × 1238
John de Chatham, [1236]-1238
Roger de la Lee, 1239–1244
Nicholas de Sandwyco, 1244–1258
Roger de St Elphege, 1258–1263
Adam de Chillenden, 1263 × 1264–1274
Thomas de Ryngmer, 1274–1285
Henry de Eastry, 1285–1331
Richard de Oxenden, 1331–1338
Robert Hathbrande, 1338–1370
Richard de Gyllyngham, 1370–1376
Stephen de Mongeham, 1376–1377
John Fynch, 1377–1391
Thomas Chillenden, 1391–1411
John Wodnesburgh, 1411–1428
William Molassh, 1428–1438
John Salisbury, 1438–1446
John Elham, 1446–1449
Thomas Goldston I, 1449–1468
John de Oxney, 1468–1471
William Pettham, 1471–1472
William Sellyng, 1472–1494
Thomas Goldston II, 1495–1517
Thomas Goldwell, 1517–1540

III COVENTRY [LICHFIELD]

i Bishops

Robert de Limesey, 1085–1117
Robert Peche, 1121–1126
Roger de Clinton, 1129–1148
Walter Durdent, 1149–1159, monk of Canterbury
Richard Peche, 1161–1182
Gerard Pucelle, 1183–1184
Hugh de Nonant, 1185–1198
Geoffrey Muschamp, 1198–1208
William Cornhill, 1214–1223
Alexander Stavensby, 1224–1238

Hugh Pattishall, 1239–1241
Roger Weseham, 1245–1256
Roger Longespee (Meuland), 1258–1295
Walter Langton, 1296–1321
Roger Northburgh, 1321–1358
Robert Stretton, 1358–1385
Walter Skirlaw, 1385–1386
Richard le Scrope, 1386–1398
John Burghill, 1398–1414
John Catterick, 1415–1419
William Heyworth, 1419–1447
William Booth, 1447–1452
Nicholas Close, 1452
Reginald Boulers, 1453–1459
John Hales, 1459–1490
William Smith, 1493–1496
John Arundel, 1496–1502
Geoffrey Blyth, 1503–1531
Rowland Lee, 1543–

ii Priors

Bruning, *c.*1102 × 1122
Hervey, *c.*1122
Leasstan, *c.*1122 × 1139 }
Owyne, *c.*1122 × 1139 } see the relevant entries
Stanulf, *c.*1122 × 1139 }
Richard, *c.*1122 × 1139 }
Laurence, 1144–1179
Moses, 1183–1198
Joybert, 1198–1216
Geoffrey, 1216–1235
Roger de Walton, 1235–1249
William de Brythwalton, 1249–1280
Thomas de Pavy, 1280–1294
Henry de Leycester I, 1294 × ?1321 }
Henry de Leycester II, 1326 or 1328 × 1342 } see the relevant entries
William Irreys, 1342–1349
William de Dunstable, 1349–1361
William de Greneburgh, 1361–1390
James de Horton, 1390–1396
Roger de Coton, 1396–1399
Richard Crosby, 1399–1437
Richard Nottingham, 1437–1453
John Shotteswell, 1453–1461
Thomas Deram, 1461–1481
Richard Coventry, 1481–1501
William Pollesworth, 1501–1516
John Impingham, 1516–1517
John Webbe, 1517–1527
Thomas Weoford, 1527–1538
Thomas Carnswell, 1538–1539

IV ELY

i Bishops

Hervey, 1109–1131
Nigel, 1133–1169
Geoffrey Ridel, 1173–1189
William de Longchamp, 1189–1197
Eustace, 1197–1215
[Robert of York, 1215–1218 × 1219]
[Geoffrey de Burgh, 1215–1218 × 1219]
John of Fountains, 1219–1225
Geoffrey de Burgh, 1225–1228
Hugh de Northwold, 1229–1254
William de Kilkenny, 1254–1256
Hugh de Balsham, 1256–1286, monk of Ely
John de Kirkeby, 1286–1290
William de Luda, 1290–1298
[John Salmon, 1298–1299, prior of Ely]
[John de Langeton, 1298–1299]
Ralph de Walpole, 1299–1302
Robert de Orford, 1302–1310, prior of Ely
John de Ketene, 1310–1316, monk of Ely
John de Hotham, 1316–1337
[John de Crauden, 1337]
Simon de Montacute, 1337–1345
[Alan de Walsingham, 1345, prior of Ely]
Thomas de Lisle, 1345–1361
[Reginald Brien, 1361]
[John Buckingham, 1362]
Simon Langham, 1362–1366
John Barnet, 1366–1373
[Henry de Wakefield, 1373]
[John Woodrowe, 1373]
Thomas Arundel, 1373–1388
John de Fordham, 1388–1425
[Peter de Ely, 1425, prior of Ely]
[William Alnwick, 1425]
Philip Morgan, 1426–1435
[Robert Fitzhugh, 1435]
[Thomas Rudborne, 1436]
[Thomas Bourgchier, 1436]
Lewis de Luxemburg, 1437–1443
Thomas Bourgchier, again, 1443–1454
William Gray, 1454–1478
John Morton, 1478–1486
John Alcock, 1486–1500
Richard Redmayn, 1501–1505
James Stanley, 1506–1515
Nicholas West, 1515–1533

[Nicholas Hawkins, 1533]
Thomas Goodrich, 1534–

ii Priors

Vincent, 1109 × *c*.1128
Henry, 1129–1133
William, 1133 × 1134/5 × 1137
Theinbert, 1144–?1151
Alexander, 1151 × 1152–*c*.1158
Salomon, 1163–1176
Richard, 1177–1189
Robert de Longchamp, 1194–1197
John de ?Strateshete, [1198–?1202]
Hugh, *c*.1203 × 1208
Roger de Bergham, 1215–1225 × 1228
Ralph, ?1229–1238
Alexander, 1151 × 1152–*c*.1158
Walter, *c*.1241–1259
Robert de Leverington, 1261–1271
Henry de Bancs, 1271–1273
John de Hemmingestone, 1273–1288
John de Shepreth, 1288–1292
John Salmon, 1292–1299
Robert de Orford, 1299–1302
William de Clare, 1303
John de Fresingfeld, 1303–1321
John de Crauden, 1321–1341
Alan de Walsingham, 1341–1363 or 1364
William de Hathfield, *c*.1363–1364
John de Bukton, 1364–1396
William de Walpole, 1396/7–1401
William Powcher, 1401–?1418
Edmund Walsingham, 1418–1424
Peter de Ely, 1425–?1430
William Wells, 1430–1461
Henry Peterborough, 1462–1478
Roger Westminster, 1478–1499
Robert Colville, *c*.1500–1510
William Wittlesey, *c*.1510–1516
John Cottenham, 1516–1522
Robert Wells, 1522–1539

V NORWICH

i Bishops

Herbert Losinga, 1094 × 1095–1119
Everard de Calne, 1121–1146
William de Turba, 1146 × 1147–1174, monk of Norwich
John de Oxford, 1175–1200
John de Grey, 1200–1214
Pandulph Masca, 1215–1226
Thomas de Blundeville, 1226–1236
[Simon de Elmham, 1236–1239, monk of Norwich]
William de Ralegh, 1239–1243
Walter de Suffield, 1244–1257
Simon de Wauton, 1257–1266
Roger de Skerning, 1266–1278, prior of Norwich
William de Middleton, 1278–1288
Ralph de Walpole, 1288–1299
John Salmon, 1299–1325, monk of Ely
[Robert de Baldock, 1325]
William de Ayermine, 1325–1336
[Thomas de Hemenhale, 1336–1337, monk of Norwich]
Anthony Bek, 1337–1343
William Bateman, 1343–1355
Thomas Percy, 1355–1369
Henry Despenser, 1369–1406
Alexander de Totyngton, 1406–1413, prior of Norwich
Richard Courtenay, 1413–1415
John Wakeryng, 1415–1425
William Alnwick, 1425–1436
Thomas Brouns, 1436–1445
[John Stanbury, 1445–1446]
Walter Lyhert, 1446–1472
James Goldwell, 1472–1499
[Thomas Savage, 1499]
Thomas Jane, 1499–1500
Richard Nikke, 1501–1535/6
William Repps, 1536– , monk of Norwich

ii Priors

Ingulph, [1106 × 1107]–c. 1136
William de Turba, c. 1136 × 1143–1146 × 1147
Elias, c. 1146–1150
Richard de Ferreres, c. 1150–1158
Ranulph, [?1161 × 1174]
John, [1153 × 1168], [1161 × 1174]
Elricus, 1172
Tancred, c. 1172–1175
Gerard, c. 1175–1202
William de Walsham, 1205–?1217
Ranulph de Wareham, ?1215–1217
William son of Odo of Norwich, c. 1220 × 1235
Simon de Elmham, 1235–1257
Roger de Skerning, 1257–1266
Nicholas de Bramertone, 1266–1269
William de Burnham, [1268/9]–1272

William de Kirkeby, 1272–1289
Henry de Lakenham, 1289–1310
Robert de Langele, 1310–1326
William de Claxton, 1326–1344
Simon Bozoun, 1344–1352
Laurence de Leck, 1352–1357
Nicholas de Hoo, 1357–1381
Alexander de Totyngton, 1381–1406
Robert de Burnham, 1407–1427
William Worstede, 1427–1436
John Heverlond, 1436–1454
John Molet, 1454–1471
Thomas Bouzon, 1471–1480
John Bonwell, 1480–1488
William Spynk, 1488–1503
William Bakonesthorp, 1503–1504
Robert Catton, 1504–?1529
William Castleton, 1529–1538

VI ROCHESTER

i Bishops

Gundulf, 1077–1108
Ralph d'Escures, 1108–1114
Ernulph, 1114–1124, prior of Canterbury
John I
John II [of Séez]
Ascelin, 1142–1148
Walter, 1148–1182
Waleran, 1182–1184
Gilbert de Glanville, 1185–1214
Benedict de Sawston, 1214–1226
Henry de Sandford, 1227–1235
Richard de Wendene, 1235–1250
Laurence de St Martin, 1250–1274
Walter de Merton, 1274–1277
John de Bradfield, 1278–1283, monk of Rochester
[John de Kirkeby, 1283]
Thomas de Ingoldisthorpe, 1283–1291
Thomas de Wouldham, 1291–1317, prior of Rochester
[John Puteoli, 1317]
Hamo de Hethe, 1317–1352, prior of Rochester
John de Shepey, 1352–1360, prior of Rochester
William Wittlesey, 1360–1364
Thomas de Trillek, 1364–1372
[John de Hertlepe, 1372, prior of Rochester]
Thomas Brinton, 1373–1389, monk of Norwich
[John Barnet, 1389]
William de Bottlesham, 1389–1400
John de Bottlesham, 1400–1404
[Thomas Chillenden, 1404, monk of Canterbury]
Richard Young, 1404–1418
John Kemp, 1419–1421
[Thomas Spofford, 1421]
John Langdon, 1421–1434, monk of Canterbury
Thomas Brouns, 1435–1436
William Wells, 1436–1444
John Lowe, 1444–1467
Thomas Rotherham, 1468–1472
John Alcock, 1472–1476
John Russell, 1476–1480
Edmund Audley, 1480–1492
Thomas Savage, 1492–1496
Richard Fitzjames, 1497–1503
John Fisher, 1504–1535
John Hilsey, 1535–1540

ii Priors

Ernulph, before 1107
Ralph, before 1107
Ordwinus, 1107 × 1108–1125
Thomas, [*c*.1128 × 1137]
Brien, *c*.1145–?1148
Reginald, 1155, 1160
William de Borstall, *c*.1160 × 1180
Silvester, *c*.1177 × 1180
Richard, 1181–1182
Alfred, *c*.1182–1186
Osbern de Shepey, 1189–1190
Ralph de Ros, *c*.1193–1203, ? before 1208
Elias, *c*.1214–1217
William, *c*.1218–1222
Richard de Darente, *c*.1225–1238
William de Hoo, 1239–1242
Alexander de Glanvill, 1242–1252
Simon de Clyve, 1252–1262
John de Reynham, 1262–1283
Thomas de Wouldham, 1283–1291
John de Reynham, again, 1292–1294
Thomas de Shelford, 1294–1301
John de Grenestrete, 1301–1314
Hamo de Hethe, 1314–1317
John de Westerham, 1320–1321
John de Speldhurst, 1321–1333
John de Shepey I, 1333–1352
Robert de Southflete, 1350–1361

John de Hertlepe, 1361–1380
John de Shepey II, 1380–1419
William Tonebregg, 1419–1445
John Clyve, 1445–1460
Richard Pecham, 1460–?1468
William Wode, ?1468 × 1475
Thomas Bourne, *c.*1480–1494
William Bisshope, 1494–1509
William Fresell, 1509–1532
Laurence Mereworth, 1532–1538
Walter Boxley, 1538–1540

VII WINCHESTER

i Bishops

Walkelin, 1070–1098
William Giffard, 1100–1129
Henry of Blois, 1129–1171
Richard of Ilchester, 1173–1188
Godfrey de Lucy, 1189–1204
[Richard Poore, 1205]
Peter des Roches, 1205–1238
[Ralph de Neville, 1238–1239]
William de Ralegh, 1239 × 1244–1250
Aymer de Valence *alias* de Lusignan, 1250–1260
[Andrew de London, 1261–1262, prior of Winchester]
[William de Taunton, 1261–1262, former prior of Winchester]
John of Exeter, 1262–1268
Nicholas of Ely, 1268–1280
[Robert Burnell, 1280]
[Richard de la More, 1280–1282]
John de Pontissara, 1282–1304
Henry Woodlock, 1304–1316, prior of Winchester
John de Sandale, 1316–1319
[Henry de Burgershe, 1319]
[Adam de Winton, 1319, monk of Winchester]
Rigaud de Asserio, 1319–1323
[Robert de Baldock, 1323]
John de Stratford, 1323–1333
Adam de Orleton, 1333–1345
[John le Devenish, 1345, monk of Winchester]
William de Edington, 1345–1366
William de Wykeham, 1366–1404
[Thomas Nevyle, 1404, prior of Winchester]
Henry Beaufort, 1404–1447
William Waynflete, 1447–1486
Peter Courtenay, 1487–1492
Thomas Langton, 1493–1501
Richard Fox, 1501–1528
Thomas Wolsey, 1529–1530
Stephen Gardiner, 1531–

ii Priors

Simeon, before 1081–1082
Godfrey, 1082–1107
Geoffrey I, 1107–1111
Geoffrey II, 1111–1126
Ingulph, *c.*1126–1130
Robert I, 1130
Geoffrey III, 1139 × 1153
William, [1165]
Robert II, 1165–1173
Walter I, *c.*1173–1175/6
John, 1185–1187
Robert III, son of Henry, 1187–1191
Stephen [de Luci], 1201–1214
Walter II, 1215/16–1238/9
Andrew, 1239–1243
John de Cauz, 1243–1244
Walter III, 1244/45–1247
John de Cauz, again, 1247–1250
William de Taunton, 1250–1255
Andrew de London, 1255–1261
Walter Rufus, 1262 × 1265
Ralph Russel, [?1261 × 1265]
Valentine [de Wherewell], 1265–1267, 1268–1276
John de Dureville, 1276–1278/9
Adam de Farnham, 1279–1283
William de Basyng I, 283 × 1284–1294 × 1295
Henry Woodlock, 1295–1304/5
Nicholas de Tarente, 1305–1309
Richard de Enford, 1309–1328
Alexander de Heriard, 1328–1349
John de Merlawe, 1349–1361
[William Thudden, 1361–1362]
Hugh de Basyng, 1362–1384
Robert de Rodebourne, 1384–1395
Thomas Nevyle, 1395–1415
Thomas Shirebourne, 1415–1433 × 1434
William Alton, 1435–1450
Richard Marleburgh, 1450–1457
Robert Westgate, 1457–1470
Thomas Hunton, 1470–1498
Thomas Silkestede, 1498–1524
Henry Broke, 1524–1536
William Basyng II, 1536–1539

VIII WORCESTER

i Bishops

Wulstan, 1062–1095
Sampson, 1096–1112
Theulf, 1113–1123
Simon, 1125–1150
John de Pagham, 1151–1157
Alfred, 1158–1160
Roger of Gloucester, 1163–1179
Baldwin, 1180–1184
William of Northolt, 1186–1190
Robert, son of William Fitz Ralph, 1190–1193
Henry de Soilli, 1193–1195
John de Coutances, 1196–1198
Mauger, 1199–1212
[Randulph de Evesham, 1213–1214, prior of Worcester]
Walter de Grey, 1214–1215
Silvester de Evesham, 1216–1218, prior of Worcester
William of Blois, 1218–1236
Walter de Cantilupe, 1236–1266
Nicholas de Ely, 1266–1268
Godfrey Giffard, 1268–1302
[John de St Germans, 1302, monk of Worcester]
William de Gainsborough, 1302–1307
Walter Reynolds, 1307–1313
Walter Maidstone, 1313–1317
Thomas de Cobham, 1317–1327
[Wulstan de Bransford, 1327, prior of Worcester]
Adam de Orleton, 1327–1333
Simon de Montacute, 1333–1337
Thomas de Hemenhale, 1337–1338, monk of Norwich
Wulstan de Bransford, again, 1338–1349, prior of Worcester
[John de Evesham, 1349, prior of Worcester]
John de Thoresby, 1349–1352
Reginald Bryan, 1352–1361
John Barnet, 1362–1363
William Wittlesey, 1364–1368
William de Lynn, 1368–1373
[Walter de Legh, 1373–1375, prior of Worcester]
Henry de Wakefield, 1375–1395
[John Grene, 1395, prior of Worcester]
Robert Tideman de Winchcombe, 1395–1401
Richard Clifford, 1401–1407
Thomas Peverel, 1407–1419
Philip Morgan, 1419–1426
Thomas Polton, 1426–1433
[Thomas Brouns, 1433]
Thomas Bourgchier, 1435–1443
John Carpenter, 1443–1476
John Alcock, 1476–1486
Robert Morton, 1486–1497
Giovanni de Gigli, 1497–1498
Silvestro de Gigli, 1498–1521
Giulio de Medici, 1521–1522
Geronimo de Ghinucci, 1522–1535
Hugh Latimer, 1535–1539
John Bell, 1539–

ii Priors

Aelfstan, ?1062–1077
Thomas I, 1080–1113
Nicholas, 1116–1124
Warinus, 1133 × 1140
Ralph de Bathonia, 1142–1143
David, 1143–1145
Osbert, 1145–1146
Ralph de Bedeford, 1146–1189
Senatus, 1189–1196
Peter, 1196–1203
Randulph de Evesham, 1203–1214
Silvester de Evesham, 1214/15–1216
Simon Pimme, 1216–1222
William Norman, 1222–1224
William de Bedeford, 1224–1242
Richard de Gundicote, 1242–1252
Thomas II, 1252–1260
Richard de Dumbleton, 1260–1272
William de Cirencester, 1272–1274
Richard de Feckenham, 1274–1286
Philip Aubyn, 1287–1296
Simon de Wyre, 1296–1301
John de Wyke, 1301–1317
Wulstan de Bransford, 1317–1339
Simon le Botiler, 1339
Simon Crompe, 1339–1340
John de Evesham, 1340–1370
Walter de Legh, 1370–1388
John Grene, 1388–1395
John de Malverne, 1395–1409
John de Fordham, 1409–1438
Thomas Ledbury, 1438–1444
John Hertilbury, 1444–1457/8
Thomas Musard, 1457/8–1469
Robert Multon, 1469–1492

William Wenlok, 1492–1499
Thomas Mildenham, 1499–1507
John Wednesbury, 1507–1518
William More, 1518–1536
Henry Holbech, 1536–1540

INDEX OF NAMES

The purpose of this index is to save the reader, whose knowledge of a monk is limited to the name, from the necessity of searching through all eight sections of the register. Since the entries are in alphabetical order within each section it has been deemed sufficient to dispense with page references and to provide key letter(s) for each: *B* (Bath); *C* (Canterbury); *Co* (Coventry); *E* (Ely); *N* (Norwich); *R* (Rochester); *W* (Winchester); *Wo* (Worcester). The diverse forms of spelling of medieval names and places often conceal the forms familiar to us; for this reason many of the variations are included here as separate entries referring the reader to the appropriate section where the form under which the name is entered will be found. In my view it is safer to cope with the problem of medieval orthography than to attempt to allocate the modern equivalents to the toponyms by which the majority of monks were known. In the case of two or more monks with the same name and of the same house or of different houses there is only one entry; this should cause no difficulty as their names in the text are prefixed by numbers in chronological order. In cases of uncertainty the reader is advised to consult the alternative spellings that follow many of the main entries below and then to check the index under the variants: e.g., under the toponym Salisbury both Sarisbury and Sarum occur, and both have their own separate entries in the index.